D1266402

PETERSON'S®
GRADUATE PROGRAMS IN THE PHYSICAL SCIENCES, MATHEMATICS, AGRICULTURAL SCIENCES, THE ENVIRONMENT & NATURAL RESOURCES

2017

 PETERSON'S®

About Peterson's®

Peterson's® provides the accurate, dependable, high-quality education content and guidance you need to succeed. No matter where you are on your academic or professional path, you can rely on Peterson's publications and its online information at www.petersons.com for the most up-to-date education exploration data, expert test-prep tools, and top-notch career success resources—everything you need to achieve your goals.

For more information, contact Peterson's, 3 Columbia Circle, Suite 205, Albany, NY 12203-5158; 800-338-3282 Ext. 54229; or find us online at **www.petersons.com.**

ISSN 1093-8443
ISBN: 978-0-7689-4095-4

Printed in the United States of America

10 9 8 7 6 5 4 3 2 1   19 18 17

Fifty-first Edition

CONTENTS

iv www.petersons.com

Peterson's Graduate Programs in the Physical Sciences, Mathematics, Agricultural Sciences, the Environment & Natural Resources 2017

A Note from the Peterson's Editors

The six volumes of Peterson's *Graduate and Professional Programs*, the only annually updated reference work of its kind, provide wide-ranging information on the graduate and professional programs offered by accredited colleges and universities in the United States, U.S. territories, and Canada and by those institutions outside the United States that are accredited by U.S. accrediting bodies. More than 44,000 individual academic and professional programs at more than 2,300 institutions are listed. Peterson's *Graduate and Professional Programs* have been used for more than fifty years by prospective graduate and professional students, placement counselors, faculty advisers, and all others interested in postbaccalaureate education.

Graduate & Professional Programs: An Overview contains information on institutions as a whole, while the other books in the series are devoted to specific academic and professional fields:

- *Graduate Programs in the Biological/Biomedical Sciences & Health-Related Medical Professions*

- *Graduate Programs in Business, Education, Information Studies, Law & Social Work*

- *Graduate Programs in Engineering & Applied Sciences*

- *Graduate Programs in the Humanities, Arts & Social Sciences*

- *Graduate Programs in the Physical Sciences, Mathematics, Agricultural Sciences, the Environment & Natural Resources*

The books may be used individually or as a set. For example, if you have chosen a field of study but do not know what institution you want to attend or if you have a college or university in mind but have not chosen an academic field of study, it is best to begin with the Overview guide.

Graduate & Professional Programs: An Overview presents several directories to help you identify programs of study that might interest you; you can then research those programs further in the other books in the series by using the Directory of Graduate and Professional Programs by Field, which lists 500 fields and gives the names of those institutions that offer graduate degree programs in each.

For geographical or financial reasons, you may be interested in attending a particular institution and will want to know what it has to offer. You should turn to the Directory of Institutions and Their Offerings, which lists the degree programs available at each institution. As in the Directory of Graduate and Professional Programs by Field, the level of degrees offered is also indicated.

All books in the series include advice on graduate education, including topics such as admissions tests, financial aid, and accreditation. **The Graduate Adviser** includes two essays and information about accreditation. The first essay, "The Admissions Process," discusses general admission requirements, admission tests, factors to consider when selecting a graduate school or program, when and how to apply, and how admission decisions are made. Special information for international students and tips for minority students are also included. The second essay, "Financial Support," is an overview of the broad range of support available at the graduate level. Fellowships, scholarships, and grants; assistantships and internships; federal and private loan programs, as well as Federal Work-Study; and the GI bill are detailed. This essay concludes with advice on applying for need-based financial aid. "Accreditation and Accrediting Agencies" gives information on accreditation and its purpose and lists institutional accrediting agencies first and then specialized accrediting agencies relevant to each volume's specific fields of study.

With information on more than 40,000 graduate programs in more than 500 disciplines, Peterson's *Graduate and Professional Programs* give you all the information you need about the programs that are of interest to you in three formats: **Profiles** (capsule summaries of basic information), **Displays** (information that an institution or program wants to emphasize), and **Close-Ups** (written by administrators, with more expansive information than the **Profiles**, emphasizing different aspects of the programs). By using these various formats of program information, coupled with **Appendixes** and **Indexes** covering directories and subject areas for all six books, you will find that these guides provide the most comprehensive, accurate, and up-to-date graduate study information available.

Peterson's publishes a full line of resources with information you need to guide you through the graduate admissions process. Peterson's publications can be found at college libraries and career centers and your local bookstore or library—or visit us on the Web at www.petersons.com.

Colleges and universities will be pleased to know that Peterson's helped you in your selection. Admissions staff members are more than happy to answer questions, address specific problems, and help in any way they can. The editors at Peterson's wish you great success in your graduate program search!

THE GRADUATE ADVISER

The Admissions Process

Generalizations about graduate admissions practices are not always helpful because each institution has its own set of guidelines and procedures. Nevertheless, some broad statements can be made about the admissions process that may help you plan your strategy.

Factors Involved in Selecting a Graduate School or Program

Selecting a graduate school and a specific program of study is a complex matter. Quality of the faculty; program and course offerings; the nature, size, and location of the institution; admission requirements; cost; and the availability of financial assistance are among the many factors that affect one's choice of institution. Other considerations are job placement and achievements of the program's graduates and the institution's resources, such as libraries, laboratories, and computer facilities. If you are to make the best possible choice, you need to learn as much as you can about the schools and programs you are considering before you apply.

The following steps may help you narrow your choices.

- Talk to alumni of the programs or institutions you are considering to get their impressions of how well they were prepared for work in their fields of study.
- Remember that graduate school requirements change, so be sure to get the most up-to-date information possible.
- Talk to department faculty members and the graduate adviser at your undergraduate institution. They often have information about programs of study at other institutions.
- Visit the websites of the graduate schools in which you are interested to request a graduate catalog. Contact the department chair in your chosen field of study for additional information about the department and the field.
- Visit as many campuses as possible. Call ahead for an appointment with the graduate adviser in your field of interest and be sure to check out the facilities and talk to students.

General Requirements

Graduate schools and departments have requirements that applicants for admission must meet. Typically, these requirements include undergraduate transcripts (which provide information about undergraduate grade point average and course work applied toward a major), admission test scores, and letters of recommendation. Most graduate programs also ask for an essay or personal statement that describes your personal reasons for seeking graduate study. In some fields, such as art and music, portfolios or auditions may be required in addition to other evidence of talent. Some institutions require that the applicant have an undergraduate degree in the same subject as the intended graduate major.

Most institutions evaluate each applicant on the basis of the applicant's total record, and the weight accorded any given factor varies widely from institution to institution and from program to program.

The Application Process

You should begin the application process at least one year before you expect to begin your graduate study. Find out the application deadline for each institution (many are provided in the **Profile** section of this guide). Go to the institution's website and find out if you can apply online. If not, request a paper application form. Fill out this form thoroughly and neatly. Assume that the school needs all the information it is requesting and that the admissions officer will be sensitive to the neatness and overall quality of what you submit. Do not supply more information than the school requires.

The institution may ask at least one question that will require a three- or four-paragraph answer. Compose your response on the assumption that the admissions officer is interested in both what you think and how you express yourself. Keep your statement brief and to the point, but, at the same time, include all pertinent information about your past experiences and your educational goals. Individual statements vary greatly in style and content, which helps admissions officers differentiate among applicants. Many graduate departments give considerable weight to the statement in making their admissions decisions, so be sure to take the time to prepare a thoughtful and concise statement.

If recommendations are a part of the admissions requirements, carefully choose the individuals you ask to write them. It is generally best to ask current or former professors to write the recommendations, provided they are able to attest to your intellectual ability and motivation for doing the work required of a graduate student. It is advisable to provide stamped, preaddressed envelopes to people being asked to submit recommendations on your behalf.

Completed applications, including references, transcripts, and admission test scores, should be received at the institution by the specified date.

Be advised that institutions do not usually make admissions decisions until all materials have been received. Enclose a self-addressed postcard with your application, requesting confirmation of receipt. Allow at least ten days for the return of the postcard before making further inquiries.

If you plan to apply for financial support, it is imperative that you file your application early.

ADMISSION TESTS

The major testing program used in graduate admissions is the Graduate Record Examinations (GRE®) testing program, sponsored by the GRE Board and administered by Educational Testing Service, Princeton, New Jersey.

The Graduate Record Examinations testing program consists of a General Test and eight Subject Tests. The General Test measures critical thinking, verbal reasoning, quantitative reasoning, and analytical writing skills. It is offered as an Internet-based test (iBT) in the United States, Canada, and many other countries.

The GRE® revised General Test's questions were designed to reflect the kind of thinking that students need to do in graduate or business school and demonstrate that students are indeed ready for graduate-level work.

- **Verbal Reasoning**—Measures ability to analyze and evaluate written material and synthesize information obtained from it, analyze relationships among component parts of sentences, and recognize relationships among words and concepts.
- **Quantitative Reasoning**—Measures problem-solving ability, focusing on basic concepts of arithmetic, algebra, geometry, and data analysis.
- **Analytical Writing**—Measures critical thinking and analytical writing skills, specifically the ability to articulate and support complex ideas clearly and effectively.

The computer-delivered GRE® revised General Test is offered year-round at Prometric™ test centers and on specific dates at testing locations outside of the Prometric test center network. Appointments are scheduled on a first-come, first-served basis. The GRE® revised General Test is also offered as a paper-based test three times a year in areas where computer-based testing is not available.

You can take the computer-delivered GRE® revised General Test once every twenty-one days, up to five times within any continuous rolling twelve-month period (365 days)—even if you canceled your

Peterson's Graduate Programs in the Physical Sciences, Mathematics, Agricultural Sciences, the Environment & Natural Resources 2017

www.petersons.com   **3**

scores on a previously taken test. You may take the paper-delivered GRE® revised General Test as often as it is offered.

Three scores are reported on the revised General Test:

1. A **Verbal Reasoning score** is reported on a 130–170 score scale, in 1-point increments.

2. A **Quantitative Reasoning score** is reported on a 130–170 score scale, in 1-point increments.

3. An **Analytical Writing score** is reported on a 0–6 score level, in half-point increments.

The GRE® Subject Tests measure achievement and assume undergraduate majors or extensive background in the following eight disciplines:

- Biochemistry, Cell and Molecular Biology
- Biology
- Chemistry
- Computer Science
- Literature in English
- Mathematics
- Physics
- Psychology

The Subject Tests are available three times per year as paper-based administrations around the world. Testing time is approximately 2 hours and 50 minutes. You can obtain more information about the GRE® by visiting the ETS website at www.ets.org or consulting the *GRE® Information and Registration Bulletin*. The *Bulletin* can be obtained at many undergraduate colleges. You can also download it from the ETS website or obtain it by contacting Graduate Record Examinations, Educational Testing Service, P.O. Box 6000, Princeton, NJ 08541-6000; phone: 609-771-7670.

If you expect to apply for admission to a program that requires any of the GRE® tests, you should select a test date well in advance of the application deadline. Scores on the computer-based General Test are reported within ten to fifteen days; scores on the paper-based Subject Tests are reported within six weeks.

Another testing program, the Miller Analogies Test® (MAT®), is administered at more than 500 Controlled Testing Centers, licensed by Harcourt Assessment, Inc., in the United States, Canada, and other countries. The MAT® computer-based test is now available. Testing time is 60 minutes. The test consists of 120 partial analogies. You can obtain the *Candidate Information Booklet,* which contains a list of test centers and instructions for taking the test, from http://www.milleranalogies.com or by calling 800-328-5999 (toll-free).

Check the specific requirements of the programs to which you are applying.

How Admission Decisions Are Made

The program you apply to is directly involved in the admissions process. Although the final decision is usually made by the graduate dean (or an associate) or the faculty admissions committee, recommendations from faculty members in your intended field are important. At some institutions, an interview is incorporated into the decision process.

A Special Note for International Students

In addition to the steps already described, there are some special considerations for international students who intend to apply for graduate study in the United States. All graduate schools require an indication of competence in English. The purpose of the Test of English as a Foreign Language (TOEFL®) is to evaluate the English proficiency of people who are nonnative speakers of English and want to study at colleges and universities where English is the language of instruction. The TOEFL® is administered by Educational Testing Service (ETS) under the general direction of a policy board established by the College Board and the Graduate Record Examinations Board.

The TOEFL® iBT assesses the four basic language skills: listening, reading, writing, and speaking. It was administered for the first time in September 2005, and ETS continues to introduce the TOEFL® iBT in selected cities. The Internet-based test is administered at secure, official test centers. The testing time is approximately 4 hours. Because the TOEFL® iBT includes a speaking section, the Test of Spoken English (TSE) is no longer needed.

The TOEFL® is also offered in the paper-based format in areas of the world where Internet-based testing is not available. The paper-based TOEFL® consists of three sections—listening comprehension, structure and written expression, and reading comprehension. The testing time is approximately 3 hours. The Test of Written English (TWE®) is also given. The TWE® is a 30-minute essay that measures the examinee's ability to compose in English. Examinees receive a TWE® score separate from their TOEFL® score. The *Information Bulletin* contains information on local fees and registration procedures.

The TOEFL® paper-based test (TOEFL® PBT) began being phased out in mid-2012. For those who may have taken the TOEFL® PBT, scores remain valid for two years after the test date. The Test of Written English (TWE®) is also given. The TWE® is a 30-minute essay that measures the examinee's ability to compose in English. Examinees receive a TWE® score separate from their TOEFL® score. The Information Bulletin contains information on local fees and registration procedures.

Additional information and registration materials are available from TOEFL® Services, Educational Testing Service, P.O. Box 6151, Princeton, New Jersey 08541-6151. Phone: 609-771-7100. Website: www.toefl.org.

International students should apply especially early because of the number of steps required to complete the admissions process. Furthermore, many United States graduate schools have a limited number of spaces for international students, and many more students apply than the schools can accommodate.

International students may find financial assistance from institutions very limited. The U.S. government requires international applicants to submit a certification of support, which is a statement attesting to the applicant's financial resources. In addition, international students *must* have health insurance coverage.

Tips for Minority Students

Indicators of a university's values in terms of diversity are found both in its recruitment programs and its resources directed to student success. Important questions: Does the institution vigorously recruit minorities for its graduate programs? Is there funding available to help with the costs associated with visiting the school? Are minorities represented in the institution's brochures or website or on their faculty rolls? What campus-based resources or services (including assistance in locating housing or career counseling and placement) are available? Is funding available to members of underrepresented groups?

At the program level, it is particularly important for minority students to investigate the "climate" of a program under consideration. How many minority students are enrolled and how many have graduated? What opportunities are there to work with diverse faculty and mentors whose research interests match yours? How are conflicts resolved or concerns addressed? How interested are faculty in building strong and supportive relations with students? "Climate" concerns should be addressed by posing questions to various individuals, including faculty members, current students, and alumni.

Information is also available through various organizations, such as the Hispanic Association of Colleges & Universities (HACU), and publications such as *Diverse Issues in Higher Education* and *Hispanic Outlook* magazine. There are also books devoted to this topic, such as *The Multicultural Student's Guide to Colleges* by Robert Mitchell.

4 www.petersons.com

Peterson's Graduate Programs in the Physical Sciences, Mathematics, Agricultural Sciences, the Environment & Natural Resources 2017

Financial Support

The range of financial support at the graduate level is very broad. The following descriptions will give you a general idea of what you might expect and what will be expected of you as a financial support recipient.

Fellowships, Scholarships, and Grants

These are usually outright awards of a few hundred to many thousands of dollars with no service to the institution required in return. Fellowships and scholarships are usually awarded on the basis of merit and are highly competitive. Grants are made on the basis of financial need or special talent in a field of study. Many fellowships, scholarships, and grants not only cover tuition, fees, and supplies but also include stipends for living expenses with allowances for dependents. However, the terms of each should be examined because some do not permit recipients to supplement their income with outside work. Fellowships, scholarships, and grants may vary in the number of years for which they are awarded.

In addition to the availability of these funds at the university or program level, many excellent fellowship programs are available at the national level and may be applied for before and during enrollment in a graduate program. A listing of many of these programs can be found at the Council of Graduate Schools' website: http://www.cgsnet.org. There is a wealth of information in the "Programs" and "Awards" sections.

Assistantships and Internships

Many graduate students receive financial support through assistantships, particularly involving teaching or research duties. It is important to recognize that such appointments should not be viewed simply as employment relationships but rather should constitute an integral and important part of a student's graduate education. As such, the appointments should be accompanied by strong faculty mentoring and increasingly responsible apprenticeship experiences. The specific nature of these appointments in a given program should be considered in selecting that graduate program.

TEACHING ASSISTANTSHIPS

These usually provide a salary and full or partial tuition remission and may also provide health benefits. Unlike fellowships, scholarships, and grants, which require no service to the institution, teaching assistantships require recipients to provide the institution with a specific amount of undergraduate teaching, ideally related to the student's field of study. Some teaching assistants are limited to grading papers, compiling bibliographies, taking notes, or monitoring laboratories. At some graduate schools, teaching assistants must carry lighter course loads than regular full-time students.

RESEARCH ASSISTANTSHIPS

These are very similar to teaching assistantships in the manner in which financial assistance is provided. The difference is that recipients are given basic research assignments in their disciplines rather than teaching responsibilities. The work required is normally related to the student's field of study; in most instances, the assistantship supports the student's thesis or dissertation research.

ADMINISTRATIVE INTERNSHIPS

These are similar to assistantships in application of financial assistance funds, but the student is given an assignment on a part-time basis, usually as a special assistant with one of the university's administrative offices. The assignment may not necessarily be directly related to the recipient's discipline.

RESIDENCE HALL AND COUNSELING ASSISTANTSHIPS

These assistantships are frequently assigned to graduate students in psychology, counseling, and social work, but they may be offered to students in other disciplines, especially if the student has worked in this capacity during his or her undergraduate years. Duties can vary from being available in a dean's office for a specific number of hours for consultation with undergraduates to living in campus residences and being responsible for both counseling and administrative tasks or advising student activity groups. Residence hall assistantships often include a room and board allowance and, in some cases, tuition assistance and stipends. Contact the Housing and Student Life Office for more information.

Health Insurance

The availability and affordability of health insurance is an important issue and one that should be considered in an applicant's choice of institution and program. While often included with assistantships and fellowships, this is not always the case and, even if provided, the benefits may be limited. It is important to note that the U.S. government requires international students to have health insurance.

The GI Bill

This provides financial assistance for students who are veterans of the United States armed forces. If you are a veteran, contact your local Veterans Administration office to determine your eligibility and to get full details about benefits. There are a number of programs that offer educational benefits to current military enlistees. Some states have tuition assistance programs for members of the National Guard. Contact the VA office at the college for more information.

Federal Work-Study Program (FWS)

Employment is another way some students finance their graduate studies. The federally funded Federal Work-Study Program provides eligible students with employment opportunities, usually in public and private nonprofit organizations. Federal funds pay up to 75 percent of the wages, with the remainder paid by the employing agency. FWS is available to graduate students who demonstrate financial need. Not all schools have these funds, and some only award them to undergraduates. Each school sets its application deadline and workstudy earnings limits. Wages vary and are related to the type of work done. You must file the Free Application for Federal Student Aid (FAFSA) to be eligible for this program.

Loans

Many graduate students borrow to finance their graduate programs when other sources of assistance (which do not have to be repaid) prove insufficient. You should always read and understand the terms of any loan program before submitting your application.

FEDERAL DIRECT LOANS

Federal Direct Loans. The Federal Direct Loan Program offers a variable-fixed interest rate loan to graduate students with the Department of Education acting as the lender. Students receive a new rate with each new loan, but that rate is fixed for the life of the loan. Beginning with loans made on or after July 1, 2013, the interest rate for loans made each July 1st to June 30th period are determined based on the last 10-year Treasury note auction prior to June 1st of that year, plus an added percentage. The interest rate can be no higher than 9.5%.

Beginning July 1, 2012, the Federal Direct Loan for graduate students is an unsubsidized loan. Under the *unsubsidized* program, the grad borrower pays the interest on the loan from the day proceeds are issued and is responsible for paying interest during all periods. If the borrower chooses not to pay the interest while in school, or during the grace periods, deferment, or forbearance, the interest accrues and will be capitalized.

Graduate students may borrow up to $20,500 per year through the Direct Loan Program, up to a cumulative maximum of $138,500, including undergraduate borrowing. No more than $65,000 of the $138,500 can be from subsidized loans, including loans the grad borrower may have received for periods of enrollment that began before July 1, 2012, or for prior undergraduate borrowing. You may borrow up to the cost of attendance at the school in which you are enrolled or will attend, minus estimated financial assistance from other federal, state, and private sources, up to a maximum of $20,500. Grad borrowers who reach the aggregate loan limit over the course of their education cannot receive additional loans; however, if they repay some of their loans to bring the outstanding balance below the aggregate limit, they could be eligible to borrow again, up to that limit.

For Unsubsidized loans first disbursed on or after July 1, 2015, and before July 1, 2016, the interest rate was 5.84%. For those first disbursed on or after July 1, 2015, and before July 1, 2017, the interest rate is 5.31%.

A fee is deducted from the loan proceeds upon disbursement. Loans with a first disbursement on or after July 1, 2010 but before July 1, 2012, have a borrower origination fee of 1 percent. For loans disbursed after July 1, 2012, these fee deductions no longer apply. The Budget Control Act of 2011, signed into law on August 2, 2011, eliminated Direct Subsidized Loan eligibility for graduate and professional students for periods of enrollment beginning on or after July 1, 2012, and terminated the authority of the Department of Education to offer most repayment incentives to Direct Loan borrowers for loans disbursed on or after July 1, 2012.

Under the *subsidized* Federal Direct Loan Program, repayment begins six months after your last date of enrollment on at least a half-time basis. Under the *unsubsidized* program, repayment of interest begins within thirty days from disbursement of the loan proceeds, and repayment of the principal begins six months after your last enrollment on at least a half-time basis. Some borrowers may choose to defer interest payments while they are in school. The accrued interest is added to the loan balance when the borrower begins repayment. There are several repayment options.

Federal Perkins Loans. The Federal Perkins Loan is available to students demonstrating financial need and is administered directly by the school. Not all schools have these funds, and some may award them to undergraduates only. Eligibility is determined from the information you provide on the FAFSA. The school will notify you of your eligibility.

Eligible graduate students may borrow up to $8,000 per year, up to a maximum of $60,000, including undergraduate borrowing (even if your previous Perkins Loans have been repaid). The interest rate for Federal Perkins Loans is 5 percent, and no interest accrues while you remain in school at least half-time. Students who are attending less than half-time need to check with their school to determine the length of their grace period. There are no guarantee, loan, or disbursement fees. Repayment begins nine months after your last date of enrollment on at least a half-time basis and may extend over a maximum of ten years with no prepayment penalty.

Federal Direct Graduate PLUS Loans. Effective July 1, 2006, graduate and professional students are eligible for Graduate PLUS loans. This program allows students to borrow up to the cost of attendance, less any other aid received. These loans have a fixed interest rate, and interest begins to accrue at the time of disbursement. Beginning with loans made on or after July 1, 2013, the interest rate for loans made each July 1st to June 30th period are determined based on the last 10-year Treasury note auction prior to June 1st of that year. The interest rate can be no higher than 10.5%. The PLUS loans do involve a credit check; a PLUS borrower may obtain a loan with a cosigner if his or her credit is not good enough. Grad PLUS loans may be deferred while a student is in school and for the six months following a drop below half-time

enrollment. For more information, you should contact a representative in your college's financial aid office.

Deferring Your Federal Loan Repayments. If you borrowed under the Federal Direct Loan Program, Federal Direct PLUS Loan Program, or the Federal Perkins Loan Program for previous undergraduate or graduate study, your payments may be deferred when you return to graduate school, depending on when you borrowed and under which program.

There are other deferment options available if you are temporarily unable to repay your loan. Information about these deferments is provided at your entrance and exit interviews. If you believe you are eligible for a deferment of your loan payments, you must contact your lender or loan servicer to request a deferment. The deferment must be filed prior to the time your payment is due, and it must be re-filed when it expires if you remain eligible for deferment at that time.

SUPPLEMENTAL (PRIVATE) LOANS

Many lending institutions offer supplemental loan programs and other financing plans, such as the ones described here, to students seeking additional assistance in meeting their education expenses. Some loan programs target all types of graduate students; others are designed specifically for business, law, or medical students. In addition, you can use private loans not specifically designed for education to help finance your graduate degree.

If you are considering borrowing through a supplemental or private loan program, you should carefully consider the terms and be sure to read the fine print. Check with the program sponsor for the most current terms that will be applicable to the amounts you intend to borrow for graduate study. Most supplemental loan programs for graduate study offer unsubsidized, credit-based loans. In general, a credit-ready borrower is one who has a satisfactory credit history or no credit history at all. A creditworthy borrower generally must pass a credit test to be eligible to borrow or act as a cosigner for the loan funds.

Many supplemental loan programs have minimum and maximum annual loan limits. Some offer amounts equal to the cost of attendance minus any other aid you will receive for graduate study. If you are planning to borrow for several years of graduate study, consider whether there is a cumulative or aggregate limit on the amount you may borrow. Often this cumulative or aggregate limit will include any amounts you borrowed and have not repaid for undergraduate or previous graduate study.

The combination of the annual interest rate, loan fees, and the repayment terms you choose will determine how much you will repay over time. Compare these features in combination before you decide which loan program to use. Some loans offer interest rates that are adjusted monthly, quarterly, or annually. Some offer interest rates that are lower during the in-school, grace, and deferment periods and then increase when you begin repayment. Some programs include a loan origination fee, which is usually deducted from the principal amount you receive when the loan is disbursed and must be repaid along with the interest and other principal when you graduate, withdraw from school, or drop below half-time study. Sometimes the loan fees are reduced if you borrow with a qualified cosigner. Some programs allow you to defer interest and/or principal payments while you are enrolled in graduate school. Many programs allow you to capitalize your interest payments; the interest due on your loan is added to the outstanding balance of your loan, so you don't have to repay immediately, but this increases the amount you owe. Other programs allow you to pay the interest as you go, which reduces the amount you later have to repay. The private loan market is very competitive, and your financial aid office can help you evaluate these programs.

Applying for Need-Based Financial Aid

Schools that award federal and institutional financial assistance based on need will require you to complete the FAFSA and, in some cases, an institutional financial aid application.

6 www.petersons.com

Peterson's Graduate Programs in the Physical Sciences, Mathematics, Agricultural Sciences, the Environment & Natural Resources 2017

If you are applying for federal student assistance, you **must** complete the FAFSA. A service of the U.S. Department of Education, the FAFSA is free to all applicants. Most applicants apply online at www.fafsa.ed.gov. Paper applications are available at the financial aid office of your local college.

After your FAFSA information has been processed, you will receive a Student Aid Report (SAR). If you provided an e-mail address on the FAFSA, this will be sent to you electronically; otherwise, it will be mailed to your home address.

Follow the instructions on the SAR if you need to correct information reported on your original application. If your situation changes after you file your FAFSA, contact your financial aid officer to discuss amending your information. You can also appeal your financial aid award if you have extenuating circumstances.

If you would like more information on federal student financial aid, visit the FAFSA website or download the most recent version of *Funding Education Beyond High School: The Guide to Federal Student Aid* at http://studentaid.ed.gov/students/publications/student_guide/index.html. This guide is also available in Spanish.

The U.S. Department of Education also has a toll-free number for questions concerning federal student aid programs. The number is 1-800-4-FED AID (1-800-433-3243). If you are hearing impaired, call toll-free, 1-800-730-8913.

Summary

Remember that these are generalized statements about financial assistance at the graduate level. Because each institution allots its aid differently, you should communicate directly with the school and the specific department of interest to you. It is not unusual, for example, to find that an endowment vested within a specific department supports one or more fellowships. You may fit its requirements and specifications precisely.

Peterson's Graduate Programs in the Physical Sciences, Mathematics, Agricultural Sciences, the Environment & Natural Resources 2017

www.petersons.com **7**

Accreditation and Accrediting Agencies

Colleges and universities in the United States, and their individual academic and professional programs, are accredited by nongovernmental agencies concerned with monitoring the quality of education in this country. Agencies with both regional and national jurisdictions grant accreditation to institutions as a whole, while specialized bodies acting on a nationwide basis—often national professional associations—grant accreditation to departments and programs in specific fields.

Institutional and specialized accrediting agencies share the same basic concerns: the purpose an academic unit—whether university or program—has set for itself and how well it fulfills that purpose, the adequacy of its financial and other resources, the quality of its academic offerings, and the level of services it provides. Agencies that grant institutional accreditation take a broader view, of course, and examine university-wide or college-wide services with which a specialized agency may not concern itself.

Both types of agencies follow the same general procedures when considering an application for accreditation. The academic unit prepares a self-evaluation, focusing on the concerns mentioned above and usually including an assessment of both its strengths and weaknesses; a team of representatives of the accrediting body reviews this evaluation, visits the campus, and makes its own report; and finally, the accrediting body makes a decision on the application. Often, even when accreditation is granted, the agency makes a recommendation regarding how the institution or program can improve. All institutions and programs are also reviewed every few years to determine whether they continue to meet established standards; if they do not, they may lose their accreditation.

Accrediting agencies themselves are reviewed and evaluated periodically by the U.S. Department of Education and the Council for Higher Education Accreditation (CHEA). Recognized agencies adhere to certain standards and practices, and their authority in matters of accreditation is widely accepted in the educational community.

This does not mean, however, that accreditation is a simple matter, either for schools wishing to become accredited or for students deciding where to apply. Indeed, in certain fields the very meaning and methods of accreditation are the subject of a good deal of debate. For their part, those applying to graduate school should be aware of the safeguards provided by regional accreditation, especially in terms of degree acceptance and institutional longevity. Beyond this, applicants should understand the role that specialized accreditation plays in their field, as this varies considerably from one discipline to another. In certain professional fields, it is necessary to have graduated from a program that is accredited in order to be eligible for a license to practice, and in some fields the federal government also makes this a hiring requirement. In other disciplines, however, accreditation is not as essential, and there can be excellent programs that are not accredited. In fact, some programs choose not to seek accreditation, although most do.

Institutions and programs that present themselves for accreditation are sometimes granted the status of candidate for accreditation, or what is known as "preaccreditation." This may happen, for example, when an academic unit is too new to have met all the requirements for accreditation. Such status signifies initial recognition and indicates that the school or program in question is working to fulfill all requirements; it does not, however, guarantee that accreditation will be granted.

Institutional Accrediting Agencies—Regional

MIDDLE STATES ASSOCIATION OF COLLEGES AND SCHOOLS

Accredits institutions in Delaware, District of Columbia, Maryland, New Jersey, New York, Pennsylvania, Puerto Rico, and the Virgin Islands.

Dr. Elizabeth Sibolski, President
Middle States Commission on Higher Education
3624 Market Street, Second Floor West
Philadelphia, Pennsylvania 19104
Phone: 267-284-5000
Fax: 215-662-5501
E-mail: info@msche.org
Website: www.msche.org

NEW ENGLAND ASSOCIATION OF SCHOOLS AND COLLEGES

Accredits institutions in Connecticut, Maine, Massachusetts, New Hampshire, Rhode Island, and Vermont.

Dr. Barbara E. Brittingham, President/Director
Commission on Institutions of Higher Education
3 Burlington Woods Drive, Suite 100
Burlington, Massachusetts 01803-4531
Phone: 855-886-3272 or 781-425-7714
Fax: 781-425-1001
E-mail: cihe@neasc.org
Website: http://cihe.neasc.org

THE HIGHER LEARNING COMMISSION

Accredits institutions in Arizona, Arkansas, Colorado, Illinois, Indiana, Iowa, Kansas, Michigan, Minnesota, Missouri, Nebraska, New Mexico, North Dakota, Ohio, Oklahoma, South Dakota, West Virginia, Wisconsin, and Wyoming.

Dr. Barbara Gellman-Danley, President
The Higher Learning Commission
230 South LaSalle Street, Suite 7-500
Chicago, Illinois 60604-1413
Phone: 800-621-7440 or 312-263-0456
Fax: 312-263-7462
E-mail: info@hlcommission.org
Website: www.hlcommission.org

NORTHWEST COMMISSION ON COLLEGES AND UNIVERSITIES

Accredits institutions in Alaska, Idaho, Montana, Nevada, Oregon, Utah, and Washington.

Dr. Sandra E. Elman, President
8060 165th Avenue, NE, Suite 100
Redmond, Washington 98052
Phone: 425-558-4224
Fax: 425-376-0596
E-mail: selman@nwccu.org
Website: www.nwccu.org

SOUTHERN ASSOCIATION OF COLLEGES AND SCHOOLS

Accredits institutions in Alabama, Florida, Georgia, Kentucky, Louisiana, Mississippi, North Carolina, South Carolina, Tennessee, Texas, and Virginia.

Dr. Belle S. Wheelan, President
Commission on Colleges
1866 Southern Lane
Decatur, Georgia 30033-4097
Phone: 404-679-4500 Ext. 4504
Fax: 404-679-4558
E-mail: questions@sacscoc.org
Website: www.sacscoc.org

WESTERN ASSOCIATION OF SCHOOLS AND COLLEGES

Accredits institutions in California, Guam, and Hawaii.

Dr. Mary Ellen Petrisko, President
Accrediting Commission for Senior Colleges and Universities
985 Atlantic Avenue, Suite 100
Alameda, California 94501
Phone: 510-748-9001
Fax: 510-748-9797
E-mail: wasc@wascsenior.org
Website: http://www.wascsenior.org/

Institutional Accrediting Agencies—Other

ACCREDITING COUNCIL FOR INDEPENDENT COLLEGES AND SCHOOLS
Anthony S. Bieda, Executive in Charge
750 First Street, NE, Suite 980
Washington, DC 20002-4241
Phone: 202-336-6780
Fax: 202-842-2593
E-mail: info@acics.org
Website: www.acics.org

DISTANCE EDUCATION AND ACCREDITING COMMISSION (DEAC)
Accrediting Commission
Leah Matthews, Executive Director
1101 17th Street, NW, Suite 808
Washington, DC 20036-4704
Phone: 202-234-5100
Fax: 202-332-1386
E-mail: info@deac.org
Website: www.deac.org

Specialized Accrediting Agencies

ACUPUNCTURE AND ORIENTAL MEDICINE
Mark S. McKenzie, LAc MsOM DiplOM, Executive Director
Accreditation Commission for Acupuncture and Oriental Medicine
8941 Aztec Drive
Eden Prairie, Minnesota 55347
Phone: 952-212-2434
Fax: 301-313-0912
E-mail: coordinator@acaom.org
Website: www.acaom.org

ALLIED HEALTH
Kathleen Megivern, Executive Director
Commission on Accreditation of Allied Health Education Programs (CAAHEP)
25400 US Hwy 19 North, Suite 158
Clearwater, Florida 33763
Phone: 727-210-2350
Fax: 727-210-2354
E-mail: mail@caahep.org
Website: www.caahep.org

ART AND DESIGN
Karen P. Moynahan, Executive Director
National Association of Schools of Art and Design (NASAD)
Commission on Accreditation
11250 Roger Bacon Drive, Suite 21
Reston, Virginia 20190-5248
Phone: 703-437-0700
Fax: 703-437-6312
E-mail: info@arts-accredit.org
Website: http://nasad.arts-accredit.org

ATHLETIC TRAINING EDUCATION
Micki Cuppett, Executive Director
Commission on Accreditation of Athletic Training Education (CAATE)
6850 Austin Center Blvd., Suite 100
Austin, Texas 78731-3184
Phone: 512-733-9700
E-mail: micki@caate.net
Website: www.caate.net

AUDIOLOGY EDUCATION
Doris Gordon, Executive Director
Accreditation Commission for Audiology Education (ACAE)
11480 Commerce Park Drive, Suite 220
Reston, Virginia 20191
Phone: 202-986-9550
Fax: 202-986-9500
E-mail: info@acaeaccred.org
Website: www.acaeaccred.org

AVIATION
Dr. Gary J. Northam, Executive Director
Aviation Accreditation Board International (AABI)
3410 Skyway Drive
Auburn, Alabama 36830
Phone: 334-844-2431
Fax: 334-844-2432
E-mail: bayenva@auburn.edu
Website: www.aabi.aero

BUSINESS
Robert D. Reid, Executive Vice President and Chief Accreditation Officer
AACSB International—The Association to Advance Collegiate Schools of Business
777 South Harbour Island Boulevard, Suite 750
Tampa, Florida 33602
Phone: 813-769-6500
Fax: 813-769-6559
E-mail: bob@aacsb.edu
Website: www.aacsb.edu

BUSINESS EDUCATION
Dennis N. Gash, President and Chief Executive Officer
International Assembly for Collegiate Business Education (IACBE)
11257 Strang Line Road
Lenexa, Kansas 66215
Phone: 913-631-3009
Fax: 913-631-9154
E-mail:iacbe@iacbe.org
Website: www.iacbe.org

CHIROPRACTIC
Craig S. Little, President
Council on Chiropractic Education (CCE)
Commission on Accreditation
8049 North 85th Way
Scottsdale, Arizona 85258-4321
Phone: 480-443-8877 or 888-443-3506
Fax: 480-483-7333
E-mail: cce@cce-usa.org
Website: www.cce-usa.org

CLINICAL LABORATORY SCIENCES
Dianne M. Cearlock, Ph.D., Chief Executive Officer
National Accrediting Agency for Clinical Laboratory Sciences
5600 North River Road, Suite 720
Rosemont, Illinois 60018-5119
Phone: 773-714-8880 or 847-939-3597
Fax: 773-714-8886
E-mail: info@naacls.org
Website: www.naacls.org

CLINICAL PASTORAL EDUCATION
Trace Haythorn, Executive Director
Association for Clinical Pastoral Education, Inc.
1549 Clairmont Road, Suite 103
Decatur, Georgia 30033-4611
Phone: 404-320-1472
Fax: 404-320-0849
E-mail: acpe@acpe.edu
Website: www.acpe.edu

10 www.petersons.com

Peterson's Graduate Programs in the Physical Sciences, Mathematics, Agricultural Sciences, the Environment & Natural Resources 2017

DANCE
Karen P. Moynahan, Executive Director
National Association of Schools of Dance (NASD)
Commission on Accreditation
11250 Roger Bacon Drive, Suite 21
Reston, Virginia 20190-5248
Phone: 703-437-0700
Fax: 703-437-6312
E-mail: info@arts-accredit.org
Website: http://nasd.arts-accredit.org

DENTISTRY
Dr. Sherin Tooks, Director
Commission on Dental Accreditation
American Dental Association
211 East Chicago Avenue, Suite 1900
Chicago, Illinois 60611
Phone: 312-440-4643 or 800-621-8099
E-mail: accreditation@ada.org
Website: www.ada.org

DIETETICS AND NUTRITION
Mary B. Gregoire, Ph.D., Executive Director; RD, FADA, FAND
Academy of Nutrition and Dietetics
Accreditation Council for Education in Nutrition and Dietetics (ACEND)
120 South Riverside Plaza, Suite 2000
Chicago, Illinois 60606-6995
Phone: 800-877-1600 Ext. 5400 or 312-899-0040
Fax: 312-899-4817
E-mail: acend@eatright.org
Website: www.eatright.org/ACEND

EDUCATION PREPARATION
Christopher Koch, President
Council for the Accreditation of Education Preparation (CAEP)
1140 19th Street NW, Suite 400
Washington, DC 20036
Phone: 202-223-0077
Fax: 202-296-6620
E-mail: caep@caepnet.org
Website: www.caepnet.org

ENGINEERING
Michael Milligan, Ph.D., PE, Executive Director
Accreditation Board for Engineering and Technology, Inc. (ABET)
415 North Charles Street
Baltimore, Maryland 21201
Phone: 410-347-7700
E-mail: accreditation@abet.org
Website: www.abet.org

FORENSIC SCIENCES
Nancy J. Jackson, Director of Development and Accreditation
American Academy of Forensic Sciences (AAFS)
Forensic Science Education Program Accreditation Commission (FEPAC)
410 North 21st Street
Colorado Springs, Colorado 80904
Phone: 719-636-1100
Fax: 719-636-1993
E-mail: njackson@aafs.org
Website: www.fepac-edu.org

FORESTRY
Carol L. Redelsheimer
Director of Science and Education
Society of American Foresters
5400 Grosvenor Lane
Bethesda, Maryland 20814-2198
Phone: 301-897-8720 or 866-897-8720
Fax: 301-897-3690
E-mail: redelsheimerc@safnet.org
Website: www.safnet.org

HEALTHCARE MANAGEMENT
Commission on Accreditation of Healthcare Management Education (CAHME)
Anthony Stanowski, President and CEO
1700 Rockville Pike
Suite 400
Rockville, Maryland 20852
Phone: 301-998-6101
E-mail: info@cahme.org
Website: www.cahme.org

HEALTH INFORMATICS AND HEALTH MANAGEMENT
Claire Dixon-Lee, Executive Director
Commission on Accreditation for Health Informatics and Information Management Education (CAHIIM)
233 North Michigan Avenue, 21st Floor
Chicago, Illinois 60601-5800
Phone: 312-233-1100
Fax: 312-233-1948
E-mail:E-mail: claire.dixon-lee@cahiim.org
Website: www.cahiim.org

HUMAN SERVICE EDUCATION
Dr. Elaine Green, President
Council for Standards in Human Service Education (CSHSE)
3337 Duke Street
Alexandria, Virginia 22314
Phone: 571-257-3959
E-mail: info@cshse.org
Web: http://www.cshse.org

INTERIOR DESIGN
Holly Mattson, Executive Director
Council for Interior Design Accreditation
206 Grandview Avenue, Suite 350
Grand Rapids, Michigan 49503-4014
Phone: 616-458-0400
Fax: 616-458-0460
E-mail: info@accredit-id.org
Website: www.accredit-id.org

JOURNALISM AND MASS COMMUNICATIONS
Susanne Shaw, Executive Director
Accrediting Council on Education in Journalism and Mass Communications (ACEJMC)
School of Journalism
Stauffer-Flint Hall
University of Kansas
1435 Jayhawk Boulevard
Lawrence, Kansas 66045-7575
Phone: 785-864-3973
Fax: 785-864-5225
E-mail: sshaw@ku.edu
Website: http://www2.ku.edu/~acejmc/

LANDSCAPE ARCHITECTURE
Kristopher D. Pritchard, Executive Director
Landscape Architectural Accreditation Board (LAAB)
American Society of Landscape Architects (ASLA)
636 Eye Street, NW
Washington, DC 20001-3736
Phone: 202-216-2359
Fax: 202-898-1185
E-mail: info@asla.org
Website: www.asla.org

Peterson's Graduate Programs in the Physical Sciences, Mathematics, Agricultural Sciences, the Environment & Natural Resources 2017

www.petersons.com   **11**

LAW
Barry Currier, Managing Director of Accreditation & Legal Education
American Bar Association
321 North Clark Street, 21st Floor
Chicago, Illinois 60654
Phone: 312-988-6738
Fax: 312-988-5681
E-mail: legaled@americanbar.org
Website: http://www.americanbar.org/groups/legal_education/
    resources/accreditation.html

LIBRARY
Karen O'Brien, Director
Office for Accreditation
American Library Association
50 East Huron Street
Chicago, Illinois 60611-2795
Phone: 312-280-2432
Fax: 312-280-2433
E-mail: accred@ala.org
Website: www.ala.org/accreditation/

MARRIAGE AND FAMILY THERAPY
Tanya A. Tamarkin, Director of Educational Affairs
Commission on Accreditation for Marriage and Family Therapy
    Education (COAMFTE)
American Association for Marriage and Family Therapy
112 South Alfred Street
Alexandria, Virginia 22314-3061
Phone: 703-838-9808
Fax: 703-838-9805
E-mail: coa@aamft.org
Website: www.aamft.org

MEDICAL ILLUSTRATION
Kathleen Megivern, Executive Director
Commission on Accreditation of Allied Health Education Programs
    (CAAHEP)
1361 Park Street
Clearwater, Florida 33756
Phone: 727-210-2350
Fax: 727-210-2354
E-mail: mail@caahep.org
Website: www.caahep.org

MEDICINE
Liaison Committee on Medical Education (LCME)
Robert B. Hash, M.D., LCME Secretary
American Medical Association
Council on Medical Education
330 North Wabash Avenue, Suite 39300
Chicago, Illinois 60611-5885
Phone: 312-464-4933
E-mail: lcme@aamc.org
Website: www.ama-assn.org

Liaison Committee on Medical Education (LCME)
Heather Lent, M.A., Director
Accreditation Services
Association of American Medical Colleges
655 K Street, NW
Washington, DC 20001-2399
Phone: 202-828-0596
E-mail: lcme@aamc.org
Website: www.lcme.org

MUSIC
Karen P. Moynahan, Executive Director
National Association of Schools of Music (NASM)
Commission on Accreditation
11250 Roger Bacon Drive, Suite 21
Reston, Virginia 20190-5248
Phone: 703-437-0700
Fax: 703-437-6312
E-mail: info@arts-accredit.org
Website: http://nasm.arts-accredit.org/

NATUROPATHIC MEDICINE
Daniel Seitz, J.D., Ed.D., Executive Director
Council on Naturopathic Medical Education
P.O. Box 178
Great Barrington, Massachusetts 01230
Phone: 413-528-8877
E-mail: www.cnme.org/contact.html
Website: www.cnme.org

NURSE ANESTHESIA
Francis R.Gerbasi, Ph.D., CRNA, COA Executive Director
Council on Accreditation of Nurse Anesthesia Educational Programs
    (CoA-NAEP)
American Association of Nurse Anesthetists
222 South Prospect Avenue, Suite 304
Park Ridge, Illinois 60068-4010
Phone: 847-655-1160
Fax: 847-692-7137
E-mail: accreditation@coa.us.com
Website: http://home.coa.us.com

NURSE EDUCATION
Jennifer L. Butlin, Executive Director
Commission on Collegiate Nursing Education (CCNE)
One Dupont Circle, NW, Suite 530
Washington, DC 20036-1120
Phone: 202-887-6791
Fax: 202-887-8476
E-mail: jbutlin@aacn.nche.edu
Website: www.aacn.nche.edu/accreditation

Marsal P. Stoll, Chief Executive Officer
Accreditation Commission for Education in Nursing (ACEN)
3343 Peachtree Road, NE, Suite 850
Atlanta, Georgia 30326
Phone: 404-975-5000
Fax: 404-975-5020
E-mail: mstoll@acenursing.org
Website: www.acenursing.org

NURSE MIDWIFERY
Heather L. Maurer, M.A., Executive Director
Accreditation Commission for Midwifery Education (ACME)
American College of Nurse-Midwives
8403 Colesville Road, Suite 1550
Silver Spring, Maryland 20910
Phone: 240-485-1800
Fax: 240-485-1818
E-mail: info@acnm.org
Website: www.midwife.org/Program-Accreditation

NURSE PRACTITIONER
Gay Johnson, CEO
National Association of Nurse Practitioners in Women's Health
Council on Accreditation
505 C Street, NE
Washington, DC 20002
Phone: 202-543-9693 Ext. 1
Fax: 202-543-9858
E-mail: info@npwh.org
Website: www.npwh.org

12 www.petersons.com

*Peterson's Graduate Programs in the Physical Sciences, Mathematics,
Agricultural Sciences, the Environment & Natural Resources 2017*

NURSING
Marsal P. Stoll, Chief Executive Director
Accreditation Commission for Education in Nursing (ACEN)
3343 Peachtree Road, NE, Suite 850
Atlanta, Georgia 30326
Phone: 404-975-5000
Fax: 404-975-5020
E-mail: info@acenursing.org
Website: www.acenursing.org

OCCUPATIONAL THERAPY
Heather Stagliano, DHSc, OTR/L, Executive Director
The American Occupational Therapy Association, Inc.
4720 Montgomery Lane, Suite 200
Bethesda, Maryland 20814-3449
Phone: 301-652-6611 Ext. 2682
TDD: 800-377-8555
Fax: 240-762-5150
E-mail: accred@aota.org
Website: www.aoteonline.org

OPTOMETRY
Joyce L. Urbeck, Administrative Director
Accreditation Council on Optometric Education (ACOE)
American Optometric Association
243 North Lindbergh Boulevard
St. Louis, Missouri 63141-7881
Phone: 314-991-4100, Ext. 4246
Fax: 314-991-4101
E-mail: accredit@aoa.org
Website: www.theacoe.org

OSTEOPATHIC MEDICINE
Director, Department of Accreditation
Commission on Osteopathic College Accreditation (COCA)
American Osteopathic Association
142 East Ontario Street
Chicago, Illinois 60611
Phone: 312-202-8048
Fax: 312-202-8202
E-mail: predoc@osteopathic.org
Website: www.aoacoca.org

PHARMACY
Peter H. Vlasses, PharmD, Executive Director
Accreditation Council for Pharmacy Education
135 South LaSalle Street, Suite 4100
Chicago, Illinois 60603-4810
Phone: 312-664-3575
Fax: 312-664-4652
E-mail: csinfo@acpe-accredit.org
Website: www.acpe-accredit.org

PHYSICAL THERAPY
Sandra Wise, Senior Director
Commission on Accreditation in Physical Therapy Education (CAPTE)
American Physical Therapy Association (APTA)
1111 North Fairfax Street
Alexandria, Virginia 22314-1488
Phone: 703-706-3245
Fax: 703-706-3387
E-mail: accreditation@apta.org
Website: www.capteonline.org

PHYSICIAN ASSISTANT STUDIES
Sharon L. Luke, Executive Director
Accredittion Review Commission on Education for the Physician
    Assistant, Inc. (ARC-PA)
12000 Findley Road, Suite 150
Johns Creek, Georgia 30097
Phone: 770-476-1224
Fax: 770-476-1738
E-mail: arc-pa@arc-pa.org
Website: www.arc-pa.org

PLANNING
Ms. Shonagh Merits, Executive Director
American Institute of Certified Planners/Association of Collegiate
    Schools of Planning/American Planning Association
Planning Accreditation Board (PAB)
2334 West Lawrence Avenue, Suite 209
Chicago, Illinois 60625
Phone: 773-334-7200
E-mail: smerits@planningaccreditationboard.org
Website: www.planningaccreditationboard.org

PODIATRIC MEDICINE
Alan R. Tinkleman, M.P.A., Executive Director
Council on Podiatric Medical Education (CPME)
American Podiatric Medical Association (APMA)
9312 Old Georgetown Road
Bethesda, Maryland 20814-1621
Phone: 301-581-9200
Fax: 301-571-4903
Website: www.cpme.org

PSYCHOLOGY AND COUNSELING
Jacqueline Remondet Wall, CEO of the Accrediting Unit,
Office of Program Consultation and Accreditation
American Psychological Association
750 First Street, NE
Washington, DC 20002-4202
Phone: 202-336-5979 or 800-374-2721
TDD/TTY: 202-336-6123
Fax: 202-336-5978
E-mail: apaaccred@apa.org
Website: www.apa.org/ed/accreditation

Carol L. Bobby, Ph.D., Executive Director
Council for Accreditation of Counseling and Related Educational
    Programs (CACREP)
1001 North Fairfax Street, Suite 510
Alexandria, Virginia 22314
Phone: 703-535-5990
Fax: 703-739-6209
E-mail: cacrep@cacrep.org
Website: www.cacrep.org

Richard M. McFall, Executive Director
Psychological Clinical Science Accreditation System (PCSAS)
1101 East Tenth Street
IU Psychology Building
Bloomington, Indiana 47405-7007
Phone: 812-856-2570
Fax: 812-322-5545
E-mail: rmmcfall@pcsas.org
Website: www.pcsas.org

PUBLIC HEALTH
Laura Rasar King, M.P.H., MCHES, Executive Director
Council on Education for Public Health
1010 Wayne Avenue, Suite 220
Silver Spring, Maryland 20910
Phone: 202-789-1050
Fax: 202-789-1895
E-mail: Lking@ceph.org
Website: www.ceph.org

PUBLIC POLICY, AFFAIRS AND ADMINISTRATION
Crystal Calarusse, Chief Accreditation Officer
Commission on Peer Review and Accreditation
Network of Schools of Public Policy, Affairs, and Administration
(NASPAA-COPRA)
1029 Vermont Avenue, NW, Suite 1100
Washington, DC 20005
Phone: 202-628-8965
Fax: 202-626-4978
E-mail: copra@naspaa.org
Website: www.naspaa.org

Peterson's Graduate Programs in the Physical Sciences, Mathematics, Agricultural Sciences, the Environment & Natural Resources 2017

www.petersons.com 13

RADIOLOGIC TECHNOLOGY
Leslie Winter, Chief Executive Officer Joint Review Committee on
Education in Radiologic Technology (JRCERT)
20 North Wacker Drive, Suite 2850
Chicago, Illinois 60606-3182
Phone: 312-704-5300
Fax: 312-704-5304
E-mail: mail@jrcert.org
Web: www.jrcert.org

REHABILITATION EDUCATION
Frank Lane, Ph.D., Executive Director
Council on Rehabilitation Education (CORE)
Commission on Standards and Accreditation
1699 Woodfield Road, Suite 300
Schaumburg, Illinois 60173
Phone: 847-944-1345
Fax: 847-944-1346
E-mail: flane@core-rehab.org
Website: www.core-rehab.org

RESPIRATORY CARE
Thomas Smalling, Executive Director
Commission on Accreditation for Respiratory Care (CoARC)
1248 Harwood Road
Bedford, Texas 76021-4244
Phone: 817-283-2835
Fax: 817-354-8519
E-mail: tom@coarc.com
Website: www.coarc.com

SOCIAL WORK
Dr. Stacey Borasky, Director of Accreditation
Office of Social Work Accreditation
Council on Social Work Education
1701 Duke Street, Suite 200
Alexandria, Virginia 22314
Phone: 703-683-8080
Fax: 703-519-2078
E-mail: info@cswe.org
Website: www.cswe.org

SPEECH-LANGUAGE PATHOLOGY AND AUDIOLOGY
Patrima L. Tice, Accreditation Executive Director
American Speech-Language-Hearing Association
Council on Academic Accreditation in Audiology and Speech-Language
    Pathology
2200 Research Boulevard #310
Rockville, Maryland 20850-3289
Phone: 301-296-5700
Fax: 301-296-8750
E-mail: accreditation@asha.org
Website: http://caa.asha.org

TEACHER EDUCATION
Christopher A. Koch, President
National Council for Accreditation of Teacher Education (NCATE)
Teacher Education Accreditation Council (TEAC)
1140 19th Street, Suite 400
Washington, DC 20036
Phone: 202-223-0077
Fax: 202-296-6620
E-mail: caep@caepnet.org
Website: www.ncate.org

TECHNOLOGY
Michale S. McComis, Ed.D., Executive Director
Accrediting Commission of Career Schools and Colleges
2101 Wilson Boulevard, Suite 302
Arlington, Virginia 22201
Phone: 703-247-4212
Fax: 703-247-4533
E-mail: mccomis@accsc.org
Website: www.accsc.org

TECHNOLOGY, MANAGEMENT, AND APPLIED ENGINEERING
Kelly Schild, Director of Accreditation
The Association of Technology, Management, and Applied Engineering
(ATMAE)
275 N. York Street, Suite 401
Elmhurst, Illinois 60126
Phone: 630-433-4514
Fax: 630-563-9181
E-mail: Kelly@atmae.org
Website: www.atmae.org

THEATER
Karen P. Moynahan, Executive Director
National Association of Schools of Theatre Commission on
    Accreditation
11250 Roger Bacon Drive, Suite 21
Reston, Virginia 20190
Phone: 703-437-0700
Fax: 703-437-6312
E-mail: info@arts-accredit.org
Website: http://nast.arts-accredit.org/

THEOLOGY
Dr. Bernard Fryshman, Executive VP
Emeritus and Interim Executive Director
Association of Advanced Rabbinical and Talmudic Schools (AARTS)
Accreditation Commission
11 Broadway, Suite 405
New York, New York 10004
Phone: 212-363-1991
Fax: 212-533-5335
E-mail: k.sharfman.aarts@gmail.com

Daniel O. Aleshire, Executive Director
Association of Theological Schools in the United States and Canada
    (ATS)
Commission on Accrediting
10 Summit Park Drive
Pittsburgh, Pennsylvania 15275
Phone: 412-788-6505
Fax: 412-788-6510
E-mail: ats@ats.edu
Website: www.ats.edu

Dr. Timothy Eaton, Interim President
Transnational Association of Christian Colleges and Schools (TRACS)
Accreditation Commission
15935 Forest Road
Forest, Virginia 24551
Phone: 434-525-9539
Fax: 434-525-9538
E-mail: info@tracs.org
Website: www.tracs.org

VETERINARY MEDICINE
Dr. Karen Brandt, Director of Education and Research
American Veterinary Medical Association (AVMA)
Council on Education
1931 North Meacham Road, Suite 100
Schaumburg, Illinois 60173-4360
Phone: 847-925-8070 Ext. 6674
Fax: 847-285-5732
E-mail: info@avma.org
Website: www.avma.org

14   www.petersons.com

*Peterson's Graduate Programs in the Physical Sciences, Mathematics,
Agricultural Sciences, the Environment & Natural Resources 2017*

How to Use These Guides

As you identify the particular programs and institutions that interest you, you can use both the *Graduate & Professional Programs: An Overview* volume and the specialized volumes in the series to obtain detailed information.

- *Graduate Programs in the Biological/Biomedical Sciences & Health-Related Professions*
- *Graduate Programs in Business, Education, Information Studies, Law & Social Work*
- *Graduate Programs in Engineering & Applied Sciences*
- *Graduate Programs the Humanities, Arts & Social Sciences*
- *Graduate Programs in the Physical Sciences, Mathematics, Agricultural Sciences, the Environment & Natural Resources*

Each of the specialized volumes in the series is divided into sections that contain one or more directories devoted to programs in a particular field. If you do not find a directory devoted to your field of interest in a specific volume, consult "Directories and Subject Areas" (located at the end of each volume). After you have identified the correct volume, consult the "Directories and Subject Areas in This Book" index, which shows (as does the more general directory) what directories cover subjects not specifically named in a directory or section title.

Each of the specialized volumes in the series has a number of general directories. These directories have entries for the largest unit at an institution granting graduate degrees in that field. For example, the general Engineering and Applied Sciences directory in the *Graduate Programs in Engineering & Applied Sciences* volume consists of **Profiles** for colleges, schools, and departments of engineering and applied sciences.

General directories are followed by other directories, or sections, that give more detailed information about programs in particular areas of the general field that has been covered. The general Engineering and Applied Sciences directory, in the previous example, is followed by nineteen sections with directories in specific areas of engineering, such as Chemical Engineering, Industrial/Management Engineering, and Mechanical Engineering.

Because of the broad nature of many fields, any system of organization is bound to involve a certain amount of overlap. Environmental studies, for example, is a field whose various aspects are studied in several types of departments and schools. Readers interested in such studies will find information on relevant programs in the *Graduate Programs in the Biological/Biomedical Sciences & Health-Related Professions* volume under Ecology and Environmental Biology and Environmental and Occupational Health; in the *Graduate Programs in the Physical Sciences, Mathematics, Agricultural Sciences, the Environment & Natural Resources* volume under Environmental Management and Policy and Natural Resources; and in the *Graduate Programs in Engineering & Applied Sciences* volume under Energy Management and Policy and Environmental Engineering. To help you find all of the programs of interest to you, the introduction to each section within the specialized volumes includes, if applicable, a paragraph suggesting other sections and directories with information on related areas of study.

Directory of Institutions with Programs in the Physical Sciences, Mathematics, Agricultural Sciences, the Environment & Natural Resources

This directory lists institutions in alphabetical order and includes beneath each name the academic fields in which each institution offers graduate programs. The degree level in each field is also indicated, provided that the institution has supplied that information in response to Peterson's Annual Survey of Graduate and Professional Institutions.

An M indicates that a master's degree program is offered; a D indicates that a doctoral degree program is offered; a P indicates that the first professional degree is offered; an O signifies that other advanced degrees (e.g., certificates or specialist degrees) are offered; and an * (asterisk) indicates that a **Close-Up** and/or **Display** is located in this volume. See the index, "Close-Ups and Displays," for the specific page number.

Profiles of Academic and Professional Programs in the Specialized Volumes

Each section of **Profiles** has a table of contents that lists the Program Directories, **Displays**, and **Close-Ups**. Program Directories consist of the **Profiles** of programs in the relevant fields, with **Displays** following if programs have chosen to include them. **Close-Ups**, which are more individualized statements, are also listed for those graduate schools or programs that have chosen to submit them.

The **Profiles** found in the 500 directories in the specialized volumes provide basic data about the graduate units in capsule form for quick reference. To make these directories as useful as possible, **Profiles** are generally listed for an institution's smallest academic unit within a subject area. In other words, if an institution has a College of Liberal Arts that administers many related programs, the **Profile** for the individual program (e.g., Program in History), not the entire College, appears in the directory.

There are some programs that do not fit into any current directory and are not given individual **Profiles**. The directory structure is reviewed annually in order to keep this number to a minimum and to accommodate major trends in graduate education.

The following outline describes the **Profile** information found in the guides and explains how best to use that information. Any item that does not apply to or was not provided by a graduate unit is omitted from its listing. The format of the **Profiles** is constant, making it easy to compare one institution with another and one program with another.

A ★ graphic next to the school's name indicates the institution has additional detailed information in a "Premium Profile" on Petersons.com. After reading their information here, you can learn more about the school by visiting www.petersons.com and searching for that particular college or university's graduate program.

Identifying Information. The institution's name, in boldface type, is followed by a complete listing of the administrative structure for that field of study. (For example, University of Akron, Buchtel College of Arts and Sciences, Department of Theoretical and Applied Mathematics, Program in Mathematics.) The last unit listed is the one to which all information in the **Profile** pertains. The institution's city, state, and zip code follow.

Offerings. Each field of study offered by the unit is listed with all postbaccalaureate degrees awarded. Degrees that are not preceded by a specific concentration are awarded in the general field listed in the unit name. Frequently, fields of study are broken down into subspecializations, and those appear following the degrees awarded; for example, "Offerings in secondary education (M.Ed.), including English education, mathematics education, science education." Students enrolled in the M.Ed. program would be able to specialize in any of the three fields mentioned.

Professional Accreditation. Some **Profiles** indicate whether a program is professionally accredited. Because it is possible for a program to receive or lose professional accreditation at any time, students entering fields in which accreditation is important to a career should verify the status of programs by contacting either the chairperson or the appropriate accrediting association.

Jointly Offered Degrees. Explanatory statements concerning programs that are offered in cooperation with other institutions are included in the list of degrees offered. This occurs most commonly on a regional basis (for example, two state universities offering a cooperative Ph.D. in special education) or where the specialized nature of the institutions encourages joint efforts (a J.D./M.B.A. offered by a law school at an institution with no formal business programs and an institution with a business school but lacking a law school). Only programs that are truly cooperative are listed; those involving only limited course work at another institution are not. Interested students should contact the heads of such units for further information.

Program Availability. This may include the following: part-time, evening/weekend, online only, 100% online, blended/hybrid learning, and/or minimal on-campus study, When information regarding the availability of part-time or evening/weekend study appears in the **Profile**, it means that students are able to earn a degree exclusively through such study. Blended/hybrid learning describe those courses in which some traditional in-class time has been replaced by online learning activities. Hybrid courses take advantage of the best features of both face-to-face and online learning.

Faculty. Figures on the number of faculty members actively involved with graduate students through teaching or research are separated into full- and part-time as well as men and women whenever the information has been supplied.

Students. Figures for the number of students enrolled in graduate and professional programs pertain to the semester of highest enrollment from the 2015–16 academic year. These figures are broken down into full- and part-time and men and women whenever the data have been supplied. Information on the number of matriculated students enrolled in the unit who are members of a minority group or are international students appears here. The average age of the matriculated students is followed by the number of applicants, the percentage accepted, and the number enrolled for fall 2015.

Degrees Awarded. The number of degrees awarded in the calendar year is listed. Many doctoral programs offer a terminal master's degree if students leave the program after completing only part of the requirements for a doctoral degree; that is indicated here. All degrees are classified into one of four types: master's, doctoral, first professional, and other advanced degrees. A unit may award one or several degrees at a given level; however, the data are only collected by type and may therefore represent several different degree programs.

Degree Requirements. The information in this section is also broken down by type of degree, and all information for a degree level pertains to all degrees of that type unless otherwise specified. Degree requirements are collected in a simplified form to provide some very basic information on the nature of the program and on foreign language, thesis or dissertation, comprehensive exam, and registration requirements. Many units also provide a short list of additional requirements, such as fieldwork or an internship. For complete information on graduation requirements, contact the graduate school or program directly.

Entrance Requirements. Entrance requirements are broken down into the four degree levels of master's, doctoral, first professional, and other advanced degrees. Within each level, information may be provided in two basic categories: entrance exams and other requirements. The entrance exams are identified by the standard acronyms used by the testing agencies, unless they are not well known. Other entrance requirements are quite varied, but they often contain an undergraduate or graduate grade point average (GPA). Unless otherwise stated, the GPA is calculated on a 4.0 scale and is listed as a minimum required for admission. Additional exam requirements/recommendations for international students may be listed here. Application deadlines for domestic and international students, the application fee, and whether electronic applications are accepted may be listed here. Note that the deadline should be used for reference only; these dates are subject to change, and students interested in applying should always contact the graduate unit directly about application procedures and deadlines.

Expenses. The typical cost of study for the 2016–2017 academic year (2015–16 if 2016–17 figures were not available) is given in two basic categories: tuition and fees. Cost of study may be quite complex at a graduate institution. There are often sliding scales for part-time study, a different cost for first-year students, and other variables that make it impossible to completely cover the cost of study for each graduate program. To provide the most usable information, figures are given for full-time study for a full year where available and for part-time study in terms of a per-unit rate (per credit, per semester hour, etc.). Occasionally, variances may be noted in tuition and fees for reasons such as the type of program, whether courses are taken during the day or evening, whether courses are at the master's or doctoral level, or other institution-specific reasons. Respondents were also given the opportunity to provide more specific and detailed tuition and fees information at the unit level. When provided, this information will appear in place of any typical costs entered elsewhere on the university-level survey. Expenses are usually subject to change; for exact costs at any given time, contact your chosen schools and programs directly. Keep in mind that the tuition of Canadian institutions is usually given in Canadian dollars.

Financial Support. This section contains data on the number of awards administered by the institution and given to graduate students during the 2015–16 academic year. The first figure given represents the total number of students receiving financial support enrolled in that unit. If the unit has provided information on graduate appointments, these are broken down into three major categories: fellowships give money to graduate students to cover the cost of study and living expenses and are not based on a work obligation or research commitment, research assistantships provide stipends to graduate students for assistance in a formal research project with a faculty member, and teaching assistantships provide stipends to graduate students for teaching or for assisting faculty members in teaching undergraduate classes. Within each category, figures are given for the total number of awards, the average yearly amount per award, and whether full or partial tuition reimbursements are awarded. In addition to graduate appointments, the availability of several other financial aid sources is covered in this section. Tuition waivers are routinely part of a graduate appointment, but units sometimes waive part or all of a student's tuition even if a graduate appointment is not available. Federal WorkStudy is made available to students who demonstrate need and meet the federal guidelines; this form of aid normally includes 10 or more hours of work per week in an office of the institution. Institutionally sponsored loans are low-interest loans available to graduate students to cover both educational and living expenses. Career-related internships or fieldwork offer money to students who are participating in a formal off-campus research project or practicum. Grants, scholarships, traineeships, unspecified assistantships, and other awards may also be noted. The availability of financial support to part-time students is also indicated here.

Some programs list the financial aid application deadline and the forms that need to be completed for students to be eligible for financial awards. There are two forms: FAFSA, the Free Application for Federal Student Aid, which is required for federal aid, and the CSS PROFILE®.

Faculty Research. Each unit has the opportunity to list several keyword phrases describing the current research involving faculty members and graduate students. Space limitations prevent the unit from listing complete information on all research programs. The total expenditure for funded research from the previous academic year may also be included.

Unit Head and Application Contact. The head of the graduate program for each unit may be listed with academic title, phone and fax numbers, and e-mail address. In addition to the unit head's contact information, many graduate programs also list a separate contact for application and admission information, followed by the graduate school, program, or department's website. If no unit head or application contact is given, you should contact the overall institution for information on graduate admissions.

Displays and Close-Ups

The **Displays** and **Close-Ups** are supplementary insertions submitted by deans, chairs, and other administrators who wish to offer an additional, more individualized statement to readers. A number of graduate school and program administrators have attached a **Display** ad near the **Profile** listing. Here you will find information that an institution or program wants to emphasize. The **Close-Ups** are by their very nature more expansive and flexible than the **Profiles**, and the administrators who have written them may emphasize different aspects of their programs. All of the **Close-Ups** are organized in the

16 www.petersons.com

*Peterson's Graduate Programs in the Physical Sciences, Mathematics,
Agricultural Sciences, the Environment & Natural Resources 2017*

same way (with the exception of a few that describe research and training opportunities instead of degree programs), and in each one you will find information on the same basic topics, such as programs of study, research facilities, tuition and fees, financial aid, and application procedures. If an institution or program has submitted a **Close-Up**, a boldface cross-reference appears below its **Profile**. As with the **Displays**, all of the **Close-Ups** in the guides have been submitted by choice; the absence of a **Display** or **Close-Up** does not reflect any type of editorial judgment on the part of Peterson's, and their presence in the guides should not be taken as an indication of status, quality, or approval. Statements regarding a university's objectives and accomplishments are a reflection of its own beliefs and are not the opinions of the Peterson's editors.

Appendixes

This section contains two appendixes. The first, "Institutional Changes Since the 2016 Edition," lists institutions that have closed, merged, or changed their name or status since the last edition of the guides. The second, "Abbreviations Used in the Guides," gives abbreviations of degree names, along with what those abbreviations stand for. These appendixes are identical in all six volumes of *Peterson's Graduate and Professional Programs*.

Indexes

There are three indexes presented here. The first index, "Close-Ups and Displays," gives page references for all programs that have chosen to place **Close-Ups** and **Displays** in this volume. It is arranged alphabetically by institution; within institutions, the arrangement is alphabetical by subject area. It is not an index to all programs in the book's directories of **Profiles**; readers must refer to the directories themselves for **Profile** information on programs that have not submitted the additional, more individualized statements. The second index, "Directories and Subject Areas in Other Books in This Series", gives book references for the directories in the specialized volumes and also includes cross-references for subject area names not used in the directory structure, for example, "Computing Technology (see Computer Science)." The third index, "Directories and Subject Areas in This Book," gives page references for the directories in this volume and cross-references for subject area names not used in this volume's directory structure.

Data Collection Procedures

The information published in the directories and Profiles of all the books is collected through Peterson's Annual Survey of Graduate and Professional Institutions. The survey is sent each spring to nearly 2,300 institutions offering postbaccalaureate degree programs, including accredited institutions in the United States, U.S. territories, and Canada and those institutions outside the United States that are accredited by U.S. accrediting bodies. Deans and other administrators complete these surveys, providing information on programs in the 500 academic and professional fields covered in the guides as well as overall institutional information. While every effort has been made to ensure the accuracy and completeness of the data, information is sometimes unavailable or changes occur after publication deadlines. All usable information received in time for publication has been included. The omission of any particular item from a directory or Profile signifies either that the item is not applicable to the institution or program or that information was not available. Profiles of programs scheduled to begin during the 2016–17 academic year cannot, obviously, include statistics on enrollment or, in many cases, the number of faculty members. If no usable data were submitted by an institution, its name, address, and program name appear in order to indicate the availability of graduate work.

Criteria for Inclusion in This Guide

To be included in this guide, an institution must have full accreditation or be a candidate for accreditation (preaccreditation) status by an institutional or specialized accrediting body recognized by the U.S. Department of Education or the Council for Higher Education Accreditation (CHEA). Institutional accrediting bodies, which review each institution as a whole, include the six regional associations of schools and colleges (Middle States, New England, North Central, Northwest, Southern, and Western), each of which is responsible for a specified portion of the United States and its territories. Other institutional accrediting bodies are national in scope and accredit specific kinds of institutions (e.g., Bible colleges, independent colleges, and rabbinical and Talmudic schools). Program registration by the New York State Board of Regents is considered to be the equivalent of institutional accreditation, since the board requires that all programs offered by an institution meet its standards before recognition is granted. A Canadian institution must be chartered and authorized to grant degrees by the provincial government, affiliated with a chartered institution, or accredited by a recognized U.S. accrediting body. This guide also includes institutions outside the United States that are accredited by these U.S. accrediting bodies. There are recognized specialized or professional accrediting bodies in more than fifty different fields, each of which is authorized to accredit institutions or specific programs in its particular field. For specialized institutions that offer programs in one field only, we designate this to be the equivalent of institutional accreditation. A full explanation of the accrediting process and complete information on recognized institutional (regional and national) and specialized accrediting bodies can be found online at www.chea.org or at www.ed.gov/admins/finaid/accred/index.html.

Peterson's Graduate Programs in the Physical Sciences, Mathematics, Agricultural Sciences, the Environment & Natural Resources 2017

www.petersons.com **17**

DIRECTORY OF INSTITUTIONS WITH PROGRAMS IN THE PHYSICAL SCIENCES, MATHEMATICS, AGRICULTURAL SCIENCES, THE ENVIRONMENT & NATURAL RESOURCES

ACADIA UNIVERSITY
Applied Mathematics	M
Chemistry	M
Geology	M
Statistics	M

ADELPHI UNIVERSITY
Environmental Management and Policy	M
Environmental Sciences	M

AIR FORCE INSTITUTE OF TECHNOLOGY
Applied Mathematics	M,D
Applied Physics	M,D
Astrophysics	M,D
Environmental Management and Policy	M
Optical Sciences	M,D
Planetary and Space Sciences	M,D

ALABAMA AGRICULTURAL AND MECHANICAL UNIVERSITY
Agricultural Sciences— General	M,D
Agronomy and Soil Sciences	M,D
Food Science and Technology	M,D
Optical Sciences	M,D
Physics	M,D
Planetary and Space Sciences	M,D
Plant Sciences	M,D

ALABAMA STATE UNIVERSITY
Mathematics	M

ALASKA PACIFIC UNIVERSITY
Environmental Sciences	M

ALBANY STATE UNIVERSITY
Water Resources	M

ALCORN STATE UNIVERSITY
Agricultural Sciences— General	M
Agronomy and Soil Sciences	M
Animal Sciences	M

AMERICAN PUBLIC UNIVERSITY SYSTEM
Environmental Management and Policy	M
Fish, Game, and Wildlife Management	M
Marine Affairs	M
Planetary and Space Sciences	M

AMERICAN UNIVERSITY
Applied Statistics	M,O
Chemistry	M
Environmental Management and Policy	M,D,O
Environmental Sciences	M,O
Mathematics	M,O
Natural Resources	M,D,O
Statistics	M,O

THE AMERICAN UNIVERSITY IN CAIRO
Chemistry	M

AMERICAN UNIVERSITY OF BEIRUT
Animal Sciences	M
Aquaculture	M
Biostatistics	M
Chemistry	M,D
Computational Sciences	M,D
Environmental Management and Policy	M,D
Environmental Sciences	M,D
Food Science and Technology	M
Geology	M,D
Mathematics	M,D
Physics	M,D
Plant Sciences	M
Statistics	M,D
Theoretical Physics	M,D

AMERICAN UNIVERSITY OF SHARJAH
Mathematics	M

ANGELO STATE UNIVERSITY
Agricultural Sciences— General	M
Animal Sciences	M

ANTIOCH UNIVERSITY NEW ENGLAND
Environmental Management and Policy	M,D
Environmental Sciences	M,D

ANTIOCH UNIVERSITY SEATTLE
Environmental Management and Policy	M

APPALACHIAN STATE UNIVERSITY
Environmental Management and Policy	M
Mathematics	M

AQUINAS COLLEGE (MI)
Environmental Management and Policy	M

ARIZONA STATE UNIVERSITY AT THE TEMPE CAMPUS
Applied Mathematics	M,D,O
Astrophysics	M,D
Chemistry	M,D
Environmental Management and Policy	M
Environmental Sciences	M,D,O
Geology	M,D
Geosciences	M,D
Mathematics	M,D,O
Physics	M,D

ARKANSAS STATE UNIVERSITY
Agricultural Sciences— General	M,O
Chemistry	M,O
Environmental Sciences	M,D
Mathematics	M

ARKANSAS TECH UNIVERSITY
Fish, Game, and Wildlife Management	M

AUBURN UNIVERSITY
Agricultural Sciences— General	M,D
Agronomy and Soil Sciences	M,D
Analytical Chemistry	M,D
Animal Sciences	M,D
Applied Mathematics	M,D
Aquaculture	M,D
Chemistry	M,D
Fish, Game, and Wildlife Management	M,D
Food Science and Technology	M,D,O
Forestry	M,D
Geology	M
Horticulture	M,D
Hydrology	M,D
Inorganic Chemistry	M,D
Mathematics	M,D
Natural Resources	M,D
Organic Chemistry	M,D
Physical Chemistry	M,D
Physics	M,D
Statistics	M,D

AURORA UNIVERSITY
Mathematics	M

BALL STATE UNIVERSITY
Chemistry	M,D
Environmental Management and Policy	M,O
Environmental Sciences	D
Geology	M
Geosciences	M
Mathematics	M
Meteorology	M,O
Natural Resources	M,O
Physics	M
Statistics	M

BARD COLLEGE
Atmospheric Sciences	M,O
Environmental Management and Policy	M,O

BARUCH COLLEGE OF THE CITY UNIVERSITY OF NEW YORK
Statistics	M

BAYLOR UNIVERSITY
Chemistry	M,D
Environmental Management and Policy	M
Environmental Sciences	D
Geophysics	M,D
Geosciences	M,D
Limnology	M,D
Mathematics	M,D
Physics	M,D
Statistics	M,D

BEMIDJI STATE UNIVERSITY
Environmental Management and Policy	M
Mathematics	M

BERGIN UNIVERSITY OF CANINE STUDIES
Animal Sciences	M

BINGHAMTON UNIVERSITY, STATE UNIVERSITY OF NEW YORK
Analytical Chemistry	M,D
Applied Physics	M,D
Chemistry	M,D
Environmental Sciences	M,D
Geology	M,D
Inorganic Chemistry	M,D
Mathematics	M,D
Organic Chemistry	M,D
Physical Chemistry	M,D
Physics	M,D

BOISE STATE UNIVERSITY
Animal Sciences	M,D
Chemistry	M
Environmental Management and Policy	M,D,O
Geophysics	M,D
Hydrology	M,D
Mathematics	M
Natural Resources	M,D,O

BOSTON COLLEGE
Chemistry	M,D
Geology	M
Geophysics	M
Inorganic Chemistry	M,D
Mathematics	D
Organic Chemistry	M,D
Physical Chemistry	M,D
Physics	M,D

BOSTON UNIVERSITY
Astronomy	M,D
Biostatistics	M,D
Chemistry	M,D
Environmental Management and Policy	M,D
Environmental Sciences	M,D
Food Science and Technology	M
Geosciences	M,D

Mathematical and Computational Finance	M,D
Mathematics	M,D
Photonics	M,D
Physics	D

BOWIE STATE UNIVERSITY
Applied Mathematics	M

BOWLING GREEN STATE UNIVERSITY
Applied Statistics	M,D
Chemistry	M,D
Geology	M
Geophysics	M
Mathematics	M,D
Physics	M
Statistics	M,D

BRADLEY UNIVERSITY
Chemistry	M

BRANDEIS UNIVERSITY
Chemistry	M,D
Inorganic Chemistry	M,D
Mathematics	M,D,O
Organic Chemistry	M,D
Physical Chemistry	M,D
Physics	M,D

BRIGHAM YOUNG UNIVERSITY
Agricultural Sciences— General	M,D
Analytical Chemistry	M,D
Animal Sciences	M,D
Applied Statistics	M
Astronomy	M,D
Chemistry	M,D
Environmental Sciences	M,D
Fish, Game, and Wildlife Management	M,D
Food Science and Technology	M
Geology	M
Mathematics	M,D
Physics	M,D
Plant Sciences	M,D
Statistics	M

BROCK UNIVERSITY
Chemistry	M,D
Geosciences	M
Mathematics	M
Physics	M
Statistics	M

BROOKLYN COLLEGE OF THE CITY UNIVERSITY OF NEW YORK
Chemistry	M,D
Geology	M,D
Geosciences	M
Mathematics	M
Physics	M

BROWN UNIVERSITY
Applied Mathematics	M,D
Biostatistics	M,D
Chemistry	D
Geosciences	D
Mathematics	D
Physics	M,D

BRYANT UNIVERSITY
Environmental Sciences	M

BRYN MAWR COLLEGE
Chemistry	M,D
Mathematics	M,D
Physics	M,D

BUCKNELL UNIVERSITY
Chemistry	M
Mathematics	M

BUFFALO STATE COLLEGE, STATE UNIVERSITY OF NEW YORK
Chemistry	M

CALIFORNIA BAPTIST UNIVERSITY
Applied Mathematics	M

CALIFORNIA INSTITUTE OF TECHNOLOGY
Applied Mathematics	M,D
Applied Physics	M,D
Astronomy	D
Chemistry	M,D
Computational Sciences	M,D
Environmental Sciences	M,D
Geochemistry	M,D
Geology	M,D
Geophysics	M,D
Mathematics	D
Physics	D
Planetary and Space Sciences	M,D

CALIFORNIA POLYTECHNIC STATE UNIVERSITY, SAN LUIS OBISPO
Agricultural Sciences— General	M
Chemistry	M
Forestry	M
Mathematics	M
Natural Resources	M

CALIFORNIA STATE POLYTECHNIC UNIVERSITY, POMONA
Agricultural Sciences— General	M
Applied Mathematics	M
Chemistry	M
Environmental Sciences	M
Geology	M
Mathematics	M

CALIFORNIA STATE UNIVERSITY, BAKERSFIELD
Geology	M
Hydrology	M

CALIFORNIA STATE UNIVERSITY CHANNEL ISLANDS
Mathematics	M

CALIFORNIA STATE UNIVERSITY, CHICO
Environmental Sciences	M
Geology	M
Geosciences	M
Hydrogeology	M
Hydrology	M

CALIFORNIA STATE UNIVERSITY, EAST BAY
Applied Mathematics	M
Applied Statistics	M
Biostatistics	M
Chemistry	M
Environmental Sciences	M
Geology	M
Marine Sciences	M
Mathematics	M
Statistics	M

CALIFORNIA STATE UNIVERSITY, FRESNO
Animal Sciences	M
Chemistry	M
Food Science and Technology	M
Geology	M
Marine Sciences	M
Mathematics	M
Physics	M
Plant Sciences	M
Viticulture and Enology	M

CALIFORNIA STATE UNIVERSITY, FULLERTON
Applied Mathematics	M
Chemistry	M
Environmental Management and Policy	M
Geochemistry	M
Geology	M
Mathematics	M
Physics	M

CALIFORNIA STATE UNIVERSITY, LONG BEACH
Applied Mathematics	M,D
Applied Statistics	M
Chemistry	M
Food Science and Technology	M
Geology	M
Geophysics	M
Mathematics	M
Physics	M

CALIFORNIA STATE UNIVERSITY, LOS ANGELES
Analytical Chemistry	M
Applied Mathematics	M
Chemistry	M
Geology	M
Inorganic Chemistry	M
Mathematics	M
Organic Chemistry	M
Physical Chemistry	M
Physics	M

CALIFORNIA STATE UNIVERSITY, MONTEREY BAY
Marine Sciences	M
Water Resources	M

CALIFORNIA STATE UNIVERSITY, NORTHRIDGE
Applied Mathematics	M
Chemistry	M
Environmental Sciences	M
Geology	M
Mathematics	M
Physics	M

CALIFORNIA STATE UNIVERSITY, SACRAMENTO
Chemistry	M
Mathematics	M

CALIFORNIA STATE UNIVERSITY, SAN BERNARDINO
Environmental Sciences	M
Geosciences	M
Mathematics	M

CALIFORNIA STATE UNIVERSITY, SAN MARCOS
Mathematics	M

CARLETON UNIVERSITY
Chemistry	M,D
Geosciences	M,D
Mathematics	M,D
Physics	M,D

CARNEGIE MELLON UNIVERSITY
Applied Physics	M,D
Atmospheric Sciences	D
Chemistry	D
Environmental Sciences	D
Mathematical and Computational Finance	M,D
Mathematics	M,D
Physics	M,D
Statistics	M,D
Theoretical Chemistry	D

CASE WESTERN RESERVE UNIVERSITY
Applied Mathematics	M,D
Astronomy	M,D
Biostatistics	M,D
Chemistry	M,D
Geology	M,D
Geosciences	M,D
Mathematics	M,D
Physics	M,D

20 www.petersons.com

Petersons Graduate Programs in the Physical Sciences, Mathematics, Agricultural Sciences, the Environment & Natural Resources 2017

THE CATHOLIC UNIVERSITY OF AMERICA

Physics	M,D

CENTRAL CONNECTICUT STATE UNIVERSITY

Mathematics	M,O
Statistics	M,O

CENTRAL EUROPEAN UNIVERSITY

Applied Mathematics	M,D
Environmental Management and Policy	M,D
Mathematics	M,D

CENTRAL MICHIGAN UNIVERSITY

Chemistry	M
Mathematics	M,D
Physics	M

CENTRAL WASHINGTON UNIVERSITY

Chemistry	M
Geology	M
Mathematics	M
Natural Resources	M

CHAPMAN UNIVERSITY

Computational Sciences	M,D*
Food Science and Technology	M

CHICAGO STATE UNIVERSITY

Mathematics	M

CHRISTOPHER NEWPORT UNIVERSITY

Applied Physics	M
Environmental Sciences	M
Physics	M

CITY COLLEGE OF THE CITY UNIVERSITY OF NEW YORK

Atmospheric Sciences	M
Chemistry	M,D
Geology	M
Geosciences	M
Mathematics	M
Physics	M,D

CLAREMONT GRADUATE UNIVERSITY

Applied Mathematics	M,D
Computational Sciences	M,D
Mathematics	M,D
Statistics	M,D

CLARK ATLANTA UNIVERSITY

Chemistry	M,D
Mathematics	M
Physics	M

CLARKSON UNIVERSITY

Chemistry	M,D
Environmental Management and Policy	M
Environmental Sciences	M,D
Mathematics	M,D
Physics	M,D

CLARK UNIVERSITY

Chemistry	M,D
Environmental Management and Policy	M
Physics	D

CLEMSON UNIVERSITY

Agricultural Sciences— General	M
Animal Sciences	M,D
Aquaculture	M,D
Chemistry	M,D
Environmental Management and Policy	M,D
Environmental Sciences	M,D
Fish, Game, and Wildlife Management	M,D
Food Science and Technology	M,D
Forestry	M,D
Hydrogeology	M
Mathematics	M,D
Plant Sciences	M,D
Statistics	M,D

CLEVELAND STATE UNIVERSITY

Analytical Chemistry	M,D
Applied Statistics	M
Chemistry	M,D
Condensed Matter Physics	M
Environmental Management and Policy	M,O
Environmental Sciences	M,D
Inorganic Chemistry	M,D
Mathematics	M
Optical Sciences	M,D
Organic Chemistry	M,D
Physical Chemistry	M,D
Physics	M,D

COASTAL CAROLINA UNIVERSITY

Marine Sciences	M,D,O

THE COLLEGE AT BROCKPORT, STATE UNIVERSITY OF NEW YORK

Chemistry	M,O
Environmental Sciences	M
Mathematics	M,O

COLLEGE OF CHARLESTON

Environmental Sciences	M
Marine Sciences	M
Mathematics	M,O

COLLEGE OF STATEN ISLAND OF THE CITY UNIVERSITY OF NEW YORK

Environmental Sciences	M

COLLEGE OF THE ATLANTIC

Environmental Management and Policy	M

THE COLLEGE OF WILLIAM AND MARY

Applied Mathematics	M,D
Applied Physics	M,D
Atmospheric Sciences	M,D
Biomathematics	M,D
Chemistry	M
Computational Sciences	M
Environmental Sciences	M
Marine Sciences	M,D
Optical Sciences	M,D
Physics	M,D

COLORADO HEIGHTS UNIVERSITY

Environmental Management and Policy	M

COLORADO SCHOOL OF MINES

Applied Mathematics	M,D
Applied Physics	M,D
Applied Statistics	M,D
Chemistry	M,D
Geochemistry	M,D
Geology	M,D
Geophysics	M,D
Hydrology	M,D
Physics	M,D

COLORADO STATE UNIVERSITY

Agricultural Sciences— General	M,D
Agronomy and Soil Sciences	M,D
Animal Sciences	M,D
Atmospheric Sciences	M,D
Chemistry	M,D
Fish, Game, and Wildlife Management	M,D
Food Science and Technology	M,D
Forestry	M,D
Geosciences	M,D
Horticulture	M,D
Mathematics	M,D
Natural Resources	M,D
Physics	M,D
Plant Sciences	M,D
Range Science	M,D
Statistics	M,D
Water Resources	M,D

COLORADO STATE UNIVERSITY–PUEBLO

Chemistry	M

COLUMBIA UNIVERSITY

Applied Mathematics	M,D
Applied Physics	M,D
Astronomy	M,D
Atmospheric Sciences	M,D
Biostatistics	M,D
Chemical Physics	M,D
Chemistry	M,D
Environmental Management and Policy	M
Environmental Sciences	M,D*
Geosciences	M,D
Mathematics	M,D
Physics	M,D
Statistics	M,D

COLUMBUS STATE UNIVERSITY

Chemistry	M,O
Environmental Management and Policy	M
Environmental Sciences	M,O
Mathematics	M,O

CONCORDIA UNIVERSITY (CANADA)

Chemistry	M,D
Environmental Management and Policy	M,D,O
Mathematics	M,D
Physics	M,D
Statistics	M,D

CORNELL UNIVERSITY

Agronomy and Soil Sciences	M,D
Analytical Chemistry	D
Animal Sciences	M,D
Applied Mathematics	M,D
Applied Physics	M,D
Applied Statistics	M,D
Astronomy	D
Astrophysics	D
Atmospheric Sciences	M,D
Biometry	M,D
Chemical Physics	D
Chemistry	D
Computational Sciences	M,D
Environmental Management and Policy	M,D
Environmental Sciences	M,D
Fish, Game, and Wildlife Management	M,D
Food Science and Technology	M,D
Forestry	M,D
Geochemistry	M,D
Geology	M,D
Geophysics	M,D
Geosciences	M,D
Horticulture	M,D
Hydrology	M,D
Inorganic Chemistry	D
Limnology	D
Marine Geology	M,D
Marine Sciences	M,D
Mathematics	D
Mineralogy	M,D
Natural Resources	M,D

Oceanography — see next column

Oceanography	D
Organic Chemistry	D
Paleontology	M,D
Physical Chemistry	D
Physics	M,D
Planetary and Space Sciences	D
Plant Sciences	M,D
Statistics	M,D
Theoretical Chemistry	D
Theoretical Physics	M,D
Water Resources	M,D

CREIGHTON UNIVERSITY

Physics	M

DALHOUSIE UNIVERSITY

Agricultural Sciences— General	M
Agronomy and Soil Sciences	M
Animal Sciences	M
Applied Mathematics	M,D
Aquaculture	M
Chemistry	M,D
Environmental Management and Policy	M
Environmental Sciences	M
Food Science and Technology	M,D
Geosciences	M,D
Horticulture	M
Marine Affairs	M
Mathematics	M,D
Natural Resources	M
Oceanography	M,D
Physics	M,D
Statistics	M,D
Water Resources	M

DARTMOUTH COLLEGE

Astronomy	D
Biostatistics	D
Chemistry	M,D
Geosciences	M,D
Mathematics	M,D
Physical Chemistry	M,D
Physics	D

DELAWARE STATE UNIVERSITY

Applied Mathematics	M,D
Chemistry	M,D
Mathematics	M
Natural Resources	M
Optical Sciences	M,D
Physics	M,D
Plant Sciences	M
Theoretical Physics	D

DEPAUL UNIVERSITY

Applied Mathematics	M,D
Applied Statistics	M,D
Chemistry	M,D
Mathematical and Computational Finance	M,D
Mathematics	M,D
Physics	M,D

DREW UNIVERSITY

Chemistry	M,D,O
Mathematics	M,D,O

DREXEL UNIVERSITY

Biostatistics	M,D,O
Chemistry	M,D
Environmental Management and Policy	M
Environmental Sciences	M,D
Food Science and Technology	M
Hydrology	M,D
Mathematics	M,D
Physics	M,D

DUKE UNIVERSITY

Biostatistics	M
Chemistry	D
Environmental Management and Policy	M,D
Environmental Sciences	M,D
Forestry	M,D
Geology	M,D
Marine Sciences	D
Mathematics	D
Natural Resources	M,D
Optical Sciences	M
Paleontology	D
Photonics	M
Physics	D
Statistics	M,D

DUQUESNE UNIVERSITY

Chemistry	D
Environmental Management and Policy	M,O
Environmental Sciences	M,O
Mathematics	M

EAST CAROLINA UNIVERSITY

Applied Physics	M,D
Chemistry	M
Geology	M,O
Hydrogeology	M,O
Mathematics	M,O
Physics	M,D
Statistics	M,O

EASTERN ILLINOIS UNIVERSITY

Chemistry	M
Mathematics	M

EASTERN KENTUCKY UNIVERSITY

Chemistry	M
Geology	M,D
Mathematics	M

EASTERN MICHIGAN UNIVERSITY

Chemistry	M
Geosciences	M
Mathematics	M
Physics	M
Water Resources	M,O

EASTERN NEW MEXICO UNIVERSITY

Analytical Chemistry	M
Chemistry	M
Inorganic Chemistry	M
Organic Chemistry	M
Physical Chemistry	M

EASTERN WASHINGTON UNIVERSITY

Mathematics	M

EAST STROUDSBURG UNIVERSITY OF PENNSYLVANIA

Physics	M

EAST TENNESSEE STATE UNIVERSITY

Chemistry	M
Geosciences	M
Mathematics	M,O
Paleontology	M

ÉCOLE POLYTECHNIQUE DE MONTRÉAL

Applied Mathematics	M,D,O
Optical Sciences	M,D,O

ELIZABETH CITY STATE UNIVERSITY

Applied Mathematics	M
Mathematics	M

EMORY UNIVERSITY

Biostatistics	M,D
Chemistry	D
Computational Sciences	D
Mathematics	M,D
Physics	D
Theoretical Physics	D

EMPORIA STATE UNIVERSITY

Geosciences	M,O
Mathematics	M

THE EVERGREEN STATE COLLEGE

Environmental Management and Policy	M

FAIRFIELD UNIVERSITY

Mathematics	M

FAIRLEIGH DICKINSON UNIVERSITY, COLLEGE AT FLORHAM

Chemistry	M

FAIRLEIGH DICKINSON UNIVERSITY, METROPOLITAN CAMPUS

Chemistry	M
Mathematics	M

FAYETTEVILLE STATE UNIVERSITY

Mathematics	M

FISK UNIVERSITY

Chemistry	M
Physics	M

FLORIDA AGRICULTURAL AND MECHANICAL UNIVERSITY

Chemistry	M
Environmental Sciences	M,D
Physics	M,D

FLORIDA ATLANTIC UNIVERSITY

Applied Mathematics	M,D
Chemistry	M,D
Environmental Management and Policy	M,O
Environmental Sciences	M,D
Geology	M,D
Geosciences	M,D
Mathematics	M,D
Physics	M,D
Statistics	M,D

FLORIDA GULF COAST UNIVERSITY

Environmental Management and Policy	M
Environmental Sciences	M
Mathematics	M

FLORIDA INSTITUTE OF TECHNOLOGY

Applied Mathematics	M,D
Chemistry	M,D
Environmental Management and Policy	M
Environmental Sciences	M,D
Geosciences	M
Marine Sciences	M,D
Meteorology	M
Oceanography	M,D
Physics	M,D
Planetary and Space Sciences	M,D

FLORIDA INTERNATIONAL UNIVERSITY

Biostatistics	M,D
Chemistry	M,D
Environmental Management and Policy	M
Environmental Sciences	M
Geosciences	M
Mathematics	M
Physics	M
Statistics	M

FLORIDA STATE UNIVERSITY

Analytical Chemistry	M,D
Applied Mathematics	M,D
Applied Statistics	M,D
Atmospheric Sciences	M,D
Biostatistics	M,D
Chemistry	M,D

---

*M—master's; D—doctorate; O—other advanced degree; *Close-Up and/or Display*

Petersons Graduate Programs in the Physical Sciences, Mathematics, Agricultural Sciences, the Environment & Natural Resources 2017

www.petersons.com **21**

Computational Sciences — M,D
Environmental Sciences — M,D
Food Science and
 Technology — M,D
Geology — M,D
Geophysics — D
Geosciences — M,D
Inorganic Chemistry — M,D
Marine Sciences — M,D
Mathematical and
 Computational Finance — M,D
Mathematics — M,D
Meteorology — M,D
Oceanography — M,D
Organic Chemistry — M,D
Physical Chemistry — M,D
Physics — M,D
Statistics — M,D

FORT HAYS STATE UNIVERSITY
Geology — M
Geosciences — M

FORT VALLEY STATE UNIVERSITY
Animal Sciences — M

FRAMINGHAM STATE UNIVERSITY
Food Science and
 Technology — M

FROSTBURG STATE UNIVERSITY
Fish, Game, and Wildlife
 Management — M

FURMAN UNIVERSITY
Chemistry — M

GANNON UNIVERSITY
Environmental Sciences — M

GEORGE MASON UNIVERSITY
Applied Physics — M,D,O
Astronomy — M,D,O
Atmospheric Sciences — D
Biostatistics — M,D,O
Chemistry — M,D
Environmental Management
 and Policy — M,D
Environmental Sciences — M,D
Geosciences — M,D,O
Mathematics — M,D,O
Physics — M,D,O
Statistics — M,D,O

GEORGETOWN UNIVERSITY
Analytical Chemistry — D
Biostatistics — M,O
Chemistry — D
Inorganic Chemistry — D
Mathematics — M
Organic Chemistry — D
Statistics — M
Theoretical Chemistry — D

THE GEORGE WASHINGTON UNIVERSITY
Analytical Chemistry — M,D
Applied Mathematics — M,D,O
Biostatistics — M,D
Chemistry — M,D
Environmental Management
 and Policy — M
Inorganic Chemistry — M,D
Mathematical and
 Computational Finance — M,D,O
Mathematics — M,D,O
Organic Chemistry — M,D
Physical Chemistry — M,D
Physics — M,D
Statistics — M,D,O

GEORGIA INSTITUTE OF TECHNOLOGY
Atmospheric Sciences — M,D
Chemistry — M,D
Computational Sciences — M,D
Environmental Management
 and Policy — M,D
Geosciences — M,D
Mathematical and
 Computational Finance — M
Mathematics — M,D
Physics — M,D
Statistics — M

GEORGIA SOUTHERN UNIVERSITY
Applied Physics — M
Biostatistics — M,D
Environmental Sciences — O
Mathematics — M

GEORGIA STATE UNIVERSITY
Analytical Chemistry — M,D
Astronomy — D
Biostatistics — M,D
Chemistry — M,D
Environmental Management
 and Policy — M,D,O
Geochemistry — M,D
Geology — M
Geosciences — M,D,O
Mathematics — M,D
Organic Chemistry — M,D
Physical Chemistry — M,D
Physics — M,D
Statistics — M,D

GOUCHER COLLEGE
Environmental Management
 and Policy — M

GOVERNORS STATE UNIVERSITY
Analytical Chemistry — M

THE GRADUATE CENTER, CITY UNIVERSITY OF NEW YORK
Chemistry — D
Environmental Sciences — D
Geosciences — D
Mathematics — D

Physics — D

GRAND VALLEY STATE UNIVERSITY
Biostatistics — M

GREEN MOUNTAIN COLLEGE
Environmental Management
 and Policy — M

HAMPTON UNIVERSITY
Applied Mathematics — M
Atmospheric Sciences — M,D
Chemistry — M
Computational Sciences — M
Physics — M,D
Planetary and Space
 Sciences — M,D
Statistics — M

HARDIN-SIMMONS UNIVERSITY
Environmental Management
 and Policy — M
Mathematics — M

HARVARD UNIVERSITY
Applied Mathematics — M,D
Applied Physics — M,D
Astronomy — D
Astrophysics — D
Biostatistics — M,D
Chemical Physics — D
Chemistry — D
Computational Sciences — M,D
Environmental Management
 and Policy — M,O
Environmental Sciences — M
Forestry — M
Geosciences — M,D
Inorganic Chemistry — D
Mathematics — D
Organic Chemistry — D
Physical Chemistry — D
Physics — D
Planetary and Space
 Sciences — M,D
Statistics — M,D
Theoretical Physics — D

HAWAIʻI PACIFIC UNIVERSITY
Marine Sciences — M

HENDERSON STATE UNIVERSITY
Mathematics — M,O

HOFSTRA UNIVERSITY
Geology — M,D,O

HOWARD UNIVERSITY
Analytical Chemistry — M,D
Applied Mathematics — M,D
Atmospheric Sciences — M,D
Chemistry — M,D
Environmental Sciences — M,D
Inorganic Chemistry — M,D
Mathematics — M,D
Organic Chemistry — M,D
Physical Chemistry — M,D
Physics — M,D

HUMBOLDT STATE UNIVERSITY
Environmental Management
 and Policy — M
Environmental Sciences — M
Fish, Game, and Wildlife
 Management — M
Forestry — M
Geology — M
Natural Resources — M
Water Resources — M

HUNTER COLLEGE OF THE CITY UNIVERSITY OF NEW YORK
Applied Mathematics — M
Biostatistics — M
Chemistry — M
Geosciences — M
Mathematics — M
Physics — M
Statistics — M

IDAHO STATE UNIVERSITY
Applied Physics — M,D
Chemistry — M
Environmental Management
 and Policy — M
Environmental Sciences — M,O
Geology — M,O
Geophysics — M,O
Geosciences — M,O
Hydrology — M,O
Mathematics — M,D
Physics — M,D

ILLINOIS INSTITUTE OF TECHNOLOGY
Analytical Chemistry — M,D
Applied Mathematics — M,D
Applied Physics — M,D
Chemistry — M,D
Environmental Management
 and Policy — M
Food Science and
 Technology — M
Inorganic Chemistry — M,D
Mathematical and
 Computational Finance — M,D
Physics — M,D

ILLINOIS STATE UNIVERSITY
Agricultural Sciences—
 General — M
Chemistry — M
Hydrogeology — M
Hydrology — M
Mathematics — M
Plant Sciences — M

INDIANA STATE UNIVERSITY
Mathematics — M

INDIANA UNIVERSITY BLOOMINGTON
Analytical Chemistry — M,D
Applied Mathematics — M,D
Applied Statistics — M,D
Astronomy — M,D
Astrophysics — M,D
Biostatistics — M,D
Chemistry — M,D
Environmental Management
 and Policy — M,D,O
Environmental Sciences — M,D,O
Geochemistry — M,D
Geology — M,D
Geophysics — M,D
Geosciences — M,D
Hydrogeology — M,D
Inorganic Chemistry — M,D
Mathematical Physics — M,D
Mathematics — M,D
Mineralogy — M,D
Organic Chemistry — M,D
Physical Chemistry — M,D
Physics — M,D
Statistics — M,D

INDIANA UNIVERSITY NORTHWEST
Environmental Management
 and Policy — M,O

INDIANA UNIVERSITY OF PENNSYLVANIA
Applied Mathematics — M
Chemistry — M
Environmental Management
 and Policy — M
Mathematics — M
Physics — M

INDIANA UNIVERSITY–PURDUE UNIVERSITY FORT WAYNE
Applied Mathematics — M,O
Applied Statistics — M,O
Mathematics — M,O

INDIANA UNIVERSITY–PURDUE UNIVERSITY INDIANAPOLIS
Applied Mathematics — M,D
Applied Statistics — M,D
Biostatistics — M,D
Chemistry — M,D
Geology — M,D
Geosciences — M,D
Mathematics — M,D
Physics — M,D
Statistics — M,D

INDIANA UNIVERSITY SOUTH BEND
Applied Mathematics — M

INSTITUTO TECNOLOGICO DE SANTO DOMINGO
Environmental Management
 and Policy — M,D,O
Environmental Sciences — M,D,O
Marine Sciences — M,D,O
Mathematics — M,D,O
Natural Resources — M,D,O

INSTITUTO TECNOLÓGICO Y DE ESTUDIOS SUPERIORES DE MONTERREY, CAMPUS CIUDAD DE MÉXICO
Environmental Sciences — M,D

INSTITUTO TECNOLÓGICO Y DE ESTUDIOS SUPERIORES DE MONTERREY, CAMPUS ESTADO DE MÉXICO
Environmental Management
 and Policy — M,D

INSTITUTO TECNOLÓGICO Y DE ESTUDIOS SUPERIORES DE MONTERREY, CAMPUS IRAPUATO
Environmental Management
 and Policy — M,D

INSTITUTO TECNOLÓGICO Y DE ESTUDIOS SUPERIORES DE MONTERREY, CAMPUS MONTERREY
Agricultural Sciences—
 General — M,D
Applied Statistics — M,D
Chemistry — M,D
Organic Chemistry — M,D

INTER AMERICAN UNIVERSITY OF PUERTO RICO, METROPOLITAN CAMPUS
Environmental Management
 and Policy — M

INTER AMERICAN UNIVERSITY OF PUERTO RICO, SAN GERMÁN CAMPUS
Applied Mathematics — M
Environmental Sciences — M

IOWA STATE UNIVERSITY OF SCIENCE AND TECHNOLOGY
Agricultural Sciences—
 General — M,D
Agronomy and Soil Sciences — M,D
Analytical Chemistry — D
Animal Sciences — M,D
Applied Mathematics — M,D
Applied Physics — M,D
Astrophysics — M,D
Biostatistics — M,D
Chemistry — M,D
Condensed Matter Physics — M,D
Environmental Sciences — M,D
Fish, Game, and Wildlife
 Management — M,D
Food Science and
 Technology — M,D
Forestry — M,D
Geology — M,D

Geosciences — M,D
Horticulture — M,D
Inorganic Chemistry — M,D
Mathematics — M,D
Meteorology — M,D
Natural Resources — M,D
Organic Chemistry — M,D
Physical Chemistry — M,D
Physics — M,D
Plant Sciences — M,D
Statistics — M,D

JACKSON STATE UNIVERSITY
Chemistry — M,D
Environmental Sciences — M,D
Mathematics — M

JACKSONVILLE STATE UNIVERSITY
Mathematics — M

JACKSONVILLE UNIVERSITY
Marine Sciences — M

JOHN CARROLL UNIVERSITY
Mathematics — M

JOHNS HOPKINS UNIVERSITY
Applied Mathematics — M,D,O
Applied Physics — M,O
Astronomy — D
Biostatistics — M,D
Chemistry — M,D
Environmental Management
 and Policy — M,O
Environmental Sciences — M,O
Geosciences — M,D
Mathematical and
 Computational Finance — M,D
Mathematics — M,D
Physics — M,D
Statistics — M,D

KANSAS STATE UNIVERSITY
Agricultural Sciences—
 General — M,D,O
Agronomy and Soil Sciences — M,D,O
Analytical Chemistry — M,D
Animal Sciences — M,D
Chemistry — M,D
Environmental Sciences — M,D,O
Food Science and
 Technology — M,D
Geology — M
Horticulture — M,D
Inorganic Chemistry — M,D
Mathematics — M,D,O
Organic Chemistry — M,D
Physical Chemistry — M,D
Physics — M,D
Plant Sciences — M,D,O
Range Science — M,D,O
Statistics — M,D,O

KENNESAW STATE UNIVERSITY
Applied Statistics — M
Chemistry — M
Physics — M

KENT STATE UNIVERSITY
Applied Mathematics — M,D
Chemical Physics — M,D
Chemistry — M,D
Geology — M,D
Mathematics — M,D
Physics — M,D

KENTUCKY STATE UNIVERSITY
Aquaculture — M
Environmental Management
 and Policy — M

LAKE FOREST COLLEGE
Environmental Management
 and Policy — M

LAKEHEAD UNIVERSITY
Chemistry — M
Forestry — M,D
Geology — M
Mathematics — M
Physics — M

LAMAR UNIVERSITY
Chemistry — M
Environmental Management
 and Policy — M,D
Mathematics — M

LAURENTIAN UNIVERSITY
Analytical Chemistry — M
Applied Physics — M
Chemistry — M
Environmental Sciences — M
Geology — M,D
Natural Resources — M,D
Organic Chemistry — M
Physical Chemistry — M
Theoretical Chemistry — M

LEE UNIVERSITY
Mathematics — M,O

LEHIGH UNIVERSITY
Applied Mathematics — M,D
Chemistry — M,D
Computational Sciences — M,D
Environmental Management
 and Policy — M,O
Environmental Sciences — M,D
Geology — M,D
Geosciences — M,D
Mathematics — M,D
Photonics — M,D
Physics — M,D
Statistics — M,D

LEHMAN COLLEGE OF THE CITY UNIVERSITY OF NEW YORK
Mathematics — M
Plant Sciences — D

LOMA LINDA UNIVERSITY
Biostatistics — M,D,O
Geosciences — M,D

LONDON METROPOLITAN UNIVERSITY
Food Science and
  Technology — M,D

LONG ISLAND UNIVERSITY–LIU BROOKLYN
Chemistry — M,D,O

LONG ISLAND UNIVERSITY–LIU POST
Applied Mathematics — M,O
Environmental Management
  and Policy — M,O
Geosciences — M,O
Mathematics — M,O

LOUISIANA STATE UNIVERSITY AND AGRICULTURAL & MECHANICAL COLLEGE
Agricultural Sciences—
  General — M,D
Animal Sciences — M,D
Applied Statistics — M
Astronomy — M,D
Astrophysics — M,D
Chemistry — M,D
Environmental Management
  and Policy — M,D
Environmental Sciences — M,D
Fish, Game, and Wildlife
  Management — M,D
Food Science and
  Technology — M,D
Forestry — M,D
Geology — M,D
Geophysics — M,D
Marine Affairs — M,D
Mathematics — M,D
Natural Resources — M,D
Oceanography — M,D
Physics — M,D
Statistics — M

LOUISIANA STATE UNIVERSITY HEALTH SCIENCES CENTER
Biostatistics — M,D

LOUISIANA TECH UNIVERSITY
Applied Physics — M
Chemistry — M
Mathematics — M,D
Physics — M
Statistics — M,D

LOYOLA MARYMOUNT UNIVERSITY
Environmental Sciences — M

LOYOLA UNIVERSITY CHICAGO
Applied Statistics — M
Chemistry — M,D
Mathematics — M
Statistics — M

MANHATTAN COLLEGE
Applied Mathematics — M
Mathematics — M

MARLBORO COLLEGE
Food Science and
  Technology — M

MARQUETTE UNIVERSITY
Analytical Chemistry — M,D
Chemical Physics — M,D
Chemistry — M,D
Computational Sciences — M,D
Inorganic Chemistry — M,D
Mathematics — M,D
Organic Chemistry — M,D
Physical Chemistry — M,D
Water Resources — M,D,O

MARSHALL UNIVERSITY
Chemistry — M
Environmental Sciences — M
Mathematics — M
Physics — M

MASSACHUSETTS INSTITUTE OF TECHNOLOGY
Atmospheric Sciences — M,D
Chemistry — D
Computational Sciences — M
Environmental Sciences — M,D,O
Geochemistry — M,D
Geology — M,D
Geophysics — M,D
Geosciences — M,D
Hydrology — M,D,O
Inorganic Chemistry — D
Marine Geology — M,D
Mathematics — D
Oceanography — M,D,O
Organic Chemistry — M,D,O
Physical Chemistry — D
Physics — M,D
Planetary and Space
  Sciences — M,D

MCGILL UNIVERSITY
Agricultural Sciences—
  General — M,D,O
Agronomy and Soil Sciences — M,D
Animal Sciences — M,D
Applied Mathematics — M,D
Atmospheric Sciences — M,D,O
Biostatistics — M,D
Chemistry — M,D
Computational Sciences — M,D
Environmental Management
  and Policy — M,D

Fish, Game, and Wildlife
  Management — M,D
Food Science and
  Technology — M,D
Forestry — M,D
Geosciences — M,D
Mathematics — M,D
Meteorology — M,D
Natural Resources — M,D
Oceanography — M,D
Physics — M,D
Planetary and Space
  Sciences — M,D
Plant Sciences — M,D,O
Statistics — M,D,O

MCMASTER UNIVERSITY
Analytical Chemistry — M,D
Applied Statistics — M
Astrophysics — D
Chemical Physics — M,D
Chemistry — M,D
Geochemistry — M,D
Geology — M,D
Geosciences — M,D
Inorganic Chemistry — M,D
Mathematics — M,D
Organic Chemistry — M,D
Physical Chemistry — M,D
Physics — D
Statistics — M

MCNEESE STATE UNIVERSITY
Agricultural Sciences—
  General — M
Chemistry — M
Environmental Sciences — M
Mathematics — M
Statistics — M

MCPHS UNIVERSITY
Chemistry — M,D

MEDICAL COLLEGE OF WISCONSIN
Biostatistics — D*

MEDICAL UNIVERSITY OF SOUTH CAROLINA
Biostatistics — M,D
Marine Sciences — D

MEMORIAL UNIVERSITY OF NEWFOUNDLAND
Aquaculture — M
Chemistry — M,D
Computational Sciences — M,D
Condensed Matter Physics — M,D
Environmental Sciences — M,D
Fish, Game, and Wildlife
  Management — M,O
Food Science and
  Technology — M,D
Geology — M,D
Geophysics — M,D
Geosciences — M,D
Marine Affairs — M,D,O
Marine Sciences — M,O
Mathematics — M,D
Oceanography — M,D
Physics — M,D
Statistics — M,D

MERCER UNIVERSITY
Environmental Sciences — M

MIAMI UNIVERSITY
Chemistry — M,D
Environmental Sciences — M,D
Geology — M,D
Mathematics — M
Physics — M
Statistics — M

MICHIGAN STATE UNIVERSITY
Agricultural Sciences—
  General — M,D
Agronomy and Soil Sciences — M,D
Animal Sciences — M,D
Applied Mathematics — M,D
Applied Statistics — M,D
Astronomy — M,D
Astrophysics — M,D
Chemical Physics — M,D
Chemistry — M,D
Environmental Sciences — M,D
Fish, Game, and Wildlife
  Management — M,D
Food Science and
  Technology — M,D
Forestry — M,D
Geosciences — M,D
Horticulture — M,D
Mathematics — M,D
Natural Resources — M,D
Physics — M,D
Plant Sciences — M,D
Statistics — M,D

MICHIGAN TECHNOLOGICAL UNIVERSITY
Applied Physics — M,D
Atmospheric Sciences — M,D,O
Chemistry — M,D,O
Computational Sciences — M,D,O
Environmental Management
  and Policy — M,D
Forestry — M,D
Geology — M,D
Geophysics — M,D
Mathematics — M,D
Physics — M,D
Water Resources — M,D,O

MIDDLEBURY INSTITUTE OF INTERNATIONAL STUDIES AT MONTEREY
Environmental Management
  and Policy — M

MIDDLE TENNESSEE STATE UNIVERSITY
Biostatistics — M
Chemistry — M
Computational Sciences — D
Geosciences — O
Mathematics — M

MILLERSVILLE UNIVERSITY OF PENNSYLVANIA
Atmospheric Sciences — M
Environmental Management
  and Policy — M
Meteorology — M

MINNESOTA STATE UNIVERSITY MANKATO
Astronomy — M
Environmental Sciences — M
Mathematics — M
Physics — M
Statistics — M

MISSISSIPPI COLLEGE
Chemistry — M
Mathematics — M

MISSISSIPPI STATE UNIVERSITY
Agricultural Sciences—
  General — M,D
Agronomy and Soil Sciences — M,D
Animal Sciences — M,D
Applied Physics — M,D
Atmospheric Sciences — M,D
Chemistry — M,D
Fish, Game, and Wildlife
  Management — M,D
Food Science and
  Technology — M,D
Forestry — M,D
Geology — M,D
Geosciences — M,D
Horticulture — M,D
Mathematics — M,D
Meteorology — M,D
Physics — M,D
Plant Sciences — M,D
Statistics — M,D

MISSOURI STATE UNIVERSITY
Agricultural Sciences—
  General — M
Chemistry — M
Environmental Management
  and Policy — M,O
Geology — M
Geosciences — M
Mathematics — M
Physics — M
Plant Sciences — M

MISSOURI UNIVERSITY OF SCIENCE AND TECHNOLOGY
Applied Mathematics — M,D
Chemistry — M,D
Geochemistry — M,D
Geology — M,D
Geophysics — M,D
Hydrology — M,D
Mathematics — M,D
Physics — M,D
Statistics — M,D
Water Resources — M,D

MISSOURI WESTERN STATE UNIVERSITY
Chemistry — M

MOLLOY COLLEGE
Mathematics — M,O

MONTANA STATE UNIVERSITY
Agricultural Sciences—
  General — M,D
Animal Sciences — M,D
Chemistry — M,D
Environmental Sciences — M,D
Fish, Game, and Wildlife
  Management — M,D
Geosciences — M,D
Mathematics — M,D
Natural Resources — M
Physics — M,D
Plant Sciences — M,D
Range Science — M,D
Statistics — M,D

MONTANA TECH OF THE UNIVERSITY OF MONTANA
Geochemistry — M
Geology — M
Geosciences — M
Hydrogeology — M

MONTCLAIR STATE UNIVERSITY
Applied Mathematics — M
Chemistry — M
Environmental Management
  and Policy — M,D
Environmental Sciences — M
Geosciences — M
Mathematics — M
Statistics — M
Water Resources — O

MOREHEAD STATE UNIVERSITY
Agricultural Sciences—
  General — M

Environmental Management
  and Policy — M

MORGAN STATE UNIVERSITY
Chemistry — M
Mathematics — M

MOUNT ALLISON UNIVERSITY
Chemistry — M

MURRAY STATE UNIVERSITY
Agricultural Sciences—
  General — M
Chemistry — M
Environmental Sciences — M
Geosciences — M
Hydrology — M
Mathematics — M
Statistics — M

NAROPA UNIVERSITY
Environmental Management
  and Policy — M

NAVAL POSTGRADUATE SCHOOL
Acoustics — M,D
Applied Mathematics — M,D
Applied Physics — M,D,O
Meteorology — M,D
Oceanography — M,D
Physics — M,D

NEW JERSEY INSTITUTE OF TECHNOLOGY
Applied Mathematics — M,D,O
Applied Physics — M,D,O
Applied Statistics — M,D,O
Biostatistics — M,D,O
Chemistry — M,D,O
Environmental Sciences — M,D,O
Mathematical and
  Computational Finance — M,D,O
Mathematics — M,D,O
Statistics — M,D,O

NEW MEXICO HIGHLANDS UNIVERSITY
Chemistry — M
Natural Resources — M

NEW MEXICO INSTITUTE OF MINING AND TECHNOLOGY
Applied Mathematics — M,D
Astrophysics — M,D
Atmospheric Sciences — M,D
Chemistry — M,D
Geochemistry — M,D
Geology — M,D
Geophysics — M,D
Geosciences — M,D
Hydrology — M,D
Mathematical Physics — M,D
Mathematics — M,D
Physics — M,D
Statistics — M,D

NEW MEXICO STATE UNIVERSITY
Animal Sciences — M,D
Applied Statistics — M,D,O
Astronomy — M,D
Astrophysics — M,D
Chemistry — M,D
Environmental Sciences — M,D
Fish, Game, and Wildlife
  Management — M
Food Science and
  Technology — M
Geology — M
Horticulture — M,D
Hydrology — M,D
Mathematics — M,D
Physics — M,D
Plant Sciences — M
Range Science — M,D
Water Resources — M,D

THE NEW SCHOOL
Environmental Management
  and Policy — M,O

NEW YORK INSTITUTE OF TECHNOLOGY
Environmental Management
  and Policy — M,O

NEW YORK MEDICAL COLLEGE
Biostatistics — M

NEW YORK UNIVERSITY
Applied Physics — M,D
Applied Statistics — M
Chemistry — M,D,O
Environmental Management
  and Policy — M,O
Environmental Sciences — M
Food Science and
  Technology — M,D
Mathematical and
  Computational Finance — M,D,O
Mathematics — M,D*
Physics — M,D,O
Statistics — M,D

NICHOLLS STATE UNIVERSITY
Mathematics — M

NORFOLK STATE UNIVERSITY
Optical Sciences — M

NORTH CAROLINA AGRICULTURAL AND TECHNICAL STATE UNIVERSITY
Agricultural Sciences—
  General — M
Agronomy and Soil Sciences — M
Animal Sciences — M
Applied Mathematics — M
Chemistry — M,D

*M—master's; D—doctorate; O—other advanced degree; *Close-Up and/or Display*

*Petersons Graduate Programs in the Physical Sciences, Mathematics,
Agricultural Sciences, the Environment & Natural Resources 2017*

www.petersons.com **23**

Computational Sciences — M
Environmental Sciences — M
Mathematics — M
Optical Sciences — M,D
Physics — M
Plant Sciences — M

NORTH CAROLINA CENTRAL UNIVERSITY
Applied Mathematics — M
Chemistry — M
Geosciences — M
Mathematics — M
Physics — M

NORTH CAROLINA STATE UNIVERSITY
Agricultural Sciences—
   General — M,D,O
Agronomy and Soil Sciences — M,D
Animal Sciences — M,D
Applied Mathematics — M,D
Atmospheric Sciences — M,D
Biomathematics — M,D
Chemistry — M,D
Fish, Game, and Wildlife
   Management — M,D
Food Science and
   Technology — M,D
Forestry — M,D
Geosciences — M,D
Horticulture — M,D,O
Marine Sciences — M,D
Mathematical and
   Computational Finance — M
Mathematics — M,D
Meteorology — M,D
Natural Resources — M,D
Oceanography — M,D
Physics — M,D
Statistics — M,D

NORTH DAKOTA STATE UNIVERSITY
Agricultural Sciences—
   General — M,D
Agronomy and Soil Sciences — M,D
Animal Sciences — M,D
Applied Mathematics — M,D
Applied Statistics — M,D,O
Chemistry — M,D
Environmental Sciences — M,D
Food Science and
   Technology — M,D,O
Mathematics — M,D
Natural Resources — M,D
Physics — M,D
Plant Sciences — M,D
Statistics — M,D,O

NORTHEASTERN ILLINOIS UNIVERSITY
Applied Mathematics — M
Chemistry — M
Environmental Management
   and Policy — M
Mathematics — M

NORTHEASTERN STATE UNIVERSITY
Environmental Management
   and Policy — M
Natural Resources — M

NORTHEASTERN UNIVERSITY
Applied Mathematics — M,D
Chemistry — M,D
Mathematics — M,D
Physics — M,D

NORTHERN ARIZONA UNIVERSITY
Applied Physics — M,D
Applied Statistics — M,O
Atmospheric Sciences — M,D
Chemistry — M
Environmental Management
   and Policy — M,D
Environmental Sciences — M,D
Forestry — M,D
Geology — M,D
Mathematics — M,O
Meteorology — M,D
Physics — M,D
Statistics — M,O

NORTHERN ILLINOIS UNIVERSITY
Chemistry — M,D
Geology — M,D
Mathematics — M,D
Physics — M,D
Statistics — M

NORTHWESTERN UNIVERSITY
Applied Mathematics — M,D
Applied Physics — D
Astronomy — D
Biostatistics — D
Chemistry — D
Geology — D
Geosciences — D
Mathematics — D
Physics — D
Statistics — D

NORTHWEST MISSOURI STATE UNIVERSITY
Agricultural Sciences—
   General — M
Mathematics — M

NOVA SOUTHEASTERN UNIVERSITY
Atmospheric Sciences — M,D,O
Environmental Sciences — M,D,O
Marine Affairs — M,D,O
Marine Sciences — M,D,O
Oceanography — M,D,O

OAKLAND UNIVERSITY
Applied Mathematics — M,D
Applied Statistics — M
Chemistry — M,D
Environmental Sciences — M,D

Mathematics — M
Physics — M,D
Statistics — O

THE OHIO STATE UNIVERSITY
Agricultural Sciences—
   General — M,D
Agronomy and Soil Sciences — M,D
Animal Sciences — M,D
Astronomy — M,D
Atmospheric Sciences — M,D
Biostatistics — M,D
Chemical Physics — M,D
Chemistry — M,D
Computational Sciences — M,D
Environmental Management
   and Policy — M,D
Environmental Sciences — M,D
Fish, Game, and Wildlife
   Management — M,D
Food Science and
   Technology — M,D
Forestry — M,D
Geodetic Sciences — M,D
Geology — M,D
Geosciences — M,D
Horticulture — M,D
Mathematics — M,D
Natural Resources — M,D
Optical Sciences — M,D
Physics — M,D
Plant Sciences — D
Statistics — M,D

OHIO UNIVERSITY
Astronomy — M,D
Environmental Management
   and Policy — M
Geochemistry — M
Geology — M
Geophysics — M
Hydrogeology — M
Mathematics — M
Physics — M,D

OKLAHOMA STATE UNIVERSITY
Agricultural Sciences—
   General — M,D
Agronomy and Soil Sciences — M,D
Animal Sciences — M,D
Applied Mathematics — M,D
Chemistry — M,D
Environmental Sciences — M,D,O
Food Science and
   Technology — M,D
Forestry — M,D
Geology — M,D
Horticulture — M,D
Mathematics — M,D
Natural Resources — M,D
Photonics — M,D
Physics — M,D
Plant Sciences — M,D
Statistics — M,D

OLD DOMINION UNIVERSITY
Analytical Chemistry — M,D
Biostatistics — M,D
Chemistry — M,D
Environmental Sciences — M,D
Inorganic Chemistry — M,D
Mathematics — M,D
Oceanography — M,D
Organic Chemistry — M,D
Physical Chemistry — M,D
Physics — M,D
Statistics — M,D
Water Resources — M

OREGON HEALTH & SCIENCE UNIVERSITY
Environmental Sciences — M,D

OREGON STATE UNIVERSITY
Agronomy and Soil Sciences — M,D
Analytical Chemistry — M,D
Animal Sciences — M,D
Applied Mathematics — M,D
Atmospheric Sciences — M,D
Biostatistics — M,D
Chemistry — M,D
Computational Sciences — M,D
Environmental Management
   and Policy — M,D
Environmental Sciences — M,D
Fish, Game, and Wildlife
   Management — M,D
Food Science and
   Technology — M,D
Forestry — M,D
Geochemistry — M,D
Geology — M,D
Geophysics — M,D
Horticulture — M,D
Inorganic Chemistry — M,D
Marine Affairs — M
Marine Sciences — M
Mathematical and
   Computational Finance — M,D
Mathematics — M,D
Natural Resources — M,D
Oceanography — M,D
Organic Chemistry — M,D
Physical Chemistry — M,D
Physics — M,D
Range Science — M,D
Statistics — M,D
Water Resources — M,D

PACE UNIVERSITY
Chemistry — M,O
Environmental Management
   and Policy — M
Environmental Sciences — M
Geosciences — M
Mathematics — M,O

Physics — M,O

PENN STATE HARRISBURG
Environmental Sciences — M,O

PENN STATE HERSHEY MEDICAL CENTER
Biostatistics — D

PENN STATE UNIVERSITY PARK
Acoustics — M,D
Agricultural Sciences—
   General — M,D,O
Agronomy and Soil Sciences — M,D
Animal Sciences — M,D
Applied Statistics — M,D
Astronomy — M,D
Astrophysics — M,D
Chemistry — M,D
Environmental Management
   and Policy — M
Environmental Sciences — M
Fish, Game, and Wildlife
   Management — M,D
Food Science and
   Technology — M,D
Forestry — M,D
Geosciences — M,D
Horticulture — M,D
Mathematics — M,D
Meteorology — M,D
Physics — M,D
Plant Sciences — M,D
Statistics — M,D

PEPPERDINE UNIVERSITY
Mathematics — M,D

PITTSBURG STATE UNIVERSITY
Chemistry — M
Mathematics — M
Physics — M

PLYMOUTH STATE UNIVERSITY
Environmental Management
   and Policy — M
Meteorology — M

POINT PARK UNIVERSITY
Environmental Management
   and Policy — M

POLYTECHNIC UNIVERSITY OF PUERTO RICO
Environmental Management
   and Policy — M

POLYTECHNIC UNIVERSITY OF PUERTO RICO, MIAMI CAMPUS
Environmental Management
   and Policy — M

POLYTECHNIC UNIVERSITY OF PUERTO RICO, ORLANDO CAMPUS
Environmental Management
   and Policy — M

PONTIFICAL CATHOLIC UNIVERSITY OF PUERTO RICO
Chemistry — M
Environmental Sciences — M

PORTLAND STATE UNIVERSITY
Chemistry — M,D
Environmental Management
   and Policy — M,D
Environmental Sciences — M,D
Geology — M,D
Mathematics — M,D,O
Physics — M,D
Statistics — M,D

PRAIRIE VIEW A&M UNIVERSITY
Agricultural Sciences—
   General — M
Chemistry — M

PRESCOTT COLLEGE
Environmental Management
   and Policy — M

PRINCETON UNIVERSITY
Applied Mathematics — D
Astronomy — D
Astrophysics — D
Atmospheric Sciences — D
Chemistry — M,D
Computational Sciences — D
Geosciences — D
Mathematics — D
Oceanography — D
Photonics — D
Physics — D
Plasma Physics — D

PURDUE UNIVERSITY
Agricultural Sciences—
   General — M,D
Agronomy and Soil Sciences — M,D
Analytical Chemistry — M,D
Animal Sciences — M,D
Applied Statistics — M,D
Aquaculture — M,D
Atmospheric Sciences — M,D
Chemistry — M,D
Computational Sciences — M,D
Environmental Management
   and Policy — M,D
Fish, Game, and Wildlife
   Management — M,D
Food Science and
   Technology — M,D
Forestry — M,D
Geosciences — M,D
Horticulture — M,D
Inorganic Chemistry — M,D
Mathematical and
   Computational Finance — M,D
Mathematics — M,D

Natural Resources — M,D
Organic Chemistry — M,D
Physical Chemistry — M,D
Physics — M,D
Plant Sciences — D
Statistics — M,D

PURDUE UNIVERSITY NORTHWEST
Mathematics — M

QUEENS COLLEGE OF THE CITY UNIVERSITY OF NEW YORK
Chemistry — M
Environmental Sciences — M
Geology — M
Geosciences — M
Mathematics — M
Physics — M

QUEEN'S UNIVERSITY AT KINGSTON
Chemistry — M,D
Geology — M,D
Mathematics — M,D
Physics — M,D
Statistics — M,D

RENSSELAER POLYTECHNIC INSTITUTE
Acoustics — M,D
Applied Mathematics — M
Chemistry — M,D
Geology — M,D
Mathematics — M,D
Physics — M,D

RHODE ISLAND COLLEGE
Mathematics — M,O

RICE UNIVERSITY
Applied Mathematics — M,D
Applied Physics — M,D
Astronomy — M,D
Biostatistics — M,D
Chemistry — M,D
Computational Sciences — M,D
Environmental Management
   and Policy — M
Environmental Sciences — M,D
Geophysics — M
Geosciences — M,D
Inorganic Chemistry — M,D
Mathematical and
   Computational Finance — M,D
Mathematics — D
Organic Chemistry — M,D
Physical Chemistry — M,D
Physics — M,D
Statistics — M,D

RIVIER UNIVERSITY
Mathematics — M

ROCHESTER INSTITUTE OF TECHNOLOGY
Applied Mathematics — M
Applied Statistics — M,O
Astrophysics — M,D
Chemistry — M
Environmental Sciences — M
Mathematical and
   Computational Finance — M
Mathematics — M,O
Optical Sciences — M,D
Statistics — O

ROOSEVELT UNIVERSITY
Chemistry — M
Mathematics — M

ROSE-HULMAN INSTITUTE OF TECHNOLOGY
Optical Sciences — M

ROWAN UNIVERSITY
Mathematics — M

ROYAL MILITARY COLLEGE OF CANADA
Chemistry — M,D
Environmental Sciences — M,D
Mathematics — M,D
Physics — M

ROYAL ROADS UNIVERSITY
Environmental Management
   and Policy — M,O

RUTGERS UNIVERSITY–CAMDEN
Applied Mathematics — M
Chemistry — M
Mathematics — M

RUTGERS UNIVERSITY–NEWARK
Analytical Chemistry — M,D
Applied Physics — M,D
Chemistry — M,D
Environmental Sciences — M,D
Geology — M
Inorganic Chemistry — M,D
Mathematics — D
Organic Chemistry — M,D
Physical Chemistry — M,D

RUTGERS UNIVERSITY–NEW BRUNSWICK
Animal Sciences — M,D
Applied Mathematics — M,D
Applied Statistics — M,D
Astronomy — M,D
Atmospheric Sciences — M,D
Biostatistics — M,D,O
Chemistry — M,D
Condensed Matter Physics — M,D
Environmental Sciences — M,D
Food Science and
   Technology — M,D
Geology — M,D
Horticulture — M,D
Inorganic Chemistry — M,D

Mathematics	M,D
Oceanography	M,D
Organic Chemistry	M,D
Physical Chemistry	M,D
Physics	M,D
Statistics	M,D
Theoretical Physics	M,D
Water Resources	M,D

SACRED HEART UNIVERSITY

Chemistry	M
Environmental Management and Policy	M

ST. CLOUD STATE UNIVERSITY

Applied Statistics	M
Environmental Management and Policy	M
Mathematics	M

ST. EDWARD'S UNIVERSITY

Environmental Management and Policy	M

ST. FRANCIS XAVIER UNIVERSITY

Chemistry	M
Geology	M
Geosciences	M
Physics	M

ST. JOHN'S UNIVERSITY (NY)

Chemistry	M

SAINT JOSEPH'S UNIVERSITY

Mathematics	M,O

SAINT LOUIS UNIVERSITY

Chemistry	M,D
Geophysics	M,D
Geosciences	M,D
Mathematics	M,D
Meteorology	M,D

SAINT MARY'S UNIVERSITY (CANADA)

Astronomy	M,D

ST. THOMAS UNIVERSITY

Geosciences	M,D,O
Planetary and Space Sciences	M,D,O

SALEM STATE UNIVERSITY

Mathematics	M

SAMFORD UNIVERSITY

Environmental Management and Policy	M
Mathematics	M,D,O

SAM HOUSTON STATE UNIVERSITY

Agricultural Sciences— General	M
Chemistry	M
Computational Sciences	M,D
Mathematics	M
Statistics	M

SAN DIEGO STATE UNIVERSITY

Applied Mathematics	M
Astronomy	M
Biometry	M
Biostatistics	M,D
Chemistry	M,D
Computational Sciences	M,D
Geology	M
Mathematics	M,D
Physics	M
Statistics	M

SAN FRANCISCO STATE UNIVERSITY

Astronomy	M
Chemistry	M
Environmental Management and Policy	M
Geosciences	M
Marine Sciences	M
Mathematics	M
Physics	M

SAN JOSE STATE UNIVERSITY

Chemistry	M,O
Computational Sciences	M,O
Environmental Management and Policy	M,O
Geology	M,O
Marine Sciences	M,O
Mathematics	M,D,O
Meteorology	M,O
Physics	M,O
Statistics	M,O

SANTA CLARA UNIVERSITY

Applied Mathematics	M,D,O

SAVANNAH STATE UNIVERSITY

Marine Sciences	M

THE SCRIPPS RESEARCH INSTITUTE

Chemistry	D

SETON HALL UNIVERSITY

Analytical Chemistry	M,D
Chemistry	M,D
Inorganic Chemistry	M,D
Organic Chemistry	M,D
Physical Chemistry	M,D

SHIPPENSBURG UNIVERSITY OF PENNSYLVANIA

Environmental Management and Policy	M

SIMON FRASER UNIVERSITY

Applied Mathematics	M,D
Chemistry	M,D
Computational Sciences	M,D
Environmental Management and Policy	M,D,O

Fish, Game, and Wildlife Management	M,D,O
Geosciences	M,D
Mathematics	M,D
Physics	M,D
Statistics	M,D

SITTING BULL COLLEGE

Environmental Sciences	M

SLIPPERY ROCK UNIVERSITY OF PENNSYLVANIA

Environmental Management and Policy	M

SMITH COLLEGE

Chemistry	O
Mathematics	O

SOUTH CAROLINA STATE UNIVERSITY

Mathematics	M

SOUTH DAKOTA SCHOOL OF MINES AND TECHNOLOGY

Atmospheric Sciences	M,D
Environmental Sciences	D
Geology	M,D
Paleontology	M,D
Physics	M,D

SOUTH DAKOTA STATE UNIVERSITY

Agricultural Sciences— General	M,D
Agronomy and Soil Sciences	M,D
Animal Sciences	M,D
Chemistry	M,D
Computational Sciences	M,D
Fish, Game, and Wildlife Management	M,D
Geosciences	D
Mathematics	M,D
Physics	M
Plant Sciences	M,D
Statistics	M,D

SOUTHEAST MISSOURI STATE UNIVERSITY

Chemistry	M
Environmental Management and Policy	M
Environmental Sciences	M
Mathematics	M

SOUTHERN ARKANSAS UNIVERSITY–MAGNOLIA

Agricultural Sciences— General	M

SOUTHERN CONNECTICUT STATE UNIVERSITY

Chemistry	M
Environmental Sciences	M,O
Marine Sciences	M,O
Mathematics	M

SOUTHERN ILLINOIS UNIVERSITY CARBONDALE

Agricultural Sciences— General	M
Agronomy and Soil Sciences	M
Animal Sciences	M
Applied Physics	M,D
Chemistry	M,D
Environmental Management and Policy	M,D
Environmental Sciences	D
Forestry	M
Geology	M,D
Geosciences	M,D
Mathematics	M,D
Physics	M,D
Plant Sciences	M

SOUTHERN ILLINOIS UNIVERSITY EDWARDSVILLE

Applied Mathematics	M
Chemistry	M
Computational Sciences	M
Environmental Management and Policy	M
Environmental Sciences	M
Mathematics	M
Statistics	M

SOUTHERN METHODIST UNIVERSITY

Applied Mathematics	M,D
Atmospheric Sciences	M,D
Chemistry	M,D
Computational Sciences	M,D
Environmental Sciences	M,D
Geology	M,D
Geophysics	M,D
Mathematics	M,D
Physics	M,D
Statistics	M,D

SOUTHERN NEW HAMPSHIRE UNIVERSITY

Environmental Management and Policy	M,O

SOUTHERN OREGON UNIVERSITY

Applied Mathematics	M

SOUTHERN UNIVERSITY AND AGRICULTURAL AND MECHANICAL COLLEGE

Agricultural Sciences— General	M
Analytical Chemistry	M
Chemistry	M
Environmental Sciences	M
Forestry	M
Inorganic Chemistry	M
Mathematics	M

Organic Chemistry	M
Physical Chemistry	M
Physics	M

STANFORD UNIVERSITY

Applied Physics	M,D
Biostatistics	M,D
Chemistry	D
Computational Sciences	M,D
Environmental Sciences	M,D,O
Geophysics	M,D
Geosciences	M,D,O
Hydrology	M,D,O
Mathematics	M,D
Physics	D
Statistics	M,D

STATE UNIVERSITY OF NEW YORK AT NEW PALTZ

Chemistry	M,O
Geosciences	M,O

STATE UNIVERSITY OF NEW YORK AT OSWEGO

Chemistry	M

STATE UNIVERSITY OF NEW YORK COLLEGE AT ONEONTA

Geosciences	M

STATE UNIVERSITY OF NEW YORK COLLEGE AT POTSDAM

Mathematics	M

STATE UNIVERSITY OF NEW YORK COLLEGE OF ENVIRONMENTAL SCIENCE AND FORESTRY

Chemistry	M,D
Environmental Management and Policy	M,D
Environmental Sciences	M,D
Fish, Game, and Wildlife Management	M,D
Forestry	M,D
Natural Resources	M,D
Organic Chemistry	M,D
Plant Sciences	M,D
Water Resources	M,D

STEPHEN F. AUSTIN STATE UNIVERSITY

Chemistry	M
Environmental Sciences	M
Forestry	M,D
Geology	M
Mathematics	M
Physics	M
Statistics	M

STEVENS INSTITUTE OF TECHNOLOGY

Analytical Chemistry	M,D,O
Applied Mathematics	M
Applied Statistics	O
Atmospheric Sciences	M,D,O
Chemistry	M,D,O
Hydrology	M,D,O
Marine Affairs	M,D
Mathematics	M,D
Photonics	M,D,O
Physics	M,D,O
Statistics	M,O

STEVENSON UNIVERSITY

Chemistry	M

STOCKTON UNIVERSITY

Computational Sciences	M
Environmental Sciences	M

STONY BROOK UNIVERSITY, STATE UNIVERSITY OF NEW YORK

Applied Mathematics	M,D,O
Astronomy	D
Atmospheric Sciences	M,D
Chemistry	M,D
Environmental Management and Policy	M,O
Geosciences	M,D
Marine Affairs	M
Marine Sciences	M,D
Mathematics	M,D
Physics	M,D
Statistics	M,D,O

SUL ROSS STATE UNIVERSITY

Animal Sciences	M
Fish, Game, and Wildlife Management	M
Geology	M
Natural Resources	M
Range Science	M

SYRACUSE UNIVERSITY

Applied Statistics	M
Chemistry	M,D
Geology	M,D
Geosciences	M,D
Mathematics	M,D
Physics	M,D

TARLETON STATE UNIVERSITY

Agricultural Sciences— General	M
Mathematics	M

TEACHERS COLLEGE, COLUMBIA UNIVERSITY

Applied Statistics	M,D
Chemistry	M,D
Geosciences	M,D
Physics	M,D

TEMPLE UNIVERSITY

Applied Mathematics	M,D
Chemistry	M,D
Computational Sciences	M,D
Geology	M,D

Hydrology	M,O
Mathematics	M,D
Physics	M,D
Statistics	M,D

TENNESSEE STATE UNIVERSITY

Agricultural Sciences— General	M,D
Agronomy and Soil Sciences	M,D
Chemistry	M
Mathematics	M,D
Plant Sciences	M,D

TENNESSEE TECHNOLOGICAL UNIVERSITY

Chemistry	M,D
Environmental Management and Policy	M
Environmental Sciences	D
Fish, Game, and Wildlife Management	M
Mathematics	M

TEXAS A&M INTERNATIONAL UNIVERSITY

Mathematics	M

TEXAS A&M UNIVERSITY

Agricultural Sciences— General	M,D
Agronomy and Soil Sciences	M,D
Animal Sciences	M,D
Applied Physics	M,D
Chemistry	M,D
Fish, Game, and Wildlife Management	M,D
Food Science and Technology	M,D
Forestry	M,D
Geology	M,D
Geophysics	M,D
Horticulture	M,D
Mathematics	M,D
Meteorology	M,D
Natural Resources	M,D
Oceanography	M,D
Physics	M,D
Range Science	M,D
Statistics	M,D

TEXAS A&M UNIVERSITY AT GALVESTON

Marine Sciences	M

TEXAS A&M UNIVERSITY–CENTRAL TEXAS

Mathematics	M,O

TEXAS A&M UNIVERSITY–COMMERCE

Agricultural Sciences— General	M

TEXAS A&M UNIVERSITY–CORPUS CHRISTI

Aquaculture	M
Environmental Sciences	M
Marine Sciences	M,D
Mathematics	M

TEXAS A&M UNIVERSITY–KINGSVILLE

Agricultural Sciences— General	M,D
Agronomy and Soil Sciences	M
Animal Sciences	M
Chemistry	M
Fish, Game, and Wildlife Management	M,D
Horticulture	M,D
Mathematics	M
Plant Sciences	M
Range Science	M
Statistics	M

TEXAS CHRISTIAN UNIVERSITY

Applied Mathematics	M,D
Astrophysics	M,D
Chemistry	M,D
Environmental Sciences	M
Geology	M
Mathematics	M,D
Physics	M,D

TEXAS SOUTHERN UNIVERSITY

Chemistry	M
Environmental Management and Policy	M,D
Mathematics	M

TEXAS STATE UNIVERSITY

Applied Mathematics	M
Chemistry	M
Environmental Management and Policy	M
Fish, Game, and Wildlife Management	M
Mathematics	M
Physics	M

TEXAS TECH UNIVERSITY

Agricultural Sciences— General	M,D
Agronomy and Soil Sciences	M,D
Animal Sciences	M,D
Applied Physics	M,D
Atmospheric Sciences	M,D
Chemistry	M,D
Environmental Management and Policy	M,D
Environmental Sciences	M,D
Fish, Game, and Wildlife Management	M,D
Food Science and Technology	M,D
Geosciences	M,D
Horticulture	M,D

*M—master's; D—doctorate; O—other advanced degree; *Close-Up and/or Display*

Petersons Graduate Programs in the Physical Sciences, Mathematics, Agricultural Sciences, the Environment & Natural Resources 2017

www.petersons.com **25**

Mathematics	M,D
Natural Resources	M,D
Physics	M,D
Plant Sciences	M,D
Statistics	M,D

TEXAS WOMAN'S UNIVERSITY

Chemistry	M
Food Science and Technology	M,D
Mathematics	M

THOMPSON RIVERS UNIVERSITY

Environmental Sciences	M

TOWSON UNIVERSITY

Applied Mathematics	M
Applied Physics	M
Environmental Management and Policy	M
Environmental Sciences	M,O

TRENT UNIVERSITY

Chemistry	M
Environmental Management and Policy	M,D
Physics	M

TROPICAL AGRICULTURE RESEARCH AND HIGHER EDUCATION CENTER

Agricultural Sciences—General	M,D
Environmental Management and Policy	M,D
Forestry	M,D
Water Resources	M,D

TROY UNIVERSITY

Environmental Management and Policy	M
Environmental Sciences	M

TUFTS UNIVERSITY

Analytical Chemistry	M,D
Animal Sciences	M
Astrophysics	M,D
Biostatistics	M,D,O
Chemical Physics	M,D
Chemistry	M,D
Environmental Management and Policy	M,D,O
Environmental Sciences	M,D
Inorganic Chemistry	M,D
Mathematics	M,D
Organic Chemistry	M,D
Physical Chemistry	M,D
Physics	M,D

TULANE UNIVERSITY

Applied Mathematics	M,D
Biostatistics	M,D
Chemistry	M,D
Mathematics	M,D
Physics	D
Statistics	M,D

TUSKEGEE UNIVERSITY

Agronomy and Soil Sciences	M
Animal Sciences	M
Chemistry	M
Environmental Sciences	M
Food Science and Technology	M
Plant Sciences	M

UNIVERSIDAD AUTONOMA DE GUADALAJARA

Environmental Management and Policy	M,D

UNIVERSIDAD DE LAS AMÉRICAS PUEBLA

Food Science and Technology	M

UNIVERSIDAD DEL TURABO

Chemistry	M,D
Environmental Management and Policy	M,D
Environmental Sciences	M,D

UNIVERSIDAD METROPOLITANA

Environmental Management and Policy	M
Natural Resources	M

UNIVERSIDAD NACIONAL PEDRO HENRIQUEZ URENA

Agricultural Sciences—General	M
Animal Sciences	M
Environmental Sciences	M
Horticulture	M
Natural Resources	M

UNIVERSITÉ DE MONCTON

Astronomy	M
Chemistry	M
Food Science and Technology	M
Mathematics	M
Physics	M

UNIVERSITÉ DE MONTRÉAL

Chemistry	M,D
Environmental Management and Policy	O
Mathematical and Computational Finance	M,D,O
Mathematics	M,D,O
Physics	M,D
Statistics	M,D,O

UNIVERSITÉ DE SHERBROOKE

Chemistry	M,D,O
Environmental Sciences	M,O
Mathematics	M,D
Physics	M,D

UNIVERSITÉ DU QUÉBEC À CHICOUTIMI

Environmental Management and Policy	M
Geosciences	M
Mineralogy	D

UNIVERSITÉ DU QUÉBEC À MONTRÉAL

Atmospheric Sciences	M,D,O
Chemistry	M
Environmental Sciences	M,D,O
Geology	M,D,O
Geosciences	M,D,O
Mathematics	M,D
Meteorology	M,D,O
Mineralogy	M,D,O
Natural Resources	M,D,O

UNIVERSITÉ DU QUÉBEC À RIMOUSKI

Fish, Game, and Wildlife Management	M,D,O
Marine Affairs	M,O
Oceanography	M,D

UNIVERSITÉ DU QUÉBEC À TROIS-RIVIÈRES

Chemistry	M
Environmental Sciences	M,D
Mathematics	M
Physics	M,D

UNIVERSITÉ DU QUÉBEC EN ABITIBI-TÉMISCAMINGUE

Environmental Sciences	M,D
Forestry	M,D
Natural Resources	M,D

UNIVERSITÉ DU QUÉBEC, INSTITUT NATIONAL DE LA RECHERCHE SCIENTIFIQUE

Environmental Management and Policy	M,D
Geosciences	M,D
Hydrology	M,D

UNIVERSITÉ LAVAL

Agricultural Sciences—General	M,D,O
Agronomy and Soil Sciences	M,D
Animal Sciences	M,D
Chemistry	M,D
Environmental Management and Policy	M,D,O
Environmental Sciences	M,D
Food Science and Technology	M,D
Forestry	M,D
Geodetic Sciences	M,D
Geology	M,D
Geosciences	M,D
Mathematics	M,D
Oceanography	D
Physics	M,D
Statistics	M

UNIVERSITY AT ALBANY, STATE UNIVERSITY OF NEW YORK

Atmospheric Sciences	M,D
Biostatistics	M,D
Chemistry	M,D
Environmental Management and Policy	M
Environmental Sciences	M
Mathematics	M,D
Physics	M,D

UNIVERSITY AT BUFFALO, THE STATE UNIVERSITY OF NEW YORK

Biostatistics	M,D
Chemistry	M,D
Computational Sciences	O
Environmental Sciences	M,D,O
Geology	M,D
Geosciences	M,D,O
Mathematics	M,D
Physics	M,D

THE UNIVERSITY OF AKRON

Applied Mathematics	M
Chemistry	M,D
Geology	M
Geophysics	M
Geosciences	M
Mathematics	M
Physics	M

THE UNIVERSITY OF ALABAMA

Applied Mathematics	M,D
Applied Statistics	M,D
Chemistry	M,D
Geology	M,D
Geosciences	M
Mathematics	M,D
Physics	M,D

THE UNIVERSITY OF ALABAMA AT BIRMINGHAM

Applied Mathematics	D
Biostatistics	M,D
Chemistry	M,D
Computational Sciences	D
Mathematics	M,D
Physics	M,D

THE UNIVERSITY OF ALABAMA IN HUNTSVILLE

Applied Mathematics	M,D
Atmospheric Sciences	M,D
Chemistry	M,D
Environmental Sciences	M,D
Geosciences	M,D
Mathematics	M,D
Optical Sciences	M,D
Photonics	M,D
Physics	M,D

UNIVERSITY OF ALASKA ANCHORAGE

Environmental Sciences	M

UNIVERSITY OF ALASKA FAIRBANKS

Astrophysics	M,D
Atmospheric Sciences	M,D
Chemistry	M,D
Computational Sciences	M,D
Environmental Management and Policy	M
Environmental Sciences	M
Geology	M,D
Geophysics	M,D
Limnology	M,D
Marine Sciences	M,D
Mathematics	M,D,O
Natural Resources	M,D
Oceanography	M,D
Physics	M,D
Statistics	M,D,O
Water Resources	M,D,O

UNIVERSITY OF ALBERTA

Agricultural Sciences—General	M,D
Agronomy and Soil Sciences	M,D
Applied Mathematics	M,D,O
Astrophysics	M,D
Biostatistics	M,D,O
Chemistry	M,D
Condensed Matter Physics	M,D
Environmental Management and Policy	M,D
Environmental Sciences	M,D
Forestry	M,D
Geophysics	M,D
Geosciences	M,D
Mathematical and Computational Finance	M,D,O
Mathematical Physics	M,D,O
Mathematics	M,D,O
Natural Resources	M,D
Physics	M,D
Statistics	M,D,O

THE UNIVERSITY OF ARIZONA

Agricultural Sciences—General	M,D,O
Agronomy and Soil Sciences	M,D,O
Animal Sciences	M,D
Applied Mathematics	M,D
Astronomy	D
Atmospheric Sciences	M,D
Biostatistics	M,D
Chemistry	M,D
Environmental Management and Policy	M,D
Environmental Sciences	M,D,O
Forestry	M,D
Geosciences	M,D
Mathematics	M,D
Optical Sciences	M,D
Physics	M,D
Planetary and Space Sciences	M,D
Range Science	M,D
Statistics	M,D
Water Resources	M,D,O

UNIVERSITY OF ARKANSAS

Agricultural Sciences—General	M,D
Agronomy and Soil Sciences	M,D
Animal Sciences	M,D
Applied Physics	M,D
Chemistry	M,D
Food Science and Technology	M,D
Geology	M
Horticulture	M
Mathematics	M,D
Photonics	M,D
Physics	M,D
Planetary and Space Sciences	M,D
Plant Sciences	D
Statistics	M,D

UNIVERSITY OF ARKANSAS AT LITTLE ROCK

Applied Mathematics	M,O
Applied Statistics	M,O
Chemistry	M
Geosciences	O
Mathematics	M,O

UNIVERSITY OF ARKANSAS AT MONTICELLO

Forestry	M
Natural Resources	M

UNIVERSITY OF ARKANSAS AT PINE BLUFF

Aquaculture	M
Fish, Game, and Wildlife Management	M

UNIVERSITY OF ARKANSAS FOR MEDICAL SCIENCES

Biostatistics	M,D,O

THE UNIVERSITY OF BRITISH COLUMBIA

Agricultural Sciences—General	M,D
Agronomy and Soil Sciences	M,D
Animal Sciences	M,D
Applied Mathematics	M,D
Astronomy	M,D
Atmospheric Sciences	M,D
Chemistry	M,D
Food Science and Technology	M,D
Forestry	M,D
Geology	M,D
Geophysics	M,D
Marine Sciences	M,D
Mathematics	M,D
Natural Resources	M,D

Oceanography	M,D
Physics	M,D
Plant Sciences	M,D
Statistics	M,D
Water Resources	M,D

UNIVERSITY OF CALGARY

Analytical Chemistry	M,D
Astronomy	M,D
Chemistry	M,D
Environmental Management and Policy	M,D,O
Geology	M,D
Geophysics	M,D
Geosciences	M,D
Hydrology	M,D
Inorganic Chemistry	M,D
Mathematics	M,D
Organic Chemistry	M,D
Physical Chemistry	M,D
Physics	M,D
Statistics	M,D
Theoretical Chemistry	M,D
Water Resources	M,D

UNIVERSITY OF CALIFORNIA, BERKELEY

Applied Mathematics	D
Astrophysics	D
Biostatistics	M,D
Chemistry	D
Environmental Management and Policy	M,D,O
Environmental Sciences	M,D
Forestry	M,D
Geology	M,D
Geophysics	M,D
Mathematics	M,D
Natural Resources	M,D
Physics	D
Range Science	M
Statistics	M,D

UNIVERSITY OF CALIFORNIA, DAVIS

Agricultural Sciences—General	M
Agronomy and Soil Sciences	M,D
Animal Sciences	M,D
Applied Mathematics	M,D
Atmospheric Sciences	M,D
Biostatistics	M,D
Chemistry	M,D
Environmental Sciences	M,D
Food Science and Technology	M,D
Geology	M,D
Horticulture	M
Hydrology	M,D
Mathematics	M,D
Physics	M,D
Statistics	M,D
Viticulture and Enology	M,D

UNIVERSITY OF CALIFORNIA, IRVINE

Applied Mathematics	M,D
Chemistry	M,D
Geosciences	M,D
Mathematics	M,D
Physics	M,D
Statistics	M,D

UNIVERSITY OF CALIFORNIA, LOS ANGELES

Astronomy	M,D
Astrophysics	M,D
Atmospheric Sciences	M,D
Biomathematics	M,D
Biostatistics	M,D
Chemistry	M,D
Environmental Sciences	M,D
Geochemistry	M,D
Geology	M,D
Geophysics	M,D
Geosciences	M,D
Mathematics	M,D
Oceanography	M,D
Physics	M,D
Planetary and Space Sciences	M,D
Statistics	M,D

UNIVERSITY OF CALIFORNIA, MERCED

Applied Mathematics	M,D
Chemistry	M,D
Physics	M,D

UNIVERSITY OF CALIFORNIA, RIVERSIDE

Agronomy and Soil Sciences	M,D
Applied Statistics	M,D
Chemistry	M,D
Environmental Sciences	M,D
Geology	M,D
Mathematics	M,D
Physics	M,D
Plant Sciences	M,D
Statistics	M,D
Water Resources	M,D

UNIVERSITY OF CALIFORNIA, SAN DIEGO

Applied Mathematics	M,D
Applied Physics	M,D
Biostatistics	D
Chemistry	M,D
Computational Sciences	M,D
Geophysics	M,D
Geosciences	M,D
Marine Sciences	M
Mathematics	M,D
Meteorology	M
Oceanography	M,D
Photonics	M,D
Physics	M,D
Statistics	M,D

26 www.petersons.com

Petersons Graduate Programs in the Physical Sciences, Mathematics, Agricultural Sciences, the Environment & Natural Resources 2017

UNIVERSITY OF CALIFORNIA, SAN FRANCISCO

Chemistry	D

UNIVERSITY OF CALIFORNIA, SANTA BARBARA

Applied Mathematics	M,D
Applied Statistics	M,D
Chemistry	M,D
Computational Sciences	M,D
Environmental Management and Policy	M,D
Environmental Sciences	M,D
Geosciences	M,D
Marine Sciences	M,D
Mathematical and Computational Finance	M,D
Mathematics	M,D
Photonics	M,D
Physics	D
Statistics	M,D

UNIVERSITY OF CALIFORNIA, SANTA CRUZ

Applied Mathematics	M,D
Astronomy	D
Astrophysics	D
Chemistry	M,D
Environmental Management and Policy	D
Geosciences	M,D
Marine Sciences	M,D
Mathematics	M,D
Physics	M,D
Planetary and Space Sciences	M,D
Statistics	M,D

UNIVERSITY OF CENTRAL ARKANSAS

Applied Mathematics	M
Mathematics	M

UNIVERSITY OF CENTRAL FLORIDA

Chemistry	M,D,O
Mathematics	M,D,O
Optical Sciences	M,D
Photonics	M,D
Physics	M,D
Statistics	M,O

UNIVERSITY OF CENTRAL MISSOURI

Applied Mathematics	M,D,O
Environmental Management and Policy	M,D,O
Mathematics	M

UNIVERSITY OF CENTRAL OKLAHOMA

Applied Mathematics	M
Mathematics	M
Statistics	M

UNIVERSITY OF CHICAGO

Applied Mathematics	D
Applied Statistics	M
Astronomy	D
Astrophysics	D
Atmospheric Sciences	D
Chemistry	D
Computational Sciences	M
Environmental Management and Policy	M
Environmental Sciences	M
Geochemistry	D
Geophysics	D
Geosciences	D
Mathematical and Computational Finance	M
Mathematics	D
Paleontology	D
Physics	M,D
Planetary and Space Sciences	D
Statistics	M,D,O

UNIVERSITY OF CINCINNATI

Analytical Chemistry	M,D
Applied Mathematics	M,D
Biostatistics	M,D
Chemistry	M,D
Environmental Sciences	M,D
Geology	M,D
Inorganic Chemistry	M,D
Mathematics	M,D
Organic Chemistry	M,D
Physical Chemistry	M,D
Physics	M,D
Statistics	M,D

UNIVERSITY OF COLORADO BOULDER

Applied Mathematics	M,D
Astrophysics	M,D
Atmospheric Sciences	M,D
Chemical Physics	M,D
Chemistry	M,D
Environmental Management and Policy	M,D
Geology	M,D
Geophysics	M,D
Hydrology	M,D
Mathematical Physics	M,D
Mathematics	M,D
Oceanography	M,D
Optical Sciences	M,D
Physics	M,D
Plasma Physics	M,D

UNIVERSITY OF COLORADO COLORADO SPRINGS

Applied Mathematics	M
Environmental Sciences	M
Mathematics	D
Physics	D

UNIVERSITY OF COLORADO DENVER

Applied Mathematics	M,D
Applied Statistics	M,D
Biostatistics	M,D
Chemistry	M
Computational Sciences	M,D
Environmental Management and Policy	M,D
Environmental Sciences	M,D
Hydrology	M,D
Mathematics	M,D
Statistics	M,D
Water Resources	M

UNIVERSITY OF CONNECTICUT

Agricultural Sciences— General	M,D
Agronomy and Soil Sciences	M,D
Animal Sciences	M,D
Applied Mathematics	M
Chemistry	M,D
Geology	M,D
Marine Sciences	M,D
Mathematical and Computational Finance	M
Mathematics	M,D
Natural Resources	M,D
Oceanography	M,D
Physics	M,D
Plant Sciences	M,D
Statistics	M,D

UNIVERSITY OF DAYTON

Applied Mathematics	M
Chemistry	M
Environmental Management and Policy	M,D
Mathematical and Computational Finance	M
Optical Sciences	M,D

UNIVERSITY OF DELAWARE

Agricultural Sciences— General	M,D
Agronomy and Soil Sciences	M,D
Animal Sciences	M,D
Applied Mathematics	M,D
Astronomy	M,D
Chemistry	M,D
Environmental Management and Policy	M,D
Fish, Game, and Wildlife Management	M,D
Food Science and Technology	M,D
Geology	M,D
Horticulture	M
Marine Affairs	M,D
Marine Geology	M,D
Marine Sciences	M,D
Mathematics	M,D
Natural Resources	M
Oceanography	M,D
Physics	M,D
Plant Sciences	M,D
Statistics	M

UNIVERSITY OF DENVER

Chemistry	M,D
Environmental Management and Policy	M,O
Mathematics	M,D
Physics	M,D
Statistics	M

UNIVERSITY OF DETROIT MERCY

Chemistry	M,D

THE UNIVERSITY OF FINDLAY

Environmental Management and Policy	M,D

UNIVERSITY OF FLORIDA

Agricultural Sciences— General	M,D,O
Agronomy and Soil Sciences	M,D
Animal Sciences	M,D
Aquaculture	M,D
Astronomy	M,D
Biostatistics	M,D,O
Chemistry	M,D
Fish, Game, and Wildlife Management	M,D,O
Food Science and Technology	M,D
Forestry	M,D
Geology	M,D
Geosciences	M,D
Horticulture	M,D
Hydrology	M,D
Limnology	M,D
Marine Sciences	M,D
Mathematics	M,D
Natural Resources	M,D
Physics	M,D
Plant Sciences	D
Statistics	M,D
Water Resources	M,D

UNIVERSITY OF GEORGIA

Agricultural Sciences— General	M,D
Agronomy and Soil Sciences	M,D
Analytical Chemistry	M,D
Animal Sciences	M,D
Applied Mathematics	M,D
Chemistry	M,D
Food Science and Technology	M,D
Forestry	M,D
Geology	M,D
Horticulture	M,D
Inorganic Chemistry	M,D

Marine Sciences	M,D
Mathematics	M,D
Natural Resources	M,D
Organic Chemistry	M,D
Physical Chemistry	M,D
Physics	M,D
Plant Sciences	M,D
Statistics	M,D

UNIVERSITY OF GUAM

Environmental Sciences	M

UNIVERSITY OF GUELPH

Agricultural Sciences— General	M,D,O
Agronomy and Soil Sciences	M,D
Animal Sciences	M,D
Applied Mathematics	M,D
Applied Statistics	M,D
Aquaculture	M
Atmospheric Sciences	M,D
Chemistry	M,D
Environmental Management and Policy	M,D
Environmental Sciences	M,D
Food Science and Technology	M,D
Horticulture	M,D
Mathematics	M,D
Natural Resources	M,D
Physics	M,D
Statistics	M,D

UNIVERSITY OF HAWAII AT HILO

Environmental Sciences	M

UNIVERSITY OF HAWAII AT MANOA

Agricultural Sciences— General	M,D
Animal Sciences	M
Astronomy	M,D
Chemistry	M,D
Environmental Management and Policy	M,D,O
Food Science and Technology	M
Geochemistry	M,D
Geology	M,D
Geophysics	M,D
Horticulture	M,D
Hydrogeology	M,D
Marine Geology	M,D
Marine Sciences	O
Mathematics	M,D
Meteorology	M,D
Natural Resources	M,D
Oceanography	M,D
Physics	M,D
Planetary and Space Sciences	M,D
Plant Sciences	M,D

UNIVERSITY OF HOUSTON

Applied Mathematics	M,D
Atmospheric Sciences	M,D
Chemistry	M,D
Geology	M,D
Geophysics	M,D
Mathematics	M,D
Physics	M,D
Planetary and Space Sciences	M,D

UNIVERSITY OF HOUSTON–CLEAR LAKE

Chemistry	M
Environmental Management and Policy	M
Environmental Sciences	M
Mathematics	M
Physics	M
Statistics	M

UNIVERSITY OF IDAHO

Agronomy and Soil Sciences	M,D
Animal Sciences	M,D
Chemistry	M,D
Environmental Sciences	M,D
Food Science and Technology	M,D
Geology	M,D
Hydrology	M,D
Mathematics	M,D
Natural Resources	M,D
Physics	M,D
Plant Sciences	M,D
Statistics	M
Water Resources	M,D

UNIVERSITY OF ILLINOIS AT CHICAGO

Biostatistics	M,D
Chemistry	M,D
Geology	M,D
Geosciences	M,D
Mathematics	M,D
Physics	M,D
Statistics	M,D

UNIVERSITY OF ILLINOIS AT SPRINGFIELD

Environmental Management and Policy	M
Environmental Sciences	M

UNIVERSITY OF ILLINOIS AT URBANA–CHAMPAIGN

Agricultural Sciences— General	M
Agronomy and Soil Sciences	M,D
Animal Sciences	M,D
Applied Mathematics	M,D
Applied Statistics	M,D
Astronomy	M,D
Atmospheric Sciences	M,D

Chemical Physics	M,D
Chemistry	M,D
Environmental Sciences	M,D
Food Science and Technology	M,D
Geology	M,D
Geosciences	M,D
Mathematics	M,D
Natural Resources	M,D
Physics	M,D
Statistics	M,D

THE UNIVERSITY OF IOWA

Agricultural Sciences— General	M,D,O
Applied Mathematics	D
Astronomy	M
Biostatistics	M,D,O
Chemistry	D
Computational Sciences	D
Geosciences	M,D
Mathematics	M,D
Physics	M,D
Statistics	M,D,O

THE UNIVERSITY OF KANSAS

Applied Statistics	M,D,O
Astronomy	M,D
Atmospheric Sciences	M,D
Biostatistics	M,D,O
Chemistry	M,D
Computational Sciences	M,D
Environmental Sciences	M,D
Geology	M,D
Mathematics	M,D
Physics	M,D
Statistics	M,D,O

UNIVERSITY OF KENTUCKY

Agricultural Sciences— General	M,D
Agronomy and Soil Sciences	M,D
Animal Sciences	M,D
Applied Mathematics	M,D
Astronomy	M,D
Biostatistics	D
Chemistry	M,D
Food Science and Technology	M,D
Forestry	M
Geology	M,D
Mathematics	M,D
Physics	M,D
Plant Sciences	M,D
Statistics	M,D

UNIVERSITY OF LETHBRIDGE

Agricultural Sciences— General	M,D
Chemistry	M,D
Computational Sciences	M,D
Environmental Sciences	M,D
Mathematics	M,D
Physics	M,D

UNIVERSITY OF LOUISIANA AT LAFAYETTE

Geology	M
Mathematics	M,D
Physics	M

UNIVERSITY OF LOUISVILLE

Analytical Chemistry	M,D
Applied Mathematics	M,D
Biostatistics	M,D
Chemical Physics	M,D
Chemistry	M,D
Inorganic Chemistry	M,D
Mathematics	M,D
Organic Chemistry	M,D
Physical Chemistry	M,D
Physics	M,D

UNIVERSITY OF MAINE

Agricultural Sciences— General	M,D,O
Animal Sciences	M,D,O
Chemistry	M,D
Environmental Management and Policy	D
Environmental Sciences	M,D
Fish, Game, and Wildlife Management	M,D
Food Science and Technology	M,D,O
Forestry	M,D
Geology	M,O
Geosciences	M,D
Horticulture	M,D,O
Marine Affairs	M,D
Marine Sciences	M,D
Natural Resources	M,D
Oceanography	M,D
Physics	M,D
Plant Sciences	M,D,O
Water Resources	M,D

THE UNIVERSITY OF MANCHESTER

Analytical Chemistry	M,D
Applied Mathematics	M,D
Astronomy	M,D
Astrophysics	M,D
Atmospheric Sciences	M,D
Chemistry	M,D
Condensed Matter Physics	M,D
Environmental Management and Policy	M,D
Environmental Sciences	M,D
Geochemistry	M,D
Geosciences	M,D
Inorganic Chemistry	M,D
Mathematical and Computational Finance	M,D

*M—master's; D—doctorate; O—other advanced degree; *Close-Up and/or Display*

Petersons Graduate Programs in the Physical Sciences, Mathematics, Agricultural Sciences, the Environment & Natural Resources 2017

www.petersons.com **27**

Mathematics M,D
Natural Resources M,D
Organic Chemistry M,D
Paleontology M,D
Physical Chemistry M,D
Physics M,D
Plant Sciences M,D
Statistics M,D
Theoretical Chemistry M,D
Theoretical Physics M,D

UNIVERSITY OF MANITOBA
Agricultural Sciences—General M,D
Agronomy and Soil Sciences M,D
Animal Sciences M,D
Chemistry M,D
Computational Sciences M
Environmental Sciences M,D
Food Science and Technology M,D
Geology M,D
Geophysics M,D
Horticulture M,D
Mathematics M,D
Natural Resources M,D
Physics M,D
Plant Sciences M,D
Statistics M,D

UNIVERSITY OF MARYLAND, BALTIMORE
Biostatistics M,D
Environmental Sciences M,D
Marine Sciences M,D

UNIVERSITY OF MARYLAND, BALTIMORE COUNTY
Applied Mathematics M,D
Atmospheric Sciences M,D
Biostatistics M,D
Chemistry M,D,O
Environmental Management and Policy M,D
Environmental Sciences M,D
Marine Sciences M,D
Physics M,D
Planetary and Space Sciences M
Statistics M,D

UNIVERSITY OF MARYLAND, COLLEGE PARK
Agricultural Sciences—General M,D
Analytical Chemistry M,D
Animal Sciences M,D
Applied Mathematics M,D
Astronomy M,D
Biostatistics M,D
Chemical Physics M,D
Chemistry M,D
Environmental Sciences M,D
Food Science and Technology M,D
Geology M,D
Horticulture M,D
Inorganic Chemistry M,D
Marine Sciences M,D
Mathematics M,D
Meteorology M,D
Natural Resources M,D
Oceanography M,D
Organic Chemistry M,D
Physical Chemistry M,D
Physics M,D
Statistics M,D

UNIVERSITY OF MARYLAND EASTERN SHORE
Agricultural Sciences—General M,D
Chemistry M,D
Environmental Management and Policy M,D
Environmental Sciences M,D
Fish, Game, and Wildlife Management M,D
Food Science and Technology M,D
Marine Sciences M,D

UNIVERSITY OF MARYLAND UNIVERSITY COLLEGE
Environmental Management and Policy M,O

UNIVERSITY OF MASSACHUSETTS AMHERST
Animal Sciences M,D
Applied Mathematics M,D
Astronomy M,D
Biostatistics M,D
Chemistry M,D
Environmental Management and Policy M,D
Fish, Game, and Wildlife Management M,D
Food Science and Technology M,D
Forestry M,D
Geosciences M,D
Marine Sciences M,D
Mathematics M,D
Physics M,D
Plant Sciences M,D
Statistics M,D
Water Resources M,D

UNIVERSITY OF MASSACHUSETTS BOSTON
Applied Physics M
Chemistry M,D
Environmental Sciences M,D
Marine Sciences M,D

UNIVERSITY OF MASSACHUSETTS DARTMOUTH
Acoustics M,D,O
Chemistry M,D
Computational Sciences D
Environmental Management and Policy M,O
Marine Affairs M,D
Marine Sciences M,D
Physics M

UNIVERSITY OF MASSACHUSETTS LOWELL
Analytical Chemistry M,D
Applied Mathematics M,D
Applied Physics M
Atmospheric Sciences M,D
Chemistry M,D
Computational Sciences M,D
Environmental Management and Policy M,D,O
Environmental Sciences M,D,O
Inorganic Chemistry M,D
Mathematics M,D
Optical Sciences M
Organic Chemistry M,D
Physics M,D*

UNIVERSITY OF MEMPHIS
Analytical Chemistry M,D
Applied Mathematics M,D
Applied Statistics M,D
Biostatistics M
Chemistry M,D
Geology M,D,O
Geophysics M,D,O
Inorganic Chemistry M,D
Mathematics M,D
Physical Chemistry M,D
Physics M
Statistics M,D

UNIVERSITY OF MIAMI
Chemistry M,D
Fish, Game, and Wildlife Management M,D
Geophysics M,D
Inorganic Chemistry M,D
Marine Affairs M
Marine Geology M,D
Marine Sciences M,D
Mathematical and Computational Finance M,D
Mathematics M,D
Meteorology M,D
Oceanography M,D
Organic Chemistry M,D
Physical Chemistry M,D
Physics M,D

UNIVERSITY OF MICHIGAN
Analytical Chemistry D
Applied Physics D
Applied Statistics M,D
Astronomy D
Astrophysics D
Atmospheric Sciences M,D
Biostatistics M,D
Chemistry D
Environmental Management and Policy M,D
Environmental Sciences M,D
Geosciences M,D
Inorganic Chemistry D
Marine Sciences M,D,O
Mathematics M,D
Natural Resources M,D
Organic Chemistry D
Physical Chemistry D
Physics D
Planetary and Space Sciences M,D
Statistics M,D,O

UNIVERSITY OF MICHIGAN–DEARBORN
Applied Mathematics M
Computational Sciences M
Environmental Sciences M

UNIVERSITY OF MICHIGAN–FLINT
Mathematics M

UNIVERSITY OF MINNESOTA, DULUTH
Applied Mathematics M
Chemistry M
Computational Sciences M
Geology M,D
Physics M

UNIVERSITY OF MINNESOTA, TWIN CITIES CAMPUS
Agricultural Sciences—General M,D
Agronomy and Soil Sciences M,D
Animal Sciences M,D
Astrophysics M,D
Biostatistics M,D
Chemical Physics M,D
Chemistry M,D
Computational Sciences M,D
Environmental Management and Policy M,D
Fish, Game, and Wildlife Management M,D
Food Science and Technology M,D
Forestry M,D
Geology M,D
Geophysics M,D
Hydrology M,D
Mathematics M,D,O
Natural Resources M,D
Physics M,D
Plant Sciences M,D
Statistics M,D
Water Resources M,D

UNIVERSITY OF MISSISSIPPI
Chemistry M,D
Food Science and Technology M,D
Mathematics M,D
Physics M,D

UNIVERSITY OF MISSOURI
Agricultural Sciences—General M,D,O
Agronomy and Soil Sciences M,D
Analytical Chemistry M,D
Animal Sciences M,D
Applied Mathematics M,D
Astronomy M,D
Atmospheric Sciences M,D
Chemistry M,D
Environmental Management and Policy M,D
Fish, Game, and Wildlife Management M,D,O
Food Science and Technology M,D
Forestry M,D,O
Geology M,D
Horticulture M,D
Inorganic Chemistry M,D
Mathematics M,D
Natural Resources M
Organic Chemistry M,D
Physical Chemistry M,D
Physics M,D
Plant Sciences M,D
Statistics M,D
Water Resources M,D

UNIVERSITY OF MISSOURI–KANSAS CITY
Analytical Chemistry M,D
Chemistry M,D
Geology M,D
Geosciences M,D
Inorganic Chemistry M,D
Mathematics M,D
Organic Chemistry M,D
Physical Chemistry M,D
Physics M,D
Statistics M,D

UNIVERSITY OF MISSOURI–ST. LOUIS
Applied Physics M,D
Astrophysics M,D
Chemistry M,D
Mathematics M,D
Physics M,D

UNIVERSITY OF MONTANA
Analytical Chemistry M,D
Chemistry M,D
Environmental Management and Policy M
Environmental Sciences M
Fish, Game, and Wildlife Management M,D
Forestry M,D
Geology M,D
Geosciences M,D
Inorganic Chemistry M,D
Mathematics M,D
Natural Resources M,D
Organic Chemistry M,D
Physical Chemistry M,D

UNIVERSITY OF NEBRASKA AT OMAHA
Mathematics M

UNIVERSITY OF NEBRASKA–LINCOLN
Agricultural Sciences—General M,D
Agronomy and Soil Sciences M,D
Analytical Chemistry M,D
Animal Sciences M,D
Astronomy M,D
Chemistry M,D
Food Science and Technology M,D
Geosciences M,D
Horticulture M,D
Inorganic Chemistry M,D
Mathematics M,D
Natural Resources M,D
Organic Chemistry M,D
Physical Chemistry M,D
Physics M,D
Statistics M,D

UNIVERSITY OF NEBRASKA MEDICAL CENTER
Biostatistics D

UNIVERSITY OF NEVADA, LAS VEGAS
Astronomy M,D
Chemistry M,D
Environmental Sciences M,D,O
Geosciences M,D
Mathematics M,D
Physics M,D
Water Resources M

UNIVERSITY OF NEVADA, RENO
Agricultural Sciences—General M,D
Animal Sciences M
Atmospheric Sciences M,D
Chemical Physics D
Chemistry M,D
Environmental Management and Policy M
Environmental Sciences M,D
Geochemistry M,D
Geology M,D
Geophysics M,D
Hydrogeology M,D
Hydrology M,D
Mathematics M
Physics M,D

UNIVERSITY OF NEW BRUNSWICK FREDERICTON
Chemistry M,D
Environmental Management and Policy M,D
Forestry M,D
Geodetic Sciences M,D
Geology M,D
Hydrology M,D
Mathematics M,D
Physics M,D
Statistics M,D
Water Resources M,D

UNIVERSITY OF NEW BRUNSWICK SAINT JOHN
Natural Resources M

UNIVERSITY OF NEW ENGLAND
Marine Sciences M

UNIVERSITY OF NEW HAMPSHIRE
Animal Sciences M,D
Chemistry M,D
Environmental Management and Policy M
Fish, Game, and Wildlife Management M
Forestry M
Geology M,D
Geosciences M,D
Hydrology M,D
Marine Sciences M
Mathematics M,D,O
Natural Resources M,D
Oceanography M,D,O
Physics M,D
Water Resources M

UNIVERSITY OF NEW HAVEN
Environmental Management and Policy M,O
Environmental Sciences M,O
Geosciences M,O

UNIVERSITY OF NEW MEXICO
Chemistry M,D
Environmental Management and Policy M
Geosciences M,D
Mathematics M,D
Natural Resources M,D
Optical Sciences M,D
Photonics M,D
Physics M,D
Planetary and Space Sciences M,D
Statistics M,D
Water Resources M

UNIVERSITY OF NEW ORLEANS
Chemistry M,D
Environmental Sciences M
Geosciences M
Mathematics M
Physics M,D

THE UNIVERSITY OF NORTH CAROLINA AT CHAPEL HILL
Astronomy M,D
Astrophysics M,D
Atmospheric Sciences M,D
Biostatistics M,D
Chemistry M,D
Environmental Management and Policy M,D
Environmental Sciences M,D
Geology M,D
Marine Sciences M,D
Mathematics M,D
Physics M,D
Statistics M,D

THE UNIVERSITY OF NORTH CAROLINA AT CHARLOTTE
Applied Mathematics M,D
Applied Physics M,D
Chemistry M,D
Geosciences M,D
Mathematical and Computational Finance M,O
Mathematics M,D,O
Optical Sciences M,D
Statistics M,O

THE UNIVERSITY OF NORTH CAROLINA AT GREENSBORO
Chemistry M
Mathematics M,D

THE UNIVERSITY OF NORTH CAROLINA WILMINGTON
Chemistry M
Environmental Management and Policy M
Geosciences M
Marine Sciences M,D,O
Mathematics M,O
Statistics M,O

UNIVERSITY OF NORTH DAKOTA
Atmospheric Sciences M,D
Chemistry M,D
Fish, Game, and Wildlife Management M,D
Geology M,D
Geosciences M,D
Mathematics M
Physics M,D
Planetary and Space Sciences M

UNIVERSITY OF NORTHERN BRITISH COLUMBIA
Environmental Management and Policy M,D,O
Mathematics M,D,O
Natural Resources M,D,O

UNIVERSITY OF NORTHERN COLORADO
Applied Statistics	M,D
Chemistry	M,D
Geosciences	M
Mathematics	M,D

UNIVERSITY OF NORTHERN IOWA
Applied Mathematics	M
Geosciences	M
Mathematics	M
Physics	M

UNIVERSITY OF NORTH FLORIDA
Mathematics	M
Statistics	M

UNIVERSITY OF NORTH TEXAS
Chemistry	M,D,O
Environmental Sciences	M,D,O
Mathematics	M,D,O

UNIVERSITY OF NORTH TEXAS HEALTH SCIENCE CENTER AT FORT WORTH
Biostatistics	M,D

UNIVERSITY OF NOTRE DAME
Applied Mathematics	M,D
Applied Statistics	M,D
Chemistry	M,D
Computational Sciences	M,D
Geosciences	M,D
Inorganic Chemistry	M,D
Mathematical and Computational Finance	M,D
Mathematics	M,D
Organic Chemistry	M,D
Physical Chemistry	M,D
Physics	M,D
Statistics	M,D

UNIVERSITY OF OKLAHOMA
Chemistry	M,D
Environmental Sciences	M,D
Geology	M,D
Geophysics	M,D
Mathematics	M,D*
Meteorology	M,D
Physics	M,D

UNIVERSITY OF OKLAHOMA HEALTH SCIENCES CENTER
Biostatistics	M,D

UNIVERSITY OF OREGON
Chemistry	M,D
Environmental Management and Policy	M,D
Geology	M,D
Mathematics	M,D
Physics	M,D

UNIVERSITY OF OTTAWA
Chemistry	M,D
Geosciences	M,D
Mathematics	M,D
Physics	M,D
Statistics	M,D

UNIVERSITY OF PENNSYLVANIA
Applied Mathematics	D
Biostatistics	M,D
Chemistry	M,D
Computational Sciences	M,D
Environmental Management and Policy	M
Environmental Sciences	M,D
Geosciences	M,D
Mathematics	M,D
Physics	M,D
Statistics	M,D

UNIVERSITY OF PITTSBURGH
Applied Mathematics	M,D
Applied Statistics	M,D
Astronomy	D
Biostatistics	M,D
Chemistry	M,D
Environmental Sciences	M,D
Geology	M,D
Mathematics	M,D
Physics	M,D*
Statistics	M,D

UNIVERSITY OF PRINCE EDWARD ISLAND
Chemistry	M

UNIVERSITY OF PUERTO RICO, MAYAGÜEZ CAMPUS
Agricultural Sciences— General	M
Agronomy and Soil Sciences	M
Animal Sciences	M
Applied Mathematics	M
Chemistry	M,D
Computational Sciences	M
Food Science and Technology	M
Geology	M
Horticulture	M
Marine Sciences	M,D
Mathematics	M
Physics	M
Statistics	M

UNIVERSITY OF PUERTO RICO, MEDICAL SCIENCES CAMPUS
Biostatistics	M

UNIVERSITY OF PUERTO RICO, RÍO PIEDRAS CAMPUS
Chemistry	M,D
Environmental Management and Policy	M

Environmental Sciences — M,D
Mathematics	M,D
Physics	M,D

UNIVERSITY OF REGINA
Analytical Chemistry	M,D
Chemistry	M,D
Geology	M,D
Inorganic Chemistry	M,D
Mathematics	M,D
Organic Chemistry	M,D
Physics	M,D
Statistics	M,D
Theoretical Chemistry	M,D

UNIVERSITY OF RHODE ISLAND
Animal Sciences	M,D
Applied Mathematics	M,D
Aquaculture	M,D
Chemistry	M,D
Environmental Management and Policy	M,D
Environmental Sciences	M,D
Fish, Game, and Wildlife Management	M,D
Food Science and Technology	M,D
Geosciences	M,D
Marine Affairs	M,D
Marine Sciences	M,D
Mathematics	M,D
Natural Resources	M,D
Oceanography	M,D
Physics	M,D
Statistics	M,D,O

UNIVERSITY OF ROCHESTER
Astronomy	M,D
Biostatistics	M
Chemistry	M,D
Environmental Management and Policy	M
Geology	M,D
Geosciences	M,D
Mathematics	M,D
Optical Sciences	M,D
Physics	M,D
Statistics	M,D

UNIVERSITY OF SAINT JOSEPH
Chemistry	M

UNIVERSITY OF SAN DIEGO
Marine Affairs	M
Marine Sciences	M

UNIVERSITY OF SAN FRANCISCO
Chemistry	M
Natural Resources	M

UNIVERSITY OF SASKATCHEWAN
Agricultural Sciences— General	M,D,O
Agronomy and Soil Sciences	M,D,O
Animal Sciences	M,D
Chemistry	M,D
Environmental Sciences	M,D
Food Science and Technology	M,D
Geology	M,D,O
Mathematics	M,D
Physics	M,D
Plant Sciences	M,D
Statistics	M,D

THE UNIVERSITY OF SCRANTON
Chemistry	M

UNIVERSITY OF SOUTH AFRICA
Agricultural Sciences— General	M,D
Environmental Management and Policy	M,D
Environmental Sciences	M,D
Horticulture	M,D
Natural Resources	M,D
Statistics	M,D

UNIVERSITY OF SOUTH ALABAMA
Marine Sciences	M,D
Mathematics	M

UNIVERSITY OF SOUTH CAROLINA
Applied Statistics	M,D,O
Astronomy	M,D
Biostatistics	M,D
Chemistry	M,D
Environmental Management and Policy	M
Geology	M,D
Geosciences	M,D
Marine Sciences	M,D
Mathematics	M,D
Physics	M,D
Statistics	M,D,O

THE UNIVERSITY OF SOUTH DAKOTA
Chemistry	M,D
Mathematics	M
Physics	M,D

UNIVERSITY OF SOUTHERN CALIFORNIA
Applied Mathematics	M,D
Biostatistics	M,D
Chemistry	D
Food Science and Technology	M,D,O
Geosciences	M,D
Marine Sciences	M,D
Mathematical and Computational Finance	M,D
Mathematics	M,D
Oceanography	M,D
Physical Chemistry	D

Physics	M,D
Statistics	M,D
Water Resources	M,D,O

UNIVERSITY OF SOUTHERN MAINE
Statistics	M,O

UNIVERSITY OF SOUTHERN MISSISSIPPI
Biostatistics	M
Chemistry	M,D
Computational Sciences	M,D
Food Science and Technology	M,D
Geology	M,D
Hydrology	M,D
Inorganic Chemistry	M,D
Marine Sciences	M,D
Mathematics	M,D
Organic Chemistry	M,D
Physical Chemistry	M,D
Physics	M,D

UNIVERSITY OF SOUTH FLORIDA
Applied Mathematics	M,D
Applied Physics	M,D
Atmospheric Sciences	M,D
Biostatistics	M,D,O
Chemistry	M,D
Environmental Management and Policy	M,D,O
Environmental Sciences	M,D
Geology	M,D,O
Geosciences	M,D
Hydrogeology	O
Marine Sciences	M,D
Mathematics	M,D,O
Oceanography	M,D
Physics	M,D
Statistics	M,D

UNIVERSITY OF SOUTH FLORIDA, ST. PETERSBURG
Environmental Management and Policy	M
Environmental Sciences	M

THE UNIVERSITY OF TENNESSEE
Agricultural Sciences— General	M,D
Analytical Chemistry	M,D
Animal Sciences	M,D
Applied Mathematics	M,D
Chemical Physics	M,D
Chemistry	M,D
Environmental Management and Policy	M,D
Fish, Game, and Wildlife Management	M
Food Science and Technology	M,D
Forestry	M
Geology	M,D
Inorganic Chemistry	M,D
Mathematics	M,D
Organic Chemistry	M,D
Physical Chemistry	M,D
Physics	M,D
Plant Sciences	M
Statistics	M,D
Theoretical Chemistry	M,D

THE UNIVERSITY OF TENNESSEE AT CHATTANOOGA
Applied Mathematics	M
Applied Statistics	M
Computational Sciences	M,D
Environmental Sciences	M
Mathematics	M

THE UNIVERSITY OF TENNESSEE AT MARTIN
Agricultural Sciences— General	M
Food Science and Technology	M

THE UNIVERSITY OF TEXAS AT ARLINGTON
Applied Mathematics	M,D
Chemistry	M,D
Environmental Sciences	M,D
Geology	M,D
Mathematics	M,D
Physics	M,D

THE UNIVERSITY OF TEXAS AT AUSTIN
Analytical Chemistry	D
Applied Mathematics	M,D
Applied Physics	M,D
Astronomy	M,D
Chemistry	D
Computational Sciences	M,D
Environmental Management and Policy	M
Geology	M,D
Geosciences	M,D
Inorganic Chemistry	D
Marine Sciences	M,D
Mathematics	M,D
Natural Resources	M
Organic Chemistry	D
Physical Chemistry	D
Physics	M,D
Statistics	M,D

THE UNIVERSITY OF TEXAS AT DALLAS
Applied Mathematics	M,D
Chemistry	M,D
Geochemistry	M,D
Geophysics	M,D
Geosciences	M,D
Hydrogeology	M,D
Mathematics	M,D

Paleontology	M,D
Physics	M,D
Statistics	M,D

THE UNIVERSITY OF TEXAS AT EL PASO
Chemistry	M,D
Computational Sciences	M,D
Environmental Sciences	M,D
Geology	M,D
Geophysics	M
Mathematics	M
Physics	M
Statistics	M

THE UNIVERSITY OF TEXAS AT SAN ANTONIO
Applied Mathematics	M,D
Applied Statistics	M,D
Chemistry	M,D
Environmental Sciences	M,D
Geology	M
Mathematics	M
Physics	M
Statistics	M,D

THE UNIVERSITY OF TEXAS AT TYLER
Mathematics	M

THE UNIVERSITY OF TEXAS HEALTH SCIENCE CENTER AT HOUSTON
Biomathematics	M,D
Biostatistics	M,D

THE UNIVERSITY OF TEXAS OF THE PERMIAN BASIN
Geology	M

THE UNIVERSITY OF TEXAS RIO GRANDE VALLEY
Chemistry	M
Mathematics	M
Physics	M
Statistics	M

UNIVERSITY OF THE DISTRICT OF COLUMBIA
Applied Statistics	M
Water Resources	M

UNIVERSITY OF THE INCARNATE WORD
Mathematics	M
Statistics	M

UNIVERSITY OF THE PACIFIC
Water Resources	M,D

UNIVERSITY OF THE SCIENCES
Chemistry	M,D

UNIVERSITY OF THE VIRGIN ISLANDS
Environmental Sciences	M
Marine Sciences	M

THE UNIVERSITY OF TOLEDO
Analytical Chemistry	M,D
Applied Mathematics	M,D
Astrophysics	M,D
Biostatistics	M,O
Chemistry	M,D
Environmental Sciences	M,D
Geology	M,D
Inorganic Chemistry	M,D
Mathematics	M,D
Organic Chemistry	M,D
Physical Chemistry	M,D
Physics	M,D
Statistics	M,D

UNIVERSITY OF TORONTO
Astronomy	M,D
Astrophysics	M,D
Biostatistics	M,D
Chemistry	M,D
Environmental Sciences	M,D
Forestry	M,D
Geology	M,D
Mathematical and Computational Finance	M
Mathematics	M,D
Physics	M,D
Statistics	M,D

THE UNIVERSITY OF TULSA
Applied Mathematics	
Chemistry	M,D
Geophysics	M,D
Geosciences	M,D
Mathematics	M,D
Physics	M,D

UNIVERSITY OF UTAH
Atmospheric Sciences	M,D
Biostatistics	M,D
Chemical Physics	M,D
Chemistry	M
Computational Sciences	M,D
Environmental Sciences	M,D
Geology	M,D
Geophysics	M,D
Mathematics	M,D
Physics	M,D
Statistics	M,D

UNIVERSITY OF VERMONT
Agricultural Sciences— General	M,D
Agronomy and Soil Sciences	M,D
Animal Sciences	M,D
Biostatistics	M
Chemistry	M,D
Food Science and Technology	M,D
Forestry	M,D
Geology	M
Horticulture	M,D

*M—master's; D—doctorate; O—other advanced degree; *Close-Up and/or Display*

Petersons Graduate Programs in the Physical Sciences, Mathematics, Agricultural Sciences, the Environment & Natural Resources 2017

www.petersons.com **29**

Mathematics	M,D
Natural Resources	M,D
Physics	M
Plant Sciences	M,D
Statistics	M

UNIVERSITY OF VICTORIA
Astronomy	M,D
Astrophysics	M,D
Chemistry	M,D
Condensed Matter Physics	M,D
Geosciences	M,D
Mathematics	M,D
Oceanography	M,D
Physics	M,D
Statistics	M,D
Theoretical Physics	M,D

UNIVERSITY OF VIRGINIA
Astronomy	M,D
Chemistry	M,D
Environmental Sciences	M,D
Mathematics	M,D
Physics	M,D
Statistics	M,D

UNIVERSITY OF WASHINGTON
Applied Mathematics	M,D
Applied Physics	M,D
Astronomy	M,D
Atmospheric Sciences	M,D
Biostatistics	M,D
Chemistry	M,D
Computational Sciences	M,D
Environmental Management and Policy	M,D
Fish, Game, and Wildlife Management	M,D
Forestry	M,D
Geology	M,D
Geophysics	M,D
Horticulture	M,D
Hydrology	M,D
Marine Affairs	M,O
Marine Geology	M,D
Mathematics	M,D
Natural Resources	M,D
Oceanography	M,D
Physics	M,D
Statistics	M,D

UNIVERSITY OF WATERLOO
Applied Mathematics	M,D
Biostatistics	M,D
Chemistry	M,D
Environmental Management and Policy	M,D
Environmental Sciences	M,D
Geosciences	M,D
Mathematics	M,D
Physics	M,D
Statistics	M,D

THE UNIVERSITY OF WESTERN ONTARIO
Applied Mathematics	M,D
Astronomy	M,D
Biostatistics	M,D
Chemistry	M,D
Environmental Sciences	M,D
Geology	M,D
Geophysics	M,D
Geosciences	M,D
Mathematics	M,D
Physics	M,D
Statistics	M,D

UNIVERSITY OF WEST FLORIDA
Applied Statistics	M
Environmental Sciences	M
Geosciences	M
Marine Affairs	M
Mathematics	M

UNIVERSITY OF WEST GEORGIA
Mathematics	M,O

UNIVERSITY OF WINDSOR
Chemistry	M,D
Environmental Sciences	M,D
Geosciences	M,D
Mathematics	M,D
Physics	M,D
Statistics	M,D

UNIVERSITY OF WISCONSIN–GREEN BAY
Environmental Management and Policy	M
Environmental Sciences	M

UNIVERSITY OF WISCONSIN–LA CROSSE
Marine Sciences	M

UNIVERSITY OF WISCONSIN–MADISON
Agricultural Sciences—General	M,D
Agronomy and Soil Sciences	M,D
Animal Sciences	M,D
Astronomy	D
Atmospheric Sciences	M,D
Biometry	M
Chemistry	M,D
Fish, Game, and Wildlife Management	M,D
Food Science and Technology	M,D
Forestry	M,D
Geology	M,D
Geophysics	M,D
Horticulture	M,D
Marine Sciences	M,D
Mathematics	D
Natural Resources	M,D
Oceanography	M,D
Physics	M,D
Plant Sciences	M,D

Statistics	M,D
Water Resources	M

UNIVERSITY OF WISCONSIN–MILWAUKEE
Chemistry	M,D
Geology	M,D
Mathematics	M,D
Physics	M,D
Water Resources	M,D

UNIVERSITY OF WISCONSIN–RIVER FALLS
Agricultural Sciences—General	M

UNIVERSITY OF WISCONSIN–STEVENS POINT
Natural Resources	M

UNIVERSITY OF WISCONSIN–STOUT
Applied Mathematics	M
Food Science and Technology	M

UNIVERSITY OF WYOMING
Agricultural Sciences—General	M,D
Agronomy and Soil Sciences	M,D
Animal Sciences	M,D
Atmospheric Sciences	M,D
Chemistry	M,D
Food Science and Technology	M
Geology	M,D
Geophysics	M,D
Mathematics	M,D
Natural Resources	M,D
Range Science	M,D
Statistics	M,D
Water Resources	M,D

UTAH STATE UNIVERSITY
Agricultural Sciences—General	M,D
Agronomy and Soil Sciences	M,D
Animal Sciences	M,D
Applied Mathematics	M,D
Chemistry	M,D
Environmental Management and Policy	M,D
Fish, Game, and Wildlife Management	M,D
Food Science and Technology	M,D
Forestry	M,D
Geology	M
Mathematics	M,D
Meteorology	M,D
Natural Resources	M
Physics	M,D
Plant Sciences	M,D
Range Science	M,D
Statistics	M,D
Water Resources	M,D

VALPARAISO UNIVERSITY
Computational Sciences	M

VANDERBILT UNIVERSITY
Analytical Chemistry	M,D
Astronomy	M,D
Chemistry	M,D
Environmental Management and Policy	M,D
Environmental Sciences	M
Geology	M
Inorganic Chemistry	M,D
Mathematics	M,D
Organic Chemistry	M,D
Physical Chemistry	M,D
Physics	M,D
Theoretical Chemistry	M,D

VERMONT LAW SCHOOL
Environmental Management and Policy	M

VILLANOVA UNIVERSITY
Applied Statistics	M
Chemistry	M
Mathematics	M

VIRGINIA COMMONWEALTH UNIVERSITY
Analytical Chemistry	M,D
Applied Mathematics	M
Applied Physics	M
Biostatistics	M,D
Chemical Physics	M,D
Chemistry	M,D
Environmental Management and Policy	M
Inorganic Chemistry	M,D
Mathematics	M
Organic Chemistry	M,D
Physical Chemistry	M,D
Physics	M,D
Statistics	M,D

VIRGINIA POLYTECHNIC INSTITUTE AND STATE UNIVERSITY
Agricultural Sciences—General	M,D,O
Agronomy and Soil Sciences	M,D
Animal Sciences	M,D
Chemistry	M,D
Environmental Management and Policy	M,D,O
Environmental Sciences	M,D,O
Fish, Game, and Wildlife Management	M,D
Forestry	M,D
Geosciences	M,D
Horticulture	M,D
Mathematics	M,D
Natural Resources	M,D,O
Physics	M,D

Statistics	M,D

VIRGINIA STATE UNIVERSITY
Mathematics	M

WAKE FOREST UNIVERSITY
Analytical Chemistry	M,D
Chemistry	M,D
Inorganic Chemistry	M,D
Mathematics	M
Organic Chemistry	M,D
Physical Chemistry	M,D
Physics	M,D

WASHINGTON STATE UNIVERSITY
Agronomy and Soil Sciences	M,D,O
Animal Sciences	M,D
Applied Mathematics	M,D
Chemistry	M,D
Environmental Sciences	M,D
Food Science and Technology	M,D
Geology	M,D
Horticulture	M,D
Mathematics	M,D
Natural Resources	M,D
Physics	M,D

WASHINGTON UNIVERSITY IN ST. LOUIS
Biostatistics	M,D,O
Chemistry	D
Geosciences	D
Mathematics	M,D
Physics	D
Planetary and Space Sciences	D
Statistics	M,D

WAYNE STATE UNIVERSITY
Analytical Chemistry	M,D
Applied Mathematics	M,D
Chemistry	M,D
Food Science and Technology	M,D,O
Geology	M
Inorganic Chemistry	M,D
Mathematics	M,D
Organic Chemistry	M,D
Physical Chemistry	M,D
Physics	M,D
Statistics	M,D

WEBSTER UNIVERSITY
Environmental Management and Policy	M

WESLEYAN UNIVERSITY
Astronomy	M
Chemical Physics	D
Chemistry	D
Environmental Sciences	M
Geosciences	M
Inorganic Chemistry	D
Mathematics	M,D
Organic Chemistry	D
Physics	D
Theoretical Chemistry	D

WESLEY COLLEGE
Environmental Management and Policy	M

WEST CHESTER UNIVERSITY OF PENNSYLVANIA
Applied Mathematics	M,O
Applied Statistics	M,O
Astronomy	M
Chemistry	O
Geology	M
Geosciences	M
Mathematics	M,O

WESTERN CAROLINA UNIVERSITY
Chemistry	M
Mathematics	M

WESTERN CONNECTICUT STATE UNIVERSITY
Environmental Sciences	M
Geosciences	M
Mathematics	M
Planetary and Space Sciences	M

WESTERN ILLINOIS UNIVERSITY
Applied Mathematics	M,O
Chemistry	M
Environmental Sciences	D
Mathematics	M,O
Physics	M

WESTERN KENTUCKY UNIVERSITY
Agricultural Sciences—General	M
Chemistry	M
Computational Sciences	M
Geology	M
Geosciences	M
Mathematics	M
Physics	M

WESTERN MICHIGAN UNIVERSITY
Applied Mathematics	M,D
Chemistry	M,D,O
Computational Sciences	M,D
Geosciences	M,D,O
Mathematics	M,D
Physics	M,D,O
Statistics	M,D,O

WESTERN STATE COLORADO UNIVERSITY
Environmental Management and Policy	M

WESTERN WASHINGTON UNIVERSITY
Chemistry	M
Environmental Sciences	M

Geology	M
Marine Sciences	M
Mathematics	M

WEST TEXAS A&M UNIVERSITY
Agricultural Sciences—General	M,D
Animal Sciences	M
Chemistry	M
Environmental Sciences	M
Mathematics	M
Plant Sciences	M

WEST VIRGINIA UNIVERSITY
Agricultural Sciences—General	M,D
Agronomy and Soil Sciences	D
Analytical Chemistry	M,D
Animal Sciences	M,D
Applied Mathematics	M,D
Applied Physics	M,D
Biostatistics	M,D
Chemical Physics	M,D
Chemistry	M,D
Condensed Matter Physics	M,D
Environmental Management and Policy	M,D
Fish, Game, and Wildlife Management	M
Food Science and Technology	M,D
Forestry	M,D
Geology	M,D
Geophysics	M,D
Horticulture	M,D
Hydrogeology	M,D
Inorganic Chemistry	M,D
Mathematics	M,D
Natural Resources	M,D
Organic Chemistry	M,D
Paleontology	M,D
Physical Chemistry	M,D
Physics	M,D
Plant Sciences	D
Plasma Physics	M,D
Statistics	M,D
Theoretical Chemistry	M,D
Theoretical Physics	M,D

WICHITA STATE UNIVERSITY
Applied Mathematics	M,D
Chemistry	M,D
Environmental Sciences	M
Geology	M
Mathematics	M,D
Physics	M,D

WILFRID LAURIER UNIVERSITY
Chemistry	M
Environmental Management and Policy	M,D
Environmental Sciences	M

WILKES UNIVERSITY
Mathematics	M

WILMINGTON UNIVERSITY
Environmental Management and Policy	M,D

WOODS HOLE OCEANOGRAPHIC INSTITUTION
Marine Geology	D
Oceanography	D

WORCESTER POLYTECHNIC INSTITUTE
Applied Mathematics	M,D,O
Applied Statistics	M,D,O
Chemistry	M,D
Mathematics	M,D,O
Physics	M,D

WRIGHT STATE UNIVERSITY
Applied Mathematics	M
Applied Statistics	M
Chemistry	M
Environmental Sciences	M,D
Geology	M
Geophysics	M
Mathematics	M
Physics	M

YALE UNIVERSITY
Applied Mathematics	M,D
Applied Physics	M,D
Astronomy	M,D
Astrophysics	M,D
Atmospheric Sciences	D
Biostatistics	M,D
Chemistry	D
Environmental Management and Policy	M,D
Environmental Sciences	M,D
Forestry	M,D
Geochemistry	D
Geology	D
Geophysics	D
Geosciences	D
Inorganic Chemistry	D
Mathematics	M,D
Meteorology	D
Oceanography	D
Organic Chemistry	D
Paleontology	D
Physical Chemistry	D
Physics	D
Planetary and Space Sciences	M,D
Statistics	M,D
Theoretical Chemistry	D

YESHIVA UNIVERSITY
Mathematics	M,D

YORK UNIVERSITY
Applied Mathematics	M,D
Astronomy	M,D

30 www.petersons.com

Petersons Graduate Programs in the Physical Sciences, Mathematics, Agricultural Sciences, the Environment & Natural Resources 2017

Chemistry	M,D		
Environmental Management			
and Policy	M,D		
Geosciences	M,D		
Mathematics	M,D		
Physics	M,D		

Planetary and Space	
Sciences	M,D
Statistics	M,D

YOUNGSTOWN STATE UNIVERSITY

Analytical Chemistry	M

Applied Mathematics	M
Chemistry	M
Environmental Management	
and Policy	M,O
Inorganic Chemistry	M
Mathematics	M

Organic Chemistry	M
Physical Chemistry	M
Statistics	M

*M—master's; D—doctorate; O—other advanced degree; *Close-Up and/or Display*

*Petersons Graduate Programs in the Physical Sciences, Mathematics,
Agricultural Sciences, the Environment & Natural Resources 2017*

www.petersons.com **31**

ACADEMIC AND PROFESSIONAL PROGRAMS IN THE PHYSICAL SCIENCES

Section 1
Astronomy and Astrophysics

This section contains a directory of institutions offering graduate work in astronomy and astrophysics. Additional information may be obtained by writing directly to the dean of a graduate school or chair of a department at the address given in the directory.

For programs offering related work, see also in this book *Geosciences, Meteorology and Atmospheric Sciences,* and *Physics.* In the other guides in this series:

Graduate Programs in the Biological/Biomedical Sciences & Health-Related Medical Professions

See *Biological and Biomedical Sciences* and *Biophysics*

Graduate Programs in Engineering & Applied Sciences

See *Aerospace/Aeronautical Engineering, Energy and Power Engineering (Nuclear Engineering), Engineering and Applied Sciences,* and *Mechanical Engineering and Mechanics*

CONTENTS

Program Directories

Astronomy

Boston University, Graduate School of Arts and Sciences, Department of Astronomy, Boston, MA 02215. Offers MA, PhD. *Students:* 32 full-time (11 women); includes 4 minority (2 Asian, non-Hispanic/Latino; 2 Hispanic/Latino), 5 international. Average age 27. 88 applicants, 24% accepted, 3 enrolled. In 2015, 6 master's, 1 doctorate awarded. Terminal master's awarded for partial completion of doctoral program. *Degree requirements:* For master's, one foreign language, comprehensive exam, thesis or alternative; for doctorate, one foreign language, comprehensive exam, thesis/dissertation. *Entrance requirements:* For master's and doctorate, GRE General Test, GRE Subject Test (physics), 3 letters of recommendation, transcripts, personal statement, curriculum vitae. Additional exam requirements/recommendations for international students: Required—TOEFL (minimum score 550 paper-based; 84 iBT). *Application deadline:* For fall admission, 12/15 for domestic and international students. Application fee: $95. Electronic applications accepted. *Financial support:* In 2015–16, 30 students received support, including 1 fellowship with full tuition reimbursement available (averaging $21,000 per year), 20 research assistantships with full tuition reimbursements available (averaging $21,000 per year), 6 teaching assistantships with full tuition reimbursements available (averaging $21,000 per year); Federal Work-Study, health care benefits, and unspecified assistantships also available. Support available to part-time students. Financial award application deadline: 12/15. *Unit head:* Alan Marscher, Chairman, 617-353-5029, Fax: 617-353-5704, E-mail: marscher@bu.edu. *Application contact:* Anne Smart, Department Administrator, 617-363-2625, Fax: 617-353-5704, E-mail: asmart@bu.edu.
Website: http://www.bu.edu/dbin/astronomy

Brigham Young University, Graduate Studies, College of Physical and Mathematical Sciences, Department of Physics and Astronomy, Provo, UT 84602-1001. Offers physics (MS, PhD); physics and astronomy (PhD). *Program availability:* Part-time. *Faculty:* 29 full-time (2 women), 1 (woman) part-time/adjunct. *Students:* 31 full-time (5 women), 3 part-time (0 women); includes 5 minority (2 Asian, non-Hispanic/Latino; 2 Hispanic/Latino; 1 Native Hawaiian or other Pacific Islander, non-Hispanic/Latino), 4 international. Average age 28. 21 applicants, 48% accepted, 9 enrolled. In 2015, 5 master's, 3 doctorates awarded. Terminal master's awarded for partial completion of doctoral program. *Degree requirements:* For master's, thesis; for doctorate, thesis/dissertation, qualifying exam, candidacy exam. *Entrance requirements:* For master's and doctorate, GRE Subject Test (physics), GRE General Test, minimum GPA of 3.0, ecclesiastical endorsement. Additional exam requirements/recommendations for international students: Required—TOEFL (minimum score 580 paper-based; 85 iBT), IELTS (minimum score 7), CAE (minimum 75 or B grade). *Application deadline:* For fall admission, 1/15 priority date for domestic and international students. Application fee: $50. Electronic applications accepted. *Financial support:* In 2015–16, 26 students received support, including 20 research assistantships with full tuition reimbursements available (averaging $20,640 per year), 6 teaching assistantships with full tuition reimbursements available (averaging $19,680 per year); institutionally sponsored loans, health care benefits, and tuition waivers (full) also available. Support available to part-time students. Financial award application deadline: 1/15. *Faculty research:* Acoustics; atomic, molecular, and optical physics; theoretical and mathematical physics; condensed matter; astrophysics and plasma. *Total annual research expenditures:* $3 million. *Unit head:* Dr. Richard R. Vanfleet, Chair, 801-422-1702, Fax: 801-422-0553, E-mail: richard_vanfleet@byu.edu. *Application contact:* Dr. Eric W. Hirschmann, Graduate Coordinator, 801-422-9271, Fax: 801-422-0553, E-mail: eric_hirschmann@byu.edu.
Website: http://physics.byu.edu/

California Institute of Technology, Division of Physics, Mathematics and Astronomy, Department of Astronomy, Pasadena, CA 91125-0001. Offers PhD. *Degree requirements:* For doctorate, one foreign language, thesis/dissertation, candidacy and final exams. *Entrance requirements:* For doctorate, GRE General Test, GRE Subject Test. Additional exam requirements/recommendations for international students: Required—TOEFL. *Faculty research:* Observational and theoretical astrophysics, cosmology, radio astronomy, solar physics.

Case Western Reserve University, School of Graduate Studies, Department of Astronomy, Cleveland, OH 44106. Offers MS, PhD. *Program availability:* Part-time. *Faculty:* 5 full-time (2 women), 1 part-time/adjunct (0 women). *Students:* 5 full-time (1 woman) 1 international. Average age 28. 13 applicants, 15% accepted. In 2015, 2 master's awarded. *Degree requirements:* For doctorate, comprehensive exam, thesis/dissertation. *Entrance requirements:* For doctorate, GRE General Test, GRE Subject Test (physics). Additional exam requirements/recommendations for international students: Required—TOEFL (minimum score 577 paper-based; 90 iBT), IELTS (minimum score 7). *Application deadline:* For fall admission, 1/15 priority date for domestic students. Applications are processed on a rolling basis. Application fee: $50. Electronic applications accepted. *Expenses: Tuition, area resident:* Full-time $41,137; part-time $1714 per credit hour. *Required fees:* $32. Tuition and fees vary according to course load and program. *Financial support:* Fellowships and research assistantships available. Financial award application deadline: 1/15; financial award applicants required to submit FAFSA. *Faculty research:* Optical observational astronomy, high- and low-dispersion spectroscopy, theoretical astrophysics, galactic structure, computational theory. *Unit head:* Prof. Stacy McGaugh, Professor and Chair, 216-368-1808, Fax: 216-368-5406, E-mail: stacy.mcgaugh@case.edu. *Application contact:* Agnes Torontalli, Department Assistant, 216-368-3728, Fax: 216-368-5406, E-mail: agnes@case.edu.
Website: http://astronomy.case.edu/

Columbia University, Graduate School of Arts and Sciences, New York, NY 10027. Offers African-American studies (MA); American studies (MA); anthropology (MA, PhD); art history and archaeology (MA, PhD); astronomy (PhD); biological sciences (PhD); biotechnology (MA); chemical physics (PhD); chemistry (PhD); classical studies (MA, PhD); classics (MA, PhD); climate and society (MA); conservation biology (MA); earth and environmental sciences (PhD); East Asia: regional studies (MA); East Asian languages and cultures (MA, PhD); ecology, evolution and environmental biology (MA), including conservation biology; ecology, evolution, and environmental biology (PhD), including ecology and evolutionary biology, evolutionary primatology; economics (MA, PhD); English and comparative literature (MA, PhD); French and Romance philology (MA, PhD); Germanic languages (MA, PhD); global French studies (MA); global thought (MA); Hispanic cultural studies (MA); history (PhD); history and literature (MA); human rights studies (MA); Islamic studies (MA); Italian (MA, PhD); Japanese pedagogy (MA); Jewish studies (MA); Latin America and the Caribbean: regional studies (MA); Latin American and Iberian cultures (PhD); mathematics (MA, PhD), including finance (MA); medieval and Renaissance studies (MA); Middle Eastern, South Asian, and African studies (MA, PhD); modern art: critical and curatorial studies (MA); modern European studies (MA); museum anthropology (MA); music (DMA, PhD); oral history (MA); philosophical foundations of physics (MA); philosophy (MA, PhD); physics (PhD); political science (MA, PhD); psychology (PhD); quantitative methods in the social sciences (MA); religion (MA, PhD); Russia, Eurasia and East Europe: regional studies (MA); Russian translation (MA); Slavic cultures (MA); Slavic languages (MA, PhD); sociology (MA, PhD); South Asian studies (MA); statistics (MA, PhD); theatre (PhD). Dual-degree programs require admission to both Graduate School of Arts and Sciences and another Columbia school. *Program availability:* Part-time. *Students:* 3,030 full-time, 235 part-time; includes 861 minority (88 Black or African American, non-Hispanic/Latino; 5 American Indian or Alaska Native, non-Hispanic/Latino; 517 Asian, non-Hispanic/Latino; 159 Hispanic/Latino; 4 Native Hawaiian or other Pacific Islander, non-Hispanic/Latino; 88 Two or more races, non-Hispanic/Latino), 1,697 international. 13,288 applicants, 21% accepted, 1162 enrolled. In 2015, 1,061 master's, 553 doctorates awarded. Terminal master's awarded for partial completion of doctoral program. *Degree requirements:* For master's, variable foreign language requirement, comprehensive exam (for some programs), thesis (for some programs); for doctorate, variable foreign language requirement, comprehensive exam (for some programs), thesis/dissertation. *Entrance requirements:* For master's and doctorate, GRE General Test, GRE Subject Test (for some programs). Additional exam requirements/recommendations for international students: Required—TOEFL, IELTS. Application fee: $105. Electronic applications accepted. *Financial support:* Fellowships, research assistantships, teaching assistantships, career-related internships or fieldwork, Federal Work-Study, institutionally sponsored loans, scholarships/grants, traineeships, health care benefits, tuition waivers, and unspecified assistantships available. Support available to part-time students. Financial award application deadline: 12/15. *Unit head:* Carlos J. Alonso, Dean of the Graduate School of Arts and Sciences, 212-854-5177. *Application contact:* GSAS Office of Admissions, 212-854-8903, E-mail: gsas-admissions@columbia.edu.
Website: http://gsas.columbia.edu/

Cornell University, Graduate School, Graduate Fields of Arts and Sciences, Field of Astronomy and Space Sciences, Ithaca, NY 14853-0001. Offers astronomy (PhD); astrophysics (PhD); general space sciences (PhD); infrared astronomy (PhD); planetary studies (PhD); radio astronomy (PhD); radiophysics (PhD); theoretical astrophysics (PhD). *Degree requirements:* For doctorate, comprehensive exam, thesis/dissertation. *Entrance requirements:* For doctorate, GRE General Test, GRE Subject Test (physics), 3 letters of recommendation. Additional exam requirements/recommendations for international students: Required—TOEFL (minimum score 600 paper-based; 77 iBT). Electronic applications accepted. *Faculty research:* Observational astrophysics, planetary sciences, cosmology, instrumentation, gravitational astrophysics.

Dartmouth College, Arts and Sciences Graduate Programs, Department of Physics and Astronomy, Hanover, NH 03755. Offers PhD. *Faculty:* 21 full-time (4 women), 4 part-time/adjunct (0 women). *Students:* 52 full-time (18 women); includes 3 minority (1 Asian, non-Hispanic/Latino; 1 Hispanic/Latino; 1 Two or more races, non-Hispanic/Latino), 24 international. Average age 26. 114 applicants, 27% accepted, 9 enrolled. In 2015, 7 doctorates awarded. *Degree requirements:* For doctorate, thesis/dissertation. *Entrance requirements:* For doctorate, GRE General Test, GRE Subject Test. Additional exam requirements/recommendations for international students: Required—TOEFL. *Application deadline:* For fall admission, 1/15 for domestic students. Application fee: $50. Electronic applications accepted. *Expenses: Tuition, area resident:* Full-time $48,120. *Required fees:* $296. One-time fee: $50 full-time. *Financial support:* Research assistantships with full tuition reimbursements, teaching assistantships with full tuition reimbursements, and scholarships/grants available. *Faculty research:* Matter physics, plasma and beam physics, space physics, astronomy, cosmology. *Unit head:* James W. LaBelle, Chair, 603-646-2973, Fax: 603-646-1446. *Application contact:* Judy Lowell, Administrative Assistant, 603-646-2359, Fax: 603-646-1446.
Website: http://www.dartmouth.edu/~physics/

George Mason University, College of Science, Department of Physics and Astronomy, Fairfax, VA 22030. Offers applied and engineering physics (MS); computational science and informatics (PhD); computational techniques and applications (Certificate). *Faculty:* 47 full-time (10 women), 11 part-time/adjunct (1 woman). *Students:* 24 full-time (3 women), 27 part-time (5 women); includes 9 minority (3 Black or African American, non-Hispanic/Latino; 1 Asian, non-Hispanic/Latino; 1 Hispanic/Latino; 4 Two or more races, non-Hispanic/Latino), 11 international. Average age 31. 53 applicants, 34% accepted, 10 enrolled. In 2015, 8 master's, 4 doctorates awarded. *Degree requirements:* For master's, thesis optional; for doctorate, comprehensive exam, thesis/dissertation. *Entrance requirements:* For master's and doctorate, GRE, baccalaureate degree in related field with minimum GPA of 3.0 in last 60 credit hours; 3 letters of recommendation; expanded goals statement; resume; 2 copies of official transcripts. Additional exam requirements/recommendations for international students: Required—TOEFL (minimum score 575 paper-based; 88 iBT), IELTS (minimum score 6.5), PTE (minimum score 59). Application fee: $75 ($80 for international students). Electronic applications accepted. *Financial support:* In 2015–16, 39 students received support, including 1 fellowship (averaging $8,000 per year), 17 research assistantships with tuition reimbursements available (averaging $17,848 per year), 5 teaching assistantships with tuition reimbursements available (averaging $17,000 per year); career-related internships or fieldwork, Federal Work-Study, scholarships/grants, unspecified assistantships, and health care benefits (for full-time research or teaching assistantship recipients) also available. Support available to part-time students. Financial award application deadline: 3/1; financial award applicants required to submit FAFSA. *Faculty research:* Particle and nuclear physics; computational statistics; astronomy, astrophysics, and space and planetary science; astronomy and physics education; atomic physics; biophysics and neuroscience; optical physics; fundamental theoretical studies; multidimensional data analysis. *Total annual research expenditures:* $3.2 million.

Georgia State University, College of Arts and Sciences, Department of Physics and Astronomy, Program in Astronomy, Atlanta, GA 30302-3083. Offers PhD. Terminal master's awarded for partial completion of doctoral program. *Degree requirements:* For doctorate, 2 foreign languages, comprehensive exam, thesis/dissertation. *Entrance requirements:* For doctorate, GRE General Test, GRE Subject Test (physics). Additional exam requirements/recommendations for international students: Required—TOEFL (minimum score 550 paper-based; 80 iBT). *Application deadline:* For fall admission, 1/15 for domestic and international students; for spring admission, 11/15 for domestic and international students. Application fee: $50. Electronic applications accepted. *Expenses: Tuition, state resident:* full-time $6876; part-time $382 per credit hour. *Tuition, nonresident:* full-time $22,374; part-time $1243 per credit hour. *Required fees:* $2128; $2128 per term. $1064 per term. Part-time tuition and fees vary according to course load and program. *Financial support:* In 2015–16, fellowships with full tuition reimbursements (averaging $22,000 per year), research assistantships with full tuition reimbursements

(averaging $22,000 per year), teaching assistantships with full tuition reimbursements (averaging $20,500 per year) were awarded; institutionally sponsored loans, scholarships/grants, and unspecified assistantships also available. Financial award application deadline: 1/15; financial award applicants required to submit FAFSA. *Faculty research:* Astrophysics, active galactic nuclei, exoplanet searches, missing mass and dark matter stellar. *Unit head:* Dr. Mike Crenshaw, Chair, 404-413-6020, E-mail: crenshaw@chara.gsu.edu. *Application contact:* Todd Henry, Graduate Director, 404-413-6054, E-mail: thenry@chara.gsu.edu.
Website: http://www.phy-astr.gsu.edu/

Harvard University, Graduate School of Arts and Sciences, Department of Astronomy, Cambridge, MA 02138. Offers astronomy (PhD); astrophysics (PhD). *Degree requirements:* For doctorate, thesis/dissertation, paper, research project, 2 semesters of teaching. *Entrance requirements:* For doctorate, GRE General Test, GRE Subject Test (physics). Additional exam requirements/recommendations for international students: Required—TOEFL. Electronic applications accepted. *Faculty research:* Atomic and molecular physics, electromagnetism, solar physics, nuclear physics, fluid dynamics.

Indiana University Bloomington, University Graduate School, College of Arts and Sciences, Department of Astronomy, Bloomington, IN 47405-7000. Offers astronomy (MA, PhD); astrophysics (PhD). Terminal master's awarded for partial completion of doctoral program. *Degree requirements:* For master's, thesis or alternative, oral exam; for doctorate, comprehensive exam, thesis/dissertation, oral defense. *Entrance requirements:* For master's and doctorate, GRE General Test, GRE Subject Test (physics), BA or BS in science. Additional exam requirements/recommendations for international students: Required—TOEFL. Electronic applications accepted. *Faculty research:* Stellar and galaxy dynamics, stellar chemical abundances, galaxy evolution, observational cosmology.

Johns Hopkins University, Zanvyl Krieger School of Arts and Sciences, Henry A. Rowland Department of Physics and Astronomy, Baltimore, MD 21218. Offers astronomy (PhD); physics (PhD). *Degree requirements:* For doctorate, comprehensive exam, thesis/dissertation, minimum B- average on required coursework. *Entrance requirements:* For doctorate, GRE General Test, GRE Subject Test. Additional exam requirements/recommendations for international students: Required—TOEFL (minimum score 600 paper-based; 100 iBT), IELTS. Electronic applications accepted. *Faculty research:* High-energy physics, condensed-matter, astrophysics, particle and experimental physics, plasma physics.

Louisiana State University and Agricultural & Mechanical College, Graduate School, College of Science, Department of Physics and Astronomy, Baton Rouge, LA 70803. Offers astronomy (PhD); astrophysics (PhD); medical physics (MS); physics (MS, PhD).

Michigan State University, The Graduate School, College of Natural Science, Department of Physics and Astronomy, East Lansing, MI 48824. Offers astrophysics and astronomy (MS, PhD); physics (MS, PhD). *Entrance requirements:* Additional exam requirements/recommendations for international students: Required—TOEFL (minimum score 550 paper-based), Michigan State University ELT (minimum score 85), Michigan English Language Assessment Battery (minimum score 83). Electronic applications accepted. *Faculty research:* Nuclear and accelerator physics, high energy physics, condensed matter physics, biophysics, astrophysics and astronomy.

Minnesota State University Mankato, College of Graduate Studies and Research, College of Science, Engineering and Technology, Department of Physics and Astronomy, Mankato, MN 56001. Offers MS. *Degree requirements:* For master's, one foreign language, comprehensive exam, thesis or alternative. *Entrance requirements:* For master's, minimum GPA of 3.0 during previous 2 years, recommendation letters. Additional exam requirements/recommendations for international students: Required—TOEFL. Electronic applications accepted.

New Mexico State University, College of Arts and Sciences, Department of Astronomy, Las Cruces, NM 88003-8001. Offers MS, PhD. *Program availability:* Part-time. *Faculty:* 10 full-time (2 women). *Students:* 25 full-time (12 women), 2 part-time (both women); includes 2 minority (both Hispanic/Latino). Average age 26. 46 applicants, 7% accepted, 3 enrolled. In 2015, 2 master's, 8 doctorates awarded. Terminal master's awarded for partial completion of doctoral program. *Degree requirements:* For master's, comprehensive exam (for some programs), thesis (for some programs); for doctorate, comprehensive exam, thesis/dissertation. *Entrance requirements:* For master's and doctorate, GRE General Test, GRE Subject Test (advanced physics). Additional exam requirements/recommendations for international students: Required—TOEFL (minimum score 550 paper-based; 79 iBT), IELTS (minimum score 6.5). *Application deadline:* For fall admission, 1/15 priority date for domestic and international students. Applications are processed on a rolling basis. Application fee: $40 ($50 for international students). Electronic applications accepted. *Expenses:* $274.50 per credit hour for in-state students, and all students enrolled in six or fewer credits; $839.30 per credit hour for out-of-state and international students enrolled in at least seven hours. *Financial support:* In 2015–16, 26 students received support, including 2 fellowships (averaging $4,088 per year), 16 research assistantships (averaging $22,403 per year), 8 teaching assistantships (averaging $16,616 per year); career-related internships or fieldwork, Federal Work-Study, scholarships/grants, traineeships, health care benefits, and unspecified assistantships also available. Support available to part-time students. Financial award application deadline: 3/1. *Faculty research:* Planetary science, solar physics, starts and stellar populations, interstellar medium, galaxies, cosmology. *Total annual research expenditures:* $5.7 million. *Unit head:* Dr. Jon Holtzman, Department Head, 575-646-8181, Fax: 575-646-1602, E-mail: jholtzma@nmsu.edu. *Application contact:* Dr. Jason Jackiewicz, Chair of Graduate Admissions, 575-646-1699, Fax: 575-646-1602, E-mail: gradapps@astronomy.nmsu.edu.
Website: http://astronomy.nmsu.edu/

Northwestern University, The Graduate School, Judd A. and Marjorie Weinberg College of Arts and Sciences, Department of Physics and Astronomy, Evanston, IL 60208. Offers PhD. Admissions and degrees offered through The Graduate School. *Degree requirements:* For doctorate, thesis/dissertation, qualifying exam. *Entrance requirements:* For doctorate, GRE General Test, GRE Subject Test. Additional exam requirements/recommendations for international students: Required—TOEFL. *Faculty research:* Nuclear and particle physics, condensed-matter physics, nonlinear physics, astrophysics.

The Ohio State University, Graduate School, College of Arts and Sciences, Division of Natural and Mathematical Sciences, Department of Astronomy, Columbus, OH 43210. Offers MS, PhD. Terminal master's awarded for partial completion of doctoral program. *Degree requirements:* For master's, comprehensive exam, thesis; for doctorate, comprehensive exam, thesis/dissertation. *Entrance requirements:* For master's and doctorate, GRE General Test, GRE Subject Test (physics). Additional exam requirements/recommendations for international students: Required—TOEFL (minimum score 550 paper-based; 79 iBT), Michigan English Language Assessment Battery (minimum score 82); Recommended—IELTS (minimum score 7). Electronic applications accepted.

Ohio University, Graduate College, College of Arts and Sciences, Department of Physics and Astronomy, Athens, OH 45701. Offers astronomy (MS, PhD); physics (MS, PhD). *Faculty:* 29 full-time (4 women), 3 part-time/adjunct (1 woman). *Students:* 75 full-time (15 women), 57 international. 90 applicants, 36% accepted, 7 enrolled. In 2015, 12 master's, 11 doctorates awarded. Terminal master's awarded for partial completion of doctoral program. *Degree requirements:* For master's, thesis or alternative; for doctorate, comprehensive exam, thesis/dissertation. *Entrance requirements:* For master's and doctorate, minimum GPA of 3.0. Additional exam requirements/recommendations for international students: Required—TOEFL (minimum score 600 paper-based; 100 iBT), IELTS (minimum score 7), TWE (minimum score 4). *Application deadline:* For fall admission, 1/15 priority date for domestic and international students. Applications are processed on a rolling basis. Application fee: $50 ($55 for international students). Electronic applications accepted. *Expenses:* $4,852 tuition and fees per term in-state, $8,848 out-of-state. *Financial support:* In 2015–16, 67 students received support, including 3 fellowships with full tuition reimbursements available (averaging $28,544 per year), 34 research assistantships with full tuition reimbursements available (averaging $25,991 per year), 32 teaching assistantships with full tuition reimbursements available (averaging $24,024 per year); scholarships/grants also available. Financial award application deadline: 1/15. *Faculty research:* Nuclear physics, condensed-matter physics, nonlinear systems, astrophysics, biophysics. *Total annual research expenditures:* $2.4 million. *Unit head:* Dr. David Ingram, Chair, 740-593-0336, Fax: 740-593-0433, E-mail: ingram@ohio.edu. *Application contact:* Dr. Alexander Neiman, Graduate Admissions Chair, 740-593-1701, Fax: 740-593-0433, E-mail: gradapp@phy.ohiou.edu.
Website: http://www.ohio.edu/physastro/

Penn State University Park, Graduate School, Eberly College of Science, Department of Astronomy and Astrophysics, University Park, PA 16802. Offers astronomy and astrophysics (MS, PhD). *Unit head:* Dr. Douglas R. Cavener, Dean, 814-865-9591, Fax: 814-865-3634. *Application contact:* Lori Stania, Director, Graduate Student Services, 814-865-1795, Fax: 814-863-4627, E-mail: l-gswww@lists.psu.edu.
Website: http://astro.psu.edu/

Princeton University, Graduate School, Department of Astrophysical Sciences, Princeton, NJ 08544-1019. Offers astronomy (PhD); plasma physics (PhD). *Degree requirements:* For doctorate, thesis/dissertation. *Entrance requirements:* For doctorate, GRE General Test, GRE Subject Test (physics). Additional exam requirements/recommendations for international students: Required—TOEFL (minimum score 600 paper-based). Electronic applications accepted. *Faculty research:* Theoretical astrophysics, cosmology, galaxy formation, galactic dynamics, interstellar and intergalactic matter.

Rice University, Graduate Programs, Wiess School of Natural Sciences, Department of Physics and Astronomy, Houston, TX 77251-1892. Offers nanoscale physics (MS); physics and astronomy (PhD); science teaching (MST). *Program availability:* Part-time. *Degree requirements:* For master's, thesis (for some programs); for doctorate, thesis/dissertation, minimum B average. *Entrance requirements:* For master's, GRE General Test; for doctorate, GRE General Test, GRE Subject Test. Additional exam requirements/recommendations for international students: Required—TOEFL (minimum score 600 paper-based; 90 iBT). Electronic applications accepted. *Faculty research:* Optical physics; ultra cold atoms; membrane electr-statics, peptides, proteins and lipids; solar astrophysics; stellar activity; magnetic fields; young stars.

Rutgers University–New Brunswick, Graduate School-New Brunswick, Department of Physics and Astronomy, Piscataway, NJ 08854-8097. Offers astronomy (MS, PhD); biophysics (PhD); condensed matter physics (MS, PhD); elementary particle physics (MS, PhD); intermediate energy nuclear physics (MS); nuclear physics (MS, PhD); physics (MST); surface science (PhD); theoretical physics (MS, PhD). *Program availability:* Part-time. Terminal master's awarded for partial completion of doctoral program. *Degree requirements:* For master's, comprehensive exam, thesis or alternative; for doctorate, comprehensive exam, thesis/dissertation. *Entrance requirements:* For master's and doctorate, GRE General Test, GRE Subject Test. Additional exam requirements/recommendations for international students: Required—TOEFL (minimum score 560 paper-based). Electronic applications accepted. *Faculty research:* Astronomy, high energy, condensed matter, surface, nuclear physics.

Saint Mary's University, Faculty of Science, Department of Astronomy and Physics, Halifax, NS B3H 3C3, Canada. Offers astronomy (M Sc, PhD). *Program availability:* Part-time. *Degree requirements:* For master's, thesis optional; for doctorate, comprehensive exam, thesis/dissertation. *Entrance requirements:* For master's, honors degree with minimum GPA of 3.0. Additional exam requirements/recommendations for international students: Required—TOEFL. *Faculty research:* Young stellar objects, interstellar medium, star clusters, galactic structure, early-type galaxies.

San Diego State University, Graduate and Research Affairs, College of Sciences, Department of Astronomy, San Diego, CA 92182. Offers MS. *Degree requirements:* For master's, thesis. *Entrance requirements:* For master's, GRE General Test, letters of reference. Additional exam requirements/recommendations for international students: Required—TOEFL. Electronic applications accepted. *Faculty research:* Classical and dwarf novae, photometry, interactive binaries.

San Francisco State University, Division of Graduate Studies, College of Science and Engineering, Department of Physics and Astronomy, San Francisco, CA 94132-1722. Offers astronomy (MS); physics and astronomy (MS). *Program availability:* Part-time. *Application deadline:* Applications are processed on a rolling basis. Electronic applications accepted. *Expenses:* Tuition, state resident: full-time $6738. Tuition, nonresident: full-time $15,666. *Required fees:* $1004 per year. *Unit head:* Dr. Maarten Golterman, Chair, 415-338-1659, Fax: 415-338-2178, E-mail: maarten@sfsu.edu. *Application contact:* Dr. Susan Lee, Graduate Advisor, 415-338-1655, Fax: 415-338-2178, E-mail: slea@sfsu.edu.
Website: http://www.physics.sfsu.edu/

Stony Brook University, State University of New York, Graduate School, College of Arts and Sciences, Department of Physics and Astronomy, Program in Astronomy, Stony Brook, NY 11794. Offers PhD. *Degree requirements:* For doctorate, thesis/dissertation. *Entrance requirements:* For doctorate, GRE General Test, minimum GPA of 3.0. Additional exam requirements/recommendations for international students: Required—TOEFL. *Application deadline:* For fall admission, 1/15 for domestic students. Application fee: $100. *Expenses:* $12,421 full-time resident tuition and fees, $453 per credit hour; $23,761 full-time nonresident tuition and fees, $925 per credit hour. *Financial support:* Fellowships, research assistantships, and teaching assistantships available. Financial award application deadline: 2/1. *Unit head:* Dr. Axel Drees, Chair, 631-632-8114, Fax: 631-632-8176, E-mail: axel.drees@stonybrook.edu. *Application contact:* Donald Sheehan, Coordinator, 631-632-1046, Fax: 631-632-8176, E-mail: donald.j.sheehan@stonybrook.edu.

Astronomy

Université de Moncton, Faculty of Sciences, Department of Physics and Astronomy, Moncton, NB E1A 3E9, Canada. Offers M Sc. *Program availability:* Part-time. *Degree requirements:* For master's, thesis. *Entrance requirements:* For master's, proficiency in French. Electronic applications accepted. *Faculty research:* Thin films, optical properties, solar selective surfaces, microgravity and photonic materials.

The University of Arizona, College of Science, Department of Astronomy, Tucson, AZ 85721. Offers PhD. *Degree requirements:* For doctorate, thesis/dissertation. *Entrance requirements:* For doctorate, GRE General Test, GRE Subject Test (physics), minimum GPA of 3.5, 3 letters of recommendation. Additional exam requirements/ recommendations for international students: Required—TOEFL (minimum score 550 paper-based; 79 iBT). *Application deadline:* For fall admission, 1/15 for domestic students, 12/1 for international students. Applications are processed on a rolling basis. Application fee: $75. Electronic applications accepted. *Financial support:* Research assistantships, teaching assistantships, scholarships/grants, health care benefits, and unspecified assistantships available. *Faculty research:* Astrophysics, submillimeter astronomy, infrared astronomy, Near Infrared Camera and Multi-Object Spectrometer (NICMOS), Spitzer Space Telescope. *Unit head:* Dr. Buell Jannuzi, Head, 520-621-2288, Fax: 520-621-1532, E-mail: buelljannuzi@email.arizona.edu.
Website: http://www.as.arizona.edu

The University of British Columbia, Faculty of Science, Program in Astronomy, Vancouver, BC V6T 1Z1, Canada. Offers M Sc, PhD.

University of Calgary, Faculty of Graduate Studies, Faculty of Science, Department of Physics and Astronomy, Calgary, AB T2N 1N4, Canada. Offers M Sc, PhD. *Program availability:* Part-time. *Degree requirements:* For master's, thesis; for doctorate, thesis/ dissertation, oral candidacy exam, written qualifying exam. *Entrance requirements:* For master's and doctorate, GRE General Test, GRE Subject Test. Additional exam requirements/recommendations for international students: Required—TOEFL (minimum score 550 paper-based). Electronic applications accepted. *Faculty research:* Astronomy and astrophysics, mass spectrometry, atmospheric physics, space physics, medical physics.

University of California, Los Angeles, Graduate Division, College of Letters and Science, Department of Physics and Astronomy, Program in Astronomy, Los Angeles, CA 90095. Offers MAT, MS, PhD. Terminal master's awarded for partial completion of doctoral program. *Degree requirements:* For master's, comprehensive exam; for doctorate, thesis/dissertation, oral and written qualifying exams; 3 quarters of teaching experience. *Entrance requirements:* For master's and doctorate, GRE General Test, GRE Subject Test (physics), bachelor's degree; minimum undergraduate GPA of 3.0 (or its equivalent if letter grade system not used). Additional exam requirements/ recommendations for international students: Required—TOEFL. Electronic applications accepted.

University of California, Santa Cruz, Division of Graduate Studies, Division of Physical and Biological Sciences, Department of Astronomy and Astrophysics, Santa Cruz, CA 95064. Offers PhD. *Degree requirements:* For doctorate, one foreign language, thesis/ dissertation, qualifying exam. *Entrance requirements:* For doctorate, GRE General Test, GRE Subject Test. Additional exam requirements/recommendations for international students: Required—TOEFL (minimum score 550 paper-based; 83 iBT); Recommended—IELTS (minimum score 8). Electronic applications accepted. *Faculty research:* Solar system and the Milky Way to the most distant galaxies in the Universe, fundamental questions of cosmology.

University of Chicago, Division of the Physical Sciences, Department of Astronomy and Astrophysics, Chicago, IL 60637. Offers PhD. Terminal master's awarded for partial completion of doctoral program. *Degree requirements:* For doctorate, comprehensive exam, thesis/dissertation, dissertation for publication. *Entrance requirements:* For doctorate, GRE General Test, GRE Subject Test. Additional exam requirements/ recommendations for international students: Required—TOEFL (minimum score 600 paper-based; 90 iBT), IELTS (minimum score 7). Electronic applications accepted. *Faculty research:* Cosmology, exoplanets, galaxy formation, interstellar and intergalactic matter, astroparticle physics, high-performance computation in astrophysics.

University of Delaware, College of Arts and Sciences, Department of Physics and Astronomy, Newark, DE 19716. Offers MS, PhD. *Program availability:* Part-time. Terminal master's awarded for partial completion of doctoral program. *Degree requirements:* For master's, thesis; for doctorate, thesis/dissertation. *Entrance requirements:* For master's and doctorate, GRE General Test, GRE Subject Test. Additional exam requirements/recommendations for international students: Required—TOEFL (minimum score 600 paper-based). Electronic applications accepted. *Faculty research:* Magnetoresistance and magnetic materials, ultrafast optical phenomena, superfluidity, elementary particle physics, stellar atmospheres and interiors.

University of Florida, Graduate School, College of Liberal Arts and Sciences, Department of Astronomy, Gainesville, FL 32611-2055. Offers MS, MST, PhD. *Degree requirements:* For doctorate, one foreign language, comprehensive exam, thesis/ dissertation. *Entrance requirements:* For master's and doctorate, GRE General Test, GRE Subject Test (physics), minimum GPA of 3.0. Additional exam requirements/ recommendations for international students: Required—TOEFL (minimum score 550 paper-based; 80 iBT), IELTS (minimum score 6). Electronic applications accepted. *Faculty research:* Solar systems, stars and stellar populations, star formation and interstellar medium, structure and evolution of galaxies, extragalactic astronomy and cosmology, extrasolar planets and instrumentation.

University of Hawaii at Manoa, Graduate Division, College of Natural Sciences, Department of Physics and Astronomy, Program in Astronomy, Honolulu, HI 96822. Offers MS, PhD. *Program availability:* Part-time. *Faculty:* 53 full-time (8 women). *Students:* 40 full-time (14 women); includes 4 minority (2 Asian, non-Hispanic/Latino; 2 Two or more races, non-Hispanic/Latino), 14 international. Average age 28. 97 applicants, 9% accepted, 8 enrolled. In 2015, 3 master's, 9 doctorates awarded. *Degree requirements:* For master's, thesis optional; for doctorate, comprehensive exam, thesis/ dissertation. *Entrance requirements:* For master's and doctorate, GRE General Test. Additional exam requirements/recommendations for international students: Required—TOEFL (minimum score 560 paper-based; 83 iBT), IELTS (minimum score 5). *Application deadline:* For fall admission, 12/31 for domestic and international students. Application fee: $100. *Financial support:* In 2015–16, 38 students received support, including 1 fellowship (averaging $1,100 per year), 33 research assistantships (averaging $24,981 per year), 4 teaching assistantships (averaging $22,140 per year). *Total annual research expenditures:* $29.3 million. *Unit head:* Pui K. Lam, Chair, 808-956-2988. *Application contact:* David Sanders, Graduate Chair, 808-956-8101, Fax: 808-956-4532, E-mail: sandersd@hawaii.edu.

University of Illinois at Urbana–Champaign, Graduate College, College of Liberal Arts and Sciences, Department of Astronomy, Champaign, IL 61820. Offers MS, PhD.

The University of Iowa, Graduate College, College of Liberal Arts and Sciences, Department of Physics and Astronomy, Program in Astronomy, Iowa City, IA 52242-1316. Offers MS. *Degree requirements:* For master's, thesis optional, exam. *Entrance requirements:* For master's, GRE General Test, minimum GPA of 3.0. Additional exam requirements/recommendations for international students: Required—TOEFL (minimum score 550 paper-based; 81 iBT). Electronic applications accepted.

The University of Kansas, Graduate Studies, College of Liberal Arts and Sciences, Department of Physics and Astronomy, Lawrence, KS 66045. Offers computational physics and astronomy (MS); physics (MS, PhD). *Students:* 54 full-time (7 women), 1 part-time (0 women); includes 5 minority (1 American Indian or Alaska Native, non-Hispanic/Latino; 1 Hispanic/Latino; 3 Two or more races, non-Hispanic/Latino), 23 international. Average age 30. 80 applicants, 14% accepted, 7 enrolled. In 2015, 4 master's, 6 doctorates awarded. Terminal master's awarded for partial completion of doctoral program. *Entrance requirements:* For master's and doctorate, GRE Subject Test (physics), undergraduate degree. Additional exam requirements/recommendations for international students: Required—TOEFL. *Application deadline:* For fall admission, 12/1 priority date for domestic and international students; for spring admission, 10/1 priority date for domestic and international students. Application fee: $65 ($85 for international students). Electronic applications accepted. *Financial support:* Fellowships, research assistantships, teaching assistantships, health care benefits, and unspecified assistantships available. Financial award application deadline: 4/1; financial award applicants required to submit FAFSA. *Faculty research:* Astrophysics, biophysics, high energy physics, nanophysics, nuclear physics. *Unit head:* Hume A. Feldman, Chair, 785-864-4740, E-mail: feldman@ku.edu. *Application contact:* Desiree Neyens, Graduate Secretary, 785-864-1225, E-mail: dneyens@ku.edu.
Website: http://www.physics.ku.edu

University of Kentucky, Graduate School, College of Arts and Sciences, Program in Physics and Astronomy, Lexington, KY 40506-0032. Offers MS, PhD. *Degree requirements:* For master's, comprehensive exam, thesis optional; for doctorate, comprehensive exam, thesis/dissertation. *Entrance requirements:* For master's, GRE General Test, minimum undergraduate GPA of 2.75; for doctorate, GRE General Test, minimum graduate GPA of 3.0. Additional exam requirements/recommendations for international students: Required—TOEFL (minimum score 550 paper-based). Electronic applications accepted. *Faculty research:* Astrophysics, active galactic nuclei, and radio astronomy; Rydbert atoms, and electron scattering; TOF spectroscopy, hyperon interactions and muons; particle theory, lattice gauge theory, quark, and skyrmion models.

The University of Manchester, School of Physics and Astronomy, Manchester, United Kingdom. Offers astronomy and astrophysics (M Sc, PhD); biological physics (M Sc, PhD); condensed matter physics (M Sc, PhD); nonlinear and liquid crystals physics (M Sc, PhD); nuclear physics (M Sc, PhD); particle physics (M Sc, PhD); photon physics (M Sc, PhD); physics (M Sc, PhD); theoretical physics (M Sc, PhD).

University of Maryland, College Park, Academic Affairs, College of Computer, Mathematical and Natural Sciences, Department of Astronomy, College Park, MD 20742. Offers MS, PhD. *Program availability:* Part-time, evening/weekend. Terminal master's awarded for partial completion of doctoral program. *Degree requirements:* For master's, thesis or alternative, written exam; for doctorate, thesis/dissertation, research project. *Entrance requirements:* For master's, GRE General Test, GRE Subject Test (physics), minimum GPA of 3.0, 3 letters of recommendation; for doctorate, GRE General Test, GRE Subject Test (physics), 3 letters of recommendation. Electronic applications accepted. *Faculty research:* Solar radio astronomy, plasma and high-energy astrophysics, galactic and extragalactic astronomy.

University of Massachusetts Amherst, Graduate School, College of Natural Sciences, Department of Astronomy, Amherst, MA 01003. Offers MS, PhD. *Program availability:* Part-time. Terminal master's awarded for partial completion of doctoral program. *Degree requirements:* For master's, thesis or alternative; for doctorate, comprehensive exam, thesis/dissertation. *Entrance requirements:* For master's and doctorate, GRE General Test, GRE Subject Test (physics). Additional exam requirements/recommendations for international students: Required—TOEFL (minimum score 550 paper-based; 80 iBT), IELTS (minimum score 6.5). Electronic applications accepted.

University of Michigan, Rackham Graduate School, College of Literature, Science, and the Arts, Department of Astronomy, Ann Arbor, MI 48109-1042. Offers astronomy and astrophysics (PhD). *Faculty:* 25 full-time (7 women). *Students:* 26 full-time (12 women); includes 6 minority (4 Asian, non-Hispanic/Latino; 2 Hispanic/Latino). 134 applicants, 22% accepted, 6 enrolled. In 2015, 5 doctorates awarded. Terminal master's awarded for partial completion of doctoral program. *Degree requirements:* For doctorate, thesis/dissertation, oral defense of dissertation. *Entrance requirements:* For doctorate, GRE General Test, GRE Subject Test (physics). Additional exam requirements/ recommendations for international students: Required—TOEFL. *Application deadline:* For fall admission, 1/1 for domestic and international students. Application fee: $75 ($90 for international students). Electronic applications accepted. *Financial support:* In 2015–16, 22 students received support. Fellowships, research assistantships, teaching assistantships, institutionally sponsored loans, scholarships/grants, health care benefits, and unspecified assistantships available. Financial award applicants required to submit FAFSA. *Faculty research:* Extragalactic and galactic astronomy, cosmology, star and planet formation, high energy astrophysics. *Unit head:* Dr. Edwin Bergin, Professor and Chair, 734-764-3440, Fax: 734-763-6317, E-mail: astrochair@umich.edu. *Application contact:* Brian Cox, Graduate Program Coordinator, 734-764-3440, Fax: 734-763-6317, E-mail: astro-phd@umich.edu.
Website: http://www.lsa.umich.edu/astro

University of Missouri, Office of Research and Graduate Studies, College of Arts and Science, Department of Physics and Astronomy, Columbia, MO 65211. Offers MS, PhD. Terminal master's awarded for partial completion of doctoral program. *Degree requirements:* For doctorate, one foreign language, comprehensive exam, thesis/ dissertation. *Entrance requirements:* For master's and doctorate, GRE General Test, minimum GPA of 3.0. Additional exam requirements/recommendations for international students: Required—TOEFL (minimum score 550 paper-based; 80 iBT). Electronic applications accepted. *Faculty research:* Experimental and theoretical condensed-matter physics, biological physics, astronomy/astrophysics.

University of Nebraska–Lincoln, Graduate College, College of Arts and Sciences, Department of Physics and Astronomy, Lincoln, NE 68588. Offers astronomy (MS, PhD); physics (MS, PhD). *Degree requirements:* For master's, thesis optional; for doctorate, comprehensive exam, thesis/dissertation. *Entrance requirements:* For master's and doctorate, GRE General Test. Additional exam requirements/ recommendations for international students: Required—TOEFL (minimum score 550 paper-based). Electronic applications accepted. *Faculty research:* Electromagnetics of solids and thin films, photoionization, ion collisions with atoms, molecules and surfaces, nanostructures.

University of Nevada, Las Vegas, Graduate College, College of Sciences, Department of Physics and Astronomy, Las Vegas, NV 89154-4002. Offers astronomy (MS, PhD); physics (MS, PhD). *Program availability:* Part-time. *Faculty:* 12 full-time (0 women).

Students: 20 full-time (3 women), 2 part-time (0 women); includes 3 minority (2 Hispanic/Latino; 1 Two or more races, non-Hispanic/Latino), 6 international. Average age 33. 14 applicants, 50% accepted, 5 enrolled. In 2015, 1 master's, 3 doctorates awarded. *Degree requirements:* For master's, comprehensive exam (for some programs), thesis (for some programs); for doctorate, comprehensive exam, thesis/dissertation. *Entrance requirements:* For master's and doctorate, GRE General Test. Additional exam requirements/recommendations for international students: Required—TOEFL (minimum score 550 paper-based; 80 iBT), IELTS (minimum score 7). *Application deadline:* For fall admission, 5/15 for domestic students, 5/1 for international students; for spring admission, 11/15 for domestic students, 10/1 for international students. Application fee: $60 ($95 for international students). Electronic applications accepted. *Expenses:* $264 per credit state resident full-time and part-time; $6,955 per semester, $264 per credit nonresident full-time; $555 per credit nonresident part-time. *Financial support:* In 2015–16, 19 students received support, including 2 research assistantships with partial tuition reimbursements available (averaging $18,150 per year), 17 teaching assistantships with partial tuition reimbursements available (averaging $16,640 per year); institutionally sponsored loans, scholarships/grants, health care benefits, and unspecified assistantships also available. Financial award application deadline: 3/1. *Faculty research:* Gamma-ray bursters astrophysics, cosmology and dark matter astrophysics, experimental high pressure physics, theoretical condensed matter physics, laser-plasma atomic physics. *Total annual research expenditures:* $3 million. *Unit head:* Stephen Lepp, Chair/Professor, 702-895-4455, E-mail: lepp@physics.unlv.edu. *Application contact:* Graduate College Admissions Evaluator, 702-895-3367, Fax: 702-895-4180, E-mail: gradadmissions@unlv.edu.
Website: http://www.physics.unlv.edu/academics.html

The University of North Carolina at Chapel Hill, Graduate School, College of Arts and Sciences, Department of Physics and Astronomy, Chapel Hill, NC 27599. Offers physics (MS, PhD). Terminal master's awarded for partial completion of doctoral program. *Degree requirements:* For master's, comprehensive exam; for doctorate, comprehensive exam, thesis/dissertation. *Entrance requirements:* For master's and doctorate, GRE General Test, minimum GPA of 3.0. Electronic applications accepted. *Faculty research:* Observational astronomy, fullerenes, polarized beams, nanotubes, nucleosynthesis in stars and supernovae, superstring theory, ballistic transport in semiconductors, gravitation.

University of Pittsburgh, Dietrich School of Arts and Sciences, Program in Computational Modeling and Simulation, Pittsburgh, PA 15260. Offers biological science (PhD); chemistry (PhD); computer science (PhD); economics (PhD); mathematics (PhD); physics and astronomy (PhD); psychology (PhD); statistics (PhD). *Program availability:* Part-time. *Faculty:* 3 full-time (0 women). *Students:* 3 full-time (1 woman); includes 2 minority (both Asian, non-Hispanic/Latino). Average age 23. 13 applicants, 31% accepted, 2 enrolled. *Degree requirements:* For doctorate, comprehensive exam, thesis/dissertation, preliminary exam. *Entrance requirements:* For doctorate, GRE, statement of purpose, transcripts for all college-level institutions attended, three letters of reference. Additional exam requirements/recommendations for international students: Required—TOEFL (minimum score 90 iBT), IELTS (minimum score 7). *Application deadline:* For fall admission, 1/15 for domestic and international students. Applications are processed on a rolling basis. Application fee: $0 ($50 for international students). Electronic applications accepted. Tuition and fees vary according to program. *Financial support:* In 2015–16, 3 students received support, including 2 fellowships with full tuition reimbursements available (averaging $27,000 per year), 1 research assistantship with full tuition reimbursement available (averaging $21,500 per year); tuition waivers (full) also available. Financial award application deadline: 4/15. *Faculty research:* Econometric modeling, developing reduced-scaling first principles approaches for expedited predictions of molecular and materials properties, developing computational models to quantitatively describe origins of reactivity and selectivity in organocatalytic reactions. *Unit head:* Dr. Kathleen Blee, Associate Dean, Graduate Studies and Research, 412-624-3939, Fax: 412-624-6855. *Application contact:* Wendy G. Janocha, Graduate Administrator, 412-648-7251, E-mail: wgj1@pitt.edu.
Website: http://cmsp.pitt.edu/

University of Rochester, School of Arts and Sciences, Department of Physics and Astronomy, Rochester, NY 14627. Offers physics (MA, MS, PhD); physics and astronomy (PhD). *Program availability:* Part-time. *Faculty:* 27 full-time (3 women). *Students:* 103 full-time (24 women), 1 (woman) part-time; includes 11 minority (5 Asian, non-Hispanic/Latino; 4 Hispanic/Latino; 2 Two or more races, non-Hispanic/Latino), 32 international. 290 applicants, 30% accepted, 27 enrolled. In 2015, 6 master's, 8 doctorates awarded. Terminal master's awarded for partial completion of doctoral program. *Degree requirements:* For master's, comprehensive exam, thesis (for some programs); for doctorate, comprehensive exam, thesis/dissertation, qualifying exam. *Entrance requirements:* For master's and doctorate, GRE General Test. Additional exam requirements/recommendations for international students: Required—TOEFL. *Application deadline:* For fall admission, 1/15 priority date for domestic students. Application fee: $60. Electronic applications accepted. *Expenses: Tuition, area resident:* Full-time $47,450; part-time $1482 per credit hour. *Required fees:* $528. Tuition and fees vary according to program. *Financial support:* Fellowships, research assistantships, teaching assistantships, and tuition waivers (full and partial) available. Financial award application deadline: 2/1. *Faculty research:* Astronomy and astrophysics, biological physics, condensed matter physics, high energy/nuclear physics, quantum optics. *Unit head:* Nicholas P. Bigelow, Chair, 585-275-4344. *Application contact:* Laura Blumkin, Graduate Coordinator, 585-275-4356, E-mail: laurablumkin@pas.rochester.edu.
Website: http://www.pas.rochester.edu/urpas/pages/graduate/gradprograms

University of South Carolina, The Graduate School, College of Arts and Sciences, Department of Physics and Astronomy, Columbia, SC 29208. Offers IMA, MAT, MS, PSM, PhD. IMA and MAT offered in cooperation with the College of Education. *Program availability:* Part-time. Terminal master's awarded for partial completion of doctoral program. *Degree requirements:* For master's, comprehensive exam, thesis; for doctorate, one foreign language, comprehensive exam, thesis/dissertation. *Entrance requirements:* For master's and doctorate, GRE General Test, GRE Subject Test. Additional exam requirements/recommendations for international students: Required—TOEFL (minimum score 570 paper-based; 75 iBT). Electronic applications accepted. *Faculty research:* Condensed matter, intermediate-energy nuclear physics, foundations of quantum mechanics, astronomy/astrophysics.

The University of Texas at Austin, Graduate School, College of Natural Sciences, Department of Astronomy, Austin, TX 78712-1111. Offers MA, PhD. *Entrance requirements:* For master's and doctorate, GRE General Test, GRE Subject Test (physics). Additional exam requirements/recommendations for international students: Required—TOEFL. Electronic applications accepted. *Faculty research:* Stars, interstellar medium, galaxies, planetary astronomy, cosmology.

University of Toronto, School of Graduate Studies, Faculty of Arts and Science, Department of Astronomy and Astrophysics, Toronto, ON M5S 1A1, Canada. Offers M Sc, PhD. *Program availability:* Part-time. *Degree requirements:* For doctorate, thesis/dissertation, qualifying exam, thesis defense. *Entrance requirements:* For master's, minimum B average, bachelor's degree in astronomy or equivalent, 3 letters of reference; for doctorate, GRE General Test, minimum B+ average, master's degree in astronomy or equivalent, demonstrated research competence, 3 letters of reference. Additional exam requirements/recommendations for international students: Required—TOEFL (minimum score 580 paper-based; 93 iBT), TWE (minimum score 4). Electronic applications accepted.

University of Victoria, Faculty of Graduate Studies, Faculty of Science, Department of Physics and Astronomy, Victoria, BC V8W 2Y2, Canada. Offers astronomy and astrophysics (M Sc, PhD); condensed matter physics (M Sc, PhD); experimental particle physics (M Sc, PhD); medical physics (M Sc, PhD); ocean physics (M Sc, PhD); theoretical physics (M Sc, PhD). *Degree requirements:* For master's, thesis; for doctorate, comprehensive exam, thesis/dissertation, candidacy exam. *Entrance requirements:* For master's and doctorate, GRE. Additional exam requirements/recommendations for international students: Required—TOEFL (minimum score 575 paper-based), IELTS (minimum score 7). Electronic applications accepted. *Faculty research:* Old stellar populations; observational cosmology and large scale structure; cp violation; atlas.

University of Virginia, College and Graduate School of Arts and Sciences, Department of Astronomy, Charlottesville, VA 22903. Offers MS, PhD. *Degree requirements:* For master's, comprehensive exam, thesis or alternative; for doctorate, comprehensive exam, thesis/dissertation. *Entrance requirements:* For master's and doctorate, GRE General Test, GRE Subject Test. Additional exam requirements/recommendations for international students: Required—TOEFL (minimum score 650 paper-based; 90 iBT), IELTS (minimum score 7). Electronic applications accepted.

University of Washington, Graduate School, College of Arts and Sciences, Department of Astronomy, Seattle, WA 98195. Offers MS, PhD. Terminal master's awarded for partial completion of doctoral program. *Degree requirements:* For doctorate, thesis/dissertation. *Entrance requirements:* For master's and doctorate, GRE General Test, GRE Subject Test, minimum GPA of 3.0. Additional exam requirements/recommendations for international students: Required—TOEFL. *Faculty research:* Solar system dust, space astronomy, high-energy astrophysics, galactic and extragalactic astronomy, stellar astrophysics.

The University of Western Ontario, Faculty of Graduate Studies, Physical Sciences Division, Department of Physics and Astronomy, Program in Astronomy, London, ON N6A 5B8, Canada. Offers M Sc, PhD. Terminal master's awarded for partial completion of doctoral program. *Degree requirements:* For master's, thesis optional; for doctorate, comprehensive exam, thesis/dissertation. *Entrance requirements:* For master's, GRE Subject Test (physics), honors B Sc degree, minimum B average (Canadian), A - (international); for doctorate, M Sc degree, minimum B average (Canadian), A - (international). Additional exam requirements/recommendations for international students: Required—TOEFL (minimum score 580 paper-based). *Faculty research:* Observational and theoretical astrophysics spectroscopy, photometry, spectro-polarimetry, variable stars, cosmology.

University of Wisconsin–Madison, Graduate School, College of Letters and Science, Department of Astronomy, Madison, WI 53706-1380. Offers PhD. *Degree requirements:* For doctorate, comprehensive exam, thesis/dissertation. *Entrance requirements:* For doctorate, GRE General Test, GRE Subject Test (physics), bachelor's degree in related field. Additional exam requirements/recommendations for international students: Required—TOEFL. Electronic applications accepted. *Expenses:* Tuition, state resident: full-time $5364. Tuition, nonresident: full-time $12,027. *Required fees:* $571. Tuition and fees vary according to campus/location, program and reciprocity agreements. *Faculty research:* Kinematics, evolution of galaxies, cosmic distance, scale and large-scale structures, interstellar intergalactic medium, star formation and evolution, solar system chemistry and dynamics.

Vanderbilt University, Department of Physics and Astronomy, Nashville, TN 37240-1001. Offers astronomy (MS); health physics (MA); physics (MAT, MS, PhD). *Faculty:* 26 full-time (3 women). *Students:* 55 full-time (9 women); includes 10 minority (2 Black or African American, non-Hispanic/Latino; 1 Asian, non-Hispanic/Latino; 6 Hispanic/Latino; 1 Two or more races, non-Hispanic/Latino), 18 international. Average age 27. 169 applicants, 19% accepted, 7 enrolled. In 2015, 4 master's, 12 doctorates awarded. *Degree requirements:* For master's, thesis; for doctorate, comprehensive exam, thesis/dissertation, final and qualifying exams. *Entrance requirements:* For master's, GRE General Test; for doctorate, GRE General Test, GRE Subject Test. Additional exam requirements/recommendations for international students: Required—TOEFL (minimum score 570 paper-based; 88 iBT). *Application deadline:* For fall admission, 1/15 for domestic and international students. Electronic applications accepted. *Financial support:* Fellowships with tuition reimbursements, research assistantships with full tuition reimbursements, teaching assistantships with full tuition reimbursements, career-related internships or fieldwork, Federal Work-Study, and institutionally sponsored loans available. Financial award application deadline: 1/15; financial award applicants required to submit CSS PROFILE or FAFSA. *Faculty research:* Experimental and theoretical physics, free electron laser, living-state physics, heavy-ion physics, nuclear structure. *Unit head:* Dr. Julia Velkovska, Director of Graduate Studies, 615-322-2828, Fax: 615-343-7263, E-mail: julia.velkovska@vanderbilt.edu. *Application contact:* Donald Pickert, Administrative Assistant, 615-343-1026, Fax: 615-343-7263, E-mail: donald.pickert@vanderbilt.edu.
Website: http://www.vanderbilt.edu/physics/

Wesleyan University, Graduate Studies, Department of Astronomy, Middletown, CT 06459-0123. Offers MA. *Faculty:* 4 full-time (1 woman). *Students:* 4 full-time (3 women); includes 1 minority (Hispanic/Latino). Average age 25. 25 applicants, 8% accepted, 2 enrolled. In 2015, 3 master's awarded. *Degree requirements:* For master's, thesis. *Entrance requirements:* For master's, GRE General Test; GRE Subject Test in physics (recommended). Additional exam requirements/recommendations for international students: Required—TOEFL. *Application deadline:* For fall admission, 3/1 for domestic and international students. Application fee: $0. Electronic applications accepted. *Financial support:* In 2015–16, 4 students received support, including 4 teaching assistantships with full tuition reimbursements available; research assistantships, tuition waivers (full), and full-year stipends also available. Financial award application deadline: 4/15. *Faculty research:* Observational-theoretical astronomy and astrophysics. *Unit head:* Dr. Edward Moran, Chair, 860-685-3739, E-mail: emoran@wesleyan.edu. *Application contact:* Linda Shettleworth, Administrative Assistant, 860-685-2130, Fax: 860-685-2131, E-mail: shettleworth@wesleyan.edu.
Website: http://www.wesleyan.edu/astro/

West Chester University of Pennsylvania, College of Arts and Sciences, Department of Geology and Astronomy, West Chester, PA 19383. Offers geoscience (MA). *Program availability:* Part-time, evening/weekend. *Faculty:* 9 full-time (4 women), 1 part-time/adjunct (0 women). *Students:* 14 full-time (7 women), 16 part-time (5 women); includes 2 minority (1 Black or African American, non-Hispanic/Latino; 1 Hispanic/Latino). Average age 33. 11 applicants, 100% accepted, 7 enrolled. In 2015, 7 degrees awarded. *Degree*

requirements: For master's, final project involving manuscript (for some programs), presentation. *Entrance requirements:* For master's, minimum GPA of 2.8 (for some programs). Additional exam requirements/recommendations for international students: Required—TOEFL or IELTS. *Application deadline:* For fall admission, 5/15 for international students; for spring admission, 10/15 for international students. Applications are processed on a rolling basis. Application fee: $50. Electronic applications accepted. *Expenses:* Tuition, state resident: full-time $8460; part-time $470 per credit. Tuition, nonresident: full-time $12,690; part-time $705 per credit. *Required fees:* $2312; $126.75 per credit. Tuition and fees vary according to campus/location and program. *Financial support:* Scholarships/grants and unspecified assistantships available. Financial award application deadline: 2/15; financial award applicants required to submit FAFSA. *Faculty research:* Geoscience education, environmental geology, energy and sustainability, astronomy, coastal geomorphology (sea level change), water and soil remediation, hydrogeology, short-term weather forecasting. *Unit head:* Dr. Martin Helmke, Chair, 610-436-3565, Fax: 610-436-3036, E-mail: mhelmke@wcupa.edu. *Application contact:* Dr. Joby Hilliker, Graduate Coordinator, 610-436-2213, Fax: 610-436-3036, E-mail: jhilliker@wcupa.edu.
Website: http://www.wcupa.edu/_academics/sch_cas.esc/

Yale University, Graduate School of Arts and Sciences, Department of Astronomy, New Haven, CT 06520. Offers astronomy (PhD); solar and terrestrial physics (PhD). *Degree requirements:* For doctorate, thesis/dissertation. *Entrance requirements:* For doctorate, GRE General Test, GRE Subject Test (physics).

York University, Faculty of Graduate Studies, Faculty of Science, Program in Physics and Astronomy, Toronto, ON M3J 1P3, Canada. Offers M Sc, PhD. *Program availability:* Part-time, evening/weekend. *Degree requirements:* For master's, thesis or alternative; for doctorate, comprehensive exam, thesis/dissertation. Electronic applications accepted.

Astrophysics

Air Force Institute of Technology, Graduate School of Engineering and Management, Department of Engineering Physics, Dayton, OH 45433-7765. Offers applied physics (MS, PhD); electro-optics (MS, PhD); materials science (PhD); nuclear engineering (MS, PhD); space physics (MS). *Program availability:* Part-time. *Degree requirements:* For master's, thesis; for doctorate, thesis/dissertation. *Entrance requirements:* For master's and doctorate, GRE General Test, minimum GPA of 3.0, U.S. citizenship. *Faculty research:* High-energy lasers, space physics, nuclear weapon effects, semiconductor physics.

Arizona State University at the Tempe campus, College of Liberal Arts and Sciences, School of Earth and Space Exploration, Tempe, AZ 85287-1404. Offers astrophysics (MS, PhD); exploration systems design (PhD); geological sciences (MS, PhD). PhD in exploration systems design is offered in collaboration with the Ira A. Fulton School of Engineering. Terminal master's awarded for partial completion of doctoral program. *Degree requirements:* For master's, thesis, interactive Program of Study (iPOS) submitted before completing 50 percent of required credit hours; for doctorate, thesis/dissertation, interactive Program of Study (iPOS) submitted before completing 50 percent of required credit hours. *Entrance requirements:* For master's and doctorate, GRE, minimum GPA of 3.0 or equivalent in last 2 years of work leading to bachelor's degree. Additional exam requirements/recommendations for international students: Required—TOEFL, IELTS, or PTE. Electronic applications accepted.

Cornell University, Graduate School, Graduate Fields of Arts and Sciences, Field of Astronomy and Space Sciences, Ithaca, NY 14853-0001. Offers astronomy (PhD); astrophysics (PhD); general space sciences (PhD); infrared astronomy (PhD); planetary studies (PhD); radio astronomy (PhD); radiophysics (PhD); theoretical astrophysics (PhD). *Degree requirements:* For doctorate, comprehensive exam, thesis/dissertation. *Entrance requirements:* For doctorate, GRE General Test, GRE Subject Test (physics), 3 letters of recommendation. Additional exam requirements/recommendations for international students: Required—TOEFL (minimum score 600 paper-based; 77 iBT). Electronic applications accepted. *Faculty research:* Observational astrophysics, planetary sciences, cosmology, instrumentation, gravitational astrophysics.

Harvard University, Graduate School of Arts and Sciences, Department of Astronomy, Cambridge, MA 02138. Offers astronomy (PhD); astrophysics (PhD). *Degree requirements:* For doctorate, thesis/dissertation, paper, research project, 2 semesters of teaching. *Entrance requirements:* For doctorate, GRE General Test, GRE Subject Test (physics). Additional exam requirements/recommendations for international students: Required—TOEFL. Electronic applications accepted. *Faculty research:* Atomic and molecular physics, electromagnetism, solar physics, nuclear physics, fluid dynamics.

Indiana University Bloomington, University Graduate School, College of Arts and Sciences, Department of Astronomy, Bloomington, IN 47405-7000. Offers astronomy (MA, PhD); astrophysics (PhD). Terminal master's awarded for partial completion of doctoral program. *Degree requirements:* For master's, thesis or alternative, oral exam; for doctorate, comprehensive exam, thesis/dissertation, oral defense. *Entrance requirements:* For master's and doctorate, GRE General Test, GRE Subject Test (physics), BA or BS in science. Additional exam requirements/recommendations for international students: Required—TOEFL. Electronic applications accepted. *Faculty research:* Stellar and galaxy dynamics, stellar chemical abundances, galaxy evolution, observational cosmology.

Iowa State University of Science and Technology, Department of Physics and Astronomy, Ames, IA 50011. Offers applied physics (MS, PhD); astrophysics (MS, PhD); condensed matter physics (MS, PhD); high energy physics (MS, PhD); nuclear physics (MS, PhD); physics (MS, PhD). *Degree requirements:* For master's, thesis (for some programs); for doctorate, thesis/dissertation. *Entrance requirements:* For master's and doctorate, GRE General Test, GRE Subject Test (physics). Additional exam requirements/recommendations for international students: Required—TOEFL (minimum score 550 paper-based; 79 iBT), IELTS (minimum score 6.5). Electronic applications accepted. *Faculty research:* Condensed-matter physics, including superconductivity and new materials; high-energy and nuclear physics; astronomy and astrophysics; atmospheric and environmental physics.

Iowa State University of Science and Technology, Program in Astrophysics, Ames, IA 50011. Offers MS, PhD. *Entrance requirements:* For master's and doctorate, GRE. Additional exam requirements/recommendations for international students: Required—TOEFL (minimum score 550 paper-based; 79 iBT), IELTS (minimum score 6.5).

Louisiana State University and Agricultural & Mechanical College, Graduate School, College of Science, Department of Physics and Astronomy, Baton Rouge, LA 70803. Offers astronomy (PhD); astrophysics (PhD); medical physics (MS); physics (MS, PhD).

McMaster University, School of Graduate Studies, Faculty of Science, Department of Physics and Astronomy, Hamilton, ON L8S 4M2, Canada. Offers astrophysics (PhD); physics (PhD). *Program availability:* Part-time. *Degree requirements:* For doctorate, comprehensive exam, thesis/dissertation. *Entrance requirements:* For doctorate, minimum B+ average. Additional exam requirements/recommendations for international students: Required—TOEFL (minimum score 550 paper-based). *Faculty research:* Condensed matter, astrophysics, nuclear, medical, nonlinear dynamics.

Michigan State University, The Graduate School, College of Natural Science, Department of Physics and Astronomy, East Lansing, MI 48824. Offers astrophysics and astronomy (MS, PhD); physics (MS, PhD). *Entrance requirements:* Additional exam requirements/recommendations for international students: Required—TOEFL (minimum score 550 paper-based), Michigan State University ELT (minimum score 85), Michigan English Language Assessment Battery (minimum score 83). Electronic applications accepted. *Faculty research:* Nuclear and accelerator physics, high energy physics, condensed matter physics, biophysics, astrophysics and astronomy.

New Mexico Institute of Mining and Technology, Center for Graduate Studies, Department of Physics, Socorro, NM 87801. Offers astrophysics (PhD); atmospheric physics (PhD); instrumentation (MS); mathematical physics (PhD); physics (MS). *Degree requirements:* For master's, thesis optional; for doctorate, thesis/dissertation. *Entrance requirements:* For master's, GRE General Test; for doctorate, GRE General Test, GRE Subject Test. Additional exam requirements/recommendations for international students: Required—TOEFL (minimum score 540 paper-based). *Expenses:* Tuition, state resident: full-time $5811; part-time $322.81 per credit. Tuition, nonresident: full-time $19,220; part-time $1067.79 per credit. *Required fees:* $1030. Tuition and fees vary according to course load. *Faculty research:* Cloud physics, stellar and extragalactic processes.

New Mexico State University, College of Arts and Sciences, Department of Physics, Las Cruces, NM 88003-8001. Offers space physics (MS). *Program availability:* Part-time. *Faculty:* 13 full-time (1 woman), 1 part-time/adjunct (0 women). *Students:* 35 full-time (8 women), 4 part-time (1 woman); includes 3 minority (all Hispanic/Latino), 28 international. Average age 30. 31 applicants, 26% accepted, 8 enrolled. In 2015, 3 master's, 5 doctorates awarded. Terminal master's awarded for partial completion of doctoral program. *Degree requirements:* For master's, comprehensive exam, thesis optional, written qualifying exam; for doctorate, comprehensive exam, thesis/dissertation. *Entrance requirements:* For master's and doctorate, GRE General Test, GRE Subject Test. Additional exam requirements/recommendations for international students: Required—TOEFL (minimum score 550 paper-based; 79 iBT), IELTS (minimum score 6.5). *Application deadline:* For fall admission, 2/15 priority date for domestic and international students; for spring admission, 11/1 priority date for domestic students, 9/1 priority date for international students. Applications are processed on a rolling basis. Application fee: $40 ($50 for international students). Electronic applications accepted. *Expenses:* $274.50 per credit hour for in-state students, and all students enrolled in six or fewer credits; $839.30 per credit hour for out-of-state and international students enrolled in at least seven hours. *Financial support:* In 2015–16, 35 students received support, including 14 research assistantships (averaging $21,107 per year), 19 teaching assistantships (averaging $18,836 per year); career-related internships or fieldwork, Federal Work-Study, scholarships/grants, traineeships, health care benefits, and unspecified assistantships also available. Support available to part-time students. Financial award application deadline: 3/1; financial award applicants required to submit FAFSA. *Faculty research:* Nuclear and particle physics, materials science, geophysics, applied physics. *Total annual research expenditures:* $2.4 million. *Unit head:* Dr. Stefan Zollner, Department Head, 575-646-7627, Fax: 575-646-1934, E-mail: zollner@nmsu.edu. *Application contact:* Dr. Vassilios Papavassiliou, Graduate Program Head, 575-646-3831, Fax: 575-646-1934, E-mail: graduate-advisor@physics.nmsu.edu.
Website: http://physics.nmsu.edu

Penn State University Park, Graduate School, Eberly College of Science, Department of Astronomy and Astrophysics, University Park, PA 16802. Offers astronomy and astrophysics (MS, PhD). *Unit head:* Dr. Douglas R. Cavener, Dean, 814-865-9591, Fax: 814-865-3634. *Application contact:* Lori Stania, Director, Graduate Student Services, 814-865-1795, Fax: 814-863-4627, E-mail: l-gswww@lists.psu.edu.
Website: http://astro.psu.edu/

Princeton University, Graduate School, Department of Astrophysical Sciences, Princeton, NJ 08544-1019. Offers astronomy (PhD); plasma physics (PhD). *Degree requirements:* For doctorate, thesis/dissertation. *Entrance requirements:* For doctorate, GRE General Test, GRE Subject Test (physics). Additional exam requirements/recommendations for international students: Required—TOEFL (minimum score 600 paper-based). Electronic applications accepted. *Faculty research:* Theoretical astrophysics, cosmology, galaxy formation, galactic dynamics, interstellar and intergalactic matter.

Rochester Institute of Technology, Graduate Enrollment Services, College of Science, School of Physics and Astronomy, MS Program in Astrophysical Science and Technology, Rochester, NY 14623-5603. Offers MS. *Program availability:* Part-time. *Students:* 6 full-time (0 women), 3 international. Average age 25. 18 applicants, 39% accepted, 2 enrolled. *Degree requirements:* For master's, thesis. *Entrance requirements:* For master's, GRE, minimum GPA of 3.0 (recommended). Additional exam requirements/recommendations for international students: Required—PTE (minimum score 58), TOEFL (minimum score 550 paper-based, 79 iBT) or IELTS (minimum score 6.5). *Application deadline:* For fall admission, 2/15 priority date for domestic and international students; for spring admission, 12/15 priority date for domestic and international students. Applications are processed on a rolling basis. Application fee: $60. Electronic applications accepted. *Expenses: Tuition, area resident:* Full-time $41,084; part-time $1742 per credit hour. *Required fees:* $274. Tuition and fees vary according to course load and program. *Financial support:* In 2015–16, 3

students received support. Research assistantships with partial tuition reimbursements available, teaching assistantships with partial tuition reimbursements available, career-related internships or fieldwork, scholarships/grants, and unspecified assistantships available. Financial award applicants required to submit FAFSA. *Faculty research:* Galaxy formation and evolution, energetic phenomena associated with supermassive black holes and theoretical studies of gravitational interactions between stars and black holes in galactic nuclei. *Unit head:* Dr. Andrew Robinson, Graduate Program Director, 585-475-2726, E-mail: axrsps@rit.edu. *Application contact:* Diane Ellison, Associate Vice President, Graduate Enrollment Services, 585-475-2229, Fax: 585-475-7164, E-mail: gradinfo@rit.edu.
Website: https://www.rit.edu/cos/physics/

Rochester Institute of Technology, Graduate Enrollment Services, College of Science, School of Physics and Astronomy, PhD Program in Astrophysical Science and Technology, Rochester, NY 14623-5603. Offers PhD. *Students:* 18 full-time (7 women), 2 part-time (0 women); includes 4 minority (1 Black or African American, non-Hispanic/Latino; 3 Hispanic/Latino), 6 international. Average age 28. 43 applicants, 21% accepted, 3 enrolled. *Degree requirements:* For doctorate, comprehensive exam, thesis/dissertation. *Entrance requirements:* For doctorate, GRE, minimum GPA of 3.0 (recommended). Additional exam requirements/recommendations for international students: Required—PTE (minimum score 58), TOEFL (minimum score 550 paper-based, 79 iBT) or IELTS (minimum score 6.5). *Application deadline:* For fall admission, 1/15 priority date for domestic and international students. Applications are processed on a rolling basis. Application fee: $60. Electronic applications accepted. *Expenses: Tuition, area resident:* Full-time $41,084; part-time $1742 per credit hour. *Required fees:* $274. Tuition and fees vary according to course load and program. *Financial support:* In 2015–16, 17 students received support. Research assistantships with full tuition reimbursements available, teaching assistantships with full tuition reimbursements available, career-related internships or fieldwork, scholarships/grants, health care benefits, and unspecified assistantships available. Financial award applicants required to submit FAFSA. *Faculty research:* Galaxy formation and evolution, energetic phenomena associated with supermassive black holes and theoretical studies of gravitational interactions between stars and black holes in galactic nuclei. *Unit head:* Dr. Andrew Robinson, Graduate Program Director, 585-475-2726, E-mail: axrsps@rit.edu. *Application contact:* Diane Ellison, Associate Vice President, Graduate Enrollment Services, 585-475-2229, Fax: 585-475-7164, E-mail: gradinfo@rit.edu.
Website: https://www.rit.edu/cos/physics/

Texas Christian University, College of Science and Engineering, Department of Physics and Astronomy, Fort Worth, TX 76129. Offers physics (MA, MS, PhD), including astrophysics (PhD), biophysics (PhD); PhD/MBA. *Program availability:* Part-time. *Faculty:* 8 full-time (2 women). *Students:* 15 full-time (5 women); includes 2 minority (both Hispanic/Latino), 9 international. Average age 32. 20 applicants, 30% accepted, 4 enrolled. In 2015, 3 master's, 2 doctorates awarded. Terminal master's awarded for partial completion of doctoral program. *Degree requirements:* For master's, one foreign language, comprehensive exam, thesis or alternative; for doctorate, comprehensive exam, thesis/dissertation. *Entrance requirements:* For master's and doctorate, GRE. Additional exam requirements/recommendations for international students: Required—TOEFL (minimum score 80 iBT). *Application deadline:* For fall admission, 2/1 for domestic and international students; for spring admission, 9/1 for domestic and international students. Applications are processed on a rolling basis. Application fee: $60. Electronic applications accepted. *Expenses:* Contact institution. *Financial support:* In 2015–16, 14 students received support, including 1 research assistantship with full tuition reimbursement available (averaging $23,000 per year), 13 teaching assistantships with full tuition reimbursements available (averaging $20,500 per year); scholarships/grants and unspecified assistantships also available. Financial award application deadline: 2/1. *Faculty research:* Nanomaterials, computer simulations of biophysical processes, nonlinear dynamics, spectra of local stellar populations, spectroscopy and fluorescence of biomolecules. *Unit head:* Dr. Yuri M. Strzhemechny, Associate Professor/Chair, 817-257-5793, Fax: 817-257-7742, E-mail: y.strzhemechny@tcu.edu. *Application contact:* Dr. Peter M. Frinchaboy, III, Associate Professor, 817-257-6387, Fax: 817-257-7742, E-mail: p.frinchaboy@tcu.edu.
Website: http://physics.tcu.edu/

Tufts University, Graduate School of Arts and Sciences, Department of Physics and Astronomy, Medford, MA 02155. Offers astrophysics (MS, PhD); chemical physics (PhD); physics (MS, PhD); physics education (PhD). Terminal master's awarded for partial completion of doctoral program. *Degree requirements:* For master's, thesis optional; for doctorate, thesis/dissertation. *Entrance requirements:* For master's and doctorate, GRE General Test. Additional exam requirements/recommendations for international students: Required—TOEFL (minimum score 550 paper-based; 80 iBT), IELTS (minimum score 6.5). Electronic applications accepted. *Expenses: Tuition, area resident:* Full-time $48,412; part-time $1210 per credit hour. *Required fees:* $806. Full-time tuition and fees vary according to degree level, program and student level. Part-time tuition and fees vary according to course load.

University of Alaska Fairbanks, College of Natural Sciences and Mathematics, Department of Physics, Fairbanks, AK 99775-5920. Offers computational physics (MS); physics (MS, PhD); space physics (MS). *Program availability:* Part-time. *Faculty:* 8 full-time (2 women). *Students:* 22 full-time (3 women), 2 part-time (0 women); includes 3 minority (1 American Indian or Alaska Native, non-Hispanic/Latino; 2 Asian, non-Hispanic/Latino), 4 international. Average age 29. 53 applicants, 17% accepted, 9 enrolled. In 2015, 1 master's, 3 doctorates awarded. *Degree requirements:* For master's, comprehensive exam, oral defense of project or thesis; for doctorate, comprehensive exam, thesis/dissertation, oral defense of dissertation. *Entrance requirements:* For master's, GRE General Test, bachelor's degree from accredited institution with minimum cumulative undergraduate and major GPA of 3.0; for doctorate, GRE General Test, minimum cumulative GPA of 3.0. Additional exam requirements/recommendations for international students: Required—TOEFL (minimum score 550 paper-based; 80 iBT). *Application deadline:* For fall admission, 6/1 for domestic students, 3/1 for international students; for spring admission, 10/15 for domestic students, 9/1 for international students. Applications are processed on a rolling basis. Application fee: $60. Electronic applications accepted. *Expenses:* Tuition, state resident: full-time $7614; part-time $423 per credit. Tuition, nonresident: full-time $15,552; part-time $864 per credit. *Required fees:* $38 per credit. $187 per semester. Tuition and fees vary according to course level, course load, program and reciprocity agreements. *Financial support:* In 2015–16, 10 research assistantships with full tuition reimbursements (averaging $16,599 per year), 11 teaching assistantships with full tuition reimbursements (averaging $16,577 per year) were awarded; fellowships with full tuition reimbursements, Federal Work-Study, scholarships/grants, health care benefits, and unspecified assistantships also available. Support available to part-time students. Financial award application deadline: 2/15; financial award applicants required to submit FAFSA. *Faculty research:* Atmospheric and ionospheric radar studies, space plasma theory, magnetospheric dynamics, space weather and auroral studies, turbulence and complex systems. *Unit head:* Renate Wackerbauer, Department Chair, 907-474-7339, Fax: 907-474-6130, E-mail: uaf-

physics@alaska.edu. *Application contact:* Mary Kreta, Director of Admissions, 907-474-7500, Fax: 907-474-7097, E-mail: admissions@uaf.edu.
Website: http://www.uaf.edu/physics/

University of Alberta, Faculty of Graduate Studies and Research, Department of Physics, Edmonton, AB T6G 2E1, Canada. Offers astrophysics (M Sc, PhD); condensed matter (M Sc, PhD); geophysics (M Sc, PhD); medical physics (M Sc, PhD); subatomic physics (M Sc, PhD). *Degree requirements:* For master's, thesis; for doctorate, thesis/dissertation. *Entrance requirements:* For master's and doctorate, minimum GPA of 7.0 on a 9.0 scale. Additional exam requirements/recommendations for international students: Required—TOEFL. *Faculty research:* Cosmology, astroparticle physics, high-intermediate energy, magnetism, superconductivity.

University of California, Berkeley, Graduate Division, College of Letters and Science, Department of Astrophysics, Berkeley, CA 94720-1500. Offers PhD. *Degree requirements:* For doctorate, thesis/dissertation, qualifying exam. *Entrance requirements:* For doctorate, GRE General Test, GRE Subject Test, minimum GPA of 3.0, 3 letters of recommendation. *Faculty research:* Theory, cosmology, radio astronomy, extra solar planets, infrared instrumentation.

University of California, Los Angeles, Graduate Division, College of Letters and Science, Department of Earth and Space Sciences, Program in Geophysics and Space Physics, Los Angeles, CA 90095. Offers MS, PhD. Terminal master's awarded for partial completion of doctoral program. *Degree requirements:* For master's, comprehensive exam or thesis; for doctorate, thesis/dissertation, oral and written qualifying exams. *Entrance requirements:* For master's and doctorate, GRE General Test, bachelor's degree; minimum undergraduate GPA of 3.0 (or its equivalent if letter grade system not used). Additional exam requirements/recommendations for international students: Required—TOEFL. Electronic applications accepted.

University of California, Santa Cruz, Division of Graduate Studies, Division of Physical and Biological Sciences, Department of Astronomy and Astrophysics, Santa Cruz, CA 95064. Offers PhD. *Degree requirements:* For doctorate, one foreign language, thesis/dissertation, qualifying exam. *Entrance requirements:* For doctorate, GRE General Test, GRE Subject Test. Additional exam requirements/recommendations for international students: Required—TOEFL (minimum score 550 paper-based; 83 iBT); Recommended—IELTS (minimum score 8). Electronic applications accepted. *Faculty research:* Solar system and the Milky Way to the most distant galaxies in the Universe, fundamental questions of cosmology.

University of Chicago, Division of the Physical Sciences, Department of Astronomy and Astrophysics, Chicago, IL 60637. Offers PhD. Terminal master's awarded for partial completion of doctoral program. *Degree requirements:* For doctorate, comprehensive exam, thesis/dissertation, dissertation for publication. *Entrance requirements:* For doctorate, GRE General Test, GRE Subject Test. Additional exam requirements/recommendations for international students: Required—TOEFL (minimum score 600 paper-based; 90 iBT), IELTS (minimum score 7). Electronic applications accepted. *Faculty research:* Cosmology, exoplanets, galaxy formation, interstellar and intergalactic matter, astroparticle physics, high-performance computation in astrophysics.

University of Colorado Boulder, Graduate School, College of Arts and Sciences, Department of Astrophysical and Planetary Sciences, Boulder, CO 80309. Offers astrophysics (MS, PhD); planetary science (MS, PhD). *Faculty:* 24 full-time (2 women). *Students:* 53 full-time (14 women); includes 2 minority (1 Black or African American, non-Hispanic/Latino; 1 Asian, non-Hispanic/Latino), 3 international. Average age 26. 159 applicants, 16% accepted, 7 enrolled. In 2015, 9 master's, 6 doctorates awarded. Terminal master's awarded for partial completion of doctoral program. *Degree requirements:* For master's, comprehensive exam, thesis or alternative; for doctorate, one foreign language, thesis/dissertation. *Entrance requirements:* For master's, GRE General Test, GRE Subject Test, minimum undergraduate GPA of 3.0; for doctorate, GRE General Test, GRE Subject Test. *Application deadline:* For fall admission, 1/15 for domestic students, 12/1 for international students. Applications are processed on a rolling basis. Application fee: $50 ($70 for international students). Electronic applications accepted. Application fee is waived when completed online. *Financial support:* In 2015–16, 109 students received support, including 25 fellowships (averaging $9,613 per year), 27 research assistantships with tuition reimbursements available (averaging $39,044 per year), 13 teaching assistantships with tuition reimbursements available (averaging $27,883 per year); institutionally sponsored loans, scholarships/grants, health care benefits, and unspecified assistantships also available. Financial award application deadline: 1/15; financial award applicants required to submit FAFSA. *Faculty research:* Astrophysics, astronomy, galaxies: stellar systems, infrared/optical astronomy, spectroscopy. *Total annual research expenditures:* $25 million. *Application contact:* E-mail: apsgradsec@colorado.edu.
Website: http://aps.colorado.edu/

The University of Manchester, School of Physics and Astronomy, Manchester, United Kingdom. Offers astronomy and astrophysics (M Sc, PhD); biological physics (M Sc, PhD); condensed matter physics (M Sc, PhD); nonlinear and liquid crystals physics (M Sc, PhD); nuclear physics (M Sc, PhD); particle physics (M Sc, PhD); photon physics (M Sc, PhD); physics (M Sc, PhD); theoretical physics (M Sc, PhD).

University of Michigan, Rackham Graduate School, College of Literature, Science, and the Arts, Department of Astronomy, Ann Arbor, MI 48109-1042. Offers astronomy and astrophysics (PhD). *Faculty:* 25 full-time (7 women). *Students:* 26 full-time (12 women); includes 6 minority (4 Asian, non-Hispanic/Latino; 2 Hispanic/Latino). 134 applicants, 22% accepted, 6 enrolled. In 2015, 5 doctorates awarded. Terminal master's awarded for partial completion of doctoral program. *Degree requirements:* For doctorate, thesis/dissertation, oral defense of dissertation. *Entrance requirements:* For doctorate, GRE General Test, GRE Subject Test (physics). Additional exam requirements/recommendations for international students: Required—TOEFL. *Application deadline:* For fall admission, 1/1 for domestic and international students. Application fee: $75 ($90 for international students). Electronic applications accepted. *Financial support:* In 2015–16, 22 students received support. Fellowships, research assistantships, teaching assistantships, institutionally sponsored loans, scholarships/grants, health care benefits, and unspecified assistantships available. Financial award applicants required to submit FAFSA. *Faculty research:* Extragalactic and galactic astronomy, cosmology, star and planet formation, high energy astrophysics. *Unit head:* Dr. Edwin Bergin, Professor and Chair, 734-764-3440, Fax: 734-763-6317, E-mail: astrochair@umich.edu. *Application contact:* Brian Cox, Graduate Program Coordinator, 734-764-3440, Fax: 734-763-6317, E-mail: astro-phd@umich.edu.
Website: http://www.lsa.umich.edu/astro

University of Minnesota, Twin Cities Campus, College of Science and Engineering, School of Physics and Astronomy, Program in Astrophysics, Minneapolis, MN 55455-0213. Offers MS, PhD. Terminal master's awarded for partial completion of doctoral program. *Degree requirements:* For master's, thesis optional; for doctorate, thesis/dissertation. *Entrance requirements:* For master's and doctorate, GRE General Test, GRE Subject Test. Additional exam requirements/recommendations for international

Peterson's Graduate Programs in the Physical Sciences, Mathematics, Agricultural Sciences, the Environment & Natural Resources 2017

www.petersons.com **41**

students: Required—TOEFL. *Faculty research:* Evolution of stars and galaxies; the interstellar medium; cosmology; observational, optical, infrared, and radio astronomy; computational astrophysics.

University of Missouri–St. Louis, College of Arts and Sciences, Department of Physics and Astronomy, St. Louis, MO 63121. Offers applied physics (MS); astrophysics (MS); physics (PhD). *Program availability:* Part-time, evening/weekend. *Faculty:* 10 full-time (2 women), 3 part-time/adjunct (0 women). *Students:* 16 full-time (4 women), 8 part-time (2 women); includes 3 minority (2 Black or African American, non-Hispanic/Latino; 1 Asian, non-Hispanic/Latino), 6 international. Average age 32. 28 applicants, 39% accepted, 6 enrolled. Terminal master's awarded for partial completion of doctoral program. *Degree requirements:* For master's, thesis optional; for doctorate, thesis/dissertation. *Entrance requirements:* For master's, GRE General Test; for doctorate, GRE General Test, 2 letters of recommendation. Additional exam requirements/recommendations for international students: Required—TOEFL (minimum score 550 paper-based; 79 iBT), IELTS (minimum score 6.5). *Application deadline:* For fall admission, 7/1 for domestic and international students; for spring admission, 12/1 for domestic students, 11/1 for international students. Application fee: $50 ($40 for international students). Electronic applications accepted. *Financial support:* Research assistantships with tuition reimbursements, teaching assistantships with tuition reimbursements, and career-related internships or fieldwork available. Financial award applicants required to submit FAFSA. *Faculty research:* Biophysics, atomic physics, nonlinear dynamics, materials science. *Unit head:* Dr. Bruce Wilking, Graduate Program Advisor, 314-516-5023, Fax: 314-516-6152, E-mail: bwilking@umsl.edu. *Application contact:* 314-516-5458, Fax: 314-516-6996, E-mail: gradadm@umsl.edu. Website: http://www.umsl.edu/~physics/

The University of North Carolina at Chapel Hill, Graduate School, College of Arts and Sciences, Department of Physics and Astronomy, Chapel Hill, NC 27599. Offers physics (MS, PhD). Terminal master's awarded for partial completion of doctoral program. *Degree requirements:* For master's, comprehensive exam; for doctorate, comprehensive exam, thesis/dissertation. *Entrance requirements:* For master's and doctorate, GRE General Test, minimum GPA of 3.0. Electronic applications accepted. *Faculty research:* Observational astronomy, fullerenes, polarized beams, nanotubes, nucleosynthesis in stars and supernovae, superstring theory, ballistic transport in semiconductors, gravitation.

The University of Toledo, College of Graduate Studies, College of Natural Sciences and Mathematics, Department of Physics and Astronomy, Toledo, OH 43606-3390.

Offers photovoltaics (PSM); physics (MS, PhD), including astrophysics (PhD), materials science, medical physics (PhD); MS/PhD. *Degree requirements:* For master's, thesis; for doctorate, thesis/dissertation, departmental qualifying exam. *Entrance requirements:* For master's and doctorate, GRE General Test, GRE Subject Test, minimum cumulative point-hour ratio of 2.7 for all previous academic work, three letters of recommendation, statement of purpose, transcripts from all prior institutions attended. Additional exam requirements/recommendations for international students: Required—TOEFL (minimum score 550 paper-based; 80 iBT). Electronic applications accepted. *Faculty research:* Atomic physics, solid-state physics, materials science, astrophysics.

University of Toronto, School of Graduate Studies, Faculty of Arts and Science, Department of Astronomy and Astrophysics, Toronto, ON M5S 1A1, Canada. Offers M Sc, PhD. *Program availability:* Part-time. *Degree requirements:* For doctorate, thesis/dissertation, qualifying exam, thesis defense. *Entrance requirements:* For master's, minimum B average, bachelor's degree in astronomy or equivalent, 3 letters of reference; for doctorate, GRE General Test, minimum B+ average, master's degree in astronomy or equivalent, demonstrated research competence, 3 letters of reference. Additional exam requirements/recommendations for international students: Required—TOEFL (minimum score 580 paper-based; 93 iBT), TWE (minimum score 4). Electronic applications accepted.

University of Victoria, Faculty of Graduate Studies, Faculty of Science, Department of Physics and Astronomy, Victoria, BC V8W 2Y2, Canada. Offers astronomy and astrophysics (M Sc, PhD); condensed matter physics (M Sc, PhD); experimental particle physics (M Sc, PhD); medical physics (M Sc, PhD); ocean physics (M Sc, PhD); theoretical physics (M Sc, PhD). *Degree requirements:* For master's, thesis; for doctorate, comprehensive exam, thesis/dissertation, candidacy exam. *Entrance requirements:* For master's and doctorate, GRE. Additional exam requirements/recommendations for international students: Required—TOEFL (minimum score 575 paper-based), IELTS (minimum score 7). Electronic applications accepted. *Faculty research:* Old stellar populations; observational cosmology and large scale structure; cp violation; atlas.

Yale University, Graduate School of Arts and Sciences, Department of Astronomy, New Haven, CT 06520. Offers astronomy (PhD); solar and terrestrial physics (PhD). *Degree requirements:* For doctorate, thesis/dissertation. *Entrance requirements:* For doctorate, GRE General Test, GRE Subject Test (physics).

42 www.petersons.com

Peterson's Graduate Programs in the Physical Sciences, Mathematics, Agricultural Sciences, the Environment & Natural Resources 2017

Section 2
Chemistry

This section contains a directory of institutions offering graduate work in chemistry. Additional information about programs listed in the directory may be obtained by writing directly to the dean of a graduate school or chair of a department at the address given in the directory.

For programs offering related work, see also in this book *Geosciences* and *Physics.* In the other guides in this series:

Graduate Programs in the Biological/Biomedical Sciences & Health-Related Medical Professions

See *Biological and Biomedical Sciences, Biochemistry, Biophysics, Nutrition, Pharmacology and Toxicology,* and *Pharmacy and Pharmaceutical Sciences*

Graduate Programs in Engineering & Applied Sciences

See *Engineering and Applied Sciences; Agricultural Engineering; Chemical Engineering; Geological, Mineral/Mining, and Petroleum Engineering; Materials Sciences and Engineering;* and *Pharmaceutical Engineering*

CONTENTS

Program Directories

Analytical Chemistry

Auburn University, Graduate School, College of Sciences and Mathematics, Department of Chemistry and Biochemistry, Auburn University, AL 36849. Offers analytical chemistry (MS, PhD); biochemistry (MS, PhD); inorganic chemistry (MS, PhD); organic chemistry (MS, PhD); physical chemistry (MS, PhD). *Program availability:* Part-time. *Faculty:* 27 full-time (4 women), 2 part-time/adjunct (0 women). *Students:* 45 full-time (17 women), 26 part-time (15 women); includes 9 minority (7 Black or African American, non-Hispanic/Latino; 1 American Indian or Alaska Native, non-Hispanic/Latino; 1 Asian, non-Hispanic/Latino), 38 international. Average age 27. 33 applicants, 52% accepted, 16 enrolled. In 2015, 1 master's, 6 doctorates awarded. *Degree requirements:* For master's, thesis (for some programs); for doctorate, thesis/dissertation, oral and written exams. *Entrance requirements:* For master's and doctorate, GRE General Test. *Application deadline:* Applications are processed on a rolling basis. Application fee: $50 ($60 for international students). Electronic applications accepted. *Expenses:* Tuition, state resident: full-time $8802; part-time $489 per credit hour. Tuition, nonresident: full-time $26,406; part-time $1467 per credit hour. *Required fees:* $808 per semester. Tuition and fees vary according to degree level and program. *Financial support:* Fellowships, research assistantships, and teaching assistantships available. Financial award application deadline: 3/15; financial award applicants required to submit FAFSA. *Unit head:* Dr. Curtis Shannon, Chair, 334-844-4043, Fax: 334-844-4043. *Application contact:* Dr. George Flowers, Dean of the Graduate School, 334-844-2125.
Website: http://www.auburn.edu/cosam/departments/chemistry/

Binghamton University, State University of New York, Graduate School, School of Arts and Sciences, Department of Chemistry, Vestal, NY 13850. Offers analytical chemistry (PhD); chemistry (MA, MS); environmental chemistry (PhD); inorganic chemistry (PhD); organic chemistry (PhD); physical chemistry (PhD). *Program availability:* Part-time. *Faculty:* 21 full-time (4 women). *Students:* 60 full-time (24 women), 1 part-time (0 women); includes 4 minority (2 Black or African American, non-Hispanic/Latino; 1 Asian, non-Hispanic/Latino; 1 Hispanic/Latino), 40 international. Average age 27. 53 applicants, 81% accepted, 16 enrolled. In 2015, 3 master's, 7 doctorates awarded. Terminal master's awarded for partial completion of doctoral program. *Degree requirements:* For master's, thesis; for doctorate, comprehensive exam, thesis/dissertation. *Entrance requirements:* For master's and doctorate, GRE General Test. Additional exam requirements/recommendations for international students: Required—TOEFL (minimum score 90 iBT). *Application deadline:* Applications are processed on a rolling basis. Application fee: $75. Electronic applications accepted. *Financial support:* In 2015–16, 53 students received support, including 8 research assistantships with full tuition reimbursements available (averaging $18,000 per year), 34 teaching assistantships with full tuition reimbursements available (averaging $18,000 per year); career-related internships or fieldwork, Federal Work-Study, institutionally sponsored loans, scholarships/grants, health care benefits, tuition waivers (full and partial), and unspecified assistantships also available. Financial award applicants required to submit FAFSA. *Unit head:* Dr. Wayne E. Jones, Chairperson, 607-777-2421, E-mail: wjones@binghamton.edu. *Application contact:* Kishan Zuber, Recruiting and Admissions Coordinator, 607-777-2151, Fax: 607-777-2501,
E-mail: kzuber@binghamton.edu.

Brigham Young University, Graduate Studies, College of Physical and Mathematical Sciences, Department of Chemistry and Biochemistry, Provo, UT 84602. Offers biochemistry (MS, PhD); chemistry (MS, PhD). *Faculty:* 30 full-time (1 woman). *Students:* 92 full-time (32 women); includes 5 minority (2 Asian, non-Hispanic/Latino; 2 Hispanic/Latino; 1 Native Hawaiian or other Pacific Islander, non-Hispanic/Latino), 47 international. Average age 28. 52 applicants, 50% accepted, 17 enrolled. In 2015, 1 master's, 14 doctorates awarded. *Degree requirements:* For master's, thesis; for doctorate, comprehensive exam, thesis/dissertation, qualifying exam. *Entrance requirements:* For master's and doctorate, GRE General Test, minimum GPA of 3.0. Additional exam requirements/recommendations for international students: Required—TOEFL (minimum score 580 paper-based; 85 iBT), IELTS (minimum score 7); Recommended—TWE. *Application deadline:* For fall admission, 2/1 priority date for domestic and international students. Applications are processed on a rolling basis. Application fee: $50. Electronic applications accepted. *Financial support:* In 2015–16, 90 students received support, including 13 fellowships with full tuition reimbursements available (averaging $21,250 per year), 39 research assistantships with full tuition reimbursements available (averaging $21,250 per year), 38 teaching assistantships with full tuition reimbursements available (averaging $21,250 per year); institutionally sponsored loans, scholarships/grants, health care benefits, unspecified assistantships, and supplementary awards also available. Financial award application deadline: 2/1. *Faculty research:* Separation science, molecular recognition, organic synthesis and biomedical application, biochemistry and molecular biology, molecular spectroscopy. *Total annual research expenditures:* $2.2 million. *Unit head:* Dr. Gregory F. Burton, Chair, 801-422-4917, Fax: 801-422-0153, E-mail: gburton@byu.edu. *Application contact:* Dr. Paul B. Farnsworth, Graduate Coordinator, 801-422-6502, Fax: 801-422-0153, E-mail: pbfarnsw@byu.edu.
Website: http://www.chem.byu.edu/

California State University, Los Angeles, Graduate Studies, College of Natural and Social Sciences, Department of Chemistry and Biochemistry, Los Angeles, CA 90032-8530. Offers analytical chemistry (MS); biochemistry (MS); chemistry (MS); inorganic chemistry (MS); organic chemistry (MS); physical chemistry (MS). *Program availability:* Part-time, evening/weekend. *Degree requirements:* For master's, one foreign language, comprehensive exam or thesis. *Entrance requirements:* Additional exam requirements/recommendations for international students: Required—TOEFL. *Faculty research:* Intercalation of heavy metal, carborane chemistry, conductive polymers and fabrics, titanium reagents, computer modeling and synthesis.

Cleveland State University, College of Graduate Studies, College of Sciences and Health Professions, Department of Chemistry, Cleveland, OH 44115. Offers analytical chemistry (MS); clinical/bioanalytical chemistry (PhD), including cellular and molecular medicine, clinical/bioanalytical chemistry; inorganic chemistry (MS); pharmaceutical/organic chemistry (MS); physical chemistry (MS). *Program availability:* Part-time, evening/weekend. *Faculty:* 17 full-time (3 women). *Students:* 63 full-time (30 women), 25 part-time (10 women); includes 4 minority (1 Black or African American, non-Hispanic/Latino; 1 Asian, non-Hispanic/Latino; 2 Hispanic/Latino), 48 international. Average age 30. 22 applicants, 64% accepted, 12 enrolled. In 2015, 16 master's, 8 doctorates awarded. *Degree requirements:* For master's, thesis optional; for doctorate, comprehensive exam, thesis/dissertation. *Entrance requirements:* For master's and doctorate, GRE General Test. Additional exam requirements/recommendations for international students: Required—TOEFL (minimum score 550 paper-based; 78 iBT). *Application deadline:* For fall admission, 1/15 priority date for domestic and international students. Applications are processed on a rolling basis. Application fee: $30. Electronic applications accepted. *Expenses:* Tuition, state resident: full-time $9565. Tuition, nonresident: full-time $17,980. Tuition and fees vary according to program. *Financial support:* In 2015–16, 44 students received support, including 10 fellowships with full tuition reimbursements available (averaging $22,500 per year), 6 research assistantships with full tuition reimbursements available (averaging $22,500 per year), 34 teaching assistantships with full tuition reimbursements available (averaging $21,000 per year); scholarships/grants and unspecified assistantships also available. Financial award application deadline: 1/15. *Faculty research:* Bioanalytical techniques and molecular diagnostics, glycoproteomics and antithrombotic agents, drug discovery and innovation, analytical pharmacology, inflammatory disease research. *Total annual research expenditures:* $3 million. *Unit head:* Dr. David W. Ball, Chair, 216-687-2467, Fax: 216-687-9298, E-mail: d.ball@csuohio.edu. *Application contact:* Richelle P. Emery, Administrative Coordinator, 216-687-2457, Fax: 216-687-9298,
E-mail: r.emery@csuohio.edu.
Website: http://www.csuohio.edu/sciences/chemistry

Cornell University, Graduate School, Graduate Fields of Arts and Sciences, Field of Chemistry and Chemical Biology, Ithaca, NY 14853-0001. Offers analytical chemistry (PhD); bio-organic chemistry (PhD); biophysical chemistry (PhD); chemical biology (PhD); chemical physics (PhD); inorganic chemistry (PhD); materials chemistry (PhD); organic chemistry (PhD); organometallic chemistry (PhD); physical chemistry (PhD); polymer chemistry (PhD); theoretical chemistry (PhD). *Degree requirements:* For doctorate, comprehensive exam, thesis/dissertation. *Entrance requirements:* For doctorate, GRE General Test, GRE Subject Test (chemistry), 3 letters of recommendation. Additional exam requirements/recommendations for international students: Required—TOEFL (minimum score 600 paper-based; 77 iBT). Electronic applications accepted. *Faculty research:* Analytical, organic, inorganic, physical, materials, chemical biology.

Eastern New Mexico University, Graduate School, College of Liberal Arts and Sciences, Department of Physical Sciences, Portales, NM 88130. Offers chemistry (MS), including analytical, biochemistry, inorganic, organic, physical. *Program availability:* Part-time. *Degree requirements:* For master's, thesis optional, seminar, oral and written comprehensive exams. *Entrance requirements:* For master's, ACS placement examination, minimum GPA of 3.0; 2 letters of recommendation; personal statement of career goals; bachelor's degree with one year minimum each of general, organic, and analytical chemistry. Additional exam requirements/recommendations for international students: Required—TOEFL (minimum score 550 paper-based; 79 iBT), IELTS (minimum score 6). Electronic applications accepted. *Faculty research:* Synfuel, electrochemistry, protein chemistry.

Florida State University, The Graduate School, College of Arts and Sciences, Department of Chemistry and Biochemistry, Tallahassee, FL 32306-4390. Offers analytical chemistry (MS, PhD); biochemistry (MS, PhD); inorganic chemistry (MS, PhD); materials chemistry (PhD); organic chemistry (MS, PhD); physical chemistry (MS, PhD). *Faculty:* 40 full-time (6 women), 4 part-time/adjunct (2 women). *Students:* 162 full-time (56 women); includes 37 minority (8 Black or African American, non-Hispanic/Latino; 6 Asian, non-Hispanic/Latino; 18 Hispanic/Latino; 1 Native Hawaiian or other Pacific Islander, non-Hispanic/Latino; 4 Two or more races, non-Hispanic/Latino), 54 international. Average age 28. 182 applicants, 47% accepted, 31 enrolled. In 2015, 6 master's, 18 doctorates awarded. Terminal master's awarded for partial completion of doctoral program. *Degree requirements:* For master's, thesis (for some programs); for doctorate, thesis/dissertation. *Entrance requirements:* For master's and doctorate, GRE General Test (minimum scores: 150 verbal, 151 quantitative; 1100 total on the old scale), minimum GPA of 3.1 in undergraduate course work. Additional exam requirements/recommendations for international students: Required—TOEFL (minimum score 90 iBT). *Application deadline:* For fall admission, 12/15 priority date for domestic and international students. Application fee: $30. Electronic applications accepted. *Expenses: Tuition, area resident:* Full-time $7263; part-time $403.50 per credit hour. Tuition, nonresident: full-time $18,087; part-time $1004.85 per credit hour. *Required fees:* $1365; $75.81 per credit hour. $20 per semester. Tuition and fees vary according to campus/location. *Financial support:* In 2015–16, 162 students received support, including 4 fellowships with tuition reimbursements available (averaging $22,000 per year), 51 research assistantships with full tuition reimbursements available (averaging $22,809 per year), 67 teaching assistantships with full tuition reimbursements available (averaging $22,809 per year). Financial award application deadline: 12/15; financial award applicants required to submit FAFSA. *Faculty research:* Bioanalytical chemistry, including separations, microfluidics, petroleomics; materials chemistry, including magnets, polymers, catalysts, nanomaterials; spectroscopy, including NMR and EPR, ultrafast, Raman, and mass spectrometry; organic synthesis, natural products, photochemistry, and supramolecular chemistry; biochemistry, with focus on structural biology, metabolomics, and anticancer drugs. *Total annual research expenditures:* $3.5 million. *Unit head:* Dr. Timothy Logan, Chairman, 850-644-3810, Fax: 850-644-8281, E-mail: gradinfo@chem.fsu.edu. *Application contact:* Dr. Geoffrey Strouse, Associate Chair for Graduate Studies, 850-445-9042, Fax: 850-644-8281,
E-mail: gradinfo@chem.fsu.edu.
Website: http://www.chem.fsu.edu/

Georgetown University, Graduate School of Arts and Sciences, Department of Chemistry, Washington, DC 20057. Offers analytical chemistry (PhD); biochemistry (PhD); computational chemistry (PhD); inorganic chemistry (PhD); materials chemistry (PhD); organic chemistry (PhD); theoretical chemistry (PhD). Terminal master's awarded for partial completion of doctoral program. *Degree requirements:* For doctorate, comprehensive exam, thesis/dissertation. *Entrance requirements:* For doctorate, GRE General Test. Additional exam requirements/recommendations for international students: Required—TOEFL.

The George Washington University, Columbian College of Arts and Sciences, Department of Chemistry, Washington, DC 20052. Offers analytical chemistry (MS, PhD); inorganic chemistry (MS, PhD); materials science (MS, PhD); organic chemistry (MS, PhD); physical chemistry (MS, PhD). *Program availability:* Part-time, evening/weekend. *Faculty:* 17 full-time (6 women), 4 part-time/adjunct (1 woman). *Students:* 25 full-time (13 women), 12 part-time (5 women); includes 2 minority (1 Asian, non-Hispanic/Latino; 1 Hispanic/Latino), 10 international. Average age 28. 60 applicants, 37% accepted, 9 enrolled. In 2015, 2 master's, 6 doctorates awarded. Terminal master's awarded for partial completion of doctoral program. *Degree requirements:* For master's, comprehensive exam, thesis or alternative; for doctorate, thesis/dissertation, general exam. *Entrance requirements:* For master's and doctorate, GRE General Test, interview, minimum GPA of 3.0. Additional exam requirements/recommendations for international students: Required—TOEFL (minimum score 550 paper-based; 80 iBT). *Application deadline:* For fall admission, 1/15 priority date for domestic and international students; for spring admission, 9/1 priority date for domestic and international students. Applications are processed on a rolling basis. Application fee: $75. Electronic applications accepted. *Financial support:* In 2015–16, 27 students received support. Fellowships with tuition reimbursements available, research assistantships, teaching assistantships with tuition reimbursements available, Federal Work-Study, and tuition waivers available. Financial award application deadline: 1/15. *Unit head:* Dr. Michael King, Chair, 202-994-6488. *Application contact:* Information Contact, 202-994-6121, E-mail: gwchem@gwu.edu.

Website: http://chemistry.columbian.gwu.edu/

Georgia State University, College of Arts and Sciences, Department of Chemistry, Atlanta, GA 30302-3083. Offers analytical chemistry (MS, PhD); biochemistry (MS, PhD); bioinformatics (MS, PhD); biophysical chemistry (PhD); computational chemistry (MS, PhD); geochemistry (PhD); organic/medicinal chemistry (MS, PhD); physical chemistry (MS). PhD in geochemistry offered jointly with Department of Geosciences. *Program availability:* Part-time. *Faculty:* 26 full-time (4 women). *Students:* 158 full-time (53 women), 4 part-time (all women); includes 43 minority (22 Black or African American, non-Hispanic/Latino; 1 American Indian or Alaska Native, non-Hispanic/Latino; 9 Asian, non-Hispanic/Latino; 7 Hispanic/Latino; 4 Two or more races, non-Hispanic/Latino), 81 international. Average age 28. 117 applicants, 50% accepted, 42 enrolled. In 2015, 28 master's, 15 doctorates awarded. Terminal master's awarded for partial completion of doctoral program. *Degree requirements:* For master's, one foreign language, comprehensive exam (for some programs), thesis (for some programs); for doctorate, one foreign language, comprehensive exam, thesis/dissertation. *Entrance requirements:* For master's and doctorate, GRE. Additional exam requirements/recommendations for international students: Required—TOEFL (minimum score 550 paper-based; 80 iBT) or IELTS (minimum score 6.5). *Application deadline:* For fall admission, 7/1 priority date for domestic and international students; for winter admission, 11/15 priority date for domestic and international students; for spring admission, 4/15 priority date for domestic and international students. Applications are processed on a rolling basis. Application fee: $50. Electronic applications accepted. *Expenses:* Tuition, state resident: full-time $6876; part-time $382 per credit hour. Tuition, nonresident: full-time $22,374; part-time $1243 per credit hour. *Required fees:* $2128; $2128 per term. $1064 per term. Part-time tuition and fees vary according to course load and program. *Financial support:* Fellowships with full tuition reimbursements, research assistantships with full tuition reimbursements, and teaching assistantships with full tuition reimbursements available. Financial award applicants required to submit FAFSA. *Faculty research:* Analytical chemistry, biological/biochemistry, biophysical/computational chemistry, chemical education, organic/medicinal chemistry. *Unit head:* Dr. Peng George Wang, Department Chair, 404-413-3591, Fax: 404-413-5505, E-mail: pwang11@gsu.edu.

Website: http://chemistry.gsu.edu/

Governors State University, College of Arts and Sciences, Program in Analytical Chemistry, University Park, IL 60484. Offers MS. *Program availability:* Part-time, evening/weekend. *Degree requirements:* For master's, thesis or alternative. *Faculty research:* Electrochemistry, photochemistry, spectrochemistry, biochemistry.

Howard University, Graduate School, Department of Chemistry, Washington, DC 20059-0002. Offers analytical chemistry (MS, PhD); atmospheric (MS, PhD); biochemistry (MS, PhD); environmental (MS, PhD); inorganic chemistry (MS, PhD); organic chemistry (MS, PhD); physical chemistry (MS, PhD). Terminal master's awarded for partial completion of doctoral program. *Degree requirements:* For master's, comprehensive exam, thesis, teaching experience; for doctorate, comprehensive exam, thesis/dissertation, teaching experience. *Entrance requirements:* For master's, GRE General Test, minimum GPA of 2.7; for doctorate, GRE General Test, minimum GPA of 3.0. Additional exam requirements/recommendations for international students: Required—TOEFL. Electronic applications accepted. *Faculty research:* Synthetic organics, materials, natural products, mass spectrometry.

Illinois Institute of Technology, Graduate College, College of Science, Department of Chemistry, Chicago, IL 60616. Offers analytical chemistry (MAS); chemistry (MAS, MS, PhD); materials chemistry (MAS), including inorganic, organic, or polymeric materials. *Program availability:* Part-time, evening/weekend, online learning. Terminal master's awarded for partial completion of doctoral program. *Degree requirements:* For master's, comprehensive exam, thesis (for some programs); for doctorate, comprehensive exam, thesis/dissertation. *Entrance requirements:* For master's, GRE General Test (minimum score 300 Quantitative and Verbal, 2.5 Analytical Writing), minimum undergraduate GPA of 3.0; for doctorate, GRE General Test (minimum score 310 Quantitative and Verbal, 3.0 Analytical Writing), GRE Subject Test, minimum undergraduate GPA of 3.0. Additional exam requirements/recommendations for international students: Required—TOEFL (minimum score 550 paper-based; 80 iBT); Recommended—IELTS. Electronic applications accepted. *Faculty research:* Materials science, biological chemistry, synthetic chemistry, computational chemistry, energy, sensor science and technology, scholarship of teaching and learning.

Indiana University Bloomington, University Graduate School, College of Arts and Sciences, Department of Chemistry, Bloomington, IN 47405. Offers analytical chemistry (PhD); chemical biology (PhD); chemistry (MAT); inorganic chemistry (PhD); materials chemistry (PhD); organic chemistry (PhD); physical chemistry (PhD); MSES/MS. Terminal master's awarded for partial completion of doctoral program. *Degree requirements:* For master's, thesis; for doctorate, thesis/dissertation. *Entrance requirements:* For master's and doctorate, GRE General Test, GRE Subject Test. Additional exam requirements/recommendations for international students: Required—TOEFL. Electronic applications accepted. *Faculty research:* Synthesis of complex natural products, organic reaction mechanisms, organic electrochemistry, transitive-metal chemistry, solid-state and surface chemistry.

Iowa State University of Science and Technology, Program in Analytical Chemistry, Ames, IA 50011. Offers PhD. *Entrance requirements:* For doctorate, official academic transcripts, resume, three letters of recommendation. Additional exam requirements/recommendations for international students: Required—TOEFL (minimum score 570 paper-based; 89 iBT), IELTS (minimum score 6.5). Electronic applications accepted.

Kansas State University, Graduate School, College of Arts and Sciences, Department of Chemistry, Manhattan, KS 66506. Offers analytical chemistry (MS); biological chemistry (MS); inorganic chemistry (MS); materials chemistry (MS); organic chemistry (MS); physical chemistry (MS). Terminal master's awarded for partial completion of doctoral program. *Degree requirements:* For master's, thesis; for doctorate, thesis/dissertation. *Entrance requirements:* For master's and doctorate, GRE, minimum GPA of 3.0. Additional exam requirements/recommendations for international students: Required—TOEFL (minimum score 550 paper-based). Electronic applications accepted. *Faculty research:* Inorganic chemistry, organic and biological chemistry, analytical chemistry, physical chemistry, materials chemistry and nanotechnology.

Laurentian University, School of Graduate Studies and Research, Programme in Chemistry and Biochemistry, Sudbury, ON P3E 2C6, Canada. Offers analytical chemistry (M Sc); biochemistry (M Sc); environmental chemistry (M Sc); organic chemistry (M Sc); physical/theoretical chemistry (M Sc). *Program availability:* Part-time. *Degree requirements:* For master's, thesis or alternative. *Entrance requirements:* For master's, honors degree with minimum second class. *Faculty research:* Cell cycle checkpoints, kinetic modeling, toxicology to metal stress, quantum chemistry, biogeochemistry metal speciation.

Marquette University, Graduate School, College of Arts and Sciences, Department of Chemistry, Milwaukee, WI 53201-1881. Offers analytical chemistry (MS, PhD); bioanalytical chemistry (MS, PhD); biophysical chemistry (MS, PhD); chemical physics (MS, PhD); inorganic chemistry (MS, PhD); organic chemistry (MS, PhD); physical chemistry (MS, PhD). *Program availability:* Part-time. *Faculty:* 19 full-time (3 women), 1 part-time/adjunct (0 women). *Students:* 43 full-time (14 women), 4 part-time (0 women); includes 2 minority (1 Asian, non-Hispanic/Latino; 1 Hispanic/Latino), 32 international. Average age 28. In 2015, 4 master's, 4 doctorates awarded. Terminal master's awarded for partial completion of doctoral program. *Degree requirements:* For master's, comprehensive exam; for doctorate, thesis/dissertation, cumulative exams. *Entrance requirements:* For master's and doctorate, official transcripts from all current and previous colleges/universities except Marquette, three letters of recommendation from individuals familiar with the applicant's academic work. Additional exam requirements/recommendations for international students: Required—TOEFL (minimum score 530 paper-based). *Application deadline:* Applications are processed on a rolling basis. Application fee: $50. Electronic applications accepted. *Financial support:* In 2015–16, 41 students received support, including 2 fellowships (averaging $17,134 per year), 30 teaching assistantships with full tuition reimbursements available (averaging $20,295 per year); research assistantships, scholarships/grants, health care benefits, tuition waivers (full and partial), and unspecified assistantships also available. Support available to part-time students. Financial award application deadline: 2/15. *Faculty research:* Inorganic complexes, laser Raman spectroscopy, organic synthesis, synthetic bioinorganic chemistry, electro-active organic molecules. *Total annual research expenditures:* $1.2 million. *Unit head:* Dr. Scott Reid, Chair, 414-288-7565, E-mail: scott.reid@marquette.edu. *Application contact:* Dr. Adam Fiedler, New and Recruiting, 414-288-1625.

Website: http://www.marquette.edu/chem/graduate.shtml

McMaster University, School of Graduate Studies, Faculty of Science, Department of Chemistry, Hamilton, ON L8S 4M2, Canada. Offers analytical chemistry (M Sc, PhD); chemical physics (M Sc, PhD); chemistry (M Sc, PhD); inorganic chemistry (M Sc, PhD); organic chemistry (M Sc, PhD); physical chemistry (M Sc, PhD); polymer chemistry (M Sc, PhD). *Program availability:* Part-time. Terminal master's awarded for partial completion of doctoral program. *Degree requirements:* For master's, thesis; for doctorate, comprehensive exam, thesis/dissertation. *Entrance requirements:* For master's, minimum B+ average. Additional exam requirements/recommendations for international students: Required—TOEFL (minimum score 550 paper-based).

Old Dominion University, College of Sciences, Program in Chemistry, Norfolk, VA 23529. Offers analytical (MS, PhD); biochemistry (MS, PhD); environmental (MS, PhD); inorganic (MS, PhD); organic (MS, PhD); physical (MS, PhD). *Program availability:* Part-time, evening/weekend. *Faculty:* 19 full-time (5 women). *Students:* 35 full-time (17 women), 6 part-time (2 women); includes 5 minority (4 Black or African American, non-Hispanic/Latino; 1 Two or more races, non-Hispanic/Latino), 16 international. Average age 27. 20 applicants, 55% accepted, 4 enrolled. In 2015, 9 master's, 9 doctorates awarded. *Degree requirements:* For master's, comprehensive exam, thesis (for some programs); for doctorate, comprehensive exam, thesis/dissertation. *Entrance requirements:* For master's and doctorate, GRE General Test, minimum GPA of 3.0 in major, 2.5 overall, transcripts, essay, three letters of recommendation, resume. Additional exam requirements/recommendations for international students: Required—TOEFL. *Application deadline:* For fall admission, 7/1 for domestic students, 1/15 for international students; for spring admission, 11/1 for domestic students, 8/15 for international students. Applications are processed on a rolling basis. Application fee: $50. Electronic applications accepted. *Expenses:* $464 per credit in-state tuition; $1,160 per credit out-of-state tuition. *Financial support:* In 2015–16, 42 students received support, including 2 fellowships with full tuition reimbursements available (averaging $18,000 per year), 10 research assistantships with full tuition reimbursements available (averaging $18,000 per year), 33 teaching assistantships with full tuition reimbursements available (averaging $18,000 per year); career-related internships or fieldwork, institutionally sponsored loans, scholarships/grants, health care benefits, and unspecified assistantships also available. Financial award application deadline: 2/15; financial award applicants required to submit FAFSA. *Faculty research:* Biogeochemistry, materials chemistry, computational chemistry, organic chemistry, biofuels. *Total annual research expenditures:* $2.6 million. *Unit head:* Dr. John R. Donat, Graduate Program Director, 757-683-4098, Fax: 757-683-4628, E-mail: chemgpd@odu.edu. *Application contact:* Kristi Rehrauer, Graduate Program Assistant, 757-683-6979, Fax: 757-683-4628, E-mail: krehraue@odu.edu.

Oregon State University, College of Science, Program in Chemistry, Corvallis, OR 97331. Offers analytical chemistry (MA, MS, PhD); inorganic chemistry (MA, MS, PhD); materials chemistry (MA, MS, PhD); nuclear chemistry (MA, MS, PhD); organic chemistry (MA, MS, PhD); physical chemistry (MA, MS, PhD). *Program availability:* Part-time. *Faculty:* 23 full-time (6 women). *Students:* 111 full-time (38 women), 4 part-time (2 women); includes 14 minority (1 Black or African American, non-Hispanic/Latino; 5 Asian, non-Hispanic/Latino; 6 Hispanic/Latino; 2 Two or more races, non-Hispanic/Latino), 49 international. Average age 28. 47 applicants, 51% accepted, 22 enrolled. In 2015, 6 master's, 12 doctorates awarded. Terminal master's awarded for partial completion of doctoral program. *Degree requirements:* For master's, one foreign language, thesis; for doctorate, one foreign language, thesis/dissertation. *Entrance requirements:* For master's and doctorate, GRE, minimum GPA of 3.0 in last 90 hours of course work. Additional exam requirements/recommendations for international students: Required—TOEFL (minimum score 80 iBT), IELTS (minimum score 6.5). *Application deadline:* For fall admission, 4/1 for domestic students. Application fee: $75 ($85 for international students). *Expenses:* Tuition, state resident: full-time $12,150; part-time $450 per credit. Tuition, nonresident: full-time $20,952; part-time $776 per credit. *Required fees:* $1572; $1443 per unit. One-time fee: $350. Tuition and fees vary according to course load, campus/location and program. *Financial support:* Fellowships, research assistantships, and teaching assistantships available. Support available to part-time students. *Faculty research:* Solid state chemistry, enzyme reaction mechanisms, structure and dynamics of gas molecules, chemiluminescence, nonlinear optical spectroscopy. *Unit head:* Dr. Rich G. Carter, Professor/Chair. *Application contact:* Sarah Burton, Chemistry Advisor, 541-737-6808, E-mail: chemadm@chem.oregonstate.edu.

Website: http://chemistry.oregonstate.edu/

Purdue University, Graduate School, College of Science, Department of Chemistry, West Lafayette, IN 47907. Offers analytical chemistry (MS, PhD); biochemistry (MS, PhD); chemical education (MS, PhD); inorganic chemistry (MS, PhD); organic chemistry

(MS, PhD); physical chemistry (MS, PhD). Terminal master's awarded for partial completion of doctoral program. *Degree requirements:* For master's, thesis; for doctorate, comprehensive exam, thesis/dissertation. *Entrance requirements:* For master's and doctorate, minimum undergraduate GPA of 3.0. Additional exam requirements/recommendations for international students: Required—TOEFL (minimum score 550 paper-based; 77 iBT); Recommended—TWE. Electronic applications accepted.

Rutgers University–Newark, Graduate School, Program in Chemistry, Newark, NJ 07102. Offers analytical chemistry (MS, PhD); biochemistry (MS, PhD); inorganic chemistry (MS, PhD); organic chemistry (MS, PhD); physical chemistry (MS, PhD). *Program availability:* Part-time, evening/weekend. Terminal master's awarded for partial completion of doctoral program. *Degree requirements:* For master's, thesis optional, cumulative exams; for doctorate, thesis/dissertation, exams, research proposal. *Entrance requirements:* For master's and doctorate, GRE General Test, minimum undergraduate B average. Additional exam requirements/recommendations for international students: Required—TOEFL. Electronic applications accepted. *Faculty research:* Medicinal chemistry, natural products, isotope effects, biophysics and biorganic approaches to enzyme mechanisms, organic and organometallic synthesis.

Seton Hall University, College of Arts and Sciences, Department of Chemistry and Biochemistry, South Orange, NJ 07079-2697. Offers analytical chemistry (MS, PhD); biochemistry (MS, PhD); chemistry (MS); inorganic chemistry (MS, PhD); organic chemistry (MS, PhD); physical chemistry (MS, PhD). *Program availability:* Part-time, evening/weekend. Terminal master's awarded for partial completion of doctoral program. *Degree requirements:* For master's, thesis optional; for doctorate, comprehensive exam, thesis/dissertation. *Entrance requirements:* Additional exam requirements/recommendations for international students: Required—TOEFL. Electronic applications accepted. *Faculty research:* DNA metal reactions; chromatography; bioinorganic, biophysical, organometallic, polymer chemistry; heterogeneous catalyst; synthetic organic and carbohydrate chemistry.

Southern University and Agricultural and Mechanical College, Graduate School, College of Sciences, Department of Chemistry, Baton Rouge, LA 70813. Offers analytical chemistry (MS); biochemistry (MS); environmental sciences (MS); inorganic chemistry (MS); organic chemistry (MS); physical chemistry (MS). *Degree requirements:* For master's, thesis. *Entrance requirements:* For master's, GMAT or GRE General Test. Additional exam requirements/recommendations for international students: Required—TOEFL (minimum score 525 paper-based). *Faculty research:* Synthesis of macrocyclic ligands, latex accelerators, anticancer drugs, biosensors, absorption isotheums, isolation of specific enzymes from plants.

Stevens Institute of Technology, Graduate School, Charles V. Schaefer Jr. School of Engineering, Department of Chemistry, Chemical Biology and Biomedical Engineering, Hoboken, NJ 07030. Offers analytical chemistry (Certificate), including analytical chemistry; bioinformatics (Certificate), including bioinformatics; biomedical chemistry (Certificate), including biomedical chemistry; biomedical engineering (M Eng, PhD); chemical biology (MS, PhD, Certificate), including chemical physiology (Certificate); chemical physiology (Certificate), including polymer chemistry; chemistry (MS, PhD); polymer chemistry (Certificate). *Program availability:* Part-time, evening/weekend, online learning. *Faculty:* 24 full-time (10 women), 8 part-time/adjunct (2 women). *Students:* 77 full-time (42 women), 14 part-time (8 women); includes 9 minority (3 Black or African American, non-Hispanic/Latino; 5 Asian, non-Hispanic/Latino; 1 Hispanic/Latino), 54 international. Average age 27. 239 applicants, 41% accepted, 27 enrolled. In 2015, 24 master's, 5 doctorates, 1 other advanced degree awarded. Terminal master's awarded for partial completion of doctoral program. *Entrance requirements:* Additional exam requirements/recommendations for international students: Required—TOEFL (minimum score 74 iBT). *Application deadline:* Applications are processed on a rolling basis. Application fee: $60. Electronic applications accepted. *Expenses: Tuition, area resident:* Full-time $32,200; part-time $1450 per credit. *Required fees:* $1150; $550 per unit. $275 per semester. *Financial support:* Fellowships, research assistantships, teaching assistantships, career-related internships or fieldwork, Federal Work-Study, scholarships/grants, and unspecified assistantships available. Financial award application deadline: 2/15; financial award applicants required to submit FAFSA. *Faculty research:* Polymerization engineering, methods of instrumental analysis, medicinal chemistry, structural chemistry, protein trafficking, proteomics. *Unit head:* Dr. Peter Tolias, Interim Director, 201-216-8253, Fax: 201-216-8196,
E-mail: ptolias@stevens.edu. *Application contact:* Graduate Admissions, 888-783-8367, Fax: 888-511-1306, E-mail: graduate@stevens.edu.

Tufts University, Graduate School of Arts and Sciences, Department of Chemistry, Medford, MA 02155. Offers analytical chemistry (MS, PhD); bioorganic chemistry (MS, PhD); environmental chemistry (MS, PhD); inorganic chemistry (MS, PhD); organic chemistry (MS, PhD); physical chemistry (MS, PhD). Terminal master's awarded for partial completion of doctoral program. *Degree requirements:* For master's, thesis optional; for doctorate, thesis/dissertation. *Entrance requirements:* For master's and doctorate, GRE General Test; GRE Subject Test (recommended). Additional exam requirements/recommendations for international students: Required—TOEFL (minimum score 600 paper-based; 80 iBT), IELTS (minimum score 6.5). Electronic applications accepted. *Expenses: Tuition, area resident:* Full-time $48,412; part-time $1210 per credit hour. *Required fees:* $806. Full-time tuition and fees vary according to degree level, program and student level. Part-time tuition and fees vary according to course load.

University of Calgary, Faculty of Graduate Studies, Faculty of Science, Department of Chemistry, Calgary, AB T2N 1N4, Canada. Offers analytical chemistry (M Sc, PhD); applied chemistry (M Sc, PhD); inorganic chemistry (M Sc, PhD); organic chemistry (M Sc, PhD); physical chemistry (M Sc, PhD); polymer chemistry (M Sc, PhD); theoretical chemistry (M Sc, PhD). *Degree requirements:* For master's, thesis; for doctorate, thesis/dissertation, candidacy exam. *Entrance requirements:* For master's, minimum GPA of 3.0; for doctorate, honors B Sc degree with minimum GPA of 3.7 or M Sc with minimum GPA of 3.3. Additional exam requirements/recommendations for international students: Required—TOEFL (minimum score 580 paper-based). Electronic applications accepted. *Faculty research:* Chemical analysis, chemical dynamics, synthesis theory.

University of Cincinnati, Graduate School, McMicken College of Arts and Sciences, Department of Chemistry, Cincinnati, OH 45221. Offers analytical chemistry (MS, PhD); biochemistry (MS, PhD); inorganic chemistry (MS, PhD); organic chemistry (MS, PhD); physical chemistry (MS, PhD); polymer chemistry (MS, PhD); sensors (PhD). *Program availability:* Part-time, evening/weekend. Terminal master's awarded for partial completion of doctoral program. *Degree requirements:* For master's, thesis optional; for doctorate, comprehensive exam, thesis/dissertation. *Entrance requirements:* For master's and doctorate, GRE General Test. Additional exam requirements/recommendations for international students: Required—TOEFL (minimum score 580 paper-based). Electronic applications accepted. *Faculty research:* Biomedical chemistry, laser chemistry, surface science, chemical sensors, synthesis.

University of Georgia, Franklin College of Arts and Sciences, Department of Chemistry, Athens, GA 30602. Offers analytical chemistry (MS, PhD); inorganic chemistry (MS, PhD); organic chemistry (MS, PhD); physical chemistry (MS, PhD). Terminal master's awarded for partial completion of doctoral program. *Degree requirements:* For master's, thesis; for doctorate, one foreign language, thesis/dissertation. *Entrance requirements:* For master's and doctorate, GRE General Test. Additional exam requirements/recommendations for international students: Required—TOEFL. Electronic applications accepted.

University of Louisville, Graduate School, College of Arts and Sciences, Department of Chemistry, Louisville, KY 40292-0001. Offers analytical chemistry (MS, PhD); biochemistry (MS, PhD); chemical physics (PhD); inorganic chemistry (MS, PhD); organic chemistry (MS, PhD); physical chemistry (MS, PhD). *Students:* 46 full-time (16 women), 8 part-time (1 woman); includes 3 minority (1 Black or African American, non-Hispanic/Latino; 1 Asian, non-Hispanic/Latino; 1 Two or more races, non-Hispanic/Latino), 36 international. Average age 29. 51 applicants, 22% accepted, 6 enrolled. In 2015, 2 master's, 1 doctorate awarded. Terminal master's awarded for partial completion of doctoral program. *Degree requirements:* For master's, variable foreign language requirement, comprehensive exam, thesis optional; for doctorate, variable foreign language requirement, comprehensive exam, thesis/dissertation. *Entrance requirements:* For master's and doctorate, GRE General Test, BA or BS coursework. Additional exam requirements/recommendations for international students: Required—TOEFL (minimum score 550 paper-based; 79 iBT). *Application deadline:* For fall admission, 3/15 for domestic students, 5/1 priority date for international students; for winter admission, 9/15 for domestic and international students; for spring admission, 11/1 priority date for international students; for summer admission, 4/1 priority date for international students. Applications are processed on a rolling basis. Application fee: $60. Electronic applications accepted. *Expenses:* Tuition, state resident: full-time $11,664; part-time $649 per credit hour. Tuition, nonresident: full-time $24,274; part-time $1350 per credit hour. *Required fees:* $196. Tuition and fees vary according to program and reciprocity agreements. *Financial support:* In 2015–16, 757,720 students received support. Fellowships with full tuition reimbursements available, research assistantships with full tuition reimbursements available, teaching assistantships with full tuition reimbursements available, career-related internships or fieldwork, scholarships/grants, traineeships, health care benefits, and unspecified assistantships available. Support available to part-time students. Financial award application deadline: 3/15. *Faculty research:* Computational chemistry, biophysics nuclear magnetic resonance, synthetic organic chemistry, synthetic inorganic chemistry, medicinal chemistry, protein chemistry, enzymology, nano chemistry, electrochemistry, analytical chemistry, synthetic biology, bioinformatics. *Total annual research expenditures:* $2.4 million. *Unit head:* Dr. Richard J. Wittebort, Professor/Chair, 502-852-6613. *Application contact:* Libby Leggett, Director, Graduate Admissions, 502-852-3101, Fax: 502-852-6536, E-mail: gradadm@louisville.edu.
Website: http://louisville.edu/chemistry

The University of Manchester, School of Chemical Engineering and Analytical Science, Manchester, United Kingdom. Offers biocatalysis (M Phil, PhD); chemical engineering (M Phil, PhD); chemical engineering and analytical science (M Phil, D Eng, PhD); colloids, crystals, interfaces and materials (M Phil, PhD); environment and sustainable technology (M Phil, PhD); instrumentation (M Phil, PhD); multi-scale modeling (M Phil, PhD); process integration (M Phil, PhD); systems biology (M Phil, PhD).

University of Maryland, College Park, Academic Affairs, College of Computer, Mathematical and Natural Sciences, Department of Chemistry and Biochemistry, Chemistry Program, College Park, MD 20742. Offers analytical chemistry (MS, PhD); inorganic chemistry (MS, PhD); organic chemistry (MS, PhD); physical chemistry (MS, PhD). *Program availability:* Part-time, evening/weekend. Terminal master's awarded for partial completion of doctoral program. *Degree requirements:* For master's, thesis optional; for doctorate, thesis/dissertation, 2 seminar presentations, oral exam. *Entrance requirements:* For master's and doctorate, GRE General Test, GRE Subject Test (recommended), minimum GPA of 3.0, 3 letters of recommendation. Additional exam requirements/recommendations for international students: Required—TOEFL. Electronic applications accepted. *Faculty research:* Environmental chemistry, nuclear chemistry, lunar and environmental analysis, X-ray crystallography.

University of Massachusetts Lowell, College of Sciences, Department of Chemistry, Lowell, MA 01854. Offers analytical chemistry (PhD); biochemistry (PhD); chemistry (MS, PhD); environmental studies (PhD); green chemistry (PhD); inorganic chemistry (PhD); organic chemistry (PhD); polymer science (MS). Terminal master's awarded for partial completion of doctoral program. *Degree requirements:* For master's, thesis; for doctorate, 2 foreign languages, thesis/dissertation. *Entrance requirements:* For master's and doctorate, GRE General Test. Electronic applications accepted.

University of Memphis, Graduate School, College of Arts and Sciences, Department of Chemistry, Memphis, TN 38152. Offers analytical chemistry (PhD); inorganic chemistry (MS); physical chemistry (MS). *Program availability:* Part-time. *Faculty:* 5 full-time (2 women), 1 part-time/adjunct (0 women). *Students:* 26 full-time (11 women), 9 part-time (2 women); includes 6 minority (2 Black or African American, non-Hispanic/Latino; 2 Asian, non-Hispanic/Latino; 2 Two or more races, non-Hispanic/Latino), 5 international. Average age 28. 19 applicants, 74% accepted, 9 enrolled. In 2015, 9 master's, 3 doctorates awarded. Terminal master's awarded for partial completion of doctoral program. *Degree requirements:* For master's, comprehensive exam, thesis or alternative; for doctorate, comprehensive exam, thesis/dissertation. *Entrance requirements:* For master's and doctorate, GRE General Test, admission to Graduate School plus 32 undergraduate hours in chemistry. Additional exam requirements/recommendations for international students: Required—TOEFL. *Application deadline:* For fall admission, 7/1 for domestic students, 5/1 for international students; for winter admission, 9/15 for international students; for spring admission, 12/1 for domestic students. Applications are processed on a rolling basis. Application fee: $35 ($60 for international students). Electronic applications accepted. *Financial support:* In 2015–16, 12 students received support. Research assistantships with full tuition reimbursements available, teaching assistantships with full tuition reimbursements available, Federal Work-Study, scholarships/grants, and unspecified assistantships available. Financial award application deadline: 2/15; financial award applicants required to submit FAFSA. *Faculty research:* Computational chemistry, materials chemistry, organic/polymer synthesis, drug design/delivery, water chemistry. *Unit head:* Dr. Abby L. Parrill, Professor and Chair, 901-678-2638, Fax: 901-678-3447, E-mail: aparrill@memphis.edu. *Application contact:* Dr. Gary Emmert, Associate Professor and Graduate Coordinator, 901-678-2636, Fax: 901-678-3447, E-mail: gemmert@memphis.edu.
Website: http://www.chem.memphis.edu/

University of Michigan, Rackham Graduate School, College of Literature, Science, and the Arts, Department of Chemistry, Ann Arbor, MI 48109-1055. Offers analytical (PhD); chemical biology (PhD); inorganic (PhD); materials (PhD); organic (PhD); physical (PhD). *Faculty:* 38 full-time (9 women), 9 part-time/adjunct (3 women). *Students:* 264 full-time (113 women). 535 applicants, 31% accepted, 54 enrolled. In

2015, 45 doctorates awarded. *Degree requirements:* For doctorate, comprehensive exam, thesis/dissertation, oral defense of dissertation, organic cumulative proficiency exams. *Entrance requirements:* For doctorate, GRE General Test, GRE Subject Test (recommended), 3 letters of recommendation. Additional exam requirements/recommendations for international students: Required—TOEFL (minimum score 560 paper-based; 84 iBT). *Application deadline:* For fall admission, 12/15 for domestic and international students. Applications are processed on a rolling basis. Application fee: $0 ($90 for international students). Electronic applications accepted. *Financial support:* In 2015–16, 264 students received support, including 40 fellowships with full tuition reimbursements available (averaging $29,000 per year), 78 research assistantships with full tuition reimbursements available (averaging $29,025 per year), 146 teaching assistantships with full tuition reimbursements available (averaging $29,025 per year); career-related internships or fieldwork, scholarships/grants, traineeships, health care benefits, and unspecified assistantships also available. *Faculty research:* Biological catalysis, protein engineering, chemical sensors, de novo metalloprotein design, supramolecular architecture. *Unit head:* Dr. Robert Kennedy, Professor of Chemistry/Chair, 734-763-9681, Fax: 734-647-4847. *Application contact:* Elizabeth Oxford, Graduate Program Coordinator, 734-764-7278, Fax: 734-647-4865,
E-mail: chemadmissions@umich.edu.
Website: http://www.lsa.umich.edu/chem/

University of Missouri, Office of Research and Graduate Studies, College of Arts and Science, Department of Chemistry, Columbia, MO 65211. Offers analytical chemistry (MS, PhD); inorganic chemistry (MS, PhD); organic chemistry (MS, PhD); physical chemistry (MS, PhD). *Degree requirements:* For master's, thesis; for doctorate, one foreign language, comprehensive exam, thesis/dissertation. *Entrance requirements:* For master's, GRE General Test, minimum GPA of 3.0; for doctorate, GRE General Test (minimum score: Verbal 450, Quantitative 600, Analytical 3), minimum GPA of 3.0. Additional exam requirements/recommendations for international students: Required—TOEFL (minimum score 600 paper-based; 100 iBT). Electronic applications accepted. *Faculty research:* Analytical, organic, biological, physical, inorganic and radiochemistry.

University of Missouri–Kansas City, College of Arts and Sciences, Department of Chemistry, Kansas City, MO 64110-2499. Offers analytical chemistry (MS, PhD); inorganic chemistry (MS, PhD); organic chemistry (MS, PhD); physical chemistry (MS, PhD); polymer chemistry (MS, PhD). PhD (interdisciplinary) offered through the School of Graduate Studies. *Program availability:* Part-time, evening/weekend. *Faculty:* 15 full-time (2 women), 1 part-time/adjunct (0 women). *Students:* 3 full-time (2 women), 4 part-time (2 women); includes 1 minority (Black or African American, non-Hispanic/Latino), 3 international. Average age 36. 35 applicants, 23% accepted, 1 enrolled. In 2015, 3 master's awarded. *Degree requirements:* For master's, thesis (for some programs); for doctorate, thesis/dissertation. *Entrance requirements:* For master's, equivalent of American Chemical Society approved bachelor's degree in chemistry; for doctorate, GRE General Test, equivalent of American Chemical Society approved bachelor's degree in chemistry. Additional exam requirements/recommendations for international students: Required—TOEFL (minimum score 550 paper-based; 80 iBT), TWE. *Application deadline:* For fall admission, 4/15 for domestic and international students; for spring admission, 10/15 for domestic and international students. Applications are processed on a rolling basis. Application fee: $45 ($50 for international students). Electronic applications accepted. *Financial support:* In 2015–16, 2 research assistantships with partial tuition reimbursements (averaging $18,000 per year), 30 teaching assistantships with partial tuition reimbursements (averaging $18,062 per year) were awarded; Federal Work-Study, institutionally sponsored loans, and scholarships/grants also available. Support available to part-time students. Financial award application deadline: 3/1; financial award applicants required to submit FAFSA. *Faculty research:* Molecular spectroscopy, characterization and synthesis of materials and compounds, computational chemistry, natural products, drug delivery systems and anti-tumor agents. *Unit head:* Dr. Kathleen V. Kilway, Chair, 816-235-2289, Fax: 816-235-5502, E-mail: kilwayk@umkc.edu. *Application contact:* Graduate Recruiting Committee, 816-235-2272, Fax: 816-235-5502, E-mail: umkc-chemdept@umkc.edu.

University of Montana, Graduate School, College of Humanities and Sciences, Department of Chemistry and Biochemistry, Missoula, MT 59812-0002. Offers chemistry (MS, PhD), including environmental/analytical chemistry, inorganic chemistry, organic chemistry, physical chemistry. Terminal master's awarded for partial completion of doctoral program. *Degree requirements:* For master's, thesis (for some programs); for doctorate, thesis/dissertation. *Entrance requirements:* For master's and doctorate, GRE General Test. Additional exam requirements/recommendations for international students: Required—TOEFL (minimum score 575 paper-based). *Faculty research:* Reaction mechanisms and kinetics, inorganic and organic synthesis, analytical chemistry, natural products.

University of Nebraska–Lincoln, Graduate College, College of Arts and Sciences, Department of Chemistry, Lincoln, NE 68588. Offers analytical chemistry (PhD); biochemistry (PhD); chemistry (MS); inorganic chemistry (PhD); materials chemistry (PhD); organic chemistry (PhD); physical chemistry (PhD). *Degree requirements:* For master's, one foreign language, thesis optional, departmental qualifying exam; for doctorate, one foreign language, comprehensive exam, thesis/dissertation, departmental qualifying exams. *Entrance requirements:* For master's and doctorate, GRE. Additional exam requirements/recommendations for international students: Required—TOEFL (minimum score 550 paper-based). Electronic applications accepted. *Faculty research:* Bioorganic and bioinorganic chemistry, biophysical and bioanalytical chemistry, structure-function of DNA and proteins, organometallics, mass spectrometry.

University of Regina, Faculty of Graduate Studies and Research, Faculty of Science, Department of Chemistry and Biochemistry, Regina, SK S4S 0A2, Canada. Offers analytical/environmental chemistry (M Sc, PhD); biophysics of biological interfaces (M Sc, PhD); enzymology/chemical biology (M Sc, PhD); inorganic/organometallic chemistry (M Sc, PhD); signal transduction and mechanisms of cancer cell regulation (M Sc, PhD); supramolecular organic photochemistry and photophysics (M Sc, PhD); synthetic organic chemistry (M Sc, PhD); theoretical/computational chemistry (M Sc, PhD). *Degree requirements:* For master's, thesis; for doctorate, thesis/dissertation. *Entrance requirements:* Additional exam requirements/recommendations for international students: Required—TOEFL (minimum score 580 paper-based; 80 iBT), IELTS (minimum score 6.5), PTE (minimum score 59). Electronic applications accepted. *Faculty research:* Asymmetric synthesis and methodology, theoretical and computational chemistry, biophysical biochemistry, analytical and environmental chemistry, chemical biology.

The University of Tennessee, Graduate School, College of Arts and Sciences, Department of Chemistry, Knoxville, TN 37996. Offers analytical chemistry (MS, PhD); chemical physics (PhD); environmental chemistry (MS, PhD); inorganic chemistry (MS, PhD); organic chemistry (MS, PhD); physical chemistry (MS, PhD); polymer chemistry (MS, PhD); theoretical chemistry (PhD). *Program availability:* Part-time. Terminal master's awarded for partial completion of doctoral program. *Degree requirements:* For master's, thesis; for doctorate, thesis/dissertation. *Entrance requirements:* For master's and doctorate, GRE General Test, minimum GPA of 2.7. Additional exam requirements/recommendations for international students: Required—TOEFL. Electronic applications accepted.

The University of Texas at Austin, Graduate School, College of Natural Sciences, Department of Chemistry and Biochemistry, Austin, TX 78712-1111. Offers analytical chemistry (PhD); biochemistry (PhD); inorganic chemistry (PhD); organic chemistry (PhD); physical chemistry (PhD). *Entrance requirements:* For doctorate, GRE General Test.

The University of Toledo, College of Graduate Studies, College of Natural Sciences and Mathematics, Department of Chemistry, Toledo, OH 43606-3390. Offers analytical chemistry (MS, PhD); biological chemistry (MS, PhD); inorganic chemistry (MS, PhD); organic chemistry (MS, PhD); physical chemistry (MS, PhD). *Program availability:* Part-time. *Degree requirements:* For master's, thesis or alternative; for doctorate, thesis/dissertation. *Entrance requirements:* For master's and doctorate, GRE General Test, GRE Subject Test, minimum cumulative point-hour ratio of 2.7 for all previous academic work, three letters of recommendation, statement of purpose, transcripts from all prior institutions attended. Additional exam requirements/recommendations for international students: Required—TOEFL (minimum score 550 paper-based; 80 iBT). Electronic applications accepted. *Faculty research:* Enzymology, materials chemistry, crystallography, theoretical chemistry.

Vanderbilt University, Department of Chemistry, Nashville, TN 37240-1001. Offers analytical chemistry (MAT, MS, PhD); inorganic chemistry (MAT, MS, PhD); organic chemistry (MAT, MS, PhD); physical chemistry (MAT, MS, PhD); theoretical chemistry (MAT, MS). *Faculty:* 19 full-time (3 women). *Students:* 114 full-time (41 women); includes 19 minority (5 Black or African American, non-Hispanic/Latino; 3 Asian, non-Hispanic/Latino; 7 Hispanic/Latino; 4 Two or more races, non-Hispanic/Latino), 8 international. Average age 26. 339 applicants, 17% accepted, 19 enrolled. In 2015, 11 master's, 13 doctorates awarded. Terminal master's awarded for partial completion of doctoral program. *Degree requirements:* For master's, thesis; for doctorate, thesis/dissertation, area, qualifying, and final exams. *Entrance requirements:* For master's and doctorate, GRE General Test, GRE Subject Test (recommended). Additional exam requirements/recommendations for international students: Required—TOEFL (minimum score 570 paper-based; 88 iBT). *Application deadline:* For fall admission, 1/15 for domestic and international students. Application fee: $0. Electronic applications accepted. *Financial support:* Fellowships with tuition reimbursements, research assistantships with full tuition reimbursements, teaching assistantships with full tuition reimbursements, Federal Work-Study, institutionally sponsored loans, scholarships/grants, traineeships, and health care benefits available. Financial award application deadline: 1/15; financial award applicants required to submit CSS PROFILE or FAFSA. *Faculty research:* Chemical synthesis; mechanistic, theoretical, bioorganic, analytical, and spectroscopic chemistry. *Unit head:* Dr. Carmello Rizzo, Director of Graduate Studies, 615-322-2861, Fax: 615-322-4936, E-mail: c.rizzo@vanderbilt.edu. *Application contact:* Sandra Ford, Administrative Assistant, 615-322-8695, Fax: 615-322-4936, E-mail: sandra.e.ford@vanderbilt.edu.
Website: http://www.vanderbilt.edu/chemistry/

Virginia Commonwealth University, Graduate School, College of Humanities and Sciences, Department of Chemistry, Richmond, VA 23284-9005. Offers analytical chemistry (MS, PhD); chemical physics (PhD); inorganic chemistry (MS, PhD); organic chemistry (MS, PhD); physical chemistry (MS, PhD). *Program availability:* Part-time. Terminal master's awarded for partial completion of doctoral program. *Degree requirements:* For master's, thesis; for doctorate, thesis/dissertation, comprehensive cumulative exams, research proposal. *Entrance requirements:* For master's, GRE General Test, 30 undergraduate credits in chemistry; for doctorate, GRE General Test. Additional exam requirements/recommendations for international students: Required—TOEFL (minimum score 600 paper-based; 100 iBT) or IELTS (minimum score 6.5). Electronic applications accepted. *Faculty research:* Physical, organic, inorganic, analytical, and polymer chemistry; chemical physics.

Wake Forest University, Graduate School of Arts and Sciences, Department of Chemistry, Winston-Salem, NC 27109. Offers analytical chemistry (MS, PhD); inorganic chemistry (MS, PhD); organic chemistry (MS, PhD); physical chemistry (MS, PhD). *Program availability:* Part-time. *Degree requirements:* For master's, one foreign language, comprehensive exam, thesis; for doctorate, 2 foreign languages, comprehensive exam, thesis/dissertation. *Entrance requirements:* For master's and doctorate, GRE General Test. Additional exam requirements/recommendations for international students: Required—TOEFL. Electronic applications accepted.

Wayne State University, College of Liberal Arts and Sciences, Department of Chemistry, Detroit, MI 48202. Offers analytical chemistry (PhD); biochemistry (PhD); chemistry (MA, MS); inorganic chemistry (PhD); organic chemistry (PhD); physical chemistry (PhD). *Faculty:* 29. *Students:* 146 full-time (61 women); includes 9 minority (2 Asian, non-Hispanic/Latino; 3 Hispanic/Latino; 4 Two or more races, non-Hispanic/Latino), 95 international. Average age 28. 280 applicants, 19% accepted, 28 enrolled. In 2015, 4 master's, 22 doctorates awarded. *Degree requirements:* For master's, thesis (for some programs), oral exam; for doctorate, thesis/dissertation, oral exam. *Entrance requirements:* For master's, GRE (strongly recommended), 1 year of physics, math through calculus, general chemistry (8 credits), organic chemistry (8 credits), physical chemistry (6 credits), quantitative analysis (4 credits), advanced chemistry (3 credits), minimum undergraduate GPA of 2.75 in chemistry and cognate sciences, statement of interest, three letters of recommendation; for doctorate, GRE (strongly recommended), minimum undergraduate GPA of 3.0 in chemistry and cognate science. Additional exam requirements/recommendations for international students: Required—TOEFL (minimum score 90 iBT), IELTS (minimum score 6.5), TWE (minimum score 5.5). *Application deadline:* For fall admission, 12/1 priority date for domestic and international students. Applications are processed on a rolling basis. Application fee: $0. Electronic applications accepted. *Expenses:* Tuition, state resident: full-time $14,165; part-time $590.20 per credit hour. Tuition, nonresident: full-time $30,682; part-time $1278.40 per credit hour. *Required fees:* $1688; $47.45 per credit hour. $274.60 per semester. Tuition and fees vary according to course load and program. *Financial support:* In 2015–16, 141 students received support, including 10 fellowships with tuition reimbursements available (averaging $23,000 per year), 54 research assistantships with tuition reimbursements available (averaging $21,609 per year), 73 teaching assistantships with tuition reimbursements available (averaging $21,363 per year); scholarships/grants and unspecified assistantships also available. Financial award application deadline: 3/31; financial award applicants required to submit FAFSA. *Faculty research:* Natural products synthesis, molecular biology, molecular mechanics calculations, organometallic chemistry, experimental physical chemistry. *Total annual research expenditures:* $7.4 million. *Unit head:* Dr. James Rigby, Chair, 313-577-3472,
E-mail: jhr@chem.wayne.edu. *Application contact:* Melissa Barton, Graduate Academic Services Officer, E-mail: melissa@chem.wayne.edu.
Website: http://chem.wayne.edu/

West Virginia University, Eberly College of Arts and Sciences, Department of Chemistry, Morgantown, WV 26506. Offers analytical chemistry (MS, PhD); inorganic chemistry (MS, PhD); organic chemistry (MS, PhD); physical chemistry (MS, PhD); theoretical chemistry (MS, PhD). *Program availability:* Part-time, online learning. Terminal master's awarded for partial completion of doctoral program. *Degree requirements:* For master's, thesis; for doctorate, thesis/dissertation. *Entrance requirements:* For master's, GRE General Test, GRE Subject Test (recommended), minimum GPA of 2.5; for doctorate, GRE General Test, GRE Subject Test (recommended), minimum GPA of 2.75. Additional exam requirements/recommendations for international students: Required—TOEFL. Electronic applications accepted. *Expenses:* Tuition, state resident: full-time $8568. Tuition, nonresident: full-time $22,140. Tuition and fees vary according to program. *Faculty research:* Analysis of proteins, drug interactions, solids and effluents by advanced separation methods; new synthetic strategies for complex organic molecules; synthesis and structural characterization of metal complexes for polymerization catalysis, nonlinear science, spectroscopy.

Youngstown State University, Graduate School, College of Science, Technology, Engineering and Mathematics, Department of Chemistry, Youngstown, OH 44555-0001. Offers analytical chemistry (MS); biochemistry (MS); chemistry education (MS); inorganic chemistry (MS); organic chemistry (MS); physical chemistry (MS). *Program availability:* Part-time. *Degree requirements:* For master's, thesis. *Entrance requirements:* For master's, bachelor's degree in chemistry, minimum GPA of 2.7. Additional exam requirements/recommendations for international students: Required—TOEFL. *Faculty research:* Analysis of antioxidants, chromatography, defects and disorder in crystalline oxides, hydrogen bonding, novel organic and organometallic materials.

Chemistry

Acadia University, Faculty of Pure and Applied Science, Department of Chemistry, Wolfville, NS B4P 2R6, Canada. Offers M Sc. *Degree requirements:* For master's, thesis. *Entrance requirements:* Additional exam requirements/recommendations for international students: Required—TOEFL (minimum score 580 paper-based; 93 iBT), IELTS (minimum score 6.5). *Faculty research:* Atmospheric chemistry, chemical kinetics, bioelectrochemistry of proteins, self-assembling monolayers.

American University, College of Arts and Sciences, Department of Chemistry, Washington, DC 20016-8014. Offers chemistry (MS). *Program availability:* Part-time, evening/weekend. *Faculty:* 12 full-time (6 women). *Students:* 2 full-time (both women), 3 part-time (2 women); includes 3 minority (2 Black or African American, non-Hispanic/Latino; 1 Two or more races, non-Hispanic/Latino). Average age 25. 7 applicants, 57% accepted, 2 enrolled. In 2015, 2 master's awarded. *Degree requirements:* For master's, comprehensive exam, thesis. *Entrance requirements:* For master's, GRE, statement of purpose, transcripts, 2 letters of recommendation, resume. Additional exam requirements/recommendations for international students: Required—TOEFL (minimum score 100 iBT), IELTS (minimum score 7), PTE (minimum score 68). *Application deadline:* For fall admission, 3/1 priority date for domestic students; for spring admission, 11/1 for domestic students. Applications are processed on a rolling basis. Application fee: $55. *Expenses: Tuition, area resident:* Full-time $27,468; part-time $1526 per credit hour. *Required fees:* $430. Tuition and fees vary according to course level and program. *Financial support:* Application deadline: 2/1. *Unit head:* Dr. Shouzhong Zou, Chair, 202-885-1763, E-mail: szou@american.edu. *Application contact:* Kathleen Clowery, Associate Director, Graduate Admissions, 202-885-3620, Fax: 202-885-1344, E-mail: clowery@american.edu.
Website: http://www.american.edu/cas/chemistry/

The American University in Cairo, School of Sciences and Engineering, Department of Chemistry, Cairo, Egypt. Offers food chemistry (M Chem). *Degree requirements:* For master's, thesis. *Entrance requirements:* For master's, bachelor's degree in chemistry or related discipline with minimum GPA of 3.0. *Expenses: Tuition, area resident:* Full-time $20,412; part-time $13,608. *Required fees:* $598; $598. Tuition and fees vary according to course load and program. *Unit head:* Dr. Tamer Shoeib, Chair, 20-2-2615-2926. *Application contact:* Wesley Clark, Director of North American Admissions and Financial Aid, 212-646-810-9433 Ext. 4547, E-mail: wclark@aucnyo.edu.
Website: http://www.aucegypt.edu/sse/chem/

American University of Beirut, Graduate Programs, Faculty of Arts and Sciences, Beirut, Lebanon. Offers anthropology (MA); Arab and Middle Eastern history (PhD); Arabic language and literature (MA, PhD); archaeology (MA); biology (MS); cell and molecular biology (PhD); chemistry (MS); clinical psychology (MA); computational sciences (MS); computer science (MS); economics (MA); English language (MA); English literature (MA); environmental policy planning (MS); financial economics (MAFE); geology (MS); history (MA); mathematics (MA, MS); media studies (MA); Middle Eastern studies (MA); physics (MS); political studies (MA); psychology (MA); public administration (MA); sociology (MA); statistics (MA, MS); theoretical physics (PhD); transnational American studies (MA). *Program availability:* Part-time. *Faculty:* 114 full-time (36 women), 4 part-time/adjunct (2 women). *Students:* 258 full-time (190 women), 207 part-time (142 women). Average age 27. 241 applicants, 71% accepted, 98 enrolled. In 2015, 47 master's, 3 doctorates awarded. *Degree requirements:* For master's, one foreign language, comprehensive exam, thesis (for some programs); for doctorate, one foreign language, comprehensive exam, thesis/dissertation. *Entrance requirements:* For master's, GRE (for some MA, MS programs), letter of recommendation; for doctorate, GRE, letters of recommendation. Additional exam requirements/recommendations for international students: Required—TOEFL (minimum score 600 paper-based; 97 iBT), IELTS (minimum score 7). *Application deadline:* For fall admission, 4/1 for domestic and international students; for spring admission, 11/1 for domestic and international students. Application fee: $50. Electronic applications accepted. *Expenses: Tuition, area resident:* Full-time $16,254; part-time $903 per credit. *Required fees:* $699. Tuition and fees vary according to course load and program. *Financial support:* Research assistantships, career-related internships or fieldwork, institutionally sponsored loans, scholarships/grants, health care benefits, and unspecified assistantships available. Financial award application deadline: 2/4; financial award applicants required to submit FAFSA. *Faculty research:* Analysis and algebra; software engineering; machine learning and big data analysis; philosophy of mind and political philosophy; anthropology of art, anthropology of migration and medical anthropology; sociology of knowledge, sociology of migration, critical theory; sociology of education; hybrid solid materials; photocatalysis; human creativity. *Total annual research expenditures:* $680,360. *Unit head:* Dr. Patrick McGreevy, Dean, 961-1374374 Ext. 3800, Fax: 961-1744461, E-mail: pm07@aub.edu.lb. *Application contact:* Dr. Salim Kanaan, Director, Admissions Office, 961-1350000 Ext. 2590, Fax: 961-1750775, E-mail: sk00@aub.edu.lb.
Website: http://www.aub.edu.lb/fas/

Arizona State University at the Tempe campus, College of Liberal Arts and Sciences, Department of Chemistry and Biochemistry, Tempe, AZ 85287-1604. Offers biochemistry (MS, PhD); chemistry (MS, PhD); nanoscience (PSM). Terminal master's awarded for partial completion of doctoral program. *Degree requirements:* For master's, thesis, interactive Program of Study (iPOS) submitted before completing 50 percent of required credit hours; for doctorate, comprehensive exam, thesis/dissertation, interactive Program of Study (iPOS) submitted before completing 50 percent of required credit hours. *Entrance requirements:* For master's and doctorate, GRE, minimum GPA of 3.0 or equivalent in last 2 years of work leading to bachelor's degree. Additional exam requirements/recommendations for international students: Required—TOEFL, IELTS, or PTE. Electronic applications accepted.

Arkansas State University, Graduate School, College of Sciences and Mathematics, Department of Chemistry and Physics, State University, AR 72467. Offers chemistry (MS); chemistry education (MSE, SCCT). *Program availability:* Part-time. *Faculty:* 12 full-time (1 woman). *Students:* 4 full-time (3 women), 5 part-time (3 women), 4 international. Average age 29. 26 applicants, 31% accepted, 4 enrolled. In 2015, 4 master's awarded. *Degree requirements:* For master's, comprehensive exam, thesis or alternative; for SCCT, comprehensive exam. *Entrance requirements:* For master's, GRE General Test or MAT, appropriate bachelor's degree, official transcript, immunization records, valid teaching certificate (for MSE); for SCCT, GRE General Test or MAT, interview, master's degree, official transcript, immunization records. Additional exam requirements/recommendations for international students: Required—TOEFL (minimum score 550 paper-based; 79 iBT), IELTS (minimum score 6), PTE (minimum score 56). *Application deadline:* For fall admission, 7/1 for domestic and international students; for spring admission, 11/15 for domestic students, 11/14 for international students. Applications are processed on a rolling basis. Application fee: $30 ($40 for international students). Electronic applications accepted. *Expenses:* Tuition, state resident: full-time $4572; part-time $254 per credit hour. Tuition, nonresident: full-time $9144; part-time $508 per credit hour. *International tuition:* $9844 full-time. *Required fees:* $1188; $66 per credit hour. $25 per term. Tuition and fees vary according to course load and program. *Financial support:* In 2015–16, 2 students received support. Teaching assistantships, career-related internships or fieldwork, scholarships/grants, and unspecified assistantships available. Financial award application deadline: 7/1; financial award applicants required to submit FAFSA. *Unit head:* Dr. William Burns, Chair, 870-972-3086, Fax: 870-972-3089, E-mail: wburns@astate.edu. *Application contact:* Vickey Ring, Graduate Admissions Coordinator, 870-972-2737, Fax: 870-972-3917, E-mail: vickeyring@astate.edu.
Website: http://www.astate.edu/college/sciences-and-mathematics/departments/chemistry-physics/

Auburn University, Graduate School, College of Sciences and Mathematics, Department of Chemistry and Biochemistry, Auburn University, AL 36849. Offers analytical chemistry (MS, PhD); biochemistry (MS, PhD); inorganic chemistry (MS, PhD); organic chemistry (MS, PhD); physical chemistry (MS, PhD). *Program availability:* Part-time. *Faculty:* 27 full-time (4 women), 2 part-time/adjunct (0 women). *Students:* 45 full-time (17 women), 26 part-time (15 women); includes 9 minority (7 Black or African American, non-Hispanic/Latino; 1 American Indian or Alaska Native, non-Hispanic/Latino; 1 Asian, non-Hispanic/Latino), 38 international. Average age 27. 33 applicants, 52% accepted, 16 enrolled. In 2015, 1 master's, 6 doctorates awarded. *Degree requirements:* For master's, thesis (for some programs); for doctorate, thesis/dissertation, oral and written exams. *Entrance requirements:* For master's and doctorate, GRE General Test. *Application deadline:* Applications are processed on a rolling basis. Application fee: $50 ($60 for international students). Electronic applications accepted. *Expenses:* Tuition, state resident: full-time $8802; part-time $489 per credit hour. Tuition, nonresident: full-time $26,406; part-time $1467 per credit hour. *Required fees:* $808 per semester. Tuition and fees vary according to degree level and program. *Financial support:* Fellowships, research assistantships, and teaching assistantships available. Financial award application deadline: 3/15; financial award applicants required to submit FAFSA. *Unit head:* Dr. Curtis Shannon, Chair, 334-844-4043, Fax: 334-844-4043. *Application contact:* Dr. George Flowers, Dean of the Graduate School, 334-844-2125.
Website: http://www.auburn.edu/cosam/departments/chemistry/

Ball State University, Graduate School, College of Sciences and Humanities, Department of Chemistry, Muncie, IN 47306. Offers chemistry (MA, MS). *Program availability:* Part-time. *Faculty:* 11 full-time (2 women). *Students:* 9 full-time (4 women), 10 part-time (4 women); includes 2 minority (both Asian, non-Hispanic/Latino), 7 international. Average age 26. 24 applicants, 54% accepted, 7 enrolled. In 2015, 6 master's awarded. *Entrance requirements:* For master's, minimum baccalaureate GPA of 2.75 or 3.0 in latter half of baccalauareate, two letters of reference, academic transcripts. Additional exam requirements/recommendations for international students: Required—TOEFL (minimum score 550 paper-based; 79 iBT), IELTS (minimum score 6.5). *Application deadline:* Applications are processed on a rolling basis. Application fee: $60. Electronic applications accepted. *Expenses: Tuition, area resident:* Full-time $6948; part-time $2316 per semester. Tuition, state resident: full-time $10,422; part-time $3474 per semester. Tuition, nonresident: full-time $19,062; part-time $6354 per semester. *Required fees:* $651 per semester. Tuition and fees vary according to campus/location, program and reciprocity agreements. *Financial support:* In 2015–16, 11 students received support, including 2 research assistantships with partial tuition reimbursements available (averaging $13,460 per year), 9 teaching assistantships with partial tuition reimbursements available (averaging $12,960 per year). Financial award application deadline: 3/1; financial award applicants required to submit FAFSA. *Faculty research:* Synthetic and analytical chemistry, biochemistry, theoretical chemistry. *Total annual research expenditures:* $124,927. *Unit head:* Dr. Robert Sammelson, Chairperson, 765-285-8060, Fax: 765-285-6505, E-mail: resammelson@bsu.edu. *Application contact:* Dr. Patricia Lang, Professor/Graduate Advisor, 765-285-5516, Fax: 765-285-6505, E-mail: plang@bsu.edu.
Website: http://www.bsu.edu/chemistry

Ball State University, Graduate School, College of Sciences and Humanities, Interdepartmental Program in Environmental Sciences, Muncie, IN 47306. Offers

environmental science (PhD), including biology, chemistry, geology. *Program availability:* Part-time. *Students:* 3 full-time (0 women), 9 part-time (3 women), 4 international. Average age 31. 4 applicants, 25% accepted, 1 enrolled. In 2015, 2 doctorates awarded. *Degree requirements:* For doctorate, thesis/dissertation. *Entrance requirements:* For doctorate, GRE General Test, minimum cumulative GPA of 3.0 (3.2 for biology and geology concentration), acknowledged arrangement for doctoral environmental sciences research with a faculty mentor (biology, chemistry, or geological sciences), three letters of recommendation. Additional exam requirements/recommendations for international students: Required—TOEFL (minimum score 550 paper-based; 79 iBT), IELTS (minimum score 6.5). *Application deadline:* Applications are processed on a rolling basis. Application fee: $60. Electronic applications accepted. *Expenses: Tuition, area resident:* Full-time $6948; part-time $2316 per semester. Tuition, state resident: full-time $10,422; part-time $3474 per semester. Tuition, nonresident: full-time $19,062; part-time $6354 per semester. *Required fees:* $651 per semester. Tuition and fees vary according to campus/location, program and reciprocity agreements. *Financial support:* In 2015–16, 9 students received support, including 5 research assistantships with partial tuition reimbursements available (averaging $13,866 per year), 4 teaching assistantships with partial tuition reimbursements available (averaging $15,142 per year). Financial award application deadline: 3/1; financial award applicants required to submit FAFSA. *Unit head:* Dr. E. Michael Perdue, Director, 765-285-8096, Fax: 765-285-6505, E-mail: emperdue@bsu.edu.
Website: http://cms.bsu.edu/Academics/CollegesandDepartments/EnvironmentalScience.aspx

Baylor University, Graduate School, College of Arts and Sciences, Department of Chemistry and Biochemistry, Waco, TX 76798. Offers chemistry (MS, PhD). *Faculty:* 18 full-time (2 women). *Students:* 56 full-time (18 women); includes 5 minority (1 Black or African American, non-Hispanic/Latino; 2 Asian, non-Hispanic/Latino; 2 Hispanic/Latino), 15 international. Average age 26. In 2015, 9 master's, 6 doctorates awarded. Terminal master's awarded for partial completion of doctoral program. *Degree requirements:* For master's, thesis or alternative; for doctorate, comprehensive exam, thesis/dissertation. *Entrance requirements:* For doctorate, GRE General Test, transcripts, 3 letters of recommendation, personal statement. Additional exam requirements/recommendations for international students: Required—TOEFL (minimum score 90 iBT). *Application deadline:* For fall admission, 3/1 for domestic and international students. Applications are processed on a rolling basis. Application fee: $50. Electronic applications accepted. *Financial support:* In 2015–16, 42 students received support. Fellowships, research assistantships, teaching assistantships, and tuition waivers (full) available. *Faculty research:* Total synthesis, proteomics, computational materials, medicinal and assay, bioorganic. *Unit head:* Dr. Charles Garner, Graduate Program Director, 254-710-6862, Fax: 254-710-2403,
E-mail: charles_garner@baylor.edu. *Application contact:* Nancy Kallas, Administrative Assistant, 254-710-6844, Fax: 254-710-2403, E-mail: nancy_kallas@baylor.edu.
Website: http://www.baylor.edu/chemistry/

Binghamton University, State University of New York, Graduate School, School of Arts and Sciences, Department of Chemistry, Vestal, NY 13850. Offers analytical chemistry (PhD); chemistry (MA, MS); environmental chemistry (PhD); inorganic chemistry (PhD); organic chemistry (PhD); physical chemistry (PhD). *Program availability:* Part-time. *Faculty:* 21 full-time (4 women). *Students:* 60 full-time (24 women), 1 part-time (0 women); includes 4 minority (2 Black or African American, non-Hispanic/Latino; 1 Asian, non-Hispanic/Latino; 1 Hispanic/Latino), 40 international. Average age 27. 53 applicants, 81% accepted, 16 enrolled. In 2015, 3 master's, 7 doctorates awarded. Terminal master's awarded for partial completion of doctoral program. *Degree requirements:* For master's, thesis; for doctorate, comprehensive exam, thesis/dissertation. *Entrance requirements:* For master's and doctorate, GRE General Test. Additional exam requirements/recommendations for international students: Required—TOEFL (minimum score 90 iBT). *Application deadline:* Applications are processed on a rolling basis. Application fee: $75. Electronic applications accepted. *Financial support:* In 2015–16, 53 students received support, including 8 research assistantships with full tuition reimbursements available (averaging $18,000 per year), 34 teaching assistantships with full tuition reimbursements available (averaging $18,000 per year); career-related internships or fieldwork, Federal Work-Study, institutionally sponsored loans, scholarships/grants, health care benefits, tuition waivers (full and partial), and unspecified assistantships also available. Financial award applicants required to submit FAFSA. *Unit head:* Dr. Wayne E. Jones, Chairperson, 607-777-2421, E-mail: wjones@binghamton.edu. *Application contact:* Kishan Zuber, Recruiting and Admissions Coordinator, 607-777-2151, Fax: 607-777-2501,
E-mail: kzuber@binghamton.edu.

Boise State University, College of Arts and Sciences, Department of Chemistry and Biochemistry, Boise, ID 83725-1520. Offers chemistry (MS). *Program availability:* Part-time. *Faculty:* 8. *Students:* 9 full-time (4 women), 4 part-time (2 women); includes 1 minority (Asian, non-Hispanic/Latino), 2 international. Average age 27. 14 applicants, 29% accepted, 4 enrolled. In 2015, 2 master's awarded. *Degree requirements:* For master's, thesis. *Entrance requirements:* For master's, GRE General Test, minimum GPA of 3.0 for all upper-division credits. Additional exam requirements/recommendations for international students: Required—TOEFL (minimum score 550 paper-based; 80 iBT), IELTS (minimum score 6). Application fee: $65 ($95 for international students). Electronic applications accepted. *Expenses:* Tuition, state resident: full-time $6058; part-time $358 per credit hour. Tuition, nonresident: full-time $20,108; part-time $608 per credit hour. *Required fees:* $2108. Tuition and fees vary according to program. *Financial support:* In 2015–16, 2 research assistantships (averaging $2,954 per year), 7 teaching assistantships (averaging $8,097 per year) were awarded; scholarships/grants and unspecified assistantships also available. Financial award applicants required to submit FAFSA. *Unit head:* Dr. Owen McDougal, Department Chair, 208-426-3964, E-mail: bbammel@boisestate.edu. *Application contact:* Dr. Don Warner, Graduate Program Coordinator, 208-426-3030,
E-mail: dwarner@boisestate.edu.
Website: http://chemistry.boisestate.edu/graduate/

Boston College, Graduate School of Arts and Sciences, Department of Chemistry, Chestnut Hill, MA 02467. Offers biochemistry (PhD); inorganic chemistry (PhD); organic chemistry (PhD); physical chemistry (PhD); science education (MST). *Faculty:* 21 full-time. *Students:* 121 full-time (57 women); includes 9 minority (6 Asian, non-Hispanic/Latino; 3 Hispanic/Latino), 53 international. 222 applicants, 50% accepted, 43 enrolled. In 2015, 2 master's, 11 doctorates awarded. *Degree requirements:* For doctorate, thesis/dissertation, qualifying exam. *Entrance requirements:* For doctorate, GRE General Test, GRE Subject Test. Additional exam requirements/recommendations for international students: Required—TOEFL (minimum score 600 paper-based; 100 iBT), IELTS (minimum score 8). *Application deadline:* For fall admission, 1/2 for domestic and international students. Application fee: $75. Electronic applications accepted. Tuition and fees vary according to program. *Financial support:* In 2015–16, 121 students received support, including fellowships with full tuition reimbursements available (averaging $30,000 per year), research assistantships with full tuition reimbursements available (averaging $30,000 per year), teaching assistantships with full tuition reimbursements available (averaging $30,000 per year); Federal Work-Study, scholarships/grants, health care benefits, and unspecified assistantships also available. Support available to part-time students. Financial award application deadline: 1/2. *Faculty research:* Organic and organometallic chemistry, chemical biology and biochemistry, physical and theoretical chemistry, inorganic chemistry. *Unit head:* Dr. Amir Hoveyda, Chairperson, 617-552-1735, E-mail: amir.hoveyda@bc.edu. *Application contact:* Dr. Jianmin Gao, Graduate Program Director, 617-552-0326, Fax: 617-552-0833, E-mail: gaojc@bc.edu.
Website: http://www.bc.edu/chemistry

Boston University, Graduate School of Arts and Sciences, Department of Chemistry, Boston, MA 02215. Offers MA, PhD. *Students:* 95 full-time (47 women); includes 18 minority (11 Asian, non-Hispanic/Latino; 5 Hispanic/Latino; 2 Two or more races, non-Hispanic/Latino), 30 international. Average age 26. 301 applicants, 23% accepted, 20 enrolled. In 2015, 14 master's, 7 doctorates awarded. Terminal master's awarded for partial completion of doctoral program. *Degree requirements:* For master's, one foreign language; for doctorate, one foreign language, comprehensive exam, thesis/dissertation. *Entrance requirements:* For master's and doctorate, GRE General Test, GRE Subject Test (recommended), 3 letters of recommendation, transcripts, personal statement. Additional exam requirements/recommendations for international students: Required—TOEFL (minimum score 550 paper-based; 84 iBT). *Application deadline:* For fall admission, 1/5 for domestic and international students. Application fee: $95. Electronic applications accepted. *Financial support:* In 2015–16, 96 students received support, including 1 fellowship with full tuition reimbursement available (averaging $21,000 per year), 36 research assistantships with full tuition reimbursements available (averaging $21,000 per year), 50 teaching assistantships with full tuition reimbursements available (averaging $21,000 per year); Federal Work-Study, scholarships/grants, health care benefits, and tuition waivers (full) also available. Support available to part-time students. Financial award application deadline: 1/5. *Unit head:* Lawrence Ziegler, Chair, 617-353-8663, Fax: 617-353-6466,
E-mail: lziegler@bu.edu. *Application contact:* Kaitlin Valli, Academic Administrator, 617-353-2503, Fax: 617-353-6466, E-mail: chemgaa@bu.edu.
Website: http://www.bu.edu/chemistry/

Bowling Green State University, Graduate College, College of Arts and Sciences, Center for Photochemical Sciences, Bowling Green, OH 43403. Offers PhD. *Degree requirements:* For doctorate, comprehensive exam, thesis/dissertation. *Entrance requirements:* For doctorate, GRE General Test. Additional exam requirements/recommendations for international students: Required—TOEFL. Electronic applications accepted. *Faculty research:* Laser-initiated photopolymerization, spectroscopic and kinetic studies, optoelectronics of semiconductor multiple quantum wells, electron transfer processes, carotenoid pigments.

Bowling Green State University, Graduate College, College of Arts and Sciences, Department of Chemistry, Bowling Green, OH 43403. Offers MAT, MS. *Program availability:* Part-time. *Degree requirements:* For master's, thesis or alternative. *Entrance requirements:* For master's, GRE General Test. Additional exam requirements/recommendations for international students: Required—TOEFL. Electronic applications accepted. *Faculty research:* Organic, inorganic, physical, and analytical chemistry; biochemistry; surface science.

Bradley University, Graduate School, College of Liberal Arts and Sciences, Department of Chemistry and Biochemistry, Peoria, IL 61625-0002. Offers chemistry (MS). *Program availability:* Part-time, evening/weekend. *Degree requirements:* For master's, comprehensive exam, thesis. *Entrance requirements:* Additional exam requirements/recommendations for international students: Required—TOEFL (minimum score 550 paper-based; 79 iBT), IELTS (minimum score 6.5). Electronic applications accepted.

Brandeis University, Graduate School of Arts and Sciences, Department of Chemistry, Waltham, MA 02454. Offers inorganic chemistry (MA, MS, PhD); organic chemistry (MA, MS, PhD); physical chemistry (MS, PhD). *Program availability:* Part-time. *Faculty:* 12 full-time (4 women), 1 part-time/adjunct (0 women). *Students:* 43 full-time (15 women); includes 2 minority (1 Black or African American, non-Hispanic/Latino; 1 Two or more races, non-Hispanic/Latino), 26 international. 102 applicants, 34% accepted, 7 enrolled. In 2015, 8 master's, 6 doctorates awarded. Terminal master's awarded for partial completion of doctoral program. *Degree requirements:* For master's, comprehensive exam, thesis (for some programs), 1 year of residency (for MA); 2 years of residency (for MS); for doctorate, comprehensive exam, thesis/dissertation, 3 years of residency, 2 seminars, qualifying exams. *Entrance requirements:* For master's and doctorate, GRE General Test, resume, statement of purpose, letters of recommendation. Additional exam requirements/recommendations for international students: Required—TOEFL (minimum score 600 paper-based; 100 iBT); Recommended—IELTS (minimum score 7), TSE (minimum score 68). *Application deadline:* For fall admission, 1/15 priority date for domestic students. Application fee: $75. Electronic applications accepted. *Financial support:* In 2015–16, 42 students received support, including 24 fellowships with full tuition reimbursements available (averaging $27,500 per year), 18 research assistantships with full tuition reimbursements available (averaging $27,500 per year); Federal Work-Study, scholarships/grants, health care benefits, tuition waivers (partial), and unspecified assistantships also available. Support available to part-time students. Financial award application deadline: 4/15; financial award applicants required to submit FAFSA. *Faculty research:* Inorganic and organic chemistry, physical chemistry, chemical biology, biophysical chemistry, materials chemistry. *Unit head:* Dr. Judith Herzfeld, Chair, Graduate Program, 781-736-2540, Fax: 781-736-2516,
E-mail: herzfeld@brandeis.edu. *Application contact:* Dr. Maryanna Aldrich, Coordinator, 781-736-2500, Fax: 781-736-2516, E-mail: scigradoffice@brandeis.edu.
Website: http://www.brandeis.edu/gsas

Brigham Young University, Graduate Studies, College of Physical and Mathematical Sciences, Department of Chemistry and Biochemistry, Provo, UT 84602. Offers biochemistry (MS, PhD); chemistry (MS, PhD). *Faculty:* 30 full-time (1 woman). *Students:* 92 full-time (32 women); includes 5 minority (2 Asian, non-Hispanic/Latino; 2 Hispanic/Latino; 1 Native Hawaiian or other Pacific Islander, non-Hispanic/Latino), 47 international. Average age 28. 52 applicants, 50% accepted, 17 enrolled. In 2015, 1 master's, 14 doctorates awarded. *Degree requirements:* For master's, thesis; for doctorate, comprehensive exam, thesis/dissertation, qualifying exam. *Entrance requirements:* For master's and doctorate, GRE General Test, minimum GPA of 3.0. Additional exam requirements/recommendations for international students: Required—TOEFL (minimum score 580 paper-based; 85 iBT), IELTS (minimum score 7); Recommended—TWE. *Application deadline:* For fall admission, 2/1 priority date for domestic and international students. Applications are processed on a rolling basis. Application fee: $50. Electronic applications accepted. *Financial support:* In 2015–16, 90 students received support, including 13 fellowships with full tuition reimbursements available (averaging $21,250 per year), 39 research assistantships with full tuition reimbursements available (averaging $21,250 per year), 38 teaching assistantships with full tuition reimbursements available (averaging $21,250 per year); institutionally sponsored loans, scholarships/grants, health care benefits, unspecified assistantships,

and supplementary awards also available. Financial award application deadline: 2/1. *Faculty research:* Separation science, molecular recognition, organic synthesis and biomedical application, biochemistry and molecular biology, molecular spectroscopy. *Total annual research expenditures:* $2.2 million. *Unit head:* Dr. Gregory F. Burton, Chair, 801-422-4917, Fax: 801-422-0153, E-mail: gburton@byu.edu. *Application contact:* Dr. Paul B. Farnsworth, Graduate Coordinator, 801-422-6502, Fax: 801-422-0153, E-mail: pbfarnsw@byu.edu.
Website: http://www.chem.byu.edu/

Brock University, Faculty of Graduate Studies, Faculty of Mathematics and Science, Program in Chemistry, St. Catharines, ON L2S 3A1, Canada. Offers M Sc, PhD. *Program availability:* Part-time. *Degree requirements:* For master's, thesis; for doctorate, thesis/dissertation. *Entrance requirements:* For master's, honors B Sc in chemistry; for doctorate, M Sc. Additional exam requirements/recommendations for international students: Required—TOEFL (minimum score 550 paper-based; 80 iBT), IELTS (minimum score 6.5), TWE (minimum score 4). Electronic applications accepted. *Faculty research:* Bioorganic chemistry, trace element analysis, organic synthesis, electrochemistry, structural inorganic chemistry.

Brooklyn College of the City University of New York, School of Education, Program in Middle Childhood Science Education, Brooklyn, NY 11210-2889. Offers biology (MA); chemistry (MA); earth science (MA); general science (MA); physics (MA). *Program availability:* Part-time, evening/weekend. *Entrance requirements:* For master's, LAST, interview, previous course work in education and mathematics, resume, 2 letters of recommendation, essay. Additional exam requirements/recommendations for international students: Required—TOEFL (minimum score 500 paper-based; 61 iBT). Electronic applications accepted. *Faculty research:* Geometric thinking, mastery of basic facts, problem-solving strategies, history of mathematics.

Brooklyn College of the City University of New York, School of Natural and Behavioral Sciences, Department of Chemistry, Brooklyn, NY 11210-2889. Offers MA, MS, PhD. *Program availability:* Part-time. *Degree requirements:* For master's, one foreign language, thesis or alternative, 30 credits. *Entrance requirements:* For master's, 2 letters of recommendation. Additional exam requirements/recommendations for international students: Required—TOEFL (minimum score 500 paper-based; 61 iBT). Electronic applications accepted.

Brown University, Graduate School, Department of Chemistry, Providence, RI 02912. Offers PhD. *Degree requirements:* For doctorate, one foreign language, thesis/dissertation, cumulative exam. *Application deadline:* For fall admission, 1/2 priority date for domestic students. Applications are processed on a rolling basis. Application fee: $60. *Financial support:* Fellowships, research assistantships, teaching assistantships, institutionally sponsored loans, tuition waivers (full and partial), and unspecified assistantships available. Financial award application deadline: 1/2. *Unit head:* Matthew Zimmt, Chairman, 401-863-2909. *Application contact:* Admission Office, 401-863-2600.

Bryn Mawr College, Graduate School of Arts and Sciences, Department of Chemistry, Bryn Mawr, PA 19010-2899. Offers MA, PhD. *Faculty:* 10 full-time (6 women), 1 part-time/adjunct (0 women). *Students:* 4 full-time (1 woman), 5 part-time (4 women); includes 1 minority (Two or more races, non-Hispanic/Latino). Average age 31. 13 applicants, 54% accepted, 1 enrolled. In 2015, 2 master's, 1 doctorate awarded. *Degree requirements:* For master's, one foreign language, thesis; for doctorate, 2 foreign languages, comprehensive exam, thesis/dissertation. *Entrance requirements:* For master's and doctorate, GRE General Test, GRE Subject Test, transcripts, three letters of recommendation, statement of interest, resume or curriculum vitae. Additional exam requirements/recommendations for international students: Required—TOEFL (minimum score 600 paper-based, 100 iBT) or IELTS (7.0). *Application deadline:* For fall admission, 1/4 for domestic and international students. Application fee: $50. *Expenses: Tuition, area resident:* Full-time $39,240; part-time $6540 per unit. *Financial support:* In 2015–16, 10 students received support, including 1 fellowship with full tuition reimbursement available (averaging $18,500 per year), 1 research assistantship with full tuition reimbursement available (averaging $18,500 per year), 6 teaching assistantships with full tuition reimbursements available (averaging $16,958 per year); Federal Work-Study, scholarships/grants, and tuition waivers (partial) also available. Support available to part-time students. Financial award application deadline: 1/3. *Unit head:* Maria Dantis, Graduate Program Administrator, 610-526-5074, E-mail: gsas@brynmawr.edu.

Bucknell University, Graduate Studies, College of Arts and Sciences, Department of Chemistry, Lewisburg, PA 17837. Offers MA, MS. *Degree requirements:* For master's, thesis. *Entrance requirements:* For master's, GRE General Test, GRE Subject Test, minimum GPA of 3.0. Additional exam requirements/recommendations for international students: Required—TOEFL (minimum score 600 paper-based).

Buffalo State College, State University of New York, The Graduate School, Faculty of Natural and Social Sciences, Department of Chemistry, Buffalo, NY 14222-1095. Offers chemistry (MA); secondary education (MS Ed), including chemistry. *Program availability:* Part-time, evening/weekend. *Degree requirements:* For master's, thesis (for some programs), project. *Entrance requirements:* For master's, minimum GPA of 2.6, New York teaching certificate (MS Ed). Additional exam requirements/recommendations for international students: Required—TOEFL (minimum score 550 paper-based).

California Institute of Technology, Division of Chemistry and Chemical Engineering, Program in Chemistry, Pasadena, CA 91125-0001. Offers MS, PhD. *Faculty:* 44 full-time (8 women). *Students:* 197 full-time (77 women); includes 52 minority (32 Asian, non-Hispanic/Latino; 13 Hispanic/Latino; 7 Two or more races, non-Hispanic/Latino), 35 international. Average age 25. 396 applicants, 29% accepted, 38 enrolled. In 2015, 5 master's, 33 doctorates awarded. Terminal master's awarded for partial completion of doctoral program. *Degree requirements:* For master's, thesis; for doctorate, thesis/dissertation. *Entrance requirements:* Additional exam requirements/recommendations for international students: Required—TOEFL; Recommended—IELTS, TWE. *Application deadline:* For fall admission, 12/15 for domestic students, 1/1 for international students. Application fee: $100. Electronic applications accepted. *Financial support:* Fellowships, research assistantships, teaching assistantships, Federal Work-Study, institutionally sponsored loans, scholarships/grants, traineeships, health care benefits, and unspecified assistantships available. Financial award application deadline: 1/1. *Faculty research:* Biochemistry and molecular biophysics, inorganic and electrochemistry, organic chemistry, physical chemistry both experimental and theoretical. *Unit head:* Prof. Jacqueline K. Barton, Chair, Chemistry and Chemical Engineering, 626-395-3646, Fax: 626-568-8824, E-mail: jkbarton@caltech.edu. *Application contact:* Agnes Tong, Graduate Program Administrator, 626-395-6110, E-mail: agnest@caltech.edu.
Website: http://chemistry.caltech.edu/

California Polytechnic State University, San Luis Obispo, College of Science and Mathematics, Department of Chemistry and Biochemistry, San Luis Obispo, CA 93407. Offers polymers and coating science (MS). *Program availability:* Part-time. *Faculty:* 3 full-time (0 women). *Students:* 8 full-time (4 women), 8 part-time (4 women); includes 4 minority (3 Asian, non-Hispanic/Latino; 1 Hispanic/Latino), 2 international. Average age 24. 14 applicants, 50% accepted, 5 enrolled. In 2015, 3 master's awarded. *Degree requirements:* For master's, comprehensive exam (for some programs), thesis (for some programs). *Application deadline:* For fall admission, 4/1 for domestic and international students; for winter admission, 11/1 for domestic students, 6/30 for international students; for spring admission, 2/1 for domestic students. Applications are processed on a rolling basis. Application fee: $55. Electronic applications accepted. *Expenses:* Tuition, state resident: full-time $6738; part-time $3906 per year. Tuition, nonresident: full-time $15,666; part-time $8370 per year. *Required fees:* $3528; $3075 per unit. $1025 per term. *Financial support:* Fellowships, research assistantships, career-related internships or fieldwork, Federal Work-Study, and scholarships/grants available. Support available to part-time students. Financial award application deadline: 3/2; financial award applicants required to submit FAFSA. *Faculty research:* Polymer physical chemistry and analysis, polymer synthesis, coatings formulation.
Website: http://www.chemistry.calpoly.edu/

California State Polytechnic University, Pomona, Program in Chemistry, Pomona, CA 91768-2557. Offers MS. *Program availability:* Part-time. *Students:* 4 full-time (2 women), 17 part-time (6 women); includes 7 minority (4 Asian, non-Hispanic/Latino; 3 Hispanic/Latino), 7 international. Average age 25. 36 applicants, 42% accepted, 6 enrolled. In 2015, 3 master's awarded. *Degree requirements:* For master's, thesis. *Entrance requirements:* For master's, GRE General Test. *Application deadline:* For fall admission, 5/1 priority date for domestic students; for winter admission, 10/15 priority date for domestic students; for spring admission, 1/20 priority date for domestic students. Applications are processed on a rolling basis. Application fee: $55. Electronic applications accepted. *Expenses:* Tuition, state resident: full-time $6738. Tuition, nonresident: full-time $13,434. *Required fees:* $1504. Tuition and fees vary according to course load, degree level and program. *Financial support:* In 2015–16, 2 students received support. Career-related internships or fieldwork, Federal Work-Study, and institutionally sponsored loans available. Support available to part-time students. Financial award application deadline: 3/2; financial award applicants required to submit FAFSA. *Unit head:* Dr. Timothy C. Corcoran, Graduate Coordinator, 909-869-3672, Fax: 909-869-4344, E-mail: tccorcoran@cpp.edu.
Website: http://www.cpp.edu/~sci/chemistry-biochemistry/graduate-students/

California State University, East Bay, Office of Graduate Studies Programs, College of Science, Department of Chemistry and Biochemistry, Hayward, CA 94542-3000. Offers chemistry (MS), including biochemistry, chemistry. *Students:* 11 full-time (7 women), 21 part-time (11 women); includes 19 minority (1 Black or African American, non-Hispanic/Latino; 15 Asian, non-Hispanic/Latino; 3 Hispanic/Latino), 5 international. Average age 30. 44 applicants, 52% accepted, 8 enrolled. In 2015, 12 master's awarded. *Degree requirements:* For master's, comprehensive exam or thesis. *Entrance requirements:* For master's, minimum GPA of 2.6 in field during previous 2 years of course work. Additional exam requirements/recommendations for international students: Required—TOEFL (minimum score 550 paper-based). *Application deadline:* For fall admission, 6/30 for domestic and international students. Application fee: $55. Electronic applications accepted. *Financial support:* Fellowships, career-related internships or fieldwork, Federal Work-Study, institutionally sponsored loans, and scholarships/grants available. Support available to part-time students. Financial award application deadline: 3/2; financial award applicants required to submit FAFSA. *Unit head:* Dr. Ann McPartland, Chair, 510-885-3452, Fax: 510-885-4675,
E-mail: ann.mcpartland@csueastbay.edu. *Application contact:* Prof. Chul Kim, Chemistry Graduate Advisor, 510-885-3490, Fax: 510-885-4675,
E-mail: chul.kim@csueastbay.edu.
Website: http://www20.csueastbay.edu/csci/departments/chemistry

California State University, Fresno, Division of Graduate Studies, College of Science and Mathematics, Department of Chemistry, Fresno, CA 93740-8027. Offers MS. *Program availability:* Part-time. *Degree requirements:* For master's, thesis or alternative. *Entrance requirements:* For master's, GRE General Test, minimum GPA of 2.5. Additional exam requirements/recommendations for international students: Required—TOEFL. Electronic applications accepted. *Faculty research:* Genetics, viticulture, DNA, soils, molecular modeling, analysis of quinone.

California State University, Fullerton, Graduate Studies, College of Natural Science and Mathematics, Department of Chemistry and Biochemistry, Fullerton, CA 92834-9480. Offers chemistry (MA, MS); geochemistry (MS). *Program availability:* Part-time. *Degree requirements:* For master's, thesis, departmental qualifying exam. *Entrance requirements:* For master's, minimum GPA of 2.5 in last 60 units of course work, major in chemistry or related field.

California State University, Long Beach, Graduate Studies, College of Natural Sciences and Mathematics, Department of Chemistry and Biochemistry, Long Beach, CA 90840. Offers biochemistry (MS); chemistry (MS). *Program availability:* Part-time. *Degree requirements:* For master's, thesis, departmental qualifying exam. Electronic applications accepted. *Faculty research:* Enzymology, organic synthesis, molecular modeling, environmental chemistry, reaction kinetics.

California State University, Los Angeles, Graduate Studies, College of Natural and Social Sciences, Department of Chemistry and Biochemistry, Los Angeles, CA 90032-8530. Offers analytical chemistry (MS); biochemistry (MS); chemistry (MS); inorganic chemistry (MS); organic chemistry (MS); physical chemistry (MS). *Program availability:* Part-time, evening/weekend. *Degree requirements:* For master's, one foreign language, comprehensive exam or thesis. *Entrance requirements:* Additional exam requirements/recommendations for international students: Required—TOEFL. *Faculty research:* Intercalation of heavy metal, carborane chemistry, conductive polymers and fabrics, titanium reagents, computer modeling and synthesis.

California State University, Northridge, Graduate Studies, College of Science and Mathematics, Department of Chemistry and Biochemistry, Northridge, CA 91330. Offers biochemistry (MS); chemistry (MS), including chemistry, environmental chemistry. *Faculty:* 14 full-time (4 women), 30 part-time/adjunct (10 women). *Students:* 2 full-time (1 woman), 30 part-time (12 women); includes 15 minority (1 Black or African American, non-Hispanic/Latino; 7 Asian, non-Hispanic/Latino; 7 Hispanic/Latino), 3 international. Average age 26. 69 applicants, 23% accepted, 8 enrolled. *Degree requirements:* For master's, thesis. *Entrance requirements:* For master's, GRE General Test or minimum GPA of 3.0. Additional exam requirements/recommendations for international students: Required—TOEFL. *Application deadline:* For fall admission, 11/30 for domestic students. Application fee: $55. Electronic applications accepted. *Financial support:* Teaching assistantships available. Support available to part-time students. Financial award application deadline: 3/1. *Unit head:* Eric Kelson, Chair, 818-677-3381.
Website: http://www.csun.edu/chemistry/

California State University, Sacramento, Office of Graduate Studies, College of Natural Sciences and Mathematics, Department of Chemistry, Sacramento, CA 95819. Offers MS. *Program availability:* Part-time. *Degree requirements:* For master's, thesis or project; qualifying exam; writing proficiency exam. *Entrance requirements:* For master's, minimum GPA of 2.5 during previous 2 years of course work, BA in chemistry or equivalent. Additional exam requirements/recommendations for international students: Required—TOEFL. Electronic applications accepted.

Carleton University, Faculty of Graduate Studies, Faculty of Science, Department of Chemistry, Ottawa, ON K1S 5B6, Canada. Offers M Sc, PhD. Programs offered jointly with University of Ottawa. *Degree requirements:* For master's, thesis; for doctorate, comprehensive exam, thesis/dissertation. *Entrance requirements:* For master's, honors degree; for doctorate, M Sc. Additional exam requirements/recommendations for international students: Required—TOEFL. *Faculty research:* Bioorganic chemistry, analytical toxicology, theoretical and physical chemistry, inorganic chemistry.

Carnegie Mellon University, Mellon College of Science, Department of Chemistry, Pittsburgh, PA 15213-3891. Offers atmospheric chemistry (PhD); bioinorganic chemistry (PhD); bioorganic chemistry and chemical biology (PhD); biophysical chemistry (PhD); catalysis (PhD); green and environmental chemistry (PhD); materials and nanoscience (PhD); renewable energy (PhD); sensors, probes, and imaging (PhD); spectroscopy and single molecule analysis (PhD); theoretical and computational chemistry (PhD). *Program availability:* Part-time. Terminal master's awarded for partial completion of doctoral program. *Degree requirements:* For doctorate, thesis/dissertation, departmental qualifying and oral exams, teaching experience. *Entrance requirements:* For doctorate, GRE General Test, GRE Subject Test. Additional exam requirements/recommendations for international students: Required—TOEFL. Electronic applications accepted. *Faculty research:* Physical and theoretical chemistry, chemical synthesis, biophysical/bioinorganic chemistry.

Case Western Reserve University, School of Graduate Studies, Department of Chemistry, Cleveland, OH 44106. Offers MS, PhD. *Program availability:* Part-time. *Faculty:* 21 full-time (6 women), 3 part-time/adjunct (1 woman). *Students:* 84 full-time (33 women), 1 (woman) part-time; includes 11 minority (3 Black or African American, non-Hispanic/Latino; 3 Asian, non-Hispanic/Latino; 5 Hispanic/Latino), 34 international. Average age 26. 153 applicants, 29% accepted, 16 enrolled. In 2015, 14 master's, 12 doctorates awarded. Terminal master's awarded for partial completion of doctoral program. *Degree requirements:* For master's, thesis optional; for doctorate, thesis/dissertation. *Entrance requirements:* For master's and doctorate, GRE General Test, GRE Subject Test. Additional exam requirements/recommendations for international students: Required—TOEFL (minimum score 577 paper-based; 90 iBT); Recommended—IELTS (minimum score 7). *Application deadline:* For fall admission, 3/1 priority date for domestic students. Applications are processed on a rolling basis. Application fee: $0. Electronic applications accepted. *Expenses: Tuition, area resident:* Full-time $41,137; part-time $1714 per credit hour. *Required fees:* $32. Tuition and fees vary according to course load and program. *Financial support:* Fellowships, research assistantships, teaching assistantships, and unspecified assistantships available. Financial award application deadline: 3/1. *Faculty research:* Electrochemistry, synthetic chemistry, chemistry of life process, spectroscopy, kinetics. *Unit head:* Prof. Mary Barkley, Chair, 216-368-0602, Fax: 216-368-3006, E-mail: mary.barkley@case.edu. *Application contact:* June Ilhan, Department Assistant, 216-368-5030, Fax: 216-368-3006, E-mail: june.ilhan@case.edu.
Website: http://chemistry.case.edu/

Central Michigan University, College of Graduate Studies, College of Science and Technology, Department of Chemistry, Mount Pleasant, MI 48859. Offers chemistry (MS); teaching chemistry (MA), including teaching college chemistry, teaching high school chemistry. *Program availability:* Part-time. *Degree requirements:* For master's, comprehensive exam, thesis or alternative. *Entrance requirements:* For master's, GRE. Electronic applications accepted. *Faculty research:* Analytical and organic-inorganic chemistry, biochemistry, catalysis, dendrimer and polymer studies, nanotechnology.

Central Washington University, Graduate Studies and Research, College of the Sciences, Department of Chemistry, Ellensburg, WA 98926. Offers MS. *Program availability:* Part-time. *Degree requirements:* For master's, thesis. *Entrance requirements:* For master's, GRE General Test, minimum GPA of 3.0. Additional exam requirements/recommendations for international students: Required—TOEFL (minimum score 550 paper-based; 79 iBT), IELTS (minimum score 6.5). Electronic applications accepted.

City College of the City University of New York, Graduate School, Division of Science, Department of Chemistry, Program in Chemistry, New York, NY 10031-9198. Offers MS, PhD. PhD program offered jointly with Graduate School and University Center of the City University of New York. Terminal master's awarded for partial completion of doctoral program. *Degree requirements:* For doctorate, one foreign language, thesis/dissertation. *Entrance requirements:* For master's and doctorate, GRE. Additional exam requirements/recommendations for international students: Required—TOEFL (minimum score 500 paper-based). *Application deadline:* For fall admission, 5/1 for domestic students; for spring admission, 11/1 for domestic students. Application fee: $125. Tuition and fees vary according to course load, degree level and program. *Financial support:* Federal Work-Study available. Financial award application deadline: 6/1. *Faculty research:* Laser spectroscopy, bioorganic chemistry, polymer chemistry and crystallography, electroanalytical chemistry, ESR of metal clusters. *Unit head:* Dr. Daniel L. Akins, Chair, 212-650-8402, Fax: 212-650-6107.

Clark Atlanta University, School of Arts and Sciences, Department of Chemistry, Atlanta, GA 30314. Offers MS, PhD. *Program availability:* Part-time. *Faculty:* 9 full-time (0 women). *Students:* 27 full-time (16 women), 13 part-time (8 women); includes 17 minority (15 Black or African American, non-Hispanic/Latino; 1 Asian, non-Hispanic/Latino; 1 Hispanic/Latino), 20 international. Average age 30. 24 applicants, 42% accepted, 4 enrolled. In 2015, 1 master's, 1 doctorate awarded. *Degree requirements:* For master's, one foreign language, thesis; for doctorate, 2 foreign languages, thesis/dissertation. *Entrance requirements:* For master's, GRE General Test, minimum GPA of 2.5; for doctorate, GRE General Test, GRE Subject Test, minimum graduate GPA of 3.0. Additional exam requirements/recommendations for international students: Required—TOEFL (minimum score 500 paper-based; 61 iBT). *Application deadline:* For fall admission, 4/1 for domestic and international students; for spring admission, 11/1 for domestic and international students. Applications are processed on a rolling basis. Application fee: $40 ($55 for international students). *Expenses: Tuition, area resident:* Full-time $15,498; part-time $861 per credit hour. *Required fees:* $1006; $1006 per unit. Tuition and fees vary according to course load. *Financial support:* Fellowships, research assistantships, teaching assistantships, career-related internships or fieldwork, Federal Work-Study, scholarships/grants, traineeships, and unspecified assistantships available. Support available to part-time students. Financial award application deadline: 4/30; financial award applicants required to submit FAFSA. *Unit head:* Dr. Eric Mintz, Interim Chairperson, 404-880-6886, E-mail: emintz@cau.edu. *Application contact:* Graduate Program Admissions, 404-880-8483, E-mail: graduateadmissions@cau.edu.

Clarkson University, Graduate School, School of Arts and Sciences, Department of Chemistry and Biomolecular Science, Potsdam, NY 13699. Offers chemistry (MS, PhD). *Program availability:* Part-time. *Faculty:* 21 full-time (8 women), 4 part-time/adjunct (1 woman). *Students:* 27 full-time (14 women); includes 1 minority (Asian, non-Hispanic/Latino), 17 international. Average age 28. 20 applicants, 50% accepted, 2 enrolled. In 2015, 3 master's, 5 doctorates awarded. *Degree requirements:* For doctorate, comprehensive exam, thesis/dissertation, departmental qualifying exam. *Entrance requirements:* For master's and doctorate, GRE, transcripts of all college coursework, resume, personal statement, three letters of recommendation. Additional exam requirements/recommendations for international students: Required—TOEFL or IELTS. *Application deadline:* For fall admission, 1/30 priority date for domestic and international students; for spring admission, 9/1 priority date for domestic and international students. Applications are processed on a rolling basis. Application fee: $25 ($35 for international students). Electronic applications accepted. *Financial support:* In 2015–16, 26 students received support, including 2 fellowships with full tuition reimbursements available (averaging $24,510 per year), 4 research assistantships with full tuition reimbursements available (averaging $24,510 per year), 19 teaching assistantships with full tuition reimbursements available (averaging $24,510 per year); scholarships/grants, tuition waivers (partial), and unspecified assistantships also available. *Faculty research:* Real-time monitoring of neurotransmitters, chemical catalysis, inorganic nanoparticles, engineered abrasives, bioelectrodes. *Total annual research expenditures:* $1.1 million. *Unit head:* Dr. Devon Shipp, Chair, 315-268-2393, Fax: 315-268-6610,
E-mail: dshipp@clarkson.edu. *Application contact:* Jennifer Reed, Graduate School Coordinator, Provost's Office, 315-268-3802, Fax: 315-268-3989,
E-mail: sciencegrad@clarkson.edu.
Website: http://www.clarkson.edu/biosci_chemistry/

Clark University, Graduate School, Gustav H. Carlson School of Chemistry, Worcester, MA 01610-1477. Offers biochemistry (MS, PhD); chemistry (MS, PhD). *Faculty:* 10 full-time (1 woman), 1 (woman) part-time/adjunct. *Students:* 17 full-time (6 women), 2 part-time (1 woman); includes 4 minority (2 Asian, non-Hispanic/Latino; 2 Hispanic/Latino), 9 international. Average age 27. 52 applicants, 23% accepted, 5 enrolled. In 2015, 5 master's awarded. Terminal master's awarded for partial completion of doctoral program. *Degree requirements:* For master's, thesis or alternative; for doctorate, one foreign language, thesis/dissertation. *Entrance requirements:* For master's and doctorate, GRE General Test. Additional exam requirements/recommendations for international students: Required—TOEFL. *Application deadline:* For fall admission, 1/15 priority date for domestic students. Applications are processed on a rolling basis. Application fee: $75. *Expenses: Tuition, area resident:* Full-time $41,590; part-time $1300 per credit hour. *Required fees:* $80. Tuition and fees vary according to course load and program. *Financial support:* In 2015–16, fellowships with tuition reimbursements (averaging $21,875 per year), 11 teaching assistantships with full tuition reimbursements (averaging $21,875 per year) were awarded; research assistantships with full tuition reimbursements and tuition waivers (full) also available. *Faculty research:* Nuclear chemistry, molecular biology simulation, NMR studies, biochemistry, protein folding mechanisms. *Total annual research expenditures:* $25,000. *Unit head:* Dr. Luis Smith, Chair, 508-793-7753. *Application contact:* Rene Baril, Managerial Secretary, 508-793-7130, Fax: 528-793-7117, E-mail: mbaril@clarku.edu.
Website: http://www.clarku.edu/departments/chemistry/graduate/index.cfm

Clemson University, Graduate School, College of Science, Department of Chemistry, Clemson, SC 29634. Offers MS, PhD. *Faculty:* 36 full-time (6 women), 1 part-time/adjunct (0 women). *Students:* 99 full-time (41 women), 6 part-time (3 women); includes 10 minority (3 Black or African American, non-Hispanic/Latino; 6 Asian, non-Hispanic/Latino; 1 Hispanic/Latino), 54 international. Average age 27. 111 applicants, 48% accepted, 22 enrolled. In 2015, 2 master's, 8 doctorates awarded. *Degree requirements:* For master's, thesis; for doctorate, comprehensive exam, thesis/dissertation. *Entrance requirements:* For master's and doctorate, GRE General Test, unofficial transcripts, letters of recommendation. Additional exam requirements/recommendations for international students: Required—TOEFL (minimum score 80 iBT), IELTS (minimum score 6.5). *Application deadline:* For fall admission, 12/31 priority date for domestic and international students. Applications are processed on a rolling basis. Application fee: $80 ($90 for international students). Electronic applications accepted. *Expenses:* $4,610 per semester full-time resident, $9,203 per semester full-time non-resident, $582 per credit hour part-time resident, $1,166 per credit hour part-time non-resident. *Financial support:* In 2015–16, 110 students received support, including 1 fellowship with partial tuition reimbursement available (averaging $5,000 per year), 30 research assistantships with partial tuition reimbursements available (averaging $22,133 per year), 79 teaching assistantships with partial tuition reimbursements available (averaging $21,962 per year); career-related internships or fieldwork, health care benefits, and unspecified assistantships also available. Financial award application deadline: 12/31. *Faculty research:* Fluorine chemistry, organic synthetic methods and natural products, metal and non-metal clusters, analytical spectroscopies, polymers. *Total annual research expenditures:* $2.3 million. *Unit head:* Dr. R. Karl Dieter, Department Chair, 864-656-5025, E-mail: dieterr@clemson.edu. *Application contact:* Dr. Bill Pennington, Graduate Program Coordinator, 864-656-4200, E-mail: billp@clemson.edu.
Website: http://www.clemson.edu/ces/departments/chemistry/

Cleveland State University, College of Graduate Studies, College of Sciences and Health Professions, Department of Chemistry, Cleveland, OH 44115. Offers analytical chemistry (MS); clinical/bioanalytical chemistry (PhD), including cellular and molecular medicine, clinical/bioanalytical chemistry; inorganic chemistry (MS); pharmaceutical/organic chemistry (MS); physical chemistry (MS). *Program availability:* Part-time, evening/weekend. *Faculty:* 17 full-time (3 women). *Students:* 63 full-time (30 women), 25 part-time (10 women); includes 4 minority (1 Black or African American, non-Hispanic/Latino; 1 Asian, non-Hispanic/Latino; 2 Hispanic/Latino), 48 international. Average age 30. 22 applicants, 64% accepted, 12 enrolled. In 2015, 16 master's, 8 doctorates awarded. *Degree requirements:* For master's, thesis optional; for doctorate, comprehensive exam, thesis/dissertation. *Entrance requirements:* For master's and doctorate, GRE General Test. Additional exam requirements/recommendations for international students: Required—TOEFL (minimum score 550 paper-based; 78 iBT). *Application deadline:* For fall admission, 1/15 priority date for domestic and international students. Applications are processed on a rolling basis. Application fee: $30. Electronic applications accepted. *Expenses:* Tuition, state resident: full-time $9565. Tuition, nonresident: full-time $17,980. Tuition and fees vary according to program. *Financial support:* In 2015–16, 44 students received support, including 10 fellowships with full tuition reimbursements available (averaging $22,500 per year), 6 research assistantships with full tuition reimbursements available (averaging $22,500 per year), 34 teaching assistantships with full tuition reimbursements available (averaging $21,000 per year); scholarships/grants and unspecified assistantships also available. Financial award application deadline: 1/15. *Faculty research:* Bioanalytical techniques and molecular diagnostics, glycoproteomics and antithrombotic agents, drug discovery and innovation, analytical pharmacology, inflammatory disease research. *Total annual research expenditures:* $3 million. *Unit head:* Dr. David W. Ball, Chair, 216-687-2467, Fax: 216-687-9298, E-mail: d.ball@csuohio.edu. *Application contact:* Richelle P. Emery, Administrative Coordinator, 216-687-2457, Fax: 216-687-9298,
E-mail: r.emery@csuohio.edu.
Website: http://www.csuohio.edu/sciences/chemistry

The College at Brockport, State University of New York, School of Education and Human Services, Department of Education and Human Development, Program in

Inclusive Generalist Education, Brockport, NY 14420-2997. Offers biology (MS Ed, AGC); chemistry (MS Ed, AGC); English (MS Ed, Advanced Certificate); mathematics (MS Ed, Advanced Certificate); science (MS Ed, Advanced Certificate); social studies (MS Ed, Advanced Certificate). *Students:* 27 full-time (16 women), 24 part-time (16 women); includes 13 minority (4 Black or African American, non-Hispanic/Latino; 3 Asian, non-Hispanic/Latino; 2 Hispanic/Latino; 4 Two or more races, non-Hispanic/Latino). 23 applicants, 57% accepted, 10 enrolled. In 2015, 13 master's, 1 AGC awarded. *Degree requirements:* For master's, thesis or alternative. *Entrance requirements:* For master's, minimum GPA of 3.0, letters of recommendation, statement of objectives, academic major (or equivalent) in program discipline, current resume. Additional exam requirements/recommendations for international students: Required—TOEFL (minimum score 550 paper-based; 79 iBT), IELTS (minimum score 6.5). *Application deadline:* For fall admission, 3/15 priority date for domestic and international students; for spring admission, 10/15 priority date for domestic and international students; for summer admission, 3/15 for domestic and international students. Application fee: $80. Electronic applications accepted. *Expenses:* $11,840 per academic year. *Financial support:* Federal Work-Study, scholarships/grants, and unspecified assistantships available. Support available to part-time students. Financial award application deadline: 3/15; financial award applicants required to submit FAFSA. *Unit head:* Dr. Sue Robb, Chairperson, 585-395-5935, Fax: 585-395-2171,
E-mail: awalton@brockport.edu. *Application contact:* Anne Walton, Coordinator of Certification and Graduate Advisement, 585-395-2326, Fax: 585-395-2172,
E-mail: awalton@brockport.edu.
Website: http://www.brockport.edu/ehd/

The College of William and Mary, Faculty of Arts and Sciences, Department of Chemistry, Williamsburg, VA 23187-8795. Offers MA, MS. *Program availability:* Part-time. *Faculty:* 17 full-time (5 women), 3 part-time/adjunct (0 women). *Students:* 5 full-time (2 women); includes 4 minority (1 Asian, non-Hispanic/Latino; 3 Hispanic/Latino), 1 international. Average age 23. 15 applicants, 40% accepted, 3 enrolled. In 2015, 8 master's awarded. *Degree requirements:* For master's, comprehensive exam, thesis (for some programs). *Entrance requirements:* For master's, GRE, minimum GPA of 2.75. Additional exam requirements/recommendations for international students: Required—TOEFL, IELTS. *Application deadline:* For fall admission, 2/15 priority date for domestic and international students; for spring admission, 9/15 priority date for domestic and international students. Applications are processed on a rolling basis. Application fee: $45. Electronic applications accepted. *Expenses:* Tuition, state resident: full-time $8009; part-time $450 per credit hour. Tuition, nonresident: full-time $23,752; part-time $1160 per credit hour. *Required fees:* $4162. One-time fee: $400 full-time. *Financial support:* In 2015–16, 8 fellowships (averaging $1,300 per year), 1 research assistantship with full tuition reimbursement (averaging $16,950 per year), 7 teaching assistantships with full tuition reimbursements (averaging $16,950 per year) were awarded; health care benefits and unspecified assistantships also available. Financial award application deadline: 2/15; financial award applicants required to submit FAFSA. *Faculty research:* Organic, physical, polymer and analytic chemistry; biochemistry. *Total annual research expenditures:* $580,941. *Unit head:* Dr. Chris Abelt, Chair, 757-221-2540, Fax: 757-221-2715, E-mail: cjabel@wm.edu. *Application contact:* Dr. Deborah C. Bebout, Graduate Director, 757-221-2558, Fax: 757-221-2715,
E-mail: dcbebo@wm.edu.
Website: http://www.wm.edu/as/chemistry

Colorado School of Mines, Office of Graduate Studies, Department of Chemistry and Geochemistry, Golden, CO 80401. Offers chemistry (MS, PhD), including applied chemistry (PhD), chemistry (MS); geochemistry (MS, PhD); materials science (MS, PhD); nuclear engineering (MS, PhD). *Program availability:* Part-time. *Faculty:* 40 full-time (12 women), 10 part-time/adjunct (3 women). *Students:* 57 full-time (22 women); includes 5 minority (1 American Indian or Alaska Native, non-Hispanic/Latino; 2 Hispanic/Latino; 2 Two or more races, non-Hispanic/Latino), 9 international. Average age 28. 76 applicants, 41% accepted, 12 enrolled. In 2015, 4 master's, 14 doctorates awarded. *Degree requirements:* For master's, thesis (for some programs); for doctorate, comprehensive exam, thesis/dissertation. *Entrance requirements:* For master's and doctorate, GRE General Test. Additional exam requirements/recommendations for international students: Required—TOEFL (minimum score 550 paper-based; 80 iBT). *Application deadline:* For fall admission, 12/15 priority date for domestic and international students; for spring admission, 9/1 priority date for domestic and international students. Application fee: $50 ($70 for international students). Electronic applications accepted. *Expenses:* Tuition, state resident: full-time $15,225. Tuition, nonresident: full-time $32,700. *Financial support:* In 2015–16, 52 students received support, including 3 fellowships with full tuition reimbursements available (averaging $21,120 per year), 27 research assistantships with full tuition reimbursements available (averaging $21,120 per year), 22 teaching assistantships with full tuition reimbursements available (averaging $21,120 per year); scholarships/grants, health care benefits, and unspecified assistantships also available. Financial award application deadline: 12/15; financial award applicants required to submit FAFSA. *Faculty research:* Environmental chemistry, exploration geochemistry, biogeochemistry, organic geochemistry, catalysis and surface chemistry. *Total annual research expenditures:* $2.5 million. *Unit head:* Dr. David Wu, Head, 303-384-2066, Fax: 303-273-3629,
E-mail: dwu@mines.edu. *Application contact:* Jeremiah Mashore, Program Coordinator, 303-273-3637, E-mail: jmashore@mines.edu.
Website: http://chemistry.mines.edu

Colorado State University, College of Natural Sciences, Department of Chemistry, Fort Collins, CO 80523-1872. Offers MS, PhD. *Faculty:* 40 full-time (11 women), 8 part-time/adjunct (1 woman). *Students:* 62 full-time (22 women), 94 part-time (42 women); includes 20 minority (7 Asian, non-Hispanic/Latino; 9 Hispanic/Latino; 4 Two or more races, non-Hispanic/Latino), 10 international. Average age 26. 35 applicants, 94% accepted, 32 enrolled. In 2015, 10 master's, 19 doctorates awarded. Terminal master's awarded for partial completion of doctoral program. *Degree requirements:* For master's, comprehensive exam, thesis (for some programs); for doctorate, comprehensive exam, thesis/dissertation. *Entrance requirements:* For master's and doctorate, GRE General Test, minimum GPA of 3.0, 3 letters of recommendation, transcripts. Additional exam requirements/recommendations for international students: Required—TOEFL (minimum score 550 paper-based; 80 iBT), IELTS (minimum score 6.5). *Application deadline:* For fall admission, 2/15 for domestic and international students; for spring admission, 9/15 for domestic and international students. Applications are processed on a rolling basis. Application fee: $60 ($70 for international students). Electronic applications accepted. *Expenses:* Tuition, state resident: full-time $9348. Tuition, nonresident: full-time $22,916. *Required fees:* $2174; $473.72 per credit hour. $236.86 per semester. Tuition and fees vary according to course load and program. *Financial support:* In 2015–16, 144 students received support, including 30 fellowships (averaging $34,860 per year), 73 research assistantships with full tuition reimbursements available (averaging $23,343 per year), 75 teaching assistantships with full tuition reimbursements available (averaging $23,840 per year); career-related internships or fieldwork, scholarships/grants, and unspecified assistantships also available. Financial award application deadline: 2/1. *Faculty research:* Atmospheric biogeochemistry and mass spectrometry; microscale bioanalytical and environmental chemistry; organic synthesis and catalysis; biomaterials and biomedical engineering; (magnetic) applications of coordination complexes. *Total annual research expenditures:* $7.8 million. *Unit head:* Dr. Chuck Henry, Department Chair and Professor, 970-491-6381, Fax: 970-491-1801,
E-mail: chuck.henry@colostate.edu. *Application contact:* Kathy Lucas, Graduate Resources Coordinator, 970-491-7966, Fax: 970-491-1801,
E-mail: kathy.lucas@colostate.edu.
Website: http://www.chem.colostate.edu/

Colorado State University–Pueblo, College of Science and Mathematics, Pueblo, CO 81001-4901. Offers applied natural science (MS), including biochemistry, biology, chemistry. *Program availability:* Part-time, evening/weekend. *Degree requirements:* For master's, comprehensive exam (for some programs), thesis (for some programs), internship report (if non-thesis). *Entrance requirements:* For master's, GRE General Test (minimum score 1000), 2 letters of reference, minimum GPA of 3.0. Additional exam requirements/recommendations for international students: Required—TOEFL (minimum score 500 paper-based), IELTS (minimum score 5). *Faculty research:* Fungal cell walls, molecular biology, bioactive materials synthesis, atomic force microscopy-surface chemistry, nanoscience.

Columbia University, Graduate School of Arts and Sciences, New York, NY 10027. Offers African-American studies (MA); American studies (MA); anthropology (MA, PhD); art history and archaeology (MA, PhD); astronomy (PhD); biological sciences (PhD); biotechnology (MA); chemical physics (PhD); chemistry (PhD); classical studies (MA, PhD); classics (MA, PhD); climate and society (MA); conservation biology (MA); earth and environmental sciences (PhD); East Asia: regional studies (MA); East Asian languages and cultures (MA, PhD); ecology, evolution and environmental biology (MA), including conservation biology; ecology, evolution, and environmental biology (PhD), including ecology and evolutionary biology, evolutionary primatology; economics (MA, PhD); English and comparative literature (MA, PhD); French and Romance philology (MA, PhD); Germanic languages (MA, PhD); global French studies (MA); global thought (MA); Hispanic cultural studies (MA); history (PhD); history and literature (MA); human rights studies (MA); Islamic studies (MA); Italian (MA, PhD); Japanese pedagogy (MA); Jewish studies (MA); Latin America and the Caribbean: regional studies (MA); Latin American and Iberian cultures (PhD); mathematics (MA, PhD), including finance (MA); medieval and Renaissance studies (MA); Middle Eastern, South Asian, and African studies (MA, PhD); modern art: critical and curatorial studies (MA); modern European studies (MA); museum anthropology (MA); music (DMA, PhD); oral history (MA); philosophical foundations of physics (MA); philosophy (MA, PhD); physics (PhD); political science (MA, PhD); psychology (PhD); quantitative methods in the social sciences (MA); religion (MA, PhD); Russia, Eurasia and East Europe: regional studies (MA); Russian translation (MA); Slavic cultures (MA); Slavic languages (MA, PhD); sociology (MA, PhD); South Asian studies (MA); statistics (MA, PhD); theatre (PhD). Dual-degree programs require admission to both Graduate School of Arts and Sciences and another Columbia school. *Program availability:* Part-time. *Students:* 3,030 full-time, 235 part-time; includes 861 minority (88 Black or African American, non-Hispanic/Latino; 5 American Indian or Alaska Native, non-Hispanic/Latino; 517 Asian, non-Hispanic/Latino; 159 Hispanic/Latino; 4 Native Hawaiian or other Pacific Islander, non-Hispanic/Latino; 88 Two or more races, non-Hispanic/Latino), 1,697 international. 13,288 applicants, 21% accepted, 1162 enrolled. In 2015, 1,061 master's, 553 doctorates awarded. Terminal master's awarded for partial completion of doctoral program. *Degree requirements:* For master's, variable foreign language requirement, comprehensive exam (for some programs), thesis (for some programs); for doctorate, variable foreign language requirement, comprehensive exam (for some programs), thesis/dissertation. *Entrance requirements:* For master's and doctorate, GRE General Test, GRE Subject Test (for some programs). Additional exam requirements/recommendations for international students: Required—TOEFL, IELTS. Application fee: $105. Electronic applications accepted. *Financial support:* Fellowships, research assistantships, teaching assistantships, career-related internships or fieldwork, Federal Work-Study, institutionally sponsored loans, scholarships/grants, traineeships, health care benefits, tuition waivers, and unspecified assistantships available. Support available to part-time students. Financial award application deadline: 12/15. *Unit head:* Carlos J. Alonso, Dean of the Graduate School of Arts and Sciences, 212-854-5177. *Application contact:* GSAS Office of Admissions, 212-854-8903, E-mail: gsas-admissions@columbia.edu.
Website: http://gsas.columbia.edu/

Columbus State University, Graduate Studies, College of Education and Health Professions, Department of Teacher Education, Columbus, GA 31907-5645. Offers curriculum and instruction in accomplished teaching (M Ed); early childhood education (M Ed, MAT, Ed S); middle grades education (M Ed, MAT, Ed S); secondary education (M Ed, MAT, Ed S), including biology (MAT), chemistry (MAT), earth and space science (MAT), English/language arts, general science (M Ed), history (MAT), mathematics, science (Ed S), social science (M Ed, Ed S); special education (M Ed, MAT, Ed S), including general curriculum (M Ed, MAT); teacher leadership (M Ed). *Accreditation:* NCATE. *Program availability:* Part-time, evening/weekend, 100% online, blended/hybrid learning. *Faculty:* 15 full-time (10 women), 26 part-time/adjunct (21 women). *Students:* 84 full-time (68 women), 199 part-time (153 women); includes 106 minority (96 Black or African American, non-Hispanic/Latino; 3 Asian, non-Hispanic/Latino; 5 Hispanic/Latino; 2 Two or more races, non-Hispanic/Latino), 6 international. Average age 35. 174 applicants, 62% accepted, 81 enrolled. In 2015, 74 master's, 10 other advanced degrees awarded. *Degree requirements:* For Ed S, thesis or alternative. *Entrance requirements:* For master's, GRE General Test, minimum undergraduate GPA of 2.75; for Ed S, GRE General Test, minimum undergraduate GPA of 2.75, graduate 3.0. Additional exam requirements/recommendations for international students: Required—TOEFL (minimum score 550 paper-based; 79 iBT). *Application deadline:* For fall admission, 6/30 for domestic students, 5/1 for international students; for spring admission, 11/1 for domestic and international students; for summer admission, 3/1 for domestic and international students. Applications are processed on a rolling basis. Application fee: $50. Electronic applications accepted. *Expenses:* Tuition, state resident: full-time $4804; part-time $2412 per semester hour. Tuition, nonresident: full-time $19,218; part-time $9612 per semester hour. *Required fees:* $1830; $1830 per unit. Tuition and fees vary according to program. *Financial support:* In 2015–16, 203 students received support, including 22 research assistantships with partial tuition reimbursements available (averaging $3,000 per year); career-related internships or fieldwork, Federal Work-Study, institutionally sponsored loans, scholarships/grants, tuition waivers (partial), and unspecified assistantships also available. Support available to part-time students. Financial award application deadline: 5/1; financial award applicants required to submit FAFSA. *Unit head:* Dr. Jan Burcham, Department Chair, 706-507-8519, Fax: 706-568-3134, E-mail: burcham_jan@columbusstate.edu. *Application contact:* Kristin Williams, Director of International and Graduate Recruitment, 706-507-8848, Fax: 706-568-5091, E-mail: williams_kristin@columbusstate.edu.
Website: http://te.columbusstate.edu/

Concordia University, School of Graduate Studies, Faculty of Arts and Science, Department of Chemistry and Biochemistry, Montréal, QC H3G 1M8, Canada. Offers chemistry (M Sc, PhD). *Degree requirements:* For master's, thesis; for doctorate, thesis/dissertation. *Entrance requirements:* For master's, honors degree in chemistry; for

doctorate, M Sc in biochemistry, biology, or chemistry. *Application deadline:* For fall admission, 6/1 priority date for domestic students; for winter admission, 10/1 for domestic students; for spring admission, 4/1 for domestic students. Application fee: $50. Tuition and fees vary according to course load, degree level and program. *Financial support:* Teaching assistantships available. *Faculty research:* Bioanalytical, bio-organic, and inorganic chemistry; materials and solid-state chemistry. *Unit head:* Dr. Christine DeWolf, Chair, 514-848-2424 Ext. 3378, Fax: 514-848-2868. *Application contact:* Dr. Peter Pawelek, Graduate Program Director, 514-848-2424 Ext. 3118, Fax: 514-848-2868.
Website: http://www.concordia.ca/artsci/chemistry.html

Cornell University, Graduate School, Graduate Fields of Arts and Sciences, Field of Chemistry and Chemical Biology, Ithaca, NY 14853-0001. Offers analytical chemistry (PhD); bio-organic chemistry (PhD); biophysical chemistry (PhD); chemical biology (PhD); chemical physics (PhD); inorganic chemistry (PhD); materials chemistry (PhD); organic chemistry (PhD); organometallic chemistry (PhD); physical chemistry (PhD); polymer chemistry (PhD); theoretical chemistry (PhD). *Degree requirements:* For doctorate, comprehensive exam, thesis/dissertation. *Entrance requirements:* For doctorate, GRE General Test, GRE Subject Test (chemistry), 3 letters of recommendation. Additional exam requirements/recommendations for international students: Required—TOEFL (minimum score 600 paper-based; 77 iBT). Electronic applications accepted. *Faculty research:* Analytical, organic, inorganic, physical, materials, chemical biology.

Dalhousie University, Faculty of Science, Department of Chemistry, Halifax, NS B3H 4R2, Canada. Offers M Sc, PhD. *Program availability:* Part-time. Terminal master's awarded for partial completion of doctoral program. *Degree requirements:* For master's, thesis; for doctorate, thesis/dissertation. *Entrance requirements:* Additional exam requirements/recommendations for international students: Required—TOEFL (minimum score 600 paper-based; 92 iBT), IELTS (minimum score 7). Electronic applications accepted. *Faculty research:* Analytical, inorganic, organic, physical, and theoretical chemistry.

Dartmouth College, Arts and Sciences Graduate Programs, Department of Chemistry, Hanover, NH 03755. Offers biophysical chemistry (MS); chemistry (PhD). *Faculty:* 19 full-time (4 women), 1 (woman) part-time/adjunct. *Students:* 47 full-time (22 women); includes 8 minority (1 American Indian or Alaska Native, non-Hispanic/Latino; 4 Asian, non-Hispanic/Latino; 3 Two or more races, non-Hispanic/Latino), 15 international. Average age 26. 97 applicants, 12% accepted, 9 enrolled. In 2015, 3 master's, 6 doctorates awarded. *Degree requirements:* For doctorate, thesis/dissertation, departmental qualifying exams, research proposal, research seminar, teaching. *Entrance requirements:* For doctorate, GRE General Test, GRE Subject Test. Additional exam requirements/recommendations for international students: Required—TOEFL. *Application deadline:* For fall admission, 1/4 for domestic students. Application fee: $45. Electronic applications accepted. *Expenses: Tuition, area resident:* Full-time $48,120. *Required fees:* $296. One-time fee: $50 full-time. *Financial support:* Fellowships with full tuition reimbursements, research assistantships with full tuition reimbursements, teaching assistantships with full tuition reimbursements, institutionally sponsored loans, scholarships/grants, traineeships, tuition waivers (full), and unspecified assistantships available. Financial award application deadline: 4/1; financial award applicants required to submit CSS PROFILE or FAFSA. *Faculty research:* Organic and polymer synthesis, bioinorganic chemistry, magnetic resonance parameters. *Unit head:* Dr. Dale F. Mierke, Chair, 603-646-1154. *Application contact:* Deborah Carr, Administrative Assistant, 603-646-2189, E-mail: deborah.a.carr@dartmouth.edu.
Website: http://www.dartmouth.edu/~chem/

Delaware State University, Graduate Programs, Department of Chemistry, Dover, DE 19901-2277. Offers applied chemistry (MS, PhD); chemistry (MS). *Program availability:* Part-time, evening/weekend. *Entrance requirements:* For master's, GRE, minimum GPA of 3.0 in major, 2.75 overall; for doctorate, GRE. Additional exam requirements/recommendations for international students: Required—TOEFL (minimum score 550 paper-based). Electronic applications accepted. *Faculty research:* Chemiluminescence, environmental chemistry, forensic chemistry, heteropoly anions anti-cancer and antiviral agents, low temperature infrared studies of lithium salts.

DePaul University, College of Science and Health, Chicago, IL 60614. Offers applied mathematics (MS); applied statistics (MS); biological sciences (MA, MS); chemistry (MS); mathematics education (MA); mathematics for teaching (MS); nursing (MS); nursing practice (DNP); physics (MS); psychology (MS); pure mathematics (MS); science education (MS); MA/PhD. Electronic applications accepted.

Drew University, Caspersen School of Graduate Studies, Madison, NJ 07940-1493. Offers conflict resolution and leadership (Certificate), including community leadership, moderation, peace building; history and culture (MA, PhD), including American history, book history, British history, European history, Holocaust and genocide (M Litt, MA, D Litt, PhD), intellectual history, Irish history, print culture, public history; K-12 education (MAT), including art, biology, chemistry, elementary education, English, French, Italian, math, secondary education, special education, teacher of students with disabilities; k-12 education (MAT), including art, biology, chemistry, elementary education, English, French, Italian, math, secondary education, special education, teacher of students with disabilities; liberal studies (M Litt, D Litt), including history, Holocaust and genocide (M Litt, MA, D Litt, PhD), Irish/Irish-American studies, literature (M Litt, MMH, D Litt, DMH, CMH), religion, spirituality, teaching in the two-year college, writing; medical humanities (MMH, DMH, CMH), including arts, health, healthcare, literature (M Litt, MMH, D Litt, DMH, CMH), scientific research; poetry and poetry in translation (MFA). *Program availability:* Part-time, evening/weekend. *Faculty:* 1 full-time, 26 part-time/adjunct. *Students:* 125 full-time (82 women), 261 part-time (164 women); includes 34 minority (17 Black or African American, non-Hispanic/Latino; 6 Asian, non-Hispanic/Latino; 11 Hispanic/Latino), 6 international. Average age 42. 120 applicants, 90% accepted, 76 enrolled. In 2015, 54 master's, 36 doctorates, 9 other advanced degrees awarded. Terminal master's awarded for partial completion of doctoral program. *Degree requirements:* For master's and other advanced degree, thesis (for some programs); for doctorate, one foreign language, comprehensive exam (for some programs), thesis/dissertation. *Entrance requirements:* For master's, GRE (MA in history and culture), PRAXIS Core and Subject Area tests (MAT), resume, transcripts, writing sample, personal statement, letters of recommendation; for doctorate, GRE (PhD in history and culture), resume, transcripts, writing sample, personal statement, letters of recommendation. Additional exam requirements/recommendations for international students: Required—TOEFL (minimum score 587 paper-based; 94 iBT), IELTS (minimum score 7), TWE (minimum score 4). *Application deadline:* Applications are processed on a rolling basis. Application fee: $35. Tuition and fees vary according to program. *Financial support:* In 2015–16, 214 students received support. Fellowships, research assistantships, teaching assistantships, career-related internships or fieldwork, Federal Work-Study, scholarships/grants, and unspecified assistantships available. Support available to part-time students. Financial award applicants required to submit FAFSA. *Unit head:* Dr. Robert Ready, Dean, 973-408-3285, Fax: 973-408-3040, E-mail: gsdean@drew.edu. *Application contact:* Leanne Horinko, Interim-Director of Admissions, 973-408-3110, Fax: 973-408-3110, E-mail: gradm@drew.edu.
Website: http://www.drew.edu/graduate

Drexel University, College of Arts and Sciences, Department of Chemistry, Philadelphia, PA 19104-2875. Offers MS, PhD. *Program availability:* Part-time. Terminal master's awarded for partial completion of doctoral program. *Degree requirements:* For master's, thesis optional; for doctorate, one foreign language, thesis/dissertation. *Entrance requirements:* For master's and doctorate, GRE. Additional exam requirements/recommendations for international students: Required—TOEFL. Electronic applications accepted. *Faculty research:* Inorganic, analytical, organic, physical, and atmospheric polymer chemistry.

Duke University, Graduate School, Department of Chemistry, Durham, NC 27708. Offers PhD. *Degree requirements:* For doctorate, one foreign language, thesis/dissertation. *Entrance requirements:* For doctorate, GRE General Test, GRE Subject Test (recommended). Additional exam requirements/recommendations for international students: Required—TOEFL (minimum score 577 paper-based; 90 iBT) or IELTS (minimum score 7). Electronic applications accepted.

Duquesne University, Bayer School of Natural and Environmental Sciences, Department of Chemistry and Biochemistry, Pittsburgh, PA 15282-0001. Offers chemistry (PhD). *Program availability:* Part-time. *Faculty:* 17 full-time (5 women), 1 (woman) part-time/adjunct. *Students:* 41 full-time (20 women), 3 part-time (all women); includes 7 minority (1 Black or African American, non-Hispanic/Latino; 4 Asian, non-Hispanic/Latino; 2 Hispanic/Latino), 5 international. Average age 27. 56 applicants, 34% accepted, 11 enrolled. In 2015, 8 doctorates awarded. Terminal master's awarded for partial completion of doctoral program. *Degree requirements:* For doctorate, thesis/dissertation. *Entrance requirements:* For doctorate, GRE General Test, BS in chemistry or related field, statement of purpose, official transcripts, 3 letters of recommendation with recommendation forms. Additional exam requirements/recommendations for international students: Required—TOEFL (minimum score 100 iBT) or IELTS. *Application deadline:* For fall admission, 1/4 priority date for domestic students, 2/15 for international students; for spring admission, 10/1 for international students. Applications are processed on a rolling basis. Application fee: $0. Electronic applications accepted. *Expenses:* $1,218 per credit. *Financial support:* In 2015–16, 39 students received support, including 1 fellowship with tuition reimbursement available (averaging $25,200 per year), 8 research assistantships with full tuition reimbursements available (averaging $24,230 per year), 30 teaching assistantships with full tuition reimbursements available (averaging $24,230 per year); scholarships/grants and unspecified assistantships also available. Financial award application deadline: 5/31. *Faculty research:* Computational physical chemistry, bioinorganic chemistry, analytical chemistry, biophysics, synthetic organic chemistry. *Total annual research expenditures:* $1.4 million. *Unit head:* Dr. Ralph Wheeler, Chair, 412-396-6341, Fax: 412-396-5683, E-mail: wheeler7@duq.edu. *Application contact:* Heather Costello, Senior Graduate Academic Advisor, 412-396-6339, E-mail: costelloh@duq.edu.
Website: http://www.duq.edu/academics/schools/natural-and-environmental-sciences/academic-programs/chemistry-and-biochemistry

East Carolina University, Graduate School, Thomas Harriot College of Arts and Sciences, Department of Chemistry, Greenville, NC 27858-4353. Offers MS. *Program availability:* Part-time. *Students:* 21 full-time (7 women), 3 part-time (2 women); includes 3 minority (1 Black or African American, non-Hispanic/Latino; 1 Hispanic/Latino; 1 Two or more races, non-Hispanic/Latino). Average age 24. 17 applicants, 94% accepted, 11 enrolled. In 2015, 5 master's awarded. *Degree requirements:* For master's, one foreign language, comprehensive exam, thesis. *Entrance requirements:* For master's, GRE General Test. Additional exam requirements/recommendations for international students: Required—TOEFL. *Application deadline:* For fall admission, 6/1 priority date for domestic students; for spring admission, 10/15 for domestic students. Applications are processed on a rolling basis. Application fee: $50. *Financial support:* Teaching assistantships and Federal Work-Study available. Financial award application deadline: 6/1. *Faculty research:* Organometallic, natural-product syntheses; chemometrics; electroanalytical method development; microcomputer adaptations for handicapped students. *Unit head:* Dr. Allison Danell, Interim Chair, 252-328-9700,
E-mail: danella@ecu.edu. *Application contact:* Dean of Graduate School, 252-328-6012, Fax: 252-328-6071, E-mail: gradschool@ecu.edu.
Website: http://www.ecu.edu/cs-cas/chem/Graduate-Program.cfm

Eastern Illinois University, Graduate School, College of Sciences, Department of Chemistry, Charleston, IL 61920. Offers MS. *Program availability:* Part-time, evening/weekend. *Degree requirements:* For master's, thesis. *Entrance requirements:* For master's, GMAT or GRE. Additional exam requirements/recommendations for international students: Required—TOEFL (minimum score 500 paper-based; 61 iBT), IELTS (minimum score 6). Electronic applications accepted.

Eastern Kentucky University, The Graduate School, College of Arts and Sciences, Department of Chemistry, Richmond, KY 40475-3102. Offers MS. *Program availability:* Part-time, evening/weekend. *Entrance requirements:* For master's, GRE General Test, minimum GPA of 2.5. *Faculty research:* Organic synthesis, surface chemistry, inorganic chemistry, analytical chemistry.

Eastern Michigan University, Graduate School, College of Arts and Sciences, Department of Chemistry, Ypsilanti, MI 48197. Offers MS. *Program availability:* Part-time, evening/weekend. *Faculty:* 22 full-time (9 women). *Students:* 5 full-time (1 woman), 23 part-time (10 women); includes 2 minority (both Black or African American, non-Hispanic/Latino), 5 international. Average age 29. 24 applicants, 71% accepted, 12 enrolled. In 2015, 15 master's awarded. *Degree requirements:* For master's, thesis. *Entrance requirements:* For master's, GRE General Test. Additional exam requirements/recommendations for international students: Required—TOEFL. *Application deadline:* For fall admission, 8/1 for domestic students, 5/1 for international students; for winter admission, 12/1 for domestic students, 8/1 for international students; for spring admission, 4/1 for domestic students, 3/1 for international students. Applications are processed on a rolling basis. Application fee: $45. *Financial support:* Fellowships, research assistantships with full tuition reimbursements, teaching assistantships with full tuition reimbursements, career-related internships or fieldwork, Federal Work-Study, institutionally sponsored loans, scholarships/grants, tuition waivers (partial), and unspecified assistantships available. Support available to part-time students. Financial award applicants required to submit FAFSA. *Unit head:* Dr. Ross Nord, Interim Department Head, 734-487-0106, Fax: 734-487-1496, E-mail: rnord@emich.edu. *Application contact:* Dr. Timothy Brewer, Graduate Coordinator, 734-487-9613, Fax: 734-487-1496, E-mail: tbrewer@emich.edu.
Website: http://www.emich.edu/chemistry/

Eastern New Mexico University, Graduate School, College of Liberal Arts and Sciences, Department of Physical Sciences, Portales, NM 88130. Offers chemistry (MS), including analytical, biochemistry, inorganic, organic, physical. *Program availability:* Part-time. *Degree requirements:* For master's, thesis optional, seminar, oral and written comprehensive exams. *Entrance requirements:* For master's, ACS placement examination, minimum GPA of 3.0; 2 letters of recommendation; personal statement of career goals; bachelor's degree with one year minimum each of general, organic, and analytical chemistry. Additional exam requirements/recommendations for international students: Required—TOEFL (minimum score 550 paper-based; 79 iBT), IELTS (minimum score 6). Electronic applications accepted. *Faculty research:* Synfuel, electrochemistry, protein chemistry.

East Tennessee State University, School of Graduate Studies, College of Arts and Sciences, Department of Chemistry, Johnson City, TN 37614. Offers MS. *Program availability:* Part-time, evening/weekend. *Faculty:* 11 full-time (4 women). *Students:* 15 full-time (5 women), 8 part-time (3 women); includes 2 minority (both Asian, non-Hispanic/Latino), 15 international. Average age 28. 64 applicants, 53% accepted, 9 enrolled. In 2015, 6 master's awarded. *Degree requirements:* For master's, comprehensive exam, thesis. *Entrance requirements:* For master's, prerequisites in physical chemistry with lab requiring calculus; two letters of recommendation. Additional exam requirements/recommendations for international students: Required—TOEFL (minimum score 550 paper-based; 79 iBT). *Application deadline:* For fall admission, 6/1 for domestic students, 4/30 for international students; for spring admission, 11/1 for domestic students, 9/30 for international students. Application fee: $35 ($45 for international students). Electronic applications accepted. *Financial support:* In 2015–16, 18 students received support, including 3 research assistantships (averaging $6,000 per year), 20 teaching assistantships with tuition reimbursements available (averaging $8,000 per year); career-related internships or fieldwork, institutionally sponsored loans, scholarships/grants, and unspecified assistantships also available. Financial award application deadline: 7/1; financial award applicants required to submit FAFSA. *Faculty research:* Analytical chemistry, inorganic chemistry, organic chemistry, physical chemistry. *Unit head:* Dr. Cassandra Eagle, Chair, 423-439-4367, Fax: 423-439-5835, E-mail: eaglec@etsu.edu. *Application contact:* Angela Edwards, Graduate Specialist, 423-439-4703, Fax: 423-439-5624, E-mail: edwardag@etsu.edu.
Website: http://www.etsu.edu/cas/chemistry/

Emory University, Laney Graduate School, Department of Chemistry, Atlanta, GA 30322-1100. Offers PhD. *Degree requirements:* For doctorate, comprehensive exam, thesis/dissertation. *Entrance requirements:* For doctorate, GRE General Test, 3 letters of recommendation, curriculum vitae. Additional exam requirements/recommendations for international students: Required—TOEFL. Electronic applications accepted. *Faculty research:* Organometallic synthesis and catalysis, synthesis of natural products, x-ray crystallography, mass spectrometry, analytical neurochemistry.

Fairleigh Dickinson University, College at Florham, Maxwell Becton College of Arts and Sciences, Department of Chemistry and Geological Sciences, Program in Chemistry, Madison, NJ 07940-1099. Offers MS.

Fairleigh Dickinson University, Metropolitan Campus, University College: Arts, Sciences, and Professional Studies, School of Natural Sciences, Program in Chemistry, Teaneck, NJ 07666-1914. Offers MS.

Fairleigh Dickinson University, Metropolitan Campus, University College: Arts, Sciences, and Professional Studies, School of Natural Sciences, Program in Cosmetic Science, Teaneck, NJ 07666-1914. Offers MS.

Fisk University, Division of Graduate Studies, Department of Chemistry, Nashville, TN 37208-3051. Offers MA. *Program availability:* Part-time. *Degree requirements:* For master's, comprehensive exam, thesis. *Entrance requirements:* For master's, GRE General Test, minimum GPA of 3.0. Electronic applications accepted. *Faculty research:* Environmental studies, lithium compound synthesis, HIU compound synthesis.

Florida Agricultural and Mechanical University, Division of Graduate Studies, Research, and Continuing Education, College of Science and Technology, Department of Chemistry, Tallahassee, FL 32307-3200. Offers MS. *Degree requirements:* For master's, comprehensive exam, thesis optional. *Entrance requirements:* For master's, GRE General Test, minimum GPA of 3.0.

Florida Atlantic University, Charles E. Schmidt College of Science, Department of Chemistry and Biochemistry, Boca Raton, FL 33431-0991. Offers chemistry (MS, MST, PhD). *Program availability:* Part-time. Terminal master's awarded for partial completion of doctoral program. *Degree requirements:* For master's, thesis; for doctorate, comprehensive exam, thesis/dissertation. *Entrance requirements:* For master's, GRE General Test, minimum GPA of 3.0; for doctorate, GRE, minimum GPA of 3.0. Additional exam requirements/recommendations for international students: Required—TOEFL (minimum score 500 paper-based; 61 iBT), IELTS (minimum score 6). *Faculty research:* Polymer synthesis and characterization, spectroscopy, geochemistry, environmental chemistry, biomedical chemistry.

Florida Institute of Technology, College of Science, Program in Chemistry, Melbourne, FL 32901-6975. Offers MS, PhD. *Program availability:* Part-time. *Students:* 29 full-time (13 women), 11 part-time (8 women); includes 1 minority (Black or African American, non-Hispanic/Latino), 32 international. Average age 29. 118 applicants, 53% accepted, 18 enrolled. In 2015, 16 master's, 2 doctorates awarded. Terminal master's awarded for partial completion of doctoral program. *Degree requirements:* For master's, thesis optional, research proposal, oral examination in defense of the thesis, or final program examination and research project, 30 credit hours; for doctorate, comprehensive exam, thesis/dissertation, six cumulative examinations, research proposal, completion of original research study, preparation and defense of dissertation, presentation of seminar on dissertation. *Entrance requirements:* For master's, undergraduate degree in chemistry, or related area; for doctorate, 3 letters of recommendation, resume, statement of objectives, minimum GPA of 3.2. Additional exam requirements/recommendations for international students: Required—TOEFL (minimum score 550 paper-based; 79 iBT). *Application deadline:* For fall admission, 4/1 for international students; for spring admission, 9/30 for international students. Applications are processed on a rolling basis. Electronic applications accepted. *Expenses: Tuition, area resident:* Full-time $21,690; part-time $1205 per credit hour. *Required fees:* $500. Tuition and fees vary according to degree level, campus/location and program. *Financial support:* Career-related internships or fieldwork, institutionally sponsored loans, tuition waivers (partial), unspecified assistantships, and tuition remissions available. Support available to part-time students. Financial award application deadline: 3/1; financial award applicants required to submit FAFSA. *Faculty research:* Energy storage applications, marine and organic chemistry, stereochemistry, medicinal chemistry, environmental chemistry. *Unit head:* Dr. Michael Freund, Department Head, 321-674-8046, Fax: 321-674-8951, E-mail: msfreund@fit.edu. *Application contact:* Cheryl A. Brown, Associate Director of Graduate Admissions, 321-674-7581, Fax: 321-723-9468, E-mail: cbrown@fit.edu.
Website: http://cos.fit.edu/chemistry/

Florida International University, College of Arts, Sciences, and Education, Department of Chemistry and Biochemistry, Chemistry Program, Miami, FL 33199. Offers MS, PhD. *Faculty:* 30 full-time (7 women), 7 part-time/adjunct (3 women). *Students:* 93 full-time (44 women), 10 part-time (6 women); includes 31 minority (2 Black or African American, non-Hispanic/Latino; 2 Asian, non-Hispanic/Latino; 27 Hispanic/Latino), 43 international. Average age 28. 79 applicants, 14% accepted, 11 enrolled. In 2015, 2 master's, 14 doctorates awarded. *Degree requirements:* For master's, thesis; for doctorate, comprehensive exam, thesis/dissertation. *Entrance requirements:* For master's and doctorate, GRE, minimum GPA of 3.0, 3 letters of recommendation. Additional exam requirements/recommendations for international students: Required—TOEFL (minimum score 550 paper-based). *Application deadline:* For fall admission, 6/1 for domestic students, 4/1 for international students; for spring admission, 10/1 for domestic students, 9/1 for international students. Applications are processed on a rolling basis. Application fee: $30. Electronic applications accepted. *Expenses:* Tuition, state resident: full-time $10,708; part-time $455.64 per credit hour. Tuition, nonresident: full-time $23,816; part-time $1001.69 per credit hour. *Required fees:* $390; $195 per semester. Tuition and fees vary according to program. *Financial support:* Fellowships, research assistantships, teaching assistantships, Federal Work-Study, institutionally sponsored loans, and scholarships/grants available. Financial award application deadline: 3/1; financial award applicants required to submit FAFSA. *Unit head:* Palmer Graves, Associate Chairman, 305-348-3496, E-mail: gravesp@fiu.edu. *Application contact:* Nanett Rojas, Manager Admissions Operations, 305-348-7464,
E-mail: gradadm@fiu.edu.

Florida State University, The Graduate School, College of Arts and Sciences, Department of Chemistry and Biochemistry, Tallahassee, FL 32306-4390. Offers analytical chemistry (MS, PhD); biochemistry (MS, PhD); inorganic chemistry (MS, PhD); materials chemistry (PhD); organic chemistry (MS, PhD); physical chemistry (MS, PhD). *Faculty:* 40 full-time (6 women), 4 part-time/adjunct (2 women). *Students:* 162 full-time (56 women); includes 37 minority (8 Black or African American, non-Hispanic/Latino; 6 Asian, non-Hispanic/Latino; 18 Hispanic/Latino; 1 Native Hawaiian or other Pacific Islander, non-Hispanic/Latino; 4 Two or more races, non-Hispanic/Latino), 54 international. Average age 28. 182 applicants, 47% accepted, 31 enrolled. In 2015, 6 master's, 18 doctorates awarded. Terminal master's awarded for partial completion of doctoral program. *Degree requirements:* For master's, thesis (for some programs); for doctorate, thesis/dissertation. *Entrance requirements:* For master's and doctorate, GRE General Test (minimum scores: 150 verbal, 151 quantitative; 1100 total on the old scale), minimum GPA of 3.1 in undergraduate course work. Additional exam requirements/recommendations for international students: Required—TOEFL (minimum score 90 iBT). *Application deadline:* For fall admission, 12/15 priority date for domestic and international students. Application fee: $30. Electronic applications accepted. *Expenses: Tuition, area resident:* Full-time $7263; part-time $403.50 per credit hour. Tuition, nonresident: full-time $18,087; part-time $1004.85 per credit hour. *Required fees:* $1365; $75.81 per credit hour. $20 per semester. Tuition and fees vary according to campus/location. *Financial support:* In 2015–16, 162 students received support, including 4 fellowships with tuition reimbursements available (averaging $22,000 per year), 51 research assistantships with full tuition reimbursements available (averaging $22,809 per year), 67 teaching assistantships with full tuition reimbursements available (averaging $22,809 per year). Financial award application deadline: 12/15; financial award applicants required to submit FAFSA. *Faculty research:* Bioanalytical chemistry, including separations, microfluidics, petroleomics; materials chemistry, including magnets, polymers, catalysts, nanomaterials; spectroscopy, including NMR and EPR, ultrafast, Raman, and mass spectrometry; organic synthesis, natural products, photochemistry, and supramolecular chemistry; biochemistry, with focus on structural biology, metabolomics, and anticancer drugs. *Total annual research expenditures:* $3.5 million. *Unit head:* Dr. Timothy Logan, Chairman, 850-644-3810, Fax: 850-644-8281, E-mail: gradinfo@chem.fsu.edu. *Application contact:* Dr. Geoffrey Strouse, Associate Chair for Graduate Studies, 850-445-9042, Fax: 850-644-8281,
E-mail: gradinfo@chem.fsu.edu.
Website: http://www.chem.fsu.edu/

Furman University, Graduate Division, Department of Chemistry, Greenville, SC 29613. Offers MS. *Degree requirements:* For master's, comprehensive exam, thesis. *Entrance requirements:* For master's, GRE General Test, GRE Subject Test. *Faculty research:* Computer-assisted chemical analysis, DNA-metal interactions, laser-initiated reactions, nucleic acid chemistry and biochemistry.

George Mason University, College of Science, Department of Chemistry and Biochemistry, Fairfax, VA 22030. Offers chemistry (MS); chemistry and biochemistry (PhD). *Faculty:* 16 full-time (5 women), 6 part-time/adjunct (4 women). *Students:* 30 full-time (20 women), 25 part-time (12 women); includes 23 minority (8 Black or African American, non-Hispanic/Latino; 7 Asian, non-Hispanic/Latino; 6 Hispanic/Latino; 2 Two or more races, non-Hispanic/Latino), 6 international. Average age 30. 41 applicants, 49% accepted, 10 enrolled. In 2015, 14 master's, 2 doctorates awarded. *Degree requirements:* For master's, thesis or alternative; for doctorate, comprehensive exam, thesis/dissertation, exit seminar. *Entrance requirements:* For master's, GRE, bachelor's degree in related field; 2 official copies of transcripts; expanded goals statement; 3 letters of recommendation; resume for those whose bachelor's degree is 5 years or older; for doctorate, GRE, undergraduate degree in related field; BS with minimum GPA of 3.0; 3 letters of recommendation; 2 copies of official transcripts; expanded goals statement; resume. Additional exam requirements/recommendations for international students: Required—TOEFL (minimum score 575 paper-based; 88 iBT), IELTS (minimum score 6.5), PTE (minimum score 59). Application fee: $75 ($80 for international students). Electronic applications accepted. *Financial support:* In 2015–16, 27 students received support, including 2 fellowships with tuition reimbursements available (averaging $12,897 per year), 5 research assistantships with tuition reimbursements available (averaging $16,420 per year), 20 teaching assistantships with tuition reimbursements available (averaging $12,752 per year); career-related internships or fieldwork, Federal Work-Study, scholarships/grants, unspecified assistantships, and health care benefits (for full-time research or teaching assistantship recipients) also available. Support available to part-time students. Financial award application deadline: 3/1; financial award applicants required to submit FAFSA. *Faculty research:* Electroanalytical techniques for the study of toxic species in the environment, problems associated with the solid-gas interface, applying peptide/protein engineering principles to investigate biomolecules, enzymes, isoprene biosynthesis, contaminants in the aquatic environment, radioactivity, middle distillate fuels. *Total annual research expenditures:* $155,380. *Unit head:* John A. Schreifels, Chair, 703-993-1082, Fax: 703-993-1055, E-mail: jschreif@gmu.edu. *Application contact:* Robert Honeychuck, Graduate Coordinator, 703-993-1076, Fax: 703-993-1055, E-mail: rhoneych@gmu.edu.
Website: http://chemistry.gmu.edu/

Georgetown University, Graduate School of Arts and Sciences, Department of Chemistry, Washington, DC 20057. Offers analytical chemistry (PhD); biochemistry (PhD); computational chemistry (PhD); inorganic chemistry (PhD); materials chemistry (PhD); organic chemistry (PhD); theoretical chemistry (PhD). Terminal master's awarded for partial completion of doctoral program. *Degree requirements:* For doctorate, comprehensive exam, thesis/dissertation. *Entrance requirements:* For doctorate, GRE General Test. Additional exam requirements/recommendations for international students: Required—TOEFL.

The George Washington University, Columbian College of Arts and Sciences, Department of Chemistry, Washington, DC 20052. Offers analytical chemistry (MS,

PhD); inorganic chemistry (MS, PhD); materials science (MS, PhD); organic chemistry (MS, PhD); physical chemistry (MS, PhD). *Program availability:* Part-time, evening/weekend. *Faculty:* 17 full-time (6 women), 4 part-time/adjunct (1 woman). *Students:* 25 full-time (13 women), 12 part-time (5 women); includes 2 minority (1 Asian, non-Hispanic/Latino; 1 Hispanic/Latino), 10 international. Average age 28. 60 applicants, 37% accepted, 9 enrolled. In 2015, 2 master's, 6 doctorates awarded. Terminal master's awarded for partial completion of doctoral program. *Degree requirements:* For master's, comprehensive exam, thesis or alternative; for doctorate, thesis/dissertation, general exam. *Entrance requirements:* For master's and doctorate, GRE General Test, interview, minimum GPA of 3.0. Additional exam requirements/recommendations for international students: Required—TOEFL (minimum score 550 paper-based; 80 iBT). *Application deadline:* For fall admission, 1/15 priority date for domestic and international students; for spring admission, 9/1 priority date for domestic and international students. Applications are processed on a rolling basis. Application fee: $75. Electronic applications accepted. *Financial support:* In 2015–16, 27 students received support. Fellowships with tuition reimbursements available, research assistantships, teaching assistantships with tuition reimbursements available, Federal Work-Study, and tuition waivers available. Financial award application deadline: 1/15. *Unit head:* Dr. Michael King, Chair, 202-994-6488. *Application contact:* Information Contact, 202-994-6121, E-mail: gwchem@gwu.edu.
Website: http://chemistry.columbian.gwu.edu/

Georgia Institute of Technology, Graduate Studies, College of Sciences, School of Chemistry and Biochemistry, Atlanta, GA 30332-0001. Offers MS, PhD. *Program availability:* Part-time. Terminal master's awarded for partial completion of doctoral program. *Degree requirements:* For master's, thesis optional; for doctorate, comprehensive exam, thesis/dissertation. *Entrance requirements:* For master's and doctorate, GRE General Test, GRE Subject Test. Additional exam requirements/recommendations for international students: Required—TOEFL (minimum score 600 paper-based; 100 iBT). Electronic applications accepted. *Faculty research:* Inorganic, organic, physical, and analytical chemistry.

Georgia State University, College of Arts and Sciences, Department of Chemistry, Atlanta, GA 30302-3083. Offers analytical chemistry (MS, PhD); biochemistry (MS, PhD); bioinformatics (MS, PhD); biophysical chemistry (PhD); computational chemistry (MS, PhD); geochemistry (PhD); organic/medicinal chemistry (MS, PhD); physical chemistry (MS). PhD in geochemistry offered jointly with Department of Geosciences. *Program availability:* Part-time. *Faculty:* 26 full-time (4 women). *Students:* 158 full-time (53 women), 4 part-time (all women); includes 43 minority (22 Black or African American, non-Hispanic/Latino; 1 American Indian or Alaska Native, non-Hispanic/Latino; 9 Asian, non-Hispanic/Latino; 7 Hispanic/Latino; 4 Two or more races, non-Hispanic/Latino), 81 international. Average age 28. 117 applicants, 50% accepted, 42 enrolled. In 2015, 28 master's, 15 doctorates awarded. Terminal master's awarded for partial completion of doctoral program. *Degree requirements:* For master's, one foreign language, comprehensive exam (for some programs), thesis (for some programs); for doctorate, one foreign language, comprehensive exam, thesis/dissertation. *Entrance requirements:* For master's and doctorate, GRE. Additional exam requirements/recommendations for international students: Required—TOEFL (minimum score 550 paper-based; 80 iBT) or IELTS (minimum score 6.5). *Application deadline:* For fall admission, 7/1 priority date for domestic and international students; for winter admission, 11/15 priority date for domestic and international students; for spring admission, 4/15 priority date for domestic and international students. Applications are processed on a rolling basis. Application fee: $50. Electronic applications accepted. *Expenses:* Tuition, state resident: full-time $6876; part-time $382 per credit hour. Tuition, nonresident: full-time $22,374; part-time $1243 per credit hour. *Required fees:* $2128; $2128 per term. $1064 per term. Part-time tuition and fees vary according to course load and program. *Financial support:* Fellowships with full tuition reimbursements, research assistantships with full tuition reimbursements, and teaching assistantships with full tuition reimbursements available. Financial award applicants required to submit FAFSA. *Faculty research:* Analytical chemistry, biological/biochemistry, biophysical/computational chemistry, chemical education, organic/medicinal chemistry. *Unit head:* Dr. Peng George Wang, Department Chair, 404-413-3591, Fax: 404-413-5505,
E-mail: pwang11@gsu.edu.
Website: http://chemistry.gsu.edu/

Georgia State University, College of Education, Department of Middle and Secondary Education, Atlanta, GA 30302-3083. Offers curriculum and instruction (Ed D); English education (MAT); mathematics education (M Ed, MAT); middle level education (MAT); reading, language and literacy education (M Ed, MAT), including reading instruction (M Ed); science education (M Ed, MAT), including biology (MAT), broad field science (MAT), chemistry (MAT), earth science (MAT), physics (MAT); social studies education (M Ed, MAT), including economics (MAT), geography (MAT), history (MAT), political science (MAT); teaching and learning (PhD), including language and literacy, mathematics education, music education, science education, social studies education, teaching and teacher education. *Accreditation:* NCATE. *Program availability:* Part-time, evening/weekend, online learning. *Faculty:* 19 full-time (15 women). *Students:* 153 full-time (109 women), 174 part-time (122 women); includes 145 minority (112 Black or African American, non-Hispanic/Latino; 1 American Indian or Alaska Native, non-Hispanic/Latino; 10 Asian, non-Hispanic/Latino; 17 Hispanic/Latino; 5 Two or more races, non-Hispanic/Latino), 9 international. Average age 35. 68 applicants, 75% accepted, 38 enrolled. In 2015, 63 master's awarded. *Degree requirements:* For master's, comprehensive exam (for some programs), thesis or alternative, exit portfolio; for doctorate, comprehensive exam, thesis/dissertation. *Entrance requirements:* For master's, GRE; GACE I (for initial teacher preparation programs), baccalaureate degree or equivalent, resume, goals statement, two letters of recommendation, minimum undergraduate GPA of 2.5; proof of initial teacher certification in the content area (for M Ed); for doctorate, GRE, resume, goals statement, writing sample, two letters of recommendation, minimum graduate GPA of 3.3, interview. Additional exam requirements/recommendations for international students: Required—TOEFL (minimum score 550 paper-based; 79 iBT) or IELTS (minimum score 6.5). *Application deadline:* For fall admission, 1/15 priority date for domestic and international students; for spring admission, 10/1 for domestic and international students. Application fee: $50. Electronic applications accepted. *Expenses:* Tuition, state resident: full-time $6876; part-time $382 per credit hour. Tuition, nonresident: full-time $22,374; part-time $1243 per credit hour. *Required fees:* $2128; $2128 per term. $1064 per term. Part-time tuition and fees vary according to course load and program. *Financial support:* In 2015–16, fellowships with full tuition reimbursements (averaging $19,667 per year), research assistantships with full tuition reimbursements (averaging $5,436 per year), teaching assistantships with full tuition reimbursements (averaging $2,779 per year) were awarded; career-related internships or fieldwork, Federal Work-Study, scholarships/grants, health care benefits, tuition waivers (full and partial), and unspecified assistantships also available. Financial award application deadline: 3/15. *Faculty research:* Teacher education in language and literacy, mathematics, science, and social studies in urban middle and secondary school settings; learning technologies in school, community, and corporate settings; multicultural education and education for social justice; urban education; international education. *Unit head:* Dr. Dana L. Fox, Chair, 404-413-8060, Fax: 404-413-8063, E-mail: dfox@gsu.edu. *Application contact:* Bobbie Turner, Administrative Coordinator I, 404-413-8405, Fax: 404-413-8063, E-mail: bnturner@gsu.edu.
Website: http://mse.education.gsu.edu/

The Graduate Center, City University of New York, Graduate Studies, Program in Chemistry, New York, NY 10016-4039. Offers PhD. *Degree requirements:* For doctorate, one foreign language, thesis/dissertation. *Entrance requirements:* For doctorate, GRE General Test. Additional exam requirements/recommendations for international students: Required—TOEFL. Electronic applications accepted.

Hampton University, School of Science, Department of Chemistry and Biochemistry, Hampton, VA 23668. Offers MS. *Degree requirements:* For master's, one foreign language, comprehensive exam, thesis. *Entrance requirements:* For master's, GRE General Test. Additional exam requirements/recommendations for international students: Required—TOEFL (minimum score 525 paper-based) or IELTS (6.5). Electronic applications accepted. *Expenses: Tuition, area resident:* Full-time $10,263; part-time $522 per credit hour. *Required fees:* $35. Tuition and fees vary according to course load and program.

Harvard University, Graduate School of Arts and Sciences, Department of Chemistry and Chemical Biology, Cambridge, MA 02138. Offers biochemical chemistry (PhD); inorganic chemistry (PhD); organic chemistry (PhD); physical chemistry (PhD). *Degree requirements:* For doctorate, thesis/dissertation, cumulative exams. *Entrance requirements:* For doctorate, GRE General Test, GRE Subject Test. Additional exam requirements/recommendations for international students: Required—TOEFL.

Howard University, Graduate School, Department of Chemistry, Washington, DC 20059-0002. Offers analytical chemistry (MS, PhD); atmospheric (MS, PhD); biochemistry (MS, PhD); environmental (MS, PhD); inorganic chemistry (MS, PhD); organic chemistry (MS, PhD); physical chemistry (MS, PhD). Terminal master's awarded for partial completion of doctoral program. *Degree requirements:* For master's, comprehensive exam, thesis, teaching experience; for doctorate, comprehensive exam, thesis/dissertation, teaching experience. *Entrance requirements:* For master's, GRE General Test, minimum GPA of 2.7; for doctorate, GRE General Test, minimum GPA of 3.0. Additional exam requirements/recommendations for international students: Required—TOEFL. Electronic applications accepted. *Faculty research:* Synthetic organics, materials, natural products, mass spectrometry.

Hunter College of the City University of New York, Graduate School, School of Arts and Sciences, Department of Chemistry, New York, NY 10065-5085. Offers biochemistry (MA). *Program availability:* Part-time. *Faculty:* 2 full-time (both women). *Students:* 2 full-time (1 woman); includes 1 minority (Asian, non-Hispanic/Latino). Average age 24. 8 applicants, 38% accepted, 2 enrolled. In 2015, 1 master's awarded. *Degree requirements:* For master's, comprehensive exam or thesis. *Entrance requirements:* For master's, GRE General Test, 1 year of course work in chemistry, quantitative analysis, organic chemistry, physical chemistry, biology, biochemistry lecture and laboratory. Additional exam requirements/recommendations for international students: Required—TOEFL. *Application deadline:* For fall admission, 4/1 for domestic students; for spring admission, 11/1 for domestic students. *Financial support:* Teaching assistantships and tuition waivers (partial) available. Support available to part-time students. *Faculty research:* Theoretical chemistry, vibrational optical activity, Raman spectroscopy. *Unit head:* Dr. Michael Drain, Chairperson, 212-650-3781,
E-mail: cdrain@hunter.cuny.edu. *Application contact:* Milena Solo, Director for Graduate Admissions, 212-772-4480, E-mail: admissions@hunter.cuny.edu.

Idaho State University, Office of Graduate Studies, College of Science and Engineering, Department of Chemistry, Pocatello, ID 83209-8023. Offers MNS, MS. MS students must enter as undergraduates. *Program availability:* Part-time. *Degree requirements:* For master's, comprehensive exam, thesis (for some programs). *Entrance requirements:* For master's, GRE General Test, minimum GPA of 3.0 in all upper-division classes; 1 semester of calculus, inorganic chemistry, and analytical chemistry; 1 year of physics, organic chemistry and physical chemistry. Additional exam requirements/recommendations for international students: Required—TOEFL (minimum score 550 paper-based; 80 iBT). Electronic applications accepted. *Faculty research:* Low temperature plasma, organic chemistry, physical chemistry, inorganic chemistry, analytical chemistry.

Illinois Institute of Technology, Graduate College, College of Science, Department of Chemistry, Chicago, IL 60616. Offers analytical chemistry (MAS); chemistry (MAS, MS, PhD); materials chemistry (MAS), including inorganic, organic, or polymeric materials. *Program availability:* Part-time, evening/weekend, online learning. Terminal master's awarded for partial completion of doctoral program. *Degree requirements:* For master's, comprehensive exam, thesis (for some programs); for doctorate, comprehensive exam, thesis/dissertation. *Entrance requirements:* For master's, GRE General Test (minimum score 300 Quantitative and Verbal, 2.5 Analytical Writing), minimum undergraduate GPA of 3.0; for doctorate, GRE General Test (minimum score 310 Quantitative and Verbal, 3.0 Analytical Writing), GRE Subject Test, minimum undergraduate GPA of 3.0. Additional exam requirements/recommendations for international students: Required—TOEFL (minimum score 550 paper-based; 80 iBT); Recommended—IELTS. Electronic applications accepted. *Faculty research:* Materials science, biological chemistry, synthetic chemistry, computational chemistry, energy, sensor science and technology, scholarship of teaching and learning.

Illinois State University, Graduate School, College of Arts and Sciences, Department of Chemistry, Normal, IL 61790-2200. Offers MS. *Degree requirements:* For master's, thesis. *Entrance requirements:* For master's, GRE General Test, minimum GPA of 2.6 in last 60 hours of course work. *Faculty research:* Solid-state and solution behavior of lanthanide scorpionates and porphyrinoids; CAREER: Versatile Vanadium: biology, materials science and education through its diverse coordinator carbaporphyrins and other highly modified porphyrinoid systems; oxadiazines: structurally novel templates for catalytic asymmetric synthesis.

Indiana University Bloomington, University Graduate School, College of Arts and Sciences, Department of Chemistry, Bloomington, IN 47405. Offers analytical chemistry (PhD); chemical biology (PhD); chemistry (MAT); inorganic chemistry (PhD); materials chemistry (PhD); organic chemistry (PhD); physical chemistry (PhD); MSES/MS. Terminal master's awarded for partial completion of doctoral program. *Degree requirements:* For master's, thesis; for doctorate, thesis/dissertation. *Entrance requirements:* For master's and doctorate, GRE General Test, GRE Subject Test. Additional exam requirements/recommendations for international students: Required—TOEFL. Electronic applications accepted. *Faculty research:* Synthesis of complex natural products, organic reaction mechanisms, organic electrochemistry, transitive-metal chemistry, solid-state and surface chemistry.

Indiana University of Pennsylvania, School of Graduate Studies and Research, College of Natural Sciences and Mathematics, Department of Chemistry, MA Program in Chemistry, Indiana, PA 15705-1087. Offers MA. *Program availability:* Part-time. *Faculty:* 6 full-time (1 woman). In 2015, 2 master's awarded. *Degree requirements:* For master's, thesis optional. *Entrance requirements:* For master's, 2 letters of recommendation.

Chemistry

Additional exam requirements/recommendations for international students: Required—TOEFL (minimum score 540 paper-based). *Application deadline:* Applications are processed on a rolling basis. Application fee: $50. Electronic applications accepted. *Financial support:* Research assistantships available. Financial award application deadline: 4/15; financial award applicants required to submit FAFSA. *Unit head:* Dr. Avijita Jain, Graduate Coordinator, 724-357-2118, E-mail: avijita.jain@iup.edu.

Indiana University of Pennsylvania, School of Graduate Studies and Research, College of Natural Sciences and Mathematics, Department of Chemistry, Program in Applied and Industrial Chemistry, Indiana, PA 15705-1087. Offers PSM. *Program availability:* Part-time. *Faculty:* 6 full-time (1 woman). *Students:* 6 full-time (2 women), 2 part-time (0 women); includes 1 minority (Asian, non-Hispanic/Latino), 4 international. Average age 27. 17 applicants, 53% accepted, 4 enrolled. In 2015, 4 master's awarded. *Degree requirements:* For master's, thesis. *Entrance requirements:* For master's, 2 letters of recommendation. Additional exam requirements/recommendations for international students: Required—TOEFL (minimum score 540 paper-based). *Application deadline:* Applications are processed on a rolling basis. Application fee: $50. Electronic applications accepted. *Financial support:* In 2015–16, 2 research assistantships with tuition reimbursements (averaging $1,000 per year) were awarded; career-related internships or fieldwork, Federal Work-Study, scholarships/grants, and unspecified assistantships also available. *Unit head:* Dr. Avijita Jain, Graduate Coordinator, 724-357-2118, E-mail: avijita.jain@iup.edu.

Indiana University–Purdue University Indianapolis, School of Science, Department of Chemistry and Chemical Biology, Indianapolis, IN 46202. Offers MS, PhD, MD/PhD. MD/PhD offered jointly with Indiana University School of Medicine and Purdue University. *Program availability:* Part-time, evening/weekend. Terminal master's awarded for partial completion of doctoral program. *Degree requirements:* For master's, thesis (for some programs); for doctorate, comprehensive exam, thesis/dissertation. *Entrance requirements:* For master's and doctorate, minimum GPA of 3.0. Additional exam requirements/recommendations for international students: Required—TOEFL (minimum score 106 iBT). Electronic applications accepted. *Faculty research:* Analytical, biological, inorganic, organic, and physical chemistry.

Instituto Tecnológico y de Estudios Superiores de Monterrey, Campus Monterrey, Graduate and Research Division, Program in Natural and Social Sciences, Monterrey, Mexico. Offers biotechnology (MS); chemistry (MS, PhD); communications (MS); education (MA). *Program availability:* Part-time. *Degree requirements:* For master's, one foreign language, thesis; for doctorate, one foreign language, thesis/dissertation. *Entrance requirements:* For master's, EXADEP; for doctorate, EXADEP, master's degree in related field. Additional exam requirements/recommendations for international students: Required—TOEFL. *Faculty research:* Cultural industries, mineral substances, bioremediation, food processing, CQ in industrial chemical processing.

Iowa State University of Science and Technology, Department of Chemistry, Ames, IA 50011. Offers MS, PhD. *Degree requirements:* For master's, thesis; for doctorate, thesis/dissertation. *Entrance requirements:* Additional exam requirements/recommendations for international students: Required—TOEFL (minimum score 570 paper-based; 89 iBT), IELTS (minimum score 6.5). Electronic applications accepted.

Jackson State University, Graduate School, College of Science, Engineering and Technology, Department of Chemistry and Biochemistry, Jackson, MS 39217. Offers MS, PhD. *Program availability:* Part-time, evening/weekend. *Degree requirements:* For master's, comprehensive exam, thesis; for doctorate, comprehensive exam, thesis/dissertation. *Entrance requirements:* For master's, GRE General Test; for doctorate, MAT. Additional exam requirements/recommendations for international students: Required—TOEFL (minimum score 520 paper-based; 67 iBT). *Faculty research:* Electrochemical and spectroscopic studies on charge transfer and energy transfer processes, spectroscopy of trapped molecular ions, respirable mine dust.

Johns Hopkins University, School of Education, Master's Programs in Education, Baltimore, MD 21218. Offers counseling (MS), including clinical mental health counseling, school counseling; education (MS), including educational studies, gifted education, reading, school administration and supervision, technology for educators; elementary education (MAT); health professions (M Ed); intelligence analysis (MS); organizational leadership (MS); secondary education (MAT), including biology, chemistry, earth/space science, English, mathematics, physics, science, social studies; special education (MS), including early childhood special education, general special education studies, mild to moderate disabilities, severe disabilities. *Program availability:* Part-time, evening/weekend, 100% online, blended/hybrid learning. *Students:* 302 full-time (241 women), 1,472 part-time (1,106 women); includes 710 minority (313 Black or African American, non-Hispanic/Latino; 6 American Indian or Alaska Native, non-Hispanic/Latino; 133 Asian, non-Hispanic/Latino; 167 Hispanic/Latino; 11 Native Hawaiian or other Pacific Islander, non-Hispanic/Latino; 80 Two or more races, non-Hispanic/Latino), 46 international. Average age 28. 1,717 applicants, 69% accepted, 904 enrolled. In 2015, 623 master's awarded. *Degree requirements:* For master's, comprehensive exam (for some programs), portfolio, capstone project and/or internship; PRAXIS II Core (for teacher preparation programs that lead to licensure). *Entrance requirements:* For master's, GRE (for full-time programs only); PRAXIS I or state approved alternative (for teacher preparation programs that lead to licensure), minimum of a bachelor's degree from regionally- or nationally-accredited institution; minimum GPA of 3.0 in all previous programs of study; official transcripts from all post-secondary institutions attended; essay; curriculum vitae/resume; letters of recommendation (3 for full-time, 2 for part-time). Additional exam requirements/recommendations for international students: Required—TOEFL (minimum score 600 paper-based; 100 iBT), IELTS (minimum score 7). *Application deadline:* For fall admission, 4/1 for domestic and international students; for spring admission, 10/1 for domestic and international students; for summer admission, 2/1 for domestic and international students. Application fee: $80. Electronic applications accepted. *Expenses:* Contact institution. *Financial support:* Applicants required to submit FAFSA. *Unit head:* Dr. Mariale M. Hardiman, Interim Dean, 410-516-7820, Fax: 410-516-6697, E-mail: mmhardiman@jhu.edu. *Application contact:* Rhodri Evans, Director of Enrollment Services, 410-516-0741, Fax: 410-516-6697, E-mail: revans@jhu.edu.

Johns Hopkins University, Zanvyl Krieger School of Arts and Sciences, Chemistry-Biology Interface Program, Baltimore, MD 21218. Offers PhD. Terminal master's awarded for partial completion of doctoral program. *Degree requirements:* For doctorate, comprehensive exam, thesis/dissertation, 8 one-semester courses, research proposal, graduate board oral exam. *Entrance requirements:* For doctorate, GRE General Test, GRE Subject Test in biochemistry, cell and molecular biology, biology or chemistry (strongly recommended), 3 letters of recommendation, transcripts, statement of purpose, interview. Additional exam requirements/recommendations for international students: Required—TOEFL. Electronic applications accepted. *Faculty research:* Enzyme mechanisms, inhibitors, and metabolic pathways; DNA replication, damaged, and repair; using small molecules to probe signal transduction, gene regulation, angiogenesis, and other biological processes; synthetic methods and medicinal chemistry; synthetic modeling of metalloenzymes.

Johns Hopkins University, Zanvyl Krieger School of Arts and Sciences, Department of Chemistry, Baltimore, MD 21218. Offers PhD. Terminal master's awarded for partial completion of doctoral program. *Degree requirements:* For doctorate, comprehensive exam, thesis/dissertation, 8 one-semester courses, literature seminar, department oral exam, graduate board oral exam. *Entrance requirements:* For doctorate, GRE General Test, GRE Subject Test, 3 letters of recommendation, transcripts, statement of purpose. Additional exam requirements/recommendations for international students: Required—TOEFL (minimum score 600 paper-based), IELTS. Electronic applications accepted. *Faculty research:* Experimental physical, biophysical, inorganic/materials, organic/bioorganic, theoretical.

Kansas State University, Graduate School, College of Arts and Sciences, Department of Chemistry, Manhattan, KS 66506. Offers analytical chemistry (MS); biological chemistry (MS); inorganic chemistry (MS); materials chemistry (MS); organic chemistry (MS); physical chemistry (MS). Terminal master's awarded for partial completion of doctoral program. *Degree requirements:* For master's, thesis; for doctorate, thesis/dissertation. *Entrance requirements:* For master's and doctorate, GRE, minimum GPA of 3.0. Additional exam requirements/recommendations for international students: Required—TOEFL (minimum score 550 paper-based). Electronic applications accepted. *Faculty research:* Inorganic chemistry, organic and biological chemistry, analytical chemistry, physical chemistry, materials chemistry and nanotechnology.

Kennesaw State University, College of Science and Mathematics, Program in Chemical Sciences, Kennesaw, GA 30144. Offers biochemistry (MS); chemistry (MS). *Degree requirements:* For master's, thesis. *Entrance requirements:* For master's, GRE. Additional exam requirements/recommendations for international students: Required—TOEFL (minimum score 550 paper-based; 80 iBT), IELTS (minimum score 6.5). Electronic applications accepted.

Kennesaw State University, Leland and Clarice C. Bagwell College of Education, Program in Teaching, Kennesaw, GA 30144. Offers art education (MAT); biology (MAT); chemistry (MAT); foreign language education (Chinese and Spanish) (MAT); physics (MAT); secondary English (MAT); secondary mathematics (MAT); special education (MAT); teaching English to speakers of other languages (MAT). *Program availability:* Part-time, evening/weekend. *Entrance requirements:* For master's, GRE, GACE I (state certificate exam), minimum GPA of 2.75, 2 recommendations, resume. Additional exam requirements/recommendations for international students: Required—TOEFL (minimum score 550 paper-based; 80 iBT), IELTS (minimum score 6.5). Electronic applications accepted.

Kent State University, College of Arts and Sciences, Department of Chemistry and Biochemistry, Kent, OH 44242-0001. Offers chemistry (MA). *Program availability:* Part-time. *Faculty:* 19 full-time (4 women). *Students:* 51 full-time (14 women), 1 part-time (0 women), 38 international. Average age 29. 269 applicants, 7% accepted, 14 enrolled. In 2015, 1 master's, 5 doctorates awarded. Terminal master's awarded for partial completion of doctoral program. *Degree requirements:* For master's, comprehensive exam, thesis; for doctorate, comprehensive exam, thesis/dissertation. *Entrance requirements:* For master's and doctorate, GRE General Test, GRE Subject Test (recommended), minimum GPA of 3.0, transcript, resume, letter of intent, curriculum vitae/resume, 3 letters of recommendation. Additional exam requirements/recommendations for international students: Required—TOEFL (minimum score: paper-based 525, iBT 71), Michigan English Language Assessment Battery (minimum score of 75), IELTS (minimum score of 6.0), PTE Academic (minimum score of 48), or completion of ELS level 112 Intensive Program. *Application deadline:* For fall admission, 1/10 for domestic and international students; for spring admission, 9/15 for domestic and international students. Application fee: $45 ($70 for international students). Electronic applications accepted. *Expenses:* Tuition, state resident: full-time $10,864; part-time $495 per credit hour. Tuition, nonresident: full-time $18,380; part-time $837 per credit hour. *Financial support:* Research assistantships with full tuition reimbursements, teaching assistantships with full tuition reimbursements, Federal Work-Study, institutionally sponsored loans, and unspecified assistantships available. Financial award application deadline: 2/1. *Unit head:* Dr. Michael Tebergen, Professor and Chair, 330-672-2032, Fax: 330-672-3816. *Application contact:* 330-672-2032, E-mail: chemgc@kent.edu.
Website: http://www.kent.edu/chemistry/

Lakehead University, Graduate Studies, Faculty of Social Sciences and Humanities, Department of Chemistry, Thunder Bay, ON P7B 5E1, Canada. Offers M Sc. *Program availability:* Part-time, evening/weekend. *Degree requirements:* For master's, thesis, oral examination. *Entrance requirements:* For master's, minimum B+ average. Additional exam requirements/recommendations for international students: Required—TOEFL. *Faculty research:* Physical inorganic chemistry, photochemistry, physical chemistry.

Lamar University, College of Graduate Studies, College of Arts and Sciences, Department of Chemistry and Biochemistry, Beaumont, TX 77710. Offers chemistry (MS). *Program availability:* Part-time. *Faculty:* 7 full-time (3 women), 1 part-time/adjunct (0 women). *Students:* 85 full-time (39 women), 37 part-time (17 women); includes 2 minority (both Black or African American, non-Hispanic/Latino), 117 international. Average age 26. 52 applicants, 87% accepted, 31 enrolled. In 2015, 58 master's awarded. *Degree requirements:* For master's, thesis, practicum. *Entrance requirements:* For master's, GRE General Test, minimum GPA of 2.5 in last 60 hours of course work. Additional exam requirements/recommendations for international students: Required—TOEFL (minimum score 550 paper-based; 79 iBT), IELTS (minimum score 6.5). *Application deadline:* For fall admission, 8/10 for domestic students, 7/1 for international students; for spring admission, 1/5 for domestic students, 12/1 for international students. Applications are processed on a rolling basis. Application fee: $25 ($50 for international students). Electronic applications accepted. *Expenses: Tuition, area resident:* Full-time $6720; part-time $4032. Tuition, nonresident: full-time $14,880; part-time $8928. *Required fees:* $1900; $950 $784. *Financial support:* Teaching assistantships with partial tuition reimbursements, tuition waivers (partial), and unspecified assistantships available. Financial award application deadline: 4/1. *Faculty research:* Environmental chemistry, surface chemistry, polymer chemistry, organic synthesis, computational chemistry. *Unit head:* Dr. Paul Bernazzani, Chair, 409-880-8267, Fax: 409-880-8270. *Application contact:* Melissa Gallien, Director, Admissions and Academic Services, 409-880-8888, Fax: 409-880-7419, E-mail: gradmissions@lamar.edu.
Website: http://artssciences.lamar.edu/chemistry-and-biochemistry/

Laurentian University, School of Graduate Studies and Research, Programme in Chemistry and Biochemistry, Sudbury, ON P3E 2C6, Canada. Offers analytical chemistry (M Sc); biochemistry (M Sc); environmental chemistry (M Sc); organic chemistry (M Sc); physical/theoretical chemistry (M Sc). *Program availability:* Part-time. *Degree requirements:* For master's, thesis or alternative. *Entrance requirements:* For master's, honors degree with minimum second class. *Faculty research:* Cell cycle checkpoints, kinetic modeling, toxicology to metal stress, quantum chemistry, biogeochemistry metal speciation.

Lehigh University, College of Arts and Sciences, Department of Chemistry, Bethlehem, PA 18015. Offers MS, PhD. *Program availability:* Part-time, online learning. *Faculty:* 18

full-time (3 women), 4 part-time/adjunct (2 women). *Students:* 37 full-time (16 women), 19 part-time (13 women); includes 5 minority (4 Asian, non-Hispanic/Latino; 1 Two or more races, non-Hispanic/Latino), 15 international. Average age 28. 42 applicants, 67% accepted, 10 enrolled. In 2015, 19 master's, 6 doctorates awarded. Terminal master's awarded for partial completion of doctoral program. *Degree requirements:* For master's, comprehensive exam, thesis; for doctorate, comprehensive exam, thesis/dissertation. *Entrance requirements:* Additional exam requirements/recommendations for international students: Required—TOEFL (minimum score 85 iBT). *Application deadline:* For fall admission, 1/15 priority date for domestic and international students. Applications are processed on a rolling basis. Application fee: $75. Electronic applications accepted. *Expenses:* Contact institution. *Financial support:* In 2015–16, 3 fellowships with full tuition reimbursements (averaging $25,000 per year), 8 research assistantships with full tuition reimbursements (averaging $25,000 per year), 19 teaching assistantships with full tuition reimbursements (averaging $25,000 per year) were awarded; career-related internships or fieldwork, Federal Work-Study, institutionally sponsored loans, scholarships/grants, and tuition waivers (full and partial) also available. Financial award application deadline: 1/15. *Faculty research:* Materials chemistry, biological chemistry, surface chemistry, nano science, organic. *Total annual research expenditures:* $2.9 million. *Unit head:* Prof. David A. Vicic, Professor/Chair, 610-758-3471, Fax: 610-758-6536, E-mail: dav512@lehigh.edu. *Application contact:* Dr. Rebecca Miller, Graduate Coordinator, 610-758-3471, Fax: 610-758-6536, E-mail: inluchem@lehigh.edu.
Website: http://www.lehigh.edu/chemistry

Long Island University–LIU Brooklyn, Richard L. Conolly College of Liberal Arts and Sciences, Brooklyn, NY 11201-8423. Offers biology (MA); chemistry (MS); clinical psychology (PhD); communication sciences and disorders (MS); creative writing (MFA); English (MA); media arts (MA, MFA); political science (MA); psychology (MA); social science (MS); speech-language pathology (MS); United Nations certificate program (Advanced Certificate); urban studies (MA); writing and production for television (MFA). *Program availability:* Part-time, evening/weekend, blended/hybrid learning. *Faculty:* 90 full-time (35 women), 125 part-time/adjunct (67 women). *Students:* 382 full-time (288 women), 223 part-time (154 women); includes 257 minority (129 Black or African American, non-Hispanic/Latino; 33 Asian, non-Hispanic/Latino; 80 Hispanic/Latino; 1 Native Hawaiian or other Pacific Islander, non-Hispanic/Latino; 14 Two or more races, non-Hispanic/Latino), 93 international. Average age 33. 801 applicants, 44% accepted, 169 enrolled. In 2015, 163 master's, 16 doctorates, 9 other advanced degrees awarded. *Degree requirements:* For doctorate, thesis/dissertation. *Entrance requirements:* Additional exam requirements/recommendations for international students: Required—TOEFL (minimum score 550 paper-based; 79 iBT). *Application deadline:* Applications are processed on a rolling basis. Application fee: $50. Electronic applications accepted. *Expenses:* $1,155 per credit tuition, $934 per term full-time fees, $442 per term part-time fees. *Financial support:* In 2015–16, 221 students received support, including 135 fellowships with full tuition reimbursements available (averaging $23,986 per year), 29 research assistantships with partial tuition reimbursements available (averaging $13,860 per year), 185 teaching assistantships with full tuition reimbursements available (averaging $20,790 per year). Financial award application deadline: 2/15; financial award applicants required to submit FAFSA. *Faculty research:* Nanocrystal polymerization of cellulose using electron microscopy. *Unit head:* Dr. David Cohen, Dean, 718-488-1003, E-mail: david.cohen@liu.edu. *Application contact:* Richard Sunday, Dean of Admissions, 718-488-1011, Fax: 718-780-6110, E-mail: bkln-admissions@liu.edu.

Louisiana State University and Agricultural & Mechanical College, Graduate School, College of Science, Department of Chemistry, Baton Rouge, LA 70803. Offers MS, PhD.

Louisiana Tech University, Graduate School, College of Engineering and Science, Department of Chemistry, Ruston, LA 71272. Offers MS. *Program availability:* Part-time. *Degree requirements:* For master's, thesis. *Entrance requirements:* For master's, GRE General Test, minimum GPA of 3.0 in last 60 hours. Additional exam requirements/recommendations for international students: Required—TOEFL. *Application deadline:* For fall admission, 8/1 for domestic students; for spring admission, 2/1 for domestic students. Applications are processed on a rolling basis. Application fee: $20 ($30 for international students). *Financial support:* Teaching assistantships and Federal Work-Study available. Financial award application deadline: 4/1. *Faculty research:* Vibrational spectroscopy, quantum studies of chemical reactions, enzyme kinetics, synthesis of transition metal compounds, nuclear magnetic resonance (NMR) spectrometry. *Unit head:* Dr. Lee Sawyer, Academic Director, 318-257-4053, Fax: 318-257-3823. *Application contact:* Marilyn J. Robinson, Assistant to the Dean, 318-257-2924, Fax: 318-257-4487.
Website: http://coes.latech.edu/chemistry/

Loyola University Chicago, Graduate School, Department of Chemistry and Biochemistry, Chicago, IL 60660. Offers MS, PhD. *Program availability:* Part-time, evening/weekend. *Faculty:* 16 full-time (2 women). *Students:* 36 full-time (17 women), 5 part-time (1 woman); includes 10 minority (4 Black or African American, non-Hispanic/Latino; 2 Asian, non-Hispanic/Latino; 3 Hispanic/Latino; 1 Two or more races, non-Hispanic/Latino), 9 international. Average age 28. 21 applicants, 90% accepted, 9 enrolled. In 2015, 4 master's, 7 doctorates awarded. Terminal master's awarded for partial completion of doctoral program. *Degree requirements:* For master's, thesis (for some programs); for doctorate, comprehensive exam, thesis/dissertation. *Entrance requirements:* For master's and doctorate, GRE General Test, GRE Subject Test. Additional exam requirements/recommendations for international students: Required—TOEFL (minimum score 550 paper-based). *Application deadline:* For fall admission, 8/1 priority date for domestic students; for spring admission, 12/1 for domestic students. Applications are processed on a rolling basis. Application fee: $50. Electronic applications accepted. Application fee is waived when completed online. *Expenses: Tuition, area resident:* Full-time $18,054; part-time $9027 per credit hour. *Required fees:* $832; $284 per credit hour. Part-time tuition and fees vary according to course load, degree level and program. *Financial support:* In 2015–16, 19 students received support, including 3 fellowships with full tuition reimbursements available (averaging $23,000 per year), 6 research assistantships with tuition reimbursements available (averaging $23,000 per year), 16 teaching assistantships with full tuition reimbursements available (averaging $23,000 per year); Federal Work-Study, scholarships/grants, traineeships, and unspecified assistantships also available. Financial award application deadline: 2/1; financial award applicants required to submit FAFSA. *Faculty research:* Magnetic resonance of membrane/protein systems, organometallic catalysis, novel synthesis of natural products. *Total annual research expenditures:* $682,510. *Unit head:* Dr. Duarte Freitas, Chair, 773-508-7045, Fax: 773-508-3086, E-mail: dfreita@luc.edu. *Application contact:* Stacey N. Lind, Graduate Program Coordinator, 773-508-3104, Fax: 773-508-3086, E-mail: slind@luc.edu.
Website: http://www.luc.edu/chemistry/

Marquette University, Graduate School, College of Arts and Sciences, Department of Chemistry, Milwaukee, WI 53201-1881. Offers analytical chemistry (MS, PhD); bioanalytical chemistry (MS, PhD); biophysical chemistry (MS, PhD); chemical physics (MS, PhD); inorganic chemistry (MS, PhD); organic chemistry (MS, PhD); physical chemistry (MS, PhD). *Program availability:* Part-time. *Faculty:* 19 full-time (3 women), 1 part-time/adjunct (0 women). *Students:* 43 full-time (14 women), 4 part-time (0 women); includes 2 minority (1 Asian, non-Hispanic/Latino; 1 Hispanic/Latino), 32 international. Average age 28. In 2015, 4 master's, 4 doctorates awarded. Terminal master's awarded for partial completion of doctoral program. *Degree requirements:* For master's, comprehensive exam; for doctorate, thesis/dissertation, cumulative exams. *Entrance requirements:* For master's and doctorate, official transcripts from all current and previous colleges/universities except Marquette, three letters of recommendation from individuals familiar with the applicant's academic work. Additional exam requirements/recommendations for international students: Required—TOEFL (minimum score 530 paper-based). *Application deadline:* Applications are processed on a rolling basis. Application fee: $50. Electronic applications accepted. *Financial support:* In 2015–16, 41 students received support, including 2 fellowships (averaging $17,134 per year), 30 teaching assistantships with full tuition reimbursements available (averaging $20,295 per year); research assistantships, scholarships/grants, health care benefits, tuition waivers (full and partial), and unspecified assistantships also available. Support available to part-time students. Financial award application deadline: 2/15. *Faculty research:* Inorganic complexes, laser Raman spectroscopy, organic synthesis, synthetic bioinorganic chemistry, electro-active organic molecules. *Total annual research expenditures:* $1.2 million. *Unit head:* Dr. Scott Reid, Chair, 414-288-7565, E-mail: scott.reid@marquette.edu. *Application contact:* Dr. Adam Fiedler, New and Recruiting, 414-288-1625.
Website: http://www.marquette.edu/chem/graduate.shtml

Marshall University, Academic Affairs Division, College of Science, Department of Chemistry, Huntington, WV 25755. Offers MS. *Students:* 1 full-time (0 women), 1 part-time (0 women), 1 international. Average age 27. In 2015, 4 master's awarded. *Degree requirements:* For master's, thesis. Application fee: $40. *Financial support:* Career-related internships or fieldwork available. *Unit head:* Dr. Michael Casteliani, Chairperson, 304-696-6486, E-mail: castella@marshall.edu. *Application contact:* Dr. John Hubbard, Information Contact, 304-696-2430, Fax: 304-746-1902, E-mail: hubbard@marshall.edu.

Massachusetts Institute of Technology, School of Science, Department of Chemistry, Cambridge, MA 02139. Offers biological chemistry (PhD); inorganic chemistry (PhD); organic chemistry (PhD); physical chemistry (PhD). *Faculty:* 29 full-time (6 women). *Students:* 236 full-time (81 women); includes 51 minority (2 Black or African American, non-Hispanic/Latino; 1 American Indian or Alaska Native, non-Hispanic/Latino; 30 Asian, non-Hispanic/Latino; 12 Hispanic/Latino; 6 Two or more races, non-Hispanic/Latino), 83 international. Average age 26. 591 applicants, 18% accepted, 38 enrolled. In 2015, 40 doctorates awarded. *Degree requirements:* For doctorate, comprehensive exam, thesis/dissertation, teaching assistantship during two semesters. *Entrance requirements:* For doctorate, GRE General Test. Additional exam requirements/recommendations for international students: Required—TOEFL (minimum score 600 paper-based), IELTS (minimum score 7). *Application deadline:* For fall admission, 12/15 for domestic and international students. Application fee: $75. Electronic applications accepted. *Expenses: Tuition:* Full-time $46,400; part-time $725 per credit. One-time fee: $304 full-time. Full-time tuition and fees vary according to course load and program. *Financial support:* In 2015–16, 218 students received support, including 62 fellowships (averaging $45,800 per year), 129 research assistantships (averaging $37,000 per year), 43 teaching assistantships (averaging $38,300 per year); Federal Work-Study, institutionally sponsored loans, scholarships/grants, traineeships, health care benefits, and unspecified assistantships also available. Support available to part-time students. Financial award application deadline: 4/15; financial award applicants required to submit FAFSA. *Faculty research:* Synthetic organic and organometallic chemistry including catalysis; biological chemistry including bioorganic chemistry; physical chemistry including chemical dynamics, theoretical chemistry and biophysical chemistry; inorganic chemistry including synthesis, catalysis, bioinorganic and physical inorganic chemistry; materials chemistry including surface science, nanoscience and polymers. *Total annual research expenditures:* $30.3 million. *Unit head:* Prof. Timothy F. Jamison, Department Head, 617-253-1803, Fax: 617-258-7500. *Application contact:* Graduate Administrator, 617-253-1845, Fax: 617-258-0241, E-mail: chemgradeducation@mit.edu.
Website: http://web.mit.edu/chemistry/

McGill University, Faculty of Graduate and Postdoctoral Studies, Faculty of Science, Department of Chemistry, Montréal, QC H3A 2T5, Canada. Offers chemical biology (M Sc, PhD); chemistry (M Sc, PhD).

McMaster University, School of Graduate Studies, Faculty of Science, Department of Chemistry, Hamilton, ON L8S 4M2, Canada. Offers analytical chemistry (M Sc, PhD); chemical physics (M Sc, PhD); chemistry (M Sc, PhD); inorganic chemistry (M Sc, PhD); organic chemistry (M Sc, PhD); physical chemistry (M Sc, PhD); polymer chemistry (M Sc, PhD). *Program availability:* Part-time. Terminal master's awarded for partial completion of doctoral program. *Degree requirements:* For master's, thesis; for doctorate, comprehensive exam, thesis/dissertation. *Entrance requirements:* For master's, minimum B+ average. Additional exam requirements/recommendations for international students: Required—TOEFL (minimum score 550 paper-based).

McNeese State University, Doré School of Graduate Studies, College of Science, Department of Chemistry, Program in Environmental and Chemical Sciences, Lake Charles, LA 70609. Offers chemistry (MS); chemistry/environmental science education (MS). *Program availability:* Evening/weekend. *Degree requirements:* For master's, comprehensive exam, thesis or alternative. *Entrance requirements:* For master's, GRE.

MCPHS University, Graduate Studies, Program in Medicinal Chemistry, Boston, MA 02115-5896. Offers MS, PhD. Terminal master's awarded for partial completion of doctoral program. *Degree requirements:* For master's, thesis, oral defense of thesis; for doctorate, one foreign language, comprehensive exam, thesis/dissertation, oral defense of dissertation, qualifying exam. *Entrance requirements:* For master's and doctorate, GRE General Test, minimum GPA of 3.0. Additional exam requirements/recommendations for international students: Required—TOEFL (minimum score 550 paper-based; 79 iBT). Electronic applications accepted. *Faculty research:* Analytical chemistry, medicinal chemistry, organic chemistry, neurochemistry.

Memorial University of Newfoundland, School of Graduate Studies, Department of Chemistry, St. John's, NL A1C 5S7, Canada. Offers chemistry (M Sc, PhD); instrumental analysis (M Sc). *Program availability:* Part-time. *Degree requirements:* For master's, thesis, research seminar, American Chemical Society Exam; for doctorate, comprehensive exam, thesis/dissertation, seminars, oral thesis defense, American Chemical Society Exam. *Entrance requirements:* For master's, B Sc or honors degree in chemistry (preferred); for doctorate, master's degree in chemistry or honors bachelor's degree. *Application deadline:* For fall admission, 3/1 for domestic students, 2/1 for international students. Applications are processed on a rolling basis. Application fee: $50 Canadian dollars ($100 Canadian dollars for international students). Electronic applications accepted. *Expenses: Tuition, area resident:* Full-time $2199 Canadian dollars. *International tuition:* $2859 Canadian dollars full-time. *Financial support:*

Chemistry

Fellowships, research assistantships, and teaching assistantships available. *Faculty research:* Analytical/environmental chemistry; medicinal electrochemistry; inorganic, marine, organic, physical, and theoretical/computational chemistry, environmental science and instrumental analysis. *Unit head:* Dr. Travis Fridgen, Head, 709-864-8772, Fax: 709-864-3702, E-mail: chemhead@mun.ca. *Application contact:* Dr. Christina Bottaro, Graduate Officer, 709-864-8088, Fax: 709-864-3702, E-mail: cbottaro@mun.ca.
Website: http://www.mun.ca/science/chemgrad/

Miami University, College of Arts and Science, Department of Chemistry and Biochemistry, Oxford, OH 45056. Offers MS, PhD. *Students:* 54 full-time (26 women), 1 part-time (0 women); includes 6 minority (3 Black or African American, non-Hispanic/Latino; 3 Hispanic/Latino), 21 international. Average age 27. In 2015, 5 master's, 10 doctorates awarded. *Entrance requirements:* For master's and doctorate, GRE General Test; GRE Subject Test (recommended), bachelor's degree in chemistry from accredited college or university; personal statement; three letters of recommendation. Additional exam requirements/recommendations for international students: Recommended—TOEFL (minimum score 80 iBT), IELTS (minimum score 6.5), TSE (minimum score 54). *Application deadline:* Applications are processed on a rolling basis. Application fee: $50. Electronic applications accepted. *Expenses:* Tuition, state resident: full-time $12,888; part-time $537 per credit hour. Tuition, nonresident: full-time $29,022; part-time $1209 per credit hour. *Required fees:* $530; $24 per credit hour. $30 per semester. Part-time tuition and fees vary according to course load and program. *Financial support:* Application deadline: 2/15; applicants required to submit FAFSA. *Unit head:* Dr. Michael Crowder, Professor and Chair, 513-529-2813, E-mail: crowdemw@miamioh.edu. *Application contact:* Dr. David Tierney, Professor, 513-529-3731, E-mail: tiernedl@miamioh.edu.
Website: http://www.miamioh.edu/cas/academics/departments/chemistry-biochemistry/

Michigan State University, The Graduate School, College of Natural Science, Department of Chemistry, East Lansing, MI 48824. Offers chemical physics (PhD); chemistry (MS, PhD); chemistry-environmental toxicology (PhD); computational chemistry (MS). *Entrance requirements:* Additional exam requirements/recommendations for international students: Required—TOEFL. Electronic applications accepted. *Faculty research:* Analytical chemistry, inorganic and organic chemistry, nuclear chemistry, physical chemistry, theoretical and computational chemistry.

Michigan State University, National Superconducting Cyclotron Laboratory, East Lansing, MI 48824. Offers chemistry (PhD); physics (PhD).

Michigan Technological University, Graduate School, College of Sciences and Arts, Department of Chemistry, Houghton, MI 49931. Offers MS, PhD. *Faculty:* 23 full-time (8 women). *Students:* 29 full-time (12 women), 4 part-time; includes 2 minority (both Black or African American, non-Hispanic/Latino), 21 international. Average age 28. 106 applicants, 7% accepted, 3 enrolled. In 2015, 2 master's, 3 doctorates awarded. Terminal master's awarded for partial completion of doctoral program. *Degree requirements:* For master's, thesis; for doctorate, comprehensive exam, thesis/dissertation. *Entrance requirements:* For master's and doctorate, GRE, statement of purpose, personal statement, official transcripts, 3 letters of recommendation, resume/curriculum vitae. Additional exam requirements/recommendations for international students: Required—TOEFL (recommended score 85 iBT) or IELTS. *Application deadline:* For fall admission, 1/1 priority date for domestic and international students. Applications are processed on a rolling basis. Electronic applications accepted. *Expenses:* Tuition, state resident: full-time $15,507; part-time $861.50 per credit. Tuition, nonresident: full-time $15,507; part-time $861.50 per credit. *Required fees:* $248; $248. Tuition and fees vary according to course load and program. *Financial support:* In 2015–16, 29 students received support, including 2 fellowships with tuition reimbursements available (averaging $14,516 per year), 1 research assistantship with tuition reimbursement available (averaging $14,516 per year), 23 teaching assistantships with tuition reimbursements available (averaging $14,516 per year); career-related internships or fieldwork, Federal Work-Study, scholarships/grants, traineeships, health care benefits, unspecified assistantships, and cooperative program also available. Financial award applicants required to submit FAFSA. *Faculty research:* Inorganic chemistry, physical/theoretical chemistry, bio/organic chemistry, polymer/materials chemistry, analytical/environmental chemistry. *Total annual research expenditures:* $200,122. *Unit head:* Dr. Cary F. Chabalowski, Chair, 906-487-2048, Fax: 906-487-2061, E-mail: cfchabal@mtu.edu. *Application contact:* Celine Grace, Office Assistant, 906-487-2048, Fax: 906-487-2061, E-mail: cegrace@mtu.edu.
Website: http://www.mtu.edu/chemistry/

Middle Tennessee State University, College of Graduate Studies, College of Basic and Applied Sciences, Department of Chemistry, Murfreesboro, TN 37132. Offers MS. *Program availability:* Part-time, evening/weekend, online learning. *Degree requirements:* For master's, comprehensive exam, thesis. *Entrance requirements:* For master's, GRE. Additional exam requirements/recommendations for international students: Required—TOEFL (minimum score 525 paper-based; 71 iBT) or IELTS (minimum score 6). Electronic applications accepted.

Mississippi College, Graduate School, College of Arts and Sciences, School of Science and Mathematics, Department of Chemistry and Biochemistry, Clinton, MS 39058. Offers MCS, MS. *Program availability:* Part-time. *Degree requirements:* For master's, comprehensive exam, thesis (for some programs). *Entrance requirements:* For master's, GRE. Additional exam requirements/recommendations for international students: Recommended—TOEFL, IELTS. Electronic applications accepted.

Mississippi State University, College of Arts and Sciences, Department of Chemistry, Mississippi State, MS 39762. Offers MA, MS, PhD. MA offered online only. *Program availability:* Online learning. *Faculty:* 12 full-time (1 woman). *Students:* 56 full-time (28 women), 2 part-time (0 women); includes 5 minority (3 Black or African American, non-Hispanic/Latino; 2 Hispanic/Latino), 37 international. Average age 28. 131 applicants, 25% accepted, 17 enrolled. In 2015, 4 master's, 10 doctorates awarded. Terminal master's awarded for partial completion of doctoral program. *Degree requirements:* For master's, thesis, comprehensive oral or written exam; for doctorate, thesis/dissertation, comprehensive oral or written exam. *Entrance requirements:* For master's, minimum GPA of 2.75 on last two years of undergraduate courses; for doctorate, minimum GPA of 2.75. Additional exam requirements/recommendations for international students: Required—TOEFL (minimum score 477 paper-based; 53 iBT); Recommended—IELTS (minimum score 4.5). *Application deadline:* For fall admission, 7/1 for domestic students, 5/1 for international students; for spring admission, 11/1 for domestic students, 9/1 for international students. Applications are processed on a rolling basis. Application fee: $60. Electronic applications accepted. *Expenses:* Tuition, area resident: Full-time $7502; part-time $833.74 per credit hour. Tuition, nonresident: full-time $20,142; part-time $2238.24 per credit hour. *Financial support:* In 2015–16, 9 research assistantships with full tuition reimbursements (averaging $18,301 per year), 44 teaching assistantships with full tuition reimbursements (averaging $18,201 per year) were awarded; Federal Work-Study, institutionally sponsored loans, scholarships/grants, and unspecified assistantships also available. Financial award application deadline: 4/1;

financial award applicants required to submit FAFSA. *Faculty research:* Spectroscopy, fluorometry, organic and inorganic synthesis, electrochemistry. *Total annual research expenditures:* $4.4 million. *Unit head:* Dr. Alan I. Marcus, Interim Department Head, 662-325-7813, Fax: 662-325-1618, E-mail: aim10@msstate.edu. *Application contact:* Meredith Nagel, Admissions Assistant, 662-325-9077, E-mail: mnagel@grad.msstate.edu.
Website: http://www.chemistry.msstate.edu/graduate/

Missouri State University, Graduate College, College of Natural and Applied Sciences, Department of Chemistry, Springfield, MO 65897. Offers chemistry (MS); natural and applied science (MNAS), including chemistry (MNAS, MS Ed); secondary education (MS Ed), including chemistry (MNAS, MS Ed). *Program availability:* Part-time. *Faculty:* 15 full-time (2 women). *Students:* 12 full-time (4 women), 11 part-time (7 women); includes 1 minority (Two or more races, non-Hispanic/Latino), 7 international. Average age 27. 22 applicants, 18% accepted, 4 enrolled. In 2015, 4 master's awarded. *Degree requirements:* For master's, comprehensive exam, thesis. *Entrance requirements:* For master's, GRE General Test (MS, MNAS), minimum undergraduate GPA of 3.0 (MS and MNAS), 9-12 teacher certification (MS Ed). Additional exam requirements/recommendations for international students: Required—TOEFL (minimum score 550 paper-based; 79 iBT), IELTS (minimum score 6). *Application deadline:* For fall admission, 7/20 priority date for domestic students, 5/1 for international students; for spring admission, 12/20 priority date for domestic students, 9/1 for international students; for summer admission, 5/20 priority date for domestic students. Applications are processed on a rolling basis. Application fee: $35 ($50 for international students). Electronic applications accepted. *Expenses:* Tuition, state resident: full-time $5500. Tuition, nonresident: full-time $10,108. *Required fees:* $1000. *Financial support:* In 2015–16, 17 teaching assistantships with full tuition reimbursements (averaging $8,732 per year) were awarded; Federal Work-Study, institutionally sponsored loans, scholarships/grants, and unspecified assistantships also available. Financial award application deadline: 3/31; financial award applicants required to submit FAFSA. *Faculty research:* Polyethylene glycol derivatives, electrochemiluminescence of environmental systems, enzymology, environmental organic pollutants, DNA repair via nuclear magnetic resonance (NMR). *Unit head:* Dr. Bryan Breyfogle, Department Head, 417-836-5601, Fax: 417-836-5507, E-mail: chemistry@missouristate.edu. *Application contact:* Michael Edwards, Coordinator of Graduate Admissions, 417-836-5330, Fax: 417-836-6200, E-mail: michaeledwards@missouristate.edu.
Website: http://chemistry.missouristate.edu

Missouri University of Science and Technology, Graduate School, Department of Chemistry, Rolla, MO 65409. Offers MS, MST, PhD. *Faculty:* 18 full-time (3 women), 1 part-time/adjunct (0 women). *Students:* 49 full-time (21 women), 7 part-time (1 woman), 40 international. Average age 28. 48 applicants, 31% accepted, 6 enrolled. In 2015, 9 master's, 10 doctorates awarded. Terminal master's awarded for partial completion of doctoral program. *Degree requirements:* For doctorate, one foreign language, thesis/dissertation. *Entrance requirements:* For master's, GRE (minimum score 600 quantitative, 3 writing), minimum GPA of 3.0; for doctorate, GRE (minimum score: quantitative 600, writing 3.5), minimum GPA of 3.0. Additional exam requirements/recommendations for international students: Required—TOEFL (minimum score 550 paper-based). *Application deadline:* For fall admission, 7/1 for domestic students. Applications are processed on a rolling basis. Application fee: $55 ($75 for international students). Electronic applications accepted. *Expenses:* Tuition, state resident: full-time $10,536. Tuition, nonresident: full-time $27,015. Full-time tuition and fees vary according to course load. *Financial support:* In 2015–16, 4 fellowships, 12 research assistantships with tuition reimbursements (averaging $1,814 per year), 22 teaching assistantships with tuition reimbursements (averaging $1,814 per year) were awarded; institutionally sponsored loans also available. *Faculty research:* Structure and properties of materials; bioanalytical, environmental, and polymer chemistry. *Total annual research expenditures:* $2.2 million. *Unit head:* Dr. Phil Whitefield, Chairman, 573-341-4340, Fax: 573-341-64891, E-mail: pwhite@mst.edu. *Application contact:* Dr. Pericles Stavropoulos, Information Contact, 573-341-7220, Fax: 573-341-6033, E-mail: pericles@mst.edu.
Website: https://chem.mst.edu/

Missouri Western State University, Program in Applied Science, St. Joseph, MO 64507-2294. Offers chemistry (MAS); engineering technology management (MAS); human factors and usability testing (MAS); industrial life science (MAS); information technology management (MAS); sport and fitness management (MAS). *Program availability:* Part-time. *Students:* 40 full-time (14 women), 38 part-time (12 women); includes 9 minority (8 Black or African American, non-Hispanic/Latino; 1 Asian, non-Hispanic/Latino), 19 international. Average age 29. 36 applicants, 92% accepted, 25 enrolled. In 2015, 28 master's awarded. *Entrance requirements:* Additional exam requirements/recommendations for international students: Recommended—TOEFL (minimum score 79 iBT), IELTS (minimum score 6). *Application deadline:* For fall admission, 7/15 for domestic and international students; for spring admission, 11/1 for domestic students, 10/15 for international students; for summer admission, 4/29 for domestic students. Applications are processed on a rolling basis. Application fee: $45 ($50 for international students). Electronic applications accepted. *Expenses:* Tuition, state resident: full-time $6290; part-time $314 per credit hour. Tuition, nonresident: full-time $11,490; part-time $574 per credit hour. *Required fees:* $542; $99 per credit hour. $176 per semester. One-time fee: $45. Tuition and fees vary according to course load and program. *Financial support:* Scholarships/grants and unspecified assistantships available. Support available to part-time students. *Unit head:* Dr. Benjamin D. Caldwell, Dean of the Graduate School, 816-271-4394, Fax: 816-271-4525, E-mail: graduate@missouriwestern.edu.

Montana State University, The Graduate School, College of Letters and Science, Department of Chemistry and Biochemistry, Bozeman, MT 59717. Offers biochemistry (MS, PhD); chemistry (MS, PhD). *Program availability:* Part-time. *Degree requirements:* For master's, comprehensive exam, thesis (for some programs); for doctorate, comprehensive exam, thesis/dissertation. *Entrance requirements:* For master's and doctorate, GRE General Test, transcripts, letter of recommendation. Additional exam requirements/recommendations for international students: Required—TOEFL (minimum score 550 paper-based). Electronic applications accepted. *Faculty research:* Proteomics, nano-materials chemistry, computational chemistry, optical spectroscopy, photochemistry.

Montclair State University, The Graduate School, College of Science and Mathematics, Program in Chemistry, Montclair, NJ 07043-1624. Offers MS. *Students:* 8 full-time (6 women), 9 part-time (6 women); includes 9 minority (4 Black or African American, non-Hispanic/Latino; 3 Asian, non-Hispanic/Latino; 2 Hispanic/Latino), 2 international. Average age 28. 9 applicants, 44% accepted, 3 enrolled. In 2015, 11 master's awarded. *Degree requirements:* For master's, thesis. *Entrance requirements:* For master's, GRE General Test, 24 undergraduate credits in chemistry, 2 letters of recommendation, essay. Additional exam requirements/recommendations for international students: Required—TOEFL (minimum score 83 iBT), IELTS (minimum score 6.5). *Application deadline:* Applications are processed on a rolling basis. Application fee: $60. Electronic applications accepted. *Expenses:* Tuition, state

resident: part-time $553 per credit. Tuition, nonresident: part-time $854 per credit. *Required fees:* $91 per credit. Tuition and fees vary according to program. *Financial support:* Federal Work-Study, scholarships/grants, and unspecified assistantships available. Support available to part-time students. Financial award application deadline: 3/1; financial award applicants required to submit FAFSA. *Faculty research:* Computational chemistry, nanochemistry, pharmaceutical biochemistry, medicinal chemistry, biophysical chemistry. *Unit head:* Dr. Marc Kasner, Chair, 973-655-6864. *Application contact:* Amy Aiello, Executive Director of The Graduate School, 973-655-5147, Fax: 973-973-7869, E-mail: graduate.school@montclair.edu.
Website: http://www.montclair.edu/catalog/view_requirements.php?CurriculumID-2913

Morgan State University, School of Graduate Studies, School of Computer, Mathematical, and Natural Sciences, Department of Chemistry, Baltimore, MD 21251. Offers MS. *Degree requirements:* For master's, comprehensive exam, thesis, oral defense of thesis. *Entrance requirements:* For master's, GRE General Test, minimum GPA of 2.5.

Mount Allison University, Department of Chemistry, Sackville, NB E4L 1E4, Canada. Offers M Sc. *Degree requirements:* For master's, thesis. *Entrance requirements:* For master's, honors degree in chemistry. *Faculty research:* Biophysical chemistry of model biomembranes, organic synthesis, fast-reaction kinetics, physical chemistry of micelles.

Murray State University, College of Science, Engineering and Technology, Program in Chemistry, Murray, KY 42071. Offers MS. *Program availability:* Part-time. *Degree requirements:* For master's, comprehensive exam (for some programs), thesis (for some programs). *Entrance requirements:* For master's, GRE General Test. Additional exam requirements/recommendations for international students: Required—TOEFL. *Faculty research:* Environmental, organic, biochemistry, analytical.

New Jersey Institute of Technology, College of Science and Liberal Arts, Newark, NJ 07102. Offers applied mathematics (MS); applied physics (M Sc, PhD); applied statistical models (Certificate); applied statistics (MS); biology (MS, PhD); biostatistics (MS); biostatistics essentials (Certificate); chemistry (MS, PhD); computational biology (MS); environmental science (MS, PhD); history (MA, MAT); materials science and engineering (MS, PhD); mathematical and computational finance (MS); mathematics science (PhD); pharmaceutical chemistry (MS); professional and technical communications (MS); technical common essentials (Certificate). *Program availability:* Part-time, evening/weekend. *Faculty:* 153 full-time (35 women), 100 part-time/adjunct (40 women). *Students:* 212 full-time (82 women), 94 part-time (37 women); includes 72 minority (22 Black or African American, non-Hispanic/Latino; 25 Asian, non-Hispanic/Latino; 19 Hispanic/Latino; 6 Two or more races, non-Hispanic/Latino), 164 international. Average age 29. 519 applicants, 62% accepted, 104 enrolled. In 2015, 98 master's, 21 doctorates, 3 other advanced degrees awarded. Terminal master's awarded for partial completion of doctoral program. *Degree requirements:* For master's, thesis optional; for doctorate, thesis/dissertation. *Entrance requirements:* For master's, GRE General Test; for doctorate, GRE General Test, minimum graduate GPA of 3.5. Additional exam requirements/recommendations for international students: Required—TOEFL (minimum score 550 paper-based; 79 iBT). *Application deadline:* For fall admission, 6/1 priority date for domestic students, 5/1 priority date for international students; for spring admission, 11/15 priority date for domestic and international students. Applications are processed on a rolling basis. Application fee: $75. Electronic applications accepted. *Expenses:* $28,800 per year non-resident full-time. *Financial support:* In 2015–16, 56 research assistantships with full tuition reimbursements (averaging $17,711 per year), 52 teaching assistantships with full tuition reimbursements (averaging $17,914 per year) were awarded; fellowships with full tuition reimbursements also available. Financial award application deadline: 1/15. *Total annual research expenditures:* $23.1 million. *Unit head:* Dr. Kevin Belfield, Dean, 973-596-3676, Fax: 973-565-0586, E-mail: kevin.d.belfield@njit.edu. *Application contact:* Stephen Eck, Director of Admissions, 973-596-3300, Fax: 973-596-3461,
E-mail: admissions@njit.edu.
Website: http://csla.njit.edu/

New Mexico Highlands University, Graduate Studies, College of Arts and Sciences, Department of Biology and Chemistry, Las Vegas, NM 87701. Offers chemistry (MS). *Program availability:* Part-time. *Degree requirements:* For master's, comprehensive exam, thesis. *Entrance requirements:* For master's, minimum undergraduate GPA of 3.0. Additional exam requirements/recommendations for international students: Required—TOEFL (minimum score 540 paper-based). *Faculty research:* Invasive organisms in managed and wildland ecosystems, juniper and pinyon ecology and management, vegetation and community structure, big game management, quantitative forestry.

New Mexico Highlands University, Graduate Studies, College of Arts and Sciences, Department of Natural Resources Management, Las Vegas, NM 87701. Offers natural science (MS), including chemistry.

New Mexico Institute of Mining and Technology, Center for Graduate Studies, Department of Chemistry, Socorro, NM 87801. Offers MS, PhD. *Program availability:* Part-time. *Degree requirements:* For master's, thesis; for doctorate, thesis/dissertation. *Entrance requirements:* For master's, GRE General Test; for doctorate, GRE General Test, GRE Subject Test. Additional exam requirements/recommendations for international students: Required—TOEFL (minimum score 540 paper-based). Electronic applications accepted. *Expenses:* Tuition, state resident: full-time $5811; part-time $322.81 per credit. Tuition, nonresident: full-time $19,220; part-time $1067.79 per credit. *Required fees:* $1030. Tuition and fees vary according to course load. *Faculty research:* Organic, analytical, environmental, and explosives chemistry.

New Mexico State University, College of Arts and Sciences, Department of Chemistry and Biochemistry, Las Cruces, NM 88003-8001. Offers chemistry (MS, PhD). *Program availability:* Part-time. *Faculty:* 19 full-time (7 women). *Students:* 37 full-time (11 women), 2 part-time (0 women); includes 6 minority (2 Asian, non-Hispanic/Latino; 3 Hispanic/Latino; 1 Two or more races, non-Hispanic/Latino), 23 international. Average age 31. 66 applicants, 14% accepted, 7 enrolled. In 2015, 6 master's, 6 doctorates awarded. *Degree requirements:* For master's, comprehensive exam, thesis; for doctorate, comprehensive exam, thesis/dissertation. *Entrance requirements:* For master's and doctorate, GRE, BS in chemistry or biochemistry, minimum GPA of 3.0. Additional exam requirements/recommendations for international students: Required—TOEFL (minimum score 550 paper-based; 79 iBT), IELTS (minimum score 6.5). *Application deadline:* For fall admission, 7/1 priority date for domestic students, 3/1 priority date for international students; for spring admission, 11/1 for domestic students, 9/1 priority date for international students. Applications are processed on a rolling basis. Application fee: $40 ($50 for international students). Electronic applications accepted. *Expenses:* Tuition, state resident: full-time $4086. Tuition, nonresident: full-time $14,254. *Required fees:* $853; $284.40. Tuition and fees vary according to course load. *Financial support:* In 2015–16, 37 students received support, including 9 research assistantships (averaging $18,901 per year), 25 teaching assistantships (averaging $17,816 per year); career-related internships or fieldwork, Federal Work-Study, scholarships/grants, traineeships, health care benefits, and unspecified assistantships also available. Support available to part-time students. Financial award application deadline: 3/1. *Faculty research:* Biochemistry, inorganic chemistry, organic chemistry, analytical chemistry, physical chemistry. *Total annual research expenditures:* $6.4 million. *Unit head:* Dr. William Quintana, Department Head, 575-646-2505, Fax: 575-646-2649, E-mail: wquintan@nmsu.edu. *Application contact:* Denise Pedraza, Administrative Assistant, 575-646-2556, Fax: 575-646-2649,
E-mail: dpedraza@nmsu.edu.
Website: http://www.chemistry.nmsu.edu/

New York University, Graduate School of Arts and Science, Department of Chemistry, New York, NY 10012-1019. Offers MS, PhD. *Degree requirements:* For master's, thesis or alternative; for doctorate, one foreign language, thesis/dissertation. *Entrance requirements:* For master's and doctorate, GRE General Test; GRE Subject Test (strongly recommended). Additional exam requirements/recommendations for international students: Required—TOEFL. *Faculty research:* Biomolecular chemistry, theoretical and computational chemistry, physical chemistry, nanotechnology, bio-organic chemistry.

New York University, Polytechnic School of Engineering, Department of Chemical and Biomolecular Engineering, Major in Chemistry, New York, NY 10012-1019. Offers MS. *Program availability:* Part-time, evening/weekend. *Degree requirements:* For master's, comprehensive exam (for some programs), thesis (for some programs). *Entrance requirements:* For master's, GRE General Test, GRE Subject Test. Additional exam requirements/recommendations for international students: Required—TOEFL (minimum score 550 paper-based; 80 iBT); Recommended—IELTS (minimum score 6.5). Electronic applications accepted. *Faculty research:* Optical rotation of light by plastic films, supramolecular chemistry, unusual stereochemical opportunities, polyaniline copolymers.

New York University, Polytechnic School of Engineering, Department of Chemical and Biomolecular Engineering, Major in Materials Chemistry, New York, NY 10012-1019. Offers PhD. *Program availability:* Part-time, evening/weekend. *Degree requirements:* For doctorate, comprehensive exam, thesis/dissertation. *Entrance requirements:* Additional exam requirements/recommendations for international students: Required—TOEFL (minimum score 550 paper-based; 80 iBT); Recommended—IELTS (minimum score 6.5). Electronic applications accepted.

New York University, Steinhardt School of Culture, Education, and Human Development, Department of Teaching and Learning, New York, NY 10003. Offers clinically rich integrated science (MA), including clinically rich integrated science, teaching biology grades 7-12, teaching chemistry 7-12, teaching physics 7-12; early childhood and childhood education (MA), including childhood education, early childhood education, early childhood education/early childhood special education; English education (MA, PhD, Advanced Certificate), including clinically-based English education, grades 7-12 (MA), English education (PhD, Advanced Certificate), English education, grades 7-12 (MA); environmental conservation education (MA); literacy education (MA), including literacy 5-12, literacy B-6; mathematics education (MA), including teachers of mathematics 7-12; multilingual/multicultural studies (MA, PhD, Advanced Certificate), including bilingual education, foreign language education (MA), teaching English to speakers of other languages (MA, PhD), teaching foreign languages, 7-12 (MA), teaching French as a foreign language (MA), teaching Spanish as a foreign language (MA); social studies education (MA), including teaching art/social studies 7-12, teaching social studies 7-12; special education (MA), including childhood, early childhood; teaching and learning (Ed D, PhD). *Program availability:* Part-time. *Degree requirements:* For doctorate, thesis/dissertation. *Entrance requirements:* For doctorate, GRE General Test, interview; for Advanced Certificate, master's degree. Additional exam requirements/recommendations for international students: Required—TOEFL (minimum score 100 iBT). Electronic applications accepted. *Faculty research:* Cultural contexts for literacy learning, school restructuring, parenting and education, teacher learning, language assessment.

North Carolina Agricultural and Technical State University, School of Graduate Studies, College of Arts and Sciences, Department of Chemistry, Greensboro, NC 27411. Offers MS, PhD. *Program availability:* Part-time, evening/weekend. *Degree requirements:* For master's, comprehensive exam, thesis or alternative, qualifying exam. *Entrance requirements:* For master's, GRE General Test, minimum GPA of 3.0. *Faculty research:* Tobacco pesticides.

North Carolina Central University, College of Science and Technology, Department of Chemistry, Durham, NC 27707-3129. Offers MS. *Degree requirements:* For master's, one foreign language, comprehensive exam, thesis. *Entrance requirements:* For master's, GRE, minimum GPA of 3.0 in major, 2.5 overall. Additional exam requirements/recommendations for international students: Required—TOEFL.

North Carolina State University, Graduate School, College of Physical and Mathematical Sciences, Department of Chemistry, Raleigh, NC 27695. Offers MS, PhD. *Program availability:* Part-time. Terminal master's awarded for partial completion of doctoral program. *Degree requirements:* For master's, thesis (for some programs); for doctorate, thesis/dissertation. *Entrance requirements:* For master's and doctorate, GRE General Test (recommended). Electronic applications accepted. *Faculty research:* Biological chemistry, electrochemistry, organic/inorganic materials, natural products, organometallics.

North Dakota State University, College of Graduate and Interdisciplinary Studies, College of Science and Mathematics, Department of Chemistry and Biochemistry, Program in Chemistry, Fargo, ND 58102. Offers MS, PhD.

Northeastern Illinois University, College of Graduate Studies and Research, College of Arts and Sciences, Program in Chemistry, Chicago, IL 60625-4699. Offers MS. *Program availability:* Part-time, evening/weekend. *Degree requirements:* For master's, comprehensive exam, final exam or thesis. *Entrance requirements:* For master's, 2 semesters of chemistry, calculus, organic chemistry, physical chemistry, and physics; 1 semester of analytic chemistry; minimum GPA of 2.75. Additional exam requirements/recommendations for international students: Required—TOEFL (minimum score 550 paper-based; 79 iBT). Electronic applications accepted. *Faculty research:* Liquid chromatographic separation of pharmaceuticals, Diels-Alder reaction products, organogermanium chemistry, mass spectroscopy.

Northeastern University, College of Science, Boston, MA 02115-5096. Offers applied mathematics (MS); bioinformatics (MS); biology (PhD); biotechnology (MS); chemistry (MS, PhD); ecology, evolution, and marine biology (PhD); marine biology (MS); mathematics (MS, PhD); network science (PhD); operations research (MSOR); physics (MS, PhD); psychology (PhD). *Program availability:* Part-time. *Faculty:* 216 full-time (70 women), 62 part-time/adjunct (20 women). *Students:* 517 full-time (252 women), 80 part-time (39 women). In 2015, 94 master's, 46 doctorates awarded. Terminal master's awarded for partial completion of doctoral program. *Degree requirements:* For master's, comprehensive exam (for some programs), thesis; for doctorate, comprehensive exam (for some programs), thesis/dissertation. *Entrance requirements:* For master's, GRE General Test. *Application deadline:* Applications are processed on a rolling basis.

Application fee: $75. Electronic applications accepted. *Expenses:* $1,325 per credit; $1,170 per credit (for marine biology). *Financial support:* Fellowships with tuition reimbursements, research assistantships with tuition reimbursements, teaching assistantships with tuition reimbursements, career-related internships or fieldwork, scholarships/grants, health care benefits, tuition waivers (full and partial), and unspecified assistantships available. Support available to part-time students. Financial award applicants required to submit FAFSA. *Unit head:* Dr. Jonathan Tilly, Interim Dean. *Application contact:* Graduate Student Services, 617-373-4275,
E-mail: gradcos@neu.edu.
Website: http://www.northeastern.edu/cos/

Northern Arizona University, Graduate College, College of Engineering, Forestry, and Natural Sciences, Department of Chemistry and Biochemistry, Flagstaff, AZ 86011. Offers chemistry (MS). *Program availability:* Part-time. *Faculty:* 11 full-time. *Degree requirements:* For master's, thesis. *Entrance requirements:* For master's, minimum GPA of 3.0. Additional exam requirements/recommendations for international students: Required—TOEFL (minimum score 550 paper-based; 80 iBT), IELTS (minimum score 7). *Application deadline:* For fall admission, 3/1 priority date for domestic and international students; for spring admission, 10/1 priority date for domestic and international students. Applications are processed on a rolling basis. Application fee: $65. Electronic applications accepted. *Expenses: Tuition, area resident:* Full-time $8710. Tuition, nonresident: full-time $20,350. *Required fees:* $896. *Financial support:* Research assistantships with full tuition reimbursements, teaching assistantships with full tuition reimbursements, Federal Work-Study, scholarships/grants, health care benefits, tuition waivers (full and partial), and unspecified assistantships available. Financial award applicants required to submit FAFSA. *Faculty research:* Biochemistry of exercise, organic and inorganic mechanism studies, inhibition of ice mutation, polymer separation. *Unit head:* Edgar Civitello, Chair, 928-523-3420,
E-mail: edgar.civitello@nau.edu. *Application contact:* Julie Gillette, Administrative Associate, 928-523-7079, Fax: 928-523-8111, E-mail: chemistry@nau.edu.
Website: http://nau.edu/cefns/natsci/chem-biochem/

Northern Illinois University, Graduate School, College of Liberal Arts and Sciences, Department of Chemistry and Biochemistry, De Kalb, IL 60115-2854. Offers chemistry (MS, PhD). *Faculty:* 16 full-time (1 woman), 3 part-time/adjunct (1 woman). *Students:* 38 full-time (14 women), 8 part-time (5 women); includes 6 minority (3 Black or African American, non-Hispanic/Latino; 2 Hispanic/Latino; 1 Two or more races, non-Hispanic/Latino), 13 international. Average age 28. 50 applicants, 44% accepted, 9 enrolled. In 2015, 4 master's, 9 doctorates awarded. Terminal master's awarded for partial completion of doctoral program. *Degree requirements:* For master's, comprehensive exam, thesis optional, research seminar; for doctorate, one foreign language, thesis/dissertation, candidacy exam, dissertation defense, research seminar. *Entrance requirements:* For master's, GRE General Test, bachelor's degree in mathematics or science, minimum GPA of 2.75; for doctorate, GRE General Test, bachelor's degree in mathematics or science; minimum undergraduate GPA of 2.75, 3.2 graduate. Additional exam requirements/recommendations for international students: Required—TOEFL (minimum score 550 paper-based). *Application deadline:* For fall admission, 6/1 for domestic students, 5/1 for international students; for spring admission, 11/1 for domestic students, 10/1 for international students. Applications are processed on a rolling basis. Application fee: $40. Electronic applications accepted. *Financial support:* In 2015–16, 9 research assistantships with full tuition reimbursements, 33 teaching assistantships with full tuition reimbursements were awarded; fellowships with full tuition reimbursements, career-related internships or fieldwork, Federal Work-Study, scholarships/grants, tuition waivers (full), and unspecified assistantships also available. Support available to part-time students. Financial award applicants required to submit FAFSA. *Faculty research:* Viscoelastic properties of polymers, lig and buding tocytochrome coxidases, computational inorganic chemistry, chemistry of organosilanes. *Unit head:* Dr. Jon Carnahan, Chair, 815-753-1181, Fax: 815-753-4802, E-mail: carnahan@niu.edu. *Application contact:* Graduate School Office, 815-753-0395, E-mail: gradsch@niu.edu.
Website: http://www.chembio.niu.edu/

Northwestern University, The Graduate School, Judd A. and Marjorie Weinberg College of Arts and Sciences, Department of Chemistry, Evanston, IL 60208. Offers PhD. Admissions and degrees offered through The Graduate School. *Degree requirements:* For doctorate, thesis/dissertation. *Entrance requirements:* For doctorate, GRE General Test, GRE Subject Test (chemistry). Additional exam requirements/recommendations for international students: Required—TOEFL. Electronic applications accepted. *Faculty research:* Inorganic, organic, physical, environmental, materials, and chemistry of life processes.

Oakland University, Graduate Study and Lifelong Learning, College of Arts and Sciences, Department of Chemistry, Rochester, MI 48309-4401. Offers biomedical sciences: health and environmental chemistry (PhD); chemistry (MS). *Faculty:* 13 full-time (5 women). *Students:* 15 full-time (5 women), 26 part-time (9 women); includes 2 minority (1 Black or African American, non-Hispanic/Latino; 1 Asian, non-Hispanic/Latino), 6 international. Average age 29. 33 applicants, 39% accepted, 10 enrolled. In 2015, 5 master's, 2 doctorates awarded. *Degree requirements:* For master's, thesis; for doctorate, thesis/dissertation. *Entrance requirements:* For master's, minimum GPA of 3.0; for doctorate, GRE Subject Test, minimum GPA of 3.0. Additional exam requirements/recommendations for international students: Required—TOEFL (minimum score 550 paper-based). *Application deadline:* Applications are processed on a rolling basis. Application fee: $0. Electronic applications accepted. *Expenses: Tuition, area resident:* Part-time $655 per credit. Tuition and fees vary according to program. *Financial support:* Federal Work-Study, institutionally sponsored loans, and tuition waivers (full) available. Financial award application deadline: 3/1; financial award applicants required to submit FAFSA. *Unit head:* Dr. Roman Dembinski, Department Chair/Professor, 248-370-2248, Fax: 248-370-2321, E-mail: dembinsk@oakland.edu. *Application contact:* Katherine Z. Rowley, Director, Graduate Admissions, 248-370-3167, Fax: 248-370-4114, E-mail: kzrowley@oakland.edu.
Website: http://www2.oakland.edu/chemistry/

The Ohio State University, Graduate School, College of Arts and Sciences, Division of Natural and Mathematical Sciences, Departments of Chemistry and Biochemistry, Columbus, OH 43210. Offers biochemistry (MS); chemistry (MS, PhD). *Degree requirements:* For master's, thesis optional; for doctorate, thesis/dissertation. *Entrance requirements:* For master's and doctorate, GRE General Test. Additional exam requirements/recommendations for international students: Required—TOEFL (minimum score 550 paper-based; 79 iBT), Michigan English Language Assessment Battery (minimum score 82); Recommended—IELTS (minimum score 7). Electronic applications accepted.

Oklahoma State University, College of Arts and Sciences, Department of Chemistry, Stillwater, OK 74078. Offers MS, PhD. *Faculty:* 27 full-time (4 women). *Students:* 19 full-time (12 women), 53 part-time (17 women); includes 7 minority (1 Black or African American, non-Hispanic/Latino; 3 Asian, non-Hispanic/Latino; 1 Hispanic/Latino; 2 Two or more races, non-Hispanic/Latino), 54 international. Average age 29. 84 applicants, 38% accepted, 15 enrolled. In 2015, 4 master's, 9 doctorates awarded. *Degree requirements:* For master's, thesis; for doctorate, comprehensive exam, thesis/dissertation. *Entrance requirements:* For master's and doctorate, GRE or GMAT. Additional exam requirements/recommendations for international students: Required—TOEFL (minimum score 550 paper-based; 79 iBT). *Application deadline:* For fall admission, 3/1 priority date for international students; for spring admission, 8/1 priority date for international students. Applications are processed on a rolling basis. Application fee: $40 ($75 for international students). Electronic applications accepted. *Expenses:* Tuition, state resident: full-time $3528; part-time $196 per credit hour. Tuition, nonresident: full-time $14,144; part-time $785.75 per credit hour. *Required fees:* $1895; $105.25 per credit hour. Tuition and fees vary according to campus/location. *Financial support:* In 2015–16, 18 research assistantships (averaging $23,179 per year), 46 teaching assistantships (averaging $22,563 per year) were awarded; career-related internships or fieldwork, Federal Work-Study, scholarships/grants, health care benefits, tuition waivers (partial), and unspecified assistantships also available. Support available to part-time students. Financial award application deadline: 3/1; financial award applicants required to submit FAFSA. *Faculty research:* Materials science, surface chemistry, and nanoparticles; theoretical physical chemistry; synthetic and medicinal chemistry; bioanalytical chemistry; electromagnetic (UV, VIS, IR, Raman), mass, and X-ray spectroscopes. *Unit head:* Dr. Frank D. Blum, Department Head, 405-744-5920, Fax: 405-744-6007, E-mail: fblum@okstate.edu. *Application contact:* Jimmie Weaver, Graduate Recruiter, 405-744-3966, E-mail: jimmie.weaver@okstate.edu.
Website: http://chemistry.okstate.edu

Old Dominion University, College of Sciences, Program in Chemistry, Norfolk, VA 23529. Offers analytical (MS, PhD); biochemistry (MS, PhD); environmental (MS, PhD); inorganic (MS, PhD); organic (MS, PhD); physical (MS, PhD). *Program availability:* Part-time, evening/weekend. *Faculty:* 19 full-time (5 women). *Students:* 35 full-time (17 women), 6 part-time (2 women); includes 5 minority (4 Black or African American, non-Hispanic/Latino; 1 Two or more races, non-Hispanic/Latino), 16 international. Average age 27. 20 applicants, 55% accepted, 4 enrolled. In 2015, 9 master's, 9 doctorates awarded. *Degree requirements:* For master's, comprehensive exam, thesis (for some programs); for doctorate, comprehensive exam, thesis/dissertation. *Entrance requirements:* For master's and doctorate, GRE General Test, minimum GPA of 3.0 in major, 2.5 overall, transcripts, essay, three letters of recommendation, resume. Additional exam requirements/recommendations for international students: Required—TOEFL. *Application deadline:* For fall admission, 7/1 for domestic students, 1/15 for international students; for spring admission, 11/1 for domestic students, 8/15 for international students. Applications are processed on a rolling basis. Application fee: $50. Electronic applications accepted. *Expenses:* $464 per credit in-state tuition; $1,160 per credit out-of-state tuition. *Financial support:* In 2015–16, 42 students received support, including 2 fellowships with full tuition reimbursements available (averaging $18,000 per year), 10 research assistantships with full tuition reimbursements available (averaging $18,000 per year), 33 teaching assistantships with full tuition reimbursements available (averaging $18,000 per year); career-related internships or fieldwork, institutionally sponsored loans, scholarships/grants, health care benefits, and unspecified assistantships also available. Financial award application deadline: 2/15; financial award applicants required to submit FAFSA. *Faculty research:* Biogeochemistry, materials chemistry, computational chemistry, organic chemistry, biofuels. *Total annual research expenditures:* $2.6 million. *Unit head:* Dr. John R. Donat, Graduate Program Director, 757-683-4098, Fax: 757-683-4628,
E-mail: chemgpd@odu.edu. *Application contact:* Kristi Rehrauer, Graduate Program Assistant, 757-683-6979, Fax: 757-683-4628, E-mail: krehraue@odu.edu.

Old Dominion University, Darden College of Education, Programs in Secondary Education, Norfolk, VA 23529. Offers chemistry (MS Ed); English (MS Ed); secondary education (MS Ed). *Accreditation:* NCATE. *Program availability:* Part-time, evening/weekend, online learning. *Faculty:* 13 full-time (7 women), 10 part-time/adjunct (7 women). *Students:* 49 full-time (32 women), 57 part-time (44 women); includes 20 minority (9 Black or African American, non-Hispanic/Latino; 3 Asian, non-Hispanic/Latino; 3 Hispanic/Latino; 5 Two or more races, non-Hispanic/Latino). Average age 32. 75 applicants, 71% accepted, 53 enrolled. In 2015, 72 master's awarded. *Degree requirements:* For master's, comprehensive exam, thesis. *Entrance requirements:* For master's, GRE General Test or MAT, PRAXIS I (for licensure), minimum GPA of 2.8, teaching certificate. Additional exam requirements/recommendations for international students: Required—TOEFL. *Application deadline:* For fall admission, 6/1 for domestic and international students; for winter admission, 11/1 for domestic and international students; for spring admission, 3/1 for domestic and international students. Applications are processed on a rolling basis. Application fee: $50. Electronic applications accepted. *Expenses:* Tuition, state resident: full-time $11,136; part-time $464 per credit hour. Tuition, nonresident: full-time $27,840; part-time $1160 per credit hour. *Required fees:* $64 per semester. Tuition and fees vary according to campus/location, program and reciprocity agreements. *Financial support:* In 2015–16, 56 students received support, including fellowships (averaging $15,000 per year), research assistantships with tuition reimbursements available (averaging $9,000 per year), teaching assistantships with tuition reimbursements available (averaging $15,000 per year). Financial award application deadline: 2/15; financial award applicants required to submit FAFSA. *Faculty research:* Use of technology, writing project for teachers, geography teaching, reading. *Unit head:* Dr. Robert Lucking, Graduate Program Director, 757-683-5545, Fax: 757-683-5862, E-mail: rlucking@odu.edu. *Application contact:* William Heffelfinger, Director of Graduate Admissions, 757-683-5554, Fax: 757-683-3255,
E-mail: gradadmit@odu.edu.
Website: http://education.odu.edu/eci/secondary/

Oregon State University, College of Science, Program in Chemistry, Corvallis, OR 97331. Offers analytical chemistry (MA, MS, PhD); inorganic chemistry (MA, MS, PhD); materials chemistry (MA, MS, PhD); nuclear chemistry (MA, MS, PhD); organic chemistry (MA, MS, PhD); physical chemistry (MA, MS, PhD). *Program availability:* Part-time. *Faculty:* 23 full-time (6 women). *Students:* 111 full-time (38 women), 4 part-time (2 women); includes 14 minority (1 Black or African American, non-Hispanic/Latino; 5 Asian, non-Hispanic/Latino; 6 Hispanic/Latino; 2 Two or more races, non-Hispanic/Latino), 49 international. Average age 28. 47 applicants, 51% accepted, 22 enrolled. In 2015, 6 master's, 12 doctorates awarded. Terminal master's awarded for partial completion of doctoral program. *Degree requirements:* For master's, one foreign language, thesis; for doctorate, one foreign language, thesis/dissertation. *Entrance requirements:* For master's and doctorate, GRE, minimum GPA of 3.0 in last 90 hours of course work. Additional exam requirements/recommendations for international students: Required—TOEFL (minimum score 80 iBT), IELTS (minimum score 6.5). *Application deadline:* For fall admission, 4/1 for domestic students. Application fee: $75 ($85 for international students). *Expenses:* Tuition, state resident: full-time $12,150; part-time $450 per credit. Tuition, nonresident: full-time $20,952; part-time $776 per credit. *Required fees:* $1572; $1443 per unit. One-time fee: $350. Tuition and fees vary according to course load, campus/location and program. *Financial support:* Fellowships, research assistantships, and teaching assistantships available. Support available to part-time students. *Faculty research:* Solid state chemistry, enzyme reaction mechanisms, structure and dynamics of gas molecules, chemiluminescence, nonlinear optical spectroscopy. *Unit head:* Dr. Rich G. Carter, Professor/Chair.

Application contact: Sarah Burton, Chemistry Advisor, 541-737-6808, E-mail: chemadm@chem.oregonstate.edu.
Website: http://chemistry.oregonstate.edu/

Pace University, School of Education, New York, NY 10038. Offers adolescent education (MST), including biology, business education, chemistry, earth science, English, foreign languages, mathematics, physics, social studies, visual arts; childhood education (MST); early childhood development, learning and intervention (MST); educational technology studies (MS); inclusive adolescent education (MST), including biology, business education, chemistry, earth science, English, foreign languages, mathematics, physics, social studies, visual arts; integrated instruction for educational technology (Certificate); integrated instruction for literacy and technology (Certificate); literacy (MS Ed); special education (MS Ed). *Accreditation:* NCATE. *Program availability:* Part-time, evening/weekend. *Faculty:* 19 full-time (13 women), 86 part-time/adjunct (49 women). *Students:* 112 full-time (95 women), 432 part-time (306 women); includes 179 minority (89 Black or African American, non-Hispanic/Latino; 1 American Indian or Alaska Native, non-Hispanic/Latino; 24 Asian, non-Hispanic/Latino; 55 Hispanic/Latino; 10 Two or more races, non-Hispanic/Latino), 9 international. Average age 30. 181 applicants, 78% accepted, 72 enrolled. In 2015, 261 master's, 11 other advanced degrees awarded. *Degree requirements:* For master's, internship. *Entrance requirements:* For master's, interview, teaching certificate. Additional exam requirements/recommendations for international students: Required—TOEFL (minimum score 88 iBT), IELTS or PTE. *Application deadline:* For fall admission, 8/1 priority date for domestic students, 6/1 for international students; for spring admission, 12/1 priority date for domestic students, 10/1 for international students. Applications are processed on a rolling basis. Application fee: $70. Electronic applications accepted. *Expenses:* Contact institution. *Financial support:* In 2015–16, 17 students received support, including 17 research assistantships with partial tuition reimbursements available (averaging $6,020 per year); career-related internships or fieldwork and Federal Work-Study also available. Financial award application deadline: 2/15; financial award applicants required to submit FAFSA. *Faculty research:* STEM education, TESOL, teacher education, special education, language and literary development. *Total annual research expenditures:* $290,153. *Unit head:* Dr. Xiao-Lei Wang, Dean, School of Education, 914-773-3876, E-mail: xwang@pace.edu. *Application contact:* Susan Ford-Goldschein, Director of Graduate Admissions, 212-346-1531, Fax: 212-346-1585, E-mail: graduateadmission@pace.edu.
Website: http://www.pace.edu/school-of-education

Penn State University Park, Graduate School, Eberly College of Science, Department of Chemistry, University Park, PA 16802. Offers chemistry (MS, PhD). *Unit head:* Dr. Douglas R. Cavener, Dean, 814-865-9591, Fax: 814-865-3634. *Application contact:* Lori Stania, Director, Graduate Student Services, 814-865-1795, Fax: 814-863-4627, E-mail: l-gswww@lists.psu.edu.
Website: http://chem.psu.edu/

Pittsburg State University, Graduate School, College of Arts and Sciences, Department of Chemistry, Pittsburg, KS 66762. Offers chemistry (MS); polymer chemistry (MS). *Students:* 20 (8 women); includes 1 minority (Hispanic/Latino), 14 international. In 2015, 4 master's awarded. *Degree requirements:* For master's, comprehensive exam (for some programs), thesis or alternative. *Entrance requirements:* Additional exam requirements/recommendations for international students: Required—TOEFL (minimum score 520 paper-based; 68 iBT), IELTS (minimum score 6), PTE (minimum score 47). *Application deadline:* For fall admission, 6/1 for international students; for spring admission, 10/15 for international students; for summer admission, 4/1 for international students. Applications are processed on a rolling basis. Application fee: $35 ($60 for international students). Electronic applications accepted. *Expenses:* $305 per credit for residents; $711 per credit for non-residents. *Financial support:* In 2015–16, 6 research assistantships with partial tuition reimbursements (averaging $5,000 per year), 4 teaching assistantships with full tuition reimbursements (averaging $5,500 per year) were awarded; career-related internships or fieldwork, Federal Work-Study, and unspecified assistantships also available. Financial award application deadline: 2/1; financial award applicants required to submit FAFSA. *Unit head:* Dr. Petar Dvornic, Chairperson, 620-235-4748, Fax: 620-235-4003, E-mail: pdvornic@pittstate.edu. *Application contact:* Lisa Allen, Assistant Director, 620-235-4223, Fax: 620-235-4219, E-mail: lallen@pittstate.edu.
Website: http://www.pittstate.edu/department/chemistry/

Pontifical Catholic University of Puerto Rico, College of Sciences, Department of Chemistry, Ponce, PR 00717-0777. Offers MS. *Program availability:* Part-time, evening/weekend. *Degree requirements:* For master's, thesis. *Entrance requirements:* For master's, GRE General Test, 2 letters of recommendation, minimum GPA of 3.0, minimum 37 credits in chemistry. Electronic applications accepted.

Portland State University, Graduate Studies, College of Liberal Arts and Sciences, Department of Chemistry, Portland, OR 97207-0751. Offers MA, MS, PhD. *Program availability:* Part-time. *Faculty:* 27 full-time (6 women), 5 part-time/adjunct (3 women). *Students:* 49 full-time (23 women), 4 part-time (2 women); includes 4 minority (1 Asian, non-Hispanic/Latino; 2 Hispanic/Latino; 1 Two or more races, non-Hispanic/Latino), 14 international. Average age 30. 75 applicants, 53% accepted, 27 enrolled. In 2015, 4 master's, 7 doctorates awarded. *Degree requirements:* For master's, one foreign language, thesis; for doctorate, one foreign language, thesis/dissertation, cumulative exams, seminar presentations. *Entrance requirements:* For master's, GRE General Test, GRE Subject Test, minimum GPA of 3.0 in upper-division course work or 2.75 overall, 2 letters of recommendation. Additional exam requirements/recommendations for international students: Required—TOEFL (minimum score 550 paper-based; 80 iBT). *Application deadline:* For fall admission, 1/1 priority date for domestic and international students; for winter admission, 9/1 for domestic and international students; for spring admission, 11/1 for domestic and international students. Application fee: $50. *Expenses:* $11,490 per year. *Financial support:* In 2015–16, 10 research assistantships with full tuition reimbursements (averaging $6,301 per year), 36 teaching assistantships with full tuition reimbursements (averaging $6,261 per year) were awarded; career-related internships or fieldwork, Federal Work-Study, scholarships/grants, tuition waivers (partial), and unspecified assistantships also available. Support available to part-time students. Financial award application deadline: 3/1; financial award applicants required to submit FAFSA. *Faculty research:* Synthetic inorganic chemistry, atmospheric chemistry, organic photochemistry, enzymology, analytical chemistry. *Total annual research expenditures:* $2.6 million. *Unit head:* Dirk Iwata-Reuyl, Chair, 503-725-5737, Fax: 503-725-3888, E-mail: iwatareuyld@pdx.edu. *Application contact:* Tam Rankin, Department Manager, 503-725-8756, Fax: 503-725-3888, E-mail: tam.rankin@pdx.edu.
Website: http://www.chem.pdx.edu/

Prairie View A&M University, College of Arts and Sciences, Department of Chemistry, Prairie View, TX 77446-0519. Offers chemistry (MS). *Program availability:* Part-time, evening/weekend. *Faculty:* 4 full-time (1 woman). *Students:* 10 full-time (7 women), 3 part-time (2 women); includes 9 minority (7 Black or African American, non-Hispanic/Latino; 1 Asian, non-Hispanic/Latino; 1 Hispanic/Latino), 3 international. Average age 28. 14 applicants, 64% accepted, 5 enrolled. *Degree requirements:* For master's, comprehensive exam, thesis. *Entrance requirements:* For master's, GRE General Test. Additional exam requirements/recommendations for international students: Required—TOEFL (minimum score 550 paper-based; 79 iBT). *Application deadline:* For fall admission, 7/1 priority date for domestic students, 6/1 priority date for international students; for spring admission, 11/1 priority date for domestic students, 10/1 priority date for international students; for summer admission, 3/1 priority date for domestic students, 2/1 priority date for international students. Applications are processed on a rolling basis. Application fee: $50. Electronic applications accepted. *Expenses:* Tuition, state resident: full-time $4243; part-time $237.29 per credit hour. Tuition, nonresident: full-time $11,798; part-time $657 per credit hour. *Required fees:* $2762; $172.10 per credit hour. *Financial support:* Research assistantships, teaching assistantships, career-related internships or fieldwork, Federal Work-Study, institutionally sponsored loans, and tuition waivers (full and partial) available. Support available to part-time students. Financial award application deadline: 4/1; financial award applicants required to submit FAFSA. *Faculty research:* Material science, environmental characterization (surface phenomena), activation of plasminogen's, polymer modifications, organic synthesis. *Unit head:* Dr. Remi R. Oki, Head, 936-261-3106, Fax: 936-261-3117, E-mail: aroki@pvamu.edu. *Application contact:* Pauline Walker, Office of Graduate Admissions, 936-261-3521, Fax: 936-261-3529, E-mail: gradadmissions@pvamu.edu.

Princeton University, Graduate School, Department of Chemistry, Princeton, NJ 08544-1019. Offers chemistry (PhD); industrial chemistry (MS). *Degree requirements:* For doctorate, thesis/dissertation, general exams. *Entrance requirements:* For master's, GRE General Test; for doctorate, GRE General Test, GRE Subject Test (recommended). Additional exam requirements/recommendations for international students: Required—TOEFL. Electronic applications accepted. *Faculty research:* Chemistry of interfaces, organic synthesis, organometallic chemistry, inorganic reactions, biostructural chemistry.

Purdue University, Graduate School, College of Science, Department of Chemistry, West Lafayette, IN 47907. Offers analytical chemistry (MS, PhD); biochemistry (MS, PhD); chemical education (MS, PhD); inorganic chemistry (MS, PhD); organic chemistry (MS, PhD); physical chemistry (MS, PhD). Terminal master's awarded for partial completion of doctoral program. *Degree requirements:* For master's, thesis; for doctorate, comprehensive exam, thesis/dissertation. *Entrance requirements:* For master's and doctorate, minimum undergraduate GPA of 3.0. Additional exam requirements/recommendations for international students: Required—TOEFL (minimum score 550 paper-based; 77 iBT); Recommended—TWE. Electronic applications accepted.

Queens College of the City University of New York, Mathematics and Natural Sciences Division, Department of Chemistry and Biochemistry, Flushing, NY 11367-1597. Offers chemistry (MA). *Program availability:* Part-time. *Faculty:* 13 full-time (3 women), 34 part-time/adjunct (11 women). *Students:* 9 full-time (4 women), 25 part-time (15 women); includes 8 minority (3 Black or African American, non-Hispanic/Latino; 3 Asian, non-Hispanic/Latino; 2 Hispanic/Latino), 16 international. Average age 27. 20 applicants, 60% accepted, 7 enrolled. In 2015, 10 master's awarded. *Degree requirements:* For master's, comprehensive exam. *Entrance requirements:* Additional exam requirements/recommendations for international students: Required—TOEFL (minimum score 61 iBT), IELTS (minimum score 5). *Application deadline:* For fall admission, 4/1 for domestic students; for spring admission, 11/1 for domestic students. Applications are processed on a rolling basis. Application fee: $125. Electronic applications accepted. *Expenses:* Tuition, state resident: full-time $5065; part-time $425 per credit. Tuition, nonresident: part-time $780 per credit. *Required fees:* $522. Part-time tuition and fees vary according to course load and program. *Financial support:* Career-related internships or fieldwork and unspecified assistantships available. Financial award application deadline: 4/1; financial award applicants required to submit FAFSA. *Unit head:* Dr. Wilma Saffran, Chairperson, 718-997-4144, E-mail: wilma.saffran@qc.cuny.edu.

Queen's University at Kingston, School of Graduate Studies, Faculty of Arts and Sciences, Department of Chemistry, Kingston, ON K7L 3N6, Canada. Offers M Sc, PhD. *Program availability:* Part-time. *Degree requirements:* For master's, thesis (for some programs); for doctorate, comprehensive exam, thesis/dissertation. *Entrance requirements:* Additional exam requirements/recommendations for international students: Required—TOEFL (minimum score 580 paper-based). *Faculty research:* Medicinal/biological chemistry, materials chemistry, environmental/analytical chemistry, theoretical/computational chemistry.

Rensselaer Polytechnic Institute, Graduate School, School of Science, Program in Chemistry, Troy, NY 12180-3590. Offers MS, PhD. *Faculty:* 28 full-time (4 women), 2 part-time/adjunct (0 women). *Students:* 37 full-time (16 women); includes 7 minority (4 Black or African American, non-Hispanic/Latino; 1 Asian, non-Hispanic/Latino; 1 Hispanic/Latino; 1 Two or more races, non-Hispanic/Latino), 14 international. Average age 25. 82 applicants, 30% accepted, 8 enrolled. In 2015, 5 master's, 3 doctorates awarded. Terminal master's awarded for partial completion of doctoral program. *Degree requirements:* For master's, thesis (for some programs); for doctorate, comprehensive exam, thesis/dissertation. *Entrance requirements:* For master's and doctorate, GRE. Additional exam requirements/recommendations for international students: Required—TOEFL (minimum score 600 paper-based; 100 iBT), IELTS (minimum score 7), PTE (minimum score 68). *Application deadline:* For fall admission, 1/1 priority date for domestic and international students; for spring admission, 8/15 priority date for domestic and international students. Applications are processed on a rolling basis. Electronic applications accepted. *Financial support:* In 2015–16, research assistantships (averaging $21,500 per year), teaching assistantships (averaging $21,500 per year) were awarded; fellowships also available. Financial award application deadline: 1/1. *Faculty research:* Analytical and bioanalytical chemistry; biotechnology; chemical biology and biochemistry; chemistry; inorganic and organometallic chemistry; nanotechnology, organic and medicinal chemistry; physical and computational chemistry; polymer and materials chemistry. *Unit head:* Dr. Peter Dinolfo, Graduate Program Director, 518-276-2326, E-mail: dinolp@rpi.edu. *Application contact:* Office of Graduate Admissions, 518-276-6216, E-mail: gradadmissions@rpi.edu.
Website: http://www.rpi.edu/dept/chem/academic/graduate.html

Rice University, Graduate Programs, Wiess School of Natural Sciences, Department of Chemistry, Houston, TX 77251-1892. Offers chemistry (MA); inorganic chemistry (PhD); organic chemistry (PhD); physical chemistry (PhD). Terminal master's awarded for partial completion of doctoral program. *Degree requirements:* For master's, thesis; for doctorate, thesis/dissertation. *Entrance requirements:* For master's and doctorate, GRE General Test, minimum GPA of 3.0. Additional exam requirements/recommendations for international students: Required—TOEFL (minimum score 600 paper-based; 90 iBT). Electronic applications accepted. *Faculty research:* Nanoscience, biomaterials, nanobioinformatics, fullerene pharmaceuticals.

Rochester Institute of Technology, Graduate Enrollment Services, College of Science, School of Chemistry and Materials Science, Rochester, NY 14623-5603. Offers chemistry (MS); materials science and engineering (MS). *Program availability:*

Part-time. *Students:* 16 full-time (6 women), 13 part-time (5 women); includes 4 minority (1 Black or African American, non-Hispanic/Latino; 2 Asian, non-Hispanic/Latino; 1 Hispanic/Latino), 11 international. Average age 26. 68 applicants, 43% accepted, 14 enrolled. In 2015, 14 master's awarded. *Degree requirements:* For master's, thesis or alternative. *Entrance requirements:* For master's, GRE (for some programs), minimum GPA of 3.0 (recommended). Additional exam requirements/recommendations for international students: Required—PTE (minimum score 58), TOEFL (minimum score 550 paper-based, 79 iBT) or IELTS (minimum score 6.5). *Application deadline:* For fall admission, 2/15 priority date for domestic and international students; for spring admission, 12/15 priority date for domestic and international students. Applications are processed on a rolling basis. Application fee: $60. Electronic applications accepted. *Expenses: Tuition, area resident:* Full-time $41,084; part-time $1742 per credit hour. *Required fees:* $274. Tuition and fees vary according to course load and program. *Financial support:* In 2015–16, 15 students received support. Research assistantships with partial tuition reimbursements available, teaching assistantships with partial tuition reimbursements available, career-related internships or fieldwork, scholarships/grants, and unspecified assistantships available. Support available to part-time students. Financial award applicants required to submit FAFSA. *Faculty research:* Organic chemistry, analytical chemistry, inorganic chemistry, physical chemistry, polymer chemistry, materials science, and biochemistry; polymer engineering, chemistry, and physics; nanomaterials; electronic materials; metallurgy; nonlinear phenomena; electronic properties of molecular crystals; experimental low temperature physics; large scale computations; parallel processing; superconductivity. *Unit head:* Dr. Paul Craig, Head, 585-475-2497, E-mail: science@rit.edu. *Application contact:* Diane Ellison, Associate Vice President, Graduate Enrollment Services, 585-475-2229, Fax: 585-475-7164, E-mail: gradinfo@rit.edu.
Website: https://www.rit.edu/cos/scms/

Roosevelt University, Graduate Division, College of Arts and Sciences, Department of Biological, Chemical, and Physical Sciences, Chicago, IL 60605. Offers biotechnology and chemical science (MS). *Program availability:* Part-time, evening/weekend. *Degree requirements:* For master's, thesis optional. *Entrance requirements:* For master's, minimum GPA of 2.7, undergraduate course work in science and mathematics. *Faculty research:* Phase-transfer catalysts, bioinorganic chemistry, long chain dicarboxylic acids, organosilicon compounds, spectroscopic studies.

Royal Military College of Canada, Division of Graduate Studies and Research, Science Division, Department of Chemistry and Chemical and Materials Engineering, Kingston, ON K7K 7B4, Canada. Offers chemical engineering (M Eng, MA Sc, PhD); chemistry (M Sc, PhD). *Degree requirements:* For master's, thesis; for doctorate, comprehensive exam, thesis/dissertation. *Entrance requirements:* For master's, honour's degree with second-class standing; for doctorate, master's degree. Electronic applications accepted.

Rutgers University–Camden, Graduate School of Arts and Sciences, Program in Chemistry, Camden, NJ 08102. Offers MS. *Program availability:* Part-time, evening/weekend. *Degree requirements:* For master's, comprehensive exam, thesis (for some programs), 30 credits. *Entrance requirements:* For master's, GRE (for assistantships), 3 letters of recommendation; statement of personal, professional and academic goals; chemistry or related undergraduate degree (preferred). Additional exam requirements/recommendations for international students: Required—TOEFL, IELTS; Recommended—TWE. Electronic applications accepted. *Faculty research:* Organic and inorganic synthesis, enzyme biochemistry, trace metal analysis, theoretical and molecular modeling.

Rutgers University–Newark, Graduate School, Program in Chemistry, Newark, NJ 07102. Offers analytical chemistry (MS, PhD); biochemistry (MS, PhD); inorganic chemistry (MS, PhD); organic chemistry (MS, PhD); physical chemistry (MS, PhD). *Program availability:* Part-time, evening/weekend. Terminal master's awarded for partial completion of doctoral program. *Degree requirements:* For master's, thesis optional, cumulative exams; for doctorate, thesis/dissertation, exams, research proposal. *Entrance requirements:* For master's and doctorate, GRE General Test, minimum undergraduate B average. Additional exam requirements/recommendations for international students: Required—TOEFL. Electronic applications accepted. *Faculty research:* Medicinal chemistry, natural products, isotope effects, biophysics and biorganic approaches to enzyme mechanisms, organic and organometallic synthesis.

Rutgers University–New Brunswick, Graduate School-New Brunswick, Department of Chemistry and Chemical Biology, Piscataway, NJ 08854-8097. Offers biological chemistry (MS, PhD); inorganic chemistry (MS, PhD); organic chemistry (MS, PhD); physical chemistry (MS, PhD). *Program availability:* Part-time, evening/weekend. Terminal master's awarded for partial completion of doctoral program. *Degree requirements:* For master's, thesis or alternative, exam; for doctorate, thesis/dissertation, 1 year residency. *Entrance requirements:* For master's and doctorate, GRE General Test, GRE Subject Test. Additional exam requirements/recommendations for international students: Required—TOEFL. Electronic applications accepted. *Faculty research:* Biophysical organic/bioorganic, inorganic/bioinorganic, theoretical, and solid-state/surface chemistry.

Rutgers University–New Brunswick, Graduate School-New Brunswick, Department of Environmental Sciences, Piscataway, NJ 08854-8097. Offers air pollution and resources (MS, PhD); aquatic biology (MS, PhD); aquatic chemistry (MS, PhD); atmospheric science (MS, PhD); chemistry and physics of aerosol and hydrosol systems (MS, PhD); environmental chemistry (MS, PhD); environmental microbiology (MS, PhD); environmental toxicology (PhD); exposure assessment (PhD); fate and effects of pollutants (MS, PhD); pollution prevention and control (MS, PhD); water and wastewater treatment (MS, PhD); water resources (MS, PhD). Terminal master's awarded for partial completion of doctoral program. *Degree requirements:* For master's, comprehensive exam, thesis or alternative, oral final exam; for doctorate, comprehensive exam, thesis/dissertation, thesis defense, qualifying exam. *Entrance requirements:* For master's and doctorate, GRE General Test. Additional exam requirements/recommendations for international students: Required—TOEFL. Electronic applications accepted. *Faculty research:* Biological waste treatment; contaminant fate and transport; air, soil and water quality.

Sacred Heart University, Graduate Programs, College of Arts and Sciences, Department of Chemistry, Fairfield, CT 06825. Offers MS. *Program availability:* Part-time, evening/weekend. *Faculty:* 4 full-time (1 woman), 2 part-time/adjunct (0 women). *Students:* 36 full-time (19 women), 5 part-time (4 women); includes 1 minority (Two or more races, non-Hispanic/Latino), 33 international. Average age 29. 116 applicants, 68% accepted, 20 enrolled. In 2015, 19 master's awarded. *Degree requirements:* For master's, thesis optional. *Entrance requirements:* For master's, bachelor's degree in related area (natural science with a heavy concentration in chemistry), minimum GPA of 2.75. Additional exam requirements/recommendations for international students: Required—PTE; Recommended—TOEFL (minimum score 570 paper-based; 80 iBT), IELTS (minimum score 6.5). *Application deadline:* For fall admission, 9/1 priority date for domestic students; for spring admission, 1/1 priority date for domestic students. Applications are processed on a rolling basis. Application fee: $75. Electronic applications accepted. *Expenses: Tuition, area resident:* Part-time $654 per credit hour. *Financial support:* Unspecified assistantships available. Financial award applicants required to submit FAFSA. *Unit head:* Dr. Eid Alkhatib, Chair, 203-365-7546, E-mail: alkhatibe@sacredheart.edu. *Application contact:* William Sweeney, Director of Graduate Admissions Operations, 203-365-7619, Fax: 203-365-4732, E-mail: gradstudies@sacredheart.edu.
Website: http://www.sacredheart.edu/academics/collegeofartssciences/academicdepartments/chemistry/graduatedegreesandcertificates/

St. Francis Xavier University, Graduate Studies, Department of Chemistry, Antigonish, NS B2G 2W5, Canada. Offers M Sc. *Degree requirements:* For master's, thesis. *Entrance requirements:* Additional exam requirements/recommendations for international students: Required—TOEFL (minimum score 580 paper-based). *Faculty research:* Photoelectron spectroscopy, synthesis and properties of surfactants, nucleic acid synthesis, transition metal chemistry, colloids.

St. John's University, St. John's College of Liberal Arts and Sciences, Department of Chemistry, Queens, NY 11439. Offers MS. *Program availability:* Part-time, evening/weekend. *Degree requirements:* For master's, comprehensive exam, thesis optional. *Entrance requirements:* For master's, GRE, minimum GPA of 3.0 (overall), 3.5 (in chemistry). Additional exam requirements/recommendations for international students: Required—TOEFL (minimum score 600 paper-based; 100 iBT), IELTS (minimum score 7). Electronic applications accepted. *Faculty research:* Synthesis and reactions of a-lactams, NMR spectroscopy or nucleosides, analytical chemistry, environment chemistry and photochemistry of transition metal complexes.

Saint Louis University, Graduate Education, College of Arts and Sciences and Graduate Education, Department of Chemistry, St. Louis, MO 63103. Offers MS, MS-R, PhD. *Program availability:* Part-time, evening/weekend. *Degree requirements:* For master's, thesis; for doctorate, comprehensive exam, thesis/dissertation. *Entrance requirements:* For master's, letters of recommendation, resume, interview; for doctorate, letters of recommendation, resumé, interview, transcripts, goal statement. Additional exam requirements/recommendations for international students: Required—TOEFL (minimum score 550 paper-based; 80 iBT). Electronic applications accepted. *Faculty research:* Photochemistry, energy, materials, biomaterials, nanomaterials.

Sam Houston State University, College of Sciences, Department of Chemistry, Huntsville, TX 77341. Offers MS. *Program availability:* Part-time. *Degree requirements:* For master's, comprehensive exam, thesis optional. *Entrance requirements:* For master's, GRE General Test, letters of recommendation. Additional exam requirements/recommendations for international students: Required—TOEFL (minimum score 550 paper-based; 79 iBT), IELTS (minimum score 6.5). Electronic applications accepted.

San Diego State University, Graduate and Research Affairs, College of Sciences, Department of Chemistry and Biochemistry, San Diego, CA 92182. Offers MA, MS, PhD. PhD offered jointly with University of California, San Diego. Terminal master's awarded for partial completion of doctoral program. *Degree requirements:* For doctorate, thesis/dissertation. *Entrance requirements:* For master's, GRE General Test, bachelor's degree in related field, 3 letters of reference; for doctorate, GRE General Test, GRE Subject Test. Additional exam requirements/recommendations for international students: Required—TOEFL. Electronic applications accepted. *Faculty research:* Nonlinear, laser, and electrochemistry; surface reaction dynamics; catalysis, synthesis, and organometallics; proteins, enzymology, and gene expression regulation.

San Francisco State University, Division of Graduate Studies, College of Science and Engineering, Department of Chemistry and Biochemistry, San Francisco, CA 94132-1722. Offers biochemistry (MS); chemistry and biochemistry (MS). *Program availability:* Part-time. *Application deadline:* Applications are processed on a rolling basis. Electronic applications accepted. *Expenses:* Tuition, state resident: full-time $6738. Tuition, nonresident: full-time $15,666. *Required fees:* $1004 per year. *Unit head:* Dr. Jane DeWitt, Chair, 415-338-1895, Fax: 415-338-2384, E-mail: dewitt@sfsu.edu. *Application contact:* Dr. Andrew Ichimura, Graduate Coordinator, 415-405-0721, Fax: 415-338-2384, E-mail: ichimura@sfsu.edu.
Website: http://www.chembiochem.sfsu.edu/0home/0layout.php

San Jose State University, Graduate Studies and Research, College of Science, San Jose, CA 95192-0001. Offers biological sciences (MA, MS), including molecular biology and microbiology (MS), organismal biology, conservation and ecology (MS), physiology (MS); chemistry (MA, MS); computer science (MS); cybersecurity (Certificate); cybersecurity: core technologies (Certificate); geology (MS); marine science (MS); master biotechnology (MBT); mathematics (MA, MS), including mathematics education (MA), science; meteorology (MS); physics (MS), including computational physics, modern optics, science (MA, MS); science education (MA); statistics (MS); unix system administration (Certificate). *Program availability:* Part-time, evening/weekend. *Students:* 118 full-time (68 women), 52 part-time (25 women); includes 125 minority (5 Black or African American, non-Hispanic/Latino; 97 Asian, non-Hispanic/Latino; 23 Hispanic/Latino), 121 international. Average age 27. 1,236 applicants, 21% accepted, 171 enrolled. In 2015, 168 master's awarded. *Entrance requirements:* For master's, GRE. *Application deadline:* For fall admission, 6/29 for domestic students; for spring admission, 11/30 for domestic students. Applications are processed on a rolling basis. Application fee: $55. Electronic applications accepted. *Financial support:* Teaching assistantships, career-related internships or fieldwork, Federal Work-Study, and institutionally sponsored loans available. Support available to part-time students. Financial award applicants required to submit FAFSA. *Faculty research:* Radiochemistry/environmental analysis, health physics, radiation effects. *Unit head:* J. Michael Parrish, Dean, 408-924-4800, Fax: 408-924-4815. *Application contact:* 408-924-2480, Fax: 408-924-2477.
Website: http://www.science.sjsu.edu/

The Scripps Research Institute, Kellogg School of Science and Technology, La Jolla, CA 92037. Offers chemical and biological sciences (PhD). *Degree requirements:* For doctorate, thesis/dissertation. *Entrance requirements:* For doctorate, GRE General Test, GRE Subject Test, 3 letters of recommendation, official transcripts. Additional exam requirements/recommendations for international students: Required—TOEFL. Electronic applications accepted. *Faculty research:* Molecular structure and function, plant biology, immunology, bioorganic chemistry and molecular design, synthetic organic chemistry and natural product synthesis.

Seton Hall University, College of Arts and Sciences, Department of Chemistry and Biochemistry, South Orange, NJ 07079-2697. Offers analytical chemistry (MS, PhD); biochemistry (MS, PhD); chemistry (MS); inorganic chemistry (MS, PhD); organic chemistry (MS, PhD); physical chemistry (MS, PhD). *Program availability:* Part-time, evening/weekend. Terminal master's awarded for partial completion of doctoral program. *Degree requirements:* For master's, thesis optional; for doctorate, comprehensive exam, thesis/dissertation. *Entrance requirements:* Additional exam requirements/recommendations for international students: Required—TOEFL. Electronic applications accepted. *Faculty research:* DNA metal reactions;

chromatography; bioinorganic, biophysical, organometallic, polymer chemistry; heterogeneous catalyst; synthetic organic and carbohydrate chemistry.

Simon Fraser University, Office of Graduate Studies, Faculty of Science, Department of Chemistry, Burnaby, BC V5A 1S6, Canada. Offers M Sc, PhD. *Degree requirements:* For master's, thesis; for doctorate, thesis/dissertation. *Entrance requirements:* For master's, minimum GPA of 3.0 (on scale of 4.33), or 3.33 based on last 60 credits of undergraduate courses; for doctorate, minimum GPA of 3.5 (on scale of 4.33). Additional exam requirements/recommendations for international students: Recommended—TOEFL (minimum score 580 paper-based; 93 iBT), IELTS (minimum score 7), TWE (minimum score 5). Electronic applications accepted. *Faculty research:* Analytical chemistry, inorganic and bioinorganic chemistry, organic and biological chemistry, physical and nuclear chemistry, chemical biology.

Smith College, Graduate and Special Programs, Department of Chemistry, Northampton, MA 01063. Offers secondary education (MAT), including chemistry. *Program availability:* Part-time. *Students:* 1 applicant, 100% accepted. *Entrance requirements:* Additional exam requirements/recommendations for international students: Required—TOEFL (minimum score 595 paper-based; 97 iBT), IELTS. *Application deadline:* For fall admission, 4/1 for domestic students, 1/15 for international students; for spring admission, 12/1 for domestic students. Application fee: $60. *Expenses: Tuition, area resident:* Full-time $34,560; part-time $1440 per credit. Tuition and fees vary according to course load and program. *Financial support:* Scholarships/grants available. Support available to part-time students. Financial award application deadline: 1/15; financial award applicants required to submit CSS PROFILE or FAFSA. *Unit head:* Cristina Suarez, Chair, 413-585-3838, E-mail: csuarez@smith.edu. *Application contact:* Ruth Morgan, Program Assistant, 413-585-3050, Fax: 413-585-3054, E-mail: gradstdy@smith.edu.
Website: http://www.science.smith.edu/departments/chem/

South Dakota State University, Graduate School, College of Arts and Science, Department of Chemistry, Brookings, SD 57007. Offers MS, PhD. *Degree requirements:* For master's, thesis, oral exam; for doctorate, thesis/dissertation, preliminary oral and written exams, research tool. *Entrance requirements:* For master's and doctorate, bachelor's degree in chemistry or closely related discipline. Additional exam requirements/recommendations for international students: Required—TOEFL (minimum score 580 paper-based; 92 iBT). *Faculty research:* Environmental chemistry, computational chemistry, organic synthesis and photochemistry, novel material development and characterization.

Southeast Missouri State University, School of Graduate Studies, Department of Chemistry, Cape Girardeau, MO 63701-4799. Offers MNS. *Program availability:* Part-time. *Faculty:* 10 full-time (4 women). *Students:* 16 full-time (11 women), 6 part-time (4 women); includes 2 minority (both Hispanic/Latino), 11 international. Average age 25. 27 applicants, 85% accepted, 11 enrolled. In 2015, 5 master's awarded. *Degree requirements:* For master's, comprehensive exam (for some programs), thesis. *Entrance requirements:* For master's, GRE General Test, minimum undergraduate GPA of 2.75 for last 30 semester hours of undergraduate science and math courses; 2 letters of recommendation from individuals competent to evaluate the candidate's potential for academic and professional success; minimum C grade in selected chemistry courses and labs. Additional exam requirements/recommendations for international students: Required—TOEFL (minimum score 550 paper-based; 79 iBT), IELTS (minimum score 6), PTE (minimum score 53). *Application deadline:* For fall admission, 4/1 for domestic and international students; for spring admission, 11/21 for domestic students, 10/1 for international students. Applications are processed on a rolling basis. Application fee: $30 ($40 for international students). Electronic applications accepted. *Expenses:* Tuition, state resident: part-time $260.80 per credit hour. Tuition, nonresident: part-time $486.80 per credit hour. *Required fees:* $33.70 per credit hour. *Financial support:* In 2015–16, 13 students received support, including 10 teaching assistantships with full tuition reimbursements available (averaging $8,467 per year); career-related internships or fieldwork, Federal Work-Study, scholarships/grants, traineeships, tuition waivers (full), and unspecified assistantships also available. Financial award application deadline: 6/30; financial award applicants required to submit FAFSA. *Faculty research:* Development of a method to identify ALS from cerebrospinal fluid using protein, electrochemistry of molecules of biological interest, environmental trace metal analysis: fingerprint age determination by chemometric analysis, green chemistry methodology and synthesis. *Unit head:* Dr. Philip W. Crawford, Chairperson and Professor, 573-651-2166, Fax: 573-651-2508, E-mail: pcrawford@semo.edu. *Application contact:* Dr. Mohammed H. Ali, Professor, 573-651-2983, Fax: 573-651-2508,
E-mail: mhali@semo.edu.
Website: http://www.semo.edu/chemistry/

Southern Connecticut State University, School of Graduate Studies, School of Arts and Sciences, Department of Chemistry, New Haven, CT 06515-1355. Offers MS. *Program availability:* Part-time, evening/weekend. *Faculty:* 6 full-time (2 women). *Students:* 9 full-time (1 woman), 7 part-time (3 women); includes 4 minority (3 Black or African American, non-Hispanic/Latino; 1 Two or more races, non-Hispanic/Latino). Average age 28. 13 applicants, 85% accepted, 8 enrolled. In 2015, 1 master's awarded. *Degree requirements:* For master's, thesis or alternative. *Entrance requirements:* For master's, interview, undergraduate work in chemistry. *Application deadline:* Applications are processed on a rolling basis. Application fee: $50. Electronic applications accepted. *Expenses:* Tuition, state resident: full-time $4968; part-time $494 per credit hour. Tuition, nonresident: full-time $16,078; part-time $509 per credit hour. *Required fees:* $4632; $55 per semester. Tuition and fees vary according to program. *Financial support:* Career-related internships or fieldwork, scholarships/grants, and unspecified assistantships available. Financial award application deadline: 4/15; financial award applicants required to submit FAFSA. *Unit head:* Dr. Jeffrey Webb, Chairperson, 203-392-5018, Fax: 203-392-6396, E-mail: webbj6@southernct.edu. *Application contact:* Lisa Galvin, Director of Graduate Admissions, 203-392-5240, Fax: 203-392-5235, E-mail: galvinl1@southernct.edu.

Southern Illinois University Carbondale, Graduate School, College of Science, Department of Chemistry and Biochemistry, Carbondale, IL 62901-4701. Offers MS, PhD. *Program availability:* Part-time. *Faculty:* 18 full-time (1 woman), 2 part-time/adjunct (0 women). *Students:* 39 full-time (19 women), 13 part-time (6 women); includes 2 minority (both Asian, non-Hispanic/Latino), 34 international. Average age 25. 31 applicants, 29% accepted, 5 enrolled. In 2015, 4 master's, 9 doctorates awarded. Terminal master's awarded for partial completion of doctoral program. *Degree requirements:* For master's, one foreign language, thesis; for doctorate, variable foreign language requirement, thesis/dissertation. *Entrance requirements:* For master's, GRE, minimum GPA of 2.7; for doctorate, GRE General Test, minimum GPA of 3.25. Additional exam requirements/recommendations for international students: Required—TOEFL. *Application deadline:* For fall admission, 1/2 for domestic students; for spring admission, 6/30 for domestic students. Applications are processed on a rolling basis. Application fee: $65. *Financial support:* In 2015–16, 38 students received support, including 8 research assistantships with full tuition reimbursements available, 30 teaching assistantships with full tuition reimbursements available; fellowships with full tuition reimbursements available, Federal Work-Study, institutionally sponsored loans, and tuition waivers (full) also available. Support available to part-time students. *Faculty research:* Materials, separations, computational chemistry, synthetics. *Total annual research expenditures:* $1 million. *Unit head:* Gary Kinsel, Chair, 618-453-6482, Fax: 618-453-6408. *Application contact:* Andrea Steen, Office Manager, 618-453-6413, E-mail: asteen@siu.edu.

Southern Illinois University Edwardsville, Graduate School, College of Arts and Sciences, Department of Chemistry, Edwardsville, IL 62026. Offers MS. *Program availability:* Part-time, evening/weekend. *Faculty:* 14. *Students:* 13 full-time (9 women), 20 part-time (12 women); includes 4 minority (1 Black or African American, non-Hispanic/Latino; 3 Asian, non-Hispanic/Latino), 13 international. 32 applicants, 59% accepted, 11 enrolled. *Degree requirements:* For master's, thesis optional, research paper. *Entrance requirements:* Additional exam requirements/recommendations for international students: Required—TOEFL (minimum score 550 paper-based; 79 iBT), IELTS (minimum score 6.5). *Application deadline:* For fall admission, 7/22 for domestic students, 7/15 for international students; for spring admission, 12/9 for domestic students, 11/15 for international students; for summer admission, 4/29 for domestic students, 4/15 for international students. Applications are processed on a rolling basis. Application fee: $30. Electronic applications accepted. *Expenses:* Tuition, state resident: full-time $5026; part-time $837 per course. Tuition, nonresident: full-time $12,566; part-time $2094 per course. *Required fees:* $1682; $474 per course. Tuition and fees vary according to course load, campus/location and program. *Financial support:* In 2015–16, 25 students received support, including 1 research assistantship with full tuition reimbursement available, 24 teaching assistantships with full tuition reimbursements available; fellowships with full tuition reimbursements available, institutionally sponsored loans, scholarships/grants, and unspecified assistantships also available. Financial award application deadline: 3/1; financial award applicants required to submit FAFSA. *Unit head:* Dr. Yun Lu, Program Director, 618-650-2042,
E-mail: yulu@siue.edu. *Application contact:* Bob Skorczewski, Coordinator of International and Graduate Recruitment, 618-650-3705, Fax: 618-650-3618,
E-mail: graduateadmissions@siue.edu.
Website: http://www.siue.edu/artsandsciences/chemistry/

Southern Methodist University, Dedman College of Humanities and Sciences, Department of Chemistry, Dallas, TX 75275-0314. Offers chemistry (MS, PhD); materials science and engineering (MS, PhD). Terminal master's awarded for partial completion of doctoral program. *Degree requirements:* For master's, thesis; for doctorate, comprehensive exam, thesis/dissertation. *Entrance requirements:* For master's, GRE General Test, bachelor's degree in chemistry, minimum GPA of 3.0; for doctorate, GRE General Test, bachelor's degree in chemistry or closely-related field, minimum GPA of 3.0. Additional exam requirements/recommendations for international students: Required—TOEFL (minimum score 550 paper-based; 80 iBT). Electronic applications accepted. *Faculty research:* Materials/polymer, medicinal/bioorganic, theoretical and computational, organic/inorganic/organometallic synthesis, inorganic polymer chemistry.

Southern University and Agricultural and Mechanical College, Graduate School, College of Sciences, Department of Chemistry, Baton Rouge, LA 70813. Offers analytical chemistry (MS); biochemistry (MS); environmental sciences (MS); inorganic chemistry (MS); organic chemistry (MS); physical chemistry (MS). *Degree requirements:* For master's, thesis. *Entrance requirements:* For master's, GMAT or GRE General Test. Additional exam requirements/recommendations for international students: Required—TOEFL (minimum score 525 paper-based). *Faculty research:* Synthesis of macrocyclic ligands, latex accelerators, anticancer drugs, biosensors, absorption isotheums, isolation of specific enzymes from plants.

Stanford University, School of Humanities and Sciences, Department of Chemistry, Stanford, CA 94305-5080. Offers PhD. *Degree requirements:* For doctorate, thesis/dissertation. *Entrance requirements:* For doctorate, GRE General Test, GRE Subject Test. Additional exam requirements/recommendations for international students: Required—TOEFL. Electronic applications accepted. *Expenses: Tuition, area resident:* Full-time $45,729. *Required fees:* $591.

State University of New York at New Paltz, Graduate School, School of Education, Department of Secondary Education, New Paltz, NY 12561. Offers adolescence education: biology (MAT, MS Ed); adolescence education: chemistry (MAT, MS Ed); adolescence education: earth science (MAT, MS Ed); adolescence education: English (MAT, MS Ed); adolescence education: French (MAT, MS Ed); adolescence education: social studies (MAT, MS Ed); adolescence education: Spanish (MAT, MS Ed); second language education (MS Ed, AC), including second language education (MS Ed), teaching English language learners (AC). *Accreditation:* NCATE. *Program availability:* Part-time, evening/weekend. *Faculty:* 11 full-time (7 women), 13 part-time/adjunct (9 women). *Students:* 46 full-time (30 women), 45 part-time (28 women); includes 28 minority (2 Black or African American, non-Hispanic/Latino; 1 Asian, non-Hispanic/Latino; 23 Hispanic/Latino; 2 Two or more races, non-Hispanic/Latino). Average age 30. 50 applicants, 62% accepted, 23 enrolled. In 2015, 33 master's awarded. *Degree requirements:* For master's, comprehensive exam (for some programs), portfolio. *Entrance requirements:* For master's, minimum GPA of 3.0, New York state teaching certificate (MS Ed). Additional exam requirements/recommendations for international students: Required—TOEFL (minimum score 550 paper-based; 80 iBT), IELTS (minimum score 6.5). *Application deadline:* For fall admission, 3/1 priority date for domestic students, 3/1 for international students; for spring admission, 10/1 priority date for domestic students, 10/1 for international students. Application fee: $50. Electronic applications accepted. *Financial support:* Application deadline: 8/1. *Unit head:* Dr. Laura Dull, Chair, 845-257-2849, E-mail: dullj@newpaltz.edu. *Application contact:* Vika Shock, Director of Graduate Admissions, 845-257-3285, Fax: 845-257-3284,
E-mail: gradschool@newpaltz.edu.
Website: http://www.newpaltz.edu/secondaryed/

State University of New York at Oswego, Graduate Studies, College of Liberal Arts and Sciences, Department of Chemistry, Oswego, NY 13126. Offers MS. *Program availability:* Part-time. *Degree requirements:* For master's, comprehensive exam, thesis. *Entrance requirements:* For master's, GRE General Test, GRE Subject Test, BA or BS in chemistry. Additional exam requirements/recommendations for international students: Required—TOEFL (minimum score 560 paper-based).

State University of New York College of Environmental Science and Forestry, Department of Chemistry, Syracuse, NY 13210-2779. Offers biochemistry (MPS, MS, PhD); environmental chemistry (MPS, MS, PhD); organic chemistry of natural products (MPS, MS, PhD); polymer chemistry (MPS, MS, PhD). *Faculty:* 17 full-time (2 women), 1 part-time/adjunct (0 women). *Students:* 33 full-time (13 women), 5 part-time (2 women); includes 2 minority (1 Black or African American, non-Hispanic/Latino; 1 Asian, non-Hispanic/Latino), 10 international. 55 applicants, 67% accepted, 12 enrolled. In 2015, 4 master's, 7 doctorates awarded. *Degree requirements:* For master's, thesis; for doctorate, comprehensive exam, thesis/dissertation. *Entrance requirements:* For master's and doctorate, GRE General Test, GRE Subject Test, minimum GPA of 3.0.

Additional exam requirements/recommendations for international students: Required—TOEFL (minimum score 550 paper-based; 80 iBT), IELTS (minimum score 6). *Application deadline:* For fall admission, 2/1 priority date for domestic and international students; for spring admission, 11/1 priority date for domestic and international students. Applications are processed on a rolling basis. Application fee: $60. Electronic applications accepted. *Expenses:* Tuition, state resident: full-time $10,870; part-time $453 per credit. Tuition, nonresident: full-time $22,210; part-time $925 per credit. *Required fees:* $1075; $89.22 per credit. *Financial support:* In 2015–16, 40 students received support, including 5 fellowships with full tuition reimbursements available (averaging $4,000 per year), 19 research assistantships with full tuition reimbursements available (averaging $20,000 per year), 44 teaching assistantships with full tuition reimbursements available (averaging $21,300 per year); Federal Work-Study, institutionally sponsored loans, scholarships/grants, health care benefits, unspecified assistantships, and departmental tuition assistance also available. Financial award application deadline: 6/30; financial award applicants required to submit FAFSA. *Faculty research:* Polymer chemistry, biochemistry, environmental chemistry, natural products chemistry. *Total annual research expenditures:* $1.8 million. *Unit head:* Prof. Ivan Gitsov, Chair, 315-470-6851, Fax: 315-470-6856, E-mail: igivanov@syr.edu. *Application contact:* Scott Shannon, Associate Provost for Instruction/Dean of the Graduate School, 315-470-6599, Fax: 315-470-6978, E-mail: sshannon@esf.edu.
Website: http://www.esf.edu/chemistry

Stephen F. Austin State University, Graduate School, College of Sciences and Mathematics, Department of Chemistry, Nacogdoches, TX 75962. Offers MS. *Program availability:* Part-time. *Degree requirements:* For master's, comprehensive exam. *Entrance requirements:* For master's, GRE General Test, minimum GPA of 2.8 in last 60 hours, 2.5 overall. Additional exam requirements/recommendations for international students: Required—TOEFL. *Faculty research:* Synthesis and chemistry of ferrate ion, properties of fluoroberyllates, polymer chemistry.

Stevens Institute of Technology, Graduate School, Charles V. Schaefer Jr. School of Engineering, Department of Chemistry, Chemical Biology and Biomedical Engineering, Program in Chemistry, Hoboken, NJ 07030. Offers MS, PhD, Certificate. *Program availability:* Part-time, evening/weekend. *Students:* 26 full-time (15 women), 1 (woman) part-time, 23 international. Average age 26. 69 applicants, 46% accepted, 7 enrolled. In 2015, 5 master's, 1 doctorate awarded. *Entrance requirements:* Additional exam requirements/recommendations for international students: Required—TOEFL (minimum score 74 iBT). *Application deadline:* For fall admission, 6/1 for domestic students, 4/15 for international students; for spring admission, 11/30 for domestic students, 11/1 for international students. Applications are processed on a rolling basis. Application fee: $60. Electronic applications accepted. *Expenses: Tuition, area resident:* Full-time $32,200; part-time $1450 per credit. *Required fees:* $1150; $550 per unit. $275 per semester. *Financial support:* Fellowships, research assistantships, teaching assistantships, career-related internships or fieldwork, Federal Work-Study, and unspecified assistantships available. Financial award application deadline: 2/15; financial award applicants required to submit FAFSA. *Unit head:* Patricia Muisener, Program Director, 201-216-3715, Fax: 201-216-8240,
E-mail: patricia.muisener@stevens.edu. *Application contact:* Graduate Admissions, 888-783-8367, Fax: 888-511-1306, E-mail: graduate@stevens.edu.

Stevenson University, Program in Forensic Science, Owings Mills, MD 21117. Offers biology (MS); chemistry (MS); crime scene investigation (MS). Program offered in partnership with Maryland State Police Forensic Sciences Division. *Program availability:* Part-time. *Faculty:* 4 full-time (3 women), 5 part-time/adjunct (2 women). *Students:* 20 full-time (14 women), 23 part-time (18 women); includes 19 minority (18 Black or African American, non-Hispanic/Latino; 1 Hispanic/Latino). Average age 27. 28 applicants, 71% accepted, 16 enrolled. In 2015, 23 master's awarded. *Degree requirements:* For master's, capstone course. *Entrance requirements:* For master's, bachelor's degree in a natural science from regionally-accredited institution; official college transcripts from all previous academic work; minimum cumulative GPA of 3.0 in past academic work. Additional exam requirements/recommendations for international students: Required—TOEFL (minimum score 550 paper-based), IELTS (minimum score 6.5). *Application deadline:* Applications are processed on a rolling basis. Application fee: $0. Electronic applications accepted. *Expenses:* $670 per credit, $125 fee per semester. *Financial support:* Applicants required to submit FAFSA. *Unit head:* John Tobin, PhD, Coordinator, 443-352-4142, Fax: 443-394-0538, E-mail: jtobin@stevenson.edu. *Application contact:* William Wellein, Enrollment Counselor, 443-352-5843, Fax: 443-394-0538, E-mail: wwellein@stevenson.edu.
Website: http://www.stevenson.edu

Stony Brook University, State University of New York, Graduate School, College of Arts and Sciences, Department of Chemistry, Stony Brook, NY 11794. Offers MS, PhD. *Faculty:* 39 full-time (9 women), 3 part-time/adjunct (0 women). *Students:* 192 full-time (92 women), 2 part-time (both women); includes 31 minority (7 Black or African American, non-Hispanic/Latino; 12 Asian, non-Hispanic/Latino; 12 Hispanic/Latino), 115 international. Average age 26. 358 applicants, 42% accepted, 48 enrolled. In 2015, 15 master's, 29 doctorates awarded. Terminal master's awarded for partial completion of doctoral program. *Degree requirements:* For master's, thesis; for doctorate, one foreign language, thesis/dissertation. *Entrance requirements:* For master's and doctorate, GRE General Test. Additional exam requirements/recommendations for international students: Required—TOEFL (minimum score 90 iBT). *Application deadline:* For fall admission, 1/15 for domestic students; for spring admission, 10/1 for domestic students. Application fee: $100. *Expenses:* $12,421 full-time resident tuition and fees, $453 per credit hour; $23,761 full-time nonresident tuition and fees, $925 per credit hour. *Financial support:* In 2015–16, 13 fellowships, 103 research assistantships, 60 teaching assistantships were awarded. *Faculty research:* Bioimaging, Chemical Sciences, Chemistry, Spectroscopy, Enzymology. *Total annual research expenditures:* $8 million. *Unit head:* Prof. Nicole Sampson, Chairman, 631-632-7952, Fax: 631-632-7960,
E-mail: nicole.sampson@stonybrook.edu. *Application contact:* Katherine Hughes, Coordinator, 631-632-7886, Fax: 631-632-7960,
E-mail: katherine.hughes@stonybrook.edu.
Website: http://ws.cc.stonybrook.edu/chemistry/

Syracuse University, College of Arts and Sciences, Programs in Chemistry, Syracuse, NY 13244. Offers chemistry (MS, PhD). *Students:* Average age 25. *Degree requirements:* For master's, comprehensive exam, thesis (for some programs); for doctorate, comprehensive exam, thesis/dissertation. *Entrance requirements:* For master's and doctorate, GRE General Test, official transcripts, three letters of recommendation, curriculum vitae, personal statement. Additional exam requirements/recommendations for international students: Required—TOEFL (minimum score 100 iBT). *Application deadline:* For fall admission, 3/15 priority date for domestic and international students. Application fee: $75. Electronic applications accepted. *Expenses: Tuition, area resident:* Full-time $25,974; part-time $1443 per credit hour. *Required fees:* $802; $50 per course. Tuition and fees vary according to course load and program. *Financial support:* Fellowships with full tuition reimbursements, research assistantships with tuition reimbursements, teaching assistantships with tuition reimbursements, and scholarships/grants available. Financial award application deadline: 1/1. *Faculty research:* Synthetic organic chemistry, biophysical spectroscopy, solid state in organic chemistry, biochemistry, organometallic chemistry. *Unit head:* Dr. Jon Zubieta, Chair, 315-443-2547, Fax: 315-443-4070, E-mail: jazubiet@syr.edu. *Application contact:* Jodi Randall, Graduate Admissions Coordinator, 315-443-5908, E-mail: chemgrad@syr.edu.
Website: http://chemistry.syr.edu

Syracuse University, School of Education, Programs in Science Education, Syracuse, NY 13244. Offers biology (MS, PhD); chemistry (MS, PhD); earth science (MS, PhD); physics (MS, PhD). *Program availability:* Part-time. *Students:* Average age 38. In 2015, 4 doctorates awarded. *Degree requirements:* For doctorate, comprehensive exam, thesis/dissertation. *Entrance requirements:* For master's, official transcripts from previous academic institutions, 3 letters of recommendation (preferably from faculty), personal statement that makes a clear and compelling argument for why applicant wants to teach secondary science; for doctorate, GRE General Test or MAT, master's degree, interview. Additional exam requirements/recommendations for international students: Required—TOEFL (minimum score 100 iBT). *Application deadline:* For fall admission, 1/15 priority date for domestic and international students; for spring admission, 10/15 priority date for domestic and international students. Applications are processed on a rolling basis. Application fee: $75. Electronic applications accepted. *Expenses: Tuition, area resident:* Full-time $25,974; part-time $1443 per credit hour. *Required fees:* $802; $50 per course. Tuition and fees vary according to course load and program. *Financial support:* Fellowships with full tuition reimbursements, research assistantships with tuition reimbursements, teaching assistantships with tuition reimbursements, and scholarships/grants available. Financial award application deadline: 1/15. *Faculty research:* Diverse field experiences and theoretical and practical knowledge in research-based science teaching, biology, chemistry, earth science, and physics.. *Unit head:* Dr. John Tillotson, Program Coordinator, 315-443-9137, E-mail: jwtillot@syr.edu. *Application contact:* Speranza Migliore, Graduate Admissions Recruiter, 315-443-2505, E-mail: gradrcrt@syr.edu.
Website: http://soeweb.syr.edu/

Teachers College, Columbia University, Department of Mathematics, Science and Technology, New York, NY 10027-6696. Offers biology 7-12 (MA); chemistry 7-12 (MA); communication and education (MA); communications (Ed M); communications and education (Ed D); computing in education (MA); computing in education-distant learning (MA); earth science 7-12 (MA); instructional technology and media (Ed M, MA, Ed D); mathematics education (Ed M, MA, Ed D, Ed DCT, PhD); physics 7-12 (MA); science and dental education (MA); science education (Ed M, MS, Ed DCT, PhD); supervisor / teacher of science education (MA); technology specialist (MA). *Program availability:* Part-time, evening/weekend. *Students:* 134 full-time (89 women), 285 part-time (168 women); includes 219 minority (49 Black or African American, non-Hispanic/Latino; 124 Asian, non-Hispanic/Latino; 31 Hispanic/Latino; 15 Two or more races, non-Hispanic/Latino), 29 international. Terminal master's awarded for partial completion of doctoral program. *Degree requirements:* For doctorate, thesis/dissertation. *Expenses: Tuition, area resident:* Part-time $1454 per credit. *Required fees:* $428 per semester. One-time fee: $475 full-time. Full-time tuition and fees vary according to course load. *Unit head:* Dr. O. Roger Anderson, Chair, 212-678-3405, Fax: 212-678-8129,
E-mail: ora@ldeo.columbia.edu. *Application contact:* David Estrella, Director of Admission, E-mail: estrella@tc.columbia.edu.
Website: http://www.tc.columbia.edu/mathematics-science-and-technology/

Temple University, College of Science and Technology, Department of Chemistry, Philadelphia, PA 19122. Offers MA, PhD. *Program availability:* Evening/weekend. *Faculty:* 35 full-time (7 women). *Students:* 122 full-time (41 women), 5 part-time (3 women); includes 10 minority (4 Black or African American, non-Hispanic/Latino; 4 Asian, non-Hispanic/Latino; 2 Hispanic/Latino), 48 international. 112 applicants, 55% accepted, 29 enrolled. In 2015, 8 master's, 9 doctorates awarded. Terminal master's awarded for partial completion of doctoral program. *Degree requirements:* For master's, thesis (for some programs); for doctorate, thesis/dissertation, teaching experience. *Entrance requirements:* For master's and doctorate, GRE General Test, minimum GPA of 3.0. Additional exam requirements/recommendations for international students: Required—TOEFL (minimum score 550 paper-based; 79 iBT). *Application deadline:* For fall admission, 1/15 for domestic students, 12/15 for international students; for spring admission, 9/15 for domestic students, 8/1 for international students. Applications are processed on a rolling basis. Application fee: $60. Electronic applications accepted. *Financial support:* Fellowships, research assistantships, and teaching assistantships available. Financial award application deadline: 1/15; financial award applicants required to submit FAFSA. *Faculty research:* Polymers, nonlinear optics, natural products, materials science, enantioselective synthesis. *Unit head:* Dr. Robert Levis, Chair, 215-204-7118, Fax: 215-204-1532, E-mail: rjlevis@temple.edu. *Application contact:* Tiffany Gilles, Program Coordinator, 215-204-7118, Fax: 215-204-1532,
E-mail: tgilles@temple.edu.
Website: http://www.temple.edu/chemistry

Tennessee State University, The School of Graduate Studies and Research, College of Agriculture, Human and Natural Sciences, Department of Chemistry, Nashville, TN 37209-1561. Offers MS. *Program availability:* Part-time. *Degree requirements:* For master's, thesis optional. *Entrance requirements:* For master's, GRE General Test. Electronic applications accepted.

Tennessee Technological University, College of Graduate Studies, College of Arts and Sciences, Department of Chemistry, Cookeville, TN 38505. Offers MS. *Program availability:* Part-time. *Faculty:* 16 full-time (1 woman). *Students:* 11 full-time (6 women), 9 part-time (2 women); includes 2 minority (1 Black or African American, non-Hispanic/Latino; 1 Two or more races, non-Hispanic/Latino), 7 international. Average age 28. 14 applicants, 43% accepted, 2 enrolled. In 2015, 4 master's awarded. *Degree requirements:* For master's, thesis. *Entrance requirements:* For master's, GRE. Additional exam requirements/recommendations for international students: Required—TOEFL (minimum score 527 paper-based; 71 iBT), IELTS (minimum score 5.5), PTE (minimum score 48), or TOEIC (Test of English as an International Communication). *Application deadline:* For fall admission, 8/1 for domestic students, 5/1 for international students; for spring admission, 12/1 for domestic students, 10/1 for international students; for summer admission, 5/1 for domestic students, 2/1 for international students. Applications are processed on a rolling basis. Application fee: $35 ($40 for international students). Electronic applications accepted. *Expenses:* Tuition, state resident: full-time $8961; part-time $6132 per credit hour. Tuition, nonresident: full-time $23,121; part-time $14,608 per credit hour. *Financial support:* In 2015–16, 1 research assistantship (averaging $10,000 per year), 6 teaching assistantships (averaging $7,500 per year) were awarded; career-related internships or fieldwork also available. Financial award application deadline: 4/1. *Unit head:* Dr. Jeffrey Boles, Interim Chairperson, 931-372-3421, Fax: 931-372-3434, E-mail: jboles@tntech.edu. *Application contact:* Shelia K. Kendrick, Coordinator of Graduate Studies, 931-372-3808, Fax: 931-372-3497,
E-mail: skendrick@tntech.edu.

Tennessee Technological University, College of Graduate Studies, School of Environmental Studies, Department of Environmental Sciences, Cookeville, TN 38505. Offers biology (PhD); chemistry (PhD). *Program availability:* Part-time. *Students:* 4 full-time (0 women), 12 part-time (5 women), 7 international. 13 applicants, 38% accepted, 2 enrolled. In 2015, 5 doctorates awarded. *Degree requirements:* For doctorate, comprehensive exam, thesis/dissertation. *Entrance requirements:* For doctorate, GRE. Additional exam requirements/recommendations for international students: Required—TOEFL (minimum score 527 paper-based; 71 iBT), IELTS (minimum score 5.5), PTE (minimum score 48), or TOEIC (Test of English as an International Communication). *Application deadline:* For fall admission, 8/1 for domestic students, 5/1 for international students; for spring admission, 12/1 for domestic students, 10/2 for international students; for summer admission, 5/1 for domestic students, 2/1 for international students. Applications are processed on a rolling basis. Application fee: $35 ($40 for international students). Electronic applications accepted. *Expenses:* Tuition, state resident: full-time $8961; part-time $6132 per credit hour. Tuition, nonresident: full-time $23,121; part-time $14,608 per credit hour. *Financial support:* In 2015–16, 5 research assistantships (averaging $10,000 per year), 3 teaching assistantships (averaging $10,000 per year) were awarded; fellowships also available. Financial award application deadline: 4/1. *Unit head:* Dr. Hayden Mattingly, Interim Director, 931-372-6246, E-mail: hmattingly@tntech.edu. *Application contact:* Shelia K. Kendrick, Coordinator of Graduate Studies, 931-372-3808, Fax: 931-372-3497, E-mail: skendrick@tntech.edu.

Texas A&M University, College of Science, Department of Chemistry, College Station, TX 77843. Offers MS, PhD. *Faculty:* 39. *Students:* 257 full-time (93 women), 11 part-time (4 women); includes 34 minority (1 Black or African American, non-Hispanic/Latino; 13 Asian, non-Hispanic/Latino; 16 Hispanic/Latino; 4 Two or more races, non-Hispanic/Latino), 140 international. Average age 27. 379 applicants, 54% accepted, 61 enrolled. In 2015, 2 master's, 43 doctorates awarded. Terminal master's awarded for partial completion of doctoral program. *Degree requirements:* For master's, thesis; for doctorate, thesis/dissertation. *Entrance requirements:* For master's and doctorate, GRE General Test. Additional exam requirements/recommendations for international students: Required—TOEFL. *Application deadline:* For fall admission, 3/1 priority date for domestic students. Applications are processed on a rolling basis. Application fee: $50 ($90 for international students). Electronic applications accepted. *Expenses:* Contact institution. *Financial support:* In 2015–16, 262 students received support, including 38 fellowships with tuition reimbursements available (averaging $11,823 per year), 140 research assistantships with tuition reimbursements available (averaging $7,896 per year), 118 teaching assistantships with tuition reimbursements available (averaging $7,705 per year); career-related internships or fieldwork, institutionally sponsored loans, scholarships/grants, traineeships, health care benefits, tuition waivers (full and partial), and unspecified assistantships also available. Support available to part-time students. Financial award application deadline: 3/1; financial award applicants required to submit FAFSA. *Faculty research:* Biological chemistry, spectroscopy, structure and bonding, reactions and mechanisms, theoretical chemistry. *Unit head:* Dr. Simon North, Interim Head, 979-845-9829, Fax: 979-845-9485, E-mail: chemhead@chem.tamu.edu. *Application contact:* Dr. Simon North, Graduate Advisor, 979-845-4947, E-mail: north@chem.tamu.edu.
Website: http://www.chem.tamu.edu/

Texas A&M University–Kingsville, College of Graduate Studies, College of Arts and Sciences, Department of Chemistry, Kingsville, TX 78363. Offers MS. *Degree requirements:* For master's, variable foreign language requirement, comprehensive exam, thesis (for some programs). *Entrance requirements:* For master's, GRE, MAT, GMAT, minimum GPA of 3.0; 20 hours of approved undergraduate chemistry, including 12 advanced; 8 hours of approved physics; 6 hours of calculus. Additional exam requirements/recommendations for international students: Required—TOEFL (minimum score 525 paper-based; 79 iBT). Electronic applications accepted. *Faculty research:* Organic heterocycles, amino alcohol complexes, rare earth arsine complexes.

Texas Christian University, College of Science and Engineering, Department of Chemistry and Biochemistry, Fort Worth, TX 76129. Offers MA, MS, PhD. *Program availability:* Part-time. *Faculty:* 12 full-time (3 women). *Students:* 22 full-time (12 women), 2 part-time (0 women); includes 4 minority (2 Asian, non-Hispanic/Latino; 1 Hispanic/Latino; 1 Two or more races, non-Hispanic/Latino), 11 international. Average age 27. 18 applicants, 33% accepted, 4 enrolled. In 2015, 1 master's, 4 doctorates awarded. Terminal master's awarded for partial completion of doctoral program. *Degree requirements:* For master's, thesis; for doctorate, thesis/dissertation, literature seminar, cumulative exams, research progress report, independent research proposal, teaching of undergraduate labs. *Entrance requirements:* For master's and doctorate, GRE General Test. Additional exam requirements/recommendations for international students: Required—TOEFL (minimum score 80 iBT). *Application deadline:* For fall admission, 2/1 for domestic and international students; for spring admission, 9/1 for domestic and international students. Application fee: $60. Electronic applications accepted. *Expenses: Tuition, area resident:* Full-time $26,640; part-time $1480 per credit hour. *Required fees:* $48; $48 per unit. Tuition and fees vary according to program. *Financial support:* In 2015–16, 18 students received support, including 18 fellowships with full tuition reimbursements available (averaging $21,000 per year); scholarships/grants, tuition waivers, and unspecified assistantships also available. Support available to part-time students. Financial award application deadline: 2/1. *Faculty research:* Bioinorganic and materials chemistry, protein folding, aggregation and transport phenomena, synthetic methodology and total synthesis, synthetic switches for sensing applications, electronic structure approximations. *Unit head:* Dr. Eric Simanek, Chair/Professor, 817-257-5355, Fax: 817-257-5851, E-mail: e.simanek@tcu.edu. *Application contact:* Dr. Benjamin G Janesko, Director of Graduate Studies/Associate Professor, 817-257-6202, Fax: 817-257-5851, E-mail: b.janesko@tcu.edu.
Website: http://www.chm.tcu.edu/

Texas Southern University, School of Science and Technology, Department of Chemistry, Houston, TX 77004-4584. Offers MS. *Degree requirements:* For master's, one foreign language, comprehensive exam, thesis. *Entrance requirements:* For master's, GRE General Test, minimum GPA of 2.5. Additional exam requirements/recommendations for international students: Required—TOEFL. Electronic applications accepted. *Faculty research:* Analytical and physical chemistry, geochemistry, inorganic chemistry, biochemistry, organic chemistry.

Texas State University, The Graduate College, College of Science and Engineering, Program in Chemistry, San Marcos, TX 78666. Offers MA, MS. *Program availability:* Part-time. *Faculty:* 11 full-time (4 women), 1 part-time/adjunct (0 women). *Students:* 10 full-time (5 women), 5 part-time (0 women); includes 5 minority (3 Black or African American, non-Hispanic/Latino; 1 American Indian or Alaska Native, non-Hispanic/Latino; 1 Asian, non-Hispanic/Latino), 3 international. Average age 27. 19 applicants, 53% accepted, 5 enrolled. In 2015, 5 master's awarded. *Degree requirements:* For master's, comprehensive exam, thesis (for some programs). *Entrance requirements:* For master's, GRE (minimum preferred score of 300), baccalaureate degree from regionally-accredited university; undergraduate major in chemistry; minimum GPA of 3.0 on last 60 undergraduate semester hours; 2 letters of reference; statement of purpose. Additional exam requirements/recommendations for international students: Required—TOEFL (minimum score 550 paper-based; 78 iBT). *Application deadline:* For fall admission, 2/1 priority date for domestic and international students; for spring admission, 10/1 for domestic and international students. Applications are processed on a rolling basis. Application fee: $40 ($90 for international students). Electronic applications accepted. *Expenses:* $3,615 in-state tuition for 12 semester credit hours (1 full-time semester), $974 in-state fees. *Financial support:* In 2015–16, 9 students received support, including 5 research assistantships (averaging $11,340 per year), 7 teaching assistantships (averaging $13,615 per year); career-related internships or fieldwork, Federal Work-Study, institutionally sponsored loans, scholarships/grants, health care benefits, and unspecified assistantships also available. Support available to part-time students. Financial award application deadline: 3/1; financial award applicants required to submit FAFSA. *Faculty research:* Chemically-modified ternary chalcogenide materials, interfaces in materials research triangle, chemistry REU on molecular innovation and entrepreneurship, stabilizing unusual main group allotropes, low-cost and scalable nono-silicon production, precise control over the assembly of metallo-supramolecular architectures, photochemical control of nanoarticle aggregation. *Total annual research expenditures:* $1.2 million. *Unit head:* Dr. Chad Booth, Graduate Advisor, 512-245-8789, Fax: 512-245-2374, E-mail: cb31@txstate.edu. *Application contact:* Dr. Andrea Golato, Dean of Graduate School, 512-245-2581, Fax: 512-245-8365, E-mail: gradcollege@txstate.edu.
Website: http://www.txstate.edu/chemistry/

Texas Tech University, Graduate School, College of Arts and Sciences, Department of Chemistry and Biochemistry, Lubbock, TX 79409. Offers chemical biology (MS); chemistry (MS, PhD). *Program availability:* Part-time. *Faculty:* 35 full-time (5 women). *Students:* 87 full-time (38 women); includes 10 minority (1 Black or African American, non-Hispanic/Latino; 1 American Indian or Alaska Native, non-Hispanic/Latino; 3 Asian, non-Hispanic/Latino; 5 Hispanic/Latino), 61 international. Average age 28. 107 applicants, 38% accepted, 20 enrolled. In 2015, 7 master's, 9 doctorates awarded. *Degree requirements:* For master's, thesis (for some programs); for doctorate, thesis/dissertation. *Entrance requirements:* For master's and doctorate, GRE General Test, diagnostic examination in area of specialization. Additional exam requirements/recommendations for international students: Required—TOEFL (minimum score 550 paper-based; 79 iBT); Recommended—IELTS (minimum score 6.5). *Application deadline:* For fall admission, 6/1 priority date for domestic students, 1/15 priority date for international students; for spring admission, 9/1 priority date for domestic students, 6/15 priority date for international students. Applications are processed on a rolling basis. Application fee: $60. Electronic applications accepted. *Expenses:* Tuition, state resident: full-time $6477; part-time $269.89 per credit hour. Tuition, nonresident: full-time $15,837; part-time $659.89 per credit hour. *Required fees:* $2751; $36.50 per credit hour. $937.50 per semester. Tuition and fees vary according to course level. *Financial support:* In 2015–16, 96 students received support, including 82 fellowships (averaging $1,487 per year), 62 research assistantships (averaging $9,090 per year), 80 teaching assistantships (averaging $14,026 per year); career-related internships or fieldwork, Federal Work-Study, scholarships/grants, and tuition waivers (partial) also available. Financial award application deadline: 4/1; financial award applicants required to submit FAFSA. *Faculty research:* Theoretical and computational chemistry, plant biochemistry and chemical biology, materials and supramolecular chemistry, nanotechnology, spectroscopic analysis. *Total annual research expenditures:* $2.2 million. *Unit head:* Dr. Louisa J. Hope-Weeks, Chair, 806-742-3067, Fax: 806-742-1289, E-mail: louisa.hope-weeks@ttu.edu. *Application contact:* Donna C. Smith, Graduate Advisor, 806-834-1906, Fax: 806-742-1289, E-mail: chemgrad@ttu.edu.
Website: http://www.depts.ttu.edu/chemistry/

Texas Woman's University, Graduate School, College of Arts and Sciences, Department of Chemistry and Biochemistry, Denton, TX 76201. Offers chemistry (MS). *Program availability:* Part-time. *Faculty:* 3 full-time. *Degree requirements:* For master's, comprehensive exam, thesis. *Entrance requirements:* For master's, GRE General Test (preferred minimum score 146 [400 old version] verbal, 146 [550 old version] quantitative), 2 reference contacts. Additional exam requirements/recommendations for international students: Required—TOEFL (minimum score 550 paper-based; 79 iBT). *Application deadline:* For fall admission, 7/1 priority date for domestic students, 3/1 for international students; for spring admission, 12/1 priority date for domestic students, 7/1 for international students. Applications are processed on a rolling basis. Application fee: $50 ($75 for international students). Electronic applications accepted. *Expenses:* Tuition, state resident: full-time $4380; part-time $243 per credit hour. Tuition, nonresident: full-time $11,400; part-time $633 per credit hour. *International tuition:* $11,465 full-time. *Required fees:* $1778; $99 per credit hour. $283 per semester. One-time fee: $50. Tuition and fees vary according to course load and program. *Financial support:* Research assistantships, teaching assistantships, career-related internships or fieldwork, Federal Work-Study, institutionally sponsored loans, scholarships/grants, traineeships, health care benefits, and unspecified assistantships available. Support available to part-time students. Financial award application deadline: 3/1; financial award applicants required to submit FAFSA. *Faculty research:* Glutathione synthetize, conformational properties of DNA quadruplexes, constriction and analysis of aqueous enzyme phase diagrams, development of metallopolymers, basic chemical research. *Unit head:* Dr. Richard Sheardy, Chair, 940-898-2551, Fax: 940-898-2548, E-mail: chemistry@twu.edu. *Application contact:* Dr. Samuel Wheeler, Assistant Director of Admissions, 940-898-3188, Fax: 940-898-3081, E-mail: wheelersr@twu.edu.
Website: http://www.twu.edu/chemistry-biochemistry/

Trent University, Graduate Studies, Program in Applications of Modeling in the Natural and Social Sciences, Department of Chemistry, Peterborough, ON K9J 7B8, Canada. Offers M Sc. *Program availability:* Part-time. *Degree requirements:* For master's, thesis. *Entrance requirements:* For master's, honours degree. *Faculty research:* Synthetic-organic chemistry, mass spectrometry and ion storage.

Tufts University, Graduate School of Arts and Sciences, Department of Chemistry, Medford, MA 02155. Offers analytical chemistry (MS, PhD); bioorganic chemistry (MS, PhD); environmental chemistry (MS, PhD); inorganic chemistry (MS, PhD); organic chemistry (MS, PhD); physical chemistry (MS, PhD). Terminal master's awarded for partial completion of doctoral program. *Degree requirements:* For master's, thesis optional; for doctorate, thesis/dissertation. *Entrance requirements:* For master's and doctorate, GRE General Test; GRE Subject Test (recommended). Additional exam requirements/recommendations for international students: Required—TOEFL (minimum score 600 paper-based; 80 iBT), IELTS (minimum score 6.5). Electronic applications accepted. *Expenses: Tuition, area resident:* Full-time $48,412; part-time $1210 per credit hour. *Required fees:* $806. Full-time tuition and fees vary according to degree level, program and student level. Part-time tuition and fees vary according to course load.

Tulane University, School of Science and Engineering, Department of Chemistry, New Orleans, LA 70118-5669. Offers MS, PhD. Terminal master's awarded for partial completion of doctoral program. *Degree requirements:* For master's, thesis; for doctorate, thesis/dissertation. *Entrance requirements:* For master's, GRE General Test, minimum B average in undergraduate course work; for doctorate, GRE General Test. Additional exam requirements/recommendations for international students: Required—TOEFL. Electronic applications accepted. *Faculty research:* Enzyme mechanisms, organic synthesis, photochemistry, theory of polymer dynamics.

Chemistry

Tuskegee University, Graduate Programs, College of Arts and Sciences, Department of Chemistry, Tuskegee, AL 36088. Offers MS. *Degree requirements:* For master's, thesis. *Entrance requirements:* For master's, GRE General Test. Additional exam requirements/recommendations for international students: Required—TOEFL (minimum score 500 paper-based).

Universidad del Turabo, Graduate Programs, Programs in Science and Technology, Gurabo, PR 00778-3030. Offers environmental analysis (MSE), including environmental chemistry; environmental management (MSE), including pollution management; environmental science (D Sc), including environmental biology. *Entrance requirements:* For master's, GRE, EXADEP, interview.

Université de Moncton, Faculty of Sciences, Department of Chemistry and Biochemistry, Moncton, NB E1A 3E9, Canada. Offers biochemistry (M Sc); chemistry (M Sc). *Program availability:* Part-time. *Degree requirements:* For master's, one foreign language, thesis. *Entrance requirements:* For master's, minimum GPA of 3.0. Electronic applications accepted. *Faculty research:* Environmental contaminants, natural products synthesis, nutraceutical, organic catalysis, molecular biology of cancer.

Université de Montréal, Faculty of Arts and Sciences, Department of Chemistry, Montréal, QC H3C 3J7, Canada. Offers M Sc, PhD. *Degree requirements:* For master's, thesis; for doctorate, thesis/dissertation, general exam. *Entrance requirements:* For master's, B Sc in chemistry or the equivalent; for doctorate, M Sc in chemistry or equivalent. Electronic applications accepted. *Faculty research:* Analytical, inorganic, physical, and organic chemistry.

Université de Sherbrooke, Faculty of Sciences, Department of Chemistry, Sherbrooke, QC J1K 2R1, Canada. Offers M Sc, PhD, Diploma. *Degree requirements:* For master's, thesis; for doctorate, thesis/dissertation. *Entrance requirements:* For doctorate, master's degree. Electronic applications accepted. *Faculty research:* Organic, electro-, theoretical, and physical chemistry.

Université du Québec à Montréal, Graduate Programs, Program in Chemistry, Montréal, QC H3C 3P8, Canada. Offers M Sc, PhD. M Sc offered jointly with Université du Québec à Trois-Rivières. *Program availability:* Part-time. *Degree requirements:* For master's, thesis. *Entrance requirements:* For master's, appropriate bachelor's degree or equivalent and proficiency in French.

Université du Québec à Trois-Rivières, Graduate Programs, Program in Chemistry, Trois-Rivières, QC G9A 5H7, Canada. Offers M Sc. *Program availability:* Part-time. *Degree requirements:* For master's, thesis. *Entrance requirements:* For master's, appropriate bachelor's degree, proficiency in French.

Université Laval, Faculty of Sciences and Engineering, Department of Chemistry, Programs in Chemistry, Québec, QC G1K 7P4, Canada. Offers M Sc, PhD. *Program availability:* Part-time. Terminal master's awarded for partial completion of doctoral program. *Degree requirements:* For master's, thesis; for doctorate, comprehensive exam, thesis/dissertation. *Entrance requirements:* For master's and doctorate, knowledge of French, comprehension of written English. Electronic applications accepted.

University at Albany, State University of New York, College of Arts and Sciences, Department of Chemistry, Albany, NY 12222-0001. Offers MS, PhD. *Degree requirements:* For master's, one foreign language, thesis, major field exam; for doctorate, 2 foreign languages, thesis/dissertation, cumulative exams, oral proposition. *Entrance requirements:* For doctorate, GRE. Additional exam requirements/recommendations for international students: Required—TOEFL (minimum score 550 paper-based). Electronic applications accepted. *Faculty research:* Synthetic, organic, and inorganic chemistry; polymer chemistry; ESR and NMR spectroscopy; theoretical chemistry; physical biochemistry.

University at Albany, State University of New York, School of Public Health, Department of Environmental Health Sciences, Albany, NY 12222-0001. Offers environmental and occupational health (MS, PhD); environmental chemistry (MS, PhD); toxicology (MS, PhD). *Degree requirements:* For master's, thesis; for doctorate, comprehensive exam, thesis/dissertation. *Entrance requirements:* For master's and doctorate, GRE General Test, GRE Subject Test, 3 letters of reference. Additional exam requirements/recommendations for international students: Required—TOEFL (minimum score 600 paper-based). Electronic applications accepted. *Faculty research:* Xenobiotic metabolism, neurotoxicity of halogenated hydrocarbons, pharmac/toxicogenomics, environmental analytical chemistry.

University at Buffalo, the State University of New York, Graduate School, College of Arts and Sciences, Department of Chemistry, Buffalo, NY 14260. Offers chemistry (MA, PhD); medicinal chemistry (MS, PhD). *Program availability:* Part-time. *Faculty:* 30 full-time (5 women), 2 part-time/adjunct (both women). *Students:* 149 full-time (60 women); includes 21 minority (8 Black or African American, non-Hispanic/Latino; 2 American Indian or Alaska Native, non-Hispanic/Latino; 3 Asian, non-Hispanic/Latino; 8 Hispanic/Latino), 38 international. Average age 26. 268 applicants, 28% accepted, 28 enrolled. In 2015, 12 master's, 20 doctorates awarded. Terminal master's awarded for partial completion of doctoral program. *Degree requirements:* For master's, thesis or alternative, project; for doctorate, thesis/dissertation, synopsis proposal. *Entrance requirements:* For master's and doctorate, GRE General Test. Additional exam requirements/recommendations for international students: Required—TOEFL (minimum score 550 paper-based; 79 iBT). *Application deadline:* For fall admission, 3/1 priority date for domestic students, 3/1 for international students; for spring admission, 11/1 priority date for domestic students. Applications are processed on a rolling basis. Application fee: $75. Electronic applications accepted. *Expenses:* $22,210; $925 per credit hour. *Financial support:* In 2015–16, 7 students received support, including 8 fellowships with full tuition reimbursements available (averaging $22,080 per year), 24 research assistantships with full tuition reimbursements available (averaging $22,080 per year), 98 teaching assistantships with full tuition reimbursements available (averaging $23,000 per year); Federal Work-Study, institutionally sponsored loans, and unspecified assistantships also available. Financial award application deadline: 6/15; financial award applicants required to submit FAFSA. *Faculty research:* Synthesis, measurements, structure theory, translation. *Total annual research expenditures:* $8 million. *Unit head:* Dr. Michael R. Detty, Chairman, 716-645-6824, Fax: 716-645-6963, E-mail: chechair@buffalo.edu. *Application contact:* Dr. Diana S. Aga, Director of Graduate Studies, 716-645-4220, Fax: 716-645-6963, E-mail: dianaaga@buffalo.edu. Website: http://www.chemistry.buffalo.edu/

The University of Akron, Graduate School, Buchtel College of Arts and Sciences, Department of Chemistry, Akron, OH 44325. Offers MS, PhD. *Program availability:* Part-time, evening/weekend. *Faculty:* 14 full-time (3 women), 2 part-time/adjunct (1 woman). *Students:* 46 full-time (21 women), 8 part-time (5 women); includes 3 minority (1 Black or African American, non-Hispanic/Latino; 2 Asian, non-Hispanic/Latino), 23 international. Average age 28. 60 applicants, 28% accepted, 10 enrolled. In 2015, 33 master's, 6 doctorates awarded. Terminal master's awarded for partial completion of doctoral program. *Degree requirements:* For master's, thesis optional, seminar presentation; for doctorate, comprehensive exam, thesis/dissertation, cumulative exams, oral exam, defense of dissertation. *Entrance requirements:* For master's, baccalaureate degree in chemistry, biochemistry, or a related field; minimum GPA of 2.75; 3 letters of recommendation; statement of purpose; research interest questionnaire; for doctorate, baccalaureate degree in chemistry, biochemistry, or a related field; minimum GPA of 2.75; three letters of recommendation; statement of purpose. Additional exam requirements/recommendations for international students: Required—TOEFL (minimum score 550 paper-based; 79 iBT), IELTS (minimum score 6.5). *Application deadline:* For fall admission, 6/1 for domestic and international students; for spring admission, 11/15 for domestic and international students. Application fee: $45 ($70 for international students). Electronic applications accepted. *Expenses:* Tuition, state resident: full-time $7958; part-time $442 per credit hour. Tuition, nonresident: full-time $13,464; part-time $748 per credit hour. *Required fees:* $1404. *Financial support:* In 2015–16, 3 research assistantships with full tuition reimbursements, 39 teaching assistantships with full tuition reimbursements were awarded. *Faculty research:* NMR and mass spectrometric characterization of biological and synthetic polymers, synthesis and characterization of new organic and inorganic material, metals in medicine, enzymology of gene regulation, high-resolution spectroscopy and ultrafast characterization of organic materials. *Total annual research expenditures:* $1.3 million. *Unit head:* Dr. Kim Calvo, Department Chair, 330-972-6078, E-mail: kcalvo@uakron.edu. Website: http://www.uakron.edu/chemistry/

The University of Alabama, Graduate School, College of Arts and Sciences, Department of Chemistry, Tuscaloosa, AL 35487-0336. Offers MS, PhD. *Faculty:* 22 full-time (2 women). *Students:* 86 full-time (37 women), 5 part-time (1 woman); includes 18 minority (8 Black or African American, non-Hispanic/Latino; 4 Asian, non-Hispanic/Latino; 3 Hispanic/Latino; 3 Two or more races, non-Hispanic/Latino), 29 international. Average age 27. 123 applicants, 32% accepted, 19 enrolled. In 2015, 3 master's, 15 doctorates awarded. Terminal master's awarded for partial completion of doctoral program. *Degree requirements:* For master's, comprehensive exam, thesis (for some programs); for doctorate, comprehensive exam, thesis/dissertation, research proposal, oral defense, research seminar. *Entrance requirements:* For master's and doctorate, GRE General Test, minimum GPA of 3.0. Additional exam requirements/recommendations for international students: Recommended—TOEFL (minimum score 550 paper-based; 79 iBT), IELTS (minimum score 6.5), TSE (minimum score 59). *Application deadline:* For fall admission, 1/15 priority date for domestic and international students. Applications are processed on a rolling basis. Application fee: $50 ($60 for international students). Electronic applications accepted. *Expenses:* Tuition, state resident: full-time $10,170. Tuition, nonresident: full-time $25,950. *Financial support:* In 2015–16, 6 fellowships with full tuition reimbursements (averaging $24,000 per year), 16 research assistantships with full tuition reimbursements (averaging $23,928 per year), 59 teaching assistantships with full tuition reimbursements (averaging $23,928 per year) were awarded; career-related internships or fieldwork, scholarships/grants, health care benefits, and unspecified assistantships also available. *Faculty research:* Molecular synthesis and assembly, materials and measurements for alternative energy, electronic and magnetic nanomaterials, biochemical processes and biomaterials, environmental and green chemistry. *Total annual research expenditures:* $3.2 million. *Unit head:* Dr. Kevin H. Shaughnessy, Associate Professor and Chair of Chemistry, 205-348-8436, Fax: 205-348-9104, E-mail: kshaughn@ua.edu. *Application contact:* Dr. Shane C. Street, Associate Professor and Director of Graduate Recruiting, 205-348-5957, Fax: 205-348-9104, E-mail: sstreet@ua.edu. Website: http://chemistry.ua.edu/

The University of Alabama at Birmingham, College of Arts and Sciences, Program in Chemistry, Birmingham, AL 35294. Offers MS, PhD. Terminal master's awarded for partial completion of doctoral program. *Degree requirements:* For master's, thesis (for some programs); for doctorate, thesis/dissertation. *Entrance requirements:* For master's and doctorate, GRE General Test, letters of recommendation. Additional exam requirements/recommendations for international students: Required—TOEFL. *Expenses:* Tuition, state resident: full-time $7340. Tuition, nonresident: full-time $16,628. Full-time tuition and fees vary according to course load and program. *Faculty research:* Drug discovery and synthesis, structural biochemistry and physical biochemistry, synthesis and characterization of advanced materials and polymers.

The University of Alabama in Huntsville, School of Graduate Studies, College of Science, Department of Chemistry, Huntsville, AL 35899. Offers biotechnology science and engineering (PhD); chemistry (MS); education (MS); materials science (PhD). *Program availability:* Part-time, evening/weekend. *Degree requirements:* For master's, comprehensive exam, thesis or alternative, oral and written exams. *Entrance requirements:* For master's, GRE General Test, minimum GPA of 3.0. Additional exam requirements/recommendations for international students: Required—TOEFL (minimum score 550 paper-based; 80 iBT), IELTS (minimum score 6.5). Electronic applications accepted. *Faculty research:* Natural products drug discovery, protein biochemistry, macromolecular biophysics, polymer synthesis, surface modification and analysis of materials.

University of Alaska Fairbanks, College of Natural Sciences and Mathematics, Department of Chemistry and Biochemistry, Fairbanks, AK 99775-6160. Offers biochemistry and neuroscience (PhD); chemistry (MA, MS), including chemistry (MS); environmental chemistry (PhD). *Program availability:* Part-time. *Faculty:* 10 full-time (3 women). *Students:* 31 full-time (17 women), 4 part-time (3 women); includes 3 minority (1 Asian, non-Hispanic/Latino; 2 Two or more races, non-Hispanic/Latino), 9 international. Average age 29. 27 applicants, 30% accepted, 7 enrolled. In 2015, 4 master's, 1 doctorate awarded. *Degree requirements:* For master's, comprehensive exam, thesis (for some programs), oral defense of project or thesis; for doctorate, comprehensive exam, thesis/dissertation, oral defense of dissertation. *Entrance requirements:* For master's, GRE General Test (for MS), bachelor's degree from accredited institution with minimum cumulative undergraduate and major GPA of 3.0; for doctorate, GRE General Test, minimum cumulative GPA of 3.0. Additional exam requirements/recommendations for international students: Required—TOEFL (minimum score 550 paper-based; 79 iBT), TWE. *Application deadline:* For fall admission, 6/1 for domestic students, 3/1 for international students; for spring admission, 10/15 for domestic students, 9/1 for international students. Applications are processed on a rolling basis. Application fee: $60. Electronic applications accepted. *Expenses:* Tuition, state resident: full-time $7614; part-time $423 per credit. Tuition, nonresident: full-time $15,552; part-time $864 per credit. *Required fees:* $38 per credit. $187 per semester. Tuition and fees vary according to course level, course load, program and reciprocity agreements. *Financial support:* In 2015–16, 14 research assistantships with full tuition reimbursements (averaging $16,421 per year), 14 teaching assistantships with full tuition reimbursements (averaging $17,322 per year) were awarded; fellowships with full tuition reimbursements, Federal Work-Study, scholarships/grants, health care benefits, and unspecified assistantships also available. Support available to part-time students. Financial award application deadline: 7/1; financial award applicants required to submit FAFSA. *Faculty research:* Atmospheric aerosols, cold adaptation, hibernation and neuroprotection, liganogated ion channels, arctic contaminants. *Unit head:* Bill Simpson, Department Chair, 907-474-5510, Fax: 907-474-5640,

E-mail: uaf-chem-biochem@alaska.edu. *Application contact:* Mary Kreta, Director of Admissions, 907-474-7500, Fax: 907-474-7097, E-mail: admissions@uaf.edu.
Website: http://www.uaf.edu/chem

University of Alberta, Faculty of Graduate Studies and Research, Department of Chemistry, Edmonton, AB T6G 2E1, Canada. Offers M Sc, PhD. *Program availability:* Part-time. Terminal master's awarded for partial completion of doctoral program. *Degree requirements:* For master's, thesis; for doctorate, thesis/dissertation. *Entrance requirements:* For master's and doctorate, minimum GPA of 6.5 on 9.0 scale. *Expenses:* Contact institution. *Faculty research:* Synthetic inorganic and organic chemistry, chemical biology and biochemical analysis, materials and surface chemistry, spectroscopy and instrumentation, computational chemistry.

The University of Arizona, College of Science, Department of Chemistry and Biochemistry, Tucson, AZ 85721. Offers biochemistry (PhD). *Program availability:* Part-time. *Degree requirements:* For doctorate, comprehensive exam, thesis/dissertation. *Entrance requirements:* For doctorate, GRE General Test, 3 letters of recommendation, statement of purpose. Additional exam requirements/recommendations for international students: Required—TOEFL (minimum score 550 paper-based; 79 iBT). *Application deadline:* For fall admission, 2/1 for domestic students, 1/1 for international students; for spring admission, 10/15 for domestic and international students. Applications are processed on a rolling basis. Application fee: $75. Electronic applications accepted. *Financial support:* Research assistantships, teaching assistantships, institutionally sponsored loans, scholarships/grants, health care benefits, tuition waivers (partial), and unspecified assistantships available. Financial award applicants required to submit FAFSA. *Faculty research:* Analytical, inorganic, organic, physical chemistry, biological chemistry. *Unit head:* Dr. Roger L. Miesfeld, Department Head, 520-626-2343, Fax: 520-621-8407, E-mail: rlm@email.arizona.edu. *Application contact:* Dr. Kriss Pope, Director, Finance and Administration, 520-621-6345, E-mail: kpope@email.arizona.edu.
Website: http://www.chem.arizona.edu/

University of Arkansas, Graduate School, J. William Fulbright College of Arts and Sciences, Department of Chemistry and Biochemistry, Fayetteville, AR 72701-1201. Offers chemistry (MS, PhD). *Students:* 22 full-time (10 women), 42 part-time (18 women); includes 3 minority (1 Black or African American, non-Hispanic/Latino; 2 Asian, non-Hispanic/Latino), 19 international. In 2015, 2 master's, 7 doctorates awarded. *Degree requirements:* For master's, one foreign language, thesis; for doctorate, one foreign language, thesis/dissertation. *Application deadline:* For fall admission, 4/1 for international students; for spring admission, 10/1 for international students. Applications are processed on a rolling basis. Application fee: $40 ($50 for international students). Electronic applications accepted. *Financial support:* In 2015–16, 17 research assistantships, 32 teaching assistantships were awarded; fellowships with tuition reimbursements, career-related internships or fieldwork, and Federal Work-Study also available. Support available to part-time students. Financial award application deadline: 4/1; financial award applicants required to submit FAFSA. *Unit head:* Dr. Wes Stites, Departmental Chairperson, 479-575-4601, Fax: 479-575-4049,
E-mail: cheminfo@uark.edu. *Application contact:* Colin Heyes, Graduate Coordinator, 479-575-5607, Fax: 479-575-4049, E-mail: cheyes@uark.edu.
Website: http://chemistry.uark.edu/

University of Arkansas at Little Rock, Graduate School, College of Arts, Letters, and Sciences, Department of Chemistry, Little Rock, AR 72204-1099. Offers MA, MS. *Program availability:* Part-time, evening/weekend. *Degree requirements:* For master's, thesis (MS). *Entrance requirements:* For master's, minimum GPA of 2.7. *Expenses:* Tuition, state resident: part-time $300 per credit hour. Tuition, nonresident: part-time $690 per credit hour. *Required fees:* $100 per credit hour. One-time fee: $40 full-time.

The University of British Columbia, Faculty of Science, Program in Chemistry, Vancouver, BC V6T 1Z1, Canada. Offers M Sc, PhD. Terminal master's awarded for partial completion of doctoral program. *Degree requirements:* For master's, thesis; for doctorate, comprehensive exam, thesis/dissertation. *Entrance requirements:* For master's and doctorate, GRE General Test, GRE Subject Test. Additional exam requirements/recommendations for international students: Required—TOEFL (minimum score 580 paper-based; 92 iBT), IELTS (minimum score 6.5). Electronic applications accepted. Application fee is waived when completed online. *Expenses:* Contact institution. *Faculty research:* Analytical chemistry, biological chemistry, environmental chemistry, inorganic chemistry, materials chemistry, organic chemistry, physical chemistry, theoretical chemistry.

University of Calgary, Faculty of Graduate Studies, Faculty of Science, Department of Chemistry, Calgary, AB T2N 1N4, Canada. Offers analytical chemistry (M Sc, PhD); applied chemistry (M Sc, PhD); inorganic chemistry (M Sc, PhD); organic chemistry (M Sc, PhD); physical chemistry (M Sc, PhD); polymer chemistry (M Sc, PhD); theoretical chemistry (M Sc, PhD). *Degree requirements:* For master's, thesis; for doctorate, thesis/dissertation, candidacy exam. *Entrance requirements:* For master's, minimum GPA of 3.0; for doctorate, honors B Sc degree with minimum GPA of 3.7 or M Sc with minimum GPA of 3.3. Additional exam requirements/recommendations for international students: Required—TOEFL (minimum score 580 paper-based). Electronic applications accepted. *Faculty research:* Chemical analysis, chemical dynamics, synthesis theory.

University of California, Berkeley, Graduate Division, College of Chemistry, Department of Chemistry, Berkeley, CA 94720-1500. Offers PhD. *Degree requirements:* For doctorate, thesis/dissertation, qualifying exam. *Entrance requirements:* For doctorate, GRE General Test, GRE Subject Test, minimum GPA of 3.0, 3 letters of recommendation. Additional exam requirements/recommendations for international students: Required—TOEFL. Electronic applications accepted. *Faculty research:* Analytical bioinorganic, bio-organic, biophysical environmental, inorganic and organometallic.

University of California, Davis, Graduate Studies, Graduate Group in Agricultural and Environmental Chemistry, Davis, CA 95616. Offers MS, PhD. *Degree requirements:* For master's, thesis; for doctorate, thesis/dissertation. *Entrance requirements:* For master's and doctorate, GRE General Test, minimum GPA of 3.0. Additional exam requirements/recommendations for international students: Required—TOEFL (minimum score 550 paper-based). Electronic applications accepted.

University of California, Davis, Graduate Studies, Program in Chemistry, Davis, CA 95616. Offers MS, PhD. Terminal master's awarded for partial completion of doctoral program. *Degree requirements:* For master's, thesis; for doctorate, thesis/dissertation. *Entrance requirements:* For master's, minimum GPA of 3.0; for doctorate, GRE, minimum GPA of 3.0. Additional exam requirements/recommendations for international students: Required—TOEFL (minimum score 550 paper-based). Electronic applications accepted. *Faculty research:* Analytical, biological, organic, inorganic, and theoretical chemistry.

University of California, Irvine, School of Physical Sciences, Department of Chemistry, Irvine, CA 92697. Offers chemistry (MS, PhD). *Students:* 219 full-time (70 women), 4 part-time (1 woman); includes 58 minority (2 Black or African American, non-Hispanic/Latino; 35 Asian, non-Hispanic/Latino; 12 Hispanic/Latino; 1 Native Hawaiian or other Pacific Islander, non-Hispanic/Latino; 8 Two or more races, non-Hispanic/Latino), 23 international. Average age 26. 344 applicants, 34% accepted, 28 enrolled. In 2015, 15 master's, 26 doctorates awarded. *Degree requirements:* For doctorate, thesis/dissertation. *Entrance requirements:* For master's and doctorate, GRE General Test, GRE Subject Test, minimum GPA of 3.0. Additional exam requirements/recommendations for international students: Required—TOEFL (minimum score 550 paper-based). *Application deadline:* For fall admission, 1/15 priority date for domestic students, 1/15 for international students. Applications are processed on a rolling basis. Application fee: $90 ($110 for international students). Electronic applications accepted. *Financial support:* Fellowships, research assistantships with full tuition reimbursements, teaching assistantships, institutionally sponsored loans, traineeships, health care benefits, and unspecified assistantships available. Financial award application deadline: 3/1; financial award applicants required to submit FAFSA. *Faculty research:* Analytical, organic, inorganic, physical, and atmospheric chemistry; biogeochemistry and climate; synthetic chemistry. *Unit head:* Dr. Reginald M. Penner, Chair, 949-824-8572, Fax: 949-824-8571, E-mail: rmpenner@uci.edu. *Application contact:* Jaime M. Albano, Graduate Affairs Manager, 949-824-4261, Fax: 949-824-8571, E-mail: jmalbano@uci.edu.
Website: http://www.chem.uci.edu/

University of California, Los Angeles, Graduate Division, College of Letters and Science, Department of Chemistry and Biochemistry, Program in Chemistry, Los Angeles, CA 90095. Offers MS, PhD. *Degree requirements:* For master's, comprehensive exam or thesis; for doctorate, thesis/dissertation, oral and written exams, 1 year of teaching experience. *Entrance requirements:* For doctorate, GRE General Test, GRE Subject Test (recommended), bachelor's degree; minimum undergraduate GPA of 3.0 (or its equivalent if letter grade system not used). Additional exam requirements/recommendations for international students: Required—TOEFL. Electronic applications accepted.

University of California, Merced, Graduate Division, School of Natural Sciences, Merced, CA 95343. Offers applied mathematics (MS, PhD); chemistry and chemical biology (MS, PhD); physics (MS, PhD); quantitative and systems biology (MS, PhD). *Faculty:* 63 full-time (25 women). *Students:* 156 full-time (64 women); includes 58 minority (3 Black or African American, non-Hispanic/Latino; 23 Asian, non-Hispanic/Latino; 22 Hispanic/Latino; 1 Native Hawaiian or other Pacific Islander, non-Hispanic/Latino; 9 Two or more races, non-Hispanic/Latino), 37 international. Average age 27. 199 applicants, 57% accepted, 45 enrolled. In 2015, 12 master's, 11 doctorates awarded. Terminal master's awarded for partial completion of doctoral program. *Degree requirements:* For master's, variable foreign language requirement, comprehensive exam, thesis or alternative; for doctorate, variable foreign language requirement, comprehensive exam, thesis/dissertation. *Entrance requirements:* For master's and doctorate, GRE. Additional exam requirements/recommendations for international students: Required—TOEFL (minimum score 550 paper-based; 80 iBT); Recommended—IELTS (minimum score 7). *Application deadline:* For fall admission, 1/15 for domestic and international students. Application fee: $90 ($110 for international students). Electronic applications accepted. *Expenses:* $11,220 per year resident tuition, $15,102 per year non-resident tuition. *Financial support:* In 2015–16, 151 students received support, including 12 fellowships with full tuition reimbursements available (averaging $23,614 per year), 37 research assistantships with full tuition reimbursements available (averaging $18,842 per year), 127 teaching assistantships with full tuition reimbursements available (averaging $18,538 per year); scholarships/grants, traineeships, and health care benefits also available. Financial award application deadline: 1/15. *Faculty research:* Computational science, soft matter physics, neurobiology, genomics, biochemistry. *Total annual research expenditures:* $5.3 million. *Unit head:* Dr. Juan C. Meza, Dean, 209-228-4487, Fax: 209-228-4060,
E-mail: jcmeza@ucmerced.edu. *Application contact:* Tsu Ya, Director of Graduate Admissions and Academic Services, 209-228-4521, Fax: 209-228-6906,
E-mail: tya@ucmerced.edu.

University of California, Riverside, Graduate Division, Department of Chemistry, Riverside, CA 92521-0403. Offers MS, PhD. Terminal master's awarded for partial completion of doctoral program. *Degree requirements:* For master's, qualifying exams or thesis; for doctorate, thesis/dissertation, qualifying exams, 3 quarters of teaching experience, research proposition. *Entrance requirements:* For master's and doctorate, GRE General Test, minimum GPA of 3.0. Additional exam requirements/recommendations for international students: Required—TOEFL (minimum score 550 paper-based; 80 iBT). Electronic applications accepted. *Faculty research:* Analytical, inorganic, organic, and physical chemistry; chemical physics.

University of California, San Diego, Graduate Division, Department of Chemistry and Biochemistry, La Jolla, CA 92093. Offers chemistry (MS, PhD). PhD offered jointly with San Diego State University. *Students:* 285 full-time (102 women), 5 part-time (1 woman); includes 99 minority (9 Black or African American, non-Hispanic/Latino; 3 American Indian or Alaska Native, non-Hispanic/Latino; 60 Asian, non-Hispanic/Latino; 26 Hispanic/Latino; 1 Native Hawaiian or other Pacific Islander, non-Hispanic/Latino), 52 international. 640 applicants, 34% accepted, 85 enrolled. In 2015, 54 master's, 44 doctorates awarded. *Degree requirements:* For master's, comprehensive exam (for some programs), thesis (for some programs); for doctorate, comprehensive exam, thesis/dissertation. *Entrance requirements:* For master's, GRE General Test; for doctorate, GRE General Test, GRE Subject Test. Additional exam requirements/recommendations for international students: Required—TOEFL (minimum score 550 paper-based; 80 iBT), IELTS. *Application deadline:* For fall admission, 12/15 priority date for domestic students. Application fee: $90 ($110 for international students). Electronic applications accepted. *Expenses:* Tuition, state resident: full-time $11,220. Tuition, nonresident: full-time $26,322. *Required fees:* $1800. *Financial support:* Fellowships, research assistantships, teaching assistantships, scholarships/grants, and traineeships available. Financial award applicants required to submit FAFSA. *Faculty research:* Analytical and atmospheric chemistry, biochemistry & biophysics, cellular and systems biochemistry, chemical biology, inorganic chemistry, organic chemistry, physical chemistry, quantitative biology, structural biology, theoretical and computational chemistry. *Unit head:* Partho Ghosh, Chair, 858-822-1339, E-mail: pghosh@ucsd.edu. *Application contact:* Jeff Rances, Admissions Coordinator, 858-534-9728, Fax: 858-534-7687, E-mail: chemgradinfo@ucsd.edu.
Website: http://chemistry.ucsd.edu

University of California, San Francisco, School of Pharmacy and Graduate Division, Chemistry and Chemical Biology Graduate Program, San Francisco, CA 94143. Offers PhD. *Degree requirements:* For doctorate, thesis/dissertation. *Entrance requirements:* For doctorate, GRE General Test, minimum GPA of 3.0, bachelor's degree. Additional exam requirements/recommendations for international students: Required—TOEFL (minimum score 550 paper-based; 80 iBT). Electronic applications accepted. *Faculty research:* Macromolecular structure function and dynamics, computational chemistry and biology, biological chemistry and synthetic biology, chemical biology and molecular design, nanomolecular design.

Chemistry

University of California, Santa Barbara, Graduate Division, College of Letters and Sciences, Division of Mathematics, Life, and Physical Sciences, Department of Chemistry and Biochemistry, Santa Barbara, CA 93106-9510. Offers chemistry (MA, MS, PhD). *Faculty:* 37 full-time (9 women), 6 part-time/adjunct (0 women). *Students:* 138 full-time (41 women); includes 34 minority (2 Black or African American, non-Hispanic/Latino; 1 American Indian or Alaska Native, non-Hispanic/Latino; 20 Asian, non-Hispanic/Latino; 9 Hispanic/Latino; 2 Native Hawaiian or other Pacific Islander, non-Hispanic/Latino), 24 international. Average age 26. 403 applicants, 28% accepted, 27 enrolled. In 2015, 9 master's, 32 doctorates awarded. Terminal master's awarded for partial completion of doctoral program. *Degree requirements:* For master's, comprehensive exam (for some programs), thesis (for some programs); for doctorate, comprehensive exam, thesis/dissertation, annual faculty committee meetings; minimum 1 year of teaching experience; proposal exam. *Entrance requirements:* For master's and doctorate, GRE General Test, GRE Subject Test in chemistry (recommended), 3 letters of recommendation, statement of purpose, personal achievements essay, resume/curriculum vitae, transcripts. Additional exam requirements/recommendations for international students: Required—TOEFL (minimum score 550 paper-based; 80 iBT), IELTS (minimum score 7). *Application deadline:* For fall admission, 12/15 for domestic and international students. Application fee: $90 ($110 for international students). Electronic applications accepted. *Financial support:* In 2015–16, 25 students received support, including 76 fellowships with tuition reimbursements available (averaging $3,280 per year), 112 research assistantships with tuition reimbursements available (averaging $10,960 per year), 109 teaching assistantships with tuition reimbursements available (averaging $13,760 per year); career-related internships or fieldwork, Federal Work-Study, institutionally sponsored loans, scholarships/grants, traineeships, health care benefits, tuition waivers (full and partial), and unspecified assistantships also available. Support available to part-time students. Financial award application deadline: 12/15; financial award applicants required to submit FAFSA. *Faculty research:* Organic, inorganic, physical, biochemistry, and materials chemistry. *Unit head:* Dr. Steve K. Buratto, Department Chair, 805-893-3393, Fax: 805-893-4120,
E-mail: buratto@chem.ucsb.edu. *Application contact:* Mallarie A. Stevens, Graduate Program Advisor/Student Affairs Manager, 805-893-5675, Fax: 805-893-4120,
E-mail: gradprog@chem.ucsb.edu.
Website: http://www.chem.ucsb.edu/

University of California, Santa Cruz, Division of Graduate Studies, Division of Physical and Biological Sciences, Department of Chemistry and Biochemistry, Santa Cruz, CA 95064. Offers MS, PhD. *Degree requirements:* For master's, thesis optional; for doctorate, one foreign language, thesis/dissertation, qualifying exam. *Entrance requirements:* For master's and doctorate, GRE General Test, GRE Subject Test. Additional exam requirements/recommendations for international students: Required—TOEFL (minimum score 570 paper-based; 89 iBT); Recommended—IELTS (minimum score 8). Electronic applications accepted. *Faculty research:* Marine chemistry; biochemistry; inorganic, organic, and physical chemistry.

University of Central Florida, College of Education and Human Performance, School of Teaching, Learning, and Leadership, Program in Teacher Education, Orlando, FL 32816. Offers art education (MAT); English language (MAT); mathematics education (MAT); middle school mathematics (MAT); science education (MAT), including biology, chemistry, physics; social science education (MAT). *Accreditation:* NCATE. *Program availability:* Part-time, evening/weekend. *Students:* 25 full-time (16 women), 43 part-time (32 women); includes 19 minority (5 Black or African American, non-Hispanic/Latino; 2 Asian, non-Hispanic/Latino; 10 Hispanic/Latino; 2 Two or more races, non-Hispanic/Latino). Average age 30. In 2015, 88 master's awarded. *Entrance requirements:* For master's, GRE General Test. Additional exam requirements/recommendations for international students: Required—TOEFL. *Application deadline:* For fall admission, 7/15 for domestic students; for spring admission, 12/1 for domestic students. Application fee: $30. Electronic applications accepted. *Expenses:* Tuition, state resident: part-time $288.16 per credit hour. Tuition, nonresident: part-time $1071.31 per credit hour. *Financial support:* Fellowships, research assistantships, teaching assistantships, career-related internships or fieldwork, Federal Work-Study, institutionally sponsored loans, tuition waivers (partial), and unspecified assistantships available. Financial award application deadline: 3/1; financial award applicants required to submit FAFSA. *Unit head:* Dr. Michael Hynes, Director, 407-823-2005, E-mail: mychael.hynes@ucf.edu. *Application contact:* Director, Admissions and Student Support, 407-823-2766, Fax: 407-823-6442, E-mail: gradadmissions@ucf.edu.

University of Central Florida, College of Sciences, Department of Chemistry, Orlando, FL 32816. Offers chemistry (MS, PhD); computer forensics (Certificate). *Program availability:* Part-time, evening/weekend. *Faculty:* 29 full-time (6 women), 4 part-time/adjunct (2 women). *Students:* 77 full-time (38 women), 11 part-time (3 women); includes 23 minority (3 Black or African American, non-Hispanic/Latino; 5 Asian, non-Hispanic/Latino; 10 Hispanic/Latino; 5 Two or more races, non-Hispanic/Latino), 24 international. Average age 29. 104 applicants, 49% accepted, 20 enrolled. In 2015, 13 master's, 17 doctorates, 4 other advanced degrees awarded. *Degree requirements:* For master's, thesis, final exam. *Entrance requirements:* For master's, GRE General Test, minimum GPA of 3.0 in last 60 hours. Additional exam requirements/recommendations for international students: Required—TOEFL. *Application deadline:* For fall admission, 7/15 for domestic students; for spring admission, 12/1 for domestic students. Application fee: $30. Electronic applications accepted. *Expenses:* Tuition, state resident: part-time $288.16 per credit hour. Tuition, nonresident: part-time $1071.31 per credit hour. *Financial support:* In 2015–16, 58 students received support, including 8 fellowships with partial tuition reimbursements available (averaging $1,500 per year), 13 research assistantships with partial tuition reimbursements available (averaging $11,200 per year), 44 teaching assistantships with partial tuition reimbursements available (averaging $12,300 per year); career-related internships or fieldwork, Federal Work-Study, institutionally sponsored loans, tuition waivers (partial), and unspecified assistantships also available. Financial award application deadline: 3/1; financial award applicants required to submit FAFSA. *Faculty research:* Physical and synthetic organic chemistry, lasers, polymers, biochemical action of pesticides, environmental analysis. *Unit head:* Dr. Cherie Yestrebsky, Interim Chair, 407-823-2135, Fax: 407-823-2252, E-mail: cherie.yestrebsky@ucf.edu. *Application contact:* Director, Admissions and Student Services, 407-823-2766, Fax: 407-823-6442, E-mail: gradadmissions@ucf.edu.
Website: http://chemistry.cos.ucf.edu/

University of Chicago, Division of the Physical Sciences, Department of Chemistry, Chicago, IL 60637. Offers PhD. *Degree requirements:* For doctorate, comprehensive exam, thesis/dissertation. *Entrance requirements:* For doctorate, GRE General Test, GRE Subject Test. Additional exam requirements/recommendations for international students: Required—TOEFL (minimum score 600 paper-based; 90 iBT), IELTS (minimum score 7). Electronic applications accepted. *Expenses:* Contact institution. *Faculty research:* Organic, inorganic, physical, biological chemistry.

University of Cincinnati, Graduate School, McMicken College of Arts and Sciences, Department of Chemistry, Cincinnati, OH 45221. Offers analytical chemistry (MS, PhD); biochemistry (MS, PhD); inorganic chemistry (MS, PhD); organic chemistry (MS, PhD); physical chemistry (MS, PhD); polymer chemistry (MS, PhD); sensors (PhD). *Program availability:* Part-time, evening/weekend. Terminal master's awarded for partial completion of doctoral program. *Degree requirements:* For master's, thesis optional; for doctorate, comprehensive exam, thesis/dissertation. *Entrance requirements:* For master's and doctorate, GRE General Test. Additional exam requirements/recommendations for international students: Required—TOEFL (minimum score 580 paper-based). Electronic applications accepted. *Faculty research:* Biomedical chemistry, laser chemistry, surface science, chemical sensors, synthesis.

University of Colorado Boulder, Graduate School, College of Arts and Sciences, Department of Chemistry and Biochemistry, Boulder, CO 80309. Offers biochemistry (PhD); chemistry (MS). *Faculty:* 46 full-time (9 women). *Students:* 222 full-time (78 women), 3 part-time (2 women); includes 33 minority (8 Asian, non-Hispanic/Latino; 18 Hispanic/Latino; 7 Two or more races, non-Hispanic/Latino), 37 international. Average age 26. 574 applicants, 27% accepted, 51 enrolled. In 2015, 9 master's, 44 doctorates awarded. Terminal master's awarded for partial completion of doctoral program. *Degree requirements:* For master's, comprehensive exam or thesis; for doctorate, comprehensive exam, thesis/dissertation, cumulative exam. *Entrance requirements:* For master's, GRE General Test, GRE Subject Test, minimum undergraduate GPA of 2.75; for doctorate, GRE General Test, GRE Subject Test, minimum GPA of 3.0. *Application deadline:* For fall admission, 12/15 for domestic and international students. Applications are processed on a rolling basis. Application fee: $50 ($70 for international students). Electronic applications accepted. Application fee is waived when completed online. *Financial support:* In 2015–16, 529 students received support, including 25 fellowships (averaging $4,975 per year), 126 research assistantships with tuition reimbursements available (averaging $33,604 per year), 98 teaching assistantships with tuition reimbursements available (averaging $33,154 per year); institutionally sponsored loans, scholarships/grants, health care benefits, and unspecified assistantships also available. Financial award applicants required to submit FAFSA. *Faculty research:* Biochemistry; physical chemistry, biochemistry: proteins, catalysis/kinetics, biochemistry: nucleic acid. *Total annual research expenditures:* $24.7 million. *Application contact:*
E-mail: chemgrad@colorado.edu.
Website: http://chem.colorado.edu

University of Colorado Denver, College of Liberal Arts and Sciences, Department of Chemistry, Denver, CO 80217. Offers MS. *Program availability:* Part-time. *Faculty:* 13 full-time (4 women), 1 part-time/adjunct (0 women). *Students:* 8 full-time (5 women), 10 part-time (3 women); includes 5 minority (1 Black or African American, non-Hispanic/Latino; 2 Asian, non-Hispanic/Latino; 2 Hispanic/Latino), 1 international. Average age 30. 13 applicants, 38% accepted, 3 enrolled. In 2015, 6 master's awarded. *Degree requirements:* For master's, comprehensive exam, thesis optional, 30-33 credit hours. *Entrance requirements:* For master's, GRE General Test and GRE Subject Test in chemistry (recommended), undergraduate degree in chemistry; minimum undergraduate GPA of 3.0. Additional exam requirements/recommendations for international students: Required—TOEFL (minimum score 550 paper-based; 79 iBT); Recommended—IELTS (minimum score 6). *Application deadline:* For fall admission, 6/15 for domestic students, 5/15 priority date for international students; for spring admission, 11/15 for domestic students, 10/15 priority date for international students. Application fee: $50 ($75 for international students). Electronic applications accepted. *Financial support:* In 2015–16, 11 students received support. Fellowships, research assistantships, teaching assistantships, Federal Work-Study, institutionally sponsored loans, scholarships/grants, and traineeships available. Financial award application deadline: 4/1; financial award applicants required to submit FAFSA. *Faculty research:* Enzymology of proteinases, computational chemistry, metal-organic coordination and materials chemistry, environmental chemistry, materials chemistry. *Unit head:* Dr. Haobin Wang, Professor and Chair, 303-556-5866,
E-mail: haobin.wang@ucdenver.edu. *Application contact:* 303-556-3259.
Website: http://www.ucdenver.edu/academics/colleges/CLAS/Departments/chemistry/Programs/Masters/Pages/Masters.aspx

University of Connecticut, Graduate School, College of Liberal Arts and Sciences, Department of Chemistry, Storrs, CT 06269. Offers MS, PhD. Terminal master's awarded for partial completion of doctoral program. *Degree requirements:* For master's, comprehensive exam; for doctorate, thesis/dissertation. *Entrance requirements:* For master's and doctorate, GRE General Test, GRE Subject Test. Additional exam requirements/recommendations for international students: Required—TOEFL (minimum score 550 paper-based). Electronic applications accepted.

University of Dayton, Department of Chemistry, Dayton, OH 45469. Offers MS. *Faculty:* 5 full-time (0 women). *Students:* 3 full-time (2 women); includes 1 minority (Asian, non-Hispanic/Latino). Average age 35. 52 applicants, 8% accepted, 4 enrolled. In 2015, 1 master's awarded. *Degree requirements:* For master's, thesis, 30 hours. *Entrance requirements:* For master's, BS in chemistry or closely-related discipline. Additional exam requirements/recommendations for international students: Required—GRE; Recommended—TOEFL (minimum score 550 paper-based; 80 iBT), IELTS. *Application deadline:* For fall admission, 5/1 priority date for domestic and international students; for winter admission, 7/1 priority date for international students; for spring admission, 11/1 priority date for international students. Applications are processed on a rolling basis. Application fee: $0 ($50 for international students). Electronic applications accepted. *Expenses:* $873 per credit hour. *Financial support:* In 2015–16, 3 students received support, including 5 teaching assistantships with full tuition reimbursements available (averaging $12,876 per year); institutionally sponsored loans and health care benefits also available. Financial award application deadline: 5/1; financial award applicants required to submit FAFSA. *Faculty research:* Nucleoside transition metal complexes; fire retardant materials, bacterial flux pump inhibitors; chiral phosphate synthesis and applications; circular dichroism of DNA-drug complexes. *Total annual research expenditures:* $85,000. *Unit head:* Dr. David Johnson, Chair, 937-229-2631, E-mail: djohnson1@udayton.edu. *Application contact:* Dr. Kevin Church, Graduate Program Director, 937-229-2659, E-mail: kchurch1@udayton.edu.
Website: https://www.udayton.edu/artssciences/academics/chemistry/welcome/index.php

University of Delaware, College of Arts and Sciences, Department of Chemistry and Biochemistry, Newark, DE 19716. Offers biochemistry (MA, MS, PhD); chemistry (MA, MS, PhD). *Program availability:* Part-time. Terminal master's awarded for partial completion of doctoral program. *Degree requirements:* For master's, one foreign language, thesis (for some programs); for doctorate, one foreign language, thesis/dissertation, cumulative exam. *Entrance requirements:* For master's and doctorate, GRE General Test. Additional exam requirements/recommendations for international students: Required—TOEFL (minimum score 600 paper-based). Electronic applications accepted. *Faculty research:* Micro-organisms, bone, cancer metastosis, developmental biology, cell biology, molecular biology.

University of Denver, Division of Natural Sciences and Mathematics, Department of Chemistry and Biochemistry, Denver, CO 80208. Offers chemistry (MA, MS, PhD). *Program availability:* Part-time. *Faculty:* 18 full-time (3 women), 2 part-time/adjunct (1 woman). *Students:* 12 full-time (2 women), 14 part-time (6 women); includes 8 minority (2 Black or African American, non-Hispanic/Latino; 5 Hispanic/Latino; 1 Two or more

races, non-Hispanic/Latino), 7 international. Average age 27. 45 applicants, 73% accepted, 12 enrolled. In 2015, 2 master's, 2 doctorates awarded. Terminal master's awarded for partial completion of doctoral program. *Degree requirements:* For master's, comprehensive exam (for some programs), thesis; for doctorate, comprehensive exam, thesis/dissertation. *Entrance requirements:* For master's and doctorate, GRE General Test, bachelor's degree in chemistry, biochemistry, or a related field; transcripts; personal statement, resume or curriculum vitae; three letters of recommendation. Additional exam requirements/recommendations for international students: Required—TOEFL (minimum score 550 paper-based; 80 iBT). *Application deadline:* For fall admission, 3/1 priority date for domestic and international students. Applications are processed on a rolling basis. Application fee: $65. Electronic applications accepted. *Expenses:* $30,477. *Financial support:* In 2015–16, 23 students received support, including 12 research assistantships with tuition reimbursements available (averaging $17,153 per year), 15 teaching assistantships with tuition reimbursements available (averaging $16,556 per year); career-related internships or fieldwork, Federal Work-Study, institutionally sponsored loans, and scholarships/grants also available. Support available to part-time students. Financial award application deadline: 2/15; financial award applicants required to submit FAFSA. *Faculty research:* Environmental analytical chemistry, protein folding, organic synthesis, biophysics, magnetic resonance. *Unit head:* Dr. Sandra S. Eaton, Professor and Chair, 303-871-3100, Fax: 303-871-2254, E-mail: seaton@du.edu. *Application contact:* Christine Stutzman, Office Assistant, 303-871-2435, Fax: 303-871-2254, E-mail: cheminfo@du.edu.
Website: http://www.du.edu/nsm/departments/chemistryandbiochemistry

University of Detroit Mercy, College of Engineering and Science, Detroit, MI 48221. Offers chemistry (MS); civil and environmental engineering (DE); electrical and computer engineering (ME); electrical engineering (DE); engineering management (M Eng Mgt); environmental engineering (MEE); mechanical engineering (MME, DE); product development (MS); software engineering (MSSE); teaching of mathematics (MATM). *Program availability:* Part-time, evening/weekend. *Faculty:* 54 full-time (16 women), 32 part-time/adjunct (8 women). *Students:* 102 full-time (20 women), 80 part-time (14 women); includes 19 minority (8 Black or African American, non-Hispanic/Latino; 9 Asian, non-Hispanic/Latino; 2 Hispanic/Latino), 112 international. Average age 30. 300 applicants, 45% accepted, 35 enrolled. In 2015, 60 master's awarded. *Degree requirements:* For doctorate, thesis/dissertation. *Application deadline:* For fall admission, 8/1 priority date for domestic students. Applications are processed on a rolling basis. Application fee: $30 ($50 for international students). Electronic applications accepted. Application fee is waived when completed online. *Expenses:* Contact institution. *Financial support:* Fellowships, teaching assistantships, career-related internships or fieldwork, and Federal Work-Study available. Financial award application deadline: 8/1; financial award applicants required to submit FAFSA. *Unit head:* Gary Kuleck, Dean, 313-993-1216, Fax: 313-993-1187, E-mail: kuleckga@udmercy.edu. *Application contact:* Matt Fortescu, Graduate Studies Coordinator, 313-993-3378, Fax: 313-993-1187, E-mail: fortesme@udmercy.edu.

University of Florida, Graduate School, College of Liberal Arts and Sciences, Department of Chemistry, Gainesville, FL 32611. Offers chemistry (MS, MST, PhD); clinical and translational science (PhD); imaging science and technology (PhD). *Faculty:* 8 full-time. *Students:* 221 full-time (73 women), 5 part-time (1 woman); includes 25 minority (7 Black or African American, non-Hispanic/Latino; 10 Asian, non-Hispanic/Latino; 8 Hispanic/Latino), 147 international. Average age 28. 449 applicants, 26% accepted, 46 enrolled. In 2015, 11 master's, 28 doctorates awarded. Terminal master's awarded for partial completion of doctoral program. *Degree requirements:* For master's, thesis; for doctorate, comprehensive exam, thesis/dissertation. *Entrance requirements:* For master's and doctorate, GRE General Test, minimum GPA of 3.0. Additional exam requirements/recommendations for international students: Required—TOEFL (minimum score 550 paper-based; 80 iBT), IELTS (minimum score 6). *Application deadline:* For fall admission, 1/1 priority date for domestic students, 1/1 for international students; for spring admission, 9/1 for domestic and international students. Applications are processed on a rolling basis. Application fee: $30. Electronic applications accepted. *Financial support:* In 2015–16, 18 fellowships, 110 research assistantships, 182 teaching assistantships were awarded; institutionally sponsored loans and unspecified assistantships also available. Financial award applicants required to submit FAFSA. *Faculty research:* Organic, analytical, physical, inorganic, and biological chemistry. *Total annual research expenditures:* $6.7 million. *Unit head:* William R. Dolbier, PhD, Professor and Chair, 352-392-0591, Fax: 352-846-1962, E-mail: wrd@chem.ufl.edu. *Application contact:* Ben W. Smith, Graduate Coordinator, 352-392-0256, Fax: 352-846-1962, E-mail: bwsmith@ufl.edu.
Website: http://web.chem.ufl.edu/

University of Georgia, Franklin College of Arts and Sciences, Department of Chemistry, Athens, GA 30602. Offers analytical chemistry (MS, PhD); inorganic chemistry (MS, PhD); organic chemistry (MS, PhD); physical chemistry (MS, PhD). Terminal master's awarded for partial completion of doctoral program. *Degree requirements:* For master's, thesis; for doctorate, one foreign language, thesis/dissertation. *Entrance requirements:* For master's and doctorate, GRE General Test. Additional exam requirements/recommendations for international students: Required—TOEFL. Electronic applications accepted.

University of Guelph, Graduate Studies, College of Physical and Engineering Science, Guelph-Waterloo Centre for Graduate Work in Chemistry and Biochemistry, Guelph, ON N1G 2W1, Canada. Offers M Sc, PhD. M Sc, PhD offered jointly with University of Waterloo. *Program availability:* Part-time. *Degree requirements:* For master's, thesis; for doctorate, thesis/dissertation. *Faculty research:* Inorganic, analytical, biological, physical/theoretical, polymer, and organic chemistry.

University of Hawaii at Manoa, Graduate Division, College of Natural Sciences, Department of Chemistry, Honolulu, HI 96822. Offers MS, PhD. *Program availability:* Part-time. *Faculty:* 14 full-time (1 woman). *Students:* 36 full-time (8 women), 1 (woman) part-time; includes 11 minority (7 Asian, non-Hispanic/Latino; 1 Hispanic/Latino; 3 Two or more races, non-Hispanic/Latino), 11 international. Average age 29. 20 applicants, 60% accepted, 7 enrolled. In 2015, 5 master's, 2 doctorates awarded. *Degree requirements:* For master's, comprehensive exam, thesis; for doctorate, comprehensive exam, thesis/dissertation. *Entrance requirements:* For master's and doctorate, GRE General Test, GRE Subject Test. Additional exam requirements/recommendations for international students: Required—TOEFL (minimum score 500 paper-based; 61 iBT), IELTS (minimum score 5). *Application deadline:* For fall admission, 5/1 for domestic students, 3/1 for international students; for spring admission, 9/1 for domestic students, 8/1 for international students. Applications are processed on a rolling basis. Application fee: $100. *Financial support:* In 2015–16, 3 fellowships (averaging $1,667 per year), 8 research assistantships (averaging $18,438 per year), 25 teaching assistantships (averaging $15,811 per year) were awarded. Support available to part-time students. *Faculty research:* Marine natural products, biophysical spectroscopy, zeolites, organometallic hydrides, new visual pigments, theory of surfaces. *Total annual research expenditures:* $2.3 million. *Unit head:* William Ditto, Dean, 808-956-6451, E-mail: wditto@hawaii.edu. *Application contact:* Thomas Hemscheidt, Graduate Chair, 808-956-7480, Fax: 808-956-5908, E-mail: hemschei@hawaii.edu.
Website: http://www.chem.hawaii.edu/

University of Houston, College of Natural Sciences and Mathematics, Department of Chemistry, Houston, TX 77204. Offers MA, PhD. *Program availability:* Part-time. Terminal master's awarded for partial completion of doctoral program. *Degree requirements:* For master's, thesis; for doctorate, thesis/dissertation, oral presentation. *Entrance requirements:* For master's and doctorate, GRE General Test. Additional exam requirements/recommendations for international students: Required—TOEFL (minimum score 79 iBT), IELTS (minimum score 6.5). Electronic applications accepted. *Faculty research:* Materials, molecular design, surface science, structural chemistry, synthesis.

University of Houston–Clear Lake, School of Science and Computer Engineering, Program in Chemistry, Houston, TX 77058-1002. Offers MS. *Program availability:* Part-time, evening/weekend. *Entrance requirements:* For master's, GRE General Test. Additional exam requirements/recommendations for international students: Required—TOEFL (minimum score 550 paper-based).

University of Idaho, College of Graduate Studies, College of Science, Department of Chemistry, Moscow, ID 83844-2343. Offers MS, PhD. *Faculty:* 8 full-time. *Students:* 21 full-time, 5 part-time. Average age 32. In 2015, 6 doctorates awarded. *Degree requirements:* For master's, thesis or alternative; for doctorate, one foreign language, thesis/dissertation. *Entrance requirements:* For master's, minimum GPA of 2.8; for doctorate, minimum undergraduate GPA of 2.8, 3.0 graduate. Additional exam requirements/recommendations for international students: Required—TOEFL. *Application deadline:* For fall admission, 8/1 for domestic students; for spring admission, 12/15 for domestic students. Applications are processed on a rolling basis. Application fee: $60. Electronic applications accepted. *Expenses:* Tuition, state resident: full-time $6205; part-time $399 per credit hour. Tuition, nonresident: full-time $20,209; part-time $1177 per credit hour. *Required fees:* $2017; $58 per credit hour. Full-time tuition and fees vary according to course load and reciprocity agreements. *Financial support:* Fellowships, research assistantships, and teaching assistantships available. Financial award applicants required to submit FAFSA. *Faculty research:* Analytical chemistry, inorganic chemistry, organic chemistry, physical chemistry. *Unit head:* Dr. Ray von Wandruszka, Chair, 208-885-6552, E-mail: chemoff@uidaho.edu. *Application contact:* Sean Scoggin, Graduate Recruitment Coordinator, 208-885-4723, Fax: 208-885-4406, E-mail: graduateadmissions@uidaho.edu.
Website: http://www.uidaho.edu/sci/chem

University of Illinois at Chicago, College of Liberal Arts and Sciences, Department of Chemistry, Chicago, IL 60607-7128. Offers MS, PhD. *Program availability:* Part-time. *Faculty:* 38 full-time (13 women), 16 part-time/adjunct (5 women). *Students:* 125 full-time (46 women), 1 part-time (0 women); includes 10 minority (1 Black or African American, non-Hispanic/Latino; 6 Asian, non-Hispanic/Latino; 3 Hispanic/Latino), 83 international. Average age 28. Terminal master's awarded for partial completion of doctoral program. *Degree requirements:* For master's, thesis or cumulative exam; for doctorate, one foreign language, thesis/dissertation, cumulative exams. *Entrance requirements:* For master's and doctorate, GRE Subject Test, minimum GPA of 3.0. Additional exam requirements/recommendations for international students: Required—TOEFL. *Application deadline:* For fall admission, 1/1 priority date for domestic students, 2/15 for international students; for spring admission, 10/1 priority date for domestic students, 7/15 for international students. Applications are processed on a rolling basis. Application fee: $60. Electronic applications accepted. *Expenses:* Contact institution. *Financial support:* In 2015–16, 1 fellowship with full tuition reimbursement was awarded; research assistantships with full tuition reimbursements, teaching assistantships with full tuition reimbursements, Federal Work-Study, institutionally sponsored loans, scholarships/grants, traineeships, tuition waivers (full), and unspecified assistantships also available. Financial award application deadline: 3/1; financial award applicants required to submit FAFSA. *Faculty research:* Analytical, biological, inorganic, organic and physical chemistry; chemical biology, nanotechnology and neurochemistry. *Unit head:* Prof. Luke Hanley, Professor and Head, 312-996-3161, E-mail: lhanley@uic.edu. *Application contact:* Receptionist, 312-413-2550, E-mail: gradcoll@uic.edu.
Website: http://www.chem.uic.edu/

University of Illinois at Chicago, College of Pharmacy and Graduate College, Graduate Programs in Pharmacy, Chicago, IL 60607-7128. Offers forensic science (MS), including forensic toxicology; medicinal chemistry (MS); pharmacognosy (MS, PhD); pharmacy administration (MS, PhD). *Faculty:* 237 full-time (137 women), 60 part-time/adjunct (32 women). *Students:* 110 full-time (62 women), 17 part-time (8 women); includes 26 minority (7 Black or African American, non-Hispanic/Latino; 15 Asian, non-Hispanic/Latino; 4 Hispanic/Latino), 54 international. Average age 28. Terminal master's awarded for partial completion of doctoral program. *Degree requirements:* For master's, variable foreign language requirement, thesis; for doctorate, variable foreign language requirement, thesis/dissertation. *Entrance requirements:* For master's and doctorate, GRE General Test. Additional exam requirements/recommendations for international students: Required—TOEFL. *Application deadline:* For fall admission, 2/1 for domestic students. Applications are processed on a rolling basis. Application fee: $60. Electronic applications accepted. *Expenses:* Tuition, state resident: full-time $11,480; part-time $3826 per credit. Tuition, nonresident: full-time $23,720; part-time $7906 per credit. *Required fees:* $1333 per semester. Part-time tuition and fees vary according to course load and program. *Financial support:* In 2015–16, 2 fellowships with full tuition reimbursements were awarded; research assistantships with full tuition reimbursements, teaching assistantships with full tuition reimbursements, career-related internships or fieldwork, Federal Work-Study, institutionally sponsored loans, traineeships, tuition waivers (full), and unspecified assistantships also available. Financial award application deadline: 3/1; financial award applicants required to submit FAFSA. *Faculty research:* Biopharmaceutical science, forensic science, forensic toxicology, medicinal chemistry, pharmacognosy. *Unit head:* Prof. Joanna Burdette, Associate Dean for Research and Graduate Education, 312-996-6153, E-mail: joannab@uic.edu. *Application contact:* Jackie Perry, Graduate College Receptionist, 312-413-2550, Fax: 312-413-0185, E-mail: gradcoll@uic.edu.
Website: http://www.uic.edu/pharmacy/education/graduatePrograms.php

University of Illinois at Urbana–Champaign, Graduate College, College of Liberal Arts and Sciences, School of Chemical Sciences, Department of Chemistry, Champaign, IL 61820. Offers astrochemistry (PhD); chemical physics (PhD); chemistry (MA, MS, PhD); teaching of chemistry (MS); MS/JD; MS/MBA.

The University of Iowa, Graduate College, College of Liberal Arts and Sciences, Department of Chemistry, Iowa City, IA 52242-1316. Offers PhD. *Degree requirements:* For doctorate, comprehensive exam, thesis/dissertation. *Entrance requirements:* For doctorate, GRE General Test, minimum GPA of 3.0. Additional exam requirements/recommendations for international students: Required—TOEFL (minimum score 550 paper-based; 81 iBT). Electronic applications accepted.

The University of Kansas, Graduate Studies, College of Liberal Arts and Sciences, Department of Chemistry, Lawrence, KS 66045. Offers MS, PhD. *Students:* 118 full-time

(53 women), 1 part-time (0 women); includes 13 minority (4 Black or African American, non-Hispanic/Latino; 4 Asian, non-Hispanic/Latino; 5 Two or more races, non-Hispanic/Latino), 47 international. Average age 27. 197 applicants, 38% accepted, 23 enrolled. In 2015, 3 master's, 11 doctorates awarded. *Entrance requirements:* For master's and doctorate, GRE General Test. Additional exam requirements/recommendations for international students: Required—TOEFL. *Application deadline:* For fall admission, 1/15 priority date for domestic and international students; for spring admission, 9/1 priority date for domestic and international students. Application fee: $65 ($85 for international students). Electronic applications accepted. *Financial support:* Fellowships, research assistantships, teaching assistantships, scholarships/grants, traineeships, tuition waivers (full), and unspecified assistantships available. Financial award application deadline: 4/15. *Faculty research:* Organometallic and inorganic synthetic methodology, bioanalytical chemistry, computational materials science, proteomics, physical chemistry. *Unit head:* Prof. Brian B. Laird, Chair, 785-864-4632, E-mail: blaird@ku.edu. *Application contact:* Ruben Leal, Graduate Affairs Administrator, 785-864-4693, E-mail: rleal@ku.edu.
Website: http://www.chem.ku.edu/

University of Kentucky, Graduate School, College of Arts and Sciences, Program in Chemistry, Lexington, KY 40506-0032. Offers MS, PhD. *Program availability:* Part-time. Terminal master's awarded for partial completion of doctoral program. *Degree requirements:* For master's, comprehensive exam, thesis optional; for doctorate, comprehensive exam, thesis/dissertation. *Entrance requirements:* For master's, GRE General Test, minimum undergraduate GPA of 2.75; for doctorate, GRE General Test, minimum graduate GPA of 3.0. Additional exam requirements/recommendations for international students: Required—TOEFL (minimum score 550 paper-based). Electronic applications accepted. *Faculty research:* Analytical, inorganic, organic, and physical chemistry; biological chemistry; nuclear chemistry; radiochemistry; materials chemistry.

University of Lethbridge, School of Graduate Studies, Lethbridge, AB T1K 3M4, Canada. Offers addictions counseling (M Sc); agricultural biotechnology (M Sc); agricultural studies (M Sc, MA); anthropology (MA); archaeology (M Sc, MA); art (MA, MFA); biochemistry (M Sc); biological sciences (M Sc); biomolecular science (PhD); biosystems and biodiversity (PhD); Canadian studies (MA); chemistry (M Sc); computer science (M Sc); computer science and geographical information science (M Sc); counseling (MC); counseling psychology (M Ed); dramatic arts (MA); earth, space, and physical science (PhD); economics (MA); education (MA, PhD); educational leadership (M Ed); English (MA); environmental science (M Sc); evolution and behavior (PhD); exercise science (M Sc); French (MA); French/German (MA); French/Spanish (MA); general education (M Ed); geography (M Sc, MA); German (MA); health sciences (M Sc); individualized multidisciplinary (M Sc, MA); kinesiology (M Sc, MA); management (M Sc), including accounting, finance, human resource management and labor relations, information systems, international management, marketing, policy and strategy; mathematics (M Sc); music (M Mus, MA); Native American studies (MA); neuroscience (M Sc, PhD); new media (MA, MFA); nursing (M Sc, MN); philosophy (MA); physics (M Sc); political science (MA); psychology (M Sc, MA); religious studies (MA); sociology (MA); theatre and dramatic arts (MFA); theoretical and computational science (PhD); urban and regional studies (MA); women and gender studies (MA). *Program availability:* Part-time, evening/weekend. *Students:* 448 full-time (249 women), 110 part-time (64 women). Average age 32. 285 applicants, 36% accepted, 96 enrolled. In 2015, 154 master's, 11 doctorates awarded. *Degree requirements:* For master's, thesis (for some programs); for doctorate, comprehensive exam, thesis/dissertation. *Entrance requirements:* For master's, GMAT (for M Sc in management), bachelor's degree in related field, minimum GPA of 3.0 during previous 20 graded semester courses, 2 years' teaching or related experience (M Ed); for doctorate, master's degree, minimum graduate GPA of 3.5. Additional exam requirements/recommendations for international students: Required—TOEFL (minimum score 580 paper-based; 93 iBT). Application fee: $100 Canadian dollars ($140 Canadian dollars for international students). Electronic applications accepted. *Financial support:* Fellowships, research assistantships, teaching assistantships, scholarships/grants, health care benefits, and unspecified assistantships available. *Faculty research:* Movement and brain plasticity, gibberellin physiology, photosynthesis, carbon cycling, molecular properties of main-group ring components. *Unit head:* Kathleen Schrage, Manager, School of Graduate Studies, 403-329-2121, E-mail: schrage@uleth.ca. *Application contact:* School of Graduate Studies, 403-329-5194, E-mail: sgsinquiries@uleth.ca.
Website: http://www.uleth.ca/graduate-studies/

University of Louisville, Graduate School, College of Arts and Sciences, Department of Chemistry, Louisville, KY 40292-0001. Offers analytical chemistry (MS, PhD); biochemistry (MS, PhD); chemical physics (PhD); inorganic chemistry (MS, PhD); organic chemistry (MS, PhD); physical chemistry (MS, PhD). *Students:* 46 full-time (16 women), 8 part-time (1 woman); includes 3 minority (1 Black or African American, non-Hispanic/Latino; 1 Asian, non-Hispanic/Latino; 1 Two or more races, non-Hispanic/Latino), 36 international. Average age 29. 51 applicants, 22% accepted, 6 enrolled. In 2015, 2 master's, 1 doctorate awarded. Terminal master's awarded for partial completion of doctoral program. *Degree requirements:* For master's, variable foreign language requirement, comprehensive exam, thesis optional; for doctorate, variable foreign language requirement, comprehensive exam, thesis/dissertation. *Entrance requirements:* For master's and doctorate, GRE General Test, BA or BS coursework. Additional exam requirements/recommendations for international students: Required—TOEFL (minimum score 550 paper-based; 79 iBT). *Application deadline:* For fall admission, 3/15 for domestic students, 5/1 priority date for international students; for winter admission, 9/15 for domestic and international students; for spring admission, 11/1 priority date for international students; for summer admission, 4/1 priority date for international students. Applications are processed on a rolling basis. Application fee: $60. Electronic applications accepted. *Expenses:* Tuition, state resident: full-time $11,664; part-time $649 per credit hour. Tuition, nonresident: full-time $24,274; part-time $1350 per credit hour. *Required fees:* $196. Tuition and fees vary according to program and reciprocity agreements. *Financial support:* In 2015–16, 757,720 students received support. Fellowships with full tuition reimbursements available, research assistantships with full tuition reimbursements available, teaching assistantships with full tuition reimbursements available, career-related internships or fieldwork, scholarships/grants, traineeships, health care benefits, and unspecified assistantships available. Support available to part-time students. Financial award application deadline: 3/15. *Faculty research:* Computational chemistry, biophysics nuclear magnetic resonance, synthetic organic chemistry, synthetic inorganic chemistry, medicinal chemistry, protein chemistry, enzymology, nano chemistry, electrochemistry, analytical chemistry, synthetic biology, bioinformatics. *Total annual research expenditures:* $2.4 million. *Unit head:* Dr. Richard J. Wittebort, Professor/Chair, 502-852-6613. *Application contact:* Libby Leggett, Director, Graduate Admissions, 502-852-3101, Fax: 502-852-6536, E-mail: gradadm@louisville.edu.
Website: http://louisville.edu/chemistry

University of Maine, Graduate School, College of Liberal Arts and Sciences, Department of Chemistry, Orono, ME 04469. Offers MS, PhD. *Faculty:* 12 full-time (3 women), 1 part-time/adjunct (0 women). *Students:* 23 full-time (9 women); includes 2 minority (1 American Indian or Alaska Native, non-Hispanic/Latino; 1 Asian, non-Hispanic/Latino), 16 international. Average age 29. 30 applicants, 43% accepted, 6 enrolled. In 2015, 4 master's, 4 doctorates awarded. Terminal master's awarded for partial completion of doctoral program. *Degree requirements:* For master's, thesis; for doctorate, comprehensive exam, thesis/dissertation. *Entrance requirements:* For master's and doctorate, GRE General Test. Additional exam requirements/recommendations for international students: Required—TOEFL. *Application deadline:* For fall admission, 2/1 priority date for domestic students. Applications are processed on a rolling basis. Application fee: $65. Electronic applications accepted. *Financial support:* In 2015–16, 27 students received support, including 5 research assistantships with full tuition reimbursements available (averaging $14,600 per year), 16 teaching assistantships with full tuition reimbursements available (averaging $14,600 per year); tuition waivers (full and partial) also available. Financial award application deadline: 3/1. *Faculty research:* Quantum mechanics, insect chemistry, organic synthesis. *Unit head:* Dr. Barbara Cole, Chair, 207-581-1196, E-mail: cole@maine.edu. *Application contact:* Scott G. Delcourt, Assistant Vice President for Graduate Studies and Senior Associate Dean, 207-581-3291, Fax: 207-581-3232, E-mail: graduate@maine.edu.
Website: http://umaine.edu/chemistry

The University of Manchester, School of Chemical Engineering and Analytical Science, Manchester, United Kingdom. Offers biocatalysis (M Phil, PhD); chemical engineering (M Phil, PhD); chemical engineering and analytical science (M Phil, D Eng, PhD); colloids, crystals, interfaces and materials (M Phil, PhD); environment and sustainable technology (M Phil, PhD); instrumentation (M Phil, PhD); multi-scale modeling (M Phil, PhD); process integration (M Phil, PhD); systems biology (M Phil, PhD).

The University of Manchester, School of Chemistry, Manchester, United Kingdom. Offers biological chemistry (PhD); chemistry (M Ent, M Phil, M Sc, D Ent, PhD); inorganic chemistry (PhD); materials chemistry (PhD); nanoscience (PhD); nuclear fission (PhD); organic chemistry (PhD); physical chemistry (PhD); theoretical chemistry (PhD).

The University of Manchester, School of Earth, Atmospheric and Environmental Sciences, Manchester, United Kingdom. Offers atmospheric sciences (M Phil, M Sc, PhD); basin studies and petroleum geosciences (M Phil, M Sc, PhD); earth, atmospheric and environmental sciences (M Phil, M Sc, PhD); environmental geochemistry and cosmochemistry (M Phil, M Sc, PhD); isotope geochemistry and cosmochemistry (M Phil, M Sc, PhD); paleontology (M Phil, M Sc, PhD); physics and chemistry of minerals and fluids (M Phil, M Sc, PhD); structural and petrological geosciences (M Phil, M Sc, PhD).

University of Manitoba, Faculty of Graduate Studies, Faculty of Science, Department of Chemistry, Winnipeg, MB R3T 2N2, Canada. Offers M Sc, PhD. *Degree requirements:* For master's, thesis; for doctorate, one foreign language, thesis/dissertation.

University of Maryland, Baltimore County, The Graduate School, College of Arts, Humanities and Social Sciences, Department of Education, Program in Teaching, Baltimore, MD 21250. Offers early childhood education (MAT); elementary education (MAT); teaching (MAT), including art, biology, chemistry, choral music, classical foreign language, dance, earth/space science, English, instrumental music, mathematics, modern foreign language, physical science, physics, social studies, theatre. *Program availability:* Part-time, evening/weekend. *Faculty:* 24 full-time (18 women), 25 part-time/adjunct (19 women). *Students:* 43 full-time (34 women), 40 part-time (27 women); includes 29 minority (9 Black or African American, non-Hispanic/Latino; 10 Asian, non-Hispanic/Latino; 9 Hispanic/Latino; 1 Two or more races, non-Hispanic/Latino), 1 international. Average age 30. 54 applicants, 69% accepted, 35 enrolled. In 2015, 106 master's awarded. *Degree requirements:* For master's, comprehensive exam (for some programs), thesis (for some programs). *Entrance requirements:* For master's, PRAXIS Core Examination or GRE (minimum score of 1000), minimum GPA of 3.0. Additional exam requirements/recommendations for international students: Required—TOEFL. *Application deadline:* For fall admission, 6/1 for domestic and international students; for spring admission, 11/1 for domestic and international students. Applications are processed on a rolling basis. Application fee: $50. Electronic applications accepted. *Expenses:* Tuition, state resident: full-time $12,816. Tuition, nonresident: full-time $19,710. *Financial support:* In 2015–16, 6 students received support, including teaching assistantships with tuition reimbursements available (averaging $12,000 per year); career-related internships or fieldwork, Federal Work-Study, scholarships/grants, tuition waivers, and unspecified assistantships also available. Financial award application deadline: 3/1. *Faculty research:* STEM teacher education, culturally sensitive pedagogy, ESOL/bilingual education, early childhood education, language, literacy and culture. *Unit head:* Dr. Susan M. Blunck, Graduate Program Director, 410-455-2869, Fax: 410-455-3986, E-mail: blunck@umbc.edu. *Application contact:* Cheryl Johnson, MAT Program Specialist, 410-455-3388, E-mail: blackwel@umbc.edu.
Website: http://www.umbc.edu/education/

University of Maryland, Baltimore County, The Graduate School, College of Natural and Mathematical Sciences, Department of Chemistry and Biochemistry, Baltimore, MD 21250. Offers biochemistry (PhD); chemistry (MS, PhD); chemistry and biochemistry (Postbaccalaureate Certificate). *Program availability:* Part-time. *Faculty:* 21 full-time (5 women), 4 part-time/adjunct (1 woman). *Students:* 44 full-time (23 women), 1 part-time (0 women); includes 11 minority (6 Black or African American, non-Hispanic/Latino; 1 American Indian or Alaska Native, non-Hispanic/Latino; 2 Asian, non-Hispanic/Latino; 2 Hispanic/Latino), 6 international. Average age 26. 59 applicants, 25% accepted, 9 enrolled. In 2015, 4 master's, 4 doctorates awarded. Terminal master's awarded for partial completion of doctoral program. *Degree requirements:* For master's, comprehensive exam (for some programs), thesis (for some programs); for doctorate, comprehensive exam, thesis/dissertation. *Entrance requirements:* For master's, GRE General Test, minimum GPA of 3.0; for doctorate, GRE General Test, GRE Subject Test (recommended), minimum GPA of 3.0. Additional exam requirements/recommendations for international students: Required—TOEFL (minimum score 550 paper-based, 80 iBT) or IELTS. *Application deadline:* For fall admission, 6/1 priority date for domestic students, 1/1 priority date for international students; for spring admission, 11/1 priority date for domestic students, 5/1 for international students. Applications are processed on a rolling basis. Application fee: $50. Electronic applications accepted. Application fee is waived when completed online. *Expenses:* Tuition, state resident: full-time $12,816. Tuition, nonresident: full-time $19,710. *Financial support:* In 2015–16, 44 students received support, including 7 fellowships with full tuition reimbursements available (averaging $24,000 per year), 12 research assistantships with full tuition reimbursements available (averaging $23,166 per year), 25 teaching assistantships with full tuition reimbursements available (averaging $23,166 per year); health care benefits also available. *Faculty research:* Protein structures, bio-organic chemistry, enzyme catalysis, molecular biology, metabolism, nanotechnology. *Total annual research expenditures:* $4.4 million. *Unit head:* Dr. Zeev Rosenzweig, Chairman, 410-455-2521, Fax: 410-455-2608, E-mail: chemgrad@umbc.edu. *Application contact:* Patricia Gagne,

Graduate Coordinator, 866-PhD-UMBC, Fax: 410-455-2608,
E-mail: pgagne1@umbc.edu.
Website: http://chemistry.umbc.edu

University of Maryland, College Park, Academic Affairs, College of Computer, Mathematical and Natural Sciences, Department of Chemistry and Biochemistry, Chemistry Program, College Park, MD 20742. Offers analytical chemistry (MS, PhD); inorganic chemistry (MS, PhD); organic chemistry (MS, PhD); physical chemistry (MS, PhD). *Program availability:* Part-time, evening/weekend. Terminal master's awarded for partial completion of doctoral program. *Degree requirements:* For master's, thesis optional; for doctorate, thesis/dissertation, 2 seminar presentations, oral exam. *Entrance requirements:* For master's and doctorate, GRE General Test, GRE Subject Test (recommended), minimum GPA of 3.0, 3 letters of recommendation. Additional exam requirements/recommendations for international students: Required—TOEFL. Electronic applications accepted. *Faculty research:* Environmental chemistry, nuclear chemistry, lunar and environmental analysis, X-ray crystallography.

University of Maryland Eastern Shore, Graduate Programs, Department of Natural Sciences, Princess Anne, MD 21853-1299. Offers chemistry (MS); marine-estuarine-environmental sciences (MS, PhD); quantitative fisheries and resource economics (PMS); toxicology (MS, PhD). *Degree requirements:* For master's, thesis; for doctorate, comprehensive exam, thesis/dissertation. *Entrance requirements:* For master's and doctorate, GRE General Test, minimum GPA of 3.0. Additional exam requirements/recommendations for international students: Required—TOEFL (minimum score 80 iBT). Electronic applications accepted. *Faculty research:* Environmental chemistry (air/water pollution), fin fish ecology.

University of Massachusetts Amherst, Graduate School, College of Natural Sciences, Department of Chemistry, Amherst, MA 01003. Offers MS, PhD. *Program availability:* Part-time. Terminal master's awarded for partial completion of doctoral program. *Degree requirements:* For master's, thesis (for some programs); for doctorate, comprehensive exam, thesis/dissertation. *Entrance requirements:* For master's and doctorate, GRE General Test. Additional exam requirements/recommendations for international students: Required—TOEFL (minimum score 550 paper-based; 80 iBT), IELTS (minimum score 6.5). Electronic applications accepted.

University of Massachusetts Boston, College of Science and Mathematics, Program in Chemistry, Boston, MA 02125-3393. Offers MS, PhD. *Program availability:* Part-time, evening/weekend. *Faculty:* 15 full-time (4 women), 4 part-time/adjunct (1 woman). *Students:* 30 full-time (13 women), 8 part-time (5 women); includes 9 minority (1 Black or African American, non-Hispanic/Latino; 6 Asian, non-Hispanic/Latino; 1 Hispanic/Latino; 1 Two or more races, non-Hispanic/Latino), 11 international. 64 applicants, 31% accepted, 10 enrolled. In 2015, 3 master's, 4 doctorates awarded. *Degree requirements:* For master's, comprehensive exam, thesis, oral exams. *Entrance requirements:* For master's, GRE General Test, GRE Subject Test, minimum GPA of 2.75. *Application deadline:* For fall admission, 3/1 for domestic students; for spring admission, 11/1 for domestic students. *Expenses:* Tuition, state resident: full-time $2590. Tuition, nonresident: full-time $9758. *Required fees:* $13,525. *Financial support:* Research assistantships with full tuition reimbursements, teaching assistantships with full tuition reimbursements, career-related internships or fieldwork, Federal Work-Study, and unspecified assistantships available. Support available to part-time students. Financial award application deadline: 3/1; financial award applicants required to submit FAFSA. *Faculty research:* Synthesis and mechanisms of organic nitrogen compounds, application of spin resonance in the study of structure and dynamics, chemical education and teacher training, new synthetic reagents, structural study of inorganic solids by infrared and Raman spectroscopy. *Unit head:* Dr. Michelle Foster, Director, 617-287-6130. *Application contact:* Peggy Roldan Patel, Graduate Admissions Coordinator, 617-287-6400, Fax: 617-287-6236, E-mail: bos.gadm@dpc.umassp.edu.

University of Massachusetts Dartmouth, Graduate School, College of Arts and Sciences, Department of Chemistry and Biochemistry, North Dartmouth, MA 02747-2300. Offers chemistry (MS, PhD). *Program availability:* Part-time. *Faculty:* 18 full-time (6 women), 4 part-time/adjunct (2 women). *Students:* 21 full-time (9 women), 17 part-time (9 women); includes 4 minority (1 Black or African American, non-Hispanic/Latino; 3 Asian, non-Hispanic/Latino), 20 international. Average age 27. 31 applicants, 84% accepted, 11 enrolled. In 2015, 8 master's awarded. *Degree requirements:* For master's, thesis or project; for doctorate, comprehensive exam, thesis/dissertation. *Entrance requirements:* For master's, GRE (recommended), statement of purpose (minimum of 300 words), resume, official transcripts, 2 letters of recommendation; for doctorate, GRE, statement of purpose (minimum of 300 words), resume, official transcripts, 2 letters of recommendation. Additional exam requirements/recommendations for international students: Required—TOEFL (minimum score 533 paper-based; 72 iBT). *Application deadline:* For fall admission, 3/15 priority date for domestic students, 2/15 priority date for international students; for spring admission, 11/1 priority date for domestic students, 10/1 priority date for international students. Applications are processed on a rolling basis. Application fee: $60. Electronic applications accepted. *Expenses:* Tuition, state resident: full-time $2071; part-time $86.29 per credit. Tuition, nonresident: full-time $8099; part-time $337.46 per credit. *Required fees:* $18,074; $762.08 per credit. Tuition and fees vary according to course load and reciprocity agreements. *Financial support:* In 2015–16, 2 fellowships (averaging $21,000 per year), 4 research assistantships (averaging $11,250 per year), 17 teaching assistantships (averaging $11,294 per year) were awarded; Federal Work-Study and unspecified assistantships also available. Support available to part-time students. Financial award application deadline: 3/1; financial award applicants required to submit FAFSA. *Total annual research expenditures:* $1.3 million. *Unit head:* Yuegang Zuo, Graduate Program Director, 508-999-8959, E-mail: yzuo@umassd.edu. *Application contact:* Steven Briggs, Director of Recruitment and Marketing for Graduate Studies, 508-999-8604, Fax: 508-999-8183, E-mail: graduate@umassd.edu.
Website: http://www.umassd.edu/cas/chemistry/

University of Massachusetts Lowell, College of Sciences, Department of Chemistry, Lowell, MA 01854. Offers analytical chemistry (PhD); biochemistry (PhD); chemistry (MS, PhD); environmental studies (PhD); green chemistry (PhD); inorganic chemistry (PhD); organic chemistry (PhD); polymer science (MS). Terminal master's awarded for partial completion of doctoral program. *Degree requirements:* For master's, thesis; for doctorate, 2 foreign languages, thesis/dissertation. *Entrance requirements:* For master's and doctorate, GRE General Test. Electronic applications accepted.

University of Memphis, Graduate School, College of Arts and Sciences, Department of Chemistry, Memphis, TN 38152. Offers analytical chemistry (PhD); inorganic chemistry (MS); physical chemistry (MS). *Program availability:* Part-time. *Faculty:* 5 full-time (2 women), 1 part-time/adjunct (0 women). *Students:* 26 full-time (11 women), 9 part-time (2 women); includes 6 minority (2 Black or African American, non-Hispanic/Latino; 2 Asian, non-Hispanic/Latino; 2 Two or more races, non-Hispanic/Latino), 5 international. Average age 28. 19 applicants, 74% accepted, 9 enrolled. In 2015, 9 master's, 3 doctorates awarded. Terminal master's awarded for partial completion of doctoral program. *Degree requirements:* For master's, comprehensive exam, thesis or alternative; for doctorate, comprehensive exam, thesis/dissertation. *Entrance requirements:* For master's and doctorate, GRE General Test, admission to Graduate School plus 32 undergraduate hours in chemistry. Additional exam requirements/recommendations for international students: Required—TOEFL. *Application deadline:* For fall admission, 7/1 for domestic students, 5/1 for international students; for winter admission, 9/15 for international students; for spring admission, 12/1 for domestic students. Applications are processed on a rolling basis. Application fee: $35 ($60 for international students). Electronic applications accepted. *Financial support:* In 2015–16, 12 students received support. Research assistantships with full tuition reimbursements available, teaching assistantships with full tuition reimbursements available, Federal Work-Study, scholarships/grants, and unspecified assistantships available. Financial award application deadline: 2/15; financial award applicants required to submit FAFSA. *Faculty research:* Computational chemistry, materials chemistry, organic/polymer synthesis, drug design/delivery, water chemistry. *Unit head:* Dr. Abby L. Parrill, Professor and Chair, 901-678-2638, Fax: 901-678-3447, E-mail: aparrill@memphis.edu. *Application contact:* Dr. Gary Emmert, Associate Professor and Graduate Coordinator, 901-678-2636, Fax: 901-678-3447, E-mail: gemmert@memphis.edu.
Website: http://www.chem.memphis.edu/

University of Miami, Graduate School, College of Arts and Sciences, Department of Chemistry, Coral Gables, FL 33124. Offers chemistry (MS); inorganic chemistry (PhD); organic chemistry (PhD); physical chemistry (PhD). Terminal master's awarded for partial completion of doctoral program. *Degree requirements:* For master's, comprehensive exam; for doctorate, comprehensive exam, thesis/dissertation. *Entrance requirements:* For master's and doctorate, GRE General Test. Additional exam requirements/recommendations for international students: Required—TOEFL (minimum score 550 paper-based). Electronic applications accepted. *Faculty research:* Supramolecular chemistry, electrochemistry, surface chemistry, catalysis, organometalic.

University of Michigan, Rackham Graduate School, College of Literature, Science, and the Arts, Department of Chemistry, Ann Arbor, MI 48109-1055. Offers analytical (PhD); chemical biology (PhD); inorganic (PhD); materials (PhD); organic (PhD); physical (PhD). *Faculty:* 38 full-time (9 women), 9 part-time/adjunct (3 women). *Students:* 264 full-time (113 women). 535 applicants, 31% accepted, 54 enrolled. In 2015, 45 doctorates awarded. *Degree requirements:* For doctorate, comprehensive exam, thesis/dissertation, oral defense of dissertation, organic cumulative proficiency exams. *Entrance requirements:* For doctorate, GRE General Test, GRE Subject Test (recommended), 3 letters of recommendation. Additional exam requirements/recommendations for international students: Required—TOEFL (minimum score 560 paper-based; 84 iBT). *Application deadline:* For fall admission, 12/15 for domestic and international students. Applications are processed on a rolling basis. Application fee: $0 ($90 for international students). Electronic applications accepted. *Financial support:* In 2015–16, 264 students received support, including 40 fellowships with full tuition reimbursements available (averaging $29,000 per year), 78 research assistantships with full tuition reimbursements available (averaging $29,025 per year), 146 teaching assistantships with full tuition reimbursements available (averaging $29,025 per year); career-related internships or fieldwork, scholarships/grants, traineeships, health care benefits, and unspecified assistantships also available. *Faculty research:* Biological catalysis, protein engineering, chemical sensors, de novo metalloprotein design, supramolecular architecture. *Unit head:* Dr. Robert Kennedy, Professor of Chemistry/Chair, 734-763-9681, Fax: 734-647-4847. *Application contact:* Elizabeth Oxford, Graduate Program Coordinator, 734-764-7278, Fax: 734-647-4865,
E-mail: chemadmissions@umich.edu.
Website: http://www.lsa.umich.edu/chem/

University of Minnesota, Duluth, Graduate School, Swenson College of Science and Engineering, Department of Chemistry and Biochemistry, Duluth, MN 55812-2496. Offers MS. *Program availability:* Part-time. *Degree requirements:* For master's, thesis. *Entrance requirements:* For master's, bachelor's degree in chemistry, minimum GPA of 3.0. Additional exam requirements/recommendations for international students: Required—TOEFL (minimum score 550 paper-based; 79 iBT), IELTS (minimum score 6.5). *Faculty research:* Physical, inorganic, organic, and analytical chemistry; biochemistry and molecular biology.

University of Minnesota, Twin Cities Campus, College of Science and Engineering, Department of Chemistry, Minneapolis, MN 55455-0213. Offers chemical physics (MS, PhD); chemistry (MS, PhD). *Program availability:* Part-time. Terminal master's awarded for partial completion of doctoral program. *Degree requirements:* For master's, thesis or alternative; for doctorate, thesis/dissertation, preliminary candidacy exams. *Entrance requirements:* For master's and doctorate, GRE General Test. Additional exam requirements/recommendations for international students: Required—TOEFL. Electronic applications accepted. *Faculty research:* Analytical chemistry, environmental chemistry, organic chemistry, inorganic chemistry, materials chemistry, polymer chemistry, computational chemistry, experimental physical chemistry, chemical biology.

University of Minnesota, Twin Cities Campus, School of Public Health, Division of Environmental Health Sciences, Area in Environmental Chemistry, Minneapolis, MN 55455-0213. Offers MS, PhD. *Degree requirements:* For doctorate, thesis/dissertation. *Entrance requirements:* For master's and doctorate, GRE General Test. Electronic applications accepted.

University of Mississippi, Graduate School, College of Liberal Arts, University, MS 38677. Offers anthropology (MA); biology (MS, PhD); chemistry (MS, PhD); clinical psychology (PhD); economics (MA, PhD); English (MA, MFA, PhD); experimental psychology (PhD); history (MA, PhD); mathematics (MS, PhD); modern languages (MA); music (MM, PhD); philosophy (MA); physics (MA, MS, PhD); political science (MA, PhD); sociology (MA); studio art (MFA). *Program availability:* Part-time. *Faculty:* 446 full-time (186 women), 84 part-time/adjunct (36 women). *Students:* 475 full-time (233 women), 79 part-time (37 women); includes 83 minority (42 Black or African American, non-Hispanic/Latino; 9 Asian, non-Hispanic/Latino; 19 Hispanic/Latino; 13 Two or more races, non-Hispanic/Latino), 107 international. *Degree requirements:* For doctorate, thesis/dissertation. *Entrance requirements:* For master's, GRE General Test, minimum GPA of 3.0; for doctorate, GRE General Test. Additional exam requirements/recommendations for international students: Required—TOEFL. *Application deadline:* For fall admission, 4/1 for domestic students; for spring admission, 10/1 for domestic students. Applications are processed on a rolling basis. Application fee: $40. Electronic applications accepted. *Financial support:* Fellowships, research assistantships, teaching assistantships, career-related internships or fieldwork, Federal Work-Study, institutionally sponsored loans, scholarships/grants, and unspecified assistantships available. Financial award application deadline: 3/1; financial award applicants required to submit FAFSA. *Unit head:* Dean, 662-915-7177, Fax: 662-915-5792, E-mail: libarts@olemiss.edu. *Application contact:* Dr. Christy M. Wyandt, Associate Dean of Graduate School, 662-915-7474, Fax: 662-915-7577, E-mail: cwyandt@olemiss.edu.

University of Missouri, Office of Research and Graduate Studies, College of Arts and Science, Department of Chemistry, Columbia, MO 65211. Offers analytical chemistry

(MS, PhD); inorganic chemistry (MS, PhD); organic chemistry (MS, PhD); physical chemistry (MS, PhD). *Degree requirements:* For master's, thesis; for doctorate, one foreign language, comprehensive exam, thesis/dissertation. *Entrance requirements:* For master's, GRE General Test, minimum GPA of 3.0; for doctorate, GRE General Test (minimum score: Verbal 450, Quantitative 600, Analytical 3), minimum GPA of 3.0. Additional exam requirements/recommendations for international students: Required—TOEFL (minimum score 600 paper-based; 100 iBT). Electronic applications accepted. *Faculty research:* Analytical, organic, biological, physical, inorganic and radiochemistry.

University of Missouri–Kansas City, College of Arts and Sciences, Department of Chemistry, Kansas City, MO 64110-2499. Offers analytical chemistry (MS, PhD); inorganic chemistry (MS, PhD); organic chemistry (MS, PhD); physical chemistry (MS, PhD); polymer chemistry (MS, PhD). PhD (interdisciplinary) offered through the School of Graduate Studies. *Program availability:* Part-time, evening/weekend. *Faculty:* 15 full-time (2 women), 1 part-time/adjunct (0 women). *Students:* 3 full-time (2 women), 4 part-time (2 women); includes 1 minority (Black or African American, non-Hispanic/Latino), 3 international. Average age 36. 35 applicants, 23% accepted, 1 enrolled. In 2015, 3 master's awarded. *Degree requirements:* For master's, thesis (for some programs); for doctorate, thesis/dissertation. *Entrance requirements:* For master's, equivalent of American Chemical Society approved bachelor's degree in chemistry; for doctorate, GRE General Test, equivalent of American Chemical Society approved bachelor's degree in chemistry. Additional exam requirements/recommendations for international students: Required—TOEFL (minimum score 550 paper-based; 80 iBT), TWE. *Application deadline:* For fall admission, 4/15 for domestic and international students; for spring admission, 10/15 for domestic and international students. Applications are processed on a rolling basis. Application fee: $45 ($50 for international students). Electronic applications accepted. *Financial support:* In 2015–16, 2 research assistantships with partial tuition reimbursements (averaging $18,000 per year), 30 teaching assistantships with partial tuition reimbursements (averaging $18,062 per year) were awarded; Federal Work-Study, institutionally sponsored loans, and scholarships/grants also available. Support available to part-time students. Financial award application deadline: 3/1; financial award applicants required to submit FAFSA. *Faculty research:* Molecular spectroscopy, characterization and synthesis of materials and compounds, computational chemistry, natural products, drug delivery systems and anti-tumor agents. *Unit head:* Dr. Kathleen V. Kilway, Chair, 816-235-2289, Fax: 816-235-5502, E-mail: kilwayk@umkc.edu. *Application contact:* Graduate Recruiting Committee, 816-235-2272, Fax: 816-235-5502, E-mail: umkc-chemdept@umkc.edu.

University of Missouri–St. Louis, College of Arts and Sciences, Department of Chemistry and Biochemistry, St. Louis, MO 63121. Offers biochemistry and biotechnology (MS); chemistry (MS, PhD). *Program availability:* Part-time, evening/weekend. *Faculty:* 21 full-time (3 women), 3 part-time/adjunct (1 woman). *Students:* 37 full-time (24 women), 21 part-time (15 women); includes 8 minority (1 Black or African American, non-Hispanic/Latino; 3 Asian, non-Hispanic/Latino; 3 Hispanic/Latino; 1 Native Hawaiian or other Pacific Islander, non-Hispanic/Latino), 20 international. 39 applicants, 64% accepted, 16 enrolled. Terminal master's awarded for partial completion of doctoral program. *Degree requirements:* For master's, thesis optional; for doctorate, thesis/dissertation. *Entrance requirements:* For master's, 2 letters of recommendation; for doctorate, GRE General Test, 3 letters of recommendation. Additional exam requirements/recommendations for international students: Required—TOEFL (minimum score 550 paper-based; 79 iBT), IELTS (minimum score 6.5). *Application deadline:* For fall admission, 7/1 priority date for domestic and international students; for spring admission, 12/1 priority date for domestic and international students. Applications are processed on a rolling basis. Application fee: $50 ($40 for international students). Electronic applications accepted. *Financial support:* Fellowships with tuition reimbursements, research assistantships with tuition reimbursements, and teaching assistantships with tuition reimbursements available. *Faculty research:* Metallaborane chemistry, serum transferrin chemistry, natural products chemistry, organic synthesis. *Unit head:* Cynthia Dupureur, Interim Chair, 314-516-4392, Fax: 314-516-5342, E-mail: cdup@umsl.edu. *Application contact:* Graduate Admissions, 314-516-5458, Fax: 314-516-6996, E-mail: gradadm@umsl.edu.
Website: http://www.umsl.edu/chemistry/

University of Montana, Graduate School, College of Humanities and Sciences, Department of Chemistry and Biochemistry, Missoula, MT 59812-0002. Offers chemistry (MS, PhD), including environmental/analytical chemistry, inorganic chemistry, organic chemistry, physical chemistry. Terminal master's awarded for partial completion of doctoral program. *Degree requirements:* For master's, thesis (for some programs); for doctorate, thesis/dissertation. *Entrance requirements:* For master's and doctorate, GRE General Test. Additional exam requirements/recommendations for international students: Required—TOEFL (minimum score 575 paper-based). *Faculty research:* Reaction mechanisms and kinetics, inorganic and organic synthesis, analytical chemistry, natural products.

University of Nebraska–Lincoln, Graduate College, College of Arts and Sciences, Department of Chemistry, Lincoln, NE 68588. Offers analytical chemistry (PhD); biochemistry (PhD); chemistry (MS); inorganic chemistry (PhD); materials chemistry (PhD); organic chemistry (PhD); physical chemistry (PhD). *Degree requirements:* For master's, one foreign language, thesis optional, departmental qualifying exam; for doctorate, one foreign language, comprehensive exam, thesis/dissertation, departmental qualifying exams. *Entrance requirements:* For master's and doctorate, GRE. Additional exam requirements/recommendations for international students: Required—TOEFL (minimum score 550 paper-based). Electronic applications accepted. *Faculty research:* Bioorganic and bioinorganic chemistry, biophysical and bioanalytical chemistry, structure-function of DNA and proteins, organometallics, mass spectrometry.

University of Nevada, Las Vegas, Graduate College, College of Sciences, Department of Chemistry and Biochemistry, Las Vegas, NV 89154-4003. Offers biochemistry (MS); chemistry (MS, PhD); radiochemistry (PhD). *Program availability:* Part-time. *Faculty:* 16 full-time (3 women). *Students:* 45 full-time (23 women), 6 part-time (1 woman); includes 12 minority (4 Black or African American, non-Hispanic/Latino; 5 Asian, non-Hispanic/Latino; 3 Hispanic/Latino), 4 international. Average age 29. 39 applicants, 31% accepted, 8 enrolled. In 2015, 1 master's, 7 doctorates awarded. *Degree requirements:* For master's, thesis, departmental seminar; for doctorate, comprehensive exam (for some programs), thesis/dissertation. *Entrance requirements:* For master's and doctorate, GRE General Test. Additional exam requirements/recommendations for international students: Required—TOEFL (minimum score 550 paper-based; 80 iBT), IELTS (minimum score 7). *Application deadline:* For fall admission, 2/1 for domestic students, 5/1 for international students; for spring admission, 10/1 for domestic and international students. Application fee: $60 ($95 for international students). Electronic applications accepted. *Expenses:* $264 per credit state resident full-time and part-time; $6,955 per semester, $264 per credit nonresident full-time; $555 per credit nonresident part-time. *Financial support:* In 2015–16, 44 students received support, including 24 research assistantships with partial tuition reimbursements available (averaging $19,528 per year), 20 teaching assistantships with partial tuition reimbursements available (averaging $19,031 per year); institutionally sponsored loans, scholarships/grants, health care benefits, and unspecified assistantships also available. Financial award application deadline: 3/1. *Faculty research:* Material science, biochemistry, chemical education, physical chemistry and theoretical computation, analytical and organic chemistry. *Total annual research expenditures:* $3 million. *Unit head:* Dr. David Hatchett, Chair/Associate Professor, 702-895-4226, Fax: 702-895-4072, E-mail: david.hatchett@unlv.edu. *Application contact:* Graduate College Admissions Evaluator, 702-895-3367, Fax: 702-895-4180, E-mail: gradadmissions@unlv.edu.
Website: http://www.unlv.edu/chemistry

University of Nevada, Reno, Graduate School, College of Science, Department of Chemistry, Reno, NV 89557. Offers MS, PhD. Terminal master's awarded for partial completion of doctoral program. *Degree requirements:* For master's, thesis; for doctorate, one foreign language, thesis/dissertation. *Entrance requirements:* For master's, GRE, minimum GPA of 2.75; for doctorate, GRE, minimum GPA of 3.0. Additional exam requirements/recommendations for international students: Required—TOEFL (minimum score 500 paper-based; 61 iBT), IELTS (minimum score 6). Electronic applications accepted. *Faculty research:* Organic/inorganic chemistry, physical chemistry, chemical chemistry, physics, organometallic chemistry.

University of New Brunswick Fredericton, School of Graduate Studies, Faculty of Science, Department of Chemistry, Fredericton, NB E3B 5A3, Canada. Offers M Sc, PhD. *Faculty:* 13 full-time (2 women). *Students:* 12 full-time (5 women), 1 (woman) part-time. In 2015, 2 master's awarded. Terminal master's awarded for partial completion of doctoral program. *Degree requirements:* For master's, thesis; for doctorate, comprehensive exam, thesis/dissertation. *Entrance requirements:* For master's, bachelor's degree in chemistry or biochemistry; minimum GPA of 3.0; for doctorate, minimum GPA of 3.0. Additional exam requirements/recommendations for international students: Required—TOEFL (minimum score 580 paper-based), IELTS (minimum score 7.5), TWE (minimum score 4). *Application deadline:* For fall admission, 3/1 for domestic students. Applications are processed on a rolling basis. Application fee: $50 Canadian dollars. Electronic applications accepted. *Financial support:* In 2015–16, fellowships (averaging $18,000 per year), research assistantships (averaging $1,595 per year), teaching assistantships (averaging $3,800 per year) were awarded; scholarships/grants also available. *Faculty research:* Analytical, inorganic, organic, bio-organic, physical chemistry, pulp and paper, theoretical and computational chemistry. *Total annual research expenditures:* $1.1 million. *Unit head:* Dr. John Neville, Director of Graduate Studies, 506-447-3115, Fax: 506-453-4981, E-mail: jneville@unb.ca. *Application contact:* Heidi Stewart, Graduate Secretary, 506-458-7488, E-mail: scigrad@unb.ca.
Website: http://go.unb.ca/gradprograms

University of New Hampshire, Graduate School, College of Engineering and Physical Sciences, Department of Chemistry, Durham, NH 03824. Offers chemistry (PhD); chemistry education (PhD). Terminal master's awarded for partial completion of doctoral program. *Degree requirements:* For master's, thesis; for doctorate, one foreign language, thesis/dissertation. *Entrance requirements:* Additional exam requirements/recommendations for international students: Required—TOEFL (minimum score 550 paper-based; 80 iBT). Electronic applications accepted. *Faculty research:* Analytical, physical, organic, and inorganic chemistry.

University of New Mexico, Graduate Studies, College of Arts and Sciences, Program in Chemistry, Albuquerque, NM 87131-2039. Offers MS, PhD. *Faculty:* 14 full-time (2 women), 1 part-time/adjunct (0 women). *Students:* 53 full-time (11 women), 2 part-time (1 woman); includes 2 minority (1 Asian, non-Hispanic/Latino; 1 Hispanic/Latino), 40 international. Average age 29. 74 applicants, 32% accepted, 17 enrolled. In 2015, 9 master's, 4 doctorates awarded. Terminal master's awarded for partial completion of doctoral program. *Degree requirements:* For master's, comprehensive exam, thesis (for some programs); for doctorate, comprehensive exam, thesis/dissertation. *Entrance requirements:* For master's and doctorate, department exams. Additional exam requirements/recommendations for international students: Required—TOEFL (minimum score 550 paper-based; 79 iBT). *Application deadline:* For fall admission, 2/1 for domestic and international students. Applications are processed on a rolling basis. Application fee: $50 ($100 for international students). *Financial support:* Fellowships, research assistantships with tuition reimbursements, teaching assistantships, scholarships/grants, health care benefits, and unspecified assistantships available. Financial award application deadline: 2/1; financial award applicants required to submit FAFSA. *Faculty research:* Materials, inorganic, organic, physical, and biological chemistry. *Total annual research expenditures:* $2.7 million. *Unit head:* Dr. Stephen Cabaniss, Chair, 505-277-6655, Fax: 505-277-2609, E-mail: cabaniss@unm.edu. *Application contact:* Coordinator, Program Advisement, 505-277-6655, Fax: 505-277-2609, E-mail: kamc@unm.edu.
Website: http://chemistry.unm.edu/

University of New Orleans, Graduate School, College of Sciences, Department of Chemistry, New Orleans, LA 70148. Offers MS, PhD. *Degree requirements:* For master's, variable foreign language requirement, thesis, departmental qualifying exam; for doctorate, variable foreign language requirement, thesis/dissertation, departmental qualifying exam. *Entrance requirements:* For master's and doctorate, GRE General Test. Additional exam requirements/recommendations for international students: Required—TOEFL (minimum score 550 paper-based; 79 iBT), IELTS (minimum score 6.5). Electronic applications accepted. *Faculty research:* Synthesis and reactions of novel compounds, high-temperature kinetics, calculations of molecular electrostatic potentials, structures and reactions of metal complexes.

The University of North Carolina at Chapel Hill, Graduate School, College of Arts and Sciences, Department of Chemistry, Chapel Hill, NC 27599. Offers MA, MS, PhD. *Degree requirements:* For master's, comprehensive exam, thesis (for some programs); for doctorate, comprehensive exam, thesis/dissertation. *Entrance requirements:* For master's and doctorate, GRE General Test, GRE Subject Test, minimum GPA of 3.0.

The University of North Carolina at Charlotte, College of Liberal Arts and Sciences, Department of Chemistry, Charlotte, NC 28223-0001. Offers chemistry (MS); nanoscale science (PhD). *Program availability:* Part-time. *Faculty:* 18 full-time (3 women), 1 (woman) part-time/adjunct. *Students:* 19 full-time (8 women), 18 part-time (6 women); includes 7 minority (4 Black or African American, non-Hispanic/Latino; 2 Hispanic/Latino; 1 Two or more races, non-Hispanic/Latino), 8 international. Average age 27. 37 applicants, 51% accepted, 10 enrolled. In 2015, 7 master's, 2 doctorates awarded. Terminal master's awarded for partial completion of doctoral program. *Degree requirements:* For master's, thesis; for doctorate, thesis/dissertation. *Entrance requirements:* For master's, GRE, minimum GPA of 3.0 in undergraduate major, 2.75 overall; for doctorate, GRE, bachelor's or master's degree in a science or engineering field relevant to nanoscale science. Additional exam requirements/recommendations for international students: Required—TOEFL (minimum score 557 paper-based, 83 iBT) or IELTS (minimum score 6.5). *Application deadline:* For fall admission, 3/1 for domestic and international students; for spring admission, 10/1 for domestic and international students; for summer admission, 4/1 for domestic and international students. Applications are processed on a rolling basis. Application fee: $75. Electronic applications accepted. *Expenses:* Tuition, state resident: full-time $4128. Tuition, nonresident: full-time $16,799. *Required fees:* $2904. Tuition and fees vary according to

course load and program. *Financial support:* In 2015–16, 32 students received support, including 1 fellowship (averaging $42,000 per year), 8 research assistantships (averaging $12,825 per year), 23 teaching assistantships (averaging $13,346 per year); career-related internships or fieldwork, Federal Work-Study, institutionally sponsored loans, scholarships/grants, and unspecified assistantships also available. Support available to part-time students. Financial award application deadline: 3/1; financial award applicants required to submit FAFSA. *Faculty research:* Organometallic reagents as chiral auxiliaries for organic synthesis, fluorinated molecular tweezers of different molecular architecture in a convergent approach from various tether scaffolds and fluoroarene building blocks, using capillary electrophoresis (CE) to analyze and characterize proteins, the synthesis and integration of organic conjugated polymers and dye molecules for solar energy conversion applications. *Total annual research expenditures:* $447,049. *Unit head:* Dr. Bernadette T. Donovan-Merkert, Chair, 704-687-1300, E-mail: bdonovan@uncc.edu. *Application contact:* Kathy B. Giddings, Director of Graduate Admissions, 704-687-5503, Fax: 704-687-1668, E-mail: gradadm@uncc.edu.
Website: http://chemistry.uncc.edu/

The University of North Carolina at Greensboro, Graduate School, College of Arts and Sciences, Department of Chemistry and Biochemistry, Greensboro, NC 27412-5001. Offers biochemistry (MS); chemistry (MS). *Degree requirements:* For master's, one foreign language, thesis. *Entrance requirements:* For master's, GRE General Test. Additional exam requirements/recommendations for international students: Required—TOEFL. Electronic applications accepted. *Faculty research:* Synthesis of novel cyclopentadienes, molybdenum hydroxylase-cata ladder polymers, vinyl silicones.

The University of North Carolina Wilmington, College of Arts and Sciences, Department of Chemistry and Biochemistry, Wilmington, NC 28403-3297. Offers chemistry (MS). *Program availability:* Part-time, 100% online. *Faculty:* 28 full-time (6 women). *Students:* 14 full-time (5 women), 64 part-time (36 women); includes 11 minority (2 Black or African American, non-Hispanic/Latino; 3 Asian, non-Hispanic/Latino; 6 Hispanic/Latino). Average age 29. 31 applicants, 22 enrolled. In 2015, 28 master's awarded. *Degree requirements:* For master's, comprehensive exam, thesis. *Entrance requirements:* For master's, GRE General Test, minimum B average in undergraduate work, 3 letters of recommendation, bachelor's degree in chemistry. Additional exam requirements/recommendations for international students: Required—TOEFL (minimum score 79 iBT), IELTS (minimum score 6.5). *Application deadline:* For fall admission, 6/15 for domestic students; for spring admission, 11/15 for domestic students. Applications are processed on a rolling basis. Application fee: $60. Electronic applications accepted. *Expenses:* $8,854 in-state full-time per year; $20,945 out-of-state full-time per year. *Financial support:* Unspecified assistantships available. Financial award application deadline: 3/15; financial award applicants required to submit FAFSA. *Unit head:* Dr. Pam Seaton, Chair, 910-962-3279, Fax: 910-962-3013, E-mail: seatonp@uncw.edu. *Application contact:* Dr. Robert Kieber, Graduate Coordinator, 910-962-3865, Fax: 910-962-3013, E-mail: kieberr@uncw.edu.
Website: http://uncw.edu/chem/grad-program.html

University of North Dakota, Graduate School, College of Arts and Sciences, Department of Chemistry, Grand Forks, ND 58202. Offers MS, PhD. Terminal master's awarded for partial completion of doctoral program. *Degree requirements:* For master's, thesis, final exam; for doctorate, comprehensive exam, thesis/dissertation, final exam. *Entrance requirements:* For master's and doctorate, GRE General Test, GRE Subject Test, minimum GPA of 3.0. Additional exam requirements/recommendations for international students: Required—TOEFL (minimum score 550 paper-based; 79 iBT), IELTS (minimum score 6.5). Electronic applications accepted. *Faculty research:* Synthetic and structural organometallic chemistry, photochemistry, theoretical chemistry, chromatographic chemistry, x-ray crystallography.

University of Northern Colorado, Graduate School, College of Natural and Health Sciences, Department of Chemistry and Biochemistry, Greeley, CO 80639. Offers chemical education (MS, PhD); chemistry (MS). *Program availability:* Part-time. *Degree requirements:* For master's, comprehensive exam, thesis or alternative; for doctorate, comprehensive exam, thesis/dissertation. *Entrance requirements:* For master's, 3 letters of reference; for doctorate, GRE General Test, 3 letters of reference. Electronic applications accepted.

University of North Texas, Robert B. Toulouse School of Graduate Studies, Denton, TX 76203-5459. Offers accounting (MS); applied anthropology (MA, MS); applied behavior analysis (Certificate); applied geography (MA); applied technology and performance improvement (M Ed, MS); art education (MA); art history (MA); art museum education (Certificate); arts leadership (Certificate); audiology (Au D); behavior analysis (MS); behavioral science (PhD); biochemistry and molecular biology (MS); biology (MA, MS); biomedical engineering (MS); business analysis (MS); chemistry (MS); clinical health psychology (PhD); communication studies (MA, MS); computer engineering (MS); computer science (MS); counseling (M Ed, MS), including clinical mental health counseling (MS), college and university counseling, elementary school counseling, secondary school counseling; creative writing (MA); criminal justice (MS); curriculum and instruction (M Ed); decision sciences (MBA); design (MA, MFA), including fashion design (MFA), innovation studies, interior design (MFA); early childhood studies (MS); economics (MS); educational leadership (M Ed, Ed D); educational psychology (MS, PhD), including family studies (MS), gifted and talented (MS), human development (MS), learning and cognition (MS), research, measurement and evaluation (MS); electrical engineering (MS); emergency management (MPA); engineering technology (MS); English (MA); English as a second language (MA); environmental science (MS); finance (MBA, MS); financial management (MPA); French (MA); health services management (MBA); higher education (M Ed, Ed D); history (MA, MS); hospitality management (MS); human resources management (MPA); information science (MS); information systems (PhD); information technologies (MBA); interdisciplinary studies (MA, MS); international studies (MA); international sustainable tourism (MS); jazz studies (MM); journalism (MA, MJ, Graduate Certificate), including interactive and virtual digital communication (Graduate Certificate), narrative journalism (Graduate Certificate), public relations (Graduate Certificate); kinesiology (MS); linguistics (MA); local government management (MPA); logistics (PhD); logistics and supply chain management (MBA); long-term care, senior housing, and aging services (MA); management (PhD); marketing (MBA); mathematics (MA, MS); mechanical and energy engineering (MS, PhD); music (MA), including ethnomusicology, music theory, musicology, performance; music composition (PhD); music education (MM Ed, PhD); nonprofit management (MPA); operations and supply chain management (MBA); performance (MM, DMA); philosophy (MA); political science (MA); professional and technical communication (MA); radio, television and film (MA, MFA); rehabilitation counseling (Certificate); sociology (MA); Spanish (MA); special education (M Ed); speech-language pathology (MA); strategic management (MBA); studio art (MFA); teaching (M Ed); MBA/MS. *Program availability:* Part-time, evening/weekend, online learning. Terminal master's awarded for partial completion of doctoral program. *Degree requirements:* For master's, variable foreign language requirement, comprehensive exam (for some programs), thesis (for some programs); for doctorate, variable foreign language requirement, comprehensive exam (for some programs), thesis/dissertation; for other advanced degree, variable foreign language requirement, comprehensive exam (for some programs). *Entrance requirements:* For master's and doctorate, GRE, GMAT. Additional exam requirements/recommendations for international students: Required—TOEFL (minimum score 550 paper-based; 79 iBT). Electronic applications accepted.

University of Notre Dame, Graduate School, College of Science, Department of Chemistry and Biochemistry, Notre Dame, IN 46556. Offers biochemistry (MS, PhD); inorganic chemistry (MS, PhD); organic chemistry (MS, PhD); physical chemistry (MS, PhD). Terminal master's awarded for partial completion of doctoral program. *Degree requirements:* For master's, comprehensive exam, thesis; for doctorate, thesis/dissertation, qualifying exam. *Entrance requirements:* For master's and doctorate, GRE General Test, GRE Subject Test (strongly recommended). Additional exam requirements/recommendations for international students: Required—TOEFL (minimum score 600 paper-based; 80 iBT). Electronic applications accepted. *Faculty research:* Reaction design and mechanistic studies; reactive intermediates; synthesis, structure and reactivity of organometallic cluster complexes and biologically active natural products; bioorganic chemistry; enzymology.

University of Oklahoma, College of Arts and Sciences, Department of Chemistry and Biochemistry, Norman, OK 73019. Offers bioinformatics (MS, PhD); chemistry (MS, PhD). *Program availability:* Part-time. *Faculty:* 30 full-time (10 women). *Students:* 65 full-time (24 women), 35 part-time (17 women); includes 14 minority (2 Black or African American, non-Hispanic/Latino; 1 American Indian or Alaska Native, non-Hispanic/Latino; 3 Asian, non-Hispanic/Latino; 7 Hispanic/Latino; 1 Two or more races, non-Hispanic/Latino), 35 international. Average age 26. 75 applicants, 36% accepted, 27 enrolled. In 2015, 16 master's, 7 doctorates awarded. Terminal master's awarded for partial completion of doctoral program. *Degree requirements:* For master's, comprehensive exam (for some programs), thesis (for some programs); for doctorate, comprehensive exam, thesis/dissertation, general exam. *Entrance requirements:* For master's and doctorate, GRE. Additional exam requirements/recommendations for international students: Required—TOEFL (minimum score 79 iBT). *Application deadline:* For fall admission, 3/1 priority date for domestic students, 3/1 for international students; for spring admission, 9/1 for domestic and international students. Application fee: $50 ($100 for international students). Electronic applications accepted. *Expenses:* Tuition, state resident: full-time $4577; part-time $190.70 per credit hour. Tuition, nonresident: full-time $17,758; part-time $739.90 per credit hour. *Required fees:* $3060; $115.70 per credit hour. $141.50 per semester. *Financial support:* In 2015–16, 92 students received support, including 4 fellowships with full tuition reimbursements available (averaging $4,375 per year), 26 research assistantships with full tuition reimbursements available (averaging $16,499 per year), 72 teaching assistantships with full tuition reimbursements available (averaging $16,613 per year); institutionally sponsored loans, scholarships/grants, health care benefits, unspecified assistantships, and full tuition with qualifying graduate assistantship also available. Support available to part-time students. Financial award application deadline: 6/1; financial award applicants required to submit FAFSA. *Faculty research:* Structural biology, synthesis and catalysis, natural products, membrane biochemistry, genomics. *Total annual research expenditures:* $7 million. *Unit head:* Dr. Ronald L. Halterman, Professor and Chair, 405-325-4812, Fax: 405-325-6111, E-mail: rhalterman@ou.edu. *Application contact:* Angelika Tietz, Graduate Program Assistant, 405-325-4811 Ext. 62946, Fax: 405-325-6111, E-mail: atietz@ou.edu.
Website: http://www.ou.edu/cas/chemistry

University of Oregon, Graduate School, College of Arts and Sciences, Department of Chemistry, Eugene, OR 97403. Offers biochemistry (MA, MS, PhD); chemistry (MA, MS, PhD). Terminal master's awarded for partial completion of doctoral program. *Degree requirements:* For doctorate, thesis/dissertation. *Entrance requirements:* For master's and doctorate, GRE General Test, minimum GPA of 3.0. Additional exam requirements/recommendations for international students: Required—TOEFL. *Faculty research:* Organic chemistry, organometallic chemistry, inorganic chemistry, physical chemistry, materials science, biochemistry, chemical physics, molecular or cell biology.

University of Ottawa, Faculty of Graduate and Postdoctoral Studies, Faculty of Science, Ottawa-Carleton Chemistry Institute, Ottawa, ON K1N 6N5, Canada. Offers M Sc, PhD. M Sc, PhD offered jointly with Carleton University. *Degree requirements:* For master's, thesis, seminar; for doctorate, comprehensive exam, thesis/dissertation, 2 seminars. *Entrance requirements:* For master's, honors B Sc degree or equivalent, minimum B average; for doctorate, honors B Sc with minimum B average or M Sc in chemistry with minimum B+ average. Electronic applications accepted. *Faculty research:* Organic chemistry, physical chemistry, inorganic chemistry.

University of Pennsylvania, School of Arts and Sciences, College of Liberal and Professional Studies, Philadelphia, PA 19104. Offers applied geosciences (MSAG); applied positive psychology (MAP); chemical sciences (MCS); environmental studies (MES); individualized study (MLA); liberal arts (M Phil); medical physics (MMP); organization dynamics (M Phil). *Students:* 135 full-time (69 women), 329 part-time (203 women); includes 85 minority (27 Black or African American, non-Hispanic/Latino; 23 Asian, non-Hispanic/Latino; 17 Hispanic/Latino; 18 Two or more races, non-Hispanic/Latino), 61 international. Average age 35. 542 applicants, 52% accepted, 173 enrolled. In 2015, 161 master's awarded. *Expenses: Tuition, area resident:* Full-time $31,068; part-time $5762 per course. *Required fees:* $3200; $336 per course. Full-time tuition and fees vary according to degree level, program and student level. Part-time tuition and fees vary according to course load, degree level and program. *Unit head:* Nora Lewis, E-mail: nlewis@sas.upenn.edu.
Website: http://www.sas.upenn.edu/lps/graduate

University of Pennsylvania, School of Arts and Sciences, Graduate Group in Chemistry, Philadelphia, PA 19104. Offers MS, PhD. *Faculty:* 31 full-time (6 women), 10 part-time/adjunct (1 woman). *Students:* 174 full-time (71 women); includes 17 minority (1 Black or African American, non-Hispanic/Latino; 11 Asian, non-Hispanic/Latino; 2 Hispanic/Latino; 3 Two or more races, non-Hispanic/Latino), 73 international. Average age 26. 436 applicants, 34% accepted, 50 enrolled. In 2015, 21 master's, 27 doctorates awarded. *Expenses: Tuition, area resident:* Full-time $31,068; part-time $5762 per course. *Required fees:* $3200; $336 per course. Full-time tuition and fees vary according to degree level, program and student level. Part-time tuition and fees vary according to course load, degree level and program. *Financial support:* Application deadline: 12/1.
Website: http://www.sas.upenn.edu/graduate-division

University of Pittsburgh, Dietrich School of Arts and Sciences, Department of Chemistry, Pittsburgh, PA 15216. Offers MS, PhD. *Program availability:* Part-time, evening/weekend. *Faculty:* 50 full-time (11 women), 21 part-time/adjunct (6 women). *Students:* 180 full-time (54 women); includes 19 minority (3 Black or African American, non-Hispanic/Latino; 12 Asian, non-Hispanic/Latino; 4 Hispanic/Latino), 57 international. Average age 25. 278 applicants, 43% accepted, 30 enrolled. In 2015, 4 master's, 23 doctorates awarded. Terminal master's awarded for partial completion of doctoral program. *Degree requirements:* For master's, comprehensive exam, thesis; for doctorate, comprehensive exam, thesis/dissertation, original research proposal. *Entrance requirements:* For master's and doctorate, GRE General Test, GRE Subject Test. Additional exam requirements/recommendations for international students: Required—TOEFL (minimum score 600 paper-based; 100 iBT), IELTS (minimum score

7). *Application deadline:* For fall admission, 1/15 for domestic and international students. Applications are processed on a rolling basis. Application fee: $0 ($50 for international students). Electronic applications accepted. Tuition and fees vary according to program. *Financial support:* In 2015–16, 173 students received support, including 28 fellowships with full tuition reimbursements available (averaging $30,381 per year), 67 research assistantships with full tuition reimbursements available (averaging $25,807 per year), 78 teaching assistantships with full tuition reimbursements available (averaging $26,858 per year); career-related internships or fieldwork, scholarships/grants, health care benefits, tuition waivers (full), and unspecified assistantships also available. Financial award application deadline: 1/15. *Faculty research:* Analytical, biological, inorganic and materials chemistry including nanostructured materials, organic, physical and theoretical chemistry. *Total annual research expenditures:* $7.1 million. *Unit head:* Dr. Kay M. Brummond, Chairman, 412-624-0415, Fax: 412-624-1649, E-mail: chemchr@pitt.edu. *Application contact:* Christie D. Hay, Graduate Program Administrator, 412-624-8501, Fax: 412-624-8611, E-mail: gradadm@pitt.edu.
Website: http://www.chem.pitt.edu

University of Pittsburgh, Dietrich School of Arts and Sciences, Program in Computational Modeling and Simulation, Pittsburgh, PA 15260. Offers biological science (PhD); chemistry (PhD); computer science (PhD); economics (PhD); mathematics (PhD); physics and astronomy (PhD); psychology (PhD); statistics (PhD). *Program availability:* Part-time. *Faculty:* 3 full-time (0 women). *Students:* 3 full-time (1 woman); includes 2 minority (both Asian, non-Hispanic/Latino). Average age 23. 13 applicants, 31% accepted, 2 enrolled. *Degree requirements:* For doctorate, comprehensive exam, thesis/dissertation, preliminary exam. *Entrance requirements:* For doctorate, GRE, statement of purpose, transcripts for all college-level institutions attended, three letters of reference. Additional exam requirements/recommendations for international students: Required—TOEFL (minimum score 90 iBT), IELTS (minimum score 7). *Application deadline:* For fall admission, 1/15 for domestic and international students. Applications are processed on a rolling basis. Application fee: $0 ($50 for international students). Electronic applications accepted. Tuition and fees vary according to program. *Financial support:* In 2015–16, 3 students received support, including 2 fellowships with full tuition reimbursements available (averaging $27,000 per year), 1 research assistantship with full tuition reimbursement available (averaging $21,500 per year); tuition waivers (full) also available. Financial award application deadline: 4/15. *Faculty research:* Econometric modeling, developing reduced-scaling first principles approaches for expedited predictions of molecular and materials properties, developing computational models to quantitatively describe origins of reactivity and selectivity in organocatalytic reactions. *Unit head:* Dr. Kathleen Blee, Associate Dean, Graduate Studies and Research, 412-624-3939, Fax: 412-624-6855. *Application contact:* Wendy G. Janocha, Graduate Administrator, 412-648-7251, E-mail: wgj1@pitt.edu.
Website: http://cmsp.pitt.edu/

University of Prince Edward Island, Faculty of Science, Charlottetown, PE C1A 4P3, Canada. Offers biology (M Sc); chemistry (M Sc). *Degree requirements:* For master's, thesis. *Entrance requirements:* Additional exam requirements/recommendations for international students: Required—TOEFL (minimum score 550 paper-based; 80 iBT), Canadian Academic English Language Assessment, Michigan English Language Assessment Battery, Canadian Test of English for Scholars and Trainees. *Faculty research:* Ecology and wildlife biology, molecular, genetics and biotechnology, organametallic, bio-organic, supramolecular and synthetic organic chemistry, neurobiology and stoke materials science.

University of Puerto Rico, Mayagüez Campus, Graduate Studies, College of Arts and Sciences, Department of Chemistry, Mayagüez, PR 00681-9000. Offers MS, PhD. *Program availability:* Part-time. *Degree requirements:* For master's, one foreign language, comprehensive exam, thesis; for doctorate, comprehensive exam, thesis/dissertation. *Entrance requirements:* For master's, GRE, BS in chemistry or the equivalent. *Faculty research:* Biochemistry, spectroscopy, food chemistry, physical chemistry, electrochemistry.

University of Puerto Rico, Río Piedras Campus, College of Natural Sciences, Department of Chemistry, San Juan, PR 00931-3300. Offers MS, PhD. *Program availability:* Part-time. *Degree requirements:* For master's, one foreign language, comprehensive exam, thesis; for doctorate, one foreign language, comprehensive exam, thesis/dissertation. *Entrance requirements:* For master's, GRE General Test, GRE Subject Test, interview, minimum GPA of 3.0, letter of recommendation; for doctorate, GRE General Test, GRE Subject Test, minimum GPA of 3.0, letter of recommendation. Additional exam requirements/recommendations for international students: Required—TOEFL.

University of Regina, Faculty of Graduate Studies and Research, Faculty of Science, Department of Chemistry and Biochemistry, Regina, SK S4S 0A2, Canada. Offers analytical/environmental chemistry (M Sc, PhD); biophysics of biological interfaces (M Sc, PhD); enzymology/chemical biology (M Sc, PhD); inorganic/organometallic chemistry (M Sc, PhD); signal transduction and mechanisms of cancer cell regulation (M Sc, PhD); supramolecular organic photochemistry and photophysics (M Sc, PhD); synthetic organic chemistry (M Sc, PhD); theoretical/computational chemistry (M Sc, PhD). *Degree requirements:* For master's, thesis; for doctorate, thesis/dissertation. *Entrance requirements:* Additional exam requirements/recommendations for international students: Required—TOEFL (minimum score 580 paper-based; 80 iBT), IELTS (minimum score 6.5), PTE (minimum score 59). Electronic applications accepted. *Faculty research:* Asymmetric synthesis and methodology, theoretical and computational chemistry, biophysical biochemistry, analytical and environmental chemistry, chemical biology.

University of Rhode Island, Graduate School, College of Arts and Sciences, Department of Chemistry, Kingston, RI 02881. Offers MS, PhD. *Program availability:* Part-time, evening/weekend. *Faculty:* 20 full-time (6 women). *Students:* 49 full-time (20 women), 2 part-time (0 women); includes 4 minority (1 Black or African American, non-Hispanic/Latino; 1 Asian, non-Hispanic/Latino; 1 Hispanic/Latino; 1 Native Hawaiian or other Pacific Islander, non-Hispanic/Latino), 16 international. In 2015, 3 master's, 7 doctorates awarded. *Degree requirements:* For master's, comprehensive exam (for some programs), thesis optional; for doctorate, comprehensive exam, thesis/dissertation, 72 credit hours of work, residency. *Entrance requirements:* For master's and doctorate, GRE General Test (for graduates of non-U.S. universities), GRE Subject Test in chemistry (recommended), 2 letters of recommendation (3 for non-U.S. graduates). Additional exam requirements/recommendations for international students: Required—TOEFL (minimum score 550 paper-based). *Application deadline:* For fall admission, 7/15 for domestic students, 1/15 for international students; for spring admission, 11/15 for domestic students, 9/15 for international students. Application fee: $65. Electronic applications accepted. *Expenses:* Tuition, state resident: full-time $11,796; part-time $655 per credit. Tuition, nonresident: full-time $24,206; part-time $1345 per credit. *Required fees:* $1546; $44 per credit. One-time fee: $155 full-time; $35 part-time. *Financial support:* In 2015–16, 13 research assistantships with tuition reimbursements (averaging $12,111 per year), 29 teaching assistantships with tuition reimbursements (averaging $12,784 per year) were awarded. Financial award application deadline: 7/15; financial award applicants required to submit FAFSA. *Faculty research:* Analytical chemistry, biochemistry, analytical/nanoscience, materials/analytical, theoretical chemistry. *Total annual research expenditures:* $4 million. *Unit head:* Dr. William Euler, Chairperson, 401-874-5090, Fax: 401-874-5072, E-mail: weuler@chm.uri.edu. *Application contact:* Dr. David Freeman, Chair of the Graduate Admissions Committee, 401-874-5093, E-mail: dfreeman@chm.uri.edu.
Website: http://www.chm.uri.edu/index.php

University of Rochester, School of Arts and Sciences, Department of Chemistry, Rochester, NY 14627. Offers MS, PhD. *Faculty:* 18 full-time (3 women). *Students:* 89 full-time (45 women); includes 9 minority (1 Black or African American, non-Hispanic/Latino; 1 Asian, non-Hispanic/Latino; 5 Hispanic/Latino; 2 Two or more races, non-Hispanic/Latino), 26 international. 297 applicants, 19% accepted, 9 enrolled. In 2015, 27 master's, 16 doctorates awarded. Terminal master's awarded for partial completion of doctoral program. *Degree requirements:* For doctorate, thesis/dissertation, qualifying exam. *Entrance requirements:* For doctorate, GRE General Test, undergraduate transcript, three letters of recommendation. Additional exam requirements/recommendations for international students: Required—TOEFL. *Application deadline:* For fall admission, 1/15 for domestic students. Application fee: $60. Electronic applications accepted. *Expenses: Tuition, area resident:* Full-time $47,450; part-time $1482 per credit hour. *Required fees:* $528. Tuition and fees vary according to program. *Financial support:* Fellowships, research assistantships, teaching assistantships, and tuition waivers (full and partial) available. Financial award application deadline: 1/15. *Faculty research:* Organic, inorganic, physical, biological, theoretical. *Unit head:* Robert K. Boeckman, Jr., Chair, 585-275-4229. *Application contact:* Robin Cooley, Graduate Studies Coordinator, 585-275-0635.
Website: http://www.chem.rochester.edu/

University of Saint Joseph, Department of Chemistry, West Hartford, CT 06117-2700. Offers biochemistry (MS); chemistry (MS). *Program availability:* Part-time, evening/weekend, online learning. *Degree requirements:* For master's, comprehensive exam, thesis optional. *Entrance requirements:* For master's, 2 letters of recommendation, official undergraduate transcript. Electronic applications accepted. Application fee is waived when completed online.

University of San Francisco, College of Arts and Sciences, Chemistry Program, San Francisco, CA 94117-1080. Offers MS. *Program availability:* Part-time, evening/weekend. *Faculty:* 1 full-time (0 women). *Students:* 11 full-time (6 women); includes 3 minority (1 Asian, non-Hispanic/Latino; 2 Hispanic/Latino), 3 international. Average age 24. 40 applicants, 18% accepted, 6 enrolled. In 2015, 3 master's awarded. *Degree requirements:* For master's, thesis. *Entrance requirements:* For master's, GRE General Test, GRE Subject Test, BS in chemistry or related field. Additional exam requirements/recommendations for international students: Required—TOEFL, IELTS, PTE. *Application deadline:* For fall admission, 2/1 for domestic and international students; for spring admission, 10/15 for domestic and international students. Applications are processed on a rolling basis. Application fee: $55 ($65 for international students). *Expenses: Tuition, area resident:* Full-time $22,410; part-time $1245 per credit. Tuition and fees vary according to course load, degree level and campus/location. *Financial support:* In 2015–16, 11 students received support. Fellowships, research assistantships, teaching assistantships, career-related internships or fieldwork, Federal Work-Study, institutionally sponsored loans, and tuition waivers (partial) available. Support available to part-time students. Financial award application deadline: 3/2; financial award applicants required to submit FAFSA. *Faculty research:* Organic photochemistry, genetics of chromatic adaptation, electron transfer processes in solution, metabolism of protein hormones. *Total annual research expenditures:* $75,000. *Unit head:* Dr. Tami Spector, Faculty Director, 415-422-6157, Fax: 415-422-5157. *Application contact:* Mark Landerghini, Information Contact, 415-422-5101, Fax: 415-422-2217, E-mail: asgraduate@usfca.edu.
Website: http://www.usfca.edu/artsci/chemg/

University of Saskatchewan, College of Graduate Studies and Research, College of Arts and Science, Department of Chemistry, Saskatoon, SK S7N 5A2, Canada. Offers M Sc, PhD. *Degree requirements:* For master's, thesis; for doctorate, comprehensive exam (for some programs), thesis/dissertation. *Entrance requirements:* Additional exam requirements/recommendations for international students: Required—TOEFL (minimum score 80 iBT); Recommended—IELTS (minimum score 6.5). Electronic applications accepted.

The University of Scranton, College of Arts and Sciences, Department of Chemistry, Program in Chemistry, Scranton, PA 18510. Offers MS. *Program availability:* Part-time, evening/weekend. *Faculty:* 3 full-time. *Students:* 7 part-time (1 woman); includes 3 minority (1 Asian, non-Hispanic/Latino; 1 Hispanic/Latino; 1 Two or more races, non-Hispanic/Latino). Average age 23. 28 applicants, 36% accepted, 7 enrolled. *Degree requirements:* For master's, comprehensive exam (for some programs), thesis (for some programs), capstone experience. *Entrance requirements:* For master's, minimum GPA of 3.0, three letters of reference. Additional exam requirements/recommendations for international students: Required—TOEFL (minimum score 500 paper-based; 80 iBT), IELTS (minimum score 6.5). *Application deadline:* For fall admission, 6/1 for international students; for spring admission, 11/1 for international students; for summer admission, 3/1 for international students. Applications are processed on a rolling basis. Application fee: $0. Electronic applications accepted. *Financial support:* Applicants required to submit FAFSA. *Unit head:* Dr. Joan Wasilewski, Director, 570-941-7705, Fax: 570-941-7510, E-mail: joan.wasilewski@scranton.edu. *Application contact:* Dr. Christopher A. Baumann, Director, 570-941-6389, Fax: 570-941-7510, E-mail: cab@scranton.edu.

The University of Scranton, College of Arts and Sciences, Department of Chemistry, Program in Clinical Chemistry, Scranton, PA 18510. Offers MS. *Program availability:* Part-time, evening/weekend. *Students:* 1 full-time (0 women), 3 part-time (2 women). Average age 23. 12 applicants, 42% accepted, 3 enrolled. *Degree requirements:* For master's, comprehensive exam (for some programs), thesis (for some programs), capstone experience. *Entrance requirements:* For master's, minimum GPA of 3.0, three letters of reference. Additional exam requirements/recommendations for international students: Required—TOEFL (minimum score 500 paper-based; 80 iBT), IELTS (minimum score 6.5). *Application deadline:* For fall admission, 6/1 for international students; for spring admission, 11/1 for international students; for summer admission, 3/1 for international students. Applications are processed on a rolling basis. Application fee: $0. Electronic applications accepted. *Financial support:* Applicants required to submit FAFSA. *Unit head:* Dr. Joan Wasilewski, Director, 570-941-7705, Fax: 570-941-7510, E-mail: joan.wasilewski@scranton.edu. *Application contact:* Dr. Christopher A. Baumann, Director, 570-941-6389, Fax: 570-941-7510, E-mail: cab@scranton.edu.

University of South Carolina, The Graduate School, College of Arts and Sciences, Department of Chemistry and Biochemistry, Columbia, SC 29208. Offers IMA, MAT, MS, PhD. IMA and MAT offered in cooperation with the College of Education. *Program availability:* Part-time. Terminal master's awarded for partial completion of doctoral program. *Degree requirements:* For master's, comprehensive exam, thesis; for doctorate, comprehensive exam, thesis/dissertation. *Entrance requirements:* For master's and doctorate, GRE General Test. Additional exam requirements/ recommendations for international students: Required—TOEFL. Electronic applications accepted. *Faculty research:* Spectroscopy, crystallography, organic and organometallic synthesis, analytical chemistry, materials.

The University of South Dakota, Graduate School, College of Arts and Sciences, Department of Chemistry, Vermillion, SD 57069-2390. Offers MS, PhD. *Degree requirements:* For master's, comprehensive exam, thesis. *Entrance requirements:* For master's, minimum GPA of 2.7; for doctorate, GRE, minimum GPA of 2.7. Additional exam requirements/recommendations for international students: Required—TOEFL (minimum score 550 paper-based; 79 iBT), GRE. *Application deadline:* For fall admission, 3/15 priority date for domestic students. Applications are processed on a rolling basis. Application fee: $35. Electronic applications accepted. *Financial support:* Research assistantships with partial tuition reimbursements, teaching assistantships with partial tuition reimbursements, Federal Work-Study, and unspecified assistantships available. Support available to part-time students. Financial award applicants required to submit FAFSA. *Faculty research:* Electrochemistry, photochemistry, inorganic synthesis, environmental and solid-state chemistry. *Unit head:* Dr. Miles Koppang, Acting Chair, 605-677-5693, Fax: 605-677-6397, E-mail: miles.koppang@usd.edu.
Website: http://www.usd.edu/chemistry/

University of Southern California, Graduate School, Dana and David Dornsife College of Letters, Arts and Sciences, Department of Chemistry, Los Angeles, CA 90089. Offers chemistry (PhD); physical chemistry (PhD). Terminal master's awarded for partial completion of doctoral program. *Degree requirements:* For doctorate, thesis/ dissertation. *Entrance requirements:* For doctorate, GRE General Test. Additional exam requirements/recommendations for international students: Required—TOEFL. Electronic applications accepted. *Faculty research:* Biological chemistry, inorganic chemistry, organic chemistry, physical chemistry, theoretical chemistry.

University of Southern Mississippi, Graduate School, College of Science and Technology, Department of Chemistry and Biochemistry, Hattiesburg, MS 39406-0001. Offers inorganic chemistry (MS); organic chemistry (MS); physical chemistry (MS). *Degree requirements:* For master's, comprehensive exam, thesis; for doctorate, comprehensive exam, thesis/dissertation. *Entrance requirements:* For master's, GRE General Test, minimum GPA of 2.75 in last 60 hours; for doctorate, GRE General Test, minimum GPA of 3.5. Additional exam requirements/recommendations for international students: Required—TOEFL, IELTS. *Faculty research:* Plant biochemistry, photo chemistry, polymer chemistry, x-ray analysis, enzyme chemistry.

University of Southern Mississippi, Graduate School, College of Science and Technology, Department of Marine Science, Stennis Space Center, MS 39529. Offers hydrographic science (MS); marine science (MS, PhD). *Program availability:* Part-time. *Faculty:* 16 full-time (1 woman). *Students:* 42 full-time (18 women), 5 part-time (2 women); includes 13 minority (7 Black or African American, non-Hispanic/Latino; 4 Asian, non-Hispanic/Latino; 1 Hispanic/Latino; 1 Two or more races, non-Hispanic/ Latino). Average age 32. 44 applicants, 61% accepted, 22 enrolled. In 2015, 15 master's, 2 doctorates awarded. *Degree requirements:* For master's, comprehensive exam, thesis, oral qualifying exam (marine science); for doctorate, 2 foreign languages, comprehensive exam, thesis/dissertation, oral qualifying exam. *Entrance requirements:* For master's, GRE General Test, minimum GPA of 3.0; for doctorate, GRE General Test, minimum GPA of 3.0 (undergraduate), 3.5 (graduate). Additional exam requirements/recommendations for international students: Required—TOEFL (minimum score 84 iBT). *Application deadline:* For fall admission, 5/1 priority date for domestic and international students; for spring admission, 10/1 for domestic and international students; for summer admission, 3/1 for domestic and international students. Application fee: $60. Electronic applications accepted. *Expenses:* Contact institution. *Financial support:* In 2015–16, 9 students received support, including 1 fellowship with full tuition reimbursement available (averaging $5,300 per year), 4 research assistantships with full tuition reimbursements available (averaging $61,200 per year), 5 teaching assistantships with full tuition reimbursements available (averaging $76,500 per year). Financial award application deadline: 5/1. *Faculty research:* Biological oceanography, geological oceanography; physical oceanography; bio-optics; hydrography; marine chemistry; marine science; numerical modeling; remote sensing; zooplankton; hydrography. *Total annual research expenditures:* $6.5 million. *Unit head:* Dr. William Montrose Graham, Chair and Professor, 228-688-3177, Fax: 228-688-1121,
E-mail: monty.graham@usm.edu. *Application contact:* Linda Downs, Senior Office Support Specialist, 228-688-7097, Fax: 228-688-1121, E-mail: linda.downs@usm.edu.
Website: http://www.usm.edu/marine/

University of South Florida, College of Arts and Sciences, Department of Chemistry, Tampa, FL 33620-9951. Offers chemistry (MS, PhD); chemistry (non-thesis) (MA). *Program availability:* Part-time. *Faculty:* 26 full-time (4 women). *Students:* 99 full-time (42 women), 11 part-time (3 women); includes 15 minority (5 Black or African American, non-Hispanic/Latino; 1 American Indian or Alaska Native, non-Hispanic/Latino; 2 Asian, non-Hispanic/Latino; 7 Hispanic/Latino), 45 international. Average age 28. 100 applicants, 53% accepted, 26 enrolled. In 2015, 6 master's, 23 doctorates awarded. Terminal master's awarded for partial completion of doctoral program. *Degree requirements:* For master's, comprehensive exam, thesis (for some programs); for doctorate, comprehensive exam, thesis/dissertation. *Entrance requirements:* For master's, GRE General Test, minimum GPA of 3.0 in last two years of undergraduate chemistry coursework, three letters of recommendation; for doctorate, GRE General Test; GRE Subject Test in chemistry (recommended), minimum GPA of 3.0 in last two years of chemistry coursework, three letters of recommendation. Additional exam requirements/recommendations for international students: Required—TOEFL (minimum score 550 paper-based; 79 iBT) or IELTS (minimum score 6.5). *Application deadline:* For fall admission, 2/15 priority date for domestic students, 1/2 priority date for international students; for spring admission, 10/1 priority date for domestic students, 6/1 priority date for international students. Applications are processed on a rolling basis. Application fee: $30. Electronic applications accepted. *Financial support:* In 2015–16, 108 students received support, including 28 research assistantships with tuition reimbursements available (averaging $15,020 per year), 108 teaching assistantships with tuition reimbursements available (averaging $15,164 per year); unspecified assistantships also available. Financial award application deadline: 6/30. *Faculty research:* Synthesis, bio-organic chemistry, bioinorganic chemistry, environmental chemistry, nuclear magnetic resonance (NMR). *Total annual research expenditures:* $1.5 million. *Unit head:* Dr. Randy Larsen, Chairperson and Professor, Chemistry Department, 813-974-7925, Fax: 813-974-3203, E-mail: rwlarsen@usf.edu. *Application contact:* Dr. Edward Turos, Professor/Graduate Program Director, 813-974-7312, Fax: 813-974-3203, E-mail: eturos@usf.edu.
Website: http://chemistry.usf.edu/

The University of Tennessee, Graduate School, College of Arts and Sciences, Department of Chemistry, Knoxville, TN 37996. Offers analytical chemistry (MS, PhD); chemical physics (PhD); environmental chemistry (MS, PhD); inorganic chemistry (MS, PhD); organic chemistry (MS, PhD); physical chemistry (MS, PhD); polymer chemistry (MS, PhD); theoretical chemistry (PhD). *Program availability:* Part-time. Terminal master's awarded for partial completion of doctoral program. *Degree requirements:* For master's, thesis; for doctorate, thesis/dissertation. *Entrance requirements:* For master's and doctorate, GRE General Test, minimum GPA of 2.7. Additional exam requirements/ recommendations for international students: Required—TOEFL. Electronic applications accepted.

The University of Texas at Arlington, Graduate School, College of Science, Department of Chemistry and Biochemistry, Arlington, TX 76019. Offers chemistry (MS, PhD). *Program availability:* Part-time. Terminal master's awarded for partial completion of doctoral program. *Degree requirements:* For master's, comprehensive exam (for some programs), thesis optional; for doctorate, comprehensive exam, thesis/ dissertation, internship, oral defense of dissertation. *Entrance requirements:* For master's and doctorate, GRE General Test, minimum GPA of 3.0 in last 60 hours of course work; BS in STEM field (preferably chemistry or biochemistry) or equivalent 4-year minimum program. Additional exam requirements/recommendations for international students: Required—TOEFL (minimum score 550 paper-based; 80 iBT). Electronic applications accepted.

The University of Texas at Austin, Graduate School, College of Natural Sciences, Department of Chemistry and Biochemistry, Austin, TX 78712-1111. Offers analytical chemistry (PhD); biochemistry (PhD); inorganic chemistry (PhD); organic chemistry (PhD); physical chemistry (PhD). *Entrance requirements:* For doctorate, GRE General Test.

The University of Texas at Dallas, School of Natural Sciences and Mathematics, Department of Chemistry, Richardson, TX 75080. Offers MS, PhD. *Program availability:* Part-time, evening/weekend. *Faculty:* 22 full-time (4 women). *Students:* 95 full-time (46 women), 1 (woman) part-time; includes 19 minority (2 Black or African American, non-Hispanic/Latino; 7 Asian, non-Hispanic/Latino; 9 Hispanic/Latino; 1 Two or more races, non-Hispanic/Latino), 52 international. Average age 28. 137 applicants, 18% accepted, 22 enrolled. In 2015, 2 master's, 10 doctorates awarded. *Degree requirements:* For master's, thesis or internship; for doctorate, comprehensive exam, thesis/dissertation, research practica. *Entrance requirements:* For master's and doctorate, GRE General Test, minimum GPA of 3.0 in upper-level course work in field. Additional exam requirements/recommendations for international students: Required—TOEFL (minimum score 600 paper-based). *Application deadline:* For fall admission, 7/15 for domestic students, 5/1 priority date for international students; for spring admission, 11/15 for domestic students, 9/1 priority date for international students. Applications are processed on a rolling basis. Application fee: $50 ($100 for international students). Electronic applications accepted. *Expenses:* Tuition, state resident: full-time $11,940; part-time $663 per semester hour. Tuition, nonresident: full-time $22,786; part-time $1266 per semester hour. Tuition and fees vary according to course load. *Financial support:* In 2015–16, 95 students received support, including 37 research assistantships with partial tuition reimbursements available (averaging $23,919 per year), 54 teaching assistantships with partial tuition reimbursements available (averaging $17,150 per year); career-related internships or fieldwork, Federal Work-Study, institutionally sponsored loans, scholarships/grants, and unspecified assistantships also available. Support available to part-time students. Financial award application deadline: 4/30; financial award applicants required to submit FAFSA. *Faculty research:* Advanced nano-materials; novel MRI agents; peptidomimetics to treat diabetes; semiconducting polymers for organic electronics; macrocyclic receptors for catalysis, medicine, materials science; electroactive polymers. *Unit head:* Dr. John P. Ferraris, Department Head, 972-883-2905, Fax: 972-883-2925,
E-mail: chemistry@utdallas.edu. *Application contact:* Dr. Inga Holl Musselman, Administrative Services Officer, 972-883-2901, Fax: 972-883-2925,
E-mail: chemistry@utdallas.edu.
Website: http://www.utdallas.edu/chemistry/

The University of Texas at El Paso, Graduate School, College of Science, Department of Chemistry, El Paso, TX 79968-0001. Offers MS, PhD. *Program availability:* Part-time, evening/weekend. *Degree requirements:* For master's, thesis; for doctorate, thesis/ dissertation. *Entrance requirements:* For master's, GRE, minimum GPA of 3.0; for doctorate, GRE, letters of recommendation. Additional exam requirements/ recommendations for international students: Required—TOEFL; Recommended—IELTS. Electronic applications accepted.

The University of Texas at San Antonio, College of Sciences, Department of Chemistry, San Antonio, TX 78249-0617. Offers MS, PhD. *Faculty:* 15 full-time (0 women), 1 part-time/adjunct (0 women). *Students:* 29 full-time (12 women), 19 part-time (9 women); includes 15 minority (3 Asian, non-Hispanic/Latino; 8 Hispanic/Latino; 4 Two or more races, non-Hispanic/Latino), 10 international. Average age 29. 55 applicants, 42% accepted, 13 enrolled. In 2015, 5 master's, 5 doctorates awarded. *Degree requirements:* For master's, comprehensive exam, thesis optional; for doctorate, comprehensive exam, thesis/dissertation. *Entrance requirements:* For master's, GRE General Test, minimum GPA of 3.0 in all undergraduate chemistry courses, 2 letters of recommendation; for doctorate, GRE, official transcripts from all colleges and universities attended, resume or curriculum vitae, at least 2 letters of recommendation, statement of purpose. Additional exam requirements/recommendations for international students: Required—TOEFL (minimum score 550 paper-based; 79 iBT), IELTS (minimum score 6.5). *Application deadline:* For fall admission, 7/1 for domestic students, 4/1 for international students; for spring admission, 11/1 for domestic students, 9/1 for international students. Application fee: $45 ($80 for international students). Electronic applications accepted. *Financial support:* Applicants required to submit FAFSA. *Faculty research:* Medicinal chemistry, biosensors, mass spectrometry, organic synthesis, enzymatic mechanisms. *Unit head:* Dr. Waldemar Gorski, Department Chair, 210-458-5469, Fax: 210-458-7428, E-mail: waldemar.gorski@utsa.edu. *Application contact:* Dr. Ghezai Musie, Graduate Advisor of Record, 210-458-5454, Fax: 210-458-7428,
E-mail: ghezai.musie@utsa.edu.
Website: http://www.utsa.edu/chem

The University of Texas Rio Grande Valley, College of Sciences, Department of Chemistry, Edinburg, TX 78539. Offers MS, MSIS. *Program availability:* Part-time, evening/weekend. *Degree requirements:* For master's, thesis optional. *Entrance requirements:* For master's, GRE General Test, minimum GPA of 3.0 in the last 32 hours of the completed undergraduate degree; 32 credit hours of undergraduate coursework in chemistry. Additional exam requirements/recommendations for international students: Required—TOEFL (minimum score 500 paper-based; 61 iBT); Recommended—IELTS (minimum score 5.5). Electronic applications accepted. Tuition and fees vary according to course load and program.

University of the Sciences, Program in Chemistry, Biochemistry and Pharmacognosy, Philadelphia, PA 19104-4495. Offers biochemistry (MS, PhD); chemistry (MS, PhD); pharmacognosy (MS, PhD). *Program availability:* Part-time. *Degree requirements:* For master's, thesis, qualifying exams; for doctorate, comprehensive exam, thesis/ dissertation, qualifying exams. *Entrance requirements:* For master's and doctorate, GRE General Test, GRE Subject Test. Additional exam requirements/recommendations for international students: Required—TOEFL, TWE. *Expenses:* Contact institution. *Faculty research:* Organic and medicinal synthesis, mass spectroscopy use in protein analysis, study of analogues of Taxol.

The University of Toledo, College of Graduate Studies, College of Natural Sciences and Mathematics, Department of Chemistry, Toledo, OH 43606-3390. Offers analytical chemistry (MS, PhD); biological chemistry (MS, PhD); inorganic chemistry (MS, PhD); organic chemistry (MS, PhD); physical chemistry (MS, PhD). *Program availability:* Part-time. *Degree requirements:* For master's, thesis or alternative; for doctorate, thesis/dissertation. *Entrance requirements:* For master's and doctorate, GRE General Test, GRE Subject Test, minimum cumulative point-hour ratio of 2.7 for all previous academic work, three letters of recommendation, statement of purpose, transcripts from all prior institutions attended. Additional exam requirements/recommendations for international students: Required—TOEFL (minimum score 550 paper-based; 80 iBT). Electronic applications accepted. *Faculty research:* Enzymology, materials chemistry, crystallography, theoretical chemistry.

University of Toronto, School of Graduate Studies, Faculty of Arts and Science, Department of Chemistry, Toronto, ON M5S 1A1, Canada. Offers M Sc, PhD. *Degree requirements:* For master's, thesis; for doctorate, thesis/dissertation, oral exam, thesis defense. *Entrance requirements:* For master's, bachelor's degree in chemistry or a related field; for doctorate, master's degree in chemistry or a related field. Additional exam requirements/recommendations for international students: Required—TOEFL (minimum score 580 paper-based; 93 iBT), TWE (minimum score 4). Electronic applications accepted.

The University of Tulsa, Graduate School, College of Engineering and Natural Sciences, Department of Chemistry and Biochemistry, Program in Chemistry, Tulsa, OK 74104-3189. Offers MS, PhD. *Program availability:* Part-time. *Faculty:* 10 full-time (1 woman). *Students:* 10 full-time (5 women), 4 part-time (2 women); includes 1 minority (American Indian or Alaska Native, non-Hispanic/Latino), 5 international. Average age 29. 21 applicants, 29% accepted, 1 enrolled. In 2015, 2 master's, 1 doctorate awarded. Terminal master's awarded for partial completion of doctoral program. *Degree requirements:* For master's, thesis (for some programs); for doctorate, comprehensive exam, thesis/dissertation. *Entrance requirements:* For master's, GRE General Test. Additional exam requirements/recommendations for international students: Required—TOEFL (minimum score 550 paper-based; 80 iBT), IELTS (minimum score 6). *Application deadline:* Applications are processed on a rolling basis. Application fee: $55. Electronic applications accepted. *Expenses: Tuition, area resident:* Full-time $22,230; part-time $1176 per credit hour. *Required fees:* $590 per semester. Tuition and fees vary according to course load. *Financial support:* In 2015–16, 15 students received support, including 5 fellowships with partial tuition reimbursements available (averaging $6,750 per year), 6 research assistantships with full tuition reimbursements available (averaging $16,141 per year), 7 teaching assistantships with full tuition reimbursements available (averaging $11,408 per year); career-related internships or fieldwork, Federal Work-Study, scholarships/grants, health care benefits, tuition waivers (full and partial), and unspecified assistantships also available. Support available to part-time students. Financial award application deadline: 2/1; financial award applicants required to submit FAFSA. *Unit head:* Dr. Dale C. Teeters, Chairperson, 918-631-2515, Fax: 918-631-3404, E-mail: dale-teeters@utulsa.edu. *Application contact:* Dr. Kenneth Roberts, Advisor, 918-631-3090, Fax: 918-631-3404, E-mail: kproberts@utulsa.edu.

University of Utah, Graduate School, College of Science, Department of Chemistry, Salt Lake City, UT 84112-0850. Offers chemistry (MS, PhD); science teacher education (MS). *Program availability:* Part-time, online learning. *Faculty:* 32 full-time (9 women), 8 part-time/adjunct (2 women). *Students:* 137 full-time (49 women), 28 part-time (9 women); includes 10 minority (2 Black or African American, non-Hispanic/Latino; 2 Asian, non-Hispanic/Latino; 6 Hispanic/Latino), 45 international. Average age 27. 256 applicants, 34% accepted, 24 enrolled. In 2015, 17 master's, 21 doctorates awarded. Terminal master's awarded for partial completion of doctoral program. *Degree requirements:* For master's, thesis optional, 20 hours of course work, 10 hours of research; for doctorate, thesis/dissertation, 18 hours of course work, 14 hours of research. *Entrance requirements:* For master's and doctorate, GRE General Test, minimum GPA of 3.0. Additional exam requirements/recommendations for international students: Required—TOEFL (minimum score 620 paper-based; 105 iBT). *Application deadline:* For fall admission, 4/1 for domestic students, 2/1 for international students; for spring admission, 11/1 for domestic and international students. Application fee: $55 ($65 for international students). Electronic applications accepted. Application fee is waived when completed online. *Financial support:* In 2015–16, 1 fellowship with tuition reimbursement (averaging $25,000 per year), 119 research assistantships with tuition reimbursements (averaging $25,500 per year), 55 teaching assistantships with tuition reimbursements (averaging $25,000 per year) were awarded; scholarships/grants and tuition waivers (full) also available. Financial award application deadline: 4/1; financial award applicants required to submit FAFSA. *Faculty research:* Analytical, biological, inorganic, materials, organic, physical and theoretical chemistry. *Unit head:* Dr. Cynthia J. Burrows, Chair, 801-585-7290, Fax: 801-581-8433,
E-mail: chair@chemistry.utah.edu. *Application contact:* Jo Hoovey, Graduate Coordinator, 801-581-4393, Fax: 801-581-5408, E-mail: jhoovey@chem.utah.edu.
Website: http://www.chem.utah.edu/

University of Vermont, Graduate College, College of Arts and Sciences, Department of Chemistry, Burlington, VT 05405. Offers MS, PhD. *Degree requirements:* For master's, one foreign language, thesis; for doctorate, 2 foreign languages, thesis/dissertation. *Entrance requirements:* For master's and doctorate, GRE General Test. Additional exam requirements/recommendations for international students: Required—TOEFL (minimum score 550 paper-based; 80 iBT). Electronic applications accepted.

University of Victoria, Faculty of Graduate Studies, Faculty of Science, Department of Chemistry, Victoria, BC V8W 2Y2, Canada. Offers M Sc, PhD. *Degree requirements:* For master's, thesis; for doctorate, thesis/dissertation, candidacy exam. *Entrance requirements:* For master's and doctorate, GRE Subject Test. Additional exam requirements/recommendations for international students: Required—TOEFL (minimum score 575 paper-based), IELTS (minimum score 7). Electronic applications accepted. *Faculty research:* Laser spectroscopy and dynamics; inorganic, organic, and organometallic synthesis; electro and surface chemistry.

University of Virginia, College and Graduate School of Arts and Sciences, Department of Chemistry, Charlottesville, VA 22903. Offers MA, MS, PhD. *Degree requirements:* For master's, comprehensive exam, thesis; for doctorate, comprehensive exam, thesis/dissertation. *Entrance requirements:* For master's and doctorate, GRE General Test; GRE Subject Test (recommended). Additional exam requirements/recommendations for international students: Required—TOEFL (minimum score 600 paper-based; 90 iBT), IELTS (minimum score 7). Electronic applications accepted.

University of Washington, Graduate School, College of Arts and Sciences, Department of Chemistry, Seattle, WA 98195. Offers MS, PhD. Terminal master's awarded for partial completion of doctoral program. *Degree requirements:* For master's, thesis (for some programs); for doctorate, thesis/dissertation. *Entrance requirements:* For master's and doctorate, GRE Subject Test, minimum GPA of 3.0. Additional exam requirements/recommendations for international students: Required—TOEFL. *Faculty research:* Biopolymers, material science and nanotechnology, organometallic chemistry, analytical chemistry, bioorganic chemistry.

University of Waterloo, Graduate Studies, Faculty of Science, Guelph-Waterloo Centre for Graduate Work in Chemistry and Biochemistry, Waterloo, ON N2L 3G1, Canada. Offers M Sc, PhD. M Sc, PhD offered jointly with University of Guelph. *Program availability:* Part-time. *Degree requirements:* For master's and doctorate, project or thesis. *Entrance requirements:* For master's, GRE, honors degree, minimum B average; for doctorate, GRE, master's degree, minimum B average. Additional exam requirements/recommendations for international students: Required—TOEFL, IELTS, PTE. *Application deadline:* Applications are processed on a rolling basis. Application fee: $100 Canadian dollars. Electronic applications accepted. *Financial support:* Research assistantships, teaching assistantships, and scholarships/grants available. *Faculty research:* Polymer, physical, inorganic, organic, and theoretical chemistry. *Unit head:* E-mail: gwc@uwaterloo.ca. *Application contact:* E-mail: gwc@uoguelph.ca.
Website: http://www.gwc2.on.ca/

The University of Western Ontario, Faculty of Graduate Studies, Physical Sciences Division, Department of Chemistry, London, ON N6A 5B8, Canada. Offers M Sc, PhD. *Degree requirements:* For master's, thesis; for doctorate, thesis/dissertation. *Entrance requirements:* For master's, minimum B+ average, honors B Sc in chemistry; for doctorate, M Sc or equivalent in chemistry. Additional exam requirements/recommendations for international students: Required—TOEFL (paper-based 570) or IELTS (6). *Faculty research:* Materials, inorganic, organic, physical and theoretical chemistry.

University of Windsor, Faculty of Graduate Studies, Faculty of Science, Department of Chemistry and Biochemistry, Windsor, ON N9B 3P4, Canada. Offers M Sc, PhD. *Program availability:* Part-time. *Degree requirements:* For master's, thesis; for doctorate, comprehensive exam, thesis/dissertation. *Entrance requirements:* For master's and doctorate, minimum B average. Additional exam requirements/recommendations for international students: Required—TOEFL (minimum score 560 paper-based). Electronic applications accepted. *Faculty research:* Molecular biology/recombinant DNA techniques (PCR, cloning mutagenesis), No/02 detectors, western immunoblotting and detection, CD/NMR protein/peptide structure determination, confocal/electron microscopes.

University of Wisconsin–Madison, Graduate School, College of Engineering, Program in Environmental Chemistry and Technology, Madison, WI 53706. Offers MS, PhD. *Program availability:* Part-time. *Faculty:* 13 full-time (3 women). *Students:* 15 full-time (10 women); includes 4 minority (1 Black or African American, non-Hispanic/Latino; 2 Hispanic/Latino; 1 Two or more races, non-Hispanic/Latino), 1 international. Average age 27. 49 applicants, 4% accepted, 2 enrolled. In 2015, 3 master's, 2 doctorates awarded. Terminal master's awarded for partial completion of doctoral program. *Degree requirements:* For master's, thesis or alternative; for doctorate, thesis/dissertation. *Entrance requirements:* For master's and doctorate, GRE General Test. Additional exam requirements/recommendations for international students: Required—TOEFL. Application fee: $54 ($62 for international students). Electronic applications accepted. *Expenses:* $5,935 resident tuition and fees; $12,598 nonresident and international; $8,493 Minnesota resident. *Financial support:* In 2015–16, 13 students received support, including 1 fellowship with full tuition reimbursement available (averaging $34,000 per year), 11 research assistantships with full tuition reimbursements available (averaging $21,885 per year); Federal Work-Study and institutionally sponsored loans also available. Financial award application deadline: 1/1. *Faculty research:* Chemical limnology, chemical remediation, geochemistry, photocatalysis, water quality. *Unit head:* Dr. Marc A. Anderson, Chair, 608-263-3264, E-mail: nanopor@wisc.edu. *Application contact:* Mary Possin, Student Services Coordinator, 608-890-2075,
E-mail: mcpossin@wisc.edu.
Website: http://www.engr.wisc.edu/interd/ect/

University of Wisconsin–Madison, Graduate School, College of Letters and Science, Department of Chemistry, Madison, WI 53706-1380. Offers MS, PhD. *Program availability:* Part-time. Terminal master's awarded for partial completion of doctoral program. *Degree requirements:* For master's, thesis (for some programs); for doctorate, thesis/dissertation, cumulative exams, research proposal, seminar. *Entrance requirements:* For master's and doctorate, GRE, minimum GPA of 3.0. Additional exam requirements/recommendations for international students: Required—TOEFL. Electronic applications accepted. *Expenses:* Tuition, state resident: full-time $5364. Tuition, nonresident: full-time $12,027. *Required fees:* $571. Tuition and fees vary according to campus/location, program and reciprocity agreements. *Faculty research:* Analytical, inorganic, organic, physical, and macromolecular chemistry.

University of Wisconsin–Milwaukee, Graduate School, College of Letters and Science, Department of Chemistry, Milwaukee, WI 53201-0413. Offers chemistry (MS, PhD). *Faculty:* 20 full-time (4 women). *Students:* 52 full-time (20 women), 12 part-time (3 women); includes 7 minority (4 Asian, non-Hispanic/Latino; 3 Two or more races, non-Hispanic/Latino), 25 international. Average age 31. 60 applicants, 30% accepted, 8 enrolled. In 2015, 14 doctorates awarded. *Degree requirements:* For master's, thesis or alternative; for doctorate, thesis/dissertation. *Entrance requirements:* For doctorate, GRE General Test. Additional exam requirements/recommendations for international students: Required—TOEFL (minimum score 600 paper-based; 79 iBT), IELTS (minimum score 6.5). *Application deadline:* For fall admission, 1/1 priority date for domestic students; for spring admission, 9/1 for domestic students. Applications are processed on a rolling basis. Application fee: $56 ($96 for international students). *Financial support:* In 2015–16, 3 fellowships, 30 research assistantships, 46 teaching assistantships were awarded; career-related internships or fieldwork, unspecified assistantships, and project assistantships also available. Support available to part-time students. Financial award application deadline: 4/15; financial award applicants required to submit FAFSA. *Faculty research:* Analytical chemistry, biochemistry, inorganic chemistry, organic chemistry, physical chemistry. *Unit head:* Peter Geissinger, Department Chair, 414-229-4098, E-mail: geissing@uwm.edu. *Application contact:* General Information Contact, 414-229-4982, Fax: 414-229-6967,
E-mail: gradschool@uwm.edu.
Website: https://uwm.edu/chemistry/

University of Wyoming, College of Arts and Sciences, Department of Chemistry, Laramie, WY 82071. Offers MS, PhD. *Degree requirements:* For master's, thesis; for doctorate, thesis/dissertation. *Entrance requirements:* For master's and doctorate, GRE General Test, minimum GPA of 3.0. Additional exam requirements/recommendations for international students: Required—TOEFL (minimum score 600 paper-based). Electronic applications accepted. *Faculty research:* Organic chemistry, inorganic chemistry, analytical chemistry, physical chemistry.

Utah State University, School of Graduate Studies, College of Science, Department of Chemistry and Biochemistry, Logan, UT 84322. Offers biochemistry (MS, PhD); chemistry (MS, PhD). *Program availability:* Part-time. Terminal master's awarded for partial completion of doctoral program. *Degree requirements:* For master's, thesis, oral and written exams; for doctorate, thesis/dissertation, oral and written exams. *Entrance requirements:* For master's and doctorate, GRE General Test, minimum GPA of 3.0. Additional exam requirements/recommendations for international students: Required—TOEFL. *Faculty research:* Analytical, inorganic, organic, and physical chemistry; iron in asbestos chemistry and carcinogenicity; dicopper complexes; photothermal spectrometry; metal molecule clusters.

Vanderbilt University, Department of Chemistry, Nashville, TN 37240-1001. Offers analytical chemistry (MAT, MS, PhD); inorganic chemistry (MAT, MS, PhD); organic chemistry (MAT, MS, PhD); physical chemistry (MAT, MS, PhD); theoretical chemistry (MAT, MS). *Faculty:* 19 full-time (3 women). *Students:* 114 full-time (41 women); includes 19 minority (5 Black or African American, non-Hispanic/Latino; 3 Asian, non-Hispanic/Latino; 7 Hispanic/Latino; 4 Two or more races, non-Hispanic/Latino), 8 international. Average age 26. 339 applicants, 17% accepted, 19 enrolled. In 2015, 11 master's, 13 doctorates awarded. Terminal master's awarded for partial completion of doctoral program. *Degree requirements:* For master's, thesis; for doctorate, thesis/dissertation, area, qualifying, and final exams. *Entrance requirements:* For master's and doctorate, GRE General Test, GRE Subject Test (recommended). Additional exam requirements/recommendations for international students: Required—TOEFL (minimum score 570 paper-based; 88 iBT). *Application deadline:* For fall admission, 1/15 for domestic and international students. Application fee: $0. Electronic applications accepted. *Financial support:* Fellowships with tuition reimbursements, research assistantships with full tuition reimbursements, teaching assistantships with full tuition reimbursements, Federal Work-Study, institutionally sponsored loans, scholarships/grants, traineeships, and health care benefits available. Financial award application deadline: 1/15; financial award applicants required to submit CSS PROFILE or FAFSA. *Faculty research:* Chemical synthesis; mechanistic, theoretical, bioorganic, analytical, and spectroscopic chemistry. *Unit head:* Dr. Carmello Rizzo, Director of Graduate Studies, 615-322-2861, Fax: 615-322-4936, E-mail: c.rizzo@vanderbilt.edu. *Application contact:* Sandra Ford, Administrative Assistant, 615-322-8695, Fax: 615-322-4936, E-mail: sandra.e.ford@vanderbilt.edu.
Website: http://www.vanderbilt.edu/chemistry/

Villanova University, Graduate School of Liberal Arts and Sciences, Department of Chemistry, Villanova, PA 19085-1699. Offers MS. *Program availability:* Part-time, evening/weekend. *Faculty:* 6. *Students:* 16 full-time (9 women), 11 part-time (6 women); includes 7 minority (1 Asian, non-Hispanic/Latino; 1 Hispanic/Latino; 5 Two or more races, non-Hispanic/Latino), 1 international. Average age 26. 18 applicants, 56% accepted, 8 enrolled. In 2015, 18 master's awarded. *Degree requirements:* For master's, comprehensive exam (for some programs), thesis (for some programs). *Entrance requirements:* For master's, GRE General Test, minimum GPA of 3.0, 3 recommendation letters, statement of goals. Additional exam requirements/recommendations for international students: Required—TOEFL. *Application deadline:* For fall admission, 5/1 priority date for international students; for spring admission, 10/15 priority date for international students. Applications are processed on a rolling basis. Application fee: $50. Electronic applications accepted. *Financial support:* Research assistantships, teaching assistantships, scholarships/grants, and unspecified assistantships available. Financial award applicants required to submit FAFSA. *Unit head:* Dr. Scott Kassell, Chair, 610-519-4842. *Application contact:* Dean, Graduate School of Liberal Arts and Sciences.
Website: http://www1.villanova.edu/villanova/artsci/chemistry/Academic_Programs/graduate.html

Virginia Commonwealth University, Graduate School, College of Humanities and Sciences, Department of Chemistry, Richmond, VA 23284-9005. Offers analytical chemistry (MS, PhD); chemical physics (PhD); inorganic chemistry (MS, PhD); organic chemistry (MS, PhD); physical chemistry (MS, PhD). *Program availability:* Part-time. Terminal master's awarded for partial completion of doctoral program. *Degree requirements:* For master's, thesis; for doctorate, thesis/dissertation, comprehensive cumulative exams, research proposal. *Entrance requirements:* For master's, GRE General Test, 30 undergraduate credits in chemistry; for doctorate, GRE General Test. Additional exam requirements/recommendations for international students: Required—TOEFL (minimum score 600 paper-based; 100 iBT) or IELTS (minimum score 6.5). Electronic applications accepted. *Faculty research:* Physical, organic, inorganic, analytical, and polymer chemistry; chemical physics.

Virginia Polytechnic Institute and State University, Graduate School, College of Science, Blacksburg, VA 24061. Offers biological sciences (MS, PhD); biomedical technology development and management (MS); chemistry (MS, PhD); economics (MA, PhD); geosciences (MS, PhD); mathematics (MS, PhD); physics (MS, PhD); psychology (MS, PhD); statistics (MS, PhD). *Degree requirements:* For master's, comprehensive exam (for some programs), thesis (for some programs); for doctorate, comprehensive exam (for some programs), thesis/dissertation (for some programs). *Entrance requirements:* For master's and doctorate, GRE/GMAT (may vary by department). Additional exam requirements/recommendations for international students: Required—TOEFL (minimum score 550 paper-based). Electronic applications accepted.

Wake Forest University, Graduate School of Arts and Sciences, Department of Chemistry, Winston-Salem, NC 27109. Offers analytical chemistry (MS, PhD); inorganic chemistry (MS, PhD); organic chemistry (MS, PhD); physical chemistry (MS, PhD). *Program availability:* Part-time. *Degree requirements:* For master's, one foreign language, comprehensive exam, thesis; for doctorate, 2 foreign languages, comprehensive exam, thesis/dissertation. *Entrance requirements:* For master's and doctorate, GRE General Test. Additional exam requirements/recommendations for international students: Required—TOEFL. Electronic applications accepted.

Washington State University, College of Arts and Sciences, Department of Chemistry, Pullman, WA 99164. Offers MS, PhD. Program applications must be made through the Pullman campus. *Program availability:* Part-time, evening/weekend. Terminal master's awarded for partial completion of doctoral program. *Degree requirements:* For master's, comprehensive exam (for some programs), thesis (for some programs), oral exam, teaching experience; for doctorate, comprehensive exam, thesis/dissertation, oral exam, written exam, teaching experience. *Entrance requirements:* For master's and doctorate, GRE General Test, GRE Subject Test (recommended), transcripts from each post-secondary school attended (photocopies acceptable); three letters of recommendation. Additional exam requirements/recommendations for international students: Required—TOEFL. Electronic applications accepted. *Faculty research:* Chemistry of biological systems, chemistry of materials, chemistry of energy and the environment, radiochemistry.

Washington University in St. Louis, Graduate School of Arts and Sciences, Department of Chemistry, St. Louis, MO 63130-4899. Offers PhD. *Students:* 97 full-time (41 women); includes 8 minority (2 Black or African American, non-Hispanic/Latino; 3 Asian, non-Hispanic/Latino; 1 Hispanic/Latino; 2 Two or more races, non-Hispanic/Latino), 47 international. 130 applicants, 39% accepted, 24 enrolled. In 2015, 18 doctorates awarded. Terminal master's awarded for partial completion of doctoral program. *Degree requirements:* For doctorate, thesis/dissertation. *Entrance requirements:* For doctorate, GRE General Test, GRE Subject Test. Additional exam requirements/recommendations for international students: Required—TOEFL. *Application deadline:* For fall admission, 1/15 for domestic students. Applications are processed on a rolling basis. Application fee: $45. Electronic applications accepted. *Financial support:* Fellowships, research assistantships, and teaching assistantships available. Financial award application deadline: 1/15. *Faculty research:* Bioinorganic; biological; biorganic; biophysical; inorganic; materials; nuclear; organic; organometallic; physical; polymer; radiochemistry; spectroscopy and theoretical. *Unit head:* Dr. William Buhro, Chair, 314-935-7316. *Application contact:* Bridget Coleman, Director of Admissions, 314-935-6880, Fax: 314-935-4887.
Website: http://www.chemistry.wustl.edu/

Wayne State University, College of Liberal Arts and Sciences, Department of Chemistry, Detroit, MI 48202. Offers analytical chemistry (PhD); biochemistry (PhD); chemistry (MA, MS); inorganic chemistry (PhD); organic chemistry (PhD); physical chemistry (PhD). *Faculty:* 29. *Students:* 146 full-time (61 women); includes 9 minority (2 Asian, non-Hispanic/Latino; 3 Hispanic/Latino; 4 Two or more races, non-Hispanic/Latino), 95 international. Average age 28. 280 applicants, 19% accepted, 28 enrolled. In 2015, 4 master's, 22 doctorates awarded. *Degree requirements:* For master's, thesis (for some programs), oral exam; for doctorate, thesis/dissertation, oral exam. *Entrance requirements:* For master's, GRE (strongly recommended), 1 year of physics, math through calculus, general chemistry (8 credits), organic chemistry (8 credits), physical chemistry (6 credits), quantitative analysis (4 credits), advanced chemistry (3 credits), minimum undergraduate GPA of 2.75 in chemistry and cognate sciences, statement of interest, three letters of recommendation; for doctorate, GRE (strongly recommended), minimum undergraduate GPA of 3.0 in chemistry and cognate science. Additional exam requirements/recommendations for international students: Required—TOEFL (minimum score 90 iBT), IELTS (minimum score 6.5), TWE (minimum score 5.5). *Application deadline:* For fall admission, 12/1 priority date for domestic and international students. Applications are processed on a rolling basis. Application fee: $0. Electronic applications accepted. *Expenses:* Tuition, state resident: full-time $14,165; part-time $590.20 per credit hour. Tuition, nonresident: full-time $30,682; part-time $1278.40 per credit hour. *Required fees:* $1688; $47.45 per credit hour. $274.60 per semester. Tuition and fees vary according to course load and program. *Financial support:* In 2015–16, 141 students received support, including 10 fellowships with tuition reimbursements available (averaging $23,000 per year), 54 research assistantships with tuition reimbursements available (averaging $21,609 per year), 73 teaching assistantships with tuition reimbursements available (averaging $21,363 per year); scholarships/grants and unspecified assistantships also available. Financial award application deadline: 3/31; financial award applicants required to submit FAFSA. *Faculty research:* Natural products synthesis, molecular biology, molecular mechanics calculations, organometallic chemistry, experimental physical chemistry. *Total annual research expenditures:* $7.4 million. *Unit head:* Dr. James Rigby, Chair, 313-577-3472,
E-mail: jhr@chem.wayne.edu. *Application contact:* Melissa Barton, Graduate Academic Services Officer, E-mail: melissa@chem.wayne.edu.
Website: http://chem.wayne.edu/

Wesleyan University, Graduate Studies, Department of Chemistry, Middletown, CT 06459. Offers biochemistry (PhD); chemical physics (PhD); inorganic chemistry (PhD); organic chemistry (PhD); physical chemistry (PhD); theoretical chemistry (PhD). *Faculty:* 13 full-time (3 women), 3 part-time/adjunct (2 women). *Students:* 20 full-time (10 women), 2 part-time (0 women); includes 4 minority (1 Black or African American, non-Hispanic/Latino; 3 Asian, non-Hispanic/Latino), 8 international. Average age 25. In 2015, 6 doctorates awarded. Terminal master's awarded for partial completion of doctoral program. *Degree requirements:* For doctorate, thesis/dissertation, proposal. *Entrance requirements:* For doctorate, GRE General Test, 3 recommendations. Additional exam requirements/recommendations for international students: Required—TOEFL, IELTS. *Application deadline:* 2/15 for domestic and international students; for summer admission, 2/15 for domestic and international students. Applications are processed on a rolling basis. Application fee: $0. Electronic applications accepted. *Financial support:* In 2015–16, 4 research assistantships with full tuition reimbursements, 21 teaching assistantships with full tuition reimbursements were awarded; institutionally sponsored loans and health care benefits also available. Financial award application deadline: 4/15; financial award applicants required to submit FAFSA. *Faculty research:* MICHELLE LOUISE PERSONICK Research in the Personick lab is focused on the synthesis of noble metal and noble metal alloy nanoparticles with well-defined shapes and catalytically active high-energy surfaces. Our research takes place at the interface between inorganic chemistry and materials science, and we combine solution-phase nanoparticle synthesis with advanced materials characterization techniques such as scanning electron microscopy (SEM). In addition, we evaluate the catalytic activity of. *Unit head:* Michael Calter, Chair, 860-685-2633, E-mail: mcalter@wesleyan.edu. *Application contact:* Roslyn Brault, Administrative Assistant/Graduate Program Coordinator, 860-685-2573, Fax: 860-685-2211, E-mail: rbrault@wesleyan.edu.
Website: http://www.wesleyan.edu/chem/

West Chester University of Pennsylvania, College of Arts and Sciences, Department of Chemistry, West Chester, PA 19383. Offers chemistry (Teaching Certificate). *Students:* 1 (woman) full-time. Average age 24. 2 applicants, 100% accepted. In 2015, 1 Teaching Certificate awarded. *Degree requirements:* For Teaching Certificate, minimum overall GPA of 3.0, Chemistry PRAXIS. *Entrance requirements:* For degree, minimum GPA of 2.8 in most recent 48 credits. Additional exam requirements/recommendations for international students: Required—TOEFL or IELTS. *Application deadline:* For fall admission, 5/15 for international students; for spring admission, 10/15 for international students. Applications are processed on a rolling basis. Application fee: $50. Electronic applications accepted. *Expenses:* Tuition, state resident: full-time $8460; part-time $470 per credit. Tuition, nonresident: full-time $12,690; part-time $705 per credit. *Required fees:* $2312; $126.75 per credit. Tuition and fees vary according to campus/location and program. *Financial support:* Scholarships/grants and unspecified assistantships available. Financial award application deadline: 2/15; financial award applicants required to submit FAFSA. *Faculty research:* Nanomaterials synthesis and characterization, medicinal chemistry synthesis, biosensor development and testing, atmospheric chemistry, forensic analysis of drug microcrystals. *Unit head:* Dr. Melissa Cichowicz, Chair, 610-436-2774, E-mail: mcichowicz@wcupa.edu. *Application contact:* Dr. John Townsend, Secondary Education Advisor, 610-436-1063,
E-mail: jtownsend@wcupa.edu.
Website: http://www.wcupa.edu/_academics/sch_cas.che/

Western Carolina University, Graduate School, College of Arts and Sciences, Department of Chemistry and Physics, Cullowhee, NC 28723. Offers chemistry (MS). *Degree requirements:* For master's, thesis. *Entrance requirements:* For master's, GRE General Test, undergraduate science degree with minimum GPA of 3.0, 3 letters of recommendation. Additional exam requirements/recommendations for international students: Required—TOEFL (minimum score 550 paper-based; 79 iBT). *Faculty research:* Trace metal analysis, metal waste reduction, supramolecular chemistry, free radical biophysical chemistry.

Chemistry

Western Illinois University, School of Graduate Studies, College of Arts and Sciences, Department of Chemistry, Macomb, IL 61455-1390. Offers MS. *Program availability:* Part-time. *Students:* 30 full-time (11 women), 6 part-time (3 women); includes 3 minority (1 Black or African American, non-Hispanic/Latino; 1 Asian, non-Hispanic/Latino; 1 Two or more races, non-Hispanic/Latino), 23 international. Average age 27. 26 applicants, 54% accepted, 10 enrolled. In 2015, 12 master's awarded. *Degree requirements:* For master's, thesis or alternative. *Entrance requirements:* Additional exam requirements/recommendations for international students: Required—TOEFL (minimum score 530 paper-based; 71 iBT). *Application deadline:* Applications are processed on a rolling basis. Application fee: $30. Electronic applications accepted. *Financial support:* In 2015–16, 21 students received support, including 17 teaching assistantships with full tuition reimbursements available (averaging $8,688 per year); unspecified assistantships also available. Financial award applicants required to submit FAFSA. *Unit head:* Dr. Rose McConnell, Chairperson, 309-298-1538. *Application contact:* Dr. Nancy Parsons, Associate Provost and Director of Graduate Studies, 309-298-1806, Fax: 309-298-2345, E-mail: grad-office@wiu.edu.
Website: http://wiu.edu/chemistry

Western Kentucky University, Graduate Studies, Ogden College of Science and Engineering, Department of Chemistry, Bowling Green, KY 42101. Offers MA Ed, MS. *Degree requirements:* For master's, comprehensive exam, thesis. *Entrance requirements:* For master's, GRE General Test, minimum GPA of 2.75. Additional exam requirements/recommendations for international students: Required—TOEFL (minimum score 555 paper-based). *Faculty research:* Catatonic surfactants, directed orthometalation reactions, thermal stability and degradation mechanisms, co-firing refused derived fuels, laser fluorescence.

Western Michigan University, Graduate College, College of Arts and Sciences, Department of Chemistry, Kalamazoo, MI 49008. Offers MS, PhD. *Degree requirements:* For master's, thesis; for doctorate, thesis/dissertation.

Western Michigan University, Graduate College, College of Arts and Sciences, Department of Interdisciplinary Arts and Sciences, Kalamazoo, MI 49008. Offers science education (MA, PhD), including biological sciences (PhD), chemistry (PhD), geosciences (PhD), physical geography (PhD), physics (PhD), science education (PhD). *Degree requirements:* For doctorate, thesis/dissertation.

Western Washington University, Graduate School, College of Sciences and Technology, Department of Chemistry, Bellingham, WA 98225-5996. Offers MS. *Program availability:* Part-time. *Degree requirements:* For master's, thesis (for some programs). *Entrance requirements:* For master's, GRE General Test, minimum GPA of 3.0 in last 60 semester hours or last 90 quarter hours. Additional exam requirements/recommendations for international students: Required—TOEFL (minimum score 567 paper-based). Electronic applications accepted. *Faculty research:* Bio-, organic, inorganic, physical, analytical chemistry.

West Texas A&M University, College of Agriculture, Science and Engineering, Department of Mathematics, Physical Sciences and Engineering Technology, Program in Chemistry, Canyon, TX 79016-0001. Offers MS. *Program availability:* Part-time. *Degree requirements:* For master's, comprehensive exam, thesis optional. *Entrance requirements:* For master's, GRE General Test. Additional exam requirements/recommendations for international students: Required—TOEFL (minimum score 550 paper-based). Electronic applications accepted. *Faculty research:* Biochemistry; inorganic, organic, and physical chemistry; vibrational spectroscopy; magnetic susceptibilities; carbene chemistry.

West Virginia University, Eberly College of Arts and Sciences, Department of Chemistry, Morgantown, WV 26506. Offers analytical chemistry (MS, PhD); inorganic chemistry (MS, PhD); organic chemistry (MS, PhD); physical chemistry (MS, PhD); theoretical chemistry (MS, PhD). *Program availability:* Part-time, online learning. Terminal master's awarded for partial completion of doctoral program. *Degree requirements:* For master's, thesis; for doctorate, thesis/dissertation. *Entrance requirements:* For master's, GRE General Test, GRE Subject Test (recommended), minimum GPA of 2.5; for doctorate, GRE General Test, GRE Subject Test (recommended), minimum GPA of 2.75. Additional exam requirements/recommendations for international students: Required—TOEFL. Electronic applications accepted. *Expenses:* Tuition, state resident: full-time $8568. Tuition, nonresident: full-time $22,140. Tuition and fees vary according to program. *Faculty research:* Analysis of proteins, drug interactions, solids and effluents by advanced separation methods; new synthetic strategies for complex organic molecules; synthesis and structural

characterization of metal complexes for polymerization catalysis, nonlinear science, spectroscopy.

Wichita State University, Graduate School, Fairmount College of Liberal Arts and Sciences, Department of Chemistry, Wichita, KS 67260. Offers MS, PhD. *Unit head:* Dr. David Eichhorn, Chair, 316-978-3120, Fax: 316-978-3431, E-mail: david.eichhorn@wichita.edu. *Application contact:* Jordan Oleson, Admission Coordinator, 316-978-3095, E-mail: jordan.oleson@wichita.edu.
Website: http://www.wichita.edu/chemistry

Wilfrid Laurier University, Faculty of Graduate and Postdoctoral Studies, Faculty of Science, Department of Chemistry, Waterloo, ON N2L 3C5, Canada. Offers M Sc. *Degree requirements:* For master's, thesis. *Entrance requirements:* For master's, honors degree or equivalent in chemistry, biochemistry or a related discipline; minimum B average in last two full-time undergraduate years. Additional exam requirements/recommendations for international students: Required—TOEFL (minimum score 89 iBT). Electronic applications accepted. *Faculty research:* Cold regions water science, biophysical methods, biochemistry, nanochemistry.

Worcester Polytechnic Institute, Graduate Studies and Research, Department of Chemistry and Biochemistry, Worcester, MA 01609-2280. Offers biochemistry (MS, PhD); chemistry (MS, PhD). *Program availability:* Evening/weekend. *Faculty:* 7 full-time (1 woman). *Students:* 16 full-time (8 women), 8 international. 44 applicants, 16% accepted, 3 enrolled. In 2015, 2 master's awarded. *Degree requirements:* For master's, thesis; for doctorate, comprehensive exam, thesis/dissertation. *Entrance requirements:* For master's and doctorate, GRE General Test, 3 letters of recommendation, statement of purpose. Additional exam requirements/recommendations for international students: Required—TOEFL (minimum score 563 paper-based; 84 iBT), IELTS (minimum score 7). *Application deadline:* For fall admission, 1/1 priority date for domestic and international students; for spring admission, 10/1 priority date for domestic and international students. Applications are processed on a rolling basis. Application fee: $70. Electronic applications accepted. *Financial support:* Research assistantships, teaching assistantships, career-related internships or fieldwork, institutionally sponsored loans, scholarships/grants, and unspecified assistantships available. Financial award application deadline: 1/1; financial award applicants required to submit FAFSA. *Unit head:* Dr. Arne Gericke, Department Head, 508-831-5371, Fax: 508-831-5933, E-mail: agericke@wpi.edu. *Application contact:* Dr. Shawn Burdette, Graduate Coordinator, 508-831-5371, Fax: 508-831-5933, E-mail: scburdette@wpi.edu.
Website: http://www.wpi.edu/academics/cbc/gradprograms.html

Wright State University, School of Graduate Studies, College of Science and Mathematics, Department of Chemistry, Dayton, OH 45435. Offers chemistry (MS); environmental sciences (MS). *Program availability:* Part-time, evening/weekend. *Degree requirements:* For master's, oral defense of thesis, seminar. *Entrance requirements:* Additional exam requirements/recommendations for international students: Required—TOEFL. *Faculty research:* Polymer synthesis and characterization, laser kinetics, organic and inorganic synthesis, analytical and environmental chemistry.

Yale University, Graduate School of Arts and Sciences, Department of Chemistry, New Haven, CT 06520. Offers biophysical chemistry (PhD); inorganic chemistry (PhD); organic chemistry (PhD); physical and theoretical chemistry (PhD). *Degree requirements:* For doctorate, thesis/dissertation. *Entrance requirements:* For doctorate, GRE General Test, GRE Subject Test. Additional exam requirements/recommendations for international students: Required—TOEFL.

York University, Faculty of Graduate Studies, Faculty of Science, Program in Chemistry, Toronto, ON M3J 1P3, Canada. Offers M Sc, PhD. *Program availability:* Part-time, evening/weekend. *Degree requirements:* For master's, thesis or alternative; for doctorate, thesis/dissertation. Electronic applications accepted.

Youngstown State University, Graduate School, College of Science, Technology, Engineering and Mathematics, Department of Chemistry, Youngstown, OH 44555-0001. Offers analytical chemistry (MS); biochemistry (MS); chemistry education (MS); inorganic chemistry (MS); organic chemistry (MS); physical chemistry (MS). *Program availability:* Part-time. *Degree requirements:* For master's, thesis. *Entrance requirements:* For master's, bachelor's degree in chemistry, minimum GPA of 2.7. Additional exam requirements/recommendations for international students: Required—TOEFL. *Faculty research:* Analysis of antioxidants, chromatography, defects and disorder in crystalline oxides, hydrogen bonding, novel organic and organometallic materials.

Inorganic Chemistry

Auburn University, Graduate School, College of Sciences and Mathematics, Department of Chemistry and Biochemistry, Auburn University, AL 36849. Offers analytical chemistry (MS, PhD); biochemistry (MS, PhD); inorganic chemistry (MS, PhD); organic chemistry (MS, PhD); physical chemistry (MS, PhD). *Program availability:* Part-time. *Faculty:* 27 full-time (4 women), 2 part-time/adjunct (0 women). *Students:* 45 full-time (17 women), 26 part-time (15 women); includes 9 minority (7 Black or African American, non-Hispanic/Latino; 1 American Indian or Alaska Native, non-Hispanic/Latino; 1 Asian, non-Hispanic/Latino), 38 international. Average age 27. 33 applicants, 52% accepted, 16 enrolled. In 2015, 1 master's, 6 doctorates awarded. *Degree requirements:* For master's, thesis (for some programs); for doctorate, thesis/dissertation, oral and written exams. *Entrance requirements:* For master's and doctorate, GRE General Test. *Application deadline:* Applications are processed on a rolling basis. Application fee: $50 ($60 for international students). Electronic applications accepted. *Expenses:* Tuition, state resident: full-time $8802; part-time $489 per credit hour. Tuition, nonresident: full-time $26,406; part-time $1467 per credit hour. *Required fees:* $808 per semester. Tuition and fees vary according to degree level and program. *Financial support:* Fellowships, research assistantships, and teaching assistantships available. Financial award application deadline: 3/15; financial award applicants required to submit FAFSA. *Unit head:* Dr. Curtis Shannon, Chair, 334-844-4043, Fax: 334-844-4043. *Application contact:* Dr. George Flowers, Dean of the Graduate School, 334-844-2125.
Website: http://www.auburn.edu/cosam/departments/chemistry/

Binghamton University, State University of New York, Graduate School, School of Arts and Sciences, Department of Chemistry, Vestal, NY 13850. Offers analytical chemistry (PhD); chemistry (MA, MS); environmental chemistry (PhD); inorganic chemistry (PhD); organic chemistry (PhD); physical chemistry (PhD). *Program availability:* Part-time. *Faculty:* 21 full-time (4 women). *Students:* 60 full-time (24 women), 1 part-time (0 women); includes 4 minority (2 Black or African American, non-Hispanic/Latino; 1 Asian, non-Hispanic/Latino; 1 Hispanic/Latino), 40 international. Average age 27. 53 applicants, 81% accepted, 16 enrolled. In 2015, 3 master's, 7 doctorates awarded. Terminal master's awarded for partial completion of doctoral program. *Degree requirements:* For master's, thesis; for doctorate, comprehensive exam, thesis/dissertation. *Entrance requirements:* For master's and doctorate, GRE General Test. Additional exam requirements/recommendations for international students: Required—TOEFL (minimum score 90 iBT). *Application deadline:* Applications are processed on a rolling basis. Application fee: $75. Electronic applications accepted. *Financial support:* In 2015–16, 53 students received support, including 8 research assistantships with full tuition reimbursements available (averaging $18,000 per year), 34 teaching assistantships with full tuition reimbursements available (averaging $18,000 per year); career-related internships or fieldwork, Federal Work-Study, institutionally sponsored loans, scholarships/grants, health care benefits, tuition waivers (full and partial), and unspecified assistantships also available. Financial award applicants required to submit FAFSA. *Unit head:* Dr. Wayne E. Jones, Chairperson, 607-777-2421, E-mail: wjones@binghamton.edu. *Application contact:* Kishan Zuber, Recruiting and Admissions Coordinator, 607-777-2151, Fax: 607-777-2501, E-mail: kzuber@binghamton.edu.

Boston College, Graduate School of Arts and Sciences, Department of Chemistry, Chestnut Hill, MA 02467. Offers biochemistry (PhD); inorganic chemistry (PhD); organic chemistry (PhD); physical chemistry (PhD); science education (MST). *Faculty:* 21 full-time. *Students:* 121 full-time (57 women); includes 9 minority (6 Asian, non-Hispanic/Latino; 3 Hispanic/Latino), 53 international. 222 applicants, 50% accepted, 43 enrolled. In 2015, 2 master's, 11 doctorates awarded. *Degree requirements:* For doctorate, thesis/

dissertation, qualifying exam. *Entrance requirements:* For doctorate, GRE General Test, GRE Subject Test. Additional exam requirements/recommendations for international students: Required—TOEFL (minimum score 600 paper-based; 100 iBT), IELTS (minimum score 8). *Application deadline:* For fall admission, 1/2 for domestic and international students. Application fee: $75. Electronic applications accepted. Tuition and fees vary according to program. *Financial support:* In 2015–16, 121 students received support, including fellowships with full tuition reimbursements available (averaging $30,000 per year), research assistantships with full tuition reimbursements available (averaging $30,000 per year), teaching assistantships with full tuition reimbursements available (averaging $30,000 per year); Federal Work-Study, scholarships/grants, health care benefits, and unspecified assistantships also available. Support available to part-time students. Financial award application deadline: 1/2. *Faculty research:* Organic and organometallic chemistry, chemical biology and biochemistry, physical and theoretical chemistry, inorganic chemistry. *Unit head:* Dr. Amir Hoveyda, Chairperson, 617-552-1735, E-mail: amir.hoveyda@bc.edu. *Application contact:* Dr. Jianmin Gao, Graduate Program Director, 617-552-0326, Fax: 617-552-0833, E-mail: gaojc@bc.edu.
Website: http://www.bc.edu/chemistry

Brandeis University, Graduate School of Arts and Sciences, Department of Chemistry, Waltham, MA 02454. Offers inorganic chemistry (MA, MS, PhD); organic chemistry (MA, MS, PhD); physical chemistry (MS, PhD). *Program availability:* Part-time. *Faculty:* 12 full-time (4 women), 1 part-time/adjunct (0 women). *Students:* 43 full-time (15 women); includes 2 minority (1 Black or African American, non-Hispanic/Latino; 1 Two or more races, non-Hispanic/Latino), 26 international. 102 applicants, 34% accepted, 7 enrolled. In 2015, 8 master's, 6 doctorates awarded. Terminal master's awarded for partial completion of doctoral program. *Degree requirements:* For master's, comprehensive exam, thesis (for some programs), 1 year of residency (for MA); 2 years of residency (for MS); for doctorate, comprehensive exam, thesis/dissertation, 3 years of residency, 2 seminars, qualifying exams. *Entrance requirements:* For master's and doctorate, GRE General Test, resume, statement of purpose, letters of recommendation. Additional exam requirements/recommendations for international students: Required—TOEFL (minimum score 600 paper-based; 100 iBT); Recommended—IELTS (minimum score 7), TSE (minimum score 68). *Application deadline:* For fall admission, 1/15 priority date for domestic students. Application fee: $75. Electronic applications accepted. *Financial support:* In 2015–16, 42 students received support, including 24 fellowships with full tuition reimbursements available (averaging $27,500 per year), 18 research assistantships with full tuition reimbursements available (averaging $27,500 per year); Federal Work-Study, scholarships/grants, health care benefits, tuition waivers (partial), and unspecified assistantships also available. Support available to part-time students. Financial award application deadline: 4/15; financial award applicants required to submit FAFSA. *Faculty research:* Inorganic and organic chemistry, physical chemistry, chemical biology, biophysical chemistry, materials chemistry. *Unit head:* Dr. Judith Herzfeld, Chair, Graduate Program, 781-736-2540, Fax: 781-736-2516,
E-mail: herzfeld@brandeis.edu. *Application contact:* Dr. Maryanna Aldrich, Coordinator, 781-736-2500, Fax: 781-736-2516, E-mail: scigradoffice@brandeis.edu.
Website: http://www.brandeis.edu/gsas

California State University, Los Angeles, Graduate Studies, College of Natural and Social Sciences, Department of Chemistry and Biochemistry, Los Angeles, CA 90032-8530. Offers analytical chemistry (MS); biochemistry (MS); chemistry (MS); inorganic chemistry (MS); organic chemistry (MS); physical chemistry (MS). *Program availability:* Part-time, evening/weekend. *Degree requirements:* For master's, one foreign language, comprehensive exam or thesis. *Entrance requirements:* Additional exam requirements/recommendations for international students: Required—TOEFL. *Faculty research:* Intercalation of heavy metal, carborane chemistry, conductive polymers and fabrics, titanium reagents, computer modeling and synthesis.

Cleveland State University, College of Graduate Studies, College of Sciences and Health Professions, Department of Chemistry, Cleveland, OH 44115. Offers analytical chemistry (MS); clinical/bioanalytical chemistry (PhD), including cellular and molecular medicine, clinical/bioanalytical chemistry; inorganic chemistry (MS); pharmaceutical/organic chemistry (MS); physical chemistry (MS). *Program availability:* Part-time, evening/weekend. *Faculty:* 17 full-time (3 women). *Students:* 63 full-time (30 women), 25 part-time (10 women); includes 4 minority (1 Black or African American, non-Hispanic/Latino; 1 Asian, non-Hispanic/Latino; 2 Hispanic/Latino), 48 international. Average age 30. 22 applicants, 64% accepted, 12 enrolled. In 2015, 16 master's, 8 doctorates awarded. *Degree requirements:* For master's, thesis optional; for doctorate, comprehensive exam, thesis/dissertation. *Entrance requirements:* For master's and doctorate, GRE General Test. Additional exam requirements/recommendations for international students: Required—TOEFL (minimum score 550 paper-based; 78 iBT). *Application deadline:* For fall admission, 1/15 priority date for domestic and international students. Applications are processed on a rolling basis. Application fee: $30. Electronic applications accepted. *Expenses:* Tuition, state resident: full-time $9565. Tuition, nonresident: full-time $17,980. Tuition and fees vary according to program. *Financial support:* In 2015–16, 44 students received support, including 10 fellowships with full tuition reimbursements available (averaging $22,500 per year), 6 research assistantships with full tuition reimbursements available (averaging $22,500 per year), 34 teaching assistantships with full tuition reimbursements available (averaging $21,000 per year); scholarships/grants and unspecified assistantships also available. Financial award application deadline: 1/15. *Faculty research:* Bioanalytical techniques and molecular diagnostics, glycoproteomics and antithrombotic agents, drug discovery and innovation, analytical pharmacology, inflammatory disease research. *Total annual research expenditures:* $3 million. *Unit head:* Dr. David W. Ball, Chair, 216-687-2467, Fax: 216-687-9298, E-mail: d.ball@csuohio.edu. *Application contact:* Richelle P. Emery, Administrative Coordinator, 216-687-2457, Fax: 216-687-9298,
E-mail: r.emery@csuohio.edu.
Website: http://www.csuohio.edu/sciences/chemistry

Cornell University, Graduate School, Graduate Fields of Arts and Sciences, Field of Chemistry and Chemical Biology, Ithaca, NY 14853-0001. Offers analytical chemistry (PhD); bio-organic chemistry (PhD); biophysical chemistry (PhD); chemical biology (PhD); chemical physics (PhD); inorganic chemistry (PhD); materials chemistry (PhD); organic chemistry (PhD); organometallic chemistry (PhD); physical chemistry (PhD); polymer chemistry (PhD); theoretical chemistry (PhD). *Degree requirements:* For doctorate, comprehensive exam, thesis/dissertation. *Entrance requirements:* For doctorate, GRE General Test, GRE Subject Test (chemistry), 3 letters of recommendation. Additional exam requirements/recommendations for international students: Required—TOEFL (minimum score 600 paper-based; 77 iBT). Electronic applications accepted. *Faculty research:* Analytical, organic, inorganic, physical, materials, chemical biology.

Eastern New Mexico University, Graduate School, College of Liberal Arts and Sciences, Department of Physical Sciences, Portales, NM 88130. Offers chemistry (MS), including analytical, biochemistry, inorganic, organic, physical. *Program availability:* Part-time. *Degree requirements:* For master's, thesis optional, seminar, oral and written comprehensive exams. *Entrance requirements:* For master's, ACS placement examination, minimum GPA of 3.0; 2 letters of recommendation; personal statement of career goals; bachelor's degree with one year minimum each of general, organic, and analytical chemistry. Additional exam requirements/recommendations for international students: Required—TOEFL (minimum score 550 paper-based; 79 iBT), IELTS (minimum score 6). Electronic applications accepted. *Faculty research:* Synfuel, electrochemistry, protein chemistry.

Florida State University, The Graduate School, College of Arts and Sciences, Department of Chemistry and Biochemistry, Tallahassee, FL 32306-4390. Offers analytical chemistry (MS, PhD); biochemistry (MS, PhD); inorganic chemistry (MS, PhD); materials chemistry (PhD); organic chemistry (MS, PhD); physical chemistry (MS, PhD). *Faculty:* 40 full-time (6 women), 4 part-time/adjunct (2 women). *Students:* 162 full-time (56 women); includes 37 minority (8 Black or African American, non-Hispanic/Latino; 6 Asian, non-Hispanic/Latino; 18 Hispanic/Latino; 1 Native Hawaiian or other Pacific Islander, non-Hispanic/Latino; 4 Two or more races, non-Hispanic/Latino), 54 international. Average age 28. 182 applicants, 47% accepted, 31 enrolled. In 2015, 6 master's, 18 doctorates awarded. Terminal master's awarded for partial completion of doctoral program. *Degree requirements:* For master's, thesis (for some programs); for doctorate, thesis/dissertation. *Entrance requirements:* For master's and doctorate, GRE General Test (minimum scores: 150 verbal, 151 quantitative; 1100 total on the old scale), minimum GPA of 3.1 in undergraduate course work. Additional exam requirements/recommendations for international students: Required—TOEFL (minimum score 90 iBT). *Application deadline:* For fall admission, 12/15 priority date for domestic and international students. Application fee: $30. Electronic applications accepted. *Expenses: Tuition, area resident:* Full-time $7263; part-time $403.50 per credit hour. Tuition, nonresident: full-time $18,087; part-time $1004.85 per credit hour. *Required fees:* $1365; $75.81 per credit hour. $20 per semester. Tuition and fees vary according to campus/location. *Financial support:* In 2015–16, 162 students received support, including 4 fellowships with tuition reimbursements available (averaging $22,000 per year), 51 research assistantships with full tuition reimbursements available (averaging $22,809 per year), 67 teaching assistantships with full tuition reimbursements available (averaging $22,809 per year). Financial award application deadline: 12/15; financial award applicants required to submit FAFSA. *Faculty research:* Bioanalytical chemistry, including separations, microfluidics, petroleomics; materials chemistry, including magnets, polymers, catalysts, nanomaterials; spectroscopy, including NMR and EPR, ultrafast, Raman, and mass spectrometry; organic synthesis, natural products, photochemistry, and supramolecular chemistry; biochemistry, with focus on structural biology, metabolomics, and anticancer drugs. *Total annual research expenditures:* $3.5 million. *Unit head:* Dr. Timothy Logan, Chairman, 850-644-3810, Fax: 850-644-8281, E-mail: gradinfo@chem.fsu.edu. *Application contact:* Dr. Geoffrey Strouse, Associate Chair for Graduate Studies, 850-445-9042, Fax: 850-644-8281,
E-mail: gradinfo@chem.fsu.edu.
Website: http://www.chem.fsu.edu/

Georgetown University, Graduate School of Arts and Sciences, Department of Chemistry, Washington, DC 20057. Offers analytical chemistry (PhD); biochemistry (PhD); computational chemistry (PhD); inorganic chemistry (PhD); materials chemistry (PhD); organic chemistry (PhD); theoretical chemistry (PhD). Terminal master's awarded for partial completion of doctoral program. *Degree requirements:* For doctorate, comprehensive exam, thesis/dissertation. *Entrance requirements:* For doctorate, GRE General Test. Additional exam requirements/recommendations for international students: Required—TOEFL.

The George Washington University, Columbian College of Arts and Sciences, Department of Chemistry, Washington, DC 20052. Offers analytical chemistry (MS, PhD); inorganic chemistry (MS, PhD); materials science (MS, PhD); organic chemistry (MS, PhD); physical chemistry (MS, PhD). *Program availability:* Part-time, evening/weekend. *Faculty:* 17 full-time (6 women), 4 part-time/adjunct (1 woman). *Students:* 25 full-time (13 women), 12 part-time (5 women); includes 2 minority (1 Asian, non-Hispanic/Latino; 1 Hispanic/Latino), 10 international. Average age 28. 60 applicants, 37% accepted, 9 enrolled. In 2015, 2 master's, 6 doctorates awarded. Terminal master's awarded for partial completion of doctoral program. *Degree requirements:* For master's, comprehensive exam, thesis or alternative; for doctorate, thesis/dissertation, general exam. *Entrance requirements:* For master's and doctorate, GRE General Test, interview, minimum GPA of 3.0. Additional exam requirements/recommendations for international students: Required—TOEFL (minimum score 550 paper-based; 80 iBT). *Application deadline:* For fall admission, 1/15 priority date for domestic and international students; for spring admission, 9/1 priority date for domestic and international students. Applications are processed on a rolling basis. Application fee: $75. Electronic applications accepted. *Financial support:* In 2015–16, 27 students received support. Fellowships with tuition reimbursements available, research assistantships, teaching assistantships with tuition reimbursements available, Federal Work-Study, and tuition waivers available. Financial award application deadline: 1/15. *Unit head:* Dr. Michael King, Chair, 202-994-6488. *Application contact:* Information Contact, 202-994-6121, E-mail: gwchem@gwu.edu.
Website: http://chemistry.columbian.gwu.edu/

Harvard University, Graduate School of Arts and Sciences, Department of Chemistry and Chemical Biology, Cambridge, MA 02138. Offers biochemical chemistry (PhD); inorganic chemistry (PhD); organic chemistry (PhD); physical chemistry (PhD). *Degree requirements:* For doctorate, thesis/dissertation, cumulative exams. *Entrance requirements:* For doctorate, GRE General Test, GRE Subject Test. Additional exam requirements/recommendations for international students: Required—TOEFL.

Howard University, Graduate School, Department of Chemistry, Washington, DC 20059-0002. Offers analytical chemistry (MS, PhD); atmospheric (MS, PhD); biochemistry (MS, PhD); environmental (MS, PhD); inorganic chemistry (MS, PhD); organic chemistry (MS, PhD); physical chemistry (MS, PhD). Terminal master's awarded for partial completion of doctoral program. *Degree requirements:* For master's, comprehensive exam, thesis, teaching experience; for doctorate, comprehensive exam, thesis/dissertation, teaching experience. *Entrance requirements:* For master's, GRE General Test, minimum GPA of 2.7; for doctorate, GRE General Test, minimum GPA of 3.0. Additional exam requirements/recommendations for international students: Required—TOEFL. Electronic applications accepted. *Faculty research:* Synthetic organics, materials, natural products, mass spectrometry.

Illinois Institute of Technology, Graduate College, College of Science, Department of Chemistry, Chicago, IL 60616. Offers analytical chemistry (MAS); chemistry (MAS, MS, PhD); materials chemistry (MAS), including inorganic, organic, or polymeric materials. *Program availability:* Part-time, evening/weekend, online learning. Terminal master's awarded for partial completion of doctoral program. *Degree requirements:* For master's, comprehensive exam, thesis (for some programs); for doctorate, comprehensive exam, thesis/dissertation. *Entrance requirements:* For master's, GRE General Test (minimum score 300 Quantitative and Verbal, 2.5 Analytical Writing), minimum undergraduate GPA of 3.0; for doctorate, GRE General Test (minimum score 310 Quantitative and Verbal, 3.0 Analytical Writing), GRE Subject Test, minimum undergraduate GPA of 3.0. Additional exam requirements/recommendations for international students: Required—

Inorganic Chemistry

TOEFL (minimum score 550 paper-based; 80 iBT); Recommended—IELTS. Electronic applications accepted. *Faculty research:* Materials science, biological chemistry, synthetic chemistry, computational chemistry, energy, sensor science and technology, scholarship of teaching and learning.

Indiana University Bloomington, University Graduate School, College of Arts and Sciences, Department of Chemistry, Bloomington, IN 47405. Offers analytical chemistry (PhD); chemical biology (PhD); chemistry (MAT); inorganic chemistry (PhD); materials chemistry (PhD); organic chemistry (PhD); physical chemistry (PhD); MSES/MS. Terminal master's awarded for partial completion of doctoral program. *Degree requirements:* For master's, thesis; for doctorate, thesis/dissertation. *Entrance requirements:* For master's and doctorate, GRE General Test, GRE Subject Test. Additional exam requirements/recommendations for international students: Required—TOEFL. Electronic applications accepted. *Faculty research:* Synthesis of complex natural products, organic reaction mechanisms, organic electrochemistry, transitive-metal chemistry, solid-state and surface chemistry.

Iowa State University of Science and Technology, Program in Inorganic Chemistry, Ames, IA 50011. Offers MS, PhD. *Entrance requirements:* Additional exam requirements/recommendations for international students: Required—TOEFL (minimum score 570 paper-based; 89 iBT), IELTS (minimum score 6.5). Electronic applications accepted.

Kansas State University, Graduate School, College of Arts and Sciences, Department of Chemistry, Manhattan, KS 66506. Offers analytical chemistry (MS); biological chemistry (MS); inorganic chemistry (MS); materials chemistry (MS); organic chemistry (MS); physical chemistry (MS). Terminal master's awarded for partial completion of doctoral program. *Degree requirements:* For master's, thesis; for doctorate, thesis/dissertation. *Entrance requirements:* For master's and doctorate, GRE, minimum GPA of 3.0. Additional exam requirements/recommendations for international students: Required—TOEFL (minimum score 550 paper-based). Electronic applications accepted. *Faculty research:* Inorganic chemistry, organic and biological chemistry, analytical chemistry, physical chemistry, materials chemistry and nanotechnology.

Marquette University, Graduate School, College of Arts and Sciences, Department of Chemistry, Milwaukee, WI 53201-1881. Offers analytical chemistry (MS, PhD); bioanalytical chemistry (MS, PhD); biophysical chemistry (MS, PhD); chemical physics (MS, PhD); inorganic chemistry (MS, PhD); organic chemistry (MS, PhD); physical chemistry (MS, PhD). *Program availability:* Part-time. *Faculty:* 19 full-time (3 women), 1 part-time/adjunct (0 women). *Students:* 43 full-time (14 women), 4 part-time (0 women); includes 2 minority (1 Asian, non-Hispanic/Latino; 1 Hispanic/Latino), 32 international. Average age 28. In 2015, 4 master's, 4 doctorates awarded. Terminal master's awarded for partial completion of doctoral program. *Degree requirements:* For master's, comprehensive exam; for doctorate, thesis/dissertation, cumulative exams. *Entrance requirements:* For master's and doctorate, official transcripts from all current and previous colleges/universities except Marquette, three letters of recommendation from individuals familiar with the applicant's academic work. Additional exam requirements/recommendations for international students: Required—TOEFL (minimum score 530 paper-based). *Application deadline:* Applications are processed on a rolling basis. Application fee: $50. Electronic applications accepted. *Financial support:* In 2015–16, 41 students received support, including 2 fellowships (averaging $17,134 per year), 30 teaching assistantships with full tuition reimbursements available (averaging $20,295 per year); research assistantships, scholarships/grants, health care benefits, tuition waivers (full and partial), and unspecified assistantships also available. Support available to part-time students. Financial award application deadline: 2/15. *Faculty research:* Inorganic complexes, laser Raman spectroscopy, organic synthesis, synthetic bioinorganic chemistry, electro-active organic molecules. *Total annual research expenditures:* $1.2 million. *Unit head:* Dr. Scott Reid, Chair, 414-288-7565, E-mail: scott.reid@marquette.edu. *Application contact:* Dr. Adam Fiedler, New and Recruiting, 414-288-1625.
Website: http://www.marquette.edu/chem/graduate.shtml

Massachusetts Institute of Technology, School of Science, Department of Chemistry, Cambridge, MA 02139. Offers biological chemistry (PhD); inorganic chemistry (PhD); organic chemistry (PhD); physical chemistry (PhD). *Faculty:* 29 full-time (6 women). *Students:* 236 full-time (81 women); includes 51 minority (2 Black or African American, non-Hispanic/Latino; 1 American Indian or Alaska Native, non-Hispanic/Latino; 30 Asian, non-Hispanic/Latino; 12 Hispanic/Latino; 6 Two or more races, non-Hispanic/Latino), 83 international. Average age 26. 591 applicants, 18% accepted, 38 enrolled. In 2015, 40 doctorates awarded. *Degree requirements:* For doctorate, comprehensive exam, thesis/dissertation, teaching assistantship during two semesters. *Entrance requirements:* For doctorate, GRE General Test. Additional exam requirements/recommendations for international students: Required—TOEFL (minimum score 600 paper-based), IELTS (minimum score 7). *Application deadline:* For fall admission, 12/15 for domestic and international students. Application fee: $75. Electronic applications accepted. *Expenses: Tuition:* Full-time $46,400; part-time $725 per credit. One-time fee: $304 full-time. Full-time tuition and fees vary according to course load and program. *Financial support:* In 2015–16, 218 students received support, including 62 fellowships (averaging $45,800 per year), 129 research assistantships (averaging $37,000 per year), 43 teaching assistantships (averaging $38,300 per year); Federal Work-Study, institutionally sponsored loans, scholarships/grants, traineeships, health care benefits, and unspecified assistantships also available. Support available to part-time students. Financial award application deadline: 4/15; financial award applicants required to submit FAFSA. *Faculty research:* Synthetic organic and organometallic chemistry including catalysis; biological chemistry including bioorganic chemistry; physical chemistry including chemical dynamics, theoretical chemistry and biophysical chemistry; inorganic chemistry including synthesis, catalysis, bioinorganic and physical inorganic chemistry; materials chemistry including surface science, nanoscience and polymers. *Total annual research expenditures:* $30.3 million. *Unit head:* Prof. Timothy F. Jamison, Department Head, 617-253-1803, Fax: 617-258-7500. *Application contact:* Graduate Administrator, 617-253-1845, Fax: 617-258-0241, E-mail: chemgradeducation@mit.edu.
Website: http://web.mit.edu/chemistry/

McMaster University, School of Graduate Studies, Faculty of Science, Department of Chemistry, Hamilton, ON L8S 4M2, Canada. Offers analytical chemistry (M Sc, PhD); chemical physics (M Sc, PhD); chemistry (M Sc, PhD); inorganic chemistry (M Sc, PhD); organic chemistry (M Sc, PhD); physical chemistry (M Sc, PhD); polymer chemistry (M Sc, PhD). *Program availability:* Part-time. Terminal master's awarded for partial completion of doctoral program. *Degree requirements:* For master's, thesis; for doctorate, comprehensive exam, thesis/dissertation. *Entrance requirements:* For master's, minimum B+ average. Additional exam requirements/recommendations for international students: Required—TOEFL (minimum score 550 paper-based).

Old Dominion University, College of Sciences, Program in Chemistry, Norfolk, VA 23529. Offers analytical (MS, PhD); biochemistry (MS, PhD); environmental (MS, PhD); inorganic (MS, PhD); organic (MS, PhD); physical (MS, PhD). *Program availability:* Part-time, evening/weekend. *Faculty:* 19 full-time (5 women). *Students:* 35 full-time (17 women), 6 part-time (2 women); includes 5 minority (4 Black or African American, non-Hispanic/Latino; 1 Two or more races, non-Hispanic/Latino), 16 international. Average age 27. 20 applicants, 55% accepted, 4 enrolled. In 2015, 9 master's, 9 doctorates awarded. *Degree requirements:* For master's, comprehensive exam, thesis (for some programs); for doctorate, comprehensive exam, thesis/dissertation. *Entrance requirements:* For master's and doctorate, GRE General Test, minimum GPA of 3.0 in major, 2.5 overall, transcripts, essay, three letters of recommendation, resume. Additional exam requirements/recommendations for international students: Required—TOEFL. *Application deadline:* For fall admission, 7/1 for domestic students, 1/15 for international students; for spring admission, 11/1 for domestic students, 8/15 for international students. Applications are processed on a rolling basis. Application fee: $50. Electronic applications accepted. *Expenses:* $464 per credit in-state tuition; $1,160 per credit out-of-state tuition. *Financial support:* In 2015–16, 42 students received support, including 2 fellowships with full tuition reimbursements available (averaging $18,000 per year), 10 research assistantships with full tuition reimbursements available (averaging $18,000 per year), 33 teaching assistantships with full tuition reimbursements available (averaging $18,000 per year); career-related internships or fieldwork, institutionally sponsored loans, scholarships/grants, health care benefits, and unspecified assistantships also available. Financial award application deadline: 2/15; financial award applicants required to submit FAFSA. *Faculty research:* Biogeochemistry, materials chemistry, computational chemistry, organic chemistry, biofuels. *Total annual research expenditures:* $2.6 million. *Unit head:* Dr. John R. Donat, Graduate Program Director, 757-683-4098, Fax: 757-683-4628, E-mail: chemgpd@odu.edu. *Application contact:* Kristi Rehrauer, Graduate Program Assistant, 757-683-6979, Fax: 757-683-4628, E-mail: krehraue@odu.edu.

Oregon State University, College of Science, Program in Chemistry, Corvallis, OR 97331. Offers analytical chemistry (MA, MS, PhD); inorganic chemistry (MA, MS, PhD); materials chemistry (MA, MS, PhD); nuclear chemistry (MA, MS, PhD); organic chemistry (MA, MS, PhD); physical chemistry (MA, MS, PhD). *Program availability:* Part-time. *Faculty:* 23 full-time (6 women). *Students:* 111 full-time (38 women), 4 part-time (2 women); includes 14 minority (1 Black or African American, non-Hispanic/Latino; 5 Asian, non-Hispanic/Latino; 6 Hispanic/Latino; 2 Two or more races, non-Hispanic/Latino), 49 international. Average age 28. 47 applicants, 51% accepted, 22 enrolled. In 2015, 6 master's, 12 doctorates awarded. Terminal master's awarded for partial completion of doctoral program. *Degree requirements:* For master's, one foreign language, thesis; for doctorate, one foreign language, thesis/dissertation. *Entrance requirements:* For master's and doctorate, GRE, minimum GPA of 3.0 in last 90 hours of course work. Additional exam requirements/recommendations for international students: Required—TOEFL (minimum score 80 iBT), IELTS (minimum score 6.5). *Application deadline:* For fall admission, 4/1 for domestic students. Application fee: $75 ($85 for international students). *Expenses:* Tuition, state resident: full-time $12,150; part-time $450 per credit. Tuition, nonresident: full-time $20,952; part-time $776 per credit. *Required fees:* $1572; $1443 per unit. One-time fee: $350. Tuition and fees vary according to course load, campus/location and program. *Financial support:* Fellowships, research assistantships, and teaching assistantships available. Support available to part-time students. *Faculty research:* Solid state chemistry, enzyme reaction mechanisms, structure and dynamics of gas molecules, chemiluminescence, nonlinear optical spectroscopy. *Unit head:* Dr. Rich G. Carter, Professor/Chair. *Application contact:* Sarah Burton, Chemistry Advisor, 541-737-6808, E-mail: chemadm@chem.oregonstate.edu.
Website: http://chemistry.oregonstate.edu/

Purdue University, Graduate School, College of Science, Department of Chemistry, West Lafayette, IN 47907. Offers analytical chemistry (MS, PhD); biochemistry (MS, PhD); chemical education (MS, PhD); inorganic chemistry (MS, PhD); organic chemistry (MS, PhD); physical chemistry (MS, PhD). Terminal master's awarded for partial completion of doctoral program. *Degree requirements:* For master's, thesis; for doctorate, comprehensive exam, thesis/dissertation. *Entrance requirements:* For master's and doctorate, minimum undergraduate GPA of 3.0. Additional exam requirements/recommendations for international students: Required—TOEFL (minimum score 550 paper-based; 77 iBT); Recommended—TWE. Electronic applications accepted.

Rice University, Graduate Programs, Wiess School of Natural Sciences, Department of Chemistry, Houston, TX 77251-1892. Offers chemistry (MA); inorganic chemistry (PhD); organic chemistry (PhD); physical chemistry (PhD). Terminal master's awarded for partial completion of doctoral program. *Degree requirements:* For master's, thesis; for doctorate, thesis/dissertation. *Entrance requirements:* For master's and doctorate, GRE General Test, minimum GPA of 3.0. Additional exam requirements/recommendations for international students: Required—TOEFL (minimum score 600 paper-based; 90 iBT). Electronic applications accepted. *Faculty research:* Nanoscience, biomaterials, nanobioinformatics, fullerene pharmaceuticals.

Rutgers University–Newark, Graduate School, Program in Chemistry, Newark, NJ 07102. Offers analytical chemistry (MS, PhD); biochemistry (MS, PhD); inorganic chemistry (MS, PhD); organic chemistry (MS, PhD); physical chemistry (MS, PhD). *Program availability:* Part-time, evening/weekend. Terminal master's awarded for partial completion of doctoral program. *Degree requirements:* For master's, thesis optional, cumulative exams; for doctorate, thesis/dissertation, exams, research proposal. *Entrance requirements:* For master's and doctorate, GRE General Test, minimum undergraduate B average. Additional exam requirements/recommendations for international students: Required—TOEFL. Electronic applications accepted. *Faculty research:* Medicinal chemistry, natural products, isotope effects, biophysics and biorganic approaches to enzyme mechanisms, organic and organometallic synthesis.

Rutgers University–New Brunswick, Graduate School-New Brunswick, Department of Chemistry and Chemical Biology, Piscataway, NJ 08854-8097. Offers biological chemistry (MS, PhD); inorganic chemistry (MS, PhD); organic chemistry (MS, PhD); physical chemistry (MS, PhD). *Program availability:* Part-time, evening/weekend. Terminal master's awarded for partial completion of doctoral program. *Degree requirements:* For master's, thesis or alternative, exam; for doctorate, thesis/dissertation, 1 year residency. *Entrance requirements:* For master's and doctorate, GRE General Test, GRE Subject Test. Additional exam requirements/recommendations for international students: Required—TOEFL. Electronic applications accepted. *Faculty research:* Biophysical organic/bioorganic, inorganic/bioinorganic, theoretical, and solid-state/surface chemistry.

Seton Hall University, College of Arts and Sciences, Department of Chemistry and Biochemistry, South Orange, NJ 07079-2697. Offers analytical chemistry (MS, PhD); biochemistry (MS, PhD); chemistry (MS); inorganic chemistry (MS, PhD); organic chemistry (MS, PhD); physical chemistry (MS, PhD). *Program availability:* Part-time, evening/weekend. Terminal master's awarded for partial completion of doctoral program. *Degree requirements:* For master's, thesis optional; for doctorate, comprehensive exam, thesis/dissertation. *Entrance requirements:* Additional exam requirements/recommendations for international students: Required—TOEFL. Electronic applications accepted. *Faculty research:* DNA metal reactions;

chromatography; bioinorganic, biophysical, organometallic, polymer chemistry; heterogeneous catalyst; synthetic organic and carbohydrate chemistry.

Southern University and Agricultural and Mechanical College, Graduate School, College of Sciences, Department of Chemistry, Baton Rouge, LA 70813. Offers analytical chemistry (MS); biochemistry (MS); environmental sciences (MS); inorganic chemistry (MS); organic chemistry (MS); physical chemistry (MS). *Degree requirements:* For master's, thesis. *Entrance requirements:* For master's, GMAT or GRE General Test. Additional exam requirements/recommendations for international students: Required—TOEFL (minimum score 525 paper-based). *Faculty research:* Synthesis of macrocyclic ligands, latex accelerators, anticancer drugs, biosensors, absorption isotheums, isolation of specific enzymes from plants.

Tufts University, Graduate School of Arts and Sciences, Department of Chemistry, Medford, MA 02155. Offers analytical chemistry (MS, PhD); bioorganic chemistry (MS, PhD); environmental chemistry (MS, PhD); inorganic chemistry (MS, PhD); organic chemistry (MS, PhD); physical chemistry (MS, PhD). Terminal master's awarded for partial completion of doctoral program. *Degree requirements:* For master's, thesis optional; for doctorate, thesis/dissertation. *Entrance requirements:* For master's and doctorate, GRE General Test; GRE Subject Test (recommended). Additional exam requirements/recommendations for international students: Required—TOEFL (minimum score 600 paper-based; 80 iBT), IELTS (minimum score 6.5). Electronic applications accepted. *Expenses: Tuition, area resident:* Full-time $48,412; part-time $1210 per credit hour. *Required fees:* $806. Full-time tuition and fees vary according to degree level, program and student level. Part-time tuition and fees vary according to course load.

University of Calgary, Faculty of Graduate Studies, Faculty of Science, Department of Chemistry, Calgary, AB T2N 1N4, Canada. Offers analytical chemistry (M Sc, PhD); applied chemistry (M Sc, PhD); inorganic chemistry (M Sc, PhD); organic chemistry (M Sc, PhD); physical chemistry (M Sc, PhD); polymer chemistry (M Sc, PhD); theoretical chemistry (M Sc, PhD). *Degree requirements:* For master's, thesis; for doctorate, thesis/dissertation, candidacy exam. *Entrance requirements:* For master's, minimum GPA of 3.0; for doctorate, honors B Sc degree with minimum GPA of 3.7 or M Sc with minimum GPA of 3.3. Additional exam requirements/recommendations for international students: Required—TOEFL (minimum score 580 paper-based). Electronic applications accepted. *Faculty research:* Chemical analysis, chemical dynamics, synthesis theory.

University of Cincinnati, Graduate School, McMicken College of Arts and Sciences, Department of Chemistry, Cincinnati, OH 45221. Offers analytical chemistry (MS, PhD); biochemistry (MS, PhD); inorganic chemistry (MS, PhD); organic chemistry (MS, PhD); physical chemistry (MS, PhD); polymer chemistry (MS, PhD); sensors (PhD). *Program availability:* Part-time, evening/weekend. Terminal master's awarded for partial completion of doctoral program. *Degree requirements:* For master's, thesis optional; for doctorate, comprehensive exam, thesis/dissertation. *Entrance requirements:* For master's and doctorate, GRE General Test. Additional exam requirements/recommendations for international students: Required—TOEFL (minimum score 580 paper-based). Electronic applications accepted. *Faculty research:* Biomedical chemistry, laser chemistry, surface science, chemical sensors, synthesis.

University of Georgia, Franklin College of Arts and Sciences, Department of Chemistry, Athens, GA 30602. Offers analytical chemistry (MS, PhD); inorganic chemistry (MS, PhD); organic chemistry (MS, PhD); physical chemistry (MS, PhD). Terminal master's awarded for partial completion of doctoral program. *Degree requirements:* For master's, thesis; for doctorate, one foreign language, thesis/dissertation. *Entrance requirements:* For master's and doctorate, GRE General Test. Additional exam requirements/recommendations for international students: Required—TOEFL. Electronic applications accepted.

University of Louisville, Graduate School, College of Arts and Sciences, Department of Chemistry, Louisville, KY 40292-0001. Offers analytical chemistry (MS, PhD); biochemistry (MS, PhD); chemical physics (PhD); inorganic chemistry (MS, PhD); organic chemistry (MS, PhD); physical chemistry (MS, PhD). *Students:* 46 full-time (16 women), 8 part-time (1 woman); includes 3 minority (1 Black or African American, non-Hispanic/Latino; 1 Asian, non-Hispanic/Latino; 1 Two or more races, non-Hispanic/Latino), 36 international. Average age 29. 51 applicants, 22% accepted, 6 enrolled. In 2015, 2 master's, 1 doctorate awarded. Terminal master's awarded for partial completion of doctoral program. *Degree requirements:* For master's, variable foreign language requirement, comprehensive exam, thesis optional; for doctorate, variable foreign language requirement, comprehensive exam, thesis/dissertation. *Entrance requirements:* For master's and doctorate, GRE General Test, BA or BS coursework. Additional exam requirements/recommendations for international students: Required—TOEFL (minimum score 550 paper-based; 79 iBT). *Application deadline:* For fall admission, 3/15 for domestic students, 5/1 priority date for international students; for winter admission, 9/15 for domestic and international students; for spring admission, 11/1 priority date for international students; for summer admission, 4/1 priority date for international students. Applications are processed on a rolling basis. Application fee: $60. Electronic applications accepted. *Expenses:* Tuition, state resident: full-time $11,664; part-time $649 per credit hour. Tuition, nonresident: full-time $24,274; part-time $1350 per credit hour. *Required fees:* $196. Tuition and fees vary according to program and reciprocity agreements. *Financial support:* In 2015–16, 757,720 students received support. Fellowships with full tuition reimbursements available, research assistantships with full tuition reimbursements available, teaching assistantships with full tuition reimbursements available, career-related internships or fieldwork, scholarships/grants, traineeships, health care benefits, and unspecified assistantships available. Support available to part-time students. Financial award application deadline: 3/15. *Faculty research:* Computational chemistry, biophysics nuclear magnetic resonance, synthetic organic chemistry, synthetic inorganic chemistry, medicinal chemistry, protein chemistry, enzymology, nano chemistry, electrochemistry, analytical chemistry, synthetic biology, bioinformatics. *Total annual research expenditures:* $2.4 million. *Unit head:* Dr. Richard J. Wittebort, Professor/Chair, 502-852-6613. *Application contact:* Libby Leggett, Director, Graduate Admissions, 502-852-3101, Fax: 502-852-6536, E-mail: gradadm@louisville.edu.
Website: http://louisville.edu/chemistry

The University of Manchester, School of Chemistry, Manchester, United Kingdom. Offers biological chemistry (PhD); chemistry (M Ent, M Phil, M Sc, D Ent, PhD); inorganic chemistry (PhD); materials chemistry (PhD); nanoscience (PhD); nuclear fission (PhD); organic chemistry (PhD); physical chemistry (PhD); theoretical chemistry (PhD).

University of Maryland, College Park, Academic Affairs, College of Computer, Mathematical and Natural Sciences, Department of Chemistry and Biochemistry, Chemistry Program, College Park, MD 20742. Offers analytical chemistry (MS, PhD); inorganic chemistry (MS, PhD); organic chemistry (MS, PhD); physical chemistry (MS, PhD). *Program availability:* Part-time, evening/weekend. Terminal master's awarded for partial completion of doctoral program. *Degree requirements:* For master's, thesis optional; for doctorate, thesis/dissertation, 2 seminar presentations, oral exam. *Entrance requirements:* For master's and doctorate, GRE General Test, GRE Subject Test (recommended), minimum GPA of 3.0, 3 letters of recommendation. Additional exam requirements/recommendations for international students: Required—TOEFL. Electronic applications accepted. *Faculty research:* Environmental chemistry, nuclear chemistry, lunar and environmental analysis, X-ray crystallography.

University of Massachusetts Lowell, College of Sciences, Department of Chemistry, Lowell, MA 01854. Offers analytical chemistry (PhD); biochemistry (PhD); chemistry (MS, PhD); environmental studies (PhD); green chemistry (PhD); inorganic chemistry (PhD); organic chemistry (PhD); polymer science (MS). Terminal master's awarded for partial completion of doctoral program. *Degree requirements:* For master's, thesis; for doctorate, 2 foreign languages, thesis/dissertation. *Entrance requirements:* For master's and doctorate, GRE General Test. Electronic applications accepted.

University of Memphis, Graduate School, College of Arts and Sciences, Department of Chemistry, Memphis, TN 38152. Offers analytical chemistry (PhD); inorganic chemistry (MS); physical chemistry (MS). *Program availability:* Part-time. *Faculty:* 5 full-time (2 women), 1 part-time/adjunct (0 women). *Students:* 26 full-time (11 women), 9 part-time (2 women); includes 6 minority (2 Black or African American, non-Hispanic/Latino; 2 Asian, non-Hispanic/Latino; 2 Two or more races, non-Hispanic/Latino), 5 international. Average age 28. 19 applicants, 74% accepted, 9 enrolled. In 2015, 9 master's, 3 doctorates awarded. Terminal master's awarded for partial completion of doctoral program. *Degree requirements:* For master's, comprehensive exam, thesis or alternative; for doctorate, comprehensive exam, thesis/dissertation. *Entrance requirements:* For master's and doctorate, GRE General Test, admission to Graduate School plus 32 undergraduate hours in chemistry. Additional exam requirements/recommendations for international students: Required—TOEFL. *Application deadline:* For fall admission, 7/1 for domestic students, 5/1 for international students; for winter admission, 9/15 for international students; for spring admission, 12/1 for domestic students. Applications are processed on a rolling basis. Application fee: $35 ($60 for international students). Electronic applications accepted. *Financial support:* In 2015–16, 12 students received support. Research assistantships with full tuition reimbursements available, teaching assistantships with full tuition reimbursements available, Federal Work-Study, scholarships/grants, and unspecified assistantships available. Financial award application deadline: 2/15; financial award applicants required to submit FAFSA. *Faculty research:* Computational chemistry, materials chemistry, organic/polymer synthesis, drug design/delivery, water chemistry. *Unit head:* Dr. Abby L. Parrill, Professor and Chair, 901-678-2638, Fax: 901-678-3447, E-mail: aparrill@memphis.edu. *Application contact:* Dr. Gary Emmert, Associate Professor and Graduate Coordinator, 901-678-2636, Fax: 901-678-3447, E-mail: gemmert@memphis.edu.
Website: http://www.chem.memphis.edu/

University of Miami, Graduate School, College of Arts and Sciences, Department of Chemistry, Coral Gables, FL 33124. Offers chemistry (MS); inorganic chemistry (PhD); organic chemistry (PhD); physical chemistry (PhD). Terminal master's awarded for partial completion of doctoral program. *Degree requirements:* For master's, comprehensive exam; for doctorate, comprehensive exam, thesis/dissertation. *Entrance requirements:* For master's and doctorate, GRE General Test. Additional exam requirements/recommendations for international students: Required—TOEFL (minimum score 550 paper-based). Electronic applications accepted. *Faculty research:* Supramolecular chemistry, electrochemistry, surface chemistry, catalysis, organometalic.

University of Michigan, Rackham Graduate School, College of Literature, Science, and the Arts, Department of Chemistry, Ann Arbor, MI 48109-1055. Offers analytical (PhD); chemical biology (PhD); inorganic (PhD); materials (PhD); organic (PhD); physical (PhD). *Faculty:* 38 full-time (9 women), 9 part-time/adjunct (3 women). *Students:* 264 full-time (113 women). 535 applicants, 31% accepted, 54 enrolled. In 2015, 45 doctorates awarded. *Degree requirements:* For doctorate, comprehensive exam, thesis/dissertation, oral defense of dissertation, organic cumulative proficiency exams. *Entrance requirements:* For doctorate, GRE General Test, GRE Subject Test (recommended), 3 letters of recommendation. Additional exam requirements/recommendations for international students: Required—TOEFL (minimum score 560 paper-based; 84 iBT). *Application deadline:* For fall admission, 12/15 for domestic and international students. Applications are processed on a rolling basis. Application fee: $0 ($90 for international students). Electronic applications accepted. *Financial support:* In 2015–16, 264 students received support, including 40 fellowships with full tuition reimbursements available (averaging $29,000 per year), 78 research assistantships with full tuition reimbursements available (averaging $29,025 per year), 146 teaching assistantships with full tuition reimbursements available (averaging $29,025 per year); career-related internships or fieldwork, scholarships/grants, traineeships, health care benefits, and unspecified assistantships also available. *Faculty research:* Biological catalysis, protein engineering, chemical sensors, de novo metalloprotein design, supramolecular architecture. *Unit head:* Dr. Robert Kennedy, Professor of Chemistry/Chair, 734-763-9681, Fax: 734-647-4847. *Application contact:* Elizabeth Oxford, Graduate Program Coordinator, 734-764-7278, Fax: 734-647-4865,
E-mail: chemadmissions@umich.edu.
Website: http://www.lsa.umich.edu/chem/

University of Missouri, Office of Research and Graduate Studies, College of Arts and Science, Department of Chemistry, Columbia, MO 65211. Offers analytical chemistry (MS, PhD); inorganic chemistry (MS, PhD); organic chemistry (MS, PhD); physical chemistry (MS, PhD). *Degree requirements:* For master's, thesis; for doctorate, one foreign language, comprehensive exam, thesis/dissertation. *Entrance requirements:* For master's, GRE General Test, minimum GPA of 3.0; for doctorate, GRE General Test (minimum score: Verbal 450, Quantitative 600, Analytical 3), minimum GPA of 3.0. Additional exam requirements/recommendations for international students: Required—TOEFL (minimum score 600 paper-based; 100 iBT). Electronic applications accepted. *Faculty research:* Analytical, organic, biological, physical, inorganic and radiochemistry.

University of Missouri–Kansas City, College of Arts and Sciences, Department of Chemistry, Kansas City, MO 64110-2499. Offers analytical chemistry (MS, PhD); inorganic chemistry (MS, PhD); organic chemistry (MS, PhD); physical chemistry (MS, PhD); polymer chemistry (MS, PhD). PhD (interdisciplinary) offered through the School of Graduate Studies. *Program availability:* Part-time, evening/weekend. *Faculty:* 15 full-time (2 women), 1 part-time/adjunct (0 women). *Students:* 3 full-time (2 women), 4 part-time (2 women); includes 1 minority (Black or African American, non-Hispanic/Latino), 3 international. Average age 36. 35 applicants, 23% accepted, 1 enrolled. In 2015, 3 master's awarded. *Degree requirements:* For master's, thesis (for some programs); for doctorate, thesis/dissertation. *Entrance requirements:* For master's, equivalent of American Chemical Society approved bachelor's degree in chemistry; for doctorate, GRE General Test, equivalent of American Chemical Society approved bachelor's degree in chemistry. Additional exam requirements/recommendations for international students: Required—TOEFL (minimum score 550 paper-based; 80 iBT), TWE. *Application deadline:* For fall admission, 4/15 for domestic and international students; for spring admission, 10/15 for domestic and international students. Applications are processed on a rolling basis. Application fee: $45 ($50 for international students). Electronic applications accepted. *Financial support:* In 2015–16, 2 research assistantships with partial tuition reimbursements (averaging $18,000 per year), 30 teaching assistantships with partial tuition reimbursements (averaging $18,062 per year) were awarded; Federal Work-Study, institutionally sponsored loans, and scholarships/grants also available. Support available to part-time students. Financial award application deadline: 3/1; financial award applicants required to submit FAFSA. *Faculty research:* Molecular spectroscopy, characterization and synthesis of materials and compounds, computational chemistry, natural products, drug delivery systems and anti-tumor agents. *Unit head:* Dr. Kathleen V. Kilway, Chair, 816-235-2289, Fax: 816-235-5502, E-mail: kilwayk@umkc.edu. *Application contact:* Graduate Recruiting Committee, 816-235-2272, Fax: 816-235-5502, E-mail: umkc-chemdept@umkc.edu.

University of Montana, Graduate School, College of Humanities and Sciences, Department of Chemistry and Biochemistry, Missoula, MT 59812-0002. Offers chemistry (MS, PhD), including environmental/analytical chemistry, inorganic chemistry, organic chemistry, physical chemistry. Terminal master's awarded for partial completion of doctoral program. *Degree requirements:* For master's, thesis (for some programs); for doctorate, thesis/dissertation. *Entrance requirements:* For master's and doctorate, GRE General Test. Additional exam requirements/recommendations for international students: Required—TOEFL (minimum score 575 paper-based). *Faculty research:* Reaction mechanisms and kinetics, inorganic and organic synthesis, analytical chemistry, natural products.

University of Nebraska–Lincoln, Graduate College, College of Arts and Sciences, Department of Chemistry, Lincoln, NE 68588. Offers analytical chemistry (PhD); biochemistry (PhD); chemistry (MS); inorganic chemistry (PhD); materials chemistry (PhD); organic chemistry (PhD); physical chemistry (PhD). *Degree requirements:* For master's, one foreign language, thesis optional, departmental qualifying exam; for doctorate, one foreign language, comprehensive exam, thesis/dissertation, departmental qualifying exams. *Entrance requirements:* For master's and doctorate, GRE. Additional exam requirements/recommendations for international students: Required—TOEFL (minimum score 550 paper-based). Electronic applications accepted. *Faculty research:* Bioorganic and bioinorganic chemistry, biophysical and bioanalytical chemistry, structure-function of DNA and proteins, organometallics, mass spectrometry.

University of Notre Dame, Graduate School, College of Science, Department of Chemistry and Biochemistry, Notre Dame, IN 46556. Offers biochemistry (MS, PhD); inorganic chemistry (MS, PhD); organic chemistry (MS, PhD); physical chemistry (MS, PhD). Terminal master's awarded for partial completion of doctoral program. *Degree requirements:* For master's, comprehensive exam, thesis; for doctorate, thesis/dissertation, qualifying exam. *Entrance requirements:* For master's and doctorate, GRE General Test, GRE Subject Test (strongly recommended). Additional exam requirements/recommendations for international students: Required—TOEFL (minimum score 600 paper-based; 80 iBT). Electronic applications accepted. *Faculty research:* Reaction design and mechanistic studies; reactive intermediates; synthesis, structure and reactivity of organometallic cluster complexes and biologically active natural products; bioorganic chemistry; enzymology.

University of Regina, Faculty of Graduate Studies and Research, Faculty of Science, Department of Chemistry and Biochemistry, Regina, SK S4S 0A2, Canada. Offers analytical/environmental chemistry (M Sc, PhD); biophysics of biological interfaces (M Sc, PhD); enzymology/chemical biology (M Sc, PhD); inorganic/organometallic chemistry (M Sc, PhD); signal transduction and mechanisms of cancer cell regulation (M Sc, PhD); supramolecular organic photochemistry and photophysics (M Sc, PhD); synthetic organic chemistry (M Sc, PhD); theoretical/computational chemistry (M Sc, PhD). *Degree requirements:* For master's, thesis; for doctorate, thesis/dissertation. *Entrance requirements:* Additional exam requirements/recommendations for international students: Required—TOEFL (minimum score 580 paper-based; 80 iBT), IELTS (minimum score 6.5), PTE (minimum score 59). Electronic applications accepted. *Faculty research:* Asymmetric synthesis and methodology, theoretical and computational chemistry, biophysical biochemistry, analytical and environmental chemistry, chemical biology.

University of Southern Mississippi, Graduate School, College of Science and Technology, Department of Chemistry and Biochemistry, Hattiesburg, MS 39406-0001. Offers inorganic chemistry (MS); organic chemistry (MS); physical chemistry (MS). *Degree requirements:* For master's, comprehensive exam, thesis; for doctorate, comprehensive exam, thesis/dissertation. *Entrance requirements:* For master's, GRE General Test, minimum GPA of 2.75 in last 60 hours; for doctorate, GRE General Test, minimum GPA of 3.5. Additional exam requirements/recommendations for international students: Required—TOEFL, IELTS. *Faculty research:* Plant biochemistry, photo chemistry, polymer chemistry, x-ray analysis, enzyme chemistry.

The University of Tennessee, Graduate School, College of Arts and Sciences, Department of Chemistry, Knoxville, TN 37996. Offers analytical chemistry (MS, PhD); chemical physics (PhD); environmental chemistry (MS, PhD); inorganic chemistry (MS, PhD); organic chemistry (MS, PhD); physical chemistry (MS, PhD); polymer chemistry (MS, PhD); theoretical chemistry (PhD). *Program availability:* Part-time. Terminal master's awarded for partial completion of doctoral program. *Degree requirements:* For master's, thesis; for doctorate, thesis/dissertation. *Entrance requirements:* For master's and doctorate, GRE General Test, minimum GPA of 2.7. Additional exam requirements/recommendations for international students: Required—TOEFL. Electronic applications accepted.

The University of Texas at Austin, Graduate School, College of Natural Sciences, Department of Chemistry and Biochemistry, Austin, TX 78712-1111. Offers analytical chemistry (PhD); biochemistry (PhD); inorganic chemistry (PhD); organic chemistry (PhD); physical chemistry (PhD). *Entrance requirements:* For doctorate, GRE General Test.

The University of Toledo, College of Graduate Studies, College of Natural Sciences and Mathematics, Department of Chemistry, Toledo, OH 43606-3390. Offers analytical chemistry (MS, PhD); biological chemistry (MS, PhD); inorganic chemistry (MS, PhD); organic chemistry (MS, PhD); physical chemistry (MS, PhD). *Program availability:* Part-time. *Degree requirements:* For master's, thesis or alternative; for doctorate, thesis/dissertation. *Entrance requirements:* For master's and doctorate, GRE General Test, GRE Subject Test, minimum cumulative point-hour ratio of 2.7 for all previous academic work, three letters of recommendation, statement of purpose, transcripts from all prior institutions attended. Additional exam requirements/recommendations for international students: Required—TOEFL (minimum score 550 paper-based; 80 iBT). Electronic applications accepted. *Faculty research:* Enzymology, materials chemistry, crystallography, theoretical chemistry.

Vanderbilt University, Department of Chemistry, Nashville, TN 37240-1001. Offers analytical chemistry (MAT, MS, PhD); inorganic chemistry (MAT, MS, PhD); organic chemistry (MAT, MS, PhD); physical chemistry (MAT, MS, PhD); theoretical chemistry (MAT, MS). *Faculty:* 19 full-time (3 women). *Students:* 114 full-time (41 women); includes 19 minority (5 Black or African American, non-Hispanic/Latino; 3 Asian, non-Hispanic/Latino; 7 Hispanic/Latino; 4 Two or more races, non-Hispanic/Latino), 8 international. Average age 26. 339 applicants, 17% accepted, 19 enrolled. In 2015, 11 master's, 13 doctorates awarded. Terminal master's awarded for partial completion of doctoral program. *Degree requirements:* For master's, thesis; for doctorate, thesis/dissertation, area, qualifying, and final exams. *Entrance requirements:* For master's and doctorate, GRE General Test, GRE Subject Test (recommended). Additional exam requirements/recommendations for international students: Required—TOEFL (minimum score 570 paper-based; 88 iBT). *Application deadline:* For fall admission, 1/15 for domestic and international students. Application fee: $0. Electronic applications accepted. *Financial support:* Fellowships with tuition reimbursements, research assistantships with full tuition reimbursements, teaching assistantships with full tuition reimbursements, Federal Work-Study, institutionally sponsored loans, scholarships/grants, traineeships, and health care benefits available. Financial award application deadline: 1/15; financial award applicants required to submit CSS PROFILE or FAFSA. *Faculty research:* Chemical synthesis; mechanistic, theoretical, bioorganic, analytical, and spectroscopic chemistry. *Unit head:* Dr. Carmello Rizzo, Director of Graduate Studies, 615-322-2861, Fax: 615-322-4936, E-mail: c.rizzo@vanderbilt.edu. *Application contact:* Sandra Ford, Administrative Assistant, 615-322-8695, Fax: 615-322-4936, E-mail: sandra.e.ford@vanderbilt.edu.
Website: http://www.vanderbilt.edu/chemistry/

Virginia Commonwealth University, Graduate School, College of Humanities and Sciences, Department of Chemistry, Richmond, VA 23284-9005. Offers analytical chemistry (MS, PhD); chemical physics (PhD); inorganic chemistry (MS, PhD); organic chemistry (MS, PhD); physical chemistry (MS, PhD). *Program availability:* Part-time. Terminal master's awarded for partial completion of doctoral program. *Degree requirements:* For master's, thesis; for doctorate, thesis/dissertation, comprehensive cumulative exams, research proposal. *Entrance requirements:* For master's, GRE General Test, 30 undergraduate credits in chemistry; for doctorate, GRE General Test. Additional exam requirements/recommendations for international students: Required—TOEFL (minimum score 600 paper-based; 100 iBT) or IELTS (minimum score 6.5). Electronic applications accepted. *Faculty research:* Physical, organic, inorganic, analytical, and polymer chemistry; chemical physics.

Wake Forest University, Graduate School of Arts and Sciences, Department of Chemistry, Winston-Salem, NC 27109. Offers analytical chemistry (MS, PhD); inorganic chemistry (MS, PhD); organic chemistry (MS, PhD); physical chemistry (MS, PhD). *Program availability:* Part-time. *Degree requirements:* For master's, one foreign language, comprehensive exam, thesis; for doctorate, 2 foreign languages, comprehensive exam, thesis/dissertation. *Entrance requirements:* For master's and doctorate, GRE General Test. Additional exam requirements/recommendations for international students: Required—TOEFL. Electronic applications accepted.

Wayne State University, College of Liberal Arts and Sciences, Department of Chemistry, Detroit, MI 48202. Offers analytical chemistry (PhD); biochemistry (PhD); chemistry (MA, MS); inorganic chemistry (PhD); organic chemistry (PhD); physical chemistry (PhD). *Faculty:* 29. *Students:* 146 full-time (61 women); includes 9 minority (2 Asian, non-Hispanic/Latino; 3 Hispanic/Latino; 4 Two or more races, non-Hispanic/Latino), 95 international. Average age 28. 280 applicants, 19% accepted, 28 enrolled. In 2015, 4 master's, 22 doctorates awarded. *Degree requirements:* For master's, thesis (for some programs), oral exam; for doctorate, thesis/dissertation, oral exam. *Entrance requirements:* For master's, GRE (strongly recommended), 1 year of physics, math through calculus, general chemistry (8 credits), organic chemistry (8 credits), physical chemistry (6 credits), quantitative analysis (4 credits), advanced chemistry (3 credits), minimum undergraduate GPA of 2.75 in chemistry and cognate sciences, statement of interest, three letters of recommendation; for doctorate, GRE (strongly recommended), minimum undergraduate GPA of 3.0 in chemistry and cognate science. Additional exam requirements/recommendations for international students: Required—TOEFL (minimum score 90 iBT), IELTS (minimum score 6.5), TWE (minimum score 5.5). *Application deadline:* For fall admission, 12/1 priority date for domestic and international students. Applications are processed on a rolling basis. Application fee: $0. Electronic applications accepted. *Expenses:* Tuition, state resident: full-time $14,165; part-time $590.20 per credit hour. Tuition, nonresident: full-time $30,682; part-time $1278.40 per credit hour. *Required fees:* $1688; $47.45 per credit hour. $274.60 per semester. Tuition and fees vary according to course load and program. *Financial support:* In 2015–16, 141 students received support, including 10 fellowships with tuition reimbursements available (averaging $23,000 per year), 54 research assistantships with tuition reimbursements available (averaging $21,609 per year), 73 teaching assistantships with tuition reimbursements available (averaging $21,363 per year); scholarships/grants and unspecified assistantships also available. Financial award application deadline: 3/31; financial award applicants required to submit FAFSA. *Faculty research:* Natural products synthesis, molecular biology, molecular mechanics calculations, organometallic chemistry, experimental physical chemistry. *Total annual research expenditures:* $7.4 million. *Unit head:* Dr. James Rigby, Chair, 313-577-3472,
E-mail: jhr@chem.wayne.edu. *Application contact:* Melissa Barton, Graduate Academic Services Officer, E-mail: melissa@chem.wayne.edu.
Website: http://chem.wayne.edu/

Wesleyan University, Graduate Studies, Department of Chemistry, Middletown, CT 06459. Offers biochemistry (PhD); chemical physics (PhD); inorganic chemistry (PhD); organic chemistry (PhD); physical chemistry (PhD); theoretical chemistry (PhD). *Faculty:* 13 full-time (3 women), 3 part-time/adjunct (2 women). *Students:* 20 full-time (10 women), 2 part-time (0 women); includes 4 minority (1 Black or African American, non-Hispanic/Latino; 3 Asian, non-Hispanic/Latino), 8 international. Average age 25. In 2015, 6 doctorates awarded. Terminal master's awarded for partial completion of doctoral program. *Degree requirements:* For doctorate, thesis/dissertation, proposal. *Entrance requirements:* For doctorate, GRE General Test, 3 recommendations. Additional exam requirements/recommendations for international students: Required—TOEFL, IELTS. *Application deadline:* 2/15 for domestic and international students; for summer admission, 2/15 for domestic and international students. Applications are processed on a rolling basis. Application fee: $0. Electronic applications accepted. *Financial support:* In 2015–16, 4 research assistantships with full tuition reimbursements, 21 teaching assistantships with full tuition reimbursements were awarded; institutionally sponsored loans and health care benefits also available. Financial award application deadline: 4/15; financial award applicants required to submit FAFSA. *Faculty research:* MICHELLE LOUISE PERSONICK Research in the Personick lab is focused on the synthesis of noble metal and noble metal alloy nanoparticles with well-defined shapes and catalytically active high-energy surfaces. Our research takes place at the interface between inorganic chemistry and materials science, and we combine solution-phase nanoparticle synthesis with advanced materials characterization techniques such as scanning electron microscopy (SEM). In addition, we evaluate the catalytic activity of. *Unit head:* Michael Calter, Chair, 860-685-2633, E-mail: mcalter@wesleyan.edu. *Application contact:* Roslyn Brault, Administrative Assistant/Graduate Program Coordinator, 860-685-2573, Fax: 860-685-2211, E-mail: rbrault@wesleyan.edu.
Website: http://www.wesleyan.edu/chem/

West Virginia University, Eberly College of Arts and Sciences, Department of Chemistry, Morgantown, WV 26506. Offers analytical chemistry (MS, PhD); inorganic chemistry (MS, PhD); organic chemistry (MS, PhD); physical chemistry (MS, PhD); theoretical chemistry (MS, PhD). *Program availability:* Part-time, online learning. Terminal master's awarded for partial completion of doctoral program. *Degree requirements:* For master's, thesis; for doctorate, thesis/dissertation. *Entrance requirements:* For master's, GRE General Test, GRE Subject Test (recommended), minimum GPA of 2.5; for doctorate, GRE General Test, GRE Subject Test (recommended), minimum GPA of 2.75. Additional exam requirements/recommendations for international students: Required—TOEFL. Electronic applications accepted. *Expenses:* Tuition, state resident: full-time $8568. Tuition, nonresident: full-time $22,140. Tuition and fees vary according to program. *Faculty research:* Analysis of proteins, drug interactions, solids and effluents by advanced separation methods; new synthetic strategies for complex organic molecules; synthesis and structural characterization of metal complexes for polymerization catalysis, nonlinear science, spectroscopy.

Yale University, Graduate School of Arts and Sciences, Department of Chemistry, New Haven, CT 06520. Offers biophysical chemistry (PhD); inorganic chemistry (PhD); organic chemistry (PhD); physical and theoretical chemistry (PhD). *Degree requirements:* For doctorate, thesis/dissertation. *Entrance requirements:* For doctorate, GRE General Test, GRE Subject Test. Additional exam requirements/recommendations for international students: Required—TOEFL.

Youngstown State University, Graduate School, College of Science, Technology, Engineering and Mathematics, Department of Chemistry, Youngstown, OH 44555-0001. Offers analytical chemistry (MS); biochemistry (MS); chemistry education (MS); inorganic chemistry (MS); organic chemistry (MS); physical chemistry (MS). *Program availability:* Part-time. *Degree requirements:* For master's, thesis. *Entrance requirements:* For master's, bachelor's degree in chemistry, minimum GPA of 2.7. Additional exam requirements/recommendations for international students: Required—TOEFL. *Faculty research:* Analysis of antioxidants, chromatography, defects and disorder in crystalline oxides, hydrogen bonding, novel organic and organometallic materials.

Organic Chemistry

Auburn University, Graduate School, College of Sciences and Mathematics, Department of Chemistry and Biochemistry, Auburn University, AL 36849. Offers analytical chemistry (MS, PhD); biochemistry (MS, PhD); inorganic chemistry (MS, PhD); organic chemistry (MS, PhD); physical chemistry (MS, PhD). *Program availability:* Part-time. *Faculty:* 27 full-time (4 women), 2 part-time/adjunct (0 women). *Students:* 45 full-time (17 women), 26 part-time (15 women); includes 9 minority (7 Black or African American, non-Hispanic/Latino; 1 American Indian or Alaska Native, non-Hispanic/Latino; 1 Asian, non-Hispanic/Latino), 38 international. Average age 27. 33 applicants, 52% accepted, 16 enrolled. In 2015, 1 master's, 6 doctorates awarded. *Degree requirements:* For master's, thesis (for some programs); for doctorate, thesis/dissertation, oral and written exams. *Entrance requirements:* For master's and doctorate, GRE General Test. *Application deadline:* Applications are processed on a rolling basis. Application fee: $50 ($60 for international students). Electronic applications accepted. *Expenses:* Tuition, state resident: full-time $8802; part-time $489 per credit hour. Tuition, nonresident: full-time $26,406; part-time $1467 per credit hour. *Required fees:* $808 per semester. Tuition and fees vary according to degree level and program. *Financial support:* Fellowships, research assistantships, and teaching assistantships available. Financial award application deadline: 3/15; financial award applicants required to submit FAFSA. *Unit head:* Dr. Curtis Shannon, Chair, 334-844-4043, Fax: 334-844-4043. *Application contact:* Dr. George Flowers, Dean of the Graduate School, 334-844-2125.
Website: http://www.auburn.edu/cosam/departments/chemistry/

Binghamton University, State University of New York, Graduate School, School of Arts and Sciences, Department of Chemistry, Vestal, NY 13850. Offers analytical chemistry (PhD); chemistry (MA, MS); environmental chemistry (PhD); inorganic chemistry (PhD); organic chemistry (PhD); physical chemistry (PhD). *Program availability:* Part-time. *Faculty:* 21 full-time (4 women). *Students:* 60 full-time (24 women), 1 part-time (0 women); includes 4 minority (2 Black or African American, non-Hispanic/Latino; 1 Asian, non-Hispanic/Latino; 1 Hispanic/Latino), 40 international. Average age 27. 53 applicants, 81% accepted, 16 enrolled. In 2015, 3 master's, 7 doctorates awarded. Terminal master's awarded for partial completion of doctoral program. *Degree requirements:* For master's, thesis; for doctorate, comprehensive exam, thesis/dissertation. *Entrance requirements:* For master's and doctorate, GRE General Test. Additional exam requirements/recommendations for international students: Required—TOEFL (minimum score 90 iBT). *Application deadline:* Applications are processed on a rolling basis. Application fee: $75. Electronic applications accepted. *Financial support:* In 2015–16, 53 students received support, including 8 research assistantships with full tuition reimbursements available (averaging $18,000 per year), 34 teaching assistantships with full tuition reimbursements available (averaging $18,000 per year); career-related internships or fieldwork, Federal Work-Study, institutionally sponsored loans, scholarships/grants, health care benefits, tuition waivers (full and partial), and unspecified assistantships also available. Financial award applicants required to submit FAFSA. *Unit head:* Dr. Wayne E. Jones, Chairperson, 607-777-2421, E-mail: wjones@binghamton.edu. *Application contact:* Kishan Zuber, Recruiting and Admissions Coordinator, 607-777-2151, Fax: 607-777-2501,
E-mail: kzuber@binghamton.edu.

Boston College, Graduate School of Arts and Sciences, Department of Chemistry, Chestnut Hill, MA 02467. Offers biochemistry (PhD); inorganic chemistry (PhD); organic chemistry (PhD); physical chemistry (PhD); science education (MST). *Faculty:* 21 full-time. *Students:* 121 full-time (57 women); includes 9 minority (6 Asian, non-Hispanic/Latino; 3 Hispanic/Latino), 53 international. 222 applicants, 50% accepted, 43 enrolled. In 2015, 2 master's, 11 doctorates awarded. *Degree requirements:* For doctorate, thesis/dissertation, qualifying exam. *Entrance requirements:* For doctorate, GRE General Test, GRE Subject Test. Additional exam requirements/recommendations for international students: Required—TOEFL (minimum score 600 paper-based; 100 iBT), IELTS (minimum score 8). *Application deadline:* For fall admission, 1/2 for domestic and international students. Application fee: $75. Electronic applications accepted. Tuition and fees vary according to program. *Financial support:* In 2015–16, 121 students received support, including fellowships with full tuition reimbursements available (averaging $30,000 per year), research assistantships with full tuition reimbursements available (averaging $30,000 per year), teaching assistantships with full tuition reimbursements available (averaging $30,000 per year); Federal Work-Study, scholarships/grants, health care benefits, and unspecified assistantships also available. Support available to part-time students. Financial award application deadline: 1/2. *Faculty research:* Organic and organometallic chemistry, chemical biology and biochemistry, physical and theoretical chemistry, inorganic chemistry. *Unit head:* Dr. Amir Hoveyda, Chairperson, 617-552-1735, E-mail: amir.hoveyda@bc.edu. *Application contact:* Dr. Jianmin Gao, Graduate Program Director, 617-552-0326, Fax: 617-552-0833, E-mail: gaojc@bc.edu.
Website: http://www.bc.edu/chemistry

Brandeis University, Graduate School of Arts and Sciences, Department of Chemistry, Waltham, MA 02454. Offers inorganic chemistry (MA, MS, PhD); organic chemistry (MA, MS, PhD); physical chemistry (MS, PhD). *Program availability:* Part-time. *Faculty:* 12 full-time (4 women), 1 part-time/adjunct (0 women). *Students:* 43 full-time (15 women); includes 2 minority (1 Black or African American, non-Hispanic/Latino; 1 Two or more races, non-Hispanic/Latino), 26 international. 102 applicants, 34% accepted, 7 enrolled. In 2015, 8 master's, 6 doctorates awarded. Terminal master's awarded for partial completion of doctoral program. *Degree requirements:* For master's, comprehensive exam, thesis (for some programs), 1 year of residency (for MA); 2 years of residency (for MS); for doctorate, comprehensive exam, thesis/dissertation, 3 years of residency, 2 seminars, qualifying exams. *Entrance requirements:* For master's and doctorate, GRE General Test, resume, statement of purpose, letters of recommendation. Additional exam requirements/recommendations for international students: Required—TOEFL (minimum score 600 paper-based; 100 iBT); Recommended—IELTS (minimum score 7), TSE (minimum score 68). *Application deadline:* For fall admission, 1/15 priority date for domestic students. Application fee: $75. Electronic applications accepted. *Financial support:* In 2015–16, 42 students received support, including 24 fellowships with full tuition reimbursements available (averaging $27,500 per year), 18 research assistantships with full tuition reimbursements available (averaging $27,500 per year); Federal Work-Study, scholarships/grants, health care benefits, tuition waivers (partial), and unspecified assistantships also available. Support available to part-time students. Financial award application deadline: 4/15; financial award applicants required to submit FAFSA. *Faculty research:* Inorganic and organic chemistry, physical chemistry, chemical biology, biophysical chemistry, materials chemistry. *Unit head:* Dr. Judith Herzfeld, Chair, Graduate Program, 781-736-2540, Fax: 781-736-2516,
E-mail: herzfeld@brandeis.edu. *Application contact:* Dr. Maryanna Aldrich, Coordinator, 781-736-2500, Fax: 781-736-2516, E-mail: scigradoffice@brandeis.edu.
Website: http://www.brandeis.edu/gsas

California State University, Los Angeles, Graduate Studies, College of Natural and Social Sciences, Department of Chemistry and Biochemistry, Los Angeles, CA 90032-8530. Offers analytical chemistry (MS); biochemistry (MS); chemistry (MS); inorganic chemistry (MS); organic chemistry (MS); physical chemistry (MS). *Program availability:* Part-time, evening/weekend. *Degree requirements:* For master's, one foreign language, comprehensive exam or thesis. *Entrance requirements:* Additional exam requirements/recommendations for international students: Required—TOEFL. *Faculty research:* Intercalation of heavy metal, carborane chemistry, conductive polymers and fabrics, titanium reagents, computer modeling and synthesis.

Cleveland State University, College of Graduate Studies, College of Sciences and Health Professions, Department of Chemistry, Cleveland, OH 44115. Offers analytical chemistry (MS); clinical/bioanalytical chemistry (PhD), including cellular and molecular medicine, clinical/bioanalytical chemistry; inorganic chemistry (MS); pharmaceutical/organic chemistry (MS); physical chemistry (MS). *Program availability:* Part-time, evening/weekend. *Faculty:* 17 full-time (3 women). *Students:* 63 full-time (30 women), 25 part-time (10 women); includes 4 minority (1 Black or African American, non-Hispanic/Latino; 1 Asian, non-Hispanic/Latino; 2 Hispanic/Latino), 48 international. Average age 30. 22 applicants, 64% accepted, 12 enrolled. In 2015, 16 master's, 8 doctorates awarded. *Degree requirements:* For master's, thesis optional; for doctorate, comprehensive exam, thesis/dissertation. *Entrance requirements:* For master's and doctorate, GRE General Test. Additional exam requirements/recommendations for international students: Required—TOEFL (minimum score 550 paper-based; 78 iBT). *Application deadline:* For fall admission, 1/15 priority date for domestic and international students. Applications are processed on a rolling basis. Application fee: $30. Electronic applications accepted. *Expenses:* Tuition, state resident: full-time $9565. Tuition, nonresident: full-time $17,980. Tuition and fees vary according to program. *Financial support:* In 2015–16, 44 students received support, including 10 fellowships with full tuition reimbursements available (averaging $22,500 per year), 6 research assistantships with full tuition reimbursements available (averaging $22,500 per year), 34 teaching assistantships with full tuition reimbursements available (averaging $21,000 per year); scholarships/grants and unspecified assistantships also available. Financial award application deadline: 1/15. *Faculty research:* Bioanalytical techniques and molecular diagnostics, glycoproteomics and antithrombotic agents, drug discovery and innovation, analytical pharmacology, inflammatory disease research. *Total annual research expenditures:* $3 million. *Unit head:* Dr. David W. Ball, Chair, 216-687-2467, Fax: 216-687-9298, E-mail: d.ball@csuohio.edu. *Application contact:* Richelle P. Emery, Administrative Coordinator, 216-687-2457, Fax: 216-687-9298,
E-mail: r.emery@csuohio.edu.
Website: http://www.csuohio.edu/sciences/chemistry

Cornell University, Graduate School, Graduate Fields of Arts and Sciences, Field of Chemistry and Chemical Biology, Ithaca, NY 14853-0001. Offers analytical chemistry (PhD); bio-organic chemistry (PhD); biophysical chemistry (PhD); chemical biology (PhD); chemical physics (PhD); inorganic chemistry (PhD); materials chemistry (PhD); organic chemistry (PhD); organometallic chemistry (PhD); physical chemistry (PhD); polymer chemistry (PhD); theoretical chemistry (PhD). *Degree requirements:* For doctorate, comprehensive exam, thesis/dissertation. *Entrance requirements:* For doctorate, GRE General Test, GRE Subject Test (chemistry), 3 letters of recommendation. Additional exam requirements/recommendations for international students: Required—TOEFL (minimum score 600 paper-based; 77 iBT). Electronic applications accepted. *Faculty research:* Analytical, organic, inorganic, physical, materials, chemical biology.

Eastern New Mexico University, Graduate School, College of Liberal Arts and Sciences, Department of Physical Sciences, Portales, NM 88130. Offers chemistry

(MS), including analytical, biochemistry, inorganic, organic, physical. *Program availability:* Part-time. *Degree requirements:* For master's, thesis optional, seminar, oral and written comprehensive exams. *Entrance requirements:* For master's, ACS placement examination, minimum GPA of 3.0; 2 letters of recommendation; personal statement of career goals; bachelor's degree with one year minimum each of general, organic, and analytical chemistry. Additional exam requirements/recommendations for international students: Required—TOEFL (minimum score 550 paper-based; 79 iBT), IELTS (minimum score 6). Electronic applications accepted. *Faculty research:* Synfuel, electrochemistry, protein chemistry.

Florida State University, The Graduate School, College of Arts and Sciences, Department of Chemistry and Biochemistry, Tallahassee, FL 32306-4390. Offers analytical chemistry (MS, PhD); biochemistry (MS, PhD); inorganic chemistry (MS, PhD); materials chemistry (PhD); organic chemistry (MS, PhD); physical chemistry (MS, PhD). *Faculty:* 40 full-time (6 women), 4 part-time/adjunct (2 women). *Students:* 162 full-time (56 women); includes 37 minority (8 Black or African American, non-Hispanic/Latino; 6 Asian, non-Hispanic/Latino; 18 Hispanic/Latino; 1 Native Hawaiian or other Pacific Islander, non-Hispanic/Latino; 4 Two or more races, non-Hispanic/Latino), 54 international. Average age 28. 182 applicants, 47% accepted, 31 enrolled. In 2015, 6 master's, 18 doctorates awarded. Terminal master's awarded for partial completion of doctoral program. *Degree requirements:* For master's, thesis (for some programs); for doctorate, thesis/dissertation. *Entrance requirements:* For master's and doctorate, GRE General Test (minimum scores: 150 verbal, 151 quantitative; 1100 total on the old scale), minimum GPA of 3.1 in undergraduate course work. Additional exam requirements/recommendations for international students: Required—TOEFL (minimum score 90 iBT). *Application deadline:* For fall admission, 12/15 priority date for domestic and international students. Application fee: $30. Electronic applications accepted. *Expenses: Tuition, area resident:* Full-time $7263; part-time $403.50 per credit hour. Tuition, nonresident: full-time $18,087; part-time $1004.85 per credit hour. *Required fees:* $1365; $75.81 per credit hour. $20 per semester. Tuition and fees vary according to campus/location. *Financial support:* In 2015–16, 162 students received support, including 4 fellowships with tuition reimbursements available (averaging $22,000 per year), 51 research assistantships with full tuition reimbursements available (averaging $22,809 per year), 67 teaching assistantships with full tuition reimbursements available (averaging $22,809 per year). Financial award application deadline: 12/15; financial award applicants required to submit FAFSA. *Faculty research:* Bioanalytical chemistry, including separations, microfluidics, petroleomics; materials chemistry, including magnets, polymers, catalysts, nanomaterials; spectroscopy, including NMR and EPR, ultrafast, Raman, and mass spectrometry; organic synthesis, natural products, photochemistry, and supramolecular chemistry; biochemistry, with focus on structural biology, metabolomics, and anticancer drugs. *Total annual research expenditures:* $3.5 million. *Unit head:* Dr. Timothy Logan, Chairman, 850-644-3810, Fax: 850-644-8281, E-mail: gradinfo@chem.fsu.edu. *Application contact:* Dr. Geoffrey Strouse, Associate Chair for Graduate Studies, 850-445-9042, Fax: 850-644-8281,
E-mail: gradinfo@chem.fsu.edu.
Website: http://www.chem.fsu.edu/

Georgetown University, Graduate School of Arts and Sciences, Department of Chemistry, Washington, DC 20057. Offers analytical chemistry (PhD); biochemistry (PhD); computational chemistry (PhD); inorganic chemistry (PhD); materials chemistry (PhD); organic chemistry (PhD); theoretical chemistry (PhD). Terminal master's awarded for partial completion of doctoral program. *Degree requirements:* For doctorate, comprehensive exam, thesis/dissertation. *Entrance requirements:* For doctorate, GRE General Test. Additional exam requirements/recommendations for international students: Required—TOEFL.

The George Washington University, Columbian College of Arts and Sciences, Department of Chemistry, Washington, DC 20052. Offers analytical chemistry (MS, PhD); inorganic chemistry (MS, PhD); materials science (MS, PhD); organic chemistry (MS, PhD); physical chemistry (MS, PhD). *Program availability:* Part-time, evening/weekend. *Faculty:* 17 full-time (6 women), 4 part-time/adjunct (1 woman). *Students:* 25 full-time (13 women), 12 part-time (5 women); includes 2 minority (1 Asian, non-Hispanic/Latino; 1 Hispanic/Latino), 10 international. Average age 28. 60 applicants, 37% accepted, 9 enrolled. In 2015, 2 master's, 6 doctorates awarded. Terminal master's awarded for partial completion of doctoral program. *Degree requirements:* For master's, comprehensive exam, thesis or alternative; for doctorate, thesis/dissertation, general exam. *Entrance requirements:* For master's and doctorate, GRE General Test, interview, minimum GPA of 3.0. Additional exam requirements/recommendations for international students: Required—TOEFL (minimum score 550 paper-based; 80 iBT). *Application deadline:* For fall admission, 1/15 priority date for domestic and international students; for spring admission, 9/1 priority date for domestic and international students. Applications are processed on a rolling basis. Application fee: $75. Electronic applications accepted. *Financial support:* In 2015–16, 27 students received support. Fellowships with tuition reimbursements available, research assistantships, teaching assistantships with tuition reimbursements available, Federal Work-Study, and tuition waivers available. Financial award application deadline: 1/15. *Unit head:* Dr. Michael King, Chair, 202-994-6488. *Application contact:* Information Contact, 202-994-6121, E-mail: gwchem@gwu.edu.
Website: http://chemistry.columbian.gwu.edu/

Georgia State University, College of Arts and Sciences, Department of Chemistry, Atlanta, GA 30302-3083. Offers analytical chemistry (MS, PhD); biochemistry (MS, PhD); bioinformatics (MS, PhD); biophysical chemistry (PhD); computational chemistry (MS, PhD); geochemistry (PhD); organic/medicinal chemistry (MS, PhD); physical chemistry (MS). PhD in geochemistry offered jointly with Department of Geosciences. *Program availability:* Part-time. *Faculty:* 26 full-time (4 women). *Students:* 158 full-time (53 women), 4 part-time (all women); includes 43 minority (22 Black or African American, non-Hispanic/Latino; 1 American Indian or Alaska Native, non-Hispanic/Latino; 9 Asian, non-Hispanic/Latino; 7 Hispanic/Latino; 4 Two or more races, non-Hispanic/Latino), 81 international. Average age 28. 117 applicants, 50% accepted, 42 enrolled. In 2015, 28 master's, 15 doctorates awarded. Terminal master's awarded for partial completion of doctoral program. *Degree requirements:* For master's, one foreign language, comprehensive exam (for some programs), thesis (for some programs); for doctorate, one foreign language, comprehensive exam, thesis/dissertation. *Entrance requirements:* For master's and doctorate, GRE. Additional exam requirements/recommendations for international students: Required—TOEFL (minimum score 550 paper-based; 80 iBT) or IELTS (minimum score 6.5). *Application deadline:* For fall admission, 7/1 priority date for domestic and international students; for winter admission, 11/15 priority date for domestic and international students; for spring admission, 4/15 priority date for domestic and international students. Applications are processed on a rolling basis. Application fee: $50. Electronic applications accepted. *Expenses:* Tuition, state resident: full-time $6876; part-time $382 per credit hour. Tuition, nonresident: full-time $22,374; part-time $1243 per credit hour. *Required fees:* $2128; $2128 per term. $1064 per term. Part-time tuition and fees vary according to course load and program. *Financial support:* Fellowships with full tuition reimbursements, research assistantships with full tuition reimbursements, and teaching assistantships with full tuition reimbursements available. Financial award applicants required to submit FAFSA. *Faculty research:* Analytical chemistry, biological/biochemistry, biophysical/computational chemistry, chemical education, organic/medicinal chemistry. *Unit head:* Dr. Peng George Wang, Department Chair, 404-413-3591, Fax: 404-413-5505,
E-mail: pwang11@gsu.edu.
Website: http://chemistry.gsu.edu/

Harvard University, Graduate School of Arts and Sciences, Department of Chemistry and Chemical Biology, Cambridge, MA 02138. Offers biochemical chemistry (PhD); inorganic chemistry (PhD); organic chemistry (PhD); physical chemistry (PhD). *Degree requirements:* For doctorate, thesis/dissertation, cumulative exams. *Entrance requirements:* For doctorate, GRE General Test, GRE Subject Test. Additional exam requirements/recommendations for international students: Required—TOEFL.

Howard University, Graduate School, Department of Chemistry, Washington, DC 20059-0002. Offers analytical chemistry (MS, PhD); atmospheric (MS, PhD); biochemistry (MS, PhD); environmental (MS, PhD); inorganic chemistry (MS, PhD); organic chemistry (MS, PhD); physical chemistry (MS, PhD). Terminal master's awarded for partial completion of doctoral program. *Degree requirements:* For master's, comprehensive exam, thesis, teaching experience; for doctorate, comprehensive exam, thesis/dissertation, teaching experience. *Entrance requirements:* For master's, GRE General Test, minimum GPA of 2.7; for doctorate, GRE General Test, minimum GPA of 3.0. Additional exam requirements/recommendations for international students: Required—TOEFL. Electronic applications accepted. *Faculty research:* Synthetic organics, materials, natural products, mass spectrometry.

Indiana University Bloomington, University Graduate School, College of Arts and Sciences, Department of Chemistry, Bloomington, IN 47405. Offers analytical chemistry (PhD); chemical biology (PhD); chemistry (MAT); inorganic chemistry (PhD); materials chemistry (PhD); organic chemistry (PhD); physical chemistry (PhD); MSES/MS. Terminal master's awarded for partial completion of doctoral program. *Degree requirements:* For master's, thesis; for doctorate, thesis/dissertation. *Entrance requirements:* For master's and doctorate, GRE General Test, GRE Subject Test. Additional exam requirements/recommendations for international students: Required—TOEFL. Electronic applications accepted. *Faculty research:* Synthesis of complex natural products, organic reaction mechanisms, organic electrochemistry, transitive-metal chemistry, solid-state and surface chemistry.

Instituto Tecnológico y de Estudios Superiores de Monterrey, Campus Monterrey, Graduate and Research Division, Program in Natural and Social Sciences, Monterrey, Mexico. Offers biotechnology (MS); chemistry (MS, PhD); communications (MS); education (MA). *Program availability:* Part-time. *Degree requirements:* For master's, one foreign language, thesis; for doctorate, one foreign language, thesis/dissertation. *Entrance requirements:* For master's, EXADEP; for doctorate, EXADEP, master's degree in related field. Additional exam requirements/recommendations for international students: Required—TOEFL. *Faculty research:* Cultural industries, mineral substances, bioremediation, food processing, CQ in industrial chemical processing.

Iowa State University of Science and Technology, Program in Organic Chemistry, Ames, IA 50011. Offers MS, PhD. *Entrance requirements:* Additional exam requirements/recommendations for international students: Required—TOEFL (minimum score 570 paper-based; 89 iBT), IELTS (minimum score 6.5). Electronic applications accepted.

Kansas State University, Graduate School, College of Arts and Sciences, Department of Chemistry, Manhattan, KS 66506. Offers analytical chemistry (MS); biological chemistry (MS); inorganic chemistry (MS); materials chemistry (MS); organic chemistry (MS); physical chemistry (MS). Terminal master's awarded for partial completion of doctoral program. *Degree requirements:* For master's, thesis; for doctorate, thesis/dissertation. *Entrance requirements:* For master's and doctorate, GRE, minimum GPA of 3.0. Additional exam requirements/recommendations for international students: Required—TOEFL (minimum score 550 paper-based). Electronic applications accepted. *Faculty research:* Inorganic chemistry, organic and biological chemistry, analytical chemistry, physical chemistry, materials chemistry and nanotechnology.

Laurentian University, School of Graduate Studies and Research, Programme in Chemistry and Biochemistry, Sudbury, ON P3E 2C6, Canada. Offers analytical chemistry (M Sc); biochemistry (M Sc); environmental chemistry (M Sc); organic chemistry (M Sc); physical/theoretical chemistry (M Sc). *Program availability:* Part-time. *Degree requirements:* For master's, thesis or alternative. *Entrance requirements:* For master's, honors degree with minimum second class. *Faculty research:* Cell cycle checkpoints, kinetic modeling, toxicology to metal stress, quantum chemistry, biogeochemistry metal speciation.

Marquette University, Graduate School, College of Arts and Sciences, Department of Chemistry, Milwaukee, WI 53201-1881. Offers analytical chemistry (MS, PhD); bioanalytical chemistry (MS, PhD); biophysical chemistry (MS, PhD); chemical physics (MS, PhD); inorganic chemistry (MS, PhD); organic chemistry (MS, PhD); physical chemistry (MS, PhD). *Program availability:* Part-time. *Faculty:* 19 full-time (3 women), 1 part-time/adjunct (0 women). *Students:* 43 full-time (14 women), 4 part-time (0 women); includes 2 minority (1 Asian, non-Hispanic/Latino; 1 Hispanic/Latino), 32 international. Average age 28. In 2015, 4 master's, 4 doctorates awarded. Terminal master's awarded for partial completion of doctoral program. *Degree requirements:* For master's, comprehensive exam; for doctorate, thesis/dissertation, cumulative exams. *Entrance requirements:* For master's and doctorate, official transcripts from all current and previous colleges/universities except Marquette, three letters of recommendation from individuals familiar with the applicant's academic work. Additional exam requirements/recommendations for international students: Required—TOEFL (minimum score 530 paper-based). *Application deadline:* Applications are processed on a rolling basis. Application fee: $50. Electronic applications accepted. *Financial support:* In 2015–16, 41 students received support, including 2 fellowships (averaging $17,134 per year), 30 teaching assistantships with full tuition reimbursements available (averaging $20,295 per year); research assistantships, scholarships/grants, health care benefits, tuition waivers (full and partial), and unspecified assistantships also available. Support available to part-time students. Financial award application deadline: 2/15. *Faculty research:* Inorganic complexes, laser Raman spectroscopy, organic synthesis, synthetic bioinorganic chemistry, electro-active organic molecules. *Total annual research expenditures:* $1.2 million. *Unit head:* Dr. Scott Reid, Chair, 414-288-7565,
E-mail: scott.reid@marquette.edu. *Application contact:* Dr. Adam Fiedler, New and Recruiting, 414-288-1625.
Website: http://www.marquette.edu/chem/graduate.shtml

Massachusetts Institute of Technology, School of Engineering, Department of Civil and Environmental Engineering, Cambridge, MA 02139. Offers biological oceanography (PhD, Sc D); chemical oceanography (PhD, Sc D); civil and environmental engineering (M Eng, SM, PhD, Sc D); civil and environmental systems (PhD, Sc D); civil engineering (PhD, Sc D, CE); coastal engineering (PhD, Sc D); construction engineering and management (PhD, Sc D); environmental biology (PhD, Sc D); environmental chemistry

(PhD, Sc D); environmental engineering (PhD, Sc D); environmental fluid mechanics (PhD, Sc D); geotechnical and geoenvironmental engineering (PhD, Sc D); hydrology (PhD, Sc D); information technology (PhD, Sc D); oceanographic engineering (PhD, Sc D); structures and materials (PhD, Sc D); transportation (PhD, Sc D); SM/MBA. *Faculty:* 27 full-time (5 women). *Students:* 183 full-time (59 women); includes 19 minority (1 Black or African American, non-Hispanic/Latino; 7 Asian, non-Hispanic/Latino; 8 Hispanic/Latino; 3 Two or more races, non-Hispanic/Latino), 106 international. Average age 27. 513 applicants, 20% accepted, 56 enrolled. In 2015, 77 master's, 18 doctorates, 1 other advanced degree awarded. *Degree requirements:* For master's, thesis; for doctorate, comprehensive exam, thesis/dissertation; for CE, comprehensive exam, thesis. *Entrance requirements:* For master's and doctorate, GRE General Test; for CE, GRE General Test. Additional exam requirements/recommendations for international students: Required—TOEFL (minimum score 577 paper-based; 100 iBT), IELTS (minimum score 7). *Application deadline:* For fall admission, 12/15 for domestic and international students. Application fee: $75. Electronic applications accepted. *Expenses: Tuition:* Full-time $46,400; part-time $725 per credit. One-time fee: $304 full-time. Full-time tuition and fees vary according to course load and program. *Financial support:* In 2015–16, 150 students received support, including 38 fellowships (averaging $38,000 per year), 111 research assistantships (averaging $35,100 per year), 9 teaching assistantships (averaging $39,900 per year); Federal Work-Study, institutionally sponsored loans, scholarships/grants, traineeships, health care benefits, and unspecified assistantships also available. Support available to part-time students. Financial award application deadline: 4/15; financial award applicants required to submit FAFSA. *Faculty research:* Environmental chemistry, environmental fluid mechanics and coastal engineering, environmental microbiology, geotechnical engineering and geomechanics, hydrology and hydroclimatology, infrastructure systems, mechanics of materials and structures, transportation systems. *Total annual research expenditures:* $24.8 million. *Unit head:* Prof. Markus Buehler, Department Head, 617-253-7101. *Application contact:* Graduate Admissions Coordinator, 617-253-7119,
E-mail: cee-admissions@mit.edu.
Website: http://cee.mit.edu/

Massachusetts Institute of Technology, School of Science, Department of Chemistry, Cambridge, MA 02139. Offers biological chemistry (PhD); inorganic chemistry (PhD); organic chemistry (PhD); physical chemistry (PhD). *Faculty:* 29 full-time (6 women). *Students:* 236 full-time (81 women); includes 51 minority (2 Black or African American, non-Hispanic/Latino; 1 American Indian or Alaska Native, non-Hispanic/Latino; 30 Asian, non-Hispanic/Latino; 12 Hispanic/Latino; 6 Two or more races, non-Hispanic/Latino), 83 international. Average age 26. 591 applicants, 18% accepted, 38 enrolled. In 2015, 40 doctorates awarded. *Degree requirements:* For doctorate, comprehensive exam, thesis/dissertation, teaching assistantship during two semesters. *Entrance requirements:* For doctorate, GRE General Test. Additional exam requirements/recommendations for international students: Required—TOEFL (minimum score 600 paper-based), IELTS (minimum score 7). *Application deadline:* For fall admission, 12/15 for domestic and international students. Application fee: $75. Electronic applications accepted. *Expenses: Tuition:* Full-time $46,400; part-time $725 per credit. One-time fee: $304 full-time. Full-time tuition and fees vary according to course load and program. *Financial support:* In 2015–16, 218 students received support, including 62 fellowships (averaging $45,800 per year), 129 research assistantships (averaging $37,000 per year), 43 teaching assistantships (averaging $38,300 per year); Federal Work-Study, institutionally sponsored loans, scholarships/grants, traineeships, health care benefits, and unspecified assistantships also available. Support available to part-time students. Financial award application deadline: 4/15; financial award applicants required to submit FAFSA. *Faculty research:* Synthetic organic and organometallic chemistry including catalysis; biological chemistry including bioorganic chemistry; physical chemistry including chemical dynamics, theoretical chemistry and biophysical chemistry; inorganic chemistry including synthesis, catalysis, bioinorganic and physical inorganic chemistry; materials chemistry including surface science, nanoscience and polymers. *Total annual research expenditures:* $30.3 million. *Unit head:* Prof. Timothy F. Jamison, Department Head, 617-253-1803, Fax: 617-258-7500. *Application contact:* Graduate Administrator, 617-253-1845, Fax: 617-258-0241, E-mail: chemgradeducation@mit.edu.
Website: http://web.mit.edu/chemistry/

McMaster University, School of Graduate Studies, Faculty of Science, Department of Chemistry, Hamilton, ON L8S 4M2, Canada. Offers analytical chemistry (M Sc, PhD); chemical physics (M Sc, PhD); chemistry (M Sc, PhD); inorganic chemistry (M Sc, PhD); organic chemistry (M Sc, PhD); physical chemistry (M Sc, PhD); polymer chemistry (M Sc, PhD). *Program availability:* Part-time. Terminal master's awarded for partial completion of doctoral program. *Degree requirements:* For master's, thesis; for doctorate, comprehensive exam, thesis/dissertation. *Entrance requirements:* For master's, minimum B+ average. Additional exam requirements/recommendations for international students: Required—TOEFL (minimum score 550 paper-based).

Old Dominion University, College of Sciences, Program in Chemistry, Norfolk, VA 23529. Offers analytical (MS, PhD); biochemistry (MS, PhD); environmental (MS, PhD); inorganic (MS, PhD); organic (MS, PhD); physical (MS, PhD). *Program availability:* Part-time, evening/weekend. *Faculty:* 19 full-time (5 women). *Students:* 35 full-time (17 women), 6 part-time (2 women); includes 5 minority (4 Black or African American, non-Hispanic/Latino; 1 Two or more races, non-Hispanic/Latino), 16 international. Average age 27. 20 applicants, 55% accepted, 4 enrolled. In 2015, 9 master's, 9 doctorates awarded. *Degree requirements:* For master's, comprehensive exam, thesis (for some programs); for doctorate, comprehensive exam, thesis/dissertation. *Entrance requirements:* For master's and doctorate, GRE General Test, minimum GPA of 3.0 in major, 2.5 overall, transcripts, essay, three letters of recommendation, resume. Additional exam requirements/recommendations for international students: Required—TOEFL. *Application deadline:* For fall admission, 7/1 for domestic students, 1/15 for international students; for spring admission, 11/1 for domestic students, 8/15 for international students. Applications are processed on a rolling basis. Application fee: $50. Electronic applications accepted. *Expenses:* $464 per credit in-state tuition; $1,160 per credit out-of-state tuition. *Financial support:* In 2015–16, 42 students received support, including 2 fellowships with full tuition reimbursements available (averaging $18,000 per year), 10 research assistantships with full tuition reimbursements available (averaging $18,000 per year), 33 teaching assistantships with full tuition reimbursements available (averaging $18,000 per year); career-related internships or fieldwork, institutionally sponsored loans, scholarships/grants, health care benefits, and unspecified assistantships also available. Financial award application deadline: 2/15; financial award applicants required to submit FAFSA. *Faculty research:* Biogeochemistry, materials chemistry, computational chemistry, organic chemistry, biofuels. *Total annual research expenditures:* $2.6 million. *Unit head:* Dr. John R. Donat, Graduate Program Director, 757-683-4098, Fax: 757-683-4628,
E-mail: chemgpd@odu.edu. *Application contact:* Kristi Rehrauer, Graduate Program Assistant, 757-683-6979, Fax: 757-683-4628, E-mail: krehraue@odu.edu.

Oregon State University, College of Science, Program in Chemistry, Corvallis, OR 97331. Offers analytical chemistry (MA, MS, PhD); inorganic chemistry (MA, MS, PhD); materials chemistry (MA, MS, PhD); nuclear chemistry (MA, MS, PhD); organic chemistry (MA, MS, PhD); physical chemistry (MA, MS, PhD). *Program availability:* Part-time. *Faculty:* 23 full-time (6 women). *Students:* 111 full-time (38 women), 4 part-time (2 women); includes 14 minority (1 Black or African American, non-Hispanic/Latino; 5 Asian, non-Hispanic/Latino; 6 Hispanic/Latino; 2 Two or more races, non-Hispanic/Latino), 49 international. Average age 28. 47 applicants, 51% accepted, 22 enrolled. In 2015, 6 master's, 12 doctorates awarded. Terminal master's awarded for partial completion of doctoral program. *Degree requirements:* For master's, one foreign language, thesis; for doctorate, one foreign language, thesis/dissertation. *Entrance requirements:* For master's and doctorate, GRE, minimum GPA of 3.0 in last 90 hours of course work. Additional exam requirements/recommendations for international students: Required—TOEFL (minimum score 80 iBT), IELTS (minimum score 6.5). *Application deadline:* For fall admission, 4/1 for domestic students. Application fee: $75 ($85 for international students). *Expenses:* Tuition, state resident: full-time $12,150; part-time $450 per credit. Tuition, nonresident: full-time $20,952; part-time $776 per credit. *Required fees:* $1572; $1443 per unit. One-time fee: $350. Tuition and fees vary according to course load, campus/location and program. *Financial support:* Fellowships, research assistantships, and teaching assistantships available. Support available to part-time students. *Faculty research:* Solid state chemistry, enzyme reaction mechanisms, structure and dynamics of gas molecules, chemiluminescence, nonlinear optical spectroscopy. *Unit head:* Dr. Rich G. Carter, Professor/Chair. *Application contact:* Sarah Burton, Chemistry Advisor, 541-737-6808,
E-mail: chemadm@chem.oregonstate.edu.
Website: http://chemistry.oregonstate.edu/

Purdue University, Graduate School, College of Science, Department of Chemistry, West Lafayette, IN 47907. Offers analytical chemistry (MS, PhD); biochemistry (MS, PhD); chemical education (MS, PhD); inorganic chemistry (MS, PhD); organic chemistry (MS, PhD); physical chemistry (MS, PhD). Terminal master's awarded for partial completion of doctoral program. *Degree requirements:* For master's, thesis; for doctorate, comprehensive exam, thesis/dissertation. *Entrance requirements:* For master's and doctorate, minimum undergraduate GPA of 3.0. Additional exam requirements/recommendations for international students: Required—TOEFL (minimum score 550 paper-based; 77 iBT); Recommended—TWE. Electronic applications accepted.

Rice University, Graduate Programs, Wiess School of Natural Sciences, Department of Chemistry, Houston, TX 77251-1892. Offers chemistry (MA); inorganic chemistry (PhD); organic chemistry (PhD); physical chemistry (PhD). Terminal master's awarded for partial completion of doctoral program. *Degree requirements:* For master's, thesis; for doctorate, thesis/dissertation. *Entrance requirements:* For master's and doctorate, GRE General Test, minimum GPA of 3.0. Additional exam requirements/recommendations for international students: Required—TOEFL (minimum score 600 paper-based; 90 iBT). Electronic applications accepted. *Faculty research:* Nanoscience, biomaterials, nanobioinformatics, fullerene pharmaceuticals.

Rutgers University–Newark, Graduate School, Program in Chemistry, Newark, NJ 07102. Offers analytical chemistry (MS, PhD); biochemistry (MS, PhD); inorganic chemistry (MS, PhD); organic chemistry (MS, PhD); physical chemistry (MS, PhD). *Program availability:* Part-time, evening/weekend. Terminal master's awarded for partial completion of doctoral program. *Degree requirements:* For master's, thesis optional, cumulative exams; for doctorate, thesis/dissertation, exams, research proposal. *Entrance requirements:* For master's and doctorate, GRE General Test, minimum undergraduate B average. Additional exam requirements/recommendations for international students: Required—TOEFL. Electronic applications accepted. *Faculty research:* Medicinal chemistry, natural products, isotope effects, biophysics and biorganic approaches to enzyme mechanisms, organic and organometallic synthesis.

Rutgers University–New Brunswick, Graduate School-New Brunswick, Department of Chemistry and Chemical Biology, Piscataway, NJ 08854-8097. Offers biological chemistry (MS, PhD); inorganic chemistry (MS, PhD); organic chemistry (MS, PhD); physical chemistry (MS, PhD). *Program availability:* Part-time, evening/weekend. Terminal master's awarded for partial completion of doctoral program. *Degree requirements:* For master's, thesis or alternative, exam; for doctorate, thesis/dissertation, 1 year residency. *Entrance requirements:* For master's and doctorate, GRE General Test, GRE Subject Test. Additional exam requirements/recommendations for international students: Required—TOEFL. Electronic applications accepted. *Faculty research:* Biophysical organic/bioorganic, inorganic/bioinorganic, theoretical, and solid-state/surface chemistry.

Seton Hall University, College of Arts and Sciences, Department of Chemistry and Biochemistry, South Orange, NJ 07079-2697. Offers analytical chemistry (MS, PhD); biochemistry (MS, PhD); chemistry (MS); inorganic chemistry (MS, PhD); organic chemistry (MS, PhD); physical chemistry (MS, PhD). *Program availability:* Part-time, evening/weekend. Terminal master's awarded for partial completion of doctoral program. *Degree requirements:* For master's, thesis optional; for doctorate, comprehensive exam, thesis/dissertation. *Entrance requirements:* Additional exam requirements/recommendations for international students: Required—TOEFL. Electronic applications accepted. *Faculty research:* DNA metal reactions; chromatography; bioinorganic, biophysical, organometallic, polymer chemistry; heterogeneous catalyst; synthetic organic and carbohydrate chemistry.

Southern University and Agricultural and Mechanical College, Graduate School, College of Sciences, Department of Chemistry, Baton Rouge, LA 70813. Offers analytical chemistry (MS); biochemistry (MS); environmental sciences (MS); inorganic chemistry (MS); organic chemistry (MS); physical chemistry (MS). *Degree requirements:* For master's, thesis. *Entrance requirements:* For master's, GMAT or GRE General Test. Additional exam requirements/recommendations for international students: Required—TOEFL (minimum score 525 paper-based). *Faculty research:* Synthesis of macrocyclic ligands, latex accelerators, anticancer drugs, biosensors, absorption isotheums, isolation of specific enzymes from plants.

State University of New York College of Environmental Science and Forestry, Department of Chemistry, Syracuse, NY 13210-2779. Offers biochemistry (MPS, MS, PhD); environmental chemistry (MPS, MS, PhD); organic chemistry of natural products (MPS, MS, PhD); polymer chemistry (MPS, MS, PhD). *Faculty:* 17 full-time (2 women), 1 part-time/adjunct (0 women). *Students:* 33 full-time (13 women), 5 part-time (2 women); includes 2 minority (1 Black or African American, non-Hispanic/Latino; 1 Asian, non-Hispanic/Latino), 10 international. 55 applicants, 67% accepted, 12 enrolled. In 2015, 4 master's, 7 doctorates awarded. *Degree requirements:* For master's, thesis; for doctorate, comprehensive exam, thesis/dissertation. *Entrance requirements:* For master's and doctorate, GRE General Test, GRE Subject Test, minimum GPA of 3.0. Additional exam requirements/recommendations for international students: Required—TOEFL (minimum score 550 paper-based; 80 iBT), IELTS (minimum score 6). *Application deadline:* For fall admission, 2/1 priority date for domestic and international students; for spring admission, 11/1 priority date for domestic and international students. Applications are processed on a rolling basis. Application fee: $60. Electronic applications accepted. *Expenses:* Tuition, state resident: full-time $10,870; part-time

$453 per credit. Tuition, nonresident: full-time $22,210; part-time $925 per credit. *Required fees:* $1075; $89.22 per credit. *Financial support:* In 2015–16, 40 students received support, including 5 fellowships with full tuition reimbursements available (averaging $4,000 per year), 19 research assistantships with full tuition reimbursements available (averaging $20,000 per year), 44 teaching assistantships with full tuition reimbursements available (averaging $21,300 per year); Federal Work-Study, institutionally sponsored loans, scholarships/grants, health care benefits, unspecified assistantships, and departmental tuition assistance also available. Financial award application deadline: 6/30; financial award applicants required to submit FAFSA. *Faculty research:* Polymer chemistry, biochemistry, environmental chemistry, natural products chemistry. *Total annual research expenditures:* $1.8 million. *Unit head:* Prof. Ivan Gitsov, Chair, 315-470-6851, Fax: 315-470-6856, E-mail: igivanov@syr.edu. *Application contact:* Scott Shannon, Associate Provost for Instruction/Dean of the Graduate School, 315-470-6599, Fax: 315-470-6978, E-mail: sshannon@esf.edu.
Website: http://www.esf.edu/chemistry

Tufts University, Graduate School of Arts and Sciences, Department of Chemistry, Medford, MA 02155. Offers analytical chemistry (MS, PhD); bioorganic chemistry (MS, PhD); environmental chemistry (MS, PhD); inorganic chemistry (MS, PhD); organic chemistry (MS, PhD); physical chemistry (MS, PhD). Terminal master's awarded for partial completion of doctoral program. *Degree requirements:* For master's, thesis optional; for doctorate, thesis/dissertation. *Entrance requirements:* For master's and doctorate, GRE General Test; GRE Subject Test (recommended). Additional exam requirements/recommendations for international students: Required—TOEFL (minimum score 600 paper-based; 80 iBT), IELTS (minimum score 6.5). Electronic applications accepted. *Expenses: Tuition, area resident:* Full-time $48,412; part-time $1210 per credit hour. *Required fees:* $806. Full-time tuition and fees vary according to degree level, program and student level. Part-time tuition and fees vary according to course load.

University of Calgary, Faculty of Graduate Studies, Faculty of Science, Department of Chemistry, Calgary, AB T2N 1N4, Canada. Offers analytical chemistry (M Sc, PhD); applied chemistry (M Sc, PhD); inorganic chemistry (M Sc, PhD); organic chemistry (M Sc, PhD); physical chemistry (M Sc, PhD); polymer chemistry (M Sc, PhD); theoretical chemistry (M Sc, PhD). *Degree requirements:* For master's, thesis; for doctorate, thesis/dissertation, candidacy exam. *Entrance requirements:* For master's, minimum GPA of 3.0; for doctorate, honors B Sc degree with minimum GPA of 3.7 or M Sc with minimum GPA of 3.3. Additional exam requirements/recommendations for international students: Required—TOEFL (minimum score 580 paper-based). Electronic applications accepted. *Faculty research:* Chemical analysis, chemical dynamics, synthesis theory.

University of Cincinnati, Graduate School, McMicken College of Arts and Sciences, Department of Chemistry, Cincinnati, OH 45221. Offers analytical chemistry (MS, PhD); biochemistry (MS, PhD); inorganic chemistry (MS, PhD); organic chemistry (MS, PhD); physical chemistry (MS, PhD); polymer chemistry (MS, PhD); sensors (PhD). *Program availability:* Part-time, evening/weekend. Terminal master's awarded for partial completion of doctoral program. *Degree requirements:* For master's, thesis optional; for doctorate, comprehensive exam, thesis/dissertation. *Entrance requirements:* For master's and doctorate, GRE General Test. Additional exam requirements/recommendations for international students: Required—TOEFL (minimum score 580 paper-based). Electronic applications accepted. *Faculty research:* Biomedical chemistry, laser chemistry, surface science, chemical sensors, synthesis.

University of Georgia, Franklin College of Arts and Sciences, Department of Chemistry, Athens, GA 30602. Offers analytical chemistry (MS, PhD); inorganic chemistry (MS, PhD); organic chemistry (MS, PhD); physical chemistry (MS, PhD). Terminal master's awarded for partial completion of doctoral program. *Degree requirements:* For master's, thesis; for doctorate, one foreign language, thesis/dissertation. *Entrance requirements:* For master's and doctorate, GRE General Test. Additional exam requirements/recommendations for international students: Required—TOEFL. Electronic applications accepted.

University of Louisville, Graduate School, College of Arts and Sciences, Department of Chemistry, Louisville, KY 40292-0001. Offers analytical chemistry (MS, PhD); biochemistry (MS, PhD); chemical physics (PhD); inorganic chemistry (MS, PhD); organic chemistry (MS, PhD); physical chemistry (MS, PhD). *Students:* 46 full-time (16 women), 8 part-time (1 woman); includes 3 minority (1 Black or African American, non-Hispanic/Latino; 1 Asian, non-Hispanic/Latino; 1 Two or more races, non-Hispanic/Latino), 36 international. Average age 29. 51 applicants, 22% accepted, 6 enrolled. In 2015, 2 master's, 1 doctorate awarded. Terminal master's awarded for partial completion of doctoral program. *Degree requirements:* For master's, variable foreign language requirement, comprehensive exam, thesis optional; for doctorate, variable foreign language requirement, comprehensive exam, thesis/dissertation. *Entrance requirements:* For master's and doctorate, GRE General Test, BA or BS coursework. Additional exam requirements/recommendations for international students: Required—TOEFL (minimum score 550 paper-based; 79 iBT). *Application deadline:* For fall admission, 3/15 for domestic students, 5/1 priority date for international students; for winter admission, 9/15 for domestic and international students; for spring admission, 11/1 priority date for international students; for summer admission, 4/1 priority date for international students. Applications are processed on a rolling basis. Application fee: $60. Electronic applications accepted. *Expenses:* Tuition, state resident: full-time $11,664; part-time $649 per credit hour. Tuition, nonresident: full-time $24,274; part-time $1350 per credit hour. *Required fees:* $196. Tuition and fees vary according to program and reciprocity agreements. *Financial support:* In 2015–16, 757,720 students received support. Fellowships with full tuition reimbursements available, research assistantships with full tuition reimbursements available, teaching assistantships with full tuition reimbursements available, career-related internships or fieldwork, scholarships/grants, traineeships, health care benefits, and unspecified assistantships available. Support available to part-time students. Financial award application deadline: 3/15. *Faculty research:* Computational chemistry, biophysics nuclear magnetic resonance, synthetic organic chemistry, synthetic inorganic chemistry, medicinal chemistry, protein chemistry, enzymology, nano chemistry, electrochemistry, analytical chemistry, synthetic biology, bioinformatics. *Total annual research expenditures:* $2.4 million. *Unit head:* Dr. Richard J. Wittebort, Professor/Chair, 502-852-6613. *Application contact:* Libby Leggett, Director, Graduate Admissions, 502-852-3101, Fax: 502-852-6536, E-mail: gradadm@louisville.edu.
Website: http://louisville.edu/chemistry

The University of Manchester, School of Chemistry, Manchester, United Kingdom. Offers biological chemistry (PhD); chemistry (M Ent, M Phil, M Sc, D Ent, PhD); inorganic chemistry (PhD); materials chemistry (PhD); nanoscience (PhD); nuclear fission (PhD); organic chemistry (PhD); physical chemistry (PhD); theoretical chemistry (PhD).

University of Maryland, College Park, Academic Affairs, College of Computer, Mathematical and Natural Sciences, Department of Chemistry and Biochemistry, Chemistry Program, College Park, MD 20742. Offers analytical chemistry (MS, PhD); inorganic chemistry (MS, PhD); organic chemistry (MS, PhD); physical chemistry (MS, PhD). *Program availability:* Part-time, evening/weekend. Terminal master's awarded for partial completion of doctoral program. *Degree requirements:* For master's, thesis optional; for doctorate, thesis/dissertation, 2 seminar presentations, oral exam. *Entrance requirements:* For master's and doctorate, GRE General Test, GRE Subject Test (recommended), minimum GPA of 3.0, 3 letters of recommendation. Additional exam requirements/recommendations for international students: Required—TOEFL. Electronic applications accepted. *Faculty research:* Environmental chemistry, nuclear chemistry, lunar and environmental analysis, X-ray crystallography.

University of Massachusetts Lowell, College of Sciences, Department of Chemistry, Lowell, MA 01854. Offers analytical chemistry (PhD); biochemistry (PhD); chemistry (MS, PhD); environmental studies (PhD); green chemistry (PhD); inorganic chemistry (PhD); organic chemistry (PhD); polymer science (MS). Terminal master's awarded for partial completion of doctoral program. *Degree requirements:* For master's, thesis; for doctorate, 2 foreign languages, thesis/dissertation. *Entrance requirements:* For master's and doctorate, GRE General Test. Electronic applications accepted.

University of Miami, Graduate School, College of Arts and Sciences, Department of Chemistry, Coral Gables, FL 33124. Offers chemistry (MS); inorganic chemistry (PhD); organic chemistry (PhD); physical chemistry (PhD). Terminal master's awarded for partial completion of doctoral program. *Degree requirements:* For master's, comprehensive exam; for doctorate, comprehensive exam, thesis/dissertation. *Entrance requirements:* For master's and doctorate, GRE General Test. Additional exam requirements/recommendations for international students: Required—TOEFL (minimum score 550 paper-based). Electronic applications accepted. *Faculty research:* Supramolecular chemistry, electrochemistry, surface chemistry, catalysis, organometalic.

University of Michigan, Rackham Graduate School, College of Literature, Science, and the Arts, Department of Chemistry, Ann Arbor, MI 48109-1055. Offers analytical (PhD); chemical biology (PhD); inorganic (PhD); materials (PhD); organic (PhD); physical (PhD). *Faculty:* 38 full-time (9 women), 9 part-time/adjunct (3 women). *Students:* 264 full-time (113 women). 535 applicants, 31% accepted, 54 enrolled. In 2015, 45 doctorates awarded. *Degree requirements:* For doctorate, comprehensive exam, thesis/dissertation, oral defense of dissertation, organic cumulative proficiency exams. *Entrance requirements:* For doctorate, GRE General Test, GRE Subject Test (recommended), 3 letters of recommendation. Additional exam requirements/recommendations for international students: Required—TOEFL (minimum score 560 paper-based; 84 iBT). *Application deadline:* For fall admission, 12/15 for domestic and international students. Applications are processed on a rolling basis. Application fee: $0 ($90 for international students). Electronic applications accepted. *Financial support:* In 2015–16, 264 students received support, including 40 fellowships with full tuition reimbursements available (averaging $29,000 per year), 78 research assistantships with full tuition reimbursements available (averaging $29,025 per year), 146 teaching assistantships with full tuition reimbursements available (averaging $29,025 per year); career-related internships or fieldwork, scholarships/grants, traineeships, health care benefits, and unspecified assistantships also available. *Faculty research:* Biological catalysis, protein engineering, chemical sensors, de novo metalloprotein design, supramolecular architecture. *Unit head:* Dr. Robert Kennedy, Professor of Chemistry/Chair, 734-763-9681, Fax: 734-647-4847. *Application contact:* Elizabeth Oxford, Graduate Program Coordinator, 734-764-7278, Fax: 734-647-4865, E-mail: chemadmissions@umich.edu.
Website: http://www.lsa.umich.edu/chem/

University of Missouri, Office of Research and Graduate Studies, College of Arts and Science, Department of Chemistry, Columbia, MO 65211. Offers analytical chemistry (MS, PhD); inorganic chemistry (MS, PhD); organic chemistry (MS, PhD); physical chemistry (MS, PhD). *Degree requirements:* For master's, thesis; for doctorate, one foreign language, comprehensive exam, thesis/dissertation. *Entrance requirements:* For master's, GRE General Test, minimum GPA of 3.0; for doctorate, GRE General Test (minimum score: Verbal 450, Quantitative 600, Analytical 3), minimum GPA of 3.0. Additional exam requirements/recommendations for international students: Required—TOEFL (minimum score 600 paper-based; 100 iBT). Electronic applications accepted. *Faculty research:* Analytical, organic, biological, physical, inorganic and radiochemistry.

University of Missouri–Kansas City, College of Arts and Sciences, Department of Chemistry, Kansas City, MO 64110-2499. Offers analytical chemistry (MS, PhD); inorganic chemistry (MS, PhD); organic chemistry (MS, PhD); physical chemistry (MS, PhD); polymer chemistry (MS, PhD). PhD (interdisciplinary) offered through the School of Graduate Studies. *Program availability:* Part-time, evening/weekend. *Faculty:* 15 full-time (2 women), 1 part-time/adjunct (0 women). *Students:* 3 full-time (2 women), 4 part-time (2 women); includes 1 minority (Black or African American, non-Hispanic/Latino), 3 international. Average age 36. 35 applicants, 23% accepted, 1 enrolled. In 2015, 3 master's awarded. *Degree requirements:* For master's, thesis (for some programs); for doctorate, thesis/dissertation. *Entrance requirements:* For master's, equivalent of American Chemical Society approved bachelor's degree in chemistry; for doctorate, GRE General Test, equivalent of American Chemical Society approved bachelor's degree in chemistry. Additional exam requirements/recommendations for international students: Required—TOEFL (minimum score 550 paper-based; 80 iBT), TWE. *Application deadline:* For fall admission, 4/15 for domestic and international students; for spring admission, 10/15 for domestic and international students. Applications are processed on a rolling basis. Application fee: $45 ($50 for international students). Electronic applications accepted. *Financial support:* In 2015–16, 2 research assistantships with partial tuition reimbursements (averaging $18,000 per year), 30 teaching assistantships with partial tuition reimbursements (averaging $18,062 per year) were awarded; Federal Work-Study, institutionally sponsored loans, and scholarships/grants also available. Support available to part-time students. Financial award application deadline: 3/1; financial award applicants required to submit FAFSA. *Faculty research:* Molecular spectroscopy, characterization and synthesis of materials and compounds, computational chemistry, natural products, drug delivery systems and anti-tumor agents. *Unit head:* Dr. Kathleen V. Kilway, Chair, 816-235-2289, Fax: 816-235-5502, E-mail: kilwayk@umkc.edu. *Application contact:* Graduate Recruiting Committee, 816-235-2272, Fax: 816-235-5502, E-mail: umkc-chemdept@umkc.edu.

University of Montana, Graduate School, College of Humanities and Sciences, Department of Chemistry and Biochemistry, Missoula, MT 59812-0002. Offers chemistry (MS, PhD), including environmental/analytical chemistry, inorganic chemistry, organic chemistry, physical chemistry. Terminal master's awarded for partial completion of doctoral program. *Degree requirements:* For master's, thesis (for some programs); for doctorate, thesis/dissertation. *Entrance requirements:* For master's and doctorate, GRE General Test. Additional exam requirements/recommendations for international students: Required—TOEFL (minimum score 575 paper-based). *Faculty research:* Reaction mechanisms and kinetics, inorganic and organic synthesis, analytical chemistry, natural products.

University of Nebraska–Lincoln, Graduate College, College of Arts and Sciences, Department of Chemistry, Lincoln, NE 68588. Offers analytical chemistry (PhD); biochemistry (PhD); chemistry (MS); inorganic chemistry (PhD); materials chemistry (PhD); organic chemistry (PhD); physical chemistry (PhD). *Degree requirements:* For master's, one foreign language, thesis optional, departmental qualifying exam; for doctorate, one foreign language, comprehensive exam, thesis/dissertation, departmental qualifying exams. *Entrance requirements:* For master's and doctorate, GRE. Additional exam requirements/recommendations for international students: Required—TOEFL (minimum score 550 paper-based). Electronic applications accepted. *Faculty research:* Bioorganic and bioinorganic chemistry, biophysical and bioanalytical chemistry, structure-function of DNA and proteins, organometallics, mass spectrometry.

University of Notre Dame, Graduate School, College of Science, Department of Chemistry and Biochemistry, Notre Dame, IN 46556. Offers biochemistry (MS, PhD); inorganic chemistry (MS, PhD); organic chemistry (MS, PhD); physical chemistry (MS, PhD). Terminal master's awarded for partial completion of doctoral program. *Degree requirements:* For master's, comprehensive exam, thesis; for doctorate, thesis/dissertation, qualifying exam. *Entrance requirements:* For master's and doctorate, GRE General Test, GRE Subject Test (strongly recommended). Additional exam requirements/recommendations for international students: Required—TOEFL (minimum score 600 paper-based; 80 iBT). Electronic applications accepted. *Faculty research:* Reaction design and mechanistic studies; reactive intermediates; synthesis, structure and reactivity of organometallic cluster complexes and biologically active natural products; bioorganic chemistry; enzymology.

University of Regina, Faculty of Graduate Studies and Research, Faculty of Science, Department of Chemistry and Biochemistry, Regina, SK S4S 0A2, Canada. Offers analytical/environmental chemistry (M Sc, PhD); biophysics of biological interfaces (M Sc, PhD); enzymology/chemical biology (M Sc, PhD); inorganic/organometallic chemistry (M Sc, PhD); signal transduction and mechanisms of cancer cell regulation (M Sc, PhD); supramolecular organic photochemistry and photophysics (M Sc, PhD); synthetic organic chemistry (M Sc, PhD); theoretical/computational chemistry (M Sc, PhD). *Degree requirements:* For master's, thesis; for doctorate, thesis/dissertation. *Entrance requirements:* Additional exam requirements/recommendations for international students: Required—TOEFL (minimum score 580 paper-based; 80 iBT), IELTS (minimum score 6.5), PTE (minimum score 59). Electronic applications accepted. *Faculty research:* Asymmetric synthesis and methodology, theoretical and computational chemistry, biophysical biochemistry, analytical and environmental chemistry, chemical biology.

University of Southern Mississippi, Graduate School, College of Science and Technology, Department of Chemistry and Biochemistry, Hattiesburg, MS 39406-0001. Offers inorganic chemistry (MS); organic chemistry (MS); physical chemistry (MS). *Degree requirements:* For master's, comprehensive exam, thesis; for doctorate, comprehensive exam, thesis/dissertation. *Entrance requirements:* For master's, GRE General Test, minimum GPA of 2.75 in last 60 hours; for doctorate, GRE General Test, minimum GPA of 3.5. Additional exam requirements/recommendations for international students: Required—TOEFL, IELTS. *Faculty research:* Plant biochemistry, photo chemistry, polymer chemistry, x-ray analysis, enzyme chemistry.

The University of Tennessee, Graduate School, College of Arts and Sciences, Department of Chemistry, Knoxville, TN 37996. Offers analytical chemistry (MS, PhD); chemical physics (PhD); environmental chemistry (MS, PhD); inorganic chemistry (MS, PhD); organic chemistry (MS, PhD); physical chemistry (MS, PhD); polymer chemistry (MS, PhD); theoretical chemistry (PhD). *Program availability:* Part-time. Terminal master's awarded for partial completion of doctoral program. *Degree requirements:* For master's, thesis; for doctorate, thesis/dissertation. *Entrance requirements:* For master's and doctorate, GRE General Test, minimum GPA of 2.7. Additional exam requirements/recommendations for international students: Required—TOEFL. Electronic applications accepted.

The University of Texas at Austin, Graduate School, College of Natural Sciences, Department of Chemistry and Biochemistry, Austin, TX 78712-1111. Offers analytical chemistry (PhD); biochemistry (PhD); inorganic chemistry (PhD); organic chemistry (PhD); physical chemistry (PhD). *Entrance requirements:* For doctorate, GRE General Test.

The University of Toledo, College of Graduate Studies, College of Natural Sciences and Mathematics, Department of Chemistry, Toledo, OH 43606-3390. Offers analytical chemistry (MS, PhD); biological chemistry (MS, PhD); inorganic chemistry (MS, PhD); organic chemistry (MS, PhD); physical chemistry (MS, PhD). *Program availability:* Part-time. *Degree requirements:* For master's, thesis or alternative; for doctorate, thesis/dissertation. *Entrance requirements:* For master's and doctorate, GRE General Test, GRE Subject Test, minimum cumulative point-hour ratio of 2.7 for all previous academic work, three letters of recommendation, statement of purpose, transcripts from all prior institutions attended. Additional exam requirements/recommendations for international students: Required—TOEFL (minimum score 550 paper-based; 80 iBT). Electronic applications accepted. *Faculty research:* Enzymology, materials chemistry, crystallography, theoretical chemistry.

Vanderbilt University, Department of Chemistry, Nashville, TN 37240-1001. Offers analytical chemistry (MAT, MS, PhD); inorganic chemistry (MAT, MS, PhD); organic chemistry (MAT, MS, PhD); physical chemistry (MAT, MS, PhD); theoretical chemistry (MAT, MS). *Faculty:* 19 full-time (3 women). *Students:* 114 full-time (41 women); includes 19 minority (5 Black or African American, non-Hispanic/Latino; 3 Asian, non-Hispanic/Latino; 7 Hispanic/Latino; 4 Two or more races, non-Hispanic/Latino), 8 international. Average age 26. 339 applicants, 17% accepted, 19 enrolled. In 2015, 11 master's, 13 doctorates awarded. Terminal master's awarded for partial completion of doctoral program. *Degree requirements:* For master's, thesis; for doctorate, thesis/dissertation, area, qualifying, and final exams. *Entrance requirements:* For master's and doctorate, GRE General Test, GRE Subject Test (recommended). Additional exam requirements/recommendations for international students: Required—TOEFL (minimum score 570 paper-based; 88 iBT). *Application deadline:* For fall admission, 1/15 for domestic and international students. Application fee: $0. Electronic applications accepted. *Financial support:* Fellowships with tuition reimbursements, research assistantships with full tuition reimbursements, teaching assistantships with full tuition reimbursements, Federal Work-Study, institutionally sponsored loans, scholarships/grants, traineeships, and health care benefits available. Financial award application deadline: 1/15; financial award applicants required to submit CSS PROFILE or FAFSA. *Faculty research:* Chemical synthesis; mechanistic, theoretical, bioorganic, analytical, and spectroscopic chemistry. *Unit head:* Dr. Carmello Rizzo, Director of Graduate Studies, 615-322-2861, Fax: 615-322-4936, E-mail: c.rizzo@vanderbilt.edu. *Application contact:* Sandra Ford, Administrative Assistant, 615-322-8695, Fax: 615-322-4936, E-mail: sandra.e.ford@vanderbilt.edu.
Website: http://www.vanderbilt.edu/chemistry/

Virginia Commonwealth University, Graduate School, College of Humanities and Sciences, Department of Chemistry, Richmond, VA 23284-9005. Offers analytical chemistry (MS, PhD); chemical physics (PhD); inorganic chemistry (MS, PhD); organic chemistry (MS, PhD); physical chemistry (MS, PhD). *Program availability:* Part-time. Terminal master's awarded for partial completion of doctoral program. *Degree requirements:* For master's, thesis; for doctorate, thesis/dissertation, comprehensive cumulative exams, research proposal. *Entrance requirements:* For master's, GRE General Test, 30 undergraduate credits in chemistry; for doctorate, GRE General Test. Additional exam requirements/recommendations for international students: Required—TOEFL (minimum score 600 paper-based; 100 iBT) or IELTS (minimum score 6.5). Electronic applications accepted. *Faculty research:* Physical, organic, inorganic, analytical, and polymer chemistry; chemical physics.

Wake Forest University, Graduate School of Arts and Sciences, Department of Chemistry, Winston-Salem, NC 27109. Offers analytical chemistry (MS, PhD); inorganic chemistry (MS, PhD); organic chemistry (MS, PhD); physical chemistry (MS, PhD). *Program availability:* Part-time. *Degree requirements:* For master's, one foreign language, comprehensive exam, thesis; for doctorate, 2 foreign languages, comprehensive exam, thesis/dissertation. *Entrance requirements:* For master's and doctorate, GRE General Test. Additional exam requirements/recommendations for international students: Required—TOEFL. Electronic applications accepted.

Wayne State University, College of Liberal Arts and Sciences, Department of Chemistry, Detroit, MI 48202. Offers analytical chemistry (PhD); biochemistry (PhD); chemistry (MA, MS); inorganic chemistry (PhD); organic chemistry (PhD); physical chemistry (PhD). *Faculty:* 29. *Students:* 146 full-time (61 women); includes 9 minority (2 Asian, non-Hispanic/Latino; 3 Hispanic/Latino; 4 Two or more races, non-Hispanic/Latino), 95 international. Average age 28. 280 applicants, 19% accepted, 28 enrolled. In 2015, 4 master's, 22 doctorates awarded. *Degree requirements:* For master's, thesis (for some programs), oral exam; for doctorate, thesis/dissertation, oral exam. *Entrance requirements:* For master's, GRE (strongly recommended), 1 year of physics, math through calculus, general chemistry (8 credits), organic chemistry (8 credits), physical chemistry (6 credits), quantitative analysis (4 credits), advanced chemistry (3 credits), minimum undergraduate GPA of 2.75 in chemistry and cognate sciences, statement of interest, three letters of recommendation; for doctorate, GRE (strongly recommended), minimum undergraduate GPA of 3.0 in chemistry and cognate science. Additional exam requirements/recommendations for international students: Required—TOEFL (minimum score 90 iBT), IELTS (minimum score 6.5), TWE (minimum score 5.5). *Application deadline:* For fall admission, 12/1 priority date for domestic and international students. Applications are processed on a rolling basis. Application fee: $0. Electronic applications accepted. *Expenses:* Tuition, state resident: full-time $14,165; part-time $590.20 per credit hour. Tuition, nonresident: full-time $30,682; part-time $1278.40 per credit hour. *Required fees:* $1688; $47.45 per credit hour. $274.60 per semester. Tuition and fees vary according to course load and program. *Financial support:* In 2015–16, 141 students received support, including 10 fellowships with tuition reimbursements available (averaging $23,000 per year), 54 research assistantships with tuition reimbursements available (averaging $21,609 per year), 73 teaching assistantships with tuition reimbursements available (averaging $21,363 per year); scholarships/grants and unspecified assistantships also available. Financial award application deadline: 3/31; financial award applicants required to submit FAFSA. *Faculty research:* Natural products synthesis, molecular biology, molecular mechanics calculations, organometallic chemistry, experimental physical chemistry. *Total annual research expenditures:* $7.4 million. *Unit head:* Dr. James Rigby, Chair, 313-577-3472,
E-mail: jhr@chem.wayne.edu. *Application contact:* Melissa Barton, Graduate Academic Services Officer, E-mail: melissa@chem.wayne.edu.
Website: http://chem.wayne.edu/

Wesleyan University, Graduate Studies, Department of Chemistry, Middletown, CT 06459. Offers biochemistry (PhD); chemical physics (PhD); inorganic chemistry (PhD); organic chemistry (PhD); physical chemistry (PhD); theoretical chemistry (PhD). *Faculty:* 13 full-time (3 women), 3 part-time/adjunct (2 women). *Students:* 20 full-time (10 women), 2 part-time (0 women); includes 4 minority (1 Black or African American, non-Hispanic/Latino; 3 Asian, non-Hispanic/Latino), 8 international. Average age 25. In 2015, 6 doctorates awarded. Terminal master's awarded for partial completion of doctoral program. *Degree requirements:* For doctorate, thesis/dissertation, proposal. *Entrance requirements:* For doctorate, GRE General Test, 3 recommendations. Additional exam requirements/recommendations for international students: Required—TOEFL, IELTS. *Application deadline:* 2/15 for domestic and international students; for summer admission, 2/15 for domestic and international students. Applications are processed on a rolling basis. Application fee: $0. Electronic applications accepted. *Financial support:* In 2015–16, 4 research assistantships with full tuition reimbursements, 21 teaching assistantships with full tuition reimbursements were awarded; institutionally sponsored loans and health care benefits also available. Financial award application deadline: 4/15; financial award applicants required to submit FAFSA. *Faculty research:* MICHELLE LOUISE PERSONICK Research in the Personick lab is focused on the synthesis of noble metal and noble metal alloy nanoparticles with well-defined shapes and catalytically active high-energy surfaces. Our research takes place at the interface between inorganic chemistry and materials science, and we combine solution-phase nanoparticle synthesis with advanced materials characterization techniques such as scanning electron microscopy (SEM). In addition, we evaluate the catalytic activity of. *Unit head:* Michael Calter, Chair, 860-685-2633, E-mail: mcalter@wesleyan.edu. *Application contact:* Roslyn Brault, Administrative Assistant/Graduate Program Coordinator, 860-685-2573, Fax: 860-685-2211, E-mail: rbrault@wesleyan.edu.
Website: http://www.wesleyan.edu/chem/

West Virginia University, Eberly College of Arts and Sciences, Department of Chemistry, Morgantown, WV 26506. Offers analytical chemistry (MS, PhD); inorganic chemistry (MS, PhD); organic chemistry (MS, PhD); physical chemistry (MS, PhD); theoretical chemistry (MS, PhD). *Program availability:* Part-time, online learning. Terminal master's awarded for partial completion of doctoral program. *Degree requirements:* For master's, thesis; for doctorate, thesis/dissertation. *Entrance requirements:* For master's, GRE General Test, GRE Subject Test (recommended), minimum GPA of 2.5; for doctorate, GRE General Test, GRE Subject Test (recommended), minimum GPA of 2.75. Additional exam requirements/recommendations for international students: Required—TOEFL. Electronic applications accepted. *Expenses:* Tuition, state resident: full-time $8568. Tuition, nonresident: full-time $22,140. Tuition and fees vary according to program. *Faculty research:* Analysis of proteins, drug interactions, solids and effluents by advanced separation methods; new synthetic strategies for complex organic molecules; synthesis and structural characterization of metal complexes for polymerization catalysis, nonlinear science, spectroscopy.

Yale University, Graduate School of Arts and Sciences, Department of Chemistry, New Haven, CT 06520. Offers biophysical chemistry (PhD); inorganic chemistry (PhD); organic chemistry (PhD); physical and theoretical chemistry (PhD). *Degree requirements:* For doctorate, thesis/dissertation. *Entrance requirements:* For doctorate, GRE General Test, GRE Subject Test. Additional exam requirements/recommendations for international students: Required—TOEFL.

Youngstown State University, Graduate School, College of Science, Technology, Engineering and Mathematics, Department of Chemistry, Youngstown, OH 44555-0001. Offers analytical chemistry (MS); biochemistry (MS); chemistry education (MS); inorganic chemistry (MS); organic chemistry (MS); physical chemistry (MS). *Program availability:* Part-time. *Degree requirements:* For master's, thesis. *Entrance requirements:* For master's, bachelor's degree in chemistry, minimum GPA of 2.7. Additional exam requirements/recommendations for international students: Required—TOEFL. *Faculty research:* Analysis of antioxidants, chromatography, defects and disorder in crystalline oxides, hydrogen bonding, novel organic and organometallic materials.

Physical Chemistry

Auburn University, Graduate School, College of Sciences and Mathematics, Department of Chemistry and Biochemistry, Auburn University, AL 36849. Offers analytical chemistry (MS, PhD); biochemistry (MS, PhD); inorganic chemistry (MS, PhD); organic chemistry (MS, PhD); physical chemistry (MS, PhD). *Program availability:* Part-time. *Faculty:* 27 full-time (4 women), 2 part-time/adjunct (0 women). *Students:* 45 full-time (17 women), 26 part-time (15 women); includes 9 minority (7 Black or African American, non-Hispanic/Latino; 1 American Indian or Alaska Native, non-Hispanic/Latino; 1 Asian, non-Hispanic/Latino), 38 international. Average age 27. 33 applicants, 52% accepted, 16 enrolled. In 2015, 1 master's, 6 doctorates awarded. *Degree requirements:* For master's, thesis (for some programs); for doctorate, thesis/dissertation, oral and written exams. *Entrance requirements:* For master's and doctorate, GRE General Test. *Application deadline:* Applications are processed on a rolling basis. Application fee: $50 ($60 for international students). Electronic applications accepted. *Expenses:* Tuition, state resident: full-time $8802; part-time $489 per credit hour. Tuition, nonresident: full-time $26,406; part-time $1467 per credit hour. *Required fees:* $808 per semester. Tuition and fees vary according to degree level and program. *Financial support:* Fellowships, research assistantships, and teaching assistantships available. Financial award application deadline: 3/15; financial award applicants required to submit FAFSA. *Unit head:* Dr. Curtis Shannon, Chair, 334-844-4043, Fax: 334-844-4043. *Application contact:* Dr. George Flowers, Dean of the Graduate School, 334-844-2125.
Website: http://www.auburn.edu/cosam/departments/chemistry/

Binghamton University, State University of New York, Graduate School, School of Arts and Sciences, Department of Chemistry, Vestal, NY 13850. Offers analytical chemistry (PhD); chemistry (MA, MS); environmental chemistry (PhD); inorganic chemistry (PhD); organic chemistry (PhD); physical chemistry (PhD). *Program availability:* Part-time. *Faculty:* 21 full-time (4 women). *Students:* 60 full-time (24 women), 1 part-time (0 women); includes 4 minority (2 Black or African American, non-Hispanic/Latino; 1 Asian, non-Hispanic/Latino; 1 Hispanic/Latino), 40 international. Average age 27. 53 applicants, 81% accepted, 16 enrolled. In 2015, 3 master's, 7 doctorates awarded. Terminal master's awarded for partial completion of doctoral program. *Degree requirements:* For master's, thesis; for doctorate, comprehensive exam, thesis/dissertation. *Entrance requirements:* For master's and doctorate, GRE General Test. Additional exam requirements/recommendations for international students: Required—TOEFL (minimum score 90 iBT). *Application deadline:* Applications are processed on a rolling basis. Application fee: $75. Electronic applications accepted. *Financial support:* In 2015–16, 53 students received support, including 8 research assistantships with full tuition reimbursements available (averaging $18,000 per year), 34 teaching assistantships with full tuition reimbursements available (averaging $18,000 per year); career-related internships or fieldwork, Federal Work-Study, institutionally sponsored loans, scholarships/grants, health care benefits, tuition waivers (full and partial), and unspecified assistantships also available. Financial award applicants required to submit FAFSA. *Unit head:* Dr. Wayne E. Jones, Chairperson, 607-777-2421, E-mail: wjones@binghamton.edu. *Application contact:* Kishan Zuber, Recruiting and Admissions Coordinator, 607-777-2151, Fax: 607-777-2501,
E-mail: kzuber@binghamton.edu.

Boston College, Graduate School of Arts and Sciences, Department of Chemistry, Chestnut Hill, MA 02467. Offers biochemistry (PhD); inorganic chemistry (PhD); organic chemistry (PhD); physical chemistry (PhD); science education (MST). *Faculty:* 21 full-time. *Students:* 121 full-time (57 women); includes 9 minority (6 Asian, non-Hispanic/Latino; 3 Hispanic/Latino), 53 international. 222 applicants, 50% accepted, 43 enrolled. In 2015, 2 master's, 11 doctorates awarded. *Degree requirements:* For doctorate, thesis/dissertation, qualifying exam. *Entrance requirements:* For doctorate, GRE General Test, GRE Subject Test. Additional exam requirements/recommendations for international students: Required—TOEFL (minimum score 600 paper-based; 100 iBT), IELTS (minimum score 8). *Application deadline:* For fall admission, 1/2 for domestic and international students. Application fee: $75. Electronic applications accepted. Tuition and fees vary according to program. *Financial support:* In 2015–16, 121 students received support, including fellowships with full tuition reimbursements available (averaging $30,000 per year), research assistantships with full tuition reimbursements available (averaging $30,000 per year), teaching assistantships with full tuition reimbursements available (averaging $30,000 per year); Federal Work-Study, scholarships/grants, health care benefits, and unspecified assistantships also available. Support available to part-time students. Financial award application deadline: 1/2. *Faculty research:* Organic and organometallic chemistry, chemical biology and biochemistry, physical and theoretical chemistry, inorganic chemistry. *Unit head:* Dr. Amir Hoveyda, Chairperson, 617-552-1735, E-mail: amir.hoveyda@bc.edu. *Application contact:* Dr. Jianmin Gao, Graduate Program Director, 617-552-0326, Fax: 617-552-0833, E-mail: gaojc@bc.edu.
Website: http://www.bc.edu/chemistry

Brandeis University, Graduate School of Arts and Sciences, Department of Chemistry, Waltham, MA 02454. Offers inorganic chemistry (MA, MS, PhD); organic chemistry (MA, MS, PhD); physical chemistry (MS, PhD). *Program availability:* Part-time. *Faculty:* 12 full-time (4 women), 1 part-time/adjunct (0 women). *Students:* 43 full-time (15 women); includes 2 minority (1 Black or African American, non-Hispanic/Latino; 1 Two or more races, non-Hispanic/Latino), 26 international. 102 applicants, 34% accepted, 7 enrolled. In 2015, 8 master's, 6 doctorates awarded. Terminal master's awarded for partial completion of doctoral program. *Degree requirements:* For master's, comprehensive exam, thesis (for some programs), 1 year of residency (for MA); 2 years of residency (for MS); for doctorate, comprehensive exam, thesis/dissertation, 3 years of residency, 2 seminars, qualifying exams. *Entrance requirements:* For master's and doctorate, GRE General Test, resume, statement of purpose, letters of recommendation. Additional exam requirements/recommendations for international students: Required—TOEFL (minimum score 600 paper-based; 100 iBT); Recommended—IELTS (minimum score 7), TSE (minimum score 68). *Application deadline:* For fall admission, 1/15 priority date for domestic students. Application fee: $75. Electronic applications accepted. *Financial support:* In 2015–16, 42 students received support, including 24 fellowships with full tuition reimbursements available (averaging $27,500 per year), 18 research assistantships with full tuition reimbursements available (averaging $27,500 per year); Federal Work-Study, scholarships/grants, health care benefits, tuition waivers (partial), and unspecified assistantships also available. Support available to part-time students. Financial award application deadline: 4/15; financial award applicants required to submit FAFSA. *Faculty research:* Inorganic and organic chemistry, physical chemistry, chemical biology, biophysical chemistry, materials chemistry. *Unit head:* Dr. Judith Herzfeld, Chair, Graduate Program, 781-736-2540, Fax: 781-736-2516,
E-mail: herzfeld@brandeis.edu. *Application contact:* Dr. Maryanna Aldrich, Coordinator, 781-736-2500, Fax: 781-736-2516, E-mail: scigradoffice@brandeis.edu.
Website: http://www.brandeis.edu/gsas

California State University, Los Angeles, Graduate Studies, College of Natural and Social Sciences, Department of Chemistry and Biochemistry, Los Angeles, CA 90032-8530. Offers analytical chemistry (MS); biochemistry (MS); chemistry (MS); inorganic chemistry (MS); organic chemistry (MS); physical chemistry (MS). *Program availability:* Part-time, evening/weekend. *Degree requirements:* For master's, one foreign language, comprehensive exam or thesis. *Entrance requirements:* Additional exam requirements/recommendations for international students: Required—TOEFL. *Faculty research:* Intercalation of heavy metal, carborane chemistry, conductive polymers and fabrics, titanium reagents, computer modeling and synthesis.

Cleveland State University, College of Graduate Studies, College of Sciences and Health Professions, Department of Chemistry, Cleveland, OH 44115. Offers analytical chemistry (MS); clinical/bioanalytical chemistry (PhD), including cellular and molecular medicine, clinical/bioanalytical chemistry; inorganic chemistry (MS); pharmaceutical/organic chemistry (MS); physical chemistry (MS). *Program availability:* Part-time, evening/weekend. *Faculty:* 17 full-time (3 women). *Students:* 63 full-time (30 women), 25 part-time (10 women); includes 4 minority (1 Black or African American, non-Hispanic/Latino; 1 Asian, non-Hispanic/Latino; 2 Hispanic/Latino), 48 international. Average age 30. 22 applicants, 64% accepted, 12 enrolled. In 2015, 16 master's, 8 doctorates awarded. *Degree requirements:* For master's, thesis optional; for doctorate, comprehensive exam, thesis/dissertation. *Entrance requirements:* For master's and doctorate, GRE General Test. Additional exam requirements/recommendations for international students: Required—TOEFL (minimum score 550 paper-based; 78 iBT). *Application deadline:* For fall admission, 1/15 priority date for domestic and international students. Applications are processed on a rolling basis. Application fee: $30. Electronic applications accepted. *Expenses:* Tuition, state resident: full-time $9565. Tuition, nonresident: full-time $17,980. Tuition and fees vary according to program. *Financial support:* In 2015–16, 44 students received support, including 10 fellowships with full tuition reimbursements available (averaging $22,500 per year), 6 research assistantships with full tuition reimbursements available (averaging $22,500 per year), 34 teaching assistantships with full tuition reimbursements available (averaging $21,000 per year); scholarships/grants and unspecified assistantships also available. Financial award application deadline: 1/15. *Faculty research:* Bioanalytical techniques and molecular diagnostics, glycoproteomics and antithrombotic agents, drug discovery and innovation, analytical pharmacology, inflammatory disease research. *Total annual research expenditures:* $3 million. *Unit head:* Dr. David W. Ball, Chair, 216-687-2467, Fax: 216-687-9298, E-mail: d.ball@csuohio.edu. *Application contact:* Richelle P. Emery, Administrative Coordinator, 216-687-2457, Fax: 216-687-9298,
E-mail: r.emery@csuohio.edu.
Website: http://www.csuohio.edu/sciences/chemistry

Cornell University, Graduate School, Graduate Fields of Arts and Sciences, Field of Chemistry and Chemical Biology, Ithaca, NY 14853-0001. Offers analytical chemistry (PhD); bio-organic chemistry (PhD); biophysical chemistry (PhD); chemical biology (PhD); chemical physics (PhD); inorganic chemistry (PhD); materials chemistry (PhD); organic chemistry (PhD); organometallic chemistry (PhD); physical chemistry (PhD); polymer chemistry (PhD); theoretical chemistry (PhD). *Degree requirements:* For doctorate, comprehensive exam, thesis/dissertation. *Entrance requirements:* For doctorate, GRE General Test, GRE Subject Test (chemistry), 3 letters of recommendation. Additional exam requirements/recommendations for international students: Required—TOEFL (minimum score 600 paper-based; 77 iBT). Electronic applications accepted. *Faculty research:* Analytical, organic, inorganic, physical, materials, chemical biology.

Dartmouth College, Arts and Sciences Graduate Programs, Department of Chemistry, Hanover, NH 03755. Offers biophysical chemistry (MS); chemistry (PhD). *Faculty:* 19 full-time (4 women), 1 (woman) part-time/adjunct. *Students:* 47 full-time (22 women); includes 8 minority (1 American Indian or Alaska Native, non-Hispanic/Latino; 4 Asian, non-Hispanic/Latino; 3 Two or more races, non-Hispanic/Latino), 15 international. Average age 26. 97 applicants, 12% accepted, 9 enrolled. In 2015, 3 master's, 6 doctorates awarded. *Degree requirements:* For doctorate, thesis/dissertation, departmental qualifying exams, research proposal, research seminar, teaching. *Entrance requirements:* For doctorate, GRE General Test, GRE Subject Test. Additional exam requirements/recommendations for international students: Required—TOEFL. *Application deadline:* For fall admission, 1/4 for domestic students. Application fee: $45. Electronic applications accepted. *Expenses: Tuition, area resident:* Full-time $48,120. *Required fees:* $296. One-time fee: $50 full-time. *Financial support:* Fellowships with full tuition reimbursements, research assistantships with full tuition reimbursements, teaching assistantships with full tuition reimbursements, institutionally sponsored loans, scholarships/grants, traineeships, tuition waivers (full), and unspecified assistantships available. Financial award application deadline: 4/1; financial award applicants required to submit CSS PROFILE or FAFSA. *Faculty research:* Organic and polymer synthesis, bioinorganic chemistry, magnetic resonance parameters. *Unit head:* Dr. Dale F. Mierke, Chair, 603-646-1154. *Application contact:* Deborah Carr, Administrative Assistant, 603-646-2189, E-mail: deborah.a.carr@dartmouth.edu.
Website: http://www.dartmouth.edu/~chem/

Eastern New Mexico University, Graduate School, College of Liberal Arts and Sciences, Department of Physical Sciences, Portales, NM 88130. Offers chemistry (MS), including analytical, biochemistry, inorganic, organic, physical. *Program* *availability:* Part-time. *Degree requirements:* For master's, thesis optional, seminar, oral and written comprehensive exams. *Entrance requirements:* For master's, ACS placement examination, minimum GPA of 3.0; 2 letters of recommendation; personal statement of career goals; bachelor's degree with one year minimum each of general, organic, and analytical chemistry. Additional exam requirements/recommendations for international students: Required—TOEFL (minimum score 550 paper-based; 79 iBT), IELTS (minimum score 6). Electronic applications accepted. *Faculty research:* Synfuel, electrochemistry, protein chemistry.

Florida State University, The Graduate School, College of Arts and Sciences, Department of Chemistry and Biochemistry, Tallahassee, FL 32306-4390. Offers analytical chemistry (MS, PhD); biochemistry (MS, PhD); inorganic chemistry (MS, PhD); materials chemistry (PhD); organic chemistry (MS, PhD); physical chemistry (MS, PhD). *Faculty:* 40 full-time (6 women), 4 part-time/adjunct (2 women). *Students:* 162 full-time (56 women); includes 37 minority (8 Black or African American, non-Hispanic/Latino; 6 Asian, non-Hispanic/Latino; 18 Hispanic/Latino; 1 Native Hawaiian or other Pacific Islander, non-Hispanic/Latino; 4 Two or more races, non-Hispanic/Latino), 54 international. Average age 28. 182 applicants, 47% accepted, 31 enrolled. In 2015, 6 master's, 18 doctorates awarded. Terminal master's awarded for partial completion of doctoral program. *Degree requirements:* For master's, thesis (for some programs); for doctorate, thesis/dissertation. *Entrance requirements:* For master's and doctorate, GRE General Test (minimum scores: 150 verbal, 151 quantitative; 1100 total on the old scale), minimum GPA of 3.1 in undergraduate course work. Additional exam requirements/recommendations for international students: Required—TOEFL (minimum score 90 iBT). *Application deadline:* For fall admission, 12/15 priority date for domestic and international students. Application fee: $30. Electronic applications accepted. *Expenses: Tuition, area resident:* Full-time $7263; part-time $403.50 per credit hour. Tuition, nonresident: full-time $18,087; part-time $1004.85 per credit hour. *Required fees:* $1365; $75.81 per credit hour. $20 per semester. Tuition and fees vary according to campus/location. *Financial support:* In 2015–16, 162 students received support, including 4 fellowships with tuition reimbursements available (averaging $22,000 per year), 51 research assistantships with full tuition reimbursements available (averaging $22,809 per year), 67 teaching assistantships with full tuition reimbursements available (averaging $22,809 per year). Financial award application deadline: 12/15; financial award applicants required to submit FAFSA. *Faculty research:* Bioanalytical chemistry, including separations, microfluidics, petroleomics; materials chemistry, including magnets, polymers, catalysts, nanomaterials; spectroscopy, including NMR and EPR, ultrafast, Raman, and mass spectrometry; organic synthesis, natural products, photochemistry, and supramolecular chemistry; biochemistry, with focus on structural biology, metabolomics, and anticancer drugs. *Total annual research expenditures:* $3.5 million. *Unit head:* Dr. Timothy Logan, Chairman, 850-644-3810, Fax: 850-644-8281, E-mail: gradinfo@chem.fsu.edu. *Application contact:* Dr. Geoffrey Strouse, Associate Chair for Graduate Studies, 850-445-9042, Fax: 850-644-8281,
E-mail: gradinfo@chem.fsu.edu.
Website: http://www.chem.fsu.edu/

The George Washington University, Columbian College of Arts and Sciences, Department of Chemistry, Washington, DC 20052. Offers analytical chemistry (MS, PhD); inorganic chemistry (MS, PhD); materials science (MS, PhD); organic chemistry (MS, PhD); physical chemistry (MS, PhD). *Program availability:* Part-time, evening/weekend. *Faculty:* 17 full-time (6 women), 4 part-time/adjunct (1 woman). *Students:* 25 full-time (13 women), 12 part-time (5 women); includes 2 minority (1 Asian, non-Hispanic/Latino; 1 Hispanic/Latino), 10 international. Average age 28. 60 applicants, 37% accepted, 9 enrolled. In 2015, 2 master's, 6 doctorates awarded. Terminal master's awarded for partial completion of doctoral program. *Degree requirements:* For master's, comprehensive exam, thesis or alternative; for doctorate, thesis/dissertation, general exam. *Entrance requirements:* For master's and doctorate, GRE General Test, interview, minimum GPA of 3.0. Additional exam requirements/recommendations for international students: Required—TOEFL (minimum score 550 paper-based; 80 iBT). *Application deadline:* For fall admission, 1/15 priority date for domestic and international students; for spring admission, 9/1 priority date for domestic and international students. Applications are processed on a rolling basis. Application fee: $75. Electronic applications accepted. *Financial support:* In 2015–16, 27 students received support. Fellowships with tuition reimbursements available, research assistantships, teaching assistantships with tuition reimbursements available, Federal Work-Study, and tuition waivers available. Financial award application deadline: 1/15. *Unit head:* Dr. Michael King, Chair, 202-994-6488. *Application contact:* Information Contact, 202-994-6121, E-mail: gwchem@gwu.edu.
Website: http://chemistry.columbian.gwu.edu/

Georgia State University, College of Arts and Sciences, Department of Chemistry, Atlanta, GA 30302-3083. Offers analytical chemistry (MS, PhD); biochemistry (MS, PhD); bioinformatics (MS, PhD); biophysical chemistry (PhD); computational chemistry (MS, PhD); geochemistry (PhD); organic/medicinal chemistry (MS, PhD); physical chemistry (MS). PhD in geochemistry offered jointly with Department of Geosciences. *Program availability:* Part-time. *Faculty:* 26 full-time (4 women). *Students:* 158 full-time (53 women), 4 part-time (all women); includes 43 minority (22 Black or African American, non-Hispanic/Latino; 1 American Indian or Alaska Native, non-Hispanic/Latino; 9 Asian, non-Hispanic/Latino; 7 Hispanic/Latino; 4 Two or more races, non-Hispanic/Latino), 81 international. Average age 28. 117 applicants, 50% accepted, 42 enrolled. In 2015, 28 master's, 15 doctorates awarded. Terminal master's awarded for partial completion of doctoral program. *Degree requirements:* For master's, one foreign language, comprehensive exam (for some programs), thesis (for some programs); for doctorate, one foreign language, comprehensive exam, thesis/dissertation. *Entrance requirements:* For master's and doctorate, GRE. Additional exam requirements/recommendations for international students: Required—TOEFL (minimum score 550 paper-based; 80 iBT) or IELTS (minimum score 6.5). *Application deadline:* For fall admission, 7/1 priority date for domestic and international students; for winter admission, 11/15 priority date for domestic and international students; for spring admission, 4/15 priority date for domestic and international students. Applications are processed on a rolling basis. Application fee: $50. Electronic applications accepted. *Expenses:* Tuition, state resident: full-time $6876; part-time $382 per credit hour. Tuition, nonresident: full-time $22,374; part-time $1243 per credit hour. *Required fees:* $2128; $2128 per term. $1064 per term. Part-time tuition and fees vary according to course load and program. *Financial support:* Fellowships with full tuition reimbursements, research assistantships with full tuition reimbursements, and teaching assistantships with full tuition reimbursements available. Financial award applicants required to submit FAFSA. *Faculty research:* Analytical chemistry, biological/biochemistry, biophysical/computational chemistry, chemical education, organic/medicinal chemistry. *Unit head:* Dr. Peng George Wang, Department Chair, 404-413-3591, Fax: 404-413-5505,
E-mail: pwang11@gsu.edu.
Website: http://chemistry.gsu.edu/

Harvard University, Graduate School of Arts and Sciences, Department of Chemistry and Chemical Biology, Cambridge, MA 02138. Offers biochemical chemistry (PhD); inorganic chemistry (PhD); organic chemistry (PhD); physical chemistry (PhD). *Degree requirements:* For doctorate, thesis/dissertation, cumulative exams. *Entrance requirements:* For doctorate, GRE General Test, GRE Subject Test. Additional exam requirements/recommendations for international students: Required—TOEFL.

Howard University, Graduate School, Department of Chemistry, Washington, DC 20059-0002. Offers analytical chemistry (MS, PhD); atmospheric (MS, PhD); biochemistry (MS, PhD); environmental (MS, PhD); inorganic chemistry (MS, PhD); organic chemistry (MS, PhD); physical chemistry (MS, PhD). Terminal master's awarded for partial completion of doctoral program. *Degree requirements:* For master's, comprehensive exam, thesis, teaching experience; for doctorate, comprehensive exam, thesis/dissertation, teaching experience. *Entrance requirements:* For master's, GRE General Test, minimum GPA of 2.7; for doctorate, GRE General Test, minimum GPA of 3.0. Additional exam requirements/recommendations for international students: Required—TOEFL. Electronic applications accepted. *Faculty research:* Synthetic organics, materials, natural products, mass spectrometry.

Indiana University Bloomington, University Graduate School, College of Arts and Sciences, Department of Chemistry, Bloomington, IN 47405. Offers analytical chemistry (PhD); chemical biology (PhD); chemistry (MAT); inorganic chemistry (PhD); materials chemistry (PhD); organic chemistry (PhD); physical chemistry (PhD); MSES/MS. Terminal master's awarded for partial completion of doctoral program. *Degree requirements:* For master's, thesis; for doctorate, thesis/dissertation. *Entrance requirements:* For master's and doctorate, GRE General Test, GRE Subject Test. Additional exam requirements/recommendations for international students: Required—TOEFL. Electronic applications accepted. *Faculty research:* Synthesis of complex natural products, organic reaction mechanisms, organic electrochemistry, transitive-metal chemistry, solid-state and surface chemistry.

Iowa State University of Science and Technology, Program in Physical Chemistry, Ames, IA 50011. Offers MS, PhD. *Entrance requirements:* Additional exam requirements/recommendations for international students: Required—TOEFL (minimum score 570 paper-based; 89 iBT), IELTS (minimum score 6.5). Electronic applications accepted.

Kansas State University, Graduate School, College of Arts and Sciences, Department of Chemistry, Manhattan, KS 66506. Offers analytical chemistry (MS); biological chemistry (MS); inorganic chemistry (MS); materials chemistry (MS); organic chemistry (MS); physical chemistry (MS). Terminal master's awarded for partial completion of doctoral program. *Degree requirements:* For master's, thesis; for doctorate, thesis/dissertation. *Entrance requirements:* For master's and doctorate, GRE, minimum GPA of 3.0. Additional exam requirements/recommendations for international students: Required—TOEFL (minimum score 550 paper-based). Electronic applications accepted. *Faculty research:* Inorganic chemistry, organic and biological chemistry, analytical chemistry, physical chemistry, materials chemistry and nanotechnology.

Laurentian University, School of Graduate Studies and Research, Programme in Chemistry and Biochemistry, Sudbury, ON P3E 2C6, Canada. Offers analytical chemistry (M Sc); biochemistry (M Sc); environmental chemistry (M Sc); organic chemistry (M Sc); physical/theoretical chemistry (M Sc). *Program availability:* Part-time. *Degree requirements:* For master's, thesis or alternative. *Entrance requirements:* For master's, honors degree with minimum second class. *Faculty research:* Cell cycle checkpoints, kinetic modeling, toxicology to metal stress, quantum chemistry, biogeochemistry metal speciation.

Marquette University, Graduate School, College of Arts and Sciences, Department of Chemistry, Milwaukee, WI 53201-1881. Offers analytical chemistry (MS, PhD); bioanalytical chemistry (MS, PhD); biophysical chemistry (MS, PhD); chemical physics (MS, PhD); inorganic chemistry (MS, PhD); organic chemistry (MS, PhD); physical chemistry (MS, PhD). *Program availability:* Part-time. *Faculty:* 19 full-time (3 women), 1 part-time/adjunct (0 women). *Students:* 43 full-time (14 women), 4 part-time (0 women); includes 2 minority (1 Asian, non-Hispanic/Latino; 1 Hispanic/Latino), 32 international. Average age 28. In 2015, 4 master's, 4 doctorates awarded. Terminal master's awarded for partial completion of doctoral program. *Degree requirements:* For master's, comprehensive exam; for doctorate, thesis/dissertation, cumulative exams. *Entrance requirements:* For master's and doctorate, official transcripts from all current and previous colleges/universities except Marquette, three letters of recommendation from individuals familiar with the applicant's academic work. Additional exam requirements/recommendations for international students: Required—TOEFL (minimum score 530 paper-based). *Application deadline:* Applications are processed on a rolling basis. Application fee: $50. Electronic applications accepted. *Financial support:* In 2015–16, 41 students received support, including 2 fellowships (averaging $17,134 per year), 30 teaching assistantships with full tuition reimbursements available (averaging $20,295 per year); research assistantships, scholarships/grants, health care benefits, tuition waivers (full and partial), and unspecified assistantships also available. Support available to part-time students. Financial award application deadline: 2/15. *Faculty research:* Inorganic complexes, laser Raman spectroscopy, organic synthesis, synthetic bioinorganic chemistry, electro-active organic molecules. *Total annual research expenditures:* $1.2 million. *Unit head:* Dr. Scott Reid, Chair, 414-288-7565,
E-mail: scott.reid@marquette.edu. *Application contact:* Dr. Adam Fiedler, New and Recruiting, 414-288-1625.
Website: http://www.marquette.edu/chem/graduate.shtml

Massachusetts Institute of Technology, School of Science, Department of Chemistry, Cambridge, MA 02139. Offers biological chemistry (PhD); inorganic chemistry (PhD); organic chemistry (PhD); physical chemistry (PhD). *Faculty:* 29 full-time (6 women). *Students:* 236 full-time (81 women); includes 51 minority (2 Black or African American, non-Hispanic/Latino; 1 American Indian or Alaska Native, non-Hispanic/Latino; 30 Asian, non-Hispanic/Latino; 12 Hispanic/Latino; 6 Two or more races, non-Hispanic/Latino), 83 international. Average age 26. 591 applicants, 18% accepted, 38 enrolled. In 2015, 40 doctorates awarded. *Degree requirements:* For doctorate, comprehensive exam, thesis/dissertation, teaching assistantship during two semesters. *Entrance requirements:* For doctorate, GRE General Test. Additional exam requirements/recommendations for international students: Required—TOEFL (minimum score 600 paper-based), IELTS (minimum score 7). *Application deadline:* For fall admission, 12/15 for domestic and international students. Application fee: $75. Electronic applications accepted. *Expenses: Tuition:* Full-time $46,400; part-time $725 per credit. One-time fee: $304 full-time. Full-time tuition and fees vary according to course load and program. *Financial support:* In 2015–16, 218 students received support, including 62 fellowships (averaging $45,800 per year), 129 research assistantships (averaging $37,000 per year), 43 teaching assistantships (averaging $38,300 per year); Federal Work-Study, institutionally sponsored loans, scholarships/grants, traineeships, health care benefits, and unspecified assistantships also available. Support available to part-time students. Financial award application deadline: 4/15; financial award applicants required to submit FAFSA. *Faculty research:* Synthetic organic and organometallic chemistry including catalysis; biological chemistry including bioorganic chemistry; physical chemistry including chemical dynamics, theoretical chemistry and biophysical chemistry; inorganic chemistry including synthesis, catalysis, bioinorganic and physical inorganic chemistry;

materials chemistry including surface science, nanoscience and polymers. *Total annual research expenditures:* $30.3 million. *Unit head:* Prof. Timothy F. Jamison, Department Head, 617-253-1803, Fax: 617-258-7500. *Application contact:* Graduate Administrator, 617-253-1845, Fax: 617-258-0241, E-mail: chemgradeducation@mit.edu.

Website: http://web.mit.edu/chemistry/

McMaster University, School of Graduate Studies, Faculty of Science, Department of Chemistry, Hamilton, ON L8S 4M2, Canada. Offers analytical chemistry (M Sc, PhD); chemical physics (M Sc, PhD); chemistry (M Sc, PhD); inorganic chemistry (M Sc, PhD); organic chemistry (M Sc, PhD); physical chemistry (M Sc, PhD); polymer chemistry (M Sc, PhD). *Program availability:* Part-time. Terminal master's awarded for partial completion of doctoral program. *Degree requirements:* For master's, thesis; for doctorate, comprehensive exam, thesis/dissertation. *Entrance requirements:* For master's, minimum B+ average. Additional exam requirements/recommendations for international students: Required—TOEFL (minimum score 550 paper-based).

Old Dominion University, College of Sciences, Program in Chemistry, Norfolk, VA 23529. Offers analytical (MS, PhD); biochemistry (MS, PhD); environmental (MS, PhD); inorganic (MS, PhD); organic (MS, PhD); physical (MS, PhD). *Program availability:* Part-time, evening/weekend. *Faculty:* 19 full-time (5 women). *Students:* 35 full-time (17 women), 6 part-time (2 women); includes 5 minority (4 Black or African American, non-Hispanic/Latino; 1 Two or more races, non-Hispanic/Latino), 16 international. Average age 27. 20 applicants, 55% accepted, 4 enrolled. In 2015, 9 master's, 9 doctorates awarded. *Degree requirements:* For master's, comprehensive exam, thesis (for some programs); for doctorate, comprehensive exam, thesis/dissertation. *Entrance requirements:* For master's and doctorate, GRE General Test, minimum GPA of 3.0 in major, 2.5 overall, transcripts, essay, three letters of recommendation, resume. Additional exam requirements/recommendations for international students: Required—TOEFL. *Application deadline:* For fall admission, 7/1 for domestic students, 1/15 for international students; for spring admission, 11/1 for domestic students, 8/15 for international students. Applications are processed on a rolling basis. Application fee: $50. Electronic applications accepted. *Expenses:* $464 per credit in-state tuition; $1,160 per credit out-of-state tuition. *Financial support:* In 2015–16, 42 students received support, including 2 fellowships with full tuition reimbursements available (averaging $18,000 per year), 10 research assistantships with full tuition reimbursements available (averaging $18,000 per year), 33 teaching assistantships with full tuition reimbursements available (averaging $18,000 per year); career-related internships or fieldwork, institutionally sponsored loans, scholarships/grants, health care benefits, and unspecified assistantships also available. Financial award application deadline: 2/15; financial award applicants required to submit FAFSA. *Faculty research:* Biogeochemistry, materials chemistry, computational chemistry, organic chemistry, biofuels. *Total annual research expenditures:* $2.6 million. *Unit head:* Dr. John R. Donat, Graduate Program Director, 757-683-4098, Fax: 757-683-4628,
E-mail: chemgpd@odu.edu. *Application contact:* Kristi Rehrauer, Graduate Program Assistant, 757-683-6979, Fax: 757-683-4628, E-mail: krehraue@odu.edu.

Oregon State University, College of Science, Program in Chemistry, Corvallis, OR 97331. Offers analytical chemistry (MA, MS, PhD); inorganic chemistry (MA, MS, PhD); materials chemistry (MA, MS, PhD); nuclear chemistry (MA, MS, PhD); organic chemistry (MA, MS, PhD); physical chemistry (MA, MS, PhD). *Program availability:* Part-time. *Faculty:* 23 full-time (6 women). *Students:* 111 full-time (38 women), 4 part-time (2 women); includes 14 minority (1 Black or African American, non-Hispanic/Latino; 5 Asian, non-Hispanic/Latino; 6 Hispanic/Latino; 2 Two or more races, non-Hispanic/Latino), 49 international. Average age 28. 47 applicants, 51% accepted, 22 enrolled. In 2015, 6 master's, 12 doctorates awarded. Terminal master's awarded for partial completion of doctoral program. *Degree requirements:* For master's, one foreign language, thesis; for doctorate, one foreign language, thesis/dissertation. *Entrance requirements:* For master's and doctorate, GRE, minimum GPA of 3.0 in last 90 hours of course work. Additional exam requirements/recommendations for international students: Required—TOEFL (minimum score 80 iBT), IELTS (minimum score 6.5). *Application deadline:* For fall admission, 4/1 for domestic students. Application fee: $75 ($85 for international students). *Expenses:* Tuition, state resident: full-time $12,150; part-time $450 per credit. Tuition, nonresident: full-time $20,952; part-time $776 per credit. *Required fees:* $1572; $1443 per unit. One-time fee: $350. Tuition and fees vary according to course load, campus/location and program. *Financial support:* Fellowships, research assistantships, and teaching assistantships available. Support available to part-time students. *Faculty research:* Solid state chemistry, enzyme reaction mechanisms, structure and dynamics of gas molecules, chemiluminescence, nonlinear optical spectroscopy. *Unit head:* Dr. Rich G. Carter, Professor/Chair. *Application contact:* Sarah Burton, Chemistry Advisor, 541-737-6808,
E-mail: chemadm@chem.oregonstate.edu.

Website: http://chemistry.oregonstate.edu/

Purdue University, Graduate School, College of Science, Department of Chemistry, West Lafayette, IN 47907. Offers analytical chemistry (MS, PhD); biochemistry (MS, PhD); chemical education (MS, PhD); inorganic chemistry (MS, PhD); organic chemistry (MS, PhD); physical chemistry (MS, PhD). Terminal master's awarded for partial completion of doctoral program. *Degree requirements:* For master's, thesis; for doctorate, comprehensive exam, thesis/dissertation. *Entrance requirements:* For master's and doctorate, minimum undergraduate GPA of 3.0. Additional exam requirements/recommendations for international students: Required—TOEFL (minimum score 550 paper-based; 77 iBT); Recommended—TWE. Electronic applications accepted.

Rice University, Graduate Programs, Wiess School of Natural Sciences, Department of Chemistry, Houston, TX 77251-1892. Offers chemistry (MA); inorganic chemistry (PhD); organic chemistry (PhD); physical chemistry (PhD). Terminal master's awarded for partial completion of doctoral program. *Degree requirements:* For master's, thesis; for doctorate, thesis/dissertation. *Entrance requirements:* For master's and doctorate, GRE General Test, minimum GPA of 3.0. Additional exam requirements/recommendations for international students: Required—TOEFL (minimum score 600 paper-based; 90 iBT). Electronic applications accepted. *Faculty research:* Nanoscience, biomaterials, nanobioinformatics, fullerene pharmaceuticals.

Rutgers University–Newark, Graduate School, Program in Chemistry, Newark, NJ 07102. Offers analytical chemistry (MS, PhD); biochemistry (MS, PhD); inorganic chemistry (MS, PhD); organic chemistry (MS, PhD); physical chemistry (MS, PhD). *Program availability:* Part-time, evening/weekend. Terminal master's awarded for partial completion of doctoral program. *Degree requirements:* For master's, thesis optional, cumulative exams; for doctorate, thesis/dissertation, exams, research proposal. *Entrance requirements:* For master's and doctorate, GRE General Test, minimum undergraduate B average. Additional exam requirements/recommendations for international students: Required—TOEFL. Electronic applications accepted. *Faculty research:* Medicinal chemistry, natural products, isotope effects, biophysics and biorganic approaches to enzyme mechanisms, organic and organometallic synthesis.

Rutgers University–New Brunswick, Graduate School-New Brunswick, Department of Chemistry and Chemical Biology, Piscataway, NJ 08854-8097. Offers biological chemistry (MS, PhD); inorganic chemistry (MS, PhD); organic chemistry (MS, PhD); physical chemistry (MS, PhD). *Program availability:* Part-time, evening/weekend. Terminal master's awarded for partial completion of doctoral program. *Degree requirements:* For master's, thesis or alternative, exam; for doctorate, thesis/dissertation, 1 year residency. *Entrance requirements:* For master's and doctorate, GRE General Test, GRE Subject Test. Additional exam requirements/recommendations for international students: Required—TOEFL. Electronic applications accepted. *Faculty research:* Biophysical organic/bioorganic, inorganic/bioinorganic, theoretical, and solid-state/surface chemistry.

Seton Hall University, College of Arts and Sciences, Department of Chemistry and Biochemistry, South Orange, NJ 07079-2697. Offers analytical chemistry (MS, PhD); biochemistry (MS, PhD); chemistry (MS); inorganic chemistry (MS, PhD); organic chemistry (MS, PhD); physical chemistry (MS, PhD). *Program availability:* Part-time, evening/weekend. Terminal master's awarded for partial completion of doctoral program. *Degree requirements:* For master's, thesis optional; for doctorate, comprehensive exam, thesis/dissertation. *Entrance requirements:* Additional exam requirements/recommendations for international students: Required—TOEFL. Electronic applications accepted. *Faculty research:* DNA metal reactions; chromatography; bioinorganic, biophysical, organometallic, polymer chemistry; heterogeneous catalyst; synthetic organic and carbohydrate chemistry.

Southern University and Agricultural and Mechanical College, Graduate School, College of Sciences, Department of Chemistry, Baton Rouge, LA 70813. Offers analytical chemistry (MS); biochemistry (MS); environmental sciences (MS); inorganic chemistry (MS); organic chemistry (MS); physical chemistry (MS). *Degree requirements:* For master's, thesis. *Entrance requirements:* For master's, GMAT or GRE General Test. Additional exam requirements/recommendations for international students: Required—TOEFL (minimum score 525 paper-based). *Faculty research:* Synthesis of macrocyclic ligands, latex accelerators, anticancer drugs, biosensors, absorption isotheums, isolation of specific enzymes from plants.

Tufts University, Graduate School of Arts and Sciences, Department of Chemistry, Medford, MA 02155. Offers analytical chemistry (MS, PhD); bioorganic chemistry (MS, PhD); environmental chemistry (MS, PhD); inorganic chemistry (MS, PhD); organic chemistry (MS, PhD); physical chemistry (MS, PhD). Terminal master's awarded for partial completion of doctoral program. *Degree requirements:* For master's, thesis optional; for doctorate, thesis/dissertation. *Entrance requirements:* For master's and doctorate, GRE General Test; GRE Subject Test (recommended). Additional exam requirements/recommendations for international students: Required—TOEFL (minimum score 600 paper-based; 80 iBT), IELTS (minimum score 6.5). Electronic applications accepted. *Expenses: Tuition, area resident:* Full-time $48,412; part-time $1210 per credit hour. *Required fees:* $806. Full-time tuition and fees vary according to degree level, program and student level. Part-time tuition and fees vary according to course load.

University of Calgary, Faculty of Graduate Studies, Faculty of Science, Department of Chemistry, Calgary, AB T2N 1N4, Canada. Offers analytical chemistry (M Sc, PhD); applied chemistry (M Sc, PhD); inorganic chemistry (M Sc, PhD); organic chemistry (M Sc, PhD); physical chemistry (M Sc, PhD); polymer chemistry (M Sc, PhD); theoretical chemistry (M Sc, PhD). *Degree requirements:* For master's, thesis; for doctorate, thesis/dissertation, candidacy exam. *Entrance requirements:* For master's, minimum GPA of 3.0; for doctorate, honors B Sc degree with minimum GPA of 3.7 or M Sc with minimum GPA of 3.3. Additional exam requirements/recommendations for international students: Required—TOEFL (minimum score 580 paper-based). Electronic applications accepted. *Faculty research:* Chemical analysis, chemical dynamics, synthesis theory.

University of Cincinnati, Graduate School, McMicken College of Arts and Sciences, Department of Chemistry, Cincinnati, OH 45221. Offers analytical chemistry (MS, PhD); biochemistry (MS, PhD); inorganic chemistry (MS, PhD); organic chemistry (MS, PhD); physical chemistry (MS, PhD); polymer chemistry (MS, PhD); sensors (PhD). *Program availability:* Part-time, evening/weekend. Terminal master's awarded for partial completion of doctoral program. *Degree requirements:* For master's, thesis optional; for doctorate, comprehensive exam, thesis/dissertation. *Entrance requirements:* For master's and doctorate, GRE General Test. Additional exam requirements/recommendations for international students: Required—TOEFL (minimum score 580 paper-based). Electronic applications accepted. *Faculty research:* Biomedical chemistry, laser chemistry, surface science, chemical sensors, synthesis.

University of Georgia, Franklin College of Arts and Sciences, Department of Chemistry, Athens, GA 30602. Offers analytical chemistry (MS, PhD); inorganic chemistry (MS, PhD); organic chemistry (MS, PhD); physical chemistry (MS, PhD). Terminal master's awarded for partial completion of doctoral program. *Degree requirements:* For master's, thesis; for doctorate, one foreign language, thesis/dissertation. *Entrance requirements:* For master's and doctorate, GRE General Test. Additional exam requirements/recommendations for international students: Required—TOEFL. Electronic applications accepted.

University of Louisville, Graduate School, College of Arts and Sciences, Department of Chemistry, Louisville, KY 40292-0001. Offers analytical chemistry (MS, PhD); biochemistry (MS, PhD); chemical physics (PhD); inorganic chemistry (MS, PhD); organic chemistry (MS, PhD); physical chemistry (MS, PhD). *Students:* 46 full-time (16 women), 8 part-time (1 woman); includes 3 minority (1 Black or African American, non-Hispanic/Latino; 1 Asian, non-Hispanic/Latino; 1 Two or more races, non-Hispanic/Latino), 36 international. Average age 29. 51 applicants, 22% accepted, 6 enrolled. In 2015, 2 master's, 1 doctorate awarded. Terminal master's awarded for partial completion of doctoral program. *Degree requirements:* For master's, variable foreign language requirement, comprehensive exam, thesis optional; for doctorate, variable foreign language requirement, comprehensive exam, thesis/dissertation. *Entrance requirements:* For master's and doctorate, GRE General Test, BA or BS coursework. Additional exam requirements/recommendations for international students: Required—TOEFL (minimum score 550 paper-based; 79 iBT). *Application deadline:* For fall admission, 3/15 for domestic students, 5/1 priority date for international students; for winter admission, 9/15 for domestic and international students; for spring admission, 11/1 priority date for international students; for summer admission, 4/1 priority date for international students. Applications are processed on a rolling basis. Application fee: $60. Electronic applications accepted. *Expenses:* Tuition, state resident: full-time $11,664; part-time $649 per credit hour. Tuition, nonresident: full-time $24,274; part-time $1350 per credit hour. *Required fees:* $196. Tuition and fees vary according to program and reciprocity agreements. *Financial support:* In 2015–16, 757,720 students received support. Fellowships with full tuition reimbursements available, research assistantships with full tuition reimbursements available, teaching assistantships with full tuition reimbursements available, career-related internships or fieldwork, scholarships/grants, traineeships, health care benefits, and unspecified assistantships available.

Support available to part-time students. Financial award application deadline: 3/15. *Faculty research:* Computational chemistry, biophysics nuclear magnetic resonance, synthetic organic chemistry, synthetic inorganic chemistry, medicinal chemistry, protein chemistry, enzymology, nano chemistry, electrochemistry, analytical chemistry, synthetic biology, bioinformatics. *Total annual research expenditures:* $2.4 million. *Unit head:* Dr. Richard J. Wittebort, Professor/Chair, 502-852-6613. *Application contact:* Libby Leggett, Director, Graduate Admissions, 502-852-3101, Fax: 502-852-6536, E-mail: gradadm@louisville.edu.
Website: http://louisville.edu/chemistry

The University of Manchester, School of Chemistry, Manchester, United Kingdom. Offers biological chemistry (PhD); chemistry (M Ent, M Phil, M Sc, D Ent, PhD); inorganic chemistry (PhD); materials chemistry (PhD); nanoscience (PhD); nuclear fission (PhD); organic chemistry (PhD); physical chemistry (PhD); theoretical chemistry (PhD).

University of Maryland, College Park, Academic Affairs, College of Computer, Mathematical and Natural Sciences, Department of Chemistry and Biochemistry, Chemistry Program, College Park, MD 20742. Offers analytical chemistry (MS, PhD); inorganic chemistry (MS, PhD); organic chemistry (MS, PhD); physical chemistry (MS, PhD). *Program availability:* Part-time, evening/weekend. Terminal master's awarded for partial completion of doctoral program. *Degree requirements:* For master's, thesis optional; for doctorate, thesis/dissertation, 2 seminar presentations, oral exam. *Entrance requirements:* For master's and doctorate, GRE General Test, GRE Subject Test (recommended), minimum GPA of 3.0, 3 letters of recommendation. Additional exam requirements/recommendations for international students: Required—TOEFL. Electronic applications accepted. *Faculty research:* Environmental chemistry, nuclear chemistry, lunar and environmental analysis, X-ray crystallography.

University of Memphis, Graduate School, College of Arts and Sciences, Department of Chemistry, Memphis, TN 38152. Offers analytical chemistry (PhD); inorganic chemistry (MS); physical chemistry (MS). *Program availability:* Part-time. *Faculty:* 5 full-time (2 women), 1 part-time/adjunct (0 women). *Students:* 26 full-time (11 women), 9 part-time (2 women); includes 6 minority (2 Black or African American, non-Hispanic/Latino; 2 Asian, non-Hispanic/Latino; 2 Two or more races, non-Hispanic/Latino), 5 international. Average age 28. 19 applicants, 74% accepted, 9 enrolled. In 2015, 9 master's, 3 doctorates awarded. Terminal master's awarded for partial completion of doctoral program. *Degree requirements:* For master's, comprehensive exam, thesis or alternative; for doctorate, comprehensive exam, thesis/dissertation. *Entrance requirements:* For master's and doctorate, GRE General Test, admission to Graduate School plus 32 undergraduate hours in chemistry. Additional exam requirements/recommendations for international students: Required—TOEFL. *Application deadline:* For fall admission, 7/1 for domestic students, 5/1 for international students; for winter admission, 9/15 for international students; for spring admission, 12/1 for domestic students. Applications are processed on a rolling basis. Application fee: $35 ($60 for international students). Electronic applications accepted. *Financial support:* In 2015–16, 12 students received support. Research assistantships with full tuition reimbursements available, teaching assistantships with full tuition reimbursements available, Federal Work-Study, scholarships/grants, and unspecified assistantships available. Financial award application deadline: 2/15; financial award applicants required to submit FAFSA. *Faculty research:* Computational chemistry, materials chemistry, organic/polymer synthesis, drug design/delivery, water chemistry. *Unit head:* Dr. Abby L. Parrill, Professor and Chair, 901-678-2638, Fax: 901-678-3447, E-mail: aparrill@memphis.edu. *Application contact:* Dr. Gary Emmert, Associate Professor and Graduate Coordinator, 901-678-2636, Fax: 901-678-3447, E-mail: gemmert@memphis.edu.
Website: http://www.chem.memphis.edu/

University of Miami, Graduate School, College of Arts and Sciences, Department of Chemistry, Coral Gables, FL 33124. Offers chemistry (MS); inorganic chemistry (PhD); organic chemistry (PhD); physical chemistry (PhD). Terminal master's awarded for partial completion of doctoral program. *Degree requirements:* For master's, comprehensive exam; for doctorate, comprehensive exam, thesis/dissertation. *Entrance requirements:* For master's and doctorate, GRE General Test. Additional exam requirements/recommendations for international students: Required—TOEFL (minimum score 550 paper-based). Electronic applications accepted. *Faculty research:* Supramolecular chemistry, electrochemistry, surface chemistry, catalysis, organometalic.

University of Michigan, Rackham Graduate School, College of Literature, Science, and the Arts, Department of Chemistry, Ann Arbor, MI 48109-1055. Offers analytical (PhD); chemical biology (PhD); inorganic (PhD); materials (PhD); organic (PhD); physical (PhD). *Faculty:* 38 full-time (9 women), 9 part-time/adjunct (3 women). *Students:* 264 full-time (113 women). 535 applicants, 31% accepted, 54 enrolled. In 2015, 45 doctorates awarded. *Degree requirements:* For doctorate, comprehensive exam, thesis/dissertation, oral defense of dissertation, organic cumulative proficiency exams. *Entrance requirements:* For doctorate, GRE General Test, GRE Subject Test (recommended), 3 letters of recommendation. Additional exam requirements/recommendations for international students: Required—TOEFL (minimum score 560 paper-based; 84 iBT). *Application deadline:* For fall admission, 12/15 for domestic and international students. Applications are processed on a rolling basis. Application fee: $0 ($90 for international students). Electronic applications accepted. *Financial support:* In 2015–16, 264 students received support, including 40 fellowships with full tuition reimbursements available (averaging $29,000 per year), 78 research assistantships with full tuition reimbursements available (averaging $29,025 per year), 146 teaching assistantships with full tuition reimbursements available (averaging $29,025 per year); career-related internships or fieldwork, scholarships/grants, traineeships, health care benefits, and unspecified assistantships also available. *Faculty research:* Biological catalysis, protein engineering, chemical sensors, de novo metalloprotein design, supramolecular architecture. *Unit head:* Dr. Robert Kennedy, Professor of Chemistry/Chair, 734-763-9681, Fax: 734-647-4847. *Application contact:* Elizabeth Oxford, Graduate Program Coordinator, 734-764-7278, Fax: 734-647-4865, E-mail: chemadmissions@umich.edu.
Website: http://www.lsa.umich.edu/chem/

University of Missouri, Office of Research and Graduate Studies, College of Arts and Science, Department of Chemistry, Columbia, MO 65211. Offers analytical chemistry (MS, PhD); inorganic chemistry (MS, PhD); organic chemistry (MS, PhD); physical chemistry (MS, PhD). *Degree requirements:* For master's, thesis; for doctorate, one foreign language, comprehensive exam, thesis/dissertation. *Entrance requirements:* For master's, GRE General Test, minimum GPA of 3.0; for doctorate, GRE General Test (minimum score: Verbal 450, Quantitative 600, Analytical 3), minimum GPA of 3.0. Additional exam requirements/recommendations for international students: Required—TOEFL (minimum score 600 paper-based; 100 iBT). Electronic applications accepted. *Faculty research:* Analytical, organic, biological, physical, inorganic and radiochemistry.

University of Missouri–Kansas City, College of Arts and Sciences, Department of Chemistry, Kansas City, MO 64110-2499. Offers analytical chemistry (MS, PhD); inorganic chemistry (MS, PhD); organic chemistry (MS, PhD); physical chemistry (MS, PhD); polymer chemistry (MS, PhD). PhD (interdisciplinary) offered through the School of Graduate Studies. *Program availability:* Part-time, evening/weekend. *Faculty:* 15 full-time (2 women), 1 part-time/adjunct (0 women). *Students:* 3 full-time (2 women), 4 part-time (2 women); includes 1 minority (Black or African American, non-Hispanic/Latino), 3 international. Average age 36. 35 applicants, 23% accepted, 1 enrolled. In 2015, 3 master's awarded. *Degree requirements:* For master's, thesis (for some programs); for doctorate, thesis/dissertation. *Entrance requirements:* For master's, equivalent of American Chemical Society approved bachelor's degree in chemistry; for doctorate, GRE General Test, equivalent of American Chemical Society approved bachelor's degree in chemistry. Additional exam requirements/recommendations for international students: Required—TOEFL (minimum score 550 paper-based; 80 iBT), TWE. *Application deadline:* For fall admission, 4/15 for domestic and international students; for spring admission, 10/15 for domestic and international students. Applications are processed on a rolling basis. Application fee: $45 ($50 for international students). Electronic applications accepted. *Financial support:* In 2015–16, 2 research assistantships with partial tuition reimbursements (averaging $18,000 per year), 30 teaching assistantships with partial tuition reimbursements (averaging $18,062 per year) were awarded; Federal Work-Study, institutionally sponsored loans, and scholarships/grants also available. Support available to part-time students. Financial award application deadline: 3/1; financial award applicants required to submit FAFSA. *Faculty research:* Molecular spectroscopy, characterization and synthesis of materials and compounds, computational chemistry, natural products, drug delivery systems and anti-tumor agents. *Unit head:* Dr. Kathleen V. Kilway, Chair, 816-235-2289, Fax: 816-235-5502, E-mail: kilwayk@umkc.edu. *Application contact:* Graduate Recruiting Committee, 816-235-2272, Fax: 816-235-5502, E-mail: umkc-chemdept@umkc.edu.

University of Montana, Graduate School, College of Humanities and Sciences, Department of Chemistry and Biochemistry, Missoula, MT 59812-0002. Offers chemistry (MS, PhD), including environmental/analytical chemistry, inorganic chemistry, organic chemistry, physical chemistry. Terminal master's awarded for partial completion of doctoral program. *Degree requirements:* For master's, thesis (for some programs); for doctorate, thesis/dissertation. *Entrance requirements:* For master's and doctorate, GRE General Test. Additional exam requirements/recommendations for international students: Required—TOEFL (minimum score 575 paper-based). *Faculty research:* Reaction mechanisms and kinetics, inorganic and organic synthesis, analytical chemistry, natural products.

University of Nebraska–Lincoln, Graduate College, College of Arts and Sciences, Department of Chemistry, Lincoln, NE 68588. Offers analytical chemistry (PhD); biochemistry (PhD); chemistry (MS); inorganic chemistry (PhD); materials chemistry (PhD); organic chemistry (PhD); physical chemistry (PhD). *Degree requirements:* For master's, one foreign language, thesis optional, departmental qualifying exam; for doctorate, one foreign language, comprehensive exam, thesis/dissertation, departmental qualifying exams. *Entrance requirements:* For master's and doctorate, GRE. Additional exam requirements/recommendations for international students: Required—TOEFL (minimum score 550 paper-based). Electronic applications accepted. *Faculty research:* Bioorganic and bioinorganic chemistry, biophysical and bioanalytical chemistry, structure-function of DNA and proteins, organometallics, mass spectrometry.

University of Notre Dame, Graduate School, College of Science, Department of Chemistry and Biochemistry, Notre Dame, IN 46556. Offers biochemistry (MS, PhD); inorganic chemistry (MS, PhD); organic chemistry (MS, PhD); physical chemistry (MS, PhD). Terminal master's awarded for partial completion of doctoral program. *Degree requirements:* For master's, comprehensive exam, thesis; for doctorate, thesis/dissertation, qualifying exam. *Entrance requirements:* For master's and doctorate, GRE General Test, GRE Subject Test (strongly recommended). Additional exam requirements/recommendations for international students: Required—TOEFL (minimum score 600 paper-based; 80 iBT). Electronic applications accepted. *Faculty research:* Reaction design and mechanistic studies; reactive intermediates; synthesis, structure and reactivity of organometallic cluster complexes and biologically active natural products; bioorganic chemistry; enzymology.

University of Southern California, Graduate School, Dana and David Dornsife College of Letters, Arts and Sciences, Department of Chemistry, Los Angeles, CA 90089. Offers chemistry (PhD); physical chemistry (PhD). Terminal master's awarded for partial completion of doctoral program. *Degree requirements:* For doctorate, thesis/dissertation. *Entrance requirements:* For doctorate, GRE General Test. Additional exam requirements/recommendations for international students: Required—TOEFL. Electronic applications accepted. *Faculty research:* Biological chemistry, inorganic chemistry, organic chemistry, physical chemistry, theoretical chemistry.

University of Southern Mississippi, Graduate School, College of Science and Technology, Department of Chemistry and Biochemistry, Hattiesburg, MS 39406-0001. Offers inorganic chemistry (MS); organic chemistry (MS); physical chemistry (MS). *Degree requirements:* For master's, comprehensive exam, thesis; for doctorate, comprehensive exam, thesis/dissertation. *Entrance requirements:* For master's, GRE General Test, minimum GPA of 2.75 in last 60 hours; for doctorate, GRE General Test, minimum GPA of 3.5. Additional exam requirements/recommendations for international students: Required—TOEFL, IELTS. *Faculty research:* Plant biochemistry, photo chemistry, polymer chemistry, x-ray analysis, enzyme chemistry.

The University of Tennessee, Graduate School, College of Arts and Sciences, Department of Chemistry, Knoxville, TN 37996. Offers analytical chemistry (MS, PhD); chemical physics (PhD); environmental chemistry (MS, PhD); inorganic chemistry (MS, PhD); organic chemistry (MS, PhD); physical chemistry (MS, PhD); polymer chemistry (MS, PhD); theoretical chemistry (PhD). *Program availability:* Part-time. Terminal master's awarded for partial completion of doctoral program. *Degree requirements:* For master's, thesis; for doctorate, thesis/dissertation. *Entrance requirements:* For master's and doctorate, GRE General Test, minimum GPA of 2.7. Additional exam requirements/recommendations for international students: Required—TOEFL. Electronic applications accepted.

The University of Texas at Austin, Graduate School, College of Natural Sciences, Department of Chemistry and Biochemistry, Austin, TX 78712-1111. Offers analytical chemistry (PhD); biochemistry (PhD); inorganic chemistry (PhD); organic chemistry (PhD); physical chemistry (PhD). *Entrance requirements:* For doctorate, GRE General Test.

The University of Toledo, College of Graduate Studies, College of Natural Sciences and Mathematics, Department of Chemistry, Toledo, OH 43606-3390. Offers analytical chemistry (MS, PhD); biological chemistry (MS, PhD); inorganic chemistry (MS, PhD); organic chemistry (MS, PhD); physical chemistry (MS, PhD). *Program availability:* Part-time. *Degree requirements:* For master's, thesis or alternative; for doctorate, thesis/dissertation. *Entrance requirements:* For master's and doctorate, GRE General Test, GRE Subject Test, minimum cumulative point-hour ratio of 2.7 for all previous academic work, three letters of recommendation, statement of purpose, transcripts from all prior institutions attended. Additional exam requirements/recommendations for international students: Required—TOEFL (minimum score 550 paper-based; 80 iBT). Electronic applications accepted. *Faculty research:* Enzymology, materials chemistry, crystallography, theoretical chemistry.

Vanderbilt University, Department of Chemistry, Nashville, TN 37240-1001. Offers analytical chemistry (MAT, MS, PhD); inorganic chemistry (MAT, MS, PhD); organic chemistry (MAT, MS, PhD); physical chemistry (MAT, MS, PhD); theoretical chemistry (MAT, MS). *Faculty:* 19 full-time (3 women). *Students:* 114 full-time (41 women); includes 19 minority (5 Black or African American, non-Hispanic/Latino; 3 Asian, non-Hispanic/Latino; 7 Hispanic/Latino; 4 Two or more races, non-Hispanic/Latino), 8 international. Average age 26. 339 applicants, 17% accepted, 19 enrolled. In 2015, 11 master's, 13 doctorates awarded. Terminal master's awarded for partial completion of doctoral program. *Degree requirements:* For master's, thesis; for doctorate, thesis/dissertation, area, qualifying, and final exams. *Entrance requirements:* For master's and doctorate, GRE General Test, GRE Subject Test (recommended). Additional exam requirements/recommendations for international students: Required—TOEFL (minimum score 570 paper-based; 88 iBT). *Application deadline:* For fall admission, 1/15 for domestic and international students. Application fee: $0. Electronic applications accepted. *Financial support:* Fellowships with tuition reimbursements, research assistantships with full tuition reimbursements, teaching assistantships with full tuition reimbursements, Federal Work-Study, institutionally sponsored loans, scholarships/grants, traineeships, and health care benefits available. Financial award application deadline: 1/15; financial award applicants required to submit CSS PROFILE or FAFSA. *Faculty research:* Chemical synthesis; mechanistic, theoretical, bioorganic, analytical, and spectroscopic chemistry. *Unit head:* Dr. Carmello Rizzo, Director of Graduate Studies, 615-322-2861, Fax: 615-322-4936, E-mail: c.rizzo@vanderbilt.edu. *Application contact:* Sandra Ford, Administrative Assistant, 615-322-8695, Fax: 615-322-4936, E-mail: sandra.e.ford@vanderbilt.edu.
Website: http://www.vanderbilt.edu/chemistry/

Virginia Commonwealth University, Graduate School, College of Humanities and Sciences, Department of Chemistry, Richmond, VA 23284-9005. Offers analytical chemistry (MS, PhD); chemical physics (PhD); inorganic chemistry (MS, PhD); organic chemistry (MS, PhD); physical chemistry (MS, PhD). *Program availability:* Part-time. Terminal master's awarded for partial completion of doctoral program. *Degree requirements:* For master's, thesis; for doctorate, thesis/dissertation, comprehensive cumulative exams, research proposal. *Entrance requirements:* For master's, GRE General Test, 30 undergraduate credits in chemistry; for doctorate, GRE General Test. Additional exam requirements/recommendations for international students: Required—TOEFL (minimum score 600 paper-based; 100 iBT) or IELTS (minimum score 6.5). Electronic applications accepted. *Faculty research:* Physical, organic, inorganic, analytical, and polymer chemistry; chemical physics.

Wake Forest University, Graduate School of Arts and Sciences, Department of Chemistry, Winston-Salem, NC 27109. Offers analytical chemistry (MS, PhD); inorganic chemistry (MS, PhD); organic chemistry (MS, PhD); physical chemistry (MS, PhD). *Program availability:* Part-time. *Degree requirements:* For master's, one foreign language, comprehensive exam, thesis; for doctorate, 2 foreign languages, comprehensive exam, thesis/dissertation. *Entrance requirements:* For master's and doctorate, GRE General Test. Additional exam requirements/recommendations for international students: Required—TOEFL. Electronic applications accepted.

Wayne State University, College of Liberal Arts and Sciences, Department of Chemistry, Detroit, MI 48202. Offers analytical chemistry (PhD); biochemistry (PhD); chemistry (MA, MS); inorganic chemistry (PhD); organic chemistry (PhD); physical chemistry (PhD). *Faculty:* 29. *Students:* 146 full-time (61 women); includes 9 minority (2 Asian, non-Hispanic/Latino; 3 Hispanic/Latino; 4 Two or more races, non-Hispanic/Latino), 95 international. Average age 28. 280 applicants, 19% accepted, 28 enrolled. In 2015, 4 master's, 22 doctorates awarded. *Degree requirements:* For master's, thesis (for some programs), oral exam; for doctorate, thesis/dissertation, oral exam. *Entrance requirements:* For master's, GRE (strongly recommended), 1 year of physics, math through calculus, general chemistry (8 credits), organic chemistry (8 credits), physical chemistry (6 credits), quantitative analysis (4 credits), advanced chemistry (3 credits), minimum undergraduate GPA of 2.75 in chemistry and cognate sciences, statement of interest, three letters of recommendation; for doctorate, GRE (strongly recommended), minimum undergraduate GPA of 3.0 in chemistry and cognate science. Additional exam requirements/recommendations for international students: Required—TOEFL (minimum score 90 iBT), IELTS (minimum score 6.5), TWE (minimum score 5.5). *Application deadline:* For fall admission, 12/1 priority date for domestic and international students. Applications are processed on a rolling basis. Application fee: $0. Electronic applications accepted. *Expenses:* Tuition, state resident: full-time $14,165; part-time $590.20 per credit hour. Tuition, nonresident: full-time $30,682; part-time $1278.40 per credit hour. *Required fees:* $1688; $47.45 per credit hour. $274.60 per semester. Tuition and fees vary according to course load and program. *Financial support:* In 2015–16, 141 students received support, including 10 fellowships with tuition reimbursements available (averaging $23,000 per year), 54 research assistantships with tuition reimbursements available (averaging $21,609 per year), 73 teaching assistantships with tuition reimbursements available (averaging $21,363 per year); scholarships/grants and unspecified assistantships also available. Financial award application deadline: 3/31; financial award applicants required to submit FAFSA. *Faculty research:* Natural products synthesis, molecular biology, molecular mechanics calculations, organometallic chemistry, experimental physical chemistry. *Total annual research expenditures:* $7.4 million. *Unit head:* Dr. James Rigby, Chair, 313-577-3472,
E-mail: jhr@chem.wayne.edu. *Application contact:* Melissa Barton, Graduate Academic Services Officer, E-mail: melissa@chem.wayne.edu.
Website: http://chem.wayne.edu/

West Virginia University, Eberly College of Arts and Sciences, Department of Chemistry, Morgantown, WV 26506. Offers analytical chemistry (MS, PhD); inorganic chemistry (MS, PhD); organic chemistry (MS, PhD); physical chemistry (MS, PhD); theoretical chemistry (MS, PhD). *Program availability:* Part-time, online learning. Terminal master's awarded for partial completion of doctoral program. *Degree requirements:* For master's, thesis; for doctorate, thesis/dissertation. *Entrance requirements:* For master's, GRE General Test, GRE Subject Test (recommended), minimum GPA of 2.5; for doctorate, GRE General Test, GRE Subject Test (recommended), minimum GPA of 2.75. Additional exam requirements/recommendations for international students: Required—TOEFL. Electronic applications accepted. *Expenses:* Tuition, state resident: full-time $8568. Tuition, nonresident: full-time $22,140. Tuition and fees vary according to program. *Faculty research:* Analysis of proteins, drug interactions, solids and effluents by advanced separation methods; new synthetic strategies for complex organic molecules; synthesis and structural characterization of metal complexes for polymerization catalysis, nonlinear science, spectroscopy.

Yale University, Graduate School of Arts and Sciences, Department of Chemistry, New Haven, CT 06520. Offers biophysical chemistry (PhD); inorganic chemistry (PhD); organic chemistry (PhD); physical and theoretical chemistry (PhD). *Degree requirements:* For doctorate, thesis/dissertation. *Entrance requirements:* For doctorate, GRE General Test, GRE Subject Test. Additional exam requirements/recommendations for international students: Required—TOEFL.

Youngstown State University, Graduate School, College of Science, Technology, Engineering and Mathematics, Department of Chemistry, Youngstown, OH 44555-0001. Offers analytical chemistry (MS); biochemistry (MS); chemistry education (MS); inorganic chemistry (MS); organic chemistry (MS); physical chemistry (MS). *Program availability:* Part-time. *Degree requirements:* For master's, thesis. *Entrance requirements:* For master's, bachelor's degree in chemistry, minimum GPA of 2.7. Additional exam requirements/recommendations for international students: Required—TOEFL. *Faculty research:* Analysis of antioxidants, chromatography, defects and disorder in crystalline oxides, hydrogen bonding, novel organic and organometallic materials.

Theoretical Chemistry

Carnegie Mellon University, Mellon College of Science, Department of Chemistry, Pittsburgh, PA 15213-3891. Offers atmospheric chemistry (PhD); bioinorganic chemistry (PhD); bioorganic chemistry and chemical biology (PhD); biophysical chemistry (PhD); catalysis (PhD); green and environmental chemistry (PhD); materials and nanoscience (PhD); renewable energy (PhD); sensors, probes, and imaging (PhD); spectroscopy and single molecule analysis (PhD); theoretical and computational chemistry (PhD). *Program availability:* Part-time. Terminal master's awarded for partial completion of doctoral program. *Degree requirements:* For doctorate, thesis/dissertation, departmental qualifying and oral exams, teaching experience. *Entrance requirements:* For doctorate, GRE General Test, GRE Subject Test. Additional exam requirements/recommendations for international students: Required—TOEFL. Electronic applications accepted. *Faculty research:* Physical and theoretical chemistry, chemical synthesis, biophysical/bioinorganic chemistry.

Cornell University, Graduate School, Graduate Fields of Arts and Sciences, Field of Chemistry and Chemical Biology, Ithaca, NY 14853-0001. Offers analytical chemistry (PhD); bio-organic chemistry (PhD); biophysical chemistry (PhD); chemical biology (PhD); chemical physics (PhD); inorganic chemistry (PhD); materials chemistry (PhD); organic chemistry (PhD); organometallic chemistry (PhD); physical chemistry (PhD); polymer chemistry (PhD); theoretical chemistry (PhD). *Degree requirements:* For doctorate, comprehensive exam, thesis/dissertation. *Entrance requirements:* For doctorate, GRE General Test, GRE Subject Test (chemistry), 3 letters of recommendation. Additional exam requirements/recommendations for international students: Required—TOEFL (minimum score 600 paper-based; 77 iBT). Electronic applications accepted. *Faculty research:* Analytical, organic, inorganic, physical, materials, chemical biology.

Georgetown University, Graduate School of Arts and Sciences, Department of Chemistry, Washington, DC 20057. Offers analytical chemistry (PhD); biochemistry (PhD); computational chemistry (PhD); inorganic chemistry (PhD); materials chemistry (PhD); organic chemistry (PhD); theoretical chemistry (PhD). Terminal master's awarded for partial completion of doctoral program. *Degree requirements:* For doctorate, comprehensive exam, thesis/dissertation. *Entrance requirements:* For doctorate, GRE General Test. Additional exam requirements/recommendations for international students: Required—TOEFL.

Laurentian University, School of Graduate Studies and Research, Programme in Chemistry and Biochemistry, Sudbury, ON P3E 2C6, Canada. Offers analytical chemistry (M Sc); biochemistry (M Sc); environmental chemistry (M Sc); organic chemistry (M Sc); physical/theoretical chemistry (M Sc). *Program availability:* Part-time. *Degree requirements:* For master's, thesis or alternative. *Entrance requirements:* For master's, honors degree with minimum second class. *Faculty research:* Cell cycle checkpoints, kinetic modeling, toxicology to metal stress, quantum chemistry, biogeochemistry metal speciation.

University of Calgary, Faculty of Graduate Studies, Faculty of Science, Department of Chemistry, Calgary, AB T2N 1N4, Canada. Offers analytical chemistry (M Sc, PhD); applied chemistry (M Sc, PhD); inorganic chemistry (M Sc, PhD); organic chemistry (M Sc, PhD); physical chemistry (M Sc, PhD); polymer chemistry (M Sc, PhD); theoretical chemistry (M Sc, PhD). *Degree requirements:* For master's, thesis; for doctorate, thesis/dissertation, candidacy exam. *Entrance requirements:* For master's, minimum GPA of 3.0; for doctorate, honors B Sc degree with minimum GPA of 3.7 or M Sc with minimum GPA of 3.3. Additional exam requirements/recommendations for international students: Required—TOEFL (minimum score 580 paper-based). Electronic applications accepted. *Faculty research:* Chemical analysis, chemical dynamics, synthesis theory.

The University of Manchester, School of Chemistry, Manchester, United Kingdom. Offers biological chemistry (PhD); chemistry (M Ent, M Phil, M Sc, D Ent, PhD); inorganic chemistry (PhD); materials chemistry (PhD); nanoscience (PhD); nuclear fission (PhD); organic chemistry (PhD); physical chemistry (PhD); theoretical chemistry (PhD).

University of Regina, Faculty of Graduate Studies and Research, Faculty of Science, Department of Chemistry and Biochemistry, Regina, SK S4S 0A2, Canada. Offers analytical/environmental chemistry (M Sc, PhD); biophysics of biological interfaces (M Sc, PhD); enzymology/chemical biology (M Sc, PhD); inorganic/organometallic chemistry (M Sc, PhD); signal transduction and mechanisms of cancer cell regulation (M Sc, PhD); supramolecular organic photochemistry and photophysics (M Sc, PhD); synthetic organic chemistry (M Sc, PhD); theoretical/computational chemistry (M Sc, PhD). *Degree requirements:* For master's, thesis; for doctorate, thesis/dissertation. *Entrance requirements:* Additional exam requirements/recommendations for international students: Required—TOEFL (minimum score 580 paper-based; 80 iBT), IELTS (minimum score 6.5), PTE (minimum score 59). Electronic applications accepted. *Faculty research:* Asymmetric synthesis and methodology, theoretical and computational chemistry, biophysical biochemistry, analytical and environmental chemistry, chemical biology.

The University of Tennessee, Graduate School, College of Arts and Sciences, Department of Chemistry, Knoxville, TN 37996. Offers analytical chemistry (MS, PhD); chemical physics (PhD); environmental chemistry (MS, PhD); inorganic chemistry (MS, PhD); organic chemistry (MS, PhD); physical chemistry (MS, PhD); polymer chemistry (MS, PhD); theoretical chemistry (PhD). *Program availability:* Part-time. Terminal master's awarded for partial completion of doctoral program. *Degree requirements:* For master's, thesis; for doctorate, thesis/dissertation. *Entrance requirements:* For master's and doctorate, GRE General Test, minimum GPA of 2.7. Additional exam requirements/recommendations for international students: Required—TOEFL. Electronic applications accepted.

Vanderbilt University, Department of Chemistry, Nashville, TN 37240-1001. Offers analytical chemistry (MAT, MS, PhD); inorganic chemistry (MAT, MS, PhD); organic chemistry (MAT, MS, PhD); physical chemistry (MAT, MS, PhD); theoretical chemistry (MAT, MS). *Faculty:* 19 full-time (3 women). *Students:* 114 full-time (41 women); includes 19 minority (5 Black or African American, non-Hispanic/Latino; 3 Asian, non-Hispanic/Latino; 7 Hispanic/Latino; 4 Two or more races, non-Hispanic/Latino), 8 international. Average age 26. 339 applicants, 17% accepted, 19 enrolled. In 2015, 11 master's, 13 doctorates awarded. Terminal master's awarded for partial completion of doctoral program. *Degree requirements:* For master's, thesis; for doctorate, thesis/dissertation, area, qualifying, and final exams. *Entrance requirements:* For master's and doctorate, GRE General Test, GRE Subject Test (recommended). Additional exam requirements/recommendations for international students: Required—TOEFL (minimum score 570 paper-based; 88 iBT). *Application deadline:* For fall admission, 1/15 for domestic and international students. Application fee: $0. Electronic applications accepted. *Financial support:* Fellowships with tuition reimbursements, research assistantships with full tuition reimbursements, teaching assistantships with full tuition reimbursements, Federal Work-Study, institutionally sponsored loans, scholarships/grants, traineeships, and health care benefits available. Financial award application deadline: 1/15; financial award applicants required to submit CSS PROFILE or FAFSA. *Faculty research:* Chemical synthesis; mechanistic, theoretical, bioorganic, analytical, and spectroscopic chemistry. *Unit head:* Dr. Carmello Rizzo, Director of Graduate Studies, 615-322-2861, Fax: 615-322-4936, E-mail: c.rizzo@vanderbilt.edu. *Application contact:* Sandra Ford, Administrative Assistant, 615-322-8695, Fax: 615-322-4936, E-mail: sandra.e.ford@vanderbilt.edu.
Website: http://www.vanderbilt.edu/chemistry/

Wesleyan University, Graduate Studies, Department of Chemistry, Middletown, CT 06459. Offers biochemistry (PhD); chemical physics (PhD); inorganic chemistry (PhD); organic chemistry (PhD); physical chemistry (PhD); theoretical chemistry (PhD). *Faculty:* 13 full-time (3 women), 3 part-time/adjunct (2 women). *Students:* 20 full-time (10 women), 2 part-time (0 women); includes 4 minority (1 Black or African American, non-

Hispanic/Latino; 3 Asian, non-Hispanic/Latino), 8 international. Average age 25. In 2015, 6 doctorates awarded. Terminal master's awarded for partial completion of doctoral program. *Degree requirements:* For doctorate, thesis/dissertation, proposal. *Entrance requirements:* For doctorate, GRE General Test, 3 recommendations. Additional exam requirements/recommendations for international students: Required—TOEFL, IELTS. *Application deadline:* 2/15 for domestic and international students; for summer admission, 2/15 for domestic and international students. Applications are processed on a rolling basis. Application fee: $0. Electronic applications accepted. *Financial support:* In 2015–16, 4 research assistantships with full tuition reimbursements, 21 teaching assistantships with full tuition reimbursements were awarded; institutionally sponsored loans and health care benefits also available. Financial award application deadline: 4/15; financial award applicants required to submit FAFSA. *Faculty research:* MICHELLE LOUISE PERSONICK Research in the Personick lab is focused on the synthesis of noble metal and noble metal alloy nanoparticles with well-defined shapes and catalytically active high-energy surfaces. Our research takes place at the interface between inorganic chemistry and materials science, and we combine solution-phase nanoparticle synthesis with advanced materials characterization techniques such as scanning electron microscopy (SEM). In addition, we evaluate the catalytic activity of. *Unit head:* Michael Calter, Chair, 860-685-2633, E-mail: mcalter@wesleyan.edu. *Application contact:* Roslyn Brault, Administrative Assistant/Graduate Program Coordinator, 860-685-2573, Fax: 860-685-2211, E-mail: rbrault@wesleyan.edu.
Website: http://www.wesleyan.edu/chem/

West Virginia University, Eberly College of Arts and Sciences, Department of Chemistry, Morgantown, WV 26506. Offers analytical chemistry (MS, PhD); inorganic chemistry (MS, PhD); organic chemistry (MS, PhD); physical chemistry (MS, PhD); theoretical chemistry (MS, PhD). *Program availability:* Part-time, online learning. Terminal master's awarded for partial completion of doctoral program. *Degree requirements:* For master's, thesis; for doctorate, thesis/dissertation. *Entrance requirements:* For master's, GRE General Test, GRE Subject Test (recommended), minimum GPA of 2.5; for doctorate, GRE General Test, GRE Subject Test (recommended), minimum GPA of 2.75. Additional exam requirements/recommendations for international students: Required—TOEFL. Electronic applications accepted. *Expenses:* Tuition, state resident: full-time $8568. Tuition, nonresident: full-time $22,140. Tuition and fees vary according to program. *Faculty research:* Analysis of proteins, drug interactions, solids and effluents by advanced separation methods; new synthetic strategies for complex organic molecules; synthesis and structural characterization of metal complexes for polymerization catalysis, nonlinear science, spectroscopy.

Yale University, Graduate School of Arts and Sciences, Department of Chemistry, New Haven, CT 06520. Offers biophysical chemistry (PhD); inorganic chemistry (PhD); organic chemistry (PhD); physical and theoretical chemistry (PhD). *Degree requirements:* For doctorate, thesis/dissertation. *Entrance requirements:* For doctorate, GRE General Test, GRE Subject Test. Additional exam requirements/recommendations for international students: Required—TOEFL.

Peterson's Graduate Programs in the Physical Sciences, Mathematics, Agricultural Sciences, the Environment & Natural Resources 2017

www.petersons.com   **93**

Section 3
Geosciences

This section contains a directory of institutions offering graduate work in geosciences. Additional information about programs listed in the directory may be obtained by writing directly to the dean of a graduate school or chair of a department at the address given in the directory.

For programs offering related work, see all other areas in this book. In the other guides in this series:

Graduate Programs in the Humanities, Arts & Social Sciences
See *Geography*

Graduate Programs in the Biological/Biomedical Sciences & Health-Related Medical Professions
See *Biological and Biomedical Sciences, Biophysics,* and *Botany and Plant Biology*

Graduate Programs in Engineering & Applied Sciences
See *Aerospace/Aeronautical Engineering; Agricultural Engineering and Bioengineering; Civil and Environmental Engineering; Energy and Power Engineering (Nuclear Engineering); Engineering and Applied Sciences; Geological, Mineral/Mining, and Petroleum Engineering;* and *Mechanical Engineering and Mechanics*

CONTENTS

Program Directories

Geochemistry

California Institute of Technology, Division of Geological and Planetary Sciences, Pasadena, CA 91125-0001. Offers environmental science and engineering (MS, PhD); geobiology (MS, PhD); geochemistry (MS, PhD); geology (MS, PhD); geophysics (MS, PhD); planetary science (MS, PhD). *Degree requirements:* For doctorate, thesis/dissertation. *Entrance requirements:* For doctorate, GRE General Test. Additional exam requirements/recommendations for international students: Required—TOEFL; Recommended—IELTS, TWE. Electronic applications accepted. *Faculty research:* Planetary surfaces, evolution of anaerobic respiratory processes, structural geology and tectonics, theoretical and numerical seismology, global biogeochemical cycles.

California State University, Fullerton, Graduate Studies, College of Natural Science and Mathematics, Department of Chemistry and Biochemistry, Fullerton, CA 92834-9480. Offers chemistry (MA, MS); geochemistry (MS). *Program availability:* Part-time. *Degree requirements:* For master's, thesis, departmental qualifying exam. *Entrance requirements:* For master's, minimum GPA of 2.5 in last 60 units of course work, major in chemistry or related field.

Colorado School of Mines, Office of Graduate Studies, Department of Chemistry and Geochemistry, Golden, CO 80401. Offers chemistry (MS, PhD), including applied chemistry (PhD), chemistry (MS); geochemistry (MS, PhD); materials science (MS, PhD); nuclear engineering (MS, PhD). *Program availability:* Part-time. *Faculty:* 40 full-time (12 women), 10 part-time/adjunct (3 women). *Students:* 57 full-time (22 women); includes 5 minority (1 American Indian or Alaska Native, non-Hispanic/Latino; 2 Hispanic/Latino; 2 Two or more races, non-Hispanic/Latino), 9 international. Average age 28. 76 applicants, 41% accepted, 12 enrolled. In 2015, 4 master's, 14 doctorates awarded. *Degree requirements:* For master's, thesis (for some programs); for doctorate, comprehensive exam, thesis/dissertation. *Entrance requirements:* For master's and doctorate, GRE General Test. Additional exam requirements/recommendations for international students: Required—TOEFL (minimum score 550 paper-based; 80 iBT). *Application deadline:* For fall admission, 12/15 priority date for domestic and international students; for spring admission, 9/1 priority date for domestic and international students. Application fee: $50 ($70 for international students). Electronic applications accepted. *Expenses:* Tuition, state resident: full-time $15,225. Tuition, nonresident: full-time $32,700. *Financial support:* In 2015–16, 52 students received support, including 3 fellowships with full tuition reimbursements available (averaging $21,120 per year), 27 research assistantships with full tuition reimbursements available (averaging $21,120 per year), 22 teaching assistantships with full tuition reimbursements available (averaging $21,120 per year); scholarships/grants, health care benefits, and unspecified assistantships also available. Financial award application deadline: 12/15; financial award applicants required to submit FAFSA. *Faculty research:* Environmental chemistry, exploration geochemistry, biogeochemistry, organic geochemistry, catalysis and surface chemistry. *Total annual research expenditures:* $2.5 million. *Unit head:* Dr. David Wu, Head, 303-384-2066, Fax: 303-273-3629, E-mail: dwu@mines.edu. *Application contact:* Jeremiah Mashore, Program Coordinator, 303-273-3637, E-mail: jmashore@mines.edu.
Website: http://chemistry.mines.edu

Colorado School of Mines, Office of Graduate Studies, Department of Geology and Geological Engineering, Golden, CO 80401. Offers geochemistry (MS, PMS, PhD); geological engineering (ME, MS, PhD); geology (MS, PhD). *Program availability:* Part-time. *Faculty:* 26 full-time (12 women), 5 part-time/adjunct (1 woman). *Students:* 165 full-time (71 women), 20 part-time (7 women); includes 8 minority (1 Asian, non-Hispanic/Latino; 6 Hispanic/Latino; 1 Two or more races, non-Hispanic/Latino), 23 international. Average age 28. 373 applicants, 32% accepted, 54 enrolled. In 2015, 44 master's, 10 doctorates awarded. *Degree requirements:* For master's, thesis (for some programs); for doctorate, comprehensive exam, thesis/dissertation. *Entrance requirements:* For master's and doctorate, GRE General Test. Additional exam requirements/recommendations for international students: Required—TOEFL (minimum score 550 paper-based; 80 iBT). *Application deadline:* For fall admission, 12/15 priority date for domestic and international students; for spring admission, 9/1 priority date for domestic and international students. Application fee: $50 ($70 for international students). Electronic applications accepted. *Expenses:* Tuition, state resident: full-time $15,225. Tuition, nonresident: full-time $32,700. *Financial support:* In 2015–16, 119 students received support, including 25 fellowships with full tuition reimbursements available (averaging $21,120 per year), 73 research assistantships with full tuition reimbursements available (averaging $21,120 per year), 21 teaching assistantships with full tuition reimbursements available (averaging $21,120 per year); scholarships/grants, health care benefits, and unspecified assistantships also available. Financial award application deadline: 12/15; financial award applicants required to submit FAFSA. *Faculty research:* Predictive sediment modeling, petrophysics, aquifer-contaminant flow modeling, water-rock interactions, geotechnical engineering. *Total annual research expenditures:* $3.7 million. *Unit head:* Dr. Paul Santi, Head, 303-273-3108, E-mail: psanti@mines.edu. *Application contact:* Dr. Christian Shorey, Lecturer/Program Manager, 303-273-3556, E-mail: cshorey@mines.edu.
Website: http://geology.mines.edu

Cornell University, Graduate School, Graduate Fields of Agriculture and Life Sciences, Field of Natural Resources, Ithaca, NY 14853-0001. Offers community-based natural resources management (MS, PhD); conservation biology (MS, PhD); ecosystem biology and biogeochemistry (MPS, MS, PhD); environmental management (MPS); fishery and aquatic science (MPS, MS, PhD); forest science (MPS, MS, PhD); human dimensions of natural resources management (MPS, MS, PhD); policy and institutional analysis (MS, PhD); program development and evaluation (MPS, MS, PhD); quantitative ecology (MS, PhD); wildlife science (MPS, MS, PhD). *Degree requirements:* For master's, thesis (MS), project paper (MPS); for doctorate, comprehensive exam, thesis/dissertation. *Entrance requirements:* For master's and doctorate, GRE General Test, 2 letters of recommendation. Additional exam requirements/recommendations for international students: Required—TOEFL (minimum score 550 paper-based; 77 iBT). Electronic applications accepted. *Faculty research:* Ecosystem-level dynamics, systems modeling, conservation biology/management, resource management's human dimensions, biogeochemistry.

Cornell University, Graduate School, Graduate Fields of Engineering, Field of Geological Sciences, Ithaca, NY 14853. Offers economic geology (M Eng, MS, PhD); engineering geology (M Eng, MS, PhD); environmental geophysics (M Eng, MS, PhD); general geology (M Eng, MS, PhD); geobiology (M Eng, MS, PhD); geochemistry and isotope geology (M Eng, MS, PhD); geohydrology (M Eng, MS, PhD); geomorphology (M Eng, MS, PhD); geophysics (M Eng, MS, PhD); geotectonics (M Eng, MS, PhD); marine geology (MS, PhD); mineralogy (M Eng, MS, PhD); paleontology (M Eng, MS, PhD); petroleum geology (M Eng, MS, PhD); petrology (M Eng, MS, PhD); planetary geology (M Eng, MS, PhD); Precambrian geology (M Eng, MS, PhD); Quaternary geology (M Eng, MS, PhD); rock mechanics (M Eng, MS, PhD); sedimentology (M Eng, MS, PhD); seismology (M Eng, MS, PhD); stratigraphy (M Eng, MS, PhD); structural geology (M Eng, MS, PhD). *Degree requirements:* For master's, thesis (MS); for doctorate, comprehensive exam, thesis/dissertation. *Entrance requirements:* For master's and doctorate, GRE General Test, 3 letters of recommendation. Additional exam requirements/recommendations for international students: Required—TOEFL (minimum score 550 paper-based; 77 iBT). Electronic applications accepted. *Faculty research:* Geophysics, structural geology, petrology, geochemistry, geodynamics.

Georgia State University, College of Arts and Sciences, Department of Chemistry, Atlanta, GA 30302-3083. Offers analytical chemistry (MS, PhD); biochemistry (MS, PhD); bioinformatics (MS, PhD); biophysical chemistry (PhD); computational chemistry (MS, PhD); geochemistry (PhD); organic/medicinal chemistry (MS, PhD); physical chemistry (MS). PhD in geochemistry offered jointly with Department of Geosciences. *Program availability:* Part-time. *Faculty:* 26 full-time (4 women). *Students:* 158 full-time (53 women), 4 part-time (all women); includes 43 minority (22 Black or African American, non-Hispanic/Latino; 1 American Indian or Alaska Native, non-Hispanic/Latino; 9 Asian, non-Hispanic/Latino; 7 Hispanic/Latino; 4 Two or more races, non-Hispanic/Latino), 81 international. Average age 28. 117 applicants, 50% accepted, 42 enrolled. In 2015, 28 master's, 15 doctorates awarded. Terminal master's awarded for partial completion of doctoral program. *Degree requirements:* For master's, one foreign language, comprehensive exam (for some programs), thesis (for some programs); for doctorate, one foreign language, comprehensive exam, thesis/dissertation. *Entrance requirements:* For master's and doctorate, GRE. Additional exam requirements/recommendations for international students: Required—TOEFL (minimum score 550 paper-based; 80 iBT) or IELTS (minimum score 6.5). *Application deadline:* For fall admission, 7/1 priority date for domestic and international students; for winter admission, 11/15 priority date for domestic and international students; for spring admission, 4/15 priority date for domestic and international students. Applications are processed on a rolling basis. Application fee: $50. Electronic applications accepted. *Expenses:* Tuition, state resident: full-time $6876; part-time $382 per credit hour. Tuition, nonresident: full-time $22,374; part-time $1243 per credit hour. *Required fees:* $2128; $2128 per term. $1064 per term. Part-time tuition and fees vary according to course load and program. *Financial support:* Fellowships with full tuition reimbursements, research assistantships with full tuition reimbursements, and teaching assistantships with full tuition reimbursements available. Financial award applicants required to submit FAFSA. *Faculty research:* Analytical chemistry, biological/biochemistry, biophysical/computational chemistry, chemical education, organic/medicinal chemistry. *Unit head:* Dr. Peng George Wang, Department Chair, 404-413-3591, Fax: 404-413-5505, E-mail: pwang11@gsu.edu.
Website: http://chemistry.gsu.edu/

Indiana University Bloomington, University Graduate School, College of Arts and Sciences, Department of Geological Sciences, Bloomington, IN 47405-7000. Offers biogeochemistry (MS, PhD); economic geology (MS, PhD); geobiology (MS, PhD); geophysics, structural geology and tectonics (MS, PhD); hydrogeology (MS, PhD); mineralogy (MS, PhD); stratigraphy and sedimentology (MS, PhD). Terminal master's awarded for partial completion of doctoral program. *Degree requirements:* For master's, thesis or alternative; for doctorate, comprehensive exam, thesis/dissertation. *Entrance requirements:* For master's and doctorate, GRE General Test. Additional exam requirements/recommendations for international students: Required—TOEFL. *Faculty research:* Geophysics, geochemistry, hydrogeology, geobiology, planetary science.

Massachusetts Institute of Technology, School of Science, Department of Earth, Atmospheric, and Planetary Sciences, Cambridge, MA 02139. Offers atmospheric chemistry (PhD, Sc D); atmospheric science (SM, PhD, Sc D); chemical oceanography (SM, PhD, Sc D); climate physics and chemistry (SM, PhD, Sc D); earth and planetary sciences (SM); geochemistry (PhD, Sc D); geology (PhD, Sc D); geophysics (PhD, Sc D); marine geology and geophysics (SM, PhD, Sc D); physical oceanography (SM, PhD, Sc D); planetary sciences (PhD, Sc D). *Faculty:* 36 full-time (8 women). *Students:* 166 full-time (75 women), 1 part-time (0 women); includes 23 minority (1 Black or African American, non-Hispanic/Latino; 7 Asian, non-Hispanic/Latino; 6 Hispanic/Latino; 9 Two or more races, non-Hispanic/Latino), 54 international. Average age 27. 228 applicants, 26% accepted, 33 enrolled. In 2015, 6 master's, 24 doctorates awarded. Terminal master's awarded for partial completion of doctoral program. *Degree requirements:* For master's, thesis; for doctorate, comprehensive exam, thesis/dissertation. *Entrance requirements:* For master's, GRE General Test; for doctorate, GRE General Test, GRE Subject Test in chemistry or physics (for planetary sciences area). Additional exam requirements/recommendations for international students: Required—TOEFL (minimum score 600 paper-based; 100 iBT), IELTS (minimum score 7). *Application deadline:* For fall admission, 1/5 for domestic and international students; for spring admission, 11/1 for domestic and international students. Application fee: $75. Electronic applications accepted. *Expenses: Tuition:* Full-time $46,400; part-time $725 per credit. One-time fee: $304 full-time. Full-time tuition and fees vary according to course load and program. *Financial support:* In 2015–16, 99 students received support, including 60 fellowships (averaging $40,700 per year), 76 research assistantships (averaging $38,000 per year), 15 teaching assistantships (averaging $36,100 per year); Federal Work-Study, institutionally sponsored loans, scholarships/grants, traineeships, health care benefits, and unspecified assistantships also available. Support available to part-time students. Financial award application deadline: 4/15; financial award applicants required to submit FAFSA. *Faculty research:* Earth: origin, composition, structure, and dynamics of (and interactions between) the atmosphere, oceans, surface, and interior of the earth; planets: formation, dynamics, and evolution of planetary systems and the characterization of exoplanets; climate: characterization of past, present, and potential future climates; studies of the causes and consequences of climate change; life: co-evolution of life and environmental systems. *Total annual research expenditures:* $25.3 million. *Unit head:* Prof. Robert van der Hilst, Department Head, 617-253-2127, Fax: 617-253-8298, E-mail: eapsinfo@mit.edu. *Application contact:* EAPS Education Office, 617-253-3381, Fax: 617-253-8298, E-mail: eapsinfo@mit.edu.
Website: http://eapsweb.mit.edu/

McMaster University, School of Graduate Studies, Faculty of Science, School of Geography and Earth Sciences, Hamilton, ON L8S 4M2, Canada. Offers geochemistry (PhD); geology (M Sc, PhD); human geography (MA, PhD); physical geography (M Sc, PhD). *Program availability:* Part-time. Terminal master's awarded for partial completion of doctoral program. *Degree requirements:* For master's, thesis; for doctorate, comprehensive exam, thesis/dissertation. *Entrance requirements:* For master's, minimum B+ average. Additional exam requirements/recommendations for international students: Required—TOEFL (minimum score 550 paper-based).

Missouri University of Science and Technology, Graduate School, Department of Geological Sciences and Engineering, Rolla, MO 65409. Offers geological engineering (MS, DE, PhD); geology and geophysics (MS, PhD), including geochemistry, geology, geophysics, groundwater and environmental geology; petroleum engineering (MS, DE, PhD). *Program availability:* Part-time. *Faculty:* 18 full-time (4 women), 1 part-time/adjunct (0 women). *Students:* 249 full-time (51 women), 93 part-time (17 women); includes 37 minority (10 Black or African American, non-Hispanic/Latino; 3 American Indian or Alaska Native, non-Hispanic/Latino; 6 Asian, non-Hispanic/Latino; 18 Hispanic/Latino), 169 international. Average age 31. 296 applicants, 58% accepted, 97 enrolled. In 2015, 17 master's, 6 doctorates awarded. *Degree requirements:* For master's, thesis optional; for doctorate, comprehensive exam, thesis/dissertation. *Entrance requirements:* For master's, GRE General Test (minimum score 600 quantitative, writing 3.5), minimum GPA of 3.0 in last 4 semesters; for doctorate, GRE General Test (minimum scores: Quantitative 600, Writing 3.5). Additional exam requirements/recommendations for international students: Required—TOEFL (minimum score 550 paper-based). *Application deadline:* For fall admission, 7/1 for domestic students; for spring admission, 12/1 for domestic students. Applications are processed on a rolling basis. Application fee: $55 ($175 for international students). Electronic applications accepted. *Expenses:* Tuition, state resident: full-time $10,536. Tuition, nonresident: full-time $27,015. Full-time tuition and fees vary according to course load. *Financial support:* In 2015–16, fellowships with full tuition reimbursements (averaging $11,250 per year), 9 research assistantships with partial tuition reimbursements (averaging $1,814 per year), 3 teaching assistantships with partial tuition reimbursements (averaging $1,814 per year) were awarded; Federal Work-Study and institutionally sponsored loans also available. Support available to part-time students. Financial award application deadline: 3/1; financial award applicants required to submit FAFSA. *Faculty research:* Digital image processing and geographic information systems, mineralogy, igneous and sedimentary petrology-geochemistry, sedimentology groundwater hydrology and contaminant transport. *Total annual research expenditures:* $2.1 million. *Unit head:* Dr. Robert Laudon, Chairman, 573-341-4466, Fax: 573-341-6935,
E-mail: rlaudon@mst.edu. *Application contact:* Debbie Schwertz, Admissions Coordinator, 573-341-6013, Fax: 573-341-6271, E-mail: schwertz@mst.edu.
Website: http://gse.umr.edu/geologicalengineering.html

Montana Tech of The University of Montana, Graduate School, Geosciences Programs, Butte, MT 59701-8997. Offers geochemistry (MS); geological engineering (MS); geology (MS); geophysical engineering (MS); hydrogeological engineering (MS); hydrogeology (MS). *Program availability:* Part-time. *Faculty:* 16 full-time (4 women), 4 part-time/adjunct (0 women). *Students:* 28 full-time (10 women), 10 part-time (5 women); includes 1 minority (Hispanic/Latino), 6 international. 25 applicants, 52% accepted, 10 enrolled. In 2015, 3 master's awarded. *Degree requirements:* For master's, comprehensive exam (for some programs), thesis (for some programs). *Entrance requirements:* For master's, GRE General Test, minimum GPA of 3.0. Additional exam requirements/recommendations for international students: Required—TOEFL (minimum score 545 paper-based; 78 iBT), IELTS (minimum score 6.5). *Application deadline:* For fall admission, 4/1 priority date for domestic students, 3/1 priority date for international students; for spring admission, 10/1 priority date for domestic students, 7/1 priority date for international students. Applications are processed on a rolling basis. Application fee: $50. Electronic applications accepted. *Expenses:* Tuition, state resident: full-time $2901; part-time $1450.68 per degree program. Tuition, nonresident: full-time $8432; part-time $4215.84 per degree program. *Required fees:* $668; $354 per degree program. Tuition and fees vary according to course load and program. *Financial support:* In 2015–16, 15 students received support, including 10 teaching assistantships with partial tuition reimbursements available (averaging $5,000 per year); research assistantships with partial tuition reimbursements available, career-related internships or fieldwork, tuition waivers (full and partial), and unspecified assistantships also available. Financial award application deadline: 4/1; financial award applicants required to submit FAFSA. *Faculty research:* Water resource development, seismic processing, petroleum reservoir characterization, environmental geochemistry, geologic mapping. *Unit head:* Dr. Chris Gammons, Department Head, 406-496-4763, Fax: 406-496-4260,
E-mail: cgammons@mtech.edu. *Application contact:* Daniel Stirling, Administrator, Graduate School, 406-496-4304, Fax: 406-496-4710, E-mail: gradschool@mtech.edu.
Website: http://www.mtech.edu/academics/gradschool/degreeprograms/degrees.htm

New Mexico Institute of Mining and Technology, Center for Graduate Studies, Department of Earth and Environmental Science, Program in Geochemistry, Socorro, NM 87801. Offers MS, PhD. *Degree requirements:* For doctorate, thesis/dissertation. *Expenses:* Tuition, state resident: full-time $5811; part-time $322.81 per credit. Tuition, nonresident: full-time $19,220; part-time $1067.79 per credit. *Required fees:* $1030. Tuition and fees vary according to course load.

Ohio University, Graduate College, College of Arts and Sciences, Department of Geological Sciences, Athens, OH 45701-2979. Offers environmental geochemistry (MS); environmental geology (MS); environmental/hydrology (MS); geology (MS); geology education (MS); geomorphology/surficial processes (MS); geophysics (MS); hydrogeology (MS); sedimentology (MS); structure/tectonics (MS). *Program availability:* Part-time. *Degree requirements:* For master's, thesis. *Entrance requirements:* Additional exam requirements/recommendations for international students: Required—TOEFL (minimum score 550 paper-based; 80 iBT) or IELTS (minimum score 6.5). Electronic applications accepted. *Faculty research:* Geoscience education, tectonics, fluvial geomorphology, invertebrate paleontology, mine/hydrology.

Oregon State University, Interdisciplinary/Institutional Programs, Program in Environmental Sciences, Corvallis, OR 97331. Offers biogeochemistry (MS, PhD); ecology (MS, PhD); environmental education (MS, PhD); environmental sciences (PSM); natural resources (MS, PhD); quantitative analysis (MS, PhD); social science (MS, PhD); water resources (MS, PhD). *Program availability:* Part-time. *Students:* 17 full-time (12 women), 12 part-time (6 women); includes 7 minority (1 Black or African American, non-Hispanic/Latino; 2 Asian, non-Hispanic/Latino; 2 Hispanic/Latino; 2 Two or more races, non-Hispanic/Latino), 3 international. Average age 34. 42 applicants, 19% accepted, 3 enrolled. In 2015, 6 master's, 4 doctorates awarded. *Entrance requirements:* For master's and doctorate, GRE. Additional exam requirements/recommendations for international students: Required—TOEFL (minimum score 80 iBT), IELTS (minimum score 6.5). *Application deadline:* For fall admission, 1/15 for domestic students. Application fee: $75 ($85 for international students). *Expenses:* Contact institution. *Unit head:* Dr. Carolyn Fonyo Boggess, Interim Director, E-mail: carolyn.fonyo@oregonstate.edu.
Website: http://envsci.science.oregonstate.edu/

University of California, Los Angeles, Graduate Division, College of Letters and Science, Department of Earth and Space Sciences, Program in Geochemistry, Los Angeles, CA 90095. Offers MS, PhD. *Degree requirements:* For master's, comprehensive exam, thesis; for doctorate, thesis/dissertation, oral and written qualifying exams. *Entrance requirements:* For master's, GRE General and Subject Tests, bachelor's degree; minimum undergraduate GPA of 3.0 (or its equivalent if letter grade system not used); for doctorate, bachelor's degree; minimum undergraduate GPA of 3.0 (or its equivalent if letter grade system not used). Additional exam requirements/recommendations for international students: Required—TOEFL. Electronic applications accepted.

University of Chicago, Division of the Physical Sciences, Department of the Geophysical Sciences, Chicago, IL 60637. Offers atmospheric sciences (PhD); cosmochemistry (PhD); earth sciences (PhD); paleobiology (PhD); planetary and space sciences (PhD). Terminal master's awarded for partial completion of doctoral program. *Degree requirements:* For doctorate, variable foreign language requirement, comprehensive exam, thesis/dissertation. *Entrance requirements:* For doctorate, GRE General Test. Additional exam requirements/recommendations for international students: Required—TOEFL (minimum score 600 paper-based; 96 iBT), IELTS (minimum score 7). Electronic applications accepted. *Faculty research:* Climatology, evolutionary paleontology, cosmochemistry, geochemistry, oceanic sciences.

University of Hawaii at Manoa, Graduate Division, School of Ocean and Earth Science and Technology, Department of Geology and Geophysics, Honolulu, HI 96822. Offers high-pressure geophysics and geochemistry (MS, PhD); hydrogeology and engineering geology (MS, PhD); marine geology and geophysics (MS, PhD); planetary geosciences and remote sensing (MS, PhD); seismology and solid-earth geophysics (MS, PhD); volcanology, petrology, and geochemistry (MS, PhD). *Program availability:* Part-time. *Faculty:* 72 full-time (15 women), 6 part-time/adjunct (3 women). *Students:* 42 full-time (26 women), 2 part-time (1 woman); includes 9 minority (2 Asian, non-Hispanic/Latino; 2 Hispanic/Latino; 5 Two or more races, non-Hispanic/Latino), 9 international. Average age 31. 78 applicants, 23% accepted, 13 enrolled. In 2015, 7 master's, 8 doctorates awarded. Terminal master's awarded for partial completion of doctoral program. *Degree requirements:* For master's, thesis optional; for doctorate, comprehensive exam, thesis/dissertation. *Entrance requirements:* For master's and doctorate, GRE General Test, minimum GPA of 3.0. Additional exam requirements/recommendations for international students: Required—TOEFL (minimum score 580 paper-based; 92 iBT), IELTS (minimum score 5). *Application deadline:* For fall admission, 1/15 for domestic students, 1/1 for international students; for spring admission, 9/1 for domestic students, 8/15 for international students. Application fee: $100. *Financial support:* In 2015–16, 7 fellowships (averaging $1,359 per year), 30 research assistantships (averaging $23,988 per year), 4 teaching assistantships (averaging $15,350 per year) were awarded. *Total annual research expenditures:* $3.8 million. *Unit head:* Brian Taylor, Dean, 808-956-6182, E-mail: taylorb@hawaii.edu. *Application contact:* Dr. Gregory Moore, Chair, 808-956-7640, Fax: 808-956-5512, E-mail: gg-dept@soest.hawaii.edu.
Website: http://www.soest.hawaii.edu/GG/

The University of Manchester, School of Earth, Atmospheric and Environmental Sciences, Manchester, United Kingdom. Offers atmospheric sciences (M Phil, M Sc, PhD); basin studies and petroleum geosciences (M Phil, M Sc, PhD); earth, atmospheric and environmental sciences (M Phil, M Sc, PhD); environmental geochemistry and cosmochemistry (M Phil, M Sc, PhD); isotope geochemistry and cosmochemistry (M Phil, M Sc, PhD); paleontology (M Phil, M Sc, PhD); physics and chemistry of minerals and fluids (M Phil, M Sc, PhD); structural and petrological geosciences (M Phil, M Sc, PhD).

University of Nevada, Reno, Graduate School, College of Science, Mackay School of Earth Sciences and Engineering, Department of Geological Sciences and Engineering, Program in Geochemistry, Reno, NV 89557. Offers MS, PhD. Terminal master's awarded for partial completion of doctoral program. *Degree requirements:* For master's, thesis optional; for doctorate, thesis/dissertation. *Entrance requirements:* For master's, GRE General Test, minimum GPA of 2.75; for doctorate, GRE General Test, minimum GPA of 3.0. Additional exam requirements/recommendations for international students: Required—TOEFL (minimum score 500 paper-based; 61 iBT), IELTS (minimum score 6). Electronic applications accepted.

The University of Texas at Dallas, School of Natural Sciences and Mathematics, Department of Geosciences, Richardson, TX 75080. Offers geochemistry (MS, PhD); geophysics (MS, PhD); geospatial information sciences (MS, PhD); hydrogeology (MS, PhD); sedimentology, stratigraphy, and paleontology (MS, PhD); structural geology and tectonics (MS, PhD). *Program availability:* Part-time, evening/weekend. *Faculty:* 9 full-time (0 women). *Students:* 57 full-time (21 women), 23 part-time (4 women); includes 12 minority (3 Black or African American, non-Hispanic/Latino; 4 Asian, non-Hispanic/Latino; 3 Hispanic/Latino; 2 Two or more races, non-Hispanic/Latino), 33 international. Average age 30. 98 applicants, 31% accepted, 20 enrolled. In 2015, 20 master's, 4 doctorates awarded. *Degree requirements:* For master's, thesis optional; for doctorate, thesis/dissertation. *Entrance requirements:* For master's and doctorate, GRE General Test, minimum GPA of 3.0 in upper-level course work in field. Additional exam requirements/recommendations for international students: Required—TOEFL (minimum score 550 paper-based). *Application deadline:* For fall admission, 7/15 for domestic students, 5/1 priority date for international students; for spring admission, 11/15 for domestic students, 9/1 priority date for international students. Applications are processed on a rolling basis. Application fee: $50 ($100 for international students). Electronic applications accepted. *Expenses:* Tuition, state resident: full-time $11,940; part-time $663 per semester hour. Tuition, nonresident: full-time $22,786; part-time $1266 per semester hour. Tuition and fees vary according to course load. *Financial support:* In 2015–16, 41 students received support, including 10 research assistantships with partial tuition reimbursements available (averaging $19,260 per year), 15 teaching assistantships with partial tuition reimbursements available (averaging $17,100 per year); career-related internships or fieldwork, Federal Work-Study, institutionally sponsored loans, scholarships/grants, and unspecified assistantships also available. Support available to part-time students. Financial award application deadline: 4/30; financial award applicants required to submit FAFSA. *Faculty research:* Cybermapping, GPS applications for geophysics and geology, seismology and ground-penetrating radar, numerical modeling, signal processing and inverse modeling techniques in seismology. *Unit head:* Dr. John Geissman, Department Head, 972-883-2454, Fax: 972-883-2537, E-mail: geosciences@utdallas.edu. *Application contact:* Gloria Eby, Graduate Support Assistant, 972-883-2404, Fax: 972-883-2537, E-mail: geosciences@utdallas.edu.
Website: http://www.utdallas.edu/geosciences

Yale University, Graduate School of Arts and Sciences, Department of Geology and Geophysics, New Haven, CT 06520. Offers biogeochemistry (PhD); climate dynamics (PhD); geochemistry (PhD); geophysics (PhD); meteorology (PhD); oceanography (PhD); paleontology (PhD); paleoceanography (PhD); petrology (PhD); tectonics (PhD). *Degree requirements:* For doctorate, thesis/dissertation. *Entrance requirements:* For doctorate, GRE General Test. Additional exam requirements/recommendations for international students: Required—TOEFL.

Geodetic Sciences

The Ohio State University, Graduate School, College of Arts and Sciences, Division of Natural and Mathematical Sciences, School of Earth Sciences, Columbus, OH 43210. Offers earth sciences (MS, PhD); geodetic science (MS, PhD); geological sciences (MS, PhD). *Degree requirements:* For master's, thesis; for doctorate, thesis/dissertation. *Entrance requirements:* For master's, GRE, undergraduate degree in biological science, geological sciences, physical science or engineering (recommended); minimum GPA of 3.2; for doctorate, GRE, undergraduate degree in biological science, geological sciences, physical science or engineering (recommended); minimum GPA of 3.4. Additional exam requirements/recommendations for international students: Required—TOEFL (minimum score 550 paper-based; 79 iBT), Michigan English Language Assessment Battery (minimum score 82); Recommended—IELTS (minimum score 8). Electronic applications accepted.

Université Laval, Faculty of Forestry, Geography and Geomatics, Department of Geomatics Sciences, Programs in Geomatics Sciences, Québec, QC G1K 7P4, Canada. Offers M Sc, PhD. Terminal master's awarded for partial completion of doctoral program. *Degree requirements:* For master's, thesis (for some programs); for doctorate, comprehensive exam, thesis/dissertation. *Entrance requirements:* For master's and doctorate, knowledge of French and English. Electronic applications accepted.

University of New Brunswick Fredericton, School of Graduate Studies, Faculty of Engineering, Department of Geodesy and Geomatics Engineering, Fredericton, NB E3B 5A3, Canada. Offers M Eng, M Sc E, PhD. *Faculty:* 9 full-time (1 woman), 11 part-time/adjunct (3 women). *Students:* 37 full-time (8 women), 11 part-time (2 women). In 2015, 18 master's, 2 doctorates awarded. *Degree requirements:* For master's, thesis; for doctorate, comprehensive exam, thesis/dissertation, qualifying exam. *Entrance requirements:* For master's and doctorate, minimum GPA of 3.0. Additional exam requirements/recommendations for international students: Required—TOEFL (minimum score 550 paper-based; 80 iBT), IELTS (minimum score 7), TWE (minimum score 4), Michigan English Language Assessment Battery (minimum score 85) or CanTest (minimum score 4.5). *Application deadline:* For fall admission, 3/1 for domestic students. Applications are processed on a rolling basis. Application fee: $50 Canadian dollars. Electronic applications accepted. *Financial support:* In 2015–16, 28 fellowships, 28 research assistantships, 27 teaching assistantships were awarded. *Faculty research:* GIS, GPS, remote sensing, ocean mapping, land administration, hydrography, engineering surveys. *Unit head:* Dr. Emmanuel Stefanakis, Director of Graduate Studies, 506-453-5137, Fax: 506-453-4943, E-mail: estef@unb.ca. *Application contact:* Sylvia Whitaker, Graduate Secretary, 506-458-7085, Fax: 506-453-4943, E-mail: swhitake@unb.ca.
Website: http://go.unb.ca/gradprograms

Geology

Acadia University, Faculty of Pure and Applied Science, Department of Earth and Environmental Science, Wolfville, NS B4P 2R6, Canada. Offers M Sc. *Degree requirements:* For master's, thesis. *Entrance requirements:* For master's, BSC (honours) in geology or equivalent. Additional exam requirements/recommendations for international students: Required—TOEFL (minimum score 580 paper-based; 93 iBT), IELTS (minimum score 6.5). *Faculty research:* Igneous, metamorphic, and Quaternary geology; stratigraphy; remote sensing; tectonics, carbonate sedimentology.

American University of Beirut, Graduate Programs, Faculty of Arts and Sciences, Beirut, Lebanon. Offers anthropology (MA); Arab and Middle Eastern history (PhD); Arabic language and literature (MA, PhD); archaeology (MA); biology (MS); cell and molecular biology (PhD); chemistry (MS); clinical psychology (MA); computational sciences (MS); computer science (MS); economics (MA); English language (MA); English literature (MA); environmental policy planning (MS); financial economics (MAFE); geology (MS); history (MA); mathematics (MA, MS); media studies (MA); Middle Eastern studies (MA); physics (MS); political studies (MA); psychology (MA); public administration (MA); sociology (MA); statistics (MA, MS); theoretical physics (PhD); transnational American studies (MA). *Program availability:* Part-time. *Faculty:* 114 full-time (36 women), 4 part-time/adjunct (2 women). *Students:* 258 full-time (190 women), 207 part-time (142 women). Average age 27. 241 applicants, 71% accepted, 98 enrolled. In 2015, 47 master's, 3 doctorates awarded. *Degree requirements:* For master's, one foreign language, comprehensive exam, thesis (for some programs); for doctorate, one foreign language, comprehensive exam, thesis/dissertation. *Entrance requirements:* For master's, GRE (for some MA, MS programs), letter of recommendation; for doctorate, GRE, letters of recommendation. Additional exam requirements/recommendations for international students: Required—TOEFL (minimum score 600 paper-based; 97 iBT), IELTS (minimum score 7). *Application deadline:* For fall admission, 4/1 for domestic and international students; for spring admission, 11/1 for domestic and international students. Application fee: $50. Electronic applications accepted. *Expenses: Tuition, area resident:* Full-time $16,254; part-time $903 per credit. *Required fees:* $699. Tuition and fees vary according to course load and program. *Financial support:* Research assistantships, career-related internships or fieldwork, institutionally sponsored loans, scholarships/grants, health care benefits, and unspecified assistantships available. Financial award application deadline: 2/4; financial award applicants required to submit FAFSA. *Faculty research:* Analysis and algebra; software engineering; machine learning and big data analysis; philosophy of mind and political philosophy; anthropology of art, anthropology of migration and medical anthropology; sociology of knowledge, sociology of migration, critical theory; sociology of education; hybrid solid materials; photocatalysis; human creativity. *Total annual research expenditures:* $680,360. *Unit head:* Dr. Patrick McGreevy, Dean, 961-1374374 Ext. 3800, Fax: 961-1744461, E-mail: pm07@aub.edu.lb. *Application contact:* Dr. Salim Kanaan, Director, Admissions Office, 961-1350000 Ext. 2590, Fax: 961-1750775, E-mail: sk00@aub.edu.lb.
Website: http://www.aub.edu.lb/fas/

Arizona State University at the Tempe campus, College of Liberal Arts and Sciences, School of Earth and Space Exploration, Tempe, AZ 85287-1404. Offers astrophysics (MS, PhD); exploration systems design (PhD); geological sciences (MS, PhD). PhD in exploration systems design is offered in collaboration with the Ira A. Fulton School of Engineering. Terminal master's awarded for partial completion of doctoral program. *Degree requirements:* For master's, thesis, interactive Program of Study (iPOS) submitted before completing 50 percent of required credit hours; for doctorate, thesis/dissertation, interactive Program of Study (iPOS) submitted before completing 50 percent of required credit hours. *Entrance requirements:* For master's and doctorate, GRE, minimum GPA of 3.0 or equivalent in last 2 years of work leading to bachelor's degree. Additional exam requirements/recommendations for international students: Required—TOEFL, IELTS, or PTE. Electronic applications accepted.

Auburn University, Graduate School, College of Sciences and Mathematics, Department of Geology and Geography, Auburn University, AL 36849. Offers geography (MS); geology (MS). *Program availability:* Part-time. *Faculty:* 16 full-time (3 women), 3 part-time/adjunct (1 woman). *Students:* 27 full-time (9 women), 5 part-time (1 woman); includes 4 minority (3 Hispanic/Latino; 1 Two or more races, non-Hispanic/Latino), 12 international. Average age 26. 46 applicants, 33% accepted, 14 enrolled. In 2015, 15 master's awarded. *Degree requirements:* For master's, computer language or geographic information systems, field camp. *Entrance requirements:* For master's, GRE General Test. *Application deadline:* Applications are processed on a rolling basis. Application fee: $50 ($60 for international students). Electronic applications accepted. *Expenses:* Tuition, state resident: full-time $8802; part-time $489 per credit hour. Tuition, nonresident: full-time $26,406; part-time $1467 per credit hour. *Required fees:* $808 per semester. Tuition and fees vary according to degree level and program. *Financial support:* Research assistantships, teaching assistantships, and Federal Work-Study available. Support available to part-time students. Financial award application deadline: 3/15; financial award applicants required to submit FAFSA. *Faculty research:* Empirical magma dynamics and melt migration, ore mineralogy, role of terrestrial plant biomass in deposition, metamorphic petrology and isotope geochemistry, reef development, crinoid topology. *Unit head:* Dr. Mark Steltenpohl, Interim Chair, 334-844-4893. *Application contact:* Dr. George Flowers, Dean of the Graduate School, 334-844-2125.

Ball State University, Graduate School, College of Sciences and Humanities, Department of Geological Sciences, Muncie, IN 47306. Offers geology (MA, MS). *Program availability:* Part-time. *Faculty:* 5 full-time (0 women). *Students:* 2 full-time (1 woman), 9 part-time (4 women). Average age 26. 14 applicants, 57% accepted, 2 enrolled. In 2015, 3 master's awarded. *Degree requirements:* For master's, thesis (for some programs). *Entrance requirements:* For master's, GRE General Test, minimum baccalaureate GPA of 2.75 or 3.0 in latter half of baccalauareate. Additional exam requirements/recommendations for international students: Required—TOEFL (minimum score 550 paper-based; 79 iBT), IELTS (minimum score 6.5). *Application deadline:* Applications are processed on a rolling basis. Application fee: $60. Electronic applications accepted. *Expenses: Tuition, area resident:* Full-time $6948; part-time $2316 per semester. Tuition, state resident: full-time $10,422; part-time $3474 per semester. Tuition, nonresident: full-time $19,062; part-time $6354 per semester. *Required fees:* $651 per semester. Tuition and fees vary according to campus/location, program and reciprocity agreements. *Financial support:* In 2015–16, 7 students received support, including 1 research assistantship with partial tuition reimbursement available (averaging $12,047 per year), 6 teaching assistantships with partial tuition reimbursements available (averaging $9,365 per year). Financial award application deadline: 3/1; financial award applicants required to submit FAFSA. *Faculty research:* Environmental geology, geophysics, stratigraphy. *Unit head:* Dr. Richard Fluegeman, Chairperson, 765-285-8267, Fax: 765-285-8265, E-mail: rfluegem@bsu.edu. *Application contact:* Dr. Klaus Neumann, Associate Professor/Graduate Advisor, 765-285-8262, Fax: 765-285-8265, E-mail: kneumann@bsu.edu.
Website: http://www.bsu.edu/geology

Binghamton University, State University of New York, Graduate School, School of Arts and Sciences, Department of Geological Sciences, Vestal, NY 13850. Offers MA, PhD. *Program availability:* Part-time. *Faculty:* 11 full-time (0 women), 1 part-time/adjunct (0 women). *Students:* 23 full-time (8 women), 5 part-time (2 women); includes 4 minority (1 Black or African American, non-Hispanic/Latino; 1 Asian, non-Hispanic/Latino; 1 Hispanic/Latino; 1 Native Hawaiian or other Pacific Islander, non-Hispanic/Latino), 3 international. Average age 29. 32 applicants, 41% accepted, 7 enrolled. In 2015, 3 master's, 1 doctorate awarded. Terminal master's awarded for partial completion of doctoral program. *Degree requirements:* For master's, thesis; for doctorate, one foreign language, comprehensive exam, thesis/dissertation. *Entrance requirements:* For master's and doctorate, GRE General Test. Additional exam requirements/recommendations for international students: Required—TOEFL (minimum score 550 paper-based; 80 iBT). *Application deadline:* For fall admission, 1/30 priority date for domestic and international students; for spring admission, 9/15 priority date for domestic and international students. Application fee: $75. Electronic applications accepted. *Financial support:* In 2015–16, 14 students received support, including 2 research assistantships with full tuition reimbursements available (averaging $15,500 per year), 10 teaching assistantships with full tuition reimbursements available (averaging $15,500 per year); career-related internships or fieldwork, Federal Work-Study, institutionally sponsored loans, scholarships/grants, health care benefits, tuition waivers (full and partial), and unspecified assistantships also available. Financial award applicants required to submit FAFSA. *Unit head:* Dr. Robert V. Demicco, Chairperson, 607-777-2604, E-mail: demicco@binghamton.edu. *Application contact:* Kishan Zuber, Recruiting and Admissions Coordinator, 607-777-2151, Fax: 607-777-2501, E-mail: kzuber@binghamton.edu.

Boston College, Graduate School of Arts and Sciences, Department of Earth and Environmental Sciences, Chestnut Hill, MA 02467. Offers MS, MBA/MS. *Faculty:* 9 full-time. *Students:* 22 full-time (15 women), 1 international. 39 applicants, 31% accepted, 7 enrolled. In 2015, 5 master's awarded. *Degree requirements:* For master's, thesis. *Entrance requirements:* For master's, GRE General Test. Additional exam requirements/recommendations for international students: Required—TOEFL (minimum score 600 paper-based; 100 iBT), IELTS (minimum score 8). *Application deadline:* For fall

admission, 1/10 priority date for domestic students, 1/10 for international students. Application fee: $75. Electronic applications accepted. Tuition and fees vary according to program. *Financial support:* In 2015–16, 22 students received support, including research assistantships with full tuition reimbursements available (averaging $19,400 per year), teaching assistantships with full tuition reimbursements available (averaging $18,400 per year); Federal Work-Study, scholarships/grants, health care benefits, and unspecified assistantships also available. Support available to part-time students. Financial award application deadline: 3/1; financial award applicants required to submit FAFSA. *Faculty research:* Coastal and estuarine processes, earthquake and exploration seismology, environmental geology and geophysics, earth surface processes, paleoclimate, groundwater hydrology, igneous and metamorphic petrology, geochemistry, dynamics and processes of sedimentary systems, plate tectonics, structural geology. *Unit head:* Dr. John Ebel, Chairperson, 617-552-3640, E-mail: ebel@bc.edu. *Application contact:* Dr. Gail Kineke, Graduate Program Director, 617-552-3640, E-mail: gail.kineke@bc.edu.
Website: http://www.bc.edu/schools/eesciences

Bowling Green State University, Graduate College, College of Arts and Sciences, Department of Geology, Bowling Green, OH 43403. Offers MS. *Program availability:* Part-time. *Degree requirements:* For master's, thesis. *Entrance requirements:* For master's, GRE General Test. Additional exam requirements/recommendations for international students: Required—TOEFL. Electronic applications accepted. *Faculty research:* Remote sensing, environmental geology, geological information systems, structural geology, geochemistry.

Brigham Young University, Graduate Studies, College of Physical and Mathematical Sciences, Department of Geological Sciences, Provo, UT 84602. Offers MS. *Faculty:* 15 full-time (1 woman), 1 part-time/adjunct (0 women). *Students:* 24 full-time (5 women), 9 part-time (2 women); includes 2 minority (1 Asian, non-Hispanic/Latino; 1 Hispanic/Latino). Average age 29. 42 applicants, 48% accepted, 16 enrolled. In 2015, 6 master's awarded. *Degree requirements:* For master's, thesis. *Entrance requirements:* For master's, GRE General Test, minimum GPA of 3.0 in last 60 hours of course work. Additional exam requirements/recommendations for international students: Required—TOEFL. *Application deadline:* For fall admission, 2/1 priority date for domestic students, 2/1 for international students; for winter admission, 9/15 for domestic and international students. Applications are processed on a rolling basis. Application fee: $50. *Financial support:* In 2015–16, 21 students received support, including 3 research assistantships with partial tuition reimbursements available (averaging $18,630 per year), 21 teaching assistantships with partial tuition reimbursements available (averaging $18,630 per year); career-related internships or fieldwork, institutionally sponsored loans, scholarships/grants, and tuition waivers (partial) also available. Financial award application deadline: 2/1. *Faculty research:* Linking structure and reactivity, geological mapping of ice cave peak, groundwater surface interactions, reservoir sequence stratigraphy, sequestration of the Cambrio-Ordovician strata of Illinois and Michigan basin. *Total annual research expenditures:* $140,015. *Unit head:* Dr. John H. McBride, Chairman, 801-422-5219, Fax: 801-422-0267, E-mail: mcbseis@gmail.com. *Application contact:* Dr. Michael J. Dorais, Graduate Coordinator, 801-422-1347, Fax: 801-422-0267, E-mail: dorais@byu.edu.
Website: http://www.geology.byu.edu/

Brooklyn College of the City University of New York, School of Natural and Behavioral Sciences, Department of Earth and Environmental Sciences, Brooklyn, NY 11210-2889. Offers MA, PhD. *Program availability:* Evening/weekend. Terminal master's awarded for partial completion of doctoral program. *Degree requirements:* For master's, comprehensive exam, thesis or alternative, qualifying exams, 30 credits. *Entrance requirements:* For master's, bachelor's degree in geology or equivalent, 2 letters of recommendation; for doctorate, GRE. Additional exam requirements/recommendations for international students: Required—TOEFL (minimum score 550 paper-based; 79 iBT). Electronic applications accepted. *Faculty research:* Geochemistry, petrology, tectonophysics, hydrogeology, sedimentary geology, environmental geology.

California Institute of Technology, Division of Geological and Planetary Sciences, Pasadena, CA 91125-0001. Offers environmental science and engineering (MS, PhD); geobiology (MS, PhD); geochemistry (MS, PhD); geology (MS, PhD); geophysics (MS, PhD); planetary science (MS, PhD). *Degree requirements:* For doctorate, thesis/dissertation. *Entrance requirements:* For doctorate, GRE General Test. Additional exam requirements/recommendations for international students: Required—TOEFL; Recommended—IELTS, TWE. Electronic applications accepted. *Faculty research:* Planetary surfaces, evolution of anaerobic respiratory processes, structural geology and tectonics, theoretical and numerical seismology, global biogeochemical cycles.

California State Polytechnic University, Pomona, Program in Geology, Pomona, CA 91768-2557. Offers MS. *Program availability:* Part-time. *Students:* 9 full-time (0 women), 18 part-time (8 women); includes 13 minority (1 Black or African American, non-Hispanic/Latino; 5 Asian, non-Hispanic/Latino; 6 Hispanic/Latino; 1 Two or more races, non-Hispanic/Latino). Average age 28. 12 applicants, 92% accepted, 6 enrolled. In 2015, 6 master's awarded. *Expenses:* Tuition, state resident: full-time $6738. Tuition, nonresident: full-time $13,434. *Required fees:* $1504. Tuition and fees vary according to course load, degree level and program. *Financial support:* Applicants required to submit FAFSA. *Unit head:* Dr. Jonathan A. Nourse, Department Chair/Graduate Coordinator, 909-869-3460, Fax: 909-869-2920, E-mail: janourse@cpp.edu.
Website: http://www.cpp.edu/~sci/geological-sciences/masters-program/

California State University, Bakersfield, Division of Graduate Studies, School of Natural Sciences, Mathematics, and Engineering, Program in Geological Sciences, Bakersfield, CA 93311. Offers geological sciences (MS); hydrogeology (MS); petroleum geology (MS); science education (MS). *Program availability:* Part-time, evening/weekend. *Degree requirements:* For master's, thesis. *Entrance requirements:* For master's, GRE General Test, BS in geology. *Application deadline:* Applications are processed on a rolling basis. Application fee: $55. *Expenses: Tuition, area resident:* Full-time $2246; part-time $1302 per semester. Tuition, state resident: full-time $2246; part-time $1302 per semester. *Financial support:* Teaching assistantships, career-related internships or fieldwork, institutionally sponsored loans, and scholarships/grants available. *Unit head:* Dr. Dirk Baron, Department Chair, 661-664-3044, Fax: 661-664-2040, E-mail: dbaron@csub.edu. *Application contact:* Debbie Blowers, Assistant Director of Admissions, 661-664-3381, E-mail: dblowers@csub.edu.

California State University, Chico, Office of Graduate Studies, College of Natural Sciences, Department of Geological and Environmental Sciences, Chico, CA 95929-0722. Offers environmental science (MS, PSM); geosciences (MS), including hydrology/hydrogeology. *Program availability:* Part-time. *Degree requirements:* For master's, thesis or project. *Entrance requirements:* For master's, GRE General Test, two letters of recommendation, faculty mentor, statement of purpose. Additional exam requirements/recommendations for international students: Required—TOEFL (minimum score 550 paper-based; 80 iBT), IELTS (minimum score 6.5), PTE (minimum score 59). *Application deadline:* For fall admission, 3/1 priority date for domestic students, 3/1 for international students; for spring admission, 9/15 priority date for domestic students, 9/15 for international students. Application fee: $55. Electronic applications accepted. *Expenses: Tuition, area resident:* Full-time $4146; part-time $2730. *Financial support:* Fellowships, teaching assistantships, career-related internships or fieldwork, and scholarships/grants available. Financial award application deadline: 3/1; financial award applicants required to submit FAFSA. *Unit head:* Dr. Russell Shapiro, Chair, 530-898-4300, Fax: 530-898-5234, E-mail: geos@csuchico.edu. *Application contact:* Judy L. Rice, Graduate Admissions Coordinator, 530-898-5416, Fax: 530-898-3342, E-mail: jlrice@csuchico.edu.
Website: http://www.csuchico.edu/geos/

California State University, East Bay, Office of Graduate Studies Programs, College of Science, Department of Earth and Environmental Sciences, Hayward, CA 94542-3000. Offers geology (MS), including environmental geology, geology. *Program availability:* Part-time, evening/weekend. *Students:* 4 full-time (2 women), 13 part-time (5 women); includes 6 minority (1 American Indian or Alaska Native, non-Hispanic/Latino; 2 Asian, non-Hispanic/Latino; 3 Hispanic/Latino), 2 international. Average age 30. 15 applicants, 73% accepted, 7 enrolled. In 2015, 8 master's awarded. *Degree requirements:* For master's, thesis or project. *Entrance requirements:* For master's, GRE, minimum GPA of 2.75 in field, 2.5 overall; 2 letters of recommendation. Additional exam requirements/recommendations for international students: Required—TOEFL (minimum score 550 paper-based). *Application deadline:* For fall admission, 6/30 for domestic and international students. Application fee: $55. Electronic applications accepted. *Financial support:* Career-related internships or fieldwork, Federal Work-Study, and institutionally sponsored loans available. Support available to part-time students. Financial award application deadline: 3/2; financial award applicants required to submit FAFSA. *Faculty research:* Hydrology, seismic activity; origins of life. *Unit head:* Jean E. Moran, Chair, 510-885-2491, E-mail: jean.moran@csueastbay.edu.
Website: http://www20.csueastbay.edu/csci/departments/earth/

California State University, Fresno, Division of Graduate Studies, College of Science and Mathematics, Department of Earth and Environmental Sciences, Fresno, CA 93740-8027. Offers geology (MS). *Program availability:* Part-time. *Degree requirements:* For master's, thesis. *Entrance requirements:* For master's, GRE General Test, undergraduate geology degree, minimum GPA of 2.7. Additional exam requirements/recommendations for international students: Required—TOEFL. Electronic applications accepted. *Faculty research:* Water drainage, pollution, cartography, creek restoration, nitrate contamination.

California State University, Fullerton, Graduate Studies, College of Natural Science and Mathematics, Department of Geological Sciences, Fullerton, CA 92834-9480. Offers MS. *Program availability:* Part-time. *Degree requirements:* For master's, thesis. *Entrance requirements:* For master's, bachelor's degree in geology, minimum GPA of 3.0 in geology courses.

California State University, Long Beach, Graduate Studies, College of Natural Sciences and Mathematics, Department of Geological Sciences, Long Beach, CA 90840. Offers geology (MS); geophysics (MS). *Program availability:* Part-time. *Degree requirements:* For master's, thesis. *Entrance requirements:* For master's, GRE General Test. Electronic applications accepted. *Faculty research:* Paleontology, geophysics, structural geology, organic geochemistry, sedimentary geology.

California State University, Los Angeles, Graduate Studies, College of Natural and Social Sciences, Department of Geological Sciences, Los Angeles, CA 90032-8530. Offers MS. Program offered jointly with California State University, Northridge. *Program availability:* Part-time, evening/weekend. *Degree requirements:* For master's, comprehensive exam or thesis. *Entrance requirements:* Additional exam requirements/recommendations for international students: Required—TOEFL (minimum score 500 paper-based). Electronic applications accepted.

California State University, Northridge, Graduate Studies, College of Science and Mathematics, Department of Geological Sciences, Northridge, CA 91330. Offers geology (MS). *Program availability:* Part-time, evening/weekend. *Faculty:* 9 full-time (3 women), 14 part-time/adjunct (6 women). *Students:* 5 full-time (3 women), 10 part-time (4 women); includes 2 minority (1 American Indian or Alaska Native, non-Hispanic/Latino; 1 Two or more races, non-Hispanic/Latino). Average age 24. 22 applicants, 23% accepted, 5 enrolled. *Degree requirements:* For master's, thesis. *Entrance requirements:* For master's, GRE General Test, minimum GPA of 2.75. Additional exam requirements/recommendations for international students: Required—TOEFL. *Application deadline:* For fall admission, 11/30 for domestic students. Application fee: $55. *Financial support:* Research assistantships, teaching assistantships, Federal Work-Study, and scholarships/grants available. Financial award application deadline: 3/1. *Faculty research:* Petrology of California Miocene volcanics, sedimentology of California Miocene formations, Eocene gastropods, structure of White/Inyo Mountains, seismology of Californian and Mexican earthquakes. *Unit head:* Doug Yule, Chair, 818-677-3541, E-mail: geology@csun.edu.
Website: http://www.csun.edu/geology/

Case Western Reserve University, School of Graduate Studies, Department of Earth, Environmental, and Planetary Sciences, Cleveland, OH 44106. Offers MS, PhD. *Program availability:* Part-time. *Faculty:* 8 full-time (1 woman), 7 part-time/adjunct (1 woman). *Students:* 8 full-time (4 women), 3 international. Average age 28. 13 applicants, 31% accepted, 2 enrolled. Terminal master's awarded for partial completion of doctoral program. *Degree requirements:* For master's, thesis or alternative; for doctorate, thesis/dissertation. *Entrance requirements:* For master's and doctorate, GRE General Test, GRE Subject Test. Additional exam requirements/recommendations for international students: Required—TOEFL (minimum score 577 paper-based; 90 iBT); Recommended—IELTS (minimum score 7). *Application deadline:* For fall admission, 1/15 priority date for domestic students; for spring admission, 11/1 for domestic students. Applications are processed on a rolling basis. Application fee: $50. Electronic applications accepted. *Expenses: Tuition, area resident:* Full-time $41,137; part-time $1714 per credit hour. *Required fees:* $32. Tuition and fees vary according to course load and program. *Financial support:* Research assistantships, teaching assistantships, Federal Work-Study, and tuition waivers (partial) available. Support available to part-time students. Financial award application deadline: 1/15; financial award applicants required to submit FAFSA. *Faculty research:* Geochemistry, hydrology, ecology, geomorphology, planetary science, stratigraphy and basin analysis, igneous petrology. *Unit head:* James Van Orman, Professor and Chair, 216-368-3765, Fax: 216-368-3691, E-mail: james.vanorman@case.edu. *Application contact:* James Van Orman, Professor and Chair, 216-368-3765, Fax: 216-368-3691, E-mail: james.vanorman@case.edu.
Website: http://geology.case.edu/

Central Washington University, Graduate Studies and Research, College of the Sciences, Department of Geological Sciences, Ellensburg, WA 98926. Offers MS. *Program availability:* Part-time. *Degree requirements:* For master's, thesis. *Entrance requirements:* For master's, GRE General Test, minimum GPA of 3.0. Additional exam requirements/recommendations for international students: Required—TOEFL (minimum score 550 paper-based; 79 iBT) or IELTS. Electronic applications accepted.

Geology

City College of the City University of New York, Graduate School, Division of Science, Department of Earth and Atmospheric Sciences, New York, NY 10031-9198. Offers geology (MS). *Degree requirements:* For master's, comprehensive exam, thesis. *Entrance requirements:* Additional exam requirements/recommendations for international students: Required—TOEFL (minimum score 500 paper-based; 61 iBT). *Application deadline:* For fall admission, 5/1 for domestic and international students; for spring admission, 11/15 for domestic and international students. Applications are processed on a rolling basis. Application fee: $125. Electronic applications accepted. Tuition and fees vary according to course load, degree level and program. *Financial support:* Fellowships, career-related internships or fieldwork, and scholarships/grants available. Financial award applicants required to submit FAFSA. *Faculty research:* Water resources, high-temperature geochemistry, sedimentary basin analysis, tectonics. *Unit head:* Pengfei Zhang, Chair, 212-650-6452, Fax: 212-650-6482, E-mail: pzhang@ccny.cuny.edu. *Application contact:* 216-650-6977, E-mail: gradadm@ccny.cuny.edu.

Website: http://www.ccny.cuny.edu/eas/

Colorado School of Mines, Office of Graduate Studies, Department of Geology and Geological Engineering, Golden, CO 80401. Offers geochemistry (MS, PMS, PhD); geological engineering (ME, MS, PhD); geology (MS, PhD). *Program availability:* Part-time. *Faculty:* 26 full-time (12 women), 5 part-time/adjunct (1 woman). *Students:* 165 full-time (71 women), 20 part-time (7 women); includes 8 minority (1 Asian, non-Hispanic/Latino; 6 Hispanic/Latino; 1 Two or more races, non-Hispanic/Latino), 23 international. Average age 28. 373 applicants, 32% accepted, 54 enrolled. In 2015, 44 master's, 10 doctorates awarded. *Degree requirements:* For master's, thesis (for some programs); for doctorate, comprehensive exam, thesis/dissertation. *Entrance requirements:* For master's and doctorate, GRE General Test. Additional exam requirements/recommendations for international students: Required—TOEFL (minimum score 550 paper-based; 80 iBT). *Application deadline:* For fall admission, 12/15 priority date for domestic and international students; for spring admission, 9/1 priority date for domestic and international students. Application fee: $50 ($70 for international students). Electronic applications accepted. *Expenses:* Tuition, state resident: full-time $15,225. Tuition, nonresident: full-time $32,700. *Financial support:* In 2015–16, 119 students received support, including 25 fellowships with full tuition reimbursements available (averaging $21,120 per year), 73 research assistantships with full tuition reimbursements available (averaging $21,120 per year), 21 teaching assistantships with full tuition reimbursements available (averaging $21,120 per year); scholarships/grants, health care benefits, and unspecified assistantships also available. Financial award application deadline: 12/15; financial award applicants required to submit FAFSA. *Faculty research:* Predictive sediment modeling, petrophysics, aquifer-contaminant flow modeling, water-rock interactions, geotechnical engineering. *Total annual research expenditures:* $3.7 million. *Unit head:* Dr. Paul Santi, Head, 303-273-3108, E-mail: psanti@mines.edu. *Application contact:* Dr. Christian Shorey, Lecturer/Program Manager, 303-273-3556, E-mail: cshorey@mines.edu.

Website: http://geology.mines.edu

Cornell University, Graduate School, Graduate Fields of Engineering, Field of Geological Sciences, Ithaca, NY 14853. Offers economic geology (M Eng, MS, PhD); engineering geology (M Eng, MS, PhD); environmental geophysics (M Eng, MS, PhD); general geology (M Eng, MS, PhD); geobiology (M Eng, MS, PhD); geochemistry and isotope geology (M Eng, MS, PhD); geohydrology (M Eng, MS, PhD); geomorphology (M Eng, MS, PhD); geophysics (M Eng, MS, PhD); geotectonics (M Eng, MS, PhD); marine geology (MS, PhD); mineralogy (M Eng, MS, PhD); paleontology (M Eng, MS, PhD); petroleum geology (M Eng, MS, PhD); petrology (M Eng, MS, PhD); planetary geology (M Eng, MS, PhD); Precambrian geology (M Eng, MS, PhD); Quaternary geology (M Eng, MS, PhD); rock mechanics (M Eng, MS, PhD); sedimentology (M Eng, MS, PhD); seismology (M Eng, MS, PhD); stratigraphy (M Eng, MS, PhD); structural geology (M Eng, MS, PhD). *Degree requirements:* For master's, thesis (MS); for doctorate, comprehensive exam, thesis/dissertation. *Entrance requirements:* For master's and doctorate, GRE General Test, 3 letters of recommendation. Additional exam requirements/recommendations for international students: Required—TOEFL (minimum score 550 paper-based; 77 iBT). Electronic applications accepted. *Faculty research:* Geophysics, structural geology, petrology, geochemistry, geodynamics.

Duke University, Graduate School, Division of Earth and Ocean Sciences, Durham, NC 27708. Offers MS, PhD. *Program availability:* Part-time. Terminal master's awarded for partial completion of doctoral program. *Degree requirements:* For master's, thesis; for doctorate, thesis/dissertation. *Entrance requirements:* For master's and doctorate, GRE General Test. Additional exam requirements/recommendations for international students: Required—TOEFL (minimum score 577 paper-based; 90 iBT) or IELTS (minimum score 7). Electronic applications accepted.

East Carolina University, Graduate School, Thomas Harriot College of Arts and Sciences, Department of Geological Sciences, Greenville, NC 27858-4353. Offers geology (MS); hydrogeology and environmental geology (Certificate). *Program availability:* Part-time. *Students:* 25 full-time (8 women), 21 part-time (7 women). Average age 27. 25 applicants, 88% accepted, 12 enrolled. In 2015, 12 master's awarded. *Degree requirements:* For master's, one foreign language, comprehensive exam, thesis. *Entrance requirements:* For master's, GRE General Test. Additional exam requirements/recommendations for international students: Required—TOEFL. *Application deadline:* For fall admission, 6/1 priority date for domestic students; for spring admission, 10/15 for domestic students. Applications are processed on a rolling basis. Application fee: $50. *Financial support:* Research assistantships with partial tuition reimbursements and teaching assistantships with partial tuition reimbursements available. Support available to part-time students. Financial award application deadline: 6/1. *Unit head:* Dr. Stephen Culver, Chair, 252-328-6360, Fax: 252-328-4391, E-mail: culvers@ecu.edu. *Application contact:* Dean of Graduate School, 252-328-6012, Fax: 252-328-6071, E-mail: gradschool@ecu.edu.

Website: http://www.ecu.edu/geology/

Eastern Kentucky University, The Graduate School, College of Arts and Sciences, Department of Earth Sciences, Richmond, KY 40475-3102. Offers geology (MS, PhD). PhD program offered jointly with University of Kentucky. *Program availability:* Part-time. *Degree requirements:* For master's, thesis. *Entrance requirements:* For master's, GRE General Test, minimum GPA of 2.5. *Faculty research:* Hydrogeology, sedimentary geology, geochemistry, environmental geology, tectonics.

Florida Atlantic University, Charles E. Schmidt College of Science, Department of Geosciences, Boca Raton, FL 33431-0991. Offers geography (MA); geology (MS); geosciences (PhD). *Program availability:* Part-time. *Degree requirements:* For master's, thesis (for some programs). *Entrance requirements:* For master's, GRE General Test, minimum GPA of 3.0. Additional exam requirements/recommendations for international students: Required—TOEFL (minimum score 500 paper-based; 61 iBT), IELTS (minimum score 6). Electronic applications accepted. *Faculty research:* GIS applications, paleontology, hydrogeology, economic development.

Florida State University, The Graduate School, College of Arts and Sciences, Department of Earth, Ocean and Atmospheric Science, Program in Geological Sciences, Tallahassee, FL 32306. Offers MS, PhD. *Faculty:* 13 full-time (1 woman). *Students:* 38 full-time (17 women), 4 part-time (3 women); includes 2 minority (both Two or more races, non-Hispanic/Latino), 15 international. Average age 26. In 2015, 10 master's, 2 doctorates awarded. *Degree requirements:* For master's, comprehensive exam, thesis; for doctorate, comprehensive exam, thesis/dissertation. *Entrance requirements:* For master's and doctorate, GRE General Test, minimum GPA of 3.0. Additional exam requirements/recommendations for international students: Required—TOEFL (minimum score 550 paper-based; 80 iBT). *Application deadline:* For fall admission, 2/15 priority date for domestic and international students; for spring admission, 9/15 priority date for domestic and international students. Applications are processed on a rolling basis. Application fee: $35. Electronic applications accepted. *Expenses: Tuition, area resident:* Full-time $7263; part-time $403.50 per credit hour. Tuition, nonresident: full-time $18,087; part-time $1004.85 per credit hour. *Required fees:* $1365; $75.81 per credit hour. $20 per semester. Tuition and fees vary according to campus/location. *Financial support:* In 2015–16, 25 students received support. Fellowships, research assistantships, teaching assistantships, career-related internships or fieldwork, and Federal Work-Study available. Financial award application deadline: 2/15; financial award applicants required to submit FAFSA. *Faculty research:* Appalachian and collisional tectonics, surface and groundwater hydrogeology, micropaleontology, isotope and trace element geochemistry, coastal and estuarine studies. *Total annual research expenditures:* $2.3 million. *Unit head:* Dr. James Tull, Chairman, 850-644-6205, Fax: 850-644-4214, E-mail: jtull@fsu.edu. *Application contact:* Michaela Lupiani, Academic Coordinator, 850-644-6205, Fax: 850-644-4214, E-mail: mlupiani@fsu.edu.

Website: http://www.eoas.fsu.edu

Fort Hays State University, Graduate School, College of Arts and Sciences, Department of Geosciences, Program in Geosciences, Hays, KS 67601-4099. Offers geography (MS); geology (MS). *Degree requirements:* For master's, comprehensive exam, thesis. *Entrance requirements:* For master's, GRE General Test. Additional exam requirements/recommendations for international students: Required—TOEFL (minimum score 550 paper-based). Electronic applications accepted. *Faculty research:* Cretaceous and late Cenozoic stratigraphy, sedimentation, paleontology.

Georgia State University, College of Arts and Sciences, Department of Geosciences, Program in Geology, Atlanta, GA 30302-3083. Offers MS. *Degree requirements:* For master's, one foreign language, comprehensive exam (for some programs), thesis or alternative. *Entrance requirements:* For master's, GRE General Test, minimum GPA of 2.75. Additional exam requirements/recommendations for international students: Required—TOEFL. *Application deadline:* For fall admission, 4/15 for domestic and international students; for spring admission, 9/15 for domestic and international students. Application fee: $50. *Expenses:* Tuition, state resident: full-time $6876; part-time $382 per credit hour. Tuition, nonresident: full-time $22,374; part-time $1243 per credit hour. *Required fees:* $2128; $2128 per term. $1064 per term. Part-time tuition and fees vary according to course load and program. *Financial support:* Research assistantships with tuition reimbursements, teaching assistantships with tuition reimbursements, and tuition waivers (partial) available. *Unit head:* Dr. W. Crawford Elliott, Chair, 404-413-5756, E-mail: wcelliott@gsu.edu.

Website: http://geosciences.gsu.edu/grad-programs/m-s-degree-in-geosciences/

Hofstra University, School of Education, Programs in Teacher Education, Hempstead, NY 11549. Offers bilingual education (MA), including biology (MA, MS Ed), geology; business education (MS Ed); early childhood and childhood education (MS Ed), including French; early childhood education (MA); education technology (Advanced Certificate); elementary education (MA), including science, technology, engineering, and mathematics (STEM); English education (MS Ed); fine arts education (MS Ed), including biology (MA, MS Ed); foreign language and TESOL (MS Ed); learning and teaching (Ed D), including applied linguistics, art education, arts and humanities, early childhood education, English education, human development, math education, math, science, and technology, multicultural education, physical education, science education, social studies education, special education; mathematics education (MA, MS Ed); secondary education (Advanced Certificate); social studies education (MA, MS Ed). *Program availability:* Part-time, evening/weekend, online learning. *Students:* 141 full-time (111 women), 119 part-time (84 women); includes 58 minority (13 Black or African American, non-Hispanic/Latino; 14 Asian, non-Hispanic/Latino; 28 Hispanic/Latino; 1 Native Hawaiian or other Pacific Islander, non-Hispanic/Latino; 2 Two or more races, non-Hispanic/Latino), 18 international. Average age 30. 301 applicants, 87% accepted, 112 enrolled. In 2015, 133 master's, 5 doctorates, 28 other advanced degrees awarded. *Degree requirements:* For master's, comprehensive exam, thesis (for some programs), exit project, student teaching, fieldwork, electronic portfolio, curriculum project, minimum GPA of 3.0; for doctorate, thesis/dissertation; for Advanced Certificate, 3 foreign languages, comprehensive exam (for some programs), thesis project. *Entrance requirements:* For master's, 2 letters of recommendation, portfolio, teacher certification (MA), interview, essay; for doctorate, GMAT, GRE, LSAT, or MAT; for Advanced Certificate, 2 letters of recommendation, essay, interview and/or portfolio, teaching certificate. Additional exam requirements/recommendations for international students: Required—TOEFL (minimum score 550 paper-based; 80 iBT). *Application deadline:* Applications are processed on a rolling basis. Application fee: $70 ($75 for international students). Electronic applications accepted. *Financial support:* In 2015–16, 153 students received support, including 60 fellowships with tuition reimbursements available (averaging $5,084 per year), 4 research assistantships with tuition reimbursements available (averaging $7,095 per year); Federal Work-Study, institutionally sponsored loans, scholarships/grants, health care benefits, and tuition waivers (full and partial) also available. Support available to part-time students. Financial award applicants required to submit FAFSA. *Faculty research:* Appropriate content in secondary school disciplines, lesson development across content, interdisciplinary curriculum, multicultural education. *Unit head:* Dr. Eustace Thompson, Chairperson, 516-463-5749, Fax: 516-463-6275, E-mail: edaegt@hofstra.edu. *Application contact:* Sunil Samuel, Assistant Vice President of Admissions, 516-463-4723, Fax: 516-463-4664, E-mail: graduateadmission@hofstra.edu.

Website: http://www.hofstra.edu/education/

Humboldt State University, Academic Programs, College of Natural Resources and Sciences, Programs in Environmental Systems, Arcata, CA 95521-8299. Offers environmental systems (MS), including energy, environment and society, environmental resources engineering, geology, math modeling. *Degree requirements:* For master's, thesis. *Entrance requirements:* For master's, GRE, appropriate bachelor's degree, minimum GPA of 2.5, 3 letters of recommendation. Additional exam requirements/recommendations for international students: Required—TOEFL. *Faculty research:* Mathematical modeling, international development technology, geology, environmental resources engineering.

Idaho State University, Office of Graduate Studies, College of Science and Engineering, Department of Geosciences, Pocatello, ID 83209-8072. Offers geographic information science (MS); geology (MNS, MS); geology with emphasis in environmental geoscience (MS); geophysics/hydrology/geology (MS); geotechnology (Postbaccalaureate Certificate). *Program availability:* Part-time. *Degree requirements:* For master's, comprehensive exam, thesis, oral colloquium; for Postbaccalaureate Certificate, thesis optional, minimum 19 credits. *Entrance requirements:* For master's, GRE General Test (minimum 50th percentile in 2 sections), 3 letters of recommendation; for Postbaccalaureate Certificate, GRE General Test, 3 letters of recommendation, bachelor's degree, statement of goals. Additional exam requirements/recommendations for international students: Required—TOEFL (minimum score 550 paper-based; 80 iBT). Electronic applications accepted. *Faculty research:* Quantitative field mapping and sampling: microscopic, geochemical, and isotopic analysis of rocks, minerals and water; remote sensing, geographic information systems, and global positioning systems: environmental and watershed management; surficial and fluvial processes: landscape change; regional tectonics, structural geology; planetary geology.

Indiana University Bloomington, University Graduate School, College of Arts and Sciences, Department of Geological Sciences, Bloomington, IN 47405-7000. Offers biogeochemistry (MS, PhD); economic geology (MS, PhD); geobiology (MS, PhD); geophysics, structural geology and tectonics (MS, PhD); hydrogeology (MS, PhD); mineralogy (MS, PhD); stratigraphy and sedimentology (MS, PhD). Terminal master's awarded for partial completion of doctoral program. *Degree requirements:* For master's, thesis or alternative; for doctorate, comprehensive exam, thesis/dissertation. *Entrance requirements:* For master's and doctorate, GRE General Test. Additional exam requirements/recommendations for international students: Required—TOEFL. *Faculty research:* Geophysics, geochemistry, hydrogeology, geobiology, planetary science.

Indiana University–Purdue University Indianapolis, School of Science, Department of Earth Sciences, Indianapolis, IN 46202-3272. Offers applied earth sciences (PhD); geology (MS). *Program availability:* Part-time, evening/weekend. *Degree requirements:* For master's, thesis (for some programs). *Entrance requirements:* For master's, GRE General Test, minimum GPA of 3.0. *Faculty research:* Wetland hydrology, groundwater contamination, soils, sedimentology, sediment chemistry.

Iowa State University of Science and Technology, Department of Geological and Atmospheric Sciences, Ames, IA 50011. Offers earth science (MS, PhD); environmental science (MS, PhD); geology (MS, PhD); meteorology (MS, PhD). *Degree requirements:* For master's, thesis (for some programs); for doctorate, thesis/dissertation. *Entrance requirements:* For master's and doctorate, GRE General Test. Additional exam requirements/recommendations for international students: Required—TOEFL (minimum score 550 paper-based; 79 iBT), IELTS (minimum score 6.5). Electronic applications accepted.

Kansas State University, Graduate School, College of Arts and Sciences, Department of Geology, Manhattan, KS 66506. Offers MS. *Degree requirements:* For master's, thesis. *Entrance requirements:* For master's, GRE General Test, minimum GPA of 3.0 in all geology undergraduate coursework, two semesters of calculus. Additional exam requirements/recommendations for international students: Required—TOEFL. Electronic applications accepted. *Faculty research:* Chemical hydrogeology, petroleum geology, exploration seismic and near surface geophysics, late Pleistocene geochronology, igneous petrology, isotope geology, volcanology, climate change, tidal sedimentation processes, luminescence dating, biomineralization.

Kent State University, College of Arts and Sciences, Department of Geology, Kent, OH 44242-0001. Offers applied geology (PhD). *Program availability:* Part-time. *Faculty:* 9 full-time (3 women). *Students:* 26 full-time (15 women), 14 part-time (4 women); includes 2 minority (both Hispanic/Latino), 6 international. Average age 29. 60 applicants, 57% accepted, 8 enrolled. In 2015, 10 master's, 5 doctorates awarded. *Degree requirements:* For master's, thesis; for doctorate, one foreign language, thesis/dissertation. *Entrance requirements:* For master's and doctorate, GRE General Test, GRE Subject Test, minimum GPA of 3.0, transcript, resume, statement of purpose, 3 letters of recommendation. Additional exam requirements/recommendations for international students: Required—TOEFL (minimum score: paper-based 525, iBT 71), Michigan English Language Assessment Battery (minimum score of 75), IELTS (minimum score of 6.0), PTE Academic (minimum score of 48), or completion of ELS level 112 Intensive Program. *Application deadline:* For fall admission, 7/1 for domestic students; for spring admission, 11/15 for domestic students. Application fee: $45 ($70 for international students). Electronic applications accepted. *Expenses:* Tuition, state resident: full-time $10,864; part-time $495 per credit hour. Tuition, nonresident: full-time $18,380; part-time $837 per credit hour. *Financial support:* In 2015–16, 17 students received support. Research assistantships with full tuition reimbursements available, teaching assistantships with full tuition reimbursements available, career-related internships or fieldwork, Federal Work-Study, scholarships/grants, and unspecified assistantships available. Financial award application deadline: 2/1. *Unit head:* Dr. Daniel Holm, Professor and Chair, 330-672-4094, E-mail: dholm@kent.edu. *Application contact:* Dr. Joseph D. Ortiz, Professor and Graduate Coordinator, 330-672-2680, E-mail: geology@kent.edu.
Website: http://www.kent.edu/geology/

Lakehead University, Graduate Studies, Department of Geology, Thunder Bay, ON P7B 5E1, Canada. Offers M Sc. *Program availability:* Part-time, evening/weekend. *Degree requirements:* For master's, thesis, department seminar, oral exam. *Entrance requirements:* For master's, minimum B average, honours bachelors degree in geology. Additional exam requirements/recommendations for international students: Required—TOEFL. *Faculty research:* Rock physics, sedimentology, mineralogy and economic geology, geochemistry, petrology of alkaline rocks.

Laurentian University, School of Graduate Studies and Research, Programme in Geology (Earth Sciences), Sudbury, ON P3E 2C6, Canada. Offers geology (M Sc); mineral deposits and precambrian geology (PhD); mineral exploration (M Sc). *Program availability:* Part-time. *Degree requirements:* For master's, thesis. *Entrance requirements:* For master's, honors degree with second class or better. *Faculty research:* Localization and metallogenesis of Ni-Cu-(PGE) sulfide mineralization in the Thompson Nickel Belt, mapping lithology and ore-grade and monitoring dissolved organic carbon in lakes using remote sensing, global reefs, volcanic effects on VMS deposits.

Lehigh University, College of Arts and Sciences, Department of Earth and Environmental Sciences, Bethlehem, PA 18015. Offers MS, PhD. *Faculty:* 14 full-time (2 women). *Students:* 21 full-time (9 women), 3 part-time (1 woman), 6 international. Average age 27. 46 applicants, 24% accepted, 8 enrolled. In 2015, 3 master's, 2 doctorates awarded. Terminal master's awarded for partial completion of doctoral program. *Degree requirements:* For master's, thesis; for doctorate, thesis/dissertation. *Entrance requirements:* For master's and doctorate, GRE General Test, transcripts, recommendation letters, research statement, faculty advocates. Additional exam requirements/recommendations for international students: Required—TOEFL (minimum score 85 iBT). *Application deadline:* For fall admission, 1/1 for domestic and international students. Application fee: $75. Electronic applications accepted. *Expenses:* $1,380 per credit. *Financial support:* In 2015–16, 14 students received support, including 5 fellowships with full tuition reimbursements available (averaging $25,377 per year), 6 research assistantships with full tuition reimbursements available (averaging $20,250 per year), 10 teaching assistantships with full tuition reimbursements available (averaging $20,250 per year); scholarships/grants also available. Financial award application deadline: 1/1. *Faculty research:* Tectonics, surficial processes, ecology, environmental change, remote sensing. *Total annual research expenditures:* $1.1 million. *Unit head:* Dr. David J. Anastasio, Chairman, 610-758-5117, Fax: 610-758-3677, E-mail: dja2@lehigh.edu. *Application contact:* Dr. Kenneth Kodama, Graduate Coordinator, 610-758-3663, Fax: 610-758-3677, E-mail: kpk0@lehigh.edu.
Website: http://www.ees.lehigh.edu/

Louisiana State University and Agricultural & Mechanical College, Graduate School, College of Science, Department of Geology and Geophysics, Baton Rouge, LA 70803. Offers MS, PhD.

Massachusetts Institute of Technology, School of Science, Department of Earth, Atmospheric, and Planetary Sciences, Cambridge, MA 02139. Offers atmospheric chemistry (PhD, Sc D); atmospheric science (SM, PhD, Sc D); chemical oceanography (SM, PhD, Sc D); climate physics and chemistry (SM, PhD, Sc D); earth and planetary sciences (SM); geochemistry (PhD, Sc D); geology (PhD, Sc D); geophysics (PhD, Sc D); marine geology and geophysics (SM, PhD, Sc D); physical oceanography (SM, PhD, Sc D); planetary sciences (PhD, Sc D). *Faculty:* 36 full-time (8 women). *Students:* 166 full-time (75 women), 1 part-time (0 women); includes 23 minority (1 Black or African American, non-Hispanic/Latino; 7 Asian, non-Hispanic/Latino; 6 Hispanic/Latino; 9 Two or more races, non-Hispanic/Latino), 54 international. Average age 27. 228 applicants, 26% accepted, 33 enrolled. In 2015, 6 master's, 24 doctorates awarded. Terminal master's awarded for partial completion of doctoral program. *Degree requirements:* For master's, thesis; for doctorate, comprehensive exam, thesis/dissertation. *Entrance requirements:* For master's, GRE General Test; for doctorate, GRE General Test, GRE Subject Test in chemistry or physics (for planetary sciences area). Additional exam requirements/recommendations for international students: Required—TOEFL (minimum score 600 paper-based; 100 iBT), IELTS (minimum score 7). *Application deadline:* For fall admission, 1/5 for domestic and international students; for spring admission, 11/1 for domestic and international students. Application fee: $75. Electronic applications accepted. *Expenses: Tuition:* Full-time $46,400; part-time $725 per credit. One-time fee: $304 full-time. Full-time tuition and fees vary according to course load and program. *Financial support:* In 2015–16, 99 students received support, including 60 fellowships (averaging $40,700 per year), 76 research assistantships (averaging $38,000 per year), 15 teaching assistantships (averaging $36,100 per year); Federal Work-Study, institutionally sponsored loans, scholarships/grants, traineeships, health care benefits, and unspecified assistantships also available. Support available to part-time students. Financial award application deadline: 4/15; financial award applicants required to submit FAFSA. *Faculty research:* Earth: origin, composition, structure, and dynamics of (and interactions between) the atmosphere, oceans, surface, and interior of the earth; planets: formation, dynamics, and evolution of planetary systems and the characterization of exoplanets; climate: characterization of past, present, and potential future climates; studies of the causes and consequences of climate change; life: co-evolution of life and environmental systems. *Total annual research expenditures:* $25.3 million. *Unit head:* Prof. Robert van der Hilst, Department Head, 617-253-2127, Fax: 617-253-8298, E-mail: eapsinfo@mit.edu. *Application contact:* EAPS Education Office, 617-253-3381, Fax: 617-253-8298, E-mail: eapsinfo@mit.edu.
Website: http://eapsweb.mit.edu/

McMaster University, School of Graduate Studies, Faculty of Science, School of Geography and Earth Sciences, Hamilton, ON L8S 4M2, Canada. Offers geochemistry (PhD); geology (M Sc, PhD); human geography (MA, PhD); physical geography (M Sc, PhD). *Program availability:* Part-time. Terminal master's awarded for partial completion of doctoral program. *Degree requirements:* For master's, thesis; for doctorate, comprehensive exam, thesis/dissertation. *Entrance requirements:* For master's, minimum B+ average. Additional exam requirements/recommendations for international students: Required—TOEFL (minimum score 550 paper-based).

Memorial University of Newfoundland, School of Graduate Studies, Department of Earth Sciences, St. John's, NL A1C 5S7, Canada. Offers geology (M Sc, PhD); geophysics (M Sc, PhD). *Program availability:* Part-time. *Degree requirements:* For master's, thesis; for doctorate, comprehensive exam, thesis/dissertation, oral thesis defense, entry evaluation. *Entrance requirements:* For master's, honors B Sc; for doctorate, M Sc. *Application deadline:* 1/15 for domestic and international students. Applications are processed on a rolling basis. Application fee: $50 Canadian dollars ($100 Canadian dollars for international students). Electronic applications accepted. *Expenses: Tuition, area resident:* Full-time $2199 Canadian dollars. *International tuition:* $2859 Canadian dollars full-time. *Financial support:* Fellowships, research assistantships, and teaching assistantships available. *Faculty research:* Geochemistry, sedimentology, paleoceanography and global change, mineral deposits, petroleum geology, hydrology. *Unit head:* Dr. John Hanchar, Head, 709-864-2334, Fax: 709-864-2589. *Application contact:* Michelle Miskell, Graduate Officer, 709-864-4464, Fax: 709-864-2589, E-mail: mmiskell@mun.ca.
Website: http://www.mun.ca/earthsciences/

Miami University, College of Arts and Science, Department of Geology, Oxford, OH 45056. Offers MA, MS, PhD. *Program availability:* Part-time. *Students:* 28 full-time (16 women); includes 1 minority (Black or African American, non-Hispanic/Latino), 10 international. Average age 28. In 2015, 8 master's, 1 doctorate awarded. *Entrance requirements:* Additional exam requirements/recommendations for international students: Recommended—TOEFL (minimum score 80 iBT), IELTS (minimum score 6.5), TSE (minimum score 54). Application fee: $50. Electronic applications accepted. *Expenses:* Tuition, state resident: full-time $12,888; part-time $537 per credit hour. Tuition, nonresident: full-time $29,022; part-time $1209 per credit hour. *Required fees:* $530; $24 per credit hour. $30 per semester. Part-time tuition and fees vary according to course load and program. *Financial support:* Application deadline: 2/1; applicants required to submit FAFSA. *Unit head:* Dr. Elisabeth Widom, Department Chair and Professor, 513-529-5048, E-mail: widome@miamioh.edu. *Application contact:* Cathy Edwards, Administrative Assistant, 513-529-3216, E-mail: edwardca@miamioh.edu.
Website: http://www.MiamiOH.edu/geology/

Michigan Technological University, Graduate School, College of Engineering, Department of Geological and Mining Engineering and Sciences, Houghton, MI 49931. Offers geological engineering (MS, PhD); geology (MS, PhD); geophysics (MS, PhD); mining engineering (MS, PhD). *Program availability:* Part-time. *Faculty:* 35 full-time, 36 part-time/adjunct. *Students:* 61 full-time (25 women), 22 part-time (8 women); includes 5 minority (1 Black or African American, non-Hispanic/Latino; 1 Asian, non-Hispanic/Latino; 2 Hispanic/Latino; 1 Two or more races, non-Hispanic/Latino), 36 international. Average age 28. 177 applicants, 25% accepted, 14 enrolled. In 2015, 9 master's, 4 doctorates awarded. Terminal master's awarded for partial completion of doctoral program. *Degree requirements:* For master's, comprehensive exam (for some programs), thesis (for some programs); for doctorate, comprehensive exam, thesis/dissertation. *Entrance requirements:* For master's and doctorate, GRE, statement of purpose, personal statement, official transcripts, 3 letters of recommendation. Additional

exam requirements/recommendations for international students: Required—TOEFL (recommended score 79 iBT) or IELTS. *Application deadline:* For fall admission, 2/1 priority date for domestic and international students. Applications are processed on a rolling basis. Electronic applications accepted. *Expenses:* Tuition, state resident: full-time $15,507; part-time $861.50 per credit. Tuition, nonresident: full-time $15,507; part-time $861.50 per credit. *Required fees:* $248; $248. Tuition and fees vary according to course load and program. *Financial support:* In 2015–16, 43 students received support, including 6 fellowships with tuition reimbursements available (averaging $14,516 per year), 11 research assistantships with tuition reimbursements available (averaging $14,516 per year), 5 teaching assistantships with tuition reimbursements available (averaging $14,516 per year); career-related internships or fieldwork, Federal Work-Study, scholarships/grants, health care benefits, unspecified assistantships, and cooperative program also available. Financial award applicants required to submit FAFSA. *Faculty research:* Volcanic hazards and volcanic clouds, oil and gas exploration and development, groundwater measurement and modeling, geophysics, environmental paleomagnetism. *Total annual research expenditures:* $1.9 million. *Unit head:* Dr. John S. Gierke, Chair, 906-487-2535, Fax: 906-487-3371, E-mail: jsgierke@mtu.edu. *Application contact:* Amie S. Ledgerwood, Assistant to the Dean, 906-487-2531, Fax: 906-487-3371, E-mail: asledger@mtu.edu.
Website: http://www.mtu.edu/geo/

Mississippi State University, College of Arts and Sciences, Department of Geosciences, Mississippi State, MS 39762. Offers applied meteorology (MS); broadcast meteorology (MS); earth and atmospheric science (PhD); environmental geoscience (MS); geography (MS); geology (MS); geospatial sciences (MS); professional meteorology/climatology (MS); teachers in geoscience (MS). *Program availability:* Online learning. *Faculty:* 18 full-time (4 women), 1 part-time/adjunct (0 women). *Students:* 53 full-time (27 women), 176 part-time (81 women); includes 26 minority (7 Black or African American, non-Hispanic/Latino; 3 Asian, non-Hispanic/Latino; 10 Hispanic/Latino; 1 Native Hawaiian or other Pacific Islander, non-Hispanic/Latino; 5 Two or more races, non-Hispanic/Latino), 5 international. Average age 33. 123 applicants, 73% accepted, 68 enrolled. In 2015, 70 master's, 3 doctorates awarded. *Degree requirements:* For master's, thesis (for some programs), comprehensive oral or written exam; for doctorate, thesis/dissertation, comprehensive oral or written exam. *Entrance requirements:* For master's, GRE (for on-campus applicants), minimum undergraduate GPA of 2.75; for doctorate, thesis-based MS with background in one department emphasis area. Additional exam requirements/recommendations for international students: Required—TOEFL (minimum score 477 paper-based; 53 iBT); Recommended—IELTS (minimum score 4.5). *Application deadline:* For fall admission, 7/1 for domestic students, 5/1 for international students; for spring admission, 11/1 for domestic students, 9/1 for international students. Applications are processed on a rolling basis. Application fee: $60. Electronic applications accepted. *Expenses: Tuition, area resident:* Full-time $7502; part-time $833.74 per credit hour. Tuition, nonresident: full-time $20,142; part-time $2238.24 per credit hour. *Financial support:* In 2015–16, 7 research assistantships with full tuition reimbursements (averaging $13,792 per year), 28 teaching assistantships with full tuition reimbursements (averaging $13,500 per year) were awarded; Federal Work-Study, institutionally sponsored loans, scholarships/grants, tuition waivers (partial), and unspecified assistantships also available. Financial award application deadline: 4/1; financial award applicants required to submit FAFSA. *Faculty research:* Climatology, hydrogeology, sedimentology, meteorology. *Total annual research expenditures:* $3.1 million. *Unit head:* Dr. William Cooke, Interim Department Head, 662-325-1393, Fax: 662-325-9423, E-mail: whc5@geosci.msstate.edu. *Application contact:* Meredith Nagel, Admissions Assistant, 662-325-9077, E-mail: mnagel@grad.msstate.edu.
Website: http://www.geosciences.msstate.edu

Missouri State University, Graduate College, College of Natural and Applied Sciences, Department of Geography, Geology, and Planning, Springfield, MO 65897. Offers natural and applied science (MNAS), including geography, geology and planning; secondary education (MS Ed), including earth science, physical geography. *Accreditation:* ACSP. *Program availability:* Part-time, evening/weekend. *Faculty:* 18 full-time (4 women), 1 part-time/adjunct (0 women). *Students:* 22 full-time (8 women), 10 part-time (7 women); includes 2 minority (1 Asian, non-Hispanic/Latino; 1 Hispanic/Latino), 4 international. Average age 30. 36 applicants, 67% accepted, 19 enrolled. In 2015, 8 master's awarded. *Degree requirements:* For master's, comprehensive exam, thesis (for some programs). *Entrance requirements:* For master's, GRE General Test (MS, MNAS), minimum undergraduate GPA of 3.0 (MS, MNAS), 9-12 teacher certification (MS Ed). Additional exam requirements/recommendations for international students: Required—TOEFL (minimum score 550 paper-based; 79 iBT), IELTS (minimum score 6). *Application deadline:* For fall admission, 7/20 priority date for domestic students, 5/1 for international students; for spring admission, 12/20 priority date for domestic students, 9/1 for international students. Applications are processed on a rolling basis. Application fee: $35 ($50 for international students). Electronic applications accepted. *Expenses:* Tuition, state resident: full-time $5500. Tuition, nonresident: full-time $10,108. *Required fees:* $1000. *Financial support:* In 2015–16, 3 research assistantships with full tuition reimbursements (averaging $11,574 per year), 15 teaching assistantships with full tuition reimbursements (averaging $9,365 per year) were awarded; career-related internships or fieldwork, Federal Work-Study, institutionally sponsored loans, scholarships/grants, and unspecified assistantships also available. Financial award application deadline: 3/31; financial award applicants required to submit FAFSA. *Faculty research:* Stratigraphy and ancient meteorite impacts, environmental geochemistry of karst, hyperspectral image processing, water quality, small town planning. *Unit head:* Dr. Toby Dogwiler, Department Head, 417-836-5800, Fax: 417-836-6934, E-mail: tobydogwiler@missouristate.edu. *Application contact:* Michael Edwards, Coordinator of Graduate Admissions, 417-836-5330, Fax: 417-836-6200, E-mail: michaeledwards@missouristate.edu.
Website: http://geosciences.missouristate.edu/

Missouri University of Science and Technology, Graduate School, Department of Geological Sciences and Engineering, Rolla, MO 65409. Offers geological engineering (MS, DE, PhD); geology and geophysics (MS, PhD), including geochemistry, geology, geophysics, groundwater and environmental geology; petroleum engineering (MS, DE, PhD). *Program availability:* Part-time. *Faculty:* 18 full-time (4 women), 1 part-time/adjunct (0 women). *Students:* 249 full-time (51 women), 93 part-time (17 women); includes 37 minority (10 Black or African American, non-Hispanic/Latino; 3 American Indian or Alaska Native, non-Hispanic/Latino; 6 Asian, non-Hispanic/Latino; 18 Hispanic/Latino), 169 international. Average age 31. 296 applicants, 58% accepted, 97 enrolled. In 2015, 17 master's, 6 doctorates awarded. *Degree requirements:* For master's, thesis optional; for doctorate, comprehensive exam, thesis/dissertation. *Entrance requirements:* For master's, GRE General Test (minimum score 600 quantitative, writing 3.5), minimum GPA of 3.0 in last 4 semesters; for doctorate, GRE General Test (minimum scores: Quantitative 600, Writing 3.5). Additional exam requirements/recommendations for international students: Required—TOEFL (minimum score 550 paper-based). *Application deadline:* For fall admission, 7/1 for domestic students; for spring admission, 12/1 for domestic students. Applications are processed on a rolling basis. Application fee: $55 ($175 for international students). Electronic applications accepted. *Expenses:* Tuition, state resident: full-time $10,536. Tuition, nonresident: full-time $27,015. Full-time tuition and fees vary according to course load. *Financial support:* In 2015–16, fellowships with full tuition reimbursements (averaging $11,250 per year), 9 research assistantships with partial tuition reimbursements (averaging $1,814 per year), 3 teaching assistantships with partial tuition reimbursements (averaging $1,814 per year) were awarded; Federal Work-Study and institutionally sponsored loans also available. Support available to part-time students. Financial award application deadline: 3/1; financial award applicants required to submit FAFSA. *Faculty research:* Digital image processing and geographic information systems, mineralogy, igneous and sedimentary petrology-geochemistry, sedimentology groundwater hydrology and contaminant transport. *Total annual research expenditures:* $2.1 million. *Unit head:* Dr. Robert Laudon, Chairman, 573-341-4466, Fax: 573-341-6935, E-mail: rlaudon@mst.edu. *Application contact:* Debbie Schwertz, Admissions Coordinator, 573-341-6013, Fax: 573-341-6271, E-mail: schwertz@mst.edu.
Website: http://gse.umr.edu/geologicalengineering.html

Montana Tech of The University of Montana, Graduate School, Geosciences Programs, Butte, MT 59701-8997. Offers geochemistry (MS); geological engineering (MS); geology (MS); geophysical engineering (MS); hydrogeological engineering (MS); hydrogeology (MS). *Program availability:* Part-time. *Faculty:* 16 full-time (4 women), 4 part-time/adjunct (0 women). *Students:* 28 full-time (10 women), 10 part-time (5 women); includes 1 minority (Hispanic/Latino), 6 international. 25 applicants, 52% accepted, 10 enrolled. In 2015, 3 master's awarded. *Degree requirements:* For master's, comprehensive exam (for some programs), thesis (for some programs). *Entrance requirements:* For master's, GRE General Test, minimum GPA of 3.0. Additional exam requirements/recommendations for international students: Required—TOEFL (minimum score 545 paper-based; 78 iBT), IELTS (minimum score 6.5). *Application deadline:* For fall admission, 4/1 priority date for domestic students, 3/1 priority date for international students; for spring admission, 10/1 priority date for domestic students, 7/1 priority date for international students. Applications are processed on a rolling basis. Application fee: $50. Electronic applications accepted. *Expenses:* Tuition, state resident: full-time $2901; part-time $1450.68 per degree program. Tuition, nonresident: full-time $8432; part-time $4215.84 per degree program. *Required fees:* $668; $354 per degree program. Tuition and fees vary according to course load and program. *Financial support:* In 2015–16, 15 students received support, including 10 teaching assistantships with partial tuition reimbursements available (averaging $5,000 per year); research assistantships with partial tuition reimbursements available, career-related internships or fieldwork, tuition waivers (full and partial), and unspecified assistantships also available. Financial award application deadline: 4/1; financial award applicants required to submit FAFSA. *Faculty research:* Water resource development, seismic processing, petroleum reservoir characterization, environmental geochemistry, geologic mapping. *Unit head:* Dr. Chris Gammons, Department Head, 406-496-4763, Fax: 406-496-4260, E-mail: cgammons@mtech.edu. *Application contact:* Daniel Stirling, Administrator, Graduate School, 406-496-4304, Fax: 406-496-4710, E-mail: gradschool@mtech.edu.
Website: http://www.mtech.edu/academics/gradschool/degreeprograms/degrees.htm

New Mexico Institute of Mining and Technology, Center for Graduate Studies, Department of Earth and Environmental Science, Program in Geology, Socorro, NM 87801. Offers MS, PhD. *Degree requirements:* For master's, thesis optional; for doctorate, thesis/dissertation. *Entrance requirements:* For master's, GRE General Test; for doctorate, GRE General Test, GRE Subject Test. Additional exam requirements/recommendations for international students: Required—TOEFL (minimum score 540 paper-based). Electronic applications accepted. *Expenses:* Tuition, state resident: full-time $5811; part-time $322.81 per credit. Tuition, nonresident: full-time $19,220; part-time $1067.79 per credit. *Required fees:* $1030. Tuition and fees vary according to course load. *Faculty research:* Care and karst topography, soil/water chemistry and properties, geochemistry of ore deposits.

New Mexico State University, College of Arts and Sciences, Department of Geological Sciences, Las Cruces, NM 88003-8001. Offers MS. *Program availability:* Part-time. *Faculty:* 5 full-time (1 woman), 1 (woman) part-time/adjunct. *Students:* 11 full-time (4 women), 7 part-time (1 woman); includes 1 minority (Two or more races, non-Hispanic/Latino). Average age 28. 26 applicants, 23% accepted, 6 enrolled. In 2015, 5 master's awarded. *Degree requirements:* For master's, thesis. *Entrance requirements:* For master's, GRE General Test, BS in geology or the equivalent. Additional exam requirements/recommendations for international students: Required—TOEFL (minimum score 550 paper-based; 79 iBT), IELTS (minimum score 6.5). *Application deadline:* For fall admission, 2/15 priority date for domestic and international students; for spring admission, 10/31 priority date for domestic and international students; for summer admission, 10/31 for domestic and international students. Applications are processed on a rolling basis. Application fee: $40 ($50 for international students). Electronic applications accepted. *Expenses:* $274.50 per credit hour for in-state students, and all students enrolled in six or fewer credits; $839.30 per credit hour for out-of-state and international students enrolled in at least seven hours. *Financial support:* In 2015–16, 17 students received support, including 1 research assistantship (averaging $17,840 per year), 10 teaching assistantships (averaging $17,840 per year); career-related internships or fieldwork, Federal Work-Study, institutionally sponsored loans, scholarships/grants, traineeships, health care benefits, and unspecified assistantships also available. Support available to part-time students. Financial award application deadline: 3/1. *Faculty research:* Geochemistry, structure/tectonics, sedimentology/stratigraphy, mineralogy/petrology, volcanology. *Total annual research expenditures:* $130,008. *Unit head:* Dr. Nancy J. McMillan, Department Head, 575-646-2708, Fax: 575-646-1056, E-mail: nmcmilla@nmsu.edu. *Application contact:* Dr. Jeff Amato, Graduate Advisor, 575-646-3017, Fax: 575-646-1056, E-mail: amato@nmsu.edu.
Website: http://geology.nmsu.edu

Northern Arizona University, Graduate College, College of Engineering, Forestry, and Natural Sciences, School of Earth Sciences and Environmental Sustainability, Flagstaff, AZ 86011. Offers climate science and solutions (MS); earth sciences and environmental sustainability (PhD); environmental sciences and policy (MS); geology (MS). *Degree requirements:* For master's, comprehensive exam (for some programs), thesis (for some programs). *Entrance requirements:* Additional exam requirements/recommendations for international students: Required—TOEFL (minimum score 550 paper-based; 80 iBT), IELTS (minimum score 7). *Application deadline:* For fall admission, 2/1 priority date for domestic and international students. Applications are processed on a rolling basis. Application fee: $65. Electronic applications accepted. *Expenses: Tuition, area resident:* Full-time $8710. Tuition, nonresident: full-time $20,350. *Required fees:* $896. *Financial support:* Fellowships, research assistantships with full tuition reimbursements, teaching assistantships with full tuition reimbursements, career-related internships or fieldwork, Federal Work-Study, scholarships/grants, health care benefits, tuition waivers (full and partial), and unspecified assistantships available. Financial award applicants required to submit FAFSA. *Unit head:* Dr. Paul Umhoefer, Director, 928-523-6464, E-mail: paul.umhoefer@nau.edu. *Application contact:* SESES Support, 928-523-9333, Fax: 928-523-7432, E-mail: seses_admin_support@nau.edu.
Website: http://nau.edu/cefns/natsci/seses/

Northern Illinois University, Graduate School, College of Liberal Arts and Sciences, Department of Geology and Environmental Geosciences, De Kalb, IL 60115-2854. Offers geology (MS, PhD). *Program availability:* Part-time. *Faculty:* 11 full-time (1 woman), 1 (woman) part-time/adjunct. *Students:* 21 full-time (8 women), 16 part-time (6 women); includes 1 minority (Asian, non-Hispanic/Latino). Average age 26. 40 applicants, 48% accepted, 8 enrolled. In 2015, 10 master's awarded. Terminal master's awarded for partial completion of doctoral program. *Degree requirements:* For master's, comprehensive exam, thesis optional, research seminar; for doctorate, thesis/dissertation, candidacy exam, dissertation defense, internship, research seminar. *Entrance requirements:* For master's, GRE General Test, bachelor's degree in engineering or science, minimum GPA of 2.75; for doctorate, GRE General Test, bachelor's or master's degree in engineering or science, minimum graduate GPA of 3.2. Additional exam requirements/recommendations for international students: Required—TOEFL (minimum score 550 paper-based). *Application deadline:* For fall admission, 6/1 for domestic students, 5/1 for international students; for spring admission, 11/1 for domestic students, 10/1 for international students. Applications are processed on a rolling basis. Application fee: $40. Electronic applications accepted. *Financial support:* In 2015–16, 5 research assistantships with full tuition reimbursements, 20 teaching assistantships with full tuition reimbursements were awarded; fellowships with full tuition reimbursements, career-related internships or fieldwork, Federal Work-Study, scholarships/grants, tuition waivers (full), and unspecified assistantships also available. Support available to part-time students. Financial award applicants required to submit FAFSA. *Faculty research:* Micropaleontology, environmental geochemistry, glacial geology, igneous petrology, statistical analyses of fracture networks. *Unit head:* Dr. Mark Fischer, Chair, 815-753-0523, Fax: 815-753-1945, E-mail: mfischer@niu.edu. *Application contact:* Dr. Mark Fischer, Graduate Program Director, 815-753-7939, E-mail: mfischer@niu.edu.

Website: http://www.niu.edu/geology/

Northwestern University, The Graduate School, Judd A. and Marjorie Weinberg College of Arts and Sciences, Department of Earth and Planetary Sciences, Evanston, IL 60208. Offers PhD. Admissions and degrees offered through The Graduate School. *Program availability:* Part-time. *Degree requirements:* For doctorate, thesis/dissertation. *Entrance requirements:* For doctorate, GRE General Test. Additional exam requirements/recommendations for international students: Required—TOEFL. Electronic applications accepted.

The Ohio State University, Graduate School, College of Arts and Sciences, Division of Natural and Mathematical Sciences, School of Earth Sciences, Columbus, OH 43210. Offers earth sciences (MS, PhD); geodetic science (MS, PhD); geological sciences (MS, PhD). *Degree requirements:* For master's, thesis; for doctorate, thesis/dissertation. *Entrance requirements:* For master's, GRE, undergraduate degree in biological science, geological sciences, physical science or engineering (recommended); minimum GPA of 3.2; for doctorate, GRE, undergraduate degree in biological science, geological sciences, physical science or engineering (recommended); minimum GPA of 3.4. Additional exam requirements/recommendations for international students: Required—TOEFL (minimum score 550 paper-based; 79 iBT), Michigan English Language Assessment Battery (minimum score 82); Recommended—IELTS (minimum score 8). Electronic applications accepted.

Ohio University, Graduate College, College of Arts and Sciences, Department of Geological Sciences, Athens, OH 45701-2979. Offers environmental geochemistry (MS); environmental geology (MS); environmental/hydrology (MS); geology (MS); geology education (MS); geomorphology/surficial processes (MS); geophysics (MS); hydrogeology (MS); sedimentology (MS); structure/tectonics (MS). *Program availability:* Part-time. *Degree requirements:* For master's, thesis. *Entrance requirements:* Additional exam requirements/recommendations for international students: Required—TOEFL (minimum score 550 paper-based; 80 iBT) or IELTS (minimum score 6.5). Electronic applications accepted. *Faculty research:* Geoscience education, tectonics, fluvial geomorphology, invertebrate paleontology, mine/hydrology.

Oklahoma State University, College of Arts and Sciences, School of Geology, Stillwater, OK 74078. Offers MS, PhD. *Faculty:* 18 full-time (4 women). *Students:* 38 full-time (11 women), 52 part-time (16 women); includes 15 minority (2 Black or African American, non-Hispanic/Latino; 3 American Indian or Alaska Native, non-Hispanic/Latino; 1 Asian, non-Hispanic/Latino; 2 Hispanic/Latino; 7 Two or more races, non-Hispanic/Latino), 19 international. Average age 30. 119 applicants, 25% accepted, 20 enrolled. In 2015, 23 master's awarded. *Degree requirements:* For master's, thesis; for doctorate, comprehensive exam, thesis/dissertation. *Entrance requirements:* For master's and doctorate, GRE. Additional exam requirements/recommendations for international students: Required—TOEFL (minimum score 550 paper-based; 79 iBT). *Application deadline:* For fall admission, 3/1 priority date for international students; for spring admission, 8/1 priority date for international students. Applications are processed on a rolling basis. Application fee: $40 ($75 for international students). Electronic applications accepted. *Expenses:* Tuition, state resident: full-time $3528; part-time $196 per credit hour. Tuition, nonresident: full-time $14,144; part-time $785.75 per credit hour. *Required fees:* $1895; $105.25 per credit hour. Tuition and fees vary according to campus/location. *Financial support:* In 2015–16, 27 research assistantships (averaging $15,707 per year), 34 teaching assistantships (averaging $10,211 per year) were awarded; career-related internships or fieldwork, Federal Work-Study, scholarships/grants, health care benefits, tuition waivers (partial), and unspecified assistantships also available. Support available to part-time students. Financial award application deadline: 3/1; financial award applicants required to submit FAFSA. *Faculty research:* Groundwater hydrology, petroleum geology. *Unit head:* Dr. Estella Atekwana, Department Head, 405-744-6358, Fax: 405-744-7841, E-mail: estella.atekwana@okstate.edu.

Website: http://geology.okstate.edu

Oregon State University, College of Earth, Ocean, and Atmospheric Sciences, Program in Geology, Corvallis, OR 97331. Offers solid earth processes and history (MA, MS, PhD); surface earth processes and history (MA, MS, PhD). *Program availability:* Part-time. *Faculty:* 24 full-time (4 women), 1 part-time/adjunct (0 women). *Students:* 40 full-time (18 women), 2 part-time (1 woman); includes 2 minority (both Hispanic/Latino), 8 international. Average age 29. 137 applicants, 11% accepted, 11 enrolled. In 2015, 3 master's, 2 doctorates awarded. Terminal master's awarded for partial completion of doctoral program. *Degree requirements:* For master's, variable foreign language requirement, thesis; for doctorate, one foreign language, thesis/dissertation. *Entrance requirements:* For master's and doctorate, GRE, minimum GPA of 3.0 in last 90 hours. Additional exam requirements/recommendations for international students: Required—TOEFL (minimum score 80 iBT), IELTS (minimum score 6.5). *Application deadline:* For fall admission, 1/5 for domestic students. Application fee: $75 ($85 for international students). *Expenses:* Tuition, state resident: full-time $12,150; part-time $450 per credit. Tuition, nonresident: full-time $20,952; part-time $776 per credit. *Required fees:* $1572; $1443 per unit. One-time fee: $350. Tuition and fees vary according to course load, campus/location and program. *Financial support:* Fellowships, research assistantships, teaching assistantships, Federal Work-Study, and institutionally sponsored loans available. Support available to part-time students. Financial award application deadline: 1/5. *Faculty research:* Hydrogeology, geomorphology, ocean geology, geochemistry, earthquake geology. *Unit head:* Dr. Ed Brook, Professor/Geology Program Director. *Application contact:* Lori Hartline, Geology Advisor, 541-737-5188, E-mail: hartline@coas.oregonstate.edu.

Website: http://ceoas.oregonstate.edu/academics/geology/

Portland State University, Graduate Studies, College of Liberal Arts and Sciences, Department of Geology, Portland, OR 97207-0751. Offers environmental sciences and resources (PhD); geology (MA, MS); science/geology (MAT, MST). *Program availability:* Part-time. *Faculty:* 10 full-time (2 women), 6 part-time/adjunct (3 women). *Students:* 19 full-time (7 women), 17 part-time (11 women); includes 5 minority (1 Asian, non-Hispanic/Latino; 4 Hispanic/Latino), 2 international. Average age 32. 33 applicants, 61% accepted, 12 enrolled. In 2015, 7 master's awarded. *Degree requirements:* For master's, comprehensive exam, thesis or alternative, field comprehensive; for doctorate, thesis/dissertation. *Entrance requirements:* For master's, GRE General Test, GRE Subject Test, BA/BS in geology, minimum GPA of 3.0 in geology-related and allied sciences, resume, statement of intent, 2 letters of recommendation. Additional exam requirements/recommendations for international students: Required—TOEFL (minimum score 550 paper-based; 80 iBT). *Application deadline:* 1/31 priority date for domestic and international students. Application fee: $50. Electronic applications accepted. *Expenses:* $11,490 per year. *Financial support:* In 2015–16, 2 research assistantships with tuition reimbursements (averaging $2,651 per year), 8 teaching assistantships with full tuition reimbursements (averaging $15,000 per year) were awarded; career-related internships or fieldwork, Federal Work-Study, scholarships/grants, and unspecified assistantships also available. Support available to part-time students. Financial award application deadline: 3/1; financial award applicants required to submit FAFSA. *Faculty research:* Sediment transport, volcanic environmental geology, coastal and fluvial processes. *Total annual research expenditures:* $1.3 million. *Unit head:* Dr. Martin Streck, Chair, 503-725-3379, Fax: 503-725-3025, E-mail: streckm@pdx.edu. *Application contact:* Dr. Andrew Fountain, Graduate Committee Chair, 503-725-3386, Fax: 503-725-3025, E-mail: andrew@pdx.edu.

Website: http://geology.pdx.edu/

Queens College of the City University of New York, Mathematics and Natural Sciences Division, School of Earth and Environmental Sciences, Flushing, NY 11367-1597. Offers applied environmental geoscience (MS); geological and environmental science (MA). *Program availability:* Part-time, evening/weekend. *Faculty:* 17 full-time (3 women), 9 part-time/adjunct (2 women). *Students:* 14 part-time (6 women); includes 2 minority (1 Black or African American, non-Hispanic/Latino; 1 Hispanic/Latino), 2 international. Average age 27. 11 applicants, 55% accepted, 3 enrolled. In 2015, 6 master's awarded. *Degree requirements:* For master's, comprehensive exam, thesis. *Entrance requirements:* For master's, previous course work in calculus, physics, and chemistry; minimum GPA of 3.0. Additional exam requirements/recommendations for international students: Required—TOEFL, IELTS. *Application deadline:* For fall admission, 4/1 for domestic students; for spring admission, 11/1 for domestic students. Applications are processed on a rolling basis. Application fee: $125. Electronic applications accepted. *Expenses:* Tuition, state resident: full-time $5065; part-time $425 per credit. Tuition, nonresident: part-time $780 per credit. *Required fees:* $522. Part-time tuition and fees vary according to course load and program. *Financial support:* Career-related internships or fieldwork and unspecified assistantships available. Financial award application deadline: 4/1; financial award applicants required to submit FAFSA. *Unit head:* Dr. George Hendrey, Chairperson, 718-997-3300, E-mail: george.hendrey@qc.cuny.edu.

Queen's University at Kingston, School of Graduate Studies, Faculty of Arts and Sciences, Department of Geological Sciences and Geological Engineering, Kingston, ON K7L 3N6, Canada. Offers M Sc, M Sc Eng, PhD. *Program availability:* Part-time. *Degree requirements:* For master's, thesis (for some programs); for doctorate, comprehensive exam, thesis/dissertation. *Entrance requirements:* Additional exam requirements/recommendations for international students: Required—TOEFL. *Faculty research:* Geochemistry, sedimentology, geophysics, economic geology, structural geology.

Rensselaer Polytechnic Institute, Graduate School, School of Science, Program in Geology, Troy, NY 12180-3590. Offers MS, PhD. *Faculty:* 9 full-time (3 women). *Students:* 16 full-time (8 women); includes 3 minority (2 Hispanic/Latino; 1 Two or more races, non-Hispanic/Latino), 2 international. Average age 24. 19 applicants, 37% accepted, 4 enrolled. In 2015, 2 doctorates awarded. Terminal master's awarded for partial completion of doctoral program. *Degree requirements:* For master's, comprehensive exam, thesis (for some programs); for doctorate, comprehensive exam, thesis/dissertation. *Entrance requirements:* For master's and doctorate, GRE. Additional exam requirements/recommendations for international students: Required—TOEFL (minimum score 570 paper-based; 88 iBT), IELTS (minimum score 6.5), PTE (minimum score 60). *Application deadline:* For fall admission, 1/1 priority date for domestic and international students; for spring admission, 8/15 priority date for domestic and international students. Applications are processed on a rolling basis. Application fee: $75. Electronic applications accepted. *Financial support:* In 2015–16, research assistantships (averaging $21,500 per year), teaching assistantships (averaging $21,500 per year) were awarded; fellowships also available. Financial award application deadline: 1/1; financial award applicants required to submit FAFSA. *Faculty research:* Astrobiology, carbon in deep earth, climate assessment, ecosystem studies, environmental and freshwater geochemistry, geoinformatics, geomicrobiology, geophysical simulation, inorganic and igneous experimental geochemistry, isotopic and organic geochemistry, lithosphere dynamics and tectonophysics, metamorphic petrology and geochemistry, microbial geochemistry, paleoceanography and micropaleontology, seismology and solid earth geophysics. *Unit head:* Dr. Mimi Katz, Graduate Program Director, 518-276-8521, E-mail: katzm@rpi.edu. *Application contact:* Office of Graduate Admissions, 518-276-6216, E-mail: gradadmissions@rpi.edu.

Website: http://www.rpi.edu/dept/geo/

Rutgers University–Newark, Graduate School, Program in Environmental Geology, Newark, NJ 07102. Offers MS. *Program availability:* Part-time, evening/weekend. *Degree requirements:* For master's, comprehensive exam, thesis optional. *Entrance requirements:* For master's, GRE General Test, minimum B average. Electronic applications accepted. *Faculty research:* Environmental geology, plate tectonics, geoarchaeology, geophysics, mineralogy-petrology.

Rutgers University–New Brunswick, Graduate School-New Brunswick, Department of Earth and Planetary Sciences, Piscataway, NJ 08854-8097. Offers geological sciences (MS, PhD). *Program availability:* Part-time. *Degree requirements:* For master's, thesis; for doctorate, comprehensive exam, thesis/dissertation. *Entrance requirements:* For master's and doctorate, GRE General Test, GRE Subject Test (recommended). Electronic applications accepted. *Faculty research:* Basin analysis, volcanology, quaternary studies, engineering geophysics, marine geology, biogeochemistry and paleoceanography.

Geology

St. Francis Xavier University, Graduate Studies, Department of Earth Sciences, Antigonish, NS B2G 2W5, Canada. Offers M Sc. *Degree requirements:* For master's, thesis. *Entrance requirements:* Additional exam requirements/recommendations for international students: Required—TOEFL (minimum score 580 paper-based). *Faculty research:* Environmental earth sciences, global change tectonics, paleoclimatology, crustal fluids.

San Diego State University, Graduate and Research Affairs, College of Sciences, Department of Geological Sciences, San Diego, CA 92182. Offers MS. *Program availability:* Part-time. *Degree requirements:* For master's, thesis. *Entrance requirements:* For master's, GRE General Test, bachelor's degree in related field, 2 letters of reference. Additional exam requirements/recommendations for international students: Required—TOEFL. Electronic applications accepted. *Faculty research:* Earthquakes, hydrology, meteorological analysis and tomography studies.

San Jose State University, Graduate Studies and Research, College of Science, San Jose, CA 95192-0001. Offers biological sciences (MA, MS), including molecular biology and microbiology (MS), organismal biology, conservation and ecology (MS), physiology (MS); chemistry (MA, MS); computer science (MS); cybersecurity (Certificate); cybersecurity: core technologies (Certificate); geology (MS); marine science (MS); master biotechnology (MBT); mathematics (MA, MS), including mathematics education (MA), science; meteorology (MS); physics (MS), including computational physics, modern optics, science (MA, MS); science education (MA); statistics (MS); unix system administration (Certificate). *Program availability:* Part-time, evening/weekend. *Students:* 118 full-time (68 women), 52 part-time (25 women); includes 125 minority (5 Black or African American, non-Hispanic/Latino; 97 Asian, non-Hispanic/Latino; 23 Hispanic/Latino), 121 international. Average age 27. 1,236 applicants, 21% accepted, 171 enrolled. In 2015, 168 master's awarded. *Entrance requirements:* For master's, GRE. *Application deadline:* For fall admission, 6/29 for domestic students; for spring admission, 11/30 for domestic students. Applications are processed on a rolling basis. Application fee: $55. Electronic applications accepted. *Financial support:* Teaching assistantships, career-related internships or fieldwork, Federal Work-Study, and institutionally sponsored loans available. Support available to part-time students. Financial award applicants required to submit FAFSA. *Faculty research:* Radiochemistry/environmental analysis, health physics, radiation effects. *Unit head:* J. Michael Parrish, Dean, 408-924-4800, Fax: 408-924-4815. *Application contact:* 408-924-2480, Fax: 408-924-2477.
Website: http://www.science.sjsu.edu/

South Dakota School of Mines and Technology, Graduate Division, Department of Geology and Geological Engineering, Rapid City, SD 57701-3995. Offers geology and geological engineering (MS, PhD); paleontology (MS). *Program availability:* Part-time. *Degree requirements:* For master's, thesis; for doctorate, thesis/dissertation. *Entrance requirements:* For master's and doctorate, GRE General Test, GRE Subject Test. Additional exam requirements/recommendations for international students: Required—TOEFL (minimum score 520 paper-based; 68 iBT), TWE. Electronic applications accepted. *Faculty research:* Contaminants in soil, nitrate leaching, environmental changes, fracture formations, greenhouse effect.

Southern Illinois University Carbondale, Graduate School, College of Science, Department of Geology, Carbondale, IL 62901-4701. Offers environmental resources and policy (PhD); geology (MS); geosciences (PhD). *Faculty:* 12 full-time (0 women). *Students:* 15 full-time (5 women), 16 part-time (2 women), 18 international. Average age 25. 34 applicants, 44% accepted, 716 enrolled. In 2015, 16 master's, 3 doctorates awarded. *Degree requirements:* For master's, thesis; for doctorate, one foreign language, thesis/dissertation. *Entrance requirements:* For master's, GRE, minimum GPA of 2.7; for doctorate, GRE General Test, minimum GPA of 3.25. Additional exam requirements/recommendations for international students: Required—TOEFL. *Application deadline:* Applications are processed on a rolling basis. Application fee: $65. *Financial support:* In 2015–16, 22 students received support, including 22 teaching assistantships with full tuition reimbursements available; fellowships with full tuition reimbursements available, research assistantships with full tuition reimbursements available, Federal Work-Study, institutionally sponsored loans, and tuition waivers (full) also available. Support available to part-time students. *Total annual research expenditures:* $720,000. *Unit head:* Dr. Steven Esling, Chair, 618-453-3351, Fax: 618-453-7393, E-mail: esling@geo.siu.edu. *Application contact:* Mona Martin, Office Support Specialist, 618-453-3351, E-mail: monamartin@siu.edu.

Southern Methodist University, Dedman College of Humanities and Sciences, Department of Earth Sciences, Dallas, TX 75275. Offers applied geophysics (MS); earth sciences (MS, PhD). *Program availability:* Part-time. *Degree requirements:* For master's, thesis (for some programs), qualifying exam; for doctorate, thesis/dissertation, qualifying exam. *Entrance requirements:* For master's and doctorate, GRE General Test, minimum GPA of 3.0, letters of recommendation. Additional exam requirements/recommendations for international students: Required—TOEFL. Electronic applications accepted. *Faculty research:* Sedimentology, geochemistry, igneous and metamorphic petrology, vertebrate paleontology, seismology.

Stephen F. Austin State University, Graduate School, College of Sciences and Mathematics, Department of Geology, Nacogdoches, TX 75962. Offers MS, MSNS. *Degree requirements:* For master's, comprehensive exam. *Entrance requirements:* For master's, GRE General Test, minimum GPA of 2.8 in last 60 hours, 2.5 overall. Additional exam requirements/recommendations for international students: Required—TOEFL. *Faculty research:* Stratigraphy of Kaibab limestone, Utah; structure of Ouachita Mountains, Arkansas; groundwater chemistry of Carrizo Sand, Texas.

Sul Ross State University, College of Arts and Sciences, Department of Earth and Physical Sciences, Alpine, TX 79832. Offers geology (MS). *Program availability:* Part-time. *Students:* 15 full-time (2 women), 9 part-time (2 women); includes 4 minority (2 Black or African American, non-Hispanic/Latino; 1 Hispanic/Latino; 1 Two or more races, non-Hispanic/Latino). Average age 30. *Degree requirements:* For master's, thesis optional. *Entrance requirements:* For master's, GRE General Test, minimum GPA of 2.5 in last 60 hours of undergraduate work. *Application deadline:* Applications are processed on a rolling basis. Application fee: $0 ($50 for international students). *Financial support:* Research assistantships, teaching assistantships, career-related internships or fieldwork, Federal Work-Study, and institutionally sponsored loans available. Support available to part-time students. Financial award application deadline: 5/1; financial award applicants required to submit FAFSA. *Unit head:* Dr. Chris Ritzi, Chairman, 432-837-8112, Fax: 432-837-8682, E-mail: critzi@sulross.edu. *Application contact:* Lonora Hunt, Department Secretary, 432-837-8112, Fax: 432-837-8692,
E-mail: lhunt@sulross.edu.
Website: http://www.sulross.edu/section/366/geology

Syracuse University, College of Arts and Sciences, Programs in Earth Sciences, Syracuse, NY 13244. Offers earth sciences (MA, MS, PhD). *Program availability:* Part-time. *Students:* Average age 27. In 2015, 6 master's, 3 doctorates awarded. *Degree requirements:* For master's, thesis (for some programs), research tool; for doctorate, comprehensive exam, thesis/dissertation, 2 research tools. *Entrance requirements:* For master's, GRE General Test, personal statement, including research and/or teaching experience, research interests, and career goals; three letters of recommendation; official transcripts; for doctorate, GRE General Test. Additional exam requirements/recommendations for international students: Required—TOEFL (minimum score 100 iBT). *Application deadline:* For fall admission, 1/15 priority date for domestic and international students. Application fee: $75. Electronic applications accepted. *Expenses: Tuition, area resident:* Full-time $25,974; part-time $1443 per credit hour. *Required fees:* $802; $50 per course. Tuition and fees vary according to course load and program. *Financial support:* Fellowships with full tuition reimbursements, research assistantships with tuition reimbursements, teaching assistantships with tuition reimbursements, and scholarships/grants available. Financial award application deadline: 1/1. *Faculty research:* Environmental geology, thermochronology, tectonics, isotope geochemistry, paleobiology. *Unit head:* Dr. Donald Siegel, Chair, 315-443-3607,
E-mail: disiegel@syr.edu. *Application contact:* Jolene Fitch, Academic Coordinator, 315-443-2674, E-mail: jofitch@syr.edu.
Website: http://earthsciences.syr.edu/Academics/GraduateStudies_EAR.html

Temple University, College of Science and Technology, Department of Earth and Environmental Sciences, Philadelphia, PA 19122. Offers MS, PhD. *Faculty:* 10 full-time (4 women). *Students:* 12 full-time (9 women); includes 2 minority (1 Asian, non-Hispanic/Latino; 1 Hispanic/Latino), 2 international. 25 applicants, 40% accepted, 8 enrolled. In 2015, 3 master's awarded. *Degree requirements:* For master's, comprehensive exam (for some programs), thesis (for some programs), qualifying exam; for doctorate, thesis/dissertation. *Entrance requirements:* For master's, GRE General Test, minimum GPA of 3.0. Additional exam requirements/recommendations for international students: Required—TOEFL (minimum score 550 paper-based; 79 iBT). *Application deadline:* For fall admission, 12/15 for domestic and international students; for spring admission, 8/1 for domestic and international students. Applications are processed on a rolling basis. Application fee: $60. Electronic applications accepted. *Financial support:* Fellowships, research assistantships with full tuition reimbursements, teaching assistantships with full tuition reimbursements, and scholarships/grants available. Financial award application deadline: 1/15; financial award applicants required to submit FAFSA. *Faculty research:* Hydraulic modeling, environmental geochemistry and geophysics, paleosas, cyclic stratigraphy, materials research. *Unit head:* Dr. Jonathan Nyquist, Chair, 215-204-7484, Fax: 215-204-3496, E-mail: ees@temple.edu. *Application contact:* Shelah Cox, Administrative Assistant, 215-204-8227, E-mail: scox@temple.edu.
Website: https://ees.cst.temple.edu/

Texas A&M University, College of Geosciences, Department of Geology and Geophysics, College Station, TX 77843. Offers geology (MS, PhD); geophysics (MS, PhD). *Faculty:* 35. *Students:* 105 full-time (36 women), 31 part-time (11 women); includes 16 minority (1 Black or African American, non-Hispanic/Latino; 6 Asian, non-Hispanic/Latino; 9 Hispanic/Latino), 49 international. Average age 29. 308 applicants, 12% accepted, 30 enrolled. In 2015, 26 master's, 10 doctorates awarded. *Degree requirements:* For master's, thesis; for doctorate, thesis/dissertation. *Entrance requirements:* For master's and doctorate, GRE General Test. Additional exam requirements/recommendations for international students: Required—TOEFL (minimum score 550 paper-based; 80 iBT), IELTS (minimum score 6), PTE (minimum score 53). *Application deadline:* For fall admission, 3/1 priority date for domestic students, 1/15 for international students; for spring admission, 10/1 priority date for domestic students, 8/15 for international students. Applications are processed on a rolling basis. Application fee: $50 ($90 for international students). Electronic applications accepted. *Expenses:* Contact institution. *Financial support:* In 2015–16, 105 students received support, including 15 fellowships with tuition reimbursements available (averaging $19,400 per year), 23 research assistantships with tuition reimbursements available (averaging $6,474 per year), 54 teaching assistantships with tuition reimbursements available (averaging $6,446 per year); career-related internships or fieldwork, institutionally sponsored loans, scholarships/grants, traineeships, health care benefits, tuition waivers (full and partial), and unspecified assistantships also available. Support available to part-time students. Financial award application deadline: 3/15; financial award applicants required to submit FAFSA. *Faculty research:* Environmental and engineering geology and geophysics, petroleum geology, tectonophysics, geochemistry. *Unit head:* Dr. Mike Pope, Professor and Department Head, 979-845-4376, E-mail: mcpope@tamu.edu. *Application contact:* Dr. Mark E. Everett, Professor and Associate Department Head for Graduate Affairs, 979-862-2129, E-mail: everett@geo.tamu.edu.
Website: http://geoweb.tamu.edu

Texas Christian University, College of Science and Engineering, School of Geology, Energy and the Environment, Fort Worth, TX 76129. Offers environmental science (MA, MEM, MS); geology (MS). *Program availability:* Part-time. *Faculty:* 13 full-time (4 women), 1 part-time/adjunct (0 women). *Students:* 32 full-time (10 women), 3 part-time (0 women); includes 5 minority (1 Black or African American, non-Hispanic/Latino; 2 Asian, non-Hispanic/Latino; 2 Hispanic/Latino), 3 international. Average age 27. 56 applicants, 25% accepted, 10 enrolled. In 2015, 15 master's awarded. *Degree requirements:* For master's, comprehensive exam (for some programs), thesis. *Entrance requirements:* For master's, GRE. Additional exam requirements/recommendations for international students: Required—TOEFL (minimum score 550 paper-based; 80 iBT). *Application deadline:* For fall admission, 2/1 for domestic and international students; for spring admission, 9/1 for domestic and international students. Application fee: $60. Electronic applications accepted. *Expenses: Tuition, area resident:* Full-time $26,640; part-time $1480 per credit hour. *Required fees:* $48; $48 per unit. Tuition and fees vary according to program. *Financial support:* In 2015–16, 15 teaching assistantships with full tuition reimbursements (averaging $16,000 per year) were awarded; unspecified assistantships also available. Financial award application deadline: 2/1. *Faculty research:* Structural geology, sedimentology, physical volcanology, geomorphology, planetary geology. *Unit head:* Dr. Helge Alsleben, Graduate Advisor, 817-257-7270, Fax: 817-257-7789, E-mail: h.alsleben@tcu.edu.
Website: http://sgee.tcu.edu

Université du Québec à Montréal, Graduate Programs, Program in Earth Sciences, Montreal, QC H3C 3P8, Canada. Offers earth sciences (M Sc); mineral resources (PhD); non-renewable resources (DESS). *Program availability:* Part-time. Terminal master's awarded for partial completion of doctoral program. *Degree requirements:* For master's, thesis (for some programs); for doctorate, thesis/dissertation. *Entrance requirements:* For master's, appropriate bachelor's degree or equivalent, proficiency in French. *Faculty research:* Economic geology, structural geology, geochemistry, Quaternary geology, isotopic geochemistry.

Université Laval, Faculty of Sciences and Engineering, Department of Geology and Geological Engineering, Québec, QC G1K 7P4, Canada. Offers earth sciences (M Sc, PhD), including earth sciences, environmental technologies (M Sc); geology (M Sc, PhD). Terminal master's awarded for partial completion of doctoral program. *Degree requirements:* For master's, thesis (for some programs); for doctorate, comprehensive exam, thesis/dissertation. *Entrance requirements:* For master's and doctorate, knowledge of French. Electronic applications accepted. *Faculty research:* Engineering, economics, regional geology.

University at Buffalo, the State University of New York, Graduate School, College of Arts and Sciences, Department of Geology, Buffalo, NY 14260. Offers MA, MS, PhD. *Program availability:* Part-time. *Faculty:* 14 full-time (6 women), 1 part-time/adjunct (0 women). *Students:* 64 full-time (25 women), 1 part-time (0 women); includes 5 minority (3 Asian, non-Hispanic/Latino; 1 Hispanic/Latino; 1 Native Hawaiian or other Pacific Islander, non-Hispanic/Latino), 13 international. Average age 26. 95 applicants, 37% accepted, 18 enrolled. *Degree requirements:* For master's, project or thesis; for doctorate, thesis/dissertation, dissertation defense. *Entrance requirements:* For master's and doctorate, GRE General Test. Additional exam requirements/recommendations for international students: Required—TOEFL (minimum score 550 paper-based; 79 iBT). *Application deadline:* For fall admission, 1/1 priority date for domestic and international students; for spring admission, 10/1 priority date for domestic and international students. Applications are processed on a rolling basis. Application fee: $75. Electronic applications accepted. *Financial support:* Fellowships with full tuition reimbursements, research assistantships with full tuition reimbursements, teaching assistantships with full tuition reimbursements, Federal Work-Study, scholarships/grants, health care benefits, and unspecified assistantships available. Financial award application deadline: 2/1; financial award applicants required to submit FAFSA. *Faculty research:* Environmental hydrogeology, volcanology, geohazards, climate change, evolution/ecology. *Total annual research expenditures:* $1.9 million. *Unit head:* Dr. Marcus Bursik, Professor and Chair, 716-645-3489, Fax: 716-645-3999, E-mail: geology@buffalo.edu. *Application contact:* Dr. Greg Valentine, Director of Graduate Studies, 716-645-4295, Fax: 716-645-3999, E-mail: gav4@buffalo.edu.
Website: http://www.geology.buffalo.edu/

The University of Akron, Graduate School, Buchtel College of Arts and Sciences, Department of Geosciences, Akron, OH 44325. Offers earth science (MS); engineering geology (MS); environmental geology (MS); geology (MS); geophysics (MS). *Program availability:* Part-time. *Faculty:* 8 full-time (1 woman), 3 part-time/adjunct (0 women). *Students:* 23 full-time (9 women), 19 part-time (6 women); includes 2 minority (both Black or African American, non-Hispanic/Latino), 15 international. Average age 27. 49 applicants, 59% accepted, 17 enrolled. In 2015, 13 master's awarded. *Degree requirements:* For master's, comprehensive exam, thesis, seminar, proficiency exam. *Entrance requirements:* For master's, minimum GPA of 2.75, three letters of recommendation, statement of purpose. Additional exam requirements/recommendations for international students: Required—TOEFL (minimum score 550 paper-based; 79 iBT), IELTS (minimum score 6.5). *Application deadline:* Applications are processed on a rolling basis. Application fee: $45 ($70 for international students). Electronic applications accepted. *Expenses:* Tuition, state resident: full-time $7958; part-time $442 per credit hour. Tuition, nonresident: full-time $13,464; part-time $748 per credit hour. *Required fees:* $1404. *Financial support:* In 2015–16, 1 research assistantship with full tuition reimbursement, 16 teaching assistantships with full tuition reimbursements were awarded. *Faculty research:* Terrestrial environmental change, karst hydrogeology, lacustrine paleo environments, environmental magnetism and geophysics. *Total annual research expenditures:* $509,174. *Unit head:* Dr. James McManus, Chair, 330-972-7991, E-mail: jmcmanus@uakron.edu. *Application contact:* Dr. John Peck, Director of Graduate Studies, 330-972-7659, E-mail: jpeck@uakron.edu.
Website: http://www.uakron.edu/geology/

The University of Alabama, Graduate School, College of Arts and Sciences, Department of Geological Sciences, Tuscaloosa, AL 35487. Offers MS, PhD. *Faculty:* 18 full-time (6 women), 1 part-time/adjunct (0 women). *Students:* 44 full-time (21 women), 12 part-time (4 women); includes 4 minority (1 Black or African American, non-Hispanic/Latino; 1 American Indian or Alaska Native, non-Hispanic/Latino; 1 Asian, non-Hispanic/Latino; 1 Hispanic/Latino), 20 international. Average age 28. 69 applicants, 39% accepted, 18 enrolled. In 2015, 11 master's, 1 doctorate awarded. Terminal master's awarded for partial completion of doctoral program. *Degree requirements:* For master's, comprehensive exam, thesis; for doctorate, comprehensive exam, thesis/dissertation. *Entrance requirements:* For master's and doctorate, GRE. Additional exam requirements/recommendations for international students: Required—TOEFL (minimum score 550 paper-based; 79 iBT). *Application deadline:* For fall admission, 3/1 priority date for domestic and international students; for spring admission, 10/1 priority date for domestic and international students. Applications are processed on a rolling basis. Application fee: $50 ($60 for international students). Electronic applications accepted. *Expenses:* Tuition, state resident: full-time $10,170. Tuition, nonresident: full-time $25,950. *Financial support:* In 2015–16, 26 students received support, including 11 research assistantships with full tuition reimbursements available (averaging $13,595 per year), 29 teaching assistantships with full tuition reimbursements available (averaging $13,365 per year); fellowships, career-related internships or fieldwork, Federal Work-Study, institutionally sponsored loans, and scholarships/grants also available. *Faculty research:* Energy, hydrology, geochemistry, structure, petrology. *Total annual research expenditures:* $504,921. *Unit head:* Dr. Fred Andrus, Chairperson and Associate Professor, 205-348-5177, E-mail: fandrus@ua.edu. *Application contact:* Dr. Delores Robinson, Graduate Program Director, 205-348-4034, E-mail: dmr@ua.edu.
Website: http://www.geo.ua.edu/

University of Alaska Fairbanks, College of Natural Sciences and Mathematics, Department of Geosciences, Fairbanks, AK 99775-5780. Offers geology (MS, PhD), including economic geology (PhD), petroleum geology (MS), quaternary geology (PhD), remote sensing (PhD), volcanology (PhD); geophysics (MS, PhD), including remote sensing geophysics, snow, ice, and permafrost geophysics (MS), solid-earth geophysics (MS). *Program availability:* Part-time. *Faculty:* 14 full-time (4 women), 1 part-time/adjunct (0 women). *Students:* 54 full-time (24 women), 14 part-time (7 women); includes 3 minority (1 Asian, non-Hispanic/Latino; 1 Hispanic/Latino; 1 Two or more races, non-Hispanic/Latino), 17 international. Average age 30. 83 applicants, 14% accepted, 12 enrolled. In 2015, 7 master's awarded. *Degree requirements:* For master's, comprehensive exam, thesis, oral defense of thesis; for doctorate, comprehensive exam, thesis/dissertation, defense of the dissertation. *Entrance requirements:* For master's, GRE General Test, bachelor's degree in geology, geophysics, or an appropriate physical science or engineering with minimum cumulative undergraduate and major GPA of 3.0; for doctorate, GRE General Test, minimum cumulative GPA of 3.0. Additional exam requirements/recommendations for international students: Required—TOEFL (minimum score 550 paper-based; 79 iBT), IELTS (minimum score 6.5). *Application deadline:* For fall admission, 6/1 for domestic students, 3/1 for international students; for spring admission, 10/15 for domestic students, 9/1 for international students. Applications are processed on a rolling basis. Application fee: $60. Electronic applications accepted. *Expenses:* Tuition, state resident: full-time $7614; part-time $423 per credit. Tuition, nonresident: full-time $15,552; part-time $864 per credit. *Required fees:* $38 per credit. $187 per semester. Tuition and fees vary according to course level, course load, program and reciprocity agreements. *Financial support:* In 2015–16, 32 research assistantships with full tuition reimbursements (averaging $15,761 per year), 15 teaching assistantships with full tuition reimbursements (averaging $12,788 per year) were awarded; fellowships with full tuition reimbursements, Federal Work-Study, scholarships/grants, health care benefits, and unspecified assistantships also available. Support available to part-time students. Financial award application deadline: 2/15; financial award applicants required to submit FAFSA. *Faculty research:* Glacial surging, volcanology, geochronology, impact cratering, permafrost geophysics. *Unit head:* Dr. Paul McCarthy, Department Co-Chair, 907-474-7565, Fax: 907-474-5163, E-mail: geology@uaf.edu. *Application contact:* Mary Kreta, Director of Admissions, 907-474-7500, Fax: 907-474-7097,
E-mail: admissions@uaf.edu.
Website: http://www.uaf.edu/geology/

University of Arkansas, Graduate School, J. William Fulbright College of Arts and Sciences, Department of Geosciences, Program in Geology, Fayetteville, AR 72701-1201. Offers MS. *Program availability:* Part-time. *Students:* 28 full-time (10 women), 19 part-time (3 women); includes 3 minority (2 Black or African American, non-Hispanic/Latino; 1 Hispanic/Latino), 5 international. In 2015, 5 master's awarded. *Degree requirements:* For master's, thesis. *Application deadline:* For fall admission, 4/1 for international students; for spring admission, 10/1 for international students. Applications are processed on a rolling basis. Application fee: $40 ($50 for international students). Electronic applications accepted. *Financial support:* In 2015–16, 1 research assistantship, 10 teaching assistantships were awarded; fellowships, career-related internships or fieldwork, and Federal Work-Study also available. Support available to part-time students. Financial award application deadline: 4/1; financial award applicants required to submit FAFSA. *Unit head:* Dr. Ralph Davis, Graduate Coordinator, 479-575-3355, Fax: 479-575-3469, E-mail: ralphd@uark.edu. *Application contact:* Dr. Celina Suarez, Graduate Admissions, 479-575-4866, E-mail: casuarez@uark.edu.
Website: http://geosciences.uark.edu/

The University of British Columbia, Faculty of Science, Department of Earth, Ocean and Atmospheric Sciences, Vancouver, BC V6T 1Z4, Canada. Offers atmospheric science (M Sc, PhD); geological engineering (M Eng, MA Sc, PhD); geological sciences (M Sc, PhD); geophysics (M Sc, MA Sc, PhD); oceanography (M Sc, PhD). *Degree requirements:* For master's, one foreign language, thesis (for some programs); for doctorate, one foreign language, comprehensive exam, thesis/dissertation. *Entrance requirements:* Additional exam requirements/recommendations for international students: Required—TOEFL (minimum score 600 paper-based; 100 iBT). *Faculty research:* Oceans and atmosphere, environmental earth science, hydro geology, mineral deposits, geophysics.

University of Calgary, Faculty of Graduate Studies, Faculty of Science, Department of Geoscience, Calgary, AB T2N 1N4, Canada. Offers geology (M Sc, PhD); geophysics (M Sc, PhD); hydrology (M Sc, PhD). *Program availability:* Part-time. Terminal master's awarded for partial completion of doctoral program. *Degree requirements:* For master's, thesis; for doctorate, thesis/dissertation, candidacy exam. *Entrance requirements:* For master's, B Sc; for doctorate, honors B Sc or M Sc. Additional exam requirements/recommendations for international students: Required—TOEFL. Electronic applications accepted. *Faculty research:* Geochemistry, petrology, paleontology, stratigraphy, exploration and solid-earth geophysics.

University of California, Berkeley, Graduate Division, College of Letters and Science, Department of Earth and Planetary Science, Berkeley, CA 94720-1500. Offers geology (MA, MS, PhD); geophysics (MA, MS, PhD). Terminal master's awarded for partial completion of doctoral program. *Degree requirements:* For master's, oral exam (MA), thesis (MS); for doctorate, comprehensive exam, thesis/dissertation, candidacy exams. *Entrance requirements:* For master's and doctorate, GRE General Test, minimum GPA of 3.0, 3 letters of recommendation. Additional exam requirements/recommendations for international students: Required—TOEFL. *Faculty research:* Tectonics, environmental geology, high-pressure geophysics and seismology, economic geology, geochemistry.

University of California, Davis, Graduate Studies, Program in Geology, Davis, CA 95616. Offers MS, PhD. Terminal master's awarded for partial completion of doctoral program. *Degree requirements:* For master's, thesis; for doctorate, thesis/dissertation. *Entrance requirements:* For master's and doctorate, GRE General Test, GRE Subject Test, minimum GPA of 3.0. Additional exam requirements/recommendations for international students: Required—TOEFL (minimum score 550 paper-based). Electronic applications accepted. *Faculty research:* Petrology, paleontology, geophysics, sedimentology, structure/tectonics.

University of California, Los Angeles, Graduate Division, College of Letters and Science, Department of Earth and Space Sciences, Program in Geology, Los Angeles, CA 90095. Offers MS, PhD. Terminal master's awarded for partial completion of doctoral program. *Degree requirements:* For master's, comprehensive exam or thesis; for doctorate, thesis/dissertation, oral and written qualifying exams. *Entrance requirements:* For master's and doctorate, GRE General Test, bachelor's degree; minimum undergraduate GPA of 3.0 (or its equivalent if letter grade system not used). Additional exam requirements/recommendations for international students: Required—TOEFL. Electronic applications accepted.

University of California, Riverside, Graduate Division, Department of Earth Sciences, Riverside, CA 92521-0102. Offers geological sciences (MS, PhD). Terminal master's awarded for partial completion of doctoral program. *Degree requirements:* For master's, thesis, final oral exam; for doctorate, thesis/dissertation, qualifying exams, final oral exam. *Entrance requirements:* For master's and doctorate, GRE General Test, minimum GPA of 3.2. Additional exam requirements/recommendations for international students: Required—TOEFL (minimum score 550 paper-based; 80 iBT). Electronic applications accepted. *Faculty research:* Applied and solid earth geophysics, tectonic geomorphology, fluid-rock interaction, paleobiology-ecology, sedimentary-geochemistry.

University of Cincinnati, Graduate School, McMicken College of Arts and Sciences, Department of Geology, Cincinnati, OH 45221. Offers MS, PhD. *Program availability:* Part-time. *Degree requirements:* For master's, thesis; for doctorate, comprehensive exam, thesis/dissertation. *Entrance requirements:* For master's and doctorate, GRE General Test, 1 year of course work in physics, chemistry, and calculus. Additional exam requirements/recommendations for international students: Required—TOEFL. Electronic applications accepted. *Faculty research:* Paleobiology, sequence stratigraphy, earth systems history, quaternary, groundwater.

University of Colorado Boulder, Graduate School, College of Arts and Sciences, Department of Geological Sciences, Boulder, CO 80309. Offers geology (MS, PhD); geophysics (PhD). *Faculty:* 30 full-time (10 women). *Students:* 64 full-time (33 women), 3 part-time (0 women); includes 6 minority (3 Hispanic/Latino; 3 Two or more races, non-Hispanic/Latino), 4 international. Average age 27. 263 applicants, 9% accepted, 22 enrolled. In 2015, 12 master's, 14 doctorates awarded. Terminal master's awarded for partial completion of doctoral program. *Degree requirements:* For master's, comprehensive exam, thesis; for doctorate, comprehensive exam, thesis/dissertation. *Entrance requirements:* For master's, GRE General Test, minimum undergraduate GPA of 3.0; for doctorate, GRE General Test, minimum GPA of 2.75. *Application deadline:* For fall admission, 1/7 for domestic students, 12/1 for international students. Application fee: $50 ($70 for international students). Electronic applications accepted. Application fee is waived when completed online. *Financial support:* In 2015–16, 177 students received support, including 46 fellowships (averaging $3,061 per year), 33 research assistantships with tuition reimbursements available (averaging $32,260 per year), 26

teaching assistantships with tuition reimbursements available (averaging $29,477 per year); institutionally sponsored loans, scholarships/grants, health care benefits, and unspecified assistantships also available. Financial award application deadline: 1/15; financial award applicants required to submit FAFSA. *Faculty research:* Geology, tectonics, earth sciences, geophysics, geosciences. *Total annual research expenditures:* $12.5 million. *Application contact:* E-mail: geolinfo@colorado.edu.
Website: http://www.colorado.edu/GeolSci

University of Connecticut, Graduate School, College of Liberal Arts and Sciences, Center for Integrative Geosciences, Storrs, CT 06269. Offers geological sciences (MS, PhD). *Degree requirements:* For doctorate, thesis/dissertation. *Entrance requirements:* For master's and doctorate, GRE General Test. Additional exam requirements/recommendations for international students: Required—TOEFL (minimum score 550 paper-based). Electronic applications accepted.

University of Delaware, College of Earth, Ocean, and Environment, Department of Geological Sciences, Newark, DE 19716. Offers MA, PhD.

University of Florida, Graduate School, College of Liberal Arts and Sciences, Department of Geological Sciences, Gainesville, FL 32611. Offers geology (MS, MST, PhD); hydrologic sciences (MS, PhD); tropical conservation and development (MS, MST, PhD); wetland sciences (MS, MST, PhD). *Faculty:* 22. *Students:* 43 full-time (19 women), 3 part-time (1 woman); includes 4 minority (1 Asian, non-Hispanic/Latino; 3 Hispanic/Latino), 18 international. Average age 29. 60 applicants, 20% accepted, 11 enrolled. In 2015, 6 master's, 1 doctorate awarded. Terminal master's awarded for partial completion of doctoral program. *Degree requirements:* For master's, thesis (for some programs); for doctorate, one foreign language, thesis/dissertation. *Entrance requirements:* For master's and doctorate, GRE General Test, minimum GPA of 3.0. Additional exam requirements/recommendations for international students: Required—TOEFL (minimum score 550 paper-based; 80 iBT), IELTS (minimum score 6). *Application deadline:* For fall admission, 1/15 for domestic students; for spring admission, 10/1 for domestic students. Applications are processed on a rolling basis. Application fee: $30. Electronic applications accepted. *Financial support:* In 2015–16, 3 fellowships, 21 research assistantships, 25 teaching assistantships were awarded; career-related internships or fieldwork, Federal Work-Study, institutionally sponsored loans, and scholarships/grants also available. Support available to part-time students. Financial award application deadline: 3/1; financial award applicants required to submit FAFSA. *Faculty research:* Paleoclimatology, tectonophysics, petrochemistry, marine geology, geochemistry, hydrology. *Total annual research expenditures:* $1.5 million. *Unit head:* Dr. David A. Foster, Professor and Chair, 352-392-7316, Fax: 352-392-9294, E-mail: dafoster@ufl.edu. *Application contact:* Dr. Raymond Russo, Associate Professor and Graduate Coordinator, 352-392-2231, Fax: 352-392-9294, E-mail: rrusso@ufl.edu.

University of Georgia, Franklin College of Arts and Sciences, Department of Geology, Athens, GA 30602. Offers MS, PhD. *Degree requirements:* For master's, thesis; for doctorate, one foreign language, thesis/dissertation. *Entrance requirements:* For master's and doctorate, GRE General Test. Electronic applications accepted.

University of Hawaii at Manoa, Graduate Division, School of Ocean and Earth Science and Technology, Department of Geology and Geophysics, Honolulu, HI 96822. Offers high-pressure geophysics and geochemistry (MS, PhD); hydrogeology and engineering geology (MS, PhD); marine geology and geophysics (MS, PhD); planetary geosciences and remote sensing (MS, PhD); seismology and solid-earth geophysics (MS, PhD); volcanology, petrology, and geochemistry (MS, PhD). *Program availability:* Part-time. *Faculty:* 72 full-time (15 women), 6 part-time/adjunct (3 women). *Students:* 42 full-time (26 women), 2 part-time (1 woman); includes 9 minority (2 Asian, non-Hispanic/Latino; 2 Hispanic/Latino; 5 Two or more races, non-Hispanic/Latino), 9 international. Average age 31. 78 applicants, 23% accepted, 13 enrolled. In 2015, 7 master's, 8 doctorates awarded. Terminal master's awarded for partial completion of doctoral program. *Degree requirements:* For master's, thesis optional; for doctorate, comprehensive exam, thesis/dissertation. *Entrance requirements:* For master's and doctorate, GRE General Test, minimum GPA of 3.0. Additional exam requirements/recommendations for international students: Required—TOEFL (minimum score 580 paper-based; 92 iBT), IELTS (minimum score 5). *Application deadline:* For fall admission, 1/15 for domestic students, 1/1 for international students; for spring admission, 9/1 for domestic students, 8/15 for international students. Application fee: $100. *Financial support:* In 2015–16, 7 fellowships (averaging $1,359 per year), 30 research assistantships (averaging $23,988 per year), 4 teaching assistantships (averaging $15,350 per year) were awarded. *Total annual research expenditures:* $3.8 million. *Unit head:* Brian Taylor, Dean, 808-956-6182, E-mail: taylorb@hawaii.edu. *Application contact:* Dr. Gregory Moore, Chair, 808-956-7640, Fax: 808-956-5512, E-mail: gg-dept@soest.hawaii.edu.
Website: http://www.soest.hawaii.edu/GG/

University of Houston, College of Natural Sciences and Mathematics, Department of Earth and Atmospheric Sciences, Houston, TX 77204. Offers atmospheric science (PhD); geology (MA, PhD); geophysics (PhD). *Program availability:* Part-time. *Degree requirements:* For master's, thesis; for doctorate, comprehensive exam, thesis/dissertation. *Entrance requirements:* For master's and doctorate, GRE General Test. Additional exam requirements/recommendations for international students: Required—TOEFL (minimum score 550 paper-based; 79 iBT), IELTS (minimum score 6.5). Electronic applications accepted. *Faculty research:* Atmospherics sciences, seismic and solid earth geophysics, tectonics, environmental hydrochemistry, carbonates, micropaleontology, structure and tectonics, petroleum geology.

University of Idaho, College of Graduate Studies, College of Science, Department of Geological Sciences, Moscow, ID 83844-3022. Offers geology (MS, PhD); hydrology (MS). *Faculty:* 12 full-time. *Students:* 20 full-time, 4 part-time. Average age 32. In 2015, 8 master's, 1 doctorate awarded. *Degree requirements:* For doctorate, one foreign language, thesis/dissertation. *Entrance requirements:* For master's, minimum GPA of 2.8; for doctorate, minimum undergraduate GPA of 2.8, 3.0 graduate. Additional exam requirements/recommendations for international students: Required—TOEFL. *Application deadline:* For fall admission, 8/1 for domestic students; for spring admission, 12/15 for domestic students. Applications are processed on a rolling basis. Application fee: $60. Electronic applications accepted. *Expenses:* Tuition, state resident: full-time $6205; part-time $399 per credit hour. Tuition, nonresident: full-time $20,209; part-time $1177 per credit hour. *Required fees:* $2017; $58 per credit hour. Full-time tuition and fees vary according to course load and reciprocity agreements. *Financial support:* Fellowships, research assistantships, and teaching assistantships available. Financial award applicants required to submit FAFSA. *Faculty research:* Health effects of mineral dust, geomicrobiology, glacial and arctic sciences, optical mineralogy, planetary and terrestrial geomechanics. *Unit head:* Dr. Mickey Gunter, Head, 208-885-6192, E-mail: geology@uidaho.edu. *Application contact:* Sean Scoggin, Graduate Recruitment Director, 208-885-4723, Fax: 208-885-4406, E-mail: graduateadmissions@uidaho.edu.
Website: http://www.uidaho.edu/sci/geology

University of Illinois at Chicago, College of Liberal Arts and Sciences, Department of Earth and Environmental Sciences, Chicago, IL 60607-7128. Offers MS, PhD. *Faculty:* 9 full-time (4 women). *Students:* 18 full-time (10 women), 1 (woman) part-time; includes 3 minority (2 Asian, non-Hispanic/Latino; 1 Hispanic/Latino), 5 international. Average age 29. *Degree requirements:* For master's, thesis; for doctorate, thesis/dissertation. *Entrance requirements:* For master's and doctorate, GRE General Test, minimum GPA of 2.75. Additional exam requirements/recommendations for international students: Required—TOEFL. *Application deadline:* For fall admission, 2/1 for domestic and international students; for spring admission, 11/15 for domestic students, 7/15 for international students. Applications are processed on a rolling basis. Application fee: $60. Electronic applications accepted. *Expenses:* Contact institution. *Financial support:* In 2015–16, 1 fellowship with full tuition reimbursement was awarded; research assistantships with full tuition reimbursements, teaching assistantships with full tuition reimbursements, Federal Work-Study, scholarships/grants, traineeships, tuition waivers (full), and unspecified assistantships also available. Financial award application deadline: 3/1; financial award applicants required to submit FAFSA. *Faculty research:* Geochemistry, mineralogy and petrology, geophysics, tectonics, global change, hydrology, geobiology. *Unit head:* Dr. Kathryn Nagy, Head, 312-355-3276,
E-mail: klnagy@uic.edu. *Application contact:* Andrew Dombard, Director of Graduate Studies, 312-996-9206, E-mail: adombard@uic.edu.
Website: http://www.uic.edu/depts/geos/

University of Illinois at Urbana–Champaign, Graduate College, College of Liberal Arts and Sciences, School of Earth, Society and Environment, Department of Geology, Champaign, IL 61820. Offers geology (MS, PhD); teaching of earth sciences (MS). Terminal master's awarded for partial completion of doctoral program.

The University of Kansas, Graduate Studies, College of Liberal Arts and Sciences, Department of Geology, Lawrence, KS 66045. Offers MS, PhD. PhD offered jointly with Kansas State University. *Students:* 65 full-time (24 women), 27 part-time (12 women); includes 8 minority (2 American Indian or Alaska Native, non-Hispanic/Latino; 4 Hispanic/Latino; 2 Two or more races, non-Hispanic/Latino), 10 international. Average age 28. 150 applicants, 20% accepted, 25 enrolled. In 2015, 18 master's, 6 doctorates awarded. *Entrance requirements:* For master's and doctorate, GRE General Test, 3 letters of recommendation. Additional exam requirements/recommendations for international students: Required—TOEFL. *Application deadline:* For fall admission, 2/1 priority date for domestic and international students; for spring admission, 10/31 priority date for domestic and international students. Application fee: $65 ($85 for international students). Electronic applications accepted. *Financial support:* Fellowships, research assistantships, teaching assistantships, and unspecified assistantships available. Financial award application deadline: 2/1. *Faculty research:* Sedimentology, paleontology, tectonics, geophysics, hydrogeology. *Unit head:* Luis A. Gonzalez, Chair, 785-864-4974, E-mail: lgonzlez@ku.edu. *Application contact:* Yolanda Balderas, Graduate Admissions Contact, 785-864-4975, Fax: 785-864-5276,
E-mail: yolanda@ku.edu.
Website: http://www.geo.ku.edu

University of Kentucky, Graduate School, College of Arts and Sciences, Program in Geology, Lexington, KY 40506-0032. Offers MS, PhD. *Degree requirements:* For master's, comprehensive exam, thesis; for doctorate, comprehensive exam, thesis/dissertation. *Entrance requirements:* For master's, GRE General Test, minimum undergraduate GPA of 2.75; for doctorate, GRE General Test, minimum graduate GPA of 3.0. Additional exam requirements/recommendations for international students: Required—TOEFL (minimum score 550 paper-based). Electronic applications accepted. *Faculty research:* Structure tectonics, geophysics, stratigraphy, hydrogeology, coal geology.

University of Louisiana at Lafayette, College of Sciences, Department of Geology, Lafayette, LA 70504. Offers MS. *Program availability:* Part-time. *Degree requirements:* For master's, comprehensive exam, thesis. *Entrance requirements:* For master's, GRE General Test, minimum GPA of 2.75. Additional exam requirements/recommendations for international students: Required—TOEFL (minimum score 550 paper-based). Electronic applications accepted. *Faculty research:* Aquifer contamination, coastal erosion, geochemistry of peat, petroleum geology and geophysics, remote sensing and geographic information systems applications.

University of Maine, Graduate School, Climate Change Institute, Orono, ME 04469. Offers MS, CGS. *Program availability:* Part-time. *Faculty:* 41 full-time (11 women). *Students:* 8 full-time (4 women), 1 (woman) part-time; includes 1 minority (American Indian or Alaska Native, non-Hispanic/Latino). Average age 33. 13 applicants, 31% accepted, 2 enrolled. In 2015, 1 master's awarded. *Degree requirements:* For master's, thesis. *Entrance requirements:* For master's, GRE General Test. Additional exam requirements/recommendations for international students: Required—TOEFL. *Application deadline:* For fall admission, 11/1 priority date for domestic and international students; for spring admission, 2/1 priority date for domestic and international students. Applications are processed on a rolling basis. Application fee: $65. Electronic applications accepted. *Financial support:* In 2015–16, 6 students received support, including 4 research assistantships with full tuition reimbursements available (averaging $14,780 per year); unspecified assistantships also available. Financial award application deadline: 3/1. *Faculty research:* Archeology and anthropology; atmospheric climate reconstruction and glaciology; glacial geology; ecosystems and environmental change; climate prediction and modeling. *Total annual research expenditures:* $17.4 million. *Unit head:* Dr. Paul Mayewski, Director, 207-581-3019, Fax: 207-581-1203,
E-mail: paul.mayewski@maine.edu. *Application contact:* Dr. Karl Kreutz, Graduate Coordinator, 207-581-3011, E-mail: karl.kreutz@maine.edu.
Website: http://climatechange.umaine.edu/

University of Manitoba, Faculty of Graduate Studies, Clayton H. Riddell Faculty of Environment, Earth, and Resources, Department of Geological Sciences, Winnipeg, MB R3T 2N2, Canada. Offers geology (M Sc, PhD); geophysics (M Sc, PhD). *Degree requirements:* For master's, thesis; for doctorate, thesis/dissertation. *Entrance requirements:* For master's and doctorate, GRE General Test, GRE Subject Test (geology), minimum GPA of 3.0. Additional exam requirements/recommendations for international students: Required—TOEFL.

University of Maryland, College Park, Academic Affairs, College of Computer, Mathematical and Natural Sciences, Department of Geology, College Park, MD 20742. Offers MS, PhD. *Degree requirements:* For master's, thesis, oral defense; for doctorate, thesis/dissertation. *Entrance requirements:* For master's, GRE General Test, minimum GPA of 3.0, 3 letters of recommendation; for doctorate, GRE General Test, 3 letters of recommendation. Additional exam requirements/recommendations for international students: Required—TOEFL. Electronic applications accepted.

University of Memphis, Graduate School, College of Arts and Sciences, Department of Earth Sciences, Memphis, TN 38152. Offers archaeology (MS); earth sciences (PhD); geographic information systems (Graduate Certificate), including geographic information systems, GIS educator, GIS planning, GIS professional; geography (MA, MS); geology (MS); geophysics (MS); interdisciplinary studies (MS). *Program availability:* Part-time, evening/weekend. *Faculty:* 14 full-time (3 women), 1 part-time/adjunct (0 women). *Students:* 37 full-time (9 women), 33 part-time (12 women); includes 7 minority (3 Black or African American, non-Hispanic/Latino; 1 Asian, non-Hispanic/Latino; 1 Hispanic/

Latino; 2 Two or more races, non-Hispanic/Latino), 25 international. Average age 33. 31 applicants, 71% accepted, 8 enrolled. In 2015, 7 master's, 5 doctorates awarded. Terminal master's awarded for partial completion of doctoral program. *Degree requirements:* For master's, comprehensive exam, thesis, seminar presentation; for doctorate, thesis/dissertation. *Entrance requirements:* For master's, GRE General Test, 3 letters of recommendation, statement of research interests; for doctorate, GRE General Test, 2 letters of recommendation, resume, personal statement. Additional exam requirements/recommendations for international students: Required—TOEFL (minimum score 550 paper-based). *Application deadline:* For fall admission, 1/31 for domestic students; for spring admission, 11/1 for domestic students. Applications are processed on a rolling basis. Application fee: $35 ($60 for international students). Electronic applications accepted. *Financial support:* In 2015–16, 18 students received support. Fellowships with full tuition reimbursements available, research assistantships with full tuition reimbursements available, teaching assistantships with full tuition reimbursements available, Federal Work-Study, scholarships/grants, and unspecified assistantships available. Financial award application deadline: 2/15; financial award applicants required to submit FAFSA. *Faculty research:* Hazards, active tectonics, geophysics, hydrology and water resources, spatial analysis. *Unit head:* Dr. M. Jerry Bartholomew, Chair, 901-678-4536, Fax: 901-678-4467,
E-mail: jbrthlm1@memphis.edu. *Application contact:* Dr. Arlene Hill, Associate Professor and Graduate Program Coordinator, 901-678-4358, Fax: 901-678-2178, E-mail: dlarsen@memphis.edu.
Website: http://www.memphis.edu/earthsciences/

University of Minnesota, Duluth, Graduate School, Swenson College of Science and Engineering, Department of Geological Sciences, Duluth, MN 55812-2496. Offers MS, PhD. PhD offered jointly with University of Minnesota, Twin Cities Campus. *Program availability:* Part-time. *Degree requirements:* For master's, thesis, final oral exam, written and oral research proposal. *Entrance requirements:* For master's, GRE General Test, minimum GPA of 3.0. Additional exam requirements/recommendations for international students: Required—TOEFL (minimum score 550 paper-based). Electronic applications accepted. *Faculty research:* Surface processes, tectonics, planetary geology, paleoclimate, petrology.

University of Minnesota, Twin Cities Campus, College of Science and Engineering, Department of Earth Sciences, Minneapolis, MN 55455-0213. Offers MS, PhD. Terminal master's awarded for partial completion of doctoral program. *Degree requirements:* For master's, thesis; for doctorate, thesis/dissertation. *Entrance requirements:* For master's and doctorate, GRE General Test, 3 letters of recommendation. Additional exam requirements/recommendations for international students: Required—TOEFL (minimum score 550 paper-based). Electronic applications accepted. *Faculty research:* Geology, geophysics, geochemistry, geobiology, climate and environmental geosciences.

University of Missouri, Office of Research and Graduate Studies, College of Arts and Science, Department of Geological Sciences, Columbia, MO 65211. Offers MS, PhD. *Degree requirements:* For master's, thesis; for doctorate, variable foreign language requirement, thesis/dissertation. *Entrance requirements:* For master's and doctorate, GRE General Test, minimum GPA of 3.0. Additional exam requirements/recommendations for international students: Required—TOEFL (minimum score 530 paper-based; 71 iBT). Electronic applications accepted. *Faculty research:* Geochemistry, tectonics, economic geology, biogeochemistry, geophysics.

University of Missouri–Kansas City, College of Arts and Sciences, Department of Geosciences, Kansas City, MO 64110-2499. Offers environmental and urban geosciences (MS); geosciences (PhD). PhD (interdisciplinary) offered through the School of Graduate Studies. *Program availability:* Part-time. *Faculty:* 6 full-time (2 women), 10 part-time/adjunct (1 woman). *Students:* 3 full-time (1 woman), 19 part-time (9 women); includes 1 minority (Hispanic/Latino), 1 international. Average age 33. 17 applicants, 82% accepted, 9 enrolled. In 2015, 4 master's awarded. *Degree requirements:* For master's, thesis; for doctorate, thesis/dissertation, qualifying exam. *Entrance requirements:* For master's, GRE General Test, minimum GPA of 3.0. Additional exam requirements/recommendations for international students: Required—TOEFL (minimum score 550 paper-based; 80 iBT). *Application deadline:* For fall admission, 3/15 priority date for domestic and international students. Applications are processed on a rolling basis. Application fee: $45 ($50 for international students). Electronic applications accepted. *Financial support:* In 2015–16, 15 teaching assistantships with partial tuition reimbursements (averaging $13,158 per year) were awarded; research assistantships with partial tuition reimbursements, Federal Work-Study, institutionally sponsored loans, and tuition waivers (full and partial) also available. Support available to part-time students. Financial award application deadline: 3/1; financial award applicants required to submit FAFSA. *Faculty research:* Neotectonics and applied geophysics, environmental geosciences, urban geoscience, geoinformatics-remote sensing, atmospheric research. *Unit head:* Dr. Michael B. Kruger, Interim Chair, 816-235-5441, Fax: 816-235-5535, E-mail: krugerm@umkc.edu. *Application contact:* Dr. Jejung Lee, Associate Professor, 816-235-6495, Fax: 816-235-5535,
E-mail: leej@umkc.edu.
Website: http://cas.umkc.edu/geo/

University of Montana, Graduate School, College of Humanities and Sciences, Department of Geosciences, Missoula, MT 59812-0002. Offers MS, PhD. *Degree requirements:* For doctorate, thesis/dissertation. *Entrance requirements:* For master's and doctorate, GRE General Test. Additional exam requirements/recommendations for international students: Required—TOEFL (minimum score 525 paper-based). *Faculty research:* Environmental geoscience, regional structure and tectonics, groundwater geology, petrology, mineral deposits.

University of Nevada, Reno, Graduate School, College of Science, Mackay School of Earth Sciences and Engineering, Department of Geological Sciences and Engineering, Program in Geology, Reno, NV 89557. Offers MS, PhD. Terminal master's awarded for partial completion of doctoral program. *Degree requirements:* For master's, thesis optional; for doctorate, thesis/dissertation. *Entrance requirements:* For master's, GRE General Test, minimum GPA of 2.75; for doctorate, GRE General Test, minimum GPA of 3.0. Additional exam requirements/recommendations for international students: Required—TOEFL (minimum score 500 paper-based; 61 iBT), IELTS (minimum score 6). Electronic applications accepted. *Faculty research:* Mineral exploration, geochemistry, hydrology.

University of New Brunswick Fredericton, School of Graduate Studies, Faculty of Science, Department of Earth Sciences, Fredericton, NB E3B 5A3, Canada. Offers M Sc, PhD. *Program availability:* Part-time. *Faculty:* 12 full-time (1 woman). *Students:* 21 full-time (12 women), 7 part-time (4 women). In 2015, 3 master's, 1 doctorate awarded. *Degree requirements:* For master's, thesis; for doctorate, thesis/dissertation. *Entrance requirements:* For master's, minimum GPA of 3.0, B Sc in earth sciences or related subject; for doctorate, minimum GPA of 3.0; M Sc in earth science or related subject. Additional exam requirements/recommendations for international students: Required—TOEFL, IELTS, TWE. *Application deadline:* For fall admission, 3/1 for domestic students. Applications are processed on a rolling basis. Application fee: $50 Canadian dollars. Electronic applications accepted. *Financial support:* Fellowships, research assistantships, and teaching assistantships available. *Faculty research:* Applied geophysics and rock physics; applied glacial and quaternary geology; aqueous and environmental geochemistry and hydrogeology; lithogeochemistry and mineral deposits; igneous, metamorphic and experimental petrology; isotope geochemistry and U-Pb geochronology; paleontology and ichnology; sedimentology, stratigraphy and petroleum geology; shock metamorphism, impact and planetary geology; structural geology and rock mechanics. *Total annual research expenditures:* $133,936. *Unit head:* Dr. David Lentz, Director of Graduate Studies, 506-447-3190, Fax: 506-453-5055,
E-mail: dlentz@unb.ca. *Application contact:* Heidi Stewart, Office Support Staff, Administrative and Graduate Services, 506-458-7488, E-mail: scigrad@unb.ca.
Website: http://go.unb.ca/gradprograms

University of New Hampshire, Graduate School, College of Engineering and Physical Sciences, Department of Earth Sciences, Durham, NH 03824. Offers earth sciences (PhD); geology (MS); hydrology (MS). *Degree requirements:* For master's, thesis. *Entrance requirements:* For master's, GRE General Test. Additional exam requirements/recommendations for international students: Required—TOEFL (minimum score 550 paper-based; 80 iBT). Electronic applications accepted.

The University of North Carolina at Chapel Hill, Graduate School, College of Arts and Sciences, Department of Geological Sciences, Chapel Hill, NC 27599. Offers MS, PhD. *Degree requirements:* For master's, comprehensive exam, thesis; for doctorate, one foreign language, comprehensive exam, thesis/dissertation. *Entrance requirements:* For master's and doctorate, GRE General Test, minimum GPA of 3.0. Electronic applications accepted. *Faculty research:* Paleoceanography, igneous petrology, paleontology, geophysics, structural geology.

University of North Dakota, Graduate School, School of Engineering and Mines, Department of Geology, Grand Forks, ND 58202. Offers MA, MS, PhD. *Degree requirements:* For master's, thesis, final exam; for doctorate, one foreign language, comprehensive exam, thesis/dissertation, final exam. *Entrance requirements:* For master's and doctorate, GRE General Test, minimum GPA of 3.0. Additional exam requirements/recommendations for international students: Required—TOEFL (minimum score 550 paper-based; 79 iBT), IELTS (minimum score 6.5). Electronic applications accepted. *Faculty research:* Hydrogeology, environmental geology, geological engineering, sedimentology, geomorphology.

University of Oklahoma, Mewbourne College of Earth and Energy, ConocoPhillips School of Geology and Geophysics, Program in Geology, Norman, OK 73019. Offers MS, PhD. *Program availability:* Part-time. *Students:* 37 full-time (16 women), 31 part-time (14 women); includes 4 minority (1 American Indian or Alaska Native, non-Hispanic/Latino; 1 Asian, non-Hispanic/Latino; 2 Hispanic/Latino), 29 international. Average age 27. 189 applicants, 11% accepted, 19 enrolled. In 2015, 27 master's, 4 doctorates awarded. *Degree requirements:* For master's, thesis; for doctorate, thesis/dissertation. *Entrance requirements:* For master's and doctorate, GRE. Additional exam requirements/recommendations for international students: Required—TOEFL (minimum score 79 iBT) or IELTS (minimum score 6.5). *Application deadline:* For fall admission, 1/10 for domestic students, 1/10 priority date for international students; for spring admission, 9/1 for domestic and international students. Application fee: $50 ($100 for international students). Electronic applications accepted. *Expenses:* Tuition, state resident: full-time $4577; part-time $190.70 per credit hour. Tuition, nonresident: full-time $17,758; part-time $739.90 per credit hour. *Required fees:* $3060; $115.70 per credit hour. $141.50 per semester. *Financial support:* In 2015–16, 55 students received support. Career-related internships or fieldwork, scholarships/grants, and unspecified assistantships available. Financial award application deadline: 6/1; financial award applicants required to submit FAFSA. *Faculty research:* Energy, geochemistry, geophysics, earth systems, lithospheric dynamics. *Unit head:* Dr. R. Douglas Elmore, Director, 405-325-3253, Fax: 405-325-3140, E-mail: delmore@ou.edu. *Application contact:* Rebecca Fay, Coordinator for Academic Student Services, 405-325-3253, Fax: 405-325-3140, E-mail: rfay@ou.edu.
Website: http://geology.ou.edu

University of Oregon, Graduate School, College of Arts and Sciences, Department of Geological Sciences, Eugene, OR 97403. Offers MA, MS, PhD. *Degree requirements:* For master's, foreign language (MA). *Entrance requirements:* For master's and doctorate, GRE General Test, GRE Subject Test.

University of Pittsburgh, Dietrich School of Arts and Sciences, Department of Geology and Environmental Science, Pittsburgh, PA 15260. Offers geographical information systems and remote sensing (Pro-MS); geology and environmental science (MS, PhD). *Program availability:* Part-time. *Faculty:* 9 full-time (3 women). *Students:* 36 full-time (15 women), 2 part-time (both women); includes 6 minority (1 Black or African American, non-Hispanic/Latino; 4 Asian, non-Hispanic/Latino; 1 Two or more races, non-Hispanic/Latino). Average age 29. 67 applicants, 36% accepted, 12 enrolled. In 2015, 7 master's, 3 doctorates awarded. *Degree requirements:* For master's, thesis, thesis defense; for doctorate, comprehensive exam, thesis/dissertation, thesis defense, public presentation. *Entrance requirements:* Additional exam requirements/recommendations for international students: Required—TOEFL (minimum score 90 iBT), IELTS (minimum score 7). *Application deadline:* For fall admission, 1/15 for domestic and international students. Applications are processed on a rolling basis. Application fee: $50. Electronic applications accepted. Tuition and fees vary according to program. *Financial support:* In 2015–16, 26 students received support, including 7 fellowships with full tuition reimbursements available (averaging $18,219 per year), 15 research assistantships with tuition reimbursements available (averaging $14,893 per year), 12 teaching assistantships with tuition reimbursements available (averaging $17,130 per year); scholarships/grants and tuition waivers (full and partial) also available. Financial award application deadline: 1/15. *Faculty research:* Tectonic, volcanic and surface processes; planetary science and astrobiology; paleoclimate and environmental change; environmental geochemistry and biogeochemistry; hydrologic processes. *Total annual research expenditures:* $1.8 million. *Unit head:* Dr. Mark Abbott, Chair, 412-624-8783, Fax: 412-624-3914, E-mail: mabbott1@pitt.edu. *Application contact:* Annemarie Vranesevic, Academic Coordinator, 412-624-8779, Fax: 412-624-3914,
E-mail: alv36@pitt.edu.
Website: http://geology.pitt.edu/

University of Puerto Rico, Mayagüez Campus, Graduate Studies, College of Arts and Sciences, Department of Geology, Mayagüez, PR 00681-9000. Offers MS. *Program availability:* Part-time. *Degree requirements:* For master's, comprehensive exam, thesis. *Entrance requirements:* For master's, GRE General Test, BS in geology or the equivalent; minimum GPA of 2.8. *Faculty research:* Seismology, applied geophysics, geographic information systems, environmental remote sensing, petrology.

University of Regina, Faculty of Graduate Studies and Research, Faculty of Science, Department of Geology, Regina, SK S4S 0A2, Canada. Offers M Sc, PhD. *Program availability:* Part-time. *Degree requirements:* For master's, thesis; for doctorate, thesis/dissertation. *Entrance requirements:* Additional exam requirements/recommendations for international students: Required—TOEFL (minimum score 580 paper-based; 80 iBT),

IELTS (minimum score 6.5), PTE (minimum score 59). Electronic applications accepted. *Faculty research:* Quaternary and economic geology; volcanology; organic, igneous, and metamorphic petrology; carbonate sedimentology and basin analysis; mineralogy.

University of Rochester, School of Arts and Sciences, Department of Earth and Environmental Sciences, Rochester, NY 14627. Offers MS, PhD. *Faculty:* 8 full-time (2 women). *Students:* 21 full-time (8 women); includes 2 minority (1 American Indian or Alaska Native, non-Hispanic/Latino; 1 Hispanic/Latino), 6 international. 17 applicants, 35% accepted, 4 enrolled. In 2015, 6 master's, 1 doctorate awarded. *Degree requirements:* For doctorate, thesis/dissertation, qualifying exam. *Entrance requirements:* For master's and doctorate, GRE General Test. Additional exam requirements/recommendations for international students: Required—TOEFL. *Application deadline:* For fall admission, 2/1 priority date for domestic students. Application fee: $60. Electronic applications accepted. *Expenses: Tuition, area resident:* Full-time $47,450; part-time $1482 per credit hour. *Required fees:* $528. Tuition and fees vary according to program. *Financial support:* Fellowships, research assistantships, teaching assistantships, career-related internships or fieldwork, and tuition waivers (full and partial) available. Financial award application deadline: 2/1. *Faculty research:* Geochemistry and environmental sciences; paleomagnetism, structure and tectonics. *Unit head:* Carmala Garzione, Chair, 585-275-5713,
E-mail: carmala.garzione@rochester.edu. *Application contact:* Kathy Lutz, Secretary, 585-275-5713, E-mail: kathy@ur.rochester.edu.
Website: http://www.ees.rochester.edu/

University of Saskatchewan, College of Graduate Studies and Research, College of Arts and Science and College of Engineering, Department of Geological Sciences, Saskatoon, SK S7N 5A2, Canada. Offers M Sc, PhD, Diploma. *Degree requirements:* For master's, thesis; for doctorate, comprehensive exam (for some programs), thesis/dissertation. *Entrance requirements:* Additional exam requirements/recommendations for international students: Required—TOEFL (minimum score 80 iBT); Recommended—IELTS (minimum score 6.5). Electronic applications accepted.

University of South Carolina, The Graduate School, College of Arts and Sciences, Department of Geological Sciences, Columbia, SC 29208. Offers MS, PhD. Terminal master's awarded for partial completion of doctoral program. *Degree requirements:* For master's, thesis; for doctorate, comprehensive exam, thesis/dissertation, published paper. *Entrance requirements:* For master's and doctorate, GRE General Test. Additional exam requirements/recommendations for international students: Required—TOEFL (minimum score 570 paper-based; 75 iBT). Electronic applications accepted. *Faculty research:* Environmental geology, tectonics, petrology, coastal processes, paleoclimatology.

University of Southern Mississippi, Graduate School, College of Science and Technology, Department of Geography and Geology, Hattiesburg, MS 39406-0001. Offers MS, PhD. *Program availability:* Part-time. *Degree requirements:* For master's, comprehensive exam, thesis (for some programs), internships; for doctorate, comprehensive exam, thesis/dissertation. *Entrance requirements:* For master's, GMAT, GRE General Test, minimum GPA of 3.0 for last 60 hours; for doctorate, GRE, minimum GPA of 3.5. Additional exam requirements/recommendations for international students: Required—TOEFL, IELTS. Electronic applications accepted. *Faculty research:* City and regional planning, geographic techniques, physical geography, human geography.

University of South Florida, College of Arts and Sciences, School of Geosciences, Tampa, FL 33620-9951. Offers environmental science and policy (MS); geography (MA), including environmental geography, geographic information science and spatial analysis, human geography; geography and environmental science and policy (PhD); geology (MS, PhD); urban and regional planning (MURP). *Program availability:* Part-time, evening/weekend. *Faculty:* 32 full-time (7 women). *Students:* 87 full-time (41 women), 45 part-time (19 women); includes 18 minority (7 Black or African American, non-Hispanic/Latino; 3 Asian, non-Hispanic/Latino; 7 Hispanic/Latino; 1 Two or more races, non-Hispanic/Latino), 29 international. Average age 34. 39 applicants, 62% accepted, 9 enrolled. In 2015, 10 master's awarded. *Degree requirements:* For master's, comprehensive exam, thesis (for some programs); for doctorate, comprehensive exam, thesis/dissertation. *Entrance requirements:* For master's, GRE General Test, minimum GPA of 3.0 for last 60 credits of undergraduate degree, letter of intent, letters of recommendation; for doctorate, GRE General Test, minimum GPA of 3.0 for all doctorate programs except for ESP/Geography which requires 3.20 GPA for all academic work, letter of intent, letters of recommendation. Additional exam requirements/recommendations for international students: Required—TOEFL (minimum score 550 paper-based; 79 iBT) or IELTS (minimum score 6.5) for MA and MURP; TOEFL (minimum score 600 paper-based) for MS and PhD. *Application deadline:* For fall admission, 2/15 for domestic students, 1/2 for international students; for spring admission, 10/15 for domestic students, 6/1 for international students. Application fee: $30. *Financial support:* In 2015–16, 26 students received support, including 3 research assistantships (averaging $12,345 per year), 25 teaching assistantships with tuition reimbursements available (averaging $12,807 per year); unspecified assistantships also available. Financial award application deadline: 3/1. *Faculty research:* Geography: human geography, environmental geography, geographic information science and spatial analysis, urban geography, social theory; environmental science, policy, and planning: water resources, wildlife ecology, Karst and wetland environments, natural hazards, soil contamination, meteorology and climatology, environmental sustainability and policy, urban and regional planning. *Total annual research expenditures:* $2.3 million. *Unit head:* Dr. Jayajit Chakraborty, Professor and Chair, Geography Division, 813-974-8188, Fax: 813-974-5911, E-mail: jchakrab@usf.edu. *Application contact:* Dr. Jennifer Collins, Associate Professor and Graduate Program Coordinator, 813-974-4242, Fax: 813-974-5911, E-mail: collinsjm@usf.edu.
Website: http://hennarot.forest.usf.edu/main/depts/geosci/

University of South Florida, Innovative Education, Tampa, FL 33620-9951. Offers adult, career and higher education (Graduate Certificate), including college teaching, leadership in developing human resources, leadership in higher education; Africana studies (Graduate Certificate), including diasporas and health disparities, genocide and human rights; aging studies (Graduate Certificate), including gerontology; art research (Graduate Certificate), including museum studies; business foundations (Graduate Certificate); chemical and biomedical engineering (Graduate Certificate), including materials science and engineering, water, health and sustainability; child and family studies (Graduate Certificate), including positive behavior support; civil and industrial engineering (Graduate Certificate), including transportation systems analysis; community and family health (Graduate Certificate), including maternal and child health, social marketing and public health, violence and injury: prevention and intervention, women's health; criminology (Graduate Certificate), including criminal justice administration; educational measurement and research (Graduate Certificate), including evaluation; English (Graduate Certificate), including comparative literary studies, creative writing, professional and technical communication; entrepreneurship (Graduate Certificate); environmental health (Graduate Certificate), including safety management; epidemiology and biostatistics (Graduate Certificate), including applied biostatistics, biostatistics, concepts and tools of epidemiology, epidemiology, epidemiology of infectious diseases; geography, environment and planning (Graduate Certificate), including community development, environmental policy and management, geographical information systems; geology (Graduate Certificate), including hydrogeology; global health (Graduate Certificate), including disaster management, global health and Latin American and Caribbean studies, global health practice, humanitarian assistance, infection control; government and international affairs (Graduate Certificate), including Cuban studies, globalization studies; health policy and management (Graduate Certificate), including health management and leadership, public health policy and programs; hearing specialist: early intervention (Graduate Certificate); industrial and management systems engineering (Graduate Certificate), including systems engineering, technology management; information studies (Graduate Certificate), including school library media specialist; information systems/decision sciences (Graduate Certificate), including analytics and business intelligence; instructional technology (Graduate Certificate), including distance education, Florida digital/virtual educator, instructional design, multimedia design, Web design; internal medicine, bioethics and medical humanities (Graduate Certificate), including biomedical ethics; Latin American and Caribbean studies (Graduate Certificate); mass communications (Graduate Certificate), including multimedia journalism; mathematics and statistics (Graduate Certificate), including mathematics; medicine (Graduate Certificate), including aging and neuroscience, bioinformatics, biotechnology, brain fitness and memory management, clinical investigation, health informatics, health sciences, integrative weight management, intellectual property, medicine and gender, metabolic and nutritional medicine, metabolic cardiology, pharmacy sciences; national and competitive intelligence (Graduate Certificate); psychological and social foundations (Graduate Certificate), including career counseling, college teaching, diversity in education, mental health counseling, school counseling; public affairs (Graduate Certificate), including nonprofit management, public management, research administration; public health (Graduate Certificate), including environmental health, health equity, public health generalist, translational research in adolescent behavioral health; public health practices (Graduate Certificate), including planning for healthy communities; rehabilitation and mental health counseling (Graduate Certificate), including integrative mental health care, marriage and family therapy, rehabilitation technology; secondary education (Graduate Certificate), including ESOL, foreign language education: culture and content, foreign language education: professional; social work (Graduate Certificate), including geriatric social work/clinical gerontology; special education (Graduate Certificate), including autism spectrum disorder, disabilities education: severe/profound; world languages (Graduate Certificate), including teaching English as a second language (TESL) or foreign language. *Unit head:* Kathy Barnes, Interdisciplinary Programs Coordinator, 813-974-8031, Fax: 813-974-7061,
E-mail: barnesk@usf.edu. *Application contact:* Karen Tylinski, Metro Initiatives, 813-974-9943, Fax: 813-974-7061, E-mail: ktylinsk@usf.edu.
Website: http://www.usf.edu/innovative-education/

The University of Tennessee, Graduate School, College of Arts and Sciences, Department of Geological Sciences, Knoxville, TN 37996. Offers geology (MS, PhD). *Program availability:* Part-time. *Degree requirements:* For master's, thesis; for doctorate, one foreign language, thesis/dissertation. *Entrance requirements:* For master's and doctorate, GRE General Test, minimum GPA of 2.7. Additional exam requirements/recommendations for international students: Required—TOEFL. Electronic applications accepted.

The University of Texas at Arlington, Graduate School, College of Science, Department of Earth and Environmental Sciences, Program in Environmental and Earth Sciences, Arlington, TX 76019. Offers environmental science (MS, PhD); geology (MS, PhD). *Program availability:* Part-time, evening/weekend. Terminal master's awarded for partial completion of doctoral program. *Degree requirements:* For master's, thesis optional; for doctorate, comprehensive exam, thesis/dissertation. *Entrance requirements:* For master's, GRE General Test. Additional exam requirements/recommendations for international students: Required—TOEFL (minimum score 550 paper-based). Electronic applications accepted.

The University of Texas at Austin, Graduate School, Jackson School of Geosciences, Austin, TX 78712-1111. Offers MA, MS, PhD. *Program availability:* Part-time. *Degree requirements:* For master's, report (MA), thesis (MS); for doctorate, thesis/dissertation. *Entrance requirements:* For master's and doctorate, GRE General Test. Electronic applications accepted. *Faculty research:* Sedimentary geology, geophysics, hydrogeology, structure/tectonics, vertebrate paleontology.

The University of Texas at El Paso, Graduate School, College of Science, Department of Geological Sciences, El Paso, TX 79968-0001. Offers geological sciences (MS, PhD); geophysics (MS). *Program availability:* Part-time, evening/weekend. *Degree requirements:* For master's, thesis; for doctorate, one foreign language, comprehensive exam, thesis/dissertation. *Entrance requirements:* For master's, GRE, minimum GPA of 3.0, BS in geology or equivalent; for doctorate, GRE, minimum GPA of 3.0, MS in geology or equivalent. Additional exam requirements/recommendations for international students: Required—TOEFL. Electronic applications accepted.

The University of Texas at San Antonio, College of Sciences, Department of Geological Sciences, San Antonio, TX 78249-0617. Offers MS. *Program availability:* Part-time. *Faculty:* 10 full-time (3 women), 1 part-time/adjunct (0 women). *Students:* 22 full-time (5 women), 19 part-time (4 women); includes 12 minority (1 Black or African American, non-Hispanic/Latino; 1 American Indian or Alaska Native, non-Hispanic/Latino; 2 Asian, non-Hispanic/Latino; 6 Hispanic/Latino; 2 Two or more races, non-Hispanic/Latino), 1 international. Average age 27. 32 applicants, 75% accepted, 17 enrolled. In 2015, 12 master's awarded. *Degree requirements:* For master's, comprehensive exam, thesis (for some programs). *Entrance requirements:* For master's, GRE General Test, three letters of recommendation, statement of research interest, undergraduate transcripts. Additional exam requirements/recommendations for international students: Required—TOEFL (minimum score 550 paper-based; 79 iBT), IELTS (minimum score 6.5). *Application deadline:* For fall admission, 7/1 for domestic students, 4/1 for international students; for spring admission, 11/1 for domestic students, 11/1 priority date for international students; for summer admission, 4/1 for domestic students, 4/1 priority date for international students. Application fee: $60 ($80 for international students). *Financial support:* In 2015–16, 6 teaching assistantships (averaging $10,578 per year) were awarded. *Faculty research:* Hydrogeology, sedimentary and stratigraphy, structure, paleontology, geographic information science. *Unit head:* Dr. Lance L. Lambert, Department Chair, 210-458-5447,
E-mail: lance.lambert@utsa.edu.
Website: http://www.utsa.edu/geosci/

The University of Texas of the Permian Basin, Office of Graduate Studies, College of Arts and Sciences, Department of Physical Sciences, Program in Geology, Odessa, TX 79762-0001. Offers MS. *Degree requirements:* For master's, comprehensive exam, thesis or alternative. *Entrance requirements:* For master's, GRE General Test. Additional exam requirements/recommendations for international students: Required—TOEFL (minimum score 550 paper-based).

The University of Toledo, College of Graduate Studies, College of Natural Sciences and Mathematics, Department of Environmental Sciences, Toledo, OH 43606-3390. Offers biology (MS, PhD), including ecology; geology (MS), including earth surface processes. *Program availability:* Part-time. *Degree requirements:* For master's, thesis or alternative. *Entrance requirements:* For master's, GRE General Test, minimum cumulative point-hour ratio of 2.7 for all previous academic work, three letters of recommendation, statement of purpose, transcripts from all prior institutions attended. Additional exam requirements/recommendations for international students: Required—TOEFL (minimum score 550 paper-based; 80 iBT). Electronic applications accepted. *Faculty research:* Environmental geochemistry, geophysics, petrology and mineralogy, paleontology, geohydrology.

University of Toronto, School of Graduate Studies, Faculty of Arts and Science, Department of Earth Sciences, Toronto, ON M5S 1A1, Canada. Offers M Sc, MA Sc, PhD. *Program availability:* Part-time. *Degree requirements:* For master's, thesis (for some programs); for doctorate, thesis/dissertation. *Entrance requirements:* For master's, B Sc, BA Sc, or equivalent; letters of reference; for doctorate, M Sc or equivalent, minimum B+ average, letters of reference. Additional exam requirements/recommendations for international students: Required—TOEFL (minimum score 580 paper-based; 93 iBT), TWE (minimum score 4). Electronic applications accepted.

University of Utah, Graduate School, College of Mines and Earth Sciences, Department of Geology and Geophysics, Salt Lake City, UT 84112. Offers environmental engineering (ME, MS, PhD); geological engineering (ME, MS, PhD); geology (MS, PhD); geophysics (MS, PhD). *Faculty:* 23 full-time (5 women), 11 part-time/adjunct (4 women). *Students:* 60 full-time (22 women), 16 part-time (6 women); includes 6 minority (1 Black or African American, non-Hispanic/Latino; 1 American Indian or Alaska Native, non-Hispanic/Latino; 4 Hispanic/Latino), 17 international. Average age 27. 228 applicants, 14% accepted, 22 enrolled. In 2015, 27 master's, 6 doctorates awarded. Terminal master's awarded for partial completion of doctoral program. *Degree requirements:* For master's, comprehensive exam, thesis; for doctorate, thesis/dissertation, qualifying exam (written and oral). *Entrance requirements:* For master's and doctorate, GRE General Test, minimum GPA of 3.25. Additional exam requirements/recommendations for international students: Required—TOEFL (minimum score 500 paper-based; 61 iBT). *Application deadline:* For fall admission, 1/15 priority date for domestic and international students. Application fee: $55 ($65 for international students). Electronic applications accepted. *Financial support:* In 2015–16, 62 students received support, including 14 fellowships with full tuition reimbursements available (averaging $17,500 per year), 32 research assistantships with full tuition reimbursements available (averaging $23,000 per year), 16 teaching assistantships with full tuition reimbursements available (averaging $17,500 per year); career-related internships or fieldwork, institutionally sponsored loans, scholarships/grants, unspecified assistantships, and stipends also available. Financial award application deadline: 1/15; financial award applicants required to submit FAFSA. *Faculty research:* Igneous, metamorphic, and sedimentary petrology; stratigraphy; paleoclimatology; hydrology; seismology. *Total annual research expenditures:* $4.1 million. *Unit head:* Dr. John Bartley, Chair, 801-585-1670, Fax: 801-581-7065, E-mail: john.bartley@utah.edu. *Application contact:* Dr. Gabriel J. Bowen, Director of Graduate Studies, 801-585-7925, Fax: 801-581-7065, E-mail: gabe.bowen@utah.edu.
Website: http://www.earth.utah.edu/

University of Vermont, Graduate College, College of Arts and Sciences, Department of Geology, Burlington, VT 05405. Offers MS. *Degree requirements:* For master's, thesis. *Entrance requirements:* For master's, GRE General Test. Additional exam requirements/recommendations for international students: Required—TOEFL (minimum score 550 paper-based; 80 iBT). Electronic applications accepted. *Faculty research:* Mineralogy, lake sediments, structural geology.

University of Washington, Graduate School, College of the Environment, Department of Earth and Space Sciences, Seattle, WA 98195. Offers geology (MS, PhD); geophysics (MS, PhD). *Degree requirements:* For master's, thesis or alternative, departmental qualifying exam, final exam; for doctorate, thesis/dissertation, departmental qualifying exam, general and final exams. *Entrance requirements:* For master's and doctorate, GRE General Test, minimum GPA of 3.0. Additional exam requirements/recommendations for international students: Required—TOEFL (minimum score 580 paper-based). Electronic applications accepted.

The University of Western Ontario, Faculty of Graduate Studies, Physical Sciences Division, Department of Earth Sciences, London, ON N6A 5B8, Canada. Offers environment and sustainability (MES); geology (M Sc, PhD); geology and environmental science (M Sc, PhD); geophysics (M Sc, PhD); geophysics and environmental science (M Sc, PhD). *Degree requirements:* For master's, thesis; for doctorate, thesis/dissertation, qualifying exam. *Entrance requirements:* For master's, honors in B Sc; for doctorate, M Sc. Additional exam requirements/recommendations for international students: Required—TOEFL. *Faculty research:* Geophysics, geochemistry, paleontology, sedimentology/stratigraphy, glaciology/quaternary.

University of Wisconsin–Madison, Graduate School, College of Letters and Science, Department of Geology and Geophysics, Program in Geology, Madison, WI 53706-1380. Offers MS, PhD. *Degree requirements:* For master's, thesis; for doctorate, one foreign language, thesis/dissertation. *Entrance requirements:* For master's and doctorate, GRE General Test. *Expenses:* Tuition, state resident: full-time $5364. Tuition, nonresident: full-time $12,027. *Required fees:* $571. Tuition and fees vary according to campus/location, program and reciprocity agreements.

University of Wisconsin–Milwaukee, Graduate School, College of Letters and Science, Department of Geosciences, Milwaukee, WI 53201-0413. Offers geological sciences (MS, PhD). *Faculty:* 8 full-time (2 women). *Students:* 10 full-time (4 women), 9 part-time (4 women), 2 international. Average age 34. 32 applicants, 41% accepted, 3 enrolled. In 2015, 8 master's, 1 doctorate awarded. *Degree requirements:* For master's, thesis; for doctorate, one foreign language, thesis/dissertation. *Entrance requirements:* For master's, GRE General Test, minimum GPA of 3.0; for doctorate, GRE General Test, master's degree. Additional exam requirements/recommendations for international students: Required—TOEFL (minimum score 550 paper-based; 79 iBT), IELTS (minimum score 6.5). *Application deadline:* For fall admission, 1/1 priority date for domestic students; for spring admission, 9/1 for domestic students. Applications are processed on a rolling basis. Application fee: $56 ($96 for international students). Electronic applications accepted. *Financial support:* In 2015–16, 4 research assistantships, 11 teaching assistantships were awarded; career-related internships or fieldwork and unspecified assistantships also available. Support available to part-time students. Financial award application deadline: 4/15; financial award applicants required to submit FAFSA. *Faculty research:* Geology, geosciences, geophysics, hydrogeology, paleontology. *Unit head:* Dr. Barry Cameron, Department Chair, 414-229-3136, E-mail: bcameron@uwm.edu. *Application contact:* General Information Contact, 414-229-4982, Fax: 414-229-6967, E-mail: gradschool@uwm.edu.
Website: http://www.uwm.edu/dept/geosciences/

University of Wyoming, College of Arts and Sciences, Department of Geology and Geophysics, Laramie, WY 82071. Offers geology (MS, PhD); geophysics (MS, PhD). *Program availability:* Part-time. *Degree requirements:* For master's, comprehensive exam, thesis; for doctorate, comprehensive exam, thesis/dissertation. *Entrance requirements:* For master's and doctorate, GRE General Test, minimum GPA of 3.0. *Faculty research:* Low-temp geochemistry, geohydrology, paleontology, structure/tectonics, sedimentation and petroleum geology, petrology, geophysics/seismology.

Utah State University, School of Graduate Studies, College of Science, Department of Geology, Logan, UT 84322. Offers MS. *Degree requirements:* For master's, thesis. *Entrance requirements:* For master's, GRE General Test, minimum GPA of 3.0. Additional exam requirements/recommendations for international students: Required—TOEFL. *Faculty research:* Sedimentary geology, structural geology, regional tectonics, hydrogeology petrology.

Vanderbilt University, Department of Earth and Environmental Sciences, Nashville, TN 37240-1001. Offers MAT, MS. *Faculty:* 10 full-time (2 women). *Students:* 7 full-time (4 women), 4 part-time (3 women); includes 1 minority (Black or African American, non-Hispanic/Latino). Average age 23. 54 applicants, 15% accepted, 5 enrolled. In 2015, 8 master's awarded. *Degree requirements:* For master's, thesis. *Entrance requirements:* For master's, GRE General Test, GRE Subject Test (recommended). Additional exam requirements/recommendations for international students: Required—TOEFL (minimum score 570 paper-based; 88 iBT). *Application deadline:* For fall admission, 1/15 for domestic and international students. Application fee: $0. Electronic applications accepted. *Financial support:* Fellowships with tuition reimbursements, research assistantships with tuition reimbursements, teaching assistantships with full tuition reimbursements, career-related internships or fieldwork, Federal Work-Study, institutionally sponsored loans, and health care benefits available. Financial award application deadline: 1/15; financial award applicants required to submit CSS PROFILE or FAFSA. *Faculty research:* Geochemical processes, magmatic processes and crustal evolution, paleoecology and paleoenvironments, sedimentary systems, transport phenomena, environmental policy. *Unit head:* Dr. Guil Gualda, Director of Graduate Studies, 615-322-2976, E-mail: g.gualda@vanderbilt.edu. *Application contact:* Teri Pugh, Office Assistant, 615-322-2976, E-mail: teri.pugh@vanderbilt.edu.
Website: http://www.vanderbilt.edu/ees/

Washington State University, College of Arts and Sciences, School of the Environment, Pullman, WA 99164. Offers environmental and natural resource sciences (PhD); environmental science (MS); geology (MS, PhD); natural resource science (MS). *Degree requirements:* For master's, comprehensive exam (for some programs), thesis (for some programs), oral exam; for doctorate, comprehensive exam, thesis/dissertation, oral exam, written exam. *Entrance requirements:* For master's, 3 undergraduate semester hours each in sociology or cultural anthropology, environmental science, biological sciences, and calculus or statistics; 4 in general ecology; and 6 in general chemistry or general physics; for doctorate, minimum GPA of 3.0. Additional exam requirements/recommendations for international students: Required—TOEFL, IELTS.

Wayne State University, College of Liberal Arts and Sciences, Department of Geology, Detroit, MI 48202. Offers MS. *Faculty:* 5. *Students:* 7 full-time (4 women). Average age 27. 20 applicants, 15% accepted, 1 enrolled. In 2015, 4 master's awarded. *Degree requirements:* For master's, thesis. *Entrance requirements:* For master's, GRE, undergraduate major in geology or strong background in geology; minimum GPA of 3.0 in major; prerequisite study in mineralogy, petrology, sedimentation, geomorphology, environmental geochemistry, and structural geology. Additional exam requirements/recommendations for international students: Required—TOEFL (minimum score 550 paper-based; 79 iBT), TWE (minimum score 5.5), Michigan English Language Assessment Battery (minimum score 85); Recommended—IELTS (minimum score 6.5). *Application deadline:* For fall admission, 6/1 for domestic students, 5/1 priority date for international students; for winter admission, 11/1 for domestic students, 9/1 priority date for international students; for spring admission, 3/15 for domestic students, 10/1 priority date for international students. Application fee: $0. Electronic applications accepted. *Expenses:* Tuition, state resident: full-time $14,165; part-time $590.20 per credit hour. Tuition, nonresident: full-time $30,682; part-time $1278.40 per credit hour. *Required fees:* $1688; $47.45 per credit hour. $274.60 per semester. Tuition and fees vary according to course load and program. *Financial support:* In 2015–16, 4 students received support, including 2 research assistantships with tuition reimbursements available (averaging $18,801 per year); fellowships with tuition reimbursements available, teaching assistantships with tuition reimbursements available, scholarships/grants, health care benefits, and unspecified assistantships also available. Financial award application deadline: 3/31; financial award applicants required to submit FAFSA. *Faculty research:* Isotope geochemistry, hydrogeology, geochronology, sedimentology/stratigraphy, quaternary geology, soils and soil pollution, contaminate fate and transport, geophysics and crustal processes. *Total annual research expenditures:* $354,506. *Unit head:* Dr. David Njus, Interim Chair and Professor, 313-577-3105, Fax: 313-577-6891, E-mail: dnjus@wayne.edu. *Application contact:* Dr. Sarah Brownlee, Graduate Program Director and Assistant Professor, E-mail: sarah.brownlee@wayne.edu.
Website: http://clas.wayne.edu/geology/

West Chester University of Pennsylvania, College of Arts and Sciences, Department of Geology and Astronomy, West Chester, PA 19383. Offers geoscience (MA). *Program availability:* Part-time, evening/weekend. *Faculty:* 9 full-time (4 women), 1 part-time/adjunct (0 women). *Students:* 14 full-time (7 women), 16 part-time (5 women); includes 2 minority (1 Black or African American, non-Hispanic/Latino; 1 Hispanic/Latino). Average age 33. 11 applicants, 100% accepted, 7 enrolled. In 2015, 7 degrees awarded. *Degree requirements:* For master's, final project involving manuscript (for some programs), presentation. *Entrance requirements:* For master's, minimum GPA of 2.8 (for some programs). Additional exam requirements/recommendations for international students: Required—TOEFL or IELTS. *Application deadline:* For fall admission, 5/15 for international students; for spring admission, 10/15 for international students. Applications are processed on a rolling basis. Application fee: $50. Electronic applications accepted. *Expenses:* Tuition, state resident: full-time $8460; part-time $470 per credit. Tuition, nonresident: full-time $12,690; part-time $705 per credit. *Required fees:* $2312; $126.75 per credit. Tuition and fees vary according to campus/location and program. *Financial support:* Scholarships/grants and unspecified assistantships available. Financial award application deadline: 2/15; financial award applicants required to submit FAFSA. *Faculty research:* Geoscience education, environmental geology, energy and sustainability, astronomy, coastal geomorphology (sea level change), water and soil remediation, hydrogeology, short-term weather forecasting. *Unit head:* Dr. Martin Helmke, Chair, 610-436-3565, Fax: 610-436-3036, E-mail: mhelmke@wcupa.edu. *Application contact:* Dr. Joby Hilliker, Graduate Coordinator, 610-436-2213, Fax: 610-436-3036, E-mail: jhilliker@wcupa.edu.
Website: http://www.wcupa.edu/_academics/sch_cas.esc/

Western Kentucky University, Graduate Studies, Ogden College of Science and Engineering, Department of Geography and Geology, Bowling Green, KY 42101. Offers geoscience (MS). *Degree requirements:* For master's, comprehensive exam, thesis or alternative. *Entrance requirements:* For master's, GRE General Test, minimum GPA of

2.75. Additional exam requirements/recommendations for international students: Required—TOEFL (minimum score 555 paper-based; 79 iBT). *Faculty research:* Hydroclimatology, electronic data sets, groundwater, sinkhole liquification potential, meteorological analysis.

Western Washington University, Graduate School, College of Sciences and Technology, Department of Geology, Bellingham, WA 98225-5996. Offers MS. *Program availability:* Part-time. *Degree requirements:* For master's, thesis. *Entrance requirements:* For master's, GRE General Test, minimum GPA of 3.0 in last 60 semester hours or last 90 quarter hours. Additional exam requirements/recommendations for international students: Required—TOEFL (minimum score 567 paper-based). Electronic applications accepted. *Faculty research:* Structure/tectonics; sedimentary, glacial and quaternary geomorphology; igneous and metamorphic petrology; hydrology, geophysics.

West Virginia University, Eberly College of Arts and Sciences, Department of Geology and Geography, Program in Geology, Morgantown, WV 26506. Offers geomorphology (MS, PhD); geophysics (MS, PhD); hydrogeology (MS, PhD); paleontology (MS, PhD); petroleum geology (PhD); petrology (MS, PhD); stratigraphy (MS, PhD); structure (MS, PhD). *Program availability:* Part-time. Terminal master's awarded for partial completion of doctoral program. *Degree requirements:* For master's, thesis (for some programs); for doctorate, comprehensive exam, thesis/dissertation. *Entrance requirements:* For master's, GRE General Test, minimum GPA of 2.5; for doctorate, GRE General Test, minimum GPA of 3.3. Additional exam requirements/recommendations for international students: Required—TOEFL. *Expenses:* Tuition, state resident: full-time $8568. Tuition, nonresident: full-time $22,140. Tuition and fees vary according to program.

Wichita State University, Graduate School, Fairmount College of Liberal Arts and Sciences, Department of Geology, Wichita, KS 67260. Offers earth, environmental, and physical sciences (MS). *Program availability:* Part-time. *Unit head:* Dr. William Parcell, Chair, 316-978-3140, E-mail: william.parcell@wichita.edu. *Application contact:* Jordan Oleson, Admissions Coordinator, 316-978-3095, Fax: 316-978-3253,
E-mail: jordan.oleson@wichita.edu.
Website: http://www.wichita.edu/geology

Wright State University, School of Graduate Studies, College of Science and Mathematics, Department of Earth and Environmental Sciences, Program in Geological Sciences, Dayton, OH 45435. Offers MS. *Program availability:* Part-time. *Degree requirements:* For master's, thesis. *Entrance requirements:* Additional exam requirements/recommendations for international students: Required—TOEFL.

Yale University, Graduate School of Arts and Sciences, Department of Geology and Geophysics, New Haven, CT 06520. Offers biogeochemistry (PhD); climate dynamics (PhD); geochemistry (PhD); geophysics (PhD); meteorology (PhD); oceanography (PhD); paleontology (PhD); paleooceanography (PhD); petrology (PhD); tectonics (PhD). *Degree requirements:* For doctorate, thesis/dissertation. *Entrance requirements:* For doctorate, GRE General Test. Additional exam requirements/recommendations for international students: Required—TOEFL.

Geophysics

Baylor University, Graduate School, College of Arts and Sciences, Department of Geosciences, Waco, TX 76798. Offers geosciences (MS, PhD), including geophysics, geology. *Faculty:* 15 full-time (1 woman). *Students:* 40 full-time (11 women), 5 part-time (3 women); includes 3 minority (2 Hispanic/Latino; 1 Two or more races, non-Hispanic/Latino), 10 international. Average age 23. 41 applicants, 51% accepted, 15 enrolled. In 2015, 4 master's, 1 doctorate awarded. *Degree requirements:* For master's, thesis, preliminary exam, thesis proposal; for doctorate, thesis/dissertation, preliminary exam, dissertation proposal. *Entrance requirements:* For master's and doctorate, GRE General Test. Additional exam requirements/recommendations for international students: Required—TOEFL (minimum score 550 paper-based; 80 iBT), IELTS (minimum score 6.5), PTE (minimum score 58). *Application deadline:* For fall admission, 1/31 priority date for domestic students, 1/15 priority date for international students; for spring admission, 10/1 priority date for domestic and international students. Applications are processed on a rolling basis. Application fee: $40. Electronic applications accepted. *Financial support:* In 2015–16, 33 students received support, including 6 research assistantships with tuition reimbursements available (averaging $17,000 per year), 18 teaching assistantships with tuition reimbursements available (averaging $21,000 per year); career-related internships or fieldwork, Federal Work-Study, institutionally sponsored loans, scholarships/grants, health care benefits, tuition waivers (full and partial), and unspecified assistantships also available. Support available to part-time students. Financial award application deadline: 2/28; financial award applicants required to submit FAFSA. *Faculty research:* Terrestrial paleoclimatology, applied petroleum studies, applied and solid earth geophysics, hydrogeoscience, high temperature geochemistry and volcanology. *Total annual research expenditures:* $800,000. *Unit head:* Dr. Steven George Driese, Graduate Program Director, 254-710-2194, Fax: 254-710-2673, E-mail: steven_driese@baylor.edu. *Application contact:* Jamie Ruth, Administrative Associate, 254-710-2361, Fax: 254-710-2673, E-mail: jamie_ruth@baylor.edu.
Website: http://www.baylor.edu/geology/

Boise State University, College of Arts and Sciences, Department of Geosciences, Boise, ID 83725-1535. Offers earth science (M E Sci); geophysics (MS, PhD); geosciences (MS, PhD); hydrology (MS). *Program availability:* Part-time. *Faculty:* 20. *Students:* 52 full-time (21 women), 13 part-time (3 women); includes 7 minority (1 Black or African American, non-Hispanic/Latino; 5 Hispanic/Latino; 1 Two or more races, non-Hispanic/Latino), 7 international. Average age 29. 73 applicants, 29% accepted, 14 enrolled. In 2015, 4 master's, 1 doctorate awarded. Terminal master's awarded for partial completion of doctoral program. *Degree requirements:* For master's, thesis (for some programs); for doctorate, thesis/dissertation. *Entrance requirements:* For master's, GRE General Test, BS in related field, minimum GPA of 3.0; for doctorate, GRE General Test. Additional exam requirements/recommendations for international students: Required—TOEFL (minimum score 550 paper-based; 80 iBT), IELTS (minimum score 6). *Application deadline:* For fall admission, 2/1 for domestic and international students; for spring admission, 10/15 for domestic and international students. Application fee: $65 ($95 for international students). Electronic applications accepted. *Expenses:* Tuition, state resident: full-time $6058; part-time $358 per credit hour. Tuition, nonresident: full-time $20,108; part-time $608 per credit hour. *Required fees:* $2108. Tuition and fees vary according to program. *Financial support:* In 2015–16, 6 students received support, including 17 research assistantships with full tuition reimbursements available (averaging $10,119 per year), 15 teaching assistantships (averaging $9,024 per year); scholarships/grants and unspecified assistantships also available. Financial award application deadline: 2/1; financial award applicants required to submit FAFSA. *Faculty research:* Seismology, geothermal aquifers, sedimentation, tectonics, seismo-acoustic propagation. *Unit head:* Dr. James McNamara, Department Chair, 208-426-1354, E-mail: jmcnamar@boisestate.edu. *Application contact:* Dr. Mark Schmitz, Graduate Program Coordinator, 208-426-5907, E-mail: markschmitz@boisestate.edu.
Website: http://earth.boisestate.edu/degrees/graduate/

Boston College, Graduate School of Arts and Sciences, Department of Earth and Environmental Sciences, Chestnut Hill, MA 02467. Offers MS, MBA/MS. *Faculty:* 9 full-time. *Students:* 22 full-time (15 women), 1 international. 39 applicants, 31% accepted, 7 enrolled. In 2015, 5 master's awarded. *Degree requirements:* For master's, thesis. *Entrance requirements:* For master's, GRE General Test. Additional exam requirements/recommendations for international students: Required—TOEFL (minimum score 600 paper-based; 100 iBT), IELTS (minimum score 8). *Application deadline:* For fall admission, 1/10 priority date for domestic students, 1/10 for international students. Application fee: $75. Electronic applications accepted. Tuition and fees vary according to program. *Financial support:* In 2015–16, 22 students received support, including research assistantships with full tuition reimbursements available (averaging $19,400 per year), teaching assistantships with full tuition reimbursements available (averaging $18,400 per year); Federal Work-Study, scholarships/grants, health care benefits, and unspecified assistantships also available. Support available to part-time students. Financial award application deadline: 3/1; financial award applicants required to submit FAFSA. *Faculty research:* Coastal and estuarine processes, earthquake and exploration seismology, environmental geology and geophysics, earth surface processes, paleoclimate, groundwater hydrology, igneous and metamorphic petrology, geochemistry, dynamics and processes of sedimentary systems, plate tectonics, structural geology. *Unit head:* Dr. John Ebel, Chairperson, 617-552-3640, E-mail: ebel@bc.edu. *Application contact:* Dr. Gail Kineke, Graduate Program Director, 617-552-3640, E-mail: gail.kineke@bc.edu.
Website: http://www.bc.edu/schools/eesciences

Bowling Green State University, Graduate College, College of Arts and Sciences, Department of Physics and Astronomy, Bowling Green, OH 43403. Offers geophysics (MS); physics (MAT, MS). *Degree requirements:* For master's, thesis or alternative. *Entrance requirements:* For master's, GRE General Test. Additional exam requirements/recommendations for international students: Required—TOEFL. Electronic applications accepted. *Faculty research:* Computational physics, solid-state physics, materials science, theoretical physics.

California Institute of Technology, Division of Geological and Planetary Sciences, Pasadena, CA 91125-0001. Offers environmental science and engineering (MS, PhD); geobiology (MS, PhD); geochemistry (MS, PhD); geology (MS, PhD); geophysics (MS, PhD); planetary science (MS, PhD). *Degree requirements:* For doctorate, thesis/dissertation. *Entrance requirements:* For doctorate, GRE General Test. Additional exam requirements/recommendations for international students: Required—TOEFL; Recommended—IELTS, TWE. Electronic applications accepted. *Faculty research:* Planetary surfaces, evolution of anaerobic respiratory processes, structural geology and tectonics, theoretical and numerical seismology, global biogeochemical cycles.

California State University, Long Beach, Graduate Studies, College of Natural Sciences and Mathematics, Department of Geological Sciences, Long Beach, CA 90840. Offers geology (MS); geophysics (MS). *Program availability:* Part-time. *Degree requirements:* For master's, thesis. *Entrance requirements:* For master's, GRE General Test. Electronic applications accepted. *Faculty research:* Paleontology, geophysics, structural geology, organic geochemistry, sedimentary geology.

Colorado School of Mines, Office of Graduate Studies, Department of Geophysics, Golden, CO 80401. Offers geophysical engineering (ME, MS, PhD); geophysics (MS, PhD); hydrology (MS, PhD); mineral exploration and mining geosciences (PMS). *Program availability:* Part-time. *Faculty:* 17 full-time (2 women), 6 part-time/adjunct (1 woman). *Students:* 77 full-time (26 women), 5 part-time (1 woman); includes 3 minority (1 American Indian or Alaska Native, non-Hispanic/Latino; 1 Asian, non-Hispanic/Latino; 1 Hispanic/Latino), 29 international. Average age 28. 195 applicants, 13% accepted, 17 enrolled. In 2015, 16 master's, 9 doctorates awarded. *Degree requirements:* For master's, thesis (for some programs); for doctorate, comprehensive exam, thesis/dissertation. *Entrance requirements:* For master's and doctorate, GRE General Test. Additional exam requirements/recommendations for international students: Required—TOEFL (minimum score 550 paper-based; 80 iBT). *Application deadline:* For fall admission, 12/15 priority date for domestic and international students; for spring admission, 9/1 priority date for domestic students, 9/1 for international students. Application fee: $50 ($70 for international students). Electronic applications accepted. *Expenses:* Tuition, state resident: full-time $15,225. Tuition, nonresident: full-time $32,700. *Financial support:* In 2015–16, 58 students received support, including 2 fellowships with full tuition reimbursements available, 52 research assistantships with full tuition reimbursements available, 4 teaching assistantships with full tuition reimbursements available; scholarships/grants, health care benefits, and unspecified assistantships also available. Financial award application deadline: 12/15; financial award applicants required to submit FAFSA. *Faculty research:* Seismic exploration, gravity and geomagnetic fields, electrical mapping and sounding, bore hole measurements, environmental physics. *Total annual research expenditures:* $5.2 million. *Unit head:* Dr. Terence K. Young, Head, 303-273-3454, E-mail: tkyoung@mines.edu. *Application contact:* Michelle Szobody, Program Assistant, 303-273-3935, E-mail: mszobody@mines.edu.
Website: http://geophysics.mines.edu

Cornell University, Graduate School, Graduate Fields of Engineering, Field of Geological Sciences, Ithaca, NY 14853. Offers economic geology (M Eng, MS, PhD); engineering geology (M Eng, MS, PhD); environmental geophysics (M Eng, MS, PhD); general geology (M Eng, MS, PhD); geobiology (M Eng, MS, PhD); geochemistry and isotope geology (M Eng, MS, PhD); geohydrology (M Eng, MS, PhD); geomorphology (M Eng, MS, PhD); geophysics (M Eng, MS, PhD); geotectonics (M Eng, MS, PhD); marine geology (MS, PhD); mineralogy (M Eng, MS, PhD); paleontology (M Eng, MS, PhD); petroleum geology (M Eng, MS, PhD); petrology (M Eng, MS, PhD); planetary geology (M Eng, MS, PhD); Precambrian geology (M Eng, MS, PhD); Quaternary geology (M Eng, MS, PhD); rock mechanics (M Eng, MS, PhD); sedimentology (M Eng, MS, PhD); seismology (M Eng, MS, PhD); stratigraphy (M Eng, MS, PhD); structural geology (M Eng, MS, PhD). *Degree requirements:* For master's, thesis (MS); for doctorate, comprehensive exam, thesis/dissertation. *Entrance requirements:* For master's and doctorate, GRE General Test, 3 letters of recommendation. Additional exam requirements/recommendations for international students: Required—TOEFL (minimum score 550 paper-based; 77 iBT). Electronic applications accepted. *Faculty research:* Geophysics, structural geology, petrology, geochemistry, geodynamics.

Florida State University, The Graduate School, College of Arts and Sciences, Interdisciplinary Program in Geophysical Fluid Dynamics, Tallahassee, FL 32306-4360. Offers PhD. *Faculty:* 23 full-time (0 women). *Students:* 12 full-time (3 women), 7 international. Average age 30. 3 applicants, 33% accepted. In 2015, 1 doctorate awarded. *Degree requirements:* For doctorate, thesis/dissertation, departmental qualifying exam. *Entrance requirements:* For doctorate, GRE General Test, GRE Subject Test, minimum GPA of 3.0. Additional exam requirements/recommendations for international students: Required—TOEFL (minimum score 550 paper-based; 80 iBT). *Application deadline:* For fall admission, 3/30 for domestic and international students; for spring admission, 9/30 for domestic and international students; for summer admission, 12/15 for domestic students, 12/17 for international students. Application fee: $30. Electronic applications accepted. *Expenses: Tuition, area resident:* Full-time $7263; part-time $403.50 per credit hour. Tuition, nonresident: full-time $18,087; part-time $1004.85 per credit hour. *Required fees:* $1365; $75.81 per credit hour. $20 per semester. Tuition and fees vary according to campus/location. *Financial support:* In 2015–16, 1 research assistantship (averaging $21,500 per year) was awarded; fellowships and unspecified assistantships also available. Financial award applicants required to submit FAFSA. *Faculty research:* Hurricane dynamics, convection, air-sea interaction, wave-mean flow interaction, numerical models, Ground water flows, Karst environmental dynamics. *Total annual research expenditures:* $408,421. *Unit head:* Dr. Kevin Speer, Director, 850-645-5625, Fax: 850-644-8972, E-mail: kspeer@fsu.edu. *Application contact:* Vijaya Challa, Academic Coordinator, 850-644-5594, Fax: 850-644-8972, E-mail: vijaya@fsu.edu.
Website: http://www.gfdi.fsu.edu/

Idaho State University, Office of Graduate Studies, College of Science and Engineering, Department of Geosciences, Pocatello, ID 83209-8072. Offers geographic information science (MS); geology (MNS, MS); geology with emphasis in environmental geoscience (MS); geophysics/hydrology/geology (MS); geotechnology (Postbaccalaureate Certificate). *Program availability:* Part-time. *Degree requirements:* For master's, comprehensive exam, thesis, oral colloquium; for Postbaccalaureate Certificate, thesis optional, minimum 19 credits. *Entrance requirements:* For master's, GRE General Test (minimum 50th percentile in 2 sections), 3 letters of recommendation; for Postbaccalaureate Certificate, GRE General Test, 3 letters of recommendation, bachelor's degree, statement of goals. Additional exam requirements/recommendations for international students: Required—TOEFL (minimum score 550 paper-based; 80 iBT). Electronic applications accepted. *Faculty research:* Quantitative field mapping and sampling: microscopic, geochemical, and isotopic analysis of rocks, minerals and water; remote sensing, geographic information systems, and global positioning systems: environmental and watershed management; surficial and fluvial processes: landscape change; regional tectonics, structural geology; planetary geology.

Indiana University Bloomington, University Graduate School, College of Arts and Sciences, Department of Geological Sciences, Bloomington, IN 47405-7000. Offers biogeochemistry (MS, PhD); economic geology (MS, PhD); geobiology (MS, PhD); geophysics, structural geology and tectonics (MS, PhD); hydrogeology (MS, PhD); mineralogy (MS, PhD); stratigraphy and sedimentology (MS, PhD). Terminal master's awarded for partial completion of doctoral program. *Degree requirements:* For master's, thesis or alternative; for doctorate, comprehensive exam, thesis/dissertation. *Entrance requirements:* For master's and doctorate, GRE General Test. Additional exam requirements/recommendations for international students: Required—TOEFL. *Faculty research:* Geophysics, geochemistry, hydrogeology, geobiology, planetary science.

Louisiana State University and Agricultural & Mechanical College, Graduate School, College of Science, Department of Geology and Geophysics, Baton Rouge, LA 70803. Offers MS, PhD.

Massachusetts Institute of Technology, School of Science, Department of Earth, Atmospheric, and Planetary Sciences, Cambridge, MA 02139. Offers atmospheric chemistry (PhD, Sc D); atmospheric science (SM, PhD, Sc D); chemical oceanography (SM, PhD, Sc D); climate physics and chemistry (SM, PhD, Sc D); earth and planetary sciences (SM); geochemistry (PhD, Sc D); geology (PhD, Sc D); geophysics (PhD, Sc D); marine geology and geophysics (SM, PhD, Sc D); physical oceanography (SM, PhD, Sc D); planetary sciences (PhD, Sc D). *Faculty:* 36 full-time (8 women). *Students:* 166 full-time (75 women), 1 part-time (0 women); includes 23 minority (1 Black or African American, non-Hispanic/Latino; 7 Asian, non-Hispanic/Latino; 6 Hispanic/Latino; 9 Two or more races, non-Hispanic/Latino), 54 international. Average age 27. 228 applicants, 26% accepted, 33 enrolled. In 2015, 6 master's, 24 doctorates awarded. Terminal master's awarded for partial completion of doctoral program. *Degree requirements:* For master's, thesis; for doctorate, comprehensive exam, thesis/dissertation. *Entrance requirements:* For master's, GRE General Test; for doctorate, GRE General Test, GRE Subject Test in chemistry or physics (for planetary sciences area). Additional exam requirements/recommendations for international students: Required—TOEFL (minimum score 600 paper-based; 100 iBT), IELTS (minimum score 7). *Application deadline:* For fall admission, 1/5 for domestic and international students; for spring admission, 11/1 for domestic and international students. Application fee: $75. Electronic applications accepted. *Expenses: Tuition:* Full-time $46,400; part-time $725 per credit. One-time fee: $304 full-time. Full-time tuition and fees vary according to course load and program. *Financial support:* In 2015–16, 99 students received support, including 60 fellowships (averaging $40,700 per year), 76 research assistantships (averaging $38,000 per year), 15 teaching assistantships (averaging $36,100 per year); Federal Work-Study, institutionally sponsored loans, scholarships/grants, traineeships, health care benefits, and unspecified assistantships also available. Support available to part-time students. Financial award application deadline: 4/15; financial award applicants required to submit FAFSA. *Faculty research:* Earth: origin, composition, structure, and dynamics of (and interactions between) the atmosphere, oceans, surface, and interior of the earth; planets: formation, dynamics, and evolution of planetary systems and the characterization of exoplanets; climate: characterization of past, present, and potential future climates; studies of the causes and consequences of climate change; life: co-evolution of life and environmental systems. *Total annual research expenditures:* $25.3 million. *Unit head:* Prof. Robert van der Hilst, Department Head, 617-253-2127, Fax: 617-253-8298, E-mail: eapsinfo@mit.edu. *Application contact:* EAPS Education Office, 617-253-3381, Fax: 617-253-8298, E-mail: eapsinfo@mit.edu.
Website: http://eapsweb.mit.edu/

Memorial University of Newfoundland, School of Graduate Studies, Department of Earth Sciences, St. John's, NL A1C 5S7, Canada. Offers geology (M Sc, PhD); geophysics (M Sc, PhD). *Program availability:* Part-time. *Degree requirements:* For master's, thesis; for doctorate, comprehensive exam, thesis/dissertation, oral thesis defense, entry evaluation. *Entrance requirements:* For master's, honors B Sc; for doctorate, M Sc. *Application deadline:* 1/15 for domestic and international students. Applications are processed on a rolling basis. Application fee: $50 Canadian dollars ($100 Canadian dollars for international students). Electronic applications accepted. *Expenses: Tuition, area resident:* Full-time $2199 Canadian dollars. *International tuition:* $2859 Canadian dollars full-time. *Financial support:* Fellowships, research assistantships, and teaching assistantships available. *Faculty research:* Geochemistry, sedimentology, paleoceanography and global change, mineral deposits, petroleum geology, hydrology. *Unit head:* Dr. John Hanchar, Head, 709-864-2334, Fax: 709-864-2589. *Application contact:* Michelle Miskell, Graduate Officer, 709-864-4464, Fax: 709-864-2589, E-mail: mmiskell@mun.ca.
Website: http://www.mun.ca/earthsciences/

Michigan Technological University, Graduate School, College of Engineering, Department of Geological and Mining Engineering and Sciences, Houghton, MI 49931. Offers geological engineering (MS, PhD); geology (MS, PhD); geophysics (MS, PhD); mining engineering (MS, PhD). *Program availability:* Part-time. *Faculty:* 35 full-time, 36 part-time/adjunct. *Students:* 61 full-time (25 women), 22 part-time (8 women); includes 5 minority (1 Black or African American, non-Hispanic/Latino; 1 Asian, non-Hispanic/Latino; 2 Hispanic/Latino; 1 Two or more races, non-Hispanic/Latino), 36 international. Average age 28. 177 applicants, 25% accepted, 14 enrolled. In 2015, 9 master's, 4 doctorates awarded. Terminal master's awarded for partial completion of doctoral program. *Degree requirements:* For master's, comprehensive exam (for some programs), thesis (for some programs); for doctorate, comprehensive exam, thesis/dissertation. *Entrance requirements:* For master's and doctorate, GRE, statement of purpose, personal statement, official transcripts, 3 letters of recommendation. Additional exam requirements/recommendations for international students: Required—TOEFL (recommended score 79 iBT) or IELTS. *Application deadline:* For fall admission, 2/1 priority date for domestic and international students. Applications are processed on a rolling basis. Electronic applications accepted. *Expenses:* Tuition, state resident: full-time $15,507; part-time $861.50 per credit. Tuition, nonresident: full-time $15,507; part-time $861.50 per credit. *Required fees:* $248; $248. Tuition and fees vary according to course load and program. *Financial support:* In 2015–16, 43 students received support, including 6 fellowships with tuition reimbursements available (averaging $14,516 per year), 11 research assistantships with tuition reimbursements available (averaging $14,516 per year), 5 teaching assistantships with tuition reimbursements available (averaging $14,516 per year); career-related internships or fieldwork, Federal Work-Study, scholarships/grants, health care benefits, unspecified assistantships, and cooperative program also available. Financial award applicants required to submit FAFSA. *Faculty research:* Volcanic hazards and volcanic clouds, oil and gas exploration and development, groundwater measurement and modeling, geophysics, environmental paleomagnetism. *Total annual research expenditures:* $1.9 million. *Unit head:* Dr. John S. Gierke, Chair, 906-487-2535, Fax: 906-487-3371, E-mail: jsgierke@mtu.edu. *Application contact:* Amie S. Ledgerwood, Assistant to the Dean, 906-487-2531, Fax: 906-487-3371, E-mail: asledger@mtu.edu.
Website: http://www.mtu.edu/geo/

Missouri University of Science and Technology, Graduate School, Department of Geological Sciences and Engineering, Rolla, MO 65409. Offers geological engineering (MS, DE, PhD); geology and geophysics (MS, PhD), including geochemistry, geology, geophysics, groundwater and environmental geology; petroleum engineering (MS, DE, PhD). *Program availability:* Part-time. *Faculty:* 18 full-time (4 women), 1 part-time/adjunct (0 women). *Students:* 249 full-time (51 women), 93 part-time (17 women); includes 37 minority (10 Black or African American, non-Hispanic/Latino; 3 American Indian or Alaska Native, non-Hispanic/Latino; 6 Asian, non-Hispanic/Latino; 18 Hispanic/Latino), 169 international. Average age 31. 296 applicants, 58% accepted, 97 enrolled. In 2015, 17 master's, 6 doctorates awarded. *Degree requirements:* For master's, thesis optional; for doctorate, comprehensive exam, thesis/dissertation. *Entrance requirements:* For master's, GRE General Test (minimum score 600 quantitative, writing 3.5), minimum GPA of 3.0 in last 4 semesters; for doctorate, GRE General Test (minimum scores: Quantitative 600, Writing 3.5). Additional exam requirements/recommendations for international students: Required—TOEFL (minimum score 550 paper-based). *Application deadline:* For fall admission, 7/1 for domestic students; for spring admission, 12/1 for domestic students. Applications are processed on a rolling basis. Application fee: $55 ($175 for international students). Electronic applications accepted. *Expenses:* Tuition, state resident: full-time $10,536. Tuition, nonresident: full-time $27,015. Full-time tuition and fees vary according to course load. *Financial support:* In 2015–16, fellowships with full tuition reimbursements (averaging $11,250 per year), 9 research assistantships with partial tuition reimbursements (averaging $1,814 per year), 3 teaching assistantships with partial tuition reimbursements (averaging $1,814 per year) were awarded; Federal Work-Study and institutionally sponsored loans also available. Support available to part-time students. Financial award application deadline: 3/1; financial award applicants required to submit FAFSA. *Faculty research:* Digital image processing and geographic information systems, mineralogy, igneous and sedimentary petrology-geochemistry, sedimentology groundwater hydrology and contaminant transport. *Total annual research expenditures:* $2.1 million. *Unit head:* Dr. Robert Laudon, Chairman, 573-341-4466, Fax: 573-341-6935, E-mail: rlaudon@mst.edu. *Application contact:* Debbie Schwertz, Admissions Coordinator, 573-341-6013, Fax: 573-341-6271, E-mail: schwertz@mst.edu.
Website: http://gse.umr.edu/geologicalengineering.html

New Mexico Institute of Mining and Technology, Center for Graduate Studies, Department of Earth and Environmental Science, Program in Geophysics, Socorro, NM 87801. Offers MS, PhD. *Degree requirements:* For master's, thesis optional; for doctorate, thesis/dissertation. *Entrance requirements:* For master's, GRE General Test; for doctorate, GRE General Test, GRE Subject Test. Additional exam requirements/recommendations for international students: Required—TOEFL (minimum score 540 paper-based). *Expenses:* Tuition, state resident: full-time $5811; part-time $322.81 per credit. Tuition, nonresident: full-time $19,220; part-time $1067.79 per credit. *Required fees:* $1030. Tuition and fees vary according to course load. *Faculty research:* Earthquake and volcanic seismology, subduction zone tectonics, network seismology, physical properties of sediments in fault zones.

Ohio University, Graduate College, College of Arts and Sciences, Department of Geological Sciences, Athens, OH 45701-2979. Offers environmental geochemistry (MS); environmental geology (MS); environmental/hydrology (MS); geology (MS); geology education (MS); geomorphology/surficial processes (MS); geophysics (MS); hydrogeology (MS); sedimentology (MS); structure/tectonics (MS). *Program availability:* Part-time. *Degree requirements:* For master's, thesis. *Entrance requirements:* Additional exam requirements/recommendations for international students: Required—TOEFL (minimum score 550 paper-based; 80 iBT) or IELTS (minimum score 6.5). Electronic applications accepted. *Faculty research:* Geoscience education, tectonics, fluvial geomorphology, invertebrate paleontology, mine/hydrology.

Geophysics

Oregon State University, College of Earth, Ocean, and Atmospheric Sciences, Program in Ocean, Earth, and Atmospheric Sciences, Corvallis, OR 97331. Offers atmospheric sciences (MA, MS, PhD); geological oceanography (MA, MS, PhD); geophysics (MA, MS, PhD); ocean ecology and biogeochemistry (MS, PhD); physical oceanography (MA, MS, PhD). *Program availability:* Part-time. *Faculty:* 38 full-time (11 women), 3 part-time/adjunct (1 woman). *Students:* 51 full-time (26 women), 4 part-time (1 woman); includes 7 minority (1 Asian, non-Hispanic/Latino; 4 Hispanic/Latino; 2 Two or more races, non-Hispanic/Latino), 12 international. Average age 29. 116 applicants, 16% accepted, 9 enrolled. In 2015, 5 master's, 1 doctorate awarded. *Entrance requirements:* For master's, GRE. Additional exam requirements/recommendations for international students: Required—TOEFL (minimum score 80 iBT), IELTS (minimum score 6.5). *Application deadline:* For fall admission, 1/5 for domestic students. Application fee: $75 ($85 for international students). *Expenses:* Tuition, state resident: full-time $12,150; part-time $450 per credit. Tuition, nonresident: full-time $20,952; part-time $776 per credit. *Required fees:* $1572; $1443 per unit. One-time fee: $350. Tuition and fees vary according to course load, campus/location and program. *Unit head:* Dr. Rob Wheatcroft, Professor/Program Head, Earth Systems. *Application contact:* Student Advisor, 541-737-5188, E-mail: student_advisor@coas.oregonstate.edu.
Website: http://ceoas.oregonstate.edu/academics/ocean/

Rice University, Graduate Programs, Wiess School–Professional Science Master's Programs, Professional Master's Program in Subsurface Geosciences, Houston, TX 77251-1892. Offers geophysics (MS). *Program availability:* Part-time. *Degree requirements:* For master's, internship. *Entrance requirements:* For master's, GRE, letters of recommendation (4). Additional exam requirements/recommendations for international students: Required—TOEFL (minimum score 600 paper-based; 90 iBT). Electronic applications accepted. *Faculty research:* Seismology, geodynamics, wave propagation, bio-geochemistry, remote sensing.

Saint Louis University, Graduate Education, College of Arts and Sciences, Department of Earth and Atmospheric Sciences, St. Louis, MO 63103. Offers geophysics (PhD); geoscience (MS); meteorology (M Pr Met, MS-R, PhD). *Program availability:* Part-time. *Degree requirements:* For master's, thesis (for some programs), comprehensive oral exam; for doctorate, thesis/dissertation, preliminary exams. *Entrance requirements:* For master's, GRE General Test, letters of recommendation, resume; for doctorate, GRE General Test, letters of recommendation, resumé, goal statement, transcripts. Additional exam requirements/recommendations for international students: Required—TOEFL (minimum score 525 paper-based). Electronic applications accepted. *Faculty research:* Structural geology, mesoscale meteorology and severe storms, weather and climate change prediction.

Southern Methodist University, Dedman College of Humanities and Sciences, Department of Earth Sciences, Dallas, TX 75275. Offers applied geophysics (MS); earth sciences (MS, PhD). *Program availability:* Part-time. *Degree requirements:* For master's, thesis (for some programs), qualifying exam; for doctorate, thesis/dissertation, qualifying exam. *Entrance requirements:* For master's and doctorate, GRE General Test, minimum GPA of 3.0, letters of recommendation. Additional exam requirements/recommendations for international students: Required—TOEFL. Electronic applications accepted. *Faculty research:* Sedimentology, geochemistry, igneous and metamorphic petrology, vertebrate paleontology, seismology.

Stanford University, School of Earth, Energy and Environmental Sciences, Department of Geophysics, Stanford, CA 94305-9991. Offers MS, PhD. Terminal master's awarded for partial completion of doctoral program. *Degree requirements:* For master's, thesis; for doctorate, thesis/dissertation. *Entrance requirements:* For master's and doctorate, GRE General Test. Additional exam requirements/recommendations for international students: Required—TOEFL. Electronic applications accepted. *Expenses: Tuition, area resident:* Full-time $45,729. *Required fees:* $591.

Texas A&M University, College of Geosciences, Department of Geology and Geophysics, College Station, TX 77843. Offers geology (MS, PhD); geophysics (MS, PhD). *Faculty:* 35. *Students:* 105 full-time (36 women), 31 part-time (11 women); includes 16 minority (1 Black or African American, non-Hispanic/Latino; 6 Asian, non-Hispanic/Latino; 9 Hispanic/Latino), 49 international. Average age 29. 308 applicants, 12% accepted, 30 enrolled. In 2015, 26 master's, 10 doctorates awarded. *Degree requirements:* For master's, thesis; for doctorate, thesis/dissertation. *Entrance requirements:* For master's and doctorate, GRE General Test. Additional exam requirements/recommendations for international students: Required—TOEFL (minimum score 550 paper-based; 80 iBT), IELTS (minimum score 6), PTE (minimum score 53). *Application deadline:* For fall admission, 3/1 priority date for domestic students, 1/15 for international students; for spring admission, 10/1 priority date for domestic students, 8/15 for international students. Applications are processed on a rolling basis. Application fee: $50 ($90 for international students). Electronic applications accepted. *Expenses:* Contact institution. *Financial support:* In 2015–16, 105 students received support, including 15 fellowships with tuition reimbursements available (averaging $19,400 per year), 23 research assistantships with tuition reimbursements available (averaging $6,474 per year), 54 teaching assistantships with tuition reimbursements available (averaging $6,446 per year); career-related internships or fieldwork, institutionally sponsored loans, scholarships/grants, traineeships, health care benefits, tuition waivers (full and partial), and unspecified assistantships also available. Support available to part-time students. Financial award application deadline: 3/15; financial award applicants required to submit FAFSA. *Faculty research:* Environmental and engineering geology and geophysics, petroleum geology, tectonophysics, geochemistry. *Unit head:* Dr. Mike Pope, Professor and Department Head, 979-845-4376, E-mail: mcpope@tamu.edu. *Application contact:* Dr. Mark E. Everett, Professor and Associate Department Head for Graduate Affairs, 979-862-2129, E-mail: everett@geo.tamu.edu.
Website: http://geoweb.tamu.edu

The University of Akron, Graduate School, Buchtel College of Arts and Sciences, Department of Geosciences, Akron, OH 44325. Offers earth science (MS); engineering geology (MS); environmental geology (MS); geology (MS); geophysics (MS). *Program availability:* Part-time. *Faculty:* 8 full-time (1 woman), 3 part-time/adjunct (0 women). *Students:* 23 full-time (9 women), 19 part-time (6 women); includes 2 minority (both Black or African American, non-Hispanic/Latino), 15 international. Average age 27. 49 applicants, 59% accepted, 17 enrolled. In 2015, 13 master's awarded. *Degree requirements:* For master's, comprehensive exam, thesis, seminar, proficiency exam. *Entrance requirements:* For master's, minimum GPA of 2.75, three letters of recommendation, statement of purpose. Additional exam requirements/recommendations for international students: Required—TOEFL (minimum score 550 paper-based; 79 iBT), IELTS (minimum score 6.5). *Application deadline:* Applications are processed on a rolling basis. Application fee: $45 ($70 for international students). Electronic applications accepted. *Expenses:* Tuition, state resident: full-time $7958; part-time $442 per credit hour. Tuition, nonresident: full-time $13,464; part-time $748 per credit hour. *Required fees:* $1404. *Financial support:* In 2015–16, 1 research assistantship with full tuition reimbursement, 16 teaching assistantships with full tuition reimbursements were awarded. *Faculty research:* Terrestrial environmental change, karst hydrogeology, lacustrine paleo environments, environmental magnetism and geophysics. *Total annual research expenditures:* $509,174. *Unit head:* Dr. James McManus, Chair, 330-972-7991, E-mail: jmcmanus@uakron.edu. *Application contact:* Dr. John Peck, Director of Graduate Studies, 330-972-7659, E-mail: jpeck@uakron.edu.
Website: http://www.uakron.edu/geology/

University of Alaska Fairbanks, College of Natural Sciences and Mathematics, Department of Geosciences, Fairbanks, AK 99775-5780. Offers geology (MS, PhD), including economic geology (PhD), petroleum geology (MS), quaternary geology (PhD), remote sensing (PhD), volcanology (PhD); geophysics (MS, PhD), including remote sensing geophysics, snow, ice, and permafrost geophysics (MS), solid-earth geophysics (MS). *Program availability:* Part-time. *Faculty:* 14 full-time (4 women), 1 part-time/adjunct (0 women). *Students:* 54 full-time (24 women), 14 part-time (7 women); includes 3 minority (1 Asian, non-Hispanic/Latino; 1 Hispanic/Latino; 1 Two or more races, non-Hispanic/Latino), 17 international. Average age 30. 83 applicants, 14% accepted, 12 enrolled. In 2015, 7 master's awarded. *Degree requirements:* For master's, comprehensive exam, thesis, oral defense of thesis; for doctorate, comprehensive exam, thesis/dissertation, defense of the dissertation. *Entrance requirements:* For master's, GRE General Test, bachelor's degree in geology, geophysics, or an appropriate physical science or engineering with minimum cumulative undergraduate and major GPA of 3.0; for doctorate, GRE General Test, minimum cumulative GPA of 3.0. Additional exam requirements/recommendations for international students: Required—TOEFL (minimum score 550 paper-based; 79 iBT), IELTS (minimum score 6.5). *Application deadline:* For fall admission, 6/1 for domestic students, 3/1 for international students; for spring admission, 10/15 for domestic students, 9/1 for international students. Applications are processed on a rolling basis. Application fee: $60. Electronic applications accepted. *Expenses:* Tuition, state resident: full-time $7614; part-time $423 per credit. Tuition, nonresident: full-time $15,552; part-time $864 per credit. *Required fees:* $38 per credit. $187 per semester. Tuition and fees vary according to course level, course load, program and reciprocity agreements. *Financial support:* In 2015–16, 32 research assistantships with full tuition reimbursements (averaging $15,761 per year), 15 teaching assistantships with full tuition reimbursements (averaging $12,788 per year) were awarded; fellowships with full tuition reimbursements, Federal Work-Study, scholarships/grants, health care benefits, and unspecified assistantships also available. Support available to part-time students. Financial award application deadline: 2/15; financial award applicants required to submit FAFSA. *Faculty research:* Glacial surging, volcanology, geochronology, impact cratering, permafrost geophysics. *Unit head:* Dr. Paul McCarthy, Department Co-Chair, 907-474-7565, Fax: 907-474-5163, E-mail: geology@uaf.edu. *Application contact:* Mary Kreta, Director of Admissions, 907-474-7500, Fax: 907-474-7097, E-mail: admissions@uaf.edu.
Website: http://www.uaf.edu/geology/

University of Alberta, Faculty of Graduate Studies and Research, Department of Physics, Edmonton, AB T6G 2E1, Canada. Offers astrophysics (M Sc, PhD); condensed matter (M Sc, PhD); geophysics (M Sc, PhD); medical physics (M Sc, PhD); subatomic physics (M Sc, PhD). *Degree requirements:* For master's, thesis; for doctorate, thesis/dissertation. *Entrance requirements:* For master's and doctorate, minimum GPA of 7.0 on a 9.0 scale. Additional exam requirements/recommendations for international students: Required—TOEFL. *Faculty research:* Cosmology, astroparticle physics, high-intermediate energy, magnetism, superconductivity.

The University of British Columbia, Faculty of Science, Department of Earth, Ocean and Atmospheric Sciences, Vancouver, BC V6T 1Z4, Canada. Offers atmospheric science (M Sc, PhD); geological engineering (M Eng, MA Sc, PhD); geological sciences (M Sc, PhD); geophysics (M Sc, MA Sc, PhD); oceanography (M Sc, PhD). *Degree requirements:* For master's, one foreign language, thesis (for some programs); for doctorate, one foreign language, comprehensive exam, thesis/dissertation. *Entrance requirements:* Additional exam requirements/recommendations for international students: Required—TOEFL (minimum score 600 paper-based; 100 iBT). *Faculty research:* Oceans and atmosphere, environmental earth science, hydro geology, mineral deposits, geophysics.

University of Calgary, Faculty of Graduate Studies, Faculty of Science, Department of Geoscience, Calgary, AB T2N 1N4, Canada. Offers geology (M Sc, PhD); geophysics (M Sc, PhD); hydrology (M Sc, PhD). *Program availability:* Part-time. Terminal master's awarded for partial completion of doctoral program. *Degree requirements:* For master's, thesis; for doctorate, thesis/dissertation, candidacy exam. *Entrance requirements:* For master's, B Sc; for doctorate, honors B Sc or M Sc. Additional exam requirements/recommendations for international students: Required—TOEFL. Electronic applications accepted. *Faculty research:* Geochemistry, petrology, paleontology, stratigraphy, exploration and solid-earth geophysics.

University of California, Berkeley, Graduate Division, College of Letters and Science, Department of Earth and Planetary Science, Berkeley, CA 94720-1500. Offers geology (MA, MS, PhD); geophysics (MA, MS, PhD). Terminal master's awarded for partial completion of doctoral program. *Degree requirements:* For master's, oral exam (MA), thesis (MS); for doctorate, comprehensive exam, thesis/dissertation, candidacy exams. *Entrance requirements:* For master's and doctorate, GRE General Test, minimum GPA of 3.0, 3 letters of recommendation. Additional exam requirements/recommendations for international students: Required—TOEFL. *Faculty research:* Tectonics, environmental geology, high-pressure geophysics and seismology, economic geology, geochemistry.

University of California, Los Angeles, Graduate Division, College of Letters and Science, Department of Earth and Space Sciences, Program in Geophysics and Space Physics, Los Angeles, CA 90095. Offers MS, PhD. Terminal master's awarded for partial completion of doctoral program. *Degree requirements:* For master's, comprehensive exam or thesis; for doctorate, thesis/dissertation, oral and written qualifying exams. *Entrance requirements:* For master's and doctorate, GRE General Test, bachelor's degree; minimum undergraduate GPA of 3.0 (or its equivalent if letter grade system not used). Additional exam requirements/recommendations for international students: Required—TOEFL. Electronic applications accepted.

University of California, San Diego, Graduate Division, Scripps Institution of Oceanography, La Jolla, CA 92093. Offers climate science and policy (MAS); earth sciences (MS, PhD); geophysics (PhD); marine biodiversity and conservation (MAS); marine biology (MS, PhD); oceanography (MS, PhD). PhD in geophysics is offered jointly with San Diego State University. *Students:* 262 full-time (137 women), 11 part-time (1 woman); includes 51 minority (11 Black or African American, non-Hispanic/Latino; 3 American Indian or Alaska Native, non-Hispanic/Latino; 21 Asian, non-Hispanic/Latino; 16 Hispanic/Latino), 56 international. 332 applicants, 24% accepted, 47 enrolled. In 2015, 38 master's, 28 doctorates awarded. Terminal master's awarded for partial completion of doctoral program. *Degree requirements:* For master's, comprehensive exam (for some programs), thesis (for some programs); for doctorate, comprehensive exam, thesis/dissertation. *Entrance requirements:* For master's and doctorate, GRE General Test, GRE Subject Test (encouraged for ocean biosciences applicants), minimum GPA of 3.0. Additional exam requirements/recommendations for international students: Required—TOEFL (minimum score 550 paper-based; 80 iBT),

IELTS (minimum score 7). *Application deadline:* For fall admission, 12/10 for domestic students. Application fee: $90 ($110 for international students). Electronic applications accepted. *Expenses:* Tuition, state resident: full-time $11,220. Tuition, nonresident: full-time $26,322. *Required fees:* $1800. *Financial support:* Fellowships, research assistantships, teaching assistantships, scholarships/grants, traineeships, and unspecified assistantships available. Financial award applicants required to submit FAFSA. *Faculty research:* Biodiversity and conservation, earth and planetary chemistry, alternative energy, global environmental monitoring, air-sea boundary, tectonic margins and the interactions between systems and environments. *Unit head:* Brian Palenik, Chair, 858-534-7505, E-mail: bpalenik@ucsd.edu. *Application contact:* Gilbert Bretado, Graduate Coordinator, 858-534-1694, E-mail: siodept@sio.ucsd.edu.
Website: https://scripps.ucsd.edu/education

University of Chicago, Division of the Physical Sciences, Department of the Geophysical Sciences, Chicago, IL 60637. Offers atmospheric sciences (PhD); cosmochemistry (PhD); earth sciences (PhD); paleobiology (PhD); planetary and space sciences (PhD). Terminal master's awarded for partial completion of doctoral program. *Degree requirements:* For doctorate, variable foreign language requirement, comprehensive exam, thesis/dissertation. *Entrance requirements:* For doctorate, GRE General Test. Additional exam requirements/recommendations for international students: Required—TOEFL (minimum score 600 paper-based; 96 iBT), IELTS (minimum score 7). Electronic applications accepted. *Faculty research:* Climatology, evolutionary paleontology, cosmochemistry, geochemistry, oceanic sciences.

University of Colorado Boulder, Graduate School, College of Arts and Sciences, Department of Geological Sciences, Boulder, CO 80309. Offers geology (MS, PhD); geophysics (PhD). *Faculty:* 30 full-time (10 women). *Students:* 64 full-time (33 women), 3 part-time (0 women); includes 6 minority (3 Hispanic/Latino; 3 Two or more races, non-Hispanic/Latino), 4 international. Average age 27. 263 applicants, 9% accepted, 22 enrolled. In 2015, 12 master's, 14 doctorates awarded. Terminal master's awarded for partial completion of doctoral program. *Degree requirements:* For master's, comprehensive exam, thesis; for doctorate, comprehensive exam, thesis/dissertation. *Entrance requirements:* For master's, GRE General Test, minimum undergraduate GPA of 3.0; for doctorate, GRE General Test, minimum GPA of 2.75. *Application deadline:* For fall admission, 1/7 for domestic students, 12/1 for international students. Application fee: $50 ($70 for international students). Electronic applications accepted. Application fee is waived when completed online. *Financial support:* In 2015–16, 177 students received support, including 46 fellowships (averaging $3,061 per year), 33 research assistantships with tuition reimbursements available (averaging $32,260 per year), 26 teaching assistantships with tuition reimbursements available (averaging $29,477 per year); institutionally sponsored loans, scholarships/grants, health care benefits, and unspecified assistantships also available. Financial award application deadline: 1/15; financial award applicants required to submit FAFSA. *Faculty research:* Geology, tectonics, earth sciences, geophysics, geosciences. *Total annual research expenditures:* $12.5 million. *Application contact:* E-mail: geolinfo@colorado.edu.
Website: http://www.colorado.edu/GeolSci

University of Colorado Boulder, Graduate School, College of Arts and Sciences, Department of Physics, Boulder, CO 80309. Offers chemical physics (PhD); geophysics (PhD); liquid crystal science and technology (PhD); mathematical physics (PhD); medical physics (PhD); optical sciences and engineering (PhD); physics (MS, PhD). *Faculty:* 48 full-time (8 women). *Students:* 131 full-time (22 women), 97 part-time (22 women); includes 14 minority (5 Asian, non-Hispanic/Latino; 4 Hispanic/Latino; 5 Two or more races, non-Hispanic/Latino), 61 international. Average age 26. 624 applicants, 24% accepted, 36 enrolled. In 2015, 24 master's, 29 doctorates awarded. Terminal master's awarded for partial completion of doctoral program. *Degree requirements:* For master's, comprehensive exam, thesis or alternative; for doctorate, comprehensive exam, thesis/dissertation. *Entrance requirements:* For master's and doctorate, GRE General Test, GRE Subject Test, minimum undergraduate GPA of 3.0. Additional exam requirements/recommendations for international students: Required—TOEFL. *Application deadline:* For fall admission, 12/15 for domestic students, 12/1 for international students. Applications are processed on a rolling basis. Application fee: $50 ($70 for international students). Electronic applications accepted. Application fee is waived when completed online. *Financial support:* In 2015–16, 521 students received support, including 7 fellowships (averaging $5,311 per year), 162 research assistantships with tuition reimbursements available (averaging $34,608 per year), 51 teaching assistantships with tuition reimbursements available (averaging $29,058 per year); institutionally sponsored loans, scholarships/grants, health care benefits, and unspecified assistantships also available. Financial award application deadline: 1/15; financial award applicants required to submit FAFSA. *Faculty research:* Physics, theoretical physics, high energy physics, experimental physics, solid state physics. *Total annual research expenditures:* $24.8 million. *Application contact:* E-mail: jeanne.nijhowne@colorado.edu.
Website: http://phys.colorado.edu/graduate-students

University of Hawaii at Manoa, Graduate Division, School of Ocean and Earth Science and Technology, Department of Geology and Geophysics, Honolulu, HI 96822. Offers high-pressure geophysics and geochemistry (MS, PhD); hydrogeology and engineering geology (MS, PhD); marine geology and geophysics (MS, PhD); planetary geosciences and remote sensing (MS, PhD); seismology and solid-earth geophysics (MS, PhD); volcanology, petrology, and geochemistry (MS, PhD). *Program availability:* Part-time. *Faculty:* 72 full-time (15 women), 6 part-time/adjunct (3 women). *Students:* 42 full-time (26 women), 2 part-time (1 woman); includes 9 minority (2 Asian, non-Hispanic/Latino; 2 Hispanic/Latino; 5 Two or more races, non-Hispanic/Latino), 9 international. Average age 31. 78 applicants, 23% accepted, 13 enrolled. In 2015, 7 master's, 8 doctorates awarded. Terminal master's awarded for partial completion of doctoral program. *Degree requirements:* For master's, thesis optional; for doctorate, comprehensive exam, thesis/dissertation. *Entrance requirements:* For master's and doctorate, GRE General Test, minimum GPA of 3.0. Additional exam requirements/recommendations for international students: Required—TOEFL (minimum score 580 paper-based; 92 iBT), IELTS (minimum score 5). *Application deadline:* For fall admission, 1/15 for domestic students, 1/1 for international students; for spring admission, 9/1 for domestic students, 8/15 for international students. Application fee: $100. *Financial support:* In 2015–16, 7 fellowships (averaging $1,359 per year), 30 research assistantships (averaging $23,988 per year), 4 teaching assistantships (averaging $15,350 per year) were awarded. *Total annual research expenditures:* $3.8 million. *Unit head:* Brian Taylor, Dean, 808-956-6182, E-mail: taylorb@hawaii.edu. *Application contact:* Dr. Gregory Moore, Chair, 808-956-7640, Fax: 808-956-5512, E-mail: gg-dept@soest.hawaii.edu.
Website: http://www.soest.hawaii.edu/GG/

University of Houston, College of Natural Sciences and Mathematics, Department of Earth and Atmospheric Sciences, Houston, TX 77204. Offers atmospheric science (PhD); geology (MA, PhD); geophysics (PhD). *Program availability:* Part-time. *Degree requirements:* For master's, thesis; for doctorate, comprehensive exam, thesis/dissertation. *Entrance requirements:* For master's and doctorate, GRE General Test. Additional exam requirements/recommendations for international students: Required—TOEFL (minimum score 550 paper-based; 79 iBT), IELTS (minimum score 6.5). Electronic applications accepted. *Faculty research:* Atmospherics sciences, seismic and solid earth geophysics, tectonics, environmental hydrochemistry, carbonates, micropaleontology, structure and tectonics, petroleum geology.

University of Manitoba, Faculty of Graduate Studies, Clayton H. Riddell Faculty of Environment, Earth, and Resources, Department of Geological Sciences, Winnipeg, MB R3T 2N2, Canada. Offers geology (M Sc, PhD); geophysics (M Sc, PhD). *Degree requirements:* For master's, thesis; for doctorate, thesis/dissertation. *Entrance requirements:* For master's and doctorate, GRE General Test, GRE Subject Test (geology), minimum GPA of 3.0. Additional exam requirements/recommendations for international students: Required—TOEFL.

University of Memphis, Graduate School, College of Arts and Sciences, Department of Earth Sciences, Memphis, TN 38152. Offers archaeology (MS); earth sciences (PhD); geographic information systems (Graduate Certificate), including geographic information systems, GIS educator, GIS planning, GIS professional; geography (MA, MS); geology (MS); geophysics (MS); interdisciplinary studies (MS). *Program availability:* Part-time, evening/weekend. *Faculty:* 14 full-time (3 women), 1 part-time/adjunct (0 women). *Students:* 37 full-time (9 women), 33 part-time (12 women); includes 7 minority (3 Black or African American, non-Hispanic/Latino; 1 Asian, non-Hispanic/Latino; 1 Hispanic/Latino; 2 Two or more races, non-Hispanic/Latino), 25 international. Average age 33. 31 applicants, 71% accepted, 8 enrolled. In 2015, 7 master's, 5 doctorates awarded. Terminal master's awarded for partial completion of doctoral program. *Degree requirements:* For master's, comprehensive exam, thesis, seminar presentation; for doctorate, thesis/dissertation. *Entrance requirements:* For master's, GRE General Test, 3 letters of recommendation, statement of research interests; for doctorate, GRE General Test, 2 letters of recommendation, resume, personal statement. Additional exam requirements/recommendations for international students: Required—TOEFL (minimum score 550 paper-based). *Application deadline:* For fall admission, 1/31 for domestic students; for spring admission, 11/1 for domestic students. Applications are processed on a rolling basis. Application fee: $35 ($60 for international students). Electronic applications accepted. *Financial support:* In 2015–16, 18 students received support. Fellowships with full tuition reimbursements available, research assistantships with full tuition reimbursements available, teaching assistantships with full tuition reimbursements available, Federal Work-Study, scholarships/grants, and unspecified assistantships available. Financial award application deadline: 2/15; financial award applicants required to submit FAFSA. *Faculty research:* Hazards, active tectonics, geophysics, hydrology and water resources, spatial analysis. *Unit head:* Dr. M. Jerry Bartholomew, Chair, 901-678-4536, Fax: 901-678-4467, E-mail: jbrthlm1@memphis.edu. *Application contact:* Dr. Arlene Hill, Associate Professor and Graduate Program Coordinator, 901-678-4358, Fax: 901-678-2178, E-mail: dlarsen@memphis.edu.
Website: http://www.memphis.edu/earthsciences/

University of Miami, Graduate School, Rosenstiel School of Marine and Atmospheric Science, Division of Marine Geology and Geophysics, Coral Gables, FL 33124. Offers MS, PhD. Terminal master's awarded for partial completion of doctoral program. *Degree requirements:* For master's, comprehensive exam, thesis; for doctorate, comprehensive exam, thesis/dissertation. *Entrance requirements:* For master's and doctorate, GRE General Test. Additional exam requirements/recommendations for international students: Required—TOEFL (minimum score 550 paper-based). Electronic applications accepted. *Faculty research:* Carbonate sedimentology, low-temperature geochemistry, paleoceanography, geodesy and tectonics.

University of Minnesota, Twin Cities Campus, College of Science and Engineering, Department of Earth Sciences, Minneapolis, MN 55455-0213. Offers MS, PhD. Terminal master's awarded for partial completion of doctoral program. *Degree requirements:* For master's, thesis; for doctorate, thesis/dissertation. *Entrance requirements:* For master's and doctorate, GRE General Test, 3 letters of recommendation. Additional exam requirements/recommendations for international students: Required—TOEFL (minimum score 550 paper-based). Electronic applications accepted. *Faculty research:* Geology, geophysics, geochemistry, geobiology, climate and environmental geosciences.

University of Nevada, Reno, Graduate School, College of Science, Mackay School of Earth Sciences and Engineering, Department of Geological Sciences and Engineering, Program in Geophysics, Reno, NV 89557. Offers MS, PhD. Terminal master's awarded for partial completion of doctoral program. *Degree requirements:* For master's, thesis optional; for doctorate, thesis/dissertation. *Entrance requirements:* For master's, GRE General Test, minimum GPA of 2.75; for doctorate, GRE General Test, minimum GPA of 3.0. Additional exam requirements/recommendations for international students: Required—TOEFL (minimum score 500 paper-based; 61 iBT), IELTS (minimum score 6). Electronic applications accepted. *Faculty research:* Geophysics exploration, seismology, remote sensing.

University of Oklahoma, Mewbourne College of Earth and Energy, ConocoPhillips School of Geology and Geophysics, Program in Geophysics, Norman, OK 73019. Offers MS, PhD. *Program availability:* Part-time. *Students:* 23 full-time (5 women), 13 part-time (4 women); includes 6 minority (1 Asian, non-Hispanic/Latino; 3 Hispanic/Latino; 2 Two or more races, non-Hispanic/Latino), 21 international. Average age 26. 76 applicants, 16% accepted, 11 enrolled. In 2015, 9 master's, 4 doctorates awarded. *Degree requirements:* For master's, thesis; for doctorate, comprehensive exam, thesis/dissertation. *Entrance requirements:* For master's and doctorate, GRE. Additional exam requirements/recommendations for international students: Required—TOEFL (minimum score 79 iBT) or IELTS (minimum score 6.5). *Application deadline:* For fall admission, 1/10 for domestic students, 1/10 priority date for international students; for spring admission, 9/1 for domestic and international students. Application fee: $50 ($100 for international students). Electronic applications accepted. *Expenses:* Tuition, state resident: full-time $4577; part-time $190.70 per credit hour. Tuition, nonresident: full-time $17,758; part-time $739.90 per credit hour. *Required fees:* $3060; $115.70 per credit hour. $141.50 per semester. *Financial support:* In 2015–16, 32 students received support. Career-related internships or fieldwork, scholarships/grants, and unspecified assistantships available. Financial award application deadline: 6/1; financial award applicants required to submit FAFSA. *Faculty research:* Lithospheric structure and evolution, basin analysis, outcrop-scale investigations of sand bodies in turbidite channels. *Unit head:* Dr. R. Douglas Elmore, Director and Associate Provost, 405-325-3253, Fax: 405-325-3140, E-mail: delmore@ou.edu. *Application contact:* Rebecca Fay, Coordinator of Academic Student Services, 405-325-3253, Fax: 405-325-3140, E-mail: rfay@ou.edu.
Website: http://geology.ou.edu

The University of Texas at Dallas, School of Natural Sciences and Mathematics, Department of Geosciences, Richardson, TX 75080. Offers geochemistry (MS, PhD); geophysics (MS, PhD); geospatial information sciences (MS, PhD); hydrogeology (MS, PhD); sedimentology, stratigraphy, and paleontology (MS, PhD); structural geology and tectonics (MS, PhD). *Program availability:* Part-time, evening/weekend. *Faculty:* 9 full-time (0 women). *Students:* 57 full-time (21 women), 23 part-time (4 women); includes 12 minority (3 Black or African American, non-Hispanic/Latino; 4 Asian, non-Hispanic/

Latino; 3 Hispanic/Latino; 2 Two or more races, non-Hispanic/Latino), 33 international. Average age 30. 98 applicants, 31% accepted, 20 enrolled. In 2015, 20 master's, 4 doctorates awarded. *Degree requirements:* For master's, thesis optional; for doctorate, thesis/dissertation. *Entrance requirements:* For master's and doctorate, GRE General Test, minimum GPA of 3.0 in upper-level course work in field. Additional exam requirements/recommendations for international students: Required—TOEFL (minimum score 550 paper-based). *Application deadline:* For fall admission, 7/15 for domestic students, 5/1 priority date for international students; for spring admission, 11/15 for domestic students, 9/1 priority date for international students. Applications are processed on a rolling basis. Application fee: $50 ($100 for international students). Electronic applications accepted. *Expenses:* Tuition, state resident: full-time $11,940; part-time $663 per semester hour. Tuition, nonresident: full-time $22,786; part-time $1266 per semester hour. Tuition and fees vary according to course load. *Financial support:* In 2015–16, 41 students received support, including 10 research assistantships with partial tuition reimbursements available (averaging $19,260 per year), 15 teaching assistantships with partial tuition reimbursements available (averaging $17,100 per year); career-related internships or fieldwork, Federal Work-Study, institutionally sponsored loans, scholarships/grants, and unspecified assistantships also available. Support available to part-time students. Financial award application deadline: 4/30; financial award applicants required to submit FAFSA. *Faculty research:* Cybermapping, GPS applications for geophysics and geology, seismology and ground-penetrating radar, numerical modeling, signal processing and inverse modeling techniques in seismology. *Unit head:* Dr. John Geissman, Department Head, 972-883-2454, Fax: 972-883-2537, E-mail: geosciences@utdallas.edu. *Application contact:* Gloria Eby, Graduate Support Assistant, 972-883-2404, Fax: 972-883-2537, E-mail: geosciences@utdallas.edu.
Website: http://www.utdallas.edu/geosciences

The University of Texas at El Paso, Graduate School, College of Science, Department of Geological Sciences, Program in Geophysics, El Paso, TX 79968-0001. Offers MS. *Program availability:* Part-time, evening/weekend. *Degree requirements:* For master's, thesis. *Entrance requirements:* For master's, minimum GPA of 3.0, letters of recommendation. Additional exam requirements/recommendations for international students: Required—TOEFL. Electronic applications accepted.

The University of Tulsa, Graduate School, College of Engineering and Natural Sciences, Department of Geosciences, Tulsa, OK 74104-3189. Offers geophysics (MS); geosciences (MS, PhD); JD/MS. *Program availability:* Part-time. *Faculty:* 8 full-time (1 woman). *Students:* 27 full-time (11 women), 9 part-time (6 women); includes 3 minority (1 Black or African American, non-Hispanic/Latino; 2 American Indian or Alaska Native, non-Hispanic/Latino), 20 international. Average age 28. 132 applicants, 30% accepted, 18 enrolled. In 2015, 26 master's, 5 doctorates awarded. Terminal master's awarded for partial completion of doctoral program. *Degree requirements:* For master's, thesis (for some programs); for doctorate, comprehensive exam, thesis/dissertation. *Entrance requirements:* For master's and doctorate, GRE General Test. Additional exam requirements/recommendations for international students: Required—TOEFL (minimum score 550 paper-based; 80 iBT), IELTS (minimum score 6). *Application deadline:* Applications are processed on a rolling basis. Application fee: $55. Electronic applications accepted. *Expenses: Tuition, area resident:* Full-time $22,230; part-time $1176 per credit hour. *Required fees:* $590 per semester. Tuition and fees vary according to course load. *Financial support:* In 2015–16, 18 students received support, including 2 fellowships with full tuition reimbursements available (averaging $3,600 per year), 7 research assistantships with full tuition reimbursements available (averaging $7,609 per year), 10 teaching assistantships with full tuition reimbursements available (averaging $11,498 per year); career-related internships or fieldwork, scholarships/grants, health care benefits, and unspecified assistantships also available. Support available to part-time students. Financial award application deadline: 2/1; financial award applicants required to submit FAFSA. *Faculty research:* Petroleum exploration/production and environmental science, including clastic sedimentology, petroleum seismology, seismic stratigraphy, structural geology, geochemistry, and biogeoscience. *Total annual research expenditures:* $409,030. *Unit head:* Dr. Peter Michael, Chairperson, 918-631-3017, Fax: 918-631-2091, E-mail: pjm@utulsa.edu. *Application contact:* Dr. Dennis Kerr, Adviser, 918-631-3020, Fax: 918-631-2156, E-mail: dennis-kerr@utulsa.edu.
Website: http://engineering.utulsa.edu/academics/geosciences/

University of Utah, Graduate School, College of Mines and Earth Sciences, Department of Geology and Geophysics, Salt Lake City, UT 84112. Offers environmental engineering (ME, MS, PhD); geological engineering (ME, MS, PhD); geology (MS, PhD); geophysics (MS, PhD). *Faculty:* 23 full-time (5 women), 11 part-time/adjunct (4 women). *Students:* 60 full-time (22 women), 16 part-time (6 women); includes 6 minority (1 Black or African American, non-Hispanic/Latino; 1 American Indian or Alaska Native, non-Hispanic/Latino; 4 Hispanic/Latino), 17 international. Average age 27. 228 applicants, 14% accepted, 22 enrolled. In 2015, 27 master's, 6 doctorates awarded. Terminal master's awarded for partial completion of doctoral program. *Degree requirements:* For master's, comprehensive exam, thesis; for doctorate, thesis/dissertation, qualifying exam (written and oral). *Entrance requirements:* For master's and doctorate, GRE General Test, minimum GPA of 3.25. Additional exam requirements/recommendations for international students: Required—TOEFL (minimum score 500 paper-based; 61 iBT). *Application deadline:* For fall admission, 1/15 priority date for domestic and international students. Application fee: $55 ($65 for international students). Electronic applications accepted. *Financial support:* In 2015–16, 62 students received support, including 14 fellowships with full tuition reimbursements available (averaging $17,500 per year), 32 research assistantships with full tuition reimbursements available (averaging $23,000 per year), 16 teaching assistantships with full tuition reimbursements available (averaging $17,500 per year); career-related internships or fieldwork, institutionally sponsored loans, scholarships/grants, unspecified assistantships, and stipends also available. Financial award application deadline: 1/15; financial award applicants required to submit FAFSA. *Faculty research:* Igneous, metamorphic, and sedimentary petrology; stratigraphy; paleoclimatology; hydrology; seismology. *Total annual research expenditures:* $4.1 million. *Unit head:* Dr. John Bartley, Chair, 801-585-1670, Fax: 801-581-7065, E-mail: john.bartley@utah.edu. *Application contact:* Dr. Gabriel J. Bowen, Director of Graduate Studies, 801-585-7925, Fax: 801-581-7065, E-mail: gabe.bowen@utah.edu.
Website: http://www.earth.utah.edu/

University of Washington, Graduate School, College of the Environment, Department of Earth and Space Sciences, Seattle, WA 98195. Offers geology (MS, PhD); geophysics (MS, PhD). *Degree requirements:* For master's, thesis or alternative, departmental qualifying exam, final exam; for doctorate, thesis/dissertation, departmental qualifying exam, general and final exams. *Entrance requirements:* For master's and doctorate, GRE General Test, minimum GPA of 3.0. Additional exam requirements/recommendations for international students: Required—TOEFL (minimum score 580 paper-based). Electronic applications accepted.

The University of Western Ontario, Faculty of Graduate Studies, Physical Sciences Division, Department of Earth Sciences, London, ON N6A 5B8, Canada. Offers environment and sustainability (MES); geology (M Sc, PhD); geology and environmental science (M Sc, PhD); geophysics (M Sc, PhD); geophysics and environmental science (M Sc, PhD). *Degree requirements:* For master's, thesis; for doctorate, thesis/dissertation, qualifying exam. *Entrance requirements:* For master's, honors in B Sc; for doctorate, M Sc. Additional exam requirements/recommendations for international students: Required—TOEFL. *Faculty research:* Geophysics, geochemistry, paleontology, sedimentology/stratigraphy, glaciology/quaternary.

University of Wisconsin–Madison, Graduate School, College of Letters and Science, Department of Geology and Geophysics, Program in Geophysics, Madison, WI 53706-1380. Offers MS, PhD. *Degree requirements:* For master's, thesis; for doctorate, one foreign language, thesis/dissertation. *Entrance requirements:* For master's and doctorate, GRE General Test. *Expenses:* Tuition, state resident: full-time $5364. Tuition, nonresident: full-time $12,027. *Required fees:* $571. Tuition and fees vary according to campus/location, program and reciprocity agreements.

University of Wyoming, College of Arts and Sciences, Department of Geology and Geophysics, Laramie, WY 82071. Offers geology (MS, PhD); geophysics (MS, PhD). *Program availability:* Part-time. *Degree requirements:* For master's, comprehensive exam, thesis; for doctorate, comprehensive exam, thesis/dissertation. *Entrance requirements:* For master's and doctorate, GRE General Test, minimum GPA of 3.0. *Faculty research:* Low-temp geochemistry, geohydrology, paleontology, structure/tectonics, sedimentation and petroleum geology, petrology, geophysics/seismology.

West Virginia University, Eberly College of Arts and Sciences, Department of Geology and Geography, Program in Geology, Morgantown, WV 26506. Offers geomorphology (MS, PhD); geophysics (MS, PhD); hydrogeology (MS, PhD); paleontology (MS, PhD); petroleum geology (PhD); petrology (MS, PhD); stratigraphy (MS, PhD); structure (MS, PhD). *Program availability:* Part-time. Terminal master's awarded for partial completion of doctoral program. *Degree requirements:* For master's, thesis (for some programs); for doctorate, comprehensive exam, thesis/dissertation. *Entrance requirements:* For master's, GRE General Test, minimum GPA of 2.5; for doctorate, GRE General Test, minimum GPA of 3.3. Additional exam requirements/recommendations for international students: Required—TOEFL. *Expenses:* Tuition, state resident: full-time $8568. Tuition, nonresident: full-time $22,140. Tuition and fees vary according to program.

Wright State University, School of Graduate Studies, College of Science and Mathematics, Department of Physics, Program in Physics, Dayton, OH 45435. Offers geophysics (MS); medical physics (MS). *Program availability:* Part-time, evening/weekend. *Degree requirements:* For master's, thesis. *Entrance requirements:* Additional exam requirements/recommendations for international students: Required—TOEFL. *Faculty research:* Solid-state physics, optics, geophysics.

Yale University, Graduate School of Arts and Sciences, Department of Geology and Geophysics, New Haven, CT 06520. Offers biogeochemistry (PhD); climate dynamics (PhD); geochemistry (PhD); geophysics (PhD); meteorology (PhD); oceanography (PhD); paleontology (PhD); paleooceanography (PhD); petrology (PhD); tectonics (PhD). *Degree requirements:* For doctorate, thesis/dissertation. *Entrance requirements:* For doctorate, GRE General Test. Additional exam requirements/recommendations for international students: Required—TOEFL.

Geosciences

Arizona State University at the Tempe campus, College of Liberal Arts and Sciences, School of Earth and Space Exploration, Tempe, AZ 85287-1404. Offers astrophysics (MS, PhD); exploration systems design (PhD); geological sciences (MS, PhD). PhD in exploration systems design is offered in collaboration with the Ira A. Fulton School of Engineering. Terminal master's awarded for partial completion of doctoral program. *Degree requirements:* For master's, thesis, interactive Program of Study (iPOS) submitted before completing 50 percent of required credit hours; for doctorate, thesis/dissertation, interactive Program of Study (iPOS) submitted before completing 50 percent of required credit hours. *Entrance requirements:* For master's and doctorate, GRE, minimum GPA of 3.0 or equivalent in last 2 years of work leading to bachelor's degree. Additional exam requirements/recommendations for international students: Required—TOEFL, IELTS, or PTE. Electronic applications accepted.

Ball State University, Graduate School, College of Sciences and Humanities, Department of Geological Sciences, Muncie, IN 47306. Offers geology (MA, MS). *Program availability:* Part-time. *Faculty:* 5 full-time (0 women). *Students:* 2 full-time (1 woman), 9 part-time (4 women). Average age 26. 14 applicants, 57% accepted, 2 enrolled. In 2015, 3 master's awarded. *Degree requirements:* For master's, thesis (for some programs). *Entrance requirements:* For master's, GRE General Test, minimum baccalaureate GPA of 2.75 or 3.0 in latter half of baccalauareate. Additional exam requirements/recommendations for international students: Required—TOEFL (minimum score 550 paper-based; 79 iBT), IELTS (minimum score 6.5). *Application deadline:* Applications are processed on a rolling basis. Application fee: $60. Electronic applications accepted. *Expenses: Tuition, area resident:* Full-time $6948; part-time $2316 per semester. Tuition, state resident: full-time $10,422; part-time $3474 per semester. Tuition, nonresident: full-time $19,062; part-time $6354 per semester. *Required fees:* $651 per semester. Tuition and fees vary according to campus/location, program and reciprocity agreements. *Financial support:* In 2015–16, 7 students received support, including 1 research assistantship with partial tuition reimbursement available (averaging $12,047 per year), 6 teaching assistantships with partial tuition reimbursements available (averaging $9,365 per year). Financial award application deadline: 3/1; financial award applicants required to submit FAFSA. *Faculty research:* Environmental geology, geophysics, stratigraphy. *Unit head:* Dr. Richard Fluegeman, Chairperson, 765-285-8267, Fax: 765-285-8265, E-mail: rfluegem@bsu.edu.

Application contact: Dr. Klaus Neumann, Associate Professor/Graduate Advisor, 765-285-8262, Fax: 765-285-8265, E-mail: kneumann@bsu.edu.
Website: http://www.bsu.edu/geology

Baylor University, Graduate School, College of Arts and Sciences, Department of Geosciences, Waco, TX 76798. Offers geosciences (MS, PhD), including geophysics, geology. *Faculty:* 15 full-time (1 woman). *Students:* 40 full-time (11 women), 5 part-time (3 women); includes 3 minority (2 Hispanic/Latino; 1 Two or more races, non-Hispanic/Latino), 10 international. Average age 23. 41 applicants, 51% accepted, 15 enrolled. In 2015, 4 master's, 1 doctorate awarded. *Degree requirements:* For master's, thesis, preliminary exam, thesis proposal; for doctorate, thesis/dissertation, preliminary exam, dissertation proposal. *Entrance requirements:* For master's and doctorate, GRE General Test. Additional exam requirements/recommendations for international students: Required—TOEFL (minimum score 550 paper-based; 80 iBT), IELTS (minimum score 6.5), PTE (minimum score 58). *Application deadline:* For fall admission, 1/31 priority date for domestic students, 1/15 priority date for international students; for spring admission, 10/1 priority date for domestic and international students. Applications are processed on a rolling basis. Application fee: $40. Electronic applications accepted. *Financial support:* In 2015–16, 33 students received support, including 6 research assistantships with tuition reimbursements available (averaging $17,000 per year), 18 teaching assistantships with tuition reimbursements available (averaging $21,000 per year); career-related internships or fieldwork, Federal Work-Study, institutionally sponsored loans, scholarships/grants, health care benefits, tuition waivers (full and partial), and unspecified assistantships also available. Support available to part-time students. Financial award application deadline: 2/28; financial award applicants required to submit FAFSA. *Faculty research:* Terrestrial paleoclimatology, applied petroleum studies, applied and solid earth geophysics, hydrogeoscience, high temperature geochemistry and volcanology. *Total annual research expenditures:* $800,000. *Unit head:* Dr. Steven George Driese, Graduate Program Director, 254-710-2194, Fax: 254-710-2673, E-mail: steven_driese@baylor.edu. *Application contact:* Jamie Ruth, Administrative Associate, 254-710-2361, Fax: 254-710-2673, E-mail: jamie_ruth@baylor.edu.
Website: http://www.baylor.edu/geology/

Baylor University, Graduate School, College of Arts and Sciences, The Institute of Ecological, Earth and Environmental Sciences, Waco, TX 76798. Offers PhD. *Degree requirements:* For doctorate, variable foreign language requirement, comprehensive exam, thesis/dissertation or alternative. *Entrance requirements:* For doctorate, GRE. Additional exam requirements/recommendations for international students: Required—TOEFL (minimum score 550 paper-based; 80 iBT); Recommended—IELTS (minimum score 6.5). Electronic applications accepted. *Faculty research:* Ecosystem processes, environmental toxicology and risk assessment, biogeochemical cycling, chemical fate and transport, conservation management.

Boston University, Graduate School of Arts and Sciences, Department of Earth and Environment, Boston, MA 02215. Offers earth sciences (MA, PhD); energy and environment (MA); geography (MA, PhD); global development policy (MA); international relations and environmental policy (MA); remote sensing and geospatial sciences (MA). *Students:* 57 full-time (25 women), 5 part-time (1 woman); includes 5 minority (2 Asian, non-Hispanic/Latino; 3 Hispanic/Latino), 23 international. Average age 28. 234 applicants, 51% accepted, 27 enrolled. In 2015, 4 master's, 12 doctorates awarded. Terminal master's awarded for partial completion of doctoral program. *Degree requirements:* For master's, comprehensive exam (for some programs), thesis (for some programs); for doctorate, comprehensive exam, thesis/dissertation. *Entrance requirements:* For master's and doctorate, GRE General Test, 3 letters of recommendation, official transcripts, personal statement, writing sample (for geography). Additional exam requirements/recommendations for international students: Required—TOEFL (minimum score 550 paper-based; 84 iBT). *Application deadline:* For fall admission, 1/31 for domestic and international students; for winter admission, 10/15 for domestic and international students. Application fee: $95. Electronic applications accepted. *Financial support:* In 2015–16, 43 students received support, including 5 fellowships with full tuition reimbursements available (averaging $21,000 per year), 17 research assistantships with full tuition reimbursements available (averaging $21,000 per year), 12 teaching assistantships with full tuition reimbursements available (averaging $21,000 per year); Federal Work-Study, scholarships/grants, traineeships, and health care benefits also available. Financial award application deadline: 1/31. *Faculty research:* Biogeosciences, climate and surface processes; energy, environment and society; geographical sciences; geology, geochemistry and geophysics. *Unit head:* David Marchant, Chair, 617-353-3236, E-mail: marchant@bu.edu. *Application contact:* Nora Watson, Graduate Program Coordinator, 617-353-2529, Fax: 617-353-8399, E-mail: norala31@bu.edu.
Website: http://www.bu.edu/earth/

Brock University, Faculty of Graduate Studies, Faculty of Mathematics and Science, Program in Earth Sciences, St. Catharines, ON L2S 3A1, Canada. Offers M Sc. *Program availability:* Part-time. *Degree requirements:* For master's, thesis. *Entrance requirements:* For master's, honors B Sc in earth sciences. Additional exam requirements/recommendations for international students: Required—TOEFL (minimum score 550 paper-based; 80 iBT), IELTS (minimum score 6.5), TWE (minimum score 4). Electronic applications accepted. *Faculty research:* Clastic sedimentology, environmental geology, geochemistry, micropaleontology, structural geology.

Brooklyn College of the City University of New York, School of Education, Program in Adolescence Science Education and Special Subjects, Brooklyn, NY 11210-2889. Offers adolescence science education (MAT); biology teacher (7-12) (MA); chemistry teacher (7-12) (MA); earth science teacher (7-12) (MAT); English teacher (7-12) (MA); French teacher (7-12) (MA); mathematics teacher (7-12) (MA); music teacher (MA); physics teacher (7-12) (MA); social studies teacher (7-12) (MA); Spanish teacher (7-12) (MA). *Program availability:* Part-time, evening/weekend. *Degree requirements:* For master's, comprehensive exam (for some programs), thesis (for some programs). *Entrance requirements:* For master's, LAST, previous course work in education, resume, 2 letters of recommendation, essay. Additional exam requirements/recommendations for international students: Required—TOEFL (minimum score 500 paper-based; 61 iBT). Electronic applications accepted. *Faculty research:* Interdisciplinary education, semiotics, discourse analysis, autobiography, teacher identity.

Brooklyn College of the City University of New York, School of Education, Program in Middle Childhood Science Education, Brooklyn, NY 11210-2889. Offers biology (MA); chemistry (MA); earth science (MA); general science (MA); physics (MA). *Program availability:* Part-time, evening/weekend. *Entrance requirements:* For master's, LAST, interview, previous course work in education and mathematics, resume, 2 letters of recommendation, essay. Additional exam requirements/recommendations for international students: Required—TOEFL (minimum score 500 paper-based; 61 iBT). Electronic applications accepted. *Faculty research:* Geometric thinking, mastery of basic facts, problem-solving strategies, history of mathematics.

Brown University, Graduate School, Department of Geological Sciences, Providence, RI 02912. Offers PhD. *Degree requirements:* For doctorate, thesis/dissertation, 1 semester of teaching experience, preliminary exam. *Faculty research:* Geochemistry, mineral kinetics, igneous and metamorphic petrology, tectonophysics including geophysics and structural geology, paleoclimatology, paleoceanography, sedimentation, planetary geology.

California State University, Chico, Office of Graduate Studies, College of Natural Sciences, Department of Geological and Environmental Sciences, Program in Geosciences, Chico, CA 95929-0722. Offers hydrology/hydrogeology (MS). *Program availability:* Part-time. *Degree requirements:* For master's, comprehensive exam, thesis. *Entrance requirements:* For master's, GRE. Additional exam requirements/recommendations for international students: Required—TOEFL (minimum score 550 paper-based; 80 iBT), IELTS (minimum score 6.5), PTE (minimum score 59). *Application deadline:* For fall admission, 3/1 priority date for domestic students, 3/1 for international students; for spring admission, 9/15 priority date for domestic students, 9/15 for international students. Application fee: $55. Electronic applications accepted. *Expenses: Tuition, area resident:* Full-time $4146; part-time $2730. *Financial support:* Fellowships, research assistantships, teaching assistantships, and career-related internships or fieldwork available. *Unit head:* Dr. David L. Brown, Chair, 530-898-1995, Fax: 530-898-5234, E-mail: geos@csuchico.edu. *Application contact:* Judy L. Rice, Graduate Admissions Coordinator, 530-898-5416, Fax: 530-898-3342, E-mail: jlrice@csuchico.edu.
Website: http://catalog.csuchico.edu/viewer/15/GEOS/

California State University, San Bernardino, Graduate Studies, College of Natural Sciences, Program in Earth and Environmental Sciences, San Bernardino, CA 92407. Offers MS. *Students:* 1 (woman) full-time, 4 part-time (1 woman); includes 1 minority (American Indian or Alaska Native, non-Hispanic/Latino). 7 applicants, 43% accepted, 1 enrolled. In 2015, 8 master's awarded. *Entrance requirements:* Additional exam requirements/recommendations for international students: Required—TOEFL. *Application deadline:* For fall admission, 7/16 for domestic students; for winter admission, 10/16 for domestic students; for spring admission, 1/22 for domestic students. Application fee: $55. *Expenses:* Tuition, state resident: full-time $7843; part-time $5011.20 per year. Tuition and fees vary according to course load, degree level, program and reciprocity agreements. *Unit head:* Dr. Joan E. Frysxell, Graduate Coordinator, 909-537-5311, E-mail: jfryxell@csusb.edu. *Application contact:* Dr. Jeffrey Thompson, Dean of Graduate Studies, 909-537-5058, E-mail: jthompso@csusb.edu.

Carleton University, Faculty of Graduate Studies, Faculty of Science, Department of Earth Sciences, Ottawa, ON K1S 5B6, Canada. Offers M Sc, PhD. Programs offered jointly with University of Ottawa. *Degree requirements:* For master's, thesis, seminar; for doctorate, comprehensive exam, thesis/dissertation, seminar. *Entrance requirements:* For master's, honors degree in science; for doctorate, M Sc. Additional exam requirements/recommendations for international students: Required—TOEFL. *Faculty research:* Resource geology, geophysics, basin analysis, lithosphere dynamics.

Case Western Reserve University, School of Graduate Studies, Department of Earth, Environmental, and Planetary Sciences, Cleveland, OH 44106. Offers MS, PhD. *Program availability:* Part-time. *Faculty:* 8 full-time (1 woman), 7 part-time/adjunct (1 woman). *Students:* 8 full-time (4 women), 3 international. Average age 28. 13 applicants, 31% accepted, 2 enrolled. Terminal master's awarded for partial completion of doctoral program. *Degree requirements:* For master's, thesis or alternative; for doctorate, thesis/dissertation. *Entrance requirements:* For master's and doctorate, GRE General Test, GRE Subject Test. Additional exam requirements/recommendations for international students: Required—TOEFL (minimum score 577 paper-based; 90 iBT); Recommended—IELTS (minimum score 7). *Application deadline:* For fall admission, 1/15 priority date for domestic students; for spring admission, 11/1 for domestic students. Applications are processed on a rolling basis. Application fee: $50. Electronic applications accepted. *Expenses: Tuition, area resident:* Full-time $41,137; part-time $1714 per credit hour. *Required fees:* $32. Tuition and fees vary according to course load and program. *Financial support:* Research assistantships, teaching assistantships, Federal Work-Study, and tuition waivers (partial) available. Support available to part-time students. Financial award application deadline: 1/15; financial award applicants required to submit FAFSA. *Faculty research:* Geochemistry, hydrology, ecology, geomorphology, planetary science, stratigraphy and basin analysis, igneous petrology. *Unit head:* James Van Orman, Professor and Chair, 216-368-3765, Fax: 216-368-3691, E-mail: james.vanorman@case.edu. *Application contact:* James Van Orman, Professor and Chair, 216-368-3765, Fax: 216-368-3691, E-mail: james.vanorman@case.edu.
Website: http://geology.case.edu/

City College of the City University of New York, Graduate School, Division of Science, Department of Earth and Atmospheric Sciences, New York, NY 10031-9198. Offers geology (MS). PhD program offered jointly with Graduate School and University Center of the City University of New York. *Degree requirements:* For master's, comprehensive exam, thesis. *Entrance requirements:* Additional exam requirements/recommendations for international students: Required—TOEFL (minimum score 500 paper-based; 61 iBT). *Application deadline:* For fall admission, 5/1 for domestic and international students; for spring admission, 11/15 for domestic and international students. Applications are processed on a rolling basis. Application fee: $125. Electronic applications accepted. Tuition and fees vary according to course load, degree level and program. *Financial support:* Fellowships, career-related internships or fieldwork, and scholarships/grants available. Financial award applicants required to submit FAFSA. *Faculty research:* Water resources, high-temperature geochemistry, sedimentary basin analysis, tectonics. *Unit head:* Pengfei Zhang, Chair, 212-650-6452, Fax: 212-650-6482, E-mail: pzhang@ccny.cuny.edu. *Application contact:* 216-650-6977, E-mail: gradadm@ccny.cuny.edu.
Website: http://www.ccny.cuny.edu/eas/

Colorado State University, Warner College of Natural Resources, Department of Geosciences, Fort Collins, CO 80523-1482. Offers earth sciences (PhD), including geosciences, watershed science; geosciences (MS). *Program availability:* Part-time. *Faculty:* 11 full-time (3 women), 4 part-time/adjunct (2 women). *Students:* 25 full-time (10 women), 48 part-time (24 women); includes 6 minority (1 Asian, non-Hispanic/Latino; 3 Hispanic/Latino; 2 Two or more races, non-Hispanic/Latino), 9 international. Average age 31. 91 applicants, 31% accepted, 17 enrolled. In 2015, 13 master's awarded. *Degree requirements:* For master's, thesis; for doctorate, comprehensive exam, thesis/dissertation. *Entrance requirements:* For master's and doctorate, GRE General Test, minimum GPA of 3.3, letters of recommendation. Additional exam requirements/recommendations for international students: Required—TOEFL (minimum score 550 paper-based; 80 iBT); Recommended—IELTS (minimum score 6). *Application deadline:* For fall admission, 1/1 priority date for domestic and international students; for spring admission, 9/1 for domestic and international students. Applications are processed on a rolling basis. Application fee: $60 ($70 for international students). Electronic applications accepted. *Expenses:* Tuition, state resident: full-time $9348. Tuition, nonresident: full-time $22,916. *Required fees:* $2174; $473.72 per credit hour. $236.86 per semester. Tuition and fees vary according to course load and program.

Financial support: In 2015–16, 4 fellowships (averaging $45,000 per year), 16 research assistantships with full tuition reimbursements (averaging $20,208 per year), 10 teaching assistantships with full tuition reimbursements (averaging $14,310 per year) were awarded; scholarships/grants also available. Financial award application deadline: 1/1; financial award applicants required to submit FAFSA. *Faculty research:* Applied geophysics, hydrogeology and hydrogeophysics, sedimentary petrology and geochemistry, seismology and tectonics, economic geology. *Total annual research expenditures:* $1.9 million. *Unit head:* Dr. Richard Aster, Professor and Department Head, 970-491-7606, Fax: 970-491-6307, E-mail: rick.aster@colostate.edu. *Application contact:* Sharon Gale, Graduate Contact, 970-491-5661, Fax: 970-491-6307, E-mail: sharon.gale@colostate.edu.
Website: http://warnercnr.colostate.edu/geosciences-home/

Columbia University, Graduate School of Arts and Sciences, New York, NY 10027. Offers African-American studies (MA); American studies (MA); anthropology (MA, PhD); art history and archaeology (MA, PhD); astronomy (PhD); biological sciences (PhD); biotechnology (MA); chemical physics (PhD); chemistry (PhD); classical studies (MA, PhD); classics (MA, PhD); climate and society (MA); conservation biology (MA); earth and environmental sciences (PhD); East Asia: regional studies (MA); East Asian languages and cultures (MA, PhD); ecology, evolution and environmental biology (MA), including conservation biology; ecology, evolution, and environmental biology (PhD), including ecology and evolutionary biology, evolutionary primatology; economics (MA, PhD); English and comparative literature (MA, PhD); French and Romance philology (MA, PhD); Germanic languages (MA, PhD); global French studies (MA); global thought (MA); Hispanic cultural studies (MA); history (PhD); history and literature (MA); human rights studies (MA); Islamic studies (MA); Italian (MA, PhD); Japanese pedagogy (MA); Jewish studies (MA); Latin America and the Caribbean: regional studies (MA); Latin American and Iberian cultures (PhD); mathematics (MA, PhD), including finance (MA); medieval and Renaissance studies (MA); Middle Eastern, South Asian, and African studies (MA, PhD); modern art: critical and curatorial studies (MA); modern European studies (MA); museum anthropology (MA); music (DMA, PhD); oral history (MA); philosophical foundations of physics (MA); philosophy (MA, PhD); physics (PhD); political science (MA, PhD); psychology (PhD); quantitative methods in the social sciences (MA); religion (MA, PhD); Russia, Eurasia and East Europe: regional studies (MA); Russian translation (MA); Slavic cultures (MA); Slavic languages (MA, PhD); sociology (MA, PhD); South Asian studies (MA); statistics (MA, PhD); theatre (PhD). Dual-degree programs require admission to both Graduate School of Arts and Sciences and another Columbia school. *Program availability:* Part-time. *Students:* 3,030 full-time, 235 part-time; includes 861 minority (88 Black or African American, non-Hispanic/Latino; 5 American Indian or Alaska Native, non-Hispanic/Latino; 517 Asian, non-Hispanic/Latino; 159 Hispanic/Latino; 4 Native Hawaiian or other Pacific Islander, non-Hispanic/Latino; 88 Two or more races, non-Hispanic/Latino), 1,697 international. 13,288 applicants, 21% accepted, 1162 enrolled. In 2015, 1,061 master's, 553 doctorates awarded. Terminal master's awarded for partial completion of doctoral program. *Degree requirements:* For master's, variable foreign language requirement, comprehensive exam (for some programs), thesis (for some programs); for doctorate, variable foreign language requirement, comprehensive exam (for some programs), thesis/dissertation. *Entrance requirements:* For master's and doctorate, GRE General Test, GRE Subject Test (for some programs). Additional exam requirements/recommendations for international students: Required—TOEFL, IELTS. Application fee: $105. Electronic applications accepted. *Financial support:* Fellowships, research assistantships, teaching assistantships, career-related internships or fieldwork, Federal Work-Study, institutionally sponsored loans, scholarships/grants, traineeships, health care benefits, tuition waivers, and unspecified assistantships available. Support available to part-time students. Financial award application deadline: 12/15. *Unit head:* Carlos J. Alonso, Dean of the Graduate School of Arts and Sciences, 212-854-5177. *Application contact:* GSAS Office of Admissions, 212-854-8903, E-mail: gsas-admissions@columbia.edu.
Website: http://gsas.columbia.edu/

Cornell University, Graduate School, Graduate Fields of Engineering, Field of Geological Sciences, Ithaca, NY 14853. Offers economic geology (M Eng, MS, PhD); engineering geology (M Eng, MS, PhD); environmental geophysics (M Eng, MS, PhD); general geology (M Eng, MS, PhD); geobiology (M Eng, MS, PhD); geochemistry and isotope geology (M Eng, MS, PhD); geohydrology (M Eng, MS, PhD); geomorphology (M Eng, MS, PhD); geophysics (M Eng, MS, PhD); geotectonics (M Eng, MS, PhD); marine geology (MS, PhD); mineralogy (M Eng, MS, PhD); paleontology (M Eng, MS, PhD); petroleum geology (M Eng, MS, PhD); petrology (M Eng, MS, PhD); planetary geology (M Eng, MS, PhD); Precambrian geology (M Eng, MS, PhD); Quaternary geology (M Eng, MS, PhD); rock mechanics (M Eng, MS, PhD); sedimentology (M Eng, MS, PhD); seismology (M Eng, MS, PhD); stratigraphy (M Eng, MS, PhD); structural geology (M Eng, MS, PhD). *Degree requirements:* For master's, thesis (MS); for doctorate, comprehensive exam, thesis/dissertation. *Entrance requirements:* For master's and doctorate, GRE General Test, 3 letters of recommendation. Additional exam requirements/recommendations for international students: Required—TOEFL (minimum score 550 paper-based; 77 iBT). Electronic applications accepted. *Faculty research:* Geophysics, structural geology, petrology, geochemistry, geodynamics.

Dalhousie University, Faculty of Science, Department of Earth Sciences, Halifax, NS B3H 4R2, Canada. Offers M Sc, PhD. *Degree requirements:* For master's, one foreign language, thesis; for doctorate, one foreign language, thesis/dissertation. *Entrance requirements:* Additional exam requirements/recommendations for international students: Required—TOEFL, IELTS, CANTEST, CAEL, or Michigan English Language Assessment Battery. *Faculty research:* Marine geology and geophysics, Appalachian and Grenville geology, micropaleontology, geodynamics and structural geology, geochronology.

Dartmouth College, Arts and Sciences Graduate Programs, Department of Earth Sciences, Hanover, NH 03755. Offers MS, PhD. *Faculty:* 11 full-time (3 women). *Students:* 23 full-time (15 women); includes 2 minority (both Asian, non-Hispanic/Latino), 4 international. Average age 26. 41 applicants, 22% accepted, 6 enrolled. In 2015, 4 master's, 2 doctorates awarded. Terminal master's awarded for partial completion of doctoral program. *Degree requirements:* For master's, thesis; for doctorate, thesis/dissertation, research project presentation and defense, qualifying exam. *Entrance requirements:* For master's and doctorate, GRE General Test, GRE Subject Test. Additional exam requirements/recommendations for international students: Required—TOEFL. *Application deadline:* For fall admission, 1/15 for domestic students. Application fee: $50. Electronic applications accepted. *Expenses: Tuition, area resident:* Full-time $48,120. *Required fees:* $296. One-time fee: $50 full-time. *Financial support:* Fellowships with full tuition reimbursements, research assistantships with full tuition reimbursements, teaching assistantships with full tuition reimbursements, career-related internships or fieldwork, institutionally sponsored loans, scholarships/grants, tuition waivers (full), and unspecified assistantships available. Financial award application deadline: 4/1; financial award applicants required to submit FAFSA. *Faculty research:* Geochemistry, remote sensing, geophysics, hydrology, economic geology. *Unit head:* Dr. William B. Dade, Chair, 603-646-0286. *Application contact:* Patty Alves, Department Administrator, 603-646-2373, Fax: 603-646-3922.
Website: http://www.dartmouth.edu/~earthsci/

Eastern Michigan University, Graduate School, College of Arts and Sciences, Department of Geography and Geology, Program in Earth Science Education, Ypsilanti, MI 48197. Offers MS. Application fee: $45.

East Tennessee State University, School of Graduate Studies, College of Arts and Sciences, Department of Geosciences, Johnson City, TN 37614. Offers geospatial analysis (MS); paleontology (MS). *Program availability:* Part-time. *Faculty:* 11 full-time (3 women). *Students:* 17 full-time (11 women), 3 part-time (2 women); includes 1 minority (Black or African American, non-Hispanic/Latino), 1 international. Average age 27. 30 applicants, 30% accepted, 5 enrolled. In 2015, 6 master's awarded. *Degree requirements:* For master's, thesis. *Entrance requirements:* For master's, bachelor's degree in geosciences or related discipline, minimum GPA of 3.0, three letters of recommendation, resume. Additional exam requirements/recommendations for international students: Required—TOEFL (minimum score 550 paper-based; 79 iBT). *Application deadline:* For fall admission, 2/1 for domestic and international students. Application fee: $35 ($45 for international students). Electronic applications accepted. *Financial support:* In 2015–16, 12 students received support, including 5 research assistantships with full tuition reimbursements available (averaging $8,000 per year), 9 teaching assistantships with full tuition reimbursements available (averaging $8,000 per year); career-related internships or fieldwork, institutionally sponsored loans, scholarships/grants, and unspecified assistantships also available. Financial award application deadline: 7/1; financial award applicants required to submit FAFSA. *Faculty research:* Vertebrate paleontology; volcanology; soils and geological engineering; geological hazards stemming from volcanoes and tsunamis and the sociological responses; applications of geospatial analysis to meteorology, weather and climate, and geomorphology/watershed management; shallow surface geophysics, sedimentology, and stratigraphy. *Unit head:* Dr. Jim Mead, Chair, 423-439-7515, Fax: 423-439-7520, E-mail: mead@etsu.edu. *Application contact:* Angela Edwards, Graduate Specialist, 423-439-4703, Fax: 423-439-5624, E-mail: edwardag@etsu.edu.
Website: http://www.etsu.edu/cas/geosciences/

Emporia State University, Department of Physical Sciences, Emporia, KS 66801-5415. Offers MS, Postbaccalaureate Certificate. *Program availability:* Part-time, online learning. *Faculty:* 15 full-time (5 women). *Students:* 16 full-time (7 women), 21 part-time (9 women); includes 1 minority (Two or more races, non-Hispanic/Latino), 17 international. 9 applicants, 100% accepted, 6 enrolled. In 2015, 12 master's, 2 other advanced degrees awarded. *Degree requirements:* For master's, comprehensive exam or thesis; qualifying exam. *Entrance requirements:* For master's, appropriate undergraduate degree. Additional exam requirements/recommendations for international students: Required—TOEFL (minimum score 520 paper-based; 68 iBT). *Application deadline:* For fall admission, 8/15 priority date for domestic students. Applications are processed on a rolling basis. Application fee: $30 ($75 for international students). Electronic applications accepted. *Expenses:* Tuition, state resident: full-time $5640; part-time $235 per credit hour. Tuition, nonresident: full-time $17,544; part-time $731 per credit hour. *Required fees:* $1848; $77 per credit hour. *Financial support:* In 2015–16, 2 research assistantships with full tuition reimbursements (averaging $7,344 per year), 8 teaching assistantships with full tuition reimbursements (averaging $7,844 per year) were awarded; Federal Work-Study, institutionally sponsored loans, health care benefits, and unspecified assistantships also available. Financial award application deadline: 3/15; financial award applicants required to submit FAFSA. *Faculty research:* Bredigite, larnite, and dicalcium silicates from Marble Canyon. *Unit head:* Dr. Kim Simons, Chair, 620-341-5330, Fax: 620-341-6055, E-mail: ksimons@emporia.edu. *Application contact:* Mary Sewell, Admissions Coordinator, 800-950-GRAD, Fax: 620-341-5909, E-mail: msewell@emporia.edu.
Website: http://www.emporia.edu/physci/

Florida Atlantic University, Charles E. Schmidt College of Science, Department of Geosciences, Boca Raton, FL 33431-0991. Offers geography (MA); geology (MS); geosciences (PhD). *Program availability:* Part-time. *Degree requirements:* For master's, thesis (for some programs). *Entrance requirements:* For master's, GRE General Test, minimum GPA of 3.0. Additional exam requirements/recommendations for international students: Required—TOEFL (minimum score 500 paper-based; 61 iBT), IELTS (minimum score 6). Electronic applications accepted. *Faculty research:* GIS applications, paleontology, hydrogeology, economic development.

Florida Institute of Technology, College of Engineering, Program in Earth Remote Sensing, Melbourne, FL 32901-6975. Offers MS. *Program availability:* Part-time. *Students:* 1 (woman) full-time. 7 applicants, 14% accepted. In 2015, 1 master's awarded. *Degree requirements:* For master's, thesis or final exam. *Entrance requirements:* For master's, GRE General Test, 3 letters of recommendation, resume, statement of objectives. Additional exam requirements/recommendations for international students: Required—TOEFL (minimum score 550 paper-based; 79 iBT). *Application deadline:* Applications are processed on a rolling basis. Electronic applications accepted. *Expenses: Tuition, area resident:* Full-time $21,690; part-time $1205 per credit hour. *Required fees:* $500. Tuition and fees vary according to degree level, campus/location and program. *Financial support:* Applicants required to submit FAFSA. *Unit head:* Dr. Thomas Waite, Department Head, 321-674-7344, E-mail: twaite@fit.edu. *Application contact:* Cheryl A. Brown, Associate Director of Graduate Admissions, 321-674-7581, Fax: 321-723-9468, E-mail: cbrown@fit.edu.
Website: http://coe.fit.edu/dmes/

Florida International University, College of Arts, Sciences, and Education, Department of Earth and Environment, Program in Geosciences, Miami, FL 33199. Offers MS, PhD. *Program availability:* Part-time, evening/weekend. *Faculty:* 26 full-time (6 women), 11 part-time/adjunct (2 women). *Students:* 38 full-time (16 women), 5 part-time (all women); includes 15 minority (14 Hispanic/Latino; 1 Two or more races, non-Hispanic/Latino), 11 international. Average age 30. 32 applicants, 28% accepted, 9 enrolled. In 2015, 6 master's, 4 doctorates awarded. *Degree requirements:* For master's, thesis optional; for doctorate, comprehensive exam, thesis/dissertation. *Entrance requirements:* For master's, GRE (minimum score of 1000), minimum GPA of 3.0 during last two years of undergraduate study, letter of intent, 3 letters of recommendation, resume; for doctorate, GRE (minimum score of 1120), minimum GPA of 3.0 during last two years of undergraduate study, letter of intent, 3 letters of recommendation, resume. Additional exam requirements/recommendations for international students: Required—TOEFL (minimum score 550 paper-based; 80 iBT). *Application deadline:* For fall admission, 2/15 for domestic and international students; for spring admission, 9/1 for domestic and international students. Application fee: $30. Electronic applications accepted. *Expenses:* Tuition, state resident: full-time $10,708; part-time $455.64 per credit hour. Tuition, nonresident: full-time $23,816; part-time $1001.69 per credit hour. *Required fees:* $390; $195 per semester. Tuition and fees vary according to program. *Financial support:* Institutionally sponsored loans and scholarships/grants available. Financial award application deadline: 3/1; financial award applicants required to submit FAFSA. *Total annual research expenditures:* $30. *Unit head:* Dr. Rene Price, Chair, 305-

348-3119, E-mail: rene.price@fiu.edu. *Application contact:* Nanett Rojas, Manager Admissions Operations, 305-348-7464, E-mail: gradadm@fiu.edu.

Florida State University, The Graduate School, College of Arts and Sciences, Department of Scientific Computing, Tallahassee, FL 32306-4120. Offers computational science (MS, PhD), including atmospheric science (PhD), biochemistry (PhD), biological science (PhD), computational science (PhD), geological science (PhD), materials science (PhD), physics (PhD). *Program availability:* Part-time. *Faculty:* 14 full-time (2 women). *Students:* 32 full-time (4 women), 7 part-time (1 woman); includes 14 minority (9 Asian, non-Hispanic/Latino; 3 Hispanic/Latino; 2 Two or more races, non-Hispanic/Latino). Average age 27. 28 applicants, 43% accepted, 7 enrolled. In 2015, 9 master's, 7 doctorates awarded. *Degree requirements:* For master's, thesis (for some programs); for doctorate, comprehensive exam, thesis/dissertation. *Entrance requirements:* For master's and doctorate, GRE General Test, knowledge of at least one object-oriented computing language, 3 letters of recommendation, resume, statement of purpose. Additional exam requirements/recommendations for international students: Required—TOEFL (minimum score 550 paper-based; 80 iBT). *Application deadline:* For fall admission, 1/15 for domestic and international students. Application fee: $30. Electronic applications accepted. *Expenses: Tuition, area resident:* Full-time $7263; part-time $403.50 per credit hour. Tuition, nonresident: full-time $18,087; part-time $1004.85 per credit hour. *Required fees:* $1365; $75.81 per credit hour. $20 per semester. Tuition and fees vary according to campus/location. *Financial support:* In 2015–16, 33 students received support, including 10 research assistantships with full tuition reimbursements available (averaging $20,000 per year), 23 teaching assistantships with full tuition reimbursements available (averaging $20,000 per year); scholarships/grants and unspecified assistantships also available. Financial award application deadline: 1/15. *Faculty research:* Morphometrics, mathematical and systems biology, mining proteomic and metabolic data, computational materials research, advanced 4-D Var data-assimilation methods in dynamic meteorology and oceanography, computational fluid dynamics, astrophysics. *Unit head:* Dr. Gordon Erlebacher, Chair, 850-644-7024, E-mail: gerlebacher@fsu.edu. *Application contact:* Mark Howard, Academic Program Specialist, 850-644-0143, Fax: 850-644-0098, E-mail: mlhoward@fsu.edu.
Website: http://www.sc.fsu.edu

Fort Hays State University, Graduate School, College of Arts and Sciences, Department of Geosciences, Program in Geosciences, Hays, KS 67601-4099. Offers geography (MS); geology (MS). *Degree requirements:* For master's, comprehensive exam, thesis. *Entrance requirements:* For master's, GRE General Test. Additional exam requirements/recommendations for international students: Required—TOEFL (minimum score 550 paper-based). Electronic applications accepted. *Faculty research:* Cretaceous and late Cenozoic stratigraphy, sedimentation, paleontology.

George Mason University, College of Science, Department of Geography and Geoinformation Science, Fairfax, VA 22030. Offers earth system science (MS); earth systems and geoinformation sciences (PhD); geography and geoinformation science (Certificate). *Faculty:* 18 full-time (3 women), 7 part-time/adjunct (1 woman). *Students:* 58 full-time (16 women), 116 part-time (33 women); includes 24 minority (6 Black or African American, non-Hispanic/Latino; 1 American Indian or Alaska Native, non-Hispanic/Latino; 9 Asian, non-Hispanic/Latino; 7 Hispanic/Latino; 1 Two or more races, non-Hispanic/Latino), 25 international. Average age 36. 92 applicants, 77% accepted, 38 enrolled. In 2015, 27 master's, 9 doctorates, 20 other advanced degrees awarded. *Degree requirements:* For master's, thesis optional. *Entrance requirements:* For master's, GRE (waived for those who have earned a master's degree from U.S. institution), bachelor's degree with minimum GPA of 3.0; 2 copies of official transcripts; current resume; expanded goals statement; 3 letters of recommendation; for doctorate, GRE (waived for those who have earned a master's degree from U.S. institution), bachelor's degree with minimum GPA of 3.0; 2 copies of official transcripts; 3 letters of recommendation; resume; expanded goals statement; for Certificate, GRE (waived for those who have earned a master's degree from U.S. institution), baccalaureate degree with minimum GPA of 3.0; 2 official copies of transcripts; expanded goals statement; 3 letters of recommendation; resume. Additional exam requirements/recommendations for international students: Required—TOEFL (minimum score 575 paper-based; 88 iBT), IELTS (minimum score 6.5), PTE (minimum score 59). *Application deadline:* For fall admission, 2/1 priority date for domestic students. Application fee: $75 ($80 for international students). Electronic applications accepted. *Financial support:* In 2015–16, 31 students received support, including 23 research assistantships with tuition reimbursements available (averaging $15,292 per year), 8 teaching assistantships with tuition reimbursements available (averaging $14,022 per year); career-related internships or fieldwork, Federal Work-Study, scholarships/grants, unspecified assistantships, and health care benefits (for full-time research or teaching assistantship recipients) also available. Support available to part-time students. Financial award application deadline: 3/1; financial award applicants required to submit FAFSA. *Faculty research:* Global environment climate monitoring, gender and earth science, earth science education, remote sensing, planetary geology, hydrology, theoretical issues of geographic information data acquisition and processing. *Total annual research expenditures:* $1.7 million. *Unit head:* Anthony Stefanidis, Acting Chair, 703-993-9237, Fax: 703-993-9230, E-mail: astefani@gmu.edu.
Website: http://ggs.gmu.edu/

Georgia Institute of Technology, Graduate Studies, College of Sciences, School of Earth and Atmospheric Sciences, Atlanta, GA 30332-0340. Offers MS, PhD. *Program availability:* Part-time. Terminal master's awarded for partial completion of doctoral program. *Degree requirements:* For master's, thesis optional; for doctorate, comprehensive exam, thesis/dissertation. *Entrance requirements:* For master's and doctorate, GRE. Additional exam requirements/recommendations for international students: Required—TOEFL (minimum score 550 paper-based; 79 iBT). Electronic applications accepted. *Faculty research:* Geophysics; atmospheric chemistry, aerosols and clouds; dynamics of weather and climate; geochemistry; oceanography; paleoclimate; planetary science; remote sensing.

Georgia State University, College of Arts and Sciences, Department of Geosciences, Atlanta, GA 30302-3083. Offers geographic information systems (Certificate); geography (MS); geology (MS). *Program availability:* Part-time. *Faculty:* 9 full-time (3 women). *Students:* 41 full-time (13 women), 7 part-time (4 women); includes 7 minority (4 Black or African American, non-Hispanic/Latino; 1 Hispanic/Latino; 2 Two or more races, non-Hispanic/Latino), 7 international. Average age 31. 25 applicants, 72% accepted, 13 enrolled. In 2015, 8 master's, 7 other advanced degrees awarded. *Degree requirements:* For master's, one foreign language, comprehensive exam (for some programs), thesis. *Entrance requirements:* For master's and Certificate, GRE. Additional exam requirements/recommendations for international students: Required—TOEFL (minimum score 550 paper-based; 80 iBT). *Application deadline:* For fall admission, 4/15 for domestic and international students; for spring admission, 11/15 for domestic and international students. Applications are processed on a rolling basis. Application fee: $50. Electronic applications accepted. *Expenses:* Tuition, state resident: full-time $6876; part-time $382 per credit hour. Tuition, nonresident: full-time $22,374; part-time $1243 per credit hour. *Required fees:* $2128; $2128 per term. $1064 per term. Part-time tuition and fees vary according to course load and program. *Financial support:* In 2015–16, research assistantships with full tuition reimbursements (averaging $12,000 per year), teaching assistantships with full tuition reimbursements (averaging $6,000 per year) were awarded; fellowships, career-related internships or fieldwork, Federal Work-Study, and unspecified assistantships also available. Support available to part-time students. Financial award application deadline: 4/15; financial award applicants required to submit FAFSA. *Faculty research:* Sedimentology, mineralogy, climatology, geographic information science, hydrology. *Unit head:* Dr. W. Crawford Elliott, Chair, 404-413-5756, Fax: 404-413-5768, E-mail: wcelliott@gsu.edu.
Website: http://geosciences.gsu.edu/

Georgia State University, College of Education, Department of Middle and Secondary Education, Atlanta, GA 30302-3083. Offers curriculum and instruction (Ed D); English education (MAT); mathematics education (M Ed, MAT); middle level education (MAT); reading, language and literacy education (M Ed, MAT), including reading instruction (M Ed); science education (M Ed, MAT), including biology (MAT), broad field science (MAT), chemistry (MAT), earth science (MAT), physics (MAT); social studies education (M Ed, MAT), including economics (MAT), geography (MAT), history (MAT), political science (MAT); teaching and learning (PhD), including language and literacy, mathematics education, music education, science education, social studies education, teaching and teacher education. *Accreditation:* NCATE. *Program availability:* Part-time, evening/weekend, online learning. *Faculty:* 19 full-time (15 women). *Students:* 153 full-time (109 women), 174 part-time (122 women); includes 145 minority (112 Black or African American, non-Hispanic/Latino; 1 American Indian or Alaska Native, non-Hispanic/Latino; 10 Asian, non-Hispanic/Latino; 17 Hispanic/Latino; 5 Two or more races, non-Hispanic/Latino), 9 international. Average age 35. 68 applicants, 75% accepted, 38 enrolled. In 2015, 63 master's awarded. *Degree requirements:* For master's, comprehensive exam (for some programs), thesis or alternative, exit portfolio; for doctorate, comprehensive exam, thesis/dissertation. *Entrance requirements:* For master's, GRE; GACE I (for initial teacher preparation programs), baccalaureate degree or equivalent, resume, goals statement, two letters of recommendation, minimum undergraduate GPA of 2.5; proof of initial teacher certification in the content area (for M Ed); for doctorate, GRE, resume, goals statement, writing sample, two letters of recommendation, minimum graduate GPA of 3.3, interview. Additional exam requirements/recommendations for international students: Required—TOEFL (minimum score 550 paper-based; 79 iBT) or IELTS (minimum score 6.5). *Application deadline:* For fall admission, 1/15 priority date for domestic and international students; for spring admission, 10/1 for domestic and international students. Application fee: $50. Electronic applications accepted. *Expenses:* Tuition, state resident: full-time $6876; part-time $382 per credit hour. Tuition, nonresident: full-time $22,374; part-time $1243 per credit hour. *Required fees:* $2128; $2128 per term. $1064 per term. Part-time tuition and fees vary according to course load and program. *Financial support:* In 2015–16, fellowships with full tuition reimbursements (averaging $19,667 per year), research assistantships with full tuition reimbursements (averaging $5,436 per year), teaching assistantships with full tuition reimbursements (averaging $2,779 per year) were awarded; career-related internships or fieldwork, Federal Work-Study, scholarships/grants, health care benefits, tuition waivers (full and partial), and unspecified assistantships also available. Financial award application deadline: 3/15. *Faculty research:* Teacher education in language and literacy, mathematics, science, and social studies in urban middle and secondary school settings; learning technologies in school, community, and corporate settings; multicultural education and education for social justice; urban education; international education. *Unit head:* Dr. Dana L. Fox, Chair, 404-413-8060, Fax: 404-413-8063, E-mail: dfox@gsu.edu. *Application contact:* Bobbie Turner, Administrative Coordinator I, 404-413-8405, Fax: 404-413-8063, E-mail: bnturner@gsu.edu.
Website: http://mse.education.gsu.edu/

The Graduate Center, City University of New York, Graduate Studies, Program in Earth and Environmental Sciences, New York, NY 10016-4039. Offers PhD. *Degree requirements:* For doctorate, one foreign language, comprehensive exam, thesis/dissertation. *Entrance requirements:* For doctorate, GRE General Test. Additional exam requirements/recommendations for international students: Required—TOEFL. Electronic applications accepted.

Harvard University, Graduate School of Arts and Sciences, Department of Earth and Planetary Sciences, Cambridge, MA 02138. Offers AM, PhD. Terminal master's awarded for partial completion of doctoral program. *Degree requirements:* For doctorate, comprehensive exam, thesis/dissertation. *Entrance requirements:* For doctorate, GRE General Test. Additional exam requirements/recommendations for international students: Required—TOEFL. Electronic applications accepted. *Faculty research:* Economic geography, geochemistry, geophysics, mineralogy, crystallography.

Hunter College of the City University of New York, Graduate School, School of Education, Programs in Secondary Education, New York, NY 10065-5085. Offers biology education (MA); chemistry education (MA); earth science (MA); English education (MA); French education (MA); Italian education (MA); mathematics education (MA); physics education (MA); social studies education (MA); Spanish education (MA). *Accreditation:* NCATE. *Degree requirements:* For master's, thesis. *Entrance requirements:* Additional exam requirements/recommendations for international students: Required—TOEFL.

Idaho State University, Office of Graduate Studies, College of Science and Engineering, Department of Geosciences, Pocatello, ID 83209-8072. Offers geographic information science (MS); geology (MNS, MS); geology with emphasis in environmental geoscience (MS); geophysics/hydrology/geology (MS); geotechnology (Postbaccalaureate Certificate). *Program availability:* Part-time. *Degree requirements:* For master's, comprehensive exam, thesis, oral colloquium; for Postbaccalaureate Certificate, thesis optional, minimum 19 credits. *Entrance requirements:* For master's, GRE General Test (minimum 50th percentile in 2 sections), 3 letters of recommendation; for Postbaccalaureate Certificate, GRE General Test, 3 letters of recommendation, bachelor's degree, statement of goals. Additional exam requirements/recommendations for international students: Required—TOEFL (minimum score 550 paper-based; 80 iBT). Electronic applications accepted. *Faculty research:* Quantitative field mapping and sampling: microscopic, geochemical, and isotopic analysis of rocks, minerals and water; remote sensing, geographic information systems, and global positioning systems: environmental and watershed management; surficial and fluvial processes: landscape change; regional tectonics, structural geology; planetary geology.

Indiana University Bloomington, University Graduate School, College of Arts and Sciences, Department of Geological Sciences, Bloomington, IN 47405-7000. Offers biogeochemistry (MS, PhD); economic geology (MS, PhD); geobiology (MS, PhD); geophysics, structural geology and tectonics (MS, PhD); hydrogeology (MS, PhD); mineralogy (MS, PhD); stratigraphy and sedimentology (MS, PhD). Terminal master's awarded for partial completion of doctoral program. *Degree requirements:* For master's, thesis or alternative; for doctorate, comprehensive exam, thesis/dissertation. *Entrance requirements:* For master's and doctorate, GRE General Test. Additional exam requirements/recommendations for international students: Required—TOEFL. *Faculty research:* Geophysics, geochemistry, hydrogeology, geobiology, planetary science.

Geosciences

Indiana University–Purdue University Indianapolis, School of Science, Department of Earth Sciences, Indianapolis, IN 46202-3272. Offers applied earth sciences (PhD); geology (MS). *Program availability:* Part-time, evening/weekend. *Degree requirements:* For master's, thesis (for some programs). *Entrance requirements:* For master's, GRE General Test, minimum GPA of 3.0. *Faculty research:* Wetland hydrology, groundwater contamination, soils, sedimentology, sediment chemistry.

Iowa State University of Science and Technology, Department of Geological and Atmospheric Sciences, Ames, IA 50011. Offers earth science (MS, PhD); environmental science (MS, PhD); geology (MS, PhD); meteorology (MS, PhD). *Degree requirements:* For master's, thesis (for some programs); for doctorate, thesis/dissertation. *Entrance requirements:* For master's and doctorate, GRE General Test. Additional exam requirements/recommendations for international students: Required—TOEFL (minimum score 550 paper-based; 79 iBT), IELTS (minimum score 6.5). Electronic applications accepted.

Iowa State University of Science and Technology, Program in Earth Science, Ames, IA 50011. Offers MS, PhD. *Entrance requirements:* For master's and doctorate, GRE. Additional exam requirements/recommendations for international students: Required—TOEFL (minimum score 550 paper-based; 79 iBT), IELTS (minimum score 6.5). Electronic applications accepted.

Johns Hopkins University, School of Education, Master's Programs in Education, Baltimore, MD 21218. Offers counseling (MS), including clinical mental health counseling, school counseling; education (MS), including educational studies, gifted education, reading, school administration and supervision, technology for educators; elementary education (MAT); health professions (M Ed); intelligence analysis (MS); organizational leadership (MS); secondary education (MAT), including biology, chemistry, earth/space science, English, mathematics, physics, science, social studies; special education (MS), including early childhood special education, general special education studies, mild to moderate disabilities, severe disabilities. *Program availability:* Part-time, evening/weekend, 100% online, blended/hybrid learning. *Students:* 302 full-time (241 women), 1,472 part-time (1,106 women); includes 710 minority (313 Black or African American, non-Hispanic/Latino; 6 American Indian or Alaska Native, non-Hispanic/Latino; 133 Asian, non-Hispanic/Latino; 167 Hispanic/Latino; 11 Native Hawaiian or other Pacific Islander, non-Hispanic/Latino; 80 Two or more races, non-Hispanic/Latino), 46 international. Average age 28. 1,717 applicants, 69% accepted, 904 enrolled. In 2015, 623 master's awarded. *Degree requirements:* For master's, comprehensive exam (for some programs), portfolio, capstone project and/or internship; PRAXIS II Core (for teacher preparation programs that lead to licensure). *Entrance requirements:* For master's, GRE (for full-time programs only); PRAXIS I or state approved alternative (for teacher preparation programs that lead to licensure), minimum of a bachelor's degree from regionally- or nationally-accredited institution; minimum GPA of 3.0 in all previous programs of study; official transcripts from all post-secondary institutions attended; essay; curriculum vitae/resume; letters of recommendation (3 for full-time, 2 for part-time). Additional exam requirements/recommendations for international students: Required—TOEFL (minimum score 600 paper-based; 100 iBT), IELTS (minimum score 7). *Application deadline:* For fall admission, 4/1 for domestic and international students; for spring admission, 10/1 for domestic and international students; for summer admission, 2/1 for domestic and international students. Application fee: $80. Electronic applications accepted. *Expenses:* Contact institution. *Financial support:* Applicants required to submit FAFSA. *Unit head:* Dr. Mariale M. Hardiman, Interim Dean, 410-516-7820, Fax: 410-516-6697, E-mail: mmhardiman@jhu.edu. *Application contact:* Rhodri Evans, Director of Enrollment Services, 410-516-0741, Fax: 410-516-6697, E-mail: revans@jhu.edu.

Johns Hopkins University, Zanvyl Krieger School of Arts and Sciences, The Morton K. Blaustein Department of Earth and Planetary Sciences, Baltimore, MD 21218. Offers MA, PhD. *Degree requirements:* For doctorate, comprehensive exam, thesis/dissertation. *Entrance requirements:* For master's and doctorate, GRE General Test. Additional exam requirements/recommendations for international students: Required—TOEFL (minimum score 600 paper-based; 100 iBT), IELTS. Electronic applications accepted. *Faculty research:* Oceanography, atmospheric sciences, geophysics, geology, geochemistry.

Lehigh University, College of Arts and Sciences, Department of Earth and Environmental Sciences, Bethlehem, PA 18015. Offers MS, PhD. *Faculty:* 14 full-time (2 women). *Students:* 21 full-time (9 women), 3 part-time (1 woman), 6 international. Average age 27. 46 applicants, 24% accepted, 8 enrolled. In 2015, 3 master's, 2 doctorates awarded. Terminal master's awarded for partial completion of doctoral program. *Degree requirements:* For master's, thesis; for doctorate, thesis/dissertation. *Entrance requirements:* For master's and doctorate, GRE General Test, transcripts, recommendation letters, research statement, faculty advocates. Additional exam requirements/recommendations for international students: Required—TOEFL (minimum score 85 iBT). *Application deadline:* For fall admission, 1/1 for domestic and international students. Application fee: $75. Electronic applications accepted. *Expenses:* $1,380 per credit. *Financial support:* In 2015–16, 14 students received support, including 5 fellowships with full tuition reimbursements available (averaging $25,377 per year), 6 research assistantships with full tuition reimbursements available (averaging $20,250 per year), 10 teaching assistantships with full tuition reimbursements available (averaging $20,250 per year); scholarships/grants also available. Financial award application deadline: 1/1. *Faculty research:* Tectonics, surficial processes, ecology, environmental change, remote sensing. *Total annual research expenditures:* $1.1 million. *Unit head:* Dr. David J. Anastasio, Chairman, 610-758-5117, Fax: 610-758-3677, E-mail: dja2@lehigh.edu. *Application contact:* Dr. Kenneth Kodama, Graduate Coordinator, 610-758-3663, Fax: 610-758-3677, E-mail: kpk0@lehigh.edu.
Website: http://www.ees.lehigh.edu/

Loma Linda University, School of Science and Technology, Department of Biological and Earth Sciences, Loma Linda, CA 92350. Offers MS, PhD. *Degree requirements:* For master's, comprehensive exam, thesis; for doctorate, comprehensive exam, thesis/dissertation. *Entrance requirements:* For master's, minimum GPA of 3.0. Additional exam requirements/recommendations for international students: Required—TOEFL (minimum score 550 paper-based).

Long Island University–LIU Post, College of Liberal Arts and Sciences, Brookville, NY 11548-1300. Offers applied mathematics (MS); behavior analysis (MA); biology (MS); criminal justice (MS); earth science (MS); English (MA); environmental studies (MS); environmental sustainability (MS); genetic counseling (MS); gerontology (Advanced Certificate); health care administration (MPA); history (MA); interdisciplinary studies (MA, MS); mathematics for secondary school teachers (MS); mobile GIS application development (Advanced Certificate); non-profit management (Advanced Certificate); political science (MA); psychology (MA); public administration (MPA). *Program availability:* Part-time, evening/weekend, online learning. *Faculty:* 77 full-time (35 women), 36 part-time/adjunct (17 women). *Students:* 254 full-time (178 women), 177 part-time (134 women); includes 104 minority (40 Black or African American, non-Hispanic/Latino; 27 Asian, non-Hispanic/Latino; 28 Hispanic/Latino; 1 Native Hawaiian or other Pacific Islander, non-Hispanic/Latino; 8 Two or more races, non-Hispanic/Latino), 44 international. Average age 31. 686 applicants, 47% accepted, 138 enrolled. In 2015, 135 master's awarded. *Degree requirements:* For master's, comprehensive exam (for some programs), thesis (for some programs). *Entrance requirements:* Additional exam requirements/recommendations for international students: Required—TOEFL (minimum score 550 paper-based; 79 iBT), IELTS (minimum score 6.5). *Application deadline:* Applications are processed on a rolling basis. Application fee: $50. Electronic applications accepted. *Expenses:* $1155 per credit; $934 full-time fees; $442 part-time fees. *Financial support:* In 2015–16, 48 fellowships (averaging $12,637 per year), 5 research assistantships with full tuition reimbursements were awarded; Federal Work-Study and institutionally sponsored loans also available. Support available to part-time students. Financial award application deadline: 2/15; financial award applicants required to submit FAFSA. *Faculty research:* Biology, criminal justice, earth and environmental science, English, health care and public administration, history, mathematics, political science, psychology, Spanish. *Unit head:* Dr. Nicholas J. Ramer, Acting Dean, 516-299-2233, Fax: 516-299-4140, E-mail: nicholas.ramer@liu.edu. *Application contact:* Carol Zerah, Director of Graduate Admissions, 516-299-2900 Ext. 3952, Fax: 516-299-2137, E-mail: enroll@cwpost.liu.edu.
Website: http://liu.edu/CWPost/Academics/Schools/CLAS

Massachusetts Institute of Technology, School of Science, Department of Earth, Atmospheric, and Planetary Sciences, Cambridge, MA 02139. Offers atmospheric chemistry (PhD, Sc D); atmospheric science (SM, PhD, Sc D); chemical oceanography (SM, PhD, Sc D); climate physics and chemistry (SM, PhD, Sc D); earth and planetary sciences (SM); geochemistry (PhD, Sc D); geology (PhD, Sc D); geophysics (PhD, Sc D); marine geology and geophysics (SM, PhD, Sc D); physical oceanography (SM, PhD, Sc D); planetary sciences (PhD, Sc D). *Faculty:* 36 full-time (8 women). *Students:* 166 full-time (75 women), 1 part-time (0 women); includes 23 minority (1 Black or African American, non-Hispanic/Latino; 7 Asian, non-Hispanic/Latino; 6 Hispanic/Latino; 9 Two or more races, non-Hispanic/Latino), 54 international. Average age 27. 228 applicants, 26% accepted, 33 enrolled. In 2015, 6 master's, 24 doctorates awarded. Terminal master's awarded for partial completion of doctoral program. *Degree requirements:* For master's, thesis; for doctorate, comprehensive exam, thesis/dissertation. *Entrance requirements:* For master's, GRE General Test; for doctorate, GRE General Test, GRE Subject Test in chemistry or physics (for planetary sciences area). Additional exam requirements/recommendations for international students: Required—TOEFL (minimum score 600 paper-based; 100 iBT), IELTS (minimum score 7). *Application deadline:* For fall admission, 1/5 for domestic and international students; for spring admission, 11/1 for domestic and international students. Application fee: $75. Electronic applications accepted. *Expenses: Tuition:* Full-time $46,400; part-time $725 per credit. One-time fee: $304 full-time. Full-time tuition and fees vary according to course load and program. *Financial support:* In 2015–16, 99 students received support, including 60 fellowships (averaging $40,700 per year), 76 research assistantships (averaging $38,000 per year), 15 teaching assistantships (averaging $36,100 per year); Federal Work-Study, institutionally sponsored loans, scholarships/grants, traineeships, health care benefits, and unspecified assistantships also available. Support available to part-time students. Financial award application deadline: 4/15; financial award applicants required to submit FAFSA. *Faculty research:* Earth: origin, composition, structure, and dynamics of (and interactions between) the atmosphere, oceans, surface, and interior of the earth; planets: formation, dynamics, and evolution of planetary systems and the characterization of exoplanets; climate: characterization of past, present, and potential future climates; studies of the causes and consequences of climate change; life: co-evolution of life and environmental systems. *Total annual research expenditures:* $25.3 million. *Unit head:* Prof. Robert van der Hilst, Department Head, 617-253-2127, Fax: 617-253-8298, E-mail: eapsinfo@mit.edu. *Application contact:* EAPS Education Office, 617-253-3381, Fax: 617-253-8298, E-mail: eapsinfo@mit.edu.
Website: http://eapsweb.mit.edu/

McGill University, Faculty of Graduate and Postdoctoral Studies, Faculty of Science, Department of Earth and Planetary Sciences, Montréal, QC H3A 2T5, Canada. Offers M Sc, PhD.

McMaster University, School of Graduate Studies, Faculty of Science, School of Geography and Earth Sciences, Hamilton, ON L8S 4M2, Canada. Offers geochemistry (PhD); geology (M Sc, PhD); human geography (MA, PhD); physical geography (M Sc, PhD). *Program availability:* Part-time. Terminal master's awarded for partial completion of doctoral program. *Degree requirements:* For master's, thesis; for doctorate, comprehensive exam, thesis/dissertation. *Entrance requirements:* For master's, minimum B+ average. Additional exam requirements/recommendations for international students: Required—TOEFL (minimum score 550 paper-based).

Memorial University of Newfoundland, School of Graduate Studies, Department of Earth Sciences, St. John's, NL A1C 5S7, Canada. Offers geology (M Sc, PhD); geophysics (M Sc, PhD). *Program availability:* Part-time. *Degree requirements:* For master's, thesis; for doctorate, comprehensive exam, thesis/dissertation, oral thesis defense, entry evaluation. *Entrance requirements:* For master's, honors B Sc; for doctorate, M Sc. *Application deadline:* 1/15 for domestic and international students. Applications are processed on a rolling basis. Application fee: $50 Canadian dollars ($100 Canadian dollars for international students). Electronic applications accepted. *Expenses: Tuition, area resident:* Full-time $2199 Canadian dollars. *International tuition:* $2859 Canadian dollars full-time. *Financial support:* Fellowships, research assistantships, and teaching assistantships available. *Faculty research:* Geochemistry, sedimentology, paleoceanography and global change, mineral deposits, petroleum geology, hydrology. *Unit head:* Dr. John Hanchar, Head, 709-864-2334, Fax: 709-864-2589. *Application contact:* Michelle Miskell, Graduate Officer, 709-864-4464, Fax: 709-864-2589, E-mail: mmiskell@mun.ca.
Website: http://www.mun.ca/earthsciences/

Michigan State University, The Graduate School, College of Natural Science, Department of Geological Sciences, East Lansing, MI 48824. Offers environmental geosciences (MS, PhD); environmental geosciences-environmental toxicology (PhD); geological sciences (MS, PhD). *Degree requirements:* For master's, thesis (for those without prior thesis work); for doctorate, thesis/dissertation. *Entrance requirements:* For master's, GRE General Test, minimum GPA of 3.0, course work in geoscience, 3 letters of recommendation; for doctorate, GRE General Test, 3 letters of recommendation. Additional exam requirements/recommendations for international students: Required—TOEFL (minimum score 550 paper-based), Michigan State University ELT (minimum score 85), Michigan English Language Assessment Battery (minimum score 83). Electronic applications accepted. *Faculty research:* Water in the environment, global and biological change, crystal dynamics.

Middle Tennessee State University, College of Graduate Studies, College of Liberal Arts, Department of Geosciences, Murfreesboro, TN 37132. Offers Graduate Certificate. *Program availability:* Part-time, evening/weekend, online learning. *Entrance requirements:* Additional exam requirements/recommendations for international students: Required—TOEFL (minimum score 525 paper-based; 71 iBT) or IELTS (minimum score 6). Electronic applications accepted.

Mississippi State University, College of Arts and Sciences, Department of Geosciences, Mississippi State, MS 39762. Offers applied meteorology (MS); broadcast meteorology (MS); earth and atmospheric science (PhD); environmental geoscience (MS); geography (MS); geology (MS); geospatial sciences (MS); professional meteorology/climatology (MS); teachers in geoscience (MS). *Program availability:* Online learning. *Faculty:* 18 full-time (4 women), 1 part-time/adjunct (0 women). *Students:* 53 full-time (27 women), 176 part-time (81 women); includes 26 minority (7 Black or African American, non-Hispanic/Latino; 3 Asian, non-Hispanic/Latino; 10 Hispanic/Latino; 1 Native Hawaiian or other Pacific Islander, non-Hispanic/Latino; 5 Two or more races, non-Hispanic/Latino), 5 international. Average age 33. 123 applicants, 73% accepted, 68 enrolled. In 2015, 70 master's, 3 doctorates awarded. *Degree requirements:* For master's, thesis (for some programs), comprehensive oral or written exam; for doctorate, thesis/dissertation, comprehensive oral or written exam. *Entrance requirements:* For master's, GRE (for on-campus applicants), minimum undergraduate GPA of 2.75; for doctorate, thesis-based MS with background in one department emphasis area. Additional exam requirements/recommendations for international students: Required—TOEFL (minimum score 477 paper-based; 53 iBT); Recommended—IELTS (minimum score 4.5). *Application deadline:* For fall admission, 7/1 for domestic students, 5/1 for international students; for spring admission, 11/1 for domestic students, 9/1 for international students. Applications are processed on a rolling basis. Application fee: $60. Electronic applications accepted. *Expenses: Tuition, area resident:* Full-time $7502; part-time $833.74 per credit hour. Tuition, nonresident: full-time $20,142; part-time $2238.24 per credit hour. *Financial support:* In 2015–16, 7 research assistantships with full tuition reimbursements (averaging $13,792 per year), 28 teaching assistantships with full tuition reimbursements (averaging $13,500 per year) were awarded; Federal Work-Study, institutionally sponsored loans, scholarships/grants, tuition waivers (partial), and unspecified assistantships also available. Financial award application deadline: 4/1; financial award applicants required to submit FAFSA. *Faculty research:* Climatology, hydrogeology, sedimentology, meteorology. *Total annual research expenditures:* $3.1 million. *Unit head:* Dr. William Cooke, Interim Department Head, 662-325-1393, Fax: 662-325-9423, E-mail: whc5@geosci.msstate.edu. *Application contact:* Meredith Nagel, Admissions Assistant, 662-325-9077, E-mail: mnagel@grad.msstate.edu.
Website: http://www.geosciences.msstate.edu

Missouri State University, Graduate College, College of Natural and Applied Sciences, Department of Geography, Geology, and Planning, Springfield, MO 65897. Offers natural and applied science (MNAS), including geography, geology and planning; secondary education (MS Ed), including earth science, physical geography. *Accreditation:* ACSP. *Program availability:* Part-time, evening/weekend. *Faculty:* 18 full-time (4 women), 1 part-time/adjunct (0 women). *Students:* 22 full-time (8 women), 10 part-time (7 women); includes 2 minority (1 Asian, non-Hispanic/Latino; 1 Hispanic/Latino), 4 international. Average age 30. 36 applicants, 67% accepted, 19 enrolled. In 2015, 8 master's awarded. *Degree requirements:* For master's, comprehensive exam, thesis (for some programs). *Entrance requirements:* For master's, GRE General Test (MS, MNAS), minimum undergraduate GPA of 3.0 (MS, MNAS), 9-12 teacher certification (MS Ed). Additional exam requirements/recommendations for international students: Required—TOEFL (minimum score 550 paper-based; 79 iBT), IELTS (minimum score 6). *Application deadline:* For fall admission, 7/20 priority date for domestic students, 5/1 for international students; for spring admission, 12/20 priority date for domestic students, 9/1 for international students. Applications are processed on a rolling basis. Application fee: $35 ($50 for international students). Electronic applications accepted. *Expenses:* Tuition, state resident: full-time $5500. Tuition, nonresident: full-time $10,108. *Required fees:* $1000. *Financial support:* In 2015–16, 3 research assistantships with full tuition reimbursements (averaging $11,574 per year), 15 teaching assistantships with full tuition reimbursements (averaging $9,365 per year) were awarded; career-related internships or fieldwork, Federal Work-Study, institutionally sponsored loans, scholarships/grants, and unspecified assistantships also available. Financial award application deadline: 3/31; financial award applicants required to submit FAFSA. *Faculty research:* Stratigraphy and ancient meteorite impacts, environmental geochemistry of karst, hyperspectral image processing, water quality, small town planning. *Unit head:* Dr. Toby Dogwiler, Department Head, 417-836-5800, Fax: 417-836-6934, E-mail: tobydogwiler@missouristate.edu. *Application contact:* Michael Edwards, Coordinator of Graduate Admissions, 417-836-5330, Fax: 417-836-6200, E-mail: michaeledwards@missouristate.edu.
Website: http://geosciences.missouristate.edu/

Montana State University, The Graduate School, College of Letters and Science, Department of Earth Sciences, Bozeman, MT 59717. Offers MS, PhD. *Program availability:* Part-time. *Degree requirements:* For master's, comprehensive exam, thesis (for some programs); for doctorate, comprehensive exam, thesis/dissertation. *Entrance requirements:* For master's and doctorate, GRE General Test, minimum GPA of 3.0. Additional exam requirements/recommendations for international students: Required—TOEFL (minimum score 550 paper-based). Electronic applications accepted. *Faculty research:* Dinosaur paleontology, climate history/geomicrobiology, stratigraphy/sedimentology/structure/carbon sequestration, igneous petrology South America, historical/urban economic geography western U. S. and China.

Montana Tech of The University of Montana, Graduate School, Geosciences Programs, Butte, MT 59701-8997. Offers geochemistry (MS); geological engineering (MS); geology (MS); geophysical engineering (MS); hydrogeological engineering (MS); hydrogeology (MS). *Program availability:* Part-time. *Faculty:* 16 full-time (4 women), 4 part-time/adjunct (0 women). *Students:* 28 full-time (10 women), 10 part-time (5 women); includes 1 minority (Hispanic/Latino), 6 international. 25 applicants, 52% accepted, 10 enrolled. In 2015, 3 master's awarded. *Degree requirements:* For master's, comprehensive exam (for some programs), thesis (for some programs). *Entrance requirements:* For master's, GRE General Test, minimum GPA of 3.0. Additional exam requirements/recommendations for international students: Required—TOEFL (minimum score 545 paper-based; 78 iBT), IELTS (minimum score 6.5). *Application deadline:* For fall admission, 4/1 priority date for domestic students, 3/1 priority date for international students; for spring admission, 10/1 priority date for domestic students, 7/1 priority date for international students. Applications are processed on a rolling basis. Application fee: $50. Electronic applications accepted. *Expenses:* Tuition, state resident: full-time $2901; part-time $1450.68 per degree program. Tuition, nonresident: full-time $8432; part-time $4215.84 per degree program. *Required fees:* $668; $354 per degree program. Tuition and fees vary according to course load and program. *Financial support:* In 2015–16, 15 students received support, including 10 teaching assistantships with partial tuition reimbursements available (averaging $5,000 per year); research assistantships with partial tuition reimbursements available, career-related internships or fieldwork, tuition waivers (full and partial), and unspecified assistantships also available. Financial award application deadline: 4/1; financial award applicants required to submit FAFSA. *Faculty research:* Water resource development, seismic processing, petroleum reservoir characterization, environmental geochemistry, geologic mapping. *Unit head:* Dr. Chris Gammons, Department Head, 406-496-4763, Fax: 406-496-4260, E-mail: cgammons@mtech.edu. *Application contact:* Daniel Stirling, Administrator, Graduate School, 406-496-4304, Fax: 406-496-4710, E-mail: gradschool@mtech.edu.
Website: http://www.mtech.edu/academics/gradschool/degreeprograms/degrees.htm

Montclair State University, The Graduate School, College of Science and Mathematics, Program in Geoscience, Montclair, NJ 07043-1624. Offers MS. *Program availability:* Part-time, evening/weekend. *Students:* 8 full-time (6 women), 7 part-time (2 women); includes 2 minority (both Hispanic/Latino). Average age 27. 10 applicants, 70% accepted, 5 enrolled. In 2015, 5 master's awarded. *Degree requirements:* For master's, thesis. *Entrance requirements:* Additional exam requirements/recommendations for international students: Required—TOEFL (minimum score 83 iBT), IELTS (minimum score 6.5). *Application deadline:* Applications are processed on a rolling basis. Application fee: $60. Electronic applications accepted. *Expenses:* Tuition, state resident: part-time $553 per credit. Tuition, nonresident: part-time $854 per credit. *Required fees:* $91 per credit. Tuition and fees vary according to program. *Financial support:* In 2015–16, 3 research assistantships with full tuition reimbursements (averaging $7,000 per year) were awarded; Federal Work-Study, scholarships/grants, and unspecified assistantships also available. Support available to part-time students. Financial award application deadline: 3/1; financial award applicants required to submit FAFSA. *Faculty research:* Environmental geochemistry, flood hydrology, geomorphology and weathering processes, regional climate modeling, remote sensing, Cenozoic marine sediment records from polar regions, igneous and metamorphic petrology. *Unit head:* Dr. Matthew Goring, Chairperson, 973-655-5409. *Application contact:* Amy Aiello, Director of Graduate Admissions and Operations, 973-655-5147, Fax: 973-655-7869, E-mail: graduate.school@montclair.edu.
Website: http://www.montclair.edu/graduate/programs-of-study/geoscience/

Murray State University, College of Science, Engineering and Technology, Program in Geosciences, Murray, KY 42071. Offers MS. *Program availability:* Part-time. *Degree requirements:* For master's, comprehensive exam, thesis optional. *Entrance requirements:* Additional exam requirements/recommendations for international students: Required—TOEFL, IELTS.

New Mexico Institute of Mining and Technology, Center for Graduate Studies, Department of Earth and Environmental Science, Socorro, NM 87801. Offers geochemistry (MS, PhD); geology (MS, PhD); geophysics (MS, PhD); hydrology (MS, PhD). *Degree requirements:* For master's, thesis optional; for doctorate, thesis/dissertation. *Entrance requirements:* For master's, GRE General Test; for doctorate, GRE General Test, GRE Subject Test. Additional exam requirements/recommendations for international students: Required—TOEFL. *Expenses:* Tuition, state resident: full-time $5811; part-time $322.81 per credit. Tuition, nonresident: full-time $19,220; part-time $1067.79 per credit. *Required fees:* $1030. Tuition and fees vary according to course load. *Faculty research:* Seismology, geochemistry, caves and karst topography, hydrology, volcanology.

North Carolina Central University, College of Science and Technology, Department of Environmental, Earth and Geospatial Sciences, Durham, NC 27707-3129. Offers earth sciences (MS). *Degree requirements:* For master's, one foreign language, comprehensive exam. *Entrance requirements:* For master's, GRE, minimum GPA of 3.0 in major, 2.5 overall. Additional exam requirements/recommendations for international students: Required—TOEFL.

North Carolina State University, Graduate School, College of Physical and Mathematical Sciences, Department of Marine, Earth, and Atmospheric Sciences, Raleigh, NC 27695. Offers marine, earth, and atmospheric sciences (MS, PhD); meteorology (MS, PhD); oceanography (MS, PhD). PhD offered jointly with The University of North Carolina Wilmington. Terminal master's awarded for partial completion of doctoral program. *Degree requirements:* For master's, thesis (for some programs), final oral exam; for doctorate, comprehensive exam, thesis/dissertation, final oral exam, preliminary oral and written exams. *Entrance requirements:* For master's, GRE General Test, minimum GPA of 3.0; for doctorate, GRE General Test, GRE Subject Test (for disciplines in biological oceanography and geology), minimum GPA of 3.0. Additional exam requirements/recommendations for international students: Required—TOEFL (minimum score 550 paper-based). Electronic applications accepted. *Faculty research:* Boundary layer and air quality meteorology; climate and mesoscale dynamics; biological, chemical, geological, and physical oceanography; hard rock, soft rock, environmental, and paleo-geology.

Northwestern University, The Graduate School, Judd A. and Marjorie Weinberg College of Arts and Sciences, Department of Earth and Planetary Sciences, Evanston, IL 60208. Offers PhD. Admissions and degrees offered through The Graduate School. *Program availability:* Part-time. *Degree requirements:* For doctorate, thesis/dissertation. *Entrance requirements:* For doctorate, GRE General Test. Additional exam requirements/recommendations for international students: Required—TOEFL. Electronic applications accepted.

The Ohio State University, Graduate School, College of Arts and Sciences, Division of Natural and Mathematical Sciences, School of Earth Sciences, Columbus, OH 43210. Offers earth sciences (MS, PhD); geodetic science (MS, PhD); geological sciences (MS, PhD). *Degree requirements:* For master's, thesis; for doctorate, thesis/dissertation. *Entrance requirements:* For master's, GRE, undergraduate degree in biological science, geological sciences, physical science or engineering (recommended); minimum GPA of 3.2; for doctorate, GRE, undergraduate degree in biological science, geological sciences, physical science or engineering (recommended); minimum GPA of 3.4. Additional exam requirements/recommendations for international students: Required—TOEFL (minimum score 550 paper-based; 79 iBT), Michigan English Language Assessment Battery (minimum score 82); Recommended—IELTS (minimum score 8). Electronic applications accepted.

Pace University, School of Education, New York, NY 10038. Offers adolescent education (MST), including biology, business education, chemistry, earth science, English, foreign languages, mathematics, physics, social studies, visual arts; childhood education (MST); early childhood development, learning and intervention (MST); educational technology studies (MS); inclusive adolescent education (MST), including biology, business education, chemistry, earth science, English, foreign languages, mathematics, physics, social studies, visual arts; integrated instruction for educational technology (Certificate); integrated instruction for literacy and technology (Certificate); literacy (MS Ed); special education (MS Ed). *Accreditation:* NCATE. *Program availability:* Part-time, evening/weekend. *Faculty:* 19 full-time (13 women), 86 part-time/adjunct (49 women). *Students:* 112 full-time (95 women), 432 part-time (306 women); includes 179 minority (89 Black or African American, non-Hispanic/Latino; 1 American Indian or Alaska Native, non-Hispanic/Latino; 24 Asian, non-Hispanic/Latino; 55 Hispanic/Latino; 10 Two or more races, non-Hispanic/Latino), 9 international. Average age 30. 181 applicants, 78% accepted, 72 enrolled. In 2015, 261 master's, 11 other advanced degrees awarded. *Degree requirements:* For master's, internship. *Entrance requirements:* For master's, interview, teaching certificate. Additional exam requirements/recommendations for international students: Required—TOEFL (minimum score 88 iBT), IELTS or PTE. *Application deadline:* For fall admission, 8/1 priority date

for domestic students, 6/1 for international students; for spring admission, 12/1 priority date for domestic students, 10/1 for international students. Applications are processed on a rolling basis. Application fee: $70. Electronic applications accepted. *Expenses:* Contact institution. *Financial support:* In 2015–16, 17 students received support, including 17 research assistantships with partial tuition reimbursements available (averaging $6,020 per year); career-related internships or fieldwork and Federal Work-Study also available. Financial award application deadline: 2/15; financial award applicants required to submit FAFSA. *Faculty research:* STEM education, TESOL, teacher education, special education, language and literary development. *Total annual research expenditures:* $290,153. *Unit head:* Dr. Xiao-Lei Wang, Dean, School of Education, 914-773-3876, E-mail: xwang@pace.edu. *Application contact:* Susan Ford-Goldschein, Director of Graduate Admissions, 212-346-1531, Fax: 212-346-1585, E-mail: graduateadmission@pace.edu.
Website: http://www.pace.edu/school-of-education

Penn State University Park, Graduate School, College of Earth and Mineral Sciences, Department of Geosciences, University Park, PA 16802. Offers earth sciences (M Ed); geosciences (MS, PhD). *Unit head:* Dr. William E. Easterling, III, Dean, 814-865-7482, Fax: 814-863-7708. *Application contact:* Lori Stania, Director, Graduate Student Services, 814-865-1795, Fax: 814-863-4627, E-mail: l-gswww@lists.psu.edu.
Website: http://www.geosc.psu.edu/

Princeton University, Graduate School, Department of Geosciences, Princeton, NJ 08544-1019. Offers atmospheric and oceanic sciences (PhD); geosciences (PhD); ocean sciences and marine biology (PhD). *Degree requirements:* For doctorate, one foreign language, thesis/dissertation. *Entrance requirements:* For doctorate, GRE General Test. Additional exam requirements/recommendations for international students: Required—TOEFL (minimum score 600 paper-based). Electronic applications accepted. *Faculty research:* Biogeochemistry, climate science, earth history, regional geology and tectonics, solid–earth geophysics.

Purdue University, Graduate School, College of Science, Department of Earth and Atmospheric Sciences, West Lafayette, IN 47907. Offers MS, PhD. *Degree requirements:* For master's, comprehensive exam, thesis; for doctorate, one foreign language, comprehensive exam, thesis/dissertation. *Entrance requirements:* For master's, GRE General Test, minimum undergraduate GPA of 3.0 or equivalent; for doctorate, GRE General Test, minimum undergraduate or master's GPA of 3.0 or equivalent. Additional exam requirements/recommendations for international students: Required—TOEFL (minimum score 550 paper-based; 77 iBT); Recommended—TWE. Electronic applications accepted. *Faculty research:* Geology, geophysics, hydrogeology, paleoclimatology, environmental science.

Queens College of the City University of New York, Mathematics and Natural Sciences Division, School of Earth and Environmental Sciences, Flushing, NY 11367-1597. Offers applied environmental geoscience (MS); geological and environmental science (MA). *Program availability:* Part-time, evening/weekend. *Faculty:* 17 full-time (3 women), 9 part-time/adjunct (2 women). *Students:* 14 part-time (6 women); includes 2 minority (1 Black or African American, non-Hispanic/Latino; 1 Hispanic/Latino), 2 international. Average age 27. 11 applicants, 55% accepted, 3 enrolled. In 2015, 6 master's awarded. *Degree requirements:* For master's, comprehensive exam, thesis. *Entrance requirements:* For master's, previous course work in calculus, physics, and chemistry; minimum GPA of 3.0. Additional exam requirements/recommendations for international students: Required—TOEFL, IELTS. *Application deadline:* For fall admission, 4/1 for domestic students; for spring admission, 11/1 for domestic students. Applications are processed on a rolling basis. Application fee: $125. Electronic applications accepted. *Expenses:* Tuition, state resident: full-time $5065; part-time $425 per credit. Tuition, nonresident: part-time $780 per credit. *Required fees:* $522. Part-time tuition and fees vary according to course load and program. *Financial support:* Career-related internships or fieldwork and unspecified assistantships available. Financial award application deadline: 4/1; financial award applicants required to submit FAFSA. *Unit head:* Dr. George Hendrey, Chairperson, 718-997-3300, E-mail: george.hendrey@qc.cuny.edu.

Rice University, Graduate Programs, Wiess School of Natural Sciences, Department of Earth Science, Houston, TX 77251-1892. Offers MS, PhD. Terminal master's awarded for partial completion of doctoral program. *Degree requirements:* For master's, comprehensive exam, thesis, annual department report and presentation, qualifying exam, orals, 2 publications; for doctorate, comprehensive exam, thesis/dissertation, annual department report and presentation, qualifying exam, orals, 3 publications. *Entrance requirements:* For master's and doctorate, GRE. Additional exam requirements/recommendations for international students: Required—TOEFL (minimum score 600 paper-based; 90 iBT), IELTS. Electronic applications accepted. *Faculty research:* Seismology, structural geology, tectonics and paleomagnetism, geodynamics, high temperature geochemistry, volcanic processes.

Rice University, Graduate Programs, Wiess School–Professional Science Master's Programs, Professional Master's Program in Subsurface Geosciences, Houston, TX 77251-1892. Offers geophysics (MS). *Program availability:* Part-time. *Degree requirements:* For master's, internship. *Entrance requirements:* For master's, GRE, letters of recommendation (4). Additional exam requirements/recommendations for international students: Required—TOEFL (minimum score 600 paper-based; 90 iBT). Electronic applications accepted. *Faculty research:* Seismology, geodynamics, wave propagation, bio-geochemistry, remote sensing.

St. Francis Xavier University, Graduate Studies, Department of Earth Sciences, Antigonish, NS B2G 2W5, Canada. Offers M Sc. *Degree requirements:* For master's, thesis. *Entrance requirements:* Additional exam requirements/recommendations for international students: Required—TOEFL (minimum score 580 paper-based). *Faculty research:* Environmental earth sciences, global change tectonics, paleoclimatology, crustal fluids.

Saint Louis University, Graduate Education, College of Arts and Sciences, Department of Earth and Atmospheric Sciences, St. Louis, MO 63103. Offers geophysics (PhD); geoscience (MS); meteorology (M Pr Met, MS-R, PhD). *Program availability:* Part-time. *Degree requirements:* For master's, thesis (for some programs), comprehensive oral exam; for doctorate, thesis/dissertation, preliminary exams. *Entrance requirements:* For master's, GRE General Test, letters of recommendation, resume; for doctorate, GRE General Test, letters of recommendation, resumé, goal statement, transcripts. Additional exam requirements/recommendations for international students: Required—TOEFL (minimum score 525 paper-based). Electronic applications accepted. *Faculty research:* Structural geology, mesoscale meteorology and severe storms, weather and climate change prediction.

St. Thomas University, School of Leadership Studies, Institute for Education, Miami Gardens, FL 33054-6459. Offers earth/space science (Certificate); educational administration (MS, Certificate); educational leadership (Ed D); elementary education (MS); ESOL (Certificate); gifted education (Certificate); instructional technology (MS, Certificate); professional/studies (Certificate); reading (MS, Certificate); special education (MS). *Program availability:* Part-time, evening/weekend. *Degree requirements:* For master's, comprehensive exam; for doctorate, comprehensive exam, thesis/dissertation. *Entrance requirements:* For master's, interview, minimum GPA of 3.0 or GRE; for doctorate, GRE or MAT. Additional exam requirements/recommendations for international students: Required—TOEFL (minimum score 550 paper-based; 79 iBT). Electronic applications accepted.

San Francisco State University, Division of Graduate Studies, College of Science and Engineering, Department of Earth and Climate Sciences, San Francisco, CA 94132-1722. Offers geosciences (MS). *Application deadline:* Applications are processed on a rolling basis. *Expenses:* Tuition, state resident: full-time $6738. Tuition, nonresident: full-time $15,666. *Required fees:* $1004 per year. *Unit head:* Dr. David Dempsey, Chair, 415-338-7716, Fax: 415-338-7705, E-mail: dempsey@sfsu.edu. *Application contact:* Dr. Petra Dekens, Graduate Coordinator, 415-338-6015, Fax: 415-338-7705, E-mail: dekens@sfsu.edu.
Website: http://tornado.sfsu.edu

Simon Fraser University, Office of Graduate Studies, Faculty of Science, Department of Earth Sciences, Burnaby, BC V5A 1S6, Canada. Offers M Sc, PhD. *Degree requirements:* For master's, thesis; for doctorate, comprehensive exam, thesis/dissertation. *Entrance requirements:* For master's, minimum GPA of 3.0 (on scale of 4.33), or 3.33 based on last 60 credits of undergraduate courses; for doctorate, minimum GPA of 3.5 (on scale of 4.33). Additional exam requirements/recommendations for international students: Recommended—TOEFL (minimum score 580 paper-based; 93 iBT), IELTS (minimum score 7), TWE (minimum score 5). Electronic applications accepted. *Faculty research:* Glaciology, structural geology, quaternary and environmental earth sciences, geochronology, and tectonics; exploration or earthquake seismology.

South Dakota State University, Graduate School, College of Engineering, Geospatial Science and Engineering Program, Brookings, SD 57007. Offers PhD. *Program availability:* Part-time. *Degree requirements:* For doctorate, comprehensive exam, thesis/dissertation. *Entrance requirements:* For doctorate, GRE. Additional exam requirements/recommendations for international students: Required—TOEFL (minimum score 525 paper-based; 71 iBT). *Faculty research:* Deforestation, land use/cover change, GIS spatial modeling.

Southern Illinois University Carbondale, Graduate School, College of Science, Department of Geology, Carbondale, IL 62901-4701. Offers environmental resources and policy (PhD); geology (MS); geosciences (PhD). *Faculty:* 12 full-time (0 women). *Students:* 15 full-time (5 women), 16 part-time (2 women), 18 international. Average age 25. 34 applicants, 44% accepted, 716 enrolled. In 2015, 16 master's, 3 doctorates awarded. *Degree requirements:* For master's, thesis; for doctorate, one foreign language, thesis/dissertation. *Entrance requirements:* For master's, GRE, minimum GPA of 2.7; for doctorate, GRE General Test, minimum GPA of 3.25. Additional exam requirements/recommendations for international students: Required—TOEFL. *Application deadline:* Applications are processed on a rolling basis. Application fee: $65. *Financial support:* In 2015–16, 22 students received support, including 22 teaching assistantships with full tuition reimbursements available; fellowships with full tuition reimbursements available, research assistantships with full tuition reimbursements available, Federal Work-Study, institutionally sponsored loans, and tuition waivers (full) also available. Support available to part-time students. *Total annual research expenditures:* $720,000. *Unit head:* Dr. Steven Esling, Chair, 618-453-3351, Fax: 618-453-7393, E-mail: esling@geo.siu.edu. *Application contact:* Mona Martin, Office Support Specialist, 618-453-3351, E-mail: monamartin@siu.edu.

Stanford University, School of Earth, Energy and Environmental Sciences, Department of Earth System Science, Stanford, CA 94305-9991. Offers MS, PhD. Students are admitted at the undergraduate level. Electronic applications accepted. *Expenses: Tuition, area resident:* Full-time $45,729. *Required fees:* $591.

Stanford University, School of Earth, Energy and Environmental Sciences, Department of Geological Sciences, Stanford, CA 94305-9991. Offers MS, PhD, Eng. Terminal master's awarded for partial completion of doctoral program. *Degree requirements:* For master's and Eng, thesis; for doctorate, thesis/dissertation. *Entrance requirements:* For master's, doctorate, and Eng, GRE General Test. Additional exam requirements/recommendations for international students: Required—TOEFL. Electronic applications accepted. *Expenses: Tuition, area resident:* Full-time $45,729. *Required fees:* $591.

State University of New York at New Paltz, Graduate School, School of Education, Department of Secondary Education, New Paltz, NY 12561. Offers adolescence education: biology (MAT, MS Ed); adolescence education: chemistry (MAT, MS Ed); adolescence education: earth science (MAT, MS Ed); adolescence education: English (MAT, MS Ed); adolescence education: French (MAT, MS Ed); adolescence education: social studies (MAT, MS Ed); adolescence education: Spanish (MAT, MS Ed); second language education (MS Ed, AC), including second language education (MS Ed), teaching English language learners (AC). *Accreditation:* NCATE. *Program availability:* Part-time, evening/weekend. *Faculty:* 11 full-time (7 women), 13 part-time/adjunct (9 women). *Students:* 46 full-time (30 women), 45 part-time (28 women); includes 28 minority (2 Black or African American, non-Hispanic/Latino; 1 Asian, non-Hispanic/Latino; 23 Hispanic/Latino; 2 Two or more races, non-Hispanic/Latino). Average age 30. 50 applicants, 62% accepted, 23 enrolled. In 2015, 33 master's awarded. *Degree requirements:* For master's, comprehensive exam (for some programs), portfolio. *Entrance requirements:* For master's, minimum GPA of 3.0, New York state teaching certificate (MS Ed). Additional exam requirements/recommendations for international students: Required—TOEFL (minimum score 550 paper-based; 80 iBT), IELTS (minimum score 6.5). *Application deadline:* For fall admission, 3/1 priority date for domestic students, 3/1 for international students; for spring admission, 10/1 priority date for domestic students, 10/1 for international students. Application fee: $50. Electronic applications accepted. *Financial support:* Application deadline: 8/1. *Unit head:* Dr. Laura Dull, Chair, 845-257-2849, E-mail: dullj@newpaltz.edu. *Application contact:* Vika Shock, Director of Graduate Admissions, 845-257-3285, Fax: 845-257-3284, E-mail: gradschool@newpaltz.edu.
Website: http://www.newpaltz.edu/secondaryed/

State University of New York College at Oneonta, Graduate Education, Department of Earth Sciences, Oneonta, NY 13820-4015. Offers MA. *Program availability:* Part-time, evening/weekend. *Degree requirements:* For master's, thesis. *Entrance requirements:* For master's, GRE General Test.

Stony Brook University, State University of New York, Graduate School, College of Arts and Sciences, Department of Geosciences, Stony Brook, NY 11794. Offers earth science (MAT); geosciences (MS, PhD). MAT offered through the School of Professional Development. *Faculty:* 14 full-time (4 women), 3 part-time/adjunct (0 women). *Students:* 34 full-time (17 women), 11 part-time (7 women); includes 9 minority (4 Black or African American, non-Hispanic/Latino; 2 Asian, non-Hispanic/Latino; 2 Hispanic/Latino; 1 Two or more races, non-Hispanic/Latino), 14 international. Average age 26. 41 applicants, 49% accepted, 12 enrolled. In 2015, 11 master's, 7 doctorates awarded. Terminal master's awarded for partial completion of doctoral program. *Degree requirements:* For master's, thesis or alternative; for doctorate, thesis/dissertation. *Entrance requirements:* For master's and doctorate, GRE General Test, minimum GPA of 3.0. Additional exam requirements/recommendations for international students: Required—TOEFL. *Application deadline:* For fall admission, 1/15 for domestic students; for spring admission, 10/1 for domestic students. Application fee: $100. *Expenses:* $12,421 full-time resident tuition and fees, $453 per credit hour; $23,761 full-time nonresident tuition and fees, $925 per credit hour. *Financial support:* In 2015–16, 5 fellowships, 17 research assistantships, 10 teaching assistantships were awarded. *Faculty research:* Geology, Petrology, Planetary Studies, Planetary Geology, Mineralogy. *Total annual research expenditures:* $3.1 million. *Unit head:* Dr. Daniel M. Davis, Chair, 631-632-8217, Fax: 631-632-8240, E-mail: rjreeder@stonybrook.edu. *Application contact:* Yvonne Barbour, Coordinator, 631-632-8554, Fax: 631-632-8240, E-mail: yvonne.barbour@stonybrook.edu.

Website: http://www.geosciences.stonybrook.edu/

Syracuse University, School of Education, Programs in Science Education, Syracuse, NY 13244. Offers biology (MS, PhD); chemistry (MS, PhD); earth science (MS, PhD); physics (MS, PhD). *Program availability:* Part-time. *Students:* Average age 38. In 2015, 4 doctorates awarded. *Degree requirements:* For doctorate, comprehensive exam, thesis/dissertation. *Entrance requirements:* For master's, official transcripts from previous academic institutions, 3 letters of recommendation (preferably from faculty), personal statement that makes a clear and compelling argument for why applicant wants to teach secondary science; for doctorate, GRE General Test or MAT, master's degree, interview. Additional exam requirements/recommendations for international students: Required—TOEFL (minimum score 100 iBT). *Application deadline:* For fall admission, 1/15 priority date for domestic and international students; for spring admission, 10/15 priority date for domestic and international students. Applications are processed on a rolling basis. Application fee: $75. Electronic applications accepted. *Expenses: Tuition, area resident:* Full-time $25,974; part-time $1443 per credit hour. *Required fees:* $802; $50 per course. Tuition and fees vary according to course load and program. *Financial support:* Fellowships with full tuition reimbursements, research assistantships with tuition reimbursements, teaching assistantships with tuition reimbursements, and scholarships/grants available. Financial award application deadline: 1/15. *Faculty research:* Diverse field experiences and theoretical and practical knowledge in research-based science teaching, biology, chemistry, earth science, and physics.. *Unit head:* Dr. John Tillotson, Program Coordinator, 315-443-9137, E-mail: jwtillot@syr.edu. *Application contact:* Speranza Migliore, Graduate Admissions Recruiter, 315-443-2505, E-mail: gradrcrt@syr.edu.

Website: http://soeweb.syr.edu/

Teachers College, Columbia University, Department of Mathematics, Science and Technology, New York, NY 10027-6696. Offers biology 7-12 (MA); chemistry 7-12 (MA); communication and education (MA); communications (Ed M); communications and education (Ed D); computing in education (MA); computing in education-distant learning (MA); earth science 7-12 (MA); instructional technology and media (Ed M, MA, Ed D); mathematics education (Ed M, MA, Ed D, Ed DCT, PhD); physics 7-12 (MA); science and dental education (MA); science education (Ed M, MS, Ed DCT, PhD); supervisor / teacher of science education (MA); technology specialist (MA). *Program availability:* Part-time, evening/weekend. *Students:* 134 full-time (89 women), 285 part-time (168 women); includes 219 minority (49 Black or African American, non-Hispanic/Latino; 124 Asian, non-Hispanic/Latino; 31 Hispanic/Latino; 15 Two or more races, non-Hispanic/Latino), 29 international. Terminal master's awarded for partial completion of doctoral program. *Degree requirements:* For doctorate, thesis/dissertation. *Expenses: Tuition, area resident:* Part-time $1454 per credit. *Required fees:* $428 per semester. One-time fee: $475 full-time. Full-time tuition and fees vary according to course load. *Unit head:* Dr. O. Roger Anderson, Chair, 212-678-3405, Fax: 212-678-8129, E-mail: ora@ldeo.columbia.edu. *Application contact:* David Estrella, Director of Admission, E-mail: estrella@tc.columbia.edu.

Website: http://www.tc.columbia.edu/mathematics-science-and-technology/

Texas Tech University, Graduate School, College of Arts and Sciences, Department of Geosciences, Lubbock, TX 79409. Offers atmospheric science (MS); geography (MS); geosciences (MS, PhD). *Program availability:* Part-time. *Faculty:* 27 full-time (3 women), 5 part-time/adjunct (1 woman). *Students:* 75 full-time (27 women), 16 part-time (6 women); includes 14 minority (2 Black or African American, non-Hispanic/Latino; 1 Asian, non-Hispanic/Latino; 7 Hispanic/Latino; 4 Two or more races, non-Hispanic/Latino), 18 international. Average age 27. 175 applicants, 19% accepted, 22 enrolled. In 2015, 19 master's, 2 doctorates awarded. *Degree requirements:* For master's, thesis; for doctorate, comprehensive exam, thesis/dissertation. *Entrance requirements:* For master's and doctorate, GRE General Test. Additional exam requirements/recommendations for international students: Required—TOEFL (minimum score 550 paper-based; 79 iBT). *Application deadline:* For fall admission, 6/1 priority date for domestic students, 1/15 priority date for international students; for spring admission, 9/1 priority date for domestic students, 6/15 priority date for international students. Applications are processed on a rolling basis. Application fee: $60. Electronic applications accepted. *Expenses:* Tuition, state resident: full-time $6477; part-time $269.89 per credit hour. Tuition, nonresident: full-time $15,837; part-time $659.89 per credit hour. *Required fees:* $2751; $36.50 per credit hour. $937.50 per semester. Tuition and fees vary according to course level. *Financial support:* In 2015–16, 87 students received support, including 68 fellowships (averaging $3,203 per year), 38 research assistantships (averaging $12,295 per year), 54 teaching assistantships (averaging $12,351 per year); Federal Work-Study, scholarships/grants, health care benefits, tuition waivers (partial), and unspecified assistantships also available. Financial award application deadline: 2/15; financial award applicants required to submit FAFSA. *Faculty research:* Geology, geophysics, geochemistry, geospatial technology, atmospheric sciences. *Total annual research expenditures:* $1.9 million. *Unit head:* Dr. Jeffrey A. Lee, Chairman, 806-834-8228, Fax: 806-742-0100, E-mail: jeff.lee@ttu.edu. *Application contact:* Dr. Callum Hetherington, Associate Professor, 806-834-3110, Fax: 806-724-0100, E-mail: callum.hetherington@ttu.edu.

Website: http://www.geosciences.ttu.edu

Université du Québec à Chicoutimi, Graduate Programs, Program in Earth Sciences, Chicoutimi, QC G7H 2B1, Canada. Offers M Sc A. *Program availability:* Part-time. *Degree requirements:* For master's, thesis. *Entrance requirements:* For master's, appropriate bachelor's degree, proficiency in French.

Université du Québec à Montréal, Graduate Programs, Program in Earth and Atmospheric Sciences, Montréal, QC H3C 3P8, Canada. Offers atmospheric sciences (M Sc); Earth and atmospheric sciences (PhD); Earth science (M Sc); meteorology (PhD, Diploma). PhD programs offered jointly with McGill University. *Program availability:* Part-time. *Degree requirements:* For master's, thesis. *Entrance requirements:* For master's and Diploma, appropriate bachelor's degree or equivalent, proficiency in French; for doctorate, appropriate master's degree or equivalent, proficiency in French.

Université du Québec à Montréal, Graduate Programs, Program in Earth Sciences, Montreal, QC H3C 3P8, Canada. Offers earth sciences (M Sc); mineral resources (PhD); non-renewable resources (DESS). *Program availability:* Part-time. Terminal master's awarded for partial completion of doctoral program. *Degree requirements:* For master's, thesis (for some programs); for doctorate, thesis/dissertation. *Entrance requirements:* For master's, appropriate bachelor's degree or equivalent, proficiency in French. *Faculty research:* Economic geology, structural geology, geochemistry, Quaternary geology, isotopic geochemistry.

Université du Québec, Institut National de la Recherche Scientifique, Graduate Programs, Research Center–Water Earth Environment, Québec, QC G1K 9A9, Canada. Offers earth sciences (M Sc, PhD); earth sciences - environmental technologies (M Sc); water sciences (M Sc, PhD). *Program availability:* Part-time. *Degree requirements:* For master's, thesis (for some programs); for doctorate, thesis/dissertation. *Entrance requirements:* For master's, appropriate bachelor's degree, proficiency in French; for doctorate, appropriate master's degree, proficiency in French. Electronic applications accepted. *Faculty research:* Land use, impacts of climate change, adaptation to climate change, integrated management of resources (mineral and water).

Université Laval, Faculty of Sciences and Engineering, Department of Geology and Geological Engineering, Programs in Earth Sciences, Québec, QC G1K 7P4, Canada. Offers earth sciences (M Sc, PhD); environmental technologies (M Sc). Offered jointly with INRS-Géressources. Terminal master's awarded for partial completion of doctoral program. *Degree requirements:* For master's, thesis (for some programs); for doctorate, comprehensive exam, thesis/dissertation. *Entrance requirements:* For master's and doctorate, knowledge of French. Electronic applications accepted.

University at Buffalo, the State University of New York, Graduate School, College of Arts and Sciences, Department of Geography, Buffalo, NY 14261. Offers Canadian studies (Certificate); earth systems science (MA, MS); economic geography and business geographics (MS); environmental modeling and analysis (MA); geographic information science (MA, MS); geography (MA, PhD); GIS and environmental analysis (Certificate); health geography (MS); international trade (MA); transportation and business geographics (MA); urban and regional analysis (MA). *Program availability:* Part-time. *Faculty:* 19 full-time (9 women), 1 part-time/adjunct (0 women). *Students:* 42 full-time (21 women), 58 part-time (18 women); includes 66 minority (1 Black or African American, non-Hispanic/Latino; 63 Asian, non-Hispanic/Latino; 2 Hispanic/Latino), 2 international. Average age 29. 163 applicants, 32% accepted, 32 enrolled. In 2015, 44 master's, 6 doctorates awarded. Terminal master's awarded for partial completion of doctoral program. *Degree requirements:* For master's, thesis (for some programs), project or portfolio; for doctorate, thesis/dissertation. *Entrance requirements:* For master's, GRE General Test, minimum GPA of 2.9; for doctorate, GRE General Test, minimum GPA of 3.0. Additional exam requirements/recommendations for international students: Required—TOEFL (minimum score 550 paper-based; 79 iBT). *Application deadline:* For fall admission, 5/1 priority date for domestic students, 3/10 priority date for international students; for spring admission, 11/1 priority date for domestic students, 9/1 priority date for international students. Applications are processed on a rolling basis. Application fee: $75. Electronic applications accepted. *Expenses:* $6,582 per semester in-state. *Financial support:* In 2015–16, 13 students received support, including 8 fellowships with full tuition reimbursements available (averaging $5,500 per year), 10 research assistantships with full tuition reimbursements available (averaging $13,000 per year), 13 teaching assistantships with full tuition reimbursements available (averaging $13,800 per year); career-related internships or fieldwork, Federal Work-Study, institutionally sponsored loans, traineeships, health care benefits, and unspecified assistantships also available. Financial award application deadline: 1/10. *Faculty research:* International business and world trade, geographic information systems and cartography, transportation, urban and regional analysis, physical and environmental geography. *Total annual research expenditures:* $2.6 million. *Unit head:* Dr. Sharmistha Bagchi-Sen, Chairman, 716-645-0473, Fax: 716-645-2329, E-mail: geosbs@buffalo.edu. *Application contact:* Betsy Crooks, Graduate Secretary, 716-645-0471, Fax: 716-645-2329, E-mail: babraham@buffalo.edu.

Website: http://www.geog.buffalo.edu/

The University of Akron, Graduate School, Buchtel College of Arts and Sciences, Department of Geosciences, Akron, OH 44325. Offers earth science (MS); engineering geology (MS); environmental geology (MS); geology (MS); geophysics (MS). *Program availability:* Part-time. *Faculty:* 8 full-time (1 woman), 3 part-time/adjunct (0 women). *Students:* 23 full-time (9 women), 19 part-time (6 women); includes 2 minority (both Black or African American, non-Hispanic/Latino), 15 international. Average age 27. 49 applicants, 59% accepted, 17 enrolled. In 2015, 13 master's awarded. *Degree requirements:* For master's, comprehensive exam, thesis, seminar, proficiency exam. *Entrance requirements:* For master's, minimum GPA of 2.75, three letters of recommendation, statement of purpose. Additional exam requirements/recommendations for international students: Required—TOEFL (minimum score 550 paper-based; 79 iBT), IELTS (minimum score 6.5). *Application deadline:* Applications are processed on a rolling basis. Application fee: $45 ($70 for international students). Electronic applications accepted. *Expenses:* Tuition, state resident: full-time $7958; part-time $442 per credit hour. Tuition, nonresident: full-time $13,464; part-time $748 per credit hour. *Required fees:* $1404. *Financial support:* In 2015–16, 1 research assistantship with full tuition reimbursement, 16 teaching assistantships with full tuition reimbursements were awarded. *Faculty research:* Terrestrial environmental change, karst hydrogeology, lacustrine paleo environments, environmental magnetism and geophysics. *Total annual research expenditures:* $509,174. *Unit head:* Dr. James McManus, Chair, 330-972-7991, E-mail: jmcmanus@uakron.edu. *Application contact:* Dr. John Peck, Director of Graduate Studies, 330-972-7659, E-mail: jpeck@uakron.edu.

Website: http://www.uakron.edu/geology/

The University of Alabama, Graduate School, College of Arts and Sciences, Department of Geography, Tuscaloosa, AL 35487. Offers earth system science (MS); geographic information science (MS); planning (MS). *Program availability:* Part-time. *Faculty:* 15 full-time (2 women), 1 (woman) part-time/adjunct. *Students:* 27 full-time (11 women), 5 part-time (1 woman), 6 international. Average age 26. 35 applicants, 54% accepted, 14 enrolled. In 2015, 11 master's awarded. *Degree requirements:* For master's, comprehensive exam (for some programs), thesis (for some programs). *Entrance requirements:* For master's, GRE, minimum GPA of 3.0. Additional exam requirements/recommendations for international students: Required—TOEFL (minimum score 550 paper-based; 79 iBT). *Application deadline:* For fall admission, 2/15 priority date for domestic and international students; for spring admission, 10/1 priority date for domestic and international students. Applications are processed on a rolling basis. Application fee: $50 ($60 for international students). Electronic applications accepted. *Expenses:* Tuition, state resident: full-time $10,170. Tuition, nonresident: full-time $25,950. *Financial support:* In 2015–16, 16 students received support, including fellowships with full tuition reimbursements available (averaging $15,000 per year), 4 research assistantships with full tuition reimbursements available (averaging $13,311 per year), 18 teaching assistantships with full tuition reimbursements available (averaging $13,311 per year); career-related internships or fieldwork, health care benefits, and unspecified assistantships also available. Financial award application deadline: 2/15. *Faculty research:* Earth system science; geographic information science; urban, regional and environmental planning; ecology. *Total annual research expenditures:* $216,364. *Unit head:* Dr. Douglas Sherman, Chair, 205-348-5047, Fax: 205-348-2278, E-mail: douglas.j.sherman@ua.edu. *Application contact:* Dr. Justin Hart, Assistant Professor, 205-348-5047, Fax: 205-348-2278, E-mail: hart013@ua.edu. Website: http://geography.ua.edu

The University of Alabama in Huntsville, School of Graduate Studies, College of Science, Department of Atmospheric Science, Huntsville, AL 35899. Offers atmospheric science (MS, PhD); earth system science (MS). *Program availability:* Part-time, evening/weekend. *Degree requirements:* For master's, comprehensive exam, thesis or alternative, oral and written exams; for doctorate, comprehensive exam, thesis/dissertation, oral and written exams. *Entrance requirements:* For master's, GRE General Test, minimum GPA of 3.0; sequence of courses in calculus (including the calculus of vector-valued functions); courses in linear algebra and ordinary differential equations; two semesters each of chemistry and calculus-based physics; proficiency in at least one high-level computer programming language; for doctorate, GRE General Test, minimum GPA of 3.0. Additional exam requirements/recommendations for international students: Required—TOEFL (minimum score 550 paper-based; 80 iBT), IELTS (minimum score 6.5). Electronic applications accepted. *Faculty research:* Severe weather, climate, satellite remote sensing, numerical modeling, air pollution.

University of Alberta, Faculty of Graduate Studies and Research, Department of Earth and Atmospheric Sciences, Edmonton, AB T6G 2E1, Canada. Offers M Sc, MA, PhD. *Degree requirements:* For master's, thesis, residency; for doctorate, thesis/dissertation, residency. *Entrance requirements:* For master's, B Sc, minimum GPA of 6.5 on a 9.0 scale; for doctorate, M Sc. Additional exam requirements/recommendations for international students: Required—TOEFL or Michigan English Language Assessment Battery. Electronic applications accepted. *Faculty research:* Geology, human geography, physical geography, meteorology.

The University of Arizona, College of Science, Department of Geosciences, Tucson, AZ 85721. Offers MS, PhD. *Program availability:* Part-time. Terminal master's awarded for partial completion of doctoral program. *Degree requirements:* For master's, thesis or prepublication; for doctorate, comprehensive exam, thesis/dissertation. *Entrance requirements:* For master's, GRE General Test, 3 letters of recommendation, curriculum vitae; for doctorate, GRE General Test, statement of purpose, 3 letters of recommendation, curriculum vitae. Additional exam requirements/recommendations for international students: Required—TOEFL (minimum score 550 paper-based; 79 iBT). Electronic applications accepted. *Faculty research:* Tectonics, geophysics, geochemistry/petrology, economic geology, Quaternary studies, stratigraphy/paleontology.

University of Arkansas at Little Rock, Graduate School, George W. Donaghey College of Engineering and Information Technology, Program in Geospatial Technology, Little Rock, AR 72204-1099. Offers Graduate Certificate. *Entrance requirements:* For degree, baccalaureate degree, minimum cumulative GPA of 2.75. *Expenses:* Tuition, state resident: part-time $300 per credit hour. Tuition, nonresident: part-time $690 per credit hour. *Required fees:* $100 per credit hour. One-time fee: $40 full-time.

University of Calgary, Faculty of Graduate Studies, Faculty of Science, Department of Geoscience, Calgary, AB T2N 1N4, Canada. Offers geology (M Sc, PhD); geophysics (M Sc, PhD); hydrology (M Sc, PhD). *Program availability:* Part-time. Terminal master's awarded for partial completion of doctoral program. *Degree requirements:* For master's, thesis; for doctorate, thesis/dissertation, candidacy exam. *Entrance requirements:* For master's, B Sc; for doctorate, honors B Sc or M Sc. Additional exam requirements/recommendations for international students: Required—TOEFL. Electronic applications accepted. *Faculty research:* Geochemistry, petrology, paleontology, stratigraphy, exploration and solid-earth geophysics.

University of California, Irvine, School of Physical Sciences, Department of Earth System Science, Irvine, CA 92697. Offers MS, PhD. *Students:* 51 full-time (24 women); includes 8 minority (1 Asian, non-Hispanic/Latino; 3 Hispanic/Latino; 4 Two or more races, non-Hispanic/Latino), 23 international. Average age 27. 6 applicants, 300% accepted, 10 enrolled. In 2015, 8 master's, 13 doctorates awarded. *Degree requirements:* For doctorate, thesis/dissertation. *Entrance requirements:* For master's and doctorate, GRE General Test, GRE Subject Test, minimum GPA of 3.0. Additional exam requirements/recommendations for international students: Required—TOEFL (minimum score 550 paper-based). *Application deadline:* For fall admission, 1/15 priority date for domestic students, 1/15 for international students. Applications are processed on a rolling basis. Application fee: $90 ($110 for international students). Electronic applications accepted. *Financial support:* Fellowships, research assistantships with full tuition reimbursements, teaching assistantships, career-related internships or fieldwork, institutionally sponsored loans, traineeships, health care benefits, and unspecified assistantships available. Financial award application deadline: 3/1; financial award applicants required to submit FAFSA. *Faculty research:* Atmospheric chemistry, climate change, isotope biogeochemistry, global environmental chemistry. *Unit head:* Gudrun Magnusdottir, Chair, 949-824-3250, Fax: 949-824-3874, E-mail: gudrun@uci.edu. *Application contact:* Morgan Sibley, Student Affairs Manager, 949-824-1604, Fax: 949-824-3874, E-mail: msibley@uci.edu.
Website: http://www.ess.uci.edu/

University of California, Los Angeles, Graduate Division, College of Letters and Science, Department of Earth and Space Sciences, Los Angeles, CA 90095. Offers geochemistry (MS, PhD); geology (MS, PhD); geophysics and space physics (MS, PhD). Terminal master's awarded for partial completion of doctoral program. *Degree requirements:* For master's, comprehensive exams or thesis; for doctorate, thesis/dissertation, oral and written qualifying exams. *Entrance requirements:* For master's, GRE General Test; GRE Subject Test, bachelor's degree; minimum undergraduate GPA of 3.0 (or its equivalent if letter grade system not used); for doctorate, GRE General Test, bachelor's degree; minimum undergraduate GPA of 3.0 (or its equivalent if letter grade system not used). Additional exam requirements/recommendations for international students: Required—TOEFL. Electronic applications accepted.

University of California, San Diego, Graduate Division, Scripps Institution of Oceanography, La Jolla, CA 92093. Offers climate science and policy (MAS); earth sciences (MS, PhD); geophysics (PhD); marine biodiversity and conservation (MAS); marine biology (MS, PhD); oceanography (MS, PhD). PhD in geophysics is offered jointly with San Diego State University. *Students:* 262 full-time (137 women), 11 part-time (1 woman); includes 51 minority (11 Black or African American, non-Hispanic/Latino; 3 American Indian or Alaska Native, non-Hispanic/Latino; 21 Asian, non-Hispanic/Latino; 16 Hispanic/Latino), 56 international. 332 applicants, 24% accepted, 47 enrolled. In 2015, 38 master's, 28 doctorates awarded. Terminal master's awarded for partial completion of doctoral program. *Degree requirements:* For master's, comprehensive exam (for some programs), thesis (for some programs); for doctorate, comprehensive exam, thesis/dissertation. *Entrance requirements:* For master's and doctorate, GRE General Test, GRE Subject Test (encouraged for ocean biosciences applicants), minimum GPA of 3.0. Additional exam requirements/recommendations for international students: Required—TOEFL (minimum score 550 paper-based; 80 iBT), IELTS (minimum score 7). *Application deadline:* For fall admission, 12/10 for domestic students. Application fee: $90 ($110 for international students). Electronic applications accepted. *Expenses:* Tuition, state resident: full-time $11,220. Tuition, nonresident: full-time $26,322. *Required fees:* $1800. *Financial support:* Fellowships, research assistantships, teaching assistantships, scholarships/grants, traineeships, and unspecified assistantships available. Financial award applicants required to submit FAFSA. *Faculty research:* Biodiversity and conservation, earth and planetary chemistry, alternative energy, global environmental monitoring, air-sea boundary, tectonic margins and the interactions between systems and environments. *Unit head:* Brian Palenik, Chair, 858-534-7505, E-mail: bpalenik@ucsd.edu. *Application contact:* Gilbert Bretado, Graduate Coordinator, 858-534-1694, E-mail: siodept@sio.ucsd.edu.
Website: https://scripps.ucsd.edu/education

University of California, Santa Barbara, Graduate Division, College of Letters and Sciences, Division of Mathematics, Life, and Physical Sciences, Department of Earth Science, Santa Barbara, CA 93106-9620. Offers MS, PhD. *Faculty:* 19 full-time (3 women), 8 part-time/adjunct (1 woman). *Students:* 41 full-time (19 women); includes 4 minority (1 American Indian or Alaska Native, non-Hispanic/Latino; 3 Hispanic/Latino), 5 international. Average age 27. 109 applicants, 16% accepted, 12 enrolled. In 2015, 10 master's, 8 doctorates awarded. Terminal master's awarded for partial completion of doctoral program. *Degree requirements:* For master's, comprehensive exam, thesis, 30 units; for doctorate, comprehensive exam, thesis/dissertation, 30 units, qualifying exam, defense. *Entrance requirements:* For master's and doctorate, GRE General Test. Additional exam requirements/recommendations for international students: Required—TOEFL (minimum score 550 paper-based; 80 iBT), IELTS (minimum score 7). *Application deadline:* For fall admission, 2/1 for domestic and international students. Application fee: $90 ($110 for international students). Electronic applications accepted. *Financial support:* In 2015–16, 28 students received support, including 8 fellowships with full tuition reimbursements available (averaging $22,000 per year), 16 research assistantships with tuition reimbursements available (averaging $16,500 per year), 19 teaching assistantships with partial tuition reimbursements available (averaging $17,655 per year); health care benefits also available. Financial award application deadline: 1/3; financial award applicants required to submit CSS PROFILE or FAFSA. *Faculty research:* Geology, geomaterials and earth's structure; geomorphology, tectonics; geophysics, seismology; paleoclimatology, paleoceanography and geochemistry; paleobiology, evolution and paleontology. *Unit head:* Dr. Douglas Burbank, Chair, 805-893-7858, Fax: 805-893-2314, E-mail: burbank@eri.ucsb.edu. *Application contact:* Hannah Smit, Graduate Program Assistant, 805-893-3329, Fax: 805-893-2314, E-mail: hsmit@geol.ucsb.edu.
Website: http://www.geol.ucsb.edu/

University of California, Santa Cruz, Division of Graduate Studies, Division of Physical and Biological Sciences, Department of Earth and Planetary Sciences, Santa Cruz, CA 95064. Offers MS, PhD. Terminal master's awarded for partial completion of doctoral program. *Degree requirements:* For master's, thesis; for doctorate, one foreign language, thesis/dissertation, qualifying exam. *Entrance requirements:* For master's and doctorate, GRE General Test. Additional exam requirements/recommendations for international students: Required—TOEFL (minimum score 550 paper-based; 83 iBT); Recommended—IELTS (minimum score 8). Electronic applications accepted. *Faculty research:* Evolution of continental margins and orogenic belts, geologic processes occurring at plate boundaries, deep-sea sediment diagenesis, paleoecology, hydrogeology.

University of Chicago, Division of the Physical Sciences, Department of the Geophysical Sciences, Chicago, IL 60637. Offers atmospheric sciences (PhD); cosmochemistry (PhD); earth sciences (PhD); paleobiology (PhD); planetary and space sciences (PhD). Terminal master's awarded for partial completion of doctoral program. *Degree requirements:* For doctorate, variable foreign language requirement, comprehensive exam, thesis/dissertation. *Entrance requirements:* For doctorate, GRE General Test. Additional exam requirements/recommendations for international students: Required—TOEFL (minimum score 600 paper-based; 96 iBT), IELTS (minimum score 7). Electronic applications accepted. *Faculty research:* Climatology, evolutionary paleontology, cosmochemistry, geochemistry, oceanic sciences.

University of Florida, Graduate School, College of Liberal Arts and Sciences, Department of Geological Sciences, Gainesville, FL 32611. Offers geology (MS, MST, PhD); hydrologic sciences (MS, PhD); tropical conservation and development (MS, MST, PhD); wetland sciences (MS, MST, PhD). *Faculty:* 22. *Students:* 43 full-time (19 women), 3 part-time (1 woman); includes 4 minority (1 Asian, non-Hispanic/Latino; 3 Hispanic/Latino), 18 international. Average age 29. 60 applicants, 20% accepted, 11 enrolled. In 2015, 6 master's, 1 doctorate awarded. Terminal master's awarded for partial completion of doctoral program. *Degree requirements:* For master's, thesis (for some programs); for doctorate, one foreign language, thesis/dissertation. *Entrance requirements:* For master's and doctorate, GRE General Test, minimum GPA of 3.0. Additional exam requirements/recommendations for international students: Required—TOEFL (minimum score 550 paper-based; 80 iBT), IELTS (minimum score 6). *Application deadline:* For fall admission, 1/15 for domestic students; for spring admission, 10/1 for domestic students. Applications are processed on a rolling basis. Application fee: $30. Electronic applications accepted. *Financial support:* In 2015–16, 3 fellowships, 21 research assistantships, 25 teaching assistantships were awarded; career-related internships or fieldwork, Federal Work-Study, institutionally sponsored loans, and scholarships/grants also available. Support available to part-time students. Financial award application deadline: 3/1; financial award applicants required to submit FAFSA. *Faculty research:* Paleoclimatology, tectonophysics, petrochemistry, marine geology, geochemistry, hydrology. *Total annual research expenditures:* $1.5 million. *Unit head:* Dr. David A. Foster, Professor and Chair, 352-392-7316, Fax: 352-392-9294, E-mail: dafoster@ufl.edu. *Application contact:* Dr. Raymond Russo, Associate Professor and Graduate Coordinator, 352-392-2231, Fax: 352-392-9294, E-mail: rrusso@ufl.edu.

University of Illinois at Chicago, College of Liberal Arts and Sciences, Department of Earth and Environmental Sciences, Chicago, IL 60607-7128. Offers MS, PhD. *Faculty:* 9 full-time (4 women). *Students:* 18 full-time (10 women), 1 (woman) part-time; includes 3 minority (2 Asian, non-Hispanic/Latino; 1 Hispanic/Latino), 5 international. Average age 29. *Degree requirements:* For master's, thesis; for doctorate, thesis/dissertation. *Entrance requirements:* For master's and doctorate, GRE General Test, minimum GPA of 2.75. Additional exam requirements/recommendations for international students: Required—TOEFL. *Application deadline:* For fall admission, 2/1 for domestic and international students; for spring admission, 11/15 for domestic students, 7/15 for international students. Applications are processed on a rolling basis. Application fee: $60. Electronic applications accepted. *Expenses:* Contact institution. *Financial support:* In 2015–16, 1 fellowship with full tuition reimbursement was awarded; research assistantships with full tuition reimbursements, teaching assistantships with full tuition reimbursements, Federal Work-Study, scholarships/grants, traineeships, tuition waivers (full), and unspecified assistantships also available. Financial award application deadline: 3/1; financial award applicants required to submit FAFSA. *Faculty research:* Geochemistry, mineralogy and petrology, geophysics, tectonics, global change,

hydrology, geobiology. *Unit head:* Dr. Kathryn Nagy, Head, 312-355-3276, E-mail: klnagy@uic.edu. *Application contact:* Andrew Dombard, Director of Graduate Studies, 312-996-9206, E-mail: adombard@uic.edu.
Website: http://www.uic.edu/depts/geos/

University of Illinois at Urbana–Champaign, Graduate College, College of Liberal Arts and Sciences, School of Earth, Society and Environment, Department of Geology, Champaign, IL 61820. Offers geology (MS, PhD); teaching of earth sciences (MS). Terminal master's awarded for partial completion of doctoral program.

The University of Iowa, Graduate College, College of Liberal Arts and Sciences, Department of Earth and Environmental Science, Iowa City, IA 52242-1316. Offers MS, PhD. *Degree requirements:* For master's, thesis optional, exam; for doctorate, comprehensive exam, thesis/dissertation. *Entrance requirements:* For master's and doctorate, GRE General Test, minimum GPA of 3.0. Additional exam requirements/recommendations for international students: Required—TOEFL (minimum score 550 paper-based; 81 iBT). Electronic applications accepted.

University of Maine, Graduate School, College of Natural Sciences, Forestry, and Agriculture, School of Earth and Climate Sciences, Orono, ME 04469. Offers MS, PhD. *Program availability:* Part-time. *Faculty:* 21 full-time (5 women). *Students:* 27 full-time (14 women); includes 1 minority (Hispanic/Latino), 4 international. Average age 31. 43 applicants, 30% accepted, 9 enrolled. In 2015, 6 master's, 2 doctorates awarded. Terminal master's awarded for partial completion of doctoral program. *Degree requirements:* For master's, thesis; for doctorate, one foreign language, comprehensive exam, thesis/dissertation. *Entrance requirements:* For master's and doctorate, GRE General Test. Additional exam requirements/recommendations for international students: Required—TOEFL (minimum score 80 iBT). *Application deadline:* For fall admission, 2/20 priority date for domestic and international students. Applications are processed on a rolling basis. Application fee: $65. Electronic applications accepted. *Financial support:* In 2015–16, 27 students received support, including 19 research assistantships with tuition reimbursements available (averaging $14,600 per year), 7 teaching assistantships with full tuition reimbursements available (averaging $14,600 per year); Federal Work-Study, institutionally sponsored loans, and tuition waivers (full and partial) also available. Financial award application deadline: 3/1. *Faculty research:* Climate change, environmental geosciences, marine geology, geodynamics and solid earth geology. *Total annual research expenditures:* $2.5 million. *Unit head:* Dr. Scott Johnson, Chair, 207-581-2142, Fax: 207-581-2202. *Application contact:* Scott G. Delcourt, Assistant Vice President for Graduate Studies and Senior Associate Dean, 207-581-3291, Fax: 207-581-3232, E-mail: graduate@maine.edu.
Website: http://umaine.edu/earthclimate/

The University of Manchester, School of Earth, Atmospheric and Environmental Sciences, Manchester, United Kingdom. Offers atmospheric sciences (M Phil, M Sc, PhD); basin studies and petroleum geosciences (M Phil, M Sc, PhD); earth, atmospheric and environmental sciences (M Phil, M Sc, PhD); environmental geochemistry and cosmochemistry (M Phil, M Sc, PhD); isotope geochemistry and cosmochemistry (M Phil, M Sc, PhD); paleontology (M Phil, M Sc, PhD); physics and chemistry of minerals and fluids (M Phil, M Sc, PhD); structural and petrological geosciences (M Phil, M Sc, PhD).

University of Massachusetts Amherst, Graduate School, College of Natural Sciences, Department of Geosciences, Program in Geosciences, Amherst, MA 01003. Offers MS, PhD. *Program availability:* Part-time. Terminal master's awarded for partial completion of doctoral program. *Degree requirements:* For master's, thesis or alternative; for doctorate, comprehensive exam, thesis/dissertation. *Entrance requirements:* For master's and doctorate, GRE General Test. Additional exam requirements/recommendations for international students: Required—TOEFL (minimum score 550 paper-based; 80 iBT), IELTS (minimum score 6.5). Electronic applications accepted.

University of Michigan, Rackham Graduate School, College of Literature, Science, and the Arts, Department of Earth and Environmental Sciences, Ann Arbor, MI 48109-1005. Offers MS, PhD. *Faculty:* 28 full-time (9 women), 6 part-time/adjunct (3 women). *Students:* 59 full-time (28 women), 1 part-time (0 women); includes 6 minority (1 Asian, non-Hispanic/Latino; 3 Hispanic/Latino; 2 Two or more races, non-Hispanic/Latino), 12 international. 131 applicants, 17% accepted, 14 enrolled. In 2015, 3 master's, 9 doctorates awarded. Terminal master's awarded for partial completion of doctoral program. *Degree requirements:* For master's, thesis; for doctorate, comprehensive exam, thesis/dissertation, oral defense of dissertation. *Entrance requirements:* For master's and doctorate, GRE General Test. Additional exam requirements/recommendations for international students: Required—TOEFL (minimum score 100 iBT). *Application deadline:* For fall admission, 1/5 for domestic and international students; for winter admission, 11/1 for domestic and international students. Application fee: $75 ($90 for international students). Electronic applications accepted. *Financial support:* Fellowships with full tuition reimbursements, research assistantships with full tuition reimbursements, teaching assistantships with full tuition reimbursements, career-related internships or fieldwork, scholarships/grants, health care benefits, and unspecified assistantships available. Financial award application deadline: 1/5; financial award applicants required to submit FAFSA. *Faculty research:* Isotope geochemistry, paleoclimatology, mineral physics, tectonics, paleontology. *Unit head:* Dr. Christopher Poulsen, Chair, 734-764-1435, Fax: 734-763-4690, E-mail: michiganearth@umich.edu. *Application contact:* Anne Hudon, Graduate Program Coordinator, 734-615-3034, Fax: 734-763-4690, E-mail: michiganearth@umich.edu.
Website: http://lsa.umich.edu/earth

University of Missouri–Kansas City, College of Arts and Sciences, Department of Geosciences, Kansas City, MO 64110-2499. Offers environmental and urban geosciences (MS); geosciences (PhD). PhD (interdisciplinary) offered through the School of Graduate Studies. *Program availability:* Part-time. *Faculty:* 6 full-time (2 women), 10 part-time/adjunct (1 woman). *Students:* 3 full-time (1 woman), 19 part-time (9 women); includes 1 minority (Hispanic/Latino), 1 international. Average age 33. 17 applicants, 82% accepted, 9 enrolled. In 2015, 4 master's awarded. *Degree requirements:* For master's, thesis; for doctorate, thesis/dissertation, qualifying exam. *Entrance requirements:* For master's, GRE General Test, minimum GPA of 3.0. Additional exam requirements/recommendations for international students: Required—TOEFL (minimum score 550 paper-based; 80 iBT). *Application deadline:* For fall admission, 3/15 priority date for domestic and international students. Applications are processed on a rolling basis. Application fee: $45 ($50 for international students). Electronic applications accepted. *Financial support:* In 2015–16, 15 teaching assistantships with partial tuition reimbursements (averaging $13,158 per year) were awarded; research assistantships with partial tuition reimbursements, Federal Work-Study, institutionally sponsored loans, and tuition waivers (full and partial) also available. Support available to part-time students. Financial award application deadline: 3/1; financial award applicants required to submit FAFSA. *Faculty research:* Neotectonics and applied geophysics, environmental geosciences, urban geoscience, geoinformatics-remote sensing, atmospheric research. *Unit head:* Dr. Michael B. Kruger, Interim Chair, 816-235-5441, Fax: 816-235-5535, E-mail: krugerm@umkc.edu. *Application contact:* Dr. Jejung Lee, Associate Professor, 816-235-6495, Fax: 816-235-5535, E-mail: leej@umkc.edu.
Website: http://cas.umkc.edu/geo/

University of Montana, Graduate School, College of Humanities and Sciences, Department of Geosciences, Missoula, MT 59812-0002. Offers MS, PhD. *Degree requirements:* For doctorate, thesis/dissertation. *Entrance requirements:* For master's and doctorate, GRE General Test. Additional exam requirements/recommendations for international students: Required—TOEFL (minimum score 525 paper-based). *Faculty research:* Environmental geoscience, regional structure and tectonics, groundwater geology, petrology, mineral deposits.

University of Nebraska–Lincoln, Graduate College, College of Arts and Sciences, Department of Geosciences, Lincoln, NE 68588. Offers MS, PhD. *Degree requirements:* For master's, thesis optional, departmental qualifying exam; for doctorate, comprehensive exam, thesis/dissertation, departmental qualifying exams. *Entrance requirements:* For master's and doctorate, GRE General Test. Additional exam requirements/recommendations for international students: Required—TOEFL (minimum score 550 paper-based). Electronic applications accepted. *Faculty research:* Hydrogeology, sedimentology, environmental geology, vertebrate paleontology.

University of Nevada, Las Vegas, Graduate College, College of Sciences, Department of Geoscience, Las Vegas, NV 89154-4010. Offers MS, PhD. *Program availability:* Part-time. *Faculty:* 6 full-time (0 women), 1 (woman) part-time/adjunct. *Students:* 35 full-time (8 women), 13 part-time (4 women); includes 5 minority (3 Asian, non-Hispanic/Latino; 1 Hispanic/Latino; 1 Two or more races, non-Hispanic/Latino), 9 international. Average age 29. 56 applicants, 36% accepted, 15 enrolled. In 2015, 10 master's, 2 doctorates awarded. *Degree requirements:* For master's, thesis; for doctorate, comprehensive exam, thesis/dissertation. *Entrance requirements:* For master's and doctorate, GRE General Test. Additional exam requirements/recommendations for international students: Required—TOEFL (minimum score 550 paper-based; 80 iBT), IELTS (minimum score 7). *Application deadline:* For fall admission, 2/1 for domestic students, 5/1 for international students; for spring admission, 10/1 for domestic and international students. Application fee: $60 ($95 for international students). Electronic applications accepted. *Expenses:* $264 per credit state resident full-time and part-time; $6,955 per semester, $264 per credit nonresident full-time; $555 per credit nonresident part-time. *Financial support:* In 2015–16, 36 students received support, including 6 research assistantships with partial tuition reimbursements available (averaging $15,444 per year), 30 teaching assistantships with partial tuition reimbursements available (averaging $17,433 per year); institutionally sponsored loans, scholarships/grants, health care benefits, and unspecified assistantships also available. Financial award application deadline: 3/1. *Faculty research:* Petrology, geochemistry and economic geology; climate and earth surface processes; structural geology and tectonics; sedimentary geology and paleontology; hydrogeological and environmental science. *Total annual research expenditures:* $2.5 million. *Unit head:* Dr. Terry Spell, Chair/Professor, 702-895-0828, E-mail: terry.spell@unlv.edu. *Application contact:* Graduate College Admissions Evaluator, 702-895-3367, Fax: 702-895-4180, E-mail: gradadmissions@unlv.edu.
Website: http://geoscience.unlv.edu/

University of New Hampshire, Graduate School, College of Engineering and Physical Sciences, Department of Earth Sciences, Durham, NH 03824. Offers earth sciences (PhD); geology (MS); hydrology (MS). *Degree requirements:* For master's, thesis. *Entrance requirements:* For master's, GRE General Test. Additional exam requirements/recommendations for international students: Required—TOEFL (minimum score 550 paper-based; 80 iBT). Electronic applications accepted.

University of New Haven, Graduate School, College of Arts and Sciences, Program in Environmental Science, West Haven, CT 06516-1916. Offers environmental ecology (MS); environmental education (MS); environmental geoscience (MS); environmental health and management (MS); environmental science (MS); geographical information systems (MS, Graduate Certificate). *Program availability:* Part-time, evening/weekend. *Students:* 20 full-time (10 women), 6 part-time (5 women); includes 2 minority (1 Black or African American, non-Hispanic/Latino; 1 Hispanic/Latino), 5 international. Average age 26. 25 applicants, 88% accepted, 13 enrolled. In 2015, 19 master's awarded. *Degree requirements:* For master's, thesis optional, research project. *Entrance requirements:* Additional exam requirements/recommendations for international students: Required—TOEFL (minimum score 80 iBT), IELTS, PTE. *Application deadline:* For fall admission, 5/31 for international students; for winter admission, 10/15 for international students; for spring admission, 1/15 for international students. Applications are processed on a rolling basis. Application fee: $75. Electronic applications accepted. Application fee is waived when completed online. *Expenses: Tuition, area resident:* Full-time $15,282; part-time $849 per credit hour. *Required fees:* $150; $60 per term. Tuition and fees vary according to program. *Financial support:* Research assistantships with partial tuition reimbursements, teaching assistantships with partial tuition reimbursements, career-related internships or fieldwork, Federal Work-Study, scholarships/grants, and unspecified assistantships available. Support available to part-time students. Financial award applicants required to submit FAFSA. *Unit head:* Dr. Roman Zajac, Coordinator, 203-932-7114, E-mail: rzajac@newhaven.edu. *Application contact:* Michelle Mason, Director of Graduate Enrollment, 203-932-7067, E-mail: mmason@newhaven.edu.
Website: http://www.newhaven.edu/4728/

University of New Mexico, Graduate Studies, College of Arts and Sciences, Program in Earth and Planetary Sciences, Albuquerque, NM 87131. Offers MS, PhD. *Program availability:* Part-time. *Faculty:* 17 full-time (5 women). *Students:* 25 full-time (10 women), 22 part-time (11 women); includes 7 minority (1 Asian, non-Hispanic/Latino; 6 Hispanic/Latino), 1 international. Average age 30. 60 applicants, 23% accepted, 14 enrolled. In 2015, 1 master's, 3 doctorates awarded. Terminal master's awarded for partial completion of doctoral program. *Degree requirements:* For master's, comprehensive exam, thesis; for doctorate, comprehensive exam, thesis/dissertation. *Entrance requirements:* For master's and doctorate, GRE General Test. Additional exam requirements/recommendations for international students: Required—TOEFL. *Application deadline:* For fall admission, 1/15 priority date for domestic and international students; for spring admission, 11/1 priority date for domestic and international students. Application fee: $50. Electronic applications accepted. *Financial support:* Fellowships with full tuition reimbursements, research assistantships with full tuition reimbursements, teaching assistantships with full tuition reimbursements, scholarships/grants, and health care benefits available. Financial award application deadline: 1/15. *Faculty research:* Climatology, experimental petrology, geochemistry, geographic information technologies, geomorphology, geophysics, hydrogeology, igneous petrology, metamorphic petrology, meteoritics, meteorology, micrometeorites, mineralogy, paleoclimatology, paleontology, pedology, petrology, physical volcanology, planetary sciences, Precambrian geology, quaternary geology, sedimentary geochemistry, sedimentology, stable isotope geochemistry, stratigraphy, structural geology, tectonics, volcanology. *Total annual research expenditures:* $2.5 million. *Unit head:* Dr. Adrian J. Brearley, Chair, 505-277-4204, Fax: 505-277-8843, E-mail: brearley@unm.edu. *Application contact:* Cindy Jaramillo, Administrative Assistant III, 505-277-1635, Fax:

505-277-8843, E-mail: epsdept@unm.edu.
Website: http://epswww.unm.edu/

University of New Orleans, Graduate School, College of Sciences, Department of Earth and Environmental Sciences, New Orleans, LA 70148. Offers MS. *Program availability:* Evening/weekend. *Degree requirements:* For master's, thesis. *Entrance requirements:* For master's, GRE General Test. Additional exam requirements/recommendations for international students: Required—TOEFL (minimum score 550 paper-based; 79 iBT), IELTS. Electronic applications accepted. *Faculty research:* Continental margin structure and seismology, burial diagenesis of siliclastic sediments, tectonics at convergent plate margins, continental shelf sediment stability, early diagenesis of carbonates.

The University of North Carolina at Charlotte, College of Liberal Arts and Sciences, Department of Geography and Earth Sciences, Charlotte, NC 28223-0001. Offers earth sciences (MS); geography (MA), including community planning, geographic information science and technologies, location analysis, transportation studies, urban-regional analysis; geography and urban regional analysis (PhD). *Program availability:* Part-time, evening/weekend. *Faculty:* 30 full-time (12 women), 1 part-time/adjunct (0 women). *Students:* 49 full-time (22 women), 22 part-time (11 women); includes 6 minority (2 Black or African American, non-Hispanic/Latino; 1 Asian, non-Hispanic/Latino; 2 Hispanic/Latino; 1 Two or more races, non-Hispanic/Latino), 18 international. Average age 30. 50 applicants, 78% accepted, 25 enrolled. In 2015, 17 master's, 9 doctorates awarded. Terminal master's awarded for partial completion of doctoral program. *Degree requirements:* For master's, comprehensive exam, thesis or alternative, project. *Entrance requirements:* For master's, GRE General Test or MAT, minimum GPA of 2.75, 3.0 for junior and senior years, transcripts, letters of recommendation, and personal essays (for MS); minimum overall GPA of 3.1 or for the last 2 years, 3.2 in major, three letters of reference, and personal essay (for MA); for doctorate, GRE, MA or MS in geography or a field related to the primary emphases of the program; minimum master's-level GPA of 3.5. Additional exam requirements/recommendations for international students: Required—TOEFL (minimum score 557 paper-based, 83 iBT) or IELTS (minimum score 6.5). *Application deadline:* For fall admission, 2/1 priority date for domestic and international students; for spring admission, 9/30 for domestic and international students; for summer admission, 4/1 for domestic and international students. Applications are processed on a rolling basis. Application fee: $75. Electronic applications accepted. *Expenses:* Tuition, state resident: full-time $4128. Tuition, nonresident: full-time $16,799. *Required fees:* $2904. Tuition and fees vary according to course load and program. *Financial support:* In 2015–16, 42 students received support, including 1 fellowship (averaging $42,000 per year), 8 research assistantships (averaging $10,025 per year), 33 teaching assistantships (averaging $9,612 per year); career-related internships or fieldwork, institutionally sponsored loans, scholarships/grants, and unspecified assistantships also available. Support available to part-time students. Financial award application deadline: 3/1; financial award applicants required to submit FAFSA. *Faculty research:* Improving geographic knowledge discovery and spatial reasoning with mobile and Web-based geographical information systems; an in-house supercomputing cluster for multi-scale science and collaborative research; feedback between a generalist pathogen, hosts and heterogeneous environments at multiple spatial and temporal scales. *Total annual research expenditures:* $348,765. *Unit head:* Dr. Craig Allan, Chair, 704-687-5999, E-mail: cjallan@uncc.edu. *Application contact:* Kathy B. Giddings, Director of Graduate Admissions, 704-687-5503, Fax: 704-687-1668, E-mail: gradadm@uncc.edu.
Website: https://geoearth.uncc.edu/

The University of North Carolina Wilmington, College of Arts and Sciences, Department of Geography and Geology, Wilmington, NC 28403-3297. Offers geoscience (MS). *Program availability:* Part-time. *Faculty:* 24 full-time (8 women). *Students:* 6 full-time (5 women), 37 part-time (9 women); includes 8 minority (5 Black or African American, non-Hispanic/Latino; 1 Asian, non-Hispanic/Latino; 2 Hispanic/Latino), 1 international. Average age 33. 46 applicants, 17 enrolled. In 2015, 14 master's awarded. *Degree requirements:* For master's, comprehensive exam, thesis or alternative. *Entrance requirements:* For master's, GRE General Test, minimum B average in undergraduate major and prerequisite geoscience courses, 3 letters of recommendation, essay. Additional exam requirements/recommendations for international students: Required—TOEFL (minimum score 79 iBT), IELTS (minimum score 6.5). *Application deadline:* For fall admission, 4/15 for domestic students; for spring admission, 10/15 for domestic students. Applications are processed on a rolling basis. Application fee: $60. Electronic applications accepted. *Expenses:* $8,854 in-state full-time per year, $20,945 out-of-state full-time per year. *Financial support:* Research assistantships, teaching assistantships, and scholarships/grants available. Financial award application deadline: 3/15; financial award applicants required to submit FAFSA. *Unit head:* Dr. Lynn Leonard, Chair, 910-962-2339, Fax: 910-962-7077, E-mail: lynnl@uncw.edu. *Application contact:* Dr. Joanne Halls, Graduate Coordinator, 910-962-7614, Fax: 910-962-7077, E-mail: hallsj@uncw.edu.
Website: http://uncw.edu/msgeoscience/index.html

University of North Dakota, Graduate School, John D. Odegard School of Aerospace Sciences, Program in Earth System Science and Policy, Grand Forks, ND 58202. Offers MEM, MS, PhD. *Program availability:* Part-time. *Degree requirements:* For master's, thesis (for some programs); for doctorate, thesis/dissertation (for some programs). *Entrance requirements:* For master's and doctorate, GRE General Test, minimum GPA of 3.0. Additional exam requirements/recommendations for international students: Required—TOEFL (minimum score 550 paper-based; 79 iBT), IELTS (minimum score 6.5). Electronic applications accepted.

University of Northern Colorado, Graduate School, College of Natural and Health Sciences, School of Chemistry, Earth Sciences and Physics, Program in Earth Sciences, Greeley, CO 80639. Offers MA. *Program availability:* Part-time. *Degree requirements:* For master's, comprehensive exam. *Entrance requirements:* For master's, GRE General Test, 3 letters of recommendation. Electronic applications accepted.

University of Northern Iowa, Graduate College, College of Humanities, Arts and Sciences, MA Program in Science Education, Cedar Falls, IA 50614. Offers earth science education (MA); physics education (MA); science education (MA). *Students:* 2 full-time (1 woman), 37 part-time (23 women); includes 1 minority (Hispanic/Latino). 3 applicants. In 2015, 1 master's awarded. *Degree requirements:* For master's, comprehensive exam (for some programs), thesis or alternative. *Entrance requirements:* For master's, minimum GPA of 3.0. Additional exam requirements/recommendations for international students: Required—TOEFL (minimum score 500 paper-based; 61 iBT). *Application deadline:* For fall admission, 8/1 priority date for domestic students. Applications are processed on a rolling basis. Application fee: $50 ($70 for international students). Electronic applications accepted. *Financial support:* Application deadline: 2/1. *Unit head:* Dr. Dawn Del Carlo, Coordinator, 319-273-3296, Fax: 319-273-7140, E-mail: sciedgradcoord@uni.edu. *Application contact:* Laurie S. Russell, Record Analyst, 319-273-2623, Fax: 319-273-2885, E-mail: laurie.russell@uni.edu.
Website: http://www.uni.edu/science-ed/graduate-program

University of Notre Dame, Graduate School, College of Engineering, Department of Civil Engineering and Geological Sciences, Notre Dame, IN 46556. Offers bioengineering (MS Bio E); civil engineering (MSCE); civil engineering and geological sciences (PhD); environmental engineering (MS Env E); geological sciences (MS). Terminal master's awarded for partial completion of doctoral program. *Degree requirements:* For master's, comprehensive exam; for doctorate, thesis/dissertation, candidacy exam. *Entrance requirements:* For master's and doctorate, GRE General Test. Additional exam requirements/recommendations for international students: Required—TOEFL (minimum score 600 paper-based; 80 iBT). Electronic applications accepted. *Faculty research:* Environmental modeling, biological-waste treatment, petrology, environmental geology, geochemistry.

University of Ottawa, Faculty of Graduate and Postdoctoral Studies, Faculty of Science, Ottawa-Carleton Geoscience Centre, Ottawa, ON K1N 6N5, Canada. Offers earth sciences (M Sc, PhD). M Sc, PhD offered jointly with Carleton University. *Degree requirements:* For master's, thesis, seminar; for doctorate, comprehensive exam, thesis/dissertation, seminar. *Entrance requirements:* For master's, honors B Sc degree or equivalent, minimum B average; for doctorate, honors B Sc with minimum B average or M Sc with minimum B+ average. Electronic applications accepted. *Faculty research:* Environmental geoscience, geochemistry/petrology, geomatics/geomathematics, mineral resource studies.

University of Pennsylvania, School of Arts and Sciences, College of Liberal and Professional Studies, Philadelphia, PA 19104. Offers applied geosciences (MSAG); applied positive psychology (MAP); chemical sciences (MCS); environmental studies (MES); individualized study (MLA); liberal arts (M Phil); medical physics (MMP); organization dynamics (M Phil). *Students:* 135 full-time (69 women), 329 part-time (203 women); includes 85 minority (27 Black or African American, non-Hispanic/Latino; 23 Asian, non-Hispanic/Latino; 17 Hispanic/Latino; 18 Two or more races, non-Hispanic/Latino), 61 international. Average age 35. 542 applicants, 52% accepted, 173 enrolled. In 2015, 161 master's awarded. *Expenses: Tuition, area resident:* Full-time $31,068; part-time $5762 per course. *Required fees:* $3200; $336 per course. Full-time tuition and fees vary according to degree level, program and student level. Part-time tuition and fees vary according to course load, degree level and program. *Unit head:* Nora Lewis, E-mail: nlewis@sas.upenn.edu.
Website: http://www.sas.upenn.edu/lps/graduate

University of Pennsylvania, School of Arts and Sciences, Graduate Group in Earth and Environmental Science, Philadelphia, PA 19104. Offers MS, PhD. *Program availability:* Part-time. *Faculty:* 9 full-time (3 women), 4 part-time/adjunct (0 women). *Students:* 14 full-time (10 women); includes 5 minority (2 Black or African American, non-Hispanic/Latino; 3 Two or more races, non-Hispanic/Latino), 3 international. Average age 27. 40 applicants, 10% accepted, 3 enrolled. In 2015, 4 doctorates awarded. *Expenses: Tuition, area resident:* Full-time $31,068; part-time $5762 per course. *Required fees:* $3200; $336 per course. Full-time tuition and fees vary according to degree level, program and student level. Part-time tuition and fees vary according to course load, degree level and program.
Website: http://www.sas.upenn.edu/graduate-division

University of Rhode Island, Graduate School, College of the Environment and Life Sciences, Department of Geosciences, Kingston, RI 02881. Offers environmental science and management (MESM); environmental sciences (MS, PhD). *Program availability:* Part-time. *Faculty:* 7 full-time (3 women), 1 part-time/adjunct (0 women). *Students:* 8 full-time (5 women), 1 part-time (0 women); includes 1 minority (Asian, non-Hispanic/Latino), 2 international. *Degree requirements:* For master's, comprehensive exam (for some programs), thesis optional; for doctorate, comprehensive exam, thesis/dissertation. *Entrance requirements:* For master's and doctorate, GRE, 2 letters of recommendation. Additional exam requirements/recommendations for international students: Required—TOEFL (minimum score 550 paper-based). *Application deadline:* For fall admission, 7/15 for domestic students, 2/1 for international students; for spring admission, 11/15 for domestic students, 7/15 for international students. Application fee: $65. Electronic applications accepted. *Expenses:* Tuition, state resident: full-time $11,796; part-time $655 per credit. Tuition, nonresident: full-time $24,206; part-time $1345 per credit. *Required fees:* $1546; $44 per credit. One-time fee: $155 full-time; $35 part-time. *Financial support:* In 2015–16, 5 research assistantships with tuition reimbursements (averaging $10,479 per year), 7 teaching assistantships (averaging $9,785 per year) were awarded. Financial award application deadline: 2/1; financial award applicants required to submit FAFSA. *Faculty research:* Hydrology and water resources, interior of the earth, quaternary and modern depositional environments, geobiology of Mesozoic terrestrial ecosystems. *Total annual research expenditures:* $2.4 million. *Unit head:* Dr. Daivd Fastovsky, Chair, 401-874-2185, Fax: 401-874-2190, E-mail: defastov@uri.edu. *Application contact:* Graduate Admissions, 401-874-2872, E-mail: gradadm@etal.uri.edu.
Website: http://web.uri.edu/geo/

University of Rochester, School of Arts and Sciences, Department of Earth and Environmental Sciences, Rochester, NY 14627. Offers MS, PhD. *Faculty:* 8 full-time (2 women). *Students:* 21 full-time (8 women); includes 2 minority (1 American Indian or Alaska Native, non-Hispanic/Latino; 1 Hispanic/Latino), 6 international. 17 applicants, 35% accepted, 4 enrolled. In 2015, 6 master's, 1 doctorate awarded. *Degree requirements:* For doctorate, thesis/dissertation, qualifying exam. *Entrance requirements:* For master's and doctorate, GRE General Test. Additional exam requirements/recommendations for international students: Required—TOEFL. *Application deadline:* For fall admission, 2/1 priority date for domestic students. Application fee: $60. Electronic applications accepted. *Expenses: Tuition, area resident:* Full-time $47,450; part-time $1482 per credit hour. *Required fees:* $528. Tuition and fees vary according to program. *Financial support:* Fellowships, research assistantships, teaching assistantships, career-related internships or fieldwork, and tuition waivers (full and partial) available. Financial award application deadline: 2/1. *Faculty research:* Geochemistry and environmental sciences; paleomagnetism, structure and tectonics. *Unit head:* Carmala Garzione, Chair, 585-275-5713, E-mail: carmala.garzione@rochester.edu. *Application contact:* Kathy Lutz, Secretary, 585-275-5713, E-mail: kathy@ur.rochester.edu.
Website: http://www.ees.rochester.edu/

University of South Carolina, The Graduate School, College of Arts and Sciences, Department of Geological Sciences, Columbia, SC 29208. Offers MS, PhD. Terminal master's awarded for partial completion of doctoral program. *Degree requirements:* For master's, thesis; for doctorate, comprehensive exam, thesis/dissertation, published paper. *Entrance requirements:* For master's and doctorate, GRE General Test. Additional exam requirements/recommendations for international students: Required—TOEFL (minimum score 570 paper-based; 75 iBT). Electronic applications accepted. *Faculty research:* Environmental geology, tectonics, petrology, coastal processes, paleoclimatology.

University of Southern California, Graduate School, Dana and David Dornsife College of Letters, Arts and Sciences, Department of Earth Sciences, Los Angeles, CA 90089.

Offers geological sciences (MS, PhD). *Program availability:* Part-time. Terminal master's awarded for partial completion of doctoral program. *Degree requirements:* For master's, thesis; for doctorate, comprehensive exam, thesis/dissertation. *Entrance requirements:* For master's and doctorate, GRE. Additional exam requirements/recommendations for international students: Required—TOEFL. Electronic applications accepted. *Faculty research:* Geophysics, paleoceanography, geochemistry, geobiology, structure, tectonics.

University of South Florida, College of Arts and Sciences, School of Geosciences, Tampa, FL 33620-9951. Offers environmental science and policy (MS); geography (MA), including environmental geography, geographic information science and spatial analysis, human geography; geography and environmental science and policy (PhD); geology (MS, PhD); urban and regional planning (MURP). *Program availability:* Part-time, evening/weekend. *Faculty:* 32 full-time (7 women). *Students:* 87 full-time (41 women), 45 part-time (19 women); includes 18 minority (7 Black or African American, non-Hispanic/Latino; 3 Asian, non-Hispanic/Latino; 7 Hispanic/Latino; 1 Two or more races, non-Hispanic/Latino), 29 international. Average age 34. 39 applicants, 62% accepted, 9 enrolled. In 2015, 10 master's awarded. *Degree requirements:* For master's, comprehensive exam, thesis (for some programs); for doctorate, comprehensive exam, thesis/dissertation. *Entrance requirements:* For master's, GRE General Test, minimum GPA of 3.0 for last 60 credits of undergraduate degree, letter of intent, letters of recommendation; for doctorate, GRE General Test, minimum GPA of 3.0 for all doctorate programs except for ESP/Geography which requires 3.20 GPA for all academic work, letter of intent, letters of recommendation. Additional exam requirements/recommendations for international students: Required—TOEFL (minimum score 550 paper-based; 79 iBT) or IELTS (minimum score 6.5) for MA and MURP; TOEFL (minimum score 600 paper-based) for MS and PhD. *Application deadline:* For fall admission, 2/15 for domestic students, 1/2 for international students; for spring admission, 10/15 for domestic students, 6/1 for international students. Application fee: $30. *Financial support:* In 2015–16, 26 students received support, including 3 research assistantships (averaging $12,345 per year), 25 teaching assistantships with tuition reimbursements available (averaging $12,807 per year); unspecified assistantships also available. Financial award application deadline: 3/1. *Faculty research:* Geography: human geography, environmental geography, geographic information science and spatial analysis, urban geography, social theory; environmental science, policy, and planning: water resources, wildlife ecology, Karst and wetland environments, natural hazards, soil contamination, meteorology and climatology, environmental sustainability and policy, urban and regional planning. *Total annual research expenditures:* $2.3 million. *Unit head:* Dr. Jayajit Chakraborty, Professor and Chair, Geography Division, 813-974-8188, Fax: 813-974-5911, E-mail: jchakrab@usf.edu. *Application contact:* Dr. Jennifer Collins, Associate Professor and Graduate Program Coordinator, 813-974-4242, Fax: 813-974-5911, E-mail: collinsjm@usf.edu.
Website: http://hennarot.forest.usf.edu/main/depts/geosci/

The University of Texas at Austin, Graduate School, Jackson School of Geosciences, Austin, TX 78712-1111. Offers MA, MS, PhD. *Program availability:* Part-time. *Degree requirements:* For master's, report (MA), thesis (MS); for doctorate, thesis/dissertation. *Entrance requirements:* For master's and doctorate, GRE General Test. Electronic applications accepted. *Faculty research:* Sedimentary geology, geophysics, hydrogeology, structure/tectonics, vertebrate paleontology.

The University of Texas at Dallas, School of Natural Sciences and Mathematics, Department of Geosciences, Richardson, TX 75080. Offers geochemistry (MS, PhD); geophysics (MS, PhD); geospatial information sciences (MS, PhD); hydrogeology (MS, PhD); sedimentology, stratigraphy, and paleontology (MS, PhD); structural geology and tectonics (MS, PhD). *Program availability:* Part-time, evening/weekend. *Faculty:* 9 full-time (0 women). *Students:* 57 full-time (21 women), 23 part-time (4 women); includes 12 minority (3 Black or African American, non-Hispanic/Latino; 4 Asian, non-Hispanic/Latino; 3 Hispanic/Latino; 2 Two or more races, non-Hispanic/Latino), 33 international. Average age 30. 98 applicants, 31% accepted, 20 enrolled. In 2015, 20 master's, 4 doctorates awarded. *Degree requirements:* For master's, thesis optional; for doctorate, thesis/dissertation. *Entrance requirements:* For master's and doctorate, GRE General Test, minimum GPA of 3.0 in upper-level course work in field. Additional exam requirements/recommendations for international students: Required—TOEFL (minimum score 550 paper-based). *Application deadline:* For fall admission, 7/15 for domestic students, 5/1 priority date for international students; for spring admission, 11/15 for domestic students, 9/1 priority date for international students. Applications are processed on a rolling basis. Application fee: $50 ($100 for international students). Electronic applications accepted. *Expenses:* Tuition, state resident: full-time $11,940; part-time $663 per semester hour. Tuition, nonresident: full-time $22,786; part-time $1266 per semester hour. Tuition and fees vary according to course load. *Financial support:* In 2015–16, 41 students received support, including 10 research assistantships with partial tuition reimbursements available (averaging $19,260 per year), 15 teaching assistantships with partial tuition reimbursements available (averaging $17,100 per year); career-related internships or fieldwork, Federal Work-Study, institutionally sponsored loans, scholarships/grants, and unspecified assistantships also available. Support available to part-time students. Financial award application deadline: 4/30; financial award applicants required to submit FAFSA. *Faculty research:* Cybermapping, GPS applications for geophysics and geology, seismology and ground-penetrating radar, numerical modeling, signal processing and inverse modeling techniques in seismology. *Unit head:* Dr. John Geissman, Department Head, 972-883-2454, Fax: 972-883-2537, E-mail: geosciences@utdallas.edu. *Application contact:* Gloria Eby, Graduate Support Assistant, 972-883-2404, Fax: 972-883-2537, E-mail: geosciences@utdallas.edu.
Website: http://www.utdallas.edu/geosciences

The University of Tulsa, Graduate School, College of Engineering and Natural Sciences, Department of Geosciences, Tulsa, OK 74104-3189. Offers geophysics (MS); geosciences (MS, PhD); JD/MS. *Program availability:* Part-time. *Faculty:* 8 full-time (1 woman). *Students:* 27 full-time (11 women), 9 part-time (6 women); includes 3 minority (1 Black or African American, non-Hispanic/Latino; 2 American Indian or Alaska Native, non-Hispanic/Latino), 20 international. Average age 28. 132 applicants, 30% accepted, 18 enrolled. In 2015, 26 master's, 5 doctorates awarded. Terminal master's awarded for partial completion of doctoral program. *Degree requirements:* For master's, thesis (for some programs); for doctorate, comprehensive exam, thesis/dissertation. *Entrance requirements:* For master's and doctorate, GRE General Test. Additional exam requirements/recommendations for international students: Required—TOEFL (minimum score 550 paper-based; 80 iBT), IELTS (minimum score 6). *Application deadline:* Applications are processed on a rolling basis. Application fee: $55. Electronic applications accepted. *Expenses: Tuition, area resident:* Full-time $22,230; part-time $1176 per credit hour. *Required fees:* $590 per semester. Tuition and fees vary according to course load. *Financial support:* In 2015–16, 18 students received support, including 2 fellowships with full tuition reimbursements available (averaging $3,600 per year), 7 research assistantships with full tuition reimbursements available (averaging $7,609 per year), 10 teaching assistantships with full tuition reimbursements available (averaging $11,498 per year); career-related internships or fieldwork, scholarships/grants, health care benefits, and unspecified assistantships also available. Support available to part-time students. Financial award application deadline: 2/1; financial award applicants required to submit FAFSA. *Faculty research:* Petroleum exploration/production and environmental science, including clastic sedimentology, petroleum seismology, seismic stratigraphy, structural geology, geochemistry, and biogeoscience. *Total annual research expenditures:* $409,030. *Unit head:* Dr. Peter Michael, Chairperson, 918-631-3017, Fax: 918-631-2091, E-mail: pjm@utulsa.edu. *Application contact:* Dr. Dennis Kerr, Adviser, 918-631-3020, Fax: 918-631-2156, E-mail: dennis-kerr@utulsa.edu.
Website: http://engineering.utulsa.edu/academics/geosciences/

University of Victoria, Faculty of Graduate Studies, Faculty of Science, School of Earth and Ocean Sciences, Victoria, BC V8W 2Y2, Canada. Offers M Sc, PhD. *Program availability:* Part-time. *Degree requirements:* For master's, thesis; for doctorate, thesis/dissertation, candidacy exam. *Entrance requirements:* For master's and doctorate, GRE. Additional exam requirements/recommendations for international students: Required—TOEFL (minimum score 575 paper-based), IELTS (minimum score 7). Electronic applications accepted. *Faculty research:* Climate modeling, geology.

University of Waterloo, Graduate Studies, Faculty of Science, Department of Earth and Environmental Sciences, Waterloo, ON N2L 3G1, Canada. Offers M Sc, PhD. *Program availability:* Part-time. *Degree requirements:* For master's, research paper or thesis; for doctorate, comprehensive exam, thesis/dissertation. *Entrance requirements:* For master's, GRE, honors degree, minimum B average; for doctorate, GRE, master's degree, minimum B average. Additional exam requirements/recommendations for international students: Required—TOEFL, IELTS, PTE. *Application deadline:* Applications are processed on a rolling basis. Application fee: $100 Canadian dollars. Electronic applications accepted. *Financial support:* Research assistantships, teaching assistantships, career-related internships or fieldwork, and institutionally sponsored loans available. *Faculty research:* Environmental geology, soil physics.
Website: https://uwaterloo.ca/earth-environmental-sciences/

The University of Western Ontario, Faculty of Graduate Studies, Physical Sciences Division, Department of Earth Sciences, London, ON N6A 5B8, Canada. Offers environment and sustainability (MES); geology (M Sc, PhD); geology and environmental science (M Sc, PhD); geophysics (M Sc, PhD); geophysics and environmental science (M Sc, PhD). *Degree requirements:* For master's, thesis; for doctorate, thesis/dissertation, qualifying exam. *Entrance requirements:* For master's, honors in B Sc; for doctorate, M Sc. Additional exam requirements/recommendations for international students: Required—TOEFL. *Faculty research:* Geophysics, geochemistry, paleontology, sedimentology/stratigraphy, glaciology/quaternary.

University of West Florida, College of Science and Engineering, Department of Earth and Environmental Sciences, Pensacola, FL 32514-5750. Offers MS. *Program availability:* Part-time. *Entrance requirements:* For master's, GRE (minimum score: 50th percentile for verbal; 40th percentile for quantitative), official transcripts; formal letter of interest, background, and professional goals; three letters of recommendation by individuals in professionally-relevant fields (waived for graduates of UWF Department of Environmental Sciences); current curriculum vitae/resume. Additional exam requirements/recommendations for international students: Required—TOEFL (minimum score 550 paper-based).

University of Windsor, Faculty of Graduate Studies, Faculty of Science, Department of Earth and Environmental Sciences, Windsor, ON N9B 3P4, Canada. Offers earth sciences (M Sc, PhD). *Program availability:* Part-time. *Degree requirements:* For master's, thesis; for doctorate, comprehensive exam, thesis/dissertation. *Entrance requirements:* For master's, minimum B average; for doctorate, minimum B average, copies of publication abstract. Additional exam requirements/recommendations for international students: Required—TOEFL (minimum score 560 paper-based). *Faculty research:* Aqueous geochemistry and hydrothermal processes, igneous petrochemistry, radiogenic isotopes, radiometric age-dating, diagenetic and sedimentary geochemistry.

Virginia Polytechnic Institute and State University, Graduate School, College of Science, Blacksburg, VA 24061. Offers biological sciences (MS, PhD); biomedical technology development and management (MS); chemistry (MS, PhD); economics (MA, PhD); geosciences (MS, PhD); mathematics (MS, PhD); physics (MS, PhD); psychology (MS, PhD); statistics (MS, PhD). *Degree requirements:* For master's, comprehensive exam (for some programs), thesis (for some programs); for doctorate, comprehensive exam (for some programs), thesis/dissertation (for some programs). *Entrance requirements:* For master's and doctorate, GRE/GMAT (may vary by department). Additional exam requirements/recommendations for international students: Required—TOEFL (minimum score 550 paper-based). Electronic applications accepted.

Washington University in St. Louis, Graduate School of Arts and Sciences, Department of Earth and Planetary Sciences, St. Louis, MO 63130-4899. Offers PhD. *Students:* 30 full-time (14 women); includes 2 minority (1 Asian, non-Hispanic/Latino; 1 Two or more races, non-Hispanic/Latino), 15 international. 61 applicants, 30% accepted, 6 enrolled. In 2015, 5 doctorates awarded. Terminal master's awarded for partial completion of doctoral program. *Degree requirements:* For doctorate, thesis/dissertation. *Entrance requirements:* For doctorate, GRE General Test. Additional exam requirements/recommendations for international students: Required—TOEFL. *Application deadline:* For fall admission, 1/15 for domestic students. Application fee: $45. Electronic applications accepted. *Financial support:* Fellowships, research assistantships, teaching assistantships, and tuition waivers (full and partial) available. Financial award application deadline: 1/15. *Faculty research:* Planetary sciences; geology; geobiology; geochemistry; geodynamics. *Unit head:* Dr. Viatcheslav Solomatov, Chairman, 314-935-5603. *Application contact:* Bridget Coleman, Director of Admissions, 314-935-6880, Fax: 314-935-4887.
Website: http://eps.wustl.edu/

Wesleyan University, Graduate Studies, Department of Earth and Environmental Sciences, Middletown, CT 06459. Offers MA. *Faculty:* 11 full-time (4 women). *Students:* 5 full-time (1 woman). Average age 24. In 2015, 3 master's awarded. *Degree requirements:* For master's, thesis. *Entrance requirements:* For master's, GRE General Test, official transcripts, three recommendation letters, essay. Additional exam requirements/recommendations for international students: Required—TOEFL; Recommended—IELTS. *Application deadline:* For fall admission, 2/15 priority date for domestic and international students. Applications are processed on a rolling basis. Application fee: $0. Electronic applications accepted. *Financial support:* In 2015–16, 2 teaching assistantships with full tuition reimbursements were awarded; scholarships/grants and tuition waivers (full and partial) also available. Financial award application deadline: 4/15; financial award applicants required to submit FAFSA. *Faculty research:* Tectonics, volcanology, stratigraphy, coastal processes, geochemistry. *Unit head:* Dr. Martha Gilmore, Chair, 860-685-3129, E-mail: mgilmore@wesleyan.edu. *Application contact:* Ginny Harris, Administrative Assistant, 860-685-2244, E-mail: vharris@wesleyan.edu.
Website: http://www.wesleyan.edu/ees/

Geosciences

West Chester University of Pennsylvania, College of Arts and Sciences, Department of Geology and Astronomy, West Chester, PA 19383. Offers geoscience (MA). *Program availability:* Part-time, evening/weekend. *Faculty:* 9 full-time (4 women), 1 part-time/adjunct (0 women). *Students:* 14 full-time (7 women), 16 part-time (5 women); includes 2 minority (1 Black or African American, non-Hispanic/Latino; 1 Hispanic/Latino). Average age 33. 11 applicants, 100% accepted, 7 enrolled. In 2015, 7 degrees awarded. *Degree requirements:* For master's, final project involving manuscript (for some programs), presentation. *Entrance requirements:* For master's, minimum GPA of 2.8 (for some programs). Additional exam requirements/recommendations for international students: Required—TOEFL or IELTS. *Application deadline:* For fall admission, 5/15 for international students; for spring admission, 10/15 for international students. Applications are processed on a rolling basis. Application fee: $50. Electronic applications accepted. *Expenses:* Tuition, state resident: full-time $8460; part-time $470 per credit. Tuition, nonresident: full-time $12,690; part-time $705 per credit. *Required fees:* $2312; $126.75 per credit. Tuition and fees vary according to campus/location and program. *Financial support:* Scholarships/grants and unspecified assistantships available. Financial award application deadline: 2/15; financial award applicants required to submit FAFSA. *Faculty research:* Geoscience education, environmental geology, energy and sustainability, astronomy, coastal geomorphology (sea level change), water and soil remediation, hydrogeology, short-term weather forecasting. *Unit head:* Dr. Martin Helmke, Chair, 610-436-3565, Fax: 610-436-3036, E-mail: mhelmke@wcupa.edu. *Application contact:* Dr. Joby Hilliker, Graduate Coordinator, 610-436-2213, Fax: 610-436-3036, E-mail: jhilliker@wcupa.edu. Website: http://www.wcupa.edu/_academics/sch_cas.esc/

Western Connecticut State University, Division of Graduate Studies, Maricostas School of Arts and Sciences, Department of Physics, Astronomy and Meteorology, Danbury, CT 06810-6885. Offers earth and planetary sciences (MA). *Program availability:* Part-time. *Degree requirements:* For master's, thesis, completion of program in 6 years. *Entrance requirements:* For master's, minimum GPA of 2.5 or GRE; one year each of calculus-based physics and calculus; semester course in differential equations. Additional exam requirements/recommendations for international students: Recommended—TOEFL (minimum score 550 paper-based; 79 iBT), IELTS (minimum score 6). *Expenses:* Contact institution. *Faculty research:* Data collection and analysis of Gulf Stream surface temperature and circulation; science for visually impaired students

including investigations of a satellite orbit, the Moon's surface, spectra of chemical elements and stars, the rotation of the Sun, and the spiral structure of our galaxy.

Western Kentucky University, Graduate Studies, Ogden College of Science and Engineering, Department of Geography and Geology, Bowling Green, KY 42101. Offers geoscience (MS). *Degree requirements:* For master's, comprehensive exam, thesis or alternative. *Entrance requirements:* For master's, GRE General Test, minimum GPA of 2.75. Additional exam requirements/recommendations for international students: Required—TOEFL (minimum score 555 paper-based; 79 iBT). *Faculty research:* Hydroclimatology, electronic data sets, groundwater, sinkhole liquification potential, meteorological analysis.

Western Michigan University, Graduate College, College of Arts and Sciences, Department of Geosciences, Kalamazoo, MI 49008. Offers earth science (MA); geosciences (MS, PhD). *Degree requirements:* For master's, thesis; for doctorate, one foreign language, thesis/dissertation.

Western Michigan University, Graduate College, College of Arts and Sciences, Department of Interdisciplinary Arts and Sciences, Kalamazoo, MI 49008. Offers science education (MA, PhD), including biological sciences (PhD), chemistry (PhD), geosciences (PhD), physical geography (PhD), physics (PhD), science education (PhD). *Degree requirements:* For doctorate, thesis/dissertation.

Yale University, Graduate School of Arts and Sciences, Department of Geology and Geophysics, New Haven, CT 06520. Offers biogeochemistry (PhD); climate dynamics (PhD); geochemistry (PhD); geophysics (PhD); meteorology (PhD); oceanography (PhD); paleontology (PhD); paleooceanography (PhD); petrology (PhD); tectonics (PhD). *Degree requirements:* For doctorate, thesis/dissertation. *Entrance requirements:* For doctorate, GRE General Test. Additional exam requirements/recommendations for international students: Required—TOEFL.

York University, Faculty of Graduate Studies, Lassonde School of Engineering, Program in Earth and Space Science, Toronto, ON M3J 1P3, Canada. Offers M Sc, PhD. *Program availability:* Part-time, evening/weekend. *Degree requirements:* For master's, thesis or alternative; for doctorate, thesis/dissertation. Electronic applications accepted.

Hydrogeology

California State University, Chico, Office of Graduate Studies, College of Natural Sciences, Department of Geological and Environmental Sciences, Program in Geosciences, Chico, CA 95929-0722. Offers hydrology/hydrogeology (MS). *Program availability:* Part-time. *Degree requirements:* For master's, comprehensive exam, thesis. *Entrance requirements:* For master's, GRE. Additional exam requirements/recommendations for international students: Required—TOEFL (minimum score 550 paper-based; 80 iBT), IELTS (minimum score 6.5), PTE (minimum score 59). *Application deadline:* For fall admission, 3/1 priority date for domestic students, 3/1 for international students; for spring admission, 9/15 priority date for domestic students, 9/15 for international students. Application fee: $55. Electronic applications accepted. *Expenses:* Tuition, area resident: Full-time $4146; part-time $2730. *Financial support:* Fellowships, research assistantships, teaching assistantships, and career-related internships or fieldwork available. *Unit head:* Dr. David L. Brown, Chair, 530-898-1995, Fax: 530-898-5234, E-mail: geos@csuchico.edu. *Application contact:* Judy L. Rice, Graduate Admissions Coordinator, 530-898-5416, Fax: 530-898-3342, E-mail: jlrice@csuchico.edu. Website: http://catalog.csuchico.edu/viewer/15/GEOS/

Clemson University, Graduate School, College of Engineering, Computing and Applied Sciences, Department of Environmental Engineering and Earth Sciences, Program in Hydrogeology, Anderson, SC 29625. Offers MS. *Program availability:* Part-time. *Faculty:* 25 full-time (6 women), 4 part-time/adjunct (2 women). *Students:* 17 full-time (4 women), 5 part-time (2 women); includes 2 minority (both Two or more races, non-Hispanic/Latino), 3 international. Average age 25. 25 applicants, 88% accepted, 9 enrolled. In 2015, 3 master's awarded. *Degree requirements:* For master's, thesis optional. *Entrance requirements:* For master's, GRE General Test, unofficial transcripts, letters of recommendation. Additional exam requirements/recommendations for international students: Required—TOEFL (minimum score 80 iBT), IELTS (minimum score 6.5). *Application deadline:* For fall admission, 2/15 for domestic and international students. Applications are processed on a rolling basis. Application fee: $80 ($90 for international students). Electronic applications accepted. *Expenses:* $4,610 per semester full-time resident, $9,203 per semester full-time non-resident, $582 per credit hour part-time resident, $1,166 per credit hour part-time non-resident. *Financial support:* In 2015–16, 12 students received support, including 4 research assistantships with partial tuition reimbursements available (averaging $18,130 per year), 8 teaching assistantships with partial tuition reimbursements available (averaging $18,130 per year); career-related internships or fieldwork and health care benefits also available. Financial award application deadline: 2/15. *Faculty research:* Groundwater, geology, environmental geology, geophysics, geochemistry, remediation, modeling, sedimentology. *Unit head:* Dr. David Freedman, Department Chair, 864-656-5566, E-mail: dfreedm@clemson.edu. *Application contact:* Dr. Jim Castle, Graduate Program Coordinator, 864-656-5015, E-mail: jcastle@clemson.edu. Website: http://www.clemson.edu/ces/eees/gradprog/hydro/index.html

East Carolina University, Graduate School, Thomas Harriot College of Arts and Sciences, Department of Geological Sciences, Greenville, NC 27858-4353. Offers geology (MS); hydrogeology and environmental geology (Certificate). *Program availability:* Part-time. *Students:* 25 full-time (8 women), 21 part-time (7 women). Average age 27. 25 applicants, 88% accepted, 12 enrolled. In 2015, 12 master's awarded. *Degree requirements:* For master's, one foreign language, comprehensive exam, thesis. *Entrance requirements:* For master's, GRE General Test. Additional exam requirements/recommendations for international students: Required—TOEFL. *Application deadline:* For fall admission, 6/1 priority date for domestic students; for spring admission, 10/15 for domestic students. Applications are processed on a rolling basis. Application fee: $50. *Financial support:* Research assistantships with partial tuition reimbursements and teaching assistantships with partial tuition reimbursements available. Support available to part-time students. Financial award application deadline: 6/1. *Unit head:* Dr. Stephen Culver, Chair, 252-328-6360, Fax: 252-328-4391, E-mail: culvers@ecu.edu. *Application contact:* Dean of Graduate School, 252-328-6012, Fax: 252-328-6071, E-mail: gradschool@ecu.edu. Website: http://www.ecu.edu/geology/

Illinois State University, Graduate School, College of Arts and Sciences, Department of Geography-Geology, Normal, IL 61790-2200. Offers hydrogeology (MS). *Degree requirements:* For master's, thesis optional. *Entrance requirements:* For master's, GRE General Test. *Faculty research:* Thermal transport within the hyporheic zone, nutrient cycling in watersheds, water quality in karst systems, ground water dating using dissolved helium.

Indiana University Bloomington, University Graduate School, College of Arts and Sciences, Department of Geological Sciences, Bloomington, IN 47405-7000. Offers biogeochemistry (MS, PhD); economic geology (MS, PhD); geobiology (MS, PhD); geophysics, structural geology and tectonics (MS, PhD); hydrogeology (MS, PhD); mineralogy (MS, PhD); stratigraphy and sedimentology (MS, PhD). Terminal master's awarded for partial completion of doctoral program. *Degree requirements:* For master's, thesis or alternative; for doctorate, comprehensive exam, thesis/dissertation. *Entrance requirements:* For master's and doctorate, GRE General Test. Additional exam requirements/recommendations for international students: Required—TOEFL. *Faculty research:* Geophysics, geochemistry, hydrogeology, geobiology, planetary science.

Montana Tech of The University of Montana, Graduate School, Geosciences Programs, Butte, MT 59701-8997. Offers geochemistry (MS); geological engineering (MS); geology (MS); geophysical engineering (MS); hydrogeological engineering (MS); hydrogeology (MS). *Program availability:* Part-time. *Faculty:* 16 full-time (4 women), 4 part-time/adjunct (0 women). *Students:* 28 full-time (10 women), 10 part-time (5 women); includes 1 minority (Hispanic/Latino), 6 international. 25 applicants, 52% accepted, 10 enrolled. In 2015, 3 master's awarded. *Degree requirements:* For master's, comprehensive exam (for some programs), thesis (for some programs). *Entrance requirements:* For master's, GRE General Test, minimum GPA of 3.0. Additional exam requirements/recommendations for international students: Required—TOEFL (minimum score 545 paper-based; 78 iBT), IELTS (minimum score 6.5). *Application deadline:* For fall admission, 4/1 priority date for domestic students, 3/1 priority date for international students; for spring admission, 10/1 priority date for domestic students, 7/1 priority date for international students. Applications are processed on a rolling basis. Application fee: $50. Electronic applications accepted. *Expenses:* Tuition, state resident: full-time $2901; part-time $1450.68 per degree program. Tuition, nonresident: full-time $8432; part-time $4215.84 per degree program. *Required fees:* $668; $354 per degree program. Tuition and fees vary according to course load and program. *Financial support:* In 2015–16, 15 students received support, including 10 teaching assistantships with partial tuition reimbursements available (averaging $5,000 per year); research assistantships with partial tuition reimbursements available, career-related internships or fieldwork, tuition waivers (full and partial), and unspecified assistantships also available. Financial award application deadline: 4/1; financial award applicants required to submit FAFSA. *Faculty research:* Water resource development, seismic processing, petroleum reservoir characterization, environmental geochemistry, geologic mapping. *Unit head:* Dr. Chris Gammons, Department Head, 406-496-4763, Fax: 406-496-4260, E-mail: cgammons@mtech.edu. *Application contact:* Daniel Stirling, Administrator, Graduate School, 406-496-4304, Fax: 406-496-4710, E-mail: gradschool@mtech.edu. Website: http://www.mtech.edu/academics/gradschool/degreeprograms/degrees.htm

Ohio University, Graduate College, College of Arts and Sciences, Department of Geological Sciences, Athens, OH 45701-2979. Offers environmental geochemistry (MS); environmental geology (MS); environmental/hydrology (MS); geology (MS); geology education (MS); geomorphology/surficial processes (MS); geophysics (MS); hydrogeology (MS); sedimentology (MS); structure/tectonics (MS). *Program availability:* Part-time. *Degree requirements:* For master's, thesis. *Entrance requirements:* Additional exam requirements/recommendations for international students: Required—TOEFL (minimum score 550 paper-based; 80 iBT) or IELTS (minimum score 6.5). Electronic applications accepted. *Faculty research:* Geoscience education, tectonics, fluvial geomorphology, invertebrate paleontology, mine/hydrology.

University of Hawaii at Manoa, Graduate Division, School of Ocean and Earth Science and Technology, Department of Geology and Geophysics, Honolulu, HI 96822. Offers

high-pressure geophysics and geochemistry (MS, PhD); hydrogeology and engineering geology (MS, PhD); marine geology and geophysics (MS, PhD); planetary geosciences and remote sensing (MS, PhD); seismology and solid-earth geophysics (MS, PhD); volcanology, petrology, and geochemistry (MS, PhD). *Program availability:* Part-time. *Faculty:* 72 full-time (15 women), 6 part-time/adjunct (3 women). *Students:* 42 full-time (26 women), 2 part-time (1 woman); includes 9 minority (2 Asian, non-Hispanic/Latino; 2 Hispanic/Latino; 5 Two or more races, non-Hispanic/Latino), 9 international. Average age 31. 78 applicants, 23% accepted, 13 enrolled. In 2015, 7 master's, 8 doctorates awarded. Terminal master's awarded for partial completion of doctoral program. *Degree requirements:* For master's, thesis optional; for doctorate, comprehensive exam, thesis/dissertation. *Entrance requirements:* For master's and doctorate, GRE General Test, minimum GPA of 3.0. Additional exam requirements/recommendations for international students: Required—TOEFL (minimum score 580 paper-based; 92 iBT), IELTS (minimum score 5). *Application deadline:* For fall admission, 1/15 for domestic students, 1/1 for international students; for spring admission, 9/1 for domestic students, 8/15 for international students. Application fee: $100. *Financial support:* In 2015–16, 7 fellowships (averaging $1,359 per year), 30 research assistantships (averaging $23,988 per year), 4 teaching assistantships (averaging $15,350 per year) were awarded. *Total annual research expenditures:* $3.8 million. *Unit head:* Brian Taylor, Dean, 808-956-6182, E-mail: taylorb@hawaii.edu. *Application contact:* Dr. Gregory Moore, Chair, 808-956-7640, Fax: 808-956-5512, E-mail: gg-dept@soest.hawaii.edu.
Website: http://www.soest.hawaii.edu/GG/

University of Nevada, Reno, Graduate School, Interdisciplinary Program in Hydrologic Sciences, Reno, NV 89557. Offers hydrogeology (MS, PhD); hydrology (MS, PhD). Offered through the M. C. Fleischmann College of Agriculture, the College of Engineering, the Mackay School of Mines, and the Desert Research Institute. Terminal master's awarded for partial completion of doctoral program. *Degree requirements:* For master's, thesis optional; for doctorate, thesis/dissertation. *Entrance requirements:* For master's and doctorate, GRE General Test, minimum GPA of 3.0. Additional exam requirements/recommendations for international students: Required—TOEFL (minimum score 500 paper-based; 61 iBT), IELTS (minimum score 6). Electronic applications accepted. *Faculty research:* Groundwater, water resources, surface water, soil science.

University of South Florida, Innovative Education, Tampa, FL 33620-9951. Offers adult, career and higher education (Graduate Certificate), including college teaching, leadership in developing human resources, leadership in higher education; Africana studies (Graduate Certificate), including diasporas and health disparities, genocide and human rights; aging studies (Graduate Certificate), including gerontology; art research (Graduate Certificate), including museum studies; business foundations (Graduate Certificate); chemical and biomedical engineering (Graduate Certificate), including materials science and engineering, water, health and sustainability; child and family studies (Graduate Certificate), including positive behavior support; civil and industrial engineering (Graduate Certificate), including transportation systems analysis; community and family health (Graduate Certificate), including maternal and child health, social marketing and public health, violence and injury: prevention and intervention, women's health; criminology (Graduate Certificate), including criminal justice administration; educational measurement and research (Graduate Certificate), including evaluation; English (Graduate Certificate), including comparative literary studies, creative writing, professional and technical communication; entrepreneurship (Graduate Certificate); environmental health (Graduate Certificate), including safety management; epidemiology and biostatistics (Graduate Certificate), including applied biostatistics, biostatistics, concepts and tools of epidemiology, epidemiology, epidemiology of infectious diseases; geography, environment and planning (Graduate Certificate), including community development, environmental policy and management, geographical information systems; geology (Graduate Certificate), including hydrogeology; global health (Graduate Certificate), including disaster management, global health and Latin American and Caribbean studies, global health practice, humanitarian assistance, infection control; government and international affairs (Graduate Certificate), including Cuban studies, globalization studies; health policy and management (Graduate Certificate), including health management and leadership, public health policy and programs; hearing specialist: early intervention (Graduate Certificate); industrial and management systems engineering (Graduate Certificate), including systems engineering, technology management; information studies (Graduate Certificate), including school library media specialist; information systems/decision sciences (Graduate Certificate), including analytics and business intelligence; instructional technology (Graduate Certificate), including distance education, Florida digital/virtual educator, instructional design, multimedia design, Web design; internal medicine, bioethics and medical humanities (Graduate Certificate), including biomedical ethics; Latin American and Caribbean studies (Graduate Certificate); mass communications (Graduate Certificate), including multimedia journalism; mathematics and statistics (Graduate Certificate), including mathematics; medicine (Graduate Certificate), including aging and neuroscience, bioinformatics, biotechnology, brain fitness and memory management, clinical investigation, health informatics, health sciences, integrative weight management, intellectual property, medicine and gender, metabolic and nutritional medicine, metabolic cardiology, pharmacy sciences; national and competitive intelligence (Graduate Certificate); psychological and social foundations (Graduate Certificate), including career counseling, college teaching, diversity in education, mental health counseling, school counseling; public affairs (Graduate Certificate), including nonprofit management, public management, research administration; public health (Graduate Certificate), including environmental health, health equity, public health generalist, translational research in adolescent behavioral health; public health practices (Graduate Certificate), including planning for healthy communities; rehabilitation and mental health counseling (Graduate Certificate), including integrative mental health care, marriage and family therapy, rehabilitation technology; secondary education (Graduate Certificate), including ESOL, foreign language education: culture and content, foreign language education: professional; social work (Graduate Certificate), including geriatric social work/clinical gerontology; special education (Graduate Certificate), including autism spectrum disorder, disabilities education: severe/profound; world languages (Graduate Certificate), including teaching English as a second language (TESL) or foreign language. *Unit head:* Kathy Barnes, Interdisciplinary Programs Coordinator, 813-974-8031, Fax: 813-974-7061, E-mail: barnesk@usf.edu. *Application contact:* Karen Tylinski, Metro Initiatives, 813-974-9943, Fax: 813-974-7061, E-mail: ktylinsk@usf.edu.
Website: http://www.usf.edu/innovative-education/

The University of Texas at Dallas, School of Natural Sciences and Mathematics, Department of Geosciences, Richardson, TX 75080. Offers geochemistry (MS, PhD); geophysics (MS, PhD); geospatial information sciences (MS, PhD); hydrogeology (MS, PhD); sedimentology, stratigraphy, and paleontology (MS, PhD); structural geology and tectonics (MS, PhD). *Program availability:* Part-time, evening/weekend. *Faculty:* 9 full-time (0 women). *Students:* 57 full-time (21 women), 23 part-time (4 women); includes 12 minority (3 Black or African American, non-Hispanic/Latino; 4 Asian, non-Hispanic/Latino; 3 Hispanic/Latino; 2 Two or more races, non-Hispanic/Latino), 33 international. Average age 30. 98 applicants, 31% accepted, 20 enrolled. In 2015, 20 master's, 4 doctorates awarded. *Degree requirements:* For master's, thesis optional; for doctorate, thesis/dissertation. *Entrance requirements:* For master's and doctorate, GRE General Test, minimum GPA of 3.0 in upper-level course work in field. Additional exam requirements/recommendations for international students: Required—TOEFL (minimum score 550 paper-based). *Application deadline:* For fall admission, 7/15 for domestic students, 5/1 priority date for international students; for spring admission, 11/15 for domestic students, 9/1 priority date for international students. Applications are processed on a rolling basis. Application fee: $50 ($100 for international students). Electronic applications accepted. *Expenses:* Tuition, state resident: full-time $11,940; part-time $663 per semester hour. Tuition, nonresident: full-time $22,786; part-time $1266 per semester hour. Tuition and fees vary according to course load. *Financial support:* In 2015–16, 41 students received support, including 10 research assistantships with partial tuition reimbursements available (averaging $19,260 per year), 15 teaching assistantships with partial tuition reimbursements available (averaging $17,100 per year); career-related internships or fieldwork, Federal Work-Study, institutionally sponsored loans, scholarships/grants, and unspecified assistantships also available. Support available to part-time students. Financial award application deadline: 4/30; financial award applicants required to submit FAFSA. *Faculty research:* Cybermapping, GPS applications for geophysics and geology, seismology and ground-penetrating radar, numerical modeling, signal processing and inverse modeling techniques in seismology. *Unit head:* Dr. John Geissman, Department Head, 972-883-2454, Fax: 972-883-2537, E-mail: geosciences@utdallas.edu. *Application contact:* Gloria Eby, Graduate Support Assistant, 972-883-2404, Fax: 972-883-2537, E-mail: geosciences@utdallas.edu.
Website: http://www.utdallas.edu/geosciences

West Virginia University, Eberly College of Arts and Sciences, Department of Geology and Geography, Program in Geology, Morgantown, WV 26506. Offers geomorphology (MS, PhD); geophysics (MS, PhD); hydrogeology (MS, PhD); paleontology (MS, PhD); petroleum geology (PhD); petrology (MS, PhD); stratigraphy (MS, PhD); structure (MS, PhD). *Program availability:* Part-time. Terminal master's awarded for partial completion of doctoral program. *Degree requirements:* For master's, thesis (for some programs); for doctorate, comprehensive exam, thesis/dissertation. *Entrance requirements:* For master's, GRE General Test, minimum GPA of 2.5; for doctorate, GRE General Test, minimum GPA of 3.3. Additional exam requirements/recommendations for international students: Required—TOEFL. *Expenses:* Tuition, state resident: full-time $8568. Tuition, nonresident: full-time $22,140. Tuition and fees vary according to program.

Hydrology

Auburn University, Graduate School, Ginn College of Engineering, Department of Civil Engineering, Auburn University, AL 36849. Offers construction engineering and management (MCE, MS, PhD); environmental engineering (MCE, MS, PhD); geotechnical/materials engineering (MCE, MS, PhD); hydraulics/hydrology (MCE, MS, PhD); structural engineering (MCE, MS, PhD); transportation engineering (MCE, MS, PhD). *Program availability:* Part-time. *Faculty:* 22 full-time (1 woman), 1 part-time/adjunct (0 women). *Students:* 76 full-time (24 women), 43 part-time (7 women); includes 8 minority (2 Black or African American, non-Hispanic/Latino; 1 Asian, non-Hispanic/Latino; 4 Hispanic/Latino; 1 Two or more races, non-Hispanic/Latino), 51 international. Average age 27. 150 applicants, 52% accepted, 25 enrolled. In 2015, 23 master's, 8 doctorates awarded. *Degree requirements:* For master's, project (MCE), thesis (MS); for doctorate, comprehensive exam, thesis/dissertation. *Entrance requirements:* For master's and doctorate, GRE General Test. *Application deadline:* Applications are processed on a rolling basis. Application fee: $50 ($60 for international students). Electronic applications accepted. *Expenses:* Tuition, state resident: full-time $8802; part-time $489 per credit hour. Tuition, nonresident: full-time $26,406; part-time $1467 per credit hour. *Required fees:* $808 per semester. Tuition and fees vary according to degree level and program. *Financial support:* Fellowships, research assistantships, teaching assistantships, and Federal Work-Study available. Support available to part-time students. Financial award application deadline: 3/15; financial award applicants required to submit FAFSA. *Unit head:* Dr. Andy Nowak, Head, 334-844-4320. *Application contact:* Dr. George Flowers, Dean of the Graduate School, 334-844-2125.

Boise State University, College of Arts and Sciences, Department of Geosciences, Boise, ID 83725-1535. Offers earth science (M E Sci); geophysics (MS, PhD); geosciences (MS, PhD); hydrology (MS). *Program availability:* Part-time. *Faculty:* 20. *Students:* 52 full-time (21 women), 13 part-time (3 women); includes 7 minority (1 Black or African American, non-Hispanic/Latino; 5 Hispanic/Latino; 1 Two or more races, non-Hispanic/Latino), 7 international. Average age 29. 73 applicants, 29% accepted, 14 enrolled. In 2015, 4 master's, 1 doctorate awarded. Terminal master's awarded for partial completion of doctoral program. *Degree requirements:* For master's, thesis (for some programs); for doctorate, thesis/dissertation. *Entrance requirements:* For master's, GRE General Test, BS in related field, minimum GPA of 3.0; for doctorate, GRE General Test. Additional exam requirements/recommendations for international students: Required—TOEFL (minimum score 550 paper-based; 80 iBT), IELTS (minimum score 6). *Application deadline:* For fall admission, 2/1 for domestic and international students; for spring admission, 10/15 for domestic and international students. Application fee: $65 ($95 for international students). Electronic applications accepted. *Expenses:* Tuition, state resident: full-time $6058; part-time $358 per credit hour. Tuition, nonresident: full-time $20,108; part-time $608 per credit hour. *Required fees:* $2108. Tuition and fees vary according to program. *Financial support:* In 2015–16, 6 students received support, including 17 research assistantships with full tuition reimbursements available (averaging $10,119 per year), 15 teaching assistantships (averaging $9,024 per year); scholarships/grants and unspecified assistantships also available. Financial award application deadline: 2/1; financial award applicants required to submit FAFSA. *Faculty research:* Seismology, geothermal aquifers, sedimentation, tectonics, seismo-acoustic propagation. *Unit head:* Dr. James McNamara, Department Chair, 208-426-1354, E-mail: jmcnamar@boisestate.edu. *Application contact:* Dr. Mark Schmitz, Graduate Program Coordinator, 208-426-5907,

Hydrology

E-mail: markschmitz@boisestate.edu.
Website: http://earth.boisestate.edu/degrees/graduate/

California State University, Bakersfield, Division of Graduate Studies, School of Natural Sciences, Mathematics, and Engineering, Program in Geological Sciences, Bakersfield, CA 93311. Offers geological sciences (MS); hydrogeology (MS); petroleum geology (MS); science education (MS). *Program availability:* Part-time, evening/weekend. *Degree requirements:* For master's, thesis. *Entrance requirements:* For master's, GRE General Test, BS in geology. *Application deadline:* Applications are processed on a rolling basis. Application fee: $55. *Expenses: Tuition, area resident:* Full-time $2246; part-time $1302 per semester. Tuition, state resident: full-time $2246; part-time $1302 per semester. *Financial support:* Teaching assistantships, career-related internships or fieldwork, institutionally sponsored loans, and scholarships/grants available. *Unit head:* Dr. Dirk Baron, Department Chair, 661-664-3044, Fax: 661-664-2040, E-mail: dbaron@csub.edu. *Application contact:* Debbie Blowers, Assistant Director of Admissions, 661-664-3381, E-mail: dblowers@csub.edu.

California State University, Chico, Office of Graduate Studies, College of Natural Sciences, Department of Geological and Environmental Sciences, Program in Geosciences, Chico, CA 95929-0722. Offers hydrology/hydrogeology (MS). *Program availability:* Part-time. *Degree requirements:* For master's, comprehensive exam, thesis. *Entrance requirements:* For master's, GRE. Additional exam requirements/recommendations for international students: Required—TOEFL (minimum score 550 paper-based; 80 iBT), IELTS (minimum score 6.5), PTE (minimum score 59). *Application deadline:* For fall admission, 3/1 priority date for domestic students, 3/1 for international students; for spring admission, 9/15 priority date for domestic students, 9/15 for international students. Application fee: $55. Electronic applications accepted. *Expenses: Tuition, area resident:* Full-time $4146; part-time $2730. *Financial support:* Fellowships, research assistantships, teaching assistantships, and career-related internships or fieldwork available. *Unit head:* Dr. David L. Brown, Chair, 530-898-1995, Fax: 530-898-5234, E-mail: geos@csuchico.edu. *Application contact:* Judy L. Rice, Graduate Admissions Coordinator, 530-898-5416, Fax: 530-898-3342, E-mail: jlrice@csuchico.edu.
Website: http://catalog.csuchico.edu/viewer/15/GEOS/

Colorado School of Mines, Office of Graduate Studies, Department of Geophysics, Golden, CO 80401. Offers geophysical engineering (ME, MS, PhD); geophysics (MS, PhD); hydrology (MS, PhD); mineral exploration and mining geosciences (PMS). *Program availability:* Part-time. *Faculty:* 17 full-time (2 women), 6 part-time/adjunct (1 woman). *Students:* 77 full-time (26 women), 5 part-time (1 woman); includes 3 minority (1 American Indian or Alaska Native, non-Hispanic/Latino; 1 Asian, non-Hispanic/Latino; 1 Hispanic/Latino), 29 international. Average age 28. 195 applicants, 13% accepted, 17 enrolled. In 2015, 16 master's, 9 doctorates awarded. *Degree requirements:* For master's, thesis (for some programs); for doctorate, comprehensive exam, thesis/dissertation. *Entrance requirements:* For master's and doctorate, GRE General Test. Additional exam requirements/recommendations for international students: Required—TOEFL (minimum score 550 paper-based; 80 iBT). *Application deadline:* For fall admission, 12/15 priority date for domestic and international students; for spring admission, 9/1 priority date for domestic students, 9/1 for international students. Application fee: $50 ($70 for international students). Electronic applications accepted. *Expenses:* Tuition, state resident: full-time $15,225. Tuition, nonresident: full-time $32,700. *Financial support:* In 2015–16, 58 students received support, including 2 fellowships with full tuition reimbursements available, 52 research assistantships with full tuition reimbursements available, 4 teaching assistantships with full tuition reimbursements available; scholarships/grants, health care benefits, and unspecified assistantships also available. Financial award application deadline: 12/15; financial award applicants required to submit FAFSA. *Faculty research:* Seismic exploration, gravity and geomagnetic fields, electrical mapping and sounding, bore hole measurements, environmental physics. *Total annual research expenditures:* $5.2 million. *Unit head:* Dr. Terence K. Young, Head, 303-273-3454, E-mail: tkyoung@mines.edu. *Application contact:* Michelle Szobody, Program Assistant, 303-273-3935, E-mail: mszobody@mines.edu.
Website: http://geophysics.mines.edu

Cornell University, Graduate School, Graduate Fields of Engineering, Field of Civil and Environmental Engineering, Ithaca, NY 14853-0001. Offers engineering management (M Eng, MS, PhD); environmental engineering (M Eng, MS, PhD); environmental fluid mechanics and hydrology (M Eng, MS, PhD); environmental systems engineering (M Eng, MS, PhD); geotechnical engineering (M Eng, MS, PhD); remote sensing (M Eng, MS, PhD); structural engineering (M Eng, MS, PhD); structural mechanics (M Eng, MS); transportation engineering (MS, PhD); transportation systems engineering (M Eng); water resource systems (M Eng, MS, PhD). Terminal master's awarded for partial completion of doctoral program. *Degree requirements:* For master's, thesis (MS); for doctorate, comprehensive exam, thesis/dissertation. *Entrance requirements:* For master's and doctorate, GRE General Test (recommended), 2 letters of recommendation. Additional exam requirements/recommendations for international students: Required—TOEFL (minimum score 600 paper-based; 77 iBT). Electronic applications accepted. *Faculty research:* Environmental engineering, geotechnical engineering, remote sensing, environmental fluid mechanics and hydrology, structural engineering.

Cornell University, Graduate School, Graduate Fields of Engineering, Field of Geological Sciences, Ithaca, NY 14853. Offers economic geology (M Eng, MS, PhD); engineering geology (M Eng, MS, PhD); environmental geophysics (M Eng, MS, PhD); general geology (M Eng, MS, PhD); geobiology (M Eng, MS, PhD); geochemistry and isotope geology (M Eng, MS, PhD); geohydrology (M Eng, MS, PhD); geomorphology (M Eng, MS, PhD); geophysics (M Eng, MS, PhD); geotectonics (M Eng, MS, PhD); marine geology (MS, PhD); mineralogy (M Eng, MS, PhD); paleontology (M Eng, MS, PhD); petroleum geology (M Eng, MS, PhD); petrology (M Eng, MS, PhD); planetary geology (M Eng, MS, PhD); Precambrian geology (M Eng, MS, PhD); Quaternary geology (M Eng, MS, PhD); rock mechanics (M Eng, MS, PhD); sedimentology (M Eng, MS, PhD); seismology (M Eng, MS, PhD); stratigraphy (M Eng, MS, PhD); structural geology (M Eng, MS, PhD). *Degree requirements:* For master's, thesis (MS); for doctorate, comprehensive exam, thesis/dissertation. *Entrance requirements:* For master's and doctorate, GRE General Test, 3 letters of recommendation. Additional exam requirements/recommendations for international students: Required—TOEFL (minimum score 550 paper-based; 77 iBT). Electronic applications accepted. *Faculty research:* Geophysics, structural geology, petrology, geochemistry, geodynamics.

Drexel University, College of Engineering, Department of Civil, Architectural, and Environmental Engineering, Philadelphia, PA 19104-2875. Offers architectural / building systems engineering (PhD); architectural/building systems engineering (MS); civil engineering (MS, PhD); environmental engineering (MS, PhD); geotechnical, geoenvironmental and geosynthetics engineering (MS, PhD); hydraulics, hydrology and water resources engineering (MS, PhD); structures (MS). *Program availability:* Part-time, evening/weekend. *Degree requirements:* For master's, thesis optional; for doctorate, thesis/dissertation. *Entrance requirements:* For master's, minimum GPA of 3.0; for doctorate, minimum GPA of 3.5, MS in civil engineering. Additional exam requirements/recommendations for international students: Required—TOEFL. Electronic applications accepted. *Faculty research:* Structural dynamics, hazardous wastes, water resources, pavement materials, groundwater.

Idaho State University, Office of Graduate Studies, College of Science and Engineering, Department of Geosciences, Pocatello, ID 83209-8072. Offers geographic information science (MS); geology (MNS, MS); geology with emphasis in environmental geoscience (MS); geophysics/hydrology/geology (MS); geotechnology (Postbaccalaureate Certificate). *Program availability:* Part-time. *Degree requirements:* For master's, comprehensive exam, thesis, oral colloquium; for Postbaccalaureate Certificate, thesis optional, minimum 19 credits. *Entrance requirements:* For master's, GRE General Test (minimum 50th percentile in 2 sections), 3 letters of recommendation; for Postbaccalaureate Certificate, GRE General Test, 3 letters of recommendation, bachelor's degree, statement of goals. Additional exam requirements/recommendations for international students: Required—TOEFL (minimum score 550 paper-based; 80 iBT). Electronic applications accepted. *Faculty research:* Quantitative field mapping and sampling: microscopic, geochemical, and isotopic analysis of rocks, minerals and water; remote sensing, geographic information systems, and global positioning systems: environmental and watershed management; surficial and fluvial processes: landscape change; regional tectonics, structural geology; planetary geology.

Illinois State University, Graduate School, College of Arts and Sciences, Department of Geography-Geology, Normal, IL 61790-2200. Offers hydrogeology (MS). *Degree requirements:* For master's, thesis optional. *Entrance requirements:* For master's, GRE General Test. *Faculty research:* Thermal transport within the hyporheic zone, nutrient cycling in watersheds, water quality in karst systems, ground water dating using dissolved helium.

Massachusetts Institute of Technology, School of Engineering, Department of Civil and Environmental Engineering, Cambridge, MA 02139. Offers biological oceanography (PhD, Sc D); chemical oceanography (PhD, Sc D); civil and environmental engineering (M Eng, SM, PhD, Sc D); civil and environmental systems (PhD, Sc D); civil engineering (PhD, Sc D, CE); coastal engineering (PhD, Sc D); construction engineering and management (PhD, Sc D); environmental biology (PhD, Sc D); environmental chemistry (PhD, Sc D); environmental engineering (PhD, Sc D); environmental fluid mechanics (PhD, Sc D); geotechnical and geoenvironmental engineering (PhD, Sc D); hydrology (PhD, Sc D); information technology (PhD, Sc D); oceanographic engineering (PhD, Sc D); structures and materials (PhD, Sc D); transportation (PhD, Sc D); SM/MBA. *Faculty:* 27 full-time (5 women). *Students:* 183 full-time (59 women); includes 19 minority (1 Black or African American, non-Hispanic/Latino; 7 Asian, non-Hispanic/Latino; 8 Hispanic/Latino; 3 Two or more races, non-Hispanic/Latino), 106 international. Average age 27. 513 applicants, 20% accepted, 56 enrolled. In 2015, 77 master's, 18 doctorates, 1 other advanced degree awarded. *Degree requirements:* For master's, thesis; for doctorate, comprehensive exam, thesis/dissertation; for CE, comprehensive exam, thesis. *Entrance requirements:* For master's and doctorate, GRE General Test; for CE, GRE General Test. Additional exam requirements/recommendations for international students: Required—TOEFL (minimum score 577 paper-based; 100 iBT), IELTS (minimum score 7). *Application deadline:* For fall admission, 12/15 for domestic and international students. Application fee: $75. Electronic applications accepted. *Expenses: Tuition:* Full-time $46,400; part-time $725 per credit. One-time fee: $304 full-time. Full-time tuition and fees vary according to course load and program. *Financial support:* In 2015–16, 150 students received support, including 38 fellowships (averaging $38,000 per year), 111 research assistantships (averaging $35,100 per year), 9 teaching assistantships (averaging $39,900 per year); Federal Work-Study, institutionally sponsored loans, scholarships/grants, traineeships, health care benefits, and unspecified assistantships also available. Support available to part-time students. Financial award application deadline: 4/15; financial award applicants required to submit FAFSA. *Faculty research:* Environmental chemistry, environmental fluid mechanics and coastal engineering, environmental microbiology, geotechnical engineering and geomechanics, hydrology and hydroclimatology, infrastructure systems, mechanics of materials and structures, transportation systems. *Total annual research expenditures:* $24.8 million. *Unit head:* Prof. Markus Buehler, Department Head, 617-253-7101. *Application contact:* Graduate Admissions Coordinator, 617-253-7119, E-mail: cee-admissions@mit.edu.
Website: http://cee.mit.edu/

Missouri University of Science and Technology, Graduate School, Department of Civil, Architectural, and Environmental Engineering, Rolla, MO 65409. Offers civil engineering (MS, DE, PhD); construction engineering (MS, DE, PhD); environmental engineering (MS); fluid mechanics (MS, DE, PhD); geotechnical engineering (MS, DE, PhD); hydrology and hydraulic engineering (MS, DE, PhD). *Program availability:* Part-time, evening/weekend. *Faculty:* 20 full-time (0 women), 4 part-time/adjunct (0 women). *Students:* 72 full-time (19 women), 58 part-time (14 women); includes 9 minority (5 Black or African American, non-Hispanic/Latino; 3 Asian, non-Hispanic/Latino; 1 Two or more races, non-Hispanic/Latino), 51 international. Average age 28. 186 applicants, 44% accepted, 33 enrolled. In 2015, 38 master's, 8 doctorates awarded. Terminal master's awarded for partial completion of doctoral program. *Degree requirements:* For master's, thesis optional; for doctorate, comprehensive exam, thesis/dissertation. *Entrance requirements:* For master's, GRE General Test (minimum combined score 1100), minimum GPA of 3.0; for doctorate, GRE General Test (minimum score: verbal and quantitative 400, writing 3.5), minimum GPA of 3.0. Additional exam requirements/recommendations for international students: Required—TOEFL (minimum score 550 paper-based). *Application deadline:* For fall admission, 7/1 for domestic students; for spring admission, 12/1 for domestic students. Applications are processed on a rolling basis. Application fee: $55 ($75 for international students). Electronic applications accepted. *Expenses:* Tuition, state resident: full-time $10,536. Tuition, nonresident: full-time $27,015. Full-time tuition and fees vary according to course load. *Financial support:* In 2015–16, 21 fellowships with full tuition reimbursements (averaging $16,357 per year), 21 research assistantships with partial tuition reimbursements (averaging $1,811 per year), 10 teaching assistantships with partial tuition reimbursements (averaging $1,814 per year) were awarded; institutionally sponsored loans also available. Support available to part-time students. Financial award application deadline: 1/1; financial award applicants required to submit FAFSA. *Faculty research:* Earthquake engineering, structural optimization and control systems, structural health monitoring/damage detection, soil-structure interaction, soil mechanics and foundation engineering. *Unit head:* Dr. William P. Schonberg, Chair, 573-341-4787, Fax: 573-341-4729, E-mail: wschon@mst.edu. *Application contact:* Dr. Rick Stephenson, Graduate Advisor, 573-341-6549, Fax: 573-341-4729, E-mail: stephens@mst.edu.
Website: http://civil.umr.edu/

Murray State University, College of Science, Engineering and Technology, Program in Water Science, Murray, KY 42071. Offers MS. *Program availability:* Part-time. *Degree requirements:* For master's, comprehensive exam, thesis. *Entrance requirements:* For master's, GRE General Test. Electronic applications accepted. *Faculty research:* Water chemistry, GIS, amphibian biology, nutrient chemistry, limnology.

New Mexico Institute of Mining and Technology, Center for Graduate Studies, Department of Earth and Environmental Science, Program in Hydrology, Socorro, NM 87801. Offers MS, PhD. *Degree requirements:* For master's, thesis; for doctorate, thesis/dissertation. *Entrance requirements:* For master's, GRE General Test; for doctorate, GRE General Test, GRE Subject Test. Additional exam requirements/recommendations for international students: Required—TOEFL (minimum score 540 paper-based). *Expenses:* Tuition, state resident: full-time $5811; part-time $322.81 per credit. Tuition, nonresident: full-time $19,220; part-time $1067.79 per credit. *Required fees:* $1030. Tuition and fees vary according to course load. *Faculty research:* Surface and subsurface hydrology, numerical simulation, stochastic hydrology, water quality, modeling.

New Mexico State University, College of Agricultural, Consumer and Environmental Sciences, Department of Agricultural Economics and Agricultural Business, Las Cruces, NM 88003-8001. Offers agribusiness (MBA); economic development (DED); water science management (MS). *Program availability:* Part-time. *Faculty:* 6 full-time (0 women), 1 part-time/adjunct (0 women). *Students:* 9 full-time (5 women); includes 3 minority (all Hispanic/Latino), 3 international. Average age 32. 9 applicants, 67% accepted, 4 enrolled. In 2015, 6 master's awarded. *Degree requirements:* For master's, thesis (for some programs); for doctorate, comprehensive exam, thesis/dissertation. *Entrance requirements:* For master's, GRE; GMAT (for MBA), previous course work in intermediate microeconomics, intermediate macroeconomics, college-level calculus, statistics; for doctorate, previous course work in intermediate microeconomics, intermediate macroeconomics, college-level calculus, statistics, related MS or equivalent, minimum GPA of 3.0. Additional exam requirements/recommendations for international students: Required—TOEFL (minimum score 550 paper-based; 79 iBT), IELTS (minimum score 6.5). *Application deadline:* For fall admission, 7/1 priority date for domestic and international students; for spring admission, 11/1 priority date for domestic and international students. Applications are processed on a rolling basis. Application fee: $40 ($50 for international students). Electronic applications accepted. *Expenses:* Tuition, state resident: full-time $4086. Tuition, nonresident: full-time $14,254. *Required fees:* $853; $284.40. Tuition and fees vary according to course load. *Financial support:* In 2015–16, 6 students received support, including 2 research assistantships (averaging $18,378 per year), 3 teaching assistantships (averaging $8,482 per year); career-related internships or fieldwork, Federal Work-Study, scholarships/grants, traineeships, health care benefits, and unspecified assistantships also available. Support available to part-time students. Financial award application deadline: 3/1. *Faculty research:* Natural resource policy, production economics and farm/ranch management, agribusiness and marketing, international marketing and trade, agricultural risk management. *Total annual research expenditures:* $846,736. *Unit head:* Dr. Jay Lillywhite, Department Head, 575-646-3215, Fax: 575-646-3808, E-mail: lillywhi@nmsu.edu. *Application contact:* Dr. L. Allen Torell, Graduate Committee Chair, 575-646-4732, Fax: 575-646-3808, E-mail: atorell@nmsu.edu.
Website: http://aces.nmsu.edu/academics/aeab/

Stanford University, School of Engineering, Department of Civil and Environmental Engineering, Stanford, CA 94305-9991. Offers atmosphere and energy (MS, PhD); construction (MS), including construction engineering and management, design-construction integration, sustainable design and construction; environmental engineering and science (MS, PhD, Eng); environmental fluid mechanics and hydrology (PhD); geomechanics (MS); structural engineering (MS). Terminal master's awarded for partial completion of doctoral program. *Degree requirements:* For doctorate, thesis/dissertation, qualifying exam; for Eng, thesis. *Entrance requirements:* For master's, doctorate, and Eng, GRE General Test. Additional exam requirements/recommendations for international students: Required—TOEFL. Electronic applications accepted. *Expenses: Tuition, area resident:* Full-time $45,729. *Required fees:* $591.

Stevens Institute of Technology, Graduate School, Charles V. Schaefer Jr. School of Engineering, Department of Civil, Environmental, and Ocean Engineering, Program in Civil Engineering, Hoboken, NJ 07030. Offers civil engineering (PhD, Certificate), including geotechnical engineering (Certificate); geotechnical/geoenvironmental engineering (M Eng, Engr); hydrologic modeling (M Eng); stormwater management (M Eng); structural engineering (M Eng, Engr); transportation engineering (M Eng); water resources engineering (M Eng). *Program availability:* Part-time, evening/weekend. *Students:* 51 full-time (11 women), 27 part-time (9 women); includes 6 minority (1 Black or African American, non-Hispanic/Latino; 5 Asian, non-Hispanic/Latino), 44 international. Average age 25. 119 applicants, 69% accepted, 29 enrolled. In 2015, 28 master's awarded. *Entrance requirements:* Additional exam requirements/recommendations for international students: Required—TOEFL (minimum score 74 iBT). *Application deadline:* For fall admission, 6/1 for domestic students, 4/15 for international students; for spring admission, 11/30 for domestic students, 11/1 for international students. Applications are processed on a rolling basis. Application fee: $60. Electronic applications accepted. *Expenses: Tuition, area resident:* Full-time $32,200; part-time $1450 per credit. *Required fees:* $1150; $550 per unit. $275 per semester. *Financial support:* Fellowships, research assistantships, teaching assistantships, career-related internships or fieldwork, Federal Work-Study, scholarships/grants, and unspecified assistantships available. Financial award application deadline: 2/15; financial award applicants required to submit FAFSA. *Unit head:* Dr. David A. Vaccari, Director, 201-216-5570, Fax: 201-216-8739, E-mail: dvaccari@stevens.edu. *Application contact:* Graduate Admission, 888-783-8367, Fax: 888-511-1306, E-mail: graduate@stevens.edu.

Temple University, College of Engineering, Department of Civil and Environmental Engineering, Philadelphia, PA 19122-6096. Offers civil engineering (MSCE); environmental engineering (MS Env E); storm water management (Graduate Certificate). *Program availability:* Part-time, evening/weekend. *Faculty:* 18 full-time (4 women), 2 part-time/adjunct (0 women). *Students:* 32 full-time (8 women), 16 part-time (4 women); includes 9 minority (5 Black or African American, non-Hispanic/Latino; 3 Asian, non-Hispanic/Latino; 1 Hispanic/Latino), 22 international. 46 applicants, 41% accepted, 7 enrolled. In 2015, 4 master's awarded. Terminal master's awarded for partial completion of doctoral program. *Degree requirements:* For master's, thesis optional. *Entrance requirements:* For master's, GRE General Test, minimum GPA of 3.0; BS in engineering from ABET-accredited or equivalent institution; resume; goals statement; three letters of reference; official transcripts. Additional exam requirements/recommendations for international students: Required—TOEFL (minimum score 550 paper-based; 79 iBT), IELTS (minimum score 6.5), PTE (minimum score 53). *Application deadline:* For fall admission, 3/1 priority date for domestic and international students; for spring admission, 11/1 priority date for domestic students, 8/1 priority date for international students. Applications are processed on a rolling basis. Application fee: $60. Electronic applications accepted. *Expenses:* $968 per credit hour in-state tuition; $1,283 per credit hour out-of-state. *Financial support:* Fellowships with tuition reimbursements, research assistantships with tuition reimbursements, teaching assistantships with tuition reimbursements, Federal Work-Study, scholarships/grants, health care benefits, and unspecified assistantships available. Financial award application deadline: 3/1; financial award applicants required to submit FAFSA. *Faculty research:* Analysis of the effect of scour on bridge stability, design of sustainable buildings, development of new highway pavement material using plastic waste, characterization of by-products and waste materials for pavement and geotechnical engineering applications, development of effective traffic signals in urban and rural settings, development of techniques for effective construction management. *Unit head:* Dr. Rominder Suri, Chair, Department of Civil & Environmental Engineering, 215-204-2378, Fax: 215-204-6936, E-mail: rominder.suri@temple.edu. *Application contact:* Leslie Levin, Assistant Director, Recruitment & Marketing, 215-204-7800, Fax: 215-204-6936, E-mail: gradengr@temple.edu.
Website: http://engineering.temple.edu/department/civil-environmental-engineering

Université du Québec, Institut National de la Recherche Scientifique, Graduate Programs, Research Center–Water Earth Environment, Québec, QC G1K 9A9, Canada. Offers earth sciences (M Sc, PhD); earth sciences - environmental technologies (M Sc); water sciences (M Sc, PhD). *Program availability:* Part-time. *Degree requirements:* For master's, thesis (for some programs); for doctorate, thesis/dissertation. *Entrance requirements:* For master's, appropriate bachelor's degree, proficiency in French; for doctorate, appropriate master's degree, proficiency in French. Electronic applications accepted. *Faculty research:* Land use, impacts of climate change, adaptation to climate change, integrated management of resources (mineral and water).

University of Calgary, Faculty of Graduate Studies, Faculty of Science, Department of Geoscience, Calgary, AB T2N 1N4, Canada. Offers geology (M Sc, PhD); geophysics (M Sc, PhD); hydrology (M Sc, PhD). *Program availability:* Part-time. Terminal master's awarded for partial completion of doctoral program. *Degree requirements:* For master's, thesis; for doctorate, thesis/dissertation, candidacy exam. *Entrance requirements:* For master's, B Sc; for doctorate, honors B Sc or M Sc. Additional exam requirements/recommendations for international students: Required—TOEFL. Electronic applications accepted. *Faculty research:* Geochemistry, petrology, paleontology, stratigraphy, exploration and solid-earth geophysics.

University of California, Davis, Graduate Studies, Graduate Group in Hydrologic Sciences, Davis, CA 95616. Offers MS, PhD. Terminal master's awarded for partial completion of doctoral program. *Degree requirements:* For master's, comprehensive exam (for some programs), thesis (for some programs); for doctorate, thesis/dissertation. *Entrance requirements:* For master's, GRE General Test, minimum GPA of 3.0; for doctorate, GRE. Additional exam requirements/recommendations for international students: Required—TOEFL (minimum score 550 paper-based). Electronic applications accepted. *Faculty research:* Pollutant transport in surface and subsurface waters, subsurface heterogeneity, micrometeorology evaporation, biodegradation.

University of Colorado Boulder, Graduate School, College of Engineering and Applied Science, Department of Civil, Environmental, and Architectural Engineering, Boulder, CO 80309. Offers building systems engineering (MS, PhD); construction engineering management (MS, PhD); environmental engineering (MS, PhD); geotechnical engineering and geomechanics (MS, PhD); hydrology, water resources and environmental fluid mechanics (MS, PhD); structural engineering and structural mechanics (MS, PhD). *Faculty:* 42 full-time (10 women). *Students:* 229 full-time (80 women), 37 part-time (9 women); includes 28 minority (1 American Indian or Alaska Native, non-Hispanic/Latino; 8 Asian, non-Hispanic/Latino; 9 Hispanic/Latino; 10 Two or more races, non-Hispanic/Latino), 76 international. Average age 28. 494 applicants, 57% accepted, 69 enrolled. In 2015, 75 master's, 22 doctorates awarded. Terminal master's awarded for partial completion of doctoral program. *Degree requirements:* For master's, comprehensive exam, thesis or alternative; for doctorate, thesis/dissertation. *Entrance requirements:* For master's, GRE General Test, minimum undergraduate GPA of 3.0. *Application deadline:* For fall admission, 1/31 for domestic and international students; for spring admission, 10/1 for domestic and international students. Application fee: $50 ($70 for international students). Electronic applications accepted. Application fee is waived when completed online. *Financial support:* In 2015–16, 365 students received support, including 50 fellowships (averaging $4,774 per year), 95 research assistantships with tuition reimbursements available (averaging $33,130 per year), 21 teaching assistantships with tuition reimbursements available (averaging $36,075 per year); institutionally sponsored loans, scholarships/grants, health care benefits, and unspecified assistantships also available. Financial award application deadline: 1/15; financial award applicants required to submit FAFSA. *Faculty research:* Civil engineering, environmental engineering, architectural engineering, solid mechanics, hydrology. *Total annual research expenditures:* $14.9 million. *Application contact:* E-mail: cvengrad@colorado.edu.
Website: http://civil.colorado.edu/

University of Colorado Denver, College of Engineering and Applied Science, Department of Civil Engineering, Denver, CO 80217. Offers civil engineering (EASPh D); civil engineering systems (PhD); environmental and sustainability engineering (MS, PhD); geographic information systems (MS); geotechnical engineering (MS, PhD); hydrology and hydraulics (MS, PhD); structural engineering (MS, PhD); transportation engineering (MS, PhD). *Program availability:* Part-time, evening/weekend. *Faculty:* 16 full-time (4 women), 10 part-time/adjunct (1 woman). *Students:* 57 full-time (17 women), 38 part-time (6 women); includes 18 minority (4 Black or African American, non-Hispanic/Latino; 3 Asian, non-Hispanic/Latino; 7 Hispanic/Latino; 4 Two or more races, non-Hispanic/Latino), 30 international. Average age 31. 107 applicants, 54% accepted, 22 enrolled. In 2015, 35 master's awarded. *Degree requirements:* For master's, comprehensive exam, 30 credit hours, project or thesis; for doctorate, comprehensive exam, thesis/dissertation, 60 credit hours (30 of which are dissertation research). *Entrance requirements:* For master's, GRE, statement of purpose, transcripts, three references; for doctorate, GRE, statement of purpose, transcripts, references, letter of support from faculty stating willingness to serve as dissertation advisor and outlining plan for financial support. Additional exam requirements/recommendations for international students: Required—TOEFL (minimum score 537 paper-based; 75 iBT); Recommended—IELTS (minimum score 6.5). *Application deadline:* For fall admission, 5/1 for domestic students, 4/1 for international students; for spring admission, 10/1 for domestic students, 9/1 for international students; for summer admission, 2/15 for domestic students, 1/15 for international students. Application fee: $50 ($75 for international students). Electronic applications accepted. *Expenses:* Contact institution. *Financial support:* In 2015–16, 89 students received support. Fellowships, research assistantships, teaching assistantships, career-related internships or fieldwork, Federal Work-Study, institutionally sponsored loans, scholarships/grants, traineeships, and unspecified assistantships available. Financial award application deadline: 4/1; financial award applicants required to submit FAFSA. *Faculty research:* Earthquake source physics, environmental biotechnology, hydrologic and hydraulic engineering, sustainability assessments, transportation energy use and greenhouse gas emissions. *Unit head:* Dr. Kevin Rens, Chair, 303-556-8017, E-mail: kevin.rens@ucdenver.edu. *Application contact:* Roxanne Pizano, Program Coordinator, 303-556-6274, E-mail: roxanne.pizano@ucdenver.edu.
Website: http://www.ucdenver.edu/academics/colleges/Engineering/Programs/Civil-Engineering/Pages/CivilEngineering.aspx

University of Florida, Graduate School, College of Liberal Arts and Sciences, Department of Geological Sciences, Gainesville, FL 32611. Offers geology (MS, MST,

Hydrology

PhD); hydrologic sciences (MS, PhD); tropical conservation and development (MS, MST, PhD); wetland sciences (MS, MST, PhD). *Faculty:* 22. *Students:* 43 full-time (19 women), 3 part-time (1 woman); includes 4 minority (1 Asian, non-Hispanic/Latino; 3 Hispanic/Latino), 18 international. Average age 29. 60 applicants, 20% accepted, 11 enrolled. In 2015, 6 master's, 1 doctorate awarded. Terminal master's awarded for partial completion of doctoral program. *Degree requirements:* For master's, thesis (for some programs); for doctorate, one foreign language, thesis/dissertation. *Entrance requirements:* For master's and doctorate, GRE General Test, minimum GPA of 3.0. Additional exam requirements/recommendations for international students: Required—TOEFL (minimum score 550 paper-based; 80 iBT), IELTS (minimum score 6). *Application deadline:* For fall admission, 1/15 for domestic students; for spring admission, 10/1 for domestic students. Applications are processed on a rolling basis. Application fee: $30. Electronic applications accepted. *Financial support:* In 2015–16, 3 fellowships, 21 research assistantships, 25 teaching assistantships were awarded; career-related internships or fieldwork, Federal Work-Study, institutionally sponsored loans, and scholarships/grants also available. Support available to part-time students. Financial award application deadline: 3/1; financial award applicants required to submit FAFSA. *Faculty research:* Paleoclimatology, tectonophysics, petrochemistry, marine geology, geochemistry, hydrology. *Total annual research expenditures:* $1.5 million. *Unit head:* Dr. David A. Foster, Professor and Chair, 352-392-7316, Fax: 352-392-9294, E-mail: dafoster@ufl.edu. *Application contact:* Dr. Raymond Russo, Associate Professor and Graduate Coordinator, 352-392-2231, Fax: 352-392-9294, E-mail: rrusso@ufl.edu.

University of Idaho, College of Graduate Studies, College of Science, Department of Geological Sciences, Moscow, ID 83844-3022. Offers geology (MS, PhD); hydrology (MS). *Faculty:* 12 full-time. *Students:* 20 full-time, 4 part-time. Average age 32. In 2015, 8 master's, 1 doctorate awarded. *Degree requirements:* For doctorate, one foreign language, thesis/dissertation. *Entrance requirements:* For master's, minimum GPA of 2.8; for doctorate, minimum undergraduate GPA of 2.8, 3.0 graduate. Additional exam requirements/recommendations for international students: Required—TOEFL. *Application deadline:* For fall admission, 8/1 for domestic students; for spring admission, 12/15 for domestic students. Applications are processed on a rolling basis. Application fee: $60. Electronic applications accepted. *Expenses:* Tuition, state resident: full-time $6205; part-time $399 per credit hour. Tuition, nonresident: full-time $20,209; part-time $1177 per credit hour. *Required fees:* $2017; $58 per credit hour. Full-time tuition and fees vary according to course load and reciprocity agreements. *Financial support:* Fellowships, research assistantships, and teaching assistantships available. Financial award applicants required to submit FAFSA. *Faculty research:* Health effects of mineral dust, geomicrobiology, glacial and arctic sciences, optical mineralogy, planetary and terrestrial geomechanics. *Unit head:* Dr. Mickey Gunter, Head, 208-885-6192, E-mail: geology@uidaho.edu. *Application contact:* Sean Scoggin, Graduate Recruitment Director, 208-885-4723, Fax: 208-885-4406, E-mail: graduateadmissions@uidaho.edu. Website: http://www.uidaho.edu/sci/geology

University of Minnesota, Twin Cities Campus, Graduate School, College of Food, Agricultural and Natural Resource Sciences, Program in Natural Resources Science and Management, St. Paul, MN 55108. Offers assessment, monitoring, and geospatial analysis (MS, PhD); economics, policy, management, and society (MS, PhD); forest hydrology and watershed management (MS, PhD); forest products (MS, PhD); forests: biology, ecology, conservation, and management (MS, PhD); natural resources science and management (MS, PhD); paper science and engineering (MS, PhD); recreation resources, tourism, and environmental education (MS, PhD); wildlife ecology and management (MS, PhD). *Program availability:* Part-time. *Faculty:* 71 full-time (28 women), 55 part-time/adjunct (7 women). *Students:* 80 full-time (45 women), 16 part-time (9 women); includes 5 minority (1 Black or African American, non-Hispanic/Latino; 2 American Indian or Alaska Native, non-Hispanic/Latino; 2 Asian, non-Hispanic/Latino), 8 international. 81 applicants, 52% accepted, 31 enrolled. In 2015, 25 master's, 8 doctorates awarded. Terminal master's awarded for partial completion of doctoral program. *Degree requirements:* For master's, comprehensive exam, thesis; for doctorate, comprehensive exam, thesis/dissertation. *Entrance requirements:* For master's and doctorate, GRE General Test. Additional exam requirements/recommendations for international students: Required—TOEFL (minimum score 550 paper-based; 79 iBT), IELTS (minimum score 6.5). *Application deadline:* For fall admission, 12/16 priority date for domestic and international students; for spring admission, 10/15 for domestic and international students. Applications are processed on a rolling basis. Application fee: $75 ($95 for international students). Electronic applications accepted. *Financial support:* In 2015–16, fellowships with full tuition reimbursements (averaging $40,000 per year), research assistantships with full tuition reimbursements (averaging $40,000 per year), teaching assistantships with full tuition reimbursements (averaging $40,000 per year) were awarded; scholarships/grants, health care benefits, tuition waivers (full and partial), and unspecified assistantships also available. *Faculty research:* Forest hydrology, biology, ecology, conservation, and management; recreation resources and environmental education; wildlife ecology; economics, policy, and society; geographic information systems (GIS); and forest products and paper science. *Unit head:* Dr. Michael Kilgore, Director of Graduate Studies, 612-624-6298, E-mail: mkilgore@umn.edu. *Application contact:* Toni Wheeler, Graduate Program Coordinator, 612-624-7683, Fax: 612-625-5212, E-mail: twheeler@umn.edu. Website: http://www.nrsm.umn.edu

University of Nevada, Reno, Graduate School, Interdisciplinary Program in Hydrologic Sciences, Reno, NV 89557. Offers hydrogeology (MS, PhD); hydrology (MS, PhD). Offered through the M. C. Fleischmann College of Agriculture, the College of Engineering, the Mackay School of Mines, and the Desert Research Institute. Terminal master's awarded for partial completion of doctoral program. *Degree requirements:* For master's, thesis optional; for doctorate, thesis/dissertation. *Entrance requirements:* For master's and doctorate, GRE General Test, minimum GPA of 3.0. Additional exam requirements/recommendations for international students: Required—TOEFL (minimum score 500 paper-based; 61 iBT), IELTS (minimum score 6). Electronic applications accepted. *Faculty research:* Groundwater, water resources, surface water, soil science.

University of New Brunswick Fredericton, School of Graduate Studies, Faculty of Engineering, Department of Civil Engineering, Fredericton, NB E3B 5A3, Canada. Offers construction engineering and management (M Eng, M Sc E, PhD); environmental engineering (M Eng, M Sc E, PhD); environmental studies (M Eng); geotechnical engineering (M Eng, M Sc E, PhD); groundwater/hydrology (M Eng, M Sc E, PhD); materials (M Eng, M Sc E, PhD); pavements (M Eng, M Sc E, PhD); structures (M Eng,

M Sc E, PhD); transportation (M Eng, M Sc E, PhD). *Program availability:* Part-time. *Faculty:* 12 full-time (1 woman), 4 part-time/adjunct (0 women). *Students:* 16 full-time (4 women), 15 part-time (5 women). In 2015, 2 master's, 4 doctorates awarded. *Degree requirements:* For master's, thesis; for doctorate, comprehensive exam, thesis/dissertation, qualifying exam; 27 credit hours of courses. *Entrance requirements:* For master's, minimum GPA of 3.0; B Sc E in civil engineering or related engineering degree; for doctorate, minimum GPA of 3.0; graduate degree in engineering or applied science. Additional exam requirements/recommendations for international students: Required—IELTS (minimum score 7.5), TWE (minimum score 4), Michigan English Language Assessment Battery (minimum score 85) or CanTest (minimum score 4.5); Recommended—TOEFL (minimum score 580 paper-based). *Application deadline:* For fall admission, 5/1 for domestic students; for winter admission, 11/1 for domestic students. Applications are processed on a rolling basis. Application fee: $50 Canadian dollars. Electronic applications accepted. *Financial support:* In 2015–16, 35 fellowships, 48 research assistantships, 35 teaching assistantships were awarded; career-related internships or fieldwork and scholarships/grants also available. *Faculty research:* Construction engineering and management; engineering materials and infrastructure renewal; highway and pavement research; structures and solid mechanics; geotechnical and geoenvironmental engineering; structure interaction; transportation and planning; environment, solid waste management; structural engineering; water and environmental engineering. *Unit head:* Dr. Kerry MacQuarrie, Director of Graduate Studies, 506-453-5121, Fax: 506-453-3568, E-mail: ktm@unb.ca. *Application contact:* Joyce Moore, Graduate Secretary, 506-452-6127, Fax: 506-453-3568, E-mail: joycem@unb.ca. Website: http://go.unb.ca/gradprograms

University of New Hampshire, Graduate School, College of Engineering and Physical Sciences, Department of Earth Sciences, Durham, NH 03824. Offers earth sciences (PhD); geology (MS); hydrology (MS). *Degree requirements:* For master's, thesis. *Entrance requirements:* For master's, GRE General Test. Additional exam requirements/recommendations for international students: Required—TOEFL (minimum score 550 paper-based; 80 iBT). Electronic applications accepted.

University of Southern Mississippi, Graduate School, College of Science and Technology, Department of Marine Science, Stennis Space Center, MS 39529. Offers hydrographic science (MS); marine science (MS, PhD). *Program availability:* Part-time. *Faculty:* 16 full-time (1 woman). *Students:* 42 full-time (18 women), 5 part-time (2 women); includes 13 minority (7 Black or African American, non-Hispanic/Latino; 4 Asian, non-Hispanic/Latino; 1 Hispanic/Latino; 1 Two or more races, non-Hispanic/Latino). Average age 32. 44 applicants, 61% accepted, 22 enrolled. In 2015, 15 master's, 2 doctorates awarded. *Degree requirements:* For master's, comprehensive exam, thesis, oral qualifying exam (marine science); for doctorate, 2 foreign languages, comprehensive exam, thesis/dissertation, oral qualifying exam. *Entrance requirements:* For master's, GRE General Test, minimum GPA of 3.0; for doctorate, GRE General Test, minimum GPA of 3.0 (undergraduate), 3.5 (graduate). Additional exam requirements/recommendations for international students: Required—TOEFL (minimum score 84 iBT). *Application deadline:* For fall admission, 5/1 priority date for domestic and international students; for spring admission, 10/1 for domestic and international students; for summer admission, 3/1 for domestic and international students. Application fee: $60. Electronic applications accepted. *Expenses:* Contact institution. *Financial support:* In 2015–16, 9 students received support, including 1 fellowship with full tuition reimbursement available (averaging $5,300 per year), 4 research assistantships with full tuition reimbursements available (averaging $61,200 per year), 5 teaching assistantships with full tuition reimbursements available (averaging $76,500 per year). Financial award application deadline: 5/1. *Faculty research:* Biological oceanography, geological oceanography; physical oceanography; bio-optics; hydrography; marine chemistry; marine science; numerical modeling; remote sensing; zooplankton; hydrography. *Total annual research expenditures:* $6.5 million. *Unit head:* Dr. William Montrose Graham, Chair and Professor, 228-688-3177, Fax: 228-688-1121, E-mail: monty.graham@usm.edu. *Application contact:* Linda Downs, Senior Office Support Specialist, 228-688-7097, Fax: 228-688-1121, E-mail: linda.downs@usm.edu. Website: http://www.usm.edu/marine/

University of Washington, Graduate School, College of Engineering, Department of Civil and Environmental Engineering, Seattle, WA 98195-2700. Offers construction engineering (MSCE, PhD); environmental engineering (MSCE, PhD); geotechnical engineering (MSCE, PhD); hydrology and hydrodynamics (MSCE, PhD); structural engineering and mechanics (MSCE, PhD); transportation engineering (MSCE, PhD). *Program availability:* Part-time, 100% online. *Faculty:* 37 full-time (10 women). *Students:* 247 full-time (97 women), 157 part-time (47 women); includes 74 minority (7 Black or African American, non-Hispanic/Latino; 35 Asian, non-Hispanic/Latino; 20 Hispanic/Latino; 12 Two or more races, non-Hispanic/Latino), 117 international. Average age 29. 853 applicants, 59% accepted, 182 enrolled. In 2015, 123 master's, 7 doctorates awarded. Terminal master's awarded for partial completion of doctoral program. *Degree requirements:* For master's, thesis optional; for doctorate, comprehensive exam, thesis/dissertation, qualifying, general and final exams; completion of degree within 10 years. *Entrance requirements:* For master's, GRE General Test, minimum GPA of 3.0, statement of purpose, letters of recommendation, transcripts; for doctorate, GRE General Test, minimum GPA of 3.5, statement of purpose, letters of recommendation, transcripts, resume. Additional exam requirements/recommendations for international students: Required—TOEFL (minimum score 580 paper-based; 92 iBT); Recommended—IELTS (minimum score 7), TSE. *Application deadline:* For fall admission, 12/15 for domestic and international students. Applications are processed on a rolling basis. Application fee: $85. Electronic applications accepted. *Expenses:* Contact institution. *Financial support:* In 2015–16, 92 students received support, including 15 fellowships with tuition reimbursements available, 53 research assistantships with full tuition reimbursements available, 24 teaching assistantships with full tuition reimbursements available; scholarships/grants also available. Financial award application deadline: 12/15; financial award applicants required to submit FAFSA. *Faculty research:* Structural and geotechnical engineering, transportation and construction engineering, water and environmental engineering. *Total annual research expenditures:* $13.4 million. *Unit head:* Dr. Gregory R. Miller, Professor/Chair, 206-543-0350, Fax: 206-543-1543, E-mail: gmiller@uw.edu. *Application contact:* Lorna Latal, Graduate Adviser, 206-543-2574, Fax: 206-543-1543, E-mail: ceginfo@u.washington.edu. Website: http://www.ce.washington.edu/

130 www.petersons.com

Peterson's Graduate Programs in the Physical Sciences, Mathematics, Agricultural Sciences, the Environment & Natural Resources 2017

Limnology

Baylor University, Graduate School, College of Arts and Sciences, Department of Biology, Waco, TX 76798. Offers biology (MA, MS, PhD); environmental biology (MS); limnology (MS). *Program availability:* Part-time. *Degree requirements:* For master's, thesis (for some programs); for doctorate, thesis/dissertation. *Entrance requirements:* For master's and doctorate, GRE General Test. Additional exam requirements/recommendations for international students: Required—TOEFL. *Faculty research:* Terrestrial ecology, aquatic ecology, genetics.

Cornell University, Graduate School, Graduate Fields of Agriculture and Life Sciences, Field of Ecology and Evolutionary Biology, Ithaca, NY 14853-0001. Offers ecology (PhD), including animal ecology, applied ecology, biogeochemistry, community and ecosystem ecology, limnology, oceanography, physiological ecology, plant ecology, population ecology, theoretical ecology, vertebrate zoology; evolutionary biology (PhD), including ecological genetics, paleobiology, population biology, systematics. *Degree requirements:* For doctorate, comprehensive exam, thesis/dissertation, 2 semesters of teaching experience. *Entrance requirements:* For doctorate, GRE General Test, GRE Subject Test (biology), 2 letters of recommendation. Additional exam requirements/recommendations for international students: Required—TOEFL (minimum score 550 paper-based; 77 iBT). Electronic applications accepted. *Faculty research:* Population and organismal biology, population and evolutionary genetics, systematics and macroevolution, biochemistry, conservation biology.

University of Alaska Fairbanks, School of Fisheries and Ocean Sciences, Program in Marine Sciences and Limnology, Fairbanks, AK 99775-7220. Offers marine biology (MS, PhD); oceanography (MS, PhD). *Program availability:* Part-time. *Faculty:* 4 full-time (1 woman). *Students:* 31 full-time (20 women), 10 part-time (7 women); includes 6 minority (1 Asian, non-Hispanic/Latino; 4 Hispanic/Latino; 1 Two or more races, non-Hispanic/Latino), 8 international. Average age 31. 26 applicants, 46% accepted, 12 enrolled. In 2015, 10 master's, 3 doctorates awarded. *Median time to degree:* Of those who began their doctoral program in fall 2007, 100% received their degree in 8 years or less. *Degree requirements:* For master's, comprehensive exam, thesis, oral defense of thesis; for doctorate, comprehensive exam, thesis/dissertation, oral defense of dissertation. *Entrance requirements:* For master's, GRE General Test, bachelor's degree from accredited institution with minimum cumulative undergraduate and major GPA of 3.0; for doctorate, GRE General Test, minimum cumulative GPA of 3.0. Additional exam requirements/recommendations for international students: Required—TOEFL (minimum score 550 paper-based; 79 iBT), IELTS (minimum score 6.5). *Application deadline:* For fall admission, 5/1 for domestic students, 4/1 for international students; for spring admission, 9/15 for domestic students, 8/15 for international students. Applications are processed on a rolling basis. Application fee: $60. Electronic applications accepted. *Expenses:* Tuition, state resident: full-time $7614; part-time $423 per credit. Tuition, nonresident: full-time $15,552; part-time $864 per credit. *Required fees:* $38 per credit. $187 per semester. Tuition and fees vary according to course level, course load, program and reciprocity agreements. *Financial support:* In 2015–16, 29 research assistantships with full tuition reimbursements (averaging $14,427 per year), 5 teaching assistantships with full tuition reimbursements (averaging $7,083 per year) were awarded; fellowships with full tuition reimbursements, career-related internships or fieldwork, Federal Work-Study, scholarships/grants, health care benefits, and unspecified assistantships also available. Support available to part-time students. Financial award application deadline: 7/1; financial award applicants required to submit FAFSA. *Total annual research expenditures:* $24.1 million. *Unit head:* Katrin Iken, Co-Chair, 907-474-7289, Fax: 907-474-5863, E-mail: info@sfos.uaf.edu. *Application contact:* Mary Kreta, Director of Admissions, 907-474-7500, Fax: 907-474-7097, E-mail: admissions@alaska.edu.
Website: http://www.uaf.edu/sfos/academics/graduate/

University of Florida, Graduate School, College of Agricultural and Life Sciences, School of Forest Resources and Conservation, Department of Fisheries and Aquatic Sciences, Gainesville, FL 32611. Offers MFAS, MS, PhD. *Program availability:* Part-time, online learning. *Faculty:* 63. *Students:* 32 full-time (15 women), 51 part-time (30 women); includes 5 minority (1 Black or African American, non-Hispanic/Latino; 1 American Indian or Alaska Native, non-Hispanic/Latino; 1 Asian, non-Hispanic/Latino; 2 Hispanic/Latino), 6 international. Average age 30. 40 applicants, 48% accepted, 18 enrolled. In 2015, 8 master's, 7 doctorates awarded. *Degree requirements:* For master's, thesis (for MS); technical paper (for MFAS); for doctorate, comprehensive exam, thesis/dissertation. *Entrance requirements:* For master's and doctorate, GRE General Test, minimum GPA of 3.0. Additional exam requirements/recommendations for international students: Required—TOEFL (minimum score 550 paper-based; 80 iBT), IELTS (minimum score 6). *Application deadline:* For fall admission, 6/1 for domestic students, 3/1 for international students; for spring admission, 10/1 for domestic students, 8/1 for international students. Applications are processed on a rolling basis. Application fee: $30. Electronic applications accepted. *Financial support:* Unspecified assistantships available. Financial award application deadline: 1/31; financial award applicants required to submit FAFSA. *Total annual research expenditures:* $1,921.
Website: http://sfrc.ufl.edu/fish/

Marine Geology

Cornell University, Graduate School, Graduate Fields of Engineering, Field of Geological Sciences, Ithaca, NY 14853. Offers economic geology (M Eng, MS, PhD); engineering geology (M Eng, MS, PhD); environmental geophysics (M Eng, MS, PhD); general geology (M Eng, MS, PhD); geobiology (M Eng, MS, PhD); geochemistry and isotope geology (M Eng, MS, PhD); geohydrology (M Eng, MS, PhD); geomorphology (M Eng, MS, PhD); geophysics (M Eng, MS, PhD); geotectonics (M Eng, MS, PhD); marine geology (MS, PhD); mineralogy (M Eng, MS, PhD); paleontology (M Eng, MS, PhD); petroleum geology (M Eng, MS, PhD); petrology (M Eng, MS, PhD); planetary geology (M Eng, MS, PhD); Precambrian geology (M Eng, MS, PhD); Quaternary geology (M Eng, MS, PhD); rock mechanics (M Eng, MS, PhD); sedimentology (M Eng, MS, PhD); seismology (M Eng, MS, PhD); stratigraphy (M Eng, MS, PhD); structural geology (M Eng, MS, PhD). *Degree requirements:* For master's, thesis (MS); for doctorate, comprehensive exam, thesis/dissertation. *Entrance requirements:* For master's and doctorate, GRE General Test, 3 letters of recommendation. Additional exam requirements/recommendations for international students: Required—TOEFL (minimum score 550 paper-based; 77 iBT). Electronic applications accepted. *Faculty research:* Geophysics, structural geology, petrology, geochemistry, geodynamics.

Massachusetts Institute of Technology, School of Science, Department of Earth, Atmospheric, and Planetary Sciences, Cambridge, MA 02139. Offers atmospheric chemistry (PhD, Sc D); atmospheric science (SM, PhD, Sc D); chemical oceanography (SM, PhD, Sc D); climate physics and chemistry (SM, PhD, Sc D); earth and planetary sciences (SM); geochemistry (PhD, Sc D); geology (PhD, Sc D); geophysics (PhD, Sc D); marine geology and geophysics (SM, PhD, Sc D); physical oceanography (SM, PhD, Sc D); planetary sciences (PhD, Sc D). *Faculty:* 36 full-time (8 women). *Students:* 166 full-time (75 women), 1 part-time (0 women); includes 23 minority (1 Black or African American, non-Hispanic/Latino; 7 Asian, non-Hispanic/Latino; 6 Hispanic/Latino; 9 Two or more races, non-Hispanic/Latino), 54 international. Average age 27. 228 applicants, 26% accepted, 33 enrolled. In 2015, 6 master's, 24 doctorates awarded. Terminal master's awarded for partial completion of doctoral program. *Degree requirements:* For master's, thesis; for doctorate, comprehensive exam, thesis/dissertation. *Entrance requirements:* For master's, GRE General Test; for doctorate, GRE General Test, GRE Subject Test in chemistry or physics (for planetary sciences area). Additional exam requirements/recommendations for international students: Required—TOEFL (minimum score 600 paper-based; 100 iBT), IELTS (minimum score 7). *Application deadline:* For fall admission, 1/5 for domestic and international students; for spring admission, 11/1 for domestic and international students. Application fee: $75. Electronic applications accepted. *Expenses: Tuition:* Full-time $46,400; part-time $725 per credit. One-time fee: $304 full-time. Full-time tuition and fees vary according to course load and program. *Financial support:* In 2015–16, 99 students received support, including 60 fellowships (averaging $40,700 per year), 76 research assistantships (averaging $38,000 per year), 15 teaching assistantships (averaging $36,100 per year); Federal Work-Study, institutionally sponsored loans, scholarships/grants, traineeships, health care benefits, and unspecified assistantships also available. Support available to part-time students. Financial award application deadline: 4/15; financial award applicants required to submit FAFSA. *Faculty research:* Earth: origin, composition, structure, and dynamics of (and interactions between) the atmosphere, oceans, surface, and interior of the earth; planets: formation, dynamics, and evolution of planetary systems and the characterization of exoplanets; climate: characterization of past, present, and potential future climates; studies of the causes and consequences of climate change; life: co-evolution of life and environmental systems. *Total annual research expenditures:* $25.3 million. *Unit head:* Prof. Robert van der Hilst, Department Head, 617-253-2127, Fax: 617-253-8298, E-mail: eapsinfo@mit.edu. *Application contact:* EAPS Education Office, 617-253-3381, Fax: 617-253-8298, E-mail: eapsinfo@mit.edu.
Website: http://eapsweb.mit.edu/

University of Delaware, College of Earth, Ocean, and Environment, Newark, DE 19716. Offers geography (MA, MS, PhD); geology (MS, PhD); marine science and policy (MMP, MS, PhD), including marine policy (MMP), marine studies (MS, PhD), oceanography (PhD); ocean engineering (MS, PhD). *Degree requirements:* For master's, thesis; for doctorate, thesis/dissertation. *Entrance requirements:* For master's and doctorate, GRE General Test. Additional exam requirements/recommendations for international students: Required—TOEFL. Electronic applications accepted. *Faculty research:* Marine biology and biochemistry, oceanography, marine policy, physical ocean science and engineering, ocean engineering.

University of Hawaii at Manoa, Graduate Division, School of Ocean and Earth Science and Technology, Department of Geology and Geophysics, Honolulu, HI 96822. Offers high-pressure geophysics and geochemistry (MS, PhD); hydrogeology and engineering geology (MS, PhD); marine geology and geophysics (MS, PhD); planetary geosciences and remote sensing (MS, PhD); seismology and solid-earth geophysics (MS, PhD); volcanology, petrology, and geochemistry (MS, PhD). *Program availability:* Part-time. *Faculty:* 72 full-time (15 women), 6 part-time/adjunct (3 women). *Students:* 42 full-time (26 women), 2 part-time (1 woman); includes 9 minority (2 Asian, non-Hispanic/Latino; 2 Hispanic/Latino; 5 Two or more races, non-Hispanic/Latino), 9 international. Average age 31. 78 applicants, 23% accepted, 13 enrolled. In 2015, 7 master's, 8 doctorates awarded. Terminal master's awarded for partial completion of doctoral program. *Degree requirements:* For master's, thesis optional; for doctorate, comprehensive exam, thesis/dissertation. *Entrance requirements:* For master's and doctorate, GRE General Test, minimum GPA of 3.0. Additional exam requirements/recommendations for international students: Required—TOEFL (minimum score 580 paper-based; 92 iBT), IELTS (minimum score 5). *Application deadline:* For fall admission, 1/15 for domestic students, 1/1 for international students; for spring admission, 9/1 for domestic students, 8/15 for international students. Application fee: $100. *Financial support:* In 2015–16, 7 fellowships (averaging $1,359 per year), 30 research assistantships (averaging $23,988 per year), 4 teaching assistantships (averaging $15,350 per year) were awarded. *Total annual research expenditures:* $3.8 million. *Unit head:* Brian Taylor, Dean, 808-956-6182, E-mail: taylorb@hawaii.edu. *Application contact:* Dr. Gregory Moore, Chair, 808-956-7640, Fax: 808-956-5512, E-mail: gg-dept@soest.hawaii.edu.
Website: http://www.soest.hawaii.edu/GG/

University of Miami, Graduate School, Rosenstiel School of Marine and Atmospheric Science, Division of Marine Geology and Geophysics, Coral Gables, FL 33124. Offers MS, PhD. Terminal master's awarded for partial completion of doctoral program. *Degree requirements:* For master's, comprehensive exam, thesis; for doctorate, comprehensive exam, thesis/dissertation. *Entrance requirements:* For master's and doctorate, GRE General Test. Additional exam requirements/recommendations for international students: Required—TOEFL (minimum score 550 paper-based). Electronic applications accepted. *Faculty research:* Carbonate sedimentology, low-temperature geochemistry, paleoceanography, geodesy and tectonics.

University of Washington, Graduate School, College of the Environment, School of Oceanography, Seattle, WA 98195. Offers biological oceanography (MS, PhD);

chemical oceanography (MS, PhD); marine geology and geophysics (MS, PhD); physical oceanography (MS, PhD). Terminal master's awarded for partial completion of doctoral program. *Degree requirements:* For master's, research project; for doctorate, thesis/dissertation. *Entrance requirements:* For master's and doctorate, GRE General Test, minimum GPA of 3.0. Additional exam requirements/recommendations for international students: Required—TOEFL. Electronic applications accepted. *Faculty research:* Global climate change, hydrothermal vent systems, marine microbiology, marine and freshwater biogeochemistry, biological-physical interactions.

Woods Hole Oceanographic Institution, MIT/WHOI Joint Program in Oceanography/Applied Ocean Science and Engineering, Woods Hole, MA 02543-1541. Offers applied ocean science and engineering (PhD); biological oceanography (PhD); chemical oceanography (PhD); marine geology and geophysics (PhD); physical oceanography (PhD). Program offered jointly with Massachusetts Institute of Technology. *Degree requirements:* For doctorate, thesis/dissertation. *Entrance requirements:* For doctorate, GRE General Test, GRE Subject Test. Additional exam requirements/recommendations for international students: Required—TOEFL. Electronic applications accepted.

Mineralogy

Cornell University, Graduate School, Graduate Fields of Engineering, Field of Geological Sciences, Ithaca, NY 14853. Offers economic geology (M Eng, MS, PhD); engineering geology (M Eng, MS, PhD); environmental geophysics (M Eng, MS, PhD); general geology (M Eng, MS, PhD); geobiology (M Eng, MS, PhD); geochemistry and isotope geology (M Eng, MS, PhD); geohydrology (M Eng, MS, PhD); geomorphology (M Eng, MS, PhD); geophysics (M Eng, MS, PhD); geotectonics (M Eng, MS, PhD); marine geology (MS, PhD); mineralogy (M Eng, MS, PhD); paleontology (M Eng, MS, PhD); petroleum geology (M Eng, MS, PhD); petrology (M Eng, MS, PhD); planetary geology (M Eng, MS, PhD); Precambrian geology (M Eng, MS, PhD); Quaternary geology (M Eng, MS, PhD); rock mechanics (M Eng, MS, PhD); sedimentology (M Eng, MS, PhD); seismology (M Eng, MS, PhD); stratigraphy (M Eng, MS, PhD); structural geology (M Eng, MS, PhD). *Degree requirements:* For master's, thesis (MS); for doctorate, comprehensive exam, thesis/dissertation. *Entrance requirements:* For master's and doctorate, GRE General Test, 3 letters of recommendation. Additional exam requirements/recommendations for international students: Required—TOEFL (minimum score 550 paper-based; 77 iBT). Electronic applications accepted. *Faculty research:* Geophysics, structural geology, petrology, geochemistry, geodynamics.

Indiana University Bloomington, University Graduate School, College of Arts and Sciences, Department of Geological Sciences, Bloomington, IN 47405-7000. Offers biogeochemistry (MS, PhD); economic geology (MS, PhD); geobiology (MS, PhD); geophysics, structural geology and tectonics (MS, PhD); hydrogeology (MS, PhD); mineralogy (MS, PhD); stratigraphy and sedimentology (MS, PhD). Terminal master's awarded for partial completion of doctoral program. *Degree requirements:* For master's, thesis or alternative; for doctorate, comprehensive exam, thesis/dissertation. *Entrance requirements:* For master's and doctorate, GRE General Test. Additional exam requirements/recommendations for international students: Required—TOEFL. *Faculty research:* Geophysics, geochemistry, hydrogeology, geobiology, planetary science.

Université du Québec à Chicoutimi, Graduate Programs, Program in Mineral Resources, Chicoutimi, QC G7H 2B1, Canada. Offers PhD. Program offered jointly with Université du Québec à Montréal. *Program availability:* Part-time. *Degree requirements:* For doctorate, thesis/dissertation. *Entrance requirements:* For doctorate, appropriate master's degree, proficiency in French.

Université du Québec à Montréal, Graduate Programs, Program in Earth Sciences, Montreal, QC H3C 3P8, Canada. Offers earth sciences (M Sc); mineral resources (PhD); non-renewable resources (DESS). *Program availability:* Part-time. Terminal master's awarded for partial completion of doctoral program. *Degree requirements:* For master's, thesis (for some programs); for doctorate, thesis/dissertation. *Entrance requirements:* For master's, appropriate bachelor's degree or equivalent, proficiency in French. *Faculty research:* Economic geology, structural geology, geochemistry, Quaternary geology, isotopic geochemistry.

Université du Québec à Montréal, Graduate Programs, Program in Mineral Resources, Montréal, QC H3C 3P8, Canada. Offers PhD. Program offered jointly with Université du Québec à Chicoutimi. *Program availability:* Part-time. *Degree requirements:* For doctorate, thesis/dissertation. *Entrance requirements:* For doctorate, appropriate master's degree or equivalent, proficiency in French.

Paleontology

Cornell University, Graduate School, Graduate Fields of Engineering, Field of Geological Sciences, Ithaca, NY 14853. Offers economic geology (M Eng, MS, PhD); engineering geology (M Eng, MS, PhD); environmental geophysics (M Eng, MS, PhD); general geology (M Eng, MS, PhD); geobiology (M Eng, MS, PhD); geochemistry and isotope geology (M Eng, MS, PhD); geohydrology (M Eng, MS, PhD); geomorphology (M Eng, MS, PhD); geophysics (M Eng, MS, PhD); geotectonics (M Eng, MS, PhD); marine geology (MS, PhD); mineralogy (M Eng, MS, PhD); paleontology (M Eng, MS, PhD); petroleum geology (M Eng, MS, PhD); petrology (M Eng, MS, PhD); planetary geology (M Eng, MS, PhD); Precambrian geology (M Eng, MS, PhD); Quaternary geology (M Eng, MS, PhD); rock mechanics (M Eng, MS, PhD); sedimentology (M Eng, MS, PhD); seismology (M Eng, MS, PhD); stratigraphy (M Eng, MS, PhD); structural geology (M Eng, MS, PhD). *Degree requirements:* For master's, thesis (MS); for doctorate, comprehensive exam, thesis/dissertation. *Entrance requirements:* For master's and doctorate, GRE General Test, 3 letters of recommendation. Additional exam requirements/recommendations for international students: Required—TOEFL (minimum score 550 paper-based; 77 iBT). Electronic applications accepted. *Faculty research:* Geophysics, structural geology, petrology, geochemistry, geodynamics.

Duke University, Graduate School, Department of Evolutionary Anthropology, Durham, NC 27708. Offers cellular and molecular biology (PhD); gross anatomy and physical anthropology (PhD), including comparative morphology of human and non-human primates, primate social behavior, vertebrate paleontology; neuroanatomy (PhD). *Degree requirements:* For doctorate, one foreign language, thesis/dissertation. *Entrance requirements:* For doctorate, GRE General Test. Additional exam requirements/recommendations for international students: Required—TOEFL (minimum score 577 paper-based; 90 iBT) or IELTS (minimum score 7). Electronic applications accepted.

East Tennessee State University, School of Graduate Studies, College of Arts and Sciences, Department of Biological Sciences, Johnson City, TN 37614. Offers paleontology (MS). *Faculty:* 21 full-time (4 women). *Students:* 33 full-time (15 women), 4 part-time (1 woman); includes 1 minority (Black or African American, non-Hispanic/Latino), 18 international. Average age 26. 67 applicants, 42% accepted, 18 enrolled. In 2015, 14 master's awarded. *Degree requirements:* For master's, comprehensive exam, thesis. *Entrance requirements:* For master's, GRE General Test or GRE Subject Test, minimum GPA of 3.0, undergraduate degree in life or physical sciences, two letters of recommendation. Additional exam requirements/recommendations for international students: Required—TOEFL (minimum score 550 paper-based; 79 iBT). *Application deadline:* For fall admission, 4/1 for domestic students, 2/1 for international students; for spring admission, 9/1 for domestic students, 7/1 for international students. Application fee: $35 ($45 for international students). Electronic applications accepted. *Financial support:* In 2015–16, 36 students received support, including 28 teaching assistantships with full tuition reimbursements available (averaging $8,000 per year); institutionally sponsored loans, scholarships/grants, and unspecified assistantships also available. Financial award application deadline: 7/1; financial award applicants required to submit FAFSA. *Faculty research:* Neuroethology, chronobiology, molecular biology, behavioral ecology, systematics, paleobotany. *Unit head:* Dr. Joseph Bidwell, Chair, 423-439-4329, Fax: 423-439-5958, E-mail: bidwell@etsu.edu. *Application contact:* Angela Edwards, Graduate Specialist, 423-439-4703, Fax: 423-439-5624, E-mail: edwardag@etsu.edu.
Website: http://www.etsu.edu/cas/biology/

East Tennessee State University, School of Graduate Studies, College of Arts and Sciences, Department of Geosciences, Johnson City, TN 37614. Offers geospatial analysis (MS); paleontology (MS). *Program availability:* Part-time. *Faculty:* 11 full-time (3 women). *Students:* 17 full-time (11 women), 3 part-time (2 women); includes 1 minority (Black or African American, non-Hispanic/Latino), 1 international. Average age 27. 30 applicants, 30% accepted, 5 enrolled. In 2015, 6 master's awarded. *Degree requirements:* For master's, thesis. *Entrance requirements:* For master's, bachelor's degree in geosciences or related discipline, minimum GPA of 3.0, three letters of recommendation, resume. Additional exam requirements/recommendations for international students: Required—TOEFL (minimum score 550 paper-based; 79 iBT). *Application deadline:* For fall admission, 2/1 for domestic and international students. Application fee: $35 ($45 for international students). Electronic applications accepted. *Financial support:* In 2015–16, 12 students received support, including 5 research assistantships with full tuition reimbursements available (averaging $8,000 per year), 9 teaching assistantships with full tuition reimbursements available (averaging $8,000 per year); career-related internships or fieldwork, institutionally sponsored loans, scholarships/grants, and unspecified assistantships also available. Financial award application deadline: 7/1; financial award applicants required to submit FAFSA. *Faculty research:* Vertebrate paleontology; volcanology; soils and geological engineering; geological hazards stemming from volcanoes and tsunamis and the sociological responses; applications of geospatial analysis to meteorology, weather and climate, and geomorphology/watershed management; shallow surface geophysics, sedimentology, and stratigraphy. *Unit head:* Dr. Jim Mead, Chair, 423-439-7515, Fax: 423-439-7520, E-mail: mead@etsu.edu. *Application contact:* Angela Edwards, Graduate Specialist, 423-439-4703, Fax: 423-439-5624, E-mail: edwardag@etsu.edu.
Website: http://www.etsu.edu/cas/geosciences/

South Dakota School of Mines and Technology, Graduate Division, Department of Geology and Geological Engineering, Rapid City, SD 57701-3995. Offers geology and geological engineering (MS, PhD); paleontology (MS). *Program availability:* Part-time. *Degree requirements:* For master's, thesis; for doctorate, thesis/dissertation. *Entrance requirements:* For master's and doctorate, GRE General Test, GRE Subject Test. Additional exam requirements/recommendations for international students: Required—TOEFL (minimum score 520 paper-based; 68 iBT), TWE. Electronic applications accepted. *Faculty research:* Contaminants in soil, nitrate leaching, environmental changes, fracture formations, greenhouse effect.

South Dakota School of Mines and Technology, Graduate Division, Program in Paleontology, Rapid City, SD 57701-3995. Offers MS. *Program availability:* Part-time. *Degree requirements:* For master's, thesis. *Entrance requirements:* For master's, GRE General Test, GRE Subject Test. Additional exam requirements/recommendations for international students: Required—TOEFL (minimum score 520 paper-based; 68 iBT), TWE. Electronic applications accepted. *Faculty research:* Cretaceous, Miocene, and Oligocene vertebrates.

University of Chicago, Division of the Physical Sciences, Department of the Geophysical Sciences, Chicago, IL 60637. Offers atmospheric sciences (PhD); cosmochemistry (PhD); earth sciences (PhD); paleobiology (PhD); planetary and space sciences (PhD). Terminal master's awarded for partial completion of doctoral program. *Degree requirements:* For doctorate, variable foreign language requirement, comprehensive exam, thesis/dissertation. *Entrance requirements:* For doctorate, GRE General Test. Additional exam requirements/recommendations for international students: Required—TOEFL (minimum score 600 paper-based; 96 iBT), IELTS (minimum score 7). Electronic applications accepted. *Faculty research:* Climatology, evolutionary paleontology, cosmochemistry, geochemistry, oceanic sciences.

The University of Manchester, School of Earth, Atmospheric and Environmental Sciences, Manchester, United Kingdom. Offers atmospheric sciences (M Phil, M Sc, PhD); basin studies and petroleum geosciences (M Phil, M Sc, PhD); earth, atmospheric and environmental sciences (M Phil, M Sc, PhD); environmental geochemistry and cosmochemistry (M Phil, M Sc, PhD); isotope geochemistry and cosmochemistry (M Phil, M Sc, PhD); paleontology (M Phil, M Sc, PhD); physics and chemistry of minerals and fluids (M Phil, M Sc, PhD); structural and petrological geosciences (M Phil, M Sc, PhD).

The University of Texas at Dallas, School of Natural Sciences and Mathematics, Department of Geosciences, Richardson, TX 75080. Offers geochemistry (MS, PhD); geophysics (MS, PhD); geospatial information sciences (MS, PhD); hydrogeology (MS, PhD); sedimentology, stratigraphy, and paleontology (MS, PhD); structural geology and tectonics (MS, PhD). *Program availability:* Part-time, evening/weekend. *Faculty:* 9 full-time (0 women). *Students:* 57 full-time (21 women), 23 part-time (4 women); includes 12 minority (3 Black or African American, non-Hispanic/Latino; 4 Asian, non-Hispanic/Latino; 3 Hispanic/Latino; 2 Two or more races, non-Hispanic/Latino), 33 international. Average age 30. 98 applicants, 31% accepted, 20 enrolled. In 2015, 20 master's, 4 doctorates awarded. *Degree requirements:* For master's, thesis optional; for doctorate, thesis/dissertation. *Entrance requirements:* For master's and doctorate, GRE General Test, minimum GPA of 3.0 in upper-level course work in field. Additional exam requirements/recommendations for international students: Required—TOEFL (minimum score 550 paper-based). *Application deadline:* For fall admission, 7/15 for domestic students, 5/1 priority date for international students; for spring admission, 11/15 for domestic students, 9/1 priority date for international students. Applications are processed on a rolling basis. Application fee: $50 ($100 for international students). Electronic applications accepted. *Expenses:* Tuition, state resident: full-time $11,940; part-time $663 per semester hour. Tuition, nonresident: full-time $22,786; part-time $1266 per semester hour. Tuition and fees vary according to course load. *Financial support:* In 2015–16, 41 students received support, including 10 research assistantships with partial tuition reimbursements available (averaging $19,260 per year), 15 teaching assistantships with partial tuition reimbursements available (averaging $17,100 per year); career-related internships or fieldwork, Federal Work-Study, institutionally sponsored loans, scholarships/grants, and unspecified assistantships also available. Support available to part-time students. Financial award application deadline: 4/30; financial award applicants required to submit FAFSA. *Faculty research:* Cybermapping, GPS applications for geophysics and geology, seismology and ground-penetrating radar, numerical modeling, signal processing and inverse modeling techniques in seismology. *Unit head:* Dr. John Geissman, Department Head, 972-883-2454, Fax: 972-883-2537, E-mail: geosciences@utdallas.edu. *Application contact:* Gloria Eby, Graduate Support Assistant, 972-883-2404, Fax: 972-883-2537, E-mail: geosciences@utdallas.edu.

Website: http://www.utdallas.edu/geosciences

West Virginia University, Eberly College of Arts and Sciences, Department of Geology and Geography, Program in Geology, Morgantown, WV 26506. Offers geomorphology (MS, PhD); geophysics (MS, PhD); hydrogeology (MS, PhD); paleontology (MS, PhD); petroleum geology (PhD); petrology (MS, PhD); stratigraphy (MS, PhD); structure (MS, PhD). *Program availability:* Part-time. Terminal master's awarded for partial completion of doctoral program. *Degree requirements:* For master's, thesis (for some programs); for doctorate, comprehensive exam, thesis/dissertation. *Entrance requirements:* For master's, GRE General Test, minimum GPA of 2.5; for doctorate, GRE General Test, minimum GPA of 3.3. Additional exam requirements/recommendations for international students: Required—TOEFL. *Expenses:* Tuition, state resident: full-time $8568. Tuition, nonresident: full-time $22,140. Tuition and fees vary according to program.

Yale University, Graduate School of Arts and Sciences, Department of Geology and Geophysics, New Haven, CT 06520. Offers biogeochemistry (PhD); climate dynamics (PhD); geochemistry (PhD); geophysics (PhD); meteorology (PhD); oceanography (PhD); paleontology (PhD); paleooceanography (PhD); petrology (PhD); tectonics (PhD). *Degree requirements:* For doctorate, thesis/dissertation. *Entrance requirements:* For doctorate, GRE General Test. Additional exam requirements/recommendations for international students: Required—TOEFL.

Planetary and Space Sciences

Air Force Institute of Technology, Graduate School of Engineering and Management, Department of Operational Sciences, Dayton, OH 45433-7765. Offers logistics management (MS); operations research (MS, PhD); space operations (MS). *Program availability:* Part-time. *Degree requirements:* For master's, thesis; for doctorate, thesis/dissertation. *Entrance requirements:* For doctorate, GRE General Test, minimum GPA of 3.0, U.S. citizenship. *Faculty research:* Optimization, simulation, combat modeling and analysis, reliability and maintainability, resource scheduling.

Alabama Agricultural and Mechanical University, School of Graduate Studies, College of Engineering, Technology, and Physical Sciences, Department of Physics, Chemistry and Mathematics, Huntsville, AL 35811. Offers physics (MS, PhD), including materials science (PhD), optics/lasers (PhD), space science (PhD). *Program availability:* Part-time, evening/weekend. *Degree requirements:* For doctorate, thesis/dissertation. *Entrance requirements:* For master's and doctorate, GRE General Test. Additional exam requirements/recommendations for international students: Required—TOEFL (minimum score 500 paper-based; 61 iBT). Electronic applications accepted.

American Public University System, AMU/APU Graduate Programs, Charles Town, WV 25414. Offers accounting (MBA, MS); criminal justice (MA), including business administration, emergency and disaster management, general (MA, MS); educational leadership (M Ed); emergency and disaster management (MA); entrepreneurship (MBA); environmental policy and management (MS), including environmental planning, environmental sustainability, fish and wildlife management, general (MA, MS), global environmental management; finance (MBA); general (MBA); global business management (MBA); history (MA), including American history, ancient and classical history, European history, global history, public history; homeland security (MA), including business administration, counter-terrorism studies, criminal justice, cyber, emergency management and public health, intelligence studies, transportation security; homeland security resource allocation (MBA); humanities (MA); information technology (MS), including digital forensics, enterprise software development, information assurance and security, IT project management; information technology management (MBA); intelligence studies (MA), including criminal intelligence, cyber, general (MA, MS), homeland security, intelligence analysis, intelligence collection, intelligence management, intelligence operations, terrorism studies; international relations and conflict resolution (MA), including comparative and security issues, conflict resolution, international and transnational security issues, peacekeeping; legal studies (MA); management (MA), including defense management, general (MA, MS), human resource management, organizational leadership, public administration; marketing (MBA); military history (MA), including American military history, American Revolution, civil war, war since 1945, World War II; military studies (MA), including joint warfare, strategic leadership; national security studies (MA), including general (MA, MS), homeland security, regional security studies, security and intelligence analysis, terrorism studies; nonprofit management (MBA); political science (MA), including American politics and government, comparative government and development, general (MA, MS), international relations, public policy; psychology (MA); public administration (MPA), including disaster management, environmental policy, health policy, human resources, national security, organizational management, security management; public health (MPH); reverse logistics management (MA); school counseling (M Ed); security management (MA); space studies (MS), including aerospace science, general (MA, MS), planetary science; sports and health sciences (MS); teaching (M Ed), including curriculum and instruction for elementary teachers, elementary reading, English language learners, instructional leadership, online learning, special education; transportation and logistics management (MA), including general (MA, MS), maritime engineering management, reverse logistics management. Programs offered via distance learning only. *Program availability:* Part-time, evening/weekend, online learning. *Faculty:* 431 full-time (241 women), 1,839 part-time/adjunct (865 women). *Students:* 531 full-time (233 women), 9,094 part-time (3,735 women); includes 3,140 minority (1,679 Black or African American, non-Hispanic/Latino; 55 American Indian or Alaska Native, non-Hispanic/Latino; 252 Asian, non-Hispanic/Latino; 773 Hispanic/Latino; 75 Native Hawaiian or other Pacific Islander, non-Hispanic/Latino; 306 Two or more races, non-Hispanic/Latino), 111 international. Average age 37. In 2015, 3,391 master's awarded. *Degree requirements:* For master's, comprehensive exam or practicum. *Entrance requirements:* For master's, official transcript showing earned bachelor's degree from institution accredited by recognized accrediting body. Additional exam requirements/recommendations for international students: Required—TOEFL (minimum score 550 paper-based), IELTS (minimum score 6.5). *Application deadline:* Applications are processed on a rolling basis. Application fee: $0. Electronic applications accepted. *Expenses: Tuition, area resident:* Part-time $350 per credit hour. *Financial support:* Applicants required to submit FAFSA. *Unit head:* Dr. Karan Powell, Executive Vice President and Provost, 877-468-6268, Fax: 304-724-3780. *Application contact:* Terry Grant, Vice President of Enrollment Management, 877-468-6268, Fax: 304-724-3780, E-mail: info@apus.edu.

Website: http://www.apus.edu

Arizona State University at the Tempe campus, College of Liberal Arts and Sciences, School of Earth and Space Exploration, Tempe, AZ 85287-1404. Offers astrophysics (MS, PhD); exploration systems design (PhD); geological sciences (MS, PhD). PhD in exploration systems design is offered in collaboration with the Ira A. Fulton School of Engineering. Terminal master's awarded for partial completion of doctoral program. *Degree requirements:* For master's, thesis, interactive Program of Study (iPOS) submitted before completing 50 percent of required credit hours; for doctorate, thesis/dissertation, interactive Program of Study (iPOS) submitted before completing 50 percent of required credit hours. *Entrance requirements:* For master's and doctorate, GRE, minimum GPA of 3.0 or equivalent in last 2 years of work leading to bachelor's degree. Additional exam requirements/recommendations for international students: Required—TOEFL, IELTS, or PTE. Electronic applications accepted.

California Institute of Technology, Division of Geological and Planetary Sciences, Pasadena, CA 91125-0001. Offers environmental science and engineering (MS, PhD); geobiology (MS, PhD); geochemistry (MS, PhD); geology (MS, PhD); geophysics (MS, PhD); planetary science (MS, PhD). *Degree requirements:* For doctorate, thesis/dissertation. *Entrance requirements:* For doctorate, GRE General Test. Additional exam requirements/recommendations for international students: Required—TOEFL; Recommended—IELTS, TWE. Electronic applications accepted. *Faculty research:* Planetary surfaces, evolution of anaerobic respiratory processes, structural geology and tectonics, theoretical and numerical seismology, global biogeochemical cycles.

Cornell University, Graduate School, Graduate Fields of Arts and Sciences, Field of Astronomy and Space Sciences, Ithaca, NY 14853-0001. Offers astronomy (PhD); astrophysics (PhD); general space sciences (PhD); infrared astronomy (PhD); planetary studies (PhD); radio astronomy (PhD); radiophysics (PhD); theoretical astrophysics (PhD). *Degree requirements:* For doctorate, comprehensive exam, thesis/dissertation. *Entrance requirements:* For doctorate, GRE General Test, GRE Subject Test (physics), 3 letters of recommendation. Additional exam requirements/recommendations for international students: Required—TOEFL (minimum score 600 paper-based; 77 iBT). Electronic applications accepted. *Faculty research:* Observational astrophysics, planetary sciences, cosmology, instrumentation, gravitational astrophysics.

Florida Institute of Technology, College of Science, Program in Space Sciences, Melbourne, FL 32901-6975. Offers MS, PhD. *Program availability:* Part-time. *Students:* 18 full-time (10 women), 4 part-time (1 woman); includes 2 minority (1 Asian, non-Hispanic/Latino; 1 Hispanic/Latino), 3 international. Average age 28. 38 applicants, 34% accepted, 7 enrolled. In 2015, 1 master's, 3 doctorates awarded. Terminal master's awarded for partial completion of doctoral program. *Degree requirements:* For master's, comprehensive exam, thesis optional, 30 credit hours, no less than a C in core courses; for doctorate, comprehensive exam, thesis/dissertation, oral defense of dissertation, 45 credit hours. *Entrance requirements:* For master's, GRE General Test, GRE Subject Test, minimum GPA of 3.0, proficiency in a computer language, 3 letters of recommendation, resume, statement of objectives; for doctorate, GRE General Test, GRE Subject Test, minimum GPA of 3.2, resume. *Application deadline:* Applications are processed on a rolling basis. Application fee: $50. Electronic applications accepted. *Expenses: Tuition, area resident:* Full-time $21,690; part-time $1205 per credit hour. *Required fees:* $500. Tuition and fees vary according to degree level, campus/location and program. *Financial support:* Research assistantships with tuition reimbursements, teaching assistantships with tuition reimbursements, and tuition remissions available. Financial award application deadline: 3/1; financial award applicants required to submit FAFSA. *Faculty research:* Observational astronomy, theoretical astrophysics, space plasma physics. *Unit head:* Dr. Daniel Batcheldor, Department Head, 321-674-7717,

Planetary and Space Sciences

Fax: 321-674-7482, E-mail: dbatcheldor@fit.edu. *Application contact:* Cheryl A Brown, Associate Director of Graduate Admissions, 321-674-7581, Fax: 321-723-9468, E-mail: cbrown@fit.edu.
Website: http://cos.fit.edu/pss/

Hampton University, School of Science, Department of Atmospheric and Planetary Sciences, Hampton, VA 23668. Offers atmospheric science (MS, PhD); planetary science (MS, PhD). *Program availability:* Part-time. Terminal master's awarded for partial completion of doctoral program. *Degree requirements:* For master's, thesis; for doctorate, comprehensive exam, thesis/dissertation. *Entrance requirements:* For master's, GRE. Additional exam requirements/recommendations for international students: Required—TOEFL (minimum score 525 paper-based) or IELTS (6.5). Electronic applications accepted. *Expenses: Tuition, area resident:* Full-time $10,263; part-time $522 per credit hour. *Required fees:* $35. Tuition and fees vary according to course load and program. *Faculty research:* Remote sensing, polar stratospheric and mesospheric clouds, lidar and related technologies, astrobiology, atmospheric dynamics.

Harvard University, Graduate School of Arts and Sciences, Department of Earth and Planetary Sciences, Cambridge, MA 02138. Offers AM, PhD. Terminal master's awarded for partial completion of doctoral program. *Degree requirements:* For doctorate, comprehensive exam, thesis/dissertation. *Entrance requirements:* For doctorate, GRE General Test. Additional exam requirements/recommendations for international students: Required—TOEFL. Electronic applications accepted. *Faculty research:* Economic geography, geochemistry, geophysics, mineralogy, crystallography.

Massachusetts Institute of Technology, School of Science, Department of Earth, Atmospheric, and Planetary Sciences, Cambridge, MA 02139. Offers atmospheric chemistry (PhD, Sc D); atmospheric science (SM, PhD, Sc D); chemical oceanography (SM, PhD, Sc D); climate physics and chemistry (SM, PhD, Sc D); earth and planetary sciences (SM); geochemistry (PhD, Sc D); geology (PhD, Sc D); geophysics (PhD, Sc D); marine geology and geophysics (SM, PhD, Sc D); physical oceanography (SM, PhD, Sc D); planetary sciences (PhD, Sc D). *Faculty:* 36 full-time (8 women). *Students:* 166 full-time (75 women), 1 part-time (0 women); includes 23 minority (1 Black or African American, non-Hispanic/Latino; 7 Asian, non-Hispanic/Latino; 6 Hispanic/Latino; 9 Two or more races, non-Hispanic/Latino), 54 international. Average age 27. 228 applicants, 26% accepted, 33 enrolled. In 2015, 6 master's, 24 doctorates awarded. Terminal master's awarded for partial completion of doctoral program. *Degree requirements:* For master's, thesis; for doctorate, comprehensive exam, thesis/dissertation. *Entrance requirements:* For master's, GRE General Test; for doctorate, GRE General Test, GRE Subject Test in chemistry or physics (for planetary sciences area). Additional exam requirements/recommendations for international students: Required—TOEFL (minimum score 600 paper-based; 100 iBT), IELTS (minimum score 7). *Application deadline:* For fall admission, 1/5 for domestic and international students; for spring admission, 11/1 for domestic and international students. Application fee: $75. Electronic applications accepted. *Expenses: Tuition:* Full-time $46,400; part-time $725 per credit. One-time fee: $304 full-time. Full-time tuition and fees vary according to course load and program. *Financial support:* In 2015–16, 99 students received support, including 60 fellowships (averaging $40,700 per year), 76 research assistantships (averaging $38,000 per year), 15 teaching assistantships (averaging $36,100 per year); Federal Work-Study, institutionally sponsored loans, scholarships/grants, traineeships, health care benefits, and unspecified assistantships also available. Support available to part-time students. Financial award application deadline: 4/15; financial award applicants required to submit FAFSA. *Faculty research:* Earth: origin, composition, structure, and dynamics of (and interactions between) the atmosphere, oceans, surface, and interior of the earth; planets: formation, dynamics, and evolution of planetary systems and the characterization of exoplanets; climate: characterization of past, present, and potential future climates; studies of the causes and consequences of climate change; life: co-evolution of life and environmental systems. *Total annual research expenditures:* $25.3 million. *Unit head:* Prof. Robert van der Hilst, Department Head, 617-253-2127, Fax: 617-253-8298, E-mail: eapsinfo@mit.edu. *Application contact:* EAPS Education Office, 617-253-3381, Fax: 617-253-8298, E-mail: eapsinfo@mit.edu.
Website: http://eapsweb.mit.edu/

McGill University, Faculty of Graduate and Postdoctoral Studies, Faculty of Science, Department of Earth and Planetary Sciences, Montréal, QC H3A 2T5, Canada. Offers M Sc, PhD.

St. Thomas University, School of Leadership Studies, Institute for Education, Miami Gardens, FL 33054-6459. Offers earth/space science (Certificate); educational administration (MS, Certificate); educational leadership (Ed D); elementary education (MS); ESOL (Certificate); gifted education (Certificate); instructional technology (MS, Certificate); professional/studies (Certificate); reading (MS, Certificate); special education (MS). *Program availability:* Part-time, evening/weekend. *Degree requirements:* For master's, comprehensive exam; for doctorate, comprehensive exam, thesis/dissertation. *Entrance requirements:* For master's, interview, minimum GPA of 3.0 or GRE; for doctorate, GRE or MAT. Additional exam requirements/recommendations for international students: Required—TOEFL (minimum score 550 paper-based; 79 iBT). Electronic applications accepted.

The University of Arizona, College of Science, Department of Planetary Sciences, Tucson, AZ 85721. Offers MS, PhD. *Degree requirements:* For master's, thesis (for some programs); for doctorate, one foreign language, thesis/dissertation. *Entrance requirements:* For master's and doctorate, 3 letters of recommendation. Additional exam requirements/recommendations for international students: Required—TOEFL (minimum score 550 paper-based; 79 iBT). *Application deadline:* For fall admission, 1/15 for domestic and international students. Applications are processed on a rolling basis. Application fee: $75. Electronic applications accepted. *Financial support:* Research assistantships, teaching assistantships, scholarships/grants, health care benefits, tuition waivers (partial), and unspecified assistantships available. Financial award application deadline: 2/15. *Faculty research:* Cosmochemistry, planetary geology, astronomy, space physics, planetary physics.
Website: http://www.lpl.arizona.edu/

University of Arkansas, Graduate School, Interdisciplinary Program in Space and Planetary Sciences, Fayetteville, AR 72701-1201. Offers MS, PhD. *Students:* 14 part-time (10 women); includes 1 minority (Two or more races, non-Hispanic/Latino), 1 international. In 2015, 1 master's, 2 doctorates awarded. *Application deadline:* For fall admission, 4/1 for international students; for spring admission, 10/1 for international students. Applications are processed on a rolling basis. Application fee: $40 ($50 for international students). Electronic applications accepted. *Financial support:* In 2015–16, 7 research assistantships, 12 teaching assistantships were awarded; fellowships also available. *Unit head:* Dr. Larry Roe, Director, 479-575-3750, E-mail: lar@uark.edu. *Application contact:* Graduate Admissions, 479-575-6246, Fax: 479-575-5908, E-mail: gradinfo@uark.edu.
Website: http://spacecenter.uark.edu

University of California, Los Angeles, Graduate Division, College of Letters and Science, Department of Earth and Space Sciences, Los Angeles, CA 90095. Offers geochemistry (MS, PhD); geology (MS, PhD); geophysics and space physics (MS, PhD). Terminal master's awarded for partial completion of doctoral program. *Degree requirements:* For master's, comprehensive exams or thesis; for doctorate, thesis/dissertation, oral and written qualifying exams. *Entrance requirements:* For master's, GRE General Test; GRE Subject Test, bachelor's degree; minimum undergraduate GPA of 3.0 (or its equivalent if letter grade system not used); for doctorate, GRE General Test, bachelor's degree; minimum undergraduate GPA of 3.0 (or its equivalent if letter grade system not used). Additional exam requirements/recommendations for international students: Required—TOEFL. Electronic applications accepted.

University of California, Santa Cruz, Division of Graduate Studies, Division of Physical and Biological Sciences, Department of Earth and Planetary Sciences, Santa Cruz, CA 95064. Offers MS, PhD. Terminal master's awarded for partial completion of doctoral program. *Degree requirements:* For master's, thesis; for doctorate, one foreign language, thesis/dissertation, qualifying exam. *Entrance requirements:* For master's and doctorate, GRE General Test. Additional exam requirements/recommendations for international students: Required—TOEFL (minimum score 550 paper-based; 83 iBT); Recommended—IELTS (minimum score 8). Electronic applications accepted. *Faculty research:* Evolution of continental margins and orogenic belts, geologic processes occurring at plate boundaries, deep-sea sediment diagenesis, paleoecology, hydrogeology.

University of Chicago, Division of the Physical Sciences, Department of the Geophysical Sciences, Chicago, IL 60637. Offers atmospheric sciences (PhD); cosmochemistry (PhD); earth sciences (PhD); paleobiology (PhD); planetary and space sciences (PhD). Terminal master's awarded for partial completion of doctoral program. *Degree requirements:* For doctorate, variable foreign language requirement, comprehensive exam, thesis/dissertation. *Entrance requirements:* For doctorate, GRE General Test. Additional exam requirements/recommendations for international students: Required—TOEFL (minimum score 600 paper-based; 96 iBT), IELTS (minimum score 7). Electronic applications accepted. *Faculty research:* Climatology, evolutionary paleontology, cosmochemistry, geochemistry, oceanic sciences.

University of Hawaii at Manoa, Graduate Division, School of Ocean and Earth Science and Technology, Department of Geology and Geophysics, Honolulu, HI 96822. Offers high-pressure geophysics and geochemistry (MS, PhD); hydrogeology and engineering geology (MS, PhD); marine geology and geophysics (MS, PhD); planetary geosciences and remote sensing (MS, PhD); seismology and solid-earth geophysics (MS, PhD); volcanology, petrology, and geochemistry (MS, PhD). *Program availability:* Part-time. *Faculty:* 72 full-time (15 women), 6 part-time/adjunct (3 women). *Students:* 42 full-time (26 women), 2 part-time (1 woman); includes 9 minority (2 Asian, non-Hispanic/Latino; 2 Hispanic/Latino; 5 Two or more races, non-Hispanic/Latino), 9 international. Average age 31. 78 applicants, 23% accepted, 13 enrolled. In 2015, 7 master's, 8 doctorates awarded. Terminal master's awarded for partial completion of doctoral program. *Degree requirements:* For master's, thesis optional; for doctorate, comprehensive exam, thesis/dissertation. *Entrance requirements:* For master's and doctorate, GRE General Test, minimum GPA of 3.0. Additional exam requirements/recommendations for international students: Required—TOEFL (minimum score 580 paper-based; 92 iBT), IELTS (minimum score 5). *Application deadline:* For fall admission, 1/15 for domestic students, 1/1 for international students; for spring admission, 9/1 for domestic students, 8/15 for international students. Application fee: $100. *Financial support:* In 2015–16, 7 fellowships (averaging $1,359 per year), 30 research assistantships (averaging $23,988 per year), 4 teaching assistantships (averaging $15,350 per year) were awarded. *Total annual research expenditures:* $3.8 million. *Unit head:* Brian Taylor, Dean, 808-956-6182, E-mail: taylorb@hawaii.edu. *Application contact:* Dr. Gregory Moore, Chair, 808-956-7640, Fax: 808-956-5512, E-mail: gg-dept@soest.hawaii.edu.
Website: http://www.soest.hawaii.edu/GG/

University of Houston, College of Liberal Arts and Social Sciences, Department of Health and Human Performance, Houston, TX 77204. Offers exercise science (MS); human nutrition (MS); human space exploration sciences (MS); kinesiology (PhD); physical education (M Ed). *Accreditation:* NCATE (one or more programs are accredited). *Program availability:* Part-time, evening/weekend. *Degree requirements:* For master's, comprehensive exam (for some programs), thesis (for some programs); for doctorate, comprehensive exam, thesis/dissertation, qualifying exam, candidacy paper. *Entrance requirements:* For master's, GRE (minimum 35th percentile on each section), minimum cumulative GPA of 3.0; for doctorate, GRE (minimum 35th percentile on each section), minimum cumulative GPA of 3.3. Additional exam requirements/recommendations for international students: Required—TOEFL (minimum score 550 paper-based; 79 iBT). Electronic applications accepted. *Faculty research:* Biomechanics, exercise physiology, obesity, nutrition, space exploration science.

University of Maryland, Baltimore County, The Graduate School, College of Arts, Humanities and Social Sciences, Department of Education, Program in Teaching, Baltimore, MD 21250. Offers early childhood education (MAT); elementary education (MAT); teaching (MAT), including art, biology, chemistry, choral music, classical foreign language, dance, earth/space science, English, instrumental music, mathematics, modern foreign language, physical science, physics, social studies, theatre. *Program availability:* Part-time, evening/weekend. *Faculty:* 24 full-time (18 women), 25 part-time/adjunct (19 women). *Students:* 43 full-time (34 women), 40 part-time (27 women); includes 29 minority (9 Black or African American, non-Hispanic/Latino; 10 Asian, non-Hispanic/Latino; 9 Hispanic/Latino; 1 Two or more races, non-Hispanic/Latino), 1 international. Average age 30. 54 applicants, 69% accepted, 35 enrolled. In 2015, 106 master's awarded. *Degree requirements:* For master's, comprehensive exam (for some programs), thesis (for some programs). *Entrance requirements:* For master's, PRAXIS Core Examination or GRE (minimum score of 1000), minimum GPA of 3.0. Additional exam requirements/recommendations for international students: Required—TOEFL. *Application deadline:* For fall admission, 6/1 for domestic and international students; for spring admission, 11/1 for domestic and international students. Applications are processed on a rolling basis. Application fee: $50. Electronic applications accepted. *Expenses:* Tuition, state resident: full-time $12,816. Tuition, nonresident: full-time $19,710. *Financial support:* In 2015–16, 6 students received support, including teaching assistantships with tuition reimbursements available (averaging $12,000 per year); career-related internships or fieldwork, Federal Work-Study, scholarships/grants, tuition waivers, and unspecified assistantships also available. Financial award application deadline: 3/1. *Faculty research:* STEM teacher education, culturally sensitive pedagogy, ESOL/bilingual education, early childhood education, language, literacy and culture. *Unit head:* Dr. Susan M. Blunck, Graduate Program Director, 410-455-2869, Fax: 410-455-3986, E-mail: blunck@umbc.edu. *Application contact:* Cheryl Johnson, MAT Program Specialist, 410-455-3388, E-mail: blackwel@umbc.edu.
Website: http://www.umbc.edu/education/

University of Michigan, College of Engineering, Department of Climate and Space Sciences and Engineering, Ann Arbor, MI 48109. Offers applied climate (M Eng); atmospheric, oceanic and space sciences (MS, PhD); geoscience and remote sensing

(PhD); space and planetary sciences (PhD); space engineering (M Eng). *Program availability:* Part-time. *Students:* 96 full-time (32 women), 2 part-time (1 woman). 125 applicants, 28% accepted, 16 enrolled. In 2015, 39 master's, 14 doctorates awarded. Terminal master's awarded for partial completion of doctoral program. *Degree requirements:* For master's, thesis (for some programs); for doctorate, thesis/ dissertation, oral defense of dissertation, preliminary exams. *Entrance requirements:* For master's and doctorate, GRE General Test. Additional exam requirements/ recommendations for international students: Required—TOEFL. *Application deadline:* Applications are processed on a rolling basis. Electronic applications accepted. *Financial support:* Fellowships, research assistantships, teaching assistantships, career-related internships or fieldwork, Federal Work-Study, institutionally sponsored loans, and health care benefits available. Support available to part-time students. Financial award applicants required to submit FAFSA. *Faculty research:* Planetary environments, space instrumentation, space weather, global climate change, sun-earth connection, space weather. *Total annual research expenditures:* $44.7 million. *Unit head:* Dr. James Slavin, Chair, 734-764-7221, Fax: 734-615-4645, E-mail: jaslavin@umich.edu. *Application contact:* Sandra Pytlinski, Graduate Student Services Coordinator, 734-936-0482, Fax: 734-763-0437, E-mail: sanpyt@umich.edu. Website: http://clasp.engin.umich.edu/

University of New Mexico, Graduate Studies, College of Arts and Sciences, Program in Earth and Planetary Sciences, Albuquerque, NM 87131. Offers MS, PhD. *Program availability:* Part-time. *Faculty:* 17 full-time (5 women). *Students:* 25 full-time (10 women), 22 part-time (11 women); includes 7 minority (1 Asian, non-Hispanic/Latino; 6 Hispanic/Latino), 1 international. Average age 30. 60 applicants, 23% accepted, 14 enrolled. In 2015, 1 master's, 3 doctorates awarded. Terminal master's awarded for partial completion of doctoral program. *Degree requirements:* For master's, comprehensive exam, thesis; for doctorate, comprehensive exam, thesis/dissertation. *Entrance requirements:* For master's and doctorate, GRE General Test. Additional exam requirements/recommendations for international students: Required—TOEFL. *Application deadline:* For fall admission, 1/15 priority date for domestic and international students; for spring admission, 11/1 priority date for domestic and international students. Application fee: $50. Electronic applications accepted. *Financial support:* Fellowships with full tuition reimbursements, research assistantships with full tuition reimbursements, teaching assistantships with full tuition reimbursements, scholarships/grants, and health care benefits available. Financial award application deadline: 1/15. *Faculty research:* Climatology, experimental petrology, geochemistry, geographic information technologies, geomorphology, geophysics, hydrogeology, igneous petrology, metamorphic petrology, meteoritics, meteorology, micrometeorites, mineralogy, paleoclimatology, paleontology, pedology, petrology, physical volcanology, planetary sciences, Precambrian geology, quaternary geology, sedimentary geochemistry, sedimentology, stable isotope geochemistry, stratigraphy, structural geology, tectonics, volcanology. *Total annual research expenditures:* $2.5 million. *Unit head:* Dr. Adrian J. Brearley, Chair, 505-277-4204, Fax: 505-277-8843, E-mail: brearley@unm.edu. *Application contact:* Cindy Jaramillo, Administrative Assistant III, 505-277-1635, Fax: 505-277-8843, E-mail: epsdept@unm.edu. Website: http://epswww.unm.edu/

University of North Dakota, Graduate School, John D. Odegard School of Aerospace Sciences, Space Studies Program, Grand Forks, ND 58202. Offers MS. *Program availability:* Part-time, online learning. *Degree requirements:* For master's, comprehensive exam, thesis or alternative. *Entrance requirements:* For master's, minimum GPA of 3.0. Additional exam requirements/recommendations for international students: Required—TOEFL (minimum score 550 paper-based; 79 iBT), IELTS (minimum score 6.5). Electronic applications accepted. *Faculty research:* Earth-approaching asteroids, international remote sensing statutes, Mercury fly-by design, origin of meteorites, craters on Venus.

Washington University in St. Louis, Graduate School of Arts and Sciences, Department of Earth and Planetary Sciences, St. Louis, MO 63130-4899. Offers PhD. *Students:* 30 full-time (14 women); includes 2 minority (1 Asian, non-Hispanic/Latino; 1 Two or more races, non-Hispanic/Latino), 15 international. 61 applicants, 30% accepted, 6 enrolled. In 2015, 5 doctorates awarded. Terminal master's awarded for partial completion of doctoral program. *Degree requirements:* For doctorate, thesis/ dissertation. *Entrance requirements:* For doctorate, GRE General Test. Additional exam requirements/recommendations for international students: Required—TOEFL. *Application deadline:* For fall admission, 1/15 for domestic students. Application fee: $45. Electronic applications accepted. *Financial support:* Fellowships, research assistantships, teaching assistantships, and tuition waivers (full and partial) available. Financial award application deadline: 1/15. *Faculty research:* Planetary sciences; geology; geobiology; geochemistry; geodynamics. *Unit head:* Dr. Viatcheslav Solomatov, Chairman, 314-935-5603. *Application contact:* Bridget Coleman, Director of Admissions, 314-935-6880, Fax: 314-935-4887. Website: http://eps.wustl.edu/

Western Connecticut State University, Division of Graduate Studies, Maricostas School of Arts and Sciences, Department of Physics, Astronomy and Meteorology, Danbury, CT 06810-6885. Offers earth and planetary sciences (MA). *Program availability:* Part-time. *Degree requirements:* For master's, thesis, completion of program in 6 years. *Entrance requirements:* For master's, minimum GPA of 2.5 or GRE; one year each of calculus-based physics and calculus; semester course in differential equations. Additional exam requirements/recommendations for international students: Recommended—TOEFL (minimum score 550 paper-based; 79 iBT), IELTS (minimum score 6). *Faculty research:* Data collection and analysis of Gulf Stream surface temperature and circulation; science for visually impaired students including investigations of a satellite orbit, the Moon's surface, spectra of chemical elements and stars, the rotation of the Sun, and the spiral structure of our galaxy.

Yale University, Graduate School of Arts and Sciences, Department of Astronomy, New Haven, CT 06520. Offers astronomy (PhD); solar and terrestrial physics (PhD). *Degree requirements:* For doctorate, thesis/dissertation. *Entrance requirements:* For doctorate, GRE General Test, GRE Subject Test (physics).

York University, Faculty of Graduate Studies, Lassonde School of Engineering, Program in Earth and Space Science, Toronto, ON M3J 1P3, Canada. Offers M Sc, PhD. *Program availability:* Part-time, evening/weekend. *Degree requirements:* For master's, thesis or alternative; for doctorate, thesis/dissertation. Electronic applications accepted.

Peterson's Graduate Programs in the Physical Sciences, Mathematics, Agricultural Sciences, the Environment & Natural Resources 2017

www.petersons.com   **135**

Section 4
Marine Sciences and Oceanography

This section contains a directory of institutions offering graduate work in marine sciences and oceanography. Additional information about programs listed in the directory may be obtained by writing directly to the dean of a graduate school or chair of a department at the address given in the directory.

For programs offering related work, see also in this book *Chemistry, Geosciences, Meteorology and Atmospheric Sciences,* and *Physics.*

In the other guides in this series:

Graduate Programs in the Biological/Biomedical Sciences & Health-Related Medical Professions

See *Biological and Biomedical Sciences; Environmental Biology, and Evolutionary Biology;* and *Marine Biology*

Graduate Programs in Engineering & Applied Sciences

See *Civil and Environmental Engineering, Engineering and Applied Sciences,* and *Ocean Engineering*

CONTENTS
Program Directories

Marine Sciences

California State University, East Bay, Office of Graduate Studies Programs, College of Science, Department of Biological Sciences, Marine Science Program, Moss Landing, CA 95039. Offers MS. *Degree requirements:* For master's, thesis. *Entrance requirements:* For master's, GRE Subject Test, minimum GPA of 3.0 in field, 2.75 overall; 3 letters of reference; statement of purpose. Additional exam requirements/recommendations for international students: Required—TOEFL. *Application deadline:* For fall admission, 3/15 for domestic students. Application fee: $55. *Financial support:* Federal Work-Study, institutionally sponsored loans, and scholarships/grants available. Support available to part-time students. Financial award application deadline: 3/1; financial award applicants required to submit FAFSA. *Unit head:* Dr. Kenneth A. Coale, Director, 831-771-4406, Fax: 831-632-4403, E-mail: coale@mlml.calstate.edu. *Application contact:* Prof. Maria Nieto, Biology Graduate Advisor, 510-885-4757, Fax: 510-885-4747, E-mail: maria.nieto@csueastbay.edu.
Website: http://www.mlml.calstate.edu

California State University, Fresno, Division of Graduate Studies, College of Science and Mathematics, Program in Marine Sciences, Fresno, CA 93740-8027. Offers MS. *Program availability:* Part-time, online learning. *Degree requirements:* For master's, thesis. *Entrance requirements:* For master's, GRE General Test, minimum GPA of 3.0. Additional exam requirements/recommendations for international students: Required—TOEFL. Electronic applications accepted. *Faculty research:* Wetlands ecology, land/water conservation, water irrigation.

California State University, Monterey Bay, College of Science, Moss Landing Marine Laboratories, Seaside, CA 93955-8001. Offers MS. *Program availability:* Part-time. *Degree requirements:* For master's, thesis, thesis defense. *Entrance requirements:* For master's, selected MLML faculty member to serve as potential thesis advisor and selected consortium institution to serve as home campus. Additional exam requirements/recommendations for international students: Required—TOEFL (minimum score 525 paper-based; 71 iBT). Electronic applications accepted. *Faculty research:* Remote sensing microbiology trace elements, chemistry ecology of birds, mammals, turtles and fish, invasive species, marine phycology.

Coastal Carolina University, College of Science, Conway, SC 29528-6054. Offers applied computing and information systems (Certificate); coastal marine and wetland studies (MS); marine science (PhD); sports management (MS). *Program availability:* Part-time, evening/weekend. *Faculty:* 21 full-time (5 women), 1 part-time/adjunct (0 women). *Students:* 29 full-time (16 women), 12 part-time (8 women), 2 international. Average age 25. 32 applicants, 63% accepted, 19 enrolled. In 2015, 11 master's awarded. *Degree requirements:* For master's, thesis or internship; for doctorate, comprehensive exam, thesis/dissertation. *Entrance requirements:* For master's, GRE, 3 letters of recommendation, resume, official transcripts, written statement of educational and career goals, baccalaureate degree; for doctorate, GRE, official transcripts; baccalaureate or master's degree; minimum GPA of 3.0 for all collegiate coursework; successful completion of at least two semesters of college-level calculus, physics, and chemistry; 3 letters of recommendation; written statement of educational and career goals; resume; for Certificate, 2 letters of reference, official transcripts, minimum GPA of 3.0 in all computing and information systems courses, documentation of graduation from accredited four-year college or university. Additional exam requirements/recommendations for international students: Required—TOEFL (minimum score 550 paper-based; 79 iBT). *Application deadline:* For fall admission, 1/15 priority date for domestic and international students; for spring admission, 11/1 priority date for domestic and international students. Applications are processed on a rolling basis. Application fee: $45. Electronic applications accepted. *Expenses:* Tuition, state resident: full-time $9666; part-time $537 per credit hour. Tuition, nonresident: full-time $17,532; part-time $974 per credit hour. *Required fees:* $90; $5 per credit hour. *Financial support:* Fellowships, research assistantships, and unspecified assistantships available. Support available to part-time students. Financial award application deadline: 3/1; financial award applicants required to submit FAFSA. *Unit head:* Dr. Michael H. Roberts, Dean, 843-349-2282, Fax: 843-349-2545, E-mail: mroberts@coastal.edu. *Application contact:* Dr. James O. Luken, Associate Provost/Director of Graduate Studies, 843-349-2235, Fax: 843-349-6444, E-mail: joluken@coastal.edu.
Website: http://www.coastal.edu/science/

College of Charleston, Graduate School, School of Sciences and Mathematics, Program in Marine Biology, Charleston, SC 29412. Offers MS. *Degree requirements:* For master's, comprehensive exam, thesis. *Entrance requirements:* For master's, GRE General Test, 3 letters of recommendation. Additional exam requirements/recommendations for international students: Required—TOEFL (minimum score 81 iBT). Electronic applications accepted. *Faculty research:* Ecology, environmental physiology, marine genomics, bioinformatics, toxicology, cell biology, population biology, fisheries science, animal physiology, biodiversity, estuarine ecology, evolution and systematics, microbial processes, plant physiology, immunology.

The College of William and Mary, Virginia Institute of Marine Science, Gloucester Point, VA 23062. Offers MS, PhD. *Faculty:* 65 full-time (20 women), 1 part-time/adjunct (0 women). *Students:* 82 full-time (48 women), 2 part-time (0 women); includes 7 minority (2 Black or African American, non-Hispanic/Latino; 2 Asian, non-Hispanic/Latino; 1 Hispanic/Latino; 2 Two or more races, non-Hispanic/Latino), 19 international. Average age 28. 116 applicants, 28% accepted, 21 enrolled. In 2015, 11 master's, 9 doctorates awarded. *Degree requirements:* For master's, thesis, qualifying exam; for doctorate, comprehensive exam, thesis/dissertation, qualifying exam. *Entrance requirements:* For master's, GRE, appropriate bachelor's degree; for doctorate, GRE, appropriate bachelor's and master's degrees. Additional exam requirements/recommendations for international students: Required—TOEFL (minimum score 94 iBT). *Application deadline:* For fall admission, 1/5 for domestic and international students. Application fee: $53. Electronic applications accepted. *Expenses:* $9,359 tuition, $4,162 general fees. *Financial support:* In 2015–16, 56 students received support, including fellowships with full tuition reimbursements available (averaging $25,000 per year), research assistantships with full tuition reimbursements available (averaging $20,452 per year), teaching assistantships with full tuition reimbursements available (averaging $20,452 per year); career-related internships or fieldwork, scholarships/grants, health care benefits, and unspecified assistantships also available. Financial award application deadline: 1/5; financial award applicants required to submit FAFSA. *Faculty research:* Marine science, oceanography, marine ecology, fisheries, environmental science and ecotoxicology. *Total annual research expenditures:* $18.7 million. *Unit head:* Dr. John T. Wells, Dean/Director, 804-684-7102, Fax: 804-684-7009, E-mail: wells@vims.edu. *Application contact:* Dr. Linda C. Schaffner, Associate Dean of Academic Studies, 804-684-7105, Fax: 804-684-7881, E-mail: admissions@vims.edu.
Website: http://www.vims.edu/

Cornell University, Graduate School, Graduate Fields of Agriculture and Life Sciences, Field of Natural Resources, Ithaca, NY 14853-0001. Offers community-based natural resources management (MS, PhD); conservation biology (MS, PhD); ecosystem biology and biogeochemistry (MPS, MS, PhD); environmental management (MPS); fishery and aquatic science (MPS, MS, PhD); forest science (MPS, MS, PhD); human dimensions of natural resources management (MPS, MS, PhD); policy and institutional analysis (MS, PhD); program development and evaluation (MPS, MS, PhD); quantitative ecology (MS, PhD); wildlife science (MPS, MS, PhD). *Degree requirements:* For master's, thesis (MS), project paper (MPS); for doctorate, comprehensive exam, thesis/dissertation. *Entrance requirements:* For master's and doctorate, GRE General Test, 2 letters of recommendation. Additional exam requirements/recommendations for international students: Required—TOEFL (minimum score 550 paper-based; 77 iBT). Electronic applications accepted. *Faculty research:* Ecosystem-level dynamics, systems modeling, conservation biology/management, resource management's human dimensions, biogeochemistry.

Duke University, Graduate School, Program in Marine Science and Conservation, Beaufort, NC 28516. Offers PhD. *Entrance requirements:* For doctorate, GRE General Test. Additional exam requirements/recommendations for international students: Required—TOEFL (minimum score 577 paper-based; 90 iBT) or IELTS.

Florida Institute of Technology, College of Engineering, Program in Oceanography, Melbourne, FL 32901-6975. Offers biological oceanography (MS); chemical oceanography (MS); coastal management (MS); geological oceanography (MS); oceanography (PhD); physical oceanography (MS). *Program availability:* Part-time. *Students:* 7 full-time (5 women), 10 part-time (5 women); includes 3 minority (1 Hispanic/Latino; 2 Two or more races, non-Hispanic/Latino), 2 international. Average age 27. 28 applicants, 29% accepted, 3 enrolled. In 2015, 3 master's, 1 doctorate awarded. *Degree requirements:* For master's, comprehensive exam (for some programs), seminar, field project, written final exam, internship, technical paper, oral presentation, thesis or final exam; for doctorate, comprehensive exam, thesis/dissertation, seminar, internships, publications, original research. *Entrance requirements:* For master's, GRE General Test, minimum GPA of 3.0, 3 letters of recommendation, resume, transcripts, statement of objectives, appropriate bachelor's degree; for doctorate, GRE General Test, minimum GPA of 3.3, resume, 3 letters of recommendation, statement of objectives, on-campus interview (highly recommended). Additional exam requirements/recommendations for international students: Required—TOEFL (minimum score 550 paper-based; 79 iBT). *Application deadline:* Applications are processed on a rolling basis. Electronic applications accepted. *Expenses: Tuition, area resident:* Full-time $21,690; part-time $1205 per credit hour. *Required fees:* $500. Tuition and fees vary according to degree level, campus/location and program. *Financial support:* Career-related internships or fieldwork, institutionally sponsored loans, tuition waivers (partial), unspecified assistantships, and tuition remissions available. Support available to part-time students. Financial award application deadline: 3/1; financial award applicants required to submit FAFSA. *Faculty research:* Marine geochemistry, ecosystem dynamics, coastal processes, marine pollution, environmental modeling. *Unit head:* Dr. John Windsor, Program Chair, 321-674-7300, E-mail: jwindsor@fit.edu. *Application contact:* Cheryl A. Brown, Associate Director of Graduate Admission, 321-674-7581, Fax: 321-723-9468, E-mail: cbrown@fit.edu.
Website: http://www.coe.fit.edu/dmes

Florida State University, The Graduate School, College of Arts and Sciences, Department of Earth, Ocean and Atmospheric Science, Program in Oceanography, Tallahassee, FL 32306-4320. Offers aquatic environmental science (MS, PSM); oceanography (MS, PhD). *Faculty:* 16 full-time (4 women). *Students:* 41 full-time (23 women); includes 4 minority (2 Asian, non-Hispanic/Latino; 1 Hispanic/Latino; 1 Two or more races, non-Hispanic/Latino), 10 international. Average age 26. 47 applicants, 23% accepted, 7 enrolled. In 2015, 3 master's, 1 doctorate awarded. *Degree requirements:* For master's, thesis; for doctorate, comprehensive exam, thesis/dissertation. *Entrance requirements:* For master's and doctorate, GRE General Test, minimum upper-division GPA of 3.0. Additional exam requirements/recommendations for international students: Required—TOEFL (minimum score 550 paper-based; 80 iBT). *Application deadline:* For fall admission, 2/15 priority date for domestic and international students; for spring admission, 9/15 priority date for domestic and international students. Applications are processed on a rolling basis. Application fee: $35. Electronic applications accepted. *Expenses: Tuition, area resident:* Full-time $7263; part-time $403.50 per credit hour. Tuition, nonresident: full-time $18,087; part-time $1004.85 per credit hour. *Required fees:* $1365; $75.81 per credit hour. $20 per semester. Tuition and fees vary according to campus/location. *Financial support:* In 2015–16, 28 students received support, including 2 fellowships with full tuition reimbursements available, 20 research assistantships with full tuition reimbursements available, 8 teaching assistantships with full tuition reimbursements available. Financial award application deadline: 2/15; financial award applicants required to submit FAFSA. *Faculty research:* Trace metals in seawater, currents and waves, modeling, benthic ecology, marine biogeochemistry. *Unit head:* Dr. Jeffrey Chanton, Area Coordinator, 850-644-6700, Fax: 850-644-2581, E-mail: jchanton@fsu.edu. *Application contact:* Michaela Lupiani, Academic Coordinator, 850-644-6205, Fax: 850-644-2581, E-mail: admissions@ocean.fsu.edu.
Website: http://www.eoas.fsu.edu

Hawai`i Pacific University, College of Natural and Computational Sciences, Program in Marine Science, Honolulu, HI 96813. Offers MS. *Program availability:* Part-time. *Faculty:* 14 full-time (5 women), 1 (woman) part-time/adjunct. *Students:* 8 full-time (4 women), 26 part-time (15 women); includes 6 minority (2 Asian, non-Hispanic/Latino; 1 Hispanic/Latino; 3 Two or more races, non-Hispanic/Latino), 3 international. Average age 27. 36 applicants, 83% accepted, 5 enrolled. In 2015, 17 master's awarded. *Entrance requirements:* For master's, GRE, baccalaureate degree in a natural science discipline, minimum undergraduate GPA of 3.0. Additional exam requirements/recommendations for international students: Recommended—TOEFL (minimum score 550 paper-based; 80 iBT), IELTS (minimum score 6), TWE (minimum score 5). *Application deadline:* For fall admission, 1/15 for domestic students. Application fee: $50. Electronic applications accepted. *Expenses:* $1,215 per credit. *Financial support:* In 2015–16, 13 students received support. Career-related internships or fieldwork, Federal Work-Study, scholarships/grants, tuition waivers, and unspecified assistantships available. Financial award application deadline: 3/1; financial award applicants required to submit FAFSA. *Unit head:* Roland L. Jenkins, Interim Dean, 808-687-7028, Fax: 808-236-5880, E-mail: rjenkins@hpu.edu. *Application contact:* Danny Lam, Assistant Director of Graduate Admissions, 808-544-1135, Fax: 808-544-0280, E-mail: graduate@hpu.edu.
Website: http://www.hpu.edu/CNCS/Departments/GradPrograms/MarineSci/index.html

Instituto Tecnologico de Santo Domingo, Graduate School, Area of Basic And Environmental Sciences, Santo Domingo, Dominican Republic. Offers environmental science (M En S), including environmental education, environmental management, marine resources, natural resources management; mathematics (MS, PhD); renewable energy technology (MS, Certificate).

Jacksonville University, Marine Science Research Institute, Jacksonville, FL 32211. Offers MA, MS. *Degree requirements:* For master's, thesis (for MS). *Expenses: Tuition, area resident:* Full-time $12,960; part-time $8640 per credit hour. One-time fee: $50. Tuition and fees vary according to course load, degree level, campus/location and program. *Unit head:* Dr. A. Quinton White, Jr., Executive Director, 904-256-7100, E-mail: qwhite@ju.edu. *Application contact:* Marisol Preston, Chief Admissions Officer, 904-256-7000, E-mail: admissions@ju.edu.
Website: http://www.ju.edu/msri/Pages/default.aspx

Medical University of South Carolina, College of Graduate Studies, Program in Molecular and Cellular Biology and Pathobiology, Charleston, SC 29425. Offers cancer biology (PhD); cardiovascular biology (PhD); cardiovascular imaging (PhD); cell regulation (PhD); craniofacial biology (PhD); genetics and development (PhD); marine biomedicine (PhD); DMD/PhD; MD/PhD. *Degree requirements:* For doctorate, thesis/dissertation, oral and written exams. *Entrance requirements:* For doctorate, GRE General Test, interview, minimum GPA of 3.0. Additional exam requirements/recommendations for international students: Required—TOEFL (minimum score 600 paper-based; 100 iBT). Electronic applications accepted.

Memorial University of Newfoundland, School of Graduate Studies, Interdisciplinary Program in Marine Studies, St. John's, NL A1C 5S7, Canada. Offers fisheries resource management (MMS, Graduate Diploma); marine spatial planning and management (MMS). *Program availability:* Part-time. *Degree requirements:* For master's, report. *Entrance requirements:* For master's, high 2nd class degree from a recognized university; demonstrated commitment to the fishery through employment or experience in a sector of the fishery, in a regulatory agency or government department connected to the fisheries, in a non-governmental agency, or through self-employment or relevant professional consulting activities; for Graduate Diploma, high 2nd class degree from a recognized university. *Application deadline:* For fall admission, 5/15 for domestic and international students; for winter admission, 10/15 for domestic and international students. Applications are processed on a rolling basis. Application fee: $50 Canadian dollars ($100 Canadian dollars for international students). Electronic applications accepted. *Expenses: Tuition, area resident:* Full-time $2199 Canadian dollars. *International tuition:* $2859 Canadian dollars full-time. *Faculty research:* Biological, ecological and oceanographic aspects of world fisheries; economics; political science; sociology. *Unit head:* Keith Rideout, Graduate Officer, 709-778-0675, Fax: 709-778-0346, E-mail: keith.rideout@mi.mun.ca.
Website: http://www.mi.mun.ca/programsandcourses/programs/

North Carolina State University, Graduate School, College of Physical and Mathematical Sciences, Department of Marine, Earth, and Atmospheric Sciences, Raleigh, NC 27695. Offers marine, earth, and atmospheric sciences (MS, PhD); meteorology (MS, PhD); oceanography (MS, PhD). PhD offered jointly with The University of North Carolina Wilmington. Terminal master's awarded for partial completion of doctoral program. *Degree requirements:* For master's, thesis (for some programs), final oral exam; for doctorate, comprehensive exam, thesis/dissertation, final oral exam, preliminary oral and written exams. *Entrance requirements:* For master's, GRE General Test, minimum GPA of 3.0; for doctorate, GRE General Test, GRE Subject Test (for disciplines in biological oceanography and geology), minimum GPA of 3.0. Additional exam requirements/recommendations for international students: Required—TOEFL (minimum score 550 paper-based). Electronic applications accepted. *Faculty research:* Boundary layer and air quality meteorology; climate and mesoscale dynamics; biological, chemical, geological, and physical oceanography; hard rock, soft rock, environmental, and paleo-geology.

Nova Southeastern University, Halmos College of Natural Sciences and Oceanography, Fort Lauderdale, FL 33314-7796. Offers biological sciences (MS); coastal studies (Certificate); coastal zone management (MS); marine and coastal climate change (Certificate); marine and coastal studies (MA); marine biology (MS); marine biology and oceanography (PhD), including marine biology, oceanography; marine environmental sciences (MS). *Program availability:* Part-time, evening/weekend, 100% online, blended/hybrid learning. *Faculty:* 17 full-time (3 women), 22 part-time/adjunct (11 women). *Students:* 100 full-time (57 women), 114 part-time (76 women); includes 32 minority (6 Black or African American, non-Hispanic/Latino; 1 American Indian or Alaska Native, non-Hispanic/Latino; 6 Asian, non-Hispanic/Latino; 10 Hispanic/Latino; 9 Two or more races, non-Hispanic/Latino), 5 international. Average age 30. 85 applicants, 60% accepted, 39 enrolled. In 2015, 47 master's, 2 doctorates, 9 other advanced degrees awarded. *Degree requirements:* For master's, thesis; for doctorate, comprehensive exam, thesis/dissertation, departmental qualifying exam. *Entrance requirements:* For master's, GRE General Test, 3 letters of recommendation, BS/BA in natural science (for marine biology program), BS/BA in biology (for biological sciences program), minor in the natural sciences or equivalent (for coastal zone management and marine environmental sciences); for doctorate, GRE General Test, master's degree. Additional exam requirements/recommendations for international students: Required—TOEFL (minimum score 550 paper-based). *Application deadline:* Applications are processed on a rolling basis. Application fee: $50. Electronic applications accepted. *Expenses:* $34,749 per year (for PhD); $3,738 per course (for MS and Graduate Certificate). *Financial support:* In 2015–16, 157 students received support, including 14 fellowships with tuition reimbursements available (averaging $25,000 per year), 42 research assistantships with tuition reimbursements available (averaging $19,000 per year); teaching assistantships, career-related internships or fieldwork, Federal Work-Study, scholarships/grants, health care benefits, tuition waivers (full and partial), and unspecified assistantships also available. Support available to part-time students. Financial award application deadline: 4/15; financial award applicants required to submit FAFSA. *Faculty research:* Physical oceanography, biological oceanography, molecular and microbiology, ecology and evolution, coral reefs. *Total annual research expenditures:* $5 million. *Unit head:* Dr. Richard Dodge, Dean, 954-262-3600, Fax: 954-262-4020, E-mail: dodge@nsu.nova.edu. *Application contact:* Dr. Bernhard Riegl, Chair, Department of Marine and Environmental Sciences, 954-262-3600, Fax: 954-262-4020, E-mail: rieglb@nova.edu.
Website: http://cnso.nova.edu

Oregon State University, College of Earth, Ocean, and Atmospheric Sciences, Program in Marine Resource Management, Corvallis, OR 97331. Offers MA, MS. *Program availability:* Part-time. *Students:* 22 full-time (18 women), 4 part-time (1 woman); includes 4 minority (1 Asian, non-Hispanic/Latino; 1 Hispanic/Latino; 2 Two or more races, non-Hispanic/Latino), 3 international. Average age 28. 30 applicants, 30% accepted, 9 enrolled. In 2015, 9 master's awarded. *Degree requirements:* For master's, thesis optional. *Entrance requirements:* For master's, GRE, minimum GPA of 3.0 in last 90 hours of course work. Additional exam requirements/recommendations for international students: Required—TOEFL (minimum score 575 paper-based). *Application deadline:* For fall admission, 1/5 for domestic students. Application fee: $75 ($85 for international students). *Expenses:* Tuition, state resident: full-time $12,150; part-time $450 per credit. Tuition, nonresident: full-time $20,952; part-time $776 per credit. *Required fees:* $1572; $1443 per unit. One-time fee: $350. Tuition and fees vary according to course load, campus/location and program. *Financial support:* Fellowships, research assistantships, teaching assistantships, career-related internships or fieldwork, Federal Work-Study, and institutionally sponsored loans available. Support available to part-time students. *Faculty research:* Ocean and coastal resources, fisheries resources, marine pollution, marine recreation and tourism. *Unit head:* Dr. Flaxen Conway, Director/Professor. *Application contact:* Lori Hartline, Marine Resource Management Advisor, 541-737-5188,
E-mail: student_advisor@coas.oregonstate.edu.
Website: http://ceoas.oregonstate.edu/mrm/

San Francisco State University, Division of Graduate Studies, College of Science and Engineering, Department of Biology, Program in Marine Science, San Francisco, CA 94132-1722. Offers MS. Program offered through the Moss Landing Marine Laboratories. *Application deadline:* Applications are processed on a rolling basis. *Expenses:* Tuition, state resident: full-time $6738. Tuition, nonresident: full-time $15,666. *Required fees:* $1004 per year. *Unit head:* Dr. Ellen Hines, Program Coordinator, 415-338-3512, Fax: 415-338-2295, E-mail: ehines@sfsu.edu.
Website: http://biology.sfsu.edu/graduate/marine_sciencesRTC

San Jose State University, Graduate Studies and Research, College of Science, San Jose, CA 95192-0001. Offers biological sciences (MA, MS), including molecular biology and microbiology (MS), organismal biology, conservation and ecology (MS), physiology (MS); chemistry (MA, MS); computer science (MS); cybersecurity (Certificate); cybersecurity: core technologies (Certificate); geology (MS); marine science (MS); master biotechnology (MBT); mathematics (MA, MS), including mathematics education (MA), science; meteorology (MS); physics (MS), including computational physics, modern optics, science (MA, MS); science education (MA); statistics (MS); unix system administration (Certificate). *Program availability:* Part-time, evening/weekend. *Students:* 118 full-time (68 women), 52 part-time (25 women); includes 125 minority (5 Black or African American, non-Hispanic/Latino; 97 Asian, non-Hispanic/Latino; 23 Hispanic/Latino), 121 international. Average age 27. 1,236 applicants, 21% accepted, 171 enrolled. In 2015, 168 master's awarded. *Entrance requirements:* For master's, GRE. *Application deadline:* For fall admission, 6/29 for domestic students; for spring admission, 11/30 for domestic students. Applications are processed on a rolling basis. Application fee: $55. Electronic applications accepted. *Financial support:* Teaching assistantships, career-related internships or fieldwork, Federal Work-Study, and institutionally sponsored loans available. Support available to part-time students. Financial award applicants required to submit FAFSA. *Faculty research:* Radiochemistry/environmental analysis, health physics, radiation effects. *Unit head:* J. Michael Parrish, Dean, 408-924-4800, Fax: 408-924-4815. *Application contact:* 408-924-2480, Fax: 408-924-2477.
Website: http://www.science.sjsu.edu/

Savannah State University, Master of Science in Marine Sciences Program, Savannah, GA 31404. Offers applied marine science (MSMS); marine science research (MSMS); professional advancement (MSMS). *Program availability:* Part-time. *Degree requirements:* For master's, comprehensive exam, field paper or thesis. *Entrance requirements:* For master's, GRE General Test, minimum GPA of 3.0, 3 letters of recommendation, essay, official transcripts, resume, immunization certificate, interview (recommended). Additional exam requirements/recommendations for international students: Required—TOEFL. Electronic applications accepted. *Expenses:* Contact institution.

Southern Connecticut State University, School of Graduate Studies, School of Arts and Sciences, Department of Environment, Geography and Marine Sciences, New Haven, CT 06515-1355. Offers environmental education (MS); science education (MS, Diploma). *Accreditation:* NCATE. *Program availability:* Part-time, evening/weekend. *Faculty:* 1 part-time/adjunct (0 women). *Students:* 4 full-time (1 woman), 32 part-time (15 women); includes 5 minority (2 Black or African American, non-Hispanic/Latino; 1 Asian, non-Hispanic/Latino; 1 Hispanic/Latino; 1 Two or more races, non-Hispanic/Latino), 1 international. Average age 33. 36 applicants, 36% accepted, 7 enrolled. In 2015, 13 master's awarded. *Degree requirements:* For master's, thesis or alternative. *Entrance requirements:* For master's, interview; for Diploma, master's degree. *Application deadline:* For fall admission, 7/15 priority date for domestic students. Applications are processed on a rolling basis. Application fee: $50. Electronic applications accepted. *Expenses:* Tuition, state resident: full-time $4968; part-time $494 per credit hour. Tuition, nonresident: full-time $16,078; part-time $509 per credit hour. *Required fees:* $4632; $55 per semester. Tuition and fees vary according to program. *Financial support:* Career-related internships or fieldwork, scholarships/grants, and unspecified assistantships available. Financial award application deadline: 4/15; financial award applicants required to submit FAFSA. *Unit head:* Dr. Patrick Heidkamp, Chairman, 203-392-5919, Fax: 203-392-5834, E-mail: heidkampc1@southernct.edu. *Application contact:* Lisa Galvin, Director of Graduate Admissions, 203-392-5240, Fax: 203-392-5235, E-mail: galvinl1@southernct.edu.

Stony Brook University, State University of New York, Graduate School, School of Marine and Atmospheric Sciences, Institute for Terrestrial and Planetary Atmospheres, Program in Marine Sciences, Stony Brook, NY 11794. Offers MS, PhD. *Program availability:* Evening/weekend. *Degree requirements:* For doctorate, one foreign language, comprehensive exam, thesis/dissertation. *Entrance requirements:* For master's, GRE General Test, official transcripts, minimum GPA of 3.0, 3 letters of recommendation; for doctorate, GRE General Test, minimum GPA of 3.0, 3 letters of recommendation. Additional exam requirements/recommendations for international students: Required—TOEFL (minimum score 600 paper-based; 90 iBT). *Application deadline:* For fall admission, 1/15 priority date for domestic students; for spring admission, 10/1 priority date for domestic students. Application fee: $100. Electronic applications accepted. *Expenses:* $12,421 full-time resident tuition and fees, $453 per credit hour; $23,761 full-time nonresident tuition and fees, $925 per credit hour. *Financial support:* Fellowships, research assistantships, teaching assistantships, and career-related internships or fieldwork available. *Unit head:* Dr. Larry Swanson, Interim Dean, 631-632-8700, Fax: 631-632-8820, E-mail: larry.swanson@stonybrook.edu. *Application contact:* Carol Dovi, 631-632-8681, Fax: 631-632-8200, E-mail: carol.dovi@stonybrook.edu.
Website: http://you.stonybrook.edu/somas/education/graduate/marine-sciences-track/

Texas A&M University at Galveston, Department of Marine Sciences, Galveston, TX 77553-1675. Offers marine resources management (MMRM). *Program availability:* Part-time. *Faculty:* 15 full-time (3 women). *Students:* 21 full-time (12 women), 10 part-time (6 women); includes 3 minority (1 Asian, non-Hispanic/Latino; 2 Two or more races, non-Hispanic/Latino), 4 international. Average age 27. 17 applicants, 88% accepted, 12 enrolled. In 2015, 15 master's awarded. Terminal master's awarded for partial completion of doctoral program. *Degree requirements:* For master's, thesis (for some programs). *Entrance requirements:* For master's, GRE, course work in economics.

Additional exam requirements/recommendations for international students: Required—TOEFL (minimum score 550 paper-based; 80 iBT), IELTS (minimum score 6). *Application deadline:* For fall admission, 6/15 for domestic students, 6/1 for international students; for spring admission, 10/15 for domestic students, 10/1 for international students. Application fee: $50 ($90 for international students). Electronic applications accepted. *Expenses:* Contact institution. *Financial support:* In 2015–16, 22 students received support, including 2 research assistantships (averaging $5,690 per year), 11 teaching assistantships (averaging $7,275 per year); scholarships/grants, health care benefits, and unspecified assistantships also available. Financial award application deadline: 3/31; financial award applicants required to submit FAFSA. *Faculty research:* Biogeochemistry, physical oceanography, theoretical chemistry, marine policy. *Unit head:* Dr. Kyeong Park, Department Head, 409-740-4710. *Application contact:* Dr. Wesley Highfield, Assistant Professor/Graduate Advisor, 409-740-4518, Fax: 409-740-4429, E-mail: schlemme@tamug.edu.
Website: http://www.tamug.edu/mars/

Texas A&M University–Corpus Christi, College of Graduate Studies, College of Science and Engineering, Program in Coastal and Marine System Science, Corpus Christi, TX 78412-5503. Offers MS, PhD. *Students:* 26 full-time (13 women), 2 part-time (0 women); includes 5 minority (1 Black or African American, non-Hispanic/Latino; 1 American Indian or Alaska Native, non-Hispanic/Latino; 1 Asian, non-Hispanic/Latino; 2 Hispanic/Latino), 7 international. Average age 31. 15 applicants, 67% accepted, 9 enrolled. In 2015, 3 doctorates awarded. *Degree requirements:* For master's, comprehensive exam, thesis; for doctorate, comprehensive exam, thesis/dissertation. *Entrance requirements:* For master's, GRE, essay (up to 1000 words), curriculum vitae, 3 letters of evaluation; for doctorate, GRE General Test (taken within 5 years), essay (up to 1000 words), curriculum vitae, 3 letters of evaluation. Additional exam requirements/recommendations for international students: Required—TOEFL (minimum score 550 paper-based; 79 iBT), IELTS (minimum score 6.5). *Application deadline:* For fall admission, 2/1 priority date for domestic and international students; for spring admission, 8/1 priority date for domestic students, 6/6 priority date for international students; for summer admission, 2/2 priority date for domestic and international students. Applications are processed on a rolling basis. Application fee: $50 ($70 for international students). Electronic applications accepted. *Financial support:* Research assistantships, teaching assistantships, institutionally sponsored loans, scholarships/grants, health care benefits, and unspecified assistantships available. Support available to part-time students. Financial award application deadline: 3/15; financial award applicants required to submit FAFSA. *Unit head:* Dr. Paul Montagna, Program Coordinator, 361-825-3216, E-mail: thomas.naehr@tamucc.edu. *Application contact:* Graduate Admissions Coordinator, 361-825-2177, Fax: 361-825-2755, E-mail: gradweb@tamucc.edu.
Website: http://www.cmss.tamucc.edu/

University of Alaska Fairbanks, School of Fisheries and Ocean Sciences, Program in Marine Sciences and Limnology, Fairbanks, AK 99775-7220. Offers marine biology (MS, PhD); oceanography (MS, PhD). *Program availability:* Part-time. *Faculty:* 4 full-time (1 woman). *Students:* 31 full-time (20 women), 10 part-time (7 women); includes 6 minority (1 Asian, non-Hispanic/Latino; 4 Hispanic/Latino; 1 Two or more races, non-Hispanic/Latino), 8 international. Average age 31. 26 applicants, 46% accepted, 12 enrolled. In 2015, 10 master's, 3 doctorates awarded. *Median time to degree:* Of those who began their doctoral program in fall 2007, 100% received their degree in 8 years or less. *Degree requirements:* For master's, comprehensive exam, thesis, oral defense of thesis; for doctorate, comprehensive exam, thesis/dissertation, oral defense of dissertation. *Entrance requirements:* For master's, GRE General Test, bachelor's degree from accredited institution with minimum cumulative undergraduate and major GPA of 3.0; for doctorate, GRE General Test, minimum cumulative GPA of 3.0. Additional exam requirements/recommendations for international students: Required—TOEFL (minimum score 550 paper-based; 79 iBT), IELTS (minimum score 6.5). *Application deadline:* For fall admission, 5/1 for domestic students, 4/1 for international students; for spring admission, 9/15 for domestic students, 8/15 for international students. Applications are processed on a rolling basis. Application fee: $60. Electronic applications accepted. *Expenses:* Tuition, state resident: full-time $7614; part-time $423 per credit. Tuition, nonresident: full-time $15,552; part-time $864 per credit. *Required fees:* $38 per credit. $187 per semester. Tuition and fees vary according to course level, course load, program and reciprocity agreements. *Financial support:* In 2015–16, 29 research assistantships with full tuition reimbursements (averaging $14,427 per year), 5 teaching assistantships with full tuition reimbursements (averaging $7,083 per year) were awarded; fellowships with full tuition reimbursements, career-related internships or fieldwork, Federal Work-Study, scholarships/grants, health care benefits, and unspecified assistantships also available. Support available to part-time students. Financial award application deadline: 7/1; financial award applicants required to submit FAFSA. *Total annual research expenditures:* $24.1 million. *Unit head:* Katrin Iken, Co-Chair, 907-474-7289, Fax: 907-474-5863, E-mail: info@sfos.uaf.edu. *Application contact:* Mary Kreta, Director of Admissions, 907-474-7500, Fax: 907-474-7097, E-mail: admissions@alaska.edu.
Website: http://www.uaf.edu/sfos/academics/graduate/

The University of British Columbia, Faculty of Science, Department of Earth, Ocean and Atmospheric Sciences, Vancouver, BC V6T 1Z4, Canada. Offers atmospheric science (M Sc, PhD); geological engineering (M Eng, MA Sc, PhD); geological sciences (M Sc, PhD); geophysics (M Sc, MA Sc, PhD); oceanography (M Sc, PhD). *Degree requirements:* For master's, one foreign language, thesis (for some programs); for doctorate, one foreign language, comprehensive exam, thesis/dissertation. *Entrance requirements:* Additional exam requirements/recommendations for international students: Required—TOEFL (minimum score 600 paper-based; 100 iBT). *Faculty research:* Oceans and atmosphere, environmental earth science, hydro geology, mineral deposits, geophysics.

University of California, San Diego, Graduate Division, Scripps Institution of Oceanography, Program in Marine Biodiversity and Conservation, La Jolla, CA 92093. Offers MAS. *Students:* 21 full-time (15 women); includes 2 minority (1 American Indian or Alaska Native, non-Hispanic/Latino; 1 Asian, non-Hispanic/Latino), 2 international. 49 applicants, 51% accepted, 19 enrolled. In 2015, 18 master's awarded. *Degree requirements:* For master's, capstone/independent study project. *Entrance requirements:* For master's, minimum GPA of 3.0. Additional exam requirements/recommendations for international students: Required—TOEFL (minimum score 550 paper-based; 80 iBT), IELTS (minimum score 7). *Application deadline:* For fall admission, 1/15 for domestic students. Application fee: $90 ($110 for international students). Electronic applications accepted. *Expenses:* Tuition, state resident: full-time $11,220. Tuition, nonresident: full-time $26,322. *Required fees:* $1800. *Financial support:* Fellowships and scholarships/grants available. Financial award applicants required to submit FAFSA. *Faculty research:* Marine ecosystems, policy analysis, economics. *Unit head:* Dr. Richard Norris, Chair, 858-822-1868, E-mail: rnorris@ucsd.edu. *Application contact:* Jane M. Weinzierl, Graduate Coordinator, 858-822-2886, E-mail: mbc@ucsd.edu.
Website: https://scripps.ucsd.edu/masters/mas/mbc

University of California, Santa Barbara, Graduate Division, College of Letters and Sciences, Division of Mathematics, Life, and Physical Sciences, Interdepartmental Graduate Program in Marine Science, Santa Barbara, CA 93106-9620. Offers MS, PhD. *Faculty:* 39 full-time (11 women). *Students:* 27 full-time (14 women); includes 2 minority (both Asian, non-Hispanic/Latino), 2 international. Average age 28. 47 applicants, 17% accepted, 6 enrolled. In 2015, 1 master's awarded. *Degree requirements:* For master's, thesis, 39 units; for doctorate, comprehensive exam, thesis/dissertation, 31 units. *Entrance requirements:* For master's and doctorate, GRE. Additional exam requirements/recommendations for international students: Required—TOEFL (minimum score 550 paper-based; 80 iBT), IELTS (minimum score 7). *Application deadline:* For fall admission, 12/15 for domestic and international students. Application fee: $90 ($110 for international students). Electronic applications accepted. *Financial support:* In 2015–16, 10 students received support, including 15 fellowships with full tuition reimbursements available (averaging $11,468 per year), 14 research assistantships with full tuition reimbursements available (averaging $10,895 per year), 10 teaching assistantships with full tuition reimbursements available (averaging $7,908 per year); career-related internships or fieldwork, Federal Work-Study, institutionally sponsored loans, scholarships/grants, health care benefits, tuition waivers (full and partial), and unspecified assistantships also available. Support available to part-time students. Financial award application deadline: 12/15; financial award applicants required to submit FAFSA. *Faculty research:* Ocean carbon cycling, paleoceanography, physiology of marine organisms, bio-optical oceanography, biological oceanography. *Unit head:* Prof. Libe Washburn, Chair/Professor of Geography, 805-893-7367, Fax: 805-893-2578, E-mail: libe.washburn@ucsb.edu. *Application contact:* Melanie Fujii, Student Affairs Officer, 805-893-2979, Fax: 805-893-5885, E-mail: fujii@lifesci.ucsb.edu.
Website: http://www.igpms.ucsb.edu/

University of California, Santa Cruz, Division of Graduate Studies, Division of Physical and Biological Sciences, Department of Ocean Sciences, Santa Cruz, CA 95064. Offers MS, PhD. Terminal master's awarded for partial completion of doctoral program. *Degree requirements:* For master's, thesis; for doctorate, comprehensive exam, thesis/dissertation, seminar, qualifying exam. *Entrance requirements:* For master's and doctorate, GRE General Test, GRE Subject Test, 3 letters of recommendation. Additional exam requirements/recommendations for international students: Required—TOEFL (minimum score 550 paper-based; 83 iBT); Recommended—IELTS (minimum score 8). Electronic applications accepted. *Faculty research:* Sediment, marine organic and trace metal biogeochemistry; paleoceanography; remote sensing (satellite oceanography); coastal circulation processes; the development of software applications for real-time data acquisition and data visualization; climatology.

University of Connecticut, Graduate School, College of Liberal Arts and Sciences, Department of Marine Sciences, Storrs, CT 06269. Offers MS, PhD. Terminal master's awarded for partial completion of doctoral program. *Degree requirements:* For master's, comprehensive exam; for doctorate, thesis/dissertation. *Entrance requirements:* Additional exam requirements/recommendations for international students: Required—TOEFL (minimum score 550 paper-based). Electronic applications accepted.

University of Delaware, College of Earth, Ocean, and Environment, School of Marine Science and Policy, Newark, DE 19716. Offers marine policy (MMP); marine studies (MS, PhD), including marine biosciences, oceanography, physical ocean science and engineering; oceanography (PhD).

University of Florida, Graduate School, College of Agricultural and Life Sciences, School of Forest Resources and Conservation, Department of Fisheries and Aquatic Sciences, Gainesville, FL 32611. Offers MFAS, MS, PhD. *Program availability:* Part-time, online learning. *Faculty:* 63. *Students:* 32 full-time (15 women), 51 part-time (30 women); includes 5 minority (1 Black or African American, non-Hispanic/Latino; 1 American Indian or Alaska Native, non-Hispanic/Latino; 1 Asian, non-Hispanic/Latino; 2 Hispanic/Latino), 6 international. Average age 30. 40 applicants, 48% accepted, 18 enrolled. In 2015, 8 master's, 7 doctorates awarded. *Degree requirements:* For master's, thesis (for MS); technical paper (for MFAS); for doctorate, comprehensive exam, thesis/dissertation. *Entrance requirements:* For master's and doctorate, GRE General Test, minimum GPA of 3.0. Additional exam requirements/recommendations for international students: Required—TOEFL (minimum score 550 paper-based; 80 iBT), IELTS (minimum score 6). *Application deadline:* For fall admission, 6/1 for domestic students, 3/1 for international students; for spring admission, 10/1 for domestic students, 8/1 for international students. Applications are processed on a rolling basis. Application fee: $30. Electronic applications accepted. *Financial support:* Unspecified assistantships available. Financial award application deadline: 1/31; financial award applicants required to submit FAFSA. *Total annual research expenditures:* $1,921.
Website: http://sfrc.ufl.edu/fish/

University of Georgia, Franklin College of Arts and Sciences, Department of Marine Sciences, Athens, GA 30602. Offers MS, PhD. *Degree requirements:* For master's, thesis; for doctorate, comprehensive exam, thesis/dissertation, teaching experience, field research experience. *Entrance requirements:* For master's and doctorate, GRE General Test. Additional exam requirements/recommendations for international students: Required—TOEFL. Electronic applications accepted. *Faculty research:* Microbial ecology, biogeochemistry, polar biology, coastal ecology, coastal circulation.

University of Hawaii at Manoa, Graduate Division, College of Social Sciences, Department of Geography, Graduate Ocean Policy Certificate Program, Honolulu, HI 96822. Offers Graduate Certificate. *Program availability:* Part-time. *Students:* 2 (1 woman), 1 international. Average age 36. In 2015, 2 Graduate Certificates awarded. *Entrance requirements:* Additional exam requirements/recommendations for international students: Required—TOEFL (minimum score 500 paper-based; 61 iBT), IELTS (minimum score 5). *Application deadline:* For fall admission, 3/1 for domestic students, 2/1 for international students; for spring admission, 9/1 for domestic students, 8/1 for international students. Application fee: $100. *Financial support:* In 2015–16, 1 fellowship (averaging $500 per year), 1 research assistantship (averaging $25,902 per year), 1 teaching assistantship (averaging $15,558 per year) were awarded. *Total annual research expenditures:* $21.4 million. *Unit head:* Richard Dubanoski, Dean, 808-956-6570, Fax: 808-956-2340, E-mail: dickd@hawaii.edu. *Application contact:* Alison Rieser, Program Director, 808-956-8467, Fax: 808-956-3512, E-mail: rieser@hawaii.edu.
Website: http://www.geography.hawaii.edu/projects/gopc/

University of Maine, Graduate School, College of Natural Sciences, Forestry, and Agriculture, School of Marine Sciences, Orono, ME 04469. Offers marine bio-resources (MS, PhD); marine biology (MS, PhD); marine policy (MS); oceanography (MS, PhD). *Program availability:* Part-time. *Faculty:* 26 full-time (9 women), 11 part-time/adjunct (0 women). *Students:* 57 full-time (38 women); includes 2 minority (1 American Indian or Alaska Native, non-Hispanic/Latino; 1 Asian, non-Hispanic/Latino), 8 international. Average age 28. 95 applicants, 19% accepted, 16 enrolled. In 2015, 9 master's, 5 doctorates awarded. *Degree requirements:* For master's, thesis; for doctorate, comprehensive exam, thesis/dissertation. *Entrance requirements:* For master's and doctorate, GRE General Test. Additional exam requirements/recommendations for

international students: Required—TOEFL (minimum score 550 paper-based; 79 iBT). *Application deadline:* Applications are processed on a rolling basis. Application fee: $65. Electronic applications accepted. *Financial support:* In 2015–16, 54 students received support, including 2 fellowships (averaging $22,400 per year), 41 research assistantships with tuition reimbursements available (averaging $14,600 per year), 10 teaching assistantships with tuition reimbursements available (averaging $14,600 per year); career-related internships or fieldwork, Federal Work-Study, and tuition waivers (full and partial) also available. Support available to part-time students. Financial award application deadline: 3/1. *Faculty research:* Oceanography, marine biology, marine policy, aquaculture and fisheries. *Total annual research expenditures:* $12 million. *Unit head:* Dr. Fei Chai, Director, 207-581-3321, Fax: 207-581-4388. *Application contact:* Scott G. Delcourt, Assistant Vice President for Graduate Studies and Senior Associate Dean, 207-581-3291, Fax: 207-581-3232, E-mail: graduate@maine.edu.
Website: http://www.umaine.edu/marine/

University of Maryland, Baltimore, Graduate School, Program in Marine-Estuarine-Environmental Sciences, College Park, MD 20742. Offers MS, PhD. *Program availability:* Part-time. Terminal master's awarded for partial completion of doctoral program. *Degree requirements:* For master's, thesis, oral defense; for doctorate, comprehensive exam, thesis/dissertation, proposal defense, oral defense. *Entrance requirements:* For master's and doctorate, GRE General Test, minimum GPA of 3.0. Additional exam requirements/recommendations for international students: Required—TOEFL. Electronic applications accepted. Tuition and fees vary according to program.

University of Maryland, Baltimore County, The Graduate School, Marine-Estuarine-Environmental Sciences Graduate Program, College Park, MD 20742. Offers MS, PhD. *Program availability:* Part-time. *Degree requirements:* For master's, thesis, oral defense; for doctorate, comprehensive exam, thesis/dissertation, proposal defense, oral defense. *Entrance requirements:* For master's and doctorate, GRE General Test, minimum GPA of 3.0. Additional exam requirements/recommendations for international students: Required—TOEFL. Electronic applications accepted. *Expenses:* Tuition, state resident: full-time $12,816. Tuition, nonresident: full-time $19,710.

University of Maryland, College Park, Academic Affairs, College of Computer, Mathematical and Natural Sciences, Program in Marine-Estuarine-Environmental Sciences, College Park, MD 20742. Offers MS, PhD. *Program availability:* Part-time. Terminal master's awarded for partial completion of doctoral program. *Degree requirements:* For master's, thesis, oral defense; for doctorate, comprehensive exam, thesis/dissertation, proposal defense, oral defense. *Entrance requirements:* For master's and doctorate, GRE General Test, minimum GPA of 3.0. Additional exam requirements/recommendations for international students: Required—TOEFL. Electronic applications accepted. *Faculty research:* Ecology, environmental chemistry, environmental molecular biology/biotechnology, environmental sciences, fisheries science, oceanography.

University of Maryland Eastern Shore, Graduate Programs, Department of Natural Sciences, Princess Anne, MD 21853-1299. Offers chemistry (MS); marine-estuarine-environmental sciences (MS, PhD); quantitative fisheries and resource economics (PMS); toxicology (MS, PhD). *Degree requirements:* For master's, thesis; for doctorate, comprehensive exam, thesis/dissertation. *Entrance requirements:* For master's and doctorate, GRE General Test, minimum GPA of 3.0. Additional exam requirements/recommendations for international students: Required—TOEFL (minimum score 80 iBT). Electronic applications accepted. *Faculty research:* Environmental chemistry (air/water pollution), fin fish ecology.

University of Maryland Eastern Shore, Graduate Programs, Program in Marine-Estuarine-Environmental Sciences, College Park, MD 20742. Offers MS, PhD. *Program availability:* Part-time. *Degree requirements:* For master's, thesis; for doctorate, comprehensive exam, thesis/dissertation, proposal defense. *Entrance requirements:* For master's and doctorate, GRE General Test, minimum GPA of 3.0. Additional exam requirements/recommendations for international students: Required—TOEFL. Electronic applications accepted.

University of Massachusetts Amherst, Graduate School, Interdisciplinary Programs, Program in Marine Science and Technology, Amherst, MA 01003. Offers MS, PhD. *Program availability:* Part-time. Terminal master's awarded for partial completion of doctoral program. *Degree requirements:* For master's, thesis or alternative; for doctorate, comprehensive exam, thesis/dissertation. *Entrance requirements:* For master's and doctorate, GRE General Test, 3 letters of recommendation. Additional exam requirements/recommendations for international students: Required—TOEFL (minimum score 550 paper-based; 80 iBT), IELTS (minimum score 6.5). Electronic applications accepted.

University of Massachusetts Boston, College of Science and Mathematics, Program in Marine Science and Technology, Boston, MA 02125-3393. Offers MS, PhD. *Students:* 12 full-time (6 women), 2 part-time (both women); includes 1 minority (Two or more races, non-Hispanic/Latino). 9 applicants, 78% accepted, 6 enrolled. In 2015, 63 master's, 13 doctorates awarded. *Expenses:* Tuition, state resident: full-time $2590. Tuition, nonresident: full-time $9758. *Required fees:* $13,525. *Unit head:* Dr. William Hagar, Interim Dean, 617-287-5777. *Application contact:* Peggy Roldan Patel, Graduate Admissions Coordinator, 617-287-6400, Fax: 617-287-6236,
E-mail: bos.gadm@dpc.umassp.edu.

University of Massachusetts Dartmouth, Graduate School, School for Marine Science and Technology, New Bedford, MA 02744-1221. Offers coastal and ocean administration science and technology (MS). *Program availability:* Part-time. *Faculty:* 13 full-time (1 woman). *Students:* 22 full-time (9 women), 34 part-time (17 women); includes 3 minority (1 Hispanic/Latino; 2 Two or more races, non-Hispanic/Latino), 15 international. Average age 31. 28 applicants, 93% accepted, 11 enrolled. In 2015, 4 master's, 10 doctorates awarded. Terminal master's awarded for partial completion of doctoral program. *Degree requirements:* For master's, thesis or research paper; for doctorate, comprehensive exam, thesis/dissertation. *Entrance requirements:* For master's and doctorate, GRE, statement of intent (minimum of 300 words), statement of interest (minimum of 300 words), resume, 3 letters of recommendation, official transcripts. Additional exam requirements/recommendations for international students: Required—TOEFL (minimum score 533 paper-based; 72 iBT), IELTS (minimum score 6). *Application deadline:* For fall admission, 2/15 priority date for domestic students, 1/15 priority date for international students; for spring admission, 11/15 priority date for domestic students, 10/15 priority date for international students. Applications are processed on a rolling basis. Application fee: $60. Electronic applications accepted. *Expenses:* Tuition, state resident: full-time $2071; part-time $86.29 per credit. Tuition, nonresident: full-time $8099; part-time $337.46 per credit. *Required fees:* $18,074; $762.08 per credit. Tuition and fees vary according to course load and reciprocity agreements. *Financial support:* In 2015–16, 24 research assistantships with full tuition reimbursements (averaging $17,721 per year), 3 teaching assistantships with full tuition reimbursements (averaging $24,667 per year) were awarded; Federal Work-Study and unspecified assistantships also available. Support available to part-time students. Financial award application deadline: 3/1; financial award applicants required to submit FAFSA. *Faculty research:* Physical oceanography, marine and environmental chemistry, ocean circulation, ocean internal waves, ocean acoustics. *Total annual research expenditures:* $9 million. *Unit head:* Steven Lohrenz, Graduate Program Director, 508-910-6550, Fax: 508-999-8197, E-mail: slohrenz@umassd.edu. *Application contact:* Steven Briggs, Director of Marketing and Recruitment for Graduate Studies, 508-999-8604, Fax: 508-999-8183, E-mail: graduate@umassd.edu.
Website: http://www.umassd.edu/smast

University of Miami, Graduate School, Rosenstiel School of Marine and Atmospheric Science, Division of Applied Marine Physics, Coral Gables, FL 33124. Offers applied marine physics (MS, PhD), including coastal ocean dynamics, underwater acoustics and geoacoustics (PhD), wave surface dynamics and air-sea interaction (PhD). *Program availability:* Part-time. Terminal master's awarded for partial completion of doctoral program. *Degree requirements:* For master's, comprehensive exam, thesis; for doctorate, comprehensive exam, thesis/dissertation. *Entrance requirements:* For master's and doctorate, GRE General Test. Additional exam requirements/recommendations for international students: Required—TOEFL (minimum score 550 paper-based). Electronic applications accepted.

University of Miami, Graduate School, Rosenstiel School of Marine and Atmospheric Science, Division of Marine and Atmospheric Chemistry, Coral Gables, FL 33124. Offers MS, PhD. Terminal master's awarded for partial completion of doctoral program. *Degree requirements:* For master's, comprehensive exam, thesis; for doctorate, comprehensive exam, thesis/dissertation. *Entrance requirements:* For master's and doctorate, GRE General Test. Additional exam requirements/recommendations for international students: Required—TOEFL (minimum score 550 paper-based). Electronic applications accepted. *Faculty research:* Global change issues, chemistry of marine waters and marine atmosphere.

University of Michigan, School of Natural Resources and Environment, Ann Arbor, MI 48109. Offers environmental justice (Certificate); industrial ecology (Certificate); landscape architecture (MLA); natural resources and environment (MS, PhD), including aquatic sciences: research and management (MS), behavior, education and communication (MS), conservation ecology (MS), environmental informatics (MS), environmental justice (MS), environmental policy and planning (MS), natural resources and environment (PhD), sustainable systems (MS); spatial analysis (Certificate); sustainability (Certificate); JD/MS; MBA/MS; MLA/M Arch; MLA/MBA; MLA/MUP; MPP/MS; MS/AM; MS/JD; MS/MBA; MS/MPP; MS/MSE; MUP/MS. *Accreditation:* ASLA (one or more programs are accredited). *Students:* 381 full-time (213 women). Average age 26. *Degree requirements:* For master's, thesis, practicum, or group project; for doctorate, comprehensive exam, thesis/dissertation, oral defense of dissertation, preliminary exam. *Entrance requirements:* For master's and doctorate, GRE General Test. Additional exam requirements/recommendations for international students: Required—TOEFL (minimum score 560 paper-based; 84 iBT). *Application deadline:* For fall admission, 4/30 for domestic and international students. Application fee: $75 ($90 for international students). Electronic applications accepted. *Financial support:* Application deadline: 1/6; applicants required to submit FAFSA. *Unit head:* Dr. Daniel Brown, Interim Dean, 734-763-5803, E-mail: danbrown@umich.edu. *Application contact:* Sara O'Brien, Director of Academic Programs, 734-764-6453, Fax: 734-936-2195,
E-mail: snre.admissions@umich.edu.
Website: http://www.snre.umich.edu/

University of New England, College of Arts and Sciences, Program in Marine Sciences, Biddeford, ME 04005-9526. Offers MS. *Faculty:* 9 full-time (4 women), 1 (woman) part-time/adjunct. *Students:* 6 full-time (3 women), 6 part-time (4 women); includes 1 minority (Asian, non-Hispanic/Latino). Average age 25. 28 applicants, 25% accepted, 6 enrolled. In 2015, 5 master's awarded. *Degree requirements:* For master's, thesis. *Entrance requirements:* For master's, GRE. *Application deadline:* For fall admission, 2/1 for domestic students. Application fee: $40. Tuition and fees vary according to degree level and program. *Financial support:* Application deadline: 5/1; applicants required to submit FAFSA. *Unit head:* Dr. Katherine Ono, Graduate Coordinator for Marine Sciences, 207-602-2814, E-mail: kono@une.edu. *Application contact:* Scott Steinberg, Dean of University Admission, 207-221-4225, Fax: 207-523-1925, E-mail: ssteinberg@une.edu.
Website: http://www.une.edu/cas/marine/graduate/

University of New Hampshire, Graduate School, College of Life Sciences and Agriculture, Department of Natural Resources and the Environment, Durham, NH 03824. Offers environmental conservation (MS); forestry (MS); integrated coastal ecosystem science, policy and management (MS); natural resources (MS); soil and water resource management (MS); wildlife and conservation biology (MS). *Program availability:* Part-time. *Degree requirements:* For master's, thesis or alternative. *Entrance requirements:* For master's, GRE General Test. Additional exam requirements/recommendations for international students: Required—TOEFL (minimum score 550 paper-based; 80 iBT). Electronic applications accepted.

The University of North Carolina at Chapel Hill, Graduate School, College of Arts and Sciences, Department of Marine Sciences, Chapel Hill, NC 27599. Offers MS, PhD. *Degree requirements:* For master's, comprehensive exam, thesis; for doctorate, comprehensive exam, thesis/dissertation. *Entrance requirements:* For master's and doctorate, GRE General Test, minimum GPA of 3.0. Additional exam requirements/recommendations for international students: Required—TOEFL. Electronic applications accepted. *Faculty research:* Physical oceanography, marine biology and ecology, marine geochemistry, marine geology and coastal meteorology.

The University of North Carolina at Chapel Hill, Graduate School, Gillings School of Global Public Health, Department of Environmental Sciences and Engineering, Chapel Hill, NC 27599. Offers air, radiation and industrial hygiene (MPH, MS, MSEE, MSPH, PhD); aquatic and atmospheric sciences (MPH, MS, MSPH, PhD); environmental engineering (MPH, MS, MSEE, MSPH, PhD); environmental health sciences (MPH, MS, MSPH, PhD); environmental management and policy (MPH, MS, MSPH, PhD). *Students:* 112 full-time (68 women); includes 20 minority (11 Asian, non-Hispanic/Latino; 4 Hispanic/Latino; 5 Two or more races, non-Hispanic/Latino), 31 international. Average age 28. 178 applicants, 37% accepted, 39 enrolled. Terminal master's awarded for partial completion of doctoral program. *Degree requirements:* For master's, comprehensive exam, thesis (for some programs), research paper; for doctorate, comprehensive exam, thesis/dissertation. *Entrance requirements:* For master's and doctorate, GRE General Test, minimum GPA of 3.0 (recommended). Additional exam requirements/recommendations for international students: Required—TOEFL. *Application deadline:* For fall admission, 12/10 priority date for domestic and international students; for spring admission, 9/10 for domestic students. Applications are processed on a rolling basis. Application fee: $85. Electronic applications accepted. *Financial support:* Fellowships with tuition reimbursements, research assistantships with tuition reimbursements, teaching assistantships with tuition reimbursements, career-related internships or fieldwork, Federal Work-Study, traineeships, health care benefits, and unspecified assistantships available. Support available to part-time students. Financial award application deadline: 12/10; financial award applicants

required to submit FAFSA. *Faculty research:* Air, radiation and industrial hygiene, aquatic and atmospheric sciences, environmental health sciences, environmental management and policy, water resources engineering. *Unit head:* Dr. Michael Aitken, Chair, 919-966-1024, Fax: 919-966-7911, E-mail: mike_aitken@unc.edu. *Application contact:* Jack Whaley, Registrar, 919-966-3844, Fax: 919-966-7911, E-mail: jack_whaley@unc.edu.
Website: http://www2.sph.unc.edu/envr/

The University of North Carolina Wilmington, Center for Marine Science, Wilmington, NC 28403-3297. Offers marine science (MS). *Program availability:* Part-time. *Faculty:* 48 full-time (12 women). *Students:* 7 full-time (4 women), 20 part-time (10 women); includes 2 minority (1 Asian, non-Hispanic/Latino; 1 Hispanic/Latino). Average age 27. 16 applicants, 7 enrolled. In 2015, 10 master's awarded. *Degree requirements:* For master's, comprehensive exam, thesis. *Entrance requirements:* For master's, GRE, minimum B average in undergraduate work, 3 recommendations, statement of interest. Additional exam requirements/recommendations for international students: Required—TOEFL (minimum score 79 iBT), IELTS (minimum score 6.5). *Application deadline:* For fall admission, 6/15 for domestic students; for spring admission, 11/15 for domestic students. Applications are processed on a rolling basis. Application fee: $60. Electronic applications accepted. *Expenses:* $8,854 in-state full-time per year; $20,945 out-of-state full-time per year. *Financial support:* Scholarships/grants and unspecified assistantships available. Financial award application deadline: 3/15; financial award applicants required to submit FAFSA. *Unit head:* Dr. Stephen Skrabal, Director, 910-962-7160, E-mail: skrabals@uncw.edu.
Website: http://www.uncw.edu/mms/

The University of North Carolina Wilmington, College of Arts and Sciences, Department of Biology and Marine Biology, Wilmington, NC 28403-3297. Offers biology (MS); marine biology (MS, PhD). *Program availability:* Part-time. *Faculty:* 38 full-time (11 women). *Students:* 2 full-time (1 woman), 65 part-time (36 women); includes 10 minority (1 Black or African American, non-Hispanic/Latino; 2 Asian, non-Hispanic/Latino; 6 Hispanic/Latino; 1 Two or more races, non-Hispanic/Latino), 4 international. Average age 31. 89 applicants, 17 enrolled. In 2015, 14 master's, 1 doctorate awarded. *Degree requirements:* For master's, comprehensive exam, thesis; for doctorate, comprehensive exam, thesis/dissertation. *Entrance requirements:* For master's, GRE General Test, minimum B average in undergraduate work, 3 recommendations, resume, statement of interest, bachelor's degree in field of biology; for doctorate, GRE General Test, minimum B average in undergraduate and graduate work, resume, summary of MS thesis research, master's degree, statement of interest. Additional exam requirements/recommendations for international students: Required—TOEFL (minimum score 79 iBT), IELTS (minimum score 6.5). *Application deadline:* For fall admission, 6/15 for domestic students; for spring admission, 11/30 for domestic students. Applications are processed on a rolling basis. Application fee: $60. Electronic applications accepted. *Expenses:* $8,854 in-state full-time per year; $20,945 out-of-state full-time per year. *Financial support:* Research assistantships with tuition reimbursements, teaching assistantships with tuition reimbursements, and scholarships/grants available. Support available to part-time students. Financial award application deadline: 3/15; financial award applicants required to submit FAFSA. *Faculty research:* Ecology, physiology, cell and molecular biology, systematics, biomechanics. *Unit head:* Dr. Chris Finelli, Chair, 910-962-3487, E-mail: finellic@uncw.edu. *Application contact:* Dr. Stephen Kinsey, Graduate Coordinator, 910-962-7398, Fax: 910-962-4066, E-mail: kinseys@uncw.edu.
Website: http://www.uncw.edu/bio/graduate.html

The University of North Carolina Wilmington, College of Arts and Sciences, Department of Environmental Studies, Wilmington, NC 28403-3297. Offers coastal management, marine and coastal education, environmental education and interpretation, environmental management (MS). *Program availability:* Part-time. *Faculty:* 5 full-time (1 woman). *Students:* 24 full-time (13 women), 6 part-time (4 women); includes 2 minority (1 Hispanic/Latino; 1 Two or more races, non-Hispanic/Latino). Average age 28. 34 applicants, 13 enrolled. In 2015, 20 master's awarded. *Degree requirements:* For master's, comprehensive exam, thesis or alternative, final project, practicum. *Entrance requirements:* For master's, GRE General Test, 3 letters of recommendation, essay, minimum GPA of 3.0 from undergraduate work. Additional exam requirements/recommendations for international students: Required—TOEFL (minimum score 79 iBT), IELTS (minimum score 6.5). *Application deadline:* For fall admission, 4/15 for domestic and international students; for spring admission, 10/15 for domestic and international students. Applications are processed on a rolling basis. Application fee: $60. Electronic applications accepted. *Expenses:* $8,854 in-state full-time per year; $20,945 out-of-state full-time per year. *Financial support:* Scholarships/grants and unspecified assistantships available. Financial award application deadline: 3/15; financial award applicants required to submit FAFSA. *Faculty research:* Coastal management, environmental management, environmental education, environmental law, natural resource management. *Unit head:* Dr. Jeffery Hill, Chair, 910-962-3264, Fax: 910-962-7634, E-mail: hillj@uncw.edu. *Application contact:* Dr. James Rotenberg, Graduate Program Coordinator, 910-962-7549, Fax: 910-962-7634, E-mail: rotenbergj@uncw.edu.
Website: http://www.uncw.edu/evs/academics-MS_Degree.html

The University of North Carolina Wilmington, College of Arts and Sciences, Department of Public and International Affairs, Wilmington, NC 28403-3297. Offers coastal and ocean policy (MS); conflict management (Graduate Certificate); conflict management and resolution (MA), including domestic social and organizational conflict transformation, national and international security; public administration (MPA), including coastal planning and management, environmental policy and management, nonprofit management, marine policy, public management, public policy analysis. *Accreditation:* NASPAA. *Program availability:* Part-time. *Faculty:* 16 full-time (6 women). *Students:* 81 full-time (48 women), 54 part-time (35 women); includes 26 minority (16 Black or African American, non-Hispanic/Latino; 1 American Indian or Alaska Native, non-Hispanic/Latino; 1 Asian, non-Hispanic/Latino; 7 Hispanic/Latino; 1 Two or more races, non-Hispanic/Latino), 2 international. Average age 32. 91 applicants, 59 enrolled. In 2015, 40 master's awarded. *Degree requirements:* For master's, comprehensive exam (for some programs), thesis or alternative, internship, practicum, capstone project. *Entrance requirements:* For master's, GRE, GMAT, 3 letters of recommendation, statement of interest, resume, essay. Additional exam requirements/recommendations for international students: Required—TOEFL (minimum score 79 iBT), IELTS (minimum score 6.5). *Application deadline:* For fall admission, 4/15 for domestic students; for spring admission, 11/15 for domestic students. Applications are processed on a rolling basis. Application fee: $60. Electronic applications accepted. *Expenses:* $8,854 in-state full-time per year; $20,945 out-of-state full-time per year. *Financial support:* Scholarships/grants and unspecified assistantships available. Financial award application deadline: 3/15; financial award applicants required to submit FAFSA. *Unit head:* Dr. Daniel Masters, Chair, 910-962-7583, Fax: 910-962-3286, E-mail: mastersd@uncw.edu. *Application contact:* Dr. Mark Imperial, MPA Program Director, 910-962-7928, Fax: 910-962-3286, E-mail: imperialm@uncw.edu.
Website: http://www.uncw.edu/pia/graduate/index.html

University of Puerto Rico, Mayagüez Campus, Graduate Studies, College of Arts and Sciences, Department of Marine Sciences, Mayagüez, PR 00681-9000. Offers MS, PhD. *Program availability:* Part-time. *Degree requirements:* For master's, one foreign language, thesis, departmental and comprehensive final exams; for doctorate, one foreign language, thesis/dissertation, qualifying, comprehensive, and final exams. *Entrance requirements:* For master's, GRE, minimum GPA of 3.0; for doctorate, GRE, minimum GPA of 3.5. *Faculty research:* Marine botany, ecology, chemistry, and parasitology; fisheries; ichthyology; aquaculture.

University of Rhode Island, Graduate School, College of the Environment and Life Sciences, Department of Fisheries, Animal and Veterinary Science, Kingston, RI 02881. Offers animal health and disease (MS); animal science (MS); aquaculture (MS); aquatic pathology (MS); environmental sciences (PhD), including animal science, aquacultural science, aquatic pathology, fisheries science; fisheries (MS). *Faculty:* 10 full-time (3 women). *Degree requirements:* For master's, comprehensive exam (for some programs), thesis optional; for doctorate, comprehensive exam, thesis/dissertation. *Entrance requirements:* For master's and doctorate, GRE, 2 letters of recommendation. Additional exam requirements/recommendations for international students: Required—TOEFL (minimum score 550 paper-based). *Application deadline:* For fall admission, 7/15 for domestic students, 2/1 for international students; for spring admission, 11/15 for domestic students, 7/15 for international students. Application fee: $65. Electronic applications accepted. *Expenses:* Tuition, state resident: full-time $11,796; part-time $655 per credit. Tuition, nonresident: full-time $24,206; part-time $1345 per credit. *Required fees:* $1546; $44 per credit. One-time fee: $155 full-time; $35 part-time. *Financial support:* Application deadline: 2/1; applicants required to submit FAFSA. *Total annual research expenditures:* $1.2 million. *Unit head:* Dr. Marta Gomez-Chiarri, Chair, 401-874-2917, Fax: 401-874-7575, E-mail: gomezchi@uri.edu. *Application contact:* Graduate Admissions, 401-874-2872, E-mail: gradadm@etal.uri.edu.
Website: http://www.uri.edu/cels/favs/

University of San Diego, College of Arts and Sciences, Marine Sciences Graduate Program, San Diego, CA 92110-2492. Offers MS. *Program availability:* Part-time. *Faculty:* 2 full-time (both women), 2 part-time/adjunct (0 women). *Students:* 9 full-time (5 women), 10 part-time (6 women); includes 4 minority (1 Black or African American, non-Hispanic/Latino; 2 Asian, non-Hispanic/Latino; 1 Two or more races, non-Hispanic/Latino). Average age 26. 35 applicants, 29% accepted, 6 enrolled. In 2015, 3 master's awarded. *Degree requirements:* For master's, thesis. *Entrance requirements:* For master's, GRE General Test, minimum GPA of 3.0; 1 semester each of biology with lab, physics with lab, and calculus; 1 year of chemistry with lab. Additional exam requirements/recommendations for international students: Required—TOEFL (minimum score 580 paper-based; 83 iBT), TWE. *Application deadline:* For fall admission, 4/1 for domestic and international students. Applications are processed on a rolling basis. Application fee: $45. Electronic applications accepted. *Financial support:* In 2015–16, 13 students received support. Teaching assistantships, career-related internships or fieldwork, Federal Work-Study, institutionally sponsored loans, and unspecified assistantships available. Support available to part-time students. Financial award application deadline: 4/1; financial award applicants required to submit FAFSA. *Faculty research:* Marine ecology, environmental geology and geochemistry, climatology, physiological ecology, fisheries and aquaculture. *Unit head:* Dr. Ronald S. Kaufmann, Director, 619-260-4795, Fax: 619-260-6874, E-mail: andrewsk@sandiego.edu. *Application contact:* Monica Mahon, Associate Director of Graduate Admissions, 619-260-4524, Fax: 619-260-4158, E-mail: grads@sandiego.edu.
Website: http://www.sandiego.edu/cas/marine_science_ms/

University of South Alabama, College of Arts and Sciences, Department of Marine Sciences, Mobile, AL 36688. Offers MS, PhD. *Faculty:* 8 full-time (2 women). *Students:* 30 full-time (19 women), 12 part-time (8 women); includes 4 minority (2 Black or African American, non-Hispanic/Latino; 1 Native Hawaiian or other Pacific Islander, non-Hispanic/Latino; 1 Two or more races, non-Hispanic/Latino), 3 international. Average age 28. 62 applicants, 27% accepted, 14 enrolled. In 2015, 5 master's, 2 doctorates awarded. *Degree requirements:* For master's, comprehensive exam, thesis optional; for doctorate, one foreign language, comprehensive exam, thesis/dissertation, research project. *Entrance requirements:* For master's, GRE, minimum GPA of 3.0, BS in marine sciences or related discipline; for doctorate, GRE, BS or MS in marine sciences or related discipline; minimum undergraduate GPA of 3.0, graduate 3.25. Additional exam requirements/recommendations for international students: Required—TOEFL (minimum score 550 paper-based; 71 iBT). *Application deadline:* For fall admission, 2/1 for domestic and international students. Application fee: $35. Electronic applications accepted. *Expenses:* Tuition, state resident: full-time $9480; part-time $395 per credit hour. Tuition, nonresident: full-time $18,960; part-time $790 per credit hour. *Financial support:* In 2015–16, fellowships with tuition reimbursements (averaging $17,000 per year), research assistantships with tuition reimbursements (averaging $20,000 per year) were awarded; teaching assistantships, career-related internships or fieldwork, Federal Work-Study, institutionally sponsored loans, scholarships/grants, and unspecified assistantships also available. Support available to part-time students. Financial award application deadline: 2/1; financial award applicants required to submit FAFSA. *Unit head:* Dr. Sean Powers, Chair, Marine Sciences, 251-460-7136, Fax: 251-460-7357, E-mail: spowers@disl.org. *Application contact:* Dr. Ronald Kiene, Graduate Coordinator, 251-861-2141, E-mail: rkiene@disl.org.
Website: http://www.southalabama.edu/marinesciences/programs.html

University of South Carolina, The Graduate School, College of Arts and Sciences, Marine Science Program, Columbia, SC 29208. Offers MS, PhD. *Degree requirements:* For master's, thesis; for doctorate, comprehensive exam, thesis/dissertation. *Entrance requirements:* For master's and doctorate, GRE General Test. Additional exam requirements/recommendations for international students: Required—TOEFL (minimum score 570 paper-based). Electronic applications accepted. *Faculty research:* Biological, chemical, geological, and physical oceanography; policy.

University of Southern California, Graduate School, Dana and David Dornsife College of Letters, Arts and Sciences, Graduate Program in Ocean Sciences, Los Angeles, CA 90089. Offers MS, PhD. Only Ph.D. and M.S./Ph.D. students are funded.. *Program availability:* Part-time. Terminal master's awarded for partial completion of doctoral program. *Degree requirements:* For master's, thesis; for doctorate, comprehensive exam, thesis/dissertation. *Entrance requirements:* For master's and doctorate, GRE. Additional exam requirements/recommendations for international students: Required—TOEFL. Electronic applications accepted. *Faculty research:* Microbial ecology, biogeochemical cycles, marine chemistry, marine biology, global change.

University of Southern Mississippi, Graduate School, College of Science and Technology, Department of Coastal Sciences, Ocean Springs, MS 39566-7000. Offers MS, PhD. *Program availability:* Part-time. Terminal master's awarded for partial completion of doctoral program. *Degree requirements:* For master's, comprehensive exam, thesis; for doctorate, comprehensive exam, thesis/dissertation. *Entrance requirements:* For master's, GRE General Test, minimum GPA of 3.0 for last 60 hours; for doctorate, GRE General Test, minimum undergraduate GPA of 3.0, graduate 3.5.

Additional exam requirements/recommendations for international students: Required—TOEFL, IELTS. Electronic applications accepted.

University of Southern Mississippi, Graduate School, College of Science and Technology, Department of Marine Science, Stennis Space Center, MS 39529. Offers hydrographic science (MS); marine science (MS, PhD). *Program availability:* Part-time. *Faculty:* 16 full-time (1 woman). *Students:* 42 full-time (18 women), 5 part-time (2 women); includes 13 minority (7 Black or African American, non-Hispanic/Latino; 4 Asian, non-Hispanic/Latino; 1 Hispanic/Latino; 1 Two or more races, non-Hispanic/Latino). Average age 32. 44 applicants, 61% accepted, 22 enrolled. In 2015, 15 master's, 2 doctorates awarded. *Degree requirements:* For master's, comprehensive exam, thesis, oral qualifying exam (marine science); for doctorate, 2 foreign languages, comprehensive exam, thesis/dissertation, oral qualifying exam. *Entrance requirements:* For master's, GRE General Test, minimum GPA of 3.0; for doctorate, GRE General Test, minimum GPA of 3.0 (undergraduate), 3.5 (graduate). Additional exam requirements/recommendations for international students: Required—TOEFL (minimum score 84 iBT). *Application deadline:* For fall admission, 5/1 priority date for domestic and international students; for spring admission, 10/1 for domestic and international students; for summer admission, 3/1 for domestic and international students. Application fee: $60. Electronic applications accepted. *Expenses:* Contact institution. *Financial support:* In 2015–16, 9 students received support, including 1 fellowship with full tuition reimbursement available (averaging $5,300 per year), 4 research assistantships with full tuition reimbursements available (averaging $61,200 per year), 5 teaching assistantships with full tuition reimbursements available (averaging $76,500 per year). Financial award application deadline: 5/1. *Faculty research:* Biological oceanography, geological oceanography; physical oceanography; bio-optics; hydrography; marine chemistry; marine science; numerical modeling; remote sensing; zooplankton; hydrography. *Total annual research expenditures:* $6.5 million. *Unit head:* Dr. William Montrose Graham, Chair and Professor, 228-688-3177, Fax: 228-688-1121, E-mail: monty.graham@usm.edu. *Application contact:* Linda Downs, Senior Office Support Specialist, 228-688-7097, Fax: 228-688-1121, E-mail: linda.downs@usm.edu.
Website: http://www.usm.edu/marine/

University of South Florida, College of Marine Science, Saint Petersburg, FL 33701. Offers marine science (MS, PhD), including biological oceanography, chemical oceanography, geological oceanography, interdisciplinary, marine resource assessment, marine science, physical oceanography. *Program availability:* Part-time. *Faculty:* 25 full-time (7 women). *Students:* 77 full-time (52 women), 21 part-time (10 women); includes 16 minority (1 Black or African American, non-Hispanic/Latino; 1 Asian, non-Hispanic/Latino; 11 Hispanic/Latino; 3 Two or more races, non-Hispanic/Latino), 10 international. Average age 31. 87 applicants, 32% accepted, 21 enrolled. In 2015, 12 master's, 8 doctorates awarded. Terminal master's awarded for partial completion of doctoral program. *Degree requirements:* For master's, comprehensive exam, thesis; for doctorate, comprehensive exam, thesis/dissertation. *Entrance requirements:* For master's and doctorate, GRE General Test, bachelor's degree from regionally-accredited university, preferably in biology, chemistry, geology, physics or math; minimum GPA of 3.0 in upper-division coursework; research interest statement; resume; three letters of recommendation. Additional exam requirements/recommendations for international students: Required—TOEFL (minimum score 550 paper-based; 79 iBT) or IELTS (minimum score 6.5). *Application deadline:* For fall admission, 1/10 for domestic students, 1/2 for international students; for spring admission, 10/1 for domestic students, 6/1 for international students. Applications are processed on a rolling basis. Application fee: $30. *Financial support:* In 2015–16, 55 students received support, including 45 research assistantships with partial tuition reimbursements available (averaging $14,199 per year), 10 teaching assistantships with partial tuition reimbursements available (averaging $14,196 per year); health care benefits and unspecified assistantships also available. Financial award application deadline: 1/15. *Faculty research:* Problems in shelf, coastal and estuarine waters, in the deep ocean, and in the watershed that drains to the coastal zone such as long-term sea-level rise, coral reef demise, recent paleo-climate change, ocean acidification, harmful algal blooms, fisheries management, water quality, shoreline change, and oil-drilling. *Total annual research expenditures:* $12 million. *Unit head:* Dr. Jacqueline E. Dixon, Dean, 727-553-3369, Fax: 727-553-1189, E-mail: jdixon@usf.edu. *Application contact:* Dr. David F. Naar, Associate Professor and Director of Academic Affairs, 727-553-1637, Fax: 727-553-1189, E-mail: naar@usf.edu.
Website: http://www.marine.usf.edu/

The University of Texas at Austin, Graduate School, College of Natural Sciences, Department of Marine Science, Austin, TX 78712-1111. Offers MS, PhD. *Degree requirements:* For master's, thesis; for doctorate, thesis/dissertation. *Entrance requirements:* For master's and doctorate, GRE General Test. Additional exam requirements/recommendations for international students: Required—TOEFL.

University of the Virgin Islands, Graduate Programs, Division of Science and Mathematics, Program in Environmental and Marine Science, Saint Thomas, VI 00802-9990. Offers MS. *Entrance requirements:* For master's, GRE. Additional exam requirements/recommendations for international students: Required—TOEFL (minimum score 550 paper-based).

University of Wisconsin–La Crosse, College of Science and Health, Department of Biology, La Crosse, WI 54601-3742. Offers aquatic sciences (MS); biology (MS); cellular and molecular biology (MS); clinical microbiology (MS); microbiology (MS); nurse anesthesia (MS); physiology (MS). *Program availability:* Part-time. *Students:* 19 full-time (12 women), 50 part-time (26 women); includes 4 minority (3 Asian, non-Hispanic/Latino; 1 Hispanic/Latino), 1 international. Average age 29. 44 applicants, 75% accepted, 27 enrolled. In 2015, 27 master's awarded. *Degree requirements:* For master's, comprehensive exam, thesis. *Entrance requirements:* For master's, GRE General Test, minimum GPA of 2.85. Additional exam requirements/recommendations for international students: Required—TOEFL (minimum score 550 paper-based; 79 iBT). *Application deadline:* For fall admission, 2/1 priority date for domestic and international students; for spring admission, 1/4 priority date for domestic and international students. Applications are processed on a rolling basis. Electronic applications accepted. *Financial support:* Research assistantships with partial tuition reimbursements, Federal Work-Study, scholarships/grants, health care benefits, and tuition waivers (partial) available. Support available to part-time students. Financial award application deadline: 3/15; financial award applicants required to submit FAFSA. *Unit head:* Dr. Mark Sandheinrich, Department Chair, 608-785-8261, E-mail: msandheinrich@uwlax.edu. *Application contact:* Brandon Schaller, Senior Graduate Student Status Examiner, 608-785-8941, E-mail: admissions@uwlax.edu.
Website: http://uwlax.edu/biology/

University of Wisconsin–Madison, Graduate School, College of Letters and Science, Department of Atmospheric and Oceanic Sciences, Madison, WI 53706-1380. Offers MS, PhD. *Program availability:* Part-time. *Degree requirements:* For master's, thesis (for some programs); for doctorate, thesis/dissertation. *Entrance requirements:* For master's and doctorate, GRE General Test, minimum GPA of 3.0; previous course work in chemistry, mathematics, and physics. Electronic applications accepted. *Expenses:* Tuition, state resident: full-time $5364. Tuition, nonresident: full-time $12,027. *Required fees:* $571. Tuition and fees vary according to campus/location, program and reciprocity agreements. *Faculty research:* Satellite meteorology, weather systems, global climate change, numerical modeling, atmosphere-ocean interaction.

Western Washington University, Graduate School, Huxley College of the Environment, Department of Environmental Sciences, Bellingham, WA 98225-5996. Offers environmental science (MS); marine and estuarine science (MS). *Program availability:* Part-time. *Degree requirements:* For master's, thesis. *Entrance requirements:* For master's, GRE General Test, minimum GPA of 3.0 in last 60 semester hours or last 90 quarter hours. Additional exam requirements/recommendations for international students: Required—TOEFL (minimum score 567 paper-based). Electronic applications accepted. *Faculty research:* Landscape ecology, climate change, watershed studies, environmental toxicology and risk assessment, aquatic toxicology, toxic algae, invasive species.

Oceanography

Cornell University, Graduate School, Graduate Fields of Agriculture and Life Sciences, Field of Ecology and Evolutionary Biology, Ithaca, NY 14853-0001. Offers ecology (PhD), including animal ecology, applied ecology, biogeochemistry, community and ecosystem ecology, limnology, oceanography, physiological ecology, plant ecology, population ecology, theoretical ecology, vertebrate zoology; evolutionary biology (PhD), including ecological genetics, paleobiology, population biology, systematics. *Degree requirements:* For doctorate, comprehensive exam, thesis/dissertation, 2 semesters of teaching experience. *Entrance requirements:* For doctorate, GRE General Test, GRE Subject Test (biology), 2 letters of recommendation. Additional exam requirements/recommendations for international students: Required—TOEFL (minimum score 550 paper-based; 77 iBT). Electronic applications accepted. *Faculty research:* Population and organismal biology, population and evolutionary genetics, systematics and macroevolution, biochemistry, conservation biology.

Dalhousie University, Faculty of Science, Department of Oceanography, Halifax, NS B3H 4R2, Canada. Offers M Sc, PhD. *Degree requirements:* For master's, thesis; for doctorate, thesis/dissertation. *Entrance requirements:* Additional exam requirements/recommendations for international students: Required—TOEFL, IELTS, CANTEST, CAEL, or Michigan English Language Assessment Battery. Electronic applications accepted. *Faculty research:* Biological and physical oceanography, chemical and geological oceanography, atmospheric sciences.

Florida Institute of Technology, College of Engineering, Program in Oceanography, Melbourne, FL 32901-6975. Offers biological oceanography (MS); chemical oceanography (MS); coastal management (MS); geological oceanography (MS); oceanography (PhD); physical oceanography (MS). *Program availability:* Part-time. *Students:* 7 full-time (5 women), 10 part-time (5 women); includes 3 minority (1 Hispanic/Latino; 2 Two or more races, non-Hispanic/Latino), 2 international. Average age 27. 28 applicants, 29% accepted, 3 enrolled. In 2015, 3 master's, 1 doctorate awarded. *Degree requirements:* For master's, comprehensive exam (for some programs), seminar, field project, written final exam, internship, technical paper, oral presentation, thesis or final exam; for doctorate, comprehensive exam, thesis/dissertation, seminar, internships, publications, original research. *Entrance requirements:* For master's, GRE General Test, minimum GPA of 3.0, 3 letters of recommendation, resume, transcripts, statement of objectives, appropriate bachelor's degree; for doctorate, GRE General Test, minimum GPA of 3.3, resume, 3 letters of recommendation, statement of objectives, on-campus interview (highly recommended). Additional exam requirements/recommendations for international students: Required—TOEFL (minimum score 550 paper-based; 79 iBT). *Application deadline:* Applications are processed on a rolling basis. Electronic applications accepted. *Expenses: Tuition, area resident:* Full-time $21,690; part-time $1205 per credit hour. *Required fees:* $500. Tuition and fees vary according to degree level, campus/location and program. *Financial support:* Career-related internships or fieldwork, institutionally sponsored loans, tuition waivers (partial), unspecified assistantships, and tuition remissions available. Support available to part-time students. Financial award application deadline: 3/1; financial award applicants required to submit FAFSA. *Faculty research:* Marine geochemistry, ecosystem dynamics, coastal processes, marine pollution, environmental modeling. *Unit head:* Dr. John Windsor, Program Chair, 321-674-7300, E-mail: jwindsor@fit.edu. *Application contact:* Cheryl A. Brown, Associate Director of Graduate Admission, 321-674-7581, Fax: 321-723-9468, E-mail: cbrown@fit.edu.
Website: http://www.coe.fit.edu/dmes

Florida State University, The Graduate School, College of Arts and Sciences, Department of Earth, Ocean and Atmospheric Science, Program in Oceanography, Tallahassee, FL 32306-4320. Offers aquatic environmental science (MS, PSM); oceanography (MS, PhD). *Faculty:* 16 full-time (4 women). *Students:* 41 full-time (23 women); includes 4 minority (2 Asian, non-Hispanic/Latino; 1 Hispanic/Latino; 1 Two or more races, non-Hispanic/Latino), 10 international. Average age 26. 47 applicants, 23% accepted, 7 enrolled. In 2015, 3 master's, 1 doctorate awarded. *Degree requirements:* For master's, thesis; for doctorate, comprehensive exam, thesis/dissertation. *Entrance requirements:* For master's and doctorate, GRE General Test, minimum upper-division GPA of 3.0. Additional exam requirements/recommendations for international students: Required—TOEFL (minimum score 550 paper-based; 80 iBT). *Application deadline:* For fall admission, 2/15 priority date for domestic and international students; for spring admission, 9/15 priority date for domestic and international students. Applications are processed on a rolling basis. Application fee: $35. Electronic applications accepted. *Expenses: Tuition, area resident:* Full-time $7263; part-time $403.50 per credit hour. Tuition, nonresident: full-time $18,087; part-time $1004.85 per credit hour. *Required fees:* $1365; $75.81 per credit hour. $20 per semester. Tuition and fees vary according to campus/location. *Financial support:* In 2015–16, 28 students received support,

including 2 fellowships with full tuition reimbursements available, 20 research assistantships with full tuition reimbursements available, 8 teaching assistantships with full tuition reimbursements available. Financial award application deadline: 2/15; financial award applicants required to submit FAFSA. *Faculty research:* Trace metals in seawater, currents and waves, modeling, benthic ecology, marine biogeochemistry. *Unit head:* Dr. Jeffrey Chanton, Area Coordinator, 850-644-6700, Fax: 850-644-2581, E-mail: jchanton@fsu.edu. *Application contact:* Michaela Lupiani, Academic Coordinator, 850-644-6205, Fax: 850-644-2581, E-mail: admissions@ocean.fsu.edu.
Website: http://www.eoas.fsu.edu

Louisiana State University and Agricultural & Mechanical College, Graduate School, School of the Coast and Environment, Department of Oceanography and Coastal Sciences, Baton Rouge, LA 70803. Offers MS, PhD.

Massachusetts Institute of Technology, School of Engineering, Department of Civil and Environmental Engineering, Cambridge, MA 02139. Offers biological oceanography (PhD, Sc D); chemical oceanography (PhD, Sc D); civil and environmental engineering (M Eng, SM, PhD, Sc D); civil and environmental systems (PhD, Sc D); civil engineering (PhD, Sc D, CE); coastal engineering (PhD, Sc D); construction engineering and management (PhD, Sc D); environmental biology (PhD, Sc D); environmental chemistry (PhD, Sc D); environmental engineering (PhD, Sc D); environmental fluid mechanics (PhD, Sc D); geotechnical and geoenvironmental engineering (PhD, Sc D); hydrology (PhD, Sc D); information technology (PhD, Sc D); oceanographic engineering (PhD, Sc D); structures and materials (PhD, Sc D); transportation (PhD, Sc D); SM/MBA. *Faculty:* 27 full-time (5 women). *Students:* 183 full-time (59 women); includes 19 minority (1 Black or African American, non-Hispanic/Latino; 7 Asian, non-Hispanic/Latino; 8 Hispanic/Latino; 3 Two or more races, non-Hispanic/Latino), 106 international. Average age 27. 513 applicants, 20% accepted, 56 enrolled. In 2015, 77 master's, 18 doctorates, 1 other advanced degree awarded. *Degree requirements:* For master's, thesis; for doctorate, comprehensive exam, thesis/dissertation; for CE, comprehensive exam, thesis. *Entrance requirements:* For master's and doctorate, GRE General Test; for CE, GRE General Test. Additional exam requirements/recommendations for international students: Required—TOEFL (minimum score 577 paper-based; 100 iBT), IELTS (minimum score 7). *Application deadline:* For fall admission, 12/15 for domestic and international students. Application fee: $75. Electronic applications accepted. *Expenses: Tuition:* Full-time $46,400; part-time $725 per credit. One-time fee: $304 full-time. Full-time tuition and fees vary according to course load and program. *Financial support:* In 2015–16, 150 students received support, including 38 fellowships (averaging $38,000 per year), 111 research assistantships (averaging $35,100 per year), 9 teaching assistantships (averaging $39,900 per year); Federal Work-Study, institutionally sponsored loans, scholarships/grants, traineeships, health care benefits, and unspecified assistantships also available. Support available to part-time students. Financial award application deadline: 4/15; financial award applicants required to submit FAFSA. *Faculty research:* Environmental chemistry, environmental fluid mechanics and coastal engineering, environmental microbiology, geotechnical engineering and geomechanics, hydrology and hydroclimatology, infrastructure systems, mechanics of materials and structures, transportation systems. *Total annual research expenditures:* $24.8 million. *Unit head:* Prof. Markus Buehler, Department Head, 617-253-7101. *Application contact:* Graduate Admissions Coordinator, 617-253-7119, E-mail: cee-admissions@mit.edu.
Website: http://cee.mit.edu/

Massachusetts Institute of Technology, School of Science, Department of Biology, Cambridge, MA 02139. Offers biochemistry (PhD); biological oceanography (PhD); biology (PhD); biophysical chemistry and molecular structure (PhD); cell biology (PhD); computational and systems biology (PhD); developmental biology (PhD); genetics (PhD); immunology (PhD); microbiology (PhD); molecular biology (PhD); neurobiology (PhD). *Faculty:* 57 full-time (14 women). *Students:* 283 full-time (137 women); includes 83 minority (3 Black or African American, non-Hispanic/Latino; 1 American Indian or Alaska Native, non-Hispanic/Latino; 38 Asian, non-Hispanic/Latino; 31 Hispanic/Latino; 10 Two or more races, non-Hispanic/Latino), 48 international. Average age 26. 673 applicants, 14% accepted, 46 enrolled. In 2015, 32 doctorates awarded. *Degree requirements:* For doctorate, comprehensive exam, thesis/dissertation, teaching assistantship during two semesters. *Entrance requirements:* For doctorate, GRE General Test. Additional exam requirements/recommendations for international students: Required—TOEFL (minimum score 577 paper-based), IELTS. *Application deadline:* For fall admission, 12/1 for domestic and international students. Application fee: $75. Electronic applications accepted. *Expenses: Tuition:* Full-time $46,400; part-time $725 per credit. One-time fee: $304 full-time. Full-time tuition and fees vary according to course load and program. *Financial support:* In 2015–16, 235 students received support, including 118 fellowships (averaging $37,500 per year), 163 research assistantships (averaging $38,900 per year), 1 teaching assistantship; Federal Work-Study, institutionally sponsored loans, scholarships/grants, traineeships, health care benefits, and unspecified assistantships also available. Support available to part-time students. Financial award application deadline: 4/15; financial award applicants required to submit FAFSA. *Faculty research:* Cellular, developmental and molecular (plant and animal) biology; biochemistry, bioengineering, biophysics and structural biology; classical and molecular genetics, stem cell and epigenetics; immunology and microbiology; cancer biology, molecular medicine, neurobiology and human disease; computational and systems biology. *Total annual research expenditures:* $42.8 million. *Unit head:* Prof. Alan Grossman, Department Head, 617-253-4701. *Application contact:* Biology Education Office, 617-253-3717, Fax: 617-258-9329, E-mail: gradbio@mit.edu.
Website: https://biology.mit.edu/

Massachusetts Institute of Technology, School of Science, Department of Earth, Atmospheric, and Planetary Sciences, Cambridge, MA 02139. Offers atmospheric chemistry (PhD, Sc D); atmospheric science (SM, PhD, Sc D); chemical oceanography (SM, PhD, Sc D); climate physics and chemistry (SM, PhD, Sc D); earth and planetary sciences (SM); geochemistry (PhD, Sc D); geology (PhD, Sc D); geophysics (PhD, Sc D); marine geology and geophysics (SM, PhD, Sc D); physical oceanography (SM, PhD, Sc D); planetary sciences (PhD, Sc D). *Faculty:* 36 full-time (8 women). *Students:* 166 full-time (75 women), 1 part-time (0 women); includes 23 minority (1 Black or African American, non-Hispanic/Latino; 7 Asian, non-Hispanic/Latino; 6 Hispanic/Latino; 9 Two or more races, non-Hispanic/Latino), 54 international. Average age 27. 228 applicants, 26% accepted, 33 enrolled. In 2015, 6 master's, 24 doctorates awarded. Terminal master's awarded for partial completion of doctoral program. *Degree requirements:* For master's, thesis; for doctorate, comprehensive exam, thesis/dissertation. *Entrance requirements:* For master's, GRE General Test; for doctorate, GRE General Test, GRE Subject Test in chemistry or physics (for planetary sciences area). Additional exam requirements/recommendations for international students: Required—TOEFL (minimum score 600 paper-based; 100 iBT), IELTS (minimum score 7). *Application deadline:* For fall admission, 1/5 for domestic and international students; for spring admission, 11/1 for domestic and international students. Application fee: $75. Electronic applications accepted. *Expenses: Tuition:* Full-time $46,400; part-time $725 per credit. One-time fee: $304 full-time. Full-time tuition and fees vary according to course load and program. *Financial support:* In 2015–16, 99 students received support, including 60 fellowships (averaging $40,700 per year), 76 research assistantships (averaging $38,000 per year), 15 teaching assistantships (averaging $36,100 per year); Federal Work-Study, institutionally sponsored loans, scholarships/grants, traineeships, health care benefits, and unspecified assistantships also available. Support available to part-time students. Financial award application deadline: 4/15; financial award applicants required to submit FAFSA. *Faculty research:* Earth: origin, composition, structure, and dynamics of (and interactions between) the atmosphere, oceans, surface, and interior of the earth; planets: formation, dynamics, and evolution of planetary systems and the characterization of exoplanets; climate: characterization of past, present, and potential future climates; studies of the causes and consequences of climate change; life: co-evolution of life and environmental systems. *Total annual research expenditures:* $25.3 million. *Unit head:* Prof. Robert van der Hilst, Department Head, 617-253-2127, Fax: 617-253-8298, E-mail: eapsinfo@mit.edu. *Application contact:* EAPS Education Office, 617-253-3381, Fax: 617-253-8298, E-mail: eapsinfo@mit.edu.
Website: http://eapsweb.mit.edu/

McGill University, Faculty of Graduate and Postdoctoral Studies, Faculty of Science, Department of Atmospheric and Oceanic Sciences, Montréal, QC H3A 2T5, Canada. Offers atmospheric science (M Sc, PhD); physical oceanography (M Sc, PhD). PhD program in physical oceanography offered jointly with Université Laval.

Memorial University of Newfoundland, School of Graduate Studies, Department of Physics and Physical Oceanography, St. John's, NL A1C 5S7, Canada. Offers atomic and molecular physics (PhD); condensed matter physics (PhD); physical oceanography (M Sc, PhD); physics (M Sc). *Program availability:* Part-time. *Degree requirements:* For master's, thesis, seminar presentation on thesis topic; for doctorate, comprehensive exam, thesis/dissertation, oral defense of thesis. *Entrance requirements:* For master's, honors B Sc or equivalent; for doctorate, M Sc or equivalent. *Application deadline:* Applications are processed on a rolling basis. Application fee: $50 Canadian dollars ($100 Canadian dollars for international students). Electronic applications accepted. *Expenses: Tuition, area resident:* Full-time $2199 Canadian dollars. *International tuition:* $2859 Canadian dollars full-time. *Financial support:* Fellowships, research assistantships, and teaching assistantships available. *Faculty research:* Experiment and theory in atomic and molecular physics, condensed matter physics, physical oceanography, theoretical geophysics and applied nuclear physics. *Unit head:* Dr. J. Lagowski, Head, 709-864-8738, Fax: 709-864-8739, E-mail: jolantal@mun.ca. *Application contact:* Dr. Stephanie Curnoe, Graduate Officer, 709-864-8888, Fax: 709-864-8739, E-mail: gradphysicsInfo@mun.ca.
Website: http://www.mun.ca/physics

Naval Postgraduate School, Departments and Academic Groups, Department of Meteorology, Monterey, CA 93943. Offers meteorology (MS, PhD); meteorology and physical oceanography (MS). Program only open to commissioned officers of the United States and friendly nations and selected United States federal civilian employees. *Program availability:* Part-time. *Degree requirements:* For master's, thesis; for doctorate, one foreign language, thesis/dissertation. *Faculty research:* Air-sea interactions, boundary layer meteorology, climate dynamics, numerical weather prediction, tropical cyclones.

Naval Postgraduate School, Departments and Academic Groups, Department of Oceanography, Monterey, CA 93943. Offers physical oceanography (MS, PhD). Program only open to commissioned officers of the United States and friendly nations and selected United States federal civilian employees. *Program availability:* Part-time. *Degree requirements:* For master's, thesis; for doctorate, thesis/dissertation. *Faculty research:* Lagrangian acoustic subsurface technology, naval ocean analysis prediction, nearshore processes, unmanned vehicles, ocean acoustics, turbulence, waves.

Naval Postgraduate School, Departments and Academic Groups, Undersea Warfare Academic Group, Monterey, CA 93943. Offers applied mathematics (MS); applied physics (MS); applied science (MS), including acoustics, operations research, physical oceanography, signal processing; electrical engineering (MS); engineering acoustics (MS, PhD); engineering science (MS), including electrical engineering, mechanical engineering; mechanical engineer (ME); mechanical engineering (MS, MSME); meteorology (MS); operations research (MS); physical oceanography (MS). Program only open to commissioned officers of the United States and friendly nations and selected United States federal civilian employees. *Program availability:* Part-time. *Degree requirements:* For master's, thesis. *Faculty research:* Unmanned/autonomous vehicles, sea mines and countermeasures, submarine warfare in the twentieth and twenty-first centuries.

North Carolina State University, Graduate School, College of Physical and Mathematical Sciences, Department of Marine, Earth, and Atmospheric Sciences, Raleigh, NC 27695. Offers marine, earth, and atmospheric sciences (MS, PhD); meteorology (MS, PhD); oceanography (MS, PhD). PhD offered jointly with The University of North Carolina Wilmington. Terminal master's awarded for partial completion of doctoral program. *Degree requirements:* For master's, thesis (for some programs), final oral exam; for doctorate, comprehensive exam, thesis/dissertation, final oral exam, preliminary oral and written exams. *Entrance requirements:* For master's, GRE General Test, minimum GPA of 3.0; for doctorate, GRE General Test, GRE Subject Test (for disciplines in biological oceanography and geology), minimum GPA of 3.0. Additional exam requirements/recommendations for international students: Required—TOEFL (minimum score 550 paper-based). Electronic applications accepted. *Faculty research:* Boundary layer and air quality meteorology; climate and mesoscale dynamics; biological, chemical, geological, and physical oceanography; hard rock, soft rock, environmental, and paleo-geology.

Nova Southeastern University, Halmos College of Natural Sciences and Oceanography, Fort Lauderdale, FL 33314-7796. Offers biological sciences (MS); coastal studies (Certificate); coastal zone management (MS); marine and coastal climate change (Certificate); marine and coastal studies (MA); marine biology (MS); marine biology and oceanography (PhD), including marine biology, oceanography; marine environmental sciences (MS). *Program availability:* Part-time, evening/weekend, 100% online, blended/hybrid learning. *Faculty:* 17 full-time (3 women), 22 part-time/adjunct (11 women). *Students:* 100 full-time (57 women), 114 part-time (76 women); includes 32 minority (6 Black or African American, non-Hispanic/Latino; 1 American Indian or Alaska Native, non-Hispanic/Latino; 6 Asian, non-Hispanic/Latino; 10 Hispanic/Latino; 9 Two or more races, non-Hispanic/Latino), 5 international. Average age 30. 85 applicants, 60% accepted, 39 enrolled. In 2015, 47 master's, 2 doctorates, 9 other advanced degrees awarded. *Degree requirements:* For master's, thesis; for doctorate, comprehensive exam, thesis/dissertation, departmental qualifying exam. *Entrance requirements:* For master's, GRE General Test, 3 letters of recommendation, BS/BA in natural science (for marine biology program), BS/BA in biology (for biological sciences program), minor in the natural sciences or equivalent (for coastal zone management and marine environmental sciences); for doctorate, GRE General Test, master's degree. Additional exam requirements/recommendations for international students: Required—TOEFL (minimum score 550 paper-based). *Application deadline:* Applications are processed on a rolling basis. Application fee: $50. Electronic applications accepted.

Expenses: $34,749 per year (for PhD); $3,738 per course (for MS and Graduate Certificate). **Financial support:** In 2015–16, 157 students received support, including 14 fellowships with tuition reimbursements available (averaging $25,000 per year), 42 research assistantships with tuition reimbursements available (averaging $19,000 per year); teaching assistantships, career-related internships or fieldwork, Federal Work-Study, scholarships/grants, health care benefits, tuition waivers (full and partial), and unspecified assistantships also available. Support available to part-time students. Financial award application deadline: 4/15; financial award applicants required to submit FAFSA. **Faculty research:** Physical oceanography, biological oceanography, molecular and microbiology, ecology and evolution, coral reefs. **Total annual research expenditures:** $5 million. **Unit head:** Dr. Richard Dodge, Dean, 954-262-3600, Fax: 954-262-4020, E-mail: dodge@nsu.nova.edu. **Application contact:** Dr. Bernhard Riegl, Chair, Department of Marine and Environmental Sciences, 954-262-3600, Fax: 954-262-4020, E-mail: rieglb@nova.edu.
Website: http://cnso.nova.edu

Old Dominion University, College of Sciences, Department of Ocean, Earth and Atmospheric Sciences, Norfolk, VA 23529. Offers ocean and earth sciences (MS); oceanography (PhD). **Program availability:** Part-time. **Faculty:** 27 full-time (8 women). **Students:** 38 full-time (21 women), 2 part-time (1 woman); includes 6 minority (1 Black or African American, non-Hispanic/Latino; 3 Asian, non-Hispanic/Latino; 2 Hispanic/Latino), 3 international. Average age 31. 29 applicants, 59% accepted, 12 enrolled. In 2015, 9 master's, 1 doctorate awarded. Terminal master's awarded for partial completion of doctoral program. **Degree requirements:** For master's, comprehensive exam (for some programs), thesis (for some programs), 10 days of ship time or fieldwork; for doctorate, comprehensive exam, thesis/dissertation, 10 days of ship time or fieldwork. **Entrance requirements:** For master's and doctorate, GRE General Test, minimum GPA of 3.0 in major, 2.8 overall. Additional exam requirements/recommendations for international students: Required—TOEFL (minimum score 550 paper-based). **Application deadline:** For fall admission, 2/1 priority date for domestic and international students. Applications are processed on a rolling basis. Application fee: $50. Electronic applications accepted. **Expenses:** Tuition, state resident: full-time $11,136; part-time $464 per credit hour. Tuition, nonresident: full-time $27,840; part-time $1160 per credit hour. **Required fees:** $64 per semester. Tuition and fees vary according to campus/location, program and reciprocity agreements. **Financial support:** In 2015–16, 21 students received support, including 1 fellowship with full tuition reimbursement available (averaging $22,500 per year), 19 teaching assistantships with full tuition reimbursements available (averaging $22,500 per year); career-related internships or fieldwork, scholarships/grants, and unspecified assistantships also available. Support available to part-time students. Financial award application deadline: 2/1; financial award applicants required to submit FAFSA. **Faculty research:** Biological, chemical, geological, and physical oceanography. **Unit head:** Dr. Rodger Harvey, Department Chair, 757-683-4285, Fax: 757-683-5303, E-mail: rharvey@odu.edu. **Application contact:** William Heffelfinger, Director of Graduate Admissions, 757-683-5554, Fax: 757-683-3255, E-mail: gradadmit@odu.edu.
Website: http://www.odu.edu/sci/oceanography/

Oregon State University, College of Earth, Ocean, and Atmospheric Sciences, Program in Ocean, Earth, and Atmospheric Sciences, Corvallis, OR 97331. Offers atmospheric sciences (MA, MS, PhD); geological oceanography (MA, MS, PhD); geophysics (MA, MS, PhD); ocean ecology and biogeochemistry (MS, PhD); physical oceanography (MA, MS, PhD). **Program availability:** Part-time. **Faculty:** 38 full-time (11 women), 3 part-time/adjunct (1 woman). **Students:** 51 full-time (26 women), 4 part-time (1 woman); includes 7 minority (1 Asian, non-Hispanic/Latino; 4 Hispanic/Latino; 2 Two or more races, non-Hispanic/Latino), 12 international. Average age 29. 116 applicants, 16% accepted, 9 enrolled. In 2015, 5 master's, 1 doctorate awarded. **Entrance requirements:** For master's, GRE. Additional exam requirements/recommendations for international students: Required—TOEFL (minimum score 80 iBT), IELTS (minimum score 6.5). **Application deadline:** For fall admission, 1/5 for domestic students. Application fee: $75 ($85 for international students). **Expenses:** Tuition, state resident: full-time $12,150; part-time $450 per credit. Tuition, nonresident: full-time $20,952; part-time $776 per credit. **Required fees:** $1572; $1443 per unit. One-time fee: $350. Tuition and fees vary according to course load, campus/location and program. **Unit head:** Dr. Rob Wheatcroft, Professor/Program Head, Earth Systems. **Application contact:** Student Advisor, 541-737-5188, E-mail: student_advisor@coas.oregonstate.edu.
Website: http://ceoas.oregonstate.edu/academics/ocean/

Princeton University, Graduate School, Department of Geosciences, Program in Atmospheric and Oceanic Sciences, Princeton, NJ 08544-1019. Offers PhD. **Degree requirements:** For doctorate, one foreign language, thesis/dissertation. **Entrance requirements:** For doctorate, GRE General Test, GRE Subject Test. Additional exam requirements/recommendations for international students: Required—TOEFL (minimum score 600 paper-based). Electronic applications accepted. **Faculty research:** Climate dynamics, middle atmosphere dynamics and chemistry, oceanic circulation, marine geochemistry, numerical modeling.

Rutgers University–New Brunswick, Graduate School-New Brunswick, Program in Oceanography, Piscataway, NJ 08854-8097. Offers MS, PhD. Terminal master's awarded for partial completion of doctoral program. **Degree requirements:** For master's, thesis; for doctorate, comprehensive exam, thesis/dissertation. **Entrance requirements:** For master's and doctorate, GRE General Test, 1 year course work in calculus, physics, chemistry. Additional exam requirements/recommendations for international students: Required—TOEFL. Electronic applications accepted. **Faculty research:** Coastal observations and modeling, estuarine ecology/fish/benthos, geochemistry, deep sea ecology/hydrothermal vents, molecular biology applications.

Texas A&M University, College of Geosciences, Department of Oceanography, College Station, TX 77843. Offers oceanography (MS, PhD). **Faculty:** 21. **Students:** 60 full-time (29 women), 10 part-time (4 women); includes 10 minority (2 Black or African American, non-Hispanic/Latino; 1 American Indian or Alaska Native, non-Hispanic/Latino; 1 Asian, non-Hispanic/Latino; 4 Hispanic/Latino; 2 Two or more races, non-Hispanic/Latino), 27 international. Average age 29. 27 applicants, 78% accepted, 16 enrolled. In 2015, 6 master's, 8 doctorates awarded. **Degree requirements:** For master's, thesis; for doctorate, thesis/dissertation. **Entrance requirements:** For master's and doctorate, GRE General Test. Additional exam requirements/recommendations for international students: Required—TOEFL (minimum score 550 paper-based; 80 iBT), IELTS (minimum score 6), PTE (minimum score 53). **Application deadline:** For fall admission, 1/15 priority date for domestic students; for spring admission, 10/1 for domestic students. Applications are processed on a rolling basis. Application fee: $50 ($90 for international students). Electronic applications accepted. **Expenses:** Contact institution. **Financial support:** In 2015–16, 67 students received support, including 11 fellowships with tuition reimbursements available (averaging $8,902 per year), 16 research assistantships with tuition reimbursements available (averaging $7,735 per year), 16 teaching assistantships with tuition reimbursements available (averaging $8,000 per year); career-related internships or fieldwork, institutionally sponsored loans, scholarships/grants, traineeships, health care benefits, tuition waivers (full and partial), and unspecified assistantships also available. Support available to part-time students.

Financial award application deadline: 3/15; financial award applicants required to submit FAFSA. **Faculty research:** Ocean circulation, climate studies, coastal and shelf dynamics, marine phytoplankton, stable isotope geochemistry. **Unit head:** Dr. Debbie Thomas, Professor and Department Head, 979-862-7248, Fax: 979-845-6331. **Application contact:** Brady Dennis, Academic Advisor II, 979-845-5346, Fax: 979-845-6331, E-mail: brady-dennis@tamu.edu.
Website: http://ocean.tamu.edu

Université du Québec à Rimouski, Graduate Programs, Program in Oceanography, Rimouski, QC G5L 3A1, Canada. Offers M Sc, PhD. **Program availability:** Part-time. **Degree requirements:** For master's, thesis; for doctorate, thesis/dissertation. **Entrance requirements:** For master's, appropriate bachelor's degree, proficiency in French; for doctorate, appropriate master's degree, proficiency in French.

Université Laval, Faculty of Sciences and Engineering, Program in Oceanography, Québec, QC G1K 7P4, Canada. Offers PhD. Program offered jointly with McGill University and Université du Québec à Rimouski. **Degree requirements:** For doctorate, comprehensive exam, thesis/dissertation. **Entrance requirements:** For doctorate, knowledge of French, knowledge of English. Additional exam requirements/recommendations for international students: Required—TOEFL. Electronic applications accepted.

University of Alaska Fairbanks, School of Fisheries and Ocean Sciences, Program in Marine Sciences and Limnology, Fairbanks, AK 99775-7220. Offers marine biology (MS, PhD); oceanography (MS, PhD). **Program availability:** Part-time. **Faculty:** 4 full-time (1 woman). **Students:** 31 full-time (20 women), 10 part-time (7 women); includes 6 minority (1 Asian, non-Hispanic/Latino; 4 Hispanic/Latino; 1 Two or more races, non-Hispanic/Latino), 8 international. Average age 31. 26 applicants, 46% accepted, 12 enrolled. In 2015, 10 master's, 3 doctorates awarded. **Median time to degree:** Of those who began their doctoral program in fall 2007, 100% received their degree in 8 years or less. **Degree requirements:** For master's, comprehensive exam, thesis, oral defense of thesis; for doctorate, comprehensive exam, thesis/dissertation, oral defense of dissertation. **Entrance requirements:** For master's, GRE General Test, bachelor's degree from accredited institution with minimum cumulative undergraduate and major GPA of 3.0; for doctorate, GRE General Test, minimum cumulative GPA of 3.0. Additional exam requirements/recommendations for international students: Required—TOEFL (minimum score 550 paper-based; 79 iBT), IELTS (minimum score 6.5). **Application deadline:** For fall admission, 5/1 for domestic students, 4/1 for international students; for spring admission, 9/15 for domestic students, 8/15 for international students. Applications are processed on a rolling basis. Application fee: $60. Electronic applications accepted. **Expenses:** Tuition, state resident: full-time $7614; part-time $423 per credit. Tuition, nonresident: full-time $15,552; part-time $864 per credit. **Required fees:** $38 per credit. $187 per semester. Tuition and fees vary according to course level, course load, program and reciprocity agreements. **Financial support:** In 2015–16, 29 research assistantships with full tuition reimbursements (averaging $14,427 per year), 5 teaching assistantships with full tuition reimbursements (averaging $7,083 per year) were awarded; fellowships with full tuition reimbursements, career-related internships or fieldwork, Federal Work-Study, scholarships/grants, health care benefits, and unspecified assistantships also available. Support available to part-time students. Financial award application deadline: 7/1; financial award applicants required to submit FAFSA. **Total annual research expenditures:** $24.1 million. **Unit head:** Katrin Iken, Co-Chair, 907-474-7289, Fax: 907-474-5863, E-mail: info@sfos.uaf.edu. **Application contact:** Mary Kreta, Director of Admissions, 907-474-7500, Fax: 907-474-7097, E-mail: admissions@alaska.edu.
Website: http://www.uaf.edu/sfos/academics/graduate/

The University of British Columbia, Faculty of Science, Department of Earth, Ocean and Atmospheric Sciences, Vancouver, BC V6T 1Z4, Canada. Offers atmospheric science (M Sc, PhD); geological engineering (M Eng, MA Sc, PhD); geological sciences (M Sc, PhD); geophysics (M Sc, MA Sc, PhD); oceanography (M Sc, PhD). **Degree requirements:** For master's, one foreign language, thesis (for some programs); for doctorate, one foreign language, comprehensive exam, thesis/dissertation. **Entrance requirements:** Additional exam requirements/recommendations for international students: Required—TOEFL (minimum score 600 paper-based; 100 iBT). **Faculty research:** Oceans and atmosphere, environmental earth science, hydro geology, mineral deposits, geophysics.

University of California, Los Angeles, Graduate Division, College of Letters and Science, Department of Atmospheric and Oceanic Sciences, Los Angeles, CA 90095. Offers MS, PhD. Terminal master's awarded for partial completion of doctoral program. **Degree requirements:** For master's, comprehensive exam or thesis; for doctorate, thesis/dissertation, oral and written qualifying exams; 2 quarters of teaching experience. **Entrance requirements:** For master's and doctorate, GRE General Test, bachelor's degree; minimum undergraduate GPA of 3.0 (or its equivalent if letter grade system not used). Additional exam requirements/recommendations for international students: Required—TOEFL. Electronic applications accepted.

University of California, San Diego, Graduate Division, Scripps Institution of Oceanography, La Jolla, CA 92093. Offers climate science and policy (MAS); earth sciences (MS, PhD); geophysics (PhD); marine biodiversity and conservation (MAS); marine biology (MS, PhD); oceanography (MS, PhD). PhD in geophysics is offered jointly with San Diego State University. **Students:** 262 full-time (137 women), 11 part-time (1 woman); includes 51 minority (11 Black or African American, non-Hispanic/Latino; 3 American Indian or Alaska Native, non-Hispanic/Latino; 21 Asian, non-Hispanic/Latino; 16 Hispanic/Latino), 56 international. 332 applicants, 24% accepted, 47 enrolled. In 2015, 38 master's, 28 doctorates awarded. Terminal master's awarded for partial completion of doctoral program. **Degree requirements:** For master's, comprehensive exam (for some programs), thesis (for some programs); for doctorate, comprehensive exam, thesis/dissertation. **Entrance requirements:** For master's and doctorate, GRE General Test, GRE Subject Test (encouraged for ocean biosciences applicants), minimum GPA of 3.0. Additional exam requirements/recommendations for international students: Required—TOEFL (minimum score 550 paper-based; 80 iBT), IELTS (minimum score 7). **Application deadline:** For fall admission, 12/10 for domestic students. Application fee: $90 ($110 for international students). Electronic applications accepted. **Expenses:** Tuition, state resident: full-time $11,220. Tuition, nonresident: full-time $26,322. **Required fees:** $1800. **Financial support:** Fellowships, research assistantships, teaching assistantships, scholarships/grants, traineeships, and unspecified assistantships available. Financial award applicants required to submit FAFSA. **Faculty research:** Biodiversity and conservation, earth and planetary chemistry, alternative energy, global environmental monitoring, air-sea boundary, tectonic margins and the interactions between systems and environments. **Unit head:** Brian Palenik, Chair, 858-534-7505, E-mail: bpalenik@ucsd.edu. **Application contact:** Gilbert Bretado, Graduate Coordinator, 858-534-1694, E-mail: siodept@sio.ucsd.edu.
Website: https://scripps.ucsd.edu/education

University of Colorado Boulder, Graduate School, College of Arts and Sciences, Department of Atmospheric and Oceanic Sciences, Boulder, CO 80309. Offers MS,

Peterson's Graduate Programs in the Physical Sciences, Mathematics, Agricultural Sciences, the Environment & Natural Resources 2017

www.petersons.com **145**

PhD. *Faculty:* 13 full-time (7 women). *Students:* 48 full-time (22 women), 3 part-time (1 woman); includes 7 minority (2 Asian, non-Hispanic/Latino; 3 Hispanic/Latino; 2 Two or more races, non-Hispanic/Latino), 9 international. Average age 30. 111 applicants, 25% accepted, 12 enrolled. In 2015, 12 master's, 12 doctorates awarded. *Entrance requirements:* For master's, minimum undergraduate GPA of 3.0. *Application deadline:* For fall admission, 1/1 for domestic students, 12/1 for international students; for spring admission, 10/1 for domestic and international students. Application fee: $50 ($70 for international students). Electronic applications accepted. Application fee is waived when completed online. *Financial support:* In 2015–16, 96 students received support, including 2 fellowships (averaging $14,657 per year), 25 research assistantships with tuition reimbursements available (averaging $37,954 per year), 14 teaching assistantships with tuition reimbursements available (averaging $34,468 per year); institutionally sponsored loans, scholarships/grants, health care benefits, and unspecified assistantships also available. Financial award applicants required to submit FAFSA. *Faculty research:* Atmospheric sciences, atmospheric physics, atmospheric structure and dynamics, global change, climatology. *Total annual research expenditures:* $12.6 million. *Application contact:* E-mail: atocasst@colorado.edu.

Website: http://atoc.colorado.edu/

University of Connecticut, Graduate School, College of Liberal Arts and Sciences, Department of Marine Sciences, Storrs, CT 06269. Offers MS, PhD. Terminal master's awarded for partial completion of doctoral program. *Degree requirements:* For master's, comprehensive exam; for doctorate, thesis/dissertation. *Entrance requirements:* Additional exam requirements/recommendations for international students: Required—TOEFL (minimum score 550 paper-based). Electronic applications accepted.

University of Delaware, College of Earth, Ocean, and Environment, School of Marine Science and Policy, Newark, DE 19716. Offers marine policy (MMP); marine studies (MS, PhD), including marine biosciences, oceanography, physical ocean science and engineering; oceanography (PhD).

University of Hawaii at Manoa, Graduate Division, School of Ocean and Earth Science and Technology, Department of Oceanography, Honolulu, HI 96822. Offers MS, PhD. *Program availability:* Part-time. *Faculty:* 60 full-time (10 women), 8 part-time/adjunct (0 women). *Students:* 53 full-time (40 women), 2 part-time (1 woman); includes 12 minority (5 Asian, non-Hispanic/Latino; 2 Hispanic/Latino; 5 Two or more races, non-Hispanic/Latino), 14 international. Average age 29. 51 applicants, 20% accepted, 6 enrolled. In 2015, 10 master's, 7 doctorates awarded. Terminal master's awarded for partial completion of doctoral program. *Degree requirements:* For master's, one foreign language, comprehensive exam, thesis, field experience; for doctorate, one foreign language, comprehensive exam, thesis/dissertation, field experience. *Entrance requirements:* For master's and doctorate, GRE General Test. Additional exam requirements/recommendations for international students: Required—TOEFL (minimum score 560 paper-based; 83 iBT), IELTS (minimum score 5). *Application deadline:* For fall admission, 1/15 for domestic and international students; for spring admission, 9/1 for domestic students, 8/15 for international students. Application fee: $100. *Financial support:* In 2015–16, 4 students received support, including 8 fellowships (averaging $1,666 per year), 63 research assistantships (averaging $23,738 per year), 8 teaching assistantships (averaging $21,931 per year); career-related internships or fieldwork, institutionally sponsored loans, and tuition waivers (full and partial) also available. Financial award applicants required to submit FAFSA. *Faculty research:* Physical oceanography, marine chemistry, biological oceanography, atmospheric chemistry, marine geology. *Unit head:* Brian Taylor, Dean, 808-956-6182, E-mail: taylorb@hawaii.edu. *Application contact:* Kelvin Richards, Graduate Chair, 808-956-2913, Fax: 808-956-5035, E-mail: rkelvin@hawaii.edu.

Website: http://imina.soest.hawaii.edu/oceanography/

University of Maine, Graduate School, College of Natural Sciences, Forestry, and Agriculture, School of Marine Sciences, Orono, ME 04469. Offers marine bio-resources (MS, PhD); marine biology (MS, PhD); marine policy (MS); oceanography (MS, PhD). *Program availability:* Part-time. *Faculty:* 26 full-time (9 women), 11 part-time/adjunct (0 women). *Students:* 57 full-time (38 women); includes 2 minority (1 American Indian or Alaska Native, non-Hispanic/Latino; 1 Asian, non-Hispanic/Latino), 8 international. Average age 28. 95 applicants, 19% accepted, 16 enrolled. In 2015, 9 master's, 5 doctorates awarded. *Degree requirements:* For master's, thesis; for doctorate, comprehensive exam, thesis/dissertation. *Entrance requirements:* For master's and doctorate, GRE General Test. Additional exam requirements/recommendations for international students: Required—TOEFL (minimum score 550 paper-based; 79 iBT). *Application deadline:* Applications are processed on a rolling basis. Application fee: $65. Electronic applications accepted. *Financial support:* In 2015–16, 54 students received support, including 2 fellowships (averaging $22,400 per year), 41 research assistantships with tuition reimbursements available (averaging $14,600 per year), 10 teaching assistantships with tuition reimbursements available (averaging $14,600 per year); career-related internships or fieldwork, Federal Work-Study, and tuition waivers (full and partial) also available. Support available to part-time students. Financial award application deadline: 3/1. *Faculty research:* Oceanography, marine biology, marine policy, aquaculture and fisheries. *Total annual research expenditures:* $12 million. *Unit head:* Dr. Fei Chai, Director, 207-581-3321, Fax: 207-581-4388. *Application contact:* Scott G. Delcourt, Assistant Vice President for Graduate Studies and Senior Associate Dean, 207-581-3291, Fax: 207-581-3232, E-mail: graduate@maine.edu.

Website: http://www.umaine.edu/marine/

University of Maryland, College Park, Academic Affairs, College of Computer, Mathematical and Natural Sciences, Department of Atmospheric and Oceanic Science, College Park, MD 20742. Offers MS, PMS, PhD. *Program availability:* Part-time, evening/weekend, online learning. Terminal master's awarded for partial completion of doctoral program. *Degree requirements:* For master's, comprehensive exam, scholarly paper, written and oral exams; for doctorate, thesis/dissertation, exam. *Entrance requirements:* For master's, GRE General Test, background in mathematics, experience in scientific computer languages, 3 letters of recommendation; for doctorate, GRE General Test. Electronic applications accepted. *Faculty research:* Weather, atmospheric chemistry, air pollution, global change, radiation.

University of Miami, Graduate School, Rosenstiel School of Marine and Atmospheric Science, Division of Meteorology and Physical Oceanography, Coral Gables, FL 33124. Offers meteorology (MS, PhD); physical oceanography (MS, PhD). Terminal master's awarded for partial completion of doctoral program. *Degree requirements:* For master's, comprehensive exam, thesis; for doctorate, comprehensive exam, thesis/dissertation. *Entrance requirements:* For master's and doctorate, GRE General Test. Additional exam requirements/recommendations for international students: Required—TOEFL (minimum score 550 paper-based). Electronic applications accepted.

University of New Hampshire, Graduate School, College of Engineering and Physical Sciences, Program in Ocean Engineering, Durham, NH 03824. Offers ocean engineering (MS, PhD); ocean mapping (MS). *Degree requirements:* For master's, thesis. *Entrance requirements:* Additional exam requirements/recommendations for international students: Required—TOEFL (minimum score 550 paper-based; 80 iBT). Electronic applications accepted.

University of Rhode Island, Graduate School, Graduate School of Oceanography, Narragansett, RI 02882. Offers biological oceanography, chemical oceanography, geological oceanography, and physical oceanography (MO, MS, PhD); MBA/MO; PhD/MA; PhD/MMA. *Program availability:* Part-time. *Faculty:* 27 full-time (9 women), 3 part-time/adjunct (1 woman). *Students:* 40 full-time (19 women), 23 part-time (11 women); includes 4 minority (all Asian, non-Hispanic/Latino), 8 international. In 2015, 11 master's, 8 doctorates awarded. *Degree requirements:* For master's, comprehensive exam (for some programs), thesis optional; for doctorate, comprehensive exam, thesis/dissertation. *Entrance requirements:* For master's, GRE, 2 letters of recommendation; for doctorate, GRE, 3 letters of recommendation. Additional exam requirements/recommendations for international students: Required—TOEFL (minimum score 600 paper-based; 100 iBT). *Application deadline:* For fall admission, 1/15 for domestic and international students; for spring admission, 11/15 for domestic students, 7/15 for international students. Application fee: $65. Electronic applications accepted. *Expenses:* Tuition, state resident: full-time $11,796; part-time $655 per credit. Tuition, nonresident: full-time $24,206; part-time $1345 per credit. *Required fees:* $1546; $44 per credit. One-time fee: $155 full-time; $35 part-time. *Financial support:* In 2015–16, 5 research assistantships with tuition reimbursements (averaging $10,914 per year), 22 teaching assistantships with tuition reimbursements (averaging $11,011 per year) were awarded. Financial award application deadline: 1/15; financial award applicants required to submit FAFSA. *Faculty research:* Subduction, life in extreme environments, the marine nitrogen cycle, hurricane prediction, Antarctic ocean circulation. *Unit head:* Dr. Bruce Corliss, Dean, 401-874-6222, Fax: 401-874-6931, E-mail: bruce.corliss@gso.uri.edu. *Application contact:* Graduate Admission, 401-874-8272, E-mail: gradadm@etal.uri.edu.

Website: http://www.gso.uri.edu/

University of Southern California, Graduate School, Dana and David Dornsife College of Letters, Arts and Sciences, Department of Biological Sciences, Program in Marine Biology and Biological Oceanography, Los Angeles, CA 90089. Offers marine and environmental biology (MS); marine biology and biological oceanography (PhD). Terminal master's awarded for partial completion of doctoral program. *Degree requirements:* For master's, research paper; for doctorate, comprehensive exam, thesis/dissertation, qualifying examination, dissertation defense. *Entrance requirements:* For master's and doctorate, GRE, 3 letters of recommendation, personal statement, resume, minimum GPA of 3.0. Additional exam requirements/recommendations for international students: Required—TOEFL (minimum score 600 paper-based; 100 iBT). Electronic applications accepted. *Faculty research:* Microbial ecology, biogeochemistry, and geobiology; biodiversity and molecular ecology; integrative organismal biology; conservation biology; marine genomics.

University of South Florida, College of Marine Science, Saint Petersburg, FL 33701. Offers marine science (MS, PhD), including biological oceanography, chemical oceanography, geological oceanography, interdisciplinary, marine resource assessment, marine science, physical oceanography. *Program availability:* Part-time. *Faculty:* 25 full-time (7 women). *Students:* 77 full-time (52 women), 21 part-time (10 women); includes 16 minority (1 Black or African American, non-Hispanic/Latino; 1 Asian, non-Hispanic/Latino; 11 Hispanic/Latino; 3 Two or more races, non-Hispanic/Latino), 10 international. Average age 31. 87 applicants, 32% accepted, 21 enrolled. In 2015, 12 master's, 8 doctorates awarded. Terminal master's awarded for partial completion of doctoral program. *Degree requirements:* For master's, comprehensive exam, thesis; for doctorate, comprehensive exam, thesis/dissertation. *Entrance requirements:* For master's and doctorate, GRE General Test, bachelor's degree from regionally-accredited university, preferably in biology, chemistry, geology, physics or math; minimum GPA of 3.0 in upper-division coursework; research interest statement; resume; three letters of recommendation. Additional exam requirements/recommendations for international students: Required—TOEFL (minimum score 550 paper-based; 79 iBT) or IELTS (minimum score 6.5). *Application deadline:* For fall admission, 1/10 for domestic students, 1/2 for international students; for spring admission, 10/1 for domestic students, 6/1 for international students. Applications are processed on a rolling basis. Application fee: $30. *Financial support:* In 2015–16, 55 students received support, including 45 research assistantships with partial tuition reimbursements available (averaging $14,199 per year), 10 teaching assistantships with partial tuition reimbursements available (averaging $14,196 per year); health care benefits and unspecified assistantships also available. Financial award application deadline: 1/15. *Faculty research:* Problems in shelf, coastal and estuarine waters, in the deep ocean, and in the watershed that drains to the coastal zone such as long-term sea-level rise, coral reef demise, recent paleo-climate change, ocean acidification, harmful algal blooms, fisheries management, water quality, shoreline change, and oil-drilling. *Total annual research expenditures:* $12 million. *Unit head:* Dr. Jacqueline E. Dixon, Dean, 727-553-3369, Fax: 727-553-1189, E-mail: jdixon@usf.edu. *Application contact:* Dr. David F. Naar, Associate Professor and Director of Academic Affairs, 727-553-1637, Fax: 727-553-1189, E-mail: naar@usf.edu.

Website: http://www.marine.usf.edu/

University of Victoria, Faculty of Graduate Studies, Faculty of Science, School of Earth and Ocean Sciences, Victoria, BC V8W 2Y2, Canada. Offers M Sc, PhD. *Program availability:* Part-time. *Degree requirements:* For master's, thesis; for doctorate, thesis/dissertation, candidacy exam. *Entrance requirements:* For master's and doctorate, GRE. Additional exam requirements/recommendations for international students: Required—TOEFL (minimum score 575 paper-based), IELTS (minimum score 7). Electronic applications accepted. *Faculty research:* Climate modeling, geology.

University of Washington, Graduate School, College of the Environment, School of Oceanography, Seattle, WA 98195. Offers biological oceanography (MS, PhD); chemical oceanography (MS, PhD); marine geology and geophysics (MS, PhD); physical oceanography (MS, PhD). Terminal master's awarded for partial completion of doctoral program. *Degree requirements:* For master's, research project; for doctorate, thesis/dissertation. *Entrance requirements:* For master's and doctorate, GRE General Test, minimum GPA of 3.0. Additional exam requirements/recommendations for international students: Required—TOEFL. Electronic applications accepted. *Faculty research:* Global climate change, hydrothermal vent systems, marine microbiology, marine and freshwater biogeochemistry, biological-physical interactions.

University of Wisconsin–Madison, Graduate School, College of Letters and Science, Department of Atmospheric and Oceanic Sciences, Madison, WI 53706-1380. Offers MS, PhD. *Program availability:* Part-time. *Degree requirements:* For master's, thesis (for some programs); for doctorate, thesis/dissertation. *Entrance requirements:* For master's and doctorate, GRE General Test, minimum GPA of 3.0; previous course work in chemistry, mathematics, and physics. Electronic applications accepted. *Expenses:* Tuition, state resident: full-time $5364. Tuition, nonresident: full-time $12,027. *Required fees:* $571. Tuition and fees vary according to campus/location, program and reciprocity agreements. *Faculty research:* Satellite meteorology, weather systems, global climate change, numerical modeling, atmosphere-ocean interaction.

Woods Hole Oceanographic Institution, MIT/WHOI Joint Program in Oceanography/Applied Ocean Science and Engineering, Woods Hole, MA 02543-1541. Offers applied ocean science and engineering (PhD); biological oceanography (PhD); chemical oceanography (PhD); marine geology and geophysics (PhD); physical oceanography (PhD). Program offered jointly with Massachusetts Institute of Technology. *Degree requirements:* For doctorate, thesis/dissertation. *Entrance requirements:* For doctorate, GRE General Test, GRE Subject Test. Additional exam requirements/recommendations for international students: Required—TOEFL. Electronic applications accepted.

Yale University, Graduate School of Arts and Sciences, Department of Geology and Geophysics, New Haven, CT 06520. Offers biogeochemistry (PhD); climate dynamics (PhD); geochemistry (PhD); geophysics (PhD); meteorology (PhD); oceanography (PhD); paleontology (PhD); paleooceanography (PhD); petrology (PhD); tectonics (PhD). *Degree requirements:* For doctorate, thesis/dissertation. *Entrance requirements:* For doctorate, GRE General Test. Additional exam requirements/recommendations for international students: Required—TOEFL.

Peterson's Graduate Programs in the Physical Sciences, Mathematics, Agricultural Sciences, the Environment & Natural Resources 2017

www.petersons.com   **147**

Section 5
Meteorology and Atmospheric Sciences

This section contains a directory of institutions offering graduate work in meteorology and atmospheric sciences. Additional information about programs listed in the directory may be obtained by writing directly to the dean of a graduate school or chair of a department at the address given in the directory.

For programs offering related work, see also in this book *Astronomy and Astrophysics, Geosciences, Marine Sciences and Oceanography,* and *Physics.* In the other guides in this series:

Graduate Programs in the Biological/Biomedical Sciences & Health-Related Medical Professions

See *Biological and Biomedical Sciences* and *Biophysics*

Graduate Programs in Engineering & Applied Sciences

See *Aerospace/Aeronautical Engineering, Civil and Environmental Engineering, Engineering and Applied Sciences,* and *Mechanical Engineering and Mechanics*

CONTENTS

Program Directories

Atmospheric Sciences

Bard College, Bard Center for Environmental Policy, Annandale-on-Hudson, NY 12504. Offers climate science and policy (MS, Professional Certificate), including agriculture (MS), ecosystems (MS); environmental policy (MS, Professional Certificate); sustainability (MBA); MS/JD; MS/MAT. *Program availability:* Part-time. *Degree requirements:* For master's, thesis, 4-month, full-time internship. *Entrance requirements:* For master's, GRE, coursework in statistics, chemistry and one other semester of college science; personal statement; curriculum vitae; 3 letters of recommendation; sample of written work. Additional exam requirements/recommendations for international students: Required—TOEFL (minimum score 600 paper-based; 100 iBT). Electronic applications accepted. *Expenses:* Contact institution. *Faculty research:* Climate and agriculture, alternative energy, environmental economics, environmental toxicology, EPA law, sustainable development, international relations, literature and composition, human rights, agronomy, advocacy, leadership.

Carnegie Mellon University, Mellon College of Science, Department of Chemistry, Pittsburgh, PA 15213-3891. Offers atmospheric chemistry (PhD); bioinorganic chemistry (PhD); bioorganic chemistry and chemical biology (PhD); biophysical chemistry (PhD); catalysis (PhD); green and environmental chemistry (PhD); materials and nanoscience (PhD); renewable energy (PhD); sensors, probes, and imaging (PhD); spectroscopy and single molecule analysis (PhD); theoretical and computational chemistry (PhD). *Program availability:* Part-time. Terminal master's awarded for partial completion of doctoral program. *Degree requirements:* For doctorate, thesis/dissertation, departmental qualifying and oral exams, teaching experience. *Entrance requirements:* For doctorate, GRE General Test, GRE Subject Test. Additional exam requirements/recommendations for international students: Required—TOEFL. Electronic applications accepted. *Faculty research:* Physical and theoretical chemistry, chemical synthesis, biophysical/bioinorganic chemistry.

City College of the City University of New York, Graduate School, Division of Science, Department of Earth and Atmospheric Sciences, New York, NY 10031-9198. Offers geology (MS). PhD program offered jointly with Graduate School and University Center of the City University of New York. *Degree requirements:* For master's, comprehensive exam, thesis. *Entrance requirements:* Additional exam requirements/recommendations for international students: Required—TOEFL (minimum score 500 paper-based; 61 iBT). *Application deadline:* For fall admission, 5/1 for domestic and international students; for spring admission, 11/15 for domestic and international students. Applications are processed on a rolling basis. Application fee: $125. Electronic applications accepted. Tuition and fees vary according to course load, degree level and program. *Financial support:* Fellowships, career-related internships or fieldwork, and scholarships/grants available. Financial award applicants required to submit FAFSA. *Faculty research:* Water resources, high-temperature geochemistry, sedimentary basin analysis, tectonics. *Unit head:* Pengfei Zhang, Chair, 212-650-6452, Fax: 212-650-6482, E-mail: pzhang@ccny.cuny.edu. *Application contact:* 216-650-6977, E-mail: gradadm@ccny.cuny.edu.
Website: http://www.ccny.cuny.edu/eas/

The College of William and Mary, Faculty of Arts and Sciences, Department of Applied Science, Williamsburg, VA 23187-8795. Offers accelerator science (PhD); applied mathematics (PhD); applied mechanics (PhD); applied robotics (PhD); applied science (MS); atmospheric and environmental science (PhD); computational neuroscience (PhD); interface, thin film and surface science (PhD); lasers and optics (PhD); magnetic resonance (PhD); materials science and engineering (PhD); mathematical and computational biology (PhD); medical imaging (PhD); nanotechnology (PhD); neuroscience (PhD); non-destructive evaluation (PhD); polymer chemistry (PhD); remote sensing (PhD). *Program availability:* Part-time. *Faculty:* 7 full-time (1 woman), 1 part-time/adjunct (0 women). *Students:* 26 full-time (9 women), 3 part-time (1 woman); includes 5 minority (2 Black or African American, non-Hispanic/Latino; 1 Asian, non-Hispanic/Latino; 2 Hispanic/Latino), 12 international. Average age 28. 24 applicants, 46% accepted, 6 enrolled. In 2015, 2 master's, 6 doctorates awarded. Terminal master's awarded for partial completion of doctoral program. *Degree requirements:* For master's, comprehensive exam, thesis; for doctorate, comprehensive exam, thesis/dissertation, 4 core courses. *Entrance requirements:* For master's and doctorate, GRE General Test, GRE Subject Test. Additional exam requirements/recommendations for international students: Required—TOEFL, TWE. *Application deadline:* For fall admission, 2/3 priority date for domestic students, 2/3 for international students; for spring admission, 10/15 priority date for domestic students, 10/14 for international students. Applications are processed on a rolling basis. Application fee: $45. Electronic applications accepted. *Expenses:* $6,550 per semester; $13,100 per year. *Financial support:* Fellowships, research assistantships, teaching assistantships, Federal Work-Study, health care benefits, tuition waivers (full), and unspecified assistantships available. Financial award application deadline: 4/15; financial award applicants required to submit FAFSA. *Faculty research:* Computational biology, non-destructive evaluation, neurophysiology, lasers and optics. *Total annual research expenditures:* $1.7 million. *Unit head:* Dr. Christopher Del Negro, Chair, 757-221-7808, Fax: 757-221-2050, E-mail: cadeln@wm.edu. *Application contact:* Lianne Rios Ashburne, Graduate Program Coordinator, 757-221-2563, Fax: 757-221-2050, E-mail: lrashburne@wm.edu.
Website: http://www.wm.edu/as/appliedscience

Colorado State University, College of Engineering, Department of Atmospheric Science, Fort Collins, CO 80523-1371. Offers MS, PhD. *Program availability:* Part-time. *Faculty:* 67 full-time (20 women), 13 part-time/adjunct (3 women). *Students:* 54 full-time (20 women), 30 part-time (11 women); includes 12 minority (2 Black or African American, non-Hispanic/Latino; 3 Asian, non-Hispanic/Latino; 6 Hispanic/Latino; 1 Two or more races, non-Hispanic/Latino), 11 international. Average age 28. 145 applicants, 12% accepted, 15 enrolled. In 2015, 10 master's, 7 doctorates awarded. *Degree requirements:* For master's, thesis (for some programs); for doctorate, comprehensive exam, thesis/dissertation. *Entrance requirements:* For master's, GRE General Test, minimum GPA of 3.0; BS in physics, math, atmospheric science, engineering, chemistry or related major; calculus-based math and differential equations; calculus-based physics; letters of recommendation; statement of purpose; curriculum vitae; for doctorate, GRE General Test, minimum GPA of 3.0; MS with thesis in atmospheric science or related field; statement of purpose; curriculum vitae; letters of recommendation. Additional exam requirements/recommendations for international students: Required—TOEFL (minimum score 550 paper-based; 80 iBT), IELTS (minimum score 6.5). *Application deadline:* For fall admission, 1/1 priority date for domestic and international students; for spring admission, 9/1 for domestic and international students. Applications are processed on a rolling basis. Application fee: $60 ($70 for international students). Electronic applications accepted. *Expenses:* $100 per credit hour. *Financial support:* In 2015–16, 78 students received support, including 11 fellowships with full tuition reimbursements available (averaging $49,403 per year), 66 research assistantships with full tuition reimbursements available (averaging $27,232 per year); teaching assistantships, scholarships/grants, traineeships, and unspecified assistantships also available. Financial award application deadline: 1/1. *Faculty research:* Radiation and remote sensing; atmospheric chemistry; climate and atmosphere; ocean dynamics; cloud microphysics, severe storms, and mesoscale meteorology; global biogeochemical cycles and ecosystems. *Total annual research expenditures:* $34 million. *Unit head:* Dr. Jeffrey L. Collett, Jr., Department Head and Professor, 970-491-8360, Fax: 970-491-8449, E-mail: jeffrey.collett@colostate.edu. *Application contact:* Sarah Tisdale, Administrative Assistant, 970-491-8382, Fax: 970-491-8449, E-mail: skt@atmos.colostate.edu.
Website: http://www.ATMOS.colostate.edu/

Columbia University, Graduate School of Arts and Sciences, New York, NY 10027. Offers African-American studies (MA); American studies (MA); anthropology (MA, PhD); art history and archaeology (MA, PhD); astronomy (PhD); biological sciences (PhD); biotechnology (MA); chemical physics (PhD); chemistry (PhD); classical studies (MA, PhD); classics (MA, PhD); climate and society (MA); conservation biology (MA); earth and environmental sciences (PhD); East Asia: regional studies (MA); East Asian languages and cultures (MA, PhD); ecology, evolution and environmental biology (MA), including conservation biology; ecology, evolution, and environmental biology (PhD), including ecology and evolutionary biology, evolutionary primatology; economics (MA, PhD); English and comparative literature (MA, PhD); French and Romance philology (MA, PhD); Germanic languages (MA, PhD); global French studies (MA); global thought (MA); Hispanic cultural studies (MA); history (PhD); history and literature (MA); human rights studies (MA); Islamic studies (MA); Italian (MA, PhD); Japanese pedagogy (MA); Jewish studies (MA); Latin America and the Caribbean: regional studies (MA); Latin American and Iberian cultures (PhD); mathematics (MA, PhD), including finance (MA); medieval and Renaissance studies (MA); Middle Eastern, South Asian, and African studies (MA, PhD); modern art: critical and curatorial studies (MA); modern European studies (MA); museum anthropology (MA); music (DMA, PhD); oral history (MA); philosophical foundations of physics (MA); philosophy (MA, PhD); physics (PhD); political science (MA, PhD); psychology (PhD); quantitative methods in the social sciences (MA); religion (MA, PhD); Russia, Eurasia and East Europe: regional studies (MA); Russian translation (MA); Slavic cultures (MA); Slavic languages (MA, PhD); sociology (MA, PhD); South Asian studies (MA); statistics (MA, PhD); theatre (PhD). Dual-degree programs require admission to both Graduate School of Arts and Sciences and another Columbia school. *Program availability:* Part-time. *Students:* 3,030 full-time, 235 part-time; includes 861 minority (88 Black or African American, non-Hispanic/Latino; 5 American Indian or Alaska Native, non-Hispanic/Latino; 517 Asian, non-Hispanic/Latino; 159 Hispanic/Latino; 4 Native Hawaiian or other Pacific Islander, non-Hispanic/Latino; 88 Two or more races, non-Hispanic/Latino), 1,697 international. 13,288 applicants, 21% accepted, 1162 enrolled. In 2015, 1,061 master's, 553 doctorates awarded. Terminal master's awarded for partial completion of doctoral program. *Degree requirements:* For master's, variable foreign language requirement, comprehensive exam (for some programs), thesis (for some programs); for doctorate, variable foreign language requirement, comprehensive exam (for some programs), thesis/dissertation. *Entrance requirements:* For master's and doctorate, GRE General Test, GRE Subject Test (for some programs). Additional exam requirements/recommendations for international students: Required—TOEFL, IELTS. Application fee: $105. Electronic applications accepted. *Financial support:* Fellowships, research assistantships, teaching assistantships, career-related internships or fieldwork, Federal Work-Study, institutionally sponsored loans, scholarships/grants, traineeships, health care benefits, tuition waivers, and unspecified assistantships available. Support available to part-time students. Financial award application deadline: 12/15. *Unit head:* Carlos J. Alonso, Dean of the Graduate School of Arts and Sciences, 212-854-5177. *Application contact:* GSAS Office of Admissions, 212-854-8903, E-mail: gsas-admissions@columbia.edu.
Website: http://gsas.columbia.edu/

Cornell University, Graduate School, Graduate Fields of Agriculture and Life Sciences, Field of Atmospheric Science, Ithaca, NY 14853-0001. Offers MS, PhD. *Degree requirements:* For master's, thesis; for doctorate, comprehensive exam, thesis/dissertation. *Entrance requirements:* For master's and doctorate, GRE General Test, 2 letters of recommendation. Additional exam requirements/recommendations for international students: Required—TOEFL (minimum score 550 paper-based; 77 iBT). Electronic applications accepted. *Faculty research:* Applied climatology, climate dynamics, statistical meteorology/climatology, synoptic meteorology, upper atmospheric science.

Florida State University, The Graduate School, College of Arts and Sciences, Department of Scientific Computing, Tallahassee, FL 32306-4120. Offers computational science (MS, PhD), including atmospheric science (PhD), biochemistry (PhD), biological science (PhD), computational science (PhD), geological science (PhD), materials science (PhD), physics (PhD). *Program availability:* Part-time. *Faculty:* 14 full-time (2 women). *Students:* 32 full-time (4 women), 7 part-time (1 woman); includes 14 minority (9 Asian, non-Hispanic/Latino; 3 Hispanic/Latino; 2 Two or more races, non-Hispanic/Latino). Average age 27. 28 applicants, 43% accepted, 7 enrolled. In 2015, 9 master's, 7 doctorates awarded. *Degree requirements:* For master's, thesis (for some programs); for doctorate, comprehensive exam, thesis/dissertation. *Entrance requirements:* For master's and doctorate, GRE General Test, knowledge of at least one object-oriented computing language, 3 letters of recommendation, resume, statement of purpose. Additional exam requirements/recommendations for international students: Required—TOEFL (minimum score 550 paper-based; 80 iBT). *Application deadline:* For fall admission, 1/15 for domestic and international students. Application fee: $30. Electronic applications accepted. *Expenses: Tuition, area resident:* Full-time $7263; part-time $403.50 per credit hour. Tuition, nonresident: full-time $18,087; part-time $1004.85 per credit hour. *Required fees:* $1365; $75.81 per credit hour. $20 per semester. Tuition and fees vary according to campus/location. *Financial support:* In 2015–16, 33 students received support, including 10 research assistantships with full tuition reimbursements available (averaging $20,000 per year), 23 teaching assistantships with full tuition reimbursements available (averaging $20,000 per year); scholarships/grants and unspecified assistantships also available. Financial award application deadline: 1/15. *Faculty research:* Morphometrics, mathematical and systems biology, mining proteomic and metabolic data, computational materials research, advanced 4-D Var data-assimilation methods in dynamic meteorology and oceanography, computational fluid dynamics, astrophysics. *Unit head:* Dr. Gordon Erlebacher, Chair, 850-644-7024, E-mail: gerlebacher@fsu.edu. *Application contact:* Mark Howard, Academic Program Specialist, 850-644-0143, Fax: 850-644-0098, E-mail: mlhoward@fsu.edu.
Website: http://www.sc.fsu.edu

George Mason University, College of Science, Program in Climate Dynamics, Fairfax, VA 22030. Offers PhD. *Faculty:* 24 full-time (5 women), 9 part-time/adjunct (2 women). *Students:* 19 full-time (10 women), 1 (woman) part-time; includes 2 minority (1 Black or African American, non-Hispanic/Latino; 1 Asian, non-Hispanic/Latino), 12 international. Average age 32. 11 applicants, 45% accepted. In 2015, 3 doctorates awarded. *Degree requirements:* For doctorate, comprehensive exam, thesis/dissertation. *Entrance requirements:* For doctorate, GRE (waived for those who have earned a master's degree from U.S. institution), undergraduate degree with minimum GPA of 3.0; 2 copies of official transcripts; current resume; expanded goals statement; 3 letters of recommendation. Additional exam requirements/recommendations for international students: Required—TOEFL (minimum score 575 paper-based; 88 iBT), IELTS (minimum score 6.5), PTE (minimum score 59). *Application deadline:* For fall admission, 12/31 priority date for domestic students. Application fee: $75 ($80 for international students). Electronic applications accepted. *Financial support:* In 2015–16, 23 students received support, including 1 fellowship (averaging $10,000 per year), 19 research assistantships with tuition reimbursements available (averaging $16,150 per year); career-related internships or fieldwork, Federal Work-Study, scholarships/grants, unspecified assistantships, and health care benefits (for full-time research or teaching assistantship recipients) also available. Support available to part-time students. Financial award application deadline: 3/1; financial award applicants required to submit FAFSA. *Faculty research:* Modeling and diagnosis of large-scale behavior of the climate system, anthropogenic climate changes, El Nino, prediction of climate events, ocean change in Antarctic. *Unit head:* Jagadish Shukla, Director, 703-993-1983, Fax: 703-993-9300, E-mail: jshukla@gmu.edu. *Application contact:* Dr. Barry Klinger, Graduate Coordinator, 703-993-9227, Fax: 703-993-9300, E-mail: bklinger@gmu.edu.
Website: https://cos.gmu.edu/aoes/academics/climate-dynamics-graduate-program/

Georgia Institute of Technology, Graduate Studies, College of Sciences, School of Earth and Atmospheric Sciences, Atlanta, GA 30332-0340. Offers MS, PhD. *Program availability:* Part-time. Terminal master's awarded for partial completion of doctoral program. *Degree requirements:* For master's, thesis optional; for doctorate, comprehensive exam, thesis/dissertation. *Entrance requirements:* For master's and doctorate, GRE. Additional exam requirements/recommendations for international students: Required—TOEFL (minimum score 550 paper-based; 79 iBT). Electronic applications accepted. *Faculty research:* Geophysics; atmospheric chemistry, aerosols and clouds; dynamics of weather and climate; geochemistry; oceanography; paleoclimate; planetary science; remote sensing.

Hampton University, School of Science, Department of Atmospheric and Planetary Sciences, Hampton, VA 23668. Offers atmospheric science (MS, PhD); planetary science (MS, PhD). *Program availability:* Part-time. Terminal master's awarded for partial completion of doctoral program. *Degree requirements:* For master's, thesis; for doctorate, comprehensive exam, thesis/dissertation. *Entrance requirements:* For master's, GRE. Additional exam requirements/recommendations for international students: Required—TOEFL (minimum score 525 paper-based) or IELTS (6.5). Electronic applications accepted. *Expenses: Tuition, area resident:* Full-time $10,263; part-time $522 per credit hour. *Required fees:* $35. Tuition and fees vary according to course load and program. *Faculty research:* Remote sensing, polar stratospheric and mesospheric clouds, lidar and related technologies, astrobiology, atmospheric dynamics.

Howard University, Graduate School and School of Engineering and Computer Science, Department of Atmospheric Sciences, Washington, DC 20059-0002. Offers MS, PhD. *Program availability:* Part-time. Terminal master's awarded for partial completion of doctoral program. *Degree requirements:* For master's, thesis; for doctorate, one foreign language, comprehensive exam, thesis/dissertation. *Entrance requirements:* For master's, GRE General Test, minimum GPA of 3.0; for doctorate, GRE General Test, minimum GPA of 3.2. Additional exam requirements/recommendations for international students: Required—TOEFL (minimum score 550 paper-based). *Faculty research:* Atmospheric chemistry, climate, atmospheric radiation, gravity waves, aerosols, extraterrestrial atmospheres, turbulence.

Howard University, Graduate School, Department of Chemistry, Washington, DC 20059-0002. Offers analytical chemistry (MS, PhD); atmospheric (MS, PhD); biochemistry (MS, PhD); environmental (MS, PhD); inorganic chemistry (MS, PhD); organic chemistry (MS, PhD); physical chemistry (MS, PhD). Terminal master's awarded for partial completion of doctoral program. *Degree requirements:* For master's, comprehensive exam, thesis, teaching experience; for doctorate, comprehensive exam, thesis/dissertation, teaching experience. *Entrance requirements:* For master's, GRE General Test, minimum GPA of 2.7; for doctorate, GRE General Test, minimum GPA of 3.0. Additional exam requirements/recommendations for international students: Required—TOEFL. Electronic applications accepted. *Faculty research:* Synthetic organics, materials, natural products, mass spectrometry.

Massachusetts Institute of Technology, School of Science, Department of Earth, Atmospheric, and Planetary Sciences, Cambridge, MA 02139. Offers atmospheric chemistry (PhD, Sc D); atmospheric science (SM, PhD, Sc D); chemical oceanography (SM, PhD, Sc D); climate physics and chemistry (SM, PhD, Sc D); earth and planetary sciences (SM); geochemistry (PhD, Sc D); geology (PhD, Sc D); geophysics (PhD, Sc D); marine geology and geophysics (SM, PhD, Sc D); physical oceanography (SM, PhD, Sc D); planetary sciences (PhD, Sc D). *Faculty:* 36 full-time (8 women). *Students:* 166 full-time (75 women), 1 part-time (0 women); includes 23 minority (1 Black or African American, non-Hispanic/Latino; 7 Asian, non-Hispanic/Latino; 6 Hispanic/Latino; 9 Two or more races, non-Hispanic/Latino), 54 international. Average age 27. 228 applicants, 26% accepted, 33 enrolled. In 2015, 6 master's, 24 doctorates awarded. Terminal master's awarded for partial completion of doctoral program. *Degree requirements:* For master's, thesis; for doctorate, comprehensive exam, thesis/dissertation. *Entrance requirements:* For master's, GRE General Test; for doctorate, GRE General Test, GRE Subject Test in chemistry or physics (for planetary sciences area). Additional exam requirements/recommendations for international students: Required—TOEFL (minimum score 600 paper-based; 100 iBT), IELTS (minimum score 7). *Application deadline:* For fall admission, 1/5 for domestic and international students; for spring admission, 11/1 for domestic and international students. Application fee: $75. Electronic applications accepted. *Expenses: Tuition:* Full-time $46,400; part-time $725 per credit. One-time fee: $304 full-time. Full-time tuition and fees vary according to course load and program. *Financial support:* In 2015–16, 99 students received support, including 60 fellowships (averaging $40,700 per year), 76 research assistantships (averaging $38,000 per year), 15 teaching assistantships (averaging $36,100 per year); Federal Work-Study, institutionally sponsored loans, scholarships/grants, traineeships, health care benefits, and unspecified assistantships also available. Support available to part-time students. Financial award application deadline: 4/15; financial award applicants required to submit FAFSA. *Faculty research:* Earth: origin, composition, structure, and dynamics of (and interactions between) the atmosphere, oceans, surface, and interior of the earth; planets: formation, dynamics, and evolution of planetary systems and the characterization of exoplanets; climate: characterization of past, present, and potential future climates; studies of the causes and consequences of climate change; life: co-evolution of life and environmental systems. *Total annual research expenditures:* $25.3 million. *Unit head:* Prof. Robert van der Hilst, Department Head, 617-253-2127, Fax: 617-253-8298, E-mail: eapsinfo@mit.edu. *Application contact:* EAPS Education Office, 617-253-3381, Fax: 617-253-8298, E-mail: eapsinfo@mit.edu.
Website: http://eapsweb.mit.edu/

McGill University, Faculty of Graduate and Postdoctoral Studies, Faculty of Science, Department of Atmospheric and Oceanic Sciences, Montréal, QC H3A 2T5, Canada. Offers atmospheric science (M Sc, PhD); physical oceanography (M Sc, PhD). PhD program in physical oceanography offered jointly with Université Laval.

Michigan Technological University, Graduate School, Interdisciplinary Programs, Houghton, MI 49931. Offers atmospheric sciences (PhD); biochemistry and molecular biology (PhD); computational science and engineering (PhD); data science (MS, Graduate Certificate); engineering (M Eng); environmental engineering (PhD); international profile (Graduate Certificate); nanotechnology (Graduate Certificate); sustainability (Graduate Certificate); sustainable water resources systems (Graduate Certificate). *Program availability:* Part-time. *Faculty:* 118 full-time (26 women), 12 part-time/adjunct. *Students:* 53 full-time (22 women), 10 part-time; includes 2 minority (1 Asian, non-Hispanic/Latino; 1 Two or more races, non-Hispanic/Latino), 44 international. Average age 30. 300 applicants, 19% accepted, 17 enrolled. In 2015, 3 master's, 7 doctorates, 4 other advanced degrees awarded. Terminal master's awarded for partial completion of doctoral program. *Degree requirements:* For master's, comprehensive exam (for some programs), thesis (for some programs); for doctorate, comprehensive exam, thesis/dissertation. *Entrance requirements:* For master's, doctorate, and Graduate Certificate, GRE, statement of purpose, personal statement, official transcripts, 2-3 letters of recommendation. Additional exam requirements/recommendations for international students: Required—TOEFL or IELTS. *Application deadline:* Applications are processed on a rolling basis. Electronic applications accepted. *Expenses:* Tuition, state resident: full-time $15,507; part-time $861.50 per credit. Tuition, nonresident: full-time $15,507; part-time $861.50 per credit. *Required fees:* $248; $248. Tuition and fees vary according to course load and program. *Financial support:* In 2015–16, 41 students received support, including 7 fellowships with tuition reimbursements available (averaging $14,516 per year), 16 research assistantships with tuition reimbursements available (averaging $14,516 per year), 9 teaching assistantships with tuition reimbursements available (averaging $14,516 per year); career-related internships or fieldwork, Federal Work-Study, scholarships/grants, health care benefits, unspecified assistantships, and cooperative program also available. Financial award applicants required to submit FAFSA. *Faculty research:* Big data, atmospheric sciences, bioinformatics and systems biology, molecular dynamics, environmental studies. *Unit head:* Dr. Jacqueline E. Huntoon, Provost and Vice President for Academic Affairs, 906-487-2440, Fax: 906-487-2284,
E-mail: jeh@mtu.edu. *Application contact:* Carol T. Wingerson, Administrative Aide, 906-487-2328, Fax: 906-487-2284, E-mail: gradadms@mtu.edu.

Millersville University of Pennsylvania, College of Graduate Studies and Adult Learning, College of Science and Technology, Department of Earth Sciences, Millersville, PA 17551-0302. Offers integrated scientific applications: climate science applications (MS); integrated scientific applications: environmental systems management (MS); integrated scientific applications: geoinformatics (MS); integrated scientific applications: weather intelligence and risk management (MS). *Program availability:* Part-time. *Faculty:* 11 full-time (2 women), 2 part-time/adjunct (0 women). *Students:* 6 full-time (0 women), 8 part-time (3 women); includes 5 minority (3 Asian, non-Hispanic/Latino; 2 Hispanic/Latino). 8 applicants, 88% accepted, 7 enrolled. In 2015, 5 master's awarded. *Degree requirements:* For master's, thesis optional, internship or applied research. *Entrance requirements:* For master's, GRE, MAT or GMAT (if cumulative GPA is lower than 3.0), three professional letters of recommendation, academic and professional goals statement, current resume. Additional exam requirements/recommendations for international students: Required—TOEFL (minimum score 600 paper-based), IELTS (minimum score 6). *Application deadline:* Applications are processed on a rolling basis. Application fee: $40. Electronic applications accepted. *Expenses:* Tuition, state resident: full-time $8460; part-time $470 per credit. Tuition, nonresident: full-time $12,690; part-time $705 per credit. *Required fees:* $2471; $133.75 per credit. Tuition and fees vary according to course load, degree level and program. *Financial support:* Application deadline: 3/15; applicants required to submit FAFSA. *Faculty research:* Meteorology, oceanography, geology, earth sciences pedagogy. *Unit head:* Dr. Richard D. Clark, Chair, 717-871-7434, Fax: 717-871-7918, E-mail: richard.clark@millersville.edu. *Application contact:* Dr. Victor S. DeSantis, Dean of College of Graduate Studies and Adult Learning/Associate Provost for Civic and Community Engagement, 717-871-7619, Fax: 717-871-7954,
E-mail: victor.desantis@millersville.edu.
Website: http://www.millersville.edu/esci/

Mississippi State University, College of Arts and Sciences, Department of Geosciences, Mississippi State, MS 39762. Offers applied meteorology (MS); broadcast meteorology (MS); earth and atmospheric science (PhD); environmental geoscience (MS); geography (MS); geology (MS); geospatial sciences (MS); professional meteorology/climatology (MS); teachers in geoscience (MS). *Program availability:* Online learning. *Faculty:* 18 full-time (4 women), 1 part-time/adjunct (0 women). *Students:* 53 full-time (27 women), 176 part-time (81 women); includes 26 minority (7 Black or African American, non-Hispanic/Latino; 3 Asian, non-Hispanic/Latino; 10 Hispanic/Latino; 1 Native Hawaiian or other Pacific Islander, non-Hispanic/Latino; 5 Two or more races, non-Hispanic/Latino), 5 international. Average age 33. 123 applicants, 73% accepted, 68 enrolled. In 2015, 70 master's, 3 doctorates awarded. *Degree requirements:* For master's, thesis (for some programs), comprehensive oral or written exam; for doctorate, thesis/dissertation, comprehensive oral or written exam. *Entrance requirements:* For master's, GRE (for on-campus applicants), minimum undergraduate GPA of 2.75; for doctorate, thesis-based MS with background in one department emphasis area. Additional exam requirements/recommendations for international students: Required—TOEFL (minimum score 477 paper-based; 53 iBT); Recommended—IELTS (minimum score 4.5). *Application deadline:* For fall admission, 7/1 for domestic students, 5/1 for international students; for spring admission, 11/1 for domestic students, 9/1 for international students. Applications are processed on a rolling basis. Application fee: $60. Electronic applications accepted. *Expenses: Tuition, area resident:* Full-time $7502; part-time $833.74 per credit hour. Tuition, nonresident: full-time $20,142; part-time $2238.24 per credit hour. *Financial support:* In 2015–16, 7 research assistantships with full tuition reimbursements (averaging $13,792 per year), 28 teaching assistantships with full tuition reimbursements (averaging $13,500 per year) were awarded; Federal Work-Study, institutionally sponsored loans, scholarships/grants, tuition waivers (partial), and unspecified assistantships also available. Financial award application deadline: 4/1; financial award applicants required to submit FAFSA. *Faculty research:* Climatology, hydrogeology, sedimentology, meteorology. *Total annual research expenditures:* $3.1 million. *Unit head:* Dr. William Cooke, Interim Department Head, 662-325-1393, Fax: 662-325-9423, E-mail: whc5@geosci.msstate.edu. *Application contact:* Meredith Nagel, Admissions Assistant, 662-325-9077,
E-mail: mnagel@grad.msstate.edu.
Website: http://www.geosciences.msstate.edu

Atmospheric Sciences

New Mexico Institute of Mining and Technology, Center for Graduate Studies, Department of Physics, Socorro, NM 87801. Offers astrophysics (PhD); atmospheric physics (PhD); instrumentation (MS); mathematical physics (PhD); physics (MS). *Degree requirements:* For master's, thesis optional; for doctorate, thesis/dissertation. *Entrance requirements:* For master's, GRE General Test; for doctorate, GRE General Test, GRE Subject Test. Additional exam requirements/recommendations for international students: Required—TOEFL (minimum score 540 paper-based). *Expenses:* Tuition, state resident: full-time $5811; part-time $322.81 per credit. Tuition, nonresident: full-time $19,220; part-time $1067.79 per credit. *Required fees:* $1030. Tuition and fees vary according to course load. *Faculty research:* Cloud physics, stellar and extragalactic processes.

North Carolina State University, Graduate School, College of Physical and Mathematical Sciences, Department of Marine, Earth, and Atmospheric Sciences, Raleigh, NC 27695. Offers marine, earth, and atmospheric sciences (MS, PhD); meteorology (MS, PhD); oceanography (MS, PhD). PhD offered jointly with The University of North Carolina Wilmington. Terminal master's awarded for partial completion of doctoral program. *Degree requirements:* For master's, thesis (for some programs), final oral exam; for doctorate, comprehensive exam, thesis/dissertation, final oral exam, preliminary oral and written exams. *Entrance requirements:* For master's, GRE General Test, minimum GPA of 3.0; for doctorate, GRE General Test, GRE Subject Test (for disciplines in biological oceanography and geology), minimum GPA of 3.0. Additional exam requirements/recommendations for international students: Required—TOEFL (minimum score 550 paper-based). Electronic applications accepted. *Faculty research:* Boundary layer and air quality meteorology; climate and mesoscale dynamics; biological, chemical, geological, and physical oceanography; hard rock, soft rock, environmental, and paleo-geology.

Northern Arizona University, Graduate College, College of Engineering, Forestry, and Natural Sciences, School of Earth Sciences and Environmental Sustainability, Flagstaff, AZ 86011. Offers climate science and solutions (MS); earth sciences and environmental sustainability (PhD); environmental sciences and policy (MS); geology (MS). *Degree requirements:* For master's, comprehensive exam (for some programs), thesis (for some programs). *Entrance requirements:* Additional exam requirements/recommendations for international students: Required—TOEFL (minimum score 550 paper-based; 80 iBT), IELTS (minimum score 7). *Application deadline:* For fall admission, 2/1 priority date for domestic and international students. Applications are processed on a rolling basis. Application fee: $65. Electronic applications accepted. *Expenses: Tuition, area resident:* Full-time $8710. Tuition, nonresident: full-time $20,350. *Required fees:* $896. *Financial support:* Fellowships, research assistantships with full tuition reimbursements, teaching assistantships with full tuition reimbursements, career-related internships or fieldwork, Federal Work-Study, scholarships/grants, health care benefits, tuition waivers (full and partial), and unspecified assistantships available. Financial award applicants required to submit FAFSA. *Unit head:* Dr. Paul Umhoefer, Director, 928-523-6464, E-mail: paul.umhoefer@nau.edu. *Application contact:* SESES Support, 928-523-9333, Fax: 928-523-7432, E-mail: seses_admin_support@nau.edu. Website: http://nau.edu/cefns/natsci/seses/

Nova Southeastern University, Halmos College of Natural Sciences and Oceanography, Fort Lauderdale, FL 33314-7796. Offers biological sciences (MS); coastal studies (Certificate); coastal zone management (MS); marine and coastal climate change (Certificate); marine and coastal studies (MA); marine biology (MS); marine biology and oceanography (PhD), including marine biology, oceanography; marine environmental sciences (MS). *Program availability:* Part-time, evening/weekend, 100% online, blended/hybrid learning. *Faculty:* 17 full-time (3 women), 22 part-time/adjunct (11 women). *Students:* 100 full-time (57 women), 114 part-time (76 women); includes 32 minority (6 Black or African American, non-Hispanic/Latino; 1 American Indian or Alaska Native, non-Hispanic/Latino; 6 Asian, non-Hispanic/Latino; 10 Hispanic/Latino; 9 Two or more races, non-Hispanic/Latino), 5 international. Average age 30. 85 applicants, 60% accepted, 39 enrolled. In 2015, 47 master's, 2 doctorates, 9 other advanced degrees awarded. *Degree requirements:* For master's, thesis; for doctorate, comprehensive exam, thesis/dissertation, departmental qualifying exam. *Entrance requirements:* For master's, GRE General Test, 3 letters of recommendation, BS/BA in natural science (for marine biology program), BS/BA in biology (for biological sciences program), minor in the natural sciences or equivalent (for coastal zone management and marine environmental sciences); for doctorate, GRE General Test, master's degree. Additional exam requirements/recommendations for international students: Required—TOEFL (minimum score 550 paper-based). *Application deadline:* Applications are processed on a rolling basis. Application fee: $50. Electronic applications accepted. *Expenses:* $34,749 per year (for PhD); $3,738 per course (for MS and Graduate Certificate). *Financial support:* In 2015–16, 157 students received support, including 14 fellowships with tuition reimbursements available (averaging $25,000 per year), 42 research assistantships with tuition reimbursements available (averaging $19,000 per year); teaching assistantships, career-related internships or fieldwork, Federal Work-Study, scholarships/grants, health care benefits, tuition waivers (full and partial), and unspecified assistantships also available. Support available to part-time students. Financial award application deadline: 4/15; financial award applicants required to submit FAFSA. *Faculty research:* Physical oceanography, biological oceanography, molecular and microbiology, ecology and evolution, coral reefs. *Total annual research expenditures:* $5 million. *Unit head:* Dr. Richard Dodge, Dean, 954-262-3600, Fax: 954-262-4020, E-mail: dodge@nsu.nova.edu. *Application contact:* Dr. Bernhard Riegl, Chair, Department of Marine and Environmental Sciences, 954-262-3600, Fax: 954-262-4020, E-mail: rieglb@nova.edu. Website: http://cnso.nova.edu

The Ohio State University, Graduate School, College of Arts and Sciences, Division of Social and Behavioral Sciences, Department of Geography, Columbus, OH 43210. Offers atmospheric sciences (MS, PhD); geography (MA, PhD). *Degree requirements:* For doctorate, variable foreign language requirement, thesis/dissertation. *Entrance requirements:* For master's and doctorate, GRE. Additional exam requirements/recommendations for international students: Required—Michigan English Language Assessment Battery (minimum score 86); Recommended—TOEFL (minimum score 600 paper-based; 100 iBT), IELTS (minimum score 8). Electronic applications accepted.

Oregon State University, College of Earth, Ocean, and Atmospheric Sciences, Program in Ocean, Earth, and Atmospheric Sciences, Corvallis, OR 97331. Offers atmospheric sciences (MA, MS, PhD); geological oceanography (MA, MS, PhD); geophysics (MA, MS, PhD); ocean ecology and biogeochemistry (MS, PhD); physical oceanography (MA, MS, PhD). *Program availability:* Part-time. *Faculty:* 38 full-time (11 women), 3 part-time/adjunct (1 woman). *Students:* 51 full-time (26 women), 4 part-time (1 woman); includes 7 minority (1 Asian, non-Hispanic/Latino; 4 Hispanic/Latino; 2 Two or more races, non-Hispanic/Latino), 12 international. Average age 29. 116 applicants, 16% accepted, 9 enrolled. In 2015, 5 master's, 1 doctorate awarded. *Entrance requirements:* For master's, GRE. Additional exam requirements/recommendations for international students: Required—TOEFL (minimum score 80 iBT), IELTS (minimum score 6.5). *Application deadline:* For fall admission, 1/5 for domestic students. Application fee: $75 ($85 for international students). *Expenses: Tuition, state resident:*

full-time $12,150; part-time $450 per credit. Tuition, nonresident: full-time $20,952; part-time $776 per credit. *Required fees:* $1572; $1443 per unit. One-time fee: $350. Tuition and fees vary according to course load, campus/location and program. *Unit head:* Dr. Rob Wheatcroft, Professor/Program Head, Earth Systems. *Application contact:* Student Advisor, 541-737-5188, E-mail: student_advisor@coas.oregonstate.edu. Website: http://ceoas.oregonstate.edu/academics/ocean/

Princeton University, Graduate School, Department of Geosciences, Program in Atmospheric and Oceanic Sciences, Princeton, NJ 08544-1019. Offers PhD. *Degree requirements:* For doctorate, one foreign language, thesis/dissertation. *Entrance requirements:* For doctorate, GRE General Test, GRE Subject Test. Additional exam requirements/recommendations for international students: Required—TOEFL (minimum score 600 paper-based). Electronic applications accepted. *Faculty research:* Climate dynamics, middle atmosphere dynamics and chemistry, oceanic circulation, marine geochemistry, numerical modeling.

Purdue University, Graduate School, College of Science, Department of Earth and Atmospheric Sciences, West Lafayette, IN 47907. Offers MS, PhD. *Degree requirements:* For master's, comprehensive exam, thesis; for doctorate, one foreign language, comprehensive exam, thesis/dissertation. *Entrance requirements:* For master's, GRE General Test, minimum undergraduate GPA of 3.0 or equivalent; for doctorate, GRE General Test, minimum undergraduate or master's GPA of 3.0 or equivalent. Additional exam requirements/recommendations for international students: Required—TOEFL (minimum score 550 paper-based; 77 iBT); Recommended—TWE. Electronic applications accepted. *Faculty research:* Geology, geophysics, hydrogeology, paleoclimatology, environmental science.

Rutgers University–New Brunswick, Graduate School-New Brunswick, Department of Environmental Sciences, Piscataway, NJ 08854-8097. Offers air pollution and resources (MS, PhD); aquatic biology (MS, PhD); aquatic chemistry (MS, PhD); atmospheric science (MS, PhD); chemistry and physics of aerosol and hydrosol systems (MS, PhD); environmental chemistry (MS, PhD); environmental microbiology (MS, PhD); environmental toxicology (PhD); exposure assessment (PhD); fate and effects of pollutants (MS, PhD); pollution prevention and control (MS, PhD); water and wastewater treatment (MS, PhD); water resources (MS, PhD). Terminal master's awarded for partial completion of doctoral program. *Degree requirements:* For master's, comprehensive exam, thesis or alternative, oral final exam; for doctorate, comprehensive exam, thesis/dissertation, thesis defense, qualifying exam. *Entrance requirements:* For master's and doctorate, GRE General Test. Additional exam requirements/recommendations for international students: Required—TOEFL. Electronic applications accepted. *Faculty research:* Biological waste treatment; contaminant fate and transport; air, soil and water quality.

South Dakota School of Mines and Technology, Graduate Division, MS Program in Atmospheric and Environmental Sciences, Rapid City, SD 57701-3995. Offers MS. *Program availability:* Part-time. *Degree requirements:* For master's, thesis. *Entrance requirements:* For master's, GRE General Test. Additional exam requirements/recommendations for international students: Required—TOEFL (minimum score 520 paper-based; 68 iBT), TWE. Electronic applications accepted. *Faculty research:* Hailstorm observations and numerical modeling, microbursts and lightning, radioactive transfer, remote sensing.

South Dakota School of Mines and Technology, Graduate Division, PhD Program in Atmospheric and Environmental Sciences, Rapid City, SD 57701-3995. Offers PhD. Program offered jointly with South Dakota State University. *Program availability:* Part-time. *Degree requirements:* For doctorate, comprehensive exam, thesis/dissertation. *Entrance requirements:* For doctorate, GRE General Test, GRE Subject Test. Additional exam requirements/recommendations for international students: Required—TOEFL (minimum score 520 paper-based; 68 iBT), TWE. Electronic applications accepted.

Southern Methodist University, Bobby B. Lyle School of Engineering, Department of Environmental and Civil Engineering, Dallas, TX 75275-0340. Offers air pollution control and atmospheric sciences (PhD); civil engineering (MS); environmental engineering (MS); environmental science (MS); structural engineering (PhD); sustainability and development (MA); water and wastewater engineering (PhD). *Program availability:* Part-time, evening/weekend, online learning. Terminal master's awarded for partial completion of doctoral program. *Degree requirements:* For master's, thesis optional; for doctorate, thesis/dissertation, oral and written qualifying exams. *Entrance requirements:* For master's, GRE General Test, minimum GPA of 3.0 in last 2 years; bachelor's degree in engineering, mathematics, or sciences; for doctorate, GRE, BS and MS in related field, minimum GPA of 3.3. Additional exam requirements/recommendations for international students: Required—TOEFL. Electronic applications accepted. *Faculty research:* Human and environmental health effects of endocrine disrupters, development of air pollution control systems for diesel engines, structural analysis and design, modeling and design of waste treatment systems.

Stevens Institute of Technology, Graduate School, Charles V. Schaefer Jr. School of Engineering, Department of Physics and Engineering Physics, Hoboken, NJ 07030. Offers applied optics (Certificate); atmospheric and environmental science and engineering (Certificate); microdevices and microsystems (Certificate); microelectronics (Certificate); photonics (Certificate); physics (M Eng, MS, PhD). *Program availability:* Part-time, evening/weekend. *Faculty:* 25 full-time (2 women), 3 part-time/adjunct (1 woman). *Students:* 32 full-time (12 women), 9 part-time (2 women); includes 4 minority (2 Black or African American, non-Hispanic/Latino; 2 Asian, non-Hispanic/Latino), 20 international. Average age 28. 63 applicants, 48% accepted, 11 enrolled. In 2015, 3 master's, 6 doctorates, 4 other advanced degrees awarded. Terminal master's awarded for partial completion of doctoral program. *Entrance requirements:* Additional exam requirements/recommendations for international students: Required—TOEFL (minimum score 74 iBT). *Application deadline:* For fall admission, 6/1 for domestic students, 4/15 for international students; for spring admission, 11/30 for domestic students, 11/1 for international students. Applications are processed on a rolling basis. Application fee: $60. Electronic applications accepted. *Expenses: Tuition, area resident:* Full-time $32,200; part-time $1450 per credit. *Required fees:* $1150; $550 per unit. $275 per semester. *Financial support:* Fellowships, research assistantships, teaching assistantships, career-related internships or fieldwork, Federal Work-Study, scholarships/grants, and unspecified assistantships available. Financial award application deadline: 2/15; financial award applicants required to submit FAFSA. *Faculty research:* Quantum systems, nanophotonics, optics. *Unit head:* Rainer Martini, Director, 201-216-5634, Fax: 201-216-5638, E-mail: rmartini@stevens.edu. *Application contact:* Graduate Admission, 888-783-8367, Fax: 888-511-1306, E-mail: graduate@stevens.edu. Website: http://www.stevens.edu/schaefer-school-engineering-science/departments/physics-engineering-physics

Stony Brook University, State University of New York, Graduate School, School of Marine and Atmospheric Sciences, Institute for Terrestrial and Planetary Atmospheres, Program in Atmospheric Sciences, Stony Brook, NY 11794. Offers MS, PhD. *Program availability:* Evening/weekend. *Degree requirements:* For doctorate, one foreign

language, comprehensive exam, thesis/dissertation. *Entrance requirements:* For master's, GRE, minimum GPA of 3.0, 3 letters of recommendation; for doctorate, GRE, official transcripts, minimum GPA of 3.0, 3 letters of recommendation. Additional exam requirements/recommendations for international students: Required—TOEFL (minimum score 600 paper-based). *Application deadline:* For fall admission, 1/15 priority date for domestic students; for spring admission, 10/1 priority date for domestic students. Application fee: $100. Electronic applications accepted. *Expenses:* $12,421 full-time resident tuition and fees, $453 per credit hour; $23,761 full-time nonresident tuition and fees, $952 per credit hour. *Financial support:* Fellowships, research assistantships, teaching assistantships, and career-related internships or fieldwork available. *Unit head:* Dr. Larry Swanson, Interim Dean, 631-632-8700, Fax: 631-632-8820, E-mail: larry.swanson@stonybrook.edu. *Application contact:* Carol Dovi, 631-632-8681, Fax: 631-632-8200, E-mail: somas@stonybrook.edu.
Website: http://you.stonybrook.edu/somas/education/graduate/atmospheric-sciences-track/

Texas Tech University, Graduate School, College of Arts and Sciences, Department of Geosciences, Lubbock, TX 79409. Offers atmospheric science (MS); geography (MS); geosciences (MS, PhD). *Program availability:* Part-time. *Faculty:* 27 full-time (3 women), 5 part-time/adjunct (1 woman). *Students:* 75 full-time (27 women), 16 part-time (6 women); includes 14 minority (2 Black or African American, non-Hispanic/Latino; 1 Asian, non-Hispanic/Latino; 7 Hispanic/Latino; 4 Two or more races, non-Hispanic/Latino), 18 international. Average age 27. 175 applicants, 19% accepted, 22 enrolled. In 2015, 19 master's, 2 doctorates awarded. *Degree requirements:* For master's, thesis; for doctorate, comprehensive exam, thesis/dissertation. *Entrance requirements:* For master's and doctorate, GRE General Test. Additional exam requirements/recommendations for international students: Required—TOEFL (minimum score 550 paper-based; 79 iBT). *Application deadline:* For fall admission, 6/1 priority date for domestic students, 1/15 priority date for international students; for spring admission, 9/1 priority date for domestic students, 6/15 priority date for international students. Applications are processed on a rolling basis. Application fee: $60. Electronic applications accepted. *Expenses:* Tuition, state resident: full-time $6477; part-time $269.89 per credit hour. Tuition, nonresident: full-time $15,837; part-time $659.89 per credit hour. *Required fees:* $2751; $36.50 per credit hour. $937.50 per semester. Tuition and fees vary according to course level. *Financial support:* In 2015–16, 87 students received support, including 68 fellowships (averaging $3,203 per year), 38 research assistantships (averaging $12,295 per year), 54 teaching assistantships (averaging $12,351 per year); Federal Work-Study, scholarships/grants, health care benefits, tuition waivers (partial), and unspecified assistantships also available. Financial award application deadline: 2/15; financial award applicants required to submit FAFSA. *Faculty research:* Geology, geophysics, geochemistry, geospatial technology, atmospheric sciences. *Total annual research expenditures:* $1.9 million. *Unit head:* Dr. Jeffrey A. Lee, Chairman, 806-834-8228, Fax: 806-742-0100, E-mail: jeff.lee@ttu.edu. *Application contact:* Dr. Callum Hetherington, Associate Professor, 806-834-3110, Fax: 806-724-0100, E-mail: callum.hetherington@ttu.edu.
Website: http://www.geosciences.ttu.edu

Université du Québec à Montréal, Graduate Programs, Program in Earth and Atmospheric Sciences, Montréal, QC H3C 3P8, Canada. Offers atmospheric sciences (M Sc); Earth and atmospheric sciences (PhD); Earth science (M Sc); meteorology (PhD, Diploma). PhD programs offered jointly with McGill University. *Program availability:* Part-time. *Degree requirements:* For master's, thesis. *Entrance requirements:* For master's and Diploma, appropriate bachelor's degree or equivalent, proficiency in French; for doctorate, appropriate master's degree or equivalent, proficiency in French.

University at Albany, State University of New York, College of Arts and Sciences, Department of Atmospheric and Environmental Sciences, Albany, NY 12222-0001. Offers atmospheric science (MS, PhD). *Degree requirements:* For master's, one foreign language, comprehensive exam, thesis; for doctorate, 2 foreign languages, comprehensive exam, thesis/dissertation, oral exams. *Entrance requirements:* For master's and doctorate, GRE General Test. Additional exam requirements/recommendations for international students: Required—TOEFL (minimum score 550 paper-based). Electronic applications accepted. *Faculty research:* Environmental geochemistry, tectonics, mesoscale meteorology, atmospheric chemistry.

The University of Alabama in Huntsville, School of Graduate Studies, College of Science, Department of Atmospheric Science, Huntsville, AL 35899. Offers atmospheric science (MS, PhD); earth system science (MS). *Program availability:* Part-time, evening/weekend. *Degree requirements:* For master's, comprehensive exam, thesis or alternative, oral and written exams; for doctorate, comprehensive exam, thesis/dissertation, oral and written exams. *Entrance requirements:* For master's, GRE General Test, minimum GPA of 3.0; sequence of courses in calculus (including the calculus of vector-valued functions); courses in linear algebra and ordinary differential equations; two semesters each of chemistry and calculus-based physics; proficiency in at least one high-level computer programming language; for doctorate, GRE General Test, minimum GPA of 3.0. Additional exam requirements/recommendations for international students: Required—TOEFL (minimum score 550 paper-based; 80 iBT), IELTS (minimum score 6.5). Electronic applications accepted. *Faculty research:* Severe weather, climate, satellite remote sensing, numerical modeling, air pollution.

University of Alaska Fairbanks, College of Natural Sciences and Mathematics, Department of Atmospheric Sciences, Fairbanks, AK 99775-7320. Offers MS, PhD. *Program availability:* Part-time. *Faculty:* 3 full-time (2 women). *Students:* 9 full-time (2 women), 4 part-time (2 women); includes 2 minority (1 American Indian or Alaska Native, non-Hispanic/Latino; 1 Asian, non-Hispanic/Latino), 7 international. Average age 31. 12 applicants, 17% accepted, 1 enrolled. In 2015, 3 master's, 1 doctorate awarded. *Degree requirements:* For master's, comprehensive exam, thesis, oral defense of thesis; for doctorate, comprehensive exam, thesis/dissertation, oral defense of dissertation. *Entrance requirements:* For master's, GRE General Test, bachelor's degree in a scientific discipline with minimum cumulative undergraduate and major GPA of 3.0; one year of calculus-based physics, math through differential equations, and one semester of chemistry; for doctorate, GRE General Test, degree in a scientific discipline with minimum GPA of 3.0; one year of calculus-based physics, math through differential equations, and one semester of chemistry. Additional exam requirements/recommendations for international students: Required—TOEFL (minimum score 550 paper-based; 80 iBT), IELTS (minimum score 6.5). *Application deadline:* For fall admission, 6/1 for domestic students, 3/1 for international students; for spring admission, 10/15 for domestic students, 9/1 for international students. Applications are processed on a rolling basis. Application fee: $60. Electronic applications accepted. *Expenses:* Tuition, state resident: full-time $7614; part-time $423 per credit. Tuition, nonresident: full-time $15,552; part-time $864 per credit. *Required fees:* $38 per credit. $187 per semester. Tuition and fees vary according to course level, course load, program and reciprocity agreements. *Financial support:* In 2015–16, 7 research assistantships with full tuition reimbursements (averaging $17,715 per year) were awarded; fellowships with full tuition reimbursements, teaching assistantships with full tuition reimbursements, Federal Work-Study, scholarships/grants, health care benefits, and unspecified assistantships also available. Support available to part-time students. Financial award application deadline: 2/15; financial award applicants required to submit FAFSA. *Faculty research:* Sea ice, climate modeling, atmospheric chemistry, global change, cloud and aerosol physics. *Unit head:* Dr. Uma Bhatt, Program Chair, 907-474-7368, Fax: 907-474-7379, E-mail: atmos@gi.alaska.edu. *Application contact:* Mary Kreta, Director of Admissions, 907-474-7500, Fax: 907-474-7097, E-mail: admissions@uaf.edu.
Website: http://www.uaf.edu/asp

The University of Arizona, College of Science, Department of Atmospheric Sciences, Tucson, AZ 85721. Offers MS, PhD. *Degree requirements:* For master's, thesis or alternative; for doctorate, comprehensive exam, thesis/dissertation. *Entrance requirements:* For master's, GRE General Test, 3 letters of recommendation; for doctorate, GRE General Test, 3 letters of recommendation, statement of purpose. Additional exam requirements/recommendations for international students: Required—TOEFL (minimum score 550 paper-based; 79 iBT). *Application deadline:* For fall admission, 2/1 for domestic students, 12/1 for international students. Applications are processed on a rolling basis. Application fee: $75. Electronic applications accepted. *Financial support:* Research assistantships, teaching assistantships, scholarships/grants, health care benefits, tuition waivers (full), and unspecified assistantships available. *Faculty research:* Climate dynamics, radiative transfer and remote sensing, atmospheric chemistry, atmosphere dynamics, atmospheric electricity. *Unit head:* Christopher L. Castro, Head, 520-626-5617. *Application contact:* Lupe Romero, Information Contact, 520-621-6831, Fax: 520-621-6833, E-mail: gradinfo@atmo.arizona.edu.
Website: http://www.atmo.arizona.edu

The University of British Columbia, Faculty of Science, Department of Earth, Ocean and Atmospheric Sciences, Vancouver, BC V6T 1Z4, Canada. Offers atmospheric science (M Sc, PhD); geological engineering (M Eng, MA Sc, PhD); geological sciences (M Sc, PhD); geophysics (M Sc, MA Sc, PhD); oceanography (M Sc, PhD). *Degree requirements:* For master's, one foreign language, thesis (for some programs); for doctorate, one foreign language, comprehensive exam, thesis/dissertation. *Entrance requirements:* Additional exam requirements/recommendations for international students: Required—TOEFL (minimum score 600 paper-based; 100 iBT). *Faculty research:* Oceans and atmosphere, environmental earth science, hydro geology, mineral deposits, geophysics.

University of California, Davis, Graduate Studies, Graduate Group in Atmospheric Sciences, Davis, CA 95616. Offers MS, PhD. *Degree requirements:* For master's, comprehensive exam or thesis; for doctorate, thesis/dissertation, 3 part qualifying exam. *Entrance requirements:* For master's and doctorate, GRE General Test, minimum GPA of 3.0. Additional exam requirements/recommendations for international students: Required—TOEFL (minimum score 550 paper-based). Electronic applications accepted. *Faculty research:* Air quality, biometeorology, climate dynamics, boundary layer large-scale dynamics.

University of California, Los Angeles, Graduate Division, College of Letters and Science, Department of Atmospheric and Oceanic Sciences, Los Angeles, CA 90095. Offers MS, PhD. Terminal master's awarded for partial completion of doctoral program. *Degree requirements:* For master's, comprehensive exam or thesis; for doctorate, thesis/dissertation, oral and written qualifying exams; 2 quarters of teaching experience. *Entrance requirements:* For master's and doctorate, GRE General Test, bachelor's degree; minimum undergraduate GPA of 3.0 (or its equivalent if letter grade system not used). Additional exam requirements/recommendations for international students: Required—TOEFL. Electronic applications accepted.

University of Chicago, Division of the Physical Sciences, Department of the Geophysical Sciences, Chicago, IL 60637. Offers atmospheric sciences (PhD); cosmochemistry (PhD); earth sciences (PhD); paleobiology (PhD); planetary and space sciences (PhD). Terminal master's awarded for partial completion of doctoral program. *Degree requirements:* For doctorate, variable foreign language requirement, comprehensive exam, thesis/dissertation. *Entrance requirements:* For doctorate, GRE General Test. Additional exam requirements/recommendations for international students: Required—TOEFL (minimum score 600 paper-based; 96 iBT), IELTS (minimum score 7). Electronic applications accepted. *Faculty research:* Climatology, evolutionary paleontology, cosmochemistry, geochemistry, oceanic sciences.

University of Colorado Boulder, Graduate School, College of Arts and Sciences, Department of Atmospheric and Oceanic Sciences, Boulder, CO 80309. Offers MS, PhD. *Faculty:* 13 full-time (7 women). *Students:* 48 full-time (22 women), 3 part-time (1 woman); includes 7 minority (2 Asian, non-Hispanic/Latino; 3 Hispanic/Latino; 2 Two or more races, non-Hispanic/Latino), 9 international. Average age 30. 111 applicants, 25% accepted, 12 enrolled. In 2015, 12 master's, 12 doctorates awarded. *Entrance requirements:* For master's, minimum undergraduate GPA of 3.0. *Application deadline:* For fall admission, 1/1 for domestic students, 12/1 for international students; for spring admission, 10/1 for domestic and international students. Application fee: $50 ($70 for international students). Electronic applications accepted. Application fee is waived when completed online. *Financial support:* In 2015–16, 96 students received support, including 2 fellowships (averaging $14,657 per year), 25 research assistantships with tuition reimbursements available (averaging $37,954 per year), 14 teaching assistantships with tuition reimbursements available (averaging $34,468 per year); institutionally sponsored loans, scholarships/grants, health care benefits, and unspecified assistantships also available. Financial award applicants required to submit FAFSA. *Faculty research:* Atmospheric sciences, atmospheric physics, atmospheric structure and dynamics, global change, climatology. *Total annual research expenditures:* $12.6 million. *Application contact:* E-mail: atocasst@colorado.edu.
Website: http://atoc.colorado.edu/

University of Guelph, Graduate Studies, Ontario Agricultural College, Department of Land Resource Science, Guelph, ON N1G 2W1, Canada. Offers atmospheric science (M Sc, PhD); environmental and agricultural earth sciences (M Sc, PhD); land resources management (M Sc, PhD); soil science (M Sc, PhD). *Program availability:* Part-time. *Degree requirements:* For master's, thesis (for some programs), research project (non-thesis track); for doctorate, comprehensive exam, thesis/dissertation. *Entrance requirements:* For master's, minimum B- average during previous 2 years of course work; for doctorate, minimum B average during previous 2 years of course work. Additional exam requirements/recommendations for international students: Required—TOEFL (minimum score 550 paper-based). Electronic applications accepted. *Faculty research:* Soil science, environmental earth science, land resource management.

University of Houston, College of Natural Sciences and Mathematics, Department of Earth and Atmospheric Sciences, Houston, TX 77204. Offers atmospheric science (PhD); geology (MA, PhD); geophysics (PhD). *Program availability:* Part-time. *Degree requirements:* For master's, thesis; for doctorate, comprehensive exam, thesis/dissertation. *Entrance requirements:* For master's and doctorate, GRE General Test. Additional exam requirements/recommendations for international students: Required—TOEFL (minimum score 550 paper-based; 79 iBT), IELTS (minimum score 6.5).

Electronic applications accepted. *Faculty research:* Atmospherics sciences, seismic and solid earth geophysics, tectonics, environmental hydrochemistry, carbonates, micropaleontology, structure and tectonics, petroleum geology.

University of Illinois at Urbana–Champaign, Graduate College, College of Liberal Arts and Sciences, School of Earth, Society and Environment, Department of Atmospheric Sciences, Champaign, IL 61820. Offers MS, PhD.

The University of Kansas, Graduate Studies, College of Liberal Arts and Sciences, Department of Geography, Lawrence, KS 66045-7613. Offers atmospheric science (MS); geography (MA, PhD); MUP/MA. *Program availability:* Part-time. *Students:* 58 full-time (22 women), 18 part-time (5 women); includes 10 minority (8 American Indian or Alaska Native, non-Hispanic/Latino; 1 Asian, non-Hispanic/Latino; 1 Hispanic/Latino), 6 international. Average age 32. 32 applicants, 50% accepted, 11 enrolled. In 2015, 10 master's, 13 doctorates awarded. *Entrance requirements:* For master's and doctorate, GRE General Test, 3 letters of reference, transcripts, statement of interests. Additional exam requirements/recommendations for international students: Required—TOEFL. *Application deadline:* For fall admission, 1/15 priority date for domestic and international students; for spring admission, 11/1 for domestic students, 10/1 for international students. Application fee: $65 ($85 for international students). Electronic applications accepted. *Financial support:* Fellowships, research assistantships, teaching assistantships, and unspecified assistantships available. Financial award application deadline: 1/15. *Faculty research:* Physical geography, human/cultural/regional geography, geographic information science, atmospheric science. *Unit head:* Johannes Feddema, Chair, 785-864-5534, E-mail: feddema@ku.edu. *Application contact:* Beverly Koerner, Administrative Associate, 785-864-7706, E-mail: koerner@ku.edu.
Website: http://www.geog.ku.edu/

The University of Manchester, School of Earth, Atmospheric and Environmental Sciences, Manchester, United Kingdom. Offers atmospheric sciences (M Phil, M Sc, PhD); basin studies and petroleum geosciences (M Phil, M Sc, PhD); earth, atmospheric and environmental sciences (M Phil, M Sc, PhD); environmental geochemistry and cosmochemistry (M Phil, M Sc, PhD); isotope geochemistry and cosmochemistry (M Phil, M Sc, PhD); paleontology (M Phil, M Sc, PhD); physics and chemistry of minerals and fluids (M Phil, M Sc, PhD); structural and petrological geosciences (M Phil, M Sc, PhD).

University of Maryland, Baltimore County, The Graduate School, College of Natural and Mathematical Sciences, Department of Physics, Program in Atmospheric Physics, Baltimore, MD 21250. Offers MS, PhD. *Program availability:* Part-time. *Faculty:* 25 full-time (5 women), 16 part-time/adjunct (4 women). *Students:* 13 full-time (1 woman), 4 international. Average age 27. 7 applicants, 86% accepted, 5 enrolled. In 2015, 1 master's, 2 doctorates awarded. Terminal master's awarded for partial completion of doctoral program. *Degree requirements:* For master's, comprehensive exam (for some programs), thesis optional; for doctorate, comprehensive exam, thesis/dissertation. *Entrance requirements:* For master's and doctorate, GRE General Test, minimum GPA of 3.0. Additional exam requirements/recommendations for international students: Required—TOEFL (minimum score 587 paper-based; 95 iBT). *Application deadline:* For fall admission, 1/1 for domestic and international students; for spring admission, 11/1 for domestic students, 5/1 for international students. Applications are processed on a rolling basis. Application fee: $50. Electronic applications accepted. *Expenses:* Tuition, state resident: full-time $12,816. Tuition, nonresident: full-time $19,710. *Financial support:* In 2015–16, 13 students received support, including 2 fellowships with full tuition reimbursements available (averaging $30,000 per year), 10 research assistantships with full tuition reimbursements available (averaging $27,000 per year), 3 teaching assistantships with full tuition reimbursements available (averaging $23,000 per year); career-related internships or fieldwork, scholarships/grants, health care benefits, and unspecified assistantships also available. Financial award application deadline: 5/31. *Faculty research:* Atmospheric dynamics, aerosols and clouds, satellite and aircraft remote sensing, optics and instrumentation development, LIDAR and in situ aerosol measurements. *Total annual research expenditures:* $4 million. *Unit head:* Dr. Zhibo Zhang, Graduate Program Director, 410-455-6315, Fax: 410-455-1072,
E-mail: zhibo.zhang@umbc.edu. *Application contact:* Dr. Lazlo Takacs, Graduate Admissions Committee Chair, 410-455-2513, Fax: 410-455-1072,
E-mail: takacs@umbc.edu.
Website: http://physics.umbc.edu/grad/degrees/atmospheric/

University of Massachusetts Lowell, College of Sciences, Department of Environmental, Earth and Atmospheric Sciences, Lowell, MA 01854. Offers atmospheric physics (PhD); atmospheric sciences (MS).

University of Michigan, College of Engineering, Department of Climate and Space Sciences and Engineering, Ann Arbor, MI 48109. Offers applied climate (M Eng); atmospheric, oceanic and space sciences (MS, PhD); geoscience and remote sensing (PhD); space and planetary sciences (PhD); space engineering (M Eng). *Program availability:* Part-time. *Students:* 96 full-time (32 women), 2 part-time (1 woman). 125 applicants, 28% accepted, 16 enrolled. In 2015, 39 master's, 14 doctorates awarded. Terminal master's awarded for partial completion of doctoral program. *Degree requirements:* For master's, thesis (for some programs); for doctorate, thesis/dissertation, oral defense of dissertation, preliminary exams. *Entrance requirements:* For master's and doctorate, GRE General Test. Additional exam requirements/recommendations for international students: Required—TOEFL. *Application deadline:* Applications are processed on a rolling basis. Electronic applications accepted. *Financial support:* Fellowships, research assistantships, teaching assistantships, career-related internships or fieldwork, Federal Work-Study, institutionally sponsored loans, and health care benefits available. Support available to part-time students. Financial award applicants required to submit FAFSA. *Faculty research:* Planetary environments, space instrumentation, air pollution meteorology, global climate change, sun-earth connection, space weather. *Total annual research expenditures:* $44.7 million. *Unit head:* Dr. James Slavin, Chair, 734-764-7221, Fax: 734-615-4645,
E-mail: jaslavin@umich.edu. *Application contact:* Sandra Pytlinski, Graduate Student Services Coordinator, 734-936-0482, Fax: 734-763-0437, E-mail: sanpyt@umich.edu.
Website: http://clasp.engin.umich.edu/

University of Missouri, Office of Research and Graduate Studies, School of Natural Resources, Department of Soil, Environmental, and Atmospheric Sciences, Columbia, MO 65211. Offers atmospheric science (MS, PhD); soil science (MS, PhD). *Degree requirements:* For doctorate, thesis/dissertation. *Entrance requirements:* For master's and doctorate, GRE General Test, minimum GPA of 3.0. Additional exam requirements/recommendations for international students: Required—TOEFL (minimum score 530 paper-based; 71 iBT). *Faculty research:* Soil physics; x-ray tomography of soil systems; use of radar in forecasting; soil and water conservation and management and applied soil physics; soil chemical and biogeochemical investigations; fresh water supply regimes (quantity, timing); water quality disturbance mechanisms; best management practices (BMP's); environmental biophysics and ecohydrology; hydrologic scaling, modeling, and change; synoptic and mesoscale dynamics.

University of Nevada, Reno, Graduate School, Interdisciplinary Program in Atmospheric Sciences, Reno, NV 89557. Offers MS, PhD. Terminal master's awarded for partial completion of doctoral program. *Degree requirements:* For master's, thesis optional; for doctorate, thesis/dissertation. *Entrance requirements:* For master's, GRE (recommended), minimum GPA of 2.75; for doctorate, GRE (recommended), minimum GPA of 3.0. Additional exam requirements/recommendations for international students: Required—TOEFL (minimum score 500 paper-based; 61 iBT), IELTS (minimum score 6). Electronic applications accepted. *Faculty research:* Atmospheric chemistry, cloud and aerosol physics, atmospheric optics, mesoscale meterology.

The University of North Carolina at Chapel Hill, Graduate School, Gillings School of Global Public Health, Department of Environmental Sciences and Engineering, Chapel Hill, NC 27599. Offers air, radiation and industrial hygiene (MPH, MS, MSEE, MSPH, PhD); aquatic and atmospheric sciences (MPH, MS, MSPH, PhD); environmental engineering (MPH, MS, MSEE, MSPH, PhD); environmental health sciences (MPH, MS, MSPH, PhD); environmental management and policy (MPH, MS, MSPH, PhD). *Students:* 112 full-time (68 women); includes 20 minority (11 Asian, non-Hispanic/Latino; 4 Hispanic/Latino; 5 Two or more races, non-Hispanic/Latino), 31 international. Average age 28. 178 applicants, 37% accepted, 39 enrolled. Terminal master's awarded for partial completion of doctoral program. *Degree requirements:* For master's, comprehensive exam, thesis (for some programs), research paper; for doctorate, comprehensive exam, thesis/dissertation. *Entrance requirements:* For master's and doctorate, GRE General Test, minimum GPA of 3.0 (recommended). Additional exam requirements/recommendations for international students: Required—TOEFL. *Application deadline:* For fall admission, 12/10 priority date for domestic and international students; for spring admission, 9/10 for domestic students. Applications are processed on a rolling basis. Application fee: $85. Electronic applications accepted. *Financial support:* Fellowships with tuition reimbursements, research assistantships with tuition reimbursements, teaching assistantships with tuition reimbursements, career-related internships or fieldwork, Federal Work-Study, traineeships, health care benefits, and unspecified assistantships available. Support available to part-time students. Financial award application deadline: 12/10; financial award applicants required to submit FAFSA. *Faculty research:* Air, radiation and industrial hygiene, aquatic and atmospheric sciences, environmental health sciences, environmental management and policy, water resources engineering. *Unit head:* Dr. Michael Aitken, Chair, 919-966-1024, Fax: 919-966-7911, E-mail: mike_aitken@unc.edu. *Application contact:* Jack Whaley, Registrar, 919-966-3844, Fax: 919-966-7911,
E-mail: jack_whaley@unc.edu.
Website: http://www2.sph.unc.edu/envr/

University of North Dakota, Graduate School, John D. Odegard School of Aerospace Sciences, Department of Atmospheric Sciences, Grand Forks, ND 58202. Offers MS, PhD. *Program availability:* Part-time. *Degree requirements:* For master's, comprehensive exam, thesis or alternative. *Entrance requirements:* For master's and doctorate, GRE General Test, minimum GPA of 3.0. Additional exam requirements/recommendations for international students: Required—TOEFL (minimum score 550 paper-based; 79 iBT), IELTS (minimum score 6.5). Electronic applications accepted.

University of South Florida, College of Arts and Sciences, Department of Physics, Tampa, FL 33620-9951. Offers applied physics (PhD); physics (MS), including applied physics, atmospheric physics, atomic and molecular physics, laser physics, materials physics, medical physics, optical physics, semiconductor physics, solid state physics. MSE offered jointly with College of Engineering. *Program availability:* Part-time. *Faculty:* 25 full-time (2 women). *Students:* 71 full-time (16 women), 6 part-time (1 woman); includes 14 minority (2 Black or African American, non-Hispanic/Latino; 12 Hispanic/Latino), 36 international. Average age 31. 97 applicants, 21% accepted, 12 enrolled. In 2015, 14 master's, 8 doctorates awarded. *Degree requirements:* For master's, comprehensive exam, thesis optional; for doctorate, comprehensive exam, thesis/dissertation. *Entrance requirements:* For master's and doctorate, GRE General Test; GRE Subject Test in physics (recommended), minimum GPA of 3.0, three letters of recommendation, statement of purpose. Additional exam requirements/recommendations for international students: Required—TOEFL (minimum score 550 paper-based; 79 iBT) or IELTS (minimum score 6.5). *Application deadline:* For fall admission, 2/15 priority date for domestic students, 1/2 for international students; for spring admission, 9/1 for domestic students, 7/1 for international students. Applications are processed on a rolling basis. Application fee: $30. Electronic applications accepted. *Financial support:* In 2015–16, 70 students received support, including 27 research assistantships with tuition reimbursements available (averaging $15,272 per year), 43 teaching assistantships with tuition reimbursements available (averaging $16,267 per year); unspecified assistantships also available. *Faculty research:* The molecular organization of collagen, lipid rafts in biological membranes, the formation of Alzheimer plaques, the role of cellular ion pumps in wound healing, carbon nanotubes as biological detectors, optical imaging of neuronal activity, three-dimensional imaging of intact tissues, motility of cancer cells, the optical detection of pathogens in water. *Total annual research expenditures:* $2.4 million. *Unit head:* Dr. Pritish Mukherjee, Professor and Chairperson, 813-974-3293, Fax: 813-974-5813, E-mail: pritish@usf.edu. *Application contact:* Dr. Lilia Woods, Professor and Graduate Program Director, 813-974-2862, Fax: 813-974-5813, E-mail: lmwoods@usf.edu.
Website: http://physics.usf.edu/

University of Utah, Graduate School, College of Mines and Earth Sciences, Department of Atmospheric Sciences, Salt Lake City, UT 84112. Offers MS, PhD. *Program availability:* Part-time. *Faculty:* 11 full-time (1 woman), 7 part-time/adjunct (2 women). *Students:* 43 full-time (19 women); includes 3 minority (1 American Indian or Alaska Native, non-Hispanic/Latino; 2 Hispanic/Latino), 9 international. Average age 26. 68 applicants, 35% accepted, 14 enrolled. In 2015, 4 master's, 1 doctorate awarded. Terminal master's awarded for partial completion of doctoral program. *Degree requirements:* For master's, comprehensive exam, thesis; for doctorate, comprehensive exam, thesis/dissertation. *Entrance requirements:* For master's and doctorate, GRE General Test, minimum GPA of 3.0, 3 letters of reference, personal statement, resume/curriculum vitae, official transcript. Additional exam requirements/recommendations for international students: Required—TOEFL (minimum score 550 paper-based; 80 iBT); Recommended—IELTS (minimum score 6.5). *Application deadline:* For fall admission, 1/7 priority date for domestic and international students. Applications are processed on a rolling basis. Application fee: $55 ($65 for international students). Electronic applications accepted. *Expenses:* Contact institution. *Financial support:* Traineeships available. Financial award application deadline: 2/15; financial award applicants required to submit FAFSA. *Faculty research:* Cloud-aerosol-climate interactions, mountain weather and climate, climate physics and dynamics, weather and climate modeling, land-atmosphere interactions, air quality, and tropical meteorology. *Total annual research expenditures:* $4.3 million. *Unit head:* Dr. Kevin D. Perry, Chair, 801-581-6138, Fax: 801-585-3681, E-mail: kevin.perry@utah.edu. *Application contact:* Michelle R. Brooks, Academic Coordinator, 801-581-6136, Fax: 801-585-3681, E-mail: atmos-advising@lists.utah.edu.
Website: http://www.atmos.utah.edu/

University of Washington, Graduate School, College of the Environment, Department of Atmospheric Sciences, Seattle, WA 98195. Offers MS, PhD. *Degree requirements:*

For master's, thesis; for doctorate, thesis/dissertation, qualifying exam. *Entrance requirements:* For master's and doctorate, GRE General Test, minimum GPA of 3.0. Additional exam requirements/recommendations for international students: Required—TOEFL. *Faculty research:* Climate change, synoptic and mesoscale meteorology, atmospheric chemistry, cloud physics, dynamics of the atmosphere.

University of Wisconsin–Madison, Graduate School, College of Letters and Science, Department of Atmospheric and Oceanic Sciences, Madison, WI 53706-1380. Offers MS, PhD. *Program availability:* Part-time. *Degree requirements:* For master's, thesis (for some programs); for doctorate, thesis/dissertation. *Entrance requirements:* For master's and doctorate, GRE General Test, minimum GPA of 3.0; previous course work in chemistry, mathematics, and physics. Electronic applications accepted. *Expenses:* Tuition, state resident: full-time $5364. Tuition, nonresident: full-time $12,027. *Required fees:* $571. Tuition and fees vary according to campus/location, program and reciprocity agreements. *Faculty research:* Satellite meteorology, weather systems, global climate change, numerical modeling, atmosphere-ocean interaction.

University of Wyoming, College of Engineering and Applied Sciences, Department of Atmospheric Science, Laramie, WY 82071. Offers MS, PhD. *Program availability:* Online learning. Terminal master's awarded for partial completion of doctoral program. *Degree requirements:* For master's, thesis; for doctorate, comprehensive exam, thesis/dissertation. *Entrance requirements:* For master's and doctorate, GRE General Test, minimum GPA of 3.0. Additional exam requirements/recommendations for international students: Required—TOEFL (minimum score 525 paper-based). Electronic applications accepted. *Expenses:* Contact institution. *Faculty research:* Cloud physics; aerosols, boundary layer processes; airborne observations; stratospheric aerosols and gases.

Yale University, Graduate School of Arts and Sciences, Department of Geology and Geophysics, New Haven, CT 06520. Offers biogeochemistry (PhD); climate dynamics (PhD); geochemistry (PhD); geophysics (PhD); meteorology (PhD); oceanography (PhD); paleontology (PhD); paleooceanography (PhD); petrology (PhD); tectonics (PhD). *Degree requirements:* For doctorate, thesis/dissertation. *Entrance requirements:* For doctorate, GRE General Test. Additional exam requirements/recommendations for international students: Required—TOEFL.

Meteorology

Ball State University, Graduate School, College of Sciences and Humanities, Department of Geography, Muncie, IN 47306. Offers geographic information science (giscience) (Certificate); geography (MS); professional meteorology and climatology (Certificate). *Program availability:* Part-time. *Faculty:* 6 full-time (2 women). *Students:* 6 full-time (1 woman), 4 part-time (2 women); includes 2 minority (1 Hispanic/Latino; 1 Two or more races, non-Hispanic/Latino). Average age 24. 8 applicants, 100% accepted, 6 enrolled. In 2015, 4 master's, 1 other advanced degree awarded. *Degree requirements:* For master's, thesis. *Entrance requirements:* For master's, minimum baccalaureate GPA of 2.75 or 3.0 in latter half of baccalauareate, letter of interest, three letters of recommendation, resume or curriculum vitae, official transcripts. Additional exam requirements/recommendations for international students: Required—TOEFL (minimum score 550 paper-based; 79 iBT), IELTS (minimum score 6.5). *Application deadline:* Applications are processed on a rolling basis. Application fee: $60. Electronic applications accepted. *Expenses: Tuition, area resident:* Full-time $6948; part-time $2316 per semester. Tuition, state resident: full-time $10,422; part-time $3474 per semester. Tuition, nonresident: full-time $19,062; part-time $6354 per semester. *Required fees:* $651 per semester. Tuition and fees vary according to campus/location, program and reciprocity agreements. *Financial support:* In 2015–16, 7 students received support, including 7 teaching assistantships with partial tuition reimbursements available (averaging $10,027 per year). Financial award application deadline: 3/1; financial award applicants required to submit FAFSA. *Faculty research:* Remote sensing, tourism and recreation, Latin American urbanization. *Unit head:* Dr. Kevin Turcotte, Chairperson/Professor, 765-285-1776, Fax: 765-285-2351,
E-mail: turk@bsu.edu. *Application contact:* Dr. Jason Yang, Associate Professor/Graduate Program Director, 765-285-1761, Fax: 765-285-2351, E-mail: jyang@bsu.edu.
Website: http://www.bsu.edu/geography/

Florida Institute of Technology, College of Engineering, Program in Meteorology, Melbourne, FL 32901-6975. Offers MS. *Program availability:* Part-time. *Students:* 11 full-time (5 women), 2 part-time (0 women); includes 1 minority (Black or African American, non-Hispanic/Latino), 4 international. Average age 30. 19 applicants, 42% accepted, 4 enrolled. In 2015, 1 master's awarded. *Degree requirements:* For master's, thesis or final exam; oral presentation of thesis results. *Entrance requirements:* For master's, GRE General Test, 3 letters of recommendation, resume, statement of objectives. Additional exam requirements/recommendations for international students: Required—TOEFL (minimum score 550 paper-based; 79 iBT). *Application deadline:* Applications are processed on a rolling basis. Electronic applications accepted. *Expenses: Tuition, area resident:* Full-time $21,690; part-time $1205 per credit hour. *Required fees:* $500. Tuition and fees vary according to degree level, campus/location and program. *Financial support:* Research assistantships and teaching assistantships available. *Unit head:* Dr. George Maul, Program Chair, 321-674-7453, E-mail: gmaul@fit.edu. *Application contact:* Cheryl A. Brown, Associate Director of Graduate Admissions, 321-674-7581, Fax: 321-723-9468, E-mail: cbrown@fit.edu.
Website: http://www.fit.edu/programs/

Florida State University, The Graduate School, College of Arts and Sciences, Department of Earth, Ocean and Atmospheric Science, Program in Meteorology, Tallahassee, FL 32306-4520. Offers MS, PhD. *Faculty:* 16 full-time (1 woman). *Students:* 53 full-time (14 women), 4 part-time (0 women); includes 4 minority (1 Black or African American, non-Hispanic/Latino; 2 Hispanic/Latino; 1 Two or more races, non-Hispanic/Latino), 8 international. Average age 24. 60 applicants, 63% accepted, 15 enrolled. In 2015, 20 master's, 2 doctorates awarded. Terminal master's awarded for partial completion of doctoral program. *Degree requirements:* For master's, thesis optional; for doctorate, comprehensive exam, thesis/dissertation. *Entrance requirements:* For master's, GRE General Test (minimum score 300 combined verbal and quantitative), minimum GPA of 3.0 in upper-division work; for doctorate, GRE General Test (minimum combined Verbal and Quantitative score: 300), minimum GPA of 3.0, faculty sponsor. Additional exam requirements/recommendations for international students: Required—TOEFL (minimum score 550 paper-based; 80 iBT). *Application deadline:* For fall admission, 1/30 priority date for domestic students, 1/30 for international students; for spring admission, 11/1 for domestic students, 6/30 for international students. Applications are processed on a rolling basis. Application fee: $35. *Expenses: Tuition, area resident:* Full-time $7263; part-time $403.50 per credit hour. Tuition, nonresident: full-time $18,087; part-time $1004.85 per credit hour. *Required fees:* $1365; $75.81 per credit hour. $20 per semester. Tuition and fees vary according to campus/location. *Financial support:* In 2015–16, 45 students received support, including 1 fellowship with full tuition reimbursement available (averaging $19,000 per year), 30 research assistantships with full tuition reimbursements available (averaging $21,500 per year), 14 teaching assistantships with full tuition reimbursements available (averaging $21,500 per year); career-related internships or fieldwork, scholarships/grants, and unspecified assistantships also available. Financial award application deadline: 1/30; financial award applicants required to submit FAFSA. *Faculty research:* Physical, dynamic, and synoptic meteorology; climatology. *Total annual research expenditures:* $600,000. *Unit head:* Dr. James Tull, Chairman, 850-644-6205, Fax: 850-644-9642, E-mail: jtull@fsu.edu. *Application contact:* Alicia Brown, Academic Program Specialist, 850-644-8582, Fax: 850-644-9642,
E-mail: ajbrown2@fsu.edu.
Website: http://www.met.fsu.edu/

Iowa State University of Science and Technology, Department of Geological and Atmospheric Sciences, Ames, IA 50011. Offers earth science (MS, PhD); environmental science (MS, PhD); geology (MS, PhD); meteorology (MS, PhD). *Degree requirements:* For master's, thesis (for some programs); for doctorate, thesis/dissertation. *Entrance requirements:* For master's and doctorate, GRE General Test. Additional exam requirements/recommendations for international students: Required—TOEFL (minimum score 550 paper-based; 79 iBT), IELTS (minimum score 6.5). Electronic applications accepted.

Iowa State University of Science and Technology, Program in Agricultural Meteorology, Ames, IA 50011. Offers MS, PhD. *Entrance requirements:* Additional exam requirements/recommendations for international students: Required—TOEFL (minimum score 550 paper-based; 79 iBT), IELTS (minimum score 6.5). Electronic applications accepted.

Iowa State University of Science and Technology, Program in Meteorology, Ames, IA 50011. Offers MS, PhD. *Entrance requirements:* For master's and doctorate, GRE. Additional exam requirements/recommendations for international students: Required—TOEFL (minimum score 550 paper-based; 79 iBT), IELTS (minimum score 6.5). Electronic applications accepted.

McGill University, Faculty of Graduate and Postdoctoral Studies, Faculty of Agricultural and Environmental Sciences, Department of Natural Resource Sciences, Montréal, QC H3A 2T5, Canada. Offers entomology (M Sc, PhD); environmental assessment (M Sc); forest science (M Sc, PhD); microbiology (M Sc, PhD); micrometeorology (M Sc, PhD); neotropical environment (M Sc, PhD); soil science (M Sc, PhD); wildlife biology (M Sc, PhD).

Millersville University of Pennsylvania, College of Graduate Studies and Adult Learning, College of Science and Technology, Department of Earth Sciences, Program in Integrated Scientific Applications: Climate Science Applications Option, Millersville, PA 17551-0302. Offers MS. *Program availability:* Part-time. *Faculty:* 11 full-time (2 women), 2 part-time/adjunct (0 women). In 2015, 1 master's awarded. *Degree requirements:* For master's, thesis optional, internship or applied research. *Entrance requirements:* For master's, GRE, MAT or GMAT (if cumulative GPA is lower than 3.0), three professional letters of recommendation, academic and professional goals statement, current resume. Additional exam requirements/recommendations for international students: Required—TOEFL (minimum score 600 paper-based), IELTS (minimum score 6). *Application deadline:* Applications are processed on a rolling basis. Application fee: $40. Electronic applications accepted. *Expenses:* Tuition, state resident: full-time $8460; part-time $470 per credit. Tuition, nonresident: full-time $12,690; part-time $705 per credit. *Required fees:* $2471; $133.75 per credit. Tuition and fees vary according to course load, degree level and program. *Financial support:* Application deadline: 3/15; applicants required to submit FAFSA. *Faculty research:* Climatology, meteorology, environmental economics. *Unit head:* Dr. Richard D. Clark, Coordinator, 717-871-7434, Fax: 717-871-7918, E-mail: richard.clark@millersville.edu. *Application contact:* Dr. Victor S. DeSantis, Dean of College of Graduate Studies and Adult Learning/Associate Provost for Civic and Community Engagement, 717-871-7619, Fax: 717-871-7954, E-mail: victor.desantis@millersville.edu.
Website: http://www.millersville.edu/esci/msisa/csa.php

Millersville University of Pennsylvania, College of Graduate Studies and Adult Learning, College of Science and Technology, Department of Earth Sciences, Program in Integrated Scientific Applications: Weather Intelligence and Risk Management Option, Millersville, PA 17551-0302. Offers MS. *Program availability:* Part-time. *Faculty:* 11 full-time (2 women), 2 part-time/adjunct (0 women). *Students:* 5 full-time (0 women), 2 part-time (0 women); includes 2 minority (1 Asian, non-Hispanic/Latino; 1 Hispanic/Latino). 4 applicants, 75% accepted, 3 enrolled. In 2015, 2 master's awarded. *Degree requirements:* For master's, thesis optional, internship, applied research. *Entrance requirements:* For master's, GRE, MAT or GMAT (if cumulative GPA is lower than 3.0), three professional letters of recommendation, academic and professional goals statement, current resume. Additional exam requirements/recommendations for international students: Required—TOEFL (minimum score 600 paper-based), IELTS (minimum score 6). *Application deadline:* Applications are processed on a rolling basis. Application fee: $40. Electronic applications accepted. *Expenses:* Tuition, state resident: full-time $8460; part-time $470 per credit. Tuition, nonresident: full-time $12,690; part-time $705 per credit. *Required fees:* $2471; $133.75 per credit. Tuition and fees vary according to course load, degree level and program. *Financial support:* Application deadline: 3/15; applicants required to submit FAFSA. *Faculty research:* Climatology and meteorology, weather derivatives, environmental economics, statistical applications. *Unit head:* Dr. Richard D. Clark, Chair, 717-871-7434, Fax: 717-871-7918, E-mail: richard.clark@millersville.edu. *Application contact:* Dr. Victor S. DeSantis, Dean of College of Graduate Studies and Adult Learning/Associate Provost for Civic and Community Engagement, 717-871-7619, Fax: 717-871-7954,
E-mail: victor.desantis@millersville.edu.
Website: http://www.millersville.edu/esci/msisa/wirm.php

Mississippi State University, College of Arts and Sciences, Department of Geosciences, Mississippi State, MS 39762. Offers applied meteorology (MS); broadcast meteorology (MS); earth and atmospheric science (PhD); environmental geoscience

(MS); geography (MS); geology (MS); geospatial sciences (MS); professional meteorology/climatology (MS); teachers in geoscience (MS). *Program availability:* Online learning. *Faculty:* 18 full-time (4 women), 1 part-time/adjunct (0 women). *Students:* 53 full-time (27 women), 176 part-time (81 women); includes 26 minority (7 Black or African American, non-Hispanic/Latino; 3 Asian, non-Hispanic/Latino; 10 Hispanic/Latino; 1 Native Hawaiian or other Pacific Islander, non-Hispanic/Latino; 5 Two or more races, non-Hispanic/Latino), 5 international. Average age 33. 123 applicants, 73% accepted, 68 enrolled. In 2015, 70 master's, 3 doctorates awarded. *Degree requirements:* For master's, thesis (for some programs), comprehensive oral or written exam; for doctorate, thesis/dissertation, comprehensive oral or written exam. *Entrance requirements:* For master's, GRE (for on-campus applicants), minimum undergraduate GPA of 2.75; for doctorate, thesis-based MS with background in one department emphasis area. Additional exam requirements/recommendations for international students: Required—TOEFL (minimum score 477 paper-based; 53 iBT); Recommended—IELTS (minimum score 4.5). *Application deadline:* For fall admission, 7/1 for domestic students, 5/1 for international students; for spring admission, 11/1 for domestic students, 9/1 for international students. Applications are processed on a rolling basis. Application fee: $60. Electronic applications accepted. *Expenses: Tuition, area resident:* Full-time $7502; part-time $833.74 per credit hour. Tuition, nonresident: full-time $20,142; part-time $2238.24 per credit hour. *Financial support:* In 2015–16, 7 research assistantships with full tuition reimbursements (averaging $13,792 per year), 28 teaching assistantships with full tuition reimbursements (averaging $13,500 per year) were awarded; Federal Work-Study, institutionally sponsored loans, scholarships/grants, tuition waivers (partial), and unspecified assistantships also available. Financial award application deadline: 4/1; financial award applicants required to submit FAFSA. *Faculty research:* Climatology, hydrogeology, sedimentology, meteorology. *Total annual research expenditures:* $3.1 million. *Unit head:* Dr. William Cooke, Interim Department Head, 662-325-1393, Fax: 662-325-9423, E-mail: whc5@geosci.msstate.edu. *Application contact:* Meredith Nagel, Admissions Assistant, 662-325-9077, E-mail: mnagel@grad.msstate.edu.
Website: http://www.geosciences.msstate.edu

Naval Postgraduate School, Departments and Academic Groups, Department of Meteorology, Monterey, CA 93943. Offers meteorology (MS, PhD); meteorology and physical oceanography (MS). Program only open to commissioned officers of the United States and friendly nations and selected United States federal civilian employees. *Program availability:* Part-time. *Degree requirements:* For master's, thesis; for doctorate, one foreign language, thesis/dissertation. *Faculty research:* Air-sea interactions, boundary layer meteorology, climate dynamics, numerical weather prediction, tropical cyclones.

Naval Postgraduate School, Departments and Academic Groups, Undersea Warfare Academic Group, Monterey, CA 93943. Offers applied mathematics (MS); applied physics (MS); applied science (MS), including acoustics, operations research, physical oceanography, signal processing; electrical engineering (MS); engineering acoustics (MS, PhD); engineering science (MS), including electrical engineering, mechanical engineering; mechanical engineer (ME); mechanical engineering (MS, MSME); meteorology (MS); operations research (MS); physical oceanography (MS). Program only open to commissioned officers of the United States and friendly nations and selected United States federal civilian employees. *Program availability:* Part-time. *Degree requirements:* For master's, thesis. *Faculty research:* Unmanned/autonomous vehicles, sea mines and countermeasures, submarine warfare in the twentieth and twenty-first centuries.

North Carolina State University, Graduate School, College of Physical and Mathematical Sciences, Department of Marine, Earth, and Atmospheric Sciences, Raleigh, NC 27695. Offers marine, earth, and atmospheric sciences (MS, PhD); meteorology (MS, PhD); oceanography (MS, PhD). PhD offered jointly with The University of North Carolina Wilmington. Terminal master's awarded for partial completion of doctoral program. *Degree requirements:* For master's, thesis (for some programs), final oral exam; for doctorate, comprehensive exam, thesis/dissertation, final oral exam, preliminary oral and written exams. *Entrance requirements:* For master's, GRE General Test, minimum GPA of 3.0; for doctorate, GRE General Test, GRE Subject Test (for disciplines in biological oceanography and geology), minimum GPA of 3.0. Additional exam requirements/recommendations for international students: Required—TOEFL (minimum score 550 paper-based). Electronic applications accepted. *Faculty research:* Boundary layer and air quality meteorology; climate and mesoscale dynamics; biological, chemical, geological, and physical oceanography; hard rock, soft rock, environmental, and paleo-geology.

Northern Arizona University, Graduate College, College of Engineering, Forestry, and Natural Sciences, School of Earth Sciences and Environmental Sustainability, Flagstaff, AZ 86011. Offers climate science and solutions (MS); earth sciences and environmental sustainability (PhD); environmental sciences and policy (MS); geology (MS). *Degree requirements:* For master's, comprehensive exam (for some programs), thesis (for some programs). *Entrance requirements:* Additional exam requirements/recommendations for international students: Required—TOEFL (minimum score 550 paper-based; 80 iBT), IELTS (minimum score 7). *Application deadline:* For fall admission, 2/1 priority date for domestic and international students. Applications are processed on a rolling basis. Application fee: $65. Electronic applications accepted. *Expenses: Tuition, area resident:* Full-time $8710. Tuition, nonresident: full-time $20,350. *Required fees:* $896. *Financial support:* Fellowships, research assistantships with full tuition reimbursements, teaching assistantships with full tuition reimbursements, career-related internships or fieldwork, Federal Work-Study, scholarships/grants, health care benefits, tuition waivers (full and partial), and unspecified assistantships available. Financial award applicants required to submit FAFSA. *Unit head:* Dr. Paul Umhoefer, Director, 928-523-6464, E-mail: paul.umhoefer@nau.edu. *Application contact:* SESES Support, 928-523-9333, Fax: 928-523-7432, E-mail: seses_admin_support@nau.edu.
Website: http://nau.edu/cefns/natsci/seses/

Penn State University Park, Graduate School, College of Earth and Mineral Sciences, Department of Meteorology, University Park, PA 16802. Offers meteorology (MS, PhD). *Unit head:* Dr. William E. Easterling, III, Dean, 814-865-7482, Fax: 814-863-7708. *Application contact:* Lori Stania, Director, Graduate Student Services, 814-865-1795, Fax: 814-863-4627, E-mail: l-gswww@lists.psu.edu.
Website: http://www.met.psu.edu/

Plymouth State University, College of Graduate Studies, Graduate Studies in Education, Program in Science, Plymouth, NH 03264-1595. Offers applied meteorology (MS); biology (MS); clinical mental health counseling (MS); environmental science and policy (MS); science education (MS).

Saint Louis University, Graduate Education, College of Arts and Sciences, Department of Earth and Atmospheric Sciences, St. Louis, MO 63103. Offers geophysics (PhD); geoscience (MS); meteorology (M Pr Met, MS-R, PhD). *Program availability:* Part-time. *Degree requirements:* For master's, thesis (for some programs), comprehensive oral exam; for doctorate, thesis/dissertation, preliminary exams. *Entrance requirements:* For master's, GRE General Test, letters of recommendation, resume; for doctorate, GRE General Test, letters of recommendation, resumé, goal statement, transcripts. Additional exam requirements/recommendations for international students: Required—TOEFL (minimum score 525 paper-based). Electronic applications accepted. *Faculty research:* Structural geology, mesoscale meteorology and severe storms, weather and climate change prediction.

San Jose State University, Graduate Studies and Research, College of Science, San Jose, CA 95192-0001. Offers biological sciences (MA, MS), including molecular biology and microbiology (MS), organismal biology, conservation and ecology (MS), physiology (MS); chemistry (MA, MS); computer science (MS); cybersecurity (Certificate); cybersecurity: core technologies (Certificate); geology (MS); marine science (MS); master biotechnology (MBT); mathematics (MA, MS), including mathematics education (MA), science; meteorology (MS); physics (MS), including computational physics, modern optics, science (MA, MS); science education (MA); statistics (MS); unix system administration (Certificate). *Program availability:* Part-time, evening/weekend. *Students:* 118 full-time (68 women), 52 part-time (25 women); includes 125 minority (5 Black or African American, non-Hispanic/Latino; 97 Asian, non-Hispanic/Latino; 23 Hispanic/Latino), 121 international. Average age 27. 1,236 applicants, 21% accepted, 171 enrolled. In 2015, 168 master's awarded. *Entrance requirements:* For master's, GRE. *Application deadline:* For fall admission, 6/29 for domestic students; for spring admission, 11/30 for domestic students. Applications are processed on a rolling basis. Application fee: $55. Electronic applications accepted. *Financial support:* Teaching assistantships, career-related internships or fieldwork, Federal Work-Study, and institutionally sponsored loans available. Support available to part-time students. Financial award applicants required to submit FAFSA. *Faculty research:* Radiochemistry/environmental analysis, health physics, radiation effects. *Unit head:* J. Michael Parrish, Dean, 408-924-4800, Fax: 408-924-4815. *Application contact:* 408-924-2480, Fax: 408-924-2477.
Website: http://www.science.sjsu.edu/

Texas A&M University, College of Geosciences, Department of Atmospheric Sciences, College Station, TX 77843. Offers atmospheric science (MS, PhD). *Faculty:* 18. *Students:* 55 full-time (18 women), 8 part-time (4 women); includes 6 minority (1 Asian, non-Hispanic/Latino; 4 Hispanic/Latino; 1 Two or more races, non-Hispanic/Latino), 25 international. Average age 27. 100 applicants, 10% accepted, 6 enrolled. In 2015, 11 master's, 2 doctorates awarded. *Degree requirements:* For master's, thesis; for doctorate, thesis/dissertation. *Entrance requirements:* For master's and doctorate, GRE General Test. Additional exam requirements/recommendations for international students: Required—TOEFL (minimum score 550 paper-based; 80 iBT), IELTS (minimum score 6), PTE (minimum score 53). *Application deadline:* For fall admission, 3/1 for domestic students; for spring admission, 10/1 for domestic students. Applications are processed on a rolling basis. Application fee: $50 ($90 for international students). Electronic applications accepted. *Expenses:* Contact institution. *Financial support:* In 2015–16, 58 students received support, including 6 fellowships with tuition reimbursements available (averaging $8,750 per year), 43 research assistantships with tuition reimbursements available (averaging $8,800 per year), 8 teaching assistantships with tuition reimbursements available (averaging $7,959 per year); career-related internships or fieldwork, institutionally sponsored loans, scholarships/grants, traineeships, health care benefits, tuition waivers (full and partial), and unspecified assistantships also available. Support available to part-time students. Financial award application deadline: 3/15; financial award applicants required to submit FAFSA. *Faculty research:* Radar and satellite rainfall relationships, mesoscale dynamics and numerical modeling, climatology. *Unit head:* Dr. Ping Yang, Department Head, 979-845-7679, E-mail: pyang@tamu.edu. *Application contact:* Roxanne R. Russell, Senior Academic Advisor II, 979-862-3240, Fax: 979-862-4466, E-mail: rrussell@tamu.edu.
Website: http://atmo.tamu.edu/

Université du Québec à Montréal, Graduate Programs, Program in Earth and Atmospheric Sciences, Montréal, QC H3C 3P8, Canada. Offers atmospheric sciences (M Sc); Earth and atmospheric sciences (PhD); Earth science (M Sc); meteorology (PhD, Diploma). PhD programs offered jointly with McGill University. *Program availability:* Part-time. *Degree requirements:* For master's, thesis. *Entrance requirements:* For master's and Diploma, appropriate bachelor's degree or equivalent, proficiency in French; for doctorate, appropriate master's degree or equivalent, proficiency in French.

University of California, San Diego, Graduate Division, Scripps Institution of Oceanography, Program in Climate Science and Policy, La Jolla, CA 92093. Offers MAS. *Program availability:* Part-time. *Students:* 7 full-time (3 women); includes 2 minority (1 Asian, non-Hispanic/Latino; 1 Hispanic/Latino), 1 international. 13 applicants, 92% accepted, 7 enrolled. *Degree requirements:* For master's, capstone project. *Entrance requirements:* For master's, minimum GPA of 3.0, resume or curriculum vitae, 3 letters of recommendation. Additional exam requirements/recommendations for international students: Required—TOEFL (minimum score 550 paper-based; 80 iBT), IELTS (minimum score 7). *Application deadline:* For summer admission, 2/28 for domestic students. Application fee: $90 ($110 for international students). Electronic applications accepted. *Expenses:* Contact institution. *Financial support:* Scholarships/grants available. Financial award applicants required to submit FAFSA. *Faculty research:* Climate, atmospheric science, policy analysis. *Unit head:* Lynn Russell, Chair, 858-534-4852, E-mail: mas-csp@sio.ucsd.edu. *Application contact:* Maureen McCormack, Graduate Coordinator, 858-534-1695, E-mail: mas-csp@sio.ucsd.edu.
Website: https://scripps.ucsd.edu/masters/mas/climate-science-and-policy

University of Hawaii at Manoa, Graduate Division, School of Ocean and Earth Science and Technology, Department of Meteorology, Honolulu, HI 96822. Offers MS, PhD. *Program availability:* Part-time. *Faculty:* 17 full-time (1 woman), 6 part-time/adjunct (0 women). *Students:* 32 full-time (15 women), 24 part-time (12 women); includes 3 minority (1 Asian, non-Hispanic/Latino; 1 Hispanic/Latino; 1 Two or more races, non-Hispanic/Latino), 17 international. Average age 30. 36 applicants, 11% accepted, 3 enrolled. In 2015, 3 master's, 2 doctorates awarded. *Degree requirements:* For master's, comprehensive exam, thesis; for doctorate, comprehensive exam, thesis/dissertation. *Entrance requirements:* For master's and doctorate, GRE General Test. Additional exam requirements/recommendations for international students: Required—TOEFL (minimum score 560 paper-based; 83 iBT), IELTS (minimum score 5). *Application deadline:* For fall admission, 3/1 for domestic students, 1/15 for international students; for spring admission, 9/1 for domestic students, 8/1 for international students. Application fee: $100. *Financial support:* In 2015–16, 25 students received support, including 2 fellowships (averaging $133 per year), 22 research assistantships (averaging $20,783 per year), 3 teaching assistantships (averaging $18,568 per year); Federal Work-Study and tuition waivers (full) also available. *Faculty research:* Tropical cyclones, air-sea interactions, mesoscale meteorology, intraseasonal oscillations, tropical climate. *Total annual research expenditures:* $6 million. *Unit head:* Brian Taylor, Dean, 808-956-6182, E-mail: taylorb@hawaii.edu. *Application contact:* Fei-Fei Jin, Graduate Chairperson, 808-956-2567, Fax: 808-956-2877, E-mail: jff@hawaii.edu.
Website: http://www.soest.hawaii.edu/met/

University of Maryland, College Park, Academic Affairs, College of Computer, Mathematical and Natural Sciences, Department of Atmospheric and Oceanic Science, College Park, MD 20742. Offers MS, PMS, PhD. *Program availability:* Part-time, evening/weekend, online learning. Terminal master's awarded for partial completion of doctoral program. *Degree requirements:* For master's, comprehensive exam, scholarly paper, written and oral exams; for doctorate, thesis/dissertation, exam. *Entrance requirements:* For master's, GRE General Test, background in mathematics, experience in scientific computer languages, 3 letters of recommendation; for doctorate, GRE General Test. Electronic applications accepted. *Faculty research:* Weather, atmospheric chemistry, air pollution, global change, radiation.

University of Miami, Graduate School, Rosenstiel School of Marine and Atmospheric Science, Division of Meteorology and Physical Oceanography, Coral Gables, FL 33124. Offers meteorology (MS, PhD); physical oceanography (MS, PhD). Terminal master's awarded for partial completion of doctoral program. *Degree requirements:* For master's, comprehensive exam, thesis; for doctorate, comprehensive exam, thesis/dissertation. *Entrance requirements:* For master's and doctorate, GRE General Test. Additional exam requirements/recommendations for international students: Required—TOEFL (minimum score 550 paper-based). Electronic applications accepted.

University of Oklahoma, College of Atmospheric and Geographic Sciences, School of Meteorology, Norman, OK 73072. Offers meteorology (PhD). *Faculty:* 44 full-time (9 women), 1 part-time/adjunct (0 women). *Students:* 56 full-time (11 women), 23 part-time (6 women); includes 4 minority (1 Asian, non-Hispanic/Latino; 1 Hispanic/Latino; 2 Two or more races, non-Hispanic/Latino), 12 international. Average age 26. 54 applicants, 26% accepted, 14 enrolled. In 2015, 14 master's, 13 doctorates awarded. Terminal master's awarded for partial completion of doctoral program. *Degree requirements:* For master's, thesis; for doctorate, thesis/dissertation, general exam. *Entrance requirements:* For master's and doctorate, GRE, transcripts with all academic work. Additional exam requirements/recommendations for international students: Required—TOEFL (minimum score 80 iBT) or IELTS (minimum score 6.5). *Application deadline:* For fall admission, 2/1 for domestic and international students; for spring admission, 10/1 for domestic and international students. Applications are processed on a rolling basis. Application fee: $50 ($100 for international students). Electronic applications accepted. *Expenses:* Tuition, state resident: full-time $4577; part-time $190.70 per credit hour. Tuition, nonresident: full-time $17,758; part-time $739.90 per credit hour. *Required fees:* $3060; $115.70 per credit hour. $141.50 per semester. *Financial support:* In 2015–16, 72 students received support, including 62 research assistantships with full tuition reimbursements available (averaging $18,667 per year), 18 teaching assistantships with full tuition reimbursements available (averaging $18,731 per year); fellowships with full tuition reimbursements available, tuition waivers (full and partial), and unspecified assistantships also available. Financial award application deadline: 6/1; financial award applicants required to submit FAFSA. *Faculty research:* High impact weather; radar; climate; atmospheric chemistry; numerical modeling. *Total annual research expenditures:* $3 million. *Unit head:* Dr. David Parsons, Director, 405-325-6561, Fax: 405-325-7689, E-mail: dparsons@ou.edu. *Application contact:* Christie Upchurch, Academic Coordinator, 405-325-6571, Fax: 405-325-7689, E-mail: cupchurch@ou.edu.

Website: http://som.ou.edu

Utah State University, School of Graduate Studies, College of Agriculture, Department of Plants, Soils, and Biometeorology, Logan, UT 84322. Offers biometeorology (MS, PhD); ecology (MS, PhD); plant science (MS, PhD); soil science (MS, PhD). *Program availability:* Part-time. Terminal master's awarded for partial completion of doctoral program. *Degree requirements:* For master's, thesis; for doctorate, thesis/dissertation. *Entrance requirements:* For master's, GRE General Test, BS in plant, soil, atmospheric science, or related field; minimum GPA of 3.0; for doctorate, GRE General Test, minimum GPA of 3.0. Additional exam requirements/recommendations for international students: Required—TOEFL. Electronic applications accepted. *Faculty research:* Biotechnology and genomics, plant physiology and biology, nutrient and water efficient landscapes, physical-chemical-biological processes in soil, environmental biophysics and climate.

Yale University, Graduate School of Arts and Sciences, Department of Geology and Geophysics, New Haven, CT 06520. Offers biogeochemistry (PhD); climate dynamics (PhD); geochemistry (PhD); geophysics (PhD); meteorology (PhD); oceanography (PhD); paleontology (PhD); paleooceanography (PhD); petrology (PhD); tectonics (PhD). *Degree requirements:* For doctorate, thesis/dissertation. *Entrance requirements:* For doctorate, GRE General Test. Additional exam requirements/recommendations for international students: Required—TOEFL.

Peterson's Graduate Programs in the Physical Sciences, Mathematics, Agricultural Sciences, the Environment & Natural Resources 2017

www.petersons.com **157**

Section 6
Physics

This section contains a directory of institutions offering graduate work in physics, followed by in-depth entries submitted by institutions that chose to prepare detailed program descriptions. Additional information about programs listed in the directory but not augmented by an in-depth entry may be obtained by writing directly to the dean of a graduate school or chair of a department at the address given in the directory.

For programs offering related work, see all other areas in this book. In the other guides in this series:

Graduate Programs in the Biological/Biomedical Sciences & Health-Related Medical Professions

See *Allied Health, Biological and Biomedical Sciences, Biophysics,* and *Vision Sciences*

Graduate Programs in Engineering & Applied Sciences

See *Aerospace/Aeronautical Engineering, Electrical and Computer Engineering, Energy and Power Engineering (Nuclear Engineering), Engineering and Applied Sciences, Engineering Physics, Materials Sciences and Engineering,* and *Mechanical Engineering and Mechanics*

CONTENTS

Acoustics

Naval Postgraduate School, Departments and Academic Groups, Undersea Warfare Academic Group, Monterey, CA 93943. Offers applied mathematics (MS); applied physics (MS); applied science (MS), including acoustics, operations research, physical oceanography, signal processing; electrical engineering (MS); engineering acoustics (MS, PhD); engineering science (MS), including electrical engineering, mechanical engineering; mechanical engineer (ME); mechanical engineering (MS, MSME); meteorology (MS); operations research (MS); physical oceanography (MS). Program only open to commissioned officers of the United States and friendly nations and selected United States federal civilian employees. *Program availability:* Part-time. *Degree requirements:* For master's, thesis. *Faculty research:* Unmanned/autonomous vehicles, sea mines and countermeasures, submarine warfare in the twentieth and twenty-first centuries.

Penn State University Park, Graduate School, Intercollege Graduate Programs and College of Engineering, Intercollege Graduate Program in Acoustics, University Park, PA 16802. Offers acoustics (M Eng, MS, PhD). *Unit head:* Dr. Regina Vasilatos-Younken, Dean, 814-865-2516, Fax: 814-863-4627. *Application contact:* Lori Stania, Director, Graduate Student Services, 814-865-1795, Fax: 814-863-4627, E-mail: l-gswww@lists.psu.edu.

Rensselaer Polytechnic Institute, Graduate School, School of Architecture, PhD Program in Architectural Sciences, Troy, NY 12180-3590. Offers architectural acoustics (PhD); built ecologies (PhD); lighting (PhD). *Faculty:* 29 full-time (6 women), 16 part-time/adjunct (4 women). *Students:* 25 full-time (8 women), 2 part-time (0 women); includes 6 minority (2 Asian, non-Hispanic/Latino; 1 Hispanic/Latino; 3 Two or more races, non-Hispanic/Latino), 10 international. Average age 30. 60 applicants, 45% accepted, 13 enrolled. In 2015, 6 doctorates awarded. *Degree requirements:* For doctorate, comprehensive exam (for some programs), thesis/dissertation. *Entrance requirements:* For doctorate, GRE. Additional exam requirements/recommendations for international students: Required—TOEFL (minimum score 570 paper-based; 88 iBT), IELTS (minimum score 6.5), PTE (minimum score 60). *Application deadline:* For fall admission, 1/1 priority date for domestic and international students; for spring admission, 8/15 priority date for domestic and international students. Applications are processed on a rolling basis. Application fee: $75. Electronic applications accepted. *Financial support:* In 2015–16, research assistantships (averaging $21,500 per year), teaching assistantships with full tuition reimbursements (averaging $21,500 per year) were awarded; fellowships also available. Financial award application deadline: 1/1. *Faculty research:* Architectural acoustics, built ecologies, lighting. *Unit head:* Chris Perry, Graduate Program Director, 518-276-3034, E-mail: perryc3@rpi.edu. *Application contact:* Office of Graduate Admissions, 518-276-6216,
E-mail: gradadmissions@rpi.edu.
Website: http://www.arch.rpi.edu/academic/graduate/phd-program/

Rensselaer Polytechnic Institute, Graduate School, School of Architecture, Program in Architectural Acoustics, Troy, NY 12180-3590. Offers architectural sciences (MS, PhD). *Faculty:* 29 full-time (6 women). *Students:* 25 full-time (8 women), 2 part-time (0 women); includes 4 minority (2 Asian, non-Hispanic/Latino; 1 Hispanic/Latino; 1 Two or more races, non-Hispanic/Latino). Average age 30. In 2015, 10 master's, 6 doctorates awarded. Terminal master's awarded for partial completion of doctoral program. *Degree requirements:* For master's, thesis; for doctorate, comprehensive exam, thesis/dissertation. *Entrance requirements:* For master's and doctorate, GRE General Test. Additional exam requirements/recommendations for international students: Required—TOEFL (minimum score 570 paper-based; 88 iBT), IELTS (minimum score 6.5), PTE (minimum score 60). *Application deadline:* For fall admission, 1/1 priority date for domestic and international students. Applications are processed on a rolling basis. Application fee: $75. Electronic applications accepted. *Financial support:* In 2015–16, fellowships (averaging $21,500 per year), research assistantships (averaging $21,500 per year), teaching assistantships (averaging $21,500 per year) were awarded. Financial award application deadline: 1/1. *Unit head:* Chris Perry, Graduate Program Director, 518-276-3034, E-mail: perryc3@rpi.edu. *Application contact:* Office of Graduate Admissions, 518-276-6216, E-mail: gradadmissions@rpi.edu.
Website: http://www.arch.rpi.edu/academic/graduate/architectural-acoustics/

University of Massachusetts Dartmouth, Graduate School, College of Engineering, Department of Electrical and Computer Engineering, North Dartmouth, MA 02747-2300. Offers acoustics (Postbaccalaureate Certificate); communications (Postbaccalaureate Certificate); computer engineering (MS, PhD); computer systems engineering (Postbaccalaureate Certificate); digital signal processing (Postbaccalaureate Certificate); electrical engineering (MS, PhD); electrical engineering systems (Postbaccalaureate Certificate). *Program availability:* Part-time. *Faculty:* 16 full-time (3 women), 1 part-time/adjunct (0 women). *Students:* 31 full-time (8 women), 52 part-time (9 women); includes 7 minority (1 Black or African American, non-Hispanic/Latino; 3 Asian, non-Hispanic/Latino; 2 Hispanic/Latino; 1 Two or more races, non-Hispanic/Latino), 50 international. Average age 27. 124 applicants, 64% accepted, 16 enrolled. In 2015, 15 master's, 2 doctorates awarded. Terminal master's awarded for partial completion of doctoral program. *Degree requirements:* For master's, thesis or project; for doctorate, comprehensive exam, thesis/dissertation. *Entrance requirements:* For master's, GRE (UMass Dartmouth electrical/computer engineering bachelor's degree recipients are exempt), statement of purpose (minimum of 300 words), resume, 3 letters of recommendation, official transcripts; for doctorate, GRE (UMASS Dartmouth electrical/computer engineering degree recipients are exempt), statement of purpose (minimum of 300 words), resume, 3 letters of recommendation, official transcripts; for Postbaccalaureate Certificate, statement of purpose (minimum of 300 words), resume, official transcripts. Additional exam requirements/recommendations for international students: Required—TOEFL (minimum score 550 paper-based; 80 iBT), IELTS (minimum score 6.5). *Application deadline:* For fall admission, 2/15 priority date for domestic students, 1/15 priority date for international students; for spring admission, 11/1 priority date for domestic students, 10/1 priority date for international students. Applications are processed on a rolling basis. Application fee: $60. Electronic applications accepted. *Expenses:* Tuition, state resident: full-time $2071; part-time $86.29 per credit. Tuition, nonresident: full-time $8099; part-time $337.46 per credit. *Required fees:* $18,074; $762.08 per credit. Tuition and fees vary according to course load and reciprocity agreements. *Financial support:* In 2015–16, 4 fellowships (averaging $15,839 per year), 10 research assistantships (averaging $14,174 per year), 11 teaching assistantships (averaging $12,136 per year) were awarded; Federal Work-Study and unspecified assistantships also available. Support available to part-time students. Financial award application deadline: 3/1; financial award applicants required to submit FAFSA. *Faculty research:* Computer engineering, cyber security, acoustics, signals and systems, electromagnetics, electronics and solid-state devices, marine systems, photonics. *Total annual research expenditures:* $3 million. *Unit head:* Dr. Karen Payton, Graduate Program Director, 508-999-8434, Fax: 508-999-8489, E-mail: kpayton@umassd.edu. *Application contact:* Steven Briggs, Director of Marketing and Recruitment for Graduate Studies, 508-999-8604, Fax: 508-999-8183,
E-mail: graduate@umassd.edu.
Website: http://www.umassd.edu/engineering/ece/

Applied Physics

Air Force Institute of Technology, Graduate School of Engineering and Management, Department of Engineering Physics, Dayton, OH 45433-7765. Offers applied physics (MS, PhD); electro-optics (MS, PhD); materials science (PhD); nuclear engineering (MS, PhD); space physics (MS). *Program availability:* Part-time. *Degree requirements:* For master's, thesis; for doctorate, thesis/dissertation. *Entrance requirements:* For master's and doctorate, GRE General Test, minimum GPA of 3.0, U.S. citizenship. *Faculty research:* High-energy lasers, space physics, nuclear weapon effects, semiconductor physics.

Binghamton University, State University of New York, Graduate School, School of Arts and Sciences, Department of Physics, Applied Physics, and Astronomy, Vestal, NY 13850. Offers MS, PhD. *Program availability:* Part-time. *Faculty:* 15 full-time (1 woman), 7 part-time/adjunct (0 women). *Students:* 14 full-time (1 woman), 26 part-time (2 women); includes 3 minority (1 Black or African American, non-Hispanic/Latino; 2 Hispanic/Latino), 16 international. Average age 29. 31 applicants, 55% accepted, 9 enrolled. In 2015, 4 master's, 2 doctorates awarded. Terminal master's awarded for partial completion of doctoral program. *Degree requirements:* For master's, comprehensive exam (for some programs), thesis or alternative; for doctorate, comprehensive exam, thesis/dissertation. *Entrance requirements:* For master's and doctorate, GRE General Test. Additional exam requirements/recommendations for international students: Required—TOEFL (minimum score 550 paper-based; 80 iBT). *Application deadline:* For fall admission, 2/15 priority date for domestic and international students; for spring admission, 10/15 priority date for domestic and international students. Application fee: $75. Electronic applications accepted. *Financial support:* In 2015–16, 37 students received support, including 5 research assistantships with full tuition reimbursements available (averaging $15,500 per year), 21 teaching assistantships with full tuition reimbursements available (averaging $17,500 per year); career-related internships or fieldwork, Federal Work-Study, institutionally sponsored loans, scholarships/grants, health care benefits, and unspecified assistantships also available. Financial award applicants required to submit FAFSA. *Unit head:* Dr. Bruce White, Chairperson, 607-777-2843, E-mail: bwhite@binghamton.edu. *Application contact:* Kishan Zuber, Recruiting and Admissions Coordinator, 607-777-2151, Fax: 607-777-2501, E-mail: kzuber@binghamton.edu.

California Institute of Technology, Division of Engineering and Applied Science, Option in Applied Physics, Pasadena, CA 91125-0001. Offers MS, PhD. *Degree requirements:* For doctorate, thesis/dissertation. Electronic applications accepted. *Faculty research:* Solid-state electronics, quantum electronics, plasmas, linear and nonlinear laser optics, electromagnetic theory.

Carnegie Mellon University, Mellon College of Science, Department of Physics, Pittsburgh, PA 15213-3891. Offers applied physics (PhD); physics (MS, PhD). *Degree requirements:* For doctorate, thesis/dissertation, qualifying exam. *Entrance requirements:* For doctorate, GRE General Test, GRE Subject Test. Additional exam requirements/recommendations for international students: Required—TOEFL. Electronic applications accepted. *Faculty research:* Astrophysics, condensed matter physics, biological physics, medium energy and nuclear physics, high-energy physics.

Christopher Newport University, Graduate Studies, Department of Physics, Computer Science, and Engineering, Newport News, VA 23606-3072. Offers applied physics and computer science (MS). *Program availability:* Part-time, evening/weekend. *Faculty:* 22 full-time (4 women), 1 part-time/adjunct (0 women). *Students:* 10 full-time (1 woman), 6 part-time (1 woman); includes 1 minority (Black or African American, non-Hispanic/Latino). Average age 24. 17 applicants, 94% accepted, 10 enrolled. In 2015, 15 master's awarded. *Degree requirements:* For master's, comprehensive exam (for some programs), thesis (for some programs). *Entrance requirements:* For master's, GRE General Test, minimum GPA of 3.0. Additional exam requirements/recommendations for international students: Required—TOEFL (minimum score 580 paper-based; 92 iBT), IELTS (minimum score 7). *Application deadline:* For fall admission, 7/15 priority date for domestic students, 4/1 for international students; for spring admission, 11/1 for domestic students, 10/1 for international students; for summer admission, 3/15 for domestic students, 3/1 for international students. Applications are processed on a rolling basis. Application fee: $50. Electronic applications accepted. *Expenses:* Tuition, state resident: full-time $6444; part-time $358 per credit hour. Tuition, nonresident: full-time $14,706; part-time $817 per credit hour. *Required fees:* $3690; $205 per credit hour. Tuition and fees vary according to course load. *Financial support:* In 2015–16, 5 students received support, including 2 research assistantships with full tuition reimbursements available (averaging $2,000 per year), 3 teaching assistantships (averaging $1,500 per year); unspecified assistantships also available. Financial award application deadline: 3/1; financial award applicants required to submit FAFSA. *Faculty research:* Advanced programming methodologies, experimental nuclear physics, computer architecture, semiconductor nanophysics, laser and optical fiber sensors. *Total annual research expenditures:* $263,552. *Unit head:* Dr. Davie Heddle, Coordinator, 757-594-8435, Fax: 757-594-7919, E-mail: heddle@cnu.edu. *Application* *contact:* Lyn Sawyer, Associate Director, Graduate Admissions and Records, 757-594-7544, Fax: 757-594-7649, E-mail: gradstdy@cnu.edu.

The College of William and Mary, Faculty of Arts and Sciences, Department of Applied Science, Williamsburg, VA 23187-8795. Offers accelerator science (PhD); applied mathematics (PhD); applied mechanics (PhD); applied robotics (PhD); applied science (MS); atmospheric and environmental science (PhD); computational neuroscience (PhD); interface, thin film and surface science (PhD); lasers and optics (PhD); magnetic resonance (PhD); materials science and engineering (PhD); mathematical and computational biology (PhD); medical imaging (PhD); nanotechnology (PhD); neuroscience (PhD); non-destructive evaluation (PhD); polymer chemistry (PhD); remote sensing (PhD). *Program availability:* Part-time. *Faculty:* 7 full-time (1 woman), 1 part-time/adjunct (0 women). *Students:* 26 full-time (9 women), 3 part-time (1 woman); includes 5 minority (2 Black or African American, non-Hispanic/Latino; 1 Asian, non-Hispanic/Latino; 2 Hispanic/Latino), 12 international. Average age 28. 24 applicants, 46% accepted, 6 enrolled. In 2015, 2 master's, 6 doctorates awarded. Terminal master's awarded for partial completion of doctoral program. *Degree requirements:* For master's, comprehensive exam, thesis; for doctorate, comprehensive exam, thesis/dissertation, 4 core courses. *Entrance requirements:* For master's and doctorate, GRE General Test, GRE Subject Test. Additional exam requirements/recommendations for international students: Required—TOEFL, TWE. *Application deadline:* For fall admission, 2/3 priority date for domestic students, 2/3 for international students; for spring admission, 10/15 priority date for domestic students, 10/14 for international students. Applications are processed on a rolling basis. Application fee: $45. Electronic applications accepted. *Expenses:* $6,550 per semester; $13,100 per year. *Financial support:* Fellowships, research assistantships, teaching assistantships, Federal Work-Study, health care benefits, tuition waivers (full), and unspecified assistantships available. Financial award application deadline: 4/15; financial award applicants required to submit FAFSA. *Faculty research:* Computational biology, non-destructive evaluation, neurophysiology, lasers and optics. *Total annual research expenditures:* $1.7 million. *Unit head:* Dr. Christopher Del Negro, Chair, 757-221-7808, Fax: 757-221-2050, E-mail: cadeln@wm.edu. *Application contact:* Lianne Rios Ashburne, Graduate Program Coordinator, 757-221-2563, Fax: 757-221-2050, E-mail: lrashburne@wm.edu.
Website: http://www.wm.edu/as/appliedscience

Colorado School of Mines, Office of Graduate Studies, Department of Physics, Golden, CO 80401. Offers applied physics (MS, PhD); materials science (MS, PhD); nuclear engineering (ME, MS, PhD). *Program availability:* Part-time. *Faculty:* 34 full-time (2 women), 15 part-time/adjunct (1 woman). *Students:* 69 full-time (18 women), 8 part-time (2 women); includes 9 minority (1 Asian, non-Hispanic/Latino; 7 Hispanic/Latino; 1 Two or more races, non-Hispanic/Latino), 14 international. Average age 28. 100 applicants, 31% accepted, 19 enrolled. In 2015, 8 master's, 7 doctorates awarded. *Degree requirements:* For master's, thesis (for some programs); for doctorate, comprehensive exam, thesis/dissertation. *Entrance requirements:* For master's and doctorate, GRE General Test, GRE Subject Test. Additional exam requirements/recommendations for international students: Required—TOEFL (minimum score 550 paper-based; 80 iBT). *Application deadline:* For fall admission, 12/15 priority date for domestic and international students; for spring admission, 9/1 priority date for domestic and international students. Application fee: $50 ($70 for international students). Electronic applications accepted. *Expenses:* Tuition, state resident: full-time $15,225. Tuition, nonresident: full-time $32,700. *Financial support:* In 2015–16, 57 students received support, including 3 fellowships with full tuition reimbursements available (averaging $21,120 per year), 37 research assistantships with full tuition reimbursements available (averaging $21,120 per year), 17 teaching assistantships with full tuition reimbursements available (averaging $21,120 per year); scholarships/grants, health care benefits, and unspecified assistantships also available. Financial award application deadline: 12/15; financial award applicants required to submit FAFSA. *Faculty research:* Light scattering, low-energy nuclear physics, high fusion plasma diagnostics, laser operations, mathematical physics. *Total annual research expenditures:* $5.9 million. *Unit head:* Dr. Jeff Squier, Head, 303-273-2385, E-mail: jsquier@mines.edu. *Application contact:* Dr. David Wood, Professor, 303-273-3853, E-mail: dwood@mines.edu.
Website: http://physics.mines.edu

Columbia University, Fu Foundation School of Engineering and Applied Science, Department of Applied Physics and Applied Mathematics, New York, NY 10027. Offers applied mathematics (MS, Eng Sc D, PhD); applied physics (MS, Eng Sc D, PhD); materials science and engineering (MS, Eng Sc D, PhD); medical physics (MS). *Program availability:* Part-time, online learning. Terminal master's awarded for partial completion of doctoral program. *Degree requirements:* For master's, comprehensive exam; for doctorate, thesis/dissertation, qualifying exam. *Entrance requirements:* For master's, GRE General Test, GRE Subject Test (strongly recommended); for doctorate, GRE General Test, GRE Subject Test (applied physics). Additional exam requirements/recommendations for international students: Required—TOEFL, IELTS, PTE. Electronic applications accepted. *Faculty research:* Plasma physics and fusion energy; optical and laser physics; atmospheric, oceanic and earth physics; applied mathematics; solid state science and processing of materials, their properties, and their structure; medical physics.

Cornell University, Graduate School, Graduate Fields of Engineering, Field of Applied Physics, Ithaca, NY 14853-0001. Offers applied physics (PhD); engineering physics (M Eng). *Degree requirements:* For doctorate, comprehensive exam, thesis/dissertation, written exams. *Entrance requirements:* For master's, GRE General Test, 3 letters of recommendation; for doctorate, GRE General Test, GRE Subject Test (physics), GRE Writing Assessment, 3 letters of recommendation. Additional exam requirements/recommendations for international students: Required—TOEFL (minimum score 600 paper-based; 77 iBT). Electronic applications accepted. *Faculty research:* Quantum and nonlinear optics, plasma physics, solid state physics, condensed matter physics and nanotechnology, electron and X-ray spectroscopy.

East Carolina University, Graduate School, Thomas Harriot College of Arts and Sciences, Department of Physics, Greenville, NC 27858-4353. Offers applied physics (MS); biomedical physics (PhD); health physics (MS); medical physics (MS). *Program availability:* Part-time. *Students:* 28 full-time (5 women), 8 part-time (3 women); includes 10 minority (4 Black or African American, non-Hispanic/Latino; 3 Asian, non-Hispanic/Latino; 1 Hispanic/Latino; 2 Two or more races, non-Hispanic/Latino), 5 international. Average age 29. 48 applicants, 60% accepted, 8 enrolled. In 2015, 6 master's, 1 doctorate awarded. *Degree requirements:* For master's, one foreign language, comprehensive exam. *Entrance requirements:* For master's, GRE General Test. Additional exam requirements/recommendations for international students: Required—TOEFL. *Application deadline:* Applications are processed on a rolling basis. Application fee: $50. *Financial support:* Research assistantships with partial tuition reimbursements, teaching assistantships with partial tuition reimbursements, and Federal Work-Study available. Support available to part-time students. Financial award application deadline: 6/1. *Unit head:* Dr. John Sutherland, Chair, 252-328-6739, E-mail: sutherlandj@ecu.edu. *Application contact:* Dean of Graduate School, 252-328-6012, Fax: 252-328-6071, E-mail: gradschool@ecu.edu.
Website: http://www.ecu.edu/cs-cas/physics/Graduate-Program.cfm#

George Mason University, College of Science, Department of Physics and Astronomy, Fairfax, VA 22030. Offers applied and engineering physics (MS); computational science and informatics (PhD); computational techniques and applications (Certificate). *Faculty:* 47 full-time (10 women), 11 part-time/adjunct (1 woman). *Students:* 24 full-time (3 women), 27 part-time (5 women); includes 9 minority (3 Black or African American, non-Hispanic/Latino; 1 Asian, non-Hispanic/Latino; 1 Hispanic/Latino; 4 Two or more races, non-Hispanic/Latino), 11 international. Average age 31. 53 applicants, 34% accepted, 10 enrolled. In 2015, 8 master's, 4 doctorates awarded. *Degree requirements:* For master's, thesis optional; for doctorate, comprehensive exam, thesis/dissertation. *Entrance requirements:* For master's and doctorate, GRE, baccalaureate degree in related field with minimum GPA of 3.0 in last 60 credit hours; 3 letters of recommendation; expanded goals statement; resume; 2 copies of official transcripts. Additional exam requirements/recommendations for international students: Required—TOEFL (minimum score 575 paper-based; 88 iBT), IELTS (minimum score 6.5), PTE (minimum score 59). Application fee: $75 ($80 for international students). Electronic applications accepted. *Financial support:* In 2015–16, 39 students received support, including 1 fellowship (averaging $8,000 per year), 17 research assistantships with tuition reimbursements available (averaging $17,848 per year), 5 teaching assistantships with tuition reimbursements available (averaging $17,000 per year); career-related internships or fieldwork, Federal Work-Study, scholarships/grants, unspecified assistantships, and health care benefits (for full-time research or teaching assistantship recipients) also available. Support available to part-time students. Financial award application deadline: 3/1; financial award applicants required to submit FAFSA. *Faculty research:* Particle and nuclear physics; computational statistics; astronomy, astrophysics, and space and planetary science; astronomy and physics education; atomic physics; biophysics and neuroscience; optical physics; fundamental theoretical studies; multidimensional data analysis. *Total annual research expenditures:* $3.2 million.

Georgia Southern University, Jack N. Averitt College of Graduate Studies, College of Science and Mathematics, Program in Applied Physical Science, Statesboro, GA 30458. Offers applied physical science (MS), including environmental science, pharmaceutical science, material and coatings science. *Students:* 19 full-time (8 women), 6 part-time (3 women); includes 9 minority (5 Black or African American, non-Hispanic/Latino; 1 Asian, non-Hispanic/Latino; 1 Hispanic/Latino; 2 Two or more races, non-Hispanic/Latino), 1 international. Average age 25. 12 applicants, 92% accepted, 10 enrolled. In 2015, 5 master's awarded. *Degree requirements:* For master's, thesis optional. *Entrance requirements:* For master's, minimum GPA of 2.75, 2 letters of recommendation, statement of purpose. Additional exam requirements/recommendations for international students: Required—TOEFL (minimum score 550 paper-based; 80 iBT), IELTS (minimum score 6). *Application deadline:* For fall admission, 3/1 priority date for domestic students; for spring admission, 10/1 for domestic students. Electronic applications accepted. *Expenses:* Tuition, state resident: full-time $7236; part-time $277 per semester hour. Tuition, nonresident: full-time $27,118; part-time $1105 per semester hour. *Required fees:* $2092. *Financial support:* In 2015–16, 12 students received support, including 3 fellowships with full tuition reimbursements available (averaging $7,750 per year), 9 teaching assistantships with full tuition reimbursements available (averaging $7,750 per year); Federal Work-Study, scholarships/grants, tuition waivers (full), and unspecified assistantships also available. Financial award application deadline: 4/20; financial award applicants required to submit FAFSA. *Faculty research:* Cancer research, coastal plain science, materials science, computational science. *Unit head:* Dr. Michele Davis McGibony, Program Director, 912-478-5919, E-mail: mdavis@georgiasouthern.edu.

Harvard University, Graduate School of Arts and Sciences, Department of Physics, Cambridge, MA 02138. Offers experimental physics (PhD); medical engineering/medical physics (PhD), including applied physics, engineering sciences, physics; theoretical physics (PhD). *Degree requirements:* For doctorate, thesis/dissertation, final exams, laboratory experience. *Entrance requirements:* For doctorate, GRE General Test, GRE Subject Test. Additional exam requirements/recommendations for international students: Required—TOEFL. *Faculty research:* Particle physics, condensed matter physics, atomic physics.

Harvard University, Graduate School of Arts and Sciences, Harvard John A. Paulson School of Engineering and Applied Sciences, Cambridge, MA 02138. Offers applied mathematics (ME, SM, PhD); applied physics (ME, SM, PhD); computational science and engineering (ME, SM); computer science (ME, SM, PhD); design engineering (MDE); engineering science (ME), including electrical engineering (ME, SM, PhD); engineering sciences (SM, PhD), including bioengineering, electrical engineering (ME, SM, PhD), environmental science and engineering, materials science and mechanical engineering. MDE offered in collaboration with Graduate School of Design. *Program availability:* Part-time. *Faculty:* 101 full-time (14 women), 10 part-time/adjunct (1 woman). *Students:* 425 full-time (109 women), 12 part-time (1 woman); includes 70 minority (1 Black or African American, non-Hispanic/Latino; 44 Asian, non-Hispanic/Latino; 17 Hispanic/Latino; 8 Two or more races, non-Hispanic/Latino), 207 international. Average age 27. 2,116 applicants, 11% accepted, 132 enrolled. In 2015, 88 master's, 64 doctorates awarded. Terminal master's awarded for partial completion of doctoral program. *Degree requirements:* For master's, thesis (for ME); for doctorate, comprehensive exam, thesis/dissertation. *Entrance requirements:* For master's and doctorate, GRE General Test, GRE Subject Test (recommended), 3 letters of recommendation. Additional exam requirements/recommendations for international students: Required—TOEFL (minimum score 80 iBT). *Application deadline:* For fall admission, 12/15 priority date for domestic and international students. Application fee: $105. Electronic applications accepted. *Expenses:* Contact institution. *Financial support:* In 2015–16, 353 students received support, including 92 fellowships with full tuition reimbursements available (averaging $25,650 per year), 213 research assistantships with tuition reimbursements available (averaging $34,200 per year), 127 teaching assistantships with tuition reimbursements available (averaging $5,775 per year); health care benefits also available. *Faculty research:* Applied mathematics, applied physics, computer science and electrical engineering, environmental engineering, mechanical and biomedical engineering. *Total annual research expenditures:* $38 million. *Unit head:* Francis J. Doyle, III, Dean, 617-495-5829, Fax: 617-495-5264, E-mail: dean@seas.harvard.edu. *Application contact:* Office of Admissions and Financial Aid, 617-495-5315, E-mail: admissions@seas.harvard.edu.
Website: http://www.seas.harvard.edu/

Idaho State University, Office of Graduate Studies, College of Science and Engineering, Department of Physics, Pocatello, ID 83209-8106. Offers applied physics (PhD); health physics (MS); physics (MNS). *Program availability:* Part-time. *Degree requirements:* For master's, comprehensive exam, thesis (for some programs), oral exam (for some programs); for doctorate, comprehensive exam, thesis/dissertation (for some programs), oral exam, written qualifying exam in physics or health physics after 1st year. *Entrance requirements:* For master's, GRE General Test, 3 letters of recommendation, BS or BA in physics, teaching certificate (MNS); for doctorate, GRE General Test (minimum 50th percentile), 3 letters of recommendation, statement of career goals. Additional exam requirements/recommendations for international students: Required—TOEFL (minimum score 550 paper-based; 80 iBT). Electronic applications accepted. *Faculty research:* Ion beam applications, low-energy nuclear physics, relativity and cosmology, observational astronomy.

Illinois Institute of Technology, Graduate College, College of Science, Department of Physics, Chicago, IL 60616. Offers applied physics (MS); health physics (MAS); physics (MS, PhD). *Program availability:* Part-time, evening/weekend, online learning. Terminal master's awarded for partial completion of doctoral program. *Degree requirements:* For master's, comprehensive exam (for some programs), thesis (for some programs); for doctorate, comprehensive exam, thesis/dissertation. *Entrance requirements:* For master's, GRE General Test (minimum score 295 Quantitative and Verbal, 2.5 Analytical Writing), minimum undergraduate GPA of 3.0; for doctorate, GRE General Test (minimum score 310 Quantitative and Verbal, 3.0 Analytical Writing); GRE Subject Test in physics (strongly recommended), minimum undergraduate GPA of 3.0. Additional exam requirements/recommendations for international students: Required—TOEFL (minimum score 550 paper-based; 80 iBT). Electronic applications accepted. *Faculty research:* Elementary particle physics, condensed matter, superconductivity, experimental and computational biophysics.

Iowa State University of Science and Technology, Department of Physics and Astronomy, Ames, IA 50011. Offers applied physics (MS, PhD); astrophysics (MS, PhD); condensed matter physics (MS, PhD); high energy physics (MS, PhD); nuclear physics (MS, PhD); physics (MS, PhD). *Degree requirements:* For master's, thesis (for some programs); for doctorate, thesis/dissertation. *Entrance requirements:* For master's and doctorate, GRE General Test, GRE Subject Test (physics). Additional exam requirements/recommendations for international students: Required—TOEFL (minimum score 550 paper-based; 79 iBT), IELTS (minimum score 6.5). Electronic applications accepted. *Faculty research:* Condensed-matter physics, including superconductivity and new materials; high-energy and nuclear physics; astronomy and astrophysics; atmospheric and environmental physics.

Iowa State University of Science and Technology, Program in Applied Physics, Ames, IA 50011. Offers MS, PhD. *Entrance requirements:* For master's and doctorate, GRE. Additional exam requirements/recommendations for international students: Required—TOEFL (minimum score 550 paper-based; 79 iBT), IELTS (minimum score 6.5). Electronic applications accepted.

Johns Hopkins University, Engineering Program for Professionals, Part-time Program in Applied Physics, Baltimore, MD 21218. Offers MS, Post-Master's Certificate. *Program availability:* Part-time, evening/weekend. Electronic applications accepted.

Laurentian University, School of Graduate Studies and Research, Programme in Physics, Sudbury, ON P3E 2C6, Canada. Offers M Sc. *Program availability:* Part-time. *Degree requirements:* For master's, thesis or alternative. *Entrance requirements:* For master's, honors degree with second class or better. *Faculty research:* Solar neutrino physics and astrophysics, applied acoustics and ultrasonics, powder science and technology, solid state physics, theoretical physics.

Louisiana Tech University, Graduate School, College of Engineering and Science, Department of Physics, Ruston, LA 71272. Offers applied physics (MS). *Program availability:* Part-time. *Degree requirements:* For master's, thesis or alternative. *Entrance requirements:* For master's, GRE General Test, minimum GPA of 3.0 in last 60 hours. Additional exam requirements/recommendations for international students: Required—TOEFL. *Application deadline:* For fall admission, 8/1 for domestic students; for spring admission, 2/1 for domestic students. Applications are processed on a rolling basis. Application fee: $40. *Financial support:* Fellowships, teaching assistantships, and tuition waivers (partial) available. Financial award application deadline: 4/1. *Faculty research:* Experimental high energy physics, laser/optics, computational physics, quantum gravity. *Unit head:* Dr. Lee Sawyer, Academic Director, 318-257-4053. *Application contact:* Marilyn J. Robinson, Assistant to the Dean of the Graduate School, 318-257-2924, Fax: 318-257-4487.

Michigan Technological University, Graduate School, College of Sciences and Arts, Department of Physics, Houghton, MI 49931. Offers applied physics (MS); engineering physics (PhD); physics (MS, PhD). *Program availability:* Part-time. *Faculty:* 33 full-time, 10 part-time/adjunct. *Students:* 31 full-time (9 women), 2 part-time; includes 1 minority (Black or African American, non-Hispanic/Latino), 24 international. Average age 29. 122 applicants, 12% accepted, 7 enrolled. In 2015, 2 master's, 2 doctorates awarded. Terminal master's awarded for partial completion of doctoral program. *Degree requirements:* For master's, comprehensive exam (for some programs), thesis (for some programs); for doctorate, comprehensive exam, thesis/dissertation, qualifying exam, research proposal. *Entrance requirements:* For master's and doctorate, GRE (recommended minimum quantitative score of 156 and analytical score of 3.0), statement of purpose, personal statement, official transcripts, 3 letters of recommendation. Additional exam requirements/recommendations for international students: Required—TOEFL (recommended score 88 iBT) or IELTS. *Application deadline:* For fall admission, 3/1 priority date for domestic students, 1/15 priority date for international students; for spring admission, 10/1 priority date for domestic students, 9/1 priority date for international students. Applications are processed on a rolling basis. Electronic applications accepted. *Expenses:* Tuition, state resident: full-time $15,507; part-time $861.50 per credit. Tuition, nonresident: full-time $15,507; part-time $861.50 per credit. *Required fees:* $248; $248. Tuition and fees vary according to course load and program. *Financial support:* In 2015–16, 30 students received support, including 1 fellowship with tuition reimbursement available (averaging $14,516 per year), 7 research assistantships with tuition reimbursements available (averaging $14,516 per year), 21 teaching assistantships with tuition reimbursements available (averaging $14,516 per year); career-related internships or fieldwork, Federal Work-Study, scholarships/grants, health care benefits, unspecified assistantships, and cooperative program also available. Financial award applicants required to submit FAFSA. *Faculty research:* Atmospheric physics, astrophysics, biophysics, materials physics, atomic/molecular physics. *Total annual research expenditures:* $1.9 million. *Unit head:* Dr. Ravindra Pandey, Chair, 906-487-2086, Fax: 906-487-2933, E-mail: physics@mtu.edu. *Application contact:* Taana Kallianen, Office Assistant 4, 906-487-2087, Fax: 906-487-2933, E-mail: taana@mtu.edu.
Website: http://www.mtu.edu/physics/

Mississippi State University, College of Arts and Sciences, Department of Physics and Astronomy, Mississippi State, MS 39762. Offers engineering (PhD), including applied physics; physics (MS, PhD). PhD in applied physics offered jointly with College of Engineering. *Program availability:* Part-time. *Faculty:* 18 full-time (3 women). *Students:* 44 full-time (8 women), 5 part-time (1 woman); includes 4 minority (1 American Indian or Alaska Native, non-Hispanic/Latino; 2 Asian, non-Hispanic/Latino; 1 Two or more races, non-Hispanic/Latino), 38 international. Average age 30. 51 applicants, 27% accepted, 10 enrolled. In 2015, 9 master's, 5 doctorates awarded. *Degree requirements:* For master's, thesis optional, comprehensive oral or written

exam; for doctorate, thesis/dissertation, comprehensive oral or written exam. *Entrance requirements:* For master's, GRE, minimum GPA of 2.75 on last two years of undergraduate courses; for doctorate, GRE. Additional exam requirements/recommendations for international students: Required—TOEFL (minimum score 477 paper-based; 53 iBT); Recommended—IELTS (minimum score 4.5). *Application deadline:* For fall admission, 7/1 priority date for domestic students, 5/1 for international students; for spring admission, 11/1 priority date for domestic students, 9/1 for international students. Applications are processed on a rolling basis. Application fee: $60. Electronic applications accepted. *Expenses: Tuition, area resident:* Full-time $7502; part-time $833.74 per credit hour. Tuition, nonresident: full-time $20,142; part-time $2238.24 per credit hour. *Financial support:* In 2015–16, 8 research assistantships with full tuition reimbursements (averaging $14,306 per year), 26 teaching assistantships with full tuition reimbursements (averaging $13,950 per year) were awarded; Federal Work-Study, institutionally sponsored loans, and unspecified assistantships also available. Financial award application deadline: 3/15; financial award applicants required to submit FAFSA. *Faculty research:* Atomic/molecular spectroscopy, theoretical optics, gamma-ray astronomy, experimental nuclear physics, computational physics. *Total annual research expenditures:* $3.2 million. *Unit head:* Dr. Mark A. Novotny, Department Head and Professor, 662-325-2688, Fax: 662-325-8898, E-mail: man40@ra.msstate.edu. *Application contact:* Meredith Nagel, Admissions Assistant, 662-325-9077, E-mail: mnagel@grad.msstate.edu.
Website: http://www.physics.msstate.edu

Naval Postgraduate School, Departments and Academic Groups, Department of Physics, Monterey, CA 93943. Offers applied physics (MS, PhD); combat systems technology (MS); engineering acoustics (MS, PhD); physics (MS, PhD). Program only open to commissioned officers of the United States and friendly nations and selected United States federal civilian employees. *Program availability:* Part-time. *Degree requirements:* For master's, thesis; for doctorate, thesis/dissertation. *Faculty research:* Acoustics, free electron laser, sensors, weapons and effects.

Naval Postgraduate School, Departments and Academic Groups, Space Systems Academic Group, Monterey, CA 93943. Offers applied physics (MS); astronautical engineering (MS); computer science (MS); electrical engineering (MS); mechanical engineering (MS); space systems (Engr); space systems operations (MS). Program only open to commissioned officers of the United States and friendly nations and selected United States federal civilian employees. *Program availability:* Part-time. *Degree requirements:* For master's and Engr, thesis; for doctorate, thesis/dissertation. *Faculty research:* Military applications for space; space reconnaissance and remote sensing; radiation-hardened electronics for space; design, construction and operations of small satellites; satellite communications systems.

Naval Postgraduate School, Departments and Academic Groups, Undersea Warfare Academic Group, Monterey, CA 93943. Offers applied mathematics (MS); applied physics (MS); applied science (MS), including acoustics, operations research, physical oceanography, signal processing; electrical engineering (MS); engineering acoustics (MS, PhD); engineering science (MS), including electrical engineering, mechanical engineering; mechanical engineer (ME); mechanical engineering (MS, MSME); meteorology (MS); operations research (MS); physical oceanography (MS). Program only open to commissioned officers of the United States and friendly nations and selected United States federal civilian employees. *Program availability:* Part-time. *Degree requirements:* For master's, thesis. *Faculty research:* Unmanned/autonomous vehicles, sea mines and countermeasures, submarine warfare in the twentieth and twenty-first centuries.

New Jersey Institute of Technology, College of Science and Liberal Arts, Newark, NJ 07102. Offers applied mathematics (MS); applied physics (M Sc, PhD); applied statistical models (Certificate); applied statistics (MS); biology (MS, PhD); biostatistics (MS); biostatistics essentials (Certificate); chemistry (MS, PhD); computational biology (MS); environmental science (MS, PhD); history (MA, MAT); materials science and engineering (MS, PhD); mathematical and computational finance (MS); mathematics science (PhD); pharmaceutical chemistry (MS); professional and technical communications (MS); technical common essentials (Certificate). *Program availability:* Part-time, evening/weekend. *Faculty:* 153 full-time (35 women), 100 part-time/adjunct (40 women). *Students:* 212 full-time (82 women), 94 part-time (37 women); includes 72 minority (22 Black or African American, non-Hispanic/Latino; 25 Asian, non-Hispanic/Latino; 19 Hispanic/Latino; 6 Two or more races, non-Hispanic/Latino), 164 international. Average age 29. 519 applicants, 62% accepted, 104 enrolled. In 2015, 98 master's, 21 doctorates, 3 other advanced degrees awarded. Terminal master's awarded for partial completion of doctoral program. *Degree requirements:* For master's, thesis optional; for doctorate, thesis/dissertation. *Entrance requirements:* For master's, GRE General Test; for doctorate, GRE General Test, minimum graduate GPA of 3.5. Additional exam requirements/recommendations for international students: Required—TOEFL (minimum score 550 paper-based; 79 iBT). *Application deadline:* For fall admission, 6/1 priority date for domestic students, 5/1 priority date for international students; for spring admission, 11/15 priority date for domestic and international students. Applications are processed on a rolling basis. Application fee: $75. Electronic applications accepted. *Expenses:* $28,800 per year non-resident full-time. *Financial support:* In 2015–16, 56 research assistantships with full tuition reimbursements (averaging $17,711 per year), 52 teaching assistantships with full tuition reimbursements (averaging $17,914 per year) were awarded; fellowships with full tuition reimbursements also available. Financial award application deadline: 1/15. *Total annual research expenditures:* $23.1 million. *Unit head:* Dr. Kevin Belfield, Dean, 973-596-3676, Fax: 973-565-0586, E-mail: kevin.d.belfield@njit.edu. *Application contact:* Stephen Eck, Director of Admissions, 973-596-3300, Fax: 973-596-3461, E-mail: admissions@njit.edu.
Website: http://csla.njit.edu/

New York University, Polytechnic School of Engineering, Department of Applied Physics, New York, NY 10012-1019. Offers MS, PhD. *Program availability:* Part-time, evening/weekend. *Degree requirements:* For master's, comprehensive exam (for some programs), thesis (for some programs); for doctorate, comprehensive exam, thesis/dissertation, departmental qualifying exam. *Entrance requirements:* For master's, BA in physics; for doctorate, BS in physics. Additional exam requirements/recommendations for international students: Required—TOEFL (minimum score 550 paper-based; 80 iBT); Recommended—IELTS (minimum score 6.5). Electronic applications accepted. *Faculty research:* Invention of cutting edge photonic techniques for individual virus particle detection, non-thermal plasmas for surfaces for medical and dental applications, dynamics of a phase qubit-resonator system.

Northern Arizona University, Graduate College, College of Engineering, Forestry, and Natural Sciences, Department of Physics and Astronomy, Flagstaff, AZ 86011. Offers applied physics (MS); astronomy (PhD). *Program availability:* Part-time. *Faculty:* 3 full-time. *Students:* 5 full-time. *Degree requirements:* For master's, thesis optional. *Entrance requirements:* Additional exam requirements/recommendations for international students: Required—TOEFL (minimum score 550 paper-based; 80 iBT), IELTS (minimum score 7). *Application deadline:* For fall admission, 1/15 priority date for

domestic and international students. Applications are processed on a rolling basis. Application fee: $65. Electronic applications accepted. *Expenses: Tuition, area resident:* Full-time $8710. Tuition, nonresident: full-time $20,350. *Required fees:* $896. *Financial support:* Research assistantships with full tuition reimbursements, teaching assistantships with full tuition reimbursements, Federal Work-Study, scholarships/grants, health care benefits, tuition waivers (full and partial), and unspecified assistantships available. Financial award applicants required to submit FAFSA. *Unit head:* Dr. Stephen Tegler, Chair, 928-523-9382, Fax: 928-523-1371, E-mail: stephen.tegler@nau.edu. *Application contact:* Jamie Housholder, Administrative Assistant, 928-523-8170, Fax: 928-523-1371, E-mail: astro.physics@nau.edu.
Website: http://www.physics.nau.edu/

Northwestern University, The Graduate School, Judd A. and Marjorie Weinberg College of Arts and Sciences and McCormick School of Engineering and Applied Science, Program in Applied Physics, Evanston, IL 60208. Offers PhD.

Rice University, Rice Quantum Institute, Houston, TX 77251-1892. Offers MS, PhD. *Degree requirements:* For master's, thesis; for doctorate, thesis/dissertation. *Entrance requirements:* For master's and doctorate, GRE General Test, GRE Subject Test (physics), minimum GPA of 3.0. Additional exam requirements/recommendations for international students: Required—TOEFL (minimum score 600 paper-based; 90 iBT). Electronic applications accepted. *Faculty research:* Nanotechnology, solid state materials, atomic physics, thin films.

Rutgers University–Newark, Graduate School, Program in Applied Physics, Newark, NJ 07102. Offers MS, PhD. MS, PhD offered jointly with New Jersey Institute of Technology. *Entrance requirements:* For master's and doctorate, GRE. Additional exam requirements/recommendations for international students: Required—TOEFL.

Southern Illinois University Carbondale, Graduate School, College of Science, Department of Physics, Carbondale, IL 62901-4701. Offers MS, PhD. *Faculty:* 9 full-time (0 women). *Students:* 5 full-time (0 women), 17 part-time (0 women); includes 4 minority (3 Asian, non-Hispanic/Latino; 1 Hispanic/Latino), 16 international. 45 applicants, 18% accepted, 4 enrolled. In 2015, 7 master's, 4 doctorates awarded. *Degree requirements:* For master's, one foreign language, thesis; for doctorate, thesis/dissertation. *Entrance requirements:* For master's, minimum GPA of 2.7; for doctorate, GRE, minimum GPA of 3.25. Additional exam requirements/recommendations for international students: Required—TOEFL. *Application deadline:* Applications are processed on a rolling basis. Application fee: $65. *Financial support:* In 2015–16, 22 students received support, including 4 research assistantships with full tuition reimbursements available, 18 teaching assistantships with full tuition reimbursements available; fellowships with full tuition reimbursements available, career-related internships or fieldwork, Federal Work-Study, institutionally sponsored loans, and tuition waivers (full) also available. Support available to part-time students. Financial award application deadline: 2/15. *Faculty research:* Atomic, molecular, nuclear, and mathematical physics; statistical mechanics; solid-state and low-temperature physics; rheology; material science. *Total annual research expenditures:* $773,352. *Unit head:* Dr. Naushad Ali, Chairperson, 618-453-1053, E-mail: nali@physics.siu.edu. *Application contact:* Suzanne McCann, Office Support Specialist, 618-453-1041, E-mail: smccann@physics.siu.edu.
Website: http://www.physics.siu.edu/

Stanford University, School of Humanities and Sciences, Department of Applied Physics, Stanford, CA 94305-9991. Offers applied and engineering physics (MS); applied physics (PhD). Terminal master's awarded for partial completion of doctoral program. *Degree requirements:* For doctorate, thesis/dissertation. *Entrance requirements:* For master's and doctorate, GRE General Test, GRE Subject Test. Additional exam requirements/recommendations for international students: Required—TOEFL. Electronic applications accepted. *Expenses: Tuition, area resident:* Full-time $45,729. *Required fees:* $591.

Texas A&M University, College of Science, Department of Physics and Astronomy, College Station, TX 77843. Offers applied physics (PhD); physics (MS, PhD). *Faculty:* 54. *Students:* 167 full-time (23 women), 6 part-time (2 women); includes 22 minority (1 Black or African American, non-Hispanic/Latino; 1 American Indian or Alaska Native, non-Hispanic/Latino; 4 Asian, non-Hispanic/Latino; 12 Hispanic/Latino; 4 Two or more races, non-Hispanic/Latino), 94 international. Average age 28. 220 applicants, 29% accepted, 23 enrolled. In 2015, 7 master's, 23 doctorates awarded. Terminal master's awarded for partial completion of doctoral program. *Degree requirements:* For master's, thesis (for some programs); for doctorate, thesis/dissertation. *Entrance requirements:* For master's and doctorate, GRE General Test, GRE Subject Test. Additional exam requirements/recommendations for international students: Required—TOEFL. *Application deadline:* For fall admission, 3/1 priority date for domestic students; for spring admission, 8/1 for domestic students. Application fee: $50 ($90 for international students). Electronic applications accepted. *Expenses:* Contact institution. *Financial support:* In 2015–16, 169 students received support, including 40 fellowships with tuition reimbursements available (averaging $13,717 per year), 82 research assistantships with tuition reimbursements available (averaging $7,892 per year), 51 teaching assistantships with tuition reimbursements available (averaging $6,927 per year); career-related internships or fieldwork, institutionally sponsored loans, scholarships/grants, traineeships, health care benefits, tuition waivers (full and partial), and unspecified assistantships also available. Support available to part-time students. Financial award application deadline: 3/1; financial award applicants required to submit FAFSA. *Faculty research:* Condensed matter, atomic/molecular, high-energy and nuclear physics, quantum optics. *Unit head:* Dr. George R. Welch, Head, 979-845-1571, E-mail: welch@physics.tamu.edu. *Application contact:* Dr. Joe Ross, Graduate Advisor, 979-845-3842, Fax: 979-845-2590, E-mail: ross@physics.tamu.edu.
Website: http://physics.tamu.edu/

Texas Tech University, Graduate School, College of Arts and Sciences, Department of Physics, Lubbock, TX 79409. Offers applied physics (MS); physics (MS, PhD). *Program availability:* Part-time. *Faculty:* 27 full-time (5 women), 2 part-time/adjunct (0 women). *Students:* 75 full-time (26 women); includes 8 minority (2 Black or African American, non-Hispanic/Latino; 1 Asian, non-Hispanic/Latino; 4 Hispanic/Latino; 1 Two or more races, non-Hispanic/Latino), 50 international. Average age 28. 57 applicants, 53% accepted, 18 enrolled. In 2015, 9 master's, 3 doctorates awarded. *Degree requirements:* For master's, variable foreign language requirement, comprehensive exam (for some programs), thesis (for some programs); for doctorate, variable foreign language requirement, comprehensive exam, thesis/dissertation, proposal presentation. *Entrance requirements:* For master's and doctorate, GRE. Additional exam requirements/recommendations for international students: Required—TOEFL (minimum score 550 paper-based; 79 iBT), IELTS (minimum score 6.5). *Application deadline:* For fall admission, 6/1 priority date for domestic students, 1/15 priority date for international students; for spring admission, 9/1 priority date for domestic students, 6/15 priority date for international students. Applications are processed on a rolling basis. Application fee: $60. Electronic applications accepted. *Expenses:* Tuition, state resident: full-time $6477; part-time $269.89 per credit hour. Tuition, nonresident: full-time $15,837; part-time $659.89 per credit hour. *Required fees:* $2751; $36.50 per credit hour. $937.50 per semester. Tuition and fees vary according to course level. *Financial support:* In 2015–16, 55 students received support, including 43 fellowships (averaging $1,904 per year), 24 research assistantships (averaging $12,122 per year), 53 teaching assistantships (averaging $16,166 per year); Federal Work-Study, scholarships/grants, health care benefits, and unspecified assistantships also available. Support available to part-time students. Financial award application deadline: 2/1; financial award applicants required to submit FAFSA. *Faculty research:* Astrophysics, condensed matter physics, nanotechnology and materials physics, high energy physics, biophysics. *Total annual research expenditures:* $3.2 million. *Unit head:* Dr. Nural Akchurin, Professor/Chair, 806-742-3767, Fax: 806-742-1182, E-mail: nural.akchurin@ttu.edu. *Application contact:* Dr. Mahdi Sanati, Graduate Recruiter, 806-834-6169, Fax: 806-742-1182, E-mail: m.sanati@ttu.edu.
Website: http://www.phys.ttu.edu/

Towson University, Program in Applied Physics, Towson, MD 21252-0001. Offers MS. *Students:* 6 full-time (1 woman), 1 part-time (0 women); includes 3 minority (2 Black or African American, non-Hispanic/Latino; 1 Two or more races, non-Hispanic/Latino). *Entrance requirements:* For master's, bachelor's degree, minimum GPA of 3.0, resume, letter of recommendation, statement of purpose. *Application deadline:* Applications are processed on a rolling basis. Application fee: $45. Electronic applications accepted. *Expenses:* Tuition, state resident: full-time $7440; part-time $372 per unit. Tuition, nonresident: full-time $15,400; part-time $770 per unit. *Required fees:* $2360; $118 per year. $354 per term. *Unit head:* Dr. Raj Kolagani, Graduate Program Director, 410-704-3134, E-mail: rkolagani@towson.edu. *Application contact:* Alicia Arkell-Kleis, University Admissions, 410-704-2113, Fax: 410-704-3030, E-mail: grads@towson.edu.
Website: http://grad.towson.edu/program/master/apph-ms/

University of Arkansas, Graduate School, J. William Fulbright College of Arts and Sciences, Department of Physics, Fayetteville, AR 72701-1201. Offers applied physics (MS); physics (MS, PhD); physics education (MA). *Students:* 3 full-time (0 women), 39 part-time (11 women); includes 4 minority (2 Asian, non-Hispanic/Latino; 1 Hispanic/Latino; 1 Two or more races, non-Hispanic/Latino), 24 international. In 2015, 3 master's, 1 doctorate awarded. *Degree requirements:* For master's, thesis; for doctorate, thesis/dissertation. *Application deadline:* For fall admission, 4/1 for international students; for spring admission, 10/1 for international students. Applications are processed on a rolling basis. Application fee: $40 ($50 for international students). Electronic applications accepted. *Financial support:* In 2015–16, 21 research assistantships, 22 teaching assistantships were awarded; fellowships with tuition reimbursements, career-related internships or fieldwork, and Federal Work-Study also available. Support available to part-time students. Financial award application deadline: 4/1; financial award applicants required to submit FAFSA. *Unit head:* Dr. Julio Gea-Banacloche, Departmental Chairperson, 479-575-2506, Fax: 479-575-4580, E-mail: jgeabana@uark.edu. *Application contact:* Dr. Surendra Singh, Graduate Coordinator, 479-575-6058, E-mail: ssingh@uark.edu.
Website: http://www.uark.edu/depts/physics/

University of California, San Diego, Graduate Division, Department of Electrical and Computer Engineering, La Jolla, CA 92093. Offers applied ocean science (MS, PhD); applied physics (MS, PhD); communication theory and systems (MS, PhD); computer engineering (MS, PhD); electronic circuits and systems (MS, PhD); intelligent systems, robotics and control (MS, PhD); medical devices and systems (MS, PhD); nanoscale devices and systems (MS, PhD); photonics (MS, PhD); signal and image processing (MS, PhD). *Students:* 503 full-time (99 women), 48 part-time (6 women); includes 79 minority (4 Black or African American, non-Hispanic/Latino; 67 Asian, non-Hispanic/Latino; 8 Hispanic/Latino), 381 international. 2,689 applicants, 21% accepted, 200 enrolled. In 2015, 97 master's, 42 doctorates awarded. *Degree requirements:* For master's, thesis or written exam; for doctorate, comprehensive exam, thesis/dissertation. *Entrance requirements:* For master's and doctorate, GRE General Test, minimum GPA of 3.0. Additional exam requirements/recommendations for international students: Required—TOEFL (minimum score 550 paper-based; 80 iBT), IELTS. *Application deadline:* For fall admission, 12/15 for domestic students. Application fee: $90 ($110 for international students). Electronic applications accepted. *Expenses:* Tuition, state resident: full-time $11,220. Tuition, nonresident: full-time $26,322. *Required fees:* $1800. *Financial support:* Fellowships, research assistantships, teaching assistantships, scholarships/grants, traineeships, and unspecified assistantships available. Financial award applicants required to submit FAFSA. *Faculty research:* Applied ocean science; applied physics; communication theory and systems; computer engineering; electronic circuits and systems; intelligent systems, robotics and control; medical devices and systems; nanoscale devices and systems; photonics; signal and image processing. *Unit head:* Truong Nguyen, Chair, 858-822-5554, E-mail: nguyent@ece.ucsd.edu. *Application contact:* Melanie Lynn, Graduate Admissions Coordinator, 858-822-3213, E-mail: ecegradapps@ece.ucsd.edu.
Website: http://ece.ucsd.edu/

University of Massachusetts Boston, College of Science and Mathematics, Program in Applied Physics, Boston, MA 02125-3393. Offers MS. *Program availability:* Part-time, evening/weekend. *Faculty:* 12 full-time (0 women), 4 part-time/adjunct (1 woman). *Students:* 4 full-time (2 women), 24 part-time (5 women); includes 4 minority (1 Asian, non-Hispanic/Latino; 3 Hispanic/Latino), 8 international. 22 applicants, 50% accepted, 11 enrolled. In 2015, 8 master's awarded. *Degree requirements:* For master's, thesis optional. *Entrance requirements:* For master's, minimum GPA of 2.75. *Application deadline:* For fall admission, 3/1 for domestic students; for spring admission, 11/1 for domestic students. *Expenses:* Tuition, state resident: full-time $2590. Tuition, nonresident: full-time $9758. *Required fees:* $13,525. *Financial support:* Research assistantships with full tuition reimbursements, teaching assistantships with full tuition reimbursements, career-related internships or fieldwork, Federal Work-Study, and unspecified assistantships available. Support available to part-time students. Financial award application deadline: 3/1; financial award applicants required to submit FAFSA. *Faculty research:* Experimental laser research, nonlinear optics, experimental and theoretical solid state physics, semiconductor devices, opto-electronics. *Unit head:* Dr. Bala Sundaram, Chair of the Department. *Application contact:* Peggy Roldan Patel, Graduate Admissions Coordinator, 617-287-6400, Fax: 617-287-6236, E-mail: bos.gadm@dpc.umassp.edu.

University of Massachusetts Lowell, College of Sciences, Department of Physics and Applied Physics, Program in Applied Physics, Lowell, MA 01854. Offers applied physics (MS), including optical sciences. Terminal master's awarded for partial completion of doctoral program. *Degree requirements:* For master's, thesis. *Entrance requirements:* For master's, GRE General Test, 3 letters of reference. Additional exam requirements/recommendations for international students: Required—TOEFL.

University of Michigan, Rackham Graduate School, College of Literature, Science, and the Arts, Applied Physics Program, Ann Arbor, MI 48109. Offers PhD. *Degree requirements:* For doctorate, oral defense of dissertation, preliminary and qualifying exams. *Entrance requirements:* For doctorate, GRE General Test. Additional exam requirements/recommendations for international students: Required—TOEFL.

Electronic applications accepted. *Faculty research:* Optical sciences, materials research, quantum structures, medical imaging, environment and science policy.

University of Missouri–St. Louis, College of Arts and Sciences, Department of Physics and Astronomy, St. Louis, MO 63121. Offers applied physics (MS); astrophysics (MS); physics (PhD). *Program availability:* Part-time, evening/weekend. *Faculty:* 10 full-time (2 women), 3 part-time/adjunct (0 women). *Students:* 16 full-time (4 women), 8 part-time (2 women); includes 3 minority (2 Black or African American, non-Hispanic/Latino; 1 Asian, non-Hispanic/Latino), 6 international. Average age 32. 28 applicants, 39% accepted, 6 enrolled. Terminal master's awarded for partial completion of doctoral program. *Degree requirements:* For master's, thesis optional; for doctorate, thesis/dissertation. *Entrance requirements:* For master's, GRE General Test; for doctorate, GRE General Test, 2 letters of recommendation. Additional exam requirements/recommendations for international students: Required—TOEFL (minimum score 550 paper-based; 79 iBT), IELTS (minimum score 6.5). *Application deadline:* For fall admission, 7/1 for domestic and international students; for spring admission, 12/1 for domestic students, 11/1 for international students. Application fee: $50 ($40 for international students). Electronic applications accepted. *Financial support:* Research assistantships with tuition reimbursements, teaching assistantships with tuition reimbursements, and career-related internships or fieldwork available. Financial award applicants required to submit FAFSA. *Faculty research:* Biophysics, atomic physics, nonlinear dynamics, materials science. *Unit head:* Dr. Bruce Wilking, Graduate Program Advisor, 314-516-5023, Fax: 314-516-6152, E-mail: bwilking@umsl.edu. *Application contact:* 314-516-5458, Fax: 314-516-6996, E-mail: gradadm@umsl.edu.
Website: http://www.umsl.edu/~physics/

The University of North Carolina at Charlotte, College of Liberal Arts and Sciences, Department of Physics and Optical Science, Charlotte, NC 28223-0001. Offers applied physics (MS); optical science and engineering (MS, PhD). *Faculty:* 18 full-time (3 women). *Students:* 48 full-time (14 women), 11 part-time (2 women); includes 3 minority (2 Hispanic/Latino; 1 Two or more races, non-Hispanic/Latino), 21 international. Average age 28. 43 applicants, 51% accepted, 12 enrolled. In 2015, 16 master's, 9 doctorates awarded. Terminal master's awarded for partial completion of doctoral program. *Degree requirements:* For master's, comprehensive exam (for some programs), thesis or comprehensive exam; for doctorate, thesis/dissertation. *Entrance requirements:* For master's, GRE; for doctorate, GRE, baccalaureate or master's degree in physics, chemistry, mathematics, engineering, optics, or related field with minimum undergraduate GPA of 3.0 overall and 3.2 in major (3.2 graduate); letters of recommendation. Additional exam requirements/recommendations for international students: Required—TOEFL (minimum score 557 paper-based, 83 iBT) or IELTS (minimum score 6.5). *Application deadline:* For fall admission, 3/1 for domestic and international students; for spring admission, 10/1 for domestic and international students; for summer admission, 4/1 for domestic and international students. Applications are processed on a rolling basis. Application fee: $75. Electronic applications accepted. *Expenses:* Tuition, state resident: full-time $4128. Tuition, nonresident: full-time $16,799. *Required fees:* $2904. Tuition and fees vary according to course load and program. *Financial support:* In 2015–16, 53 students received support, including 2 fellowships (averaging $46,875 per year), 20 research assistantships (averaging $11,315 per year), 31 teaching assistantships (averaging $7,408 per year); career-related internships or fieldwork, institutionally sponsored loans, scholarships/grants, and unspecified assistantships also available. Support available to part-time students. Financial award application deadline: 3/1; financial award applicants required to submit FAFSA. *Faculty research:* Experimental and computational material sciences, optoelectronics, quantum structures, electronic and electromagnetic waves in anisotropic media, nanoscale smart devices, infrared (IR) transmitting optical materials, low loss IR transmitting glass optical fibers and rugged transparent ceramic spinel windows. *Total annual research expenditures:* $2.3 million. *Unit head:* Dr. Glen Boreman, Chair, 704-687-8173, E-mail: gboreman@uncc.edu. *Application contact:* Kathy B. Giddings, Director of Graduate Admissions, 704-687-5503, Fax: 704-687-1668, E-mail: gradadm@uncc.edu.
Website: http://physics.uncc.edu/

University of South Florida, College of Arts and Sciences, Department of Physics, Tampa, FL 33620-9951. Offers applied physics (PhD); physics (MS), including applied physics, atmospheric physics, atomic and molecular physics, laser physics, materials physics, medical physics, optical physics, semiconductor physics, solid state physics. MSE offered jointly with College of Engineering. *Program availability:* Part-time. *Faculty:* 25 full-time (2 women). *Students:* 71 full-time (16 women), 6 part-time (1 woman); includes 14 minority (2 Black or African American, non-Hispanic/Latino; 12 Hispanic/Latino), 36 international. Average age 31. 97 applicants, 21% accepted, 12 enrolled. In 2015, 14 master's, 8 doctorates awarded. *Degree requirements:* For master's, comprehensive exam, thesis optional; for doctorate, comprehensive exam, thesis/dissertation. *Entrance requirements:* For master's and doctorate, GRE General Test; GRE Subject Test in physics (recommended), minimum GPA of 3.0, three letters of recommendation, statement of purpose. Additional exam requirements/recommendations for international students: Required—TOEFL (minimum score 550 paper-based; 79 iBT) or IELTS (minimum score 6.5). *Application deadline:* For fall admission, 2/15 priority date for domestic students, 1/2 for international students; for spring admission, 9/1 for domestic students, 7/1 for international students. Applications are processed on a rolling basis. Application fee: $30. Electronic applications accepted. *Financial support:* In 2015–16, 70 students received support, including 27 research assistantships with tuition reimbursements available (averaging $15,272 per year), 43 teaching assistantships with tuition reimbursements available (averaging $16,267 per year); unspecified assistantships also available. *Faculty research:* The molecular organization of collagen, lipid rafts in biological membranes, the formation of Alzheimer plaques, the role of cellular ion pumps in wound healing, carbon nanotubes as biological detectors, optical imaging of neuronal activity, three-dimensional imaging of intact tissues, motility of cancer cells, the optical detection of pathogens in water. *Total annual research expenditures:* $2.4 million. *Unit head:* Dr. Pritish Mukherjee, Professor and Chairperson, 813-974-3293, Fax: 813-974-5813, E-mail: pritish@usf.edu. *Application contact:* Dr. Lilia Woods, Professor and Graduate Program Director, 813-974-2862, Fax: 813-974-5813, E-mail: lmwoods@usf.edu.
Website: http://physics.usf.edu/

The University of Texas at Austin, Graduate School, College of Natural Sciences, Department of Physics, Austin, TX 78712-1111. Offers MA, MS, PhD. *Degree requirements:* For master's, thesis; for doctorate, thesis/dissertation. *Entrance requirements:* For master's and doctorate, GRE General Test, GRE Subject Test (physics). Electronic applications accepted.

University of Washington, Graduate School, College of Arts and Sciences, Department of Physics, Seattle, WA 98195. Offers MS, PhD. *Program availability:* Part-time, evening/weekend. Terminal master's awarded for partial completion of doctoral program. *Degree requirements:* For doctorate, thesis/dissertation. *Entrance requirements:* For master's, GRE; for doctorate, GRE General Test, GRE Subject Test. Additional exam requirements/recommendations for international students: Required—TOEFL. Electronic applications accepted. *Faculty research:* Astro-, atomic, condensed-matter, nuclear, and particle physics; physics education.

Virginia Commonwealth University, Graduate School, College of Humanities and Sciences, Department of Physics, Program in Physics and Applied Physics, Richmond, VA 23284-9005. Offers MS. *Entrance requirements:* For master's, GRE. Additional exam requirements/recommendations for international students: Required—TOEFL (minimum score 600 paper-based; 100 iBT); Recommended—IELTS (minimum score 6.5). Electronic applications accepted. *Faculty research:* Theoretical and experimental condensed matter physics, general relativity and cosmology, physics education.

West Virginia University, Eberly College of Arts and Sciences, Department of Physics, Morgantown, WV 26506. Offers applied physics (MS, PhD); astrophysics (MS, PhD); chemical physics (MS, PhD); condensed matter physics (MS, PhD); elementary particle physics (MS, PhD); materials physics (MS, PhD); plasma physics (MS, PhD); solid state physics (MS, PhD); statistical physics (MS, PhD); theoretical physics (MS, PhD). Terminal master's awarded for partial completion of doctoral program. *Degree requirements:* For master's, thesis or alternative, qualifying exam; for doctorate, thesis/dissertation, qualifying exam. *Entrance requirements:* For master's and doctorate, GRE General Test, minimum GPA of 3.0. Additional exam requirements/recommendations for international students: Required—TOEFL. *Expenses:* Tuition, state resident: full-time $8568. Tuition, nonresident: full-time $22,140. Tuition and fees vary according to program. *Faculty research:* Experimental and theoretical condensed-matter, plasma, high-energy theory, nonlinear dynamics, space physics.

Yale University, Graduate School of Arts and Sciences, School of Engineering and Applied Science, Department of Applied Physics, New Haven, CT 06520. Offers MS, PhD. Terminal master's awarded for partial completion of doctoral program. *Degree requirements:* For doctorate, thesis/dissertation, area exam. *Entrance requirements:* For master's and doctorate, GRE General Test. Additional exam requirements/recommendations for international students: Required—TOEFL. *Faculty research:* Condensed-matter physics, optical physics, materials science.

Chemical Physics

Columbia University, Graduate School of Arts and Sciences, New York, NY 10027. Offers African-American studies (MA); American studies (MA); anthropology (MA, PhD); art history and archaeology (MA, PhD); astronomy (PhD); biological sciences (PhD); biotechnology (MA); chemical physics (PhD); chemistry (PhD); classical studies (MA, PhD); classics (MA, PhD); climate and society (MA); conservation biology (MA); earth and environmental sciences (PhD); East Asia: regional studies (MA); East Asian languages and cultures (MA, PhD); ecology, evolution and environmental biology (MA), including conservation biology; ecology, evolution, and environmental biology (PhD), including ecology and evolutionary biology, evolutionary primatology; economics (MA, PhD); English and comparative literature (MA, PhD); French and Romance philology (MA, PhD); Germanic languages (MA, PhD); global French studies (MA); global thought (MA); Hispanic cultural studies (MA); history (PhD); history and literature (MA); human rights studies (MA); Islamic studies (MA); Italian (MA, PhD); Japanese pedagogy (MA); Jewish studies (MA); Latin America and the Caribbean: regional studies (MA); Latin American and Iberian cultures (PhD); mathematics (MA, PhD), including finance (MA); medieval and Renaissance studies (MA); Middle Eastern, South Asian, and African studies (MA, PhD); modern art: critical and curatorial studies (MA); modern European studies (MA); museum anthropology (MA); music (DMA, PhD); oral history (MA); philosophical foundations of physics (MA); philosophy (MA, PhD); physics (PhD); political science (MA, PhD); psychology (PhD); quantitative methods in the social sciences (MA); religion (MA, PhD); Russia, Eurasia and East Europe: regional studies (MA); Russian translation (MA); Slavic cultures (MA); Slavic languages (MA, PhD); sociology (MA, PhD); South Asian studies (MA); statistics (MA, PhD); theatre (PhD). Dual-degree programs require admission to both Graduate School of Arts and Sciences and another Columbia school. *Program availability:* Part-time. *Students:* 3,030 full-time, 235 part-time; includes 861 minority (88 Black or African American, non-Hispanic/Latino; 5 American Indian or Alaska Native, non-Hispanic/Latino; 517 Asian, non-Hispanic/Latino; 159 Hispanic/Latino; 4 Native Hawaiian or other Pacific Islander, non-Hispanic/Latino; 88 Two or more races, non-Hispanic/Latino), 1,697 international. 13,288 applicants, 21% accepted, 1162 enrolled. In 2015, 1,061 master's, 553 doctorates awarded. Terminal master's awarded for partial completion of doctoral program. *Degree requirements:* For master's, variable foreign language requirement, comprehensive exam (for some programs), thesis (for some programs); for doctorate, variable foreign language requirement, comprehensive exam (for some programs), thesis/dissertation. *Entrance requirements:* For master's and doctorate, GRE General Test, GRE Subject Test (for some programs). Additional exam requirements/recommendations for international students: Required—TOEFL, IELTS. Application fee: $105. Electronic applications accepted. *Financial support:* Fellowships, research assistantships, teaching assistantships, career-related internships or fieldwork, Federal Work-Study, institutionally sponsored loans, scholarships/grants, traineeships, health care benefits, tuition waivers, and unspecified assistantships available. Support available to part-time students. Financial award application deadline: 12/15. *Unit head:* Carlos J. Alonso, Dean of the Graduate School of Arts and Sciences, 212-854-5177. *Application contact:* GSAS Office of Admissions, 212-854-8903, E-mail: gsas-admissions@columbia.edu.
Website: http://gsas.columbia.edu/

Cornell University, Graduate School, Graduate Fields of Arts and Sciences, Field of Chemistry and Chemical Biology, Ithaca, NY 14853-0001. Offers analytical chemistry (PhD); bio-organic chemistry (PhD); biophysical chemistry (PhD); chemical biology (PhD); chemical physics (PhD); inorganic chemistry (PhD); materials chemistry (PhD); organic chemistry (PhD); organometallic chemistry (PhD); physical chemistry (PhD); polymer chemistry (PhD); theoretical chemistry (PhD). *Degree requirements:* For doctorate, comprehensive exam, thesis/dissertation. *Entrance requirements:* For doctorate, GRE General Test, GRE Subject Test (chemistry), 3 letters of recommendation. Additional exam requirements/recommendations for international students: Required—TOEFL (minimum score 600 paper-based; 77 iBT). Electronic applications accepted. *Faculty research:* Analytical, organic, inorganic, physical, materials, chemical biology.

Harvard University, Graduate School of Arts and Sciences, Committee on Chemical Physics, Cambridge, MA 02138. Offers PhD. *Degree requirements:* For doctorate, one foreign language, thesis/dissertation, cumulative exams. *Entrance requirements:* For doctorate, GRE General Test, GRE Subject Test. Additional exam requirements/ recommendations for international students: Required—TOEFL.

Kent State University, College of Arts and Sciences, Chemical Physics Interdisciplinary Program, Kent, OH 44242-0001. Offers MS, PhD. Program offered in cooperation with the Departments of Chemistry, Mathematics and Computer Science, and Physics and the Liquid Crystal Institute. *Faculty:* 12 full-time (2 women). *Students:* 51 full-time (16 women), 9 part-time (5 women); includes 1 minority (Black or African American, non-Hispanic/Latino), 35 international. Average age 30. 59 applicants, 44% accepted, 14 enrolled. In 2015, 1 master's, 5 doctorates awarded. Terminal master's awarded for partial completion of doctoral program. *Degree requirements:* For master's, thesis optional; for doctorate, comprehensive exam, thesis/dissertation. *Entrance requirements:* For master's and doctorate, GRE (recommended), minimum GPA of 3.0, transcript, statement of purpose, curriculum vitae/resume, 3 letters of recommendation. Additional exam requirements/recommendations for international students: Required—TOEFL (minimum score: paper-based 525, iBT 71), Michigan English Language Assessment Battery (minimum score of 75), IELTS (minimum score of 6.0), PTE Academic (minimum score of 48), or completion of ELS level 112 Intensive Program. *Application deadline:* For fall admission, 1/31 for domestic and international students. Application fee: $45 ($70 for international students). Electronic applications accepted. *Expenses:* Tuition, state resident: full-time $10,864; part-time $495 per credit hour. Tuition, nonresident: full-time $18,380; part-time $837 per credit hour. *Financial support:* Research assistantships with full tuition reimbursements, teaching assistantships with full tuition reimbursements, Federal Work-Study, and unspecified assistantships available. Financial award application deadline: 3/31; financial award applicants required to submit FAFSA. *Unit head:* Dr. Hiroshi Yokoyama, Acting Director, 330-672-2633, E-mail: hyokoyam@kent.edu. *Application contact:* Dr. Antal Jakli, Graduate Coordinator and Professor, 330-672-2654, E-mail: cpipgrad@kent.edu.
Website: http://www.kent.edu/cas/cpip/

Marquette University, Graduate School, College of Arts and Sciences, Department of Chemistry, Milwaukee, WI 53201-1881. Offers analytical chemistry (MS, PhD); bioanalytical chemistry (MS, PhD); biophysical chemistry (MS, PhD); chemical physics (MS, PhD); inorganic chemistry (MS, PhD); organic chemistry (MS, PhD); physical chemistry (MS, PhD). *Program availability:* Part-time. *Faculty:* 19 full-time (3 women), 1 part-time/adjunct (0 women). *Students:* 43 full-time (14 women), 4 part-time (0 women); includes 2 minority (1 Asian, non-Hispanic/Latino; 1 Hispanic/Latino), 32 international. Average age 28. In 2015, 4 master's, 4 doctorates awarded. Terminal master's awarded for partial completion of doctoral program. *Degree requirements:* For master's, comprehensive exam; for doctorate, thesis/dissertation, cumulative exams. *Entrance requirements:* For master's and doctorate, official transcripts from all current and previous colleges/universities except Marquette, three letters of recommendation from individuals familiar with the applicant's academic work. Additional exam requirements/ recommendations for international students: Required—TOEFL (minimum score 530 paper-based). *Application deadline:* Applications are processed on a rolling basis. Application fee: $50. Electronic applications accepted. *Financial support:* In 2015–16, 41 students received support, including 2 fellowships (averaging $17,134 per year), 30 teaching assistantships with full tuition reimbursements available (averaging $20,295 per year); research assistantships, scholarships/grants, health care benefits, tuition waivers (full and partial), and unspecified assistantships also available. Support available to part-time students. Financial award application deadline: 2/15. *Faculty research:* Inorganic complexes, laser Raman spectroscopy, organic synthesis, synthetic bioinorganic chemistry, electro-active organic molecules. *Total annual research expenditures:* $1.2 million. *Unit head:* Dr. Scott Reid, Chair, 414-288-7565, E-mail: scott.reid@marquette.edu. *Application contact:* Dr. Adam Fiedler, New and Recruiting, 414-288-1625.
Website: http://www.marquette.edu/chem/graduate.shtml

McMaster University, School of Graduate Studies, Faculty of Science, Department of Chemistry, Hamilton, ON L8S 4M2, Canada. Offers analytical chemistry (M Sc, PhD); chemical physics (M Sc, PhD); chemistry (M Sc, PhD); inorganic chemistry (M Sc, PhD); organic chemistry (M Sc, PhD); physical chemistry (M Sc, PhD); polymer chemistry (M Sc, PhD). *Program availability:* Part-time. Terminal master's awarded for partial completion of doctoral program. *Degree requirements:* For master's, thesis; for doctorate, comprehensive exam, thesis/dissertation. *Entrance requirements:* For master's, minimum B+ average. Additional exam requirements/recommendations for international students: Required—TOEFL (minimum score 550 paper-based).

Michigan State University, The Graduate School, College of Natural Science, Department of Chemistry, East Lansing, MI 48824. Offers chemical physics (PhD); chemistry (MS, PhD); chemistry-environmental toxicology (PhD); computational chemistry (MS). *Entrance requirements:* Additional exam requirements/ recommendations for international students: Required—TOEFL. Electronic applications accepted. *Faculty research:* Analytical chemistry, inorganic and organic chemistry, nuclear chemistry, physical chemistry, theoretical and computational chemistry.

The Ohio State University, Graduate School, College of Arts and Sciences, Division of Natural and Mathematical Sciences, Program in Chemical Physics, Columbus, OH 43210. Offers MS, PhD. *Degree requirements:* For master's, thesis optional; for doctorate, thesis/dissertation. *Entrance requirements:* For doctorate, GRE General Test, GRE Subject Test in chemistry or physics (recommended). Additional exam requirements/recommendations for international students: Required—Michigan English Language Assessment Battery (minimum score 86); Recommended—TOEFL (minimum score 600 paper-based; 100 iBT), IELTS (minimum score 8). Electronic applications accepted.

Tufts University, Graduate School of Arts and Sciences, Department of Physics and Astronomy, Medford, MA 02155. Offers astrophysics (MS, PhD); chemical physics (PhD); physics (MS, PhD); physics education (PhD). Terminal master's awarded for partial completion of doctoral program. *Degree requirements:* For master's, thesis optional; for doctorate, thesis/dissertation. *Entrance requirements:* For master's and doctorate, GRE General Test. Additional exam requirements/recommendations for international students: Required—TOEFL (minimum score 550 paper-based; 80 iBT), IELTS (minimum score 6.5). Electronic applications accepted. *Expenses: Tuition, area resident:* Full-time $48,412; part-time $1210 per credit hour. *Required fees:* $806. Full-time tuition and fees vary according to degree level, program and student level. Part-time tuition and fees vary according to course load.

University of Colorado Boulder, Graduate School, College of Arts and Sciences, Department of Physics, Boulder, CO 80309. Offers chemical physics (PhD); geophysics (PhD); liquid crystal science and technology (PhD); mathematical physics (PhD); medical physics (PhD); optical sciences and engineering (PhD); physics (MS, PhD). *Faculty:* 48 full-time (8 women). *Students:* 131 full-time (22 women), 97 part-time (22 women); includes 14 minority (5 Asian, non-Hispanic/Latino; 4 Hispanic/Latino; 5 Two or more races, non-Hispanic/Latino), 61 international. Average age 26. 624 applicants, 24% accepted, 36 enrolled. In 2015, 24 master's, 29 doctorates awarded. Terminal master's awarded for partial completion of doctoral program. *Degree requirements:* For master's, comprehensive exam, thesis or alternative; for doctorate, comprehensive exam, thesis/dissertation. *Entrance requirements:* For master's and doctorate, GRE General Test, GRE Subject Test, minimum undergraduate GPA of 3.0. Additional exam requirements/recommendations for international students: Required—TOEFL. *Application deadline:* For fall admission, 12/15 for domestic students, 12/1 for international students. Applications are processed on a rolling basis. Application fee: $50 ($70 for international students). Electronic applications accepted. Application fee is waived when completed online. *Financial support:* In 2015–16, 521 students received support, including 7 fellowships (averaging $5,311 per year), 162 research assistantships with tuition reimbursements available (averaging $34,608 per year), 51 teaching assistantships with tuition reimbursements available (averaging $29,058 per year); institutionally sponsored loans, scholarships/grants, health care benefits, and unspecified assistantships also available. Financial award application deadline: 1/15; financial award applicants required to submit FAFSA. *Faculty research:* Physics, theoretical physics, high energy physics, experimental physics, solid state physics. *Total annual research expenditures:* $24.8 million. *Application contact:* E-mail: jeanne.nijhowne@colorado.edu.
Website: http://phys.colorado.edu/graduate-students

University of Illinois at Urbana–Champaign, Graduate College, College of Liberal Arts and Sciences, School of Chemical Sciences, Department of Chemistry, Champaign, IL 61820. Offers astrochemistry (PhD); chemical physics (PhD); chemistry (MA, MS, PhD); teaching of chemistry (MS); MS/JD; MS/MBA.

University of Louisville, Graduate School, College of Arts and Sciences, Department of Chemistry, Louisville, KY 40292-0001. Offers analytical chemistry (MS, PhD); biochemistry (MS, PhD); chemical physics (PhD); inorganic chemistry (MS, PhD); organic chemistry (MS, PhD); physical chemistry (MS, PhD). *Students:* 46 full-time (16 women), 8 part-time (1 woman); includes 3 minority (1 Black or African American, non-Hispanic/Latino; 1 Asian, non-Hispanic/Latino; 1 Two or more races, non-Hispanic/ Latino), 36 international. Average age 29. 51 applicants, 22% accepted, 6 enrolled. In 2015, 2 master's, 1 doctorate awarded. Terminal master's awarded for partial completion of doctoral program. *Degree requirements:* For master's, variable foreign language requirement, comprehensive exam, thesis optional; for doctorate, variable foreign language requirement, comprehensive exam, thesis/dissertation. *Entrance requirements:* For master's and doctorate, GRE General Test, BA or BS coursework. Additional exam requirements/recommendations for international students: Required—TOEFL (minimum score 550 paper-based; 79 iBT). *Application deadline:* For fall admission, 3/15 for domestic students, 5/1 priority date for international students; for winter admission, 9/15 for domestic and international students; for spring admission, 11/ 1 priority date for international students; for summer admission, 4/1 priority date for international students. Applications are processed on a rolling basis. Application fee: $60. Electronic applications accepted. *Expenses:* Tuition, state resident: full-time $11,664; part-time $649 per credit hour. Tuition, nonresident: full-time $24,274; part-time $1350 per credit hour. *Required fees:* $196. Tuition and fees vary according to program and reciprocity agreements. *Financial support:* In 2015–16, 757,720 students received support. Fellowships with full tuition reimbursements available, research assistantships with full tuition reimbursements available, teaching assistantships with full tuition reimbursements available, career-related internships or fieldwork, scholarships/ grants, traineeships, health care benefits, and unspecified assistantships available. Support available to part-time students. Financial award application deadline: 3/15. *Faculty research:* Computational chemistry, biophysics nuclear magnetic resonance, synthetic organic chemistry, synthetic inorganic chemistry, medicinal chemistry, protein chemistry, enzymology, nano chemistry, electrochemistry, analytical chemistry, synthetic biology, bioinformatics. *Total annual research expenditures:* $2.4 million. *Unit head:* Dr. Richard J. Wittebort, Professor/Chair, 502-852-6613. *Application contact:* Libby Leggett, Director, Graduate Admissions, 502-852-3101, Fax: 502-852-6536, E-mail: gradadm@louisville.edu.
Website: http://louisville.edu/chemistry

University of Maryland, College Park, Academic Affairs, College of Computer, Mathematical and Natural Sciences, Institute for Physical Science and Technology, Program in Chemical Physics, College Park, MD 20742. Offers MS, PhD. *Program availability:* Part-time, evening/weekend. Terminal master's awarded for partial completion of doctoral program. *Degree requirements:* For master's, thesis optional, paper, qualifying exam; for doctorate, thesis/dissertation, seminars. *Entrance requirements:* For master's, GRE General Test, GRE Subject Test (chemistry, math or physics), minimum GPA of 3.3, 3 letters of recommendation; for doctorate, GRE Subject Test (chemistry, math, or physics), GRE General Test, minimum GPA of 3.3, 3 letters of recommendation. Electronic applications accepted. *Faculty research:* Discrete molecules and gases; dynamic phenomena; thermodynamics, statistical mechanical theory and quantum mechanical theory; atmospheric physics; biophysics.

University of Minnesota, Twin Cities Campus, College of Science and Engineering, Department of Chemistry, Minneapolis, MN 55455-0213. Offers chemical physics (MS, PhD); chemistry (MS, PhD). *Program availability:* Part-time. Terminal master's awarded for partial completion of doctoral program. *Degree requirements:* For master's, thesis or alternative; for doctorate, thesis/dissertation, preliminary candidacy exams. *Entrance requirements:* For master's and doctorate, GRE General Test. Additional exam requirements/recommendations for international students: Required—TOEFL. Electronic applications accepted. *Faculty research:* Analytical chemistry, environmental chemistry, organic chemistry, inorganic chemistry, materials chemistry, polymer chemistry, computational chemistry, experimental physical chemistry, chemical biology.

University of Nevada, Reno, Graduate School, Interdisciplinary Program in Chemical Physics, Reno, NV 89557. Offers PhD. *Degree requirements:* For doctorate, thesis/ dissertation. *Entrance requirements:* For doctorate, GRE, minimum GPA of 3.0. Additional exam requirements/recommendations for international students: Required—TOEFL (minimum score 500 paper-based; 61 iBT). Electronic applications accepted. *Faculty research:* Atomic and molecular physics, physical chemistry.

The University of Tennessee, Graduate School, College of Arts and Sciences, Department of Chemistry, Knoxville, TN 37996. Offers analytical chemistry (MS, PhD); chemical physics (PhD); environmental chemistry (MS, PhD); inorganic chemistry (MS, PhD); organic chemistry (MS, PhD); physical chemistry (MS, PhD); polymer chemistry (MS, PhD); theoretical chemistry (PhD). *Program availability:* Part-time. Terminal master's awarded for partial completion of doctoral program. *Degree requirements:* For master's, thesis; for doctorate, thesis/dissertation. *Entrance requirements:* For master's and doctorate, GRE General Test, minimum GPA of 2.7. Additional exam requirements/

recommendations for international students: Required—TOEFL. Electronic applications accepted.

University of Utah, Graduate School, College of Science, Department of Physics and Astronomy, Salt Lake City, UT 84112. Offers chemical physics (PhD); medical physics (MS, PhD); physics (MA, MS, PhD); physics teaching (PhD). *Program availability:* Part-time. *Faculty:* 34 full-time (4 women), 16 part-time/adjunct (1 woman). *Students:* 79 full-time (26 women), 19 part-time (7 women); includes 7 minority (3 Asian, non-Hispanic/Latino; 4 Hispanic/Latino), 51 international. Average age 28. 141 applicants, 30% accepted, 19 enrolled. In 2015, 13 master's, 10 doctorates awarded. Terminal master's awarded for partial completion of doctoral program. *Degree requirements:* For master's, comprehensive exam (for some programs), thesis or alternative, teaching experience, departmental exam; for doctorate, comprehensive exam, thesis/dissertation, departmental qualifying exam. *Entrance requirements:* For master's and doctorate, GRE Subject Test, minimum GPA of 3.0. Additional exam requirements/recommendations for international students: Required—TOEFL (minimum score 550 paper-based; 85 iBT). *Application deadline:* For fall admission, 4/1 priority date for domestic and international students. Applications are processed on a rolling basis. Application fee: $55 ($65 for international students). Electronic applications accepted. *Financial support:* In 2015–16, 23 research assistantships with full tuition reimbursements (averaging $23,500 per year), 52 teaching assistantships with full tuition reimbursements (averaging $20,641 per year) were awarded; institutionally sponsored loans, scholarships/grants, and unspecified assistantships also available. Financial award application deadline: 2/15; financial award applicants required to submit FAFSA. *Faculty research:* High-energy, cosmic-ray, astrophysics, medical physics, condensed matter, relativity applied physics, biophysics, astronomy. *Total annual research expenditures:* $5.2 million. *Unit head:* Dr. Carleton DeTar, Chair, 801-581-3538, Fax: 801-581-4801, E-mail: detar@physics.utah.edu. *Application contact:* Jackie Hadley, Graduate Secretary, 801-581-6861, Fax: 801-581-4801, E-mail: jackie@physics.utah.edu.
Website: http://www.physics.utah.edu/

Virginia Commonwealth University, Graduate School, College of Humanities and Sciences, Department of Chemistry, Richmond, VA 23284-9005. Offers analytical chemistry (MS, PhD); chemical physics (PhD); inorganic chemistry (MS, PhD); organic chemistry (MS, PhD); physical chemistry (MS, PhD). *Program availability:* Part-time. Terminal master's awarded for partial completion of doctoral program. *Degree requirements:* For master's, thesis; for doctorate, thesis/dissertation, comprehensive cumulative exams, research proposal. *Entrance requirements:* For master's, GRE General Test, 30 undergraduate credits in chemistry; for doctorate, GRE General Test. Additional exam requirements/recommendations for international students: Required—TOEFL (minimum score 600 paper-based; 100 iBT) or IELTS (minimum score 6.5). Electronic applications accepted. *Faculty research:* Physical, organic, inorganic, analytical, and polymer chemistry; chemical physics.

Wesleyan University, Graduate Studies, Department of Chemistry, Middletown, CT 06459. Offers biochemistry (PhD); chemical physics (PhD); inorganic chemistry (PhD); organic chemistry (PhD); physical chemistry (PhD); theoretical chemistry (PhD). *Faculty:* 13 full-time (3 women), 3 part-time/adjunct (2 women). *Students:* 20 full-time (10 women), 2 part-time (0 women); includes 4 minority (1 Black or African American, non-Hispanic/Latino; 3 Asian, non-Hispanic/Latino), 8 international. Average age 25. In 2015, 6 doctorates awarded. Terminal master's awarded for partial completion of doctoral program. *Degree requirements:* For doctorate, thesis/dissertation, proposal. *Entrance requirements:* For doctorate, GRE General Test, 3 recommendations. Additional exam requirements/recommendations for international students: Required—TOEFL, IELTS. *Application deadline:* 2/15 for domestic and international students; for summer admission, 2/15 for domestic and international students. Applications are processed on a rolling basis. Application fee: $0. Electronic applications accepted. *Financial support:* In 2015–16, 4 research assistantships with full tuition reimbursements, 21 teaching assistantships with full tuition reimbursements were awarded; institutionally sponsored loans and health care benefits also available. Financial award application deadline: 4/15; financial award applicants required to submit FAFSA. *Faculty research:* MICHELLE LOUISE PERSONICK Research in the Personick lab is focused on the synthesis of noble metal and noble metal alloy nanoparticles with well-defined shapes and catalytically active high-energy surfaces. Our research takes place at the interface between inorganic chemistry and materials science, and we combine solution-phase nanoparticle synthesis with advanced materials characterization techniques such as scanning electron microscopy (SEM). In addition, we evaluate the catalytic activity of. *Unit head:* Michael Calter, Chair, 860-685-2633, E-mail: mcalter@wesleyan.edu. *Application contact:* Roslyn Brault, Administrative Assistant/Graduate Program Coordinator, 860-685-2573, Fax: 860-685-2211, E-mail: rbrault@wesleyan.edu.
Website: http://www.wesleyan.edu/chem/

West Virginia University, Eberly College of Arts and Sciences, Department of Physics, Morgantown, WV 26506. Offers applied physics (MS, PhD); astrophysics (MS, PhD); chemical physics (MS, PhD); condensed matter physics (MS, PhD); elementary particle physics (MS, PhD); materials physics (MS, PhD); plasma physics (MS, PhD); solid state physics (MS, PhD); statistical physics (MS, PhD); theoretical physics (MS, PhD). Terminal master's awarded for partial completion of doctoral program. *Degree requirements:* For master's, thesis or alternative, qualifying exam; for doctorate, thesis/dissertation, qualifying exam. *Entrance requirements:* For master's and doctorate, GRE General Test, minimum GPA of 3.0. Additional exam requirements/recommendations for international students: Required—TOEFL. *Expenses:* Tuition, state resident: full-time $8568. Tuition, nonresident: full-time $22,140. Tuition and fees vary according to program. *Faculty research:* Experimental and theoretical condensed-matter, plasma, high-energy theory, nonlinear dynamics, space physics.

Condensed Matter Physics

Cleveland State University, College of Graduate Studies, College of Sciences and Health Professions, Department of Physics, Cleveland, OH 44115. Offers applied optics (MS); condensed matter physics (MS); medical physics (MS); optics and materials (MS); optics and medical imaging (MS). *Program availability:* Part-time, evening/weekend. *Faculty:* 4 full-time (0 women), 1 part-time/adjunct (0 women). *Students:* 10 full-time (5 women), 9 part-time (1 woman); includes 5 minority (2 Black or African American, non-Hispanic/Latino; 1 Asian, non-Hispanic/Latino; 2 Hispanic/Latino), 2 international. Average age 28. 23 applicants, 78% accepted, 6 enrolled. In 2015, 10 master's awarded. *Entrance requirements:* For master's, undergraduate degree in engineering, physics, chemistry or mathematics. Additional exam requirements/recommendations for international students: Required—TOEFL (minimum score 550 paper-based; 78 iBT). *Application deadline:* For fall admission, 7/1 priority date for domestic students, 4/1 priority date for international students. Applications are processed on a rolling basis. Application fee: $30. Electronic applications accepted. *Expenses:* Tuition, state resident: full-time $9565. Tuition, nonresident: full-time $17,980. Tuition and fees vary according to program. *Financial support:* In 2015–16, 1 research assistantship with tuition reimbursement (averaging $5,666 per year) was awarded; fellowships with tuition reimbursements, teaching assistantships, and tuition waivers (full) also available. Financial award applicants required to submit FAFSA. *Faculty research:* Statistical physics, experimental solid-state physics, theoretical optics, experimental biological physics (macromolecular crystallography), experimental optics. *Total annual research expenditures:* $350,000. *Unit head:* Dr. Miron Kaufman, Chairperson, 216-687-2436, Fax: 216-523-7268, E-mail: m.kaufman@csuohio.edu. *Application contact:* Dr. James A. Lock, Director, 216-687-2420, Fax: 216-523-7268, E-mail: j.lock@csuohio.edu.
Website: http://www.csuohio.edu/sciences/physics/physics

Iowa State University of Science and Technology, Department of Physics and Astronomy, Ames, IA 50011. Offers applied physics (MS, PhD); astrophysics (MS, PhD); condensed matter physics (MS, PhD); high energy physics (MS, PhD); nuclear physics (MS, PhD); physics (MS, PhD). *Degree requirements:* For master's, thesis (for some programs); for doctorate, thesis/dissertation. *Entrance requirements:* For master's and doctorate, GRE General Test, GRE Subject Test (physics). Additional exam requirements/recommendations for international students: Required—TOEFL (minimum score 550 paper-based; 79 iBT), IELTS (minimum score 6.5). Electronic applications accepted. *Faculty research:* Condensed-matter physics, including superconductivity and new materials; high-energy and nuclear physics; astronomy and astrophysics; atmospheric and environmental physics.

Iowa State University of Science and Technology, Program in Condensed Matter Physics, Ames, IA 50011. Offers MS, PhD. *Entrance requirements:* For master's and doctorate, GRE. Additional exam requirements/recommendations for international students: Required—TOEFL (minimum score 550 paper-based; 79 iBT), IELTS (minimum score 6.5). Electronic applications accepted.

Memorial University of Newfoundland, School of Graduate Studies, Department of Physics and Physical Oceanography, St. John's, NL A1C 5S7, Canada. Offers atomic and molecular physics (PhD); condensed matter physics (PhD); physical oceanography (M Sc, PhD); physics (M Sc). *Program availability:* Part-time. *Degree requirements:* For master's, thesis, seminar presentation on thesis topic; for doctorate, comprehensive exam, thesis/dissertation, oral defense of thesis. *Entrance requirements:* For master's, honors B Sc or equivalent; for doctorate, M Sc or equivalent. *Application deadline:* Applications are processed on a rolling basis. Application fee: $50 Canadian dollars ($100 Canadian dollars for international students). Electronic applications accepted. *Expenses: Tuition, area resident:* Full-time $2199 Canadian dollars. *International tuition:* $2859 Canadian dollars full-time. *Financial support:* Fellowships, research assistantships, and teaching assistantships available. *Faculty research:* Experiment and theory in atomic and molecular physics, condensed matter physics, physical oceanography, theoretical geophysics and applied nuclear physics. *Unit head:* Dr. J. Lagowski, Head, 709-864-8738, Fax: 709-864-8739, E-mail: jolantal@mun.ca. *Application contact:* Dr. Stephanie Curnoe, Graduate Officer, 709-864-8888, Fax: 709-864-8739, E-mail: gradphysicsInfo@mun.ca.
Website: http://www.mun.ca/physics

Rutgers University–New Brunswick, Graduate School-New Brunswick, Department of Physics and Astronomy, Piscataway, NJ 08854-8097. Offers astronomy (MS, PhD); biophysics (PhD); condensed matter physics (MS, PhD); elementary particle physics (MS, PhD); intermediate energy nuclear physics (MS); nuclear physics (MS, PhD); physics (MST); surface science (PhD); theoretical physics (MS, PhD). *Program availability:* Part-time. Terminal master's awarded for partial completion of doctoral program. *Degree requirements:* For master's, comprehensive exam, thesis or alternative; for doctorate, comprehensive exam, thesis/dissertation. *Entrance requirements:* For master's and doctorate, GRE General Test, GRE Subject Test. Additional exam requirements/recommendations for international students: Required—TOEFL (minimum score 560 paper-based). Electronic applications accepted. *Faculty research:* Astronomy, high energy, condensed matter, surface, nuclear physics.

University of Alberta, Faculty of Graduate Studies and Research, Department of Physics, Edmonton, AB T6G 2E1, Canada. Offers astrophysics (M Sc, PhD); condensed matter (M Sc, PhD); geophysics (M Sc, PhD); medical physics (M Sc, PhD); subatomic physics (M Sc, PhD). *Degree requirements:* For master's, thesis; for doctorate, thesis/dissertation. *Entrance requirements:* For master's and doctorate, minimum GPA of 7.0 on a 9.0 scale. Additional exam requirements/recommendations for international students: Required—TOEFL. *Faculty research:* Cosmology, astroparticle physics, high-intermediate energy, magnetism, superconductivity.

The University of Manchester, School of Physics and Astronomy, Manchester, United Kingdom. Offers astronomy and astrophysics (M Sc, PhD); biological physics (M Sc, PhD); condensed matter physics (M Sc, PhD); nonlinear and liquid crystals physics (M Sc, PhD); nuclear physics (M Sc, PhD); particle physics (M Sc, PhD); photon physics (M Sc, PhD); physics (M Sc, PhD); theoretical physics (M Sc, PhD).

University of Victoria, Faculty of Graduate Studies, Faculty of Science, Department of Physics and Astronomy, Victoria, BC V8W 2Y2, Canada. Offers astronomy and astrophysics (M Sc, PhD); condensed matter physics (M Sc, PhD); experimental particle physics (M Sc, PhD); medical physics (M Sc, PhD); ocean physics (M Sc, PhD); theoretical physics (M Sc, PhD). *Degree requirements:* For master's, thesis; for doctorate, comprehensive exam, thesis/dissertation, candidacy exam. *Entrance requirements:* For master's and doctorate, GRE. Additional exam requirements/recommendations for international students: Required—TOEFL (minimum score 575 paper-based), IELTS (minimum score 7). Electronic applications accepted. *Faculty research:* Old stellar populations; observational cosmology and large scale structure; cp violation; atlas.

West Virginia University, Eberly College of Arts and Sciences, Department of Physics, Morgantown, WV 26506. Offers applied physics (MS, PhD); astrophysics (MS, PhD); chemical physics (MS, PhD); condensed matter physics (MS, PhD); elementary particle physics (MS, PhD); materials physics (MS, PhD); plasma physics (MS, PhD); solid state physics (MS, PhD); statistical physics (MS, PhD); theoretical physics (MS, PhD). Terminal master's awarded for partial completion of doctoral program. *Degree requirements:* For master's, thesis or alternative, qualifying exam; for doctorate, thesis/dissertation, qualifying exam. *Entrance requirements:* For master's and doctorate, GRE General Test, minimum GPA of 3.0. Additional exam requirements/recommendations for international students: Required—TOEFL. *Expenses:* Tuition, state resident: full-time $8568. Tuition, nonresident: full-time $22,140. Tuition and fees vary according to program. *Faculty research:* Experimental and theoretical condensed-matter, plasma, high-energy theory, nonlinear dynamics, space physics.

Mathematical Physics

Indiana University Bloomington, University Graduate School, College of Arts and Sciences, Department of Mathematics, Bloomington, IN 47405-7000. Offers applied mathematics (MA); mathematical physics (PhD); mathematics education (MAT); pure mathematics (MA, PhD). Terminal master's awarded for partial completion of doctoral program. *Degree requirements:* For doctorate, one foreign language, thesis/dissertation. *Entrance requirements:* For master's and doctorate, GRE General Test, GRE Subject Test. Additional exam requirements/recommendations for international students: Required—TOEFL. Electronic applications accepted. *Faculty research:* Topology, geometry, algebra, applied, analysis.

New Mexico Institute of Mining and Technology, Center for Graduate Studies, Department of Physics, Socorro, NM 87801. Offers astrophysics (PhD); atmospheric physics (PhD); instrumentation (MS); mathematical physics (PhD); physics (MS). *Degree requirements:* For master's, thesis optional; for doctorate, thesis/dissertation. *Entrance requirements:* For master's, GRE General Test; for doctorate, GRE General Test, GRE Subject Test. Additional exam requirements/recommendations for international students: Required—TOEFL (minimum score 540 paper-based). *Expenses:* Tuition, state resident: full-time $5811; part-time $322.81 per credit. Tuition, nonresident: full-time $19,220; part-time $1067.79 per credit. *Required fees:* $1030. Tuition and fees vary according to course load. *Faculty research:* Cloud physics, stellar and extragalactic processes.

University of Alberta, Faculty of Graduate Studies and Research, Department of Mathematical and Statistical Sciences, Edmonton, AB T6G 2E1, Canada. Offers applied mathematics (M Sc, PhD); biostatistics (M Sc); mathematical finance (M Sc, PhD); mathematical physics (M Sc, PhD); mathematics (M Sc, PhD); statistics (M Sc, PhD, Postgraduate Diploma). *Program availability:* Part-time. Terminal master's awarded for partial completion of doctoral program. *Degree requirements:* For master's, thesis (for some programs); for doctorate, comprehensive exam, thesis/dissertation. *Entrance requirements:* Additional exam requirements/recommendations for international students: Required—TOEFL (minimum score 580 paper-based). Electronic applications accepted. *Faculty research:* Classical and functional analysis, algebra, differential equations, geometry.

University of Colorado Boulder, Graduate School, College of Arts and Sciences, Department of Physics, Boulder, CO 80309. Offers chemical physics (PhD); geophysics (PhD); liquid crystal science and technology (PhD); mathematical physics (PhD); medical physics (PhD); optical sciences and engineering (PhD); physics (MS, PhD). *Faculty:* 48 full-time (8 women). *Students:* 131 full-time (22 women), 97 part-time (22 women); includes 14 minority (5 Asian, non-Hispanic/Latino; 4 Hispanic/Latino; 5 Two or more races, non-Hispanic/Latino), 61 international. Average age 26. 624 applicants, 24% accepted, 36 enrolled. In 2015, 24 master's, 29 doctorates awarded. Terminal master's awarded for partial completion of doctoral program. *Degree requirements:* For master's, comprehensive exam, thesis or alternative; for doctorate, comprehensive exam, thesis/dissertation. *Entrance requirements:* For master's and doctorate, GRE General Test, GRE Subject Test, minimum undergraduate GPA of 3.0. Additional exam requirements/recommendations for international students: Required—TOEFL. *Application deadline:* For fall admission, 12/15 for domestic students, 12/1 for international students. Applications are processed on a rolling basis. Application fee: $50 ($70 for international students). Electronic applications accepted. Application fee is waived when completed online. *Financial support:* In 2015–16, 521 students received support, including 7 fellowships (averaging $5,311 per year), 162 research assistantships with tuition reimbursements available (averaging $34,608 per year), 51 teaching assistantships with tuition reimbursements available (averaging $29,058 per year); institutionally sponsored loans, scholarships/grants, health care benefits, and unspecified assistantships also available. Financial award application deadline: 1/15; financial award applicants required to submit FAFSA. *Faculty research:* Physics, theoretical physics, high energy physics, experimental physics, solid state physics. *Total annual research expenditures:* $24.8 million. *Application contact:*
E-mail: jeanne.nijhowne@colorado.edu.
Website: http://phys.colorado.edu/graduate-students

Optical Sciences

Air Force Institute of Technology, Graduate School of Engineering and Management, Department of Electrical and Computer Engineering, Dayton, OH 45433-7765. Offers computer engineering (MS, PhD); computer systems/science (MS); electrical engineering (MS, PhD); electro-optics (MS, PhD). *Accreditation:* ABET (one or more programs are accredited). *Program availability:* Part-time. *Degree requirements:* For master's, thesis; for doctorate, thesis/dissertation. *Entrance requirements:* For master's and doctorate, GRE General Test, minimum GPA of 3.0, U.S. citizenship. *Faculty research:* Remote sensing, information survivability, microelectronics, computer networks, artificial intelligence.

Air Force Institute of Technology, Graduate School of Engineering and Management, Department of Engineering Physics, Dayton, OH 45433-7765. Offers applied physics (MS, PhD); electro-optics (MS, PhD); materials science (PhD); nuclear engineering (MS, PhD); space physics (MS). *Program availability:* Part-time. *Degree requirements:* For master's, thesis; for doctorate, thesis/dissertation. *Entrance requirements:* For master's and doctorate, GRE General Test, minimum GPA of 3.0, U.S. citizenship. *Faculty research:* High-energy lasers, space physics, nuclear weapon effects, semiconductor physics.

Alabama Agricultural and Mechanical University, School of Graduate Studies, College of Engineering, Technology, and Physical Sciences, Department of Physics, Chemistry and Mathematics, Huntsville, AL 35811. Offers physics (MS, PhD), including materials science (PhD), optics/lasers (PhD), space science (PhD). *Program availability:* Part-time, evening/weekend. *Degree requirements:* For doctorate, thesis/dissertation. *Entrance requirements:* For master's and doctorate, GRE General Test. Additional exam requirements/recommendations for international students: Required—TOEFL (minimum score 500 paper-based; 61 iBT). Electronic applications accepted.

Cleveland State University, College of Graduate Studies, College of Sciences and Health Professions, Department of Physics, Cleveland, OH 44115. Offers applied optics (MS); condensed matter physics (MS); medical physics (MS); optics and materials (MS); optics and medical imaging (MS). *Program availability:* Part-time, evening/weekend. *Faculty:* 4 full-time (0 women), 1 part-time/adjunct (0 women). *Students:* 10 full-time (5 women), 9 part-time (1 woman); includes 5 minority (2 Black or African American, non-Hispanic/Latino; 1 Asian, non-Hispanic/Latino; 2 Hispanic/Latino), 2 international. Average age 28. 23 applicants, 78% accepted, 6 enrolled. In 2015, 10 master's awarded. *Entrance requirements:* For master's, undergraduate degree in engineering, physics, chemistry or mathematics. Additional exam requirements/recommendations for international students: Required—TOEFL (minimum score 550 paper-based; 78 iBT). *Application deadline:* For fall admission, 7/1 priority date for domestic students, 4/1 priority date for international students. Applications are processed on a rolling basis. Application fee: $30. Electronic applications accepted. *Expenses:* Tuition, state resident: full-time $9565. Tuition, nonresident: full-time $17,980. Tuition and fees vary according to program. *Financial support:* In 2015–16, 1 research assistantship with tuition reimbursement (averaging $5,666 per year) was awarded; fellowships with tuition reimbursements, teaching assistantships, and tuition waivers (full) also available. Financial award applicants required to submit FAFSA. *Faculty research:* Statistical physics, experimental solid-state physics, theoretical optics, experimental biological physics (macromolecular crystallography), experimental optics. *Total annual research expenditures:* $350,000. *Unit head:* Dr. Miron Kaufman, Chairperson, 216-687-2436, Fax: 216-523-7268, E-mail: m.kaufman@csuohio.edu. *Application contact:* Dr. James A. Lock, Director, 216-687-2420, Fax: 216-523-7268, E-mail: j.lock@csuohio.edu.
Website: http://www.csuohio.edu/sciences/physics/physics

The College of William and Mary, Faculty of Arts and Sciences, Department of Applied Science, Williamsburg, VA 23187-8795. Offers accelerator science (PhD); applied mathematics (PhD); applied mechanics (PhD); applied robotics (PhD); applied science (MS); atmospheric and environmental science (PhD); computational neuroscience (PhD); interface, thin film and surface science (PhD); lasers and optics (PhD); magnetic resonance (PhD); materials science and engineering (PhD); mathematical and computational biology (PhD); medical imaging (PhD); nanotechnology (PhD); neuroscience (PhD); non-destructive evaluation (PhD); polymer chemistry (PhD); remote sensing (PhD). *Program availability:* Part-time. *Faculty:* 7 full-time (1 woman), 1 part-time/adjunct (0 women). *Students:* 26 full-time (9 women), 3 part-time (1 woman); includes 5 minority (2 Black or African American, non-Hispanic/Latino; 1 Asian, non-Hispanic/Latino; 2 Hispanic/Latino), 12 international. Average age 28. 24 applicants, 46% accepted, 6 enrolled. In 2015, 2 master's, 6 doctorates awarded. Terminal master's awarded for partial completion of doctoral program. *Degree requirements:* For master's, comprehensive exam, thesis; for doctorate, comprehensive exam, thesis/dissertation, 4 core courses. *Entrance requirements:* For master's and doctorate, GRE General Test, GRE Subject Test. Additional exam requirements/recommendations for international students: Required—TOEFL, TWE. *Application deadline:* For fall admission, 2/3 priority date for domestic students, 2/3 for international students; for spring admission, 10/15 priority date for domestic students, 10/14 for international students. Applications are processed on a rolling basis. Application fee: $45. Electronic applications accepted. *Expenses:* $6,550 per semester; $13,100 per year. *Financial support:* Fellowships, research assistantships, teaching assistantships, Federal Work-Study, health care benefits, tuition waivers (full), and unspecified assistantships available. Financial award application deadline: 4/15; financial award applicants required to submit FAFSA. *Faculty research:* Computational biology, non-destructive evaluation, neurophysiology, lasers and optics. *Total annual research expenditures:* $1.7 million. *Unit head:* Dr. Christopher Del Negro, Chair, 757-221-7808, Fax: 757-221-2050, E-mail: cadeln@wm.edu. *Application contact:* Lianne Rios Ashburne, Graduate Program Coordinator, 757-221-2563, Fax: 757-221-2050, E-mail: lrashburne@wm.edu.
Website: http://www.wm.edu/as/appliedscience

Delaware State University, Graduate Programs, Department of Physics, Dover, DE 19901-2277. Offers applied optics (MS); optics (PhD); physics (MS); physics teaching (MS). *Program availability:* Part-time, evening/weekend. *Entrance requirements:* For master's, minimum GPA of 3.0 in major, 2.75 overall. Additional exam requirements/recommendations for international students: Required—TOEFL. Electronic applications accepted. *Faculty research:* Thermal properties of solids, nuclear physics, radiation damage in solids.

Duke University, Graduate School, Pratt School of Engineering, Master of Engineering Program, Durham, NC 27708-0271. Offers biomedical engineering (M Eng); civil engineering (M Eng); electrical and computer engineering (M Eng); environmental engineering (M Eng); materials science and engineering (M Eng); mechanical engineering (M Eng); photonics and optical sciences (M Eng). *Program availability:* Part-time. *Entrance requirements:* For master's, GRE General Test, resume, 3 letters of recommendation, statement of purpose, transcripts. Additional exam requirements/ recommendations for international students: Required—TOEFL.

École Polytechnique de Montréal, Graduate Programs, Department of Engineering Physics, Montréal, QC H3C 3A7, Canada. Offers optical engineering (M Eng, M Sc A, PhD); solid-state physics and engineering (M Eng, M Sc A, PhD). *Program availability:* Part-time. *Degree requirements:* For master's, one foreign language, thesis; for doctorate, one foreign language, thesis/dissertation. *Entrance requirements:* For master's, minimum GPA of 2.75; for doctorate, minimum GPA of 3.0. *Faculty research:* Optics, thin-film physics, laser spectroscopy, plasmas, photonic devices.

Norfolk State University, School of Graduate Studies, School of Science and Technology, Program in Optical Engineering, Norfolk, VA 23504. Offers MS.

North Carolina Agricultural and Technical State University, School of Graduate Studies, College of Engineering, Department of Electrical and Computer Engineering, Greensboro, NC 27411. Offers electrical engineering (MSEE, PhD), including communications and signal processing, computer engineering, electronic and optical materials and devices, power systems and control. *Program availability:* Part-time. *Degree requirements:* For master's, project, thesis defense; for doctorate, thesis/ dissertation. *Entrance requirements:* For master's, GRE General Test, GRE Subject Test, minimum GPA of 2.8; for doctorate, GRE General Test, minimum GPA of 3.0. *Faculty research:* Semiconductor compounds, VLSI design, image processing, optical systems and devices, fault-tolerant computing.

The Ohio State University, College of Optometry, Columbus, OH 43210. Offers optometry (OD); vision science (MS, PhD); OD/MS. *Accreditation:* AOA (one or more programs are accredited). *Degree requirements:* For master's, thesis; for doctorate, thesis/dissertation. *Entrance requirements:* For master's, GRE; for doctorate, GRE (for PhD); OAT (for OD). Additional exam requirements/recommendations for international students: Required—TOEFL (minimum score 550 paper-based, 79 iBT), Michigan English Language Assessment Battery (minimum score 82), IELTS (minimum score 7) for MS and PhD; TOEFL (minimum score 577 paper-based; 90 iBT), Michigan English Language Assessment Battery (minimum score 84), IELTS (minimum score 7.5) for OD. Electronic applications accepted. *Expenses:* Contact institution.

Rochester Institute of Technology, Graduate Enrollment Services, College of Science, Center for Imaging Science, MS Program in Imaging Science, Rochester, NY 14623-5603. Offers MS. *Program availability:* Part-time, evening/weekend, 100% online. *Students:* 11 full-time (4 women), 10 part-time (3 women); includes 1 minority (Two or more races, non-Hispanic/Latino), 13 international. Average age 29. 33 applicants, 36% accepted, 5 enrolled. In 2015, 6 master's awarded. *Degree requirements:* For master's, thesis. *Entrance requirements:* For master's, GRE, minimum GPA of 3.0 (recommended). Additional exam requirements/recommendations for international students: Required—PTE (minimum score 58), TOEFL (minimum score 550 paper-based, 79 iBT) or IELTS (minimum score 6.5). *Application deadline:* For fall admission, 2/15 priority date for domestic and international students; for spring admission, 12/15 priority date for domestic students, 12/14 priority date for international students. Applications are processed on a rolling basis. Application fee: $60. Electronic applications accepted. *Expenses: Tuition, area resident:* Full-time $41,084; part-time $1742 per credit hour. *Required fees:* $274. Tuition and fees vary according to course load and program. *Financial support:* In 2015–16, 8 students received support. Research assistantships with partial tuition reimbursements available, teaching assistantships with partial tuition reimbursements available, career-related internships or fieldwork, scholarships/grants, and unspecified assistantships available. Support available to part-time students. Financial award applicants required to submit FAFSA. *Faculty research:* Biomedical imaging, astronomy and space science, cultural artifact and document imaging detector research, disaster response, nano-imaging and materials, optics, printing, remote sensing, vision, document library. *Unit head:* Dr. John Kerekes, Graduate Program Director, 585-475-6996, Fax: 585-475-5988, E-mail: kerekes@cis.rit.edu. *Application contact:* Diane Ellison, Associate Vice President, Graduate Enrollment Services, 585-475-2229, Fax: 585-475-7164, E-mail: gradinfo@rit.edu.
Website: http://cis.rit.edu/graduate-programs/master-science

Rochester Institute of Technology, Graduate Enrollment Services, College of Science, Center for Imaging Science, PhD Program in Imaging Science, Rochester, NY 14623. Offers PhD. *Program availability:* Part-time. *Students:* 58 full-time (17 women), 14 part-time (2 women); includes 2 minority (1 Asian, non-Hispanic/Latino; 1 Two or more races, non-Hispanic/Latino), 46 international. Average age 28. 39 applicants, 51% accepted, 10 enrolled. In 2015, 7 doctorates awarded. Terminal master's awarded for partial completion of doctoral program. *Degree requirements:* For doctorate, comprehensive exam, thesis/dissertation. *Entrance requirements:* For doctorate, GRE, minimum GPA of 3.0 (recommended). Additional exam requirements/recommendations for international students: Required—PTE (minimum score 58), TOEFL (minimum score 550 paper-based, 79 iBT) or IELTS (minimum score 6.5). *Application deadline:* For fall admission, 1/15 priority date for domestic and international students. Applications are processed on a rolling basis. Application fee: $60. Electronic applications accepted. *Expenses: Tuition, area resident:* Full-time $41,084; part-time $1742 per credit hour. *Required fees:* $274. Tuition and fees vary according to course load and program. *Financial support:* In 2015–16, 72 students received support. Research assistantships with full tuition reimbursements available, teaching assistantships with partial tuition reimbursements available, career-related internships or fieldwork, scholarships/grants, health care benefits, and unspecified assistantships available. Support available to part-time students. Financial award applicants required to submit FAFSA. *Faculty research:* Biomedical imaging, astronomy and space science, cultural artifact and document imaging detector research, disaster response, nano-imaging and materials, optics, printing, remote sensing, vision, document library. *Unit head:* Dr. John Kerekes, Graduate Program Director, 585-475-6996, Fax: 585-475-5988, E-mail: kerekes@cis.rit.edu. *Application contact:* Diane Ellison, Associate Vice President, Graduate Enrollment Services, 585-475-2229, Fax: 585-475-7164, E-mail: gradinfo@rit.edu.
Website: http://www.cis.rit.edu/

Rose-Hulman Institute of Technology, Faculty of Engineering and Applied Sciences, Department of Physics and Optical Engineering, Terre Haute, IN 47803-3999. Offers optical engineering (MS). *Program availability:* Part-time. *Faculty:* 16 full-time (2 women), 1 part-time/adjunct (0 women). *Students:* 9 full-time (1 woman), 9 part-time (1 woman); includes 1 minority (Black or African American, non-Hispanic/Latino), 10 international. Average age 25. 11 applicants, 64% accepted, 5 enrolled. In 2015, 6 master's awarded. *Degree requirements:* For master's, thesis. *Entrance requirements:* For master's, GRE, minimum GPA of 3.0. Additional exam requirements/ recommendations for international students: Required—TOEFL (minimum score 580 paper-based; 92 iBT). *Application deadline:* For fall admission, 2/1 priority date for domestic students. Applications are processed on a rolling basis. Application fee: $0. Electronic applications accepted. *Expenses: Tuition, area resident:* Full-time $43,122. *Financial support:* In 2015–16, 16 students received support. Fellowships with tuition reimbursements available, research assistantships with tuition reimbursements available, teaching assistantships, institutionally sponsored loans, scholarships/grants, and tuition waivers (full and partial) available. Financial award application deadline: 2/1. *Faculty research:* Non-linear optics/laser physics and photo refractive materials; integrated optics and optical MEMS; fiber optics, fiber optic communications, and optical system design; semi-conductor materials, acoustics, and asteroid photometry; holography and speckles; micro and Nano technology and nanomedicine. *Total annual research expenditures:* $131,186. *Unit head:* Dr. Galen Duree, Chairman, 812-872-6025, Fax: 812-877-8023, E-mail: duree@rose-hulman.edu. *Application contact:* Dr. Azad Siahmakoun, Associate Dean of the Faculty, 812-877-8400, Fax: 812-877-8061, E-mail: siahmako@rose-hulman.edu.
Website: http://www.rose-hulman.edu/academics/academic-departments/physics-optical-engineering.aspx

The University of Alabama in Huntsville, School of Graduate Studies, College of Engineering, Department of Electrical and Computer Engineering, Huntsville, AL 35899. Offers computer engineering (MSE, PhD); electrical engineering (MSE, PhD), including optics and photonics technology (MSE), opto-electronics (MSE); information assurance (MS); optical science and engineering (PhD); optics and photonics (MSE); software engineering (MSSE). *Program availability:* Part-time, evening/weekend. *Degree requirements:* For master's, comprehensive exam, thesis or alternative, oral and written exams; for doctorate, comprehensive exam, thesis/dissertation, oral and written exams. *Entrance requirements:* For master's, GRE General Test, appropriate bachelor's degree, minimum GPA of 3.0; for doctorate, GRE General Test, minimum GPA of 3.0. Additional exam requirements/recommendations for international students: Required—TOEFL (minimum score 500 paper-based; 80 iBT), IELTS (minimum score 6.5). Electronic applications accepted. *Faculty research:* Advanced computer architecture and systems, fault tolerant computing and verification, computational electro-magnetics, nano-photonics and plasmonics, micro electro-mechanical (MEMS) systems.

The University of Alabama in Huntsville, School of Graduate Studies, Interdisciplinary Studies, Interdisciplinary Program in Optical Science and Engineering, Huntsville, AL 35899. Offers PhD. *Program availability:* Part-time, evening/weekend. *Degree requirements:* For doctorate, comprehensive exam, thesis/dissertation, written and oral exams. *Entrance requirements:* For doctorate, GRE General Test, minimum GPA of 3.0, BS in physical science or engineering. Additional exam requirements/recommendations for international students: Required—TOEFL (minimum score 550 paper-based; 80 iBT), IELTS (minimum score 6.5). Electronic applications accepted. *Faculty research:* Optoelectronics, optical communications, digital signal/image processing, computer-generated holography, semiconductor device modeling.

The University of Arizona, College of Optical Sciences, Tucson, AZ 85721. Offers MS, PhD. *Program availability:* Part-time. *Degree requirements:* For master's, thesis (for some programs), exam; for doctorate, thesis/dissertation, oral and written exams. *Entrance requirements:* For master's, GRE General Test, GRE Subject Test (recommended), minimum GPA of 3.0, 2 letters of recommendation, resume; for doctorate, GRE General Test, GRE Subject Test (recommended), minimum GPA of 3.0, 2 letters of recommendation, statement of purpose, resume. Additional exam requirements/recommendations for international students: Required—TOEFL. Electronic applications accepted. *Faculty research:* Medical optics, medical imaging, optical data storage, optical bistability, nonlinear optical effects.

University of Central Florida, College of Optics and Photonics, Orlando, FL 32816. Offers MS, PhD. *Program availability:* Part-time, evening/weekend. *Faculty:* 40 full-time (6 women), 17 part-time/adjunct (1 woman). *Students:* 106 full-time (19 women), 10 part-time (1 woman); includes 8 minority (1 Asian, non-Hispanic/Latino; 6 Hispanic/ Latino; 1 Two or more races, non-Hispanic/Latino), 71 international. Average age 26. 186 applicants, 32% accepted, 29 enrolled. In 2015, 16 master's, 22 doctorates awarded. *Degree requirements:* For master's, thesis or alternative; for doctorate, thesis/ dissertation, departmental qualifying exam, candidacy exam. *Entrance requirements:* For master's, GRE General Test, minimum GPA of 3.0 in last 60 hours; for doctorate, GRE General Test, minimum GPA of 3.5 in last 60 hours. Additional exam requirements/ recommendations for international students: Required—TOEFL. *Application deadline:* For fall admission, 2/1 priority date for domestic students; for spring admission, 12/1 for domestic students. Application fee: $30. Electronic applications accepted. *Expenses:* Tuition, state resident: part-time $288.16 per credit hour. Tuition, nonresident: part-time $1071.31 per credit hour. *Financial support:* In 2015–16, 74 students received support, including 20 fellowships with partial tuition reimbursements available (averaging $7,800 per year), 74 research assistantships with partial tuition reimbursements available (averaging $12,400 per year), 5 teaching assistantships with partial tuition reimbursements available (averaging $8,000 per year); career-related internships or fieldwork, Federal Work-Study, institutionally sponsored loans, tuition waivers (partial), and unspecified assistantships also available. Financial award application deadline: 3/1; financial award applicants required to submit FAFSA. *Unit head:* Dr. Bahaa E. Saleh, Dean and Director, 407-823-6817, E-mail: besaleh@creol.ucf.edu. *Application contact:* Director, Admissions and Student Services, 407-823-2766, Fax: 407-823-6442, E-mail: gradadmissions@ucf.edu.
Website: http://www.creol.ucf.edu/

University of Colorado Boulder, Graduate School, College of Arts and Sciences, Department of Physics, Boulder, CO 80309. Offers chemical physics (PhD); geophysics (PhD); liquid crystal science and technology (PhD); mathematical physics (PhD); medical physics (PhD); optical sciences and engineering (PhD); physics (MS, PhD). *Faculty:* 48 full-time (8 women). *Students:* 131 full-time (22 women), 97 part-time (22 women); includes 14 minority (5 Asian, non-Hispanic/Latino; 4 Hispanic/Latino; 5 Two or more races, non-Hispanic/Latino), 61 international. Average age 26. 624 applicants, 24% accepted, 36 enrolled. In 2015, 24 master's, 29 doctorates awarded. Terminal master's awarded for partial completion of doctoral program. *Degree requirements:* For master's, comprehensive exam, thesis or alternative; for doctorate, comprehensive exam, thesis/dissertation. *Entrance requirements:* For master's and doctorate, GRE General Test, GRE Subject Test, minimum undergraduate GPA of 3.0. Additional exam requirements/recommendations for international students: Required—TOEFL. *Application deadline:* For fall admission, 12/15 for domestic students, 12/1 for international students. Applications are processed on a rolling basis. Application fee: $50 ($70 for international students). Electronic applications accepted. Application fee is waived when completed online. *Financial support:* In 2015–16, 521 students received support, including 7 fellowships (averaging $5,311 per year), 162 research assistantships with tuition reimbursements available (averaging $34,608 per year), 51 teaching assistantships with tuition reimbursements available (averaging $29,058 per year); institutionally sponsored loans, scholarships/grants, health care benefits, and unspecified assistantships also available. Financial award application deadline: 1/15; financial award applicants required to submit FAFSA. *Faculty research:* Physics, theoretical physics, high energy physics, experimental physics, solid state physics. *Total annual research expenditures:* $24.8 million. *Application contact:* E-mail: jeanne.nijhowne@colorado.edu.
Website: http://phys.colorado.edu/graduate-students

University of Dayton, Program in Electro-Optics, Dayton, OH 45469. Offers MSEO, PhD. *Program availability:* Part-time. *Faculty:* 4 full-time (0 women), 4 part-time/adjunct (0 women). *Students:* 43 full-time (7 women), 9 part-time (4 women); includes 3 minority (2 Black or African American, non-Hispanic/Latino; 1 Asian, non-Hispanic/Latino), 29 international. Average age 29. 99 applicants, 42% accepted, 18 enrolled. In 2015, 14 master's, 4 doctorates awarded. *Degree requirements:* For master's, thesis (for some programs); for doctorate, comprehensive exam (for some programs), thesis/dissertation (for some programs), 6 credits of math. *Entrance requirements:* For master's, Applicants must have a Master's degree to be admitted to the PhD program. Additional exam requirements/recommendations for international students: Required—TOEFL (minimum score 550 paper-based; 80 iBT). *Application deadline:* Applications are processed on a rolling basis. Application fee: $0 ($50 for international students). Electronic applications accepted. *Financial support:* In 2015–16, 17 research assistantships with full tuition reimbursements (averaging $21,000 per year), 7 teaching assistantships with full tuition reimbursements (averaging $21,000 per year) were awarded; institutionally sponsored loans, health care benefits, and unspecified assistantships also available. Financial award applicants required to submit FAFSA. *Faculty research:* Holography, nanofabrication, physical optics, laser beam control, nonlinear optics. *Total annual research expenditures:* $2 million. *Unit head:* Dr. Partha P. Banerjee, Director, 937-229-2797, Fax: 937-229-2099, E-mail: pbanerjee1@udayton.edu. *Application contact:* 937-229-4462, E-mail: graduateadmission@udayton.edu.
Website: https://www.udayton.edu/engineering/departments/electrooptics_grad/index.php

University of Massachusetts Lowell, College of Sciences, Department of Physics and Applied Physics, Program in Applied Physics, Lowell, MA 01854. Offers applied physics (MS), including optical sciences. Terminal master's awarded for partial completion of doctoral program. *Degree requirements:* For master's, thesis. *Entrance requirements:* For master's, GRE General Test, 3 letters of reference. Additional exam requirements/recommendations for international students: Required—TOEFL.

University of New Mexico, Graduate Studies, College of Arts and Sciences, Program in Optical Science and Engineering, Albuquerque, NM 87131. Offers imaging science (MS, PhD); optical science and engineering (MS, PhD); photonics (MS, PhD). Program held jointly with the Department of Physics and Astronomy and the Department of Electrical and Computer Engineering. *Program availability:* Part-time. *Faculty:* 7 full-time (0 women), 1 part-time/adjunct (0 women). *Students:* 23 full-time (8 women), 37 part-time (1 woman); includes 6 minority (1 Black or African American, non-Hispanic/Latino; 4 Hispanic/Latino; 1 Two or more races, non-Hispanic/Latino), 45 international. Average age 33. 65 applicants, 34% accepted, 6 enrolled. In 2015, 4 master's, 8 doctorates awarded. Terminal master's awarded for partial completion of doctoral program. *Degree requirements:* For master's, comprehensive exam (for some programs), thesis (for some programs); for doctorate, comprehensive exam, thesis/dissertation. *Entrance requirements:* For master's, GRE General Test, GRE Subject Test in physics (preferred), relevant undergraduate coursework, curriculum vitae, letters of recommendation, letter of intent/personal statement; for doctorate, GRE General Test, GRE Subject Test in physics (preferred), relevant undergraduate coursework, curriculum vitae, letters of recommendation. Additional exam requirements/recommendations for international students: Required—TOEFL (minimum score 575 paper-based; 79 iBT), IELTS (minimum score 7). *Application deadline:* For fall admission, 1/15 priority date for domestic and international students; for spring admission, 8/1 priority date for domestic and international students. Application fee: $50. Electronic applications accepted. *Financial support:* Fellowships with full tuition reimbursements, research assistantships with full tuition reimbursements, teaching assistantships with full tuition reimbursements, career-related internships or fieldwork, scholarships/grants, health care benefits, and unspecified assistantships available. Support available to part-time students. Financial award application deadline: 2/1; financial award applicants required to submit FAFSA. *Faculty research:* Advanced materials, atom optics, biomedical optics, fiber optics, laser cooling, high intensity interactions, lithography, nano photonics, nonlinear optics, optical imaging, optical sensors, optoelectronics, quantum optics, spectroscopy, ultrafast phenomena. *Unit head:* Dr. Majeed Hayat, Chair, 505-272-7095, Fax: 505-277-7801, E-mail: hayat@ece.unm.edu. *Application contact:* Doris Williams, Advisor, 505-277-7764, Fax: 505-277-7801, E-mail: dorisw@chtm.unm.edu.
Website: http://www.optics.unm.edu/

The University of North Carolina at Charlotte, College of Liberal Arts and Sciences, Department of Physics and Optical Science, Charlotte, NC 28223-0001. Offers applied physics (MS); optical science and engineering (MS, PhD). *Faculty:* 18 full-time (3 women). *Students:* 48 full-time (14 women), 11 part-time (2 women); includes 3 minority (2 Hispanic/Latino; 1 Two or more races, non-Hispanic/Latino), 21 international. Average age 28. 43 applicants, 51% accepted, 12 enrolled. In 2015, 16 master's, 9 doctorates awarded. Terminal master's awarded for partial completion of doctoral program. *Degree requirements:* For master's, comprehensive exam (for some programs), thesis or comprehensive exam; for doctorate, thesis/dissertation. *Entrance requirements:* For master's, GRE; for doctorate, GRE, baccalaureate or master's degree in physics, chemistry, mathematics, engineering, optics, or related field with minimum undergraduate GPA of 3.0 overall and 3.2 in major (3.2 graduate); letters of recommendation. Additional exam requirements/recommendations for international students: Required—TOEFL (minimum score 557 paper-based, 83 iBT) or IELTS (minimum score 6.5). *Application deadline:* For fall admission, 3/1 for domestic and international students; for spring admission, 10/1 for domestic and international students; for summer admission, 4/1 for domestic and international students. Applications are processed on a rolling basis. Application fee: $75. Electronic applications accepted. *Expenses:* Tuition, state resident: full-time $4128. Tuition, nonresident: full-time $16,799. *Required fees:* $2904. Tuition and fees vary according to course load and program. *Financial support:* In 2015–16, 53 students received support, including 2 fellowships (averaging $46,875 per year), 20 research assistantships (averaging $11,315 per year), 31 teaching assistantships (averaging $7,408 per year); career-related internships or fieldwork, institutionally sponsored loans, scholarships/grants, and unspecified assistantships also available. Support available to part-time students. Financial award application deadline: 3/1; financial award applicants required to submit FAFSA. *Faculty research:* Experimental and computational material sciences, optoelectronics, quantum structures, electronic and electromagnetic waves in anisotropic media, nanoscale smart devices, infrared (IR) transmitting optical materials, low loss IR transmitting glass optical fibers and rugged transparent ceramic spinel windows. *Total annual research expenditures:* $2.3 million. *Unit head:* Dr. Glen Boreman, Chair, 704-687-8173, E-mail: gboreman@uncc.edu. *Application contact:* Kathy B. Giddings, Director of Graduate Admissions, 704-687-5503, Fax: 704-687-1668, E-mail: gradadm@uncc.edu.
Website: http://physics.uncc.edu/

University of Rochester, Hajim School of Engineering and Applied Sciences, Institute of Optics, Rochester, NY 14627. Offers MS, PhD. *Faculty:* 16 full-time (1 woman). *Students:* 116 full-time (26 women), 4 part-time (1 woman); includes 10 minority (1 Black or African American, non-Hispanic/Latino; 5 Asian, non-Hispanic/Latino; 2 Hispanic/Latino; 2 Two or more races, non-Hispanic/Latino), 53 international. 233 applicants, 51% accepted, 44 enrolled. In 2015, 21 master's, 13 doctorates awarded. Terminal master's awarded for partial completion of doctoral program. *Degree requirements:* For master's, comprehensive exam; for doctorate, thesis/dissertation, preliminary and qualifying exams. *Entrance requirements:* For master's and doctorate, GRE. Additional exam requirements/recommendations for international students: Required—TOEFL. *Application deadline:* For fall admission, 2/1 priority date for domestic students. Application fee: $60. Electronic applications accepted. *Expenses: Tuition, area resident:* Full-time $47,450; part-time $1482 per credit hour. *Required fees:* $528. Tuition and fees vary according to program. *Financial support:* Fellowships, research assistantships, teaching assistantships, and tuition waivers (full and partial) available. Financial award application deadline: 2/1. *Faculty research:* Biomedical, fiber and optical communication; image science and systems; ultrafast optics and High Field sciences. *Unit head:* Xi-Cheng Zhang, Interim Director, 585-275-0333. *Application contact:* Betsy Benedict, Graduate Program Coordinator, 585-275-7720.
Website: http://www.optics.rochester.edu/

University of Rochester, Hajim School of Engineering and Applied Sciences, Master of Science in Technical Entrepreneurship and Management Program, Rochester, NY 14642. Offers biomedical engineering (MS); chemical engineering (MS); computer science (MS); electrical and computer engineering (MS); energy and the environment (MS); materials science (MS); mechanical engineering (MS); optics (MS). Program offered in collaboration with the Simon School of Business. *Program availability:* Part-time. *Students:* 43 full-time (14 women), 10 part-time (3 women); includes 7 minority (2 Asian, non-Hispanic/Latino; 3 Hispanic/Latino; 2 Two or more races, non-Hispanic/Latino), 39 international. 168 applicants, 70% accepted, 26 enrolled. In 2015, 23 master's awarded. *Degree requirements:* For master's, comprehensive exam. *Entrance requirements:* For master's, GRE or GMAT, 3 letters of recommendation; personal statement; official transcript; bachelor's degree (or equivalent for international students) in engineering, science, or mathematics. Additional exam requirements/recommendations for international students: Required—TOEFL or IELTS. *Application deadline:* For fall admission, 2/1 for domestic and international students. Applications are processed on a rolling basis. Application fee: $60. Electronic applications accepted. *Expenses: Tuition, area resident:* Full-time $47,450; part-time $1482 per credit hour. *Required fees:* $528. Tuition and fees vary according to program. *Financial support:* Career-related internships or fieldwork and scholarships/grants available. Financial award application deadline: 2/1. *Faculty research:* High efficiency solar cells, macromolecular self-assembly, digital signal processing, memory hierarchy management, molecular and physical mechanisms in cell migration, optical imaging systems. *Unit head:* Duncan T. Moore, Vice Provost for Entrepreneurship, 585-275-5248, Fax: 585-473-6745, E-mail: moore@optics.rochester.edu. *Application contact:* Andrea M. Galati, Executive Director, 585-276-3407, Fax: 585-276-2357, E-mail: andrea.galati@rochester.edu.
Website: http://www.rochester.edu/team

Photonics

Boston University, College of Engineering, Department of Electrical and Computer Engineering, Boston, MA 02215. Offers computer engineering (M Eng, MS, PhD); electrical engineering (M Eng, MS, PhD); photonics (MS). *Program availability:* Part-time. *Faculty:* 40 full-time (3 women), 5 part-time/adjunct (0 women). *Students:* 256 full-time (67 women), 72 part-time (14 women); includes 36 minority (3 Black or African American, non-Hispanic/Latino; 1 American Indian or Alaska Native, non-Hispanic/Latino; 23 Asian, non-Hispanic/Latino; 8 Hispanic/Latino; 1 Two or more races, non-Hispanic/Latino), 239 international. Average age 25. 1,121 applicants, 27% accepted, 158 enrolled. In 2015, 114 master's, 11 doctorates awarded. Terminal master's awarded for partial completion of doctoral program. *Degree requirements:* For master's, thesis (for some programs); for doctorate, comprehensive exam, thesis/dissertation. *Entrance requirements:* For master's and doctorate, GRE General Test. Additional exam requirements/recommendations for international students: Required—TOEFL (minimum score 550 paper-based; 84 iBT), IELTS (minimum score 7). *Application deadline:* For fall admission, 3/15 for domestic and international students; for spring admission, 10/1 for domestic and international students. Applications are processed on a rolling basis. Application fee: $80. Electronic applications accepted. *Expenses:* $47,422 per year; $1,428 per credit. *Financial support:* In 2015–16, 100 students received support, including 8 fellowships with full tuition reimbursements available (averaging $28,950 per year), 82 research assistantships with full tuition reimbursements available (averaging $19,300 per year), 18 teaching assistantships with full tuition reimbursements available (averaging $19,300 per year); career-related internships or fieldwork, Federal Work-Study, scholarships/grants, and tuition waivers (partial) also available. Financial award application deadline: 1/15; financial award applicants required to submit FAFSA. *Faculty research:* Communications and computer networks; signal, image, video, and multimedia processing; solid-state materials, devices, and photonics; systems, control, and reliable computing; VLSI, computer engineering and high-performance computing. *Unit head:* Dr. William C. Karl, Interim Chairman, 617-353-9880, Fax: 617-353-6440, E-mail: wckarl@bu.edu. *Application contact:* Dr. Solomon Eisenberg, Senior Associate Dean of Academic Programs, 617-353-9760, Fax: 617-353-0259, E-mail: enggrad@bu.edu.
Website: http://www.bu.edu/ece/

Duke University, Graduate School, Pratt School of Engineering, Master of Engineering Program, Durham, NC 27708-0271. Offers biomedical engineering (M Eng); civil engineering (M Eng); electrical and computer engineering (M Eng); environmental engineering (M Eng); materials science and engineering (M Eng); mechanical engineering (M Eng); photonics and optical sciences (M Eng). *Program availability:* Part-time. *Entrance requirements:* For master's, GRE General Test, resume, 3 letters of recommendation, statement of purpose, transcripts. Additional exam requirements/recommendations for international students: Required—TOEFL.

Lehigh University, College of Arts and Sciences, Department of Physics, Bethlehem, PA 18015. Offers photonics (MS); physics (MS, PhD). *Program availability:* Part-time. *Faculty:* 16 full-time (3 women). *Students:* 43 full-time (19 women), 2 part-time (1 woman); includes 2 minority (both Asian, non-Hispanic/Latino), 15 international. Average age 25. 111 applicants, 20% accepted, 11 enrolled. In 2015, 6 master's, 6 doctorates awarded. *Degree requirements:* For doctorate, comprehensive exam, thesis/dissertation. *Entrance requirements:* For master's and doctorate, GRE General Test. Additional exam requirements/recommendations for international students: Required—TOEFL (minimum score 85 iBT). *Application deadline:* For fall admission, 2/15 for domestic and international students. Application fee: $75. Electronic applications accepted. *Financial support:* In 2015–16, 39 students received support, including 12 research assistantships with full tuition reimbursements available (averaging $27,784 per year), 26 teaching assistantships with full tuition reimbursements available (averaging $27,784 per year); fellowships also available. Support available to part-time students. Financial award application deadline: 2/15. *Faculty research:* Condensed matter physics; atomic, molecular and optical physics; biophysics; nonlinear optics and photonics; astronomy and astrophysics; high energy nuclear physics. *Total annual research expenditures:* $1.9 million. *Unit head:* Dr. Volkmar Dierolf, Chair, 610-758-3909, Fax: 610-758-5730, E-mail: vod2@lehigh.edu. *Application contact:* Dr. Joshua Pepper, Graduate Admissions Officer, 610-758-3724, Fax: 610-758-3649,
E-mail: jap612@lehigh.edu.
Website: http://www.physics.lehigh.edu/

Lehigh University, P.C. Rossin College of Engineering and Applied Science, Department of Materials Science and Engineering, Bethlehem, PA 18015. Offers materials science and engineering (M Eng, MS, PhD); photonics (MS); polymer science/engineering (M Eng, MS, PhD); MBA/E. *Program availability:* Part-time. *Faculty:* 12 full-time (3 women). *Students:* 29 full-time (7 women); includes 4 minority (3 Asian, non-Hispanic/Latino; 1 Two or more races, non-Hispanic/Latino), 10 international. Average age 26. 210 applicants, 7% accepted, 4 enrolled. In 2015, 4 master's, 5 doctorates awarded. *Degree requirements:* For master's, thesis; for doctorate, comprehensive exam, thesis/dissertation. *Entrance requirements:* For master's and doctorate, GRE General Test, minimum GPA of 3.0. Additional exam requirements/recommendations for international students: Required—TOEFL (minimum score 487 paper-based; 85 iBT). *Application deadline:* For fall admission, 1/15 priority date for domestic students, 1/15 for international students; for spring admission, 12/1 priority date for domestic students, 12/1 for international students. Applications are processed on a rolling basis. Application fee: $75. Electronic applications accepted. *Expenses:* Contact institution. *Financial support:* In 2015–16, 23 students received support, including 3 fellowships with tuition reimbursements available (averaging $19,920 per year), 22 research assistantships with tuition reimbursements available (averaging $25,550 per year), 6 teaching assistantships with tuition reimbursements available (averaging $20,490 per year); scholarships/grants and health care benefits also available. Financial award application deadline: 1/15. *Faculty research:* Metals, ceramics, crystals, polymers, fatigue crack propagation, biomaterials. *Total annual research expenditures:* $3.3 million. *Unit head:* Dr. Helen Chan, Chairperson, 610-758-5554, Fax: 610-758-4244,
E-mail: hmc0@lehigh.edu. *Application contact:* Lisa Carreras Arechiga, Graduate Administrative Coordinator, 610-758-4222, Fax: 610-758-4244, E-mail: lia4@lehigh.edu.
Website: http://www.lehigh.edu/~inmatsci/

Oklahoma State University, College of Arts and Sciences, Department of Physics, Stillwater, OK 74078. Offers photonics (MS, PhD); physics (MS, PhD). *Faculty:* 23 full-time (4 women). *Students:* 4 full-time (2 women), 34 part-time (3 women); includes 1 minority (Two or more races, non-Hispanic/Latino), 22 international. Average age 29. 115 applicants, 15% accepted, 6 enrolled. In 2015, 2 master's, 5 doctorates awarded. *Degree requirements:* For master's, thesis; for doctorate, comprehensive exam, thesis/dissertation, oral defense of dissertation, preliminary exam, qualifying exam. *Entrance requirements:* For master's and doctorate, GRE. Additional exam requirements/recommendations for international students: Required—TOEFL (minimum score 550 paper-based; 79 iBT). *Application deadline:* For fall admission, 3/1 priority date for international students; for spring admission, 8/1 priority date for international students. Applications are processed on a rolling basis. Application fee: $40 ($75 for international students). Electronic applications accepted. *Expenses:* Tuition, state resident: full-time $3528; part-time $196 per credit hour. Tuition, nonresident: full-time $14,144; part-time $785.75 per credit hour. *Required fees:* $1895; $105.25 per credit hour. Tuition and fees vary according to campus/location. *Financial support:* In 2015–16, 7 research assistantships (averaging $21,591 per year), 39 teaching assistantships (averaging $21,415 per year) were awarded; career-related internships or fieldwork, Federal Work-Study, scholarships/grants, health care benefits, tuition waivers (partial), and unspecified assistantships also available. Support available to part-time students. Financial award application deadline: 3/1; financial award applicants required to submit FAFSA. *Faculty research:* Lasers and photonics, non-linear optical materials, turbulence, structure and function of biological membranes, particle theory. *Unit head:* Dr. John Mintmire, Department Head, 405-744-5796, Fax: 405-744-6811,
E-mail: john.mintmire@okstate.edu. *Application contact:* Dr. Albert T. Rosenberger, Graduate Coordinator, 405-744-6742, Fax: 405-744-6811,
E-mail: physics.grad.coordinator@okstate.edu.
Website: http://physics.okstate.edu/

Princeton University, Princeton Institute for the Science and Technology of Materials (PRISM), Princeton, NJ 08544-1019. Offers materials (PhD).

Stevens Institute of Technology, Graduate School, Charles V. Schaefer Jr. School of Engineering, Department of Electrical and Computer Engineering, Program in Electrical Engineering, Hoboken, NJ 07030. Offers autonomous robotics (Certificate); electrical engineering (M Eng, PhD, Certificate), including computer architecture and digital systems (M Eng), microelectronics and photonics science and technology (M Eng), signal processing for communications (M Eng), telecommunications systems engineering (M Eng), wireless communications (M Eng, Certificate). *Program availability:* Part-time, evening/weekend. *Students:* 264 full-time (69 women), 28 part-time (6 women); includes 10 minority (2 Black or African American, non-Hispanic/Latino; 6 Asian, non-Hispanic/Latino; 1 Hispanic/Latino; 1 Two or more races, non-Hispanic/Latino), 257 international. Average age 25. 869 applicants, 54% accepted, 113 enrolled. In 2015, 146 master's, 3 doctorates awarded. *Entrance requirements:* Additional exam requirements/recommendations for international students: Required—TOEFL (minimum score 74 iBT). *Application deadline:* For fall admission, 6/1 for domestic students, 4/15 for international students; for spring admission, 11/30 for domestic students, 11/1 for international students. Applications are processed on a rolling basis. Application fee: $60. Electronic applications accepted. *Expenses: Tuition, area resident:* Full-time $32,200; part-time $1450 per credit. *Required fees:* $1150; $550 per unit. $275 per semester. *Financial support:* Fellowships, research assistantships, teaching assistantships, career-related internships or fieldwork, Federal Work-Study, scholarships/grants, and unspecified assistantships available. Financial award application deadline: 2/15; financial award applicants required to submit FAFSA. *Unit head:* Cristina Comaniciu, Program Director, 201-216-5606, Fax: 201-216-8246,
E-mail: ccomanic@stevens.edu. *Application contact:* Graduate Admissions, 888-783-8367, Fax: 888-511-1306, E-mail: graduate@stevens.edu.

Stevens Institute of Technology, Graduate School, Charles V. Schaefer Jr. School of Engineering, Interdisciplinary Program in Microelectronics and Photonics, Hoboken, NJ 07030. Offers M Eng, MS, PhD. *Program availability:* Part-time, evening/weekend. *Faculty:* 3 full-time (0 women). *Students:* 8 full-time (0 women), 3 part-time (0 women); includes 1 minority (Asian, non-Hispanic/Latino), 5 international. Average age 37. 8 applicants, 25% accepted. In 2015, 1 master's awarded. *Entrance requirements:* Additional exam requirements/recommendations for international students: Required—TOEFL (minimum score 74 iBT). *Application deadline:* For fall admission, 6/1 for domestic students, 4/15 for international students; for spring admission, 11/30 for domestic students, 11/1 for international students. Applications are processed on a rolling basis. Application fee: $60. Electronic applications accepted. *Expenses: Tuition, area resident:* Full-time $32,200; part-time $1450 per credit. *Required fees:* $1150; $550 per unit. $275 per semester. *Financial support:* Fellowships, research assistantships, teaching assistantships, career-related internships or fieldwork, Federal Work-Study, scholarships/grants, and unspecified assistantships available. Financial award application deadline: 2/15; financial award applicants required to submit FAFSA. *Unit head:* Dr. Keith G. Sheppard, Interim Dean, 201-216-5260, Fax: 201-216-8372
E-mail: keith.sheppard@stevens.edu. *Application contact:* Graduate Admissions, 888-783-8367, Fax: 888-511-1306, E-mail: graduate@stevens.edu.

The University of Alabama in Huntsville, School of Graduate Studies, College of Engineering, Department of Electrical and Computer Engineering, Huntsville, AL 35899. Offers computer engineering (MSE, PhD); electrical engineering (MSE, PhD), including optics and photonics technology (MSE), opto-electronics (MSE); information assurance (MS); optical science and engineering (PhD); optics and photonics (MSE); software engineering (MSSE). *Program availability:* Part-time, evening/weekend. *Degree requirements:* For master's, comprehensive exam, thesis or alternative, oral and written exams; for doctorate, comprehensive exam, thesis/dissertation, oral and written exams. *Entrance requirements:* For master's, GRE General Test, appropriate bachelor's degree, minimum GPA of 3.0; for doctorate, GRE General Test, minimum GPA of 3.0. Additional exam requirements/recommendations for international students: Required—TOEFL (minimum score 500 paper-based; 80 iBT), IELTS (minimum score 6.5). Electronic applications accepted. *Faculty research:* Advanced computer architecture and systems, fault tolerant computing and verification, computational electro-magnetics, nano-photonics and plasmonics, micro electro-mechanical (MEMS) systems.

The University of Alabama in Huntsville, School of Graduate Studies, College of Science, Department of Physics, Huntsville, AL 35899. Offers education (MS); optics and photonics technology (MS); physics (MS, PhD). *Program availability:* Part-time, evening/weekend. *Degree requirements:* For master's, comprehensive exam, thesis or alternative, oral and written exams; for doctorate, comprehensive exam, thesis/dissertation, oral and written exams. *Entrance requirements:* For master's and doctorate, GRE General Test, minimum GPA of 3.0. Additional exam requirements/recommendations for international students: Required—TOEFL (minimum score 550 paper-based; 80 iBT), IELTS (minimum score 6.5). Electronic applications accepted. *Faculty research:* Space and solar physics, computational physics, optics, high energy astrophysics.

University of Arkansas, Graduate School, Interdisciplinary Program in Microelectronics and Photonics, Fayetteville, AR 72701-1201. Offers MS, PhD. *Students:* 17 full-time (6 women), 44 part-time (13 women); includes 3 minority (2 Black or African American, non-Hispanic/Latino; 1 Asian, non-Hispanic/Latino), 34 international. In 2015, 9 master's, 3 doctorates awarded. *Degree requirements:* For doctorate, thesis/dissertation. *Application deadline:* For fall admission, 4/1 for international students; for spring admission, 10/1 for international students. Applications are processed on a rolling basis. Application fee: $40 ($50 for international students). Electronic applications accepted. *Financial support:* In 2015–16, 25 research assistantships, 4 teaching assistantships were awarded; fellowships with tuition reimbursements also available. Financial award application deadline: 4/1; financial award applicants required to submit FAFSA. *Unit head:* Dr. Rick Wise, Head, 479-575-2875, Fax: 479-575-4580, E-mail: rickwise@uark.edu. *Application contact:* Graduate Admissions, 479-575-6246, Fax: 479-575-5908, E-mail: gradinfo@uark.edu.
Website: http://microep.uark.edu

University of California, San Diego, Graduate Division, Department of Electrical and Computer Engineering, La Jolla, CA 92093. Offers applied ocean science (MS, PhD); applied physics (MS, PhD); communication theory and systems (MS, PhD); computer engineering (MS, PhD); electronic circuits and systems (MS, PhD); intelligent systems, robotics and control (MS, PhD); medical devices and systems (MS, PhD); nanoscale devices and systems (MS, PhD); photonics (MS, PhD); signal and image processing (MS, PhD). *Students:* 503 full-time (99 women), 48 part-time (6 women); includes 79 minority (4 Black or African American, non-Hispanic/Latino; 67 Asian, non-Hispanic/Latino; 8 Hispanic/Latino), 381 international. 2,689 applicants, 21% accepted, 200 enrolled. In 2015, 97 master's, 42 doctorates awarded. *Degree requirements:* For master's, thesis or written exam; for doctorate, comprehensive exam, thesis/dissertation. *Entrance requirements:* For master's and doctorate, GRE General Test, minimum GPA of 3.0. Additional exam requirements/recommendations for international students: Required—TOEFL (minimum score 550 paper-based; 80 iBT), IELTS. *Application deadline:* For fall admission, 12/15 for domestic students. Application fee: $90 ($110 for international students). Electronic applications accepted. *Expenses:* Tuition, state resident: full-time $11,220. Tuition, nonresident: full-time $26,322. *Required fees:* $1800. *Financial support:* Fellowships, research assistantships, teaching assistantships, scholarships/grants, traineeships, and unspecified assistantships available. Financial award applicants required to submit FAFSA. *Faculty research:* Applied ocean science; applied physics; communication theory and systems; computer engineering; electronic circuits and systems; intelligent systems, robotics and control; medical devices and systems; nanoscale devices and systems; photonics; signal and image processing. *Unit head:* Truong Nguyen, Chair, 858-822-5554,
E-mail: nguyent@ece.ucsd.edu. *Application contact:* Melanie Lynn, Graduate Admissions Coordinator, 858-822-3213, E-mail: ecegradapps@ece.ucsd.edu.
Website: http://ece.ucsd.edu/

University of California, Santa Barbara, Graduate Division, College of Engineering, Department of Electrical and Computer Engineering, Santa Barbara, CA 93106-2014. Offers communications, control and signal processing (MS, PhD); computer engineering (MS, PhD); electronics and photonics (MS, PhD); MS/PhD. *Faculty:* 35 full-time (4 women), 1 part-time/adjunct (0 women). *Students:* 253 full-time (55 women); includes 22 minority (1 Black or African American, non-Hispanic/Latino; 2 American Indian or Alaska Native, non-Hispanic/Latino; 18 Asian, non-Hispanic/Latino; 1 Hispanic/Latino), 173 international. Average age 28. 1,550 applicants, 17% accepted, 72 enrolled. In 2015, 77 master's, 27 doctorates awarded. *Degree requirements:* For master's, comprehensive exam, thesis; for doctorate, thesis/dissertation. *Entrance requirements:* For master's and doctorate, GRE General Test. Additional exam requirements/recommendations for

170 www.petersons.com

Peterson's Graduate Programs in the Physical Sciences, Mathematics, Agricultural Sciences, the Environment & Natural Resources 2017

international students: Required—TOEFL (minimum score 550 paper-based; 80 iBT), IELTS (minimum score 7). *Application deadline:* For fall admission, 12/15 for domestic and international students; for winter admission, 11/1 for domestic and international students; for spring admission, 1/2 for domestic and international students. Application fee: $90 ($110 for international students). Electronic applications accepted. *Financial support:* In 2015–16, 183 students received support, including 65 fellowships with tuition reimbursements available (averaging $8,114 per year), 98 research assistantships with tuition reimbursements available (averaging $20,684 per year), 48 teaching assistantships with tuition reimbursements available (averaging $10,644 per year). Financial award application deadline: 12/15; financial award applicants required to submit FAFSA. *Faculty research:* Communications, signal processing, computer engineering, control, electronics and photonics. *Total annual research expenditures:* $25.4 million. *Unit head:* Prof. Joao Hespanha, Chair, 805-893-7042, Fax: 805-893-3262, E-mail: hespanha@ece.ucsb.edu. *Application contact:* Erika Klukovich, Graduate Admissions Coordinator, 805-893-3114, Fax: 805-893-5402, E-mail: erika@ece.ucsb.edu.
Website: http://www.ece.ucsb.edu/

University of Central Florida, College of Optics and Photonics, Orlando, FL 32816. Offers MS, PhD. *Program availability:* Part-time, evening/weekend. *Faculty:* 40 full-time (6 women), 17 part-time/adjunct (1 woman). *Students:* 106 full-time (19 women), 10 part-time (1 woman); includes 8 minority (1 Asian, non-Hispanic/Latino; 6 Hispanic/Latino; 1 Two or more races, non-Hispanic/Latino), 71 international. Average age 26. 186 applicants, 32% accepted, 29 enrolled. In 2015, 16 master's, 22 doctorates awarded. *Degree requirements:* For master's, thesis or alternative; for doctorate, thesis/dissertation, departmental qualifying exam, candidacy exam. *Entrance requirements:* For master's, GRE General Test, minimum GPA of 3.0 in last 60 hours; for doctorate, GRE General Test, minimum GPA of 3.5 in last 60 hours. Additional exam requirements/recommendations for international students: Required—TOEFL. *Application deadline:* For fall admission, 2/1 priority date for domestic students; for spring admission, 12/1 for domestic students. Application fee: $30. Electronic applications accepted. *Expenses:* Tuition, state resident: part-time $288.16 per credit hour. Tuition, nonresident: part-time $1071.31 per credit hour. *Financial support:* In 2015–16, 74 students received support, including 20 fellowships with partial tuition reimbursements available (averaging $7,800 per year), 74 research assistantships with partial tuition reimbursements available (averaging $12,400 per year), 5 teaching assistantships with partial tuition reimbursements available (averaging $8,000 per year); career-related internships or fieldwork, Federal Work-Study, institutionally sponsored loans, tuition waivers (partial), and unspecified assistantships also available. Financial award application deadline: 3/1; financial award applicants required to submit FAFSA. *Unit head:* Dr. Bahaa E. Saleh, Dean and Director, 407-823-6817, E-mail: besaleh@creol.ucf.edu. *Application contact:* Director, Admissions and Student Services, 407-823-2766, Fax: 407-823-6442, E-mail: gradadmissions@ucf.edu.
Website: http://www.creol.ucf.edu/

University of New Mexico, Graduate Studies, College of Arts and Sciences, Program in Optical Science and Engineering, Albuquerque, NM 87131. Offers imaging science (MS, PhD); optical science and engineering (MS, PhD); photonics (MS, PhD). Program held jointly with the Department of Physics and Astronomy and the Department of Electrical and Computer Engineering. *Program availability:* Part-time. *Faculty:* 7 full-time (0 women), 1 part-time/adjunct (0 women). *Students:* 23 full-time (8 women), 37 part-time (1 woman); includes 6 minority (1 Black or African American, non-Hispanic/Latino; 4 Hispanic/Latino; 1 Two or more races, non-Hispanic/Latino), 45 international. Average age 33. 65 applicants, 34% accepted, 6 enrolled. In 2015, 4 master's, 8 doctorates awarded. Terminal master's awarded for partial completion of doctoral program. *Degree requirements:* For master's, comprehensive exam (for some programs), thesis (for some programs); for doctorate, comprehensive exam, thesis/dissertation. *Entrance requirements:* For master's, GRE General Test, GRE Subject Test in physics (preferred), relevant undergraduate coursework, curriculum vitae, letters of recommendation, letter of intent/personal statement; for doctorate, GRE General Test, GRE Subject Test in physics (preferred), relevant undergraduate coursework, curriculum vitae, letters of recommendation. Additional exam requirements/recommendations for international students: Required—TOEFL (minimum score 575 paper-based; 79 iBT), IELTS (minimum score 7). *Application deadline:* For fall admission, 1/15 priority date for domestic and international students; for spring admission, 8/1 priority date for domestic and international students. Application fee: $50. Electronic applications accepted. *Financial support:* Fellowships with full tuition reimbursements, research assistantships with full tuition reimbursements, teaching assistantships with full tuition reimbursements, career-related internships or fieldwork, scholarships/grants, health care benefits, and unspecified assistantships available. Support available to part-time students. Financial award application deadline: 2/1; financial award applicants required to submit FAFSA. *Faculty research:* Advanced materials, atom optics, biomedical optics, fiber optics, laser cooling, high intensity interactions, lithography, nano photonics, nonlinear optics, optical imaging, optical sensors, optoelectronics, quantum optics, spectroscopy, ultrafast phenomena. *Unit head:* Dr. Majeed Hayat, Chair, 505-272-7095, Fax: 505-277-7801, E-mail: hayat@ece.unm.edu. *Application contact:* Doris Williams, Advisor, 505-277-7764, Fax: 505-277-7801, E-mail: dorisw@chtm.unm.edu.
Website: http://www.optics.unm.edu/

Physics

Alabama Agricultural and Mechanical University, School of Graduate Studies, College of Engineering, Technology, and Physical Sciences, Department of Physics, Chemistry and Mathematics, Huntsville, AL 35811. Offers physics (MS, PhD), including materials science (PhD), optics/lasers (PhD), space science (PhD). *Program availability:* Part-time, evening/weekend. *Degree requirements:* For doctorate, thesis/dissertation. *Entrance requirements:* For master's and doctorate, GRE General Test. Additional exam requirements/recommendations for international students: Required—TOEFL (minimum score 500 paper-based; 61 iBT). Electronic applications accepted.

American University of Beirut, Graduate Programs, Faculty of Arts and Sciences, Beirut, Lebanon. Offers anthropology (MA); Arab and Middle Eastern history (PhD); Arabic language and literature (MA, PhD); archaeology (MA); biology (MS); cell and molecular biology (PhD); chemistry (MS); clinical psychology (MA); computational sciences (MS); computer science (MS); economics (MA); English language (MA); English literature (MA); environmental policy planning (MS); financial economics (MAFE); geology (MS); history (MA); mathematics (MA, MS); media studies (MA); Middle Eastern studies (MA); physics (MS); political studies (MA); psychology (MA); public administration (MA); sociology (MA); statistics (MA, MS); theoretical physics (PhD); transnational American studies (MA). *Program availability:* Part-time. *Faculty:* 114 full-time (36 women), 4 part-time/adjunct (2 women). *Students:* 258 full-time (190 women), 207 part-time (142 women). Average age 27. 241 applicants, 71% accepted, 98 enrolled. In 2015, 47 master's, 3 doctorates awarded. *Degree requirements:* For master's, one foreign language, comprehensive exam, thesis (for some programs); for doctorate, one foreign language, comprehensive exam, thesis/dissertation. *Entrance requirements:* For master's, GRE (for some MA, MS programs), letter of recommendation; for doctorate, GRE, letters of recommendation. Additional exam requirements/recommendations for international students: Required—TOEFL (minimum score 600 paper-based; 97 iBT), IELTS (minimum score 7). *Application deadline:* For fall admission, 4/1 for domestic and international students; for spring admission, 11/1 for domestic and international students. Application fee: $50. Electronic applications accepted. *Expenses: Tuition, area resident:* Full-time $16,254; part-time $903 per credit. *Required fees:* $699. Tuition and fees vary according to course load and program. *Financial support:* Research assistantships, career-related internships or fieldwork, institutionally sponsored loans, scholarships/grants, health care benefits, and unspecified assistantships available. Financial award application deadline: 2/4; financial award applicants required to submit FAFSA. *Faculty research:* Analysis and algebra; software engineering; machine learning and big data analysis; philosophy of mind and political philosophy; anthropology of art, anthropology of migration and medical anthropology; sociology of knowledge, sociology of migration, critical theory; sociology of education; hybrid solid materials; photocatalysis; human creativity. *Total annual research expenditures:* $680,360. *Unit head:* Dr. Patrick McGreevy, Dean, 961-1374374 Ext. 3800, Fax: 961-1744461, E-mail: pm07@aub.edu.lb. *Application contact:* Dr. Salim Kanaan, Director, Admissions Office, 961-1350000 Ext. 2590, Fax: 961-1750775, E-mail: sk00@aub.edu.lb.
Website: http://www.aub.edu.lb/fas/

Arizona State University at the Tempe campus, College of Liberal Arts and Sciences, Department of Physics, Tempe, AZ 85287-1504. Offers nanoscience (PSM); physics (MNS, PhD). *Program availability:* Part-time. Terminal master's awarded for partial completion of doctoral program. *Degree requirements:* For master's, comprehensive exam, thesis or alternative, interactive Program of Study (iPOS) submitted before completing 50 percent of required credit hours; for doctorate, comprehensive exam, thesis/dissertation, interactive Program of Study (iPOS) submitted before completing 50 percent of required credit hours. *Entrance requirements:* For master's and doctorate, GRE, minimum GPA of 3.0 or equivalent in last 2 years of work leading to bachelor's degree. Additional exam requirements/recommendations for international students: Required—TOEFL, IELTS, or PTE. Electronic applications accepted. *Expenses:* Contact institution.

Auburn University, Graduate School, College of Sciences and Mathematics, Department of Physics, Auburn University, AL 36849. Offers MS, PhD. *Program availability:* Part-time. *Faculty:* 24 full-time (1 woman), 5 part-time/adjunct (0 women). *Students:* 22 full-time (4 women), 29 part-time (2 women); includes 1 minority (Hispanic/Latino), 21 international. Average age 29. 18 applicants, 39% accepted, 7 enrolled. In 2015, 14 master's, 1 doctorate awarded. *Degree requirements:* For doctorate, thesis/dissertation, oral and written exams. *Entrance requirements:* For master's and doctorate, GRE General Test. *Application deadline:* Applications are processed on a rolling basis. Application fee: $50 ($60 for international students). Electronic applications accepted. *Expenses:* Tuition, state resident: full-time $8802; part-time $489 per credit hour. Tuition, nonresident: full-time $26,406; part-time $1467 per credit hour. *Required fees:* $808 per semester. Tuition and fees vary according to degree level and program. *Financial support:* Research assistantships, teaching assistantships, career-related internships or fieldwork, and Federal Work-Study available. Support available to part-time students. Financial award application deadline: 3/15; financial award applicants required to submit FAFSA. *Faculty research:* Atomic/radioactive physics, plasma physics, condensed matter physics, space physics, nonlinear dynamics. *Unit head:* Dr. James D. Hanson, Chair, 334-844-4264. *Application contact:* Dr. George Flowers, Dean of the Graduate School, 334-844-2125.
Website: http://www.physics.auburn.edu/

Ball State University, Graduate School, College of Sciences and Humanities, Department of Physics and Astronomy, Muncie, IN 47306. Offers physics (MA, MAE, MS). *Program availability:* Part-time. *Faculty:* 9 full-time (0 women). *Students:* 16 full-time (6 women), 7 part-time (2 women), 7 international. Average age 27. 22 applicants, 55% accepted, 6 enrolled. In 2015, 5 master's awarded. *Entrance requirements:* For master's, GRE General Test, minimum baccalaureate GPA of 2.75 or 3.0 in latter half of baccalauareate. Additional exam requirements/recommendations for international students: Required—TOEFL (minimum score 550 paper-based; 79 iBT), IELTS (minimum score 6.5). *Application deadline:* For fall admission, 3/1 priority date for domestic students; for spring admission, 6/1 for domestic students. Applications are processed on a rolling basis. Application fee: $60. Electronic applications accepted. *Expenses: Tuition, area resident:* Full-time $6948; part-time $2316 per semester. Tuition, state resident: full-time $10,422; part-time $3474 per semester. Tuition, nonresident: full-time $19,062; part-time $6354 per semester. *Required fees:* $651 per semester. Tuition and fees vary according to campus/location, program and reciprocity agreements. *Financial support:* In 2015–16, 10 students received support, including 2 research assistantships with partial tuition reimbursements available (averaging $13,934 per year), 8 teaching assistantships with partial tuition reimbursements available (averaging $13,438 per year). Financial award application deadline: 3/1; financial award applicants required to submit FAFSA. *Unit head:* Dr. Thomas Jordan, Chairperson, 765-285-8867, Fax: 765-285-5674, E-mail: tjordan@bsu.edu. *Application contact:* Dr. Ranjith Wijesinghe, Associate Professor/Graduate Advisor, 765-285-8811, Fax: 765-285-5674, E-mail: rswijesinghe@bsu.edu.
Website: http://www.bsu.edu/physics

Baylor University, Graduate School, College of Arts and Sciences, Department of Physics, Waco, TX 76798. Offers MA, MS, PhD. *Faculty:* 15 full-time (3 women). *Students:* 30 full-time (6 women), 8 part-time (2 women); includes 3 minority (1 Asian, non-Hispanic/Latino; 2 Hispanic/Latino), 22 international. 93 applicants, 26% accepted, 8 enrolled. In 2015, 4 master's, 3 doctorates awarded. Terminal master's awarded for partial completion of doctoral program. *Degree requirements:* For master's, comprehensive exam (for some programs), thesis or alternative; for doctorate,

comprehensive exam, thesis/dissertation. *Entrance requirements:* For master's and doctorate, GRE General Test, GRE Subject Test (physics). Additional exam requirements/recommendations for international students: Required—TOEFL (minimum score 80 iBT), IELTS (minimum score 6.5), or PTE. *Application deadline:* For fall admission, 2/1 for domestic and international students; for spring admission, 12/1 for domestic and international students. Application fee: $50. Electronic applications accepted. *Financial support:* In 2015–16, 38 students received support, including 11 research assistantships with full tuition reimbursements available (averaging $23,402 per year), 27 teaching assistantships with full tuition reimbursements available (averaging $23,402 per year); health care benefits also available. *Faculty research:* Elementary particle physics and cosmology, condensed matter physics, space science physics, nonlinear dynamics, atomic and molecular physics. *Total annual research expenditures:* $545,988. *Unit head:* Prof. Gerald B. Cleaver, Graduate Program Director, 254-710-2283, Fax: 254-710-3878, E-mail: gerald_cleaver@baylor.edu. *Application contact:* Marian Nunn-Graves, Administrative Assistant, 254-710-2511, Fax: 254-710-3878, E-mail: marian_nunn-graves@baylor.edu.
Website: http://www.baylor.edu/physics/

Binghamton University, State University of New York, Graduate School, School of Arts and Sciences, Department of Physics, Applied Physics, and Astronomy, Vestal, NY 13850. Offers MS, PhD. *Program availability:* Part-time. *Faculty:* 15 full-time (1 woman), 7 part-time/adjunct (0 women). *Students:* 14 full-time (1 woman), 26 part-time (2 women); includes 3 minority (1 Black or African American, non-Hispanic/Latino; 2 Hispanic/Latino), 16 international. Average age 29. 31 applicants, 55% accepted, 9 enrolled. In 2015, 4 master's, 2 doctorates awarded. Terminal master's awarded for partial completion of doctoral program. *Degree requirements:* For master's, comprehensive exam (for some programs), thesis or alternative; for doctorate, comprehensive exam, thesis/dissertation. *Entrance requirements:* For master's and doctorate, GRE General Test. Additional exam requirements/recommendations for international students: Required—TOEFL (minimum score 550 paper-based; 80 iBT). *Application deadline:* For fall admission, 2/15 priority date for domestic and international students; for spring admission, 10/15 priority date for domestic and international students. Application fee: $75. Electronic applications accepted. *Financial support:* In 2015–16, 37 students received support, including 5 research assistantships with full tuition reimbursements available (averaging $15,500 per year), 21 teaching assistantships with full tuition reimbursements available (averaging $17,500 per year); career-related internships or fieldwork, Federal Work-Study, institutionally sponsored loans, scholarships/grants, health care benefits, and unspecified assistantships also available. Financial award applicants required to submit FAFSA. *Unit head:* Dr. Bruce White, Chairperson, 607-777-2843, E-mail: bwhite@binghamton.edu. *Application contact:* Kishan Zuber, Recruiting and Admissions Coordinator, 607-777-2151, Fax: 607-777-2501, E-mail: kzuber@binghamton.edu.

Boston College, Graduate School of Arts and Sciences, Department of Physics, Chestnut Hill, MA 02467. Offers MS, PhD. *Faculty:* 16 full-time. *Students:* 47 full-time (4 women); includes 4 minority (2 Asian, non-Hispanic/Latino; 2 Hispanic/Latino), 25 international. 61 applicants, 16% accepted, 8 enrolled. In 2015, 1 doctorate awarded. Terminal master's awarded for partial completion of doctoral program. *Degree requirements:* For master's, thesis (for some programs); for doctorate, thesis/dissertation. *Entrance requirements:* For master's and doctorate, GRE General Test, GRE Subject Test. Additional exam requirements/recommendations for international students: Required—TOEFL (minimum score 600 paper-based; 100 iBT), IELTS (minimum score 8). *Application deadline:* For fall admission, 1/2 for domestic and international students. Application fee: $75. Electronic applications accepted. Tuition and fees vary according to program. *Financial support:* In 2015–16, 47 students received support, including fellowships with full tuition reimbursements available (averaging $27,000 per year), research assistantships with full tuition reimbursements available (averaging $27,000 per year), teaching assistantships with full tuition reimbursements available (averaging $27,000 per year); Federal Work-Study, scholarships/grants, and unspecified assistantships also available. Support available to part-time students. Financial award application deadline: 3/1; financial award applicants required to submit FAFSA. *Faculty research:* Superconductivity, photovoltaics, metamaterials, thermoelectrics, nanostructures and nanomaterials for biosensing, plasmonics, plasmas, topological insulators, and novel electronic materials. *Unit head:* Dr. Michael Naughton, Chairperson, 617-552-3576, E-mail: michael.naughton@bc.edu. *Application contact:* Dr. Ziqiang Wang, Graduate Program Director, 617-552-0687, E-mail: ziqiang.wang@bc.edu.
Website: http://www.bc.edu/physics

Boston University, Graduate School of Arts and Sciences, Department of Physics, Boston, MA 02215. Offers PhD. *Students:* 90 full-time (8 women), 1 part-time (0 women); includes 9 minority (6 Asian, non-Hispanic/Latino; 3 Hispanic/Latino), 51 international. Average age 26. 280 applicants, 21% accepted, 15 enrolled. In 2015, 16 doctorates awarded. Terminal master's awarded for partial completion of doctoral program. *Degree requirements:* For doctorate, one foreign language, comprehensive exam, thesis/dissertation. *Entrance requirements:* For doctorate, GRE General Test, GRE Subject Test, 3 letters of recommendation, transcripts, personal statement, curriculum vitae. Additional exam requirements/recommendations for international students: Required—TOEFL (minimum score 600 paper-based; 84 iBT). *Application deadline:* For fall admission, 1/8 for domestic and international students. Application fee: $95. Electronic applications accepted. *Financial support:* In 2015–16, 90 students received support, including 2 fellowships with full tuition reimbursements available (averaging $21,000 per year), 40 research assistantships with full tuition reimbursements available (averaging $21,000 per year), 44 teaching assistantships with full tuition reimbursements available (averaging $21,000 per year); Federal Work-Study, scholarships/grants, and health care benefits also available. Support available to part-time students. Financial award application deadline: 1/8. *Unit head:* Dr. Karl Ludwig, Chair, 617-353-9346, Fax: 617-353-9393, E-mail: ludwig@bu.edu. *Application contact:* Mirtha M. Cabello, Administrative Coordinator, 617-353-2623, Fax: 617-353-9393, E-mail: cabello@bu.edu.
Website: http://buphy.bu.edu/

Bowling Green State University, Graduate College, College of Arts and Sciences, Department of Physics and Astronomy, Bowling Green, OH 43403. Offers geophysics (MS); physics (MAT, MS). *Degree requirements:* For master's, thesis or alternative. *Entrance requirements:* For master's, GRE General Test. Additional exam requirements/recommendations for international students: Required—TOEFL. Electronic applications accepted. *Faculty research:* Computational physics, solid-state physics, materials science, theoretical physics.

Brandeis University, Graduate School of Arts and Sciences, Department of Physics, Waltham, MA 02454-9110. Offers physics (MS, PhD); quantitative biology (PhD). *Program availability:* Part-time. *Faculty:* 15 full-time (3 women), 1 part-time/adjunct (0 women). *Students:* 47 full-time (12 women); includes 2 minority (1 Asian, non-Hispanic/Latino; 1 Hispanic/Latino), 19 international. 147 applicants, 14% accepted, 7 enrolled. In 2015, 3 master's, 10 doctorates awarded. Terminal master's awarded for partial completion of doctoral program. *Degree requirements:* For master's, thesis optional, qualifying exam, 1-year residency; for doctorate, comprehensive exam, thesis/dissertation, qualifying and advanced exams. *Entrance requirements:* For master's and doctorate, GRE General Test; GRE Subject Test (recommended), resume, 2 letters of recommendation, statement of purpose, transcript(s). Additional exam requirements/recommendations for international students: Required—TOEFL (minimum score 600 paper-based; 100 iBT); Recommended—IELTS (minimum score 7), TSE (minimum score 68). *Application deadline:* For fall admission, 1/15 priority date for domestic students. Application fee: $75. Electronic applications accepted. *Financial support:* In 2015–16, 56 students received support, including 22 fellowships with full tuition reimbursements available (averaging $26,000 per year), 22 research assistantships with full tuition reimbursements available (averaging $26,000 per year), 12 teaching assistantships with partial tuition reimbursements available (averaging $2,500 per year); Federal Work-Study, scholarships/grants, health care benefits, and tuition waivers (full and partial) also available. Support available to part-time students. Financial award application deadline: 1/15; financial award applicants required to submit FAFSA. *Faculty research:* Astrophysics, condensed-matter and biophysics, high energy and gravitational theory, particle physics, microfluidics, radio astronomy, string theory. *Unit head:* Dr. Jane' Kondev, Department Chair, 781-736-2800, E-mail: kondev@brandeis.edu. *Application contact:* Catherine Broderick, Department Administrator, 781-736-2800, E-mail: cbroderi@brandeis.edu.
Website: http://www.brandeis.edu/gsas

Brigham Young University, Graduate Studies, College of Physical and Mathematical Sciences, Department of Physics and Astronomy, Provo, UT 84602-1001. Offers physics (MS, PhD); physics and astronomy (PhD). *Program availability:* Part-time. *Faculty:* 29 full-time (2 women), 1 (woman) part-time/adjunct. *Students:* 31 full-time (5 women), 3 part-time (0 women); includes 5 minority (2 Asian, non-Hispanic/Latino; 2 Hispanic/Latino; 1 Native Hawaiian or other Pacific Islander, non-Hispanic/Latino), 4 international. Average age 28. 21 applicants, 48% accepted, 9 enrolled. In 2015, 5 master's, 3 doctorates awarded. Terminal master's awarded for partial completion of doctoral program. *Degree requirements:* For master's, thesis; for doctorate, thesis/dissertation, qualifying exam, candidacy exam. *Entrance requirements:* For master's and doctorate, GRE Subject Test (physics), GRE General Test, minimum GPA of 3.0, ecclesiastical endorsement. Additional exam requirements/recommendations for international students: Required—TOEFL (minimum score 580 paper-based; 85 iBT), IELTS (minimum score 7), CAE (minimum 75 or B grade). *Application deadline:* For fall admission, 1/15 priority date for domestic and international students. Application fee: $50. Electronic applications accepted. *Financial support:* In 2015–16, 26 students received support, including 20 research assistantships with full tuition reimbursements available (averaging $20,640 per year), 6 teaching assistantships with full tuition reimbursements available (averaging $19,680 per year); institutionally sponsored loans, health care benefits, and tuition waivers (full) also available. Support available to part-time students. Financial award application deadline: 1/15. *Faculty research:* Acoustics; atomic, molecular, and optical physics; theoretical and mathematical physics; condensed matter; astrophysics and plasma. *Total annual research expenditures:* $3 million. *Unit head:* Dr. Richard R. Vanfleet, Chair, 801-422-1702, Fax: 801-422-0553, E-mail: richard_vanfleet@byu.edu. *Application contact:* Dr. Eric W. Hirschmann, Graduate Coordinator, 801-422-9271, Fax: 801-422-0553,
E-mail: eric_hirschmann@byu.edu.
Website: http://physics.byu.edu/

Brock University, Faculty of Graduate Studies, Faculty of Mathematics and Science, Program in Physics, St. Catharines, ON L2S 3A1, Canada. Offers M Sc. *Program availability:* Part-time. *Degree requirements:* For master's, thesis. *Entrance requirements:* For master's, honors B Sc in physics. Additional exam requirements/recommendations for international students: Required—TOEFL (minimum score 550 paper-based; 80 iBT), IELTS (minimum score 6.5), TWE (minimum score 4). Electronic applications accepted. *Faculty research:* Quantum physics, optical properties, non-crystalline materials, condensed matter physics, biophysics.

Brooklyn College of the City University of New York, School of Education, Program in Middle Childhood Science Education, Brooklyn, NY 11210-2889. Offers biology (MA); chemistry (MA); earth science (MA); general science (MA); physics (MA). *Program availability:* Part-time, evening/weekend. *Entrance requirements:* For master's, LAST, interview, previous course work in education and mathematics, resume, 2 letters of recommendation, essay. Additional exam requirements/recommendations for international students: Required—TOEFL (minimum score 500 paper-based; 61 iBT). Electronic applications accepted. *Faculty research:* Geometric thinking, mastery of basic facts, problem-solving strategies, history of mathematics.

Brooklyn College of the City University of New York, School of Natural and Behavioral Sciences, Department of Physics, Brooklyn, NY 11210-2889. Offers MA. *Program availability:* Part-time. Terminal master's awarded for partial completion of doctoral program. *Degree requirements:* For master's, comprehensive exam, thesis or alternative, 30 credits. *Entrance requirements:* For master's, 2 letters of recommendation, 12 credits in advanced physics. Additional exam requirements/recommendations for international students: Required—TOEFL (minimum score 500 paper-based; 61 iBT). Electronic applications accepted.

Brown University, Graduate School, Department of Physics, Providence, RI 02912. Offers Sc M, PhD. *Degree requirements:* For doctorate, thesis/dissertation, qualifying and oral exams.

Bryn Mawr College, Graduate School of Arts and Sciences, Department of Physics, Bryn Mawr, PA 19010-2899. Offers MA, PhD. *Faculty:* 7 full-time (2 women), 2 part-time/adjunct (0 women). *Students:* 3 full-time (1 woman), 2 part-time (0 women); includes 2 minority (1 Asian, non-Hispanic/Latino; 1 Hispanic/Latino). Average age 25. 5 applicants, 40% accepted, 2 enrolled. *Degree requirements:* For master's, one foreign language, thesis; for doctorate, one foreign language, thesis/dissertation. *Entrance requirements:* For master's and doctorate, GRE General Test, GRE Subject Test, transcripts, three letters of recommendation, statement of interest, resume or curriculum vitae. Additional exam requirements/recommendations for international students: Required—TOEFL (minimum score 600 paper-based, 100 iBT) or IELTS (7.0). *Application deadline:* For fall admission, 1/4 for domestic and international students. Application fee: $50. *Expenses: Tuition, area resident:* Full-time $39,240; part-time $6540 per unit. *Financial support:* In 2015–16, 5 students received support, including 4 fellowships with full tuition reimbursements available (averaging $23,200 per year), 1 research assistantship with partial tuition reimbursement available (averaging $23,200 per year), 2 teaching assistantships with full tuition reimbursements available (averaging $18,500 per year); Federal Work-Study, scholarships/grants, health care benefits, tuition waivers (partial), and tuition awards also available. Support available to part-time students. Financial award application deadline: 1/4. *Unit head:* Maria Dantis, Graduate Program Administrator, 610-526-5074, E-mail: gsas@brynmawr.edu.

California Institute of Technology, Division of Physics, Mathematics and Astronomy, Department of Physics, Pasadena, CA 91125-0001. Offers PhD. *Degree requirements:* For doctorate, thesis/dissertation, candidacy and final exams. *Entrance requirements:*

For doctorate, GRE General Test, GRE Subject Test. Additional exam requirements/recommendations for international students: Required—TOEFL. *Faculty research:* High-energy physics, nuclear physics, condensed-matter physics, theoretical physics and astrophysics, gravity physics.

California State University, Fresno, Division of Graduate Studies, College of Science and Mathematics, Department of Physics, Fresno, CA 93740-8027. Offers MS. *Program availability:* Part-time. *Degree requirements:* For master's, thesis or alternative. *Entrance requirements:* For master's, GRE General Test, minimum GPA of 2.5. Additional exam requirements/recommendations for international students: Required—TOEFL. Electronic applications accepted. *Faculty research:* Energy, astronomy, silicon vertex detector, neuroimaging, particle physics.

California State University, Fullerton, Graduate Studies, College of Natural Science and Mathematics, Department of Physics, Fullerton, CA 92834-9480. Offers MS. *Program availability:* Part-time.

California State University, Long Beach, Graduate Studies, College of Natural Sciences and Mathematics, Department of Physics and Astronomy, Long Beach, CA 90840. Offers physics (MS). *Program availability:* Part-time. *Degree requirements:* For master's, comprehensive exam or thesis. Electronic applications accepted. *Faculty research:* Musical acoustics, modern optics, neutrino physics, quantum gravity, atomic physics.

California State University, Los Angeles, Graduate Studies, College of Natural and Social Sciences, Department of Physics and Astronomy, Los Angeles, CA 90032-8530. Offers physics (MS). *Program availability:* Part-time, evening/weekend. *Degree requirements:* For master's, comprehensive exam or thesis. *Entrance requirements:* Additional exam requirements/recommendations for international students: Required—TOEFL (minimum score 500 paper-based). Electronic applications accepted. *Faculty research:* Intermediate energy, nuclear physics, condensed-matter physics, biophysics.

California State University, Northridge, Graduate Studies, College of Science and Mathematics, Department of Physics and Astronomy, Northridge, CA 91330. Offers physics (MS). *Program availability:* Part-time, evening/weekend. *Faculty:* 14 full-time (3 women), 25 part-time/adjunct (8 women). *Students:* 15 full-time (7 women), 20 part-time (5 women); includes 13 minority (8 Asian, non-Hispanic/Latino; 5 Hispanic/Latino), 11 international. Average age 29. 35 applicants, 66% accepted, 12 enrolled. *Degree requirements:* For master's, thesis or comprehensive exam. *Entrance requirements:* For master's, GRE General Test or minimum GPA of 3.0. Additional exam requirements/recommendations for international students: Required—TOEFL. *Application deadline:* For fall admission, 11/30 for domestic students. Application fee: $55. *Financial support:* Teaching assistantships available. Financial award application deadline: 3/1. *Unit head:* Dr. Say-Peng Lim, 818-677-2171, E-mail: physics@csun.edu.
Website: http://www.csun.edu/physics/

Carleton University, Faculty of Graduate Studies, Faculty of Science, Department of Physics, Ottawa, ON K1S 5B6, Canada. Offers M Sc, PhD. Programs offered jointly with University of Ottawa. *Degree requirements:* For master's, thesis optional, seminar; for doctorate, comprehensive exam, thesis/dissertation, seminar. *Entrance requirements:* For master's, honors degree in science; for doctorate, M Sc. Additional exam requirements/recommendations for international students: Required—TOEFL. *Faculty research:* Experimental and theoretical elementary particle physics, medical physics.

Carnegie Mellon University, Mellon College of Science, Department of Physics, Pittsburgh, PA 15213-3891. Offers applied physics (PhD); physics (MS, PhD). *Degree requirements:* For doctorate, thesis/dissertation, qualifying exam. *Entrance requirements:* For doctorate, GRE General Test, GRE Subject Test. Additional exam requirements/recommendations for international students: Required—TOEFL. Electronic applications accepted. *Faculty research:* Astrophysics, condensed matter physics, biological physics, medium energy and nuclear physics, high-energy physics.

Case Western Reserve University, School of Graduate Studies, Department of Physics, Cleveland, OH 44106. Offers MS, PhD. *Program availability:* Part-time. *Faculty:* 24 full-time (3 women), 19 part-time/adjunct (2 women). *Students:* 70 full-time (12 women), 2 part-time (1 woman); includes 1 minority (Two or more races, non-Hispanic/Latino), 29 international. Average age 27. 170 applicants, 35% accepted, 19 enrolled. In 2015, 3 master's, 4 doctorates awarded. Terminal master's awarded for partial completion of doctoral program. *Degree requirements:* For master's, comprehensive exam, exam; for doctorate, thesis/dissertation, qualifying exam, topical exam. *Entrance requirements:* For master's and doctorate, GRE General Test, GRE Subject Test (physics), statement of objectives; letters of recommendation. Additional exam requirements/recommendations for international students: Required—TOEFL (minimum score 577 paper-based; 90 iBT); Recommended—IELTS (minimum score 7). *Application deadline:* For fall admission, 1/15 priority date for domestic students. Electronic applications accepted. *Expenses: Tuition, area resident:* Full-time $41,137; part-time $1714 per credit hour. *Required fees:* $32. Tuition and fees vary according to course load and program. *Financial support:* Research assistantships, teaching assistantships, tuition waivers, and unspecified assistantships available. Financial award application deadline: 1/15; financial award applicants required to submit FAFSA. *Faculty research:* Condensed-matter, optics and optical materials, cosmology and astrophysics, and biophysics, medical and imaging physics. *Unit head:* Prof. Kathleen Kash, Professor of Physics - Chair, Department of Physics, 216-368-4000, E-mail: kathleen.kash@case.edu. *Application contact:* Prof. Corbin Covault, Professor of Physics, 216-368-4000, Fax: 216-368-4671, E-mail: grad_dir@phys.case.edu.
Website: http://www.phys.cwru.edu/

The Catholic University of America, School of Arts and Sciences, Department of Physics, Washington, DC 20064. Offers MS, PhD. *Program availability:* Part-time. *Faculty:* 10 full-time (2 women). *Students:* 8 full-time (2 women), 27 part-time (13 women); includes 5 minority (1 Asian, non-Hispanic/Latino; 2 Hispanic/Latino; 2 Two or more races, non-Hispanic/Latino), 12 international. Average age 29. 22 applicants, 59% accepted, 7 enrolled. In 2015, 7 master's, 4 doctorates awarded. *Degree requirements:* For master's, comprehensive exam, thesis or alternative; for doctorate, comprehensive exam, thesis/dissertation, oral exam. *Entrance requirements:* For master's and doctorate, GRE General Test, statement of purpose, official copies of academic transcripts, three letters of recommendation. Additional exam requirements/recommendations for international students: Required—TOEFL (minimum score 550 paper-based; 80 iBT). *Application deadline:* For fall admission, 7/15 priority date for domestic students, 7/1 for international students; for spring admission, 11/15 priority date for domestic students, 11/1 for international students. Applications are processed on a rolling basis. Application fee: $55. Electronic applications accepted. *Expenses:* $20,700 per semester full-time tuition, $200 per semester full-time fees; $1,650 per credit hour part-time tuition, $145 per semester part-time fees. *Financial support:* Fellowships, research assistantships, teaching assistantships, Federal Work-Study, scholarships/grants, tuition waivers (full and partial), and unspecified assistantships available. Financial award application deadline: 2/1; financial award applicants required to submit FAFSA. *Faculty research:* Glass and ceramics technologies, astrophysics and computational sciences, the role of evolution in galaxy properties, nuclear physics, biophysics. *Total annual research expenditures:* $7.6 million. *Unit head:* Dr. Steve Kraemer, Chair, 202-319-5856, Fax: 202-319-4448, E-mail: kraemer@cua.edu. *Application contact:* Director of Graduate Admissions, 202-319-5057, Fax: 202-319-6533, E-mail: cua-admissions@cua.edu.
Website: http://physics.cua.edu/

Central Michigan University, College of Graduate Studies, College of Science and Technology, Department of Physics, Mount Pleasant, MI 48859. Offers physics (MS); science of advanced materials (PhD). PhD is an interdisciplinary program. *Program availability:* Part-time. *Degree requirements:* For master's, thesis or alternative; for doctorate, comprehensive exam, thesis/dissertation. *Entrance requirements:* For doctorate, GRE, bachelor's degree in physics, chemistry, biochemistry, biology, geology, engineering, mathematics, or other relevant area. Electronic applications accepted. *Faculty research:* Science of advanced materials, polymer physics, laser spectroscopy, observational astronomy, nuclear physics.

Christopher Newport University, Graduate Studies, Department of Physics, Computer Science, and Engineering, Newport News, VA 23606-3072. Offers applied physics and computer science (MS). *Program availability:* Part-time, evening/weekend. *Faculty:* 22 full-time (4 women), 1 part-time/adjunct (0 women). *Students:* 10 full-time (1 woman), 6 part-time (1 woman); includes 1 minority (Black or African American, non-Hispanic/Latino). Average age 24. 17 applicants, 94% accepted, 10 enrolled. In 2015, 15 master's awarded. *Degree requirements:* For master's, comprehensive exam (for some programs), thesis (for some programs). *Entrance requirements:* For master's, GRE General Test, minimum GPA of 3.0. Additional exam requirements/recommendations for international students: Required—TOEFL (minimum score 580 paper-based; 92 iBT), IELTS (minimum score 7). *Application deadline:* For fall admission, 7/15 priority date for domestic students, 4/1 for international students; for spring admission, 11/1 for domestic students, 10/1 for international students; for summer admission, 3/15 for domestic students, 3/1 for international students. Applications are processed on a rolling basis. Application fee: $50. Electronic applications accepted. *Expenses:* Tuition, state resident: full-time $6444; part-time $358 per credit hour. Tuition, nonresident: full-time $14,706; part-time $817 per credit hour. *Required fees:* $3690; $205 per credit hour. Tuition and fees vary according to course load. *Financial support:* In 2015–16, 5 students received support, including 2 research assistantships with full tuition reimbursements available (averaging $2,000 per year), 3 teaching assistantships (averaging $1,500 per year); unspecified assistantships also available. Financial award application deadline: 3/1; financial award applicants required to submit FAFSA. *Faculty research:* Advanced programming methodologies, experimental nuclear physics, computer architecture, semiconductor nanophysics, laser and optical fiber sensors. *Total annual research expenditures:* $263,552. *Unit head:* Dr. Davie Heddle, Coordinator, 757-594-8435, Fax: 757-594-7919, E-mail: heddle@cnu.edu. *Application contact:* Lyn Sawyer, Associate Director, Graduate Admissions and Records, 757-594-7544, Fax: 757-594-7649, E-mail: gradstdy@cnu.edu.

City College of the City University of New York, Graduate School, Division of Science, Department of Physics, New York, NY 10031-9198. Offers MS, PhD. PhD program offered jointly with Graduate School and University Center of the City University of New York. *Students:* 1 part-time. Terminal master's awarded for partial completion of doctoral program. *Degree requirements:* For master's, comprehensive exam; for doctorate, thesis/dissertation. *Entrance requirements:* For doctorate, GRE. Additional exam requirements/recommendations for international students: Required—TOEFL (minimum score 500 paper-based; 61 iBT). *Application deadline:* For fall admission, 5/1 for domestic and international students; for spring admission, 11/15 for domestic and international students. Applications are processed on a rolling basis. Application fee: $125. Electronic applications accepted. Tuition and fees vary according to course load, degree level and program. *Financial support:* Fellowships and scholarships/grants available. Financial award applicants required to submit FAFSA. *Unit head:* Prof. Alexios Polychronakos, Chair, 212-650-6832. *Application contact:* Prof. Timothy Boyer, Advisor, 212-650-5585, Fax: 212-650-6940, E-mail: tboyer@ccny.cuny.edu.
Website: http://www.ccny.cuny.edu/physics/

Clark Atlanta University, School of Arts and Sciences, Department of Physics, Atlanta, GA 30314. Offers MS. *Program availability:* Part-time. *Faculty:* 6 full-time (0 women). *Students:* 6 full-time (3 women), 3 part-time (0 women); includes 2 minority (both Asian, non-Hispanic/Latino), 6 international. Average age 30. 13 applicants, 46% accepted, 4 enrolled. In 2015, 1 master's awarded. *Degree requirements:* For master's, one foreign language, comprehensive exam, thesis optional. *Entrance requirements:* For master's, GRE General Test, minimum GPA of 2.5. Additional exam requirements/recommendations for international students: Required—TOEFL (minimum score 500 paper-based; 61 iBT). *Application deadline:* For fall admission, 4/1 for domestic and international students; for spring admission, 11/1 for domestic and international students. Applications are processed on a rolling basis. Application fee: $40 ($55 for international students). *Expenses: Tuition, area resident:* Full-time $15,498; part-time $861 per credit hour. *Required fees:* $1006; $1006 per unit. Tuition and fees vary according to course load. *Financial support:* Scholarships/grants and unspecified assistantships available. Financial award application deadline: 4/30; financial award applicants required to submit FAFSA. *Faculty research:* Fusion energy, investigations of nonlinear differential equations, difference schemes, collisions in dense plasma. *Unit head:* Dr. Swaraj Tayal, Chairperson, 404-880-6877, E-mail: stayal@cau.edu. *Application contact:* Graduate Program Admissions, 404-880-8483, E-mail: graduateadmissions@cau.edu.

Clarkson University, Graduate School, School of Arts and Sciences, Department of Physics, Potsdam, NY 13699. Offers MS, PhD. *Program availability:* Part-time. *Faculty:* 9 full-time (1 woman), 1 (woman) part-time/adjunct. *Students:* 17 full-time (1 woman); includes 1 minority (Two or more races, non-Hispanic/Latino), 6 international. Average age 28. 15 applicants, 67% accepted, 6 enrolled. In 2015, 4 master's, 1 doctorate awarded. Terminal master's awarded for partial completion of doctoral program. *Degree requirements:* For doctorate, thesis/dissertation, departmental qualifying exam. *Entrance requirements:* For master's and doctorate, GRE, transcripts of all college coursework, resume, personal statement, three letters of recommendation. Additional exam requirements/recommendations for international students: Required—TOEFL or IELTS. *Application deadline:* For fall admission, 1/30 priority date for domestic and international students; for spring admission, 9/1 priority date for domestic and international students. Applications are processed on a rolling basis. Application fee: $25 ($35 for international students). Electronic applications accepted. *Financial support:* In 2015–16, 16 students received support, including fellowships with full tuition reimbursements available (averaging $24,510 per year), 4 research assistantships with full tuition reimbursements available (averaging $24,510 per year), 12 teaching assistantships with full tuition reimbursements available (averaging $24,510 per year); scholarships/grants, tuition waivers (partial), and unspecified assistantships also available. *Faculty research:* Multi input sensors, built-in logic, patterns in proteins, coupling nanoscale, sense-and-act. *Total annual research expenditures:* $285,559. *Unit head:* Dr. Dipankar Roy, Chair, 315-268-6676, Fax: 315-268-7754, E-mail: droy@clarkson.edu. *Application contact:* Jennifer Reed, Graduate School

Physics

Coordinator, Provost's Office, 315-268-3802, Fax: 315-268-3989,
E-mail: sciencegrad@clarkson.edu.
Website: http://www.clarkson.edu/physics/

Clark University, Graduate School, Department of Physics, Worcester, MA 01610-1477. Offers PhD. *Program availability:* Part-time. *Faculty:* 6 full-time (1 woman), 1 part-time/adjunct (0 women). *Students:* 8 full-time (1 woman), 2 part-time (0 women); includes 2 minority (1 Black or African American, non-Hispanic/Latino; 1 Hispanic/Latino), 5 international. Average age 33. 29 applicants, 10% accepted, 1 enrolled. Terminal master's awarded for partial completion of doctoral program. *Degree requirements:* For doctorate, one foreign language, thesis/dissertation. *Entrance requirements:* Additional exam requirements/recommendations for international students: Required—TOEFL. *Application deadline:* For fall admission, 2/1 for domestic students. Application fee: $75. *Expenses: Tuition, area resident:* Full-time $41,590; part-time $1300 per credit hour. *Required fees:* $80. Tuition and fees vary according to course load and program. *Financial support:* In 2015–16, 2 research assistantships with full tuition reimbursements (averaging $20,170 per year), 5 teaching assistantships with full tuition reimbursements (averaging $20,170 per year) were awarded; fellowships with tuition reimbursements, Federal Work-Study, and tuition waivers (full and partial) also available. Financial award application deadline: 4/1. *Faculty research:* Statistical and thermal physics, magnetic properties of materials, computer simulation, particle diffusion. *Total annual research expenditures:* $391,618. *Unit head:* Dr. Charles Agosta, Chair, 508-793-7736, Fax: 508-793-8861, E-mail: cagosta@clarku.edu. *Application contact:* Sujata Davis, Secretary, 508-793-7169, Fax: 508-793-8861,
E-mail: sudavis@clarku.edu.
Website: http://www.clarku.edu/departments/physics/graduate/index.cfm

Cleveland State University, College of Graduate Studies, College of Sciences and Health Professions, Department of Physics, Cleveland, OH 44115. Offers applied optics (MS); condensed matter physics (MS); medical physics (MS); optics and materials (MS); optics and medical imaging (MS). *Program availability:* Part-time, evening/weekend. *Faculty:* 4 full-time (0 women), 1 part-time/adjunct (0 women). *Students:* 10 full-time (5 women), 9 part-time (1 woman); includes 5 minority (2 Black or African American, non-Hispanic/Latino; 1 Asian, non-Hispanic/Latino; 2 Hispanic/Latino), 2 international. Average age 28. 23 applicants, 78% accepted, 6 enrolled. In 2015, 10 master's awarded. *Entrance requirements:* For master's, undergraduate degree in engineering, physics, chemistry or mathematics. Additional exam requirements/recommendations for international students: Required—TOEFL (minimum score 550 paper-based; 78 iBT). *Application deadline:* For fall admission, 7/1 priority date for domestic students, 4/1 priority date for international students. Applications are processed on a rolling basis. Application fee: $30. Electronic applications accepted. *Expenses:* Tuition, state resident: full-time $9565. Tuition, nonresident: full-time $17,980. Tuition and fees vary according to program. *Financial support:* In 2015–16, 1 research assistantship with tuition reimbursement (averaging $5,666 per year) was awarded; fellowships with tuition reimbursements, teaching assistantships, and tuition waivers (full) also available. Financial award applicants required to submit FAFSA. *Faculty research:* Statistical physics, experimental solid-state physics, theoretical optics, experimental biological physics (macromolecular crystallography), experimental optics. *Total annual research expenditures:* $350,000. *Unit head:* Dr. Miron Kaufman, Chairperson, 216-687-2436, Fax: 216-523-7268, E-mail: m.kaufman@csuohio.edu. *Application contact:* Dr. James A. Lock, Director, 216-687-2420, Fax: 216-523-7268, E-mail: j.lock@csuohio.edu.
Website: http://www.csuohio.edu/sciences/physics/physics

The College of William and Mary, Faculty of Arts and Sciences, Department of Physics, Williamsburg, VA 23187-8795. Offers MS, PhD. *Faculty:* 29 full-time (5 women). *Students:* 81 full-time (18 women); includes 7 minority (4 Asian, non-Hispanic/Latino; 2 Hispanic/Latino; 1 Two or more races, non-Hispanic/Latino), 31 international. Average age 27. 119 applicants, 39% accepted, 14 enrolled. In 2015, 5 master's, 7 doctorates awarded. Terminal master's awarded for partial completion of doctoral program. *Degree requirements:* For master's, minimum GPA of 3.0, 32 credit hours; for doctorate, comprehensive exam, thesis/dissertation, 1-year residency, 2 semesters of physics teaching, minimum GPA of 3.0. *Entrance requirements:* For doctorate, GRE General Test, GRE Subject Test, minimum GPA of 3.0. Additional exam requirements/recommendations for international students: Required—TOEFL. *Application deadline:* For fall admission, 1/15 priority date for domestic and international students. Applications are processed on a rolling basis. Application fee: $45. Electronic applications accepted. *Expenses:* Tuition, state resident: full-time $8009; part-time $450 per credit hour. Tuition, nonresident: full-time $23,752; part-time $1160 per credit hour. *Required fees:* $4162. One-time fee: $400 full-time. *Financial support:* In 2015–16, 65 students received support, including 50 research assistantships with full tuition reimbursements available (averaging $24,000 per year), 31 teaching assistantships with full tuition reimbursements available (averaging $24,000 per year); career-related internships or fieldwork, health care benefits, tuition waivers (full), and unspecified assistantships also available. *Faculty research:* Nuclear/particle, condensed-matter, atomic, and plasma physics; accelerator physics; molecular/optical physics; computational/nonlinear physics. *Total annual research expenditures:* $4.4 million. *Unit head:* Dr. Eugene K. Tracy, Chair, 757-221-3500, Fax: 757-221-3540,
E-mail: chair@physics.wm.edu. *Application contact:* Dr. Michael A. Kordosky, Chair of Admissions, 757-221-3500, Fax: 757-221-3540, E-mail: grad@physics.wm.edu.
Website: http://www.wm.edu/physics/

Colorado School of Mines, Office of Graduate Studies, Department of Physics, Golden, CO 80401. Offers applied physics (MS, PhD); materials science (MS, PhD); nuclear engineering (ME, MS, PhD). *Program availability:* Part-time. *Faculty:* 34 full-time (2 women), 15 part-time/adjunct (1 woman). *Students:* 69 full-time (18 women), 8 part-time (2 women); includes 9 minority (1 Asian, non-Hispanic/Latino; 7 Hispanic/Latino; 1 Two or more races, non-Hispanic/Latino), 14 international. Average age 28. 100 applicants, 31% accepted, 19 enrolled. In 2015, 8 master's, 7 doctorates awarded. *Degree requirements:* For master's, thesis (for some programs); for doctorate, comprehensive exam, thesis/dissertation. *Entrance requirements:* For master's and doctorate, GRE General Test, GRE Subject Test. Additional exam requirements/recommendations for international students: Required—TOEFL (minimum score 550 paper-based; 80 iBT). *Application deadline:* For fall admission, 12/15 priority date for domestic and international students; for spring admission, 9/1 priority date for domestic and international students. Application fee: $50 ($70 for international students). Electronic applications accepted. *Expenses:* Tuition, state resident: full-time $15,225. Tuition, nonresident: full-time $32,700. *Financial support:* In 2015–16, 57 students received support, including 3 fellowships with full tuition reimbursements available (averaging $21,120 per year), 37 research assistantships with full tuition reimbursements available (averaging $21,120 per year), 17 teaching assistantships with full tuition reimbursements available (averaging $21,120 per year); scholarships/grants, health care benefits, and unspecified assistantships also available. Financial award application deadline: 12/15; financial award applicants required to submit FAFSA. *Faculty research:* Light scattering, low-energy nuclear physics, high fusion plasma diagnostics, laser operations, mathematical physics. *Total annual research expenditures:* $5.9 million. *Unit head:* Dr. Jeff Squier, Head, 303-273-2385,
E-mail: jsquier@mines.edu. *Application contact:* Dr. David Wood, Professor, 303-273-3853, E-mail: dwood@mines.edu.
Website: http://physics.mines.edu

Colorado State University, College of Natural Sciences, Department of Physics, Fort Collins, CO 80523-1875. Offers MS, PhD. *Faculty:* 17 full-time (3 women). *Students:* 23 full-time (3 women), 38 part-time (3 women); includes 3 minority (1 Asian, non-Hispanic/Latino; 1 Hispanic/Latino; 1 Two or more races, non-Hispanic/Latino), 10 international. Average age 27. 35 applicants, 74% accepted, 7 enrolled. In 2015, 9 master's, 5 doctorates awarded. Terminal master's awarded for partial completion of doctoral program. *Degree requirements:* For master's, comprehensive exam, thesis; for doctorate, comprehensive exam, thesis/dissertation. *Entrance requirements:* For master's, GRE General Test, GRE Subject Test (physics), minimum GPA of 3.0; transcripts; 3 letters of recommendation; curriculum vitae/resume; personal statement; for doctorate, GRE General Test, GRE Subject Test (physics), minimum GPA of 3.0; transcripts; 3 letters of recommendation; BA (for domestic students only); personal statement. Additional exam requirements/recommendations for international students: Required—TOEFL (minimum score 600 paper-based; 100 iBT), IELTS (minimum score 8). *Application deadline:* For fall admission, 2/1 priority date for domestic and international students. Application fee: $60 ($70 for international students). Electronic applications accepted. *Expenses:* Tuition, state resident: full-time $9348. Tuition, nonresident: full-time $22,916. *Required fees:* $2174; $473.72 per credit hour. $236.86 per semester. Tuition and fees vary according to course load and program. *Financial support:* In 2015–16, 60 students received support, including 4 fellowships (averaging $44,750 per year), 21 research assistantships with full tuition reimbursements available (averaging $17,559 per year), 31 teaching assistantships with full tuition reimbursements available (averaging $16,830 per year); scholarships/grants and unspecified assistantships also available. Financial award application deadline: 2/1. *Faculty research:* Atomic, molecular and optical physics; condensed matter; theory and experiment; high energy particles; particle astrophysics. *Total annual research expenditures:* $3.5 million. *Unit head:* Dr. Jacob Roberts, Professor and Chair, 970-491-0578, Fax: 970-491-7947, E-mail: jacob.roberts@colostate.edu. *Application contact:* Veronica Nicholson, Graduate Coordinator, 970-491-6207, Fax: 970-491-7947,
E-mail: veronica.nicholson@colostate.edu.
Website: http://www.physics.colostate.edu/

Columbia University, Graduate School of Arts and Sciences, New York, NY 10027. Offers African-American studies (MA); American studies (MA); anthropology (MA, PhD); art history and archaeology (MA, PhD); astronomy (PhD); biological sciences (PhD); biotechnology (MA); chemical physics (PhD); chemistry (PhD); classical studies (MA, PhD); classics (MA, PhD); climate and society (MA); conservation biology (MA); earth and environmental sciences (PhD); East Asia: regional studies (MA); East Asian languages and cultures (MA, PhD); ecology, evolution and environmental biology (MA), including conservation biology; ecology, evolution, and environmental biology (PhD), including ecology and evolutionary biology, evolutionary primatology; economics (MA, PhD); English and comparative literature (MA, PhD); French and Romance philology (MA, PhD); Germanic languages (MA, PhD); global French studies (MA); global thought (MA); Hispanic cultural studies (MA); history (PhD); history and literature (MA); human rights studies (MA); Islamic studies (MA); Italian (MA, PhD); Japanese pedagogy (MA); Jewish studies (MA); Latin America and the Caribbean: regional studies (MA); Latin American and Iberian cultures (PhD); mathematics (MA, PhD), including finance (MA); medieval and Renaissance studies (MA); Middle Eastern, South Asian, and African studies (MA, PhD); modern art: critical and curatorial studies (MA); modern European studies (MA); museum anthropology (MA); music (DMA, PhD); oral history (MA); philosophical foundations of physics (MA); philosophy (MA, PhD); physics (PhD); political science (MA, PhD); psychology (PhD); quantitative methods in the social sciences (MA); religion (MA, PhD); Russia, Eurasia and East Europe: regional studies (MA); Russian translation (MA); Slavic cultures (MA); Slavic languages (MA, PhD); sociology (MA, PhD); South Asian studies (MA); statistics (MA, PhD); theatre (PhD). Dual-degree programs require admission to both Graduate School of Arts and Sciences and another Columbia school. *Program availability:* Part-time. *Students:* 3,030 full-time, 235 part-time; includes 861 minority (88 Black or African American, non-Hispanic/Latino; 5 American Indian or Alaska Native, non-Hispanic/Latino; 517 Asian, non-Hispanic/Latino; 159 Hispanic/Latino; 4 Native Hawaiian or other Pacific Islander, non-Hispanic/Latino; 88 Two or more races, non-Hispanic/Latino), 1,697 international. 13,288 applicants, 21% accepted, 1162 enrolled. In 2015, 1,061 master's, 553 doctorates awarded. Terminal master's awarded for partial completion of doctoral program. *Degree requirements:* For master's, variable foreign language requirement, comprehensive exam (for some programs), thesis (for some programs); for doctorate, variable foreign language requirement, comprehensive exam (for some programs), thesis/dissertation. *Entrance requirements:* For master's and doctorate, GRE General Test, GRE Subject Test (for some programs). Additional exam requirements/recommendations for international students: Required—TOEFL, IELTS. Application fee: $105. Electronic applications accepted. *Financial support:* Fellowships, research assistantships, teaching assistantships, career-related internships or fieldwork, Federal Work-Study, institutionally sponsored loans, scholarships/grants, traineeships, health care benefits, tuition waivers, and unspecified assistantships available. Support available to part-time students. Financial award application deadline: 12/15. *Unit head:* Carlos J. Alonso, Dean of the Graduate School of Arts and Sciences, 212-854-5177. *Application contact:* GSAS Office of Admissions, 212-854-8903, E-mail: gsas-admissions@columbia.edu.
Website: http://gsas.columbia.edu/

Concordia University, School of Graduate Studies, Faculty of Arts and Science, Department of Physics, Montréal, QC H3G 1M8, Canada. Offers M Sc, PhD. *Students:* 1 full-time. *Application deadline:* For fall admission, 2/1 for domestic students; for winter admission, 8/1 for domestic students. Application fee: $50. Tuition and fees vary according to course load, degree level and program. *Unit head:* Alexandre Champagne, Chair, 514-848-2424 Ext. 3264.
Website: http://www.concordia.ca/artsci/physics.html

Cornell University, Graduate School, Graduate Fields of Arts and Sciences, Field of Physics, Ithaca, NY 14853-0001. Offers experimental physics (MS, PhD); physics (MS, PhD); theoretical physics (MS, PhD). *Degree requirements:* For doctorate, comprehensive exam, thesis/dissertation. *Entrance requirements:* For doctorate, GRE General Test, GRE Subject Test (physics), 3 letters of recommendation. Additional exam requirements/recommendations for international students: Required—TOEFL (minimum score 620 paper-based; 105 iBT). Electronic applications accepted. *Faculty research:* Experimental condensed matter physics, theoretical condensed matter physics, experimental high energy particle physics, theoretical particle physics and field theory, theoretical astrophysics.

Creighton University, Graduate School, College of Arts and Sciences, Program in Physics, Omaha, NE 68178-0001. Offers MS. *Program availability:* Part-time. *Faculty:* 11 full-time (2 women). *Students:* 10 full-time (1 woman), 1 part-time (0 women), 3 international. Average age 27. 22 applicants, 59% accepted, 5 enrolled. In 2015, 2 master's awarded. *Degree requirements:* For master's, comprehensive exam, thesis (for some programs). *Entrance requirements:* For master's, GRE General Test, 3 letters of recommendation. Additional exam requirements/recommendations for international students: Required—TOEFL (minimum score 90 iBT). *Application deadline:* For fall admission, 3/1 for domestic and international students. Applications are processed on a rolling basis. Application fee: $50. Electronic applications accepted. *Expenses: Tuition, area resident:* Full-time $14,400; part-time $800 per credit hour. *Required fees:* $158 per semester. Tuition and fees vary according to course load, campus/location, program, reciprocity agreements and student's religious affiliation. *Financial support:* In 2015–16, 8 students received support, including 8 teaching assistantships with full tuition reimbursements available (averaging $11,865 per year). Financial award applicants required to submit FAFSA. *Unit head:* Dr. Michael Nichols, Chair, 402-280-2159, E-mail: mnichols@creighton.edu. *Application contact:* Lindsay Johnson, Director of Graduate and Adult Recruitment, 402-280-2703, Fax: 402-280-2423, E-mail: gradschool@creighton.edu.

Dalhousie University, Faculty of Science, Department of Physics and Atmospheric Science, Halifax, NS B3H 4R2, Canada. Offers M Sc, PhD. *Degree requirements:* For master's, thesis; for doctorate, thesis/dissertation. *Entrance requirements:* Additional exam requirements/recommendations for international students: Required—TOEFL, IELTS, CANTEST, CAEL, or Michigan English Language Assessment Battery. Electronic applications accepted. *Faculty research:* Applied, experimental, and solid-state physics.

Dartmouth College, Arts and Sciences Graduate Programs, Department of Physics and Astronomy, Hanover, NH 03755. Offers PhD. *Faculty:* 21 full-time (4 women), 4 part-time/adjunct (0 women). *Students:* 52 full-time (18 women); includes 3 minority (1 Asian, non-Hispanic/Latino; 1 Hispanic/Latino; 1 Two or more races, non-Hispanic/Latino), 24 international. Average age 26. 114 applicants, 27% accepted, 9 enrolled. In 2015, 7 doctorates awarded. *Degree requirements:* For doctorate, thesis/dissertation. *Entrance requirements:* For doctorate, GRE General Test, GRE Subject Test. Additional exam requirements/recommendations for international students: Required—TOEFL. *Application deadline:* For fall admission, 1/15 for domestic students. Application fee: $50. Electronic applications accepted. *Expenses: Tuition, area resident:* Full-time $48,120. *Required fees:* $296. One-time fee: $50 full-time. *Financial support:* Research assistantships with full tuition reimbursements, teaching assistantships with full tuition reimbursements, and scholarships/grants available. *Faculty research:* Matter physics, plasma and beam physics, space physics, astronomy, cosmology. *Unit head:* James W. LaBelle, Chair, 603-646-2973, Fax: 603-646-1446. *Application contact:* Judy Lowell, Administrative Assistant, 603-646-2359, Fax: 603-646-1446.
Website: http://www.dartmouth.edu/~physics/

Delaware State University, Graduate Programs, Department of Physics, Dover, DE 19901-2277. Offers applied optics (MS); optics (PhD); physics (MS); physics teaching (MS). *Program availability:* Part-time, evening/weekend. *Entrance requirements:* For master's, minimum GPA of 3.0 in major, 2.75 overall. Additional exam requirements/recommendations for international students: Required—TOEFL. Electronic applications accepted. *Faculty research:* Thermal properties of solids, nuclear physics, radiation damage in solids.

DePaul University, College of Science and Health, Chicago, IL 60614. Offers applied mathematics (MS); applied statistics (MS); biological sciences (MA, MS); chemistry (MS); mathematics education (MA); mathematics for teaching (MS); nursing (MS); nursing practice (DNP); physics (MS); psychology (MS); pure mathematics (MS); science education (MS); MA/PhD. Electronic applications accepted.

Drexel University, College of Arts and Sciences, Department of Physics, Philadelphia, PA 19104-2875. Offers MS, PhD. Terminal master's awarded for partial completion of doctoral program. *Degree requirements:* For doctorate, thesis/dissertation. *Entrance requirements:* For master's and doctorate, GRE. Additional exam requirements/recommendations for international students: Required—TOEFL. Electronic applications accepted. *Faculty research:* Nuclear structure, mesoscale meteorology, numerical astrophysics, numerical weather prediction, earth energy radiation budget.

Duke University, Graduate School, Department of Physics, Durham, NC 27708. Offers PhD. *Degree requirements:* For doctorate, thesis/dissertation. *Entrance requirements:* For doctorate, GRE General Test, GRE Subject Test. Additional exam requirements/recommendations for international students: Required—TOEFL (minimum score 577 paper-based; 90 iBT) or IELTS (minimum score 7).

East Carolina University, Graduate School, Thomas Harriot College of Arts and Sciences, Department of Physics, Greenville, NC 27858-4353. Offers applied physics (MS); biomedical physics (PhD); health physics (MS); medical physics (MS). *Program availability:* Part-time. *Students:* 28 full-time (5 women), 8 part-time (3 women); includes 10 minority (4 Black or African American, non-Hispanic/Latino; 3 Asian, non-Hispanic/Latino; 1 Hispanic/Latino; 2 Two or more races, non-Hispanic/Latino), 5 international. Average age 29. 48 applicants, 60% accepted, 8 enrolled. In 2015, 6 master's, 1 doctorate awarded. *Degree requirements:* For master's, one foreign language, comprehensive exam. *Entrance requirements:* For master's, GRE General Test. Additional exam requirements/recommendations for international students: Required—TOEFL. *Application deadline:* Applications are processed on a rolling basis. Application fee: $50. *Financial support:* Research assistantships with partial tuition reimbursements, teaching assistantships with partial tuition reimbursements, and Federal Work-Study available. Support available to part-time students. Financial award application deadline: 6/1. *Unit head:* Dr. John Sutherland, Chair, 252-328-6739, E-mail: sutherlandj@ecu.edu. *Application contact:* Dean of Graduate School, 252-328-6012, Fax: 252-328-6071, E-mail: gradschool@ecu.edu.
Website: http://www.ecu.edu/cs-cas/physics/Graduate-Program.cfm#

Eastern Michigan University, Graduate School, College of Arts and Sciences, Department of Physics and Astronomy, Ypsilanti, MI 48197. Offers general science (MS); physics (MS). *Program availability:* Part-time, evening/weekend, online learning. *Faculty:* 13 full-time (2 women). *Students:* 3 full-time (1 woman), 8 part-time (2 women); includes 1 minority (Two or more races, non-Hispanic/Latino), 2 international. Average age 27. 17 applicants, 59% accepted, 10 enrolled. In 2015, 5 master's awarded. *Entrance requirements:* Additional exam requirements/recommendations for international students: Required—TOEFL. *Application deadline:* Applications are processed on a rolling basis. Application fee: $45. *Financial support:* Fellowships, research assistantships with full tuition reimbursements, teaching assistantships with full tuition reimbursements, career-related internships or fieldwork, Federal Work-Study, institutionally sponsored loans, scholarships/grants, tuition waivers, and unspecified assistantships available. Support available to part-time students. Financial award applicants required to submit FAFSA. *Unit head:* Dr. Alexandria Oakes, Department Head, 734-487-4144, Fax: 734-487-0989, E-mail: aoakes@emich.edu.
Website: http://www.emich.edu/physics/

East Stroudsburg University of Pennsylvania, Graduate College, College of Arts and Sciences, Department of Physics, East Stroudsburg, PA 18301-2999. Offers MS. *Program availability:* Part-time, evening/weekend. *Entrance requirements:* Additional exam requirements/recommendations for international students: Required—TOEFL (minimum score 560 paper-based; 83 iBT) or IELTS. Electronic applications accepted.

Emory University, Laney Graduate School, Department of Physics, Atlanta, GA 30322-1100. Offers biophysics (PhD); experimental condensed matter physics (PhD); theoretical and computational statistical physics (PhD); MS/PhD. *Degree requirements:* For doctorate, thesis/dissertation, qualifier proposal. *Entrance requirements:* For doctorate, GRE General Test, minimum GPA of 3.0. Additional exam requirements/recommendations for international students: Required—TOEFL (minimum score 600 paper-based). Electronic applications accepted. *Faculty research:* Experimental studies of the structure and function of metalloproteins, soft condensed matter, granular materials, biophotonics and fluorescence correlation spectroscopy, single molecule studies of DNA-protein systems.

Fisk University, Division of Graduate Studies, Department of Physics, Nashville, TN 37208-3051. Offers MA. *Degree requirements:* For master's, thesis. *Entrance requirements:* For master's, GRE General Test, GRE Subject Test, minimum GPA of 3.0. Electronic applications accepted. *Faculty research:* Molecular physics, astrophysics, surface physics, nanobase materials, optical processing.

Florida Agricultural and Mechanical University, Division of Graduate Studies, Research, and Continuing Education, College of Science and Technology, Department of Physics, Tallahassee, FL 32307-3200. Offers MS, PhD. *Degree requirements:* For master's, comprehensive exam, thesis optional; for doctorate, comprehensive exam, thesis/dissertation. *Entrance requirements:* For master's, GRE General Test, minimum GPA of 3.0; for doctorate, GRE General Test, minimum GPA of 3.0, letters of recommendation (2). Additional exam requirements/recommendations for international students: Required—TOEFL (minimum score 550 paper-based). *Faculty research:* Plasma physics, quantum mechanics, condensed matter physics, astrophysics, laser ablation.

Florida Atlantic University, Charles E. Schmidt College of Science, Department of Physics, Boca Raton, FL 33431-0991. Offers medical physics (MSMP); physics (MS, MST, PhD). *Program availability:* Part-time. *Degree requirements:* For master's, thesis; for doctorate, thesis/dissertation. *Entrance requirements:* For master's, GRE General Test, minimum GPA of 3.0; for doctorate, GRE General Test. Additional exam requirements/recommendations for international students: Required—TOEFL (minimum score 500 paper-based; 61 iBT), IELTS (minimum score 6). *Faculty research:* Astrophysics, spectroscopy, mathematical physics, theory of metals, superconductivity.

Florida Institute of Technology, College of Science, Program in Physics, Melbourne, FL 32901-6975. Offers MS, PhD. *Program availability:* Part-time. *Students:* 8 full-time (4 women), 8 part-time (3 women), 9 international. Average age 28. 63 applicants, 30% accepted, 6 enrolled. In 2015, 3 master's, 5 doctorates awarded. Terminal master's awarded for partial completion of doctoral program. *Degree requirements:* For master's, comprehensive exam, thesis optional, minimum of 30 credit hours; for doctorate, comprehensive exam, thesis/dissertation, oral defense of dissertation, 45 credit hours. *Entrance requirements:* For master's, 3 letters of recommendations, resume, statement of objectives, undergraduate degree in physics or related field. Additional exam requirements/recommendations for international students: Required—TOEFL (minimum score 550 paper-based; 79 iBT). *Application deadline:* For fall admission, 4/1 for international students; for spring admission, 9/30 for international students. Applications are processed on a rolling basis. Application fee: $50. Electronic applications accepted. *Expenses: Tuition, area resident:* Full-time $21,690; part-time $1205 per credit hour. *Required fees:* $500. Tuition and fees vary according to degree level, campus/location and program. *Financial support:* Research assistantships, teaching assistantships with tuition reimbursements, career-related internships or fieldwork, and tuition remissions available. Financial award application deadline: 3/1; financial award applicants required to submit FAFSA. *Faculty research:* Lasers, semiconductors, magnetism, quantum devices, solid state physics, optics. *Unit head:* Dr. Daniel Batcheldor, Department Head, 321-674-7717, Fax: 321-674-7482, E-mail: dbatcheldor@fit.edu. *Application contact:* Cheryl A Brown, Associate Director of Graduate Admissions, 321-674-7581, Fax: 321-723-9468, E-mail: cbrown@fit.edu.
Website: http://cos.fit.edu/pss/

Florida International University, College of Arts, Sciences, and Education, Department of Physics, Miami, FL 33199. Offers MS, PhD. *Program availability:* Part-time, evening/weekend. *Faculty:* 27 full-time (4 women), 14 part-time/adjunct (3 women). *Students:* 38 full-time (6 women), 2 part-time (0 women); includes 23 minority (11 Black or African American, non-Hispanic/Latino; 12 Hispanic/Latino), 17 international. Average age 30. 71 applicants, 21% accepted, 9 enrolled. In 2015, 2 master's, 4 doctorates awarded. *Degree requirements:* For master's, one foreign language, thesis; for doctorate, one foreign language, comprehensive exam, thesis/dissertation. *Entrance requirements:* For master's and doctorate, GRE General Test, 2 letters of recommendation. Additional exam requirements/recommendations for international students: Required—TOEFL (minimum score 550 paper-based; 80 iBT). *Application deadline:* For fall admission, 6/1 for domestic students, 4/1 for international students; for spring admission, 10/1 for domestic students, 9/1 for international students. Applications are processed on a rolling basis. Application fee: $30. Electronic applications accepted. *Expenses:* Tuition, state resident: full-time $10,708; part-time $455.64 per credit hour. Tuition, nonresident: full-time $23,816; part-time $1001.69 per credit hour. *Required fees:* $390; $195 per semester. Tuition and fees vary according to program. *Financial support:* Institutionally sponsored loans and scholarships/grants available. Financial award application deadline: 3/1; financial award applicants required to submit FAFSA. *Faculty research:* Molecular collision processes (molecular beams), biophysical optics. *Unit head:* Dr. Bernard Gerstman, Chair, 305-348-3115, E-mail: gerstman@fiu.edu. *Application contact:* Nanett Rojas, Manager Admissions Operations, 305-348-7464, Fax: 305-348-7441, E-mail: gradadm@fiu.edu.

Florida State University, The Graduate School, College of Arts and Sciences, Department of Physics, Tallahassee, FL 32306. Offers MS, PhD. *Faculty:* 47 full-time (5 women). *Students:* 150 full-time (43 women); includes 22 minority (1 Black or African American, non-Hispanic/Latino; 3 Asian, non-Hispanic/Latino; 7 Hispanic/Latino; 1 Native Hawaiian or other Pacific Islander, non-Hispanic/Latino; 10 Two or more races, non-Hispanic/Latino), 70 international. Average age 28. 275 applicants, 16% accepted, 25 enrolled. In 2015, 36 master's, 16 doctorates awarded. *Degree requirements:* For doctorate, comprehensive exam, thesis/dissertation. *Entrance requirements:* For master's and doctorate, GRE General Test, minimum GPA of 3.0. Additional exam requirements/recommendations for international students: Required—TOEFL (minimum score 550 paper-based; 80 iBT). *Application deadline:* For fall admission, 4/15 for domestic and international students. Application fee: $30. Electronic applications accepted. *Expenses:* Contact institution. *Financial support:* In 2015–16, 150 students received support, including 4 fellowships (averaging $3,000 per year), 125 research assistantships with full tuition reimbursements available (averaging $24,900 per year), 25 teaching assistantships with full tuition reimbursements available (averaging $21,900 per year); career-related internships or fieldwork, Federal Work-Study, scholarships/grants, and health care benefits also available. Financial award application deadline: 1/

15; financial award applicants required to submit FAFSA. *Faculty research:* High energy physics, computational physics, biophysics, condensed matter physics, nuclear physics, astrophysics. *Total annual research expenditures:* $4.1 million. *Unit head:* Dr. Horst Wahl, Chairman, 850-644-2836, Fax: 850-644-8630, E-mail: wahl@hep.fsu.edu. *Application contact:* Jonathan D. Henry, Graduate Student Affairs Coordinator, 850-644-4473, Fax: 850-644-8630, E-mail: jdhenry@physics.fsu.edu.
Website: http://www.physics.fsu.edu/

Florida State University, The Graduate School, College of Arts and Sciences, Department of Scientific Computing, Tallahassee, FL 32306-4120. Offers computational science (MS, PhD), including atmospheric science (PhD), biochemistry (PhD), biological science (PhD), computational science (PhD), geological science (PhD), materials science (PhD), physics (PhD). *Program availability:* Part-time. *Faculty:* 14 full-time (2 women). *Students:* 32 full-time (4 women), 7 part-time (1 woman); includes 14 minority (9 Asian, non-Hispanic/Latino; 3 Hispanic/Latino; 2 Two or more races, non-Hispanic/Latino). Average age 27. 28 applicants, 43% accepted, 7 enrolled. In 2015, 9 master's, 7 doctorates awarded. *Degree requirements:* For master's, thesis (for some programs); for doctorate, comprehensive exam, thesis/dissertation. *Entrance requirements:* For master's and doctorate, GRE General Test, knowledge of at least one object-oriented computing language, 3 letters of recommendation, resume, statement of purpose. Additional exam requirements/recommendations for international students: Required—TOEFL (minimum score 550 paper-based; 80 iBT). *Application deadline:* For fall admission, 1/15 for domestic and international students. Application fee: $30. Electronic applications accepted. *Expenses: Tuition, area resident:* Full-time $7263; part-time $403.50 per credit hour. Tuition, nonresident: full-time $18,087; part-time $1004.85 per credit hour. *Required fees:* $1365; $75.81 per credit hour. $20 per semester. Tuition and fees vary according to campus/location. *Financial support:* In 2015–16, 33 students received support, including 10 research assistantships with full tuition reimbursements available (averaging $20,000 per year), 23 teaching assistantships with full tuition reimbursements available (averaging $20,000 per year); scholarships/grants and unspecified assistantships also available. Financial award application deadline: 1/15. *Faculty research:* Morphometrics, mathematical and systems biology, mining proteomic and metabolic data, computational materials research, advanced 4-D Var data-assimilation methods in dynamic meteorology and oceanography, computational fluid dynamics, astrophysics. *Unit head:* Dr. Gordon Erlebacher, Chair, 850-644-7024, E-mail: gerlebacher@fsu.edu. *Application contact:* Mark Howard, Academic Program Specialist, 850-644-0143, Fax: 850-644-0098, E-mail: mlhoward@fsu.edu.
Website: http://www.sc.fsu.edu

George Mason University, College of Science, Department of Physics and Astronomy, Fairfax, VA 22030. Offers applied and engineering physics (MS); computational science and informatics (PhD); computational techniques and applications (Certificate). *Faculty:* 47 full-time (10 women), 11 part-time/adjunct (1 woman). *Students:* 24 full-time (3 women), 27 part-time (5 women); includes 9 minority (3 Black or African American, non-Hispanic/Latino; 1 Asian, non-Hispanic/Latino; 1 Hispanic/Latino; 4 Two or more races, non-Hispanic/Latino), 11 international. Average age 31. 53 applicants, 34% accepted, 10 enrolled. In 2015, 8 master's, 4 doctorates awarded. *Degree requirements:* For master's, thesis optional; for doctorate, comprehensive exam, thesis/dissertation. *Entrance requirements:* For master's and doctorate, GRE, baccalaureate degree in related field with minimum GPA of 3.0 in last 60 credit hours; 3 letters of recommendation; expanded goals statement; resume; 2 copies of official transcripts. Additional exam requirements/recommendations for international students: Required—TOEFL (minimum score 575 paper-based; 88 iBT), IELTS (minimum score 6.5), PTE (minimum score 59). Application fee: $75 ($80 for international students). Electronic applications accepted. *Financial support:* In 2015–16, 39 students received support, including 1 fellowship (averaging $8,000 per year), 17 research assistantships with tuition reimbursements available (averaging $17,848 per year), 5 teaching assistantships with tuition reimbursements available (averaging $17,000 per year); career-related internships or fieldwork, Federal Work-Study, scholarships/grants, unspecified assistantships, and health care benefits (for full-time research or teaching assistantship recipients) also available. Support available to part-time students. Financial award application deadline: 3/1; financial award applicants required to submit FAFSA. *Faculty research:* Particle and nuclear physics; computational statistics; astronomy, astrophysics, and space and planetary science; astronomy and physics education; atomic physics; biophysics and neuroscience; optical physics; fundamental theoretical studies; multidimensional data analysis. *Total annual research expenditures:* $3.2 million.

The George Washington University, Columbian College of Arts and Sciences, Department of Physics, Washington, DC 20052. Offers MA, PhD. *Program availability:* Part-time, evening/weekend. *Faculty:* 22 full-time (4 women), 6 part-time/adjunct (2 women). *Students:* 25 full-time (5 women), 8 part-time (1 woman); includes 3 minority (1 Black or African American, non-Hispanic/Latino; 1 Asian, non-Hispanic/Latino; 1 Two or more races, non-Hispanic/Latino), 19 international. Average age 27. 48 applicants, 48% accepted, 5 enrolled. In 2015, 1 master's, 4 doctorates awarded. *Degree requirements:* For doctorate, thesis/dissertation, general exam. *Entrance requirements:* For master's and doctorate, GRE General Test, minimum GPA of 3.0. Additional exam requirements/recommendations for international students: Required—TOEFL (minimum score 550 paper-based; 80 iBT). *Application deadline:* For fall admission, 1/15 priority date for domestic and international students; for spring admission, 10/1 priority date for domestic students, 9/1 priority date for international students. Applications are processed on a rolling basis. Application fee: $75. Electronic applications accepted. *Financial support:* In 2015–16, 24 students received support. Fellowships with full tuition reimbursements available, research assistantships, teaching assistantships with tuition reimbursements available, Federal Work-Study, and tuition waivers available. Financial award application deadline: 1/15. *Unit head:* Dr. Cornelius Bennhold, Chair, 202-994-6274. *Application contact:* Dr. Mark Reeves, Director, 202-994-6279, Fax: 202-994-3001,
E-mail: reevesme@gwu.edu.
Website: http://www.gwu.edu/~physics/

Georgia Institute of Technology, Graduate Studies, College of Sciences, School of Physics, Atlanta, GA 30332-0001. Offers MS, PhD. *Program availability:* Part-time. Terminal master's awarded for partial completion of doctoral program. *Degree requirements:* For doctorate, comprehensive exam, thesis/dissertation. *Entrance requirements:* For master's and doctorate, GRE General Test, GRE Subject Test. Additional exam requirements/recommendations for international students: Required—TOEFL (minimum score 625 paper-based; 106 iBT). Electronic applications accepted. *Faculty research:* Atomic and molecular physics, chemical physics, condensed matter, optics, nonlinear physics and chaos.

Georgia State University, College of Arts and Sciences, Department of Physics and Astronomy, Program in Physics, Atlanta, GA 30302-3083. Offers MS, PhD. *Program availability:* Part-time, evening/weekend. Terminal master's awarded for partial completion of doctoral program. *Degree requirements:* For master's, one foreign language, thesis optional; for doctorate, 2 foreign languages, comprehensive exam, thesis/dissertation. *Entrance requirements:* For master's and doctorate, GRE General Test, GRE Subject Test. Additional exam requirements/recommendations for international students: Required—TOEFL (minimum score 550 paper-based; 80 iBT). *Application deadline:* For fall admission, 7/1 for domestic and international students; for spring admission, 11/15 for domestic and international students. Applications are processed on a rolling basis. Application fee: $50. Electronic applications accepted. *Expenses:* Tuition, state resident: full-time $6876; part-time $382 per credit hour. Tuition, nonresident: full-time $22,374; part-time $1243 per credit hour. *Required fees:* $2128; $2128 per term. $1064 per term. Part-time tuition and fees vary according to course load and program. *Financial support:* In 2015–16, fellowships with full tuition reimbursements (averaging $21,000 per year), research assistantships with full tuition reimbursements (averaging $20,000 per year), teaching assistantships with full tuition reimbursements (averaging $20,000 per year) were awarded; scholarships/grants and unspecified assistantships also available. Financial award application deadline: 2/15; financial award applicants required to submit FAFSA. *Faculty research:* Experimental and theoretical condensed matter physics, nuclear physics (relativistic heavy ion collisions, proton and neutron spin, cosmic ray radiation), biophysics and brain sciences, theoretical atomic and molecular structure and collisions, physics education research. *Unit head:* Dr. Xiaochun He, Physics Graduate Director, 404-413-6051, Fax: 404-413-6025, E-mail: xhe@gsu.edu. *Application contact:* Amber Amari, Director, Graduate and Scheduling Services, 404-413-5037, E-mail: aamari@gsu.edu.
Website: http://www.phy-astr.gsu.edu/

Georgia State University, College of Education, Department of Middle and Secondary Education, Atlanta, GA 30302-3083. Offers curriculum and instruction (Ed D); English education (MAT); mathematics education (M Ed, MAT); middle level education (MAT); reading, language and literacy education (M Ed, MAT), including reading instruction (M Ed); science education (M Ed, MAT), including biology (MAT), broad field science (MAT), chemistry (MAT), earth science (MAT), physics (MAT); social studies education (M Ed, MAT), including economics (MAT), geography (MAT), history (MAT), political science (MAT); teaching and learning (PhD), including language and literacy, mathematics education, music education, science education, social studies education, teaching and teacher education. *Accreditation:* NCATE. *Program availability:* Part-time, evening/weekend, online learning. *Faculty:* 19 full-time (15 women). *Students:* 153 full-time (109 women), 174 part-time (122 women); includes 145 minority (112 Black or African American, non-Hispanic/Latino; 1 American Indian or Alaska Native, non-Hispanic/Latino; 10 Asian, non-Hispanic/Latino; 17 Hispanic/Latino; 5 Two or more races, non-Hispanic/Latino), 9 international. Average age 35. 68 applicants, 75% accepted, 38 enrolled. In 2015, 63 master's awarded. *Degree requirements:* For master's, comprehensive exam (for some programs), thesis or alternative, exit portfolio; for doctorate, comprehensive exam, thesis/dissertation. *Entrance requirements:* For master's, GRE; GACE I (for initial teacher preparation programs), baccalaureate degree or equivalent, resume, goals statement, two letters of recommendation, minimum undergraduate GPA of 2.5; proof of initial teacher certification in the content area (for M Ed); for doctorate, GRE, resume, goals statement, writing sample, two letters of recommendation, minimum graduate GPA of 3.3, interview. Additional exam requirements/recommendations for international students: Required—TOEFL (minimum score 550 paper-based; 79 iBT) or IELTS (minimum score 6.5). *Application deadline:* For fall admission, 1/15 priority date for domestic and international students; for spring admission, 10/1 for domestic and international students. Application fee: $50. Electronic applications accepted. *Expenses:* Tuition, state resident: full-time $6876; part-time $382 per credit hour. Tuition, nonresident: full-time $22,374; part-time $1243 per credit hour. *Required fees:* $2128; $2128 per term. $1064 per term. Part-time tuition and fees vary according to course load and program. *Financial support:* In 2015–16, fellowships with full tuition reimbursements (averaging $19,667 per year), research assistantships with full tuition reimbursements (averaging $5,436 per year), teaching assistantships with full tuition reimbursements (averaging $2,779 per year) were awarded; career-related internships or fieldwork, Federal Work-Study, scholarships/grants, health care benefits, tuition waivers (full and partial), and unspecified assistantships also available. Financial award application deadline: 3/15. *Faculty research:* Teacher education in language and literacy, mathematics, science, and social studies in urban middle and secondary school settings; learning technologies in school, community, and corporate settings; multicultural education and education for social justice; urban education; international education. *Unit head:* Dr. Dana L. Fox, Chair, 404-413-8060, Fax: 404-413-8063, E-mail: dfox@gsu.edu. *Application contact:* Bobbie Turner, Administrative Coordinator I, 404-413-8405, Fax: 404-413-8063, E-mail: bnturner@gsu.edu.
Website: http://mse.education.gsu.edu/

The Graduate Center, City University of New York, Graduate Studies, Program in Physics, New York, NY 10016-4039. Offers PhD. *Degree requirements:* For doctorate, thesis/dissertation. *Entrance requirements:* For doctorate, GRE General Test. Additional exam requirements/recommendations for international students: Required—TOEFL. Electronic applications accepted. *Faculty research:* Condensed-matter, particle, nuclear, and atomic physics.

Hampton University, School of Science, Department of Physics, Hampton, VA 23668. Offers medical physics (MS, PhD); nuclear physics (MS, PhD); optical physics (MS, PhD). *Degree requirements:* For master's, thesis optional; for doctorate, thesis/dissertation, oral defense, qualifying exam. *Entrance requirements:* For master's, GRE General Test; for doctorate, GRE General Test, minimum GPA of 3.0 or master's degree in physics or related field. Additional exam requirements/recommendations for international students: Required—TOEFL (minimum score 525 paper-based) or IELTS (6.5). Electronic applications accepted. *Expenses: Tuition, area resident:* Full-time $10,263; part-time $522 per credit hour. *Required fees:* $35. Tuition and fees vary according to course load and program. *Faculty research:* Laser optics, remote sensing.

Harvard University, Graduate School of Arts and Sciences, Department of Physics, Cambridge, MA 02138. Offers experimental physics (PhD); medical engineering/medical physics (PhD), including applied physics, engineering sciences, physics; theoretical physics (PhD). *Degree requirements:* For doctorate, thesis/dissertation, final exams, laboratory experience. *Entrance requirements:* For doctorate, GRE General Test, GRE Subject Test. Additional exam requirements/recommendations for international students: Required—TOEFL. *Faculty research:* Particle physics, condensed matter physics, atomic physics.

Howard University, Graduate School, Department of Physics and Astronomy, Washington, DC 20059-0002. Offers physics (MS, PhD). *Degree requirements:* For master's, comprehensive exam (for some programs), thesis (for some programs); for doctorate, comprehensive exam, thesis/dissertation, departmental qualifying exam. *Entrance requirements:* For master's, GRE General Test, bachelor's degree in physics or related field, minimum GPA of 3.0; for doctorate, GRE General Test, bachelor's or master's degree in physics or related field, minimum GPA of 3.0. Additional exam requirements/recommendations for international students: Required—TOEFL (minimum score 550 paper-based). Electronic applications accepted. *Faculty research:* Atmospheric physics, spectroscopy and optical physics, high energy physics, condensed matter.

Hunter College of the City University of New York, Graduate School, School of Arts and Sciences, Department of Physics, New York, NY 10065-5085. Offers MA, PhD. PhD

offered jointly with The Graduate Center, City University of New York. *Program availability:* Part-time. *Faculty:* 2 full-time (1 woman). *Students:* 4 full-time (2 women), 4 part-time (1 woman); includes 3 minority (1 Black or African American, non-Hispanic/Latino; 2 Hispanic/Latino). Average age 27. 3 applicants, 67% accepted, 1 enrolled. In 2015, 6 master's awarded. Terminal master's awarded for partial completion of doctoral program. *Degree requirements:* For master's, comprehensive exam or thesis. *Entrance requirements:* For master's, minimum 36 credits of course work in mathematics and physics. Additional exam requirements/recommendations for international students: Required—TOEFL. *Application deadline:* For fall admission, 4/1 for domestic students, 2/1 for international students; for spring admission, 11/1 for domestic students, 9/1 for international students. *Financial support:* In 2015–16, research assistantships (averaging $20,000 per year), teaching assistantships (averaging $9,000 per year) were awarded; Federal Work-Study, scholarships/grants, and tuition waivers (partial) also available. Support available to part-time students. *Faculty research:* Experimental and theoretical quantum optics, experimental and theoretical condensed matter, mathematical physics. *Unit head:* Godfrey Gumbs, Chairperson, 212-772-5248, Fax: 212-772-5390, E-mail: physicsinfo@hunter.cuny.edu. *Application contact:* Hyungsik Lim, Admissions, 212-772-4806, E-mail: hyungsik.lim@hunter.cuny.edu.
Website: http://www.hunter.cuny.edu/physics/

Idaho State University, Office of Graduate Studies, College of Science and Engineering, Department of Physics, Pocatello, ID 83209-8106. Offers applied physics (PhD); health physics (MS); physics (MNS). *Program availability:* Part-time. *Degree requirements:* For master's, comprehensive exam, thesis (for some programs), oral exam (for some programs); for doctorate, comprehensive exam, thesis/dissertation (for some programs), oral exam, written qualifying exam in physics or health physics after 1st year. *Entrance requirements:* For master's, GRE General Test, 3 letters of recommendation, BS or BA in physics, teaching certificate (MNS); for doctorate, GRE General Test (minimum 50th percentile), 3 letters of recommendation, statement of career goals. Additional exam requirements/recommendations for international students: Required—TOEFL (minimum score 550 paper-based; 80 iBT). Electronic applications accepted. *Faculty research:* Ion beam applications, low-energy nuclear physics, relativity and cosmology, observational astronomy.

Illinois Institute of Technology, Graduate College, College of Science, Department of Physics, Chicago, IL 60616. Offers applied physics (MS); health physics (MAS); physics (MS, PhD). *Program availability:* Part-time, evening/weekend, online learning. Terminal master's awarded for partial completion of doctoral program. *Degree requirements:* For master's, comprehensive exam (for some programs), thesis (for some programs); for doctorate, comprehensive exam, thesis/dissertation. *Entrance requirements:* For master's, GRE General Test (minimum score 295 Quantitative and Verbal, 2.5 Analytical Writing), minimum undergraduate GPA of 3.0; for doctorate, GRE General Test (minimum score 310 Quantitative and Verbal, 3.0 Analytical Writing); GRE Subject Test in physics (strongly recommended), minimum undergraduate GPA of 3.0. Additional exam requirements/recommendations for international students: Required—TOEFL (minimum score 550 paper-based; 80 iBT). Electronic applications accepted. *Faculty research:* Elementary particle physics, condensed matter, superconductivity, experimental and computational biophysics.

Indiana University Bloomington, University Graduate School, College of Arts and Sciences, Department of Physics, Bloomington, IN 47405. Offers medical physics (MS); physics (MAT, MS, PhD). *Program availability:* Part-time, online learning. Terminal master's awarded for partial completion of doctoral program. *Degree requirements:* For master's, comprehensive exam (for some programs), thesis (for some programs), qualifying exam; for doctorate, comprehensive exam, thesis/dissertation, qualifying exam. *Entrance requirements:* For master's and doctorate, GRE General Test, GRE Subject Test (physics), minimum GPA of 3.0. Additional exam requirements/recommendations for international students: Required—TOEFL (minimum score 550 paper-based; 80 iBT) or IELTS (minimum score 6.5). Electronic applications accepted. *Faculty research:* Accelerator physics, astrophysics and cosmology, biophysics (biocomplexity, neural networks, visual systems, chemical signaling), condensed matter physics (neutron scattering, complex fluids, quantum computing), particle physics (collider physics, hybrid mesons, lattice gauge, symmetries, collider phenomenology), neutrino physics, nuclear physics (proton and neutron physics, neutrinos, symmetries, nuclear astrophysics, hadron structure).

Indiana University of Pennsylvania, School of Graduate Studies and Research, College of Natural Sciences and Mathematics, Department of Physics, Program in Physics, Indiana, PA 15705-1087. Offers PSM. *Faculty:* 3 full-time (0 women). In 2015, 5 master's awarded. *Degree requirements:* For master's, thesis optional. *Entrance requirements:* Additional exam requirements/recommendations for international students: Required—TOEFL (minimum score 540 paper-based). *Application deadline:* Applications are processed on a rolling basis. Electronic applications accepted. *Financial support:* Fellowships with full tuition reimbursements available. Financial award application deadline: 4/15; financial award applicants required to submit FAFSA. *Unit head:* Dr. John Bradshaw, Graduate Coordinator, 724-357-7731,
E-mail: bradshaw@iup.edu.
Website: http://www.iup.edu/physics/grad/physics-psm/

Indiana University–Purdue University Indianapolis, School of Science, Department of Physics, Indianapolis, IN 46202. Offers MS, PhD. PhD offered jointly with Purdue University. *Program availability:* Part-time. Terminal master's awarded for partial completion of doctoral program. *Degree requirements:* For master's, thesis optional; for doctorate, thesis/dissertation. *Entrance requirements:* For master's and doctorate, GRE. Additional exam requirements/recommendations for international students: Required—TOEFL (minimum score 79 iBT). *Faculty research:* Magnetic resonance, photosynthesis, optical physics, biophysics, physics of materials.

Iowa State University of Science and Technology, Department of Physics and Astronomy, Ames, IA 50011. Offers applied physics (MS, PhD); astrophysics (MS, PhD); condensed matter physics (MS, PhD); high energy physics (MS, PhD); nuclear physics (MS, PhD); physics (MS, PhD). *Degree requirements:* For master's, thesis (for some programs); for doctorate, thesis/dissertation. *Entrance requirements:* For master's and doctorate, GRE General Test, GRE Subject Test (physics). Additional exam requirements/recommendations for international students: Required—TOEFL (minimum score 550 paper-based; 79 iBT), IELTS (minimum score 6.5). Electronic applications accepted. *Faculty research:* Condensed-matter physics, including superconductivity and new materials; high-energy and nuclear physics; astronomy and astrophysics; atmospheric and environmental physics.

Iowa State University of Science and Technology, Program in High Energy Physics, Ames, IA 50011. Offers MS, PhD. *Entrance requirements:* For master's and doctorate, GRE. Additional exam requirements/recommendations for international students: Required—TOEFL (minimum score 550 paper-based; 79 iBT), IELTS (minimum score 6.5). Electronic applications accepted.

Iowa State University of Science and Technology, Program in Nuclear Physics, Ames, IA 50011. Offers MS, PhD. *Entrance requirements:* For master's and doctorate, GRE. Additional exam requirements/recommendations for international students: Required—TOEFL (minimum score 550 paper-based; 79 iBT), IELTS (minimum score 6.5). Electronic applications accepted.

Johns Hopkins University, School of Education, Master's Programs in Education, Baltimore, MD 21218. Offers counseling (MS), including clinical mental health counseling, school counseling; education (MS), including educational studies, gifted education, reading, school administration and supervision, technology for educators; elementary education (MAT); health professions (M Ed); intelligence analysis (MS); organizational leadership (MS); secondary education (MAT), including biology, chemistry, earth/space science, English, mathematics, physics, science, social studies; special education (MS), including early childhood special education, general special education studies, mild to moderate disabilities, severe disabilities. *Program availability:* Part-time, evening/weekend, 100% online, blended/hybrid learning. *Students:* 302 full-time (241 women), 1,472 part-time (1,106 women); includes 710 minority (313 Black or African American, non-Hispanic/Latino; 6 American Indian or Alaska Native, non-Hispanic/Latino; 133 Asian, non-Hispanic/Latino; 167 Hispanic/Latino; 11 Native Hawaiian or other Pacific Islander, non-Hispanic/Latino; 80 Two or more races, non-Hispanic/Latino), 46 international. Average age 28. 1,717 applicants, 69% accepted, 904 enrolled. In 2015, 623 master's awarded. *Degree requirements:* For master's, comprehensive exam (for some programs), portfolio, capstone project and/or internship; PRAXIS II Core (for teacher preparation programs that lead to licensure). *Entrance requirements:* For master's, GRE (for full-time programs only); PRAXIS I or state approved alternative (for teacher preparation programs that lead to licensure), minimum of a bachelor's degree from regionally- or nationally-accredited institution; minimum GPA of 3.0 in all previous programs of study; official transcripts from all post-secondary institutions attended; essay; curriculum vitae/resume; letters of recommendation (3 for full-time, 2 for part-time). Additional exam requirements/recommendations for international students: Required—TOEFL (minimum score 600 paper-based; 100 iBT), IELTS (minimum score 7). *Application deadline:* For fall admission, 4/1 for domestic and international students; for spring admission, 10/1 for domestic and international students; for summer admission, 2/1 for domestic and international students. Application fee: $80. Electronic applications accepted. *Expenses:* Contact institution. *Financial support:* Applicants required to submit FAFSA. *Unit head:* Dr. Mariale M. Hardiman, Interim Dean, 410-516-7820, Fax: 410-516-6697,
E-mail: mmhardiman@jhu.edu. *Application contact:* Rhodri Evans, Director of Enrollment Services, 410-516-0741, Fax: 410-516-6697, E-mail: revans@jhu.edu.

Johns Hopkins University, Zanvyl Krieger School of Arts and Sciences, Henry A. Rowland Department of Physics and Astronomy, Baltimore, MD 21218. Offers astronomy (PhD); physics (PhD). *Degree requirements:* For doctorate, comprehensive exam, thesis/dissertation, minimum B- average on required coursework. *Entrance requirements:* For doctorate, GRE General Test, GRE Subject Test. Additional exam requirements/recommendations for international students: Required—TOEFL (minimum score 600 paper-based; 100 iBT), IELTS. Electronic applications accepted. *Faculty research:* High-energy physics, condensed-matter, astrophysics, particle and experimental physics, plasma physics.

Kansas State University, Graduate School, College of Arts and Sciences, Department of Physics, Manhattan, KS 66506. Offers MS, PhD. Terminal master's awarded for partial completion of doctoral program. *Degree requirements:* For master's, thesis; for doctorate, comprehensive exam, thesis/dissertation, preliminary exams, thesis defense. *Entrance requirements:* For master's and doctorate, BS in physics, minimum GPA of 3.0. Additional exam requirements/recommendations for international students: Required—TOEFL (minimum score 550 paper-based; 79 iBT). Electronic applications accepted. *Faculty research:* Atomic, molecular, optical physics; soft matter and biological physics; high energy physics; physics education; cosmology.

Kennesaw State University, Leland and Clarice C. Bagwell College of Education, Program in Teaching, Kennesaw, GA 30144. Offers art education (MAT); biology (MAT); chemistry (MAT); foreign language education (Chinese and Spanish) (MAT); physics (MAT); secondary English (MAT); secondary mathematics (MAT); special education (MAT); teaching English to speakers of other languages (MAT). *Program availability:* Part-time, evening/weekend. *Entrance requirements:* For master's, GRE, GACE I (state certificate exam), minimum GPA of 2.75, 2 recommendations, resume. Additional exam requirements/recommendations for international students: Required—TOEFL (minimum score 550 paper-based; 80 iBT), IELTS (minimum score 6.5). Electronic applications accepted.

Kent State University, College of Arts and Sciences, Department of Physics, Kent, OH 44242-0001. Offers MA, MS, PhD. *Program availability:* Part-time. *Faculty:* 21 full-time (5 women). *Students:* 72 full-time (18 women), 2 part-time (0 women); includes 2 minority (both Hispanic/Latino), 55 international. Average age 30. 134 applicants, 13% accepted, 8 enrolled. In 2015, 12 master's, 6 doctorates awarded. Terminal master's awarded for partial completion of doctoral program. *Degree requirements:* For master's, thesis; for doctorate, comprehensive exam, thesis/dissertation. *Entrance requirements:* For master's, GRE General Test, minimum GPA of 3.0, transcript, resume, statement of purpose, 3 letters of recommendation; for doctorate, GRE General Test, minimum GPA of 3.0, transcript, resume, goal statement, 3 letters of recommendation. Additional exam requirements/recommendations for international students: Required—TOEFL (minimum score: paper-based 525, iBT 71), Michigan English Language Assessment Battery (minimum score of 75), IELTS (minimum score of 6.0), PTE Academic (minimum score of 48), or completion of ELS level 112 Intensive Program. *Application deadline:* For fall admission, 1/31 for domestic students. Application fee: $45 ($70 for international students). Electronic applications accepted. *Expenses:* Tuition, state resident: full-time $10,864; part-time $495 per credit hour. Tuition, nonresident: full-time $18,380; part-time $837 per credit hour. *Financial support:* Research assistantships with full tuition reimbursements, teaching assistantships with full tuition reimbursements, Federal Work-Study, scholarships/grants, and unspecified assistantships available. Financial award application deadline: 2/1. *Unit head:* Dr. James Gleeson, Professor and Chair, 330-672-2246, E-mail: jgleeson@kent.edu. *Application contact:* Dr. John Portman, Associate Professor and Graduate Coordinator, 330-672-9518, E-mail: jportman@kent.edu.
Website: http://www.kent.edu/cas/physics/

Lakehead University, Graduate Studies, Department of Physics, Thunder Bay, ON P7B 5E1, Canada. Offers M Sc. *Degree requirements:* For master's, thesis or alternative. *Entrance requirements:* For master's, minimum B average. Additional exam requirements/recommendations for international students: Required—TOEFL. *Faculty research:* Absorbed water, radiation reaction, superlattices and quantum well structures, polaron interactions.

Lehigh University, College of Arts and Sciences, Department of Physics, Bethlehem, PA 18015. Offers photonics (MS); physics (MS, PhD). *Program availability:* Part-time. *Faculty:* 16 full-time (3 women). *Students:* 43 full-time (19 women), 2 part-time (1 woman); includes 2 minority (both Asian, non-Hispanic/Latino), 15 international. Average age 25. 111 applicants, 20% accepted, 11 enrolled. In 2015, 6 master's, 6 doctorates awarded. *Degree requirements:* For doctorate, comprehensive exam, thesis/

dissertation. *Entrance requirements:* For master's and doctorate, GRE General Test. Additional exam requirements/recommendations for international students: Required—TOEFL (minimum score 85 iBT). *Application deadline:* For fall admission, 2/15 for domestic and international students. Application fee: $75. Electronic applications accepted. *Financial support:* In 2015–16, 39 students received support, including 12 research assistantships with full tuition reimbursements available (averaging $27,784 per year), 26 teaching assistantships with full tuition reimbursements available (averaging $27,784 per year); fellowships also available. Support available to part-time students. Financial award application deadline: 2/15. *Faculty research:* Condensed matter physics; atomic, molecular and optical physics; biophysics; nonlinear optics and photonics; astronomy and astrophysics; high energy nuclear physics. *Total annual research expenditures:* $1.9 million. *Unit head:* Dr. Volkmar Dierolf, Chair, 610-758-3909, Fax: 610-758-5730, E-mail: vod2@lehigh.edu. *Application contact:* Dr. Joshua Pepper, Graduate Admissions Officer, 610-758-3724, Fax: 610-758-3649,
E-mail: jap612@lehigh.edu.
Website: http://www.physics.lehigh.edu/

Louisiana State University and Agricultural & Mechanical College, Graduate School, College of Science, Department of Physics and Astronomy, Baton Rouge, LA 70803. Offers astronomy (PhD); astrophysics (PhD); medical physics (MS); physics (MS, PhD).

Louisiana Tech University, Graduate School, College of Engineering and Science, Department of Physics, Ruston, LA 71272. Offers applied physics (MS). *Program availability:* Part-time. *Degree requirements:* For master's, thesis or alternative. *Entrance requirements:* For master's, GRE General Test, minimum GPA of 3.0 in last 60 hours. Additional exam requirements/recommendations for international students: Required—TOEFL. *Application deadline:* For fall admission, 8/1 for domestic students; for spring admission, 2/1 for domestic students. Applications are processed on a rolling basis. Application fee: $40. *Financial support:* Fellowships, teaching assistantships, and tuition waivers (partial) available. Financial award application deadline: 4/1. *Faculty research:* Experimental high energy physics, laser/optics, computational physics, quantum gravity. *Unit head:* Dr. Lee Sawyer, Academic Director, 318-257-4053. *Application contact:* Marilyn J. Robinson, Assistant to the Dean of the Graduate School, 318-257-2924, Fax: 318-257-4487.

Marshall University, Academic Affairs Division, College of Science, Department of Physical and Applied Science, Huntington, WV 25755. Offers MS. *Students:* 2 full-time (0 women), 3 part-time (0 women). Average age 36. In 2015, 2 master's awarded. *Degree requirements:* For master's, thesis optional. Application fee: $40. *Unit head:* Dr. Nicola Orsini, Chairperson, 304-696-2756, E-mail: orsini@marshall.edu. *Application contact:* Dr. Ralph Oberly, Information Contact, 304-696-2757, Fax: 304-746-1902, E-mail: oberly@marshall.edu.

Massachusetts Institute of Technology, School of Science, Department of Physics, Cambridge, MA 02139. Offers SM, PhD. *Faculty:* 68 full-time (7 women). *Students:* 239 full-time (44 women); includes 37 minority (17 Asian, non-Hispanic/Latino; 13 Hispanic/Latino; 7 Two or more races, non-Hispanic/Latino), 117 international. Average age 26. 821 applicants, 10% accepted, 30 enrolled. In 2015, 6 master's, 39 doctorates awarded. Terminal master's awarded for partial completion of doctoral program. *Degree requirements:* For master's, thesis; for doctorate, comprehensive exam, thesis/dissertation. *Entrance requirements:* For master's and doctorate, GRE General Test, GRE Subject Test. Additional exam requirements/recommendations for international students: Required—TOEFL (minimum score 600 paper-based; 100 iBT), IELTS (minimum score 7). *Application deadline:* For fall admission, 12/15 for domestic and international students; for spring admission, 11/1 for domestic and international students. Application fee: $75. Electronic applications accepted. *Expenses: Tuition:* Full-time $46,400; part-time $725 per credit. One-time fee: $304 full-time. Full-time tuition and fees vary according to course load and program. *Financial support:* In 2015–16, 223 students received support, including 63 fellowships (averaging $43,000 per year), 141 research assistantships (averaging $38,700 per year), 35 teaching assistantships (averaging $38,100 per year); Federal Work-Study, institutionally sponsored loans, scholarships/grants, traineeships, health care benefits, and unspecified assistantships also available. Support available to part-time students. Financial award application deadline: 4/15; financial award applicants required to submit FAFSA. *Faculty research:* High-energy and nuclear physics, condensed matter physics, astrophysics, atomic physics, biophysics, plasma physics. *Total annual research expenditures:* $97.4 million. *Unit head:* Prof. Peter Fisher, Department Head, 617-253-4800, Fax: 617-253-8554, E-mail: physics@mit.edu. *Application contact:* Graduate Admissions, 617-253-4851, Fax: 617-258-8319, E-mail: physics-grad@mit.edu.
Website: http://web.mit.edu/physics/

McGill University, Faculty of Graduate and Postdoctoral Studies, Faculty of Science, Department of Physics, Montréal, QC H3A 2T5, Canada. Offers M Sc, PhD.

McMaster University, School of Graduate Studies, Faculty of Science, Department of Physics and Astronomy, Hamilton, ON L8S 4M2, Canada. Offers astrophysics (PhD); physics (PhD). *Program availability:* Part-time. *Degree requirements:* For doctorate, comprehensive exam, thesis/dissertation. *Entrance requirements:* For doctorate, minimum B+ average. Additional exam requirements/recommendations for international students: Required—TOEFL (minimum score 550 paper-based). *Faculty research:* Condensed matter, astrophysics, nuclear, medical, nonlinear dynamics.

Memorial University of Newfoundland, School of Graduate Studies, Department of Physics and Physical Oceanography, St. John's, NL A1C 5S7, Canada. Offers atomic and molecular physics (PhD); condensed matter physics (PhD); physical oceanography (M Sc, PhD); physics (M Sc). *Program availability:* Part-time. *Degree requirements:* For master's, thesis, seminar presentation on thesis topic; for doctorate, comprehensive exam, thesis/dissertation, oral defense of thesis. *Entrance requirements:* For master's, honors B Sc or equivalent; for doctorate, M Sc or equivalent. *Application deadline:* Applications are processed on a rolling basis. Application fee: $50 Canadian dollars ($100 Canadian dollars for international students). Electronic applications accepted. *Expenses: Tuition, area resident:* Full-time $2199 Canadian dollars. *International tuition:* $2859 Canadian dollars full-time. *Financial support:* Fellowships, research assistantships, and teaching assistantships available. *Faculty research:* Experiment and theory in atomic and molecular physics, condensed matter physics, physical oceanography, theoretical geophysics and applied nuclear physics. *Unit head:* Dr. J. Lagowski, Head, 709-864-8738, Fax: 709-864-8739, E-mail: jolantal@mun.ca. *Application contact:* Dr. Stephanie Curnoe, Graduate Officer, 709-864-8888, Fax: 709-864-8739, E-mail: gradphysicsInfo@mun.ca.
Website: http://www.mun.ca/physics

Miami University, College of Arts and Science, Department of Physics, Oxford, OH 45056. Offers MS. *Students:* 24 full-time (4 women); includes 1 minority (Asian, non-Hispanic/Latino), 15 international. Average age 27. In 2015, 9 master's awarded. *Entrance requirements:* For master's, GRE (recommended), minimum undergraduate cumulative GPA of 2.75, bachelor's degree in physics or a cognate discipline. Additional exam requirements/recommendations for international students: Recommended—TOEFL (minimum score 80 iBT), IELTS (minimum score 6.5), TSE (minimum score 54). *Application deadline:* For fall admission, 1/15 for domestic and international students. Applications are processed on a rolling basis. Application fee: $50. Electronic applications accepted. *Expenses:* Tuition, state resident: full-time $12,888; part-time $537 per credit hour. Tuition, nonresident: full-time $29,022; part-time $1209 per credit hour. *Required fees:* $530; $24 per credit hour. $30 per semester. Part-time tuition and fees vary according to course load and program. *Financial support:* Application deadline: 2/15; applicants required to submit FAFSA. *Unit head:* Dr. Herbert Jaeger, Chair, 513-529-5515, E-mail: jaegerh@miamioh.edu. *Application contact:* Dr. Khalid Eid, Graduate Director, 513-529-1933, E-mail: eidkf@miamioh.edu.
Website: http://www.MiamiOH.edu/physics

Michigan State University, The Graduate School, College of Natural Science, Department of Physics and Astronomy, East Lansing, MI 48824. Offers astrophysics and astronomy (MS, PhD); physics (MS, PhD). *Entrance requirements:* Additional exam requirements/recommendations for international students: Required—TOEFL (minimum score 550 paper-based), Michigan State University ELT (minimum score 85), Michigan English Language Assessment Battery (minimum score 83). Electronic applications accepted. *Faculty research:* Nuclear and accelerator physics, high energy physics, condensed matter physics, biophysics, astrophysics and astronomy.

Michigan State University, National Superconducting Cyclotron Laboratory, East Lansing, MI 48824. Offers chemistry (PhD); physics (PhD).

Michigan Technological University, Graduate School, College of Sciences and Arts, Department of Physics, Houghton, MI 49931. Offers applied physics (MS); engineering physics (PhD); physics (MS, PhD). *Program availability:* Part-time. *Faculty:* 33 full-time, 10 part-time/adjunct. *Students:* 31 full-time (9 women), 2 part-time; includes 1 minority (Black or African American, non-Hispanic/Latino), 24 international. Average age 29. 122 applicants, 12% accepted, 7 enrolled. In 2015, 2 master's, 2 doctorates awarded. Terminal master's awarded for partial completion of doctoral program. *Degree requirements:* For master's, comprehensive exam (for some programs), thesis (for some programs); for doctorate, comprehensive exam, thesis/dissertation, qualifying exam, research proposal. *Entrance requirements:* For master's and doctorate, GRE (recommended minimum quantitative score of 156 and analytical score of 3.0), statement of purpose, personal statement, official transcripts, 3 letters of recommendation. Additional exam requirements/recommendations for international students: Required—TOEFL (recommended score 88 iBT) or IELTS. *Application deadline:* For fall admission, 3/1 priority date for domestic students, 1/15 priority date for international students; for spring admission, 10/1 priority date for domestic students, 9/1 priority date for international students. Applications are processed on a rolling basis. Electronic applications accepted. *Expenses:* Tuition, state resident: full-time $15,507; part-time $861.50 per credit. Tuition, nonresident: full-time $15,507; part-time $861.50 per credit. *Required fees:* $248; $248. Tuition and fees vary according to course load and program. *Financial support:* In 2015–16, 30 students received support, including 1 fellowship with tuition reimbursement available (averaging $14,516 per year), 7 research assistantships with tuition reimbursements available (averaging $14,516 per year), 21 teaching assistantships with tuition reimbursements available (averaging $14,516 per year); career-related internships or fieldwork, Federal Work-Study, scholarships/grants, health care benefits, unspecified assistantships, and cooperative program also available. Financial award applicants required to submit FAFSA. *Faculty research:* Atmospheric physics, astrophysics, biophysics, materials physics, atomic/molecular physics. *Total annual research expenditures:* $1.9 million. *Unit head:* Dr. Ravindra Pandey, Chair, 906-487-2086, Fax: 906-487-2933, E-mail: physics@mtu.edu. *Application contact:* Taana Kallianen, Office Assistant 4, 906-487-2087, Fax: 906-487-2933, E-mail: taana@mtu.edu.
Website: http://www.mtu.edu/physics/

Minnesota State University Mankato, College of Graduate Studies and Research, College of Science, Engineering and Technology, Department of Physics and Astronomy, Mankato, MN 56001. Offers MS. *Degree requirements:* For master's, one foreign language, comprehensive exam, thesis or alternative. *Entrance requirements:* For master's, minimum GPA of 3.0 during previous 2 years, recommendation letters. Additional exam requirements/recommendations for international students: Required—TOEFL. Electronic applications accepted.

Mississippi State University, College of Arts and Sciences, Department of Physics and Astronomy, Mississippi State, MS 39762. Offers engineering (PhD), including applied physics; physics (MS, PhD). PhD in applied physics offered jointly with College of Engineering. *Program availability:* Part-time. *Faculty:* 18 full-time (3 women). *Students:* 44 full-time (8 women), 5 part-time (1 woman); includes 4 minority (1 American Indian or Alaska Native, non-Hispanic/Latino; 2 Asian, non-Hispanic/Latino; 1 Two or more races, non-Hispanic/Latino), 38 international. Average age 30. 51 applicants, 27% accepted, 10 enrolled. In 2015, 9 master's, 5 doctorates awarded. *Degree requirements:* For master's, thesis optional, comprehensive oral or written exam; for doctorate, thesis/dissertation, comprehensive oral or written exam. *Entrance requirements:* For master's, GRE, minimum GPA of 2.75 on last two years of undergraduate courses; for doctorate, GRE. Additional exam requirements/recommendations for international students: Required—TOEFL (minimum score 477 paper-based; 53 iBT); Recommended—IELTS (minimum score 4.5). *Application deadline:* For fall admission, 7/1 priority date for domestic students, 5/1 for international students; for spring admission, 11/1 priority date for domestic students, 9/1 for international students. Applications are processed on a rolling basis. Application fee: $60. Electronic applications accepted. *Expenses: Tuition, area resident:* Full-time $7502; part-time $833.74 per credit hour. Tuition, nonresident: full-time $20,142; part-time $2238.24 per credit hour. *Financial support:* In 2015–16, 8 research assistantships with full tuition reimbursements (averaging $14,306 per year), 26 teaching assistantships with full tuition reimbursements (averaging $13,950 per year) were awarded; Federal Work-Study, institutionally sponsored loans, and unspecified assistantships also available. Financial award application deadline: 3/15; financial award applicants required to submit FAFSA. *Faculty research:* Atomic/molecular spectroscopy, theoretical optics, gamma-ray astronomy, experimental nuclear physics, computational physics. *Total annual research expenditures:* $3.2 million. *Unit head:* Dr. Mark A. Novotny, Department Head and Professor, 662-325-2688, Fax: 662-325-8898,
E-mail: man40@ra.msstate.edu. *Application contact:* Meredith Nagel, Admissions Assistant, 662-325-9077, E-mail: mnagel@grad.msstate.edu.
Website: http://www.physics.msstate.edu

Missouri State University, Graduate College, College of Natural and Applied Sciences, Department of Physics, Astronomy, and Materials Science, Springfield, MO 65897. Offers materials science (MS); natural and applied science (MNAS), including physics (MNAS, MS Ed); secondary education (MS Ed), including physics (MNAS, MS Ed). *Program availability:* Part-time. *Faculty:* 9 full-time (0 women). *Students:* 12 full-time (3 women), 6 part-time (0 women), 10 international. Average age 26. 36 applicants, 44% accepted, 7 enrolled. In 2015, 6 master's awarded. *Degree requirements:* For master's, comprehensive exam, thesis. *Entrance requirements:* For master's, GRE (MS, MNAS), minimum undergraduate GPA of 3.0 (MS and MNAS), 9-12 teaching certification (MS

Ed). Additional exam requirements/recommendations for international students: Required—TOEFL (minimum score 550 paper-based; 79 iBT), IELTS (minimum score 6). *Application deadline:* For fall admission, 7/20 priority date for domestic students, 5/1 for international students; for spring admission, 12/20 priority date for domestic students, 9/1 for international students. Applications are processed on a rolling basis. Application fee: $35 ($50 for international students). Electronic applications accepted. *Expenses:* Tuition, state resident: full-time $5500. Tuition, nonresident: full-time $10,108. *Required fees:* $1000. *Financial support:* In 2015–16, 6 research assistantships with full tuition reimbursements (averaging $10,464 per year), 11 teaching assistantships with full tuition reimbursements (averaging $10,464 per year) were awarded; Federal Work-Study, institutionally sponsored loans, scholarships/grants, and unspecified assistantships also available. Financial award application deadline: 3/31; financial award applicants required to submit FAFSA. *Faculty research:* Nanocomposites, ferroelectricity, infrared focal plane array sensors, biosensors, pulsating stars. *Unit head:* Dr. David Cornelison, Department Head, 417-836-4467, Fax: 417-836-6226, E-mail: physics@missouristate.edu. *Application contact:* Michael Edwards, Coordinator of Graduate Admissions, 417-836-5330, Fax: 417-836-6200,
E-mail: michaeledwards@missouristate.edu.
Website: http://physics.missouristate.edu/

Missouri University of Science and Technology, Graduate School, Department of Physics, Rolla, MO 65409. Offers MS, MST, PhD. *Faculty:* 19 full-time (2 women), 1 (woman) part-time/adjunct. *Students:* 32 full-time (4 women), 2 part-time (1 woman); includes 1 minority (Hispanic/Latino), 25 international. Average age 30. 16 applicants, 38% accepted, 3 enrolled. In 2015, 6 master's, 2 doctorates awarded. *Entrance requirements:* For master's, GRE (minimum score 600 quantitative, 3 writing); for doctorate, GRE (minimum score: 600 quantitative, 3.5 writing). Additional exam requirements/recommendations for international students: Required—TOEFL (minimum score 550 paper-based). Application fee: $55 ($75 for international students). Electronic applications accepted. *Expenses:* Tuition, state resident: full-time $10,536. Tuition, nonresident: full-time $27,015. Full-time tuition and fees vary according to course load. *Financial support:* In 2015–16, 13 research assistantships (averaging $1,814 per year), 8 teaching assistantships (averaging $1,814 per year) were awarded. Financial award applicants required to submit FAFSA. *Total annual research expenditures:* $11.1 million. *Unit head:* Dr. Dan Waddill, Chairman, 573-341-4797, Fax: 573-341-4715,
E-mail: waddill@mst.edu. *Application contact:* Debbie Schwertz, Admissions Coordinator, 573-341-6013, Fax: 573-341-6271, E-mail: schwertz@mst.edu.
Website: http://www.physics.mst.edu

Montana State University, The Graduate School, College of Letters and Science, Department of Physics, Bozeman, MT 59717. Offers MS, PhD. *Program availability:* Part-time. *Degree requirements:* For master's, comprehensive exam, thesis (for some programs); for doctorate, comprehensive exam, thesis/dissertation. *Entrance requirements:* For master's and doctorate, GRE General Test, GRE Subject Test (physics). Additional exam requirements/recommendations for international students: Required—TOEFL (minimum score 550 paper-based). Electronic applications accepted. *Faculty research:* Nanotechnology, gravitational wave, astronomy, photodynamic theory, diode laser development, solar radiation transfer.

Naval Postgraduate School, Departments and Academic Groups, Department of Physics, Monterey, CA 93943. Offers applied physics (MS, PhD); combat systems technology (MS); engineering acoustics (MS, PhD); physics (MS, PhD). Program only open to commissioned officers of the United States and friendly nations and selected United States federal civilian employees. *Program availability:* Part-time. *Degree requirements:* For master's, thesis; for doctorate, thesis/dissertation. *Faculty research:* Acoustics, free electron laser, sensors, weapons and effects.

New Mexico Institute of Mining and Technology, Center for Graduate Studies, Department of Physics, Socorro, NM 87801. Offers astrophysics (PhD); atmospheric physics (PhD); instrumentation (MS); mathematical physics (PhD); physics (MS). *Degree requirements:* For master's, thesis optional; for doctorate, thesis/dissertation. *Entrance requirements:* For master's, GRE General Test; for doctorate, GRE General Test, GRE Subject Test. Additional exam requirements/recommendations for international students: Required—TOEFL (minimum score 540 paper-based). *Expenses:* Tuition, state resident: full-time $5811; part-time $322.81 per credit. Tuition, nonresident: full-time $19,220; part-time $1067.79 per credit. *Required fees:* $1030. Tuition and fees vary according to course load. *Faculty research:* Cloud physics, stellar and extragalactic processes.

New Mexico State University, College of Arts and Sciences, Department of Physics, Las Cruces, NM 88003-8001. Offers space physics (MS). *Program availability:* Part-time. *Faculty:* 13 full-time (1 woman), 1 part-time/adjunct (0 women). *Students:* 35 full-time (8 women), 4 part-time (1 woman); includes 3 minority (all Hispanic/Latino), 28 international. Average age 30. 31 applicants, 26% accepted, 8 enrolled. In 2015, 3 master's, 5 doctorates awarded. Terminal master's awarded for partial completion of doctoral program. *Degree requirements:* For master's, comprehensive exam, thesis optional, written qualifying exam; for doctorate, comprehensive exam, thesis/dissertation. *Entrance requirements:* For master's and doctorate, GRE General Test, GRE Subject Test. Additional exam requirements/recommendations for international students: Required—TOEFL (minimum score 550 paper-based; 79 iBT), IELTS (minimum score 6.5). *Application deadline:* For fall admission, 2/15 priority date for domestic and international students; for spring admission, 11/1 priority date for domestic students, 9/1 priority date for international students. Applications are processed on a rolling basis. Application fee: $40 ($50 for international students). Electronic applications accepted. *Expenses:* $274.50 per credit hour for in-state students, and all students enrolled in six or fewer credits; $839.30 per credit hour for out-of-state and international students enrolled in at least seven hours. *Financial support:* In 2015–16, 35 students received support, including 14 research assistantships (averaging $21,107 per year), 19 teaching assistantships (averaging $18,836 per year); career-related internships or fieldwork, Federal Work-Study, scholarships/grants, traineeships, health care benefits, and unspecified assistantships also available. Support available to part-time students. Financial award application deadline: 3/1; financial award applicants required to submit FAFSA. *Faculty research:* Nuclear and particle physics, materials science, geophysics, applied physics. *Total annual research expenditures:* $2.4 million. *Unit head:* Dr. Stefan Zollner, Department Head, 575-646-7627, Fax: 575-646-1934,
E-mail: zollner@nmsu.edu. *Application contact:* Dr. Vassilios Papavassiliou, Graduate Program Head, 575-646-3831, Fax: 575-646-1934, E-mail: graduate-advisor@physics.nmsu.edu.
Website: http://physics.nmsu.edu

New York University, Graduate School of Arts and Science, Department of Physics, New York, NY 10012-1019. Offers MS, PhD. *Program availability:* Part-time. Terminal master's awarded for partial completion of doctoral program. *Degree requirements:* For master's, thesis (for some programs); for doctorate, one foreign language, thesis/dissertation, research seminar, teaching experience. *Entrance requirements:* For master's, GRE General Test, GRE Subject Test, bachelor's degree in physics; for doctorate, GRE General Test, GRE Subject Test. Additional exam requirements/recommendations for international students: Required—TOEFL. *Faculty research:* Atomic physics, elementary particles and fields, astrophysics, condensed-matter physics, neuromagnetism.

New York University, Steinhardt School of Culture, Education, and Human Development, Department of Teaching and Learning, New York, NY 10003. Offers clinically rich integrated science (MA), including clinically rich integrated science, teaching biology grades 7-12, teaching chemistry 7-12, teaching physics 7-12; early childhood and childhood education (MA), including childhood education, early childhood education, early childhood education/early childhood special education; English education (MA, PhD, Advanced Certificate), including clinically-based English education, grades 7-12 (MA), English education (PhD, Advanced Certificate), English education, grades 7-12 (MA); environmental conservation education (MA); literacy education (MA), including literacy 5-12, literacy B-6; mathematics education (MA), including teachers of mathematics 7-12; multilingual/multicultural studies (MA, PhD, Advanced Certificate), including bilingual education, foreign language education (MA), teaching English to speakers of other languages (MA, PhD), teaching foreign languages, 7-12 (MA), teaching French as a foreign language (MA), teaching Spanish as a foreign language (MA); social studies education (MA), including teaching art/social studies 7-12, teaching social studies 7-12; special education (MA), including childhood, early childhood; teaching and learning (Ed D, PhD). *Program availability:* Part-time. *Degree requirements:* For doctorate, thesis/dissertation. *Entrance requirements:* For doctorate, GRE General Test, interview; for Advanced Certificate, master's degree. Additional exam requirements/recommendations for international students: Required—TOEFL (minimum score 100 iBT). Electronic applications accepted. *Faculty research:* Cultural contexts for literacy learning, school restructuring, parenting and education, teacher learning, language assessment.

North Carolina Agricultural and Technical State University, School of Graduate Studies, College of Arts and Sciences, Department of Physics, Greensboro, NC 27411. Offers computational sciences (MS); physics (MS).

North Carolina Central University, College of Science and Technology, Department of Physics, Durham, NC 27707-3129. Offers MS.

North Carolina State University, Graduate School, College of Physical and Mathematical Sciences, Department of Physics, Raleigh, NC 27695. Offers MS, PhD. *Program availability:* Part-time. Terminal master's awarded for partial completion of doctoral program. *Degree requirements:* For master's, thesis (for some programs); for doctorate, thesis/dissertation. *Entrance requirements:* For master's and doctorate, GRE General Test, GRE Subject Test. Electronic applications accepted. *Faculty research:* Astrophysics, optics, physics education, biophysics, geophysics.

North Dakota State University, College of Graduate and Interdisciplinary Studies, College of Science and Mathematics, Department of Physics, Fargo, ND 58102. Offers MS, PhD. *Program availability:* Part-time. Terminal master's awarded for partial completion of doctoral program. *Degree requirements:* For master's, thesis; for doctorate, comprehensive exam, thesis/dissertation. *Entrance requirements:* Additional exam requirements/recommendations for international students: Required—TOEFL (minimum score 550 paper-based; 79 iBT). Electronic applications accepted. *Faculty research:* Biophysics; condensed matter; surface physics; general relativity, gravitation, and space physics; nonlinear physics.

Northeastern University, College of Science, Boston, MA 02115-5096. Offers applied mathematics (MS); bioinformatics (MS); biology (PhD); biotechnology (MS); chemistry (MS, PhD); ecology, evolution, and marine biology (PhD); marine biology (MS); mathematics (MS, PhD); network science (PhD); operations research (MSOR); physics (MS, PhD); psychology (PhD). *Program availability:* Part-time. *Faculty:* 216 full-time (70 women), 62 part-time/adjunct (20 women). *Students:* 517 full-time (252 women), 80 part-time (39 women). In 2015, 94 master's, 46 doctorates awarded. Terminal master's awarded for partial completion of doctoral program. *Degree requirements:* For master's, comprehensive exam (for some programs), thesis; for doctorate, comprehensive exam (for some programs), thesis/dissertation. *Entrance requirements:* For master's, GRE General Test. *Application deadline:* Applications are processed on a rolling basis. Application fee: $75. Electronic applications accepted. *Expenses:* $1,325 per credit; $1,170 per credit (for marine biology). *Financial support:* Fellowships with tuition reimbursements, research assistantships with tuition reimbursements, teaching assistantships with tuition reimbursements, career-related internships or fieldwork, scholarships/grants, health care benefits, tuition waivers (full and partial), and unspecified assistantships available. Support available to part-time students. Financial award applicants required to submit FAFSA. *Unit head:* Dr. Jonathan Tilly, Interim Dean. *Application contact:* Graduate Student Services, 617-373-4275,
E-mail: gradcos@neu.edu.
Website: http://www.northeastern.edu/cos/

Northern Arizona University, Graduate College, College of Engineering, Forestry, and Natural Sciences, Department of Physics and Astronomy, Flagstaff, AZ 86011. Offers applied physics (MS); astronomy (PhD). *Program availability:* Part-time. *Faculty:* 3 full-time. *Students:* 5 full-time. *Degree requirements:* For master's, thesis optional. *Entrance requirements:* Additional exam requirements/recommendations for international students: Required—TOEFL (minimum score 550 paper-based; 80 iBT), IELTS (minimum score 7). *Application deadline:* For fall admission, 1/15 priority date for domestic and international students. Applications are processed on a rolling basis. Application fee: $65. Electronic applications accepted. *Expenses: Tuition, area resident:* Full-time $8710. Tuition, nonresident: full-time $20,350. *Required fees:* $896. *Financial support:* Research assistantships with full tuition reimbursements, teaching assistantships with full tuition reimbursements, Federal Work-Study, scholarships/grants, health care benefits, tuition waivers (full and partial), and unspecified assistantships available. Financial award applicants required to submit FAFSA. *Unit head:* Dr. Stephen Tegler, Chair, 928-523-9382, Fax: 928-523-1371,
E-mail: stephen.tegler@nau.edu. *Application contact:* Jamie Housholder, Administrative Assistant, 928-523-8170, Fax: 928-523-1371, E-mail: astro.physics@nau.edu.
Website: http://www.physics.nau.edu/

Northern Illinois University, Graduate School, College of Liberal Arts and Sciences, Department of Physics, De Kalb, IL 60115-2854. Offers MS, PhD. *Program availability:* Part-time. *Faculty:* 18 full-time (3 women), 3 part-time/adjunct (0 women). *Students:* 29 full-time (8 women), 23 part-time (1 woman); includes 3 minority (2 Asian, non-Hispanic/Latino; 1 Hispanic/Latino), 20 international. Average age 29. 55 applicants, 44% accepted, 9 enrolled. In 2015, 6 master's, 5 doctorates awarded. Terminal master's awarded for partial completion of doctoral program. *Degree requirements:* For master's, comprehensive exam, thesis or alternative, research seminar; for doctorate, thesis/dissertation, candidacy exam, dissertation defense, research seminar. *Entrance requirements:* For master's, GRE General Test, minimum GPA of 2.75; for doctorate, GRE General Test, GRE Subject Test (physics), bachelor's degree in physics or related field; minimum undergraduate GPA of 2.75, graduate 3.2. Additional exam requirements/recommendations for international students: Required—TOEFL (minimum score 550 paper-based). *Application deadline:* For fall admission, 6/1 for domestic

students, 5/1 for international students; for spring admission, 11/1 for domestic students, 10/1 for international students. Applications are processed on a rolling basis. Application fee: $40. Electronic applications accepted. *Financial support:* In 2015–16, 18 research assistantships with full tuition reimbursements, 21 teaching assistantships with full tuition reimbursements were awarded; fellowships with full tuition reimbursements, career-related internships or fieldwork, Federal Work-Study, scholarships/grants, and unspecified assistantships also available. Support available to part-time students. Financial award applicants required to submit FAFSA. *Faculty research:* Band-structure interpolation schemes, nonlinear procession beams, Mossbauer spectroscopy, beam physics. *Unit head:* Dr. Laurence Lurio, Chair, 815-753-6470, Fax: 815-753-8565, E-mail: lluio@niu.edu. *Application contact:* Graduate School Office, 815-753-0395, E-mail: gradsch@niu.edu.
Website: http://www.physics.niu.edu/

Northwestern University, The Graduate School, Judd A. and Marjorie Weinberg College of Arts and Sciences, Department of Physics and Astronomy, Evanston, IL 60208. Offers PhD. Admissions and degrees offered through The Graduate School. *Degree requirements:* For doctorate, thesis/dissertation, qualifying exam. *Entrance requirements:* For doctorate, GRE General Test, GRE Subject Test. Additional exam requirements/recommendations for international students: Required—TOEFL. *Faculty research:* Nuclear and particle physics, condensed-matter physics, nonlinear physics, astrophysics.

Oakland University, Graduate Study and Lifelong Learning, College of Arts and Sciences, Department of Physics, Rochester, MI 48309-4401. Offers medical physics (PhD); physics (MS). *Faculty:* 6 full-time (0 women). *Students:* 10 full-time (5 women), 5 part-time (2 women); includes 3 minority (1 Black or African American, non-Hispanic/Latino; 2 Asian, non-Hispanic/Latino), 6 international. Average age 33. 28 applicants, 7% accepted. In 2015, 1 doctorate awarded. *Degree requirements:* For doctorate, thesis/dissertation. *Entrance requirements:* For master's, minimum GPA of 3.0; for doctorate, GRE Subject Test, GRE General Test, minimum GPA of 3.0. Additional exam requirements/recommendations for international students: Required—TOEFL (minimum score 550 paper-based). *Application deadline:* For fall admission, 7/15 priority date for domestic students, 5/1 priority date for international students; for winter admission, 12/1 priority date for domestic students, 9/1 priority date for international students; for spring admission, 3/15 priority date for domestic students. Applications are processed on a rolling basis. Application fee: $0. Electronic applications accepted. *Expenses:* Contact institution. *Financial support:* Fellowships, career-related internships or fieldwork, Federal Work-Study, institutionally sponsored loans, and tuition waivers (full) available. Financial award application deadline: 3/1; financial award applicants required to submit FAFSA. *Unit head:* Dr. Andrei Slavin, Chair, 248-370-3401, Fax: 248-370-3401, E-mail: slavin@oakland.edu.

The Ohio State University, Graduate School, College of Arts and Sciences, Division of Natural and Mathematical Sciences, Department of Physics, Columbus, OH 43210. Offers MS, PhD. *Degree requirements:* For master's, thesis optional; for doctorate, thesis/dissertation. *Entrance requirements:* For doctorate, GRE General Test, GRE Subject Test (physics). Additional exam requirements/recommendations for international students: Required—TOEFL (minimum score 550 paper-based; 79 iBT), Michigan English Language Assessment Battery (minimum score 82); Recommended—IELTS (minimum score 7). Electronic applications accepted.

Ohio University, Graduate College, College of Arts and Sciences, Department of Physics and Astronomy, Athens, OH 45701. Offers astronomy (MS, PhD); physics (MS, PhD). *Faculty:* 29 full-time (4 women), 3 part-time/adjunct (1 woman). *Students:* 75 full-time (15 women), 57 international. 90 applicants, 36% accepted, 7 enrolled. In 2015, 12 master's, 11 doctorates awarded. Terminal master's awarded for partial completion of doctoral program. *Degree requirements:* For master's, thesis or alternative; for doctorate, comprehensive exam, thesis/dissertation. *Entrance requirements:* For master's and doctorate, minimum GPA of 3.0. Additional exam requirements/recommendations for international students: Required—TOEFL (minimum score 600 paper-based; 100 iBT), IELTS (minimum score 7), TWE (minimum score 4). *Application deadline:* For fall admission, 1/15 priority date for domestic and international students. Applications are processed on a rolling basis. Application fee: $50 ($55 for international students). Electronic applications accepted. *Expenses:* $4,852 tuition and fees per term in-state, $8,848 out-of-state. *Financial support:* In 2015–16, 67 students received support, including 3 fellowships with full tuition reimbursements available (averaging $28,544 per year), 34 research assistantships with full tuition reimbursements available (averaging $25,991 per year), 32 teaching assistantships with full tuition reimbursements available (averaging $24,024 per year); scholarships/grants also available. Financial award application deadline: 1/15. *Faculty research:* Nuclear physics, condensed-matter physics, nonlinear systems, astrophysics, biophysics. *Total annual research expenditures:* $2.4 million. *Unit head:* Dr. David Ingram, Chair, 740-593-0336, Fax: 740-593-0433, E-mail: ingram@ohio.edu. *Application contact:* Dr. Alexander Neiman, Graduate Admissions Chair, 740-593-1701, Fax: 740-593-0433, E-mail: gradapp@phy.ohiou.edu.
Website: http://www.ohio.edu/physastro/

Oklahoma State University, College of Arts and Sciences, Department of Physics, Stillwater, OK 74078. Offers photonics (MS, PhD); physics (MS, PhD). *Faculty:* 23 full-time (4 women). *Students:* 4 full-time (2 women), 34 part-time (3 women); includes 1 minority (Two or more races, non-Hispanic/Latino), 22 international. Average age 29. 115 applicants, 15% accepted, 6 enrolled. In 2015, 2 master's, 5 doctorates awarded. *Degree requirements:* For master's, thesis; for doctorate, comprehensive exam, thesis/dissertation, oral defense of dissertation, preliminary exam, qualifying exam. *Entrance requirements:* For master's and doctorate, GRE. Additional exam requirements/recommendations for international students: Required—TOEFL (minimum score 550 paper-based; 79 iBT). *Application deadline:* For fall admission, 3/1 priority date for international students; for spring admission, 8/1 priority date for international students. Applications are processed on a rolling basis. Application fee: $40 ($75 for international students). Electronic applications accepted. *Expenses:* Tuition, state resident: full-time $3528; part-time $196 per credit hour. Tuition, nonresident: full-time $14,144; part-time $785.75 per credit hour. *Required fees:* $1895; $105.25 per credit hour. Tuition and fees vary according to campus/location. *Financial support:* In 2015–16, 7 research assistantships (averaging $21,591 per year), 39 teaching assistantships (averaging $21,415 per year) were awarded; career-related internships or fieldwork, Federal Work-Study, scholarships/grants, health care benefits, tuition waivers (partial), and unspecified assistantships also available. Support available to part-time students. Financial award application deadline: 3/1; financial award applicants required to submit FAFSA. *Faculty research:* Lasers and photonics, non-linear optical materials, turbulence, structure and function of biological membranes, particle theory. *Unit head:* Dr. John Mintmire, Department Head, 405-744-5796, Fax: 405-744-6811, E-mail: john.mintmire@okstate.edu. *Application contact:* Dr. Albert T. Rosenberger, Graduate Coordinator, 405-744-6742, Fax: 405-744-6811, E-mail: physics.grad.coordinator@okstate.edu.
Website: http://physics.okstate.edu/

Old Dominion University, College of Sciences, Program in Physics, Norfolk, VA 23529. Offers MS, PhD. *Faculty:* 22 full-time (2 women), 3 part-time/adjunct (1 woman). *Students:* 14 full-time (4 women), 33 part-time (9 women); includes 5 minority (1 Black or African American, non-Hispanic/Latino; 4 Asian, non-Hispanic/Latino), 20 international. Average age 29. 48 applicants, 46% accepted, 9 enrolled. In 2015, 6 master's, 8 doctorates awarded. Terminal master's awarded for partial completion of doctoral program. *Degree requirements:* For master's, comprehensive exam, thesis optional; for doctorate, comprehensive exam, thesis/dissertation. *Entrance requirements:* For master's, GRE General Test, BS in physics or related field, minimum GPA of 3.0 in major, 2 reference letters; for doctorate, GRE General Test; GRE Subject Test (strongly recommended), minimum GPA of 3.0; three reference letters. Additional exam requirements/recommendations for international students: Required—TOEFL (minimum score 550 paper-based, 79 iBT) or IELTS (6.5). *Application deadline:* For fall admission, 1/15 for domestic and international students. Applications are processed on a rolling basis. Application fee: $50. Electronic applications accepted. *Expenses:* Tuition, state resident: full-time $11,136; part-time $464 per credit hour. Tuition, nonresident: full-time $27,840; part-time $1160 per credit hour. *Required fees:* $64 per semester. Tuition and fees vary according to campus/location, program and reciprocity agreements. *Financial support:* In 2015–16, 39 students received support, including 27 research assistantships with tuition reimbursements available (averaging $25,500 per year), 12 teaching assistantships with full tuition reimbursements available (averaging $24,000 per year); fellowships with full tuition reimbursements available and scholarships/grants also available. Financial award application deadline: 2/15; financial award applicants required to submit FAFSA. *Faculty research:* Nuclear and particle physics, atomic physics, condensed-matter physics, plasma physics, accelerator physics. *Unit head:* Dr. Lepsha Vuskovic, Graduate Program Director, 757-683-4611, Fax: 757-683-3038, E-mail: vuskovic@odu.edu. *Application contact:* Dr. Mark Havey, Graduate Recruitment and Admissions Director, 757-683-4612, Fax: 757-683-3038, E-mail: mhavey@odu.edu.
Website: https://www.odu.edu/physics/academics/graduate

Oregon State University, College of Science, Program in Physics, Corvallis, OR 97331. Offers atomic physics (MA, MS, PhD); computational physics (MA, MS, PhD); nuclear physics (MA, MS, PhD); optical physics (MA, MS, PhD); particle physics (MA, MS, PhD); physics education (MA, MS, PhD); relativity (MA, MS, PhD); solid state physics (MA, MS, PhD). *Faculty:* 15 full-time (4 women), 1 (woman) part-time/adjunct. *Students:* 40 full-time (12 women), 4 part-time (0 women); includes 5 minority (2 Hispanic/Latino; 3 Two or more races, non-Hispanic/Latino), 13 international. Average age 28. 111 applicants, 15% accepted, 7 enrolled. In 2015, 15 master's, 3 doctorates awarded. *Entrance requirements:* Additional exam requirements/recommendations for international students: Required—TOEFL (minimum score 600 paper-based; 100 iBT). Application fee: $75 ($85 for international students). *Expenses:* Tuition, state resident: full-time $12,150; part-time $450 per credit. Tuition, nonresident: full-time $20,952; part-time $776 per credit. *Required fees:* $1572; $1443 per unit. One-time fee: $350. Tuition and fees vary according to course load, campus/location and program. *Financial support:* Application deadline: 1/15. *Unit head:* Dr. Heidi Schellman, Professor and Department Head. *Application contact:* Kelly Carter, Graduate Student Support, 541-737-1674, E-mail: gradinfo@physics.oregonstate.edu.
Website: http://www.physics.oregonstate.edu/

Pace University, School of Education, New York, NY 10038. Offers adolescent education (MST), including biology, business education, chemistry, earth science, English, foreign languages, mathematics, physics, social studies, visual arts; childhood education (MST); early childhood development, learning and intervention (MST); educational technology studies (MS); inclusive adolescent education (MST), including biology, business education, chemistry, earth science, English, foreign languages, mathematics, physics, social studies, visual arts; integrated instruction for educational technology (Certificate); integrated instruction for literacy and technology (Certificate); literacy (MS Ed); special education (MS Ed). *Accreditation:* NCATE. *Program availability:* Part-time, evening/weekend. *Faculty:* 19 full-time (13 women), 86 part-time/adjunct (49 women). *Students:* 112 full-time (95 women), 432 part-time (306 women); includes 179 minority (89 Black or African American, non-Hispanic/Latino; 1 American Indian or Alaska Native, non-Hispanic/Latino; 24 Asian, non-Hispanic/Latino; 55 Hispanic/Latino; 10 Two or more races, non-Hispanic/Latino), 9 international. Average age 30. 181 applicants, 78% accepted, 72 enrolled. In 2015, 261 master's, 11 other advanced degrees awarded. *Degree requirements:* For master's, internship. *Entrance requirements:* For master's, interview, teaching certificate. Additional exam requirements/recommendations for international students: Required—TOEFL (minimum score 88 iBT), IELTS or PTE. *Application deadline:* For fall admission, 8/1 priority date for domestic students, 6/1 for international students; for spring admission, 12/1 priority date for domestic students, 10/1 for international students. Applications are processed on a rolling basis. Application fee: $70. Electronic applications accepted. *Expenses:* Contact institution. *Financial support:* In 2015–16, 17 students received support, including 17 research assistantships with partial tuition reimbursements available (averaging $6,020 per year); career-related internships or fieldwork and Federal Work-Study also available. Financial award application deadline: 2/15; financial award applicants required to submit FAFSA. *Faculty research:* STEM education, TESOL, teacher education, special education, language and literary development. *Total annual research expenditures:* $290,153. *Unit head:* Dr. Xiao-Lei Wang, Dean, School of Education, 914-773-3876, E-mail: xwang@pace.edu. *Application contact:* Susan Ford-Goldschein, Director of Graduate Admissions, 212-346-1531, Fax: 212-346-1585, E-mail: graduateadmission@pace.edu.
Website: http://www.pace.edu/school-of-education

Penn State University Park, Graduate School, Eberly College of Science, Department of Physics, University Park, PA 16802. Offers physics (M Ed, MS, PhD). *Unit head:* Dr. Douglas R. Cavener, Dean, 814-865-9591, Fax: 814-865-3634. *Application contact:* Lori Stania, Director, Graduate Student Services, 814-865-1795, Fax: 814-863-4627, E-mail: l-gswww@lists.psu.edu.
Website: http://www.phys.psu.edu/

Pittsburg State University, Graduate School, College of Arts and Sciences, Department of Physics, Pittsburg, KS 66762. Offers physics (MS). *Students:* 10 (2 women), 6 international. In 2015, 4 master's awarded. *Degree requirements:* For master's, thesis or alternative. *Entrance requirements:* Additional exam requirements/recommendations for international students: Required—TOEFL (minimum score 520 paper-based; 68 iBT), IELTS (minimum score 6), PTE (minimum score 47). *Application deadline:* For fall admission, 6/1 for international students; for spring admission, 10/15 for international students; for summer admission, 4/1 for international students. Applications are processed on a rolling basis. Application fee: $35 ($60 for international students). Electronic applications accepted. *Expenses:* $305 per credit hour for residents; $711 per credit hour for non-residents. *Financial support:* In 2015–16, 4 teaching assistantships with full tuition reimbursements (averaging $8,000 per year) were awarded; career-related internships or fieldwork, Federal Work-Study, and unspecified assistantships also available. Financial award application deadline: 2/1; financial award applicants required to submit FAFSA. *Unit head:* Dr. David Kuehn, Chairperson, 620-235-4391, E-mail: dkuehn@pittstate.edu. *Application contact:* Lisa

Allen, Assistant Director, 620-235-4223, Fax: 620-235-4219, E-mail: lallen@pittstate.edu.

Portland State University, Graduate Studies, College of Liberal Arts and Sciences, Department of Physics, Portland, OR 97207-0751. Offers MA, MS, PhD. *Program availability:* Part-time. *Faculty:* 18 full-time (3 women). *Students:* 31 full-time (4 women), 12 part-time (1 woman); includes 4 minority (2 Hispanic/Latino; 2 Two or more races, non-Hispanic/Latino), 4 international. Average age 32. 66 applicants, 41% accepted, 12 enrolled. In 2015, 3 master's awarded. *Degree requirements:* For master's, variable foreign language requirement, thesis, oral exam, written report; for doctorate, thesis/dissertation. *Entrance requirements:* For master's, GRE General Test, minimum GPA of 3.0 in upper-division course work or 2.75 overall, 2 letters of recommendation. Additional exam requirements/recommendations for international students: Required—TOEFL (minimum score 550 paper-based). *Application deadline:* For fall admission, 3/15 priority date for domestic students, 3/15 for international students; for winter admission, 11/1 for domestic and international students; for spring admission, 1/15 for domestic and international students. Applications are processed on a rolling basis. Application fee: $50. *Expenses:* $11,490 per year. *Financial support:* In 2015–16, 1 research assistantship with full tuition reimbursement (averaging $5,000 per year), 18 teaching assistantships with tuition reimbursements (averaging $9,222 per year) were awarded; career-related internships or fieldwork, Federal Work-Study, and unspecified assistantships also available. Support available to part-time students. Financial award application deadline: 3/1; financial award applicants required to submit FAFSA. *Faculty research:* Statistical physics, membrane biophysics, low-temperature physics, electron microscopy, atmospheric physics. *Total annual research expenditures:* $616,278. *Unit head:* Dr. John L. Freeouf, Chair, 503-725-9876, Fax: 503-725-3815, E-mail: jfreeouf@pdx.edu. *Application contact:* Dr. Erik Sanchez, Professor, 503-725-3819, Fax: 503-725-3815, E-mail: esanchez@pdx.edu.
Website: http://www.pdx.edu/physics/

Princeton University, Graduate School, Department of Physics, Princeton, NJ 08544-1019. Offers PhD. *Degree requirements:* For doctorate, thesis/dissertation, qualifying exam. *Entrance requirements:* For doctorate, GRE General Test, GRE Subject Test. Additional exam requirements/recommendations for international students: Required—TOEFL (minimum score 600 paper-based). Electronic applications accepted.

Purdue University, Graduate School, College of Science, Department of Physics, West Lafayette, IN 47907. Offers MS, PhD. *Program availability:* Part-time. Terminal master's awarded for partial completion of doctoral program. *Degree requirements:* For master's, thesis optional, qualifying exam; for doctorate, thesis/dissertation, qualifying exam. *Entrance requirements:* For master's and doctorate, GRE General Test, GRE Subject Test (physics), minimum undergraduate GPA of 3.0 or equivalent. Additional exam requirements/recommendations for international students: Required—TOEFL (minimum score 550 paper-based; 77 iBT); Recommended—TWE. Electronic applications accepted. *Faculty research:* Solid-state, elementary particle, and nuclear physics; biological physics; acoustics; astrophysics.

Queens College of the City University of New York, Mathematics and Natural Sciences Division, Department of Physics, Flushing, NY 11367-1597. Offers physics (MA). *Program availability:* Part-time. *Faculty:* 12 full-time (1 woman), 11 part-time/adjunct (0 women). *Students:* 4 full-time (0 women), 24 part-time (12 women); includes 8 minority (2 Black or African American, non-Hispanic/Latino; 4 Asian, non-Hispanic/Latino; 2 Hispanic/Latino), 13 international. Average age 30. 18 applicants, 83% accepted, 12 enrolled. In 2015, 2 master's awarded. *Degree requirements:* For master's, comprehensive exam. *Entrance requirements:* For master's, previous course work in calculus, minimum GPA of 3.0. Additional exam requirements/recommendations for international students: Required—TOEFL (minimum score 61 iBT), IELTS (minimum score 5). *Application deadline:* For fall admission, 4/1 for domestic students; for spring admission, 11/1 for domestic students. Applications are processed on a rolling basis. Application fee: $125. Electronic applications accepted. *Expenses:* Tuition, state resident: full-time $5065; part-time $425 per credit. Tuition, nonresident: part-time $780 per credit. *Required fees:* $522. Part-time tuition and fees vary according to course load and program. *Financial support:* Career-related internships or fieldwork, Federal Work-Study, institutionally sponsored loans, and tuition waivers (partial) available. Support available to part-time students. Financial award application deadline: 4/1; financial award applicants required to submit FAFSA. *Unit head:* Dr. Alexander Lisyansky, Chairperson, 718-997-3350, E-mail: alexander.lisyansky@qc.cuny.edu.

Queen's University at Kingston, School of Graduate Studies, Faculty of Arts and Sciences, Department of Physics, Kingston, ON K7L 3N6, Canada. Offers M Sc, M Sc Eng, PhD. *Program availability:* Part-time. *Degree requirements:* For master's, thesis; for doctorate, comprehensive exam, thesis/dissertation. *Entrance requirements:* For master's, first or upper second class honours in Physics; for doctorate, M Sc or M Sc Eng. Additional exam requirements/recommendations for international students: Required—TOEFL (minimum score 550 paper-based). *Faculty research:* Theoretical physics, astronomy and astrophysics, subatomic, condensed matter, applied and engineering.

Rensselaer Polytechnic Institute, Graduate School, School of Science, Department of Physics, Applied Physics and Astronomy, Troy, NY 12180-3590. Offers MS, PhD. *Faculty:* 29 full-time (5 women), 2 part-time/adjunct (1 woman). *Students:* 53 full-time (4 women), 3 part-time (0 women); includes 4 minority (1 Black or African American, non-Hispanic/Latino; 1 Hispanic/Latino; 2 Two or more races, non-Hispanic/Latino), 13 international. Average age 25. 117 applicants, 40% accepted, 19 enrolled. In 2015, 12 master's, 11 doctorates awarded. *Degree requirements:* For doctorate, thesis/dissertation. *Entrance requirements:* For master's and doctorate, GRE General Test, GRE Subject Test (physics). Additional exam requirements/recommendations for international students: Required—TOEFL (minimum score 600 paper-based; 100 iBT), IELTS (minimum score 7), PTE (minimum score 68). *Application deadline:* For fall admission, 1/1 priority date for domestic and international students; for spring admission, 8/15 priority date for domestic and international students. Applications are processed on a rolling basis. Application fee: $75. Electronic applications accepted. *Financial support:* In 2015–16, 44 students received support, including research assistantships (averaging $18,500 per year), teaching assistantships (averaging $18,500 per year); fellowships also available. Financial award application deadline: 1/1. *Faculty research:* Astronomy and astrophysics, biological physics, condensed matter physics, optical physics, particle physics, stochastic dynamic on complex networks. *Total annual research expenditures:* $9.7 million. *Unit head:* Dr. Joel Giedt, Graduate Program Director, 518-276-6455, E-mail: giedtj@rpi.edu. *Application contact:* Office of Graduate Admissions, 518-276-6216, E-mail: gradadmissions@rpi.edu.
Website: http://www.rpi.edu/dept/phys/graduate/index.html

Rice University, Graduate Programs, Wiess School of Natural Sciences, Department of Physics and Astronomy, Houston, TX 77251-1892. Offers nanoscale physics (MS); physics and astronomy (PhD); science teaching (MST). *Program availability:* Part-time. *Degree requirements:* For master's, thesis (for some programs); for doctorate, thesis/dissertation, minimum B average. *Entrance requirements:* For master's, GRE General Test; for doctorate, GRE General Test, GRE Subject Test. Additional exam requirements/recommendations for international students: Required—TOEFL (minimum score 600 paper-based; 90 iBT). Electronic applications accepted. *Faculty research:* Optical physics; ultra cold atoms; membrane electr-statics, peptides, proteins and lipids; solar astrophysics; stellar activity; magnetic fields; young stars.

Rice University, Graduate Programs, Wiess School–Professional Science Master's Programs, Professional Master's Program in Nanoscale Physics, Houston, TX 77251-1892. Offers MS. *Degree requirements:* For master's, internship. *Entrance requirements:* For master's, GRE General Test, bachelor's degree in physics and related field, 4 letters of recommendation. Additional exam requirements/recommendations for international students: Required—TOEFL (minimum score 600 paper-based; 90 iBT). Electronic applications accepted. *Faculty research:* Atomic, molecular, and applied physics, surface and condensed matter physics.

Royal Military College of Canada, Division of Graduate Studies and Research, Science Division, Department of Physics, Kingston, ON K7K 7B4, Canada. Offers M Sc. *Degree requirements:* For master's, thesis. *Entrance requirements:* For master's, honour's degree with second-class standing. Electronic applications accepted.

Rutgers University–New Brunswick, Graduate School-New Brunswick, Department of Physics and Astronomy, Piscataway, NJ 08854-8097. Offers astronomy (MS, PhD); biophysics (PhD); condensed matter physics (MS, PhD); elementary particle physics (MS, PhD); intermediate energy nuclear physics (MS); nuclear physics (MS, PhD); physics (MST); surface science (PhD); theoretical physics (MS, PhD). *Program availability:* Part-time. Terminal master's awarded for partial completion of doctoral program. *Degree requirements:* For master's, comprehensive exam, thesis or alternative; for doctorate, comprehensive exam, thesis/dissertation. *Entrance requirements:* For master's and doctorate, GRE General Test, GRE Subject Test. Additional exam requirements/recommendations for international students: Required—TOEFL (minimum score 560 paper-based). Electronic applications accepted. *Faculty research:* Astronomy, high energy, condensed matter, surface, nuclear physics.

St. Francis Xavier University, Graduate Studies, Department of Physics, Antigonish, NS B2G 2W5, Canada. Offers M Sc. *Degree requirements:* For master's, thesis. *Entrance requirements:* For master's, minimum B average in undergraduate course work, honors degree in physics or related area. Additional exam requirements/recommendations for international students: Required—TOEFL (minimum score 580 paper-based). *Faculty research:* Atomic and molecular spectroscopy, quantum theory, many body theory, mathematical physics, phase transitions.

San Diego State University, Graduate and Research Affairs, College of Sciences, Department of Physics, Program in Physics, San Diego, CA 92182. Offers MA, MS. *Program availability:* Part-time. *Degree requirements:* For master's, thesis, oral exam. *Entrance requirements:* For master's, GRE General Test, GRE Subject Test (physics), 2 letters of recommendation. Additional exam requirements/recommendations for international students: Required—TOEFL. Electronic applications accepted.

San Francisco State University, Division of Graduate Studies, College of Science and Engineering, Department of Physics and Astronomy, San Francisco, CA 94132-1722. Offers astronomy (MS); physics and astronomy (MS). *Program availability:* Part-time. *Application deadline:* Applications are processed on a rolling basis. Electronic applications accepted. *Expenses:* Tuition, state resident: full-time $6738. Tuition, nonresident: full-time $15,666. *Required fees:* $1004 per year. *Unit head:* Dr. Maarten Golterman, Chair, 415-338-1659, Fax: 415-338-2178, E-mail: maarten@sfsu.edu. *Application contact:* Dr. Susan Lee, Graduate Advisor, 415-338-1655, Fax: 415-338-2178, E-mail: slea@sfsu.edu.
Website: http://www.physics.sfsu.edu/

San Jose State University, Graduate Studies and Research, College of Science, San Jose, CA 95192-0001. Offers biological sciences (MA, MS), including molecular biology and microbiology (MS), organismal biology, conservation and ecology (MS), physiology (MS); chemistry (MA, MS); computer science (MS); cybersecurity (Certificate); cybersecurity: core technologies (Certificate); geology (MS); marine science (MS); master biotechnology (MBT); mathematics (MA, MS), including mathematics education (MA), science; meteorology (MS); physics (MS), including computational physics, modern optics, science (MA, MS); science education (MA); statistics (MS); unix system administration (Certificate). *Program availability:* Part-time, evening/weekend. *Students:* 118 full-time (68 women), 52 part-time (25 women); includes 125 minority (5 Black or African American, non-Hispanic/Latino; 97 Asian, non-Hispanic/Latino; 23 Hispanic/Latino), 121 international. Average age 27. 1,236 applicants, 21% accepted, 171 enrolled. In 2015, 168 master's awarded. *Entrance requirements:* For master's, GRE. *Application deadline:* For fall admission, 6/29 for domestic students; for spring admission, 11/30 for domestic students. Applications are processed on a rolling basis. Application fee: $55. Electronic applications accepted. *Financial support:* Teaching assistantships, career-related internships or fieldwork, Federal Work-Study, and institutionally sponsored loans available. Support available to part-time students. Financial award applicants required to submit FAFSA. *Faculty research:* Radiochemistry/environmental analysis, health physics, radiation effects. *Unit head:* J. Michael Parrish, Dean, 408-924-4800, Fax: 408-924-4815. *Application contact:* 408-924-2480, Fax: 408-924-2477.
Website: http://www.science.sjsu.edu/

Simon Fraser University, Office of Graduate Studies, Faculty of Science, Department of Physics, Burnaby, BC V5A 1S6, Canada. Offers M Sc, PhD. *Degree requirements:* For master's, thesis; for doctorate, thesis/dissertation. *Entrance requirements:* For master's, minimum GPA of 3.0 (on scale of 4.33), or 3.33 based on last 60 credits of undergraduate courses; for doctorate, minimum GPA of 3.5 (on scale of 4.33). Additional exam requirements/recommendations for international students: Recommended—TOEFL (minimum score 580 paper-based; 93 iBT), IELTS (minimum score 7), TWE (minimum score 5). Electronic applications accepted. *Faculty research:* Biophysics and soft condensed matter, particle physics, quantum matter, superconductivity, theoretical physics.

South Dakota School of Mines and Technology, Graduate Division, Program in Physics, Rapid City, SD 57701-3995. Offers MS, PhD. *Program availability:* Part-time. *Degree requirements:* For master's, thesis (for some programs). *Entrance requirements:* Additional exam requirements/recommendations for international students: Required—TOEFL (minimum score 520 paper-based; 68 iBT). Electronic applications accepted.

South Dakota State University, Graduate School, College of Engineering, Department of Physics, Brookings, SD 57007. Offers engineering (MS). *Program availability:* Part-time. *Degree requirements:* For master's, comprehensive exam (for some programs), thesis (for some programs), oral exam. *Entrance requirements:* Additional exam requirements/recommendations for international students: Required—TOEFL (minimum score 580 paper-based). *Faculty research:* Materials science, astrophysics, remote sensing and atmospheric corrections, theoretical and computational physics, applied physics.

Physics

Southern Illinois University Carbondale, Graduate School, College of Science, Department of Physics, Carbondale, IL 62901-4701. Offers MS, PhD. *Faculty:* 9 full-time (0 women). *Students:* 5 full-time (0 women), 17 part-time (0 women); includes 4 minority (3 Asian, non-Hispanic/Latino; 1 Hispanic/Latino), 16 international. 45 applicants, 18% accepted, 4 enrolled. In 2015, 7 master's, 4 doctorates awarded. *Degree requirements:* For master's, one foreign language, thesis; for doctorate, thesis/dissertation. *Entrance requirements:* For master's, minimum GPA of 2.7; for doctorate, GRE, minimum GPA of 3.25. Additional exam requirements/recommendations for international students: Required—TOEFL. *Application deadline:* Applications are processed on a rolling basis. Application fee: $65. *Financial support:* In 2015–16, 22 students received support, including 4 research assistantships with full tuition reimbursements available, 18 teaching assistantships with full tuition reimbursements available; fellowships with full tuition reimbursements available, career-related internships or fieldwork, Federal Work-Study, institutionally sponsored loans, and tuition waivers (full) also available. Support available to part-time students. Financial award application deadline: 2/15. *Faculty research:* Atomic, molecular, nuclear, and mathematical physics; statistical mechanics; solid-state and low-temperature physics; rheology; material science. *Total annual research expenditures:* $773,352. *Unit head:* Dr. Naushad Ali, Chairperson, 618-453-1053, E-mail: nali@physics.siu.edu. *Application contact:* Suzanne McCann, Office Support Specialist, 618-453-1041, E-mail: smccann@physics.siu.edu.
Website: http://www.physics.siu.edu/

Southern Methodist University, Dedman College of Humanities and Sciences, Department of Physics, Dallas, TX 75275. Offers MS, PhD. *Program availability:* Part-time. Terminal master's awarded for partial completion of doctoral program. *Degree requirements:* For master's, thesis optional, oral exam; for doctorate, thesis/dissertation, written exam. *Entrance requirements:* For master's and doctorate, GRE General Test, GRE Subject Test (physics), minimum GPA of 3.0. Additional exam requirements/recommendations for international students: Required—TOEFL. Electronic applications accepted. *Faculty research:* Particle physics, cosmology, astrophysics, mathematics physics, computational physics.

Southern University and Agricultural and Mechanical College, Graduate School, College of Sciences, Department of Physics, Baton Rouge, LA 70813. Offers MS. *Degree requirements:* For master's, thesis. *Entrance requirements:* For master's, GMAT or GRE General Test. Additional exam requirements/recommendations for international students: Required—TOEFL (minimum score 525 paper-based). *Faculty research:* Piezoelectric materials and devices, predictive ab-instio calculations, high energy physics, surface growth studies, semiconductor and intermetallics.

Stanford University, School of Humanities and Sciences, Department of Physics, Stanford, CA 94305-9991. Offers PhD. *Degree requirements:* For doctorate, thesis/dissertation, oral exam, qualifying exam. *Entrance requirements:* For doctorate, GRE General Test, GRE Subject Test. Additional exam requirements/recommendations for international students: Required—TOEFL. Electronic applications accepted. *Expenses: Tuition, area resident:* Full-time $45,729. *Required fees:* $591.

Stephen F. Austin State University, Graduate School, College of Sciences and Mathematics, Department of Physics and Astronomy, Nacogdoches, TX 75962. Offers physics (MS). *Program availability:* Part-time. *Degree requirements:* For master's, comprehensive exam. *Entrance requirements:* For master's, GRE General Test, minimum GPA of 2.8 in last 60 hours, 2.5 overall. Additional exam requirements/recommendations for international students: Required—TOEFL. *Faculty research:* Low-temperature physics, x-ray spectroscopy and metallic glasses, infrared spectroscopy.

Stevens Institute of Technology, Graduate School, Charles V. Schaefer Jr. School of Engineering, Department of Physics and Engineering Physics, Hoboken, NJ 07030. Offers applied optics (Certificate); atmospheric and environmental science and engineering (Certificate); microdevices and microsystems (Certificate); microelectronics (Certificate); photonics (Certificate); physics (M Eng, MS, PhD). *Program availability:* Part-time, evening/weekend. *Faculty:* 25 full-time (2 women), 3 part-time/adjunct (1 woman). *Students:* 32 full-time (12 women), 9 part-time (2 women); includes 4 minority (2 Black or African American, non-Hispanic/Latino; 2 Asian, non-Hispanic/Latino), 20 international. Average age 28. 63 applicants, 48% accepted, 11 enrolled. In 2015, 3 master's, 6 doctorates, 4 other advanced degrees awarded. Terminal master's awarded for partial completion of doctoral program. *Entrance requirements:* Additional exam requirements/recommendations for international students: Required—TOEFL (minimum score 74 iBT). *Application deadline:* For fall admission, 6/1 for domestic students, 4/15 for international students; for spring admission, 11/30 for domestic students, 11/1 for international students. Applications are processed on a rolling basis. Application fee: $60. Electronic applications accepted. *Expenses: Tuition, area resident:* Full-time $32,200; part-time $1450 per credit. *Required fees:* $1150; $550 per unit. $275 per semester. *Financial support:* Fellowships, research assistantships, teaching assistantships, career-related internships or fieldwork, Federal Work-Study, scholarships/grants, and unspecified assistantships available. Financial award application deadline: 2/15; financial award applicants required to submit FAFSA. *Faculty research:* Quantum systems, nanophotonics, optics. *Unit head:* Rainer Martini, Director, 201-216-5634, Fax: 201-216-5638, E-mail: rmartini@stevens.edu. *Application contact:* Graduate Admission, 888-783-8367, Fax: 888-511-1306,
E-mail: graduate@stevens.edu.
Website: http://www.stevens.edu/schaefer-school-engineering-science/departments/physics-engineering-physics

Stony Brook University, State University of New York, Graduate School, College of Arts and Sciences, Department of Physics and Astronomy, Program in Physics, Stony Brook, NY 11794. Offers modern research instrumentation (MS); physics (MA, PhD); physics education (MAT). *Students:* 191 full-time (38 women), 2 part-time (1 woman); includes 19 minority (2 Black or African American, non-Hispanic/Latino; 11 Asian, non-Hispanic/Latino; 4 Hispanic/Latino; 2 Two or more races, non-Hispanic/Latino), 127 international. *Degree requirements:* For doctorate, one foreign language, thesis/dissertation. *Entrance requirements:* For master's and doctorate, GRE General Test. Additional exam requirements/recommendations for international students: Required—TOEFL (minimum score 90 iBT). *Application deadline:* For fall admission, 1/15 for domestic students; for spring admission, 10/1 for domestic students. Application fee: $100. *Expenses:* $12,421 full-time in-state tuition and fees, $453 per credit hour; $23,761 full-time out-of-state tuition and fees, $925 per credit hour. *Financial support:* Fellowships, research assistantships, and teaching assistantships available. Financial award application deadline: 2/1. *Unit head:* Dr. Axel Drees, Chair, 631-632-8114, Fax: 631-632-8176, E-mail: axel.drees@stonybrook.edu. *Application contact:* Donald Sheehan, Coordinator, 631-632-1046, Fax: 631-632-8176,
E-mail: donald.j.sheehan@stonybrook.edu.

Syracuse University, College of Arts and Sciences, Programs in Physics, Syracuse, NY 13244. Offers physics (MS, PhD). *Program availability:* Part-time. *Students:* Average age 26. Terminal master's awarded for partial completion of doctoral program. *Degree requirements:* For master's, thesis or alternative; for doctorate, comprehensive exam, thesis/dissertation. *Entrance requirements:* For master's and doctorate, GRE General Test, GRE Subject Test, three letters of recommendation, statement of purpose, transcripts. Additional exam requirements/recommendations for international students: Required—TOEFL (minimum score 100 iBT). *Application deadline:* For fall admission, 1/1 priority date for domestic and international students. Application fee: $75. Electronic applications accepted. *Expenses: Tuition, area resident:* Full-time $25,974; part-time $1443 per credit hour. *Required fees:* $802; $50 per course. Tuition and fees vary according to course load and program. *Financial support:* Fellowships with full tuition reimbursements, research assistantships with tuition reimbursements, teaching assistantships with tuition reimbursements, and scholarships/grants available. Financial award application deadline: 1/1. *Faculty research:* Methods of theoretical physics, classical mechanics, quantum mechanics, thermodynamics and statistical mechanics, electromagnetic theory. *Unit head:* Dr. A. Alan Middleton, Director, Graduate Studies, 315-443-2408, E-mail: aamiddle@syr.edu. *Application contact:* Tomasz Skwarnicki, Graduate Admissions Coordinator, 315-443-5973, E-mail: graduate@physics.syr.edu.
Website: http://www.physics.syr.edu/

Syracuse University, School of Education, Programs in Science Education, Syracuse, NY 13244. Offers biology (MS, PhD); chemistry (MS, PhD); earth science (MS, PhD); physics (MS, PhD). *Program availability:* Part-time. *Students:* Average age 38. In 2015, 4 doctorates awarded. *Degree requirements:* For doctorate, comprehensive exam, thesis/dissertation. *Entrance requirements:* For master's, official transcripts from previous academic institutions, 3 letters of recommendation (preferably from faculty), personal statement that makes a clear and compelling argument for why applicant wants to teach secondary science; for doctorate, GRE General Test or MAT, master's degree, interview. Additional exam requirements/recommendations for international students: Required—TOEFL (minimum score 100 iBT). *Application deadline:* For fall admission, 1/15 priority date for domestic and international students; for spring admission, 10/15 priority date for domestic and international students. Applications are processed on a rolling basis. Application fee: $75. Electronic applications accepted. *Expenses: Tuition, area resident:* Full-time $25,974; part-time $1443 per credit hour. *Required fees:* $802; $50 per course. Tuition and fees vary according to course load and program. *Financial support:* Fellowships with full tuition reimbursements, research assistantships with tuition reimbursements, teaching assistantships with tuition reimbursements, and scholarships/grants available. Financial award application deadline: 1/15. *Faculty research:* Diverse field experiences and theoretical and practical knowledge in research-based science teaching, biology, chemistry, earth science, and physics.. *Unit head:* Dr. John Tillotson, Program Coordinator, 315-443-9137, E-mail: jwtillot@syr.edu. *Application contact:* Speranza Migliore, Graduate Admissions Recruiter, 315-443-2505, E-mail: gradrcrt@syr.edu.
Website: http://soeweb.syr.edu/

Teachers College, Columbia University, Department of Mathematics, Science and Technology, New York, NY 10027-6696. Offers biology 7-12 (MA); chemistry 7-12 (MA); communication and education (MA); communications (Ed M); communications and education (Ed D); computing in education (MA); computing in education-distant learning (MA); earth science 7-12 (MA); instructional technology and media (Ed M, MA, Ed D); mathematics education (Ed M, MA, Ed D, Ed DCT, PhD); physics 7-12 (MA); science and dental education (MA); science education (Ed M, MS, Ed DCT, PhD); supervisor / teacher of science education (MA); technology specialist (MA). *Program availability:* Part-time, evening/weekend. *Students:* 134 full-time (89 women), 285 part-time (168 women); includes 219 minority (49 Black or African American, non-Hispanic/Latino; 124 Asian, non-Hispanic/Latino; 31 Hispanic/Latino; 15 Two or more races, non-Hispanic/Latino), 29 international. Terminal master's awarded for partial completion of doctoral program. *Degree requirements:* For doctorate, thesis/dissertation. *Expenses: Tuition, area resident:* Part-time $1454 per credit. *Required fees:* $428 per semester. One-time fee: $475 full-time. Full-time tuition and fees vary according to course load. *Unit head:* Dr. O. Roger Anderson, Chair, 212-678-3405, Fax: 212-678-8129, E-mail: ora@ldeo.columbia.edu. *Application contact:* David Estrella, Director of Admission, E-mail: estrella@tc.columbia.edu.
Website: http://www.tc.columbia.edu/mathematics-science-and-technology/

Temple University, College of Science and Technology, Department of Physics, Philadelphia, PA 19122. Offers MA, PhD. *Faculty:* 31 full-time (5 women). *Students:* 60 full-time (13 women), 2 part-time (0 women); includes 9 minority (1 Black or African American, non-Hispanic/Latino; 5 Asian, non-Hispanic/Latino; 1 Hispanic/Latino; 2 Two or more races, non-Hispanic/Latino), 34 international. 66 applicants, 47% accepted, 15 enrolled. In 2015, 3 master's, 7 doctorates awarded. Terminal master's awarded for partial completion of doctoral program. *Degree requirements:* For master's, comprehensive exam, thesis or alternative; for doctorate, thesis/dissertation, 2 comprehensive exams. *Entrance requirements:* For master's and doctorate, GRE General Test, minimum GPA of 3.0. Additional exam requirements/recommendations for international students: Required—TOEFL (minimum score 550 paper-based; 79 iBT). *Application deadline:* For fall admission, 7/15 for domestic students, 12/15 for international students; for spring admission, 11/15 for domestic students, 8/1 for international students. Applications are processed on a rolling basis. Application fee: $60. Electronic applications accepted. *Financial support:* Fellowships, research assistantships, teaching assistantships, and tuition waivers (full and partial) available. Financial award application deadline: 1/15; financial award applicants required to submit FAFSA. *Faculty research:* Laser-based molecular spectroscopy, elementary particle physics, statistical mechanics, solid-state physics. *Unit head:* Dr. Xiaoxing Xi, Chair, 215-204-7634, Fax: 215-204-5652, E-mail: physics@temple.edu. *Application contact:* Karen E. Woods-Wilson, Department Administrative Specialist, 215-204-4770, E-mail: karen.woods-wilson@temple.edu.
Website: http://www.temple.edu/physics/

Texas A&M University, College of Science, Department of Physics and Astronomy, College Station, TX 77843. Offers applied physics (PhD); physics (MS, PhD). *Faculty:* 54. *Students:* 167 full-time (23 women), 6 part-time (2 women); includes 22 minority (1 Black or African American, non-Hispanic/Latino; 1 American Indian or Alaska Native, non-Hispanic/Latino; 4 Asian, non-Hispanic/Latino; 12 Hispanic/Latino; 4 Two or more races, non-Hispanic/Latino), 94 international. Average age 28. 220 applicants, 29% accepted, 23 enrolled. In 2015, 7 master's, 23 doctorates awarded. Terminal master's awarded for partial completion of doctoral program. *Degree requirements:* For master's, thesis (for some programs); for doctorate, thesis/dissertation. *Entrance requirements:* For master's and doctorate, GRE General Test, GRE Subject Test. Additional exam requirements/recommendations for international students: Required—TOEFL. *Application deadline:* For fall admission, 3/1 priority date for domestic students; for spring admission, 8/1 for domestic students. Application fee: $50 ($90 for international students). Electronic applications accepted. *Expenses:* Contact institution. *Financial support:* In 2015–16, 169 students received support, including 40 fellowships with tuition reimbursements available (averaging $13,717 per year), 82 research assistantships with tuition reimbursements available (averaging $7,892 per year), 51 teaching assistantships with tuition reimbursements available (averaging $6,927 per year); career-related internships or fieldwork, institutionally sponsored loans, scholarships/grants, traineeships, health care benefits, tuition waivers (full and partial), and unspecified assistantships also available. Support available to part-time students.

Financial award application deadline: 3/1; financial award applicants required to submit FAFSA. *Faculty research:* Condensed matter, atomic/molecular, high-energy and nuclear physics, quantum optics. *Unit head:* Dr. George R. Welch, Head, 979-845-1571, E-mail: welch@physics.tamu.edu. *Application contact:* Dr. Joe Ross, Graduate Advisor, 979-845-3842, Fax: 979-845-2590, E-mail: ross@physics.tamu.edu.
Website: http://physics.tamu.edu/

Texas Christian University, College of Science and Engineering, Department of Physics and Astronomy, Fort Worth, TX 76129. Offers physics (MA, MS, PhD), including astrophysics (PhD), biophysics (PhD); PhD/MBA. *Program availability:* Part-time. *Faculty:* 8 full-time (2 women). *Students:* 15 full-time (5 women); includes 2 minority (both Hispanic/Latino), 9 international. Average age 32. 20 applicants, 30% accepted, 4 enrolled. In 2015, 3 master's, 2 doctorates awarded. Terminal master's awarded for partial completion of doctoral program. *Degree requirements:* For master's, one foreign language, comprehensive exam, thesis or alternative; for doctorate, comprehensive exam, thesis/dissertation. *Entrance requirements:* For master's and doctorate, GRE. Additional exam requirements/recommendations for international students: Required—TOEFL (minimum score 80 iBT). *Application deadline:* For fall admission, 2/1 for domestic and international students; for spring admission, 9/1 for domestic and international students. Applications are processed on a rolling basis. Application fee: $60. Electronic applications accepted. *Expenses:* Contact institution. *Financial support:* In 2015–16, 14 students received support, including 1 research assistantship with full tuition reimbursement available (averaging $23,000 per year), 13 teaching assistantships with full tuition reimbursements available (averaging $20,500 per year); scholarships/grants and unspecified assistantships also available. Financial award application deadline: 2/1. *Faculty research:* Nanomaterials, computer simulations of biophysical processes, nonlinear dynamics, spectra of local stellar populations, spectroscopy and fluorescence of biomolecules. *Unit head:* Dr. Yuri M. Strzhemechny, Associate Professor/Chair, 817-257-5793, Fax: 817-257-7742,
E-mail: y.strzhemechny@tcu.edu. *Application contact:* Dr. Peter M. Frinchaboy, III, Associate Professor, 817-257-6387, Fax: 817-257-7742, E-mail: p.frinchaboy@tcu.edu.
Website: http://physics.tcu.edu/

Texas State University, The Graduate College, College of Science and Engineering, Program in Physics, San Marcos, TX 78666. Offers MS. *Program availability:* Part-time, evening/weekend. *Faculty:* 12 full-time (3 women), 1 part-time/adjunct (0 women). *Students:* 12 full-time (1 woman), 3 part-time (1 woman); includes 4 minority (2 Black or African American, non-Hispanic/Latino; 1 Hispanic/Latino; 1 Two or more races, non-Hispanic/Latino), 1 international. Average age 29. 26 applicants, 50% accepted, 8 enrolled. In 2015, 1 master's awarded. *Degree requirements:* For master's, comprehensive exam, thesis optional. *Entrance requirements:* For master's, baccalaureate degree from regionally-accredited university with minimum GPA of 2.75 on last 60 undergraduate semester hours, statement of purpose, resume/vitae, 3 letters of recommendation. Additional exam requirements/recommendations for international students: Required—TOEFL (minimum score 550 paper-based; 78 iBT). *Application deadline:* For fall admission, 2/15 priority date for domestic and international students; for spring admission, 10/15 for domestic students, 10/1 for international students. Applications are processed on a rolling basis. Application fee: $40 ($90 for international students). Electronic applications accepted. *Expenses:* $3,615 in-state tuition for 12 semester credit hours (1 full-time semester), $974 in-state fees. *Financial support:* In 2015–16, 14 students received support, including 4 research assistantships (averaging $14,170 per year), 7 teaching assistantships (averaging $12,464 per year); career-related internships or fieldwork, Federal Work-Study, institutionally sponsored loans, scholarships/grants, health care benefits, and unspecified assistantships also available. Support available to part-time students. Financial award application deadline: 3/1; financial award applicants required to submit FAFSA. *Faculty research:* Thermal transport in diamond films electronics thermal management. *Total annual research expenditures:* $281,549. *Unit head:* Dr. Wihelmus Geerts, Graduate Advisor, 512-245-1821, E-mail: wg06@txstate.edu. *Application contact:* Dr. Andrea Golato, Dean of Graduate School, 512-245-2581, Fax: 512-245-8365, E-mail: gradcollege@txstate.edu.

Texas Tech University, Graduate School, College of Arts and Sciences, Department of Physics, Lubbock, TX 79409. Offers applied physics (MS); physics (MS, PhD). *Program availability:* Part-time. *Faculty:* 27 full-time (5 women), 2 part-time/adjunct (0 women). *Students:* 75 full-time (26 women); includes 8 minority (2 Black or African American, non-Hispanic/Latino; 1 Asian, non-Hispanic/Latino; 4 Hispanic/Latino; 1 Two or more races, non-Hispanic/Latino), 50 international. Average age 28. 57 applicants, 53% accepted, 18 enrolled. In 2015, 9 master's, 3 doctorates awarded. *Degree requirements:* For master's, variable foreign language requirement, comprehensive exam (for some programs), thesis (for some programs); for doctorate, variable foreign language requirement, comprehensive exam, thesis/dissertation, proposal presentation. *Entrance requirements:* For master's and doctorate, GRE. Additional exam requirements/recommendations for international students: Required—TOEFL (minimum score 550 paper-based; 79 iBT), IELTS (minimum score 6.5). *Application deadline:* For fall admission, 6/1 priority date for domestic students, 1/15 priority date for international students; for spring admission, 9/1 priority date for domestic students, 6/15 priority date for international students. Applications are processed on a rolling basis. Application fee: $60. Electronic applications accepted. *Expenses:* Tuition, state resident: full-time $6477; part-time $269.89 per credit hour. Tuition, nonresident: full-time $15,837; part-time $659.89 per credit hour. *Required fees:* $2751; $36.50 per credit hour. $937.50 per semester. Tuition and fees vary according to course level. *Financial support:* In 2015–16, 55 students received support, including 43 fellowships (averaging $1,904 per year), 24 research assistantships (averaging $12,122 per year), 53 teaching assistantships (averaging $16,166 per year); Federal Work-Study, scholarships/grants, health care benefits, and unspecified assistantships also available. Support available to part-time students. Financial award application deadline: 2/1; financial award applicants required to submit FAFSA. *Faculty research:* Astrophysics, condensed matter physics, nanotechnology and materials physics, high energy physics, biophysics. *Total annual research expenditures:* $3.2 million. *Unit head:* Dr. Nural Akchurin, Professor/Chair, 806-742-3767, Fax: 806-742-1182, E-mail: nural.akchurin@ttu.edu. *Application contact:* Dr. Mahdi Sanati, Graduate Recruiter, 806-834-6169, Fax: 806-742-1182,
E-mail: m.sanati@ttu.edu.
Website: http://www.phys.ttu.edu/

Trent University, Graduate Studies, Program in Applications of Modeling in the Natural and Social Sciences, Department of Physics, Peterborough, ON K9J 7B8, Canada. Offers M Sc. *Program availability:* Part-time. *Degree requirements:* For master's, thesis. *Entrance requirements:* For master's, honours degree. *Faculty research:* Radiation physics, chemical physics.

Tufts University, Graduate School of Arts and Sciences, Department of Physics and Astronomy, Medford, MA 02155. Offers astrophysics (MS, PhD); chemical physics (PhD); physics (MS, PhD); physics education (PhD). Terminal master's awarded for partial completion of doctoral program. *Degree requirements:* For master's, thesis optional; for doctorate, thesis/dissertation. *Entrance requirements:* For master's and doctorate, GRE General Test. Additional exam requirements/recommendations for international students: Required—TOEFL (minimum score 550 paper-based; 80 iBT), IELTS (minimum score 6.5). Electronic applications accepted. *Expenses: Tuition, area resident:* Full-time $48,412; part-time $1210 per credit hour. *Required fees:* $806. Full-time tuition and fees vary according to degree level, program and student level. Part-time tuition and fees vary according to course load.

Tulane University, School of Science and Engineering, Department of Physics and Engineering Physics, New Orleans, LA 70118-5669. Offers physics (PhD). *Degree requirements:* For doctorate, thesis/dissertation. *Entrance requirements:* For doctorate, GRE General Test. Additional exam requirements/recommendations for international students: Required—TOEFL. Electronic applications accepted. *Faculty research:* Surface physics, condensed-matter experiment, condensed-matter theory, nuclear theory, polymers.

Université de Moncton, Faculty of Sciences, Department of Physics and Astronomy, Moncton, NB E1A 3E9, Canada. Offers M Sc. *Program availability:* Part-time. *Degree requirements:* For master's, thesis. *Entrance requirements:* For master's, proficiency in French. Electronic applications accepted. *Faculty research:* Thin films, optical properties, solar selective surfaces, microgravity and photonic materials.

Université de Montréal, Faculty of Arts and Sciences, Department of Physics, Montréal, QC H3C 3J7, Canada. Offers M Sc, PhD. *Degree requirements:* For doctorate, thesis/dissertation, general exam. Electronic applications accepted. *Faculty research:* Astronomy; biophysics; solid-state, plasma, and nuclear physics.

Université de Sherbrooke, Faculty of Sciences, Department of Physics, Sherbrooke, QC J1K 2R1, Canada. Offers M Sc, PhD. *Degree requirements:* For master's, thesis; for doctorate, comprehensive exam, thesis/dissertation. *Entrance requirements:* For doctorate, master's degree. Electronic applications accepted. *Faculty research:* Solid-state physics, quantum computing.

Université du Québec à Trois-Rivières, Graduate Programs, Program in Physics, Trois-Rivières, QC G9A 5H7, Canada. Offers matter and energy (MS, PhD).

Université Laval, Faculty of Sciences and Engineering, Department of Physics, Physical Engineering, and Optics, Programs in Physics, Québec, QC G1K 7P4, Canada. Offers M Sc, PhD. Terminal master's awarded for partial completion of doctoral program. *Degree requirements:* For master's, thesis; for doctorate, comprehensive exam, thesis/dissertation. *Entrance requirements:* For master's and doctorate, knowledge of French, comprehension of written English. Electronic applications accepted.

University at Albany, State University of New York, College of Arts and Sciences, Department of Physics, Albany, NY 12222-0001. Offers MS, PhD. *Degree requirements:* For master's, one foreign language; for doctorate, one foreign language, thesis/dissertation. *Entrance requirements:* Additional exam requirements/recommendations for international students: Required—TOEFL (minimum score 550 paper-based). Electronic applications accepted. *Faculty research:* Condensed-matter physics, high-energy physics, applied physics, electronic materials, theoretical particle physics.

University at Buffalo, the State University of New York, Graduate School, College of Arts and Sciences, Department of Physics, Buffalo, NY 14260-1500. Offers MS, PhD. Terminal master's awarded for partial completion of doctoral program. *Degree requirements:* For master's, thesis optional; for doctorate, comprehensive exam, thesis/dissertation. *Entrance requirements:* For master's and doctorate, GRE General Test, GRE Subject Test (physics), undergraduate degree, letters of recommendation, statement of purpose. Additional exam requirements/recommendations for international students: Required—TOEFL (minimum score 550 paper-based; 79 iBT). Electronic applications accepted. *Faculty research:* Condensed-matter physics (experimental and theoretical), cosmology (theoretical), high energy and particle physics (experimental and theoretical), computational physics, biophysics (experimental and theoretical), materials physics.

The University of Akron, Graduate School, Buchtel College of Arts and Sciences, Department of Physics, Akron, OH 44325. Offers MS. *Program availability:* Part-time, evening/weekend. *Faculty:* 9 full-time (2 women). *Students:* 18 full-time (5 women), 3 part-time (2 women); includes 2 minority (1 Asian, non-Hispanic/Latino; 1 Hispanic/Latino), 16 international. Average age 30. 21 applicants, 48% accepted, 5 enrolled. In 2015, 4 master's awarded. *Degree requirements:* For master's, thesis, written exam or formal report. *Entrance requirements:* For master's, baccalaureate degree in physics or related field, three letters of recommendation, resume, statement of purpose. Additional exam requirements/recommendations for international students: Required—TOEFL (minimum score 550 paper-based; 79 iBT), IELTS (minimum score 6.5). *Application deadline:* For fall admission, 3/15 for domestic and international students. Applications are processed on a rolling basis. Application fee: $45 ($70 for international students). Electronic applications accepted. *Expenses:* Tuition, state resident: full-time $7958; part-time $442 per credit hour. Tuition, nonresident: full-time $13,464; part-time $748 per credit hour. *Required fees:* $1404. *Financial support:* In 2015–16, 17 teaching assistantships with full tuition reimbursements were awarded. *Faculty research:* Materials physics, surface physics, nanotechnology, polymer physics, condensed matter physics. *Total annual research expenditures:* $6,620. *Unit head:* Dr. David Steer, Interim Department Chair, 330-972-2099, E-mail: steer@uakron.edu. *Application contact:* Dr. Ang Chen, Graduate Director, 330-972-6657, E-mail: ang@uakron.edu.
Website: http://www.uakron.edu/physics/

The University of Alabama, Graduate School, College of Arts and Sciences, Department of Physics and Astronomy, Tuscaloosa, AL 35487-0324. Offers physics (MS, PhD), including astronomy. *Faculty:* 27 full-time (3 women). *Students:* 47 full-time (7 women); includes 4 minority (1 Black or African American, non-Hispanic/Latino; 1 American Indian or Alaska Native, non-Hispanic/Latino; 1 Asian, non-Hispanic/Latino; 1 Hispanic/Latino), 30 international. Average age 29. 85 applicants, 31% accepted, 9 enrolled. In 2015, 7 master's, 3 doctorates awarded. Terminal master's awarded for partial completion of doctoral program. *Degree requirements:* For master's, thesis optional, oral exam; for doctorate, thesis/dissertation, oral and written exams. *Entrance requirements:* For master's and doctorate, GRE General Test (minimum score of 300), minimum GPA of 3.0. Additional exam requirements/recommendations for international students: Required—TOEFL (minimum score 550 paper-based; 79 iBT). *Application deadline:* For fall admission, 2/15 priority date for domestic and international students; for spring admission, 11/1 for domestic students, 6/1 for international students. Applications are processed on a rolling basis. Electronic applications accepted. *Expenses:* Tuition, state resident: full-time $10,170. Tuition, nonresident: full-time $25,950. *Financial support:* In 2015–16, 45 students received support, including 11 research assistantships with full tuition reimbursements available (averaging $24,996 per year), 33 teaching assistantships with full tuition reimbursements available (averaging $24,996 per year); career-related internships or fieldwork, institutionally sponsored loans, and health care benefits also available. Financial award application deadline: 2/15. *Faculty research:* Condensed matter, particle physics, astrophysics, particle astrophysics, collider physics. *Total annual research expenditures:* $2.6 million. *Unit head:* Dr. Raymond E. White, III, Chairman and Professor, 205-348-5050, Fax: 205-348-5051, E-mail: rwhite@ua.edu. *Application contact:* Patrick D. Fuller, Senior

Peterson's Graduate Programs in the Physical Sciences, Mathematics, Agricultural Sciences, the Environment & Natural Resources 2017

www.petersons.com **183**

Physics

Graduate Admissions Counselor, 205-348-5923, Fax: 205-348-0400,
E-mail: patrick.d.fuller@ua.edu.
Website: http://physics.ua.edu/

The University of Alabama at Birmingham, College of Arts and Sciences, Program in Physics, Birmingham, AL 35294. Offers MS, PhD. Terminal master's awarded for partial completion of doctoral program. *Degree requirements:* For master's, thesis optional; for doctorate, thesis/dissertation. *Entrance requirements:* For master's and doctorate, GRE General Test; GRE Subject Test (recommended), minimum GPA of 3.0. Additional exam requirements/recommendations for international students: Required—TOEFL, TWE. Electronic applications accepted. *Expenses:* Tuition, state resident: full-time $7340. Tuition, nonresident: full-time $16,628. Full-time tuition and fees vary according to course load and program. *Faculty research:* Condensed matter physics, material physics, laser physics, optics, biophysics, computational physics.

The University of Alabama in Huntsville, School of Graduate Studies, College of Science, Department of Physics, Huntsville, AL 35899. Offers education (MS); optics and photonics technology (MS); physics (MS, PhD). *Program availability:* Part-time, evening/weekend. *Degree requirements:* For master's, comprehensive exam, thesis or alternative, oral and written exams; for doctorate, comprehensive exam, thesis/ dissertation, oral and written exams. *Entrance requirements:* For master's and doctorate, GRE General Test, minimum GPA of 3.0. Additional exam requirements/ recommendations for international students: Required—TOEFL (minimum score 550 paper-based; 80 iBT), IELTS (minimum score 6.5). Electronic applications accepted. *Faculty research:* Space and solar physics, computational physics, optics, high energy astrophysics.

University of Alaska Fairbanks, College of Natural Sciences and Mathematics, Department of Physics, Fairbanks, AK 99775-5920. Offers computational physics (MS); physics (MS, PhD); space physics (MS). *Program availability:* Part-time. *Faculty:* 8 full-time (2 women). *Students:* 22 full-time (3 women), 2 part-time (0 women); includes 3 minority (1 American Indian or Alaska Native, non-Hispanic/Latino; 2 Asian, non-Hispanic/Latino), 4 international. Average age 29. 53 applicants, 17% accepted, 9 enrolled. In 2015, 1 master's, 3 doctorates awarded. *Degree requirements:* For master's, comprehensive exam, oral defense of project or thesis; for doctorate, comprehensive exam, thesis/dissertation, oral defense of dissertation. *Entrance requirements:* For master's, GRE General Test, bachelor's degree from accredited institution with minimum cumulative undergraduate and major GPA of 3.0; for doctorate, GRE General Test, minimum cumulative GPA of 3.0. Additional exam requirements/recommendations for international students: Required—TOEFL (minimum score 550 paper-based; 80 iBT). *Application deadline:* For fall admission, 6/1 for domestic students, 3/1 for international students; for spring admission, 10/15 for domestic students, 9/1 for international students. Applications are processed on a rolling basis. Application fee: $60. Electronic applications accepted. *Expenses:* Tuition, state resident: full-time $7614; part-time $423 per credit. Tuition, nonresident: full-time $15,552; part-time $864 per credit. *Required fees:* $38 per credit. $187 per semester. Tuition and fees vary according to course level, course load, program and reciprocity agreements. *Financial support:* In 2015–16, 10 research assistantships with full tuition reimbursements (averaging $16,599 per year), 11 teaching assistantships with full tuition reimbursements (averaging $16,577 per year) were awarded; fellowships with full tuition reimbursements, Federal Work-Study, scholarships/grants, health care benefits, and unspecified assistantships also available. Support available to part-time students. Financial award application deadline: 2/15; financial award applicants required to submit FAFSA. *Faculty research:* Atmospheric and ionospheric radar studies, space plasma theory, magnetospheric dynamics, space weather and auroral studies, turbulence and complex systems. *Unit head:* Renate Wackerbauer, Department Chair, 907-474-7339, Fax: 907-474-6130, E-mail: uaf-physics@alaska.edu. *Application contact:* Mary Kreta, Director of Admissions, 907-474-7500, Fax: 907-474-7097, E-mail: admissions@uaf.edu.
Website: http://www.uaf.edu/physics/

University of Alberta, Faculty of Graduate Studies and Research, Department of Physics, Edmonton, AB T6G 2E1, Canada. Offers astrophysics (M Sc, PhD); condensed matter (M Sc, PhD); geophysics (M Sc, PhD); medical physics (M Sc, PhD); subatomic physics (M Sc, PhD). *Degree requirements:* For master's, thesis; for doctorate, thesis/ dissertation. *Entrance requirements:* For master's and doctorate, minimum GPA of 7.0 on a 9.0 scale. Additional exam requirements/recommendations for international students: Required—TOEFL. *Faculty research:* Cosmology, astroparticle physics, high-intermediate energy, magnetism, superconductivity.

The University of Arizona, College of Science, Department of Physics, Tucson, AZ 85721. Offers medical physics (PSM); physics (PhD). *Program availability:* Part-time. Terminal master's awarded for partial completion of doctoral program. *Degree requirements:* For master's, comprehensive exam (for some programs), thesis optional; for doctorate, comprehensive exam, thesis/dissertation. *Entrance requirements:* For master's and doctorate, GRE General Test, GRE Subject Test, minimum GPA of 3.2, 3 letters of recommendation. Additional exam requirements/recommendations for international students: Required—TOEFL (minimum score 550 paper-based; 79 iBT). *Application deadline:* For fall admission, 2/1 for domestic students, 12/1 for international students. Applications are processed on a rolling basis. Application fee: $75. Electronic applications accepted. *Financial support:* Research assistantships, teaching assistantships, career-related internships or fieldwork, scholarships/grants, health care benefits, tuition waivers (full and partial), and unspecified assistantships available. Financial award application deadline: 5/1. *Faculty research:* Astrophysics; high-energy, condensed-matter, atomic and molecular physics; optics. *Unit head:* Dr. Sumitendra Mazumdar, Head, E-mail: sumit@physics.arizona.edu.
Website: http://www.physics.arizona.edu

University of Arkansas, Graduate School, J. William Fulbright College of Arts and Sciences, Department of Physics, Fayetteville, AR 72701-1201. Offers applied physics (MS); physics (MS, PhD); physics education (MA). *Students:* 3 full-time (0 women), 39 part-time (11 women); includes 4 minority (2 Asian, non-Hispanic/Latino; 1 Hispanic/ Latino; 1 Two or more races, non-Hispanic/Latino), 24 international. In 2015, 3 master's, 1 doctorate awarded. *Degree requirements:* For master's, thesis; for doctorate, thesis/ dissertation. *Application deadline:* For fall admission, 4/1 for international students; for spring admission, 10/1 for international students. Applications are processed on a rolling basis. Application fee: $40 ($50 for international students). Electronic applications accepted. *Financial support:* In 2015–16, 21 research assistantships, 22 teaching assistantships were awarded; fellowships with tuition reimbursements, career-related internships or fieldwork, and Federal Work-Study also available. Support available to part-time students. Financial award application deadline: 4/1; financial award applicants required to submit FAFSA. *Unit head:* Dr. Julio Gea-Banacloche, Departmental Chairperson, 479-575-2506, Fax: 479-575-4580, E-mail: jgeabana@uark.edu. *Application contact:* Dr. Surendra Singh, Graduate Coordinator, 479-575-6058, E-mail: ssingh@uark.edu.
Website: http://www.uark.edu/depts/physics/

The University of British Columbia, Faculty of Science, Program in Physics, Vancouver, BC V6T 1Z1, Canada. Offers M Sc, PhD. *Degree requirements:* For master's, thesis; for doctorate, comprehensive exam, thesis/dissertation. *Entrance requirements:* For master's, GRE General Test, honors degree; for doctorate, GRE General Test, master's degree. Additional exam requirements/recommendations for international students: Required—TOEFL. *Faculty research:* Applied physics, astrophysics, condensed matter, plasma physics, subatomic physics, astronomy.

University of Calgary, Faculty of Graduate Studies, Faculty of Science, Department of Physics and Astronomy, Calgary, AB T2N 1N4, Canada. Offers M Sc, PhD. *Program availability:* Part-time. *Degree requirements:* For master's, thesis; for doctorate, thesis/ dissertation, oral candidacy exam, written qualifying exam. *Entrance requirements:* For master's and doctorate, GRE General Test, GRE Subject Test. Additional exam requirements/recommendations for international students: Required—TOEFL (minimum score 550 paper-based). Electronic applications accepted. *Faculty research:* Astronomy and astrophysics, mass spectrometry, atmospheric physics, space physics, medical physics.

University of California, Berkeley, Graduate Division, College of Letters and Science, Department of Physics, Berkeley, CA 94720-1500. Offers PhD. *Degree requirements:* For doctorate, thesis/dissertation, qualifying exam. *Entrance requirements:* For doctorate, GRE General Test, GRE Subject Test, minimum GPA of 3.0, 3 letters of recommendation. Additional exam requirements/recommendations for international students: Required—TOEFL (minimum score 570 paper-based). *Faculty research:* Astrophysics (experimental and theoretical), condensed matter physics (experimental and theoretical), particle physics (experimental and theoretical), atomic/molecular physics, biophysics and complex systems.

University of California, Davis, Graduate Studies, Program in Physics, Davis, CA 95616. Offers MS, PhD. Terminal master's awarded for partial completion of doctoral program. *Degree requirements:* For master's, comprehensive exam (for some programs), thesis (for some programs); for doctorate, thesis/dissertation. *Entrance requirements:* For master's and doctorate, GRE General Test, GRE Subject Test, minimum GPA of 3.0. Additional exam requirements/recommendations for international students: Required—TOEFL (minimum score 550 paper-based). Electronic applications accepted. *Faculty research:* Astrophysics, condensed-matter physics, nuclear physics, particle physics, quantum optics.

University of California, Irvine, School of Physical Sciences, Department of Physics and Astronomy, Irvine, CA 92697. Offers physics (MS, PhD); MD/PhD. *Students:* 84 full-time (13 women), 1 part-time (0 women); includes 21 minority (12 Asian, non-Hispanic/ Latino; 7 Hispanic/Latino; 2 Two or more races, non-Hispanic/Latino), 10 international. Average age 27. 302 applicants, 16% accepted, 16 enrolled. In 2015, 10 master's, 11 doctorates awarded. Terminal master's awarded for partial completion of doctoral program. *Degree requirements:* For doctorate, thesis/dissertation. *Entrance requirements:* For master's and doctorate, GRE General Test, GRE Subject Test, minimum GPA of 3.0. Additional exam requirements/recommendations for international students: Required—TOEFL (minimum score 550 paper-based). *Application deadline:* For fall admission, 1/15 priority date for domestic and international students. Application fee: $90 ($110 for international students). Electronic applications accepted. *Financial support:* Fellowships with full tuition reimbursements, research assistantships with full tuition reimbursements, teaching assistantships with partial tuition reimbursements, institutionally sponsored loans, traineeships, health care benefits, and unspecified assistantships available. Financial award application deadline: 3/1; financial award applicants required to submit FAFSA. *Faculty research:* Condensed-matter physics, plasma physics, astrophysics, particle physics, chemical and materials physics, biophysics. *Unit head:* Peter Taborek, Chair, 949-824-2254, Fax: 949-824-2174, E-mail: ptaborek@uci.edu. *Application contact:* My Banh, Graduate Student Affairs Officer, 949-824-3496, Fax: 949-824-7988, E-mail: mbanh@uci.edu.
Website: http://www.physics.uci.edu/

University of California, Los Angeles, Graduate Division, College of Letters and Science, Department of Physics and Astronomy, Program in Physics, Los Angeles, CA 90095. Offers MS, PhD. Terminal master's awarded for partial completion of doctoral program. *Degree requirements:* For master's, comprehensive exam, thesis; for doctorate, thesis/dissertation, oral and written qualifying exams. *Entrance requirements:* For master's and doctorate, GRE General Test; GRE Subject Test (physics), bachelor's degree; minimum undergraduate GPA of 3.0 (or its equivalent if letter grade system not used). Additional exam requirements/recommendations for international students: Required—TOEFL. Electronic applications accepted.

University of California, Merced, Graduate Division, School of Natural Sciences, Merced, CA 95343. Offers applied mathematics (MS, PhD); chemistry and chemical biology (MS, PhD); physics (MS, PhD); quantitative and systems biology (MS, PhD). *Faculty:* 63 full-time (25 women). *Students:* 156 full-time (64 women); includes 58 minority (3 Black or African American, non-Hispanic/Latino; 23 Asian, non-Hispanic/ Latino; 22 Hispanic/Latino; 1 Native Hawaiian or other Pacific Islander, non-Hispanic/ Latino; 9 Two or more races, non-Hispanic/Latino), 37 international. Average age 27. 199 applicants, 57% accepted, 45 enrolled. In 2015, 12 master's, 11 doctorates awarded. Terminal master's awarded for partial completion of doctoral program. *Degree requirements:* For master's, variable foreign language requirement, comprehensive exam, thesis or alternative; for doctorate, variable foreign language requirement, comprehensive exam, thesis/dissertation. *Entrance requirements:* For master's and doctorate, GRE. Additional exam requirements/recommendations for international students: Required—TOEFL (minimum score 550 paper-based; 80 iBT); Recommended—IELTS (minimum score 7). *Application deadline:* For fall admission, 1/ 15 for domestic and international students. Application fee: $90 ($110 for international students). Electronic applications accepted. *Expenses:* $11,220 per year resident tuition, $15,102 per year non-resident tuition. *Financial support:* In 2015–16, 151 students received support, including 12 fellowships with full tuition reimbursements available (averaging $23,614 per year), 37 research assistantships with full tuition reimbursements available (averaging $18,842 per year), 127 teaching assistantships with full tuition reimbursements available (averaging $18,538 per year); scholarships/ grants, traineeships, and health care benefits also available. Financial award application deadline: 1/15. *Faculty research:* Computational science, soft matter physics, neurobiology, genomics, biochemistry. Total annual research expenditures: $5.3 million. *Unit head:* Dr. Juan C. Meza, Dean, 209-228-4487, Fax: 209-228-4060, E-mail: jcmeza@ucmerced.edu. *Application contact:* Tsu Ya, Director of Graduate Admissions and Academic Services, 209-228-4521, Fax: 209-228-6906, E-mail: tya@ucmerced.edu.

University of California, Riverside, Graduate Division, Department of Physics and Astronomy, Riverside, CA 92521-0102. Offers physics (MS, PhD). *Degree requirements:* For master's, comprehensive exams or thesis; for doctorate, thesis/ dissertation, qualifying exams. *Entrance requirements:* For master's and doctorate, GRE General Test, GRE Subject Test, minimum GPA of 3.0. Additional exam requirements/ recommendations for international students: Required—TOEFL (minimum score 550 paper-based; 80 iBT). Electronic applications accepted. *Faculty research:* Laser physics and surface science, elementary particle and heavy ion physics, plasma physics, optical physics, astrophysics.

University of California, San Diego, Graduate Division, Department of Physics, La Jolla, CA 92093. Offers biophysics (PhD); multi-scale biology (PhD); physics (MS, PhD). *Students:* 154 full-time (18 women); includes 26 minority (3 Black or African American, non-Hispanic/Latino; 15 Asian, non-Hispanic/Latino; 8 Hispanic/Latino), 52 international. 481 applicants, 13% accepted, 17 enrolled. In 2015, 13 master's, 27 doctorates awarded. *Degree requirements:* For doctorate, comprehensive exam, thesis/ dissertation, 1-quarter teaching assistantship. *Entrance requirements:* For doctorate, GRE General Test, GRE Subject Test. Additional exam requirements/recommendations for international students: Required—TOEFL (minimum score 550 paper-based; 80 iBT), IELTS (minimum score 7). *Application deadline:* For fall admission, 12/23 for domestic students. Application fee: $90 ($110 for international students). Electronic applications accepted. *Expenses:* Tuition, state resident: full-time $11,220. Tuition, nonresident: full-time $26,322. *Required fees:* $1800. *Financial support:* Fellowships, research assistantships, teaching assistantships, scholarships/grants, and unspecified assistantships available. Financial award applicants required to submit FAFSA. *Faculty research:* Astrophysics/astronomy, biological physics, condensed matter/material science, elementary particles, plasma physics. *Unit head:* Benjamin Grinstein, Chair, 858-534-6857, E-mail: chair@physics.ucsd.edu. *Application contact:* Sharmila Poddar, Graduate Coordinator, 858-822-1074, E-mail: shpoddar@ucsd.edu. Website: http://physics.ucsd.edu/

University of California, Santa Barbara, Graduate Division, College of Letters and Sciences, Division of Mathematics, Life, and Physical Sciences, Department of Physics, Santa Barbara, CA 93106-9530. Offers astrophysics (PhD); physics (PhD). *Faculty:* 49 full-time (6 women), 3 part-time/adjunct (0 women). *Students:* 140 full-time (21 women); includes 30 minority (1 American Indian or Alaska Native, non-Hispanic/Latino; 19 Asian, non-Hispanic/Latino; 10 Hispanic/Latino), 20 international. Average age 26. 640 applicants, 15% accepted, 26 enrolled. In 2015, 20 doctorates awarded. Terminal master's awarded for partial completion of doctoral program. *Degree requirements:* For doctorate, comprehensive exam, thesis/dissertation. *Entrance requirements:* For doctorate, GRE General Test, GRE Subject Test (physics). Additional exam requirements/recommendations for international students: Required—TOEFL (minimum score 550 paper-based; 80 iBT), IELTS (minimum score 7). *Application deadline:* For fall admission, 12/15 priority date for domestic students, 12/15 for international students. Application fee: $90 ($110 for international students). Electronic applications accepted. *Financial support:* In 2015–16, 53 students received support, including 6 fellowships with full tuition reimbursements available (averaging $30,000 per year), 66 research assistantships with full tuition reimbursements available (averaging $21,888 per year), 39 teaching assistantships with partial tuition reimbursements available (averaging $17,655 per year); Federal Work-Study, scholarships/grants, health care benefits, and unspecified assistantships also available. Financial award application deadline: 12/15; financial award applicants required to submit FAFSA. *Faculty research:* High energy theoretical/experimental physics, condensed matter theoretical/experimental physics, astrophysics and cosmology, biophysics, gravity and relativity. *Total annual research expenditures:* $20.3 million. *Unit head:* Prof. Philip Pincus, Chair/Professor, 805-893-4685, Fax: 805-893-4685, E-mail: fyl@mrl.ucsb.edu. *Application contact:* Jennifer Farrar, Staff Graduate Advisor, 805-893-4646, Fax: 805-893-4646, E-mail: jennifer@physics.ucsb.edu. Website: http://www.physics.ucsb.edu

University of California, Santa Cruz, Division of Graduate Studies, Division of Physical and Biological Sciences, Department of Physics, Santa Cruz, CA 95064. Offers MS, PhD. Terminal master's awarded for partial completion of doctoral program. *Degree requirements:* For master's, thesis; for doctorate, one foreign language, thesis/ dissertation, qualifying exam. *Entrance requirements:* For master's and doctorate, GRE General Test, GRE Subject Test. Additional exam requirements/recommendations for international students: Required—TOEFL (minimum score 550 paper-based; 83 iBT); Recommended—IELTS (minimum score 8). Electronic applications accepted. *Faculty research:* Theoretical and experimental particle physics, astrophysics and cosmology, condensed matter physics.

University of Central Florida, College of Education and Human Performance, School of Teaching, Learning, and Leadership, Program in Teacher Education, Orlando, FL 32816. Offers art education (MAT); English language (MAT); mathematics education (MAT); middle school mathematics (MAT); science education (MAT), including biology, chemistry, physics; social science education (MAT). Accreditation: NCATE. *Program availability:* Part-time, evening/weekend. *Students:* 25 full-time (16 women), 43 part-time (32 women); includes 19 minority (5 Black or African American, non-Hispanic/Latino; 2 Asian, non-Hispanic/Latino; 10 Hispanic/Latino; 2 Two or more races, non-Hispanic/ Latino). Average age 30. In 2015, 88 master's awarded. *Entrance requirements:* For master's, GRE General Test. Additional exam requirements/recommendations for international students: Required—TOEFL. *Application deadline:* For fall admission, 7/15 for domestic students; for spring admission, 12/1 for domestic students. Application fee: $30. Electronic applications accepted. *Expenses:* Tuition, state resident: part-time $288.16 per credit hour. Tuition, nonresident: part-time $1071.31 per credit hour. *Financial support:* Fellowships, research assistantships, teaching assistantships, career-related internships or fieldwork, Federal Work-Study, institutionally sponsored loans, tuition waivers (partial), and unspecified assistantships available. Financial award application deadline: 3/1; financial award applicants required to submit FAFSA. *Unit head:* Dr. Michael Hynes, Director, 407-823-2005, E-mail: mychael.hynes@ucf.edu. *Application contact:* Director, Admissions and Student Support, 407-823-2766, Fax: 407-823-6442, E-mail: gradadmissions@ucf.edu.

University of Central Florida, College of Sciences, Department of Physics, Orlando, FL 32816. Offers MS, PhD. *Program availability:* Part-time, evening/weekend. *Faculty:* 41 full-time (8 women), 3 part-time/adjunct (1 woman). *Students:* 91 full-time (24 women), 7 part-time (3 women); includes 13 minority (2 Black or African American, non-Hispanic/Latino; 2 Asian, non-Hispanic/Latino; 7 Hispanic/Latino; 2 Two or more races, non-Hispanic/Latino), 44 international. Average age 29. 151 applicants, 32% accepted, 22 enrolled. In 2015, 4 master's, 21 doctorates awarded. *Degree requirements:* For master's, thesis or alternative; for doctorate, thesis/dissertation, candidacy and qualifying exams. *Entrance requirements:* For master's, GRE General Test, minimum GPA of 3.0 in last 60 hours of course work; for doctorate, GRE General Test, GRE Subject Test, minimum GPA of 3.0 in last 60 hours or master's qualifying exam. Additional exam requirements/recommendations for international students: Required— TOEFL. *Application deadline:* For fall admission, 2/15 priority date for domestic students. Application fee: $30. Electronic applications accepted. *Expenses:* Tuition, state resident: part-time $288.16 per credit hour. Tuition, nonresident: part-time $1071.31 per credit hour. *Financial support:* In 2015–16, 75 students received support, including 24 fellowships with partial tuition reimbursements available (averaging $3,600 per year), 45 research assistantships with partial tuition reimbursements available (averaging $11,900 per year), 39 teaching assistantships with partial tuition reimbursements available (averaging $10,700 per year); career-related internships or

fieldwork, Federal Work-Study, institutionally sponsored loans, tuition waivers (partial), and unspecified assistantships also available. Financial award application deadline: 3/1; financial award applicants required to submit FAFSA. *Faculty research:* Atomic-molecular physics, condensed-matter physics, biophysics of proteins, laser physics. *Unit head:* Dr. Joshua Colwell, Interim Chair, 407-823-2021, E-mail: jec@ucf.edu. *Application contact:* Director, Admissions and Student Services, 407-823-2766, Fax: 407-823-6442, E-mail: gradadmissions@ucf.edu. Website: http://www.physics.ucf.edu/

University of Chicago, Division of the Physical Sciences, Department of Physics, Chicago, IL 60637. Offers PhD. *Degree requirements:* For doctorate, comprehensive exam, thesis/dissertation. *Entrance requirements:* For doctorate, GRE General Test, GRE Subject Test. Additional exam requirements/recommendations for international students: Required—TOEFL (minimum score 90 iBT), IELTS (minimum score 7). Electronic applications accepted. *Faculty research:* High energy physics experiment and theory; condensed matter experiment and theory; astrophysics; atomic, molecular, and optical physics; general relativity.

University of Chicago, Division of the Physical Sciences, Master of Science in Physical Sciences Programs, Chicago, IL 60637. Offers MS. *Program availability:* Part-time. *Degree requirements:* For master's, thesis. *Entrance requirements:* For master's, GRE General Test. Additional exam requirements/recommendations for international students: Required—TOEFL (minimum score 90 iBT), IELTS (minimum score 7). Electronic applications accepted.

University of Cincinnati, Graduate School, McMicken College of Arts and Sciences, Department of Physics, Cincinnati, OH 45221. Offers MS, PhD. Terminal master's awarded for partial completion of doctoral program. *Degree requirements:* For master's, thesis optional; for doctorate, thesis/dissertation. *Entrance requirements:* For master's and doctorate, GRE General Test, GRE Subject Test. Additional exam requirements/ recommendations for international students: Required—TOEFL (minimum score 540 paper-based). Electronic applications accepted. *Faculty research:* Condensed matter physics, experimental particle physics, theoretical high energy physics, astronomy and astrophysics, computational physics.

University of Colorado Boulder, Graduate School, College of Arts and Sciences, Department of Physics, Boulder, CO 80309. Offers chemical physics (PhD); geophysics (PhD); liquid crystal science and technology (PhD); mathematical physics (PhD); medical physics (PhD); optical sciences and engineering (PhD); physics (MS, PhD). *Faculty:* 48 full-time (8 women). *Students:* 131 full-time (22 women), 97 part-time (22 women); includes 14 minority (5 Asian, non-Hispanic/Latino; 4 Hispanic/Latino; 5 Two or more races, non-Hispanic/Latino), 61 international. Average age 26. 624 applicants, 24% accepted, 36 enrolled. In 2015, 24 master's, 29 doctorates awarded. Terminal master's awarded for partial completion of doctoral program. *Degree requirements:* For master's, comprehensive exam, thesis or alternative; for doctorate, comprehensive exam, thesis/dissertation. *Entrance requirements:* For master's and doctorate, GRE General Test, GRE Subject Test, minimum undergraduate GPA of 3.0. Additional exam requirements/recommendations for international students: Required—TOEFL. *Application deadline:* For fall admission, 12/15 for domestic students, 12/1 for international students. Applications are processed on a rolling basis. Application fee: $50 ($70 for international students). Electronic applications accepted. Application fee is waived when completed online. *Financial support:* In 2015–16, 521 students received support, including 7 fellowships (averaging $5,311 per year), 162 research assistantships with tuition reimbursements available (averaging $34,608 per year), 51 teaching assistantships with tuition reimbursements available (averaging $29,058 per year); institutionally sponsored loans, scholarships/grants, health care benefits, and unspecified assistantships also available. Financial award application deadline: 1/15; financial award applicants required to submit FAFSA. *Faculty research:* Physics, theoretical physics, high energy physics, experimental physics, solid state physics. *Total annual research expenditures:* $24.8 million. *Application contact:* E-mail: jeanne.nijhowne@colorado.edu. Website: http://phys.colorado.edu/graduate-students

University of Colorado Colorado Springs, College of Letters, Arts and Sciences, Program in Interdisciplinary Applied Sciences, Colorado Springs, CO 80918. Offers mathematics (PhD); physics (PhD). *Program availability:* Part-time, evening/weekend. *Faculty:* 16 full-time (3 women), 6 part-time/adjunct (2 women). *Students:* 2 full-time (both women), 31 part-time (6 women); includes 3 minority (1 American Indian or Alaska Native, non-Hispanic/Latino; 1 Hispanic/Latino; 1 Two or more races, non-Hispanic/ Latino), 3 international. Average age 34. 12 applicants, 92% accepted, 5 enrolled. *Degree requirements:* For doctorate, comprehensive exam, thesis/dissertation. *Entrance requirements:* For doctorate, GRE or minimum GPA of 3.0 and hold a baccalaureate degree in biological sciences, mathematics, physics or equivalents from an accredited college or university and have an appropriate background of undergraduate physics courses. Additional exam requirements/recommendations for international students: Required—TOEFL (minimum score 560 paper-based; 83 iBT), IELTS (minimum score 6.5). *Application deadline:* Applications are processed on a rolling basis. Application fee: $60 ($100 for international students). Electronic applications accepted. *Expenses:* Tuition, state resident: full-time $9914. Tuition, nonresident: full-time $19,330. Tuition and fees vary according to course load, degree level, program and reciprocity agreements. *Financial support:* In 2015–16, 13 students received support. Federal Work-Study and scholarships/grants available. Support available to part-time students. Financial award application deadline: 3/1; financial award applicants required to submit FAFSA. *Faculty research:* Solid-state/condensed-matter physics, surface science, electron spectroscopies, nonlinear physics. *Total annual research expenditures:* $821,552. *Unit head:* Dr. Robert Camley, Distinguished Professor, 719-255-3512, E-mail: rcamley@uccs.edu. *Application contact:* Dr. Karen Livesey, Assistant Professor, 719-255-5116, E-mail: klivesey@uccs.edu.

University of Connecticut, Graduate School, College of Liberal Arts and Sciences, Department of Physics, Storrs, CT 06269. Offers MS, PhD. *Degree requirements:* For master's, comprehensive exam; for doctorate, thesis/dissertation. *Entrance requirements:* For master's and doctorate, GRE General Test, GRE Subject Test. Additional exam requirements/recommendations for international students: Required— TOEFL (minimum score 550 paper-based). Electronic applications accepted.

University of Delaware, College of Arts and Sciences, Department of Physics and Astronomy, Newark, DE 19716. Offers MS, PhD. *Program availability:* Part-time. Terminal master's awarded for partial completion of doctoral program. *Degree requirements:* For master's, thesis; for doctorate, thesis/dissertation. *Entrance requirements:* For master's and doctorate, GRE General Test, GRE Subject Test. Additional exam requirements/recommendations for international students: Required— TOEFL (minimum score 600 paper-based). Electronic applications accepted. *Faculty research:* Magnetoresistance and magnetic materials, ultrafast optical phenomena, superfluidity, elementary particle physics, stellar atmospheres and interiors.

University of Denver, Division of Natural Sciences and Mathematics, Department of Physics and Astronomy, Denver, CO 80208. Offers physics (MS, PhD). *Program*

Peterson's Graduate Programs in the Physical Sciences, Mathematics, Agricultural Sciences, the Environment & Natural Resources 2017

www.petersons.com   **185**

availability: Part-time. *Faculty:* 11 full-time (3 women), 5 part-time/adjunct (0 women). *Students:* 8 part-time (4 women); includes 1 minority (Two or more races, non-Hispanic/Latino), 3 international. Average age 25. 43 applicants, 19% accepted, 4 enrolled. In 2015, 1 master's, 1 doctorate awarded. Terminal master's awarded for partial completion of doctoral program. *Degree requirements:* For master's, comprehensive exam, thesis optional; for doctorate, comprehensive exam, thesis/dissertation. *Entrance requirements:* For master's, GRE General Test, GRE Subject Test in physics (strongly preferred), bachelor's degree, transcripts, personal statement, three letters of recommendation; for doctorate, GRE General Test, GRE Subject Test in physics (strongly preferred), master's degree, transcripts, personal statement, three letters of recommendation. Additional exam requirements/recommendations for international students: Required—TOEFL (minimum score 550 paper-based; 80 iBT). *Application deadline:* For fall admission, 2/1 priority date for domestic and international students. Applications are processed on a rolling basis. Application fee: $65. Electronic applications accepted. *Expenses:* $30,477. *Financial support:* In 2015–16, 8 students received support, including 2 research assistantships with tuition reimbursements available (averaging $20,001 per year), 3 teaching assistantships with tuition reimbursements available (averaging $20,001 per year); career-related internships or fieldwork, Federal Work-Study, institutionally sponsored loans, scholarships/grants, and unspecified assistantships also available. Support available to part-time students. Financial award application deadline: 2/15; financial award applicants required to submit FAFSA. *Faculty research:* Astronomy and astrophysics, biophysics, condensed matter and materials physics. *Total annual research expenditures:* $1.1 million. *Unit head:* Dr. Davor Balzar, Associate Professor and Chair, 303-871-2137, Fax: 303-871-4405, E-mail: davor.balzar@du.edu. *Application contact:* Barbara Stephen, Assistant to the Chair, 303-871-2238, Fax: 303-871-4405, E-mail: barbara.stephen@du.edu.

Website: http://www.du.edu/nsm/departments/physicsandastronomy

University of Florida, Graduate School, College of Liberal Arts and Sciences, Department of Physics, Gainesville, FL 32611. Offers imaging science and technology (PhD); physics (MS, MST, PhD). *Faculty:* 49. *Students:* 134 full-time (23 women), 2 part-time (0 women); includes 12 minority (1 Black or African American, non-Hispanic/Latino; 8 Asian, non-Hispanic/Latino; 3 Hispanic/Latino), 62 international. Average age 28. 244 applicants, 27% accepted, 31 enrolled. In 2015, 9 master's, 19 doctorates awarded. Terminal master's awarded for partial completion of doctoral program. *Degree requirements:* For doctorate, comprehensive exam, thesis/dissertation. *Entrance requirements:* For master's and doctorate, GRE General Test, minimum GPA of 3.0. Additional exam requirements/recommendations for international students: Required—TOEFL (minimum score 550 paper-based; 80 iBT), IELTS (minimum score 6). *Application deadline:* For spring admission, 2/1 for domestic students, 1/1 for international students. Applications are processed on a rolling basis. Application fee: $30. Electronic applications accepted. *Financial support:* In 2015–16, 15 fellowships, 59 research assistantships, 76 teaching assistantships were awarded; unspecified assistantships also available. Financial award applicants required to submit FAFSA. *Faculty research:* Astrophysics, biological physics (molecular, magnetic resonance imaging, spectroscopy, biomagnetism), chemical physics (molecular, nano-scale physics, solid state, surface physics, quantum chemistry, quantum electron dynamics, molecular biology), experimental and theory condensed matter physics, low temperature physics (theory and experimental, mathematical physics. *Total annual research expenditures:* $10.5 million. *Unit head:* Kevin Ingersent, PhD, Professor and Chair, 352-392-0521, Fax: 352-392-0524, E-mail: kevin@phys.ufl.edu. *Application contact:* Dmitrii Maslov, PhD, Professor and Graduate Coordinator, 352-392-0513, Fax: 352-392-0524, E-mail: maslov@ufl.edu.

Website: http://www.phys.ufl.edu/

University of Georgia, Franklin College of Arts and Sciences, Department of Physics and Astronomy, Athens, GA 30602. Offers physics (MS, PhD). *Degree requirements:* For master's, thesis; for doctorate, one foreign language, thesis/dissertation. *Entrance requirements:* For master's and doctorate, GRE General Test. Electronic applications accepted.

University of Guelph, Graduate Studies, College of Physical and Engineering Science, Guelph-Waterloo Physics Institute, Guelph, ON N1G 2W1, Canada. Offers M Sc, PhD. M Sc, PhD offered jointly with University of Waterloo. *Program availability:* Part-time. *Degree requirements:* For master's, project or thesis; for doctorate, comprehensive exam, thesis/dissertation. *Entrance requirements:* For master's, GRE Subject Test, minimum B average for honors degree; for doctorate, GRE Subject Test, minimum B average. Additional exam requirements/recommendations for international students: Required—TOEFL (minimum score 550 paper-based), TWE (minimum score 4). *Faculty research:* Condensed matter and material physics, quantum computing, astrophysics and gravitation, industrial and applied physics, subatomic physics.

University of Hawaii at Manoa, Graduate Division, College of Natural Sciences, Department of Physics and Astronomy, Program in Physics, Honolulu, HI 96822. Offers MS, PhD. *Program availability:* Part-time. *Faculty:* 23 full-time (0 women), 5 part-time/adjunct (0 women). *Students:* 41 full-time (12 women), 1 part-time; includes 8 minority (4 Asian, non-Hispanic/Latino; 3 Hispanic/Latino; 1 Two or more races, non-Hispanic/Latino), 7 international. Average age 30. 25 applicants, 40% accepted, 4 enrolled. In 2015, 5 master's, 1 doctorate awarded. *Degree requirements:* For master's, thesis optional; for doctorate, comprehensive exam, thesis/dissertation. *Entrance requirements:* For master's and doctorate, GRE General Test. Additional exam requirements/recommendations for international students: Required—TOEFL (minimum score 560 paper-based; 83 iBT), IELTS (minimum score 5). *Application deadline:* For fall admission, 1/15 for domestic and international students; for spring admission, 8/1 for domestic and international students. Application fee: $100. *Financial support:* In 2015–16, 1 student received support, including 9 fellowships (averaging $989 per year), 15 research assistantships (averaging $19,034 per year), 9 teaching assistantships (averaging $15,767 per year). *Total annual research expenditures:* $2.5 million. *Unit head:* Pui K. Lam, Chair, 808-956-2988. *Application contact:* Pui K. Lam, Graduate Chairperson, 808-956-7087, Fax: 808-956-7107, E-mail: plam@hawaii.edu.

Website: http://www.hawaii.edu/graduatestudies/fields/html/departments/pr/physics/physics.htm

University of Houston, College of Natural Sciences and Mathematics, Department of Physics, Houston, TX 77204. Offers MA, PhD. *Program availability:* Part-time. Terminal master's awarded for partial completion of doctoral program. *Entrance requirements:* For master's and doctorate, GRE General Test. Electronic applications accepted. *Faculty research:* Condensed-matter, particle physics; high-temperature superconductivity; material/space physics; chaos.

University of Houston–Clear Lake, School of Science and Computer Engineering, Program in Physics, Houston, TX 77058-1002. Offers MS. *Program availability:* Part-time, evening/weekend. *Entrance requirements:* For master's, GRE General Test. Additional exam requirements/recommendations for international students: Required—TOEFL (minimum score 550 paper-based).

University of Idaho, College of Graduate Studies, College of Science, Department of Physics, Moscow, ID 83844-0903. Offers MS, PhD. *Faculty:* 8 full-time. *Students:* 18 full-time. Average age 35. In 2015, 3 master's, 2 doctorates awarded. *Degree requirements:* For master's, thesis; for doctorate, thesis/dissertation. *Entrance requirements:* For master's, GRE, minimum GPA of 2.8; for doctorate, GRE, minimum undergraduate GPA of 2.8, 3.0 graduate. Additional exam requirements/recommendations for international students: Required—TOEFL. *Application deadline:* For fall admission, 8/1 for domestic students; for spring admission, 12/15 for domestic students. Applications are processed on a rolling basis. Application fee: $60. Electronic applications accepted. *Expenses:* Tuition, state resident: full-time $6205; part-time $399 per credit hour. Tuition, nonresident: full-time $20,209; part-time $1177 per credit hour. *Required fees:* $2017; $58 per credit hour. Full-time tuition and fees vary according to course load and reciprocity agreements. *Financial support:* Research assistantships and teaching assistantships available. Financial award applicants required to submit FAFSA. *Faculty research:* Condensed matter physics, nuclear physics, biological physics, astronomy/planetary science. *Unit head:* Dr. Jo Ellen Force, Interim Chair, 208-885-6380, E-mail: physics@uidaho.edu. *Application contact:* Sean Scoggin, Graduate Recruitment Coordinator, 208-885-4723, Fax: 208-885-4406, E-mail: graduateadmissions@uidaho.edu.

Website: http://www.uidaho.edu/sci/physics

University of Illinois at Chicago, College of Liberal Arts and Sciences, Department of Physics, Chicago, IL 60607-7128. Offers MS, PhD. *Faculty:* 31 full-time (5 women), 24 part-time/adjunct (3 women). *Students:* 74 full-time (19 women), 8 part-time (3 women); includes 9 minority (5 Asian, non-Hispanic/Latino; 1 Hispanic/Latino; 3 Two or more races, non-Hispanic/Latino), 52 international. Average age 28. Terminal master's awarded for partial completion of doctoral program. *Degree requirements:* For doctorate, thesis/dissertation. *Entrance requirements:* For master's and doctorate, GRE General Test, minimum GPA of 3.0. Additional exam requirements/recommendations for international students: Required—TOEFL. *Application deadline:* For fall admission, 5/15 for domestic students, 2/15 for international students; for spring admission, 11/1 for domestic students, 7/15 for international students. Applications are processed on a rolling basis. Application fee: $60. Electronic applications accepted. *Expenses:* Contact institution. *Financial support:* Fellowships with full tuition reimbursements, research assistantships with full tuition reimbursements, teaching assistantships with full tuition reimbursements, Federal Work-Study, scholarships/grants, traineeships, tuition waivers (full), and unspecified assistantships available. Financial award application deadline: 3/1; financial award applicants required to submit FAFSA. *Faculty research:* High-energy, laser, and solid-state physics. *Unit head:* Prof. David Jonathan Hofman, Acting Head, 312-413-2798, E-mail: hofman@uic.edu. *Application contact:* Receptionist, 312-413-2550, E-mail: gradcoll@uic.edu.

Website: http://physicsweb.phy.uic.edu/

University of Illinois at Urbana–Champaign, Graduate College, College of Engineering, Department of Physics, Champaign, IL 61820. Offers physics (MS, PhD); teaching of physics (MS).

The University of Iowa, Graduate College, College of Liberal Arts and Sciences, Department of Physics and Astronomy, Program in Physics, Iowa City, IA 52242-1316. Offers MS, PhD. *Degree requirements:* For master's, thesis optional, exam; for doctorate, comprehensive exam, thesis/dissertation. *Entrance requirements:* For master's and doctorate, GRE General Test, minimum GPA of 3.0. Additional exam requirements/recommendations for international students: Required—TOEFL (minimum score 550 paper-based; 81 iBT). Electronic applications accepted.

The University of Kansas, Graduate Studies, College of Liberal Arts and Sciences, Department of Physics and Astronomy, Lawrence, KS 66045. Offers computational physics and astronomy (MS); physics (MS, PhD). *Students:* 54 full-time (7 women), 1 part-time (0 women); includes 5 minority (1 American Indian or Alaska Native, non-Hispanic/Latino; 1 Hispanic/Latino; 3 Two or more races, non-Hispanic/Latino), 23 international. Average age 30. 80 applicants, 14% accepted, 7 enrolled. In 2015, 4 master's, 6 doctorates awarded. Terminal master's awarded for partial completion of doctoral program. *Entrance requirements:* For master's and doctorate, GRE Subject Test (physics), undergraduate degree. Additional exam requirements/recommendations for international students: Required—TOEFL. *Application deadline:* For fall admission, 12/1 priority date for domestic and international students; for spring admission, 10/1 priority date for domestic and international students. Application fee: $65 ($85 for international students). Electronic applications accepted. *Financial support:* Fellowships, research assistantships, teaching assistantships, health care benefits, and unspecified assistantships available. Financial award application deadline: 4/1; financial award applicants required to submit FAFSA. *Faculty research:* Astrophysics, biophysics, high energy physics, nanophysics, nuclear physics. *Unit head:* Hume A. Feldman, Chair, 785-864-4740, E-mail: feldman@ku.edu. *Application contact:* Desiree Neyens, Graduate Secretary, 785-864-1225, E-mail: dneyens@ku.edu.

Website: http://www.physics.ku.edu

University of Kentucky, Graduate School, College of Arts and Sciences, Program in Physics and Astronomy, Lexington, KY 40506-0032. Offers MS, PhD. *Degree requirements:* For master's, comprehensive exam, thesis optional; for doctorate, comprehensive exam, thesis/dissertation. *Entrance requirements:* For master's, GRE General Test, minimum undergraduate GPA of 2.75; for doctorate, GRE General Test, minimum graduate GPA of 3.0. Additional exam requirements/recommendations for international students: Required—TOEFL (minimum score 550 paper-based). Electronic applications accepted. *Faculty research:* Astrophysics, active galactic nuclei, and radio astronomy; Rydbert atoms, and electron scattering; TOF spectroscopy, hyperon interactions and muons; particle theory, lattice gauge theory, quark, and skyrmion models.

University of Lethbridge, School of Graduate Studies, Lethbridge, AB T1K 3M4, Canada. Offers addictions counseling (M Sc); agricultural biotechnology (M Sc); agricultural studies (M Sc, MA); anthropology (MA); archaeology (M Sc, MA); art (MA, MFA); biochemistry (M Sc); biological sciences (M Sc); biomolecular science (PhD); biosystems and biodiversity (PhD); Canadian studies (MA); chemistry (M Sc); computer science (M Sc); computer science and geographical information science (M Sc); counseling (MC); counseling psychology (M Ed); dramatic arts (MA); earth, space, and physical science (PhD); economics (MA); education (MA, PhD); educational leadership (M Ed); English (MA); environmental science (M Sc); evolution and behavior (PhD); exercise science (M Sc); French (MA); French/German (MA); French/Spanish (MA); general education (M Ed); geography (M Sc, MA); German (MA); health sciences (M Sc); individualized multidisciplinary (M Sc, MA); kinesiology (M Sc, MA); management (M Sc), including accounting, finance, human resource management and labor relations, information systems, international management, marketing, policy and strategy; mathematics (M Sc); music (M Mus, MA); Native American studies (MA); neuroscience (M Sc, PhD); new media (MA, MFA); nursing (M Sc, MN); philosophy (MA); physics (M Sc); political science (MA); psychology (M Sc, MA); religious studies (MA); sociology (MA); theatre and dramatic arts (MFA); theoretical and computational science (PhD); urban and regional studies (MA); women and gender studies (MA).

Program availability: Part-time, evening/weekend. *Students:* 448 full-time (249 women), 110 part-time (64 women). Average age 32. 285 applicants, 36% accepted, 96 enrolled. In 2015, 154 master's, 11 doctorates awarded. *Degree requirements:* For master's, thesis (for some programs); for doctorate, comprehensive exam, thesis/dissertation. *Entrance requirements:* For master's, GMAT (for M Sc in management), bachelor's degree in related field, minimum GPA of 3.0 during previous 20 graded semester courses, 2 years' teaching or related experience (M Ed); for doctorate, master's degree, minimum graduate GPA of 3.5. Additional exam requirements/recommendations for international students: Required—TOEFL (minimum score 580 paper-based; 93 iBT). Application fee: $100 Canadian dollars ($140 Canadian dollars for international students). Electronic applications accepted. *Financial support:* Fellowships, research assistantships, teaching assistantships, scholarships/grants, health care benefits, and unspecified assistantships available. *Faculty research:* Movement and brain plasticity, gibberellin physiology, photosynthesis, carbon cycling, molecular properties of main-group ring components. *Unit head:* Kathleen Schrage, Manager, School of Graduate Studies, 403-329-2121, E-mail: schrage@uleth.ca. *Application contact:* School of Graduate Studies, 403-329-5194, E-mail: sgsinquiries@uleth.ca.
Website: http://www.uleth.ca/graduate-studies/

University of Louisiana at Lafayette, College of Sciences, Department of Physics, Lafayette, LA 70504. Offers MS. *Program availability:* Part-time. *Degree requirements:* For master's, thesis. *Entrance requirements:* For master's, GRE General Test, minimum GPA of 2.75. Additional exam requirements/recommendations for international students: Required—TOEFL (minimum score 550 paper-based). Electronic applications accepted. *Faculty research:* Environmental physics, geophysics, astrophysics, acoustics, atomic physics.

University of Louisville, Graduate School, College of Arts and Sciences, Department of Physics and Astronomy, Louisville, KY 40292. Offers physics (MS, PhD). *Program availability:* Part-time. *Students:* 37 full-time (4 women), 3 part-time (0 women); includes 3 minority (1 Black or African American, non-Hispanic/Latino; 2 Two or more races, non-Hispanic/Latino), 16 international. Average age 30. 48 applicants, 42% accepted, 15 enrolled. In 2015, 7 master's, 1 doctorate awarded. Terminal master's awarded for partial completion of doctoral program. *Degree requirements:* For master's, thesis optional; for doctorate, comprehensive exam, thesis/dissertation. *Entrance requirements:* For master's, GRE General Test. Additional exam requirements/recommendations for international students: Required—TOEFL (minimum score 550 paper-based; 80 iBT). *Application deadline:* For fall admission, 3/1 for domestic students, 5/1 priority date for international students; for spring admission, 11/1 priority date for international students; for summer admission, 4/1 priority date for international students. Applications are processed on a rolling basis. Application fee: $60. Electronic applications accepted. *Expenses:* Tuition, state resident: full-time $11,664; part-time $649 per credit hour. Tuition, nonresident: full-time $24,274; part-time $1350 per credit hour. *Required fees:* $196. Tuition and fees vary according to program and reciprocity agreements. *Financial support:* In 2015–16, 338,017 students received support. Fellowships, research assistantships, and teaching assistantships available. *Faculty research:* Condensed matter physics; atmospheric science; high energy physics; astrophysics; atomic, molecular, and optical physics. *Total annual research expenditures:* $435,503. *Unit head:* Dr. Chakram S. Jayanthi, Professor/Chair, 502-852-6790, Fax: 502-852-0742, E-mail: csjaya01@louisville.edu. *Application contact:* Libby Leggett, Director, Graduate Admissions, 502-852-3101,
E-mail: gradadm@louisville.edu.
Website: http://www.physics.louisville.edu/

University of Maine, Graduate School, College of Liberal Arts and Sciences, Department of Physics and Astronomy, Orono, ME 04469. Offers engineering physics (ME); physics (MS, PhD). *Faculty:* 13 full-time (1 woman), 1 part-time/adjunct (0 women). *Students:* 59 full-time (18 women), 5 part-time (3 women); includes 9 minority (1 American Indian or Alaska Native, non-Hispanic/Latino; 4 Asian, non-Hispanic/Latino; 1 Hispanic/Latino; 3 Two or more races, non-Hispanic/Latino), 4 international. Average age 29. 51 applicants, 49% accepted, 19 enrolled. In 2015, 8 master's, 4 doctorates awarded. Terminal master's awarded for partial completion of doctoral program. *Degree requirements:* For master's, thesis; for doctorate, comprehensive exam, thesis/dissertation. *Entrance requirements:* For master's, GRE General Test, GRE Subject Test; for doctorate, GRE General Test. Additional exam requirements/recommendations for international students: Required—TOEFL. *Application deadline:* For fall admission, 1/15 priority date for domestic students. Applications are processed on a rolling basis. Application fee: $65. Electronic applications accepted. *Financial support:* In 2015–16, 68 students received support, including 11 research assistantships with full tuition reimbursements available (averaging $14,600 per year), 47 teaching assistantships with full tuition reimbursements available (averaging $14,600 per year); tuition waivers (full and partial) also available. Financial award application deadline: 3/1. *Faculty research:* Physics education research, experimental and theoretical biophysics, surface/nano physics, extragalactic astrophysics, environmental/nuclear physics, thermal/statistical physics theory. *Total annual research expenditures:* $4.7 million. *Unit head:* Dr. David Batuski, Chair, 207-581-1015, Fax: 207-581-3410. *Application contact:* Scott G. Delcourt, Associate Dean of the Graduate School, 207-581-3291, Fax: 207-581-3232, E-mail: graduate@maine.edu.
Website: http://www.physics.umaine.edu/

The University of Manchester, School of Earth, Atmospheric and Environmental Sciences, Manchester, United Kingdom. Offers atmospheric sciences (M Phil, M Sc, PhD); basin studies and petroleum geosciences (M Phil, M Sc, PhD); earth, atmospheric and environmental sciences (M Phil, M Sc, PhD); environmental geochemistry and cosmochemistry (M Phil, M Sc, PhD); isotope geochemistry and cosmochemistry (M Phil, M Sc, PhD); paleontology (M Phil, M Sc, PhD); physics and chemistry of minerals and fluids (M Phil, M Sc, PhD); structural and petrological geosciences (M Phil, M Sc, PhD).

The University of Manchester, School of Physics and Astronomy, Manchester, United Kingdom. Offers astronomy and astrophysics (M Sc, PhD); biological physics (M Sc, PhD); condensed matter physics (M Sc, PhD); nonlinear and liquid crystals physics (M Sc, PhD); nuclear physics (M Sc, PhD); particle physics (M Sc, PhD); photon physics (M Sc, PhD); physics (M Sc, PhD); theoretical physics (M Sc, PhD).

University of Manitoba, Faculty of Graduate Studies, Faculty of Science, Department of Physics and Astronomy, Winnipeg, MB R3T 2N2, Canada. Offers M Sc, PhD. *Degree requirements:* For master's, thesis; for doctorate, one foreign language, thesis/dissertation.

University of Maryland, Baltimore County, The Graduate School, College of Arts, Humanities and Social Sciences, Department of Education, Program in Teaching, Baltimore, MD 21250. Offers early childhood education (MAT); elementary education (MAT); teaching (MAT), including art, biology, chemistry, choral music, classical foreign language, dance, earth/space science, English, instrumental music, mathematics, modern foreign language, physical science, physics, social studies, theatre. *Program availability:* Part-time, evening/weekend. *Faculty:* 24 full-time (18 women), 25 part-time/adjunct (19 women). *Students:* 43 full-time (34 women), 40 part-time (27 women); includes 29 minority (9 Black or African American, non-Hispanic/Latino; 10 Asian, non-Hispanic/Latino; 9 Hispanic/Latino; 1 Two or more races, non-Hispanic/Latino), 1 international. Average age 30. 54 applicants, 69% accepted, 35 enrolled. In 2015, 106 master's awarded. *Degree requirements:* For master's, comprehensive exam (for some programs), thesis (for some programs). *Entrance requirements:* For master's, PRAXIS Core Examination or GRE (minimum score of 1000), minimum GPA of 3.0. Additional exam requirements/recommendations for international students: Required—TOEFL. *Application deadline:* For fall admission, 6/1 for domestic and international students; for spring admission, 11/1 for domestic and international students. Applications are processed on a rolling basis. Application fee: $50. Electronic applications accepted. *Expenses:* Tuition, state resident: full-time $12,816. Tuition, nonresident: full-time $19,710. *Financial support:* In 2015–16, 6 students received support, including teaching assistantships with tuition reimbursements available (averaging $12,000 per year); career-related internships or fieldwork, Federal Work-Study, scholarships/grants, tuition waivers, and unspecified assistantships also available. Financial award application deadline: 3/1. *Faculty research:* STEM teacher education, culturally sensitive pedagogy, ESOL/bilingual education, early childhood education, language, literacy and culture. *Unit head:* Dr. Susan M. Blunck, Graduate Program Director, 410-455-2869, Fax: 410-455-3986, E-mail: blunck@umbc.edu. *Application contact:* Cheryl Johnson, MAT Program Specialist, 410-455-3388, E-mail: blackwel@umbc.edu.
Website: http://www.umbc.edu/education/

University of Maryland, Baltimore County, The Graduate School, College of Natural and Mathematical Sciences, Department of Physics, Program in Physics, Baltimore, MD 21250. Offers MS, PhD. *Program availability:* Part-time. *Faculty:* 21 full-time (3 women), 16 part-time/adjunct (2 women). *Students:* 28 full-time (8 women), 1 part-time (0 women); includes 1 minority (Black or African American, non-Hispanic/Latino), 7 international. Average age 24. 37 applicants, 84% accepted, 11 enrolled. In 2015, 6 master's, 5 doctorates awarded. Terminal master's awarded for partial completion of doctoral program. *Degree requirements:* For master's, thesis optional; for doctorate, comprehensive exam, thesis/dissertation. *Entrance requirements:* For master's and doctorate, GRE General Test, GRE Subject Test (recommended), minimum GPA of 3.0. Additional exam requirements/recommendations for international students: Required—TOEFL. *Application deadline:* For fall admission, 1/1 for domestic and international students; for spring admission, 11/30 for domestic students. Applications are processed on a rolling basis. Application fee: $50. Electronic applications accepted. *Expenses:* Tuition, state resident: full-time $12,816. Tuition, nonresident: full-time $19,710. *Financial support:* In 2015–16, 28 students received support, including 3 fellowships with full tuition reimbursements available (averaging $30,000 per year), 13 research assistantships with full tuition reimbursements available (averaging $26,000 per year), 12 teaching assistantships with full tuition reimbursements available (averaging $24,000 per year); career-related internships or fieldwork, scholarships/grants, health care benefits, and unspecified assistantships also available. Support available to part-time students. Financial award application deadline: 1/1. *Faculty research:* Astrophysics, atmospheric physics, condensed matter physics, quantum optics and quantum information. *Total annual research expenditures:* $4.8 million. *Unit head:* Dr. Todd Pittman, Graduate Program Director, 410-455-2513, Fax: 410-455-1072,
E-mail: todd.pittman@umbc.edu. *Application contact:* Dr. Lazlo Takacs, Graduate Admissions Committee Chair, 410-455-2513, Fax: 410-455-1072,
E-mail: takacs@umbc.edu.
Website: http://physics.umbc.edu/

University of Maryland, College Park, Academic Affairs, College of Computer, Mathematical and Natural Sciences, Department of Physics, College Park, MD 20742. Offers MS, PhD. *Program availability:* Part-time, evening/weekend. Terminal master's awarded for partial completion of doctoral program. *Degree requirements:* For master's, thesis optional; for doctorate, thesis/dissertation. *Entrance requirements:* For master's, GRE General Test, GRE Subject Test (physics), minimum GPA of 3.0, 3 letters of recommendation; for doctorate, GRE General Test, GRE Subject Test (physics), 3 letters of recommendation. Electronic applications accepted. *Faculty research:* Astrometeorology, superconductivity, particle astrophysics, plasma physics, elementary particle theory.

University of Massachusetts Amherst, Graduate School, College of Natural Sciences, Department of Physics, Amherst, MA 01003. Offers MS, PhD. *Program availability:* Part-time. Terminal master's awarded for partial completion of doctoral program. *Degree requirements:* For master's, thesis or alternative; for doctorate, comprehensive exam, thesis/dissertation. *Entrance requirements:* For master's and doctorate, GRE General Test, GRE Subject Test (physics). Additional exam requirements/recommendations for international students: Required—TOEFL (minimum score 550 paper-based; 80 iBT), IELTS (minimum score 6.5). Electronic applications accepted.

University of Massachusetts Dartmouth, Graduate School, College of Engineering, Department of Physics, North Dartmouth, MA 02747-2300. Offers physics (MS). *Program availability:* Part-time. *Faculty:* 9 full-time (1 woman). *Students:* 11 full-time (4 women), 5 part-time (0 women), 5 international. Average age 28. 19 applicants, 79% accepted, 8 enrolled. In 2015, 4 master's awarded. *Degree requirements:* For master's, thesis or project. *Entrance requirements:* For master's, GRE (recommended), statement of purpose (minimum of 300 words), resume, 3 letters of recommendation, official transcripts. Additional exam requirements/recommendations for international students: Required—TOEFL (minimum score 533 paper-based; 72 iBT), IELTS (minimum score 6). *Application deadline:* For fall admission, 3/31 priority date for domestic students, 2/28 priority date for international students; for spring admission, 11/15 priority date for domestic students, 10/15 priority date for international students. Applications are processed on a rolling basis. Application fee: $60. Electronic applications accepted. *Expenses:* Tuition, state resident: full-time $2071; part-time $86.29 per credit. Tuition, nonresident: full-time $8099; part-time $337.46 per credit. *Required fees:* $18,074; $762.08 per credit. Tuition and fees vary according to course load and reciprocity agreements. *Financial support:* In 2015–16, 1 research assistantship (averaging $16,000 per year), 8 teaching assistantships (averaging $12,656 per year) were awarded; Federal Work-Study and unspecified assistantships also available. Support available to part-time students. Financial award application deadline: 3/1; financial award applicants required to submit FAFSA. *Faculty research:* Amophysics, astrophysics, computational and theoretical physics, ocean physics traffic engineering. *Total annual research expenditures:* $603,000. *Unit head:* Gaurav Khanna, Graduate Program Director, 508-910-6605, Fax: 508-999-9115, E-mail: gkhanna@umassd.edu. *Application contact:* Steven Briggs, Director of Marketing and Recruitment for Graduate Studies, 508-999-8604, Fax: 508-999-8183, E-mail: graduate@umassd.edu.
Website: http://www.umassd.edu/engineering/phy/

University of Massachusetts Lowell, College of Sciences, Department of Physics and Applied Physics, Program in Physics, Lowell, MA 01854. Offers MS, PhD. *Degree requirements:* For master's, thesis; for doctorate, 2 foreign languages, thesis/dissertation. *Entrance requirements:* For master's, GRE General Test, 3 letters of reference; for doctorate, GRE General Test, transcripts, 3

Physics

letters of reference. Additional exam requirements/recommendations for international students: Required—TOEFL.

See Display on this page and Close-Up on page 197.

University of Memphis, Graduate School, College of Arts and Sciences, Department of Physics, Memphis, TN 38152. Offers MS. *Program availability:* Part-time. *Faculty:* 4 full-time (0 women). *Students:* 10 full-time (4 women), 3 part-time (1 woman); includes 2 minority (1 American Indian or Alaska Native, non-Hispanic/Latino; 1 Asian, non-Hispanic/Latino), 9 international. Average age 26. 18 applicants, 39% accepted, 3 enrolled. In 2015, 2 master's awarded. *Degree requirements:* For master's, comprehensive exam, thesis or alternative. *Entrance requirements:* For master's, GRE General Test or MAT, 20 undergraduate hours of course work in physics. *Application deadline:* For fall admission, 8/1 for domestic students; for spring admission, 12/1 for domestic students. Applications are processed on a rolling basis. Application fee: $35 ($60 for international students). Electronic applications accepted. *Financial support:* In 2015–16, 5 students received support. Research assistantships with full tuition reimbursements available, teaching assistantships with full tuition reimbursements available, Federal Work-Study, institutionally sponsored loans, scholarships/grants, and unspecified assistantships available. Financial award application deadline: 2/15; financial award applicants required to submit FAFSA. *Faculty research:* Solid-state physics, materials science, biophysics, astrophysics, physics education. *Unit head:* Dr. M. Shah Jahan, Chair, 901-678-2620, Fax: 901-678-4733, E-mail: mjahan@memphis.edu. *Application contact:* Dr. Sanjay Mishra, Coordinator of Graduate Studies, 901-678-3115, Fax: 901-678-4733, E-mail: srmishra@memphis.edu. Website: http://www.memphis.edu/physics/index.php

University of Miami, Graduate School, College of Arts and Sciences, Department of Physics, Coral Gables, FL 33124. Offers MS, PhD. Terminal master's awarded for partial completion of doctoral program. *Degree requirements:* For master's, comprehensive exam; for doctorate, comprehensive exam, thesis/dissertation. *Entrance requirements:* For master's and doctorate, GRE General Test, GRE Subject Test. Additional exam requirements/recommendations for international students: Required—TOEFL (minimum score 550 paper-based; 80 iBT). Electronic applications accepted. *Faculty research:* High-energy theory, marine and atmospheric optics, plasma physics, solid-state physics.

University of Michigan, Rackham Graduate School, College of Literature, Science, and the Arts, Department of Physics, Ann Arbor, MI 48109. Offers PhD. *Faculty:* 68 full-time (14 women). *Students:* 141 full-time (41 women); includes 42 minority (36 Asian, non-Hispanic/Latino; 6 Hispanic/Latino), 42 international. Average age 27. 541 applicants, 20% accepted, 34 enrolled. In 2015, 17 doctorates awarded. Terminal master's awarded for partial completion of doctoral program. *Degree requirements:* For doctorate, thesis/dissertation, oral defense of dissertation, preliminary exam. *Entrance requirements:* For doctorate, GRE General Test, GRE Subject Test (physics). Additional exam requirements/recommendations for international students: Required—TOEFL (minimum score 600 paper-based; 100 iBT). *Application deadline:* For fall admission, 12/15 for domestic and international students. Application fee: $75 ($90 for international students). Electronic applications accepted. *Financial support:* In 2015–16, fellowships with full tuition reimbursements (averaging $60,000 per year), research assistantships with full tuition reimbursements (averaging $60,000 per year), teaching assistantships with full tuition reimbursements (averaging $60,000 per year) were awarded. *Faculty research:* Elementary particle, solid-state, atomic, and molecular physics (theoretical and experimental). *Total annual research expenditures:* $250,000. *Unit head:* Dr. Bradford Orr, Chair, 734-764-4437. *Application contact:* Christina A. Zigulis, Graduate Coordinator, 734-936-0658, Fax: 734-763-9694, E-mail: physics.inquiries@umich.edu. Website: http://www.lsa.umich.edu/physics/

University of Minnesota, Duluth, Graduate School, Swenson College of Science and Engineering, Department of Physics, Duluth, MN 55812-2496. Offers MS. *Program availability:* Part-time. *Degree requirements:* For master's, thesis optional, final oral exam. *Entrance requirements:* For master's, minimum GPA of 3.0 (preferred). Additional exam requirements/recommendations for international students: Required—TOEFL (minimum score 550 paper-based; 79 iBT), IELTS (minimum score 6.5), or Michigan English Language Assessment Battery (minimum score 80). Electronic applications accepted. *Faculty research:* Computational physics, neutrino physics, oceanography, computational particle physics, optics, condensed matter.

University of Minnesota, Twin Cities Campus, College of Science and Engineering, School of Physics and Astronomy, Program in Physics, Minneapolis, MN 55455-0213. Offers MS, PhD. *Program availability:* Part-time. *Degree requirements:* For master's, thesis; for doctorate, thesis/dissertation. *Entrance requirements:* For master's and doctorate, GRE General Test, GRE Subject Test. Additional exam requirements/recommendations for international students: Required—TOEFL. Electronic applications accepted. *Faculty research:* Elementary particles, condensed matter, cosmology, nuclear physics, space physics, biological physics, physics education.

University of Mississippi, Graduate School, College of Liberal Arts, University, MS 38677. Offers anthropology (MA); biology (MS, PhD); chemistry (MS, PhD); clinical psychology (PhD); economics (MA, PhD); English (MA, MFA, PhD); experimental psychology (PhD); history (MA, PhD); mathematics (MS); modern languages (MA); music (MM, PhD); philosophy (MA); physics (MA, MS, PhD); political science (MA, PhD); sociology (MA); studio art (MFA). *Program availability:* Part-time. *Faculty:* 446 full-time (186 women), 84 part-time/adjunct (36 women). *Students:* 475 full-time (233 women), 79 part-time (37 women); includes 83 minority (42 Black or African American, non-Hispanic/Latino; 9 Asian, non-Hispanic/Latino; 19 Hispanic/Latino; 13 Two or more races, non-Hispanic/Latino), 107 international. *Degree requirements:* For doctorate, thesis/dissertation. *Entrance requirements:* For master's, GRE General Test, minimum GPA of 3.0; for doctorate, GRE General Test. Additional exam requirements/recommendations for international students: Required—TOEFL. *Application deadline:* For fall admission, 4/1 for domestic students; for spring admission, 10/1 for domestic students. Applications are processed on a rolling basis. Application fee: $40. Electronic applications accepted. *Financial support:* Fellowships, research assistantships, teaching assistantships, career-related internships or fieldwork, Federal Work-Study, institutionally sponsored loans, scholarships/grants, and unspecified assistantships available. Financial award application deadline: 3/1; financial award applicants required to submit FAFSA. *Unit head:* Dean, 662-915-7177, Fax: 662-915-5792, E-mail: libarts@olemiss.edu. *Application contact:* Dr. Christy M. Wyandt, Associate Dean of Graduate School, 662-915-7474, Fax: 662-915-7577, E-mail: cwyandt@olemiss.edu.

University of Missouri, Office of Research and Graduate Studies, College of Arts and Science, Department of Physics and Astronomy, Columbia, MO 65211. Offers MS, PhD. Terminal master's awarded for partial completion of doctoral program. *Degree requirements:* For doctorate, one foreign language, comprehensive exam, thesis/dissertation. *Entrance requirements:* For master's and doctorate, GRE General Test, minimum GPA of 3.0. Additional exam requirements/recommendations for international students: Required—TOEFL (minimum score 550 paper-based; 80 iBT). Electronic

Peterson's Graduate Programs in the Physical Sciences, Mathematics, Agricultural Sciences, the Environment & Natural Resources 2017

applications accepted. *Faculty research:* Experimental and theoretical condensed-matter physics, biological physics, astronomy/astrophysics.

University of Missouri–Kansas City, College of Arts and Sciences, Department of Physics and Astronomy, Kansas City, MO 64110-2499. Offers physics (MS, PhD). PhD (interdisciplinary) offered through the School of Graduate Studies. *Program availability:* Part-time, evening/weekend. *Faculty:* 11 full-time (2 women). *Students:* 23 full-time (7 women), 12 part-time (2 women); includes 2 minority (1 Asian, non-Hispanic/Latino; 1 Hispanic/Latino), 21 international. Average age 29. 46 applicants, 30% accepted, 4 enrolled. In 2015, 13 master's awarded. Terminal master's awarded for partial completion of doctoral program. *Degree requirements:* For master's, comprehensive exam, thesis optional; for doctorate, comprehensive exam, thesis/dissertation. *Entrance requirements:* For master's and doctorate, GRE General Test. Additional exam requirements/recommendations for international students: Required—TOEFL (minimum score 550 paper-based; 80 iBT). *Application deadline:* For fall admission, 4/1 priority date for domestic and international students; for spring admission, 11/1 priority date for domestic and international students. Applications are processed on a rolling basis. Application fee: $45 ($50 for international students). Electronic applications accepted. *Financial support:* In 2015–16, 15 research assistantships with tuition reimbursements (averaging $19,102 per year), 9 teaching assistantships with tuition reimbursements (averaging $14,091 per year) were awarded; Federal Work-Study, institutionally sponsored loans, and tuition waivers (full and partial) also available. Support available to part-time students. Financial award application deadline: 3/1; financial award applicants required to submit FAFSA. *Faculty research:* Surface physics, material science, statistical mechanics, computational physics, relativity and quantum theory. *Unit head:* Dr. Jerzy M. Wrobel, Chair, 816-235-1686, E-mail: wrobelj@umkc.edu. *Application contact:* Anthony Caruso, Principal Graduate Advisor, 816-235-2505, Fax: 816-235-5221, E-mail: carusoan@umkc.edu.
Website: http://cas.umkc.edu/physics/

University of Missouri–St. Louis, College of Arts and Sciences, Department of Physics and Astronomy, St. Louis, MO 63121. Offers applied physics (MS); astrophysics (MS); physics (PhD). *Program availability:* Part-time, evening/weekend. *Faculty:* 10 full-time (2 women), 3 part-time/adjunct (0 women). *Students:* 16 full-time (4 women), 8 part-time (2 women); includes 3 minority (2 Black or African American, non-Hispanic/Latino; 1 Asian, non-Hispanic/Latino), 6 international. Average age 32. 28 applicants, 39% accepted, 6 enrolled. Terminal master's awarded for partial completion of doctoral program. *Degree requirements:* For master's, thesis optional; for doctorate, thesis/dissertation. *Entrance requirements:* For master's, GRE General Test; for doctorate, GRE General Test, 2 letters of recommendation. Additional exam requirements/recommendations for international students: Required—TOEFL (minimum score 550 paper-based; 79 iBT), IELTS (minimum score 6.5). *Application deadline:* For fall admission, 7/1 for domestic and international students; for spring admission, 12/1 for domestic students, 11/1 for international students. Application fee: $50 ($40 for international students). Electronic applications accepted. *Financial support:* Research assistantships with tuition reimbursements, teaching assistantships with tuition reimbursements, and career-related internships or fieldwork available. Financial award applicants required to submit FAFSA. *Faculty research:* Biophysics, atomic physics, nonlinear dynamics, materials science. *Unit head:* Dr. Bruce Wilking, Graduate Program Advisor, 314-516-5023, Fax: 314-516-6152, E-mail: bwilking@umsl.edu. *Application contact:* 314-516-5458, Fax: 314-516-6996, E-mail: gradadm@umsl.edu.
Website: http://www.umsl.edu/~physics/

University of Nebraska–Lincoln, Graduate College, College of Arts and Sciences, Department of Physics and Astronomy, Lincoln, NE 68588. Offers astronomy (MS, PhD); physics (MS, PhD). *Degree requirements:* For master's, thesis optional; for doctorate, comprehensive exam, thesis/dissertation. *Entrance requirements:* For master's and doctorate, GRE General Test. Additional exam requirements/recommendations for international students: Required—TOEFL (minimum score 550 paper-based). Electronic applications accepted. *Faculty research:* Electromagnetics of solids and thin films, photoionization, ion collisions with atoms, molecules and surfaces, nanostructures.

University of Nevada, Las Vegas, Graduate College, College of Sciences, Department of Physics and Astronomy, Las Vegas, NV 89154-4002. Offers astronomy (MS, PhD); physics (MS, PhD). *Program availability:* Part-time. *Faculty:* 12 full-time (0 women). *Students:* 20 full-time (3 women), 2 part-time (0 women); includes 3 minority (2 Hispanic/Latino; 1 Two or more races, non-Hispanic/Latino), 6 international. Average age 33. 14 applicants, 50% accepted, 5 enrolled. In 2015, 1 master's, 3 doctorates awarded. *Degree requirements:* For master's, comprehensive exam (for some programs), thesis (for some programs); for doctorate, comprehensive exam, thesis/dissertation. *Entrance requirements:* For master's and doctorate, GRE General Test. Additional exam requirements/recommendations for international students: Required—TOEFL (minimum score 550 paper-based; 80 iBT), IELTS (minimum score 7). *Application deadline:* For fall admission, 5/15 for domestic students, 5/1 for international students; for spring admission, 11/15 for domestic students, 10/1 for international students. Application fee: $60 ($95 for international students). Electronic applications accepted. *Expenses:* $264 per credit state resident full-time and part-time; $6,955 per semester, $264 per credit nonresident full-time; $555 per credit nonresident part-time. *Financial support:* In 2015–16, 19 students received support, including 2 research assistantships with partial tuition reimbursements available (averaging $18,150 per year), 17 teaching assistantships with partial tuition reimbursements available (averaging $16,640 per year); institutionally sponsored loans, scholarships/grants, health care benefits, and unspecified assistantships also available. Financial award application deadline: 3/1. *Faculty research:* Gamma-ray bursters astrophysics, cosmology and dark matter astrophysics, experimental high pressure physics, theoretical condensed matter physics, laser-plasma atomic physics. *Total annual research expenditures:* $3 million. *Unit head:* Stephen Lepp, Chair/Professor, 702-895-4455, E-mail: lepp@physics.unlv.edu. *Application contact:* Graduate College Admissions Evaluator, 702-895-3367, Fax: 702-895-4180, E-mail: gradadmissions@unlv.edu.
Website: http://www.physics.unlv.edu/academics.html

University of Nevada, Reno, Graduate School, College of Science, Department of Physics, Reno, NV 89557. Offers MS, PhD. Terminal master's awarded for partial completion of doctoral program. *Degree requirements:* For master's, thesis optional; for doctorate, thesis/dissertation. *Entrance requirements:* For master's, GRE General Test, GRE Subject Test, minimum GPA of 2.75; for doctorate, GRE General Test, GRE Subject Test, minimum GPA of 3.0. Additional exam requirements/recommendations for international students: Required—TOEFL (minimum score 500 paper-based; 61 iBT), IELTS (minimum score 6). Electronic applications accepted. *Faculty research:* Atomic and molecular physics.

University of New Brunswick Fredericton, School of Graduate Studies, Faculty of Science, Department of Physics, Fredericton, NB E3B 5A3, Canada. Offers M Sc, PhD. *Program availability:* Part-time. *Faculty:* 11 full-time (2 women), 1 part-time/adjunct (0 women). *Students:* 20 full-time (6 women). In 2015, 1 master's, 2 doctorates awarded. *Degree requirements:* For master's, thesis; for doctorate, comprehensive exam, thesis/dissertation. *Entrance requirements:* For master's, B Sc with minimum B average; for doctorate, M Sc, minimum GPA of 3.0. Additional exam requirements/recommendations for international students: Required—TOEFL, TWE. *Application deadline:* For fall admission, 3/1 for domestic students. Applications are processed on a rolling basis. Application fee: $50 Canadian dollars. Electronic applications accepted. *Financial support:* In 2015–16, 17 fellowships with tuition reimbursements, 31 research assistantships, 49 teaching assistantships were awarded. *Faculty research:* Optical and laser spectroscopy, infrared and microwave spectroscopy, magnetic resonance and magnetic resonance imaging, space and atmospheric physics, theoretical atomic and molecular physics, space plasma theory, theoretical molecular spectroscopy. *Unit head:* Dr. Igor Mastikhin, Director of Graduate Studies, 506-458-7927, Fax: 506-453-4581, E-mail: mast@unb.ca. *Application contact:* Heidi Stewart, Graduate Secretary, 506-458-7488, E-mail: scigrad@unb.ca.
Website: http://go.unb.ca/gradprograms

University of New Hampshire, Graduate School, College of Engineering and Physical Sciences, Department of Physics, Durham, NH 03824. Offers MS, PhD. Terminal master's awarded for partial completion of doctoral program. *Degree requirements:* For master's, thesis or alternative; for doctorate, thesis/dissertation. *Entrance requirements:* For master's and doctorate, GRE General Test. Additional exam requirements/recommendations for international students: Required—TOEFL (minimum score 550 paper-based; 80 iBT). Electronic applications accepted. *Faculty research:* Astrophysics and space physics, nuclear physics, atomic and molecular physics, nonlinear dynamical systems.

University of New Mexico, Graduate Studies, College of Arts and Sciences, Program in Physics, Albuquerque, NM 87131. Offers MS, PhD. *Program availability:* Part-time. *Faculty:* 28 full-time (2 women), 1 part-time/adjunct (0 women). *Students:* 55 full-time (9 women), 15 part-time (1 woman); includes 10 minority (4 Asian, non-Hispanic/Latino; 6 Hispanic/Latino), 25 international. Average age 27. 86 applicants, 12% accepted, 10 enrolled. In 2015, 12 master's, 9 doctorates awarded. Terminal master's awarded for partial completion of doctoral program. *Degree requirements:* For master's, comprehensive exam (for some programs), preliminary exams or thesis; for doctorate, comprehensive exam, thesis/dissertation. *Entrance requirements:* For master's and doctorate, GRE General Test; GRE Subject Test (physics). Additional exam requirements/recommendations for international students: Required—TOEFL (minimum score 550 paper-based; 80 iBT), IELTS (minimum score 7). *Application deadline:* For fall admission, 1/15 for domestic students, 1/15 priority date for international students; for spring admission, 8/1 for domestic students, 8/1 priority date for international students. Application fee: $50. Electronic applications accepted. *Financial support:* Fellowships, research assistantships with full tuition reimbursements, teaching assistantships with full tuition reimbursements, career-related internships or fieldwork, scholarships/grants, traineeships, health care benefits, and unspecified assistantships available. Support available to part-time students. Financial award application deadline: 2/1; financial award applicants required to submit FAFSA. *Faculty research:* Astronomy and astrophysics, biological physics, condensed-matter physics, nonlinear science and complexity, optics and photonics, quantum information, subatomic physics. *Unit head:* Dr. Wolfgang Rudolph, Chair, 505-277-1517, Fax: 505-277-1520, E-mail: wrudolph@unm.edu. *Application contact:* Alisa Gibson, Coordinator, Academic Programs, 505-277-1514, Fax: 505-277-1520, E-mail: agibson@unm.edu.
Website: http://panda.unm.edu

University of New Orleans, Graduate School, College of Sciences, Department of Physics, New Orleans, LA 70148. Offers MS, PhD. *Program availability:* Part-time, evening/weekend. *Degree requirements:* For master's, thesis (for some programs). *Entrance requirements:* For master's, GRE General Test. Additional exam requirements/recommendations for international students: Required—TOEFL (minimum score 550 paper-based; 79 iBT), IELTS. Electronic applications accepted. *Faculty research:* Underwater acoustics, applied electromagnetics, experimental atomic beams, digital signal processing, astrophysics.

The University of North Carolina at Chapel Hill, Graduate School, College of Arts and Sciences, Department of Physics and Astronomy, Chapel Hill, NC 27599. Offers physics (MS, PhD). Terminal master's awarded for partial completion of doctoral program. *Degree requirements:* For master's, comprehensive exam; for doctorate, comprehensive exam, thesis/dissertation. *Entrance requirements:* For master's and doctorate, GRE General Test, minimum GPA of 3.0. Electronic applications accepted. *Faculty research:* Observational astronomy, fullerenes, polarized beams, nanotubes, nucleosynthesis in stars and supernovae, superstring theory, ballistic transport in semiconductors, gravitation.

University of North Dakota, Graduate School, College of Arts and Sciences, Department of Physics, Grand Forks, ND 58202. Offers MS, PhD. *Degree requirements:* For master's, thesis, final exam; for doctorate, comprehensive exam, thesis/dissertation, final exam. *Entrance requirements:* For master's, minimum GPA of 3.0; for doctorate, minimum GPA of 3.5. Additional exam requirements/recommendations for international students: Required—TOEFL (minimum score 550 paper-based; 79 iBT), IELTS (minimum score 6.5). Electronic applications accepted. *Faculty research:* Solid state physics, atomic and molecular physics, astrophysics, health physics.

University of Northern Iowa, Graduate College, College of Humanities, Arts and Sciences, MA Program in Science Education, Cedar Falls, IA 50614. Offers earth science education (MA); physics education (MA); science education (MA). *Students:* 2 full-time (1 woman), 37 part-time (23 women); includes 1 minority (Hispanic/Latino). 3 applicants.. In 2015, 1 master's awarded. *Degree requirements:* For master's, comprehensive exam (for some programs), thesis or alternative. *Entrance requirements:* For master's, minimum GPA of 3.0. Additional exam requirements/recommendations for international students: Required—TOEFL (minimum score 500 paper-based; 61 iBT). *Application deadline:* For fall admission, 8/1 priority date for domestic students. Applications are processed on a rolling basis. Application fee: $50 ($70 for international students). Electronic applications accepted. *Financial support:* Application deadline: 2/1. *Unit head:* Dr. Dawn Del Carlo, Coordinator, 319-273-3296, Fax: 319-273-7140, E-mail: sciedgradcoord@uni.edu. *Application contact:* Laurie S. Russell, Record Analyst, 319-273-2623, Fax: 319-273-2885, E-mail: laurie.russell@uni.edu.
Website: http://www.uni.edu/science-ed/graduate-program

University of Notre Dame, Graduate School, College of Science, Department of Physics, Notre Dame, IN 46556. Offers MS, PhD. *Degree requirements:* For doctorate, thesis/dissertation, candidacy exam. *Entrance requirements:* For doctorate, GRE General Test, GRE Subject Test. Additional exam requirements/recommendations for international students: Required—TOEFL (minimum score 600 paper-based; 80 iBT). Electronic applications accepted. *Faculty research:* High energy, nuclear, atomic, condensed-matter physics; astrophysics; biophysics.

University of Oklahoma, College of Arts and Sciences, Department of Physics and Astronomy, Norman, OK 73019. Offers physics (MS, PhD). *Program availability:* Part-time. *Faculty:* 32 full-time (3 women). *Students:* 57 full-time (13 women), 23 part-time (7 women); includes 2 minority (1 Asian, non-Hispanic/Latino; 1 Hispanic/Latino), 39

Peterson's Graduate Programs in the Physical Sciences, Mathematics, Agricultural Sciences, the Environment & Natural Resources 2017

www.petersons.com **189**

Physics

international. Average age 27. 78 applicants, 27% accepted, 19 enrolled. In 2015, 8 master's, 11 doctorates awarded. Terminal master's awarded for partial completion of doctoral program. *Degree requirements:* For master's, comprehensive exam, thesis (for some programs); for doctorate, comprehensive exam, thesis/dissertation. *Entrance requirements:* Additional exam requirements/recommendations for international students: Required—TOEFL (minimum score 80 iBT) or IELTS (minimum score 6.5). *Application deadline:* For fall admission, 4/1 for domestic students, 5/31 for international students; for spring admission, 11/15 for international students; for summer admission, 11/1 for domestic students. Application fee: $50 ($100 for international students). Electronic applications accepted. *Expenses:* Tuition, state resident: full-time $4577; part-time $190.70 per credit hour. Tuition, nonresident: full-time $17,758; part-time $739.90 per credit hour. *Required fees:* $3060; $115.70 per credit hour. $141.50 per semester. *Financial support:* In 2015–16, 72 students received support, including 30 research assistantships with tuition reimbursements available (averaging $15,860 per year), 48 teaching assistantships with tuition reimbursements available (averaging $14,250 per year); fellowships, institutionally sponsored loans, scholarships/grants, health care benefits, and unspecified assistantships also available. Financial award application deadline: 6/1; financial award applicants required to submit FAFSA. *Faculty research:* Astrophysics; atomic, molecular, and optical physics; high energy physics; condensed matter physics. *Total annual research expenditures:* $3.5 million. *Unit head:* Dr. Gregory A. Parker, Chair, 405-325-3961, Fax: 405-325-7557, E-mail: office@nhn.ou.edu. *Application contact:* Dr. Lloyd Bumm, Professor, 405-325-3961 Ext. 36123, Fax: 405-325-7557, E-mail: grad@nhn.ou.edu. Website: http://www.nhn.ou.edu

University of Oregon, Graduate School, College of Arts and Sciences, Department of Physics, Eugene, OR 97403. Offers MA, MS, PhD. Terminal master's awarded for partial completion of doctoral program. *Degree requirements:* For doctorate, thesis/dissertation. *Entrance requirements:* For master's and doctorate, GRE General Test, GRE Subject Test, minimum GPA of 3.0. Additional exam requirements/recommendations for international students: Required—TOEFL. *Faculty research:* Solid-state and chemical physics, optical physics, elementary particle physics, astrophysics, atomic and molecular physics.

University of Ottawa, Faculty of Graduate and Postdoctoral Studies, Faculty of Science, Ottawa-Carleton Institute for Physics, Ottawa, ON K1N 6N5, Canada. Offers M Sc, PhD. M Sc, PhD offered jointly with Carleton University. *Degree requirements:* For master's, thesis or alternative; for doctorate, comprehensive exam, thesis/dissertation, seminar. *Entrance requirements:* For master's, honors B Sc degree or equivalent, minimum B average; for doctorate, M Sc, minimum B+ average. Electronic applications accepted. *Faculty research:* Condensed matter physics and statistical physics (CMS), subatomic physics (SAP), medical physics (Med).

University of Pennsylvania, School of Arts and Sciences, Graduate Group in Physics and Astronomy, Philadelphia, PA 19104. Offers medical physics (MS); physics (PhD). *Program availability:* Part-time. *Faculty:* 43 full-time (7 women), 11 part-time/adjunct (0 women). *Students:* 100 full-time (28 women), 1 part-time (0 women); includes 18 minority (1 Black or African American, non-Hispanic/Latino; 9 Asian, non-Hispanic/Latino; 6 Hispanic/Latino; 2 Two or more races, non-Hispanic/Latino), 20 international. Average age 26. 371 applicants, 20% accepted, 28 enrolled. In 2015, 35 master's, 24 doctorates awarded. *Expenses:* Tuition, area resident: Full-time $31,068; part-time $5762 per course. *Required fees:* $3200; $336 per course. Full-time tuition and fees vary according to degree level, program and student level. Part-time tuition and fees vary according to course load, degree level and program. *Financial support:* Application deadline: 12/1. Website: http://www.physics.upenn.edu/graduate/

University of Pittsburgh, Dietrich School of Arts and Sciences, Department of Physics and Astronomy, Pittsburgh, PA 15260. Offers MS, PhD. *Faculty:* 45 full-time (4 women), 2 part-time/adjunct (both women). *Students:* 95 full-time (20 women), 3 part-time (2 women); includes 4 minority (1 Asian, non-Hispanic/Latino; 2 Hispanic/Latino; 1 Two or more races, non-Hispanic/Latino), 63 international. Average age 25. 249 applicants, 26% accepted, 16 enrolled. In 2015, 6 master's, 12 doctorates awarded. Terminal master's awarded for partial completion of doctoral program. *Degree requirements:* For master's, comprehensive exam, thesis or alternative; for doctorate, comprehensive exam, thesis/dissertation, preliminary evaluation, student teaching, admission to candidacy, minimum of 72 credits. *Entrance requirements:* For master's, GRE General Test, minimum GPA of 3.0; for doctorate, GRE General Test; GRE Subject Test (recommended), minimum GPA of 3.0. Additional exam requirements/recommendations for international students: Required—TOEFL (minimum score 90 iBT, 22 in each component) or IELTS (minimum score 6.5 in each section). *Application deadline:* For fall admission, 1/15 priority date for domestic and international students. Applications are processed on a rolling basis. Application fee: $0 ($50 for international students). Electronic applications accepted. *Expenses:* $21,260 in-state per year, $34,944 out-of-state per year; $800 fees. *Financial support:* In 2015–16, 92 students received support, including 14 fellowships with tuition reimbursements available (averaging $30,257 per year), 42 research assistantships with tuition reimbursements available (averaging $26,340 per year), 34 teaching assistantships with tuition reimbursements available (averaging $26,340 per year); scholarships/grants, health care benefits, and tuition waivers (full and partial) also available. Financial award application deadline: 4/15. *Faculty research:* Astrophysics and cosmology, particle physics, condensed matter and solid-state physics, biological physics, nanoscience, physics education research. *Total annual research expenditures:* $9.5 million. *Unit head:* Dr. Adam Leibovich, Department Chair, 412-624-6381, Fax: 412-624-9163, E-mail: adaml@pitt.edu. *Application contact:* Dr. Robert P. Devaty, Admissions Committee Chair, 412-624-9009, Fax: 412-624-9163, E-mail: devaty@pitt.edu. Website: http://www.physicsandastronomy.pitt.edu/

See Display below and Close-Up on page 199.

University of Pittsburgh, Dietrich School of Arts and Sciences, Program in Computational Modeling and Simulation, Pittsburgh, PA 15260. Offers biological science (PhD); chemistry (PhD); computer science (PhD); economics (PhD); mathematics (PhD); physics and astronomy (PhD); psychology (PhD); statistics (PhD). *Program availability:* Part-time. *Faculty:* 3 full-time (0 women). *Students:* 3 full-time (1 woman); includes 2 minority (both Asian, non-Hispanic/Latino). Average age 23. 13 applicants, 31% accepted, 2 enrolled. *Degree requirements:* For doctorate, comprehensive exam, thesis/dissertation, preliminary exam. *Entrance requirements:* For doctorate, GRE, statement of purpose, transcripts for all college-level institutions attended, three letters of reference. Additional exam requirements/recommendations for international students: Required—TOEFL (minimum score 90 iBT), IELTS (minimum score 7). *Application deadline:* For fall admission, 1/15 for domestic and international students. Applications are processed on a rolling basis. Application fee: $0 ($50 for international students). Electronic applications accepted. Tuition and fees vary according to program. *Financial support:* In 2015–16, 3 students received support, including 2 fellowships with full tuition reimbursements available (averaging $27,000 per year), 1 research assistantship with full tuition reimbursement available (averaging $21,500 per year); tuition waivers (full) also available. Financial award application deadline: 4/15. *Faculty research:* Econometric modeling, developing reduced-scaling first principles approaches for expedited predictions of molecular and materials properties, developing computational models to quantitatively describe origins of reactivity and selectivity in organocatalytic

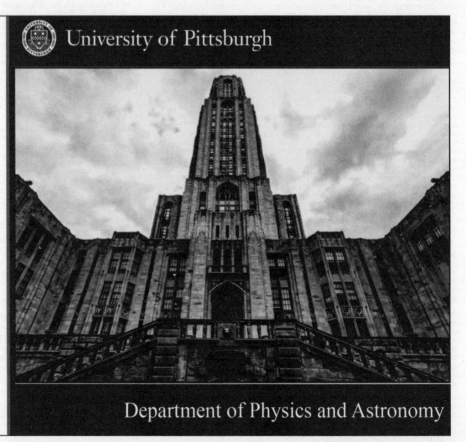
190 www.petersons.com

Peterson's Graduate Programs in the Physical Sciences, Mathematics, Agricultural Sciences, the Environment & Natural Resources 2017

reactions. *Unit head:* Dr. Kathleen Blee, Associate Dean, Graduate Studies and Research, 412-624-3939, Fax: 412-624-6855. *Application contact:* Wendy G. Janocha, Graduate Administrator, 412-648-7251, E-mail: wgj1@pitt.edu.
Website: http://cmsp.pitt.edu/

University of Puerto Rico, Mayagüez Campus, Graduate Studies, College of Arts and Sciences, Department of Physics, Mayagüez, PR 00681-9000. Offers MS. *Program availability:* Part-time. *Degree requirements:* For master's, comprehensive exam, thesis. *Entrance requirements:* For master's, bachelor's degree in physics or its equivalent. *Faculty research:* Atomic and molecular physics, nuclear physics, nonlinear thermostatics, fluid dynamics, molecular spectroscopy.

University of Puerto Rico, Río Piedras Campus, College of Natural Sciences, Department of Physics, San Juan, PR 00931-3300. Offers chemical physics (PhD); physics (MS). *Program availability:* Part-time. *Degree requirements:* For master's, comprehensive exam, thesis; for doctorate, comprehensive exam, thesis/dissertation. *Entrance requirements:* For master's, GRE General Test, GRE Subject Test, interview, minimum GPA of 3.0, letter of recommendation (3); for doctorate, GRE, master's degree, minimum GPA of 3.0, letter of recommendation (3). Additional exam requirements/recommendations for international students: Required—TOEFL. *Faculty research:* Energy transfer process through Van der Vacqs interactions, study of the photodissociation of ketene.

University of Regina, Faculty of Graduate Studies and Research, Faculty of Science, Department of Physics, Regina, SK S4S 0A2, Canada. Offers M Sc, PhD. *Program availability:* Part-time. *Degree requirements:* For master's, thesis; for doctorate, thesis/dissertation. *Entrance requirements:* For master's, honors degree in physics or engineering physics; for doctorate, M Sc or equivalent. Additional exam requirements/recommendations for international students: Required—TOEFL (minimum score 580 paper-based; 80 iBT), IELTS (minimum score 6.5), PTE (minimum score 59). Electronic applications accepted. *Faculty research:* Quantum mechanics, theoretical nuclear physics, quantum field theory, relativistic astrophysics and cosmology, classical electrodynamics.

University of Rhode Island, Graduate School, College of Arts and Sciences, Department of Physics, Kingston, RI 02881. Offers MS, PhD. *Program availability:* Part-time, evening/weekend. *Faculty:* 17 full-time (1 woman). *Students:* 17 full-time (2 women), 1 (woman) part-time; includes 2 minority (both Black or African American, non-Hispanic/Latino), 6 international. In 2015, 4 master's, 2 doctorates awarded. *Degree requirements:* For master's, comprehensive exam (for some programs), thesis optional; for doctorate, comprehensive exam, thesis/dissertation. *Entrance requirements:* For master's and doctorate, 2 letters of recommendation. Additional exam requirements/recommendations for international students: Required—TOEFL (minimum score 550 paper-based). *Application deadline:* For fall admission, 4/15 for domestic students, 2/1 for international students. Application fee: $65. Electronic applications accepted. *Expenses:* Tuition, state resident: full-time $11,796; part-time $655 per credit. Tuition, nonresident: full-time $24,206; part-time $1345 per credit. *Required fees:* $1546; $44 per credit. One-time fee: $155 full-time; $35 part-time. *Financial support:* In 2015–16, 8 research assistantships with tuition reimbursements (averaging $16,243 per year), 10 teaching assistantships with tuition reimbursements (averaging $15,361 per year) were awarded. Financial award application deadline: 3/1; financial award applicants required to submit FAFSA. *Total annual research expenditures:* $825,653. *Unit head:* Dr. Oleg Andreev, Chair, 401-874-2060, Fax: 401-874-2380, E-mail: andreev@mail.uri.edu. *Application contact:* Dr. Leonard M. Kahn, Director of Graduate Studies, 401-874-2503, Fax: 401-874-2380, E-mail: lkahn@uri.edu.
Website: http://www.phys.uri.edu/index.html

University of Rochester, School of Arts and Sciences, Department of Physics and Astronomy, Rochester, NY 14627. Offers physics (MA, MS, PhD); physics and astronomy (PhD). *Program availability:* Part-time. *Faculty:* 27 full-time (3 women). *Students:* 103 full-time (24 women), 1 (woman) part-time; includes 11 minority (5 Asian, non-Hispanic/Latino; 4 Hispanic/Latino; 2 Two or more races, non-Hispanic/Latino), 32 international. 290 applicants, 30% accepted, 27 enrolled. In 2015, 6 master's, 8 doctorates awarded. Terminal master's awarded for partial completion of doctoral program. *Degree requirements:* For master's, comprehensive exam, thesis (for some programs); for doctorate, comprehensive exam, thesis/dissertation, qualifying exam. *Entrance requirements:* For master's and doctorate, GRE General Test. Additional exam requirements/recommendations for international students: Required—TOEFL. *Application deadline:* For fall admission, 1/15 priority date for domestic students. Application fee: $60. Electronic applications accepted. *Expenses: Tuition, area resident:* Full-time $47,450; part-time $1482 per credit hour. *Required fees:* $528. Tuition and fees vary according to program. *Financial support:* Fellowships, research assistantships, teaching assistantships, and tuition waivers (full and partial) available. Financial award application deadline: 2/1. *Faculty research:* Astronomy and astrophysics, biological physics, condensed matter physics, high energy/nuclear physics, quantum optics. *Unit head:* Nicholas P. Bigelow, Chair, 585-275-4344. *Application contact:* Laura Blumkin, Graduate Coordinator, 585-275-4356, E-mail: laurablumkin@pas.rochester.edu.
Website: http://www.pas.rochester.edu/urpas/pages/graduate/gradprograms

University of Saskatchewan, College of Graduate Studies and Research, College of Arts and Science, Department of Physics and Engineering Physics, Saskatoon, SK S7N 5A2, Canada. Offers M Sc, PhD. *Degree requirements:* For master's, thesis; for doctorate, comprehensive exam (for some programs), thesis/dissertation. *Entrance requirements:* Additional exam requirements/recommendations for international students: Required—TOEFL (minimum score 80 iBT); Recommended—IELTS (minimum score 6.5). Electronic applications accepted.

University of South Carolina, The Graduate School, College of Arts and Sciences, Department of Physics and Astronomy, Columbia, SC 29208. Offers IMA, MAT, MS, PSM, PhD. IMA and MAT offered in cooperation with the College of Education. *Program availability:* Part-time. Terminal master's awarded for partial completion of doctoral program. *Degree requirements:* For master's, comprehensive exam, thesis; for doctorate, one foreign language, comprehensive exam, thesis/dissertation. *Entrance requirements:* For master's and doctorate, GRE General Test, GRE Subject Test. Additional exam requirements/recommendations for international students: Required—TOEFL (minimum score 570 paper-based; 75 iBT). Electronic applications accepted. *Faculty research:* Condensed matter, intermediate-energy nuclear physics, foundations of quantum mechanics, astronomy/astrophysics.

The University of South Dakota, Graduate School, College of Arts and Sciences, Department of Physics, Vermillion, SD 57069-2390. Offers MS, PhD. PhD program offered jointly with South Dakota School of Mines and Technology and South Dakota State University. *Entrance requirements:* For master's and doctorate, GRE. Additional exam requirements/recommendations for international students: Required—TOEFL (minimum score 550 paper-based; 79 iBT). *Financial support:* Unspecified assistantships available.
Website: http://www.usd.edu/arts-and-sciences/physics/

University of Southern California, Graduate School, Dana and David Dornsife College of Letters, Arts and Sciences, Department of Physics and Astronomy, Los Angeles, CA 90089. Offers physics (MA, MS, PhD). *Program availability:* Part-time. Terminal master's awarded for partial completion of doctoral program. *Degree requirements:* For master's, comprehensive exam, thesis (for some programs); for doctorate, comprehensive exam, thesis/dissertation. *Entrance requirements:* For doctorate, GRE General Test, GRE Subject Test (physics), 3 letters of recommendation, statement of purpose. Additional exam requirements/recommendations for international students: Required—TOEFL (minimum score 550 paper-based; 80 iBT). Electronic applications accepted. *Faculty research:* High-energy particle theory, condensed matter physics, astrophysics, solar and cosmology, biophysics, computational physics.

University of Southern Mississippi, Graduate School, College of Science and Technology, Department of Physics and Astronomy, Hattiesburg, MS 39406-0001. Offers computational science (PhD); physics (MS). *Degree requirements:* For master's, comprehensive exam, thesis; for doctorate, comprehensive exam, thesis/dissertation. *Entrance requirements:* For master's, GRE General Test, minimum GPA of 2.75 in last 60 hours; for doctorate, GRE General Test, minimum GPA of 3.5. Additional exam requirements/recommendations for international students: Required—TOEFL, IELTS. *Faculty research:* Polymers, atomic physics, fluid mechanics, liquid crystals, refractory materials.

University of South Florida, College of Arts and Sciences, Department of Physics, Tampa, FL 33620-9951. Offers applied physics (PhD); physics (MS), including applied physics, atmospheric physics, atomic and molecular physics, laser physics, materials physics, medical physics, optical physics, semiconductor physics, solid state physics. MSE offered jointly with College of Engineering. *Program availability:* Part-time. *Faculty:* 25 full-time (2 women). *Students:* 71 full-time (16 women), 6 part-time (1 woman); includes 14 minority (2 Black or African American, non-Hispanic/Latino; 12 Hispanic/Latino), 36 international. Average age 31. 97 applicants, 21% accepted, 12 enrolled. In 2015, 14 master's, 8 doctorates awarded. *Degree requirements:* For master's, comprehensive exam, thesis optional; for doctorate, comprehensive exam, thesis/dissertation. *Entrance requirements:* For master's and doctorate, GRE General Test; GRE Subject Test in physics (recommended), minimum GPA of 3.0, three letters of recommendation, statement of purpose. Additional exam requirements/recommendations for international students: Required—TOEFL (minimum score 550 paper-based; 79 iBT) or IELTS (minimum score 6.5). *Application deadline:* For fall admission, 2/15 priority date for domestic students, 1/2 for international students; for spring admission, 9/1 for domestic students, 7/1 for international students. Applications are processed on a rolling basis. Application fee: $30. Electronic applications accepted. *Financial support:* In 2015–16, 70 students received support, including 27 research assistantships with tuition reimbursements available (averaging $15,272 per year), 43 teaching assistantships with tuition reimbursements available (averaging $16,267 per year); unspecified assistantships also available. *Faculty research:* The molecular organization of collagen, lipid rafts in biological membranes, the formation of Alzheimer plaques, the role of cellular ion pumps in wound healing, carbon nanotubes as biological detectors, optical imaging of neuronal activity, three-dimensional imaging of intact tissues, motility of cancer cells, the optical detection of pathogens in water. *Total annual research expenditures:* $2.4 million. *Unit head:* Dr. Pritish Mukherjee, Professor and Chairperson, 813-974-3293, Fax: 813-974-5813, E-mail: pritish@usf.edu. *Application contact:* Dr. Lilia Woods, Professor and Graduate Program Director, 813-974-2862, Fax: 813-974-5813, E-mail: lmwoods@usf.edu.
Website: http://physics.usf.edu/

The University of Tennessee, Graduate School, College of Arts and Sciences, Department of Physics and Astronomy, Knoxville, TN 37996. Offers physics (MS, PhD). *Program availability:* Part-time. *Degree requirements:* For master's, thesis or alternative; for doctorate, thesis/dissertation. *Entrance requirements:* For master's and doctorate, minimum GPA of 2.7. Additional exam requirements/recommendations for international students: Required—TOEFL. Electronic applications accepted.

The University of Tennessee, The University of Tennessee Space Institute, Tullahoma, TN 37388. Offers aerospace engineering (MS, PhD); biomedical engineering (MS, PhD); engineering science (MS, PhD); industrial and systems engineering/engineering management (MS, PhD); mechanical engineering (MS, PhD); physics (MS, PhD). *Program availability:* Part-time, blended/hybrid learning. *Faculty:* 27 full-time (1 woman), 12 part-time/adjunct (1 woman). *Students:* 32 full-time (7 women), 71 part-time (10 women); includes 10 minority (5 Black or African American, non-Hispanic/Latino; 1 American Indian or Alaska Native, non-Hispanic/Latino; 3 Asian, non-Hispanic/Latino; 1 Hispanic/Latino), 11 international. In 2015, 26 master's, 2 doctorates awarded. Terminal master's awarded for partial completion of doctoral program. *Degree requirements:* For doctorate, one foreign language, thesis/dissertation. *Entrance requirements:* Additional exam requirements/recommendations for international students: Required—TOEFL (minimum score 550 paper-based; 80 iBT), IELTS (minimum score 6.5). *Application deadline:* For fall admission, 2/1 for international students; for spring admission, 6/15 for international students. Applications are processed on a rolling basis. Application fee: $60. Electronic applications accepted. *Expenses:* $5,309 in-state tuition per semester full-time, $75 per semester activity fee. *Financial support:* In 2015–16, 2 fellowships with full tuition reimbursements (averaging $2,496 per year), 24 research assistantships with full tuition reimbursements (averaging $22,872 per year) were awarded; career-related internships or fieldwork, Federal Work-Study, institutionally sponsored loans, health care benefits, and unspecified assistantships also available. *Faculty research:* Fluid mechanics/aerodynamics, chemical and electric propulsion and laser diagnostics, computational mechanics and simulations, carbon fiber production and composite materials. *Total annual research expenditures:* $1.2 million. *Unit head:* Dr. James Simonton, Associate Executive Director, 931-393-7319, Fax: 931-393-7211, E-mail: jsimonto@utsi.edu. *Application contact:* Dee Merriman, Director, 931-393-7213, Fax: 931-393-7211, E-mail: dmerrima@utsi.edu.
Website: http://www.utsi.edu/

The University of Texas at Arlington, Graduate School, College of Science, Department of Physics, Arlington, TX 76019. Offers physics (MS); physics and applied physics (PhD). *Program availability:* Part-time. Terminal master's awarded for partial completion of doctoral program. *Degree requirements:* For master's, thesis optional; for doctorate, comprehensive exam, thesis/dissertation, internship or substitute. *Entrance requirements:* For master's, GRE General Test, minimum GPA of 3.0 in last 60 hours of course work; for doctorate, GRE General Test, minimum GPA of 3.0 in last 60 hours of course work, 30 hours graduate course work in physics. Additional exam requirements/recommendations for international students: Required—TOEFL (minimum score 550 paper-based; 79 iBT). *Faculty research:* Particle physics, astrophysics, condensed matter theory and experiment.

The University of Texas at Austin, Graduate School, College of Natural Sciences, Department of Physics, Austin, TX 78712-1111. Offers MA, MS, PhD. *Degree requirements:* For master's, thesis; for doctorate, thesis/dissertation. *Entrance* *requirements:* For master's and doctorate, GRE General Test, GRE Subject Test (physics). Electronic applications accepted.

The University of Texas at Dallas, School of Natural Sciences and Mathematics, Department of Physics, Richardson, TX 75080. Offers MS, PhD. *Program availability:* Part-time, evening/weekend. *Faculty:* 26 full-time (1 woman). *Students:* 58 full-time (11 women), 2 part-time (1 woman); includes 6 minority (1 Asian, non-Hispanic/Latino; 4 Hispanic/Latino; 1 Two or more races, non-Hispanic/Latino), 30 international. Average age 29. 73 applicants, 36% accepted, 14 enrolled. In 2015, 14 master's, 8 doctorates awarded. *Degree requirements:* For master's, thesis optional, industrial internship; for doctorate, thesis/dissertation, publishable paper. *Entrance requirements:* For master's and doctorate, GRE General Test, minimum GPA of 3.0 in upper-level coursework in field. Additional exam requirements/recommendations for international students: Required—TOEFL (minimum score 550 paper-based). *Application deadline:* For fall admission, 7/15 for domestic students, 5/1 priority date for international students; for spring admission, 11/15 for domestic students, 9/1 priority date for international students. Applications are processed on a rolling basis. Application fee: $50 ($100 for international students). Electronic applications accepted. *Expenses:* Tuition, state resident: full-time $11,940; part-time $663 per semester hour. Tuition, nonresident: full-time $22,786; part-time $1266 per semester hour. Tuition and fees vary according to course load. *Financial support:* In 2015–16, 58 students received support, including 1 fellowship with partial tuition reimbursement available (averaging $350 per year), 19 research assistantships with partial tuition reimbursements available (averaging $23,274 per year), 39 teaching assistantships with partial tuition reimbursements available (averaging $17,100 per year); career-related internships or fieldwork, Federal Work-Study, institutionally sponsored loans, scholarships/grants, and unspecified assistantships also available. Support available to part-time students. Financial award application deadline: 4/30; financial award applicants required to submit FAFSA. *Faculty research:* Ionospheric and magnetospheric electrodynamics; high-energy proton collisions and muon detector design and construction; condensed matter physics with emphasis on nanoscience; optical properties of solids including semiconductors, thermoelectric materials and nanomaterials; gravitational lensing and applications to cosmology. *Unit head:* Dr. Mark Lee, Department Head, 972-883-2835, Fax: 972-883-2848, E-mail: physdept@exchange.utdallas.edu. *Application contact:* Dr. Phillip Charles Anderson, Graduate Advisor, 972-883-2875, Fax: 972-883-2848, E-mail: physdept@exchange.utdallas.edu.
Website: http://www.utdallas.edu/physics/

The University of Texas at El Paso, Graduate School, College of Science, Department of Physics, El Paso, TX 79968-0001. Offers MS. *Program availability:* Part-time, evening/weekend. *Degree requirements:* For master's, thesis optional. *Entrance requirements:* For master's, GRE, minimum GPA of 3.0. Additional exam requirements/recommendations for international students: Required—TOEFL; Recommended—IELTS. Electronic applications accepted.

The University of Texas at San Antonio, College of Sciences, Department of Physics and Astronomy, San Antonio, TX 78249-0617. Offers physics (MS, PhD). *Program availability:* Part-time. *Faculty:* 14 full-time (3 women), 13 part-time/adjunct (0 women). *Students:* 53 full-time (14 women), 15 part-time (5 women); includes 17 minority (1 Black or African American, non-Hispanic/Latino; 3 Asian, non-Hispanic/Latino; 9 Hispanic/Latino; 4 Two or more races, non-Hispanic/Latino), 25 international. Average age 30. 38 applicants, 50% accepted, 11 enrolled. In 2015, 5 master's, 13 doctorates awarded. Terminal master's awarded for partial completion of doctoral program. *Degree requirements:* For master's, comprehensive exam, thesis; for doctorate, comprehensive exam, thesis/dissertation, at least 1 publication. *Entrance requirements:* For master's, GRE, resume, two letters of recommendation, statement of purpose; for doctorate, GRE, minimum GPA of 3.0 on last 60 hours of undergraduate or graduate coursework, resume, two letters of recommendation, statement of purpose. Additional exam requirements/recommendations for international students: Required—TOEFL (minimum score 550 paper-based; 79 iBT), IELTS (minimum score 6.5). *Application deadline:* For fall admission, 7/1 for domestic students, 4/1 for international students; for spring admission, 11/1 for domestic students, 9/1 for international students. Application fee: $45 ($80 for international students). Electronic applications accepted. *Expenses:* Contact institution. *Financial support:* In 2015–16, 36 students received support, including 18 fellowships with tuition reimbursements available (averaging $25,000 per year), 7 research assistantships with tuition reimbursements available (averaging $27,000 per year), 22 teaching assistantships with full tuition reimbursements available (averaging $27,000 per year); Federal Work-Study, scholarships/grants, health care benefits, and unspecified assistantships also available. Financial award applicants required to submit FAFSA. *Faculty research:* Ultramicroscopy, computational physics, terahertz spectroscopy, space physics, biophysics, nanotechnology materials, physics, astrophysics and cosmology, theoretical condensed matter and experimental condensed matter. *Total annual research expenditures:* $2.5 million. *Unit head:* Dr. Miguel Yacaman, Chair, 210-458-6954, Fax: 210-458-4919, E-mail: miguel.yacaman@utsa.edu. *Application contact:* Dr. Lorenzo Brancaleon, Graduate Advisor of Record, 210-458-5694, Fax: 210-458-4919, E-mail: lorenzo.brancaleon@utsa.edu.
Website: http://physics.utsa.edu/

The University of Texas Rio Grande Valley, College of Sciences, Department of Physics, Edinburg, TX 78539. Offers MS. *Program availability:* Part-time. *Faculty:* 14 full-time (2 women). *Students:* 15 full-time (4 women), 2 part-time; includes 5 minority (2 Asian, non-Hispanic/Latino; 3 Hispanic/Latino). Average age 28. 7 applicants, 100% accepted, 6 enrolled. Terminal master's awarded for partial completion of doctoral program. *Degree requirements:* For master's, thesis optional. *Entrance requirements:* For master's, GRE, three letters of recommendation. Application fee: $100. Tuition and fees vary according to course load and program. *Faculty research:* Gravitational wave astronomy, nano-photonics, modern optics and lasers, radio astronomy, nano technology, experimental and nano-scale biophysics, astrophysics, computational physics, applied and experimental physics, condensed matter physics, medical physics. *Unit head:* Dr. Soma Mukherjee, Chair, 956-665-2041, E-mail: soma.mukherjee@utrgv.edu. *Application contact:* Stephanie Ozuna, Graduate Recruiter, 956-665-3558, Fax: 956-665-2863, E-mail: stephanie.ozuna@utrgv.edu.
Website: http://portal.utpa.edu/utpa_main/daa_home/cosm_home/physics_home

The University of Toledo, College of Graduate Studies, College of Natural Sciences and Mathematics, Department of Physics and Astronomy, Toledo, OH 43606-3390. Offers photovoltaics (PSM); physics (MS, PhD), including astrophysics (PhD), materials science, medical physics (PhD); MS/PhD. *Degree requirements:* For master's, thesis; for doctorate, thesis/dissertation, departmental qualifying exam. *Entrance requirements:* For master's and doctorate, GRE General Test, GRE Subject Test, minimum cumulative point-hour ratio of 2.7 for all previous academic work, three letters of recommendation, statement of purpose, transcripts from all prior institutions attended. Additional exam requirements/recommendations for international students: Required—TOEFL (minimum score 550 paper-based; 80 iBT). Electronic applications accepted. *Faculty research:* Atomic physics, solid-state physics, materials science, astrophysics.

University of Toronto, School of Graduate Studies, Faculty of Arts and Science, Department of Physics, Toronto, ON M5S 1A1, Canada. Offers M Sc, PhD. *Degree requirements:* For master's, thesis optional; for doctorate, thesis/dissertation. *Entrance requirements:* For master's, minimum B+ average in an honors physics program or equivalent, 2 letters of reference; for doctorate, M Sc in physics or related field, 2 letters of reference. Additional exam requirements/recommendations for international students: Required—TOEFL (minimum score 580 paper-based; 93 iBT), TWE (minimum score 4). Electronic applications accepted.

The University of Tulsa, Graduate School, College of Engineering and Natural Sciences, Department of Physics and Engineering Physics, Program in Physics, Tulsa, OK 74104-3189. Offers MS, PhD. *Program availability:* Part-time. *Students:* 12 full-time (5 women), 3 part-time (0 women); includes 2 minority (1 American Indian or Alaska Native, non-Hispanic/Latino; 1 Two or more races, non-Hispanic/Latino), 12 international. Average age 30. 26 applicants, 62% accepted, 4 enrolled. Terminal master's awarded for partial completion of doctoral program. *Degree requirements:* For master's, thesis. *Entrance requirements:* For master's, GRE General Test. Additional exam requirements/recommendations for international students: Required—TOEFL (minimum score 550 paper-based; 80 iBT), IELTS (minimum score 6). *Application deadline:* Applications are processed on a rolling basis. Application fee: $55. Electronic applications accepted. *Expenses: Tuition, area resident:* Full-time $22,230; part-time $1176 per credit hour. *Required fees:* $590 per semester. Tuition and fees vary according to course load. *Financial support:* In 2015–16, 15 students received support, including 9 fellowships with full tuition reimbursements available (averaging $596 per year), 8 research assistantships with full tuition reimbursements available (averaging $14,304 per year), 9 teaching assistantships with full tuition reimbursements available (averaging $11,853 per year); career-related internships or fieldwork, Federal Work-Study, scholarships/grants, health care benefits, tuition waivers (full and partial), and unspecified assistantships also available. Support available to part-time students. Financial award application deadline: 2/1. *Faculty research:* Nanotechnology, theoretical plasma physics, theoretical and experimental condensed matter, optics, applications of laser spectroscopy to environmental applications. *Unit head:* Dr. George Miller, Program Chair, 918-631-3021, Fax: 918-631-2995, E-mail: george-miller@utulsa.edu.

University of Utah, Graduate School, College of Science, Department of Physics and Astronomy, Salt Lake City, UT 84112. Offers chemical physics (PhD); medical physics (MS, PhD); physics (MA, MS, PhD); physics teaching (PhD). *Program availability:* Part-time. *Faculty:* 34 full-time (4 women), 16 part-time/adjunct (1 woman). *Students:* 79 full-time (26 women), 19 part-time (7 women); includes 7 minority (3 Asian, non-Hispanic/Latino; 4 Hispanic/Latino), 51 international. Average age 28. 141 applicants, 30% accepted, 19 enrolled. In 2015, 13 master's, 10 doctorates awarded. Terminal master's awarded for partial completion of doctoral program. *Degree requirements:* For master's, comprehensive exam (for some programs), thesis or alternative, teaching experience, departmental exam; for doctorate, comprehensive exam, thesis/dissertation, departmental qualifying exam. *Entrance requirements:* For master's and doctorate, GRE Subject Test, minimum GPA of 3.0. Additional exam requirements/recommendations for international students: Required—TOEFL (minimum score 550 paper-based; 85 iBT). *Application deadline:* For fall admission, 4/1 priority date for domestic and international students. Applications are processed on a rolling basis. Application fee: $55 ($65 for international students). Electronic applications accepted. *Financial support:* In 2015–16, 23 research assistantships with full tuition reimbursements (averaging $23,500 per year), 52 teaching assistantships with full tuition reimbursements (averaging $20,641 per year) were awarded; institutionally sponsored loans, scholarships/grants, and unspecified assistantships also available. Financial award application deadline: 2/15; financial award applicants required to submit FAFSA. *Faculty research:* High-energy, cosmic-ray, astrophysics, medical physics, condensed matter, relativity applied physics, biophysics, astronomy. *Total annual research expenditures:* $5.2 million. *Unit head:* Dr. Carleton DeTar, Chair, 801-581-3538, Fax: 801-581-4801, E-mail: detar@physics.utah.edu. *Application contact:* Jackie Hadley, Graduate Secretary, 801-581-6861, Fax: 801-581-4801, E-mail: jackie@physics.utah.edu.
Website: http://www.physics.utah.edu/

University of Vermont, Graduate College, College of Arts and Sciences, Department of Physics, Burlington, VT 05405. Offers MS. *Entrance requirements:* For master's, GRE General Test. Additional exam requirements/recommendations for international students: Required—TOEFL (minimum score 550 paper-based; 80 iBT). Electronic applications accepted.

University of Victoria, Faculty of Graduate Studies, Faculty of Science, Department of Physics and Astronomy, Victoria, BC V8W 2Y2, Canada. Offers astronomy and astrophysics (M Sc, PhD); condensed matter physics (M Sc, PhD); experimental particle physics (M Sc, PhD); medical physics (M Sc, PhD); ocean physics (M Sc, PhD); theoretical physics (M Sc, PhD). *Degree requirements:* For master's, thesis; for doctorate, comprehensive exam, thesis/dissertation, candidacy exam. *Entrance requirements:* For master's and doctorate, GRE. Additional exam requirements/recommendations for international students: Required—TOEFL (minimum score 575 paper-based), IELTS (minimum score 7). Electronic applications accepted. *Faculty research:* Old stellar populations; observational cosmology and large scale structure; cp violation; atlas.

University of Virginia, College and Graduate School of Arts and Sciences, Department of Physics, Charlottesville, VA 22903. Offers physics (MA, MS, PhD); physics education (MAPE). *Degree requirements:* For master's, thesis (for some programs); for doctorate, comprehensive exam, thesis/dissertation. *Entrance requirements:* For master's and doctorate, GRE General Test, GRE Subject Test, 2 or more letters of recommendation. Additional exam requirements/recommendations for international students: Required—TOEFL (minimum score 600 paper-based; 90 iBT), IELTS. Electronic applications accepted.

University of Washington, Graduate School, College of Arts and Sciences, Department of Physics, Seattle, WA 98195. Offers MS, PhD. *Program availability:* Part-time, evening/weekend. Terminal master's awarded for partial completion of doctoral program. *Degree requirements:* For doctorate, thesis/dissertation. *Entrance requirements:* For master's, GRE; for doctorate, GRE General Test, GRE Subject Test. Additional exam requirements/recommendations for international students: Required—TOEFL. Electronic applications accepted. *Faculty research:* Astro-, atomic, condensed-matter, nuclear, and particle physics; physics education.

University of Waterloo, Graduate Studies, Faculty of Science, Guelph-Waterloo Physics Institute, Waterloo, ON N2L 3G1, Canada. Offers M Sc, PhD. M Sc, PhD offered jointly with University of Guelph. *Program availability:* Part-time. *Degree requirements:* For master's, project or thesis; for doctorate, thesis/dissertation. *Entrance requirements:* For master's, GRE Subject Test, honors degree, minimum B average; for doctorate, GRE Subject Test, master's degree, minimum B average. Additional exam requirements/recommendations for international students: Required—TOEFL, IELTS, PTE. *Application deadline:* Applications are processed on a rolling basis. Application fee: $100 Canadian dollars. Electronic applications accepted. *Financial support:*

Research assistantships, teaching assistantships, career-related internships or fieldwork, scholarships/grants, and unspecified assistantships available. *Faculty research:* Condensed-matter and materials physics; industrial and applied physics; subatomic physics; astrophysics and gravitation; atomic, molecular, and optical physics. Website: https://uwaterloo.ca/guelph-waterloo-physics-institute/

The University of Western Ontario, Faculty of Graduate Studies, Physical Sciences Division, Department of Applied Mathematics, London, ON N6A 5B8, Canada. Offers applied mathematics (M Sc, PhD); theoretical physics (PhD). *Degree requirements:* For master's, thesis or alternative; for doctorate, comprehensive exam, thesis/dissertation. *Entrance requirements:* For master's and doctorate, minimum B average. Additional exam requirements/recommendations for international students: Required—TOEFL. *Faculty research:* Fluid dynamics, mathematical and computational methods, theoretical physics.

The University of Western Ontario, Faculty of Graduate Studies, Physical Sciences Division, Department of Physics and Astronomy, Program in Physics, London, ON N6A 5B8, Canada. Offers M Sc, PhD. Terminal master's awarded for partial completion of doctoral program. *Degree requirements:* For master's, thesis; for doctorate, comprehensive exam, thesis/dissertation. *Entrance requirements:* For master's, GRE Subject Test (physics), honors B Sc degree, minimum B average (Canadian), A- (international); for doctorate, minimum B average (Canadian), A- (international). Additional exam requirements/recommendations for international students: Required—TOEFL (minimum score 580 paper-based). *Faculty research:* Condensed-matter and surface science, space and atmospheric physics, atomic and molecular physics, medical physics, theoretical physics.

University of Windsor, Faculty of Graduate Studies, Faculty of Science, Department of Physics, Windsor, ON N9B 3P4, Canada. Offers M Sc, PhD. *Program availability:* Part-time. *Degree requirements:* For master's, thesis or alternative; for doctorate, thesis/dissertation. *Entrance requirements:* For master's, GRE General Test, minimum B average; for doctorate, GRE General Test, master's degree. Additional exam requirements/recommendations for international students: Required—TOEFL (minimum score 560 paper-based). Electronic applications accepted. *Faculty research:* Electrodynamics, plasma physics, atomic structure/particles, spectroscopy, quantum mechanics.

University of Wisconsin–Madison, Graduate School, College of Letters and Science, Department of Physics, Madison, WI 53706-1380. Offers MA, MS, PhD. Terminal master's awarded for partial completion of doctoral program. *Degree requirements:* For master's, qualifying exam, thesis (MS); for doctorate, thesis/dissertation, preliminary and qualifying exams. *Entrance requirements:* For master's and doctorate, GRE, minimum GPA of 3.0. Additional exam requirements/recommendations for international students: Required—TOEFL. Electronic applications accepted. *Expenses:* Tuition, state resident: full-time $5364. Tuition, nonresident: full-time $12,027. *Required fees:* $571. Tuition and fees vary according to campus/location, program and reciprocity agreements. *Faculty research:* Atomic, physics, condensed matter, astrophysics, particles and fields.

University of Wisconsin–Milwaukee, Graduate School, College of Letters and Science, Department of Physics, Milwaukee, WI 53201-0413. Offers MS, PhD. *Faculty:* 19 full-time (2 women), 1 (woman) part-time/adjunct. *Students:* 33 full-time (1 woman), 17 part-time (5 women); includes 1 minority (Two or more races, non-Hispanic/Latino), 27 international. Average age 29. 124 applicants, 4% accepted, 4 enrolled. In 2015, 17 master's, 6 doctorates awarded. *Degree requirements:* For master's, thesis or alternative; for doctorate, one foreign language, thesis/dissertation. *Entrance requirements:* For master's, GRE General Test, curriculum vitae; for doctorate, GRE General Test. Additional exam requirements/recommendations for international students: Required—TOEFL (minimum score 550 paper-based; 79 iBT), IELTS (minimum score 6.5). *Application deadline:* For fall admission, 1/1 priority date for domestic students; for spring admission, 9/1 for domestic students. Applications are processed on a rolling basis. Application fee: $56 ($96 for international students). Electronic applications accepted. *Financial support:* In 2015–16, 1 fellowship, 14 research assistantships, 20 teaching assistantships were awarded; career-related internships or fieldwork and unspecified assistantships also available. Support available to part-time students. Financial award application deadline: 4/15; financial award applicants required to submit FAFSA. *Faculty research:* Gravitation, biophysics, condensed matter, optics. *Unit head:* Valerica Raicu, Department Chair, 414-229-4969, E-mail: vraicu@uwm.edu. *Application contact:* General Information Contact, 414-229-4982, Fax: 414-229-6967, E-mail: gradschool@uwm.edu. Website: http://www.uwm.edu/dept/physics/

Utah State University, School of Graduate Studies, College of Science, Department of Physics, Logan, UT 84322. Offers MS, PhD. *Program availability:* Part-time. Terminal master's awarded for partial completion of doctoral program. *Degree requirements:* For master's, thesis; for doctorate, comprehensive exam, thesis/dissertation. *Entrance requirements:* For master's and doctorate, GRE General Test, minimum GPA of 3.0. Additional exam requirements/recommendations for international students: Required—TOEFL (minimum score 550 paper-based). Electronic applications accepted. *Faculty research:* Upper-atmosphere physics, relativity, gravitational magnetism, particle physics, nanotechnology.

Vanderbilt University, Department of Physics and Astronomy, Nashville, TN 37240-1001. Offers astronomy (MS); health physics (MA); physics (MAT, MS, PhD). *Faculty:* 26 full-time (3 women). *Students:* 55 full-time (9 women); includes 10 minority (2 Black or African American, non-Hispanic/Latino; 1 Asian, non-Hispanic/Latino; 6 Hispanic/Latino; 1 Two or more races, non-Hispanic/Latino), 18 international. Average age 27. 169 applicants, 19% accepted, 7 enrolled. In 2015, 4 master's, 12 doctorates awarded. *Degree requirements:* For master's, thesis; for doctorate, comprehensive exam, thesis/dissertation, final and qualifying exams. *Entrance requirements:* For master's, GRE General Test; for doctorate, GRE General Test, GRE Subject Test. Additional exam requirements/recommendations for international students: Required—TOEFL (minimum score 570 paper-based; 88 iBT). *Application deadline:* For fall admission, 1/15 for domestic and international students. Electronic applications accepted. *Financial support:* Fellowships with tuition reimbursements, research assistantships with full tuition reimbursements, teaching assistantships with full tuition reimbursements, career-related internships or fieldwork, Federal Work-Study, and institutionally sponsored loans available. Financial award application deadline: 1/15; financial award applicants required to submit CSS PROFILE or FAFSA. *Faculty research:* Experimental and theoretical physics, free electron laser, living-state physics, heavy-ion physics, nuclear structure. *Unit head:* Dr. Julia Velkovska, Director of Graduate Studies, 615-322-2828, Fax: 615-343-7263, E-mail: julia.velkovska@vanderbilt.edu. *Application contact:* Donald Pickert, Administrative Assistant, 615-343-1026, Fax: 615-343-7263, E-mail: donald.pickert@vanderbilt.edu. Website: http://www.vanderbilt.edu/physics/

Virginia Commonwealth University, Graduate School, College of Humanities and Sciences, Department of Physics, Program in Physics and Applied Physics, Richmond, VA 23284-9005. Offers MS. *Entrance requirements:* For master's, GRE. Additional

exam requirements/recommendations for international students: Required—TOEFL (minimum score 600 paper-based; 100 iBT); Recommended—IELTS (minimum score 6.5). Electronic applications accepted. *Faculty research:* Theoretical and experimental condensed matter physics, general relativity and cosmology, physics education.

Virginia Polytechnic Institute and State University, Graduate School, College of Science, Blacksburg, VA 24061. Offers biological sciences (MS, PhD); biomedical technology development and management (MS); chemistry (MS, PhD); economics (MA, PhD); geosciences (MS, PhD); mathematics (MS, PhD); physics (MS, PhD); psychology (MS, PhD); statistics (MS, PhD). *Degree requirements:* For master's, comprehensive exam (for some programs), thesis (for some programs); for doctorate, comprehensive exam (for some programs), thesis/dissertation (for some programs). *Entrance requirements:* For master's and doctorate, GRE/GMAT (may vary by department). Additional exam requirements/recommendations for international students: Required—TOEFL (minimum score 550 paper-based). Electronic applications accepted.

Wake Forest University, Graduate School of Arts and Sciences, Department of Physics, Winston-Salem, NC 27109. Offers MS, PhD. *Program availability:* Part-time. *Degree requirements:* For master's, thesis; for doctorate, comprehensive exam, thesis/dissertation. *Entrance requirements:* For master's and doctorate, GRE General Test. Additional exam requirements/recommendations for international students: Required—TOEFL (minimum score 79 iBT). Electronic applications accepted.

Washington State University, College of Arts and Sciences, Department of Physics and Astronomy, Pullman, WA 99164-2814. Offers MS, PhD. Programs offered at the Pullman campus. Terminal master's awarded for partial completion of doctoral program. *Degree requirements:* For master's, comprehensive exam (for some programs), thesis (for some programs), oral exam; for doctorate, comprehensive exam, thesis/dissertation, oral exam, written exam. *Entrance requirements:* For master's and doctorate, GRE General Test, GRE Subject Test (recommended), minimum GPA of 3.0. Additional exam requirements/recommendations for international students: Required—TOEFL (minimum score 550 paper-based; 80 iBT), IELTS. Electronic applications accepted. *Faculty research:* Astrophysics, matters under extreme conditions, materials and optical physics, novel states of matter.

Washington University in St. Louis, Graduate School of Arts and Sciences, Department of Physics, St. Louis, MO 63130-4899. Offers PhD. *Students:* 84 full-time (14 women); includes 4 minority (3 Asian, non-Hispanic/Latino; 1 Two or more races, non-Hispanic/Latino), 44 international. 135 applicants, 19% accepted, 11 enrolled. In 2015, 14 doctorates awarded. Terminal master's awarded for partial completion of doctoral program. *Degree requirements:* For doctorate, thesis/dissertation. *Entrance requirements:* For doctorate, GRE General Test. Additional exam requirements/recommendations for international students: Required—TOEFL. *Application deadline:* For fall admission, 12/31 for domestic students. Application fee: $45. Electronic applications accepted. *Financial support:* Fellowships, research assistantships, teaching assistantships, and tuition waivers (full and partial) available. Financial award application deadline: 1/15. *Unit head:* Dr. Mark Alford, Chair, 314-935-6250. *Application contact:* Bridget Coleman, Director of Admissions, 314-935-6880, Fax: 314-935-4887. Website: http://physics.wustl.edu/

Wayne State University, College of Liberal Arts and Sciences, Department of Physics and Astronomy, Detroit, MI 48202. Offers physics (MA, MS, PhD). *Faculty:* 28 full-time (2 women), 13 part-time/adjunct (4 women). *Students:* 56 full-time (14 women), 6 part-time (3 women); includes 10 minority (3 Black or African American, non-Hispanic/Latino; 5 Asian, non-Hispanic/Latino; 2 Two or more races, non-Hispanic/Latino), 28 international. Average age 29. 112 applicants, 13% accepted, 11 enrolled. In 2015, 13 master's, 6 doctorates awarded. Terminal master's awarded for partial completion of doctoral program. *Degree requirements:* For master's, comprehensive exam (for some programs), thesis (for some programs); for doctorate, thesis/dissertation. *Entrance requirements:* For master's and doctorate, GRE General Test; GRE Subject Test in physics (recommended), bachelor's degree from recognized college or university, completion of general college physics with laboratory, fifteen credits in intermediate physics courses, general chemistry and lab, calculus 3 and differential equations and matrix algebra. Additional exam requirements/recommendations for international students: Required—TOEFL (minimum score 550 paper-based; 79 iBT), TWE (minimum score 5.5), Michigan English Language Assessment Battery (minimum score 85); Recommended—IELTS (minimum score 6.5). *Application deadline:* For fall admission, 1/15 priority date for domestic and international students; for winter admission, 10/1 priority date for domestic students, 9/1 priority date for international students; for spring admission, 2/1 priority date for domestic students, 1/1 priority date for international students. Applications are processed on a rolling basis. Application fee: $0. Electronic applications accepted. *Expenses:* Tuition, state resident: full-time $14,165; part-time $590.20 per credit hour. Tuition, nonresident: full-time $30,682; part-time $1278.40 per credit hour. *Required fees:* $1688; $47.45 per credit hour. $274.60 per semester. Tuition and fees vary according to course load and program. *Financial support:* In 2015–16, 56 students received support, including 7 fellowships with tuition reimbursements available (averaging $15,221 per year), 19 research assistantships with tuition reimbursements available (averaging $19,273 per year), 26 teaching assistantships with tuition reimbursements available (averaging $18,852 per year); scholarships/grants, health care benefits, and unspecified assistantships also available. Financial award application deadline: 3/31; financial award applicants required to submit FAFSA. *Faculty research:* Applied physics and optics, astrophysics, atomic physics, biomedical physics, condensed matter and materials physics, nuclear physics, high energy particle physics, energy materials research. *Total annual research expenditures:* $2.5 million. *Unit head:* Dr. David Cinabro, Professor and Chair, 313-577-2918, Fax: 313-577-2918, E-mail: cinabro@physics.wayne.edu. *Application contact:* Dr. Claude Pruneau, Chair of the Graduate Admissions Committee, 313-577-1813, Fax: 313-577-3932, E-mail: pruneau@physics.wayne.edu. Website: http://physics.clas.wayne.edu/

Wesleyan University, Graduate Studies, Department of Physics, Middletown, CT 06459. Offers PhD. *Faculty:* 10 full-time (2 women), 1 part-time/adjunct. *Students:* 19 full-time (4 women), 13 international. Average age 25. Terminal master's awarded for partial completion of doctoral program. *Degree requirements:* For doctorate, thesis/dissertation. *Entrance requirements:* For doctorate, GRE General and Subject Tests (recommended). Additional exam requirements/recommendations for international students: Required—TOEFL (minimum score 550 paper-based; 80 iBT). *Application deadline:* For fall admission, 1/31 for domestic and international students. Application fee: $0. Electronic applications accepted. *Financial support:* In 2015–16, 19 students received support. Fellowships, research assistantships, teaching assistantships, institutionally sponsored loans, health care benefits, and tuition waivers (full) available. Financial award application deadline: 4/15; financial award applicants required to submit FAFSA. *Faculty research:* Fluid dynamics and soft condensed matter, quantum fluids, protein dynamics, high energy molecular spectroscopy, molecular photophysics, molecular collisions, quantum computing and computational physics, soft matter and biological physics, wave transport in complex systems. *Unit head:* Reinhold Blumel, Chair, 860-685-2032, E-mail: rblumel@wesleyan.edu. *Application contact:* Janet

Peterson's Graduate Programs in the Physical Sciences, Mathematics, Agricultural Sciences, the Environment & Natural Resources 2017

www.petersons.com   **193**

Desmarais, Administrative Assistant, 860-685-2223, Fax: 860-685-2030, E-mail: jdesmarais01@wesleyan.edu.

Website: http://www.wesleyan.edu/physics/

Western Illinois University, School of Graduate Studies, College of Arts and Sciences, Department of Physics, Macomb, IL 61455-1390. Offers MS. *Program availability:* Part-time. *Students:* 28 full-time (7 women), 4 part-time (0 women); includes 2 minority (1 Black or African American, non-Hispanic/Latino; 1 Two or more races, non-Hispanic/Latino), 25 international. Average age 29. 18 applicants, 44% accepted, 7 enrolled. In 2015, 18 master's awarded. *Degree requirements:* For master's, thesis or alternative. *Entrance requirements:* Additional exam requirements/recommendations for international students: Required—TOEFL (minimum score 550 paper-based; 80 iBT). *Application deadline:* Applications are processed on a rolling basis. Application fee: $30. Electronic applications accepted. *Financial support:* In 2015–16, 14 students received support. Unspecified assistantships available. Financial award applicants required to submit FAFSA. *Unit head:* Dr. Mark Boley, Interim Chairperson, 309-298-1538. *Application contact:* Dr. Nancy Parsons, Associate Provost and Director of Graduate Studies, 309-298-1806, Fax: 309-298-2345, E-mail: grad-office@wiu.edu.

Website: http://wiu.edu/physics

Western Kentucky University, Graduate Studies, Ogden College of Science and Engineering, Department of Physics and Astronomy, Bowling Green, KY 42101. Offers homeland security sciences (MS); physics (MA Ed).

Western Michigan University, Graduate College, College of Arts and Sciences, Department of Interdisciplinary Arts and Sciences, Kalamazoo, MI 49008. Offers science education (MA, PhD), including biological sciences (PhD), chemistry (PhD), geosciences (PhD), physical geography (PhD), physics (PhD), science education (PhD). *Degree requirements:* For doctorate, thesis/dissertation.

Western Michigan University, Graduate College, College of Arts and Sciences, Department of Physics, Kalamazoo, MI 49008. Offers MA, PhD. *Degree requirements:* For master's, thesis; for doctorate, thesis/dissertation.

West Virginia University, Eberly College of Arts and Sciences, Department of Physics, Morgantown, WV 26506. Offers applied physics (MS, PhD); astrophysics (MS, PhD); chemical physics (MS, PhD); condensed matter physics (MS, PhD); elementary particle physics (MS, PhD); materials physics (MS, PhD); plasma physics (MS, PhD); solid state physics (MS, PhD); statistical physics (MS, PhD); theoretical physics (MS, PhD). Terminal master's awarded for partial completion of doctoral program. *Degree requirements:* For master's, thesis or alternative, qualifying exam; for doctorate, thesis/dissertation, qualifying exam. *Entrance requirements:* For master's and doctorate, GRE General Test, minimum GPA of 3.0. Additional exam requirements/recommendations for international students: Required—TOEFL. *Expenses:* Tuition, state resident: full-time $8568. Tuition, nonresident: full-time $22,140. Tuition and fees vary according to program. *Faculty research:* Experimental and theoretical condensed-matter, plasma, high-energy theory, nonlinear dynamics, space physics.

Wichita State University, Graduate School, Fairmount College of Liberal Arts and Sciences, Department of Mathematics, Statistics and Physics, Wichita, KS 67260. Offers applied mathematics (PhD); mathematics (MS); physics (MS). *Program availability:* Part-time. *Unit head:* Dr. Thomas DeLillo, Chair, 316-978-3160, Fax: 316-978-3748, E-mail: thomas.delillo@wichita.edu. *Application contact:* Jordan Oleson, Admissions Coordinator, 316-978-3095, Fax: 316-978-3253, E-mail: jordan.oleson@wichita.edu.

Website: http://www.wichita.edu/math

Worcester Polytechnic Institute, Graduate Studies and Research, Department of Physics, Worcester, MA 01609-2280. Offers physics (MS, PhD); physics for educators (MS). *Faculty:* 9 full-time (2 women), 3 part-time/adjunct (1 woman). *Students:* 23 full-time (5 women), 4 part-time (2 women); includes 1 minority (Hispanic/Latino), 8 international. 25 applicants, 56% accepted, 7 enrolled. In 2015, 4 master's, 1 doctorate awarded. *Degree requirements:* For master's, thesis; for doctorate, comprehensive exam, thesis/dissertation. *Entrance requirements:* For master's, GRE (recommended), 3 letters of recommendation; for doctorate, GRE General Test (recommended), GRE Subject Test (physics), 3 letters of recommendation, statement of purpose (recommended). Additional exam requirements/recommendations for international students: Required—TOEFL (minimum score 563 paper-based; 84 iBT), IELTS (minimum score 7). *Application deadline:* For fall admission, 1/1 priority date for domestic students, 1/1 for international students; for spring admission, 10/1 priority date for domestic students, 10/1 for international students. Applications are processed on a rolling basis. Application fee: $70. Electronic applications accepted. *Financial support:* Research assistantships, teaching assistantships, career-related internships or fieldwork, institutionally sponsored loans, scholarships/grants, and unspecified assistantships available. Financial award application deadline: 1/1; financial award applicants required to submit FAFSA. *Unit head:* Dr. Germano S. Iannacchione, Head, 508-831-5258, Fax: 508-831-5886, E-mail: gsiannac@wpi.edu. *Application contact:* Dr. Erkan Tuzel, Graduate Coordinator, 508-831-5258, Fax: 508-831-5886, E-mail: etuzel@wpi.edu.

Website: http://www.wpi.edu/academics/physics

Wright State University, School of Graduate Studies, College of Science and Mathematics, Department of Physics, Program in Physics, Dayton, OH 45435. Offers geophysics (MS); medical physics (MS). *Program availability:* Part-time, evening/weekend. *Degree requirements:* For master's, thesis. *Entrance requirements:* Additional exam requirements/recommendations for international students: Required—TOEFL. *Faculty research:* Solid-state physics, optics, geophysics.

Yale University, Graduate School of Arts and Sciences, Department of Physics, New Haven, CT 06520. Offers PhD. *Degree requirements:* For doctorate, thesis/dissertation. *Entrance requirements:* For doctorate, GRE General Test, GRE Subject Test.

York University, Faculty of Graduate Studies, Faculty of Science, Program in Physics and Astronomy, Toronto, ON M3J 1P3, Canada. Offers M Sc, PhD. *Program availability:* Part-time, evening/weekend. *Degree requirements:* For master's, thesis or alternative; for doctorate, comprehensive exam, thesis/dissertation. Electronic applications accepted.

Plasma Physics

Princeton University, Graduate School, Department of Astrophysical Sciences, Program in Plasma Physics, Princeton, NJ 08544-1019. Offers PhD. *Degree requirements:* For doctorate, thesis/dissertation. *Entrance requirements:* For doctorate, GRE General Test, GRE Subject Test. Additional exam requirements/recommendations for international students: Required—TOEFL (minimum score 600 paper-based). *Faculty research:* Magnetic fusion energy research, plasma physics, x-ray laser studies.

University of Colorado Boulder, Graduate School, College of Arts and Sciences, Department of Astrophysical and Planetary Sciences, Boulder, CO 80309. Offers astrophysics (MS, PhD); planetary science (MS, PhD). *Faculty:* 24 full-time (2 women). *Students:* 53 full-time (14 women); includes 2 minority (1 Black or African American, non-Hispanic/Latino; 1 Asian, non-Hispanic/Latino), 3 international. Average age 26. 159 applicants, 16% accepted, 7 enrolled. In 2015, 9 master's, 6 doctorates awarded. Terminal master's awarded for partial completion of doctoral program. *Degree requirements:* For master's, comprehensive exam, thesis or alternative; for doctorate, one foreign language, thesis/dissertation. *Entrance requirements:* For master's, GRE General Test, GRE Subject Test, minimum undergraduate GPA of 3.0; for doctorate, GRE General Test, GRE Subject Test. *Application deadline:* For fall admission, 1/15 for domestic students, 12/1 for international students. Applications are processed on a rolling basis. Application fee: $50 ($70 for international students). Electronic applications accepted. Application fee is waived when completed online. *Financial support:* In 2015–16, 109 students received support, including 25 fellowships (averaging $9,613 per year), 27 research assistantships with tuition reimbursements available (averaging $39,044 per year), 13 teaching assistantships with tuition reimbursements available (averaging $27,883 per year); institutionally sponsored loans, scholarships/grants, health care benefits, and unspecified assistantships also available. Financial award application deadline: 1/15; financial award applicants required to submit FAFSA. *Faculty research:* Astrophysics, astronomy, galaxies: stellar systems, infrared/optical astronomy, spectroscopy. *Total annual research expenditures:* $25 million. *Application contact:* E-mail: apsgradsec@colorado.edu.

Website: http://aps.colorado.edu/

West Virginia University, Eberly College of Arts and Sciences, Department of Physics, Morgantown, WV 26506. Offers applied physics (MS, PhD); astrophysics (MS, PhD); chemical physics (MS, PhD); condensed matter physics (MS, PhD); elementary particle physics (MS, PhD); materials physics (MS, PhD); plasma physics (MS, PhD); solid state physics (MS, PhD); statistical physics (MS, PhD); theoretical physics (MS, PhD). Terminal master's awarded for partial completion of doctoral program. *Degree requirements:* For master's, thesis or alternative, qualifying exam; for doctorate, thesis/dissertation, qualifying exam. *Entrance requirements:* For master's and doctorate, GRE General Test, minimum GPA of 3.0. Additional exam requirements/recommendations for international students: Required—TOEFL. *Expenses:* Tuition, state resident: full-time $8568. Tuition, nonresident: full-time $22,140. Tuition and fees vary according to program. *Faculty research:* Experimental and theoretical condensed-matter, plasma, high-energy theory, nonlinear dynamics, space physics.

Theoretical Physics

American University of Beirut, Graduate Programs, Faculty of Arts and Sciences, Beirut, Lebanon. Offers anthropology (MA); Arab and Middle Eastern history (PhD); Arabic language and literature (MA, PhD); archaeology (MA); biology (MS); cell and molecular biology (PhD); chemistry (MS); clinical psychology (MA); computational sciences (MS); computer science (MS); economics (MA); English language (MA); English literature (MA); environmental policy planning (MS); financial economics (MAFE); geology (MS); history (MA); mathematics (MA, MS); media studies (MA); Middle Eastern studies (MA); physics (MS); political studies (MA); psychology (MA); public administration (MA); sociology (MA); statistics (MA, MS); theoretical physics (PhD); transnational American studies (MA). *Program availability:* Part-time. *Faculty:* 114 full-time (36 women), 4 part-time/adjunct (2 women). *Students:* 258 full-time (190 women), 207 part-time (142 women). Average age 27. 241 applicants, 71% accepted, 98 enrolled. In 2015, 47 master's, 3 doctorates awarded. *Degree requirements:* For master's, one foreign language, comprehensive exam, thesis (for some programs); for doctorate, one foreign language, comprehensive exam, thesis/dissertation. *Entrance requirements:* For master's, GRE (for some MA, MS programs), letter of recommendation; for doctorate, GRE, letters of recommendation. Additional exam requirements/recommendations for international students: Required—TOEFL (minimum score 600 paper-based; 97 iBT), IELTS (minimum score 7). *Application deadline:* For fall admission, 4/1 for domestic and international students; for spring admission, 11/1 for domestic and international students. Application fee: $50. Electronic applications accepted. *Expenses: Tuition, area resident:* Full-time $16,254; part-time $903 per credit. *Required fees:* $699. Tuition and fees vary according to course load and program. *Financial support:* Research assistantships, career-related internships or fieldwork, institutionally sponsored loans, scholarships/grants, health care benefits, and unspecified assistantships available. Financial award application deadline: 2/4; financial award applicants required to submit FAFSA. *Faculty research:* Analysis and algebra; software engineering; machine learning and big data analysis; philosophy of mind and

political philosophy; anthropology of art, anthropology of migration and medical anthropology; sociology of knowledge, sociology of migration, critical theory; sociology of education; hybrid solid materials; photocatalysis; human creativity. *Total annual research expenditures:* $680,360. *Unit head:* Dr. Patrick McGreevy, Dean, 961-1374374 Ext. 3800, Fax: 961-1744461, E-mail: pm07@aub.edu.lb. *Application contact:* Dr. Salim Kanaan, Director, Admissions Office, 961-1350000 Ext. 2590, Fax: 961-1750775, E-mail: sk00@aub.edu.lb.
Website: http://www.aub.edu.lb/fas/

Cornell University, Graduate School, Graduate Fields of Arts and Sciences, Field of Physics, Ithaca, NY 14853-0001. Offers experimental physics (MS, PhD); physics (MS, PhD); theoretical physics (MS, PhD). *Degree requirements:* For doctorate, comprehensive exam, thesis/dissertation. *Entrance requirements:* For doctorate, GRE General Test, GRE Subject Test (physics), 3 letters of recommendation. Additional exam requirements/recommendations for international students: Required—TOEFL (minimum score 620 paper-based; 105 iBT). Electronic applications accepted. *Faculty research:* Experimental condensed matter physics, theoretical condensed matter physics, experimental high energy particle physics, theoretical particle physics and field theory, theoretical astrophysics.

Delaware State University, Graduate Programs, Department of Mathematics, Interdisciplinary Program in Applied Mathematics and Theoretical Physics, Dover, DE 19901-2277. Offers PhD. *Degree requirements:* For doctorate, one foreign language, thesis defense. *Entrance requirements:* For doctorate, GRE General Test, MS degree in physics or mathematics. Additional exam requirements/recommendations for international students: Required—TOEFL (minimum score 550 paper-based).

Emory University, Laney Graduate School, Department of Physics, Atlanta, GA 30322-1100. Offers biophysics (PhD); experimental condensed matter physics (PhD); theoretical and computational statistical physics (PhD); MS/PhD. *Degree requirements:* For doctorate, thesis/dissertation, qualifier proposal. *Entrance requirements:* For doctorate, GRE General Test, minimum GPA of 3.0. Additional exam requirements/recommendations for international students: Required—TOEFL (minimum score 600 paper-based). Electronic applications accepted. *Faculty research:* Experimental studies of the structure and function of metalloproteins, soft condensed matter, granular materials, biophotonics and fluorescence correlation spectroscopy, single molecule studies of DNA-protein systems.

Harvard University, Graduate School of Arts and Sciences, Department of Physics, Cambridge, MA 02138. Offers experimental physics (PhD); medical engineering/medical physics (PhD), including applied physics, engineering sciences, physics; theoretical physics (PhD). *Degree requirements:* For doctorate, thesis/dissertation, final exams, laboratory experience. *Entrance requirements:* For doctorate, GRE General Test, GRE Subject Test. Additional exam requirements/recommendations for international students: Required—TOEFL. *Faculty research:* Particle physics, condensed matter physics, atomic physics.

Rutgers University–New Brunswick, Graduate School-New Brunswick, Department of Physics and Astronomy, Piscataway, NJ 08854-8097. Offers astronomy (MS, PhD); biophysics (PhD); condensed matter physics (MS, PhD); elementary particle physics (MS, PhD); intermediate energy nuclear physics (MS); nuclear physics (MS, PhD); physics (MST); surface science (PhD); theoretical physics (MS, PhD). *Program availability:* Part-time. Terminal master's awarded for partial completion of doctoral program. *Degree requirements:* For master's, comprehensive exam, thesis or alternative; for doctorate, comprehensive exam, thesis/dissertation. *Entrance requirements:* For master's and doctorate, GRE General Test, GRE Subject Test. Additional exam requirements/recommendations for international students: Required—TOEFL (minimum score 560 paper-based). Electronic applications accepted. *Faculty research:* Astronomy, high energy, condensed matter, surface, nuclear physics.

The University of Manchester, School of Physics and Astronomy, Manchester, United Kingdom. Offers astronomy and astrophysics (M Sc, PhD); biological physics (M Sc, PhD); condensed matter physics (M Sc, PhD); nonlinear and liquid crystals physics (M Sc, PhD); nuclear physics (M Sc, PhD); particle physics (M Sc, PhD); photon physics (M Sc, PhD); physics (M Sc, PhD); theoretical physics (M Sc, PhD).

University of Victoria, Faculty of Graduate Studies, Faculty of Science, Department of Physics and Astronomy, Victoria, BC V8W 2Y2, Canada. Offers astronomy and astrophysics (M Sc, PhD); condensed matter physics (M Sc, PhD); experimental particle physics (M Sc, PhD); medical physics (M Sc, PhD); ocean physics (M Sc, PhD); theoretical physics (M Sc, PhD). *Degree requirements:* For master's, thesis; for doctorate, comprehensive exam, thesis/dissertation. *Entrance requirements:* For master's and doctorate, GRE. Additional exam requirements/recommendations for international students: Required—TOEFL (minimum score 575 paper-based), IELTS (minimum score 7). Electronic applications accepted. *Faculty research:* Old stellar populations; observational cosmology and large scale structure; cp violation; atlas.

West Virginia University, Eberly College of Arts and Sciences, Department of Physics, Morgantown, WV 26506. Offers applied physics (MS, PhD); astrophysics (MS, PhD); chemical physics (MS, PhD); condensed matter physics (MS, PhD); elementary particle physics (MS, PhD); materials physics (MS, PhD); plasma physics (MS, PhD); solid state physics (MS, PhD); statistical physics (MS, PhD); theoretical physics (MS, PhD). Terminal master's awarded for partial completion of doctoral program. *Degree requirements:* For master's, thesis or alternative, qualifying exam; for doctorate, thesis/dissertation, qualifying exam. *Entrance requirements:* For master's and doctorate, GRE General Test, minimum GPA of 3.0. Additional exam requirements/recommendations for international students: Required—TOEFL. *Expenses:* Tuition, state resident: full-time $8568. Tuition, nonresident: full-time $22,140. Tuition and fees vary according to program. *Faculty research:* Experimental and theoretical condensed-matter, plasma, high-energy theory, nonlinear dynamics, space physics.

Peterson's Graduate Programs in the Physical Sciences, Mathematics, Agricultural Sciences, the Environment & Natural Resources 2017

www.petersons.com   **195**

UNIVERSITY OF MASSACHUSETTS LOWELL
Department of Physics and Applied Physics

 For more information, visit http://petersons.to/umasslowell_physics

Programs of Study

Merging science with technology—that's the mission of the UMass Lowell Department of Physics and Applied Physics. Leading-edge research lies at heart of graduate programs in physics. With over $8 million annually in funded research, the department was recently ranked by the National Science Foundation in the top 50 nationwide in research and development expenditures. The department has 23 full-time faculty members, approximately 80 graduate students (M.S. and Ph.D.), and 80 undergraduate majors. The reasonably small faculty size coupled to the high commitment to research, both in fundamental and applied physics, allows quality interactions and mentoring of graduate students. Departmental faculty members are world leaders in their disciplines, and new hires are expanding existing research strengths. Specific areas of research expertise are described below.

The M.S. degree is offered in physics, radiological sciences and protection (health physics), and medical physics. M.S. programs require 30 credits, including a thesis or project. The M.S. may serve as a basis for further study toward a Ph.D. A Professional Science master's option is offered in the radiological science and protection degree program.

The Ph.D. degree is offered in physics, medical physics, and physics with a radiological science option. The program requires 60 credits beyond the bachelor's degree, including dissertation research. A prior master's degree is not required for admission into the Ph.D. program.

The M.S. degree can typically be completed in three to four semesters. A typical timeline for the Ph.D. degree includes two years of graduate coursework, passing a comprehensive exam at the beginning of the third semester (two chances are allowed; the exam is offered twice a year), and then three more years to complete, culminating in a dissertation with original publishable research work.

More information is available at http://www.uml.edu/physics.

Research Centers and Programs

The **Astrophysics Group** develops instruments used on suborbital sounding rockets to study the structure of galaxies and interstellar media, investigates atmospheres and environments of planets and exoplanets, studies neutron stars and black holes in X-ray binaries and pulsars, and carries out research in multi-wavelength astronomy and time-domain astrophysics.

The **Center for Advanced Materials** designs, synthesizes, characterizes, and processes materials for application in new technologies. Research includes nonlinear optics, dielectric behavior of materials, polymeric and biomolecular systems, and nanoscale materials.

The **Photonics Center** has design and fabrication facilities to support innovative semiconductor-based photonic and electronic device technologies for defense, medical, and commercial applications. Equipment includes molecular beam epitaxy machines and concomitant lithography and epilayer characterization facilities.

The **Submillimeter-Wave Technology Laboratory** builds and maintains high-performance solid-state and laser-based measurement systems to generate terahertz frequency radiation, resulting in the development of a wide range of materials characterization techniques and high-resolution imaging systems for industry, defense, and medical applications.

The **Radiation Laboratory,** with a 1-MW research reactor, an intense Co-60 gamma source, and a 5.5-MV Van de Graaff accelerator, is a unique interdisciplinary research center for nuclear science and applications. Fundamental nuclear structure and astrophysics research are carried out at national labs. In-house research includes advanced detector development for nuclear science and applications.

The **Multiscale Electromagnetics Group** specializes in computational and theoretical photonics and plasmonics in composites, metamaterials, and multi-scale systems.

The **Advanced Biophotonics Laboratory** provides fundamental expertise on the structural and functional characterization of pathology for exploratory efforts in medical and bioengineering applications, integrating multiple optical imaging and spectroscopic approaches.

The **Laboratory for Nanoscience and Laser Applications** uses intense femtosecond lasers to study light-matter interactions in material structures and chemical reactions at the molecular level, as well as facilitate the manufacture of micro- and nanostructure materials.

The **Space Physics Team** studies and models solar winds, magnetospheres, plasmaspheres, ionospheres, radiation belts, and antenna radiation theory and experiment.

The research expertise of recent faculty hires includes theory and computation in soft condensed matter, plasma physics, quantum information, and cosmology.

The Medical Physics program is CAMPEP accredited. The Health Physics program is ABET accredited and has a separate Professional Science master's program. Research efforts include aerosol transport, dosimetry, medical imaging, diagnostics and therapeutics with nanoparticles, and research on radiation mitigating drugs.

More information can be found online at https://www.uml.edu/Sciences/physics/Research/Research.aspx.

Financial Aid

Essentially all Ph.D. candidates receive full financial support throughout their graduate career, starting with a departmental teaching assistantship for two years and then moving on to a research assistantship. Both TA and RA appointments include full waiver of tuition and fees. TAs and RAs must be full-time students carrying at least 9 credit hours per semester. M.S. students are NOT eligible for TA/RA appointments.

The guaranteed 12-month stipend for physics Ph.D. students is $25,000, which includes a TA/RA stipend for the academic semesters and research stipends outside academic semesters from research groups. With the tuition and fees waiver, the total out-of-state compensation package for 2016–17 is $48,000. Additional $3,000 merit scholarships are awarded on a competitive basis.

TA duties during the academic year involve 18 hours per week teaching introductory physics labs, grading, and assisting faculty in large enrollment courses or in upper division labs. RA duties involve working in the departmental research labs as part of one's graduate research, and are typically funded through external grants and contracts.

Other financial aid for grading and tutoring may be available at an hourly rate. These are not accompanied by a waiver of tuition and fees and are available to M.S. students as well.

Cost of Study

For full-time students who are Massachusetts residents, in-state tuition and fees for the 2015–16 academic year was $13,799. Part-time in-state students paid $1,533 per credit. For full-time students who are not Massachusetts residents, the out-of-state tuition and fees for the academic year was $24,478. Part-time out-of-state students paid $2,720 per credit.

Living and Housing

UMass Lowell does not provide graduate student housing; however, there are numerous housing options available in the nearby area.

Student Outcomes

Graduates from the M.S. and Ph.D. programs in physics and applied physics at UMass Lowell have obtained leading positions in academia, government research laboratories, major medical facilities, and industry. They have obtained postdoctoral, research scientist, or faculty appointments at major research universities such as Princeton, Yale, Chicago, Duke, and UC Santa Barbara; national laboratories such as Los Alamos, Pacific Northwest, and Naval Research Labs; research positions at companies such as Raytheon and Schlumberger; and positions at top medical institutions such as Massachusetts General Hospital and Mayo Clinic.

Applying

The application process for the graduate program is fully online and is available at the Graduate Admissions website (http://www.uml.edu/grad). Ph.D. applications are only considered for the fall semester, other than in exceptional circumstances. The deadline for Ph.D. applications, which automatically includes full financial aid considerations, is January 15 for the upcoming fall semester. The deadline for M.S. applications, is March 15 for fall and November 15 for spring applications.

Admission to the graduate programs requires the equivalent of 4 years of undergraduate course work. The general GRE is required for all M.S. and Ph.D. graduate applications. In addition, the subject GRE in physics is required for applicants to the physics Ph.D. program. Other required application material includes relevant transcripts, a personal statement, and three letters of recommendation. In addition, TOEFL exam scores are required from international students whose native language is not English, except in cases in which an international applicant has received an advanced degree from a U.S. institution. The minimum cutoff for the TOEFL is 550 on the paper-based exam, and 79 on the Internet-based test. There is no specified minimum cutoff for the GRE. While copies of transcripts are acceptable during the application process, certified transcripts of all undergraduate and graduate study are required prior to enrollment.

Additional information is available on the Physics Graduate Program website at http://www.uml.edu/Sciences/physics/Programs-of-Study/Graduate-Program.aspx.

Peterson's Graduate Programs in the Physical Sciences, Mathematics, Agricultural Sciences, the Environment & Natural Resources 2017

www.petersons.com **197**

University of Massachusetts Lowell

Correspondence and Information

Professor Partha Chowdhury
Graduate Coordinator
Department of Physics and Applied Physics
University of Massachusetts Lowell
Lowell, Massachusetts 01854
United States
Phone: 978-934-3730
E-mail: Partha_Chowdhury@uml.edu
Website: http://www.uml.edu/physics

THE FACULTY AND THEIR RESEARCH

Supriya Chakrabarti, Professor; Ph.D., Berkeley, 1982. Space experiments, hyperspectral imaging, LIDAR.

Partha Chowdhury, Professor; Ph.D., SUNY at Stony Brook, 1979. Nuclear structure, novel radiation detectors, neutron spectroscopy, applied nuclear science.

Timothy A. Cook, Assistant Professor, Ph.D.), Colorado, 1991. Visible and UV instrumentation, sounding rockets, small satellites, tomography.

Andriy Danylov, Lecturer; Ph.D., Massachusetts, Lowell, 2010. Submillimeter wave technology.

Clayton S. French, Professor; Ph.D., Massachusetts, Lowell, 1985. Health physics, radiological science and protection.

Robert Giles, Professor; Ph.D., Massachusetts, Lowell, 1986. Terahertz laser physics, imaging, biomedical applications.

Wei Guo, Assistant Professor; Ph.D., Brown, 2008. Photonics and optoelectronics, nanomaterial growth.

Jayant Kumar, Professor; Ph.D., Rutgers, 1983. Polymer science, optical and electronic properties of materials.

Silas Laycock, Assistant Professor; Ph.D., Southampton (UK), 2002. Neutron stars and black holes in X-ray binaries, pulsars, multi-wavelength astronomy, time-domain astrophysics.

Nikolay Lepeshkin, Lecturer; Ph.D., New Mexico State, 2001. Optics, physics education.

Christopher J. (Kim) Lister, Professor; Ph.D., Liverpool (UK), 1977. Nuclear structure, detector development and instrumentation, applied nuclear science.

Arthur Mittler, Professor; Ph.D., Kentucky, 1970. Physics education.

Wilfred F. Ngwa, Assistant Professor; Ph.D., Leipzig (Germany), 2004. Medical physics, radiation oncology, nanoparticle therapy.

Viktor Podolskiy, Professor; Ph.D., New Mexico State, 2002. Computational physics, photonics, plasmonics, metamaterials.

Xifeng,Qian, Assistant Professor; Ph.D., Massachusetts, Lowell, 2009. Photonic devices, epi-growth, nanofabrication.

Andrew Rogers, Assistant Professor; Ph.D., Michigan State, 2009. Nuclear structure, nuclear astrophysics, applied nuclear science.

Erno Sajo, Professor; Massachusetts, Lowell, 1990. Medical physics, health physics, radiation transport, radiation biology.

Kunnat J. Sebastian, Professor; Ph.D., Maryland, 1969. Theoretical atomic and particle physics.

Paul Song, Professor; Ph.D., UCLA, 1991. Plasma physics, space weather, solar system.

Mengyan Shen, Associate Professor; Ph.D., Science and Technology (China), 1990. Nanoscience and technology, femtosecond lasers.

Mark A. Tries, Associate Professor; Ph.D., Massachusetts, Lowell, 1999. Health physics, radiological science and protection.

Anna Yaroslavsky, Associate Professor; Ph.D., Saratov State (Russia), 1999. Advanced biophotonics, medical imaging.

Johannes (Jos) Zwanikken, Assistant Professor; Ph.D., Utrecht (Netherlands), 2009. Theory and computation in soft matter and dynamic systems, polymers and biological ensembles.

EMERITUS FACULTY

Albert Altman, Professor Emeritus; Ph.D., Maryland, 1962. Physics education.

James J. Egan, Professor Emeritus; Ph.D., Kentucky, 1969. Nuclear physics, neutron scattering.

William D. Goodhue, Professor Emeritus; Ph.D., Massachusetts, Lowell, 1982. Photonics, molecular beam epitaxy.

F. Raymond Hardy, Professor Emeritus; M.S., Massachusetts, Lowell, 1962. Physics education.

Aram S. Karakashian, Professor Emeritus; Ph.D., Maryland, 1970. Computational solid-state, optics, photonics.

Lloyd C. Kannenberg, Professor Emeritus; Ph.D., Northeastern, 1966. Relativity, cosmology, radiation theory.

Gunter H. R. Kegel, Professor Emeritus; Ph.D., MIT, 1961. Accelerator, neutron physics.

David J. Pullen, Professor Emeritus; Ph.D., Oxford (UK), 1963. Nuclear physics, physics education.

Walter Schier, Professor Emeritus; Ph.D., Notre Dame, 1964. Nuclear physics, physics education.

Richard W. Stimets, Professor Emeritus; Ph.D., MIT, 1969. Astronomy, optics, image processing.

Jerry Waldman, Professor Emeritus; Ph.D., MIT, 1970. Experimental terahertz laser physics.

Martin Wilner, Professor Emeritus; Ph.D., MIT, 1964. Theoretical solid state physics, optics.

The bluish glow of Cerenkov radiation, emitted by charged particles from fission traveling faster than the speed of light in water, lights up the core of the 1 MW research reactor in operation. *Photo courtesy Imelda Joson/Joson Images.*

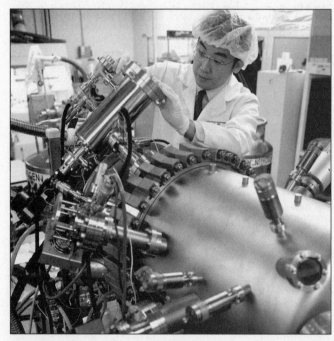

The molecular beam epitaxy system at the Photonics Center is used to grow nano-materials for fabricating terahertz quantum-cascade lasers and quantum-nanodot detectors. *Photo courtesy Imelda Joson/Joson Images.*

198 www.petersons.com

Peterson's Graduate Programs in the Physical Sciences, Mathematics, Agricultural Sciences, the Environment & Natural Resources 2017

UNIVERSITY OF PITTSBURGH

Department of Physics and Astronomy

★ For more information, visit http://petersons.to/upitt-physics_astrononomy

Programs of Study

The graduate programs in the Department of Physics and Astronomy are designed primarily for students who wish to obtain the Ph.D. degree, although the M.S. degree is also offered. The Ph.D. program provides high-quality training for students without excessive emphasis on formal requirements. Prior to arrival, each graduate student is appointed a faculty academic adviser to provide personalized guidance through the core curriculum. A set of basic courses is to be taken by all graduate students unless the equivalent material has been demonstrably mastered in other ways. These basic courses include mathematical methods, dynamical systems, quantum mechanics, electromagnetic theory, and statistical physics and thermodynamics. More advanced courses are offered in a range of areas, including, but not limited to, condensed matter, statistical, solid-state, and biological physics; high-energy and particle physics; nanoscience; astrophysics; cosmology; particle astrophysics; relativity; and astronomical techniques.

Students have a wide variety of research programs from which to choose a thesis topic. Faculty members maintain active research programs in astrophysics, condensed matter physics, cosmology, particle physics, and physics education research. Topics in astrophysics and cosmology include: observational, numerical, and theoretical cosmology; dark matter and dark energy; galaxy formation and evolution; active galactic nuclei and quasars; galactic and intergalactic medium; stellar atmospheres and massive stars; supernovae; and physics of the early universe. Topics in condensed matter physics include: biological physics; nanoscience; quantum information; quantum kinetics; quantum optics; quantum states of matter; semiconductor physics; soft condensed matter physics; statistical physics; superconductivity and superfluidity; and ultrafast optics. Topics in particle physics include: the origin of mass and flavor; the search for new symmetries of nature; neutrino physics; CP violation; heavy quarks; leptoquarks; supersymmetry; extra dimensions; baryogenesis; effective field theory; and strongly interacting field theory. Topics in physics education research include: cognitive issues in learning physics; and development and evaluation of research-based curricula for introductory and advanced physics courses. Multidisciplinary thesis research may also be carried out in, for example, particle astrophysics, biophysics, chemical physics, laser physics, materials science, nanoscience, and surface science. This research may be done in collaboration with faculty from other departments within the University.

Interdisciplinary research programs may be arranged on a case-by-case basis. Previous students have performed their thesis research in collaboration with faculty members in the Department of Biological Sciences, the Department of Chemistry, the Department of Mathematics, the Department of Mechanical Engineering and Materials Science, the Departments of Electrical and Chemical Engineering, the Department of Computational Biology, the Department of Radiological Sciences, and the Department of Radiology in the School of Medicine, among others.

Research Facilities

The Department of Physics and Astronomy is located on the University of Pittsburgh's main campus and housed in a complex of five interconnecting buildings containing numerous cutting-edge research laboratories and other educational facilities. The Department also houses a number of cross-disciplinary centers including the PITTsburgh Particle physics, Astrophysics, and Cosmology Center (PITT PACC, http://www.physicsandastronomy.pitt.edu/pittpacc), the Discipline Based Science Education Research Center (dB-SERC, www.dbserc.pitt.edu) and the Pittsburgh Quantum Institute (PQI, www.pqi.org). The Department also has access to a number of facilities, including machine, electronic, and glass shops, the Gertrude E. and John M. Peterson Institute of NanoScience and Engineering (PINSE, www.nano.pitt.edu), the Nano Fabrication and Characterization Facility (NFCF, www.nano.pitt.edu/nfcf.html), the Center for Simulation and Modeling (SAM, www.sam.pitt.edu), and the Pittsburgh Supercomputing Center (PSC, www.psc.edu). Other local facilities include University of Pittsburgh's Allegheny Observatory (AO, www.pitt.edu/~aobsvtry). Experiments in particle physics are carried out at national and international facilities such as Fermilab near Chicago, CERN in Switzerland and J–PARC in Japan. This includes, for example, the Large Hadron Collider ATLAS experiment at CERN and various neutrino experiments (MINOS, MINERvA, and T2K).

Similarly, observational programs in astrophysics and cosmology are conducted at national and international ground-based observatories located at, for example, Kitt Peak and Mount Hopkins in Arizona, Cerro Tololo in Chile, Mauna Kea in Hawaii, and Apache Point in New Mexico for collection of Sloan Digital Sky Survey data. Faculty also makes use of space-based telescopes, for example, the Hubble Space Telescope, the Chandra X-Ray Telescope, and the GALEX UV Telescope. University of Pittsburgh faculty are also members of several current and/or future large-telescope consortia: the Sloan Digital Sky Survey (SDSS, www.sdss.org), the Atacama Cosmology Telescope (ACT, www.physics.princeton.edu/act/), the Panoramic Survey Telescope and Rapid Response System (Pan-STARRS, www.ps1sc.org), and the Large Synoptic Survey Telescope (LSST, www.lsst.org). Many members of the Department play a significant leadership role in the LSST project. More information is available at http://www.gradschoolshopper.com/gradschool/sclisting.jsp?rec=353#equipment.

Financial Aid

Financial aid is normally provided through teaching assistantships during the first year and through research assistantships thereafter. These awards carry benefits as well as tuition and fee merit scholarships. The University provides individual health insurance under the Graduate Student Medical Plan, with options for spouse or family upgrades, with additional cost to the student, as well as dental and vision options. In addition to several University competitive predoctoral fellowships, the Department's predoctoral fellowships include the Dietrich School of Arts and Sciences Graduate Fellowships, the Dietrich School of Arts and Sciences Summer Research Fellowship, the K. Leroy Irvis Predoctoral Fellowship, and the Warga Predoctoral Fellowship for entering graduate students. They are awarded on a competitive basis with all qualified applicants automatically considered. These also carry tuition and fee scholarships. Currently, the University provides health insurance for fellows to purchase. The University's financial support package generally covers five consecutive years of graduate study, provided they maintain good academic standing, make progress toward their degree, and are in residence in the Department or at an appropriate research facility. Teaching and research assistantship appointments carried a stipend of $8,780 per term in 2015, bringing the annual stipend to $26,125 for students supported throughout the year. This includes a full-tuition scholarship and benefits. Research assistantship appointments may be held in connection with most of the Department's research programs.

Cost of Study

For full-time students who are not Pennsylvania residents, tuition per term in 2016–17 is $17,952, including fees. Part-time students pay $1,468 per credit. Full-time students who are Pennsylvania residents pay $10,874 per term, including fees, and part-time students who are Pennsylvania residents pay $877 per credit. Fees for all part-time students are $205 per term.

Living and Housing Costs

Housing is particularly reasonable in both quality and price. Most University of Pittsburgh students live in apartments in the Oakland and surrounding areas. The typical cost of apartments ranges from $400 to $800 per month for housing. Pittsburgh's low cost of living affords extremely reasonable and numerous food and beverage prices. Further information may be found online at http://www.ocl.pitt.edu. A valid PITT student ID serves many purposes, including free transportation around campus and in and around the city.

Student Group

The Department's graduate student body for the fall of 2016 consists of approximately 118 students, all of whom receive financial support.

Student Outcomes

Many Ph.D. graduates accept postdoctoral positions at major research universities, often leading to teaching and research positions at outstanding universities in the United States and around the world. Other recent graduates have entered research careers in the private sector and national labs. One former graduate, Patrick D. Gallagher, recently became the eighteenth Chancellor and Chief Executive Officer of the University of Pittsburgh.

Location

Pittsburgh, nicknamed the City of Bridges, with a network of bike trains, is a hilly urban center located in western Pennsylvania and was ranked the Most Livable City in the U.S. in 2013 by Forbes.com. Surrounded by nine state parks, the woodland city offers a variety of outdoor activities including cycling, hiking, downhill and cross-country skiing, white-water rafting and kayaking, rock climbing, hunting, and fishing. It is a culturally vibrant city, easily accessible, with many museums, an internationally renowned symphony orchestra, opera, and many theaters. It possesses multiple major league sports teams, along with the exciting University of Pittsburgh football and basketball teams as well as numerous athletic programs. The region boasts several smaller cultural centers with their own intrinsic character, including Oakland, where the University is based. The University is located about 3 miles east of downtown Pittsburgh in the city's cultural center. Adjacent to the campus are Carnegie Mellon University and the Carnegie Museum, comprising the Museum of Art, the Museum of Natural History, the Carnegie Library, and the Carnegie Music Hall. Schenley Park adjoins the campus; it has picnic areas, playing fields, jogging trails, and an excellent botanical conservatory. For detailed information, students should visit http://www.pitt.edu/about.html.

The Department

The Department has a long history of high-impact research and is internationally recognized for its excellence in research and education. With accessibility to more than 40 core faculty members and lecturers, students have an unparalleled opportunity for individualized training, interaction, and mentorship. The Department has guided Ph.D. candidates to success for more than 80 years. In that time, many alumni have gone on to build distinguished careers as researchers at major academic and industrial laboratories, educators at universities and colleges, and independent scientific entrepreneurs. Close cooperation exists between this Department and the physics department of Carnegie Mellon University; all seminars, colloquiums, and advanced courses are shared. The graduate students of both institutions benefit from belonging to one of the largest communities of active physicists in the country. Furthermore, basic research, conducted at the University of Pittsburgh Medical Center and the School of Medicine, provides additional opportunities for research with multidisciplinary perspectives.

Applying

Students who wish to apply for admission or financial aid should apply online and take the GRE (the Subject Test in physics is strongly recommended), and have a cumulative grade point average of at least 3.0 on a 4.0 scale. Applicants should upload copies of their undergraduate transcripts and when applicable, graduate transcripts, with their online application. Include translations if applicable. Certified transcripts (with final grades and degrees posted) of all undergraduate and graduate study are required no later than time of enrollment. Three letters of recommendation are required for admission with aid. Unless English is the applicant's native language, the TOEFL (IBT) or IELTS exam is required, except in cases in which an international applicant has received an advanced degree from a U.S. institution. Acceptable minimum scores are listed in the application instructions. The application deadline is January 15. The application fee is waived for U.S. citizens and permanent residents (refer to instructions). Through early March, late applications are accepted on the basis of space availability.

Correspondence and Information

Professor Robert P. Devaty
Admissions Committee
Department of Physics and Astronomy
University of Pittsburgh
Pittsburgh, Pennsylvania 15260
United States
Phone: 412-624-9009
Website: http://www.physicsandastronomy.pitt.edu/

THE FACULTY AND THEIR RESEARCH

Carles Badeness, Assistant Professor; Ph.D., Politecnia de Catalunya (Spain). Type 1a supernovae, supernova remnants, large astronomoical data bases, extragalactic astronomy, observational cosmology.

Brian Batell, Assistant Professor; Ph.D., Minnesota. Theoretical particle physics.

Rachel Bezanson, Assistant Professor (starting 2017); Ph.D., Yale. Observational astronomy, galaxy evolution in the early universe, the evolution of black holes in galaxies.

Joseph Boudreau, Professor; Ph.D., Wisconsin. Experimental particle physics.

Daniel Boyanovsky, Professor; Ph.D., California, Santa Barbara. Theoretical condensed matter physics, particle astrophysics, astrophysics and cosmology.

Matteo Broccio, Lecturer; Ph.D., Messina (Italy). Biophysics, physics, physics education research.

Guanglei Cheng, Research Assistant Professor; Ph.D., Pittsburgh. Experimental condensed matter physics.

Wolfgang J. Choyke, Research Professor; Ph.D., Ohio State. Experimental solid-state physics, defect states in semiconductors, large-bandgap spectroscopy.

Russell Clark, Senior Lecturer/Lab Supervisor; Ph.D., LSU. Physics education research, neutrino physics.

Rob Coalson, Professor; Ph.D., Harvard. Chemical physics.

Istvan Danko, Lab Instructor; Ph.D., Vanderbilt. Experimental particle physics.

Robert P. Devaty, Associate Professor and Chair of the Graduate Admissions Committee; Ph.D., Cornell. Experimental solid-state physics, semiconductor physics.

Brian D'Urso, Assistant Professor; Ph.D., Harvard. Experimental condensed matter physics, nanoscience.

Gurudev Dutt, Associate Professor; Ph.D., Michigan. Quantum optics, quantum information.

Steven A. Dytman, Professor; Ph.D., Carnegie Mellon. Experimental particle physics, neutrino physics.

Min Feng, Adjunct Research Professor; Ph.D., Chinese Academy of Sciences (Beijing). Experimental condensed matter.

Ayres Freitas, Associate Professor; Ph.D., Hamburg. Theoretical particle physics.

Sergey Frolov, Assistant Professor and member of the Peterson Institute of Nanoscience and Engineering Executive Committee (PINSE); Ph.D., Illinois. Experimental condensed matter physics, quantum nanowires, Majorana fermions in nanowires, nanowire quantum bits.

Tao Han, Distinguished Professor and Director of the PITTsburgh Particle physics, Astrophysics, and Cosmology Center (PITT PACC); Ph.D., Wisconsin. Theoretical particle physics.

Michael Hatridge, Assistant Professor; Ph.D., Berkeley. Experimental condensed matter, superconducting qubits and amplifier, quantum-limited measurement, quantum information.

D. John Hillier, Professor; Ph.D., Australian National. Theoretical and observational astrophysics, computational physics.

Tae Min Hong, Assistant Professor; Ph.D., California, Santa Barbara. Experimental high energy physics, dark matter, supersymmetry.

Kunie Ishioka, Adjunct Research Professor; Ph.D., Kyoto (Japan). Experimental condensed matter.

Patrick Irvin, Research Assistant Professor; Ph.D., Pittsburgh. Experimental condensed matter physics.

Arthur Kosowsky, Professor and Associate Director of the PITTsburgh Particle physics, Astrophysics, and Cosmology Center (PITT PACC); Ph.D., Chicago. Theoretical and experimental cosmology and astrophysics.

Sangyeop Lee, Assistant Professor; Ph.D., MIT. Mechanical engineering, material science.

Adam Leibovich, Professor and Department Chair; Ph.D., Caltech. Theoretical particle physics.

Jeremy Levy, Distinguished Professor and Director of the Pittsburgh Quantum Institute (PQI); Ph.D., California, Santa Barbara. Experimental condensed matter, nanoscience, quantum information.

W. Vincent Liu, Professor; Ph.D., Texas at Austin. Theoretical condensed matter physics, cold atoms.

James V. Maher, Professor; Ph.D., Yale. Experimental statistical physics, critical phenomena, physics of fluids.

Roger Mong, Assistant Professor; Ph.D., Berkeley. Theoretical condensed matter physics, topological insulators and superconductors, fractional quantum Hall, quantum information, disorder and transport in topological systems.

James Mueller, Associate Professor and Undergraduate Program Director; Ph.D., Cornell. Experimental particle physics.

Donna Naples, Professor; Ph.D., Maryland. Experimental neutrino physics.

Thomas Nelson, Research Assistant Professor; Ph.D., Wisconsin–Madison. Multi-wavelength observations of novae in outburst, x-ray observations of symbiotic stars, astronomy education research.

David Nero, Lecturer; Ph.D., Toledo. Astronomy, physics, physics education research.

Jeffrey Newman, Associate Professor; Ph.D., Berkeley. Astrophysics, extragalactic astronomy, observational cosmology.

Max Niedermaier, Research Associate Professor; Ph.D., Hamburg (Germany). Theoretical particle physics.

Vittorio Paolone, Professor; Ph.D., California, Davis. Experimental particle physics, neutrino physics.

David Pekker, Assistant Professor; Ph.D., Illinois at Urbana-Champaign. Atomic, molecular, and optical physics; computational physics; condensed matter physics.

Hrvoje Petek, Mellon Professor; Ph.D., Berkeley. Experimental condensed matter/AMO physics, nanoscience, solid-state physics.

Sandhya Rao, Research Professor; Ph.D., Pittsburgh. Astrophysics, extragalactic astronomy, observational cosmology.

Ralph Z. Roskies, Professor and Scientific Director of the Pittsburgh Supercomputing Center; Ph.D., Princeton. Theoretical particle physics, use of computers in theoretical physics.

Hanna Salman, Associate Professor; Ph.D., Weizmann Institute (Israel). Experimental biological physics.

Vladimir Savinov, Professor; Ph.D., Minnesota. Experimental particle physics.

Regina E. Schulte-Ladbeck, Professor; Ph.D., Heidelberg. Extragalactic astronomy, observational cosmology.

Chandralekha Singh, Professor and Director of the Discipline Based Science Education Research Center (dB SERC); Ph.D., California, Santa Barbara. Physics education research, polymer physics.

David Snoke, Professor; Ph.D., Illinois at Urbana-Champaign. Experimental condensed matter physics, nanoscience, solid-state physics.

Eric Swanson, Professor; Ph.D., Toronto. Theoretical particle physics.

David A. Turnshek, Professor and Director of Allegheny Observatory; Ph.D., Arizona. Astrophysics, extragalactic astronomy, observational cosmology.

Michael Wood-Vasey, Associate Professor; Ph.D., Berkeley. Astrophysics, extragalactic astronomy, observational cosmology.

Xiao-Lun Wu, Professor; Ph.D., Cornell. Experimental condensed matter physics, biological physics.

Yan Xu, Professor; Ph.D., Stony Brook, SUNY. Biophysics.

Judith Yang, Professor; Ph.D., Cornell. Materials science and engineering.

Andrew Zentner, Associate Professor and Director of the Graduate Program; Ph.D., Ohio State. Theoretical cosmology.

Jin Zhao, Adjunct Research Professor; Ph.D., University of Sciences and Technology of China. Theoretical condensed matter.

EMERITUS FACULTY

Wilfred W. Cleland, Professor; Ph.D., Yale. Experimental particle physics.

H. E. Anthony Duncan, Professor; Ph.D., MIT. Theoretical particle physics.

Eugene Engels Jr., Professor; Ph.D., Princeton. Experimental particle physics.

Edward Gerjuoy, Professor; Ph.D., Berkeley. Theoretical atomic physics.

Walter I. Goldburg, Professor; Ph.D., Duke. Experimental solid-state physics, phase transitions, light scattering, turbulence.

Allen I. Janis, Professor; Ph.D., Syracuse. General relativity, philosophy of science.

David M. Jasnow, Professor; Ph.D., Illinois at Urbana–Champaign. Theory of phase transitions, statistical physics, biological physics.

Rainer Johnsen, Professor; Ph.D., Kiel (Germany). Experimental atomic and plasma physics.

Peter F. M. Koehler, Professor and Academic Assistant to Dean of University Honors College; Ph.D., Rochester. Experimental high-energy physics, physics education research.

Ezra T. Newman, Professor; Ph.D., Syracuse. General relativity, gravitational lensing.

Richard H. Pratt, Professor; Ph.D., Chicago. Theoretical atomic physics.

Paul Shepard, Professor; Ph.D., Princeton. Experimental particle physics.

C. Martin Vincent, Professor; Ph.D., Witwatersrand (South Africa). Theoretical intermediate-energy physics.

Jeffrey Winicour, Professor; Ph.D., Syracuse. General relativity, numerical relativity.

Allen Hall, home to the Department.

Research collaboration.

200   www.petersons.com

Peterson's Graduate Programs in the Physical Sciences, Mathematics, Agricultural Sciences, the Environment & Natural Resources 2017

ACADEMIC AND PROFESSIONAL PROGRAMS IN MATHEMATICS

Section 7
Mathematical Sciences

This section contains a directory of institutions offering graduate work in mathematical sciences, followed by in-depth entries submitted by institutions that chose to prepare detailed program descriptions. Additional information about programs listed in the directory but not augmented by an in-depth entry may be obtained by writing directly to the dean of a graduate school or chair of a department at the address given in the directory.

For programs offering work in related fields, see all other areas in this book. In the other guides in this series:

Graduate Programs in the Humanities, Arts & Social Sciences

See *Economics* and *Psychology and Counseling*

Graduate Programs in the Biological/Biomedical Sciences & Health-Related Medical Professions

See *Biological and Biomedical Sciences; Biophysics; Genetics, Developmental Biology, and Reproductive Biology; Pharmacology and Toxicology* and *Public Health*

Graduate Programs in Engineering & Applied Sciences

See *Biomedical Engineering and Biotechnology; Chemical Engineering (Biochemical Engineering); Computer Science and Information Technology; Electrical and Computer Engineering; Engineering and Applied Sciences;* and *Industrial Engineering*

Graduate Programs in Business, Education, Information Studies, Law & Social Work

See *Business Administration and Management* and *Library and Information Studies*

CONTENTS

Program Directories

Featured Schools: Displays and Close-Ups

Applied Mathematics

Acadia University, Faculty of Pure and Applied Science, Department of Mathematics and Statistics, Wolfville, NS B4P 2R6, Canada. Offers applied mathematics and statistics (M Sc). *Degree requirements:* For master's, thesis. *Entrance requirements:* For master's, honors degree in mathematics, statistics or equivalent. Additional exam requirements/recommendations for international students: Required—TOEFL (minimum score 580 paper-based; 93 iBT), IELTS (minimum score 6.5). *Faculty research:* Geophysical fluid dynamics, machine scheduling problems, control theory, stochastic optimization, survival analysis.

Air Force Institute of Technology, Graduate School of Engineering and Management, Department of Mathematics and Statistics, Dayton, OH 45433-7765. Offers applied mathematics (MS, PhD). *Program availability:* Part-time. *Degree requirements:* For master's, thesis; for doctorate, thesis/dissertation. *Entrance requirements:* For master's, GRE General Test, minimum GPA of 3.0, U.S. citizenship or permanent U.S. residency; for doctorate, GRE General Test, minimum GPA of 3.5, U.S. citizenship or permanent U.S. residency. *Faculty research:* Electromagnetics, groundwater modeling, nonlinear diffusion, goodness of fit, finite element analysis.

Arizona State University at the Tempe campus, College of Liberal Arts and Sciences, School of Human Evolution and Social Change, Tempe, AZ 85287-2402. Offers anthropology (MA, PhD), including anthropology (PhD), archaeology (PhD), bioarchaeology (PhD), evolutionary (PhD), museum studies (MA), sociocultural (PhD); applied mathematics for the life and social sciences (PhD); environmental social science (PhD), including environmental social science, urbanism; global health (MA, PhD), including complex adaptive systems science (PhD), evolutionary global health sciences (PhD), health and culture (PhD), urbanism (PhD); immigration studies (Graduate Certificate). Terminal master's awarded for partial completion of doctoral program. *Degree requirements:* For master's, thesis or alternative, interactive Program of Study (iPOS) submitted before completing 50 percent of required credit hours; for doctorate, comprehensive exam, thesis/dissertation, interactive Program of Study (iPOS) submitted before completing 50 percent of required credit hours. *Entrance requirements:* For master's and doctorate, GRE, minimum GPA of 3.0 or equivalent in last 2 years of work leading to bachelor's degree. Additional exam requirements/recommendations for international students: Required—TOEFL, IELTS, or PTE. Electronic applications accepted.

Arizona State University at the Tempe campus, College of Liberal Arts and Sciences, School of Mathematical and Statistical Sciences, Tempe, AZ 85287-1804. Offers applied mathematics (PhD); mathematics (MA, PhD); mathematics education (PhD); statistics (MS, PhD, Graduate Certificate). *Program availability:* Part-time. Terminal master's awarded for partial completion of doctoral program. *Degree requirements:* For master's, thesis or alternative, interactive Program of Study (iPOS) submitted before completing 50 percent of required credit hours; for doctorate, comprehensive exam, thesis/dissertation, interactive Program of Study (iPOS) submitted before completing 50 percent of required credit hours. *Entrance requirements:* For master's and doctorate, GRE General Test, minimum GPA of 3.0 or equivalent in last 2 years of work leading to bachelor's degree. Additional exam requirements/recommendations for international students: Required—TOEFL, IELTS, or PTE. Electronic applications accepted. *Expenses:* Contact institution.

Auburn University, Graduate School, College of Sciences and Mathematics, Department of Mathematics and Statistics, Auburn University, AL 36849. Offers applied mathematics (MAM, MS); mathematics (MS, PhD); probability and statistics (M Prob S); statistics (MS). *Faculty:* 57 full-time (12 women), 8 part-time/adjunct (2 women). *Students:* 64 full-time (18 women), 36 part-time (11 women); includes 10 minority (9 Asian, non-Hispanic/Latino; 1 Two or more races, non-Hispanic/Latino), 57 international. Average age 29. 123 applicants, 54% accepted, 15 enrolled. In 2015, 23 master's, 14 doctorates awarded. *Degree requirements:* For doctorate, thesis/dissertation. *Entrance requirements:* For master's, GRE General Test, undergraduate mathematics background; for doctorate, GRE General Test, GRE Subject Test. *Application deadline:* Applications are processed on a rolling basis. Application fee: $50 ($60 for international students). Electronic applications accepted. *Expenses:* Tuition, state resident: full-time $8802; part-time $489 per credit hour. Tuition, nonresident: full-time $26,406; part-time $1467 per credit hour. *Required fees:* $808 per semester. Tuition and fees vary according to degree level and program. *Financial support:* Fellowships and teaching assistantships available. Financial award applicants required to submit FAFSA. *Faculty research:* Pure and applied mathematics. *Unit head:* Dr. Tin Yau Tam, Chair, 334-844-6572, Fax: 334-844-6655. *Application contact:* Dr. George Flowers, Dean of the Graduate School, 334-844-2125.
Website: http://www.auburn.edu/~math/

Bowie State University, Graduate Programs, Program in Applied and Computational Mathematics, Bowie, MD 20715-9465. Offers MS. *Program availability:* Part-time, evening/weekend. *Degree requirements:* For master's, comprehensive exam. *Entrance requirements:* For master's, calculus sequence, differential equations, linear algebra, mathematical probability and statistics. Electronic applications accepted. *Expenses:* Tuition, state resident: full-time $9384; part-time $2346 per year. Tuition, nonresident: full-time $16,344; part-time $4086 per year. *Required fees:* $2552; $325 per semester.

Brown University, Graduate School, Division of Applied Mathematics, Providence, RI 02912. Offers Sc M, PhD. *Degree requirements:* For master's, thesis or alternative; for doctorate, one foreign language, thesis/dissertation, oral exam. *Entrance requirements:* For master's and doctorate, GRE General Test.

California Baptist University, Program in Applied Mathematics, Riverside, CA 92504-3206. Offers MS. *Program availability:* Part-time. *Faculty:* 4 full-time (1 woman). *Students:* 2 full-time (1 woman), 6 part-time (2 women); includes 3 minority (1 Black or African American, non-Hispanic/Latino; 2 Hispanic/Latino), 1 international. Average age 25. 8 applicants, 100% accepted, 7 enrolled. *Entrance requirements:* For master's, minimum undergraduate GPA of 3.0, two letters of recommendation, essay, interview. Additional exam requirements/recommendations for international students: Required—TOEFL (minimum score 80 iBT). *Application deadline:* For fall admission, 8/1 priority date for domestic students, 7/1 priority date for international students; for spring admission, 12/1 priority date for domestic students, 11/1 priority date for international students. Applications are processed on a rolling basis. Application fee: $45. Electronic applications accepted. *Expenses:* $544 per unit plus $355 fee per semester. *Financial support:* Applicants required to submit CSS PROFILE or FAFSA. *Faculty research:* Time-dependent Schrodinger equations, knot theory, strategic analysis. *Application contact:* Taylor Neece, Director of Graduate Admissions, 951-343-4871, Fax: 877-228-8877, E-mail: graduateadmissions@calbaptist.edu.

California Institute of Technology, Division of Engineering and Applied Science, Option in Applied and Computational Mathematics, Pasadena, CA 91125-0001. Offers MS, PhD. *Degree requirements:* For doctorate, thesis/dissertation. *Entrance requirements:* For doctorate, GRE Subject Test. Electronic applications accepted. *Faculty research:* Theoretical and computational fluid mechanics, numerical analysis, ordinary and partial differential equations, linear and nonlinear wave propagation, perturbation and asymptotic methods.

California State Polytechnic University, Pomona, Program in Mathematics, Pomona, CA 91768-2557. Offers applied mathematics (MS); pure mathematics (MS). *Program availability:* Part-time. *Students:* 13 full-time (4 women), 26 part-time (7 women); includes 25 minority (3 Black or African American, non-Hispanic/Latino; 8 Asian, non-Hispanic/Latino; 13 Hispanic/Latino; 1 Two or more races, non-Hispanic/Latino), 2 international. Average age 26. 66 applicants, 38% accepted, 11 enrolled. In 2015, 17 master's awarded. *Degree requirements:* For master's, thesis or alternative. *Entrance requirements:* For master's, GRE General Test. *Application deadline:* For fall admission, 5/1 priority date for domestic students; for winter admission, 10/15 priority date for domestic students; for spring admission, 1/20 priority date for domestic students. Applications are processed on a rolling basis. Application fee: $55. Electronic applications accepted. *Expenses:* Tuition, state resident: full-time $6738. Tuition, nonresident: full-time $13,434. *Required fees:* $1504. Tuition and fees vary according to course load, degree level and program. *Financial support:* Career-related internships or fieldwork, Federal Work-Study, and institutionally sponsored loans available. Support available to part-time students. Financial award application deadline: 3/2; financial award applicants required to submit FAFSA. *Unit head:* Dr. John Rock, Graduate Coordinator, 909-869-2404, Fax: 909-869-4904, E-mail: jarock@cpp.edu.
Website: http://www.cpp.edu/~sci/mathematics-statistics/graduate-students/

California State University, East Bay, Office of Graduate Studies Programs, College of Science, Department of Mathematics and Computer Science, Mathematics Program, Hayward, CA 94542-3000. Offers applied mathematics (MS); mathematics (MS); mathematics teaching (MS). *Program availability:* Part-time, evening/weekend. *Students:* 19 full-time (5 women), 27 part-time (14 women); includes 25 minority (2 Black or African American, non-Hispanic/Latino; 13 Asian, non-Hispanic/Latino; 6 Hispanic/Latino; 2 Native Hawaiian or other Pacific Islander, non-Hispanic/Latino; 2 Two or more races, non-Hispanic/Latino), 3 international. Average age 36. 25 applicants, 80% accepted, 10 enrolled. In 2015, 22 master's awarded. *Degree requirements:* For master's, comprehensive exam or thesis. *Entrance requirements:* For master's, minimum GPA of 3.0 in field. Additional exam requirements/recommendations for international students: Required—TOEFL (minimum score 550 paper-based). *Application deadline:* For fall admission, 6/30 for domestic and international students. Application fee: $55. Electronic applications accepted. *Financial support:* Fellowships, teaching assistantships, Federal Work-Study, institutionally sponsored loans, and scholarships/grants available. Support available to part-time students. Financial award application deadline: 3/1; financial award applicants required to submit FAFSA. *Unit head:* Matthew Johnson, Chair, 510-885-3414, E-mail: matt.johnson@csueastbay.edu. *Application contact:* Dr. Donald Wolitzer, Math Graduate Advisor, 510-885-3467, E-mail: donald.wolitzer@csueastbay.edu.
Website: http://www20.csueastbay.edu/csci/departments/math-cs/

California State University, Fullerton, Graduate Studies, College of Natural Science and Mathematics, Department of Mathematics, Fullerton, CA 92834-9480. Offers applied mathematics (MA); mathematics (MA); teaching (MA). *Program availability:* Part-time. *Degree requirements:* For master's, comprehensive exam or project. *Entrance requirements:* For master's, minimum GPA of 2.5 in last 60 units of course work, major in mathematics or related field.

California State University, Long Beach, Graduate Studies, College of Engineering, Department of Mechanical and Aerospace Engineering, Long Beach, CA 90840. Offers aerospace engineering (MSAE); engineering and industrial applied mathematics (PhD); interdisciplinary engineering (MSE); management engineering (MSE); mechanical engineering (MSME). *Program availability:* Part-time. *Entrance requirements:* Additional exam requirements/recommendations for international students: Required—TOEFL. Electronic applications accepted. *Faculty research:* Unsteady turbulent flows, solar energy, energy conversion, CAD/CAM, computer-assisted instruction.

California State University, Long Beach, Graduate Studies, College of Natural Sciences and Mathematics, Department of Mathematics and Statistics, Long Beach, CA 90840. Offers mathematics (MS), including applied mathematics, applied statistics, mathematics education for secondary school teachers. *Program availability:* Part-time. *Degree requirements:* For master's, comprehensive exam or thesis. Electronic applications accepted. *Faculty research:* Algebra, functional analysis, partial differential equations, operator theory, numerical analysis.

California State University, Los Angeles, Graduate Studies, College of Natural and Social Sciences, Department of Mathematics, Los Angeles, CA 90032-8530. Offers mathematics (MS), including applied mathematics, mathematics. *Program availability:* Part-time, evening/weekend. *Degree requirements:* For master's, comprehensive exam or thesis. *Entrance requirements:* For master's, previous course work in mathematics. Additional exam requirements/recommendations for international students: Required—TOEFL (minimum score 500 paper-based). Electronic applications accepted. *Faculty research:* Group theory, functional analysis, convexity theory, ordered geometry.

California State University, Northridge, Graduate Studies, College of Science and Mathematics, Department of Mathematics, Northridge, CA 91330. Offers applied mathematics (MS); mathematics (MS); mathematics for educational careers (MS). *Program availability:* Part-time, evening/weekend. *Faculty:* 33 full-time (7 women), 54 part-time/adjunct (27 women). *Students:* 16 full-time (8 women), 36 part-time (12 women); includes 13 minority (8 Asian, non-Hispanic/Latino; 5 Hispanic/Latino), 11 international. Average age 29. 62 applicants, 60% accepted, 17 enrolled. *Degree requirements:* For master's, thesis (for some programs). *Entrance requirements:* For master's, GRE (if cumulative undergraduate GPA less than 3.0). Additional exam requirements/recommendations for international students: Required—TOEFL. *Application deadline:* For fall admission, 4/15 priority date for domestic students. Application fee: $55. *Financial support:* Teaching assistantships, Federal Work-Study, and institutionally sponsored loans available. Support available to part-time students. Financial award application deadline: 3/1. *Unit head:* Dr. Rabia Djellouli, 818-677-7794.
Website: http://www.csun.edu/~hfmth009/

Case Western Reserve University, School of Graduate Studies, Department of Mathematics, Applied Mathematics and Statistics, Cleveland, OH 44106. Offers applied

mathematics (MS, PhD); mathematics (MS, PhD). *Program availability:* Part-time. *Faculty:* 23 full-time (10 women), 5 part-time/adjunct (0 women). *Students:* 33 full-time (13 women), 1 part-time (0 women); includes 4 minority (1 Black or African American, non-Hispanic/Latino; 1 Asian, non-Hispanic/Latino; 2 Two or more races, non-Hispanic/Latino), 17 international. Average age 27. 58 applicants, 22% accepted, 10 enrolled. In 2015, 1 master's, 1 doctorate awarded. Terminal master's awarded for partial completion of doctoral program. *Degree requirements:* For master's, thesis (for applied mathematics); for doctorate, comprehensive exam, thesis/dissertation. *Entrance requirements:* For master's and doctorate, GRE General Test, 3 letters of recommendation. Additional exam requirements/recommendations for international students: Required—TOEFL (minimum score 577 paper-based; 90 iBT); Recommended—IELTS (minimum score 7). *Application deadline:* For fall admission, 4/1 priority date for domestic students; for spring admission, 11/1 priority date for domestic students. Applications are processed on a rolling basis. Application fee: $50. Electronic applications accepted. *Expenses: Tuition, area resident:* Full-time $41,137; part-time $1714 per credit hour. *Required fees:* $32. Tuition and fees vary according to course load and program. *Financial support:* Research assistantships, teaching assistantships, institutionally sponsored loans, and unspecified assistantships available. Financial award application deadline: 12/15; financial award applicants required to submit CSS PROFILE or FAFSA. *Faculty research:* Probability theory, convexity and high-dimensional phenomena, imaging, geometric evaluation of curves, dynamical systems, large scale scientific computing, life sciences. *Unit head:* David Singer, Professor and Interim Chair, 216-368-2892, Fax: 216-368-5163, E-mail: david.singer@case.edu. *Application contact:* Sakeenah Bari-Harold, Department Administrator, 216-368-0463, Fax: 216-368-5163, E-mail: sakeenah.bari-harold@case.edu.
Website: http://math.case.edu/

Central European University, Graduate Studies, Department of Mathematics and its Applications, Budapest, Hungary. Offers applied mathematics (MS); mathematics and its applications (PhD). *Faculty:* 2 full-time (0 women), 10 part-time/adjunct (0 women). *Students:* 39 full-time (9 women). Average age 26. 87 applicants, 25% accepted, 15 enrolled. In 2015, 7 master's, 3 doctorates awarded. *Degree requirements:* For master's, one foreign language, thesis (for some programs); for doctorate, comprehensive exam, thesis/dissertation. *Entrance requirements:* For master's and doctorate, entrance exam or GRE, statement of purpose. Additional exam requirements/recommendations for international students: Required—TOEFL (minimum score 570 paper-based); Recommended—IELTS (minimum score 6.5). *Application deadline:* For fall admission, 2/4 for domestic and international students. Application fee: $40. Electronic applications accepted. *Expenses: Tuition, area resident:* Full-time 12,000 euros. Tuition and fees vary according to degree level, program and student level. *Financial support:* In 2015–16, 39 students received support. Fellowships, career-related internships or fieldwork, scholarships/grants, health care benefits, and tuition waivers (full and partial) available. Financial award application deadline: 2/4. *Faculty research:* Algebra, algebraic geometry, bioinformatics, calculus of variations, computational biology, cryptography, discrete mathematics, evolutions equations, fluid mechanics, geometry, number theory, numerical analysis, optimization, ordinary and partial differential equations, probability theory, quantum mechanics, statistics, stochastic processes. *Unit head:* Dr. Karoly Boroczky, Head, 36 1 327-3053, E-mail: mathematics@ceu.edu. *Application contact:* Zsuzsanna Jaszberenyi, Admissions Officer, 361-324-3009, Fax: 367-327-3211, E-mail: admissions@ceu.edu.
Website: http://mathematics.ceu.hu/

Claremont Graduate University, Graduate Programs, Institute of Mathematical Sciences, Claremont, CA 91711-6160. Offers computational and systems biology (PhD); computational mathematics and numerical analysis (MA, MS); computational science (PhD); engineering and industrial applied mathematics (PhD); mathematics (PhD); operations research and statistics (MA, MS); physical applied mathematics (MA, MS); pure mathematics (MA, MS); scientific computing (MA, MS); systems and control theory (MA, MS). *Program availability:* Part-time. *Faculty:* 6 full-time (1 woman), 2 part-time/adjunct (0 women). *Students:* 74 full-time (19 women), 35 part-time (12 women); includes 23 minority (2 Black or African American, non-Hispanic/Latino; 12 Asian, non-Hispanic/Latino; 8 Hispanic/Latino; 1 Two or more races, non-Hispanic/Latino), 51 international. Average age 30. In 2015, 25 master's, 10 doctorates awarded. Terminal master's awarded for partial completion of doctoral program. *Entrance requirements:* For master's and doctorate, GRE General Test. Additional exam requirements/recommendations for international students: Required—TOEFL (minimum score 75 iBT). *Application deadline:* For fall admission, 2/1 priority date for domestic and international students. Applications are processed on a rolling basis. Application fee: $80. Electronic applications accepted. *Expenses: Tuition, area resident:* Full-time $43,032; part-time $1793 per unit. *Required fees:* $600; $300 per semester. $300 per semester. Tuition and fees vary according to course load and program. *Financial support:* Fellowships, research assistantships, Federal Work-Study, institutionally sponsored loans, scholarships/grants, and tuition waivers (full and partial) available. Support available to part-time students. Financial award application deadline: 2/15; financial award applicants required to submit FAFSA. *Unit head:* Ali Nadim, Director, 909-607-9413, E-mail: ali.nadim@cgu.edu. *Application contact:* Jake Campbell, Assistant Director of Admissions, 909-607-3024, E-mail: jake.campbell@cgu.edu.
Website: http://www.cgu.edu/pages/168.asp

The College of William and Mary, Faculty of Arts and Sciences, Department of Applied Science, Williamsburg, VA 23187-8795. Offers accelerator science (PhD); applied mathematics (PhD); applied mechanics (PhD); applied robotics (PhD); applied science (MS); atmospheric and environmental science (PhD); computational neuroscience (PhD); interface, thin film and surface science (PhD); lasers and optics (PhD); magnetic resonance (PhD); materials science and engineering (PhD); mathematical and computational biology (PhD); medical imaging (PhD); nanotechnology (PhD); neuroscience (PhD); non-destructive evaluation (PhD); polymer chemistry (PhD); remote sensing (PhD). *Program availability:* Part-time. *Faculty:* 7 full-time (1 woman), 1 part-time/adjunct (0 women). *Students:* 26 full-time (9 women), 3 part-time (1 woman); includes 5 minority (2 Black or African American, non-Hispanic/Latino; 1 Asian, non-Hispanic/Latino; 2 Hispanic/Latino), 12 international. Average age 28. 24 applicants, 46% accepted, 6 enrolled. In 2015, 2 master's, 6 doctorates awarded. Terminal master's awarded for partial completion of doctoral program. *Degree requirements:* For master's, comprehensive exam, thesis; for doctorate, comprehensive exam, thesis/dissertation, 4 core courses. *Entrance requirements:* For master's and doctorate, GRE General Test, GRE Subject Test. Additional exam requirements/recommendations for international students: Required—TOEFL, TWE. *Application deadline:* For fall admission, 2/3 priority date for domestic students, 2/3 for international students; for spring admission, 10/15 priority date for domestic students, 10/14 for international students. Applications are processed on a rolling basis. Application fee: $45. Electronic applications accepted. *Expenses:* $6,550 per semester; $13,100 per year. *Financial support:* Fellowships, research assistantships, teaching assistantships, Federal Work-Study, health care benefits, tuition waivers (full), and unspecified assistantships available. Financial award application deadline: 4/15; financial award applicants required to submit FAFSA. *Faculty research:* Computational biology, non-destructive evaluation, neurophysiology, lasers and optics. *Total annual research expenditures:* $1.7 million. *Unit head:* Dr. Christopher Del Negro, Chair, 757-221-7808, Fax: 757-221-2050, E-mail: cadeln@wm.edu. *Application contact:* Lianne Rios Ashburne, Graduate Program Coordinator, 757-221-2563, Fax: 757-221-2050, E-mail: lrashburne@wm.edu.
Website: http://www.wm.edu/as/appliedscience

Colorado School of Mines, Office of Graduate Studies, Department of Applied Mathematics and Statistics, Golden, CO 80401. Offers nuclear engineering (MS, PhD). *Program availability:* Part-time. *Faculty:* 25 full-time (10 women), 7 part-time/adjunct (4 women). *Students:* 33 full-time (14 women), 7 part-time (3 women); includes 6 minority (1 Black or African American, non-Hispanic/Latino; 1 American Indian or Alaska Native, non-Hispanic/Latino; 3 Hispanic/Latino; 1 Two or more races, non-Hispanic/Latino). Average age 28. 64 applicants, 77% accepted, 16 enrolled. In 2015, 12 master's, 2 doctorates awarded. *Degree requirements:* For master's, thesis (for some programs); for doctorate, comprehensive exam, thesis/dissertation. *Entrance requirements:* For master's and doctorate, GRE General Test. Additional exam requirements/recommendations for international students: Required—TOEFL (minimum score 550 paper-based; 80 iBT). *Application deadline:* For fall admission, 12/15 priority date for domestic and international students; for spring admission, 9/1 priority date for domestic and international students. Application fee: $50 ($70 for international students). Electronic applications accepted. *Expenses:* Tuition, state resident: full-time $15,225. Tuition, nonresident: full-time $32,700. *Financial support:* In 2015–16, 20 students received support, including 4 fellowships with full tuition reimbursements available (averaging $21,120 per year), 9 teaching assistantships with full tuition reimbursements available (averaging $21,120 per year); scholarships/grants, health care benefits, and unspecified assistantships also available. Financial award application deadline: 12/15; financial award applicants required to submit FAFSA. *Faculty research:* Applied statistics, numerical computation, artificial intelligence, linear optimization. *Total annual research expenditures:* $669,371. *Unit head:* Dr. Willy Hereman, Head, 303-273-3881, E-mail: whereman@mines.edu. *Application contact:* Dr. William Navidi, Professor, 303-273-3489, E-mail: wnavidi@mines.edu.
Website: http://ams.mines.edu/

Columbia University, Fu Foundation School of Engineering and Applied Science, Department of Applied Physics and Applied Mathematics, New York, NY 10027. Offers applied mathematics (MS, Eng Sc D, PhD); applied physics (MS, Eng Sc D, PhD); materials science and engineering (MS, Eng Sc D, PhD); medical physics (MS). *Program availability:* Part-time, online learning. Terminal master's awarded for partial completion of doctoral program. *Degree requirements:* For master's, comprehensive exam; for doctorate, thesis/dissertation, qualifying exam. *Entrance requirements:* For master's, GRE General Test, GRE Subject Test (strongly recommended); for doctorate, GRE General Test, GRE Subject Test (applied physics). Additional exam requirements/recommendations for international students: Required—TOEFL, IELTS, PTE. Electronic applications accepted. *Faculty research:* Plasma physics and fusion energy; optical and laser physics; atmospheric, oceanic and earth physics; applied mathematics; solid state science and processing of materials, their properties, and their structure; medical physics.

Cornell University, Graduate School, Graduate Fields of Arts and Sciences, Center for Applied Mathematics, Ithaca, NY 14853-0001. Offers PhD. *Degree requirements:* For doctorate, one foreign language, comprehensive exam, thesis/dissertation. *Entrance requirements:* For doctorate, GRE General Test, GRE Subject Test in mathematics (recommended), 3 letters of recommendation. Additional exam requirements/recommendations for international students: Required—TOEFL (minimum score 550 paper-based; 77 iBT). Electronic applications accepted. *Faculty research:* Nonlinear systems and PDEs, numerical methods, signal and image processing, mathematical biology, discrete mathematics and optimization.

Cornell University, Graduate School, Graduate Fields of Engineering, Field of Chemical Engineering, Ithaca, NY 14853-0001. Offers advanced materials processing (M Eng, MS, PhD); applied mathematics and computational methods (M Eng, MS, PhD); biochemical engineering (M Eng, MS, PhD); chemical reaction engineering (M Eng, MS, PhD); classical and statistical thermodynamics (M Eng, MS, PhD); fluid dynamics, rheology and biorheology (M Eng, MS, PhD); heat and mass transfer (M Eng, MS, PhD); kinetics and catalysis (M Eng, MS, PhD); polymers (M Eng, MS, PhD); surface science (M Eng, MS, PhD). *Degree requirements:* For master's, thesis (MS); for doctorate, comprehensive exam, thesis/dissertation. *Entrance requirements:* For master's and doctorate, GRE General Test, 2 letters of recommendation. Additional exam requirements/recommendations for international students: Required—TOEFL (minimum score 600 paper-based; 77 iBT). Electronic applications accepted. *Faculty research:* Biochemical, biomedical and metabolic engineering; fluid and polymer dynamics; surface science and chemical kinetics; electronics materials; microchemical systems and nanotechnology.

Cornell University, Graduate School, Graduate Fields of Engineering, Field of Operations Research and Information Engineering, Ithaca, NY 14853. Offers applied probability and statistics (PhD); manufacturing systems engineering (PhD); mathematical programming (PhD); operations research and industrial engineering (M Eng). *Degree requirements:* For doctorate, comprehensive exam, thesis/dissertation. *Entrance requirements:* For master's and doctorate, GRE General Test, 3 letters of recommendation. Additional exam requirements/recommendations for international students: Required—TOEFL (minimum score 600 paper-based; 100 iBT). Electronic applications accepted. *Faculty research:* Mathematical programming and combinatorial optimization, statistics, stochastic processes, mathematical finance, simulation, manufacturing, e-commerce.

Dalhousie University, Faculty of Engineering, Department of Engineering Mathematics, Halifax, NS B3J 2X4, Canada. Offers M Sc, PhD. *Degree requirements:* For master's, thesis; for doctorate, thesis/dissertation. *Entrance requirements:* Additional exam requirements/recommendations for international students: Required—TOEFL, IELTS, CANTEST, CAEL, or Michigan English Language Assessment Battery. Electronic applications accepted. *Faculty research:* Piecewise regression and robust statistics, random field theory, dynamical systems, wave loads on offshore structures, digital signal processing.

Delaware State University, Graduate Programs, Department of Mathematics, Interdisciplinary Program in Applied Mathematics and Theoretical Physics, Dover, DE 19901-2277. Offers PhD. *Degree requirements:* For doctorate, one foreign language, thesis defense. *Entrance requirements:* For doctorate, GRE General Test, MS degree in physics or mathematics. Additional exam requirements/recommendations for international students: Required—TOEFL (minimum score 550 paper-based).

Delaware State University, Graduate Programs, Department of Mathematics, Program in Applied Mathematics, Dover, DE 19901-2277. Offers MS. *Entrance requirements:* Additional exam requirements/recommendations for international students: Required—TOEFL (minimum score 550 paper-based). Electronic applications accepted.

DePaul University, College of Science and Health, Chicago, IL 60614. Offers applied mathematics (MS); applied statistics (MS); biological sciences (MA, MS); chemistry

(MS); mathematics education (MA); mathematics for teaching (MS); nursing (MS); nursing practice (DNP); physics (MS); psychology (MS); pure mathematics (MS); science education (MS); MA/PhD. Electronic applications accepted.

École Polytechnique de Montréal, Graduate Programs, Department of Mathematics and Industrial Engineering, Montréal, QC H3C 3A7, Canada. Offers ergonomy (M Eng, M Sc A, DESS); mathematical method in CA engineering (M Eng, M Sc A, PhD); operational research (M Eng, M Sc A, PhD); production (M Eng, M Sc A); technology management (M Eng, M Sc A). DESS program offered jointly with HEC Montreal and Université de Montréal. *Program availability:* Part-time. *Degree requirements:* For master's, one foreign language, thesis. *Entrance requirements:* For master's, minimum GPA of 2.75. *Faculty research:* Use of computers in organizations.

Elizabeth City State University, School of Mathematics, Science and Technology, Master of Science in Mathematics Program, Elizabeth City, NC 27909-7806. Offers applied mathematics (MS); community college teaching (MS); mathematics education (MS); remote sensing (MS). *Program availability:* Part-time, evening/weekend. *Degree requirements:* For master's, thesis. *Entrance requirements:* For master's, MAT and/or GRE, minimum GPA of 3.0, 3 letters of recommendation, two official transcripts from all undergraduate/graduate schools attended, typewritten one-page request for entry into program that includes description of student's educational preparation. Additional exam requirements/recommendations for international students: Required—TOEFL (minimum score 550 paper-based, 80 iBT) or IELTS (minimum score 6.5). Electronic applications accepted. *Faculty research:* Oceanic temperature effects, mathematics strategies in elementary schools, multimedia, Antarctic temperature mapping, computer networks, water quality, remote sensing, polar ice, satellite imagery.

Florida Atlantic University, Charles E. Schmidt College of Science, Department of Mathematical Sciences, Boca Raton, FL 33431-0991. Offers applied mathematics and statistics (MS); mathematics (MS, MST, PhD). *Program availability:* Part-time. Terminal master's awarded for partial completion of doctoral program. *Degree requirements:* For master's, comprehensive exam (for some programs), thesis (for some programs); for doctorate, comprehensive exam, thesis/dissertation. *Entrance requirements:* For master's and doctorate, GRE General Test, minimum GPA of 3.0. Additional exam requirements/recommendations for international students: Required—TOEFL (minimum score 500 paper-based; 61 iBT), IELTS (minimum score 6). Electronic applications accepted. *Faculty research:* Cryptography, statistics, algebra, analysis, combinatorics.

Florida Institute of Technology, College of Science, Program in Applied Mathematics, Melbourne, FL 32901-6975. Offers MS, PhD. *Program availability:* Part-time. *Students:* 28 full-time (6 women), 6 part-time (2 women); includes 3 minority (1 Black or African American, non-Hispanic/Latino; 1 Asian, non-Hispanic/Latino; 1 Hispanic/Latino), 19 international. Average age 31. 63 applicants, 56% accepted, 6 enrolled. In 2015, 5 master's, 1 doctorate awarded. Terminal master's awarded for partial completion of doctoral program. *Degree requirements:* For master's, comprehensive exam (for some programs), thesis (for some programs), 30 credit hours; for doctorate, comprehensive exam, thesis/dissertation, 75 credit hours. *Entrance requirements:* For master's, minimum GPA of 3.0, proficiency in a computer language, FORTRAN or C programming language; for doctorate, GRE General Test, minimum GPA of 3.2, resume, 3 letters of recommendation, statement of objectives, good English-speaking skills. Additional exam requirements/recommendations for international students: Required—TOEFL (minimum score 550 paper-based; 79 iBT). *Application deadline:* For fall admission, 4/1 for international students; for spring admission, 9/30 for international students. Applications are processed on a rolling basis. Application fee: $50. Electronic applications accepted. *Expenses: Tuition, area resident:* Full-time $21,690; part-time $1205 per credit hour. *Required fees:* $500. Tuition and fees vary according to degree level, campus/location and program. *Financial support:* In 2015–16, 17 students received support. Research assistantships with tuition reimbursements available, teaching assistantships with tuition reimbursements available, career-related internships or fieldwork, and tuition remissions available. Financial award application deadline: 3/1; financial award applicants required to submit FAFSA. *Faculty research:* Methods of nonlinear analysis, spectral theory of operators, reaction diffusion equations, mathematical modeling. *Unit head:* Dr. Ugur Abdulla, Department Head, 321-674-8765, Fax: 321-674-7412, E-mail: abdulla@fit.edu. *Application contact:* Cheryl A Brown, Associate Director of Graduate Admissions, 321-674-7581, Fax: 321-723-9468, E-mail: cbrown@fit.edu.
Website: http://cos.fit.edu/math/programs/applied_mathematics.php

Florida State University, The Graduate School, College of Arts and Sciences, Department of Mathematics, Tallahassee, FL 32306-4510. Offers applied computational mathematics (MS, PhD); biomathematics (MS, PhD); financial mathematics (MS, PhD); pure mathematics (MS, PhD). *Program availability:* Part-time. *Faculty:* 34 full-time (4 women). *Students:* 145 full-time (43 women), 4 part-time (1 woman); includes 18 minority (2 Black or African American, non-Hispanic/Latino; 5 Asian, non-Hispanic/Latino; 2 Hispanic/Latino; 9 Two or more races, non-Hispanic/Latino), 87 international. 300 applicants, 41% accepted, 39 enrolled. In 2015, 44 master's, 14 doctorates awarded. Terminal master's awarded for partial completion of doctoral program. *Degree requirements:* For master's, comprehensive exam (for some programs), thesis optional; for doctorate, comprehensive exam (for some programs), thesis/dissertation, candidacy exam (including written qualifying examinations which differ by degree concentration). *Entrance requirements:* For master's and doctorate, GRE General Test, minimum upper-division GPA of 3.0, 4-year bachelor's degree. Additional exam requirements/recommendations for international students: Required—TOEFL (minimum score 550 paper-based; 80 iBT), IELTS (minimum score 6.5). *Application deadline:* For fall admission, 1/15 priority date for domestic and international students. Applications are processed on a rolling basis. Application fee: $30. Electronic applications accepted. *Expenses: Tuition, area resident:* Full-time $7263; part-time $403.50 per credit hour. Tuition, nonresident: full-time $18,087; part-time $1004.85 per credit hour. *Required fees:* $1365; $75.81 per credit hour. $20 per semester. Tuition and fees vary according to campus/location. *Financial support:* In 2015–16, 106 students received support, including 1 fellowship with full tuition reimbursement available (averaging $22,600 per year), 11 research assistantships with full tuition reimbursements available (averaging $22,000 per year), 83 teaching assistantships with full tuition reimbursements available (averaging $20,650 per year); career-related internships or fieldwork, institutionally sponsored loans, scholarships/grants, health care benefits, tuition waivers (full and partial), and unspecified assistantships also available. Financial award application deadline: 1/30. *Faculty research:* Low-dimensional and geometric topology, mathematical modeling in neuroscience, computational stochastics and Monte Carlo methods, mathematical physics, applied analysis. *Total annual research expenditures:* $1.4 million. *Unit head:* Dr. Xiaoming Wang, Chairperson, 850-645-3338, Fax: 850-644-4053, E-mail: wxm@math.fsu.edu. *Application contact:* Kari Aime, Graduate Advisor and Admissions Coordinator, 850-644-2278, Fax: 850-644-4053,
E-mail: aime@math.fsu.edu.
Website: http://www.math.fsu.edu/

The George Washington University, Columbian College of Arts and Sciences, Department of Mathematics, Washington, DC 20052. Offers applied mathematics (MS); financial mathematics (Graduate Certificate); mathematics (MA, PhD, Graduate Certificate). *Program availability:* Part-time, evening/weekend. *Faculty:* 19 full-time (3 women), 11 part-time/adjunct (4 women). *Students:* 33 full-time (8 women), 17 part-time (5 women); includes 4 minority (1 Black or African American, non-Hispanic/Latino; 1 American Indian or Alaska Native, non-Hispanic/Latino; 2 Hispanic/Latino), 29 international. Average age 26. 107 applicants, 55% accepted, 23 enrolled. In 2015, 7 master's, 5 doctorates, 1 other advanced degree awarded. Terminal master's awarded for partial completion of doctoral program. *Degree requirements:* For master's, comprehensive exam; for doctorate, one foreign language, thesis/dissertation, general exam. *Entrance requirements:* For master's and doctorate, GRE General Test, minimum GPA of 3.0, interview. Additional exam requirements/recommendations for international students: Required—TOEFL (minimum score 550 paper-based; 80 iBT). *Application deadline:* For fall admission, 1/15 priority date for domestic and international students; for spring admission, 10/1 priority date for domestic students, 9/1 priority date for international students. Applications are processed on a rolling basis. Application fee: $75. Electronic applications accepted. *Financial support:* In 2015–16, 17 students received support. Fellowships with full tuition reimbursements available, teaching assistantships with tuition reimbursements available, Federal Work-Study, and tuition waivers available. Financial award application deadline: 1/15. *Unit head:* Yongwu Rong, Chair, 202-994-6890, E-mail: rong@gwu.edu. *Application contact:* 202-994-6210, Fax: 202-994-6213, E-mail: askccas@gwu.edu.
Website: http://math.columbian.gwu.edu/

Hampton University, School of Science, Program in Applied Mathematics, Hampton, VA 23668. Offers computational mathematics (MS); nonlinear science (MS); statistics and probability (MS). *Program availability:* Part-time. *Degree requirements:* For master's, thesis optional. *Entrance requirements:* For master's, GRE General Test. Additional exam requirements/recommendations for international students: Required—TOEFL (minimum score 525 paper-based) or IELTS (6.5). Electronic applications accepted. *Expenses: Tuition, area resident:* Full-time $10,263; part-time $522 per credit hour. *Required fees:* $35. Tuition and fees vary according to course load and program. *Faculty research:* Stochastic processes, nonlinear dynamics, approximation theory, prediction theory, hydrodynamical stability.

Harvard University, Graduate School of Arts and Sciences, Harvard John A. Paulson School of Engineering and Applied Sciences, Cambridge, MA 02138. Offers applied mathematics (ME, SM, PhD); applied physics (ME, SM, PhD); computational science and engineering (ME, SM); computer science (ME, SM, PhD); design engineering (MDE); engineering science (ME), including electrical engineering (ME, SM, PhD); engineering sciences (SM, PhD), including bioengineering, electrical engineering (ME, SM, PhD), environmental science and engineering, materials science and mechanical engineering. MDE offered in collaboration with Graduate School of Design. *Program availability:* Part-time. *Faculty:* 101 full-time (14 women), 10 part-time/adjunct (1 woman). *Students:* 425 full-time (109 women), 12 part-time (1 woman); includes 70 minority (1 Black or African American, non-Hispanic/Latino; 44 Asian, non-Hispanic/Latino; 17 Hispanic/Latino; 8 Two or more races, non-Hispanic/Latino), 207 international. Average age 27. 2,116 applicants, 11% accepted, 132 enrolled. In 2015, 88 master's, 64 doctorates awarded. Terminal master's awarded for partial completion of doctoral program. *Degree requirements:* For master's, thesis (for ME); for doctorate, comprehensive exam, thesis/dissertation. *Entrance requirements:* For master's and doctorate, GRE General Test, GRE Subject Test (recommended), 3 letters of recommendation. Additional exam requirements/recommendations for international students: Required—TOEFL (minimum score 80 iBT). *Application deadline:* For fall admission, 12/15 priority date for domestic and international students. Application fee: $105. Electronic applications accepted. *Expenses:* Contact institution. *Financial support:* In 2015–16, 353 students received support, including 92 fellowships with full tuition reimbursements available (averaging $25,650 per year), 213 research assistantships with tuition reimbursements available (averaging $34,200 per year), 127 teaching assistantships with tuition reimbursements available (averaging $5,775 per year); health care benefits also available. *Faculty research:* Applied mathematics, applied physics, computer science and electrical engineering, environmental engineering, mechanical and biomedical engineering. *Total annual research expenditures:* $38 million. *Unit head:* Francis J. Doyle, III, Dean, 617-495-5829, Fax: 617-495-5264,
E-mail: dean@seas.harvard.edu. *Application contact:* Office of Admissions and Financial Aid, 617-495-5315, E-mail: admissions@seas.harvard.edu.
Website: http://www.seas.harvard.edu/

Howard University, Graduate School, Department of Mathematics, Washington, DC 20059-0002. Offers applied mathematics (MS, PhD); mathematics (MS, PhD). *Program availability:* Part-time. Terminal master's awarded for partial completion of doctoral program. *Degree requirements:* For master's, comprehensive exam, thesis or alternative, qualifying exam; for doctorate, 2 foreign languages, comprehensive exam, thesis/dissertation, qualifying exams. *Entrance requirements:* For master's, GRE General Test, minimum GPA of 3.0; for doctorate, GRE General Test. Additional exam requirements/recommendations for international students: Required—TOEFL. Electronic applications accepted.

Hunter College of the City University of New York, Graduate School, School of Arts and Sciences, Department of Mathematics and Statistics, New York, NY 10065-5085. Offers adolescent mathematics education (MA); applied mathematics (MA); pure mathematics (MA); statistics (MA). *Program availability:* Part-time, evening/weekend. *Faculty:* 3 full-time (1 woman). *Students:* 8 full-time (1 woman), 18 part-time (5 women); includes 13 minority (4 Black or African American, non-Hispanic/Latino; 6 Asian, non-Hispanic/Latino; 3 Hispanic/Latino), 2 international. Average age 29. 52 applicants, 67% accepted, 21 enrolled. In 2015, 21 master's awarded. *Degree requirements:* For master's, one foreign language, comprehensive exam, thesis (for some programs). *Entrance requirements:* For master's, GRE General Test, 24 credits in mathematics. Additional exam requirements/recommendations for international students: Required—TOEFL. *Application deadline:* For fall admission, 4/1 for domestic students, 2/1 for international students; for spring admission, 11/1 for domestic students, 9/1 for international students. *Financial support:* Federal Work-Study, institutionally sponsored loans, scholarships/grants, and tuition waivers (partial) available. Support available to part-time students. *Faculty research:* Data analysis, dynamical systems, computer graphics, topology, statistical decision theory. *Unit head:* Robert Thompson, Chair, 212-772-5300, Fax: 212-772-4858, E-mail: robert.thompson@hunter.cuny.edu. *Application contact:* Ada Peluso, Director for Graduate Admissions, 212-772-4632, Fax: 212-772-4858, E-mail: peluso@math.hunter.cuny.edu.
Website: http://math.hunter.cuny.edu/

Illinois Institute of Technology, Graduate College, College of Science, Department of Applied Mathematics, Chicago, IL 60616. Offers applied mathematics (MS, PhD); data science (MAS); mathematical finance (MAS). MAS in mathematical finance program held jointly with Stuart School of Business. Terminal master's awarded for partial completion of doctoral program. *Degree requirements:* For master's, comprehensive exam, thesis; for doctorate, comprehensive exam, thesis/dissertation. *Entrance requirements:* For master's, GRE General Test (minimum scores: 304 Quantitative and Verbal, 2.5 Analytical Writing), minimum undergraduate GPA of 3.0; three letters of recommendation; for doctorate, GRE General Test (minimum scores: 304 Quantitative and Verbal, 3.0 Analytical Writing), minimum undergraduate GPA of 3.5; three letters of recommendation. Additional exam requirements/recommendations for international students: Required—TOEFL (minimum score 550 paper-based; 80 iBT). Electronic applications accepted. *Faculty research:* Applied analysis, computational mathematics, discrete applied mathematics, stochastics (including financial mathematics).

Indiana University Bloomington, University Graduate School, College of Arts and Sciences, Department of Mathematics, Bloomington, IN 47405-7000. Offers applied mathematics (MA); mathematical physics (PhD); mathematics education (MAT); pure mathematics (MA, PhD). Terminal master's awarded for partial completion of doctoral program. *Degree requirements:* For doctorate, one foreign language, thesis/dissertation. *Entrance requirements:* For master's and doctorate, GRE General Test, GRE Subject Test. Additional exam requirements/recommendations for international students: Required—TOEFL. Electronic applications accepted. *Faculty research:* Topology, geometry, algebra, applied, analysis.

Indiana University of Pennsylvania, School of Graduate Studies and Research, College of Natural Sciences and Mathematics, Department of Mathematics, Program in Applied Mathematics, Indiana, PA 15705-1087. Offers MS. *Program availability:* Part-time. *Faculty:* 8 full-time (3 women). *Students:* 14 full-time (8 women), 3 part-time (1 woman); includes 1 minority (Black or African American, non-Hispanic/Latino), 5 international. Average age 28. 33 applicants, 45% accepted, 5 enrolled. In 2015, 3 master's awarded. *Degree requirements:* For master's, thesis optional. *Entrance requirements:* For master's, 2 letters of recommendation. Additional exam requirements/recommendations for international students: Required—TOEFL (minimum score 540 paper-based). *Application deadline:* Applications are processed on a rolling basis. Application fee: $50. Electronic applications accepted. *Financial support:* In 2015–16, 9 research assistantships with tuition reimbursements (averaging $3,998 per year) were awarded; fellowships with full tuition reimbursements, Federal Work-Study, scholarships/grants, and unspecified assistantships also available. Support available to part-time students. Financial award application deadline: 4/15; financial award applicants required to submit FAFSA. *Unit head:* Dr. Yu-Ju Kuo, Graduate Co-Coordinator, 724-357-4765, E-mail: yjkuo@iup.edu. *Application contact:* Dr. Rick Adkins, Graduate Co-Coordinator, 724-357-3790, E-mail: fadkins@iup.edu.
Website: http://www.iup.edu/grad/appliedmath/default.aspx

Indiana University–Purdue University Fort Wayne, College of Arts and Sciences, Department of Mathematical Sciences, Fort Wayne, IN 46805-1499. Offers applied mathematics (MS); applied statistics (Certificate); mathematics (MS); operations research (MS); teaching (MAT). *Program availability:* Part-time, evening/weekend. *Faculty:* 18 full-time (5 women). *Students:* 2 full-time (1 woman), 9 part-time (2 women); includes 1 minority (Hispanic/Latino), 1 international. Average age 31. 6 applicants, 100% accepted, 4 enrolled. In 2015, 5 master's, 1 other advanced degree awarded. *Entrance requirements:* For master's, minimum GPA of 3.0, major or minor in mathematics, three letters of recommendation. Additional exam requirements/recommendations for international students: Required—TOEFL (minimum score 550 paper-based; 79 iBT); Recommended—TWE. *Application deadline:* For fall admission, 8/1 priority date for domestic students, 7/1 priority date for international students; for spring admission, 12/1 for domestic students, 10/1 for international students. Applications are processed on a rolling basis. Application fee: $55 ($60 for international students). Electronic applications accepted. *Financial support:* In 2015–16, 5 teaching assistantships with partial tuition reimbursements (averaging $13,522 per year) were awarded; scholarships/grants and unspecified assistantships also available. Support available to part-time students. Financial award application deadline: 3/1; financial award applicants required to submit FAFSA. *Faculty research:* Eves' Theorem, paired-placements for student teaching, holomorphic maps. *Total annual research expenditures:* $56,223. *Unit head:* Dr. Peter Dragnev, Chair/Professor, 260-481-6382, Fax: 260-481-0155, E-mail: dragnevp@ipfw.edu. *Application contact:* Dr. W. Douglas Weakley, Director of Graduate Studies, 260-481-6233, Fax: 260-481-0155,
E-mail: weakley@ipfw.edu.
Website: http://www.ipfw.edu/math/

Indiana University–Purdue University Indianapolis, School of Science, Department of Mathematical Sciences, Indianapolis, IN 46202-3216. Offers mathematics (MS, PhD), including applied mathematics, applied statistics (MS), mathematical statistics (PhD), mathematics, mathematics education (MS). *Program availability:* Part-time. Terminal master's awarded for partial completion of doctoral program. *Degree requirements:* For master's, thesis optional; for doctorate, one foreign language, thesis/dissertation. *Entrance requirements:* For doctorate, GRE General Test. Additional exam requirements/recommendations for international students: Required—TOEFL. *Faculty research:* Mathematical physics, integral systems, partial differential equations, noncommutative geometry, biomathematics, computational neurosciences.

Indiana University South Bend, College of Liberal Arts and Sciences, South Bend, IN 46634-7111. Offers applied mathematics and computer science (MS); English (MA); liberal studies (MLS); public affairs (MPA). *Program availability:* Part-time, evening/weekend. *Degree requirements:* For master's, thesis (for some programs). *Entrance requirements:* For master's, minimum GPA of 3.0. Additional exam requirements/recommendations for international students: Required—TOEFL. *Faculty research:* Artificial intelligence, bioinformatics, English language and literature, creative writing, computer networks.

Inter American University of Puerto Rico, San Germán Campus, Graduate Studies Center, Program in Mathematics Education, San Germán, PR 00683-5008. Offers applied mathematics (MA). *Program availability:* Part-time, evening/weekend. *Degree requirements:* For master's, comprehensive exam. *Entrance requirements:* For master's, EXADEP or GRE General Test, minimum GPA of 3.0.

Iowa State University of Science and Technology, Department of Mathematics, Ames, IA 50011. Offers applied mathematics (MS, PhD); mathematics (MS, PhD); school mathematics (MSM). *Degree requirements:* For master's, thesis or alternative; for doctorate, thesis/dissertation. *Entrance requirements:* For master's and doctorate, GRE General Test. Additional exam requirements/recommendations for international students: Required—TOEFL (minimum score 550 paper-based; 79 iBT), IELTS (minimum score 6.5). Electronic applications accepted.

Iowa State University of Science and Technology, Program in Applied Mathematics, Ames, IA 50011. Offers MS, PhD. *Entrance requirements:* For master's and doctorate, GRE. Additional exam requirements/recommendations for international students: Required—TOEFL (minimum score 550 paper-based; 79 iBT), IELTS (minimum score 6.5). Electronic applications accepted.

Johns Hopkins University, Engineering Program for Professionals, Part-time Program in Applied and Computational Mathematics, Baltimore, MD 21218. Offers MS, Post-Master's Certificate. *Program availability:* Part-time, evening/weekend. Electronic applications accepted.

Johns Hopkins University, G. W. C. Whiting School of Engineering, Department of Applied Mathematics and Statistics, Baltimore, MD 21218. Offers computational medicine (PhD); discrete mathematics (MA, MSE, PhD); financial mathematics (MSE); operations research/optimization (MA, MSE, PhD); statistics/probability (MA, MSE, PhD). Terminal master's awarded for partial completion of doctoral program. *Degree requirements:* For master's, thesis (for some programs); for doctorate, thesis/dissertation, oral exam, introductory exam. *Entrance requirements:* For master's and doctorate, GRE General Test, GRE Subject Test. Additional exam requirements/recommendations for international students: Required—TOEFL (minimum score 600 paper-based; 100 iBT). Electronic applications accepted. *Faculty research:* Discrete mathematics, probability, statistics, optimization and operations research, scientific computation, financial mathematics.

Kent State University, College of Arts and Sciences, Department of Mathematical Sciences, Kent, OH 44242-0001. Offers applied mathematics (MA, MS, PhD); pure mathematics (MA, MS, PhD). *Program availability:* Part-time. *Faculty:* 42 full-time (17 women). *Students:* 61 full-time (21 women), 40 part-time (19 women); includes 3 minority (2 Asian, non-Hispanic/Latino; 1 Two or more races, non-Hispanic/Latino), 50 international. Average age 30. 205 applicants, 58% accepted, 38 enrolled. In 2015, 6 master's, 6 doctorates awarded. *Degree requirements:* For master's, comprehensive exam (for some programs), thesis (for MS); for doctorate, one foreign language, comprehensive exam, thesis/dissertation, qualifying exam. *Entrance requirements:* For master's and doctorate, GRE General Test, minimum GPA of 3.0, transcript, goal statement, resume, 3 letters of recommendation. Additional exam requirements/recommendations for international students: Required—TOEFL (minimum score: paper-based 525, iBT 71), Michigan English Language Assessment Battery (minimum score of 75), IELTS (minimum score of 6.0), PTE Academic (minimum score of 48), or completion of ELS level 112 Intensive Program. *Application deadline:* For fall admission, 7/12 for domestic students; for spring admission, 11/29 for domestic students. Applications are processed on a rolling basis. Application fee: $45 ($70 for international students). Electronic applications accepted. *Expenses:* Tuition, state resident: full-time $10,864; part-time $495 per credit hour. Tuition, nonresident: full-time $18,380; part-time $837 per credit hour. *Financial support:* Research assistantships with full tuition reimbursements, teaching assistantships with full tuition reimbursements, career-related internships or fieldwork, Federal Work-Study, scholarships/grants, and unspecified assistantships available. Financial award application deadline: 2/1. *Unit head:* Dr. Andrew Tonge, Chairman, 330-672-9046, E-mail: tonge@math.kent.edu. *Application contact:* Artem Zvavitch, Professor and Graduate Coordinator, 330-672-2430, Fax: 330-672-2209, E-mail: math-gradinfo@math.kent.edu.
Website: http://www.kent.edu/math/

Lehigh University, College of Arts and Sciences, Department of Mathematics, Bethlehem, PA 18015. Offers applied mathematics (MS, PhD); mathematics (MS, PhD); statistics (MS). *Program availability:* Part-time. *Faculty:* 24 full-time (3 women), 1 part-time/adjunct (0 women). *Students:* 38 full-time (11 women), 8 part-time (3 women); includes 1 minority (Hispanic/Latino), 17 international. Average age 25. 147 applicants, 39% accepted, 11 enrolled. In 2015, 17 master's, 3 doctorates awarded. Terminal master's awarded for partial completion of doctoral program. *Degree requirements:* For master's, comprehensive exam, thesis optional; for doctorate, comprehensive exam, thesis/dissertation, qualifying examination, general examination, advanced topic examination. *Entrance requirements:* For master's and doctorate, GRE General Test (strongly recommended), minimum undergraduate GPA of 2.75, 3.0 for last two semesters; adequate background in math. Additional exam requirements/recommendations for international students: Required—TOEFL (minimum score 85 iBT). *Application deadline:* For fall admission, 1/1 for domestic and international students; for spring admission, 12/1 for domestic and international students. Application fee: $75. Electronic applications accepted. *Financial support:* In 2015–16, 31 students received support, including 1 fellowship with full tuition reimbursement available (averaging $25,000 per year), 1 research assistantship with full tuition reimbursement available (averaging $20,000 per year), 25 teaching assistantships with full tuition reimbursements available (averaging $20,000 per year); tuition waivers (partial) also available. Financial award application deadline: 1/1. *Faculty research:* Probability and statistics, geometry and topology, algebra, discrete mathematics, differential equations. *Total annual research expenditures:* $182,459. *Unit head:* Dr. Wei-Min Huang, Chairman, 610-758-3730, Fax: 610-758-3767, E-mail: wh02@lehigh.edu. *Application contact:* Dr. Terry Napier, Graduate Director, 610-758-3755,
E-mail: mathgrad@lehigh.edu.
Website: http://www.lehigh.edu/~math/grad.html

Long Island University–LIU Post, College of Liberal Arts and Sciences, Brookville, NY 11548-1300. Offers applied mathematics (MS); behavior analysis (MA); biology (MS); criminal justice (MS); earth science (MS); English (MA); environmental studies (MS); environmental sustainability (MS); genetic counseling (MS); gerontology (Advanced Certificate); health care administration (MPA); history (MA); interdisciplinary studies (MA, MS); mathematics for secondary school teachers (MS); mobile GIS application development (Advanced Certificate); non-profit management (Advanced Certificate); political science (MA); psychology (MA); public administration (MPA). *Program availability:* Part-time, evening/weekend, online learning. *Faculty:* 77 full-time (35 women), 36 part-time/adjunct (17 women). *Students:* 254 full-time (178 women), 177 part-time (134 women); includes 104 minority (40 Black or African American, non-Hispanic/Latino; 27 Asian, non-Hispanic/Latino; 28 Hispanic/Latino; 1 Native Hawaiian or other Pacific Islander, non-Hispanic/Latino; 8 Two or more races, non-Hispanic/Latino), 44 international. Average age 31. 686 applicants, 47% accepted, 138 enrolled. In 2015, 135 master's awarded. *Degree requirements:* For master's, comprehensive exam (for some programs), thesis (for some programs). *Entrance requirements:* Additional exam requirements/recommendations for international students: Required—TOEFL (minimum score 550 paper-based; 79 iBT), IELTS (minimum score 6.5). *Application deadline:* Applications are processed on a rolling basis. Application fee: $50. Electronic applications accepted. *Expenses:* $1155 per credit; $934 full-time fees; $442 part-time fees. *Financial support:* In 2015–16, 48 fellowships (averaging $12,637 per year), 5 research assistantships with full tuition reimbursements were awarded; Federal Work-Study and institutionally sponsored loans also available. Support available to part-time students. Financial award application deadline: 2/15; financial award applicants required to submit FAFSA. *Faculty research:* Biology, criminal justice, earth and environmental science, English, health care and public administration, history, mathematics, political science, psychology, Spanish. *Unit head:* Dr. Nicholas J. Ramer, Acting Dean, 516-299-2233, Fax: 516-299-4140, E-mail: nicholas.ramer@liu.edu. *Application contact:* Carol Zerah, Director of Graduate Admissions, 516-299-2900 Ext. 3952, Fax: 516-299-2137, E-mail: enroll@cwpost.liu.edu.
Website: http://liu.edu/CWPost/Academics/Schools/CLAS

Manhattan College, Graduate Programs, School of Science, Program in Applied Mathematics-Data Analytics, Riverdale, NY 10471. Offers MS.

McGill University, Faculty of Graduate and Postdoctoral Studies, Faculty of Science, Department of Mathematics and Statistics, Montréal, QC H3A 2T5, Canada. Offers computational science and engineering (M Sc); mathematics and statistics (M Sc, MA, PhD), including applied mathematics (M Sc, MA), pure mathematics (M Sc, MA), statistics (M Sc, MA).

Applied Mathematics

Michigan State University, The Graduate School, College of Natural Science, Department of Mathematics, East Lansing, MI 48824. Offers applied mathematics (MS, PhD); industrial mathematics (MS); mathematics (MAT, MS, PhD). *Entrance requirements:* Additional exam requirements/recommendations for international students: Required—TOEFL. Electronic applications accepted.

Missouri University of Science and Technology, Graduate School, Department of Mathematics and Statistics, Rolla, MO 65409. Offers applied mathematics (MS); mathematics (MST, PhD), including mathematics (PhD), mathematics education (MST), statistics (PhD). *Faculty:* 21 full-time (9 women), 1 part-time/adjunct (0 women). *Students:* 38 full-time (16 women), 5 part-time (0 women), 33 international. Average age 29. 37 applicants, 68% accepted, 8 enrolled. In 2015, 5 master's, 3 doctorates awarded. Terminal master's awarded for partial completion of doctoral program. *Degree requirements:* For master's, thesis or alternative; for doctorate, one foreign language, thesis/dissertation. *Entrance requirements:* For master's and doctorate, GRE General Test, GRE Subject Test. Additional exam requirements/recommendations for international students: Required—TOEFL (minimum score 550 paper-based). *Application deadline:* For fall admission, 7/1 for domestic students. Applications are processed on a rolling basis. Application fee: $55 ($75 for international students). Electronic applications accepted. *Expenses:* Tuition, state resident: full-time $10,536. Tuition, nonresident: full-time $27,015. Full-time tuition and fees vary according to course load. *Financial support:* In 2015–16, 5 fellowships, 1 research assistantship with partial tuition reimbursement (averaging $1,814 per year), 19 teaching assistantships with partial tuition reimbursements (averaging $1,813 per year) were awarded; institutionally sponsored loans also available. *Faculty research:* Analysis, differential equations, topology, statistics. *Total annual research expenditures:* $223,299. *Unit head:* Dr. Leon M. Hall, Chair, 573-341-4641, Fax: 573-341-4741, E-mail: lmhall@mst.edu. *Application contact:* Dr. V. A. Samaranayake, Director of Graduate Studies, 573-341-4658, Fax: 573-341-4741, E-mail: vsam@mst.edu.
Website: http://math.mst.edu/

Montclair State University, The Graduate School, College of Science and Mathematics, Program in Mathematics, Montclair, NJ 07043-1624. Offers mathematics education (MS); pure and applied mathematics (MS). *Program availability:* Part-time, evening/weekend. *Students:* 9 full-time (4 women), 53 part-time (27 women); includes 16 minority (2 Black or African American, non-Hispanic/Latino; 4 Asian, non-Hispanic/Latino; 8 Hispanic/Latino; 2 Two or more races, non-Hispanic/Latino), 1 international. Average age 33. 22 applicants, 82% accepted, 14 enrolled. In 2015, 17 master's awarded. *Degree requirements:* For master's, comprehensive exam. *Entrance requirements:* For master's, GRE General Test, 2 letters of recommendation, essay. Additional exam requirements/recommendations for international students: Required—TOEFL (minimum score 83 iBT), IELTS (minimum score 6.5). *Application deadline:* Applications are processed on a rolling basis. Application fee: $60. Electronic applications accepted. *Expenses:* Tuition, state resident: part-time $553 per credit. Tuition, nonresident: part-time $854 per credit. *Required fees:* $91 per credit. Tuition and fees vary according to program. *Financial support:* In 2015–16, 9 research assistantships with full tuition reimbursements (averaging $7,000 per year) were awarded; Federal Work-Study, scholarships/grants, and unspecified assistantships also available. Support available to part-time students. Financial award application deadline: 3/1; financial award applicants required to submit FAFSA. *Faculty research:* Computation, applied analysis. *Unit head:* Dr. Helen Roberts, Chairperson, 973-655-5132. *Application contact:* Amy Aiello, Director of Graduate Admissions and Operations, 973-655-5147, Fax: 973-655-7869, E-mail: graduate.school@montclair.edu.

Naval Postgraduate School, Departments and Academic Groups, Department of Applied Mathematics, Monterey, CA 93943. Offers MS, PhD. Program only open to commissioned officers of the United States and friendly nations and selected United States federal civilian employees. *Program availability:* Part-time. *Degree requirements:* For master's, thesis; for doctorate, one foreign language, thesis/dissertation. *Faculty research:* Compact S-box for Advanced Encryption Standard (AES), rotation symmetric Boolean functions - count and crytograhic properties, pseudospectral method for the optimal control of constrained feedback linearizable systems, nodal triangle-based spectral element method for the shallow water equations on the sphere, axisymmetric equilibria of three-dimensional Smoluchowski equation.

Naval Postgraduate School, Departments and Academic Groups, Undersea Warfare Academic Group, Monterey, CA 93943. Offers applied mathematics (MS); applied physics (MS); applied science (MS), including acoustics, operations research, physical oceanography, signal processing; electrical engineering (MS); engineering acoustics (MS, PhD); engineering science (MS), including electrical engineering, mechanical engineering; mechanical engineer (ME); mechanical engineering (MS, MSME); meteorology (MS); operations research (MS); physical oceanography (MS). Program only open to commissioned officers of the United States and friendly nations and selected United States federal civilian employees. *Program availability:* Part-time. *Degree requirements:* For master's, thesis. *Faculty research:* Unmanned/autonomous vehicles, sea mines and countermeasures, submarine warfare in the twentieth and twenty-first centuries.

New Jersey Institute of Technology, College of Science and Liberal Arts, Newark, NJ 07102. Offers applied mathematics (MS); applied physics (M Sc, PhD); applied statistical models (Certificate); applied statistics (MS); biology (MS, PhD); biostatistics (MS); biostatistics essentials (Certificate); chemistry (MS, PhD); computational biology (MS); environmental science (MS, PhD); history (MA, MAT); materials science and engineering (MS, PhD); mathematical and computational finance (MS); mathematics science (PhD); pharmaceutical chemistry (MS); professional and technical communications (MS); technical common essentials (Certificate). *Program availability:* Part-time, evening/weekend. *Faculty:* 153 full-time (35 women), 100 part-time/adjunct (40 women). *Students:* 212 full-time (82 women), 94 part-time (37 women); includes 72 minority (22 Black or African American, non-Hispanic/Latino; 25 Asian, non-Hispanic/Latino; 19 Hispanic/Latino; 6 Two or more races, non-Hispanic/Latino), 164 international. Average age 29. 519 applicants, 62% accepted, 104 enrolled. In 2015, 98 master's, 21 doctorates, 3 other advanced degrees awarded. Terminal master's awarded for partial completion of doctoral program. *Degree requirements:* For master's, thesis optional; for doctorate, thesis/dissertation. *Entrance requirements:* For master's, GRE General Test; for doctorate, GRE General Test, minimum graduate GPA of 3.5. Additional exam requirements/recommendations for international students: Required—TOEFL (minimum score 550 paper-based; 79 iBT). *Application deadline:* For fall admission, 6/1 priority date for domestic students, 5/1 priority date for international students; for spring admission, 11/15 priority date for domestic and international students. Applications are processed on a rolling basis. Application fee: $75. Electronic applications accepted. *Expenses:* $28,800 per year non-resident full-time. *Financial support:* In 2015–16, 56 research assistantships with full tuition reimbursements (averaging $17,711 per year), 52 teaching assistantships with full tuition reimbursements (averaging $17,914 per year) were awarded; fellowships with full tuition reimbursements also available. Financial award application deadline: 1/15. *Total annual research expenditures:* $23.1 million. *Unit head:* Dr. Kevin Belfield, Dean, 973-596-3676, Fax: 973-565-0586, E-mail: kevin.d.belfield@njit.edu. *Application contact:* Stephen Eck, Director of Admissions, 973-596-3300, Fax: 973-596-3461, E-mail: admissions@njit.edu.
Website: http://csla.njit.edu/

New Mexico Institute of Mining and Technology, Center for Graduate Studies, Department of Mathematics, Socorro, NM 87801. Offers applied and industrial mathematics (PhD); industrial mathematics (MS); mathematics (MS); operations research and statistics (MS). *Degree requirements:* For master's, thesis optional; for doctorate, thesis/dissertation. *Entrance requirements:* For master's, GRE General Test. Additional exam requirements/recommendations for international students: Required—TOEFL (minimum score 540 paper-based). *Expenses:* Tuition, state resident: full-time $5811; part-time $322.81 per credit. Tuition, nonresident: full-time $19,220; part-time $1067.79 per credit. *Required fees:* $1030. Tuition and fees vary according to course load. *Faculty research:* Applied mathematics, differential equations, industrial mathematics, numerical analysis, stochastic processes.

North Carolina Agricultural and Technical State University, School of Graduate Studies, College of Arts and Sciences, Department of Mathematics, Greensboro, NC 27411. Offers applied mathematics (MS), including secondary education. *Accreditation:* NCATE. *Program availability:* Part-time, evening/weekend. *Degree requirements:* For master's, comprehensive exam, thesis or alternative, qualifying exam. *Entrance requirements:* For master's, GRE General Test, minimum GPA of 3.0.

North Carolina Central University, College of Science and Technology, Department of Mathematics and Computer Science, Durham, NC 27707-3129. Offers applied mathematics (MS); mathematics education (MS); pure mathematics (MS). *Program availability:* Part-time, evening/weekend. *Degree requirements:* For master's, one foreign language, comprehensive exam, thesis. *Entrance requirements:* For master's, minimum GPA of 3.0 in major, 2.5 overall. Additional exam requirements/recommendations for international students: Required—TOEFL. *Faculty research:* Structure theorems for Lie algebra, Kleene monoids and semi-groups, theoretical computer science, mathematics education.

North Carolina State University, Graduate School, College of Physical and Mathematical Sciences, Department of Mathematics, Program in Applied Mathematics, Raleigh, NC 27695. Offers MS, PhD. *Degree requirements:* For master's, thesis (for some programs); for doctorate, thesis/dissertation. *Entrance requirements:* For master's and doctorate, GRE, GRE Subject Test. Electronic applications accepted. *Faculty research:* Biological and physical modeling, numerical analysis, control, stochastic processes, industrial mathematics.

North Dakota State University, College of Graduate and Interdisciplinary Studies, College of Science and Mathematics, Department of Mathematics, Fargo, ND 58102. Offers applied mathematics (MS, PhD); mathematics (MS, PhD). *Degree requirements:* For master's, comprehensive exam, thesis; for doctorate, one foreign language, comprehensive exam, thesis/dissertation, computer proficiency. *Entrance requirements:* For master's and doctorate, GRE General Test. Additional exam requirements/recommendations for international students: Required—TOEFL (minimum score 525 paper-based; 71 iBT), IELTS. Electronic applications accepted. *Faculty research:* Discrete mathematics, number theory, analysis theory, algebra, applied math.

Northeastern Illinois University, College of Graduate Studies and Research, College of Arts and Sciences, Program in Applied Mathematics, Chicago, IL 60625-4699. Offers MS.

Northeastern University, College of Science, Boston, MA 02115-5096. Offers applied mathematics (MS); bioinformatics (MS); biology (PhD); biotechnology (MS); chemistry (MS, PhD); ecology, evolution, and marine biology (PhD); marine biology (MS); mathematics (MS, PhD); network science (PhD); operations research (MSOR); physics (MS, PhD); psychology (PhD). *Program availability:* Part-time. *Faculty:* 216 full-time (70 women), 62 part-time/adjunct (20 women). *Students:* 517 full-time (252 women), 80 part-time (39 women). In 2015, 94 master's, 46 doctorates awarded. Terminal master's awarded for partial completion of doctoral program. *Degree requirements:* For master's, comprehensive exam (for some programs), thesis; for doctorate, comprehensive exam (for some programs), thesis/dissertation. *Entrance requirements:* For master's, GRE General Test. *Application deadline:* Applications are processed on a rolling basis. Application fee: $75. Electronic applications accepted. *Expenses:* $1,325 per credit; $1,170 per credit (for marine biology). *Financial support:* Fellowships with tuition reimbursements, research assistantships with tuition reimbursements, teaching assistantships with tuition reimbursements, career-related internships or fieldwork, scholarships/grants, health care benefits, tuition waivers (full and partial), and unspecified assistantships available. Support available to part-time students. Financial award applicants required to submit FAFSA. *Unit head:* Dr. Jonathan Tilly, Interim Dean. *Application contact:* Graduate Student Services, 617-373-4275, E-mail: gradcos@neu.edu.
Website: http://www.northeastern.edu/cos/

Northwestern University, McCormick School of Engineering and Applied Science, Department of Engineering Sciences and Applied Mathematics, Evanston, IL 60208. Offers MS, PhD. Admissions and degrees offered through The Graduate School. *Program availability:* Part-time. *Faculty:* 12 full-time (1 woman). *Students:* 58 full-time (16 women), 2 part-time (1 woman); includes 13 minority (1 Black or African American, non-Hispanic/Latino; 9 Asian, non-Hispanic/Latino; 1 Hispanic/Latino; 2 Two or more races, non-Hispanic/Latino), 24 international. 159 applicants, 28% accepted, 13 enrolled. In 2015, 12 master's, 4 doctorates awarded. Terminal master's awarded for partial completion of doctoral program. *Degree requirements:* For master's, comprehensive exam; for doctorate, comprehensive exam, thesis/dissertation. *Entrance requirements:* For master's and doctorate, GRE General Test. Additional exam requirements/recommendations for international students: Required—TOEFL (minimum score 577 paper-based; 90 iBT), IELTS (minimum score 7). *Application deadline:* For fall admission, 1/12 for domestic and international students. Application fee: $95. Electronic applications accepted. *Financial support:* In 2015–16, fellowships with full tuition reimbursements (averaging $29,000 per year), research assistantships with full tuition reimbursements (averaging $29,000 per year), teaching assistantships with full tuition reimbursements (averaging $29,000 per year) were awarded; career-related internships or fieldwork, institutionally sponsored loans, health care benefits, and unspecified assistantships also available. Financial award application deadline: 1/15; financial award applicants required to submit FAFSA. *Faculty research:* Acoustics, asymptotic analysis, bifurcation theory, combustion theory, fluid dynamics, information technology, math biology, microfluidics, moving boundary problems, nonlinear dynamics, pattern formation, waves. *Total annual research expenditures:* $1.8 million. *Unit head:* Dr. David Chopp, Chair, 847-491-8391, Fax: 847-491-2178, E-mail: chopp@northwestern.edu. *Application contact:* Dr. David Chopp, Chair, 847-491-8391, Fax: 847-491-2178, E-mail: chopp@northwestern.edu.
Website: http://www.mccormick.northwestern.edu/applied-math/index.html

Oakland University, Graduate Study and Lifelong Learning, College of Arts and Sciences, Department of Mathematics and Statistics, Program in Applied Mathematical

Sciences, Rochester, MI 48309-4401. Offers PhD. *Students:* 16 full-time (10 women), 5 part-time (1 woman); includes 3 minority (2 Asian, non-Hispanic/Latino; 1 Hispanic/Latino), 7 international. Average age 34. 21 applicants, 19% accepted, 2 enrolled. Application fee: $0. *Expenses: Tuition, area resident:* Part-time $655 per credit. Tuition and fees vary according to program. *Unit head:* Dr. Louis J. Nachman, Chair, Department of Mathematics and Statistics, 248-370-3439, Fax: 248-370-4184, E-mail: nachman@oakland.edu. *Application contact:* Dr. Robert Kushler, Coordinator, Graduate Programs, 248-370-3445, Fax: 248-370-4184, E-mail: kushler@oakland.edu.

Oakland University, Graduate Study and Lifelong Learning, College of Arts and Sciences, Department of Mathematics and Statistics, Program in Industrial Applied Mathematics, Rochester, MI 48309-4401. Offers MS. *Program availability:* Part-time, evening/weekend. *Students:* 1 (woman) full-time, 1 (woman) part-time. Average age 28. 3 applicants.. *Entrance requirements:* For master's, minimum GPA of 3.0. Additional exam requirements/recommendations for international students: Required—TOEFL (minimum score 550 paper-based). *Application deadline:* For fall admission, 7/15 priority date for domestic students, 5/1 priority date for international students; for winter admission, 12/1 priority date for domestic students, 9/1 priority date for international students; for spring admission, 3/15 priority date for domestic students. Applications are processed on a rolling basis. Application fee: $0. Electronic applications accepted. *Expenses:* Contact institution. *Financial support:* Federal Work-Study, institutionally sponsored loans, and tuition waivers (full) available. Financial award application deadline: 3/1; financial award applicants required to submit FAFSA. *Unit head:* Dr. Laszlo Liptak, Chair, Department of Mathematics and Statistics, 248-370-4054, Fax: 248-370-4184, E-mail: liptak@oakland.edu. *Application contact:* Dr. Meir Shillor, Coordinator, Graduate Programs, 248-370-3439, Fax: 248-370-4184, E-mail: shillor@oakland.edu.

Oklahoma State University, College of Arts and Sciences, Department of Mathematics, Stillwater, OK 74078. Offers applied mathematics (MS, PhD); mathematics education (MS, PhD); pure mathematics (MS, PhD). *Faculty:* 43 full-time (9 women), 9 part-time/adjunct (5 women). *Students:* 5 full-time (3 women), 36 part-time (14 women); includes 4 minority (1 Black or African American, non-Hispanic/Latino; 2 Hispanic/Latino; 1 Two or more races, non-Hispanic/Latino), 17 international. Average age 30. 52 applicants, 35% accepted, 11 enrolled. In 2015, 8 master's, 3 doctorates awarded. *Degree requirements:* For master's, thesis, creative component, or report; for doctorate, comprehensive exam, thesis/dissertation. *Entrance requirements:* For master's and doctorate, GRE (recommended). Additional exam requirements/recommendations for international students: Required—TOEFL (minimum score 550 paper-based; 79 iBT). *Application deadline:* For fall admission, 3/1 for domestic and international students; for spring admission, 10/15 for domestic students, 10/15 priority date for international students. Applications are processed on a rolling basis. Application fee: $40 ($75 for international students). Electronic applications accepted. *Expenses:* Tuition, state resident: full-time $3528; part-time $196 per credit hour. Tuition, nonresident: full-time $14,144; part-time $785.75 per credit hour. *Required fees:* $1895; $105.25 per credit hour. Tuition and fees vary according to campus/location. *Financial support:* In 2015–16, 2 research assistantships (averaging $17,172 per year), 40 teaching assistantships (averaging $21,173 per year) were awarded; health care benefits and tuition waivers (partial) also available. Financial award application deadline: 3/1; financial award applicants required to submit FAFSA. *Unit head:* Dr. Willam Jaco, Department Head, 405-744-5688, Fax: 405-744-8225, E-mail: william.jaco@okstate.edu. Website: http://math.okstate.edu/

Oregon State University, College of Science, Program in Mathematics, Corvallis, OR 97331. Offers actuarial science (MA, MS, PhD); algebra (MA, MS, PhD); analysis (MA, MS, PhD); applied mathematics (MA, MS, PhD); computational mathematics (MA, MS, PhD); differential equations (MA, MS, PhD); financial mathematics (MA, MS, PhD); geometry (MA, MS, PhD); mathematics education (MA). *Faculty:* 26 full-time (8 women), 4 part-time/adjunct (1 woman). *Students:* 68 full-time (16 women), 2 part-time (0 women); includes 10 minority (1 Black or African American, non-Hispanic/Latino; 3 Asian, non-Hispanic/Latino; 2 Hispanic/Latino; 1 Native Hawaiian or other Pacific Islander, non-Hispanic/Latino; 3 Two or more races, non-Hispanic/Latino), 15 international. Average age 29. 117 applicants, 34% accepted, 17 enrolled. In 2015, 13 master's, 2 doctorates awarded. Terminal master's awarded for partial completion of doctoral program. *Median time to degree:* Of those who began their doctoral program in fall 2007, 40% received their degree in 8 years or less. *Degree requirements:* For master's, variable foreign language requirement, thesis or alternative; for doctorate, one foreign language, thesis/dissertation, qualifying exams. *Entrance requirements:* For master's and doctorate, GRE. Additional exam requirements/recommendations for international students: Required—TOEFL (minimum score 100 iBT). *Application deadline:* For fall admission, 1/15 for domestic students. Application fee: $75 ($85 for international students). *Expenses:* Tuition, state resident: full-time $12,150; part-time $450 per credit. Tuition, nonresident: full-time $20,952; part-time $776 per credit. *Required fees:* $1572; $1443 per unit. One-time fee: $350. Tuition and fees vary according to course load, campus/location and program. *Financial support:* Research assistantships, teaching assistantships, Federal Work-Study, and institutionally sponsored loans available. Support available to part-time students. Financial award application deadline: 1/15. *Unit head:* Dr. Enrique A. Thomann, Professor and Interim Department Head. *Application contact:* Mathematics Advisor, 541-737-4686, E-mail: gradinfo@math.oregonstate.edu. Website: http://www.math.oregonstate.edu/

Princeton University, Graduate School, Program in Applied and Computational Mathematics, Princeton, NJ 08544-1019. Offers PhD. *Degree requirements:* For doctorate, thesis/dissertation. *Entrance requirements:* For doctorate, GRE General Test, GRE Subject Test. Additional exam requirements/recommendations for international students: Required—TOEFL (minimum score 600 paper-based). Electronic applications accepted.

Rensselaer Polytechnic Institute, Graduate School, School of Science, Program in Applied Mathematics, Troy, NY 12180-3590. Offers MS. *Program availability:* Part-time. *Faculty:* 56 full-time (10 women), 4 part-time/adjunct (0 women). *Students:* 4 full-time (1 woman); includes 1 minority (Black or African American, non-Hispanic/Latino), 1 international. Average age 25. 23 applicants, 22% accepted, 1 enrolled. In 2015, 2 master's awarded. *Entrance requirements:* For master's, GRE. Additional exam requirements/recommendations for international students: Required—TOEFL (minimum score 600 paper-based; 100 iBT), IELTS (minimum score 7), PTE (minimum score 68). *Application deadline:* For fall admission, 1/1 priority date for domestic and international students; for spring admission, 8/15 priority date for domestic and international students. Applications are processed on a rolling basis. Application fee: $75. Electronic applications accepted. *Financial support:* In 2015–16, 8 students received support, including teaching assistantships with full tuition reimbursements available (averaging $21,500 per year). Financial award application deadline: 1/1. *Total annual research expenditures:* $2.5 million. *Unit head:* Dr. John Mitchell, Graduate Program Director,

518-276-6519, E-mail: mitchj@rpi.edu. *Application contact:* Office of Graduate Admissions, 518-276-6216, E-mail: gradadmissions@rpi.edu. Website: https://www.rpi.edu/dept/math/ms_graduate/index.html

Rice University, Graduate Programs, George R. Brown School of Engineering, Department of Computational and Applied Mathematics, Houston, TX 77251-1892. Offers computational and applied mathematics (MA, MCAM, PhD); computational science and engineering (PhD). *Degree requirements:* For master's, comprehensive exam (for some programs), thesis (for some programs); for doctorate, comprehensive exam, thesis/dissertation. *Entrance requirements:* For master's and doctorate, GRE General Test, minimum GPA of 3.0. Additional exam requirements/recommendations for international students: Required—TOEFL (minimum score 600 paper-based; 90 iBT). Electronic applications accepted. *Faculty research:* Inverse problems, partial differential equations, computer algorithms, computational modeling, optimization theory.

Rochester Institute of Technology, Graduate Enrollment Services, College of Science, School of Mathematical Sciences, MS Program in Applied and Computational Mathematics, Rochester, NY 14623-5603. Offers MS. *Program availability:* Part-time. *Students:* 17 full-time (9 women), 12 part-time (1 woman); includes 2 minority (1 Black or African American, non-Hispanic/Latino; 1 Hispanic/Latino), 8 international. Average age 26. 33 applicants, 55% accepted, 9 enrolled. In 2015, 2 master's awarded. *Degree requirements:* For master's, thesis. *Entrance requirements:* For master's, GRE or GMAT, minimum GPA of 3.0 (recommended). Additional exam requirements/recommendations for international students: Required—PTE (minimum score 58), TOEFL (minimum score 550 paper-based, 79 iBT) or IELTS (minimum score 6.5). *Application deadline:* For fall admission, 2/15 priority date for domestic and international students; for spring admission, 12/15 priority date for domestic and international students. Applications are processed on a rolling basis. Application fee: $60. Electronic applications accepted. *Expenses: Tuition, area resident:* Full-time $41,084; part-time $1742 per credit hour. *Required fees:* $274. Tuition and fees vary according to course load and program. *Financial support:* In 2015–16, 16 students received support. Teaching assistantships with partial tuition reimbursements available, career-related internships or fieldwork, scholarships/grants, and unspecified assistantships available. Support available to part-time students. Financial award applicants required to submit FAFSA. *Faculty research:* Fluid mechanics, nonlinear dynamics, image processing, inverse problems, condensed matter, mathematical biology, solid mechanics and materials science, microelectromechanical systems (MEMS), network analysis, data assimilation. *Unit head:* Dr. Nathan Cahill, Head, 585-475-5144, E-mail: ndcsma@rit.edu. *Application contact:* Diane Ellison, Associate Vice President, Graduate Enrollment Services, 585-475-2229, Fax: 585-475-7164, E-mail: gradinfo@rit.edu. Website: https://www.rit.edu/science/programs/ms/applied-and-computational-mathematics

Rutgers University–Camden, Graduate School of Arts and Sciences, Program in Mathematical Sciences, Camden, NJ 08102. Offers industrial mathematics (MBS); industrial/applied mathematics (MS); mathematical computer science (MS); pure mathematics (MS); teaching in mathematical sciences (MS). *Program availability:* Part-time, evening/weekend. *Degree requirements:* For master's, comprehensive exam, thesis optional, survey paper, 30 credits. *Entrance requirements:* For master's, GRE, BS/BA in math or related subject, 2 letters of recommendation. Additional exam requirements/recommendations for international students: Required—TOEFL (minimum score 550 paper-based), IELTS. Electronic applications accepted. *Faculty research:* Differential geometry, dynamical systems, vertex operator algebra, automorphic forms, CR-structures.

Rutgers University–New Brunswick, Graduate School-New Brunswick, Department of Mathematics, Piscataway, NJ 08854-8097. Offers applied mathematics (MS, PhD); mathematics (MS, PhD). *Program availability:* Part-time. *Degree requirements:* For doctorate, one foreign language, comprehensive exam, thesis/dissertation. *Entrance requirements:* For master's and doctorate, GRE General Test, GRE Subject Test. Additional exam requirements/recommendations for international students: Required—TOEFL. *Faculty research:* Logic and set theory, number theory, mathematical physics, control theory, partial differential equations.

San Diego State University, Graduate and Research Affairs, College of Sciences, Department of Mathematics and Statistics, Program in Applied Mathematics, San Diego, CA 92182. Offers MS. *Program availability:* Part-time. *Degree requirements:* For master's, comprehensive exam. *Entrance requirements:* For master's, GRE General Test. Additional exam requirements/recommendations for international students: Required—TOEFL. Electronic applications accepted. *Faculty research:* Modeling, computational fluid dynamics, biomathematics, thermodynamics.

Santa Clara University, School of Engineering, Santa Clara, CA 95053. Offers applied mathematics (MS); bioengineering (MS); civil engineering (MS); computer science and engineering (MS, PhD); electrical engineering (MS, PhD); engineering (Engineer); engineering management and leadership (MS); mechanical engineering (MS, PhD); software engineering (MS); sustainable energy (MS); thermofluids (Certificate). *Program availability:* Part-time, evening/weekend. *Faculty:* 63 full-time (24 women), 6 part-time/adjunct (4 women). *Students:* 544 full-time (237 women), 364 part-time (103 women); includes 215 minority (7 Black or African American, non-Hispanic/Latino; 149 Asian, non-Hispanic/Latino; 42 Hispanic/Latino; 1 Native Hawaiian or other Pacific Islander, non-Hispanic/Latino; 16 Two or more races, non-Hispanic/Latino), 529 international. Average age 28. 1,335 applicants, 38% accepted, 243 enrolled. In 2015, 343 master's, 2 doctorates awarded. *Entrance requirements:* For master's, GRE, transcript; for doctorate, GRE, master's degree or equivalent; for other advanced degree, master's degree, published paper. Additional exam requirements/recommendations for international students: Required—TOEFL (minimum score 79 iBT) or IELTS (6.5). *Application deadline:* For fall admission, 4/1 for domestic and international students; for winter admission, 9/9 for domestic students, 9/2 for international students; for spring admission, 2/17 for domestic students, 12/9 for international students. Application fee: $60. Electronic applications accepted. *Expenses:* $892 per unit. *Financial support:* In 2015–16, 89 students received support. Fellowships, research assistantships, teaching assistantships, career-related internships or fieldwork, Federal Work-Study, scholarships/grants, traineeships, health care benefits, tuition waivers, and unspecified assistantships available. Support available to part-time students. Financial award applicants required to submit FAFSA. *Total annual research expenditures:* $1 million. *Unit head:* Dr. Alex Zecevic, Associate Dean for Graduate Studies, 408-554-2394, E-mail: azecevic@scu.edu. *Application contact:* Stacey Tinker, Director of Admissions and Marketing, 408-554-4748, Fax: 408-554-4323, E-mail: stinker@scu.edu. Website: http://www.scu.edu/engineering/graduate/

Simon Fraser University, Office of Graduate Studies, Faculty of Science, Department of Mathematics, Burnaby, BC V5A 1S6, Canada. Offers applied and computational mathematics (M Sc, PhD); mathematics (M Sc, PhD); operations research (M Sc, PhD). *Degree requirements:* For master's, thesis or alternative; for doctorate, comprehensive exam, thesis/dissertation. *Entrance requirements:* For master's, GRE General Test,

Peterson's Graduate Programs in the Physical Sciences, Mathematics, Agricultural Sciences, the Environment & Natural Resources 2017

www.petersons.com　209

GRE Subject Test (mathematics), minimum GPA of 3.0 (on scale of 4.33), or 3.33 based on last 60 credits of undergraduate courses; for doctorate, GRE General Test, GRE Subject Test (mathematics), minimum GPA of 3.5 (on scale of 4.33). Additional exam requirements/recommendations for international students: Recommended—TOEFL (minimum score 580 paper-based; 93 iBT), IELTS (minimum score 7), TWE (minimum score 5). Electronic applications accepted. *Faculty research:* Computer algebra, discrete mathematics, fluid dynamics, nonlinear partial differential equations and variation methods, numerical analysis and scientific computing.

Southern Illinois University Edwardsville, Graduate School, College of Arts and Sciences, Department of Mathematics and Statistics, Program in Computational and Applied Mathematics, Edwardsville, IL 62026. Offers MS. *Program availability:* Part-time. *Degree requirements:* For master's, thesis (for some programs), research paper. *Entrance requirements:* Additional exam requirements/recommendations for international students: Required—TOEFL (minimum score 550 paper-based, 79 iBT), IELTS (minimum score 6.5), Michigan Test of English Language Proficiency or PTE. *Application deadline:* For fall admission, 7/22 for domestic students, 7/15 for international students; for spring admission, 12/9 for domestic students, 11/15 for international students; for summer admission, 4/29 for domestic students, 4/15 for international students. Applications are processed on a rolling basis. Application fee: $30. Electronic applications accepted. *Expenses:* Tuition, state resident: full-time $5026; part-time $837 per course. Tuition, nonresident: full-time $12,566; part-time $2094 per course. *Required fees:* $1682; $474 per course. Tuition and fees vary according to course load, campus/location and program. *Financial support:* Fellowships, research assistantships, teaching assistantships, and unspecified assistantships available. *Unit head:* Dr. Myung Sin Song, Program Director, 618-650-2580, E-mail: msong@siue.edu. *Application contact:* Bob Skorczewski, Coordinator of International and Graduate Recruitment, 618-650-3705, Fax: 618-650-3618,
E-mail: graduateadmissions@siue.edu.
Website: http://www.siue.edu/artsandsciences/math/

Southern Methodist University, Dedman College of Humanities and Sciences, Department of Mathematics, Dallas, TX 75275. Offers computational and applied mathematics (MS, PhD). *Degree requirements:* For master's, oral exams; for doctorate, thesis/dissertation, oral and written exams. *Entrance requirements:* For master's and doctorate, GRE General Test, minimum GPA of 3.0, 18 undergraduate hours in mathematics beyond first- and second-year calculus. Additional exam requirements/recommendations for international students: Required—TOEFL. Electronic applications accepted. *Faculty research:* Numerical analysis and scientific computation, fluid dynamics, optics, wave propagation, mathematical biology.

Southern Oregon University, Graduate Studies, Department of Mathematics, Ashland, OR 97520. Offers applied mathematics (PSM). *Program availability:* Part-time, online learning. *Degree requirements:* For master's, thesis (for some programs). *Entrance requirements:* For master's, GRE General Test, minimum cumulative GPA of 3.0 in the last 90 quarter credits (60 semester credits) of undergraduate coursework. Additional exam requirements/recommendations for international students: Required—TOEFL (minimum score 540 paper-based; 76 iBT), IELTS (minimum score 6), ELPT (minimum score 964) or ELS (minimum score 112). Electronic applications accepted.

Stevens Institute of Technology, Graduate School, Charles V. Schaefer Jr. School of Engineering, Department of Mathematical Sciences, Program in Applied Mathematics, Hoboken, NJ 07030. Offers MS. *Program availability:* Part-time, evening/weekend. *Students:* 7 full-time (2 women), 1 (woman) part-time; includes 2 minority (1 Asian, non-Hispanic/Latino; 1 Two or more races, non-Hispanic/Latino), 5 international. Average age 26. 34 applicants, 71% accepted, 5 enrolled. In 2015, 4 master's awarded. *Entrance requirements:* Additional exam requirements/recommendations for international students: Required—TOEFL (minimum score 74 iBT). *Application deadline:* For fall admission, 6/1 for domestic students, 4/15 for international students; for spring admission, 11/30 for domestic students, 11/1 for international students. Applications are processed on a rolling basis. Application fee: $60. Electronic applications accepted. *Expenses: Tuition, area resident:* Full-time $32,200; part-time $1450 per credit. *Required fees:* $1150; $550 per unit. $275 per semester. *Financial support:* Fellowships, research assistantships, teaching assistantships, career-related internships or fieldwork, Federal Work-Study, scholarships/grants, and unspecified assistantships available. Financial award application deadline: 2/15; financial award applicants required to submit FAFSA. *Unit head:* Dr. Alexei Miasnikov, Director, 201-216-8598, Fax: 201-216-8321, E-mail: amiasnik@stevens.edu. *Application contact:* Graduate Admission, 888-783-8367, Fax: 888-511-1306,
E-mail: graduate@stevens.edu.

Stony Brook University, State University of New York, Graduate School, College of Engineering and Applied Sciences, Department of Applied Mathematics and Statistics, Stony Brook, NY 11794. Offers MS, PhD, Advanced Certificate. *Faculty:* 30 full-time (7 women), 2 part-time/adjunct (0 women). *Students:* 279 full-time (97 women), 20 part-time (10 women); includes 24 minority (2 Black or African American, non-Hispanic/Latino; 18 Asian, non-Hispanic/Latino; 4 Hispanic/Latino), 239 international. Average age 26. 564 applicants, 72% accepted, 97 enrolled. In 2015, 72 master's, 26 doctorates awarded. *Degree requirements:* For master's, thesis or alternative; for doctorate, one foreign language, comprehensive exam, thesis/dissertation. *Entrance requirements:* For master's and doctorate, GRE General Test. Additional exam requirements/recommendations for international students: Required—TOEFL (minimum score 90 iBT). *Application deadline:* For fall admission, 1/15 for domestic students; for spring admission, 10/1 for domestic students. Application fee: $100. *Expenses:* $12,421 full-time resident tuition and fees, $453 per credit hour; $23,761 full-time nonresident tuition and fees, $925 per credit hour. *Financial support:* In 2015–16, 1 fellowship, 44 research assistantships, 39 teaching assistantships were awarded. *Faculty research:* Computational Mathematics, Computational modeling, Applied Mathematics, Computational Physics, Computational Chemistry. *Total annual research expenditures:* $2.5 million. *Unit head:* Dr. Joseph Mitchell, Chair, 631-632-8366, Fax: 631-632-8490, E-mail: joseph.mitchell@stonybrook.edu. *Application contact:* Christine Rota, Coordinator, 631-632-8360, Fax: 631-632-8490, E-mail: christine.rota@stonybrook.edu.

Temple University, College of Science and Technology, Department of Mathematics, Philadelphia, PA 19122. Offers applied mathematics (MA); mathematics (PhD); pure mathematics (MA). *Program availability:* Part-time, evening/weekend. *Faculty:* 27 full-time (6 women). *Students:* 34 full-time (10 women), 3 part-time (0 women); includes 3 minority (all Asian, non-Hispanic/Latino), 18 international. 57 applicants, 46% accepted, 9 enrolled. In 2015, 8 master's, 5 doctorates awarded. Terminal master's awarded for partial completion of doctoral program. *Degree requirements:* For master's, thesis optional, written exam; for doctorate, 2 foreign languages, thesis/dissertation, oral and written exams. *Entrance requirements:* For master's, GRE General Test, minimum GPA of 3.0; for doctorate, GRE General Test, GRE Subject Test, minimum GPA of 3.0. Additional exam requirements/recommendations for international students: Required—TOEFL (minimum score 550 paper-based; 79 iBT). *Application deadline:* For fall admission, 2/15 priority date for domestic students, 12/15 for international students; for spring admission, 11/15 for domestic students, 8/1 for international students. Applications are processed on a rolling basis. Application fee: $60. Electronic applications accepted. *Financial support:* Fellowships, research assistantships, teaching assistantships, Federal Work-Study, and institutionally sponsored loans available. Financial award application deadline: 1/15; financial award applicants required to submit FAFSA. *Faculty research:* Differential geometry, numerical analysis. *Unit head:* Edward Letzter, Department Chair, 215-204-7841, Fax: 215-204-6433,
E-mail: mathematics@temple.edu. *Application contact:* Alexis Cogan, Administrative Assistant, 215-204-7840, E-mail: cogana@temple.edu.
Website: http://math.temple.edu/

Texas Christian University, College of Science and Engineering, Department of Mathematics, Fort Worth, TX 76129. Offers applied mathematics (MS); mathematics (MAT, PhD); pure mathematics (MS). *Program availability:* Part-time, evening/weekend. *Faculty:* 13 full-time (2 women). *Students:* 14 full-time (3 women), 1 part-time (0 women); includes 4 minority (1 Asian, non-Hispanic/Latino; 2 Hispanic/Latino; 1 Two or more races, non-Hispanic/Latino), 3 international. Average age 26. 20 applicants, 30% accepted, 6 enrolled. In 2015, 2 master's awarded. Terminal master's awarded for partial completion of doctoral program. *Degree requirements:* For master's, thesis optional; for doctorate, comprehensive exam, thesis/dissertation. *Entrance requirements:* For master's and doctorate, GRE General Test, 24 hours of math, including courses in elementary calculus of one and several variables, linear algebra, abstract algebra and real analysis. Additional exam requirements/recommendations for international students: Recommended—TOEFL (minimum score 550 paper-based; 80 iBT), IELTS (minimum score 6.5). *Application deadline:* For fall admission, 2/15 for domestic and international students; for spring admission, 10/15 for domestic and international students. Application fee: $60. Electronic applications accepted. *Expenses: Tuition, area resident:* Full-time $26,640; part-time $1480 per credit hour. *Required fees:* $48; $48 per unit. Tuition and fees vary according to program. *Financial support:* In 2015–16, 15 students received support, including 9 teaching assistantships with full tuition reimbursements available (averaging $17,500 per year); tuition waivers also available. Support available to part-time students. Financial award application deadline: 2/15. *Faculty research:* Algebraic geometry, differential geometry and global analysis, algebraic topology, K-theory and operator algebras, number theory. *Total annual research expenditures:* $60,000. *Unit head:* Dr. George Gilbert, Associate Professor/Chair, 817-257-6061, Fax: 817-257-7766, E-mail: g.gilbert@tcu.edu. *Application contact:* Dr. Ken Richardson, Professor/Director, Graduate Program, 817-257-6128, E-mail: k.richardson@tcu.edu.
Website: http://mathematics.tcu.edu/

Texas State University, The Graduate College, College of Science and Engineering, Program in Applied Mathematics, San Marcos, TX 78666. Offers MS. *Program availability:* Part-time. *Faculty:* 2 full-time (0 women). *Students:* 1 full-time (0 women), 2 part-time (0 women); includes 1 minority (Black or African American, non-Hispanic/Latino), 1 international. Average age 34. 8 applicants, 50% accepted, 2 enrolled. In 2015, 2 master's awarded. *Degree requirements:* For master's, comprehensive exam, thesis. *Entrance requirements:* For master's, GRE (minimum preferred score of 300 verbal and quantitative combined), baccalaureate degree in mathematics or related field from regionally-accredited university with minimum GPA of 2.75 on last 60 undergraduate semester hours. Additional exam requirements/recommendations for international students: Required—TOEFL (minimum score 550 paper-based; 78 iBT). *Application deadline:* For fall admission, 6/15 for domestic students, 6/1 for international students; for spring admission, 10/15 for domestic students, 10/1 for international students; for summer admission, 4/15 for domestic students, 3/15 for international students. Applications are processed on a rolling basis. Application fee: $40 ($90 for international students). Electronic applications accepted. *Expenses:* $3,615 in-state tuition for 12 semester credit hours (1 full-time semester), $974 in-state fees. *Financial support:* In 2015–16, 1 student received support, including 1 teaching assistantship (averaging $14,514 per year); research assistantships, Federal Work-Study, institutionally sponsored loans, scholarships/grants, health care benefits, and unspecified assistantships also available. Support available to part-time students. Financial award application deadline: 3/1; financial award applicants required to submit FAFSA. *Faculty research:* Modeling and simulations of complex fluids and atomistic strain. *Total annual research expenditures:* $29,567. *Unit head:* Dr. Gregory Passty, Graduate Advisor, 512-245-2551, Fax: 512-245-3425, E-mail: gp02@txstate.edu. *Application contact:* Dr. Andrea Golato, Dean of Graduate College, 512-245-2581, E-mail: gradcollege@txstate.edu.
Website: http://www.math.txstate.edu/degrees-programs/masters/applied-math.html

Towson University, Program in Applied and Industrial Mathematics, Towson, MD 21252-0001. Offers MS. *Program availability:* Part-time, evening/weekend. *Students:* 9 full-time (4 women), 16 part-time (6 women); includes 5 minority (4 Black or African American, non-Hispanic/Latino; 1 Two or more races, non-Hispanic/Latino), 3 international. *Entrance requirements:* For master's, bachelor's degree in mathematics or related field; minimum GPA of 3.0 over last 60 credits, including 3 terms of calculus, course in differential equations, course in linear algebra. *Application deadline:* Applications are processed on a rolling basis. Application fee: $45. Electronic applications accepted. *Expenses:* Tuition, state resident: full-time $7440; part-time $372 per unit. Tuition, nonresident: full-time $15,400; part-time $770 per unit. *Required fees:* $2360; $118 per year. $354 per term. *Financial support:* Application deadline: 4/1; applicants required to submit FAFSA. *Unit head:* Dr. Moustapha Pemy, Graduate Program Director, 410-704-3585, E-mail: mpemy@towson.edu. *Application contact:* Alicia Arkell-Kleis, University Admissions, 410-704-2113, Fax: 410-704-3030,
E-mail: grads@towson.edu.
Website: http://grad.towson.edu/program/master/apim-ms/

Tulane University, School of Science and Engineering, Department of Mathematics, New Orleans, LA 70118-5669. Offers applied mathematics (MS); mathematics (MS, PhD); statistics (MS). *Degree requirements:* For master's, thesis (for some programs); for doctorate, thesis/dissertation. *Entrance requirements:* For master's, GRE General Test, minimum B average in undergraduate course work; for doctorate, GRE General Test. Additional exam requirements/recommendations for international students: Required—TOEFL. Electronic applications accepted.

The University of Akron, Graduate School, Buchtel College of Arts and Sciences, Department of Mathematics, Program in Applied Mathematics, Akron, OH 44325. Offers MS. *Students:* 11 full-time (5 women), 1 (woman) part-time. Average age 25. 6 applicants, 100% accepted, 1 enrolled. In 2015, 6 master's awarded. *Degree requirements:* For master's, seminar and comprehensive exam or thesis. *Entrance requirements:* For master's, minimum GPA of 2.75, three letters of recommendation, statement of purpose. Additional exam requirements/recommendations for international students: Required—TOEFL (minimum score 550 paper-based; 79 iBT), IELTS (minimum score 6.5). *Application deadline:* Applications are processed on a rolling basis. Application fee: $45 ($70 for international students). Electronic applications accepted. *Expenses:* Tuition, state resident: full-time $7958; part-time $442 per credit hour. Tuition, nonresident: full-time $13,464; part-time $748 per credit hour. *Required fees:* $1404. *Faculty research:* Analysis of nonlinear partial differential equations, finite groups and character theory, mathematics education, modeling and simulation of

continuum and nanoscale systems, numerical analysis and scientific computation. *Unit head:* Dr. Timothy Norfolk, Chair, 330-972-6121. *Application contact:* Dr. J. Patrick Wilber, Graduate Director, 330-972-6964, E-mail: jw50@uakron.edu.
Website: http://www.uakron.edu/math/academics/graduate/applied-mathematics-program.dot

The University of Alabama, Graduate School, College of Arts and Sciences, Department of Mathematics, Tuscaloosa, AL 35487-0350. Offers applied mathematics (PhD); mathematics (MA, PhD); pure mathematics (PhD). *Faculty:* 27 full-time (3 women). *Students:* 38 full-time (18 women), 3 part-time (2 women); includes 5 minority (4 Black or African American, non-Hispanic/Latino; 1 Two or more races, non-Hispanic/Latino), 21 international. Average age 27. 34 applicants, 44% accepted, 5 enrolled. In 2015, 5 master's, 5 doctorates awarded. Terminal master's awarded for partial completion of doctoral program. *Degree requirements:* For master's, thesis or alternative; for doctorate, comprehensive exam, thesis/dissertation. *Entrance requirements:* For master's and doctorate, GRE General Test, minimum GPA of 3.0. Additional exam requirements/recommendations for international students: Required—TOEFL, IELTS or PTE (minimum score 59); Recommended—TOEFL (minimum score 550 paper-based; 79 iBT), IELTS (minimum score 6.5). *Application deadline:* For fall admission, 6/1 for domestic students, 12/1 for international students; for spring admission, 10/15 for domestic students, 5/1 for international students. Applications are processed on a rolling basis. Application fee: $50 ($60 for international students). Electronic applications accepted. *Expenses:* Tuition, state resident: full-time $10,170. Tuition, nonresident: full-time $25,950. *Financial support:* In 2015–16, 1 fellowship with full tuition reimbursement (averaging $30,000 per year), 35 teaching assistantships with full tuition reimbursements (averaging $12,258 per year) were awarded; research assistantships with full tuition reimbursements, Federal Work-Study, institutionally sponsored loans, scholarships/grants, and unspecified assistantships also available. Financial award application deadline: 1/15. *Faculty research:* Algebra, analysis, topology, mathematics education, applied and computational mathematics, statistics. *Unit head:* Dr. David Cruz-Uribe, Professor and Chair, 205-348-5074, Fax: 205-348-7067, E-mail: dcruzuribe@ua.edu. *Application contact:* Dr. David Halpern, Graduate Program Director, 205-348-1977, Fax: 205-348-7067, E-mail: dhalpern@ua.edu.
Website: http://math.ua.edu/

The University of Alabama at Birmingham, College of Arts and Sciences, Program in Applied Mathematics, Birmingham, AL 35294. Offers PhD. Program offered jointly with The University of Alabama (Tuscaloosa) and The University of Alabama in Huntsville. *Degree requirements:* For doctorate, comprehensive exam, thesis/dissertation. *Entrance requirements:* For doctorate, GRE General Test (minimum score of 150 on Quantitative Reasoning portion), minimum B average in previous coursework, letters of recommendation. Additional exam requirements/recommendations for international students: Required—TOEFL. Electronic applications accepted. *Expenses:* Tuition, state resident: full-time $7340. Tuition, nonresident: full-time $16,628. Full-time tuition and fees vary according to course load and program. *Faculty research:* Inverse problems, mathematical modeling, mathematical biology.

The University of Alabama in Huntsville, School of Graduate Studies, College of Science, Department of Mathematical Sciences, Huntsville, AL 35899. Offers applied mathematics (PhD); education (MA, MS); mathematics (MA, MS). PhD offered jointly with The University of Alabama (Tuscaloosa) and The University of Alabama at Birmingham. *Program availability:* Part-time, evening/weekend. *Degree requirements:* For master's, comprehensive exam, thesis or alternative, oral and written exams; for doctorate, comprehensive exam, thesis/dissertation, oral and written exams. *Entrance requirements:* For master's and doctorate, GRE General Test, minimum GPA of 3.0. Additional exam requirements/recommendations for international students: Required—TOEFL (minimum score 550 paper-based; 80 iBT), IELTS (minimum score 6.5). Electronic applications accepted. *Faculty research:* Combinatorics and graph theory, computational mathematics, differential equations and applications, mathematical biology, probability and stochastic processes.

University of Alberta, Faculty of Graduate Studies and Research, Department of Mathematical and Statistical Sciences, Edmonton, AB T6G 2E1, Canada. Offers applied mathematics (M Sc, PhD); biostatistics (M Sc); mathematical finance (M Sc, PhD); mathematical physics (M Sc, PhD); mathematics (M Sc, PhD); statistics (M Sc, PhD, Postgraduate Diploma). *Program availability:* Part-time. Terminal master's awarded for partial completion of doctoral program. *Degree requirements:* For master's, thesis (for some programs); for doctorate, comprehensive exam, thesis/dissertation. *Entrance requirements:* Additional exam requirements/recommendations for international students: Required—TOEFL (minimum score 580 paper-based). Electronic applications accepted. *Faculty research:* Classical and functional analysis, algebra, differential equations, geometry.

The University of Arizona, Graduate Interdisciplinary Programs, Graduate Interdisciplinary Program in Applied Mathematics, Tucson, AZ 85721. Offers applied mathematics (MS, PhD); mathematical sciences (PMS). Terminal master's awarded for partial completion of doctoral program. *Degree requirements:* For master's, thesis (for some programs); for doctorate, comprehensive exam, thesis/dissertation. *Entrance requirements:* For master's, GRE, 3 letters of recommendation; for doctorate, GRE, 3 letters of recommendation, statement of purpose. Additional exam requirements/recommendations for international students: Required—TOEFL (minimum score 575 paper-based; 80 iBT). *Application deadline:* For fall admission, 1/15 for domestic students, 1/30 for international students. Applications are processed on a rolling basis. Application fee: $75. Electronic applications accepted. *Financial support:* Research assistantships, institutionally sponsored loans, scholarships/grants, health care benefits, tuition waivers (full), and unspecified assistantships available. Financial award application deadline: 3/1; financial award applicants required to submit FAFSA. *Faculty research:* Dynamical systems and chaos, partial differential equations, pattern formation, fluid dynamics and turbulence, scientific computation, mathematical physics, mathematical biology, medical imaging, applied probability and stochastic processes. *Unit head:* Dr. Michael Tabor, Chair, 520-621-4664, Fax: 520-626-5048,
E-mail: tabor@math.arizona.edu. *Application contact:* Nellie Rios, Graduate Coordinator, 520-621-2016, Fax: 520-626-5048, E-mail: applmath@u.arizona.edu.
Website: http://appliedmath.arizona.edu/

University of Arkansas at Little Rock, Graduate School, College of Arts, Letters, and Sciences, Department of Mathematics and Statistics, Little Rock, AR 72204-1099. Offers applied statistics (Graduate Certificate); mathematical sciences (MS). *Program availability:* Part-time, evening/weekend. *Degree requirements:* For master's, comprehensive exam. *Entrance requirements:* For master's, GRE General Test, GRE Subject Test, minimum GPA of 2.7, previous course work in advanced mathematics. *Expenses:* Tuition, state resident: part-time $300 per credit hour. Tuition, nonresident: part-time $690 per credit hour. *Required fees:* $100 per credit hour. One-time fee: $40 full-time.

The University of British Columbia, Institute of Applied Mathematics, Vancouver, BC V6T 1Z1, Canada. Offers M Sc, PhD. *Degree requirements:* For master's, thesis (for some programs); for doctorate, comprehensive exam, thesis/dissertation. *Entrance requirements:* For doctorate, master's degree. Additional exam requirements/recommendations for international students: Required—TOEFL. *Faculty research:* Applied analysis, optimization, mathematical biology, numerical analysis, fluid mechanics.

University of California, Berkeley, Graduate Division, College of Letters and Science, Department of Mathematics, Program in Applied Mathematics, Berkeley, CA 94720-1500. Offers PhD. *Degree requirements:* For doctorate, 2 foreign languages, thesis/dissertation, qualifying exam. *Entrance requirements:* For doctorate, GRE General Test, GRE Subject Test, minimum GPA of 3.0, 3 letters of recommendation.

University of California, Davis, Graduate Studies, Graduate Group in Applied Mathematics, Davis, CA 95616. Offers MS, PhD. Terminal master's awarded for partial completion of doctoral program. *Degree requirements:* For master's, thesis; for doctorate, one foreign language, thesis/dissertation. *Entrance requirements:* For master's, GRE General Test, GRE Subject Test, minimum GPA of 3.0; for doctorate, GRE General Test, GRE Subject Test, master's degree, minimum GPA of 3.0. Additional exam requirements/recommendations for international students: Required—TOEFL (minimum score 550 paper-based). Electronic applications accepted. *Faculty research:* Mathematical biology, control and optimization, atmospheric sciences, theoretical chemistry, mathematical physics.

University of California, Irvine, School of Social Sciences, Institute for Mathematical Behavioral Sciences, Irvine, CA 92697. Offers games, decisions, and dynamical systems (PhD); mathematical behavioral sciences (MA). *Students:* 9 full-time (2 women); includes 3 minority (1 Asian, non-Hispanic/Latino; 1 Hispanic/Latino; 1 Two or more races, non-Hispanic/Latino), 2 international. Average age 32. 10 applicants, 40% accepted, 3 enrolled. In 2015, 2 master's, 1 doctorate awarded. *Degree requirements:* For doctorate, thesis/dissertation. *Entrance requirements:* For master's and doctorate, GRE General Test, minimum GPA of 3.0. *Application deadline:* For fall admission, 1/15 priority date for domestic students, 1/15 for international students. Applications are processed on a rolling basis. Application fee: $90 ($110 for international students). Electronic applications accepted. *Financial support:* Fellowships, research assistantships with full tuition reimbursements, teaching assistantships, institutionally sponsored loans, traineeships, health care benefits, and unspecified assistantships available. Financial award application deadline: 3/1; financial award applicants required to submit FAFSA. *Faculty research:* Representational measurement theory, mathematical models of learning and memory, mathematical psychology, utility theory, artificial intelligence. *Unit head:* Louis Narens, Graduate Program Director, 949-824-5360, E-mail: lnarens@uci.edu. *Application contact:* John Sommerhauser, Director of Graduate Affairs, 949-824-4074, E-mail: john.sommerhauser@uci.edu.
Website: http://www.imbs.uci.edu/

University of California, Merced, Graduate Division, School of Natural Sciences, Merced, CA 95343. Offers applied mathematics (MS, PhD); chemistry and chemical biology (MS, PhD); physics (MS, PhD); quantitative and systems biology (MS, PhD). *Faculty:* 63 full-time (25 women). *Students:* 156 full-time (64 women); includes 58 minority (3 Black or African American, non-Hispanic/Latino; 23 Asian, non-Hispanic/Latino; 22 Hispanic/Latino; 1 Native Hawaiian or other Pacific Islander, non-Hispanic/Latino; 9 Two or more races, non-Hispanic/Latino), 37 international. Average age 27. 199 applicants, 57% accepted, 45 enrolled. In 2015, 12 master's, 11 doctorates awarded. Terminal master's awarded for partial completion of doctoral program. *Degree requirements:* For master's, variable foreign language requirement, comprehensive exam, thesis or alternative; for doctorate, variable foreign language requirement, comprehensive exam, thesis/dissertation. *Entrance requirements:* For master's and doctorate, GRE. Additional exam requirements/recommendations for international students: Required—TOEFL (minimum score 550 paper-based; 80 iBT); Recommended—IELTS (minimum score 7). *Application deadline:* For fall admission, 1/15 for domestic and international students. Application fee: $90 ($110 for international students). Electronic applications accepted. *Expenses:* $11,220 per year resident tuition, $15,102 per year non-resident tuition. *Financial support:* In 2015–16, 151 students received support, including 12 fellowships with full tuition reimbursements available (averaging $23,614 per year), 37 research assistantships with full tuition reimbursements available (averaging $18,842 per year), 127 teaching assistantships with full tuition reimbursements available (averaging $18,538 per year); scholarships/grants, traineeships, and health care benefits also available. Financial award application deadline: 1/15. *Faculty research:* Computational science, soft matter physics, neurobiology, genomics, biochemistry. *Total annual research expenditures:* $5.3 million. *Unit head:* Dr. Juan C. Meza, Dean, 209-228-4487, Fax: 209-228-4060,
E-mail: jcmeza@ucmerced.edu. *Application contact:* Tsu Ya, Director of Graduate Admissions and Academic Services, 209-228-4521, Fax: 209-228-6906,
E-mail: tya@ucmerced.edu.

University of California, San Diego, Graduate Division, Department of Mathematics, La Jolla, CA 92093. Offers applied mathematics (MA); computational science (PhD); mathematics (MA, PhD); statistics (MS, PhD). *Students:* 130 full-time (32 women), 3 part-time (0 women); includes 18 minority (13 Asian, non-Hispanic/Latino; 5 Hispanic/Latino), 72 international. 777 applicants, 16% accepted, 35 enrolled. In 2015, 18 master's, 16 doctorates awarded. *Degree requirements:* For master's, comprehensive exam; for doctorate, comprehensive exam, thesis/dissertation. *Entrance requirements:* For master's, GRE General Test; GRE Subject Test (for MA), minimum GPA of 3.0; for doctorate, GRE General Test, GRE Subject Test, minimum GPA of 3.0. Additional exam requirements/recommendations for international students: Required—TOEFL (minimum score 550 paper-based; 80 iBT), IELTS. *Application deadline:* For fall admission, 1/4 for domestic and international students. Application fee: $90 ($110 for international students). Electronic applications accepted. *Expenses:* Tuition, state resident: full-time $11,220. Tuition, nonresident: full-time $26,322. *Required fees:* $1800. *Financial support:* Fellowships, research assistantships, teaching assistantships, and scholarships/grants available. Financial award applicants required to submit FAFSA. *Faculty research:* Combinatorics, bioinformatics, differential equations, logic and computational complexity, probability theory and statistics. *Unit head:* Peter Ebenfelt, Chair, 858-822-4961, E-mail: pebenfelt@ucsd.edu. *Application contact:* Debra Shon, Admissions Contact, 858-534-9056, E-mail: mathgradadmissions@math.ucsd.edu.
Website: http://math.ucsd.edu/

University of California, Santa Barbara, Graduate Division, College of Letters and Sciences, Division of Mathematics, Life, and Physical Sciences, Department of Mathematics, Santa Barbara, CA 93106-3080. Offers applied mathematics (MA), including computational science and engineering; mathematics (MA, PhD), including computational science and engineering (PhD), mathematics (MA); MA/PhD. *Faculty:* 23 full-time (2 women). *Students:* 64 full-time (15 women); includes 17 minority (1 Black or African American, non-Hispanic/Latino; 1 American Indian or Alaska Native, non-Hispanic/Latino; 6 Asian, non-Hispanic/Latino; 7 Hispanic/Latino; 2 Native Hawaiian or other Pacific Islander, non-Hispanic/Latino), 9 international. Average age 26. 189 applicants, 21% accepted, 11 enrolled. In 2015, 16 master's, 7 doctorates awarded. Terminal master's awarded for partial completion of doctoral program. *Degree*

requirements: For master's, comprehensive exam (for some programs), thesis (for some programs); for doctorate, comprehensive exam, thesis/dissertation. *Entrance requirements:* For master's and doctorate, GRE General Test, GRE Subject Test (math). Additional exam requirements/recommendations for international students: Required—TOEFL (minimum score 575 paper-based; 80 iBT), IELTS (minimum score 7). *Application deadline:* For fall admission, 1/2 for domestic and international students. Application fee: $90 ($110 for international students). Electronic applications accepted. *Financial support:* In 2015–16, 53 students received support, including 15 fellowships with full tuition reimbursements available (averaging $15,000 per year), 5 research assistantships with full tuition reimbursements available (averaging $19,000 per year), 52 teaching assistantships with partial tuition reimbursements available (averaging $18,880 per year); Federal Work-Study, institutionally sponsored loans, health care benefits, and tuition waivers (full and partial) also available. Financial award application deadline: 3/2; financial award applicants required to submit FAFSA. *Faculty research:* Topology, differential geometry, algebra, applied mathematics, partial differential equations. *Total annual research expenditures:* $205,000. *Unit head:* Prof. Darren Long, Chair, 805-893-8340, Fax: 805-893-2385, E-mail: chair@math.ucsb.edu. *Application contact:* Medina Price, Student Affairs Manager, 805-893-8192, Fax: 805-893-2385, E-mail: price@math.ucsb.edu.
Website: http://www.math.ucsb.edu/

University of California, Santa Cruz, Division of Graduate Studies, Jack Baskin School of Engineering, Program in Statistics and Applied Mathematics, Santa Cruz, CA 95064. Offers MS, PhD. Terminal master's awarded for partial completion of doctoral program. *Degree requirements:* For master's, seminar, qualifying exam, capstone project; for doctorate, thesis/dissertation, seminar, qualifying exam. *Entrance requirements:* For master's and doctorate, GRE General Test; GRE Subject Test in math (recommended). Additional exam requirements/recommendations for international students: Required—TOEFL (minimum score 570 paper-based; 89 iBT); Recommended—IELTS (minimum score 8). Electronic applications accepted. *Faculty research:* Bayesian nonparametric methods; computationally intensive Bayesian inference, prediction, and decision-making; envirometrics; fluid mechanics; mathematical biology.

University of Central Arkansas, Graduate School, College of Natural Sciences and Math, Department of Mathematics, Conway, AR 72035-0001. Offers applied mathematics (MS); math education (MA). *Program availability:* Part-time. *Degree requirements:* For master's, comprehensive exam, thesis optional. *Entrance requirements:* For master's, GRE General Test, minimum GPA of 2.7. Additional exam requirements/recommendations for international students: Required—TOEFL (minimum score 550 paper-based; 80 iBT). Electronic applications accepted.

University of Central Missouri, The Graduate School, Warrensburg, MO 64093. Offers accountancy (MA); accounting (MBA); applied mathematics (MS); aviation safety (MA); biology (MS); business administration (MBA); career and technical education leadership (MS); college student personnel administration (MS); communication (MA); computer science (MS); counseling (MS); criminal justice (MS); educational leadership (Ed D); educational technology (MS); elementary and early childhood education (MSE); English (MA); environmental studies (MA); finance (MBA); history (MA); human services/educational technology (Ed S); human services/learning resources (Ed S); human services/professional counseling (Ed S); industrial hygiene (MS); industrial management (MS); information systems (MBA); information technology (MS); kinesiology (MS); library science and information services (MS); literacy education (MSE); marketing (MBA); mathematics (MS); music (MA); occupational safety management (MS); psychology (MS); rural family nursing (MS); school administration (MSE); social gerontology (MS); sociology (MA); special education (MSE); speech language pathology (MS); superintendency (Ed S); teaching (MAT); teaching English as a second language (MA); technology (MS); technology management (PhD); theatre (MA). *Program availability:* Part-time, 100% online, blended/hybrid learning. *Faculty:* 336 full-time (145 women), 39 part-time/adjunct (25 women). *Students:* 2,161 full-time (723 women), 2,077 part-time (1,061 women); includes 188 minority (93 Black or African American, non-Hispanic/Latino; 4 American Indian or Alaska Native, non-Hispanic/Latino; 15 Asian, non-Hispanic/Latino; 32 Hispanic/Latino; 1 Native Hawaiian or other Pacific Islander, non-Hispanic/Latino; 43 Two or more races, non-Hispanic/Latino), 2,514 international. Average age 28. 3,454 applicants, 68% accepted, 1632 enrolled. In 2015, 1,530 master's, 53 other advanced degrees awarded. *Degree requirements:* For master's and Ed S, comprehensive exam (for some programs), thesis (for some programs). *Entrance requirements:* Additional exam requirements/recommendations for international students: Required—TOEFL (minimum score 550 paper-based; 79 iBT). *Application deadline:* For fall admission, 6/1 priority date for domestic and international students; for spring admission, 10/1 priority date for domestic and international students; for summer admission, 4/1 priority date for domestic and international students. Applications are processed on a rolling basis. Application fee: $30 ($75 for international students). Electronic applications accepted. *Expenses:* Tuition, state resident: full-time $6683; part-time $278.45 per credit hour. Tuition, nonresident: full-time $13,366; part-time $556.90 per credit hour. *Required fees:* $701; $29.20 per credit hour. Tuition and fees vary according to degree level and campus/location. *Financial support:* In 2015–16, 97 students received support, including 146 research assistantships with partial tuition reimbursements available (averaging $7,500 per year), 73 teaching assistantships with partial tuition reimbursements available (averaging $7,500 per year); career-related internships or fieldwork, Federal Work-Study, scholarships/grants, and administrative and laboratory assistantships also available. Support available to part-time students. Financial award application deadline: 3/1; financial award applicants required to submit FAFSA. *Unit head:* Tina Church-Hockett, Director of Graduate School and International Admissions, 660-543-4621, Fax: 660-543-4778, E-mail: church@ucmo.edu. *Application contact:* Brittany Lawrence, Graduate Student Services Coordinator, 660-543-4621, Fax: 660-543-4778, E-mail: gradinfo@ucmo.edu.
Website: http://www.ucmo.edu/graduate/

University of Central Oklahoma, The Jackson College of Graduate Studies, College of Mathematics and Science, Department of Mathematics and Statistics, Edmond, OK 73034-5209. Offers applied mathematical sciences (MS), including computer science, mathematics, statistics, teaching. *Program availability:* Part-time. *Degree requirements:* For master's, comprehensive exam (for some programs), thesis (for some programs). *Entrance requirements:* For master's, GRE. Additional exam requirements/recommendations for international students: Required—TOEFL (minimum score 550 paper-based; 79 iBT), IELTS (minimum score 6.5). Electronic applications accepted.

University of Chicago, Division of the Physical Sciences, Department of Mathematics, Chicago, IL 60637. Offers applied mathematics (PhD); mathematics (PhD). *Degree requirements:* For doctorate, one foreign language, thesis/dissertation, 2 qualifying exams, oral topic presentation. *Entrance requirements:* For doctorate, GRE General Test, GRE Subject Test. Additional exam requirements/recommendations for international students: Required—TOEFL (minimum score 600 paper-based; 90 iBT), IELTS (minimum score 7). Electronic applications accepted. *Faculty research:* Analysis, differential geometry, algebra number theory, topology, algebraic geometry.

University of Cincinnati, Graduate School, McMicken College of Arts and Sciences, Department of Mathematical Sciences, Cincinnati, OH 45221. Offers applied mathematics (MS, PhD); mathematics education (MAT); pure mathematics (MS, PhD); statistics (MS, PhD). *Program availability:* Part-time. Terminal master's awarded for partial completion of doctoral program. *Degree requirements:* For master's, comprehensive exam, thesis or alternative; for doctorate, one foreign language, comprehensive exam, thesis/dissertation. *Entrance requirements:* For master's, GRE, teacher certification (for MAT); for doctorate, GRE. Additional exam requirements/recommendations for international students: Required—TOEFL. Electronic applications accepted. *Faculty research:* Algebra, analysis, differential equations, numerical analysis, statistics.

University of Colorado Boulder, Graduate School, College of Arts and Sciences, Department of Applied Mathematics, Boulder, CO 80309. Offers MS, PhD. *Faculty:* 19 full-time (2 women). *Students:* 77 full-time (21 women), 4 part-time (1 woman); includes 12 minority (5 Asian, non-Hispanic/Latino; 4 Hispanic/Latino; 3 Two or more races, non-Hispanic/Latino), 16 international. Average age 27. 97 applicants, 43% accepted, 19 enrolled. In 2015, 12 master's, 9 doctorates awarded. Terminal master's awarded for partial completion of doctoral program. *Degree requirements:* For master's, comprehensive exam, thesis or alternative; for doctorate, one foreign language, comprehensive exam, thesis/dissertation. *Entrance requirements:* For master's, GRE General Test, minimum undergraduate GPA of 2.75; for doctorate, GRE General Test. Additional exam requirements/recommendations for international students: Required—TOEFL. *Application deadline:* For fall admission, 12/15 for domestic students, 12/1 for international students. Applications are processed on a rolling basis. Application fee: $50 ($70 for international students). Electronic applications accepted. Application fee is waived when completed online. *Financial support:* In 2015–16, 152 students received support, including 9 fellowships (averaging $6,880 per year), 19 research assistantships with tuition reimbursements available (averaging $37,844 per year), 41 teaching assistantships with tuition reimbursements available (averaging $35,263 per year); institutionally sponsored loans, scholarships/grants, health care benefits, and unspecified assistantships also available. Financial award applicants required to submit FAFSA. *Faculty research:* Applied mathematics, numerical analysis, nonlinear dynamics, wave equations, computer simulation/modeling. *Total annual research expenditures:* $2.1 million. *Application contact:* E-mail: amgradco@colorado.edu.
Website: http://amath.colorado.edu/

University of Colorado Colorado Springs, College of Letters, Arts and Sciences, Department of Mathematics, Colorado Springs, CO 80918. Offers applied mathematics (MS). *Program availability:* Part-time, evening/weekend. *Faculty:* 14 full-time (3 women), 10 part-time/adjunct (6 women). *Students:* 1 (woman) full-time, 12 part-time (4 women); includes 2 minority (both Asian, non-Hispanic/Latino). Average age 31. 6 applicants, 83% accepted, 1 enrolled. *Degree requirements:* For master's, thesis, qualifying exam. *Entrance requirements:* For master's, minimum GPA of 3.0. Additional exam requirements/recommendations for international students: Required—TOEFL (minimum score 550 paper-based; 92 iBT); Recommended—IELTS (minimum score 6.5). *Application deadline:* Applications are processed on a rolling basis. Application fee: $60 ($100 for international students). Electronic applications accepted. *Expenses:* Tuition, state resident: full-time $9914. Tuition, nonresident: full-time $19,330. Tuition and fees vary according to course load, degree level, program and reciprocity agreements. *Financial support:* In 2015–16, 3 students received support. Federal Work-Study, scholarships/grants, and unspecified assistantships available. Support available to part-time students. Financial award application deadline: 3/1; financial award applicants required to submit FAFSA. *Faculty research:* Associative rings and modules, spectral theory for quantum graphs, spectral theory of integrable systems, percolation theory, interacting particle systems, Abelian groups. *Total annual research expenditures:* $113,295. *Unit head:* Dr. Sarbarish Chakravarty, Chair, 719-255-3549, Fax: 719-255-3605, E-mail: schakrav@uccs.edu. *Application contact:* Emanuelita Martinez, Department Assistant, 719-255-3311, Fax: 719-255-3605, E-mail: emartine@uccs.edu.
Website: http://www.uccs.edu/math

University of Colorado Denver, College of Liberal Arts and Sciences, Department of Mathematical and Statistical Sciences, Denver, CO 80217. Offers applied mathematics (MS, PhD), including applied mathematics, applied probability (MS), applied statistics (MS), computational biology, computational mathematics (PhD), discrete mathematics, finite geometry (PhD), mathematics education (PhD), mathematics of engineering and science (MS), numerical analysis, operations research (MS), optimization and operations research (PhD), probability (PhD), statistics (PhD). *Program availability:* Part-time. *Faculty:* 18 full-time (4 women), 5 part-time/adjunct (0 women). *Students:* 48 full-time (16 women), 15 part-time (6 women); includes 7 minority (1 Black or African American, non-Hispanic/Latino; 2 Asian, non-Hispanic/Latino; 3 Hispanic/Latino; 1 Two or more races, non-Hispanic/Latino), 12 international. Average age 32. 105 applicants, 70% accepted, 21 enrolled. In 2015, 10 master's, 3 doctorates awarded. *Degree requirements:* For master's, comprehensive exam, thesis optional, 30 hours of course work with minimum GPA of 3.0; for doctorate, comprehensive exam, thesis/dissertation, 42 hours of course work with minimum GPA of 3.25. *Entrance requirements:* For master's, GRE General Test; GRE Subject Test in math (recommended), 30 hours of course work in mathematics (24 of which must be upper-division mathematics), bachelor's degree with minimum GPA of 3.0; for doctorate, GRE General Test; GRE Subject Test in math (recommended), 30 hours of course work in mathematics (24 of which must be upper-division mathematics), master's degree with minimum GPA of 3.25. Additional exam requirements/recommendations for international students: Required—TOEFL (minimum score 537 paper-based; 75 iBT); Recommended—IELTS (minimum score 6.5). *Application deadline:* For fall admission, 4/1 for domestic and international students; for spring admission, 10/1 for domestic and international students; for summer admission, 4/1 for domestic and international students. Application fee: $50 ($75 for international students). Electronic applications accepted. *Financial support:* In 2015–16, 46 students received support. Fellowships with partial tuition reimbursements available, research assistantships with full tuition reimbursements available, teaching assistantships with full tuition reimbursements available, Federal Work-Study, institutionally sponsored loans, scholarships/grants, and traineeships available. Financial award application deadline: 4/1; financial award applicants required to submit FAFSA. *Faculty research:* Computational mathematics, computational biology, discrete mathematics and geometry, probability and statistics, optimization. *Unit head:* Dr. Michael Ferrara, Graduate Chair, 303-315-1705,
E-mail: michael.ferrara@ucdenver.edu. *Application contact:* Julie Blunck, Program Assistant, 303-315-1743, E-mail: julie.blunck@ucdenver.edu.
Website: http://www.ucdenver.edu/academics/colleges/CLAS/Departments/math/Pages/MathStats.aspx

University of Connecticut, Graduate School, College of Liberal Arts and Sciences, Department of Mathematics, Field of Applied Financial Mathematics, Storrs, CT 06269. Offers MS. *Degree requirements:* For master's, comprehensive exam. *Entrance requirements:* Additional exam requirements/recommendations for international students: Required—TOEFL (minimum score 550 paper-based). Electronic applications accepted.

University of Dayton, Department of Mathematics, Dayton, OH 45469. Offers applied mathematics (MAS); financial mathematics (MFM); mathematics education (MME). *Program availability:* Part-time. *Faculty:* 19 full-time (7 women). *Students:* 31 full-time (13 women), 5 part-time (2 women); includes 3 minority (2 Black or African American, non-Hispanic/Latino; 1 Hispanic/Latino), 27 international. Average age 26. 121 applicants, 29% accepted, 10 enrolled. In 2015, 26 master's awarded. *Entrance requirements:* For master's, minimum undergraduate GPA of 2.8 (MAS), 3.0 (MFM, MME). Additional exam requirements/recommendations for international students: Required—TOEFL (minimum score 550 paper-based; 80 iBT). *Application deadline:* Applications are processed on a rolling basis. Application fee: $0 ($50 for international students). Electronic applications accepted. *Expenses:* $873 per credit hour. *Financial support:* In 2015–16, 6 students received support, including 6 teaching assistantships with full tuition reimbursements available (averaging $14,750 per year); institutionally sponsored loans and health care benefits also available. Financial award application deadline: 3/1; financial award applicants required to submit FAFSA. *Faculty research:* Jump diffusion with regime switching in finance models, dynamical systems, boundary value problems for ordinary differential equations, decompositions of graphs and multigraphs. *Unit head:* Dr. Joe D. Mashburn, Chair, 937-229-2511, Fax: 937-229-2566, E-mail: jmashburn1@udayton.edu. *Application contact:* Dr. Paul W. Eloe, Graduate Program Director/Professor, 937-229-2016, E-mail: peloe1@udayton.edu.
Website: https://www.udayton.edu/artssciences/academics/mathematics/welcome/index.php

University of Delaware, College of Arts and Sciences, Department of Mathematical Sciences, Newark, DE 19716. Offers applied mathematics (MS, PhD); mathematics (MS, PhD). *Program availability:* Part-time. Terminal master's awarded for partial completion of doctoral program. *Degree requirements:* For master's, thesis (for some programs); for doctorate, one foreign language, thesis/dissertation, qualifying exam. *Entrance requirements:* For master's and doctorate, GRE General Test. Additional exam requirements/recommendations for international students: Required—TOEFL. Electronic applications accepted. *Faculty research:* Scattering theory, inverse problems, fluid dynamics, numerical analysis, combinatorics.

University of Georgia, Franklin College of Arts and Sciences, Department of Mathematics, Athens, GA 30602. Offers applied mathematical science (MAMS); mathematics (MA, PhD). *Degree requirements:* For master's, one foreign language, thesis (for some programs); for doctorate, 2 foreign languages, thesis/dissertation. *Entrance requirements:* For master's and doctorate, GRE General Test. Electronic applications accepted.

University of Guelph, Graduate Studies, College of Physical and Engineering Science, Department of Mathematics and Statistics, Guelph, ON N1G 2W1, Canada. Offers applied mathematics (PhD); applied statistics (PhD); mathematics and statistics (M Sc). *Program availability:* Part-time. *Degree requirements:* For master's, thesis (for some programs); for doctorate, thesis/dissertation. *Entrance requirements:* For master's, minimum B- average during previous 2 years of course work; for doctorate, minimum B average. Additional exam requirements/recommendations for international students: Required—TOEFL (minimum score 550 paper-based; 89 iBT), IELTS (minimum score 6.5). *Faculty research:* Dynamical systems, mathematical biology, numerical analysis, linear and nonlinear models, reliability and bioassay.

University of Houston, College of Natural Sciences and Mathematics, Department of Mathematics, Houston, TX 77204. Offers applied mathematics (MS); mathematics (MA, PhD). *Program availability:* Part-time. *Degree requirements:* For master's, thesis optional. *Entrance requirements:* For master's and doctorate, GRE (Verbal and Quantitative). Additional exam requirements/recommendations for international students: Required—TOEFL (minimum score 550 paper-based; 79 iBT), IELTS (minimum score 6.5). Electronic applications accepted. *Faculty research:* Applied mathematics, modern analysis, computational science, geometry, dynamical systems.

University of Illinois at Urbana–Champaign, Graduate College, College of Liberal Arts and Sciences, Department of Mathematics, Champaign, IL 61820. Offers applied mathematics (MS); applied mathematics: actuarial science (MS); mathematics (MS, PhD); teaching of mathematics (MS).

The University of Iowa, Graduate College, Program in Applied Mathematical and Computational Sciences, Iowa City, IA 52242-1316. Offers PhD. *Degree requirements:* For doctorate, comprehensive exam, thesis/dissertation. *Entrance requirements:* For doctorate, GRE General Test, minimum GPA of 3.0. Additional exam requirements/recommendations for international students: Required—TOEFL (minimum score 620 paper-based; 105 iBT). Electronic applications accepted.

University of Kentucky, Graduate School, College of Arts and Sciences, Program in Mathematics, Lexington, KY 40506-0032. Offers applied mathematics (MS); mathematics (MA, MS, PhD). *Degree requirements:* For master's, comprehensive exam, thesis optional; for doctorate, one foreign language, comprehensive exam, thesis/dissertation. *Entrance requirements:* For master's, GRE General Test, minimum undergraduate GPA of 2.75; for doctorate, GRE General Test, minimum graduate GPA of 3.0. Additional exam requirements/recommendations for international students: Required—TOEFL (minimum score 550 paper-based). Electronic applications accepted. *Faculty research:* Numerical analysis, combinatorics, partial differential equations, algebra and number theory, real and complex analysis.

University of Louisville, Graduate School, College of Arts and Sciences, Department of Mathematics, Louisville, KY 40292. Offers applied and industrial mathematics (PhD); mathematics (MA). *Program availability:* Part-time. *Students:* 33 full-time (14 women), 2 part-time (1 woman), 12 international. Average age 30. 40 applicants, 65% accepted, 8 enrolled. In 2015, 5 master's, 1 doctorate awarded. Terminal master's awarded for partial completion of doctoral program. *Median time to degree:* Of those who began their doctoral program in fall 2007, 64% received their degree in 8 years or less. *Degree requirements:* For master's, variable foreign language requirement, thesis or alternative; for doctorate, comprehensive exam, thesis/dissertation. *Entrance requirements:* For master's and doctorate, GRE. Additional exam requirements/recommendations for international students: Required—TOEFL (minimum score 550 paper-based; 79 iBT), IELTS (minimum score 6.5). *Application deadline:* For fall admission, 3/1 priority date for domestic and international students; for winter admission, 11/1 priority date for domestic and international students; for spring admission, 11/1 priority date for domestic and international students; for summer admission, 3/1 priority date for domestic and international students. Applications are processed on a rolling basis. Application fee: $60. Electronic applications accepted. *Expenses:* Tuition, state resident: full-time $11,664; part-time $649 per credit hour. Tuition, nonresident: full-time $24,274; part-time $1350 per credit hour. *Required fees:* $196. Tuition and fees vary according to program and reciprocity agreements. *Financial support:* In 2015–16, 1 fellowship with full tuition reimbursement (averaging $22,000 per year), 1 research assistantship with partial tuition reimbursement (averaging $20,000 per year), 24 teaching assistantships with full tuition reimbursements (averaging $20,000 per year) were awarded; health care benefits and unspecified assistantships also available. Financial award application deadline: 2/3. *Faculty research:* Mathematical biology, partial differential equations, statistics, combinatorics, analysis. *Total annual research expenditures:* $125,277. *Unit head:* Dr. Thomas Riedel, Chair, 502-852-6826, Fax: 502-852-7132,
E-mail: thomas.riedel@louisville.edu. *Application contact:* Dr. Andre Kezdy, Graduate Director and Professor, 502-852-5986, Fax: 502-852-7132,
E-mail: kezdy@louisville.edu.
Website: http://www.math.louisville.edu

The University of Manchester, School of Mathematics, Manchester, United Kingdom. Offers actuarial science (PhD); applied mathematics (M Phil, PhD); applied numerical computing (M Phil, PhD); financial mathematics (M Phil, PhD); mathematical logic (M Phil); probability (M Phil, PhD); pure mathematics (M Phil, PhD); statistics (M Phil, PhD).

University of Maryland, Baltimore County, The Graduate School, College of Natural and Mathematical Sciences, Department of Mathematics and Statistics, Program in Applied Mathematics, Baltimore, MD 21250. Offers MS, PhD. *Program availability:* Part-time, evening/weekend. *Faculty:* 29 full-time (3 women). *Students:* 23 full-time (10 women), 13 part-time (2 women); includes 5 minority (1 Black or African American, non-Hispanic/Latino; 3 Asian, non-Hispanic/Latino; 1 Hispanic/Latino), 9 international. Average age 29. 31 applicants, 68% accepted, 3 enrolled. In 2015, 2 master's, 2 doctorates awarded. Terminal master's awarded for partial completion of doctoral program. *Degree requirements:* For master's, comprehensive exam (for some programs), thesis (for some programs); for doctorate, comprehensive exam, thesis/dissertation. *Entrance requirements:* For master's and doctorate, GRE General Test, minimum GPA of 3.0. Additional exam requirements/recommendations for international students: Required—TOEFL (minimum score 600 paper-based; 100 iBT). *Application deadline:* For fall admission, 2/15 priority date for domestic students, 1/1 priority date for international students; for spring admission, 10/15 priority date for domestic students, 5/1 priority date for international students. Applications are processed on a rolling basis. Application fee: $50. Electronic applications accepted. *Expenses:* Tuition, state resident: full-time $12,816. Tuition, nonresident: full-time $19,710. *Financial support:* In 2015–16, 13 students received support, including fellowships with full tuition reimbursements available (averaging $17,000 per year), 3 research assistantships with full tuition reimbursements available (averaging $17,000 per year), 10 teaching assistantships with tuition reimbursements available (averaging $17,000 per year); career-related internships or fieldwork, scholarships/grants, health care benefits, tuition waivers (full and partial), and unspecified assistantships also available. Support available to part-time students. Financial award application deadline: 2/15. *Faculty research:* Numerical analysis and scientific computation, optimization theory and algorithms, differential equations and mathematical modeling, mathematical biology and bioinformatics. *Total annual research expenditures:* $380,765. *Unit head:* Dr. Animikh Biswas, Graduate Program Director, Applied Mathematics Program, 410-455-3029, Fax: 410-455-1066, E-mail: abiswas@umbc.edu. *Application contact:* Janet Burgee, Program Coordinator, Mathematics and Statistics, 410-455-2401, Fax: 410-455-1066,
E-mail: jburgee@umbc.edu.
Website: http://www.math.umbc.edu

University of Maryland, College Park, Academic Affairs, College of Computer, Mathematical and Natural Sciences, Department of Mathematics, Applied Mathematics Program, College Park, MD 20742. Offers MS, PhD. *Program availability:* Part-time, evening/weekend. Terminal master's awarded for partial completion of doctoral program. *Degree requirements:* For master's, thesis optional, seminar, scholarly paper; for doctorate, comprehensive exam, thesis/dissertation, exams, seminars. *Entrance requirements:* For master's and doctorate, GRE General Test, GRE Subject Test, minimum GPA of 3.0, 3 letters of recommendation. Electronic applications accepted.

University of Massachusetts Amherst, Graduate School, College of Natural Sciences, Department of Mathematics and Statistics, Amherst, MA 01003. Offers applied mathematics (MS); mathematics (MS, PhD); statistics (MS, PhD). Terminal master's awarded for partial completion of doctoral program. *Degree requirements:* For master's, thesis or alternative; for doctorate, comprehensive exam, thesis/dissertation. *Entrance requirements:* For master's and doctorate, GRE General Test, GRE Subject Test (mathematics). Additional exam requirements/recommendations for international students: Required—TOEFL (minimum score 550 paper-based; 80 iBT), IELTS (minimum score 6.5). Electronic applications accepted.

University of Massachusetts Lowell, College of Sciences, Department of Mathematical Sciences, Lowell, MA 01854. Offers applied mathematics (MS); computational mathematics (PhD); mathematics (MS). *Program availability:* Part-time. *Entrance requirements:* For master's, GRE General Test.

University of Memphis, Graduate School, College of Arts and Sciences, Department of Mathematical Sciences, Memphis, TN 38152. Offers applied mathematics (MS); applied statistics (PhD); bioinformatics (MS); computer sciences (MS); statistics (MS). *Program availability:* Part-time. *Faculty:* 18 full-time (7 women). *Students:* 36 full-time (9 women), 22 part-time (9 women); includes 15 minority (9 Black or African American, non-Hispanic/Latino; 3 Asian, non-Hispanic/Latino; 3 Hispanic/Latino), 17 international. Average age 34. 50 applicants, 92% accepted, 12 enrolled. In 2015, 10 master's, 9 doctorates awarded. Terminal master's awarded for partial completion of doctoral program. *Degree requirements:* For master's, comprehensive exam; for doctorate, one foreign language, thesis/dissertation, oral exams. *Entrance requirements:* For master's and doctorate, GRE General Test, minimum GPA of 2.5. Additional exam requirements/recommendations for international students: Required—TOEFL (minimum score 550 paper-based). *Application deadline:* For fall admission, 8/1 for domestic students, 5/1 priority date for international students; for spring admission, 12/1 for domestic students, 9/1 priority date for international students. Applications are processed on a rolling basis. Application fee: $35 ($60 for international students). Electronic applications accepted. *Financial support:* In 2015–16, 22 students received support. Fellowships with full tuition reimbursements available, research assistantships with full tuition reimbursements available, teaching assistantships with full tuition reimbursements available, career-related internships or fieldwork, Federal Work-Study, scholarships/grants, and unspecified assistantships available. Financial award application deadline: 2/15; financial award applicants required to submit FAFSA. *Faculty research:* Combinatorics, ergodic theory, graph theory, Ramsey theory, applied statistics. *Unit head:* Dr. Irena Lasiecka, Chairman, 901-678-2482, Fax: 901-678-2480,
E-mail: lasiecka@memphis.edu. *Application contact:* Dr. Fernanda Botelho, Coordinator of Graduate Studies, 901-678-3131, Fax: 901-678-2480,
E-mail: mbotelho@memphis.edu.
Website: http://www.MSCI.memphis.edu/

University of Michigan–Dearborn, College of Arts, Sciences, and Letters, Master of Science in Applied and Computational Mathematics Program, Dearborn, MI 48128. Offers MS. *Program availability:* Part-time, evening/weekend. *Faculty:* 8 full-time (4 women). *Students:* 1 full-time (0 women), 12 part-time (5 women); includes 5 minority (1 Black or African American, non-Hispanic/Latino; 4 Hispanic/Latino). 7 applicants, 86% accepted, 3 enrolled. In 2015, 3 master's awarded. *Degree requirements:* For master's, thesis or alternative, project. *Entrance requirements:* For master's, 3 letters of

recommendation, minimum GPA of 3.0, 2 years of course work in math. Additional exam requirements/recommendations for international students: Required—TOEFL (minimum score 560 paper-based; 84 iBT), IELTS (minimum score 6.5). *Application deadline:* For fall admission, 8/1 priority date for domestic students, 5/1 priority date for international students; for winter admission, 12/1 priority date for domestic students, 9/1 priority date for international students; for spring admission, 4/1 priority date for domestic students, 1/1 priority date for international students. Applications are processed on a rolling basis. Application fee: $60. Electronic applications accepted. *Expenses:* $633 per credit hour in-state; $363 per credit hour for ninth credit hour and beyond in-state; $1,133 per credit hour out-of-state; $736 per credit hour for ninth credit hour and beyond out-of-state; $277 fees per term part-time, $342 fees per term full-time. *Financial support:* In 2015–16, 4 students received support. Scholarships/grants and non-resident tuition scholarships available. Financial award application deadline: 3/1; financial award applicants required to submit FAFSA. *Faculty research:* Numerical analysis, stochastic differential equations, inverse problems and medical imaging, time series forecasting, Markov processes. *Unit head:* Dr. Joan Remski, Director, 313-593-4994, E-mail: remski@umich.edu. *Application contact:* Carol Ligienza, Coordinator, CASL Graduate Programs, 313-593-1183, Fax: 313-583-6700, E-mail: caslgrad@umich.edu.
Website: http://umdearborn.edu/casl/666301/

University of Minnesota, Duluth, Graduate School, Swenson College of Science and Engineering, Department of Mathematics and Statistics, Duluth, MN 55812-2496. Offers applied and computational mathematics (MS). *Program availability:* Part-time. *Degree requirements:* For master's, thesis or alternative. *Entrance requirements:* For master's, GRE General Test, minimum GPA of 3.0. Additional exam requirements/recommendations for international students: Required—TOEFL (minimum score 550 paper-based; 79 iBT); Recommended—TWE. Electronic applications accepted. *Faculty research:* Discrete mathematics, diagnostic markers, combinatorics, biostatistics, mathematical modeling and scientific computation.

University of Missouri, Office of Research and Graduate Studies, College of Arts and Science, Department of Mathematics, Columbia, MO 65211. Offers applied mathematics (MS); mathematics (MA, MST, PhD). *Degree requirements:* For doctorate, 2 foreign languages, comprehensive exam, thesis/dissertation. *Entrance requirements:* For master's and doctorate, GRE General Test, minimum GPA of 3.0; bachelor's degree from accredited institution. Additional exam requirements/recommendations for international students: Required—TOEFL (minimum score 500 paper-based; 61 iBT). Electronic applications accepted. *Faculty research:* Algebraic geometry, analysis (real, complex, functional and harmonic), analytic functions, applied mathematics, financial mathematics and mathematics of insurance, commutative rings, scattering theory, differential equations (ordinary and partial), differential geometry, dynamical systems, general relativity, mathematical physics, number theory, probabilistic analysis and topology.

The University of North Carolina at Charlotte, College of Liberal Arts and Sciences, Department of Mathematics and Statistics, Charlotte, NC 28223-0001. Offers applied mathematics (PhD); mathematics (MS); mathematics education (MA). *Program availability:* Part-time, evening/weekend. *Faculty:* 41 full-time (10 women). *Students:* 51 full-time (24 women), 25 part-time (12 women); includes 10 minority (3 Black or African American, non-Hispanic/Latino; 2 Asian, non-Hispanic/Latino; 4 Hispanic/Latino; 1 Two or more races, non-Hispanic/Latino), 40 international. Average age 29. 59 applicants, 80% accepted, 17 enrolled. In 2015, 11 master's, 4 doctorates awarded. Terminal master's awarded for partial completion of doctoral program. *Degree requirements:* For master's, comprehensive exam, thesis, research project or portfolio; for doctorate, comprehensive exam, thesis/dissertation. *Entrance requirements:* For master's, GRE General Test, bachelor's degree, or its U.S. equivalent, from regionally-accredited college or university; minimum overall GPA of 3.0 on all previous work beyond high school; for doctorate, GRE General Test, at least 27 hours of courses in the mathematical sciences, as approved by the department Graduate Committee, with grades of C or better and minimum overall GPA in mathematics or statistics courses of 3.0. Additional exam requirements/recommendations for international students: Required—TOEFL (minimum score 557 paper-based, 83 iBT) or IELTS (minimum score 6.5). *Application deadline:* For fall admission, 3/1 priority date for domestic and international students; for spring admission, 10/1 priority date for domestic and international students; for summer admission, 4/1 priority date for domestic and international students. Applications are processed on a rolling basis. Application fee: $75. Electronic applications accepted. *Expenses:* Tuition, state resident: full-time $4128. Tuition, nonresident: full-time $16,799. *Required fees:* $2904. Tuition and fees vary according to course load and program. *Financial support:* In 2015–16, 38 students received support, including 2 fellowships (averaging $24,355 per year), 3 research assistantships (averaging $11,380 per year), 33 teaching assistantships (averaging $13,930 per year); career-related internships or fieldwork, Federal Work-Study, institutionally sponsored loans, scholarships/grants, and unspecified assistantships also available. Support available to part-time students. Financial award application deadline: 3/1; financial award applicants required to submit FAFSA. *Faculty research:* Numerical analysis and scientific computation, probability and stochastic processes, partial differential equations and mathematical physics, algebra and combinatorics, analysis, biostatistics, topology. *Total annual research expenditures:* $717,296. *Unit head:* Dr. Yuanan Diao, Chair, 704-687-0620, E-mail: ydiao@uncc.edu. *Application contact:* Kathy B. Giddings, Director of Graduate Admissions, 704-687-5503, Fax: 704-687-1668, E-mail: gradadm@uncc.edu.
Website: http://math.uncc.edu/

University of Northern Iowa, Graduate College, College of Humanities, Arts and Sciences, Department of Mathematics, PSM Program in Industrial Mathematics, Cedar Falls, IA 50614. Offers PSM. *Students:* 3 full-time (0 women), 1 part-time (0 women), 3 international. 9 applicants, 56% accepted, 2 enrolled. Application fee: $50 ($70 for international students). *Unit head:* Dr. Syed Kirmani, Coordinator, 319-273-2940, Fax: 319-273-2546, E-mail: syed.kirmani@uni.edu. *Application contact:* Laurie S. Russell, Record Analyst, 319-273-2623, Fax: 319-273-2885, E-mail: laurie.russell@uni.edu.
Website: https://www.uni.edu/math/academics/master-arts-degrees-mathematics

University of Notre Dame, Graduate School, College of Science, Department of Mathematics, Notre Dame, IN 46556. Offers algebra (PhD); algebraic geometry (PhD); applied mathematics (MSAM); complex analysis (PhD); differential geometry (PhD); logic (PhD); partial differential equations (PhD); topology (PhD). Terminal master's awarded for partial completion of doctoral program. *Degree requirements:* For doctorate, one foreign language, thesis/dissertation, qualifying exam. *Entrance requirements:* For master's and doctorate, GRE General Test, GRE Subject Test. Additional exam requirements/recommendations for international students: Required—TOEFL (minimum score 600 paper-based; 80 iBT). Electronic applications accepted. *Faculty research:* Algebra, analysis, geometry/topology, logic, applied math.

University of Pennsylvania, School of Arts and Sciences, Graduate Group in Applied Mathematics and Computational Science, Philadelphia, PA 19104. Offers PhD. *Faculty:* 28 full-time (3 women), 2 part-time/adjunct (0 women). *Students:* 31 full-time (5 women), 26 international. Average age 25. 101 applicants, 27% accepted, 10 enrolled. In 2015, 3 doctorates awarded. *Expenses: Tuition, area resident:* Full-time $31,068; part-time $5762 per course. *Required fees:* $3200; $336 per course. Full-time tuition and fees vary according to degree level, program and student level. Part-time tuition and fees vary according to course load, degree level and program.
Website: http://www.amcs.upenn.edu

University of Pittsburgh, Dietrich School of Arts and Sciences, Department of Mathematics, Pittsburgh, PA 15260. Offers applied mathematics (MA, MS); mathematics (MA, MS, PhD). *Program availability:* Part-time. *Faculty:* 31 full-time (2 women). *Students:* 86 full-time (29 women); includes 36 minority (2 Black or African American, non-Hispanic/Latino; 31 Asian, non-Hispanic/Latino; 2 Hispanic/Latino; 1 Two or more races, non-Hispanic/Latino). Average age 29. 175 applicants, 24% accepted, 16 enrolled. In 2015, 7 master's, 7 doctorates awarded. Terminal master's awarded for partial completion of doctoral program. *Degree requirements:* For master's, thesis (for some programs); for doctorate, comprehensive exam, thesis/dissertation, preliminary exams, defense of dissertation. *Entrance requirements:* For master's and doctorate, GRE General Test, GRE Subject Test (recommended), minimum GPA of 3.0. Additional exam requirements/recommendations for international students: Required—TOEFL (minimum score 90 iBT), IELTS (minimum score 7). *Application deadline:* For fall admission, 1/15 for domestic and international students; for spring admission, 11/1 for domestic and international students. Applications are processed on a rolling basis. Application fee: $50. Electronic applications accepted. Application fee is waived when completed online. Tuition and fees vary according to program. *Financial support:* In 2015–16, 75 students received support, including 12 fellowships with full tuition reimbursements available (averaging $21,712 per year), 10 research assistantships with full tuition reimbursements available (averaging $16,766 per year), 53 teaching assistantships with full tuition reimbursements available (averaging $17,464 per year); tuition waivers (full) also available. Financial award application deadline: 4/1; financial award applicants required to submit FAFSA. *Faculty research:* Algebra, combinatorics, and geometry; analysis and partial differential equations; applied analysis; complex biological systems; mathematical finance. *Total annual research expenditures:* $859,802. *Unit head:* Dr. Ivan Yotov, Chair, 412-624-8361, Fax: 412-624-8397, E-mail: yotov@math.pitt.edu. *Application contact:* Pat Markham, Graduate Administrator, 412-624-1175, Fax: 412-624-8397, E-mail: pam131@pitt.edu.
Website: http://www.mathematics.pitt.edu

University of Puerto Rico, Mayagüez Campus, Graduate Studies, College of Arts and Sciences, Department of Mathematical Sciences, Mayagüez, PR 00681-9000. Offers applied mathematics (MS); pure mathematics (MS); scientific computation (MS); statistics (MS). *Program availability:* Part-time. *Degree requirements:* For master's, one foreign language, comprehensive exam, thesis optional. *Entrance requirements:* For master's, undergraduate degree in mathematics or its equivalent. *Faculty research:* Automata theory, linear algebra, logic.

University of Rhode Island, Graduate School, College of Arts and Sciences, Department of Mathematics, Kingston, RI 02881. Offers applied mathematical sciences (MS, PhD); mathematics (MS, PhD). *Program availability:* Part-time. *Faculty:* 20 full-time (6 women). *Students:* 15 full-time (6 women), 5 part-time (2 women); includes 1 minority (Black or African American, non-Hispanic/Latino), 1 international. In 2015, 2 master's, 2 doctorates awarded. *Degree requirements:* For master's, comprehensive exam (for some programs), thesis optional; for doctorate, one foreign language, comprehensive exam, thesis/dissertation. *Entrance requirements:* For master's and doctorate, 2 letters of recommendation, 3 for international candidates (one of which must address the candidate's abilities to teach in English). Additional exam requirements/recommendations for international students: Required—TOEFL (minimum score 550 paper-based). *Application deadline:* For fall admission, 7/15 for domestic students, 2/1 for international students; for spring admission, 11/15 for domestic students, 7/15 for international students. Application fee: $65. Electronic applications accepted. *Expenses:* Tuition, state resident: full-time $11,796; part-time $655 per credit. Tuition, nonresident: full-time $24,206; part-time $1345 per credit. *Required fees:* $1546; $44 per credit. One-time fee: $155 full-time; $35 part-time. *Financial support:* In 2015–16, 5 research assistantships (averaging $16,081 per year), 8 teaching assistantships with tuition reimbursements (averaging $16,186 per year) were awarded. Financial award application deadline: 2/1; financial award applicants required to submit FAFSA. *Unit head:* Dr. James Baglama, Chair, 401-874-2709, Fax: 401-874-4454, E-mail: jbaglama@math.uri.edu. *Application contact:* Graduate Admission, 401-874-2872, E-mail: gradadm@etal.uri.edu.
Website: http://www.math.uri.edu/

University of Southern California, Graduate School, Dana and David Dornsife College of Letters, Arts and Sciences, Department of Mathematics, Los Angeles, CA 90089. Offers applied mathematics (MA, MS, PhD); mathematical finance (MS); mathematics (MA, PhD); statistics (MS). *Program availability:* Part-time. Terminal master's awarded for partial completion of doctoral program. *Degree requirements:* For master's, comprehensive exam (for some programs), thesis (for some programs); for doctorate, one foreign language, comprehensive exam, thesis/dissertation. *Entrance requirements:* For master's, GRE General Test, GMAT; for doctorate, GRE General Test, GRE Subject Test (mathematics). Additional exam requirements/recommendations for international students: Required—TOEFL (minimum score 100 iBT). Electronic applications accepted. *Faculty research:* Algebra, algebraic geometry and number theory, analysis/partial differential equations, applied mathematics, financial mathematics, probability, combinatorics and statistics.

University of South Florida, College of Arts and Sciences, Department of Mathematics and Statistics, Tampa, FL 33620-9951. Offers mathematics (MA, PhD), including pure and applied, statistics (PhD); statistics (MA). *Program availability:* Part-time, evening/weekend. *Faculty:* 22 full-time (2 women). *Students:* 70 full-time (25 women), 21 part-time (7 women); includes 9 minority (2 Black or African American, non-Hispanic/Latino; 3 Asian, non-Hispanic/Latino; 2 Hispanic/Latino; 2 Two or more races, non-Hispanic/Latino), 46 international. Average age 31. 88 applicants, 69% accepted, 16 enrolled. In 2015, 25 master's, 6 doctorates awarded. Terminal master's awarded for partial completion of doctoral program. *Degree requirements:* For master's, comprehensive exam, thesis (for some programs); for doctorate, comprehensive exam, thesis/dissertation. *Entrance requirements:* For master's, GRE General Test, minimum GPA of 3.0 in undergraduate mathematics courses, bachelor's degree in mathematical sciences or related field, and statement of goals (for mathematics); minimum GPA of 3.5 in upper-division undergraduate coursework and BA or BS in statistics, mathematics, physical sciences, engineering, or business (for statistics); for doctorate, GRE General Test, minimum GPA of 3.5 in graduate mathematics courses, three letters of recommendation, statement of goals, master's or bachelor's degree in mathematical sciences or related field. Additional exam requirements/recommendations for international students: Required—TOEFL (minimum score 550 paper-based; 79 iBT) or IELTS (minimum score 6.5). *Application deadline:* For fall admission, 2/1 for domestic students, 1/2 for international students; for spring admission, 8/1 for domestic students, 6/1 for international students. Application fee: $30. Electronic applications accepted. *Financial support:* In 2015–16, 61 students received support, including 6 research assistantships (averaging $16,990 per year), 55 teaching assistantships with partial

tuition reimbursements available (averaging $13,742 per year); unspecified assistantships also available. Financial award application deadline: 2/1. *Faculty research:* Mathematics: algebra and number theory, harmonic and complex analysis, approximation theory, theory of orthogonal polynomials, Banach space theory and operator theory, differential equations and nonlinear analysis, discrete mathematics, geometry and topology; statistics: linear and nonlinear statistical models for health sciences, operations research problems, economic systems; stochastic control problems; dynamic reliability analysis and control. *Total annual research expenditures:* $661,309. *Unit head:* Dr. Leslaw Skrzypek, Associate Professor and Chairperson, 813-974-1268, Fax: 813-974-2700, E-mail: skrzypek@usf.edu. *Application contact:* Dr. Xiang-Dong Hou, Professor/Director of Graduate Mathematics Program, 813-974-2561, Fax: 813-974-2700, E-mail: xhou@cas.usf.edu.
Website: http://math.usf.edu/

The University of Tennessee, Graduate School, College of Arts and Sciences, Department of Mathematics, Knoxville, TN 37996. Offers applied mathematics (MS); mathematical ecology (PhD); mathematics (M Math, MS, PhD). *Program availability:* Part-time. *Degree requirements:* For master's, thesis or alternative; for doctorate, one foreign language, thesis/dissertation. *Entrance requirements:* For master's and doctorate, minimum GPA of 2.7. Additional exam requirements/recommendations for international students: Required—TOEFL. Electronic applications accepted.

The University of Tennessee at Chattanooga, Program in Mathematics, Chattanooga, TN 37403-2598. Offers applied mathematics (MS); applied statistics (MS); mathematics (MS); mathematics education (MS); preprofessional (MS). *Program availability:* Part-time. *Faculty:* 8 full-time (1 woman). *Students:* 14 full-time (4 women), 3 part-time (2 women); includes 4 minority (1 Asian, non-Hispanic/Latino; 2 Hispanic/Latino; 1 Two or more races, non-Hispanic/Latino), 1 international. Average age 27. In 2015, 7 master's awarded. *Entrance requirements:* For master's, two letters of recommendation. Additional exam requirements/recommendations for international students: Required—TOEFL (minimum score 61 iBT), IELTS (minimum score 5.5). *Application deadline:* For fall admission, 6/13 for domestic students, 6/1 for international students; for spring admission, 10/15 for domestic students, 10/1 for international students. Applications are processed on a rolling basis. Application fee: $30 ($35 for international students). Electronic applications accepted. *Expenses:* Tuition, state resident: full-time $7938; part-time $441 per credit hour. Tuition, nonresident: full-time $24,056; part-time $1336 per credit hour. *Required fees:* $1732; $253 per credit hour. *Financial support:* Research assistantships available. Financial award applicants required to submit FAFSA. *Unit head:* Dr. Francesco Barioli, Graduate Program Coordinator, 423-425-2198, E-mail: francesco-barioli@utc.edu. *Application contact:* Dr. J. Randy Walker, Interim Dean of Graduate Studies, 423-425-4478, Fax: 423-425-5223, E-mail: randy-walker@utc.edu.
Website: http://www.utc.edu/Academic/Mathematics/

The University of Texas at Arlington, Graduate School, College of Science, Department of Mathematics, Arlington, TX 76019. Offers applied math (MS); mathematics (PhD); mathematics education (MA). *Program availability:* Part-time, evening/weekend. *Degree requirements:* For master's, comprehensive exam, thesis or alternative; for doctorate, comprehensive exam, thesis/dissertation, preliminary examinations. *Entrance requirements:* For master's, GRE General Test (minimum score 350 verbal, 650 quantitative); for doctorate, GRE General Test (minimum score 350 verbal, 700 quantitative), 30 hours of graduate course work in mathematics, minimum GPA of 3.0 in last 60 hours of course work. Additional exam requirements/recommendations for international students: Required—TOEFL (minimum score 550 paper-based; 79 iBT). Electronic applications accepted. *Faculty research:* Algebra, combinatorics and geometry, applied mathematics and mathematical biology, computational mathematics, mathematics education, probability and statistics.

The University of Texas at Austin, Graduate School, Program in Computational Science, Engineering, and Mathematics, Austin, TX 78712-1111. Offers MS, PhD. Terminal master's awarded for partial completion of doctoral program. *Degree requirements:* For master's, thesis optional; for doctorate, thesis/dissertation, 3 area qualifying exams. Electronic applications accepted.

The University of Texas at Dallas, School of Natural Sciences and Mathematics, Department of Mathematical Sciences, Richardson, TX 75080. Offers actuarial science (MS); mathematics (MS); mathematics (MS, PhD), including applied mathematics, engineering mathematics (MS); statistics (MS, PhD). *Program availability:* Part-time, evening/weekend. *Faculty:* 31 full-time (6 women), 1 part-time/adjunct (0 women). *Students:* 133 full-time (57 women), 26 part-time (9 women); includes 33 minority (6 Black or African American, non-Hispanic/Latino; 17 Asian, non-Hispanic/Latino; 8 Hispanic/Latino; 2 Two or more races, non-Hispanic/Latino), 94 international. Average age 30. 204 applicants, 51% accepted, 58 enrolled. In 2015, 13 master's, 6 doctorates awarded. *Median time to degree:* Of those who began their doctoral program in fall 2007, 44% received their degree in 8 years or less. *Degree requirements:* For master's, thesis optional; for doctorate, thesis/dissertation. *Entrance requirements:* For master's, GRE General Test, minimum GPA of 3.0 in upper-level course work in field; for doctorate, GRE General Test, minimum GPA of 3.5 in upper-level course work in field. Additional exam requirements/recommendations for international students: Required—TOEFL (minimum score 550 paper-based). *Application deadline:* For fall admission, 7/15 for domestic students, 5/1 priority date for international students; for spring admission, 11/15 for domestic students, 9/1 priority date for international students. Applications are processed on a rolling basis. Application fee: $50 ($100 for international students). Electronic applications accepted. *Expenses:* Tuition, state resident: full-time $11,940; part-time $663 per semester hour. Tuition, nonresident: full-time $22,786; part-time $1266 per semester hour. Tuition and fees vary according to course load. *Financial support:* In 2015–16, 108 students received support, including 8 research assistantships (averaging $23,025 per year), 64 teaching assistantships with partial tuition reimbursements available (averaging $17,283 per year); career-related internships or fieldwork, Federal Work-Study, institutionally sponsored loans, scholarships/grants, and unspecified assistantships also available. Support available to part-time students. Financial award application deadline: 4/30; financial award applicants required to submit FAFSA. *Faculty research:* Sequential analysis, applications in semiconductor manufacturing, medical image analysis, computational anatomy, information theory, probability theory. *Unit head:* Dr. Vladimir Dragovic, Department Head, 972-883-2161, Fax: 972-883-6622, E-mail: utdmath@utdallas.edu. *Application contact:* Olivia Dao, Graduate Support Assistant, 972-883-2163, Fax: 972-883-6622, E-mail: utdmath@utdallas.edu.
Website: http://www.utdallas.edu/math

The University of Texas at San Antonio, College of Sciences, Department of Mathematics, San Antonio, TX 78249-0617. Offers applied mathematics (MS), including industrial mathematics; mathematics (MS); mathematics education (MS). *Program availability:* Part-time, evening/weekend. *Faculty:* 11 full-time (2 women). *Students:* 14 full-time (5 women), 25 part-time (13 women); includes 26 minority (3 Black or African American, non-Hispanic/Latino; 6 Asian, non-Hispanic/Latino; 16 Hispanic/Latino; 1 Two or more races, non-Hispanic/Latino), 1 international. Average age 31. 13 applicants, 77% accepted, 7 enrolled. In 2015, 21 master's awarded. *Degree requirements:* For master's, comprehensive exam (for some programs), thesis or alternative. *Entrance requirements:* For master's, GRE General Test, minimum GPA of 3.0 in last 60 hours. Additional exam requirements/recommendations for international students: Required—TOEFL (minimum score 550 paper-based; 79 iBT), IELTS (minimum score 6.5). *Application deadline:* For fall admission, 7/1 for domestic students, 4/1 for international students; for spring admission, 11/1 for domestic students, 9/1 for international students. Applications are processed on a rolling basis. Application fee: $45 ($80 for international students). Electronic applications accepted. *Financial support:* Applicants required to submit FAFSA. *Faculty research:* Differential equations, functional analysis, numerical analysis, number theory, logic. *Unit head:* Dr. F. Alexander Norman, Department Chair, 210-458-7254, Fax: 210-458-4439, E-mail: sandy.norman@utsa.edu. *Application contact:* Monica Rodriguez, Director of Graduate Admissions, 210-458-4331, Fax: 210-458-4332, E-mail: graduatestudies@utsa.edu.
Website: http://math.utsa.edu/

The University of Toledo, College of Graduate Studies, College of Natural Sciences and Mathematics, Department of Mathematics, Toledo, OH 43606-3390. Offers applied mathematics (MS, PhD); statistics (MS, PhD). *Program availability:* Part-time. *Degree requirements:* For master's, comprehensive exam (for some programs), thesis (for some programs); for doctorate, 2 foreign languages, thesis/dissertation. *Entrance requirements:* For master's and doctorate, GRE General Test, GRE Subject Test, minimum cumulative point-hour ratio of 2.7 for all previous academic work, three letters of recommendation, statement of purpose, transcripts from all prior institutions attended. Additional exam requirements/recommendations for international students: Required—TOEFL (minimum score 550 paper-based; 80 iBT). Electronic applications accepted.

The University of Tulsa, Graduate School, Collins College of Business, Finance/Applied Mathematics Program, Tulsa, OK 74104-3189. Offers MS/MS. *Program availability:* Part-time. *Students:* 2 full-time (0 women); includes 1 minority (Asian, non-Hispanic/Latino). Average age 26. 2 applicants, 100% accepted, 1 enrolled. *Entrance requirements:* Additional exam requirements/recommendations for international students: Required—TOEFL (minimum score 577 paper-based; 91 iBT), IELTS (minimum score 6.5). *Application deadline:* Applications are processed on a rolling basis. Application fee: $55. Electronic applications accepted. *Expenses: Tuition, area resident:* Full-time $22,230; part-time $1176 per credit hour. *Required fees:* $590 per semester. Tuition and fees vary according to course load. *Financial support:* Fellowships, teaching assistantships, career-related internships or fieldwork, Federal Work-Study, institutionally sponsored loans, scholarships/grants, health care benefits, tuition waivers (full and partial), and unspecified assistantships available. Support available to part-time students. Financial award application deadline: 2/1; financial award applicants required to submit FAFSA. *Unit head:* Dr. Ralph Jackson, Associate Dean, 918-631-2242, Fax: 918-631-2142, E-mail: ralph-jackson@utulsa.edu. *Application contact:* Information Contact, 918-631-2242,
E-mail: graduate-business@utulsa.edu.

University of Washington, Graduate School, College of Arts and Sciences, Department of Applied Mathematics, Seattle, WA 98195. Offers MS, PhD. Terminal master's awarded for partial completion of doctoral program. *Degree requirements:* For master's, thesis optional; for doctorate, thesis/dissertation. *Entrance requirements:* For master's and doctorate, GRE, minimum GPA of 3.0. Additional exam requirements/recommendations for international students: Required—TOEFL. Electronic applications accepted. *Faculty research:* Mathematical modeling for physical, biological, social, and engineering sciences; development of mathematical methods for analysis, including perturbation, asymptotic, transform, vocational, and numerical methods.

University of Washington, Graduate School, College of Arts and Sciences, Department of Mathematics, Seattle, WA 98195. Offers mathematics (MA, MS, PhD); numerical analysis (MS); optimization (MS). *Program availability:* Part-time. Terminal master's awarded for partial completion of doctoral program. *Degree requirements:* For master's, thesis optional; for doctorate, 2 foreign languages, thesis/dissertation. *Entrance requirements:* For master's, GRE, minimum GPA of 3.0; for doctorate, GRE General Test, GRE Subject Test (mathematics), minimum GPA of 3.0. Additional exam requirements/recommendations for international students: Required—TOEFL. Electronic applications accepted. *Faculty research:* Algebra, analysis, probability, combinatorics and geometry.

University of Waterloo, Graduate Studies, Faculty of Mathematics, Department of Applied Mathematics, Waterloo, ON N2L 3G1, Canada. Offers M Math, PhD. *Program availability:* Part-time. *Degree requirements:* For master's, research paper or thesis; for doctorate, thesis/dissertation. *Entrance requirements:* For master's, honors degree in field, minimum B+ average; for doctorate, master's degree, minimum B+ average. Additional exam requirements/recommendations for international students: Required—TOEFL, IELTS, PTE. *Application deadline:* For fall admission, 2/1 for domestic and international students. Applications are processed on a rolling basis. Application fee: $100 Canadian dollars. Electronic applications accepted. *Financial support:* Research assistantships and teaching assistantships available. *Faculty research:* Differential equations, quantum theory, statistical mechanics, fluid mechanics, relativity, control theory.
Website: https://uwaterloo.ca/applied-mathematics/

The University of Western Ontario, Faculty of Graduate Studies, Physical Sciences Division, Department of Applied Mathematics, London, ON N6A 5B8, Canada. Offers applied mathematics (M Sc, PhD); theoretical physics (PhD). *Degree requirements:* For master's, thesis or alternative; for doctorate, comprehensive exam, thesis/dissertation. *Entrance requirements:* For master's and doctorate, minimum B average. Additional exam requirements/recommendations for international students: Required—TOEFL. *Faculty research:* Fluid dynamics, mathematical and computational methods, theoretical physics.

University of Wisconsin–Stout, Graduate School, College of Science, Technology, Engineering and Mathematics, Program in Industrial and Applied Mathematics, Menomonie, WI 54751. Offers PSM. *Program availability:* Online learning.

Utah State University, School of Graduate Studies, College of Science, Department of Mathematics and Statistics, Logan, UT 84322. Offers industrial mathematics (MS); mathematical sciences (PhD); mathematics (M Math, MS); statistics (MS). *Program availability:* Part-time. Terminal master's awarded for partial completion of doctoral program. *Degree requirements:* For master's, thesis optional, qualifying exam; for doctorate, one foreign language, comprehensive exam, thesis/dissertation. *Entrance requirements:* For master's and doctorate, GRE General Test, minimum GPA of 3.0. Additional exam requirements/recommendations for international students: Required—TOEFL. *Faculty research:* Differential equations, computational mathematics, dynamical systems, probability and statistics, pure mathematics.

Virginia Commonwealth University, Graduate School, College of Humanities and Sciences, Department of Mathematics and Applied Mathematics, Richmond, VA 23284-9005. Offers applied mathematics (MS); mathematics (MS). *Degree requirements:* For master's, thesis optional. *Entrance requirements:* For master's, GRE General Test, GRE Subject Test, 30 undergraduate semester credits in the mathematical sciences or closely-related fields. Additional exam requirements/recommendations for international students: Required—TOEFL (minimum score 600 paper-based; 100 iBT); Recommended—IELTS (minimum score 6.5). Electronic applications accepted. *Faculty research:* Mathematics, applied mathematics.

Washington State University, College of Arts and Sciences, Department of Mathematics, Pullman, WA 99164. Offers applied mathematics (MS, PhD); mathematics (MS, PhD); mathematics teaching (MS, PhD). Programs offered at the Pullman campus. *Program availability:* Part-time. Terminal master's awarded for partial completion of doctoral program. *Degree requirements:* For master's, comprehensive exam (for some programs), thesis or alternative, oral exam, project; for doctorate, 2 foreign languages, comprehensive exam, thesis/dissertation, oral exam, written exam. *Entrance requirements:* For master's and doctorate, minimum GPA of 3.0, 3 letters of recommendation. Additional exam requirements/recommendations for international students: Required—TOEFL (minimum score 600 paper-based; 100 iBT) or IELTS (minimum score 7). Electronic applications accepted. *Faculty research:* Computational mathematics, operations research, modeling in the natural sciences, applied statistics.

Wayne State University, College of Liberal Arts and Sciences, Department of Mathematics, Detroit, MI 48202. Offers applied mathematics (MA, PhD); mathematical statistics (MA, PhD); mathematics (MA, MS); pure mathematics (PhD). *Faculty:* 26. *Students:* 42 full-time (10 women), 29 part-time (10 women); includes 10 minority (3 Black or African American, non-Hispanic/Latino; 5 Asian, non-Hispanic/Latino; 2 Hispanic/Latino), 31 international. Average age 30. 94 applicants, 41% accepted, 9 enrolled. In 2015, 10 master's, 3 doctorates awarded. *Degree requirements:* For master's, thesis (for some programs), essays, oral exams; for doctorate, thesis/dissertation, oral exams; French, German, Russian, or Chinese. *Entrance requirements:* For master's, twelve semester credits in mathematics beyond sophomore calculus; for doctorate, master's degree in mathematics or equivalent level of advancement. Additional exam requirements/recommendations for international students: Required—TOEFL (minimum score 550 paper-based; 79 iBT), TWE (minimum score 5.5), Michigan English Language Assessment Battery (minimum score 85); Recommended—IELTS (minimum score 6.5). *Application deadline:* For fall admission, 6/1 priority date for domestic students, 5/1 priority date for international students; for winter admission, 10/1 priority date for domestic students, 9/1 priority date for international students; for spring admission, 2/1 priority date for domestic students, 1/1 priority date for international students. Application fee: $0. Electronic applications accepted. *Expenses:* Tuition, state resident: full-time $14,165; part-time $590.20 per credit hour. Tuition, nonresident: full-time $30,682; part-time $1278.40 per credit hour. *Required fees:* $1688; $47.45 per credit hour. $274.60 per semester. Tuition and fees vary according to course load and program. *Financial support:* In 2015–16, 43 students received support, including 5 fellowships with tuition reimbursements available (averaging $20,135 per year), 2 research assistantships with tuition reimbursements available (averaging $18,801 per year), 25 teaching assistantships with tuition reimbursements available (averaging $18,801 per year); scholarships/grants, health care benefits, and unspecified assistantships also available. Financial award application deadline: 3/31; financial award applicants required to submit FAFSA. *Faculty research:* Harmonic analysis and partial differential equations, group theory and non-commutative ring theory, homotopy theory and applications to topology and geometry, numerical analysis, control and optimization, statistical estimation theory. *Total annual research expenditures:* $807,813. *Unit head:* Dr. Daniel Frohardt, Professor and Chair, 313-577-6163,
E-mail: danf@math.wayne.edu. *Application contact:* Mary Klamo, Academic Services Officer, E-mail: gradsecretary@math.wayne.edu.
Website: http://clas.wayne.edu/math/

West Chester University of Pennsylvania, College of Arts and Sciences, Department of Mathematics, West Chester, PA 19383. Offers applied and computational mathematics (MS); applied statistics (MS, Certificate); mathematics (MA, Teaching Certificate); mathematics education (MA). *Program availability:* Part-time, evening/weekend. *Faculty:* 10 full-time (0 women), 2 part-time/adjunct (0 women). *Students:* 11 full-time (5 women), 92 part-time (46 women); includes 19 minority (4 Black or African American, non-Hispanic/Latino; 14 Asian, non-Hispanic/Latino; 1 Hispanic/Latino), 15 international. Average age 30. 68 applicants, 97% accepted, 48 enrolled. In 2015, 34 master's awarded. *Degree requirements:* For master's, thesis (for all but MS in applied mathematics). *Entrance requirements:* For master's, GMAT or GRE General Test (for MA in mathematics), interview (for MA in mathematics); for other advanced degree, GMAT or GRE General Test (for Teaching Certificate). Additional exam requirements/recommendations for international students: Required—TOEFL or IELTS. *Application deadline:* For fall admission, 5/15 for international students; for spring admission, 10/15 for international students. Applications are processed on a rolling basis. Application fee: $50. Electronic applications accepted. *Expenses:* Tuition, state resident: full-time $8460; part-time $470 per credit. Tuition, nonresident: full-time $12,690; part-time $705 per credit. *Required fees:* $2312; $126.75 per credit. Tuition and fees vary according to campus/location and program. *Financial support:* Scholarships/grants and unspecified assistantships available. Financial award application deadline: 2/15; financial award applicants required to submit FAFSA. *Faculty research:* Teachers teaching with technology in service training program, biostatistics, hierarchical linear models, clustered binary outcome date, mathematics biology. *Unit head:* Dr. Peter Glidden, Chair, 610-436-2440, Fax: 610-738-0578, E-mail: pglidden@wcupa.edu. *Application contact:* Dr. Gail Gallitano, Graduate Coordinator, 610-436-2452, Fax: 610-738-0578, E-mail: ggallitano@wcupa.edu.
Website: http://www.wcupa.edu/_academics/sch_cas.mat/

Western Illinois University, School of Graduate Studies, College of Arts and Sciences, Department of Mathematics, Macomb, IL 61455-1390. Offers applied math (Certificate); mathematics (MS). *Program availability:* Part-time. *Students:* 18 full-time (9 women), 2 part-time (both women); includes 1 minority (Asian, non-Hispanic/Latino), 12 international. Average age 29. 18 applicants, 67% accepted, 9 enrolled. In 2015, 9 master's awarded. *Degree requirements:* For master's, thesis or alternative. *Entrance requirements:* Additional exam requirements/recommendations for international students: Required—TOEFL (minimum score 500 paper-based; 61 iBT). *Application deadline:* Applications are processed on a rolling basis. Application fee: $30. Electronic applications accepted. *Financial support:* In 2015–16, 12 students received support, including 2 teaching assistantships with full tuition reimbursements available (averaging $8,688 per year). Financial award applicants required to submit FAFSA. *Unit head:* Dr. Iraj Kalantari, Chairperson, 309-298-1054. *Application contact:* Dr. Nancy Parsons, Associate Provost and Director of Graduate Studies, 309-298-1806, Fax: 309-298-2345, E-mail: grad-office@wiu.edu.
Website: http://wiu.edu/mathematics

Western Michigan University, Graduate College, College of Arts and Sciences, Department of Mathematics, Kalamazoo, MI 49008. Offers applied and computational mathematics (MS); mathematics education (MA, PhD), including collegiate mathematics education (PhD). *Degree requirements:* For doctorate, one foreign language, thesis/dissertation.

West Virginia University, Eberly College of Arts and Sciences, Department of Mathematics, Morgantown, WV 26506. Offers applied mathematics (MS, PhD); discrete mathematics (PhD); interdisciplinary mathematics (MS); mathematics for secondary education (MS); pure mathematics (MS). *Program availability:* Part-time. Terminal master's awarded for partial completion of doctoral program. *Degree requirements:* For master's, comprehensive exam (for some programs), thesis optional; for doctorate, one foreign language, comprehensive exam, thesis/dissertation. *Entrance requirements:* For master's, GRE Subject Test (recommended), minimum GPA of 2.5; for doctorate, GRE Subject Test (recommended), master's degree in mathematics. Additional exam requirements/recommendations for international students: Required—TOEFL (paper-based 550) or IELTS (6). *Expenses:* Tuition, state resident: full-time $8568. Tuition, nonresident: full-time $22,140. Tuition and fees vary according to program. *Faculty research:* Combinatorics and graph theory, differential equations, applied and computational mathematics.

Wichita State University, Graduate School, Fairmount College of Liberal Arts and Sciences, Department of Mathematics, Statistics and Physics, Wichita, KS 67260. Offers applied mathematics (PhD); mathematics (MS); physics (MS). *Program availability:* Part-time. *Unit head:* Dr. Thomas DeLillo, Chair, 316-978-3160, Fax: 316-978-3748, E-mail: thomas.delillo@wichita.edu. *Application contact:* Jordan Oleson, Admissions Coordinator, 316-978-3095, Fax: 316-978-3253,
E-mail: jordan.oleson@wichita.edu.
Website: http://www.wichita.edu/math

Worcester Polytechnic Institute, Graduate Studies and Research, Department of Mathematical Sciences, Worcester, MA 01609-2280. Offers applied mathematics (MS); applied statistics (MS); financial mathematics (MS); industrial mathematics (MS); mathematical sciences (PhD, Graduate Certificate); mathematics (MME). *Program availability:* Part-time, evening/weekend. *Faculty:* 19 full-time (2 women), 10 part-time/adjunct (1 woman). *Students:* 93 full-time (35 women), 24 part-time (14 women); includes 11 minority (3 Black or African American, non-Hispanic/Latino; 4 Asian, non-Hispanic/Latino; 2 Hispanic/Latino; 2 Two or more races, non-Hispanic/Latino), 71 international. 303 applicants, 57% accepted, 47 enrolled. In 2015, 47 master's awarded. *Degree requirements:* For master's, thesis (for some programs); for doctorate, comprehensive exam, thesis/dissertation. *Entrance requirements:* For master's, GRE General Test, GRE Subject Test in math (recommended), 3 letters of recommendation; for doctorate, GRE General Test, GRE Subject Test (math), 3 letters of recommendation. Additional exam requirements/recommendations for international students: Required—TOEFL (minimum score 563 paper-based; 84 iBT), IELTS (minimum score 7). *Application deadline:* For fall admission, 1/1 priority date for domestic students, 1/1 for international students; for spring admission, 10/1 priority date for domestic students, 10/1 for international students. Applications are processed on a rolling basis. Application fee: $70. Electronic applications accepted. *Financial support:* Research assistantships, teaching assistantships, career-related internships or fieldwork, institutionally sponsored loans, scholarships/grants, and unspecified assistantships available. Financial award application deadline: 1/1; financial award applicants required to submit FAFSA. *Unit head:* Dr. Luca Capogna, Head, 508-831-5241, Fax: 508-831-5824, E-mail: lcapogna@wpi.edu. *Application contact:* Dr. Joseph Fehribach, Graduate Coordinator, 508-831-5241, Fax: 508-831-5824,
E-mail: bach@wpi.edu.
Website: http://www.wpi.edu/academics/math/

Wright State University, School of Graduate Studies, College of Science and Mathematics, Department of Mathematics and Statistics, Program in Applied Mathematics, Dayton, OH 45435. Offers MS. *Degree requirements:* For master's, comprehensive exam. *Entrance requirements:* For master's, bachelor's degree in mathematics or related field. Additional exam requirements/recommendations for international students: Required—TOEFL. *Faculty research:* Control theory, ordinary differential equations, partial differential equations, numerical analysis, mathematical modeling.

Yale University, Graduate School of Arts and Sciences, Program in Applied Mathematics, New Haven, CT 06520. Offers M Phil, MS, PhD. *Entrance requirements:* For doctorate, GRE General Test.

York University, Faculty of Graduate Studies, Faculty of Science, Program in Mathematics and Statistics, Toronto, ON M3J 1P3, Canada. Offers industrial and applied mathematics (M Sc); mathematics and statistics (MA, PhD). *Program availability:* Part-time. *Degree requirements:* For master's, thesis optional; for doctorate, one foreign language, comprehensive exam, thesis/dissertation. Electronic applications accepted.

Youngstown State University, Graduate School, College of Science, Technology, Engineering and Mathematics, Department of Mathematics and Statistics, Youngstown, OH 44555-0001. Offers applied mathematics (MS); computer science (MS); secondary mathematics (MS); statistics (MS). *Program availability:* Part-time. *Degree requirements:* For master's, comprehensive exam, thesis optional. *Entrance requirements:* For master's, minimum GPA of 2.7 in computer science and mathematics. Additional exam requirements/recommendations for international students: Required—TOEFL. *Faculty research:* Regression analysis, numerical analysis, statistics, Markov chain, topology and fuzzy sets.

Applied Statistics

American University, College of Arts and Sciences, Department of Mathematics and Statistics, Washington, DC 22016-8050. Offers applied statistics (Certificate); mathematics (MA); professional science: quantitative analysis (MS); statistics (MS). *Program availability:* Part-time, evening/weekend. *Faculty:* 34 full-time (11 women), 10

part-time/adjunct (3 women). *Students:* 19 full-time (12 women), 13 part-time (7 women); includes 5 minority (4 Black or African American, non-Hispanic/Latino; 1 Two or more races, non-Hispanic/Latino), 6 international. Average age 26. 54 applicants, 93% accepted, 15 enrolled. In 2015, 12 master's awarded. *Degree requirements:* For master's, comprehensive exam, thesis or alternative. *Entrance requirements:* For master's, GRE, statement of purpose, transcripts, 2 letters of recommendation, resume; for Certificate, bachelor's degree, statement of purpose, transcripts, resume. Additional exam requirements/recommendations for international students: Required—TOEFL (minimum score 100 iBT), IELTS (minimum score 7), PTE (minimum score 68). *Application deadline:* For fall admission, 2/1 priority date for domestic students; for spring admission, 11/1 for domestic students. Application fee: $55. *Expenses: Tuition, area resident:* Full-time $27,468; part-time $1526 per credit hour. *Required fees:* $430. Tuition and fees vary according to course level and program. *Financial support:* Application deadline: 2/1. *Unit head:* Dr. Joshua D. Lansky, department Chair, 202-885-3687, Fax: 202-885-3155, E-mail: lansky@american.edu. *Application contact:* Kathleen Clowery, Associate Director, Graduate Admissions, 202-885-3620, Fax: 202-885-1344, E-mail: clowery@american.edu.
Website: http://www.american.edu/cas/mathstat/

Bowling Green State University, Graduate College, College of Arts and Sciences, Department of Mathematics and Statistics, Bowling Green, OH 43403. Offers applied statistics (MS); mathematics (MA, MAT, PhD); statistics (PhD). *Program availability:* Part-time. *Degree requirements:* For master's, thesis or alternative; for doctorate, comprehensive exam, thesis/dissertation. *Entrance requirements:* For master's and doctorate, GRE General Test. Additional exam requirements/recommendations for international students: Required—TOEFL. Electronic applications accepted. *Faculty research:* Statistics and probability, algebra, analysis.

Bowling Green State University, Graduate College, College of Business Administration, Department of Applied Statistics and Operations Research, Bowling Green, OH 43403. Offers applied statistics (MS). *Program availability:* Part-time. *Degree requirements:* For master's, thesis or alternative. *Entrance requirements:* For master's, GRE General Test. Additional exam requirements/recommendations for international students: Required—TOEFL. Electronic applications accepted. *Faculty research:* Reliability, linear models, time series, statistical quality control.

Brigham Young University, Graduate Studies, College of Physical and Mathematical Sciences, Department of Statistics, Provo, UT 84602-1001. Offers applied statistics (MS). *Faculty:* 18 full-time (3 women). *Students:* 30 full-time (8 women); includes 2 minority (1 Asian, non-Hispanic/Latino; 1 Hispanic/Latino). Average age 24. 38 applicants, 47% accepted, 15 enrolled. In 2015, 13 master's awarded. *Degree requirements:* For master's, comprehensive exam, thesis (for some programs). *Entrance requirements:* For master's, GRE General Test, minimum undergraduate GPA of 3.3; course work in statistical methods, theory, multivariable calculus and linear algebra with minimum B- average. Additional exam requirements/recommendations for international students: Required—TOEFL (minimum score 580 paper-based; 85 iBT). *Application deadline:* For fall admission, 2/1 for domestic and international students. Application fee: $50. Electronic applications accepted. *Financial support:* In 2015–16, 22 students received support, including 1 fellowship (averaging $27,000 per year), 13 research assistantships with tuition reimbursements available (averaging $10,000 per year), 9 teaching assistantships with tuition reimbursements available (averaging $10,000 per year); scholarships/grants and unspecified assistantships also available. Financial award application deadline: 2/1. *Faculty research:* Statistical genetics, reliability and pollution monitoring, Bayesian methods. *Total annual research expenditures:* $580,272. *Unit head:* Dr. Harold Dennis Tolley, Chair, 801-422-6668, Fax: 801-422-0635, E-mail: tolley@byu.edu. *Application contact:* Dr. Gilbert W. Fellingham, Graduate Coordinator, 801-422-2806, Fax: 801-422-0635, E-mail: gwf@stat.byu.edu.
Website: http://statistics.byu.edu/

California State University, East Bay, Office of Graduate Studies Programs, College of Science, Department of Statistics and Biostatistics, Statistics Program, Hayward, CA 94542-3000. Offers actuarial science (MS); applied statistics (MS); computational statistics (MS); mathematical statistics (MS). *Program availability:* Part-time, evening/weekend. *Students:* 27 full-time (10 women), 80 part-time (38 women); includes 33 minority (4 Black or African American, non-Hispanic/Latino; 20 Asian, non-Hispanic/Latino; 7 Hispanic/Latino; 2 Two or more races, non-Hispanic/Latino), 44 international. Average age 30. 85 applicants, 79% accepted, 39 enrolled. In 2015, 38 master's awarded. *Degree requirements:* For master's, comprehensive exam. *Entrance requirements:* For master's, letters of recommendation, minimum GPA of 3.0, math through lower-division calculus. Additional exam requirements/recommendations for international students: Required—TOEFL (minimum score 550 paper-based). *Application deadline:* For fall admission, 6/30 for domestic and international students. Application fee: $55. Electronic applications accepted. *Financial support:* Fellowships, career-related internships or fieldwork, Federal Work-Study, institutionally sponsored loans, scholarships/grants, and unspecified assistantships available. Support available to part-time students. Financial award application deadline: 3/2; financial award applicants required to submit FAFSA. *Unit head:* Dr. Mitchell Watnik, Chair, 510-885-3435, Fax: 510-885-4714.
Website: http://www20.csueastbay.edu/csci/departments/statistics/

California State University, Long Beach, Graduate Studies, College of Natural Sciences and Mathematics, Department of Mathematics and Statistics, Long Beach, CA 90840. Offers mathematics (MS), including applied mathematics, applied statistics, mathematics education for secondary school teachers. *Program availability:* Part-time. *Degree requirements:* For master's, comprehensive exam or thesis. Electronic applications accepted. *Faculty research:* Algebra, functional analysis, partial differential equations, operator theory, numerical analysis.

Cleveland State University, College of Graduate Studies, College of Sciences and Health Professions, Department of Mathematics, Cleveland, OH 44115. Offers applied statistics (MS); mathematics (MS). *Program availability:* Part-time, evening/weekend. *Faculty:* 17 full-time (7 women), 1 part-time/adjunct (0 women). *Students:* 24 full-time (13 women), 21 part-time (12 women); includes 2 minority (1 Asian, non-Hispanic/Latino; 1 Hispanic/Latino), 17 international. Average age 31. 30 applicants, 87% accepted, 13 enrolled. In 2015, 19 master's awarded. *Degree requirements:* For master's, thesis, exit project. *Entrance requirements:* Additional exam requirements/recommendations for international students: Required—TOEFL (minimum score 550 paper-based; 78 iBT). *Application deadline:* For fall admission, 7/1 priority date for domestic students, 6/15 priority date for international students; for spring admission, 11/15 for domestic students, 11/1 for international students; for summer admission, 4/1 for domestic students, 3/15 for international students. Applications are processed on a rolling basis. Application fee: $30. Electronic applications accepted. *Expenses:* Tuition, state resident: full-time $9565. Tuition, nonresident: full-time $17,980. Tuition and fees vary according to program. *Financial support:* In 2015–16, 14 students received support, including 9 teaching assistantships with full tuition reimbursements available (averaging $21,115 per year); unspecified assistantships also available. Financial award application deadline: 3/15. *Faculty research:* Algebraic topology, algebraic geometry, statistics, mathematical biology, applied mathematics. *Total annual research expenditures:* $132,202. *Unit head:* Dr. John Peter Holcomb, Jr., Chairperson/Professor, 216-687-4681, Fax: 216-523-7340, E-mail: j.p.holcomb@csuohio.edu. *Application contact:* Dr. John F. Oprea, Graduate Program Coordinator, 216-687-4702, Fax: 216-523-7340, E-mail: j.oprea@csuohio.edu.
Website: http://www.csuohio.edu/sciences/dept/mathematics/

Colorado School of Mines, Office of Graduate Studies, Department of Applied Mathematics and Statistics, Golden, CO 80401. Offers nuclear engineering (MS, PhD). *Program availability:* Part-time. *Faculty:* 25 full-time (10 women), 7 part-time/adjunct (4 women). *Students:* 33 full-time (14 women), 7 part-time (3 women); includes 6 minority (1 Black or African American, non-Hispanic/Latino; 1 American Indian or Alaska Native, non-Hispanic/Latino; 3 Hispanic/Latino; 1 Two or more races, non-Hispanic/Latino). Average age 28. 64 applicants, 77% accepted, 16 enrolled. In 2015, 12 master's, 2 doctorates awarded. *Degree requirements:* For master's, thesis (for some programs); for doctorate, comprehensive exam, thesis/dissertation. *Entrance requirements:* For master's and doctorate, GRE General Test. Additional exam requirements/recommendations for international students: Required—TOEFL (minimum score 550 paper-based; 80 iBT). *Application deadline:* For fall admission, 12/15 priority date for domestic and international students; for spring admission, 9/1 priority date for domestic and international students. Application fee: $50 ($70 for international students). Electronic applications accepted. *Expenses:* Tuition, state resident: full-time $15,225. Tuition, nonresident: full-time $32,700. *Financial support:* In 2015–16, 20 students received support, including 4 fellowships with full tuition reimbursements available (averaging $21,120 per year), 9 teaching assistantships with full tuition reimbursements available (averaging $21,120 per year); scholarships/grants, health care benefits, and unspecified assistantships also available. Financial award application deadline: 12/15; financial award applicants required to submit FAFSA. *Faculty research:* Applied statistics, numerical computation, artificial intelligence, linear optimization. *Total annual research expenditures:* $669,371. *Unit head:* Dr. Willy Hereman, Head, 303-273-3881, E-mail: whereman@mines.edu. *Application contact:* Dr. William Navidi, Professor, 303-273-3489, E-mail: wnavidi@mines.edu.
Website: http://ams.mines.edu/

Cornell University, Graduate School, Graduate Fields of Engineering, Field of Statistics, Ithaca, NY 14853-0001. Offers applied statistics (MPS); biometry (MS, PhD); decision theory (MS, PhD); economic and social statistics (MS, PhD); engineering statistics (MS, PhD); experimental design (MS, PhD); mathematical statistics (MS, PhD); probability (MS, PhD); sampling (MS, PhD); statistical computing (MS, PhD); stochastic processes (MS, PhD). Terminal master's awarded for partial completion of doctoral program. *Degree requirements:* For master's, project (MPS), thesis (MS); for doctorate, one foreign language, thesis/dissertation. *Entrance requirements:* For master's, GRE General Test (for MS), 2 letters of recommendation (MS, MPS); for doctorate, GRE General Test, 2 letters of recommendation. Additional exam requirements/recommendations for international students: Required—TOEFL (minimum score 550 paper-based; 77 iBT). Electronic applications accepted. *Faculty research:* Bayesian analysis, survival analysis, nonparametric statistics, stochastic processes, mathematical statistics.

DePaul University, College of Science and Health, Chicago, IL 60614. Offers applied mathematics (MS); applied statistics (MS); biological sciences (MA, MS); chemistry (MS); mathematics education (MA); mathematics for teaching (MS); nursing (MS); nursing practice (DNP); physics (MS); psychology (MS); pure mathematics (MS); science education (MS); MA/PhD. Electronic applications accepted.

Florida State University, The Graduate School, College of Arts and Sciences, Department of Statistics, Tallahassee, FL 32306-4330. Offers applied statistics (MS); applied statistics - thesis option (MS); biostatistics (MS, PhD); biostatistics - thesis option (MS); mathematical statistics (MS, PhD); mathematical statistics - thesis option (MS); statistical data science (MS). *Program availability:* Part-time. *Faculty:* 18 full-time (3 women), 1 (woman) part-time/adjunct. *Students:* 149 full-time (77 women), 13 part-time (5 women); includes 19 minority (6 Black or African American, non-Hispanic/Latino; 8 Asian, non-Hispanic/Latino; 5 Hispanic/Latino), 117 international. Average age 27. 353 applicants, 40% accepted, 56 enrolled. In 2015, 44 master's, 6 doctorates awarded. Terminal master's awarded for partial completion of doctoral program. *Degree requirements:* For master's, thesis optional; for doctorate, comprehensive exam, thesis/dissertation, departmental qualifying exam. *Entrance requirements:* For master's, GRE General Test, calculus 1-3, linear algebra, one course each in applied statistics and probability, minimum GPA of 3.0; for doctorate, GRE General Test, minimum GPA of 3.0, two semesters of advanced calculus (intermediate analysis, real analysis with proofs). Additional exam requirements/recommendations for international students: Required—TOEFL (minimum score 80 iBT). *Application deadline:* For fall admission, 7/1 for domestic and international students. Application fee: $30. Electronic applications accepted. *Expenses: Tuition, area resident:* Full-time $7263; part-time $403.50 per credit hour. Tuition, nonresident: full-time $18,087; part-time $1004.85 per credit hour. *Required fees:* $1365; $75.81 per credit hour. $20 per semester. Tuition and fees vary according to campus/location. *Financial support:* In 2015–16, 83 students received support, including 4 fellowships with full tuition reimbursements available (averaging $10,000 per year), 11 research assistantships with full tuition reimbursements available (averaging $19,380 per year), 56 teaching assistantships with full tuition reimbursements available (averaging $20,432 per year); institutionally sponsored loans, scholarships/grants, health care benefits, tuition waivers (partial), and unspecified assistantships also available. Financial award application deadline: 2/1; financial award applicants required to submit FAFSA. *Faculty research:* Statistical inference, probability theory, biostatistics, nonparametric estimation, automatic target recognition. *Total annual research expenditures:* $861,615. *Unit head:* Dr. Xufeng Niu, Chairman, 850-644-4008, Fax: 850-644-5271, E-mail: niu@stat.fsu.edu. *Application contact:* Sarah English, Academic Program Specialist, 850-644-3514, Fax: 850-644-5271, E-mail: sarah.english@stat.fsu.edu.
Website: http://www.stat.fsu.edu/

Indiana University Bloomington, University Graduate School, College of Arts and Sciences, Department of Statistics, Bloomington, IN 47408. Offers applied statistics (MS); statistical science (MS, PhD). *Program availability:* Part-time. Terminal master's awarded for partial completion of doctoral program. *Degree requirements:* For master's, thesis or alternative; for doctorate, comprehensive exam, thesis/dissertation. *Entrance requirements:* For master's and doctorate, GRE. Additional exam requirements/recommendations for international students: Required—TOEFL (minimum score 100 iBT). Electronic applications accepted. *Faculty research:* Spatial statistics, Bayesian statistics, statistical learning, network science, applied statistics.

Indiana University–Purdue University Fort Wayne, College of Arts and Sciences, Department of Mathematical Sciences, Fort Wayne, IN 46805-1499. Offers applied mathematics (MS); applied statistics (Certificate); mathematics (MS); operations research (MS); teaching (MAT). *Program availability:* Part-time, evening/weekend. *Faculty:* 18 full-time (5 women). *Students:* 2 full-time (1 woman), 9 part-time (2 women); includes 1 minority (Hispanic/Latino), 1 international. Average age 31. 6 applicants,

100% accepted, 4 enrolled. In 2015, 5 master's, 1 other advanced degree awarded. *Entrance requirements:* For master's, minimum GPA of 3.0, major or minor in mathematics, three letters of recommendation. Additional exam requirements/ recommendations for international students: Required—TOEFL (minimum score 550 paper-based; 79 iBT); Recommended—TWE. *Application deadline:* For fall admission, 8/1 priority date for domestic students, 7/1 priority date for international students; for spring admission, 12/1 for domestic students, 10/1 for international students. Applications are processed on a rolling basis. Application fee: $55 ($60 for international students). Electronic applications accepted. *Financial support:* In 2015–16, 5 teaching assistantships with partial tuition reimbursements (averaging $13,522 per year) were awarded; scholarships/grants and unspecified assistantships also available. Support available to part-time students. Financial award application deadline: 3/1; financial award applicants required to submit FAFSA. *Faculty research:* Eves' Theorem, paired-placements for student teaching, holomorphic maps. *Total annual research expenditures:* $56,223. *Unit head:* Dr. Peter Dragnev, Chair/Professor, 260-481-6382, Fax: 260-481-0155, E-mail: dragnevp@ipfw.edu. *Application contact:* Dr. W. Douglas Weakley, Director of Graduate Studies, 260-481-6233, Fax: 260-481-0155,
E-mail: weakley@ipfw.edu.
Website: http://www.ipfw.edu/math/

Indiana University–Purdue University Indianapolis, School of Science, Department of Mathematical Sciences, Indianapolis, IN 46202-3216. Offers mathematics (MS, PhD), including applied mathematics, applied statistics (MS), mathematical statistics (PhD), mathematics, mathematics education (MS). *Program availability:* Part-time. Terminal master's awarded for partial completion of doctoral program. *Degree requirements:* For master's, thesis optional; for doctorate, one foreign language, thesis/dissertation. *Entrance requirements:* For doctorate, GRE General Test. Additional exam requirements/recommendations for international students: Required—TOEFL. *Faculty research:* Mathematical physics, integral systems, partial differential equations, noncommutative geometry, biomathematics, computational neurosciences.

Instituto Tecnológico y de Estudios Superiores de Monterrey, Campus Monterrey, Graduate and Research Division, Programs in Engineering, Monterrey, Mexico. Offers applied statistics (M Eng); artificial intelligence (PhD); automation engineering (M Eng); chemical engineering (M Eng); civil engineering (M Eng); electrical engineering (M Eng); electronic engineering (M Eng); environmental engineering (M Eng); industrial engineering (M Eng, PhD); manufacturing engineering (M Eng); mechanical engineering (M Eng); systems and quality engineering (M Eng). M Eng program offered jointly with University of Waterloo; PhD in industrial engineering with Texas A&M University. *Program availability:* Part-time, evening/weekend. Terminal master's awarded for partial completion of doctoral program. *Degree requirements:* For master's, one foreign language, thesis; for doctorate, one foreign language, thesis/dissertation. *Entrance requirements:* For master's, EXADEP; for doctorate, GRE, master's degree in related field. Additional exam requirements/recommendations for international students: Required—TOEFL. *Faculty research:* Flexible manufacturing cells, materials, statistical methods, environmental prevention, control and evaluation.

Kennesaw State University, College of Science and Mathematics, Program in Applied Statistics, Kennesaw, GA 30144. Offers MSAS. *Program availability:* Part-time, evening/ weekend. *Entrance requirements:* For master's, GRE, minimum GPA of 2.75, resume. Additional exam requirements/recommendations for international students: Required—TOEFL (minimum score 550 paper-based; 80 iBT), IELTS (minimum score 6.5). Electronic applications accepted.

Louisiana State University and Agricultural & Mechanical College, Graduate School, College of Agriculture, Department of Experimental Statistics, Baton Rouge, LA 70803. Offers applied statistics (M App St).

Loyola University Chicago, Graduate School, Department of Mathematics and Statistics, Chicago, IL 60660. Offers applied statistics (MS); mathematics (MS). *Program availability:* Part-time. *Faculty:* 19 full-time (3 women). *Students:* 36 full-time (21 women), 9 part-time (4 women); includes 9 minority (2 Black or African American, non-Hispanic/Latino; 3 Asian, non-Hispanic/Latino; 4 Hispanic/Latino), 18 international. Average age 27. 54 applicants, 91% accepted, 18 enrolled. In 2015, 25 master's awarded. *Entrance requirements:* For master's, GRE General Test. Additional exam requirements/recommendations for international students: Required—TOEFL. *Application deadline:* For fall admission, 8/1 for domestic students; for spring admission, 12/1 for domestic students. Applications are processed on a rolling basis. Application fee: $0. Electronic applications accepted. *Expenses: Tuition, area resident:* Full-time $18,054; part-time $9027 per credit hour. *Required fees:* $832; $284 per credit hour. Part-time tuition and fees vary according to course load, degree level and program. *Financial support:* In 2015–16, 13 students received support, including 6 teaching assistantships with tuition reimbursements available (averaging $10,000 per year); fellowships with tuition reimbursements available, career-related internships or fieldwork, Federal Work-Study, institutionally sponsored loans, and tuition waivers (partial) also available. Financial award application deadline: 3/15. *Faculty research:* Nonlinear analysis and partial differential equations, algebra and combinatorics, knot theory, control theory and engineering, probability and applied statistics. *Total annual research expenditures:* $70,000. *Unit head:* Dr. Anthony Giaquinto, Chair, 773-508-3578, Fax: 773-508-2123, E-mail: agiaqui@luc.edu. *Application contact:* Dr. Rafal Goebel, Graduate Program Director for Mathematics, 773-508-3558, E-mail: rgoebel1@luc.edu.
Website: http://math.luc.edu/

McMaster University, School of Graduate Studies, Faculty of Science, Department of Mathematics and Statistics, Program in Statistics, Hamilton, ON L8S 4M2, Canada. Offers applied statistics (M Sc); medical statistics (M Sc); statistical theory (M Sc). *Degree requirements:* For master's, thesis or alternative. *Entrance requirements:* For master's, honors degree background in mathematics and statistics. Additional exam requirements/recommendations for international students: Required—TOEFL (minimum score 550 paper-based). *Faculty research:* Development of polymer production technology, quality of life in patients who use pharmaceutical agents, mathematical modeling, order statistics from progressively censored samples, nonlinear stochastic model in genetics.

Michigan State University, The Graduate School, College of Natural Science, Department of Statistics and Probability, East Lansing, MI 48824. Offers applied statistics (MS); statistics (MS, PhD). *Entrance requirements:* Additional exam requirements/recommendations for international students: Required—TOEFL. Electronic applications accepted.

New Jersey Institute of Technology, College of Science and Liberal Arts, Newark, NJ 07102. Offers applied mathematics (MS); applied physics (M Sc, PhD); applied statistical models (Certificate); applied statistics (MS); biology (MS, PhD); biostatistics (MS); biostatistics essentials (Certificate); chemistry (MS, PhD); computational biology (MS); environmental science (MS, PhD); history (MA, MAT); materials science and engineering (MS, PhD); mathematical and computational finance (MS); mathematics science (PhD); pharmaceutical chemistry (MS); professional and technical communications (MS); technical common essentials (Certificate). *Program availability:* Part-time, evening/weekend. *Faculty:* 153 full-time (35 women), 100 part-time/adjunct (40 women). *Students:* 212 full-time (82 women), 94 part-time (37 women); includes 72 minority (22 Black or African American, non-Hispanic/Latino; 25 Asian, non-Hispanic/ Latino; 19 Hispanic/Latino; 6 Two or more races, non-Hispanic/Latino), 164 international. Average age 29. 519 applicants, 62% accepted, 104 enrolled. In 2015, 98 master's, 21 doctorates, 3 other advanced degrees awarded. Terminal master's awarded for partial completion of doctoral program. *Degree requirements:* For master's, thesis optional; for doctorate, thesis/dissertation. *Entrance requirements:* For master's, GRE General Test; for doctorate, GRE General Test, minimum graduate GPA of 3.5. Additional exam requirements/recommendations for international students: Required—TOEFL (minimum score 550 paper-based; 79 iBT). *Application deadline:* For fall admission, 6/1 priority date for domestic students, 5/1 priority date for international students; for spring admission, 11/15 priority date for domestic and international students. Applications are processed on a rolling basis. Application fee: $75. Electronic applications accepted. *Expenses:* $28,800 per year non-resident full-time. *Financial support:* In 2015–16, 56 research assistantships with full tuition reimbursements (averaging $17,711 per year), 52 teaching assistantships with full tuition reimbursements (averaging $17,914 per year) were awarded; fellowships with full tuition reimbursements also available. Financial award application deadline: 1/15. *Total annual research expenditures:* $23.1 million. *Unit head:* Dr. Kevin Belfield, Dean, 973-596-3676, Fax: 973-565-0586, E-mail: kevin.d.belfield@njit.edu. *Application contact:* Stephen Eck, Director of Admissions, 973-596-3300, Fax: 973-596-3461,
E-mail: admissions@njit.edu.
Website: http://csla.njit.edu/

New Mexico State University, College of Business, Department of Economics, Applied Statistics and International Business, Las Cruces, NM 88003. Offers applied statistics (MS); economic development (DED); economics (MA); public utility regulation and economics (Graduate Certificate). *Program availability:* Part-time. *Faculty:* 16 full-time (5 women). *Students:* 39 full-time (15 women), 26 part-time (11 women); includes 21 minority (3 Black or African American, non-Hispanic/Latino; 1 Asian, non-Hispanic/ Latino; 17 Hispanic/Latino), 24 international. Average age 35. 70 applicants, 51% accepted, 16 enrolled. In 2015, 15 master's, 3 doctorates, 12 other advanced degrees awarded. Terminal master's awarded for partial completion of doctoral program. *Degree requirements:* For master's, comprehensive exam, thesis or alternative; for doctorate, comprehensive exam, thesis/dissertation, internship. *Entrance requirements:* For master's, minimum GPA of 3.0; for doctorate, appropriate master's degree, minimum GPA of 3.0. Additional exam requirements/recommendations for international students: Required—TOEFL (minimum score 550 paper-based; 79 iBT), IELTS (minimum score 6.5). *Application deadline:* For fall admission, 3/1 priority date for domestic and international students. Applications are processed on a rolling basis. Application fee: $40 ($50 for international students). Electronic applications accepted. *Expenses:* $274.50 per credit hour for in-state students, and all students enrolled in six or fewer credits; $839.30 per credit hour for out-of-state and international students enrolled in at least seven hours. *Financial support:* In 2015–16, 37 students received support, including 1 research assistantship (averaging $8,482 per year), 27 teaching assistantships (averaging $13,471 per year); career-related internships or fieldwork, Federal Work-Study, scholarships/grants, traineeships, health care benefits, and unspecified assistantships also available. Support available to part-time students. Financial award application deadline: 3/1. *Faculty research:* Public utilities, environment, linear models, biological sampling, public policy, economic development, energy, regional economics. *Unit head:* Dr. Richard V. Adkisson, Department Head, 575-646-4988, Fax: 575-646-1915, E-mail: radkisso@nmsu.edu. *Application contact:* 575-646-2113, Fax: 575-646-1915.
Website: http://business.nmsu.edu/departments/economics

New York University, Steinhardt School of Culture, Education, and Human Development, Department of Humanities and Social Sciences in the Professions, Program in Applied Statistics for Social Science Research, New York, NY 10012-1019. Offers MS. *Entrance requirements:* For master's, GRE, statement of purpose, resume/ curriculum vitae, two letters of recommendation, transcripts. Additional exam requirements/recommendations for international students: Required—TOEFL. Electronic applications accepted. *Faculty research:* Causal inference, multi-level models, multivariate analysis, psychometrics, survey research and design.

North Dakota State University, College of Graduate and Interdisciplinary Studies, College of Science and Mathematics, Department of Statistics, Fargo, ND 58102. Offers applied statistics (MS, Certificate); statistics (PhD); MS/MS. *Degree requirements:* For master's, comprehensive exam, thesis; for doctorate, comprehensive exam, thesis/ dissertation. *Entrance requirements:* For master's and doctorate, minimum GPA of 3.0. Additional exam requirements/recommendations for international students: Required—TOEFL (minimum score 550 paper-based; 79 iBT). Electronic applications accepted. *Faculty research:* Nonparametric statistics, survival analysis, multivariate analysis, distribution theory, inference modeling, biostatistics.

Northern Arizona University, Graduate College, College of Engineering, Forestry, and Natural Sciences, Department of Mathematics and Statistics, Flagstaff, AZ 86011. Offers applied statistics (Certificate); mathematics (MS); mathematics education (MS); statistics (MS). *Program availability:* Part-time. *Degree requirements:* For master's, comprehensive exam (for some programs), thesis (for some programs). *Entrance requirements:* For master's, minimum GPA of 3.0. Additional exam requirements/ recommendations for international students: Required—TOEFL (minimum score 550 paper-based; 80 iBT), IELTS (minimum score 7). *Application deadline:* For fall admission, 3/15 priority date for domestic and international students; for spring admission, 10/15 priority date for domestic and international students. Applications are processed on a rolling basis. Application fee: $65. Electronic applications accepted. *Expenses: Tuition, area resident:* Full-time $8710. Tuition, nonresident: full-time $20,350. *Required fees:* $896. *Financial support:* Teaching assistantships with full tuition reimbursements, Federal Work-Study, scholarships/grants, health care benefits, tuition waivers (full and partial), and unspecified assistantships available. Financial award applicants required to submit FAFSA. *Faculty research:* Topology, statistics, groups, ring theory, number theory. *Unit head:* Dr. Michael J. Falk, Chair, 928-523-6891, Fax: 928-523-5847, E-mail: michael.falk@nau.edu. *Application contact:* Melinda Miller, Administrative Assistant, 928-523-6228, Fax: 928-523-5847,
E-mail: math.grad@nau.edu.
Website: http://nau.edu/CEFNS/NatSci/Math/

Oakland University, Graduate Study and Lifelong Learning, College of Arts and Sciences, Department of Mathematics and Statistics, Program in Applied Statistics, Rochester, MI 48309-4401. Offers MS. *Program availability:* Part-time, evening/ weekend. *Students:* 7 full-time (2 women), 6 part-time (4 women); includes 2 minority (both Asian, non-Hispanic/Latino), 1 international. Average age 33. 13 applicants, 31% accepted, 4 enrolled. In 2015, 3 master's awarded. *Entrance requirements:* For master's, minimum GPA of 3.0. Additional exam requirements/recommendations for international students: Required—TOEFL (minimum score 550 paper-based). *Application deadline:* For fall admission, 7/15 priority date for domestic students, 5/1 priority date for international students; for winter admission, 12/1 priority date for domestic students, 9/1 priority date for international students; for spring admission, 3/15 priority date for domestic students. Applications are processed on a rolling basis. Application fee: $0. Electronic applications accepted. *Expenses:* Contact institution. *Financial support:* Career-related internships or fieldwork and tuition waivers (full) available. Financial award application deadline: 3/1; financial award applicants required to submit FAFSA. *Unit head:* Dr. Laszlo Liptak, Chair, Department of Mathematics and Statistics, 248-370-4054, Fax: 248-370-4184, E-mail: liptak@oakland.edu. *Application contact:* Dr. Meir Shillor, Coordinator, Graduate Programs, 248-370-3439, Fax: 248-370-4184, E-mail: shillor@oakland.edu.

Penn State University Park, Graduate School, Eberly College of Science, Department of Statistics, University Park, PA 16802. Offers applied statistics (MAS); statistics (MA, MS, PhD). *Unit head:* Dr. Douglas R. Cavener, Dean, 814-865-9591, Fax: 814-865-3634. *Application contact:* Lori Stania, Director, Graduate Student Services, 814-865-1795, Fax: 814-865-4627, E-mail: l-gswww@lists.psu.edu.
Website: http://stat.psu.edu/

Purdue University, Graduate School, College of Science, Department of Statistics, West Lafayette, IN 47909. Offers applied statistics (MS); computational finance (MS); computational science and engineering (MS); statistics (PhD). *Program availability:* Part-time. *Faculty:* 71 full-time (22 women). *Students:* 102 full-time (36 women); includes 71 minority (8 Black or African American, non-Hispanic/Latino; 1 American Indian or Alaska Native, non-Hispanic/Latino; 55 Asian, non-Hispanic/Latino; 4 Hispanic/Latino; 3 Native Hawaiian or other Pacific Islander, non-Hispanic/Latino). Average age 25. 505 applicants, 9% accepted, 29 enrolled. In 2015, 29 master's, 14 doctorates awarded. Terminal master's awarded for partial completion of doctoral program. *Degree requirements:* For master's, comprehensive exam; for doctorate, thesis/dissertation, qualifying exams. *Entrance requirements:* For master's and doctorate, GRE General Test. Additional exam requirements/recommendations for international students: Required—TOEFL (minimum score 80 iBT); Recommended—IELTS (minimum score 7). *Application deadline:* For fall admission, 1/15 for domestic and international students; for spring admission, 10/15 for domestic students, 9/15 for international students. Application fee: $60 ($75 for international students). Electronic applications accepted. *Expenses:* Contact institution. *Financial support:* In 2015–16, 5 students received support, including 5 fellowships with full tuition reimbursements available (averaging $20,000 per year), research assistantships with full tuition reimbursements available (averaging $20,000 per year), 10 teaching assistantships with full tuition reimbursements available (averaging $20,000 per year); career-related internships or fieldwork and unspecified assistantships also available. Support available to part-time students. Financial award application deadline: 1/15; financial award applicants required to submit FAFSA. *Faculty research:* Nonparametric models, computational finance, design of experiments, probability theory, bioinformatics. *Unit head:* Dr. Hao Zhang, Head, 765-494-3141, Fax: 765-494-0558, E-mail: zhanghao@purdue.edu. *Application contact:* Anna Hook, Graduate Coordinator, 765-494-5794, Fax: 765-494-0558,
E-mail: hook6@purdue.edu.
Website: http://www.stat.purdue.edu/

Rochester Institute of Technology, Graduate Enrollment Services, College of Science, School of Mathematical Sciences, Advanced Certificate Program in Applied Statistics, Rochester, NY 14623-5603. Offers Advanced Certificate. *Program availability:* Part-time, evening/weekend, 100% online. *Students:* 1 (woman) full-time, 2 part-time (both women). *Entrance requirements:* For degree, GRE, minimum GPA of 3.0 (recommended). Additional exam requirements/recommendations for international students: Required—PTE (minimum score 58), TOEFL (minimum score 550 paper-based, 79 iBT) or IELTS (minimum score 6.5). *Application deadline:* Applications are processed on a rolling basis. Application fee: $60. Electronic applications accepted. *Expenses: Tuition, area resident:* Full-time $41,084; part-time $1742 per credit hour. *Required fees:* $274. Tuition and fees vary according to course load and program. *Financial support:* In 2015–16, 1 student received support. Scholarships/grants available. Support available to part-time students. Financial award applicants required to submit FAFSA. *Unit head:* Dr. Peter Bajorski, Director, 585-475-7889,
E-mail: pxbeqa@rit.edu. *Application contact:* Diane Ellison, Associate Vice President, Graduate Enrollment Services, 585-475-2229, Fax: 585-475-7164,
E-mail: gradinfo@rit.edu.

Rochester Institute of Technology, Graduate Enrollment Services, College of Science, School of Mathematical Sciences, MS Program in Applied Statistics, Rochester, NY 14623-5603. Offers MS. *Program availability:* Part-time, evening/weekend, 100% online, blended/hybrid learning. *Students:* 29 full-time (10 women), 47 part-time (21 women); includes 14 minority (1 Black or African American, non-Hispanic/Latino; 8 Asian, non-Hispanic/Latino; 1 Hispanic/Latino; 4 Two or more races, non-Hispanic/Latino), 21 international. Average age 30. 67 applicants, 43% accepted, 14 enrolled. In 2015, 20 master's awarded. *Degree requirements:* For master's, thesis or alternative, capstone. *Entrance requirements:* For master's, minimum GPA of 3.0 (recommended). Additional exam requirements/recommendations for international students: Required—PTE (minimum score 58), TOEFL (minimum score 550 paper-based, 79 iBT) or IELTS (minimum score 6.5). *Application deadline:* Applications are processed on a rolling basis. Application fee: $60. Electronic applications accepted. *Expenses: Tuition, area resident:* Full-time $41,084; part-time $1742 per credit hour. *Required fees:* $274. Tuition and fees vary according to course load and program. *Financial support:* In 2015–16, 40 students received support. Research assistantships with partial tuition reimbursements available, teaching assistantships with partial tuition reimbursements available, career-related internships or fieldwork, scholarships/grants, and unspecified assistantships available. Support available to part-time students. Financial award applicants required to submit FAFSA. *Faculty research:* Enterprising culture, corporate tax avoidance, deaf entrepreneurship, digital and accessibility entrepreneurship; sentiment and big data analytics; global Internet marketing; international accounting and auditing; integration of technology, business, and design thinking. *Unit head:* Dr. Peter Bajorski, Director, 585-475-7889, E-mail: pxbeqa@rit.edu. *Application contact:* Diane Ellison, Associate Vice President, Graduate Enrollment Services, 585-475-2229, Fax: 585-475-7164, E-mail: gradinfo@rit.edu.

Rutgers University–New Brunswick, Graduate School-New Brunswick, Program in Statistics, Piscataway, NJ 08854-8097. Offers applied statistics (MS); biostatistics (MS); data mining (MS); quality and productivity management (MS); statistics (MS, PhD). *Program availability:* Part-time. Terminal master's awarded for partial completion of doctoral program. *Degree requirements:* For master's, comprehensive exam, essay, exam, non-thesis essay paper; for doctorate, one foreign language, thesis/dissertation, qualifying oral and written exams. *Entrance requirements:* For master's, GRE General Test; for doctorate, GRE General Test, GRE Subject Test (recommended). Additional exam requirements/recommendations for international students: Required—TOEFL (minimum score 550 paper-based). Electronic applications accepted. *Faculty research:* Probability, decision theory, linear models, multivariate statistics, statistical computing.

St. Cloud State University, School of Graduate Studies, College of Science and Engineering, Program in Applied Statistics, St. Cloud, MN 56301-4498. Offers MS.

Stevens Institute of Technology, Graduate School, Charles V. Schaefer Jr. School of Engineering, Department of Mathematical Sciences, Program in Applied Statistics, Hoboken, NJ 07030. Offers Certificate. *Program availability:* Part-time, evening/weekend. *Entrance requirements:* Additional exam requirements/recommendations for international students: Required—TOEFL (minimum score 74 iBT). *Application deadline:* For fall admission, 6/1 for domestic students, 4/15 for international students; for spring admission, 11/30 for domestic students, 11/1 for international students. Applications are processed on a rolling basis. Application fee: $60. Electronic applications accepted. *Expenses: Tuition, area resident:* Full-time $32,200; part-time $1450 per credit. *Required fees:* $1150; $550 per unit. $275 per semester. *Financial support:* Fellowships, research assistantships, teaching assistantships, career-related internships or fieldwork, Federal Work-Study, scholarships/grants, and unspecified assistantships available. Financial award application deadline: 2/15; financial award applicants required to submit FAFSA. *Unit head:* Dr. Alexei Miasnikov, Director, 201-216-8598, Fax: 201-216-8321, E-mail: amiasnik@stevens.edu. *Application contact:* Graduate Admission, 888-783-8367, Fax: 888-511-1306,
E-mail: graduate@stevens.edu.

Syracuse University, College of Arts and Sciences, MS Program in Applied Statistics, Syracuse, NY 13244. Offers applied statistics (MS). *Program availability:* Part-time. *Students:* Average age 23. *Entrance requirements:* For master's, GRE General Test, letters of recommendation, personal statement, resume. Additional exam requirements/recommendations for international students: Required—TOEFL (minimum score 100 iBT). *Application deadline:* For fall admission, 3/15 for domestic and international students. Applications are processed on a rolling basis. Application fee: $75. Electronic applications accepted. *Expenses: Tuition, area resident:* Full-time $25,974; part-time $1443 per credit hour. *Required fees:* $802; $50 per course. Tuition and fees vary according to course load and program. *Financial support:* Fellowships with full tuition reimbursements, teaching assistantships with tuition reimbursements, and tuition waivers available. Financial award application deadline: 1/1; financial award applicants required to submit FAFSA. *Faculty research:* Cutting-edge statistical methodologies, statistical theory, applied statistics, mathematical Statistics, statistical consulting. *Unit head:* Dr. Pinyuen Chen, Graduate Contact, 315-443-1577, E-mail: pinchen@syr.edu. *Application contact:* Cassidy Perreault, Administrative Specialist, 315-443-4322,
E-mail: clperrea@syr.edu.
Website: http://thecollege.syr.edu/students/undergraduate/interdisciplinary/applied-statistics/graduate_study.html

Teachers College, Columbia University, Department of Human Development, New York, NY 10027-6696. Offers applied psychology: measurement and evaluation (ME, Ed D, PhD); applied statistics (MS, ND); cognitive studies in education (MA, Ed D, PhD); developmental psychology (MA, Ed D, PhD); educational psychology-human cognition and learning (Ed M, MA, Ed D, PhD); educational psychology: cognitive behavior development analysis (ME); learning analytics (MS); measurement, evaluation, and statistics (MA, MS, Ed D, PhD). *Program availability:* Part-time. *Students:* 140 full-time (97 women), 167 part-time (125 women); includes 170 minority (18 Black or African American, non-Hispanic/Latino; 123 Asian, non-Hispanic/Latino; 22 Hispanic/Latino; 7 Two or more races, non-Hispanic/Latino), 51 international. *Expenses: Tuition, area resident:* Part-time $1454 per credit. *Required fees:* $428 per semester. One-time fee: $475 full-time. Full-time tuition and fees vary according to course load. *Unit head:* Prof. Matthew S. Johnson, Chair, 212-678-3882, Fax: 212-678-3837,
E-mail: johnson@tc.columbia.edu. *Application contact:* David Estrella, Director of Admission, 212-678-3305, E-mail: estrella@tc.columbia.edu.

The University of Alabama, Graduate School, Manderson Graduate School of Business, Department of Information Systems, Statistics, and Management Science, Program in Applied Statistics, Tuscaloosa, AL 35487. Offers MS, PhD. *Program availability:* Part-time. *Students:* 22 full-time (11 women), 3 part-time (1 woman); includes 4 minority (3 Black or African American, non-Hispanic/Latino; 1 Asian, non-Hispanic/Latino), 13 international. Average age 28. 62 applicants, 45% accepted, 11 enrolled. In 2015, 15 master's, 2 doctorates awarded. Terminal master's awarded for partial completion of doctoral program. *Degree requirements:* For master's, comprehensive exam; for doctorate, comprehensive exam, thesis/dissertation. *Entrance requirements:* For master's and doctorate, GMAT or GRE, 3 semesters of calculus and linear algebra. Additional exam requirements/recommendations for international students: Required—TOEFL (minimum score 550 paper-based; 100 iBT), IELTS (minimum score 6.5). *Application deadline:* For fall admission, 1/15 priority date for domestic and international students; for spring admission, 10/15 priority date for domestic and international students. Applications are processed on a rolling basis. Application fee: $50 ($60 for international students). Electronic applications accepted. *Expenses:* Tuition, state resident: full-time $10,170. Tuition, nonresident: full-time $25,950. *Financial support:* In 2015–16, 9 students received support, including 7 teaching assistantships with tuition reimbursements available (averaging $13,500 per year); scholarships/grants and health care benefits also available. Financial award application deadline: 1/15. *Faculty research:* Data mining, regression analysis, statistical quality control, nonparametric statistics, design of experiments. *Unit head:* Dr. Charles R. Sox, Professor and Department Head, 205-348-8992, E-mail: csox@cba.ua.edu. *Application contact:* Sarah Schmidt, Program Assistant, 205-348-8904, E-mail: sschmidt@cba.ua.edu.
Website: http://www.cba.ua.edu/stats

University of Arkansas at Little Rock, Graduate School, College of Arts, Letters, and Sciences, Department of Mathematics and Statistics, Little Rock, AR 72204-1099. Offers applied statistics (Graduate Certificate); mathematical sciences (MS). *Program availability:* Part-time, evening/weekend. *Degree requirements:* For master's, comprehensive exam. *Entrance requirements:* For master's, GRE General Test, GRE Subject Test, minimum GPA of 2.7, previous course work in advanced mathematics. *Expenses:* Tuition, state resident: part-time $300 per credit hour. Tuition, nonresident: part-time $690 per credit hour. *Required fees:* $100 per credit hour. One-time fee: $40 full-time.

University of California, Riverside, Graduate Division, Department of Statistics, Riverside, CA 92521-0219. Offers applied statistics (PhD); statistics (MS). Terminal master's awarded for partial completion of doctoral program. *Degree requirements:* For master's, comprehensive exam; for doctorate, comprehensive exam, thesis/dissertation. *Entrance requirements:* For master's, GRE (minimum score 300), strong background in statistics and sufficient training in mathematics or upper-division statistical courses to meet deficiencies; minimum GPA of 3.0; for doctorate, GRE (minimum score 300), BS in statistics, computer science, mathematics, or other quantitatively-based discipline; minimum GPA of 3.25. Additional exam requirements/recommendations for international students: Required—TOEFL (minimum score 550 paper-based; 80 iBT); Recommended—IELTS. Electronic applications accepted. *Faculty research:* Design and analysis of gene expression experiments using DNA microarrays, statistical design and analysis of experiments, linear models, probability models and statistical inference, SNP/SFP discovery using DNA microarray, genetic mapping.

Applied Statistics

University of California, Santa Barbara, Graduate Division, College of Letters and Sciences, Division of Mathematics, Life, and Physical Sciences, Department of Statistics and Applied Probability, Santa Barbara, CA 93106-3110. Offers bioengineering (PhD); financial mathematics and statistics (PhD); quantitative methods in the social sciences (PhD); statistics (MA), including applied statistics, mathematical statistics; statistics and applied probability (PhD); MA/PhD. *Faculty:* 11 full-time (2 women), 8 part-time/adjunct (0 women). *Students:* 65 full-time (32 women); includes 8 minority (1 Black or African American, non-Hispanic/Latino; 5 Asian, non-Hispanic/Latino; 1 Hispanic/Latino; 1 Native Hawaiian or other Pacific Islander, non-Hispanic/Latino), 47 international. Average age 27. 452 applicants, 9% accepted, 12 enrolled. In 2015, 18 master's, 8 doctorates awarded. Terminal master's awarded for partial completion of doctoral program. *Degree requirements:* For master's, comprehensive exam, thesis optional; for doctorate, comprehensive exam, thesis/dissertation. *Entrance requirements:* For master's and doctorate, GRE General Test. Additional exam requirements/recommendations for international students: Required—TOEFL (minimum score 550 paper-based; 80 iBT), IELTS (minimum score 7). *Application deadline:* For fall admission, 12/15 priority date for domestic students, 12/1 priority date for international students; for winter admission, 11/1 priority date for domestic and international students; for spring admission, 2/1 priority date for domestic and international students. Application fee: $90 ($110 for international students). Electronic applications accepted. *Financial support:* In 2015–16, 23 students received support, including 6 fellowships with full tuition reimbursements available (averaging $11,285 per year), 1 research assistantship with tuition reimbursement available (averaging $2,790 per year), 28 teaching assistantships with partial tuition reimbursements available (averaging $14,557 per year); Federal Work-Study, scholarships/grants, and health care benefits also available. Financial award application deadline: 12/15; financial award applicants required to submit FAFSA. *Faculty research:* Bayesian inference, financial mathematics, stochastic processes, environmental statistics, biostatistical modeling. *Total annual research expenditures:* $139,480. *Unit head:* Dr. John Hsu, Chair, 805-893-4055, E-mail: hsu@pstat.ucsb.edu. *Application contact:* Angelina M. Toporov, Graduate Program Assistant, 805-893-2129, Fax: 805-893-2334,
E-mail: toporov@pstat.ucsb.edu.
Website: http://www.pstat.ucsb.edu/

University of Chicago, Graham School of Continuing Liberal and Professional Studies, Program in Analytics, Chicago, IL 60637. Offers M Sc. *Program availability:* Part-time. *Degree requirements:* For master's, capstone project. *Entrance requirements:* For master's, baccalaureate degree from accredited college or university, three letters of recommendation, official transcripts, resume or curriculum vitae, interview. Additional exam requirements/recommendations for international students: Required—TOEFL (minimum score 104 iBT), IELTS (minimum score 7). Electronic applications accepted.

University of Colorado Denver, College of Liberal Arts and Sciences, Department of Mathematical and Statistical Sciences, Denver, CO 80217. Offers applied mathematics (MS, PhD), including applied mathematics, applied probability (MS), applied statistics (MS), computational biology, computational mathematics (PhD), discrete mathematics, finite geometry (PhD), mathematics education (PhD), mathematics of engineering and science (MS), numerical analysis, operations research (MS), optimization and operations research (PhD), probability (PhD), statistics (PhD). *Program availability:* Part-time. *Faculty:* 18 full-time (4 women), 5 part-time/adjunct (0 women). *Students:* 48 full-time (16 women), 15 part-time (6 women); includes 7 minority (1 Black or African American, non-Hispanic/Latino; 2 Asian, non-Hispanic/Latino; 3 Hispanic/Latino; 1 Two or more races, non-Hispanic/Latino), 12 international. Average age 32. 105 applicants, 70% accepted, 21 enrolled. In 2015, 10 master's, 3 doctorates awarded. *Degree requirements:* For master's, comprehensive exam, thesis optional, 30 hours of course work with minimum GPA of 3.0; for doctorate, comprehensive exam, thesis/dissertation, 42 hours of course work with minimum GPA of 3.25. *Entrance requirements:* For master's, GRE General Test; GRE Subject Test in math (recommended), 30 hours of course work in mathematics (24 of which must be upper-division mathematics), bachelor's degree with minimum GPA of 3.0; for doctorate, GRE General Test; GRE Subject Test in math (recommended), 30 hours of course work in mathematics (24 of which must be upper-division mathematics), master's degree with minimum GPA of 3.25. Additional exam requirements/recommendations for international students: Required—TOEFL (minimum score 537 paper-based; 75 iBT); Recommended—IELTS (minimum score 6.5). *Application deadline:* For fall admission, 4/1 for domestic and international students; for spring admission, 10/1 for domestic and international students; for summer admission, 4/1 for domestic and international students. Application fee: $50 ($75 for international students). Electronic applications accepted. *Financial support:* In 2015–16, 46 students received support. Fellowships with partial tuition reimbursements available, research assistantships with full tuition reimbursements available, teaching assistantships with full tuition reimbursements available, Federal Work-Study, institutionally sponsored loans, scholarships/grants, and traineeships available. Financial award application deadline: 4/1; financial award applicants required to submit FAFSA. *Faculty research:* Computational mathematics, computational biology, discrete mathematics and geometry, probability and statistics, optimization. *Unit head:* Dr. Michael Ferrara, Graduate Chair, 303-315-1705,
E-mail: michael.ferrara@ucdenver.edu. *Application contact:* Julie Blunck, Program Assistant, 303-315-1743, E-mail: julie.blunck@ucdenver.edu.
Website: http://www.ucdenver.edu/academics/colleges/CLAS/Departments/math/Pages/MathStats.aspx

University of Guelph, Graduate Studies, College of Physical and Engineering Science, Department of Mathematics and Statistics, Guelph, ON N1G 2W1, Canada. Offers applied mathematics (PhD); applied statistics (PhD); mathematics and statistics (M Sc). *Program availability:* Part-time. *Degree requirements:* For master's, thesis (for some programs); for doctorate, thesis/dissertation. *Entrance requirements:* For master's, minimum B- average during previous 2 years of course work; for doctorate, minimum B average. Additional exam requirements/recommendations for international students: Required—TOEFL (minimum score 550 paper-based; 89 iBT), IELTS (minimum score 6.5). *Faculty research:* Dynamical systems, mathematical biology, numerical analysis, linear and nonlinear models, reliability and bioassay.

University of Illinois at Urbana–Champaign, Graduate College, College of Liberal Arts and Sciences, Department of Statistics, Champaign, IL 61820. Offers analytics (MS); applied statistics (MS); statistics (MS, PhD).

The University of Kansas, University of Kansas Medical Center, School of Medicine, Department of Biostatistics, Kansas City, KS 66160. Offers applied statistics and analytics (MS); biostatistics (MS, PhD, Graduate Certificate); statistical applications (Graduate Certificate). *Faculty:* 16. *Students:* 25 full-time (7 women), 13 part-time (5 women); includes 9 minority (3 Black or African American, non-Hispanic/Latino; 5 Asian, non-Hispanic/Latino; 1 Two or more races, non-Hispanic/Latino), 13 international. Average age 31. 52 applicants, 94% accepted, 18 enrolled. In 2015, 4 master's, 2 doctorates awarded. *Degree requirements:* For master's, comprehensive exam; for doctorate, comprehensive exam, thesis/dissertation. *Entrance requirements:* For master's, GRE, coursework in calculus, computer programming, linear algebra, differential equations, and numerical analysis; for doctorate, master's degree. Additional exam requirements/recommendations for international students: Required—TOEFL. Application fee: $60. Electronic applications accepted. *Expenses:* Contact institution. *Financial support:* Research assistantships with full tuition reimbursements, scholarships/grants, traineeships, and unspecified assistantships available. Financial award application deadline: 3/1; financial award applicants required to submit FAFSA. *Faculty research:* Biostatistics, clinical trials. *Total annual research expenditures:* $774,141. *Unit head:* Dr. Matthew Mayo, Professor and Chair, 913-588-4735 Ext. 913, Fax: 913-588-0252, E-mail: mmayo@kumc.edu. *Application contact:* Dr. Jo A. Wick, Assistant Director of Graduate Education, 913-588-4790, Fax: 913-588-0252,
E-mail: jwick@kumc.edu.
Website: http://www.kumc.edu/school-of-medicine/department-of-biostatistics.html

University of Memphis, Graduate School, College of Arts and Sciences, Department of Mathematical Sciences, Memphis, TN 38152. Offers applied mathematics (MS); applied statistics (PhD); bioinformatics (MS); computer sciences (MS); statistics (MS). *Program availability:* Part-time. *Faculty:* 18 full-time (7 women). *Students:* 36 full-time (9 women), 22 part-time (9 women); includes 15 minority (9 Black or African American, non-Hispanic/Latino; 3 Asian, non-Hispanic/Latino; 3 Hispanic/Latino), 17 international. Average age 34. 50 applicants, 92% accepted, 12 enrolled. In 2015, 10 master's, 9 doctorates awarded. Terminal master's awarded for partial completion of doctoral program. *Degree requirements:* For master's, comprehensive exam; for doctorate, one foreign language, thesis/dissertation, oral exams. *Entrance requirements:* For master's and doctorate, GRE General Test, minimum GPA of 2.5. Additional exam requirements/recommendations for international students: Required—TOEFL (minimum score 550 paper-based). *Application deadline:* For fall admission, 8/1 for domestic students, 5/1 priority date for international students; for spring admission, 12/1 for domestic students, 9/1 priority date for international students. Applications are processed on a rolling basis. Application fee: $35 ($60 for international students). Electronic applications accepted. *Financial support:* In 2015–16, 22 students received support. Fellowships with full tuition reimbursements available, research assistantships with full tuition reimbursements available, teaching assistantships with full tuition reimbursements available, career-related internships or fieldwork, Federal Work-Study, scholarships/grants, and unspecified assistantships available. Financial award application deadline: 2/15; financial award applicants required to submit FAFSA. *Faculty research:* Combinatorics, ergodic theory, graph theory, Ramsey theory, applied statistics. *Unit head:* Dr. Irena Lasiecka, Chairman, 901-678-2482, Fax: 901-678-2480, E-mail: lasiecka@memphis.edu. *Application contact:* Dr. Fernanda Botelho, Coordinator of Graduate Studies, 901-678-3131, Fax: 901-678-2480, E-mail: mbotelho@memphis.edu.
Website: http://www.MSCI.memphis.edu/

University of Michigan, Rackham Graduate School, College of Literature, Science, and the Arts, Department of Statistics, Ann Arbor, MI 48109. Offers applied statistics (MS); statistics (AM, PhD). *Faculty:* 20 full-time (4 women). *Students:* 156 full-time (62 women); includes 122 minority (3 Black or African American, non-Hispanic/Latino; 115 Asian, non-Hispanic/Latino; 4 Hispanic/Latino). Average age 27. 960 applicants, 20% accepted, 59 enrolled. In 2015, 35 master's, 9 doctorates awarded. Terminal master's awarded for partial completion of doctoral program. *Degree requirements:* For master's, thesis; for doctorate, thesis/dissertation, oral defense of dissertation, preliminary exam. *Entrance requirements:* For master's and doctorate, GRE General Test. Additional exam requirements/recommendations for international students: Required—TOEFL (minimum score 560 paper-based; 84 iBT), IELTS (minimum score 6.5). *Application deadline:* For fall admission, 12/31 priority date for domestic and international students. Applications are processed on a rolling basis. Application fee: $75 ($90 for international students). Electronic applications accepted. *Expenses:* $40,892 per year tuition and fees (for master's program). *Financial support:* In 2015–16, 83 students received support, including 12 fellowships with full tuition reimbursements available (averaging $25,000 per year), 27 research assistantships with full tuition reimbursements available (averaging $19,000 per year), 41 teaching assistantships with full tuition reimbursements available (averaging $19,000 per year); career-related internships or fieldwork, Federal Work-Study, institutionally sponsored loans, scholarships/grants, health care benefits, and unspecified assistantships also available. Financial award application deadline: 12/31. *Faculty research:* Reliability and degradation modeling, biological and legal applications, bioinformatics, statistical computing, covariance estimation. *Unit head:* Prof. Xuming He, Chair, 734-647-8192,
E-mail: statchair@umich.edu. *Application contact:* Judy McDonald, Graduate Program Coordinator, 734-763-3520, Fax: 734-763-4676,
E-mail: stat-grad-coordinator@umich.edu.
Website: http://www.lsa.umich.edu/stats/

University of Northern Colorado, Graduate School, College of Education and Behavioral Sciences, Department of Applied Statistics and Research Methods, Greeley, CO 80639. Offers MS, PhD. *Program availability:* Part-time. *Degree requirements:* For master's, comprehensive exam; for doctorate, comprehensive exam, thesis/dissertation. *Entrance requirements:* For master's, 3 letters of reference; for doctorate, GRE General Test, 3 letters of reference. Electronic applications accepted.

University of Notre Dame, Graduate School, College of Science, Department of Applied and Computational Mathematics and Statistics, Notre Dame, IN 46556. Offers applied and computational mathematics and statistics (PhD); applied statistics (MS); computational finance (MS).

University of Pittsburgh, Dietrich School of Arts and Sciences, Department of Statistics, Pittsburgh, PA 15260. Offers applied statistics (MA, MS); statistics (MA, MS, PhD). *Program availability:* Part-time. *Faculty:* 11 full-time (3 women), 5 part-time/adjunct (3 women). *Students:* 35 full-time (12 women); includes 21 minority (1 Black or African American, non-Hispanic/Latino; 20 Asian, non-Hispanic/Latino). Average age 26. 324 applicants, 9% accepted, 14 enrolled. In 2015, 13 master's, 8 doctorates awarded. Terminal master's awarded for partial completion of doctoral program. *Degree requirements:* For master's, comprehensive exam, thesis (for some programs); for doctorate, comprehensive exam, thesis/dissertation. *Entrance requirements:* For master's and doctorate, 3 semesters of calculus, 1 semester of linear algebra, 1 year of mathematical statistics. Additional exam requirements/recommendations for international students: Required—TOEFL (minimum score 90 iBT), IELTS, GRE. *Application deadline:* For fall admission, 1/15 priority date for domestic and international students; for spring admission, 10/1 priority date for domestic and international students. Application fee: $50. Electronic applications accepted. *Expenses:* $21,260 per year in-state, $34,944 per year out-of-state. *Financial support:* In 2015–16, 23 students received support, including 3 fellowships with full tuition reimbursements available (averaging $18,250 per year), 4 research assistantships with full tuition reimbursements available (averaging $17,800 per year), 12 teaching assistantships with full tuition reimbursements available (averaging $17,560 per year); scholarships/grants and health care benefits also available. Financial award application deadline: 1/15. *Faculty research:* Multivariate analysis, time series, quantile association analysis, stochastic models, high dimensional statistical inference. *Total annual research expenditures:* $347,794. *Unit head:* Dr. Allan R. Sampson, Acting Chair, 412-624-8372, Fax: 412-648-8814, E-mail: asampson@pitt.edu. *Application contact:* Dr. Yu Cheng, Director of Graduate Studies, 412-624-1851, Fax: 412-648-8814, E-mail: yucheng@pitt.edu.
Website: http://www.stat.pitt.edu/

University of South Carolina, The Graduate School, College of Arts and Sciences, Department of Statistics, Columbia, SC 29208. Offers applied statistics (CAS); industrial statistics (MIS); statistics (MS, PhD). *Program availability:* Part-time, evening/weekend, online learning. Terminal master's awarded for partial completion of doctoral program. *Degree requirements:* For master's, thesis; for doctorate, comprehensive exam, thesis/dissertation. *Entrance requirements:* For master's, GRE General Test or GMAT, 2 years of work experience (MIS); for doctorate, GRE General Test; for CAS, GRE General Test or GMAT. Additional exam requirements/recommendations for international students: Required—TOEFL (minimum score 600 paper-based; 100 iBT). Electronic applications accepted. *Expenses:* Contact institution. *Faculty research:* Reliability, environmentrics, statistics computing, psychometrics, bioinformatics.

The University of Tennessee at Chattanooga, Program in Mathematics, Chattanooga, TN 37403-2598. Offers applied mathematics (MS); applied statistics (MS); mathematics (MS); mathematics education (MS); preprofessional (MS). *Program availability:* Part-time. *Faculty:* 8 full-time (1 woman). *Students:* 14 full-time (4 women), 3 part-time (2 women); includes 4 minority (1 Asian, non-Hispanic/Latino; 2 Hispanic/Latino; 1 Two or more races, non-Hispanic/Latino), 1 international. Average age 27. In 2015, 7 master's awarded. *Entrance requirements:* For master's, two letters of recommendation. Additional exam requirements/recommendations for international students: Required—TOEFL (minimum score 61 iBT), IELTS (minimum score 5.5). *Application deadline:* For fall admission, 6/13 for domestic students, 6/1 for international students; for spring admission, 10/15 for domestic students, 10/1 for international students. Applications are processed on a rolling basis. Application fee: $30 ($35 for international students). Electronic applications accepted. *Expenses:* Tuition, state resident: full-time $7938; part-time $441 per credit hour. Tuition, nonresident: full-time $24,056; part-time $1336 per credit hour. *Required fees:* $1732; $253 per credit hour. *Financial support:* Research assistantships available. Financial award applicants required to submit FAFSA. *Unit head:* Dr. Francesco Barioli, Graduate Program Coordinator, 423-425-2198, E-mail: francesco-barioli@utc.edu. *Application contact:* Dr. J. Randy Walker, Interim Dean of Graduate Studies, 423-425-4478, Fax: 423-425-5223,
E-mail: randy-walker@utc.edu.
Website: http://www.utc.edu/Academic/Mathematics/

The University of Texas at San Antonio, College of Business, Department of Management Science and Statistics, San Antonio, TX 78249-0617. Offers applied statistics (MS, PhD); management science (MBA). *Accreditation:* AACSB. *Program availability:* Part-time, evening/weekend. *Faculty:* 14 full-time (2 women), 2 part-time/adjunct (0 women). *Students:* 41 full-time (15 women), 35 part-time (14 women); includes 20 minority (2 Black or African American, non-Hispanic/Latino; 6 Asian, non-Hispanic/Latino; 12 Hispanic/Latino), 26 international. Average age 31. 91 applicants, 32% accepted, 20 enrolled. In 2015, 21 master's awarded. *Degree requirements:* For master's, comprehensive exam (for some programs), thesis or alternative; for doctorate, comprehensive exam, thesis/dissertation. *Entrance requirements:* For master's, GMAT, minimum of 36 semester credit hours of coursework beyond any hours acquired in the MBA-leveling courses; statement of purpose; for doctorate, GRE, minimum cumulative GPA of 3.3 in the last 60 hours of coursework; transcripts from all colleges and universities attended; curriculum vitae; statement of academic work experiences, interests, and goals; three letters of recommendation; BA, BS, or MS in mathematics, statistics, or closely-related field. Additional exam requirements/recommendations for international students: Required—TOEFL (minimum score 550 paper-based; 79 iBT), IELTS (minimum score 6.5). *Application deadline:* For fall admission, 7/1 for domestic students, 4/1 for international students; for spring admission, 11/1 for domestic students, 9/1 for international students. Applications are processed on a rolling basis. Application fee: $45 ($80 for international students). Electronic applications accepted. *Faculty research:* Statistical signal processing, reliability and life-testing experiments, modeling decompression sickness using survival analysis. *Unit head:* Dr. Raydel Tullous, Chair, 210-458-6345, Fax: 210-458-6350, E-mail: raydel.tullous@utsa.edu. *Application contact:* Katherine Pope, Graduate Assistant of Record, 210-458-7316, Fax: 210-458-4398, E-mail: katherine.pope@utsa.edu.
Website: http://business.utsa.edu/mss/

University of the District of Columbia, College of Arts and Sciences, Program in Applied Statistics, Washington, DC 20008-1175. Offers MS. *Degree requirements:* For master's, internship or thesis.

University of West Florida, College of Science and Engineering, Department of Mathematics and Statistics, Pensacola, FL 32514-5750. Offers applied statistics (MS); mathematical sciences (MS). *Program availability:* Part-time, evening/weekend. *Degree requirements:* For master's, thesis optional. *Entrance requirements:* For master's, GRE (minimum score: verbal 420; quantitative 580), minimum GPA of 3.0; official transcripts. Additional exam requirements/recommendations for international students: Required—TOEFL (minimum score 550 paper-based).

Villanova University, Graduate School of Liberal Arts and Sciences, Department of Mathematical Sciences, Program in Applied Statistics, Villanova, PA 19085-1699. Offers MS. *Program availability:* Part-time, evening/weekend. *Students:* 33 full-time (19 women), 10 part-time (3 women); includes 7 minority (3 Asian, non-Hispanic/Latino; 2 Hispanic/Latino; 2 Two or more races, non-Hispanic/Latino), 4 international. Average age 28. 33 applicants, 88% accepted, 15 enrolled. In 2015, 21 master's awarded. *Degree requirements:* For master's, comprehensive exam. *Entrance requirements:* For master's, GRE, minimum GPA of 3.0, 3 letters of recommendation. Additional exam requirements/recommendations for international students: Required—TOEFL. *Application deadline:* For fall admission, 5/1 for international students; for spring admission, 10/15 for international students. Applications are processed on a rolling basis. Application fee: $50. Electronic applications accepted. *Financial support:* Research assistantships, teaching assistantships, scholarships/grants, and unspecified assistantships available. Financial award applicants required to submit FAFSA. *Unit head:* Dr. Michael Levitan, Director, 610-519-4818.
Website: http://www.villanova.edu/artsci/mathematics/graduate/msapplied/

West Chester University of Pennsylvania, College of Arts and Sciences, Department of Mathematics, West Chester, PA 19383. Offers applied and computational mathematics (MS); applied statistics (MS, Certificate); mathematics (MA, Teaching Certificate); mathematics education (MA). *Program availability:* Part-time, evening/weekend. *Faculty:* 10 full-time (0 women), 2 part-time/adjunct (0 women). *Students:* 11 full-time (5 women), 92 part-time (46 women); includes 19 minority (4 Black or African American, non-Hispanic/Latino; 14 Asian, non-Hispanic/Latino; 1 Hispanic/Latino), 15 international. Average age 30. 68 applicants, 97% accepted, 48 enrolled. In 2015, 34 master's awarded. *Degree requirements:* For master's, thesis (for all but MS in applied mathematics). *Entrance requirements:* For master's, GMAT or GRE General Test (for MA in mathematics), interview (for MA in mathematics); for other advanced degree, GMAT or GRE General Test (for Teaching Certificate). Additional exam requirements/recommendations for international students: Required—TOEFL or IELTS. *Application deadline:* For fall admission, 5/15 for international students; for spring admission, 10/15 for international students. Applications are processed on a rolling basis. Application fee: $50. Electronic applications accepted. *Expenses:* Tuition, state resident: full-time $8460; part-time $470 per credit. Tuition, nonresident: full-time $12,690; part-time $705 per credit. *Required fees:* $2312; $126.75 per credit. Tuition and fees vary according to campus/location and program. *Financial support:* Scholarships/grants and unspecified assistantships available. Financial award application deadline: 2/15; financial award applicants required to submit FAFSA. *Faculty research:* Teachers teaching with technology in service training program, biostatistics, hierarchical linear models, clustered binary outcome date, mathematics biology. *Unit head:* Dr. Peter Glidden, Chair, 610-436-2440, Fax: 610-738-0578, E-mail: pglidden@wcupa.edu. *Application contact:* Dr. Gail Gallitano, Graduate Coordinator, 610-436-2452, Fax: 610-738-0578, E-mail: ggallitano@wcupa.edu.
Website: http://www.wcupa.edu/_academics/sch_cas.mat/

Worcester Polytechnic Institute, Graduate Studies and Research, Department of Mathematical Sciences, Worcester, MA 01609-2280. Offers applied mathematics (MS); applied statistics (MS); financial mathematics (MS); industrial mathematics (MS); mathematical sciences (PhD, Graduate Certificate); mathematics (MME). *Program availability:* Part-time, evening/weekend. *Faculty:* 19 full-time (2 women), 10 part-time/adjunct (1 woman). *Students:* 93 full-time (35 women), 24 part-time (14 women); includes 11 minority (3 Black or African American, non-Hispanic/Latino; 4 Asian, non-Hispanic/Latino; 2 Hispanic/Latino; 2 Two or more races, non-Hispanic/Latino), 71 international. 303 applicants, 57% accepted, 47 enrolled. In 2015, 47 master's awarded. *Degree requirements:* For master's, thesis (for some programs); for doctorate, comprehensive exam, thesis/dissertation. *Entrance requirements:* For master's, GRE General Test, GRE Subject Test in math (recommended), 3 letters of recommendation; for doctorate, GRE General Test, GRE Subject Test (math), 3 letters of recommendation. Additional exam requirements/recommendations for international students: Required—TOEFL (minimum score 563 paper-based; 84 iBT), IELTS (minimum score 7). *Application deadline:* For fall admission, 1/1 priority date for domestic students, 1/1 for international students; for spring admission, 10/1 priority date for domestic students, 10/1 for international students. Applications are processed on a rolling basis. Application fee: $70. Electronic applications accepted. *Financial support:* Research assistantships, teaching assistantships, career-related internships or fieldwork, institutionally sponsored loans, scholarships/grants, and unspecified assistantships available. Financial award application deadline: 1/1; financial award applicants required to submit FAFSA. *Unit head:* Dr. Luca Capogna, Head, 508-831-5241, Fax: 508-831-5824, E-mail: lcapogna@wpi.edu. *Application contact:* Dr. Joseph Fehribach, Graduate Coordinator, 508-831-5241, Fax: 508-831-5824,
E-mail: bach@wpi.edu.
Website: http://www.wpi.edu/academics/math/

Wright State University, School of Graduate Studies, College of Science and Mathematics, Department of Mathematics and Statistics, Program in Applied Statistics, Dayton, OH 45435. Offers MS. *Degree requirements:* For master's, comprehensive exam. *Entrance requirements:* For master's, 1 year of course work in calculus and matrix algebra, previous course work in computer programming and statistics. Additional exam requirements/recommendations for international students: Required—TOEFL. *Faculty research:* Reliability theory, stochastic process, nonparametric statistics, design of experiments, multivariate statistics.

Biomathematics

The College of William and Mary, Faculty of Arts and Sciences, Department of Applied Science, Williamsburg, VA 23187-8795. Offers accelerator science (PhD); applied mathematics (PhD); applied mechanics (PhD); applied robotics (PhD); applied science (MS); atmospheric and environmental science (PhD); computational neuroscience (PhD); interface, thin film and surface science (PhD); lasers and optics (PhD); magnetic resonance (PhD); materials science and engineering (PhD); mathematical and computational biology (PhD); medical imaging (PhD); nanotechnology (PhD); neuroscience (PhD); non-destructive evaluation (PhD); polymer chemistry (PhD); remote sensing (PhD). *Program availability:* Part-time. *Faculty:* 7 full-time (1 woman), 1 part-time/adjunct (0 women). *Students:* 26 full-time (9 women), 3 part-time (1 woman); includes 5 minority (2 Black or African American, non-Hispanic/Latino; 1 Asian, non-Hispanic/Latino; 2 Hispanic/Latino), 12 international. Average age 28. 24 applicants, 46% accepted, 6 enrolled. In 2015, 2 master's, 6 doctorates awarded. Terminal master's awarded for partial completion of doctoral program. *Degree requirements:* For master's, comprehensive exam, thesis; for doctorate, comprehensive exam, thesis/dissertation, 4 core courses. *Entrance requirements:* For master's and doctorate, GRE General Test, GRE Subject Test. Additional exam requirements/recommendations for international students: Required—TOEFL, TWE. *Application deadline:* For fall admission, 2/3 priority date for domestic students, 2/3 for international students; for spring admission, 10/15 priority date for domestic students, 10/14 for international students. Applications are processed on a rolling basis. Application fee: $45. Electronic applications accepted. *Expenses:* $6,550 per semester; $13,100 per year. *Financial support:* Fellowships, research assistantships, teaching assistantships, Federal Work-Study, health care benefits, tuition waivers (full), and unspecified assistantships available. Financial award application deadline: 4/15; financial award applicants required to submit FAFSA. *Faculty research:* Computational biology, non-destructive evaluation, neurophysiology, lasers and optics. *Total annual research expenditures:* $1.7 million. *Unit head:* Dr. Christopher Del Negro, Chair, 757-221-7808, Fax: 757-221-2050, E-mail: cadeln@wm.edu. *Application contact:* Lianne Rios Ashburne, Graduate Program Coordinator, 757-221-2563, Fax: 757-221-2050, E-mail: lrashburne@wm.edu.
Website: http://www.wm.edu/as/appliedscience

North Carolina State University, Graduate School, College of Physical and Mathematical Sciences, Program in Biomathematics, Raleigh, NC 27695. Offers M Biomath, MS, PhD. *Program availability:* Part-time. Terminal master's awarded for partial completion of doctoral program. *Degree requirements:* For master's, thesis (for some programs); for doctorate, thesis/dissertation. *Entrance requirements:* For master's and doctorate, GRE General Test. Additional exam requirements/recommendations for international students: Required—TOEFL. Electronic applications accepted. *Faculty research:* Theory and methods of biological modeling, theoretical biology (genetics, ecology, neurobiology), applied biology (wildlife).

University of California, Los Angeles, David Geffen School of Medicine and Graduate Division, Graduate Programs in Medicine, Department of Biomathematics, Program in Biomathematics, Los Angeles, CA 90095. Offers MS, PhD. *Degree requirements:* For master's, comprehensive exam, thesis; for doctorate, thesis/dissertation, written and oral qualifying exams; 2 quarters of teaching experience. *Entrance requirements:* For master's and doctorate, GRE General and Subject Tests, bachelor's degree; minimum undergraduate GPA of 3.0 (or its equivalent if letter grade system not used). Additional exam requirements/recommendations for international students: Required—TOEFL. Electronic applications accepted.

The University of Texas Health Science Center at Houston, Graduate School of Biomedical Sciences, Program in Biomathematics and Biostatistics, Houston, TX 77225-0036. Offers MS, PhD, MD/PhD. Terminal master's awarded for partial completion of doctoral program. *Degree requirements:* For master's, thesis; for doctorate, thesis/dissertation. *Entrance requirements:* For master's and doctorate, GRE General Test. Additional exam requirements/recommendations for international students: Required—TOEFL. Electronic applications accepted. *Faculty research:* Biostatistics, biomarkers, epidemiology, bioinformatics, computational biology.

Biometry

Cornell University, Graduate School, Graduate Fields of Agriculture and Life Sciences, Field of Biometry, Ithaca, NY 14853-0001. Offers MS, PhD. Terminal master's awarded for partial completion of doctoral program. *Degree requirements:* For master's, thesis; for doctorate, comprehensive exam, thesis/dissertation. *Entrance requirements:* For master's and doctorate, GRE General Test, 2 letters of recommendation. Additional exam requirements/recommendations for international students: Required—TOEFL (minimum score 550 paper-based; 77 iBT). Electronic applications accepted. *Faculty research:* Environmental, agricultural, and biological statistics; biomathematics; modern nonparametric statistics; statistical genetics; computational statistics.

Cornell University, Graduate School, Graduate Fields of Engineering, Field of Statistics, Ithaca, NY 14853-0001. Offers applied statistics (MPS); biometry (MS, PhD); decision theory (MS, PhD); economic and social statistics (MS, PhD); engineering statistics (MS, PhD); experimental design (MS, PhD); mathematical statistics (MS, PhD); probability (MS, PhD); sampling (MS, PhD); statistical computing (MS, PhD); stochastic processes (MS, PhD). Terminal master's awarded for partial completion of doctoral program. *Degree requirements:* For master's, project (MPS), thesis (MS); for doctorate, one foreign language, thesis/dissertation. *Entrance requirements:* For master's, GRE General Test (for MS), 2 letters of recommendation (MS, MPS); for doctorate, GRE General Test, 2 letters of recommendation. Additional exam requirements/recommendations for international students: Required—TOEFL (minimum score 550 paper-based; 77 iBT). Electronic applications accepted. *Faculty research:* Bayesian analysis, survival analysis, nonparametric statistics, stochastic processes, mathematical statistics.

San Diego State University, Graduate and Research Affairs, College of Health and Human Services, Program in Biostatistics and Biometry, San Diego, CA 92182. Offers biometry (MPH). Electronic applications accepted.

University of Wisconsin–Madison, Graduate School, College of Letters and Science, Department of Statistics, Biometry Program, Madison, WI 53706-1380. Offers MS. *Expenses:* Tuition, state resident: full-time $5364. Tuition, nonresident: full-time $12,027. *Required fees:* $571. Tuition and fees vary according to campus/location, program and reciprocity agreements.

Biostatistics

American University of Beirut, Graduate Programs, Faculty of Health Sciences, Beirut, Lebanon. Offers environmental sciences (MS), including environmental health; epidemiology (MS); epidemiology and biostatistics (MPH); health management and policy (MPH); health promotion and community health (MPH). *Program availability:* Part-time. *Faculty:* 30 full-time (21 women), 3 part-time/adjunct (1 woman). *Students:* 49 full-time (38 women), 99 part-time (81 women). Average age 27. 115 applicants, 71% accepted, 40 enrolled. In 2015, 51 master's awarded. *Degree requirements:* For master's, one foreign language, comprehensive exam (for some programs), thesis (for some programs). *Entrance requirements:* For master's, 2 letters of recommendation, personal statement, transcripts. Additional exam requirements/recommendations for international students: Required—TOEFL (minimum score 583 paper-based; 97 iBT), IELTS (minimum score 7). *Application deadline:* For fall admission, 1/4 priority date for domestic and international students; for spring admission, 11/1 for domestic and international students. Application fee: $50. Electronic applications accepted. *Expenses: Tuition, area resident:* Full-time $16,254; part-time $903 per credit. *Required fees:* $699. Tuition and fees vary according to course load and program. *Financial support:* In 2015–16, 70 students received support. Scholarships/grants, health care benefits, and unspecified assistantships available. Financial award application deadline: 4/1. *Faculty research:* Tobacco control; health of the elderly; youth health; mental health; women's health; reproductive and sexual health, including HIV/AIDS; water quality; health systems; quality in health care delivery; health human resources; health policy; occupational and environmental health; social inequality; social determinants of health; non-communicable diseases; nutrition; refugees health; conflict and health.. *Total annual research expenditures:* $2 million. *Unit head:* Iman Adel Nuwayhid, Dean, 961-1759683, Fax: 961-1744470, E-mail: nuwayhid@aub.edu.lb. *Application contact:* Mitra Tauk, Administrative Coordinator, 961-1350000 Ext. 4687, Fax: 961-1744470,
E-mail: mt12@aub.edu.lb.

Boston University, Graduate School of Arts and Sciences, Intercollegiate Program in Biostatistics, Boston, MA 02215. Offers MA, PhD. *Students:* 36 full-time (25 women), 13 part-time (9 women); includes 9 minority (6 Asian, non-Hispanic/Latino; 1 Hispanic/Latino; 2 Two or more races, non-Hispanic/Latino), 15 international. Average age 28. 224 applicants, 16% accepted, 12 enrolled. In 2015, 37 master's, 8 doctorates awarded. Terminal master's awarded for partial completion of doctoral program. *Degree requirements:* For master's, one foreign language, comprehensive exam; for doctorate, one foreign language, comprehensive exam, thesis/dissertation. *Entrance requirements:* For master's and doctorate, GRE General Test, 3 letters of recommendation, transcripts, personal statement, curriculum vitae/resume, previous coursework document. Additional exam requirements/recommendations for international students: Required—TOEFL (minimum score 550 paper-based; 84 iBT). *Application deadline:* For fall admission, 12/15 for domestic and international students. Application fee: $95. Electronic applications accepted. *Financial support:* In 2015–16, 31 students received support, including 6 fellowships with full tuition reimbursements available (averaging $21,000 per year), 25 research assistantships with full tuition reimbursements available (averaging $21,000 per year); traineeships and health care benefits also available. Support available to part-time students. Financial award application deadline: 12/15. *Unit head:* Josee Dupuis, Interim Chair, 617-638-5880, E-mail: dupuis@bu.edu. *Application contact:* Marisa Crowley, Program Manager, 617-638-5207, Fax: 617-638-6484,
E-mail: marisac@bu.edu.
Website: http://sph.bu.edu/Biostatistics/department-of-biostatistics/menu-id-617603.html

Boston University, School of Public Health, Biostatistics Department, Boston, MA 02215. Offers MA, MPH, PhD. *Program availability:* Part-time, evening/weekend. *Faculty:* 26 full-time, 18 part-time/adjunct. *Students:* 33 full-time (25 women), 14 part-time (9 women); includes 14 minority (4 Black or African American, non-Hispanic/Latino; 7 Asian, non-Hispanic/Latino; 2 Hispanic/Latino; 1 Two or more races, non-Hispanic/Latino), 15 international. Average age 26. 79 applicants, 46% accepted, 14 enrolled. In 2015, 37 master's, 8 doctorates awarded. *Entrance requirements:* For master's, GRE, GMAT, MCAT; for doctorate, GRE. Additional exam requirements/recommendations for international students: Required—TOEFL (minimum score 600 paper-based; 100 iBT), IELTS (minimum score 7). *Application deadline:* For fall admission, 12/1 priority date for domestic and international students; for spring admission, 10/1 priority date for domestic students. Applications are processed on a rolling basis. Application fee: $120. Electronic applications accepted. *Financial support:* Fellowships, research assistantships, teaching assistantships, career-related internships or fieldwork, Federal Work-Study, institutionally sponsored loans, scholarships/grants, traineeships, health care benefits, and unspecified assistantships available. Support available to part-time students. Financial award application deadline: 3/1; financial award applicants required to submit FAFSA. *Faculty research:* Statistical genetics, clinical trials, research methods. *Unit head:* Dr. Josee Dupuis, Chair - Ad Interim, 617-638-5880, Fax: 617-638-4458,
E-mail: dupuis@bu.edu. *Application contact:* Marisa Crowley, Educational Program Manager, 617-638-4640, Fax: 617-638-5207, E-mail: marisac@bu.edu.
Website: http://www.bu.edu/sph/bio

Brown University, Graduate School, Division of Biology and Medicine, School of Public Health, Department of Biostatistics, Providence, RI 02912. Offers AM, Sc M, PhD. *Degree requirements:* For doctorate, thesis/dissertation, preliminary exam. *Entrance requirements:* For master's and doctorate, GRE General Test.

California State University, East Bay, Office of Graduate Studies Programs, College of Science, Department of Statistics and Biostatistics, Biostatistics Program, Hayward, CA 94542-3000. Offers MS. *Program availability:* Part-time, evening/weekend. *Students:* 8 full-time (4 women), 16 part-time (6 women); includes 13 minority (3 Black or African American, non-Hispanic/Latino; 6 Asian, non-Hispanic/Latino; 4 Hispanic/Latino), 3 international. Average age 30. 34 applicants, 76% accepted, 14 enrolled. In 2015, 17 master's awarded. *Degree requirements:* For master's, comprehensive exam. *Entrance requirements:* For master's, minimum GPA of 3.0; math through lower-division calculus; statement of purpose; 2-3 letters of recommendation or GRE. Additional exam requirements/recommendations for international students: Required—TOEFL (minimum score 550 paper-based). *Application deadline:* For fall admission, 6/30 for domestic and international students. Application fee: $55. Electronic applications accepted. *Financial support:* Fellowships, career-related internships or fieldwork, Federal Work-Study, scholarships/grants, and unspecified assistantships available. Support available to part-time students. Financial award application deadline: 3/1; financial award applicants required to submit FAFSA. *Unit head:* Dr. Mitchell Watnik, Chair, 510-885-3879. *Application contact:* Prof. Lynn Eudey, Graduate Advisor, 510-885-3617, Fax: 510-885-4714, E-mail: lynn.eudey@csueastbay.edu.
Website: http://www20.csueastbay.edu/csci/departments/statistics/

Case Western Reserve University, School of Medicine and School of Graduate Studies, Graduate Programs in Medicine, Department of Epidemiology and Biostatistics, Program in Biostatistics, Cleveland, OH 44106. Offers MS, PhD. *Program availability:* Part-time. Terminal master's awarded for partial completion of doctoral program. *Degree requirements:* For master's, comprehensive exam, thesis, exam/practicum; for doctorate, comprehensive exam, thesis/dissertation. *Entrance requirements:* For master's, GRE General Test or MCAT, 3 recommendations; for doctorate, GRE General Test, 3 recommendations. Additional exam requirements/recommendations for international students: Required—TOEFL (minimum score 550 paper-based). Electronic applications accepted. *Expenses: Tuition, area resident:* Full-time $41,137; part-time $1714 per credit hour. *Required fees:* $32. Tuition and fees vary according to course load and program. *Faculty research:* Survey sampling and statistical computing, generalized linear models, statistical modeling, models in breast cancer survival.

Columbia University, Columbia University Mailman School of Public Health, Department of Biostatistics, New York, NY 10032. Offers MPH, MS, Dr PH, PhD. PhD

offered in cooperation with the Graduate School of Arts and Sciences. *Program availability:* Part-time. *Students:* 68 full-time (48 women), 85 part-time (55 women); includes 18 minority (2 Black or African American, non-Hispanic/Latino; 13 Asian, non-Hispanic/Latino; 2 Hispanic/Latino; 1 Two or more races, non-Hispanic/Latino), 97 international. Average age 27. 298 applicants, 52% accepted, 57 enrolled. In 2015, 53 master's, 6 doctorates awarded. *Degree requirements:* For doctorate, thesis/dissertation. *Entrance requirements:* For master's, GRE General Test; for doctorate, GRE General Test, MPH or equivalent (for Dr PH). Additional exam requirements/recommendations for international students: Required—TOEFL (minimum score 600 paper-based; 100 iBT). *Application deadline:* For fall admission, 12/1 priority date for domestic and international students. Applications are processed on a rolling basis. Application fee: $120. Electronic applications accepted. *Financial support:* Research assistantships, teaching assistantships, career-related internships or fieldwork, and Federal Work-Study available. Financial award application deadline: 2/1; financial award applicants required to submit FAFSA. *Faculty research:* Statistical methods and public health implications of biomedical experiments, clinical trials, functional data analysis, statistical genetics, observational studies. *Unit head:* Dr. F. Dubois Bowman, Chairperson, 212-342-2271, Fax: 212-305-9408. *Application contact:* Dr. Joseph Korevec, Senior Director of Admissions and Financial Aid, 212-305-8698, Fax: 212-342-1861, E-mail: ph-admit@columbia.edu.
Website: https://www.mailman.columbia.edu/become-student/departments/biostatistics

Dartmouth College, Arts and Sciences Graduate Programs, Institute for Quantitative Biomedical Sciences, Hanover, NH 03755. Offers PhD. Program offered in collaboration with the Department of Genetics and the Department of Community and Family Medicine. *Students:* 16 full-time (9 women); includes 3 minority (1 Black or African American, non-Hispanic/Latino; 2 Asian, non-Hispanic/Latino), 3 international. Average age 28. 39 applicants, 31% accepted, 5 enrolled. In 2015, 1 doctorate awarded. *Entrance requirements:* For doctorate, GRE (minimum scores: 1200 old scoring, 308 new scoring verbal and quantitative; analytical writing 4.5; verbal 500 old scoring, 153 new scoring). *Application deadline:* For fall admission, 3/1 for domestic students. Application fee: $75. Electronic applications accepted. *Expenses:* Tuition, area resident: Full-time $48,120. *Required fees:* $296. One-time fee: $50 full-time. *Financial support:* In 2015–16, fellowships with tuition reimbursements (averaging $28,200 per year) were awarded. *Unit head:* Krissy Giffin, Director. *Application contact:* Gary Hutchins, Assistant Dean, School of Arts and Sciences, 603-646-2107, Fax: 603-646-3488, E-mail: g.hutchins@dartmouth.edu.
Website: https://www.dartmouth.edu/~qbs/index.html

Drexel University, School of Biomedical Engineering, Science and Health Systems, Philadelphia, PA 19104-2875. Offers biomedical engineering (MS, PhD); biomedical science (MS, PhD); biostatistics (MS); clinical/rehabilitation engineering (MS); MD/PhD. *Degree requirements:* For doctorate, thesis/dissertation, 1 year of residency, qualifying exam. *Entrance requirements:* For master's, minimum GPA of 3.0; for doctorate, minimum GPA of 3.0, MS. Additional exam requirements/recommendations for international students: Required—TOEFL. Electronic applications accepted. *Faculty research:* Cardiovascular dynamics, diagnostic and therapeutic ultrasound.

Drexel University, School of Public Health, Department of Epidemiology and Biostatistics, Philadelphia, PA 19104-2875. Offers biostatistics (MS); epidemiology (PhD); epidemiology and biostatistics (Certificate).

Duke University, School of Medicine, Program in Biostatistics, Durham, NC 27710. Offers MS. *Program availability:* Part-time. *Faculty:* 53 full-time (24 women), 1 (woman) part-time/adjunct. *Students:* 46 full-time (23 women); includes 12 minority (2 Black or African American, non-Hispanic/Latino; 9 Asian, non-Hispanic/Latino; 1 Hispanic/Latino), 5 international. 114 applicants, 56% accepted, 28 enrolled. In 2015, 16 master's awarded. *Degree requirements:* For master's, project. *Entrance requirements:* For master's, GRE. Additional exam requirements/recommendations for international students: Required—TOEFL. *Application deadline:* For fall admission, 1/15 for domestic students. Application fee: $75. *Financial support:* In 2015–16, 20 students received support. Scholarships/grants available. Financial award application deadline: 5/1; financial award applicants required to submit FAFSA. *Unit head:* Dr. Gregory P. Samsa, Associate Professor, 919-613-5212, Fax: 919-660-7040, E-mail: samsa001@mc.duke.edu. *Application contact:* Rob Hirtz, Program Coordinator, 919-668-5876, Fax: 919-681-4569, E-mail: rob.hirtz@duke.edu.
Website: http://biostat.duke.edu/master-biostatistics-program/program-overview

Emory University, Rollins School of Public Health, Department of Biostatistics and Bioinformatics, Atlanta, GA 30322-1100. Offers bioinformatics (PhD); biostatistics (MPH, MSPH); public health informatics (MSPH). PhD offered through the Graduate School of Arts and Sciences. *Program availability:* Part-time. *Degree requirements:* For master's, thesis, practicum. *Entrance requirements:* For master's, GRE General Test. Additional exam requirements/recommendations for international students: Required—TOEFL (minimum score 550 paper-based; 80 iBT). Electronic applications accepted.

Florida International University, Robert Stempel College of Public Health and Social Work, Programs in Public Health, Miami, FL 33199. Offers biostatistics (MPH); environmental and occupational health (MPH, PhD); epidemiology (MPH, PhD); health policy and management (MPH); health promotion and disease prevention (PhD); health promotion and diseases prevention (MPH). Ph D program has fall admissions only; MPH offered jointly with University of Miami. *Accreditation:* CEPH. *Program availability:* Part-time, evening/weekend, online learning. *Faculty:* 27 full-time (12 women), 2 part-time/adjunct (1 woman). *Students:* 126 full-time (80 women), 62 part-time (46 women); includes 129 minority (47 Black or African American, non-Hispanic/Latino; 10 Asian, non-Hispanic/Latino; 69 Hispanic/Latino; 3 Two or more races, non-Hispanic/Latino), 32 international. Average age 30. 298 applicants, 35% accepted, 68 enrolled. In 2015, 67 master's, 10 doctorates awarded. *Degree requirements:* For master's, thesis optional; for doctorate, comprehensive exam, thesis/dissertation. *Entrance requirements:* For master's, minimum GPA of 3.0, letters of recommendation; for doctorate, GRE, resume, minimum GPA of 3.0, letters of recommendation, letter of intent. Additional exam requirements/recommendations for international students: Required—TOEFL (minimum score 550 paper-based; 80 iBT). *Application deadline:* For fall admission, 6/1 for domestic students, 4/1 for international students; for spring admission, 10/1 for domestic students, 9/1 for international students. Applications are processed on a rolling basis. Application fee: $30. Electronic applications accepted. *Expenses:* Contact institution. *Financial support:* Institutionally sponsored loans, scholarships/grants, and tuition waivers (full) available. Financial award application deadline: 3/1; financial award applicants required to submit FAFSA. *Faculty research:* Drugs/AIDS intervention among migrant workers, provision of services for active/recovering drug users with HIV. *Unit head:* Dr. Benjamin C. Amick, III, Chair, 305-348-4903, E-mail: benjamin.amickiii@fiu.edu. *Application contact:* Dr. Vukosava Pekovic, Director, 305-348-1823, Fax: 305-348-4901, E-mail: pekovic@fiu.edu.

Florida State University, The Graduate School, College of Arts and Sciences, Department of Statistics, Tallahassee, FL 32306-4330. Offers applied statistics (MS); applied statistics - thesis option (MS); biostatistics (MS, PhD); biostatistics - thesis

option (MS); mathematical statistics (MS, PhD); mathematical statistics - thesis option (MS); statistical data science (MS). *Program availability:* Part-time. *Faculty:* 18 full-time (3 women), 1 (woman) part-time/adjunct. *Students:* 149 full-time (77 women), 13 part-time (5 women); includes 19 minority (6 Black or African American, non-Hispanic/Latino; 8 Asian, non-Hispanic/Latino; 5 Hispanic/Latino), 117 international. Average age 27. 353 applicants, 40% accepted, 56 enrolled. In 2015, 44 master's, 6 doctorates awarded. Terminal master's awarded for partial completion of doctoral program. *Degree requirements:* For master's, thesis optional; for doctorate, comprehensive exam, thesis/dissertation, departmental qualifying exam. *Entrance requirements:* For master's, GRE General Test, calculus 1-3, linear algebra, one course each in applied statistics and probability, minimum GPA of 3.0; for doctorate, GRE General Test, minimum GPA of 3.0, two semesters of advanced calculus (intermediate analysis, real analysis with proofs). Additional exam requirements/recommendations for international students: Required—TOEFL (minimum score 80 iBT). *Application deadline:* For fall admission, 7/1 for domestic and international students. Application fee: $30. Electronic applications accepted. *Expenses:* Tuition, area resident: Full-time $7263; part-time $403.50 per credit hour. Tuition, nonresident: full-time $18,087; part-time $1004.85 per credit hour. *Required fees:* $1365; $75.81 per credit hour. $20 per semester. Tuition and fees vary according to campus/location. *Financial support:* In 2015–16, 83 students received support, including 4 fellowships with full tuition reimbursements available (averaging $10,000 per year), 11 research assistantships with full tuition reimbursements available (averaging $19,380 per year), 56 teaching assistantships with full tuition reimbursements available (averaging $20,432 per year); institutionally sponsored loans, scholarships/grants, health care benefits, tuition waivers (partial), and unspecified assistantships also available. Financial award application deadline: 2/1; financial award applicants required to submit FAFSA. *Faculty research:* Statistical inference, probability theory, biostatistics, nonparametric estimation, automatic target recognition. *Total annual research expenditures:* $861,615. *Unit head:* Dr. Xufeng Niu, Chairman, 850-644-4008, Fax: 850-644-5271, E-mail: niu@stat.fsu.edu. *Application contact:* Sarah English, Academic Program Specialist, 850-644-3514, Fax: 850-644-5271, E-mail: sarah.english@stat.fsu.edu.
Website: http://www.stat.fsu.edu/

George Mason University, Volgenau School of Engineering, Department of Statistics, Fairfax, VA 22030. Offers biostatistics (MS); statistical science (MS, PhD); statistics (Certificate). *Faculty:* 15 full-time (3 women), 2 part-time/adjunct (0 women). *Students:* 31 full-time (13 women), 36 part-time (13 women); includes 25 minority (5 Black or African American, non-Hispanic/Latino; 14 Asian, non-Hispanic/Latino; 4 Hispanic/Latino; 1 Native Hawaiian or other Pacific Islander, non-Hispanic/Latino; 1 Two or more races, non-Hispanic/Latino), 17 international. Average age 32. 78 applicants, 67% accepted, 19 enrolled. In 2015, 18 master's, 5 doctorates, 7 other advanced degrees awarded. *Degree requirements:* For master's, comprehensive exam, thesis optional, qualifying exams; for doctorate, comprehensive exam, thesis/dissertation, qualifying exams. *Entrance requirements:* For master's, GRE/GMAT, bachelor's degree from accredited institution with minimum of GPA of 3.0 in a major that includes calculus, matrix algebra, calculus-based probability and statistics; personal goal statement; 2 official copies of transcripts; 3 letters of recommendation; resume; official bank statement; proof of financial support; photocopy of passport; for doctorate, GRE, MS in math-intensive discipline with minimum GPA of 3.5, personal goals statement, 2 official copies of transcripts, 3 letters of recommendation, resume, official bank statement, proof of financial support, photocopy of passport; for Certificate, bachelor's degree with 2 courses in calculus and probability or statistics, personal goals statement, 2 official copies of transcripts, 1-3 letters of recommendation (depending on program), resume, official bank statement, proof of financial support, photocopy of passport. Additional exam requirements/recommendations for international students: Required—TOEFL (minimum score 575 paper-based; 80 iBT), IELTS (minimum score 6.5), PTE. *Application deadline:* For fall admission, 1/15 priority date for domestic students. Application fee: $65 ($80 for international students). Electronic applications accepted. *Expenses:* Contact institution. *Financial support:* In 2015–16, 17 students received support, including 4 research assistantships with tuition reimbursements available (averaging $16,250 per year), 15 teaching assistantships with tuition reimbursements available (averaging $16,772 per year); career-related internships or fieldwork, Federal Work-Study, scholarships/grants, unspecified assistantships, and health care benefits (for full-time research or teaching assistantship recipients) also available. Support available to part-time students. Financial award application deadline: 3/1; financial award applicants required to submit FAFSA. *Faculty research:* Computational statistics, nonparametric function estimation, scientific and statistical visualization, statistical applications to engineering, survey research. *Total annual research expenditures:* $231,752. *Unit head:* William F. Rosenberger, Chair, 703-993-3645, Fax: 703-993-1700, E-mail: wrosenbe@gmu.edu. *Application contact:* Elizabeth Quigley, Administrative Assistant, 703-993-9107, Fax: 703-993-1700, E-mail: equigley@gmu.edu.
Website: http://statistics.gmu.edu/

Georgetown University, Graduate School of Arts and Sciences, Department of Biostatistics, Bioinformatics and Biomathematics, Washington, DC 20057-1484. Offers biostatistics (MS, Certificate), including bioinformatics (MS), epidemiology (MS); epidemiology (Certificate). *Entrance requirements:* For master's, GRE General Test. Additional exam requirements/recommendations for international students: Required—TOEFL. *Faculty research:* Occupation epidemiology, cancer.

The George Washington University, Columbian College of Arts and Sciences, Program in Biostatistics, Washington, DC 20052. Offers MS, PhD. *Students:* 15 full-time (11 women), 10 part-time (7 women); includes 3 minority (all Asian, non-Hispanic/Latino), 16 international. Average age 28. 84 applicants, 58% accepted, 10 enrolled. In 2015, 7 master's awarded. *Degree requirements:* For master's, comprehensive exam; for doctorate, thesis/dissertation, general exam. *Entrance requirements:* For master's and doctorate, GRE General Test, minimum GPA of 3.0. Additional exam requirements/recommendations for international students: Required—TOEFL (minimum score 550 paper-based; 80 iBT). *Application deadline:* For fall admission, 1/15 priority date for domestic and international students; for spring admission, 10/1 priority date for domestic students, 9/1 priority date for international students. Applications are processed on a rolling basis. Application fee: $75. Electronic applications accepted. *Financial support:* In 2015–16, 1 student received support. Fellowships with full tuition reimbursements available, teaching assistantships, and tuition waivers available. *Unit head:* Dr. Zhaohai Li, Director, 202-994-7844, Fax: 202-994-6917, E-mail: zli@gwu.edu. *Application contact:* 202-994-6210, Fax: 202-994-6213, E-mail: askccas@gwu.edu.

The George Washington University, Milken Institute School of Public Health, Department of Epidemiology and Biostatistics, Washington, DC 20052. Offers biostatistics (MPH); epidemiology (MPH); microbiology and emerging infectious diseases (MSPH). *Faculty:* 30 full-time (20 women), 9 part-time/adjunct (7 women). *Students:* 65 full-time (49 women), 70 part-time (54 women); includes 40 minority (12 Black or African American, non-Hispanic/Latino; 15 Asian, non-Hispanic/Latino; 8 Hispanic/Latino; 5 Two or more races, non-Hispanic/Latino), 12 international. Average age 29. 493 applicants, 55% accepted, 47 enrolled. In 2015, 56 master's awarded. *Degree requirements:* For master's, case study or special project. *Entrance*

Peterson's Graduate Programs in the Physical Sciences, Mathematics, Agricultural Sciences, the Environment & Natural Resources 2017

www.petersons.com **223**

requirements: For master's, GMAT, GRE General Test, or MCAT. Additional exam requirements/recommendations for international students: Required—TOEFL. *Application deadline:* For fall admission, 4/15 priority date for domestic students, 4/15 for international students; for spring admission, 11/1 for domestic and international students. Applications are processed on a rolling basis. Application fee: $75. *Financial support:* In 2015–16, 6 students received support. Tuition waivers available. Financial award application deadline: 2/15. *Unit head:* Dr. Alan E. Greenberg, Chair, 202-994-0612, E-mail: aeg1@gwu.edu. *Application contact:* Jane Smith, Director of Admissions, 202-994-0248, Fax: 202-994-1860, E-mail: sphhsinfo@gwumc.edu.

Georgia Southern University, Jack N. Averitt College of Graduate Studies, Jiann-Ping Hsu College of Public Health, Program in Public Health, Statesboro, GA 30460. Offers biostatistics (MPH, Dr PH); community health behavior and education (Dr PH); community health education (MPH); environmental health sciences (MPH); epidemiology (MPH); health policy and management (MPH, Dr PH). *Accreditation:* CEPH. *Program availability:* Part-time. *Students:* 129 full-time (86 women), 41 part-time (32 women); includes 87 minority (67 Black or African American, non-Hispanic/Latino; 6 Asian, non-Hispanic/Latino; 8 Hispanic/Latino; 6 Two or more races, non-Hispanic/Latino), 30 international. Average age 30. 218 applicants, 63% accepted, 41 enrolled. In 2015, 37 master's, 8 doctorates awarded. *Degree requirements:* For master's, thesis optional, practicum; for doctorate, comprehensive exam, thesis/dissertation, practicum. *Entrance requirements:* For master's, GRE General Test, minimum GPA of 2.75, resume, 3 letters of reference; for doctorate, GRE, GMAT, MCAT, LSAT, 3 letters of reference, statement of purpose, resume or curriculum vitae. Additional exam requirements/recommendations for international students: Required—TOEFL (minimum score 550 paper-based; 80 iBT), IELTS (minimum score 6). *Application deadline:* For fall admission, 6/1 priority date for domestic and international students; for spring admission, 10/1 priority date for domestic students, 10/1 for international students. Applications are processed on a rolling basis. Application fee: $50. Electronic applications accepted. *Expenses:* $335.00 per credit hour. *Financial support:* In 2015–16, 93 students received support, including 23 fellowships with full tuition reimbursements available (averaging $7,750 per year), 1 research assistantship with full tuition reimbursement available (averaging $7,750 per year), 1 teaching assistantship with full tuition reimbursement available (averaging $7,750 per year); career-related internships or fieldwork, Federal Work-Study, scholarships/grants, tuition waivers (full), and unspecified assistantships also available. Support available to part-time students. Financial award application deadline: 4/15; financial award applicants required to submit FAFSA. *Faculty research:* Rural public health best practices, health disparity elimination, community initiatives to enhance public health, cost effectiveness analysis, epidemiology of rural public health, environmental health issues, health care system assessment, rural health care, health policy and healthcare financing, survival analysis, nonparametric statistics and resampling methods, micro-arrays and genomics, data imputation techniques and clinical trial methodology. *Total annual research expenditures:* $281,707. *Unit head:* Dr. Shamia Garrett, Program Coordinator, 912-478-2393, E-mail: sgarrett@georgiasouthern.edu.
Website: http://chhs.georgiasouthern.edu/health/

Georgia State University, College of Arts and Sciences, Department of Mathematics and Statistics, Atlanta, GA 30302-3083. Offers bioinformatics (MS, PhD); biostatistics (MS, PhD); discrete mathematics (MS); mathematics (MS, PhD); scientific computing (MS); statistics (MS). *Program availability:* Part-time. *Faculty:* 22 full-time (7 women). *Students:* 97 full-time (44 women), 20 part-time (5 women); includes 40 minority (14 Black or African American, non-Hispanic/Latino; 23 Asian, non-Hispanic/Latino; 3 Hispanic/Latino), 50 international. Average age 32. 80 applicants, 51% accepted, 23 enrolled. In 2015, 22 master's, 4 doctorates awarded. Terminal master's awarded for partial completion of doctoral program. *Degree requirements:* For master's, comprehensive exam (for some programs), thesis optional; for doctorate, comprehensive exam, thesis/dissertation. *Entrance requirements:* For master's and doctorate, GRE. Additional exam requirements/recommendations for international students: Required—TOEFL (minimum score 550 paper-based; 80 iBT). *Application deadline:* For fall admission, 7/1 priority date for domestic and international students; for spring admission, 11/15 priority date for domestic and international students. Application fee: $50. Electronic applications accepted. *Expenses:* Tuition, state resident: full-time $6876; part-time $382 per credit hour. Tuition, nonresident: full-time $22,374; part-time $1243 per credit hour. *Required fees:* $2128; $2128 per term. $1064 per term. Part-time tuition and fees vary according to course load and program. *Financial support:* In 2015–16, fellowships with full tuition reimbursements (averaging $22,000 per year), research assistantships with full tuition reimbursements (averaging $9,000 per year), teaching assistantships with full tuition reimbursements (averaging $9,000 per year) were awarded; institutionally sponsored loans, scholarships/grants, health care benefits, and unspecified assistantships also available. Financial award application deadline: 2/1. *Faculty research:* Algebra, matrix theory, graph theory and combinatorics; applied mathematics and analysis; collegiate mathematics education; statistics, biostatistics and applications; bioinformatics, dynamical systems. *Unit head:* Dr. Guantao Chen, Chair, 404-413-6436, Fax: 404-413-6403, E-mail: gchen@gsu.edu.
Website: http://www2.gsu.edu/~wwwmat/

Grand Valley State University, College of Liberal Arts and Sciences, Program in Biostatistics, Allendale, MI 49401-9403. Offers MS. *Students:* 38 full-time (21 women), 17 part-time (11 women); includes 4 minority (2 Black or African American, non-Hispanic/Latino; 1 Asian, non-Hispanic/Latino; 1 Hispanic/Latino), 2 international. Average age 27. 31 applicants, 74% accepted, 22 enrolled. In 2015, 15 master's awarded. *Entrance requirements:* For master's, minimum GPA of 3.0. Application fee: $30. *Financial support:* In 2015–16, 24 students received support, including 1 fellowship (averaging $2,517 per year), 23 research assistantships with tuition reimbursements available (averaging $7,761 per year); unspecified assistantships also available. *Faculty research:* Biometrical models, spatial methods, medical statistics, design of experiments. *Unit head:* Dr. Paul Stephenson, Department Chair, 616-331-2081, E-mail: stephenp@gvsu.edu. *Application contact:* Dr. Robert Downer, Graduate Program Director, 616-331-2247, E-mail: downerr@gvsu.edu.

Harvard University, Cyprus International Institute for the Environment and Public Health in Association with Harvard School of Public Health, Cambridge, MA 02138. Offers environmental health (MS); environmental/public health (PhD); epidemiology and biostatistics (MS). *Entrance requirements:* For master's and doctorate, GRE, resume/curriculum vitae, 3 letters of recommendation, BA or BS (including diploma and official transcripts). Additional exam requirements/recommendations for international students: Required—TOEFL, IELTS (minimum score 7). Electronic applications accepted. *Faculty research:* Air pollution, climate change, biostatistics, sustainable development, environmental management.

Harvard University, Graduate School of Arts and Sciences, Department of Biostatistics, Cambridge, MA 02138. Offers PhD.

Harvard University, Harvard T.H. Chan School of Public Health, Department of Biostatistics, Boston, MA 02115-6096. Offers SM, PhD. *Program availability:* Part-time. *Faculty:* 60 full-time (18 women), 7 part-time/adjunct (3 women). *Students:* 170 full-time (86 women), 18 part-time (9 women); includes 48 minority (11 Black or African American, non-Hispanic/Latino; 23 Asian, non-Hispanic/Latino; 5 Hispanic/Latino; 9 Two or more races, non-Hispanic/Latino), 86 international. Average age 28. 397 applicants, 27% accepted, 77 enrolled. In 2015, 69 master's, 11 doctorates awarded. *Degree requirements:* For doctorate, thesis/dissertation, oral and written qualifying exams. *Entrance requirements:* For master's, GRE, MCAT, prior training in mathematics and/or statistics; for doctorate, GRE, prior training in mathematics and/or statistics. Additional exam requirements/recommendations for international students: Recommended—TOEFL (minimum score 600 paper-based; 100 iBT), IELTS (minimum score 7). *Application deadline:* For fall admission, 12/15 for domestic and international students. Application fee: $120. Electronic applications accepted. Application fee is waived when completed online. *Financial support:* Fellowships, research assistantships, teaching assistantships, Federal Work-Study, scholarships/grants, traineeships, and unspecified assistantships available. Support available to part-time students. Financial award application deadline: 2/15; financial award applicants required to submit FAFSA. *Faculty research:* Statistical genetics, clinical trials, cancer and AIDS research, environmental and mental health, dose response modeling. *Unit head:* Dr. Xihong Lin, Chair, Henry Pickering Walcott Professor of Biostatistics, 617-432-1056, Fax: 617-432-5619, E-mail: xlin@hsph.harvard.edu. *Application contact:* Vincent W. James, Director of Admissions, 617-432-1031, Fax: 617-432-7080, E-mail: admissions@hsph.harvard.edu.
Website: http://www.hsph.harvard.edu/biostatistics/

Hunter College of the City University of New York, Graduate School, Schools of the Health Professions, School of Health Sciences, Programs in Urban Public Health, Program in Epidemiology and Biostatistics, New York, NY 10065-5085. Offers MPH. *Accreditation:* CEPH. *Program availability:* Part-time, evening/weekend. *Students:* 75 applicants, 55% accepted, 21 enrolled. *Degree requirements:* For master's, comprehensive exam, thesis optional, internship. *Entrance requirements:* For master's, GRE General Test, previous course work in calculus and statistics. Additional exam requirements/recommendations for international students: Required—TOEFL. *Application deadline:* For fall admission, 4/1 for domestic students; for spring admission, 11/1 for domestic students. *Financial support:* In 2015–16, 6 fellowships were awarded; career-related internships or fieldwork, Federal Work-Study, institutionally sponsored loans, and tuition waivers (partial) also available. Support available to part-time students. Financial award application deadline: 3/1. *Unit head:* Prof. Lorna Thorpe, Program Director, 212-396-7746, Fax: 212-481-5260, E-mail: lthor@hunter.cuny.edu. *Application contact:* Milena Solo, Director for Graduate Admissions, 212-772-4288, Fax: 212-650-3336, E-mail: milena.solo@hunter.cuny.edu.
Website: http://cuny.edu/site/sph/hunter-college/a-programs/graduate/eb-mph.html

Indiana University Bloomington, School of Public Health, Department of Epidemiology and Biostatistics, Bloomington, IN 47405. Offers biostatistics (MPH); epidemiology (MPH, PhD). *Degree requirements:* For master's, thesis or alternative; for doctorate, comprehensive exam, thesis/dissertation. *Entrance requirements:* For master's, GRE (for applicants with cumulative undergraduate GPA less than 2.8); for doctorate, GRE. Additional exam requirements/recommendations for international students: Required—TOEFL (minimum score 550 paper-based; 80 iBT). Electronic applications accepted. *Faculty research:* Nutritional epidemiology, cancer epidemiology, global health, biostatistics.

Indiana University–Purdue University Indianapolis, Indiana University School of Medicine, Department of Biostatistics, Indianapolis, IN 46202. Offers PhD. Program offered jointly with Purdue University Department of Mathematical Sciences. *Degree requirements:* For doctorate, thesis/dissertation. *Entrance requirements:* For doctorate, GRE General Test. Additional exam requirements/recommendations for international students: Required—TOEFL. Electronic applications accepted.

Indiana University–Purdue University Indianapolis, School of Public Health, Indianapolis, IN 46202. Offers biostatistics (MPH); environmental health science (MPH); epidemiology (MPH, PhD); health administration (MHA); health policy and management (MPH, PhD); social and behavioral sciences (MPH). *Accreditation:* CEPH. *Expenses:* Contact institution.

Iowa State University of Science and Technology, Bioinformatics and Computational Biology Program, Ames, IA 50011. Offers MS, PhD. *Degree requirements:* For doctorate, thesis/dissertation. *Entrance requirements:* For master's and doctorate, GRE General Test. Additional exam requirements/recommendations for international students: Recommended—TOEFL, IELTS. Electronic applications accepted. *Faculty research:* Functional and structural genomics, genome evolution, macromolecular structure and function, mathematical biology and biological statistics, metabolic and developmental networks.

Johns Hopkins University, Bloomberg School of Public Health, Department of Biostatistics, Baltimore, MD 21205-2179. Offers bioinformatics (MHS); biostatistics (MHS, Sc M, PhD). *Program availability:* Part-time. *Degree requirements:* For master's, comprehensive exam (for some programs), thesis (for some programs), written exam, final project; for doctorate, comprehensive exam, thesis/dissertation, 1-year full-time residency, oral and written exams. *Entrance requirements:* For master's and doctorate, GRE General Test, course work in calculus and matrix algebra, 3 letters of recommendation, curriculum vitae. Additional exam requirements/recommendations for international students: Required—TOEFL (minimum score 600 paper-based). Electronic applications accepted. *Faculty research:* Statistical genetics, bioinformatics, statistical computing, statistical methods, environmental statistics.

Loma Linda University, School of Public Health, Programs in Epidemiology and Biostatistics, Loma Linda, CA 92350. Offers MPH, MSPH, Dr PH, Postbaccalaureate Certificate. *Entrance requirements:* Additional exam requirements/recommendations for international students: Required—Michigan English Language Assessment Battery or TOEFL.

Louisiana State University Health Sciences Center, School of Public Health, New Orleans, LA 70112. Offers behavioral and community health sciences (MPH); biostatistics (MPH, MS, PhD); community health sciences (PhD); environmental and occupational health sciences (MPH); epidemiology (MPH, PhD); health policy and systems management (MPH). *Accreditation:* CEPH. *Program availability:* Part-time. *Entrance requirements:* For master's, GRE General Test.

McGill University, Faculty of Graduate and Postdoctoral Studies, Faculty of Medicine, Department of Epidemiology and Biostatistics, Montréal, QC H3A 2T5, Canada. Offers community health (M Sc); environmental health (M Sc); epidemiology and biostatistics (M Sc, PhD, Diploma); health care evaluation (M Sc); medical statistics (M Sc). *Accreditation:* CEPH (one or more programs are accredited).

★ **Medical College of Wisconsin,** Graduate School of Biomedical Sciences, Department of Population Health, Division of Biostatistics, Milwaukee, WI 53226-0509. Offers PhD. *Program availability:* Part-time. *Degree requirements:* For doctorate, comprehensive exam, thesis/dissertation.

Entrance requirements: For doctorate, GRE, official transcripts, three letters of recommendation. Additional exam requirements/recommendations for international students: Required—TOEFL. Electronic applications accepted. *Faculty research:* Survival analysis, spatial statistics, time series, genetic statistics, Bayesian statistics.
See Display below and Close-Up on page 293.

Medical University of South Carolina, College of Graduate Studies, Division of Biostatistics and Epidemiology, Charleston, SC 29425. Offers biostatistics (MS, PhD); epidemiology (MS, PhD); DMD/PhD; MD/PhD. Terminal master's awarded for partial completion of doctoral program. *Degree requirements:* For master's, comprehensive exam, thesis (for some programs); for doctorate, comprehensive exam, oral and written exams. *Entrance requirements:* For master's, GRE General Test, two semesters of college-level calculus; for doctorate, GRE General Test, interview, minimum GPA of 3.0, two semesters of college-level calculus. Additional exam requirements/recommendations for international students: Required—TOEFL (minimum score 600 paper-based; 100 iBT). Electronic applications accepted. *Faculty research:* Health disparities, central nervous system injuries, radiation exposure, analysis of clinical trial data, biomedical information.

Middle Tennessee State University, College of Graduate Studies, College of Basic and Applied Sciences, Program in Professional Science, Murfreesboro, TN 37132. Offers actuarial sciences (MS); biostatistics (MS); biotechnology (MS); engineering management (MS); health care informatics (MS). *Program availability:* Part-time, evening/weekend, online learning. *Degree requirements:* For master's, comprehensive exam. *Entrance requirements:* For master's, GRE. Additional exam requirements/recommendations for international students: Required—TOEFL (minimum score 525 paper-based; 71 iBT) or IELTS (minimum score 6).

New Jersey Institute of Technology, College of Science and Liberal Arts, Newark, NJ 07102. Offers applied mathematics (MS); applied physics (M Sc, PhD); applied statistical models (Certificate); applied statistics (MS); biology (MS, PhD); biostatistics (MS); biostatistics essentials (Certificate); chemistry (MS, PhD); computational biology (MS); environmental science (MS, PhD); history (MA, MAT); materials science and engineering (MS, PhD); mathematical and computational finance (MS); mathematics science (PhD); pharmaceutical chemistry (MS); professional and technical communications (MS); technical common essentials (Certificate). *Program availability:* Part-time, evening/weekend. *Faculty:* 153 full-time (35 women), 100 part-time/adjunct (40 women). *Students:* 212 full-time (82 women), 94 part-time (37 women); includes 72 minority (22 Black or African American, non-Hispanic/Latino; 25 Asian, non-Hispanic/Latino; 19 Hispanic/Latino; 6 Two or more races, non-Hispanic/Latino), 164 international. Average age 29. 519 applicants, 62% accepted, 104 enrolled. In 2015, 98 master's, 21 doctorates, 3 other advanced degrees awarded. Terminal master's awarded for partial completion of doctoral program. *Degree requirements:* For master's, thesis optional; for doctorate, thesis/dissertation. *Entrance requirements:* For master's, GRE General Test; for doctorate, GRE General Test, minimum graduate GPA of 3.5. Additional exam requirements/recommendations for international students: Required—TOEFL (minimum score 550 paper-based; 79 iBT). *Application deadline:* For fall admission, 6/1 priority date for domestic students, 5/1 priority date for international students; for spring admission, 11/15 priority date for domestic and international students. Applications are processed on a rolling basis. Application fee: $75. Electronic applications accepted. *Expenses:* $28,800 per year non-resident full-time. *Financial support:* In 2015–16, 56 research assistantships with full tuition reimbursements (averaging $17,711 per year), 52 teaching assistantships with full tuition reimbursements (averaging $17,914 per year) were awarded; fellowships with full tuition reimbursements also available. Financial award application deadline: 1/15. *Total annual research expenditures:* $23.1 million. *Unit head:* Dr. Kevin Belfield, Dean, 973-596-3676, Fax: 973-565-0586, E-mail: kevin.d.belfield@njit.edu. *Application contact:* Stephen Eck, Director of Admissions, 973-596-3300, Fax: 973-596-3461, E-mail: admissions@njit.edu. Website: http://csla.njit.edu/

New York Medical College, School of Health Sciences and Practice, Program in Biostatistics, Valhalla, NY 10595-1691. Offers MS. *Program availability:* Part-time, evening/weekend. *Degree requirements:* For master's, thesis. *Entrance requirements:* For master's, minimum undergraduate GPA of 3.0. Additional exam requirements/recommendations for international students: Required—TOEFL (minimum score 600 paper-based). Electronic applications accepted. *Expenses: Tuition, area resident:* Full-time $44,355; part-time $1025 per credit. *Required fees:* $500; $95 per year. One-time fee: $140 part-time. Tuition and fees vary according to course load and program.

Northwestern University, Feinberg School of Medicine and Interdepartmental Programs, Integrated Graduate Programs in the Life Sciences, Chicago, IL 60611. Offers biostatistics (PhD); epidemiology (PhD); health and biomedical informatics (PhD); health services and outcomes research (PhD); healthcare quality and patient safety (PhD); translational outcomes in science (PhD). *Degree requirements:* For doctorate, comprehensive exam, thesis/dissertation, written and oral qualifying exams. *Entrance requirements:* For doctorate, GRE General Test. Additional exam requirements/recommendations for international students: Required—TOEFL (minimum score 600 paper-based). Electronic applications accepted.

The Ohio State University, Graduate School, College of Arts and Sciences, Division of Natural and Mathematical Sciences, Department of Statistics, Columbus, OH 43210. Offers biostatistics (PhD); statistics (M Appl Stat, MS, PhD). *Program availability:* Part-time. Terminal master's awarded for partial completion of doctoral program. *Degree requirements:* For master's, thesis optional; for doctorate, thesis/dissertation. *Entrance requirements:* For master's and doctorate, GRE General Test. Additional exam requirements/recommendations for international students: Required—TOEFL (minimum score 600 paper-based; 100 iBT); Recommended—IELTS (minimum score 8). Electronic applications accepted.

The Ohio State University, Graduate School, Program in Biostatistics, Columbus, OH 43210. Offers PhD. *Degree requirements:* For doctorate, thesis/dissertation. *Entrance requirements:* For doctorate, GRE General Test. Additional exam requirements/recommendations for international students: Required—TOEFL (minimum score 600 paper-based; 100 iBT), IELTS (minimum score 8), Michigan English Language Assessment Battery (minimum score 86). Electronic applications accepted.

Old Dominion University, College of Sciences, Programs in Computational and Applied Mathematics, Norfolk, VA 23529. Offers applied mathematics (MS, PhD), including statistics and biostatistics. *Program availability:* Part-time. *Faculty:* 19 full-time (3 women), 1 part-time/adjunct (0 women). *Students:* 27 full-time (10 women), 13 part-time (3 women); includes 5 minority (1 Black or African American, non-Hispanic/Latino; 3 Asian, non-Hispanic/Latino; 1 Two or more races, non-Hispanic/Latino), 11 international. Average age 30. 31 applicants, 55% accepted, 8 enrolled. In 2015, 8 master's, 3 doctorates awarded. Terminal master's awarded for partial completion of doctoral program. *Degree requirements:* For master's, project; for doctorate, comprehensive exam, thesis/dissertation, candidacy exam. *Entrance requirements:* For master's, minimum GPA of 3.0 in major, 2.8 overall; for doctorate, GRE General Test, 3 recommendation letters, transcripts, essay. Additional exam requirements/recommendations for international students: Required—TOEFL (minimum score 550 paper-based; 79 iBT); Recommended—IELTS (minimum score 6.5). *Application deadline:* For fall admission, 6/1 for domestic students, 5/15 for international students; for winter admission, 11/1 for domestic students, 10/1 for international students; for

Peterson's Graduate Programs in the Physical Sciences, Mathematics, Agricultural Sciences, the Environment & Natural Resources 2017

www.petersons.com **225**

spring admission, 3/1 for domestic students, 2/1 for international students. Applications are processed on a rolling basis. Application fee: $50. Electronic applications accepted. *Expenses:* Tuition, state resident: full-time $11,136; part-time $464 per credit hour. Tuition, nonresident: full-time $27,840; part-time $1160 per credit hour. *Required fees:* $64 per semester. Tuition and fees vary according to campus/location, program and reciprocity agreements. *Financial support:* In 2015–16, 21 students received support, including 6 fellowships with full tuition reimbursements available (averaging $18,000 per year), 3 research assistantships with full tuition reimbursements available (averaging $16,000 per year), 12 teaching assistantships with full tuition reimbursements available (averaging $15,000 per year); scholarships/grants also available. Financial award application deadline: 2/15; financial award applicants required to submit FAFSA. *Faculty research:* Numerical analysis, integral equations, continuum mechanics, statistics, direct and inverse scattering. *Total annual research expenditures:* $506,890. *Unit head:* Dr. Raymond Cheng, Graduate Program Director, 757-683-3882, Fax: 757-683-3885, E-mail: rcheng@odu.edu. *Application contact:* William Heffelfinger, Director of Graduate Admissions, 757-683-5554, Fax: 757-683-3255, E-mail: gradadmit@odu.edu.

Website: http://sci.odu.edu/math/academics/grad.shtml

Oregon State University, College of Public Health and Human Sciences, Program in Public Health, Corvallis, OR 97331. Offers biostatistics (MPH); environmental and occupational health and safety (MPH, PhD); epidemiology (MPH, PhD); health management and policy (MPH); health policy (PhD); health promotion and health behavior (MPH, PhD); international health (MPH). *Accreditation:* CEPH. *Program availability:* Part-time. *Faculty:* 32 full-time (18 women), 3 part-time/adjunct (0 women). *Students:* 123 full-time (91 women), 20 part-time (14 women); includes 43 minority (2 Black or African American, non-Hispanic/Latino; 2 American Indian or Alaska Native, non-Hispanic/Latino; 9 Asian, non-Hispanic/Latino; 18 Hispanic/Latino; 1 Native Hawaiian or other Pacific Islander, non-Hispanic/Latino; 11 Two or more races, non-Hispanic/Latino), 18 international. Average age 31. 276 applicants, 65% accepted, 45 enrolled. In 2015, 59 master's, 6 doctorates awarded. Terminal master's awarded for partial completion of doctoral program. *Degree requirements:* For doctorate, one foreign language, thesis/dissertation. *Entrance requirements:* For master's and doctorate, GRE, minimum GPA of 3.0 in last 90 hours. Additional exam requirements/recommendations for international students: Required—TOEFL (minimum score 80 iBT), IELTS (minimum score 6.5). *Application deadline:* For fall admission, 12/1 priority date for domestic students. Applications are processed on a rolling basis. *Expenses:* $13,851 full-time resident tuition, $23,679 full-time non-resident tuition, $1,572 fees. *Financial support:* Fellowships, research assistantships, teaching assistantships, career-related internships or fieldwork, Federal Work-Study, and institutionally sponsored loans available. Support available to part-time students. Financial award application deadline: 12/1. *Faculty research:* Traffic safety, health safety, injury control, health promotion. *Unit head:* Dr. Sheryl Thorburn, Professor/Co-Director. *Application contact:* Amanda Armington, Public Health Program Manager, 541-737-3825,
E-mail: amanda.armington@oregonstate.edu.

Penn State Hershey Medical Center, College of Medicine, Graduate School Programs in the Biomedical Sciences, Program in Biostatistics, Hershey, PA 17033. Offers PhD. *Students:* 5 full-time (3 women); includes 1 minority (Black or African American, non-Hispanic/Latino), 3 international. 26 applicants, 12% accepted, 3 enrolled. *Entrance requirements:* For doctorate, GRE General Test, previous coursework or master's degree in biostatistics or statistics. Additional exam requirements/recommendations for international students: Required—TOEFL (minimum score 550 paper-based; 80 iBT). *Application deadline:* For fall admission, 1/15 for domestic and international students. Applications are processed on a rolling basis. Application fee: $65. Electronic applications accepted. *Financial support:* In 2015–16, research assistantships (averaging $24,544 per year) were awarded; scholarships/grants, health care benefits, and unspecified assistantships also available. *Unit head:* Dr. Arthur Berg, Director, 717-531-3039, Fax: 717-531-5779, E-mail: asb17@psu.edu. *Application contact:* Mardi Sawyer, Program Administrator, 717-531-7178, Fax: 717-531-5779,
E-mail: hes-grad-hmc@psu.edu.

Website: https://www2.med.psu.edu/phs/graduate-programs/phd-in-biostatistics/

Rice University, Graduate Programs, George R. Brown School of Engineering, Department of Statistics, Houston, TX 77251-1892. Offers bioinformatics (PhD); biostatistics (PhD); computational finance (PhD); general statistics (PhD); statistics (M Stat, MA); MBA/M Stat. *Program availability:* Part-time. *Degree requirements:* For master's, comprehensive exam; for doctorate, comprehensive exam, thesis/dissertation. *Entrance requirements:* For master's and doctorate, GRE General Test, minimum GPA of 3.0. Additional exam requirements/recommendations for international students: Required—TOEFL (minimum score 630 paper-based; 90 iBT). Electronic applications accepted. *Faculty research:* Statistical genetics, non parametric function estimation, computational statistics and visualization, stochastic processes.

Rutgers University–New Brunswick, Graduate School-New Brunswick, BioMaPS Institute for Quantitative Biology, Piscataway, NJ 08854-8097. Offers computational biology and molecular biophysics (PhD). *Degree requirements:* For doctorate, comprehensive exam, thesis/dissertation. *Entrance requirements:* For doctorate, GRE. Additional exam requirements/recommendations for international students: Required—TOEFL. Electronic applications accepted. *Faculty research:* Structural biology, systems biology, bioinformatics, translational medicine, genomics.

Rutgers University–New Brunswick, Graduate School-New Brunswick, Program in Statistics, Piscataway, NJ 08854-8097. Offers applied statistics (MS); biostatistics (MS); data mining (MS); quality and productivity management (MS); statistics (MS, PhD). *Program availability:* Part-time. Terminal master's awarded for partial completion of doctoral program. *Degree requirements:* For master's, comprehensive exam, essay, exam, non-thesis essay paper; for doctorate, one foreign language, thesis/dissertation, qualifying oral and written exams. *Entrance requirements:* For master's, GRE General Test; for doctorate, GRE General Test, GRE Subject Test (recommended). Additional exam requirements/recommendations for international students: Required—TOEFL (minimum score 550 paper-based). Electronic applications accepted. *Faculty research:* Probability, decision theory, linear models, multivariate statistics, statistical computing.

Rutgers University–New Brunswick, School of Public Health, Piscataway, NJ 08854. Offers biostatistics (MPH, MS, Dr PH, PhD); clinical epidemiology (Certificate); environmental and occupational health (MPH, Dr PH, PhD, Certificate); epidemiology (MPH, Dr PH, PhD); general public health (Certificate); health education and behavioral science (MPH, Dr PH, PhD); health systems and policy (MPH, PhD); public health (MPH, Dr PH, PhD); public health preparedness (Certificate); DO/MPH; JD/MPH; MBA/MPH; MD/MPH; MPH/MBA; MPH/MSPA; MS/MPH; Psy D/MPH. *Accreditation:* CEPH. *Program availability:* Part-time, evening/weekend. *Degree requirements:* For master's, thesis, internship; for doctorate, comprehensive exam, thesis/dissertation. *Entrance requirements:* For master's, GRE General Test; for doctorate, GRE General Test, MPH (Dr PH); MA, MPH, or MS (PhD). Additional exam requirements/recommendations for international students: Required—TOEFL. Electronic applications accepted.

San Diego State University, Graduate and Research Affairs, College of Health and Human Services, Graduate School of Public Health, San Diego, CA 92182. Offers environmental health (MPH); epidemiology (MPH, PhD), including biostatistics (MPH); global emergency preparedness and response (MS); global health (PhD); health behavior (PhD); health promotion (MPH); health services administration (MPH); toxicology (MS); MPH/MA; MSW/MPH. *Accreditation:* CAHME (one or more programs are accredited); CEPH (one or more programs are accredited). *Program availability:* Part-time. *Degree requirements:* For master's, comprehensive exam (for some programs), thesis (for some programs); for doctorate, thesis/dissertation. *Entrance requirements:* For master's, GMAT (MPH in health services administration), GRE General Test; for doctorate, GRE General Test. Additional exam requirements/recommendations for international students: Required—TOEFL. *Faculty research:* Evaluation of tobacco, AIDS prevalence and prevention, mammography, infant death project, Alzheimer's in elderly Chinese.

Stanford University, School of Medicine, Graduate Programs in Medicine, Department of Health Research and Policy, Stanford, CA 94305-9991. Offers biostatistics (PhD); epidemiology and clinical research (MS, PhD); health policy (MS, PhD). *Degree requirements:* For master's, thesis. Electronic applications accepted. *Expenses: Tuition, area resident:* Full-time $45,729. *Required fees:* $591. *Faculty research:* Cost and quality of life in cardiovascular disease, technology assessment, physician decision-making.

Tufts University, Sackler School of Graduate Biomedical Sciences, Clinical and Translational Science Program, Medford, MA 02155. Offers MS, PhD, Certificate. *Faculty:* 34 full-time (10 women). *Students:* 20 full-time (13 women), 1 part-time; includes 4 minority (1 Black or African American, non-Hispanic/Latino; 3 Asian, non-Hispanic/Latino), 4 international. Average age 37. 34 applicants, 47% accepted, 11 enrolled. In 2015, 3 master's, 3 doctorates, 4 other advanced degrees awarded. *Degree requirements:* For master's, thesis; for doctorate, comprehensive exam, thesis/dissertation. *Entrance requirements:* For master's, MD or PhD, strong clinical research background. Additional exam requirements/recommendations for international students: Required—TOEFL (minimum score 600 paper-based; 100 iBT). *Application deadline:* For fall admission, 4/15 for domestic and international students. Applications are processed on a rolling basis. Application fee: $90. Electronic applications accepted. *Expenses:* $26,964 per year tuition and fees. *Faculty research:* Clinical study design, mathematical modeling, meta analysis, epidemiologic research, coronary heart disease. *Unit head:* Dr. David Kent, Program Director, 617-636-3234, Fax: 617-636-8023,
E-mail: dkent@tuftsmedicalcenter.edu. *Application contact:* Kellie Melchin, Associate Director of Admissions, 617-636-6767, Fax: 617-636-0375,
E-mail: sackler-school@tufts.edu.
Website: http://sackler.tufts.edu/Academics/Degree-Programs/Clinical-and-Translational-Science

Tufts University, School of Medicine, Public Health and Professional Degree Programs, Boston, MA 02111. Offers biomedical sciences (MS); development and regulation of medicines and devices (MS, Certificate); health communication (MS, Certificate); pain research, education and policy (MS, Certificate); physician assistant (MS); public health (MPH, Dr PH), including biostatistics (MPH), epidemiology (MPH), global health (MPH), health communication (MPH), health services (MPH), management and policy (MPH), nutrition (MPH); DMD/MPH; DVM/MPH; JD/MPH; MD/MPH; MS/MBA; MS/MPH. MS programs offered jointly with Emerson College. *Accreditation:* CEPH (one or more programs are accredited). *Program availability:* Part-time, evening/weekend. *Faculty:* 78 full-time (29 women), 42 part-time/adjunct (20 women). *Students:* 457 full-time (266 women), 61 part-time (46 women); includes 187 minority (21 Black or African American, non-Hispanic/Latino; 107 Asian, non-Hispanic/Latino; 37 Hispanic/Latino; 22 Two or more races, non-Hispanic/Latino), 24 international. Average age 27. 1,599 applicants, 48% accepted, 222 enrolled. In 2015, 219 master's awarded. *Degree requirements:* For master's, thesis (for some programs); for doctorate, thesis/dissertation. *Entrance requirements:* For master's, GRE General Test, MCAT, or GMAT; for doctorate, GRE General Test or MCAT. Additional exam requirements/recommendations for international students: Required—TOEFL (minimum score 100 iBT). *Application deadline:* For fall admission, 1/15 priority date for domestic students, 12/15 priority date for international students; for spring admission, 10/25 priority date for domestic and international students. Applications are processed on a rolling basis. Application fee: $70. Electronic applications accepted. *Expenses:* Contact institution. *Financial support:* In 2015–16, 12 students received support, including 1 fellowship (averaging $3,000 per year), 50 research assistantships (averaging $1,000 per year), 65 teaching assistantships (averaging $2,000 per year); Federal Work-Study and scholarships/grants also available. Support available to part-time students. Financial award application deadline: 2/19; financial award applicants required to submit FAFSA. *Faculty research:* Environmental and occupational health, nutrition, epidemiology, health communication, biostatics, obesity/chronic disease, health policy and health care delivery, global health, health inequality and social determinants of health. *Unit head:* Dr. Aviva Must, Dean, 617-636-0935, Fax: 617-636-0898, E-mail: aviva.must@tufts.edu. *Application contact:* Emily Keily, Director of Admissions, 617-636-0935, Fax: 617-636-0898, E-mail: med-phpd@tufts.edu.
Website: http://publichealth.tufts.edu

Tulane University, School of Public Health and Tropical Medicine, Department of Biostatistics and Bioinformatics, New Orleans, LA 70118-5669. Offers MS, MSPH, PhD. MS and PhD offered through the Graduate School. *Program availability:* Part-time. *Degree requirements:* For doctorate, comprehensive exam, thesis/dissertation. *Entrance requirements:* For master's and doctorate, GRE General Test. Additional exam requirements/recommendations for international students: Required—TOEFL. Electronic applications accepted. *Faculty research:* Clinical trials, measurement, longitudinal analyses.

University at Albany, State University of New York, School of Public Health, Department of Epidemiology and Biostatistics, Albany, NY 12222-0001. Offers epidemiology and biostatistics (MS, PhD); public health (MPH, Dr PH). *Degree requirements:* For master's, thesis; for doctorate, thesis/dissertation. *Entrance requirements:* For master's and doctorate, GRE General Test. Additional exam requirements/recommendations for international students: Required—TOEFL (minimum score 550 paper-based). Electronic applications accepted.

University at Buffalo, the State University of New York, Graduate School, School of Public Health and Health Professions, Department of Biostatistics, Buffalo, NY 14260. Offers MA, MPH, PhD. *Faculty:* 11 full-time (3 women), 2 part-time/adjunct (0 women). *Students:* 66 full-time (36 women), 15 part-time (6 women); includes 7 minority (1 Black or African American, non-Hispanic/Latino; 6 Asian, non-Hispanic/Latino), 57 international. Average age 28. 184 applicants, 61% accepted, 35 enrolled. In 2015, 16 master's, 3 doctorates awarded. Terminal master's awarded for partial completion of doctoral program. *Degree requirements:* For master's, comprehensive exam, thesis optional, final oral exam, practical data analysis experience; for doctorate, comprehensive exam, thesis/dissertation, final oral exam. *Entrance requirements:* For master's, GRE, 3 semesters of course work in calculus (for mathematics), course work

in real analysis (preferred), course work in linear algebra; for doctorate, GRE, master's degree in statistics, biostatistics or equivalent. Additional exam requirements/recommendations for international students: Required—TOEFL (minimum score 640 paper-based; 79 iBT). *Application deadline:* For fall admission, 4/1 priority date for domestic and international students. Application fee: $50. Electronic applications accepted. *Financial support:* In 2015–16, 12 students received support, including 1 fellowship with full tuition reimbursement available (averaging $4,000 per year), 4 research assistantships with full tuition reimbursements available (averaging $24,000 per year), 4 teaching assistantships with full tuition reimbursements available (averaging $20,000 per year); institutionally sponsored loans, scholarships/grants, and tuition waivers (partial) also available. Financial award application deadline: 2/1; financial award applicants required to submit FAFSA. *Faculty research:* Biostatistics, longitudinal data analysis, nonparametrics, statistical genetics, epidemiology. *Unit head:* Dr. Gregory Wilding, Interim Chair, 716-829-2594, Fax: 716-829-2200,
E-mail: gwilding@buffalo.edu. *Application contact:* Dr. Lili Tian, Director of Graduate Studies/Professor, 716-829-2715, Fax: 716-829-2200, E-mail: ltian@buffalo.edu.
Website: http://sphhp.buffalo.edu/biostat/index.php

The University of Alabama at Birmingham, School of Public Health, Program in Biostatistics, Birmingham, AL 35294-0022. Offers biostatistics (MPH, MS, MSPH, PhD), including clinical and translational science (MSPH). *Program availability:* Part-time. *Faculty:* 16 full-time (7 women), 2 part-time/adjunct (0 women). *Students:* 26 full-time (20 women), 17 part-time (8 women); includes 22 minority (5 Black or African American, non-Hispanic/Latino; 16 Asian, non-Hispanic/Latino; 1 Two or more races, non-Hispanic/Latino), 11 international. Average age 35. 63 applicants, 35% accepted, 15 enrolled. In 2015, 6 master's, 7 doctorates awarded. Terminal master's awarded for partial completion of doctoral program. *Degree requirements:* For master's, variable foreign language requirement, comprehensive exam (for some programs), thesis (for some programs), research project; for doctorate, variable foreign language requirement, comprehensive exam, thesis/dissertation. *Entrance requirements:* For master's, GRE General Test (minimum scores: 147 on verbal and 150 on quantitative sections), minimum undergraduate GPA of 3.0; for doctorate, GRE General Test (minimum scores: 70th percentile on both verbal and quantitative sections), master's degree, minimum GPA of 3.0, interview. Additional exam requirements/recommendations for international students: Required—TOEFL (minimum score 550 paper-based; 79 iBT). *Application deadline:* For fall admission, 5/1 for domestic and international students. Application fee: $60 ($75 for international students). Electronic applications accepted. *Expenses:* $12,000 in-state, $26,000 out-of-state. *Financial support:* In 2015–16, 15 students received support, including 8 fellowships with full tuition reimbursements available (averaging $22,476 per year), 4 research assistantships with partial tuition reimbursements available (averaging $21,000 per year), 3 teaching assistantships with partial tuition reimbursements available (averaging $21,000 per year); career-related internships or fieldwork, scholarships/grants, health care benefits, tuition waivers (full and partial), and unspecified assistantships also available. Financial award application deadline: 5/1. *Faculty research:* Statistical genetics and genomics, bioinformatics, clinical trials, linear model, survival analysis. *Total annual research expenditures:* $5.1 million. *Unit head:* Dr. Nianjun Liu, Program Director, 205-934-4905, Fax: 205-975-2540, E-mail: nliu@uab.edu. *Application contact:* Holly Hebard, Director of Graduate School Operations, 205-934-8227, Fax: 205-934-8413, E-mail: gradschool@uab.edu.
Website: http://www.soph.uab.edu/bst

The University of Alabama at Birmingham, School of Public Health, Program in Public Health, Birmingham, AL 35294. Offers applied epidemiology and pharmacoepidemiology (MSPH); biostatistics (MPH); clinical and translational science (MSPH); environmental health (MPH); environmental health and toxicology (MSPH); epidemiology (MPH); general theory and practice (MPH); health behavior (MPH); health care organization (MPH); health policy quantitative policy analysis (MPH); industrial hygiene (MPH, MSPH); maternal and child health policy (Dr PH); maternal and child health policy and leadership (MPH); occupational health and safety (MPH); outcomes research (MSPH, Dr PH); public health (PhD); public health management (Dr PH); public health preparedness management (MPH). *Accreditation:* CEPH. *Program availability:* Part-time, online learning. *Degree requirements:* For doctorate, comprehensive exam, thesis/dissertation. *Entrance requirements:* For master's and doctorate, GRE. Additional exam requirements/recommendations for international students: Recommended—TOEFL (minimum score 550 paper-based; 79 iBT), IELTS (minimum score 6.5). Electronic applications accepted. *Expenses:* Tuition, state resident: full-time $7340. Tuition, nonresident: full-time $16,628. Full-time tuition and fees vary according to course load and program.

University of Alberta, Faculty of Graduate Studies and Research, Department of Mathematical and Statistical Sciences, Edmonton, AB T6G 2E1, Canada. Offers applied mathematics (M Sc, PhD); biostatistics (M Sc); mathematical finance (M Sc, PhD); mathematical physics (M Sc, PhD); mathematics (M Sc, PhD); statistics (M Sc, PhD, Postgraduate Diploma). *Program availability:* Part-time. Terminal master's awarded for partial completion of doctoral program. *Degree requirements:* For master's, thesis (for some programs); for doctorate, comprehensive exam, thesis/dissertation. *Entrance requirements:* Additional exam requirements/recommendations for international students: Required—TOEFL (minimum score 580 paper-based). Electronic applications accepted. *Faculty research:* Classical and functional analysis, algebra, differential equations, geometry.

The University of Arizona, Mel and Enid Zuckerman College of Public Health, Program in Biostatistics, Tucson, AZ 85721. Offers MS, PhD. *Entrance requirements:* Additional exam requirements/recommendations for international students: Required—TOEFL (minimum score 550 paper-based; 79 iBT). *Application deadline:* For fall admission, 1/1 for domestic and international students. Applications are processed on a rolling basis. Application fee: $75. Electronic applications accepted. *Financial support:* Research assistantships and teaching assistantships available. *Unit head:* Denise Roe, Dean, 520-626-2281. *Application contact:* Amy Glicken, Special Assistant to the Dean, 520-626-3201, E-mail: coph-admit@email.arizona.edu.

University of Arkansas for Medical Sciences, College of Public Health, Little Rock, AR 72205-7199. Offers biostatistics (MPH); environmental and occupational health (MPH, Certificate); epidemiology (MPH, PhD); health behavior and health education (MPH); health policy and management (MPH); health promotion and prevention research (PhD); health services administration (MHSA); health systems research (PhD); public health (Certificate); public health leadership (Dr PH). *Program availability:* Part-time. *Degree requirements:* For master's, preceptorship, culminating experience, internship; for doctorate, comprehensive exam, capstone. *Entrance requirements:* For master's, GRE, GMAT, LSAT, PCAT, MCAT, DAT; for doctorate, GRE. Additional exam requirements/recommendations for international students: Required—TOEFL (minimum score 80 iBT), IELTS. Electronic applications accepted. *Expenses:* Contact institution. *Faculty research:* Health systems, tobacco prevention control, obesity prevention, environmental and occupational exposure, cancer prevention.

University of California, Berkeley, Graduate Division, School of Public Health, Group in Biostatistics, Berkeley, CA 94720-1500. Offers MA, PhD. *Accreditation:* CEPH (one or more programs are accredited). *Degree requirements:* For master's, oral exam; for doctorate, thesis/dissertation, oral exam. *Entrance requirements:* For master's and doctorate, GRE General Test, minimum GPA of 3.0, 3 letters of recommendation. Additional exam requirements/recommendations for international students: Required—TOEFL.

University of California, Davis, Graduate Studies, Graduate Group in Biostatistics, Davis, CA 95616. Offers MS, PhD. *Degree requirements:* For master's, comprehensive exam; for doctorate, thesis/dissertation. *Entrance requirements:* Additional exam requirements/recommendations for international students: Required—TOEFL (minimum score 550 paper-based). Electronic applications accepted.

University of California, Los Angeles, Graduate Division, School of Public Health, Department of Biostatistics, Los Angeles, CA 90095. Offers MPH, MS, Dr PH, PhD. *Degree requirements:* For master's, comprehensive exam; for doctorate, thesis/dissertation, oral and written qualifying exams. *Entrance requirements:* For master's, GRE General Test, minimum GPA of 3.0; for doctorate, GRE General Test, minimum undergraduate GPA of 3.0. Electronic applications accepted.

University of California, San Diego, School of Medicine, Program in Biostatistics, La Jolla, CA 92093. Offers PhD. *Entrance requirements:* For doctorate, GRE, 3 letters of recommendation, statement of purpose, resume/curriculum vitae, official transcripts with minimum GPA of 3.0. Additional exam requirements/recommendations for international students: Required—TOEFL (minimum score 550 paper-based; 80 iBT). *Application deadline:* For fall admission, 1/6 for domestic students. Application fee: $90 ($110 for international students). Electronic applications accepted. *Expenses:* Tuition, state resident: full-time $11,220. Tuition, nonresident: full-time $26,322. *Required fees:* $1800. *Financial support:* Applicants required to submit FAFSA. *Faculty research:* Biostatistics, mathematical statistics, computer sciences, survival analysis, prognostic modeling, longitudinal data analysis, statistical genetics. *Unit head:* Dr. Karen Messer, Director, 858-822-1073. *Application contact:* Melody Bazyar, 858-822-1073,
E-mail: somadmissions@ucsd.edu.
Website: http://biostat.ucsd.edu/phd-program/index.html

University of Cincinnati, Graduate School, College of Medicine, Graduate Programs in Biomedical Sciences, Department of Environmental Health, Cincinnati, OH 45221. Offers environmental and industrial hygiene (MS, PhD); environmental and occupational medicine (MS); environmental genetics and molecular toxicology (MS, PhD); epidemiology and biostatistics (MS, PhD); occupational safety and ergonomics (MS, PhD). *Accreditation:* ABET (one or more programs are accredited). Terminal master's awarded for partial completion of doctoral program. *Degree requirements:* For master's, thesis; for doctorate, thesis/dissertation, qualifying exam. *Entrance requirements:* For master's, GRE General Test, bachelor's degree in science; for doctorate, GRE General Test. Additional exam requirements/recommendations for international students: Required—TOEFL (minimum score 600 paper-based; 100 iBT). Electronic applications accepted. *Faculty research:* Carcinogens and mutagenesis, pulmonary studies, reproduction and development.

University of Colorado Denver, Colorado School of Public Health, Department of Biostatistics and Informatics, Aurora, CO 80045. Offers MS, PhD. *Program availability:* Part-time. *Faculty:* 24 full-time (14 women), 4 part-time/adjunct (2 women). *Students:* 25 full-time (17 women), 15 part-time (8 women); includes 6 minority (5 Asian, non-Hispanic/Latino; 1 Two or more races, non-Hispanic/Latino), 3 international. Average age 32. 65 applicants, 18% accepted, 11 enrolled. In 2015, 2 master's awarded. Terminal master's awarded for partial completion of doctoral program. *Degree requirements:* For master's, 34 credit hours, project or thesis; for doctorate, comprehensive exam, thesis/dissertation, 78 credit hours (25 of which can be completed while completing a master's degree). *Entrance requirements:* For master's, GRE General Test, baccalaureate degree in scientific field, minimum GPA of 3.0, math course work through integral calculus, two official copies of all academic transcripts, four letters of recommendation/reference, essays describing the applicant's career goals and reasons for applying to the program, resume; for doctorate, GRE General Test, baccalaureate degree in scientific field; master's degree in biostatistics, statistics or equivalent; minimum GPA of 3.0; math course work through integral calculus; two official copies of all academic transcripts; four letters of recommendation/reference; essays; resume. Additional exam requirements/recommendations for international students: Required—TOEFL (minimum score 550 paper-based; 80 iBT). *Application deadline:* For fall admission, 2/1 for domestic students. Application fee: $65 ($75 for international students). Electronic applications accepted. *Expenses:* Contact institution. *Financial support:* In 2015–16, 25 students received support. Fellowships, research assistantships, teaching assistantships, Federal Work-Study, institutionally sponsored loans, scholarships/grants, traineeships, and unspecified assistantships available. Financial award application deadline: 3/1; financial award applicants required to submit FAFSA. *Faculty research:* Health policy research, nonlinear mixed effects models for longitudinal data, statistical methods in nutrition, clinical trials. *Unit head:* Dr. Debashis Ghosh, Chair, 303-724-4365, Fax: 303-724-4620,
E-mail: debashis.ghosh@ucdenver.edu. *Application contact:* Crystal Alvarado, Department Assistant, 303-724-8618, E-mail: crystal.alvarado@ucdenver.edu.
Website: http://www.ucdenver.edu/academics/colleges/PublicHealth/departments/Biostatistics/Pages/welcome.aspx

University of Florida, Graduate School, College of Public Health and Health Professions, Department of Biostatistics, Gainesville, FL 32611. Offers MS, PhD. *Faculty:* 19. *Students:* 41 full-time (26 women), 1 part-time (0 women); includes 2 minority (1 Black or African American, non-Hispanic/Latino; 1 Asian, non-Hispanic/Latino), 30 international. Average age 28. 149 applicants, 22% accepted, 13 enrolled. In 2015, 7 master's, 2 doctorates awarded. *Degree requirements:* For doctorate, comprehensive exam, thesis/dissertation. *Entrance requirements:* For master's, GRE General Test, minimum GPA of 3.0. Additional exam requirements/recommendations for international students: Required—TOEFL (minimum score 550 paper-based; 80 iBT), IELTS (minimum score 6). *Application deadline:* For fall admission, 1/15 for domestic and international students. Application fee: $30. *Financial support:* In 2015–16, 1 fellowship, 21 teaching assistantships were awarded; research assistantships also available. *Faculty research:* Stochastic modeling of infectious diseases, medical image processing and jump regression analysis, causal modeling and inference for clinical trials and observational studies, modeling of dose-response curves, simultaneous statistical inference. *Total annual research expenditures:* $9.6 million. *Unit head:* Peihua Qiu, PhD, Chair and Professor, 352-294-5911, E-mail: pqiu@ufl.edu. *Application contact:* Office of Admissions, 352-392-1365, E-mail: webrequests@admissions.ufl.edu.
Website: http://biostat.ufl.edu/

University of Florida, Graduate School, College of Public Health and Health Professions, Programs in Public Health, Gainesville, FL 32611. Offers biostatistics (MPH); clinical and translational science (PhD); environmental health (MPH); epidemiology (MPH); health management and policy (MPH); public health (MPH, PhD, Certificate); public health practice (MPH); rehabilitation science (PhD); social and behavioral sciences (MPH); DPT/MPH; DVM/MPH; JD/MPH; MD/MPH; Pharm D/MPH.

Biostatistics

Accreditation: CEPH. *Program availability:* Online learning. *Faculty:* 31. *Students:* 205 full-time (154 women), 60 part-time (42 women); includes 67 minority (27 Black or African American, non-Hispanic/Latino; 1 American Indian or Alaska Native, non-Hispanic/Latino; 25 Asian, non-Hispanic/Latino; 14 Hispanic/Latino), 24 international. Average age 30. 385 applicants, 44% accepted, 75 enrolled. In 2015, 81 master's, 6 doctorates awarded. *Degree requirements:* For master's, internship. *Entrance requirements:* For master's, GRE General Test, minimum GPA of 3.0. Additional exam requirements/recommendations for international students: Required—TOEFL (minimum score 550 paper-based; 80 iBT), IELTS (minimum score 6). *Application deadline:* For fall admission, 7/1 for domestic students, 4/1 for international students. Application fee: $30. *Financial support:* In 2015–16, 5 research assistantships, 10 teaching assistantships were awarded; fellowships also available. Financial award applicants required to submit FAFSA. *Unit head:* Sarah L. McKune, PhD, Program Director, 352-328-0615, Fax: 352-273-6448, E-mail: smckune@ufl.edu. *Application contact:* Telisha Martin, PhD, Associate Director, MPH Program, 352-273-6444, E-mail: martints@ufl.edu.
Website: http://www.mph.ufl.edu/

University of Illinois at Chicago, School of Public Health, Epidemiology and Biostatistics Division, Chicago, IL 60607-7128. Offers biostatistics (MPH, MS, PhD); epidemiology (MPH, MS, PhD). *Program availability:* Part-time. *Faculty:* 17 full-time (7 women), 12 part-time/adjunct (5 women). *Students:* 132 full-time (93 women), 58 part-time (43 women); includes 50 minority (12 Black or African American, non-Hispanic/Latino; 26 Asian, non-Hispanic/Latino; 10 Hispanic/Latino; 2 Two or more races, non-Hispanic/Latino), 32 international. Average age 30. Terminal master's awarded for partial completion of doctoral program. *Degree requirements:* For master's, thesis, field practicum; for doctorate, thesis/dissertation, independent research, internship. *Entrance requirements:* For master's and doctorate, GRE General Test, minimum GPA of 2.75. Additional exam requirements/recommendations for international students: Required—TOEFL. *Application deadline:* For fall admission, 2/1 for domestic students, 1/1 priority date for international students. Application fee: $60. Electronic applications accepted. *Expenses:* Contact institution. *Financial support:* In 2015–16, 17 students received support. Fellowships with full tuition reimbursements available, research assistantships with full tuition reimbursements available, teaching assistantships with full tuition reimbursements available, career-related internships or fieldwork, Federal Work-Study, institutionally sponsored loans, scholarships/grants, traineeships, tuition waivers (full), and unspecified assistantships available. Support available to part-time students. Financial award application deadline: 3/1; financial award applicants required to submit FAFSA. *Faculty research:* Quantitative methods. *Unit head:* Dr. Ronald Hershow, Division Director, 312-996-4759, E-mail: rchersho@uic.edu.
Website: http://publichealth.uic.edu/departments/epidemiologyandbiostatistics/

The University of Iowa, Graduate College, College of Public Health, Department of Biostatistics, Iowa City, IA 52242-1316. Offers biostatistics (MS, PhD, Certificate); quantitative methods (MPH). *Degree requirements:* For master's, thesis optional, exam; for doctorate, comprehensive exam, thesis/dissertation. *Entrance requirements:* For master's and doctorate, GRE General Test, minimum GPA of 3.0. Additional exam requirements/recommendations for international students: Required—TOEFL (minimum score 600 paper-based; 100 iBT). Electronic applications accepted.

The University of Kansas, University of Kansas Medical Center, School of Medicine, Department of Biostatistics, Kansas City, KS 66160. Offers applied statistics and analytics (MS); biostatistics (MS, PhD, Graduate Certificate); statistical applications (Graduate Certificate). *Faculty:* 16. *Students:* 25 full-time (7 women), 13 part-time (5 women); includes 9 minority (3 Black or African American, non-Hispanic/Latino; 5 Asian, non-Hispanic/Latino; 1 Two or more races, non-Hispanic/Latino), 13 international. Average age 31. 52 applicants, 94% accepted, 18 enrolled. In 2015, 4 master's, 2 doctorates awarded. *Degree requirements:* For master's, comprehensive exam; for doctorate, comprehensive exam, thesis/dissertation. *Entrance requirements:* For master's, GRE, coursework in calculus, computer programming, linear algebra, differential equations, and numerical analysis; for doctorate, master's degree. Additional exam requirements/recommendations for international students: Required—TOEFL. Application fee: $60. Electronic applications accepted. *Expenses:* Contact institution. *Financial support:* Research assistantships with full tuition reimbursements, scholarships/grants, traineeships, and unspecified assistantships available. Financial award application deadline: 3/1; financial award applicants required to submit FAFSA. *Faculty research:* Biostatistics, clinical trials. *Total annual research expenditures:* $774,141. *Unit head:* Dr. Matthew Mayo, Professor and Chair, 913-588-4735 Ext. 913, Fax: 913-588-0252, E-mail: mmayo@kumc.edu. *Application contact:* Dr. Jo A. Wick, Assistant Director of Graduate Education, 913-588-4790, Fax: 913-588-0252,
E-mail: jwick@kumc.edu.
Website: http://www.kumc.edu/school-of-medicine/department-of-biostatistics.html

University of Kentucky, Graduate School, College of Public Health, Program in Epidemiology and Biostatistics, Lexington, KY 40506-0032. Offers PhD.

University of Louisville, Graduate School, School of Public Health and Information Sciences, Department of Bioinformatics and Biostatistics, Louisville, KY 40292-0001. Offers biostatistics (MS, PhD); decision science (MS). *Program availability:* Part-time. *Students:* 21 full-time (9 women), 4 part-time (3 women); includes 3 minority (all Asian, non-Hispanic/Latino), 12 international. Average age 32. 25 applicants, 72% accepted, 7 enrolled. In 2015, 2 master's, 1 doctorate awarded. *Degree requirements:* For master's, thesis optional; for doctorate, comprehensive exam, thesis/dissertation. *Entrance requirements:* For master's and doctorate, GRE General Test. Additional exam requirements/recommendations for international students: Required—TOEFL (minimum score 600 paper-based; 100 iBT). *Application deadline:* For fall admission, 3/1 for domestic and international students. Application fee: $60. Electronic applications accepted. *Expenses:* Tuition, state resident: full-time $11,664; part-time $649 per credit hour. Tuition, nonresident: full-time $24,274; part-time $1350 per credit hour. *Required fees:* $196. Tuition and fees vary according to program and reciprocity agreements. *Financial support:* In 2015–16, 229,582 students received support. Research assistantships with full tuition reimbursements available, health care benefits, and unspecified assistantships available. Financial award applicants required to submit FAFSA. *Faculty research:* Survival analysis, bioinformatics, bootstrap methods, Bayesian analysis, clinical trials. *Total annual research expenditures:* $1.3 million. *Unit head:* Dr. Karunarathna Kulasekera, Interim Department Chair, 502-852-1827, Fax: 502-852-3294, E-mail: kb.kulasekera@louisville.edu. *Application contact:* Lynne Dosker, Administrative Assistant, 502-852-1827, Fax: 502-852-3294,
E-mail: lcdosk01@louisville.edu.
Website: http://www.louisville.edu/sphis

University of Louisville, Graduate School, School of Public Health and Information Sciences, Department of Public Health and Information Sciences, Louisville, KY 40202. Offers biostatistics (MS, PhD); clinical investigation (M Sc); epidemiology (MS); health management and systems sciences (MPH); public health sciences (PhD), including environmental health, epidemiology, health management, health promotion; public health sciences - health management (PhD). *Program availability:* Part-time. *Students:* 92 full-time (60 women), 33 part-time (19 women); includes 37 minority (16 Black or African American, non-Hispanic/Latino; 12 Asian, non-Hispanic/Latino; 6 Hispanic/Latino; 3 Two or more races, non-Hispanic/Latino), 19 international. Average age 32. 128 applicants, 77% accepted, 56 enrolled. In 2015, 38 master's, 6 doctorates awarded. *Degree requirements:* For master's, thesis optional; for doctorate, comprehensive exam, thesis/dissertation. *Entrance requirements:* For master's and doctorate, GRE General Test. Additional exam requirements/recommendations for international students: Required—TOEFL (minimum score 600 paper-based; 100 iBT). *Application deadline:* For fall admission, 5/1 for domestic and international students. Application fee: $60. Electronic applications accepted. *Expenses:* Tuition, state resident: full-time $11,664; part-time $649 per credit hour. Tuition, nonresident: full-time $24,274; part-time $1350 per credit hour. *Required fees:* $196. Tuition and fees vary according to program and reciprocity agreements. *Financial support:* In 2015–16, 718,988 students received support. Research assistantships with full tuition reimbursements available, scholarships/grants, health care benefits, and unspecified assistantships available. Financial award applicants required to submit FAFSA. *Faculty research:* Department of environmental and occupational health sciences department of health management and systems sciences department of health promotion and behavioral sciences. *Total annual research expenditures:* $2.1 million. *Unit head:* Dr. Craig Blakely, Dean, 502-852-3297, Fax: 502-852-3291, E-mail: chblak01@louisville.edu.
Website: http://louisville.edu/sphis/departments/health-management-systems-science

University of Maryland, Baltimore, School of Medicine, Department of Epidemiology and Public Health, Baltimore, MD 21201. Offers biostatistics (MS); clinical research (MS); epidemiology and preventive medicine (MPH, MS, PhD); gerontology (PhD); human genetics and genomic medicine (MS, PhD); molecular epidemiology (MS, PhD); toxicology (MS, PhD); JD/MS; MD/PhD; MS/PhD. *Accreditation:* CEPH. *Program availability:* Part-time. *Students:* 73 full-time (58 women), 56 part-time (32 women); includes 45 minority (23 Black or African American, non-Hispanic/Latino; 12 Asian, non-Hispanic/Latino; 5 Hispanic/Latino; 5 Two or more races, non-Hispanic/Latino), 17 international. Average age 31. In 2015, 34 master's, 17 doctorates awarded. *Degree requirements:* For doctorate, comprehensive exam, thesis/dissertation. *Entrance requirements:* For master's and doctorate, GRE General Test. Additional exam requirements/recommendations for international students: Required—TOEFL (minimum score 550 paper-based; 80 iBT); Recommended—IELTS (minimum score 7). *Application deadline:* For fall admission, 1/15 for domestic and international students. Application fee: $75. Electronic applications accepted. *Expenses:* Contact institution. *Financial support:* In 2015–16, research assistantships with partial tuition reimbursements (averaging $26,000 per year) were awarded; fellowships, Federal Work-Study, scholarships/grants, and unspecified assistantships also available. Financial award application deadline: 3/1; financial award applicants required to submit FAFSA. *Unit head:* Dr. Laura Hungerford, Program Director, 410-706-8492, Fax: 410-706-4225. *Application contact:* Jessica Kelley, Program Coordinator, 410-706-8492, Fax: 410-706-4225, E-mail: jkelley@som.umaryland.edu.
Website: http://lifesciences.umaryland.edu/epidemiology/

University of Maryland, Baltimore County, The Graduate School, College of Natural and Mathematical Sciences, Department of Mathematics and Statistics, Program in Statistics, Baltimore, MD 21250. Offers biostatistics (PhD); environmental statistics (MS); statistics (MS, PhD). *Program availability:* Part-time, evening/weekend. *Faculty:* 10 full-time (3 women). *Students:* 21 full-time (11 women), 16 part-time (7 women); includes 5 minority (4 Asian, non-Hispanic/Latino; 1 Hispanic/Latino), 16 international. Average age 34. 36 applicants, 39% accepted, 6 enrolled. In 2015, 9 master's, 5 doctorates awarded. Terminal master's awarded for partial completion of doctoral program. *Degree requirements:* For master's, comprehensive exam (for some programs), thesis (for some programs); for doctorate, comprehensive exam, thesis/dissertation. *Entrance requirements:* For master's and doctorate, GRE General Test, minimum GPA of 3.0. Additional exam requirements/recommendations for international students: Required—TOEFL (minimum score 600 paper-based; 100 iBT). *Application deadline:* For fall admission, 2/15 priority date for domestic students, 1/1 priority date for international students; for spring admission, 10/15 priority date for domestic students, 5/1 priority date for international students. Applications are processed on a rolling basis. Application fee: $50. Electronic applications accepted. *Expenses:* Tuition, state resident: full-time $12,816. Tuition, nonresident: full-time $19,710. *Financial support:* In 2015–16, 14 students received support, including 1 fellowship with full tuition reimbursement available (averaging $17,000 per year), 1 research assistantship with full tuition reimbursement available (averaging $17,000 per year), 10 teaching assistantships with tuition reimbursements available (averaging $17,000 per year); career-related internships or fieldwork, scholarships/grants, traineeships, health care benefits, tuition waivers (full and partial), and unspecified assistantships also available. Support available to part-time students. Financial award application deadline: 2/15. *Faculty research:* Design of experiments, statistical decision theory and inference, time series analysis, biostatistics and environmental statistics, bioinformatics. *Total annual research expenditures:* $578,449. *Unit head:* Dr. Junyong Park, Graduate Program Director, 410-455-2407, Fax: 410-455-1066, E-mail: junpark@umbc.edu. *Application contact:* Janet Burgee, Program Coordinator, Mathematics and Statistics, 410-455-2401, Fax: 410-455-1066, E-mail: jburgee@umbc.edu.
Website: http://www.math.umbc.edu

University of Maryland, College Park, Academic Affairs, School of Public Health, Department of Epidemiology and Biostatistics, College Park, MD 20742. Offers biostatistics (MPH); epidemiology (MPH, PhD).

University of Massachusetts Amherst, Graduate School, School of Public Health and Health Sciences, Department of Public Health, Amherst, MA 01003. Offers biostatistics (MPH, MS, PhD); community health education (MPH, MS, PhD); environmental health sciences (MPH, MS, PhD); epidemiology (MPH, MS, PhD); health policy and management (MPH, MS, PhD); nutrition (MPH, PhD); public health practice (MPH); MPH/MPPA. *Accreditation:* CEPH (one or more programs are accredited). *Program availability:* Part-time, evening/weekend, online learning. Terminal master's awarded for partial completion of doctoral program. *Degree requirements:* For master's, thesis (for some programs); for doctorate, comprehensive exam, thesis/dissertation. *Entrance requirements:* For master's and doctorate, GRE General Test. Additional exam requirements/recommendations for international students: Required—TOEFL (minimum score 550 paper-based; 80 iBT), IELTS (minimum score 6.5). Electronic applications accepted.

University of Memphis, Graduate School, School of Public Health, Memphis, TN 38152. Offers biostatistics (MPH); environmental health (MPH); epidemiology (MPH); health systems management (MPH); public health (MHA); social and behavioral sciences (MPH). *Program availability:* Part-time, evening/weekend, online learning. *Faculty:* 117 full-time (5 women), 5 part-time/adjunct (1 woman). *Students:* 100 full-time (68 women), 48 part-time (35 women); includes 63 minority (33 Black or African American, non-Hispanic/Latino; 20 Asian, non-Hispanic/Latino; 7 Hispanic/Latino; 3 Two or more races, non-Hispanic/Latino), 17 international. Average age 30. 114 applicants, 83% accepted, 37 enrolled. In 2015, 55 master's awarded. *Degree requirements:* For master's, comprehensive exam, thesis. *Entrance requirements:* For master's, GRE, letters of recommendation. Additional exam requirements/recommendations for

international students: Required—TOEFL. *Application deadline:* For fall admission, 4/1 for domestic students; for spring admission, 11/1 for domestic students. Application fee: $35 ($60 for international students). Electronic applications accepted. *Financial support:* In 2015–16, 46 students received support. Research assistantships with full tuition reimbursements available, Federal Work-Study, scholarships/grants, and unspecified assistantships available. Financial award application deadline: 2/15; financial award applicants required to submit FAFSA. *Faculty research:* Health and medical savings accounts, adoption rates, health informatics, Telehealth technologies, biostatistics, environmental health, epidemiology, health systems management, social and behavioral sciences. *Unit head:* Dr. Lisa M. Klesges, Director, 901-678-4637,
E-mail: lmklsges@memphis.edu. *Application contact:* Dr. Karen Weddle-West, Information Contact, 901-678-2531, Fax: 901-678-5023,
E-mail: gradsch@memphis.edu.
Website: http://www.memphis.edu/sph/

University of Michigan, School of Public Health, Department of Biostatistics, Ann Arbor, MI 48109. Offers MPH, MS, PhD. MS and PhD offered through the Horace H. Rackham School of Graduate Studies. *Faculty:* 32 full-time (13 women), 17 part-time/adjunct (5 women). *Students:* 133 full-time (61 women), 9 part-time (4 women); includes 12 minority (10 Asian, non-Hispanic/Latino; 2 Two or more races, non-Hispanic/Latino), 79 international. Average age 27. 537 applicants, 34% accepted, 61 enrolled. In 2015, 69 master's, 12 doctorates awarded. Terminal master's awarded for partial completion of doctoral program. *Degree requirements:* For doctorate, oral defense of dissertation, qualifying exam. *Entrance requirements:* For master's, GRE General Test; for doctorate, GRE General Test, master's degree. Additional exam requirements/recommendations for international students: Required—TOEFL (minimum score 100 iBT). *Application deadline:* For fall admission, 12/15 priority date for domestic students, 1/15 for international students. Applications are processed on a rolling basis. Application fee: $75. Electronic applications accepted. *Financial support:* Fellowships, research assistantships, teaching assistantships, career-related internships or fieldwork, Federal Work-Study, institutionally sponsored loans, scholarships/grants, traineeships, health care benefits, and unspecified assistantships available. Financial award application deadline: 12/15. *Faculty research:* Statistical genetics, categorical data analysis, incomplete data, survival analysis, modeling. *Unit head:* Dr. Goncalo Abecasis, Chair, 734-763-4901, Fax: 734-615-8322, E-mail: goncalo@umich.edu. *Application contact:* Nicole Fenech, Student Services Coordinator, 734-615-9817, Fax: 734-763-2215, E-mail: sph.bio.inquiries@umich.edu.
Website: http://www.sph.umich.edu/biostat/

University of Michigan, School of Public Health, Program in Clinical Research Design and Statistical Analysis, Ann Arbor, MI 48109. Offers MS. Offered through the Horace H. Rackham School of Graduate Studies; program admits applicants in odd-numbered calendar years only. *Program availability:* Evening/weekend. *Students:* 20 full-time (4 women); includes 2 minority (both Asian, non-Hispanic/Latino), 5 international. Average age 35. In 2015, 26 master's awarded. *Degree requirements:* For master's, comprehensive exam. *Entrance requirements:* For master's, GRE General Test or MCAT. Additional exam requirements/recommendations for international students: Recommended—TOEFL (minimum score 560 paper-based; 100 iBT). *Application deadline:* For fall admission, 1/15 priority date for domestic and international students. Applications are processed on a rolling basis. Application fee: $75. Electronic applications accepted. *Expenses:* Contact institution. *Financial support:* Application deadline: 3/15; applicants required to submit FAFSA. *Faculty research:* Survival analysis, missing data, Bayesian inference, health economics, quality of life. *Unit head:* Dr. Trivellore Raghunathan, Director, 734-615-9832, E-mail: teraghu@umich.edu. *Application contact:* Fatma Nedjari, Information Contact, 734-615-9812, Fax: 734-763-2215, E-mail: sph.bio.inquiries@umich.edu.
Website: http://www.sph.umich.edu/biostat/programs/clinical-stat/

University of Minnesota, Twin Cities Campus, School of Public Health, Major in Biostatistics, Minneapolis, MN 55455-0213. Offers MPH, MS, PhD. *Program availability:* Part-time. Terminal master's awarded for partial completion of doctoral program. *Degree requirements:* For master's, comprehensive exam; for doctorate, comprehensive exam, thesis/dissertation. *Entrance requirements:* For master's, GRE General Test, course work in applied statistics, computer programming, multivariable calculus, linear algebra; for doctorate, GRE General Test, bachelor's or master's degree in statistics, biostatistics or mathematics. Additional exam requirements/recommendations for international students: Required—TOEFL (minimum score 600 paper-based; 90 iBT). Electronic applications accepted. *Faculty research:* Analysis of spatial and longitudinal data, Bayes/Empirical Bayes methods, survival analysis, longitudinal models, generalized linear models.

University of Nebraska Medical Center, Department of Biostatistics, Omaha, NE 68198. Offers PhD. *Program availability:* Part-time, online learning. *Faculty:* 8 full-time (5 women). *Students:* 5 full-time (0 women), 3 part-time (2 women); includes 1 minority (Asian, non-Hispanic/Latino), 4 international. Average age 34. 9 applicants, 44% accepted, 4 enrolled. *Degree requirements:* For doctorate, comprehensive exam, thesis/dissertation. *Entrance requirements:* For doctorate, GRE. Additional exam requirements/recommendations for international students: Required—TOEFL (minimum score 550 paper-based). *Application deadline:* For fall admission, 4/1 for domestic and international students. Application fee: $45. Electronic applications accepted. *Expenses:* Tuition, state resident: full-time $7830; part-time $3915 per credit hour. Tuition, nonresident: full-time $22,410; part-time $11,205 per credit hour. *Required fees:* $521. *Financial support:* In 2015–16, research assistantships with full tuition reimbursements (averaging $23,100 per year), teaching assistantships with full tuition reimbursements (averaging $23,100 per year) were awarded. Financial award application deadline: 2/1; financial award applicants required to submit FAFSA. *Unit head:* Dr. Gleb Haynatzki, Professor, 402-559-3294, E-mail: ghaynatzki@unmc.edu. *Application contact:* Mary Morris, Coordinator, 402-559-4112, E-mail: mary.morris@unmc.edu.
Website: http://www.unmc.edu/publichealth/departments/biostatistics/

The University of North Carolina at Chapel Hill, Graduate School, Gillings School of Global Public Health, Department of Biostatistics, Chapel Hill, NC 27599. Offers MPH, MS, Dr PH, PhD. *Students:* 146 full-time (64 women); includes 43 minority (4 Black or African American, non-Hispanic/Latino; 26 Asian, non-Hispanic/Latino; 5 Hispanic/Latino; 1 Native Hawaiian or other Pacific Islander, non-Hispanic/Latino; 7 Two or more races, non-Hispanic/Latino), 50 international. Average age 29. 306 applicants, 26% accepted, 32 enrolled. In 2015, 13 master's, 14 doctorates awarded. *Degree requirements:* For master's, comprehensive exam, thesis, major paper; for doctorate, comprehensive exam, thesis/dissertation. *Entrance requirements:* For master's and doctorate, GRE General Test, minimum GPA of 3.0 (recommended). Additional exam requirements/recommendations for international students: Required—TOEFL, IELTS. *Application deadline:* For fall admission, 12/10 priority date for domestic and international students. Applications are processed on a rolling basis. Application fee: $85. Electronic applications accepted. *Financial support:* Fellowships with tuition reimbursements, research assistantships with tuition reimbursements, teaching assistantships with tuition reimbursements, Federal Work-Study, institutionally sponsored loans, traineeships, health care benefits, and unspecified assistantships available. Financial award application deadline: 1/1; financial award applicants required to submit FAFSA. *Faculty research:* Cancer, cardiovascular, environmental biostatistics; AIDS and other infectious diseases; statistical genetics; demography and population studies. *Unit head:* Dr. Michael R. Kosorok, Chair, 919-966-7254, Fax: 919-966-3804. *Application contact:* Melissa Hobgood, Student Services Manager, 919-966-7256, Fax: 919-966-3804, E-mail: hobgood@unc.edu.
Website: http://www2.sph.unc.edu/bios/

University of North Texas Health Science Center at Fort Worth, School of Public Health, Fort Worth, TX 76107-2699. Offers biostatistics (MPH); community health (MPH); disease control and prevention (Dr PH); environmental and occupational health sciences (MPH); epidemiology (MPH); health administration (MHA); health policy and management (MPH, Dr PH); DO/MPH; MS/MPH; MSN/MPH. MPH offered jointly with University of North Texas; DO/MPH with Texas College of Osteopathic Medicine. *Accreditation:* CEPH. *Program availability:* Part-time, evening/weekend. *Degree requirements:* For master's, thesis or alternative, supervised internship; for doctorate, thesis/dissertation, supervised internship. *Entrance requirements:* For master's, GRE General Test. Additional exam requirements/recommendations for international students: Required—TOEFL. Electronic applications accepted.

University of Oklahoma Health Sciences Center, Graduate College, College of Public Health, Program in Biostatistics and Epidemiology, Oklahoma City, OK 73190. Offers biostatistics (MPH, MS, Dr PH, PhD); epidemiology (MPH, MS, Dr PH, PhD). *Accreditation:* CEPH (one or more programs are accredited). *Program availability:* Part-time. *Degree requirements:* For master's, comprehensive exam, thesis (for some programs); for doctorate, comprehensive exam, thesis/dissertation. *Entrance requirements:* For master's, 3 letters of recommendation, resume; for doctorate, GRE General Test, letters of recommendation. Additional exam requirements/recommendations for international students: Required—TOEFL (minimum score 570 paper-based), TWE. *Faculty research:* Statistical methodology, applied statistics, acute and chronic disease epidemiology.

University of Pennsylvania, Perelman School of Medicine, Biomedical Graduate Studies, Graduate Group in Epidemiology and Biostatistics, Philadelphia, PA 19104. Offers biostatistics (MS, PhD); epidemiology (PhD). *Faculty:* 97 full-time (47 women), 11 part-time/adjunct (1 woman). *Students:* 43 full-time (23 women), 6 part-time (all women); includes 5 minority (1 Black or African American, non-Hispanic/Latino; 3 Asian, non-Hispanic/Latino; 1 Hispanic/Latino), 18 international. Average age 30. 129 applicants, 16% accepted, 12 enrolled. In 2015, 3 master's, 6 doctorates awarded. Terminal master's awarded for partial completion of doctoral program. *Degree requirements:* For master's, thesis; for doctorate, thesis/dissertation. *Entrance requirements:* For master's, GRE, 1 year of course work in calculus, 1 semester of course work in linear algebra, working knowledge of programming language; for doctorate, GRE, 1 year of course work in calculus, 1 semester of course work in linear algebra, and working knowledge of programming language (for biostatistics); training and experience in epidemiology, clinical sciences or a public health-related field (for epidemiology). Additional exam requirements/recommendations for international students: Required—TOEFL. *Application deadline:* For fall admission, 12/1 for domestic and international students. Application fee: $80. *Expenses: Tuition, area resident:* Full-time $31,068; part-time $5762 per course. *Required fees:* $3200; $336 per course. Full-time tuition and fees vary according to degree level, program and student level. Part-time tuition and fees vary according to course load, degree level and program. *Financial support:* In 2015–16, 42 students received support, including 12 fellowships with tuition reimbursements available (averaging $31,000 per year), 28 research assistantships with tuition reimbursements available (averaging $31,000 per year), 1 teaching assistantship with tuition reimbursement available (averaging $31,000 per year); career-related internships or fieldwork, institutionally sponsored loans, scholarships/grants, traineeships, health care benefits, and unspecified assistantships also available. Financial award application deadline: 12/1. *Faculty research:* Biostatistics: randomized clinical trials, data coordinating centers, methodological approaches to non-experimental epidemiologic studies, theoretical research in biostatistics; epidemiology: epidemiologic research designs including randomized clinical trials, cohort and case-control studies, surveys and quasi-experiments, health measurements, clinical economics and clinical decision making as applied to epidemiologic research. *Total annual research expenditures:* $28.8 million. *Unit head:* Dr. John H. Holmes, Graduate Group Chair, 215-898-4833,
E-mail: jhholmes@mail.med.upenn.edu. *Application contact:* Catherine Vallejo, Coordinator, 215-573-3881, E-mail: vallejo@mail.med.upenn.edu.
Website: http://www.med.upenn.edu/ggeb

University of Pittsburgh, Graduate School of Public Health, Department of Biostatistics, Pittsburgh, PA 15261. Offers MPH, MS, PhD. *Program availability:* Part-time. *Faculty:* 23 full-time (9 women), 5 part-time/adjunct (3 women). *Students:* 52 full-time (26 women), 14 part-time (9 women); includes 10 minority (9 Asian, non-Hispanic/Latino; 1 Hispanic/Latino), 32 international. Average age 29. 295 applicants, 37% accepted, 19 enrolled. In 2015, 17 master's, 15 doctorates awarded. Terminal master's awarded for partial completion of doctoral program. *Degree requirements:* For master's, comprehensive exam, thesis (for MS); essay or thesis (for MPH); for doctorate, comprehensive exam, thesis/dissertation. *Entrance requirements:* For master's, GRE General Test, previous course work in biology, calculus, computer science, and social science (for MPH); prior professional degree; for doctorate, GRE General Test, previous course work in biology, calculus, and computer science. Additional exam requirements/recommendations for international students: Required—TOEFL (minimum score 550 paper-based, 80 iBT) or IELTS (minimum score 6.5). *Application deadline:* For fall admission, 1/15 for domestic and international students. Applications are processed on a rolling basis. Application fee: $120. Electronic applications accepted. *Expenses:* $24,826 tuition and fees per year full-time in-state; $41,804 tuition and fees per year full-time out-of-state; $1,016 per credit plus $205 fees part-time in-state; $1,680 per credit plus $205 fees part-time out-of-state. *Financial support:* In 2015–16, 34 students received support, including 1 fellowship (averaging $12,864 per year), 29 research assistantships (averaging $20,907 per year), 10 teaching assistantships (averaging $16,377 per year); scholarships/grants, health care benefits, and unspecified assistantships also available. Financial award application deadline: 1/15. *Faculty research:* Survival analysis, statistical genetics, clinical trials, stochastic modeling. *Total annual research expenditures:* $3.7 million. *Unit head:* Dr. Sally C. Morton, Chair, 412-624-9939, Fax: 412-624-2183, E-mail: scmorton@pitt.edu. *Application contact:* Renee Valenti, Academic Affairs Administrator, 412-624-3023, Fax: 412-624-0184,
E-mail: rmn4@pitt.edu.
Website: http://www.publichealth.pitt.edu/biostatistics

University of Puerto Rico, Medical Sciences Campus, Graduate School of Public Health, Department of Social Sciences, Program in Biostatistics, San Juan, PR 00936-5067. Offers MPH. *Program availability:* Part-time. *Entrance requirements:* For master's, GRE, previous course work in algebra. *Expenses:* Contact institution.

University of Rochester, School of Medicine and Dentistry, Graduate Programs in Medicine and Dentistry, Department of Biostatistics and Computational Biology, Program in Medical Statistics, Rochester, NY 14627. Offers MS. *Degree requirements:*

Biostatistics

For master's, internship/applied project. *Expenses: Tuition, area resident:* Full-time $47,450; part-time $1482 per credit hour. *Required fees:* $528. Tuition and fees vary according to program.

University of South Carolina, The Graduate School, Arnold School of Public Health, Department of Epidemiology and Biostatistics, Program in Biostatistics, Columbia, SC 29208. Offers MPH, MSPH, Dr PH, PhD. *Program availability:* Part-time. *Degree requirements:* For master's, comprehensive exam, thesis (for some programs), practicum (MPH); for doctorate, comprehensive exam, thesis/dissertation (for some programs), practicum (Dr PH). *Entrance requirements:* For master's, GRE General Test; for doctorate, GRE General Test, master's degree. Additional exam requirements/recommendations for international students: Required—TOEFL (minimum score 570 paper-based; 88 iBT). Electronic applications accepted. *Faculty research:* Bayesian methods, biometric modeling, nonlinear regression, health survey methodology, measurement of health status.

University of Southern California, Keck School of Medicine and Graduate School, Graduate Programs in Medicine, Department of Preventive Medicine, Division of Biostatistics, Los Angeles, CA 90089. Offers applied biostatistics and epidemiology (MS); biostatistics (MS, PhD); epidemiology (PhD); molecular epidemiology (MS). *Faculty:* 47 full-time (8 women), 7 part-time/adjunct (3 women). *Students:* 122 full-time (69 women); includes 22 minority (2 Black or African American, non-Hispanic/Latino; 1 American Indian or Alaska Native, non-Hispanic/Latino; 13 Asian, non-Hispanic/Latino; 4 Hispanic/Latino; 2 Native Hawaiian or other Pacific Islander, non-Hispanic/Latino), 76 international. Average age 29. 116 applicants, 51% accepted, 36 enrolled. In 2015, 21 master's, 13 doctorates awarded. Terminal master's awarded for partial completion of doctoral program. *Degree requirements:* For master's, thesis; for doctorate, thesis/dissertation. *Entrance requirements:* For master's, GRE General Test, minimum scores of 150 on each Verbal and Quantitative sections, minimum GPA of 3.0; for doctorate, GRE General Test, minimum scores of 160 on each Verbal and Quantitative sections, minimum GPA of 3.5. Additional exam requirements/recommendations for international students: Required—TOEFL (minimum score 600 paper-based; 100 iBT), IELTS (minimum score 7). *Application deadline:* For fall admission, 12/1 priority date for domestic and international students; for winter admission, 5/15 priority date for domestic and international students; for spring admission, 11/1 priority date for domestic and international students; for summer admission, 3/1 priority date for domestic and international students. Applications are processed on a rolling basis. Application fee: $85. Electronic applications accepted. *Expenses:* Contact institution. *Financial support:* In 2015–16, 38 students received support, including 10 fellowships with full tuition reimbursements available (averaging $32,000 per year), 36 research assistantships with tuition reimbursements available (averaging $32,000 per year), 15 teaching assistantships with tuition reimbursements available (averaging $32,000 per year); career-related internships or fieldwork, Federal Work-Study, institutionally sponsored loans, scholarships/grants, traineeships, health care benefits, and unspecified assistantships also available. Financial award application deadline: 12/1; financial award applicants required to submit CSS PROFILE or FAFSA. *Faculty research:* Clinical trials in ophthalmology and cancer research, methods of analysis for epidemiological studies, genetic epidemiology. *Total annual research expenditures:* $1.3 million. *Unit head:* Dr. Kiros Berhane, Director, Graduate Programs in Biostatistics and Epidemiology, 323-442-1994, Fax: 323-442-2993, E-mail: kiros@usc.edu. *Application contact:* Mary L. Trujillo, Student Advisor/Program Manager, 323-442-2633, Fax: 323-442-2993, E-mail: mtrujill@usc.edu.
Website: https://biostatepi.usc.edu/

University of Southern California, Keck School of Medicine and Graduate School, Graduate Programs in Medicine, Department of Preventive Medicine, Master of Public Health Program, Los Angeles, CA 91803. Offers biostatistics and epidemiology (MPH); child and family health (MPH); environmental health (MPH); global health leadership (MPH); health communication (MPH); health education and promotion (MPH); public health policy (MPH). *Accreditation:* CEPH. *Program availability:* Part-time, evening/weekend. *Faculty:* 22 full-time (12 women), 3 part-time/adjunct (0 women). *Students:* 182 full-time (142 women), 35 part-time (25 women); includes 120 minority (19 Black or African American, non-Hispanic/Latino; 64 Asian, non-Hispanic/Latino; 37 Hispanic/Latino), 33 international. Average age 24. 236 applicants, 70% accepted, 71 enrolled. In 2015, 99 master's awarded. *Degree requirements:* For master's, practicum, final report, oral presentation. *Entrance requirements:* For master's, GRE General Test, MCAT, GMAT, minimum GPA of 3.0. Additional exam requirements/recommendations for international students: Required—TOEFL (minimum score 600 paper-based; 90 iBT). *Application deadline:* For fall admission, 6/1 priority date for domestic and international students; for spring admission, 10/1 priority date for domestic and international students; for summer admission, 3/1 for domestic and international students. Applications are processed on a rolling basis. Application fee: $85. Electronic applications accepted. *Expenses:* Contact institution. *Financial support:* Career-related internships or fieldwork, Federal Work-Study, institutionally sponsored loans, and scholarships/grants available. Support available to part-time students. Financial award application deadline: 5/4; financial award applicants required to submit CSS PROFILE or FAFSA. *Faculty research:* Substance abuse prevention, cancer and heart disease prevention, mass media and health communication research, health promotion, treatment compliance. *Unit head:* Dr. Louise A. Rohrbach, Director, 323-442-8237, Fax: 323-442-8297, E-mail: rohrbac@usc.edu. *Application contact:* Valerie Burris, Admissions Counselor, 323-442-7257, Fax: 323-442-8297, E-mail: valeriem@usc.edu.
Website: http://mph.usc.edu/

University of Southern Mississippi, Graduate School, College of Health, Department of Public Health, Hattiesburg, MS 39406-0001. Offers epidemiology and biostatistics (MPH); health education (MPH); health policy and administration (MPH). *Accreditation:* CEPH. *Program availability:* Part-time, evening/weekend. *Degree requirements:* For master's, comprehensive exam, thesis (for some programs). *Entrance requirements:* For master's, GRE General Test, minimum GPA of 2.75 in last 60 hours. Additional exam requirements/recommendations for international students: Required—TOEFL, IELTS. Electronic applications accepted. *Faculty research:* Rural health care delivery, school health, nutrition of pregnant teens, risk factor reduction, sexually transmitted diseases.

University of South Florida, College of Public Health, Department of Epidemiology and Biostatistics, Tampa, FL 33620-9951. Offers MPH, MSPH, PhD. *Accreditation:* CEPH (one or more programs are accredited). *Program availability:* Part-time, evening/weekend. *Degree requirements:* For master's, comprehensive exam, thesis (for some programs); for doctorate, comprehensive exam, thesis/dissertation. *Entrance requirements:* For master's, GRE General Test, minimum GPA of 3.0 in upper-level course work, goal statement letter, two professional letters of recommendation, resume/curriculum vitae; for doctorate, GRE General Test, minimum GPA of 3.0 in upper-level course work, 3 professional letters of recommendation, resume/curriculum vitae, writing sample. Additional exam requirements/recommendations for international students: Required—TOEFL (minimum score 550 paper-based; 79 iBT). Electronic applications accepted. *Faculty research:* Dementia, mental illness, mental health preventative trails, rural health outreach, clinical and administrative studies.

University of South Florida, Innovative Education, Tampa, FL 33620-9951. Offers adult, career and higher education (Graduate Certificate), including college teaching, leadership in developing human resources, leadership in higher education; Africana studies (Graduate Certificate), including diasporas and health disparities, genocide and human rights; aging studies (Graduate Certificate), including gerontology; art research (Graduate Certificate), including museum studies; business foundations (Graduate Certificate); chemical and biomedical engineering (Graduate Certificate), including materials science and engineering, water, health and sustainability; child and family studies (Graduate Certificate), including positive behavior support; civil and industrial engineering (Graduate Certificate), including transportation systems analysis; community and family health (Graduate Certificate), including maternal and child health, social marketing and public health, violence and injury: prevention and intervention, women's health; criminology (Graduate Certificate), including criminal justice administration; educational measurement and research (Graduate Certificate), including evaluation; English (Graduate Certificate), including comparative literary studies, creative writing, professional and technical communication; entrepreneurship (Graduate Certificate); environmental health (Graduate Certificate), including safety management; epidemiology and biostatistics (Graduate Certificate), including applied biostatistics, biostatistics, concepts and tools of epidemiology, epidemiology, epidemiology of infectious diseases; geography, environment and planning (Graduate Certificate), including community development, environmental policy and management, geographical information systems; geology (Graduate Certificate), including hydrogeology; global health (Graduate Certificate), including disaster management, global health and Latin American and Caribbean studies, global health practice, humanitarian assistance, infection control; government and international affairs (Graduate Certificate), including Cuban studies, globalization studies; health policy and management (Graduate Certificate), including health management and leadership, public health policy and programs; hearing specialist: early intervention (Graduate Certificate); industrial and management systems engineering (Graduate Certificate), including systems engineering, technology management; information studies (Graduate Certificate), including school library media specialist; information systems/decision sciences (Graduate Certificate), including analytics and business intelligence; instructional technology (Graduate Certificate), including distance education, Florida digital/virtual educator, instructional design, multimedia design, Web design; internal medicine, bioethics and medical humanities (Graduate Certificate), including biomedical ethics; Latin American and Caribbean studies (Graduate Certificate); mass communications (Graduate Certificate), including multimedia journalism; mathematics and statistics (Graduate Certificate), including mathematics; medicine (Graduate Certificate), including aging and neuroscience, bioinformatics, biotechnology, brain fitness and memory management, clinical investigation, health informatics, health sciences, integrative weight management, intellectual property, medicine and gender, metabolic and nutritional medicine, metabolic cardiology, pharmacy sciences; national and competitive intelligence (Graduate Certificate); psychological and social foundations (Graduate Certificate), including career counseling, college teaching, diversity in education, mental health counseling, school counseling; public affairs (Graduate Certificate), including nonprofit management, public management, research administration; public health (Graduate Certificate), including environmental health, health equity, public health generalist, translational research in adolescent behavioral health; public health practices (Graduate Certificate), including planning for healthy communities; rehabilitation and mental health counseling (Graduate Certificate), including integrative mental health care, marriage and family therapy, rehabilitation technology; secondary education (Graduate Certificate), including ESOL, foreign language education: culture and content, foreign language education: professional; social work (Graduate Certificate), including geriatric social work/clinical gerontology; special education (Graduate Certificate), including autism spectrum disorder, disabilities education: severe/profound; world languages (Graduate Certificate), including teaching English as a second language (TESL) or foreign language. *Unit head:* Kathy Barnes, Interdisciplinary Programs Coordinator, 813-974-8031, Fax: 813-974-7061, E-mail: barnesk@usf.edu. *Application contact:* Karen Tylinski, Metro Initiatives, 813-974-9943, Fax: 813-974-7061, E-mail: ktylinsk@usf.edu.
Website: http://www.usf.edu/innovative-education/

The University of Texas Health Science Center at Houston, Graduate School of Biomedical Sciences, Program in Biomathematics and Biostatistics, Houston, TX 77225-0036. Offers MS, PhD, MD/PhD. Terminal master's awarded for partial completion of doctoral program. *Degree requirements:* For master's, thesis; for doctorate, thesis/dissertation. *Entrance requirements:* For master's and doctorate, GRE General Test. Additional exam requirements/recommendations for international students: Required—TOEFL. Electronic applications accepted. *Faculty research:* Biostatistics, biomarkers, epidemiology, bioinformatics, computational biology.

The University of Toledo, College of Graduate Studies, College of Medicine and Life Sciences, Department of Public Health and Preventative Medicine, Toledo, OH 43606-3390. Offers biostatistics and epidemiology (Certificate); contemporary gerontological practice (Certificate); environmental and occupational health and safety (MPH); epidemiology (Certificate); global public health (Certificate); health promotion and education (MPH); industrial hygiene (MSOH); medical and health science teaching and learning (Certificate); occupational health (Certificate); public health administration (MPH); public health and emergency response (Certificate); public health epidemiology (MPH); public health nutrition (MPH); MD/MPH. *Program availability:* Part-time, evening/weekend. *Degree requirements:* For master's, thesis or alternative. *Entrance requirements:* For master's, GRE, minimum undergraduate GPA of 3.0, three letters of recommendation, statement of purpose, transcripts from all prior institutions attended, resume; for Certificate, minimum undergraduate GPA of 3.0, three letters of recommendation, statement of purpose, transcripts from all prior institutions attended, resume. Additional exam requirements/recommendations for international students: Required—TOEFL (minimum score 550 paper-based; 80 iBT), IELTS (minimum score 6.5). Electronic applications accepted.

University of Toronto, School of Graduate Studies, Department of Public Health Sciences, Toronto, ON M5S 1A1, Canada. Offers biostatistics (M Sc, PhD); community health (M Sc); community nutrition (MPH), including nutrition and dietetics; epidemiology (MPH, PhD); family and community medicine (MPH); occupational and environmental health (MPH); social and behavioral health science (PhD); social and behavioral health sciences (MPH), including health promotion. *Accreditation:* CAHME (one or more programs are accredited); CEPH (one or more programs are accredited). *Program availability:* Part-time. *Degree requirements:* For master's, thesis (for some programs), practicum; for doctorate, comprehensive exam, thesis/dissertation, oral thesis defense. *Entrance requirements:* For master's, 2 letters of reference, relevant professional/research experience, minimum B average in final year; for doctorate, 2 letters of reference, relevant professional/research experience, minimum B+ average. Additional exam requirements/recommendations for international students: Required—TOEFL (minimum score 580 paper-based; 93 iBT), TWE (minimum score 5). Electronic applications accepted. *Expenses:* Contact institution.

University of Utah, Graduate School, Interdepartmental Program in Statistics, Salt Lake City, UT 84112-1107. Offers biostatistics (M Stat); econometrics (M Stat); educational psychology (M Stat); mathematics (M Stat); sociology (M Stat). *Program availability:* Part-time. *Students:* 61 full-time (34 women), 45 part-time (13 women); includes 18 minority (3 Black or African American, non-Hispanic/Latino; 10 Asian, non-Hispanic/Latino; 3 Hispanic/Latino; 2 Two or more races, non-Hispanic/Latino), 30 international. Average age 32. 50 applicants, 70% accepted, 27 enrolled. In 2015, 18 master's awarded. *Degree requirements:* For master's, comprehensive exam (for some programs), projects. *Entrance requirements:* For master's, GRE General Test (for all but biostatistics); GRE Subject Test (for mathematics), minimum GPA of 3.0; course work in calculus, matrix theory, statistics. Additional exam requirements/recommendations for international students: Required—TOEFL (minimum score 500 paper-based; 61 iBT). *Application deadline:* For fall admission, 7/1 for domestic students, 4/1 for international students. Applications are processed on a rolling basis. Application fee: $55 ($65 for international students). Electronic applications accepted. *Financial support:* In 2015–16, 10 students received support, including 10 research assistantships with tuition reimbursements available (averaging $1,000 per year); career-related internships or fieldwork, scholarships/grants, and unspecified assistantships also available. *Faculty research:* Biostatistics, sociology, economics, educational psychology, mathematics. *Unit head:* Xiaoming Sheng, Chair, University Statistics Committee, 801-213-3729, E-mail: xiaoming.sheng@utah.edu. *Application contact:* Laura Egbert, Coordinator, 801-585-6853, E-mail: laura.egbert@utah.edu.
Website: http://www.mstat.utah.edu

University of Utah, School of Medicine and Graduate School, Graduate Programs in Medicine, Programs in Public Health, Salt Lake City, UT 84112-1107. Offers biostatistics (M Stat); public health (MPH, MSPH, PhD). *Accreditation:* CEPH (one or more programs are accredited). *Program availability:* Part-time. *Degree requirements:* For master's, comprehensive exam, thesis or project (MSPH); for doctorate, comprehensive exam, thesis/dissertation. *Entrance requirements:* For master's and doctorate, GRE General Test, 3 letters of reference, in-person interviews, minimum GPA of 3.0. Additional exam requirements/recommendations for international students: Required—TOEFL (minimum score 550 paper-based). Electronic applications accepted. *Faculty research:* Health services, health policy, epidemiology of chronic disease, infectious disease epidemiology, cancer epidemiology.

University of Vermont, Graduate College, College of Engineering and Mathematics, Department of Mathematics and Statistics, Program in Biostatistics, Burlington, VT 05405. Offers MS. *Degree requirements:* For master's, thesis or alternative. *Entrance requirements:* For master's, GRE General Test. Additional exam requirements/recommendations for international students: Required—TOEFL (minimum score 90 iBT). Electronic applications accepted.

University of Washington, Graduate School, Interdisciplinary Graduate Program in Quantitative Ecology and Resource Management, Seattle, WA 98195. Offers MS, PhD. *Degree requirements:* For master's, thesis; for doctorate, thesis/dissertation. *Entrance requirements:* For master's and doctorate, GRE General Test, minimum GPA of 3.0. Additional exam requirements/recommendations for international students: Required—TOEFL. Electronic applications accepted. *Faculty research:* Population dynamics, statistical analysis, ecological modeling and systems analysis of aquatic and terrestrial ecosystems.

University of Washington, Graduate School, School of Public Health, Department of Biostatistics, Seattle, WA 98195. Offers biostatistics (MPH, MS, PhD); clinical research (MS), including biostatistics; statistical genetics (PhD). *Program availability:* Part-time. Terminal master's awarded for partial completion of doctoral program. *Degree requirements:* For master's, comprehensive exam, thesis, practicum (MPH); for doctorate, comprehensive exam, thesis/dissertation. *Entrance requirements:* For master's and doctorate, GRE General Test, coursework on multivariate calculus, linear algebra and probability; minimum GPA of 3.0. Additional exam requirements/recommendations for international students: Required—TOEFL. Electronic applications accepted. *Expenses:* Contact institution. *Faculty research:* Statistical methods for survival data analysis, clinical trials, epidemiological case control and cohort studies, statistical genetics.

University of Waterloo, Graduate Studies, Faculty of Mathematics, Department of Statistics and Actuarial Science, Waterloo, ON N2L 3G1, Canada. Offers actuarial science (M Math, MAS, PhD); biostatistics (PhD); statistics (M Math, PhD); statistics-biostatistics (M Math); statistics-computing (M Math); statistics-finance (M Math). *Degree requirements:* For master's, research paper or thesis; for doctorate, comprehensive exam, thesis/dissertation. *Entrance requirements:* For master's, honors degree in field, minimum B+ average; for doctorate, master's degree, minimum B+ average. Additional exam requirements/recommendations for international students: Required—TOEFL, IELTS, PTE. *Application deadline:* Applications are processed on a rolling basis. Application fee: $100 Canadian dollars. Electronic applications accepted. *Financial support:* Fellowships, research assistantships, teaching assistantships, career-related internships or fieldwork, and scholarships/grants available. *Faculty research:* Data analysis, risk theory, inference, stochastic processes, quantitative finance.
Website: https://uwaterloo.ca/statistics-and-actuarial-science/

The University of Western Ontario, Faculty of Graduate Studies, Biosciences Division, Department of Epidemiology and Biostatistics, London, ON N6A 5B8, Canada. Offers M Sc, PhD. *Accreditation:* CEPH (one or more programs are accredited). *Program availability:* Part-time. *Degree requirements:* For master's, thesis; for doctorate, comprehensive exam, thesis proposal defense. *Entrance requirements:* For master's, BA or B Sc honors degree, minimum B+ average in last 10 courses; for doctorate, M Sc or equivalent, minimum B+ average in last 10 courses. *Faculty research:* Chronic disease epidemiology, clinical epidemiology.

Virginia Commonwealth University, Medical College of Virginia-Professional Programs, School of Medicine, School of Medicine Graduate Programs, Department of Biostatistics, Richmond, VA 23284-9005. Offers MS, PhD, MD/PhD. *Program availability:* Part-time. Terminal master's awarded for partial completion of doctoral program. *Degree requirements:* For master's, thesis; for doctorate, thesis/dissertation, comprehensive oral and written exams. *Entrance requirements:* For master's and doctorate, GRE, MCAT or DAT. Additional exam requirements/recommendations for international students: Required—TOEFL (minimum score 600 paper-based; 100 iBT). Electronic applications accepted. *Faculty research:* Health services, linear models, response surfaces, design and analysis of drug/chemical combinations, clinical trials.

Washington University in St. Louis, Brown School, St. Louis, MO 63130. Offers affordable housing and mixed-income community management (Certificate); American Indian and Alaska native (MSW); children, youth and families (MSW); health (MSW); individualized (MSW), including health; mental health (MSW); older adults and aging societies (MSW); public health (MPH), including epidemiology/biostatistics, global health, health policy analysis, urban design; public health sciences (PhD); social and economic development (MSW); social work (MSW, PhD), including management (MSW), policy (MSW), research (MSW), sexual health and education (MSW), social entrepreneurship (MSW), system dynamics (MSW); violence and injury prevention (MSW, Certificate); JD/MSW; M Arch/MSW; MPH/MBA; MPH/MS; MSW/M Div; MSW/M Ed; MSW/MAPS; MSW/MBA; MSW/MPH; MUD/MSW. MSW/M Div and MSW/MAPS offered in partnership with Eden Theological Seminary. *Accreditation:* CSWE (one or more programs are accredited). *Faculty:* 54 full-time (31 women), 87 part-time/adjunct (61 women). *Students:* 303 full-time (256 women); includes 125 minority (42 Black or African American, non-Hispanic/Latino; 16 American Indian or Alaska Native, non-Hispanic/Latino; 47 Asian, non-Hispanic/Latino; 9 Hispanic/Latino; 11 Two or more races, non-Hispanic/Latino), 71 international. Average age 26. 923 applicants, 322 enrolled. In 2015, 239 master's, 5 doctorates awarded. *Degree requirements:* For master's, 60 credit hours (for MSW), 52 credit hours (for MPH); practicum; for doctorate, comprehensive exam, thesis/dissertation. *Entrance requirements:* For master's, GRE, GMAT, LSAT, or MCAT (for MPH); for doctorate, GRE, MA or MSW. Additional exam requirements/recommendations for international students: Required—TOEFL (minimum score 100 iBT) or IELTS. *Application deadline:* For fall admission, 12/15 priority date for domestic and international students; for winter admission, 3/1 priority date for domestic and international students. Applications are processed on a rolling basis. Application fee: $50. Electronic applications accepted. *Expenses:* Contact institution. *Financial support:* In 2015–16, 267 students received support. Fellowships, research assistantships, Federal Work-Study, institutionally sponsored loans, scholarships/grants, health care benefits, tuition waivers (partial), and unspecified assistantships available. Support available to part-time students. Financial award application deadline: 3/1; financial award applicants required to submit FAFSA. *Faculty research:* Mental health services, social development, child welfare, at-risk teens, autism, environmental health, health policy, health communications, obesity, gender and sexuality, violence and injury prevention, chronic disease prevention, poverty, older adults/aging societies, civic engagement, school social work, program evaluation, health disparities. *Unit head:* Jamie L. Adkisson, Director of Admissions & Recruitment, 314-935-3524, Fax: 314-935-4859, E-mail: jadkisson@wustl.edu. *Application contact:* Office of Admissions & Recruitment, 314-935-6676, Fax: 314-935-4859, E-mail: brownadmissions@wustl.ed.
Website: http://brownschool.wustl.edu

Washington University in St. Louis, School of Medicine, Division of Biostatistics, St. Louis, MO 63110. Offers biostatistics (MS); genetic epidemiology (Certificate). *Program availability:* Part-time. *Entrance requirements:* For master's, GRE, proficiency in computer programming, statistics and biology/genetics. Additional exam requirements/recommendations for international students: Required—TOEFL (minimum score 600 paper-based; 100 iBT), TWE. Electronic applications accepted. *Expenses:* Contact institution. *Faculty research:* Biostatistics, clinical trials, cardiovascular diseases, genetics, genetic epidemiology.

West Virginia University, School of Public Health, Morgantown, WV 26506-9190. Offers biostatistics; community health promotion (MS); community health/preventative medicine (MPH); public health sciences (PhD). *Accreditation:* CEPH. *Program availability:* Part-time, online learning. *Faculty:* 37 full-time (17 women), 3 part-time/adjunct (2 women). *Students:* 85 full-time (55 women), 52 part-time (34 women); includes 28 minority (8 Black or African American, non-Hispanic/Latino; 1 American Indian or Alaska Native, non-Hispanic/Latino; 13 Asian, non-Hispanic/Latino; 3 Hispanic/Latino; 3 Two or more races, non-Hispanic/Latino), 10 international. Average age 31. In 2015, 11 doctorates awarded. *Degree requirements:* For master's, practicum, project. *Entrance requirements:* For master's, GRE General Test, MCAT, medical degree, medical internship. Additional exam requirements/recommendations for international students: Required—TOEFL (minimum score 550 paper-based; 80 iBT). *Application deadline:* For fall admission, 4/15 priority date for domestic students; for spring admission, 12/1 for domestic students. Applications are processed on a rolling basis. Application fee: $60. *Expenses:* Contact institution. *Financial support:* Research assistantships, teaching assistantships, scholarships/grants, and health care benefits available. Financial award application deadline: 2/1; financial award applicants required to submit FAFSA. *Faculty research:* Occupational health, environmental health, clinical epidemiology, health care management, prevention. *Unit head:* Dr. Gregory A. Hand, Dean, School of Public Health, 304-293-2502, Fax: 304-293-6685, E-mail: gahand@hsc.wvu.edu. *Application contact:* Sherry Kuhl, Director, Office of Student Services, 304-293-1795, Fax: 304-293-6685, E-mail: skuhl@hsc.wvu.edu.
Website: http://pubichealth.hsc.wvu.edu

Yale University, School of Medicine, Yale School of Public Health, New Haven, CT 06520. Offers applied biostatistics and epidemiology (APMPH); biostatistics (MPH, MS, PhD), including global health (MPH); chronic disease epidemiology (MPH, PhD), including global health (MPH); environmental health sciences (MPH, PhD), including global health (MPH); epidemiology of microbial diseases (MPH, PhD), including global health (MPH); global health (APMPH); health management (MPH), including global health; health policy (MPH), including global health; health policy and administration (APMPH, PhD); occupational and environmental medicine (APMPH); preventive medicine (APMPH); social and behavioral sciences (APMPH, MPH), including global health (MPH); JD/MPH; M Div/MPH; MBA/MPH; MD/MPH; MEM/MPH; MFS/MPH; MM Sc/MPH; MPH/MA; MSN/MPH. MS and PhD offered through the Graduate School. *Accreditation:* CEPH. *Program availability:* Part-time. Terminal master's awarded for partial completion of doctoral program. *Degree requirements:* For master's, thesis, summer internship; for doctorate, comprehensive exam, thesis/dissertation, residency. *Entrance requirements:* For master's, GMAT, GRE, or MCAT, two years of undergraduate coursework in math and science; for doctorate, GRE General Test. Additional exam requirements/recommendations for international students: Required—TOEFL (minimum score 100 iBT). Electronic applications accepted. *Expenses:* Contact institution. *Faculty research:* Genetic and emerging infections epidemiology, virology, cost/quality, vector biology, quantitative methods, aging, asthma, cancer.

Computational Sciences

American University of Beirut, Graduate Programs, Faculty of Arts and Sciences, Beirut, Lebanon. Offers anthropology (MA); Arab and Middle Eastern history (PhD); Arabic language and literature (MA, PhD); archaeology (MA); biology (MS); cell and molecular biology (PhD); chemistry (MS); clinical psychology (MA); computational sciences (MS); computer science (MS); economics (MA); English language (MA); English literature (MA); environmental policy planning (MA); financial economics (MAFE); geology (MS); history (MA); mathematics (MA, MS); media studies (MA); Middle Eastern studies (MA); physics (MS); political studies (MA); psychology (MA); public administration (MA); sociology (MA); statistics (MA, MS); theoretical physics (PhD); transnational American studies (MA). *Program availability:* Part-time. *Faculty:* 114 full-time (36 women), 4 part-time/adjunct (2 women). *Students:* 258 full-time (190 women), 207 part-time (142 women). Average age 27. 241 applicants, 71% accepted, 98 enrolled. In 2015, 47 master's, 3 doctorates awarded. *Degree requirements:* For master's, one foreign language, comprehensive exam, thesis (for some programs); for doctorate, one foreign language, comprehensive exam, thesis/dissertation. *Entrance requirements:* For master's, GRE (for some MA, MS programs), letter of recommendation; for doctorate, GRE, letters of recommendation. Additional exam requirements/recommendations for international students: Required—TOEFL (minimum score 600 paper-based; 97 iBT), IELTS (minimum score 7). *Application deadline:* For fall admission, 4/1 for domestic and international students; for spring admission, 11/1 for domestic and international students. Application fee: $50. Electronic applications accepted. *Expenses: Tuition, area resident:* Full-time $16,254; part-time $903 per credit. *Required fees:* $699. Tuition and fees vary according to course load and program. *Financial support:* Research assistantships, career-related internships or fieldwork, institutionally sponsored loans, scholarships/grants, health care benefits, and unspecified assistantships available. Financial award application deadline: 2/4; financial award applicants required to submit FAFSA. *Faculty research:* Analysis and algebra; software engineering; machine learning and big data analysis; philosophy of mind and political philosophy; anthropology of art, anthropology of migration and medical anthropology; sociology of knowledge, sociology of migration, critical theory; sociology of education; hybrid solid materials; photocatalysis; human creativity. *Total annual research expenditures:* $680,360. *Unit head:* Dr. Patrick McGreevy, Dean, 961-1374374 Ext. 3800, Fax: 961-1744461, E-mail: pm07@aub.edu.lb. *Application contact:* Dr. Salim Kanaan, Director, Admissions Office, 961-1350000 Ext. 2590, Fax: 961-1750775, E-mail: sk00@aub.edu.lb.
Website: http://www.aub.edu.lb/fas/

California Institute of Technology, Division of Engineering and Applied Science, Option in Computation and Neural Systems, Pasadena, CA 91125-0001. Offers MS, PhD. Terminal master's awarded for partial completion of doctoral program. *Degree requirements:* For doctorate, thesis/dissertation, qualifying exam. *Entrance requirements:* For doctorate, GRE General Test. *Faculty research:* Biological and artificial computational devices, modeling of sensory processes and learning, theory of collective computation.

Chapman University, Schmid College of Science and Technology, Computational and Data Sciences Program, Orange, CA 92866. Offers MS, PhD. *Program availability:* Part-time. *Faculty:* 11 full-time (1 woman), 1 part-time/adjunct (0 women). *Students:* 17 full-time (5 women), 19 part-time (3 women); includes 15 minority (1 Black or African American, non-Hispanic/Latino; 7 Asian, non-Hispanic/Latino; 7 Hispanic/Latino), 7 international. Average age 31. 44 applicants, 82% accepted, 19 enrolled. In 2015, 11 master's, 1 doctorate awarded. *Degree requirements:* For master's, thesis or alternative; for doctorate, thesis/dissertation. *Entrance requirements:* For master's and doctorate, GRE. Additional exam requirements/recommendations for international students: Required—TOEFL (minimum score 600 paper-based; 100 iBT), IELTS (minimum score 7), PTE (minimum score 68), CAE: Level C1. *Application deadline:* For fall admission, 5/1 for domestic students. Application fee: $60. Electronic applications accepted. *Expenses:* $1,445 per unit. *Financial support:* Fellowships, research assistantships, teaching assistantships, Federal Work-Study, and scholarships/grants available. Financial award applicants required to submit FAFSA. *Unit head:* Dr. Hesham El-Askary, Director, 714-289-2053, E-mail: eleskary@chapman.edu. *Application contact:* Monica Chen, Graduate Admission Counselor, 714-289-3590, E-mail: mchen@chapman.edu.
See Display below and Close-Up on page 291.

Claremont Graduate University, Graduate Programs, Institute of Mathematical Sciences, Claremont, CA 91711-6160. Offers computational and systems biology (PhD); computational mathematics and numerical analysis (MA, MS); computational science (PhD); engineering and industrial applied mathematics (PhD); mathematics (PhD); operations research and statistics (MA, MS); physical applied mathematics (MA, MS); pure mathematics (MA, MS); scientific computing (MA, MS); systems and control theory (MA, MS). *Program availability:* Part-time. *Faculty:* 6 full-time (1 woman), 2 part-time/adjunct (0 women). *Students:* 74 full-time (19 women), 35 part-time (12 women); includes 23 minority (2 Black or African American, non-Hispanic/Latino; 12 Asian, non-Hispanic/Latino; 8 Hispanic/Latino; 1 Two or more races, non-Hispanic/Latino), 51 international. Average age 30. In 2015, 25 master's, 10 doctorates awarded. Terminal master's awarded for partial completion of doctoral program. *Entrance requirements:* For master's and doctorate, GRE General Test. Additional exam requirements/recommendations for international students: Required—TOEFL (minimum score 75 iBT). *Application deadline:* For fall admission, 2/1 priority date for domestic and international students. Applications are processed on a rolling basis. Application fee: $80. Electronic applications accepted. *Expenses: Tuition, area resident:* Full-time $43,032; part-time $1793 per unit. *Required fees:* $600; $300 per semester. $300 per semester. Tuition and fees vary according to course load and program. *Financial support:* Fellowships, research assistantships, Federal Work-Study, institutionally sponsored loans, scholarships/grants, and tuition waivers (full and partial) available. Support available to part-time students. Financial award application deadline: 2/15; financial award applicants required to submit FAFSA. *Unit head:* Ali Nadim, Director, 909-607-9413, E-mail: ali.nadim@cgu.edu. *Application contact:* Jake Campbell, Assistant Director of Admissions, 909-607-3024, E-mail: jake.campbell@cgu.edu.
Website: http://www.cgu.edu/pages/168.asp

232 www.petersons.com

Peterson's Graduate Programs in the Physical Sciences, Mathematics, Agricultural Sciences, the Environment & Natural Resources 2017

The College of William and Mary, Faculty of Arts and Sciences, Department of Computer Science, Program in Computational Operations Research, Williamsburg, VA 23187-8795. Offers MS. *Program availability:* Part-time. *Faculty:* 5 full-time (1 woman), 1 part-time/adjunct (0 women). *Students:* 17 full-time (6 women); includes 1 minority (Black or African American, non-Hispanic/Latino), 6 international. Average age 24. 17 applicants, 76% accepted, 5 enrolled. In 2015, 10 master's awarded. *Degree requirements:* For master's, research project. *Entrance requirements:* For master's, GRE General Test, minimum GPA of 3.0. Additional exam requirements/recommendations for international students: Required—TOEFL. *Application deadline:* For fall admission, 3/1 priority date for domestic students, 3/15 priority date for international students; for spring admission, 11/1 for domestic and international students. Applications are processed on a rolling basis. Application fee: $45. Electronic applications accepted. *Expenses:* Tuition, state resident: full-time $8009; part-time $450 per credit hour. Tuition, nonresident: full-time $23,752; part-time $1160 per credit hour. *Required fees:* $4162. One-time fee: $400 full-time. *Financial support:* In 2015–16, 13 students received support, including 6 fellowships (averaging $9,000 per year), 7 teaching assistantships with full tuition reimbursements available (averaging $13,500 per year); scholarships/grants, tuition waivers (full), and unspecified assistantships also available. Financial award application deadline: 3/1; financial award applicants required to submit FAFSA. *Faculty research:* Metaheuristics, reliability, optimization, statistics, networks. *Unit head:* Dr. Rex Kincaid, Professor, 757-221-2038, E-mail: rrkinc@math.wm.edu. *Application contact:* Vanessa Godwin, Administrative Director, 757-221-3455, Fax: 757-221-1717, E-mail: cor@cs.wm.edu.
Website: http://www.wm.edu/as/mathematics/graduate/cor/index.php

Cornell University, Graduate School, Graduate Fields of Engineering, Field of Chemical Engineering, Ithaca, NY 14853-0001. Offers advanced materials processing (M Eng, MS, PhD); applied mathematics and computational methods (M Eng, MS, PhD); biochemical engineering (M Eng, MS, PhD); chemical reaction engineering (M Eng, MS, PhD); classical and statistical thermodynamics (M Eng, MS, PhD); fluid dynamics, rheology and biorheology (M Eng, MS, PhD); heat and mass transfer (M Eng, MS, PhD); kinetics and catalysis (M Eng, MS, PhD); polymers (M Eng, MS, PhD); surface science (M Eng, MS, PhD). *Degree requirements:* For master's, thesis (MS); for doctorate, comprehensive exam, thesis/dissertation. *Entrance requirements:* For master's and doctorate, GRE General Test, 2 letters of recommendation. Additional exam requirements/recommendations for international students: Required—TOEFL (minimum score 600 paper-based; 77 iBT). Electronic applications accepted. *Faculty research:* Biochemical, biomedical and metabolic engineering; fluid and polymer dynamics; surface science and chemical kinetics; electronics materials; microchemical systems and nanotechnology.

Emory University, Laney Graduate School, Department of Physics, Atlanta, GA 30322-1100. Offers biophysics (PhD); experimental condensed matter physics (PhD); theoretical and computational statistical physics (PhD); MS/PhD. *Degree requirements:* For doctorate, thesis/dissertation, qualifier proposal. *Entrance requirements:* For doctorate, GRE General Test, minimum GPA of 3.0. Additional exam requirements/recommendations for international students: Required—TOEFL (minimum score 600 paper-based). Electronic applications accepted. *Faculty research:* Experimental studies of the structure and function of metalloproteins, soft condensed matter, granular materials, biophotonics and fluorescence correlation spectroscopy, single molecule studies of DNA-protein systems.

Florida State University, The Graduate School, College of Arts and Sciences, Department of Scientific Computing, Tallahassee, FL 32306-4120. Offers computational science (MS, PhD), including atmospheric science (PhD), biochemistry (PhD), biological science (PhD), computational science (PhD), geological science (PhD), materials science (PhD), physics (PhD). *Program availability:* Part-time. *Faculty:* 14 full-time (2 women). *Students:* 32 full-time (4 women), 7 part-time (1 woman); includes 14 minority (9 Asian, non-Hispanic/Latino; 3 Hispanic/Latino; 2 Two or more races, non-Hispanic/Latino). Average age 27. 28 applicants, 43% accepted, 7 enrolled. In 2015, 9 master's, 7 doctorates awarded. *Degree requirements:* For master's, thesis (for some programs); for doctorate, comprehensive exam, thesis/dissertation. *Entrance requirements:* For master's and doctorate, GRE General Test, knowledge of at least one object-oriented computing language, 3 letters of recommendation, resume, statement of purpose. Additional exam requirements/recommendations for international students: Required—TOEFL (minimum score 550 paper-based; 80 iBT). *Application deadline:* For fall admission, 1/15 for domestic and international students. Application fee: $30. Electronic applications accepted. *Expenses: Tuition, area resident:* Full-time $7263; part-time $403.50 per credit hour. Tuition, nonresident: full-time $18,087; part-time $1004.85 per credit hour. *Required fees:* $1365; $75.81 per credit hour. $20 per semester. Tuition and fees vary according to campus/location. *Financial support:* In 2015–16, 33 students received support, including 10 research assistantships with full tuition reimbursements available (averaging $20,000 per year), 23 teaching assistantships with full tuition reimbursements available (averaging $20,000 per year); scholarships/grants and unspecified assistantships also available. Financial award application deadline: 1/15. *Faculty research:* Morphometrics, mathematical and systems biology, mining proteomic and metabolic data, computational materials research, advanced 4-D Var data-assimilation methods in dynamic meteorology and oceanography, computational fluid dynamics, astrophysics. *Unit head:* Dr. Gordon Erlebacher, Chair, 850-644-7024, E-mail: gerlebacher@fsu.edu. *Application contact:* Mark Howard, Academic Program Specialist, 850-644-0143, Fax: 850-644-0098, E-mail: mlhoward@fsu.edu.
Website: http://www.sc.fsu.edu

Georgia Institute of Technology, Graduate Studies, Multidisciplinary Program in Computational Science and Engineering, Atlanta, GA 30332-0001. Offers MS, PhD. *Program availability:* Part-time, online learning. Terminal master's awarded for partial completion of doctoral program. *Degree requirements:* For master's, thesis optional; for doctorate, comprehensive exam, thesis/dissertation. *Entrance requirements:* For master's and doctorate, GRE General Test. Additional exam requirements/recommendations for international students: Required—TOEFL (minimum score 600 paper-based; 100 iBT). Electronic applications accepted.

Hampton University, School of Science, Program in Applied Mathematics, Hampton, VA 23668. Offers computational mathematics (MS); nonlinear science (MS); statistics and probability (MS). *Program availability:* Part-time. *Degree requirements:* For master's, thesis optional. *Entrance requirements:* For master's, GRE General Test. Additional exam requirements/recommendations for international students: Required—TOEFL (minimum score 525 paper-based) or IELTS (6.5). Electronic applications accepted. *Expenses: Tuition, area resident:* Full-time $10,263; part-time $522 per credit hour. *Required fees:* $35. Tuition and fees vary according to course load and program. *Faculty research:* Stochastic processes, nonlinear dynamics, approximation theory, prediction theory, hydrodynamical stability.

Harvard University, Graduate School of Arts and Sciences, Harvard John A. Paulson School of Engineering and Applied Sciences, Cambridge, MA 02138. Offers applied mathematics (ME, SM, PhD); applied physics (ME, SM, PhD); computational science and engineering (ME, SM); computer science (ME, SM, PhD); design engineering (MDE); engineering science (ME), including electrical engineering (ME, SM, PhD); engineering sciences (SM, PhD), including bioengineering, electrical engineering (ME, SM, PhD), environmental science and engineering, materials science and mechanical engineering. MDE offered in collaboration with Graduate School of Design. *Program availability:* Part-time. *Faculty:* 101 full-time (14 women), 10 part-time/adjunct (1 woman). *Students:* 425 full-time (109 women), 12 part-time (1 woman); includes 70 minority (1 Black or African American, non-Hispanic/Latino; 44 Asian, non-Hispanic/Latino; 17 Hispanic/Latino; 8 Two or more races, non-Hispanic/Latino), 207 international. Average age 27. 2,116 applicants, 11% accepted, 132 enrolled. In 2015, 88 master's, 64 doctorates awarded. Terminal master's awarded for partial completion of doctoral program. *Degree requirements:* For master's, thesis (for ME); for doctorate, comprehensive exam, thesis/dissertation. *Entrance requirements:* For master's and doctorate, GRE General Test, GRE Subject Test (recommended), 3 letters of recommendation. Additional exam requirements/recommendations for international students: Required—TOEFL (minimum score 80 iBT). *Application deadline:* For fall admission, 12/15 priority date for domestic and international students. Application fee: $105. Electronic applications accepted. *Expenses:* Contact institution. *Financial support:* In 2015–16, 353 students received support, including 92 fellowships with full tuition reimbursements available (averaging $25,650 per year), 213 research assistantships with tuition reimbursements available (averaging $34,200 per year), 127 teaching assistantships with tuition reimbursements available (averaging $5,775 per year); health care benefits also available. *Faculty research:* Applied mathematics, applied physics, computer science and electrical engineering, environmental engineering, mechanical and biomedical engineering. *Total annual research expenditures:* $38 million. *Unit head:* Francis J. Doyle, III, Dean, 617-495-5829, Fax: 617-495-5264,
E-mail: dean@seas.harvard.edu. *Application contact:* Office of Admissions and Financial Aid, 617-495-5315, E-mail: admissions@seas.harvard.edu.
Website: http://www.seas.harvard.edu/

Lehigh University, P.C. Rossin College of Engineering and Applied Science, Department of Mechanical Engineering and Mechanics, Bethlehem, PA 18015. Offers computational and engineering mechanics (MS, PhD); mechanical engineering (M Eng, MS, PhD); MBA/E. *Program availability:* Part-time, 100% online, blended/hybrid learning. *Faculty:* 28 full-time (2 women), 1 part-time/adjunct (0 women). *Students:* 141 full-time (19 women), 33 part-time (3 women); includes 10 minority (1 Black or African American, non-Hispanic/Latino; 4 Asian, non-Hispanic/Latino; 4 Hispanic/Latino; 1 Two or more races, non-Hispanic/Latino), 104 international. Average age 26. 624 applicants, 17% accepted, 40 enrolled. In 2015, 41 master's, 14 doctorates awarded. Terminal master's awarded for partial completion of doctoral program. *Degree requirements:* For master's, thesis (for MS); for doctorate, thesis/dissertation, general exam. *Entrance requirements:* Additional exam requirements/recommendations for international students: Required—TOEFL (minimum score 550 paper-based; 79 iBT). *Application deadline:* For fall admission, 7/15 for domestic and international students; for spring admission, 12/1 for domestic and international students. Application fee: $75. Electronic applications accepted. *Expenses:* $1,380 per credit on-campus; $1,190 per credit plus $100 technology fee online. *Financial support:* In 2015–16, 59 students received support, including 5 fellowships with full tuition reimbursements available (averaging $27,319 per year), 57 research assistantships with full tuition reimbursements available (averaging $24,300 per year), 14 teaching assistantships with full tuition reimbursements available (averaging $28,140 per year); dean's doctoral assistantships also available. Financial award application deadline: 1/15. *Faculty research:* Thermofluids, dynamic systems, CAD/CAM, computational mechanics, solid mechanics. *Total annual research expenditures:* $4 million. *Unit head:* Dr. D. Gary Harlow, Chairman, 610-758-4102, Fax: 610-758-6224, E-mail: dgh0@lehigh.edu. *Application contact:* Jo Ann M. Casciano, Graduate Coordinator, 610-758-4107, Fax: 610-758-6224, E-mail: jmc4@lehigh.edu.
Website: http://www.lehigh.edu/~inmem/

Marquette University, Graduate School, College of Arts and Sciences, Department of Mathematics, Statistics, and Computer Science, Milwaukee, WI 53201-1881. Offers bioinformatics (MS); computational sciences (MS, PhD); computing (MS); mathematics education (MS). *Program availability:* Part-time, evening/weekend, online learning. *Faculty:* 30 full-time (8 women), 12 part-time/adjunct (3 women). *Students:* 22 full-time (7 women), 22 part-time (10 women); includes 10 minority (2 Black or African American, non-Hispanic/Latino; 6 Asian, non-Hispanic/Latino; 2 Two or more races, non-Hispanic/Latino), 19 international. Average age 30. 45 applicants, 62% accepted, 10 enrolled. In 2015, 6 master's, 3 doctorates awarded. Terminal master's awarded for partial completion of doctoral program. *Degree requirements:* For master's, thesis (for some programs), essay with oral presentation; for doctorate, comprehensive exam, thesis/dissertation, qualifying examination. *Entrance requirements:* For master's, official transcripts from all current and previous colleges/universities except Marquette, three letters of recommendation; for doctorate, GRE General Test, official transcripts from all current and previous colleges/universities except Marquette, three letters of recommendation. Additional exam requirements/recommendations for international students: Required—TOEFL (minimum score 530 paper-based). *Application deadline:* For fall admission, 1/15 for domestic and international students. Applications are processed on a rolling basis. Application fee: $50. Electronic applications accepted. *Financial support:* In 2015–16, 23 students received support, including 4 fellowships (averaging $1,375 per year), 5 research assistantships with full tuition reimbursements available (averaging $17,000 per year), 15 teaching assistantships with full tuition reimbursements available (averaging $17,000 per year); scholarships/grants, health care benefits, tuition waivers (full and partial), and unspecified assistantships also available. Support available to part-time students. Financial award application deadline: 2/15. *Faculty research:* Models of physiological systems, mathematical immunology, computational group theory, mathematical logic, computational science. *Unit head:* Dr. Rebecca Sanders, Chair, 414-288-7573, Fax: 414-288-1578. *Application contact:* Dr. Stephen Merrill, Professor, 414-288-5237.
Website: http://www.marquette.edu/mscs/grad.shtml

Massachusetts Institute of Technology, School of Engineering and School of Science and MIT Sloan School of Management, Program in Computation for Design and Optimization, Cambridge, MA 02139. Offers SM. *Faculty:* 68 full-time (11 women), 1 part-time/adjunct (0 women). *Students:* 24 full-time (2 women); includes 4 minority (3 Asian, non-Hispanic/Latino; 1 Two or more races, non-Hispanic/Latino), 18 international. Average age 25. 95 applicants, 15% accepted, 9 enrolled. In 2015, 12 master's awarded. *Degree requirements:* For master's, thesis. *Entrance requirements:* For master's, GRE General Test. Additional exam requirements/recommendations for international students: Required—IELTS. *Application deadline:* For fall admission, 1/10 for domestic and international students. Application fee: $75. Electronic applications accepted. *Expenses: Tuition:* Full-time $46,400; part-time $725 per credit. One-time fee: $304 full-time. Full-time tuition and fees vary according to course load and program. *Financial support:* In 2015–16, 14 students received support, including 1 fellowship, 15 research assistantships (averaging $33,700 per year), 3 teaching assistantships (averaging $32,300 per year); Federal Work-Study, institutionally sponsored loans, scholarships/grants, traineeships, health care benefits, and unspecified assistantships also available. Support available to part-time students. Financial award application

deadline: 4/15; financial award applicants required to submit FAFSA. *Faculty research:* Computational methods; partial differential equations; optimization; uncertainty quantification; computational mechanics and materials. *Unit head:* Prof. Nicolas Hadjiconstantinou, Co-Director, 617-253-3725, E-mail: cdo_info@mit.edu. *Application contact:* 617-253-3725, E-mail: cdo_info@mit.edu.
Website: http://computationalengineering.mit.edu/education/

McGill University, Faculty of Graduate and Postdoctoral Studies, Faculty of Science, Department of Mathematics and Statistics, Montréal, QC H3A 2T5, Canada. Offers computational science and engineering (M Sc); mathematics and statistics (M Sc, MA, PhD), including applied mathematics (M Sc, MA), pure mathematics (M Sc, MA), statistics (M Sc, MA).

Memorial University of Newfoundland, School of Graduate Studies, Interdisciplinary Program in Scientific Computing, St. John's, NL A1C 5S7, Canada. Offers scientific computing (M Sc). *Degree requirements:* For master's, thesis. *Entrance requirements:* For master's, honors B Sc or significant background in the field. *Application deadline:* Applications are processed on a rolling basis. Application fee: $50 Canadian dollars ($100 Canadian dollars for international students). Electronic applications accepted. *Expenses: Tuition, area resident:* Full-time $2199 Canadian dollars. *International tuition:* $2859 Canadian dollars full-time. *Financial support:* Fellowships, research assistantships, and teaching assistantships available. *Faculty research:* Scientific computing, modeling and simulation, computational fluid dynamics, polymer physics, computational chemistry. *Unit head:* Dr. Mark Abrams, Dean, 709-864-8153, Fax: 709-864-3316. *Application contact:* Gail Kenny, Secretary, 709-864-8154, Fax: 709-864-3316, E-mail: gkenny@mun.ca.

Michigan Technological University, Graduate School, Interdisciplinary Programs, Houghton, MI 49931. Offers atmospheric sciences (PhD); biochemistry and molecular biology (PhD); computational science and engineering (PhD); data science (MS, Graduate Certificate); engineering (M Eng); environmental engineering (PhD); international profile (Graduate Certificate); nanotechnology (Graduate Certificate); sustainability (Graduate Certificate); sustainable water resources systems (Graduate Certificate). *Program availability:* Part-time. *Faculty:* 118 full-time (26 women), 12 part-time/adjunct. *Students:* 53 full-time (22 women), 10 part-time; includes 2 minority (1 Asian, non-Hispanic/Latino; 1 Two or more races, non-Hispanic/Latino), 44 international. Average age 30. 300 applicants, 19% accepted, 17 enrolled. In 2015, 3 master's, 7 doctorates, 4 other advanced degrees awarded. Terminal master's awarded for partial completion of doctoral program. *Degree requirements:* For master's, comprehensive exam (for some programs), thesis (for some programs); for doctorate, comprehensive exam, thesis/dissertation. *Entrance requirements:* For master's, doctorate, and Graduate Certificate, GRE, statement of purpose, personal statement, official transcripts, 2-3 letters of recommendation. Additional exam requirements/recommendations for international students: Required—TOEFL or IELTS. *Application deadline:* Applications are processed on a rolling basis. Electronic applications accepted. *Expenses:* Tuition, state resident: full-time $15,507; part-time $861.50 per credit. Tuition, nonresident: full-time $15,507; part-time $861.50 per credit. *Required fees:* $248; $248. Tuition and fees vary according to course load and program. *Financial support:* In 2015–16, 41 students received support, including 7 fellowships with tuition reimbursements available (averaging $14,516 per year), 16 research assistantships with tuition reimbursements available (averaging $14,516 per year), 9 teaching assistantships with tuition reimbursements available (averaging $14,516 per year); career-related internships or fieldwork, Federal Work-Study, scholarships/grants, health care benefits, unspecified assistantships, and cooperative program also available. Financial award applicants required to submit FAFSA. *Faculty research:* Big data, atmospheric sciences, bioinformatics and systems biology, molecular dynamics, environmental studies. *Unit head:* Dr. Jacqueline E. Huntoon, Provost and Vice President for Academic Affairs, 906-487-2440, Fax: 906-487-2284,
E-mail: jeh@mtu.edu. *Application contact:* Carol T. Wingerson, Administrative Aide, 906-487-2328, Fax: 906-487-2284, E-mail: gradadms@mtu.edu.

Middle Tennessee State University, College of Graduate Studies, College of Basic and Applied Sciences, Interdisciplinary Program in Computational Science, Murfreesboro, TN 37132. Offers PhD. *Entrance requirements:* For doctorate, GRE. Additional exam requirements/recommendations for international students: Required—TOEFL (minimum score 525 paper-based; 71 iBT) or IELTS (minimum score 6).

North Carolina Agricultural and Technical State University, School of Graduate Studies, College of Arts and Sciences, Department of Physics, Greensboro, NC 27411. Offers computational sciences (MS); physics (MS).

The Ohio State University, Graduate School, College of Arts and Sciences, Division of Natural and Mathematical Sciences, Department of Mathematics, Columbus, OH 43210. Offers computational sciences (MMS); mathematical biosciences (MMS); mathematics (PhD); mathematics for educators (MMS). *Degree requirements:* For master's, thesis optional; for doctorate, one foreign language, thesis/dissertation. *Entrance requirements:* For master's, GRE General Test; for doctorate, GRE General Test (recommended), GRE Subject Test (mathematics). Additional exam requirements/recommendations for international students: Required—TOEFL (minimum score 550 paper-based; 79 iBT), Michigan English Language Assessment Battery (minimum score 82); Recommended—IELTS (minimum score 7). Electronic applications accepted.

Oregon State University, College of Science, Program in Physics, Corvallis, OR 97331. Offers atomic physics (MA, MS, PhD); computational physics (MA, MS, PhD); nuclear physics (MA, MS, PhD); optical physics (MA, MS, PhD); particle physics (MA, MS, PhD); physics education (MA, MS, PhD); relativity (MA, MS, PhD); solid state physics (MA, MS, PhD). *Faculty:* 15 full-time (4 women), 1 (woman) part-time/adjunct. *Students:* 40 full-time (12 women), 4 part-time (0 women); includes 5 minority (2 Hispanic/Latino; 3 Two or more races, non-Hispanic/Latino), 13 international. Average age 28. 111 applicants, 15% accepted, 7 enrolled. In 2015, 15 master's, 3 doctorates awarded. *Entrance requirements:* Additional exam requirements/recommendations for international students: Required—TOEFL (minimum score 600 paper-based; 100 iBT). Application fee: $75 ($85 for international students). *Expenses:* Tuition, state resident: full-time $12,150; part-time $450 per credit. Tuition, nonresident: full-time $20,952; part-time $776 per credit. *Required fees:* $1572; $1443 per unit. One-time fee: $350. Tuition and fees vary according to course load, campus/location and program. *Financial support:* Application deadline: 1/15. *Unit head:* Dr. Heidi Schellman, Professor and Department Head. *Application contact:* Kelly Carter, Graduate Student Support, 541-737-1674, E-mail: gradinfo@physics.oregonstate.edu.
Website: http://www.physics.oregonstate.edu/

Princeton University, Graduate School, Program in Applied and Computational Mathematics, Princeton, NJ 08544-1019. Offers PhD. *Degree requirements:* For doctorate, thesis/dissertation. *Entrance requirements:* For doctorate, GRE General Test, GRE Subject Test. Additional exam requirements/recommendations for international students: Required—TOEFL (minimum score 600 paper-based). Electronic applications accepted.

Purdue University, Graduate School, College of Health and Human Sciences, Department of Psychological Sciences, West Lafayette, IN 47907. Offers behavioral neuroscience (PhD); clinical psychology (PhD); cognitive psychology (PhD); industrial/organizational psychology (PhD); mathematical and computational cognitive science (PhD). *Accreditation:* APA. Terminal master's awarded for partial completion of doctoral program. *Degree requirements:* For doctorate, thesis/dissertation. *Entrance requirements:* For doctorate, GRE General Test, minimum undergraduate GPA of 3.0 or equivalent. Additional exam requirements/recommendations for international students: Required—TOEFL (minimum score 550 paper-based; 77 iBT); Recommended—TWE. Electronic applications accepted. *Faculty research:* Career development of women in science, development of friendships during childhood and adolescence, social competence, human information processing.

Purdue University, Graduate School, College of Science, Department of Statistics, West Lafayette, IN 47909. Offers applied statistics (MS); computational finance (MS); computational science and engineering (MS); statistics (PhD). *Program availability:* Part-time. *Faculty:* 71 full-time (22 women). *Students:* 102 full-time (36 women); includes 71 minority (8 Black or African American, non-Hispanic/Latino; 1 American Indian or Alaska Native, non-Hispanic/Latino; 55 Asian, non-Hispanic/Latino; 4 Hispanic/Latino; 3 Native Hawaiian or other Pacific Islander, non-Hispanic/Latino). Average age 25. 505 applicants, 9% accepted, 29 enrolled. In 2015, 29 master's, 14 doctorates awarded. Terminal master's awarded for partial completion of doctoral program. *Degree requirements:* For master's, comprehensive exam; for doctorate, thesis/dissertation, qualifying exams. *Entrance requirements:* For master's and doctorate, GRE General Test. Additional exam requirements/recommendations for international students: Required—TOEFL (minimum score 80 iBT); Recommended—IELTS (minimum score 7). *Application deadline:* For fall admission, 1/15 for domestic and international students; for spring admission, 10/15 for domestic students, 9/15 for international students. Application fee: $60 ($75 for international students). Electronic applications accepted. *Expenses:* Contact institution. *Financial support:* In 2015–16, 5 students received support, including 5 fellowships with full tuition reimbursements available (averaging $20,000 per year), research assistantships with full tuition reimbursements available (averaging $20,000 per year), 10 teaching assistantships with full tuition reimbursements available (averaging $20,000 per year); career-related internships or fieldwork and unspecified assistantships also available. Support available to part-time students. Financial award application deadline: 1/15; financial award applicants required to submit FAFSA. *Faculty research:* Nonparametric models, computational finance, design of experiments, probability theory, bioinformatics. *Unit head:* Dr. Hao Zhang, Head, 765-494-3141, Fax: 765-494-0558, E-mail: zhanghao@purdue.edu. *Application contact:* Anna Hook, Graduate Coordinator, 765-494-5794, Fax: 765-494-0558,
E-mail: hook6@purdue.edu.
Website: http://www.stat.purdue.edu/

Rice University, Graduate Programs, George R. Brown School of Engineering, Department of Computational and Applied Mathematics, Houston, TX 77251-1892. Offers computational and applied mathematics (MA, MCAM, PhD); computational science and engineering (PhD). *Degree requirements:* For master's, comprehensive exam (for some programs), thesis (for some programs); for doctorate, comprehensive exam, thesis/dissertation. *Entrance requirements:* For master's and doctorate, GRE General Test, minimum GPA of 3.0. Additional exam requirements/recommendations for international students: Required—TOEFL (minimum score 600 paper-based; 90 iBT). Electronic applications accepted. *Faculty research:* Inverse problems, partial differential equations, computer algorithms, computational modeling, optimization theory.

Rice University, Graduate Programs, George R. Brown School of Engineering, Program in Computational Science and Engineering, Houston, TX 77251-1892. Offers MCSE.

Sam Houston State University, College of Sciences, Department of Computer Science, Huntsville, TX 77341. Offers computing and information science (MS); digital forensics (MS); information assurance and security (MS). *Program availability:* Part-time. *Degree requirements:* For master's, comprehensive exam, thesis optional, internship; for doctorate, comprehensive exam, thesis/dissertation. *Entrance requirements:* For master's, GRE General Test, letters of recommendation. Additional exam requirements/recommendations for international students: Required—TOEFL (minimum score 550 paper-based; 79 iBT), IELTS (minimum score 6.5). Electronic applications accepted.

San Diego State University, Graduate and Research Affairs, College of Sciences, Program in Computational Science, San Diego, CA 92182. Offers MS, PhD. *Degree requirements:* For master's, thesis; for doctorate, thesis/dissertation. *Entrance requirements:* For master's, GRE General Test, 3 letters of recommendation; for doctorate, GRE, 3 letters of recommendation. Additional exam requirements/recommendations for international students: Required—TOEFL. Electronic applications accepted.

San Jose State University, Graduate Studies and Research, College of Science, San Jose, CA 95192-0001. Offers biological sciences (MA, MS), including molecular biology and microbiology (MS), organismal biology, conservation and ecology (MS), physiology (MS); chemistry (MA, MS); computer science (MS); cybersecurity (Certificate); cybersecurity: core technologies (Certificate); geology (MS); marine science (MS); master biotechnology (MBT); mathematics (MA, MS), including mathematics education (MA), science; meteorology (MS); physics (MS), including computational physics, modern optics, science (MA, MS); science education (MA); statistics (MS); unix system administration (Certificate). *Program availability:* Part-time, evening/weekend. *Students:* 118 full-time (68 women), 52 part-time (25 women); includes 125 minority (5 Black or African American, non-Hispanic/Latino; 97 Asian, non-Hispanic/Latino; 23 Hispanic/Latino), 121 international. Average age 27. 1,236 applicants, 21% accepted, 171 enrolled. In 2015, 168 master's awarded. *Entrance requirements:* For master's, GRE. *Application deadline:* For fall admission, 6/29 for domestic students; for spring admission, 11/30 for domestic students. Applications are processed on a rolling basis. Application fee: $55. Electronic applications accepted. *Financial support:* Teaching assistantships, career-related internships or fieldwork, Federal Work-Study, and institutionally sponsored loans available. Support available to part-time students. Financial award applicants required to submit FAFSA. *Faculty research:* Radiochemistry/environmental analysis, health physics, radiation effects. *Unit head:* J. Michael Parrish, Dean, 408-924-4800, Fax: 408-924-4815. *Application contact:* 408-924-2480, Fax: 408-924-2477.
Website: http://www.science.sjsu.edu/

Simon Fraser University, Office of Graduate Studies, Faculty of Science, Department of Mathematics, Burnaby, BC V5A 1S6, Canada. Offers applied and computational mathematics (M Sc, PhD); mathematics (M Sc, PhD); operations research (M Sc, PhD). *Degree requirements:* For master's, thesis or alternative; for doctorate, comprehensive exam, thesis/dissertation. *Entrance requirements:* For master's, GRE General Test, GRE Subject Test (mathematics), minimum GPA of 3.0 (on scale of 4.33), or 3.33 based on last 60 credits of undergraduate courses; for doctorate, GRE General Test, GRE

Subject Test (mathematics), minimum GPA of 3.5 (on scale of 4.33). Additional exam requirements/recommendations for international students: Recommended—TOEFL (minimum score 580 paper-based; 93 iBT), IELTS (minimum score 7), TWE (minimum score 5). Electronic applications accepted. *Faculty research:* Computer algebra, discrete mathematics, fluid dynamics, nonlinear partial differential equations and variation methods, numerical analysis and scientific computing.

South Dakota State University, Graduate School, College of Engineering, Department of Mathematics and Statistics, Brookings, SD 57007. Offers computational science and statistics (PhD); mathematics (MS); statistics (MS). *Program availability:* Part-time. Terminal master's awarded for partial completion of doctoral program. *Degree requirements:* For master's, thesis (for some programs), oral exam; for doctorate, comprehensive exam, thesis/dissertation, oral and written exams. *Entrance requirements:* Additional exam requirements/recommendations for international students: Required—TOEFL (minimum score 550 paper-based; 80 iBT); Recommended—IELTS. *Faculty research:* Financial mathematics, predictive analytics, operations research, bioinformatics, biostatistics, computational science, statistics, number theory, abstract algebra.

Southern Illinois University Edwardsville, Graduate School, College of Arts and Sciences, Department of Mathematics and Statistics, Program in Computational and Applied Mathematics, Edwardsville, IL 62026. Offers MS. *Program availability:* Part-time. *Degree requirements:* For master's, thesis (for some programs), research paper. *Entrance requirements:* Additional exam requirements/recommendations for international students: Required—TOEFL (minimum score 550 paper-based, 79 iBT), IELTS (minimum score 6.5), Michigan Test of English Language Proficiency or PTE. *Application deadline:* For fall admission, 7/22 for domestic students, 7/15 for international students; for spring admission, 12/9 for domestic students, 11/15 for international students; for summer admission, 4/29 for domestic students, 4/15 for international students. Applications are processed on a rolling basis. Application fee: $30. Electronic applications accepted. *Expenses:* Tuition, state resident: full-time $5026; part-time $837 per course. Tuition, nonresident: full-time $12,566; part-time $2094 per course. *Required fees:* $1682; $474 per course. Tuition and fees vary according to course load, campus/location and program. *Financial support:* Fellowships, research assistantships, teaching assistantships, and unspecified assistantships available. *Unit head:* Dr. Myung Sin Song, Program Director, 618-650-2580, E-mail: msong@siue.edu. *Application contact:* Bob Skorczewski, Coordinator of International and Graduate Recruitment, 618-650-3705, Fax: 618-650-3618, E-mail: graduateadmissions@siue.edu.
Website: http://www.siue.edu/artsandsciences/math/

Southern Methodist University, Dedman College of Humanities and Sciences, Department of Mathematics, Dallas, TX 75275. Offers computational and applied mathematics (MS, PhD). *Degree requirements:* For master's, oral exams; for doctorate, thesis/dissertation, oral and written exams. *Entrance requirements:* For master's and doctorate, GRE General Test, minimum GPA of 3.0, 18 undergraduate hours in mathematics beyond first- and second-year calculus. Additional exam requirements/recommendations for international students: Required—TOEFL. Electronic applications accepted. *Faculty research:* Numerical analysis and scientific computation, fluid dynamics, optics, wave propagation, mathematical biology.

Stanford University, School of Engineering, Institute for Computational and Mathematical Engineering, Stanford, CA 94305-9991. Offers MS, PhD. Terminal master's awarded for partial completion of doctoral program. *Degree requirements:* For doctorate, thesis/dissertation, qualifying exam. *Entrance requirements:* For master's, GRE General Test; for doctorate, GRE General Test, GRE Subject Test. Additional exam requirements/recommendations for international students: Required—TOEFL. Electronic applications accepted. *Expenses: Tuition, area resident:* Full-time $45,729. *Required fees:* $591.

Stockton University, Office of Graduate Studies, Program in Computational Science, Galloway, NJ 08205-9441. Offers MS. *Program availability:* Part-time, evening/weekend, online learning. *Faculty:* 1 full-time (0 women), 1 part-time/adjunct (0 women). *Students:* 3 full-time (2 women), 9 part-time (3 women); includes 4 minority (1 Black or African American, non-Hispanic/Latino; 2 Asian, non-Hispanic/Latino; 1 Two or more races, non-Hispanic/Latino). Average age 29. 6 applicants, 83% accepted, 3 enrolled. In 2015, 13 master's awarded. *Degree requirements:* For master's, thesis optional. *Entrance requirements:* For master's, GRE. Additional exam requirements/recommendations for international students: Required—TOEFL. *Application deadline:* For fall admission, 7/1 for domestic and international students; for spring admission, 12/1 for domestic students, 11/1 for international students. Applications are processed on a rolling basis. Application fee: $50. Electronic applications accepted. *Expenses:* Tuition, state resident: full-time $13,968; part-time $582 per credit. Tuition, nonresident: full-time $21,502; part-time $895 per credit. *Required fees:* $4200; $175 per credit. $90. Tuition and fees vary according to degree level. *Financial support:* Fellowships, research assistantships with partial tuition reimbursements, career-related internships or fieldwork, Federal Work-Study, scholarships/grants, and unspecified assistantships available. Financial award application deadline: 3/1; financial award applicants required to submit FAFSA. *Unit head:* Dr. J. Russell Manson, Program Director, 609-626-3640, E-mail: gradschool@stockton.edu. *Application contact:* Tara Williams, Assistant Director of Enrollment Management, 609-626-3640, Fax: 609-626-6050, E-mail: gradschool@stockton.edu.
Website: http://www.stockton.edu/grad

Temple University, College of Science and Technology, Department of Mathematics, Philadelphia, PA 19122. Offers applied mathematics (MA); mathematics (PhD); pure mathematics (MA). *Program availability:* Part-time, evening/weekend. *Faculty:* 27 full-time (6 women). *Students:* 34 full-time (10 women), 3 part-time (0 women); includes 3 minority (all Asian, non-Hispanic/Latino), 18 international. 57 applicants, 46% accepted, 9 enrolled. In 2015, 8 master's, 5 doctorates awarded. Terminal master's awarded for partial completion of doctoral program. *Degree requirements:* For master's, thesis optional, written exam; for doctorate, 2 foreign languages, thesis/dissertation, oral and written exams. *Entrance requirements:* For master's, GRE General Test, minimum GPA of 3.0; for doctorate, GRE General Test, GRE Subject Test, minimum GPA of 3.0. Additional exam requirements/recommendations for international students: Required—TOEFL (minimum score 550 paper-based; 79 iBT). *Application deadline:* For fall admission, 2/15 priority date for domestic students, 12/15 for international students; for spring admission, 11/15 for domestic students, 8/1 for international students. Applications are processed on a rolling basis. Application fee: $60. Electronic applications accepted. *Financial support:* Fellowships, research assistantships, teaching assistantships, Federal Work-Study, and institutionally sponsored loans available. Financial award application deadline: 1/15; financial award applicants required to submit FAFSA. *Faculty research:* Differential geometry, numerical analysis. *Unit head:* Edward Letzter, Department Chair, 215-204-7841, Fax: 215-204-6433, E-mail: mathematics@temple.edu. *Application contact:* Alexis Cogan, Administrative Assistant, 215-204-7840, E-mail: cogana@temple.edu.
Website: http://math.temple.edu/

University at Buffalo, the State University of New York, Graduate School, College of Arts and Sciences, Center for Computational Research, Buffalo, NY 14260. Offers computational science (Advanced Certificate).

The University of Alabama at Birmingham, School of Engineering, Program in Interdisciplinary Engineering, Birmingham, AL 35294. Offers computational engineering (PhD); environmental health and safety engineering (PhD). *Degree requirements:* For doctorate, comprehensive exam, thesis/dissertation. *Entrance requirements:* For doctorate, GRE (minimum rank 50% in both Quantitative Reasoning and Verbal Reasoning sections), undergraduate degree in a supporting field, official transcripts, minimum undergraduate GPA of 3.0. Additional exam requirements/recommendations for international students: Required—TOEFL (minimum score 100 iBT). *Expenses:* Tuition, state resident: full-time $7340. Tuition, nonresident: full-time $16,628. Full-time tuition and fees vary according to course load and program.

University of Alaska Fairbanks, College of Natural Sciences and Mathematics, Department of Physics, Fairbanks, AK 99775-5920. Offers computational physics (MS); physics (MS, PhD); space physics (MS). *Program availability:* Part-time. *Faculty:* 8 full-time (2 women). *Students:* 22 full-time (3 women), 2 part-time (0 women); includes 3 minority (1 American Indian or Alaska Native, non-Hispanic/Latino; 2 Asian, non-Hispanic/Latino), 4 international. Average age 29. 53 applicants, 17% accepted, 9 enrolled. In 2015, 1 master's, 3 doctorates awarded. *Degree requirements:* For master's, comprehensive exam, oral defense of project or thesis; for doctorate, comprehensive exam, thesis/dissertation, oral defense of dissertation. *Entrance requirements:* For master's, GRE General Test, bachelor's degree from accredited institution with minimum cumulative undergraduate and major GPA of 3.0; for doctorate, GRE General Test, minimum cumulative GPA of 3.0. Additional exam requirements/recommendations for international students: Required—TOEFL (minimum score 550 paper-based; 80 iBT). *Application deadline:* For fall admission, 6/1 for domestic students, 3/1 for international students; for spring admission, 10/15 for domestic students, 9/1 for international students. Applications are processed on a rolling basis. Application fee: $60. Electronic applications accepted. *Expenses:* Tuition, state resident: full-time $7614; part-time $423 per credit. Tuition, nonresident: full-time $15,552; part-time $864 per credit. *Required fees:* $38 per credit. $187 per semester. Tuition and fees vary according to course level, course load, program and reciprocity agreements. *Financial support:* In 2015–16, 10 research assistantships with full tuition reimbursements (averaging $16,599 per year), 11 teaching assistantships with full tuition reimbursements (averaging $16,577 per year) were awarded; fellowships with full tuition reimbursements, Federal Work-Study, scholarships/grants, health care benefits, and unspecified assistantships also available. Support available to part-time students. Financial award application deadline: 2/15; financial award applicants required to submit FAFSA. *Faculty research:* Atmospheric and ionospheric radar studies, space plasma theory, magnetospheric dynamics, space weather and auroral studies, turbulence and complex systems. *Unit head:* Renate Wackerbauer, Department Chair, 907-474-7339, Fax: 907-474-6130, E-mail: uaf-physics@alaska.edu. *Application contact:* Mary Kreta, Director of Admissions, 907-474-7500, Fax: 907-474-7097, E-mail: admissions@uaf.edu.
Website: http://www.uaf.edu/physics/

University of California, San Diego, Graduate Division, Department of Mathematics, La Jolla, CA 92093. Offers applied mathematics (MA); computational science (PhD); mathematics (MA, PhD); statistics (MS, PhD). *Students:* 130 full-time (32 women), 3 part-time (0 women); includes 18 minority (13 Asian, non-Hispanic/Latino; 5 Hispanic/Latino), 72 international. 777 applicants, 16% accepted, 35 enrolled. In 2015, 18 master's, 16 doctorates awarded. *Degree requirements:* For master's, comprehensive exam; for doctorate, comprehensive exam, thesis/dissertation. *Entrance requirements:* For master's, GRE General Test; GRE Subject Test (for MA), minimum GPA of 3.0; for doctorate, GRE General Test, GRE Subject Test, minimum GPA of 3.0. Additional exam requirements/recommendations for international students: Required—TOEFL (minimum score 550 paper-based; 80 iBT), IELTS. *Application deadline:* For fall admission, 1/4 for domestic and international students. Application fee: $90 ($110 for international students). Electronic applications accepted. *Expenses:* Tuition, state resident: full-time $11,220. Tuition, nonresident: full-time $26,322. *Required fees:* $1800. *Financial support:* Fellowships, research assistantships, teaching assistantships, and scholarships/grants available. Financial award applicants required to submit FAFSA. *Faculty research:* Combinatorics, bioinformatics, differential equations, logic and computational complexity, probability theory and statistics. *Unit head:* Peter Ebenfelt, Chair, 858-822-4961, E-mail: pebenfelt@ucsd.edu. *Application contact:* Debra Shon, Admissions Contact, 858-534-9056, E-mail: mathgradadmissions@math.ucsd.edu.
Website: http://math.ucsd.edu/

University of California, San Diego, Graduate Division, Department of Mechanical and Aerospace Engineering, La Jolla, CA 92023-0515. Offers aerospace engineering (MS, PhD); applied mechanics (MS, PhD); applied ocean science (MS, PhD); engineering physics (MS, PhD); engineering sciences (PhD), including computational science, multi-scale biology; mechanical engineering (MS, PhD). PhD in engineering sciences offered jointly with San Diego State University. *Students:* 229 full-time (41 women), 36 part-time (9 women); includes 44 minority (2 Black or African American, non-Hispanic/Latino; 2 American Indian or Alaska Native, non-Hispanic/Latino; 29 Asian, non-Hispanic/Latino; 11 Hispanic/Latino), 156 international. 883 applicants, 35% accepted, 106 enrolled. In 2015, 30 master's, 26 doctorates awarded. *Degree requirements:* For master's, comprehensive exam or thesis; for doctorate, comprehensive exam, thesis/dissertation. *Entrance requirements:* For master's and doctorate, GRE General Test, minimum GPA of 3.0. Additional exam requirements/recommendations for international students: Required—TOEFL (minimum score 550 paper-based), IELTS (minimum score 7). *Application deadline:* For fall admission, 12/15 for domestic students. Application fee: $90 ($110 for international students). Electronic applications accepted. *Expenses:* Tuition, state resident: full-time $11,220. Tuition, nonresident: full-time $26,322. *Required fees:* $1800. *Financial support:* Fellowships, research assistantships, teaching assistantships, scholarships/grants, and traineeships available. Financial award application deadline: 1/1; financial award applicants required to submit FAFSA. *Faculty research:* Solid mechanics; materials; fluid mechanics and heat transfer; dynamics, systems and controls; energy, including combustion and renewables, plasmas. *Unit head:* Vitali Nesterenko, Chair, 858-534-0113, E-mail: mae-chair-l@ucsd.edu. *Application contact:* Lydia Ramirez, Graduate Coordinator, 858-534-4387, E-mail: mae-gradadm-l@ucsd.edu.
Website: http://maeweb.ucsd.edu/

University of California, San Diego, Graduate Division, Program in Computational Science, Mathematics and Engineering, La Jolla, CA 92093. Offers MS. *Students:* 19 full-time (6 women); includes 1 minority (Asian, non-Hispanic/Latino), 15 international. 122 applicants, 39% accepted, 15 enrolled. In 2015, 4 master's awarded. *Degree requirements:* For master's, comprehensive exam. *Entrance requirements:* For master's, GRE General Test, 3 letters of recommendation, statement of purpose, minimum GPA of 3.0, 2 years of calculus. Additional exam requirements/recommendations for international students: Required—TOEFL (minimum score 550 paper-based; 80 iBT), IELTS (minimum score 7). Application fee: $90 ($110 for international students). Electronic applications accepted. *Expenses:* Tuition, state

resident: full-time $11,220. Tuition, nonresident: full-time $26,322. *Required fees:* $1800. *Financial support:* Teaching assistantships available. Financial award applicants required to submit FAFSA. *Faculty research:* Computational fluid dynamics, atmospheric science, climate modeling, particle physics, multi-scale and multi-physics modeling. *Unit head:* Michael Holst, Co-Director, 858-534-4899, E-mail: mholst@ucsd.edu. *Application contact:* Terry Le, Program Coordinator, 858-534-6887, E-mail: tele@ucsd.edu.
Website: http://csme.ucsd.edu

University of California, Santa Barbara, Graduate Division, College of Engineering, Department of Computer Science, Santa Barbara, CA 93106-5110. Offers computer science (PhD), including cognitive science, computational science and engineering, technology and society. *Faculty:* 32 full-time (5 women), 2 part-time/adjunct (0 women). *Students:* 158 full-time (29 women); includes 16 minority (1 Black or African American, non-Hispanic/Latino; 1 American Indian or Alaska Native, non-Hispanic/Latino; 12 Asian, non-Hispanic/Latino; 2 Hispanic/Latino), 100 international. Average age 26. 1,286 applicants, 11% accepted, 53 enrolled. In 2015, 33 master's, 16 doctorates awarded. Terminal master's awarded for partial completion of doctoral program. *Degree requirements:* For master's, comprehensive exam (for some programs), thesis (for some programs), project (for some programs); for doctorate, thesis/dissertation. *Entrance requirements:* For master's and doctorate, GRE. Additional exam requirements/recommendations for international students: Required—TOEFL (minimum score 600 paper-based; 100 iBT), IELTS (minimum score 7). *Application deadline:* For fall admission, 12/15 for domestic and international students. Application fee: $90 ($110 for international students). Electronic applications accepted. *Financial support:* In 2015–16, 8 fellowships with tuition reimbursements (averaging $25,666 per year), 225 research assistantships with tuition reimbursements (averaging $20,480 per year), 120 teaching assistantships with tuition reimbursements (averaging $18,538 per year) were awarded; Federal Work-Study, scholarships/grants, health care benefits, unspecified assistantships, and course reader appointments also available. Financial award application deadline: 12/15; financial award applicants required to submit FAFSA. *Faculty research:* Algorithms and theory, computational science and engineering, computer architecture, database and information systems, machine learning and data mining, networking, operating systems and distributed systems, programming languages and software engineering, security and cryptography, social computing, visual computing and interaction. *Total annual research expenditures:* $10.4 million. *Unit head:* Prof. Ambuj Singh, Chair, 805-893-5334, Fax: 805-893-8553,
E-mail: ambuj@cs.ucsb.edu. *Application contact:* Jillian Title, Graduate Advisor, 805-893-4322, E-mail: jillian.title@cs.ucsb.edu.
Website: http://www.cs.ucsb.edu/

University of California, Santa Barbara, Graduate Division, College of Letters and Sciences, Division of Mathematics, Life, and Physical Sciences, Department of Ecology, Evolution, and Marine Biology, Santa Barbara, CA 93106-9620. Offers computational science and engineering (MA); computational sciences and engineering (PhD); ecology, evolution, and marine biology (MA, PhD); MA/PhD. *Faculty:* 33 full-time (8 women). *Students:* 69 full-time (44 women); includes 15 minority (2 Black or African American, non-Hispanic/Latino; 5 Asian, non-Hispanic/Latino; 6 Hispanic/Latino; 2 Native Hawaiian or other Pacific Islander, non-Hispanic/Latino), 3 international. Average age 29. 157 applicants, 14% accepted, 17 enrolled. In 2015, 7 master's, 8 doctorates awarded. *Degree requirements:* For master's, comprehensive exam (for some programs), thesis (for some programs); for doctorate, comprehensive exam, thesis/dissertation. *Entrance requirements:* For master's and doctorate, GRE General Test. Additional exam requirements/recommendations for international students: Required—TOEFL (minimum score 550 paper-based; 80 iBT), IELTS. *Application deadline:* For fall admission, 12/15 for domestic and international students. Application fee: $90 ($110 for international students). Electronic applications accepted. *Financial support:* In 2015–16, 50 students received support, including 55 fellowships with tuition reimbursements available (averaging $10,812 per year), 24 research assistantships with tuition reimbursements available (averaging $8,441 per year), 97 teaching assistantships with partial tuition reimbursements available (averaging $9,346 per year); Federal Work-Study, scholarships/grants, traineeships, health care benefits, and tuition waivers (full and partial) also available. Financial award application deadline: 12/15; financial award applicants required to submit FAFSA. *Faculty research:* Community ecology, evolution, marine biology, population genetics, stream ecology. *Unit head:* Dr. Craig Carlson, Chair, 805-893-2415, Fax: 805-893-5885, E-mail: eembchair@lifesci.ucsb.edu. *Application contact:* Melanie Fujii, Student Affairs Officer, 805-893-2979, Fax: 805-893-5885, E-mail: eemb-info@lifesci.ucsb.edu.
Website: http://www.lifesci.ucsb.edu/EEMB/index.html

University of California, Santa Barbara, Graduate Division, College of Letters and Sciences, Division of Mathematics, Life, and Physical Sciences, Department of Mathematics, Santa Barbara, CA 93106-3080. Offers applied mathematics (MA), including computational science and engineering; mathematics (MA, PhD), including computational science and engineering (PhD), mathematics (MA); MA/PhD. *Faculty:* 23 full-time (2 women). *Students:* 64 full-time (15 women); includes 17 minority (1 Black or African American, non-Hispanic/Latino; 1 American Indian or Alaska Native, non-Hispanic/Latino; 6 Asian, non-Hispanic/Latino; 7 Hispanic/Latino; 2 Native Hawaiian or other Pacific Islander, non-Hispanic/Latino), 9 international. Average age 26. 189 applicants, 21% accepted, 11 enrolled. In 2015, 16 master's, 7 doctorates awarded. Terminal master's awarded for partial completion of doctoral program. *Degree requirements:* For master's, comprehensive exam (for some programs), thesis (for some programs); for doctorate, comprehensive exam, thesis/dissertation. *Entrance requirements:* For master's and doctorate, GRE General Test, GRE Subject Test (math). Additional exam requirements/recommendations for international students: Required—TOEFL (minimum score 575 paper-based; 80 iBT), IELTS (minimum score 7). *Application deadline:* For fall admission, 1/2 for domestic and international students. Application fee: $90 ($110 for international students). Electronic applications accepted. *Financial support:* In 2015–16, 53 students received support, including 15 fellowships with full tuition reimbursements available (averaging $15,000 per year), 5 research assistantships with full tuition reimbursements available (averaging $19,000 per year), 52 teaching assistantships with partial tuition reimbursements available (averaging $18,880 per year); Federal Work-Study, institutionally sponsored loans, health care benefits, and tuition waivers (full and partial) also available. Financial award application deadline: 3/2; financial award applicants required to submit FAFSA. *Faculty research:* Topology, differential geometry, algebra, applied mathematics, partial differential equations. *Total annual research expenditures:* $205,000. *Unit head:* Prof. Darren Long, Chair, 805-893-8340, Fax: 805-893-2385, E-mail: chair@math.ucsb.edu. *Application contact:* Medina Price, Student Affairs Manager, 805-893-8192, Fax: 805-893-2385, E-mail: price@math.ucsb.edu.
Website: http://www.math.ucsb.edu/

University of Chicago, Division of the Social Sciences, Master of Arts Program in Computational Social Science, Chicago, IL 60637. Offers MA. *Degree requirements:* For master's, thesis. *Entrance requirements:* For master's, GRE General Test. Additional exam requirements/recommendations for international students: Required—TOEFL (minimum score 104 iBT), IELTS (minimum score 7). *Application deadline:* For fall admission, 1/5 priority date for domestic students, 1/5 for international students. Application fee: $90. Electronic applications accepted. *Financial support:* Federal Work-Study, institutionally sponsored loans, and scholarships/grants available. Financial award application deadline: 1/5. *Faculty research:* Social science data analytics, modeling social systems, cognitive neuroimaging, quantitative social science. *Unit head:* Dr. James Evans, Director, 773-702-5885, E-mail: jevans@uchicago.edu. *Application contact:* Office of the Dean of Students, 773-702-8415,
E-mail: admissions@ssd.uchicago.edu.
Website: http://macss.uchicago.edu/

University of Chicago, Harris School of Public Policy, Program in Computational Analysis and Public Policy, Chicago, IL 60637. Offers MS. Offered jointly with Department of Computer Science. *Entrance requirements:* For master's, GRE General Test. Additional exam requirements/recommendations for international students: Required—TOEFL (minimum score 104 iBT), IELTS (minimum score 7). Electronic applications accepted.

University of Colorado Denver, College of Liberal Arts and Sciences, Department of Mathematical and Statistical Sciences, Denver, CO 80217. Offers applied mathematics (MS, PhD), including applied mathematics, applied probability (MS), applied statistics (MS), computational biology, computational mathematics (PhD), discrete mathematics, finite geometry (PhD), mathematics education (PhD), mathematics of engineering and science (MS), numerical analysis, operations research (MS), optimization and operations research (PhD), probability (PhD), statistics (PhD). *Program availability:* Part-time. *Faculty:* 18 full-time (4 women), 5 part-time/adjunct (0 women). *Students:* 48 full-time (16 women), 15 part-time (6 women); includes 7 minority (1 Black or African American, non-Hispanic/Latino; 2 Asian, non-Hispanic/Latino; 3 Hispanic/Latino; 1 Two or more races, non-Hispanic/Latino), 12 international. Average age 32. 105 applicants, 70% accepted, 21 enrolled. In 2015, 10 master's, 3 doctorates awarded. *Degree requirements:* For master's, comprehensive exam, thesis optional, 30 hours of course work with minimum GPA of 3.0; for doctorate, comprehensive exam, thesis/dissertation, 42 hours of course work with minimum GPA of 3.25. *Entrance requirements:* For master's, GRE General Test; GRE Subject Test in math (recommended), 30 hours of course work in mathematics (24 of which must be upper-division mathematics), bachelor's degree with minimum GPA of 3.0; for doctorate, GRE General Test; GRE Subject Test in math (recommended), 30 hours of course work in mathematics (24 of which must be upper-division mathematics), master's degree with minimum GPA of 3.25. Additional exam requirements/recommendations for international students: Required—TOEFL (minimum score 537 paper-based; 75 iBT); Recommended—IELTS (minimum score 6.5). *Application deadline:* For fall admission, 4/1 for domestic and international students; for spring admission, 10/1 for domestic and international students; for summer admission, 4/1 for domestic and international students. Application fee: $50 ($75 for international students). Electronic applications accepted. *Financial support:* In 2015–16, 46 students received support. Fellowships with partial tuition reimbursements available, research assistantships with full tuition reimbursements available, teaching assistantships with full tuition reimbursements available, Federal Work-Study, institutionally sponsored loans, scholarships/grants, and traineeships available. Financial award application deadline: 4/1; financial award applicants required to submit FAFSA. *Faculty research:* Computational mathematics, computational biology, discrete mathematics and geometry, probability and statistics, optimization. *Unit head:* Dr. Michael Ferrara, Graduate Chair, 303-315-1705,
E-mail: michael.ferrara@ucdenver.edu. *Application contact:* Julie Blunck, Program Assistant, 303-315-1743, E-mail: julie.blunck@ucdenver.edu.
Website: http://www.ucdenver.edu/academics/colleges/CLAS/Departments/math/Pages/MathStats.aspx

The University of Iowa, Graduate College, Program in Applied Mathematical and Computational Sciences, Iowa City, IA 52242-1316. Offers PhD. *Degree requirements:* For doctorate, comprehensive exam, thesis/dissertation. *Entrance requirements:* For doctorate, GRE General Test, minimum GPA of 3.0. Additional exam requirements/recommendations for international students: Required—TOEFL (minimum score 620 paper-based; 105 iBT). Electronic applications accepted.

The University of Kansas, Graduate Studies, College of Liberal Arts and Sciences, Department of Physics and Astronomy, Lawrence, KS 66045. Offers computational physics and astronomy (MS); physics (MS, PhD). *Students:* 54 full-time (7 women), 1 part-time (0 women); includes 5 minority (1 American Indian or Alaska Native, non-Hispanic/Latino; 1 Hispanic/Latino; 3 Two or more races, non-Hispanic/Latino), 23 international. Average age 30. 80 applicants, 14% accepted, 7 enrolled. In 2015, 4 master's, 6 doctorates awarded. Terminal master's awarded for partial completion of doctoral program. *Entrance requirements:* For master's and doctorate, GRE Subject Test (physics), undergraduate degree. Additional exam requirements/recommendations for international students: Required—TOEFL. *Application deadline:* For fall admission, 12/1 priority date for domestic and international students; for spring admission, 10/1 priority date for domestic and international students. Application fee: $65 ($85 for international students). Electronic applications accepted. *Financial support:* Fellowships, research assistantships, teaching assistantships, health care benefits, and unspecified assistantships available. Financial award application deadline: 4/1; financial award applicants required to submit FAFSA. *Faculty research:* Astrophysics, biophysics, high energy physics, nanophysics, nuclear physics. *Unit head:* Hume A. Feldman, Chair, 785-864-4740, E-mail: feldman@ku.edu. *Application contact:* Desiree Neyens, Graduate Secretary, 785-864-1225, E-mail: dneyens@ku.edu.
Website: http://www.physics.ku.edu

University of Lethbridge, School of Graduate Studies, Lethbridge, AB T1K 3M4, Canada. Offers addictions counseling (M Sc); agricultural biotechnology (M Sc); agricultural studies (M Sc, MA); anthropology (MA); archaeology (M Sc, MA); art (MA, MFA); biochemistry (M Sc); biological sciences (M Sc); biomolecular science (PhD); biosystems and biodiversity (PhD); Canadian studies (MA); chemistry (M Sc); computer science (M Sc); computer science and geographical information science (M Sc); counseling (MC); counseling psychology (M Ed); dramatic arts (MA); earth, space, and physical science (PhD); economics (MA); education (MA, PhD); educational leadership (M Ed); English (MA); environmental science (M Sc); evolution and behavior (PhD); exercise science (M Sc); French (MA); French/German (MA); French/Spanish (MA); general education (M Ed); geography (M Sc, MA); German (MA); health sciences (M Sc); individualized multidisciplinary (M Sc, MA); kinesiology (M Sc, MA); management (M Sc), including accounting, finance, human resource management and labor relations, information systems, international management, marketing, policy and strategy; mathematics (M Sc); music (M Mus, MA); Native American studies (MA); neuroscience (M Sc, PhD); new media (MA, MFA); nursing (M Sc, MN); philosophy (MA); physics (M Sc); political science (MA); psychology (M Sc, MA); religious studies (MA); sociology (MA); theatre and dramatic arts (MFA); theoretical and computational science (PhD); urban and regional studies (MA); women and gender studies (MA). *Program availability:* Part-time, evening/weekend. *Students:* 448 full-time (249 women), 110 part-time (64 women). Average age 32. 285 applicants, 36% accepted, 96 enrolled. In 2015, 154 master's, 11 doctorates awarded. *Degree requirements:* For master's, thesis (for some programs); for doctorate, comprehensive exam, thesis/dissertation.

Entrance requirements: For master's, GMAT (for M Sc in management), bachelor's degree in related field, minimum GPA of 3.0 during previous 20 graded semester courses, 2 years' teaching or related experience (M Ed); for doctorate, master's degree, minimum graduate GPA of 3.5. Additional exam requirements/recommendations for international students: Required—TOEFL (minimum score 580 paper-based; 93 iBT). Application fee: $100 Canadian dollars ($140 Canadian dollars for international students). Electronic applications accepted. *Financial support:* Fellowships, research assistantships, teaching assistantships, scholarships/grants, health care benefits, and unspecified assistantships available. *Faculty research:* Movement and brain plasticity, gibberellin physiology, photosynthesis, carbon cycling, molecular properties of main-group ring components. *Unit head:* Kathleen Schrage, Manager, School of Graduate Studies, 403-329-2121, E-mail: schrage@uleth.ca. *Application contact:* School of Graduate Studies, 403-329-5194, E-mail: sgsinquiries@uleth.ca.
Website: http://www.uleth.ca/graduate-studies/

University of Manitoba, Faculty of Graduate Studies, Faculty of Science, Program in Mathematical, Computational and Statistical Sciences, Winnipeg, MB R3T 2N2, Canada. Offers MMCSS.

University of Massachusetts Dartmouth, Graduate School, College of Engineering, Program in Engineering and Applied Science, North Dartmouth, MA 02747-2300. Offers applied mechanics and materials (PhD); computational science and engineering (PhD); computer science and information systems (PhD); industrial and systems engineering (PhD). *Program availability:* Part-time. *Students:* 20 full-time (6 women), 5 part-time (2 women); includes 1 minority (Black or African American, non-Hispanic/Latino), 13 international. Average age 30. 23 applicants, 78% accepted, 3 enrolled. In 2015, 1 doctorate awarded. *Degree requirements:* For doctorate, comprehensive exam, thesis/dissertation. *Entrance requirements:* For doctorate, GRE, statement of purpose (minimum of 300 words), resume, 3 letters of recommendation, official transcripts. Additional exam requirements/recommendations for international students: Required—TOEFL (minimum score 550 paper-based; 79 iBT). *Application deadline:* For fall admission, 2/15 priority date for domestic students, 1/15 priority date for international students; for spring admission, 11/15 priority date for domestic students, 10/15 priority date for international students. Applications are processed on a rolling basis. Application fee: $60. Electronic applications accepted. *Expenses:* Tuition, state resident: full-time $2071; part-time $86.29 per credit. Tuition, nonresident: full-time $8099; part-time $337.46 per credit. *Required fees:* $18,074; $762.08 per credit. Tuition and fees vary according to course load and reciprocity agreements. *Financial support:* In 2015–16, 4 fellowships (averaging $20,654 per year), 8 research assistantships (averaging $12,739 per year), 6 teaching assistantships (averaging $13,333 per year) were awarded; Federal Work-Study and unspecified assistantships also available. Support available to part-time students. Financial award application deadline: 3/1; financial award applicants required to submit FAFSA. *Faculty research:* Tissue/cell engineering, biotransport sensors/networks, marine systems biomimetic materials, composite/polymeric materials, resilient infrastructure robotics, renewable energy. *Total annual research expenditures:* $263,000. *Unit head:* Gaurav Khanna, Graduate Program Director, 508-910-6605, Fax: 508-999-9115, E-mail: gkhanna@umassd.edu. *Application contact:* Steven Briggs, Director of Marketing and Recruitment for Graduate Studies, 508-999-8604, Fax: 508-999-8183, E-mail: graduate@umassd.edu.
Website: http://www.umassd.edu/engineering/graduate/doctoraldegreeprograms/egrandappliedsciencephd/

University of Massachusetts Lowell, College of Sciences, Department of Mathematical Sciences, Lowell, MA 01854. Offers applied mathematics (MS); computational mathematics (PhD); mathematics (MS). *Program availability:* Part-time. *Entrance requirements:* For master's, GRE General Test.

University of Michigan–Dearborn, College of Arts, Sciences, and Letters, Master of Science in Applied and Computational Mathematics Program, Dearborn, MI 48128. Offers MS. *Program availability:* Part-time, evening/weekend. *Faculty:* 8 full-time (4 women). *Students:* 1 full-time (0 women), 12 part-time (5 women); includes 5 minority (1 Black or African American, non-Hispanic/Latino; 4 Hispanic/Latino). 7 applicants, 86% accepted, 3 enrolled. In 2015, 3 master's awarded. *Degree requirements:* For master's, thesis or alternative, project. *Entrance requirements:* For master's, 3 letters of recommendation, minimum GPA of 3.0, 2 years of course work in math. Additional exam requirements/recommendations for international students: Required—TOEFL (minimum score 560 paper-based; 84 iBT), IELTS (minimum score 6.5). *Application deadline:* For fall admission, 8/1 priority date for domestic students, 5/1 priority date for international students; for winter admission, 12/1 priority date for domestic students, 9/1 priority date for international students; for spring admission, 4/1 priority date for domestic students, 1/1 priority date for international students. Applications are processed on a rolling basis. Application fee: $60. Electronic applications accepted. *Expenses:* $633 per credit hour in-state; $363 per credit hour for ninth credit hour and beyond in-state; $1,133 per credit hour out-of-state; $736 per credit hour for ninth credit hour and beyond out-of-state; $277 fees per term part-time, $342 fees per term full-time. *Financial support:* In 2015–16, 4 students received support. Scholarships/grants and non-resident tuition scholarships available. Financial award application deadline: 3/1; financial award applicants required to submit FAFSA. *Faculty research:* Numerical analysis, stochastic differential equations, inverse problems and medical imaging, time series forecasting, Markov processes. *Unit head:* Dr. Joan Remski, Director, 313-593-4994, E-mail: remski@umich.edu. *Application contact:* Carol Ligienza, Coordinator, CASL Graduate Programs, 313-593-1183, Fax: 313-583-6700, E-mail: caslgrad@umich.edu.
Website: http://umdearborn.edu/casl/666301/

University of Minnesota, Duluth, Graduate School, Swenson College of Science and Engineering, Department of Mathematics and Statistics, Duluth, MN 55812-2496. Offers applied and computational mathematics (MS). *Program availability:* Part-time. *Degree requirements:* For master's, thesis or alternative. *Entrance requirements:* For master's, GRE General Test, minimum GPA of 3.0. Additional exam requirements/recommendations for international students: Required—TOEFL (minimum score 550 paper-based; 79 iBT); Recommended—TWE. Electronic applications accepted. *Faculty research:* Discrete mathematics, diagnostic markers, combinatorics, biostatistics, mathematical modeling and scientific computation.

University of Minnesota, Twin Cities Campus, College of Science and Engineering, Scientific Computation Program, Minneapolis, MN 55455-0213. Offers MS, PhD. *Program availability:* Part-time. *Degree requirements:* For master's, thesis; for doctorate, thesis/dissertation. *Entrance requirements:* For master's and doctorate, GRE General Test. Additional exam requirements/recommendations for international students: Required—TOEFL (minimum score 550 paper-based; 79 iBT), IELTS (minimum score 6.5). Electronic applications accepted. *Faculty research:* Parallel computations, quantum mechanical dynamics, computational materials science, computational fluid dynamics, computational neuroscience.

University of Notre Dame, Graduate School, College of Science, Department of Applied and Computational Mathematics and Statistics, Notre Dame, IN 46556. Offers applied and computational mathematics and statistics (PhD); applied statistics (MS); computational finance (MS).

University of Pennsylvania, School of Arts and Sciences, Graduate Group in Applied Mathematics and Computational Science, Philadelphia, PA 19104. Offers PhD. *Faculty:* 28 full-time (3 women), 2 part-time/adjunct (0 women). *Students:* 31 full-time (5 women), 26 international. Average age 25. 101 applicants, 27% accepted, 10 enrolled. In 2015, 3 doctorates awarded. *Expenses: Tuition, area resident:* Full-time $31,068; part-time $5762 per course. *Required fees:* $3200; $336 per course. Full-time tuition and fees vary according to degree level, program and student level. Part-time tuition and fees vary according to course load, degree level and program.
Website: http://www.amcs.upenn.edu

University of Pennsylvania, School of Engineering and Applied Science, Penn Institute for Computational Science, Philadelphia, PA 19104. Offers scientific computing (MSE). *Students:* 1 full-time (0 women), 2 part-time (1 woman); includes 1 minority (Two or more races, non-Hispanic/Latino), 1 international. Average age 24. 23 applicants, 43% accepted, 5 enrolled. *Degree requirements:* For master's, independent study or thesis. *Expenses: Tuition, area resident:* Full-time $31,068; part-time $5762 per course. *Required fees:* $3200; $336 per course. Full-time tuition and fees vary according to degree level, program and student level. Part-time tuition and fees vary according to course load, degree level and program.

University of Puerto Rico, Mayagüez Campus, Graduate Studies, College of Arts and Sciences, Department of Mathematical Sciences, Mayagüez, PR 00681-9000. Offers applied mathematics (MS); pure mathematics (MS); scientific computation (MS); statistics (MS). *Program availability:* Part-time. *Degree requirements:* For master's, one foreign language, comprehensive exam, thesis optional. *Entrance requirements:* For master's, undergraduate degree in mathematics or its equivalent. *Faculty research:* Automata theory, linear algebra, logic.

University of Southern Mississippi, Graduate School, College of Science and Technology, Department of Mathematics, Hattiesburg, MS 39406-0001. Offers computational science (PhD); mathematics (MS). *Program availability:* Part-time. *Degree requirements:* For master's, comprehensive exam, thesis or alternative; for doctorate, comprehensive exam, thesis/dissertation. *Entrance requirements:* For master's, GRE General Test, minimum GPA of 2.75 in last 60 hours; for doctorate, GRE General Test, minimum GPA of 3.5. Additional exam requirements/recommendations for international students: Required—TOEFL, IELTS. Electronic applications accepted. *Faculty research:* Dynamical systems, numerical analysis and multigrid methods, random number generation, matrix theory, group theory.

University of Southern Mississippi, Graduate School, College of Science and Technology, Department of Physics and Astronomy, Hattiesburg, MS 39406-0001. Offers computational science (PhD); physics (MS). *Degree requirements:* For master's, comprehensive exam, thesis; for doctorate, comprehensive exam, thesis/dissertation. *Entrance requirements:* For master's, GRE General Test, minimum GPA of 2.75 in last 60 hours; for doctorate, GRE General Test, minimum GPA of 3.5. Additional exam requirements/recommendations for international students: Required—TOEFL, IELTS. *Faculty research:* Polymers, atomic physics, fluid mechanics, liquid crystals, refractory materials.

University of Southern Mississippi, Graduate School, College of Science and Technology, School of Computing, Hattiesburg, MS 39406-0001. Offers computational science (MS, PhD); computer science (MS). *Degree requirements:* For master's, comprehensive exam, thesis; for doctorate, comprehensive exam, thesis/dissertation. *Entrance requirements:* For master's, GRE General Test, minimum GPA of 2.75 in last 60 hours; for doctorate, GRE General Test, minimum GPA of 3.5. Additional exam requirements/recommendations for international students: Required—TOEFL, IELTS. Electronic applications accepted. *Faculty research:* Satellite telecommunications, advanced life-support systems, artificial intelligence.

The University of Tennessee at Chattanooga, Program in Computational Science, Chattanooga, TN 37403. Offers PhD. *Faculty:* 7 full-time (0 women). *Students:* 4 full-time (2 women), 18 part-time (3 women); includes 2 minority (1 Black or African American, non-Hispanic/Latino; 1 Two or more races, non-Hispanic/Latino), 14 international. Average age 31. In 2015, 2 doctorates awarded. *Degree requirements:* For doctorate, comprehensive exam, thesis/dissertation. *Entrance requirements:* For doctorate, GRE General Test. Additional exam requirements/recommendations for international students: Required—TOEFL (minimum score 550 paper-based; 79 iBT), IELTS (minimum score 6). *Application deadline:* For fall admission, 6/13 priority date for domestic students, 6/1 for international students; for spring admission, 10/15 priority date for domestic students, 10/1 for international students. Applications are processed on a rolling basis. Application fee: $30 ($35 for international students). Electronic applications accepted. *Expenses:* Tuition, state resident: full-time $7938; part-time $441 per credit hour. Tuition, nonresident: full-time $24,056; part-time $1336 per credit hour. *Required fees:* $1732; $253 per credit hour. *Financial support:* Research assistantships, career-related internships or fieldwork, scholarships/grants, and unspecified assistantships available. Support available to part-time students. *Faculty research:* Computational fluid dynamics, design optimization, solution algorithms, hydronamics and propulsion. *Unit head:* Dr. Tim W. Swafford, Dean, 423-425-5507, Fax: 423-425-5517, E-mail: tim-swafford@utc.edu. *Application contact:* Dr. J. Randy Walker, Interim Dean of Graduate Studies, 423-425-4478, Fax: 423-425-5223, E-mail: randy-walker@utc.edu.
Website: http://www.utc.edu/college-engineering-computer-science/programs/computational-engineering/

The University of Tennessee at Chattanooga, Program in Engineering, Chattanooga, TN 37403. Offers automotive systems (MS Engr); chemical engineering (MS Engr); civil engineering (MS Engr); computational engineering (MS Engr); electrical engineering (MS Engr); industrial engineering (MS Engr); mechanical engineering (MS Engr). *Program availability:* Part-time. *Faculty:* 20 full-time (3 women), 3 part-time/adjunct (0 women). *Students:* 36 full-time (13 women), 39 part-time (6 women); includes 8 minority (3 Black or African American, non-Hispanic/Latino; 4 Asian, non-Hispanic/Latino; 1 Hispanic/Latino), 32 international. Average age 29. In 2015, 29 master's awarded. *Degree requirements:* For master's, comprehensive exam, thesis or alternative, engineering project. *Entrance requirements:* For master's, GRE General Test, minimum undergraduate GPA of 2.5 or 3.0 in last 30 hours of coursework. Additional exam requirements/recommendations for international students: Required—TOEFL (minimum score 550 paper-based; 79 iBT), IELTS (minimum score 6). *Application deadline:* For fall admission, 6/13 priority date for domestic students, 6/1 for international students; for spring admission, 10/15 priority date for domestic students, 10/1 for international students. Applications are processed on a rolling basis. Application fee: $30 ($35 for international students). Electronic applications accepted. *Expenses:* Tuition, state resident: full-time $7938; part-time $441 per credit hour. Tuition, nonresident: full-time $24,056; part-time $1336 per credit hour. *Required fees:* $1732; $253 per credit hour. *Financial support:* Research assistantships, teaching assistantships, career-related internships or fieldwork, scholarships/grants, health care benefits, and unspecified

Peterson's Graduate Programs in the Physical Sciences, Mathematics, Agricultural Sciences, the Environment & Natural Resources 2017

www.petersons.com 237

assistantships available. Support available to part-time students. *Faculty research:* Quality control and reliability engineering, financial management, thermal science, energy conservation, structural analysis. *Total annual research expenditures:* $1.5 million. *Unit head:* Dr. Daniel Pack, Dean, 423-425-2256, Fax: 423-425-5311, E-mail: daniel-pack@utc.edu. *Application contact:* Dr. J. Randy Walker, Interim Dean of Graduate Studies, 423-425-4478, Fax: 423-425-5223, E-mail: randy-walker@utc.edu. Website: http://www.utc.edu/Departments/engrcs/ms_engr.php

The University of Texas at Austin, Graduate School, Program in Computational Science, Engineering, and Mathematics, Austin, TX 78712-1111. Offers MS, PhD. Terminal master's awarded for partial completion of doctoral program. *Degree requirements:* For master's, thesis optional; for doctorate, thesis/dissertation, 3 area qualifying exams. Electronic applications accepted.

The University of Texas at El Paso, Graduate School, College of Science, Computational Science Program, El Paso, TX 79968-0001. Offers MS, PMS, PhD. *Program availability:* Part-time. Terminal master's awarded for partial completion of doctoral program. *Degree requirements:* For master's, thesis (for some programs), thesis or internship; for doctorate, thesis/dissertation. *Entrance requirements:* For master's and doctorate, GRE, statement of purpose, 3 letters of recommendation. Additional exam requirements/recommendations for international students: Required—TOEFL (minimum score 79 iBT); Recommended—IELTS (minimum score 6.5). Electronic applications accepted. *Expenses:* Contact institution. *Faculty research:* Numerical optimization; vibrational properties of biological molecules, interval computations, intelligent control, reasoning under certainty; probabilistic modeling and statistical bioinformatics; high-performance computing; biomedical engineering.

University of Utah, Graduate School, College of Engineering, School of Computing, Computational Engineering and Science Program, Salt Lake City, UT 84112. Offers MS. *Students:* 4 full-time (0 women), 6 part-time (2 women); includes 2 minority (1 Asian, non-Hispanic/Latino; 1 Two or more races, non-Hispanic/Latino), 5 international. Average age 31. 12 applicants, 83% accepted, 3 enrolled. In 2015, 4 master's awarded. *Degree requirements:* For master's, comprehensive exam, thesis (for some programs). *Entrance requirements:* For master's, minimum GPA of 3.0. Additional exam requirements/recommendations for international students: Required—TOEFL (minimum score 550 paper-based; 80 iBT), IELTS (minimum score 6). *Application deadline:* For fall admission, 1/15 priority date for domestic and international students. Application fee: $55 ($65 for international students). Electronic applications accepted. *Expenses:* Contact institution. *Financial support:* In 2015–16, 1 student received support, including 2 research assistantships with full tuition reimbursements available (averaging $14,000 per year), 2 teaching assistantships with full tuition reimbursements available (averaging $14,000 per year); fellowships, health care benefits, and unspecified assistantships also available. Financial award application deadline: 12/15; financial award applicants required to submit FAFSA. *Faculty research:* Mathematical modeling, the formulation of the numerical methodology for solving the problem, the selection of the appropriate computer architecture and algorithms, the effective interpretation of the results through visualization and/or statistical reduction. *Unit head:* Dr. Martin Berzins, Director, 801-581-8224, Fax: 801-581-5843, E-mail: berzins@cs.utah.edu. *Application contact:* Vicki Jackson, Graduate Advisor, 801-581-8224, Fax: 801-581-5843, E-mail: vicki@cs.utah.edu.
Website: http://www.ces.utah.edu

University of Utah, Graduate School, Professional Master of Science and Technology Program, Salt Lake City, UT 84112. Offers biotechnology (PSM); computational science (PSM); environmental science (PSM); science instrumentation (PSM). *Program availability:* Part-time. *Students:* 21 full-time (9 women), 35 part-time (12 women); includes 3 minority (2 Asian, non-Hispanic/Latino; 1 Two or more races, non-Hispanic/Latino), 2 international. Average age 32. 55 applicants, 67% accepted, 23 enrolled. In 2015, 11 master's awarded. *Degree requirements:* For master's, internship. *Entrance requirements:* For master's, GRE (recommended), minimum undergraduate GPA of 3.0, bachelor's degree from accredited university or college. Additional exam requirements/recommendations for international students: Required—TOEFL (minimum score 550 paper-based; 80 iBT), IELTS (minimum score 6.5). *Application deadline:* For fall admission, 2/1 for domestic and international students. Application fee: $55 ($65 for international students). Electronic applications accepted. *Expenses:* Contact institution. *Financial support:* Fellowships, research assistantships, teaching assistantships, and unspecified assistantships available. *Unit head:* Ray Hoobler, Program Director, 801-585-5630, E-mail: ray.hoobler@utah.edu. *Application contact:* Jay Derek Payne, Project Coordinator, 801-585-3650, E-mail: derek.payne@gradschool.utah.edu.
Website: http://pmst.utah.edu/

University of Washington, Graduate School, College of Arts and Sciences, Department of Mathematics, Seattle, WA 98195. Offers mathematics (MA, MS, PhD); numerical analysis (MS); optimization (MS). *Program availability:* Part-time. Terminal master's awarded for partial completion of doctoral program. *Degree requirements:* For master's, thesis optional; for doctorate, 2 foreign languages, thesis/dissertation. *Entrance requirements:* For master's, GRE, minimum GPA of 3.0; for doctorate, GRE General Test, GRE Subject Test (mathematics), minimum GPA of 3.0. Additional exam requirements/recommendations for international students: Required—TOEFL. Electronic applications accepted. *Faculty research:* Algebra, analysis, probability, combinatorics and geometry.

Valparaiso University, Graduate School, Program in Analytics and Modeling, Valparaiso, IN 46383. Offers MS. *Program availability:* Part-time, evening/weekend. *Students:* 3 full-time (0 women), 3 part-time (1 woman), 5 international. Average age 29. In 2015, 1 master's awarded. *Degree requirements:* For master's, internship or research project. *Entrance requirements:* For master's, minimum GPA of 3.0; letters of recommendation; transcripts; personal essay; equivalent of minor in a science or engineering field; coursework in mathematics, statistics, and computer science. Additional exam requirements/recommendations for international students: Required—TOEFL (minimum score 550 paper-based; 80 iBT), IELTS (minimum score 6). *Application deadline:* Applications are processed on a rolling basis. Application fee: $30 ($50 for international students). Electronic applications accepted. *Financial support:* Available to part-time students. Applicants required to submit FAFSA. *Unit head:* Dr. Jennifer A. Ziegler, Dean, Graduate School and Continuing Education, 219-464-5313, Fax: 219-464-5381, E-mail: jennifer.ziegler@valpo.edu. *Application contact:* Jessica Choquette, Graduate Admissions Specialist, 219-464-6510, Fax: 219-464-5381, E-mail: jessica.choquette@valpo.edu.
Website: http://www.valpo.edu/grad/compsci/index.php

Western Kentucky University, Graduate Studies, Ogden College of Science and Engineering, Department of Mathematics and Computer Science, Bowling Green, KY 42101. Offers computational mathematics (MS); computer science (MS); mathematics (MA, MS). *Degree requirements:* For master's, comprehensive exam, thesis optional, written exam. *Entrance requirements:* For master's, GRE General Test, minimum GPA of 2.75. Additional exam requirements/recommendations for international students: Required—TOEFL (minimum score 555 paper-based; 79 iBT). *Faculty research:* Differential equations numerical analysis, probability statistics, algebra, typology, knot theory.

Western Michigan University, Graduate College, College of Arts and Sciences, Department of Mathematics, Kalamazoo, MI 49008. Offers applied and computational mathematics (MS); mathematics education (MA, PhD), including collegiate mathematics education (PhD). *Degree requirements:* For doctorate, one foreign language, thesis/dissertation.

Mathematical and Computational Finance

Boston University, Questrom School of Business, Boston, MA 02215. Offers business (EMBA); business administration (MBA); management (PhD); management studies (MSMS); mathematical finance (MS, PhD); JD/MBA; MBA/MA; MBA/MPH; MBA/MS; MBA/MSIS; MD/MBA; MS/MBA. *Accreditation:* AACSB. *Program availability:* Part-time, evening/weekend. *Faculty:* 95 full-time (27 women), 49 part-time/adjunct (13 women). *Students:* 561 full-time (234 women), 676 part-time (278 women); includes 191 minority (24 Black or African American, non-Hispanic/Latino; 1 American Indian or Alaska Native, non-Hispanic/Latino; 96 Asian, non-Hispanic/Latino; 50 Hispanic/Latino; 1 Native Hawaiian or other Pacific Islander, non-Hispanic/Latino; 19 Two or more races, non-Hispanic/Latino), 321 international. Average age 29. 1,094 applicants, 35% accepted, 146 enrolled. In 2015, 489 master's, 9 doctorates awarded. *Degree requirements:* For doctorate, comprehensive exam, thesis/dissertation. *Entrance requirements:* For master's, GMAT or GRE (for applications to the MBA and MS in mathematical finance programs), essay, resume, 2 letters of recommendation, official transcript; for doctorate, GMAT or GRE, personal statement, resume, 3 letters of recommendation, official transcripts. Additional exam requirements/recommendations for international students: Required—TOEFL (minimum score 600 paper-based; 90 iBT). *Application deadline:* For fall admission, 3/22 for domestic and international students; for spring admission, 11/9 for domestic students. Application fee: $125. Electronic applications accepted. *Financial support:* Career-related internships or fieldwork, Federal Work-Study, institutionally sponsored loans, scholarships/grants, and tuition waivers (partial) available. Support available to part-time students. Financial award applicants required to submit FAFSA. *Faculty research:* Entrepreneurship, sustainable energy, corporate social responsibility, risk management, information systems. *Unit head:* Kenneth W. Freeman, Allen Questrom Professor and Dean, 617-353-9720, Fax: 617-353-5581, E-mail: kfreeman@bu.edu. *Application contact:* Meredith C. Siegel, Assistant Dean, Graduate Admission, 617-353-2670, Fax: 617-353-7368, E-mail: mba@bu.edu.
Website: http://www.bu.edu/questrom/

Carnegie Mellon University, Mellon College of Science, Department of Mathematical Sciences, Pittsburgh, PA 15213-3891. Offers algorithms, combinatorics, and optimization (PhD); computational finance (MS); mathematical finance (PhD); mathematical sciences (DA, PhD); pure and applied logic (PhD). *Program availability:* Part-time. Terminal master's awarded for partial completion of doctoral program. *Degree requirements:* For doctorate, thesis/dissertation. *Entrance requirements:* For master's and doctorate, GRE General Test, GRE Subject Test. Additional exam requirements/recommendations for international students: Required—TOEFL. Electronic applications accepted. *Faculty research:* Continuum mechanics, discrete mathematics, applied and computational mathematics.

Carnegie Mellon University, Tepper School of Business, Pittsburgh, PA 15213-3891. Offers accounting (PhD); business management and software engineering (MBMSE); business technologies (PhD); civil engineering and industrial management (MS); computational finance (MSCF); economics (PhD); environmental engineering and management (MEEM); financial economics (PhD); industrial administration (MBA), including administration and public management; marketing (PhD); mathematical finance (PhD); operations management (PhD); operations research (PhD); organizational behavior and theory (PhD); production and operations management (PhD); public policy and management (MS, MSED); software engineering and business management (MS); JD/MS; JD/MSIA; M Div/MS; MOM/MSIA; MSCF/MSIA. JD/MSIA offered jointly with University of Pittsburgh. *Program availability:* Part-time. Terminal master's awarded for partial completion of doctoral program. *Degree requirements:* For doctorate, thesis/dissertation. *Entrance requirements:* For master's, GMAT. Additional exam requirements/recommendations for international students: Required—TOEFL. *Expenses:* Contact institution.

DePaul University, Charles H. Kellstadt Graduate School of Business, Chicago, IL 60604. Offers accountancy (M Acc, MS, MSA); applied economics (MBA); banking (MBA); behavioral finance (MBA); brand and product management (MBA); business development (MBA); business information technology (MS); business strategy and decision-making (MBA); computational finance (MS); consumer insights (MBA); corporate finance (MBA); economic policy analysis (MS); entrepreneurship (MBA, MS); finance (MBA, MS); financial analysis (MBA); general business (MBA); health sector management (MBA); hospitality leadership (MBA); hospitality leadership and operational performance (MS); human resource management (MBA); human resources (MS); investment management (MBA); leadership and change management (MBA); management accounting (MBA); marketing (MBA, MS); marketing analysis (MS); marketing strategy and planning (MBA); operations management (MBA); organizational diversity (MBA); real estate (MS); real estate finance and investment (MBA); revenue management (MBA); sports management (MBA); strategic global marketing (MBA); strategy, execution and valuation (MBA); sustainable management (MBA, MS); taxation (MS); wealth management (MS); JD/MBA. *Accreditation:* AACSB. *Program availability:* Part-time, evening/weekend, online learning. *Entrance requirements:* For master's, GMAT, 2 letters of recommendation, resume, essay, official transcripts. Additional exam requirements/recommendations for international students: Required—TOEFL (minimum score 550 paper-based; 80 iBT). Electronic applications accepted. *Expenses:* Contact institution.

DePaul University, College of Computing and Digital Media, Chicago, IL 60604. Offers animation (MA, MFA); business information technology (MS); cinema (MFA); cinema production (MS); computational finance (MS); computer and information sciences (PhD); computer game development (MS); computer information and network security (MS); computer science (MS); e-commerce technology (MS); health informatics (MS); human-computer interaction (MS); information systems (MS); information technology project management (MS); network engineering and management (MS); predictive analytics (MS); screenwriting (MFA); software engineering (MS); JD/MS. *Program availability:* Part-time, evening/weekend, online learning. *Degree requirements:* For master's, thesis (for some programs); for doctorate, comprehensive exam, thesis/dissertation. *Entrance requirements:* For master's, GRE or GMAT (for MS in computational finance only), bachelor's degree, resume (MS in predictive analytics only), IT experience (MS in information technology project management only), portfolio review (all MFA programs and MA in animation); for doctorate, GRE, master's degree in computer science. Additional exam requirements/recommendations for international students: Required—TOEFL (minimum score 590 paper-based; 80 iBT), IELTS (minimum score 6.5), PTE (minimum score 53). Electronic applications accepted. *Expenses:* Contact institution. *Faculty research:* Data mining, computer science, human-computer interaction, security, animation and film.

Florida State University, The Graduate School, College of Arts and Sciences, Department of Mathematics, Tallahassee, FL 32306-4510. Offers applied computational mathematics (MS, PhD); biomathematics (MS, PhD); financial mathematics (MS, PhD); pure mathematics (MS, PhD). *Program availability:* Part-time. *Faculty:* 34 full-time (4 women). *Students:* 145 full-time (43 women), 4 part-time (1 woman); includes 18 minority (2 Black or African American, non-Hispanic/Latino; 5 Asian, non-Hispanic/Latino; 2 Hispanic/Latino; 9 Two or more races, non-Hispanic/Latino), 87 international. 300 applicants, 41% accepted, 39 enrolled. In 2015, 44 master's, 14 doctorates awarded. Terminal master's awarded for partial completion of doctoral program. *Degree requirements:* For master's, comprehensive exam (for some programs), thesis optional; for doctorate, comprehensive exam (for some programs), thesis/dissertation, candidacy exam (including written qualifying examinations which differ by degree concentration). *Entrance requirements:* For master's and doctorate, GRE General Test, minimum upper-division GPA of 3.0, 4-year bachelor's degree. Additional exam requirements/recommendations for international students: Required—TOEFL (minimum score 550 paper-based; 80 iBT), IELTS (minimum score 6.5). *Application deadline:* For fall admission, 1/15 priority date for domestic and international students. Applications are processed on a rolling basis. Application fee: $30. Electronic applications accepted. *Expenses: Tuition, area resident:* Full-time $7263; part-time $403.50 per credit hour. Tuition, nonresident: full-time $18,087; part-time $1004.85 per credit hour. *Required fees:* $1365; $75.81 per credit hour. $20 per semester. Tuition and fees vary according to campus/location. *Financial support:* In 2015–16, 106 students received support, including 1 fellowship with full tuition reimbursement available (averaging $22,600 per year), 11 research assistantships with full tuition reimbursements available (averaging $22,000 per year), 83 teaching assistantships with full tuition reimbursements available (averaging $20,650 per year); career-related internships or fieldwork, institutionally sponsored loans, scholarships/grants, health care benefits, tuition waivers (full and partial), and unspecified assistantships also available. Financial award application deadline: 1/30. *Faculty research:* Low-dimensional and geometric topology, mathematical modeling in neuroscience, computational stochastics and Monte Carlo methods, mathematical physics, applied analysis. *Total annual research expenditures:* $1.4 million. *Unit head:* Dr. Xiaoming Wang, Chairperson, 850-645-3338, Fax: 850-644-4053, E-mail: wxm@math.fsu.edu. *Application contact:* Kari Aime, Graduate Advisor and Admissions Coordinator, 850-644-2278, Fax: 850-644-4053,
E-mail: aime@math.fsu.edu.
Website: http://www.math.fsu.edu/

The George Washington University, Columbian College of Arts and Sciences, Department of Mathematics, Washington, DC 20052. Offers applied mathematics (MS); financial mathematics (Graduate Certificate); mathematics (MA, PhD, Graduate Certificate). *Program availability:* Part-time, evening/weekend. *Faculty:* 19 full-time (3 women), 11 part-time/adjunct (4 women). *Students:* 33 full-time (8 women), 17 part-time (5 women); includes 4 minority (1 Black or African American, non-Hispanic/Latino; 1 American Indian or Alaska Native, non-Hispanic/Latino; 2 Hispanic/Latino), 29 international. Average age 26. 107 applicants, 55% accepted, 23 enrolled. In 2015, 7 master's, 5 doctorates, 1 other advanced degree awarded. Terminal master's awarded for partial completion of doctoral program. *Degree requirements:* For master's, comprehensive exam; for doctorate, one foreign language, thesis/dissertation, general exam. *Entrance requirements:* For master's and doctorate, GRE General Test, minimum GPA of 3.0, interview. Additional exam requirements/recommendations for international students: Required—TOEFL (minimum score 550 paper-based; 80 iBT). *Application deadline:* For fall admission, 1/15 priority date for domestic and international students; for spring admission, 10/1 priority date for domestic students, 9/1 priority date for international students. Applications are processed on a rolling basis. Application fee: $75. Electronic applications accepted. *Financial support:* In 2015–16, 17 students received support. Fellowships with full tuition reimbursements available, teaching assistantships with tuition reimbursements available, Federal Work-Study, and tuition waivers available. Financial award application deadline: 1/15. *Unit head:* Yongwu Rong, Chair, 202-994-6890, E-mail: rong@gwu.edu. *Application contact:* 202-994-6210, Fax: 202-994-6213, E-mail: askccas@gwu.edu.
Website: http://math.columbian.gwu.edu/

Georgia Institute of Technology, Graduate Studies, Multidisciplinary Program in Quantitative and Computational Finance, Atlanta, GA 30332-0001. Offers MS. Program offered jointly with Scheller College of Business, School of Industrial and Systems Engineering, and School of Mathematics. *Program availability:* Part-time. *Entrance requirements:* For master's, GRE General Test or GMAT. Additional exam requirements/recommendations for international students: Required—TOEFL (minimum score 570 paper-based; 95 iBT). Electronic applications accepted. *Expenses:* Contact institution.

Illinois Institute of Technology, Graduate College, College of Science, Department of Applied Mathematics, Chicago, IL 60616. Offers applied mathematics (MS, PhD); data science (MAS); mathematical finance (MAS). MAS in mathematical finance program held jointly with Stuart School of Business. Terminal master's awarded for partial completion of doctoral program. *Degree requirements:* For master's, comprehensive exam, thesis; for doctorate, comprehensive exam, thesis/dissertation. *Entrance requirements:* For master's, GRE General Test (minimum scores: 304 Quantitative and Verbal, 2.5 Analytical Writing), minimum undergraduate GPA of 3.0; three letters of recommendation; for doctorate, GRE General Test (minimum scores: 304 Quantitative and Verbal, 3.0 Analytical Writing), minimum undergraduate GPA of 3.5; three letters of recommendation. Additional exam requirements/recommendations for international students: Required—TOEFL (minimum score 550 paper-based; 80 iBT). Electronic applications accepted. *Faculty research:* Applied analysis, computational mathematics, discrete applied mathematics, stochastics (including financial mathematics).

Illinois Institute of Technology, Stuart School of Business, Program in Mathematical Finance, Chicago, IL 60661. Offers MMF. *Program availability:* Part-time, evening/weekend. *Entrance requirements:* For master's, GRE (minimum score 1200 old scoring, 310 new scoring), essay. Additional exam requirements/recommendations for international students: Required—TOEFL (minimum score 600 paper-based; 100 iBT); Recommended—IELTS (minimum score 7). Electronic applications accepted. *Expenses:* Contact institution. *Faculty research:* Factor models for investment management, credit rating and credit risk management, hedge fund performance analysis, option trading and risk management, global asset allocation strategies.

Johns Hopkins University, G. W. C. Whiting School of Engineering, Department of Applied Mathematics and Statistics, Baltimore, MD 21218. Offers computational medicine (PhD); discrete mathematics (MA, MSE, PhD); financial mathematics (MSE); operations research/optimization (MA, MSE, PhD); statistics/probability (MA, MSE, PhD). Terminal master's awarded for partial completion of doctoral program. *Degree requirements:* For master's, thesis (for some programs); for doctorate, thesis/dissertation, oral exam, introductory exam. *Entrance requirements:* For master's and doctorate, GRE General Test, GRE Subject Test. Additional exam requirements/recommendations for international students: Required—TOEFL (minimum score 600 paper-based; 100 iBT). Electronic applications accepted. *Faculty research:* Discrete mathematics, probability, statistics, optimization and operations research, scientific computation, financial mathematics.

New Jersey Institute of Technology, College of Science and Liberal Arts, Newark, NJ 07102. Offers applied mathematics (MS); applied physics (M Sc, PhD); applied statistical models (Certificate); applied statistics (MS); biology (MS, PhD); biostatistics (MS); biostatistics essentials (Certificate); chemistry (MS, PhD); computational biology (MS); environmental science (MS, PhD); history (MA, MAT); materials science and engineering (MS, PhD); mathematical and computational finance (MS); mathematics science (PhD); pharmaceutical chemistry (MS); professional and technical communications (MS); technical common essentials (Certificate). *Program availability:* Part-time, evening/weekend. *Faculty:* 153 full-time (35 women), 100 part-time/adjunct (40 women). *Students:* 212 full-time (82 women), 94 part-time (37 women); includes 72 minority (22 Black or African American, non-Hispanic/Latino; 25 Asian, non-Hispanic/Latino; 19 Hispanic/Latino; 6 Two or more races, non-Hispanic/Latino), 164 international. Average age 29. 519 applicants, 62% accepted, 104 enrolled. In 2015, 98 master's, 21 doctorates, 3 other advanced degrees awarded. Terminal master's awarded for partial completion of doctoral program. *Degree requirements:* For master's, thesis optional; for doctorate, thesis/dissertation. *Entrance requirements:* For master's, GRE General Test; for doctorate, GRE General Test, minimum graduate GPA of 3.5. Additional exam requirements/recommendations for international students: Required—TOEFL (minimum score 550 paper-based; 79 iBT). *Application deadline:* For fall admission, 6/1 priority date for domestic students, 5/1 priority date for international students; for spring admission, 11/15 priority date for domestic and international students. Applications are processed on a rolling basis. Application fee: $75. Electronic applications accepted. *Expenses:* $28,800 per year non-resident full-time. *Financial support:* In 2015–16, 56 research assistantships with full tuition reimbursements (averaging $17,711 per year), 52 teaching assistantships with full tuition reimbursements (averaging $17,914 per year) were awarded; fellowships with full tuition reimbursements also available. Financial award application deadline: 1/15. *Total annual research expenditures:* $23.1 million. *Unit head:* Dr. Kevin Belfield, Dean, 973-596-3676, Fax: 973-565-0586, E-mail: kevin.d.belfield@njit.edu. *Application contact:* Stephen Eck, Director of Admissions, 973-596-3300, Fax: 973-596-3461,
E-mail: admissions@njit.edu.
Website: http://csla.njit.edu/

★ **New York University,** Graduate School of Arts and Science, Courant Institute of Mathematical Sciences, Department of Mathematics, New York, NY 10012-1019. Offers atmosphere ocean science and mathematics (PhD); mathematics (MS, PhD); mathematics and statistics/operations research (MS); mathematics in finance (MS); scientific computing (MS). *Program availability:* Part-time, evening/weekend. *Degree requirements:* For master's, thesis optional; for doctorate, one foreign language, thesis/dissertation, oral and written exams. *Entrance requirements:* For master's, GRE General Test, GRE Subject Test; for doctorate, GRE General Test, GRE Subject Test (recommended). Additional exam requirements/recommendations for international students: Required—TOEFL. *Faculty research:* Partial differential equations, computational science, applied mathematics, geometry and topology, probability and stochastic processes.

See Close-Up on page 295.

New York University, Polytechnic School of Engineering, Department of Finance and Risk Engineering, New York, NY 10012-1019. Offers financial engineering (MS, Advanced Certificate), including capital markets (MS), computational finance (MS), financial technology (MS); financial technology management (Advanced Certificate); organizational behavior (Advanced Certificate); risk management (Advanced Certificate); technology management (Advanced Certificate). MS program also offered in Manhattan. *Program availability:* Part-time, evening/weekend. *Degree requirements:* For master's, comprehensive exam (for some programs), thesis (for some programs). *Entrance requirements:* For master's, GMAT, minimum B average in undergraduate course work. Additional exam requirements/recommendations for international students: Required—TOEFL (minimum score 550 paper-based; 80 iBT); Recommended—IELTS (minimum score 6.5). Electronic applications accepted. *Faculty research:* Optimal control theory, general modeling and analysis, risk parity optimality, a new algorithmic approach to entangled political economy.

North Carolina State University, Graduate School, College of Agriculture and Life Sciences and College of Engineering and College of Physical and Mathematical Sciences, Program in Financial Mathematics, Raleigh, NC 27695. Offers MFM. *Program availability:* Part-time. *Degree requirements:* For master's, thesis optional, project/internship. *Entrance requirements:* For master's, GRE General Test. Additional exam requirements/recommendations for international students: Required—TOEFL (minimum score 550 paper-based). Electronic applications accepted. *Faculty research:* Financial mathematics modeling and computation, futures, options and commodities markets, real options, credit risk, portfolio optimization.

Oregon State University, College of Science, Program in Mathematics, Corvallis, OR 97331. Offers actuarial science (MA, MS, PhD); algebra (MA, MS, PhD); analysis (MA, MS, PhD); applied mathematics (MA, MS, PhD); computational mathematics (MA, MS, PhD); differential equations (MA, MS, PhD); financial mathematics (MA, MS, PhD); geometry (MA, MS, PhD); mathematics education (MA). *Faculty:* 26 full-time (8 women), 4 part-time/adjunct (1 woman). *Students:* 68 full-time (16 women), 2 part-time (0 women); includes 10 minority (1 Black or African American, non-Hispanic/Latino; 3 Asian, non-Hispanic/Latino; 2 Hispanic/Latino; 1 Native Hawaiian or other Pacific

Islander, non-Hispanic/Latino; 3 Two or more races, non-Hispanic/Latino), 15 international. Average age 29. 117 applicants, 34% accepted, 17 enrolled. In 2015, 13 master's, 2 doctorates awarded. Terminal master's awarded for partial completion of doctoral program. *Median time to degree:* Of those who began their doctoral program in fall 2007, 40% received their degree in 8 years or less. *Degree requirements:* For master's, variable foreign language requirement, thesis or alternative; for doctorate, one foreign language, thesis/dissertation, qualifying exams. *Entrance requirements:* For master's and doctorate, GRE. Additional exam requirements/recommendations for international students: Required—TOEFL (minimum score 100 iBT). *Application deadline:* For fall admission, 1/15 for domestic students. Application fee: $75 ($85 for international students). *Expenses:* Tuition, state resident: full-time $12,150; part-time $450 per credit. Tuition, nonresident: full-time $20,952; part-time $776 per credit. *Required fees:* $1572; $1443 per unit. One-time fee: $350. Tuition and fees vary according to course load, campus/location and program. *Financial support:* Research assistantships, teaching assistantships, Federal Work-Study, and institutionally sponsored loans available. Support available to part-time students. Financial award application deadline: 1/15. *Unit head:* Dr. Enrique A. Thomann, Professor and Interim Department Head. *Application contact:* Mathematics Advisor, 541-737-4686, E-mail: gradinfo@math.oregonstate.edu.
Website: http://www.math.oregonstate.edu/

Purdue University, Graduate School, College of Science, Department of Statistics, West Lafayette, IN 47909. Offers applied statistics (MS); computational finance (MS); computational science and engineering (MS); statistics (PhD). *Program availability:* Part-time. *Faculty:* 71 full-time (22 women). *Students:* 102 full-time (36 women); includes 71 minority (8 Black or African American, non-Hispanic/Latino; 1 American Indian or Alaska Native, non-Hispanic/Latino; 55 Asian, non-Hispanic/Latino; 4 Hispanic/Latino; 3 Native Hawaiian or other Pacific Islander, non-Hispanic/Latino). Average age 25. 505 applicants, 9% accepted, 29 enrolled. In 2015, 29 master's, 14 doctorates awarded. Terminal master's awarded for partial completion of doctoral program. *Degree requirements:* For master's, comprehensive exam; for doctorate, thesis/dissertation, qualifying exams. *Entrance requirements:* For master's and doctorate, GRE General Test. Additional exam requirements/recommendations for international students: Required—TOEFL (minimum score 80 iBT); Recommended—IELTS (minimum score 7). *Application deadline:* For fall admission, 1/15 for domestic and international students; for spring admission, 10/15 for domestic students, 9/15 for international students. Application fee: $60 ($75 for international students). Electronic applications accepted. *Expenses:* Contact institution. *Financial support:* In 2015–16, 5 students received support, including 5 fellowships with full tuition reimbursements available (averaging $20,000 per year), research assistantships with full tuition reimbursements available (averaging $20,000 per year), 10 teaching assistantships with full tuition reimbursements available (averaging $20,000 per year); career-related internships or fieldwork and unspecified assistantships also available. Support available to part-time students. Financial award application deadline: 1/15; financial award applicants required to submit FAFSA. *Faculty research:* Nonparametric models, computational finance, design of experiments, probability theory, bioinformatics. *Unit head:* Dr. Hao Zhang, Head, 765-494-3141, Fax: 765-494-0558, E-mail: zhanghao@purdue.edu. *Application contact:* Anna Hook, Graduate Coordinator, 765-494-5794, Fax: 765-494-0558, E-mail: hook6@purdue.edu.
Website: http://www.stat.purdue.edu/

Rice University, Graduate Programs, George R. Brown School of Engineering, Department of Statistics, Houston, TX 77251-1892. Offers bioinformatics (PhD); biostatistics (PhD); computational finance (PhD); general statistics (PhD); statistics (M Stat, MA); MBA/M Stat. *Program availability:* Part-time. *Degree requirements:* For master's, comprehensive exam; for doctorate, comprehensive exam, thesis/dissertation. *Entrance requirements:* For master's and doctorate, GRE General Test, minimum GPA of 3.0. Additional exam requirements/recommendations for international students: Required—TOEFL (minimum score 630 paper-based; 90 iBT). Electronic applications accepted. *Faculty research:* Statistical genetics, non parametric function estimation, computational statistics and visualization, stochastic processes.

Rochester Institute of Technology, Graduate Enrollment Services, Saunders College of Business, Accounting and Finance Department, MS Program in Computational Finance, Rochester, NY 14623-5603. Offers MS. Program offered jointly with Saunders College of Business. *Program availability:* Part-time. *Students:* 3 full-time (2 women). 25 applicants, 40% accepted, 3 enrolled. *Degree requirements:* For master's, thesis or alternative. *Entrance requirements:* For master's, GRE or GMAT, minimum GPA of 3.0 (recommended). Additional exam requirements/recommendations for international students: Required—PTE (minimum score 58), TOEFL (minimum score 550 paper-based, 79 iBT) or IELTS (minimum score 6.5). *Application deadline:* For fall admission, 2/15 priority date for domestic and international students; for spring admission, 12/15 priority date for domestic and international students. Applications are processed on a rolling basis. Application fee: $60. Electronic applications accepted. *Expenses: Tuition, area resident:* Full-time $41,084; part-time $1742 per credit hour. *Required fees:* $274. Tuition and fees vary according to course load and program. *Financial support:* In 2015–16, 2 students received support. Teaching assistantships with partial tuition reimbursements available, career-related internships or fieldwork, scholarships/grants, and unspecified assistantships available. Support available to part-time students. Financial award applicants required to submit FAFSA. *Unit head:* Jenna Lenhardt, Assistant Director, 585-475-6916, E-mail: jlenhardt@saunders.rit.edu. *Application contact:* Diane Ellison, Associate Vice President, Graduate Enrollment Services, 585-475-2229, Fax: 585-475-7164, E-mail: gradinfo@rit.edu.
Website: http://saunders.rit.edu/programs/graduate/ms_compfin.php

Université de Montréal, Faculty of Arts and Sciences, Department of Economic Sciences, Montréal, QC H3C 3J7, Canada. Offers economics (M Sc, PhD); mathematical and computational finance (M Sc). *Degree requirements:* For master's, one foreign language, thesis; for doctorate, one foreign language, thesis/dissertation, general exam. Electronic applications accepted. *Faculty research:* Applied and economic theory, public choice, international trade, labor economics, industrial organization.

Université de Montréal, Faculty of Arts and Sciences, Department of Mathematics and Statistics, Montréal, QC H3C 3J7, Canada. Offers mathematical and computational finance (M Sc, DESS); mathematics (M Sc, PhD); statistics (M Sc, PhD). *Degree requirements:* For master's, thesis; for doctorate, thesis/dissertation, general exam. *Entrance requirements:* For master's and doctorate, proficiency in French. Electronic applications accepted. *Faculty research:* Pure and applied mathematics, actuarial mathematics.

University of Alberta, Faculty of Graduate Studies and Research, Department of Mathematical and Statistical Sciences, Edmonton, AB T6G 2E1, Canada. Offers applied mathematics (M Sc, PhD); biostatistics (M Sc); mathematical finance (M Sc, PhD); mathematical physics (M Sc, PhD); mathematics (M Sc, PhD); statistics (M Sc, PhD, Postgraduate Diploma). *Program availability:* Part-time. Terminal master's awarded for partial completion of doctoral program. *Degree requirements:* For master's, thesis (for some programs); for doctorate, comprehensive exam, thesis/dissertation. *Entrance requirements:* Additional exam requirements/recommendations for international students: Required—TOEFL (minimum score 580 paper-based). Electronic applications accepted. *Faculty research:* Classical and functional analysis, algebra, differential equations, geometry.

University of California, Santa Barbara, Graduate Division, College of Letters and Sciences, Division of Mathematics, Life, and Physical Sciences, Department of Statistics and Applied Probability, Santa Barbara, CA 93106-3110. Offers bioengineering (PhD); financial mathematics and statistics (PhD); quantitative methods in the social sciences (PhD); statistics (MA), including applied statistics, mathematical statistics; statistics and applied probability (PhD); MA/PhD. *Faculty:* 11 full-time (2 women), 8 part-time/adjunct (0 women). *Students:* 65 full-time (32 women); includes 8 minority (1 Black or African American, non-Hispanic/Latino; 5 Asian, non-Hispanic/Latino; 1 Hispanic/Latino; 1 Native Hawaiian or other Pacific Islander, non-Hispanic/Latino), 47 international. Average age 27. 452 applicants, 9% accepted, 12 enrolled. In 2015, 18 master's, 8 doctorates awarded. Terminal master's awarded for partial completion of doctoral program. *Degree requirements:* For master's, comprehensive exam, thesis optional; for doctorate, comprehensive exam, thesis/dissertation. *Entrance requirements:* For master's and doctorate, GRE General Test. Additional exam requirements/recommendations for international students: Required—TOEFL (minimum score 550 paper-based; 80 iBT), IELTS (minimum score 7). *Application deadline:* For fall admission, 12/15 priority date for domestic students, 12/1 priority date for international students; for winter admission, 11/1 priority date for domestic and international students; for spring admission, 2/1 priority date for domestic and international students. Application fee: $90 ($110 for international students). Electronic applications accepted. *Financial support:* In 2015–16, 23 students received support, including 6 fellowships with full tuition reimbursements available (averaging $11,285 per year), 1 research assistantship with tuition reimbursement available (averaging $2,790 per year), 28 teaching assistantships with partial tuition reimbursements available (averaging $14,557 per year); Federal Work-Study, scholarships/grants, and health care benefits also available. Financial award application deadline: 12/15; financial award applicants required to submit FAFSA. *Faculty research:* Bayesian inference, financial mathematics, stochastic processes, environmental statistics, biostatistical modeling. *Total annual research expenditures:* $139,480. *Unit head:* Dr. John Hsu, Chair, 805-893-4055, E-mail: hsu@pstat.ucsb.edu. *Application contact:* Angelina M. Toporov, Graduate Program Assistant, 805-893-2129, Fax: 805-893-2334, E-mail: toporov@pstat.ucsb.edu.
Website: http://www.pstat.ucsb.edu/

University of Chicago, Division of the Physical Sciences, Master of Science in Financial Mathematics Program, Chicago, IL 60637. Offers MS. *Program availability:* Part-time, evening/weekend. *Entrance requirements:* For master's, GRE General Test. Additional exam requirements/recommendations for international students: Required—TOEFL (minimum score 600 paper-based; 90 iBT), IELTS (minimum score 7). Electronic applications accepted.

University of Connecticut, Graduate School, College of Liberal Arts and Sciences, Department of Mathematics, Field of Applied Financial Mathematics, Storrs, CT 06269. Offers MS. *Degree requirements:* For master's, comprehensive exam. *Entrance requirements:* Additional exam requirements/recommendations for international students: Required—TOEFL (minimum score 550 paper-based). Electronic applications accepted.

University of Dayton, Department of Mathematics, Dayton, OH 45469. Offers applied mathematics (MAS); financial mathematics (MFM); mathematics education (MME). *Program availability:* Part-time. *Faculty:* 19 full-time (7 women). *Students:* 31 full-time (13 women), 5 part-time (2 women); includes 3 minority (2 Black or African American, non-Hispanic/Latino; 1 Hispanic/Latino), 27 international. Average age 26. 121 applicants, 29% accepted, 10 enrolled. In 2015, 26 master's awarded. *Entrance requirements:* For master's, minimum undergraduate GPA of 2.8 (MAS), 3.0 (MFM, MME). Additional exam requirements/recommendations for international students: Required—TOEFL (minimum score 550 paper-based; 80 iBT). *Application deadline:* Applications are processed on a rolling basis. Application fee: $0 ($50 for international students). Electronic applications accepted. *Expenses:* $873 per credit hour. *Financial support:* In 2015–16, 6 students received support, including 6 teaching assistantships with full tuition reimbursements available (averaging $14,750 per year); institutionally sponsored loans and health care benefits also available. Financial award application deadline: 3/1; financial award applicants required to submit FAFSA. *Faculty research:* Jump diffusion with regime switching in finance models, dynamical systems, boundary value problems for ordinary differential equations, decompositions of graphs and multigraphs. *Unit head:* Dr. Joe D. Mashburn, Chair, 937-229-2511, Fax: 937-229-2566, E-mail: jmashburn1@udayton.edu. *Application contact:* Dr. Paul W. Eloe, Graduate Program Director/Professor, 937-229-2016, E-mail: peloe1@udayton.edu.
Website: https://www.udayton.edu/artssciences/academics/mathematics/welcome/index.php

The University of Manchester, School of Mathematics, Manchester, United Kingdom. Offers actuarial science (PhD); applied mathematics (M Phil, PhD); applied numerical computing (M Phil, PhD); financial mathematics (M Phil, PhD); mathematical logic (M Phil); probability (M Phil, PhD); pure mathematics (M Phil, PhD); statistics (M Phil, PhD).

University of Miami, Graduate School, College of Arts and Sciences, Department of Mathematics, Coral Gables, FL 33124. Offers mathematical finance (MS); mathematics (MA, MS, PhD). *Program availability:* Part-time, evening/weekend. Terminal master's awarded for partial completion of doctoral program. *Degree requirements:* For master's, comprehensive exam, qualifying exams; for doctorate, one foreign language, thesis/dissertation, qualifying exams. *Entrance requirements:* For master's and doctorate, GRE General Test, minimum GPA of 3.0. Additional exam requirements/recommendations for international students: Required—TOEFL (minimum score 550 paper-based; 59 iBT). Electronic applications accepted. *Faculty research:* Applied mathematics, probability, geometric analysis, differential equations, algebraic combinatorics.

The University of North Carolina at Charlotte, Belk College of Business, Interdisciplinary Business Programs, Charlotte, NC 28223-0001. Offers mathematical finance (MS); real estate (MS, Graduate Certificate). *Program availability:* Part-time, evening/weekend. *Faculty:* 15 full-time (4 women), 3 part-time/adjunct (0 women). *Students:* 43 full-time (15 women), 50 part-time (11 women); includes 17 minority (8 Black or African American, non-Hispanic/Latino; 7 Asian, non-Hispanic/Latino; 2 Hispanic/Latino), 25 international. Average age 30. 105 applicants, 70% accepted, 38 enrolled. In 2015, 60 master's, 1 other advanced degree awarded. *Degree requirements:* For master's, comprehensive exam (for some programs). *Entrance requirements:* For master's, GRE or GMAT, baccalaureate degree in a related field with minimum GPA of 3.0 overall and in junior and senior years; transcript of all previous academic work; for Graduate Certificate, basic proficiency in using spreadsheet computer software, to be demonstrated by past project or certificate from completion of

training course in Excel; previous coursework in financial management. Additional exam requirements/recommendations for international students: Required—TOEFL (minimum score 557 paper-based, 83 iBT) or IELTS (minimum score 6.5). *Application deadline:* For fall admission, 3/1 priority date for domestic and international students; for spring admission, 10/1 priority date for domestic and international students; for summer admission, 4/1 priority date for domestic and international students. Application fee: $75. Electronic applications accepted. *Expenses:* Contact institution. *Financial support:* Career-related internships or fieldwork, scholarships/grants, and unspecified assistantships available. Support available to part-time students. Financial award application deadline: 3/1; financial award applicants required to submit FAFSA. *Unit head:* Dr. Steven Ott, Dean, 704-687-7577, Fax: 704-687-1393, E-mail: cob-dean@uncc.edu. *Application contact:* Kathy B. Giddings, Director of Graduate Admissions, 704-687-5503, Fax: 704-687-1668, E-mail: gradadm@uncc.edu.
Website: http://belkcollege.uncc.edu/

University of Notre Dame, Graduate School, College of Science, Department of Applied and Computational Mathematics and Statistics, Notre Dame, IN 46556. Offers applied and computational mathematics and statistics (PhD); applied statistics (MS); computational finance (MS).

University of Southern California, Graduate School, Dana and David Dornsife College of Letters, Arts and Sciences, Department of Economics, Los Angeles, CA 90089. Offers economic development programming (MA, PhD); mathematical finance (MS); M Pl/MA; MA/JD. Terminal master's awarded for partial completion of doctoral program. *Degree requirements:* For master's, comprehensive exam; for doctorate, comprehensive exam, thesis/dissertation. *Entrance requirements:* For master's and doctorate, GRE. Additional exam requirements/recommendations for international students: Required—TOEFL (minimum score 93 iBT). Electronic applications accepted. *Faculty research:* Macro theory, development economics, econometrics.

University of Southern California, Graduate School, Dana and David Dornsife College of Letters, Arts and Sciences, Department of Mathematics, Los Angeles, CA 90089. Offers applied mathematics (MA, MS, PhD); mathematical finance (MS); mathematics (MA, PhD); statistics (MS). *Program availability:* Part-time. Terminal master's awarded for partial completion of doctoral program. *Degree requirements:* For master's, comprehensive exam (for some programs), thesis (for some programs); for doctorate, one foreign language, comprehensive exam, thesis/dissertation. *Entrance requirements:* For master's, GRE General Test, GMAT; for doctorate, GRE General Test, GRE Subject Test (mathematics). Additional exam requirements/recommendations for international students: Required—TOEFL (minimum score 100 iBT). Electronic applications accepted. *Faculty research:* Algebra, algebraic geometry and number theory, analysis/partial differential equations, applied mathematics, financial mathematics, probability, combinatorics and statistics.

University of Toronto, School of Graduate Studies, Faculty of Arts and Science, Department of Mathematics, Program in Mathematical Finance, Toronto, ON M5S 1A1, Canada. Offers MMF. *Entrance requirements:* For master's, four-year bachelor's degree in a quantitative, technical discipline from recognized university with minimum of the equivalent of the University of Toronto mid-B (75%) standing in final two years of program or equivalent number of most senior courses. Additional exam requirements/recommendations for international students: Required—TOEFL (minimum score 580 paper-based; 93 iBT), TWE (minimum score 5). Electronic applications accepted.

Mathematics

Alabama State University, College of Science, Mathematics and Technology, Department of Mathematics and Computer Science, Montgomery, AL 36101-0271. Offers mathematics (MS). *Program availability:* Part-time. *Faculty:* 4 full-time (1 woman). *Students:* 1 full-time (0 women), 3 part-time (2 women); includes 3 minority (all Black or African American, non-Hispanic/Latino). Average age 25. 4 applicants.. In 2015, 1 master's awarded. *Degree requirements:* For master's, comprehensive exam. *Entrance requirements:* For master's, GRE General Test, GRE Subject Test, writing competency test. Additional exam requirements/recommendations for international students: Required—TOEFL (minimum score 500 paper-based). *Application deadline:* For fall admission, 7/15 for domestic students; for spring admission, 12/15 for domestic students. Applications are processed on a rolling basis. Application fee: $25. *Expenses: Tuition, area resident:* Full-time $3087; part-time $2744 per credit. Tuition, nonresident: full-time $6174; part-time $5488 per credit. *Required fees:* $2284; $1142 per credit. $571 per semester. Tuition and fees vary according to class time, course level, course load, degree level, program and student level. *Financial support:* Applicants required to submit FAFSA. *Faculty research:* Discrete mathematics, mathematical social sciences. *Unit head:* Dr. Carl S. Pettis, Chair, 334-229-4484, Fax: 334-229-4902,
E-mail: cpettis@alasu.edu. *Application contact:* Dr. William Person, Dean of Graduate Studies, 334-229-4274, Fax: 334-229-4928, E-mail: wperson@alasu.edu.
Website: http://www.alasu.edu/academics/colleges—departments/science-mathematics-technology/mathematics-computer-science/index.aspx

American University, College of Arts and Sciences, Department of Mathematics and Statistics, Washington, DC 22016-8050. Offers applied statistics (Certificate); mathematics (MA); professional science: quantitative analysis (MS); statistics (MS). *Program availability:* Part-time, evening/weekend. *Faculty:* 34 full-time (11 women), 10 part-time/adjunct (3 women). *Students:* 19 full-time (12 women), 13 part-time (7 women); includes 5 minority (4 Black or African American, non-Hispanic/Latino; 1 Two or more races, non-Hispanic/Latino), 6 international. Average age 26. 54 applicants, 93% accepted, 15 enrolled. In 2015, 12 master's awarded. *Degree requirements:* For master's, comprehensive exam, thesis or alternative. *Entrance requirements:* For master's, GRE, statement of purpose, transcripts, 2 letters of recommendation, resume; for Certificate, bachelor's degree, statement of purpose, transcripts, resume. Additional exam requirements/recommendations for international students: Required—TOEFL (minimum score 100 iBT), IELTS (minimum score 7), PTE (minimum score 68). *Application deadline:* For fall admission, 2/1 priority date for domestic students; for spring admission, 11/1 for domestic students. Application fee: $55. *Expenses: Tuition, area resident:* Full-time $27,468; part-time $1526 per credit hour. *Required fees:* $430. Tuition and fees vary according to course level and program. *Financial support:* Application deadline: 2/1. *Unit head:* Dr. Joshua D. Lansky, department Chair, 202-885-3687, Fax: 202-885-3155, E-mail: lansky@american.edu. *Application contact:* Kathleen Clowery, Associate Director, Graduate Admissions, 202-885-3620, Fax: 202-885-1344, E-mail: clowery@american.edu.
Website: http://www.american.edu/cas/mathstat/

American University of Beirut, Graduate Programs, Faculty of Arts and Sciences, Beirut, Lebanon. Offers anthropology (MA); Arab and Middle Eastern history (PhD); Arabic language and literature (MA, PhD); archaeology (MA); biology (MS); cell and molecular biology (PhD); chemistry (MS); clinical psychology (MA); computational sciences (MS); computer science (MS); economics (MA); English language (MA); English literature (MA); environmental policy planning (MS); financial economics (MAFE); geology (MS); history (MA); mathematics (MA, MS); media studies (MA); Middle Eastern studies (MA); physics (MS); political studies (MA); psychology (MA); public administration (MA); sociology (MA); statistics (MA, MS); theoretical physics (PhD); transnational American studies (MA). *Program availability:* Part-time. *Faculty:* 114 full-time (36 women), 4 part-time/adjunct (2 women). *Students:* 258 full-time (190 women), 207 part-time (142 women). Average age 27. 241 applicants, 71% accepted, 98 enrolled. In 2015, 47 master's, 3 doctorates awarded. *Degree requirements:* For master's, one foreign language, comprehensive exam, thesis (for some programs); for doctorate, one foreign language, comprehensive exam, thesis/dissertation. *Entrance requirements:* For master's, GRE (for some MA, MS programs), letter of recommendation; for doctorate, GRE, letters of recommendation. Additional exam requirements/recommendations for international students: Required—TOEFL (minimum score 600 paper-based; 97 iBT), IELTS (minimum score 7). *Application deadline:* For fall admission, 4/1 for domestic and international students; for spring admission, 11/1 for domestic and international students. Application fee: $50. Electronic applications accepted. *Expenses: Tuition, area resident:* Full-time $16,254; part-time $903 per credit. *Required fees:* $699. Tuition and fees vary according to course load and program. *Financial support:* Research assistantships, career-related internships or fieldwork, institutionally sponsored loans, scholarships/grants, health care benefits, and unspecified assistantships available. Financial award application deadline: 2/4; financial award applicants required to submit FAFSA. *Faculty research:* Analysis and algebra; software engineering; machine learning and big data analysis; philosophy of mind and political philosophy; anthropology of art, anthropology of migration and medical anthropology; sociology of knowledge, sociology of migration, critical theory; sociology of education; hybrid solid materials; photocatalysis; human creativity. *Total annual research expenditures:* $680,360. *Unit head:* Dr. Patrick McGreevy, Dean, 961-1374374 Ext. 3800, Fax: 961-1744461, E-mail: pm07@aub.edu.lb. *Application contact:* Dr. Salim Kanaan, Director, Admissions Office, 961-1350000 Ext. 2590, Fax: 961-1750775, E-mail: sk00@aub.edu.lb.
Website: http://www.aub.edu.lb/fas/

American University of Sharjah, Graduate Programs, Sharjah, United Arab Emirates. Offers accounting (MS); business (EMBA, MBA); chemical engineering (MS Ch E); civil engineering (MSCE); computer engineering (MS); electrical engineering (MSEE); engineering systems management (MS); mathematics (MS); mechanical engineering (MSME); mechatronics engineering (MS); teaching English to speakers of other languages (MA); translation and interpreting (MA); urban planning (MUP). *Program availability:* Part-time, evening/weekend. *Degree requirements:* For master's, thesis (for some programs). *Entrance requirements:* For master's, GMAT (for MBA). Additional exam requirements/recommendations for international students: Required—TOEFL (minimum score 550 paper-based; 80 iBT), TWE (minimum score 5); Recommended—IELTS (minimum score 6.5). Electronic applications accepted. *Faculty research:* Water pollution, management and waste water treatment, energy and sustainability, air pollution, Islamic finance, family business and small and medium enterprises.

Appalachian State University, Cratis D. Williams Graduate School, Department of Mathematical Sciences, Boone, NC 28608. Offers mathematics (MA); mathematics education (MA). *Program availability:* Part-time, online learning. *Degree requirements:* For master's, comprehensive exam, thesis optional. *Entrance requirements:* For master's, GRE General Test, 3 letters of recommendation. Additional exam requirements/recommendations for international students: Required—TOEFL (minimum score 570 paper-based; 79 iBT), IELTS (minimum score 6.5). Electronic applications accepted. *Faculty research:* Graph theory, differential equations, logic, geometry, complex analysis, topology, algebra, mathematics education.

Arizona State University at the Tempe campus, College of Liberal Arts and Sciences, School of Mathematical and Statistical Sciences, Tempe, AZ 85287-1804. Offers applied mathematics (PhD); mathematics (MA, PhD); mathematics education (PhD); statistics (MS, PhD, Graduate Certificate). *Program availability:* Part-time. Terminal master's awarded for partial completion of doctoral program. *Degree requirements:* For master's, thesis or alternative, interactive Program of Study (iPOS) submitted before completing 50 percent of required credit hours; for doctorate, comprehensive exam, thesis/dissertation, interactive Program of Study (iPOS) submitted before completing 50 percent of required credit hours. *Entrance requirements:* For master's and doctorate, GRE General Test, minimum GPA of 3.0 or equivalent in last 2 years of work leading to bachelor's degree. Additional exam requirements/recommendations for international students: Required—TOEFL, IELTS, or PTE. Electronic applications accepted. *Expenses:* Contact institution.

Arkansas State University, Graduate School, College of Sciences and Mathematics, Department of Mathematics and Statistics, State University, AR 72467. Offers mathematics (MS); mathematics education (MSE). *Program availability:* Part-time. *Faculty:* 11 full-time (5 women). *Students:* 13 full-time (6 women), 5 part-time (4 women); includes 5 minority (2 Black or African American, non-Hispanic/Latino; 1 Hispanic/Latino; 2 Two or more races, non-Hispanic/Latino), 4 international. Average age 26. 16 applicants, 56% accepted, 6 enrolled. In 2015, 11 master's awarded. *Degree requirements:* For master's, comprehensive exam, thesis or alternative. *Entrance requirements:* For master's, GRE General Test or MAT, appropriate bachelor's degree, official transcripts, immunization records, valid teaching certificate (for MSE). Additional exam requirements/recommendations for international students: Required—TOEFL (minimum score 550 paper-based; 79 iBT), IELTS (minimum score 6), PTE (minimum score 56). *Application deadline:* For fall admission, 7/1 for domestic and international students; for spring admission, 11/15 for domestic students, 11/14 for international students. Applications are processed on a rolling basis. Application fee: $30 ($40 for international students). Electronic applications accepted. *Expenses:* Tuition, state resident: full-time $4572; part-time $254 per credit hour. Tuition, nonresident: full-time $9144; part-time $508 per credit hour. *International tuition:* $9844 full-time. *Required fees:* $1188; $66 per credit hour. $25 per term. Tuition and fees vary according to course load and program. *Financial support:* In 2015–16, 10 students received support. Teaching assistantships, career-related internships or fieldwork, scholarships/grants,

and unspecified assistantships available. Financial award application deadline: 7/1; financial award applicants required to submit FAFSA. *Unit head:* Dr. Debra Ingram, Chair, 870-972-3090, Fax: 870-972-3950, E-mail: dingram@astate.edu. *Application contact:* Vickey Ring, Graduate Admissions Coordinator, 870-972-2737, Fax: 870-972-3917, E-mail: vickeyring@astate.edu.
Website: http://www.astate.edu/college/sciences-and-mathematics/departments/math-statistics/

Auburn University, Graduate School, College of Sciences and Mathematics, Department of Mathematics and Statistics, Auburn University, AL 36849. Offers applied mathematics (MAM, MS); mathematics (MS, PhD); probability and statistics (M Prob S); statistics (MS). *Faculty:* 57 full-time (12 women), 8 part-time/adjunct (2 women). *Students:* 64 full-time (18 women), 36 part-time (11 women); includes 10 minority (9 Asian, non-Hispanic/Latino; 1 Two or more races, non-Hispanic/Latino), 57 international. Average age 29. 123 applicants, 54% accepted, 15 enrolled. In 2015, 23 master's, 14 doctorates awarded. *Degree requirements:* For doctorate, thesis/dissertation. *Entrance requirements:* For master's, GRE General Test, undergraduate mathematics background; for doctorate, GRE General Test, GRE Subject Test. *Application deadline:* Applications are processed on a rolling basis. Application fee: $50 ($60 for international students). Electronic applications accepted. *Expenses:* Tuition, state resident: full-time $8802; part-time $489 per credit hour. Tuition, nonresident: full-time $26,406; part-time $1467 per credit hour. *Required fees:* $808 per semester. Tuition and fees vary according to degree level and program. *Financial support:* Fellowships and teaching assistantships available. Financial award applicants required to submit FAFSA. *Faculty research:* Pure and applied mathematics. *Unit head:* Dr. Tin Yau Tam, Chair, 334-844-6572, Fax: 334-844-6655. *Application contact:* Dr. George Flowers, Dean of the Graduate School, 334-844-2125.
Website: http://www.auburn.edu/~math/

Aurora University, College of Arts and Sciences, Aurora, IL 60506-4892. Offers mathematics (MS). *Program availability:* Part-time, evening/weekend. *Faculty:* 3 full-time (1 woman), 5 part-time/adjunct (0 women). *Students:* 27 part-time (18 women); includes 1 minority (Black or African American, non-Hispanic/Latino). Average age 32. 9 applicants, 100% accepted, 7 enrolled. In 2015, 7 master's awarded. *Degree requirements:* For master's, research seminars. *Entrance requirements:* For master's, For the MS in Mathematics, students must hold a bachelor's degree in mathematics or a bachelor's degree in some other field with extensive course work in mathematics. Additional exam requirements/recommendations for international students: Required—TOEFL (minimum score 550 paper-based; 79 iBT). *Application deadline:* For fall admission, 6/1 for international students; for spring admission, 10/1 for international students. Applications are processed on a rolling basis. Application fee: $0. Electronic applications accepted. *Expenses:* Contact institution. *Financial support:* Federal Work-Study, scholarships/grants, and unspecified assistantships available. Support available to part-time students. Financial award application deadline: 4/1; financial award applicants required to submit FAFSA. *Unit head:* Dr. Regina Rahn, Chair, 630-844-5651, E-mail: rrahn@aurora.edu. *Application contact:* Jason Harmon, Director of Orchard Center & Graduate Enrollment, 630-947-8905, E-mail: jharmon@aurora.edu.

Ball State University, Graduate School, College of Sciences and Humanities, Department of Mathematical Sciences, Program in Mathematics, Muncie, IN 47306. Offers MA, MS. *Program availability:* Part-time. *Students:* 6 full-time (1 woman), 6 part-time (3 women), 6 international. Average age 25. 12 applicants, 83% accepted, 4 enrolled. In 2015, 4 master's awarded. *Degree requirements:* For master's, thesis (for some programs). *Entrance requirements:* For master's, minimum baccalaureate GPA of 2.75 or 3.0 in latter half of baccalauareate. Additional exam requirements/recommendations for international students: Required—TOEFL (minimum score 550 paper-based; 79 iBT), IELTS (minimum score 6.5). *Application deadline:* Applications are processed on a rolling basis. Application fee: $60. Electronic applications accepted. *Expenses: Tuition, area resident:* Full-time $6948; part-time $2316 per semester. Tuition, state resident: full-time $10,422; part-time $3474 per semester. Tuition, nonresident: full-time $19,062; part-time $6354 per semester. *Required fees:* $651 per semester. Tuition and fees vary according to campus/location, program and reciprocity agreements. *Financial support:* In 2015–16, 5 students received support, including 5 teaching assistantships with partial tuition reimbursements available (averaging $11,600 per year). Financial award application deadline: 3/1; financial award applicants required to submit FAFSA. *Unit head:* Dr. John Lorch, Chairperson, 765-285-8640, Fax: 765-285-1721, E-mail: jlorch@bsu.edu. *Application contact:* Dr. Hanspeter Fischer, Director of Graduate Programs, 765-285-8640, Fax: 765-285-1721, E-mail: hfischer@bsu.edu.
Website: http://www.bsu.edu/math

Baylor University, Graduate School, College of Arts and Sciences, Department of Mathematics, Waco, TX 76798. Offers MS, PhD. *Faculty:* 23 full-time (1 woman). *Students:* 26 full-time (5 women), 1 (woman) part-time; includes 3 minority (1 American Indian or Alaska Native, non-Hispanic/Latino; 2 Asian, non-Hispanic/Latino), 1 international. Average age 26. 39 applicants, 18% accepted, 5 enrolled. In 2015, 2 master's, 4 doctorates awarded. Terminal master's awarded for partial completion of doctoral program. *Degree requirements:* For master's, comprehensive exam, final oral exam; for doctorate, comprehensive exam, thesis/dissertation. *Entrance requirements:* For master's and doctorate, GRE General Test. Additional exam requirements/recommendations for international students: Required—TOEFL (minimum score 80 iBT). *Application deadline:* For fall admission, 1/31 for domestic and international students. Applications are processed on a rolling basis. Application fee: $50. Electronic applications accepted. *Financial support:* In 2015–16, 27 students received support, including 2 research assistantships with full tuition reimbursements available (averaging $22,000 per year), 25 teaching assistantships with full tuition reimbursements available (averaging $22,000 per year). Financial award application deadline: 5/1. *Faculty research:* Algebra, statistics, probability, applied mathematics, numerical analysis. *Unit head:* Dr. Mark Spenski, Graduate Program Director, 254-710-6577, Fax: 254-710-3569, E-mail: mark_sepanski@baylor.edu. *Application contact:* Rita Massey, Graduate Program Coordinator, 254-710-3146, Fax: 254-710-3569,
E-mail: rita_massey@baylor.edu.
Website: http://www.baylor.edu/math/

Bemidji State University, School of Graduate Studies, Bemidji, MN 56601. Offers biology (MS); education (MS); English (MA, MS); environmental studies (MS); mathematics (MS); mathematics (elementary and middle level education) (MS); special education (M Sp Ed). *Program availability:* Part-time, online learning. *Degree requirements:* For master's, comprehensive exam, thesis (for some programs). *Entrance requirements:* For master's, GRE; GMAT, letters of recommendation, letters of interest. Additional exam requirements/recommendations for international students: Required—TOEFL (minimum score 550 paper-based; 80 iBT). Electronic applications accepted. *Expenses:* Contact institution. *Faculty research:* Human performance, sport, and health: physical education teacher education, continuum models, spiritual health, intellectual health, resiliency, health priorities; psychology: health psychology, college student drinking behavior, micro-aggressions, infant cognition, false memories, leadership assessment; biology: structure and dynamics of forest communities, aquatic and riverine ecology, interaction between animal populations and aquatic environments, cellular motility.

Binghamton University, State University of New York, Graduate School, School of Arts and Sciences, Department of Mathematical Sciences, Vestal, NY 13850. Offers MA, PhD. *Program availability:* Part-time. *Faculty:* 35 full-time (3 women), 21 part-time/adjunct (4 women). *Students:* 44 full-time (12 women), 25 part-time (5 women); includes 4 minority (1 Asian, non-Hispanic/Latino; 3 Hispanic/Latino), 38 international. Average age 27. 83 applicants, 69% accepted, 18 enrolled. In 2015, 15 master's, 4 doctorates awarded. Terminal master's awarded for partial completion of doctoral program. *Degree requirements:* For master's, comprehensive exam (for some programs), thesis or alternative; for doctorate, 2 foreign languages, thesis/dissertation. *Entrance requirements:* For master's and doctorate, GRE General Test. Additional exam requirements/recommendations for international students: Required—TOEFL (minimum score 550 paper-based; 80 iBT). *Application deadline:* For fall admission, 4/15 priority date for domestic and international students; for spring admission, 11/30 priority date for domestic and international students. Application fee: $75. Electronic applications accepted. *Financial support:* In 2015–16, 45 students received support, including 1 research assistantship with full tuition reimbursement available (averaging $17,000 per year), 44 teaching assistantships with full tuition reimbursements available (averaging $16,500 per year); career-related internships or fieldwork, Federal Work-Study, institutionally sponsored loans, scholarships/grants, health care benefits, tuition waivers (full and partial), and unspecified assistantships also available. Financial award application deadline: 1/30; financial award applicants required to submit FAFSA. *Unit head:* Dr. Ross Geoghegan, Chairperson, 607-777-2540,
E-mail: ross@math.binghamton.edu. *Application contact:* Kishan Zuber, Recruiting and Admissions Coordinator, 607-777-2151, Fax: 607-777-2501,
E-mail: kzuber@binghamton.edu.

Boise State University, College of Arts and Sciences, Department of Mathematics, Boise, ID 83725-1555. Offers mathematics (MS); mathematics education (MS). *Program availability:* Part-time. *Faculty:* 12. *Students:* 16 full-time (8 women), 9 part-time (5 women); includes 3 minority (all Asian, non-Hispanic/Latino), 3 international. Average age 31. 33 applicants, 33% accepted, 10 enrolled. In 2015, 4 master's awarded. *Degree requirements:* For master's, thesis optional. *Entrance requirements:* For master's, GRE General Test. Additional exam requirements/recommendations for international students: Required—TOEFL (minimum score 550 paper-based; 80 iBT), IELTS (minimum score 6). *Application deadline:* For fall admission, 2/1 priority date for domestic and international students. Application fee: $65 ($95 for international students). Electronic applications accepted. *Expenses:* Tuition, state resident: full-time $6058; part-time $358 per credit hour. Tuition, nonresident: full-time $20,108; part-time $608 per credit hour. *Required fees:* $2108. Tuition and fees vary according to program. *Financial support:* In 2015–16, 8 students received support, including 12 teaching assistantships (averaging $8,314 per year); scholarships/grants and unspecified assistantships also available. Financial award application deadline: 2/1; financial award applicants required to submit FAFSA. *Unit head:* Dr. Leming Qu, Chair, 208-426-1172, E-mail: lqu@boisestate.edu. *Application contact:* Dr. Jodi Mead, Graduate Program Coordinator, 208-426-2432, E-mail: jmead@boisestate.edu.
Website: http://math.boisestate.edu/

Boston College, Graduate School of Arts and Sciences, Department of Mathematics, Chestnut Hill, MA 02467. Offers PhD, MBA/MA. *Faculty:* 34 full-time. *Students:* 27 full-time (6 women); includes 5 minority (2 Asian, non-Hispanic/Latino; 2 Hispanic/Latino; 1 Two or more races, non-Hispanic/Latino), 11 international. 63 applicants, 29% accepted, 6 enrolled. In 2015, 3 doctorates awarded. Terminal master's awarded for partial completion of doctoral program. *Degree requirements:* For doctorate, comprehensive exam, thesis/dissertation. *Entrance requirements:* Additional exam requirements/recommendations for international students: Required—TOEFL (minimum score 600 paper-based; 100 iBT), IELTS (minimum score 8). *Application deadline:* For fall admission, 1/15 priority date for domestic students, 1/15 for international students. Application fee: $75. Electronic applications accepted. Tuition and fees vary according to program. *Financial support:* In 2015–16, 27 students received support, including fellowships with full tuition reimbursements available (averaging $22,250 per year), teaching assistantships with full tuition reimbursements available (averaging $22,250 per year); Federal Work-Study, scholarships/grants, health care benefits, and unspecified assistantships also available. Support available to part-time students. Financial award application deadline: 3/1; financial award applicants required to submit FAFSA. *Faculty research:* Number theory, algebraic geometry, representation theory, topology, geometry. *Unit head:* Dr. Sol Friedberg, Chairperson, 917-552-3750. *Application contact:* Dr. Robert Meyerhoff, Graduate Program Director, 617-552-3759, E-mail: meyerhog@bc.edu.
Website: http://www.bc.edu/math

Boston University, Graduate School of Arts and Sciences, Department of Mathematics and Statistics, Boston, MA 02215. Offers mathematics (MA, PhD); statistical practice (MS). *Students:* 257 full-time (113 women), 10 part-time (6 women); includes 14 minority (9 Asian, non-Hispanic/Latino; 4 Hispanic/Latino; 1 Two or more races, non-Hispanic/Latino), 219 international. Average age 24. 676 applicants, 19% accepted, 35 enrolled. In 2015, 11 master's, 6 doctorates awarded. Terminal master's awarded for partial completion of doctoral program. *Degree requirements:* For master's, one foreign language, comprehensive exam; for doctorate, one foreign language, comprehensive exam, thesis/dissertation. *Entrance requirements:* For master's and doctorate, GRE General Test, GRE Subject Test (for mathematics including probability), 3 letters of recommendation, transcripts, personal statement. Additional exam requirements/recommendations for international students: Required—TOEFL (minimum score 550 paper-based; 84 iBT). *Application deadline:* For fall admission, 12/31 for domestic and international students; for spring admission, 9/30 for domestic and international students. Application fee: $95. Electronic applications accepted. *Financial support:* In 2015–16, 48 students received support, including 3 fellowships with full tuition reimbursements available (averaging $21,000 per year), 7 research assistantships with full tuition reimbursements available (averaging $21,000 per year), 30 teaching assistantships with full tuition reimbursements available (averaging $21,000 per year); Federal Work-Study, scholarships/grants, and health care benefits also available. Support available to part-time students. Financial award application deadline: 12/31. *Unit head:* Tasso Kaper, Chair, 617-353-9552, Fax: 617-353-8100,
E-mail: tasso@bu.edu. *Application contact:* Marisa DiSarno, Graduate Program Administrator, 617-353-2560, Fax: 617-353-8100, E-mail: mdisarno@bu.edu.
Website: http://math.bu.edu/

Bowling Green State University, Graduate College, College of Arts and Sciences, Department of Mathematics and Statistics, Bowling Green, OH 43403. Offers applied statistics (MS); mathematics (MA, MAT, PhD); statistics (PhD). *Program availability:* Part-time. *Degree requirements:* For master's, thesis or alternative; for doctorate, comprehensive exam, thesis/dissertation. *Entrance requirements:* For master's and doctorate, GRE General Test. Additional exam requirements/recommendations for international students: Required—TOEFL. Electronic applications accepted. *Faculty research:* Statistics and probability, algebra, analysis.

Brandeis University, Graduate School of Arts and Sciences, Department of Mathematics, Waltham, MA 02454-9110. Offers MA, PhD, Postbaccalaureate Certificate. *Program availability:* Part-time. *Faculty:* 13 full-time (4 women), 4 part-time/adjunct (2 women). *Students:* 35 full-time (5 women), 1 part-time (0 women); includes 7 minority (4 Asian, non-Hispanic/Latino; 2 Hispanic/Latino; 1 Two or more races, non-Hispanic/Latino), 17 international. 167 applicants, 22% accepted, 11 enrolled. In 2015, 5 master's, 3 doctorates awarded. Terminal master's awarded for partial completion of doctoral program. *Degree requirements:* For master's, one foreign language; for doctorate, one foreign language, comprehensive exam, thesis/dissertation, qualifying exam. *Entrance requirements:* For master's, resume, 2 letters of recommendation, statement of purpose, transcript(s); for doctorate, GRE General Test and GRE Subject Test (recommended), resume, 3 letters of recommendation, statement of purpose, transcript(s); for Postbaccalaureate Certificate, resume, letter of recommendation, statement of purpose, transcript(s). Additional exam requirements/recommendations for international students: Required—TOEFL (minimum score 600 paper-based; 100 iBT); Recommended—IELTS (minimum score 7), TSE (minimum score 68). *Application deadline:* For fall admission, 1/15 priority date for domestic students. Application fee: $75. Electronic applications accepted. *Financial support:* In 2015–16, 40 students received support, including 26 fellowships with full tuition reimbursements available (averaging $22,000 per year), 5 research assistantships with full tuition reimbursements available (averaging $22,000 per year), 9 teaching assistantships with partial tuition reimbursements available (averaging $1,000 per year); Federal Work-Study, scholarships/grants, health care benefits, and tuition waivers (partial) also available. Support available to part-time students. Financial award application deadline: 4/15; financial award applicants required to submit FAFSA. *Faculty research:* Algebra, analysis, topology, combinatorics. *Unit head:* Prof. Daniel Ruberman, Department Chair, 781-736-3050, Fax: 781-736-3085, E-mail: ruberman@brandeis.edu. *Application contact:* Catherine Broderick, Department Administrator, 781-736-3050, Fax: 781-736-3085, E-mail: cbroderi@brandeis.edu.
Website: http://www.brandeis.edu/gsas

Brigham Young University, Graduate Studies, College of Physical and Mathematical Sciences, Department of Mathematics, Provo, UT 84602. Offers MS, PhD. *Program availability:* Part-time. *Faculty:* 30 full-time (2 women). *Students:* 19 full-time (1 woman), 16 part-time (2 women); includes 4 minority (all Asian, non-Hispanic/Latino). Average age 24. 12 applicants, 92% accepted, 9 enrolled. In 2015, 13 master's, 1 doctorate awarded. Terminal master's awarded for partial completion of doctoral program. *Degree requirements:* For master's, comprehensive exam, thesis, project; qualifying exams in algebra and analysis; for doctorate, comprehensive exam, thesis/dissertation, qualifying exams. *Entrance requirements:* For master's, GRE General Test, GRE Subject Test (math; minimum score of 600), minimum GPA of 3.0 in last 60 hours, bachelor's degree in mathematics; for doctorate, GRE General Test, GRE Subject Test (math; minimum score of 600), master's degree in mathematics or related field. Additional exam requirements/recommendations for international students: Required—TOEFL (minimum score 600 paper-based; 85 iBT). *Application deadline:* For fall admission, 1/15 priority date for domestic and international students; for winter admission, 9/16 priority date for domestic and international students; for spring admission, 1/15 priority date for domestic and international students; for summer admission, 1/15 priority date for domestic and international students. Applications are processed on a rolling basis. Application fee: $50. Electronic applications accepted. *Expenses:* $13,000 full-time tuition. *Financial support:* In 2015–16, 34 students received support, including 7 research assistantships with full tuition reimbursements available (averaging $17,400 per year), 32 teaching assistantships with full tuition reimbursements available (averaging $17,400 per year); institutionally sponsored loans also available. Support available to part-time students. Financial award application deadline: 1/15. *Faculty research:* Algebraic geometry/number theory, applied math/nonlinear PDEs, combinatorics/matrix theory, geometric group theory/topology. *Total annual research expenditures:* $123,600. *Unit head:* Dr. Michael J. Dorff, Chairperson, 801-422-1752, Fax: 801-422-0504,
E-mail: mdorff@mathematics.byu.edu. *Application contact:* Lonette Stoddard, Graduate Secretary, 801-422-2062, Fax: 801-422-0504, E-mail: lonettes@byu.edu.
Website: https://math.byu.edu

Brock University, Faculty of Graduate Studies, Faculty of Mathematics and Science, Program in Mathematics and Statistics, St. Catharines, ON L2S 3A1, Canada. Offers M Sc. *Program availability:* Part-time. *Degree requirements:* For master's, thesis or project. *Entrance requirements:* For master's, honors degree. Additional exam requirements/recommendations for international students: Required—TOEFL (minimum score 550 paper-based; 80 iBT), IELTS (minimum score 6.5), TWE (minimum score 4). Electronic applications accepted.

Brooklyn College of the City University of New York, School of Natural and Behavioral Sciences, Department of Mathematics, Brooklyn, NY 11210-2889. Offers MA. *Program availability:* Part-time, evening/weekend. *Degree requirements:* For master's, comprehensive exam (for mathematics). *Entrance requirements:* For master's, minimum GPA of 3.0, 2 letters of recommendation. Additional exam requirements/recommendations for international students: Required—TOEFL (minimum score 500 paper-based; 61 iBT). Electronic applications accepted. *Faculty research:* Differential geometry, gauge theory, complex analysis, orthogonal functions.

Brown University, Graduate School, Department of Mathematics, Providence, RI 02912. Offers PhD. *Faculty:* 18 full-time (1 woman). *Students:* 48 full-time (18 women); includes 3 minority (1 Asian, non-Hispanic/Latino; 1 Hispanic/Latino; 1 Two or more races, non-Hispanic/Latino), 28 international. Average age 25. 192 applicants, 13% accepted, 8 enrolled. In 2015, 10 doctorates awarded. *Degree requirements:* For doctorate, one foreign language, thesis/dissertation. *Entrance requirements:* For doctorate, GRE. Additional exam requirements/recommendations for international students: Required—TOEFL (minimum score 600 paper-based; 100 iBT) or IELTS (minimum score 7). *Application deadline:* For fall admission, 1/1 priority date for domestic and international students. Application fee: $75. Electronic applications accepted. *Expenses:* $48,272 tuition; $752 health fee. *Financial support:* In 2015–16, 9 fellowships (averaging $24,200 per year), 6 research assistantships (averaging $23,700 per year), 33 teaching assistantships (averaging $23,700 per year) were awarded; Federal Work-Study, institutionally sponsored loans, and tuition waivers (full and partial) also available. Financial award application deadline: 1/1; financial award applicants required to submit FAFSA. *Faculty research:* Algebraic geometry, number theory, functional analysis, geometry, topology. *Total annual research expenditures:* $1.2 million. *Unit head:* Prof. Jeffrey F. Brock, Chair, 401-863-1867, Fax: 401-863-9013, E-mail: jeff_brock@brown.edu. *Application contact:* Prof. Justin Holmer, Director of Graduate Studies, 401-863-1123, Fax: 401-863-9013, E-mail: holmer@math.brown.edu.
Website: http://www.math.brown.edu/

Bryn Mawr College, Graduate School of Arts and Sciences, Department of Mathematics, Bryn Mawr, PA 19010-2899. Offers MA, PhD. *Program availability:* Part-time. *Faculty:* 10 full-time (6 women). *Students:* 4 full-time (all women), 2 part-time (both women). Average age 27. 22 applicants, 5% accepted. In 2015, 2 master's, 1 doctorate awarded. *Degree requirements:* For master's, one foreign language, thesis; for doctorate, 2 foreign languages, comprehensive exam, thesis/dissertation. *Entrance requirements:* For master's and doctorate, GRE General Test, transcripts, three letters of recommendation, statement of interest, resume or curriculum vitae. Additional exam requirements/recommendations for international students: Required—TOEFL (minimum score 600 paper-based, 100 iBT) or IELTS (7.0). *Application deadline:* For fall admission, 1/4 for domestic and international students. Application fee: $50. *Expenses: Tuition, area resident:* Full-time $39,240; part-time $6540 per unit. *Financial support:* In 2015–16, 6 students received support, including 1 fellowship with full tuition reimbursement available (averaging $21,583 per year), 5 teaching assistantships with full tuition reimbursements available (averaging $18,500 per year); research assistantships, Federal Work-Study, scholarships/grants, health care benefits, tuition waivers (full and partial), unspecified assistantships, and tuition awards also available. Support available to part-time students. Financial award application deadline: 1/4. *Unit head:* Maria Dantis, Graduate Program Administrator, 610-526-5074,
E-mail: gsas@brynmawr.edu.

Bucknell University, Graduate Studies, College of Arts and Sciences, Department of Mathematics, Lewisburg, PA 17837. Offers MA, MS. *Degree requirements:* For master's, comprehensive exam, thesis or alternative. *Entrance requirements:* For master's, GRE General Test, GRE Subject Test, minimum GPA of 3.0. Additional exam requirements/recommendations for international students: Required—TOEFL (minimum score 600 paper-based).

California Institute of Technology, Division of Physics, Mathematics and Astronomy, Department of Mathematics, Pasadena, CA 91125-0001. Offers PhD. *Degree requirements:* For doctorate, one foreign language, thesis/dissertation, candidacy and final exams. *Entrance requirements:* For doctorate, GRE General Test, GRE Subject Test. Additional exam requirements/recommendations for international students: Required—TOEFL. *Faculty research:* Number theory, combinatorics, differential geometry, dynamical systems, finite groups.

California Polytechnic State University, San Luis Obispo, College of Science and Mathematics, Department of Mathematics, San Luis Obispo, CA 93407. Offers MS. *Program availability:* Part-time. *Faculty:* 10 full-time (0 women), 1 part-time/adjunct (0 women). *Students:* 15 full-time (3 women), 7 part-time (3 women); includes 8 minority (1 Asian, non-Hispanic/Latino; 4 Hispanic/Latino; 3 Two or more races, non-Hispanic/Latino), 1 international. Average age 24. 28 applicants, 46% accepted, 10 enrolled. In 2015, 7 master's awarded. *Degree requirements:* For master's, comprehensive exam. *Application deadline:* For fall admission, 4/1 for domestic and international students; for winter admission, 11/1 for domestic students, 6/30 for international students; for spring admission, 2/1 for domestic students. Applications are processed on a rolling basis. Application fee: $55. *Expenses:* Tuition, state resident: full-time $6738; part-time $3906 per year. Tuition, nonresident: full-time $15,666; part-time $8370 per year. *Required fees:* $3528; $3075 per unit. $1025 per term. *Financial support:* Fellowships, teaching assistantships, career-related internships or fieldwork, Federal Work-Study, and scholarships/grants available. Support available to part-time students. Financial award application deadline: 3/2; financial award applicants required to submit FAFSA. *Faculty research:* Combinatorics, dynamical systems, ordinary and partial differential equations, operator theory, topology. *Unit head:* Dr. Morgan Sherman, Graduate Coordinator, E-mail: sherman1@calpoly.edu.
Website: http://math.calpoly.edu/

California State Polytechnic University, Pomona, Program in Mathematics, Pomona, CA 91768-2557. Offers applied mathematics (MS); pure mathematics (MS). *Program availability:* Part-time. *Students:* 13 full-time (4 women), 26 part-time (7 women); includes 25 minority (3 Black or African American, non-Hispanic/Latino; 8 Asian, non-Hispanic/Latino; 13 Hispanic/Latino; 1 Two or more races, non-Hispanic/Latino), 2 international. Average age 26. 66 applicants, 38% accepted, 11 enrolled. In 2015, 17 master's awarded. *Degree requirements:* For master's, thesis or alternative. *Entrance requirements:* For master's, GRE General Test. *Application deadline:* For fall admission, 5/1 priority date for domestic students; for winter admission, 10/15 priority date for domestic students; for spring admission, 1/20 priority date for domestic students. Applications are processed on a rolling basis. Application fee: $55. Electronic applications accepted. *Expenses:* Tuition, state resident: full-time $6738. Tuition, nonresident: full-time $13,434. *Required fees:* $1504. Tuition and fees vary according to course load, degree level and program. *Financial support:* Career-related internships or fieldwork, Federal Work-Study, and institutionally sponsored loans available. Support available to part-time students. Financial award application deadline: 3/2; financial award applicants required to submit FAFSA. *Unit head:* Dr. John Rock, Graduate Coordinator, 909-869-2404, Fax: 909-869-4904, E-mail: jarock@cpp.edu.
Website: http://www.cpp.edu/~sci/mathematics-statistics/graduate-students/

California State University Channel Islands, Extended University and International Programs, Program in Mathematics, Camarillo, CA 93012. Offers MS. *Program availability:* Part-time, evening/weekend. *Degree requirements:* For master's, thesis. *Entrance requirements:* For master's, BA in math. Additional exam requirements/recommendations for international students: Required—TOEFL (minimum score 550 paper-based; 80 iBT), IELTS (minimum score 6).

California State University, East Bay, Office of Graduate Studies Programs, College of Science, Department of Mathematics and Computer Science, Mathematics Program, Hayward, CA 94542-3000. Offers applied mathematics (MS); mathematics (MS); mathematics teaching (MS). *Program availability:* Part-time, evening/weekend. *Students:* 19 full-time (5 women), 27 part-time (14 women); includes 25 minority (2 Black or African American, non-Hispanic/Latino; 13 Asian, non-Hispanic/Latino; 6 Hispanic/Latino; 2 Native Hawaiian or other Pacific Islander, non-Hispanic/Latino; 2 Two or more races, non-Hispanic/Latino), 3 international. Average age 36. 25 applicants, 80% accepted, 10 enrolled. In 2015, 22 master's awarded. *Degree requirements:* For master's, comprehensive exam or thesis. *Entrance requirements:* For master's, minimum GPA of 3.0 in field. Additional exam requirements/recommendations for international students: Required—TOEFL (minimum score 550 paper-based). *Application deadline:* For fall admission, 6/30 for domestic and international students. Application fee: $55. Electronic applications accepted. *Financial support:* Fellowships, teaching assistantships, Federal Work-Study, institutionally sponsored loans, and scholarships/grants available. Support available to part-time students. Financial award application deadline: 3/1; financial award applicants required to submit FAFSA. *Unit head:* Matthew Johnson, Chair, 510-885-3414, E-mail: matt.johnson@csueastbay.edu. *Application contact:* Dr. Donald Wolitzer, Math Graduate Advisor, 510-885-3467, E-mail: donald.wolitzer@csueastbay.edu.
Website: http://www20.csueastbay.edu/csci/departments/math-cs/

California State University, Fresno, Division of Graduate Studies, College of Science and Mathematics, Department of Mathematics, Fresno, CA 93740-8027. Offers mathematics (MA); teaching (MA). *Program availability:* Part-time. *Degree requirements:* For master's, thesis or alternative. *Entrance requirements:* For master's, GRE General Test. Additional exam requirements/recommendations for international students:

Required—TOEFL. Electronic applications accepted. *Faculty research:* Diagnostic testing project.

California State University, Fullerton, Graduate Studies, College of Natural Science and Mathematics, Department of Mathematics, Fullerton, CA 92834-9480. Offers applied mathematics (MA); mathematics (MA); teaching (MA). *Program availability:* Part-time. *Degree requirements:* For master's, comprehensive exam or project. *Entrance requirements:* For master's, minimum GPA of 2.5 in last 60 units of course work, major in mathematics or related field.

California State University, Long Beach, Graduate Studies, College of Natural Sciences and Mathematics, Department of Mathematics and Statistics, Long Beach, CA 90840. Offers mathematics (MS), including applied mathematics, applied statistics, mathematics education for secondary school teachers. *Program availability:* Part-time. *Degree requirements:* For master's, comprehensive exam or thesis. Electronic applications accepted. *Faculty research:* Algebra, functional analysis, partial differential equations, operator theory, numerical analysis.

California State University, Los Angeles, Graduate Studies, College of Natural and Social Sciences, Department of Mathematics, Los Angeles, CA 90032-8530. Offers mathematics (MS), including applied mathematics, mathematics. *Program availability:* Part-time, evening/weekend. *Degree requirements:* For master's, comprehensive exam or thesis. *Entrance requirements:* For master's, previous course work in mathematics. Additional exam requirements/recommendations for international students: Required—TOEFL (minimum score 500 paper-based). Electronic applications accepted. *Faculty research:* Group theory, functional analysis, convexity theory, ordered geometry.

California State University, Northridge, Graduate Studies, College of Science and Mathematics, Department of Mathematics, Northridge, CA 91330. Offers applied mathematics (MS); mathematics (MS); mathematics for educational careers (MS). *Program availability:* Part-time, evening/weekend. *Faculty:* 33 full-time (7 women), 54 part-time/adjunct (27 women). *Students:* 16 full-time (8 women), 36 part-time (12 women); includes 13 minority (8 Asian, non-Hispanic/Latino; 5 Hispanic/Latino), 11 international. Average age 29. 62 applicants, 60% accepted, 17 enrolled. *Degree requirements:* For master's, thesis (for some programs). *Entrance requirements:* For master's, GRE (if cumulative undergraduate GPA less than 3.0). Additional exam requirements/recommendations for international students: Required—TOEFL. *Application deadline:* For fall admission, 4/15 priority date for domestic students. Application fee: $55. *Financial support:* Teaching assistantships, Federal Work-Study, and institutionally sponsored loans available. Support available to part-time students. Financial award application deadline: 3/1. *Unit head:* Dr. Rabia Djellouli, 818-677-7794. Website: http://www.csun.edu/~hfmth009/

California State University, Sacramento, Office of Graduate Studies, College of Natural Sciences and Mathematics, Department of Mathematics and Statistics, Sacramento, CA 95819. Offers mathematics (MA). *Program availability:* Part-time. *Degree requirements:* For master's, thesis or alternative, directed reading program preparing for written proficiency exam. *Entrance requirements:* For master's, minimum GPA of 3.0 in mathematics, 2.5 overall during previous 2 years; BA in mathematics or equivalent. Additional exam requirements/recommendations for international students: Required—TOEFL. Electronic applications accepted. *Faculty research:* Algebra, applied mathematics, methods in mathematical finance, subelliptic analysis, topology.

California State University, San Bernardino, Graduate Studies, College of Natural Sciences, Program in Mathematics, San Bernardino, CA 92407. Offers mathematics (MA); teaching mathematics (MAT). *Program availability:* Part-time. *Students:* 4 full-time (0 women), 41 part-time (20 women); includes 28 minority (1 Black or African American, non-Hispanic/Latino; 4 Asian, non-Hispanic/Latino; 21 Hispanic/Latino; 2 Two or more races, non-Hispanic/Latino), 1 international. 18 applicants, 56% accepted, 8 enrolled. In 2015, 11 master's awarded. *Degree requirements:* For master's, advancement to candidacy. *Entrance requirements:* Additional exam requirements/recommendations for international students: Required—TOEFL. *Application deadline:* For fall admission, 7/16 for domestic students; for winter admission, 10/16 for domestic students; for spring admission, 1/22 for domestic students. Application fee: $55. *Expenses:* Tuition, state resident: full-time $7843; part-time $5011.20 per year. Tuition and fees vary according to course load, degree level, program and reciprocity agreements. *Faculty research:* Mathematics education, technology in education, algebra, combinatorics, real analysis. *Unit head:* Dr. Charles Stanton, Interim Chair, 909-537-5376, E-mail: cstanton@csusb.edu. *Application contact:* Dr. Jeffrey Thompson, Assistant Dean of Graduate Studies, 909-537-5058, E-mail: jthompso@csusb.edu.

California State University, San Marcos, College of Science and Mathematics, Program in Mathematics, San Marcos, CA 92096-0001. Offers MS. *Program availability:* Part-time, evening/weekend. *Degree requirements:* For master's, comprehensive exam, thesis optional. *Entrance requirements:* Additional exam requirements/recommendations for international students: Required—TOEFL, TWE. *Faculty research:* Combinatorics, graph theory, partial differential equations, numerical analysis, computational linear algebra.

Carleton University, Faculty of Graduate Studies, Faculty of Science, School of Mathematics and Statistics, Ottawa, ON K1S 5B6, Canada. Offers mathematics (M Sc, PhD). Programs offered jointly with University of Ottawa. *Degree requirements:* For master's, thesis optional; for doctorate, one foreign language, comprehensive exam, thesis/dissertation. *Entrance requirements:* For master's, honors degree; for doctorate, master's degree. Additional exam requirements/recommendations for international students: Required—TOEFL. *Faculty research:* Pure mathematics, applied mathematics, probability and statistics.

Carnegie Mellon University, Mellon College of Science, Department of Mathematical Sciences, Pittsburgh, PA 15213-3891. Offers algorithms, combinatorics, and optimization (PhD); computational finance (MS); mathematical finance (PhD); mathematical sciences (DA, PhD); pure and applied logic (PhD). *Program availability:* Part-time. Terminal master's awarded for partial completion of doctoral program. *Degree requirements:* For doctorate, thesis/dissertation. *Entrance requirements:* For master's and doctorate, GRE General Test, GRE Subject Test. Additional exam requirements/recommendations for international students: Required—TOEFL. Electronic applications accepted. *Faculty research:* Continuum mechanics, discrete mathematics, applied and computational mathematics.

Case Western Reserve University, School of Graduate Studies, Department of Mathematics, Applied Mathematics and Statistics, Cleveland, OH 44106. Offers applied mathematics (MS, PhD); mathematics (MS, PhD). *Program availability:* Part-time. *Faculty:* 23 full-time (10 women), 5 part-time/adjunct (0 women). *Students:* 33 full-time (13 women), 1 part-time (0 women); includes 4 minority (1 Black or African American, non-Hispanic/Latino; 1 Asian, non-Hispanic/Latino; 2 Two or more races, non-Hispanic/Latino), 17 international. Average age 27. 58 applicants, 22% accepted, 10 enrolled. In 2015, 1 master's, 1 doctorate awarded. Terminal master's awarded for partial completion of doctoral program. *Degree requirements:* For master's, thesis (for applied mathematics); for doctorate, comprehensive exam, thesis/dissertation. *Entrance requirements:* For master's and doctorate, GRE General Test, 3 letters of recommendation. Additional exam requirements/recommendations for international students: Required—TOEFL (minimum score 577 paper-based; 90 iBT); Recommended—IELTS (minimum score 7). *Application deadline:* For fall admission, 4/1 priority date for domestic students; for spring admission, 11/1 priority date for domestic students. Applications are processed on a rolling basis. Application fee: $50. Electronic applications accepted. *Expenses: Tuition, area resident:* Full-time $41,137; part-time $1714 per credit hour. *Required fees:* $32. Tuition and fees vary according to course load and program. *Financial support:* Research assistantships, teaching assistantships, institutionally sponsored loans, and unspecified assistantships available. Financial award application deadline: 12/15; financial award applicants required to submit CSS PROFILE or FAFSA. *Faculty research:* Probability theory, convexity and high-dimensional phenomena, imaging, geometric evaluation of curves, dynamical systems, large scale scientific computing, life sciences. *Unit head:* David Singer, Professor and Interim Chair, 216-368-2892, Fax: 216-368-5163, E-mail: david.singer@case.edu. *Application contact:* Sakeenah Bari-Harold, Department Administrator, 216-368-0463, Fax: 216-368-5163, E-mail: sakeenah.bari-harold@case.edu.
Website: http://math.case.edu/

Central Connecticut State University, School of Graduate Studies, School of Engineering, Science and Technology, Department of Mathematical Sciences, New Britain, CT 06050-4010. Offers data mining (MS, Certificate); mathematics (MA, MS, Certificate, Sixth Year Certificate), including actuarial science (MA), computer science (MA), statistics (MA). *Program availability:* Part-time, evening/weekend. *Faculty:* 14 full-time (3 women). *Students:* 11 full-time (5 women), 72 part-time (35 women); includes 21 minority (5 Black or African American, non-Hispanic/Latino; 1 American Indian or Alaska Native, non-Hispanic/Latino; 7 Asian, non-Hispanic/Latino; 6 Hispanic/Latino; 2 Two or more races, non-Hispanic/Latino), 4 international. Average age 35. 67 applicants, 55% accepted, 23 enrolled. In 2015, 23 master's, 1 other advanced degree awarded. *Degree requirements:* For master's, comprehensive exam, thesis or alternative, special project; for other advanced degree, qualifying exam. *Entrance requirements:* For master's, minimum undergraduate GPA of 2.7; for other advanced degree, minimum undergraduate GPA of 3.0, essay, letters of recommendation. Additional exam requirements/recommendations for international students: Required—TOEFL (minimum score 550 paper-based; 79 iBT). *Application deadline:* For fall admission, 5/1 for domestic and international students; for spring admission, 11/1 for domestic and international students. Applications are processed on a rolling basis. Application fee: $50. Electronic applications accepted. *Expenses: Tuition, area resident:* Full-time $6188. Tuition, state resident: full-time $9284; part-time $577 per credit. Tuition, nonresident: full-time $17,240; part-time $592 per credit. *Required fees:* $4266; $234 per credit. *Financial support:* In 2015–16, 28 students received support, including 1 research assistantship; career-related internships or fieldwork, Federal Work-Study, scholarships/grants, and unspecified assistantships also available. Support available to part-time students. Financial award application deadline: 3/1; financial award applicants required to submit FAFSA. *Faculty research:* Statistics, actuarial mathematics, computer systems and engineering, computer programming techniques, operations research. *Unit head:* Dr. Philip Halloran, Chair, 860-832-2835, E-mail: halloranp@ccsu.edu. *Application contact:* Patricia Gardner, Associate Director of Graduate Studies, 860-832-2350, Fax: 860-832-2362, E-mail: graduateadmissions@ccsu.edu.
Website: http://www.ccsu.edu/math/

Central European University, Graduate Studies, Department of Mathematics and its Applications, Budapest, Hungary. Offers applied mathematics (MS); mathematics and its applications (PhD). *Faculty:* 2 full-time (0 women), 10 part-time/adjunct (0 women). *Students:* 39 full-time (9 women). Average age 26. 87 applicants, 25% accepted, 15 enrolled. In 2015, 7 master's, 3 doctorates awarded. *Degree requirements:* For master's, one foreign language, thesis (for some programs); for doctorate, comprehensive exam, thesis/dissertation. *Entrance requirements:* For master's and doctorate, entrance exam or GRE, statement of purpose. Additional exam requirements/recommendations for international students: Required—TOEFL (minimum score 570 paper-based); Recommended—IELTS (minimum score 6.5). *Application deadline:* For fall admission, 2/4 for domestic and international students. Application fee: $40. Electronic applications accepted. *Expenses: Tuition, area resident:* Full-time 12,000 euros. Tuition and fees vary according to degree level, program and student level. *Financial support:* In 2015–16, 39 students received support. Fellowships, career-related internships or fieldwork, scholarships/grants, health care benefits, and tuition waivers (full and partial) available. Financial award application deadline: 2/4. *Faculty research:* Algebra, algebraic geometry, bioinformatics, calculus of variations, computational biology, cryptography, discrete mathematics, evolutions equations, fluid mechanics, geometry, number theory, numerical analysis, optimization, ordinary and partial differential equations, probability theory, quantum mechanics, statistics, stochastic processes. *Unit head:* Dr. Karoly Boroczky, Head, 36 1 327-3053, E-mail: mathematics@ceu.edu. *Application contact:* Zsuzsanna Jaszberenyi, Admissions Officer, 361-324-3009, Fax: 367-327-3211, E-mail: admissions@ceu.edu.
Website: http://mathematics.ceu.hu/

Central Michigan University, College of Graduate Studies, College of Science and Technology, Department of Mathematics, Mount Pleasant, MI 48859. Offers mathematics (MA, PhD), including teaching of college mathematics (PhD). *Program availability:* Part-time. *Degree requirements:* For master's, thesis or alternative; for doctorate, thesis/dissertation. *Entrance requirements:* For master's, minimum GPA of 2.7, 20 hours of course work in mathematics; for doctorate, GRE, minimum GPA of 3.0, 20 hours of course work in mathematics. Electronic applications accepted. *Faculty research:* Combinatorics, approximation theory, applied mathematics, statistics, functional analysis and operator theory.

Central Washington University, Graduate Studies and Research, College of the Sciences, Department of Mathematics, Ellensburg, WA 98926. Offers MAT. Program offered during summer only. *Degree requirements:* For master's, thesis or alternative. *Entrance requirements:* For master's, minimum GPA of 3.0. Additional exam requirements/recommendations for international students: Required—TOEFL (minimum score 550 paper-based; 79 iBT). Electronic applications accepted.

Chicago State University, School of Graduate and Professional Studies, College of Arts and Sciences, Department of Mathematics and Computer Science, Chicago, IL 60628. Offers computer science (MS); mathematics (MS). *Degree requirements:* For master's, thesis optional, oral exam. *Entrance requirements:* For master's, minimum GPA of 2.75.

City College of the City University of New York, Graduate School, Division of Science, Department of Mathematics, New York, NY 10031-9198. Offers MS. *Program availability:* Part-time. *Degree requirements:* For master's, one foreign language. *Entrance requirements:* Additional exam requirements/recommendations for international students: Required—TOEFL (minimum score 500 paper-based; 61 iBT). *Application deadline:* For fall admission, 5/1 for domestic and international students; for spring admission, 11/15 for domestic and international students. Applications are processed on a rolling basis. Application fee: $125. Electronic applications accepted.

Tuition and fees vary according to course load, degree level and program. *Financial support:* Teaching assistantships, Federal Work-Study, and scholarships/grants available. Support available to part-time students. Financial award application deadline: 5/1; financial award applicants required to submit FAFSA. *Faculty research:* Group theory, number theory, logic, statistics, computational geometry. *Unit head:* Dr. Christian Wolf, Chair, 212-650-5346. *Application contact:* Sean Cleary, Graduate Advisor, 212-650-5122, Fax: 212-862-0004, E-mail: scleary@ccny.cuny.edu.
Website: http://www.ccny.cuny.edu/mathematics

Claremont Graduate University, Graduate Programs, Institute of Mathematical Sciences, Claremont, CA 91711-6160. Offers computational and systems biology (PhD); computational mathematics and numerical analysis (MA, MS); computational science (PhD); engineering and industrial applied mathematics (PhD); mathematics (PhD); operations research and statistics (MA, MS); physical applied mathematics (MA, MS); pure mathematics (MA, MS); scientific computing (MA, MS); systems and control theory (MA, MS). *Program availability:* Part-time. *Faculty:* 6 full-time (1 woman), 2 part-time/adjunct (0 women). *Students:* 74 full-time (19 women), 35 part-time (12 women); includes 23 minority (2 Black or African American, non-Hispanic/Latino; 12 Asian, non-Hispanic/Latino; 8 Hispanic/Latino; 1 Two or more races, non-Hispanic/Latino), 51 international. Average age 30. In 2015, 25 master's, 10 doctorates awarded. Terminal master's awarded for partial completion of doctoral program. *Entrance requirements:* For master's and doctorate, GRE General Test. Additional exam requirements/recommendations for international students: Required—TOEFL (minimum score 75 iBT). *Application deadline:* For fall admission, 2/1 priority date for domestic and international students. Applications are processed on a rolling basis. Application fee: $80. Electronic applications accepted. *Expenses: Tuition, area resident:* Full-time $43,032; part-time $1793 per unit. *Required fees:* $600; $300 per semester. $300 per semester. Tuition and fees vary according to course load and program. *Financial support:* Fellowships, research assistantships, Federal Work-Study, institutionally sponsored loans, scholarships/grants, and tuition waivers (full and partial) available. Support available to part-time students. Financial award application deadline: 2/15; financial award applicants required to submit FAFSA. *Unit head:* Ali Nadim, Director, 909-607-9413, E-mail: ali.nadim@cgu.edu. *Application contact:* Jake Campbell, Assistant Director of Admissions, 909-607-3024, E-mail: jake.campbell@cgu.edu.
Website: http://www.cgu.edu/pages/168.asp

Clark Atlanta University, School of Arts and Sciences, Department of Mathematical Sciences, Atlanta, GA 30314. Offers MS. *Program availability:* Part-time. *Faculty:* 4 full-time (2 women), 2 part-time/adjunct (0 women). *Students:* 8 full-time (6 women), 1 (woman) part-time; includes 5 minority (all Black or African American, non-Hispanic/Latino), 2 international. Average age 30. 16 applicants, 31% accepted, 4 enrolled. In 2015, 4 master's awarded. *Degree requirements:* For master's, one foreign language, thesis optional. *Entrance requirements:* For master's, GRE General Test, minimum GPA of 2.5. Additional exam requirements/recommendations for international students: Required—TOEFL (minimum score 500 paper-based; 61 iBT). *Application deadline:* For fall admission, 4/1 for domestic and international students; for spring admission, 11/1 for domestic and international students. Applications are processed on a rolling basis. Application fee: $40 ($55 for international students). *Expenses: Tuition, area resident:* Full-time $15,498; part-time $861 per credit hour. *Required fees:* $1006; $1006 per unit. Tuition and fees vary according to course load. *Financial support:* Fellowships, scholarships/grants, and unspecified assistantships available. Financial award application deadline: 4/30; financial award applicants required to submit FAFSA. *Faculty research:* Numerical methods for operator equations, ADA language development. *Unit head:* Dr. Charles Pierre, Chairperson, 404-880-8195, E-mail: cpierre@cau.edu. *Application contact:* Graduate Program Admissions, 404-880-8483,
E-mail: graduateadmissions@cau.edu.

Clarkson University, Graduate School, School of Arts and Sciences, Department of Mathematics, Potsdam, NY 13699. Offers MS, PhD. *Program availability:* Part-time. *Faculty:* 15 full-time (5 women), 1 part-time/adjunct (0 women). *Students:* 22 full-time (6 women); includes 1 minority (Asian, non-Hispanic/Latino), 14 international. Average age 30. 14 applicants, 64% accepted, 4 enrolled. In 2015, 8 master's, 1 doctorate awarded. Terminal master's awarded for partial completion of doctoral program. *Degree requirements:* For doctorate, thesis/dissertation, departmental qualifying exam. *Entrance requirements:* For master's and doctorate, GRE, transcripts of all college coursework, resume, personal statement, three letters of recommendation. Additional exam requirements/recommendations for international students: Required—TOEFL or IELTS. *Application deadline:* For fall admission, 1/30 priority date for domestic and international students; for spring admission, 9/1 priority date for domestic and international students. Applications are processed on a rolling basis. Application fee: $25 ($35 for international students). Electronic applications accepted. *Financial support:* In 2015–16, 21 students received support, including fellowships with full tuition reimbursements available (averaging $24,510 per year), 4 research assistantships with full tuition reimbursements available (averaging $24,510 per year), 16 teaching assistantships with full tuition reimbursements available (averaging $24,510 per year); scholarships/grants, tuition waivers (partial), and unspecified assistantships also available. *Faculty research:* Hierarchical scales, balanced motions, LIDAR System, reduced order basis. *Total annual research expenditures:* $779,611. *Unit head:* Dr. Jospeh Skufca, Chair, 315-268-2399, Fax: 315-268-2371,
E-mail: jskufca@clarkson.edu. *Application contact:* Jennifer Reed, Graduate School Coordinator, Provost's Office, 315-268-3802, Fax: 315-268-3989,
E-mail: sciencegrad@clarkson.edu.
Website: http://www.clarkson.edu/math/

Clemson University, Graduate School, College of Science, Department of Mathematical Sciences, Clemson, SC 29634. Offers MS, PhD. *Program availability:* Part-time. *Faculty:* 74 full-time (29 women), 12 part-time/adjunct (7 women). *Students:* 107 full-time (43 women), 2 part-time (both women); includes 5 minority (1 Black or African American, non-Hispanic/Latino; 1 Asian, non-Hispanic/Latino; 2 Hispanic/Latino; 1 Two or more races, non-Hispanic/Latino), 51 international. Average age 27. 124 applicants, 74% accepted, 17 enrolled. In 2015, 30 master's, 11 doctorates awarded. *Degree requirements:* For master's, thesis or alternative; for doctorate, comprehensive exam, thesis/dissertation, 3 qualifying exams. *Entrance requirements:* For master's and doctorate, GRE General Test, GRE Subject Test (mathematics), unofficial transcripts, letters of recommendation, statement of purpose. Additional exam requirements/recommendations for international students: Required—TOEFL (minimum score 90 iBT), IELTS (minimum score 6.5). *Application deadline:* For fall admission, 1/15 priority date for domestic and international students; for spring admission, 10/1 priority date for domestic students, 9/15 priority date for international students. Applications are processed on a rolling basis. Application fee: $80 ($90 for international students). Electronic applications accepted. *Expenses:* $4,610 per semester full-time resident, $9,203 per semester full-time non-resident, $582 per credit hour part-time resident, $1,166 per credit hour part-time non-resident. *Financial support:* In 2015–16, 100 students received support, including 3 fellowships with partial tuition reimbursements available (averaging $3,333 per year), 5 research assistantships with partial tuition reimbursements available (averaging $19,141 per year), 71 teaching assistantships with partial tuition reimbursements available (averaging $21,878 per year); career-related internships or fieldwork, health care benefits, and unspecified assistantships also available. Financial award application deadline: 1/15. *Faculty research:* Pure and applied analysis, algebra and discrete mathematics, computational mathematics, operations research, statistics. *Total annual research expenditures:* $852,523. *Unit head:* Dr. Chris Cox, Interim Department Chair, 864-656-0862,
E-mail: clcox@clemson.edu. *Application contact:* Dr. Kevin James, Graduate Coordinator, 864-656-1516, Fax: 864-656-5230, E-mail: mthgrad@clemson.edu.
Website: http://www.clemson.edu/ces/departments/math/academics/index.html

Cleveland State University, College of Graduate Studies, College of Sciences and Health Professions, Department of Mathematics, Cleveland, OH 44115. Offers applied statistics (MS); mathematics (MS). *Program availability:* Part-time, evening/weekend. *Faculty:* 17 full-time (7 women), 1 part-time/adjunct (0 women). *Students:* 24 full-time (13 women), 21 part-time (12 women); includes 2 minority (1 Asian, non-Hispanic/Latino; 1 Hispanic/Latino), 17 international. Average age 31. 30 applicants, 87% accepted, 13 enrolled. In 2015, 19 master's awarded. *Degree requirements:* For master's, thesis, exit project. *Entrance requirements:* Additional exam requirements/recommendations for international students: Required—TOEFL (minimum score 550 paper-based; 78 iBT). *Application deadline:* For fall admission, 7/1 priority date for domestic students, 6/15 priority date for international students; for spring admission, 11/15 for domestic students, 11/1 for international students; for summer admission, 4/1 for domestic students, 3/15 for international students. Applications are processed on a rolling basis. Application fee: $30. Electronic applications accepted. *Expenses:* Tuition, state resident: full-time $9565. Tuition, nonresident: full-time $17,980. Tuition and fees vary according to program. *Financial support:* In 2015–16, 14 students received support, including 9 teaching assistantships with full tuition reimbursements available (averaging $21,115 per year); unspecified assistantships also available. Financial award application deadline: 3/15. *Faculty research:* Algebraic topology, algebraic geometry, statistics, mathematical biology, applied mathematics. *Total annual research expenditures:* $132,202. *Unit head:* Dr. John Peter Holcomb, Jr., Chairperson/Professor, 216-687-4681, Fax: 216-523-7340, E-mail: j.p.holcomb@csuohio.edu. *Application contact:* Dr. John F. Oprea, Graduate Program Coordinator, 216-687-4702, Fax: 216-523-7340, E-mail: j.oprea@csuohio.edu.
Website: http://www.csuohio.edu/sciences/dept/mathematics/

The College at Brockport, State University of New York, School of Education and Human Services, Department of Education and Human Development, Program in Inclusive Generalist Education, Brockport, NY 14420-2997. Offers biology (MS Ed, AGC); chemistry (MS Ed, AGC); English (MS Ed, Advanced Certificate); mathematics (MS Ed, Advanced Certificate); science (MS Ed, Advanced Certificate); social studies (MS Ed, Advanced Certificate). *Students:* 27 full-time (16 women), 24 part-time (16 women); includes 13 minority (4 Black or African American, non-Hispanic/Latino; 3 Asian, non-Hispanic/Latino; 2 Hispanic/Latino; 4 Two or more races, non-Hispanic/Latino). 23 applicants, 57% accepted, 10 enrolled. In 2015, 13 master's, 1 AGC awarded. *Degree requirements:* For master's, thesis or alternative. *Entrance requirements:* For master's, minimum GPA of 3.0, letters of recommendation, statement of objectives, academic major (or equivalent) in program discipline, current resume. Additional exam requirements/recommendations for international students: Required—TOEFL (minimum score 550 paper-based; 79 iBT), IELTS (minimum score 6.5). *Application deadline:* For fall admission, 3/15 priority date for domestic and international students; for spring admission, 10/15 priority date for domestic and international students; for summer admission, 3/15 for domestic and international students. Application fee: $80. Electronic applications accepted. *Expenses:* $11,840 per academic year. *Financial support:* Federal Work-Study, scholarships/grants, and unspecified assistantships available. Support available to part-time students. Financial award application deadline: 3/15; financial award applicants required to submit FAFSA. *Unit head:* Dr. Sue Robb, Chairperson, 585-395-5935, Fax: 585-395-2171,
E-mail: awalton@brockport.edu. *Application contact:* Anne Walton, Coordinator of Certification and Graduate Advisement, 585-395-2326, Fax: 585-395-2172,
E-mail: awalton@brockport.edu.
Website: http://www.brockport.edu/ehd/

The College at Brockport, State University of New York, School of Science and Mathematics, Department of Mathematics, Brockport, NY 14420-2997. Offers MA. *Program availability:* Part-time. *Faculty:* 9 full-time (4 women). *Students:* 6 full-time (3 women), 7 part-time (1 woman); includes 4 minority (1 Black or African American, non-Hispanic/Latino; 1 Asian, non-Hispanic/Latino; 2 Two or more races, non-Hispanic/Latino). 11 applicants, 73% accepted, 2 enrolled. In 2015, 8 master's awarded. *Degree requirements:* For master's, comprehensive exam. *Entrance requirements:* For master's, minimum GPA of 3.0, letters of recommendation, statement of objectives. Additional exam requirements/recommendations for international students: Required—TOEFL (minimum score 550 paper-based; 79 iBT), IELTS (minimum score 6.5). *Application deadline:* For fall admission, 4/15 priority date for domestic and international students; for spring admission, 11/15 priority date for domestic and international students; for summer admission, 4/15 for domestic and international students. Application fee: $50. Electronic applications accepted. *Expenses:* $11,840 per academic year. *Financial support:* In 2015–16, 4 teaching assistantships with full tuition reimbursements (averaging $6,000 per year) were awarded; Federal Work-Study, scholarships/grants, and unspecified assistantships also available. Support available to part-time students. Financial award application deadline: 3/15; financial award applicants required to submit FAFSA. *Faculty research:* Mathematical modeling, dynamical systems, complex/functional analysis, graph theory and combinations, algebra and number theory. *Unit head:* Dr. Mihail Barbosu, Chairperson, 585-395-5675, Fax: 585-395-2304, E-mail: mbarbosu@brockport.edu. *Application contact:* Dr. Howard Skogman, Graduate Director, 585-395-2046, Fax: 585-395-2304,
E-mail: hskogman@brockport.edu.
Website: http://www.brockport.edu/math/grad/

College of Charleston, Graduate School, School of Sciences and Mathematics, Program in Mathematics, Charleston, SC 29424-0001. Offers mathematics (MS). *Program availability:* Part-time, evening/weekend. *Degree requirements:* For master's, thesis optional. *Entrance requirements:* For master's, GRE, BS in mathematics or equivalent, 2 letters of recommendation. Additional exam requirements/recommendations for international students: Required—TOEFL (minimum score 81 iBT). Electronic applications accepted. *Faculty research:* Algebra, dynamical systems, probability, analysis and topology, combinatorics.

Colorado State University, College of Natural Sciences, Department of Mathematics, Fort Collins, CO 80523-1874. Offers MS, PhD. *Program availability:* Part-time. *Faculty:* 20 full-time (7 women), 1 part-time/adjunct (0 women). *Students:* 38 full-time (11 women), 14 part-time (5 women); includes 7 minority (2 Asian, non-Hispanic/Latino; 3 Hispanic/Latino; 2 Two or more races, non-Hispanic/Latino), 9 international. Average age 28. 121 applicants, 39% accepted, 18 enrolled. In 2015, 5 master's, 11 doctorates awarded. Terminal master's awarded for partial completion of doctoral program. *Degree requirements:* For master's, comprehensive exam (for some programs), thesis or alternative; for doctorate, comprehensive exam, thesis/dissertation. *Entrance*

requirements: For master's and doctorate, GRE, minimum GPA of 3.0. Additional exam requirements/recommendations for international students: Required—TOEFL (minimum score 550 paper-based; 80 iBT); Recommended—IELTS (minimum score 6.5). *Application deadline:* For fall admission, 2/1 priority date for domestic and international students; for spring admission, 9/1 priority date for domestic and international students. Application fee: $60 ($70 for international students). Electronic applications accepted. *Expenses:* Tuition, state resident: full-time $9348. Tuition, nonresident: full-time $22,916. *Required fees:* $2174; $473.72 per credit hour. $236.86 per semester. Tuition and fees vary according to course load and program. *Financial support:* In 2015–16, 2 fellowships with full tuition reimbursements (averaging $54,750 per year), 9 research assistantships with full tuition reimbursements (averaging $19,187 per year), 40 teaching assistantships with full tuition reimbursements (averaging $18,825 per year) were awarded; scholarships/grants also available. Financial award application deadline: 2/1. *Faculty research:* Applied analysis; differential equations and dynamical systems; inverse problems and control theory; computational algebra, combinatorics and number theory; topology, computational geometry and data science. *Total annual research expenditures:* $1.4 million. *Unit head:* Dr. Gerhard Dangelmayr, Department Chair, 970-491-6452, Fax: 970-491-2161, E-mail: gerhard@math.colostate.edu. *Application contact:* Bryan Elder, Graduate Program Coordinator, 970-491-7925, Fax: 970-491-2161, E-mail: elder@math.colostate.edu.
Website: http://www.math.colostate.edu/

Columbia University, Graduate School of Arts and Sciences, New York, NY 10027. Offers African-American studies (MA); American studies (MA); anthropology (MA, PhD); art history and archaeology (MA, PhD); astronomy (PhD); biological sciences (PhD); biotechnology (MA); chemical physics (PhD); chemistry (PhD); classical studies (MA, PhD); classics (MA, PhD); climate and society (MA); conservation biology (MA); earth and environmental sciences (PhD); East Asia: regional studies (MA); East Asian languages and cultures (MA, PhD); ecology, evolution and environmental biology (MA), including conservation biology; ecology, evolution, and environmental biology (PhD), including ecology and evolutionary biology, evolutionary primatology; economics (MA, PhD); English and comparative literature (MA, PhD); French and Romance philology (MA, PhD); Germanic languages (MA, PhD); global French studies (MA); global thought (MA); Hispanic cultural studies (MA); history (PhD); history and literature (MA); human rights studies (MA); Islamic studies (MA); Italian (MA, PhD); Japanese pedagogy (MA); Jewish studies (MA); Latin America and the Caribbean: regional studies (MA); Latin American and Iberian cultures (PhD); mathematics (MA, PhD), including finance (MA); medieval and Renaissance studies (MA); Middle Eastern, South Asian, and African studies (MA, PhD); modern art: critical and curatorial studies (MA); modern European studies (MA); museum anthropology (MA); music (DMA, PhD); oral history (MA); philosophical foundations of physics (MA); philosophy (MA, PhD); physics (PhD); political science (MA, PhD); psychology (PhD); quantitative methods in the social sciences (MA); religion (MA, PhD); Russia, Eurasia and East Europe: regional studies (MA); Russian translation (MA); Slavic cultures (MA); Slavic languages (MA, PhD); sociology (MA, PhD); South Asian studies (MA); statistics (MA, PhD); theatre (PhD). Dual-degree programs require admission to both Graduate School of Arts and Sciences and another Columbia school. *Program availability:* Part-time. *Students:* 3,030 full-time, 235 part-time; includes 861 minority (88 Black or African American, non-Hispanic/Latino; 5 American Indian or Alaska Native, non-Hispanic/Latino; 517 Asian, non-Hispanic/Latino; 159 Hispanic/Latino; 4 Native Hawaiian or other Pacific Islander, non-Hispanic/Latino; 88 Two or more races, non-Hispanic/Latino), 1,697 international. 13,288 applicants, 21% accepted, 1162 enrolled. In 2015, 1,061 master's, 553 doctorates awarded. Terminal master's awarded for partial completion of doctoral program. *Degree requirements:* For master's, variable foreign language requirement, comprehensive exam (for some programs), thesis (for some programs); for doctorate, variable foreign language requirement, comprehensive exam (for some programs), thesis/dissertation. *Entrance requirements:* For master's and doctorate, GRE General Test, GRE Subject Test (for some programs). Additional exam requirements/recommendations for international students: Required—TOEFL, IELTS. Application fee: $105. Electronic applications accepted. *Financial support:* Fellowships, research assistantships, teaching assistantships, career-related internships or fieldwork, Federal Work-Study, institutionally sponsored loans, scholarships/grants, traineeships, health care benefits, tuition waivers, and unspecified assistantships available. Support available to part-time students. Financial award application deadline: 12/15. *Unit head:* Carlos J. Alonso, Dean of the Graduate School of Arts and Sciences, 212-854-5177. *Application contact:* GSAS Office of Admissions, 212-854-8903, E-mail: gsas-admissions@columbia.edu.
Website: http://gsas.columbia.edu/

Columbus State University, Graduate Studies, College of Education and Health Professions, Department of Teacher Education, Columbus, GA 31907-5645. Offers curriculum and instruction in accomplished teaching (M Ed); early childhood education (M Ed, MAT, Ed S); middle grades education (M Ed, MAT, Ed S); secondary education (M Ed, MAT, Ed S), including biology (MAT), chemistry (MAT), earth and space science (MAT), English/language arts, general science (M Ed), history (MAT), mathematics, science (Ed S), social science (M Ed, Ed S); special education (M Ed, MAT, Ed S), including general curriculum (M Ed, MAT); teacher leadership (M Ed). *Accreditation:* NCATE. *Program availability:* Part-time, evening/weekend, 100% online, blended/hybrid learning. *Faculty:* 15 full-time (10 women), 26 part-time/adjunct (21 women). *Students:* 84 full-time (68 women), 199 part-time (153 women); includes 106 minority (96 Black or African American, non-Hispanic/Latino; 3 Asian, non-Hispanic/Latino; 5 Hispanic/Latino; 2 Two or more races, non-Hispanic/Latino), 6 international. Average age 35. 174 applicants, 62% accepted, 81 enrolled. In 2015, 74 master's, 10 other advanced degrees awarded. *Degree requirements:* For Ed S, thesis or alternative. *Entrance requirements:* For master's, GRE General Test, minimum undergraduate GPA of 2.75; for Ed S, GRE General Test, minimum undergraduate GPA of 2.75, graduate 3.0. Additional exam requirements/recommendations for international students: Required—TOEFL (minimum score 550 paper-based; 79 iBT). *Application deadline:* For fall admission, 6/30 for domestic students, 5/1 for international students; for spring admission, 11/1 for domestic and international students; for summer admission, 3/1 for domestic and international students. Applications are processed on a rolling basis. Application fee: $50. Electronic applications accepted. *Expenses:* Tuition, state resident: full-time $4804; part-time $2412 per semester hour. Tuition, nonresident: full-time $19,218; part-time $9612 per semester hour. *Required fees:* $1830; $1830 per unit. Tuition and fees vary according to program. *Financial support:* In 2015–16, 203 students received support, including 22 research assistantships with partial tuition reimbursements available (averaging $3,000 per year); career-related internships or fieldwork, Federal Work-Study, institutionally sponsored loans, scholarships/grants, tuition waivers (partial), and unspecified assistantships also available. Support available to part-time students. Financial award application deadline: 5/1; financial award applicants required to submit FAFSA. *Unit head:* Dr. Jan Burcham, Department Chair, 706-507-8519, Fax: 706-568-3134, E-mail: burcham_jan@columbusstate.edu. *Application contact:* Kristin Williams, Director of International and Graduate Recruitment, 706-507-8848, Fax: 706-568-5091, E-mail: williams_kristin@columbusstate.edu.
Website: http://te.columbusstate.edu/

Concordia University, School of Graduate Studies, Faculty of Arts and Science, Department of Mathematics and Statistics, Montréal, QC H3G 1M8, Canada. Offers mathematics (PhD); mathematics and statistics (M Sc, MA); teaching of mathematics (MTM). *Degree requirements:* For master's, thesis optional; for doctorate, comprehensive exam, thesis/dissertation. *Entrance requirements:* For master's, honors degree in mathematics or equivalent. *Application deadline:* For fall admission, 5/1 for domestic students; for winter admission, 3/31 for domestic students; for spring admission, 10/31 for domestic students. Application fee: $50. Tuition and fees vary according to course load, degree level and program. *Financial support:* Fellowships, research assistantships, and teaching assistantships available. Financial award application deadline: 2/1. *Faculty research:* Number theory, computational algebra, mathematical physics, differential geometry, dynamical systems and statistics. *Unit head:* Dr. Nadia Hardy, Chair, 514-848-2424 Ext. 3235, Fax: 514-848-2831. *Application contact:* Dr. Hal Proppe, Associate Chair, 514-848-3257 Ext. 3217, Fax: 514-848-2831.
Website: http://www.concordia.ca/artsci/math-stats.html

Cornell University, Graduate School, Graduate Fields of Arts and Sciences, Field of Mathematics, Ithaca, NY 14853-0001. Offers PhD. *Degree requirements:* For doctorate, one foreign language, comprehensive exam, thesis/dissertation, teaching experience. *Entrance requirements:* For doctorate, GRE General Test, GRE Subject Test (mathematics), 3 letters of recommendation. Additional exam requirements/recommendations for international students: Required—TOEFL (minimum score 600 paper-based; 95 iBT). Electronic applications accepted. *Faculty research:* Analysis, dynamical systems, Lie theory, logic, topology and geometry.

Dalhousie University, Faculty of Science, Department of Mathematics and Statistics, Program in Mathematics, Halifax, NS B3H 4R2, Canada. Offers M Sc, PhD. *Degree requirements:* For master's, thesis; for doctorate, thesis/dissertation. *Entrance requirements:* Additional exam requirements/recommendations for international students: Required—TOEFL, IELTS, CANTEST, CAEL, or Michigan English Language Assessment Battery. Electronic applications accepted. *Faculty research:* Applied mathematics, category theory, algebra, analysis, graph theory.

Dartmouth College, Arts and Sciences Graduate Programs, Department of Mathematics, Hanover, NH 03755. Offers AM, PhD. *Faculty:* 18 full-time (4 women), 4 part-time/adjunct (1 woman). *Students:* 27 full-time (8 women); includes 2 minority (1 Black or African American, non-Hispanic/Latino; 1 Two or more races, non-Hispanic/Latino), 5 international. Average age 26. 91 applicants, 23% accepted, 6 enrolled. In 2015, 4 master's, 5 doctorates awarded. Terminal master's awarded for partial completion of doctoral program. *Degree requirements:* For master's, comprehensive exam; for doctorate, 2 foreign languages, thesis/dissertation, teaching of three classes. *Entrance requirements:* For doctorate, GRE General Test, GRE Subject Test. Additional exam requirements/recommendations for international students: Required—TOEFL. *Application deadline:* For fall admission, 2/15 priority date for domestic students. Application fee: $25. Electronic applications accepted. *Expenses: Tuition, area resident:* Full-time $48,120. *Required fees:* $296. One-time fee: $50 full-time. *Financial support:* Fellowships with full tuition reimbursements, research assistantships with full tuition reimbursements, teaching assistantships with full tuition reimbursements, institutionally sponsored loans, scholarships/grants, tuition waivers (full), and unspecified assistantships available. *Faculty research:* Mathematical logic, set theory, combinations, number theory. *Unit head:* Dr. Dana P. Williams, Chair, 603-646-2990, Fax: 603-646-1312. *Application contact:* Traci Flynn-Moloney, Department Administrator, 603-646-3723, Fax: 603-646-1312.
Website: http://math.dartmouth.edu/

Delaware State University, Graduate Programs, Department of Mathematics, Program in Mathematics, Dover, DE 19901-2277. Offers MS. *Entrance requirements:* Additional exam requirements/recommendations for international students: Required—TOEFL (minimum score 550 paper-based). Electronic applications accepted.

DePaul University, College of Science and Health, Chicago, IL 60614. Offers applied mathematics (MS); applied statistics (MS); biological sciences (MA, MS); chemistry (MS); mathematics education (MA); mathematics for teaching (MS); nursing (MS); nursing practice (DNP); physics (MS); psychology (MS); pure mathematics (MS); science education (MS); MA/PhD. Electronic applications accepted.

Drew University, Caspersen School of Graduate Studies, Madison, NJ 07940-1493. Offers conflict resolution and leadership (Certificate), including community leadership, moderation, peace building; history and culture (MA, PhD), including American history, book history, British history, European history, Holocaust and genocide (M Litt, MA, D Litt, PhD), intellectual history, Irish history, print culture, public history; K-12 education (MAT), including art, biology, chemistry, elementary education, English, French, Italian, math, secondary education, special education, teacher of students with disabilities; k-12 education (MAT), including art, biology, chemistry, elementary education, English, French, Italian, math, secondary education, special education, teacher of students with disabilities; liberal studies (M Litt, D Litt), including history, Holocaust and genocide (M Litt, MA, D Litt, PhD), Irish/Irish-American studies, literature (M Litt, MMH, D Litt, DMH, CMH), religion, spirituality, teaching in the two-year college, writing; medical humanities (MMH, DMH, CMH), including arts, health, healthcare, literature (M Litt, MMH, D Litt, DMH, CMH), scientific research; poetry and poetry in translation (MFA). *Program availability:* Part-time, evening/weekend. *Faculty:* 1 full-time, 26 part-time/adjunct. *Students:* 125 full-time (82 women), 261 part-time (164 women); includes 34 minority (17 Black or African American, non-Hispanic/Latino; 6 Asian, non-Hispanic/Latino; 11 Hispanic/Latino), 6 international. Average age 42. 120 applicants, 90% accepted, 76 enrolled. In 2015, 54 master's, 36 doctorates, 9 other advanced degrees awarded. Terminal master's awarded for partial completion of doctoral program. *Degree requirements:* For master's and other advanced degree, thesis (for some programs); for doctorate, one foreign language, comprehensive exam (for some programs), thesis/dissertation. *Entrance requirements:* For master's, GRE (MA in history and culture), PRAXIS Core and Subject Area tests (MAT), resume, transcripts, writing sample, personal statement, letters of recommendation; for doctorate, GRE (PhD in history and culture), resume, transcripts, writing sample, personal statement, letters of recommendation. Additional exam requirements/recommendations for international students: Required—TOEFL (minimum score 587 paper-based; 94 iBT), IELTS (minimum score 7), TWE (minimum score 4). *Application deadline:* Applications are processed on a rolling basis. Application fee: $35. Tuition and fees vary according to program. *Financial support:* In 2015–16, 214 students received support. Fellowships, research assistantships, teaching assistantships, career-related internships or fieldwork, Federal Work-Study, scholarships/grants, and unspecified assistantships available. Support available to part-time students. Financial award applicants required to submit FAFSA. *Unit head:* Dr. Robert Ready, Dean, 973-408-3285, Fax: 973-408-3040, E-mail: gsdean@drew.edu. *Application contact:* Leanne Horinko, Interim-Director of Admissions, 973-408-3110, Fax: 973-408-3110, E-mail: gradm@drew.edu.
Website: http://www.drew.edu/graduate

Drexel University, College of Arts and Sciences, Department of Mathematics, Program in Mathematics, Philadelphia, PA 19104-2875. Offers MS, PhD. *Degree requirements:*

For doctorate, one foreign language, thesis/dissertation. *Entrance requirements:* For master's and doctorate, GRE. Additional exam requirements/recommendations for international students: Required—TOEFL. Electronic applications accepted.

Duke University, Graduate School, Department of Mathematics, Durham, NC 27708. Offers PhD. *Degree requirements:* For doctorate, 2 foreign languages, thesis/dissertation. *Entrance requirements:* For doctorate, GRE General Test, GRE Subject Test. Additional exam requirements/recommendations for international students: Required—TOEFL (minimum score 577 paper-based; 90 iBT) or IELTS (minimum score 7). Electronic applications accepted.

Duquesne University, Graduate School of Liberal Arts, Program in Computational Mathematics, Pittsburgh, PA 15282-0001. Offers MA, MS. *Faculty:* 26 full-time (8 women), 11 part-time/adjunct (5 women). *Students:* 10 full-time (2 women), 1 part-time (0 women); includes 1 minority (Asian, non-Hispanic/Latino), 2 international. Average age 26. 26 applicants, 54% accepted, 4 enrolled. In 2015, 7 master's awarded. *Degree requirements:* For master's, thesis. *Entrance requirements:* For master's, GRE General Test. Additional exam requirements/recommendations for international students: Required—TOEFL. *Application deadline:* For fall admission, 8/1 for domestic students, 5/1 for international students. Applications are processed on a rolling basis. Application fee: $0. Electronic applications accepted. *Expenses:* $1,189 per credit. *Financial support:* In 2015–16, 5 teaching assistantships with full tuition reimbursements (averaging $10,000 per year) were awarded; Federal Work-Study, institutionally sponsored loans, scholarships/grants, and unspecified assistantships also available. Financial award application deadline: 5/1. *Unit head:* Dr. John Kern, Chair, 412-396-6468. *Application contact:* Linda Rendulic, Assistant to the Dean, 412-396-6400, Fax: 412-396-5197, E-mail: rendulic@duq.edu.
Website: http://www.duq.edu/academics/schools/liberal-arts/graduate-school/programs/computational-math

East Carolina University, Graduate School, Thomas Harriot College of Arts and Sciences, Department of Mathematics, Greenville, NC 27858-4353. Offers mathematics (MA); mathematics in the community college (MA); statistics (MA, Certificate). *Program availability:* Part-time, evening/weekend. *Students:* 8 full-time (3 women), 3 part-time (0 women); includes 1 minority (Black or African American, non-Hispanic/Latino), 1 international. Average age 26. 7 applicants, 100% accepted, 3 enrolled. In 2015, 2 master's awarded. *Degree requirements:* For master's, comprehensive exam. *Entrance requirements:* For master's, GRE General Test, MAT. Additional exam requirements/recommendations for international students: Required—TOEFL. *Application deadline:* For fall admission, 6/1 for domestic students; for spring admission, 10/15 for domestic students. Applications are processed on a rolling basis. Application fee: $50. *Financial support:* Research assistantships with partial tuition reimbursements and teaching assistantships with partial tuition reimbursements available. Financial award application deadline: 6/1. *Unit head:* Dr. Johannes H. Hattingh, Chair, 252-328-6461, E-mail: hattinghj@ecu.edu. *Application contact:* Dean of Graduate School, 252-328-6012, Fax: 252-328-6071, E-mail: gradschool@ecu.edu.
Website: http://www.ecu.edu/cs-cas/math/graduateprogram.cfm

Eastern Illinois University, Graduate School, College of Sciences, Department of Mathematics and Computer Science, Charleston, IL 61920. Offers elementary/middle school mathematics education (MA); mathematics (MA). *Program availability:* Part-time, evening/weekend. *Degree requirements:* For master's, comprehensive exam (for some programs), thesis (for some programs). *Entrance requirements:* For master's, GMAT or GRE. Additional exam requirements/recommendations for international students: Required—TOEFL (minimum score 500 paper-based; 61 iBT), IELTS (minimum score 6). Electronic applications accepted.

Eastern Kentucky University, The Graduate School, College of Arts and Sciences, Department of Mathematics and Statistics, Richmond, KY 40475-3102. Offers mathematical sciences (MS). *Program availability:* Part-time. *Degree requirements:* For master's, comprehensive exam. *Entrance requirements:* For master's, GRE General Test, minimum GPA of 2.5. *Faculty research:* Graph theory, number theory, ring theory, topology, statistics, Abstract Algebra.

Eastern Michigan University, Graduate School, College of Arts and Sciences, Department of Mathematics, Ypsilanti, MI 48197. Offers MA. *Program availability:* Part-time, evening/weekend, online learning. *Faculty:* 23 full-time (9 women). *Students:* 8 full-time (5 women), 21 part-time (13 women); includes 6 minority (1 Black or African American, non-Hispanic/Latino; 3 Asian, non-Hispanic/Latino; 1 Hispanic/Latino; 1 Two or more races, non-Hispanic/Latino), 2 international. Average age 30. 32 applicants, 72% accepted, 10 enrolled. In 2015, 10 master's awarded. *Degree requirements:* For master's, thesis optional. *Entrance requirements:* Additional exam requirements/recommendations for international students: Required—TOEFL. *Application deadline:* Applications are processed on a rolling basis. Application fee: $45. *Financial support:* Fellowships, research assistantships with full tuition reimbursements, teaching assistantships with full tuition reimbursements, career-related internships or fieldwork, Federal Work-Study, institutionally sponsored loans, scholarships/grants, tuition waivers (partial), and unspecified assistantships available. Support available to part-time students. Financial award applicants required to submit FAFSA. *Unit head:* Dr. Christopher Gardiner, Department Head, 734-487-1444, Fax: 734-487-2489, E-mail: cgardiner@emich.edu. *Application contact:* Dr. Bingwu Wang, Graduate Advisor, 734-487-5044, Fax: 734-487-2489, E-mail: bwang@emich.edu.
Website: http://www.math.emich.edu

Eastern Washington University, Graduate Studies, College of Science, Health and Engineering, Department of Mathematics, Cheney, WA 99004-2431. Offers mathematics (MS); teaching mathematics (MA). *Program availability:* Part-time. *Degree requirements:* For master's, comprehensive exam, thesis (for some programs). *Entrance requirements:* For master's, GRE General Test, departmental qualifying exam, minimum GPA of 3.0.

East Tennessee State University, School of Graduate Studies, College of Arts and Sciences, Department of Mathematics and Statistics, Johnson City, TN 37614. Offers mathematical sciences (MS). *Program availability:* Part-time, evening/weekend. *Faculty:* 12 full-time (5 women). *Students:* 27 full-time (6 women), 3 part-time (0 women); includes 5 minority (1 Black or African American, non-Hispanic/Latino; 2 Asian, non-Hispanic/Latino; 1 Hispanic/Latino; 1 Two or more races, non-Hispanic/Latino), 13 international. Average age 28. 33 applicants, 73% accepted, 13 enrolled. In 2015, 9 master's awarded. *Degree requirements:* For master's, comprehensive exam, thesis. *Entrance requirements:* For master's, GRE General Test, bachelor's degree in math or related area, three letters of recommendation. Additional exam requirements/recommendations for international students: Required—TOEFL (minimum score 550 paper-based; 79 iBT). *Application deadline:* For fall admission, 6/1 for domestic students, 4/30 for international students; for spring admission, 11/1 for domestic students, 11/30 for international students. Application fee: $35 ($45 for international students). Electronic applications accepted. *Financial support:* In 2015–16, 18 students received support, including 1 research assistantship with full tuition reimbursement available (averaging $7,000 per year), 18 teaching assistantships with tuition reimbursements available (averaging $8,300 per year); career-related internships or fieldwork, institutionally sponsored loans, scholarships/grants, unspecified assistantships, and laboratory assistantships also available. Financial award application deadline: 7/1; financial award applicants required to submit FAFSA. *Faculty research:* Applied mathematics, applied statistics, discrete mathematics, graph theory, mathematics education, mathematical epidemiology, probability. *Unit head:* Dr. Robert Price, Chair, 423-439-4349, Fax: 423-439-8361, E-mail: pricejr@etsu.edu. *Application contact:* Kimberly Brockman, Graduate Specialist, 423-439-6165, Fax: 423-439-5624, E-mail: brockmank@etsu.edu.
Website: http://www.etsu.edu/cas/math/

Elizabeth City State University, School of Mathematics, Science and Technology, Master of Science in Mathematics Program, Elizabeth City, NC 27909-7806. Offers applied mathematics (MS); community college teaching (MS); mathematics education (MS); remote sensing (MS). *Program availability:* Part-time, evening/weekend. *Degree requirements:* For master's, thesis. *Entrance requirements:* For master's, MAT and/or GRE, minimum GPA of 3.0, 3 letters of recommendation, two official transcripts from all undergraduate/graduate schools attended, typewritten one-page request for entry into program that includes description of student's educational preparation. Additional exam requirements/recommendations for international students: Required—TOEFL (minimum score 550 paper-based, 80 iBT) or IELTS (minimum score 6.5). Electronic applications accepted. *Faculty research:* Oceanic temperature effects, mathematics strategies in elementary schools, multimedia, Antarctic temperature mapping, computer networks, water quality, remote sensing, polar ice, satellite imagery.

Emory University, Laney Graduate School, Department of Mathematics and Computer Science, Atlanta, GA 30322-1100. Offers computer science (MS); computer science and informatics (PhD); mathematics (MS, PhD). Terminal master's awarded for partial completion of doctoral program. *Degree requirements:* For master's, thesis; for doctorate, one foreign language, comprehensive exam, thesis/dissertation. *Entrance requirements:* For master's and doctorate, GRE General Test. Additional exam requirements/recommendations for international students: Recommended—TOEFL. Electronic applications accepted.

Emporia State University, Department of Mathematics and Economics, Emporia, KS 66801-5415. Offers mathematics (MS). *Program availability:* Part-time, evening/weekend, online learning. *Faculty:* 14 full-time (3 women). *Students:* 15 full-time (9 women), 112 part-time (53 women); includes 18 minority (5 Black or African American, non-Hispanic/Latino; 3 Asian, non-Hispanic/Latino; 6 Hispanic/Latino; 1 Native Hawaiian or other Pacific Islander, non-Hispanic/Latino; 3 Two or more races, non-Hispanic/Latino), 9 international. 39 applicants, 79% accepted, 25 enrolled. In 2015, 14 master's awarded. *Degree requirements:* For master's, comprehensive exam or thesis. *Entrance requirements:* For master's, appropriate undergraduate degree. Additional exam requirements/recommendations for international students: Required—TOEFL (minimum score 520 paper-based; 68 iBT). *Application deadline:* For fall admission, 8/15 priority date for domestic students. Applications are processed on a rolling basis. Application fee: $30 ($75 for international students). Electronic applications accepted. *Expenses:* Tuition, state resident: full-time $5640; part-time $235 per credit hour. Tuition, nonresident: full-time $17,544; part-time $731 per credit hour. *Required fees:* $1848; $77 per credit hour. *Financial support:* In 2015–16, 5 teaching assistantships with full tuition reimbursements (averaging $7,844 per year) were awarded; research assistantships, career-related internships or fieldwork, Federal Work-Study, institutionally sponsored loans, health care benefits, and unspecified assistantships also available. Financial award application deadline: 3/15; financial award applicants required to submit FAFSA. *Unit head:* Dr. H. Joe Yanik, Chair, 620-341-5281, Fax: 620-341-6055, E-mail: hyanik@emporia.edu. *Application contact:* Mary Sewell, Admissions Coordinator, 800-950-GRAD, Fax: 620-341-5909, E-mail: msewell@emporia.edu.
Website: http://www.emporia.edu/mathcsecon/

Fairfield University, College of Arts and Sciences, Fairfield, CT 06824. Offers American studies (MA); communication (MA); creative writing (MFA); mathematics (MS); public administration (MPA). *Program availability:* Part-time, evening/weekend, online learning. *Faculty:* 16 full-time (10 women), 3 part-time/adjunct (0 women). *Students:* 22 full-time (7 women), 87 part-time (42 women); includes 12 minority (3 Black or African American, non-Hispanic/Latino; 1 Asian, non-Hispanic/Latino; 4 Hispanic/Latino; 1 Native Hawaiian or other Pacific Islander, non-Hispanic/Latino; 3 Two or more races, non-Hispanic/Latino), 10 international. Average age 34. 77 applicants, 69% accepted, 27 enrolled. In 2015, 44 master's awarded. *Degree requirements:* For master's, capstone research course. *Entrance requirements:* For master's, minimum GPA of 3.0, 2 letters of recommendation, resume, personal statement. Additional exam requirements/recommendations for international students: Required—TOEFL (minimum score 550 paper-based; 80 iBT) or IELTS (minimum score 6.5). *Application deadline:* For fall admission, 5/15 for international students; for spring admission, 10/15 for international students. Applications are processed on a rolling basis. Application fee: $60. Electronic applications accepted. *Expenses:* $725 per credit hour. *Financial support:* In 2015–16, 14 students received support. Scholarships/grants and unspecified assistantships available. Financial award applicants required to submit FAFSA. *Faculty research:* Ethical theory, media industries, community-based teaching and learning, non commutative algebra and partial differential equations, cancer research in biology and physics. *Unit head:* Dr. Yohuru Williams, Dean, 203-254-4000 Ext. 2221, Fax: 203-254-4119, E-mail: ywilliams@fairfield.edu. *Application contact:* Marianne Gumpper, Director of Graduate Admission, 203-254-4184, Fax: 203-254-4073, E-mail: gradadmis@fairfield.edu.
Website: http://www.fairfield.edu/cas

Fairleigh Dickinson University, Metropolitan Campus, University College: Arts, Sciences, and Professional Studies, School of Computer Sciences and Engineering, Program in Mathematical Foundation, Teaneck, NJ 07666-1914. Offers MS.

Fayetteville State University, Graduate School, Department of Mathematics and Computer Science, Fayetteville, NC 28301-4298. Offers MS. *Program availability:* Part-time, evening/weekend. *Faculty:* 9 full-time (3 women). *Students:* 1 full-time (0 women); minority (Black or African American, non-Hispanic/Latino). Average age 35. In 2015, 4 master's awarded. *Degree requirements:* For master's, comprehensive exam, thesis or alternative, internship. *Entrance requirements:* For master's, GRE General Test. Additional exam requirements/recommendations for international students: Required—TOEFL. *Application deadline:* For fall admission, 4/15 for domestic students; for spring admission, 10/15 for domestic students. Applications are processed on a rolling basis. Application fee: $35. Electronic applications accepted. *Financial support:* Applicants required to submit FAFSA. *Faculty research:* Mathematical modeling in medicine: derivation of mathematical criteria for cure of cancer, AIDS, diabetes; error correcting codes and cryptography; qualitative properties of dynamical systems: ODE, FDE, PDE; homeomorphisms: ring, group; mathematical modeling of military strategy and outcomes for symmetrical warfare. *Unit head:* Dr. Radoslav Nickolov, Chairperson, 910-672- 2053, Fax: 910-672-1070, E-mail: rnickolov@uncfsu.edu. *Application contact:* Denise Williams, Administrative Support Associate, 910-672-2265, Fax: 910-672-1070, E-mail: dwill184@uncfsu.edu.

Mathematics

Florida Atlantic University, Charles E. Schmidt College of Science, Department of Mathematical Sciences, Boca Raton, FL 33431-0991. Offers applied mathematics and statistics (MS); mathematics (MS, MST, PhD). *Program availability:* Part-time. Terminal master's awarded for partial completion of doctoral program. *Degree requirements:* For master's, comprehensive exam (for some programs), thesis (for some programs); for doctorate, comprehensive exam, thesis/dissertation. *Entrance requirements:* For master's and doctorate, GRE General Test, minimum GPA of 3.0. Additional exam requirements/recommendations for international students: Required—TOEFL (minimum score 500 paper-based; 61 iBT), IELTS (minimum score 6). Electronic applications accepted. *Faculty research:* Cryptography, statistics, algebra, analysis, combinatorics.

Florida Gulf Coast University, College of Arts and Sciences, Program in Mathematics, Fort Myers, FL 33965-6565. Offers MS. *Faculty:* 235 full-time (96 women), 142 part-time/adjunct (60 women). *Students:* 5 full-time (3 women), 11 part-time (8 women); includes 5 minority (1 Black or African American, non-Hispanic/Latino; 2 Asian, non-Hispanic/Latino; 2 Hispanic/Latino). Average age 33. 9 applicants, 78% accepted, 6 enrolled. In 2015, 1 master's awarded. *Entrance requirements:* For master's, GRE. *Application deadline:* Applications are processed on a rolling basis. Application fee: $30. Electronic applications accepted. *Expenses:* Tuition, state resident: full-time $6974. Tuition, nonresident: full-time $28,170. *Required fees:* $1987. One-time fee: $10 full-time. Tuition and fees vary according to course load and degree level. *Financial support:* In 2015–16, 2 students received support. Application deadline: 6/1; applicants required to submit FAFSA. *Unit head:* Dr. Robert Gregerson, Dean, 239-590-7156, Fax: 239-590-7200, E-mail: rgregerson@fgcu.edu. *Application contact:* Patricia Rice, Executive Secretary, 239-590-7196, Fax: 239-590-7200, E-mail: price@fgcu.edu.

Florida International University, College of Arts, Sciences, and Education, Department of Mathematics and Statistics, Program in Mathematical Sciences, Miami, FL 33199. Offers MS. *Program availability:* Part-time, evening/weekend. *Faculty:* 50 full-time (16 women), 38 part-time/adjunct (14 women). *Students:* 7 full-time (1 woman), 2 part-time (1 woman); includes 5 minority (all Hispanic/Latino), 2 international. Average age 26. 20 applicants, 30% accepted, 4 enrolled. In 2015, 5 master's awarded. *Entrance requirements:* For master's, GRE, letter of intent; three letters of recommendation; minimum GPA of 3.0 in upper-division mathematics courses. Additional exam requirements/recommendations for international students: Required—TOEFL (minimum score 550 paper-based; 80 iBT). *Application deadline:* For fall admission, 6/1 for domestic students, 3/1 for international students; for spring admission, 10/1 for domestic students, 9/1 for international students. Applications are processed on a rolling basis. Application fee: $30. Electronic applications accepted. *Expenses:* Tuition, state resident: full-time $10,708; part-time $455.64 per credit hour. Tuition, nonresident: full-time $23,816; part-time $1001.69 per credit hour. *Required fees:* $390; $195 per semester. Tuition and fees vary according to program. *Financial support:* Institutionally sponsored loans and scholarships/grants available. Financial award application deadline: 3/1; financial award applicants required to submit FAFSA. *Unit head:* Dr. Abdelhamid Meziani, Chair, 305-348-2957, E-mail: meziani@fiu.edu. *Application contact:* Dr. Zhenmin Chen, Graduate Director, 305-348-1081,
E-mail: gradadm@fiu.edu.

Florida State University, The Graduate School, College of Arts and Sciences, Department of Mathematics, Tallahassee, FL 32306-4510. Offers applied computational mathematics (MS, PhD); biomathematics (MS, PhD); financial mathematics (MS, PhD); pure mathematics (MS, PhD). *Program availability:* Part-time. *Faculty:* 34 full-time (4 women). *Students:* 145 full-time (43 women), 4 part-time (1 woman); includes 18 minority (2 Black or African American, non-Hispanic/Latino; 5 Asian, non-Hispanic/Latino; 2 Hispanic/Latino; 9 Two or more races, non-Hispanic/Latino), 87 international. 300 applicants, 41% accepted, 39 enrolled. In 2015, 44 master's, 14 doctorates awarded. Terminal master's awarded for partial completion of doctoral program. *Degree requirements:* For master's, comprehensive exam (for some programs), thesis optional; for doctorate, comprehensive exam (for some programs), thesis/dissertation, candidacy exam (including written qualifying examinations which differ by degree concentration). *Entrance requirements:* For master's and doctorate, GRE General Test, minimum upper-division GPA of 3.0, 4-year bachelor's degree. Additional exam requirements/recommendations for international students: Required—TOEFL (minimum score 550 paper-based; 80 iBT), IELTS (minimum score 6.5). *Application deadline:* For fall admission, 1/15 priority date for domestic and international students. Applications are processed on a rolling basis. Application fee: $30. Electronic applications accepted. *Expenses: Tuition, area resident:* Full-time $7263; part-time $403.50 per credit hour. Tuition, nonresident: full-time $18,087; part-time $1004.85 per credit hour. *Required fees:* $1365; $75.81 per credit hour. $20 per semester. Tuition and fees vary according to campus/location. *Financial support:* In 2015–16, 106 students received support, including 1 fellowship with full tuition reimbursement available (averaging $22,600 per year), 11 research assistantships with full tuition reimbursements available (averaging $22,000 per year), 83 teaching assistantships with full tuition reimbursements available (averaging $20,650 per year); career-related internships or fieldwork, institutionally sponsored loans, scholarships/grants, health care benefits, tuition waivers (full and partial), and unspecified assistantships also available. Financial award application deadline: 1/30. *Faculty research:* Low-dimensional and geometric topology, mathematical modeling in neuroscience, computational stochastics and Monte Carlo methods, mathematical physics, applied analysis. *Total annual research expenditures:* $1.4 million. *Unit head:* Dr. Xiaoming Wang, Chairperson, 850-645-3338, Fax: 850-644-4053, E-mail: wxm@math.fsu.edu. *Application contact:* Kari Aime, Graduate Advisor and Admissions Coordinator, 850-644-2278, Fax: 850-644-4053,
E-mail: aime@math.fsu.edu.
Website: http://www.math.fsu.edu/

George Mason University, College of Science, Department of Mathematical Sciences, Fairfax, VA 22030. Offers MS, PhD, Certificate. *Faculty:* 38 full-time (10 women), 15 part-time/adjunct (4 women). *Students:* 34 full-time (12 women), 35 part-time (12 women); includes 16 minority (2 Black or African American, non-Hispanic/Latino; 1 American Indian or Alaska Native, non-Hispanic/Latino; 8 Asian, non-Hispanic/Latino; 5 Hispanic/Latino), 8 international. Average age 32. 80 applicants, 61% accepted, 16 enrolled. In 2015, 14 master's, 2 doctorates awarded. *Degree requirements:* For master's, comprehensive exam, thesis optional; for doctorate, comprehensive exam, thesis/dissertation. *Entrance requirements:* For master's, GRE, 3 letters of recommendation; official college transcripts; expanded goals statement; resume; for doctorate, GRE (recommended), master's degree in math or undergraduate coursework with math preparation with minimum GPA of 3.0 in last 60 credits; 2 copies of official transcripts; 3 letters of recommendation; expanded goals statement; for Certificate, 3 letters of recommendation; official transcripts. Additional exam requirements/recommendations for international students: Required—TOEFL (minimum score 575 paper-based; 88 iBT), IELTS (minimum score 6.5), PTE (minimum score 59). Application fee: $75 ($80 for international students). Electronic applications accepted. *Financial support:* In 2015–16, 29 students received support, including 3 fellowships (averaging $14,376 per year), 2 research assistantships with tuition reimbursements available (averaging $20,000 per year), 21 teaching assistantships with tuition reimbursements available (averaging $17,038 per year); career-related internships or fieldwork, Federal Work-Study, scholarships/grants, unspecified assistantships, and health care benefits (for full-time research or teaching assistantship recipients) also available. Support available to part-time students. Financial award application deadline: 3/1; financial award applicants required to submit FAFSA. *Faculty research:* Nonlinear dynamics and topology, with an emphasis on global bifurcations and chaos; numerical and theoretical methods of dynamical systems. *Total annual research expenditures:* $779,421. *Unit head:* David Walnut, Chair, 703-993-1478, Fax: 703-993-1491,
E-mail: dwalnut@gmu.edu. *Application contact:* Rebecca Goldin, Graduate Coordinator, 703-993-1480, Fax: 703-993-1491, E-mail: rgoldin@gmu.edu.
Website: http://math.gmu.edu/

Georgetown University, Graduate School of Arts and Sciences, Department of Mathematics and Statistics, Washington, DC 20057. Offers MS.

The George Washington University, Columbian College of Arts and Sciences, Department of Mathematics, Washington, DC 20052. Offers applied mathematics (MS); financial mathematics (Graduate Certificate); mathematics (MA, PhD, Graduate Certificate). *Program availability:* Part-time, evening/weekend. *Faculty:* 19 full-time (3 women), 11 part-time/adjunct (4 women). *Students:* 33 full-time (8 women), 17 part-time (5 women); includes 4 minority (1 Black or African American, non-Hispanic/Latino; 1 American Indian or Alaska Native, non-Hispanic/Latino; 2 Hispanic/Latino), 29 international. Average age 26. 107 applicants, 55% accepted, 23 enrolled. In 2015, 7 master's, 5 doctorates, 1 other advanced degree awarded. Terminal master's awarded for partial completion of doctoral program. *Degree requirements:* For master's, comprehensive exam; for doctorate, one foreign language, thesis/dissertation, general exam. *Entrance requirements:* For master's and doctorate, GRE General Test, minimum GPA of 3.0, interview. Additional exam requirements/recommendations for international students: Required—TOEFL (minimum score 550 paper-based; 80 iBT). *Application deadline:* For fall admission, 1/15 priority date for domestic and international students; for spring admission, 10/1 priority date for domestic students, 9/1 priority date for international students. Applications are processed on a rolling basis. Application fee: $75. Electronic applications accepted. *Financial support:* In 2015–16, 17 students received support. Fellowships with full tuition reimbursements available, teaching assistantships with tuition reimbursements available, Federal Work-Study, and tuition waivers available. Financial award application deadline: 1/15. *Unit head:* Yongwu Rong, Chair, 202-994-6890, E-mail: rong@gwu.edu. *Application contact:* 202-994-6210, Fax: 202-994-6213, E-mail: askccas@gwu.edu.
Website: http://math.columbian.gwu.edu/

Georgia Institute of Technology, Graduate Studies, College of Sciences, School of Mathematics, Atlanta, GA 30332-0001. Offers MS, PhD. *Program availability:* Part-time. Terminal master's awarded for partial completion of doctoral program. *Degree requirements:* For master's, thesis optional; for doctorate, one foreign language, comprehensive exam, thesis/dissertation. *Entrance requirements:* For master's, GRE General Test; for doctorate, GRE General Test, GRE Subject Test. Additional exam requirements/recommendations for international students: Required—TOEFL (minimum score 590 paper-based; 96 iBT). Electronic applications accepted. *Faculty research:* Dynamical systems, discrete mathematics, probability and statistics, mathematical physics.

Georgia Institute of Technology, Graduate Studies, Multidisciplinary Program in Algorithms, Combinatorics, and Optimization, Atlanta, GA 30332-0001. Offers PhD. Program offered jointly with College of Computing, School of Mathematics, and School of Industrial and Systems Engineering. *Program availability:* Part-time. *Degree requirements:* For doctorate, comprehensive exam, thesis/dissertation. *Entrance requirements:* For doctorate, GRE General Test, GRE Subject Test (computer science, mathematics or physics). Additional exam requirements/recommendations for international students: Required—TOEFL (minimum score 600 paper-based; 100 iBT). Electronic applications accepted. *Faculty research:* Complexity, graph minors, combinatorial optimization, mathematical programming, probabilistic methods.

Georgia Southern University, Jack N. Averitt College of Graduate Studies, College of Science and Mathematics, Program in Mathematics, Statesboro, GA 30460. Offers mathematics (MS). *Program availability:* Part-time. *Students:* 25 full-time (8 women), 1 part-time (0 women); includes 4 minority (1 Black or African American, non-Hispanic/Latino; 1 Hispanic/Latino; 2 Two or more races, non-Hispanic/Latino), 6 international. Average age 26. 23 applicants, 87% accepted, 8 enrolled. In 2015, 19 master's awarded. *Degree requirements:* For master's, comprehensive exam, thesis, terminal exam, project. *Entrance requirements:* For master's, GRE, BS in engineering, science, or mathematics; course work in calculus, probability, linear algebra; proficiency in a computer programming language. Additional exam requirements/recommendations for international students: Required—TOEFL (minimum score 550 paper-based; 80 iBT), IELTS (minimum score 6). *Application deadline:* For fall admission, 3/1 priority date for domestic and international students; for spring admission, 10/1 priority date for domestic students, 10/1 for international students. Applications are processed on a rolling basis. Application fee: $50. Electronic applications accepted. *Expenses:* Tuition, state resident: full-time $7236; part-time $277 per semester hour. Tuition, nonresident: full-time $27,118; part-time $1105 per semester hour. *Required fees:* $2092. *Financial support:* In 2015–16, 23 students received support, including 23 teaching assistantships with full tuition reimbursements available (averaging $7,750 per year); career-related internships or fieldwork, Federal Work-Study, scholarships/grants, tuition waivers (full), and unspecified assistantships also available. Support available to part-time students. Financial award application deadline: 4/15; financial award applicants required to submit FAFSA. *Faculty research:* Algebra, number theory, and combinatorics; analysis and differential equations, approximation, optimization and computational mathematics; geometry and topology; mathematics education; statistics. *Total annual research expenditures:* $21,950. *Unit head:* Dr. Sharon Taylor, Chair, 912-478-0266,
Fax: 912-478-0654, E-mail: taylors@georgiasouthern.edu.
Website: http://cosm.georgiasouthern.edu/math/student-resources/graduate-degree/

Georgia State University, College of Arts and Sciences, Department of Mathematics and Statistics, Atlanta, GA 30302-3083. Offers bioinformatics (MS, PhD); biostatistics (MS, PhD); discrete mathematics (MS); mathematics (MS, PhD); scientific computing (MS); statistics (MS). *Program availability:* Part-time. *Faculty:* 22 full-time (7 women). *Students:* 97 full-time (44 women), 20 part-time (5 women); includes 40 minority (14 Black or African American, non-Hispanic/Latino; 23 Asian, non-Hispanic/Latino; 3 Hispanic/Latino), 50 international. Average age 32. 80 applicants, 51% accepted, 23 enrolled. In 2015, 22 master's, 4 doctorates awarded. Terminal master's awarded for partial completion of doctoral program. *Degree requirements:* For master's, comprehensive exam (for some programs), thesis optional; for doctorate, comprehensive exam, thesis/dissertation. *Entrance requirements:* For master's and doctorate, GRE. Additional exam requirements/recommendations for international students: Required—TOEFL (minimum score 550 paper-based; 80 iBT). *Application deadline:* For fall admission, 7/1 priority date for domestic and international students; for spring admission, 11/15 priority date for domestic and international students. Application fee: $50. Electronic applications accepted. *Expenses:* Tuition, state resident: full-time $6876; part-time $382 per credit hour. Tuition, nonresident: full-time $22,374; part-time

$1243 per credit hour. *Required fees:* $2128; $2128 per term. $1064 per term. Part-time tuition and fees vary according to course load and program. *Financial support:* In 2015–16, fellowships with full tuition reimbursements (averaging $22,000 per year), research assistantships with full tuition reimbursements (averaging $9,000 per year), teaching assistantships with full tuition reimbursements (averaging $9,000 per year) were awarded; institutionally sponsored loans, scholarships/grants, health care benefits, and unspecified assistantships also available. Financial award application deadline: 2/1. *Faculty research:* Algebra, matrix theory, graph theory and combinatorics; applied mathematics and analysis; collegiate mathematics education; statistics, biostatistics and applications; bioinformatics, dynamical systems. *Unit head:* Dr. Guantao Chen, Chair, 404-413-6436, Fax: 404-413-6403, E-mail: gchen@gsu.edu.
Website: http://www2.gsu.edu/~wwwmat/

The Graduate Center, City University of New York, Graduate Studies, Program in Mathematics, New York, NY 10016-4039. Offers PhD. *Degree requirements:* For doctorate, 2 foreign languages, thesis/dissertation. *Entrance requirements:* For doctorate, GRE General Test. Additional exam requirements/recommendations for international students: Required—TOEFL. Electronic applications accepted.

Hardin-Simmons University, Graduate School, Holland School of Sciences and Mathematics, Program in Mathematics, Abilene, TX 79698-0001. Offers MS. *Program availability:* Part-time. *Faculty:* 2 full-time (0 women). *Students:* 6 part-time (5 women). Average age 35. *Degree requirements:* For master's, comprehensive exam. *Application deadline:* For fall admission, 8/5 priority date for domestic students, 4/1 for international students; for spring admission, 1/5 priority date for domestic students, 9/1 for international students. Applications are processed on a rolling basis. Application fee: $50. Electronic applications accepted. *Expenses: Tuition, area resident:* Full-time $12,060; part-time $670 per credit hour. *Required fees:* $325; $110 per semester. *Financial support:* Fellowships, career-related internships or fieldwork, and scholarships/grants available. Support available to part-time students. Financial award application deadline: 6/30; financial award applicants required to submit FAFSA. *Unit head:* Dr. Kenneth Davis, Director, 325-670-1388, Fax: 325-370-1385, E-mail: kdavis@hsutx.edu. *Application contact:* Dr. Nancy Kucinski, Dean of Graduate Studies, 325-670-1298, Fax: 325-670-1564, E-mail: gradoff@hsutx.edu.
Website: http://www.hsutx.edu/academics/holland/graduate/math/

Harvard University, Graduate School of Arts and Sciences, Department of Mathematics, Cambridge, MA 02138. Offers PhD. *Degree requirements:* For doctorate, 2 foreign languages, thesis/dissertation, qualifying exam. *Entrance requirements:* For doctorate, GRE General Test, GRE Subject Test. Additional exam requirements/recommendations for international students: Required—TOEFL.

Henderson State University, Graduate Studies, Teachers College, Department of Advanced Instructional Studies, Arkadelphia, AR 71999-0001. Offers advanced instructional studies - English (MSE); advanced instructional studies - English as second language (MSE); advanced instructional studies - instructional facilitator (MSE); advanced instructional studies - inter studies (MSE); advanced instructional studies - math (MSE); advanced instructional studies - middle school (MSE); advanced instructional studies - physical education (MSE); advanced instructional studies - reading (MSE); developmental therapy (MSE); dyslexia therapy (Graduate Certificate); education (MAT); educational technology leadership (Graduate Certificate); elementary education, special education (MSE); English as a second language (Graduate Certificate); instructional facilitator (Graduate Certificate); middle level education (MAT); special education (MSE); special education, k-12 (MAT, MSE); special education/early childhood (MAT). *Accreditation:* NCATE. *Program availability:* Part-time. *Faculty:* 6 full-time (4 women), 2 part-time/adjunct (both women). *Students:* 2 full-time (both women), 139 part-time (113 women); includes 25 minority (18 Black or African American, non-Hispanic/Latino; 1 American Indian or Alaska Native, non-Hispanic/Latino; 3 Hispanic/Latino; 3 Two or more races, non-Hispanic/Latino). Average age 36. 7 applicants, 100% accepted, 7 enrolled. In 2015, 50 master's awarded. *Entrance requirements:* For master's, GRE General Test or MAT, minimum GPA of 2.7, teacher certification. Additional exam requirements/recommendations for international students: Required—TOEFL (minimum score 600 paper-based); Recommended—IELTS (minimum score 6.5). *Application deadline:* For fall admission, 8/1 priority date for domestic students, 6/30 priority date for international students; for spring admission, 1/1 priority date for domestic students, 11/30 priority date for international students. Applications are processed on a rolling basis. Application fee: $25 ($75 for international students). *Expenses:* Tuition, state resident: full-time $6096; part-time $3048 per credit hour. Tuition, nonresident: full-time $12,504; part-time $6252 per credit hour. *Required fees:* $1447; $1024 per unit. Tuition and fees vary according to course load and student level. *Financial support:* In 2015–16, 1 teaching assistantship with partial tuition reimbursement (averaging $4,000 per year) was awarded; scholarships/grants and unspecified assistantships also available. Financial award application deadline: 4/15; financial award applicants required to submit FAFSA. *Unit head:* Dr. Gary Smithey, Coordinator of MSE in AIS, 870-230-5361, Fax: 870-230-5455, E-mail: smitheg@hsu.edu. *Application contact:* Dr. Ken Taylor, Graduate Dean, 870-230-5126, Fax: 870-230-5479, E-mail: taylorke@hsu.edu.
Website: http://www.hsu.edu/Academics/TeachersCollege/AIS/index.html

Howard University, Graduate School, Department of Mathematics, Washington, DC 20059-0002. Offers applied mathematics (MS, PhD); mathematics (MS, PhD). *Program availability:* Part-time. Terminal master's awarded for partial completion of doctoral program. *Degree requirements:* For master's, comprehensive exam, thesis or alternative, qualifying exam; for doctorate, 2 foreign languages, comprehensive exam, thesis/dissertation, qualifying exams. *Entrance requirements:* For master's, GRE General Test, minimum GPA of 3.0; for doctorate, GRE General Test. Additional exam requirements/recommendations for international students: Required—TOEFL. Electronic applications accepted.

Hunter College of the City University of New York, Graduate School, School of Arts and Sciences, Department of Mathematics and Statistics, New York, NY 10065-5085. Offers adolescent mathematics education (MA); applied mathematics (MA); pure mathematics (MA); statistics (MA). *Program availability:* Part-time, evening/weekend. *Faculty:* 3 full-time (1 woman). *Students:* 8 full-time (1 woman), 18 part-time (5 women); includes 13 minority (4 Black or African American, non-Hispanic/Latino; 6 Asian, non-Hispanic/Latino; 3 Hispanic/Latino), 2 international. Average age 29. 52 applicants, 67% accepted, 21 enrolled. In 2015, 21 master's awarded. *Degree requirements:* For master's, one foreign language, comprehensive exam, thesis (for some programs). *Entrance requirements:* For master's, GRE General Test, 24 credits in mathematics. Additional exam requirements/recommendations for international students: Required—TOEFL. *Application deadline:* For fall admission, 4/1 for domestic students, 2/1 for international students; for spring admission, 11/1 for domestic students, 9/1 for international students. *Financial support:* Federal Work-Study, institutionally sponsored loans, scholarships/grants, and tuition waivers (partial) available. Support available to part-time students. *Faculty research:* Data analysis, dynamical systems, computer graphics, topology, statistical decision theory. *Unit head:* Robert Thompson, Chair, 212-772-5300, Fax: 212-772-4858, E-mail: robert.thompson@hunter.cuny.edu. *Application contact:* Ada Peluso, Director for Graduate Admissions, 212-772-4632, Fax: 212-772-4858, E-mail: peluso@math.hunter.cuny.edu.
Website: http://math.hunter.cuny.edu/

Idaho State University, Office of Graduate Studies, College of Science and Engineering, Department of Mathematics, Pocatello, ID 83209-8085. Offers mathematics (MS, DA); mathematics for secondary teachers (MA). *Program availability:* Part-time. *Degree requirements:* For master's, comprehensive exam, thesis (for some programs), oral and written exams; for doctorate, comprehensive exam, thesis/dissertation, teaching internships. *Entrance requirements:* For master's, GRE General Test, GRE Subject Test, course work in modern algebra, differential equations, advanced calculus, introductory analysis; for doctorate, GRE General Test, GRE Subject Test, minimum graduate GPA of 3.5, MS in mathematics, teaching experience, 3 letters of recommendation. Additional exam requirements/recommendations for international students: Required—TOEFL (minimum score 550 paper-based; 80 iBT). Electronic applications accepted. *Faculty research:* Algebra, analysis geometry, statistics, applied mathematics.

Illinois State University, Graduate School, College of Arts and Sciences, Department of Mathematics, Program in Mathematics, Normal, IL 61790-2200. Offers MA, MS. *Degree requirements:* For master's, thesis or alternative. *Entrance requirements:* For master's, GRE General Test, minimum GPA of 2.8 in last 60 hours of course work.

Indiana State University, College of Graduate and Professional Studies, College of Arts and Sciences, Department of Mathematics and Computer Science, Terre Haute, IN 47809. Offers computer science (MS); mathematics (MA, MS). *Program availability:* Part-time. *Degree requirements:* For master's, thesis or alternative. *Entrance requirements:* For master's, 24 semester hours of course work in undergraduate mathematics. Electronic applications accepted.

Indiana University Bloomington, University Graduate School, College of Arts and Sciences, Department of Mathematics, Bloomington, IN 47405-7000. Offers applied mathematics (MA); mathematical physics (PhD); mathematics education (MAT); pure mathematics (MA, PhD). Terminal master's awarded for partial completion of doctoral program. *Degree requirements:* For doctorate, one foreign language, thesis/dissertation. *Entrance requirements:* For master's and doctorate, GRE General Test, GRE Subject Test. Additional exam requirements/recommendations for international students: Required—TOEFL. Electronic applications accepted. *Faculty research:* Topology, geometry, algebra, applied, analysis.

Indiana University of Pennsylvania, School of Graduate Studies and Research, College of Natural Sciences and Mathematics, Department of Mathematics, Indiana, PA 15705-1087. Offers applied mathematics (MS); elementary and middle school mathematics education (M Ed). *Program availability:* Part-time. *Faculty:* 8 full-time (3 women). *Students:* 17 full-time (9 women), 24 part-time (18 women); includes 2 minority (both Black or African American, non-Hispanic/Latino), 5 international. Average age 28. 55 applicants, 53% accepted, 15 enrolled. In 2015, 5 master's awarded. *Degree requirements:* For master's, thesis optional. *Entrance requirements:* For master's, 2 letters of recommendation. Additional exam requirements/recommendations for international students: Required—TOEFL (minimum score 540 paper-based). *Application deadline:* Applications are processed on a rolling basis. Application fee: $50. Electronic applications accepted. *Financial support:* In 2015–16, 2 fellowships with partial tuition reimbursements, 11 research assistantships with tuition reimbursements (averaging $4,427 per year) were awarded; career-related internships or fieldwork, Federal Work-Study, scholarships/grants, and unspecified assistantships also available. Support available to part-time students. Financial award application deadline: 4/15; financial award applicants required to submit FAFSA. *Unit head:* Dr. Edel M Reilly, Chairperson, 724-357-2608, E-mail: ereilly@iup.edu. *Application contact:* Dr. Yu-Ju Kuo, Graduate Coordinator, 724-357-3797, E-mail: yjkuo@iup.edu.
Website: http://www.iup.edu/math

Indiana University–Purdue University Fort Wayne, College of Arts and Sciences, Department of Mathematical Sciences, Fort Wayne, IN 46805-1499. Offers applied mathematics (MS); applied statistics (Certificate); mathematics (MS); operations research (MS); teaching (MAT). *Program availability:* Part-time, evening/weekend. *Faculty:* 18 full-time (5 women). *Students:* 2 full-time (1 woman), 9 part-time (2 women); includes 1 minority (Hispanic/Latino), 1 international. Average age 31. 6 applicants, 100% accepted, 4 enrolled. In 2015, 5 master's, 1 other advanced degree awarded. *Entrance requirements:* For master's, minimum GPA of 3.0, major or minor in mathematics, three letters of recommendation. Additional exam requirements/recommendations for international students: Required—TOEFL (minimum score 550 paper-based; 79 iBT); Recommended—TWE. *Application deadline:* For fall admission, 8/1 priority date for domestic students, 7/1 priority date for international students; for spring admission, 12/1 for domestic students, 10/1 for international students. Applications are processed on a rolling basis. Application fee: $55 ($60 for international students). Electronic applications accepted. *Financial support:* In 2015–16, 5 teaching assistantships with partial tuition reimbursements (averaging $13,522 per year) were awarded; scholarships/grants and unspecified assistantships also available. Support available to part-time students. Financial award application deadline: 3/1; financial award applicants required to submit FAFSA. *Faculty research:* Eves' Theorem, paired-placements for student teaching, holomorphic maps. *Total annual research expenditures:* $56,223. *Unit head:* Dr. Peter Dragnev, Chair/Professor, 260-481-6382, Fax: 260-481-0155, E-mail: dragnevp@ipfw.edu. *Application contact:* Dr. W. Douglas Weakley, Director of Graduate Studies, 260-481-6233, Fax: 260-481-0155, E-mail: weakley@ipfw.edu.
Website: http://www.ipfw.edu/math/

Indiana University–Purdue University Indianapolis, School of Science, Department of Mathematical Sciences, Indianapolis, IN 46202-3216. Offers mathematics (MS, PhD), including applied mathematics, applied statistics (MS), mathematical statistics (PhD), mathematics, mathematics education (MS). *Program availability:* Part-time. Terminal master's awarded for partial completion of doctoral program. *Degree requirements:* For master's, thesis optional; for doctorate, one foreign language, thesis/dissertation. *Entrance requirements:* For doctorate, GRE General Test. Additional exam requirements/recommendations for international students: Required—TOEFL. *Faculty research:* Mathematical physics, integral systems, partial differential equations, noncommutative geometry, biomathematics, computational neurosciences.

Instituto Tecnologico de Santo Domingo, Graduate School, Area of Basic And Environmental Sciences, Santo Domingo, Dominican Republic. Offers environmental science (M En S), including environmental education, environmental management, marine resources, natural resources management; mathematics (MS, PhD); renewable energy technology (MS, Certificate).

Iowa State University of Science and Technology, Department of Mathematics, Ames, IA 50011. Offers applied mathematics (MS, PhD); mathematics (MS, PhD); school mathematics (MSM). *Degree requirements:* For master's, thesis or alternative; for doctorate, thesis/dissertation. *Entrance requirements:* For master's and doctorate,

GRE General Test. Additional exam requirements/recommendations for international students: Required—TOEFL (minimum score 550 paper-based; 79 iBT), IELTS (minimum score 6.5). Electronic applications accepted.

Jackson State University, Graduate School, College of Science, Engineering and Technology, Department of Mathematics, Jackson, MS 39217. Offers mathematics (MS). *Program availability:* Part-time, evening/weekend. *Degree requirements:* For master's, comprehensive exam, thesis (for some programs). *Entrance requirements:* For master's, GRE General Test. Additional exam requirements/recommendations for international students: Required—TOEFL (minimum score 520 paper-based; 67 iBT).

Jacksonville State University, College of Graduate Studies and Continuing Education, College of Arts and Sciences, Department of Mathematics, Jacksonville, AL 36265-1602. Offers MS. *Program availability:* Part-time, evening/weekend. *Faculty:* 12 full-time (4 women). *Students:* 2 full-time (both women), 5 part-time (1 woman), 2 international. Average age 32. 7 applicants, 71% accepted, 2 enrolled. In 2015, 2 master's awarded. *Degree requirements:* For master's, comprehensive exam, thesis (for some programs). *Entrance requirements:* For master's, GRE General Test or MAT. Additional exam requirements/recommendations for international students: Required—TOEFL (minimum score 500 paper-based; 61 iBT). *Application deadline:* Applications are processed on a rolling basis. Application fee: $35. Electronic applications accepted. *Financial support:* In 2015–16, 5 students received support. Available to part-time students. Application deadline: 4/1; applicants required to submit FAFSA. *Unit head:* Dr. David Thornton, Head, 256-782-5359, E-mail: thornton@jsu.edu. *Application contact:* Dr. Jean Pugliese, Associate Dean, 256-782-8278, Fax: 256-782-5321, E-mail: pugliese@jsu.edu.

John Carroll University, Graduate School, Department of Mathematics, University Heights, OH 44118-4581. Offers MA, MS. *Program availability:* Part-time, evening/weekend. *Degree requirements:* For master's, comprehensive exam, thesis (for some programs), research essay. *Entrance requirements:* For master's, minimum GPA of 2.5, teaching certificate (MA). Electronic applications accepted. *Faculty research:* Algebraic topology, algebra, differential geometry, combinatorics, Lie groups.

Johns Hopkins University, School of Education, Master's Programs in Education, Baltimore, MD 21218. Offers counseling (MS), including clinical mental health counseling, school counseling; education (MS), including educational studies, gifted education, reading, school administration and supervision, technology for educators; elementary education (MAT); health professions (M Ed); intelligence analysis (MS); organizational leadership (MS); secondary education (MAT), including biology, chemistry, earth/space science, English, mathematics, physics, science, social studies; special education (MS), including early childhood special education, general special education studies, mild to moderate disabilities, severe disabilities. *Program availability:* Part-time, evening/weekend, 100% online, blended/hybrid learning. *Students:* 302 full-time (241 women), 1,472 part-time (1,106 women); includes 710 minority (313 Black or African American, non-Hispanic/Latino; 6 American Indian or Alaska Native, non-Hispanic/Latino; 133 Asian, non-Hispanic/Latino; 167 Hispanic/Latino; 11 Native Hawaiian or other Pacific Islander, non-Hispanic/Latino; 80 Two or more races, non-Hispanic/Latino), 46 international. Average age 28. 1,717 applicants, 69% accepted, 904 enrolled. In 2015, 623 master's awarded. *Degree requirements:* For master's, comprehensive exam (for some programs), portfolio, capstone project and/or internship; PRAXIS II Core (for teacher preparation programs that lead to licensure). *Entrance requirements:* For master's, GRE (for full-time programs only); PRAXIS I or state approved alternative (for teacher preparation programs that lead to licensure), minimum of a bachelor's degree from regionally- or nationally-accredited institution; minimum GPA of 3.0 in all previous programs of study; official transcripts from all post-secondary institutions attended; essay; curriculum vitae/resume; letters of recommendation (3 for full-time, 2 for part-time). Additional exam requirements/recommendations for international students: Required—TOEFL (minimum score 600 paper-based; 100 iBT), IELTS (minimum score 7). *Application deadline:* For fall admission, 4/1 for domestic and international students; for spring admission, 10/1 for domestic and international students; for summer admission, 2/1 for domestic and international students. Application fee: $80. Electronic applications accepted. *Expenses:* Contact institution. *Financial support:* Applicants required to submit FAFSA. *Unit head:* Dr. Mariale M. Hardiman, Interim Dean, 410-516-7820, Fax: 410-516-6697, E-mail: mmhardiman@jhu.edu. *Application contact:* Rhodri Evans, Director of Enrollment Services, 410-516-0741, Fax: 410-516-6697, E-mail: revans@jhu.edu.

Johns Hopkins University, Zanvyl Krieger School of Arts and Sciences, Department of Mathematics, Baltimore, MD 21218. Offers PhD. *Degree requirements:* For doctorate, one foreign language, thesis/dissertation, 3 qualifying exams. *Entrance requirements:* For doctorate, GRE General Test, GRE Subject Test. Additional exam requirements/recommendations for international students: Required—TOEFL (minimum score 600 paper-based; 100 iBT), IELTS. Electronic applications accepted. *Faculty research:* Algebraic geometry, number theory, algebraic topology, differential geometry, partial differential equations.

Kansas State University, Graduate School, College of Arts and Sciences, Department of Mathematics, Manhattan, KS 66506. Offers MS, PhD, Graduate Certificate. *Program availability:* Part-time. Terminal master's awarded for partial completion of doctoral program. *Degree requirements:* For master's, thesis or alternative; for doctorate, one foreign language, thesis/dissertation. *Entrance requirements:* For master's and doctorate, bachelor's degree in mathematics; 21 semester hours of work beyond the calculus level; minimum B average in courses taken in mathematics and in all work taken during one's last two years of university study. Additional exam requirements/recommendations for international students: Required—TOEFL (minimum score 550 paper-based; 79 iBT); Recommended—IELTS (minimum score 6.5), TSE (minimum score 58). Electronic applications accepted. *Faculty research:* Low-dimensional topology, geometry, complex and harmonic analysis, group and representation theory, noncommunicative spaces.

Kent State University, College of Arts and Sciences, Department of Mathematical Sciences, Kent, OH 44242-0001. Offers applied mathematics (MA, MS, PhD); pure mathematics (MA, MS, PhD). *Program availability:* Part-time. *Faculty:* 42 full-time (17 women). *Students:* 61 full-time (21 women), 40 part-time (19 women); includes 3 minority (2 Asian, non-Hispanic/Latino; 1 Two or more races, non-Hispanic/Latino), 50 international. Average age 30. 205 applicants, 58% accepted, 38 enrolled. In 2015, 6 master's, 6 doctorates awarded. *Degree requirements:* For master's, comprehensive exam (for some programs), thesis (for MS); for doctorate, one foreign language, comprehensive exam, thesis/dissertation, qualifying exam. *Entrance requirements:* For master's and doctorate, GRE General Test, minimum GPA of 3.0, transcript, goal statement, resume, 3 letters of recommendation. Additional exam requirements/recommendations for international students: Required—TOEFL (minimum score: paper-based 525, iBT 71), Michigan English Language Assessment Battery (minimum score of 75), IELTS (minimum score of 6.0), PTE Academic (minimum score of 48), or completion of ELS level 112 Intensive Program. *Application deadline:* For fall admission, 7/12 for domestic students; for spring admission, 11/29 for domestic students. Applications are processed on a rolling basis. Application fee: $45 ($70 for international students). Electronic applications accepted. *Expenses:* Tuition, state resident: full-time $10,864; part-time $495 per credit hour. Tuition, nonresident: full-time $18,380; part-time $837 per credit hour. *Financial support:* Research assistantships with full tuition reimbursements, teaching assistantships with full tuition reimbursements, career-related internships or fieldwork, Federal Work-Study, scholarships/grants, and unspecified assistantships available. Financial award application deadline: 2/1. *Unit head:* Dr. Andrew Tonge, Chairman, 330-672-9046, E-mail: tonge@math.kent.edu. *Application contact:* Artem Zvavitch, Professor and Graduate Coordinator, 330-672-2430, Fax: 330-672-2209, E-mail: math-gradinfo@math.kent.edu.
Website: http://www.kent.edu/math/

Kent State University, College of Education, Health and Human Services, School of Teaching, Learning and Curriculum Studies, Program in Math Specialization, Kent, OH 44242-0001. Offers M Ed, MA. *Program availability:* Part-time. *Entrance requirements:* For master's, 2 letters of reference, goals statement. Additional exam requirements/recommendations for international students: Required—TOEFL (minimum score 550 paper-based; 80 iBT). Electronic applications accepted. *Expenses:* Tuition, state resident: full-time $10,864; part-time $495 per credit hour. Tuition, nonresident: full-time $18,380; part-time $837 per credit hour.

Lakehead University, Graduate Studies, School of Mathematical Sciences, Thunder Bay, ON P7B 5E1, Canada. Offers computer science (M Sc); mathematical science (MA). *Program availability:* Part-time, evening/weekend. *Degree requirements:* For master's, thesis optional. *Entrance requirements:* For master's, minimum B average, honours degree in mathematics or computer science. Additional exam requirements/recommendations for international students: Required—TOEFL. *Faculty research:* Numerical analysis, classical analysis, theoretical computer science, abstract harmonic analysis, functional analysis.

Lamar University, College of Graduate Studies, College of Arts and Sciences, Department of Mathematics, Beaumont, TX 77710. Offers MS. *Faculty:* 5 full-time (4 women). *Students:* 9 full-time (3 women), 2 part-time (1 woman); includes 1 minority (Black or African American, non-Hispanic/Latino), 2 international. Average age 31. 12 applicants, 75% accepted, 5 enrolled. In 2015, 10 master's awarded. *Degree requirements:* For master's, comprehensive exam (for some programs), thesis optional. *Entrance requirements:* For master's, GRE General Test, minimum GPA of 2.5 in last 60 hours of undergraduate course work. Additional exam requirements/recommendations for international students: Required—TOEFL (minimum score 550 paper-based; 79 iBT), IELTS (minimum score 6.5). *Application deadline:* For fall admission, 8/1 for domestic students, 7/1 for international students; for spring admission, 1/5 for domestic students, 12/5 for international students. Applications are processed on a rolling basis. Application fee: $25 ($50 for international students). Electronic applications accepted. *Expenses: Tuition, area resident:* Full-time $6720; part-time $4032. Tuition, nonresident: full-time $14,880; part-time $8928. *Required fees:* $1900; $950 $784. *Financial support:* Fellowships, research assistantships, and teaching assistantships available. Financial award application deadline: 4/1. *Faculty research:* Complex analysis, differential equations, algebra, topology statistics. *Total annual research expenditures:* $43,585. *Unit head:* Dr. MaryE Wilkinson, Chair, 409-880-8792, Fax: 409-880-8794, E-mail: chair@math.lamar.edu. *Application contact:* Melissa Gallien, Director, Admissions and Academic Services, 409-880-8888, Fax: 409-880-7419, E-mail: gradmissions@lamar.edu.
Website: http://artssciences.lamar.edu/mathematics

Lee University, Program in Education, Cleveland, TN 37320-3450. Offers art (MAT); curriculum and instruction (M Ed, Ed S); early childhood (MAT); educational leadership (M Ed, Ed S); elementary education (MAT); English and math (MAT); English and science (MAT); English and social studies (MAT); higher education administration (MS); history (MAT); history and economics (MAT); math and science (MAT); math and social studies (MAT); middle grades (MAT); science and social studies (MASW); secondary education (MAT); Spanish (MAT); special education (M Ed, MAT); TESOL (MAT). *Accreditation:* NCATE. *Program availability:* Part-time. *Faculty:* 12 full-time (6 women), 7 part-time/adjunct (2 women). *Students:* 39 full-time (28 women), 57 part-time (37 women); includes 13 minority (7 Black or African American, non-Hispanic/Latino; 4 Hispanic/Latino; 1 Native Hawaiian or other Pacific Islander, non-Hispanic/Latino; 1 Two or more races, non-Hispanic/Latino), 5 international. Average age 30. 46 applicants, 76% accepted, 29 enrolled. In 2015, 45 master's, 10 other advanced degrees awarded. *Degree requirements:* For master's, variable foreign language requirement, thesis optional, internship. *Entrance requirements:* For master's, MAT or GRE General Test, minimum undergraduate GPA of 2.75, 3 letters of recommendation, interview, writing sample, official transcripts, background check; for Ed S, minimum undergraduate and master's GPA of 2.75, official transcripts for undergraduate and master's degrees. Additional exam requirements/recommendations for international students: Required—TOEFL (minimum score 450 paper-based). *Application deadline:* For fall admission, 6/1 priority date for domestic and international students; for spring admission, 11/1 priority date for domestic and international students; for summer admission, 4/1 priority date for domestic and international students. Applications are processed on a rolling basis. Application fee: $25. Electronic applications accepted. *Expenses: Tuition, area resident:* Full-time $10,800; part-time $600 per credit hour. *Required fees:* $35 per term. One-time fee: $25. Tuition and fees vary according to program. *Financial support:* In 2015–16, 52 students received support. Career-related internships or fieldwork, Federal Work-Study, institutionally sponsored loans, scholarships/grants, and unspecified assistantships available. Financial award application deadline: 3/1; financial award applicants required to submit FAFSA. *Unit head:* Dr. William Kamm, Director, 423-614-8544, E-mail: wkamm@leeuniversity.edu. *Application contact:* Crystal Keeter, Graduate Education Secretary, 423-614-8544, E-mail: ckeeter@leeuniversity.edu.
Website: http://www.leeuniversity.edu/academics/graduate/education

Lehigh University, College of Arts and Sciences, Department of Mathematics, Bethlehem, PA 18015. Offers applied mathematics (MS, PhD); mathematics (MS, PhD); statistics (MS). *Program availability:* Part-time. *Faculty:* 24 full-time (3 women), 1 part-time/adjunct (0 women). *Students:* 38 full-time (11 women), 8 part-time (3 women); includes 1 minority (Hispanic/Latino), 17 international. Average age 25. 147 applicants, 39% accepted, 11 enrolled. In 2015, 17 master's, 3 doctorates awarded. Terminal master's awarded for partial completion of doctoral program. *Degree requirements:* For master's, comprehensive exam, thesis optional; for doctorate, comprehensive exam, thesis/dissertation, qualifying examination, general examination, advanced topic examination. *Entrance requirements:* For master's and doctorate, GRE General Test (strongly recommended), minimum undergraduate GPA of 2.75, 3.0 for last two semesters; adequate background in math. Additional exam requirements/recommendations for international students: Required—TOEFL (minimum score 85 iBT). *Application deadline:* For fall admission, 1/1 for domestic and international students; for spring admission, 12/1 for domestic and international students. Application fee: $75. Electronic applications accepted. *Financial support:* In 2015–16, 31 students received support, including 1 fellowship with full tuition reimbursement available (averaging $25,000 per year), 1 research assistantship with full tuition reimbursement available (averaging $20,000 per year), 25 teaching assistantships with full tuition reimbursements available (averaging $20,000 per year); tuition waivers (partial) also

available. Financial award application deadline: 1/1. *Faculty research:* Probability and statistics, geometry and topology, algebra, discrete mathematics, differential equations. *Total annual research expenditures:* $182,459. *Unit head:* Dr. Wei-Min Huang, Chairman, 610-758-3730, Fax: 610-758-3767, E-mail: wh02@lehigh.edu. *Application contact:* Dr. Terry Napier, Graduate Director, 610-758-3755,
E-mail: mathgrad@lehigh.edu.
Website: http://www.lehigh.edu/~math/grad.html

Lehman College of the City University of New York, School of Natural and Social Sciences, Department of Mathematics and Computer Science, Program in Mathematics, Bronx, NY 10468-1589. Offers MA. *Program availability:* Part-time, evening/weekend. *Degree requirements:* For master's, one foreign language, thesis or alternative.

Long Island University–LIU Post, College of Liberal Arts and Sciences, Brookville, NY 11548-1300. Offers applied mathematics (MS); behavior analysis (MA); biology (MS); criminal justice (MS); earth science (MS); English (MA); environmental studies (MS); environmental sustainability (MS); genetic counseling (MS); gerontology (Advanced Certificate); health care administration (MPA); history (MA); interdisciplinary studies (MA, MS); mathematics for secondary school teachers (MS); mobile GIS application development (Advanced Certificate); non-profit management (Advanced Certificate); political science (MA); psychology (MA); public administration (MPA). *Program availability:* Part-time, evening/weekend, online learning. *Faculty:* 77 full-time (35 women), 36 part-time/adjunct (17 women). *Students:* 254 full-time (178 women), 177 part-time (134 women); includes 104 minority (40 Black or African American, non-Hispanic/Latino; 27 Asian, non-Hispanic/Latino; 28 Hispanic/Latino; 1 Native Hawaiian or other Pacific Islander, non-Hispanic/Latino; 8 Two or more races, non-Hispanic/Latino), 44 international. Average age 31. 686 applicants, 47% accepted, 138 enrolled. In 2015, 135 master's awarded. *Degree requirements:* For master's, comprehensive exam (for some programs), thesis (for some programs). *Entrance requirements:* Additional exam requirements/recommendations for international students: Required—TOEFL (minimum score 550 paper-based; 79 iBT), IELTS (minimum score 6.5). *Application deadline:* Applications are processed on a rolling basis. Application fee: $50. Electronic applications accepted. *Expenses:* $1155 per credit; $934 full-time fees; $442 part-time fees. *Financial support:* In 2015–16, 48 fellowships (averaging $12,637 per year), 5 research assistantships with full tuition reimbursements were awarded; Federal Work-Study and institutionally sponsored loans also available. Support available to part-time students. Financial award application deadline: 2/15; financial award applicants required to submit FAFSA. *Faculty research:* Biology, criminal justice, earth and environmental science, English, health care and public administration, history, mathematics, political science, psychology, Spanish. *Unit head:* Dr. Nicholas J. Ramer, Acting Dean, 516-299-2233, Fax: 516-299-4140, E-mail: nicholas.ramer@liu.edu. *Application contact:* Carol Zerah, Director of Graduate Admissions, 516-299-2900 Ext. 3952, Fax: 516-299-2137, E-mail: enroll@cwpost.liu.edu.
Website: http://liu.edu/CWPost/Academics/Schools/CLAS

Louisiana State University and Agricultural & Mechanical College, Graduate School, College of Science, Department of Mathematics, Baton Rouge, LA 70803. Offers MS, PhD.

Louisiana Tech University, Graduate School, College of Engineering and Science, Department of Mathematics and Statistics, Ruston, LA 71272. Offers computational analysis and modeling (PhD); mathematics and statistics (MS). *Program availability:* Part-time. *Degree requirements:* For master's, thesis or alternative. *Entrance requirements:* For master's, GRE General Test, minimum GPA of 3.0 in last 60 hours. Additional exam requirements/recommendations for international students: Required—TOEFL. *Application deadline:* For fall admission, 8/1 for domestic students; for spring admission, 2/1 for domestic students. Applications are processed on a rolling basis. Application fee: $20 ($30 for international students). *Financial support:* Teaching assistantships and Federal Work-Study available. Financial award application deadline: 4/1. *Application contact:* Marilyn J. Robinson, Assistant to the Dean, 318-257-2924, Fax: 318-257-4487.
Website: http://coes.latech.edu/mathematics-and-statistics/

Loyola University Chicago, Graduate School, Department of Mathematics and Statistics, Chicago, IL 60660. Offers applied statistics (MS); mathematics (MS). *Program availability:* Part-time. *Faculty:* 19 full-time (3 women). *Students:* 36 full-time (21 women), 9 part-time (4 women); includes 9 minority (2 Black or African American, non-Hispanic/Latino; 3 Asian, non-Hispanic/Latino; 4 Hispanic/Latino), 18 international. Average age 27. 54 applicants, 91% accepted, 18 enrolled. In 2015, 25 master's awarded. *Entrance requirements:* For master's, GRE General Test. Additional exam requirements/recommendations for international students: Required—TOEFL. *Application deadline:* For fall admission, 8/1 for domestic students; for spring admission, 12/1 for domestic students. Applications are processed on a rolling basis. Application fee: $0. Electronic applications accepted. *Expenses: Tuition, area resident:* Full-time $18,054; part-time $9027 per credit hour. *Required fees:* $832; $284 per credit hour. Part-time tuition and fees vary according to course load, degree level and program. *Financial support:* In 2015–16, 13 students received support, including 6 teaching assistantships with tuition reimbursements available (averaging $10,000 per year); fellowships with tuition reimbursements available, career-related internships or fieldwork, Federal Work-Study, institutionally sponsored loans, and tuition waivers (partial) also available. Financial award application deadline: 3/15. *Faculty research:* Nonlinear analysis and partial differential equations, algebra and combinatorics, knot theory, control theory and engineering, probability and applied statistics. *Total annual research expenditures:* $70,000. *Unit head:* Dr. Anthony Giaquinto, Chair, 773-508-3578, Fax: 773-508-2123, E-mail: agiaqui@luc.edu. *Application contact:* Dr. Rafal Goebel, Graduate Program Director for Mathematics, 773-508-3558,
E-mail: rgoebel1@luc.edu.
Website: http://math.luc.edu/

Manhattan College, Graduate Programs, School of Science, Program in Mathematics, Riverdale, NY 10471. Offers MS. *Program availability:* Part-time. *Faculty:* 14 full-time (6 women). *Students:* 2 applicants, 100% accepted. *Degree requirements:* For master's, comprehensive exam, research seminar. *Entrance requirements:* Additional exam requirements/recommendations for international students: Required—TOEFL. *Application deadline:* For fall admission, 4/15 priority date for domestic and international students; for spring admission, 10/30 priority date for domestic and international students. Applications are processed on a rolling basis. Electronic applications accepted. *Financial support:* Unspecified assistantships available. *Faculty research:* Algebra, topology, hyperbolic geometry, operations research, statistics and modeling. *Unit head:* Dr. Constantine Theodosiou, Dean, 718-862-7368,
E-mail: constantine.theodosiou@manhattan.edu. *Application contact:* William Bisset, Vice President for Enrollment, 718-862-7199, Fax: 718-862-8019,
E-mail: william.bisset@manhattan.edu.

Marquette University, Graduate School, College of Arts and Sciences, Department of Mathematics, Statistics, and Computer Science, Milwaukee, WI 53201-1881. Offers bioinformatics (MS); computational sciences (MS, PhD); computing (MS); mathematics education (MS). *Program availability:* Part-time, evening/weekend, online learning. *Faculty:* 30 full-time (8 women), 12 part-time/adjunct (3 women). *Students:* 22 full-time (7 women), 22 part-time (10 women); includes 10 minority (2 Black or African American, non-Hispanic/Latino; 6 Asian, non-Hispanic/Latino; 2 Two or more races, non-Hispanic/Latino), 19 international. Average age 30. 45 applicants, 62% accepted, 10 enrolled. In 2015, 6 master's, 3 doctorates awarded. Terminal master's awarded for partial completion of doctoral program. *Degree requirements:* For master's, thesis (for some programs), essay with oral presentation; for doctorate, comprehensive exam, thesis/dissertation, qualifying examination. *Entrance requirements:* For master's, official transcripts from all current and previous colleges/universities except Marquette, three letters of recommendation; for doctorate, GRE General Test, official transcripts from all current and previous colleges/universities except Marquette, three letters of recommendation. Additional exam requirements/recommendations for international students: Required—TOEFL (minimum score 530 paper-based). *Application deadline:* For fall admission, 1/15 for domestic and international students. Applications are processed on a rolling basis. Application fee: $50. Electronic applications accepted. *Financial support:* In 2015–16, 23 students received support, including 4 fellowships (averaging $1,375 per year), 5 research assistantships with full tuition reimbursements available (averaging $17,000 per year), 15 teaching assistantships with full tuition reimbursements available (averaging $17,000 per year); scholarships/grants, health care benefits, tuition waivers (full and partial), and unspecified assistantships also available. Support available to part-time students. Financial award application deadline: 2/15. *Faculty research:* Models of physiological systems, mathematical immunology, computational group theory, mathematical logic, computational science. *Unit head:* Dr. Rebecca Sanders, Chair, 414-288-7573, Fax: 414-288-1578. *Application contact:* Dr. Stephen Merrill, Professor, 414-288-5237.
Website: http://www.marquette.edu/mscs/grad.shtml

Marshall University, Academic Affairs Division, College of Science, Department of Mathematics, Huntington, WV 25755. Offers MA. *Students:* 17 full-time (5 women), 1 (woman) part-time; includes 2 minority (1 Black or African American, non-Hispanic/Latino; 1 Two or more races, non-Hispanic/Latino), 3 international. Average age 27. In 2015, 5 master's awarded. *Degree requirements:* For master's, thesis (for some programs). *Entrance requirements:* For master's, GRE General Test. Application fee: $40. *Unit head:* Dr. Peter Saveliev, Chairperson, 304-696-4639,
E-mail: saveliev@marshall.edu. *Application contact:* Dr. Peter Savaliev, Information Contact, 304-696-4639, Fax: 304-746-1902.

Massachusetts Institute of Technology, School of Science, Department of Mathematics, Cambridge, MA 02139. Offers PhD. *Faculty:* 44 full-time (4 women), 3 part-time/adjunct (1 woman). *Students:* 125 full-time (23 women); includes 20 minority (12 Asian, non-Hispanic/Latino; 4 Hispanic/Latino; 4 Two or more races, non-Hispanic/Latino), 65 international. Average age 25. 433 applicants, 15% accepted, 33 enrolled. In 2015, 21 doctorates awarded. *Degree requirements:* For doctorate, one foreign language, comprehensive exam, thesis/dissertation. *Entrance requirements:* For doctorate, GRE General Test, GRE Subject Test. Additional exam requirements/recommendations for international students: Required—IELTS (minimum score 6). *Application deadline:* For fall admission, 12/15 for domestic and international students. Application fee: $75. Electronic applications accepted. *Expenses: Tuition:* Full-time $46,400; part-time $725 per credit. One-time fee: $304 full-time. Full-time tuition and fees vary according to course load and program. *Financial support:* In 2015–16, 123 students received support, including 57 fellowships (averaging $40,300 per year), 14 research assistantships (averaging $38,600 per year), 53 teaching assistantships (averaging $42,300 per year); Federal Work-Study, institutionally sponsored loans, scholarships/grants, traineeships, health care benefits, and unspecified assistantships also available. Support available to part-time students. Financial award application deadline: 4/15; financial award applicants required to submit FAFSA. *Faculty research:* Analysis, geometry and topology; algebra and number theory; representation theory; combinatorics, theoretical computer science and computational biology; physical applied mathematics and computational science. *Total annual research expenditures:* $8.7 million. *Unit head:* Prof. Tomasz Mrowka, Department Head, 617-253-4381, Fax: 617-253-4358, E-mail: math@mit.edu. *Application contact:* Graduate Education, 617-452-2007, Fax: 617-253-4358, E-mail: gradofc@math.mit.edu.
Website: http://math.mit.edu/

McGill University, Faculty of Graduate and Postdoctoral Studies, Faculty of Science, Department of Mathematics and Statistics, Montréal, QC H3A 2T5, Canada. Offers computational science and engineering (M Sc); mathematics and statistics (M Sc, MA, PhD), including applied mathematics (M Sc, MA), pure mathematics (M Sc, MA), statistics (M Sc, MA).

McMaster University, School of Graduate Studies, Faculty of Science, Department of Mathematics and Statistics, Hamilton, ON L8S 4M2, Canada. Offers mathematics (M Sc, PhD); statistics (M Sc), including applied statistics, medical statistics, statistical theory. *Program availability:* Part-time. *Degree requirements:* For master's, thesis or alternative, oral exam; for doctorate, comprehensive exam, thesis/dissertation. *Entrance requirements:* For master's, minimum B+ average in last year of honors degree; for doctorate, minimum B+ average, M Sc in mathematics or statistics. Additional exam requirements/recommendations for international students: Required—TOEFL (minimum score 550 paper-based). *Faculty research:* Algebra, analysis, applied mathematics, geometry and topology, probability and statistics.

McNeese State University, Doré School of Graduate Studies, College of Science, Department of Mathematics, Computer Science, and Statistics, Lake Charles, LA 70609. Offers computer science (MS); mathematics (MS); statistics (MS). *Program availability:* Evening/weekend. *Degree requirements:* For master's, comprehensive exam, thesis or alternative, written exam. *Entrance requirements:* For master's, GRE.

Memorial University of Newfoundland, School of Graduate Studies, Department of Mathematics and Statistics, St. John's, NL A1C 5S7, Canada. Offers mathematics (M Sc, PhD); statistics (M Sc, MAS, PhD). *Program availability:* Part-time. *Degree requirements:* For master's, thesis, practicum and report (MAS); for doctorate, comprehensive exam, thesis/dissertation, oral defense of thesis. *Entrance requirements:* For master's, 2nd class honors degree (MAS, M Sc); for doctorate, MAS or M Sc in mathematics and statistics. *Application deadline:* For fall admission, 1/31 for domestic and international students. Applications are processed on a rolling basis. Application fee: $50 Canadian dollars ($100 Canadian dollars for international students). Electronic applications accepted. *Expenses: Tuition, area resident:* Full-time $2199 Canadian dollars. *International tuition:* $2859 Canadian dollars full-time. *Financial support:* Fellowships and teaching assistantships available. Financial award application deadline: 1/31. *Faculty research:* Algebra, topology, applied mathematics, mathematical statistics, applied statistics and probability. *Unit head:* Dr. Chris Radford, Head, 709-864-8783, Fax: 709-864-3010, E-mail: head@math.mun.ca. *Application contact:* Dr. J.C. Loredo-Osti, Graduate Officer, 709-864-8729, Fax: 709-864-3010,
E-mail: mathgrad@mun.ca.
Website: http://www.mun.ca/math

Mathematics

Miami University, College of Arts and Science, Department of Mathematics, Oxford, OH 45056. Offers MA, MAT, MS. *Students:* 20 full-time (3 women), 1 (woman) part-time; includes 1 minority (Asian, non-Hispanic/Latino), 4 international. Average age 25. In 2015, 10 master's awarded. *Entrance requirements:* For master's, three letters of recommendation. Additional exam requirements/recommendations for international students: Recommended—TOEFL (minimum score 550 paper-based; 80 iBT), IELTS (minimum score 6.5), TSE (minimum score 54). *Application deadline:* For fall admission, 2/1 for domestic and international students. Application fee: $50. Electronic applications accepted. *Expenses:* Tuition, state resident: full-time $12,888; part-time $537 per credit hour. Tuition, nonresident: full-time $29,022; part-time $1209 per credit hour. *Required fees:* $530; $24 per credit hour. $30 per semester. Part-time tuition and fees vary according to course load and program. *Financial support:* Application deadline: 2/1; applicants required to submit FAFSA. *Unit head:* Dr. Patrick Dowling, Department Chair, 513-529-5818, E-mail: dowlinpn@miamioh.edu. *Application contact:* Dr. Doug Ward, Director of Graduate Studies, 513-529-3534, E-mail: wardde@miamioh.edu. Website: http://www.MiamiOH.edu/mathematics

Michigan State University, The Graduate School, College of Natural Science, Department of Mathematics, East Lansing, MI 48824. Offers applied mathematics (MS, PhD); industrial mathematics (MS); mathematics (MAT, MS, PhD). *Entrance requirements:* Additional exam requirements/recommendations for international students: Required—TOEFL. Electronic applications accepted.

Michigan Technological University, Graduate School, College of Sciences and Arts, Department of Mathematical Sciences, Houghton, MI 49931. Offers MS, PhD. *Program availability:* Part-time. *Faculty:* 35 full-time (9 women), 9 part-time/adjunct. *Students:* 42 full-time (18 women), 2 part-time, 25 international. Average age 28. 83 applicants, 35% accepted, 12 enrolled. In 2015, 12 master's awarded. Terminal master's awarded for partial completion of doctoral program. *Degree requirements:* For master's, comprehensive exam (for some programs), thesis (for some programs); for doctorate, comprehensive exam, thesis/dissertation, proficiency exam. *Entrance requirements:* For master's and doctorate, GRE (Michigan Tech students exempt), statement of purpose, personal statement, official transcripts, 3 letters of recommendation, resume/curriculum vitae. Additional exam requirements/recommendations for international students: Required—TOEFL (recommended score 79 iBT) or IELTS. *Application deadline:* For fall admission, 2/15 priority date for domestic and international students. Applications are processed on a rolling basis. Electronic applications accepted. *Expenses:* Tuition, state resident: full-time $15,507; part-time $861.50 per credit. Tuition, nonresident: full-time $15,507; part-time $861.50 per credit. *Required fees:* $248; $248. Tuition and fees vary according to course load and program. *Financial support:* In 2015–16, 39 students received support, including 1 fellowship with tuition reimbursement available (averaging $14,516 per year), 5 research assistantships with tuition reimbursements available (averaging $14,516 per year), 30 teaching assistantships with tuition reimbursements available (averaging $14,516 per year); career-related internships or fieldwork, Federal Work-Study, scholarships/grants, health care benefits, unspecified assistantships, and cooperative program also available. Financial award applicants required to submit FAFSA. *Faculty research:* Fluid dynamics, mathematical modeling, design theory, coding theory, statistical genetics. *Total annual research expenditures:* $285,781. *Unit head:* Dr. Mark S. Gockenbach, Chair, 906-487-2068, Fax: 906-487-3133, E-mail: msgocken@mtu.edu. *Application contact:* Dr. Jianping Dong, Director of Graduate Studies, 906-487-2928, Fax: 906-487-3133, E-mail: jdong@mtu.edu. Website: http://www.mtu.edu/math/

Middle Tennessee State University, College of Graduate Studies, College of Basic and Applied Sciences, Department of Mathematical Sciences, Murfreesboro, TN 37132. Offers mathematics (MS, MST). *Program availability:* Part-time, evening/weekend, online learning. *Degree requirements:* For master's, comprehensive exam, thesis optional. *Entrance requirements:* For master's, GRE General Test or MAT. Additional exam requirements/recommendations for international students: Required—TOEFL (minimum score 525 paper-based; 71 iBT) or IELTS (minimum score 6). Electronic applications accepted.

Minnesota State University Mankato, College of Graduate Studies and Research, College of Science, Engineering and Technology, Department of Mathematics and Statistics, Program in Mathematics, Mankato, MN 56001. Offers MA, MS. *Degree requirements:* For master's, one foreign language, comprehensive exam, thesis or alternative. *Entrance requirements:* For master's, GRE General Test, minimum GPA of 3.0 during previous 2 years. Additional exam requirements/recommendations for international students: Required—TOEFL. Electronic applications accepted.

Mississippi College, Graduate School, College of Arts and Sciences, School of Science and Mathematics, Department of Mathematics, Clinton, MS 39058. Offers M Ed, MCS, MS. *Program availability:* Part-time. *Degree requirements:* For master's, comprehensive exam, thesis optional. *Entrance requirements:* For master's, GRE or NTE, minimum GPA of 2.5. Additional exam requirements/recommendations for international students: Recommended—TOEFL, IELTS. Electronic applications accepted.

Mississippi State University, College of Arts and Sciences, Department of Mathematics and Statistics, Mississippi State, MS 39762. Offers mathematical sciences (PhD); mathematics (MS); statistics (MS). *Program availability:* Part-time. *Faculty:* 25 full-time (5 women). *Students:* 35 full-time (13 women), 5 part-time (3 women); includes 7 minority (all Black or African American, non-Hispanic/Latino), 21 international. Average age 28. 49 applicants, 71% accepted, 13 enrolled. In 2015, 12 master's, 3 doctorates awarded. Terminal master's awarded for partial completion of doctoral program. *Degree requirements:* For master's, thesis optional, comprehensive oral or written exam; for doctorate, one foreign language, thesis/dissertation, comprehensive oral and written exam. *Entrance requirements:* For master's, minimum GPA of 2.75 on last two years of undergraduate courses; for doctorate, GRE. Additional exam requirements/recommendations for international students: Required—TOEFL (minimum score 477 paper-based; 53 iBT); Recommended—IELTS (minimum score 4.5). *Application deadline:* For fall admission, 3/15 priority date for domestic students, 5/1 for international students; for spring admission, 11/1 for domestic students, 9/1 for international students. Applications are processed on a rolling basis. Application fee: $60. Electronic applications accepted. *Expenses:* Tuition, area resident: Full-time $7502; part-time $833.74 per credit hour. Tuition, nonresident: full-time $20,142; part-time $2238.24 per credit hour. *Financial support:* In 2015–16, 25 teaching assistantships with full tuition reimbursements (averaging $14,656 per year) were awarded; Federal Work-Study, institutionally sponsored loans, tuition waivers (partial), and unspecified assistantships also available. Financial award application deadline: 4/1; financial award applicants required to submit FAFSA. *Faculty research:* Differential equations, algebra, numerical analysis, functional analysis, applied statistics. *Total annual research expenditures:* $1.3 million. *Unit head:* Dr. Mohsen Razzaghi, Department Head, 662-325-3414, Fax: 662-325-0005, E-mail: razzaghi@math.msstate.edu. *Application contact:* Meredith Nagel, Admissions Assistant, 662-325-9077, E-mail: mnagel@grad.msstate.edu. Website: http://www.math.msstate.edu

Missouri State University, Graduate College, College of Natural and Applied Sciences, Department of Mathematics, Springfield, MO 65897. Offers mathematics (MS); natural and applied science (MNAS), including mathematics (MNAS, MS Ed); secondary education (MS Ed), including mathematics (MNAS, MS Ed). *Program availability:* Part-time. *Faculty:* 21 full-time (4 women). *Students:* 11 full-time (3 women), 23 part-time (13 women); includes 2 minority (both Black or African American, non-Hispanic/Latino), 7 international. Average age 27. 23 applicants, 43% accepted, 3 enrolled. In 2015, 8 master's awarded. *Degree requirements:* For master's, comprehensive exam, thesis or alternative. *Entrance requirements:* For master's, GRE (MS, MNAS), minimum undergraduate GPA of 3.0 (MS, MNAS), 9-12 teacher certification (MS Ed). Additional exam requirements/recommendations for international students: Required—TOEFL (minimum score 550 paper-based; 79 iBT), IELTS (minimum score 6). *Application deadline:* For fall admission, 7/20 priority date for domestic students, 5/1 for international students; for spring admission, 12/20 priority date for domestic students, 9/1 for international students. Applications are processed on a rolling basis. Application fee: $35 ($50 for international students). Electronic applications accepted. *Expenses:* Tuition, state resident: full-time $5500. Tuition, nonresident: full-time $10,108. *Required fees:* $1000. *Financial support:* In 2015–16, 11 teaching assistantships with full tuition reimbursements (averaging $10,464 per year) were awarded; Federal Work-Study, institutionally sponsored loans, scholarships/grants, and unspecified assistantships also available. Financial award application deadline: 3/31; financial award applicants required to submit FAFSA. *Faculty research:* Harmonic analysis, commutative algebra, number theory, K-theory, probability. *Unit head:* Dr. William Bray, Department Head, 417-836-5112, Fax: 417-836-6966, E-mail: mathematics@missouristate.edu. *Application contact:* Michael Edwards, Coordinator of Graduate Admissions, 417-836-5330, Fax: 417-836-6200, E-mail: michaeledwards@missouristate.edu. Website: http://math.missouristate.edu/

Missouri University of Science and Technology, Graduate School, Department of Mathematics and Statistics, Rolla, MO 65409. Offers applied mathematics (MS); mathematics (MST, PhD), including mathematics (PhD), mathematics education (MST), statistics (PhD). *Faculty:* 21 full-time (9 women), 1 part-time/adjunct (0 women). *Students:* 38 full-time (16 women), 5 part-time (0 women), 33 international. Average age 29. 37 applicants, 68% accepted, 8 enrolled. In 2015, 5 master's, 3 doctorates awarded. Terminal master's awarded for partial completion of doctoral program. *Degree requirements:* For master's, thesis or alternative; for doctorate, one foreign language, thesis/dissertation. *Entrance requirements:* For master's and doctorate, GRE General Test, GRE Subject Test. Additional exam requirements/recommendations for international students: Required—TOEFL (minimum score 550 paper-based). *Application deadline:* For fall admission, 7/1 for domestic students. Applications are processed on a rolling basis. Application fee: $55 ($75 for international students). Electronic applications accepted. *Expenses:* Tuition, state resident: full-time $10,536. Tuition, nonresident: full-time $27,015. Full-time tuition and fees vary according to course load. *Financial support:* In 2015–16, 5 fellowships, 1 research assistantship with partial tuition reimbursement (averaging $1,814 per year), 19 teaching assistantships with partial tuition reimbursements (averaging $1,813 per year) were awarded; institutionally sponsored loans also available. *Faculty research:* Analysis, differential equations, topology, statistics. *Total annual research expenditures:* $223,299. *Unit head:* Dr. Leon M. Hall, Chair, 573-341-4641, Fax: 573-341-4741, E-mail: lmhall@mst.edu. *Application contact:* Dr. V. A. Samaranayake, Director of Graduate Studies, 573-341-4658, Fax: 573-341-4741, E-mail: vsam@mst.edu. Website: http://math.mst.edu/

Molloy College, Graduate Education Program, Rockville Centre, NY 11571-5002. Offers adolescent education in biology (MS Ed); bilingual extension (Advanced Certificate); childhood education (MS Ed); early childhood education (MS Ed); English (MS Ed); mathematics (MS Ed); social studies (MS Ed); Spanish (MS Ed); special education adolescent (Advanced Certificate); special education childhood (Advanced Certificate); special education on both childhood and adolescent levels (MS Ed); teaching English to speakers of other languages (TESOL) in grades Pre-K to 12 (MS Ed); TESOL (Advanced Certificate). *Accreditation:* NCATE. *Program availability:* Part-time, evening/weekend. *Faculty:* 18 full-time (16 women), 29 part-time/adjunct (26 women). *Students:* 84 full-time (66 women), 176 part-time (133 women); includes 35 minority (8 Black or African American, non-Hispanic/Latino; 4 Asian, non-Hispanic/Latino; 23 Hispanic/Latino). Average age 27. 116 applicants, 79% accepted, 83 enrolled. In 2015, 85 master's, 5 Advanced Certificates awarded. *Entrance requirements:* Additional exam requirements/recommendations for international students: Required—TOEFL (minimum score 550 paper-based; 79 iBT). *Application deadline:* Applications are processed on a rolling basis. Application fee: $60. Electronic applications accepted. *Expenses:* Tuition, area resident: Full-time $18,450; part-time $1025 per credit. *Required fees:* $900; $740 per unit. Tuition and fees vary according to course load. *Financial support:* Applicants required to submit FAFSA. *Faculty research:* TESOL education, bilingual education, meeting the needs of students with disabilities, teacher collaboration, public policy issues. *Unit head:* Joanne O'Brien, Associate Dean/Director, 516-323-3116, E-mail: jobrien@molloy.edu. *Application contact:* Jaclyn Machowicz, Assistant Director for Admissions, 516-323-4010, E-mail: jmachowicz@molloy.edu.

Montana State University, The Graduate School, College of Letters and Science, Department of Mathematical Sciences, Bozeman, MT 59717. Offers mathematics (MS, PhD), including mathematics education option (MS); statistics (MS, PhD). *Program availability:* Part-time, online learning. *Degree requirements:* For master's, comprehensive exam, thesis (for some programs); for doctorate, comprehensive exam, thesis/dissertation. *Entrance requirements:* For master's and doctorate, GRE General Test. Additional exam requirements/recommendations for international students: Required—TOEFL (minimum score 550 paper-based). Electronic applications accepted. *Faculty research:* Applied mathematics, dynamical systems, statistics, mathematics education, mathematical and computational biology.

Montclair State University, The Graduate School, College of Science and Mathematics, Program in Mathematics, Montclair, NJ 07043-1624. Offers mathematics education (MS); pure and applied mathematics (MS). *Program availability:* Part-time, evening/weekend. *Students:* 9 full-time (4 women), 53 part-time (27 women); includes 16 minority (2 Black or African American, non-Hispanic/Latino; 4 Asian, non-Hispanic/Latino; 8 Hispanic/Latino; 2 Two or more races, non-Hispanic/Latino), 1 international. Average age 33. 22 applicants, 82% accepted, 14 enrolled. In 2015, 17 master's awarded. *Degree requirements:* For master's, comprehensive exam. *Entrance requirements:* For master's, GRE General Test, 2 letters of recommendation, essay. Additional exam requirements/recommendations for international students: Required—TOEFL (minimum score 83 iBT), IELTS (minimum score 6.5). *Application deadline:* Applications are processed on a rolling basis. Application fee: $60. Electronic applications accepted. *Expenses:* Tuition, state resident: part-time $553 per credit. Tuition, nonresident: part-time $854 per credit. *Required fees:* $91 per credit. Tuition and fees vary according to program. *Financial support:* In 2015–16, 9 research assistantships with full tuition reimbursements (averaging $7,000 per year) were awarded; Federal Work-Study, scholarships/grants, and unspecified assistantships also available. Support available to part-time students. Financial award application deadline:

3/1; financial award applicants required to submit FAFSA. *Faculty research:* Computation, applied analysis. *Unit head:* Dr. Helen Roberts, Chairperson, 973-655-5132. *Application contact:* Amy Aiello, Director of Graduate Admissions and Operations, 973-655-5147, Fax: 973-655-7869, E-mail: graduate.school@montclair.edu.

Morgan State University, School of Graduate Studies, School of Computer, Mathematical, and Natural Sciences, Department of Mathematics, Baltimore, MD 21251. Offers MA. *Program availability:* Part-time, evening/weekend. *Degree requirements:* For master's, comprehensive exam, thesis. *Entrance requirements:* For master's, GRE. Additional exam requirements/recommendations for international students: Required—TOEFL (minimum score 550 paper-based). *Faculty research:* Number theory, semigroups, analysis, operations research.

Murray State University, College of Science, Engineering and Technology, Program in Mathematics and Statistics, Murray, KY 42071. Offers MA, MAT, MS. *Program availability:* Part-time. *Degree requirements:* For master's, comprehensive exam, thesis optional. *Entrance requirements:* For master's, GRE General Test. Additional exam requirements/recommendations for international students: Required—TOEFL. *Faculty research:* Algebraic structures, mathematical biology, topolgy.

New Jersey Institute of Technology, College of Science and Liberal Arts, Newark, NJ 07102. Offers applied mathematics (MS); applied physics (M Sc, PhD); applied statistical models (Certificate); applied statistics (MS); biology (MS, PhD); biostatistics (MS); biostatistics essentials (Certificate); chemistry (MS, PhD); computational biology (MS); environmental science (MS, PhD); history (MA, MAT); materials science and engineering (MS, PhD); mathematical and computational finance (MS); mathematics science (PhD); pharmaceutical chemistry (MS); professional and technical communications (MS); technical common essentials (Certificate). *Program availability:* Part-time, evening/weekend. *Faculty:* 153 full-time (35 women), 100 part-time/adjunct (40 women). *Students:* 212 full-time (82 women), 94 part-time (37 women); includes 72 minority (22 Black or African American, non-Hispanic/Latino; 25 Asian, non-Hispanic/Latino; 19 Hispanic/Latino; 6 Two or more races, non-Hispanic/Latino), 164 international. Average age 29. 519 applicants, 62% accepted, 104 enrolled. In 2015, 98 master's, 21 doctorates, 3 other advanced degrees awarded. Terminal master's awarded for partial completion of doctoral program. *Degree requirements:* For master's, thesis optional; for doctorate, thesis/dissertation. *Entrance requirements:* For master's, GRE General Test; for doctorate, GRE General Test, minimum graduate GPA of 3.5. Additional exam requirements/recommendations for international students: Required—TOEFL (minimum score 550 paper-based; 79 iBT). *Application deadline:* For fall admission, 6/1 priority date for domestic students, 5/1 priority date for international students; for spring admission, 11/15 priority date for domestic and international students. Applications are processed on a rolling basis. Application fee: $75. Electronic applications accepted. *Expenses:* $28,800 per year non-resident full-time. *Financial support:* In 2015–16, 56 research assistantships with full tuition reimbursements (averaging $17,711 per year), 52 teaching assistantships with full tuition reimbursements (averaging $17,914 per year) were awarded; fellowships with full tuition reimbursements also available. Financial award application deadline: 1/15. *Total annual research expenditures:* $23.1 million. *Unit head:* Dr. Kevin Belfield, Dean, 973-596-3676, Fax: 973-565-0586, E-mail: kevin.d.belfield@njit.edu. *Application contact:* Stephen Eck, Director of Admissions, 973-596-3300, Fax: 973-596-3461,
E-mail: admissions@njit.edu.
Website: http://csla.njit.edu/

New Mexico Institute of Mining and Technology, Center for Graduate Studies, Department of Mathematics, Socorro, NM 87801. Offers applied and industrial mathematics (PhD); industrial mathematics (MS); mathematics (MS); operations research and statistics (MS). *Degree requirements:* For master's, thesis optional; for doctorate, thesis/dissertation. *Entrance requirements:* For master's, GRE General Test. Additional exam requirements/recommendations for international students: Required—TOEFL (minimum score 540 paper-based). *Expenses:* Tuition, state resident: full-time $5811; part-time $322.81 per credit. Tuition, nonresident: full-time $19,220; part-time $1067.79 per credit. *Required fees:* $1030. Tuition and fees vary according to course load. *Faculty research:* Applied mathematics, differential equations, industrial mathematics, numerical analysis, stochastic processes.

New Mexico State University, College of Arts and Sciences, Department of Mathematical Sciences, Las Cruces, NM 88003-8001. Offers MS, PhD. *Program availability:* Part-time. *Faculty:* 22 full-time (5 women). *Students:* 29 full-time (10 women), 2 part-time (0 women); includes 3 minority (2 Asian, non-Hispanic/Latino; 1 Hispanic/Latino), 25 international. Average age 30. 56 applicants, 38% accepted, 6 enrolled. In 2015, 8 master's, 5 doctorates awarded. *Degree requirements:* For master's, thesis optional, final oral exam; for doctorate, comprehensive exam, thesis/dissertation, final oral exam. *Entrance requirements:* For master's, GRE Subject Test (preferred), 24 credits of upper-division math/statistics, including real analysis and modern algebra. Additional exam requirements/recommendations for international students: Required—TOEFL (minimum score 550 paper-based; 79 iBT), IELTS (minimum score 6.5). *Application deadline:* For fall admission, 2/1 priority date for domestic and international students; for spring admission, 10/1 for domestic and international students. Applications are processed on a rolling basis. Application fee: $40 ($50 for international students). Electronic applications accepted. *Expenses:* $274.50 per credit hour for in-state students, and all students enrolled in six or fewer credits; $839.30 per credit hour for out-of-state and international students enrolled in at least seven hours. *Financial support:* In 2015–16, 28 students received support, including 1 fellowship (averaging $4,088 per year), 1 research assistantship (averaging $13,200 per year), 27 teaching assistantships (averaging $18,059 per year); career-related internships or fieldwork, Federal Work-Study, scholarships/grants, traineeships, health care benefits, and unspecified assistantships also available. Support available to part-time students. Financial award application deadline: 3/1. *Faculty research:* Applied analysis, commutative algebra, logic and foundations, mathematical biology, mathematics education, partial differential equations, probability and statistics, topology. *Total annual research expenditures:* $180,001. *Unit head:* Dr. Joseph Lakey, Department Head, 575-646-3901, Fax: 575-646-1064, E-mail: jlakey@nmsu.edu. *Application contact:* Elizabeth Eres, 575-646-3901, Fax: 575-646-1064, E-mail: gradcomm@nmsu.edu.
Website: http://www.math.nmsu.edu/

★ **New York University,** Graduate School of Arts and Science, Courant Institute of Mathematical Sciences, Department of Mathematics, New York, NY 10012-1019. Offers atmosphere ocean science and mathematics (PhD); mathematics (MS, PhD); mathematics and statistics/operations research (MS); mathematics in finance (MS); scientific computing (MS). *Program availability:* Part-time, evening/weekend. *Degree requirements:* For master's, thesis optional; for doctorate, one foreign language, thesis/dissertation, oral and written exams. *Entrance requirements:* For master's, GRE General Test, GRE Subject Test; for doctorate, GRE General Test, GRE Subject Test (recommended). Additional exam requirements/recommendations for international students: Required—TOEFL. *Faculty research:* Partial differential equations, computational science, applied mathematics, geometry and topology, probability and stochastic processes.

See Close-Up on page 295.

New York University, Polytechnic School of Engineering, Department of Mathematics, New York, NY 10012-1019. Offers MS, PhD. *Program availability:* Part-time, evening/weekend. *Degree requirements:* For master's, comprehensive exam (for some programs), thesis (for some programs); for doctorate, comprehensive exam, thesis/dissertation. *Entrance requirements:* Additional exam requirements/recommendations for international students: Required—TOEFL (minimum score 550 paper-based; 80 iBT); Recommended—IELTS (minimum score 6.5). Electronic applications accepted. *Faculty research:* Applied super-computing, convex geometric analysis, applications of partial differential equations to mathematical physics, differential topology.

Nicholls State University, Graduate Studies, College of Arts and Sciences, Department of Mathematics, Thibodaux, LA 70310. Offers community/technical college mathematics (MS). *Program availability:* Part-time, evening/weekend. *Degree requirements:* For master's, comprehensive exam. *Entrance requirements:* For master's, GRE General Test. Electronic applications accepted. *Faculty research:* Operations research, statistics, numerical analysis, algebra, topology.

North Carolina Agricultural and Technical State University, School of Graduate Studies, College of Arts and Sciences, Department of Mathematics, Greensboro, NC 27411. Offers applied mathematics (MS), including secondary education. *Accreditation:* NCATE. *Program availability:* Part-time, evening/weekend. *Degree requirements:* For master's, comprehensive exam, thesis or alternative, qualifying exam. *Entrance requirements:* For master's, GRE General Test, minimum GPA of 3.0.

North Carolina Central University, College of Science and Technology, Department of Mathematics and Computer Science, Durham, NC 27707-3129. Offers applied mathematics (MS); mathematics education (MS); pure mathematics (MS). *Program availability:* Part-time, evening/weekend. *Degree requirements:* For master's, one foreign language, comprehensive exam, thesis. *Entrance requirements:* For master's, minimum GPA of 3.0 in major, 2.5 overall. Additional exam requirements/recommendations for international students: Required—TOEFL. *Faculty research:* Structure theorems for Lie algebra, Kleene monoids and semi-groups, theoretical computer science, mathematics education.

North Carolina State University, Graduate School, College of Agriculture and Life Sciences and College of Engineering and College of Physical and Mathematical Sciences, Program in Financial Mathematics, Raleigh, NC 27695. Offers MFM. *Program availability:* Part-time. *Degree requirements:* For master's, thesis optional, project/internship. *Entrance requirements:* For master's, GRE General Test. Additional exam requirements/recommendations for international students: Required—TOEFL (minimum score 550 paper-based). Electronic applications accepted. *Faculty research:* Financial mathematics modeling and computation, futures, options and commodities markets, real options, credit risk, portfolio optimization.

North Carolina State University, Graduate School, College of Physical and Mathematical Sciences, Department of Mathematics, Program in Mathematics, Raleigh, NC 27695. Offers MS, PhD. *Degree requirements:* For master's, thesis (for some programs); for doctorate, thesis/dissertation. *Entrance requirements:* For master's and doctorate, GRE, GRE Subject Test (recommended). Electronic applications accepted.

North Dakota State University, College of Graduate and Interdisciplinary Studies, College of Science and Mathematics, Department of Mathematics, Fargo, ND 58102. Offers applied mathematics (MS, PhD); mathematics (MS, PhD). *Degree requirements:* For master's, comprehensive exam, thesis; for doctorate, one foreign language, comprehensive exam, thesis/dissertation, computer proficiency. *Entrance requirements:* For master's and doctorate, GRE General Test. Additional exam requirements/recommendations for international students: Required—TOEFL (minimum score 525 paper-based; 71 iBT), IELTS. Electronic applications accepted. *Faculty research:* Discrete mathematics, number theory, analysis theory, algebra, applied math.

Northeastern Illinois University, College of Graduate Studies and Research, College of Arts and Sciences, Program in Mathematics, Chicago, IL 60625-4699. Offers MS. *Program availability:* Part-time, evening/weekend. *Degree requirements:* For master's, comprehensive exam, thesis optional, project. *Entrance requirements:* For master's, minimum GPA of 2.75, 6 undergraduate courses in mathematics. Additional exam requirements/recommendations for international students: Required—TOEFL (minimum score 550 paper-based; 79 iBT). Electronic applications accepted. *Faculty research:* Numerical analysis, mathematical biology, operations research, statistics, geometry and mathematics of finance.

Northeastern University, College of Science, Boston, MA 02115-5096. Offers applied mathematics (MS); bioinformatics (MS); biology (PhD); biotechnology (MS); chemistry (MS, PhD); ecology, evolution, and marine biology (PhD); marine biology (MS); mathematics (MS, PhD); network science (PhD); operations research (MSOR); physics (MS, PhD); psychology (PhD). *Program availability:* Part-time. *Faculty:* 216 full-time (70 women), 62 part-time/adjunct (20 women). *Students:* 517 full-time (252 women), 80 part-time (39 women). In 2015, 94 master's, 46 doctorates awarded. Terminal master's awarded for partial completion of doctoral program. *Degree requirements:* For master's, comprehensive exam (for some programs), thesis; for doctorate, comprehensive exam (for some programs), thesis/dissertation. *Entrance requirements:* For master's, GRE General Test. *Application deadline:* Applications are processed on a rolling basis. Application fee: $75. Electronic applications accepted. *Expenses:* $1,325 per credit; $1,170 per credit (for marine biology). *Financial support:* Fellowships with tuition reimbursements, research assistantships with tuition reimbursements, teaching assistantships with tuition reimbursements, career-related internships or fieldwork, scholarships/grants, health care benefits, tuition waivers (full and partial), and unspecified assistantships available. Support available to part-time students. Financial award applicants required to submit FAFSA. *Unit head:* Dr. Jonathan Tilly, Interim Dean. *Application contact:* Graduate Student Services, 617-373-4275,
E-mail: gradcos@neu.edu.
Website: http://www.northeastern.edu/cos/

Northern Arizona University, Graduate College, College of Engineering, Forestry, and Natural Sciences, Department of Mathematics and Statistics, Flagstaff, AZ 86011. Offers applied statistics (Certificate); mathematics (MS); mathematics education (MS); statistics (MS). *Program availability:* Part-time. *Degree requirements:* For master's, comprehensive exam (for some programs), thesis (for some programs). *Entrance requirements:* For master's, minimum GPA of 3.0. Additional exam requirements/recommendations for international students: Required—TOEFL (minimum score 550 paper-based; 80 iBT), IELTS (minimum score 7). *Application deadline:* For fall admission, 3/15 priority date for domestic and international students; for spring admission, 10/15 priority date for domestic and international students. Applications are processed on a rolling basis. Application fee: $65. Electronic applications accepted. *Expenses: Tuition, area resident:* Full-time $8710. Tuition, nonresident: full-time

$20,350. *Required fees:* $896. *Financial support:* Teaching assistantships with full tuition reimbursements, Federal Work-Study, scholarships/grants, health care benefits, tuition waivers (full and partial), and unspecified assistantships available. Financial award applicants required to submit FAFSA. *Faculty research:* Topology, statistics, groups, ring theory, number theory. *Unit head:* Dr. Michael J. Falk, Chair, 928-523-6891, Fax: 928-523-5847, E-mail: michael.falk@nau.edu. *Application contact:* Melinda Miller, Administrative Assistant, 928-523-6228, Fax: 928-523-5847, E-mail: math.grad@nau.edu.
Website: http://nau.edu/CEFNS/NatSci/Math/

Northern Illinois University, Graduate School, College of Liberal Arts and Sciences, Department of Mathematical Sciences, De Kalb, IL 60115-2854. Offers mathematical sciences (PhD); mathematics (MS); statistics (MS). *Program availability:* Part-time. *Faculty:* 43 full-time (10 women), 4 part-time/adjunct (0 women). *Students:* 64 full-time (23 women), 26 part-time (10 women); includes 10 minority (1 Black or African American, non-Hispanic/Latino; 8 Asian, non-Hispanic/Latino; 1 Hispanic/Latino), 31 international. Average age 30. 69 applicants, 83% accepted, 22 enrolled. In 2015, 33 master's, 4 doctorates awarded. Terminal master's awarded for partial completion of doctoral program. *Degree requirements:* For master's, comprehensive exam, thesis optional; for doctorate, one foreign language, thesis/dissertation, candidacy exam, dissertation defense, internship. *Entrance requirements:* For master's, GRE General Test, minimum GPA of 2.75; for doctorate, GRE General Test, minimum GPA of 2.75 (undergraduate), 3.2 (graduate). Additional exam requirements/recommendations for international students: Required—TOEFL (minimum score 550 paper-based). *Application deadline:* For fall admission, 6/1 for domestic students, 5/1 for international students; for spring admission, 11/1 for domestic students, 10/1 for international students. Applications are processed on a rolling basis. Application fee: $40. Electronic applications accepted. *Financial support:* In 2015–16, 39 teaching assistantships with full tuition reimbursements were awarded; fellowships with full tuition reimbursements, research assistantships with full tuition reimbursements, career-related internships or fieldwork, Federal Work-Study, scholarships/grants, tuition waivers (full), and unspecified assistantships also available. Support available to part-time students. Financial award applicants required to submit FAFSA. *Faculty research:* Numerical linear algebra, noncommutative rings, nonlinear partial differential equations, finite group theory, abstract harmonic analysis. *Unit head:* Dr. Bernard Harris, Chair, 815-753-0566, Fax: 815-753-1112, E-mail: harris@math.niu.edu. *Application contact:* Dr. John Ye, Director, Graduate Studies, 815-753-0568, E-mail: ye@math.niu.edu.
Website: http://www.math.niu.edu/

Northwestern University, The Graduate School, Judd A. and Marjorie Weinberg College of Arts and Sciences, Department of Mathematics, Evanston, IL 60208. Offers PhD. Admissions and degrees offered through The Graduate School. *Program availability:* Part-time. *Degree requirements:* For doctorate, thesis/dissertation, preliminary exam. *Entrance requirements:* For doctorate, GRE General Test, GRE Subject Test. Additional exam requirements/recommendations for international students: Required—TOEFL. *Faculty research:* Algebra, algebraic topology, analysis dynamical systems, partial differential equations.

Northwest Missouri State University, Graduate School, College of Arts and Sciences, Department of Mathematics, Computer Science and Information Systems, Maryville, MO 64468-6001. Offers applied computer science (MS); instructional technology (MS); mathematics (MS); teaching mathematics (MS Ed). *Program availability:* Part-time. *Students:* 399 full-time (89 women), 157 part-time (63 women). *Degree requirements:* For master's, comprehensive exam. *Entrance requirements:* For master's, GRE General Test, minimum undergraduate GPA of 2.5, writing sample. Additional exam requirements/recommendations for international students: Required—TOEFL (minimum score 550 paper-based). *Application deadline:* For fall admission, 7/1 for domestic and international students; for spring admission, 11/15 for domestic and international students. Applications are processed on a rolling basis. Application fee: $0 ($50 for international students). *Expenses:* Tuition, state resident: part-time $359 per credit hour. Tuition, nonresident: part-time $612 per credit hour. *Required fees:* $106 per credit hour. *Financial support:* Teaching assistantships with full tuition reimbursements available. Financial award application deadline: 4/1; financial award applicants required to submit FAFSA. *Application contact:* Jeanne Crawford, Office Manager, 660-562-1600, Fax: 660-562-1963, E-mail: jcrawfo@nwmissouri.edu.
Website: http://www.nwmissouri.edu/mathcsis/

Oakland University, Graduate Study and Lifelong Learning, College of Arts and Sciences, Department of Mathematics and Statistics, Program in Mathematics, Rochester, MI 48309-4401. Offers MA. *Students:* 4 full-time (2 women), 5 part-time (1 woman). Average age 30. 15 applicants, 33% accepted, 4 enrolled. In 2015, 4 master's awarded. *Entrance requirements:* Additional exam requirements/recommendations for international students: Required—TOEFL (minimum score 550 paper-based). *Application deadline:* For fall admission, 7/15 priority date for domestic students, 5/1 priority date for international students; for winter admission, 12/1 priority date for domestic students, 9/1 priority date for international students; for spring admission, 3/15 priority date for domestic students. Applications are processed on a rolling basis. Application fee: $0. Electronic applications accepted. *Expenses:* Contact institution. *Financial support:* Application deadline: 3/1; applicants required to submit FAFSA. *Unit head:* Dr. Laszlo Liptak, Chair, Department of Mathematics and Statistics, 248-370-4054, Fax: 248-370-4184, E-mail: liptak@oakland.edu. *Application contact:* Dr. Meir Shillor, Coordinator, Graduate Programs, 248-370-3439, Fax: 248-370-4184, E-mail: shillor@oakland.edu.

The Ohio State University, Graduate School, College of Arts and Sciences, Division of Natural and Mathematical Sciences, Department of Mathematics, Columbus, OH 43210. Offers computational sciences (MMS); mathematical biosciences (MMS); mathematics (PhD); mathematics for educators (MMS). *Degree requirements:* For master's, thesis optional; for doctorate, one foreign language, thesis/dissertation. *Entrance requirements:* For master's, GRE General Test; for doctorate, GRE General Test (recommended), GRE Subject Test (mathematics). Additional exam requirements/recommendations for international students: Required—TOEFL (minimum score 550 paper-based; 79 iBT), Michigan English Language Assessment Battery (minimum score 82); Recommended—IELTS (minimum score 7). Electronic applications accepted.

Ohio University, Graduate College, College of Arts and Sciences, Department of Mathematics, Athens, OH 45701-2979. Offers MS, PhD. *Program availability:* Part-time, evening/weekend. Terminal master's awarded for partial completion of doctoral program. *Degree requirements:* For master's, thesis optional; for doctorate, comprehensive exam, thesis/dissertation. *Entrance requirements:* For master's and doctorate, minimum GPA of 3.0. Additional exam requirements/recommendations for international students: Required—TOEFL (minimum score 550 paper-based; 80 iBT) or IELTS (minimum score 6.5). Electronic applications accepted. *Faculty research:* Algebra (group and ring theory), functional analysis, topology, differential equations, computational math.

Oklahoma State University, College of Arts and Sciences, Department of Mathematics, Stillwater, OK 74078. Offers applied mathematics (MS, PhD); mathematics education (MS, PhD); pure mathematics (MS, PhD). *Faculty:* 43 full-time (9 women), 9 part-time/adjunct (5 women). *Students:* 5 full-time (3 women), 36 part-time (14 women); includes 4 minority (1 Black or African American, non-Hispanic/Latino; 2 Hispanic/Latino; 1 Two or more races, non-Hispanic/Latino), 17 international. Average age 30. 52 applicants, 35% accepted, 11 enrolled. In 2015, 8 master's, 3 doctorates awarded. *Degree requirements:* For master's, thesis, creative component, or report; for doctorate, comprehensive exam, thesis/dissertation. *Entrance requirements:* For master's and doctorate, GRE (recommended). Additional exam requirements/recommendations for international students: Required—TOEFL (minimum score 550 paper-based; 79 iBT). *Application deadline:* For fall admission, 3/1 for domestic and international students; for spring admission, 10/15 for domestic students, 10/15 priority date for international students. Applications are processed on a rolling basis. Application fee: $40 ($75 for international students). Electronic applications accepted. *Expenses:* Tuition, state resident: full-time $3528; part-time $196 per credit hour. Tuition, nonresident: full-time $14,144; part-time $785.75 per credit hour. *Required fees:* $1895; $105.25 per credit hour. Tuition and fees vary according to campus/location. *Financial support:* In 2015–16, 2 research assistantships (averaging $17,172 per year), 40 teaching assistantships (averaging $21,173 per year) were awarded; health care benefits and tuition waivers (partial) also available. Financial award application deadline: 3/1; financial award applicants required to submit FAFSA. *Unit head:* Dr. Willam Jaco, Department Head, 405-744-5688, Fax: 405-744-8225, E-mail: william.jaco@okstate.edu.
Website: http://math.okstate.edu/

Old Dominion University, College of Sciences, Programs in Computational and Applied Mathematics, Norfolk, VA 23529. Offers applied mathematics (MS, PhD), including statistics and biostatistics. *Program availability:* Part-time. *Faculty:* 19 full-time (3 women), 1 part-time/adjunct (0 women). *Students:* 27 full-time (10 women), 13 part-time (3 women); includes 5 minority (1 Black or African American, non-Hispanic/Latino; 3 Asian, non-Hispanic/Latino; 1 Two or more races, non-Hispanic/Latino), 11 international. Average age 30. 31 applicants, 55% accepted, 8 enrolled. In 2015, 8 master's, 3 doctorates awarded. Terminal master's awarded for partial completion of doctoral program. *Degree requirements:* For master's, project; for doctorate, comprehensive exam, thesis/dissertation, candidacy exam. *Entrance requirements:* For master's, minimum GPA of 3.0 in major, 2.8 overall; for doctorate, GRE General Test, 3 recommendation letters, transcripts, essay. Additional exam requirements/recommendations for international students: Required—TOEFL (minimum score 550 paper-based; 79 iBT); Recommended—IELTS (minimum score 6.5). *Application deadline:* For fall admission, 6/1 for domestic students, 5/15 for international students; for winter admission, 11/1 for domestic students, 10/1 for international students; for spring admission, 3/1 for domestic students, 2/1 for international students. Applications are processed on a rolling basis. Application fee: $50. Electronic applications accepted. *Expenses:* Tuition, state resident: full-time $11,136; part-time $464 per credit hour. Tuition, nonresident: full-time $27,840; part-time $1160 per credit hour. *Required fees:* $64 per semester. Tuition and fees vary according to campus/location, program and reciprocity agreements. *Financial support:* In 2015–16, 21 students received support, including 6 fellowships with full tuition reimbursements available (averaging $18,000 per year), 3 research assistantships with full tuition reimbursements available (averaging $16,000 per year), 12 teaching assistantships with full tuition reimbursements available (averaging $15,000 per year); scholarships/grants also available. Financial award application deadline: 2/15; financial award applicants required to submit FAFSA. *Faculty research:* Numerical analysis, integral equations, continuum mechanics, statistics, direct and inverse scattering. *Total annual research expenditures:* $506,890. *Unit head:* Dr. Raymond Cheng, Graduate Program Director, 757-683-3882, Fax: 757-683-3885, E-mail: rcheng@odu.edu. *Application contact:* William Heffelfinger, Director of Graduate Admissions, 757-683-5554, Fax: 757-683-3255, E-mail: gradadmit@odu.edu.
Website: http://sci.odu.edu/math/academics/grad.shtml

Oregon State University, College of Science, Program in Mathematics, Corvallis, OR 97331. Offers actuarial science (MA, MS, PhD); algebra (MA, MS, PhD); analysis (MA, MS, PhD); applied mathematics (MA, MS, PhD); computational mathematics (MA, MS, PhD); differential equations (MA, MS, PhD); financial mathematics (MA, MS, PhD); geometry (MA, MS, PhD); mathematics education (MA). *Faculty:* 26 full-time (8 women), 4 part-time/adjunct (1 woman). *Students:* 68 full-time (16 women), 2 part-time (0 women); includes 10 minority (1 Black or African American, non-Hispanic/Latino; 3 Asian, non-Hispanic/Latino; 2 Hispanic/Latino; 1 Native Hawaiian or other Pacific Islander, non-Hispanic/Latino; 3 Two or more races, non-Hispanic/Latino), 15 international. Average age 29. 117 applicants, 34% accepted, 17 enrolled. In 2015, 13 master's, 2 doctorates awarded. Terminal master's awarded for partial completion of doctoral program. *Median time to degree:* Of those who began their doctoral program in fall 2007, 40% received their degree in 8 years or less. *Degree requirements:* For master's, variable foreign language requirement, thesis or alternative; for doctorate, one foreign language, thesis/dissertation, qualifying exams. *Entrance requirements:* For master's and doctorate, GRE. Additional exam requirements/recommendations for international students: Required—TOEFL (minimum score 100 iBT). *Application deadline:* For fall admission, 1/15 for domestic students. Application fee: $75 ($85 for international students). *Expenses:* Tuition, state resident: full-time $12,150; part-time $450 per credit. Tuition, nonresident: full-time $20,952; part-time $776 per credit. *Required fees:* $1572; $1443 per unit. One-time fee: $350. Tuition and fees vary according to course load, campus/location and program. *Financial support:* Research assistantships, teaching assistantships, Federal Work-Study, and institutionally sponsored loans available. Support available to part-time students. Financial award application deadline: 1/15. *Unit head:* Dr. Enrique A. Thomann, Professor and Interim Department Head. *Application contact:* Mathematics Advisor, 541-737-4686, E-mail: gradinfo@math.oregonstate.edu.
Website: http://www.math.oregonstate.edu/

Pace University, School of Education, New York, NY 10038. Offers adolescent education (MST), including biology, business education, chemistry, earth science, English, foreign languages, mathematics, physics, social studies, visual arts; childhood education (MST); early childhood development, learning and intervention (MST); educational technology studies (MS); inclusive adolescent education (MST), including biology, business education, chemistry, earth science, English, foreign languages, mathematics, physics, social studies, visual arts; integrated instruction for educational technology (Certificate); integrated instruction for literacy and technology (Certificate); literacy (MS Ed); special education (MS Ed). *Accreditation:* NCATE. *Program availability:* Part-time, evening/weekend. *Faculty:* 19 full-time (13 women), 86 part-time/adjunct (49 women). *Students:* 112 full-time (95 women), 432 part-time (306 women); includes 179 minority (89 Black or African American, non-Hispanic/Latino; 1 American Indian or Alaska Native, non-Hispanic/Latino; 24 Asian, non-Hispanic/Latino; 55 Hispanic/Latino; 10 Two or more races, non-Hispanic/Latino), 9 international. Average age 30. 181 applicants, 78% accepted, 72 enrolled. In 2015, 261 master's, 11 other advanced degrees awarded. *Degree requirements:* For master's, internship. *Entrance requirements:* For master's, interview, teaching certificate. Additional exam

254 www.petersons.com

Peterson's Graduate Programs in the Physical Sciences, Mathematics, Agricultural Sciences, the Environment & Natural Resources 2017

requirements/recommendations for international students: Required—TOEFL (minimum score 88 iBT), IELTS or PTE. *Application deadline:* For fall admission, 8/1 priority date for domestic students, 6/1 for international students; for spring admission, 12/1 priority date for domestic students, 10/1 for international students. Applications are processed on a rolling basis. Application fee: $70. Electronic applications accepted. *Expenses:* Contact institution. *Financial support:* In 2015–16, 17 students received support, including 17 research assistantships with partial tuition reimbursements available (averaging $6,020 per year); career-related internships or fieldwork and Federal Work-Study also available. Financial award application deadline: 2/15; financial award applicants required to submit FAFSA. *Faculty research:* STEM education, TESOL, teacher education, special education, language and literary development. *Total annual research expenditures:* $290,153. *Unit head:* Dr. Xiao-Lei Wang, Dean, School of Education, 914-773-3876, E-mail: xwang@pace.edu. *Application contact:* Susan Ford-Goldschein, Director of Graduate Admissions, 212-346-1531, Fax: 212-346-1585, E-mail: graduateadmission@pace.edu.
Website: http://www.pace.edu/school-of-education

Penn State University Park, Graduate School, Eberly College of Science, Department of Mathematics, University Park, PA 16802. Offers mathematics (M Ed, MA, D Ed, PhD). *Unit head:* Dr. Douglas R. Cavener, Dean, 814-865-9591, Fax: 814-865-3634. *Application contact:* Lori Stania, Director, Graduate Student Services, 814-865-1795, Fax: 814-863-4627, E-mail: l-gswww@lists.psu.edu.
Website: http://www.math.psu.edu/

Pepperdine University, Graduate School of Education and Psychology, Division of Education, Malibu, CA 90263. Offers administration and preliminary administrative services (MS); education (MA); educational leadership, administration, and policy (Ed D); learning technologies (MA, Ed D); organization change (Ed D); organizational leadership (Ed D); social entrepreneurship and change (MA); teachering (MA); teaching: TESOL (MA). *Program availability:* Part-time, evening/weekend, online learning. *Faculty:* 16 full-time (8 women), 2 part-time/adjunct (both women). *Students:* 272 full-time (187 women), 386 part-time (265 women); includes 276 minority (124 Black or African American, non-Hispanic/Latino; 6 American Indian or Alaska Native, non-Hispanic/Latino; 52 Asian, non-Hispanic/Latino; 72 Hispanic/Latino; 5 Native Hawaiian or other Pacific Islander, non-Hispanic/Latino; 17 Two or more races, non-Hispanic/Latino), 36 international. Average age 39. 333 applicants, 94% accepted, 175 enrolled. In 2015, 143 master's, 84 doctorates awarded. *Degree requirements:* For doctorate, thesis/dissertation. *Entrance requirements:* For master's, GRE General Test; for doctorate, GRE General Test, MAT. Additional exam requirements/recommendations for international students: Required—TOEFL. *Application deadline:* Applications are processed on a rolling basis. Application fee: $55. *Expenses:* Contact institution. *Financial support:* Research assistantships, teaching assistantships, career-related internships or fieldwork, institutionally sponsored loans, and scholarships/grants available. Support available to part-time students. Financial award application deadline: 7/1; financial award applicants required to submit FAFSA. *Unit head:* Dr. Martine Jago, Associate Dean, Education Division, 310-568-2828,
E-mail: martine.jago@pepperdine.edu. *Application contact:* Melissa Mansfield, Admissions Manager, Education Division, 310-568-5786,
E-mail: jennifer.agatep@pepperdine.edu.
Website: http://gsep.pepperdine.edu/masters-education/

Pittsburg State University, Graduate School, College of Arts and Sciences, Department of Mathematics, Pittsburg, KS 66762. Offers mathematics (MS). *Program availability:* Part-time. *Students:* 12 (5 women); includes 2 minority (1 American Indian or Alaska Native, non-Hispanic/Latino; 1 Two or more races, non-Hispanic/Latino), 1 international. In 2015, 5 master's awarded. *Degree requirements:* For master's, thesis or alternative. *Entrance requirements:* Additional exam requirements/recommendations for international students: Required—TOEFL (minimum score 520 paper-based; 68 iBT), IELTS (minimum score 6), PTE (minimum score 47). *Application deadline:* For fall admission, 6/1 for international students; for spring admission, 10/15 for international students; for summer admission, 4/1 for international students. Applications are processed on a rolling basis. Application fee: $35 ($60 for international students). Electronic applications accepted. *Expenses:* $305 per credit hour for residents; $711 per credit hour for non-residents. *Financial support:* In 2015–16, 5 teaching assistantships with full tuition reimbursements (averaging $5,500 per year) were awarded; career-related internships or fieldwork, Federal Work-Study, and unspecified assistantships also available. Financial award application deadline: 2/1; financial award applicants required to submit FAFSA. *Faculty research:* Operations research, numerical analysis, applied analysis, applied algebra. *Unit head:* Dr. Tim Flood, Chairperson, 620-235-4401. *Application contact:* Lisa Allen, Assistant Director, 620-235-4223, Fax: 620-235-4219, E-mail: lallen@pittstate.edu.

Portland State University, Graduate Studies, College of Liberal Arts and Sciences, Department of Mathematics and Statistics, Portland, OR 97207-0751. Offers mathematical sciences (PhD); mathematics education (PhD); statistics (MS); MA/MS. *Faculty:* 33 full-time (8 women), 15 part-time/adjunct (3 women). *Students:* 73 full-time (30 women), 53 part-time (20 women); includes 20 minority (2 American Indian or Alaska Native, non-Hispanic/Latino; 8 Asian, non-Hispanic/Latino; 7 Hispanic/Latino; 3 Two or more races, non-Hispanic/Latino), 14 international. Average age 33. 110 applicants, 71% accepted, 38 enrolled. In 2015, 26 master's, 1 doctorate awarded. *Degree requirements:* For master's, thesis or alternative, exams; for doctorate, 2 foreign languages, thesis/dissertation, exams. *Entrance requirements:* For master's, GRE General Test, GRE Subject Test, minimum GPA of 3.0 in upper-division course work or 2.75 overall; for doctorate, GRE General Test. Additional exam requirements/recommendations for international students: Required—TOEFL (minimum score 550 paper-based; 80 iBT). *Application deadline:* For fall admission, 4/1 for domestic students, 3/1 for international students; for winter admission, 9/1 for domestic students, 7/1 for international students; for spring admission, 11/1 for domestic and international students; for summer admission, 2/1 for domestic and international students. Applications are processed on a rolling basis. Application fee: $50. *Expenses:* $11,490 per year. *Financial support:* In 2015–16, 9 research assistantships with full tuition reimbursements (averaging $16,360 per year), 31 teaching assistantships with full tuition reimbursements (averaging $13,597 per year) were awarded; Federal Work-Study, scholarships/grants, tuition waivers (partial), and unspecified assistantships also available. Support available to part-time students. Financial award application deadline: 3/1; financial award applicants required to submit FAFSA. *Faculty research:* Algebra, topology, statistical distribution theory, control theory, statistical robustness. *Total annual research expenditures:* $518,084. *Unit head:* Dr. Marek Elzanowski, Chair, 503-725-3647, Fax: 503-725-3661, E-mail: elzanowskim@pdx.edu. *Application contact:* Katie Gettling, Administrative Assistant, 503-725-3604, Fax: 503-725-3661,
E-mail: ekatie@pdx.edu.
Website: http://www.mth.pdx.edu/

Portland State University, Graduate Studies, College of Liberal Arts and Sciences, Systems Science Program, Portland, OR 97207-0751. Offers computational intelligence (Certificate); computer modeling and simulation (Certificate); systems science (MS); systems science/anthropology (PhD); systems science/business administration (PhD); systems science/civil engineering (PhD); systems science/economics (PhD); systems science/engineering management (PhD); systems science/general (PhD); systems science/mathematical sciences (PhD); systems science/mechanical engineering (PhD); systems science/psychology (PhD); systems science/sociology (PhD). *Faculty:* 3 full-time (1 woman), 2 part-time/adjunct (1 woman). *Students:* 11 full-time (1 woman), 20 part-time (5 women); includes 8 minority (1 Black or African American, non-Hispanic/Latino; 1 Asian, non-Hispanic/Latino; 3 Hispanic/Latino; 3 Two or more races, non-Hispanic/Latino). Average age 40. 33 applicants, 30% accepted, 8 enrolled. In 2015, 10 master's, 3 doctorates awarded. *Degree requirements:* For master's, comprehensive exam (for some programs), thesis optional; for doctorate, variable foreign language requirement, comprehensive exam (for some programs), thesis/dissertation. *Entrance requirements:* For master's, GRE/GMAT (recommended), minimum GPA of 3.0 undergraduate or graduate work, 2 letters of recommendation, statement of interest; for doctorate, GMAT, GRE General Test, minimum GPA of 3.0 undergraduate, 3.25 graduate; 2 letters of recommendation; statement of interest. Additional exam requirements/recommendations for international students: Required—TOEFL (minimum score 550 paper-based; 80 iBT). *Application deadline:* For fall admission, 1/15 for domestic and international students; for spring admission, 11/1 for domestic students. Application fee: $50. Electronic applications accepted. *Expenses:* $11,490 per year. *Financial support:* In 2015–16, 1 research assistantship with tuition reimbursement (averaging $6,264 per year) was awarded; teaching assistantships, career-related internships or fieldwork, Federal Work-Study, scholarships/grants, and unspecified assistantships also available. Support available to part-time students. Financial award application deadline: 3/1; financial award applicants required to submit FAFSA. *Faculty research:* Systems theory and methodology, artificial intelligence neural networks, information theory, nonlinear dynamics/chaos, modeling and simulation. *Total annual research expenditures:* $133,497. *Unit head:* Dr. Wayne Wakeland, Chair, 503-725-4975, E-mail: wakeland@pdx.edu.
Website: http://www.pdx.edu/sysc/

Princeton University, Graduate School, Department of Mathematics, Princeton, NJ 08544-1019. Offers PhD. *Degree requirements:* For doctorate, 2 foreign languages, thesis/dissertation. *Entrance requirements:* For doctorate, GRE General Test, GRE Subject Test, 3 letters of recommendation. Additional exam requirements/recommendations for international students: Required—TOEFL (minimum score 600 paper-based). Electronic applications accepted.

Purdue University, Graduate School, College of Science, Department of Mathematics, West Lafayette, IN 47907. Offers MS, PhD. Terminal master's awarded for partial completion of doctoral program. *Degree requirements:* For doctorate, one foreign language, thesis/dissertation, oral and written exams. *Entrance requirements:* For master's and doctorate, GRE General Test, GRE Subject Test in advanced mathematics (strongly recommended), minimum undergraduate GPA of 3.0 or equivalent. Additional exam requirements/recommendations for international students: Required—TOEFL (minimum score 570 paper-based; 77 iBT). Electronic applications accepted. *Faculty research:* Algebra, analysis, topology, differential equations, applied mathematics.

Purdue University Northwest, Graduate Studies Office, School of Engineering, Mathematics, and Science, Department of Mathematics, Computer Science, and Statistics, Hammond, IN 46323-2094. Offers computer science (MS); mathematics (MAT, MS). *Program availability:* Part-time. *Entrance requirements:* Additional exam requirements/recommendations for international students: Required—TOEFL. *Faculty research:* Topology, analysis, algebra, mathematics education.

Queens College of the City University of New York, Mathematics and Natural Sciences Division, Department of Mathematics, Flushing, NY 11367-1597. Offers mathematics (MA). *Program availability:* Part-time, evening/weekend. *Faculty:* 36 full-time (8 women), 54 part-time/adjunct (19 women). *Students:* 3 full-time (2 women), 44 part-time (20 women); includes 23 minority (8 Black or African American, non-Hispanic/Latino; 11 Asian, non-Hispanic/Latino; 4 Hispanic/Latino), 4 international. Average age 31. 33 applicants, 64% accepted, 13 enrolled. In 2015, 10 master's awarded. *Degree requirements:* For master's, comprehensive exam. *Entrance requirements:* For master's, minimum GPA of 3.0. Additional exam requirements/recommendations for international students: Required—TOEFL (minimum score 61 iBT), IELTS (minimum score 5). *Application deadline:* For fall admission, 4/1 for domestic students; for spring admission, 11/1 for domestic students. Applications are processed on a rolling basis. Application fee: $125. Electronic applications accepted. *Expenses:* Tuition, state resident: full-time $5065; part-time $425 per credit. Tuition, nonresident: part-time $780 per credit. *Required fees:* $522. Part-time tuition and fees vary according to course load and program. *Financial support:* Career-related internships or fieldwork available. Financial award application deadline: 4/1; financial award applicants required to submit FAFSA. *Unit head:* Dr. Wallace Goldberg, Chairperson, 718-997-5800,
E-mail: wallace.goldberg@qc.cuny.edu.

Queen's University at Kingston, School of Graduate Studies, Faculty of Arts and Sciences, Department of Mathematics and Statistics, Kingston, ON K7L 3N6, Canada. Offers mathematics (M Sc, M Sc Eng, PhD); statistics (M Sc, M Sc Eng, PhD). *Program availability:* Part-time. *Degree requirements:* For master's, thesis; for doctorate, comprehensive exam, thesis/dissertation. *Entrance requirements:* Additional exam requirements/recommendations for international students: Required—TOEFL. *Faculty research:* Algebra, analysis, applied mathematics, statistics.

Rensselaer Polytechnic Institute, Graduate School, School of Science, Program in Mathematics, Troy, NY 12180-3590. Offers MS, PhD. *Faculty:* 18 full-time (7 women). *Students:* 39 full-time (8 women), 3 part-time (0 women); includes 8 minority (1 Black or African American, non-Hispanic/Latino; 3 Asian, non-Hispanic/Latino; 4 Hispanic/Latino), 6 international. Average age 26. 83 applicants, 47% accepted, 11 enrolled. In 2015, 14 master's, 8 doctorates awarded. Terminal master's awarded for partial completion of doctoral program. *Degree requirements:* For doctorate, comprehensive exam, thesis/dissertation. *Entrance requirements:* For master's and doctorate, GRE. Additional exam requirements/recommendations for international students: Required—TOEFL (minimum score 600 paper-based; 100 iBT), IELTS (minimum score 7), PTE (minimum score 68). *Application deadline:* For fall admission, 1/1 priority date for domestic and international students; for spring admission, 8/15 priority date for domestic and international students. Applications are processed on a rolling basis. Application fee: $75. Electronic applications accepted. *Financial support:* In 2015–16, 43 students received support, including research assistantships (averaging $21,500 per year), teaching assistantships (averaging $21,500 per year); fellowships also available. Financial award application deadline: 1/1. *Faculty research:* Acoustics, applied geometry, approximation theory, bioinformatics, biomathematics, chemically-reacting flows, data-driven modeling, dynamical systems, environmental problems, fluid dynamics, inverse problem, machine learning, math education, mathematical physics, multiphase flows, nonlinear analysis, nonlinear materials, nonlinear waves, operations research and mathematical programming, optimization, perturbation methods, scientific computing. *Unit head:* Dr. John Mitchell, Graduate Program Director, 518-276-6519,

E-mail: mitchj@rpi.edu. *Application contact:* Office of Graduate Admissions, 518-276-6216, E-mail: gradadmissions@rpi.edu.
Website: https://www.rpi.edu/dept/math/ms_graduate/index.html

Rhode Island College, School of Graduate Studies, Faculty of Arts and Sciences, Department of Mathematics and Computer Science, Providence, RI 02908-1991. Offers mathematics (MA); mathematics content specialist (CGS). *Program availability:* Part-time, evening/weekend. *Faculty:* 5 full-time (2 women). *Students:* 5 part-time (2 women). Average age 28. In 2015, 6 master's awarded. *Degree requirements:* For master's, comprehensive exam. *Entrance requirements:* For master's, GRE General Test or MAT, minimum of 30 hours beyond pre-calculus math, 3 letters of recommendation, interview. Additional exam requirements/recommendations for international students: Recommended—TOEFL (minimum score 550 paper-based; 79 iBT). *Application deadline:* For fall admission, 3/1 for domestic students; for spring admission, 11/1 for domestic students. Applications are processed on a rolling basis. Application fee: $50. Electronic applications accepted. *Expenses:* Tuition, state resident: full-time $8928; part-time $372 per credit. Tuition, nonresident: full-time $17,376; part-time $724 per credit. *Required fees:* $604; $22 per credit. One-time fee: $74. *Financial support:* In 2015–16, 2 teaching assistantships with full tuition reimbursements (averaging $3,500 per year) were awarded; Federal Work-Study, scholarships/grants, health care benefits, and unspecified assistantships also available. Support available to part-time students. Financial award application deadline: 5/15; financial award applicants required to submit FAFSA. *Unit head:* Dr. Christopher Teixeira, Chair, 401-456-8038. *Application contact:* Graduate Studies, 401-456-8700.
Website: http://www.ric.edu/mathComputerScience/index.php

Rice University, Graduate Programs, Wiess School of Natural Sciences, Department of Mathematics, Houston, TX 77251-1892. Offers PhD. Terminal master's awarded for partial completion of doctoral program. *Degree requirements:* For doctorate, one foreign language, comprehensive exam, thesis/dissertation. *Entrance requirements:* For doctorate, GRE Subject Test, GRE General Test. Additional exam requirements/recommendations for international students: Required—TOEFL (minimum score 600 paper-based; 90 iBT). Electronic applications accepted. *Faculty research:* Algebraic geometry/algebra, complex analysis and Teichmuller theory, dynamical systems and Ergodic theory, topology, differential geometry and geometric analysis.

Rivier University, School of Graduate Studies, Department of Computer Science and Mathematics, Nashua, NH 03060. Offers computer science (MS); mathematics (MAT). *Program availability:* Part-time, evening/weekend. *Entrance requirements:* For master's, GRE Subject Test. Electronic applications accepted.

Rochester Institute of Technology, Graduate Enrollment Services, College of Science, School of Mathematical Sciences, Rochester, NY 14623. Offers applied and computational mathematics (MS); applied statistics (MS, Advanced Certificate). *Program availability:* Part-time, evening/weekend. *Students:* 48 full-time (20 women), 61 part-time (24 women); includes 16 minority (2 Black or African American, non-Hispanic/Latino; 8 Asian, non-Hispanic/Latino; 2 Hispanic/Latino; 4 Two or more races, non-Hispanic/Latino), 31 international. Average age 29. 125 applicants, 46% accepted, 26 enrolled. In 2015, 22 master's, 2 other advanced degrees awarded. *Degree requirements:* For master's, thesis. *Entrance requirements:* For master's, minimum GPA of 3.0 (recommended). Additional exam requirements/recommendations for international students: Required—PTE (minimum score 58), TOEFL (minimum score 550 paper-based, 79 iBT) or IELTS (minimum score 6.5). *Application deadline:* For fall admission, 2/15 priority date for domestic and international students; for spring admission, 12/15 priority date for domestic and international students. Applications are processed on a rolling basis. Application fee: $60. Electronic applications accepted. *Expenses: Tuition, area resident:* Full-time $41,084; part-time $1742 per credit hour. *Required fees:* $274. Tuition and fees vary according to course load and program. *Financial support:* In 2015–16, 18 students received support. Research assistantships with partial tuition reimbursements available, teaching assistantships with partial tuition reimbursements available, career-related internships or fieldwork, scholarships/grants, and unspecified assistantships available. Support available to part-time students. Financial award applicants required to submit FAFSA. *Faculty research:* Fluid mechanics, nonlinear dynamics, image processing, inverse problems, condensed matter, mathematical biology, solid mechanics and materials science, microelectromechanical systems (MEMS), network analysis, data assimilation. *Unit head:* Dr. Mihail Barbosu, School Head, 585-475-2498, Fax: 585-475-6627, E-mail: tmwbkg@rit.edu. *Application contact:* Diane Ellison, Associate Vice President, Graduate Enrollment Services, 585-475-2229, Fax: 585-475-7164, E-mail: gradinfo@rit.edu.
Website: http://www.rit.edu/cos/sms/

Roosevelt University, Graduate Division, College of Arts and Sciences, Department of Mathematics and Actuarial Science, Program in Mathematics, Chicago, IL 60605. Offers mathematical sciences (MS), including actuarial science. *Program availability:* Part-time, evening/weekend. *Faculty research:* Statistics, mathematics education, finite groups, computers in mathematics.

Rowan University, Graduate School, College of Science and Mathematics, Department of Mathematics, Program in Mathematics, Glassboro, NJ 08028-1701. Offers MA. Electronic applications accepted.

Royal Military College of Canada, Division of Graduate Studies and Research, Science Division, Department of Mathematics and Computer Science, Kingston, ON K7K 7B4, Canada. Offers computer science (M Sc); mathematics (M Sc). *Degree requirements:* For master's, thesis. *Entrance requirements:* For master's, honours degree with second-class standing. Electronic applications accepted.

Rutgers University–Camden, Graduate School of Arts and Sciences, Program in Mathematical Sciences, Camden, NJ 08102. Offers industrial mathematics (MBS); industrial/applied mathematics (MS); mathematical computer science (MS); pure mathematics (MS); teaching in mathematical sciences (MS). *Program availability:* Part-time, evening/weekend. *Degree requirements:* For master's, comprehensive exam, thesis optional, survey paper, 30 credits. *Entrance requirements:* For master's, GRE, BS/BA in math or related subject, 2 letters of recommendation. Additional exam requirements/recommendations for international students: Required—TOEFL (minimum score 550 paper-based), IELTS. Electronic applications accepted. *Faculty research:* Differential geometry, dynamical systems, vertex operator algebra, automorphic forms, CR-structures.

Rutgers University–Newark, Graduate School, Program in Mathematical Sciences, Newark, NJ 07102. Offers PhD. *Degree requirements:* For doctorate, thesis/dissertation, written qualifying exam. *Entrance requirements:* For doctorate, GRE General Test, minimum B average. Additional exam requirements/recommendations for international students: Required—TOEFL. Electronic applications accepted. *Faculty research:* Number theory, automorphic form, low-dimensional topology, Kleinian groups, representation theory.

Rutgers University–New Brunswick, Graduate School-New Brunswick, Department of Mathematics, Piscataway, NJ 08854-8097. Offers applied mathematics (MS, PhD); mathematics (MS, PhD). *Program availability:* Part-time. *Degree requirements:* For doctorate, one foreign language, comprehensive exam, thesis/dissertation. *Entrance requirements:* For master's and doctorate, GRE General Test, GRE Subject Test. Additional exam requirements/recommendations for international students: Required—TOEFL. *Faculty research:* Logic and set theory, number theory, mathematical physics, control theory, partial differential equations.

St. Cloud State University, School of Graduate Studies, College of Science and Engineering, Program in Mathematics, St. Cloud, MN 56301-4498. Offers MS. *Degree requirements:* For master's, comprehensive exam (for some programs), thesis or alternative. *Entrance requirements:* For master's, GRE General Test, minimum GPA of 2.75. Additional exam requirements/recommendations for international students: Required—Michigan English Language Assessment Battery; Recommended—TOEFL (minimum score 550 paper-based), IELTS (minimum score 6.5). Electronic applications accepted.

Saint Joseph's University, College of Arts and Sciences, Department of Mathematics and Computer Science, Philadelphia, PA 19131-1395. Offers computer science (MS); mathematics and computer science (Post-Master's Certificate). *Program availability:* Part-time, evening/weekend. *Entrance requirements:* For master's, 2 letters of recommendation, resume, personal statement, official transcripts. Additional exam requirements/recommendations for international students: Required—TOEFL (minimum score 550 paper-based; 80 iBT), IELTS (minimum score 6.2). Electronic applications accepted. *Faculty research:* Enhancing the 5-year Math and Science Education program, nonnegative curvature on lie groups and bundles, Regional Noyce Partnership, PACMACS Bridge Expansion Program, STEM teacher preparation.

Saint Louis University, Graduate Education, College of Arts and Sciences and Graduate Education, Department of Mathematics and Computer Science, St. Louis, MO 63103. Offers mathematics (MA, MA-R, PhD). *Program availability:* Part-time. *Degree requirements:* For master's, comprehensive exam, thesis (for some programs); for doctorate, one foreign language, thesis/dissertation, preliminary exams. *Entrance requirements:* For master's, GRE General Test, letters of recommendation, resume, interview; for doctorate, GRE General Test, letters of recommendation, resumé, interview, transcripts, goal statement. Additional exam requirements/recommendations for international students: Required—TOEFL (minimum score 525 paper-based). Electronic applications accepted. *Faculty research:* Algebra, groups and rings, analysis, differential geometry, topology.

Salem State University, School of Graduate Studies, Program in Mathematics, Salem, MA 01970-5353. Offers MAT, MS. *Program availability:* Part-time, evening/weekend. *Entrance requirements:* For master's, GRE or MAT. Additional exam requirements/recommendations for international students: Required—TOEFL (minimum score 550 paper-based; 80 iBT) or IELTS (minimum score 5.5).

Samford University, Orlean Bullard Beeson School of Education, Birmingham, AL 35229. Offers early childhood/elementary education (MS Ed); education with gifted certificate (MS Ed); educational leadership (MS Ed, Ed D); elementary education (MS Ed); gifted (Certificate); gifted education (MS Ed); instructional design and technology (MS Ed); instructional leadership (MS Ed, Certificate, Ed S); K-12 collaborative special education (MS Ed); secondary education (MS Ed), including biology, general science, general social science, history, mathematics, physical education, Spanish. *Accreditation:* NCATE. *Program availability:* Part-time, evening/weekend, blended/hybrid learning. *Faculty:* 20 full-time (14 women), 41 part-time/adjunct (32 women). *Students:* 194 full-time (146 women), 98 part-time (69 women); includes 61 minority (54 Black or African American, non-Hispanic/Latino; 4 American Indian or Alaska Native, non-Hispanic/Latino; 1 Asian, non-Hispanic/Latino; 2 Hispanic/Latino), 1 international. Average age 36. 113 applicants, 96% accepted, 80 enrolled. In 2015, 60 master's, 19 doctorates, 3 Certificates awarded. *Degree requirements:* For master's, comprehensive exam (for some programs); for doctorate, comprehensive exam, thesis/dissertation; for other advanced degree, comprehensive exam. *Entrance requirements:* For master's, GRE (minimum score of 295) or MAT (minimum score of 396); Alabama Educator Certification Testing Program (AECTP); PRAXIS, transcripts, essays, recommendations; for doctorate, professional resume, writing sample, letter of recommendation, original copy of all transcripts, interview; for other advanced degree, letter of recommendation, original copy of all transcripts. Additional exam requirements/recommendations for international students: Required—TOEFL (minimum score 90 iBT), IELTS (minimum score 6.5). *Application deadline:* For fall admission, 7/15 for domestic students, 7/1 for international students; for spring admission, 11/15 for domestic and international students; for summer admission, 4/15 for domestic and international students. Application fee: $35. Electronic applications accepted. *Expenses: Tuition, area resident:* Full-time $18,673; part-time $766 per credit hour. *Required fees:* $550. Tuition and fees vary according to course load, degree level and student level. *Financial support:* In 2015–16, 229 students received support. Scholarships/grants available. Financial award application deadline: 3/1; financial award applicants required to submit FAFSA. *Faculty research:* Computer-mediated learning, educational administration assessment and accreditation, gifted children, contributions to the Alabama Veterans to state history. *Total annual research expenditures:* $11,000. *Unit head:* Dr. Jean Box, Dean, 205-726-2565, Fax: 205-726-4233,
E-mail: jabox@samford.edu. *Application contact:* Brooke Karr, Graduate Admissions Coordinator, 205-729-2783, Fax: 205-726-4233, E-mail: kbgilrea@samford.edu.
Website: http://www.samford.edu/education/

Sam Houston State University, College of Sciences, Department of Mathematics and Statistics, Huntsville, TX 77341. Offers mathematics (MA, MS); statistics (MS). *Program availability:* Part-time. *Degree requirements:* For master's, comprehensive exam, thesis optional. *Entrance requirements:* For master's, GRE General Test, letters of recommendation. Additional exam requirements/recommendations for international students: Required—TOEFL (minimum score 550 paper-based; 79 iBT), IELTS (minimum score 6.5). Electronic applications accepted.

San Diego State University, Graduate and Research Affairs, College of Sciences, Department of Mathematics and Statistics, San Diego, CA 92182. Offers applied mathematics (MS); mathematics (MA); mathematics and science education (PhD); statistics (MS). PhD offered jointly wtih University of California, San Diego. *Program availability:* Part-time. *Degree requirements:* For doctorate, thesis/dissertation. *Entrance requirements:* For master's, GRE General Test; for doctorate, GRE, minimum GPA of 3.25 in last 30 undergraduate semester units, minimum graduate GPA of 3.5, MSE recommendation form, 3 letters of recommendation. Additional exam requirements/recommendations for international students: Required—TOEFL. Electronic applications accepted. *Faculty research:* Teacher education in mathematics.

San Francisco State University, Division of Graduate Studies, College of Science and Engineering, Department of Mathematics, San Francisco, CA 94132-1722. Offers MA. *Application deadline:* Applications are processed on a rolling basis. *Expenses:* Tuition, state resident: full-time $6738. Tuition, nonresident: full-time $15,666. *Required fees:* $1004 per year. *Unit head:* Dr. David Bao, Chair, 415-338-2251, Fax: 415-338-1461,

E-mail: dbao@sfsu.edu. *Application contact:* Dr. Matthias Beck, Graduate Coordinator, 415-405-3473, Fax: 415-338-1461, E-mail: mattbeck@sfsu.edu.
Website: http://math.sfsu.edu

San Jose State University, Graduate Studies and Research, College of Science, San Jose, CA 95192-0001. Offers biological sciences (MA, MS), including molecular biology and microbiology (MS), organismal biology, conservation and ecology (MS), physiology (MS); chemistry (MA, MS); computer science (MS); cybersecurity (Certificate); cybersecurity: core technologies (Certificate); geology (MS); marine science (MS); master biotechnology (MBT); mathematics (MA, MS), including mathematics education (MA), science; meteorology (MS); physics (MS), including computational physics, modern optics, science (MA, MS); science education (MA); statistics (MS); unix system administration (Certificate). *Program availability:* Part-time, evening/weekend. *Students:* 118 full-time (68 women), 52 part-time (25 women); includes 125 minority (5 Black or African American, non-Hispanic/Latino; 97 Asian, non-Hispanic/Latino; 23 Hispanic/ Latino), 121 international. Average age 27. 1,236 applicants, 21% accepted, 171 enrolled. In 2015, 168 master's awarded. *Entrance requirements:* For master's, GRE. *Application deadline:* For fall admission, 6/29 for domestic students; for spring admission, 11/30 for domestic students. Applications are processed on a rolling basis. Application fee: $55. Electronic applications accepted. *Financial support:* Teaching assistantships, career-related internships or fieldwork, Federal Work-Study, and institutionally sponsored loans available. Support available to part-time students. Financial award applicants required to submit FAFSA. *Faculty research:* Radiochemistry/environmental analysis, health physics, radiation effects. *Unit head:* J. Michael Parrish, Dean, 408-924-4800, Fax: 408-924-4815. *Application contact:* 408-924-2480, Fax: 408-924-2477.
Website: http://www.science.sjsu.edu/

San Jose State University, Graduate Studies and Research, Connie L. Lurie College of Education, San Jose, CA 95192-0001. Offers child and adolescent development (MA); common core mathematics (k-8) (Certificate, Credential); education (MA, Credential), including counseling and student personnel (MA), speech pathology (MA); education specialist preliminary teaching credential: early childhood special (Credential); educational leadership (MA, Ed D, Credential), including administration and supervision (MA), higher education (MA), preliminary administrative services credential (Credential), professional administrative services credential (Credential); elementary education (MA), including curriculum and instruction; k-12 school counseling internship (Credential); k-12 school counseling specialization (Credential); school child welfare attendance specialization (Credential); single subject (Credential); theory (Certificate), including knowledge and practice about autism spectrum disorders. *Accreditation:* NCATE. *Program availability:* Evening/weekend. *Students:* 146 full-time (117 women), 28 part-time (25 women); includes 253 minority (18 Black or African American, non-Hispanic/ Latino; 80 Asian, non-Hispanic/Latino; 155 Hispanic/Latino), 22 international. Average age 29. 579 applicants, 39% accepted, 175 enrolled. In 2015, 218 master's awarded. *Application deadline:* For fall admission, 6/29 for domestic students; for spring admission, 11/30 for domestic students. Applications are processed on a rolling basis. Application fee: $55. Electronic applications accepted. *Financial support:* Career-related internships or fieldwork available. Financial award applicants required to submit FAFSA. *Unit head:* Elaine Chin, Dean, 408-924-3600, Fax: 408-924-3713. *Application contact:* 408-924-2480, Fax: 408-924-2477.
Website: http://www1.coe.sjsu.edu/

Simon Fraser University, Office of Graduate Studies, Faculty of Science, Department of Mathematics, Burnaby, BC V5A 1S6, Canada. Offers applied and computational mathematics (M Sc, PhD); mathematics (M Sc, PhD); operations research (M Sc, PhD). *Degree requirements:* For master's, thesis or alternative; for doctorate, comprehensive exam, thesis/dissertation. *Entrance requirements:* For master's, GRE General Test, GRE Subject Test (mathematics), minimum GPA of 3.0 (on scale of 4.33), or 3.33 based on last 60 credits of undergraduate courses; for doctorate, GRE General Test, GRE Subject Test (mathematics), minimum GPA of 3.5 (on scale of 4.33). Additional exam requirements/recommendations for international students: Recommended—TOEFL (minimum score 580 paper-based; 93 iBT), IELTS (minimum score 7), TWE (minimum score 5). Electronic applications accepted. *Faculty research:* Computer algebra, discrete mathematics, fluid dynamics, nonlinear partial differential equations and variation methods, numerical analysis and scientific computing.

Smith College, Graduate and Special Programs, Center for Women in Mathematics Post-Baccalaureate Program, Northampton, MA 01063. Offers Postbaccalaureate Certificate. *Students:* 12 full-time (all women), 1 (woman) part-time; includes 2 minority (both Asian, non-Hispanic/Latino), 2 international. Average age 24. 30 applicants, 50% accepted, 13 enrolled. In 2015, 8 Postbaccalaureate Certificates awarded. *Entrance requirements:* Additional exam requirements/recommendations for international students: Required—TOEFL (minimum score 595 paper-based; 97 iBT), IELTS (minimum score 7.5). *Application deadline:* For fall admission, 3/15 for domestic students; for spring admission, 10/15 for domestic students. Application fee: $60. *Expenses: Tuition, area resident:* Full-time $34,560; part-time $1440 per credit. Tuition and fees vary according to course load and program. *Financial support:* In 2015–16, 13 students received support. Scholarships/grants and tuition waivers (full) available. *Unit head:* Ruth Haas, Director, 413-585-3872, E-mail: rhaas@smith.edu. *Application contact:* Ruth Morgan, Program Assistant, 413-585-3050, Fax: 413-585-3054,
E-mail: rmorgan@smith.edu.
Website: http://www.smith.edu/gradstudy/nondegree_math.php

South Carolina State University, College of Graduate and Professional Studies, Department of Education, Orangeburg, SC 29117-0001. Offers early childhood education (MAT); education (M Ed); elementary education (M Ed, MAT); English (MAT); general science/biology (MAT); mathematics (MAT); secondary education (M Ed), including biology education, business education, counselor education, English education, home economics education, industrial education, mathematics education, science education, social studies education; special education (M Ed), including emotionally handicapped, learning disabilities, mentally handicapped. *Accreditation:* NCATE. *Program availability:* Part-time, evening/weekend. *Faculty:* 17 full-time (12 women), 3 part-time/adjunct (1 woman). *Students:* 30 full-time (20 women), 32 part-time (23 women); all minorities (all Black or African American, non-Hispanic/Latino). Average age 31. 22 applicants, 95% accepted, 19 enrolled. In 2015, 13 master's awarded. *Degree requirements:* For master's, thesis optional, departmental qualifying exam. *Entrance requirements:* For master's, GRE General Test, NTE, interview, teaching certificate. *Application deadline:* For fall admission, 6/15 priority date for domestic students, 6/15 for international students; for spring admission, 11/1 for domestic and international students. Applications are processed on a rolling basis. Application fee: $25. Electronic applications accepted. *Expenses:* Tuition, state resident: full-time $8906; part-time $495 per credit hour. Tuition, nonresident: full-time $18,674; part-time $1037 per credit hour. *Required fees:* $2497; $66 per credit hour. *Financial support:* Fellowships, career-related internships or fieldwork, Federal Work-Study, and scholarships/grants available. Financial award application deadline: 6/1. *Unit head:* Dr. Charlie Spell, Interim Chair, Department of Education, 803-536-8963, Fax: 803-516-4568, E-mail: cspell@scsu.edu. *Application contact:* Curtis Foskey, Coordinator of Graduate Studies, 803-536-8419, Fax: 803-536-8812, E-mail: cfoskey@scsu.edu.

South Dakota State University, Graduate School, College of Engineering, Department of Mathematics and Statistics, Brookings, SD 57007. Offers computational science and statistics (PhD); mathematics (MS); statistics (MS). *Program availability:* Part-time. Terminal master's awarded for partial completion of doctoral program. *Degree requirements:* For master's, thesis (for some programs), oral exam; for doctorate, comprehensive exam, thesis/dissertation, oral and written exams. *Entrance requirements:* Additional exam requirements/recommendations for international students: Required—TOEFL (minimum score 550 paper-based; 80 iBT); Recommended—IELTS. *Faculty research:* Financial mathematics, predictive analytics, operations research, bioinformatics, biostatistics, computational science, statistics, number theory, abstract algebra.

Southeast Missouri State University, School of Graduate Studies, Department of Mathematics, Cape Girardeau, MO 63701-4799. Offers MNS. *Program availability:* Part-time, evening/weekend, online learning. *Faculty:* 16 full-time (6 women). *Students:* 4 full-time (0 women), 5 part-time (1 woman), 4 international. Average age 26. 7 applicants, 57% accepted, 2 enrolled. In 2015, 2 master's awarded. *Degree requirements:* For master's, paper and comprehensive exam, or thesis. *Entrance requirements:* For master's, minimum undergraduate GPA of 2.76. Additional exam requirements/ recommendations for international students: Required—TOEFL (minimum score 550 paper-based; 79 iBT), IELTS (minimum score 6), PTE (minimum score 53). *Application deadline:* For fall admission, 8/1 for domestic students, 6/1 for international students; for spring admission, 11/21 for domestic students, 10/1 for international students; for summer admission, 5/15 for domestic students. Applications are processed on a rolling basis. Application fee: $30 ($40 for international students). Electronic applications accepted. *Expenses:* Tuition, state resident: part-time $260.80 per credit hour. Tuition, nonresident: part-time $486.80 per credit hour. *Required fees:* $33.70 per credit hour. *Financial support:* In 2015–16, 6 students received support, including 8 teaching assistantships with full tuition reimbursements available (averaging $8,467 per year); career-related internships or fieldwork, Federal Work-Study, scholarships/grants, traineeships, tuition waivers (full), and unspecified assistantships also available. Financial award application deadline: 6/30; financial award applicants required to submit FAFSA. *Faculty research:* Algebraic geometry, combinatorics, differential equations, mathematics education, statistics. *Unit head:* Dr. Tamela Randolph, Chairperson, 573-651-2164, Fax: 573-986-6811, E-mail: trandolph@semo.edu. *Application contact:* Dr. Daniel Daly, Graduate Program Coordinator, 573-651-2565, Fax: 573-986-6811,
E-mail: ddaly@semo.edu.
Website: http://www.semo.edu/math/

Southern Connecticut State University, School of Graduate Studies, School of Arts and Sciences, Department of Mathematics, New Haven, CT 06515-1355. Offers MS. *Program availability:* Part-time, evening/weekend. *Faculty:* 5 full-time (0 women). *Students:* 1 full-time (0 women), 15 part-time (11 women); includes 2 minority (1 Asian, non-Hispanic/Latino; 1 Two or more races, non-Hispanic/Latino). Average age 34. 12 applicants, 50% accepted, 5 enrolled. In 2015, 7 master's awarded. *Degree requirements:* For master's, thesis or alternative. *Entrance requirements:* For master's, interview. *Application deadline:* For fall admission, 7/15 priority date for domestic students. Applications are processed on a rolling basis. Application fee: $50. Electronic applications accepted. *Expenses:* Tuition, state resident: full-time $4968; part-time $494 per credit hour. Tuition, nonresident: full-time $16,078; part-time $509 per credit hour. *Required fees:* $4632; $55 per semester. Tuition and fees vary according to program. *Financial support:* Career-related internships or fieldwork, scholarships/grants, and unspecified assistantships available. Financial award application deadline: 4/15; financial award applicants required to submit FAFSA. *Unit head:* Dr. Therese Bennett, Chairperson, 203-392-6997, Fax: 203-392-6805, E-mail: bennettt1@southernct.edu. *Application contact:* Lisa Galvin, Director of Graduate Admissions, 203-392-5240, Fax: 203-392-5235, E-mail: galvinl1@southernct.edu.

Southern Illinois University Carbondale, Graduate School, College of Science, Department of Mathematics, Carbondale, IL 62901-4701. Offers MA, MS, PhD. PhD offered jointly with Southeast Missouri State University. *Program availability:* Part-time. *Faculty:* 32 full-time (2 women), 1 part-time/adjunct (0 women). *Students:* 35 full-time (11 women), 10 part-time (2 women); includes 3 minority (all Asian, non-Hispanic/ Latino), 35 international. Average age 26. 45 applicants, 49% accepted, 711 enrolled. In 2015, 4 master's, 3 doctorates awarded. *Degree requirements:* For master's, thesis; for doctorate, 2 foreign languages, thesis/dissertation. *Entrance requirements:* For master's, GRE General Test, minimum GPA of 2.7; for doctorate, GRE General Test, minimum GPA of 3.25. Additional exam requirements/recommendations for international students: Required—TOEFL. *Application deadline:* For fall admission, 1/31 for domestic students; for spring admission, 10/1 for domestic students; for summer admission, 1/15 for domestic students. Applications are processed on a rolling basis. Application fee: $65. *Financial support:* In 2015–16, 36 students received support, including 1 fellowship with full tuition reimbursement available, 1 research assistantship with full tuition reimbursement available, 34 teaching assistantships with full tuition reimbursements available; Federal Work-Study, institutionally sponsored loans, and tuition waivers (full) also available. Support available to part-time students. *Faculty research:* Differential equations, combinatorics, probability, algebra, numerical analysis. *Unit head:* Dr. Gregory Budzban, Chair, 618-453-6522, E-mail: gbudzban@siu.edu. *Application contact:* Diane Fritcher, Office Manager, 618-453-6523, E-mail: dfritcher@siu.edu.
Website: http://www.math.siu.edu/

Southern Illinois University Edwardsville, Graduate School, College of Arts and Sciences, Department of Mathematics and Statistics, Program in Pure Mathematics, Edwardsville, IL 62026. Offers MS. *Program availability:* Part-time. *Students:* 1 full-time (0 women), 2 part-time (1 woman). *Degree requirements:* For master's, thesis (for some programs), special project. *Entrance requirements:* Additional exam requirements/ recommendations for international students: Required—TOEFL (minimum score 550 paper-based, 79 iBT), IELTS (minimum score 6.5), Michigan Test of English Language Proficiency or PTE. *Application deadline:* For fall admission, 7/22 for domestic students, 7/15 for international students; for spring admission, 12/9 for domestic students, 11/15 for international students; for summer admission, 4/29 for domestic students, 4/15 for international students. Applications are processed on a rolling basis. Application fee: $30. Electronic applications accepted. *Expenses:* Tuition, state resident: full-time $5026; part-time $837 per course. Tuition, nonresident: full-time $12,566; part-time $2094 per course. *Required fees:* $1682; $474 per course. Tuition and fees vary according to course load, campus/location and program. *Financial support:* Fellowships, research assistantships, teaching assistantships, institutionally sponsored loans, scholarships/grants, and unspecified assistantships available. Financial award application deadline: 3/1; financial award applicants required to submit FAFSA. *Unit head:* Dr. Adam Weyhaupt, Chair, 618-650-2200, E-mail: aweyhau@siue.edu. *Application contact:* Bob Skorczewski, Coordinator of International and Graduate Recruitment, 618-650-3705, Fax: 618-650-3618,
E-mail: graduateadmissions@siue.edu.
Website: http://www.siue.edu/artsandsciences/math/

Mathematics

Southern Methodist University, Dedman College of Humanities and Sciences, Department of Mathematics, Dallas, TX 75275. Offers computational and applied mathematics (MS, PhD). *Degree requirements:* For master's, oral exams; for doctorate, thesis/dissertation, oral and written exams. *Entrance requirements:* For master's and doctorate, GRE General Test, minimum GPA of 3.0, 18 undergraduate hours in mathematics beyond first- and second-year calculus. Additional exam requirements/recommendations for international students: Required—TOEFL. Electronic applications accepted. *Faculty research:* Numerical analysis and scientific computation, fluid dynamics, optics, wave propagation, mathematical biology.

Southern University and Agricultural and Mechanical College, Graduate School, College of Sciences, Department of Mathematics, Baton Rouge, LA 70813. Offers MS. *Degree requirements:* For master's, comprehensive exam, thesis optional. *Entrance requirements:* For master's, GMAT, GRE General Test. Additional exam requirements/recommendations for international students: Required—TOEFL. *Faculty research:* Algebraic number theory, abstract algebra, computer analysis, probability, mathematics education.

Stanford University, School of Engineering, Institute for Computational and Mathematical Engineering, Stanford, CA 94305-9991. Offers MS, PhD. Terminal master's awarded for partial completion of doctoral program. *Degree requirements:* For doctorate, thesis/dissertation, qualifying exam. *Entrance requirements:* For master's, GRE General Test; for doctorate, GRE General Test, GRE Subject Test. Additional exam requirements/recommendations for international students: Required—TOEFL. Electronic applications accepted. *Expenses: Tuition, area resident:* Full-time $45,729. *Required fees:* $591.

Stanford University, School of Humanities and Sciences, Department of Mathematics, Stanford, CA 94305-9991. Offers PhD. Terminal master's awarded for partial completion of doctoral program. *Degree requirements:* For doctorate, 2 foreign languages, thesis/dissertation, oral exam. *Entrance requirements:* For doctorate, GRE General Test, GRE Subject Test. Additional exam requirements/recommendations for international students: Required—TOEFL. Electronic applications accepted. *Expenses: Tuition, area resident:* Full-time $45,729. *Required fees:* $591.

State University of New York College at Potsdam, School of Arts and Sciences, Department of Mathematics, Potsdam, NY 13676. Offers MA. *Program availability:* Part-time, evening/weekend. *Entrance requirements:* For master's, minimum GPA of 3.0 in all undergraduate math courses, 2.75 in last 60 hours of undergraduate coursework. Additional exam requirements/recommendations for international students: Required—TOEFL (minimum score 550 paper-based; 80 iBT), IELTS (minimum score 6). Electronic applications accepted.

Stephen F. Austin State University, Graduate School, College of Sciences and Mathematics, Department of Mathematics and Statistics, Nacogdoches, TX 75962. Offers mathematics (MS); mathematics education (MS); statistics (MS). *Degree requirements:* For master's, comprehensive exam, thesis optional. *Entrance requirements:* For master's, GRE General Test, minimum GPA of 2.8 in last 60 hours, 2.5 overall. Additional exam requirements/recommendations for international students: Required—TOEFL. *Faculty research:* Kernel type estimators, fractal mappings, spline curve fitting, robust regression continua theory.

Stevens Institute of Technology, Graduate School, Charles V. Schaefer Jr. School of Engineering, Department of Mathematical Sciences, Program in Mathematics, Hoboken, NJ 07030. Offers MS, PhD. *Program availability:* Part-time, evening/weekend. *Students:* 20 full-time (4 women), 6 part-time (2 women); includes 2 minority (1 Asian, non-Hispanic/Latino; 1 Hispanic/Latino), 8 international. Average age 31. 38 applicants, 58% accepted, 5 enrolled. In 2015, 5 master's, 3 doctorates awarded. *Entrance requirements:* Additional exam requirements/recommendations for international students: Required—TOEFL (minimum score 74 iBT). *Application deadline:* For fall admission, 6/1 for domestic students, 4/15 for international students; for spring admission, 11/30 for domestic students, 11/1 for international students. Applications are processed on a rolling basis. Application fee: $60. Electronic applications accepted. *Expenses: Tuition, area resident:* Full-time $32,200; part-time $1450 per credit. *Required fees:* $1150; $550 per unit. $275 per semester. *Financial support:* Fellowships, research assistantships, teaching assistantships, career-related internships or fieldwork, Federal Work-Study, scholarships/grants, and unspecified assistantships available. Financial award application deadline: 2/15; financial award applicants required to submit FAFSA. *Unit head:* Dr. Alexei Miasnikov, Director, 201-216-8598, Fax: 201-216-8321, E-mail: amiasnik@stevens.edu. *Application contact:* Graduate Admission, 888-783-8367, Fax: 888-511-1306, E-mail: graduate@stevens.edu.

Stony Brook University, State University of New York, Graduate School, College of Arts and Sciences, Department of Mathematics, Stony Brook, NY 11794. Offers MA, MAT, PhD. *Faculty:* 37 full-time (9 women), 21 part-time/adjunct (8 women). *Students:* 60 full-time (9 women), 17 part-time (8 women); includes 10 minority (3 Asian, non-Hispanic/Latino; 4 Hispanic/Latino; 3 Two or more races, non-Hispanic/Latino), 38 international. Average age 26. 295 applicants, 9% accepted, 17 enrolled. In 2015, 18 master's, 10 doctorates awarded. *Degree requirements:* For doctorate, 2 foreign languages, thesis/dissertation. *Entrance requirements:* For master's and doctorate, GRE General Test. Additional exam requirements/recommendations for international students: Required—TOEFL (minimum score 90 iBT). *Application deadline:* For fall admission, 1/15 for domestic students; for spring admission, 10/1 for domestic students. Application fee: $100. *Expenses:* $12,421 full-time in-state tuition and fees, $453 per credit hour; $23,761 full-time out-of-state tuition and fees, $925 per credit hour. *Financial support:* In 2015–16, 8 fellowships, 8 research assistantships, 34 teaching assistantships were awarded. *Faculty research:* Mathematics, Algebra, Topology, Polynomials, Geometry. *Total annual research expenditures:* $2 million. *Unit head:* Dr. Mikhail Lyubich, Chair, 631-632-8280, E-mail: mikhail.lyubich@stonybrook.edu. *Application contact:* Donna McWilliams, Coordinator, 631-632-8282, Fax: 631-632-7631, E-mail: donna.mcwilliams@stonybrook.edu. Website: http://www.math.sunysb.edu/html/index.shtml

Syracuse University, College of Arts and Sciences, Programs in Mathematics, Syracuse, NY 13244. Offers mathematics (MS, PhD); mathematics education (MS, PhD). *Program availability:* Part-time. *Students:* Average age 26. In 2015, 11 master's, 3 doctorates awarded. Terminal master's awarded for partial completion of doctoral program. *Degree requirements:* For doctorate, 2 foreign languages, comprehensive exam, thesis/dissertation. *Entrance requirements:* For master's and doctorate, GRE General Test, GRE Subject Test (recommended), brief (about 500 words) statement indicating why applicant wishes to pursue graduate study and why Syracuse is a good fit, curriculum vitae or resume, transcripts from each post-secondary institution, three letters of recommendation. Additional exam requirements/recommendations for international students: Required—TOEFL (minimum score 100 iBT). *Application deadline:* For fall admission, 1/15 priority date for domestic and international students. Application fee: $75. Electronic applications accepted. *Expenses: Tuition, area resident:* Full-time $25,974; part-time $1443 per credit hour. *Required fees:* $802; $50 per course.

Tuition and fees vary according to course load and program. *Financial support:* Fellowships with full tuition reimbursements, research assistantships with tuition reimbursements, teaching assistantships with tuition reimbursements, and scholarships/grants available. Financial award application deadline: 1/1; financial award applicants required to submit FAFSA. *Faculty research:* Pure mathematics, numerical mathematics, computing statistics. *Unit head:* Dr. Uday Banerjee, Chair, 315-443-1471, E-mail: banerjee@syr.edu. *Application contact:* Henry Barwotoe, Office Coordinator, 315-443-1474, E-mail: hlbywoto@syr.edu. Website: http://math.syr.edu

Tarleton State University, College of Graduate Studies, College of Science and Technology, Department of Mathematics, Stephenville, TX 76402. Offers mathematics (MS). *Program availability:* Part-time, evening/weekend. *Faculty:* 11 full-time (3 women), 2 part-time/adjunct (0 women). *Students:* 12 full-time (5 women), 10 part-time (5 women); includes 4 minority (1 Hispanic/Latino; 3 Two or more races, non-Hispanic/Latino), 2 international. 12 applicants, 67% accepted, 7 enrolled. In 2015, 13 master's awarded. *Degree requirements:* For master's, comprehensive exam, thesis (for some programs). *Entrance requirements:* For master's, GRE General Test, minimum GPA of 3.0. Additional exam requirements/recommendations for international students: Required—TOEFL (minimum score 550 paper-based; 80 iBT). *Application deadline:* For fall admission, 8/15 priority date for domestic students; for spring admission, 1/7 for domestic students. Applications are processed on a rolling basis. Application fee: $45 ($145 for international students). Electronic applications accepted. *Expenses:* Tuition, state resident: part-time $204 per credit hour. Tuition, nonresident: part-time $594 per credit hour. *Required fees:* $1994 per unit. *Financial support:* Research assistantships, teaching assistantships, career-related internships or fieldwork, and Federal Work-Study available. Support available to part-time students. Financial award application deadline: 5/1; financial award applicants required to submit FAFSA. *Unit head:* Dr. Bowen Brawner, Department Head, 254-968-9168, Fax: 254-968-9534, E-mail: brawner@tarleton.edu. *Application contact:* Information Contact, 254-968-9104, Fax: 254-968-9670, E-mail: gradoffice@tarleton.edu. Website: http://www.tarleton.edu/degrees/masters/ms-mathematics/

Temple University, College of Science and Technology, Department of Mathematics, Philadelphia, PA 19122. Offers applied mathematics (MA); mathematics (PhD); pure mathematics (MA). *Program availability:* Part-time, evening/weekend. *Faculty:* 27 full-time (6 women). *Students:* 34 full-time (10 women), 3 part-time (0 women); includes 3 minority (all Asian, non-Hispanic/Latino), 18 international. 57 applicants, 46% accepted, 9 enrolled. In 2015, 8 master's, 5 doctorates awarded. Terminal master's awarded for partial completion of doctoral program. *Degree requirements:* For master's, thesis optional, written exam; for doctorate, 2 foreign languages, thesis/dissertation, oral and written exams. *Entrance requirements:* For master's, GRE General Test, minimum GPA of 3.0; for doctorate, GRE General Test, GRE Subject Test, minimum GPA of 3.0. Additional exam requirements/recommendations for international students: Required—TOEFL (minimum score 550 paper-based; 79 iBT). *Application deadline:* For fall admission, 2/15 priority date for domestic students, 12/15 for international students; for spring admission, 11/15 for domestic students, 8/1 for international students. Applications are processed on a rolling basis. Application fee: $60. Electronic applications accepted. *Financial support:* Fellowships, research assistantships, teaching assistantships, Federal Work-Study, and institutionally sponsored loans available. Financial award application deadline: 1/15; financial award applicants required to submit FAFSA. *Faculty research:* Differential geometry, numerical analysis. *Unit head:* Edward Letzter, Department Chair, 215-204-7841, Fax: 215-204-6433, E-mail: mathematics@temple.edu. *Application contact:* Alexis Cogan, Administrative Assistant, 215-204-7840, E-mail: cogana@temple.edu. Website: http://math.temple.edu/

Tennessee State University, The School of Graduate Studies and Research, College of Engineering, Nashville, TN 37209-1561. Offers biomedical engineering (ME); civil engineering (ME); computer and information systems engineering (MS, PhD); electrical engineering (ME); environmental engineering (ME); manufacturing engineering (ME); mathematical sciences (MS); mechanical engineering (ME). *Program availability:* Part-time, evening/weekend. *Degree requirements:* For master's, project; for doctorate, comprehensive exam, thesis/dissertation. *Entrance requirements:* For doctorate, minimum GPA of 3.3. *Faculty research:* Robotics, intelligent systems, human-computer interaction software systems, biomedical engineering, signal/image processing, probabilistic design, intelligent manufacturing, cooperative mobile robots, condition based maintenance, sensor fusion.

Tennessee Technological University, College of Graduate Studies, College of Arts and Sciences, Department of Mathematics, Cookeville, TN 38505. Offers MS. *Program availability:* Part-time. *Faculty:* 17 full-time (4 women). *Students:* 12 full-time (5 women), 6 part-time (4 women); includes 1 minority (Two or more races, non-Hispanic/Latino), 1 international. Average age 27. 19 applicants, 58% accepted, 7 enrolled. In 2015, 6 degrees awarded. *Degree requirements:* For master's, thesis or alternative. *Entrance requirements:* For master's, GRE General Test. Additional exam requirements/recommendations for international students: Required—TOEFL (minimum score 527 paper-based; 71 iBT), IELTS (minimum score 5.5), PTE (minimum score 48), or TOEIC (Test of English as an International Communication). *Application deadline:* For fall admission, 8/1 for domestic students, 5/1 for international students; for spring admission, 12/1 for domestic students, 10/1 for international students; for summer admission, 5/1 for domestic students, 2/1 for international students. Applications are processed on a rolling basis. Application fee: $35 ($40 for international students). Electronic applications accepted. *Expenses:* Tuition, state resident: full-time $8961; part-time $6132 per credit hour. Tuition, nonresident: full-time $23,121; part-time $14,608 per credit hour. *Financial support:* In 2015–16, 3 research assistantships (averaging $7,500 per year), 7 teaching assistantships (averaging $7,500 per year) were awarded. Financial award application deadline: 4/1. *Unit head:* Dr. Allan Mills, Interim Chairperson, 931-372-3441, Fax: 931-372-6353, E-mail: amills@tntech.edu. *Application contact:* Shelia K. Kendrick, Coordinator of Graduate Studies, 931-372-3808, Fax: 931-372-3497, E-mail: skendrick@tntech.edu.

Texas A&M International University, Office of Graduate Studies and Research, College of Arts and Sciences, Department of Engineering, Mathematics, and Physics, Laredo, TX 78041-1900. Offers mathematics (MS). *Degree requirements:* For master's, comprehensive exam, thesis (for some programs). *Entrance requirements:* For master's, GRE General Test. Additional exam requirements/recommendations for international students: Required—TOEFL (minimum score 550 paper-based; 79 iBT).

Texas A&M University, College of Science, Department of Mathematics, College Station, TX 77843. Offers MS, PhD. *Program availability:* Part-time, online learning. *Faculty:* 54. *Students:* 138 full-time (35 women), 47 part-time (23 women); includes 15 minority (4 Black or African American, non-Hispanic/Latino; 4 Asian, non-Hispanic/Latino; 6 Hispanic/Latino; 1 Two or more races, non-Hispanic/Latino), 86 international. Average age 29. 182 applicants, 48% accepted, 43 enrolled. In 2015, 24 master's, 16 doctorates awarded. Terminal master's awarded for partial completion of doctoral program. *Degree requirements:* For master's, comprehensive exam, thesis optional; for

doctorate, one foreign language, comprehensive exam, thesis/dissertation. *Entrance requirements:* For master's and doctorate, GRE General Test. Additional exam requirements/recommendations for international students: Required—TOEFL (minimum score 550 paper-based). *Application deadline:* For fall admission, 3/1 for domestic and international students; for spring admission, 8/1 for domestic and international students. Applications are processed on a rolling basis. Application fee: $50 ($90 for international students). Electronic applications accepted. *Expenses:* Contact institution. *Financial support:* In 2015–16, 146 students received support, including 17 fellowships with tuition reimbursements available (averaging $8,853 per year), 39 research assistantships with tuition reimbursements available (averaging $7,932 per year), 81 teaching assistantships with tuition reimbursements available (averaging $7,246 per year); career-related internships or fieldwork, institutionally sponsored loans, scholarships/grants, traineeships, health care benefits, tuition waivers (full and partial), and unspecified assistantships also available. Support available to part-time students. Financial award application deadline: 3/1; financial award applicants required to submit FAFSA. *Faculty research:* Algebra and combinatorics, applied mathematics and interdisciplinary research, approximation theory, functional analysis, geometry and topology. *Unit head:* Dr. Emil Straube, Head, 979-845-9424, Fax: 979-845-6028, E-mail: straube@math.tamu.edu. *Application contact:* Monique Stewart, Academic Advisor I, 979-862-4137, Fax: 979-862-4190, E-mail: stewart@math.tamu.edu.
Website: http://www.math.tamu.edu/

Texas A&M University–Central Texas, Graduate Studies and Research, Killeen, TX 76549. Offers accounting (MS); business administration (MBA); clinical mental health counseling (MS); criminal justice (MCJ); curriculum and instruction (M Ed); educational administration (M Ed); educational psychology - experimental psychology (MS); history (MA); human resource management (MS); information systems (MS); liberal studies (MS); management and leadership (MS); marriage and family therapy (MS); mathematics (MS); political science (MA); school counseling (M Ed); school psychology (Ed S).

Texas A&M University–Corpus Christi, College of Graduate Studies, College of Science and Engineering, Program in Mathematics, Corpus Christi, TX 78412-5503. Offers MS. *Program availability:* Part-time. *Students:* 7 full-time (5 women), 4 part-time (all women); includes 3 minority (1 Asian, non-Hispanic/Latino; 2 Hispanic/Latino), 7 international. Average age 33. 10 applicants, 60% accepted, 3 enrolled. In 2015, 7 master's awarded. *Degree requirements:* For master's, thesis (for some programs), capstone. *Entrance requirements:* For master's, essay (300-500 words). Additional exam requirements/recommendations for international students: Required—TOEFL (minimum score 550 paper-based; 79 iBT), IELTS (minimum score 6.5). *Application deadline:* For fall admission, 7/15 priority date for domestic students, 5/1 priority date for international students; for spring admission, 11/15 priority date for domestic students, 10/31 priority date for international students; for summer admission, 4/15 priority date for domestic students, 2/1 priority date for international students. Applications are processed on a rolling basis. Application fee: $50 ($70 for international students). Electronic applications accepted. *Financial support:* Research assistantships, teaching assistantships, and scholarships/grants available. Financial award application deadline: 3/15; financial award applicants required to submit FAFSA. *Unit head:* Dr. Jose Guardiola, Associate Professor, 361-825-5544, E-mail: jose.guardiola@tamucc.edu. *Application contact:* Graduate Admissions Coordinator, 361-825-2177, Fax: 361-825-2755, E-mail: gradweb@tamucc.edu.
Website: http://gradschool.tamucc.edu/degrees/science/mathematics.html

Texas A&M University–Kingsville, College of Graduate Studies, College of Arts and Sciences, Department of Mathematics, Program in Mathematics, Kingsville, TX 78363. Offers MS.

Texas Christian University, College of Science and Engineering, Department of Mathematics, Fort Worth, TX 76129. Offers applied mathematics (MS); mathematics (MAT, PhD); pure mathematics (MS). *Program availability:* Part-time, evening/weekend. *Faculty:* 13 full-time (2 women). *Students:* 14 full-time (3 women), 1 part-time (0 women); includes 4 minority (1 Asian, non-Hispanic/Latino; 2 Hispanic/Latino; 1 Two or more races, non-Hispanic/Latino), 3 international. Average age 26. 20 applicants, 30% accepted, 6 enrolled. In 2015, 2 master's awarded. Terminal master's awarded for partial completion of doctoral program. *Degree requirements:* For master's, thesis optional; for doctorate, comprehensive exam, thesis/dissertation. *Entrance requirements:* For master's and doctorate, GRE General Test, 24 hours of math, including courses in elementary calculus of one and several variables, linear algebra, abstract algebra and real analysis. Additional exam requirements/recommendations for international students: Recommended—TOEFL (minimum score 550 paper-based; 80 iBT), IELTS (minimum score 6.5). *Application deadline:* For fall admission, 2/15 for domestic and international students; for spring admission, 10/15 for domestic and international students. Application fee: $60. Electronic applications accepted. *Expenses: Tuition, area resident:* Full-time $26,640; part-time $1480 per credit hour. *Required fees:* $48; $48 per unit. Tuition and fees vary according to program. *Financial support:* In 2015–16, 15 students received support, including 9 teaching assistantships with full tuition reimbursements available (averaging $17,500 per year); tuition waivers also available. Support available to part-time students. Financial award application deadline: 2/15. *Faculty research:* Algebraic geometry, differential geometry and global analysis, algebraic topology, K-theory and operator algebras, number theory. *Total annual research expenditures:* $60,000. *Unit head:* Dr. George Gilbert, Associate Professor/Chair, 817-257-6061, Fax: 817-257-7766, E-mail: g.gilbert@tcu.edu. *Application contact:* Dr. Ken Richardson, Professor/Director, Graduate Program, 817-257-6128, E-mail: k.richardson@tcu.edu.
Website: http://mathematics.tcu.edu/

Texas Southern University, School of Science and Technology, Department of Mathematics, Houston, TX 77004-4584. Offers MS. *Program availability:* Part-time, evening/weekend. *Degree requirements:* For master's, comprehensive exam, thesis. *Entrance requirements:* For master's, GRE General Test, minimum GPA of 2.5. Additional exam requirements/recommendations for international students: Required—TOEFL. Electronic applications accepted. *Faculty research:* Statistics, number theory, topology, differential equations, numerical analysis.

Texas State University, The Graduate College, College of Science and Engineering, Program in Mathematics, San Marcos, TX 78666. Offers M Ed, MS. *Program availability:* Part-time. *Faculty:* 18 full-time (6 women). *Students:* 11 full-time (4 women), 7 part-time (2 women); includes 2 minority (1 Black or African American, non-Hispanic/Latino; 1 Hispanic/Latino), 1 international. Average age 30. 11 applicants, 82% accepted, 5 enrolled. In 2015, 6 master's awarded. *Degree requirements:* For master's, comprehensive exam, thesis (for some programs). *Entrance requirements:* For master's, GRE (minimum preferred score of 300 verbal and quantitative combined), baccalaureate degree in mathematics or related field from regionally-accredited university with minimum GPA of 2.75 on last 60 undergraduate semester hours. Additional exam requirements/recommendations for international students: Required—TOEFL (minimum score 550 paper-based; 78 iBT). *Application deadline:* For fall admission, 6/15 for domestic students, 6/1 for international students; for spring admission, 10/15 for domestic students, 10/1 for international students; for summer admission, 4/15 for domestic students, 3/15 for international students. Applications are processed on a rolling basis. Application fee: $40 ($90 for international students). Electronic applications accepted. *Expenses:* $3,615 in-state tuition for 12 semester credit hours (1 full-time semester), $974 in-state fees. *Financial support:* In 2015–16, 11 students received support, including 1 research assistantship (averaging $14,514 per year), 4 teaching assistantships (averaging $13,958 per year); Federal Work-Study, institutionally sponsored loans, scholarships/grants, health care benefits, and unspecified assistantships also available. Support available to part-time students. Financial award application deadline: 3/1; financial award applicants required to submit FAFSA. *Faculty research:* Evaluation of comprehensive student success program, orbits in finite group actions, advanced caminos with focus elements. *Total annual research expenditures:* $6,930. *Unit head:* Dr. Gregory Passty, Graduate Advisor, 512-245-2551, Fax: 512-245-3425, E-mail: gp02@txstate.edu. *Application contact:* Dr. Andrea Golato, Dean of the Graduate College, 512-245-3446, Fax: 512-245-3425, E-mail: gp02@txstate.edu.
Website: http://www.math.txstate.edu/degrees-programs/masters/master-math.html

Texas Tech University, Graduate School, College of Arts and Sciences, Department of Mathematics and Statistics, Lubbock, TX 79409. Offers mathematics (MA, MS, PhD); statistics (MS). *Program availability:* Part-time, 100% online. *Faculty:* 58 full-time (19 women), 4 part-time/adjunct (1 woman). *Students:* 119 full-time (58 women), 20 part-time (10 women); includes 14 minority (2 Black or African American, non-Hispanic/Latino; 4 Asian, non-Hispanic/Latino; 7 Hispanic/Latino; 1 Two or more races, non-Hispanic/Latino), 82 international. Average age 30. 95 applicants, 68% accepted, 38 enrolled. In 2015, 27 master's, 9 doctorates awarded. Terminal master's awarded for partial completion of doctoral program. *Degree requirements:* For master's, comprehensive exam (for some programs), thesis (for some programs); for doctorate, comprehensive exam, thesis/dissertation. *Entrance requirements:* For master's, GRE (for MS and assistantship applications only), MS (official transcripts, 3 letters of recommendation, statement of purpose), MA (official transcripts); for doctorate, GRE General Test, official transcripts, 3 letters of recommendation, resume/curriculum vitae, statement of purpose. Additional exam requirements/recommendations for international students: Required—TOEFL (minimum score 550 paper-based; 79 iBT), IELTS (minimum score 6.5). *Application deadline:* For fall admission, 6/1 priority date for domestic students, 1/15 priority date for international students; for spring admission, 9/1 priority date for domestic students, 6/15 priority date for international students. Applications are processed on a rolling basis. Application fee: $60. Electronic applications accepted. *Expenses:* Tuition, state resident: full-time $6477; part-time $269.89 per credit hour. Tuition, nonresident: full-time $15,837; part-time $659.89 per credit hour. *Required fees:* $2751; $36.50 per credit hour. $937.50 per semester. Tuition and fees vary according to course level. *Financial support:* In 2015–16, 116 students received support, including 91 fellowships (averaging $2,766 per year), 12 research assistantships (averaging $8,527 per year), 100 teaching assistantships (averaging $16,914 per year). Financial award application deadline: 2/15; financial award applicants required to submit FAFSA. *Faculty research:* Applied math, biomath, complex analysis, computational mathematics, statistics. *Total annual research expenditures:* $1.1 million. *Unit head:* Dr. Magdalena Toda, Professor and Chair, 806-834-7944, Fax: 806-742-1112, E-mail: magda.toda@ttu.edu. *Application contact:* Gene Gray, Senior Graduate Academic Advisor, 806-834-1269, Fax: 806-742-1112, E-mail: gene.gray@ttu.edu.
Website: http://www.math.ttu.edu/

Texas Woman's University, Graduate School, College of Arts and Sciences, Department of Mathematics and Computer Science, Denton, TX 76201. Offers informatics (MS); mathematics (MS); mathematics teaching (MS). *Program availability:* Part-time, evening/weekend. *Faculty:* 9 full-time. *Degree requirements:* For master's, comprehensive exam, thesis. *Entrance requirements:* For master's, 2 letters of reference. Additional exam requirements/recommendations for international students: Required—TOEFL (minimum score 550 paper-based; 79 iBT). *Application deadline:* For fall admission, 7/1 priority date for domestic students, 3/1 for international students; for spring admission, 12/1 priority date for domestic students, 7/1 for international students. Applications are processed on a rolling basis. Application fee: $50 ($75 for international students). Electronic applications accepted. *Expenses:* Tuition, state resident: full-time $4380; part-time $243 per credit hour. Tuition, nonresident: full-time $11,400; part-time $633 per credit hour. *International tuition:* $11,465 full-time. *Required fees:* $1778; $99 per credit hour. $283 per semester. One-time fee: $50. Tuition and fees vary according to course load and program. *Financial support:* Research assistantships, teaching assistantships, career-related internships or fieldwork, Federal Work-Study, institutionally sponsored loans, scholarships/grants, traineeships, health care benefits, and unspecified assistantships available. Support available to part-time students. Financial award application deadline: 3/1; financial award applicants required to submit FAFSA. *Faculty research:* Biopharmaceutical statistics, dynamic systems and control theory, Bayesian inference, math and computer science curriculum innovation, computer modeling of physical phenomenon. *Unit head:* Dr. Don E. Edwards, Chair, 940-898-3275, Fax: 940-898-2179, E-mail: mathcs@twu.edu. *Application contact:* Dr. Samuel Wheeler, Assistant Director of Admissions, 940-898-3188, Fax: 940-898-3081, E-mail: wheelersr@twu.edu.
Website: http://www.twu.edu/math-computer-science/

Tufts University, Graduate School of Arts and Sciences, Department of Mathematics, Medford, MA 02155. Offers mathematics (MS, PhD); soft materials robotics (PhD). Terminal master's awarded for partial completion of doctoral program. *Degree requirements:* For master's, one foreign language, thesis; for doctorate, 2 foreign languages, thesis/dissertation. *Entrance requirements:* For master's, GRE General Test; for doctorate, GRE General Test, GRE Subject Test. Additional exam requirements/recommendations for international students: Required—TOEFL (minimum score 550 paper-based; 80 iBT), IELTS (minimum score 6.5). Electronic applications accepted. *Expenses: Tuition, area resident:* Full-time $48,412; part-time $1210 per credit hour. *Required fees:* $806. Full-time tuition and fees vary according to degree level, program and student level. Part-time tuition and fees vary according to course load.

Tulane University, School of Science and Engineering, Department of Mathematics, New Orleans, LA 70118-5669. Offers applied mathematics (MS); mathematics (MS, PhD); statistics (MS). *Degree requirements:* For master's, thesis (for some programs); for doctorate, thesis/dissertation. *Entrance requirements:* For master's, GRE General Test, minimum B average in undergraduate course work; for doctorate, GRE General Test. Additional exam requirements/recommendations for international students: Required—TOEFL. Electronic applications accepted.

Université de Moncton, Faculty of Sciences, Department of Mathematics and Statistics, Moncton, NB E1A 3E9, Canada. Offers mathematics (M Sc). *Degree requirements:* For master's, one foreign language, thesis. *Entrance requirements:* For master's, minimum GPA of 3.0. Electronic applications accepted. *Faculty research:* Statistics, numerical analysis, fixed point theory, mathematical physics.

Université de Montréal, Faculty of Arts and Sciences, Department of Mathematics and Statistics, Montréal, QC H3C 3J7, Canada. Offers mathematical and computational finance (M Sc, DESS); mathematics (M Sc, PhD); statistics (M Sc, PhD). *Degree* *requirements:* For master's, thesis; for doctorate, thesis/dissertation, general exam. *Entrance requirements:* For master's and doctorate, proficiency in French. Electronic applications accepted. *Faculty research:* Pure and applied mathematics, actuarial mathematics.

Université de Sherbrooke, Faculty of Sciences, Department of Mathematics, Sherbrooke, QC J1K 2R1, Canada. Offers M Sc, PhD. *Degree requirements:* For master's, thesis; for doctorate, comprehensive exam, thesis/dissertation. *Entrance requirements:* For doctorate, master's degree. Electronic applications accepted. *Faculty research:* Measure theory, differential equations, probability, statistics, error control codes.

Université du Québec à Montréal, Graduate Programs, Program in Mathematics, Montréal, QC H3C 3P8, Canada. Offers M Sc, PhD. *Program availability:* Part-time. *Degree requirements:* For master's, thesis; for doctorate, thesis/dissertation. *Entrance requirements:* For master's, appropriate bachelor's degree or equivalent, proficiency in French; for doctorate, appropriate master's degree or equivalent, proficiency in French.

Université du Québec à Trois-Rivières, Graduate Programs, Program in Mathematics and Computer Science, Trois-Rivières, QC G9A 5H7, Canada. Offers M Sc. *Faculty research:* Probability, statistics.

Université Laval, Faculty of Sciences and Engineering, Department of Mathematics and Statistics, Programs in Mathematics, Québec, QC G1K 7P4, Canada. Offers M Sc, PhD. Terminal master's awarded for partial completion of doctoral program. *Degree requirements:* For master's, thesis (for some programs); for doctorate, comprehensive exam, thesis/dissertation. *Entrance requirements:* For master's and doctorate, knowledge of French and English. Electronic applications accepted.

University at Albany, State University of New York, College of Arts and Sciences, Department of Mathematics and Statistics, Albany, NY 12222-0001. Offers mathematics (MA, PhD). *Degree requirements:* For doctorate, one foreign language, thesis/dissertation. *Entrance requirements:* For doctorate, GRE General Test. Additional exam requirements/recommendations for international students: Required—TOEFL (minimum score 550 paper-based). Electronic applications accepted.

University at Buffalo, the State University of New York, Graduate School, College of Arts and Sciences, Department of Mathematics, Buffalo, NY 14260. Offers MA, PhD. *Faculty:* 32 full-time (4 women), 24 part-time/adjunct (7 women). *Students:* 82 full-time (19 women), 5 part-time (1 woman); includes 43 minority (41 Asian, non-Hispanic/Latino; 2 Hispanic/Latino). Average age 29. 118 applicants, 52% accepted, 22 enrolled. In 2015, 13 master's, 4 doctorates awarded. Terminal master's awarded for partial completion of doctoral program. *Degree requirements:* For master's, comprehensive exam (for some programs), thesis (for some programs), project (for some programs); for doctorate, comprehensive exam, thesis/dissertation. *Entrance requirements:* Additional exam requirements/recommendations for international students: Required—TOEFL (minimum score 550 paper-based, 79 iBT), IELTS (minimum score 6.5), or PTE (minimum score 55 with all areas not less than 50). *Application deadline:* For fall admission, 4/15 priority date for domestic and international students; for spring admission, 10/1 priority date for domestic students, 9/15 priority date for international students. Applications are processed on a rolling basis. Application fee: $75. Electronic applications accepted. *Expenses:* Contact institution. *Financial support:* In 2015–16, 50 students received support, including fellowships with full tuition reimbursements available (averaging $4,000 per year), 50 teaching assistantships with full tuition reimbursements available (averaging $16,400 per year); research assistantships and institutionally sponsored loans also available. Financial award application deadline: 1/15; financial award applicants required to submit FAFSA. *Faculty research:* Algebra, analysis, applied mathematics, logic, number theory, topology. *Total annual research expenditures:* $367,931. *Unit head:* Dr. David Hemmer, Chairman, 716-645-8780, Fax: 716-645-5039, E-mail: chair@math.buffalo.edu. *Application contact:* Dr. William W. Menasco, Director of Graduate Studies, 716-645-8783, Fax: 716-645-5039,
E-mail: gsdmath@buffalo.edu.
Website: http://www.math.buffalo.edu/

The University of Akron, Graduate School, Buchtel College of Arts and Sciences, Department of Mathematics, Program in Mathematics, Akron, OH 44325. Offers MS. *Program availability:* Part-time, evening/weekend. *Students:* 2 full-time (1 woman). Average age 22. In 2015, 1 master's awarded. *Degree requirements:* For master's, seminar and comprehensive exam or thesis. *Entrance requirements:* For master's, minimum GPA of 2.75, three letters of recommendation, statement of purpose. Additional exam requirements/recommendations for international students: Required—TOEFL (minimum score 550 paper-based; 79 iBT), IELTS (minimum score 6.5). *Application deadline:* Applications are processed on a rolling basis. Application fee: $45 ($70 for international students). Electronic applications accepted. *Expenses:* Tuition, state resident: full-time $7958; part-time $442 per credit hour. Tuition, nonresident: full-time $13,464; part-time $748 per credit hour. *Required fees:* $1404. *Unit head:* Dr. Timothy Norfolk, Chair, 330-972-6121, E-mail: tnorfolk@uakron.edu. *Application contact:* Dr. J. Patrick Wilber, Graduate Director, 330-972-6964,
E-mail: jw50@uakron.edu.
Website: http://www.uakron.edu/math/academics/graduate/index.dot

The University of Alabama, Graduate School, College of Arts and Sciences, Department of Mathematics, Tuscaloosa, AL 35487-0350. Offers applied mathematics (PhD); mathematics (MA, PhD); pure mathematics (PhD). *Faculty:* 27 full-time (3 women). *Students:* 38 full-time (18 women), 3 part-time (2 women); includes 5 minority (4 Black or African American, non-Hispanic/Latino; 1 Two or more races, non-Hispanic/Latino), 21 international. Average age 27. 34 applicants, 44% accepted, 5 enrolled. In 2015, 5 master's, 5 doctorates awarded. Terminal master's awarded for partial completion of doctoral program. *Degree requirements:* For master's, thesis or alternative; for doctorate, comprehensive exam, thesis/dissertation. *Entrance requirements:* For master's and doctorate, GRE General Test, minimum GPA of 3.0. Additional exam requirements/recommendations for international students: Required—TOEFL, IELTS or PTE (minimum score 59); Recommended—TOEFL (minimum score 550 paper-based; 79 iBT), IELTS (minimum score 6.5). *Application deadline:* For fall admission, 6/1 for domestic students, 12/1 for international students; for spring admission, 10/15 for domestic students, 5/1 for international students. Applications are processed on a rolling basis. Application fee: $50 ($60 for international students). Electronic applications accepted. *Expenses:* Tuition, state resident: full-time $10,170. Tuition, nonresident: full-time $25,950. *Financial support:* In 2015–16, 1 fellowship with full tuition reimbursement (averaging $30,000 per year), 35 teaching assistantships with full tuition reimbursements (averaging $12,258 per year) were awarded; research assistantships with full tuition reimbursements, Federal Work-Study, institutionally sponsored loans, scholarships/grants, and unspecified assistantships also available. Financial award application deadline: 1/15. *Faculty research:* Algebra, analysis, topology, mathematics education, applied and computational mathematics, statistics. *Unit head:* Dr. David Cruz-Uribe, Professor and Chair, 205-348-5074, Fax: 205-348-7067, E-mail: dcruzuribe@ua.edu. *Application contact:* Dr. David Halpern, Graduate Program Director, 205-348-1977, Fax: 205-348-7067, E-mail: dhalpern@ua.edu.
Website: http://math.ua.edu/

The University of Alabama at Birmingham, College of Arts and Sciences, Program in Mathematics, Birmingham, AL 35294. Offers MS. Terminal master's awarded for partial completion of doctoral program. *Degree requirements:* For master's, thesis or alternative. *Entrance requirements:* For master's, GRE General Test, minimum GPA of 3.0, letters of recommendation. Additional exam requirements/recommendations for international students: Required—TOEFL, TWE. Electronic applications accepted. *Expenses:* Tuition, state resident: full-time $7340. Tuition, nonresident: full-time $16,628. Full-time tuition and fees vary according to course load and program. *Faculty research:* Differential equations, topology, mathematical physics, dynamic systems.

The University of Alabama in Huntsville, School of Graduate Studies, College of Science, Department of Mathematical Sciences, Huntsville, AL 35899. Offers applied mathematics (PhD); education (MA, MS); mathematics (MA, MS). PhD offered jointly with The University of Alabama (Tuscaloosa) and The University of Alabama at Birmingham. *Program availability:* Part-time, evening/weekend. *Degree requirements:* For master's, comprehensive exam, thesis or alternative, oral and written exams; for doctorate, comprehensive exam, thesis/dissertation, oral and written exams. *Entrance requirements:* For master's and doctorate, GRE General Test, minimum GPA of 3.0. Additional exam requirements/recommendations for international students: Required—TOEFL (minimum score 550 paper-based; 80 iBT), IELTS (minimum score 6.5). Electronic applications accepted. *Faculty research:* Combinatorics and graph theory, computational mathematics, differential equations and applications, mathematical biology, probability and stochastic processes.

University of Alaska Fairbanks, College of Natural Sciences and Mathematics, Department of Mathematics and Statistics, Fairbanks, AK 99775-6660. Offers mathematics (PhD); statistics (MS, Graduate Certificate). *Program availability:* Part-time. *Faculty:* 20 full-time (10 women). *Students:* 12 full-time (2 women), 3 part-time (1 woman), 6 international. Average age 29. 19 applicants, 47% accepted, 5 enrolled. In 2015, 4 master's awarded. *Degree requirements:* For master's, comprehensive exam, thesis (for some programs), oral defense of project or thesis; for doctorate, comprehensive exam, thesis/dissertation, oral defense of dissertation. *Entrance requirements:* For master's, GRE General Test, bachelor's degree from accredited institution with minimum cumulative undergraduate and major GPA of 3.0; for doctorate, GRE Subject Test (mathematics), bachelor's degree from accredited institution with minimum cumulative undergraduate and major GPA of 3.0. Additional exam requirements/recommendations for international students: Required—TOEFL (minimum score 550 paper-based; 79 iBT), IELTS (minimum score 6.5). *Application deadline:* For fall admission, 6/1 for domestic students, 3/1 for international students; for spring admission, 10/15 for domestic students, 9/1 for international students. Applications are processed on a rolling basis. Application fee: $60. Electronic applications accepted. *Expenses:* Tuition, state resident: full-time $7614; part-time $423 per credit. Tuition, nonresident: full-time $15,552; part-time $864 per credit. *Required fees:* $38 per credit. $187 per semester. Tuition and fees vary according to course level, course load, program and reciprocity agreements. *Financial support:* In 2015–16, 1 research assistantship with full tuition reimbursement (averaging $16,834 per year), 11 teaching assistantships with full tuition reimbursements (averaging $18,239 per year) were awarded; fellowships with full tuition reimbursements, career-related internships or fieldwork, Federal Work-Study, scholarships/grants, health care benefits, and unspecified assistantships also available. Support available to part-time students. Financial award application deadline: 2/15; financial award applicants required to submit FAFSA. *Faculty research:* Kriging, arrangements of hyperplanes, bifurcation analysis of time-periodic differential-delay equations, inverse problems, phylogenic tree construction. *Unit head:* Dr. John Rhodes, Department Chair, 907-474-7332, Fax: 907-474-5394, E-mail: uaf-mathandstat-dept@alaska.edu. *Application contact:* Mary Kreta, Director of Admissions, 907-474-7500, Fax: 907-474-7097,
E-mail: admissions@uaf.edu.
Website: http://www.uaf.edu/dms/

University of Alberta, Faculty of Graduate Studies and Research, Department of Mathematical and Statistical Sciences, Edmonton, AB T6G 2E1, Canada. Offers applied mathematics (M Sc, PhD); biostatistics (M Sc); mathematical finance (M Sc, PhD); mathematical physics (M Sc, PhD); mathematics (M Sc, PhD); statistics (M Sc, PhD, Postgraduate Diploma). *Program availability:* Part-time. Terminal master's awarded for partial completion of doctoral program. *Degree requirements:* For master's, thesis (for some programs); for doctorate, comprehensive exam, thesis/dissertation. *Entrance requirements:* Additional exam requirements/recommendations for international students: Required—TOEFL (minimum score 580 paper-based). Electronic applications accepted. *Faculty research:* Classical and functional analysis, algebra, differential equations, geometry.

The University of Arizona, College of Science, Department of Mathematics, Tucson, AZ 85721. Offers mathematics (MA, MS, PhD). *Program availability:* Part-time. *Degree requirements:* For master's, thesis; for doctorate, 2 foreign languages, thesis/dissertation. *Entrance requirements:* For master's, GRE; for doctorate, GRE, statement of purpose. Additional exam requirements/recommendations for international students: Required—TOEFL (minimum score 550 paper-based; 79 iBT). *Application deadline:* For fall admission, 2/1 for domestic students, 12/1 for international students; for spring admission, 10/1 for domestic students, 6/1 for international students. Applications are processed on a rolling basis. Application fee: $75. Electronic applications accepted. *Financial support:* Research assistantships, teaching assistantships, scholarships/grants, health care benefits, tuition waivers (full and partial), and unspecified assistantships available. Financial award application deadline: 3/5. *Faculty research:* Algebra/number theory, computational science, dynamical systems, geometry, analysis. *Unit head:* Dr. Ken McLaughlin, Department Head, E-mail: mcl@math.arizona.edu.
Website: http://math.arizona.edu/

The University of Arizona, Graduate Interdisciplinary Programs, Graduate Interdisciplinary Program in Applied Mathematics, Tucson, AZ 85721. Offers applied mathematics (MS, PhD); mathematical sciences (PMS). Terminal master's awarded for partial completion of doctoral program. *Degree requirements:* For master's, thesis (for some programs); for doctorate, comprehensive exam, thesis/dissertation. *Entrance requirements:* For master's, GRE, 3 letters of recommendation; for doctorate, GRE, 3 letters of recommendation, statement of purpose. Additional exam requirements/recommendations for international students: Required—TOEFL (minimum score 575 paper-based; 80 iBT). *Application deadline:* For fall admission, 1/15 for domestic students, 1/30 for international students. Applications are processed on a rolling basis. Application fee: $75. Electronic applications accepted. *Financial support:* Research assistantships, institutionally sponsored loans, scholarships/grants, health care benefits, tuition waivers (full), and unspecified assistantships available. Financial award application deadline: 3/1; financial award applicants required to submit FAFSA. *Faculty research:* Dynamical systems and chaos, partial differential equations, pattern formation, fluid dynamics and turbulence, scientific computation, mathematical physics,

mathematical biology, medical imaging, applied probability and stochastic processes. *Unit head:* Dr. Michael Tabor, Chair, 520-621-4664, Fax: 520-626-5048, E-mail: tabor@math.arizona.edu. *Application contact:* Nellie Rios, Graduate Coordinator, 520-621-2016, Fax: 520-626-5048, E-mail: applmath@u.arizona.edu.
Website: http://appliedmath.arizona.edu/

University of Arkansas, Graduate School, J. William Fulbright College of Arts and Sciences, Department of Mathematical Sciences, Program in Mathematics, Fayetteville, AR 72701-1201. Offers MS, PhD. *Students:* 19 full-time (6 women), 29 part-time (13 women); includes 7 minority (1 Black or African American, non-Hispanic/Latino; 1 American Indian or Alaska Native, non-Hispanic/Latino; 3 Asian, non-Hispanic/Latino; 2 Two or more races, non-Hispanic/Latino), 14 international. In 2015, 7 master's, 5 doctorates awarded. *Degree requirements:* For master's, thesis or alternative; for doctorate, 2 foreign languages, thesis/dissertation. *Application deadline:* For fall admission, 4/1 for international students; for spring admission, 10/1 for international students. Applications are processed on a rolling basis. Application fee: $40 ($50 for international students). Electronic applications accepted. *Financial support:* In 2015–16, 2 research assistantships, 44 teaching assistantships were awarded; fellowships with tuition reimbursements, career-related internships or fieldwork, and Federal Work-Study also available. Support available to part-time students. Financial award application deadline: 4/1; financial award applicants required to submit FAFSA. *Unit head:* Dr. Mark Johnson, Chair, 479-575-3351, Fax: 479-575-8630, E-mail: markj@uark.edu. *Application contact:* Dr. Dan Lueking, Graduate Coordinator, 479-575-6327, Fax: 479-575-8630, E-mail: lueking@uark.edu.
Website: http://math.uark.edu/

University of Arkansas at Little Rock, Graduate School, College of Arts, Letters, and Sciences, Department of Mathematics and Statistics, Little Rock, AR 72204-1099. Offers applied statistics (Graduate Certificate); mathematical sciences (MS). *Program availability:* Part-time, evening/weekend. *Degree requirements:* For master's, comprehensive exam. *Entrance requirements:* For master's, GRE General Test, GRE Subject Test, minimum GPA of 2.7, previous course work in advanced mathematics. *Expenses:* Tuition, state resident: part-time $300 per credit hour. Tuition, nonresident: part-time $690 per credit hour. *Required fees:* $100 per credit hour. One-time fee: $40 full-time.

The University of British Columbia, Faculty of Science, Program in Mathematics, Vancouver, BC V6T 1Z2, Canada. Offers M Sc, MA, PhD. *Program availability:* Part-time. *Degree requirements:* For master's, thesis or alternative, essay, qualifying exam; for doctorate, comprehensive exam, thesis/dissertation, qualifying exam, thesis proposal. *Entrance requirements:* Additional exam requirements/recommendations for international students: Required—TOEFL (minimum score 600 paper-based; 100 iBT). Electronic applications accepted. *Faculty research:* Applied mathematics, financial mathematics, pure mathematics.

University of Calgary, Faculty of Graduate Studies, Faculty of Science, Department of Mathematics and Statistics, Calgary, AB T2N 1N4, Canada. Offers M Sc, PhD. *Degree requirements:* For master's, comprehensive exam, thesis; for doctorate, thesis/dissertation, candidacy exam, preliminary exams. *Entrance requirements:* For master's, honors degree in applied math, pure math, or statistics; for doctorate, MA or M Sc. Additional exam requirements/recommendations for international students: Required—TOEFL (minimum score 600 paper-based) or IELTS (minimum score 7). *Faculty research:* Combinatorics, applied mathematics, statistics, probability, analysis.

University of California, Berkeley, Graduate Division, College of Letters and Science, Department of Mathematics, Berkeley, CA 94720-1500. Offers applied mathematics (PhD); mathematics (MA, PhD). Terminal master's awarded for partial completion of doctoral program. *Degree requirements:* For master's, exam or thesis; for doctorate, 2 foreign languages, thesis/dissertation, qualifying exam. *Entrance requirements:* For master's and doctorate, GRE General Test, GRE Subject Test, minimum GPA of 3.0, 3 letters of recommendation. *Faculty research:* Algebra, analysis, logic, geometry/topology.

University of California, Davis, Graduate Studies, Program in Mathematics, Davis, CA 95616. Offers MA, MAT, PhD. Terminal master's awarded for partial completion of doctoral program. *Degree requirements:* For master's, comprehensive exam; for doctorate, one foreign language, thesis/dissertation. *Entrance requirements:* For master's and doctorate, GRE General Test, GRE Subject Test, minimum GPA of 3.0. Additional exam requirements/recommendations for international students: Required—TOEFL (minimum score 550 paper-based). Electronic applications accepted. *Faculty research:* Mathematical physics, geometric topology, probability, partial differential equations, applied mathematics.

University of California, Irvine, School of Physical Sciences, Department of Mathematics, Irvine, CA 92697. Offers MS, PhD. *Students:* 102 full-time (20 women), 5 part-time (1 woman); includes 26 minority (1 American Indian or Alaska Native, non-Hispanic/Latino; 15 Asian, non-Hispanic/Latino; 7 Hispanic/Latino; 3 Two or more races, non-Hispanic/Latino), 38 international. Average age 27. 257 applicants, 33% accepted, 22 enrolled. In 2015, 23 master's, 11 doctorates awarded. *Degree requirements:* For doctorate, thesis/dissertation. *Entrance requirements:* For master's and doctorate, GRE General Test, GRE Subject Test, minimum GPA of 3.0. Additional exam requirements/recommendations for international students: Required—TOEFL (minimum score 550 paper-based). *Application deadline:* For fall admission, 1/15 priority date for domestic and international students. Applications are processed on a rolling basis. Application fee: $90 ($110 for international students). Electronic applications accepted. *Financial support:* Fellowships, research assistantships with full tuition reimbursements, teaching assistantships, institutionally sponsored loans, traineeships, health care benefits, and unspecified assistantships available. Financial award application deadline: 3/1; financial award applicants required to submit FAFSA. *Faculty research:* Algebra and logic, geometry and topology, probability, mathematical physics. *Unit head:* Karl Rubin, Chair, 949-824-1645, Fax: 949-824-7993, E-mail: krubin@math.uci.edu. *Application contact:* Donna M. McConnell, Graduate Affairs Officer, 949-824-5544, Fax: 949-824-7993, E-mail: dmcconne@uci.edu.
Website: http://www.math.uci.edu/

University of California, Los Angeles, Graduate Division, College of Letters and Science, Department of Mathematics, Los Angeles, CA 90095. Offers MA, MAT, PhD. Terminal master's awarded for partial completion of doctoral program. *Degree requirements:* For master's, comprehensive exam or thesis; for doctorate, one foreign language, thesis/dissertation, oral and written qualifying exams. *Entrance requirements:* For master's, GRE General Test; GRE Subject Test (mathematics), bachelor's degree; minimum undergraduate GPA of 3.0, 3.2 in upper-division mathematics courses (or its equivalent if letter grade system not used); for doctorate, GRE General Test; GRE Subject Test (mathematics), bachelor's degree; minimum undergraduate GPA of 3.0, 3.5 in upper-division mathematics courses (or its equivalent if letter grade system not used). Additional exam requirements/recommendations for international students: Required—TOEFL. Electronic applications accepted.

University of California, Riverside, Graduate Division, Department of Mathematics, Riverside, CA 92521-0102. Offers MA, MS, PhD. *Program availability:* Part-time. Terminal master's awarded for partial completion of doctoral program. *Degree requirements:* For master's, comprehensive exam; for doctorate, thesis/dissertation, qualifying exams. *Entrance requirements:* For master's and doctorate, GRE General Test, minimum GPA of 3.2. Additional exam requirements/recommendations for international students: Required—TOEFL (minimum score 550 paper-based; 80 iBT). Electronic applications accepted. *Faculty research:* Algebraic geometry, commutative algebra, Lie algebra, differential equations, differential geometry.

University of California, San Diego, Graduate Division, Department of Mathematics, La Jolla, CA 92093. Offers applied mathematics (MA); computational science (PhD); mathematics (MA, PhD); statistics (MS, PhD). *Students:* 130 full-time (32 women), 3 part-time (0 women); includes 18 minority (13 Asian, non-Hispanic/Latino; 5 Hispanic/Latino), 72 international. 777 applicants, 16% accepted, 35 enrolled. In 2015, 18 master's, 16 doctorates awarded. *Degree requirements:* For master's, comprehensive exam; for doctorate, comprehensive exam, thesis/dissertation. *Entrance requirements:* For master's, GRE General Test; GRE Subject Test (for MA), minimum GPA of 3.0; for doctorate, GRE General Test, GRE Subject Test, minimum GPA of 3.0. Additional exam requirements/recommendations for international students: Required—TOEFL (minimum score 550 paper-based; 80 iBT), IELTS. *Application deadline:* For fall admission, 1/4 for domestic and international students. Application fee: $90 ($110 for international students). Electronic applications accepted. *Expenses:* Tuition, state resident: full-time $11,220. Tuition, nonresident: full-time $26,322. *Required fees:* $1800. *Financial support:* Fellowships, research assistantships, teaching assistantships, and scholarships/grants available. Financial award applicants required to submit FAFSA. *Faculty research:* Combinatorics, bioinformatics, differential equations, logic and computational complexity, probability theory and statistics. *Unit head:* Peter Ebenfelt, Chair, 858-822-4961, E-mail: pebenfelt@ucsd.edu. *Application contact:* Debra Shon, Admissions Contact, 858-534-9056, E-mail: mathgradadmissions@math.ucsd.edu.
Website: http://math.ucsd.edu/

University of California, Santa Barbara, Graduate Division, College of Letters and Sciences, Division of Mathematics, Life, and Physical Sciences, Department of Mathematics, Santa Barbara, CA 93106-3080. Offers applied mathematics (MA), including computational science and engineering; mathematics (MA, PhD), including computational science and engineering (PhD), mathematics (MA); MA/PhD. *Faculty:* 23 full-time (2 women). *Students:* 64 full-time (15 women); includes 17 minority (1 Black or African American, non-Hispanic/Latino; 1 American Indian or Alaska Native, non-Hispanic/Latino; 6 Asian, non-Hispanic/Latino; 7 Hispanic/Latino; 2 Native Hawaiian or other Pacific Islander, non-Hispanic/Latino), 9 international. Average age 26. 189 applicants, 21% accepted, 11 enrolled. In 2015, 16 master's, 7 doctorates awarded. Terminal master's awarded for partial completion of doctoral program. *Degree requirements:* For master's, comprehensive exam (for some programs), thesis (for some programs); for doctorate, comprehensive exam, thesis/dissertation. *Entrance requirements:* For master's and doctorate, GRE General Test, GRE Subject Test (math). Additional exam requirements/recommendations for international students: Required—TOEFL (minimum score 575 paper-based; 80 iBT), IELTS (minimum score 7). *Application deadline:* For fall admission, 1/2 for domestic and international students. Application fee: $90 ($110 for international students). Electronic applications accepted. *Financial support:* In 2015–16, 53 students received support, including 15 fellowships with full tuition reimbursements available (averaging $15,000 per year), 5 research assistantships with full tuition reimbursements available (averaging $19,000 per year), 52 teaching assistantships with partial tuition reimbursements available (averaging $18,880 per year); Federal Work-Study, institutionally sponsored loans, health care benefits, and tuition waivers (full and partial) also available. Financial award application deadline: 3/2; financial award applicants required to submit FAFSA. *Faculty research:* Topology, differential geometry, algebra, applied mathematics, partial differential equations. *Total annual research expenditures:* $205,000. *Unit head:* Prof. Darren Long, Chair, 805-893-8340, Fax: 805-893-2385, E-mail: chair@math.ucsb.edu. *Application contact:* Medina Price, Student Affairs Manager, 805-893-8192, Fax: 805-893-2385, E-mail: price@math.ucsb.edu.
Website: http://www.math.ucsb.edu/

University of California, Santa Cruz, Division of Graduate Studies, Division of Physical and Biological Sciences, Department of Mathematics, Santa Cruz, CA 95064. Offers MA, PhD. Terminal master's awarded for partial completion of doctoral program. *Degree requirements:* For master's, thesis; for doctorate, one foreign language, thesis/dissertation, qualifying exam. *Entrance requirements:* For doctorate, GRE General Test, GRE Subject Test. Additional exam requirements/recommendations for international students: Required—TOEFL (minimum score 550 paper-based; 83 iBT); Recommended—IELTS (minimum score 8). Electronic applications accepted. *Faculty research:* Vertex operator algebras, algebraic topology, elliptic cohomology, quantum field theory, automorphic forms, dynamical systems, celestial mechanics, geometric mechanics, bifurcation theory, control theory, representations of Lie and p-adic groups, applications to number theory, Bessel functions, Rankin-Selberg integrals, Gelfand-Graev models, differential geometry, nonlinear analysis, harmonic maps, Ginzburg-Landau problem.

University of Central Arkansas, Graduate School, College of Natural Sciences and Math, Department of Mathematics, Conway, AR 72035-0001. Offers applied mathematics (MS); math education (MA). *Program availability:* Part-time. *Degree requirements:* For master's, comprehensive exam, thesis optional. *Entrance requirements:* For master's, GRE General Test, minimum GPA of 2.7. Additional exam requirements/recommendations for international students: Required—TOEFL (minimum score 550 paper-based; 80 iBT). Electronic applications accepted.

University of Central Florida, College of Sciences, Department of Mathematics, Orlando, FL 32816. Offers mathematical science (MS, PhD, Certificate). *Program availability:* Part-time, evening/weekend. *Faculty:* 46 full-time (9 women), 3 part-time/adjunct (0 women). *Students:* 56 full-time (18 women), 19 part-time (8 women); includes 15 minority (2 Black or African American, non-Hispanic/Latino; 7 Asian, non-Hispanic/Latino; 5 Hispanic/Latino; 1 Two or more races, non-Hispanic/Latino), 23 international. Average age 30. 95 applicants, 60% accepted, 25 enrolled. In 2015, 9 master's, 7 doctorates, 2 other advanced degrees awarded. *Degree requirements:* For master's, thesis or alternative; for doctorate, thesis/dissertation, candidacy exam. *Entrance requirements:* For master's, GRE General Test, minimum GPA of 3.0 in last 60 hours; for doctorate, GRE Subject Test, minimum GPA of 3.0 in last 60 hours or master's qualifying exam. Additional exam requirements/recommendations for international students: Required—TOEFL. *Application deadline:* For fall admission, 7/15 for domestic students; for spring admission, 12/1 for domestic students. Application fee: $30. Electronic applications accepted. *Expenses:* Tuition, state resident: part-time $288.16 per credit hour. Tuition, nonresident: part-time $1071.31 per credit hour. *Financial support:* In 2015–16, 48 students received support, including 5 fellowships with partial tuition reimbursements available (averaging $7,700 per year), 4 research assistantships with partial tuition reimbursements available (averaging $3,400 per year), 50 teaching assistantships with partial tuition reimbursements available (averaging $13,400 per year); career-related internships or fieldwork, Federal Work-Study, institutionally sponsored loans, tuition waivers (partial), and unspecified assistantships also available. Financial award application deadline: 3/1; financial award applicants required to submit FAFSA. *Faculty research:* Applied mathematics, analysis, approximation theory, graph theory, mathematical statistics. *Unit head:* Dr. Xin Li, Chair, 407-823-2826, Fax: 407-823-6253, E-mail: xin.li@mail.ucf.edu. *Application contact:* Director, Admissions and Student Services, 407-823-2766, Fax: 407-823-6442, E-mail: gradadmissions@ucf.edu. Website: http://www.math.ucf.edu/

University of Central Missouri, The Graduate School, Warrensburg, MO 64093. Offers accountancy (MA); accounting (MBA); applied mathematics (MS); aviation safety (MA); biology (MS); business administration (MBA); career and technical education leadership (MS); college student personnel administration (MS); communication (MA); computer science (MS); counseling (MS); criminal justice (MS); educational leadership (Ed D); educational technology (MS); elementary and early childhood education (MSE); English (MA); environmental studies (MA); finance (MBA); history (MA); human services/educational technology (Ed S); human services/learning resources (Ed S); human services/professional counseling (Ed S); industrial hygiene (MS); industrial management (MS); information systems (MBA); information technology (MS); kinesiology (MS); library science and information services (MS); literacy education (MSE); marketing (MBA); mathematics (MS); music (MA); occupational safety management (MS); psychology (MS); rural family nursing (MS); school administration (MSE); social gerontology (MS); sociology (MA); special education (MSE); speech language pathology (MS); superintendency (Ed S); teaching (MAT); teaching English as a second language (MA); technology (MS); technology management (PhD); theatre (MA). *Program availability:* Part-time, 100% online, blended/hybrid learning. *Faculty:* 336 full-time (145 women), 39 part-time/adjunct (25 women). *Students:* 2,161 full-time (723 women), 2,077 part-time (1,061 women); includes 188 minority (93 Black or African American, non-Hispanic/Latino; 4 American Indian or Alaska Native, non-Hispanic/Latino; 15 Asian, non-Hispanic/Latino; 32 Hispanic/Latino; 1 Native Hawaiian or other Pacific Islander, non-Hispanic/Latino; 43 Two or more races, non-Hispanic/Latino), 2,514 international. Average age 28. 3,454 applicants, 68% accepted, 1632 enrolled. In 2015, 1,530 master's, 53 other advanced degrees awarded. *Degree requirements:* For master's and Ed S, comprehensive exam (for some programs), thesis (for some programs). *Entrance requirements:* Additional exam requirements/recommendations for international students: Required—TOEFL (minimum score 550 paper-based; 79 iBT). *Application deadline:* For fall admission, 6/1 priority date for domestic and international students; for spring admission, 10/1 priority date for domestic and international students; for summer admission, 4/1 priority date for domestic and international students. Applications are processed on a rolling basis. Application fee: $30 ($75 for international students). Electronic applications accepted. *Expenses:* Tuition, state resident: full-time $6683; part-time $278.45 per credit hour. Tuition, nonresident: full-time $13,366; part-time $556.90 per credit hour. *Required fees:* $701; $29.20 per credit hour. Tuition and fees vary according to degree level and campus/location. *Financial support:* In 2015–16, 97 students received support, including 146 research assistantships with partial tuition reimbursements available (averaging $7,500 per year), 73 teaching assistantships with partial tuition reimbursements available (averaging $7,500 per year); career-related internships or fieldwork, Federal Work-Study, scholarships/grants, and administrative and laboratory assistantships also available. Support available to part-time students. Financial award application deadline: 3/1; financial award applicants required to submit FAFSA. *Unit head:* Tina Church-Hockett, Director of Graduate School and International Admissions, 660-543-4621, Fax: 660-543-4778, E-mail: church@ucmo.edu. *Application contact:* Brittany Lawrence, Graduate Student Services Coordinator, 660-543-4621, Fax: 660-543-4778, E-mail: gradinfo@ucmo.edu.
Website: http://www.ucmo.edu/graduate/

University of Central Oklahoma, The Jackson College of Graduate Studies, College of Mathematics and Science, Department of Mathematics and Statistics, Edmond, OK 73034-5209. Offers applied mathematical sciences (MS), including computer science, mathematics, statistics, teaching. *Program availability:* Part-time. *Degree requirements:* For master's, comprehensive exam (for some programs), thesis (for some programs). *Entrance requirements:* For master's, GRE. Additional exam requirements/recommendations for international students: Required—TOEFL (minimum score 550 paper-based; 79 iBT), IELTS (minimum score 6.5). Electronic applications accepted.

University of Chicago, Division of the Physical Sciences, Department of Mathematics, Chicago, IL 60637. Offers applied mathematics (PhD); mathematics (PhD). *Degree requirements:* For doctorate, one foreign language, thesis/dissertation, 2 qualifying exams, oral topic presentation. *Entrance requirements:* For doctorate, GRE General Test, GRE Subject Test. Additional exam requirements/recommendations for international students: Required—TOEFL (minimum score 600 paper-based; 90 iBT), IELTS (minimum score 7). Electronic applications accepted. *Faculty research:* Analysis, differential geometry, algebra number theory, topology, algebraic geometry.

University of Cincinnati, Graduate School, McMicken College of Arts and Sciences, Department of Mathematical Sciences, Cincinnati, OH 45221. Offers applied mathematics (MS, PhD); mathematics education (MAT); pure mathematics (MS, PhD); statistics (MS, PhD). *Program availability:* Part-time. Terminal master's awarded for partial completion of doctoral program. *Degree requirements:* For master's, comprehensive exam, thesis or alternative; for doctorate, one foreign language, comprehensive exam, thesis/dissertation. *Entrance requirements:* For master's, GRE, teacher certification (for MAT); for doctorate, GRE. Additional exam requirements/recommendations for international students: Required—TOEFL. Electronic applications accepted. *Faculty research:* Algebra, analysis, differential equations, numerical analysis, statistics.

University of Colorado Boulder, Graduate School, College of Arts and Sciences, Department of Mathematics, Boulder, CO 80309. Offers MA, MS, PhD. *Faculty:* 25 full-time (5 women). *Students:* 67 full-time (18 women); includes 8 minority (1 Black or African American, non-Hispanic/Latino; 4 Asian, non-Hispanic/Latino; 2 Hispanic/Latino; 1 Two or more races, non-Hispanic/Latino), 9 international. Average age 27. 125 applicants, 32% accepted, 10 enrolled. In 2015, 2 master's, 4 doctorates awarded. Terminal master's awarded for partial completion of doctoral program. *Degree requirements:* For master's, comprehensive exam, thesis or alternative; for doctorate, one foreign language, comprehensive exam, thesis/dissertation, 2 preliminary exams. *Entrance requirements:* For master's and doctorate, minimum undergraduate GPA of 3.0. *Application deadline:* For fall admission, 1/2 for domestic students, 12/16 for international students; for spring admission, 10/1 for domestic students, 9/15 for international students. Applications are processed on a rolling basis. Application fee: $50 ($70 for international students). Electronic applications accepted. Application fee is waived when completed online. *Financial support:* In 2015–16, 162 students received support, including 22 fellowships (averaging $3,000 per year), 1 research assistantship with tuition reimbursement available (averaging $38,618 per year), 61 teaching assistantships with tuition reimbursements available (averaging $36,350 per year); institutionally sponsored loans, scholarships/grants, health care benefits, and unspecified assistantships also available. Financial award application deadline: 2/1; financial award applicants required to submit FAFSA. *Faculty research:* Analysis and functional analysis, mathematics, geometry, algebra, number theory. *Total annual research expenditures:* $242,741. *Application contact:* E-mail: gradmath@colorado.edu. Website: http://math.colorado.edu/

University of Colorado Colorado Springs, College of Letters, Arts and Sciences, Program in Interdisciplinary Applied Sciences, Colorado Springs, CO 80918. Offers mathematics (PhD); physics (PhD). *Program availability:* Part-time, evening/weekend. *Faculty:* 16 full-time (3 women), 6 part-time/adjunct (2 women). *Students:* 2 full-time (both women), 31 part-time (6 women); includes 3 minority (1 American Indian or Alaska Native, non-Hispanic/Latino; 1 Hispanic/Latino; 1 Two or more races, non-Hispanic/Latino), 3 international. Average age 34. 12 applicants, 92% accepted, 5 enrolled. *Degree requirements:* For doctorate, comprehensive exam, thesis/dissertation. *Entrance requirements:* For doctorate, GRE or minimum GPA of 3.0 and hold a baccalaureate degree in biological sciences, mathematics, physics or equivalents from an accredited college or university and have an appropriate background of undergraduate physics courses. Additional exam requirements/recommendations for international students: Required—TOEFL (minimum score 560 paper-based; 83 iBT), IELTS (minimum score 6.5). *Application deadline:* Applications are processed on a rolling basis. Application fee: $60 ($100 for international students). Electronic applications accepted. *Expenses:* Tuition, state resident: full-time $9914. Tuition, nonresident: full-time $19,330. Tuition and fees vary according to course load, degree level, program and reciprocity agreements. *Financial support:* In 2015–16, 13 students received support. Federal Work-Study and scholarships/grants available. Support available to part-time students. Financial award application deadline: 3/1; financial award applicants required to submit FAFSA. *Faculty research:* Solid-state/condensed-matter physics, surface science, electron spectroscopies, nonlinear physics. *Total annual research expenditures:* $821,552. *Unit head:* Dr. Robert Camley, Distinguished Professor, 719-255-3512, E-mail: rcamley@uccs.edu. *Application contact:* Dr. Karen Livesey, Assistant Professor, 719-255-5116, E-mail: klivesey@uccs.edu.

University of Colorado Denver, College of Liberal Arts and Sciences, Department of Mathematical and Statistical Sciences, Denver, CO 80217. Offers applied mathematics (MS, PhD), including applied mathematics, applied probability (MS), applied statistics (MS), computational biology, computational mathematics (PhD), discrete mathematics, finite geometry (PhD), mathematics education (PhD), mathematics of engineering and science (MS), numerical analysis, operations research (MS), optimization and operations research (PhD), probability (PhD), statistics (PhD). *Program availability:* Part-time. *Faculty:* 18 full-time (4 women), 5 part-time/adjunct (0 women). *Students:* 48 full-time (16 women), 15 part-time (6 women); includes 7 minority (1 Black or African American, non-Hispanic/Latino; 2 Asian, non-Hispanic/Latino; 3 Hispanic/Latino; 1 Two or more races, non-Hispanic/Latino), 12 international. Average age 32. 105 applicants, 70% accepted, 21 enrolled. In 2015, 10 master's, 3 doctorates awarded. *Degree requirements:* For master's, comprehensive exam, thesis optional, 30 hours of course work with minimum GPA of 3.0; for doctorate, comprehensive exam, thesis/dissertation, 42 hours of course work with minimum GPA of 3.25. *Entrance requirements:* For master's, GRE General Test; GRE Subject Test in math (recommended), 30 hours of course work in mathematics (24 of which must be upper-division mathematics), bachelor's degree with minimum GPA of 3.0; for doctorate, GRE General Test; GRE Subject Test in math (recommended), 30 hours of course work in mathematics (24 of which must be upper-division mathematics), master's degree with minimum GPA of 3.25. Additional exam requirements/recommendations for international students: Required—TOEFL (minimum score 537 paper-based; 75 iBT); Recommended—IELTS (minimum score 6.5). *Application deadline:* For fall admission, 4/1 for domestic and international students; for spring admission, 10/1 for domestic and international students; for summer admission, 4/1 for domestic and international students. Application fee: $50 ($75 for international students). Electronic applications accepted. *Financial support:* In 2015–16, 46 students received support. Fellowships with partial tuition reimbursements available, research assistantships with full tuition reimbursements available, teaching assistantships with full tuition reimbursements available, Federal Work-Study, institutionally sponsored loans, scholarships/grants, and traineeships available. Financial award application deadline: 4/1; financial award applicants required to submit FAFSA. *Faculty research:* Computational mathematics, computational biology, discrete mathematics and geometry, probability and statistics, optimization. *Unit head:* Dr. Michael Ferrara, Graduate Chair, 303-315-1705,
E-mail: michael.ferrara@ucdenver.edu. *Application contact:* Julie Blunck, Program Assistant, 303-315-1743, E-mail: julie.blunck@ucdenver.edu.
Website: http://www.ucdenver.edu/academics/colleges/CLAS/Departments/math/Pages/MathStats.aspx

University of Colorado Denver, College of Liberal Arts and Sciences, Program in Integrated Sciences, Denver, CO 80217. Offers applied science (MIS); computer science (MIS); mathematics (MIS). *Program availability:* Part-time, evening/weekend. *Faculty:* 1 (woman) full-time. *Students:* 6 full-time (4 women), 5 part-time (2 women); includes 3 minority (1 Asian, non-Hispanic/Latino; 2 Hispanic/Latino), 2 international. Average age 34. 10 applicants, 80% accepted, 4 enrolled. In 2015, 2 master's awarded. *Degree requirements:* For master's, 30 credit hours; thesis or project. *Entrance requirements:* For master's, GRE if undergraduate GPA is 3.0 or less, minimum of 40 semester hours in mathematics, computer science, physics, biology, chemistry and/or geology; essay; three letters of recommendation. Additional exam requirements/recommendations for international students: Required—TOEFL (minimum score 537 paper-based; 75 iBT); Recommended—IELTS (minimum score 6.5). *Application deadline:* For fall admission, 4/15 for domestic students, 4/15 priority date for international students; for spring admission, 10/15 for domestic students, 10/15 priority date for international students. Application fee: $50 ($75 for international students). Electronic applications accepted. *Financial support:* In 2015–16, 3 students received support. Fellowships, research assistantships, teaching assistantships, Federal Work-Study, institutionally sponsored loans, scholarships/grants, and traineeships available. Financial award application deadline: 4/1; financial award applicants required to submit FAFSA. *Faculty research:* Computer science, applied science, mathematics. *Unit head:* E-mail: integrated.sciences@ucdenver.edu. *Application contact:* Marissa Tornatore, Graduate School Application Specialist, 303-315-0049,
E-mail: marissa.tornatore@ucdenver.edu.
Website: http://www.ucdenver.edu/academics/colleges/CLAS/Programs/MastersofIntegratedSciences/Pages/ProgramOverview.aspx

University of Connecticut, Graduate School, College of Liberal Arts and Sciences, Department of Mathematics, Field of Mathematics, Storrs, CT 06269. Offers actuarial science (MS, PhD); mathematics (MS, PhD). Terminal master's awarded for partial completion of doctoral program. *Degree requirements:* For master's, comprehensive exam; for doctorate, thesis/dissertation. *Entrance requirements:* For master's and doctorate, GRE General Test. Additional exam requirements/recommendations for international students: Required—TOEFL (minimum score 550 paper-based). Electronic applications accepted.

University of Delaware, College of Arts and Sciences, Department of Mathematical Sciences, Newark, DE 19716. Offers applied mathematics (MS, PhD); mathematics (MS, PhD). *Program availability:* Part-time. Terminal master's awarded for partial completion of doctoral program. *Degree requirements:* For master's, thesis (for some programs); for doctorate, one foreign language, thesis/dissertation, qualifying exam. *Entrance requirements:* For master's and doctorate, GRE General Test. Additional exam requirements/recommendations for international students: Required—TOEFL. Electronic applications accepted. *Faculty research:* Scattering theory, inverse problems, fluid dynamics, numerical analysis, combinatorics.

University of Denver, Division of Natural Sciences and Mathematics, Department of Mathematics, Denver, CO 80208. Offers MA, MS, PhD. *Program availability:* Part-time. *Faculty:* 16 full-time (6 women). *Students:* 1 (woman) full-time, 26 part-time (8 women); includes 2 minority (both Hispanic/Latino), 10 international. Average age 28. 55 applicants, 78% accepted, 6 enrolled. In 2015, 3 master's, 1 doctorate awarded. Terminal master's awarded for partial completion of doctoral program. *Degree requirements:* For doctorate, 2 foreign languages, comprehensive exam, thesis/dissertation, oral and written exams. *Entrance requirements:* For master's and doctorate, GRE General Test, bachelor's degree in mathematics or related field, transcripts, personal statement, three letters of recommendation. Additional exam requirements/recommendations for international students: Required—TOEFL (minimum score 550 paper-based; 80 iBT). *Application deadline:* For fall admission, 2/16 priority date for domestic and international students. Applications are processed on a rolling basis. Application fee: $65. Electronic applications accepted. *Expenses:* $30,477. *Financial support:* In 2015–16, 18 students received support, including 15 teaching assistantships with tuition reimbursements available (averaging $19,556 per year); career-related internships or fieldwork, Federal Work-Study, institutionally sponsored loans, scholarships/grants, and unspecified assistantships also available. Support available to part-time students. Financial award application deadline: 2/15; financial award applicants required to submit FAFSA. *Faculty research:* Foundations of mathematics, dynamical systems, functional analysis, nonassociative algebra, probabilistic combinatorics. *Unit head:* Dr. Michael Kinyon, Professor and Chair, 303-871-3288, Fax: 303-871-3173, E-mail: mkinyon@math.du.edu. *Application contact:* Liane Beights, Assistant to the Chair, 303-871-2911, Fax: 303-871-3173,
E-mail: math-info@math.du.edu.
Website: http://www.du.edu/nsm/departments/mathematics

University of Florida, Graduate School, College of Liberal Arts and Sciences, Department of Mathematics, Gainesville, FL 32611. Offers mathematics (MAT, MS, MST, PhD), including imaging science and technology (PhD), mathematics (PhD), quantitative finance (PhD). *Program availability:* Part-time. *Faculty:* 3 full-time. *Students:* 89 full-time (21 women), 2 part-time (0 women); includes 17 minority (1 Black or African American, non-Hispanic/Latino; 8 Asian, non-Hispanic/Latino; 8 Hispanic/Latino), 25 international. Average age 29. 93 applicants, 47% accepted, 22 enrolled. In 2015, 6 master's, 7 doctorates awarded. Terminal master's awarded for partial completion of doctoral program. *Degree requirements:* For master's, comprehensive exam, thesis optional, first-year exam; for doctorate, one foreign language, comprehensive exam, thesis/dissertation. *Entrance requirements:* For master's and doctorate, GRE General Test, GRE Subject Test (math), minimum GPA of 3.0. Additional exam requirements/recommendations for international students: Required—TOEFL (minimum score 550 paper-based; 80 iBT), IELTS (minimum score 6). *Application deadline:* For fall admission, 2/1 priority date for domestic students. Applications are processed on a rolling basis. Application fee: $30. Electronic applications accepted. *Financial support:* In 2015–16, 5 fellowships, 5 research assistantships, 63 teaching assistantships were awarded; career-related internships or fieldwork and unspecified assistantships also available. Financial award applicants required to submit FAFSA. *Faculty research:* Applied mathematics, including imaging, optimization and biomathematics; analysis and probability; combinatorics and number theory; topology and foundations; group theory. *Total annual research expenditures:* $804,200. *Unit head:* Douglas Cenzer, PhD, Chairman, 352-294-2313, Fax: 352-392-8357, E-mail: cenzer@ufl.edu. *Application contact:* Jean Larson, Associate Chair and Graduate Coordinator, 352-294-2317,
Fax: 352-392-8357, E-mail: jal@ufl.edu.
Website: http://www.math.ufl.edu/gradprog/

University of Georgia, Franklin College of Arts and Sciences, Department of Mathematics, Athens, GA 30602. Offers applied mathematical science (MAMS); mathematics (MA, PhD). *Degree requirements:* For master's, one foreign language, thesis (for some programs); for doctorate, 2 foreign languages, thesis/dissertation. *Entrance requirements:* For master's and doctorate, GRE General Test. Electronic applications accepted.

University of Guelph, Graduate Studies, College of Physical and Engineering Science, Department of Mathematics and Statistics, Guelph, ON N1G 2W1, Canada. Offers applied mathematics (PhD); applied statistics (PhD); mathematics and statistics (M Sc). *Program availability:* Part-time. *Degree requirements:* For master's, thesis (for some programs); for doctorate, thesis/dissertation. *Entrance requirements:* For master's, minimum B- average during previous 2 years of course work; for doctorate, minimum B average. Additional exam requirements/recommendations for international students: Required—TOEFL (minimum score 550 paper-based; 89 iBT), IELTS (minimum score 6.5). *Faculty research:* Dynamical systems, mathematical biology, numerical analysis, linear and nonlinear models, reliability and bioassay.

University of Hawaii at Manoa, Graduate Division, College of Natural Sciences, Department of Mathematics, Honolulu, HI 96822. Offers MA, PhD. *Program availability:* Part-time. *Faculty:* 31 full-time (4 women). *Students:* 38 full-time (11 women), 3 part-time; includes 16 minority (1 Black or African American, non-Hispanic/Latino; 3 Asian, non-Hispanic/Latino; 5 Hispanic/Latino; 7 Two or more races, non-Hispanic/Latino), 4 international. Average age 30. 35 applicants, 60% accepted, 9 enrolled. In 2015, 5 master's, 1 doctorate awarded. *Degree requirements:* For doctorate, one foreign language, comprehensive exam, thesis/dissertation. *Entrance requirements:* For master's and doctorate, GRE General Test, minimum GPA of 3.0. Additional exam requirements/recommendations for international students: Required—TOEFL (minimum score 500 paper-based; 61 iBT), IELTS (minimum score 5). *Application deadline:* For fall admission, 3/1 for domestic students, 2/1 for international students; for spring admission, 9/1 for domestic students, 8/1 for international students. Applications are processed on a rolling basis. Application fee: $100. *Financial support:* In 2015–16, 8 fellowships (averaging $2,000 per year), 1 research assistantship (averaging $16,176 per year), 17 teaching assistantships (averaging $16,154 per year) were awarded; institutionally sponsored loans, tuition waivers (full and partial), and unspecified assistantships also available. Support available to part-time students. Financial award application deadline: 3/1. *Faculty research:* Analysis, algebra, lattice theory, logic topology, differential geometry. *Total annual research expenditures:* $492,000. *Unit head:* William Ditto, Dean, 808-956-6451, E-mail: wditto@hawaii.edu. *Application contact:* James Nation, Graduate Chair, 808-956-7951, Fax: 808-956-9139,
E-mail: jb@math.hawaii.edu.
Website: http://hawaii.edu/graduatestudies/fields/html/departments/mno/math/math.htm

University of Houston, College of Natural Sciences and Mathematics, Department of Mathematics, Houston, TX 77204. Offers applied mathematics (MS); mathematics (MA, PhD). *Program availability:* Part-time. *Degree requirements:* For master's, thesis optional. *Entrance requirements:* For master's and doctorate, GRE (Verbal and Quantitative). Additional exam requirements/recommendations for international students: Required—TOEFL (minimum score 550 paper-based; 79 iBT), IELTS (minimum score 6.5). Electronic applications accepted. *Faculty research:* Applied mathematics, modern analysis, computational science, geometry, dynamical systems.

University of Houston–Clear Lake, School of Science and Computer Engineering, Program in Mathematical Sciences, Houston, TX 77058-1002. Offers MS. *Program availability:* Part-time, evening/weekend. *Entrance requirements:* For master's, GRE General Test. Additional exam requirements/recommendations for international students: Required—TOEFL (minimum score 550 paper-based).

University of Idaho, College of Graduate Studies, College of Science, Department of Mathematics, Moscow, ID 83844-1103. Offers MAT, MS, PhD. *Faculty:* 8 full-time. *Students:* 14 full-time, 7 part-time. Average age 33. In 2015, 7 master's, 1 doctorate awarded. *Degree requirements:* For doctorate, 2 foreign languages, thesis/dissertation. *Entrance requirements:* For master's, minimum GPA of 2.8; for doctorate, minimum undergraduate GPA of 2.8, 3.0 graduate. Additional exam requirements/recommendations for international students: Required—TOEFL. *Application deadline:* For fall admission, 8/1 for domestic students; for spring admission, 12/15 for domestic students. Applications are processed on a rolling basis. Application fee: $60. Electronic applications accepted. *Expenses:* Tuition, state resident: full-time $6205; part-time $399 per credit hour. Tuition, nonresident: full-time $20,209; part-time $1177 per credit hour. *Required fees:* $2017; $58 per credit hour. Full-time tuition and fees vary according to course load and reciprocity agreements. *Financial support:* Research assistantships and teaching assistantships available. Financial award applicants required to submit FAFSA. *Faculty research:* Bioinformatics and mathematical biology, analysis and differential equations, combinatorics, probability and stochastic processes, discrete geometry. *Unit head:* Dr. Christopher Williams, Chair, 208-885-6742,
E-mail: math@uidaho.edu. *Application contact:* Sean Scoggin, Graduate Recruitment Coordinator, 208-885-4723, Fax: 208-885-4406,
E-mail: graduateadmissions@uidaho.edu.
Website: http://www.uidaho.edu/sci/math

University of Illinois at Chicago, College of Liberal Arts and Sciences, Department of Mathematics, Statistics, and Computer Science, Chicago, IL 60607-7128. Offers mathematics (DA); probability and statistics (PhD); secondary school mathematics (MST); statistics (MS). *Program availability:* Part-time. *Faculty:* 73 full-time (20 women), 3 part-time/adjunct (0 women). *Students:* 118 full-time (30 women), 19 part-time (9 women); includes 19 minority (7 Asian, non-Hispanic/Latino; 9 Hispanic/Latino; 3 Two or more races, non-Hispanic/Latino), 51 international. Average age 28. *Degree requirements:* For master's, comprehensive exam; for doctorate, one foreign language, thesis/dissertation. *Entrance requirements:* For master's and doctorate, GRE General Test, minimum GPA of 3.0. Additional exam requirements/recommendations for international students: Required—TOEFL (minimum score 100 iBT). *Application deadline:* For fall admission, 1/1 for domestic and international students; for spring admission, 10/1 for domestic students, 7/15 for international students. Applications are processed on a rolling basis. Application fee: $60. Electronic applications accepted. *Expenses:* Tuition, state resident: full-time $11,480; part-time $3826 per credit. Tuition, nonresident: full-time $23,720; part-time $7906 per credit. *Required fees:* $1333 per semester. Part-time tuition and fees vary according to course load and program. *Financial support:* In 2015–16, 109 students received support, including 2 fellowships with full tuition reimbursements available (averaging $20,000 per year), 8 research assistantships with full tuition reimbursements available (averaging $17,000 per year), 87 teaching assistantships with full tuition reimbursements available (averaging $17,000 per year); Federal Work-Study, scholarships/grants, and tuition waivers (full) also available. Financial award application deadline: 1/1. *Unit head:* Prof. Brooke Shipley, Head, 312-996-3044, E-mail: shipley@math.uic.edu. *Application contact:* Ramin Takloo-Bighash, Director of Graduate Studies, 312-996-5119, E-mail: dgs@math.uic.edu.
Website: http://www.math.uic.edu/

University of Illinois at Urbana–Champaign, Graduate College, College of Liberal Arts and Sciences, Department of Mathematics, Champaign, IL 61820. Offers applied mathematics (MS); applied mathematics: actuarial science (MS); mathematics (MS, PhD); teaching of mathematics (MS).

The University of Iowa, Graduate College, College of Liberal Arts and Sciences, Department of Mathematics, Iowa City, IA 52242-1316. Offers MS, PhD. *Degree requirements:* For master's, thesis optional, exam; for doctorate, comprehensive exam, thesis/dissertation. *Entrance requirements:* For master's and doctorate, GRE General Test, minimum GPA of 3.0. Additional exam requirements/recommendations for international students: Required—TOEFL (minimum score 620 paper-based; 105 iBT). Electronic applications accepted.

The University of Kansas, Graduate Studies, College of Liberal Arts and Sciences, Department of Mathematics, Lawrence, KS 66045. Offers MA, PhD. *Students:* 72 full-time (22 women), 3 part-time (1 woman); includes 7 minority (1 Black or African American, non-Hispanic/Latino; 5 Asian, non-Hispanic/Latino; 1 Two or more races, non-Hispanic/Latino), 44 international. Average age 28. 105 applicants, 32% accepted, 16 enrolled. In 2015, 18 master's, 5 doctorates awarded. Terminal master's awarded for partial completion of doctoral program. *Entrance requirements:* For master's and doctorate, GRE. Additional exam requirements/recommendations for international students: Required—TOEFL. *Application deadline:* For fall admission, 8/4 priority date for domestic students, 5/2 priority date for international students; for spring admission, 1/4 priority date for domestic students, 10/15 priority date for international students. Application fee: $65 ($85 for international students). Electronic applications accepted. *Financial support:* Fellowships, research assistantships, teaching assistantships, institutionally sponsored loans, scholarships/grants, health care benefits, and unspecified assistantships available. Support available to part-time students. Financial award application deadline: 1/31. *Faculty research:* Algebra and algebraic geometry; analysis, partial differential equations and dynamical systems; probability, stochastic analysis and stochastic control; numerical analysis; geometry. *Unit head:* Daniel Katz, Chair, 785-864-3651, E-mail: dlk@math.ku.edu. *Application contact:* Lori Springs, Graduate Admissions Contact, 785-864-7300, E-mail: lsprings@ku.edu.
Website: http://www.math.ku.edu/

University of Kentucky, Graduate School, College of Arts and Sciences, Program in Mathematics, Lexington, KY 40506-0032. Offers applied mathematics (MS); mathematics (MA, MS, PhD). *Degree requirements:* For master's, comprehensive exam, thesis optional; for doctorate, one foreign language, comprehensive exam, thesis/dissertation. *Entrance requirements:* For master's, GRE General Test, minimum undergraduate GPA of 2.75; for doctorate, GRE General Test, minimum graduate GPA of 3.0. Additional exam requirements/recommendations for international students: Required—TOEFL (minimum score 550 paper-based). Electronic applications accepted. *Faculty research:* Numerical analysis, combinatorics, partial differential equations, algebra and number theory, real and complex analysis.

Mathematics

University of Lethbridge, School of Graduate Studies, Lethbridge, AB T1K 3M4, Canada. Offers addictions counseling (M Sc); agricultural biotechnology (M Sc); agricultural studies (M Sc, MA); anthropology (MA); archaeology (M Sc, MA); art (MA, MFA); biochemistry (M Sc); biological sciences (M Sc); biomolecular science (PhD); biosystems and biodiversity (PhD); Canadian studies (MA); chemistry (M Sc); computer science (M Sc); computer science and geographical information science (M Sc); counseling (MC); counseling psychology (M Ed); dramatic arts (MA); earth, space, and physical science (PhD); economics (MA); education (MA, PhD); educational leadership (M Ed); English (MA); environmental science (M Sc); evolution and behavior (PhD); exercise science (M Sc); French (MA); French/German (MA); French/Spanish (MA); general education (M Ed); geography (M Sc, MA); German (MA); health sciences (M Sc); individualized multidisciplinary (M Sc, MA); kinesiology (M Sc, MA); management (M Sc), including accounting, finance, human resource management and labor relations, information systems, international management, marketing, policy and strategy; mathematics (M Sc); music (M Mus, MA); Native American studies (MA); neuroscience (M Sc, PhD); new media (MA, MFA); nursing (M Sc, MN); philosophy (MA); physics (M Sc); political science (MA); psychology (M Sc, MA); religious studies (MA); sociology (MA); theatre and dramatic arts (MFA); theoretical and computational science (PhD); urban and regional studies (MA); women and gender studies (MA). *Program availability:* Part-time, evening/weekend. *Students:* 448 full-time (249 women), 110 part-time (64 women). Average age 32. 285 applicants, 36% accepted, 96 enrolled. In 2015, 154 master's, 11 doctorates awarded. *Degree requirements:* For master's, thesis (for some programs); for doctorate, comprehensive exam, thesis/dissertation. *Entrance requirements:* For master's, GMAT (for M Sc in management), bachelor's degree in related field, minimum GPA of 3.0 during previous 20 graded semester courses, 2 years' teaching or related experience (M Ed); for doctorate, master's degree, minimum graduate GPA of 3.5. Additional exam requirements/recommendations for international students: Required—TOEFL (minimum score 580 paper-based; 93 iBT). Application fee: $100 Canadian dollars ($140 Canadian dollars for international students). Electronic applications accepted. *Financial support:* Fellowships, research assistantships, teaching assistantships, scholarships/grants, health care benefits, and unspecified assistantships available. *Faculty research:* Movement and brain plasticity, gibberellin physiology, photosynthesis, carbon cycling, molecular properties of main-group ring components. *Unit head:* Kathleen Schrage, Manager, School of Graduate Studies, 403-329-2121, E-mail: schrage@uleth.ca. *Application contact:* School of Graduate Studies, 403-329-5194, E-mail: sgsinquiries@uleth.ca.
Website: http://www.uleth.ca/graduate-studies/

University of Louisiana at Lafayette, College of Sciences, Department of Mathematics, Lafayette, LA 70504. Offers MS, PhD. Terminal master's awarded for partial completion of doctoral program. *Degree requirements:* For master's, thesis or alternative; for doctorate, 2 foreign languages, comprehensive exam, thesis/dissertation. *Entrance requirements:* For master's, GRE General Test, minimum GPA of 2.75; for doctorate, GRE General Test, minimum GPA of 3.0. Additional exam requirements/recommendations for international students: Required—TOEFL (minimum score 550 paper-based). Electronic applications accepted. *Faculty research:* Topology, algebra, applied mathematics, analysis.

University of Louisville, Graduate School, College of Arts and Sciences, Department of Mathematics, Louisville, KY 40292. Offers applied and industrial mathematics (PhD); mathematics (MA). *Program availability:* Part-time. *Students:* 33 full-time (14 women), 2 part-time (1 woman), 12 international. Average age 30. 40 applicants, 65% accepted, 8 enrolled. In 2015, 5 master's, 1 doctorate awarded. Terminal master's awarded for partial completion of doctoral program. *Median time to degree:* Of those who began their doctoral program in fall 2007, 64% received their degree in 8 years or less. *Degree requirements:* For master's, variable foreign language requirement, thesis or alternative; for doctorate, comprehensive exam, thesis/dissertation. *Entrance requirements:* For master's and doctorate, GRE. Additional exam requirements/recommendations for international students: Required—TOEFL (minimum score 550 paper-based; 79 iBT), IELTS (minimum score 6.5). *Application deadline:* For fall admission, 3/1 priority date for domestic and international students; for winter admission, 11/1 priority date for domestic and international students; for spring admission, 11/1 priority date for domestic and international students; for summer admission, 3/1 priority date for domestic and international students. Applications are processed on a rolling basis. Application fee: $60. Electronic applications accepted. *Expenses:* Tuition, state resident: full-time $11,664; part-time $649 per credit hour. Tuition, nonresident: full-time $24,274; part-time $1350 per credit hour. *Required fees:* $196. Tuition and fees vary according to program and reciprocity agreements. *Financial support:* In 2015–16, 1 fellowship with full tuition reimbursement (averaging $22,000 per year), 1 research assistantship with partial tuition reimbursement (averaging $20,000 per year), 24 teaching assistantships with full tuition reimbursements (averaging $20,000 per year) were awarded; health care benefits and unspecified assistantships also available. Financial award application deadline: 2/3. *Faculty research:* Mathematical biology, partial differential equations, statistics, combinatorics, analysis. *Total annual research expenditures:* $125,277. *Unit head:* Dr. Thomas Riedel, Chair, 502-852-6826, Fax: 502-852-7132,
E-mail: thomas.riedel@louisville.edu. *Application contact:* Dr. Andre Kezdy, Graduate Director and Professor, 502-852-5986, Fax: 502-852-7132,
E-mail: kezdy@louisville.edu.
Website: http://www.math.louisville.edu

The University of Manchester, School of Mathematics, Manchester, United Kingdom. Offers actuarial science (PhD); applied mathematics (M Phil, PhD); applied numerical computing (M Phil, PhD); financial mathematics (M Phil, PhD); mathematical logic (M Phil); probability (M Phil, PhD); pure mathematics (M Phil, PhD); statistics (M Phil, PhD).

University of Manitoba, Faculty of Graduate Studies, Faculty of Science, Department of Mathematics, Winnipeg, MB R3T 2N2, Canada. Offers M Sc, PhD. *Degree requirements:* For master's, one foreign language, thesis or alternative; for doctorate, one foreign language, thesis/dissertation.

University of Manitoba, Faculty of Graduate Studies, Faculty of Science, Program in Mathematical, Computational and Statistical Sciences, Winnipeg, MB R3T 2N2, Canada. Offers MMCSS.

University of Maryland, College Park, Academic Affairs, College of Computer, Mathematical and Natural Sciences, Department of Mathematics, Program in Mathematics, College Park, MD 20742. Offers MA, PhD. *Program availability:* Part-time, evening/weekend. Terminal master's awarded for partial completion of doctoral program. *Degree requirements:* For master's, thesis or alternative; for doctorate, one foreign language, thesis/dissertation, written exam, oral exam. *Entrance requirements:* For master's, GRE General Test, GRE Subject Test, minimum GPA of 3.0, 3 letters of recommendation; for doctorate, GRE General Test, GRE Subject Test, 3 letters of recommendation. Electronic applications accepted.

University of Massachusetts Amherst, Graduate School, College of Natural Sciences, Department of Mathematics and Statistics, Amherst, MA 01003. Offers applied mathematics (MS); mathematics (MS, PhD); statistics (MS, PhD). Terminal master's awarded for partial completion of doctoral program. *Degree requirements:* For master's, thesis or alternative; for doctorate, comprehensive exam, thesis/dissertation. *Entrance requirements:* For master's and doctorate, GRE General Test, GRE Subject Test (mathematics). Additional exam requirements/recommendations for international students: Required—TOEFL (minimum score 550 paper-based; 80 iBT), IELTS (minimum score 6.5). Electronic applications accepted.

University of Massachusetts Lowell, College of Sciences, Department of Mathematical Sciences, Lowell, MA 01854. Offers applied mathematics (MS); computational mathematics (PhD); mathematics (MS). *Program availability:* Part-time. *Entrance requirements:* For master's, GRE General Test.

University of Memphis, Graduate School, College of Arts and Sciences, Department of Mathematical Sciences, Memphis, TN 38152. Offers applied mathematics (MS); applied statistics (PhD); bioinformatics (MS); computer sciences (MS); statistics (MS). *Program availability:* Part-time. *Faculty:* 18 full-time (7 women). *Students:* 36 full-time (9 women), 22 part-time (9 women); includes 15 minority (9 Black or African American, non-Hispanic/Latino; 3 Asian, non-Hispanic/Latino; 3 Hispanic/Latino), 17 international. Average age 34. 50 applicants, 92% accepted, 12 enrolled. In 2015, 10 master's, 9 doctorates awarded. Terminal master's awarded for partial completion of doctoral program. *Degree requirements:* For master's, comprehensive exam; for doctorate, one foreign language, thesis/dissertation, oral exams. *Entrance requirements:* For master's and doctorate, GRE General Test, minimum GPA of 2.5. Additional exam requirements/recommendations for international students: Required—TOEFL (minimum score 550 paper-based). *Application deadline:* For fall admission, 8/1 for domestic students, 5/1 priority date for international students; for spring admission, 12/1 for domestic students, 9/1 priority date for international students. Applications are processed on a rolling basis. Application fee: $35 ($60 for international students). Electronic applications accepted. *Financial support:* In 2015–16, 22 students received support. Fellowships with full tuition reimbursements available, research assistantships with full tuition reimbursements available, teaching assistantships with full tuition reimbursements available, career-related internships or fieldwork, Federal Work-Study, scholarships/grants, and unspecified assistantships available. Financial award application deadline: 2/15; financial award applicants required to submit FAFSA. *Faculty research:* Combinatorics, ergodic theory, graph theory, Ramsey theory, applied statistics. *Unit head:* Dr. Irena Lasiecka, Chairman, 901-678-2482, Fax: 901-678-2480,
E-mail: lasiecka@memphis.edu. *Application contact:* Dr. Fernanda Botelho, Coordinator of Graduate Studies, 901-678-3131, Fax: 901-678-2480,
E-mail: mbotelho@memphis.edu.
Website: http://www.MSCI.memphis.edu/

University of Miami, Graduate School, College of Arts and Sciences, Department of Mathematics, Coral Gables, FL 33124. Offers mathematical finance (MS); mathematics (MA, MS, PhD). *Program availability:* Part-time, evening/weekend. Terminal master's awarded for partial completion of doctoral program. *Degree requirements:* For master's, comprehensive exam, qualifying exams; for doctorate, one foreign language, thesis/dissertation, qualifying exams. *Entrance requirements:* For master's and doctorate, GRE General Test, minimum GPA of 3.0. Additional exam requirements/recommendations for international students: Required—TOEFL (minimum score 550 paper-based; 59 iBT). Electronic applications accepted. *Faculty research:* Applied mathematics, probability, geometric analysis, differential equations, algebraic combinatorics.

University of Michigan, Rackham Graduate School, College of Literature, Science, and the Arts, Department of Mathematics, Ann Arbor, MI 48109. Offers applied and interdisciplinary mathematics (AM, MS, PhD); mathematics (AM, MS, PhD). *Program availability:* Part-time. *Faculty:* 64 full-time (12 women). *Students:* 158 full-time (37 women), 5 part-time (2 women); includes 22 minority (2 Black or African American, non-Hispanic/Latino; 6 Asian, non-Hispanic/Latino; 7 Hispanic/Latino; 1 Native Hawaiian or other Pacific Islander, non-Hispanic/Latino; 6 Two or more races, non-Hispanic/Latino), 83 international. Average age 26. 691 applicants, 24% accepted, 58 enrolled. In 2015, 20 master's, 21 doctorates awarded. *Degree requirements:* For doctorate, one foreign language, comprehensive exam, thesis/dissertation, oral defense of dissertation, preliminary exam. *Entrance requirements:* For master's and doctorate, GRE General Test, GRE Subject Test. Additional exam requirements/recommendations for international students: Required—TOEFL (minimum score 560 paper-based; 84 iBT). *Application deadline:* For fall admission, 1/1 for domestic and international students. Applications are processed on a rolling basis. Application fee: $75 ($90 for international students). Electronic applications accepted. *Expenses:* Contact institution. *Financial support:* In 2015–16, 118 students received support, including 15 fellowships with full tuition reimbursements available (averaging $25,000 per year), 15 research assistantships with full tuition reimbursements available (averaging $19,350 per year), 88 teaching assistantships with full tuition reimbursements available (averaging $19,350 per year). Financial award application deadline: 3/15. *Faculty research:* Algebra, analysis, topology, applied mathematics, geometry. *Unit head:* Prof. Mel Hochster, Chair, 734-936-1310, Fax: 734-763-0937, E-mail: math-chair@umich.edu. *Application contact:* Prof. Kartik Prasanna, Admissions Director, 734-615-3439, Fax: 734-763-0937, E-mail: math-admissionsdir@umich.edu.
Website: http://www.lsa.umich.edu/math/

University of Michigan–Flint, College of Arts and Sciences, Program in Mathematics, Flint, MI 48502-1950. Offers mathematics (MA). *Program availability:* Part-time. *Faculty:* 13 full-time (4 women), 8 part-time/adjunct (3 women). *Students:* 9 part-time (6 women); includes 1 minority (Hispanic/Latino). Average age 33. 7 applicants, 100% accepted, 3 enrolled. In 2015, 6 master's awarded. *Entrance requirements:* For master's, bachelor's degree in mathematics or related field (physics, chemistry, computer science) from accredited institution including coursework through at least multivariate calculus and some proof-oriented courses; minimum overall undergraduate GPA of 3.0. Additional exam requirements/recommendations for international students: Required—TOEFL (minimum score 560 paper-based; 84 iBT), IELTS (minimum score 6.5). *Application deadline:* For fall admission, 8/1 for domestic students, 5/1 for international students; for winter admission, 11/15 for domestic students, 9/1 for international students; for spring admission, 3/15 for domestic students, 1/1 for international students. Applications are processed on a rolling basis. Application fee: $55. Electronic applications accepted. *Financial support:* Federal Work-Study, scholarships/grants, and unspecified assistantships available. Support available to part-time students. Financial award application deadline: 3/1; financial award applicants required to submit FAFSA. *Unit head:* Dr. Cam McLeman, Director, 810-767-6689, E-mail: mclemanc@umflint.edu. *Application contact:* Bradley T. Maki, Director of Graduate Admissions, 810-762-3171, Fax: 810-766-6789, E-mail: bmaki@umflint.edu.
Website: https://www.umflint.edu/graduateprograms/mathematics-ma

University of Minnesota, Twin Cities Campus, College of Science and Engineering, School of Mathematics, Minneapolis, MN 55455-0213. Offers mathematics (MS, PhD); quantitative finance (Certificate). *Program availability:* Part-time. Terminal master's awarded for partial completion of doctoral program. *Degree requirements:* For master's, thesis (for some programs); for doctorate, 2 foreign languages, thesis/dissertation.

Entrance requirements: For master's, GRE Subject Test (recommended); for doctorate, GRE Subject Test. Additional exam requirements/recommendations for international students: Required—TOEFL. Electronic applications accepted. *Faculty research:* Partial and ordinary differential equations, algebra and number theory, geometry, combinatorics, numerical analysis, probability, financial mathematics.

University of Mississippi, Graduate School, College of Liberal Arts, University, MS 38677. Offers anthropology (MA); biology (MS, PhD); chemistry (MS, PhD); clinical psychology (PhD); economics (MA, PhD); English (MA, MFA, PhD); experimental psychology (PhD); history (MA, PhD); mathematics (MS, PhD); modern languages (MA); music (MM, PhD); philosophy (MA); physics (MA, MS, PhD); political science (MA, PhD); sociology (MA); studio art (MFA). *Program availability:* Part-time. *Faculty:* 446 full-time (186 women), 84 part-time/adjunct (36 women). *Students:* 475 full-time (233 women), 79 part-time (37 women); includes 83 minority (42 Black or African American, non-Hispanic/Latino; 9 Asian, non-Hispanic/Latino; 19 Hispanic/Latino; 13 Two or more races, non-Hispanic/Latino), 107 international. *Degree requirements:* For doctorate, thesis/dissertation. *Entrance requirements:* For master's, GRE General Test, minimum GPA of 3.0; for doctorate, GRE General Test. Additional exam requirements/recommendations for international students: Required—TOEFL. *Application deadline:* For fall admission, 4/1 for domestic students; for spring admission, 10/1 for domestic students. Applications are processed on a rolling basis. Application fee: $40. Electronic applications accepted. *Financial support:* Fellowships, research assistantships, teaching assistantships, career-related internships or fieldwork, Federal Work-Study, institutionally sponsored loans, scholarships/grants, and unspecified assistantships available. Financial award application deadline: 3/1; financial award applicants required to submit FAFSA. *Unit head:* Dean, 662-915-7177, Fax: 662-915-5792, E-mail: libarts@olemiss.edu. *Application contact:* Dr. Christy M. Wyandt, Associate Dean of Graduate School, 662-915-7474, Fax: 662-915-7577, E-mail: cwyandt@olemiss.edu.

University of Missouri, Office of Research and Graduate Studies, College of Arts and Science, Department of Mathematics, Columbia, MO 65211. Offers applied mathematics (MS); mathematics (MA, MST, PhD). *Degree requirements:* For doctorate, 2 foreign languages, comprehensive exam, thesis/dissertation. *Entrance requirements:* For master's and doctorate, GRE General Test, minimum GPA of 3.0; bachelor's degree from accredited institution. Additional exam requirements/recommendations for international students: Required—TOEFL (minimum score 500 paper-based; 61 iBT). Electronic applications accepted. *Faculty research:* Algebraic geometry, analysis (real, complex, functional and harmonic), analytic functions, applied mathematics, financial mathematics and mathematics of insurance, commutative rings, scattering theory, differential equations (ordinary and partial), differential geometry, dynamical systems, general relativity, mathematical physics, number theory, probabilistic analysis and topology.

University of Missouri–Kansas City, College of Arts and Sciences, Department of Mathematics and Statistics, Kansas City, MO 64110-2499. Offers MA, MS, PhD. PhD (interdisciplinary) offered through the School of Graduate Studies. *Program availability:* Part-time. *Faculty:* 15 full-time (3 women), 4 part-time/adjunct (1 woman). *Students:* 15 full-time (9 women), 7 part-time (3 women); includes 2 minority (1 Asian, non-Hispanic/Latino; 1 Hispanic/Latino), 13 international. Average age 29. 38 applicants, 34% accepted, 3 enrolled. In 2015, 13 master's awarded. Terminal master's awarded for partial completion of doctoral program. *Degree requirements:* For master's, written exam; for doctorate, 2 foreign languages, thesis/dissertation, oral and written exams. *Entrance requirements:* For master's, bachelor's degree in mathematics, minimum GPA of 3.0; for doctorate, GMAT or GRE General Test. Additional exam requirements/recommendations for international students: Required—TOEFL (minimum score 550 paper-based; 80 iBT). *Application deadline:* For fall admission, 3/15 for domestic students, 3/15 priority date for international students; for spring admission, 10/15 for domestic and international students. Applications are processed on a rolling basis. Application fee: $45 ($50 for international students). Electronic applications accepted. *Financial support:* In 2015–16, 11 teaching assistantships with full tuition reimbursements (averaging $16,234 per year) were awarded; research assistantships, Federal Work-Study, institutionally sponsored loans, and tuition waivers (full and partial) also available. Support available to part-time students. Financial award application deadline: 3/1; financial award applicants required to submit FAFSA. *Faculty research:* Numerical analysis, statistics, biostatistics, commutative algebra, differential equations. *Unit head:* Eric Hall, Chair, 816-235-5852, Fax: 816-235-5517, E-mail: halle@umkc.edu. *Application contact:* Dr. Hristo Voulov, Associate Professor, 816-235-1641, Fax: 816-235-5517, E-mail: umkcmathdept@umkc.edu.
Website: http://cas.umkc.edu/math/

University of Missouri–St. Louis, College of Arts and Sciences, Department of Mathematics and Computer Science, St. Louis, MO 63121. Offers computer science (MS); mathematical and computational sciences (PhD); mathematics (MA). *Program availability:* Part-time, evening/weekend. *Faculty:* 14 full-time (1 woman), 1 part-time/adjunct (0 women). *Students:* 42 full-time (19 women), 43 part-time (10 women); includes 7 minority (1 Black or African American, non-Hispanic/Latino; 5 Asian, non-Hispanic/Latino; 1 Hispanic/Latino), 38 international. Average age 31. 137 applicants, 62% accepted, 32 enrolled. *Degree requirements:* For master's, thesis optional; for doctorate, thesis/dissertation. *Entrance requirements:* For master's, GRE (for teaching assistantships), 2 letters of recommendation; C programming, C++ or Java (for computer science); for doctorate, GRE General Test, 3 letters of recommendation. Additional exam requirements/recommendations for international students: Required—TOEFL (minimum score 550 paper-based; 79 iBT), IELTS (minimum score 6.5). *Application deadline:* For fall admission, 7/1 priority date for domestic and international students; for spring admission, 12/1 priority date for domestic and international students. Applications are processed on a rolling basis. Application fee: $50 ($40 for international students). Electronic applications accepted. *Financial support:* Research assistantships with tuition reimbursements and teaching assistantships with tuition reimbursements available. Financial award applicants required to submit FAFSA. *Faculty research:* Statistics, algebra, analysis. *Unit head:* Dr. Qingtang Jiang, Director of Graduate Studies, 314-516-6358, Fax: 314-516-5400, E-mail: jiangq@umsl.edu. *Application contact:* 314-516-5458, Fax: 314-516-6996, E-mail: gradadm@umsl.edu.
Website: http://umsl.edu/divisions/artscience/math_cs/

University of Montana, Graduate School, College of Humanities and Sciences, Department of Mathematical Sciences, Missoula, MT 59812-0002. Offers mathematics (MA, PhD), including college mathematics teaching (PhD), mathematical sciences research (PhD); mathematics education (MA). *Program availability:* Part-time. Terminal master's awarded for partial completion of doctoral program. *Degree requirements:* For doctorate, thesis/dissertation. *Entrance requirements:* For master's and doctorate, GRE General Test. Additional exam requirements/recommendations for international students: Required—TOEFL (minimum score 525 paper-based).

University of Nebraska at Omaha, Graduate Studies, College of Arts and Sciences, Department of Mathematics, Omaha, NE 68182. Offers MA, MAT, MS. *Program availability:* Part-time. *Faculty:* 9 full-time (3 women). *Students:* 13 full-time (7 women), 32 part-time (17 women); includes 9 minority (3 Black or African American, non-

Hispanic/Latino; 1 Asian, non-Hispanic/Latino; 4 Hispanic/Latino; 1 Two or more races, non-Hispanic/Latino), 10 international. Average age 31. 32 applicants, 50% accepted, 11 enrolled. In 2015, 18 master's awarded. *Degree requirements:* For master's, comprehensive exam, thesis (for some programs). *Entrance requirements:* For master's, minimum GPA of 3.0, 15 undergraduate math hours beyond calculus, official transcripts. Additional exam requirements/recommendations for international students: Required—TOEFL, IELTS, PTE. *Application deadline:* For fall admission, 7/31 priority date for domestic and international students; for spring admission, 11/30 priority date for domestic and international students; for summer admission, 4/15 for domestic and international students. Applications are processed on a rolling basis. Application fee: $45. Electronic applications accepted. *Financial support:* In 2015–16, 11 students received support, including 1 research assistantship with tuition reimbursement available, 10 teaching assistantships with tuition reimbursements available; Federal Work-Study, institutionally sponsored loans, traineeships, health care benefits, tuition waivers (partial), and unspecified assistantships also available. Support available to part-time students. Financial award application deadline: 3/1; financial award applicants required to submit FAFSA. *Unit head:* Dr. John Konvalina, Chairperson, 402-554-2341, E-mail: graduate@unomaha.edu. *Application contact:* Dr. Andrew Swift, Graduate Program Chair, 402-554-2341, E-mail: graduate@unomaha.edu.

University of Nebraska–Lincoln, Graduate College, College of Arts and Sciences, Department of Mathematics, Lincoln, NE 68588. Offers mathematics (MA, MAT, MS, PhD); mathematics and computer science (PhD). *Degree requirements:* For master's, thesis optional; for doctorate, variable foreign language requirement, comprehensive exam, thesis/dissertation. *Entrance requirements:* Additional exam requirements/recommendations for international students: Required—TOEFL (minimum score 550 paper-based). Electronic applications accepted. *Faculty research:* Applied mathematics, commutative algebra, algebraic geometry, Bayesian statistics, biostatistics.

University of Nevada, Las Vegas, Graduate College, College of Sciences, Department of Mathematical Sciences, Las Vegas, NV 89154-4020. Offers MS, PhD. *Program availability:* Part-time. *Faculty:* 20 full-time (4 women), 1 part-time/adjunct. *Students:* 46 full-time (10 women), 10 part-time (5 women); includes 9 minority (1 Black or African American, non-Hispanic/Latino; 4 Asian, non-Hispanic/Latino; 4 Hispanic/Latino), 15 international. Average age 31. 45 applicants, 64% accepted, 16 enrolled. In 2015, 14 master's, 7 doctorates awarded. *Degree requirements:* For master's, comprehensive exam (for some programs), thesis (for some programs); for doctorate, comprehensive exam, thesis/dissertation. *Entrance requirements:* For master's, GRE General Test; for doctorate, GRE General Test (minimum scores: quantitative 770 or 115 on the new scale, verbal and quantitative 1100 or 305 on the new scale). Additional exam requirements/recommendations for international students: Required—TOEFL (minimum score 550 paper-based; 79 iBT), IELTS (minimum score 7). *Application deadline:* For fall admission, 2/1 for domestic students, 5/1 for international students; for spring admission, 10/1 for domestic and international students. Application fee: $60 ($95 for international students). Electronic applications accepted. *Expenses:* $264 per credit state resident full-time and part-time; $6,955 per semester, $264 per credit nonresident full-time; $555 per credit nonresident part-time. *Financial support:* In 2015–16, 48 students received support, including 48 teaching assistantships with partial tuition reimbursements available (averaging $13,490 per year); institutionally sponsored loans, scholarships/grants, health care benefits, and unspecified assistantships also available. Financial award application deadline: 3/1. *Faculty research:* Scientific computing, computer simulation, numerical analysis for differential equations; partial differential equations (PDEs); mathematical logic, foundations of mathematics, set theory, large cardinals; statistics, biostatistics, statistical computing; number theory, arithmetic geometry, algebraic geometry. Total annual research expenditures: $6,947. *Unit head:* Dr. Derrick Dubose, Chair/Professor, 702-895-0382, Fax: 702-895-4343, E-mail: derrick.dubose@unlv.edu. *Application contact:* Graduate College Admissions Evaluator, 702-895-3367, Fax: 702-895-4180, E-mail: gradadmissions@unlv.edu.
Website: http://math.unlv.edu/

University of Nevada, Reno, Graduate School, College of Science, Department of Mathematics and Statistics, Reno, NV 89557. Offers mathematics (MS); teaching mathematics (MATM). *Degree requirements:* For master's, thesis optional. *Entrance requirements:* For master's, GRE General Test, minimum GPA of 2.75. Additional exam requirements/recommendations for international students: Required—TOEFL (minimum score 500 paper-based; 61 iBT), IELTS (minimum score 6). Electronic applications accepted. *Faculty research:* Operator algebra, nonlinear systems, differential equations.

University of New Brunswick Fredericton, School of Graduate Studies, Faculty of Science, Department of Mathematics and Statistics, Fredericton, NB E3B 5A3, Canada. Offers M Sc, PhD. *Faculty:* 15 full-time (0 women), 1 part-time/adjunct (0 women). *Students:* 22 full-time (7 women), 1 (woman) part-time. In 2015, 1 master's, 1 doctorate awarded. *Degree requirements:* For master's, thesis; for doctorate, comprehensive exam, thesis/dissertation. *Entrance requirements:* For master's and doctorate, minimum GPA of 3.0. Additional exam requirements/recommendations for international students: Required—TOEFL (minimum score 550 paper-based), TWE (minimum score 4); Recommended—IELTS (minimum score 7). *Application deadline:* For fall admission, 3/1 for domestic students. Applications are processed on a rolling basis. Application fee: $50 Canadian dollars. Electronic applications accepted. *Financial support:* In 2015–16, 35 research assistantships, 21 teaching assistantships were awarded; fellowships also available. *Faculty research:* Commutative and non-commutative algebra, combinatorics, mathematical modeling and computation, mathematical biology, classical and quantum gravity, multivariate statistics and spatial statistics. *Unit head:* Dr. James Watmough, Director of Graduate Studies, 506-458-7363, Fax: 506-453-4705, E-mail: watmough@unb.ca. *Application contact:* Heidi Stewart, Graduate Secretary, 506-458-7488, E-mail: scigrad@unb.ca.
Website: http://go.unb.ca/gradprograms

University of New Hampshire, Graduate School, College of Engineering and Physical Sciences, Department of Mathematics and Statistics, Durham, NH 03824. Offers MS, MST, PhD, Postbaccalaureate Certificate. Terminal master's awarded for partial completion of doctoral program. *Degree requirements:* For doctorate, 2 foreign languages, thesis/dissertation. *Entrance requirements:* Additional exam requirements/recommendations for international students: Required—TOEFL (minimum score 550 paper-based; 80 iBT). Electronic applications accepted. *Faculty research:* Operator theory, complex analysis, algebra, nonlinear dynamics, statistics.

University of New Mexico, Graduate Studies, College of Arts and Sciences, Department of Mathematics and Statistics, Albuquerque, NM 87131-2039. Offers mathematics (MS, PhD); statistics (MS, PhD). *Program availability:* Part-time. *Faculty:* 20 full-time (6 women). *Students:* 55 full-time (20 women), 32 part-time (14 women); includes 18 minority (4 Black or African American, non-Hispanic/Latino; 3 Asian, non-Hispanic/Latino; 10 Hispanic/Latino; 1 Two or more races, non-Hispanic/Latino), 29 international. Average age 31. 107 applicants, 55% accepted, 35 enrolled. In 2015, 19 master's, 13 doctorates awarded. Terminal master's awarded for partial completion of doctoral program. *Degree requirements:* For master's, comprehensive exam (for some programs), thesis or alternative; for doctorate, one foreign language, comprehensive

Peterson's Graduate Programs in the Physical Sciences, Mathematics, Agricultural Sciences, the Environment & Natural Resources 2017

www.petersons.com **265**

exam, thesis/dissertation, 4 department seminars. *Entrance requirements:* For master's and doctorate, minimum GPA of 3.0, 3 letters of recommendation, letter of intent. Additional exam requirements/recommendations for international students: Required—TOEFL (minimum score 550 paper-based). *Application deadline:* For fall admission, 2/15 priority date for domestic and international students; for spring admission, 11/1 priority date for domestic and international students. Application fee: $50. Electronic applications accepted. *Financial support:* Research assistantships with tuition reimbursements, teaching assistantships with tuition reimbursements, health care benefits, and unspecified assistantships available. Financial award application deadline: 2/15; financial award applicants required to submit FAFSA. *Faculty research:* Pure and applied mathematics, applied statistics, numerical analysis, biostatistics, differential geometry, fluid dynamics, nonparametric curve estimation. *Total annual research expenditures:* $1.2 million. *Unit head:* Dr. Terry Loring, Chair, 505-277-4613, Fax: 505-277-5505, E-mail: loring@math.unm.edu. *Application contact:* Ana Parra Lombard, Coordinator, Program Advisement, 505-277-5250, Fax: 505-277-5505, E-mail: aparra@math.unm.edu.
Website: http://math.unm.edu/

University of New Orleans, Graduate School, College of Sciences, Department of Mathematics, New Orleans, LA 70148. Offers MS. *Program availability:* Part-time. *Entrance requirements:* For master's, BA or BS in mathematics. Additional exam requirements/recommendations for international students: Required—TOEFL (minimum score 550 paper-based; 79 iBT), IELTS (minimum score 6.5). Electronic applications accepted. *Faculty research:* Differential equations, combinatorics, statistics, complex analysis, algebra.

The University of North Carolina at Chapel Hill, Graduate School, College of Arts and Sciences, Department of Mathematics, Chapel Hill, NC 27599. Offers MA, MS, PhD. *Degree requirements:* For master's, comprehensive exam, thesis or alternative, computer language proficiency; for doctorate, one foreign language, thesis/dissertation, 3 comprehensive exams, computer language proficiency, instructional service. *Entrance requirements:* For master's and doctorate, GRE General Test, minimum GPA of 3.0. Additional exam requirements/recommendations for international students: Required—TOEFL. Electronic applications accepted. *Faculty research:* Algebraic geometry, topology, analysis, lie theory, applied math.

The University of North Carolina at Charlotte, College of Education, Department of Reading and Elementary Education, Charlotte, NC 28223-0001. Offers elementary education (M Ed, Graduate Certificate); elementary mathematics education (Graduate Certificate); reading, language and literacy (M Ed). *Program availability:* Part-time, evening/weekend, 100% online, blended/hybrid learning. *Faculty:* 25 full-time (12 women), 5 part-time/adjunct (4 women). *Students:* 2 full-time (both women), 52 part-time (50 women); includes 8 minority (7 Black or African American, non-Hispanic/Latino; 1 Two or more races, non-Hispanic/Latino). Average age 29. 25 applicants, 96% accepted, 24 enrolled. In 2015, 29 master's awarded. *Degree requirements:* For master's, thesis or alternative, capstone project. *Entrance requirements:* For master's, GRE or MAT, three letters of recommendation, official transcripts, academic and professional goals statement, valid teacher's license, bachelor's degree in elementary education. Applicants to the Reading Education Masters program must hold an A level license from NCDPI or its equivalent in another state. Additional exam requirements/recommendations for international students: Required—TOEFL (minimum score 557 paper-based, 83 iBT) or IELTS (minimum score 6.5). *Application deadline:* For fall admission, 3/1 priority date for domestic students, 3/1 for international students; for spring admission, 10/1 priority date for domestic students, 10/1 for international students; for summer admission, 4/1 priority date for domestic students, 4/1 for international students. Application fee: $75. Electronic applications accepted. *Expenses:* Tuition, state resident: full-time $4128. Tuition, nonresident: full-time $16,799. *Required fees:* $2904. Tuition and fees vary according to course load and program. *Financial support:* In 2015–16, 3 students received support, including 3 research assistantships (averaging $12,500 per year); career-related internships or fieldwork, institutionally sponsored loans, scholarships/grants, and unspecified assistantships also available. Support available to part-time students. Financial award application deadline: 3/1; financial award applicants required to submit FAFSA. *Total annual research expenditures:* $11,193. *Unit head:* Mike Putman, Interim Chair, 704-687-8019, E-mail: michael.putman@uncc.edu. *Application contact:* Kathy B. Giddings, Director of Graduate Admissions, 704-687-5503, Fax: 704-687-1668, E-mail: gradadm@uncc.edu.
Website: http://reel.uncc.edu/

The University of North Carolina at Charlotte, College of Liberal Arts and Sciences, Department of Mathematics and Statistics, Charlotte, NC 28223-0001. Offers applied mathematics (PhD); mathematics (MS); mathematics education (MA). *Program availability:* Part-time, evening/weekend. *Faculty:* 41 full-time (10 women). *Students:* 51 full-time (24 women), 25 part-time (12 women); includes 10 minority (3 Black or African American, non-Hispanic/Latino; 2 Asian, non-Hispanic/Latino; 4 Hispanic/Latino; 1 Two or more races, non-Hispanic/Latino), 40 international. Average age 29. 59 applicants, 80% accepted, 17 enrolled. In 2015, 11 master's, 4 doctorates awarded. Terminal master's awarded for partial completion of doctoral program. *Degree requirements:* For master's, comprehensive exam, thesis, research project or portfolio; for doctorate, comprehensive exam, thesis/dissertation. *Entrance requirements:* For master's, GRE General Test, bachelor's degree, or its U.S. equivalent, from regionally-accredited college or university; minimum overall GPA of 3.0 on all previous work beyond high school; for doctorate, GRE General Test, at least 27 hours of courses in the mathematical sciences, as approved by the department Graduate Committee, with grades of C or better and minimum overall GPA in mathematics or statistics courses of 3.0. Additional exam requirements/recommendations for international students: Required—TOEFL (minimum score 557 paper-based, 83 iBT) or IELTS (minimum score 6.5). *Application deadline:* For fall admission, 3/1 priority date for domestic and international students; for spring admission, 10/1 priority date for domestic and international students; for summer admission, 4/1 priority date for domestic and international students. Applications are processed on a rolling basis. Application fee: $75. Electronic applications accepted. *Expenses:* Tuition, state resident: full-time $4128. Tuition, nonresident: full-time $16,799. *Required fees:* $2904. Tuition and fees vary according to course load and program. *Financial support:* In 2015–16, 38 students received support, including 2 fellowships (averaging $24,355 per year), 3 research assistantships (averaging $11,380 per year), 33 teaching assistantships (averaging $13,930 per year); career-related internships or fieldwork, Federal Work-Study, institutionally sponsored loans, scholarships/grants, and unspecified assistantships also available. Support available to part-time students. Financial award application deadline: 3/1; financial award applicants required to submit FAFSA. *Faculty research:* Numerical analysis and scientific computation, probability and stochastic processes, partial differential equations and mathematical physics, algebra and combinatorics, analysis, biostatistics, topology. *Total annual research expenditures:* $717,296. *Unit head:* Dr. Yuanan Diao, Chair, 704-687-0620, E-mail: ydiao@uncc.edu. *Application contact:* Kathy B. Giddings, Director of Graduate Admissions, 704-687-5503, Fax: 704-687-1668, E-mail: gradadm@uncc.edu.
Website: http://math.uncc.edu/

The University of North Carolina at Greensboro, Graduate School, College of Arts and Sciences, Department of Mathematics and Statistics, Greensboro, NC 27412-5001. Offers mathematics (MA, PhD). *Program availability:* Part-time. *Degree requirements:* For master's, comprehensive exam, thesis (for some programs). *Entrance requirements:* For master's, GRE General Test. Additional exam requirements/recommendations for international students: Required—TOEFL. Electronic applications accepted. *Faculty research:* General and geometric topology, statistics, computer networks, symbolic logic, mathematics education.

The University of North Carolina Wilmington, College of Arts and Sciences, Department of Mathematical Sciences, Wilmington, NC 28403-3297. Offers mathematics (MS); statistics (Graduate Certificate). *Program availability:* Part-time. *Faculty:* 16 full-time (6 women). *Students:* 12 full-time (6 women), 7 part-time (2 women), 3 international. Average age 26. 15 applicants, 10 enrolled. In 2015, 11 master's awarded. *Degree requirements:* For master's, comprehensive exam, thesis or alternative. *Entrance requirements:* For master's, GRE General Test, minimum B average in undergraduate work, 3 letters of recommendation. Additional exam requirements/recommendations for international students: Required—TOEFL (minimum score 79 iBT), IELTS (minimum score 6.5). *Application deadline:* For fall admission, 6/15 for domestic students; for spring admission, 11/30 for domestic students; for summer admission, 4/1 for domestic students. Applications are processed on a rolling basis. Application fee: $60. Electronic applications accepted. *Expenses:* $8,854 in-state full-time per year, $20,945 out-of-state full-time per year. *Financial support:* Teaching assistantships, scholarships/grants, and in- and out-of-state tuition remission available. Financial award application deadline: 3/15; financial award applicants required to submit FAFSA. *Unit head:* Dr. Susan Simmons, Interim Department Chair, 910-962-3296, Fax: 910-962-7107, E-mail: simmonssj@uncw.edu. *Application contact:* Dr. Mark Lammers, Graduate Coordinator, 910-962-3958, Fax: 910-962-7107, E-mail: lammersm@uncw.edu.
Website: http://www.uncw.edu/mathgrad/

University of North Dakota, Graduate School, College of Arts and Sciences, Department of Mathematics, Grand Forks, ND 58202. Offers M Ed, MS. *Program availability:* Part-time. *Degree requirements:* For master's, thesis or alternative, final exam. *Entrance requirements:* For master's, minimum GPA of 3.0. Additional exam requirements/recommendations for international students: Required—TOEFL (minimum score 550 paper-based; 79 iBT), IELTS (minimum score 6.5). Electronic applications accepted. *Faculty research:* Statistics, measure theory, topological vector spaces, algebra, applied math.

University of Northern British Columbia, Office of Graduate Studies, Prince George, BC V2N 4Z9, Canada. Offers business administration (Diploma); community health science (M Sc); disability management (MA); education (M Ed); first nations studies (MA); gender studies (MA); history (MA); interdisciplinary studies (MA); international studies (MA); mathematical, computer and physical sciences (M Sc); natural resources and environmental studies (M Sc, MA, MNRES, PhD); political science (MA); psychology (M Sc, PhD); social work (MSW). *Program availability:* Part-time, evening/weekend, online learning. *Degree requirements:* For master's, thesis; for doctorate, thesis/dissertation. *Entrance requirements:* For master's, GRE, minimum B average in undergraduate course work; for doctorate, candidacy exam, minimum A average in graduate course work.

University of Northern Colorado, Graduate School, College of Natural and Health Sciences, School of Mathematical Sciences, Greeley, CO 80639. Offers mathematical teaching (MA); mathematics (MA, PhD); mathematics education (PhD); mathematics: liberal arts (MA). *Program availability:* Part-time. *Degree requirements:* For master's, comprehensive exam, thesis or alternative; for doctorate, comprehensive exam, thesis/dissertation. *Entrance requirements:* For master's, GRE General Test (liberal arts), 3 letters of recommendation; for doctorate, GRE General Test, 3 letters of recommendation. Electronic applications accepted.

University of Northern Iowa, Graduate College, College of Humanities, Arts and Sciences, Department of Mathematics, MA Program in Mathematics, Cedar Falls, IA 50614. Offers community college teaching (MA); mathematics (MA); secondary teaching (MA). *Students:* 4 full-time (1 woman), 29 part-time (16 women); includes 1 minority (Black or African American, non-Hispanic/Latino), 1 international. 9 applicants, 22% accepted, 2 enrolled. In 2015, 2 master's awarded. Application fee: $50 ($70 for international students). *Unit head:* Dr. Michael Prophet, Coordinator, 319-273-2104, Fax: 319-273-2546, E-mail: mike.prophet@uni.edu. *Application contact:* Laurie S. Russell, Record Analyst, 319-273-2623, Fax: 319-273-2885, E-mail: laurie.russell@uni.edu.
Website: http://www.uni.edu/math/academics/master-arts-degrees-mathematics

University of North Florida, College of Arts and Sciences, Department of Mathematics and Statistics, Jacksonville, FL 32224. Offers mathematical sciences (MS); statistics (MS). *Program availability:* Part-time, evening/weekend. *Faculty:* 14 full-time (7 women). *Students:* 13 full-time (6 women), 11 part-time (5 women); includes 6 minority (2 Black or African American, non-Hispanic/Latino; 1 Asian, non-Hispanic/Latino; 3 Hispanic/Latino), 6 international. Average age 28. 22 applicants, 64% accepted, 8 enrolled. In 2015, 6 master's awarded. *Degree requirements:* For master's, comprehensive exam, thesis optional. *Entrance requirements:* For master's, GRE General Test, minimum GPA of 3.0 in last 60 hours of course work. Additional exam requirements/recommendations for international students: Required—TOEFL (minimum score 500 paper-based; 61 iBT). *Application deadline:* For fall admission, 7/1 priority date for domestic students, 6/1 for international students; for spring admission, 11/1 priority date for domestic students, 10/1 for international students. Application fee: $30. Electronic applications accepted. *Expenses:* Tuition, state resident: part-time $408.10 per credit hour. Tuition, nonresident: part-time $932.61 per credit hour. *Required fees:* $111.81 per credit hour. Tuition and fees vary according to course load, campus/location and program. *Financial support:* In 2015–16, 16 students received support, including 6 teaching assistantships (averaging $6,214 per year); Federal Work-Study, scholarships/grants, tuition waivers (partial), and unspecified assistantships also available. Support available to part-time students. Financial award application deadline: 4/1; financial award applicants required to submit FAFSA. *Faculty research:* Real analysis, number theory, Euclidean geometry. *Total annual research expenditures:* $3,573. *Unit head:* Dr. Scott H. Hochwald, Chair, 904-620-2653, Fax: 904-620-2818, E-mail: shochwal@unf.edu. *Application contact:* Dr. Amanda Pascale, Director, The Graduate School, 904-620-1360, Fax: 904-620-1362, E-mail: graduateschool@unf.edu.
Website: http://www.unf.edu/coas/math-stat/

University of North Texas, Robert B. Toulouse School of Graduate Studies, Denton, TX 76203-5459. Offers accounting (MS); applied anthropology (MA, MS); applied behavior analysis (Certificate); applied geography (MA); applied technology and performance improvement (M Ed, MS); art education (MA); art history (MA); art museum education (Certificate); arts leadership (Certificate); audiology (Au D); behavior analysis (MS); behavioral science (PhD); biochemistry and molecular biology (MS); biology (MA, MS); biomedical engineering (MS); business analysis (MS); chemistry (MS); clinical health psychology (PhD); communication studies (MA, MS); computer engineering (MS); computer science (MS); counseling (M Ed, MS), including clinical mental health counseling (MS), college and university counseling, elementary school counseling, secondary school counseling; creative writing (MA); criminal justice (MS); curriculum and instruction (M Ed); decision sciences (MBA); design (MA, MFA), including fashion design (MFA), innovation studies, interior design (MFA); early childhood studies (MS); economics (MS); educational leadership (M Ed, Ed D); educational psychology (MS, PhD), including family studies (MS), gifted and talented (MS), human development (MS), learning and cognition (MS), research, measurement and evaluation (MS); electrical engineering (MS); emergency management (MPA); engineering technology (MS); English (MA); English as a second language (MA); environmental science (MS); finance (MBA, MS); financial management (MPA); French (MA); health services management (MBA); higher education (M Ed, Ed D); history (MA, MS); hospitality management (MS); human resources management (MPA); information science (MS); information systems (PhD); information technologies (MBA); interdisciplinary studies (MA, MS); international studies (MA); international sustainable tourism (MS); jazz studies (MM); journalism (MA, MJ, Graduate Certificate), including interactive and virtual digital communication (Graduate Certificate), narrative journalism (Graduate Certificate), public relations (Graduate Certificate); kinesiology (MS); linguistics (MA); local government management (MPA); logistics (PhD); logistics and supply chain management (MBA); long-term care, senior housing, and aging services (MA); management (PhD); marketing (MBA); mathematics (MA, MS); mechanical and energy engineering (MS, PhD); music (MA), including ethnomusicology, music theory, musicology, performance; music composition (PhD); music education (MM Ed, PhD); nonprofit management (MPA); operations and supply chain management (MBA); performance (MM, DMA); philosophy (MA); political science (MA); professional and technical communication (MA); radio, television and film (MA, MFA); rehabilitation counseling (Certificate); sociology (MA); Spanish (MA); special education (M Ed); speech-language pathology (MA); strategic management (MBA); studio art (MFA); teaching (M Ed); MBA/MS. *Program availability:* Part-time, evening/weekend, online learning. Terminal master's awarded for partial completion of doctoral program. *Degree requirements:* For master's, variable foreign language requirement, comprehensive exam (for some programs), thesis (for some programs); for doctorate, variable foreign language requirement, comprehensive exam (for some programs), thesis/dissertation; for other advanced degree, variable foreign language requirement, comprehensive exam (for some programs). *Entrance requirements:* For master's and doctorate, GRE, GMAT. Additional exam requirements/recommendations for international students: Required—TOEFL (minimum score 550 paper-based; 79 iBT). Electronic applications accepted.

University of Notre Dame, Graduate School, College of Science, Department of Mathematics, Notre Dame, IN 46556. Offers algebra (PhD); algebraic geometry (PhD); applied mathematics (MSAM); complex analysis (PhD); differential geometry (PhD); logic (PhD); partial differential equations (PhD); topology (PhD). Terminal master's awarded for partial completion of doctoral program. *Degree requirements:* For doctorate, one foreign language, thesis/dissertation, qualifying exam. *Entrance requirements:* For master's and doctorate, GRE General Test, GRE Subject Test. Additional exam requirements/recommendations for international students: Required—TOEFL (minimum score 600 paper-based; 80 iBT). Electronic applications accepted. *Faculty research:* Algebra, analysis, geometry/topology, logic, applied math.

University of Oklahoma, College of Arts and Sciences, Department of Mathematics, Norman, OK 73019. Offers MA, MS, PhD, MBA/MS. *Faculty:* 36 full-time (5 women). *Students:* 51 full-time (23 women), 17 part-time (6 women); includes 10 minority (1 American Indian or Alaska Native, non-Hispanic/Latino; 3 Asian, non-Hispanic/Latino; 4 Hispanic/Latino; 2 Two or more races, non-Hispanic/Latino), 13 international. Average age 28. 54 applicants, 31% accepted, 16 enrolled. In 2015, 5 master's, 7 doctorates awarded. Terminal master's awarded for partial completion of doctoral program. *Degree*

requirements: For master's, comprehensive exam, thesis optional; for doctorate, 2 foreign languages, comprehensive exam, thesis/dissertation. *Entrance requirements:* Additional exam requirements/recommendations for international students: Required—TOEFL (minimum score 79 iBT) or IELTS (minimum score 6.5). *Application deadline:* For fall admission, 1/31 for domestic and international students; for spring admission, 11/1 for domestic students, 9/1 for international students. Application fee: $50 ($100 for international students). Electronic applications accepted. *Expenses:* Tuition, state resident: full-time $4577; part-time $190.70 per credit hour. Tuition, nonresident: full-time $17,758; part-time $739.90 per credit hour. *Required fees:* $3060; $115.70 per credit hour. $141.50 per semester. *Financial support:* In 2015–16, 64 students received support, including 3 fellowships with full tuition reimbursements available (averaging $3,167 per year), 2 research assistantships (averaging $15,706 per year), 61 teaching assistantships with partial tuition reimbursements available (averaging $15,452 per year); scholarships/grants and unspecified assistantships also available. Financial award application deadline: 6/1; financial award applicants required to submit FAFSA. *Faculty research:* Representation theory, number theory, topology, geometry, analysis. *Total annual research expenditures:* $381,530. *Unit head:* Dr. Andy Miller, Chair, 405-325-6711, Fax: 405-325-7484, E-mail: amiller@ou.edu. *Application contact:* Cristin Sloan, Assistant to the Graduate Director, 405-325-2719, Fax: 405-325-7484, E-mail: csloan@math.ou.edu.
Website: http://www.math.ou.edu/grad

See Display below and Close-Up on page 297.

University of Oregon, Graduate School, College of Arts and Sciences, Department of Mathematics, Eugene, OR 97403. Offers MA, MS, PhD. *Program availability:* Part-time. Terminal master's awarded for partial completion of doctoral program. *Degree requirements:* For doctorate, 2 foreign languages, thesis/dissertation. *Entrance requirements:* For master's and doctorate, GRE General Test, GRE Subject Test. Additional exam requirements/recommendations for international students: Required—TOEFL. *Faculty research:* Algebra, topology, analytic geometry, numerical analysis, statistics.

University of Ottawa, Faculty of Graduate and Postdoctoral Studies, Faculty of Science, Ottawa-Carleton Institute of Mathematics and Statistics, Ottawa, ON K1N 6N5, Canada. Offers M Sc, PhD. M Sc, PhD offered jointly with Carleton University. *Program availability:* Part-time. *Degree requirements:* For master's, thesis optional; for doctorate, one foreign language, comprehensive exam, thesis/dissertation. *Entrance requirements:* For master's, honors B Sc degree or equivalent, minimum B average; for doctorate, M Sc, minimum B+ average. Electronic applications accepted. *Faculty research:* Pure mathematics, applied mathematics, probability and statistics.

University of Pennsylvania, School of Arts and Sciences, Graduate Group in Mathematics, Philadelphia, PA 19104. Offers AM, PhD. *Faculty:* 30 full-time (3 women), 6 part-time/adjunct (0 women). *Students:* 48 full-time (14 women), 2 part-time (0 women); includes 6 minority (4 Asian, non-Hispanic/Latino; 2 Hispanic/Latino), 27 international. Average age 26. 226 applicants, 18% accepted, 13 enrolled. In 2015, 5 master's, 4 doctorates awarded. Terminal master's awarded for partial completion of doctoral program. *Degree requirements:* For master's, thesis or alternative; for doctorate, thesis/dissertation. Application fee: $70. *Expenses:* Tuition, area resident: Full-time $31,068; part-time $5762 per course. *Required fees:* $3200; $336 per course. Full-time tuition and fees vary according to degree level, program and student level. Part-time tuition and fees vary according to course load, degree level and program. *Financial support:* Application deadline: 12/15.
Website: http://www.sas.upenn.edu/graduate-division

University of Pittsburgh, Dietrich School of Arts and Sciences, Department of Mathematics, Pittsburgh, PA 15260. Offers applied mathematics (MA, MS); mathematics (MA, MS, PhD). *Program availability:* Part-time. *Faculty:* 31 full-time (2

Department of Mathematics
The University of Oklahoma

Thank you for your interest in our department and in the University of Oklahoma! The **Mathematics Department** at the University of Oklahoma has a long and rich academic tradition dating back to the mid-1890s. We awarded our first master's degree in 1927 and our first doctorate in 1947. We offer a wide range of options leading to the Master of Arts, Master of Science, and Ph.D. degrees. You will be able to select from a broad **range of options** in pure and applied mathematics and in research in mathematics education for your graduate degree:

1. **Algebra and Number Theory.** Algebraic Geometry, Algebraic Groups, Combinatorics, Modular Forms, Representation Theory (real, p-adic, Lie, automorphic).
2. **Analysis.** Global Analysis, Harmonic Analysis, Integrable Systems, PDEs, Signal Processing, Spectral Theory, Wavelets and Frames.
3. **Applied Mathematics and Mathematical Physics.** Control Theory, Dynamical Systems, Modeling.
4. **Geometry.** Convexity, Harmonic Maps, Riemannian Geometry, Group Actions and Non-negative Curvature.
5. **RUME.** Research in Undergraduate Mathematics Education, Diversity and Equity, International Comparative Education.
6. **Topology.** Algebraic and Geometric Topology, Dimension Theory, Geometric Group Theory, Hyperbolic Geometry, Low Dimensional Topology, Teichmuller Theory.

For more information, contact:
Cristin Sloan, Assistant to the Graduate Director
Department of Mathematics
The University of Oklahoma
Norman, OK 73019
csloan@math.ou.edu
www.math.ou.edu/grad/

Peterson's Graduate Programs in the Physical Sciences, Mathematics, Agricultural Sciences, the Environment & Natural Resources 2017

www.petersons.com   **267**

women). *Students:* 86 full-time (29 women); includes 36 minority (2 Black or African American, non-Hispanic/Latino; 31 Asian, non-Hispanic/Latino; 2 Hispanic/Latino; 1 Two or more races, non-Hispanic/Latino). Average age 29. 175 applicants, 24% accepted, 16 enrolled. In 2015, 7 master's, 7 doctorates awarded. Terminal master's awarded for partial completion of doctoral program. *Degree requirements:* For master's, thesis (for some programs); for doctorate, comprehensive exam, thesis/dissertation, preliminary exams, defense of dissertation. *Entrance requirements:* For master's and doctorate, GRE General Test, GRE Subject Test (recommended), minimum GPA of 3.0. Additional exam requirements/recommendations for international students: Required—TOEFL (minimum score 90 iBT), IELTS (minimum score 7). *Application deadline:* For fall admission, 1/15 for domestic and international students; for spring admission, 11/1 for domestic and international students. Applications are processed on a rolling basis. Application fee: $50. Electronic applications accepted. Application fee is waived when completed online. Tuition and fees vary according to program. *Financial support:* In 2015–16, 75 students received support, including 12 fellowships with full tuition reimbursements available (averaging $21,712 per year), 10 research assistantships with full tuition reimbursements available (averaging $16,766 per year), 53 teaching assistantships with full tuition reimbursements available (averaging $17,464 per year); tuition waivers (full) also available. Financial award application deadline: 4/1; financial award applicants required to submit FAFSA. *Faculty research:* Algebra, combinatorics, and geometry; analysis and partial differential equations; applied analysis; complex biological systems; mathematical finance. *Total annual research expenditures:* $859,802. *Unit head:* Dr. Ivan Yotov, Chair, 412-624-8361, Fax: 412-624-8397, E-mail: yotov@math.pitt.edu. *Application contact:* Pat Markham, Graduate Administrator, 412-624-1175, Fax: 412-624-8397, E-mail: pam131@pitt.edu.
Website: http://www.mathematics.pitt.edu

University of Pittsburgh, Dietrich School of Arts and Sciences, Program in Computational Modeling and Simulation, Pittsburgh, PA 15260. Offers biological science (PhD); chemistry (PhD); computer science (PhD); economics (PhD); mathematics (PhD); physics and astronomy (PhD); psychology (PhD); statistics (PhD). *Program availability:* Part-time. *Faculty:* 3 full-time (0 women). *Students:* 3 full-time (1 woman); includes 2 minority (both Asian, non-Hispanic/Latino). Average age 23. 13 applicants, 31% accepted, 2 enrolled. *Degree requirements:* For doctorate, comprehensive exam, thesis/dissertation, preliminary exam. *Entrance requirements:* For doctorate, GRE, statement of purpose, transcripts for all college-level institutions attended, three letters of reference. Additional exam requirements/recommendations for international students: Required—TOEFL (minimum score 90 iBT), IELTS (minimum score 7). *Application deadline:* For fall admission, 1/15 for domestic and international students. Applications are processed on a rolling basis. Application fee: $0 ($50 for international students). Electronic applications accepted. Tuition and fees vary according to program. *Financial support:* In 2015–16, 3 students received support, including 2 fellowships with full tuition reimbursements available (averaging $27,000 per year), 1 research assistantship with full tuition reimbursement available (averaging $21,500 per year); tuition waivers (full) also available. Financial award application deadline: 4/15. *Faculty research:* Econometric modeling, developing reduced-scaling first principles approaches for expedited predictions of molecular and materials properties, developing computational models to quantitatively describe origins of reactivity and selectivity in organocatalytic reactions. *Unit head:* Dr. Kathleen Blee, Associate Dean, Graduate Studies and Research, 412-624-3939, Fax: 412-624-6855. *Application contact:* Wendy G. Janocha, Graduate Administrator, 412-648-7251, E-mail: wgj1@pitt.edu.
Website: http://cmsp.pitt.edu/

University of Puerto Rico, Mayagüez Campus, Graduate Studies, College of Arts and Sciences, Department of Mathematical Sciences, Mayagüez, PR 00681-9000. Offers applied mathematics (MS); pure mathematics (MS); scientific computation (MS); statistics (MS). *Program availability:* Part-time. *Degree requirements:* For master's, one foreign language, comprehensive exam, thesis optional. *Entrance requirements:* For master's, undergraduate degree in mathematics or its equivalent. *Faculty research:* Automata theory, linear algebra, logic.

University of Puerto Rico, Río Piedras Campus, College of Natural Sciences, Department of Mathematics, San Juan, PR 00931-3300. Offers MS, PhD. *Program availability:* Part-time. *Degree requirements:* For master's, comprehensive exam, thesis; for doctorate, comprehensive exam, thesis/dissertation. *Entrance requirements:* For master's and doctorate, GRE General Test and GRE Subject Test, interview, minimum GPA of 3.0, 3 letters of recommendation. *Faculty research:* Investigation of database logistics, cryptograph systems, distribution and spectral theory, Boolean function, differential equations.

University of Regina, Faculty of Graduate Studies and Research, Faculty of Science, Department of Mathematics and Statistics, Regina, SK S4S 0A2, Canada. Offers mathematics (M Sc, PhD); statistics (M Sc, PhD). *Program availability:* Part-time. *Degree requirements:* For master's, thesis (for some programs), major essay; for doctorate, comprehensive exam, thesis/dissertation. *Entrance requirements:* Additional exam requirements/recommendations for international students: Required—TOEFL (minimum score 580 paper-based; 80 iBT), IELTS (minimum score 6.5), PTE (minimum score 59). Electronic applications accepted. *Faculty research:* Discrete mathematics, actuarial science and statistics, matrix theory, mathematical science, numerical analysis.

University of Rhode Island, Graduate School, College of Arts and Sciences, Department of Mathematics, Kingston, RI 02881. Offers applied mathematical sciences (MS, PhD); mathematics (MS, PhD). *Program availability:* Part-time. *Faculty:* 20 full-time (6 women). *Students:* 15 full-time (6 women), 5 part-time (2 women); includes 1 minority (Black or African American, non-Hispanic/Latino), 1 international. In 2015, 2 master's, 2 doctorates awarded. *Degree requirements:* For master's, comprehensive exam (for some programs), thesis optional; for doctorate, one foreign language, comprehensive exam, thesis/dissertation. *Entrance requirements:* For master's and doctorate, 2 letters of recommendation, 3 for international candidates (one of which must address the candidate's abilities to teach in English). Additional exam requirements/recommendations for international students: Required—TOEFL (minimum score 550 paper-based). *Application deadline:* For fall admission, 7/15 for domestic students, 2/1 for international students; for spring admission, 11/15 for domestic students, 7/15 for international students. Application fee: $65. Electronic applications accepted. *Expenses:* Tuition, state resident: full-time $11,796; part-time $655 per credit. Tuition, nonresident: full-time $24,206; part-time $1345 per credit. *Required fees:* $1546; $44 per credit. One-time fee: $155 full-time; $35 part-time. *Financial support:* In 2015–16, 5 research assistantships (averaging $16,081 per year), 8 teaching assistantships with tuition reimbursements (averaging $16,186 per year) were awarded. Financial award application deadline: 2/1; financial award applicants required to submit FAFSA. *Unit head:* Dr. James Baglama, Chair, 401-874-2709, Fax: 401-874-4454, E-mail: jbaglama@math.uri.edu. *Application contact:* Graduate Admission, 401-874-2872, E-mail: gradadm@etal.uri.edu.
Website: http://www.math.uri.edu/

University of Rochester, School of Arts and Sciences, Department of Mathematics, Rochester, NY 14627. Offers MS, PhD. *Faculty:* 22 full-time (2 women). *Students:* 37 full-time (6 women); includes 1 minority (Asian, non-Hispanic/Latino), 20 international. 43 applicants, 23% accepted, 6 enrolled. In 2015, 16 master's, 6 doctorates awarded. Terminal master's awarded for partial completion of doctoral program. *Degree requirements:* For doctorate, thesis/dissertation, qualifying exam. *Entrance requirements:* For doctorate, GRE General Test. Additional exam requirements/recommendations for international students: Required—TOEFL. *Application deadline:* For fall admission, 1/15 priority date for domestic students. Application fee: $60. Electronic applications accepted. *Expenses: Tuition, area resident:* Full-time $47,450; part-time $1482 per credit hour. *Required fees:* $528. Tuition and fees vary according to program. *Financial support:* Fellowships, research assistantships, teaching assistantships, and tuition waivers (full and partial) available. Financial award application deadline: 1/15. *Faculty research:* Algebra and number theory, analysis, geometry, mathematical physics and probability, topology. *Unit head:* Allan Greenleaf, Chair, 585-275-9421. *Application contact:* Joan Robinson, Administrative Assistant, Graduate Program, 585-275-9422.
Website: http://www.math.rochester.edu/

University of Saskatchewan, College of Graduate Studies and Research, College of Arts and Science, Department of Mathematics and Statistics, Saskatoon, SK S7N 5A2, Canada. Offers M Math, MA, PhD. *Degree requirements:* For master's, thesis (for some programs); for doctorate, comprehensive exam (for some programs), thesis/dissertation. *Entrance requirements:* Additional exam requirements/recommendations for international students: Required—TOEFL (minimum score 80 iBT); Recommended—IELTS (minimum score 6.5). Electronic applications accepted.

University of South Alabama, College of Arts and Sciences, Department of Mathematics and Statistics, Mobile, AL 36688. Offers mathematics (MS). *Program availability:* Part-time, evening/weekend. *Faculty:* 10 full-time (2 women), 1 (woman) part-time/adjunct. *Students:* 7 full-time (3 women), 4 part-time (1 woman); includes 4 minority (1 Black or African American, non-Hispanic/Latino; 3 Asian, non-Hispanic/Latino), 1 international. Average age 34. 11 applicants, 82% accepted, 4 enrolled. In 2015, 4 master's awarded. *Degree requirements:* For master's, comprehensive exam, thesis optional. *Entrance requirements:* For master's, GRE, BS in mathematics or a mathematics-related field. Additional exam requirements/recommendations for international students: Required—TOEFL. *Application deadline:* For fall admission, 7/1 priority date for domestic students, 6/15 priority date for international students; for spring admission, 12/1 priority date for domestic students, 11/1 priority date for international students; for summer admission, 5/1 for domestic students. Applications are processed on a rolling basis. Application fee: $35. Electronic applications accepted. *Expenses:* Tuition, state resident: full-time $9480; part-time $395 per credit hour. Tuition, nonresident: full-time $18,960; part-time $790 per credit hour. *Financial support:* Fellowships, research assistantships, teaching assistantships, career-related internships or fieldwork, Federal Work-Study, institutionally sponsored loans, scholarships/grants, and unspecified assistantships available. Support available to part-time students. Financial award application deadline: 5/31; financial award applicants required to submit FAFSA. *Faculty research:* Knot theory, chaos theory, algebraic groups, finite groups, quantum groups. *Unit head:* Dr. Madhuri Mulekar, Chair, Mathematics, 251-460-6264, Fax: 251-460-7969, E-mail: mathstat@southalabama.edu. *Application contact:* Dr. Cornelius Pillen, Graduate Coordinator, Mathematics, 251-460-7293, Fax: 251-460-7969, E-mail: pillen@southalabama.edu.
Website: http://www.southalabama.edu/colleges/artsandsci/mathstat/

University of South Carolina, The Graduate School, College of Arts and Sciences, Department of Mathematics, Columbia, SC 29208. Offers mathematics (MA, MS, PhD); mathematics education (M Math, MAT). MAT offered in cooperation with the College of Education. *Program availability:* Part-time. Terminal master's awarded for partial completion of doctoral program. *Degree requirements:* For master's, comprehensive exam, thesis (for some programs); for doctorate, one foreign language, comprehensive exam, thesis/dissertation, admission to candidacy exam, residency. *Entrance requirements:* For master's and doctorate, GRE General Test. Additional exam requirements/recommendations for international students: Required—TOEFL (minimum score 600 paper-based; 100 iBT). Electronic applications accepted. *Faculty research:* Computational mathematics, analysis (classical/modern), discrete mathematics, algebra, number theory.

The University of South Dakota, Graduate School, College of Arts and Sciences, Department of Mathematics, Vermillion, SD 57069-2390. Offers MA, MS. *Program availability:* Part-time. *Degree requirements:* For master's, thesis (for some programs). *Entrance requirements:* For master's, GRE, minimum GPA of 2.7. Additional exam requirements/recommendations for international students: Required—TOEFL (minimum score 550 paper-based; 79 iBT). *Application deadline:* Applications are processed on a rolling basis. Application fee: $35. Electronic applications accepted. *Financial support:* Teaching assistantships with partial tuition reimbursements available. Financial award applicants required to submit FAFSA. *Unit head:* Dr. Dan Van Peursem, Chair, 605-677-5995, E-mail: dan.vanpeursem@usd.edu.
Website: http://www.usd.edu/math/

The University of South Dakota, Graduate School, School of Education, Division of Curriculum and Instruction, Program in Elementary Education, Vermillion, SD 57069-2390. Offers elementary education (MA), including early childhood education, English learning language, reading specialist/literacy coach, science, technology or math (stm). *Accreditation:* NCATE. *Program availability:* Part-time, 100% online, blended/hybrid learning. *Degree requirements:* For master's, comprehensive exam, thesis or alternative. *Entrance requirements:* For master's, GRE General Test, MAT, minimum GPA of 2.7. Additional exam requirements/recommendations for international students: Required—TOEFL (minimum score 550 paper-based; 79 iBT). *Application deadline:* Applications are processed on a rolling basis. Application fee: $35. Electronic applications accepted. *Financial support:* Research assistantships with partial tuition reimbursements, teaching assistantships with partial tuition reimbursements, career-related internships or fieldwork, Federal Work-Study, and unspecified assistantships available. Financial award applicants required to submit FAFSA. *Unit head:* Dr. Nicholas Shudak, Division Chair, 605-677-5207, Fax: 605-677-3102, E-mail: nicholas.shudak@usd.edu. *Application contact:* Graduate School, 605-658-6140, Fax: 605-677-6118, E-mail: cde@usd.edu.
Website: http://www.usd.edu/education/curriculum-and-instruction/graduate

The University of South Dakota, Graduate School, School of Education, Division of Curriculum and Instruction, Program in Secondary Education, Vermillion, SD 57069-2390. Offers secondary education (MA), including early childhood education, English language learning, reading specialist/literacy coach, science, technology and math (stm), secondary education plus certification. *Accreditation:* NCATE. *Program availability:* Part-time, online learning. *Degree requirements:* For master's, comprehensive exam, thesis or alternative. *Entrance requirements:* For master's, GRE General Test, MAT, minimum GPA of 2.7. Additional exam requirements/recommendations for international students: Required—TOEFL (minimum score 550 paper-based; 79 iBT). *Application deadline:* Applications are processed on a rolling basis. Application fee: $35. Electronic applications accepted. *Financial support:*

Research assistantships with partial tuition reimbursements, teaching assistantships with partial tuition reimbursements, career-related internships or fieldwork, Federal Work-Study, and unspecified assistantships available. Financial award applicants required to submit FAFSA. *Unit head:* Dr. Nicholas Shudak, Division Chair, 605-677-5207, Fax: 605-677-3102, E-mail: nicholas.shudak@usd.edu.

Website: http://www.usd.edu/education/curriculum-and-instruction/graduate

University of Southern California, Graduate School, Dana and David Dornsife College of Letters, Arts and Sciences, Department of Mathematics, Los Angeles, CA 90089. Offers applied mathematics (MA, MS, PhD); mathematical finance (MS); mathematics (MA, PhD); statistics (MS). *Program availability:* Part-time. Terminal master's awarded for partial completion of doctoral program. *Degree requirements:* For master's, comprehensive exam (for some programs), thesis (for some programs); for doctorate, one foreign language, comprehensive exam, thesis/dissertation. *Entrance requirements:* For master's, GRE General Test, GMAT; for doctorate, GRE General Test, GRE Subject Test (mathematics). Additional exam requirements/recommendations for international students: Required—TOEFL (minimum score 100 iBT). Electronic applications accepted. *Faculty research:* Algebra, algebraic geometry and number theory, analysis/partial differential equations, applied mathematics, financial mathematics, probability, combinatorics and statistics.

University of Southern Mississippi, Graduate School, College of Science and Technology, Department of Mathematics, Hattiesburg, MS 39406-0001. Offers computational science (PhD); mathematics (MS). *Program availability:* Part-time. *Degree requirements:* For master's, comprehensive exam, thesis or alternative; for doctorate, comprehensive exam, thesis/dissertation. *Entrance requirements:* For master's, GRE General Test, minimum GPA of 2.75 in last 60 hours; for doctorate, GRE General Test, minimum GPA of 3.5. Additional exam requirements/recommendations for international students: Required—TOEFL, IELTS. Electronic applications accepted. *Faculty research:* Dynamical systems, numerical analysis and multigrid methods, random number generation, matrix theory, group theory.

University of South Florida, College of Arts and Sciences, Department of Mathematics and Statistics, Tampa, FL 33620-9951. Offers mathematics (MA, PhD), including pure and applied, statistics (PhD); statistics (MA). *Program availability:* Part-time, evening/weekend. *Faculty:* 22 full-time (2 women). *Students:* 70 full-time (25 women), 21 part-time (7 women); includes 9 minority (2 Black or African American, non-Hispanic/Latino; 3 Asian, non-Hispanic/Latino; 2 Hispanic/Latino; 2 Two or more races, non-Hispanic/Latino), 46 international. Average age 31. 88 applicants, 69% accepted, 16 enrolled. In 2015, 25 master's, 6 doctorates awarded. Terminal master's awarded for partial completion of doctoral program. *Degree requirements:* For master's, comprehensive exam, thesis (for some programs); for doctorate, comprehensive exam, thesis/dissertation. *Entrance requirements:* For master's, GRE General Test, minimum GPA of 3.0 in undergraduate mathematics courses, bachelor's degree in mathematical sciences or related field, and statement of goals (for mathematics); minimum GPA of 3.5 in upper-division undergraduate coursework and BA or BS in statistics, mathematics, physical sciences, engineering, or business (for statistics); for doctorate, GRE General Test, minimum GPA of 3.5 in graduate mathematics courses, three letters of recommendation, statement of goals, master's or bachelor's degree in mathematical sciences or related field. Additional exam requirements/recommendations for international students: Required—TOEFL (minimum score 550 paper-based; 79 iBT) or IELTS (minimum score 6.5). *Application deadline:* For fall admission, 2/1 for domestic students, 1/2 for international students; for spring admission, 8/1 for domestic students, 6/1 for international students. Application fee: $30. Electronic applications accepted. *Financial support:* In 2015–16, 61 students received support, including 6 research assistantships (averaging $16,990 per year), 55 teaching assistantships with partial tuition reimbursements available (averaging $13,742 per year); unspecified assistantships also available. Financial award application deadline: 2/1. *Faculty research:* Mathematics: algebra and number theory, harmonic and complex analysis, approximation theory, theory of orthogonal polynomials, Banach space theory and operator theory, differential equations and nonlinear analysis, discrete mathematics, geometry and topology; statistics: linear and nonlinear statistical models for health sciences, operations research problems, economic systems; stochastic control problems; dynamic reliability analysis and control. *Total annual research expenditures:* $661,309. *Unit head:* Dr. Leslaw Skrzypek, Associate Professor and Chairperson, 813-974-1268, Fax: 813-974-2700, E-mail: skrzypek@usf.edu. *Application contact:* Dr. Xiang-Dong Hou, Professor/Director of Graduate Mathematics Program, 813-974-2561, Fax: 813-974-2700, E-mail: xhou@cas.usf.edu.

Website: http://math.usf.edu/

University of South Florida, Innovative Education, Tampa, FL 33620-9951. Offers adult, career and higher education (Graduate Certificate), including college teaching, leadership in developing human resources, leadership in higher education; Africana studies (Graduate Certificate), including diasporas and health disparities, genocide and human rights; aging studies (Graduate Certificate), including gerontology; art research (Graduate Certificate), including museum studies; business foundations (Graduate Certificate); chemical and biomedical engineering (Graduate Certificate), including materials science and engineering, water, health and sustainability; child and family studies (Graduate Certificate), including positive behavior support; civil and industrial engineering (Graduate Certificate), including transportation systems analysis; community and family health (Graduate Certificate), including maternal and child health, social marketing and public health, violence and injury: prevention and intervention, women's health; criminology (Graduate Certificate), including criminal justice administration; educational measurement and research (Graduate Certificate), including evaluation; English (Graduate Certificate), including comparative literary studies, creative writing, professional and technical communication; entrepreneurship (Graduate Certificate); environmental health (Graduate Certificate), including safety management; epidemiology and biostatistics (Graduate Certificate), including applied biostatistics, biostatistics, concepts and tools of epidemiology, epidemiology, epidemiology of infectious diseases; geography, environment and planning (Graduate Certificate), including community development, environmental policy and management, geographical information systems; geology (Graduate Certificate), including hydrogeology; global health (Graduate Certificate), including disaster management, global health and Latin American and Caribbean studies, global health practice, humanitarian assistance, infection control; government and international affairs (Graduate Certificate), including Cuban studies, globalization studies; health policy and management (Graduate Certificate), including health management and leadership, public health policy and programs; hearing specialist: early intervention (Graduate Certificate); industrial and management systems engineering (Graduate Certificate), including systems engineering, technology management; information studies (Graduate Certificate), including school library media specialist; information systems/decision sciences (Graduate Certificate), including analytics and business intelligence; instructional technology (Graduate Certificate), including distance education, Florida digital/virtual educator, instructional design, multimedia design, Web design; internal medicine, bioethics and medical humanities (Graduate Certificate), including biomedical ethics; Latin American and Caribbean studies (Graduate Certificate); mass communications (Graduate Certificate), including multimedia journalism; mathematics and statistics (Graduate Certificate), including mathematics; medicine (Graduate Certificate), including aging and neuroscience, bioinformatics, biotechnology, brain fitness and memory management, clinical investigation, health informatics, health sciences, integrative weight management, intellectual property, medicine and gender, metabolic and nutritional medicine, metabolic cardiology, pharmacy sciences; national and competitive intelligence (Graduate Certificate); psychological and social foundations (Graduate Certificate), including career counseling, college teaching, diversity in education, mental health counseling, school counseling; public affairs (Graduate Certificate), including nonprofit management, public management, research administration; public health (Graduate Certificate), including environmental health, health equity, public health generalist, translational research in adolescent behavioral health; public health practices (Graduate Certificate), including planning for healthy communities; rehabilitation and mental health counseling (Graduate Certificate), including integrative mental health care, marriage and family therapy, rehabilitation technology; secondary education (Graduate Certificate), including ESOL, foreign language education: culture and content, foreign language education: professional; social work (Graduate Certificate), including geriatric social work/clinical gerontology; special education (Graduate Certificate), including autism spectrum disorder, disabilities education: severe/profound; world languages (Graduate Certificate), including teaching English as a second language (TESL) or foreign language. *Unit head:* Kathy Barnes, Interdisciplinary Programs Coordinator, 813-974-8031, Fax: 813-974-7061, E-mail: barnesk@usf.edu. *Application contact:* Karen Tylinski, Metro Initiatives, 813-974-9943, Fax: 813-974-7061, E-mail: ktylinsk@usf.edu.

Website: http://www.usf.edu/innovative-education/

The University of Tennessee, Graduate School, College of Arts and Sciences, Department of Mathematics, Knoxville, TN 37996. Offers applied mathematics (MS); mathematical ecology (PhD); mathematics (M Math, MS, PhD). *Program availability:* Part-time. *Degree requirements:* For master's, thesis or alternative; for doctorate, one foreign language, thesis/dissertation. *Entrance requirements:* For master's and doctorate, minimum GPA of 2.7. Additional exam requirements/recommendations for international students: Required—TOEFL. Electronic applications accepted.

The University of Tennessee at Chattanooga, Program in Mathematics, Chattanooga, TN 37403-2598. Offers applied mathematics (MS); applied statistics (MS); mathematics (MS); mathematics education (MS); preprofessional (MS). *Program availability:* Part-time. *Faculty:* 8 full-time (1 woman). *Students:* 14 full-time (4 women), 3 part-time (2 women); includes 4 minority (1 Asian, non-Hispanic/Latino; 2 Hispanic/Latino; 1 Two or more races, non-Hispanic/Latino), 1 international. Average age 27. In 2015, 7 master's awarded. *Entrance requirements:* For master's, two letters of recommendation. Additional exam requirements/recommendations for international students: Required—TOEFL (minimum score 61 iBT), IELTS (minimum score 5.5). *Application deadline:* For fall admission, 6/13 for domestic students, 6/1 for international students; for spring admission, 10/15 for domestic students, 10/1 for international students. Applications are processed on a rolling basis. Application fee: $30 ($35 for international students). Electronic applications accepted. *Expenses:* Tuition, state resident: full-time $7938; part-time $441 per credit hour. Tuition, nonresident: full-time $24,056; part-time $1336 per credit hour. *Required fees:* $1732; $253 per credit hour. *Financial support:* Research assistantships available. Financial award applicants required to submit FAFSA. *Unit head:* Dr. Francesco Barioli, Graduate Program Coordinator, 423-425-2198, E-mail: francesco-barioli@utc.edu. *Application contact:* Dr. J. Randy Walker, Interim Dean of Graduate Studies, 423-425-4478, Fax: 423-425-5223, E-mail: randy-walker@utc.edu.

Website: http://www.utc.edu/Academic/Mathematics/

The University of Texas at Arlington, Graduate School, College of Engineering, Department of Computer Science and Engineering, Arlington, TX 76019. Offers computer engineering (MS, PhD); computer science (MS, PhD); mathematical sciences, computer science (PhD); software engineering (MS). *Program availability:* Part-time, online learning. Terminal master's awarded for partial completion of doctoral program. *Degree requirements:* For master's, comprehensive exam (for some programs), thesis; for doctorate, comprehensive exam, thesis/dissertation. *Entrance requirements:* For master's, GRE General Test, minimum GPA of 3.0 (3.2 in computer science-related classes); for doctorate, GRE General Test, minimum GPA of 3.5. Additional exam requirements/recommendations for international students: Required—TOEFL (minimum score 550 paper-based; 92 iBT), IELTS (minimum score 6.5). *Faculty research:* Algorithms, homeland security, mobile pervasive computing, high performance computing bioinformation.

The University of Texas at Arlington, Graduate School, College of Science, Department of Mathematics, Arlington, TX 76019. Offers applied math (MS); mathematics (PhD); mathematics education (MA). *Program availability:* Part-time, evening/weekend. *Degree requirements:* For master's, comprehensive exam, thesis or alternative; for doctorate, comprehensive exam, thesis/dissertation, preliminary examinations. *Entrance requirements:* For master's, GRE General Test (minimum score 350 verbal, 650 quantitative); for doctorate, GRE General Test (minimum score 350 verbal, 700 quantitative), 30 hours of graduate course work in mathematics, minimum GPA of 3.0 in last 60 hours of course work. Additional exam requirements/recommendations for international students: Required—TOEFL (minimum score 550 paper-based; 79 iBT). Electronic applications accepted. *Faculty research:* Algebra, combinatorics and geometry, applied mathematics and mathematical biology, computational mathematics, mathematics education, probability and statistics.

The University of Texas at Austin, Graduate School, College of Natural Sciences, Department of Mathematics, Austin, TX 78712-1111. Offers MA, PhD. *Entrance requirements:* For master's and doctorate, GRE General Test. Electronic applications accepted.

The University of Texas at Dallas, School of Natural Sciences and Mathematics, Department of Mathematical Sciences, Richardson, TX 75080. Offers actuarial science (MS); mathematics (MS); mathematics (MS, PhD), including applied mathematics, engineering mathematics (MS); statistics (MS, PhD). *Program availability:* Part-time, evening/weekend. *Faculty:* 31 full-time (6 women), 1 part-time/adjunct (0 women). *Students:* 133 full-time (57 women), 26 part-time (9 women); includes 33 minority (6 Black or African American, non-Hispanic/Latino; 17 Asian, non-Hispanic/Latino; 8 Hispanic/Latino; 2 Two or more races, non-Hispanic/Latino), 94 international. Average age 30. 204 applicants, 51% accepted, 58 enrolled. In 2015, 13 master's, 6 doctorates awarded. *Median time to degree:* Of those who began their doctoral program in fall 2007, 44% received their degree in 8 years or less. *Degree requirements:* For master's, thesis optional; for doctorate, thesis/dissertation. *Entrance requirements:* For master's, GRE General Test, minimum GPA of 3.0 in upper-level course work in field; for doctorate, GRE General Test, minimum GPA of 3.5 in upper-level course work in field. Additional exam requirements/recommendations for international students: Required—TOEFL (minimum score 550 paper-based). *Application deadline:* For fall admission, 7/15 for domestic students, 5/1 priority date for international students; for spring admission, 11/15 for domestic students, 9/1 priority date for international students.

Applications are processed on a rolling basis. Application fee: $50 ($100 for international students). Electronic applications accepted. *Expenses:* Tuition, state resident: full-time $11,940; part-time $663 per semester hour. Tuition, nonresident: full-time $22,786; part-time $1266 per semester hour. Tuition and fees vary according to course load. *Financial support:* In 2015–16, 108 students received support, including 8 research assistantships (averaging $23,025 per year), 64 teaching assistantships with partial tuition reimbursements available (averaging $17,283 per year); career-related internships or fieldwork, Federal Work-Study, institutionally sponsored loans, scholarships/grants, and unspecified assistantships also available. Support available to part-time students. Financial award application deadline: 4/30; financial award applicants required to submit FAFSA. *Faculty research:* Sequential analysis, applications in semiconductor manufacturing, medical image analysis, computational anatomy, information theory, probability theory. *Unit head:* Dr. Vladimir Dragovic, Department Head, 972-883-2161, Fax: 972-883-6622, E-mail: utdmath@utdallas.edu. *Application contact:* Olivia Dao, Graduate Support Assistant, 972-883-2163, Fax: 972-883-6622, E-mail: utdmath@utdallas.edu.
Website: http://www.utdallas.edu/math

The University of Texas at El Paso, Graduate School, College of Science, Department of Mathematical Sciences, El Paso, TX 79968-0001. Offers mathematical sciences (MS); mathematics (teaching) (MAT); statistics (MS). *Program availability:* Part-time, evening/weekend. *Degree requirements:* For master's, thesis optional. *Entrance requirements:* For master's, minimum GPA of 3.0, letters of recommendation. Additional exam requirements/recommendations for international students: Required—TOEFL; Recommended—IELTS. Electronic applications accepted.

The University of Texas at San Antonio, College of Sciences, Department of Mathematics, San Antonio, TX 78249-0617. Offers applied mathematics (MS), including industrial mathematics; mathematics (MS); mathematics education (MS). *Program availability:* Part-time, evening/weekend. *Faculty:* 11 full-time (2 women). *Students:* 14 full-time (5 women), 25 part-time (13 women); includes 26 minority (3 Black or African American, non-Hispanic/Latino; 6 Asian, non-Hispanic/Latino; 16 Hispanic/Latino; 1 Two or more races, non-Hispanic/Latino), 1 international. Average age 31. 13 applicants, 77% accepted, 7 enrolled. In 2015, 21 master's awarded. *Degree requirements:* For master's, comprehensive exam (for some programs), thesis or alternative. *Entrance requirements:* For master's, GRE General Test, minimum GPA of 3.0 in last 60 hours. Additional exam requirements/recommendations for international students: Required—TOEFL (minimum score 550 paper-based; 79 iBT), IELTS (minimum score 6.5). *Application deadline:* For fall admission, 7/1 for domestic students, 4/1 for international students; for spring admission, 11/1 for domestic students, 9/1 for international students. Applications are processed on a rolling basis. Application fee: $45 ($80 for international students). Electronic applications accepted. *Financial support:* Applicants required to submit FAFSA. *Faculty research:* Differential equations, functional analysis, numerical analysis, number theory, logic. *Unit head:* Dr. F. Alexander Norman, Department Chair, 210-458-7254, Fax: 210-458-4439, E-mail: sandy.norman@utsa.edu. *Application contact:* Monica Rodriguez, Director of Graduate Admissions, 210-458-4331, Fax: 210-458-4332, E-mail: graduatestudies@utsa.edu.
Website: http://math.utsa.edu/

The University of Texas at Tyler, College of Arts and Sciences, Department of Mathematics, Tyler, TX 75799-0001. Offers MS, MSIS. *Degree requirements:* For master's, comprehensive exam, thesis optional. *Entrance requirements:* For master's, GRE General Test. Additional exam requirements/recommendations for international students: Required—TOEFL. *Faculty research:* Discrete geometry, knot theory, commutative algebra, noncommutative rings, group theory, mathematical biology, mathematical physics.

The University of Texas Rio Grande Valley, College of Sciences, School of Mathematical and Statistical Science, Edinburg, TX 78539. Offers mathematical sciences (MS); mathematics (MS). *Program availability:* Part-time, evening/weekend, online learning. *Faculty:* 16 full-time (1 woman). *Students:* 27 full-time (10 women), 36 part-time (17 women); includes 37 minority (1 Black or African American, non-Hispanic/Latino; 5 Asian, non-Hispanic/Latino; 31 Hispanic/Latino), 9 international. Average age 33. 23 applicants, 96% accepted, 17 enrolled. *Entrance requirements:* For master's, GRE General Test, bachelor's degree in mathematics or related field with minimum of 12 hours of upper-division mathematics or statistics course work and minimum GPA of 3.0; official transcripts from each institution attended. Additional exam requirements/recommendations for international students: Required—TOEFL (minimum score 550 paper-based, 61 iBT) or IELTS (6.5). *Application deadline:* Applications are processed on a rolling basis. Application fee: $50 ($100 for international students). Electronic applications accepted. Tuition and fees vary according to course load and program. *Financial support:* Teaching assistantships, institutionally sponsored loans, and unspecified assistantships available. *Faculty research:* Differential equations, group theory, functional analysis, analytic number theory, combinatorics and discrete geometry. *Unit head:* Dr. Cristina Villalobos, E-mail: cristina.villalobos@utrgv.edu. *Application contact:* Dr. Tim Huber, Graduate Program Coordinator, 956-665-2173, E-mail: timothy.huber@utrgv.edu.
Website: http://portal.utpa.edu/utpa_main/daa_home/cosm_home/math_home

University of the Incarnate Word, School of Graduate Studies and Research, School of Mathematics, Science, and Engineering, Program in Mathematics, San Antonio, TX 78209-6397. Offers mathematics teaching (MA); research statistics (MS). *Program availability:* Part-time, evening/weekend. *Faculty:* 8 full-time (4 women), 1 (woman) part-time/adjunct. *Students:* 3 full-time (all women), 1 (woman) part-time; includes 1 minority (Hispanic/Latino), 3 international. Average age 28. 2 applicants, 50% accepted, 1 enrolled. In 2015, 10 master's awarded. *Degree requirements:* For master's, capstone or prerequisite knowledge (for research statistics). *Entrance requirements:* For master's, GRE (minimum score 800 verbal and quantitative), 18 hours of undergraduate mathematics with minimum GPA of 3.0, letter of recommendation by a professional in the field, writing sample, teaching experience at the precollege level. Additional exam requirements/recommendations for international students: Required—TOEFL (minimum score 560 paper-based; 83 iBT). *Application deadline:* Applications are processed on a rolling basis. Application fee: $20. Electronic applications accepted. *Expenses: Tuition, area resident:* Part-time $885 per credit hour. *Required fees:* $40 per credit hour. Tuition and fees vary according to course load, degree level, campus/location, program and student level. *Financial support:* Federal Work-Study, scholarships/grants, tuition waivers (partial), and unspecified assistantships available. Financial award applicants required to submit FAFSA. *Faculty research:* Scholarship and career development for undergraduate mathematics majors. *Total annual research expenditures:* $140,844. *Unit head:* Dr. Zhanbo Yang, Mathematics Graduate Program Coordinator, 210-283-5008, Fax: 210-829-3153, E-mail: yang@uiwtx.edu. *Application contact:* Johnny Garcia, Assistant Director of Graduate Admissions, 210-805-3554, Fax: 210-829-3921, E-mail: jsgarcia@uiwtx.edu.
Website: http://www.uiw.edu/math/mathprogramsgrad.html

The University of Toledo, College of Graduate Studies, College of Natural Sciences and Mathematics, Department of Mathematics, Toledo, OH 43606-3390. Offers applied mathematics (MS, PhD); statistics (MS, PhD). *Program availability:* Part-time. *Degree requirements:* For master's, comprehensive exam (for some programs), thesis (for some programs); for doctorate, 2 foreign languages, thesis/dissertation. *Entrance requirements:* For master's and doctorate, GRE General Test, GRE Subject Test, minimum cumulative point-hour ratio of 2.7 for all previous academic work, three letters of recommendation, statement of purpose, transcripts from all prior institutions attended. Additional exam requirements/recommendations for international students: Required—TOEFL (minimum score 550 paper-based; 80 iBT). Electronic applications accepted.

University of Toronto, School of Graduate Studies, Faculty of Arts and Science, Department of Mathematics, Toronto, ON M5S 1A1, Canada. Offers mathematical finance (MMF); mathematics (M Sc, PhD). *Program availability:* Part-time. *Degree requirements:* For master's, thesis optional, research project; for doctorate, thesis/dissertation. *Entrance requirements:* For master's, minimum B average in final year, bachelor's degree in mathematics or a related area, 3 letters of reference; for doctorate, master's degree in mathematics or a related area, minimum A- average, 3 letters of reference. Additional exam requirements/recommendations for international students: Required—TOEFL (minimum score 580 paper-based; 93 iBT), TWE (minimum score 4). Electronic applications accepted.

The University of Tulsa, Graduate School, College of Engineering and Natural Sciences, Department of Mathematics, Tulsa, OK 74104-3189. Offers MS, MTA, PhD, MSF/MSAM. *Program availability:* Part-time. *Faculty:* 12 full-time (1 woman). *Students:* 13 full-time (7 women), 2 part-time (1 woman); includes 5 minority (1 Asian, non-Hispanic/Latino; 2 Hispanic/Latino; 1 Native Hawaiian or other Pacific Islander, non-Hispanic/Latino; 1 Two or more races, non-Hispanic/Latino), 3 international. Average age 28. 12 applicants, 42% accepted, 3 enrolled. In 2015, 2 master's awarded. Terminal master's awarded for partial completion of doctoral program. *Degree requirements:* For master's, thesis (for some programs). *Entrance requirements:* For master's, GRE General Test. Additional exam requirements/recommendations for international students: Required—TOEFL (minimum score 550 paper-based; 80 iBT), IELTS (minimum score 6). *Application deadline:* Applications are processed on a rolling basis. Application fee: $55. Electronic applications accepted. *Expenses: Tuition, area resident:* Full-time $22,230; part-time $1176 per credit hour. *Required fees:* $590 per semester. Tuition and fees vary according to course load. *Financial support:* In 2015–16, 5 students received support, including 1 fellowship with full tuition reimbursement available (averaging $1,250 per year), 1 research assistantship with full tuition reimbursement available (averaging $4,606 per year), 5 teaching assistantships with full tuition reimbursements available (averaging $13,444 per year); career-related internships or fieldwork, Federal Work-Study, scholarships/grants, health care benefits, tuition waivers (full and partial), and unspecified assistantships also available. Support available to part-time students. Financial award application deadline: 2/1; financial award applicants required to submit FAFSA. *Faculty research:* Optimization theory, numerical analysis, mathematical physics, modeling, Bayesian statistical inference. *Total annual research expenditures:* $48,922. *Unit head:* Dr. Bill Coberly, Department Chair, 918-631-3119, Fax: 918-631-3077, E-mail: coberly@utulsa.edu. *Application contact:* Dr. Dale Doty, Advisor, 918-631-2983, Fax: 918-631-3077, E-mail: dale-doty@utulsa.edu.
Website: http://engineering.utulsa.edu/academics/mathematics/

The University of Tulsa, Graduate School, Kendall College of Arts and Sciences, School of Urban Education, Program in Teaching Arts, Tulsa, OK 74104-3189. Offers art (MTA); biology (MTA); English (MTA); history (MTA); mathematics (MTA). *Program availability:* Part-time. *Students:* 1 (woman) full-time. Average age 25. In 2015, 1 master's awarded. *Entrance requirements:* For master's, GRE General Test. Additional exam requirements/recommendations for international students: Required—TOEFL (minimum score 577 paper-based), IELTS (minimum score 6.5). *Application deadline:* Applications are processed on a rolling basis. Application fee: $55. Electronic applications accepted. *Expenses: Tuition, area resident:* Full-time $22,230; part-time $1176 per credit hour. *Required fees:* $590 per semester. Tuition and fees vary according to course load. *Financial support:* In 2015–16, 2 students received support, including 1 teaching assistantship with full tuition reimbursement available (averaging $13,410 per year); fellowships with tuition reimbursements available, research assistantships with tuition reimbursements available, career-related internships or fieldwork, Federal Work-Study, scholarships/grants, health care benefits, tuition waivers (full and partial), and unspecified assistantships also available. Support available to part-time students. Financial award application deadline: 2/1; financial award applicants required to submit FAFSA. *Unit head:* Dr. Sharon Baker, Chair, 918-631-2238, Fax: 918-631-3721, E-mail: sharon-baker@utulsa.edu. *Application contact:* Dr. David Brown, Advisor, 918-631-2719, Fax: 918-631-2133, E-mail: david-brown@utulsa.edu.

University of Utah, Graduate School, College of Science, Department of Mathematics, Salt Lake City, UT 84112-0090. Offers mathematics (MA, MS, PhD); mathematics teaching (MS); statistics (M Stat). *Program availability:* Part-time. *Faculty:* 41 full-time (4 women), 37 part-time/adjunct (9 women). *Students:* 110 full-time (36 women), 28 part-time (12 women); includes 8 minority (5 Asian, non-Hispanic/Latino; 2 Hispanic/Latino; 1 Two or more races, non-Hispanic/Latino), 44 international. Average age 27. 195 applicants, 32% accepted, 27 enrolled. In 2015, 39 master's, 12 doctorates awarded. *Degree requirements:* For master's, comprehensive exam, thesis or alternative, written or oral exam; for doctorate, comprehensive exam, thesis/dissertation, written and oral exams. *Entrance requirements:* For master's and doctorate, GRE Subject Test in math (recommended), minimum undergraduate GPA of 3.0. Additional exam requirements/recommendations for international students: Required—TOEFL (minimum score 550 paper-based; 80 iBT), GRE (recommended). *Application deadline:* For fall admission, 3/15 for domestic and international students; for spring admission, 11/1 for domestic and international students; for summer admission, 3/15 for domestic and international students. Application fee: $55 ($65 for international students). Electronic applications accepted. *Expenses:* 17,000 per year. *Financial support:* In 2015–16, 118 students received support, including 1 fellowship (averaging $34,000 per year), 29 research assistantships with full tuition reimbursements available (averaging $19,350 per year), 81 teaching assistantships with full tuition reimbursements available (averaging $17,000 per year); health care benefits and unspecified assistantships also available. Financial award application deadline: 1/1; financial award applicants required to submit FAFSA. *Faculty research:* Algebraic geometry, geometry and topology materials and microstructure, mathematical biology, probability and statistics. *Total annual research expenditures:* $3.4 million. *Unit head:* Dr. Peter Trapa, Chairman, 801-581-6851, Fax: 801-581-4148, E-mail: ptrapa@math.utah.edu. *Application contact:* Dr. Karl Schwede, Director of Graduate Studies, 801-581-7916, Fax: 801-581-6841, E-mail: schwede@math.utah.edu.
Website: http://www.math.utah.edu/

University of Utah, Graduate School, Interdepartmental Program in Statistics, Salt Lake City, UT 84112-1107. Offers biostatistics (M Stat); econometrics (M Stat); educational psychology (M Stat); mathematics (M Stat); sociology (M Stat). *Program availability:* Part-time. *Students:* 61 full-time (34 women), 45 part-time (13 women); includes 18 minority (3 Black or African American, non-Hispanic/Latino; 10 Asian, non-Hispanic/Latino; 3 Hispanic/Latino; 2 Two or more races, non-Hispanic/Latino), 30

international. Average age 32. 50 applicants, 70% accepted, 27 enrolled. In 2015, 18 master's awarded. *Degree requirements:* For master's, comprehensive exam (for some programs), projects. *Entrance requirements:* For master's, GRE General Test (for all but biostatistics); GRE Subject Test (for mathematics), minimum GPA of 3.0; course work in calculus, matrix theory, statistics. Additional exam requirements/recommendations for international students: Required—TOEFL (minimum score 500 paper-based; 61 iBT). *Application deadline:* For fall admission, 7/1 for domestic students, 4/1 for international students. Applications are processed on a rolling basis. Application fee: $55 ($65 for international students). Electronic applications accepted. *Financial support:* In 2015–16, 10 students received support, including 10 research assistantships with tuition reimbursements available (averaging $1,000 per year); career-related internships or fieldwork, scholarships/grants, and unspecified assistantships also available. *Faculty research:* Biostatistics, sociology, economics, educational psychology, mathematics. *Unit head:* Xiaoming Sheng, Chair, University Statistics Committee, 801-213-3729, E-mail: xiaoming.sheng@utah.edu. *Application contact:* Laura Egbert, Coordinator, 801-585-6853, E-mail: laura.egbert@utah.edu.
Website: http://www.mstat.utah.edu

University of Vermont, Graduate College, College of Engineering and Mathematics, Department of Mathematics and Statistics, Program in Mathematics, Burlington, VT 05405. Offers mathematics (MS, PhD); mathematics education (MST). *Degree requirements:* For doctorate, thesis/dissertation. *Entrance requirements:* For master's and doctorate, GRE General Test. Additional exam requirements/recommendations for international students: Required—TOEFL (minimum score 550 paper-based; 80 iBT). Electronic applications accepted.

University of Victoria, Faculty of Graduate Studies, Faculty of Science, Department of Mathematics and Statistics, Victoria, BC V8W 2Y2, Canada. Offers M Sc, MA, PhD. *Program availability:* Part-time. *Degree requirements:* For master's, thesis; for doctorate, one foreign language, thesis/dissertation, 3 qualifying exams, candidacy exam. *Entrance requirements:* Additional exam requirements/recommendations for international students: Required—TOEFL (minimum score 575 paper-based), IELTS (minimum score 7). Electronic applications accepted. *Faculty research:* Functional analysis and operator theory, applied ordinary and partial differential equations, discrete mathematics and graph theory.

University of Virginia, College and Graduate School of Arts and Sciences, Department of Mathematics, Charlottesville, VA 22903. Offers math education (MA); mathematics (MA, MS, PhD). *Degree requirements:* For master's, one foreign language, comprehensive exam, thesis optional; for doctorate, one foreign language, comprehensive exam, thesis/dissertation. *Entrance requirements:* For master's and doctorate, GRE General Test, GRE Subject Test, 2-3 letters of recommendation. Additional exam requirements/recommendations for international students: Required—TOEFL (minimum score 600 paper-based; 90 iBT), IELTS. Electronic applications accepted.

University of Washington, Graduate School, College of Arts and Sciences, Department of Mathematics, Seattle, WA 98195. Offers mathematics (MA, MS, PhD); numerical analysis (MS); optimization (MS). *Program availability:* Part-time. Terminal master's awarded for partial completion of doctoral program. *Degree requirements:* For master's, thesis optional; for doctorate, 2 foreign languages, thesis/dissertation. *Entrance requirements:* For master's, GRE, minimum GPA of 3.0; for doctorate, GRE General Test, GRE Subject Test (mathematics), minimum GPA of 3.0. Additional exam requirements/recommendations for international students: Required—TOEFL. Electronic applications accepted. *Faculty research:* Algebra, analysis, probability, combinatorics and geometry.

University of Washington, Graduate School, Interdisciplinary Graduate Program in Quantitative Ecology and Resource Management, Seattle, WA 98195. Offers MS, PhD. *Degree requirements:* For master's, thesis; for doctorate, thesis/dissertation. *Entrance requirements:* For master's and doctorate, GRE General Test, minimum GPA of 3.0. Additional exam requirements/recommendations for international students: Required—TOEFL. Electronic applications accepted. *Faculty research:* Population dynamics, statistical analysis, ecological modeling and systems analysis of aquatic and terrestrial ecosystems.

University of Waterloo, Graduate Studies, Faculty of Mathematics, Department of Combinatorics and Optimization, Waterloo, ON N2L 3G1, Canada. Offers M Math, PhD. *Degree requirements:* For master's, research paper or thesis; for doctorate, comprehensive exam, thesis/dissertation. *Entrance requirements:* For master's, GRE General Test, honors degree in field, minimum B+ average; for doctorate, GRE General Test, master's degree, minimum A average. Additional exam requirements/recommendations for international students: Required—TOEFL, IELTS, PTE. *Application deadline:* Applications are processed on a rolling basis. Application fee: $100 Canadian dollars. Electronic applications accepted. *Financial support:* Research assistantships, teaching assistantships, career-related internships or fieldwork, and scholarships/grants available. *Faculty research:* Algebraic and enumerative combinatorics, continuous optimization, cryptography, discrete optimization and graph theory.
Website: https://uwaterloo.ca/combinatorics-and-optimization/

University of Waterloo, Graduate Studies, Faculty of Mathematics, Department of Pure Mathematics, Waterloo, ON N2L 3G1, Canada. Offers M Math, PhD. *Program availability:* Part-time. Terminal master's awarded for partial completion of doctoral program. *Degree requirements:* For master's, thesis optional; for doctorate, comprehensive exam, thesis/dissertation. *Entrance requirements:* For master's, honors degree in field, minimum B+ average; for doctorate, master's degree, minimum B+ average. Additional exam requirements/recommendations for international students: Required—TOEFL, IELTS, PTE. *Application deadline:* Applications are processed on a rolling basis. Application fee: $100 Canadian dollars. Electronic applications accepted. *Financial support:* In 2015–16, 4 teaching assistantships were awarded; research assistantships, scholarships/grants, and unspecified assistantships also available. *Faculty research:* Algebra, algebraic and differential geometry, functional and harmonic analysis, logic and universal algebra, number theory.
Website: https://uwaterloo.ca/pure-mathematics/

The University of Western Ontario, Faculty of Graduate Studies, Physical Sciences Division, Department of Mathematics, London, ON N6A 5B8, Canada. Offers M Sc, PhD. Terminal master's awarded for partial completion of doctoral program. *Degree requirements:* For master's, thesis or alternative; for doctorate, one foreign language, comprehensive exam, thesis/dissertation, qualifying exam. *Entrance requirements:* For master's, minimum B average, honors degree; for doctorate, master's degree. Additional exam requirements/recommendations for international students: Required—TOEFL (minimum score 550 paper-based). *Faculty research:* Algebra and number theory, analysis, geometry and topology.

University of West Florida, College of Science and Engineering, Department of Mathematics and Statistics, Pensacola, FL 32514-5750. Offers applied statistics (MS); mathematical sciences (MS). *Program availability:* Part-time, evening/weekend. *Degree requirements:* For master's, thesis optional. *Entrance requirements:* For master's, GRE (minimum score: verbal 420; quantitative 580), minimum GPA of 3.0; official transcripts. Additional exam requirements/recommendations for international students: Required—TOEFL (minimum score 550 paper-based).

University of West Georgia, College of Science and Mathematics, Carrollton, GA 30118. Offers biology (MS); computer science (MS); geographic information systems (Postbaccalaureate Certificate); mathematics (MS). *Program availability:* Part-time, evening/weekend, 100% online. *Faculty:* 54 full-time (19 women). *Students:* 20 full-time (8 women), 69 part-time (18 women); includes 15 minority (10 Black or African American, non-Hispanic/Latino; 2 Asian, non-Hispanic/Latino; 1 Hispanic/Latino; 1 Native Hawaiian or other Pacific Islander, non-Hispanic/Latino; 1 Two or more races, non-Hispanic/Latino), 9 international. Average age 35. 75 applicants, 88% accepted, 53 enrolled. In 2015, 21 master's, 4 other advanced degrees awarded. *Entrance requirements:* Additional exam requirements/recommendations for international students: Required—TOEFL (minimum score 523 paper-based; 69 iBT); Recommended—IELTS (minimum score 6.5). *Application deadline:* For fall admission, 6/1 for domestic and international students; for spring admission, 11/15 for domestic students, 10/15 for international students; for summer admission, 4/1 for domestic students, 3/30 for international students. Applications are processed on a rolling basis. Application fee: $40. Electronic applications accepted. *Expenses:* Contact institution. *Financial support:* Fellowships, research assistantships, teaching assistantships, career-related internships or fieldwork, Federal Work-Study, institutionally sponsored loans, scholarships/grants, and unspecified assistantships available. Support available to part-time students. Financial award application deadline: 4/1; financial award applicants required to submit FAFSA. *Unit head:* Dr. Scott Gordon, Interim Dean, 678-839-5190, Fax: 678-839-5191, E-mail: sgordon@westga.edu. *Application contact:* Dr. Toby Ziglar, Director of Graduate Studies and International Admissions, 678-839-1394, Fax: 678-839-1395, E-mail: graduate@westga.edu.
Website: http://www.westga.edu/cosm

University of Windsor, Faculty of Graduate Studies, Faculty of Science, Department of Mathematics and Statistics, Windsor, ON N9B 3P4, Canada. Offers mathematics (M Sc); statistics (M Sc, PhD). *Degree requirements:* For master's, thesis or alternative; for doctorate, comprehensive exam, thesis/dissertation. *Entrance requirements:* For master's, minimum B average; for doctorate, minimum A average. Additional exam requirements/recommendations for international students: Required—TOEFL (minimum score 560 paper-based). Electronic applications accepted. *Faculty research:* Applied mathematics, operational research, fluid dynamics.

University of Wisconsin–Madison, Graduate School, College of Letters and Science, Department of Mathematics, Madison, WI 53706. Offers PhD. *Degree requirements:* For doctorate, comprehensive exam, thesis/dissertation, classes in a minor field; minimum GPA of 3.3. *Entrance requirements:* For doctorate, GRE General Test, GRE Subject Test (math). Additional exam requirements/recommendations for international students: Required—TOEFL (minimum score 580 paper-based; 92 iBT), IELTS. Electronic applications accepted. *Expenses:* Tuition, state resident: full-time $5364. Tuition, nonresident: full-time $12,027. *Required fees:* $571. Tuition and fees vary according to campus/location, program and reciprocity agreements. *Faculty research:* Analysis, applied/computational mathematics, geometry/topology, logic, algebra/number theory, probability.

University of Wisconsin–Milwaukee, Graduate School, College of Letters and Science, Department of Mathematical Sciences, Milwaukee, WI 53201-0413. Offers mathematics (MS, PhD). *Faculty:* 32 full-time (3 women), 2 part-time/adjunct (1 woman). *Students:* 77 full-time (20 women), 12 part-time (1 woman); includes 5 minority (1 Black or African American, non-Hispanic/Latino; 2 Asian, non-Hispanic/Latino; 2 Two or more races, non-Hispanic/Latino), 40 international. Average age 29. 144 applicants, 30% accepted, 27 enrolled. In 2015, 14 master's, 12 doctorates awarded. *Degree requirements:* For master's, comprehensive exam, thesis optional; for doctorate, 2 foreign languages, thesis/dissertation. *Entrance requirements:* Additional exam requirements/recommendations for international students: Required—TOEFL (minimum score 550 paper-based; 79 iBT), IELTS (minimum score 6.5). *Application deadline:* For fall admission, 1/1 priority date for domestic students; for spring admission, 9/1 for domestic students. Applications are processed on a rolling basis. Application fee: $56 ($96 for international students). Electronic applications accepted. *Financial support:* In 2015–16, 23 fellowships, 9 research assistantships, 56 teaching assistantships were awarded; career-related internships or fieldwork, health care benefits, and unspecified assistantships also available. Support available to part-time students. Financial award application deadline: 4/15; financial award applicants required to submit FAFSA. *Faculty research:* Algebra, applied mathematics, atmospheric science, probability and statistics, topology. *Unit head:* Richard Stockbridge, Department Chair, 414-229-4568, E-mail: stockbri@uwm.edu. *Application contact:* General Information Contact, 414-229-4982, Fax: 414-229-6967, E-mail: gradschool@uwm.edu.
Website: http://www.uwm.edu/dept/math/

University of Wyoming, College of Arts and Sciences, Department of Mathematics, Laramie, WY 82071. Offers mathematics (MA, MAT, MS, MST, PhD); mathematics/computer science (PhD). *Program availability:* Part-time. Terminal master's awarded for partial completion of doctoral program. *Degree requirements:* For master's, comprehensive exam, thesis, qualifying exam; for doctorate, comprehensive exam, thesis/dissertation, preliminary exam. *Entrance requirements:* For master's and doctorate, GRE General Test, minimum GPA of 3.0. Additional exam requirements/recommendations for international students: Required—TOEFL (minimum score 540 paper-based; 76 iBT). *Faculty research:* Numerical analysis, classical analysis, mathematical modeling, algebraic combinations.

Utah State University, School of Graduate Studies, College of Science, Department of Mathematics and Statistics, Logan, UT 84322. Offers industrial mathematics (MS); mathematical sciences (PhD); mathematics (M Math, MS); statistics (MS). *Program availability:* Part-time. Terminal master's awarded for partial completion of doctoral program. *Degree requirements:* For master's, thesis optional, qualifying exam; for doctorate, one foreign language, comprehensive exam, thesis/dissertation. *Entrance requirements:* For master's and doctorate, GRE General Test, minimum GPA of 3.0. Additional exam requirements/recommendations for international students: Required—TOEFL. *Faculty research:* Differential equations, computational mathematics, dynamical systems, probability and statistics, pure mathematics.

Vanderbilt University, Department of Mathematics, Nashville, TN 37240-1001. Offers MA, MAT, MS, PhD. *Faculty:* 31 full-time (1 woman). *Students:* 32 full-time (1 woman); includes 2 minority (1 Black or African American, non-Hispanic/Latino; 1 Asian, non-Hispanic/Latino), 21 international. Average age 25. 93 applicants, 30% accepted, 4 enrolled. In 2015, 11 master's, 5 doctorates awarded. *Degree requirements:* For master's, one foreign language, thesis or alternative; for doctorate, one foreign language, comprehensive exam, thesis/dissertation. *Entrance requirements:* For master's and doctorate, GRE General Test, GRE Subject Test. Additional exam

requirements/recommendations for international students: Required—TOEFL (minimum score 570 paper-based; 88 iBT). *Application deadline:* For fall admission, 1/15 for domestic and international students. Application fee: $0. Electronic applications accepted. *Financial support:* Fellowships with tuition reimbursements, research assistantships with full tuition reimbursements, teaching assistantships with full tuition reimbursements, Federal Work-Study, institutionally sponsored loans, scholarships/ grants, and health care benefits available. Financial award application deadline: 1/15; financial award applicants required to submit CSS PROFILE or FAFSA. *Faculty research:* Algebra, topology, applied mathematics, graph theory, analytical mathematics. *Unit head:* Dr. Denis Osin, Director of Graduate Studies, 615-322-6672, Fax: 615-343-0215, E-mail: denis.v.osin@vanderbilt.edu. *Application contact:* Laura Rongione, Office Assistant, 615-322-6672, Fax: 315-343-0215, E-mail: laura.rongione@vanderbilt.edu.
Website: http://www.vanderbilt.edu/math/

Villanova University, Graduate School of Liberal Arts and Sciences, Department of Mathematical Sciences, Program in Mathematical Sciences, Villanova, PA 19085-1699. Offers MA. *Program availability:* Part-time, evening/weekend. *Students:* 14 full-time (7 women), 14 part-time (8 women); includes 1 minority (Asian, non-Hispanic/Latino), 1 international. Average age 34. 9 applicants, 67% accepted, 4 enrolled. In 2015, 16 master's awarded. *Degree requirements:* For master's, comprehensive exam. *Entrance requirements:* For master's, GRE, minimum GPA of 3.0, 3 letters of recommendation. Additional exam requirements/recommendations for international students: Required—TOEFL. *Application deadline:* For fall admission, 5/1 priority date for international students; for spring admission, 10/15 priority date for international students. Applications are processed on a rolling basis. Application fee: $50. Electronic applications accepted. *Financial support:* Research assistantships, scholarships/grants, and unspecified assistantships available. Financial award applicants required to submit FAFSA. *Unit head:* Dr. David Sprows, Chair, 610-519-4850.
Website: http://www.villanova.edu/artsci/mathematics/graduate/mamath.htm

Virginia Commonwealth University, Graduate School, College of Humanities and Sciences, Department of Mathematics and Applied Mathematics, Richmond, VA 23284-9005. Offers applied mathematics (MS); mathematics (MS). *Degree requirements:* For master's, thesis optional. *Entrance requirements:* For master's, GRE General Test, GRE Subject Test, 30 undergraduate semester credits in the mathematical sciences or closely-related fields. Additional exam requirements/recommendations for international students: Required—TOEFL (minimum score 600 paper-based; 100 iBT); Recommended—IELTS (minimum score 6.5). Electronic applications accepted. *Faculty research:* Mathematics, applied mathematics.

Virginia Polytechnic Institute and State University, Graduate School, College of Science, Blacksburg, VA 24061. Offers biological sciences (MS, PhD); biomedical technology development and management (MS); chemistry (MS, PhD); economics (MA, PhD); geosciences (MS, PhD); mathematics (MS, PhD); physics (MS, PhD); psychology (MS, PhD); statistics (MS, PhD). *Degree requirements:* For master's, comprehensive exam (for some programs), thesis (for some programs); for doctorate, comprehensive exam (for some programs), thesis/dissertation (for some programs). *Entrance requirements:* For master's and doctorate, GRE/GMAT (may vary by department). Additional exam requirements/recommendations for international students: Required—TOEFL (minimum score 550 paper-based). Electronic applications accepted.

Virginia State University, College of Graduate Studies, College of Engineering and Technology, Department of Mathematics and Computer Science, Petersburg, VA 23806-0001. Offers computer science (MS); mathematics (MS); mathematics education (MS). *Degree requirements:* For master's, thesis (for some programs).

Wake Forest University, Graduate School of Arts and Sciences, Department of Mathematics, Winston-Salem, NC 27109. Offers MA. *Program availability:* Part-time. *Degree requirements:* For master's, one foreign language, thesis optional. *Entrance requirements:* For master's, GRE General Test. Additional exam requirements/ recommendations for international students: Required—TOEFL (minimum score 79 iBT). Electronic applications accepted. *Faculty research:* Algebra, ring theory, topology, differential equations.

Washington State University, College of Arts and Sciences, Department of Mathematics, Pullman, WA 99164. Offers applied mathematics (MS, PhD); mathematics (MS, PhD); mathematics teaching (MS, PhD). Programs offered at the Pullman campus. *Program availability:* Part-time. Terminal master's awarded for partial completion of doctoral program. *Degree requirements:* For master's, comprehensive exam (for some programs), thesis or alternative, oral exam, project; for doctorate, 2 foreign languages, comprehensive exam, thesis/dissertation, oral exam, written exam. *Entrance requirements:* For master's and doctorate, minimum GPA of 3.0, 3 letters of recommendation. Additional exam requirements/recommendations for international students: Required—TOEFL (minimum score 600 paper-based; 100 iBT) or IELTS (minimum score 7). Electronic applications accepted. *Faculty research:* Computational mathematics, operations research, modeling in the natural sciences, applied statistics.

Washington University in St. Louis, Graduate School of Arts and Sciences, Department of Mathematics, St. Louis, MO 63130-4899. Offers mathematics (MA, PhD); statistics (MA, PhD). *Students:* 45 full-time (13 women); includes 2 minority (1 Black or African American, non-Hispanic/Latino; 1 Asian, non-Hispanic/Latino), 31 international. 300 applicants, 31% accepted, 24 enrolled. In 2015, 6 master's, 7 doctorates awarded. Terminal master's awarded for partial completion of doctoral program. *Degree requirements:* For master's, thesis or alternative; for doctorate, thesis/dissertation. *Entrance requirements:* For master's and doctorate, GRE General Test. Additional exam requirements/recommendations for international students: Required—TOEFL. *Application deadline:* For fall admission, 1/15 for domestic students. Application fee: $45. Electronic applications accepted. *Financial support:* Fellowships, research assistantships, teaching assistantships, and tuition waivers (full and partial) available. Financial award application deadline: 1/15. *Faculty research:* Algebra, algebraic geometry, real and complex analysis, differential geometry, topology, statistics, mathematical statistics, survival analysis, modeling, statistical computing for massive data, Bayesian regularization, bioinformatics, longitudinal and functional data analysis, statistical computation, application of statistics to medicine. *Unit head:* Dr. David Wright, Chairman, 314-935-6726. *Application contact:* Bridget Coleman, Director of Admissions, 314-935-6880, Fax: 314-935-4887.
Website: http://wumath.wustl.edu/

Wayne State University, College of Liberal Arts and Sciences, Department of Mathematics, Detroit, MI 48202. Offers applied mathematics (MA, PhD); mathematical statistics (MA, PhD); mathematics (MA, MS); pure mathematics (PhD). *Faculty:* 26. *Students:* 42 full-time (10 women), 29 part-time (10 women); includes 10 minority (3 Black or African American, non-Hispanic/Latino; 5 Asian, non-Hispanic/Latino; 2 Hispanic/Latino), 31 international. Average age 30. 94 applicants, 41% accepted, 9 enrolled. In 2015, 10 master's, 3 doctorates awarded. *Degree requirements:* For master's, thesis (for some programs), essays, oral exams; for doctorate, thesis/ dissertation, oral exams; French, German, Russian, or Chinese. *Entrance requirements:* For master's, twelve semester credits in mathematics beyond sophomore calculus; for doctorate, master's degree in mathematics or equivalent level of advancement. Additional exam requirements/recommendations for international students: Required—TOEFL (minimum score 550 paper-based; 79 iBT), TWE (minimum score 5.5), Michigan English Language Assessment Battery (minimum score 85); Recommended—IELTS (minimum score 6.5). *Application deadline:* For fall admission, 6/1 priority date for domestic students, 5/1 priority date for international students; for winter admission, 10/1 priority date for domestic students, 9/1 priority date for international students; for spring admission, 2/1 priority date for domestic students, 1/1 priority date for international students. Application fee: $0. Electronic applications accepted. *Expenses:* Tuition, state resident: full-time $14,165; part-time $590.20 per credit hour. Tuition, nonresident: full-time $30,682; part-time $1278.40 per credit hour. *Required fees:* $1688; $47.45 per credit hour. $274.60 per semester. Tuition and fees vary according to course load and program. *Financial support:* In 2015–16, 43 students received support, including 5 fellowships with tuition reimbursements available (averaging $20,135 per year), 2 research assistantships with tuition reimbursements available (averaging $18,801 per year), 25 teaching assistantships with tuition reimbursements available (averaging $18,801 per year); scholarships/grants, health care benefits, and unspecified assistantships also available. Financial award application deadline: 3/31; financial award applicants required to submit FAFSA. *Faculty research:* Harmonic analysis and partial differential equations, group theory and non-commutative ring theory, homotopy theory and applications to topology and geometry, numerical analysis, control and optimization, statistical estimation theory. *Total annual research expenditures:* $807,813. *Unit head:* Dr. Daniel Frohardt, Professor and Chair, 313-577-6163, E-mail: danf@math.wayne.edu. *Application contact:* Mary Klamo, Academic Services Officer, E-mail: gradsecretary@math.wayne.edu.
Website: http://clas.wayne.edu/math/

Wesleyan University, Graduate Studies, Department of Mathematics and Computer Science, Middletown, CT 06459. Offers computer science (MA); mathematics (MA, PhD). *Faculty:* 17 full-time (3 women), 5 part-time/adjunct (1 woman). *Students:* 20 full-time (10 women); includes 1 minority (Asian, non-Hispanic/Latino), 3 international. Average age 25. 71 applicants, 11% accepted, 5 enrolled. In 2015, 2 master's, 2 doctorates awarded. Terminal master's awarded for partial completion of doctoral program. *Degree requirements:* For master's, one foreign language, thesis; for doctorate, one foreign language, comprehensive exam, thesis/dissertation. *Entrance requirements:* For master's, GRE General Test, GRE Subject Test; for doctorate, GRE Subject Test. Additional exam requirements/recommendations for international students: Recommended—TOEFL. *Application deadline:* For fall admission, 2/15 for domestic and international students. Applications are processed on a rolling basis. Application fee: $0. Electronic applications accepted. *Financial support:* In 2015–16, 20 teaching assistantships with full tuition reimbursements (averaging $23,000 per year) were awarded; tuition waivers (full) also available. Financial award application deadline: 4/15. *Faculty research:* Topology, analysis, algebra, geometry, number theory. *Unit head:* Dr. Wai Kiu Chan, Chair, 860-685-2197, E-mail: wkchan@wesleyan.edu. *Application contact:* Caryn Canalia, Administrative Assistant, 860-685-2182, Fax: 860-685-2571, E-mail: ccanalia@wesleyan.edu.
Website: http://www.wesleyan.edu/mathcs/index.html

West Chester University of Pennsylvania, College of Arts and Sciences, Department of Mathematics, West Chester, PA 19383. Offers applied and computational mathematics (MS); applied statistics (MS, Certificate); mathematics (MA, Teaching Certificate); mathematics education (MA). *Program availability:* Part-time, evening/ weekend. *Faculty:* 10 full-time (0 women), 2 part-time/adjunct (0 women). *Students:* 11 full-time (5 women), 92 part-time (46 women); includes 19 minority (4 Black or African American, non-Hispanic/Latino; 14 Asian, non-Hispanic/Latino; 1 Hispanic/Latino), 15 international. Average age 30. 68 applicants, 97% accepted, 48 enrolled. In 2015, 34 master's awarded. *Degree requirements:* For master's, thesis (for all but MS in applied mathematics). *Entrance requirements:* For master's, GMAT or GRE General Test (for MA in mathematics), interview (for MA in mathematics); for other advanced degree, GMAT or GRE General Test (for Teaching Certificate). Additional exam requirements/ recommendations for international students: Required—TOEFL or IELTS. *Application deadline:* For fall admission, 5/15 for international students; for spring admission, 10/15 for international students. Applications are processed on a rolling basis. Application fee: $50. Electronic applications accepted. *Expenses:* Tuition, state resident: full-time $8460; part-time $470 per credit. Tuition, nonresident: full-time $12,690; part-time $705 per credit. *Required fees:* $2312; $126.75 per credit. Tuition and fees vary according to campus/location and program. *Financial support:* Scholarships/grants and unspecified assistantships available. Financial award application deadline: 2/15; financial award applicants required to submit FAFSA. *Faculty research:* Teachers teaching with technology in service training program, biostatistics, hierarchical linear models, clustered binary outcome date, mathematics biology. *Unit head:* Dr. Peter Glidden, Chair, 610-436-2440, Fax: 610-738-0578, E-mail: pglidden@wcupa.edu. *Application contact:* Dr. Gail Gallitano, Graduate Coordinator, 610-436-2452, Fax: 610-738-0578, E-mail: ggallitano@wcupa.edu.
Website: http://www.wcupa.edu/_academics/sch_cas.mat/

Western Carolina University, Graduate School, College of Arts and Sciences, Department of Mathematics and Computer Science, Cullowhee, NC 28723. Offers applied mathematics (MS). *Program availability:* Part-time, evening/weekend. *Degree requirements:* For master's, thesis or alternative. *Entrance requirements:* For master's, GRE General Test, appropriate undergraduate degree, 3 letters of recommendation. Additional exam requirements/recommendations for international students: Required—TOEFL (minimum score 550 paper-based; 79 iBT).

Western Connecticut State University, Division of Graduate Studies, Maricostas School of Arts and Sciences, Department of Mathematics, Danbury, CT 06810-6885. Offers MA. *Program availability:* Part-time. *Degree requirements:* For master's, comprehensive exam, thesis, completion of program in 6 years. *Entrance requirements:* For master's, minimum GPA of 2.5. Additional exam requirements/recommendations for international students: Recommended—TOEFL (minimum score 550 paper-based; 79 iBT), IELTS (minimum score 6). *Expenses:* Tuition, state resident: full-time $6188; part-time $343 per credit hour. Tuition, nonresident: full-time $17,240; part-time $350 per credit hour. *Required fees:* $4399; $173 per credit hour. One-time fee: $60 part-time. Tuition and fees vary according to degree level and program. *Faculty research:* Eulerian mathematical principles.

Western Illinois University, School of Graduate Studies, College of Arts and Sciences, Department of Mathematics, Macomb, IL 61455-1390. Offers applied math (Certificate); mathematics (MS). *Program availability:* Part-time. *Students:* 18 full-time (9 women), 2 part-time (both women); includes 1 minority (Asian, non-Hispanic/Latino), 12 international. Average age 29. 18 applicants, 67% accepted, 9 enrolled. In 2015, 9 master's awarded. *Degree requirements:* For master's, thesis or alternative. *Entrance requirements:* Additional exam requirements/recommendations for international students: Required—TOEFL (minimum score 500 paper-based; 61 iBT). *Application deadline:* Applications are processed on a rolling basis. Application fee: $30. Electronic applications accepted. *Financial support:* In 2015–16, 12 students received support,

including 2 teaching assistantships with full tuition reimbursements available (averaging $8,688 per year). Financial award applicants required to submit FAFSA. *Unit head:* Dr. Iraj Kalantari, Chairperson, 309-298-1054. *Application contact:* Dr. Nancy Parsons, Associate Provost and Director of Graduate Studies, 309-298-1806, Fax: 309-298-2345, E-mail: grad-office@wiu.edu.
Website: http://wiu.edu/mathematics

Western Kentucky University, Graduate Studies, Ogden College of Science and Engineering, Department of Mathematics and Computer Science, Bowling Green, KY 42101. Offers computational mathematics (MS); computer science (MS); mathematics (MA, MS). *Degree requirements:* For master's, comprehensive exam, thesis optional, written exam. *Entrance requirements:* For master's, GRE General Test, minimum GPA of 2.75. Additional exam requirements/recommendations for international students: Required—TOEFL (minimum score 555 paper-based; 79 iBT). *Faculty research:* Differential equations numerical analysis, probability statistics, algebra, typology, knot theory.

Western Michigan University, Graduate College, College of Arts and Sciences, Department of Mathematics, Kalamazoo, MI 49008. Offers applied and computational mathematics (MS); mathematics education (MA, PhD), including collegiate mathematics education (PhD). *Degree requirements:* For doctorate, one foreign language, thesis/dissertation.

Western Washington University, Graduate School, College of Sciences and Technology, Department of Mathematics, Bellingham, WA 98225-5996. Offers MS. *Program availability:* Part-time. *Degree requirements:* For master's, thesis (for some programs), project, qualifying examination. *Entrance requirements:* For master's, GRE General Test, minimum GPA of 3.0 in last 60 semester hours or last 90 quarter hours. Additional exam requirements/recommendations for international students: Required—TOEFL (minimum score 567 paper-based). Electronic applications accepted. *Faculty research:* Numerical analysis, combinatorics, harmonic analysis, inverse problems, reliability testing.

West Texas A&M University, College of Agriculture, Science and Engineering, Department of Mathematics, Physical Sciences and Engineering Technology, Program in Mathematics, Canyon, TX 79016-0001. Offers MS. *Program availability:* Part-time. *Degree requirements:* For master's, comprehensive exam, thesis optional. *Entrance requirements:* For master's, GRE General Test. Additional exam requirements/recommendations for international students: Required—TOEFL (minimum score 550 paper-based). Electronic applications accepted.

West Virginia University, Eberly College of Arts and Sciences, Department of Mathematics, Morgantown, WV 26506. Offers applied mathematics (MS, PhD); discrete mathematics (PhD); interdisciplinary mathematics (MS); mathematics for secondary education (MS); pure mathematics (MS). *Program availability:* Part-time. Terminal master's awarded for partial completion of doctoral program. *Degree requirements:* For master's, comprehensive exam (for some programs), thesis optional; for doctorate, one foreign language, comprehensive exam, thesis/dissertation. *Entrance requirements:* For master's, GRE Subject Test (recommended), minimum GPA of 2.5; for doctorate, GRE Subject Test (recommended), master's degree in mathematics. Additional exam requirements/recommendations for international students: Required—TOEFL (paper-based 550) or IELTS (6). *Expenses:* Tuition, state resident: full-time $8568. Tuition, nonresident: full-time $22,140. Tuition and fees vary according to program. *Faculty research:* Combinatorics and graph theory, differential equations, applied and computational mathematics.

Wichita State University, Graduate School, Fairmount College of Liberal Arts and Sciences, Department of Mathematics, Statistics and Physics, Wichita, KS 67260. Offers applied mathematics (PhD); mathematics (MS); physics (MS). *Program availability:* Part-time. *Unit head:* Dr. Thomas DeLillo, Chair, 316-978-3160, Fax: 316-978-3748, E-mail: thomas.delillo@wichita.edu. *Application contact:* Jordan Oleson, Admissions Coordinator, 316-978-3095, Fax: 316-978-3253,
E-mail: jordan.oleson@wichita.edu.
Website: http://www.wichita.edu/math

Wilfrid Laurier University, Faculty of Graduate and Postdoctoral Studies, Faculty of Science, Department of Mathematics, Waterloo, ON N2L 3C5, Canada. Offers mathematics for science and finance (M Sc). *Program availability:* Part-time. *Degree requirements:* For master's, thesis optional. *Entrance requirements:* For master's, 4-year honors degree in mathematics, minimum B+ average. Additional exam requirements/recommendations for international students: Required—TOEFL (minimum score 89 iBT). Electronic applications accepted. *Faculty research:* Modeling, analysis, resolution, and generalization of financial and scientific problems.

Wilkes University, College of Graduate and Professional Studies, College of Science and Engineering, Department of Mathematics and Computer Science, Wilkes-Barre, PA 18766-0002. Offers mathematics (MS). *Program availability:* Part-time. *Students:* 1 (woman) full-time, 3 part-time (1 woman). Average age 29. In 2015, 1 master's awarded. *Degree requirements:* For master's, thesis or alternative. *Entrance requirements:* For master's, GRE General Test. Additional exam requirements/recommendations for international students: Required—TOEFL (minimum score 550 paper-based; 79 iBT). *Application deadline:* Applications are processed on a rolling basis. Application fee: $45 ($65 for international students). Electronic applications accepted. *Financial support:* Unspecified assistantships available. Financial award application deadline: 3/1; financial award applicants required to submit FAFSA. *Unit head:* Dr. Terese Wignot, Interim Dean, 570-408-4600, Fax: 570-408-7883, E-mail: terese.wignot@wilkes.edu. *Application contact:* Joanne Thomas, Director of Graduate Enrollment, 570-408-4234, Fax: 570-408-7846, E-mail: joanne.thomas1@wilkes.edu.
Website: http://www.wilkes.edu/academics/colleges/science-and-engineering/mathematics-computer-science/index.aspx

Worcester Polytechnic Institute, Graduate Studies and Research, Department of Mathematical Sciences, Worcester, MA 01609-2280. Offers applied mathematics (MS); applied statistics (MS); financial mathematics (MS); industrial mathematics (MS); mathematical sciences (PhD, Graduate Certificate); mathematics (MME). *Program availability:* Part-time, evening/weekend. *Faculty:* 19 full-time (2 women), 10 part-time/adjunct (1 woman). *Students:* 93 full-time (35 women), 24 part-time (14 women); includes 11 minority (3 Black or African American, non-Hispanic/Latino; 4 Asian, non-Hispanic/Latino; 2 Hispanic/Latino; 2 Two or more races, non-Hispanic/Latino), 71 international. 303 applicants, 57% accepted, 47 enrolled. In 2015, 47 master's awarded. *Degree requirements:* For master's, thesis (for some programs); for doctorate, comprehensive exam, thesis/dissertation. *Entrance requirements:* For master's, GRE General Test, GRE Subject Test in math (recommended), 3 letters of recommendation; for doctorate, GRE General Test, GRE Subject Test (math), 3 letters of recommendation. Additional exam requirements/recommendations for international students: Required—TOEFL (minimum score 563 paper-based; 84 iBT), IELTS (minimum score 7). *Application deadline:* For fall admission, 1/1 priority date for domestic students, 1/1 for international students; for spring admission, 10/1 priority date for domestic students, 10/1 for international students. Applications are processed on a rolling basis. Application fee: $70. Electronic applications accepted. *Financial support:* Research assistantships, teaching assistantships, career-related internships or fieldwork, institutionally sponsored loans, scholarships/grants, and unspecified assistantships available. Financial award application deadline: 1/1; financial award applicants required to submit FAFSA. *Unit head:* Dr. Luca Capogna, Head, 508-831-5241, Fax: 508-831-5824, E-mail: lcapogna@wpi.edu. *Application contact:* Dr. Joseph Fehribach, Graduate Coordinator, 508-831-5241, Fax: 508-831-5824,
E-mail: bach@wpi.edu.
Website: http://www.wpi.edu/academics/math/

Wright State University, School of Graduate Studies, College of Science and Mathematics, Department of Mathematics and Statistics, Program in Mathematics, Dayton, OH 45435. Offers MS. *Degree requirements:* For master's, comprehensive exam. *Entrance requirements:* For master's, previous course work in mathematics beyond calculus. Additional exam requirements/recommendations for international students: Required—TOEFL. *Faculty research:* Analysis, algebraic combinatorics, graph theory, operator theory.

Yale University, Graduate School of Arts and Sciences, Department of Mathematics, New Haven, CT 06520. Offers M Phil, MS, PhD. *Degree requirements:* For doctorate, 2 foreign languages, thesis/dissertation. *Entrance requirements:* For doctorate, GRE General Test, GRE Subject Test.

Yeshiva University, Graduate Programs in Arts and Sciences, New York, NY 10033-3201. Offers mathematical sciences (PhD); mathematics (MA); quantitative economics (MS); speech-language pathology (MS).

York University, Faculty of Graduate Studies, Faculty of Science, Program in Mathematics and Statistics, Toronto, ON M3J 1P3, Canada. Offers industrial and applied mathematics (M Sc); mathematics and statistics (MA, PhD). *Program availability:* Part-time. *Degree requirements:* For master's, thesis optional; for doctorate, one foreign language, comprehensive exam, thesis/dissertation. Electronic applications accepted.

Youngstown State University, Graduate School, College of Science, Technology, Engineering and Mathematics, Department of Mathematics and Statistics, Youngstown, OH 44555-0001. Offers applied mathematics (MS); computer science (MS); secondary mathematics (MS); statistics (MS). *Program availability:* Part-time. *Degree requirements:* For master's, comprehensive exam, thesis optional. *Entrance requirements:* For master's, minimum GPA of 2.7 in computer science and mathematics. Additional exam requirements/recommendations for international students: Required—TOEFL. *Faculty research:* Regression analysis, numerical analysis, statistics, Markov chain, topology and fuzzy sets.

Statistics

Acadia University, Faculty of Pure and Applied Science, Department of Mathematics and Statistics, Wolfville, NS B4P 2R6, Canada. Offers applied mathematics and statistics (M Sc). *Degree requirements:* For master's, thesis. *Entrance requirements:* For master's, honors degree in mathematics, statistics or equivalent. Additional exam requirements/recommendations for international students: Required—TOEFL (minimum score 580 paper-based; 93 iBT), IELTS (minimum score 6.5). *Faculty research:* Geophysical fluid dynamics, machine scheduling problems, control theory, stochastic optimization, survival analysis.

American University, College of Arts and Sciences, Department of Mathematics and Statistics, Washington, DC 22016-8050. Offers applied statistics (Certificate); mathematics (MA); professional science: quantitative analysis (MS); statistics (MS). *Program availability:* Part-time, evening/weekend. *Faculty:* 34 full-time (11 women), 10 part-time/adjunct (3 women). *Students:* 19 full-time (12 women), 13 part-time (7 women); includes 5 minority (4 Black or African American, non-Hispanic/Latino; 1 Two or more races, non-Hispanic/Latino), 6 international. Average age 26. 54 applicants, 93% accepted, 15 enrolled. In 2015, 12 master's awarded. *Degree requirements:* For master's, comprehensive exam, thesis or alternative. *Entrance requirements:* For master's, GRE, statement of purpose, transcripts, 2 letters of recommendation, resume; for Certificate, bachelor's degree, statement of purpose, transcripts, resume. Additional exam requirements/recommendations for international students: Required—TOEFL (minimum score 100 iBT), IELTS (minimum score 7), PTE (minimum score 68). *Application deadline:* For fall admission, 2/1 priority date for domestic students; for spring admission, 11/1 for domestic students. Application fee: $55. *Expenses: Tuition, area resident:* Full-time $27,468; part-time $1526 per credit hour. *Required fees:* $430. Tuition and fees vary according to course level and program. *Financial support:* Application deadline: 2/1. *Unit head:* Dr. Joshua D. Lansky, department Chair, 202-885-3687, Fax: 202-885-3155, E-mail: lansky@american.edu. *Application contact:* Kathleen Clowery, Associate Director, Graduate Admissions, 202-885-3620, Fax: 202-885-1344, E-mail: clowery@american.edu.
Website: http://www.american.edu/cas/mathstat/

American University of Beirut, Graduate Programs, Faculty of Arts and Sciences, Beirut, Lebanon. Offers anthropology (MA); Arab and Middle Eastern history (PhD); Arabic language and literature (MA, PhD); archaeology (MA); biology (MS); cell and molecular biology (PhD); chemistry (MS); clinical psychology (MA); computational sciences (MS); computer science (MS); economics (MA); English language (MA); English literature (MA); environmental policy planning (MS); financial economics (MAFE); geology (MS); history (MA); mathematics (MA, MS); media studies (MA); Middle Eastern studies (MA); physics (MS); political studies (MA); psychology (MA); public administration (MA); sociology (MA); statistics (MA, MS); theoretical physics (PhD); transnational American studies (MA). *Program availability:* Part-time. *Faculty:*

114 full-time (36 women), 4 part-time/adjunct (2 women). *Students:* 258 full-time (190 women), 207 part-time (142 women). Average age 27. 241 applicants, 71% accepted, 98 enrolled. In 2015, 47 master's, 3 doctorates awarded. *Degree requirements:* For master's, one foreign language, comprehensive exam, thesis (for some programs); for doctorate, one foreign language, comprehensive exam, thesis/dissertation. *Entrance requirements:* For master's, GRE (for some MA, MS programs), letter of recommendation; for doctorate, GRE, letters of recommendation. Additional exam requirements/recommendations for international students: Required—TOEFL (minimum score 600 paper-based; 97 iBT), IELTS (minimum score 7). *Application deadline:* For fall admission, 4/1 for domestic and international students; for spring admission, 11/1 for domestic and international students. Application fee: $50. Electronic applications accepted. *Expenses: Tuition, area resident:* Full-time $16,254; part-time $903 per credit. *Required fees:* $699. Tuition and fees vary according to course load and program. *Financial support:* Research assistantships, career-related internships or fieldwork, institutionally sponsored loans, scholarships/grants, health care benefits, and unspecified assistantships available. Financial award application deadline: 2/4; financial award applicants required to submit FAFSA. *Faculty research:* Analysis and algebra; software engineering; machine learning and big data analysis; philosophy of mind and political philosophy; anthropology of art, anthropology of migration and medical anthropology; sociology of knowledge, sociology of migration, critical theory; sociology of education; hybrid solid materials; photocatalysis; human creativity. *Total annual research expenditures:* $680,360. *Unit head:* Dr. Patrick McGreevy, Dean, 961-1374374 Ext. 3800, Fax: 961-1744461, E-mail: pm07@aub.edu.lb. *Application contact:* Dr. Salim Kanaan, Director, Admissions Office, 961-1350000 Ext. 2590, Fax: 961-1750775, E-mail: sk00@aub.edu.lb.
Website: http://www.aub.edu.lb/fas/

Arizona State University at the Tempe campus, College of Liberal Arts and Sciences, School of Mathematical and Statistical Sciences, Tempe, AZ 85287-1804. Offers applied mathematics (PhD); mathematics (MA, PhD); mathematics education (PhD); statistics (MS, PhD, Graduate Certificate). *Program availability:* Part-time. Terminal master's awarded for partial completion of doctoral program. *Degree requirements:* For master's, thesis or alternative, interactive Program of Study (iPOS) submitted before completing 50 percent of required credit hours; for doctorate, comprehensive exam, thesis/dissertation, interactive Program of Study (iPOS) submitted before completing 50 percent of required credit hours. *Entrance requirements:* For master's and doctorate, GRE General Test, minimum GPA of 3.0 or equivalent in last 2 years of work leading to bachelor's degree. Additional exam requirements/recommendations for international students: Required—TOEFL, IELTS, or PTE. Electronic applications accepted. *Expenses:* Contact institution.

Auburn University, Graduate School, College of Sciences and Mathematics, Department of Mathematics and Statistics, Auburn University, AL 36849. Offers applied mathematics (MAM, MS); mathematics (MS, PhD); probability and statistics (M Prob S); statistics (MS). *Faculty:* 57 full-time (12 women), 8 part-time/adjunct (2 women). *Students:* 64 full-time (18 women), 36 part-time (11 women); includes 10 minority (9 Asian, non-Hispanic/Latino; 1 Two or more races, non-Hispanic/Latino), 57 international. Average age 29. 123 applicants, 54% accepted, 15 enrolled. In 2015, 23 master's, 14 doctorates awarded. *Degree requirements:* For doctorate, thesis/dissertation. *Entrance requirements:* For master's, GRE General Test, undergraduate mathematics background; for doctorate, GRE General Test, GRE Subject Test. *Application deadline:* Applications are processed on a rolling basis. Application fee: $50 ($60 for international students). Electronic applications accepted. *Expenses:* Tuition, state resident: full-time $8802; part-time $489 per credit hour. Tuition, nonresident: full-time $26,406; part-time $1467 per credit hour. *Required fees:* $808 per semester. Tuition and fees vary according to degree level and program. *Financial support:* Fellowships and teaching assistantships available. Financial award applicants required to submit FAFSA. *Faculty research:* Pure and applied mathematics. *Unit head:* Dr. Tin Yau Tam, Chair, 334-844-6572, Fax: 334-844-6655. *Application contact:* Dr. George Flowers, Dean of the Graduate School, 334-844-2125.
Website: http://www.auburn.edu/~math/

Ball State University, Graduate School, College of Sciences and Humanities, Department of Mathematical Sciences, Program in Statistics, Muncie, IN 47306. Offers statistics (MA, MS). *Program availability:* Part-time. *Students:* 11 full-time (5 women), 8 part-time (3 women), 15 international. Average age 27. 16 applicants, 75% accepted, 4 enrolled. In 2015, 9 master's awarded. *Degree requirements:* For master's, thesis (for some programs). *Entrance requirements:* For master's, minimum baccalaureate GPA of 2.75 or 3.0 in latter half of baccalauareate. Additional exam requirements/ recommendations for international students: Required—TOEFL (minimum score 550 paper-based; 79 iBT), IELTS (minimum score 6.5). *Application deadline:* Applications are processed on a rolling basis. Application fee: $60. Electronic applications accepted. *Expenses: Tuition, area resident:* Full-time $6948; part-time $2316 per semester. Tuition, state resident: full-time $10,422; part-time $3474 per semester. Tuition, nonresident: full-time $19,062; part-time $6354 per semester. *Required fees:* $651 per semester. Tuition and fees vary according to campus/location, program and reciprocity agreements. *Financial support:* In 2015–16, 10 students received support, including 10 teaching assistantships with partial tuition reimbursements available (averaging $10,868 per year). Financial award application deadline: 3/1; financial award applicants required to submit FAFSA. *Faculty research:* Robust methods. *Unit head:* Dr. John Lorch, Chairperson/Professor, 765-285-8640, Fax: 765-285-1721, E-mail: jlorch@bsu.edu. *Application contact:* Dr. Hanspeter Fischer, Professor/Graduate Advisor, 765-285-8680, Fax: 765-285-1721, E-mail: hfischer@bsu.edu.
Website: http://cms.bsu.edu/Academics/CollegesandDepartments/Math/AcademicsAdmissions/Programs/Masters/MAorMSinStatistics.aspx

Baruch College of the City University of New York, Zicklin School of Business, Department of Statistics and Computer Information Systems, Program in Statistics, New York, NY 10010-5585. Offers MBA, MS. *Program availability:* Part-time, evening/ weekend. *Entrance requirements:* For master's, GMAT, 2 letters of recommendation, resume, 2 years of work experience. Additional exam requirements/recommendations for international students: Required—TOEFL (minimum score 590 paper-based), TWE.

Baylor University, Graduate School, College of Arts and Sciences, Department of Statistical Science, Waco, TX 76798. Offers MA, PhD. *Faculty:* 7 full-time (1 woman), 4 part-time/adjunct (1 woman). *Students:* 24 full-time (9 women), 7 part-time (3 women); includes 3 minority (1 Asian, non-Hispanic/Latino; 1 Hispanic/Latino; 1 Two or more races, non-Hispanic/Latino), 7 international. Average age 24. 38 applicants, 16% accepted. In 2015, 2 master's, 4 doctorates awarded. *Degree requirements:* For doctorate, thesis/dissertation. *Entrance requirements:* For master's, GRE General Test, 3 semesters of course work in calculus, linear algebra; for doctorate, GRE General Test. *Application deadline:* Applications are processed on a rolling basis. Application fee: $25. *Financial support:* In 2015–16, 1 fellowship, 5 research assistantships, 7 teaching assistantships were awarded; institutionally sponsored loans also available. *Faculty research:* Mathematical statistics, Bayesian methods, probability theory, biostatistics, linear models, time series. *Unit head:* Dr. Larry Lyon, Dean, 254-710-3588, Fax: 254-710-3870, E-mail: larry_lyon@baylor.edu. *Application contact:* Dr. James Stamey, Graduate Program Director, 254-710-7405, E-mail: james_stamey@baylor.edu.
Website: http://www.baylor.edu/statistics/

Bowling Green State University, Graduate College, College of Arts and Sciences, Department of Mathematics and Statistics, Bowling Green, OH 43403. Offers applied statistics (MS); mathematics (MA, MAT, PhD); statistics (PhD). *Program availability:* Part-time. *Degree requirements:* For master's, thesis or alternative; for doctorate, comprehensive exam, thesis/dissertation. *Entrance requirements:* For master's and doctorate, GRE General Test. Additional exam requirements/recommendations for international students: Required—TOEFL. Electronic applications accepted. *Faculty research:* Statistics and probability, algebra, analysis.

Brigham Young University, Graduate Studies, College of Physical and Mathematical Sciences, Department of Statistics, Provo, UT 84602-1001. Offers applied statistics (MS). *Faculty:* 18 full-time (3 women). *Students:* 30 full-time (8 women); includes 2 minority (1 Asian, non-Hispanic/Latino; 1 Hispanic/Latino). Average age 24. 38 applicants, 47% accepted, 15 enrolled. In 2015, 13 master's awarded. *Degree requirements:* For master's, comprehensive exam, thesis (for some programs). *Entrance requirements:* For master's, GRE General Test, minimum undergraduate GPA of 3.3; course work in statistical methods, theory, multivariable calculus and linear algebra with minimum B- average. Additional exam requirements/recommendations for international students: Required—TOEFL (minimum score 580 paper-based; 85 iBT). *Application deadline:* For fall admission, 2/1 for domestic and international students. Application fee: $50. Electronic applications accepted. *Financial support:* In 2015–16, 22 students received support, including 1 fellowship (averaging $27,000 per year), 13 research assistantships with tuition reimbursements available (averaging $10,000 per year), 9 teaching assistantships with tuition reimbursements available (averaging $10,000 per year); scholarships/grants and unspecified assistantships also available. Financial award application deadline: 2/1. *Faculty research:* Statistical genetics, reliability and pollution monitoring, Bayesian methods. *Total annual research expenditures:* $580,272. *Unit head:* Dr. Harold Dennis Tolley, Chair, 801-422-6668, Fax: 801-422-0635, E-mail: tolley@byu.edu. *Application contact:* Dr. Gilbert W. Fellingham, Graduate Coordinator, 801-422-2806, Fax: 801-422-0635, E-mail: gwf@stat.byu.edu.
Website: http://statistics.byu.edu/

Brock University, Faculty of Graduate Studies, Faculty of Mathematics and Science, Program in Mathematics and Statistics, St. Catharines, ON L2S 3A1, Canada. Offers M Sc. *Program availability:* Part-time. *Degree requirements:* For master's, thesis or project. *Entrance requirements:* For master's, honors degree. Additional exam requirements/recommendations for international students: Required—TOEFL (minimum score 550 paper-based; 80 iBT), IELTS (minimum score 6.5), TWE (minimum score 4). Electronic applications accepted.

California State University, East Bay, Office of Graduate Studies Programs, College of Science, Department of Statistics and Biostatistics, Statistics Program, Hayward, CA 94542-3000. Offers actuarial science (MS); applied statistics (MS); computational statistics (MS); mathematical statistics (MS). *Program availability:* Part-time, evening/ weekend. *Students:* 27 full-time (10 women), 80 part-time (38 women); includes 33 minority (4 Black or African American, non-Hispanic/Latino; 20 Asian, non-Hispanic/ Latino; 7 Hispanic/Latino; 2 Two or more races, non-Hispanic/Latino), 44 international. Average age 30. 85 applicants, 79% accepted, 39 enrolled. In 2015, 38 master's awarded. *Degree requirements:* For master's, comprehensive exam. *Entrance requirements:* For master's, letters of recommendation, minimum GPA of 3.0, math through lower-division calculus. Additional exam requirements/recommendations for international students: Required—TOEFL (minimum score 550 paper-based). *Application deadline:* For fall admission, 6/30 for domestic and international students. Application fee: $55. Electronic applications accepted. *Financial support:* Fellowships, career-related internships or fieldwork, Federal Work-Study, institutionally sponsored loans, scholarships/grants, and unspecified assistantships available. Support available to part-time students. Financial award application deadline: 3/2; financial award applicants required to submit FAFSA. *Unit head:* Dr. Mitchell Watnik, Chair, 510-885-3435, Fax: 510-885-4714.
Website: http://www20.csueastbay.edu/csci/departments/statistics/

Carnegie Mellon University, Dietrich College of Humanities and Social Sciences, Department of Statistics, Pittsburgh, PA 15213-3891. Offers machine learning and statistics (PhD); mathematical finance (PhD); statistics (MS, PhD), including applied statistics (PhD), computational statistics (PhD), theoretical statistics (PhD); statistics and public policy (PhD). Terminal master's awarded for partial completion of doctoral program. *Degree requirements:* For doctorate, comprehensive exam, thesis/ dissertation. *Entrance requirements:* For master's and doctorate, GRE General Test. Additional exam requirements/recommendations for international students: Required—TOEFL. *Faculty research:* Stochastic processes, Bayesian statistics, statistical computing, decision theory, psychiatric statistics.

Central Connecticut State University, School of Graduate Studies, School of Engineering, Science and Technology, Department of Mathematical Sciences, New Britain, CT 06050-4010. Offers data mining (MS, Certificate); mathematics (MA, MS, Certificate, Sixth Year Certificate), including actuarial science (MA), computer science (MA), statistics (MA). *Program availability:* Part-time, evening/weekend. *Faculty:* 14 full-time (3 women). *Students:* 11 full-time (5 women), 72 part-time (35 women); includes 21 minority (5 Black or African American, non-Hispanic/Latino; 1 American Indian or Alaska Native, non-Hispanic/Latino; 7 Asian, non-Hispanic/Latino; 6 Hispanic/Latino; 2 Two or more races, non-Hispanic/Latino), 4 international. Average age 35. 67 applicants, 55% accepted, 23 enrolled. In 2015, 23 master's, 1 other advanced degree awarded. *Degree requirements:* For master's, comprehensive exam, thesis or alternative, special project; for other advanced degree, qualifying exam. *Entrance requirements:* For master's, minimum undergraduate GPA of 2.7; for other advanced degree, minimum undergraduate GPA of 3.0, essay, letters of recommendation. Additional exam requirements/recommendations for international students: Required—TOEFL (minimum score 550 paper-based; 79 iBT). *Application deadline:* For fall admission, 5/1 for domestic and international students; for spring admission, 11/1 for domestic and international students. Applications are processed on a rolling basis. Application fee: $50. Electronic applications accepted. *Expenses: Tuition, area resident:* Full-time $6188. Tuition, state resident: full-time $9284; part-time $577 per credit. Tuition, nonresident: full-time $17,240; part-time $592 per credit. *Required fees:* $4266; $234 per credit. *Financial support:* In 2015–16, 28 students received support, including 1 research assistantship; career-related internships or fieldwork, Federal Work-Study, scholarships/grants, and unspecified assistantships also available. Support available to part-time students. Financial award application deadline: 3/1; financial award applicants required to submit FAFSA. *Faculty research:* Statistics, actuarial mathematics, computer systems and engineering, computer programming techniques, operations research. *Unit head:* Dr. Philip Halloran, Chair, 860-832-2835, E-mail: halloranp@ccsu.edu. *Application contact:* Patricia Gardner, Associate Director of Graduate Studies, 860-832-2350, Fax: 860-832-2362, E-mail: graduateadmissions@ccsu.edu.
Website: http://www.ccsu.edu/math/

Claremont Graduate University, Graduate Programs, Institute of Mathematical Sciences, Claremont, CA 91711-6160. Offers computational and systems biology (PhD); computational mathematics and numerical analysis (MA, MS); computational science (PhD); engineering and industrial applied mathematics (PhD); mathematics (PhD); operations research and statistics (MA, MS); physical applied mathematics (MA, MS); pure mathematics (MA, MS); scientific computing (MA, MS); systems and control theory (MA, MS). *Program availability:* Part-time. *Faculty:* 6 full-time (1 woman), 2 part-time/adjunct (0 women). *Students:* 74 full-time (19 women), 35 part-time (12 women); includes 23 minority (2 Black or African American, non-Hispanic/Latino; 12 Asian, non-Hispanic/Latino; 8 Hispanic/Latino; 1 Two or more races, non-Hispanic/Latino), 51 international. Average age 30. In 2015, 25 master's, 10 doctorates awarded. Terminal master's awarded for partial completion of doctoral program. *Entrance requirements:* For master's and doctorate, GRE General Test. Additional exam requirements/recommendations for international students: Required—TOEFL (minimum score 75 iBT). *Application deadline:* For fall admission, 2/1 priority date for domestic and international students. Applications are processed on a rolling basis. Application fee: $80. Electronic applications accepted. *Expenses: Tuition, area resident:* Full-time $43,032; part-time $1793 per unit. *Required fees:* $600; $300 per semester. $300 per semester. Tuition and fees vary according to course load and program. *Financial support:* Fellowships, research assistantships, Federal Work-Study, institutionally sponsored loans, scholarships/grants, and tuition waivers (full and partial) available. Support available to part-time students. Financial award application deadline: 2/15; financial award applicants required to submit FAFSA. *Unit head:* Ali Nadim, Director, 909-607-9413, E-mail: ali.nadim@cgu.edu. *Application contact:* Jake Campbell, Assistant Director of Admissions, 909-607-3024, E-mail: jake.campbell@cgu.edu.
Website: http://www.cgu.edu/pages/168.asp

Clemson University, Graduate School, College of Business, John E. Walker Department of Economics, Clemson, SC 29634. Offers applied economics (PhD); applied economics and statistics (MS); economics (MA, PhD). *Faculty:* 23 full-time (2 women), 4 part-time/adjunct (1 woman). *Students:* 93 full-time (31 women), 11 part-time (3 women); includes 10 minority (3 Black or African American, non-Hispanic/Latino; 1 Asian, non-Hispanic/Latino; 2 Hispanic/Latino; 4 Two or more races, non-Hispanic/Latino), 57 international. Average age 27. 184 applicants, 60% accepted, 28 enrolled. In 2015, 15 master's, 11 doctorates awarded. Terminal master's awarded for partial completion of doctoral program. *Degree requirements:* For master's, thesis (for some programs), technical paper; for doctorate, comprehensive exam, thesis/dissertation. *Entrance requirements:* For master's and doctorate, GRE General Test or GMAT, unofficial transcripts, letters of recommendation. Additional exam requirements/recommendations for international students: Required—TOEFL (minimum score 80 iBT), IELTS (minimum score 6.5). *Application deadline:* For fall admission, 1/15 priority date for domestic and international students. Applications are processed on a rolling basis. Application fee: $80 ($90 for international students). Electronic applications accepted. *Expenses:* $4,060 per semester full-time resident, $8,103 per semester full-time non-resident, $448 per credit hour part-time resident, $898 per credit hour part-time non-resident. *Financial support:* In 2015–16, 74 students received support, including 13 fellowships with partial tuition reimbursements available (averaging $3,692 per year), 19 teaching assistantships with partial tuition reimbursements available (averaging $14,116 per year); health care benefits and unspecified assistantships also available. Financial award application deadline: 1/15. *Faculty research:* Public economics, public choice and political economy; econometrics (focus on data envelope analysis), industrial organization (focus on pricing), labor and development economics, international economics (focus on free trade agreements). *Total annual research expenditures:* $50,317. *Unit head:* Dr. Raymond Sauer, Department Chair, 864-656-3969,
E-mail: sauerr@clemson.edu. *Application contact:* Dr. Curtis Simon, Graduate Program Coordinator, 864-656-3966, E-mail: cjsmn@clemson.edu.
Website: http://economics.clemson.edu/

Colorado State University, College of Natural Sciences, Department of Statistics, Fort Collins, CO 80523-1877. Offers MAS, MS, PhD. *Program availability:* 100% online. *Faculty:* 12 full-time (2 women), 2 part-time/adjunct (both women). *Students:* 30 full-time (12 women), 80 part-time (27 women); includes 14 minority (1 Black or African American, non-Hispanic/Latino; 1 American Indian or Alaska Native, non-Hispanic/Latino; 5 Asian, non-Hispanic/Latino; 4 Hispanic/Latino; 3 Two or more races, non-Hispanic/Latino), 30 international. Average age 33. 66 applicants, 91% accepted, 41 enrolled. In 2015, 32 master's, 2 doctorates awarded. Terminal master's awarded for partial completion of doctoral program. *Degree requirements:* For master's, comprehensive exam (for some programs), thesis (for some programs), project, seminar; for doctorate, comprehensive exam, thesis/dissertation, candidacy exam, preliminary exam, seminar. *Entrance requirements:* For master's and doctorate, GRE General Test, minimum GPA of 3.0, background in math and statistics, personal statement, curriculum vitae/resume, 3 letters of recommendation. Additional exam requirements/recommendations for international students: Required—TOEFL (minimum score 550 paper-based; 80 iBT). *Application deadline:* For fall admission, 2/1 priority date for domestic and international students. Application fee: $60 ($70 for international students). Electronic applications accepted. *Expenses:* $1,000 per semester on-campus; $749 per credit hour online. *Financial support:* In 2015–16, 2 fellowships (averaging $63,000 per year), 6 research assistantships with full tuition reimbursements (averaging $17,981 per year), 21 teaching assistantships with full tuition reimbursements (averaging $20,500 per year) were awarded; scholarships/grants and health care benefits also available. Financial award application deadline: 2/1; financial award applicants required to submit FAFSA. *Faculty research:* Applied probability, linear models and experimental design, time-series analysis, non-parametric statistical inference, space-time aquatic resources modeling and analysis. *Total annual research expenditures:* $1.5 million. *Unit head:* Dr. Jean Opsomer, Professor and Department Chair, 970-491-5269, Fax: 970-491-7895, E-mail: jopsomer@stat.colostate.edu. *Application contact:* Kristin Stephens, Graduate Coordinator, 970-491-5269, Fax: 970-491-7895, E-mail: stephens@stat.colostate.edu.
Website: http://www.stat.colostate.edu/

Columbia University, Graduate School of Arts and Sciences, New York, NY 10027. Offers African-American studies (MA); American studies (MA); anthropology (MA, PhD); art history and archaeology (MA, PhD); astronomy (PhD); biological sciences (PhD); biotechnology (MA); chemical physics (PhD); chemistry (PhD); classical studies (MA, PhD); classics (MA, PhD); climate and society (MA); conservation biology (MA); earth and environmental sciences (PhD); East Asia: regional studies (MA); East Asian languages and cultures (MA, PhD); ecology, evolution and environmental biology (MA), including conservation biology; ecology, evolution, and environmental biology (PhD), including ecology and evolutionary biology, evolutionary primatology; economics (MA, PhD); English and comparative literature (MA, PhD); French and Romance philology (MA, PhD); Germanic languages (MA, PhD); global French studies (MA); global thought (MA); Hispanic cultural studies (MA); history (PhD); history and literature (MA); human rights studies (MA); Islamic studies (MA); Italian (MA, PhD); Japanese pedagogy (MA); Jewish studies (MA); Latin America and the Caribbean: regional studies (MA); Latin American and Iberian cultures (PhD); mathematics (MA, PhD), including finance (MA); medieval and Renaissance studies (MA); Middle Eastern, South Asian, and African studies (MA, PhD); modern art: critical and curatorial studies (MA); modern European studies (MA); museum anthropology (MA); music (DMA, PhD); oral history (MA); philosophical foundations of physics (MA); philosophy (MA, PhD); physics (PhD); political science (MA, PhD); psychology (PhD); quantitative methods in the social sciences (MA); religion (MA, PhD); Russia, Eurasia and East Europe: regional studies (MA); Russian translation (MA); Slavic cultures (MA); Slavic languages (MA, PhD); sociology (MA, PhD); South Asian studies (MA); statistics (MA, PhD); theatre (PhD). Dual-degree programs require admission to both Graduate School of Arts and Sciences and another Columbia school. *Program availability:* Part-time. *Students:* 3,030 full-time, 235 part-time; includes 861 minority (88 Black or African American, non-Hispanic/Latino; 5 American Indian or Alaska Native, non-Hispanic/Latino; 517 Asian, non-Hispanic/Latino; 159 Hispanic/Latino; 4 Native Hawaiian or other Pacific Islander, non-Hispanic/Latino; 88 Two or more races, non-Hispanic/Latino), 1,697 international. 13,288 applicants, 21% accepted, 1162 enrolled. In 2015, 1,061 master's, 553 doctorates awarded. Terminal master's awarded for partial completion of doctoral program. *Degree requirements:* For master's, variable foreign language requirement, comprehensive exam (for some programs), thesis (for some programs); for doctorate, variable foreign language requirement, comprehensive exam (for some programs), thesis/dissertation. *Entrance requirements:* For master's and doctorate, GRE General Test, GRE Subject Test (for some programs). Additional exam requirements/recommendations for international students: Required—TOEFL, IELTS. Application fee: $105. Electronic applications accepted. *Financial support:* Fellowships, research assistantships, teaching assistantships, career-related internships or fieldwork, Federal Work-Study, institutionally sponsored loans, scholarships/grants, traineeships, health care benefits, tuition waivers, and unspecified assistantships available. Support available to part-time students. Financial award application deadline: 12/15. *Unit head:* Carlos J. Alonso, Dean of the Graduate School of Arts and Sciences, 212-854-5177. *Application contact:* GSAS Office of Admissions, 212-854-8903, E-mail: gsas-admissions@columbia.edu.
Website: http://gsas.columbia.edu/

Concordia University, School of Graduate Studies, Faculty of Arts and Science, Department of Mathematics and Statistics, Montréal, QC H3G 1M8, Canada. Offers mathematics (PhD); mathematics and statistics (M Sc, MA); teaching of mathematics (MTM). *Degree requirements:* For master's, thesis optional; for doctorate, comprehensive exam, thesis/dissertation. *Entrance requirements:* For master's, honors degree in mathematics or equivalent. *Application deadline:* For fall admission, 5/1 for domestic students; for winter admission, 3/31 for domestic students; for spring admission, 10/31 for domestic students. Application fee: $50. Tuition and fees vary according to course load, degree level and program. *Financial support:* Fellowships, research assistantships, and teaching assistantships available. Financial award application deadline: 2/1. *Faculty research:* Number theory, computational algebra, mathematical physics, differential geometry, dynamical systems and statistics. *Unit head:* Dr. Nadia Hardy, Chair, 514-848-2424 Ext. 3235, Fax: 514-848-2831. *Application contact:* Dr. Hal Proppe, Associate Chair, 514-848-3257 Ext. 3217, Fax: 514-848-2831.
Website: http://www.concordia.ca/artsci/math-stats.html

Cornell University, Graduate School, Graduate Fields of Engineering, Field of Operations Research and Information Engineering, Ithaca, NY 14853. Offers applied probability and statistics (PhD); manufacturing systems engineering (PhD); mathematical programming (PhD); operations research and industrial engineering (M Eng). *Degree requirements:* For doctorate, comprehensive exam, thesis/dissertation. *Entrance requirements:* For master's and doctorate, GRE General Test, 3 letters of recommendation. Additional exam requirements/recommendations for international students: Required—TOEFL (minimum score 600 paper-based; 100 iBT). Electronic applications accepted. *Faculty research:* Mathematical programming and combinatorial optimization, statistics, stochastic processes, mathematical finance, simulation, manufacturing, e-commerce.

Cornell University, Graduate School, Graduate Fields of Engineering, Field of Statistics, Ithaca, NY 14853-0001. Offers applied statistics (MPS); biometry (MS, PhD); decision theory (MS, PhD); economic and social statistics (MS, PhD); engineering statistics (MS, PhD); experimental design (MS, PhD); mathematical statistics (MS, PhD); probability (MS, PhD); sampling (MS, PhD); statistical computing (MS, PhD); stochastic processes (MS, PhD). Terminal master's awarded for partial completion of doctoral program. *Degree requirements:* For master's, project (MPS), thesis (MS); for doctorate, one foreign language, thesis/dissertation. *Entrance requirements:* For master's, GRE General Test (for MS), 2 letters of recommendation (MS, MPS); for doctorate, GRE General Test, 2 letters of recommendation. Additional exam requirements/recommendations for international students: Required—TOEFL (minimum score 550 paper-based; 77 iBT). Electronic applications accepted. *Faculty research:* Bayesian analysis, survival analysis, nonparametric statistics, stochastic processes, mathematical statistics.

Dalhousie University, Faculty of Science, Department of Mathematics and Statistics, Program in Statistics, Halifax, NS B3H 4R2, Canada. Offers M Sc, PhD. *Degree requirements:* For master's, thesis, 50 hours of consulting; for doctorate, thesis/dissertation, 50 hours of consulting. *Entrance requirements:* Additional exam requirements/recommendations for international students: Required—TOEFL, IELTS, CANTEST, CAEL, or Michigan English Language Assessment Battery. Electronic applications accepted. *Faculty research:* Data analysis, multivariate analysis, robustness, time series, statistical genetics.

Duke University, Graduate School, Department of Statistical Science, Durham, NC 27708. Offers MSS, PhD. *Program availability:* Part-time. *Degree requirements:* For doctorate, thesis/dissertation. *Entrance requirements:* For doctorate, GRE General Test. Additional exam requirements/recommendations for international students: Required—TOEFL (minimum score 577 paper-based; 90 iBT) or IELTS (minimum score 7). Electronic applications accepted.

Duke University, Graduate School, Program in Statistical and Economic Modeling, Durham, NC 27708. Offers econometrics (MS); financial economics (MS). Program offered jointly by the Departments of Statistical Science and Economics. *Entrance requirements:* For master's, GRE General Test. Additional exam requirements/recommendations for international students: Required—TOEFL (minimum score 577 paper-based; 90 iBT) or IELTS (minimum score 7). Electronic applications accepted.

East Carolina University, Graduate School, Thomas Harriot College of Arts and Sciences, Department of Mathematics, Greenville, NC 27858-4353. Offers mathematics (MA); mathematics in the community college (MA); statistics (MA, Certificate). *Program availability:* Part-time, evening/weekend. *Students:* 8 full-time (3 women), 3 part-time (0 women); includes 1 minority (Black or African American, non-Hispanic/Latino), 1 international. Average age 26. 7 applicants, 100% accepted, 3 enrolled. In 2015, 2 master's awarded. *Degree requirements:* For master's, comprehensive exam. *Entrance requirements:* For master's, GRE General Test, MAT. Additional exam requirements/recommendations for international students: Required—TOEFL. *Application deadline:* For fall admission, 6/1 for domestic students; for spring admission, 10/15 for domestic students. Applications are processed on a rolling basis. Application fee: $50. *Financial*

support: Research assistantships with partial tuition reimbursements and teaching assistantships with partial tuition reimbursements available. Financial award application deadline: 6/1. *Unit head:* Dr. Johannes H. Hattingh, Chair, 252-328-6461, E-mail: hattinghj@ecu.edu. *Application contact:* Dean of Graduate School, 252-328-6012, Fax: 252-328-6071, E-mail: gradschool@ecu.edu.
Website: http://www.ecu.edu/cs-cas/math/graduateprogram.cfm

Florida Atlantic University, Charles E. Schmidt College of Science, Department of Mathematical Sciences, Boca Raton, FL 33431-0991. Offers applied mathematics and statistics (MS); mathematics (MS, MST, PhD). *Program availability:* Part-time. Terminal master's awarded for partial completion of doctoral program. *Degree requirements:* For master's, comprehensive exam (for some programs), thesis (for some programs); for doctorate, comprehensive exam, thesis/dissertation. *Entrance requirements:* For master's and doctorate, GRE General Test, minimum GPA of 3.0. Additional exam requirements/recommendations for international students: Required—TOEFL (minimum score 500 paper-based; 61 iBT), IELTS (minimum score 6). Electronic applications accepted. *Faculty research:* Cryptography, statistics, algebra, analysis, combinatorics.

Florida International University, College of Arts, Sciences, and Education, Department of Mathematics and Statistics, Program in Statistics, Miami, FL 33199. Offers MS. *Program availability:* Part-time, evening/weekend. *Faculty:* 8 full-time (2 women). *Students:* 7 full-time (3 women), 4 part-time (0 women); includes 6 minority (3 Black or African American, non-Hispanic/Latino; 3 Hispanic/Latino), 4 international. Average age 29. 18 applicants, 50% accepted, 4 enrolled. In 2015, 7 master's awarded. *Degree requirements:* For master's, thesis optional. *Entrance requirements:* For master's, GRE General Test, minimum GPA of 3.0, 3 letters of recommendation, resume. Additional exam requirements/recommendations for international students: Required—TOEFL (minimum score 550 paper-based; 80 iBT). *Application deadline:* For fall admission, 6/1 for domestic students, 4/1 for international students; for spring admission, 10/1 for domestic students, 9/1 for international students. Applications are processed on a rolling basis. Application fee: $30. Electronic applications accepted. *Expenses:* Tuition, state resident: full-time $10,708; part-time $455.64 per credit hour. Tuition, nonresident: full-time $23,816; part-time $1001.69 per credit hour. *Required fees:* $390; $195 per semester. Tuition and fees vary according to program. *Financial support:* Institutionally sponsored loans and scholarships/grants available. Financial award application deadline: 3/1; financial award applicants required to submit FAFSA. *Unit head:* Dr. Abdelhamid Meziani, Chair, 305-348-2957, E-mail: abdelhamid.meziani@fiu.edu. *Application contact:* Dr. Zhenmin Chen, Director of Graduate Programs, 305-348-1081, E-mail: chenzh@fiu.edu.

Florida State University, The Graduate School, College of Arts and Sciences, Department of Statistics, Tallahassee, FL 32306-4330. Offers applied statistics (MS); applied statistics - thesis option (MS); biostatistics (MS, PhD); biostatistics - thesis option (MS); mathematical statistics (MS, PhD); mathematical statistics - thesis option (MS); statistical data science (MS). *Program availability:* Part-time. *Faculty:* 18 full-time (3 women), 1 (woman) part-time/adjunct. *Students:* 149 full-time (77 women), 13 part-time (5 women); includes 19 minority (6 Black or African American, non-Hispanic/Latino; 8 Asian, non-Hispanic/Latino; 5 Hispanic/Latino), 117 international. Average age 27. 353 applicants, 40% accepted, 56 enrolled. In 2015, 44 master's, 6 doctorates awarded. Terminal master's awarded for partial completion of doctoral program. *Degree requirements:* For master's, thesis optional; for doctorate, comprehensive exam, thesis/dissertation, departmental qualifying exam. *Entrance requirements:* For master's, GRE General Test, calculus 1-3, linear algebra, one course each in applied statistics and probability, minimum GPA of 3.0; for doctorate, GRE General Test, minimum GPA of 3.0, two semesters of advanced calculus (intermediate analysis, real analysis with proofs). Additional exam requirements/recommendations for international students: Required—TOEFL (minimum score 80 iBT). *Application deadline:* For fall admission, 7/1 for domestic and international students. Application fee: $30. Electronic applications accepted. *Expenses: Tuition, area resident:* Full-time $7263; part-time $403.50 per credit hour. Tuition, nonresident: full-time $18,087; part-time $1004.85 per credit hour. *Required fees:* $1365; $75.81 per credit hour. $20 per semester. Tuition and fees vary according to campus/location. *Financial support:* In 2015–16, 83 students received support, including 4 fellowships with full tuition reimbursements available (averaging $10,000 per year), 11 research assistantships with full tuition reimbursements available (averaging $19,380 per year), 56 teaching assistantships with full tuition reimbursements available (averaging $20,432 per year); institutionally sponsored loans, scholarships/grants, health care benefits, tuition waivers (partial), and unspecified assistantships also available. Financial award application deadline: 2/1; financial award applicants required to submit FAFSA. *Faculty research:* Statistical inference, probability theory, biostatistics, nonparametric estimation, automatic target recognition. *Total annual research expenditures:* $861,615. *Unit head:* Dr. Xufeng Niu, Chairman, 850-644-4008, Fax: 850-644-5271, E-mail: niu@stat.fsu.edu. *Application contact:* Sarah English, Academic Program Specialist, 850-644-3514, Fax: 850-644-5271, E-mail: sarah.english@stat.fsu.edu.
Website: http://www.stat.fsu.edu/

George Mason University, Volgenau School of Engineering, Department of Statistics, Fairfax, VA 22030. Offers biostatistics (MS); statistical science (MS, PhD); statistics (Certificate). *Faculty:* 15 full-time (3 women), 2 part-time/adjunct (0 women). *Students:* 31 full-time (13 women), 36 part-time (13 women); includes 25 minority (5 Black or African American, non-Hispanic/Latino; 14 Asian, non-Hispanic/Latino; 4 Hispanic/Latino; 1 Native Hawaiian or other Pacific Islander, non-Hispanic/Latino; 1 Two or more races, non-Hispanic/Latino), 17 international. Average age 32. 78 applicants, 67% accepted, 19 enrolled. In 2015, 18 master's, 5 doctorates, 7 other advanced degrees awarded. *Degree requirements:* For master's, comprehensive exam, thesis optional, qualifying exams; for doctorate, comprehensive exam, thesis/dissertation, qualifying exams. *Entrance requirements:* For master's, GRE/GMAT, bachelor's degree from accredited institution with minimum of GPA of 3.0 in a major that includes calculus, matrix algebra, calculus-based probability and statistics; personal goal statement; 2 official copies of transcripts; 3 letters of recommendation; resume; official bank statement; proof of financial support; photocopy of passport; for doctorate, GRE, MS in math-intensive discipline with minimum GPA of 3.5, personal goals statement, 2 official copies of transcripts, 3 letters of recommendation, resume, official bank statement, proof of financial support, photocopy of passport; for Certificate, bachelor's degree with 2 courses in calculus and probability or statistics, personal goals statement, 2 official copies of transcripts, 1-3 letters of recommendation (depending on program), resume, official bank statement, proof of financial support, photocopy of passport. Additional exam requirements/recommendations for international students: Required—TOEFL (minimum score 575 paper-based; 80 iBT), IELTS (minimum score 6.5), PTE. *Application deadline:* For fall admission, 1/15 priority date for domestic students. Application fee: $65 ($80 for international students). Electronic applications accepted. *Expenses:* Contact institution. *Financial support:* In 2015–16, 17 students received support, including 4 research assistantships with tuition reimbursements available (averaging $16,250 per year), 15 teaching assistantships with tuition reimbursements available (averaging $16,772 per year); career-related internships or fieldwork, Federal Work-Study, scholarships/grants, unspecified assistantships, and health care benefits (for full-time research or teaching assistantship recipients) also available. Support available to part-time students. Financial award application deadline: 3/1; financial award applicants required to submit FAFSA. *Faculty research:* Computational statistics, nonparametric function estimation, scientific and statistical visualization, statistical applications to engineering, survey research. *Total annual research expenditures:* $231,752. *Unit head:* William F. Rosenberger, Chair, 703-993-3645, Fax: 703-993-1700, E-mail: wrosenbe@gmu.edu. *Application contact:* Elizabeth Quigley, Administrative Assistant, 703-993-9107, Fax: 703-993-1700, E-mail: equigley@gmu.edu.
Website: http://statistics.gmu.edu/

George Mason University, Volgenau School of Engineering, Program in Data Analytics Engineering, Fairfax, VA 22030. Offers MS. *Faculty:* 1 part-time/adjunct (0 women). *Students:* 41 full-time (14 women), 84 part-time (28 women); includes 34 minority (5 Black or African American, non-Hispanic/Latino; 16 Asian, non-Hispanic/Latino; 11 Hispanic/Latino; 2 Two or more races, non-Hispanic/Latino), 33 international. Average age 31. 173 applicants, 66% accepted, 67 enrolled. In 2015, 1 master's awarded. *Entrance requirements:* For master's, three letters of recommendation; detailed statement of career goals and professional aspiration; self-evaluation form. Additional exam requirements/recommendations for international students: Required—TOEFL (minimum score 575 paper-based; 88 iBT), IELTS (minimum score 6.5), PTE (minimum score 59). *Application deadline:* For fall admission, 1/15 priority date for domestic students. Application fee: $75 ($80 for international students). Electronic applications accepted. *Financial support:* Career-related internships or fieldwork, Federal Work-Study, and scholarships/grants available. Support available to part-time students. Financial award applicants required to submit FAFSA. *Unit head:* Bob Osgood, Director, 703-993-5443, Fax: 703-993-6137, E-mail: rosgood@gmu.edu. *Application contact:* Shukri Abdi, Graduate Admissions Specialist, 703-993-1830, Fax: 703-993-1242, E-mail: sabdi2@gmu.edu.
Website: http://volgenau.gmu.edu/data-analytics-engineering

Georgetown University, Graduate School of Arts and Sciences, Department of Mathematics and Statistics, Washington, DC 20057. Offers MS.

The George Washington University, Columbian College of Arts and Sciences, Department of Statistics, Washington, DC 20052. Offers statistics (MS, PhD); survey design and data analysis (Graduate Certificate). *Program availability:* Part-time, evening/weekend. *Faculty:* 19 full-time (4 women), 18 part-time/adjunct (4 women). *Students:* 254 full-time (137 women), 54 part-time (22 women); includes 7 minority (1 Black or African American, non-Hispanic/Latino; 4 Asian, non-Hispanic/Latino; 2 Hispanic/Latino), 276 international. Average age 25. 822 applicants, 65% accepted, 125 enrolled. In 2015, 113 master's, 2 doctorates, 18 other advanced degrees awarded. Terminal master's awarded for partial completion of doctoral program. *Degree requirements:* For master's, comprehensive exam; for doctorate, thesis/dissertation, general exam. *Entrance requirements:* For master's and doctorate, GRE General Test, interview, minimum GPA of 3.0. Additional exam requirements/recommendations for international students: Required—TOEFL (minimum score 550 paper-based; 80 iBT). *Application deadline:* For fall admission, 1/15 priority date for domestic and international students; for spring admission, 10/1 priority date for domestic students, 9/1 priority date for international students. Applications are processed on a rolling basis. Application fee: $75. Electronic applications accepted. *Financial support:* In 2015–16, 13 students received support. Fellowships with tuition reimbursements available, teaching assistantships with tuition reimbursements available, Federal Work-Study, and tuition waivers available. Financial award application deadline: 1/15. *Unit head:* Dr. Zhaohai Li, Chair, 202-994-6888, E-mail: zli@gwu.edu. *Application contact:* Information Contact, 202-994-6356, Fax: 202-994-6917.
Website: http://www.gwu.edu/~stat/

Georgia Institute of Technology, Graduate Studies, Multidisciplinary Program in Analytics, Atlanta, GA 30332-0001. Offers MS. Program offered jointly with Scheller College of Business, College of Computing, and College of Engineering. *Program availability:* Part-time. *Degree requirements:* For master's, applied analytics practicum or approved internship. *Entrance requirements:* For master's, GRE or GMAT. Additional exam requirements/recommendations for international students: Required—TOEFL (minimum score 600 paper-based; 100 iBT). Electronic applications accepted. *Expenses:* Contact institution.

Georgia Institute of Technology, Graduate Studies, Multidisciplinary Program in Statistics, Atlanta, GA 30332-0001. Offers MS. Program offered jointly with School of Mathematics and School of Industrial and Systems Engineering. *Program availability:* Part-time. *Degree requirements:* For master's, thesis optional. *Entrance requirements:* For master's, GRE General Test. Additional exam requirements/recommendations for international students: Required—TOEFL (minimum score 590 paper-based; 96 iBT). Electronic applications accepted. *Faculty research:* Statistical control procedures, statistical modeling of transportation systems.

Georgia State University, College of Arts and Sciences, Department of Mathematics and Statistics, Atlanta, GA 30302-3083. Offers bioinformatics (MS, PhD); biostatistics (MS, PhD); discrete mathematics (MS); mathematics (MS, PhD); scientific computing (MS); statistics (MS). *Program availability:* Part-time. *Faculty:* 22 full-time (7 women). *Students:* 97 full-time (44 women), 20 part-time (5 women); includes 40 minority (14 Black or African American, non-Hispanic/Latino; 23 Asian, non-Hispanic/Latino; 3 Hispanic/Latino), 50 international. Average age 32. 80 applicants, 51% accepted, 23 enrolled. In 2015, 22 master's, 4 doctorates awarded. Terminal master's awarded for partial completion of doctoral program. *Degree requirements:* For master's, comprehensive exam (for some programs), thesis optional; for doctorate, comprehensive exam, thesis/dissertation. *Entrance requirements:* For master's and doctorate, GRE. Additional exam requirements/recommendations for international students: Required—TOEFL (minimum score 550 paper-based; 80 iBT). *Application deadline:* For fall admission, 7/1 priority date for domestic and international students; for spring admission, 11/15 priority date for domestic and international students. Application fee: $50. Electronic applications accepted. *Expenses:* Tuition, state resident: full-time $6876; part-time $382 per credit hour. Tuition, nonresident: full-time $22,374; part-time $1243 per credit hour. *Required fees:* $2128; $2128 per term. $1064 per term. Part-time tuition and fees vary according to course load and program. *Financial support:* In 2015–16, fellowships with full tuition reimbursements (averaging $22,000 per year), research assistantships with full tuition reimbursements (averaging $9,000 per year), teaching assistantships with full tuition reimbursements (averaging $9,000 per year) were awarded; institutionally sponsored loans, scholarships/grants, health care benefits, and unspecified assistantships also available. Financial award application deadline: 2/1. *Faculty research:* Algebra, matrix theory, graph theory and combinatorics; applied mathematics and analysis; collegiate mathematics education; statistics, biostatistics and applications; bioinformatics, dynamical systems. *Unit head:* Dr. Guantao Chen, Chair, 404-413-6436, Fax: 404-413-6403, E-mail: gchen@gsu.edu.
Website: http://www2.gsu.edu/~wwwmat/

Hampton University, School of Science, Program in Applied Mathematics, Hampton, VA 23668. Offers computational mathematics (MS); nonlinear science (MS); statistics

276 www.petersons.com

Peterson's Graduate Programs in the Physical Sciences, Mathematics, Agricultural Sciences, the Environment & Natural Resources 2017

and probability (MS). *Program availability:* Part-time. *Degree requirements:* For master's, thesis optional. *Entrance requirements:* For master's, GRE General Test. Additional exam requirements/recommendations for international students: Required—TOEFL (minimum score 525 paper-based) or IELTS (6.5). Electronic applications accepted. *Expenses: Tuition, area resident:* Full-time $10,263; part-time $522 per credit hour. *Required fees:* $35. Tuition and fees vary according to course load and program. *Faculty research:* Stochastic processes, nonlinear dynamics, approximation theory, prediction theory, hydrodynamical stability.

Harvard University, Graduate School of Arts and Sciences, Department of Statistics, Cambridge, MA 02138. Offers AM, PhD. Terminal master's awarded for partial completion of doctoral program. *Degree requirements:* For master's, one foreign language; for doctorate, one foreign language, thesis/dissertation, exam, qualifying paper. *Entrance requirements:* For master's and doctorate, GRE General Test, GRE Subject Test (recommended). Additional exam requirements/recommendations for international students: Required—TOEFL. *Faculty research:* Interactive graphic analysis of multidimensional data, data analysis, modeling and inference, statistical modeling of U.S. economic time series.

Hunter College of the City University of New York, Graduate School, School of Arts and Sciences, Department of Mathematics and Statistics, New York, NY 10065-5085. Offers adolescent mathematics education (MA); applied mathematics (MA); pure mathematics (MA); statistics (MA). *Program availability:* Part-time, evening/weekend. *Faculty:* 3 full-time (1 woman). *Students:* 8 full-time (1 woman), 18 part-time (5 women); includes 13 minority (4 Black or African American, non-Hispanic/Latino; 6 Asian, non-Hispanic/Latino; 3 Hispanic/Latino), 2 international. Average age 29. 52 applicants, 67% accepted, 21 enrolled. In 2015, 21 master's awarded. *Degree requirements:* For master's, one foreign language, comprehensive exam, thesis (for some programs). *Entrance requirements:* For master's, GRE General Test, 24 credits in mathematics. Additional exam requirements/recommendations for international students: Required—TOEFL. *Application deadline:* For fall admission, 4/1 for domestic students, 2/1 for international students; for spring admission, 11/1 for domestic students, 9/1 for international students. *Financial support:* Federal Work-Study, institutionally sponsored loans, scholarships/grants, and tuition waivers (partial) available. Support available to part-time students. *Faculty research:* Data analysis, dynamical systems, computer graphics, topology, statistical decision theory. *Unit head:* Robert Thompson, Chair, 212-772-5300, Fax: 212-772-4858, E-mail: robert.thompson@hunter.cuny.edu. *Application contact:* Ada Peluso, Director for Graduate Admissions, 212-772-4632, Fax: 212-772-4858, E-mail: peluso@math.hunter.cuny.edu.
Website: http://math.hunter.cuny.edu/

Indiana University Bloomington, University Graduate School, College of Arts and Sciences, Department of Statistics, Bloomington, IN 47408. Offers applied statistics (MS); statistical science (MS, PhD). *Program availability:* Part-time. Terminal master's awarded for partial completion of doctoral program. *Degree requirements:* For master's, thesis or alternative; for doctorate, comprehensive exam, thesis/dissertation. *Entrance requirements:* For master's and doctorate, GRE. Additional exam requirements/recommendations for international students: Required—TOEFL (minimum score 100 iBT). Electronic applications accepted. *Faculty research:* Spatial statistics, Bayesian statistics, statistical learning, network science, applied statistics.

Indiana University–Purdue University Indianapolis, School of Science, Department of Mathematical Sciences, Indianapolis, IN 46202-3216. Offers mathematics (MS, PhD), including applied mathematics, applied statistics (MS), mathematical statistics (PhD), mathematics, mathematics education (MS). *Program availability:* Part-time. Terminal master's awarded for partial completion of doctoral program. *Degree requirements:* For master's, thesis optional; for doctorate, one foreign language, thesis/dissertation. *Entrance requirements:* For doctorate, GRE General Test. Additional exam requirements/recommendations for international students: Required—TOEFL. *Faculty research:* Mathematical physics, integral systems, partial differential equations, noncommutative geometry, biomathematics, computational neurosciences.

Iowa State University of Science and Technology, Department of Statistics, Ames, IA 50011. Offers MS, PhD, MBA/MS. *Entrance requirements:* For master's and doctorate, GRE General Test. Additional exam requirements/recommendations for international students: Required—TOEFL (minimum score 570 paper-based; 79 iBT), IELTS (minimum score 6.5). Electronic applications accepted.

Johns Hopkins University, G. W. C. Whiting School of Engineering, Department of Applied Mathematics and Statistics, Baltimore, MD 21218. Offers computational medicine (PhD); discrete mathematics (MA, MSE, PhD); financial mathematics (MSE); operations research/optimization (MA, MSE, PhD); statistics/probability (MA, MSE, PhD). Terminal master's awarded for partial completion of doctoral program. *Degree requirements:* For master's, thesis (for some programs); for doctorate, thesis/dissertation, oral exam, introductory exam. *Entrance requirements:* For master's and doctorate, GRE General Test, GRE Subject Test. Additional exam requirements/recommendations for international students: Required—TOEFL (minimum score 600 paper-based; 100 iBT). Electronic applications accepted. *Faculty research:* Discrete mathematics, probability, statistics, optimization and operations research, scientific computation, financial mathematics.

Johns Hopkins University, G. W. C. Whiting School of Engineering, Master of Science in Engineering Management Program, Baltimore, MD 21218. Offers biomaterials (MSEM); civil engineering (MSEM); communications science (MSEM); computer science (MSEM); environmental systems analysis, economics and public policy (MSEM); fluid mechanics (MSEM); materials science and engineering (MSEM); mechanical engineering (MSEM); mechanics and materials (MSEM); nanobiotechnology (MSEM); nanomaterials and nanotechnology (MSEM); operations research (MSEM); probability and statistics (MSEM); smart product and device design (MSEM). *Entrance requirements:* For master's, GRE, 3 letters of recommendation, resume. Additional exam requirements/recommendations for international students: Required—TOEFL (minimum score 600 paper-based; 100 iBT) or IELTS (minimum score 7). Electronic applications accepted.

Kansas State University, Graduate School, College of Arts and Sciences, Department of Statistics, Manhattan, KS 66506. Offers MS, PhD, Graduate Certificate. Terminal master's awarded for partial completion of doctoral program. *Degree requirements:* For master's, thesis or alternative, exam or research paper; for doctorate, comprehensive exam, thesis/dissertation, qualifying and preliminary exams. *Entrance requirements:* For master's and doctorate, previous course work in statistics and mathematics; for Graduate Certificate, brief statement of objectives, transcripts. Additional exam requirements/recommendations for international students: Required—TOEFL (minimum score 550 paper-based; 79 iBT), IELTS (minimum score 6.5), PTE (minimum score 58). Electronic applications accepted. *Faculty research:* Linear and nonlinear statistical models, design analysis of experiments, nonparametric methods, high-dimensional data, Bayesian methods, categorical data analysis.

Lehigh University, College of Arts and Sciences, Department of Mathematics, Bethlehem, PA 18015. Offers applied mathematics (MS, PhD); mathematics (MS, PhD); statistics (MS). *Program availability:* Part-time. *Faculty:* 24 full-time (3 women), 1 part-time/adjunct (0 women). *Students:* 38 full-time (11 women), 8 part-time (3 women); includes 1 minority (Hispanic/Latino), 17 international. Average age 25. 147 applicants, 39% accepted, 11 enrolled. In 2015, 17 master's, 3 doctorates awarded. Terminal master's awarded for partial completion of doctoral program. *Degree requirements:* For master's, comprehensive exam, thesis optional; for doctorate, comprehensive exam, thesis/dissertation, qualifying examination, general examination, advanced topic examination. *Entrance requirements:* For master's and doctorate, GRE General Test (strongly recommended), minimum undergraduate GPA of 2.75, 3.0 for last two semesters; adequate background in math. Additional exam requirements/recommendations for international students: Required—TOEFL (minimum score 85 iBT). *Application deadline:* For fall admission, 1/1 for domestic and international students; for spring admission, 12/1 for domestic and international students. Application fee: $75. Electronic applications accepted. *Financial support:* In 2015–16, 31 students received support, including 1 fellowship with full tuition reimbursement available (averaging $25,000 per year), 1 research assistantship with full tuition reimbursement available (averaging $20,000 per year), 25 teaching assistantships with full tuition reimbursements available (averaging $20,000 per year); tuition waivers (partial) also available. Financial award application deadline: 1/1. *Faculty research:* Probability and statistics, geometry and topology, algebra, discrete mathematics, differential equations. *Total annual research expenditures:* $182,459. *Unit head:* Dr. Wei-Min Huang, Chairman, 610-758-3730, Fax: 610-758-3767, E-mail: wh02@lehigh.edu. *Application contact:* Dr. Terry Napier, Graduate Director, 610-758-3755,
E-mail: mathgrad@lehigh.edu.
Website: http://www.lehigh.edu/~math/grad.html

Louisiana State University and Agricultural & Mechanical College, Graduate School, College of Agriculture, Department of Experimental Statistics, Baton Rouge, LA 70803. Offers applied statistics (M App St).

Louisiana Tech University, Graduate School, College of Engineering and Science, Department of Mathematics and Statistics, Ruston, LA 71272. Offers computational analysis and modeling (PhD); mathematics and statistics (MS). *Program availability:* Part-time. *Degree requirements:* For master's, thesis or alternative. *Entrance requirements:* For master's, GRE General Test, minimum GPA of 3.0 in last 60 hours. Additional exam requirements/recommendations for international students: Required—TOEFL. *Application deadline:* For fall admission, 8/1 for domestic students; for spring admission, 2/1 for domestic students. Applications are processed on a rolling basis. Application fee: $20 ($30 for international students). *Financial support:* Teaching assistantships and Federal Work-Study available. Financial award application deadline: 4/1. *Application contact:* Marilyn J. Robinson, Assistant to the Dean, 318-257-2924, Fax: 318-257-4487.
Website: http://coes.latech.edu/mathematics-and-statistics/

Loyola University Chicago, Graduate School, Department of Mathematics and Statistics, Chicago, IL 60660. Offers applied statistics (MS); mathematics (MS). *Program availability:* Part-time. *Faculty:* 19 full-time (3 women). *Students:* 36 full-time (21 women), 9 part-time (4 women); includes 9 minority (2 Black or African American, non-Hispanic/Latino; 3 Asian, non-Hispanic/Latino; 4 Hispanic/Latino), 18 international. Average age 27. 54 applicants, 91% accepted, 18 enrolled. In 2015, 25 master's awarded. *Entrance requirements:* For master's, GRE General Test. Additional exam requirements/recommendations for international students: Required—TOEFL. *Application deadline:* For fall admission, 8/1 for domestic students; for spring admission, 12/1 for domestic students. Applications are processed on a rolling basis. Application fee: $0. Electronic applications accepted. *Expenses: Tuition, area resident:* Full-time $18,054; part-time $9027 per credit hour. *Required fees:* $832; $284 per credit hour. Part-time tuition and fees vary according to course load, degree level and program. *Financial support:* In 2015–16, 13 students received support, including 6 teaching assistantships with tuition reimbursements available (averaging $10,000 per year); fellowships with tuition reimbursements available, career-related internships or fieldwork, Federal Work-Study, institutionally sponsored loans, and tuition waivers (partial) also available. Financial award application deadline: 3/15. *Faculty research:* Nonlinear analysis and partial differential equations, algebra and combinatorics, knot theory, control theory and engineering, probability and applied statistics. *Total annual research expenditures:* $70,000. *Unit head:* Dr. Anthony Giaquinto, Chair, 773-508-3578, Fax: 773-508-2123, E-mail: agiaqui@luc.edu. *Application contact:* Dr. Rafal Goebel, Graduate Program Director for Mathematics, 773-508-3558,
E-mail: rgoebel1@luc.edu.
Website: http://math.luc.edu/

McGill University, Faculty of Graduate and Postdoctoral Studies, Faculty of Arts, Department of Economics, Montréal, QC H3A 2T5, Canada. Offers economics (MA, PhD); social statistics (MA).

McGill University, Faculty of Graduate and Postdoctoral Studies, Faculty of Arts, Department of Sociology, Montréal, QC H3A 2T5, Canada. Offers medical sociology (MA); neo-tropical environment (MA); social statistics (MA); sociology (MA, PhD, Diploma).

McGill University, Faculty of Graduate and Postdoctoral Studies, Faculty of Science, Department of Mathematics and Statistics, Montréal, QC H3A 2T5, Canada. Offers computational science and engineering (M Sc); mathematics and statistics (M Sc, MA, PhD), including applied mathematics (M Sc, MA), pure mathematics (M Sc, MA), statistics (M Sc, MA).

McMaster University, School of Graduate Studies, Faculty of Science, Department of Mathematics and Statistics, Program in Statistics, Hamilton, ON L8S 4M2, Canada. Offers applied statistics (M Sc); medical statistics (M Sc); statistical theory (M Sc). *Degree requirements:* For master's, thesis or alternative. *Entrance requirements:* For master's, honors degree background in mathematics and statistics. Additional exam requirements/recommendations for international students: Required—TOEFL (minimum score 550 paper-based). *Faculty research:* Development of polymer production technology, quality of life in patients who use pharmaceutical agents, mathematical modeling, order statistics from progressively censored samples, nonlinear stochastic model in genetics.

McNeese State University, Doré School of Graduate Studies, College of Science, Department of Mathematics, Computer Science, and Statistics, Lake Charles, LA 70609. Offers computer science (MS); mathematics (MS); statistics (MS). *Program availability:* Evening/weekend. *Degree requirements:* For master's, comprehensive exam, thesis or alternative, written exam. *Entrance requirements:* For master's, GRE.

Memorial University of Newfoundland, School of Graduate Studies, Department of Mathematics and Statistics, St. John's, NL A1C 5S7, Canada. Offers mathematics (M Sc, PhD); statistics (M Sc, MAS, PhD). *Program availability:* Part-time. *Degree requirements:* For master's, thesis, practicum and report (MAS); for doctorate,

comprehensive exam, thesis/dissertation, oral defense of thesis. *Entrance requirements:* For master's, 2nd class honors degree (MAS, M Sc); for doctorate, MAS or M Sc in mathematics and statistics. *Application deadline:* For fall admission, 1/31 for domestic and international students. Applications are processed on a rolling basis. Application fee: $50 Canadian dollars ($100 Canadian dollars for international students). Electronic applications accepted. *Expenses: Tuition, area resident:* Full-time $2199 Canadian dollars. *International tuition:* $2859 Canadian dollars full-time. *Financial support:* Fellowships and teaching assistantships available. Financial award application deadline: 1/31. *Faculty research:* Algebra, topology, applied mathematics, mathematical statistics, applied statistics and probability. *Unit head:* Dr. Chris Radford, Head, 709-864-8783, Fax: 709-864-3010, E-mail: head@math.mun.ca. *Application contact:* Dr. J.C. Loredo-Osti, Graduate Officer, 709-864-8729, Fax: 709-864-3010,
E-mail: mathgrad@mun.ca.
Website: http://www.mun.ca/math

Miami University, College of Arts and Science, Department of Statistics, Oxford, OH 45056. Offers MS Stat. *Students:* 18 full-time (5 women), 1 part-time (0 women); includes 2 minority (both Asian, non-Hispanic/Latino), 7 international. Average age 26. In 2015, 13 master's awarded. *Entrance requirements:* For master's, minimum undergraduate GPA of 3.0 overall; strong performance in three semesters of calculus, one semester of linear algebra, and a probability/mathematical statistics course. Additional exam requirements/recommendations for international students: Recommended—TOEFL (minimum score 80 iBT), IELTS (minimum score 6.5), TSE (minimum score 54). *Application deadline:* For fall admission, 2/1 for domestic and international students. Application fee: $50. Electronic applications accepted. *Expenses:* Tuition, state resident: full-time $12,888; part-time $537 per credit hour. Tuition, nonresident: full-time $29,022; part-time $1209 per credit hour. *Required fees:* $530; $24 per credit hour. $30 per semester. Part-time tuition and fees vary according to course load and program. *Financial support:* Application deadline: 2/1; applicants required to submit FAFSA. *Unit head:* Dr. A. John Bailer, Professor/Chair, 513-529-7828, E-mail: baileraj@miamioh.edu. *Application contact:* Dr. Doug Noe, Graduate Director, 513-529-5838, E-mail: noeda@miamioh.edu.
Website: http://www.MiamiOH.edu/sta/

Michigan State University, The Graduate School, College of Natural Science, Department of Statistics and Probability, East Lansing, MI 48824. Offers applied statistics (MS); statistics (MS, PhD). *Entrance requirements:* Additional exam requirements/recommendations for international students: Required—TOEFL. Electronic applications accepted.

Minnesota State University Mankato, College of Graduate Studies and Research, College of Science, Engineering and Technology, Department of Mathematics and Statistics, Program in Statistics, Mankato, MN 56001. Offers MS. *Degree requirements:* For master's, one foreign language, comprehensive exam, thesis or alternative. *Entrance requirements:* For master's, GRE General Test, minimum GPA of 3.0 during previous 2 years. Additional exam requirements/recommendations for international students: Required—TOEFL. Electronic applications accepted.

Mississippi State University, College of Arts and Sciences, Department of Mathematics and Statistics, Mississippi State, MS 39762. Offers mathematical sciences (PhD); mathematics (MS); statistics (MS). *Program availability:* Part-time. *Faculty:* 25 full-time (5 women). *Students:* 35 full-time (13 women), 5 part-time (3 women); includes 7 minority (all Black or African American, non-Hispanic/Latino), 21 international. Average age 28. 49 applicants, 71% accepted, 13 enrolled. In 2015, 12 master's, 3 doctorates awarded. Terminal master's awarded for partial completion of doctoral program. *Degree requirements:* For master's, thesis optional, comprehensive oral or written exam; for doctorate, one foreign language, thesis/dissertation, comprehensive oral and written exam. *Entrance requirements:* For master's, minimum GPA of 2.75 on last two years of undergraduate courses; for doctorate, GRE. Additional exam requirements/recommendations for international students: Required—TOEFL (minimum score 477 paper-based; 53 iBT); Recommended—IELTS (minimum score 4.5). *Application deadline:* For fall admission, 3/15 priority date for domestic students, 5/1 for international students; for spring admission, 11/1 for domestic students, 9/1 for international students. Applications are processed on a rolling basis. Application fee: $60. Electronic applications accepted. *Expenses: Tuition, area resident:* Full-time $7502; part-time $833.74 per credit hour. Tuition, nonresident: full-time $20,142; part-time $2238.24 per credit hour. *Financial support:* In 2015–16, 25 teaching assistantships with full tuition reimbursements (averaging $14,656 per year) were awarded; Federal Work-Study, institutionally sponsored loans, tuition waivers (partial), and unspecified assistantships also available. Financial award application deadline: 4/1; financial award applicants required to submit FAFSA. *Faculty research:* Differential equations, algebra, numerical analysis, functional analysis, applied statistics. *Total annual research expenditures:* $1.3 million. *Unit head:* Dr. Mohsen Razzaghi, Department Head, 662-325-3414, Fax: 662-325-0005,
E-mail: razzaghi@math.msstate.edu. *Application contact:* Meredith Nagel, Admissions Assistant, 662-325-9077, E-mail: mnagel@grad.msstate.edu.
Website: http://www.math.msstate.edu

Missouri University of Science and Technology, Graduate School, Department of Mathematics and Statistics, Rolla, MO 65409. Offers applied mathematics (MS); mathematics (MST, PhD), including mathematics (PhD), mathematics education (MST), statistics (PhD). *Faculty:* 21 full-time (9 women), 1 part-time/adjunct (0 women). *Students:* 38 full-time (16 women), 5 part-time (0 women), 33 international. Average age 29. 37 applicants, 68% accepted, 8 enrolled. In 2015, 5 master's, 3 doctorates awarded. Terminal master's awarded for partial completion of doctoral program. *Degree requirements:* For master's, thesis or alternative; for doctorate, one foreign language, thesis/dissertation. *Entrance requirements:* For master's and doctorate, GRE General Test, GRE Subject Test. Additional exam requirements/recommendations for international students: Required—TOEFL (minimum score 550 paper-based). *Application deadline:* For fall admission, 7/1 for domestic students. Applications are processed on a rolling basis. Application fee: $55 ($75 for international students). Electronic applications accepted. *Expenses:* Tuition, state resident: full-time $10,536. Tuition, nonresident: full-time $27,015. Full-time tuition and fees vary according to course load. *Financial support:* In 2015–16, 5 fellowships, 1 research assistantship with partial tuition reimbursement (averaging $1,814 per year), 19 teaching assistantships with partial tuition reimbursements (averaging $1,813 per year) were awarded; institutionally sponsored loans also available. *Faculty research:* Analysis, differential equations, topology, statistics. *Total annual research expenditures:* $223,299. *Unit head:* Dr. Leon M. Hall, Chair, 573-341-4641, Fax: 573-341-4741,
E-mail: lmhall@mst.edu. *Application contact:* Dr. V. A. Samaranayake, Director of Graduate Studies, 573-341-4658, Fax: 573-341-4741, E-mail: vsam@mst.edu.
Website: http://math.mst.edu/

Montana State University, The Graduate School, College of Letters and Science, Department of Ecology, Bozeman, MT 59717. Offers ecological and environmental statistics (MS); ecology and environmental sciences (PhD); fish and wildlife biology (PhD); fish and wildlife management (MS). *Program availability:* Part-time. *Degree requirements:* For master's, comprehensive exam, thesis (for some programs); for doctorate, comprehensive exam, thesis/dissertation. *Entrance requirements:* For master's and doctorate, GRE, minimum GPA of 3.0, letters of recommendation, essay. Additional exam requirements/recommendations for international students: Required—TOEFL (minimum score 550 paper-based). Electronic applications accepted. *Faculty research:* Community ecology, population ecology, land-use effects, management and conservation, environmental modeling.

Montana State University, The Graduate School, College of Letters and Science, Department of Mathematical Sciences, Bozeman, MT 59717. Offers mathematics (MS, PhD), including mathematics education option (MS); statistics (MS, PhD). *Program availability:* Part-time, online learning. *Degree requirements:* For master's, comprehensive exam, thesis (for some programs); for doctorate, comprehensive exam, thesis/dissertation. *Entrance requirements:* For master's and doctorate, GRE General Test. Additional exam requirements/recommendations for international students: Required—TOEFL (minimum score 550 paper-based). Electronic applications accepted. *Faculty research:* Applied mathematics, dynamical systems, statistics, mathematics education, mathematical and computational biology.

Montclair State University, The Graduate School, College of Science and Mathematics, Program in Statistics, Montclair, NJ 07043-1624. Offers MS. *Program availability:* Part-time, evening/weekend. *Students:* 7 full-time (5 women), 14 part-time (7 women); includes 7 minority (3 Asian, non-Hispanic/Latino; 4 Hispanic/Latino), 5 international. Average age 34. 8 applicants, 63% accepted, 5 enrolled. *Degree requirements:* For master's, comprehensive exam, thesis or alternative. *Entrance requirements:* For master's, GRE General Test, 2 letters of recommendation, essay. Additional exam requirements/recommendations for international students: Required—TOEFL (minimum score 83 iBT), IELTS (minimum score 6.5). *Application deadline:* Applications are processed on a rolling basis. Application fee: $60. Electronic applications accepted. *Expenses:* Tuition, state resident: part-time $553 per credit. Tuition, nonresident: part-time $854 per credit. *Required fees:* $91 per credit. Tuition and fees vary according to program. *Financial support:* Federal Work-Study, scholarships/grants, and unspecified assistantships available. Support available to part-time students. Financial award application deadline: 3/1; financial award applicants required to submit FAFSA. *Faculty research:* Biostatistics, time series. *Unit head:* Dr. Helen Roberts, Chairperson, 973-655-5132. *Application contact:* Amy Aiello, Executive Director of The Graduate School, 973-655-5147, Fax: 973-655-7869,
E-mail: graduate.school@montclair.edu.
Website: http://www.montclair.edu/graduate/programs-of-study/statistics/

Murray State University, College of Science, Engineering and Technology, Program in Mathematics and Statistics, Murray, KY 42071. Offers MA, MAT, MS. *Program availability:* Part-time. *Degree requirements:* For master's, comprehensive exam, thesis optional. *Entrance requirements:* For master's, GRE General Test. Additional exam requirements/recommendations for international students: Required—TOEFL. *Faculty research:* Algebraic structures, mathematical biology, topolgy.

New Jersey Institute of Technology, College of Computing Science, Newark, NJ 07102. Offers big data management and mining (Certificate); business and information systems (Certificate); computer science (MS, PhD), including bioinformatics (MS), computer science, computing and business (MS), cyber security and privacy (MS), software engineering (MS); data mining (Certificate); information security (Certificate); information systems (MS, PhD), including business and information systems (MS), emergency management and business continuity (MS), information systems; information technology administration and security (MS); it administration (Certificate); network security and information assurance (Certificate); software engineering analysis/design (Certificate); Web systems development (Certificate). *Program availability:* Part-time, evening/weekend. *Faculty:* 55 full-time (7 women), 43 part-time/adjunct (4 women). *Students:* 750 full-time (227 women), 242 part-time (55 women); includes 154 minority (29 Black or African American, non-Hispanic/Latino; 68 Asian, non-Hispanic/Latino; 46 Hispanic/Latino; 11 Two or more races, non-Hispanic/Latino), 723 international. Average age 27. 2,549 applicants, 56% accepted, 440 enrolled. In 2015, 312 master's, 13 doctorates, 14 other advanced degrees awarded. Terminal master's awarded for partial completion of doctoral program. *Degree requirements:* For master's, thesis optional; for doctorate, thesis/dissertation. *Entrance requirements:* For master's, GRE General Test; for doctorate, GRE General Test, minimum graduate GPA of 3.5. Additional exam requirements/recommendations for international students: Required—TOEFL (minimum score 550 paper-based; 79 iBT). *Application deadline:* For fall admission, 6/1 priority date for domestic students, 5/1 priority date for international students; for spring admission, 11/15 priority date for domestic and international students. Applications are processed on a rolling basis. Application fee: $75. Electronic applications accepted. *Expenses:* $28,800 per year non-resident full-time. *Financial support:* In 2015–16, 3 fellowships with partial tuition reimbursements (averaging $3,600 per year), 33 research assistantships with partial tuition reimbursements (averaging $17,359 per year), 19 teaching assistantships with partial tuition reimbursements (averaging $11,225 per year) were awarded; career-related internships or fieldwork, Federal Work-Study, institutionally sponsored loans, and unspecified assistantships also available. Financial award application deadline: 1/15. *Faculty research:* Computer systems, communications and networking, artificial intelligence, database engineering, systems analysis. *Total annual research expenditures:* $2.1 million. *Unit head:* Dr. Marek Rusinkiewicz, Dean, 973-542-3383, Fax: 973-596-5777, E-mail: marek.rusinkiewicz@njit.edu. *Application contact:* Kathryn Kelly, Director of Admissions, 973-596-3300, Fax: 973-596-3461, E-mail: admissions@njit.edu.
Website: http://ccs.njit.edu

New Mexico Institute of Mining and Technology, Center for Graduate Studies, Department of Mathematics, Socorro, NM 87801. Offers applied and industrial mathematics (PhD); industrial mathematics (MS); mathematics (MS); operations research and statistics (MS). *Degree requirements:* For master's, thesis optional; for doctorate, thesis/dissertation. *Entrance requirements:* For master's, GRE General Test. Additional exam requirements/recommendations for international students: Required—TOEFL (minimum score 540 paper-based). *Expenses:* Tuition, state resident: full-time $5811; part-time $322.81 per credit. Tuition, nonresident: full-time $19,220; part-time $1067.79 per credit. *Required fees:* $1030. Tuition and fees vary according to course load. *Faculty research:* Applied mathematics, differential equations, industrial mathematics, numerical analysis, stochastic processes.

New York University, Leonard N. Stern School of Business, Department of Information, Operations and Management Sciences, New York, NY 10012-1019. Offers information systems (MBA, PhD); operations management (MBA, PhD); statistics (MBA, PhD). *Faculty research:* Knowledge management, economics of information, computer-supported groups and communities financial information systems, data mining and business intelligence.

North Carolina State University, Graduate School, College of Physical and Mathematical Sciences, Department of Statistics, Raleigh, NC 27695. Offers M Stat, MS, PhD. *Program availability:* Part-time. *Degree requirements:* For master's, comprehensive exam, thesis (for some programs), final oral exam; for doctorate, thesis/dissertation, final oral and written exams, written and oral preliminary exams. *Entrance requirements:* For master's and doctorate, GRE General Test. Additional exam requirements/recommendations for international students: Required—TOEFL. Electronic applications accepted. *Faculty research:* Biostatistics; time series; spatial, inference, environmental, industrial, genetics applications; nonlinear models; DOE.

North Dakota State University, College of Graduate and Interdisciplinary Studies, College of Science and Mathematics, Department of Statistics, Fargo, ND 58102. Offers applied statistics (MS, Certificate); statistics (PhD); MS/MS. *Degree requirements:* For master's, comprehensive exam, thesis; for doctorate, comprehensive exam, thesis/dissertation. *Entrance requirements:* For master's and doctorate, minimum GPA of 3.0. Additional exam requirements/recommendations for international students: Required—TOEFL (minimum score 550 paper-based; 79 iBT). Electronic applications accepted. *Faculty research:* Nonparametric statistics, survival analysis, multivariate analysis, distribution theory, inference modeling, biostatistics.

Northern Arizona University, Graduate College, College of Engineering, Forestry, and Natural Sciences, Department of Mathematics and Statistics, Flagstaff, AZ 86011. Offers applied statistics (Certificate); mathematics (MS); mathematics education (MS); statistics (MS). *Program availability:* Part-time. *Degree requirements:* For master's, comprehensive exam (for some programs), thesis (for some programs). *Entrance requirements:* For master's, minimum GPA of 3.0. Additional exam requirements/recommendations for international students: Required—TOEFL (minimum score 550 paper-based; 80 iBT), IELTS (minimum score 7). *Application deadline:* For fall admission, 3/15 priority date for domestic and international students; for spring admission, 10/15 priority date for domestic and international students. Applications are processed on a rolling basis. Application fee: $65. Electronic applications accepted. *Expenses: Tuition, area resident:* Full-time $8710. Tuition, nonresident: full-time $20,350. *Required fees:* $896. *Financial support:* Teaching assistantships with full tuition reimbursements, Federal Work-Study, scholarships/grants, health care benefits, tuition waivers (full and partial), and unspecified assistantships available. Financial award applicants required to submit FAFSA. *Faculty research:* Topology, statistics, groups, ring theory, number theory. *Unit head:* Dr. Michael J. Falk, Chair, 928-523-6891, Fax: 928-523-5847, E-mail: michael.falk@nau.edu. *Application contact:* Melinda Miller, Administrative Assistant, 928-523-6228, Fax: 928-523-5847,
E-mail: math.grad@nau.edu.
Website: http://nau.edu/CEFNS/NatSci/Math/

Northern Illinois University, Graduate School, College of Liberal Arts and Sciences, Department of Mathematical Sciences, Division of Statistics, De Kalb, IL 60115-2854. Offers MS. *Program availability:* Part-time. *Faculty:* 8 full-time (1 woman), 1 part-time/adjunct (0 women). *Students:* 14 full-time (4 women), 12 part-time (5 women); includes 5 minority (all Asian, non-Hispanic/Latino), 12 international. Average age 28. 27 applicants, 93% accepted, 11 enrolled. In 2015, 17 master's awarded. *Degree requirements:* For master's, comprehensive exam, thesis optional. *Entrance requirements:* For master's, GRE General Test, minimum GPA of 2.75, course work in statistics, calculus, linear algebra. Additional exam requirements/recommendations for international students: Required—TOEFL (minimum score 550 paper-based). *Application deadline:* For fall admission, 6/1 for domestic students, 5/1 for international students; for spring admission, 11/1 for domestic students, 10/1 for international students. Applications are processed on a rolling basis. Application fee: $40. Electronic applications accepted. *Financial support:* In 2015–16, 2 research assistantships with full tuition reimbursements, 18 teaching assistantships with full tuition reimbursements were awarded; fellowships with full tuition reimbursements, career-related internships or fieldwork, Federal Work-Study, scholarships/grants, tuition waivers (full), and unspecified assistantships also available. Support available to part-time students. Financial award applicants required to submit FAFSA. *Faculty research:* Reality and life testing, quality control, statistical inference from stochastic process, nonparametric statistics. *Unit head:* Dr. Sanjib Basu, Director, 815-753-6773, Fax: 815-753-6776.
Website: http://www.niu.edu/stat/

Northwestern University, The Graduate School, Judd A. and Marjorie Weinberg College of Arts and Sciences, Department of Statistics, Evanston, IL 60208. Offers MS, PhD. Admissions and degrees offered through The Graduate School. *Program availability:* Part-time. Terminal master's awarded for partial completion of doctoral program. *Degree requirements:* For master's, final exam; for doctorate, thesis/dissertation, preliminary exam, final exam. *Entrance requirements:* For master's and doctorate, GRE General Test. Additional exam requirements/recommendations for international students: Required—TOEFL. *Faculty research:* Theoretical statistics, applied statistics, computational methods, statistical designs, complex models.

Northwestern University, McCormick School of Engineering and Applied Science, Department of Industrial Engineering and Management Sciences, MS in Analytics Program, Evanston, IL 60208. Offers MS. *Students:* 70 full-time (26 women); includes 8 minority (2 Asian, non-Hispanic/Latino; 6 Hispanic/Latino), 41 international. 720 applicants, 11% accepted, 38 enrolled. In 2015, 31 master's awarded. *Entrance requirements:* For master's, GRE or GMAT. Additional exam requirements/recommendations for international students: Required—TOEFL (minimum score 80 iBT), IELTS (minimum score 7). *Application deadline:* For fall admission, 1/15 for domestic and international students. Application fee: $50. Electronic applications accepted. *Financial support:* Institutionally sponsored loans and scholarships/grants available. Financial award application deadline: 1/15; financial award applicants required to submit FAFSA. *Unit head:* Dr. Diego Klabjan, Director, 847-491-7205,
E-mail: d-klabjan@northwestern.edu. *Application contact:* Lindsay N. Montanari, Associate Director, 847-491-7205, Fax: 847-491-8005,
E-mail: lindsaymontanari@northwestern.edu.
Website: http://www.mccormick.northwestern.edu/analytics/index.html

Northwestern University, School of Professional Studies, Program in Predictive Analytics, Evanston, IL 60208. Offers computer-based data mining (MS); marketing analytics (MS); predictive modeling (MS); risk analytics (MS); Web analytics (MS). *Program availability:* Online learning. *Entrance requirements:* For master's, official transcripts, two letters of recommendation, statement of purpose, current resume or curriculum vitae. Additional exam requirements/recommendations for international students: Required—TOEFL (minimum score 600 paper-based; 100 iBT) or IELTS (minimum score 7).

Oakland University, Graduate Study and Lifelong Learning, College of Arts and Sciences, Department of Mathematics and Statistics, Program in Statistical Methods, Rochester, MI 48309-4401. Offers Certificate. *Students:* 3 applicants, 33% accepted. In 2015, 3 Certificates awarded. *Entrance requirements:* Additional exam requirements/recommendations for international students: Required—TOEFL (minimum score 550 paper-based). *Application deadline:* For fall admission, 7/15 priority date for domestic students, 5/1 priority date for international students; for winter admission, 12/1 priority date for domestic students, 9/1 priority date for international students; for spring admission, 3/15 priority date for domestic students. Application fee: $0. *Expenses:* Contact institution. *Financial support:* Federal Work-Study, institutionally sponsored loans, and tuition waivers (full) available. Financial award application deadline: 3/1; financial award applicants required to submit FAFSA. *Unit head:* Dr. Laszlo Liptak, Chair, Department of Mathematics and Statistics, 248-370-4054, Fax: 248-370-4184, E-mail: liptak@oakland.edu. *Application contact:* Dr. Meir Shillor, Coordinator of Graduate Programs, Department of Mathematics and Statistics, 248-370-3439, Fax: 248-370-4184, E-mail: shillor@oakland.edu.

The Ohio State University, Graduate School, College of Arts and Sciences, Division of Natural and Mathematical Sciences, Department of Statistics, Columbus, OH 43210. Offers biostatistics (PhD); statistics (M Appl Stat, MS, PhD). *Program availability:* Part-time. Terminal master's awarded for partial completion of doctoral program. *Degree requirements:* For master's, thesis optional; for doctorate, thesis/dissertation. *Entrance requirements:* For master's and doctorate, GRE General Test. Additional exam requirements/recommendations for international students: Required—TOEFL (minimum score 600 paper-based; 100 iBT); Recommended—IELTS (minimum score 8). Electronic applications accepted.

Oklahoma State University, College of Arts and Sciences, Department of Statistics, Stillwater, OK 74078. Offers MS, PhD. *Faculty:* 11 full-time (3 women). *Students:* 15 full-time (7 women), 4 part-time (0 women); includes 1 minority (Asian, non-Hispanic/Latino), 10 international. Average age 27. 57 applicants, 19% accepted, 5 enrolled. In 2015, 4 master's, 1 doctorate awarded. *Degree requirements:* For master's, comprehensive exam, thesis optional; for doctorate, comprehensive exam, thesis/dissertation. *Entrance requirements:* For master's and doctorate, GRE. Additional exam requirements/recommendations for international students: Required—TOEFL (minimum score 550 paper-based), IELTS (minimum score 7). *Application deadline:* For fall admission, 3/1 priority date for international students; for spring admission, 8/1 priority date for international students. Applications are processed on a rolling basis. Application fee: $40 ($75 for international students). Electronic applications accepted. *Expenses:* Tuition, state resident: full-time $3528; part-time $196 per credit hour. Tuition, nonresident: full-time $14,144; part-time $785.75 per credit hour. *Required fees:* $1895; $105.25 per credit hour. Tuition and fees vary according to campus/location. *Financial support:* In 2015–16, 1 research assistantship (averaging $19,674 per year), 15 teaching assistantships (averaging $20,454 per year) were awarded; career-related internships or fieldwork, Federal Work-Study, scholarships/grants, health care benefits, tuition waivers (partial), and unspecified assistantships also available. Support available to part-time students. Financial award application deadline: 3/1; financial award applicants required to submit FAFSA. *Faculty research:* Linear models, sampling methods, ranking and selections procedures, categorical data, multiple comparisons. *Unit head:* Dr. Mark Payton, Department Head, 405-744-5684, Fax: 405-744-3533, E-mail: mark.payton@okstate.edu. *Application contact:* Dr. Melinda H. McCann, Graduate Coordinator, 405-744-5684, Fax: 405-744-3533,
E-mail: mindy.mccann@okstate.edu.
Website: http://statistics.okstate.edu

Old Dominion University, College of Sciences, Programs in Computational and Applied Mathematics, Norfolk, VA 23529. Offers applied mathematics (MS, PhD), including statistics and biostatistics. *Program availability:* Part-time. *Faculty:* 19 full-time (3 women), 1 part-time/adjunct (0 women). *Students:* 27 full-time (10 women), 13 part-time (3 women); includes 5 minority (1 Black or African American, non-Hispanic/Latino; 3 Asian, non-Hispanic/Latino; 1 Two or more races, non-Hispanic/Latino), 11 international. Average age 30. 31 applicants, 55% accepted, 8 enrolled. In 2015, 8 master's, 3 doctorates awarded. Terminal master's awarded for partial completion of doctoral program. *Degree requirements:* For master's, project; for doctorate, comprehensive exam, thesis/dissertation, candidacy exam. *Entrance requirements:* For master's, minimum GPA of 3.0 in major, 2.8 overall; for doctorate, GRE General Test, 3 recommendation letters, transcripts, essay. Additional exam requirements/recommendations for international students: Required—TOEFL (minimum score 550 paper-based; 79 iBT); Recommended—IELTS (minimum score 6.5). *Application deadline:* For fall admission, 6/1 for domestic students, 5/15 for international students; for winter admission, 11/1 for domestic students, 10/1 for international students; for spring admission, 3/1 for domestic students, 2/1 for international students. Applications are processed on a rolling basis. Application fee: $50. Electronic applications accepted. *Expenses:* Tuition, state resident: full-time $11,136; part-time $464 per credit hour. Tuition, nonresident: full-time $27,840; part-time $1160 per credit hour. *Required fees:* $64 per semester. Tuition and fees vary according to campus/location, program and reciprocity agreements. *Financial support:* In 2015–16, 21 students received support, including 6 fellowships with full tuition reimbursements available (averaging $18,000 per year), 3 research assistantships with full tuition reimbursements available (averaging $16,000 per year), 12 teaching assistantships with full tuition reimbursements available (averaging $15,000 per year); scholarships/grants also available. Financial award application deadline: 2/15; financial award applicants required to submit FAFSA. *Faculty research:* Numerical analysis, integral equations, continuum mechanics, statistics, direct and inverse scattering. *Total annual research expenditures:* $506,890. *Unit head:* Dr. Raymond Cheng, Graduate Program Director, 757-683-3882, Fax: 757-683-3885, E-mail: rcheng@odu.edu. *Application contact:* William Heffelfinger, Director of Graduate Admissions, 757-683-5554, Fax: 757-683-3255, E-mail: gradadmit@odu.edu.
Website: http://sci.odu.edu/math/academics/grad.shtml

Oregon State University, College of Science, Program in Statistics, Corvallis, OR 97331. Offers MA, MS, PhD. *Program availability:* Part-time. *Faculty:* 14 full-time (8 women), 2 part-time/adjunct (1 woman). *Students:* 59 full-time (19 women), 2 part-time (1 woman); includes 7 minority (2 Asian, non-Hispanic/Latino; 1 Hispanic/Latino; 4 Two or more races, non-Hispanic/Latino), 23 international. Average age 28. 188 applicants, 20% accepted, 17 enrolled. In 2015, 15 master's, 3 doctorates awarded. *Degree requirements:* For master's, consulting experience; for doctorate, thesis/dissertation, consulting experience. *Entrance requirements:* For master's and doctorate, GRE. Additional exam requirements/recommendations for international students: Required—TOEFL (minimum score 80 iBT), IELTS (minimum score 6.5). *Application deadline:* For fall admission, 6/1 for domestic students. Application fee: $75 ($85 for international students). *Expenses:* Tuition, state resident: full-time $12,150; part-time $450 per credit. Tuition, nonresident: full-time $20,952; part-time $776 per credit. *Required fees:* $1572; $1443 per unit. One-time fee: $350. Tuition and fees vary according to course load, campus/location and program. *Financial support:* Research assistantships, teaching assistantships, Federal Work-Study, and institutionally sponsored loans available. Financial award application deadline: 1/15. *Faculty research:* Analysis of enumerative data, nonparametric statistics, asymptotics, experimental design, generalized regression models, linear model theory, reliability theory, survival analysis, wildlife and general survey methodology. *Unit head:* Dr. Virginia Lesser, Professor and Chair, 541-737-3584. *Application contact:* Department Office, 541-737-3366,
E-mail: stat-statoff@science.oregonstate.edu.
Website: http://www.stat.oregonstate.edu

Penn State University Park, Graduate School, Eberly College of Science, Department of Statistics, University Park, PA 16802. Offers applied statistics (MAS); statistics (MA, MS, PhD). *Unit head:* Dr. Douglas R. Cavener, Dean, 814-865-9591, Fax: 814-865-

3634. *Application contact:* Lori Stania, Director, Graduate Student Services, 814-865-1795, Fax: 814-865-4627, E-mail: l-gswww@lists.psu.edu.
Website: http://stat.psu.edu/

Portland State University, Graduate Studies, College of Liberal Arts and Sciences, Department of Mathematics and Statistics, Portland, OR 97207-0751. Offers mathematical sciences (PhD); mathematics education (PhD); statistics (MS); MA/MS. *Faculty:* 33 full-time (8 women), 15 part-time/adjunct (3 women). *Students:* 73 full-time (30 women), 53 part-time (20 women); includes 20 minority (2 American Indian or Alaska Native, non-Hispanic/Latino; 8 Asian, non-Hispanic/Latino; 7 Hispanic/Latino; 3 Two or more races, non-Hispanic/Latino), 14 international. Average age 33. 110 applicants, 71% accepted, 38 enrolled. In 2015, 26 master's, 1 doctorate awarded. *Degree requirements:* For master's, thesis or alternative, exams; for doctorate, 2 foreign languages, thesis/dissertation, exams. *Entrance requirements:* For master's, GRE General Test, GRE Subject Test, minimum GPA of 3.0 in upper-division course work or 2.75 overall; for doctorate, GRE General Test. Additional exam requirements/recommendations for international students: Required—TOEFL (minimum score 550 paper-based; 80 iBT). *Application deadline:* For fall admission, 4/1 for domestic students, 3/1 for international students; for winter admission, 9/1 for domestic students, 7/1 for international students; for spring admission, 11/1 for domestic and international students; for summer admission, 2/1 for domestic and international students. Applications are processed on a rolling basis. Application fee: $50. *Expenses:* $11,490 per year. *Financial support:* In 2015–16, 9 research assistantships with full tuition reimbursements (averaging $16,360 per year), 31 teaching assistantships with full tuition reimbursements (averaging $13,597 per year) were awarded; Federal Work-Study, scholarships/grants, tuition waivers (partial), and unspecified assistantships also available. Support available to part-time students. Financial award application deadline: 3/1; financial award applicants required to submit FAFSA. *Faculty research:* Algebra, topology, statistical distribution theory, control theory, statistical robustness. *Total annual research expenditures:* $518,084. *Unit head:* Dr. Marek Elzanowski, Chair, 503-725-3647, Fax: 503-725-3661, E-mail: elzanowskim@pdx.edu. *Application contact:* Katie Gettling, Administrative Assistant, 503-725-3604, Fax: 503-725-3661,
E-mail: ekatie@pdx.edu.
Website: http://www.mth.pdx.edu/

Purdue University, Graduate School, College of Science, Department of Statistics, West Lafayette, IN 47909. Offers applied statistics (MS); computational finance (MS); computational science and engineering (MS); statistics (PhD). *Program availability:* Part-time. *Faculty:* 71 full-time (22 women). *Students:* 102 full-time (36 women); includes 71 minority (8 Black or African American, non-Hispanic/Latino; 1 American Indian or Alaska Native, non-Hispanic/Latino; 55 Asian, non-Hispanic/Latino; 4 Hispanic/Latino; 3 Native Hawaiian or other Pacific Islander, non-Hispanic/Latino). Average age 25. 505 applicants, 9% accepted, 29 enrolled. In 2015, 29 master's, 14 doctorates awarded. Terminal master's awarded for partial completion of doctoral program. *Degree requirements:* For master's, comprehensive exam; for doctorate, thesis/dissertation, qualifying exams. *Entrance requirements:* For master's and doctorate, GRE General Test. Additional exam requirements/recommendations for international students: Required—TOEFL (minimum score 80 iBT); Recommended—IELTS (minimum score 7). *Application deadline:* For fall admission, 1/15 for domestic and international students; for spring admission, 10/15 for domestic students, 9/15 for international students. Application fee: $60 ($75 for international students). Electronic applications accepted. *Expenses:* Contact institution. *Financial support:* In 2015–16, 5 students received support, including 5 fellowships with full tuition reimbursements available (averaging $20,000 per year), research assistantships with full tuition reimbursements available (averaging $20,000 per year), 10 teaching assistantships with full tuition reimbursements available (averaging $20,000 per year); career-related internships or fieldwork and unspecified assistantships also available. Support available to part-time students. Financial award application deadline: 1/15; financial award applicants required to submit FAFSA. *Faculty research:* Nonparametric models, computational finance, design of experiments, probability theory, bioinformatics. *Unit head:* Dr. Hao Zhang, Head, 765-494-3141, Fax: 765-494-0558, E-mail: zhanghao@purdue.edu. *Application contact:* Anna Hook, Graduate Coordinator, 765-494-5794, Fax: 765-494-0558,
E-mail: hook6@purdue.edu.
Website: http://www.stat.purdue.edu/

Queen's University at Kingston, School of Graduate Studies, Faculty of Arts and Sciences, Department of Mathematics and Statistics, Kingston, ON K7L 3N6, Canada. Offers mathematics (M Sc, M Sc Eng, PhD); statistics (M Sc, M Sc Eng, PhD). *Program availability:* Part-time. *Degree requirements:* For master's, thesis; for doctorate, comprehensive exam, thesis/dissertation. *Entrance requirements:* Additional exam requirements/recommendations for international students: Required—TOEFL. *Faculty research:* Algebra, analysis, applied mathematics, statistics.

Rice University, Graduate Programs, George R. Brown School of Engineering, Department of Statistics, Houston, TX 77251-1892. Offers bioinformatics (PhD); biostatistics (PhD); computational finance (PhD); general statistics (PhD); statistics (M Stat, MA); MBA/M Stat. *Program availability:* Part-time. *Degree requirements:* For master's, comprehensive exam; for doctorate, comprehensive exam, thesis/dissertation. *Entrance requirements:* For master's and doctorate, GRE General Test, minimum GPA of 3.0. Additional exam requirements/recommendations for international students: Required—TOEFL (minimum score 630 paper-based; 90 iBT). Electronic applications accepted. *Faculty research:* Statistical genetics, non parametric function estimation, computational statistics and visualization, stochastic processes.

Rochester Institute of Technology, Graduate Enrollment Services, Kate Gleason College of Engineering, Center for Quality and Applied Statistics, Advanced Certificate Program in Lean Six Sigma, Rochester, NY 14623-5603. Offers Advanced Certificate. *Program availability:* Part-time, evening/weekend, 100% online. *Students:* 1 (woman) full-time, 1 part-time (0 women). 8 applicants, 38% accepted, 2 enrolled. In 2015, 2 Advanced Certificates awarded. *Entrance requirements:* For degree, GRE, baccalaureate degree from accredited institution with minimum GPA of 3.0, satisfactory background in statistics, official transcripts, two letters of recommendation, current resume. Additional exam requirements/recommendations for international students: Required—PTE (minimum score 58), TOEFL (minimum score 550 paper-based, 79 iBT) or IELTS (minimum score 6.5). *Application deadline:* Applications are processed on a rolling basis. Application fee: $60. Electronic applications accepted. *Expenses: Tuition, area resident:* Full-time $41,084; part-time $1742 per credit hour. *Required fees:* $274. Tuition and fees vary according to course load and program. *Financial support:* In 2015–16, 2 students received support. Available to part-time students. Applicants required to submit FAFSA. *Unit head:* Mark Smith, Director, 585-475- 7102,
E-mail: pxbeqa@rit.edu. *Application contact:* Diane Ellison, Associate Vice President, Graduate Enrollment Services, 585-475-2229, Fax: 585-475-7164,
E-mail: gradinfo@rit.edu.
Website: http://www.rit.edu/kgcoe/cqas/academics/advanced-certificate-in-lean-six-sigma

Rutgers University–New Brunswick, Graduate School-New Brunswick, Program in Statistics, Piscataway, NJ 08854-8097. Offers applied statistics (MS); biostatistics (MS); data mining (MS); quality and productivity management (MS); statistics (MS, PhD). *Program availability:* Part-time. Terminal master's awarded for partial completion of doctoral program. *Degree requirements:* For master's, comprehensive exam, essay, exam, non-thesis essay paper; for doctorate, one foreign language, thesis/dissertation, qualifying oral and written exams. *Entrance requirements:* For master's, GRE General Test; for doctorate, GRE General Test, GRE Subject Test (recommended). Additional exam requirements/recommendations for international students: Required—TOEFL (minimum score 550 paper-based). Electronic applications accepted. *Faculty research:* Probability, decision theory, linear models, multivariate statistics, statistical computing.

Sam Houston State University, College of Sciences, Department of Mathematics and Statistics, Huntsville, TX 77341. Offers mathematics (MA, MS); statistics (MS). *Program availability:* Part-time. *Degree requirements:* For master's, comprehensive exam, thesis optional. *Entrance requirements:* For master's, GRE General Test, letters of recommendation. Additional exam requirements/recommendations for international students: Required—TOEFL (minimum score 550 paper-based; 79 iBT), IELTS (minimum score 6.5). Electronic applications accepted.

San Diego State University, Graduate and Research Affairs, College of Sciences, Department of Mathematics and Statistics, Program in Statistics, San Diego, CA 92182. Offers MS. *Program availability:* Part-time. *Degree requirements:* For master's, comprehensive exam. *Entrance requirements:* For master's, GRE General Test. Additional exam requirements/recommendations for international students: Required—TOEFL. Electronic applications accepted.

San Jose State University, Graduate Studies and Research, College of Science, San Jose, CA 95192-0001. Offers biological sciences (MA, MS), including molecular biology and microbiology (MS), organismal biology, conservation and ecology (MS), physiology (MS); chemistry (MA, MS); computer science (MS); cybersecurity (Certificate); cybersecurity: core technologies (Certificate); geology (MS); marine science (MS); master biotechnology (MBT); mathematics (MA, MS), including mathematics education (MA), science; meteorology (MS); physics (MS), including computational physics, modern optics, science (MA, MS); science education (MA); statistics (MS); unix system administration (Certificate). *Program availability:* Part-time, evening/weekend. *Students:* 118 full-time (68 women), 52 part-time (25 women); includes 125 minority (5 Black or African American, non-Hispanic/Latino; 97 Asian, non-Hispanic/Latino; 23 Hispanic/Latino), 121 international. Average age 27. 1,236 applicants, 21% accepted, 171 enrolled. In 2015, 168 master's awarded. *Entrance requirements:* For master's, GRE. *Application deadline:* For fall admission, 6/29 for domestic students; for spring admission, 11/30 for domestic students. Applications are processed on a rolling basis. Application fee: $55. Electronic applications accepted. *Financial support:* Teaching assistantships, career-related internships or fieldwork, Federal Work-Study, and institutionally sponsored loans available. Support available to part-time students. Financial award applicants required to submit FAFSA. *Faculty research:* Radiochemistry/environmental analysis, health physics, radiation effects. *Unit head:* J. Michael Parrish, Dean, 408-924-4800, Fax: 408-924-4815. *Application contact:* 408-924-2480, Fax: 408-924-2477.
Website: http://www.science.sjsu.edu/

Simon Fraser University, Office of Graduate Studies, Faculty of Science, Department of Statistics and Actuarial Science, Burnaby, BC V5A 1S6, Canada. Offers actuarial science (M Sc); statistics (M Sc, PhD). *Degree requirements:* For master's, participation in consulting, project; for doctorate, comprehensive exam, thesis/dissertation. *Entrance requirements:* For master's, minimum GPA of 3.0 (on scale of 4.33), or 3.33 based on last 60 credits of undergraduate courses; for doctorate, minimum GPA of 3.5 (on scale of 4.33). Additional exam requirements/recommendations for international students: Recommended—TOEFL (minimum score 580 paper-based; 93 iBT), IELTS (minimum score 7), TWE (minimum score 5). Electronic applications accepted. *Faculty research:* Biostatistics, experimental design, envirometrics, statistical computing, statistical theory.

South Dakota State University, Graduate School, College of Engineering, Department of Mathematics and Statistics, Brookings, SD 57007. Offers computational science and statistics (PhD); mathematics (MS); statistics (MS). *Program availability:* Part-time. Terminal master's awarded for partial completion of doctoral program. *Degree requirements:* For master's, thesis (for some programs), oral exam; for doctorate, comprehensive exam, thesis/dissertation, oral and written exams. *Entrance requirements:* Additional exam requirements/recommendations for international students: Required—TOEFL (minimum score 550 paper-based; 80 iBT); Recommended—IELTS. *Faculty research:* Financial mathematics, predictive analytics, operations research, bioinformatics, biostatistics, computational science, statistics, number theory, abstract algebra.

Southern Illinois University Edwardsville, Graduate School, College of Arts and Sciences, Department of Mathematics and Statistics, Program in Statistics and Operations Research, Edwardsville, IL 62026. Offers MS. *Program availability:* Part-time. *Students:* 2 full-time (0 women), 11 part-time (7 women); includes 3 minority (1 Asian, non-Hispanic/Latino; 2 Hispanic/Latino), 3 international. *Degree requirements:* For master's, thesis (for some programs), special project. *Entrance requirements:* Additional exam requirements/recommendations for international students: Required—TOEFL (minimum score 550 paper-based, 79 iBT), IELTS (minimum score 6.5), Michigan Test of English Language Proficiency or PTE. *Application deadline:* For fall admission, 7/22 for domestic students, 7/15 for international students; for spring admission, 12/9 for domestic students, 11/15 for international students; for summer admission, 4/29 for domestic students, 4/15 for international students. Applications are processed on a rolling basis. Application fee: $30. Electronic applications accepted. *Expenses:* Tuition, state resident: full-time $5026; part-time $837 per course. Tuition, nonresident: full-time $12,566; part-time $2094 per course. *Required fees:* $1682; $474 per course. Tuition and fees vary according to course load, campus/location and program. *Financial support:* Fellowships, research assistantships, teaching assistantships, institutionally sponsored loans, scholarships/grants, and unspecified assistantships available. *Unit head:* Dr. Adam Weyhaupt, Chair, 618-650-2200, E-mail: aweyhau@siue.edu. *Application contact:* Bob Skorczewski, Coordinator of International and Graduate Recruitment, 618-650-3705, Fax: 618-650-3618,
E-mail: graduateadmissions@siue.edu.
Website: http://www.siue.edu/artsandsciences/math/

Southern Methodist University, Dedman College of Humanities and Sciences, Department of Statistical Science, Dallas, TX 75275-0332. Offers MS, PhD. *Program availability:* Part-time. *Degree requirements:* For master's, thesis, oral and written exams; for doctorate, thesis/dissertation, oral and written exams. *Entrance requirements:* For master's, GRE General Test, 12 hours of advanced math courses; for doctorate, GRE General Test, minimum GPA of 3.0. Additional exam requirements/recommendations for international students: Required—TOEFL. Electronic applications accepted. *Faculty research:* Regression, time series, linear models sampling, nonparametrics, biostatistics.

Stanford University, School of Humanities and Sciences, Department of Statistics, Stanford, CA 94305-9991. Offers data science (MS); financial mathematics (MS);

statistics (PhD). Terminal master's awarded for partial completion of doctoral program. *Degree requirements:* For doctorate, thesis/dissertation, oral exam, qualifying exams. *Entrance requirements:* For master's, GRE General Test; for doctorate, GRE General Test, GRE Subject Test. Additional exam requirements/recommendations for international students: Required—TOEFL. Electronic applications accepted. *Expenses: Tuition, area resident:* Full-time $45,729. *Required fees:* $591.

Stephen F. Austin State University, Graduate School, College of Sciences and Mathematics, Department of Mathematics and Statistics, Nacogdoches, TX 75962. Offers mathematics (MS); mathematics education (MS); statistics (MS). *Degree requirements:* For master's, comprehensive exam, thesis optional. *Entrance requirements:* For master's, GRE General Test, minimum GPA of 2.8 in last 60 hours, 2.5 overall. Additional exam requirements/recommendations for international students: Required—TOEFL. *Faculty research:* Kernel type estimators, fractal mappings, spline curve fitting, robust regression continua theory.

Stevens Institute of Technology, Graduate School, Charles V. Schaefer Jr. School of Engineering, Department of Mathematical Sciences, Program in Stochastic Systems, Hoboken, NJ 07030. Offers MS, Certificate. *Program availability:* Part-time, evening/weekend. *Students:* 2 full-time (0 women), 1 part-time (0 women); includes 1 minority (Hispanic/Latino). Average age 23. 16 applicants, 63% accepted, 3 enrolled. In 2015, 1 master's awarded. *Entrance requirements:* Additional exam requirements/recommendations for international students: Required—TOEFL (minimum score 74 iBT). *Application deadline:* For fall admission, 6/1 for domestic students, 4/15 for international students; for spring admission, 11/30 for domestic students, 11/1 for international students. Applications are processed on a rolling basis. Application fee: $60. Electronic applications accepted. *Expenses: Tuition, area resident:* Full-time $32,200; part-time $1450 per credit. *Required fees:* $1150; $550 per unit. $275 per semester. *Financial support:* Fellowships, research assistantships, teaching assistantships, career-related internships or fieldwork, Federal Work-Study, scholarships/grants, and unspecified assistantships available. Financial award application deadline: 2/15; financial award applicants required to submit FAFSA. *Unit head:* Darinka Dentcheva, Director, 201-216-8640, Fax: 201-216-8321, E-mail: ddentche@stevens.edu. *Application contact:* Graduate Admission, 888-783-8367, Fax: 888-511-1306, E-mail: graduate@stevens.edu.

Stony Brook University, State University of New York, Graduate School, College of Engineering and Applied Sciences, Department of Applied Mathematics and Statistics, Stony Brook, NY 11794. Offers MS, PhD, Advanced Certificate. *Faculty:* 30 full-time (7 women), 2 part-time/adjunct (0 women). *Students:* 279 full-time (97 women), 20 part-time (10 women); includes 24 minority (2 Black or African American, non-Hispanic/Latino; 18 Asian, non-Hispanic/Latino; 4 Hispanic/Latino), 239 international. Average age 26. 564 applicants, 72% accepted, 97 enrolled. In 2015, 72 master's, 26 doctorates awarded. *Degree requirements:* For master's, thesis or alternative; for doctorate, one foreign language, comprehensive exam, thesis/dissertation. *Entrance requirements:* For master's and doctorate, GRE General Test. Additional exam requirements/recommendations for international students: Required—TOEFL (minimum score 90 iBT). *Application deadline:* For fall admission, 1/15 for domestic students; for spring admission, 10/1 for domestic students. Application fee: $100. *Expenses:* $12,421 full-time resident tuition and fees, $453 per credit hour; $23,761 full-time nonresident tuition and fees, $925 per credit hour. *Financial support:* In 2015–16, 1 fellowship, 44 research assistantships, 39 teaching assistantships were awarded. *Faculty research:* Computational Mathematics, Computational modeling, Applied Mathematics, Computational Physics, Computational Chemistry. *Total annual research expenditures:* $2.5 million. *Unit head:* Dr. Joseph Mitchell, Chair, 631-632-8366, Fax: 631-632-8490, E-mail: joseph.mitchell@stonybrook.edu. *Application contact:* Christine Rota, Coordinator, 631-632-8360, Fax: 631-632-8490, E-mail: christine.rota@stonybrook.edu.

Temple University, Fox School of Business, Doctoral Programs in Business, Philadelphia, PA 19122-6096. Offers accounting (PhD); entrepreneurship (PhD); finance (PhD); international business (PhD); management information systems (PhD); marketing (PhD); risk management and insurance (PhD); statistics (PhD); strategic management (PhD); tourism and sport (PhD). *Accreditation:* AACSB. *Degree requirements:* For doctorate, thesis/dissertation. *Entrance requirements:* For doctorate, GRE General Test, GMAT, minimum GPA of 3.0, master's degree. Additional exam requirements/recommendations for international students: Required—TOEFL (minimum score 600 paper-based; 100 iBT), IELTS (minimum score 7.5). Electronic applications accepted.

Temple University, Fox School of Business, Specialized Master's Programs, Philadelphia, PA 19122-6096. Offers accountancy (MS); actuarial science (MS); finance (MS); financial engineering (MS); human resource management (MS); innovation management and entrepreneurship (MS); marketing (MS); statistics (MS). MS in innovation management and entrepreneurship delivered jointly with College of Engineering. *Accreditation:* AACSB. *Program availability:* Part-time. *Entrance requirements:* For master's, GRE General Test or GMAT, minimum undergraduate GPA of 3.0. Additional exam requirements/recommendations for international students: Required—TOEFL (minimum score 600 paper-based; 100 iBT), IELTS (minimum score 7.5).

Texas A&M University, College of Science, Department of Statistics, College Station, TX 77843. Offers analytics (MS); statistics (MS, PhD). MS in analytics offered in partnership with Mays Business School. *Program availability:* Part-time. *Faculty:* 28. *Students:* 58 full-time (21 women), 279 part-time (77 women); includes 86 minority (12 Black or African American, non-Hispanic/Latino; 1 American Indian or Alaska Native, non-Hispanic/Latino; 45 Asian, non-Hispanic/Latino; 21 Hispanic/Latino; 7 Two or more races, non-Hispanic/Latino), 43 international. Average age 35. 130 applicants, 100% accepted, 101 enrolled. In 2015, 59 master's, 10 doctorates awarded. Terminal master's awarded for partial completion of doctoral program. *Degree requirements:* For doctorate, thesis/dissertation. *Entrance requirements:* For master's and doctorate, GRE General Test. Additional exam requirements/recommendations for international students: Required—TOEFL. *Application deadline:* For fall admission, 3/1 priority date for domestic students; for spring admission, 8/1 for domestic students. Applications are processed on a rolling basis. Application fee: $50 ($90 for international students). *Expenses:* Contact institution. *Financial support:* In 2015–16, 93 students received support, including 10 fellowships with tuition reimbursements available (averaging $5,740 per year), 24 research assistantships with tuition reimbursements available (averaging $9,118 per year), 28 teaching assistantships with tuition reimbursements available (averaging $10,127 per year); career-related internships or fieldwork, institutionally sponsored loans, scholarships/grants, traineeships, health care benefits, tuition waivers (full and partial), and unspecified assistantships also available. Support available to part-time students. Financial award application deadline: 3/1; financial award applicants required to submit FAFSA. *Faculty research:* Time series, applied probability and stochastic processes, factor models, statistics education, microarrays. *Unit head:* Dr. Valen E. Johnson, Department Head, 979-845-3141, Fax: 979-845-3144, E-mail: vjohnson@stat.tamu.edu. *Application contact:* Dr. Jianhua Huang, Graduate Director, 979-845-3141, Fax: 979-845-3144, E-mail: grecruiting@stat.tamu.edu.
Website: http://www.stat.tamu.edu/

Texas A&M University–Kingsville, College of Graduate Studies, College of Arts and Sciences, Department of Mathematics, Program in Statistical Analytics, Computing and Modeling, Kingsville, TX 78363. Offers MS. *Degree requirements:* For master's, thesis or project. *Entrance requirements:* For master's, GRE. Additional exam requirements/recommendations for international students: Required—TOEFL (minimum score 550 paper-based; 79 iBT), IELTS (minimum score 6).

Texas Tech University, Graduate School, College of Arts and Sciences, Department of Mathematics and Statistics, Lubbock, TX 79409. Offers mathematics (MA, MS, PhD); statistics (MS). *Program availability:* Part-time, 100% online. *Faculty:* 58 full-time (19 women), 4 part-time/adjunct (1 woman). *Students:* 119 full-time (58 women), 20 part-time (10 women); includes 14 minority (2 Black or African American, non-Hispanic/Latino; 4 Asian, non-Hispanic/Latino; 7 Hispanic/Latino; 1 Two or more races, non-Hispanic/Latino), 82 international. Average age 30. 95 applicants, 68% accepted, 38 enrolled. In 2015, 27 master's, 9 doctorates awarded. Terminal master's awarded for partial completion of doctoral program. *Degree requirements:* For master's, comprehensive exam (for some programs), thesis (for some programs); for doctorate, comprehensive exam, thesis/dissertation. *Entrance requirements:* For master's, GRE (for MS and assistantship applications only), MS (official transcripts, 3 letters of recommendation, statement of purpose), MA (official transcripts); for doctorate, GRE General Test, official transcripts, 3 letters of recommendation, resume/curriculum vitae, statement of purpose. Additional exam requirements/recommendations for international students: Required—TOEFL (minimum score 550 paper-based; 79 iBT), IELTS (minimum score 6.5). *Application deadline:* For fall admission, 6/1 priority date for domestic students, 1/15 priority date for international students; for spring admission, 9/1 priority date for domestic students, 6/15 priority date for international students. Applications are processed on a rolling basis. Application fee: $60. Electronic applications accepted. *Expenses:* Tuition, state resident: full-time $6477; part-time $269.89 per credit hour. Tuition, nonresident: full-time $15,837; part-time $659.89 per credit hour. *Required fees:* $2751; $36.50 per credit hour. $937.50 per semester. Tuition and fees vary according to course level. *Financial support:* In 2015–16, 116 students received support, including 91 fellowships (averaging $2,766 per year), 12 research assistantships (averaging $8,527 per year), 100 teaching assistantships (averaging $16,914 per year). Financial award application deadline: 2/15; financial award applicants required to submit FAFSA. *Faculty research:* Applied math, biomath, complex analysis, computational mathematics, statistics. *Total annual research expenditures:* $1.1 million. *Unit head:* Dr. Magdalena Toda, Professor and Chair, 806-834-7944, Fax: 806-742-1112, E-mail: magda.toda@ttu.edu. *Application contact:* Gene Gray, Senior Graduate Academic Advisor, 806-834-1269, Fax: 806-742-1112, E-mail: gene.gray@ttu.edu.
Website: http://www.math.ttu.edu/

Tulane University, School of Science and Engineering, Department of Mathematics, New Orleans, LA 70118-5669. Offers applied mathematics (MS); mathematics (MS, PhD); statistics (MS). *Degree requirements:* For master's, thesis (for some programs); for doctorate, thesis/dissertation. *Entrance requirements:* For master's, GRE General Test, minimum B average in undergraduate course work; for doctorate, GRE General Test. Additional exam requirements/recommendations for international students: Required—TOEFL. Electronic applications accepted.

Université de Montréal, Faculty of Arts and Sciences, Department of Mathematics and Statistics, Montréal, QC H3C 3J7, Canada. Offers mathematical and computational finance (M Sc, DESS); mathematics (M Sc, PhD); statistics (M Sc, PhD). *Degree requirements:* For master's, thesis; for doctorate, thesis/dissertation, general exam. *Entrance requirements:* For master's and doctorate, proficiency in French. Electronic applications accepted. *Faculty research:* Pure and applied mathematics, actuarial mathematics.

Université Laval, Faculty of Sciences and Engineering, Department of Mathematics and Statistics, Program in Statistics, Québec, QC G1K 7P4, Canada. Offers M Sc. *Degree requirements:* For master's, thesis (for some programs). *Entrance requirements:* For master's, knowledge of French and English. Electronic applications accepted.

University of Alaska Fairbanks, College of Natural Sciences and Mathematics, Department of Mathematics and Statistics, Fairbanks, AK 99775-6660. Offers mathematics (PhD); statistics (MS, Graduate Certificate). *Program availability:* Part-time. *Faculty:* 20 full-time (10 women). *Students:* 12 full-time (2 women), 3 part-time (1 woman), 6 international. Average age 29. 19 applicants, 47% accepted, 5 enrolled. In 2015, 4 master's awarded. *Degree requirements:* For master's, comprehensive exam, thesis (for some programs), oral defense of project or thesis; for doctorate, comprehensive exam, thesis/dissertation, oral defense of dissertation. *Entrance requirements:* For master's, GRE General Test, bachelor's degree from accredited institution with minimum cumulative undergraduate and major GPA of 3.0; for doctorate, GRE Subject Test (mathematics), bachelor's degree from accredited institution with minimum cumulative undergraduate and major GPA of 3.0. Additional exam requirements/recommendations for international students: Required—TOEFL (minimum score 550 paper-based; 79 iBT), IELTS (minimum score 6.5). *Application deadline:* For fall admission, 6/1 for domestic students, 3/1 for international students; for spring admission, 10/15 for domestic students, 9/1 for international students. Applications are processed on a rolling basis. Application fee: $60. Electronic applications accepted. *Expenses:* Tuition, state resident: full-time $7614; part-time $423 per credit. Tuition, nonresident: full-time $15,552; part-time $864 per credit. *Required fees:* $38 per credit. $187 per semester. Tuition and fees vary according to course level, course load, program and reciprocity agreements. *Financial support:* In 2015–16, 1 research assistantship with full tuition reimbursement (averaging $16,834 per year), 11 teaching assistantships with full tuition reimbursements (averaging $18,239 per year) were awarded; fellowships with full tuition reimbursements, career-related internships or fieldwork, Federal Work-Study, scholarships/grants, health care benefits, and unspecified assistantships also available. Support available to part-time students. Financial award application deadline: 2/15; financial award applicants required to submit FAFSA. *Faculty research:* Kriging, arrangements of hyperplanes, bifurcation analysis of time-periodic differential-delay equations, inverse problems, phylogenic tree construction. *Unit head:* Dr. John Rhodes, Department Chair, 907-474-7332, Fax: 907-474-5394, E-mail: uaf-mathandstat-dept@alaska.edu. *Application contact:* Mary Kreta, Director of Admissions, 907-474-7500, Fax: 907-474-7097,
E-mail: admissions@uaf.edu.
Website: http://www.uaf.edu/dms/

University of Alberta, Faculty of Graduate Studies and Research, Department of Mathematical and Statistical Sciences, Edmonton, AB T6G 2E1, Canada. Offers applied mathematics (M Sc, PhD); biostatistics (M Sc); mathematical finance (M Sc, PhD); mathematical physics (M Sc, PhD); mathematics (M Sc, PhD); statistics (M Sc, PhD, Postgraduate Diploma). *Program availability:* Part-time. Terminal master's awarded for partial completion of doctoral program. *Degree requirements:* For master's, thesis (for some programs); for doctorate, comprehensive exam, thesis/dissertation. *Entrance requirements:* Additional exam requirements/recommendations for international students: Required—TOEFL (minimum score 580 paper-based). Electronic applications accepted. *Faculty research:* Classical and functional analysis, algebra, differential equations, geometry.

The University of Arizona, Graduate Interdisciplinary Programs, Graduate Interdisciplinary Program in Statistics, Tucson, AZ 85721. Offers MS, PhD. *Entrance requirements:* Additional exam requirements/recommendations for international students: Required—TOEFL, IELTS. *Application deadline:* For fall admission, 2/1 for domestic and international students; for spring admission, 8/1 for domestic and international students. Application fee: $75. *Unit head:* Dr. Joseph Watkins, Chair, 520-621-5245, Fax: 520-621-4101, E-mail: gwatkins@math.arizona.edu. *Application contact:* Rachel Mattull, Faculty Director, 520-621-0847,
E-mail: gidp@email.arizona.edu.
Website: http://stat.arizona.edu

University of Arkansas, Graduate School, J. William Fulbright College of Arts and Sciences, Department of Mathematical Sciences, Program in Statistics, Fayetteville, AR 72701-1201. Offers MS. *Students:* 11 full-time (6 women), 8 part-time (6 women); includes 2 minority (1 Black or African American, non-Hispanic/Latino; 1 Asian, non-Hispanic/Latino), 9 international. In 2015, 8 master's awarded. *Degree requirements:* For master's, thesis. *Application deadline:* For fall admission, 4/1 for international students; for spring admission, 10/1 for international students. Applications are processed on a rolling basis. Application fee: $40 ($50 for international students). Electronic applications accepted. *Financial support:* In 2015–16, 4 research assistantships, 65 teaching assistantships were awarded; fellowships, career-related internships or fieldwork, and Federal Work-Study also available. Support available to part-time students. Financial award application deadline: 4/1; financial award applicants required to submit FAFSA. *Application contact:* Dr. Mark Arnold, Graduate Coordinator, 479-575-3351, Fax: 479-575-8630, E-mail: arnold@uark.edu.
Website: http://stat.uark.edu/

The University of British Columbia, Faculty of Science, Department of Statistics, Vancouver, BC V6T 1Z4, Canada. Offers M Sc, PhD. *Degree requirements:* For master's, thesis or alternative, seminar; for doctorate, comprehensive exam, thesis/dissertation. *Entrance requirements:* Additional exam requirements/recommendations for international students: Required—TOEFL (minimum score 600 paper-based; 100 iBT), IELTS (minimum score 7.5). Electronic applications accepted. *Faculty research:* Theoretical statistics, applied statistics, biostatistics, computational statistics, data science.

University of Calgary, Faculty of Graduate Studies, Faculty of Science, Department of Mathematics and Statistics, Calgary, AB T2N 1N4, Canada. Offers M Sc, PhD. *Degree requirements:* For master's, comprehensive exam, thesis; for doctorate, thesis/dissertation, candidacy exam, preliminary exams. *Entrance requirements:* For master's, honors degree in applied math, pure math, or statistics; for doctorate, MA or M Sc. Additional exam requirements/recommendations for international students: Required—TOEFL (minimum score 600 paper-based) or IELTS (minimum score 7). *Faculty research:* Combinatorics, applied mathematics, statistics, probability, analysis.

University of California, Berkeley, Graduate Division, College of Letters and Science, Department of Statistics, Berkeley, CA 94720-1500. Offers MA, PhD. *Degree requirements:* For doctorate, thesis/dissertation, qualifying exam, written preliminary exam. *Entrance requirements:* For master's and doctorate, GRE General Test, minimum GPA of 3.0, 3 letters of recommendation.

University of California, Davis, Graduate Studies, Program in Statistics, Davis, CA 95616. Offers MS, PhD. Terminal master's awarded for partial completion of doctoral program. *Degree requirements:* For master's, comprehensive exam; for doctorate, thesis/dissertation. *Entrance requirements:* For master's and doctorate, GRE General Test, minimum GPA of 3.0. Additional exam requirements/recommendations for international students: Required—TOEFL (minimum score 550 paper-based). Electronic applications accepted. *Faculty research:* Nonparametric analysis, time series analysis, biostatistics, curve estimation, reliability.

University of California, Irvine, Donald Bren School of Information and Computer Sciences, Department of Statistics, Irvine, CA 92697. Offers MS, PhD. *Students:* 55 full-time (25 women), 4 part-time (1 woman); includes 4 minority (2 Asian, non-Hispanic/Latino; 1 Hispanic/Latino; 1 Two or more races, non-Hispanic/Latino), 37 international. Average age 26. 276 applicants, 27% accepted, 23 enrolled. In 2015, 18 master's, 7 doctorates awarded. Application fee: $90 ($110 for international students). *Unit head:* Jessica M. Utts, Chair, 949-824-0649, Fax: 949-824-9863, E-mail: jutts@uci.edu. *Application contact:* Kris Bolcer, Student Affairs Director, 949-824-5156,
E-mail: kris@ics.uci.edu.
Website: http://www.stat.uci.edu/

University of California, Los Angeles, Graduate Division, College of Letters and Science, Department of Statistics, Los Angeles, CA 90095. Offers MS, PhD. Terminal master's awarded for partial completion of doctoral program. *Degree requirements:* For master's, comprehensive exam, thesis; for doctorate, thesis/dissertation, oral and written qualifying exams; 1 quarter of teaching experience. *Entrance requirements:* For master's, GRE General Test, bachelor's degree; minimum undergraduate GPA of 3.0, 3.2 in upper-division courses (or its equivalent if letter grade system not used); for doctorate, GRE General Test, bachelor's degree; minimum GPA of 3.5 (or its equivalent if letter grade system not used). Additional exam requirements/recommendations for international students: Required—TOEFL. Electronic applications accepted.

University of California, Riverside, Graduate Division, Department of Statistics, Riverside, CA 92521-0219. Offers applied statistics (PhD); statistics (MS). Terminal master's awarded for partial completion of doctoral program. *Degree requirements:* For master's, comprehensive exam; for doctorate, comprehensive exam, thesis/dissertation. *Entrance requirements:* For master's, GRE (minimum score 300), strong background in statistics and sufficient training in mathematics or upper-division statistical courses to meet deficiencies; minimum GPA of 3.0; for doctorate, GRE (minimum score 300), BS in statistics, computer science, mathematics, or other quantitatively-based discipline; minimum GPA of 3.25. Additional exam requirements/recommendations for international students: Required—TOEFL (minimum score 550 paper-based; 80 iBT); Recommended—IELTS. Electronic applications accepted. *Faculty research:* Design and analysis of gene expression experiments using DNA microarrays, statistical design and analysis of experiments, linear models, probability models and statistical inference, SNP/SFP discovery using DNA microarray, genetic mapping.

University of California, San Diego, Graduate Division, Department of Mathematics, La Jolla, CA 92093. Offers applied mathematics (MA); computational science (PhD); mathematics (MA, PhD); statistics (MS, PhD). *Students:* 130 full-time (32 women), 3 part-time (0 women); includes 18 minority (13 Asian, non-Hispanic/Latino; 5 Hispanic/Latino), 72 international. 777 applicants, 16% accepted, 35 enrolled. In 2015, 18 master's, 16 doctorates awarded. *Degree requirements:* For master's, comprehensive exam; for doctorate, comprehensive exam, thesis/dissertation. *Entrance requirements:* For master's, GRE General Test; GRE Subject Test (for MA), minimum GPA of 3.0; for doctorate, GRE General Test, GRE Subject Test, minimum GPA of 3.0. Additional exam requirements/recommendations for international students: Required—TOEFL (minimum score 550 paper-based; 80 iBT), IELTS. *Application deadline:* For fall admission, 1/4 for domestic and international students. Application fee: $90 ($110 for international students). Electronic applications accepted. *Expenses:* Tuition, state resident: full-time $11,220. Tuition, nonresident: full-time $26,322. *Required fees:* $1800. *Financial support:* Fellowships, research assistantships, teaching assistantships, and scholarships/grants available. Financial award applicants required to submit FAFSA. *Faculty research:* Combinatorics, bioinformatics, differential equations, logic and computational complexity, probability theory and statistics. *Unit head:* Peter Ebenfelt, Chair, 858-822-4961, E-mail: pebenfelt@ucsd.edu. *Application contact:* Debra Shon, Admissions Contact, 858-534-9056, E-mail: mathgradadmissions@math.ucsd.edu.
Website: http://math.ucsd.edu/

University of California, Santa Barbara, Graduate Division, College of Letters and Sciences, Division of Mathematics, Life, and Physical Sciences, Department of Statistics and Applied Probability, Santa Barbara, CA 93106-3110. Offers bioengineering (PhD); financial mathematics and statistics (PhD); quantitative methods in the social sciences (PhD); statistics (MA), including applied statistics, mathematical statistics; statistics and applied probability (PhD); MA/PhD. *Faculty:* 11 full-time (2 women), 8 part-time/adjunct (0 women). *Students:* 65 full-time (32 women); includes 8 minority (1 Black or African American, non-Hispanic/Latino; 5 Asian, non-Hispanic/Latino; 1 Hispanic/Latino; 1 Native Hawaiian or other Pacific Islander, non-Hispanic/Latino), 47 international. Average age 27. 452 applicants, 9% accepted, 12 enrolled. In 2015, 18 master's, 8 doctorates awarded. Terminal master's awarded for partial completion of doctoral program. *Degree requirements:* For master's, comprehensive exam, thesis optional; for doctorate, comprehensive exam, thesis/dissertation. *Entrance requirements:* For master's and doctorate, GRE General Test. Additional exam requirements/recommendations for international students: Required—TOEFL (minimum score 550 paper-based; 80 iBT), IELTS (minimum score 7). *Application deadline:* For fall admission, 12/15 priority date for domestic students, 12/1 priority date for international students; for winter admission, 11/1 priority date for domestic and international students; for spring admission, 2/1 priority date for domestic and international students. Application fee: $90 ($110 for international students). Electronic applications accepted. *Financial support:* In 2015–16, 23 students received support, including 6 fellowships with full tuition reimbursements available (averaging $11,285 per year), 1 research assistantship with tuition reimbursement available (averaging $2,790 per year), 28 teaching assistantships with partial tuition reimbursements available (averaging $14,557 per year); Federal Work-Study, scholarships/grants, and health care benefits also available. Financial award application deadline: 12/15; financial award applicants required to submit FAFSA. *Faculty research:* Bayesian inference, financial mathematics, stochastic processes, environmental statistics, biostatistical modeling. *Total annual research expenditures:* $139,480. *Unit head:* Dr. John Hsu, Chair, 805-893-4055, E-mail: hsu@pstat.ucsb.edu. *Application contact:* Angelina M. Toporov, Graduate Program Assistant, 805-893-2129, Fax: 805-893-2334,
E-mail: toporov@pstat.ucsb.edu.
Website: http://www.pstat.ucsb.edu/

University of California, Santa Cruz, Division of Graduate Studies, Jack Baskin School of Engineering, Program in Statistics and Applied Mathematics, Santa Cruz, CA 95064. Offers MS, PhD. Terminal master's awarded for partial completion of doctoral program. *Degree requirements:* For master's, seminar, qualifying exam, capstone project; for doctorate, thesis/dissertation, seminar, qualifying exam. *Entrance requirements:* For master's and doctorate, GRE General Test; GRE Subject Test in math (recommended). Additional exam requirements/recommendations for international students: Required—TOEFL (minimum score 570 paper-based; 89 iBT); Recommended—IELTS (minimum score 8). Electronic applications accepted. *Faculty research:* Bayesian nonparametric methods; computationally intensive Bayesian inference, prediction, and decision-making; envirometrics; fluid mechanics; mathematical biology.

University of Central Florida, College of Sciences, Department of Statistics, Orlando, FL 32816. Offers SAS data mining (Certificate); statistical computing (MS). *Program availability:* Part-time, evening/weekend. *Faculty:* 12 full-time (2 women), 1 part-time/adjunct (0 women). *Students:* 41 full-time (17 women), 18 part-time (7 women); includes 19 minority (2 Black or African American, non-Hispanic/Latino; 1 American Indian or Alaska Native, non-Hispanic/Latino; 9 Asian, non-Hispanic/Latino; 6 Hispanic/Latino; 1 Two or more races, non-Hispanic/Latino), 15 international. Average age 29. 94 applicants, 61% accepted, 35 enrolled. In 2015, 25 master's, 4 other advanced degrees awarded. *Degree requirements:* For master's, comprehensive exam. *Entrance requirements:* For master's, GRE General Test, minimum GPA of 3.0 in last 60 hours. Additional exam requirements/recommendations for international students: Required—TOEFL. *Application deadline:* For fall admission, 7/15 for domestic students; for spring admission, 12/1 for domestic students. Application fee: $30. Electronic applications accepted. *Expenses:* Tuition, state resident: part-time $288.16 per credit hour. Tuition, nonresident: part-time $1071.31 per credit hour. *Financial support:* In 2015–16, 17 students received support, including 1 fellowship with partial tuition reimbursement available (averaging $4,000 per year), 18 teaching assistantships with partial tuition reimbursements available (averaging $9,600 per year); research assistantships with partial tuition reimbursements available, career-related internships or fieldwork, Federal Work-Study, institutionally sponsored loans, tuition waivers (partial), and unspecified assistantships also available. Financial award application deadline: 3/1; financial award applicants required to submit FAFSA. *Faculty research:* Multivariate analysis, quality control, shrinkage estimation. *Unit head:* Dr. Shunpu Zhang, Chair, 407-823-1566, Fax: 407-823-5419, E-mail: shunpu.zhang@ucf.edu. *Application contact:* Director, Admissions and Student Services, 407-823-2766, Fax: 407-823-6442,
E-mail: gradadmissions@ucf.edu.
Website: http://statistics.cos.ucf.edu/

University of Central Oklahoma, The Jackson College of Graduate Studies, College of Mathematics and Science, Department of Mathematics and Statistics, Edmond, OK 73034-5209. Offers applied mathematical sciences (MS), including computer science, mathematics, statistics, teaching. *Program availability:* Part-time. *Degree requirements:* For master's, comprehensive exam (for some programs), thesis (for some programs). *Entrance requirements:* For master's, GRE. Additional exam requirements/recommendations for international students: Required—TOEFL (minimum score 550 paper-based; 79 iBT), IELTS (minimum score 6.5). Electronic applications accepted.

University of Chicago, Booth School of Business, Full-Time MBA Program, Chicago, IL 60637. Offers accounting (MBA); analytic finance (MBA); analytic management (MBA); econometrics and statistics (MBA); economics (MBA); entrepreneurship (MBA); finance (MBA); general management (MBA); health administration and policy (Certificate); international business (MBA); managerial and organizational behavior (MBA); marketing management (MBA); operations management (MBA); strategic management (MBA); MBA/AM; MBA/JD; MBA/MA; MBA/MD; MBA/MPP. *Accreditation:* AACSB. *Students:*

1,151 full-time (443 women), 17 part-time (9 women). Terminal master's awarded for partial completion of doctoral program. *Entrance requirements:* For master's, GMAT or GRE, transcripts, resume, 2 letters of recommendation, essay, interview. Additional exam requirements/recommendations for international students: Required—TOEFL (minimum score 600 paper-based; 104 iBT), IELTS (minimum score 7), PTE (minimum score 70). *Application deadline:* For spring admission, 4/1 for domestic and international students. Electronic applications accepted. *Expenses:* Contact institution. *Unit head:* Stacey Kole, Deputy Dean, 773-702-7121. *Application contact:* Full-time MBA Program Admissions, 773-702-7369, Fax: 773-702-9085,
E-mail: admissions@chicagobooth.edu.
Website: https://www.chicagobooth.edu/programs/full-time

University of Chicago, Division of the Physical Sciences, Department of Statistics, Chicago, IL 60637. Offers MS, PhD. *Program availability:* Part-time. Terminal master's awarded for partial completion of doctoral program. *Degree requirements:* For master's, thesis; for doctorate, thesis/dissertation. *Entrance requirements:* For master's and doctorate, GRE General Test. Additional exam requirements/recommendations for international students: Required—TOEFL. Electronic applications accepted. *Faculty research:* Genetics, econometrics, generalized linear models, history of statistics, probability theory.

University of Cincinnati, Graduate School, McMicken College of Arts and Sciences, Department of Mathematical Sciences, Cincinnati, OH 45221. Offers applied mathematics (MS, PhD); mathematics education (MAT); pure mathematics (MS, PhD); statistics (MS, PhD). *Program availability:* Part-time. Terminal master's awarded for partial completion of doctoral program. *Degree requirements:* For master's, comprehensive exam, thesis or alternative; for doctorate, one foreign language, comprehensive exam, thesis/dissertation. *Entrance requirements:* For master's, GRE, teacher certification (for MAT); for doctorate, GRE. Additional exam requirements/recommendations for international students: Required—TOEFL. Electronic applications accepted. *Faculty research:* Algebra, analysis, differential equations, numerical analysis, statistics.

University of Colorado Denver, College of Liberal Arts and Sciences, Department of Mathematical and Statistical Sciences, Denver, CO 80217. Offers applied mathematics (MS, PhD), including applied mathematics, applied probability (MS), applied statistics (MS), computational biology, computational mathematics (PhD), discrete mathematics, finite geometry (PhD), mathematics education (PhD), mathematics of engineering and science (MS), numerical analysis, operations research (MS), optimization and operations research (PhD), probability (PhD), statistics (PhD). *Program availability:* Part-time. *Faculty:* 18 full-time (4 women), 5 part-time/adjunct (0 women). *Students:* 48 full-time (16 women), 15 part-time (6 women); includes 7 minority (1 Black or African American, non-Hispanic/Latino; 2 Asian, non-Hispanic/Latino; 3 Hispanic/Latino; 1 Two or more races, non-Hispanic/Latino), 12 international. Average age 32. 105 applicants, 70% accepted, 21 enrolled. In 2015, 10 master's, 3 doctorates awarded. *Degree requirements:* For master's, comprehensive exam, thesis optional, 30 hours of course work with minimum GPA of 3.0; for doctorate, comprehensive exam, thesis/dissertation, 42 hours of course work with minimum GPA of 3.25. *Entrance requirements:* For master's, GRE General Test; GRE Subject Test in math (recommended), 30 hours of course work in mathematics (24 of which must be upper-division mathematics), bachelor's degree with minimum GPA of 3.0; for doctorate, GRE General Test; GRE Subject Test in math (recommended), 30 hours of course work in mathematics (24 of which must be upper-division mathematics), master's degree with minimum GPA of 3.25. Additional exam requirements/recommendations for international students: Required—TOEFL (minimum score 537 paper-based; 75 iBT); Recommended—IELTS (minimum score 6.5). *Application deadline:* For fall admission, 4/1 for domestic and international students; for spring admission, 10/1 for domestic and international students; for summer admission, 4/1 for domestic and international students. Application fee: $50 ($75 for international students). Electronic applications accepted. *Financial support:* In 2015–16, 46 students received support. Fellowships with partial tuition reimbursements available, research assistantships with full tuition reimbursements available, teaching assistantships with full tuition reimbursements available, Federal Work-Study, institutionally sponsored loans, scholarships/grants, and traineeships available. Financial award application deadline: 4/1; financial award applicants required to submit FAFSA. *Faculty research:* Computational mathematics, computational biology, discrete mathematics and geometry, probability and statistics, optimization. *Unit head:* Dr. Michael Ferrara, Graduate Chair, 303-315-1705,
E-mail: michael.ferrara@ucdenver.edu. *Application contact:* Julie Blunck, Program Assistant, 303-315-1743, E-mail: julie.blunck@ucdenver.edu.
Website: http://www.ucdenver.edu/academics/colleges/CLAS/Departments/math/Pages/MathStats.aspx

University of Connecticut, Graduate School, College of Liberal Arts and Sciences, Department of Statistics, Storrs, CT 06269. Offers MS, PhD. Terminal master's awarded for partial completion of doctoral program. *Degree requirements:* For master's, comprehensive exam; for doctorate, thesis/dissertation. *Entrance requirements:* For master's and doctorate, GRE General Test. Additional exam requirements/recommendations for international students: Required—TOEFL (minimum score 550 paper-based). Electronic applications accepted.

University of Delaware, College of Agriculture and Natural Resources, Department of Food and Resource Economics, Program in Statistics, Newark, DE 19716. Offers MS. *Program availability:* Part-time. *Entrance requirements:* For master's, GRE General Test, 3 letters of recommendation. Additional exam requirements/recommendations for international students: Required—TOEFL (minimum score 550 paper-based). Electronic applications accepted.

University of Denver, Daniels College of Business, Department of Business Information and Analytics, Denver, CO 80208. Offers business analytics (MBA, MS). *Faculty:* 14 full-time (3 women), 9 part-time/adjunct (4 women). *Students:* 26 full-time (8 women), 24 part-time (13 women); includes 4 minority (1 Black or African American, non-Hispanic/Latino; 1 Asian, non-Hispanic/Latino; 2 Two or more races, non-Hispanic/Latino), 23 international. Average age 28. 66 applicants, 64% accepted, 18 enrolled. In 2015, 19 master's awarded. *Entrance requirements:* For master's, GRE General Test or GMAT, bachelor's degree, transcripts, essays, resume, interview. Additional exam requirements/recommendations for international students: Required—TOEFL (minimum score 570 paper-based; 88 iBT). *Application deadline:* For fall admission, 11/15 priority date for domestic and international students; for spring admission, 10/1 priority date for domestic and international students. Applications are processed on a rolling basis. Application fee: $100. Electronic applications accepted. *Expenses:* $45,621. *Financial support:* In 2015–16, 38 students received support, including 9 teaching assistantships with tuition reimbursements available (averaging $1,738 per year); career-related internships or fieldwork, Federal Work-Study, institutionally sponsored loans, scholarships/grants, and unspecified assistantships also available. Support available to part-time students. Financial award application deadline: 2/15; financial award applicants required to submit FAFSA. *Faculty research:* Information technology strategy, project management, healthcare information systems, distributed knowledge work, complex adaptive systems. *Unit head:* Dr. Andrew Urbaczewski, Associate Professor and Chair, 303-871-4802, Fax: 303-871-2067, E-mail: andrew.urbaczewski@du.edu.
Website: http://daniels.du.edu/masters-degrees/business-analytics/

University of Florida, Graduate School, College of Liberal Arts and Sciences, Department of Statistics, Gainesville, FL 32611. Offers quantitative finance (PhD); statistics (M Stat, MS Stat, PhD). *Program availability:* Part-time. *Students:* 47 full-time (16 women), 7 part-time (6 women); includes 4 minority (2 Asian, non-Hispanic/Latino; 2 Hispanic/Latino), 56 international. Average age 29. 394 applicants, 6% accepted, 15 enrolled. In 2015, 9 master's, 4 doctorates awarded. Terminal master's awarded for partial completion of doctoral program. *Degree requirements:* For master's, variable foreign language requirement, comprehensive exam, final oral exam; thesis (for MS Stat); for doctorate, comprehensive exam, thesis/dissertation. *Entrance requirements:* For master's and doctorate, GRE General Test, minimum GPA of 3.0. Additional exam requirements/recommendations for international students: Required—TOEFL (minimum score 550 paper-based; 80 iBT), IELTS (minimum score 6). *Application deadline:* For fall admission, 2/1 priority date for domestic students, 2/1 for international students. Applications are processed on a rolling basis. Application fee: $30. Electronic applications accepted. *Financial support:* In 2015–16, 13 fellowships, 5 research assistantships, 41 teaching assistantships were awarded; unspecified assistantships also available. Financial award application deadline: 2/1; financial award applicants required to submit FAFSA. *Faculty research:* Bayesian statistics, biostatistics, Markov Chain Monte Carlo (MCMC), nonparametric statistics, statistical genetics/genomics. *Total annual research expenditures:* $81,514. *Unit head:* Brett Presnell, PhD, Associate Professor and Department Chair, 352-273-2989, Fax: 352-392-5175,
E-mail: presnell@stat.ufl.edu. *Application contact:* James P. Hobert, PhD, Professor and Graduate Coordinator, 352-273-2990, Fax: 352-392-5175, E-mail: jhobert@stat.ufl.edu.
Website: http://www.stat.ufl.edu/

University of Georgia, Franklin College of Arts and Sciences, Department of Statistics, Athens, GA 30602. Offers MS, PhD. *Degree requirements:* For master's, thesis (for some programs); for doctorate, one foreign language, thesis/dissertation. *Entrance requirements:* For master's and doctorate, GRE General Test. Electronic applications accepted.

University of Guelph, Graduate Studies, College of Physical and Engineering Science, Department of Mathematics and Statistics, Guelph, ON N1G 2W1, Canada. Offers applied mathematics (PhD); applied statistics (PhD); mathematics and statistics (M Sc). *Program availability:* Part-time. *Degree requirements:* For master's, thesis (for some programs); for doctorate, thesis/dissertation. *Entrance requirements:* For master's, minimum B- average during previous 2 years of course work; for doctorate, minimum B average. Additional exam requirements/recommendations for international students: Required—TOEFL (minimum score 550 paper-based; 89 iBT), IELTS (minimum score 6.5). *Faculty research:* Dynamical systems, mathematical biology, numerical analysis, linear and nonlinear models, reliability and bioassay.

University of Houston–Clear Lake, School of Science and Computer Engineering, Program in Statistics, Houston, TX 77058-1002. Offers MS. *Entrance requirements:* For master's, GRE General Test. Additional exam requirements/recommendations for international students: Required—TOEFL (minimum score 550 paper-based).

University of Idaho, College of Graduate Studies, College of Science, Department of Statistical Science, Moscow, ID 83844-1104. Offers MS. *Faculty:* 7 full-time. *Students:* 23 full-time, 17 part-time. Average age 33. In 2015, 8 master's awarded. *Degree requirements:* For master's, thesis or alternative. *Entrance requirements:* For master's, minimum GPA of 2.8. Additional exam requirements/recommendations for international students: Required—TOEFL. *Application deadline:* For fall admission, 8/1 for domestic students; for spring admission, 12/15 for domestic students. Applications are processed on a rolling basis. Application fee: $60. Electronic applications accepted. *Expenses:* Tuition, state resident: full-time $6205; part-time $399 per credit hour. Tuition, nonresident: full-time $20,209; part-time $1177 per credit hour. *Required fees:* $2017; $58 per credit hour. Full-time tuition and fees vary according to course load and reciprocity agreements. *Financial support:* Research assistantships and teaching assistantships available. Financial award applicants required to submit FAFSA. *Faculty research:* Statistical genetics, biostatistics, nonlinear population dynamics, multivariate and computational statistics, Six Sigma innovation and design. *Unit head:* Dr. Christopher J. Williams, Chair, 208-885-2929, E-mail: stat@uidaho.edu. *Application contact:* Sean Scoggin, Graduate Recruitment Coordinator, 208-885-4723, Fax: 208-885-4406, E-mail: graduateadmissions@uidaho.edu.
Website: http://www.uidaho.edu/sci/stat/

University of Illinois at Chicago, College of Liberal Arts and Sciences, Department of Mathematics, Statistics, and Computer Science, Chicago, IL 60607-7128. Offers mathematics (DA); probability and statistics (PhD); secondary school mathematics (MST); statistics (MS). *Program availability:* Part-time. *Faculty:* 73 full-time (20 women), 3 part-time/adjunct (0 women). *Students:* 118 full-time (30 women), 19 part-time (9 women); includes 19 minority (7 Asian, non-Hispanic/Latino; 9 Hispanic/Latino; 3 Two or more races, non-Hispanic/Latino), 51 international. Average age 28. *Degree requirements:* For master's, comprehensive exam; for doctorate, one foreign language, thesis/dissertation. *Entrance requirements:* For master's and doctorate, GRE General Test, minimum GPA of 3.0. Additional exam requirements/recommendations for international students: Required—TOEFL (minimum score 100 iBT). *Application deadline:* For fall admission, 1/1 for domestic and international students; for spring admission, 10/1 for domestic students, 7/15 for international students. Applications are processed on a rolling basis. Application fee: $60. Electronic applications accepted. *Expenses:* Tuition, state resident: full-time $11,480; part-time $3826 per credit. Tuition, nonresident: full-time $23,720; part-time $7906 per credit. *Required fees:* $1333 per semester. Part-time tuition and fees vary according to course load and program. *Financial support:* In 2015–16, 109 students received support, including 2 fellowships with full tuition reimbursements available (averaging $20,000 per year), 8 research assistantships with full tuition reimbursements available (averaging $17,000 per year), 87 teaching assistantships with full tuition reimbursements available (averaging $17,000 per year); Federal Work-Study, scholarships/grants, and tuition waivers (full) also available. Financial award application deadline: 1/1. *Unit head:* Prof. Brooke Shipley, Head, 312-996-3044, E-mail: shipley@math.uic.edu. *Application contact:* Ramin Takloo-Bighash, Director of Graduate Studies, 312-996-5119, E-mail: dgs@math.uic.edu.
Website: http://www.math.uic.edu/

University of Illinois at Urbana–Champaign, Graduate College, College of Liberal Arts and Sciences, Department of Statistics, Champaign, IL 61820. Offers analytics (MS); applied statistics (MS); statistics (MS, PhD).

The University of Iowa, Graduate College, College of Education, Department of Psychological and Quantitative Foundations, Iowa City, IA 52242-1316. Offers counseling psychology (PhD); educational measurement and statistics (MA, PhD); educational psychology (MA, PhD); school psychology (PhD, Ed S). *Accreditation:* APA. *Degree requirements:* For master's, thesis optional, exam; for doctorate, comprehensive exam, thesis/dissertation; for Ed S, exam. *Entrance requirements:* For master's, doctorate, and Ed S, GRE General Test, minimum GPA of 3.0. Additional exam requirements/recommendations for international students: Required—TOEFL (minimum score 550 paper-based; 81 iBT). Electronic applications accepted.

The University of Iowa, Graduate College, College of Liberal Arts and Sciences, Department of Statistics and Actuarial Science, Iowa City, IA 52242-1316. Offers actuarial science (MS); statistics (MS, PhD). *Degree requirements:* For master's, thesis optional, exam; for doctorate, comprehensive exam, thesis/dissertation. *Entrance requirements:* For master's and doctorate, GRE General Test, minimum GPA of 3.0. Additional exam requirements/recommendations for international students: Required—TOEFL (minimum score 550 paper-based; 81 iBT). Electronic applications accepted.

The University of Kansas, University of Kansas Medical Center, School of Medicine, Department of Biostatistics, Kansas City, KS 66160. Offers applied statistics and analytics (MS); biostatistics (MS, PhD, Graduate Certificate); statistical applications (Graduate Certificate). *Faculty:* 16. *Students:* 25 full-time (7 women), 13 part-time (5 women); includes 9 minority (3 Black or African American, non-Hispanic/Latino; 5 Asian, non-Hispanic/Latino; 1 Two or more races, non-Hispanic/Latino), 13 international. Average age 31. 52 applicants, 94% accepted, 18 enrolled. In 2015, 4 master's, 2 doctorates awarded. *Degree requirements:* For master's, comprehensive exam; for doctorate, comprehensive exam, thesis/dissertation. *Entrance requirements:* For master's, GRE, coursework in calculus, computer programming, linear algebra, differential equations, and numerical analysis; for doctorate, master's degree. Additional exam requirements/recommendations for international students: Required—TOEFL. Application fee: $60. Electronic applications accepted. *Expenses:* Contact institution. *Financial support:* Research assistantships with full tuition reimbursements, scholarships/grants, traineeships, and unspecified assistantships available. Financial award application deadline: 3/1; financial award applicants required to submit FAFSA. *Faculty research:* Biostatistics, clinical trials. *Total annual research expenditures:* $774,141. *Unit head:* Dr. Matthew Mayo, Professor and Chair, 913-588-4735 Ext. 913, Fax: 913-588-0252, E-mail: mmayo@kumc.edu. *Application contact:* Dr. Jo A. Wick, Assistant Director of Graduate Education, 913-588-4790, Fax: 913-588-0252, E-mail: jwick@kumc.edu.
Website: http://www.kumc.edu/school-of-medicine/department-of-biostatistics.html

University of Kentucky, Graduate School, College of Arts and Sciences, Program in Statistics, Lexington, KY 40506-0032. Offers MS, PhD. *Degree requirements:* For master's, comprehensive exam, thesis optional; for doctorate, comprehensive exam, thesis/dissertation. *Entrance requirements:* For master's, GRE General Test, minimum undergraduate GPA of 2.75; for doctorate, GRE General Test, minimum graduate GPA of 3.0. Additional exam requirements/recommendations for international students: Required—TOEFL (minimum score 550 paper-based). Electronic applications accepted. *Faculty research:* Computer intensive statistical inference, biostatistics, mathematical and applied statistics, applied probability.

The University of Manchester, School of Mathematics, Manchester, United Kingdom. Offers actuarial science (PhD); applied mathematics (M Phil, PhD); applied numerical computing (M Phil, PhD); financial mathematics (M Phil, PhD); mathematical logic (M Phil); probability (M Phil, PhD); pure mathematics (M Phil, PhD); statistics (M Phil, PhD).

The University of Manchester, School of Social Sciences, Manchester, United Kingdom. Offers ethnographic documentary (M Phil); interdisciplinary study of culture (PhD); philosophy (PhD); politics (PhD); social anthropology (PhD); social anthropology with visual media (PhD); social change (PhD); social statistics (PhD); sociology (PhD); visual anthropology (M Phil).

University of Manitoba, Faculty of Graduate Studies, Faculty of Science, Department of Statistics, Winnipeg, MB R3T 2N2, Canada. Offers M Sc, PhD. *Degree requirements:* For master's, thesis or alternative; for doctorate, one foreign language, thesis/dissertation.

University of Manitoba, Faculty of Graduate Studies, Faculty of Science, Program in Mathematical, Computational and Statistical Sciences, Winnipeg, MB R3T 2N2, Canada. Offers MMCSS.

University of Maryland, Baltimore County, The Graduate School, College of Natural and Mathematical Sciences, Department of Mathematics and Statistics, Program in Statistics, Baltimore, MD 21250. Offers biostatistics (PhD); environmental statistics (MS); statistics (MS, PhD). *Program availability:* Part-time, evening/weekend. *Faculty:* 10 full-time (3 women). *Students:* 21 full-time (11 women), 16 part-time (7 women); includes 5 minority (4 Asian, non-Hispanic/Latino; 1 Hispanic/Latino), 16 international. Average age 34. 36 applicants, 39% accepted, 6 enrolled. In 2015, 9 master's, 5 doctorates awarded. Terminal master's awarded for partial completion of doctoral program. *Degree requirements:* For master's, comprehensive exam (for some programs), thesis (for some programs); for doctorate, comprehensive exam, thesis/dissertation. *Entrance requirements:* For master's and doctorate, GRE General Test, minimum GPA of 3.0. Additional exam requirements/recommendations for international students: Required—TOEFL (minimum score 600 paper-based; 100 iBT). *Application deadline:* For fall admission, 2/15 priority date for domestic students, 1/1 priority date for international students; for spring admission, 10/15 priority date for domestic students, 5/1 priority date for international students. Applications are processed on a rolling basis. Application fee: $50. Electronic applications accepted. *Expenses:* Tuition, state resident: full-time $12,816. Tuition, nonresident: full-time $19,710. *Financial support:* In 2015–16, 14 students received support, including 1 fellowship with full tuition reimbursement available (averaging $17,000 per year), 1 research assistantship with full tuition reimbursement available (averaging $17,000 per year), 10 teaching assistantships with tuition reimbursements available (averaging $17,000 per year); career-related internships or fieldwork, scholarships/grants, traineeships, health care benefits, tuition waivers (full and partial), and unspecified assistantships also available. Support available to part-time students. Financial award application deadline: 2/15. *Faculty research:* Design of experiments, statistical decision theory and inference, time series analysis, biostatistics and environmental statistics, bioinformatics. *Total annual research expenditures:* $578,449. *Unit head:* Dr. Junyong Park, Graduate Program Director, 410-455-2407, Fax: 410-455-1066, E-mail: junpark@umbc.edu. *Application contact:* Janet Burgee, Program Coordinator, Mathematics and Statistics, 410-455-2401, Fax: 410-455-1066, E-mail: jburgee@umbc.edu.
Website: http://www.math.umbc.edu

University of Maryland, College Park, Academic Affairs, College of Computer, Mathematical and Natural Sciences, Department of Mathematics, Program in Mathematical Statistics, College Park, MD 20742. Offers MA, PhD. *Program availability:* Part-time, evening/weekend. Terminal master's awarded for partial completion of doctoral program. *Degree requirements:* For master's, thesis or comprehensive exams, scholarly paper; for doctorate, one foreign language, thesis/dissertation, written and oral exams. *Entrance requirements:* For master's and doctorate, GRE General Test, GRE Subject Test (mathematics), minimum GPA of 3.0, 3 letters of recommendation.

Electronic applications accepted. *Faculty research:* Statistics and probability, stochastic processes, nonparametric statistics, space-time statistics.

University of Massachusetts Amherst, Graduate School, College of Natural Sciences, Department of Mathematics and Statistics, Amherst, MA 01003. Offers applied mathematics (MS); mathematics (MS, PhD); statistics (MS, PhD). Terminal master's awarded for partial completion of doctoral program. *Degree requirements:* For master's, thesis or alternative; for doctorate, comprehensive exam, thesis/dissertation. *Entrance requirements:* For master's and doctorate, GRE General Test, GRE Subject Test (mathematics). Additional exam requirements/recommendations for international students: Required—TOEFL (minimum score 550 paper-based; 80 iBT), IELTS (minimum score 6.5). Electronic applications accepted.

University of Memphis, Graduate School, College of Arts and Sciences, Department of Mathematical Sciences, Memphis, TN 38152. Offers applied mathematics (MS); applied statistics (PhD); bioinformatics (MS); computer sciences (MS); statistics (MS). *Program availability:* Part-time. *Faculty:* 18 full-time (7 women). *Students:* 36 full-time (9 women), 22 part-time (9 women); includes 15 minority (9 Black or African American, non-Hispanic/Latino; 3 Asian, non-Hispanic/Latino; 3 Hispanic/Latino), 17 international. Average age 34. 50 applicants, 92% accepted, 12 enrolled. In 2015, 10 master's, 9 doctorates awarded. Terminal master's awarded for partial completion of doctoral program. *Degree requirements:* For master's, comprehensive exam; for doctorate, one foreign language, thesis/dissertation, oral exams. *Entrance requirements:* For master's and doctorate, GRE General Test, minimum GPA of 2.5. Additional exam requirements/recommendations for international students: Required—TOEFL (minimum score 550 paper-based). *Application deadline:* For fall admission, 8/1 for domestic students, 5/1 priority date for international students; for spring admission, 12/1 for domestic students, 9/1 priority date for international students. Applications are processed on a rolling basis. Application fee: $35 ($60 for international students). Electronic applications accepted. *Financial support:* In 2015–16, 22 students received support. Fellowships with full tuition reimbursements available, research assistantships with full tuition reimbursements available, teaching assistantships with full tuition reimbursements available, career-related internships or fieldwork, Federal Work-Study, scholarships/grants, and unspecified assistantships available. Financial award application deadline: 2/15; financial award applicants required to submit FAFSA. *Faculty research:* Combinatorics, ergodic theory, graph theory, Ramsey theory, applied statistics. *Unit head:* Dr. Irena Lasiecka, Chairman, 901-678-2482, Fax: 901-678-2480, E-mail: lasiecka@memphis.edu. *Application contact:* Dr. Fernanda Botelho, Coordinator of Graduate Studies, 901-678-3131, Fax: 901-678-2480, E-mail: mbotelho@memphis.edu.
Website: http://www.MSCI.memphis.edu/

University of Michigan, Rackham Graduate School, College of Literature, Science, and the Arts, Department of Statistics, Ann Arbor, MI 48109. Offers applied statistics (MS); statistics (AM, PhD). *Faculty:* 20 full-time (4 women). *Students:* 156 full-time (62 women); includes 122 minority (3 Black or African American, non-Hispanic/Latino; 115 Asian, non-Hispanic/Latino; 4 Hispanic/Latino). Average age 27. 960 applicants, 20% accepted, 59 enrolled. In 2015, 35 master's, 9 doctorates awarded. Terminal master's awarded for partial completion of doctoral program. *Degree requirements:* For master's, thesis; for doctorate, thesis/dissertation, oral defense of dissertation, preliminary exam. *Entrance requirements:* For master's and doctorate, GRE General Test. Additional exam requirements/recommendations for international students: Required—TOEFL (minimum score 560 paper-based; 84 iBT), IELTS (minimum score 6.5). *Application deadline:* For fall admission, 12/31 priority date for domestic and international students. Applications are processed on a rolling basis. Application fee: $75 ($90 for international students). Electronic applications accepted. *Expenses:* $40,892 per year tuition and fees (for master's program). *Financial support:* In 2015–16, 83 students received support, including 12 fellowships with full tuition reimbursements available (averaging $25,000 per year), 27 research assistantships with full tuition reimbursements available (averaging $19,000 per year), 41 teaching assistantships with full tuition reimbursements available (averaging $19,000 per year); career-related internships or fieldwork, Federal Work-Study, institutionally sponsored loans, scholarships/grants, health care benefits, and unspecified assistantships also available. Financial award application deadline: 12/31. *Faculty research:* Reliability and degradation modeling, biological and legal applications, bioinformatics, statistical computing, covariance estimation. *Unit head:* Prof. Xuming He, Chair, 734-647-8192, E-mail: statchair@umich.edu. *Application contact:* Judy McDonald, Graduate Program Coordinator, 734-763-3520, Fax: 734-763-4676, E-mail: stat-grad-coordinator@umich.edu.
Website: http://www.lsa.umich.edu/stats/

University of Michigan, Rackham Graduate School, Program in Survey Methodology, Ann Arbor, MI 48106. Offers data science (MS, PhD); social and psychological (MS, PhD); statistical (MS, PhD); survey methodology (Certificate). *Program availability:* Part-time. *Faculty:* 12 full-time (2 women), 8 part-time/adjunct (3 women). *Students:* 28 full-time (19 women), 8 part-time (3 women); includes 21 minority (1 Black or African American, non-Hispanic/Latino; 10 Asian, non-Hispanic/Latino; 10 Two or more races, non-Hispanic/Latino). Average age 24. 42 applicants, 48% accepted, 13 enrolled. In 2015, 6 master's, 3 doctorates, 2 other advanced degrees awarded. Terminal master's awarded for partial completion of doctoral program. *Degree requirements:* For master's, internships; for doctorate, comprehensive exam, thesis/dissertation. *Entrance requirements:* For master's and doctorate, GRE, 3 letters of recommendation, academic statement of purpose, personal statement, resume or curriculum vitae, academic transcripts; for Certificate, 3 letters of recommendation, academic statement of purpose, personal statement, resume or curriculum vitae, academic transcripts. Additional exam requirements/recommendations for international students: Required—TOEFL (minimum score 560 paper-based; 84 iBT). *Application deadline:* For fall admission, 1/1 for domestic and international students. Application fee: $75 ($90 for international students). Electronic applications accepted. *Expenses:* $10,319 per term in-state, $20,844 per term out-of-state, plus $165 per term mandatory fees. *Financial support:* In 2015–16, 29 students received support, including 10 fellowships (averaging $14,500 per year), 9 research assistantships with full tuition reimbursements available (averaging $21,000 per year); teaching assistantships, career-related internships or fieldwork, institutionally sponsored loans, scholarships/grants, traineeships, health care benefits, and unspecified assistantships also available. Financial award application deadline: 1/1. *Faculty research:* Survey methodology, web surveys, survey non-response, sample design methods, adaptive survey design. *Total annual research expenditures:* $2.5 million. *Unit head:* Dr. Frederick Conrad, Director, 734-936-1019, Fax: 734-764-8263, E-mail: fconrad@umich.edu. *Application contact:* Jill Esau, Educational Programs Administrator, 734-647-4620, Fax: 734-764-8263, E-mail: jesau@umich.edu.
Website: http://psm.isr.umich.edu/

University of Minnesota, Twin Cities Campus, Graduate School, College of Liberal Arts, School of Statistics, Minneapolis, MN 55455-0213. Offers MS, PhD. *Program availability:* Part-time. Terminal master's awarded for partial completion of doctoral program. *Degree requirements:* For doctorate, comprehensive exam, thesis/dissertation. *Entrance requirements:* For master's and doctorate, GRE General Test.

Additional exam requirements/recommendations for international students: Required—TOEFL (minimum score 100 iBT). Electronic applications accepted. *Faculty research:* Data analysis, statistical computing, experimental design, probability theory, Bayesian inference, risk analysis.

University of Missouri, Office of Research and Graduate Studies, College of Arts and Science, Department of Statistics, Columbia, MO 65211. Offers MA, PhD. *Degree requirements:* For doctorate, comprehensive exam, thesis/dissertation. *Entrance requirements:* For master's, GRE General Test, minimum GPA of 3.0 in math and statistics courses; bachelor's degree from accredited college/university in related area; for doctorate, GRE General Test, minimum GPA of 3.0, 3.5 in math/statistics. Additional exam requirements/recommendations for international students: Required—TOEFL (minimum score 535 paper-based; 73 iBT). Electronic applications accepted. *Faculty research:* Statistical problems in the fields of ecology, genetics, economics, meteorology, wildlife management, epidemiology, AIDS research, geophysics, climatology.

University of Missouri–Kansas City, College of Arts and Sciences, Department of Mathematics and Statistics, Kansas City, MO 64110-2499. Offers MA, MS, PhD. PhD (interdisciplinary) offered through the School of Graduate Studies. *Program availability:* Part-time. *Faculty:* 15 full-time (3 women), 4 part-time/adjunct (1 woman). *Students:* 15 full-time (9 women), 7 part-time (3 women); includes 2 minority (1 Asian, non-Hispanic/Latino; 1 Hispanic/Latino), 13 international. Average age 29. 38 applicants, 34% accepted, 3 enrolled. In 2015, 13 master's awarded. Terminal master's awarded for partial completion of doctoral program. *Degree requirements:* For master's, written exam; for doctorate, 2 foreign languages, thesis/dissertation, oral and written exams. *Entrance requirements:* For master's, bachelor's degree in mathematics, minimum GPA of 3.0; for doctorate, GMAT or GRE General Test. Additional exam requirements/recommendations for international students: Required—TOEFL (minimum score 550 paper-based; 80 iBT). *Application deadline:* For fall admission, 3/15 for domestic students, 3/15 priority date for international students; for spring admission, 10/15 for domestic and international students. Applications are processed on a rolling basis. Application fee: $45 ($50 for international students). Electronic applications accepted. *Financial support:* In 2015–16, 11 teaching assistantships with full tuition reimbursements (averaging $16,234 per year) were awarded; research assistantships, Federal Work-Study, institutionally sponsored loans, and tuition waivers (full and partial) also available. Support available to part-time students. Financial award application deadline: 3/1; financial award applicants required to submit FAFSA. *Faculty research:* Numerical analysis, statistics, biostatistics, commutative algebra, differential equations. *Unit head:* Eric Hall, Chair, 816-235-5852, Fax: 816-235-5517, E-mail: halle@umkc.edu. *Application contact:* Dr. Hristo Voulov, Associate Professor, 816-235-1641, Fax: 816-235-5517, E-mail: umkcmathdept@umkc.edu.
Website: http://cas.umkc.edu/math/

University of Nebraska–Lincoln, Graduate College, College of Agricultural Sciences and Natural Resources, Department of Statistics, Lincoln, NE 68588. Offers MS, PhD. *Degree requirements:* For master's, thesis optional. *Entrance requirements:* For master's, GRE General Test. Additional exam requirements/recommendations for international students: Required—TOEFL (minimum score 550 paper-based). Electronic applications accepted. *Faculty research:* Design of experiments, linear models, spatial variability, statistical modeling and inference, sampling.

University of New Brunswick Fredericton, School of Graduate Studies, Faculty of Science, Department of Mathematics and Statistics, Fredericton, NB E3B 5A3, Canada. Offers M Sc, PhD. *Faculty:* 15 full-time (0 women), 1 part-time/adjunct (0 women). *Students:* 22 full-time (7 women), 1 (woman) part-time. In 2015, 1 master's, 1 doctorate awarded. *Degree requirements:* For master's, thesis; for doctorate, comprehensive exam, thesis/dissertation. *Entrance requirements:* For master's and doctorate, minimum GPA of 3.0. Additional exam requirements/recommendations for international students: Required—TOEFL (minimum score 550 paper-based), TWE (minimum score 4); Recommended—IELTS (minimum score 7). *Application deadline:* For fall admission, 3/1 for domestic students. Applications are processed on a rolling basis. Application fee: $50 Canadian dollars. Electronic applications accepted. *Financial support:* In 2015–16, 35 research assistantships, 21 teaching assistantships were awarded; fellowships also available. *Faculty research:* Commutative and non-commutative algebra, combinatorics, mathematical modeling and computation, mathematical biology, classical and quantum gravity, multivariate statistics and spatial statistics. *Unit head:* Dr. James Watmough, Director of Graduate Studies, 506-458-7363, Fax: 506-453-4705,
E-mail: watmough@unb.ca. *Application contact:* Heidi Stewart, Graduate Secretary, 506-458-7488, E-mail: scigrad@unb.ca.
Website: http://go.unb.ca/gradprograms

University of New Mexico, Graduate Studies, College of Arts and Sciences, Department of Mathematics and Statistics, Albuquerque, NM 87131-2039. Offers mathematics (MS, PhD); statistics (MS, PhD). *Program availability:* Part-time. *Faculty:* 20 full-time (6 women). *Students:* 55 full-time (20 women), 32 part-time (14 women); includes 18 minority (4 Black or African American, non-Hispanic/Latino; 3 Asian, non-Hispanic/Latino; 10 Hispanic/Latino; 1 Two or more races, non-Hispanic/Latino), 29 international. Average age 31. 107 applicants, 55% accepted, 35 enrolled. In 2015, 19 master's, 13 doctorates awarded. Terminal master's awarded for partial completion of doctoral program. *Degree requirements:* For master's, comprehensive exam (for some programs), thesis or alternative; for doctorate, one foreign language, comprehensive exam, thesis/dissertation, 4 department seminars. *Entrance requirements:* For master's and doctorate, minimum GPA of 3.0, 3 letters of recommendation, letter of intent. Additional exam requirements/recommendations for international students: Required—TOEFL (minimum score 550 paper-based). *Application deadline:* For fall admission, 2/15 priority date for domestic and international students; for spring admission, 11/1 priority date for domestic and international students. Application fee: $50. Electronic applications accepted. *Financial support:* Research assistantships with tuition reimbursements, teaching assistantships with tuition reimbursements, health care benefits, and unspecified assistantships available. Financial award application deadline: 2/15; financial award applicants required to submit FAFSA. *Faculty research:* Pure and applied mathematics, applied statistics, numerical analysis, biostatistics, differential geometry, fluid dynamics, nonparametric curve estimation. *Total annual research expenditures:* $1.2 million. *Unit head:* Dr. Terry Loring, Chair, 505-277-4613, Fax: 505-277-5505, E-mail: loring@math.unm.edu. *Application contact:* Ana Parra Lombard, Coordinator, Program Advisement, 505-277-5250, Fax: 505-277-5505,
E-mail: aparra@math.unm.edu.
Website: http://math.unm.edu/

The University of North Carolina at Chapel Hill, Graduate School, College of Arts and Sciences, Department of Statistics, Chapel Hill, NC 27599. Offers MS, PhD. *Degree requirements:* For master's, comprehensive exam, essay or thesis; for doctorate, comprehensive exam, thesis/dissertation. *Entrance requirements:* For master's and doctorate, GRE General Test, GRE Subject Test, minimum GPA of 3.0. Additional exam requirements/recommendations for international students: Required—TOEFL.

The University of North Carolina at Charlotte, The Graduate School, Program in Data Science and Business Analytics, Charlotte, NC 28223-0001. Offers PSM, Graduate Certificate. Program offered jointly between College of Computing and Informatics and Belk College of Business. *Program availability:* Part-time, evening/weekend. *Faculty:* 2 full-time (0 women). *Students:* 39 full-time (17 women), 50 part-time (19 women); includes 22 minority (6 Black or African American, non-Hispanic/Latino; 10 Asian, non-Hispanic/Latino; 5 Hispanic/Latino; 1 Two or more races, non-Hispanic/Latino), 30 international. Average age 32. 171 applicants, 42% accepted, 34 enrolled. In 2015, 1 master's, 3 Graduate Certificates awarded. *Degree requirements:* For master's, thesis or alternative, internship, practicum. *Entrance requirements:* For master's, GRE, GMAT, undergraduate degree in any scientific, engineering or business discipline or a closely-related field; minimum undergraduate GPA of 3.0; three letters of recommendation; statement of purpose outlining goals for pursuing graduate education; current working knowledge of at least one higher-level (procedural) language; for Graduate Certificate, undergraduate degree in any scientific, engineering or business discipline or a closely-related field; minimum undergraduate GPA of 3.0; statement of purpose outlining goals for pursuing graduate education; current working knowledge of at least one higher-level (procedural) language; familiarity with computer applications. Additional exam requirements/recommendations for international students: Required—TOEFL (minimum score 557 paper-based, 83 iBT) or IELTS (minimum score 6.5). *Application deadline:* For fall admission, 3/1 priority date for domestic and international students; for spring admission, 10/1 priority date for domestic and international students. Application fee: $75. *Expenses:* Contact institution. *Financial support:* Career-related internships or fieldwork, institutionally sponsored loans, scholarships/grants, and unspecified assistantships available. Support available to part-time students. Financial award application deadline: 3/1; financial award applicants required to submit FAFSA. *Unit head:* Carly Mahedy, Director of Student Services, Data Science Initiative, 704-687-0068, E-mail: cfletcher@uncc.edu. *Application contact:* Kathy B. Giddings, Director of Graduate Admissions, 704-687-5503, Fax: 704-687-1668, E-mail: gradadm@uncc.edu.
Website: http://www.analytics.uncc.edu/

The University of North Carolina Wilmington, College of Arts and Sciences, Department of Mathematical Sciences, Wilmington, NC 28403-3297. Offers mathematics (MS); statistics (Graduate Certificate). *Program availability:* Part-time. *Faculty:* 16 full-time (6 women). *Students:* 12 full-time (6 women), 7 part-time (2 women), 3 international. Average age 26. 15 applicants, 10 enrolled. In 2015, 11 master's awarded. *Degree requirements:* For master's, comprehensive exam, thesis or alternative. *Entrance requirements:* For master's, GRE General Test, minimum B average in undergraduate work, 3 letters of recommendation. Additional exam requirements/recommendations for international students: Required—TOEFL (minimum score 79 iBT), IELTS (minimum score 6.5). *Application deadline:* For fall admission, 6/15 for domestic students; for spring admission, 11/30 for domestic students; for summer admission, 4/1 for domestic students. Applications are processed on a rolling basis. Application fee: $60. Electronic applications accepted. *Expenses:* $8,854 in-state full-time per year, $20,945 out-of-state full-time per year. *Financial support:* Teaching assistantships, scholarships/grants, and in- and out-of-state tuition remission available. Financial award application deadline: 3/15; financial award applicants required to submit FAFSA. *Unit head:* Dr. Susan Simmons, Interim Department Chair, 910-962-3296, Fax: 910-962-7107, E-mail: simmonssj@uncw.edu. *Application contact:* Dr. Mark Lammers, Graduate Coordinator, 910-962-3958, Fax: 910-962-7107,
E-mail: lammersm@uncw.edu.
Website: http://www.uncw.edu/mathgrad/

University of North Florida, College of Arts and Sciences, Department of Mathematics and Statistics, Jacksonville, FL 32224. Offers mathematical sciences (MS); statistics (MS). *Program availability:* Part-time, evening/weekend. *Faculty:* 14 full-time (7 women). *Students:* 13 full-time (6 women), 11 part-time (5 women); includes 6 minority (2 Black or African American, non-Hispanic/Latino; 1 Asian, non-Hispanic/Latino; 3 Hispanic/Latino), 6 international. Average age 28. 22 applicants, 64% accepted, 8 enrolled. In 2015, 6 master's awarded. *Degree requirements:* For master's, comprehensive exam, thesis optional. *Entrance requirements:* For master's, GRE General Test, minimum GPA of 3.0 in last 60 hours of course work. Additional exam requirements/recommendations for international students: Required—TOEFL (minimum score 500 paper-based; 61 iBT). *Application deadline:* For fall admission, 7/1 priority date for domestic students, 6/1 for international students; for spring admission, 11/1 priority date for domestic students, 10/1 for international students. Application fee: $30. Electronic applications accepted. *Expenses:* Tuition, state resident: part-time $408.10 per credit hour. Tuition, nonresident: part-time $932.61 per credit hour. *Required fees:* $111.81 per credit hour. Tuition and fees vary according to course load, campus/location and program. *Financial support:* In 2015–16, 16 students received support, including 6 teaching assistantships (averaging $6,214 per year); Federal Work-Study, scholarships/grants, tuition waivers (partial), and unspecified assistantships also available. Support available to part-time students. Financial award application deadline: 4/1; financial award applicants required to submit FAFSA. *Faculty research:* Real analysis, number theory, Euclidean geometry. *Total annual research expenditures:* $3,573. *Unit head:* Dr. Scott H. Hochwald, Chair, 904-620-2653, Fax: 904-620-2818, E-mail: shochwal@unf.edu. *Application contact:* Dr. Amanda Pascale, Director, The Graduate School, 904-620-1360, Fax: 904-620-1362, E-mail: graduateschool@unf.edu.
Website: http://www.unf.edu/coas/math-stat/

University of Notre Dame, Graduate School, College of Science, Department of Applied and Computational Mathematics and Statistics, Notre Dame, IN 46556. Offers applied and computational mathematics and statistics (PhD); applied statistics (MS); computational finance (MS).

University of Ottawa, Faculty of Graduate and Postdoctoral Studies, Faculty of Science, Ottawa-Carleton Institute of Mathematics and Statistics, Ottawa, ON K1N 6N5, Canada. Offers M Sc, PhD. M Sc, PhD offered jointly with Carleton University. *Program availability:* Part-time. *Degree requirements:* For master's, thesis optional; for doctorate, one foreign language, comprehensive exam, thesis/dissertation. *Entrance requirements:* For master's, honors B Sc degree or equivalent, minimum B average; for doctorate, M Sc, minimum B+ average. Electronic applications accepted. *Faculty research:* Pure mathematics, applied mathematics, probability and statistics.

University of Pennsylvania, Wharton School, Department of Statistics, Philadelphia, PA 19104. Offers MBA, PhD. *Degree requirements:* For doctorate, comprehensive exam, thesis/dissertation. *Entrance requirements:* For master's and doctorate, GRE. Additional exam requirements/recommendations for international students: Required—TOEFL, TWE. *Expenses: Tuition, area resident:* Full-time $31,068; part-time $5762 per course. *Required fees:* $3200; $336 per course. Full-time tuition and fees vary according to degree level, program and student level. Part-time tuition and fees vary according to course load, degree level and program. *Faculty research:* Nonparametric function estimation, analysis of algorithms, time series analysis, observational studies, inference.

University of Pittsburgh, Dietrich School of Arts and Sciences, Department of Statistics, Pittsburgh, PA 15260. Offers applied statistics (MA, MS); statistics (MA, MS, PhD). *Program availability:* Part-time. *Faculty:* 11 full-time (3 women), 5 part-time/

adjunct (3 women). *Students:* 35 full-time (12 women); includes 21 minority (1 Black or African American, non-Hispanic/Latino; 20 Asian, non-Hispanic/Latino). Average age 26. 324 applicants, 9% accepted, 14 enrolled. In 2015, 13 master's, 8 doctorates awarded. Terminal master's awarded for partial completion of doctoral program. *Degree requirements:* For master's, comprehensive exam, thesis (for some programs); for doctorate, comprehensive exam, thesis/dissertation. *Entrance requirements:* For master's and doctorate, 3 semesters of calculus, 1 semester of linear algebra, 1 year of mathematical statistics. Additional exam requirements/recommendations for international students: Required—TOEFL (minimum score 90 iBT), IELTS, GRE. *Application deadline:* For fall admission, 1/15 priority date for domestic and international students; for spring admission, 10/1 priority date for domestic and international students. Application fee: $50. Electronic applications accepted. *Expenses:* $21,260 per year in-state, $34,944 per year out-of-state. *Financial support:* In 2015–16, 23 students received support, including 3 fellowships with full tuition reimbursements available (averaging $18,250 per year), 4 research assistantships with full tuition reimbursements available (averaging $17,800 per year), 12 teaching assistantships with full tuition reimbursements available (averaging $17,560 per year); scholarships/grants and health care benefits also available. Financial award application deadline: 1/15. *Faculty research:* Multivariate analysis, time series, quantile association analysis, stochastic models, high dimensional statistical inference. *Total annual research expenditures:* $347,794. *Unit head:* Dr. Allan R. Sampson, Acting Chair, 412-624-8372, Fax: 412-648-8814, E-mail: asampson@pitt.edu. *Application contact:* Dr. Yu Cheng, Director of Graduate Studies, 412-624-1851, Fax: 412-648-8814, E-mail: yucheng@pitt.edu.
Website: http://www.stat.pitt.edu/

University of Pittsburgh, Dietrich School of Arts and Sciences, Program in Computational Modeling and Simulation, Pittsburgh, PA 15260. Offers biological science (PhD); chemistry (PhD); computer science (PhD); economics (PhD); mathematics (PhD); physics and astronomy (PhD); psychology (PhD); statistics (PhD). *Program availability:* Part-time. *Faculty:* 3 full-time (0 women). *Students:* 3 full-time (1 woman); includes 2 minority (both Asian, non-Hispanic/Latino). Average age 23. 13 applicants, 31% accepted, 2 enrolled. *Degree requirements:* For doctorate, comprehensive exam, thesis/dissertation, preliminary exam. *Entrance requirements:* For doctorate, GRE, statement of purpose, transcripts for all college-level institutions attended, three letters of reference. Additional exam requirements/recommendations for international students: Required—TOEFL (minimum score 90 iBT), IELTS (minimum score 7). *Application deadline:* For fall admission, 1/15 for domestic and international students. Applications are processed on a rolling basis. Application fee: $0 ($50 for international students). Electronic applications accepted. Tuition and fees vary according to program. *Financial support:* In 2015–16, 3 students received support, including 2 fellowships with full tuition reimbursements available (averaging $27,000 per year), 1 research assistantship with full tuition reimbursement available (averaging $21,500 per year); tuition waivers (full) also available. Financial award application deadline: 4/15. *Faculty research:* Econometric modeling, developing reduced-scaling first principles approaches for expedited predictions of molecular and materials properties, developing computational models to quantitatively describe origins of reactivity and selectivity in organocatalytic reactions. *Unit head:* Dr. Kathleen Blee, Associate Dean, Graduate Studies and Research, 412-624-3939, Fax: 412-624-6855. *Application contact:* Wendy G. Janocha, Graduate Administrator, 412-648-7251, E-mail: wgj1@pitt.edu.
Website: http://cmsp.pitt.edu/

University of Puerto Rico, Mayagüez Campus, Graduate Studies, College of Arts and Sciences, Department of Mathematical Sciences, Mayagüez, PR 00681-9000. Offers applied mathematics (MS); pure mathematics (MS); scientific computation (MS); statistics (MS). *Program availability:* Part-time. *Degree requirements:* For master's, one foreign language, comprehensive exam, thesis optional. *Entrance requirements:* For master's, undergraduate degree in mathematics or its equivalent. *Faculty research:* Automata theory, linear algebra, logic.

University of Regina, Faculty of Graduate Studies and Research, Faculty of Science, Department of Mathematics and Statistics, Regina, SK S4S 0A2, Canada. Offers mathematics (M Sc, PhD); statistics (M Sc, PhD). *Program availability:* Part-time. *Degree requirements:* For master's, thesis (for some programs), major essay; for doctorate, comprehensive exam, thesis/dissertation. *Entrance requirements:* Additional exam requirements/recommendations for international students: Required—TOEFL (minimum score 580 paper-based; 80 iBT), IELTS (minimum score 6.5), PTE (minimum score 59). Electronic applications accepted. *Faculty research:* Discrete mathematics, actuarial science and statistics, matrix theory, mathematical science, numerical analysis.

University of Rhode Island, Graduate School, College of Arts and Sciences, Department of Computer Science and Statistics, Kingston, RI 02881. Offers computer science (MS, PhD); digital forensics (Graduate Certificate); professional science masters in cyber security (completely online) (MS); statistics (MS). *Program availability:* Part-time. *Faculty:* 15 full-time (5 women). *Students:* 28 full-time (10 women), 72 part-time (13 women); includes 16 minority (5 Black or African American, non-Hispanic/Latino; 6 Asian, non-Hispanic/Latino; 4 Hispanic/Latino; 1 Two or more races, non-Hispanic/Latino), 20 international. In 2015, 11 master's, 1 doctorate awarded. *Degree requirements:* For master's, comprehensive exam (for some programs), thesis optional; for doctorate, comprehensive exam, thesis/dissertation. *Entrance requirements:* For master's and doctorate, GRE, 2 letters of recommendation. Additional exam requirements/recommendations for international students: Required—TOEFL (minimum score 550 paper-based). *Application deadline:* For fall admission, 7/15 for domestic students, 2/1 for international students; for spring admission, 11/15 for domestic students, 7/15 for international students. Application fee: $65. Electronic applications accepted. *Expenses:* Tuition, state resident: full-time $11,796; part-time $655 per credit. Tuition, nonresident: full-time $24,206; part-time $1345 per credit. *Required fees:* $1546; $44 per credit. One-time fee: $155 full-time; $35 part-time. *Financial support:* In 2015–16, 4 research assistantships with tuition reimbursements (averaging $14,035 per year), 11 teaching assistantships with tuition reimbursements (averaging $15,331 per year) were awarded. Financial award application deadline: 2/1; financial award applicants required to submit FAFSA. *Faculty research:* Bioinformatics, computer and digital forensics, behavioral model of pedestrian dynamics, real-time distributed object computing, cryptography. *Unit head:* Dr. Joan Peckham, Chair, 401-874-2701, Fax: 401-874-4617, E-mail: joan@cs.uri.edu. *Application contact:*
E-mail: grad-inquiries@cs.uri.edu.
Website: http://www.cs.uri.edu/

University of Rochester, School of Medicine and Dentistry, Graduate Programs in Medicine and Dentistry, Department of Biostatistics and Computational Biology, Programs in Statistics, Rochester, NY 14627. Offers MA, PhD. *Expenses: Tuition, area resident:* Full-time $47,450; part-time $1482 per credit hour. *Required fees:* $528. Tuition and fees vary according to program.

University of Saskatchewan, College of Graduate Studies and Research, College of Arts and Science, Department of Mathematics and Statistics, Saskatoon, SK S7N 5A2, Canada. Offers M Math, MA, PhD. *Degree requirements:* For master's, thesis (for some programs); for doctorate, comprehensive exam (for some programs), thesis/dissertation. *Entrance requirements:* Additional exam requirements/recommendations for international students: Required—TOEFL (minimum score 80 iBT); Recommended—IELTS (minimum score 6.5). Electronic applications accepted.

University of South Africa, College of Economic and Management Sciences, Pretoria, South Africa. Offers accounting (D Admin, D Com); accounting science (DA); auditing (D Admin, D Com); business administration (M Tech); business economics (D Admin); business leadership (DBL); business management (D Admin, D Com); economic management analysis (M Tech); economics (D Admin, D Com, PhD); human resource development (M Tech); industrial psychology (D Admin, D Com, PhD); logistics (D Com); marketing (M Tech); public administration (D Admin, D Com, DPA, PhD); public management (M Tech); quantitative management (D Admin, D Com); real estate (M Tech); statistics (D Admin, PhD); tourism management (D Admin, D Com); transport economics (D Admin, D Com).

University of South Carolina, The Graduate School, College of Arts and Sciences, Department of Statistics, Columbia, SC 29208. Offers applied statistics (CAS); industrial statistics (MIS); statistics (MS, PhD). *Program availability:* Part-time, evening/weekend, online learning. Terminal master's awarded for partial completion of doctoral program. *Degree requirements:* For master's, thesis; for doctorate, comprehensive exam, thesis/dissertation. *Entrance requirements:* For master's, GRE General Test or GMAT, 2 years of work experience (MIS); for doctorate, GRE General Test; for CAS, GRE General Test or GMAT. Additional exam requirements/recommendations for international students: Required—TOEFL (minimum score 600 paper-based; 100 iBT). Electronic applications accepted. *Expenses:* Contact institution. *Faculty research:* Reliability, environmentrics, statistics computing, psychometrics, bioinformatics.

University of Southern California, Graduate School, Dana and David Dornsife College of Letters, Arts and Sciences, Department of Mathematics, Los Angeles, CA 90089. Offers applied mathematics (MA, MS, PhD); mathematical finance (MS); mathematics (MA, PhD); statistics (MS). *Program availability:* Part-time. Terminal master's awarded for partial completion of doctoral program. *Degree requirements:* For master's, comprehensive exam (for some programs), thesis (for some programs); for doctorate, one foreign language, comprehensive exam, thesis/dissertation. *Entrance requirements:* For master's, GRE General Test, GMAT; for doctorate, GRE General Test, GRE Subject Test (mathematics). Additional exam requirements/recommendations for international students: Required—TOEFL (minimum score 100 iBT). Electronic applications accepted. *Faculty research:* Algebra, algebraic geometry and number theory, analysis/partial differential equations, applied mathematics, financial mathematics, probability, combinatorics and statistics.

University of Southern Maine, College of Science, Technology, and Health, Program in Statistics, Portland, ME 04104-9300. Offers MS, CGS. *Expenses: Tuition, area resident:* Full-time $6840; part-time $380 per credit hour. Tuition, state resident: full-time $10,260; part-time $570 per credit hour. Tuition, nonresident: full-time $18,468; part-time $1026 per credit hour. *Required fees:* $830; $83 per credit hour. Tuition and fees vary according to course load and program. *Faculty research:* Environmental statistics, statistical quality control, survival and reliability analysis, design of experiments, statistical data mining, queueing system, operations research, generalized linear models.

University of South Florida, College of Arts and Sciences, Department of Mathematics and Statistics, Tampa, FL 33620-9951. Offers mathematics (MA, PhD), including pure and applied, statistics (PhD); statistics (MA). *Program availability:* Part-time, evening/weekend. *Faculty:* 22 full-time (2 women). *Students:* 70 full-time (25 women), 21 part-time (7 women); includes 9 minority (2 Black or African American, non-Hispanic/Latino; 3 Asian, non-Hispanic/Latino; 2 Hispanic/Latino; 2 Two or more races, non-Hispanic/Latino), 46 international. Average age 31. 88 applicants, 69% accepted, 16 enrolled. In 2015, 25 master's, 6 doctorates awarded. Terminal master's awarded for partial completion of doctoral program. *Degree requirements:* For master's, comprehensive exam, thesis (for some programs); for doctorate, comprehensive exam, thesis/dissertation. *Entrance requirements:* For master's, GRE General Test, minimum GPA of 3.0 in undergraduate mathematics courses, bachelor's degree in mathematical sciences or related field, and statement of goals (for mathematics); minimum GPA of 3.5 in upper-division undergraduate coursework and BA or BS in statistics, mathematics, physical sciences, engineering, or business (for statistics); for doctorate, GRE General Test, minimum GPA of 3.5 in graduate mathematics courses, three letters of recommendation, statement of goals, master's or bachelor's degree in mathematical sciences or related field. Additional exam requirements/recommendations for international students: Required—TOEFL (minimum score 550 paper-based; 79 iBT) or IELTS (minimum score 6.5). *Application deadline:* For fall admission, 2/1 for domestic students, 1/2 for international students; for spring admission, 8/1 for domestic students, 6/1 for international students. Application fee: $30. Electronic applications accepted. *Financial support:* In 2015–16, 61 students received support, including 6 research assistantships (averaging $16,990 per year), 55 teaching assistantships with partial tuition reimbursements available (averaging $13,742 per year); unspecified assistantships also available. Financial award application deadline: 2/1. *Faculty research:* Mathematics: algebra and number theory, harmonic and complex analysis, approximation theory, theory of orthogonal polynomials, Banach space theory and operator theory, differential equations and nonlinear analysis, discrete mathematics, geometry and topology; statistics: linear and nonlinear statistical models for health sciences, operations research problems, economic systems; stochastic control problems; dynamic reliability analysis and control. *Total annual research expenditures:* $661,309. *Unit head:* Dr. Leslaw Skrzypek, Associate Professor and Chairperson, 813-974-1268, Fax: 813-974-2700, E-mail: skrzypek@usf.edu. *Application contact:* Dr. Xiang-Dong Hou, Professor/Director of Graduate Mathematics Program, 813-974-2561, Fax: 813-974-2700, E-mail: xhou@cas.usf.edu.
Website: http://math.usf.edu/

The University of Tennessee, Graduate School, College of Business Administration, Department of Statistics, Knoxville, TN 37996. Offers industrial statistics (MS); statistics (MS). *Program availability:* Part-time. *Degree requirements:* For master's, thesis or alternative. *Entrance requirements:* For master's, GMAT or GRE General Test, minimum GPA of 2.7. Additional exam requirements/recommendations for international students: Required—TOEFL. Electronic applications accepted.

The University of Tennessee, Graduate School, College of Business Administration, Program in Business Administration, Knoxville, TN 37996. Offers accounting (PhD); finance (MBA, PhD); logistics and transportation (MBA, PhD); management (PhD); marketing (MBA, PhD); operations management (MBA); professional business administration (MBA); statistics (PhD); JD/MBA; MS/MBA; Pharm D/MBA. Pharm D/MBA offered jointly with The University of Tennessee Health Science Center. *Accreditation:* AACSB. *Program availability:* Online learning. *Degree requirements:* For master's, thesis or alternative; for doctorate, thesis/dissertation. *Entrance requirements:* For master's and doctorate, GMAT, minimum GPA of 2.7. Additional exam requirements/recommendations for international students: Required—TOEFL. Electronic applications accepted.

The University of Texas at Austin, Graduate School, College of Natural Sciences, Division of Statistics and Scientific Computation, Austin, TX 78712-1111. Offers statistics (MS, PhD). *Entrance requirements:* For master's, GRE General Test; for doctorate, GRE General Test, letters of recommendation, bachelor's degree from accredited college or university, minimum GPA of 3.0, statement of purpose, curriculum vitae or resume. Additional exam requirements/recommendations for international students: Required—TOEFL or IELTS.

The University of Texas at Dallas, School of Natural Sciences and Mathematics, Department of Mathematical Sciences, Richardson, TX 75080. Offers actuarial science (MS); mathematics (MS); mathematics (MS, PhD), including applied mathematics, engineering mathematics (MS); statistics (MS, PhD). *Program availability:* Part-time, evening/weekend. *Faculty:* 31 full-time (6 women), 1 part-time/adjunct (0 women). *Students:* 133 full-time (57 women), 26 part-time (9 women); includes 33 minority (6 Black or African American, non-Hispanic/Latino; 17 Asian, non-Hispanic/Latino; 8 Hispanic/Latino; 2 Two or more races, non-Hispanic/Latino), 94 international. Average age 30. 204 applicants, 51% accepted, 58 enrolled. In 2015, 13 master's, 6 doctorates awarded. *Median time to degree:* Of those who began their doctoral program in fall 2007, 44% received their degree in 8 years or less. *Degree requirements:* For master's, thesis optional; for doctorate, thesis/dissertation. *Entrance requirements:* For master's, GRE General Test, minimum GPA of 3.0 in upper-level course work in field; for doctorate, GRE General Test, minimum GPA of 3.5 in upper-level course work in field. Additional exam requirements/recommendations for international students: Required—TOEFL (minimum score 550 paper-based). *Application deadline:* For fall admission, 7/15 for domestic students, 5/1 priority date for international students; for spring admission, 11/15 for domestic students, 9/1 priority date for international students. Applications are processed on a rolling basis. Application fee: $50 ($100 for international students). Electronic applications accepted. *Expenses:* Tuition, state resident: full-time $11,940; part-time $663 per semester hour. Tuition, nonresident: full-time $22,786; part-time $1266 per semester hour. Tuition and fees vary according to course load. *Financial support:* In 2015–16, 108 students received support, including 8 research assistantships (averaging $23,025 per year), 64 teaching assistantships with partial tuition reimbursements available (averaging $17,283 per year); career-related internships or fieldwork, Federal Work-Study, institutionally sponsored loans, scholarships/grants, and unspecified assistantships also available. Support available to part-time students. Financial award application deadline: 4/30; financial award applicants required to submit FAFSA. *Faculty research:* Sequential analysis, applications in semiconductor manufacturing, medical image analysis, computational anatomy, information theory, probability theory. *Unit head:* Dr. Vladimir Dragovic, Department Head, 972-883-2161, Fax: 972-883-6622, E-mail: utdmath@utdallas.edu. *Application contact:* Olivia Dao, Graduate Support Assistant, 972-883-2163, Fax: 972-883-6622, E-mail: utdmath@utdallas.edu.
Website: http://www.utdallas.edu/math

The University of Texas at El Paso, Graduate School, College of Science, Department of Mathematical Sciences, El Paso, TX 79968-0001. Offers mathematical sciences (MS); mathematics (teaching) (MAT); statistics (MS). *Program availability:* Part-time, evening/weekend. *Degree requirements:* For master's, thesis optional. *Entrance requirements:* For master's, minimum GPA of 3.0, letters of recommendation. Additional exam requirements/recommendations for international students: Required—TOEFL; Recommended—IELTS. Electronic applications accepted.

The University of Texas at San Antonio, College of Business, Department of Management Science and Statistics, San Antonio, TX 78249-0617. Offers applied statistics (MS, PhD); management science (MBA). *Accreditation:* AACSB. *Program availability:* Part-time, evening/weekend. *Faculty:* 14 full-time (2 women), 2 part-time/adjunct (0 women). *Students:* 41 full-time (15 women), 35 part-time (14 women); includes 20 minority (2 Black or African American, non-Hispanic/Latino; 6 Asian, non-Hispanic/Latino; 12 Hispanic/Latino), 26 international. Average age 31. 91 applicants, 32% accepted, 20 enrolled. In 2015, 21 master's awarded. *Degree requirements:* For master's, comprehensive exam (for some programs), thesis or alternative; for doctorate, comprehensive exam, thesis/dissertation. *Entrance requirements:* For master's, GMAT, minimum of 36 semester credit hours of coursework beyond any hours acquired in the MBA-leveling courses; statement of purpose; for doctorate, GRE, minimum cumulative GPA of 3.3 in the last 60 hours of coursework; transcripts from all colleges and universities attended; curriculum vitae; statement of academic work experiences, interests, and goals; three letters of recommendation; BA, BS, or MS in mathematics, statistics, or closely-related field. Additional exam requirements/recommendations for international students: Required—TOEFL (minimum score 550 paper-based; 79 iBT), IELTS (minimum score 6.5). *Application deadline:* For fall admission, 7/1 for domestic students, 4/1 for international students; for spring admission, 11/1 for domestic students, 9/1 for international students. Applications are processed on a rolling basis. Application fee: $45 ($80 for international students). Electronic applications accepted. *Faculty research:* Statistical signal processing, reliability and life-testing experiments, modeling decompression sickness using survival analysis. *Unit head:* Dr. Raydel Tullous, Chair, 210-458-6345, Fax: 210-458-6350, E-mail: raydel.tullous@utsa.edu. *Application contact:* Katherine Pope, Graduate Assistant of Record, 210-458-7316, Fax: 210-458-4398, E-mail: katherine.pope@utsa.edu.
Website: http://business.utsa.edu/mss/

The University of Texas Rio Grande Valley, College of Sciences, School of Mathematical and Statistical Science, Edinburg, TX 78539. Offers mathematical sciences (MS); mathematics (MS). *Program availability:* Part-time, evening/weekend, online learning. *Faculty:* 16 full-time (1 woman). *Students:* 27 full-time (10 women), 36 part-time (17 women); includes 37 minority (1 Black or African American, non-Hispanic/Latino; 5 Asian, non-Hispanic/Latino; 31 Hispanic/Latino), 9 international. Average age 33. 23 applicants, 96% accepted, 17 enrolled. *Entrance requirements:* For master's, GRE General Test, bachelor's degree in mathematics or related field with minimum of 12 hours of upper-division mathematics or statistics course work and minimum GPA of 3.0; official transcripts from each institution attended. Additional exam requirements/recommendations for international students: Required—TOEFL (minimum score 550 paper-based, 61 iBT) or IELTS (6.5). *Application deadline:* Applications are processed on a rolling basis. Application fee: $50 ($100 for international students). Electronic applications accepted. Tuition and fees vary according to course load and program. *Financial support:* Teaching assistantships, institutionally sponsored loans, and unspecified assistantships available. *Faculty research:* Differential equations, group theory, functional analysis, analytic number theory, combinatorics and discrete geometry. *Unit head:* Dr. Cristina Villalobos, E-mail: cristina.villalobos@utrgv.edu. *Application contact:* Dr. Tim Huber, Graduate Program Coordinator, 956-665-2173, E-mail: timothy.huber@utrgv.edu.
Website: http://portal.utpa.edu/utpa_main/daa_home/cosm_home/math_home

University of the Incarnate Word, School of Graduate Studies and Research, School of Mathematics, Science, and Engineering, Program in Mathematics, San Antonio, TX 78209-6397. Offers mathematics teaching (MA); research statistics (MS). *Program availability:* Part-time, evening/weekend. *Faculty:* 8 full-time (4 women), 1 (woman) part-time/adjunct. *Students:* 3 full-time (all women), 1 (woman) part-time; includes 1 minority (Hispanic/Latino), 3 international. Average age 28. 2 applicants, 50% accepted, 1 enrolled. In 2015, 10 master's awarded. *Degree requirements:* For master's, capstone or prerequisite knowledge (for research statistics). *Entrance requirements:* For master's, GRE (minimum score 800 verbal and quantitative), 18 hours of undergraduate mathematics with minimum GPA of 3.0, letter of recommendation by a professional in the field, writing sample, teaching experience at the precollege level. Additional exam requirements/recommendations for international students: Required—TOEFL (minimum score 560 paper-based; 83 iBT). *Application deadline:* Applications are processed on a rolling basis. Application fee: $20. Electronic applications accepted. *Expenses: Tuition, area resident:* Part-time $885 per credit hour. *Required fees:* $40 per credit hour. Tuition and fees vary according to course load, degree level, campus/location, program and student level. *Financial support:* Federal Work-Study, scholarships/grants, tuition waivers (partial), and unspecified assistantships available. Financial award applicants required to submit FAFSA. *Faculty research:* Scholarship and career development for undergraduate mathematics majors. *Total annual research expenditures:* $140,844. *Unit head:* Dr. Zhanbo Yang, Mathematics Graduate Program Coordinator, 210-283-5008, Fax: 210-829-3153, E-mail: yang@uiwtx.edu. *Application contact:* Johnny Garcia, Assistant Director of Graduate Admissions, 210-805-3554, Fax: 210-829-3921, E-mail: jsgarcia@uiwtx.edu.
Website: http://www.uiw.edu/math/mathprogramsgrad.html

The University of Toledo, College of Graduate Studies, College of Natural Sciences and Mathematics, Department of Mathematics, Toledo, OH 43606-3390. Offers applied mathematics (MS, PhD); statistics (MS, PhD). *Program availability:* Part-time. *Degree requirements:* For master's, comprehensive exam (for some programs), thesis (for some programs); for doctorate, 2 foreign languages, thesis/dissertation. *Entrance requirements:* For master's and doctorate, GRE General Test, GRE Subject Test, minimum cumulative point-hour ratio of 2.7 for all previous academic work, three letters of recommendation, statement of purpose, transcripts from all prior institutions attended. Additional exam requirements/recommendations for international students: Required—TOEFL (minimum score 550 paper-based; 80 iBT). Electronic applications accepted.

University of Toronto, School of Graduate Studies, Faculty of Arts and Science, Department of Statistical Sciences, Toronto, ON M5S 1A1, Canada. Offers M Sc, PhD. *Program availability:* Part-time. *Degree requirements:* For doctorate, comprehensive exam, thesis/dissertation. *Entrance requirements:* For master's, GRE (recommended for students educated outside of Canada), 3 letters of reference; for doctorate, GRE (recommended for students educated outside of Canada), 3 letters of reference, M Stat or equivalent, minimum B+ average. Additional exam requirements/recommendations for international students: Required—TOEFL (minimum score 580 paper-based; 93 iBT), TWE (minimum score 4). Electronic applications accepted.

University of Utah, Graduate School, College of Education, Department of Educational Psychology, Salt Lake City, UT 84112. Offers clinical mental health counseling (M Ed); counseling psychology (PhD); elementary education (M Ed); instructional design and educational technology (M Ed); instructional design and technology (MS); learning and cognition (MS, PhD); reading and literacy (M Ed, PhD); school counseling (M Ed); school psychology (M Ed, PhD); statistics (M Stat). *Accreditation:* APA (one or more programs are accredited). *Faculty:* 23 full-time (12 women), 15 part-time/adjunct (10 women). *Students:* 216 full-time (162 women), 1 part-time (0 women); includes 28 minority (2 Black or African American, non-Hispanic/Latino; 3 American Indian or Alaska Native, non-Hispanic/Latino; 9 Asian, non-Hispanic/Latino; 9 Hispanic/Latino; 2 Native Hawaiian or other Pacific Islander, non-Hispanic/Latino; 3 Two or more races, non-Hispanic/Latino), 5 international. Average age 34. 296 applicants, 27% accepted, 73 enrolled. In 2015, 59 master's, 14 doctorates awarded. Terminal master's awarded for partial completion of doctoral program. *Degree requirements:* For master's, variable foreign language requirement, comprehensive exam (for some programs), thesis (for some programs), projects; for doctorate, variable foreign language requirement, comprehensive exam, thesis/dissertation, oral exam. *Entrance requirements:* For master's and doctorate, GRE General Test, minimum GPA of 3.0. Additional exam requirements/recommendations for international students: Required—TOEFL (minimum score 80 iBT). *Application deadline:* For fall admission, 12/15 for domestic and international students; for winter admission, 11/1 for domestic and international students; for spring admission, 3/15 for domestic and international students. Application fee: $55 ($65 for international students). Electronic applications accepted. *Expenses:* Contact institution. *Financial support:* In 2015–16, 82 students received support, including 12 fellowships with tuition reimbursements available (averaging $18,000 per year), 12 research assistantships with tuition reimbursements available (averaging $14,000 per year), 60 teaching assistantships with tuition reimbursements available (averaging $14,000 per year); career-related internships or fieldwork, Federal Work-Study, institutionally sponsored loans, scholarships/grants, health care benefits, and unspecified assistantships also available. Financial award application deadline: 4/1; financial award applicants required to submit FAFSA. *Faculty research:* Autism, computer technology and instruction, cognitive behavior, aging, group counseling. *Total annual research expenditures:* $620,935. *Unit head:* Dr. Anne E. Cook, Chair, 801-581-7148, Fax: 801-581-5566, E-mail: anne.cook@utah.edu. *Application contact:* JoLynn N. Yates, Academic Coordinator, 801-581-7148, Fax: 801-581-5566, E-mail: jo.yates@utah.edu.
Website: http://www.ed.utah.edu/edps/

University of Utah, Graduate School, College of Science, Department of Mathematics, Salt Lake City, UT 84112-0090. Offers mathematics (MA, MS, PhD); mathematics teaching (MS); statistics (M Stat). *Program availability:* Part-time. *Faculty:* 41 full-time (4 women), 37 part-time/adjunct (9 women). *Students:* 110 full-time (36 women), 28 part-time (12 women); includes 8 minority (5 Asian, non-Hispanic/Latino; 2 Hispanic/Latino; 1 Two or more races, non-Hispanic/Latino), 44 international. Average age 27. 195 applicants, 32% accepted, 27 enrolled. In 2015, 39 master's, 12 doctorates awarded. *Degree requirements:* For master's, comprehensive exam, thesis or alternative, written or oral exam; for doctorate, comprehensive exam, thesis/dissertation, written and oral exams. *Entrance requirements:* For master's and doctorate, GRE Subject Test in math (recommended), minimum undergraduate GPA of 3.0. Additional exam requirements/recommendations for international students: Required—TOEFL (minimum score 550 paper-based; 80 iBT), GRE (recommended). *Application deadline:* For fall admission, 3/15 for domestic and international students; for spring admission, 11/1 for domestic and international students; for summer admission, 3/15 for domestic and international students. Application fee: $55 ($65 for international students). Electronic applications accepted. *Expenses:* 17,000 per year. *Financial support:* In 2015–16, 118 students received support, including 1 fellowship (averaging $34,000 per year), 29 research assistantships with full tuition reimbursements available (averaging $19,350 per year), 81 teaching assistantships with full tuition reimbursements available (averaging $17,000 per year); health care benefits and unspecified assistantships also available. Financial award application deadline: 1/1; financial award applicants required to submit FAFSA. *Faculty research:* Algebraic geometry, geometry and topology materials and microstructure, mathematical biology, probability and statistics. *Total annual research expenditures:* $3.4 million. *Unit head:* Dr. Peter Trapa, Chairman, 801-581-6851, Fax: 801-581-4148, E-mail: ptrapa@math.utah.edu. *Application contact:* Dr. Karl Schwede,

Director of Graduate Studies, 801-581-7916, Fax: 801-581-6841, E-mail: schwede@math.utah.edu.
Website: http://www.math.utah.edu/

University of Utah, Graduate School, Interdepartmental Program in Statistics, Salt Lake City, UT 84112-1107. Offers biostatistics (M Stat); econometrics (M Stat); educational psychology (M Stat); mathematics (M Stat); sociology (M Stat). *Program availability:* Part-time. *Students:* 61 full-time (34 women), 45 part-time (13 women); includes 18 minority (3 Black or African American, non-Hispanic/Latino; 10 Asian, non-Hispanic/Latino; 3 Hispanic/Latino; 2 Two or more races, non-Hispanic/Latino), 30 international. Average age 32. 50 applicants, 70% accepted, 27 enrolled. In 2015, 18 master's awarded. *Degree requirements:* For master's, comprehensive exam (for some programs), projects. *Entrance requirements:* For master's, GRE General Test (for all but biostatistics); GRE Subject Test (for mathematics), minimum GPA of 3.0; course work in calculus, matrix theory, statistics. Additional exam requirements/recommendations for international students: Required—TOEFL (minimum score 500 paper-based; 61 iBT). *Application deadline:* For fall admission, 7/1 for domestic students, 4/1 for international students. Applications are processed on a rolling basis. Application fee: $55 ($65 for international students). Electronic applications accepted. *Financial support:* In 2015–16, 10 students received support, including 10 research assistantships with tuition reimbursements available (averaging $1,000 per year); career-related internships or fieldwork, scholarships/grants, and unspecified assistantships also available. *Faculty research:* Biostatistics, sociology, economics, educational psychology, mathematics. *Unit head:* Xiaoming Sheng, Chair, University Statistics Committee, 801-213-3729, E-mail: xiaoming.sheng@utah.edu. *Application contact:* Laura Egbert, Coordinator, 801-585-6853, E-mail: laura.egbert@utah.edu.
Website: http://www.mstat.utah.edu

University of Utah, Graduate School, Professional Master of Science and Technology Program, Salt Lake City, UT 84112. Offers biotechnology (PSM); computational science (PSM); environmental science (PSM); science instrumentation (PSM). *Program availability:* Part-time. *Students:* 21 full-time (9 women), 35 part-time (12 women); includes 3 minority (2 Asian, non-Hispanic/Latino; 1 Two or more races, non-Hispanic/Latino), 2 international. Average age 32. 55 applicants, 67% accepted, 23 enrolled. In 2015, 11 master's awarded. *Degree requirements:* For master's, internship. *Entrance requirements:* For master's, GRE (recommended), minimum undergraduate GPA of 3.0, bachelor's degree from accredited university or college. Additional exam requirements/recommendations for international students: Required—TOEFL (minimum score 550 paper-based; 80 iBT), IELTS (minimum score 6.5). *Application deadline:* For fall admission, 2/1 for domestic and international students. Application fee: $55 ($65 for international students). Electronic applications accepted. *Expenses:* Contact institution. *Financial support:* Fellowships, research assistantships, teaching assistantships, and unspecified assistantships available. *Unit head:* Ray Hoobler, Program Director, 801-585-5630, E-mail: ray.hoobler@utah.edu. *Application contact:* Jay Derek Payne, Project Coordinator, 801-585-3650, E-mail: derek.payne@gradschool.utah.edu.
Website: http://pmst.utah.edu/

University of Vermont, Graduate College, College of Engineering and Mathematics, Department of Mathematics and Statistics, Program in Statistics, Burlington, VT 05405. Offers MS. *Entrance requirements:* For master's, GRE General Test. Additional exam requirements/recommendations for international students: Required—TOEFL (minimum score 550 paper-based; 90 iBT). Electronic applications accepted. *Faculty research:* Applied statistics.

University of Victoria, Faculty of Graduate Studies, Faculty of Science, Department of Mathematics and Statistics, Victoria, BC V8W 2Y2, Canada. Offers M Sc, MA, PhD. *Program availability:* Part-time. *Degree requirements:* For master's, thesis; for doctorate, one foreign language, thesis/dissertation, 3 qualifying exams, candidacy exam. *Entrance requirements:* Additional exam requirements/recommendations for international students: Required—TOEFL (minimum score 575 paper-based), IELTS (minimum score 7). Electronic applications accepted. *Faculty research:* Functional analysis and operator theory, applied ordinary and partial differential equations, discrete mathematics and graph theory.

University of Virginia, College and Graduate School of Arts and Sciences, Department of Statistics, Charlottesville, VA 22903. Offers MS, PhD. *Degree requirements:* For master's, exam; for doctorate, comprehensive exam, thesis/dissertation. *Entrance requirements:* For master's and doctorate, GRE General Test, 3 letters of recommendation. Additional exam requirements/recommendations for international students: Required—TOEFL (minimum score 600 paper-based; 90 iBT), IELTS (minimum score 7). Electronic applications accepted.

University of Washington, Graduate School, College of Arts and Sciences, Department of Statistics, Seattle, WA 98195. Offers MS, PhD. Terminal master's awarded for partial completion of doctoral program. *Degree requirements:* For master's, thesis optional; for doctorate, one foreign language, thesis/dissertation. *Entrance requirements:* For master's and doctorate, GRE General Test, minimum GPA of 3.0. Additional exam requirements/recommendations for international students: Required—TOEFL. *Faculty research:* Mathematical statistics, stochastic modeling, spatial statistics, statistical computing.

University of Washington, Graduate School, School of Public Health, Department of Biostatistics, Seattle, WA 98195. Offers biostatistics (MPH, MS, PhD); clinical research (MS), including biostatistics; statistical genetics (PhD). *Program availability:* Part-time. Terminal master's awarded for partial completion of doctoral program. *Degree requirements:* For master's, comprehensive exam, thesis, practicum (MPH); for doctorate, comprehensive exam, thesis/dissertation. *Entrance requirements:* For master's and doctorate, GRE General Test, coursework on multivariate calculus, linear algebra and probability; minimum GPA of 3.0. Additional exam requirements/recommendations for international students: Required—TOEFL. Electronic applications accepted. *Expenses:* Contact institution. *Faculty research:* Statistical methods for survival data analysis, clinical trials, epidemiological case control and cohort studies, statistical genetics.

University of Waterloo, Graduate Studies, Faculty of Mathematics, Department of Statistics and Actuarial Science, Waterloo, ON N2L 3G1, Canada. Offers actuarial science (M Math, MAS, PhD); biostatistics (PhD); statistics (M Math, PhD); statistics-biostatistics (M Math); statistics-computing (M Math); statistics-finance (M Math). *Degree requirements:* For master's, research paper or thesis; for doctorate, comprehensive exam, thesis/dissertation. *Entrance requirements:* For master's, honors degree in field, minimum B+ average; for doctorate, master's degree, minimum B+ average. Additional exam requirements/recommendations for international students: Required—TOEFL, IELTS, PTE. *Application deadline:* Applications are processed on a rolling basis. Application fee: $100 Canadian dollars. Electronic applications accepted. *Financial support:* Fellowships, research assistantships, teaching assistantships, career-related internships or fieldwork, and scholarships/grants available. *Faculty research:* Data analysis, risk theory, inference, stochastic processes, quantitative finance.
Website: https://uwaterloo.ca/statistics-and-actuarial-science/

The University of Western Ontario, Faculty of Graduate Studies, Physical Sciences Division, Department of Statistical and Actuarial Sciences, London, ON N6A 5B8, Canada. Offers M Sc, PhD. *Degree requirements:* For master's, thesis (for some programs); for doctorate, comprehensive exam, thesis/dissertation. *Entrance requirements:* For master's, honours BA with B+ average. Additional exam requirements/recommendations for international students: Required—TOEFL. *Faculty research:* Statistical theory, statistical applications, probability, actuarial science.

University of Windsor, Faculty of Graduate Studies, Faculty of Science, Department of Mathematics and Statistics, Windsor, ON N9B 3P4, Canada. Offers mathematics (M Sc); statistics (M Sc, PhD). *Degree requirements:* For master's, thesis or alternative; for doctorate, comprehensive exam, thesis/dissertation. *Entrance requirements:* For master's, minimum B average; for doctorate, minimum A average. Additional exam requirements/recommendations for international students: Required—TOEFL (minimum score 560 paper-based). Electronic applications accepted. *Faculty research:* Applied mathematics, operational research, fluid dynamics.

University of Wisconsin–Madison, Graduate School, College of Letters and Science, Department of Statistics, Madison, WI 53706-1380. Offers biometry (MS); statistics (MS, PhD). *Program availability:* Part-time. *Degree requirements:* For master's, exam; for doctorate, thesis/dissertation. *Entrance requirements:* For master's and doctorate, GRE. Additional exam requirements/recommendations for international students: Required—TOEFL. Electronic applications accepted. *Expenses:* Tuition, state resident: full-time $5364. Tuition, nonresident: full-time $12,027. *Required fees:* $571. Tuition and fees vary according to campus/location, program and reciprocity agreements. *Faculty research:* Biostatistics, bootstrap and other resampling theory and methods, linear and nonlinear models, nonparametrics, time series and stochastic processes.

University of Wyoming, College of Arts and Sciences, Department of Statistics, Laramie, WY 82071. Offers MS, PhD. Terminal master's awarded for partial completion of doctoral program. *Degree requirements:* For master's, comprehensive exam (for some programs), thesis (for some programs); for doctorate, comprehensive exam, thesis/dissertation. *Entrance requirements:* For master's, GMAT, GRE General Test, minimum GPA of 3.0; for doctorate, GRE General Test, minimum GPA of 3.0. Additional exam requirements/recommendations for international students: Required—TOEFL; Recommended—TWE. Electronic applications accepted. *Faculty research:* Linear models categorical, Baysain, spatial biological sciences and engineering, multi-variate.

Utah State University, School of Graduate Studies, College of Science, Department of Mathematics and Statistics, Logan, UT 84322. Offers industrial mathematics (MS); mathematical sciences (PhD); mathematics (M Math, MS); statistics (MS). *Program availability:* Part-time. Terminal master's awarded for partial completion of doctoral program. *Degree requirements:* For master's, thesis optional, qualifying exam; for doctorate, one foreign language, comprehensive exam, thesis/dissertation. *Entrance requirements:* For master's and doctorate, GRE General Test, minimum GPA of 3.0. Additional exam requirements/recommendations for international students: Required—TOEFL. *Faculty research:* Differential equations, computational mathematics, dynamical systems, probability and statistics, pure mathematics.

Virginia Commonwealth University, Graduate School, College of Humanities and Sciences, Department of Statistical Sciences and Operations Research, Richmond, VA 23284-9005. Offers operations research (MS); statistics (MS); systems modeling and analysis (PhD). *Entrance requirements:* For master's, GRE General Test, 30 undergraduate credits in mathematics, statistics, or operations research, including calculus I and II, multivariate calculus, linear algebra, probability and statistics. Additional exam requirements/recommendations for international students: Required—TOEFL (minimum score 600 paper-based; 100 iBT); Recommended—IELTS (minimum score 6.5). Electronic applications accepted.

Virginia Polytechnic Institute and State University, Graduate School, College of Science, Blacksburg, VA 24061. Offers biological sciences (MS, PhD); biomedical technology development and management (MS); chemistry (MS, PhD); economics (MA, PhD); geosciences (MS, PhD); mathematics (MS, PhD); physics (MS, PhD); psychology (MS, PhD); statistics (MS, PhD). *Degree requirements:* For master's, comprehensive exam (for some programs), thesis (for some programs); for doctorate, comprehensive exam (for some programs), thesis/dissertation (for some programs). *Entrance requirements:* For master's and doctorate, GRE/GMAT (may vary by department). Additional exam requirements/recommendations for international students: Required—TOEFL (minimum score 550 paper-based). Electronic applications accepted.

Washington University in St. Louis, Graduate School of Arts and Sciences, Department of Mathematics, St. Louis, MO 63130-4899. Offers mathematics (MA, PhD); statistics (MA, PhD). *Students:* 45 full-time (13 women); includes 2 minority (1 Black or African American, non-Hispanic/Latino; 1 Asian, non-Hispanic/Latino), 31 international. 300 applicants, 31% accepted, 24 enrolled. In 2015, 6 master's, 7 doctorates awarded. Terminal master's awarded for partial completion of doctoral program. *Degree requirements:* For master's, thesis or alternative; for doctorate, thesis/dissertation. *Entrance requirements:* For master's and doctorate, GRE General Test. Additional exam requirements/recommendations for international students: Required—TOEFL. *Application deadline:* For fall admission, 1/15 for domestic students. Application fee: $45. Electronic applications accepted. *Financial support:* Fellowships, research assistantships, teaching assistantships, and tuition waivers (full and partial) available. Financial award application deadline: 1/15. *Faculty research:* Algebra, algebraic geometry, real and complex analysis, differential geometry, topology, statistics, mathematical statistics, survival analysis, modeling, statistical computing for massive data, Bayesian regularization, bioinformatics, longitudinal and functional data analysis, statistical computation, application of statistics to medicine. *Unit head:* Dr. David Wright, Chairman, 314-935-6726. *Application contact:* Bridget Coleman, Director of Admissions, 314-935-6880, Fax: 314-935-4887.
Website: http://wumath.wustl.edu/

Wayne State University, College of Liberal Arts and Sciences, Department of Mathematics, Detroit, MI 48202. Offers applied mathematics (MA, PhD); mathematical statistics (MA, PhD); mathematics (MA, MS); pure mathematics (PhD). *Faculty:* 26. *Students:* 42 full-time (10 women), 29 part-time (10 women); includes 10 minority (3 Black or African American, non-Hispanic/Latino; 5 Asian, non-Hispanic/Latino; 2 Hispanic/Latino), 31 international. Average age 30. 94 applicants, 41% accepted, 9 enrolled. In 2015, 10 master's, 3 doctorates awarded. *Degree requirements:* For master's, thesis (for some programs), essays, oral exams; for doctorate, thesis/dissertation, oral exams; French, German, Russian, or Chinese. *Entrance requirements:* For master's, twelve semester credits in mathematics beyond sophomore calculus; for doctorate, master's degree in mathematics or equivalent level of advancement. Additional exam requirements/recommendations for international students: Required—TOEFL (minimum score 550 paper-based; 79 iBT), TWE (minimum score 5.5), Michigan

English Language Assessment Battery (minimum score 85); Recommended—IELTS (minimum score 6.5). *Application deadline:* For fall admission, 6/1 priority date for domestic students, 5/1 priority date for international students; for winter admission, 10/1 priority date for domestic students, 9/1 priority date for international students; for spring admission, 2/1 priority date for domestic students, 1/1 priority date for international students. Application fee: $0. Electronic applications accepted. *Expenses:* Tuition, state resident: full-time $14,165; part-time $590.20 per credit hour. Tuition, nonresident: full-time $30,682; part-time $1278.40 per credit hour. *Required fees:* $1688; $47.45 per credit hour. $274.60 per semester. Tuition and fees vary according to course load and program. *Financial support:* In 2015–16, 43 students received support, including 5 fellowships with tuition reimbursements available (averaging $20,135 per year), 2 research assistantships with tuition reimbursements available (averaging $18,801 per year), 25 teaching assistantships with tuition reimbursements available (averaging $18,801 per year); scholarships/grants, health care benefits, and unspecified assistantships also available. Financial award application deadline: 3/31; financial award applicants required to submit FAFSA. *Faculty research:* Harmonic analysis and partial differential equations, group theory and non-commutative ring theory, homotopy theory and applications to topology and geometry, numerical analysis, control and optimization, statistical estimation theory. *Total annual research expenditures:* $807,813. *Unit head:* Dr. Daniel Frohardt, Professor and Chair, 313-577-6163, E-mail: danf@math.wayne.edu. *Application contact:* Mary Klamo, Academic Services Officer, E-mail: gradsecretary@math.wayne.edu.
Website: http://clas.wayne.edu/math/

Western Michigan University, Graduate College, College of Arts and Sciences, Department of Statistics, Kalamazoo, MI 49008. Offers MS, PhD, Graduate Certificate.

West Virginia University, College of Business and Economics, Division of Economics and Finance, Morgantown, WV 26506. Offers business analysis (MA); developmental financial economics (PhD); environmental and resource economics (PhD); international economics (PhD); mathematical economics (MA); monetary economics (PhD); public finance (PhD); public policy (MA); regional and urban economics (PhD); statistics and economics (MA). Terminal master's awarded for partial completion of doctoral program. *Degree requirements:* For master's, thesis optional; for doctorate, comprehensive exam, thesis/dissertation. *Entrance requirements:* For master's and doctorate, GRE General Test, minimum GPA of 3.0; course work in intermediate microeconomics, intermediate macroeconomics, calculus, and statistics. Additional exam requirements/

recommendations for international students: Required—TOEFL. Electronic applications accepted. *Expenses:* Tuition, state resident: full-time $8568. Tuition, nonresident: full-time $22,140. Tuition and fees vary according to program. *Faculty research:* Financial economics, regional/urban development, public economics, international trade/international finance/development economics, monetary economics.

West Virginia University, Eberly College of Arts and Sciences, Department of Statistics, Morgantown, WV 26506. Offers MS. *Degree requirements:* For master's, comprehensive exam, thesis. *Entrance requirements:* For master's, minimum GPA of 3.0, course work in linear algebra and multivariable calculus. Additional exam requirements/recommendations for international students: Required—TOEFL. *Expenses:* Tuition, state resident: full-time $8568. Tuition, nonresident: full-time $22,140. Tuition and fees vary according to program. *Faculty research:* Linear models, categorical data analysis, statistical computing, experimental design, non parametric analysis.

Yale University, Graduate School of Arts and Sciences, Department of Statistics, New Haven, CT 06520. Offers MA, PhD. Terminal master's awarded for partial completion of doctoral program. *Degree requirements:* For doctorate, thesis/dissertation. *Entrance requirements:* For doctorate, GRE General Test, GRE Subject Test.

York University, Faculty of Graduate Studies, Faculty of Science, Program in Mathematics and Statistics, Toronto, ON M3J 1P3, Canada. Offers industrial and applied mathematics (M Sc); mathematics and statistics (MA, PhD). *Program availability:* Part-time. *Degree requirements:* For master's, thesis optional; for doctorate, one foreign language, comprehensive exam, thesis/dissertation. Electronic applications accepted.

Youngstown State University, Graduate School, College of Science, Technology, Engineering and Mathematics, Department of Mathematics and Statistics, Youngstown, OH 44555-0001. Offers applied mathematics (MS); computer science (MS); secondary mathematics (MS); statistics (MS). *Program availability:* Part-time. *Degree requirements:* For master's, comprehensive exam, thesis optional. *Entrance requirements:* For master's, minimum GPA of 2.7 in computer science and mathematics. Additional exam requirements/recommendations for international students: Required—TOEFL. *Faculty research:* Regression analysis, numerical analysis, statistics, Markov chain, topology and fuzzy sets.

Peterson's Graduate Programs in the Physical Sciences, Mathematics, Agricultural Sciences, the Environment & Natural Resources 2017

www.petersons.com **289**

CHAPMAN UNIVERSITY

Schmid College of Science and Technology
Computational and Data Sciences Program
Food Sciences Program

 For more information, visit http://petersons.to/chapmanu_schmid

Programs of Study

Computational and Data Sciences: Chapman University's M.S. and Ph.D. in Computational and Data Sciences programs follow a uniquely interdisciplinary approach to solving critically important problems, using mathematics, physics, chemistry, biology, statistics, and computing. Through modeling, simulation, data mining, and study of specific phenomena via computer analysis and engineering, students learn to apply extraordinary technology and processes to answer the world's most complex questions, such as predictive analytics, earth systems science, bioinformatics and biotechnology, genomics and drug design, population genetics, and economic science.

Whereas computer science involves the pursuit of new frontiers chiefly within the realm of computer software and hardware, computational science practitioners apply the knowledge and power of computing to other science disciplines, whether it be running a costly physics experiment through a computer simulation to save millions, or creating new software that can sift through raw data with a far more strategic and sophisticated eye.

According to academic forecasters and business analysts, computational and data science is one of the most rapidly emerging areas of study in the nation. Chapman University's graduate programs in computational and data science help students find their place in this ever-growing field. Upon graduation, students are greeted with a diverse range of career options: graduates go on to work in aerospace engineering, data science, environmental modeling, medical development, gene sequencing, geology, and meteorology.

More information about this cutting-edge program is available online at graduate.chapman.edu/computational-science.

Food Science: Chapman University's M.S. in Food Science program is the perfect graduate degree program to help turn a student's passion, knowledge, and experience into a rewarding career. Chapman University students benefit from convenient evening classes, industry-informed curriculum, and numerous research and internships opportunities.

Food Science uses biology, chemistry, physical sciences, psychology, and engineering to study the properties of foods. Food scientists develop innovative ways to process, preserve, or package food, thereby making the food supply safer, sustainable, and more nutritious. Food science represents one of the healthiest industries in the world, with the various food industries—from processing to sales—contributing close to $42.2 billion to the U.S. national economy.

More than 1,500 food-processing companies are located within a 90-mile radius of Chapman University's campus. In fact, most students obtain work experience via internships and Chapman's job-placement rate is close to 100 percent. Graduates have found employment with Con-Agra, Contessa Foods, Dean Foods, Dole, Dr Pepper/Seven-Up, Carl Karcher Enterprises, Inc., Fresh Express, Golden Cheese Company, Hain Celestial, and many more.

More information is available at graduate.chapman.edu/ms-food-science.

Research Facilities

Chapman University's Schmid College of Science and Technology, which houses the Computational and Data Sciences and Food Science programs, is in a period of significant expansion. To further distinguish itself as a preeminent institution of higher education and advance its science programs, Chapman University is investing in the construction of a new, 140,000 square-foot Center for Science and Technology. Scheduled to open in 2018, the Center will feature research and teaching labs, a specialized computational sciences laboratory with super-computing room, collaboration areas for student/faculty exchange, high-tech equipment to support molecular biology, microbiology, organic and physical chemistry and biogeochemistry, graduate student lounges, and much more. (chapman.edu/forward).

Faculty in the Schmid College of Science and Technology conduct high-quality research and run several research labs that not only produce excellent research, but also actively involve students in the research process. Students receive first-hand experience in funded research projects of societal importance, have the chance to co-author papers in national recognized journals, and are able to present at national conferences.

Schmid College is also home to various centers for research, including the Center of Excellence in Computation, Algebra, and Topology (CECAT); the Center of Excellence in Complex and Hyper-complex Analysis (CECHA); and the Center of Excellence in Earth Systems Modeling and Observations (CEESMO). Schmid College is also affiliated with the Institute for Quantum Studies, which hosts a distinguished list of world-renowned physicists, including a 2013 Nobel Prize recipient and a 2010 Presidential Medal of Honor winner.

Financial Aid

Financial assistance is available in the form of federal loans, department scholarships, teaching assistantships and research assistantships. Most students receive some form of financial support from the University, and some receive additional aid through the School's industry partnerships that provide scholarship funding as well as internship opportunities.

Schmid College offers tuition support for its programs to a select number of students each semester (fees and other university charges are not covered). All students who submit a complete application are automatically considered for a department scholarship. Admitted students are notified of scholarships soon after receiving confirmation of admission.

More information can be found on the financial aid website (chapman.edu/students/tuition-and-aid/financial-aid) or by contacting Graduate Financial Aid at gradfinaid@chapman.edu or 714-628-2730.

Cost of Study

For the 2016–17 academic year, tuition for both the M.S. and Ph.D. programs in Computational and Data Science is $1,445 per credit. Tuition for the M.S. in Food Science program is $940 per credit, and it is $1,320 per credit for the MBA/M.S. Food Science program.

Living and Housing Costs

Information on graduate student housing options can be found on the Housing and Residence Life website (chapman.edu/students/services/housing-and-residence/on-campus/applying-housing) or by contacting the housing department at 714-997-6603.

Location

The Computational and Data Sciences and Food Sciences programs are offered at the Chapman campus located in Orange, California. Orange County has been rated by *Places Rated Almanac* as the number-one place to live in North America, citing superior climate, cultural, recreational, educational, and career-entree opportunities. In addition, Orange County is one of California's most important business and financial centers. Students have the opportunity to work part-time or intern at high-powered companies, and the area has many career opportunities available to students after graduation.

Orange County's central location between Los Angeles and San Diego means there is no shortage of entertainment options. Spectacular beaches, mountains for hiking and skiing, and desert landscapes compete with a wide variety of cultural attractions and sports venues. The historic district is full of cafes and shopping in a relaxed atmosphere, making it the perfect setting for college students.

The University occupies 76 park-like acres lined with palm and shade trees. A mix of historical and modern buildings makes Chapman one of the most beautiful university campuses in the nation.

The University and The College

The mission of Chapman University's Schmid College of Science and Technology is to mentor and grow leaders through a curriculum that develops outstanding problem-solving skills in the context of the grand, interdisciplinary challenges facing the world today. As the world becomes more interconnected a background in science and technology has become crucial, and as Chapman University moves towards the future, the Schmid College of Science and Technology will be leading the pack with innovative research and hands-on learning experiences.

Since its establishment, Schmid College has enjoyed significant growth, which is projected to continue. The college emphasizes a personalized, faculty-led,

Peterson's Graduate Programs in the Physical Sciences, Mathematics, Agricultural Sciences, the Environment & Natural Resources 2017

www.petersons.com   **291**

hands-on education, with opportunities for both undergraduate and graduate students to conduct and present research in their fields of study.

Faculty

In their research, Schmid College faculty members approach grand challenges by combining interdisciplinary breadth and collaboration with rigorous disciplinary depth and scholarship. This approach provides students with a modern view of problem solving in today's technologically focused world. Students are encouraged to partner with faculty in research, and to experience the exhilaration of making new discoveries or developing advanced software and hardware tools.

The following link provides a list of faculty members in mathematics, physics, and computation and their areas of research: chapman.edu/scst/core-faculty/physics-math-computation.aspx.

The following link provides a list of faculty members in the M.S. in Food Sciences program and their areas of research: chapman.edu/food-science.

Admission Requirements

Applicants to the M.S. and Ph.D. programs in Computational and Data Sciences and the M.S. in Food Science program must submit the following:

- Online application for admission ($60 nonrefundable application fee).

- Official transcript from degree-granting institution, as well as any other institutions where any program prerequisites were taken. View program prerequisites at chapman.edu/scst/graduate.

- Graduate admission test scores—the Graduate Record Examination (GRE) general test scores are required and must have been taken within the last five years. Visit chapman.edu/scst/graduate for minimum scores for each program.

- Letters of recommendation—two letters of recommendation are required, including one from an academic source for the food science program application, which describes the applicant's professional and academic abilities.

- Statement of Intent—a 750-word essay. Visit chapman.edu/scst/graduate for each program's specifications.

- Resume—a resume or curriculum vitae is required.

Applicants whose first language is not English or who have completed their undergraduate degree outside of the United States are required to achieve an acceptable score on one of the following English language proficiency exams, which must have been taken within two years of the date of application for admission: Test of English as a Foreign Language (TOEFL); International English Language Testing System (IELTS); Pearson Test of English (PTE Academic); or Cambridge English Advanced Exam (CAE). They must also submit the International Graduate Student Supplemental form.

Further information regarding application requirements can be found at chapman.edu/admission/graduate/applynow.aspx.

Applying

The application deadline is May 1 for fall semester enrollment. Prospective students should contact the Office of Graduate Admission at 714-997-6711 or gradadmit@chapman.edu with questions or for more information.

Correspondence and Information:

Schmid College of Science and Technology
Chapman University
One University Drive
Orange, California 92866
United States
Phone: 714-997-6730
E-mail: SchmidCollege@chapman.edu
Website: www.chapman.edu/scst/graduate

Food science graduate students working in the lab.

Hesham El-Askary, Ph.D., Director of Computational and Data Sciences Graduate Programs, works with a student in Chapman University's Samueli Laboratory in Computational Sciences.

292 www.petersons.com

Peterson's Graduate Programs in the Physical Sciences, Mathematics, Agricultural Sciences, the Environment & Natural Resources 2017

MEDICAL COLLEGE OF WISCONSIN
Ph.D. in Biostatistics Programs

 For more information, visit http://petersons.to/med-coll-wisconsin_biostat

Programs of Study

The Medical College of Wisconsin's (MCW) Division of Biostatistics offers a Ph.D. degree program designed for students with strong undergraduate preparation in mathematics and trains students in biostatistical methodology, theory, and practice. Emphasis is placed on sound theoretical understanding of statistical principles, research in the development of applied methodology, and collaborative research with biomedical scientists and clinicians. In addition, students gain substantial training and experience in statistical computing and in the use of software packages. Courses in the program are offered in collaboration with the Department of Mathematics at the University of Wisconsin–Milwaukee. The degree requirements, including dissertation research, are typically completed in five years beyond a bachelor's degree.

The program is designed for students with strong undergraduate preparation in mathematics and trains students in biostatistical methodology, theory, and practice. The degree requires that students earn 133 credits and can usually be completed in four to five years. It involves training in statistical computing and in the use of state-of-the-art software packages. Classes are small, allowing for considerable individual attention. The program also includes several electives, reading and research, and a dissertation.

Research Facilities

Faculty members are engaged in a number of collaborative research projects at the Center for International Blood and Marrow Transplant Research, the Clinical and Translational Science Institute, the Center for Patient Care and Outcomes Research, the Human and Molecular Genetics Center, the Clinical Cancer Center, and Marquette University.

Student Research

Dissertation research topics in statistical methodology often evolve from the faculty collaborative research projects, and students usually become coauthors on professional periodicals. The Division of Biostatistics has up-to-date networks of Sun workstations, PCs, and peripherals. The division's network is equipped with all leading statistical software and tools needed for the development of statistical methodology. Students are afforded access to multiple library collections to include MCW, the University of Wisconsin–Milwaukee, and the Division of Biostatistics.

The Epidemiology Data Service provides access to national data on health, health care, and special clinical data sets collected locally. The Medical College is a repository for the National Center for Health Statistics. The biostatistics program also houses the Biostatistics Consulting Service, which affords students the opportunity to experience extensive biomedical research.

Financial Aid and Cost of Study

Students are supported by fellowships for the first 18 months and then by research assistantships. The research assistantships provide students with the opportunity to gain experience in statistical consulting and collaborative research. Each includes tuition, stipend, and health insurance.

Living and Housing Costs

Many rental units are available in pleasant residential neighborhoods surrounding the Medical College. Housing costs begin at about $550 per month for a shared apartment.

Student Group

There are more than 1,265 students enrolled in educational programs at the Medical College. This includes 816 medical students and more than 450 graduate students. A low student-faculty ratio fosters individual attention and a close working relationship between students and faculty members.

Employment Opportunities and Alumni Achievements

Alumni of the MCW Biostatistics program are typically employed in academic institutions, government and nonprofit agencies, and pharmaceutical and consultant industries. Alumni are employed at Georgia State University, Johns Hopkins University, University of Pittsburgh, the Medical College of Wisconsin, SAS, GlaxoSmithKline, Takeda Global Research and Development, and Teva Pharmaceuticals to name a few.

Location

Milwaukee has long been noted for its old-world image. Its many ethnic traditions, especially from Middle Europe, give the city this distinction. Cultural opportunities are numerous and include museums, concert halls, art centers, and theaters. Milwaukee has a well-administered government, a low crime rate, and excellent schools. It borders Lake Michigan and lies within commuting distance of 200 inland lakes. Outdoor activities may be pursued year-round.

The College

The Medical College of Wisconsin is a private, national, freestanding institution. Founded in 1893, the College became

Peterson's Graduate Programs in the Physical Sciences, Mathematics, Agricultural Sciences, the Environment & Natural Resources 2017

www.petersons.com **293**

Medical College of Wisconsin

the Marquette University School of Medicine in 1913. It was reorganized in 1967 as an independent corporation and renamed the Medical College of Wisconsin in 1970. There are more than 1,500 faculty members. MCW is part of the Milwaukee Regional Medical Complex (MRMC) campus. Full-time students in any department may enroll in graduate courses in other departments and in programs of the University of Wisconsin-Milwaukee and Marquette University without any increase in tuition.

The College ranks in the top 34 percent of U.S. medical schools in National Institute of Health research funding.

The Faculty

Kwang Woo Ahn, Associate Professor; Ph.D., University of Iowa. *Website:* http://www.mcw.edu/Biostatistics/Faculty-Staff/Kwang-Woo-Ahn-PhD.htm.

Anjishnu Banerjee, Assistant Professor; Ph.D., Duke University. *Website:* http://www.mcw.edu/Biostatistics/Faculty-Staff/Banerjee-Anjishnu-PhD.htm.

Ruta Brazauskas, Assistant Professor; Ph.D., Medical College of Wisconsin. *Website:* http://www.mcw.edu/Biostatistics/Faculty-Staff/Ruta-Brazauskas-PhD.htm.

Raphael Fraser, Assistant Professor; Ph.D., Florida State University. *Website:* http://www.mcw.edu/Biostatistics/Faculty-Staff/Fraser-Raphael-PhD.htm.

Soyoung Kim, Assistant Professor; Ph.D., University of North Carolina. *Website:* http://www.mcw.edu/Biostatistics/Faculty-Staff/Kim-Soyoung-PhD.htm.

Purushottam (Prakash) W. Laud, Professor; Ph.D., University of Missouri. *Website:*.http://www.mcw.edu/Biostatistics/Faculty-Staff/Prakash-Laud-PhD.htm.

Brent R. Logan, Professor; Ph.D., Northwestern University. *Website:* http://www.mcw.edu/Biostatistics/Faculty-Staff/Brent-Logan-PhD.htm.

Rodney Sparapani, Assistant Professor; Ph.D., Medical College of Wisconsin. *Website:* http://www.mcw.edu/Biostatistics/Faculty-Staff/Rodney-Sparapani-PhD.htm.

Aniko Szabo, Associate Professor and Director of the Biostatistical Consulting Center; Ph.D., University of Memphis. *Website:* http://www.mcw.edu/Biostatistics/Faculty-Staff/Aniko-Szabo-PhD.htm.

Sergey Tarima, Assistant Professor; Ph.D., University of Kentucky. *Website:* http://www.mcw.edu/Biostatistics/Faculty-Staff/Sergey-Tarima-PhD.htm.

Tao Wang, Associate Professor; Ph.D., North Carolina State University. *Website:* http://www.mcw.edu/Biostatistics/Faculty-Staff/Tao-Wang-PhD.htm.

Mei-Jie Zhang, Professor; Ph.D., Florida State University. *Website:* http://www.mcw.edu/Biostatistics/Faculty-Staff/Mei-Jie-Zhang-PhD.htm.

Adjunct Faculty (University of Wisconsin-Milwaukee and Marquette University)

Jay Beder, Professor; Ph.D., George Washington University. *Website:* https://pantherfile.uwm.edu/beder/www/.

Vytaras Brazauskas, Associate Professor; Ph.D., University of Texas-Dallas. *Website:* https://pantherfile.uwm.edu/vytaras/www/.

Daniel Gervini, Associate Professor; Ph.D., University of Buenos Aires. *Website:* https://pantherfile.uwm.edu/gervini/www/.

Jugal Ghorai, Professor; Ph.D., Purdue University. *Website:* https://pantherfile.uwm.edu/jugal/www/.

Eric Key, Professor; Ph.D., Cornell University. *Website:* https://pantherfile.uwm.edu/ericskey/www/.

Thomas O'Bryan, Associate Professor Emeritus; Ph.D., Michigan State University. *Website:* https://uwm.edu/math/people/obryan-thomas-1/.

Dan Rowe, Associate Professor; Ph.D., University of California, Riverside. *Website:* http://www.mscs.mu.edu/~dbrowe/.

Gil Walter, Professor Emeritus; Ph.D., University of Wisconsin. Website: https://pantherfile.uwm.edu/ggw/www/.

Applying

Prerequisites include an undergraduate degree in mathematics or closely related fields, an overall grade point average of B or better, and a B average or better in mathematics and science. GRE requirements include an average of 60 percent or greater on the quantitative and verbal components of the GRE and a 3.5 or greater on the analytical writing component of the GRE. Foreign students are also required to submit their TOEFL score.

Application forms are available online at http://www.mcw.edu/graduateschool.htm, or by e-mail at gradschool@mcw.edu, or phone at 414-955-8218. The application deadline is January 15.

Correspondence and Information:

Division of Biostatistics
Medical College of Wisconsin
8701 Watertown Plank Road
Milwaukee, Wisconsin 53226
United States
Phone: 414-955-8280
E-mail: phdbiostatistics@mcw.edu
Website: http://www.mcw.edu/biostatistics.htm

294 www.petersons.com

Peterson's Graduate Programs in the Physical Sciences, Mathematics, Agricultural Sciences, the Environment & Natural Resources 2017

NEW YORK UNIVERSITY
Courant Institute of Mathematical Sciences
Department of Mathematics

 For more information, visit http://petersons.to/nyu-mathematics

Programs of Study

New York University's (NYU) Courant Institute of Mathematical Sciences (CIMS) is a highly respected center for research and advanced training in mathematics and computer science. NYU's world-class interdisciplinary graduate programs are known for their cutting-edge training in analysis and applied mathematics, including partial differential equations, differential geometry, dynamical systems, probability and stochastic processes, scientific computation, mathematical physics, and fluid dynamics.

The interdisciplinary focus is one of the greatest strengths of the Courant Institute's graduate programs. Courses, seminars, and research collaborations go far beyond traditional areas of pure and applied mathematics, covering diverse areas such as visual neural science, materials science, atmosphere/ocean science, cardiac fluid dynamics, plasma physics, mathematical genomics, and mathematical finance. Analysis plays a central role that provides a natural bridge between these subjects.

The Mathematics Department at the Courant Institute offers programs leading to Ph.D. degrees in mathematics and atmosphere/ocean science. It also offers Master of Science degrees in mathematics, scientific computing, and mathematical finance.

The Ph.D. degrees in mathematics and in atmosphere/ocean science and mathematics are open to students who wish to pursue a career in academic research and teaching, as well as in the private and public sectors. Consistent with its scientific breadth, the Institute welcomes applicants whose primary background is in quantitative fields such as economics, engineering, physics, or biology, as well as mathematics. Doctoral students take advanced courses in their areas of specialization, followed by a period of research and the preparation and defense of the doctoral thesis. Detailed information about the Ph.D. program in mathematics is available at http://math.nyu.edu/degree/phd/phd.html.

The M.S. degree in mathematics encompasses the basic graduate curriculum in mathematics, and also offers the opportunity of some more specialized training in an area of interest. A typical master's program involves basic courses in real analysis, complex analysis, and linear algebra, followed by other fundamental courses such as probability, scientific computing, and differential equations. Depending on their mathematical interests, students will then be able to take more advanced graduate courses in pure and applied mathematics.

The M.S. degree in scientific computing program provides broad yet rigorous training in areas of mathematics and computer science related to scientific computing. It aims to prepare students with the right talents and background for a technical career doing practical computing. The program accommodates both full-time and part-time students, with most courses meeting in the evening. The program is self-contained and terminal, providing a complete set of skills in a field where the need is greater than the supply. The masters program focuses on computational science, which includes modeling and numerical simulation as used in engineering design, development, and optimization.

The master's degree in mathematics in finance has a strong pragmatic component, including practically oriented courses and student mentoring by finance professionals. Graduates of the program know more finance than most science graduates and have stronger quantitative skills than most business graduates. They start with undergraduate degrees in quantitative subjects such as mathematics, physics, or engineering and are admitted to the program through a highly selective process. Courant's tightly integrated curriculum provides an efficient introduction to the theoretical and computational skills that are genuinely used and valued in the financial industry. The programs special strengths include its ensemble of courses, most created specifically for this program; great depth in relevant areas of applied mathematics; its extensive involvement of Fellows and other finance professionals; and strong participation by permanent faculty in teaching and mentoring students. Response from the finance industry has been very encouraging, with graduates finding excellent jobs in a wide range of quantitative areas.

Areas of Research

The Courant Institute has a tradition of research, which combines pure and applied mathematics, with a high level of interaction between different areas. Below are some of the current areas of research. The choice of categories is somewhat arbitrary, as many faculty have interests that cut across boundaries, and the fields continue to evolve.

- **Algebraic Geometry:** The research focus of the algebraic geometry group at Courant lies at the interface of geometry, topology, and number theory. Of particular interest are problems concerning the existence and distribution of rational points and rational curves on higher-dimensional varieties, group actions and hidden symmetries, as well as rationality, unirationality, and hyperbolicity properties of algebraic varieties.

- **Analysis and PDE:** Most, if not all, physical systems can be modeled by partial differential equations (PDE)—from continuum mechanics (including fluid mechanics and material science) to quantum mechanics or general relativity. The study of PDE has been a central research theme at the Courant Institute since its foundation. Themes are extremely varied, ranging from abstract questions (existence, uniqueness of solutions) to more concrete ones (qualitative or quantitative information on the behavior of solutions, often in relation with simulations).

- **Computational and Mathematical Biology:** Biological applications of mathematics and computing at Courant include genome analysis, biomolecular structure and dynamics, systems biology, embryology, immunology, neuroscience, heart physiology, biofluid dynamics, and medical imaging. The students, researchers, and faculty who work on these questions are pure and applied mathematicians and computer scientists working in close collaboration with biological and medical colleagues at NYU and elsewhere.

- **Dynamical Systems and Ergodic Theory:** The subject of dynamical systems is concerned with systems that evolve over time according to a well-defined rule, which could be either deterministic or probabilistic; examples of such systems arise in almost any field of science. Ergodic theory is a branch of dynamical systems concerned with measure preserving transformation of measure spaces, such as the dynamical systems associated with Hamiltonian mechanics. The theory of dynamical systems has applications in many areas of mathematics, including number theory, PDE, geometry, topology, and mathematical physics.

- **Geometry:** Geometry research at Courant blends differential and metric geometry with analysis and topology. The geometry group has strong ties with analysis and partial differential equations, as there are many PDEs and techniques of interest to both groups, such as Einstein's equations, the minimal surface equation, calculus of variations, and geometric measure theory.

- **Physical Applied Mathematics:** A central theme at the Courant Institute is the study of physical systems using advanced methods of applied mathematics. Currently, areas of focus include fluid dynamics, plasma physics, statistical mechanics, molecular dynamics and dynamical systems. The tradition at the Institute is to investigate fundamental questions as well as to solve problems with direct, real-world applications. In doing so, the people looking into these questions build on the strong synergies and fresh ideas that emerge in the frequent collaboration with analysis and PDE specialists as well as experts in scientific computing at the institute.

- **Probability Theory:** Domains of interest range from stochastic processes to random discrete structures to statistical physics (percolation, random matrices, etc.), which has become more and more central in recent years. Probability theory has natural connections with a number of fields (computational methods, financial mathematics, mathematical physics, dynamical systems, graph theory) since a great number of phenomena can be best modeled or understood by probabilistic means.

- **Scientific Computing:** Courant faculty have interests in stochastic modeling in statistical and quantum mechanics, nonlinear optimization, matrix analysis, high-dimensional data analysis, and numerical solutions of the partial differential equations that lie at the heart of fluid and solid mechanics, plasma physics, acoustics, and electromagnetism. Central to much of this work is the development of robust and efficient algorithms. As these algorithms are applied to increasingly complex problems, significant attention is being devoted to the design of effective and supportable software.

Research Facilities

The Courant Institute Library has one of the nation's most complete and retrospectively rich mathematics collections, including many hard-to-obtain items in languages other than English. Its collection comprises more than 64,000 volumes, including a burgeoning spectrum of electronic books and journals. The library is a campus wireless access point, and has a campus network-compatible printing facility.

Peterson's Graduate Programs in the Physical Sciences, Mathematics, Agricultural Sciences, the Environment & Natural Resources 2017

www.petersons.com   **295**

New York University

Financial Support

Financial support is awarded to students engaging in full-time Ph.D. study, covering tuition, fees, and NYU's individual comprehensive student insurance. In the 2016–17 academic year, it offers a 9-month stipend of $28,690. Summer positions involving teaching, research, or computational projects are available to a number of the Ph.D. students.

Cost of Study

In 2015–16, tuition was calculated at $1,608 per point. Associated fees were $500 for the first point in fall 2015 and spring 2016, and $66 per point thereafter. A full-time program of study normally consists of 24 points per year (four 3-credit courses per term).

Living and Housing Costs

University housing for graduate students is limited. It consists mainly of shared studio apartments in buildings on campus and shared suites in residence halls within walking distance of the University. Information about University housing, including location options and current costs, can be found online at http://www.nyu.edu/life/living-at-nyu.html.

Student Group

In 2015–16, the department had 299 graduate students. Sixty percent were full-time students.

Faculty

A detailed list of the faculty members and their research can be found at http://www.math.nyu.edu/people/.

Location

The graduate programs at the Courant Institute are offered in the very heart of the world's leading artistic and financial center in downtown Manhattan. The NYU campus is located in historic Greenwich Village, the long-time creative magnet for artists, writers, actors, musicians, and free thinkers.

Applying

The online application can be accessed at http://gsas.nyu.edu/object/grad.admissions.onlineapp. Specific information about admission requirements and applying to the Ph.D. programs in mathematics can be found at http://www.math.nyu.edu/degree/phd/application.html. Application details and admission requirements for the master's degree programs are available at http://www.math.nyu.edu/degree/ms/application.html.

Correspondence and Information

For questions regarding the graduate admissions process:

Graduate School of Arts and Science
Graduate Enrollment Services
New York University
Post Office Box 907, Cooper Station
New York, New York 10276-0907
Phone: 212-998-8050

For further information and questions regarding the programs:

Department of Mathematics
Courant Institute of Mathematical Sciences
New York University
251 Mercer Street
New York, New York 10012-1110
Phone: 212 998-3005
E-mail: admissions@math.nyu.edu
Website: http://www.math.nyu.edu/

296 www.petersons.com

Peterson's Graduate Programs in the Physical Sciences, Mathematics, Agricultural Sciences, the Environment & Natural Resources 2017

UNIVERSITY OF OKLAHOMA
Department of Mathematics

Programs of Study

While the Mathematics Department at the University of Oklahoma (OU) offers three different graduate degrees—M.S., M.A., and Ph.D.—students are considered to be on either two tracks, the M.S. track or the M.A./Ph.D. track.

The M.A./Ph.D track is the standard program for most students seeking a Ph.D. in mathematics. All students in the program (regardless of their future specialization) need to pass the three Ph.D. qualifying examinations in algebra, analysis, and topology. Each of these exams is associated with a two-semester graduate course sequence that forms the core of the M.A. degree and also count toward the Ph.D. degree. Students who pass all three qualifying examinations can go into the Ph.D. program in one of the following two options.

Ph.D. program (traditional option): This is essentially the same as the M.A./Ph.D. program above. The main difference is that students who already have a master's degree in mathematics may apply directly to this program. Students with a baccalaureate degree apply to the M.A./Ph.D. program and move into to the Ph.D. program on successful completion of the Ph.D. qualifying examinations. The student's ultimate goal in this program is to write and defend a dissertation representing an original contribution to research in mathematics.

Ph.D. program (RUME—research in undergraduate mathematics—option): As is the case with the traditional option, students who already have a master's degree in mathematics may apply to this program, while students with a baccalaureate degree apply to the M.A./Ph.D. program. The student's ultimate goal in this program is to write and defend a dissertation representing an original contribution to research in undergraduate mathematics education.

Students with strong mathematical backgrounds are encouraged to take "free shot" attempts at the Ph.D. qualifying examinations, usually held in August, the week before classes start. These attempts are only offered to students when they first enter the program, and results do not go on the student's record unless they pass.

The M.S. track (Master of Science program) is offered by the Mathematics Department for students who want to pursue studies in mathematics beyond the undergraduate level, but who do not plan to obtain a doctorate in mathematics. Recent graduates of the M.S. program have gone on to careers as actuaries, statistical analysts, and software engineers. Some become mathematics teachers in settings ranging from middle school to two- and four-year colleges. Still others have gone on to obtain doctorates and academic positions in fields other than mathematics, such as economics, mathematics education, and computer science.

Students will be able to select from a broad range of options in pure and applied mathematics and in research in undergraduate mathematics education as they pursue their graduate degree, including: (1) Algebra and Number Theory: algebraic geometry, algebraic groups, combinatorics, modular forms, representation theory (real, p-adic, Lie, automorphic); (2) Analysis: global analysis, harmonic analysis, integrable systems, PDEs, signal processing, spectral theory, wavelets and frames; (3) Applied Mathematics and Mathematical Physics: control theory, dynamical systems, modeling; (4) Geometry: convexity, harmonic maps, Riemannian geometry, group actions, non-negative curvature; (5) RUME: research in undergraduate mathematics education, diversity and equity, international comparative education; (6) Topology: algebraic and geometric topology, dimension theory, geometric group theory, hyperbolic geometry, low-dimensional topology, Teichmuller theory.

Additional information about the University's graduate programs in mathematics can be found at http://math.ou.edu/grad/programs.html.

Research Facilities

Students in the Department have a wide range of facilities and resources to support their study and research efforts. The department maintains two servers, Aftermath and Zeus, both of which run the Linux operating system. The Aftermath server hosts login shells and some software, while Zeus is the primary file server and provides NFS service to workstations throughout the department. The file system is protected by a RAID backup system. The systems manager should be able to recover a user's lost data for up to three or four weeks. There are two workstation clusters for graduate students in the department.

The library's LORA system gives students access to MathSciNet, the definitive database of mathematics literature reviews and bibliographical information (available in BibTeX format); JSTOR, and numerous other online databases and resources from off-campus locations.

Financial Aid

Most students are employed as graduate teaching assistants while earning their degrees. The students' transition into their new roles as educators is facilitated by a lighter course load in the first year and participation in the Department's graduate teaching seminar. Other graduate teaching assistant duties include grading, working in the Mathematics Help Center, and assisting in multisection courses.

In recent years, stipends for graduate teaching assistants who were fully English-language qualified to teach ranged from $15,038 to $16,187. Stipends for graduate teaching assistants who were not fully English-language qualified started at $14,030.

Other opportunities include graduate assistantships. A variable number of teaching assistantships are available for the summer semester in June and July each year, with a stipend of approximately $2,500. Several faculty members also provide support for research assistants using funds from research grants. Research assistants usually participate in research-related projects under the supervision of the faculty member.

Further details regarding financial support for graduate students can be found at http://math.ou.edu/grad/finance.html.

Cost of Study

For the 2016–17 academic year, tuition and fees for graduate students are $329.85 per credit hour for Oklahoma students and $917.45 per credit hour for nonresident students.

Living and Housing Costs

The University offers several on-campus apartment choices. In addition, there are a large number of privately owned apartments, duplexes, and houses available in Norman. Many off-campus

Peterson's Graduate Programs in the Physical Sciences, Mathematics, Agricultural Sciences, the Environment & Natural Resources 2017

www.petersons.com **297**

housing locations are served by CART, the Cleveland Area Rapid Transit system, which is free for OU students.

Student Group

The OU mathematics graduate program is composed of about 70 students, representing over a dozen different countries from around the globe. There is an active Mathematics Graduate Student Association which provides guidance and mentoring and organizes various events for graduate students. Additional details about the association can be found online at http://math.ou.edu/~mgsa/.

Location

As part of the dynamic Southwest, Oklahoma benefits from both its rich historic heritage and the vital and modern growth of its metropolitan areas. Although by location a suburb of Oklahoma City, Norman is an independent community with a permanent population of more than 95,000. Norman residents enjoy extensive parks and recreation programs and a 10,000-acre lake and park area. *Money* magazine named Norman as the nation's sixth best place to live in the 2008 edition of its annual rankings.

The University and The Department

The Mathematics Department at the University of Oklahoma has a long and rich academic tradition dating back to the mid-1890s. Students who pursue a graduate degree in mathematics at OU become part of a team that is responsible for the instruction of 10,000–12,000 OU undergraduate students annually. The Department's faculty members strive to maintain a vibrant and collegial research atmosphere and also serve as sources of inspiration, mentoring, and advice. The strong sense of community is enhanced by having faculty, postdoctoral, and student offices, as well as a common room and instructional classrooms, all housed in the same building. Prospective graduate students can experience the Mathematics Department in person during OU MathFest, an annual two-day open house for prospective graduate students. Dates, schedules, and a registration form for MathFest are available at http://math.ou.edu/grad/mathfest/.

Applying

Prospective students should submit the Mathematics Department graduate application form online, or may also download, print, and mail the form with the required materials listed below to the Mathematics Department. To ensure full consideration, the complete application and all supporting material needs to be received by the Department by January 31. The Department will forward everything to the Office of Admissions. Applications after this date will be considered, but those received after May 31 are rarely considered. International applicants are subject to the University's April 1 deadline.

In addition to the application form, students must submit official transcripts from all colleges and universities attended, GRE scores, TOEFL scores (if English is not the student's native language), and letters of reference from 3 people familiar with the student's work in mathematics (using the form found at http://math.ou.edu/grad/gradapp/Reference_Request.pdf). While the University's forms indicate an application fee is necessary, the Mathematics Department prescreens all applications and makes qualified applicants an offer; the application fee can be submitted then.

Correspondence and Information

Director of Graduate Studies
University of Oklahoma
Department of Mathematics
601 Elm Street, PHSC 423
Norman, Oklahoma 73019
Phone: 800-522-0772 (toll-free)
E-mail: mathgraddir@ou.edu
Website: http://www.math.ou.edu

THE FACULTY

The Mathematics Department at the University of Oklahoma has 34 permanent faculty members, 8 visiting faculty members, and a support staff of 6 (including a full-time undergraduate adviser). Virtually all of the department's faculty have active research programs (many externally funded) and regularly publish articles in mathematical journals and participate in conferences around the world.

Additional details regarding the Mathematics Department faculty can be found at http://www.math.ou.edu/people/faculty_research.html.

Students walk to class on the Norman campus.

298 www.petersons.com

Peterson's Graduate Programs in the Physical Sciences, Mathematics, Agricultural Sciences, the Environment & Natural Resources 2017

ACADEMIC AND PROFESSIONAL PROGRAMS IN THE AGRICULTURAL SCIENCES

Section 8
Agricultural and Food Sciences

This section contains a directory of institutions offering graduate work in agricultural and food sciences. Additional information about programs listed in the directory may be obtained by writing directly to the dean of a graduate school or chair of a department at the address given in the directory.

For programs offering related work, see also in this book *Natural Resources.* In the other guides in this series:

Graduate Programs in the Humanities, Arts & Social Sciences

See *Architecture (Landscape Architecture)* and *Economics (Agricultural Economics and Agribusiness)*

Graduate Programs in the Biological/Biomedical Sciences & Health-Related Medical Professions

See *Biological and Biomedical Sciences; Botany and Plant Biology; Ecology, Environmental Biology, and Evolutionary Biology; Entomology; Genetics, Developmental Biology, and Reproductive Biology; Nutrition; Pathology and Pathobiology; Physiology; Veterinary Medicine and Sciences;* and *Zoology*

Graduate Programs in Engineering & Applied Sciences

See *Agricultural Engineering and Bioengineering* and *Biomedical Engineering and Biotechnology*

Graduate Programs in Business, Education, Information Studies, Law & Social Work

See *Education (Agricultural Education)*

CONTENTS

Program Directories

Agricultural Sciences—General

Alabama Agricultural and Mechanical University, School of Graduate Studies, College of Agricultural, Life and Natural Sciences, Huntsville, AL 35811. Offers MS, MURP, PhD. *Program availability:* Part-time, evening/weekend. Terminal master's awarded for partial completion of doctoral program. *Degree requirements:* For doctorate, one foreign language, thesis/dissertation. *Entrance requirements:* For master's, GRE General Test; for doctorate, GRE General Test, MS. Additional exam requirements/recommendations for international students: Required—TOEFL (minimum score 500 paper-based; 61 iBT). Electronic applications accepted. *Faculty research:* Remote sensing, environmental pollutants, food biotechnology, plant growth.

Alcorn State University, School of Graduate Studies, School of Agriculture and Applied Science, Lorman, MS 39096-7500. Offers agricultural economics (MS Ag); agronomy (MS Ag); animal science (MS Ag). *Degree requirements:* For master's, thesis optional. *Faculty research:* Aquatic systems, dairy herd improvement, fruit production, alternative farming practices.

Angelo State University, College of Graduate Studies, College of Arts and Sciences, Department of Agriculture, San Angelo, TX 76909. Offers animal science (MS). *Program availability:* Part-time, evening/weekend. *Degree requirements:* For master's, comprehensive exam, thesis optional. *Entrance requirements:* For master's, GRE General Test, essay. Additional exam requirements/recommendations for international students: Required—TOEFL or IELTS. Electronic applications accepted. *Faculty research:* Effect of protein and energy on feedlot performance, bitterweed toxicosis in sheep, meat laboratory, North Concho Watershed Project, baseline vegetation.

Arkansas State University, Graduate School, College of Agriculture and Technology, State University, AR 72467. Offers agricultural education (SCCT); agriculture (MSA); vocational-technical administration (SCCT). *Program availability:* Part-time. *Faculty:* 15 full-time (3 women). *Students:* 14 full-time (7 women), 27 part-time (8 women); includes 11 minority (8 Black or African American, non-Hispanic/Latino; 3 Asian, non-Hispanic/Latino), 3 international. Average age 32. 34 applicants, 59% accepted, 13 enrolled. In 2015, 12 master's awarded. *Degree requirements:* For master's, comprehensive exam, thesis or alternative; for SCCT, comprehensive exam. *Entrance requirements:* For master's, GRE General Test or MAT, appropriate bachelor's degree, official transcripts, immunization records; for SCCT, GRE General Test or MAT, interview, master's degree, official transcript, immunization records. Additional exam requirements/recommendations for international students: Required—TOEFL (minimum score 550 paper-based; 79 iBT), IELTS (minimum score 6), PTE (minimum score 56). *Application deadline:* For fall admission, 7/1 for domestic and international students; for spring admission, 11/15 for domestic students, 11/14 for international students. Applications are processed on a rolling basis. Application fee: $30 ($40 for international students). Electronic applications accepted. *Expenses:* Tuition, state resident: full-time $4572; part-time $254 per credit hour. Tuition, nonresident: full-time $9144; part-time $508 per credit hour. *International tuition:* $9844 full-time. *Required fees:* $1188; $66 per credit hour. $25 per term. Tuition and fees vary according to course load and program. *Financial support:* In 2015–16, 8 students received support. Teaching assistantships, career-related internships or fieldwork, scholarships/grants, and unspecified assistantships available. Financial award application deadline: 7/1; financial award applicants required to submit FAFSA. *Unit head:* Dr. Timothy Burcham, Dean, 870-972-2085, Fax: 870-972-3885, E-mail: tburcham@astate.edu. *Application contact:* Vickey Ring, Graduate Admissions Coordinator, 870-972-2737, Fax: 870-972-3917, E-mail: vickeyring@astate.edu.
Website: http://www.astate.edu/college/agriculture-and-technology/index.dot

Auburn University, Graduate School, College of Agriculture, Auburn University, AL 36849. Offers M Ag, M Aq, MS, PhD. *Program availability:* Part-time. *Faculty:* 120 full-time (34 women), 13 part-time/adjunct (1 woman). *Students:* 142 full-time (68 women), 132 part-time (50 women); includes 17 minority (6 Black or African American, non-Hispanic/Latino; 2 American Indian or Alaska Native, non-Hispanic/Latino; 2 Asian, non-Hispanic/Latino; 5 Hispanic/Latino; 2 Two or more races, non-Hispanic/Latino), 114 international. Average age 28. 175 applicants, 52% accepted, 78 enrolled. In 2015, 51 master's, 19 doctorates awarded. *Degree requirements:* For doctorate, thesis/dissertation. *Entrance requirements:* For master's and doctorate, GRE General Test. *Application deadline:* Applications are processed on a rolling basis. Application fee: $50 ($60 for international students). Electronic applications accepted. *Expenses:* Tuition, state resident: full-time $8802; part-time $489 per credit hour. Tuition, nonresident: full-time $26,406; part-time $1467 per credit hour. *Required fees:* $808 per semester. Tuition and fees vary according to degree level and program. *Financial support:* Fellowships, research assistantships, teaching assistantships, and Federal Work-Study available. Support available to part-time students. Financial award application deadline: 3/15; financial award applicants required to submit FAFSA. *Unit head:* William Batchelor, Dean, 334-844-2345. *Application contact:* Dr. George Flowers, Dean of the Graduate School, 334-844-2125.
Website: http://www.ag.auburn.edu/

Brigham Young University, Graduate Studies, College of Life Sciences, Provo, UT 84602-1001. Offers MPH, MS, PhD. *Faculty:* 133 full-time (20 women), 5 part-time/adjunct (4 women). *Students:* 184 full-time (101 women), 57 part-time (22 women); includes 39 minority (2 Black or African American, non-Hispanic/Latino; 1 American Indian or Alaska Native, non-Hispanic/Latino; 16 Asian, non-Hispanic/Latino; 14 Hispanic/Latino; 3 Native Hawaiian or other Pacific Islander, non-Hispanic/Latino; 3 Two or more races, non-Hispanic/Latino), 19 international. Average age 27. 155 applicants, 51% accepted, 69 enrolled. In 2015, 56 master's, 14 doctorates awarded. *Degree requirements:* For master's, comprehensive exam, thesis, prospectus, defense of research, defense of thesis; for doctorate, comprehensive exam, thesis/dissertation, prospectus, defense of research, defense of dissertation. *Entrance requirements:* For master's, GRE General Test, minimum GPA of 3.2 for last 60 hours of course work; for doctorate, GRE General Test, GRE Subject Test (biology), minimum GPA of 3.2 for last 60 hours of course work. Additional exam requirements/recommendations for international students: Required—TOEFL (minimum score 580 paper-based; 85 iBT), IELTS (minimum score 7). *Application deadline:* For fall admission, 2/1 for domestic and international students; for winter admission, 2/1 for international students. Application fee: $50. Electronic applications accepted. *Financial support:* In 2015–16, 216 students received support, including 38 fellowships with tuition reimbursements available (averaging $10,700 per year), 181 research assistantships with tuition reimbursements available (averaging $12,578 per year), 136 teaching assistantships with tuition reimbursements available (averaging $12,310 per year); career-related internships or fieldwork, institutionally sponsored loans, scholarships/grants, health care benefits, tuition waivers (full and partial), and unspecified assistantships also available. Financial award application deadline: 2/1; financial award applicants required to submit FAFSA. *Total annual research expenditures:* $6.4 million. *Unit head:* James P. Porter, Dean, 801-422-3963, Fax: 801-422-0050. *Application contact:* Sue Pratley, Application Contact, 801-422-3963, Fax: 801-422-0050, E-mail: sue_pratley@byu.edu.
Website: http://lifesciences.byu.edu/home/

California Polytechnic State University, San Luis Obispo, College of Agriculture, Food and Environmental Sciences, Program in Agriculture, San Luis Obispo, CA 93407. Offers MS. *Program availability:* Part-time. *Faculty:* 14 full-time (6 women), 1 (woman) part-time/adjunct. *Students:* 21 full-time (17 women), 20 part-time (16 women); includes 11 minority (4 Asian, non-Hispanic/Latino; 5 Hispanic/Latino; 2 Two or more races, non-Hispanic/Latino), 5 international. Average age 26. 71 applicants, 25% accepted, 15 enrolled. In 2015, 22 master's awarded. *Degree requirements:* For master's, comprehensive exam, thesis. *Application deadline:* For fall admission, 4/1 for domestic and international students; for winter admission, 10/1 for domestic students, 6/30 for international students; for spring admission, 10/1 for domestic students. Applications are processed on a rolling basis. Application fee: $55. Electronic applications accepted. *Expenses:* Tuition, state resident: full-time $6738; part-time $3906 per year. Tuition, nonresident: full-time $15,666; part-time $8370 per year. *Required fees:* $3528; $3075 per unit. $1025 per term. *Financial support:* Fellowships, research assistantships, teaching assistantships, career-related internships or fieldwork, Federal Work-Study, institutionally sponsored loans, scholarships/grants, and unspecified assistantships available. Support available to part-time students. Financial award application deadline: 3/2; financial award applicants required to submit FAFSA. *Faculty research:* Sustainability; specialty crops; dairy products technology; irrigation training; recreation, parks, and tourism management. *Unit head:* Dr. Andrew Thulin, Dean, 805-756-2161, E-mail: athulin@calpoly.edu. *Application contact:* Dr. Chris Dicus, Interim Associate Dean, Research and Graduate Programs, 805-756-5104, E-mail: cdicus@calpoly.edu.

California State Polytechnic University, Pomona, Program in Agriculture, Pomona, CA 91768-2557. Offers agricultural science (MS); nutrition and food science (MS). *Program availability:* Part-time. *Students:* 13 full-time (9 women), 23 part-time (15 women); includes 16 minority (3 Black or African American, non-Hispanic/Latino; 4 Asian, non-Hispanic/Latino; 9 Hispanic/Latino), 3 international. Average age 28. 64 applicants, 42% accepted, 13 enrolled. In 2015, 12 master's awarded. *Degree requirements:* For master's, thesis or alternative. *Application deadline:* For fall admission, 5/1 priority date for domestic students; for winter admission, 10/15 priority date for domestic students; for spring admission, 1/2 priority date for domestic students. Applications are processed on a rolling basis. Application fee: $55. Electronic applications accepted. *Expenses:* Tuition, state resident: full-time $6738. Tuition, nonresident: full-time $13,434. *Required fees:* $1504. Tuition and fees vary according to course load, degree level and program. *Financial support:* Career-related internships or fieldwork, Federal Work-Study, and institutionally sponsored loans available. Support available to part-time students. Financial award application deadline: 3/2; financial award applicants required to submit FAFSA. *Faculty research:* Equine nutrition, physiology, and reproduction; leadership development; bioartificial pancreas; plant science; ruminant and human nutrition. *Unit head:* Dr. Harmit Singh, Director of Research and Graduate Studies, 909-869-3023, Fax: 909-869-5078, E-mail: harmitsingh@cpp.edu.
Website: http://www.cpp.edu/~agri/agmasters/index.shtml

Clemson University, Graduate School, College of Agriculture, Forestry and Life Sciences, Department of Agricultural Sciences, Clemson, SC 29634. Offers agricultural education (M Ag Ed). *Program availability:* Part-time. *Faculty:* 50 full-time (11 women), 2 part-time/adjunct (1 woman). *Students:* 58 full-time (28 women), 28 part-time (9 women); includes 5 minority (1 Black or African American, non-Hispanic/Latino; 1 Asian, non-Hispanic/Latino; 1 Hispanic/Latino; 2 Two or more races, non-Hispanic/Latino), 27 international. Average age 26. 63 applicants, 43% accepted, 19 enrolled. In 2015, 21 master's awarded. *Degree requirements:* For master's, thesis optional. *Entrance requirements:* For master's, GRE General Test, unofficial transcripts, letters of recommendation. Additional exam requirements/recommendations for international students: Required—TOEFL (minimum score 80 iBT), IELTS (minimum score 6.5). *Application deadline:* For fall admission, 6/1 for domestic students, 7/1 for international students; for spring admission, 10/1 for domestic students, 11/1 for international students. Applications are processed on a rolling basis. Application fee: $80 ($90 for international students). Electronic applications accepted. *Expenses:* $4,060 per semester full-time resident, $8,103 per semester full-time non-resident, $448 per credit hour part-time resident, $898 per credit hour part-time non-resident. *Financial support:* In 2015–16, 62 students received support, including 3 fellowships with partial tuition reimbursements available (averaging $5,000 per year), 37 research assistantships with partial tuition reimbursements available (averaging $18,210 per year), 22 teaching assistantships with partial tuition reimbursements available (averaging $17,496 per year); career-related internships or fieldwork and health care benefits also available. Financial award application deadline: 6/1. *Unit head:* Dr. George Askew, Dean, 864-656-3013, E-mail: caflsdean-l@clemson.edu. *Application contact:* Dr. Joseph Culin, Associate Dean for Research and Graduate Studies, 864-656-2810, E-mail: jculin@clemson.edu.
Website: http://www.clemson.edu/cafls/departments/agricultural-sciences/index.html

Colorado State University, College of Agricultural Sciences, Fort Collins, CO 80523-1101. Offers M Agr, MAEE, MLA, MS, PhD. *Program availability:* Part-time, evening/weekend. *Faculty:* 84 full-time (22 women), 16 part-time/adjunct (9 women). *Students:* 123 full-time (64 women), 221 part-time (121 women); includes 20 minority (1 Black or African American, non-Hispanic/Latino; 1 American Indian or Alaska Native, non-Hispanic/Latino; 9 Hispanic/Latino; 9 Two or more races, non-Hispanic/Latino), 64 international. Average age 32. 168 applicants, 65% accepted, 72 enrolled. In 2015, 81 master's, 15 doctorates awarded. *Degree requirements:* For master's, comprehensive exam (for some programs), thesis (for some programs), publication; for doctorate, comprehensive exam, thesis/dissertation, publication. *Entrance requirements:* For master's, GRE/GMAT, minimum GPA of 3.0, 3 letters of recommendation, bachelor's degree; for doctorate, GRE General Test, minimum GPA of 3.0, 3 letters of recommendation, bachelor's degree. Additional exam requirements/recommendations for international students: Required—TOEFL (minimum score 550 paper-based; 80 iBT); Recommended—IELTS (minimum score 6.5). *Application deadline:* Applications are processed on a rolling basis. Application fee: $60 ($70 for international students). Electronic applications accepted. *Expenses:* Tuition, state resident: full-time $9348. Tuition, nonresident: full-time $22,916. *Required fees:* $2174; $473.72 per credit hour. $236.86 per semester. Tuition and fees vary according to course load and program. *Financial support:* In 2015–16, 9 fellowships with full tuition reimbursements (averaging $49,223 per year), 75 research assistantships with tuition reimbursements (averaging $19,688 per year), 34 teaching assistantships (averaging $16,031 per year) were

awarded; Federal Work-Study, scholarships/grants, tuition waivers, and unspecified assistantships also available. Financial award application deadline: 1/15; financial award applicants required to submit FAFSA. *Faculty research:* Plant and animal breeding; food safety, economics and policy; water and environmental economics; plant protection; livestock management systems. *Total annual research expenditures:* $14.2 million. *Unit head:* Dr. Ajay Menon, Dean, 970-491-6274, Fax: 970-491-4895, E-mail: ajay.menon@colostate.edu. *Application contact:* Pam Schell, Administrative Assistant III, 970-491-2410, Fax: 970-491-4895, E-mail: pam.schell@colostate.edu.
Website: http://home.agsci.colostate.edu/

Dalhousie University, Faculty of Agriculture, Halifax, NS B3H 4R2, Canada. Offers agriculture (M Sc), including air quality, animal behavior, animal molecular genetics, animal nutrition, animal technology, aquaculture, botany, crop management, crop physiology, ecology, environmental microbiology, food science, horticulture, nutrient management, pest management, physiology, plant biotechnology, plant pathology, soil chemistry, soil fertility, waste management and composting, water quality. *Program availability:* Part-time. *Degree requirements:* For master's, thesis, ATC Exam Teaching Assistantship. *Entrance requirements:* For master's, honors B Sc, minimum GPA of 3.0. Additional exam requirements/recommendations for international students: Required—TOEFL (minimum score 580 paper-based; 92 iBT), IELTS, Michigan English Language Assessment Battery, CanTEST, CAEL. *Faculty research:* Bio-product development, organic agriculture, nutrient management, air and water quality, agricultural biotechnology.

Illinois State University, Graduate School, College of Applied Science and Technology, Department of Agriculture, Normal, IL 61790-2200. Offers agribusiness (MS). *Degree requirements:* For master's, thesis optional. *Entrance requirements:* For master's, GRE General Test, minimum GPA of 3.0 in last 60 hours. *Faculty research:* Engineering-economic system models for rural ethanol production facilities, development and evaluation of a propane-fueled, production scale, on-site thermal destruction system C-FAR 2007; field scale evaluation and technology transfer of economically, ecologically systems; sound liquid swine manure treatment and application.

Instituto Tecnológico y de Estudios Superiores de Monterrey, Campus Monterrey, Graduate and Research Division, Program in Agriculture, Monterrey, Mexico. Offers agricultural parasitology (PhD); agricultural sciences (MS); farming productivity (MS); food processing engineering (MS); phytopathology (MS). *Program availability:* Part-time. *Degree requirements:* For master's, one foreign language, thesis; for doctorate, one foreign language, thesis/dissertation. *Entrance requirements:* For master's, EXADEP; for doctorate, GMAT or GRE, master's degree in related field. Additional exam requirements/recommendations for international students: Required—TOEFL. *Faculty research:* Animal embryos and reproduction, crop entomology, tropical agriculture, agricultural productivity, induced mutation in oleaginous plants.

Iowa State University of Science and Technology, Program in Sustainable Agriculture, Ames, IA 50011. Offers MS, PhD. *Entrance requirements:* For master's and doctorate, GRE General Test. Additional exam requirements/recommendations for international students: Required—TOEFL (minimum score 570 paper-based; 80 iBT), IELTS (minimum score 6.5). Electronic applications accepted.

Kansas State University, Graduate School, College of Agriculture, Manhattan, KS 66506. Offers MAB, MS, PhD, Certificate. *Program availability:* Part-time, online learning. Terminal master's awarded for partial completion of doctoral program. *Degree requirements:* For doctorate, thesis/dissertation. *Entrance requirements:* For master's, GRE, minimum undergraduate GPA of 3.0; for doctorate, GRE, minimum undergraduate GPA of 3.5. Additional exam requirements/recommendations for international students: Required—TOEFL (minimum score 550 paper-based). Electronic applications accepted.

Louisiana State University and Agricultural & Mechanical College, Graduate School, College of Agriculture, Baton Rouge, LA 70803. Offers M App St, MS, PhD. *Total annual research expenditures:* $426,961.

McGill University, Faculty of Graduate and Postdoctoral Studies, Faculty of Agricultural and Environmental Sciences, Montréal, QC H3A 2T5, Canada. Offers M Sc, M Sc A, PhD, Certificate, Graduate Diploma.

McNeese State University, Doré School of Graduate Studies, College of Science, Dripps Department of Agricultural Sciences, Program in Environmental and Chemical Sciences, Lake Charles, LA 70609. Offers agricultural sciences (MS); environmental science (MS). *Program availability:* Evening/weekend. *Degree requirements:* For master's, comprehensive exam, thesis or alternative. *Entrance requirements:* For master's, GRE.

Michigan State University, The Graduate School, College of Agriculture and Natural Resources, East Lansing, MI 48824. Offers MA, MIPS, MS, MURP, PhD. *Faculty research:* Plant science, animal sciences, forestry, fisheries and wildlife, recreation and tourism.

Mississippi State University, College of Agriculture and Life Sciences, Department of Animal Dairy Sciences, Mississippi State, MS 39762. Offers agricultural life sciences (MS), including animal physiology (MS, PhD), genetics (MS, PhD); agricultural science (PhD), including animal dairy sciences, animal nutrition (MS, PhD); agriculture (MS), including animal nutrition (MS, PhD), animal science; life sciences (PhD), including animal physiology (MS, PhD), genetics (MS, PhD). *Faculty:* 18 full-time (6 women). *Students:* 15 full-time (10 women), 10 part-time (4 women); includes 1 minority (Black or African American, non-Hispanic/Latino), 7 international. Average age 28. 27 applicants, 44% accepted, 9 enrolled. In 2015, 7 master's, 2 doctorates awarded. *Degree requirements:* For master's, comprehensive exam (for some programs), thesis, written proposal of intended research area; for doctorate, comprehensive exam, thesis/dissertation, written proposal of intended research area. *Entrance requirements:* For master's, GRE General Test, minimum GPA of 3.0; for doctorate, GRE General Test. Additional exam requirements/recommendations for international students: Required—TOEFL (minimum score 575 paper-based; 84 iBT), IELTS (minimum score 7). *Application deadline:* For fall admission, 7/1 for domestic students, 5/1 for international students; for spring admission, 11/1 for domestic students, 9/1 for international students. Applications are processed on a rolling basis. Application fee: $60. Electronic applications accepted. *Expenses: Tuition, area resident:* Full-time $7502; part-time $833.74 per credit hour. Tuition, nonresident: full-time $20,142; part-time $2238.24 per credit hour. *Financial support:* In 2015–16, 10 research assistantships (averaging $13,661 per year) were awarded; Federal Work-Study, institutionally sponsored loans, and unspecified assistantships also available. Financial award application deadline: 4/1; financial award applicants required to submit FAFSA. *Faculty research:* Ecology and population dynamics, physiology, biochemistry and behavior, systematics. *Unit head:* Dr. John Blanton, Department Head, 662-325-2935, Fax: 662-325-8873, E-mail: jblanton@ads.msstate.edu. *Application contact:* Marina Hunt, Admissions Assistant, 662-325-5188, E-mail: mhunt@grad.msstate.edu.
Website: http://www.ads.msstate.edu/

Mississippi State University, College of Agriculture and Life Sciences, Department of Biochemistry, Molecular Biology, Entomology and Plant Pathology, Mississippi State, MS 39762. Offers agriculture life sciences (MS), including biochemistry (MS, PhD), entomology (MS, PhD), plant pathology (MS, PhD); life science (PhD), including biochemistry (MS, PhD), entomology (MS, PhD), plant pathology (MS, PhD); molecular biology (PhD). *Faculty:* 32 full-time (6 women), 2 part-time/adjunct (1 woman). *Students:* 44 full-time (20 women), 11 part-time (6 women); includes 6 minority (3 Black or African American, non-Hispanic/Latino; 1 Asian, non-Hispanic/Latino; 1 Hispanic/Latino; 1 Two or more races, non-Hispanic/Latino), 12 international. Average age 29. 35 applicants, 40% accepted, 12 enrolled. In 2015, 12 master's, 7 doctorates awarded. Terminal master's awarded for partial completion of doctoral program. *Degree requirements:* For master's, thesis (for some programs), final oral exam; for doctorate, thesis/dissertation, preliminary oral and written exam. *Entrance requirements:* For master's, GRE General Test, minimum GPA of 2.75; for doctorate, GRE. Additional exam requirements/recommendations for international students: Required—TOEFL (minimum score 500 paper-based; 61 iBT); Recommended—IELTS (minimum score 5.5). *Application deadline:* For fall admission, 7/1 for domestic students, 5/1 for international students; for spring admission, 11/1 for domestic students, 9/1 for international students. Applications are processed on a rolling basis. Application fee: $60. Electronic applications accepted. *Expenses: Tuition, area resident:* Full-time $7502; part-time $833.74 per credit hour. Tuition, nonresident: full-time $20,142; part-time $2238.24 per credit hour. *Financial support:* In 2015–16, 40 research assistantships with full tuition reimbursements (averaging $16,730 per year) were awarded; Federal Work-Study, institutionally sponsored loans, and unspecified assistantships also available. Financial award application deadline: 4/1; financial award applicants required to submit FAFSA. *Faculty research:* Fish nutrition, plant and animal molecular biology, plant biochemistry, enzymology, lipid metabolism, chromatin, cell wall synthesis in rice, a model grass bioenergy species and the source of rice Stover residues using reverse genetic and functional genomic and proteomic approaches. *Unit head:* Dr. Jeffrey Dean, Professor and Department Head, 662-325-0643, Fax: 662-325-8664, E-mail: jd1891@msstate.edu. *Application contact:* Marina Hunt, Admissions Assistant, 662-325-5188, E-mail: mhunt@grad.msstate.edu.
Website: http://www.biochemistry.msstate.edu

Mississippi State University, College of Agriculture and Life Sciences, Department of Plant and Soil Sciences, Mississippi State, MS 39762. Offers agriculture (MS, PhD), including agronomy, horticulture, weed science. *Faculty:* 49 full-time (5 women). *Students:* 45 full-time (11 women), 33 part-time (6 women); includes 2 minority (1 American Indian or Alaska Native, non-Hispanic/Latino; 1 Asian, non-Hispanic/Latino), 20 international. Average age 27. 26 applicants, 46% accepted, 11 enrolled. In 2015, 16 master's, 7 doctorates awarded. *Degree requirements:* For master's, comprehensive exam, thesis, oral and/or written exams; for doctorate, comprehensive exam, thesis/dissertation, minimum of 20 semester hours of research for dissertation. *Entrance requirements:* For master's, GRE (for weed science), minimum GPA of 2.75 (agronomy/horticulture), 3.0 (weed science); for doctorate, GRE (for weed science), minimum GPA of 3.0 (agronomy/horticulture), 3.25 (weed science). Additional exam requirements/recommendations for international students: Required—TOEFL (minimum score 500 paper-based; 61 iBT), TOEFL (minimum score 550 paper-based, 79 iBT) or IELTS (minimum score 6.5) for weed science; Recommended—IELTS (minimum score 5.5). *Application deadline:* For fall admission, 7/1 for domestic students, 5/1 for international students; for spring admission, 10/1 for domestic students, 9/1 for international students. Applications are processed on a rolling basis. Application fee: $60. Electronic applications accepted. *Expenses: Tuition, area resident:* Full-time $7502; part-time $833.74 per credit hour. Tuition, nonresident: full-time $20,142; part-time $2238.24 per credit hour. *Financial support:* In 2015–16, 31 research assistantships (averaging $14,967 per year), 3 teaching assistantships (averaging $15,951 per year) were awarded; Federal Work-Study, institutionally sponsored loans, scholarships/grants, and unspecified assistantships also available. Financial award application deadline: 4/1; financial award applicants required to submit FAFSA. *Faculty research:* Bioenergy crops, cotton breeding, environmental plant pathology, row crop weed control, genomics. *Unit head:* Dr. Mike Phillips, Professor and Head, 662-325-2311, Fax: 662-325-8742, E-mail: jmp657@msstate.edu. *Application contact:* Marina Hunt, Admissions Assistant, 662-325-5188, E-mail: mhunt@grad.msstate.edu.
Website: http://www.pss.msstate.edu/

Mississippi State University, College of Agriculture and Life Sciences, Department of Poultry Science, Mississippi State, MS 39762. Offers agricultural sciences (PhD), including poultry science (MS, PhD); agriculture (MS), including poultry science (MS, PhD). *Faculty:* 9 full-time (3 women). *Students:* 16 full-time (10 women), 2 part-time (1 woman); includes 1 minority (Black or African American, non-Hispanic/Latino), 10 international. Average age 27. 14 applicants, 64% accepted, 9 enrolled. In 2015, 4 master's, 1 doctorate awarded. *Degree requirements:* For master's, comprehensive exam, thesis optional; for doctorate, comprehensive exam, thesis/dissertation. *Entrance requirements:* Additional exam requirements/recommendations for international students: Required—TOEFL (minimum score 477 paper-based; 53 iBT); Recommended—IELTS (minimum score 4.5). *Application deadline:* For fall admission, 7/1 for domestic students, 5/1 for international students; for spring admission, 10/1 for domestic students, 11/1 for international students. Applications are processed on a rolling basis. Application fee: $60. Electronic applications accepted. *Expenses: Tuition, area resident:* Full-time $7502; part-time $833.74 per credit hour. Tuition, nonresident: full-time $20,142; part-time $2238.24 per credit hour. *Financial support:* In 2015–16, 17 research assistantships with partial tuition reimbursements (averaging $13,560 per year) were awarded; Federal Work-Study, institutionally sponsored loans, scholarships/grants, and unspecified assistantships also available. Financial award application deadline: 4/1; financial award applicants required to submit FAFSA. *Unit head:* Dr. Mary Beck, Professor and Head, 662-325-5430, Fax: 662-325-8292, E-mail: mbeck@poultry.msstate.edu. *Application contact:* Marina Hunt, Admissions Assistant, 662-325-5188, E-mail: mhunt@grad.msstate.edu.
Website: http://www.poultry.msstate.edu/

Mississippi State University, College of Agriculture and Life Sciences, School of Human Sciences, Mississippi State, MS 39762. Offers agricultural sciences (PhD), including agriculture and extension education; agriculture and extension education (MS); human development and family studies (MS, PhD). *Accreditation:* NCATE (one or more programs are accredited). *Program availability:* Part-time. *Faculty:* 24 full-time (15 women), 1 part-time/adjunct (0 women). *Students:* 32 full-time (23 women), 63 part-time (42 women); includes 17 minority (15 Black or African American, non-Hispanic/Latino; 1 Hispanic/Latino; 1 Two or more races, non-Hispanic/Latino), 5 international. Average age 35. 18 applicants, 78% accepted, 11 enrolled. In 2015, 16 master's, 1 doctorate awarded. *Degree requirements:* For master's, thesis optional, comprehensive oral or written exam. *Entrance requirements:* For master's, GRE, minimum GPA of 2.75 in last 4 semesters of course work; for doctorate, minimum GPA of 3.0 on prior graduate work. Additional exam requirements/recommendations for international students: Required—TOEFL (minimum score 477 paper-based; 53 iBT); Recommended—IELTS (minimum score 4.5). *Application deadline:* For fall admission, 7/1 for domestic students, 5/1 for international students; for spring admission, 11/1 for domestic students, 9/1 for

international students. Applications are processed on a rolling basis. Application fee: $60. Electronic applications accepted. *Expenses: Tuition, area resident:* Full-time $7502; part-time $833.74 per credit hour. Tuition, nonresident: full-time $20,142; part-time $2238.24 per credit hour. *Financial support:* In 2015–16, 15 research assistantships (averaging $13,002 per year) were awarded; Federal Work-Study, institutionally sponsored loans, and unspecified assistantships also available. Financial award application deadline: 4/1; financial award applicants required to submit FAFSA. *Faculty research:* Animal welfare, agroscience, information technology, learning styles, problem solving. *Unit head:* Dr. Michael Newman, Director and Professor, 662-325-2950, E-mail: mnewman@humansci.msstate.edu. *Application contact:* Marina Hunt, Admissions Assistant, 662-325-5188, E-mail: mhunt@grad.msstate.edu.
Website: http://www.humansci.msstate.edu

Missouri State University, Graduate College, William H. Darr School of Agriculture, Springfield, MO 65897. Offers plant science (MS); secondary education (MS Ed), including agriculture. *Program availability:* Part-time. *Faculty:* 16 full-time (5 women), 1 part-time/adjunct (0 women). *Students:* 17 full-time (9 women), 26 part-time (17 women); includes 3 minority (1 Black or African American, non-Hispanic/Latino; 1 Hispanic/Latino; 1 Two or more races, non-Hispanic/Latino), 1 international. Average age 27. 28 applicants, 64% accepted, 17 enrolled. In 2015, 21 master's awarded. *Degree requirements:* For master's, comprehensive exam, thesis or alternative. *Entrance requirements:* For master's, GRE (MS in plant science, MNAS), 9-12 teacher certification (MS Ed), minimum GPA of 3.0 (MS plant science, MNAS). Additional exam requirements/recommendations for international students: Required—TOEFL (minimum score 550 paper-based; 79 iBT), IELTS (minimum score 6). *Application deadline:* For fall admission, 7/20 priority date for domestic students, 5/1 for international students; for spring admission, 12/20 priority date for domestic students, 9/1 for international students; for summer admission, 5/20 priority date for domestic students. Applications are processed on a rolling basis. Application fee: $35 ($50 for international students). Electronic applications accepted. *Expenses:* Tuition, state resident: full-time $5500. Tuition, nonresident: full-time $10,108. *Required fees:* $1000. *Financial support:* In 2015–16, 7 research assistantships with full tuition reimbursements (averaging $9,365 per year), 6 teaching assistantships with full tuition reimbursements (averaging $8,450 per year) were awarded; Federal Work-Study, institutionally sponsored loans, scholarships/grants, and unspecified assistantships also available. Financial award application deadline: 3/31; financial award applicants required to submit FAFSA. *Faculty research:* Grapevine biotechnology, agricultural marketing, Asian elephant reproduction, poultry science, integrated pest management. *Unit head:* Dr. W. Anson Elliott, Head, 417-836-5638, E-mail: ansonelliot@missouristate.edu. *Application contact:* Michael Edwards, Coordinator of Graduate Admissions, 417-836-5330, Fax: 417-836-6200, E-mail: michaeledwards@missouristate.edu.
Website: http://ag.missouristate.edu/

Montana State University, The Graduate School, College of Agriculture, Bozeman, MT 59717. Offers MS, PhD. *Program availability:* Part-time, online learning. *Degree requirements:* For master's, comprehensive exam; for doctorate, comprehensive exam, thesis/dissertation. *Entrance requirements:* For master's and doctorate, GRE General Test. Additional exam requirements/recommendations for international students: Required—TOEFL (minimum score 550 paper-based). Electronic applications accepted.

Morehead State University, Graduate Programs, College of Science and Technology, Department of Agricultural Sciences, Morehead, KY 40351. Offers career and technical agricultural education (MS). *Program availability:* Part-time, evening/weekend. *Degree requirements:* For master's, comprehensive exam, thesis or alternative, exit exam. *Entrance requirements:* For master's, GRE, minimum GPA of 3.0 for undergraduate major. Additional exam requirements/recommendations for international students: Required—TOEFL (minimum score 500 paper-based). Electronic applications accepted.

Murray State University, School of Agriculture, Murray, KY 42071. Offers agriculture (MS); agriculture education (MS). *Program availability:* Evening/weekend, online learning. *Degree requirements:* For master's, comprehensive exam, thesis (for some programs). *Entrance requirements:* Additional exam requirements/recommendations for international students: Required—TOEFL. *Faculty research:* Ultrasound in beef, corn and soybean research, tobacco research.

North Carolina Agricultural and Technical State University, School of Graduate Studies, School of Agriculture and Environmental Sciences, Greensboro, NC 27411. Offers MAT, MS. *Program availability:* Part-time, evening/weekend. *Degree requirements:* For master's, comprehensive exam, qualifying exam. *Entrance requirements:* For master's, GRE General Test. *Faculty research:* Aid for small farmers, agricultural technology, housing, food science, nutrition.

North Carolina State University, Graduate School, College of Agriculture and Life Sciences, Raleigh, NC 27695. Offers M Tox, MAE, MB, MBAE, MFG, MFM, MFS, MG, MMB, MN, MP, MS, MZS, Ed D, PhD, Certificate. *Program availability:* Part-time. Electronic applications accepted.

North Dakota State University, College of Graduate and Interdisciplinary Studies, College of Agriculture, Food Systems, and Natural Resources, Fargo, ND 58102. Offers MS, PhD. *Program availability:* Part-time. *Degree requirements:* For doctorate, thesis/dissertation. *Entrance requirements:* Additional exam requirements/recommendations for international students: Required—TOEFL. Electronic applications accepted. *Faculty research:* Horticulture and forestry, plant and wheat breeding, diseases of insects, animal and range sciences, soil science, veterinary medicine.

Northwest Missouri State University, Graduate School, Melvin and Valorie Booth College of Business and Professional Studies, School of Agricultural Sciences, Maryville, MO 64468-6001. Offers agricultural economics (MBA); agriculture (MS); teaching agriculture (MS Ed). *Program availability:* Part-time. *Students:* 5 full-time (3 women), 5 part-time (2 women). *Degree requirements:* For master's, comprehensive exam, thesis (for some programs). *Entrance requirements:* For master's, GRE General Test, minimum undergraduate GPA of 2.5, writing sample. Additional exam requirements/recommendations for international students: Required—TOEFL (minimum score 550 paper-based). *Application deadline:* For fall admission, 7/1 for domestic and international students; for spring admission, 11/15 for domestic and international students. Applications are processed on a rolling basis. Application fee: $0 ($50 for international students). *Expenses:* Tuition, state resident: part-time $359 per credit hour. Tuition, nonresident: part-time $612 per credit hour. *Required fees:* $106 per credit hour. *Financial support:* Research assistantships with full tuition reimbursements, teaching assistantships with full tuition reimbursements, and unspecified assistantships available. Financial award application deadline: 4/1; financial award applicants required to submit FAFSA. *Unit head:* Rodney Barr, Director, 660-562-1620.
Website: http://www.nwmissouri.edu/ag/

The Ohio State University, Graduate School, College of Food, Agricultural, and Environmental Sciences, Columbus, OH 43210. Offers M Ed, MAS, MENR, MPHM, MS, PhD. *Program availability:* Part-time. *Degree requirements:* For master's, thesis (for some programs); for doctorate, thesis/dissertation. *Entrance requirements:* Additional exam requirements/recommendations for international students: Required—TOEFL (minimum score 550 paper-based; 79 iBT), Michigan English Language Assessment Battery (minimum score 82); Recommended—IELTS (minimum score 7). Electronic applications accepted.

Oklahoma State University, College of Agricultural Science and Natural Resources, Stillwater, OK 74078. Offers M Ag, MS, PhD. *Program availability:* Online learning. *Faculty:* 220 full-time (51 women), 8 part-time/adjunct (0 women). *Students:* 136 full-time (63 women), 351 part-time (170 women); includes 64 minority (3 Black or African American, non-Hispanic/Latino; 14 American Indian or Alaska Native, non-Hispanic/Latino; 3 Asian, non-Hispanic/Latino; 14 Hispanic/Latino; 30 Two or more races, non-Hispanic/Latino), 149 international. Average age 29. 265 applicants, 57% accepted, 95 enrolled. In 2015, 114 master's, 36 doctorates awarded. *Degree requirements:* For master's, thesis (for some programs); for doctorate, comprehensive exam, thesis/dissertation. *Entrance requirements:* For master's and doctorate, GRE or GMAT. Additional exam requirements/recommendations for international students: Required—TOEFL (minimum score 550 paper-based; 79 iBT). *Application deadline:* For fall admission, 3/1 priority date for domestic and international students; for spring admission, 8/1 priority date for domestic and international students. Applications are processed on a rolling basis. Application fee: $40 ($75 for international students). Electronic applications accepted. *Expenses:* Tuition, state resident: full-time $3528; part-time $196 per credit hour. Tuition, nonresident: full-time $14,144; part-time $785.75 per credit hour. *Required fees:* $1895; $105.25 per credit hour. Tuition and fees vary according to campus/location. *Financial support:* In 2015–16, 246 research assistantships (averaging $17,794 per year), 51 teaching assistantships (averaging $15,582 per year) were awarded; fellowships, career-related internships or fieldwork, Federal Work-Study, scholarships/grants, health care benefits, tuition waivers (partial), and unspecified assistantships also available. Support available to part-time students. Financial award application deadline: 3/1; financial award applicants required to submit FAFSA. *Unit head:* Dr. Thomas Coon, Vice President/Dean, 405-744-5395, E-mail: thomas.coon@okstate.edu.
Website: http://casnr.okstate.edu

Penn State University Park, Graduate School, College of Agricultural Sciences, University Park, PA 16802. Offers M Ed, MPS, MS, PhD, Certificate. *Program availability:* Part-time, evening/weekend, online learning. *Students:* 398 full-time (241 women), 21 part-time (10 women). Average age 29. 576 applicants, 18% accepted, 69 enrolled. *Entrance requirements:* Additional exam requirements/recommendations for international students: Required—TOEFL (minimum score 550 paper-based; 80 iBT), IELTS. *Application deadline:* Applications are processed on a rolling basis. Application fee: $65. Electronic applications accepted. *Financial support:* Fellowships, research assistantships, teaching assistantships, career-related internships or fieldwork, Federal Work-Study, scholarships/grants, traineeships, health care benefits, and unspecified assistantships available. Support available to part-time students. Financial award application deadline: 3/1; financial award applicants required to submit FAFSA. *Unit head:* Dr. Richard T. Roush, Dean, 814-865-2541, Fax: 814-865-3103. *Application contact:* Lori Stania, Director, Graduate Student Services, 814-865-1795, Fax: 814-863-4627, E-mail: l-gswww@lists.psu.edu.
Website: http://agsci.psu.edu/

Prairie View A&M University, College of Agriculture and Human Sciences, Prairie View, TX 77446-0519. Offers interdisciplinary human sciences (MS). *Program availability:* Part-time, evening/weekend. *Faculty:* 4 full-time (2 women). *Students:* 51 full-time (43 women), 26 part-time (23 women); includes 71 minority (65 Black or African American, non-Hispanic/Latino; 2 Asian, non-Hispanic/Latino; 4 Hispanic/Latino), 2 international. Average age 32. 52 applicants, 63% accepted, 26 enrolled. In 2015, 25 master's awarded. *Degree requirements:* For master's, comprehensive exam, thesis (for some programs), field placement. *Entrance requirements:* For master's, GRE General Test, minimum GPA of 2.45. Additional exam requirements/recommendations for international students: Required—TOEFL (minimum score 550 paper-based; 79 iBT). *Application deadline:* For fall admission, 7/1 priority date for domestic students, 6/1 priority date for international students; for spring admission, 11/1 priority date for domestic students, 10/1 priority date for international students; for summer admission, 3/1 priority date for domestic students, 2/1 priority date for international students. Applications are processed on a rolling basis. Application fee: $50. Electronic applications accepted. *Expenses:* Tuition, state resident: full-time $4243; part-time $237.29 per credit hour. Tuition, nonresident: full-time $11,798; part-time $657 per credit hour. *Required fees:* $2762; $172.10 per credit hour. *Financial support:* In 2015–16, 12 students received support, including 12 research assistantships (averaging $14,400 per year); career-related internships or fieldwork, Federal Work-Study, institutionally sponsored loans, scholarships/grants, tuition waivers (full and partial), and unspecified assistantships also available. Support available to part-time students. Financial award application deadline: 4/1; financial award applicants required to submit FAFSA. *Faculty research:* Domestic violence prevention, water quality, food growth regulators, wetland dynamics, biochemistry, obesity and nutrition, family therapy. *Unit head:* Dr. James Palmer, Interim Dean and Director of Land-Grant Programs, 936-261-2214, E-mail: jmpalmer@pvamu.edu. *Application contact:* Pauline Walker, Administrative Assistant II, 936-261-3521, Fax: 936-261-3529, E-mail: gradadmissions@pvamu.edu.

Purdue University, Graduate School, College of Agriculture, West Lafayette, IN 47907. Offers EMBA, M Agr, MA, MS, MSF, PhD. *Program availability:* Part-time. *Degree requirements:* For doctorate, thesis/dissertation. *Entrance requirements:* Additional exam requirements/recommendations for international students: Required—TOEFL. Electronic applications accepted.

Sam Houston State University, College of Sciences, Department of Agricultural Sciences and Engineering Technology, Huntsville, TX 77341. Offers agriculture (MS). *Program availability:* Part-time. *Degree requirements:* For master's, comprehensive exam, thesis optional. *Entrance requirements:* For master's, GRE General Test, letters of recommendation. Additional exam requirements/recommendations for international students: Required—TOEFL (minimum score 550 paper-based; 79 iBT), IELTS (minimum score 6.5). Electronic applications accepted.

South Dakota State University, Graduate School, College of Agriculture and Biological Sciences, Brookings, SD 57007. Offers MS, PhD. *Program availability:* Part-time. *Degree requirements:* For master's, thesis, oral exam; for doctorate, thesis/dissertation, preliminary oral and written exams. *Entrance requirements:* Additional exam requirements/recommendations for international students: Required—TOEFL.

Southern Arkansas University–Magnolia, School of Graduate Studies, Magnolia, AR 71753. Offers agriculture (MS); business administration (MBA), including agri-business, supply chain management; computer and information sciences (MS); elementary or secondary education (M Ed), including curriculum and instruction, educational administration and supervision, gifted and talented P-8/7-12, instructional specialist 4-12, instructional specialist P-4; higher, adult and lifelong education (M Ed); kinesiology (M Ed), including coaching; library media and information specialist (M Ed); mental

health and clinical counseling (MS); public administration (MPA); school counseling K-12 (M Ed); student affairs and college counseling (M Ed); teaching (MAT). *Accreditation:* NCATE. *Program availability:* Part-time, 100% online, blended/hybrid learning. *Faculty:* 33 full-time (17 women), 25 part-time/adjunct (11 women). *Students:* 336 full-time (69 women), 636 part-time (292 women); includes 124 minority (109 Black or African American, non-Hispanic/Latino; 6 American Indian or Alaska Native, non-Hispanic/Latino; 5 Asian, non-Hispanic/Latino; 1 Hispanic/Latino; 3 Two or more races, non-Hispanic/Latino), 554 international. Average age 28. 531 applicants, 88% accepted, 345 enrolled. In 2015, 155 master's awarded. *Degree requirements:* For master's, comprehensive exam (for some programs), thesis optional. *Entrance requirements:* For master's, GRE, MAT or GMAT, minimum GPA of 2.5. Additional exam requirements/recommendations for international students: Required—TOEFL (minimum score 550 paper-based), IELTS (minimum score 6). *Application deadline:* For fall admission, 7/20 for domestic students, 7/5 for international students; for spring admission, 12/1 for domestic students, 11/15 for international students; for summer admission, 6/1 for domestic students, 5/1 for international students. Applications are processed on a rolling basis. Application fee: $25 ($50 for international students). Electronic applications accepted. *Expenses:* Tuition, state resident: part-time $217 per credit hour. Tuition, nonresident: part-time $403 per credit hour. *Required fees:* $769 per semester. Tuition and fees vary according to course load and program. *Financial support:* Career-related internships or fieldwork, Federal Work-Study, scholarships/grants, tuition waivers (full), and unspecified assistantships available. Financial award applicants required to submit FAFSA. *Faculty research:* Alternative certification for teachers, supervision of instruction, instructional leadership, counseling. *Unit head:* Dr. Kim Bloss, Dean, School of Graduate Studies, 870-235-4150, Fax: 870-235-5227, E-mail: kkbloss@saumag.edu. *Application contact:* Shrijana Malakar, Admissions Specialist, 870-235-4150, Fax: 870-235-5227, E-mail: smalakar@saumag.edu.
Website: http://www.saumag.edu/graduate

Southern Illinois University Carbondale, Graduate School, College of Agriculture, Carbondale, IL 62901-4701. Offers MS, MBA/MS. *Program availability:* Part-time. *Faculty:* 41 full-time (8 women). *Students:* 67 full-time (32 women), 38 part-time (12 women); includes 5 minority (4 Black or African American, non-Hispanic/Latino; 1 Hispanic/Latino), 15 international. 66 applicants, 45% accepted, 27 enrolled. In 2015, 29 master's awarded. *Entrance requirements:* For master's, minimum GPA of 2.7. Additional exam requirements/recommendations for international students: Required—TOEFL. *Application deadline:* Applications are processed on a rolling basis. Application fee: $50. *Financial support:* In 2015–16, 35 students received support. Fellowships, research assistantships, teaching assistantships, career-related internships or fieldwork, Federal Work-Study, institutionally sponsored loans, and tuition waivers (full) available. Support available to part-time students. *Faculty research:* Production and studies in crops, animal nutrition, agribusiness economics and management, forest biology and ecology, microcomputers in agriculture. *Unit head:* Mickey A. Latour, Dean, 618-453-2469. *Application contact:* Associate Dean of the Graduate School, 618-536-7791.

Southern University and Agricultural and Mechanical College, Graduate School, College of Agricultural, Family and Consumer Sciences, Baton Rouge, LA 70813. Offers urban forestry (MS). *Degree requirements:* For master's, thesis. *Entrance requirements:* For master's, GRE, minimum GPA of 3.0. Additional exam requirements/recommendations for international students: Required—TOEFL (minimum score 525 paper-based). *Faculty research:* Urban forest interactions with environment, social and economic impacts of urban forests, tree biology/pathology, development of urban forest management tools.

Tarleton State University, College of Graduate Studies, College of Agricultural and Environmental Sciences, Department of Agricultural and Consumer Sciences, Stephenville, TX 76402. Offers agricultural and consumer resources (MS). *Program availability:* Part-time, evening/weekend, 100% online. *Faculty:* 11 full-time (2 women), 1 part-time/adjunct (0 women). *Students:* 42 full-time (27 women), 29 part-time (22 women); includes 8 minority (1 Black or African American, non-Hispanic/Latino; 1 American Indian or Alaska Native, non-Hispanic/Latino; 4 Hispanic/Latino; 2 Two or more races, non-Hispanic/Latino). 16 applicants, 88% accepted, 13 enrolled. In 2015, 28 master's awarded. *Degree requirements:* For master's, comprehensive exam. *Entrance requirements:* For master's, GRE General Test, minimum GPA of 3.0. Additional exam requirements/recommendations for international students: Required—TOEFL (minimum score 550 paper-based; 80 iBT). *Application deadline:* For fall admission, 8/5 priority date for domestic students; for spring admission, 12/1 for domestic students. Applications are processed on a rolling basis. Application fee: $45 ($145 for international students). Electronic applications accepted. *Expenses:* Tuition, state resident: part-time $204 per credit hour. Tuition, nonresident: part-time $594 per credit hour. *Required fees:* $1994 per unit. *Financial support:* Research assistantships, Federal Work-Study, institutionally sponsored loans, scholarships/grants, and unspecified assistantships available. Financial award application deadline: 5/1; financial award applicants required to submit FAFSA. *Unit head:* Dr. Rudy Tarpley, Department Head, 254-968-9201, Fax: 254-968-9199, E-mail: tarpley@tarleton.edu. *Application contact:* Information Contact, 254-968-9104, Fax: 254-968-9670, E-mail: gradoffice@tarleton.edu.
Website: http://www.tarleton.edu/agservices/

Tennessee State University, The School of Graduate Studies and Research, College of Agriculture, Human and Natural Sciences, Nashville, TN 37209-1561. Offers agricultural sciences (MS), including agribusiness, agricultural and extension education, animal science, plant and soil science; biological sciences (MS, PhD); biotechnology (PhD); chemistry (MS). *Program availability:* Part-time, evening/weekend. *Degree requirements:* For master's, thesis. *Entrance requirements:* For master's, GRE General Test, GRE Subject Test, MAT. *Faculty research:* Small farm economics, ornamental horticulture, beef cattle production, rural elderly.

Texas A&M University, College of Agriculture and Life Sciences, College Station, TX 77843. Offers M Agr, M Ed, M Engr, MEIM, MRRD, MS, MWSc, Ed D, PhD. *Program availability:* Part-time, blended/hybrid learning. *Faculty:* 292. *Students:* 1,030 full-time (539 women), 331 part-time (165 women); includes 232 minority (36 Black or African American, non-Hispanic/Latino; 3 American Indian or Alaska Native, non-Hispanic/Latino; 33 Asian, non-Hispanic/Latino; 145 Hispanic/Latino; 15 Two or more races, non-Hispanic/Latino), 426 international. Average age 30. 763 applicants, 52% accepted, 289 enrolled. In 2015, 197 master's, 106 doctorates awarded. *Entrance requirements:* Additional exam requirements/recommendations for international students: Required—TOEFL (minimum score 550 paper-based; 80 iBT), IELTS (minimum score 6), PTE (minimum score 53). *Application deadline:* For fall admission, 7/21 priority date for domestic students, 6/1 priority date for international students; for spring admission, 12/1 priority date for domestic students, 10/1 priority date for international students. Applications are processed on a rolling basis. Application fee: $50 ($90 for international students). Electronic applications accepted. *Expenses:* Contact institution. *Financial support:* In 2015–16, 1,042 students received support, including 159 fellowships with tuition reimbursements available (averaging $11,771 per year), 398 research assistantships with tuition reimbursements available (averaging $6,966 per year), 262 teaching assistantships with tuition reimbursements available (averaging $6,226 per year); career-related internships or fieldwork, institutionally sponsored loans, scholarships/grants, traineeships, health care benefits, tuition waivers (full and partial), and unspecified assistantships also available. Support available to part-time students. Financial award application deadline: 3/15; financial award applicants required to submit FAFSA. *Faculty research:* Plant sciences, animal sciences, environmental natural resources, biological and agricultural engineering, agricultural economics. *Unit head:* Dr. Mark A. Hussey, Vice Chancellor and Dean for Agriculture and Life Sciences, 979-845-4747, Fax: 979-845-9938, E-mail: mhussey@tamu.edu. *Application contact:* Graduate Admissions, 979-845-1044, E-mail: graduate-admissions@tamu.edu.
Website: http://aglifesciences.tamu.edu/

Texas A&M University–Commerce, School of Agriculture, Commerce, TX 75429-3011. Offers MS. *Program availability:* Part-time. *Faculty:* 9 full-time (1 woman). *Students:* 4 full-time (2 women), 30 part-time (18 women); includes 9 minority (1 Black or African American, non-Hispanic/Latino; 1 Asian, non-Hispanic/Latino; 5 Hispanic/Latino; 2 Two or more races, non-Hispanic/Latino), 3 international. Average age 29. 22 applicants, 50% accepted, 9 enrolled. In 2015, 13 master's awarded. *Degree requirements:* For master's, comprehensive exam, thesis optional. *Entrance requirements:* For master's, GRE General Test. Additional exam requirements/recommendations for international students: Required—TOEFL (minimum score 79 iBT), IELTS (minimum score 6). *Application deadline:* Applications are processed on a rolling basis. Application fee: $50. Electronic applications accepted. *Expenses:* Tuition, state resident: full-time $3630. Tuition, nonresident: full-time $10,650. *Required fees:* $1870. Tuition and fees vary according to course load, degree level and program. *Financial support:* In 2015–16, 6 research assistantships with partial tuition reimbursements (averaging $8,000 per year), 6 teaching assistantships with partial tuition reimbursements (averaging $8,000 per year) were awarded; Federal Work-Study, institutionally sponsored loans, scholarships/grants, health care benefits, and unspecified assistantships also available. Financial award application deadline: 5/1; financial award applicants required to submit FAFSA. *Unit head:* Dr. Derald Harp, Interim Director, 903-886-5351, Fax: 903-886-5990, E-mail: derald.harp@tamuc.edu. *Application contact:* Vicky Turner, Doctoral Degree and Special Programs Coordinator, 903-886-5167, E-mail: vicky.turner@tamuc.edu.
Website: http://www.tamuc.edu/academics/graduateSchool/programs/agriculture/default.aspx

Texas A&M University–Kingsville, College of Graduate Studies, Dick and Mary Lewis Kleberg College of Agriculture, Natural Resources and Human Sciences, Kingsville, TX 78363. Offers MS, PhD. *Degree requirements:* For master's, variable foreign language requirement, comprehensive exam, thesis (for some programs); for doctorate, variable foreign language requirement, comprehensive exam, thesis/dissertation. *Entrance requirements:* For master's and doctorate, GRE, GMAT, MAT. Additional exam requirements/recommendations for international students: Required—TOEFL. Electronic applications accepted. *Faculty research:* Mesquite cloning; genesis of soil salinity; dove management; bone development; egg, meat, and milk consumption versus price.

Texas A&M University–Kingsville, College of Graduate Studies, Dick and Mary Lewis Kleberg College of Agriculture, Natural Resources and Human Sciences, Department of Agriculture, Agribusiness, and Environmental Sciences, Program in Agricultural Science, Kingsville, TX 78363. Offers MS. *Degree requirements:* For master's, variable foreign language requirement, comprehensive exam, thesis (for some programs). *Entrance requirements:* For master's, GRE (minimum combined Math & Verbal score of 290), MAT, GMAT, minimum GPA of 2.5. Additional exam requirements/recommendations for international students: Required—TOEFL (minimum score 550 paper-based; 79 iBT). Electronic applications accepted.

Texas Tech University, Graduate School, College of Agricultural Sciences and Natural Resources, Lubbock, TX 79409. Offers MAB, MLA, MS, Ed D, PhD, JD/MS. *Program availability:* 100% online, blended/hybrid learning. *Faculty:* 98 full-time (30 women), 18 part-time/adjunct (4 women). *Students:* 274 full-time (135 women), 116 part-time (51 women); includes 39 minority (6 Black or African American, non-Hispanic/Latino; 1 Asian, non-Hispanic/Latino; 26 Hispanic/Latino; 6 Two or more races, non-Hispanic/Latino), 105 international. Average age 29. 260 applicants, 53% accepted, 95 enrolled. In 2015, 88 master's, 31 doctorates awarded. *Degree requirements:* For master's, thesis or alternative; for doctorate, comprehensive exam, thesis/dissertation. *Entrance requirements:* For master's and doctorate, GRE General Test, formal approval from departmental committee. Additional exam requirements/recommendations for international students: Required—TOEFL (minimum score 550 paper-based; 79 iBT). *Application deadline:* For fall admission, 6/1 priority date for domestic students, 1/15 priority date for international students; for spring admission, 9/1 priority date for domestic students, 6/15 priority date for international students. Applications are processed on a rolling basis. Application fee: $60. Electronic applications accepted. *Expenses:* Tuition, state resident: full-time $6477; part-time $269.89 per credit hour. Tuition, nonresident: full-time $15,837; part-time $659.89 per credit hour. *Required fees:* $2751; $36.50 per credit hour. $937.50 per semester. Tuition and fees vary according to course level. *Financial support:* In 2015–16, 341 students received support, including 273 fellowships (averaging $3,021 per year), 241 research assistantships (averaging $12,172 per year), 57 teaching assistantships (averaging $6,700 per year); health care benefits and unspecified assistantships also available. Financial award application deadline: 12/1; financial award applicants required to submit FAFSA. *Faculty research:* Biopolymers, sustainable land and water use, food safety, agricultural policy, ecology and land management. *Total annual research expenditures:* $9.7 million. *Unit head:* Dr. Michael L. Galyean, Professor/Dean, 806-742-2808, Fax: 806-742-2836, E-mail: michael.galyean@ttu.edu. *Application contact:* Dr. Michael Ballou, Associate Dean for Research, 806-834-6513, Fax: 806-742-2836, E-mail: michael.ballou@ttu.edu.
Website: http://www.depts.ttu.edu/agriculturalsciences/

Tropical Agriculture Research and Higher Education Center, Graduate School, Turrialba, Costa Rica. Offers agribusiness management (MS); agroforestry systems (PhD); development practices (MS); ecological agriculture (MS); environmental socioeconomics (MS); forestry in tropical and subtropical zones (PhD); integrated watershed management (MS); international sustainable tourism (MS); management and conservation of tropical rainforests and biodiversity (MS); tropical agriculture (PhD); tropical agroforestry (MS). *Entrance requirements:* For master's, GRE, 2 years of related professional experience, letters of recommendation; for doctorate, GRE, 4 letters of recommendation, letter of support from employing organization, master's degree in agronomy, biological sciences, forestry, natural resources or related field. Additional exam requirements/recommendations for international students: Required—TOEFL (minimum score 550 paper-based). Electronic applications accepted. *Faculty research:* Biodiversity in fragmented landscapes, ecosystem management, integrated pest management, environmental livestock production, biotechnology carbon balances in diverse land uses.

Universidad Nacional Pedro Henriquez Urena, Graduate School, Santo Domingo, Dominican Republic. Offers agricultural diversity (MS), including horticultural/fruit production, tropical animal production; conservation of monuments and cultural assets (M Arch); ecology and environment (MS); environmental engineering (MEE);

international relations (MA); natural resource management (MS); political science (MA); project optimization (MPM); project feasibility (MPM); project management (MPM); sanitation engineering (ME); science for teachers (MS); tropical Caribbean architecture (M Arch).

Université Laval, Faculty of Agricultural and Food Sciences, Québec, QC G1K 7P4, Canada. Offers M Sc, PhD, Diploma. *Program availability:* Part-time. *Degree requirements:* For doctorate, comprehensive exam, thesis/dissertation. Electronic applications accepted.

University of Alberta, Faculty of Graduate Studies and Research, Department of Agricultural, Food and Nutritional Science, Edmonton, AB T6G 2E1, Canada. Offers M Ag, M Eng, M Sc, PhD, MBA/M Ag. *Degree requirements:* For master's, thesis; for doctorate, comprehensive exam, thesis/dissertation. *Entrance requirements:* For master's, minimum GPA of 3.3; for doctorate, minimum GPA of 3.5. Additional exam requirements/recommendations for international students: Required—IELTS (minimum score 6.5), TOEFL (minimum score of 550 paper-based or a total iBT score of 88 with a score of at least 20 on each of the individual skill areas), Michigan English Language Assessment Battery (minimum score 85); CAEL (overall minimum score 60). *Faculty research:* Animal science, food science, nutrition and metabolism, bioresource engineering, plant science and range management.

The University of Arizona, College of Agriculture and Life Sciences, Tucson, AZ 85721. Offers MAE, MHE Ed, MS, PhD, Graduate Certificate. *Program availability:* Part-time. *Degree requirements:* For doctorate, thesis/dissertation. *Entrance requirements:* For master's, GRE, GMAT, or MAT, bachelor's degree or equivalent, minimum GPA of 3.0. Additional exam requirements/recommendations for international students: Required—TOEFL (minimum score 550 paper-based; 79 iBT). *Application deadline:* For fall admission, 1/1 for domestic students, 12/1 for international students. Applications are processed on a rolling basis. Application fee: $75. Electronic applications accepted. *Financial support:* In 2015–16, 108 research assistantships with tuition reimbursements (averaging $16,433 per year), 49 teaching assistantships with tuition reimbursements (averaging $16,636 per year) were awarded; fellowships with tuition reimbursements, career-related internships or fieldwork, Federal Work-Study, institutionally sponsored loans, scholarships/grants, traineeships, health care benefits, tuition waivers (full and partial), and unspecified assistantships also available. *Faculty research:* Regulation of skeletal muscle mass during growth, bone health and osteoporosis prevention, regulation of gene expression, development of new crops for arid and semi-arid lands, molecular genetics and pathogenesis of the opportunistic pathogen. *Unit head:* Dr. Shane Burgess, Dean, 520-621-7621, Fax: 520-621-7196, E-mail: dean@cals.arizona.edu. *Application contact:* 520-621-3612, Fax: 520-621-7196.
Website: http://www.ag.arizona.edu/

University of Arkansas, Graduate School, Dale Bumpers College of Agricultural, Food and Life Sciences, Fayetteville, AR 72701-1201. Offers MS, PhD. *Students:* 103 full-time (55 women), 207 part-time (98 women); includes 28 minority (9 Black or African American, non-Hispanic/Latino; 5 Asian, non-Hispanic/Latino; 9 Hispanic/Latino; 5 Two or more races, non-Hispanic/Latino), 88 international. 164 applicants, 59% accepted. In 2015, 82 master's, 13 doctorates awarded. *Degree requirements:* For doctorate, thesis/dissertation. *Application deadline:* For fall admission, 4/1 for international students; for spring admission, 10/1 for international students. Applications are processed on a rolling basis. Application fee: $40 ($50 for international students). Electronic applications accepted. *Financial support:* In 2015–16, 167 research assistantships, 7 teaching assistantships were awarded; fellowships with tuition reimbursements, career-related internships or fieldwork, Federal Work-Study, scholarships/grants, and unspecified assistantships also available. Support available to part-time students. Financial award application deadline: 4/1; financial award applicants required to submit FAFSA. *Unit head:* Dr. Michael E. Vayda, Dean, 479-575-2034, Fax: 479-575-7273, E-mail: mvayda@uark.edu. *Application contact:* Graduate Admissions, 479-575-6246, Fax: 479-575-5908, E-mail: gradinfo@uark.edu.
Website: http://bumperscollege.uark.edu/

The University of British Columbia, Faculty of Land and Food Systems, Vancouver, BC V6T 1Z4, Canada. Offers M Sc, MFRE, MFS, MLWS, PhD. *Program availability:* Part-time. *Degree requirements:* For master's, thesis; for doctorate, comprehensive exam, thesis/dissertation. *Entrance requirements:* Additional exam requirements/recommendations for international students: Required—TOEFL (minimum score 577 paper-based; 90 iBT), IELTS (minimum score 6.5). Electronic applications accepted.

University of California, Davis, Graduate Studies, Graduate Group in International Agricultural Development, Davis, CA 95616. Offers MS. *Degree requirements:* For master's, comprehensive exam (for some programs), thesis (for some programs). *Entrance requirements:* For master's, GRE General Test, minimum GPA of 3.0. Additional exam requirements/recommendations for international students: Required—TOEFL (minimum score 550 paper-based). Electronic applications accepted. *Faculty research:* Aspects of agricultural, environmental and social sciences on agriculture and related issues in developing countries.

University of Connecticut, Graduate School, College of Agriculture and Natural Resources, Storrs, CT 06269. Offers MS, PhD. Terminal master's awarded for partial completion of doctoral program. *Degree requirements:* For master's, comprehensive exam; for doctorate, comprehensive exam, thesis/dissertation. *Entrance requirements:* For master's and doctorate, GRE General Test. Additional exam requirements/recommendations for international students: Required—TOEFL (minimum score 550 paper-based). Electronic applications accepted.

University of Delaware, College of Agriculture and Natural Resources, Newark, DE 19716. Offers MA, MS, PhD. *Program availability:* Part-time. *Degree requirements:* For master's, thesis; for doctorate, thesis/dissertation. *Entrance requirements:* For master's and doctorate, GRE General Test. Electronic applications accepted.

University of Florida, Graduate School, College of Agricultural and Life Sciences, Gainesville, FL 32611. Offers MAB, MFAS, MFRC, MS, DPM, PhD, Certificate, JD/MFRC, JD/MS, JD/PhD. *Program availability:* Part-time. *Faculty:* 346 full-time (93 women), 12 part-time/adjunct (4 women). *Students:* 951 full-time (499 women), 370 part-time (213 women); includes 160 minority (35 Black or African American, non-Hispanic/Latino; 7 American Indian or Alaska Native, non-Hispanic/Latino; 29 Asian, non-Hispanic/Latino; 89 Hispanic/Latino), 433 international. Average age 31. 921 applicants, 36% accepted, 255 enrolled. In 2015, 208 master's, 129 doctorates awarded. *Degree requirements:* For master's, comprehensive exam (for some programs), thesis (for some programs); for doctorate, comprehensive exam, thesis/dissertation. *Entrance requirements:* For master's and doctorate, GRE General Test, minimum GPA of 3.0; for Certificate, GRE. Additional exam requirements/recommendations for international students: Required—TOEFL (minimum score 550 paper-based; 80 iBT), IELTS (minimum score 6). *Application deadline:* Applications are processed on a rolling basis. Application fee: $30. Electronic applications accepted. *Financial support:* Career-related internships or fieldwork, Federal Work-Study, institutionally sponsored loans, and unspecified assistantships available. Support available to part-time students. Financial award application deadline: 2/1; financial award applicants required to submit FAFSA. *Faculty research:* Agriculture, human and natural resources, the life sciences. *Total annual research expenditures:* $145.9 million. *Unit head:* Dr. Teresa Balser, Dean, 352-392-1961, E-mail: tcbalser@ufl.edu. *Application contact:* Office of Admissions, 352-392-1365, E-mail: webrequests@admissions.ufl.edu.
Website: http://www.cals.ufl.edu/

University of Georgia, College of Agricultural and Environmental Sciences, Athens, GA 30602. Offers MA Ext, MADS, MAE, MAL, MFT, MPPPM, MS, PhD. *Degree requirements:* For doctorate, thesis/dissertation. *Entrance requirements:* For master's and doctorate, GRE General Test. Electronic applications accepted.

University of Guelph, Graduate Studies, Ontario Agricultural College, Guelph, ON N1G 2W1, Canada. Offers M Sc, MLA, PhD, Diploma, MA/M Sc. *Program availability:* Part-time, online learning. *Degree requirements:* For doctorate, thesis/dissertation.

University of Hawaii at Manoa, Graduate Division, College of Tropical Agriculture and Human Resources, Honolulu, HI 96822. Offers MS, PhD. *Program availability:* Part-time. *Students:* 99 full-time, 28 part-time. Average age 34. 137 applicants, 60% accepted, 44 enrolled. In 2015, 30 master's, 10 doctorates awarded. *Entrance requirements:* Additional exam requirements/recommendations for international students: Required—TOEFL or IELTS. Application fee: $100. *Financial support:* In 2015–16, 12 students received support, including 37 fellowships, 129 research assistantships, 16 teaching assistantships; career-related internships or fieldwork, Federal Work-Study, institutionally sponsored loans, tuition waivers (full and partial), and unspecified assistantships also available. *Total annual research expenditures:* $11.7 million. *Unit head:* Sylvia Yuen, Interim Dean, 808-956-8234, Fax: 808-956-9105, E-mail: syuen@hawaii.edu. *Application contact:* Graduate Division, 808-956-8544.
Website: http://www.ctahr.hawaii.edu/site/

University of Illinois at Urbana–Champaign, Graduate College, College of Agricultural, Consumer and Environmental Sciences, Program in Agricultural Production, Champaign, IL 61820. Offers MS. Applications accepted for Fall semester only.

The University of Iowa, Graduate College, College of Public Health, Department of Occupational and Environmental Health, Iowa City, IA 52242-1316. Offers agricultural safety and health (MS, PhD); ergonomics (MPH); industrial hygiene (MS, PhD); occupational and environmental health (MPH, MS, PhD, Certificate); MS/MA; MS/MS. *Accreditation:* ABET (one or more programs are accredited); CEPH. *Degree requirements:* For master's, thesis optional, exam; for doctorate, comprehensive exam, thesis/dissertation. *Entrance requirements:* For master's and doctorate, GRE General Test, minimum GPA of 3.0. Additional exam requirements/recommendations for international students: Required—TOEFL (minimum score 600 paper-based; 100 iBT). Electronic applications accepted.

University of Kentucky, Graduate School, College of Agriculture, Food and Environment, Lexington, KY 40506-0032. Offers MS, MSFOR, PhD. *Program availability:* Part-time. Terminal master's awarded for partial completion of doctoral program. *Degree requirements:* For master's, comprehensive exam, thesis (for some programs); for doctorate, comprehensive exam, thesis/dissertation. *Entrance requirements:* For master's, GRE General Test, minimum undergraduate GPA of 2.75; for doctorate, GRE General Test, minimum undergraduate GPA of 2.75, graduate 3.0. Additional exam requirements/recommendations for international students: Required—TOEFL (minimum score 550 paper-based). Electronic applications accepted.

University of Lethbridge, School of Graduate Studies, Lethbridge, AB T1K 3M4, Canada. Offers addictions counseling (M Sc); agricultural biotechnology (M Sc); agricultural studies (M Sc, MA); anthropology (MA); archaeology (M Sc, MA); art (MA, MFA); biochemistry (M Sc); biological sciences (M Sc); biomolecular science (PhD); biosystems and biodiversity (PhD); Canadian studies (MA); chemistry (M Sc); computer science (M Sc); computer science and geographical information science (M Sc); counseling (MC); counseling psychology (M Ed); dramatic arts (MA); earth, space, and physical science (PhD); economics (MA); education (MA, PhD); educational leadership (M Ed); English (MA); environmental science (M Sc); evolution and behavior (PhD); exercise science (M Sc); French (MA); French/German (MA); French/Spanish (MA); general education (M Ed); geography (M Sc, MA); German (MA); health sciences (M Sc); individualized multidisciplinary (M Sc, MA); kinesiology (M Sc, MA); management (M Sc), including accounting, finance, human resource management and labor relations, information systems, international management, marketing, policy and strategy; mathematics (M Sc); music (M Mus, MA); Native American studies (MA); neuroscience (M Sc, PhD); new media (MA, MFA); nursing (M Sc, MN); philosophy (MA); physics (M Sc); political science (MA); psychology (M Sc, MA); religious studies (MA); sociology (MA); theatre and dramatic arts (MFA); theoretical and computational science (PhD); urban and regional studies (MA); women and gender studies (MA). *Program availability:* Part-time, evening/weekend. *Students:* 448 full-time (249 women), 110 part-time (64 women). Average age 32. 285 applicants, 36% accepted, 96 enrolled. In 2015, 154 master's, 11 doctorates awarded. *Degree requirements:* For master's, thesis (for some programs); for doctorate, comprehensive exam, thesis/dissertation. *Entrance requirements:* For master's, GMAT (for M Sc in management), bachelor's degree in related field, minimum GPA of 3.0 during previous 20 graded semester courses, 2 years' teaching or related experience (M Ed); for doctorate, master's degree, minimum graduate GPA of 3.5. Additional exam requirements/recommendations for international students: Required—TOEFL (minimum score 580 paper-based; 93 iBT). Application fee: $100 Canadian dollars ($140 Canadian dollars for international students). Electronic applications accepted. *Financial support:* Fellowships, research assistantships, teaching assistantships, scholarships/grants, health care benefits, and unspecified assistantships available. *Faculty research:* Movement and brain plasticity, gibberellin physiology, photosynthesis, carbon cycling, molecular properties of main-group ring components. *Unit head:* Kathleen Schrage, Manager, School of Graduate Studies, 403-329-2121, E-mail: schrage@uleth.ca. *Application contact:* School of Graduate Studies, 403-329-5194, E-mail: sgsinquiries@uleth.ca.
Website: http://www.uleth.ca/graduate-studies/

University of Maine, Graduate School, College of Natural Sciences, Forestry, and Agriculture, Orono, ME 04469. Offers MA, MF, MPS, MS, MSW, MWC, PSM, PhD, CAS, CGS. *Accreditation:* SAF (one or more programs are accredited). *Program availability:* Part-time, evening/weekend. *Faculty:* 285 full-time (104 women), 182 part-time/adjunct (50 women). *Students:* 471 full-time (295 women), 14 part-time (12 women); includes 30 minority (2 Black or African American, non-Hispanic/Latino; 9 American Indian or Alaska Native, non-Hispanic/Latino; 6 Asian, non-Hispanic/Latino; 6 Hispanic/Latino; 7 Two or more races, non-Hispanic/Latino), 74 international. Average age 30. 746 applicants, 38% accepted, 164 enrolled. In 2015, 129 master's, 27 doctorates, 9 other advanced degrees awarded. Terminal master's awarded for partial completion of doctoral program. *Degree requirements:* For master's, thesis (for some programs); for doctorate, comprehensive exam, thesis/dissertation. *Entrance requirements:* For master's and doctorate, GRE General Test. Additional exam requirements/recommendations for international students: Required—TOEFL.

Application deadline: For fall admission, 2/1 priority date for domestic students. Applications are processed on a rolling basis. Application fee: $65. Electronic applications accepted. *Financial support:* In 2015–16, 304 students received support, including 4 fellowships (averaging $25,000 per year), 204 research assistantships (averaging $14,600 per year), 77 teaching assistantships (averaging $14,600 per year); career-related internships or fieldwork, Federal Work-Study, institutionally sponsored loans, scholarships/grants, health care benefits, tuition waivers (full and partial), and unspecified assistantships also available. Support available to part-time students. Financial award application deadline: 3/1. *Unit head:* Dr. Edward Ashworth, Dean, 207-581-3206, Fax: 207-581-3207. *Application contact:* Scott G. Delcourt, Assistant Vice President for Graduate Studies and Senior Associate Dean, 207-581-3291, Fax: 207-581-3232, E-mail: graduate@maine.edu.
Website: http://nsfa.umaine.edu

University of Manitoba, Faculty of Graduate Studies, Faculty of Agricultural and Food Sciences, Winnipeg, MB R3T 2N2, Canada. Offers M Sc, PhD. *Degree requirements:* For master's, thesis or alternative; for doctorate, variable foreign language requirement, thesis/dissertation.

University of Maryland, College Park, Academic Affairs, College of Agriculture and Natural Resources, College Park, MD 20742. Offers MS, DVM, PhD. *Program availability:* Part-time, evening/weekend. *Degree requirements:* For doctorate, thesis/dissertation. *Entrance requirements:* For master's, minimum GPA of 3.0. Additional exam requirements/recommendations for international students: Required—TOEFL. Electronic applications accepted.

University of Maryland Eastern Shore, Graduate Programs, Department of Agriculture, Princess Anne, MD 21853-1299. Offers food and agricultural sciences (MS); food science and technology (PhD). *Degree requirements:* For master's, comprehensive exam, thesis (for some programs), oral exam; for doctorate, comprehensive exam, thesis/dissertation. *Entrance requirements:* For master's, GRE, minimum GPA of 3.0. Additional exam requirements/recommendations for international students: Required—TOEFL (minimum score 80 iBT). Electronic applications accepted. *Faculty research:* Poultry and swine nutrition and management, soybean specialty products, farm management practices, aquaculture technology.

University of Minnesota, Twin Cities Campus, Graduate School, College of Food, Agricultural and Natural Resource Sciences, Saint Paul, MN 55108. Offers MS, PhD. *Program availability:* Part-time. *Faculty:* 741 full-time (180 women). *Students:* 532 full-time (260 women), 63 part-time (30 women); includes 40 minority (4 Black or African American, non-Hispanic/Latino; 2 American Indian or Alaska Native, non-Hispanic/Latino; 14 Asian, non-Hispanic/Latino; 9 Hispanic/Latino; 1 Native Hawaiian or other Pacific Islander, non-Hispanic/Latino; 10 Two or more races, non-Hispanic/Latino), 183 international. Average age 30. 772 applicants, 40% accepted, 191 enrolled. In 2015, 103 master's, 64 doctorates awarded. Terminal master's awarded for partial completion of doctoral program. *Degree requirements:* For master's, comprehensive exam, thesis; for doctorate, comprehensive exam, thesis/dissertation. *Entrance requirements:* For master's and doctorate, GRE General Test. Additional exam requirements/recommendations for international students: Required—TOEFL (minimum score 550 paper-based; 79 iBT), IELTS (minimum score 6.5). *Application deadline:* For fall admission, 12/15 priority date for domestic and international students; for spring admission, 10/15 priority date for domestic and international students. Applications are processed on a rolling basis. Application fee: $75 ($95 for international students). Electronic applications accepted. *Expenses:* Contact institution. *Financial support:* In 2015–16, 500 students received support, including 100 fellowships with full tuition reimbursements available (averaging $43,000 per year), 200 research assistantships with tuition reimbursements available (averaging $40,000 per year), 200 teaching assistantships with tuition reimbursements available (averaging $40,000 per year); career-related internships or fieldwork, institutionally sponsored loans, scholarships/grants, health care benefits, tuition waivers (full), and unspecified assistantships also available. Support available to part-time students. Financial award application deadline: 12/15. *Faculty research:* All aspects of agriculture: forestry, soils, ento, plant path, agron/hort, nutrition, food science, animal science, applied econ, bioproducts/systems engineering/management, water resources, cons bio. *Total annual research expenditures:* $44.3 million. *Unit head:* Dr. Gregory J. Cuomo, Associate Dean for Research and Graduate Programs, 612-625-1158, Fax: 612-625-1260, E-mail: cuomogj@umn.edu. *Application contact:* Lisa Wiley, Coordinator of Graduate Student Services, 612-624-2748, Fax: 612-625-1260, E-mail: lwiley@umn.edu.
Website: http://www.cfans.umn.edu/GraduateStudents/index.htm

University of Missouri, Office of Research and Graduate Studies, College of Agriculture, Food and Natural Resources, Columbia, MO 65211. Offers MS, PhD, Graduate Certificate. *Program availability:* Part-time. Terminal master's awarded for partial completion of doctoral program. *Degree requirements:* For master's, thesis (for some programs); for doctorate, variable foreign language requirement, comprehensive exam (for some programs), thesis/dissertation. *Entrance requirements:* For master's and doctorate, GRE General Test, minimum GPA of 3.0. Additional exam requirements/recommendations for international students: Required—TOEFL (minimum score 500 paper-based; 61 iBT), IELTS (minimum score 5.5). Electronic applications accepted.

University of Nebraska–Lincoln, Graduate College, College of Agricultural Sciences and Natural Resources, Lincoln, NE 68588. Offers M Ag, MA, MBA, MS, PhD. *Degree requirements:* For doctorate, comprehensive exam, thesis/dissertation. *Entrance requirements:* Additional exam requirements/recommendations for international students: Required—TOEFL. Electronic applications accepted. *Faculty research:* Environmental sciences, animal sciences, human resources and family sciences, plant breeding and genetics, food and nutrition.

University of Nevada, Reno, Graduate School, College of Agriculture, Biotechnology and Natural Resources, Reno, NV 89557. Offers MS, PhD. Terminal master's awarded for partial completion of doctoral program. *Degree requirements:* For master's, thesis optional; for doctorate, thesis/dissertation. *Entrance requirements:* For master's, GRE General Test, minimum GPA of 2.75; for doctorate, GRE General Test, minimum GPA of 3.0. Additional exam requirements/recommendations for international students: Required—TOEFL (minimum score 500 paper-based; 61 iBT), IELTS (minimum score 6). Electronic applications accepted.

University of Puerto Rico, Mayagüez Campus, Graduate Studies, College of Agricultural Sciences, Mayagüez, PR 00681-9000. Offers MS. *Program availability:* Part-time. *Degree requirements:* For master's, comprehensive exam, thesis.

University of Saskatchewan, College of Graduate Studies and Research, College of Agriculture, Saskatoon, SK S7N 5A2, Canada. Offers M Ag, M Sc, MA, PhD, Diploma, PGD. *Program availability:* Part-time. *Degree requirements:* For master's, thesis (for some programs); for doctorate, comprehensive exam (for some programs), thesis/dissertation. *Entrance requirements:* Additional exam requirements/recommendations for international students: Required—TOEFL (minimum score 80 iBT); Recommended—IELTS (minimum score 6.5).

University of South Africa, College of Agriculture and Environmental Sciences, Pretoria, South Africa. Offers agriculture (MS); consumer science (MCS); environmental management (MA, MS, PhD); environmental science (MA, MS, PhD); geography (MA, MS, PhD); horticulture (M Tech); human ecology (MHE); life sciences (MS); nature conservation (M Tech).

The University of Tennessee, Graduate School, College of Agricultural Sciences and Natural Resources, Knoxville, TN 37996. Offers MS, PhD. *Program availability:* Part-time, online learning. *Degree requirements:* For master's, thesis (for some programs); for doctorate, thesis/dissertation. *Entrance requirements:* For master's and doctorate, minimum GPA of 2.7. Additional exam requirements/recommendations for international students: Required—TOEFL. Electronic applications accepted.

The University of Tennessee at Martin, Graduate Programs, College of Agriculture and Applied Sciences, Program in Agricultural and Natural Resources Management, Martin, TN 38238. Offers MSANR. *Program availability:* Part-time, online only, 100% online. *Faculty:* 20. *Students:* 6 full-time (2 women), 26 part-time (8 women). Average age 31. 14 applicants, 64% accepted, 7 enrolled. In 2015, 12 master's awarded. *Degree requirements:* For master's, comprehensive exam, thesis optional. *Entrance requirements:* For master's, GRE General Test, minimum GPA of 2.5. Additional exam requirements/recommendations for international students: Required—TOEFL (minimum score 525 paper-based; 71 iBT). *Application deadline:* For fall admission, 7/27 priority date for domestic and international students; for spring admission, 12/17 priority date for domestic and international students; for summer admission, 5/10 priority date for domestic and international students. Applications are processed on a rolling basis. Application fee: $30 ($130 for international students). Electronic applications accepted. *Expenses:* Tuition, state resident: full-time $8254; part-time $459 per credit hour. Tuition, nonresident: full-time $22,198; part-time $1234 per credit hour. *Required fees:* $79 per credit hour. Part-time tuition and fees vary according to course load and campus/location. *Financial support:* In 2015–16, 2 students received support, including 1 research assistantship with full tuition reimbursement available (averaging $9,802 per year); teaching assistantships with tuition reimbursements available, scholarships/grants, and unspecified assistantships also available. Financial award application deadline: 2/1; financial award applicants required to submit FAFSA. *Unit head:* Dr. Joey Mehlhorn, Interim Coordinator, 731-881-7275, Fax: 731-881-7968, E-mail: mehlhorn@utm.edu. *Application contact:* Jolene L. Cunningham, Student Services Specialist, 731-881-7012, Fax: 731-881-7499, E-mail: jcunningham@utm.edu.
Website: http://www.utm.edu/departments/caas/msanr

University of Vermont, Graduate College, College of Agriculture and Life Sciences, Burlington, VT 05405. Offers MPA, MS, MSD, PhD. *Program availability:* Part-time. *Degree requirements:* For doctorate, one foreign language, thesis/dissertation. *Entrance requirements:* For master's and doctorate, GRE General Test. Additional exam requirements/recommendations for international students: Required—TOEFL (minimum score 550 paper-based; 80 iBT). Electronic applications accepted.

University of Wisconsin–Madison, Graduate School, College of Agricultural and Life Sciences, Madison, WI 53706-1380. Offers MA, MPS, MS, PhD. *Program availability:* Part-time. *Entrance requirements:* For master's and doctorate, GRE. Additional exam requirements/recommendations for international students: Required—TOEFL. Electronic applications accepted. *Expenses:* Tuition, state resident: full-time $5364. Tuition, nonresident: full-time $12,027. *Required fees:* $571. Tuition and fees vary according to campus/location, program and reciprocity agreements.

University of Wisconsin–River Falls, Outreach and Graduate Studies, College of Agriculture, Food, and Environmental Sciences, River Falls, WI 54022. Offers MS. *Program availability:* Part-time. *Degree requirements:* For master's, comprehensive exam, thesis (for some programs). *Entrance requirements:* For master's, minimum GPA of 2.75. Additional exam requirements/recommendations for international students: Required—TOEFL (minimum score 500 paper-based; 65 iBT), IELTS (minimum score 5.4). Electronic applications accepted.

University of Wyoming, College of Agriculture and Natural Resources, Laramie, WY 82071. Offers MA, MS, PhD. *Program availability:* Part-time. Terminal master's awarded for partial completion of doctoral program. *Degree requirements:* For doctorate, thesis/dissertation. *Entrance requirements:* For master's and doctorate, GRE General Test, minimum GPA of 3.0. Electronic applications accepted. *Faculty research:* Nutrition, molecular biology, animal science, plant science, entomology.

Utah State University, School of Graduate Studies, College of Agriculture, Logan, UT 84322. Offers MDA, MS, PhD. *Program availability:* Part-time, online learning. Terminal master's awarded for partial completion of doctoral program. *Degree requirements:* For doctorate, thesis/dissertation. *Entrance requirements:* For master's and doctorate, GRE General Test, minimum GPA of 3.0. Additional exam requirements/recommendations for international students: Required—TOEFL. *Faculty research:* Low-input agriculture, anti-viral chemotherapy, lactic culture, environmental biophysics and climate.

Virginia Polytechnic Institute and State University, Graduate School, College of Agriculture and Life Sciences, Blacksburg, VA 24061. Offers agricultural and applied economics (MS); agricultural and life sciences (MS); animal and poultry science (MS, PhD); crop and soil environmental sciences (MS, PhD); dairy science (MS); entomology (PhD); horticulture (MS, PhD); human nutrition, foods and exercise (MS, PhD); life sciences (MS, PhD); plant pathology, physiology and weed science (PhD). *Degree requirements:* For master's, comprehensive exam (for some programs), thesis (for some programs); for doctorate, comprehensive exam (for some programs), thesis/dissertation (for some programs). *Entrance requirements:* For master's and doctorate, GRE/GMAT (may vary by department). Additional exam requirements/recommendations for international students: Required—TOEFL (minimum score 550 paper-based). Electronic applications accepted.

Virginia Polytechnic Institute and State University, VT Online, Blacksburg, VA 24061. Offers advanced transportation systems (Certificate); aerospace engineering (MS); agricultural and life sciences (MSLFS); business information systems (Graduate Certificate); career and technical education (MS); civil engineering (MS); computer engineering (M Eng, MS); decision support systems (Graduate Certificate); eLearning leadership (MA); electrical engineering (M Eng, MS); engineering administration (MEA); environmental engineering (Certificate); environmental politics and policy (Graduate Certificate); environmental sciences and engineering (MS); foundations of political analysis (Graduate Certificate); health product risk management (Graduate Certificate); industrial and systems engineering (MS); information policy and society (Graduate Certificate); information security (Graduate Certificate); information technology (MIT); instructional technology (MA); integrative STEM education (MA Ed); liberal arts (Graduate Certificate); life sciences: health product risk management (MS); natural resources (MNR, Graduate Certificate); networking (Graduate Certificate); nonprofit and nongovernmental organization management (Graduate Certificate); ocean engineering (MS); political science (MA); security studies (Graduate Certificate); software development (Graduate Certificate).

Agricultural Scienes—General

Western Kentucky University, Graduate Studies, Ogden College of Science and Engineering, Department of Agriculture, Bowling Green, KY 42101. Offers MA Ed, MS. *Program availability:* Part-time, evening/weekend. *Degree requirements:* For master's, comprehensive exam, thesis optional. *Entrance requirements:* For master's, GRE General Test, minimum GPA of 2.75. Additional exam requirements/recommendations for international students: Required—TOEFL (minimum score 555 paper-based; 79 iBT). *Faculty research:* Establishment of warm season grasses, heat composting, enrichment activities in agricultural education.

West Texas A&M University, College of Agriculture, Science and Engineering, Department of Agricultural Sciences, Canyon, TX 79016-0001. Offers agricultural business and economics (MS); agriculture (MS, PhD); animal science (MS); plant, soil and environmental science (MS). *Program availability:* Part-time. *Degree requirements:* For master's, comprehensive exam, thesis optional. *Entrance requirements:* For master's, GRE General Test. Additional exam requirements/recommendations for international students: Required—TOEFL (minimum score 550 paper-based). Electronic applications accepted.

West Virginia University, Davis College of Agriculture, Forestry and Consumer Sciences, Morgantown, WV 26506-6108. Offers M Agr, MLA, MS, MSF, PhD. *Program availability:* Part-time. *Faculty:* 72 full-time (15 women). *Students:* 212 full-time (117 women), 53 part-time (29 women); includes 28 minority (10 Black or African American, non-Hispanic/Latino; 4 Asian, non-Hispanic/Latino; 7 Hispanic/Latino; 7 Two or more races, non-Hispanic/Latino), 65 international. Average age 29. In 2015, 65 master's, 20 doctorates awarded. *Degree requirements:* For master's, thesis; for doctorate, thesis/dissertation. *Entrance requirements:* Additional exam requirements/recommendations for international students: Required—TOEFL (minimum score 550 paper-based; 213 iBT). *Application deadline:* For fall admission, 6/1 priority date for domestic students, 6/1 for international students; for spring admission, 1/5 for domestic and international students. Applications are processed on a rolling basis. Application fee: $60. Electronic applications accepted. *Expenses:* Tuition, state resident: full-time $8568. Tuition, nonresident: full-time $22,140. Tuition and fees vary according to program. *Financial support:* Fellowships, research assistantships, teaching assistantships, career-related internships or fieldwork, Federal Work-Study, institutionally sponsored loans, tuition waivers (full and partial), and unspecified assistantships available. Financial award application deadline: 2/1; financial award applicants required to submit FAFSA. *Faculty research:* Reproductive physiology, soil and water quality, human nutrition, aquaculture, wildlife management. *Unit head:* Dr. Dan J. Robison, Dean, 304-293-2395, Fax: 304-293-3740, E-mail: dan.robison@mail.wvu.edu. *Application contact:* Dr. Dennis K. Smith, Associate Dean, 304-293-2275, Fax: 304-293-3740, E-mail: denny.smith@mail.wvu.edu.
Website: https://www.davis.wvu.edu

Agronomy and Soil Sciences

Alabama Agricultural and Mechanical University, School of Graduate Studies, College of Agricultural, Life and Natural Sciences, Department of Biological and Environmental Sciences, Huntsville, AL 35811. Offers biology (MS, PhD); plant and soil science (MS, PhD). *Program availability:* Evening/weekend. Terminal master's awarded for partial completion of doctoral program. *Degree requirements:* For master's, thesis optional; for doctorate, one foreign language, thesis/dissertation optional. *Entrance requirements:* For master's, GRE General Test, BS in agriculture; for doctorate, GRE General Test, master's degree. Additional exam requirements/recommendations for international students: Required—TOEFL (minimum score 500 paper-based; 61 iBT). Electronic applications accepted. *Faculty research:* Plant breeding, cytogenetics, crop production, soil chemistry and fertility, remote sensing.

Alcorn State University, School of Graduate Studies, School of Agriculture and Applied Science, Lorman, MS 39096-7500. Offers agricultural economics (MS Ag); agronomy (MS Ag); animal science (MS Ag). *Degree requirements:* For master's, thesis optional. *Faculty research:* Aquatic systems, dairy herd improvement, fruit production, alternative farming practices.

Auburn University, Graduate School, College of Agriculture, Department of Agronomy and Soils, Auburn University, AL 36849. Offers M Ag, MS, PhD. *Program availability:* Part-time. *Faculty:* 21 full-time (7 women). *Students:* 20 full-time (8 women), 28 part-time (7 women); includes 6 minority (2 Black or African American, non-Hispanic/Latino; 1 American Indian or Alaska Native, non-Hispanic/Latino; 1 Asian, non-Hispanic/Latino; 2 Hispanic/Latino), 16 international. Average age 30. 31 applicants, 55% accepted, 14 enrolled. In 2015, 7 master's, 4 doctorates awarded. *Degree requirements:* For master's, thesis (for some programs); for doctorate, thesis/dissertation. *Entrance requirements:* For master's and doctorate, GRE General Test. *Application deadline:* Applications are processed on a rolling basis. Application fee: $50 ($60 for international students). Electronic applications accepted. *Expenses:* Tuition, state resident: full-time $8802; part-time $489 per credit hour. Tuition, nonresident: full-time $26,406; part-time $1467 per credit hour. *Required fees:* $808 per semester. Tuition and fees vary according to degree level and program. *Financial support:* Research assistantships, teaching assistantships, and Federal Work-Study available. Support available to part-time students. Financial award application deadline: 3/15; financial award applicants required to submit FAFSA. *Faculty research:* Plant breeding and genetics; weed science; crop production; soil fertility and plant nutrition; soil genesis, morphology, and classification. *Unit head:* Dr. John Beasley, Head, 334-844-4100, E-mail: jtouchto@ag.auburn.edu. *Application contact:* Dr. George Flowers, Dean of the Graduate School, 334-844-2125.

Colorado State University, College of Agricultural Sciences, Department of Soil and Crop Sciences, Fort Collins, CO 80523-1170. Offers MS, PhD. *Program availability:* Part-time. *Faculty:* 19 full-time (6 women), 3 part-time/adjunct (2 women). *Students:* 14 full-time (7 women), 30 part-time (20 women); includes 3 minority (all Hispanic/Latino), 15 international. Average age 34. 14 applicants, 79% accepted, 7 enrolled. In 2015, 4 master's, 4 doctorates awarded. Terminal master's awarded for partial completion of doctoral program. *Degree requirements:* For master's, thesis; for doctorate, comprehensive exam, thesis/dissertation, student teaching. *Entrance requirements:* For master's and doctorate, GRE, minimum GPA of 3.0, transcripts, personal statement, resume/curriculum vitae, letters of recommendation. Additional exam requirements/recommendations for international students: Required—TOEFL (minimum score 550 paper-based; 80 iBT); Recommended—IELTS (minimum score 6.5). *Application deadline:* For fall admission, 4/1 priority date for domestic students, 5/1 priority date for international students; for spring admission, 9/1 priority date for domestic students, 10/1 priority date for international students. Application fee: $60 ($70 for international students). Electronic applications accepted. *Expenses:* Tuition, state resident: full-time $9348. Tuition, nonresident: full-time $22,916. *Required fees:* $2174; $473.72 per credit hour. $236.86 per semester. Tuition and fees vary according to course load and program. *Financial support:* In 2015–16, 2 fellowships with full tuition reimbursements (averaging $42,812 per year), 18 research assistantships with full tuition reimbursements (averaging $23,343 per year), 1 teaching assistantship with full tuition reimbursement (averaging $16,380 per year) were awarded; scholarships/grants and unspecified assistantships also available. Financial award application deadline: 2/15; financial award applicants required to submit FAFSA. *Faculty research:* Water quality, soil fertility, agroecosystems management, plant breeding and genetics, soil science and crop systems. *Total annual research expenditures:* $5.4 million. *Unit head:* Dr. Eugene Kelly, Department Head and Professor, 970-491-6501, Fax: 970-491-5676, E-mail: eugene.kelly@colostate.edu. *Application contact:* Karen Allison, Student Coordinator, 970-491-6295, Fax: 970-491-5676, E-mail: karen.allison@colostate.edu. Website: http://www.soilcrop.colostate.edu/

Cornell University, Graduate School, Graduate Fields of Agriculture and Life Sciences, Field of Soil and Crop Sciences, Ithaca, NY 14853-0001. Offers agronomy (MS, PhD); environmental information science (MS, PhD); environmental management (MPS); field crop science (MS, PhD); soil science (MS, PhD). *Degree requirements:* For master's, thesis (MS); for doctorate, comprehensive exam, thesis/dissertation. *Entrance*

requirements: For master's and doctorate, GRE General Test, 2 letters of recommendation. Additional exam requirements/recommendations for international students: Required—TOEFL (minimum score 550 paper-based; 77 iBT). Electronic applications accepted. *Faculty research:* Soil chemistry, physics and biology; crop physiology and management; environmental information science and modeling; international agriculture; weed science.

Dalhousie University, Faculty of Agriculture, Halifax, NS B3H 4R2, Canada. Offers agriculture (M Sc), including air quality, animal behavior, animal molecular genetics, animal nutrition, animal technology, aquaculture, botany, crop management, crop physiology, ecology, environmental microbiology, food science, horticulture, nutrient management, pest management, physiology, plant biotechnology, plant pathology, soil chemistry, soil fertility, waste management and composting, water quality. *Program availability:* Part-time. *Degree requirements:* For master's, thesis, ATC Exam Teaching Assistantship. *Entrance requirements:* For master's, honors B Sc, minimum GPA of 3.0. Additional exam requirements/recommendations for international students: Required—TOEFL (minimum score 580 paper-based; 92 iBT), IELTS, Michigan English Language Assessment Battery, CanTEST, CAEL. *Faculty research:* Bio-product development, organic agriculture, nutrient management, air and water quality, agricultural biotechnology.

Iowa State University of Science and Technology, Department of Agronomy, Ames, IA 50011. Offers agricultural meteorology (MS, PhD); agronomy (MS); crop production and physiology (MS, PhD); plant breeding (MS, PhD); soil science (MS, PhD). *Degree requirements:* For master's, thesis or alternative. *Entrance requirements:* Additional exam requirements/recommendations for international students: Recommended—TOEFL (minimum score 550 paper-based; 79 iBT), IELTS (minimum score 6.5). Electronic applications accepted.

Iowa State University of Science and Technology, Program in Crop Production and Physiology, Ames, IA 50011. Offers MS, PhD. *Entrance requirements:* Additional exam requirements/recommendations for international students: Required—TOEFL (minimum score 550 paper-based; 79 iBT), IELTS (minimum score 6.5). Electronic applications accepted.

Iowa State University of Science and Technology, Program in Soil Science, Ames, IA 50011. Offers MS, PhD. *Entrance requirements:* Additional exam requirements/recommendations for international students: Required—TOEFL (minimum score 550 paper-based; 79 iBT), IELTS (minimum score 6.5). Electronic applications accepted.

Kansas State University, Graduate School, College of Agriculture, Department of Agronomy, Manhattan, KS 66506. Offers crop science (MS, PhD); plant breeding and genetics (MS); range and forage science (MS, PhD); soil and environmental science (PhD); weed science (MS, PhD). *Program availability:* Part-time. *Degree requirements:* For master's, thesis or alternative, oral exam; for doctorate, thesis/dissertation, preliminary exams. *Entrance requirements:* For master's, minimum GPA of 3.0 in BS; for doctorate, minimum GPA of 3.0 in master's program. Additional exam requirements/recommendations for international students: Required—TOEFL (minimum score 550 paper-based; 79 iBT). Electronic applications accepted. *Faculty research:* Range and forage science; soil and environmental science; weed science; plant breeding and genetics; crop physiology, ecology and production.

McGill University, Faculty of Graduate and Postdoctoral Studies, Faculty of Agricultural and Environmental Sciences, Department of Bioresource Engineering, Montréal, QC H3A 2T5, Canada. Offers computer applications (M Sc, M Sc A, PhD); food engineering (M Sc, M Sc A, PhD); grain drying (M Sc, M Sc A, PhD); irrigation and drainage (M Sc, M Sc A, PhD); machinery (M Sc, M Sc A, PhD); pollution control (M Sc, M Sc A, PhD); post-harvest technology (M Sc, M Sc A, PhD); soil dynamics (M Sc, M Sc A, PhD); structure and environment (M Sc, M Sc A, PhD); vegetable and fruit storage (M Sc, M Sc A, PhD).

McGill University, Faculty of Graduate and Postdoctoral Studies, Faculty of Agricultural and Environmental Sciences, Department of Natural Resource Sciences, Montréal, QC H3A 2T5, Canada. Offers entomology (M Sc, PhD); environmental assessment (M Sc); forest science (M Sc, PhD); microbiology (M Sc, PhD); micrometeorology (M Sc, PhD); neotropical environment (M Sc, PhD); soil science (M Sc, PhD); wildlife biology (M Sc, PhD).

Michigan State University, The Graduate School, College of Agriculture and Natural Resources, Department of Crop and Soil Sciences, East Lansing, MI 48824. Offers crop and soil sciences (MS, PhD); crop and soil sciences-environmental toxicology (PhD); plant breeding and genetics-crop and soil sciences (MS); plant breeding, genetics and biotechnology-crop and soil sciences (PhD). *Entrance requirements:* Additional exam requirements/recommendations for international students: Required—TOEFL (minimum score 550 paper-based), Michigan State University ELT (minimum score 85), Michigan

Michigan English Language Assessment Battery (minimum score 83). Electronic applications accepted.

Michigan State University, The Graduate School, College of Agriculture and Natural Resources, MSU-DOE Plant Research Laboratory, East Lansing, MI 48824. Offers biochemistry and molecular biology (PhD); cellular and molecular biology (PhD); crop and soil sciences (PhD); genetics (PhD); microbiology and molecular genetics (PhD); plant biology (PhD); plant physiology (PhD). Offered jointly with the Department of Energy. *Degree requirements:* For doctorate, comprehensive exam, thesis/dissertation, laboratory rotation, defense of dissertation. *Entrance requirements:* For doctorate, GRE General Test, acceptance into one of the affiliated department programs; 3 letters of recommendation; bachelor's degree or equivalent in life sciences, chemistry, biochemistry, or biophysics; research experience. Electronic applications accepted. *Faculty research:* Role of hormones in the regulation of plant development and physiology, molecular mechanisms associated with signal recognition, development and application of genetic methods and materials, protein routing and function.

Mississippi State University, College of Agriculture and Life Sciences, Department of Plant and Soil Sciences, Mississippi State, MS 39762. Offers agriculture (MS, PhD), including agronomy, horticulture, weed science. *Faculty:* 49 full-time (5 women). *Students:* 45 full-time (11 women), 33 part-time (6 women); includes 2 minority (1 American Indian or Alaska Native, non-Hispanic/Latino; 1 Asian, non-Hispanic/Latino), 20 international. Average age 27. 26 applicants, 46% accepted, 11 enrolled. In 2015, 16 master's, 7 doctorates awarded. *Degree requirements:* For master's, comprehensive exam, thesis, oral and/or written exams; for doctorate, comprehensive exam, thesis/dissertation, minimum of 20 semester hours of research for dissertation. *Entrance requirements:* For master's, GRE (for weed science), minimum GPA of 2.75 (agronomy/horticulture), 3.0 (weed science); for doctorate, GRE (for weed science), minimum GPA of 3.0 (agronomy/horticulture), 3.25 (weed science). Additional exam requirements/recommendations for international students: Required—TOEFL (minimum score 500 paper-based; 61 iBT), TOEFL (minimum score 550 paper-based, 79 iBT) or IELTS (minimum score 6.5) for weed science; Recommended—IELTS (minimum score 5.5). *Application deadline:* For fall admission, 7/1 for domestic students, 5/1 for international students; for spring admission, 10/1 for domestic students, 9/1 for international students. Applications are processed on a rolling basis. Application fee: $60. Electronic applications accepted. *Expenses: Tuition, area resident:* Full-time $7502; part-time $833.74 per credit hour. Tuition, nonresident: full-time $20,142; part-time $2238.24 per credit hour. *Financial support:* In 2015–16, 31 research assistantships (averaging $14,967 per year), 3 teaching assistantships (averaging $15,951 per year) were awarded; Federal Work-Study, institutionally sponsored loans, scholarships/grants, and unspecified assistantships also available. Financial award application deadline: 4/1; financial award applicants required to submit FAFSA. *Faculty research:* Bioenergy crops, cotton breeding, environmental plant pathology, row crop weed control, genomics. *Unit head:* Dr. Mike Phillips, Professor and Head, 662-325-2311, Fax: 662-325-8742, E-mail: jmp657@msstate.edu. *Application contact:* Marina Hunt, Admissions Assistant, 662-325-5188, E-mail: mhunt@grad.msstate.edu.
Website: http://www.pss.msstate.edu/

North Carolina Agricultural and Technical State University, School of Graduate Studies, School of Agriculture and Environmental Sciences, Department of Natural Resources and Environmental Design, Greensboro, NC 27411. Offers plant, soil and environmental science (MS). *Program availability:* Part-time, evening/weekend. *Degree requirements:* For master's, comprehensive exam, thesis optional, qualifying exam. *Entrance requirements:* For master's, GRE General Test, minimum GPA of 3.0. *Faculty research:* Soil parameters and compaction of forest site, controlled traffic effects on soil, improving soybean and vegetable crops.

North Carolina State University, Graduate School, College of Agriculture and Life Sciences, Department of Crop Science, Raleigh, NC 27695. Offers MS, PhD. *Program availability:* Part-time. Terminal master's awarded for partial completion of doctoral program. *Degree requirements:* For master's, thesis; for doctorate, thesis/dissertation. *Entrance requirements:* For master's and doctorate, GRE. Electronic applications accepted. *Faculty research:* Crop breeding and genetics, application of biotechnology to crop improvement, plant physiology, crop physiology and management, agroecology.

North Carolina State University, Graduate School, College of Agriculture and Life Sciences, Department of Soil Science, Raleigh, NC 27695. Offers MS, PhD. *Program availability:* Part-time, online learning. *Degree requirements:* For master's, thesis (for some programs); for doctorate, thesis/dissertation. *Entrance requirements:* For master's and doctorate, GRE, minimum GPA of 3.0. Additional exam requirements/recommendations for international students: Required—TOEFL (minimum score 75 iBT). Electronic applications accepted. *Faculty research:* Soil management, soil-environmental relations, chemical and physical properties of soils, nutrient and water management, land use.

North Dakota State University, College of Graduate and Interdisciplinary Studies, College of Agriculture, Food Systems, and Natural Resources, Department of Soil Science, Fargo, ND 58102. Offers soil sciences (MS, PhD). *Program availability:* Part-time. *Degree requirements:* For master's, comprehensive exam, thesis, classroom teaching; for doctorate, comprehensive exam, thesis/dissertation, classroom teaching. *Entrance requirements:* Additional exam requirements/recommendations for international students: Required—TOEFL (minimum score 525 paper-based; 71 iBT). Electronic applications accepted. *Faculty research:* Microclimate, nitrogen management, landscape studies, water quality, soil management.

The Ohio State University, Graduate School, College of Food, Agricultural, and Environmental Sciences, School of Environment and Natural Resources, Program in Soil Science, Columbus, OH 43210. Offers MS, PhD. *Degree requirements:* For doctorate, thesis/dissertation. *Entrance requirements:* For master's and doctorate, GRE General Test. Electronic applications accepted.

Oklahoma State University, College of Agricultural Science and Natural Resources, Department of Horticulture and Landscape Architecture, Stillwater, OK 74078. Offers crop science (PhD); environmental science (PhD); horticulture (M Ag, MS); plant science (PhD). *Faculty:* 17 full-time (4 women). *Students:* 3 full-time (1 woman), 9 part-time (3 women); includes 2 minority (1 Black or African American, non-Hispanic/Latino; 1 Asian, non-Hispanic/Latino), 5 international. Average age 30. 8 applicants, 63% accepted, 5 enrolled. In 2015, 3 master's awarded. *Degree requirements:* For master's, thesis (for some programs); for doctorate, comprehensive exam, thesis/dissertation. *Entrance requirements:* For master's and doctorate, GRE or GMAT. Additional exam requirements/recommendations for international students: Required—TOEFL (minimum score 550 paper-based; 79 iBT). *Application deadline:* For fall admission, 3/1 priority date for international students; for spring admission, 8/1 priority date for international students. Applications are processed on a rolling basis. Application fee: $40 ($75 for international students). Electronic applications accepted. *Expenses:* Tuition, state resident: full-time $3528; part-time $196 per credit hour. Tuition, nonresident: full-time $14,144; part-time $785.75 per credit hour. *Required fees:* $1895; $105.25 per credit hour. Tuition and fees vary according to campus/location. *Financial support:* In 2015–16, 9 research assistantships (averaging $10,469 per year), 3 teaching assistantships (averaging $12,261 per year) were awarded; career-related internships or fieldwork, Federal Work-Study, scholarships/grants, health care benefits, tuition waivers (partial), and unspecified assistantships also available. Support available to part-time students. Financial award application deadline: 3/1; financial award applicants required to submit FAFSA. *Faculty research:* Stress and postharvest physiology; water utilization and runoff; integrated pest management (IPM) systems and nursery, turf, floriculture, vegetable, net and fruit produces and natural resources, food extraction, and processing; public garden management. *Unit head:* Dr. Janet Cole, Department Head, 405-744-5414, Fax: 405-744-9709. *Application contact:* Dr. Sheryl Tucker, Dean, 405-744-7099, Fax: 405-744-0355, E-mail: gradi@okstate.edu.
Website: http://www.hortla.okstate.edu/

Oklahoma State University, College of Agricultural Science and Natural Resources, Department of Plant and Soil Sciences, Stillwater, OK 74078. Offers crop science (PhD); plant and soil sciences (MS); soil science (M Ag, PhD). *Faculty:* 28 full-time (3 women). *Students:* 13 full-time (6 women), 37 part-time (12 women); includes 5 minority (4 American Indian or Alaska Native, non-Hispanic/Latino; 1 Two or more races, non-Hispanic/Latino), 28 international. Average age 28. 26 applicants, 50% accepted, 8 enrolled. In 2015, 10 master's, 6 doctorates awarded. *Degree requirements:* For master's, thesis; for doctorate, comprehensive exam, thesis/dissertation. *Entrance requirements:* For master's and doctorate, GRE or GMAT. Additional exam requirements/recommendations for international students: Required—TOEFL (minimum score 550 paper-based; 79 iBT). *Application deadline:* For fall admission, 3/1 priority date for international students; for spring admission, 8/1 priority date for international students. Applications are processed on a rolling basis. Application fee: $40 ($75 for international students). Electronic applications accepted. *Expenses:* Tuition, state resident: full-time $3528; part-time $196 per credit hour. Tuition, nonresident: full-time $14,144; part-time $785.75 per credit hour. *Required fees:* $1895; $105.25 per credit hour. Tuition and fees vary according to campus/location. *Financial support:* In 2015–16, 36 research assistantships (averaging $19,087 per year), 2 teaching assistantships (averaging $17,400 per year) were awarded; career-related internships or fieldwork, Federal Work-Study, scholarships/grants, health care benefits, tuition waivers (partial), and unspecified assistantships also available. Support available to part-time students. Financial award application deadline: 3/1; financial award applicants required to submit FAFSA. *Faculty research:* Crop science, weed science, rangeland ecology and management, biotechnology, breeding and genetics. *Unit head:* Dr. Jeff Edwards, Department Head, 405-744-6130, Fax: 405-744-0354, E-mail: jeff.edwards@okstate.edu.
Website: http://pss.okstate.edu

Oregon State University, College of Agricultural Sciences, Program in Crop Science, Corvallis, OR 97331. Offers M Ag, MS, PhD. *Program availability:* Part-time. *Faculty:* 25 full-time (8 women), 4 part-time/adjunct (3 women). *Students:* 25 full-time (11 women), 1 part-time (0 women), 10 international. Average age 31. 16 applicants, 19% accepted, 3 enrolled. In 2015, 6 master's awarded. *Degree requirements:* For master's, thesis (for some programs); for doctorate, variable foreign language requirement, thesis/dissertation. *Entrance requirements:* For master's and doctorate, GRE, minimum GPA of 3.0 in last 90 hours of course work. Additional exam requirements/recommendations for international students: Required—TOEFL (minimum score 80 iBT), IELTS (minimum score 6.5). *Application deadline:* For fall admission, 4/1 for international students; for winter admission, 7/1 for international students; for spring admission, 10/1 for international students; for summer admission, 1/1 for international students. Application fee: $75 ($85 for international students). *Expenses:* Tuition, state resident: full-time $12,150; part-time $450 per credit. Tuition, nonresident: full-time $20,952; part-time $776 per credit. *Required fees:* $1572; $1443 per unit. One-time fee: $350. Tuition and fees vary according to course load, campus/location and program. *Financial support:* Fellowships, research assistantships, teaching assistantships, career-related internships or fieldwork, Federal Work-Study, and institutionally sponsored loans available. Support available to part-time students. Financial award application deadline: 2/1. *Faculty research:* Cereal and new crops breeding and genetics; weed science; seed technology and production; potato, new crops, and general crop production; plant physiology. *Unit head:* Dr. Jay Noller, Department Head and Professor. *Application contact:* E-mail: emmalie.goodwin@oregonstate.edu.
Website: http://cropandsoil.oregonstate.edu/content/crop-science

Oregon State University, College of Agricultural Sciences, Program in Soil Science, Corvallis, OR 97331. Offers M Ag, MS, PhD. *Program availability:* Part-time. *Faculty:* 24 full-time (8 women), 4 part-time/adjunct (3 women). *Students:* 24 full-time (11 women), 1 part-time (0 women); includes 4 minority (2 Hispanic/Latino; 2 Two or more races, non-Hispanic/Latino), 5 international. Average age 31. 32 applicants, 38% accepted, 7 enrolled. In 2015, 6 master's, 2 doctorates awarded. *Degree requirements:* For master's, thesis (for some programs); for doctorate, variable foreign language requirement, thesis/dissertation. *Entrance requirements:* Additional exam requirements/recommendations for international students: Required—TOEFL (minimum score 80 iBT), IELTS (minimum score 6.5). *Application deadline:* For fall admission, 8/1 for domestic students, 4/1 for international students; for winter admission, 9/1 for domestic students, 7/1 for international students; for spring admission, 12/1 for domestic students, 10/1 for international students; for summer admission, 3/1 for domestic students, 1/1 for international students. Application fee: $75 ($85 for international students). *Expenses:* Tuition, state resident: full-time $12,150; part-time $450 per credit. Tuition, nonresident: full-time $20,952; part-time $776 per credit. *Required fees:* $1572; $1443 per unit. One-time fee: $350. Tuition and fees vary according to course load, campus/location and program. *Financial support:* Fellowships, research assistantships, teaching assistantships, career-related internships or fieldwork, Federal Work-Study, and institutionally sponsored loans available. Support available to part-time students. Financial award application deadline: 2/1. *Faculty research:* Soil physics, chemistry, biology, fertility, and genesis. *Unit head:* Dr. Jay Noller, Department Head/Professor, E-mail: jay.noller@oregonstate.edu. *Application contact:* Maria Dragila, Soil Science Advisor, 541-737-5739, E-mail: maria.dragila@oregonstate.edu.
Website: http://cropandsoil.oregonstate.edu/content/soil-science-graduate-program

Penn State University Park, Graduate School, College of Agricultural Sciences, Department of Ecosystem Science and Management, University Park, PA 16802. Offers forest resources (MS, PhD); soil science (MS, PhD); wildlife and fisheries science (MS, PhD). *Unit head:* Dr. Richard T. Roush, Dean, 814-865-2541, Fax: 814-865-3103. *Application contact:* Lori Stania, Director, Graduate Student Services, 814-865-1795, Fax: 814-863-4627, E-mail: l-gswww@lists.psu.edu.
Website: http://ecosystems.psu.edu/

Purdue University, Graduate School, College of Agriculture, Department of Agronomy, West Lafayette, IN 47907. Offers MS, PhD. *Program availability:* Part-time. *Degree requirements:* For doctorate, thesis/dissertation. *Entrance requirements:* For master's and doctorate, GRE General Test, minimum undergraduate GPA of 3.0 or equivalent. Additional exam requirements/recommendations for international students: Required—TOEFL (minimum score 550 paper-based, 77 iBT), IELTS (minimum score 6.5) or PTE (minimum score 58). Electronic applications accepted. *Faculty research:* Plant genetics and breeding, crop physiology and ecology, agricultural meteorology, soil microbiology.

South Dakota State University, Graduate School, College of Agriculture and Biological Sciences, Department of Plant Science, Brookings, SD 57007. Offers agronomy (PhD); biological sciences (PhD); plant science (MS). *Degree requirements:* For master's, thesis (for some programs), oral exam; for doctorate, comprehensive exam, thesis/dissertation, preliminary oral and written exams. *Entrance requirements:* Additional exam requirements/recommendations for international students: Required—TOEFL (minimum score 560 paper-based; 83 iBT).

Southern Illinois University Carbondale, Graduate School, College of Agriculture, Department of Plant, Soil, and General Agriculture, Carbondale, IL 62901-4701. Offers MS. *Faculty:* 12 full-time (1 woman), 8 part-time/adjunct (0 women). *Students:* 3 full-time (0 women), 25 part-time (8 women); includes 1 minority (Asian, non-Hispanic/Latino), 5 international. 11 applicants, 45% accepted, 5 enrolled. In 2015, 8 master's awarded. *Degree requirements:* For master's, thesis. *Entrance requirements:* For master's, minimum GPA of 2.7. Additional exam requirements/recommendations for international students: Required—TOEFL. *Application deadline:* Applications are processed on a rolling basis. Application fee: $65. *Financial support:* In 2015–16, 14 students received support, including 8 research assistantships with full tuition reimbursements available, 6 teaching assistantships with full tuition reimbursements available; fellowships with full tuition reimbursements available, Federal Work-Study, institutionally sponsored loans, and tuition waivers (full) also available. Support available to part-time students. *Faculty research:* Herbicides, fertilizers, agriculture education, landscape design, plant breeding. *Total annual research expenditures:* $2 million. *Unit head:* Dr. Karen Jones, Interim Chair, 618-453-2469, E-mail: kljones@siu.edu. *Application contact:* Mary Dunmyer, Office Support Specialist, 618-453-1770, E-mail: marya@siu.edu.

Tennessee State University, The School of Graduate Studies and Research, College of Agriculture, Human and Natural Sciences, Nashville, TN 37209-1561. Offers agricultural sciences (MS), including agribusiness, agricultural and extension education, animal science, plant and soil science; biological sciences (MS, PhD); biotechnology (PhD); chemistry (MS). *Program availability:* Part-time, evening/weekend. *Degree requirements:* For master's, thesis. *Entrance requirements:* For master's, GRE General Test, GRE Subject Test, MAT. *Faculty research:* Small farm economics, ornamental horticulture, beef cattle production, rural elderly.

Texas A&M University, College of Agriculture and Life Sciences, Department of Soil and Crop Sciences, College Station, TX 77843. Offers agronomy (MS, PhD); soil science (MS, PhD). *Faculty:* 31. *Students:* 97 full-time (40 women), 39 part-time (15 women); includes 24 minority (2 Black or African American, non-Hispanic/Latino; 2 Asian, non-Hispanic/Latino; 16 Hispanic/Latino; 4 Two or more races, non-Hispanic/Latino), 49 international. Average age 30. 22 applicants, 100% accepted, 17 enrolled. In 2015, 14 master's, 13 doctorates awarded. *Degree requirements:* For master's, thesis; for doctorate, thesis/dissertation. *Entrance requirements:* For master's and doctorate, GRE General Test. Additional exam requirements/recommendations for international students: Required—TOEFL (minimum score 550 paper-based; 80 iBT), IELTS (minimum score 6), PTE (minimum score 53). *Application deadline:* For fall admission, 3/1 priority date for domestic students; for spring admission, 8/1 for domestic students. Applications are processed on a rolling basis. Application fee: $50 ($90 for international students). Electronic applications accepted. *Expenses:* Contact institution. *Financial support:* In 2015–16, 111 students received support, including 14 fellowships with tuition reimbursements available (averaging $18,305 per year), 54 research assistantships with tuition reimbursements available (averaging $5,903 per year), 12 teaching assistantships with tuition reimbursements available (averaging $6,297 per year); career-related internships or fieldwork, institutionally sponsored loans, scholarships/grants, traineeships, health care benefits, tuition waivers (full and partial), and unspecified assistantships also available. Support available to part-time students. Financial award application deadline: 3/15; financial award applicants required to submit FAFSA. *Faculty research:* Soil and crop management, turfgrass science, weed science, cereal chemistry, food protein chemistry. *Unit head:* Dr. David D. Baltensperger, Department Head, 979-845-3041, E-mail: dbaltensperger@ag.tamu.edu. *Application contact:* Megan Teel, Academic Advisor, 979-862-4165, Fax: 979-458-0533, E-mail: megan_teel@tamu.edu.
Website: http://soilcrop.tamu.edu

Texas A&M University–Kingsville, College of Graduate Studies, Dick and Mary Lewis Kleberg College of Agriculture, Natural Resources and Human Sciences, Department of Agriculture, Agribusiness, and Environmental Sciences, Program in Plant and Soil Science, Kingsville, TX 78363. Offers MS. *Degree requirements:* For master's, variable foreign language requirement, comprehensive exam, thesis (for some programs). *Entrance requirements:* For master's, GRE (minimum combined Math & Verbal score of 290), MAT, GMAT, minimum GPA of 2.5. Additional exam requirements/recommendations for international students: Required—TOEFL (minimum score 550 paper-based; 79 iBT). Electronic applications accepted.

Texas Tech University, Graduate School, College of Agricultural Sciences and Natural Resources, Department of Plant and Soil Science, Lubbock, TX 79409. Offers horticulture science (MS); plant and soil science (MS, PhD). *Program availability:* Part-time, evening/weekend, 100% online, blended/hybrid learning. *Faculty:* 16 full-time (4 women), 14 part-time/adjunct (4 women). *Students:* 57 full-time (24 women), 34 part-time (6 women); includes 7 minority (1 Black or African American, non-Hispanic/Latino; 1 Asian, non-Hispanic/Latino; 3 Hispanic/Latino; 2 Two or more races, non-Hispanic/Latino), 33 international. Average age 30. 55 applicants, 51% accepted, 21 enrolled. In 2015, 22 master's, 7 doctorates awarded. Terminal master's awarded for partial completion of doctoral program. *Degree requirements:* For master's, comprehensive exam (for some programs), thesis (for some programs); for doctorate, comprehensive exam, thesis/dissertation. *Entrance requirements:* For master's and doctorate, GRE. Additional exam requirements/recommendations for international students: Required—TOEFL (minimum score 550 paper-based; 79 iBT). *Application deadline:* For fall admission, 6/1 priority date for domestic students, 1/15 priority date for international students; for spring admission, 9/1 priority date for domestic students, 6/15 priority date for international students. Applications are processed on a rolling basis. Application fee: $60. Electronic applications accepted. *Expenses:* Tuition, state resident: full-time $6477; part-time $269.89 per credit hour. Tuition, nonresident: full-time $15,837; part-time $659.89 per credit hour. *Required fees:* $2751; $36.50 per credit hour. $937.50 per semester. Tuition and fees vary according to course level. *Financial support:* In 2015–16, 78 students received support, including 71 fellowships (averaging $2,923 per year), 55 research assistantships (averaging $13,035 per year), 31 teaching assistantships (averaging $4,062 per year); scholarships/grants, health care benefits, and unspecified assistantships also available. Financial award application deadline: 4/15; financial award applicants required to submit FAFSA. *Faculty research:* Crop protection, crop science, fibers and biopolymers, soil science, horticulture. *Total annual research expenditures:* $3 million. *Unit head:* Dr. Eric Hequet, Department Chair, 806-742-2838, Fax: 806-742-0775, E-mail: eric.hequet@ttu.edu. *Application contact:* Christi Chadwell, Communication and Recruiting Coordinator, 806-834-8124, E-mail: christi.chadwell@ttu.edu.
Website: http://www.pssc.ttu.edu

Tuskegee University, Graduate Programs, College of Agriculture, Environment and Nutrition Sciences, Department of Agricultural and Environmental Sciences, Program in Plant and Soil Sciences, Tuskegee, AL 36088. Offers MS. *Degree requirements:* For master's, thesis. *Entrance requirements:* For master's, GRE General Test. Additional exam requirements/recommendations for international students: Required—TOEFL (minimum score 500 paper-based).

Université Laval, Faculty of Agricultural and Food Sciences, Department of Soils and Agricultural Engineering, Programs in Soils and Environment Science, Québec, QC G1K 7P4, Canada. Offers environmental technology (M Sc); soils and environment science (M Sc, PhD). Terminal master's awarded for partial completion of doctoral program. *Degree requirements:* For master's, thesis (for some programs); for doctorate, comprehensive exam, thesis/dissertation. *Entrance requirements:* For master's and doctorate, knowledge of French and English. Electronic applications accepted.

Université Laval, Faculty of Forestry, Geography and Geomatics, Program in Agroforestry, Québec, QC G1K 7P4, Canada. Offers M Sc. *Degree requirements:* For master's, thesis (for some programs). *Entrance requirements:* For master's, English exam (comprehension of English), knowledge of French, knowledge of a third language. Electronic applications accepted.

University of Alberta, Faculty of Graduate Studies and Research, Department of Renewable Resources, Edmonton, AB T6G 2E1, Canada. Offers agroforestry (M Ag, M Sc, MF); conservation biology (M Sc, PhD); forest biology and management (M Sc, PhD); land reclamation and remediation (M Sc, PhD); protected areas and wildlands management (M Sc, PhD); soil science (M Ag, M Sc, PhD); water and land resources (M Ag, M Sc, PhD); wildlife ecology and management (M Sc, PhD); MBA/M Ag; MBA/MF. *Program availability:* Part-time. *Degree requirements:* For master's, thesis (for some programs); for doctorate, comprehensive exam, thesis/dissertation. *Entrance requirements:* For master's, minimum 2 years of relevant professional experiences, minimum GPA of 3.0; for doctorate, minimum GPA of 3.0. Additional exam requirements/recommendations for international students: Required—TOEFL (minimum score 550 paper-based). Electronic applications accepted. *Faculty research:* Natural and managed landscapes.

The University of Arizona, College of Agriculture and Life Sciences, Department of Soil, Water and Environmental Science, Tucson, AZ 85721. Offers MS, PhD, Graduate Certificate. *Degree requirements:* For master's, thesis; for doctorate, comprehensive exam, thesis/dissertation. *Entrance requirements:* For master's, GRE (recommended), minimum GPA of 3.0, letter of interest, 3 letters of recommendation; for doctorate, GRE (recommended), MS, minimum GPA of 3.0, letter of interest, 3 letters of recommendation. Additional exam requirements/recommendations for international students: Required—TOEFL (minimum score 550 paper-based; 80 iBT). *Application deadline:* For fall admission, 6/1 for domestic students, 12/1 for international students; for spring admission, 10/1 for domestic students, 6/1 for international students. Applications are processed on a rolling basis. Application fee: $75. Electronic applications accepted. *Financial support:* Fellowships, research assistantships, teaching assistantships, Federal Work-Study, institutionally sponsored loans, scholarships/grants, health care benefits, tuition waivers (full and partial), and unspecified assistantships available. Financial award application deadline: 5/1. *Faculty research:* Plant production, environmental microbiology, contaminant flow and transport, aquaculture. *Unit head:* Dr. Jonathan D. Chorover, Department Head, E-mail: chorover@cals.arizona.edu.
Website: http://swes.cals.arizona.edu/

University of Arkansas, Graduate School, Dale Bumpers College of Agricultural, Food and Life Sciences, Department of Crop, Soil and Environmental Sciences, Fayetteville, AR 72701-1201. Offers agronomy (MS, PhD). *Students:* 12 full-time (7 women), 50 part-time (15 women); includes 2 minority (1 American Indian or Alaska Native, non-Hispanic/Latino; 1 Hispanic/Latino), 22 international. In 2015, 10 master's, 4 doctorates awarded. *Degree requirements:* For master's, thesis optional; for doctorate, variable foreign language requirement, thesis/dissertation. *Application deadline:* For fall admission, 4/1 for international students; for spring admission, 10/1 for international students. Applications are processed on a rolling basis. Application fee: $40 ($50 for international students). Electronic applications accepted. *Financial support:* In 2015–16, 36 research assistantships were awarded; fellowships with tuition reimbursements, teaching assistantships, career-related internships or fieldwork, and Federal Work-Study also available. Support available to part-time students. Financial award application deadline: 4/1; financial award applicants required to submit FAFSA. *Unit head:* Dr. Robert Bacon, Interim Departmental Chairperson, 479-575-2347, Fax: 479-575-7465, E-mail: rbacon@uark.edu. *Application contact:* Dr. Thad Scott, Graduate Coordinator, 479-575-6337, E-mail: jts004@uark.edu.
Website: http://cses.uark.edu

The University of British Columbia, Faculty of Land and Food Systems, Program in Soil Science, Vancouver, BC V6T 1Z1, Canada. Offers land and water systems (MLWS); soil science (M Sc, PhD). *Degree requirements:* For master's, thesis; for doctorate, comprehensive exam, thesis/dissertation. *Entrance requirements:* Additional exam requirements/recommendations for international students: Required—TOEFL (minimum score 577 paper-based; 90 iBT), IELTS (minimum score 6.5). Electronic applications accepted. *Faculty research:* Soil and water conservation, land use, land use and land classification, soil physics, soil chemistry and mineralogy.

University of California, Davis, Graduate Studies, Graduate Group in Horticulture and Agronomy, Davis, CA 95616. Offers MS. *Degree requirements:* For master's, comprehensive exam (for some programs), thesis (for some programs). *Entrance requirements:* For master's, GRE General Test. Additional exam requirements/recommendations for international students: Required—TOEFL (minimum score 550 paper-based). Electronic applications accepted. *Faculty research:* Postharvest physiology, mineral nutrition, crop improvement, plant growth and development.

University of California, Davis, Graduate Studies, Graduate Group in Soils and Biogeochemistry, Davis, CA 95616. Offers MS, PhD. Terminal master's awarded for partial completion of doctoral program. *Degree requirements:* For master's, comprehensive exam (for some programs), thesis (for some programs); for doctorate, thesis/dissertation. *Entrance requirements:* For master's, minimum GPA of 3.3; for doctorate, GRE, minimum GPA of 3.3. Additional exam requirements/recommendations for international students: Required—TOEFL (minimum score 550 paper-based). Electronic applications accepted. *Faculty research:* Rhizosphere ecology, soil transport processes, biogeochemical cycling, sustainable agriculture.

University of California, Riverside, Graduate Division, Environmental Sciences Department, Riverside, CA 92521-0102. Offers MS, PhD. *Degree requirements:* For doctorate, thesis/dissertation. *Entrance requirements:* For master's and doctorate, minimum GPA of 3.2. Additional exam requirements/recommendations for international students: Required—TOEFL (minimum score 550 paper-based; 80 iBT). Electronic applications accepted. *Faculty research:* Environmental chemistry and ecotoxicology, environmental microbiology, environmental and natural resource economics and policy, soil and water science, environmental sciences and management.

University of Connecticut, Graduate School, College of Agriculture and Natural Resources, Department of Plant Science, Storrs, CT 06269. Offers plant and soil sciences (MS, PhD). Terminal master's awarded for partial completion of doctoral program. *Degree requirements:* For master's, comprehensive exam; for doctorate, thesis/dissertation. *Entrance requirements:* For master's and doctorate, GRE General Test, GRE Subject Test. Additional exam requirements/recommendations for international students: Required—TOEFL (minimum score 550 paper-based). Electronic applications accepted.

University of Delaware, College of Agriculture and Natural Resources, Department of Plant and Soil Sciences, Newark, DE 19716. Offers MS, PhD. *Program availability:* Part-time. Terminal master's awarded for partial completion of doctoral program. *Degree requirements:* For master's, thesis; for doctorate, thesis/dissertation. *Entrance requirements:* For master's and doctorate, GRE General Test. Additional exam requirements/recommendations for international students: Required—TOEFL (minimum score 550 paper-based). Electronic applications accepted. *Faculty research:* Soil chemistry, plant and cell tissue culture, plant breeding and genetics, soil physics, soil biochemistry, plant molecular biology, soil microbiology.

University of Florida, Graduate School, College of Agricultural and Life Sciences, Department of Agronomy, Gainesville, FL 32611. Offers agroecology (MS); agronomy (MS, PhD); geographic information systems (MS); toxicology (PhD); tropical conservation and development (MS, PhD). *Program availability:* Part-time, online learning. *Faculty:* 6 full-time. *Students:* 50 full-time (15 women), 19 part-time (7 women); includes 6 minority (1 American Indian or Alaska Native, non-Hispanic/Latino; 2 Asian, non-Hispanic/Latino; 3 Hispanic/Latino), 24 international. Average age 30. 33 applicants, 48% accepted, 12 enrolled. In 2015, 5 master's, 5 doctorates awarded. Terminal master's awarded for partial completion of doctoral program. *Degree requirements:* For master's, thesis (for some programs); for doctorate, comprehensive exam, thesis/dissertation (for some programs). *Entrance requirements:* For master's and doctorate, GRE General Test, minimum GPA of 3.0, statement of purpose, 3 letters of recommendation. Additional exam requirements/recommendations for international students: Required—TOEFL (minimum score 550 paper-based; 80 iBT), IELTS (minimum score 6). *Application deadline:* For fall admission, 5/1 priority date for domestic students, 4/1 for international students; for spring admission, 10/1 for domestic students, 9/1 for international students; for summer admission, 1/1 for domestic and international students. Applications are processed on a rolling basis. Application fee: $30. Electronic applications accepted. *Financial support:* In 2015–16, 2 fellowships, 39 research assistantships, 3 teaching assistantships were awarded; career-related internships or fieldwork, institutionally sponsored loans, and unspecified assistantships also available. Financial award application deadline: 1/1; financial award applicants required to submit FAFSA. *Faculty research:* Invasive and aquatic weed ecology, grassland ecology and management, genomics and molecular genetics, plant drought stress tolerance, sustainable food production systems. *Total annual research expenditures:* $3.8 million. *Unit head:* Robert Gilbert, PhD, Professor and Department Chair, 352-392-1811, Fax: 352-392-1840, E-mail: ragilber@ufl.edu. *Application contact:* Jerry M. Bennett, PhD, Graduate Coordinator, 352-294-1591, Fax: 352-392-1840, E-mail: jmbt@ufl.edu.
Website: http://agronomy.ifas.ufl.edu/

University of Florida, Graduate School, College of Agricultural and Life Sciences, Department of Soil and Water Science, Gainesville, FL 32611. Offers soil and water science (MS, PhD), including agroecology (MS), geographic information systems, hydrologic sciences, tropical conservation and development, wetland sciences. *Program availability:* Part-time, evening/weekend, online learning. *Faculty:* 24 full-time, 7 part-time/adjunct. *Students:* 58 full-time (28 women), 51 part-time (25 women); includes 15 minority (1 Black or African American, non-Hispanic/Latino; 2 Asian, non-Hispanic/Latino; 12 Hispanic/Latino), 37 international. Average age 32. 29 applicants, 66% accepted, 17 enrolled. In 2015, 16 master's, 12 doctorates awarded. Terminal master's awarded for partial completion of doctoral program. *Degree requirements:* For master's, thesis optional; for doctorate, comprehensive exam, thesis/dissertation. *Entrance requirements:* For master's and doctorate, GRE General Test, minimum GPA of 3.0. Additional exam requirements/recommendations for international students: Required—TOEFL (minimum score 550 paper-based; 80 iBT), IELTS (minimum score 6). *Application deadline:* For fall admission, 2/1 priority date for domestic students, 2/1 for international students; for spring admission, 10/1 for domestic and international students; for summer admission, 2/1 for domestic and international students. Applications are processed on a rolling basis. Application fee: $30. Electronic applications accepted. *Financial support:* In 2015–16, 5 fellowships, 38 research assistantships, 14 teaching assistantships were awarded; career-related internships or fieldwork, Federal Work-Study, institutionally sponsored loans, and unspecified assistantships also available. Support available to part-time students. Financial award applicants required to submit FAFSA. *Faculty research:* Carbon dynamics and ecosystem services; landscape analysis and modeling; nutrient pesticide and waste management; soil, water, and aquifer remediation; wetlands and aquatic ecosystems. *Total annual research expenditures:* $4.4 million. *Unit head:* K. Ramesh Reddy, PhD, Graduate Research Professor and Department Chairman, 352-294-3154, Fax: 352-392-3399, E-mail: krr@ufl.edu. *Application contact:* Max Teplitski, PhD, Associate Professor and Graduate Coordinator, 352-273-8189 Ext. 211, Fax: 352-392-3902, E-mail: maxtep@ufl.edu.
Website: http://soils.ifas.ufl.edu/

University of Georgia, College of Agricultural and Environmental Sciences, Department of Crop and Soil Sciences, Athens, GA 30602. Offers crop and soil sciences (MS, PhD); plant protection and pest management (MPPPM). *Program availability:* Part-time. *Degree requirements:* For master's, thesis (MS); for doctorate, comprehensive exam, thesis/dissertation. *Entrance requirements:* For master's and doctorate, GRE General Test. Additional exam requirements/recommendations for international students: Required—TOEFL (minimum score 550 paper-based). Electronic applications accepted. *Faculty research:* Plant breeding, genomics, nutrient management, water quality, soil chemistry.

University of Guelph, Graduate Studies, Ontario Agricultural College, Department of Land Resource Science, Guelph, ON N1G 2W1, Canada. Offers atmospheric science (M Sc, PhD); environmental and agricultural earth sciences (M Sc, PhD); land resources management (M Sc, PhD); soil science (M Sc, PhD). *Program availability:* Part-time. *Degree requirements:* For master's, thesis (for some programs), research project (non-thesis track); for doctorate, comprehensive exam, thesis/dissertation. *Entrance requirements:* For master's, minimum B- average during previous 2 years of course work; for doctorate, minimum B average during previous 2 years of course work. Additional exam requirements/recommendations for international students: Required—TOEFL (minimum score 550 paper-based). Electronic applications accepted. *Faculty research:* Soil science, environmental earth science, land resource management.

University of Idaho, College of Graduate Studies, College of Agricultural and Life Sciences, Department of Plant, Soil, and Entomological Sciences, Moscow, ID 83844-2339. Offers entomology (MS, PhD); plant science (MS, PhD); soil and land resources (MS, PhD). *Faculty:* 30 full-time. *Students:* 28 full-time (9 women), 19 part-time (9 women). Average age 32. In 2015, 5 master's, 2 doctorates awarded. *Degree requirements:* For doctorate, thesis/dissertation. *Entrance requirements:* For master's and doctorate, GRE General Test, minimum GPA of 3.0. *Application deadline:* For fall admission, 7/1 for domestic students; for spring admission, 11/1 for domestic students. Applications are processed on a rolling basis. Application fee: $60. Electronic applications accepted. *Expenses:* Tuition, state resident: full-time $6205; part-time $399 per credit hour. Tuition, nonresident: full-time $20,209; part-time $1177 per credit hour. *Required fees:* $2017; $58 per credit hour. Full-time tuition and fees vary according to course load and reciprocity agreements. *Financial support:* Research assistantships and teaching assistantships available. Financial award applicants required to submit FAFSA. *Faculty research:* Entomological sciences, crop and weed science, horticultural science, soil and land resources. *Unit head:* Dr. Paul McDaniel, Department Head, 208-885-6274, Fax: 208-885-7760, E-mail: pses@uidaho.edu. *Application contact:* Sean Scoggin, Graduate Recruitment Coordinator, 208-885-4001, Fax: 208-885-4406, E-mail: graduateadmissions@uidaho.edu.
Website: http://www.uidaho.edu/cals/pses/

University of Illinois at Urbana–Champaign, Graduate College, College of Agricultural, Consumer and Environmental Sciences, Department of Crop Sciences, Champaign, IL 61820. Offers bioinformatics: crop sciences (MS); crop sciences (MS, PhD). *Program availability:* Online learning.

University of Kentucky, Graduate School, College of Agriculture, Food and Environment, Program in Plant and Soil Science, Lexington, KY 40506-0032. Offers integrated plant and soil sciences (MS, PhD). *Degree requirements:* For master's, comprehensive exam, thesis optional. *Entrance requirements:* For master's, GRE General Test, minimum undergraduate GPA of 2.75, graduate 3.0. Additional exam requirements/recommendations for international students: Required—TOEFL (minimum score 550 paper-based). Electronic applications accepted.

University of Manitoba, Faculty of Graduate Studies, Faculty of Agricultural and Food Sciences, Department of Plant Science, Winnipeg, MB R3T 2N2, Canada. Offers agronomy and plant protection (M Sc, PhD); horticulture (M Sc, PhD); plant breeding and genetics (M Sc, PhD); plant physiology-biochemistry (M Sc, PhD). *Degree requirements:* For master's, thesis; for doctorate, one foreign language, thesis/dissertation.

University of Manitoba, Faculty of Graduate Studies, Faculty of Agricultural and Food Sciences, Department of Soil Science, Winnipeg, MB R3T 2N2, Canada. Offers M Sc, PhD. *Degree requirements:* For master's, thesis; for doctorate, one foreign language, thesis/dissertation.

University of Minnesota, Twin Cities Campus, Graduate School, College of Food, Agricultural and Natural Resource Sciences, Land and Atmospheric Science Graduate Program, Saint Paul, MN 55108. Offers MS, PhD. Terminal master's awarded for partial completion of doctoral program. *Degree requirements:* For master's, comprehensive exam, thesis; for doctorate, comprehensive exam, thesis/dissertation. *Entrance requirements:* For master's and doctorate, GRE General Test, minimum GPA of 3.0. Additional exam requirements/recommendations for international students: Required—TOEFL (minimum score 550 paper-based; 79 iBT), IELTS (minimum score 6.5). Electronic applications accepted. *Faculty research:* Soil water and atmospheric resources, soil physical management, agricultural chemicals and their management, plant nutrient management, biological nitrogen fixation.

University of Missouri, Office of Research and Graduate Studies, College of Agriculture, Food and Natural Resources, Division of Plant Sciences, Columbia, MO 65211. Offers crop, soil and pest management (MS, PhD); entomology (MS, PhD); horticulture (MS, PhD); plant biology and genetics (MS, PhD); plant stress biology (MS, PhD). Terminal master's awarded for partial completion of doctoral program. *Degree requirements:* For master's, thesis; for doctorate, comprehensive exam, thesis/dissertation. *Entrance requirements:* For master's and doctorate, GRE General Test, minimum GPA of 3.0; bachelor's degree from accredited college. Additional exam requirements/recommendations for international students: Required—TOEFL (minimum score 500 paper-based; 61 iBT), IELTS (minimum score 5.5). Electronic applications accepted. *Faculty research:* Crop, soil and pest management; entomology; horticulture; plant biology and genetics; plant microbiology and pathology.

University of Missouri, Office of Research and Graduate Studies, School of Natural Resources, Department of Soil, Environmental, and Atmospheric Sciences, Columbia, MO 65211. Offers atmospheric science (MS, PhD); soil science (MS, PhD). *Degree requirements:* For doctorate, thesis/dissertation. *Entrance requirements:* For master's and doctorate, GRE General Test, minimum GPA of 3.0. Additional exam requirements/recommendations for international students: Required—TOEFL (minimum score 530 paper-based; 71 iBT). *Faculty research:* Soil physics; x-ray tomography of soil systems; use of radar in forecasting; soil and water conservation and management and applied soil physics; soil chemical and biogeochemical investigations; fresh water supply regimes (quantity, timing); water quality disturbance mechanisms; best management practices (BMP's); environmental biophysics and ecohydrology; hydrologic scaling, modeling, and change; synoptic and mesoscale dynamics.

University of Nebraska–Lincoln, Graduate College, College of Agricultural Sciences and Natural Resources, Department of Agronomy and Horticulture, Program in Agronomy, Lincoln, NE 68588. Offers MS, PhD. *Degree requirements:* For master's, thesis; for doctorate, comprehensive exam, thesis/dissertation. *Entrance requirements:* Additional exam requirements/recommendations for international students: Required—TOEFL (minimum score 500 paper-based). Electronic applications accepted. *Faculty research:* Crop physiology and production, plant breeding and genetics, range and forage management, soil and water science, weed science.

University of Puerto Rico, Mayagüez Campus, Graduate Studies, College of Agricultural Sciences, Department of Crops and Agroenvironmental Sciences, Mayagüez, PR 00681-9000. Offers agronomy (MS); crop protection (MS); horticulture (MS); soils (MS). *Program availability:* Part-time. *Degree requirements:* For master's, comprehensive exam, thesis.

University of Saskatchewan, College of Graduate Studies and Research, College of Agriculture, Department of Soil Science, Saskatoon, SK S7N 5A2, Canada. Offers M Ag, M Sc, PhD, Diploma. *Degree requirements:* For master's, thesis (for some programs); for doctorate, comprehensive exam (for some programs), thesis/dissertation. *Entrance requirements:* Additional exam requirements/recommendations for international students: Required—TOEFL (minimum score 80 iBT); Recommended—IELTS (minimum score 6.5).

Agronomy and Soil Science

University of Vermont, Graduate College, College of Agriculture and Life Sciences, Department of Plant and Soil Science, Burlington, VT 05405. Offers MS, PhD. *Degree requirements:* For master's, thesis; for doctorate, one foreign language, thesis/dissertation. *Entrance requirements:* For master's and doctorate, GRE General Test. Additional exam requirements/recommendations for international students: Required—TOEFL (minimum score 550 paper-based; 80 iBT). Electronic applications accepted. *Faculty research:* Soil chemistry, plant nutrition.

University of Wisconsin–Madison, Graduate School, College of Agricultural and Life Sciences, Department of Agronomy, Madison, WI 53706-1380. Offers agronomy (MS, PhD); plant breeding and plant genetics (MS, PhD). *Degree requirements:* For master's, thesis or alternative; for doctorate, thesis/dissertation. *Entrance requirements:* For master's and doctorate, GRE, minimum GPA of 3.0. Additional exam requirements/recommendations for international students: Required—TOEFL (minimum score 580 paper-based). Electronic applications accepted. *Expenses:* Tuition, state resident: full-time $5364. Tuition, nonresident: full-time $12,027. *Required fees:* $571. Tuition and fees vary according to campus/location, program and reciprocity agreements. *Faculty research:* Plant breeding and genetics, plant molecular biology and physiology, cropping systems and management, weed science.

University of Wisconsin–Madison, Graduate School, College of Agricultural and Life Sciences, Department of Soil Science, Madison, WI 53706. Offers MS, PhD. *Degree requirements:* For master's, comprehensive exam, thesis; for doctorate, comprehensive exam, thesis/dissertation. *Entrance requirements:* For master's and doctorate, GRE General Test. Additional exam requirements/recommendations for international students: Required—TOEFL. Electronic applications accepted. *Expenses:* Tuition, state resident: full-time $5364. Tuition, nonresident: full-time $12,027. *Required fees:* $571. Tuition and fees vary according to campus/location, program and reciprocity agreements. *Faculty research:* Soil characterization and mapping, fate of toxicants in the environment, soil microbiology, permafrost, water quality and quantity.

University of Wyoming, College of Agriculture and Natural Resources, Department of Plant Sciences, Laramie, WY 82071. Offers agronomy (MS, PhD). *Degree requirements:* For master's, thesis; for doctorate, thesis/dissertation. *Entrance requirements:* For master's and doctorate, GRE General Test, minimum GPA of 3.0. Additional exam requirements/recommendations for international students: Required—TOEFL (minimum score 525 paper-based). Electronic applications accepted. *Faculty research:* Crops, weeds, plant diseases.

University of Wyoming, College of Agriculture and Natural Resources, Department of Renewable Resources, Laramie, WY 82071. Offers agroecology (MS); entomology (MS, PhD); entomology/water resources (MS, PhD); rangeland ecology and watershed management (MS, PhD), including soil sciences (PhD), soil sciences and water resources (MS); rangeland ecology and watershed management/water resources (MS, PhD); soil science (MS); soil science/water resources (PhD). *Program availability:* Part-time. *Degree requirements:* For master's, comprehensive exam, thesis, oral examination; for doctorate, comprehensive exam, thesis/dissertation, preliminary oral and written exam, oral final exam. *Entrance requirements:* For master's and doctorate, GRE General Test, minimum GPA of 3.0. Additional exam requirements/recommendations for international students: Required—TOEFL. Electronic applications accepted. *Faculty research:* Plant control, grazing management, riparian restoration, riparian management, reclamation.

Utah State University, School of Graduate Studies, College of Agriculture, Department of Plants, Soils, and Biometeorology, Logan, UT 84322. Offers biometeorology (MS, PhD); ecology (MS, PhD); plant science (MS, PhD); soil science (MS, PhD). *Program availability:* Part-time. Terminal master's awarded for partial completion of doctoral program. *Degree requirements:* For master's, thesis; for doctorate, thesis/dissertation. *Entrance requirements:* For master's, GRE General Test, BS in plant, soil, atmospheric science, or related field; minimum GPA of 3.0; for doctorate, GRE General Test, minimum GPA of 3.0. Additional exam requirements/recommendations for international students: Required—TOEFL. Electronic applications accepted. *Faculty research:* Biotechnology and genomics, plant physiology and biology, nutrient and water efficient landscapes, physical-chemical-biological processes in soil, environmental biophysics and climate.

Virginia Polytechnic Institute and State University, Graduate School, College of Agriculture and Life Sciences, Blacksburg, VA 24061. Offers agricultural and applied economics (MS); agricultural and life sciences (MS); animal and poultry science (MS, PhD); crop and soil environmental sciences (MS, PhD); dairy science (MS); entomology (PhD); horticulture (MS, PhD); human nutrition, foods and exercise (MS, PhD); life sciences (MS, PhD); plant pathology, physiology and weed science (PhD). *Degree requirements:* For master's, comprehensive exam (for some programs), thesis (for some programs); for doctorate, comprehensive exam (for some programs), thesis/dissertation (for some programs). *Entrance requirements:* For master's and doctorate, GRE/GMAT (may vary by department). Additional exam requirements/recommendations for international students: Required—TOEFL (minimum score 550 paper-based). Electronic applications accepted.

Washington State University, College of Agricultural, Human, and Natural Resource Sciences, Department of Crop and Soil Sciences, Pullman, WA 99164. Offers crop sciences (MS, PhD); soil sciences (MS, PhD). Programs offered at the Pullman campus. Terminal master's awarded for partial completion of doctoral program. *Degree requirements:* For master's, comprehensive exam (for some programs), thesis (for some programs), oral exam; for doctorate, comprehensive exam, thesis/dissertation, oral exam, written exam. *Entrance requirements:* For master's, GRE, personal statement of educational goals and professional expectations, minimum GPA of 3.0, 3 letters of recommendation; for doctorate, GRE, personal statement of educational goals and professional expectations, minimum GPA of 3.0. Additional exam requirements/recommendations for international students: Required—TOEFL (minimum score 550 paper-based), IELTS. Electronic applications accepted. *Faculty research:* Environmental soils, soil/water quality, plant breeding genetics, plant nutrition/nutrient cycling, plant/seed metabolism.

West Virginia University, Davis College of Agriculture, Forestry and Consumer Sciences, Division of Plant and Soil Sciences, Program in Agricultural Sciences, Morgantown, WV 26506. Offers animal and food sciences (PhD); plant and soil sciences (PhD). *Degree requirements:* For doctorate, thesis/dissertation, oral and written exams. *Entrance requirements:* Additional exam requirements/recommendations for international students: Required—TOEFL. *Expenses:* Tuition, state resident: full-time $8568. Tuition, nonresident: full-time $22,140. Tuition and fees vary according to program. *Faculty research:* Ruminant nutrition, metabolism, forage utilization, physiology, reproduction.

Animal Sciences

Alcorn State University, School of Graduate Studies, School of Agriculture and Applied Science, Lorman, MS 39096-7500. Offers agricultural economics (MS Ag); agronomy (MS Ag); animal science (MS Ag). *Degree requirements:* For master's, thesis optional. *Faculty research:* Aquatic systems, dairy herd improvement, fruit production, alternative farming practices.

American University of Beirut, Graduate Programs, Faculty of Agricultural and Food Sciences, Beirut, Lebanon. Offers agricultural economics (MS); animal sciences (MS); ecosystem management (MSES); food technology (MS); irrigation (MS); nutrition (MS); plant protection (MS); plant science (MS); poultry science (MS); rural community development (MS). *Program availability:* Part-time. *Faculty:* 19 full-time (4 women). *Students:* 13 full-time (5 women), 55 part-time (41 women). Average age 26. 93 applicants, 52% accepted, 25 enrolled. In 2015, 27 master's awarded. *Degree requirements:* For master's, one foreign language, comprehensive exam, thesis (for some programs). *Entrance requirements:* Additional exam requirements/recommendations for international students: Required—TOEFL (minimum score 600 paper-based; 100 iBT), IELTS (minimum score 7.5). *Application deadline:* For fall admission, 2/10 for domestic and international students; for spring admission, 11/2 for domestic and international students. Application fee: $50. Electronic applications accepted. *Expenses:* Tuition, area resident: Full-time $16,254; part-time $903 per credit. *Required fees:* $699. Tuition and fees vary according to course load and program. *Financial support:* In 2015–16, 1 research assistantship with partial tuition reimbursement (averaging $1,800 per year), 48 teaching assistantships with tuition reimbursements (averaging $1,400 per year) were awarded; scholarships/grants, health care benefits, and unspecified assistantships also available. Financial award application deadline: 2/2. *Faculty research:* Developing skills in the field of integrated energy planning in med landscaper; profiling refugee households in Lebanon; Improving the nutrition of Syrian refugees and host communities though garden walls; monitoring and evaluation of salt iodization in Lebanon; mother and child cohorts: towards curbing the epidemic of non-communicable diseases in Qatar and Lebanon.. *Total annual research expenditures:* $852,730. *Unit head:* Prof. Nahla Hwalla, Dean, 961-1343002 Ext. 4400, Fax: 961-1744460, E-mail: nahla@aub.edu.lb. *Application contact:* Dr. Rabih Talhouk, Director, Graduate Council, 961-1350000 Ext. 4386, Fax: 961-1374374, E-mail: graduate.council@aub.edu.lb.
Website: http://www.aub.edu.lb/fafs/fafs_home/Pages/index.aspx

Angelo State University, College of Graduate Studies, College of Arts and Sciences, Department of Agriculture, San Angelo, TX 76909. Offers animal science (MS). *Program availability:* Part-time, evening/weekend. *Degree requirements:* For master's, comprehensive exam, thesis optional. *Entrance requirements:* For master's, GRE General Test, essay. Additional exam requirements/recommendations for international students: Required—TOEFL or IELTS. Electronic applications accepted. *Faculty research:* Effect of protein and energy on feedlot performance, bitterweed toxicosis in sheep, meat laboratory, North Concho Watershed Project, baseline vegetation.

Auburn University, Graduate School, College of Agriculture, Department of Animal Sciences, Auburn University, AL 36849. Offers M Ag, MS, PhD. *Program availability:* Part-time. *Faculty:* 18 full-time (7 women). *Students:* 14 full-time (7 women), 10 part-time (8 women); includes 1 minority (American Indian or Alaska Native, non-Hispanic/Latino), 4 international. Average age 24. 26 applicants, 50% accepted, 11 enrolled. In 2015, 8 master's, 2 doctorates awarded. *Degree requirements:* For master's, thesis (for some programs); for doctorate, thesis/dissertation. *Entrance requirements:* For master's and doctorate, GRE General Test. *Application deadline:* Applications are processed on a rolling basis. Application fee: $50 ($60 for international students). Electronic applications accepted. *Expenses:* Tuition, state resident: full-time $8802; part-time $489 per credit hour. Tuition, nonresident: full-time $26,406; part-time $1467 per credit hour. *Required fees:* $808 per semester. Tuition and fees vary according to degree level and program. *Financial support:* Research assistantships, teaching assistantships, and Federal Work-Study available. Support available to part-time students. Financial award application deadline: 3/15; financial award applicants required to submit FAFSA. *Faculty research:* Animal breeding and genetics, animal biochemistry and nutrition, physiology of reproduction, animal production. *Unit head:* Dr. L. Wayne Greene, Head, 334-844-1528. *Application contact:* Dr. George Flowers, Dean of the Graduate School, 334-844-2125.

Auburn University, Graduate School, College of Agriculture, Department of Poultry Science, Auburn University, AL 36849. Offers M Ag, MS, PhD. *Program availability:* Part-time. *Faculty:* 15 full-time (4 women). *Students:* 13 full-time (5 women), 12 part-time (8 women); includes 3 minority (1 Black or African American, non-Hispanic/Latino; 1 Asian, non-Hispanic/Latino; 1 Hispanic/Latino), 7 international. Average age 28. 25 applicants, 44% accepted, 6 enrolled. In 2015, 4 master's, 2 doctorates awarded. *Degree requirements:* For master's, thesis (for some programs); for doctorate, thesis/dissertation. *Entrance requirements:* For master's, GRE General Test; for doctorate, GRE General Test, MS. *Application deadline:* Applications are processed on a rolling basis. Application fee: $50 ($60 for international students). Electronic applications accepted. *Expenses:* Tuition, state resident: full-time $8802; part-time $489 per credit hour. Tuition, nonresident: full-time $26,406; part-time $1467 per credit hour. *Required fees:* $808 per semester. Tuition and fees vary according to degree level and program. *Financial support:* Research assistantships and Federal Work-Study available. Support available to part-time students. Financial award application deadline: 3/15; financial award applicants required to submit FAFSA. *Faculty research:* Poultry nutrition, poultry breeding, poultry physiology, poultry diseases and parasites, processing/food science. *Unit head:* Dr. Donald E. Conner, Head, 334-844-4133, E-mail: connede@auburn.edu. *Application contact:* Dr. George Flowers, Dean of the Graduate School, 334-844-2125. Website: http://www.ag.auburn.edu/poul/

Bergin University of Canine Studies, Program in Canine Life Sciences, Rohnert Park, CA 94928. Offers MS. *Program availability:* Online learning. *Degree requirements:* For master's, thesis or culminating project. *Expenses:* Tuition, area resident: Full-time $18,375. *Required fees:* $600. One-time fee: $300 full-time.

Boise State University, College of Arts and Sciences, Department of Biological Sciences, Boise, ID 83725-1515. Offers biology (MA, MS); biomolecular sciences (PhD); raptor biology (MS). *Program availability:* Part-time. *Faculty:* 26. *Students:* 51 full-time (23 women), 10 part-time (5 women); includes 7 minority (1 Black or African American, non-Hispanic/Latino; 1 American Indian or Alaska Native, non-Hispanic/Latino; 1 Asian, non-Hispanic/Latino; 3 Hispanic/Latino; 1 Native Hawaiian or other Pacific Islander, non-Hispanic/Latino), 6 international. Average age 30. 45 applicants, 27% accepted, 10 enrolled. In 2015, 13 master's awarded. *Degree requirements:* For master's, thesis. *Entrance requirements:* For master's, GRE General Test, minimum GPA of 3.0. Additional exam requirements/recommendations for international students: Required—TOEFL (minimum score 550 paper-based; 80 iBT), IELTS (minimum score 6). *Application deadline:* For fall admission, 1/15 for domestic and international students; for spring admission, 10/1 for domestic and international students. Application fee: $65 ($95 for international students). Electronic applications accepted. *Expenses:* Tuition, state resident: full-time $6058; part-time $358 per credit hour. Tuition, nonresident: full-time $20,108; part-time $608 per credit hour. *Required fees:* $2108. Tuition and fees vary according to program. *Financial support:* In 2015–16, 6 students received support, including 18 research assistantships (averaging $7,534 per year), 29 teaching assistantships (averaging $8,918 per year); institutionally sponsored loans and unspecified assistantships also available. Financial award application deadline: 1/15; financial award applicants required to submit FAFSA. *Faculty research:* Soil and stream microbial ecology, avian ecology. *Unit head:* Dr. Kevin Feris, Chair, 208-426-5498, E-mail: kevinferis@boisestate.edu. *Application contact:* Dr. Julie Heath, Graduate Coordinator, 208-426-3208, E-mail: julieheath@boisestate.edu.
Website: http://biology.boisestate.edu/graduate-programs/

Brigham Young University, Graduate Studies, College of Life Sciences, Department of Plant and Wildlife Sciences, Provo, UT 84604. Offers environmental science (MS); genetics and biotechnology (MS); wildlife and wildlands conservation (MS, PhD). *Faculty:* 24 full-time (1 woman), 1 (woman) part-time/adjunct. *Students:* 12 full-time (6 women), 31 part-time (9 women); includes 4 minority (1 Asian, non-Hispanic/Latino; 3 Hispanic/Latino). Average age 25. 25 applicants, 40% accepted, 9 enrolled. In 2015, 15 master's awarded. *Degree requirements:* For master's, thesis; for doctorate, comprehensive exam, thesis/dissertation, minimum GPA of 3.2, 54 hours (18 dissertation, 36 coursework). *Entrance requirements:* For master's, GRE General Test, minimum GPA of 3.2; for doctorate, GRE, minimum GPA of 3.2. Additional exam requirements/recommendations for international students: Required—TOEFL (minimum score 580 paper-based; 85 iBT). *Application deadline:* 2/1 for domestic and international students. Applications are processed on a rolling basis. Application fee: $50. Electronic applications accepted. *Financial support:* In 2015–16, 42 students received support, including 64 research assistantships with partial tuition reimbursements available (averaging $19,000 per year), 52 teaching assistantships with partial tuition reimbursements available (averaging $19,000 per year); scholarships/grants and tuition waivers (partial) also available. Financial award application deadline: 2/1. *Faculty research:* Environmental science, plant genetics, plant ecology, plant nutrition and pathology, wildlife and wildlands conservation. *Total annual research expenditures:* $2.8 million. *Unit head:* Brock R. McMillan, Chair, 801-422-3527, Fax: 801-422-0008, E-mail: brock_mcmillan@byu.edu. *Application contact:* Bradley D. Geary, Graduate Coordinator, 801-422-1228, Fax: 801-422-0008, E-mail: bradley_geary@byu.edu.
Website: http://pws.byu.edu/home/

California State University, Fresno, Division of Graduate Studies, College of Agricultural Sciences and Technology, Department of Animal Science and Agricultural Education, Fresno, CA 93740-8027. Offers animal science (MS). *Program availability:* Part-time, evening/weekend. *Degree requirements:* For master's, thesis. *Entrance requirements:* For master's, GRE General Test, minimum GPA of 3.0 in last 60 hours. Additional exam requirements/recommendations for international students: Required—TOEFL. Electronic applications accepted. *Faculty research:* Horse nutrition, animal health and welfare, electronic monitoring.

Clemson University, Graduate School, College of Agriculture, Forestry and Life Sciences, Department of Animal and Veterinary Sciences, Clemson, SC 29634-0311. Offers animal and veterinary sciences (MS, PhD). *Program availability:* Part-time. *Faculty:* 16 full-time (9 women), 1 part-time/adjunct (0 women). *Students:* 17 full-time (10 women), 7 part-time (4 women); includes 2 minority (1 Hispanic/Latino; 1 Two or more races, non-Hispanic/Latino), 4 international. Average age 29. 9 applicants, 78% accepted, 7 enrolled. In 2015, 5 master's, 1 doctorate awarded. *Degree requirements:* For master's, thesis (for some programs); for doctorate, comprehensive exam, thesis/dissertation. *Entrance requirements:* For master's and doctorate, GRE General Test, unofficial transcripts, letters of recommendation. Additional exam requirements/recommendations for international students: Required—TOEFL, IELTS (minimum score 7). *Application deadline:* For fall admission, 4/15 for domestic and international students; for spring admission, 10/15 for domestic students, 9/15 for international students. Applications are processed on a rolling basis. Application fee: $80 ($90 for international students). Electronic applications accepted. *Expenses:* $4,060 per semester full-time resident, $8,103 per semester full-time non-resident, $448 per credit hour part-time resident, $898 per credit hour part-time non-resident. *Financial support:* In 2015–16, 25 students received support, including 1 fellowship with partial tuition reimbursement available (averaging $5,000 per year), 12 research assistantships with partial tuition reimbursements available (averaging $13,792 per year), 12 teaching assistantships with partial tuition reimbursements available (averaging $10,714 per year); career-related internships or fieldwork and health care benefits also available. Financial award application deadline: 4/15. *Total annual research expenditures:* $265,131. *Unit head:* Dr. James Strickland, Department Chair, 864-656-3138, E-mail: jrstric@clemson.edu. *Application contact:* Dr. Peter Skewes, Graduate Program Coordinator, 864-656-4026, E-mail: pskewes@clemson.edu.

Colorado State University, College of Agricultural Sciences, Department of Animal Sciences, Fort Collins, CO 80523-1171. Offers MS, PhD. *Faculty:* 22 full-time (3 women), 1 (woman) part-time/adjunct. *Students:* 35 full-time (23 women), 14 part-time (9 women); includes 2 minority (both Hispanic/Latino), 11 international. Average age 28. 35 applicants, 34% accepted, 9 enrolled. In 2015, 11 master's, 1 doctorate awarded. *Degree requirements:* For master's, comprehensive exam, thesis, one article prepared for publication in a refereed scientific journal with degree candidate as senior author and approval of on-campus graduate committee consisting of three faculty members; for doctorate, comprehensive exam, thesis/dissertation, two articles prepared for publication in refereed scientific publication with degree candidate as senior author and approval of on-campus graduate committee consisting of three faculty members. *Entrance requirements:* For master's and doctorate, GRE General Test, minimum GPA of 3.0; reference letters; transcripts. Additional exam requirements/recommendations for international students: Required—TOEFL (minimum score 550 paper-based; 80 iBT), IELTS (minimum score 6.5). *Application deadline:* For fall admission, 4/1 priority date for domestic and international students; for spring admission, 9/1 for domestic and international students. Applications are processed on a rolling basis. Application fee: $60 ($70 for international students). Electronic applications accepted. *Expenses:* Tuition, state resident: full-time $9348. Tuition, nonresident: full-time $22,916. *Required fees:* $2174; $473.72 per credit hour. $236.86 per semester. Tuition and fees vary according to course load and program. *Financial support:* In 2015–16, 22 research assistantships with full tuition reimbursements (averaging $17,825 per year), 11 teaching assistantships with full tuition reimbursements (averaging $17,572 per year) were awarded; scholarships/grants and unspecified assistantships also available. Financial award application deadline: 2/15. *Faculty research:* Breeding and genetics, ruminant animal and equine reproduction, meat science and food safety, livestock/beef/dairy management systems, livestock behavior and welfare. *Total annual research expenditures:* $1.2 million. *Unit head:* Dr. Kevin Pond, Department Head, 970-491-7295, Fax: 970-491-5326, E-mail: kevin.pond@colostate.edu. *Application contact:* Melissa Harmon, Administrative Assistant III, 970-491-1442, Fax: 970-491-5326, E-mail: melissa.harmon@colostate.edu.
Website: http://ansci.agsci.colostate.edu/

Cornell University, Graduate School, Graduate Fields of Agriculture and Life Sciences, Field of Animal Science, Ithaca, NY 14853-0001. Offers animal genetics (MPS, MS, PhD); animal genomics (MPS, MS, PhD); animal nutrition (MPS, MS, PhD); animal science (MPS, MS); physiology of reproduction (MPS, MS, PhD). *Degree requirements:* For master's, thesis, teaching experience; for doctorate, comprehensive exam, thesis/dissertation, teaching experience. *Entrance requirements:* For master's and doctorate, 2 letters of recommendation. Additional exam requirements/recommendations for international students: Required—TOEFL (minimum score 550 paper-based; 77 iBT). Electronic applications accepted. *Faculty research:* Quantitative genetics, genetic improvement of animal populations, statistical genetics.

Dalhousie University, Faculty of Agriculture, Halifax, NS B3H 4R2, Canada. Offers agriculture (M Sc), including air quality, animal behavior, animal molecular genetics, animal nutrition, animal technology, aquaculture, botany, crop management, crop physiology, ecology, environmental microbiology, food science, horticulture, nutrient management, pest management, physiology, plant biotechnology, plant pathology, soil chemistry, soil fertility, waste management and composting, water quality. *Program availability:* Part-time. *Degree requirements:* For master's, thesis, ATC Exam Teaching Assistantship. *Entrance requirements:* For master's, honors B Sc, minimum GPA of 3.0. Additional exam requirements/recommendations for international students: Required—TOEFL (minimum score 580 paper-based; 92 iBT), IELTS, Michigan English Language Assessment Battery, CanTEST, CAEL. *Faculty research:* Bio-product development, organic agriculture, nutrient management, air and water quality, agricultural biotechnology.

Fort Valley State University, College of Graduate Studies and Extended Education, Program in Animal Science, Fort Valley, GA 31030. Offers MS. *Degree requirements:* For master's, thesis. *Entrance requirements:* For master's, GRE General Test. Additional exam requirements/recommendations for international students: Recommended—TOEFL.

Iowa State University of Science and Technology, Department of Animal Science, Ames, IA 50011. Offers animal breeding and genetics (MS, PhD); animal physiology (MS); animal psychology (PhD); animal science (MS, PhD); meat science (MS, PhD). *Degree requirements:* For master's, thesis or alternative; for doctorate, thesis/dissertation. *Entrance requirements:* For master's and doctorate, GRE General Test. Additional exam requirements/recommendations for international students: Required—TOEFL (minimum score 550 paper-based; 80 iBT), IELTS (minimum score 6.5). Electronic applications accepted. *Faculty research:* Animal breeding, animal nutrition, meat science, muscle biology, nutritional physiology.

Iowa State University of Science and Technology, Program in Animal Breeding and Genetics, Ames, IA 50011. Offers animal breeding and genetics (MS); immunogenetics (PhD); molecular genetics (PhD); quantitative genetics (PhD). *Entrance requirements:* For master's and doctorate, GRE. Additional exam requirements/recommendations for international students: Required—TOEFL (minimum score 550 paper-based; 80 iBT), IELTS (minimum score 6.5). Electronic applications accepted.

Iowa State University of Science and Technology, Program in Animal Physiology, Ames, IA 50011. Offers MS, PhD. *Entrance requirements:* For master's and doctorate, GRE. Additional exam requirements/recommendations for international students: Required—TOEFL (minimum score 550 paper-based; 80 iBT), IELTS (minimum score 6.5). Electronic applications accepted.

Iowa State University of Science and Technology, Program in Meat Science, Ames, IA 50011. Offers MS, PhD. *Entrance requirements:* For master's and doctorate, GRE. Additional exam requirements/recommendations for international students: Required—TOEFL (minimum score 550 paper-based; 80 iBT), IELTS (minimum score 6.5). Electronic applications accepted.

Kansas State University, Graduate School, College of Agriculture, Department of Animal Sciences and Industry, Manhattan, KS 66506. Offers meat science (PhD); monogastric nutrition (PhD); ruminant nutrition (MS, PhD). *Degree requirements:* For master's, comprehensive exam, thesis, oral exam; for doctorate, comprehensive exam, thesis/dissertation, preliminary exams. *Entrance requirements:* Additional exam requirements/recommendations for international students: Required—TOEFL (minimum score 550 paper-based; 79 iBT). Electronic applications accepted. *Faculty research:* Animal nutrition, animal physiology, meat science, animal genetics.

Louisiana State University and Agricultural & Mechanical College, Graduate School, College of Agriculture, School of Animal Sciences, Baton Rouge, LA 70803. Offers MS, PhD.

McGill University, Faculty of Graduate and Postdoctoral Studies, Faculty of Agricultural and Environmental Sciences, Department of Animal Science, Montréal, QC H3A 2T5, Canada. Offers M Sc, M Sc A, PhD.

Michigan State University, College of Veterinary Medicine and The Graduate School, Graduate Programs in Veterinary Medicine, Department of Large Animal Clinical Sciences, East Lansing, MI 48824. Offers MS, PhD. *Entrance requirements:* Additional exam requirements/recommendations for international students: Required—TOEFL (minimum score 550 paper-based), Michigan State University ELT (minimum score 85), Michigan English Language Assessment Battery (minimum score 83). Electronic applications accepted.

Michigan State University, College of Veterinary Medicine and The Graduate School, Graduate Programs in Veterinary Medicine, Department of Small Animal Clinical Sciences, East Lansing, MI 48824. Offers MS. *Degree requirements:* For master's, thesis. *Entrance requirements:* Additional exam requirements/recommendations for international students: Required—TOEFL, Michigan State University ELT (minimum score 85), Michigan English Language Assessment Battery (minimum score 83).

Michigan State University, The Graduate School, College of Agriculture and Natural Resources, Department of Animal Science, East Lansing, MI 48824. Offers animal science (MS, PhD); animal science-environmental toxicology (PhD). *Entrance requirements:* Additional exam requirements/recommendations for international

Animal Sciences

students: Required—TOEFL (minimum score 550 paper-based), Michigan State University ELT (minimum score 85), Michigan English Language Assessment Battery (minimum score 83). Electronic applications accepted.

Mississippi State University, College of Agriculture and Life Sciences, Department of Animal Dairy Sciences, Mississippi State, MS 39762. Offers agricultural life sciences (MS), including animal physiology (MS, PhD), genetics (MS, PhD); agricultural science (PhD), including animal dairy sciences, animal nutrition (MS, PhD); agriculture (MS), including animal nutrition (MS, PhD), animal science; life sciences (PhD), including animal physiology (MS, PhD), genetics (MS, PhD). *Faculty:* 18 full-time (6 women). *Students:* 15 full-time (10 women), 10 part-time (4 women); includes 1 minority (Black or African American, non-Hispanic/Latino), 7 international. Average age 28. 27 applicants, 44% accepted, 9 enrolled. In 2015, 7 master's, 2 doctorates awarded. *Degree requirements:* For master's, comprehensive exam (for some programs), thesis, written proposal of intended research area; for doctorate, comprehensive exam, thesis/dissertation, written proposal of intended research area. *Entrance requirements:* For master's, GRE General Test, minimum GPA of 3.0; for doctorate, GRE General Test. Additional exam requirements/recommendations for international students: Required— TOEFL (minimum score 575 paper-based; 84 iBT), IELTS (minimum score 7). *Application deadline:* For fall admission, 7/1 for domestic students, 5/1 for international students; for spring admission, 11/1 for domestic students, 9/1 for international students. Applications are processed on a rolling basis. Application fee: $60. Electronic applications accepted. *Expenses: Tuition,* area resident: Full-time $7502; part-time $833.74 per credit hour. Tuition, nonresident: full-time $20,142; part-time $2238.24 per credit hour. *Financial support:* In 2015–16, 10 research assistantships (averaging $13,661 per year) were awarded; Federal Work-Study, institutionally sponsored loans, and unspecified assistantships also available. Financial award application deadline: 4/1; financial award applicants required to submit FAFSA. *Faculty research:* Ecology and population dynamics, physiology, biochemistry and behavior, systematics. *Unit head:* Dr. John Blanton, Department Head, 662-325-2935, Fax: 662-325-8873, E-mail: jblanton@ads.msstate.edu. *Application contact:* Marina Hunt, Admissions Assistant, 662-325-5188, E-mail: mhunt@grad.msstate.edu.

Website: http://www.ads.msstate.edu/

Mississippi State University, College of Agriculture and Life Sciences, Department of Poultry Science, Mississippi State, MS 39762. Offers agricultural sciences (PhD), including poultry science (MS, PhD); agriculture (MS), including poultry science (MS, PhD). *Faculty:* 9 full-time (3 women). *Students:* 16 full-time (10 women), 2 part-time (1 woman); includes 1 minority (Black or African American, non-Hispanic/Latino), 10 international. Average age 27. 14 applicants, 64% accepted, 9 enrolled. In 2015, 4 master's, 1 doctorate awarded. *Degree requirements:* For master's, comprehensive exam, thesis optional; for doctorate, comprehensive exam, thesis/dissertation. *Entrance requirements:* Additional exam requirements/recommendations for international students: Required—TOEFL (minimum score 477 paper-based; 53 iBT); Recommended—IELTS (minimum score 4.5). *Application deadline:* For fall admission, 7/1 for domestic students, 5/1 for international students; for spring admission, 10/1 for domestic students, 11/1 for international students. Applications are processed on a rolling basis. Application fee: $60. Electronic applications accepted. *Expenses: Tuition, area resident:* Full-time $7502; part-time $833.74 per credit hour. Tuition, nonresident: full-time $20,142; part-time $2238.24 per credit hour. *Financial support:* In 2015–16, 17 research assistantships with partial tuition reimbursements (averaging $13,560 per year) were awarded; Federal Work-Study, institutionally sponsored loans, scholarships/ grants, and unspecified assistantships also available. Financial award application deadline: 4/1; financial award applicants required to submit FAFSA. *Unit head:* Dr. Mary Beck, Professor and Head, 662-325-5430, Fax: 662-325-8292, E-mail: mbeck@poultry.msstate.edu. *Application contact:* Marina Hunt, Admissions Assistant, 662-325-5188, E-mail: mhunt@grad.msstate.edu.

Website: http://www.poultry.msstate.edu/

Montana State University, The Graduate School, College of Agriculture, Department of Animal and Range Sciences, Bozeman, MT 59717. Offers MS, PhD. *Program availability:* Part-time. *Degree requirements:* For master's, comprehensive exam; for doctorate, comprehensive exam, thesis/dissertation. *Entrance requirements:* For master's, GRE, minimum GPA of 3.0; undergraduate coursework in animal science, range science or closely-related field; faculty adviser; for doctorate, GRE. Additional exam requirements/recommendations for international students: Required—TOEFL (minimum score 550 paper-based; 80 iBT). Electronic applications accepted. *Faculty research:* Rangeland ecology, wildlife habitat management, residual feed intake, post-partum effect of bulls, increasing efficiency of sheep production systems.

New Mexico State University, College of Agricultural, Consumer and Environmental Sciences, Department of Animal and Range Sciences, Las Cruces, NM 88003. Offers animal science (MS, PhD). *Program availability:* Part-time. *Faculty:* 16 full-time (4 women). *Students:* 28 full-time (21 women), 6 part-time (4 women); includes 6 minority (all Hispanic/Latino), 6 international. Average age 28. 34 applicants, 38% accepted, 11 enrolled. In 2015, 6 master's, 3 doctorates awarded. *Degree requirements:* For master's, thesis, seminar, experimental statistics; for doctorate, thesis/dissertation, research tool. *Entrance requirements:* For master's, minimum GPA of 3.0 in last 60 hours of undergraduate course work (MS), 3 reference letters, personal statement, resume, BS in animal science; for doctorate, minimum graduate GPA of 3.2, MS with thesis, 3 reference letters, personal statement, resume, BS in animal science. Additional exam requirements/recommendations for international students: Required—TOEFL (minimum score 550 paper-based; 79 iBT), IELTS (minimum score 6.5). *Application deadline:* For fall admission, 2/15 priority date for domestic and international students; for spring admission, 10/1 priority date for domestic and international students. Applications are processed on a rolling basis. Application fee: $40 ($50 for international students). Electronic applications accepted. *Expenses:* $274.50 per credit hour for in-state students, and all students enrolled in six or fewer credits; $839.30 per credit hour for out-of-state and international students enrolled in at least seven hours. *Financial support:* In 2015–16, 28 students received support, including 1 fellowship (averaging $4,088 per year), 5 research assistantships (averaging $18,803 per year), 19 teaching assistantships (averaging $17,702 per year); career-related internships or fieldwork, Federal Work-Study, scholarships/grants, traineeships, health care benefits, and unspecified assistantships also available. Support available to part-time students. Financial award application deadline: 3/1. *Faculty research:* Reproductive physiology, ruminant nutrition, nutrition toxicology, range ecology, land use hydrology. *Total annual research expenditures:* $3.4 million. *Unit head:* Dr. Glenn Duff, Department Head, 575-646-2515, Fax: 575-646-5441, E-mail: glennd@nmsu.edu. *Application contact:* Jenny Castillo, Graduate Advising, 575-646-2515, Fax: 575-646-5441, E-mail: cjenny@nmsu.edu.

Website: http://aces.nmsu.edu/academics/anrs

North Carolina Agricultural and Technical State University, School of Graduate Studies, School of Agriculture and Environmental Sciences, Department of Animal Sciences, Greensboro, NC 27411. Offers animal health science (MS).

North Carolina State University, Graduate School, College of Agriculture and Life Sciences, Department of Animal Science, Raleigh, NC 27695. Offers animal and poultry science (PhD); animal science (MS). *Degree requirements:* For master's, thesis optional. *Entrance requirements:* For master's, GRE, minimum GPA of 3.0. Electronic applications accepted. *Faculty research:* Nutrient utilization, mineral nutrition, genomics, endocrinology, reproductive physiology.

North Carolina State University, Graduate School, College of Agriculture and Life Sciences, Department of Poultry Science, Raleigh, NC 27695. Offers MS. *Program availability:* Part-time. *Degree requirements:* For master's, thesis. Electronic applications accepted. *Faculty research:* Reproductive physiology, nutrition, toxicology, immunology, molecular biology.

North Dakota State University, College of Graduate and Interdisciplinary Studies, College of Agriculture, Food Systems, and Natural Resources, Department of Animal Sciences, Fargo, ND 58102. Offers MS, PhD. *Degree requirements:* For master's, thesis; for doctorate, comprehensive exam, thesis/dissertation. *Entrance requirements:* For master's and doctorate, GRE General Test. Additional exam requirements/ recommendations for international students: Required—TOEFL (minimum score 71 iBT). *Faculty research:* Reproduction, nutrition, meat and muscle biology, breeding/ genetics.

The Ohio State University, Graduate School, College of Food, Agricultural, and Environmental Sciences, Department of Animal Sciences, Columbus, OH 43210. Offers MAS, MS, PhD. *Degree requirements:* For master's, thesis; for doctorate, thesis/ dissertation. *Entrance requirements:* For master's and doctorate, GRE General Test. Additional exam requirements/recommendations for international students: Required— TOEFL (minimum score 550 paper-based; 79 iBT), Michigan English Language Assessment Battery (minimum score 82); Recommended—IELTS (minimum score 7). Electronic applications accepted.

Oklahoma State University, College of Agricultural Science and Natural Resources, Department of Animal Science, Stillwater, OK 74078. Offers animal sciences (M Ag, MS); food science (MS, PhD). *Faculty:* 29 full-time (7 women), 1 part-time/adjunct (0 women). *Students:* 15 full-time (7 women), 55 part-time (24 women); includes 9 minority (1 American Indian or Alaska Native, non-Hispanic/Latino; 5 Hispanic/Latino; 3 Two or more races, non-Hispanic/Latino), 24 international. Average age 26. 54 applicants, 39% accepted, 17 enrolled. In 2015, 18 master's, 8 doctorates awarded. *Degree requirements:* For master's, thesis; for doctorate, comprehensive exam, thesis/ dissertation. *Entrance requirements:* For master's and doctorate, GRE or GMAT. Additional exam requirements/recommendations for international students: Required— TOEFL (minimum score 550 paper-based; 79 iBT). *Application deadline:* For fall admission, 3/1 priority date for international students; for spring admission, 8/1 priority date for international students. Applications are processed on a rolling basis. Application fee: $40 ($75 for international students). Electronic applications accepted. *Expenses:* Tuition, state resident: full-time $3528; part-time $196 per credit hour. Tuition, nonresident: full-time $14,144; part-time $785.75 per credit hour. *Required fees:* $1895; $105.25 per credit hour. Tuition and fees vary according to campus/location. *Financial support:* In 2015–16, 34 research assistantships (averaging $16,299 per year), 9 teaching assistantships (averaging $15,069 per year) were awarded; career-related internships or fieldwork, Federal Work-Study, scholarships/grants, health care benefits, tuition waivers (partial), and unspecified assistantships also available. Support available to part-time students. Financial award application deadline: 3/1; financial award applicants required to submit FAFSA. *Faculty research:* Quantitative trait loci identification for economical traits in swing/beef; waste management strategies in livestock; endocrine control of reproductive processes in farm animals; cholesterol synthesis, inhibition, and reduction; food safety research. *Unit head:* Dr. Clint Rusk, Department Head, 405-744-6062, Fax: 405-744-7390, E-mail: clint.rusk@okstate.edu.

Website: http://www.ansi.okstate.edu

Oregon State University, College of Agricultural Sciences, Program in Animal Sciences, Corvallis, OR 97331. Offers M Ag, MS, PhD. *Program availability:* Part-time. *Faculty:* 13 full-time (4 women). *Students:* 22 full-time (18 women), 2 part-time (0 women), 5 international. Average age 27. 33 applicants, 24% accepted, 6 enrolled. In 2015, 11 master's awarded. *Entrance requirements:* For master's and doctorate, GRE. Additional exam requirements/recommendations for international students: Required— TOEFL (minimum score 80 iBT), IELTS (minimum score 6.5). *Application deadline:* For fall admission, 4/1 for international students; for winter admission, 7/1 for international students; for spring admission, 10/1 for international students; for summer admission, 1/ 1 for international students. Application fee: $75 ($85 for international students). *Expenses:* Tuition, state resident: full-time $12,150; part-time $450 per credit. Tuition, nonresident: full-time $20,952; part-time $776 per credit. *Required fees:* $1572; $1443 per unit. One-time fee: $350. Tuition and fees vary according to course load, campus/ location and program. *Unit head:* Dr. John Killefer, Professor and Department Head, 541-737-1981.

Website: http://ans.oregonstate.edu/content/graduate-student-information

Penn State University Park, Graduate School, College of Agricultural Sciences, Department of Animal Science, University Park, PA 16802. Offers animal science (MPS, MS, PhD). *Unit head:* Dr. Richard T. Roush, Dean, 814-865-2541, Fax: 814-865-3103. *Application contact:* Lori Stania, Director, Graduate Student Services, 814-865-1795, Fax: 814-863-4627, E-mail: l-gswww@lists.psu.edu.

Website: http://animalscience.psu.edu/

Purdue University, Graduate School, College of Agriculture, Department of Animal Sciences, West Lafayette, IN 47907. Offers MS, PhD. *Program availability:* Part-time. Terminal master's awarded for partial completion of doctoral program. *Degree requirements:* For master's, thesis optional; for doctorate, thesis/dissertation. *Entrance requirements:* For master's, GRE General Test, minimum undergraduate GPA of 3.0 or equivalent; for doctorate, GRE General Test, minimum undergraduate GPA of 3.0 or equivalent; master's degree with minimum GPA of 3.0 or equivalent. Additional exam requirements/recommendations for international students: Required—TOEFL (minimum score 550 paper-based; 77 iBT), TWE. Electronic applications accepted. *Faculty research:* Genetics, meat science, nutrition, management, ethology.

Purdue University, Graduate School, College of Health and Human Sciences, Department of Nutrition Science, West Lafayette, IN 47907. Offers animal health (MS, PhD); biochemical and molecular nutrition (MS, PhD); growth and development (MS, PhD); human and clinical nutrition (MS, PhD); public health and education (MS, PhD). *Degree requirements:* For master's, thesis; for doctorate, thesis/dissertation. *Entrance requirements:* For master's and doctorate, GRE General Test (minimum scores in verbal and quantitative areas of 1000 or 300 on new scoring), minimum undergraduate GPA of 3.0 or equivalent. Additional exam requirements/recommendations for international students: Required—TOEFL (minimum score 600 paper-based; 77 iBT). Electronic applications accepted. *Faculty research:* Nutrient requirements, nutrient metabolism, nutrition and disease prevention.

Rutgers University–New Brunswick, Graduate School-New Brunswick, Program in Endocrinology and Animal Biosciences, Piscataway, NJ 08854-8097. Offers MS, PhD. Terminal master's awarded for partial completion of doctoral program. *Degree requirements:* For master's, thesis; for doctorate, comprehensive exam, thesis/dissertation. *Entrance requirements:* For master's and doctorate, GRE General Test. Additional exam requirements/recommendations for international students: Required—TOEFL. Electronic applications accepted. *Faculty research:* Comparative and behavioral endocrinology, epigenetic regulation of the endocrine system, exercise physiology and immunology, fetal and neonatal developmental programming, mammary gland biology and breast cancer, neuroendocrinology and alcohol studies, reproductive and developmental toxicology.

South Dakota State University, Graduate School, College of Agriculture and Biological Sciences, Department of Animal and Range Sciences, Brookings, SD 57007. Offers animal science (MS, PhD); biological sciences (PhD). *Program availability:* Part-time. *Degree requirements:* For master's, thesis, oral exam; for doctorate, comprehensive exam, thesis/dissertation, preliminary oral and written exams. *Entrance requirements:* Additional exam requirements/recommendations for international students: Required—TOEFL (minimum score 550 paper-based; 79 iBT). *Faculty research:* Ruminant and nonruminant nutrition, meat science, reproductive physiology, range utilization, ecology genetics, muscle biology, animal production.

South Dakota State University, Graduate School, College of Agriculture and Biological Sciences, Department of Dairy Science, Brookings, SD 57007. Offers animal sciences (MS, PhD); biological sciences (MS, PhD). *Program availability:* Part-time. *Degree requirements:* For master's, thesis, oral exam; for doctorate, comprehensive exam, thesis/dissertation, preliminary oral and written exams. *Entrance requirements:* Additional exam requirements/recommendations for international students: Required—TOEFL (minimum score 550 paper-based). *Faculty research:* Dairy cattle nutrition, energy metabolism, food safety, dairy processing technology.

Southern Illinois University Carbondale, Graduate School, College of Agriculture, Department of Animal Science, Food and Nutrition, Program in Animal Science, Carbondale, IL 62901-4701. Offers MS. *Faculty:* 12 full-time (4 women). *Students:* 11 full-time (7 women), 4 part-time (all women), 2 international. Average age 29. 13 applicants, 38% accepted, 5 enrolled. In 2015, 5 master's awarded. *Degree requirements:* For master's, thesis. *Entrance requirements:* For master's, GRE, minimum GPA of 2.7. Additional exam requirements/recommendations for international students: Required—TOEFL. *Application deadline:* For fall admission, 3/1 for domestic students; for spring admission, 9/2 for domestic students. Applications are processed on a rolling basis. Application fee: $65. *Financial support:* In 2015–16, 7 research assistantships with full tuition reimbursements, 2 teaching assistantships with full tuition reimbursements were awarded; fellowships with full tuition reimbursements, career-related internships or fieldwork, Federal Work-Study, institutionally sponsored loans, and tuition waivers (full) also available. Support available to part-time students. *Faculty research:* Nutrition, reproductive physiology, animal biotechnology, phytoestrogens and animal reproduction. *Unit head:* Dr. William Banz, Chair, 618-453-1763, E-mail: banz@siu.edu. *Application contact:* Terry Richardson, Administrative Clerk, 618-453-2329, E-mail: cerebus@siu.edu.
Website: http://coas.siu.edu/academics/departments/animal-science-food-nutrition/index.html

Sul Ross State University, Division of Agricultural and Natural Resource Science, Program in Animal Science, Alpine, TX 79832. Offers equine (M Ag, MS). *Program availability:* Part-time. *Students:* 17 full-time (9 women), 12 part-time (10 women); includes 8 minority (1 Black or African American, non-Hispanic/Latino; 1 American Indian or Alaska Native, non-Hispanic/Latino; 6 Hispanic/Latino). Average age 29. *Degree requirements:* For master's, thesis (for some programs). *Entrance requirements:* For master's, GRE General Test, minimum GPA of 2.5 in last 60 hours of undergraduate work. *Application deadline:* Applications are processed on a rolling basis. Application fee: $0 ($50 for international students). *Financial support:* Research assistantships, teaching assistantships, career-related internships or fieldwork, Federal Work-Study, and institutionally sponsored loans available. Support available to part-time students. Financial award application deadline: 5/1; financial award applicants required to submit FAFSA. *Faculty research:* Reproductive physiology, meat processing, animal nutrition, equine foot and motion studies, Spanish goat and Barbado sheep studies. *Unit head:* Dr. Paul Will, Chair, 432-837-8200, Fax: 432-837-8409, E-mail: pwill@sulross.edu. *Application contact:* Rose Enos, Administrative Secretary, 432-837-8201, Fax: 432-837-8409, E-mail: renos@sulross.edu.
Website: http://www.sulross.edu/pages/3222.asp

Texas A&M University, College of Agriculture and Life Sciences, Department of Animal Science, College Station, TX 77843. Offers animal breeding (MS, PhD); animal science (M Agr, MS, PhD); equine industry management (MEIM); physiology of reproduction (MS, PhD). *Faculty:* 29. *Students:* 107 full-time (74 women), 29 part-time (15 women); includes 17 minority (4 Black or African American, non-Hispanic/Latino; 1 American Indian or Alaska Native, non-Hispanic/Latino; 11 Hispanic/Latino; 1 Two or more races, non-Hispanic/Latino), 20 international. Average age 28. 61 applicants, 75% accepted, 38 enrolled. In 2015, 22 master's, 6 doctorates awarded. *Degree requirements:* For master's, thesis; for doctorate, thesis/dissertation. *Entrance requirements:* For master's and doctorate, GRE General Test. Additional exam requirements/recommendations for international students: Required—TOEFL (minimum score 550 paper-based; 80 iBT), IELTS (minimum score 6), PTE (minimum score 53). *Application deadline:* For fall admission, 2/1 priority date for domestic students; for spring admission, 10/1 priority date for domestic students. Applications are processed on a rolling basis. Application fee: $50 ($90 for international students). Electronic applications accepted. *Expenses:* Contact institution. *Financial support:* In 2015–16, 104 students received support, including 31 fellowships with tuition reimbursements available (averaging $5,417 per year), 35 research assistantships with tuition reimbursements available (averaging $5,181 per year), 29 teaching assistantships with tuition reimbursements available (averaging $5,060 per year); career-related internships or fieldwork, institutionally sponsored loans, scholarships/grants, traineeships, health care benefits, tuition waivers (full and partial), and unspecified assistantships also available. Support available to part-time students. Financial award application deadline: 3/15; financial award applicants required to submit FAFSA. *Faculty research:* Genetic engineering/gene markers, dietary effects on colon cancer, biotechnology. *Unit head:* Dr. H. Russell Cross, Professor and Head, 979-845-1543, Fax: 979-845-6433, E-mail: hrcross@tamu.edu. *Application contact:* Dr. David Forrest, Professor and Associate Head for Academic Programs, 979-845-1542, E-mail: d-forrest@tamu.edu.
Website: http://animalscience.tamu.edu/

Texas A&M University, College of Agriculture and Life Sciences, Department of Poultry Science, College Station, TX 77843. Offers poultry science (M Agr, MS, PhD). *Program availability:* Part-time, evening/weekend, blended/hybrid learning. *Faculty:* 11. *Students:* 34 full-time (13 women), 13 part-time (8 women); includes 10 minority (1 Black or African American, non-Hispanic/Latino; 1 Asian, non-Hispanic/Latino; 7 Hispanic/Latino; 1 Two or more races, non-Hispanic/Latino), 10 international. Average age 31. 12 applicants, 83% accepted, 9 enrolled. In 2015, 6 master's, 1 doctorate awarded. Terminal master's awarded for partial completion of doctoral program. *Degree requirements:* For master's, thesis (for some programs); for doctorate, thesis/dissertation. *Entrance requirements:* For master's and doctorate, GRE General Test. Additional exam requirements/recommendations for international students: Required—TOEFL (minimum score 550 paper-based; 80 iBT), IELTS (minimum score 6), PTE (minimum score 53). *Application deadline:* Applications are processed on a rolling basis. Application fee: $50 ($90 for international students). Electronic applications accepted. *Expenses:* Contact institution. *Financial support:* In 2015–16, 34 students received support, including 12 fellowships with tuition reimbursements available (averaging $14,333 per year), 10 research assistantships with tuition reimbursements available (averaging $5,094 per year), 1 teaching assistantship with tuition reimbursement available (averaging $5,400 per year); career-related internships or fieldwork, institutionally sponsored loans, scholarships/grants, traineeships, health care benefits, tuition waivers (full and partial), and unspecified assistantships also available. Support available to part-time students. Financial award application deadline: 3/15; financial award applicants required to submit FAFSA. *Faculty research:* Poultry diseases and immunology, avian genetics and physiology, nutrition and metabolism, poultry processing and food safety, waste management. *Unit head:* Dr. David Caldwell, Department Head/Professor, 979-845-1931, E-mail: caldwell@tamu.edu. *Application contact:* Graduate Admissions, 979-845-1060, E-mail: admissions@tamu.edu.
Website: http://posc.tamu.edu/

Texas A&M University–Kingsville, College of Graduate Studies, Dick and Mary Lewis Kleberg College of Agriculture, Natural Resources and Human Sciences, Department of Animal, Rangeland, and Wildlife Sciences, Program in Animal Science, Kingsville, TX 78363. Offers MS. *Degree requirements:* For master's, variable foreign language requirement, comprehensive exam, thesis or alternative. *Entrance requirements:* For master's, GRE (minimum score of 150 for each of the math and verbal sections), MAT, GMAT, minimum GPA of 3.0 for coursework from a previous degree. Additional exam requirements/recommendations for international students: Required—TOEFL (minimum score 550 paper-based; 79 iBT). Electronic applications accepted.

Texas Tech University, Graduate School, College of Agricultural Sciences and Natural Resources, Department of Animal and Food Sciences, Lubbock, TX 79409-2141. Offers animal science (MS, PhD); food science (MS). *Faculty:* 28 full-time (10 women). *Students:* 56 full-time (30 women), 17 part-time (8 women); includes 6 minority (5 Hispanic/Latino; 1 Two or more races, non-Hispanic/Latino), 20 international. Average age 27. 56 applicants, 20% accepted, 7 enrolled. In 2015, 14 master's, 11 doctorates awarded. *Degree requirements:* For master's, thesis or alternative; for doctorate, thesis/dissertation. *Entrance requirements:* For master's and doctorate, GRE. Additional exam requirements/recommendations for international students: Required—TOEFL (minimum score 550 paper-based; 79 iBT). *Application deadline:* For fall admission, 6/1 priority date for domestic students, 1/15 priority date for international students; for spring admission, 9/1 priority date for domestic students, 6/15 priority date for international students. Applications are processed on a rolling basis. Application fee: $60. Electronic applications accepted. *Expenses:* Tuition, state resident: full-time $6477; part-time $269.89 per credit hour. Tuition, nonresident: full-time $15,837; part-time $659.89 per credit hour. *Required fees:* $2751; $36.50 per credit hour. $937.50 per semester. Tuition and fees vary according to course level. *Financial support:* In 2015–16, 69 students received support, including 53 fellowships (averaging $2,744 per year), 59 research assistantships (averaging $11,622 per year), 6 teaching assistantships (averaging $14,378 per year); scholarships/grants and unspecified assistantships also available. Financial award applicants required to submit FAFSA. *Faculty research:* Nutrition, welfare and behavior, physiology and reproduction, muscle and meat biology, food safety, food security, companion animal, health and well-being. *Total annual research expenditures:* $3.6 million. *Unit head:* Dr. Michael Orth, Chair and Professor, 806-834-5653, Fax: 806-742-0898, E-mail: michael.orth@ttu.edu. *Application contact:* Sandra Gellner, Administrative Business Assistant, 806-834-0608, Fax: 806-742-0898, E-mail: sandra.gellner@ttu.edu.
Website: http://www.depts.ttu.edu/afs

Tufts University, Cummings School of Veterinary Medicine, Program in Conservation Medicine, Medford, MA 02155. Offers MS. *Degree requirements:* For master's, case study, preceptorship. *Entrance requirements:* For master's, GRE, official transcripts, curriculum vitae. Additional exam requirements/recommendations for international students: Required—TOEFL or IELTS. Electronic applications accepted. *Expenses: Tuition, area resident:* Full-time $48,412; part-time $1210 per credit hour. *Required fees:* $806. Full-time tuition and fees vary according to degree level, program and student level. Part-time tuition and fees vary according to course load. *Faculty research:* Non-invasive saliva collection techniques for free-ranging mountain gorillas and captive eastern gorillas, animal sentinels for infectious diseases.

Tuskegee University, Graduate Programs, College of Agriculture, Environment and Nutrition Sciences, Department of Agricultural and Environmental Sciences, Program in Animal and Poultry Sciences, Tuskegee, AL 36088. Offers animal and poultry breeding (MS); animal and poultry nutrition (MS); animal and poultry physiology (MS). *Degree requirements:* For master's, thesis. *Entrance requirements:* For master's, GRE General Test. Additional exam requirements/recommendations for international students: Required—TOEFL (minimum score 500 paper-based).

Universidad Nacional Pedro Henriquez Urena, Graduate School, Santo Domingo, Dominican Republic. Offers agricultural diversity (MS), including horticultural/fruit production, tropical animal production; conservation of monuments and cultural assets (M Arch); ecology and environment (MS); environmental engineering (MEE); international relations (MA); natural resource management (MS); political science (MA); project optimization (MPM); project feasibility (MPM); project management (MPM); sanitation engineering (ME); science for teachers (MS); tropical Caribbean architecture (M Arch).

Université Laval, Faculty of Agricultural and Food Sciences, Department of Animal Sciences, Programs in Animal Sciences, Québec, QC G1K 7P4, Canada. Offers M Sc, PhD. *Program availability:* Part-time. Terminal master's awarded for partial completion of doctoral program. *Degree requirements:* For master's, thesis; for doctorate, comprehensive exam, thesis/dissertation. *Entrance requirements:* For master's and doctorate, knowledge of French and English. Electronic applications accepted.

The University of Arizona, College of Agriculture and Life Sciences, Department of Animal Sciences, Tucson, AZ 85721. Offers MS, PhD. *Program availability:* Part-time. *Degree requirements:* For master's, thesis; for doctorate, thesis/dissertation. *Entrance requirements:* For master's, GRE Subject Test, 3 letters of recommendation, minimum GPA of 3.0; for doctorate, GRE Subject Test (biology or chemistry recommended), 3 letters of recommendation, statement of purpose, minimum GPA of 3.0. Additional exam requirements/recommendations for international students: Required—TOEFL (minimum score 550 paper-based; 79 iBT). *Application deadline:* Applications are processed on a rolling basis. Application fee: $75. Electronic applications accepted. *Financial support:* Fellowships, research assistantships, teaching assistantships, scholarships/grants,

health care benefits, and unspecified assistantships available. Financial award application deadline: 4/1. *Faculty research:* Nutrition of beef and dairy cattle, reproduction and breeding, muscle growth and function, animal stress, meat science. *Application contact:* 520-621-7623, E-mail: ans@ag.arizona.edu.
Website: http://animal.cals.arizona.edu/

University of Arkansas, Graduate School, Dale Bumpers College of Agricultural, Food and Life Sciences, Department of Animal Science, Fayetteville, AR 72701-1201. Offers MS, PhD. *Students:* 12 full-time (4 women), 15 part-time (7 women); includes 3 minority (1 Black or African American, non-Hispanic/Latino; 1 American Indian or Alaska Native, non-Hispanic/Latino; 1 Two or more races, non-Hispanic/Latino), 4 international. In 2015, 11 master's, 1 doctorate awarded. *Degree requirements:* For master's, thesis; for doctorate, variable foreign language requirement, thesis/dissertation. *Entrance requirements:* For master's, GRE General Test or minimum GPA of 2.7. *Application deadline:* For fall admission, 4/1 for international students; for spring admission, 10/1 for international students. Applications are processed on a rolling basis. Application fee: $40 ($50 for international students). Electronic applications accepted. *Financial support:* In 2015–16, 11 research assistantships, 2 teaching assistantships were awarded; fellowships with tuition reimbursements, career-related internships or fieldwork, and Federal Work-Study also available. Support available to part-time students. Financial award application deadline: 4/1; financial award applicants required to submit FAFSA. *Unit head:* Dr. Michael Looper, Chair, 479-575-4351, E-mail: looper@uark.edu. *Application contact:* Dr. Charles Rosenkrans, Graduate Coordinator, 479-575-4376, E-mail: crosenkr@uark.edu.
Website: http://animalscience.uark.edu

University of Arkansas, Graduate School, Dale Bumpers College of Agricultural, Food and Life Sciences, Department of Poultry Science, Fayetteville, AR 72701-1201. Offers MS, PhD. *Students:* 8 full-time (5 women), 39 part-time (17 women); includes 1 minority (Two or more races, non-Hispanic/Latino), 19 international. In 2015, 5 master's, 4 doctorates awarded. *Degree requirements:* For master's, thesis; for doctorate, variable foreign language requirement, thesis/dissertation. *Application deadline:* For fall admission, 4/1 for international students; for spring admission, 10/1 for international students. Applications are processed on a rolling basis. Application fee: $40 ($50 for international students). Electronic applications accepted. *Financial support:* In 2015–16, 25 research assistantships were awarded; fellowships with tuition reimbursements, teaching assistantships, career-related internships or fieldwork, and Federal Work-Study also available. Support available to part-time students. Financial award application deadline: 4/1; financial award applicants required to submit FAFSA. *Unit head:* Dr. Mike Kidd, Department Head, 479-575-4952, E-mail: mkidd@uark.edu. *Application contact:* Dr. John Marcy, Graduate Coordinator, 479-575-4952, E-mail: jmarcy@uark.edu.
Website: http://www.poultryscience.uark.edu/

The University of British Columbia, Faculty of Land and Food Systems, Applied Animal Biology Program, Vancouver, BC V6T 1Z1, Canada. Offers M Sc, PhD. *Degree requirements:* For master's, thesis; for doctorate, comprehensive exam, thesis/dissertation. *Entrance requirements:* Additional exam requirements/recommendations for international students: Required—TOEFL (minimum score 577 paper-based; 90 iBT), IELTS (minimum score 6.5). Electronic applications accepted. *Faculty research:* Animal production, animal behavior and welfare, reproductive physiology, animal genetics, aquaculture and fish physiology.

University of California, Davis, Graduate Studies, Graduate Group in Animal Biology, Davis, CA 95616. Offers MAM, MS, PhD. Terminal master's awarded for partial completion of doctoral program. *Degree requirements:* For master's, comprehensive exam (for some programs), thesis (for some programs); for doctorate, thesis/dissertation. *Entrance requirements:* For master's, GRE General Test, minimum GPA of 3.0. Additional exam requirements/recommendations for international students: Required—TOEFL (minimum score 550 paper-based). Electronic applications accepted. *Faculty research:* Genetics, nutrition, physiology and behavior in domestic and aquatic animals.

University of Connecticut, Graduate School, College of Agriculture and Natural Resources, Department of Animal Science, Storrs, CT 06269. Offers MS, PhD. Terminal master's awarded for partial completion of doctoral program. *Degree requirements:* For master's, comprehensive exam, thesis; for doctorate, comprehensive exam, thesis/dissertation. *Entrance requirements:* For master's and doctorate, GRE General Test, GRE Subject Test. Additional exam requirements/recommendations for international students: Required—TOEFL (minimum score 550 paper-based). Electronic applications accepted.

University of Delaware, College of Agriculture and Natural Resources, Department of Animal and Food Sciences, Newark, DE 19716. Offers animal sciences (MS, PhD); food sciences (MS). *Program availability:* Part-time. Terminal master's awarded for partial completion of doctoral program. *Degree requirements:* For master's, thesis; for doctorate, comprehensive exam, thesis/dissertation. *Entrance requirements:* For master's and doctorate, GRE General Test. Additional exam requirements/recommendations for international students: Required—TOEFL. Electronic applications accepted. *Faculty research:* Food chemistry, food microbiology, process engineering technology, packaging, food analysis, microbial genetics, molecular endocrinology, growth physiology, avian immunology and virology, monogastric nutrition, avian genomics.

University of Florida, Graduate School, College of Agricultural and Life Sciences, Department of Animal Sciences, Gainesville, FL 32611. Offers animal molecular and cellular biology (MS, PhD); animal sciences (MS, PhD). *Program availability:* Part-time. *Faculty:* 20 full-time, 1 part-time/adjunct. *Students:* 55 full-time (34 women), 4 part-time (3 women); includes 5 minority (all Hispanic/Latino), 24 international. Average age 28. 60 applicants, 32% accepted, 16 enrolled. In 2015, 13 master's, 3 doctorates awarded. *Degree requirements:* For master's, variable foreign language requirement, comprehensive exam (for some programs), thesis optional, one departmental and one exit seminar; for doctorate, comprehensive exam, thesis/dissertation, two departmental seminars, one exit seminar. *Entrance requirements:* For master's and doctorate, GRE General Test, minimum GPA of 3.0, 3 letters of recommendation. Additional exam requirements/recommendations for international students: Required—TOEFL (minimum score 550 paper-based; 80 iBT), IELTS (minimum score 6). *Application deadline:* For fall admission, 5/31 priority date for domestic students, 2/1 for international students; for winter admission, 9/1 for domestic students, 8/1 for international students; for spring admission, 10/31 priority date for domestic students, 12/1 for international students. Applications are processed on a rolling basis. Application fee: $30. Electronic applications accepted. *Financial support:* In 2015–16, 3 fellowships, 33 research assistantships were awarded; teaching assistantships also available. Financial award applicants required to submit FAFSA. *Faculty research:* Improving the quality, preservation and utilization of livestock feeds; reducing effects of stress on embryonic function, growth and lactation; optimizing muscle growth and composition and meat palatability and quality; improving lactation performance, health and fertility of beef and dairy cows; genetic and genomic analysis of production, reproduction, and health traits in livestock. *Total annual research expenditures:* $6.6 million. *Unit head:* Geoffrey E. Dahl, PhD, Professor and Department Chair, 352-392-1981, Fax: 352-392-5595, E-mail: gdahl@ufl.edu. *Application contact:* Adegbola Adesogan, PhD, Professor and Graduate Coordinator, 352-392-7527, E-mail: adesogan@ufl.edu.
Website: http://animal.ufl.edu/

University of Georgia, College of Agricultural and Environmental Sciences, Department of Animal and Dairy Sciences, Athens, GA 30602. Offers animal and dairy science (PhD); animal and dairy sciences (MADS); animal science (MS); dairy science (MS). *Degree requirements:* For master's, thesis; for doctorate, one foreign language, thesis/dissertation. *Entrance requirements:* For master's and doctorate, GRE General Test. Electronic applications accepted.

University of Georgia, College of Agricultural and Environmental Sciences, Department of Poultry Science, Athens, GA 30602. Offers animal nutrition (PhD); poultry science (MS, PhD). *Degree requirements:* For master's, thesis; for doctorate, one foreign language, thesis/dissertation. *Entrance requirements:* For master's and doctorate, GRE General Test. Electronic applications accepted.

University of Guelph, Graduate Studies, Ontario Agricultural College, Department of Animal and Poultry Science, Guelph, ON N1G 2W1, Canada. Offers M Sc, PhD. *Program availability:* Part-time. *Degree requirements:* For master's, thesis (for some programs); for doctorate, comprehensive exam, thesis/dissertation. *Entrance requirements:* For master's, minimum B- average during previous 2 years of course work; for doctorate, minimum B- average. Additional exam requirements/recommendations for international students: Required—TOEFL (minimum score 550 paper-based; 89 iBT), IELTS (minimum score 6.5). *Faculty research:* Animal breeding and genetics (quantitative or molecular), animal nutrition (monogastric or ruminant), animal physiology (environmental, reproductive or behavioral), behavior and welfare.

University of Hawaii at Manoa, Graduate Division, College of Tropical Agriculture and Human Resources, Department of Human Nutrition, Food and Animal Sciences, Program in Animal Sciences, Honolulu, HI 96822. Offers MS. *Program availability:* Part-time. *Faculty:* 19 full-time (6 women), 4 part-time/adjunct (2 women). *Students:* 8 full-time (7 women), 1 (woman) part-time; includes 7 minority (1 Asian, non-Hispanic/Latino; 1 Hispanic/Latino; 2 Native Hawaiian or other Pacific Islander, non-Hispanic/Latino; 3 Two or more races, non-Hispanic/Latino), 2 international. Average age 28. 5 applicants, 80% accepted, 4 enrolled. In 2015, 1 master's awarded. *Entrance requirements:* For master's, GRE General Test. Additional exam requirements/recommendations for international students: Required—TOEFL (minimum score 580 paper-based; 100 iBT), IELTS (minimum score 5). *Application deadline:* For fall admission, 2/1 for domestic and international students; for spring admission, 9/1 for domestic and international students. Application fee: $100. *Financial support:* In 2015–16, 6 students received support, including 2 fellowships (averaging $1,250 per year), 2 research assistantships with full tuition reimbursements available (averaging $16,824 per year); tuition waivers (full) also available. Financial award applicants required to submit FAFSA. *Faculty research:* Nutritional biochemistry, food composition, nutrition education, nutritional epidemiology, international nutrition, food toxicology. *Total annual research expenditures:* $413,000. *Unit head:* Douglas Vincent, Chair, 808-956-8393, E-mail: vincent@hawaii.edu. *Application contact:* Jinzeng Yang, Graduate Chairperson, 808-956-7095, Fax: 808-956-4024, E-mail: jinzeng@hawaii.edu.
Website: http://www.hawaii.edu/HIMB/

University of Idaho, College of Graduate Studies, College of Agricultural and Life Sciences, Department of Animal and Veterinary Science, Moscow, ID 83844-2330. Offers animal physiology (PhD); animal science (MS), including production. *Faculty:* 3 full-time. *Students:* 8 full-time, 8 part-time. Average age 30. In 2015, 6 master's, 1 doctorate awarded. *Degree requirements:* For doctorate, thesis/dissertation. *Entrance requirements:* For master's, GRE General Test, minimum GPA of 2.8; for doctorate, minimum undergraduate GPA of 2.8, graduate 3.0. *Application deadline:* For fall admission, 8/1 for domestic students; for spring admission, 12/15 for domestic students. Applications are processed on a rolling basis. Application fee: $60. Electronic applications accepted. *Expenses:* Tuition, state resident: full-time $6205; part-time $399 per credit hour. Tuition, nonresident: full-time $20,209; part-time $1177 per credit hour. *Required fees:* $2017; $58 per credit hour. Full-time tuition and fees vary according to course load and reciprocity agreements. *Financial support:* Research assistantships and teaching assistantships available. Financial award applicants required to submit FAFSA. *Faculty research:* Reproductive biology, muscle and growth physiology, meat science, aquaculture, ruminant nutrition. *Unit head:* Dr. Amin Ahmadzadeh, Interim Department Co-Chair, 208-885-6345, E-mail: avs-students@uidaho.edu. *Application contact:* Sean Scoggin, Graduate Recruitment Coordinator, 208-885-4001, Fax: 208-885-4406, E-mail: graduateadmissions@uidaho.edu.
Website: http://www.uidaho.edu/cals/avs

University of Illinois at Urbana–Champaign, Graduate College, College of Agricultural, Consumer and Environmental Sciences, Department of Animal Sciences, Champaign, IL 61820. Offers animal sciences (MS, PhD); bioinformatics: animal sciences (MS).

University of Kentucky, Graduate School, College of Agriculture, Food and Environment, Program in Animal and Food Sciences, Lexington, KY 40506-0032. Offers MS, PhD. Terminal master's awarded for partial completion of doctoral program. *Degree requirements:* For master's, comprehensive exam, thesis optional; for doctorate, comprehensive exam, thesis/dissertation. *Entrance requirements:* For master's, GRE General Test, minimum undergraduate GPA of 2.75; for doctorate, GRE General Test, minimum graduate GPA of 3.0. Additional exam requirements/recommendations for international students: Required—TOEFL (minimum score 550 paper-based). Electronic applications accepted. *Faculty research:* Nutrition of horses, cattle, swine, poultry, and sheep; physiology of reproduction and lactation; food science; microbiology.

University of Maine, Graduate School, College of Natural Sciences, Forestry, and Agriculture, School of Food and Agriculture, Orono, ME 04469. Offers animal sciences (MPS, MS); food and human nutrition (PhD); food science and human nutrition (MS); horticulture (MS); plant science (PhD). *Program availability:* Part-time. *Faculty:* 30 full-time (15 women). *Students:* 50 full-time (29 women), 2 part-time (both women); includes 3 minority (2 American Indian or Alaska Native, non-Hispanic/Latino; 1 Asian, non-Hispanic/Latino), 15 international. Average age 28. 81 applicants, 48% accepted, 20 enrolled. In 2015, 18 master's, 3 doctorates, 3 other advanced degrees awarded. *Degree requirements:* For master's, thesis (for some programs); for doctorate, comprehensive exam, thesis/dissertation. *Entrance requirements:* For master's and doctorate, GRE General Test. Additional exam requirements/recommendations for international students: Required—TOEFL. *Application deadline:* For fall admission, 2/1 priority date for domestic students. Applications are processed on a rolling basis. Application fee: $65. Electronic applications accepted. *Financial support:* In 2015–16, 36 students received support, including 1 fellowship (averaging $20,000 per year), 25 research assistantships with full tuition reimbursements available (averaging $14,600 per year), 7 teaching assistantships with full tuition reimbursements available (averaging $14,600 per year); Federal Work-Study, institutionally sponsored loans, and tuition

waivers (full and partial) also available. Financial award application deadline: 3/1. *Faculty research:* Nutrition education for adults and children, food processing, food safety, sustainable crop and soil management, animal health and nutrition. *Total annual research expenditures:* $1.9 million. *Unit head:* Dr. Sue Erich, Chair, 207-581-2947, Fax: 207-581-2770. *Application contact:* Scott G. Delcourt, Assistant Vice President for Graduate Studies and Senior Associate Dean, 207-581-3291, Fax: 207-581-3232, E-mail: graduate@maine.edu.
Website: http://umaine.edu/foodandagriculture

University of Manitoba, Faculty of Graduate Studies, Faculty of Agricultural and Food Sciences, Department of Animal Science, Winnipeg, MB R3T 2N2, Canada. Offers M Sc, PhD. *Degree requirements:* For master's, thesis; for doctorate, one foreign language, thesis/dissertation.

University of Maryland, College Park, Academic Affairs, College of Agriculture and Natural Resources, Department of Animal and Avian Sciences, Program in Animal Sciences, College Park, MD 20742. Offers MS, PhD. *Degree requirements:* For master's, thesis, oral exam or written comprehensive exam; for doctorate, thesis/dissertation, journal publication, scientific paper. *Entrance requirements:* For master's, GRE General Test, minimum GPA of 3.0; for doctorate, GRE General Test. Additional exam requirements/recommendations for international students: Required—TOEFL. Electronic applications accepted. *Faculty research:* Animal physiology, cell biology and biochemistry, reproduction, biometrics, animal behavior.

University of Massachusetts Amherst, Graduate School, College of Natural Sciences, Department of Animal Biotechnology and Biomedical Sciences, Amherst, MA 01003. Offers MS, PhD. *Program availability:* Part-time. Terminal master's awarded for partial completion of doctoral program. *Degree requirements:* For master's, thesis or alternative; for doctorate, comprehensive exam, thesis/dissertation. *Entrance requirements:* For doctorate, GRE General Test. Additional exam requirements/recommendations for international students: Required—TOEFL (minimum score 550 paper-based; 80 iBT), IELTS (minimum score 6.5). Electronic applications accepted.

University of Minnesota, Twin Cities Campus, Graduate School, College of Food, Agricultural and Natural Resource Sciences, Animal Sciences Graduate Program, St. Paul, MN 55108. Offers MS, PhD. *Program availability:* Part-time. Terminal master's awarded for partial completion of doctoral program. *Degree requirements:* For master's, comprehensive exam, thesis; for doctorate, comprehensive exam, thesis/dissertation. *Entrance requirements:* For master's and doctorate, GRE. Additional exam requirements/recommendations for international students: Required—TOEFL (minimum score 550 paper-based; 79 iBT), IELTS (minimum score 6.5). Electronic applications accepted. *Faculty research:* Physiology, growth biology, nutrition, genetics, production systems.

University of Missouri, Office of Research and Graduate Studies, College of Agriculture, Food and Natural Resources, Department of Animal Sciences, Columbia, MO 65211. Offers MS, PhD. Terminal master's awarded for partial completion of doctoral program. *Degree requirements:* For doctorate, 2 foreign languages, comprehensive exam, thesis/dissertation. *Entrance requirements:* For master's, GRE General Test (minimum scores: 146 verbal and 146 quantitative), minimum GPA of 3.0; for doctorate, GRE General Test (minimum score: Verbal 146, Quantitative 146), minimum GPA of 3.0; MS with thesis; 3 letters of recommendation. Additional exam requirements/recommendations for international students: Required—TOEFL (minimum score 500 paper-based; 61 iBT), IELTS (minimum score 5.5). Electronic applications accepted. *Faculty research:* Reproductive and environmental physiology; ruminant and monogastric nutrition; genetics/genomics; meat science and livestock production across swine, dairy cattle, beef cattle, poultry, companion animals and horses.

University of Nebraska–Lincoln, Graduate College, College of Agricultural Sciences and Natural Resources, Department of Animal Science, Lincoln, NE 68588. Offers MS, PhD. *Degree requirements:* For master's, thesis; for doctorate, comprehensive exam, thesis/dissertation. *Entrance requirements:* For master's and doctorate, GRE General Test. Additional exam requirements/recommendations for international students: Required—TOEFL (minimum score 525 paper-based). Electronic applications accepted. *Faculty research:* Animal breeding and genetics, meat and poultry products, nonruminant and ruminant nutrition, physiology.

University of Nevada, Reno, Graduate School, College of Agriculture, Biotechnology and Natural Resources, Department of Animal Science, Reno, NV 89557. Offers MS. *Degree requirements:* For master's, thesis optional. *Entrance requirements:* For master's, GRE, minimum GPA of 2.75. Additional exam requirements/recommendations for international students: Required—TOEFL (minimum score 500 paper-based; 61 iBT), IELTS (minimum score 6). Electronic applications accepted. *Faculty research:* Sperm fertility, embryo development, ruminant utilization of forages.

University of New Hampshire, Graduate School, College of Life Sciences and Agriculture, Department of Biological Sciences, Program in Animal Science, Durham, NH 03824. Offers MS. *Program availability:* Part-time. *Entrance requirements:* For master's, GRE General Test. Additional exam requirements/recommendations for international students: Required—TOEFL (minimum score 550 paper-based; 80 iBT). Electronic applications accepted.

University of New Hampshire, Graduate School, College of Life Sciences and Agriculture, Department of Molecular, Cellular and Biomedical Sciences, Program in Animal and Nutritional Sciences, Durham, NH 03824. Offers PhD. *Program availability:* Part-time. *Entrance requirements:* For doctorate, GRE. Additional exam requirements/recommendations for international students: Required—TOEFL (minimum score 550 paper-based; 80 iBT). Electronic applications accepted.

University of Puerto Rico, Mayagüez Campus, Graduate Studies, College of Agricultural Sciences, Department of Animal Industries, Mayagüez, PR 00681-9000. Offers MS. *Program availability:* Part-time. *Degree requirements:* For master's, comprehensive exam, thesis. *Entrance requirements:* For master's, minimum GPA of 2.75, BS in agricultural science or closely-related field. *Faculty research:* Swine production and nutrition, poultry production, dairy science and technology, microbiology.

University of Rhode Island, Graduate School, College of the Environment and Life Sciences, Department of Fisheries, Animal and Veterinary Science, Kingston, RI 02881. Offers animal health and disease (MS); animal science (MS); aquaculture (MS); aquatic pathology (MS); environmental sciences (PhD), including animal science, aquacultural science, aquatic pathology, fisheries science; fisheries (MS). *Faculty:* 10 full-time (3 women). *Degree requirements:* For master's, comprehensive exam (for some programs), thesis optional; for doctorate, comprehensive exam, thesis/dissertation. *Entrance requirements:* For master's and doctorate, GRE, 2 letters of recommendation. Additional exam requirements/recommendations for international students: Required—TOEFL (minimum score 550 paper-based). *Application deadline:* For fall admission, 7/15 for domestic students, 2/1 for international students; for spring admission, 11/15 for domestic students, 7/15 for international students. Application fee: $65. Electronic applications accepted. *Expenses:* Tuition, state resident: full-time $11,796; part-time $655 per credit. Tuition, nonresident: full-time $24,206; part-time $1345 per credit. *Required fees:* $1546; $44 per credit. One-time fee: $155 full-time; $35 part-time. *Financial support:* Application deadline: 2/1; applicants required to submit FAFSA. *Total annual research expenditures:* $1.2 million. *Unit head:* Dr. Marta Gomez-Chiarri, Chair, 401-874-2917, Fax: 401-874-7575, E-mail: gomezchi@uri.edu. *Application contact:* Graduate Admissions, 401-874-2872, E-mail: gradadm@etal.uri.edu.
Website: http://www.uri.edu/cels/favs/

University of Saskatchewan, College of Graduate Studies and Research, College of Agriculture, Department of Animal and Poultry Science, Saskatoon, SK S7N 5A2, Canada. Offers M Ag, M Sc, PhD. *Degree requirements:* For master's, thesis; for doctorate, thesis/dissertation. *Entrance requirements:* Additional exam requirements/recommendations for international students: Required—TOEFL.

University of Saskatchewan, Western College of Veterinary Medicine and College of Graduate Studies and Research, Graduate Programs in Veterinary Medicine, Department of Large Animal Clinical Sciences, Saskatoon, SK S7N 5A2, Canada. Offers M Sc, M Vet Sc, PhD. *Degree requirements:* For master's, thesis (for some programs); for doctorate, comprehensive exam (for some programs), thesis/dissertation. *Entrance requirements:* Additional exam requirements/recommendations for international students: Required—TOEFL (minimum score 80 iBT); Recommended—IELTS (minimum score 6.5). Electronic applications accepted. *Faculty research:* Reproduction, infectious diseases, epidemiology, food safety.

University of Saskatchewan, Western College of Veterinary Medicine and College of Graduate Studies and Research, Graduate Programs in Veterinary Medicine, Department of Small Animal Clinical Sciences, Saskatoon, SK S7N 5A2, Canada. Offers small animal clinical sciences (M Sc, PhD); veterinary anesthesiology, radiology and surgery (M Vet Sc); veterinary internal medicine (M Vet Sc). *Degree requirements:* For master's, thesis (for some programs); for doctorate, comprehensive exam (for some programs), thesis/dissertation. *Entrance requirements:* Additional exam requirements/recommendations for international students: Required—TOEFL (minimum score 80 iBT); Recommended—IELTS (minimum score 6.5). Electronic applications accepted. *Faculty research:* Orthopedics, wildlife, cardiovascular exercise/myelopathy, ophthalmology.

The University of Tennessee, Graduate School, College of Agricultural Sciences and Natural Resources, Department of Animal Science, Knoxville, TN 37996. Offers animal anatomy (PhD); breeding (MS, PhD); management (MS, PhD); nutrition (MS, PhD); physiology (MS, PhD). *Program availability:* Part-time. *Degree requirements:* For master's, thesis; for doctorate, thesis/dissertation. *Entrance requirements:* For master's and doctorate, GRE General Test, minimum GPA of 2.7. Additional exam requirements/recommendations for international students: Required—TOEFL. Electronic applications accepted.

University of Vermont, Graduate College, College of Agriculture and Life Sciences, Department of Animal Sciences, Burlington, VT 05405. Offers MS. *Degree requirements:* For master's, thesis. *Entrance requirements:* For master's, GRE General Test. Additional exam requirements/recommendations for international students: Required—TOEFL (minimum score 550 paper-based; 80 iBT). Electronic applications accepted. *Faculty research:* Animal nutrition, dairy production.

University of Vermont, Graduate College, College of Agriculture and Life Sciences, Program in Animal, Nutrition and Food Sciences, Burlington, VT 05405. Offers PhD. *Degree requirements:* For doctorate, one foreign language, thesis/dissertation. *Entrance requirements:* For doctorate, GRE General Test. Additional exam requirements/recommendations for international students: Required—TOEFL (minimum score 550 paper-based; 80 iBT). Electronic applications accepted.

University of Wisconsin–Madison, Graduate School, College of Agricultural and Life Sciences, Department of Animal Sciences, Madison, WI 53706-1380. Offers MS, PhD. *Program availability:* Part-time. Terminal master's awarded for partial completion of doctoral program. *Degree requirements:* For master's, thesis; for doctorate, thesis/dissertation. *Entrance requirements:* For master's and doctorate, GRE General Test. Additional exam requirements/recommendations for international students: Required—TOEFL (minimum score 550 paper-based; 80 iBT). Electronic applications accepted. *Expenses:* Tuition, state resident: full-time $5364. Tuition, nonresident: full-time $12,027. *Required fees:* $571. Tuition and fees vary according to campus/location, program and reciprocity agreements. *Faculty research:* Animal biology, immunity and toxicology, endocrinology and reproductive physiology, genetics-animal breeding, meat science, muscle biology.

University of Wisconsin–Madison, Graduate School, College of Agricultural and Life Sciences, Department of Dairy Science, Madison, WI 53706-1380. Offers MS, PhD. *Program availability:* Part-time. Terminal master's awarded for partial completion of doctoral program. *Degree requirements:* For master's, thesis; for doctorate, thesis/dissertation. *Entrance requirements:* For master's and doctorate, GRE General Test. Additional exam requirements/recommendations for international students: Required—TOEFL (minimum score 550 paper-based; 80 iBT). Electronic applications accepted. *Expenses:* Tuition, state resident: full-time $5364. Tuition, nonresident: full-time $12,027. *Required fees:* $571. Tuition and fees vary according to campus/location, program and reciprocity agreements. *Faculty research:* Genetics, nutrition, lactation, reproduction, management of dairy cattle.

University of Wyoming, College of Agriculture and Natural Resources, Department of Animal Sciences, Program in Animal Sciences, Laramie, WY 82071. Offers MS, PhD. *Degree requirements:* For master's, comprehensive exam, thesis; for doctorate, comprehensive exam, thesis/dissertation. *Entrance requirements:* For master's, GRE General Test, minimum GPA of 3.0; for doctorate, GRE General Test or MS degree, minimum GPA of 3.0. Additional exam requirements/recommendations for international students: Required—TOEFL (minimum score 525 paper-based). *Faculty research:* Reproductive biology, ruminant nutrition meat science, muscle biology, food microbiology, lipid metabolism.

Utah State University, School of Graduate Studies, College of Agriculture, Department of Animal, Dairy and Veterinary Sciences, Logan, UT 84322. Offers animal science (MS, PhD); bioveterinary science (MS, PhD); dairy science (MS). *Program availability:* Part-time. *Degree requirements:* For master's, thesis (for some programs); for doctorate, comprehensive exam, thesis/dissertation. *Entrance requirements:* For master's and doctorate, GRE General Test, minimum GPA of 3.0. Additional exam requirements/recommendations for international students: Required—TOEFL. Electronic applications accepted. *Faculty research:* Monoclonal antibodies, antiviral chemotherapy, management systems, biotechnology, rumen fermentation manipulation.

Virginia Polytechnic Institute and State University, Graduate School, College of Agriculture and Life Sciences, Blacksburg, VA 24061. Offers agricultural and applied economics (MS); agricultural and life sciences (MS); animal and poultry science (MS, PhD); crop and soil environmental sciences (MS, PhD); dairy science (MS); entomology (PhD); horticulture (MS, PhD); human nutrition, foods and exercise (MS, PhD); life

Animal Sciences

sciences (MS, PhD); plant pathology, physiology and weed science (PhD). *Degree requirements:* For master's, comprehensive exam (for some programs), thesis (for some programs); for doctorate, comprehensive exam (for some programs), thesis/dissertation (for some programs). *Entrance requirements:* For master's and doctorate, GRE/GMAT (may vary by department). Additional exam requirements/recommendations for international students: Required—TOEFL (minimum score 550 paper-based). Electronic applications accepted.

Washington State University, College of Agricultural, Human, and Natural Resource Sciences, Department of Animal Sciences, Pullman, WA 99164. Offers MS, PhD. Programs offered at the Pullman campus. *Program availability:* Part-time. *Degree requirements:* For master's, comprehensive exam, thesis, oral exam; for doctorate, comprehensive exam, thesis/dissertation, oral and written exam. *Entrance requirements:* For master's, GRE, minimum GPA of 3.0, 3 letters of recommendation, department questionnaire; for doctorate, GRE General Test, minimum GPA of 3.0. Additional exam requirements/recommendations for international students: Required—TOEFL, IELTS. Electronic applications accepted. *Faculty research:* Animal genomics, nutrition, reproduction, muscle biology and growth.

Washington State University, College of Veterinary Medicine, Paul G. Allen School for Global Animal Health, Pullman, WA 99164. Offers immunology and infectious diseases (MS, PhD). *Program availability:* Part-time. *Faculty:* 14 full-time (4 women), 13 part-time/ adjunct (6 women). *Students:* 20 full-time (9 women); includes 2 minority (1 Black or African American, non-Hispanic/Latino; 1 Native Hawaiian or other Pacific Islander, non-Hispanic/Latino). Average age 30. 2 applicants, 100% accepted, 2 enrolled. In 2015, 1 doctorate awarded. Terminal master's awarded for partial completion of doctoral program. *Degree requirements:* For master's, thesis, 30 credits of course work; for doctorate, thesis/dissertation, 15 credits of course work. *Entrance requirements:* Additional exam requirements/recommendations for international students: Required— TOEFL (minimum score 550 paper-based, 80 iBT), IELTS (7.0), or Michigan English Language Assessment Battery. *Application deadline:* For fall admission, 1/10 priority date for domestic and international students; for spring admission, 7/1 priority date for domestic and international students. Application fee: $75. Electronic applications accepted. *Financial support:* In 2015–16, 13 students received support, including 2 fellowships with full tuition reimbursements available (averaging $7,000 per year), 10 research assistantships with full tuition reimbursements available (averaging $23,544 per year), 1 teaching assistantship (averaging $21,738 per year); scholarships/grants and health care benefits also available. Financial award application deadline: 1/1;

financial award applicants required to submit FAFSA. *Faculty research:* Immunology, infectious disease, virology, disease surveillance, vaccine development. *Total annual research expenditures:* $6.8 million. *Unit head:* Dr. Guy H. Palmer, Director, Paul G. Allen School for Global Animal Health, 509-335-5861, Fax: 509-335-6328, E-mail: gpalmer@vetmed.wsu.edu. *Application contact:* Jill Griffin, Administrative Manager, 509-335-5861, Fax: 509-335-6328, E-mail: griffinj@vetmed.wsu.edu. Website: http://globalhealth.wsu.edu/

West Texas A&M University, College of Agriculture, Science and Engineering, Department of Agricultural Sciences, Emphasis in Animal Science, Canyon, TX 79016-0001. Offers MS. *Program availability:* Part-time. *Degree requirements:* For master's, comprehensive exam, thesis optional. *Entrance requirements:* For master's, GRE General Test. Additional exam requirements/recommendations for international students: Required—TOEFL (minimum score 550 paper-based). Electronic applications accepted. *Faculty research:* Nutrition, animal breeding, meat science, reproduction physiology, feedlots.

West Virginia University, Davis College of Agriculture, Forestry and Consumer Sciences, Division of Animal and Nutritional Sciences, Program in Animal and Nutritional Sciences, Morgantown, WV 26506. Offers breeding (MS); food sciences (MS); nutrition (MS); physiology (MS); production management (MS); reproduction (MS). *Program availability:* Part-time. *Degree requirements:* For master's, thesis, oral and written exams. *Entrance requirements:* For master's, GRE, minimum GPA of 2.5. Additional exam requirements/recommendations for international students: Required—TOEFL. *Expenses:* Tuition, state resident: full-time $8568. Tuition, nonresident: full-time $22,140. Tuition and fees vary according to program. *Faculty research:* Animal nutrition, reproductive physiology, food science.

West Virginia University, Davis College of Agriculture, Forestry and Consumer Sciences, Division of Plant and Soil Sciences, Program in Agricultural Sciences, Morgantown, WV 26506. Offers animal and food sciences (PhD); plant and soil sciences (PhD). *Degree requirements:* For doctorate, thesis/dissertation, oral and written exams. *Entrance requirements:* Additional exam requirements/recommendations for international students: Required—TOEFL. *Expenses:* Tuition, state resident: full-time $8568. Tuition, nonresident: full-time $22,140. Tuition and fees vary according to program. *Faculty research:* Ruminant nutrition, metabolism, forage utilization, physiology, reproduction.

Aquaculture

American University of Beirut, Graduate Programs, Faculty of Agricultural and Food Sciences, Beirut, Lebanon. Offers agricultural economics (MS); animal sciences (MS); ecosystem management (MSES); food technology (MS); irrigation (MS); nutrition (MS); plant protection (MS); plant science (MS); poultry science (MS); rural community development (MS). *Program availability:* Part-time. *Faculty:* 19 full-time (4 women). *Students:* 13 full-time (5 women), 55 part-time (41 women). Average age 26. 93 applicants, 52% accepted, 25 enrolled. In 2015, 27 master's awarded. *Degree requirements:* For master's, one foreign language, comprehensive exam, thesis (for some programs). *Entrance requirements:* Additional exam requirements/ recommendations for international students: Required—TOEFL (minimum score 600 paper-based; 100 iBT), IELTS (minimum score 7.5). *Application deadline:* For fall admission, 2/10 for domestic and international students; for spring admission, 11/2 for domestic and international students. Application fee: $50. Electronic applications accepted. *Expenses:* Tuition, area resident: Full-time $16,254; part-time $903 per credit. *Required fees:* $699. Tuition and fees vary according to course load and program. *Financial support:* In 2015–16, 1 research assistantship with partial tuition reimbursement (averaging $1,800 per year), 48 teaching assistantships with tuition reimbursements (averaging $1,400 per year) were awarded; scholarships/grants, health care benefits, and unspecified assistantships also available. Financial award application deadline: 2/2. *Faculty research:* Developing skills in the field of integrated energy planning in med landscaper; profiling refugee households in Lebanon; Improving the nutrition of Syrian refugees and host communities though garden walls; monitoring and evaluation of salt iodization in Lebanon; mother and child cohorts: towards curbing the epidemic of non-communicable diseases in Qatar and Lebanon.. *Total annual research expenditures:* $852,730. *Unit head:* Prof. Nahla Hwalla, Dean, 961-1343002 Ext. 4400, Fax: 961-1744460, E-mail: nahla@aub.edu.lb. *Application contact:* Dr. Rabih Talhouk, Director, Graduate Council, 961-1350000 Ext. 4386, Fax: 961-1374374, E-mail: graduate.council@aub.edu.lb.
Website: http://www.aub.edu.lb/fafs/fafs_home/Pages/index.aspx

Auburn University, Graduate School, College of Agriculture, Department of Fisheries and Allied Aquacultures, Auburn University, AL 36849. Offers M Aq, MS, PhD. *Program availability:* Part-time. *Faculty:* 19 full-time (2 women). *Students:* 46 full-time (19 women), 47 part-time (17 women); includes 3 minority (1 Hispanic/Latino; 2 Two or more races, non-Hispanic/Latino), 51 international. Average age 28. 31 applicants, 55% accepted, 15 enrolled. In 2015, 18 master's, 8 doctorates awarded. *Degree requirements:* For master's, thesis (for some programs); for doctorate, 2 foreign languages, thesis/dissertation. *Entrance requirements:* For master's and doctorate, GRE General Test. *Application deadline:* Applications are processed on a rolling basis. Application fee: $50 ($60 for international students). Electronic applications accepted. *Expenses:* Tuition, state resident: full-time $8802; part-time $489 per credit hour. Tuition, nonresident: full-time $26,406; part-time $1467 per credit hour. *Required fees:* $808 per semester. Tuition and fees vary according to degree level and program. *Financial support:* Fellowships, research assistantships, teaching assistantships, and Federal Work-Study available. Support available to part-time students. Financial award application deadline: 3/15; financial award applicants required to submit FAFSA. *Faculty research:* Channel catfish production; aquatic animal health; community and population ecology; pond management; production hatching, breeding and genetics. *Total annual research expenditures:* $8 million. *Unit head:* Dr. John Jensen, Interim Director/ Professor, 334-844-4786. *Application contact:* Dr. George Flowers, Dean of the Graduate School, 334-844-2125.
Website: http://www.ag.auburn.edu/fish/

Clemson University, Graduate School, College of Agriculture, Forestry and Life Sciences, Department of Forestry and Environmental Conservation, Program in Wildlife and Fisheries Biology, Clemson, SC 29634-0317. Offers MS, PhD. *Faculty:* 15 full-time (0 women). *Students:* 30 full-time (17 women), 6 part-time (3 women); includes 3 minority (1 Hispanic/Latino; 2 Two or more races, non-Hispanic/Latino), 4 international.

Average age 30. 19 applicants, 53% accepted, 9 enrolled. In 2015, 5 master's, 4 doctorates awarded. *Degree requirements:* For master's, thesis; for doctorate, thesis/ dissertation. *Entrance requirements:* For master's and doctorate, GRE General Test, unofficial transcripts, letters of recommendation. Additional exam requirements/ recommendations for international students: Required—TOEFL (minimum score 80 iBT), IELTS (minimum score 6.5). *Application deadline:* For fall admission, 4/15 for domestic and international students; for spring admission, 9/15 for domestic and international students. Applications are processed on a rolling basis. Application fee: $80 ($90 for international students). Electronic applications accepted. *Expenses:* $4,060 per semester full-time resident, $8,103 per semester full-time non-resident, $448 per credit hour part-time resident, $898 per credit hour part-time non-resident. *Financial support:* In 2015–16, 2 fellowships with partial tuition reimbursements (averaging $5,000 per year), 27 research assistantships with partial tuition reimbursements (averaging $16,856 per year), 7 teaching assistantships with partial tuition reimbursements (averaging $14,433 per year) were awarded; health care benefits also available. Financial award application deadline: 4/15. *Faculty research:* Intensive freshwater culture systems, conservation biology, stream management, applied wildlife management. *Unit head:* Dr. Gregg Yarrow, Department Chair, 864-656-3302, Fax: 864-656-3304, E-mail: gyarrow@clemson.edu. *Application contact:* Dr. Robert Baldwin, Graduate Program Coordinator, 864-656-3302, E-mail: baldwi6@clemson.edu. Website: http://www.clemson.edu/cafls/departments/fec/index.html

Dalhousie University, Faculty of Agriculture, Halifax, NS B3H 4R2, Canada. Offers agriculture (M Sc), including air quality, animal behavior, animal molecular genetics, animal nutrition, animal technology, aquaculture, botany, crop management, crop physiology, ecology, environmental microbiology, food science, horticulture, nutrient management, pest management, physiology, plant biotechnology, plant pathology, soil chemistry, soil fertility, waste management and composting, water quality. *Program availability:* Part-time. *Degree requirements:* For master's, thesis, ATC Exam Teaching Assistantship. *Entrance requirements:* For master's, honors B Sc, minimum GPA of 3.0. Additional exam requirements/recommendations for international students: Required— TOEFL (minimum score 580 paper-based; 92 iBT), IELTS, Michigan English Language Assessment Battery, CanTEST, CAEL. *Faculty research:* Bio-product development, organic agriculture, nutrient management, air and water quality, agricultural biotechnology.

Kentucky State University, College of Agriculture, Food Science and Sustainable Systems, Frankfort, KY 40601. Offers aquaculture (MS); environmental studies (MS). *Program availability:* Part-time, evening/weekend. *Faculty:* 11 full-time (1 woman). *Students:* 24 full-time (10 women), 9 part-time (6 women); includes 9 minority (6 Black or African American, non-Hispanic/Latino; 1 Asian, non-Hispanic/Latino; 1 Hispanic/Latino; 1 Two or more races, non-Hispanic/Latino), 1 international. Average age 30. 25 applicants, 84% accepted, 17 enrolled. In 2015, 12 master's awarded. *Degree requirements:* For master's, comprehensive exam, thesis. *Entrance requirements:* For master's, GRE, GMAT. Additional exam requirements/recommendations for international students: Required—TOEFL (minimum score 525 paper-based). *Application deadline:* Applications are processed on a rolling basis. Application fee: $30 ($100 for international students). Electronic applications accepted. *Expenses:* Tuition, state resident: full-time $7524; part-time $418 per credit hour. Tuition, nonresident: full-time $11,322; part-time $629 per credit hour. Tuition and fees vary according to course load. *Financial support:* In 2015–16, 11 students received support, including 24 research assistantships (averaging $21,061 per year); scholarships/grants, tuition waivers (partial), and unspecified assistantships also available. Financial award application deadline: 4/15; financial award applicants required to submit FAFSA. *Faculty research:* Nutritional requirements of fish and shrimp dex manipulation and ploidy manipulation of fishes. development of alternative aquaculture species. development of alternative aquaculture production system, genetics and molecular markers. *Total annual research expenditures:* $4.5 million. *Unit head:* Dr. Kirk Pomper, Interim Director

of Land Grant Programs, 502-597-5942, E-mail: kirk.pomper@kysu.edu. *Application contact:* Dr. James Obielodan, Director of Graduate Studies, 502-597-4723, E-mail: james.obielodan@kysu.edu.
Website: http://www.kysu.edu/academics/CAFSSS/

Memorial University of Newfoundland, School of Graduate Studies, Interdisciplinary Program in Aquaculture, St. John's, NL A1C 5S7, Canada. Offers M Sc. *Program availability:* Part-time. *Degree requirements:* For master's, thesis, seminar or thesis topic. *Entrance requirements:* For master's, honors B Sc or diploma in aquaculture from the Marine Institute of Memorial University of Newfoundland. *Application deadline:* For fall admission, 2/1 priority date for domestic students, 2/1 for international students; for winter admission, 4/1 priority date for domestic students, 4/1 for international students. Applications are processed on a rolling basis. Application fee: $50 Canadian dollars ($100 Canadian dollars for international students). Electronic applications accepted. *Expenses: Tuition, area resident:* Full-time $2199 Canadian dollars. *International tuition:* $2859 Canadian dollars full-time. *Financial support:* Fellowships, research assistantships, and teaching assistantships available. *Faculty research:* Marine fish larval biology, fin fish nutrition, shellfish culture, fin fish virology, fin fish reproductive biology. *Unit head:* Cyr Couturier, Graduate Officer, 709-778-0609, Fax: 709-778-3316, E-mail: cyr@mi.mun.ca. *Application contact:* Gail Kenny, Secretary, 709-864-8154, Fax: 709-864-3316, E-mail: gkenny@mun.ca.

Purdue University, Graduate School, College of Agriculture, Department of Forestry and Natural Resources, West Lafayette, IN 47907. Offers fisheries and aquatic sciences (MS, MSF, PhD); forest biology (MS, MSF, PhD); natural resource social science (MS, PhD); natural resources social science (MSF); quantitative ecology (MS, MSF, PhD); wildlife science (MS, MSF, PhD); wood products and wood products manufacturing (MS, MSF, PhD). *Degree requirements:* For master's, thesis; for doctorate, thesis/dissertation. *Entrance requirements:* For master's and doctorate, GRE General Test (minimum score: verbal 50th percentile; quantitative 50th percentile; analytical writing 4.0), minimum undergraduate GPA of 3.2 or equivalent. Additional exam requirements/recommendations for international students: Required—TOEFL (minimum score 550 paper-based; 77 iBT). Electronic applications accepted. *Faculty research:* Wildlife management, forest management, forest ecology, forest soils, limnology.

Texas A&M University–Corpus Christi, College of Graduate Studies, College of Science and Engineering, Program in Fisheries and Mariculture, Corpus Christi, TX 78412-5503. Offers MS. *Students:* 17 full-time (8 women), 6 part-time (3 women); includes 6 minority (1 Black or African American, non-Hispanic/Latino; 5 Hispanic/Latino), 2 international. Average age 28. 10 applicants, 30% accepted, 3 enrolled. In 2015, 3 master's awarded. *Degree requirements:* For master's, comprehensive exam, thesis (for some programs), thesis or project. *Entrance requirements:* For master's, GRE (taken within 5 years), essay (300-400 words), 3 letters of evaluation. Additional exam requirements/recommendations for international students: Required—TOEFL (minimum score 550 paper-based; 79 iBT), IELTS (minimum score 6.5). *Application deadline:* For fall admission, 2/1 priority date for domestic and international students; for spring admission, 8/1 priority date for domestic students, 6/1 priority date for international students; for summer admission, 2/1 priority date for domestic and international students. Applications are processed on a rolling basis. Application fee: $50 ($70 for international students). Electronic applications accepted. *Financial support:* Research assistantships, teaching assistantships, institutionally sponsored loans, scholarships/grants, health care benefits, and unspecified assistantships available. Support available to part-time students. Financial award application deadline: 3/15; financial award applicants required to submit FAFSA. *Unit head:* Dr. John Scarpa, Program Coordinator, 361-825-2369, E-mail: john.scarpa@tamucc.edu. *Application contact:* Graduate Admissions Coordinator, 361-825-2177, Fax: 361-825-2755, E-mail: gradweb@tamucc.edu.
Website: http://fama.tamucc.edu/

University of Arkansas at Pine Bluff, School of Agriculture, Fisheries and Human Sciences, Pine Bluff, AR 71601-2799. Offers aquaculture and fisheries (MS).

University of Florida, Graduate School, College of Agricultural and Life Sciences, School of Forest Resources and Conservation, Department of Fisheries and Aquatic Sciences, Gainesville, FL 32611. Offers MFAS, MS, PhD. *Program availability:* Part-time, online learning. *Faculty:* 63. *Students:* 32 full-time (15 women), 51 part-time (30 women); includes 5 minority (1 Black or African American, non-Hispanic/Latino; 1 American Indian or Alaska Native, non-Hispanic/Latino; 1 Asian, non-Hispanic/Latino; 2 Hispanic/Latino), 6 international. Average age 30. 40 applicants, 48% accepted, 18 enrolled. In 2015, 8 master's, 7 doctorates awarded. *Degree requirements:* For master's, thesis (for MS); technical paper (for MFAS); for doctorate, comprehensive exam, thesis/dissertation. *Entrance requirements:* For master's and doctorate, GRE General Test, minimum GPA of 3.0. Additional exam requirements/recommendations for international students: Required—TOEFL (minimum score 550 paper-based; 80 iBT), IELTS (minimum score 6). *Application deadline:* For fall admission, 6/1 for domestic students, 3/1 for international students; for spring admission, 10/1 for domestic students, 8/1 for international students. Applications are processed on a rolling basis. Application fee: $30. Electronic applications accepted. *Financial support:* Unspecified assistantships available. Financial award application deadline: 1/31; financial award applicants required to submit FAFSA. *Total annual research expenditures:* $1,921.
Website: http://sfrc.ufl.edu/fish/

University of Guelph, Graduate Studies, Ontario Agricultural College, Program in Aquaculture, Guelph, ON N1G 2W1, Canada. Offers M Sc. *Degree requirements:* For master's, practicum, research project. *Entrance requirements:* For master's, minimum B-average during previous 2 years of course work. *Faculty research:* Protein and amino acid metabolism, genetics, gamete cryogenics, pathology, epidemiology.

University of Rhode Island, Graduate School, College of the Environment and Life Sciences, Department of Fisheries, Animal and Veterinary Science, Kingston, RI 02881. Offers animal health and disease (MS); animal science (MS); aquaculture (MS); aquatic pathology (MS); environmental sciences (PhD), including animal science, aquacultural science, aquatic pathology, fisheries science; fisheries (MS). *Faculty:* 10 full-time (3 women). *Degree requirements:* For master's, comprehensive exam (for some programs), thesis optional; for doctorate, comprehensive exam, thesis/dissertation. *Entrance requirements:* For master's and doctorate, GRE, 2 letters of recommendation. Additional exam requirements/recommendations for international students: Required—TOEFL (minimum score 550 paper-based). *Application deadline:* For fall admission, 7/15 for domestic students, 2/1 for international students; for spring admission, 11/15 for domestic students, 7/15 for international students. Application fee: $65. Electronic applications accepted. *Expenses:* Tuition, state resident: full-time $11,796; part-time $655 per credit. Tuition, nonresident: full-time $24,206; part-time $1345 per credit. *Required fees:* $1546; $44 per credit. One-time fee: $155 full-time; $35 part-time. *Financial support:* Application deadline: 2/1; applicants required to submit FAFSA. *Total annual research expenditures:* $1.2 million. *Unit head:* Dr. Marta Gomez-Chiarri, Chair, 401-874-2917, Fax: 401-874-7575, E-mail: gomezchi@uri.edu. *Application contact:* Graduate Admissions, 401-874-2872, E-mail: gradadm@etal.uri.edu.
Website: http://www.uri.edu/cels/favs/

Food Science and Technology

Alabama Agricultural and Mechanical University, School of Graduate Studies, College of Agricultural, Life and Natural Sciences, Department of Food and Animal Sciences, Huntsville, AL 35811. Offers food science (MS, PhD). *Entrance requirements:* Additional exam requirements/recommendations for international students: Required—TOEFL (minimum score 500 paper-based; 61 iBT).

American University of Beirut, Graduate Programs, Faculty of Agricultural and Food Sciences, Beirut, Lebanon. Offers agricultural economics (MS); animal sciences (MS); ecosystem management (MSES); food technology (MS); irrigation (MS); nutrition (MS); plant protection (MS); plant science (MS); poultry science (MS); rural community development (MS). *Program availability:* Part-time. *Faculty:* 19 full-time (4 women). *Students:* 13 full-time (5 women), 55 part-time (41 women). Average age 26. 93 applicants, 52% accepted, 25 enrolled. In 2015, 27 master's awarded. *Degree requirements:* For master's, one foreign language, comprehensive exam, thesis (for some programs). *Entrance requirements:* Additional exam requirements/recommendations for international students: Required—TOEFL (minimum score 600 paper-based; 100 iBT), IELTS (minimum score 7.5). *Application deadline:* For fall admission, 2/10 for domestic and international students; for spring admission, 11/2 for domestic and international students. Application fee: $50. Electronic applications accepted. *Expenses: Tuition, area resident:* Full-time $16,254; part-time $903 per credit. *Required fees:* $699. Tuition and fees vary according to course load and program. *Financial support:* In 2015–16, 1 research assistantship with partial tuition reimbursement (averaging $1,800 per year), 48 teaching assistantships with tuition reimbursements (averaging $1,400 per year) were awarded; scholarships/grants, health care benefits, and unspecified assistantships also available. Financial award application deadline: 2/2. *Faculty research:* Developing skills in the field of integrated energy planning in med landscaper; profiling refugee households in Lebanon; Improving the nutrition of Syrian refugees and host communities though garden walls; monitoring and evaluation of salt iodization in Lebanon; mother and child cohorts: towards curbing the epidemic of non-communicable diseases in Qatar and Lebanon.. *Total annual research expenditures:* $852,730. *Unit head:* Prof. Nahla Hwalla, Dean, 961-1343002 Ext. 4400, Fax: 961-1744460, E-mail: nahla@aub.edu.lb. *Application contact:* Dr. Rabih Talhouk, Director, Graduate Council, 961-1350000 Ext. 4386, Fax: 961-1374374, E-mail: graduate.council@aub.edu.lb.
Website: http://www.aub.edu.lb/fafs/fafs_home/Pages/index.aspx

Auburn University, Graduate School, College of Human Sciences, Department of Nutrition and Food Science, Auburn University, AL 36849. Offers global hospitality and retailing (Graduate Certificate); nutrition (MS, PhD). *Program availability:* Part-time. *Faculty:* 14 full-time (6 women). *Students:* 38 full-time (33 women), 36 part-time (21 women); includes 11 minority (4 Black or African American, non-Hispanic/Latino; 1 American Indian or Alaska Native, non-Hispanic/Latino; 1 Asian, non-Hispanic/Latino; 3 Hispanic/Latino; 2 Two or more races, non-Hispanic/Latino), 22 international. Average age 30. 73 applicants, 64% accepted, 33 enrolled. In 2015, 7 master's, 5 doctorates awarded. *Degree requirements:* For master's, thesis (for some programs); for doctorate, thesis/dissertation. *Entrance requirements:* For master's and doctorate, GRE General Test. *Application deadline:* Applications are processed on a rolling basis. Application fee: $50 ($60 for international students). Electronic applications accepted. *Expenses:* Tuition, state resident: full-time $8802; part-time $489 per credit hour. Tuition, nonresident: full-time $26,406; part-time $1467 per credit hour. *Required fees:* $808 per semester. Tuition and fees vary according to degree level and program. *Financial support:* Research assistantships, teaching assistantships, career-related internships or fieldwork, and Federal Work-Study available. Support available to part-time students. Financial award application deadline: 3/15; financial award applicants required to submit FAFSA. *Faculty research:* Food quality and safety, diet, food supply, physical activity in maintenance of health, prevention of selected chronic disease states. *Unit head:* Dr. Martin O'Neill, Head, 334-844-3266. *Application contact:* Dr. George Flowers, Dean of the Graduate School, 334-844-2125.
Website: http://www.humsci.auburn.edu/ndhm/grad.php

Boston University, Metropolitan College, Program in Gastronomy, Boston, MA 02215. Offers business (MLA); communications (MLA); food policy (MLA); history and culture (MLA). *Program availability:* Part-time, evening/weekend. *Faculty:* 3 full-time (2 women), 14 part-time/adjunct (8 women). *Students:* 3 full-time (all women), 66 part-time (56 women); includes 9 minority (3 Asian, non-Hispanic/Latino; 5 Hispanic/Latino; 1 Two or more races, non-Hispanic/Latino), 6 international. Average age 30. 58 applicants, 76% accepted, 27 enrolled. In 2015, 34 master's awarded. *Degree requirements:* For master's, thesis optional. *Entrance requirements:* Additional exam requirements/recommendations for international students: Required—TOEFL. *Application deadline:* Applications are processed on a rolling basis. Application fee: $85. Electronic applications accepted. *Expenses:* Contact institution. *Financial support:* In 2015–16, 4 research assistantships (averaging $4,200 per year) were awarded; career-related internships or fieldwork, scholarships/grants, and unspecified assistantships also available. Support available to part-time students. Financial award applicants required to submit FAFSA. *Faculty research:* Food studies. *Unit head:* Dr. Ari Ariel, Assistant Professor & Faculty Coordinator, 617-353-6916, Fax: 617-353-4130, E-mail: gastrmla@bu.edu. *Application contact:* Barbara Rotger, Program Manager, 617-353-6916, Fax: 617-353-4130, E-mail: brotger@bu.edu.
Website: http://www.bu.edu/met/gastronomy

Brigham Young University, Graduate Studies, College of Life Sciences, Department of Nutrition, Dietetics and Food Science, Provo, UT 84602. Offers food science (MS); nutrition (MS). *Faculty:* 12 full-time (5 women). *Students:* 16 full-time (8 women); includes 1 minority (Asian, non-Hispanic/Latino). Average age 24. 12 applicants, 50%

accepted, 6 enrolled. In 2015, 2 master's awarded. *Degree requirements:* For master's, comprehensive exam, thesis. *Entrance requirements:* For master's, GRE General Test. Additional exam requirements/recommendations for international students: Required—TOEFL; Recommended—TSE. *Application deadline:* For fall admission, 2/1 priority date for domestic and international students; for winter admission, 6/30 priority date for domestic and international students. Application fee: $50. Electronic applications accepted. *Financial support:* In 2015–16, 6 students received support, including 6 research assistantships (averaging $20,325 per year), 6 teaching assistantships (averaging $20,325 per year); career-related internships or fieldwork, institutionally sponsored loans, and scholarships/grants also available. Financial award application deadline: 4/1. *Faculty research:* Dairy foods, lipid oxidation, food processes, magnesium and selenium nutrition, nutrient effect on gene expression. *Total annual research expenditures:* $326,945. *Unit head:* Dr. Michael L. Dunn, Chair, 801-422-6670, Fax: 801-422-0258, E-mail: michael_dunn@byu.edu. *Application contact:* Dr. Susan Fullmer, Graduate Coordinator, 801-422-3349, Fax: 801-422-0258, E-mail: susan_fullmer@byu.edu.
Website: http://ndfs.byu.edu/

California State University, Fresno, Division of Graduate Studies, College of Agricultural Sciences and Technology, Department of Food Science and Nutritional Sciences, Fresno, CA 93740-8027. Offers MS. *Program availability:* Part-time. *Degree requirements:* For master's, thesis. *Entrance requirements:* For master's, GRE General Test, minimum GPA of 3.0 in last 60 units. Additional exam requirements/recommendations for international students: Required—TOEFL. Electronic applications accepted. *Faculty research:* Liquid foods, analysis, mushrooms, gaseous ozone, natamycin.

California State University, Long Beach, Graduate Studies, College of Health and Human Services, Department of Family and Consumer Sciences, Master of Science in Nutritional Science Program, Long Beach, CA 90840. Offers food science (MS); hospitality foodservice and hotel management (MS); nutritional science (MS). *Program availability:* Part-time. *Degree requirements:* For master's, thesis, oral presentation of thesis or directed project. *Entrance requirements:* For master's, GRE, minimum GPA of 2.5 in last 60 units. Electronic applications accepted. *Faculty research:* Protein and water-soluble vitamins, sensory evaluation of foods, mineral deficiencies in humans, child nutrition, minerals and blood pressure.

Chapman University, Schmid College of Science and Technology, Food Science Program, Orange, CA 92866. Offers MS, MS/MBA. *Program availability:* Part-time, evening/weekend. *Faculty:* 4 full-time (3 women), 8 part-time/adjunct (6 women). *Students:* 12 full-time (9 women), 31 part-time (22 women); includes 12 minority (1 Black or African American, non-Hispanic/Latino; 10 Asian, non-Hispanic/Latino; 1 Hispanic/Latino), 10 international. Average age 26. 38 applicants, 71% accepted, 19 enrolled. In 2015, 22 master's awarded. *Degree requirements:* For master's, thesis or alternative. *Entrance requirements:* For master's, GRE or GMAT. Additional exam requirements/recommendations for international students: Required—TOEFL (minimum score 550 paper-based; 80 iBT). *Application deadline:* For fall admission, 5/1 priority date for domestic students. Applications are processed on a rolling basis. Application fee: $60. Electronic applications accepted. *Expenses:* $940 per unit. *Financial support:* Fellowships, research assistantships, teaching assistantships, Federal Work-Study, and scholarships/grants available. Financial award applicants required to submit FAFSA. *Unit head:* Dr. Anuradha Prakash, Program Director, 714-744-7895, E-mail: prakash@chapman.edu. *Application contact:* Monica Chen, Graduate Admission Counselor, 714-289-3590, E-mail: mchen@chapman.edu.

Clemson University, Graduate School, College of Agriculture, Forestry and Life Sciences, Department of Food, Nutrition and Packaging Sciences, Program in Food, Nutrition and Culinary Sciences, Clemson, SC 29634-0316. Offers MS. *Program availability:* Part-time. *Faculty:* 19 full-time (8 women). *Students:* 18 full-time (14 women), 3 part-time (all women); includes 3 minority (2 Black or African American, non-Hispanic/Latino; 1 Hispanic/Latino), 4 international. Average age 25. 42 applicants, 17% accepted, 5 enrolled. In 2015, 20 master's awarded. *Degree requirements:* For master's, thesis. *Entrance requirements:* For master's, GRE General Test, unofficial transcripts, letters of recommendation. Additional exam requirements/recommendations for international students: Required—TOEFL (minimum score 80 iBT), IELTS (minimum score 6.5). *Application deadline:* For fall admission, 6/1 for domestic students, 4/15 for international students; for spring admission, 9/15 for international students. Applications are processed on a rolling basis. Application fee: $80 ($90 for international students). Electronic applications accepted. *Expenses:* $4,060 per semester full-time resident, $8,103 per semester full-time non-resident, $448 per credit hour part-time resident, $898 per credit hour part-time non-resident. *Financial support:* In 2015–16, 16 students received support, including 8 research assistantships with partial tuition reimbursements available (averaging $12,450 per year), 7 teaching assistantships with partial tuition reimbursements available (averaging $14,142 per year); health care benefits and unspecified assistantships also available. Financial award application deadline: 2/15. *Unit head:* Dr. E. Jeffery Rhodehamel, Department Chair, 864-656-1211, Fax: 864-656-0331, E-mail: jrhode@clemson.edu. *Application contact:* Dr. Paul Dawson, Graduate Coordinator, 864-656-1138, E-mail: pdawson@clemson.edu.
Website: http://www.clemson.edu/cafls/departments/fnps/graduate/

Clemson University, Graduate School, College of Agriculture, Forestry and Life Sciences, Department of Food, Nutrition and Packaging Sciences and Department of Animal and Veterinary Sciences, Program in Food Technology, Clemson, SC 29634-0316. Offers PhD. *Program availability:* Part-time. *Faculty:* 19 full-time (8 women). *Students:* 19 full-time (15 women), 7 part-time (4 women); includes 4 minority (2 Black or African American, non-Hispanic/Latino; 2 Hispanic/Latino), 12 international. Average age 33. 15 applicants, 27% accepted, 3 enrolled. In 2015, 3 doctorates awarded. *Degree requirements:* For doctorate, comprehensive exam, thesis/dissertation. *Entrance requirements:* For doctorate, GRE General Test, unofficial transcripts, letters of recommendation. Additional exam requirements/recommendations for international students: Required—TOEFL (minimum score 80 iBT), IELTS (minimum score 6.5). *Application deadline:* For fall admission, 6/1 for domestic students, 4/15 for international students. Applications are processed on a rolling basis. Application fee: $80 ($90 for international students). Electronic applications accepted. *Expenses:* $4,060 per semester full-time resident, $8,103 per semester full-time non-resident, $448 per credit hour part-time resident, $898 per credit hour part-time non-resident. *Financial support:* In 2015–16, 15 students received support, including 2 fellowships with partial tuition reimbursements available (averaging $2,500 per year), 8 research assistantships with partial tuition reimbursements available (averaging $14,435 per year), 5 teaching assistantships with partial tuition reimbursements available (averaging $14,800 per year); institutionally sponsored loans and health care benefits also available. Financial award application deadline: 2/15. *Unit head:* Dr. E. Jeffery Rhodehamel, Department Chair, 864-656-1211, Fax: 864-656-0331, E-mail: jrhode@clemson.edu. *Application contact:* Dr. Paul Dawson, Graduate Coordinator, 864-656-1138, E-mail: pdawson@clemson.edu.
Website: http://www.clemson.edu/cafls/departments/fnps/graduate/

Colorado State University, College of Health and Human Sciences, Department of Food Science and Human Nutrition, Fort Collins, CO 80523-1571. Offers MS, PhD. *Accreditation:* AND. *Program availability:* Part-time, 100% online, blended/hybrid learning. *Faculty:* 18 full-time (11 women). *Students:* 40 full-time (31 women), 54 part-time (48 women); includes 11 minority (1 American Indian or Alaska Native, non-Hispanic/Latino; 2 Asian, non-Hispanic/Latino; 5 Hispanic/Latino; 3 Two or more races, non-Hispanic/Latino), 1 international. Average age 32. 124 applicants, 36% accepted, 29 enrolled. In 2015, 24 master's, 5 doctorates awarded. Terminal master's awarded for partial completion of doctoral program. *Degree requirements:* For master's, thesis; for doctorate, thesis/dissertation. *Entrance requirements:* For master's, GRE (minimum 50th percentile), minimum GPA of 3.0 overall and in science classes, transcripts, three letters of recommendation, statement of purpose, resume; for doctorate, GRE (minimum 50th percentile), minimum GPA of 3.0, transcripts, three letters of recommendation, statement of purpose, resume. Additional exam requirements/recommendations for international students: Required—TOEFL (minimum score 550 paper-based; 80 iBT), IELTS (minimum score 6.5). *Application deadline:* For fall admission, 2/1 priority date for domestic and international students. Application fee: $60 ($70 for international students). Electronic applications accepted. *Expenses:* $545 per credit hour tuition for online program. *Financial support:* In 2015–16, 21 students received support, including 1 fellowship with partial tuition reimbursement available (averaging $34,848 per year), 13 research assistantships with partial tuition reimbursements available (averaging $13,608 per year), 11 teaching assistantships with partial tuition reimbursements available (averaging $11,815 per year); Federal Work-Study, scholarships/grants, and unspecified assistantships also available. Financial award application deadline: 2/1; financial award applicants required to submit FAFSA. *Faculty research:* Community nutrition, bioactive compounds, nutrition and obesity, nutrition and health disparities, fatty acids and obesity-related disorders. *Total annual research expenditures:* $1.7 million. *Unit head:* Dr. Michael Pagliassotti, Professor and Department Head, 970-491-1390, Fax: 970-491-3875, E-mail: michael.pagliassotti@colostate.edu. *Application contact:* Paula Coleman, Administrative Assistant, 970-491-3819, Fax: 970-491-3875, E-mail: paula.coleman@colostate.edu.
Website: http://www.fshn.chhs.colostate.edu/

Cornell University, Graduate School, Graduate Fields of Agriculture and Life Sciences, Field of Food Science and Technology, Ithaca, NY 14853-0001. Offers dairy science (MPS, MS, PhD); enology (MS, PhD); food chemistry (MPS, MS, PhD); food engineering (MPS, MS, PhD); food microbiology (MPS, MS, PhD); food processing waste technology (MPS, MS, PhD); food science (MFS, MPS, MS, PhD); international food science (MPS, MS, PhD); sensory evaluation (MPS, MS, PhD). Terminal master's awarded for partial completion of doctoral program. *Degree requirements:* For master's, thesis (MS), teaching experience; for doctorate, comprehensive exam, thesis/dissertation, teaching experience. *Entrance requirements:* For master's and doctorate, GRE General Test, 3 letters of recommendation. Additional exam requirements/recommendations for international students: Required—TOEFL (minimum score 550 paper-based; 77 iBT). Electronic applications accepted. *Faculty research:* Food microbiology/biotechnology, food engineering/processing, food safety/toxicology, sensory science/flavor chemistry, food packaging.

Dalhousie University, Faculty of Agriculture, Halifax, NS B3H 4R2, Canada. Offers agriculture (M Sc), including air quality, animal behavior, animal molecular genetics, animal nutrition, animal technology, aquaculture, botany, crop management, crop physiology, ecology, environmental microbiology, food science, horticulture, nutrient management, pest management, physiology, plant biotechnology, plant pathology, soil chemistry, soil fertility, waste management and composting, water quality. *Program availability:* Part-time. *Degree requirements:* For master's, thesis, ATC Exam Teaching Assistantship. *Entrance requirements:* For master's, honors B Sc, minimum GPA of 3.0. Additional exam requirements/recommendations for international students: Required—TOEFL (minimum score 580 paper-based; 92 iBT), IELTS, Michigan English Language Assessment Battery, CanTEST, CAEL. *Faculty research:* Bio-product development, organic agriculture, nutrient management, air and water quality, agricultural biotechnology.

Dalhousie University, Faculty of Engineering, Department of Food Science and Technology, Halifax, NS B3J 1Z1, Canada. Offers M Sc, PhD. *Degree requirements:* For master's, thesis; for doctorate, thesis/dissertation. *Entrance requirements:* Additional exam requirements/recommendations for international students: Required—TOEFL, IELTS, CANTEST, CAEL, or Michigan English Language Assessment Battery. Electronic applications accepted. *Faculty research:* Food microbiology, food safety/HALLP, rheology and rheometry, food processing, seafood processing.

Drexel University, Goodwin College of Professional Studies, School of Technology and Professional Studies, Philadelphia, PA 19104-2875. Offers construction management (MS); creativity and innovation (MS); engineering technology (MS); food science (MS); hospitality management (MS); professional studies: creativity studies (MS); professional studies: e-learning leadership (MS); professional studies: homeland security management (MS); project management (MS); property management (MS); sport management (MS). *Program availability:* Part-time, evening/weekend. *Entrance requirements:* Additional exam requirements/recommendations for international students: Required—TOEFL, IELTS. Electronic applications accepted. Application fee is waived when completed online.

Florida State University, The Graduate School, College of Human Sciences, Department of Nutrition, Food and Exercise Sciences, Tallahassee, FL 32306-1493. Offers exercise physiology (MS, PhD); nutrition and food science (MS, PhD), including clinical nutrition (MS), food science, human nutrition (PhD), nutrition education and health promotion (MS), nutrition science (MS); sports nutrition (MS); sports sciences (MS). *Program availability:* Part-time. *Faculty:* 20 full-time (9 women). *Students:* 89 full-time (51 women), 5 part-time (3 women); includes 12 minority (2 Black or African American, non-Hispanic/Latino; 1 Asian, non-Hispanic/Latino; 4 Hispanic/Latino; 5 Two or more races, non-Hispanic/Latino), 17 international. Average age 28. 185 applicants, 40% accepted, 31 enrolled. In 2015, 38 master's, 3 doctorates awarded. *Degree requirements:* For master's, comprehensive exam (for some programs), thesis optional; for doctorate, thesis/dissertation. *Entrance requirements:* For master's, GRE General Test, minimum upper-division GPA of 3.0; for doctorate, GRE General Test, minimum upper-division GPA of 3.0, MS. Additional exam requirements/recommendations for international students: Required—TOEFL (minimum score 550 paper-based; 80 iBT). *Application deadline:* For fall admission, 4/1 for domestic and international students; for spring admission, 10/1 for domestic and international students. Applications are processed on a rolling basis. Application fee: $30. Electronic applications accepted. *Expenses: Tuition, area resident:* Full-time $7263; part-time $403.50 per credit hour. Tuition, nonresident: full-time $18,087; part-time $1004.85 per credit hour. *Required fees:* $1365; $75.81 per credit hour. $20 per semester. Tuition and fees vary according to campus/location. *Financial support:* In 2015–16, 48 students received support, including 20 research assistantships with full tuition reimbursements available (averaging $5,975 per year), 37 teaching assistantships with full tuition reimbursements available (averaging $9,477 per year); career-related internships or fieldwork, Federal Work-Study, institutionally sponsored loans, scholarships/grants, and unspecified

assistantships also available. Financial award application deadline: 2/1; financial award applicants required to submit FAFSA. *Faculty research:* Body composition, functional food, chronic disease and aging response; food safety, food allergy, and safety/quality detection methods; sports nutrition, energy and human performance; strength training, functional performance, cardiovascular physiology, sarcopenia. *Total annual research expenditures:* $543,728. *Unit head:* Dr. Robert J. Moffatt, Professor/Interim Chair, 850-644-1520, Fax: 850-645-5000, E-mail: rmoffatt@fsu.edu. *Application contact:* Ann R. Smith, Office Administrator, 850-644-1828, Fax: 850-645-5000, E-mail: asmith@fsu.edu.
Website: http://www.chs.fsu.edu/Departments/Nutrition-Food-Exercise-Sciences

Framingham State University, Continuing Education, Programs in Food and Nutrition, Food Science and Nutrition Science Program, Framingham, MA 01701-9101. Offers MS. *Program availability:* Part-time, evening/weekend. *Entrance requirements:* For master's, GRE General Test.

Illinois Institute of Technology, Graduate College, School of Applied Technology, Institute for Food Safety and Health, Bedford Park, IL 60501-1957. Offers food process engineering (MFPE, MS); food safety and technology (MFST, MS). *Program availability:* Part-time. *Degree requirements:* For master's, comprehensive exam (for some programs), thesis (for some programs). *Entrance requirements:* For master's, GRE (minimum score 304), minimum undergraduate GPA of 3.0. Additional exam requirements/recommendations for international students: Required—TOEFL (minimum score 550 paper-based; 80 iBT). Electronic applications accepted. *Faculty research:* Microbial food safety and security, food virology, interfacial colloidal phenomena, development of DNA-based methods for detection, differentiation and tracking of food borne pathogens in food systems and environment, appetite and obesity management and vascular disease.

Iowa State University of Science and Technology, Department of Food Science and Human Nutrition, Ames, IA 50011. Offers food science and technology (MS, PhD); nutrition (MS, PhD). *Degree requirements:* For master's, thesis; for doctorate, thesis/dissertation. *Entrance requirements:* For master's and doctorate, GRE General Test. Additional exam requirements/recommendations for international students: Required—TOEFL (minimum score 550 paper-based; 79 iBT), IELTS (minimum score 6.5). Electronic applications accepted.

Kansas State University, Graduate School, College of Agriculture, Food Science Institute, Manhattan, KS 66506. Offers MS, PhD. *Program availability:* Part-time, online learning. *Degree requirements:* For master's, thesis, residency; for doctorate, thesis/dissertation, preliminary exams, residency. *Entrance requirements:* For master's, GRE General Test, minimum undergraduate GPA of 3.0, course work in mathematics; for doctorate, GRE General Test, minimum GPA of 3.5 in master's course work. Additional exam requirements/recommendations for international students: Required—TOEFL (minimum score 550 paper-based; 90 iBT), IELTS (minimum score 7). Electronic applications accepted. *Faculty research:* Food safety and defense, food chemistry, ingredient technology, food nutrients and bioactive compounds, new product development, meat and dairy technology, sensory evaluation, food microbiology.

London Metropolitan University, Graduate Programs, London, United Kingdom. Offers applied psychology (M Sc); architecture (MA); biomedical science (M Sc); blood science (M Sc); cancer pharmacology (M Sc); computer networking and cyber security (M Sc); computing and information systems (M Sc); conference interpreting (MA); counter-terrorism studies (M Sc); creative, digital and professional writing (MA); crime, violence and prevention (M Sc); criminology (M Sc); curating contemporary art (MA); data analytics (M Sc); digital media (MA); early childhood studies (MA); education (MA, Ed D); financial services law, regulation and compliance (LL M); food science (M Sc); forensic psychology (M Sc); health and social care management and policy (M Sc); human nutrition (M Sc); human resource management (MA); human rights and international conflict (MA); information technology (M Sc); intelligence and security studies (M Sc); international oil, gas and energy law (LL M); international relations (MA); interpreting (MA); learning and teaching in higher education (MA); legal practice (LL M); media and entertainment law (LL M); organizational and consumer psychology (M Sc); psychological therapy (M Sc); psychology of mental health (M Sc); public health (M Sc); public policy and management (MPA); security studies (M Sc); social work (M Sc); spatial planning and urban design (MA); sports therapy (M Sc); supporting older children and young people with dyslexia (MA); teaching languages (MA), including Arabic, English; translation (MA); woman and child abuse (MA).

Louisiana State University and Agricultural & Mechanical College, Graduate School, College of Agriculture, Department of Food Science, Baton Rouge, LA 70803. Offers MS, PhD.

Marlboro College, Graduate and Professional Studies, Program in Business Administration, Marlboro, VT 05344. Offers collaborative leadership (MBA); conscious business (MBA); mission driven organizations (MBA); project management (MBA); social innovation (MBA); sustainable food systems (MBA). *Program availability:* Part-time, evening/weekend, blended/hybrid learning. *Faculty:* 12 part-time/adjunct (5 women). *Students:* 4 full-time (3 women), 7 part-time (3 women). Average age 38. 10 applicants, 50% accepted, 4 enrolled. In 2015, 7 master's awarded. *Degree requirements:* For master's, 60 credits including capstone project. *Entrance requirements:* For master's, letter of intent, essay, transcripts, 2 letters of recommendation. *Application deadline:* For fall admission, 7/1 priority date for domestic students; for winter admission, 11/1 priority date for domestic students. Applications are processed on a rolling basis. Application fee: $0. Electronic applications accepted. *Expenses:* $765 per credit. *Financial support:* Applicants required to submit FAFSA. *Unit head:* Patricia Daniel, Degree Chair, 802-451-7511, Fax: 802-258-9201, E-mail: pdaniel@gradschool.marlboro.edu. *Application contact:* Matthew Livingston, Assistant Director of Graduate Admissions, 802-258-9209, Fax: 802-258-9201, E-mail: bmcneice@marlboro.edu.
Website: https://www.marlboro.edu/academics/graduate/mba

McGill University, Faculty of Graduate and Postdoctoral Studies, Faculty of Agricultural and Environmental Sciences, Department of Food Science and Agricultural Chemistry, Montréal, QC H3A 2T5, Canada. Offers M Sc, PhD.

Memorial University of Newfoundland, School of Graduate Studies, Department of Biochemistry, St. John's, NL A1C 5S7, Canada. Offers biochemistry (M Sc, PhD); food science (M Sc, PhD). *Program availability:* Part-time. *Degree requirements:* For master's, thesis; for doctorate, comprehensive exam, thesis/dissertation, oral defense of thesis. *Entrance requirements:* For master's, 2nd class degree in related field; for doctorate, M Sc. *Application deadline:* For fall admission, 3/1 for domestic and international students; for winter admission, 7/1 for domestic and international students; for spring admission, 11/1 for domestic and international students. Applications are processed on a rolling basis. Application fee: $50 Canadian dollars ($100 Canadian dollars for international students). Electronic applications accepted. *Expenses: Tuition, area resident:* Full-time $2199 Canadian dollars. *International tuition:* $2859 Canadian dollars full-time. *Financial support:* Fellowships, research assistantships, and teaching assistantships available. *Faculty research:* Toxicology, cell and molecular biology, food engineering, marine biotechnology, lipid biology. *Total annual research expenditures:* $1.1 million. *Unit head:* Dr. Mark D. Berry, Head, 709-864-8529, E-mail: biochead@mun.ca. *Application contact:* Dr. Robert Bertolo, Graduate Officer, 709-864-7954, Fax: 709-864-2422, E-mail: biochem@mun.ca.
Website: http://www.mun.ca/biochem

Michigan State University, College of Veterinary Medicine and The Graduate School, Graduate Programs in Veterinary Medicine, National Food Safety and Toxicology Center, East Lansing, MI 48824. Offers food safety (MS). *Entrance requirements:* Additional exam requirements/recommendations for international students: Required—TOEFL, Michigan State University ELT (minimum score 85), Michigan English Language Assessment Battery (minimum score 83). Electronic applications accepted.

Michigan State University, The Graduate School, College of Agriculture and Natural Resources and College of Natural Science, Department of Food Science and Human Nutrition, East Lansing, MI 48824. Offers food science (MS, PhD); food science - environmental toxicology (PhD); human nutrition (MS, PhD); human nutrition-environmental toxicology (PhD). *Entrance requirements:* Additional exam requirements/recommendations for international students: Required—TOEFL (minimum score 550 paper-based), Michigan State University ELT (minimum score 85), Michigan English Language Assessment Battery (minimum score 83). Electronic applications accepted.

Mississippi State University, College of Agriculture and Life Sciences, Department of Food Science, Nutrition and Health Promotion, Mississippi State, MS 39762. Offers food science and technology (MS); food science and technology (PhD); health promotion (MS); nutrition (MS, PhD). *Program availability:* Online learning. *Faculty:* 18 full-time (6 women), 2 part-time/adjunct (both women). *Students:* 55 full-time (40 women), 40 part-time (33 women); includes 25 minority (16 Black or African American, non-Hispanic/Latino; 2 Asian, non-Hispanic/Latino; 6 Hispanic/Latino; 1 Two or more races, non-Hispanic/Latino), 25 international. Average age 28. 105 applicants, 47% accepted, 29 enrolled. In 2015, 27 master's, 6 doctorates awarded. *Degree requirements:* For master's, comprehensive exam, thesis; for doctorate, comprehensive exam, thesis/dissertation. *Entrance requirements:* For master's, GRE General Test, minimum GPA of 2.75; for doctorate, GRE General Test, minimum GPA of 2.75 undergraduate, 3.0 graduate. Additional exam requirements/recommendations for international students: Required—TOEFL (minimum score 550 paper-based; 79 iBT); Recommended—IELTS (minimum score 6.5). *Application deadline:* For fall admission, 7/1 for domestic students, 5/1 for international students; for spring admission, 11/1 for domestic students, 9/1 for international students. Applications are processed on a rolling basis. Application fee: $60. Electronic applications accepted. *Expenses: Tuition, area resident:* Full-time $7502; part-time $833.74 per credit hour. Tuition, nonresident: full-time $20,142; part-time $2238.24 per credit hour. *Financial support:* In 2015–16, 17 research assistantships with full tuition reimbursements (averaging $15,465 per year), 4 teaching assistantships with full tuition reimbursements (averaging $11,861 per year) were awarded; Federal Work-Study, institutionally sponsored loans, scholarships/grants, and unspecified assistantships also available. Financial award application deadline: 4/1; financial award applicants required to submit FAFSA. *Faculty research:* Food preservation, food chemistry, food safety, food processing, product development. *Unit head:* Dr. Will Evans, Professor and Head, 662-325-5055, Fax: 662-325-8728, E-mail: mwe59@msstate.edu. *Application contact:* Marina Hunt, Admissions Assistant, 662-325-5188, E-mail: mhunt@grad.msstate.edu.
Website: http://www.fsnhp.msstate.edu

New Mexico State University, College of Agricultural, Consumer and Environmental Sciences, Department of Family and Consumer Sciences, Las Cruces, NM 88003. Offers family and child science (MS); family and consumer science education (MS); food science and technology (MS); human nutrition and dietetic science (MS); marriage and family therapy (MS). *Program availability:* Part-time. *Faculty:* 11 full-time (9 women), 1 (woman) part-time/adjunct. *Students:* 31 full-time (26 women), 6 part-time (3 women); includes 16 minority (1 Black or African American, non-Hispanic/Latino; 1 Asian, non-Hispanic/Latino; 14 Hispanic/Latino), 2 international. Average age 27. 16 applicants, 75% accepted, 11 enrolled. In 2015, 15 master's awarded. *Degree requirements:* For master's, comprehensive exam (for some programs), thesis (for some programs), oral exam. *Entrance requirements:* For master's, GRE, 3 letters of reference, resume, letter of interest. Additional exam requirements/recommendations for international students: Required—TOEFL (minimum score 550 paper-based; 79 iBT), IELTS (minimum score 6.5). *Application deadline:* For fall admission, 3/1 priority date for domestic and international students; for spring admission, 11/30 for domestic and international students. Applications are processed on a rolling basis. Application fee: $40 ($50 for international students). Electronic applications accepted. *Expenses:* $274.50 per credit hour for in-state students, and all students enrolled in six or fewer credits; $839.30 per credit hour for out-of-state and international students enrolled in at least seven hours. *Financial support:* In 2015–16, 28 students received support, including 2 fellowships (averaging $4,088 per year), 9 teaching assistantships (averaging $13,666 per year); career-related internships or fieldwork, Federal Work-Study, scholarships/grants, traineeships, health care benefits, and unspecified assistantships also available. Support available to part-time students. Financial award application deadline: 3/1. *Faculty research:* Food product analysis, childhood obesity, couple relationship education, military families, Latino college students. *Total annual research expenditures:* $476,012. *Unit head:* Dr. Esther Lynn Devall, Department Head, 575-646-1161, Fax: 575-646-1889, E-mail: edevall@nmsu.edu. *Application contact:* Dr. Margaret Ann Bock, Graduate Program Contact, 575-646-3936, Fax: 575-646-1889, E-mail: marbock@nmsu.edu.
Website: http://aces.nmsu.edu/academics/fcs

New York University, Steinhardt School of Culture, Education, and Human Development, Department of Nutrition, Food Studies, and Public Health, Program in Food Studies, New York, NY 10010. Offers food studies (MA, PhD), including food culture (MA), food systems (MA). *Program availability:* Part-time. *Degree requirements:* For master's, thesis (for some programs); for doctorate, thesis/dissertation. *Entrance requirements:* For doctorate, GRE General Test, interview. Additional exam requirements/recommendations for international students: Required—TOEFL (minimum score 100 iBT). Electronic applications accepted. *Faculty research:* Cultural and social history of food, food systems and agriculture, food and aesthetics, political economy of food.

North Carolina State University, Graduate School, College of Agriculture and Life Sciences, Department of Food Science, Raleigh, NC 27695. Offers MFS, MS, PhD. *Degree requirements:* For master's, thesis (for some programs); for doctorate, thesis/dissertation. *Entrance requirements:* For master's and doctorate, GRE. Electronic applications accepted. *Faculty research:* Food safety, value-added food products, environmental quality, nutrition and health, biotechnology.

North Dakota State University, College of Graduate and Interdisciplinary Studies, College of Agriculture, Food Systems, and Natural Resources, Program in Cereal Science, Fargo, ND 58102. Offers MS, PhD. *Program availability:* Part-time. Terminal master's awarded for partial completion of doctoral program. *Degree requirements:* For master's, comprehensive exam, thesis; for doctorate, comprehensive exam, thesis/dissertation. *Entrance requirements:* Additional exam requirements/recommendations for international students: Required—TOEFL (minimum score 550 paper-based; 79 iBT), IELTS (minimum score 6). *Faculty research:* Legume food products, cereal proteins and product quality, oilseeds functional components.

North Dakota State University, College of Graduate and Interdisciplinary Studies, Interdisciplinary Program in Food Safety, Fargo, ND 58102. Offers food protection (Certificate); food safety (MS, PhD). *Program availability:* Part-time, online learning. Terminal master's awarded for partial completion of doctoral program. *Degree requirements:* For master's, thesis; for doctorate, comprehensive exam, thesis/dissertation. *Entrance requirements:* Additional exam requirements/recommendations for international students: Required—TOEFL (minimum score 525 paper-based; 71 iBT), TWE (minimum score 5). Electronic applications accepted. *Faculty research:* Mycotoxins in grain, pathogens in meat systems, sensor development for food pathogens.

The Ohio State University, Graduate School, College of Food, Agricultural, and Environmental Sciences, Department of Food Science and Technology, Columbus, OH 43210. Offers MS, PhD. *Accreditation:* AND. *Degree requirements:* For master's, thesis optional; for doctorate, thesis/dissertation. *Entrance requirements:* For master's and doctorate, GRE General Test. Additional exam requirements/recommendations for international students: Required—TOEFL (minimum score 550 paper-based; 79 iBT), Michigan English Language Assessment Battery (minimum score 82); Recommended—IELTS (minimum score 7). Electronic applications accepted.

Oklahoma State University, College of Agricultural Science and Natural Resources, Department of Animal Science, Stillwater, OK 74078. Offers animal sciences (M Ag, MS); food science (MS, PhD). *Faculty:* 29 full-time (7 women), 1 part-time/adjunct (0 women). *Students:* 15 full-time (7 women), 55 part-time (24 women); includes 9 minority (1 American Indian or Alaska Native, non-Hispanic/Latino; 5 Hispanic/Latino; 3 Two or more races, non-Hispanic/Latino), 24 international. Average age 26. 54 applicants, 39% accepted, 17 enrolled. In 2015, 18 master's, 8 doctorates awarded. *Degree requirements:* For master's, thesis; for doctorate, comprehensive exam, thesis/dissertation. *Entrance requirements:* For master's and doctorate, GRE or GMAT. Additional exam requirements/recommendations for international students: Required—TOEFL (minimum score 550 paper-based; 79 iBT). *Application deadline:* For fall admission, 3/1 priority date for international students; for spring admission, 8/1 priority date for international students. Applications are processed on a rolling basis. Application fee: $40 ($75 for international students). Electronic applications accepted. *Expenses:* Tuition, state resident: full-time $3528; part-time $196 per credit hour. Tuition, nonresident: full-time $14,144; part-time $785.75 per credit hour. *Required fees:* $1895; $105.25 per credit hour. Tuition and fees vary according to campus/location. *Financial support:* In 2015–16, 34 research assistantships (averaging $16,299 per year), 9 teaching assistantships (averaging $15,069 per year) were awarded; career-related internships or fieldwork, Federal Work-Study, scholarships/grants, health care benefits, tuition waivers (partial), and unspecified assistantships also available. Support available to part-time students. Financial award application deadline: 3/1; financial award applicants required to submit FAFSA. *Faculty research:* Quantitative trait loci identification for economical traits in swing/beef; waste management strategies in livestock; endocrine control of reproductive processes in farm animals; cholesterol synthesis, inhibition, and reduction; food safety research. *Unit head:* Dr. Clint Rusk, Department Head, 405-744-6062, Fax: 405-744-7390, E-mail: clint.rusk@okstate.edu.
Website: http://www.ansi.okstate.edu

Oregon State University, College of Agricultural Sciences, Program in Food Science and Technology, Corvallis, OR 97331. Offers MS, PhD. *Faculty:* 15 full-time (5 women). *Students:* 38 full-time (25 women), 2 part-time (1 woman); includes 2 minority (1 Hispanic/Latino; 1 Two or more races, non-Hispanic/Latino), 21 international. Average age 28. 127 applicants, 5% accepted, 6 enrolled. In 2015, 15 master's, 1 doctorate awarded. *Degree requirements:* For master's, thesis (for some programs); for doctorate, thesis/dissertation. *Entrance requirements:* For master's and doctorate, GRE (minimum Verbal and Quantitative scores of 300), minimum GPA of 3.0 in last 90 hours. Additional exam requirements/recommendations for international students: Required—TOEFL (minimum score 80 iBT), IELTS (minimum score 6.5). *Application deadline:* For fall admission, 4/1 for international students; for winter admission, 7/1 for international students; for spring admission, 10/1 for international students; for summer admission, 1/1 for international students. Application fee: $75 ($85 for international students). *Expenses:* Tuition, state resident: full-time $12,150; part-time $450 per credit. Tuition, nonresident: full-time $20,952; part-time $776 per credit. *Required fees:* $1572; $1443 per unit. One-time fee: $350. Tuition and fees vary according to course load, campus/location and program. *Financial support:* Fellowships, research assistantships, teaching assistantships, career-related internships or fieldwork, Federal Work-Study, and institutionally sponsored loans available. Support available to part-time students. Financial award application deadline: 2/1. *Faculty research:* Diet, cancer, and anticarcinogenesis; sensory analysis; chemistry and biochemistry. *Unit head:* Dr. Robert McGorrin, Department Head and Professor. *Application contact:* Linda Dunn, Academic Programs Coordinator, 541-737-6486, E-mail: linda.dunn@oregonstate.edu.
Website: http://oregonstate.edu/foodsci/graduate-program

Penn State University Park, Graduate School, College of Agricultural Sciences, Department of Food Science, University Park, PA 16802. Offers food science (MS). *Unit head:* Dr. Richard T. Roush, Dean, 814-865-2541, Fax: 814-865-3103. *Application contact:* Lori Stania, Director, Graduate Student Services, 814-865-1795, Fax: 814-863-4627, E-mail: l-gswww@lists.psu.edu.
Website: http://foodscience.psu.edu/

Purdue University, Graduate School, College of Agriculture, Department of Food Science, West Lafayette, IN 47907. Offers MS, PhD. *Degree requirements:* For master's, thesis (for some programs); for doctorate, thesis/dissertation, teaching assistantship. *Entrance requirements:* For master's, GRE General Test (minimum score Verbal 400, Quantitative 500, Analytical 4.0 old scoring; 146/144/4.0 new scoring), minimum undergraduate GPA of 3.0 or equivalent; for doctorate, GRE General Test (minimum score Verbal 400, Quantitative 500, Analytical 4.0 old scoring; 146/144/4.0 new scoring), minimum undergraduate GPA of 3.0 or equivalent; master's degree with minimum GPA of 3.0 or equivalent. Additional exam requirements/recommendations for international students: Required—TOEFL (minimum score 575 paper-based; 77 iBT). Electronic applications accepted. *Faculty research:* Processing, technology, microbiology, chemistry of foods, carbohydrate chemistry.

Purdue University, Graduate School, Food Science Interdepartmental Program, West Lafayette, IN 47907. Offers MS, PhD. *Degree requirements:* For master's, thesis (for some programs); for doctorate, thesis/dissertation, teaching assistantship. *Entrance requirements:* For master's, GRE General Test (minimum scores: Verbal 400, Quantitative 500, Analytical 4.0 old scoring; 146/144/4.0 new scoring), minimum undergraduate GPA of 3.0 or equivalent; for doctorate, GRE General Test (minimum scores: Verbal 400, Quantitative 500, Analytical 4.0 old scoring; 146/144/4.0 new scoring), minimum undergraduate GPA of 3.0 or equivalent; master's degree with minimum GPA of 3.0 or equivalent. Additional exam requirements/recommendations for international students: Required—TOEFL (minimum score 575 paper-based; 77 iBT). Electronic applications accepted.

Rutgers University–New Brunswick, Graduate School-New Brunswick, Program in Food Science, Piscataway, NJ 08854-8097. Offers M Phil, MS, PhD. *Program availability:* Part-time, evening/weekend, online learning. *Degree requirements:* For master's, thesis or alternative; for doctorate, thesis/dissertation. *Entrance requirements:* For master's and doctorate, GRE General Test. *Faculty research:* Nutraceuticals and functional foods, food and flavor analysis, food chemistry and biochemistry, food nanotechnology, food engineering and processing.

Texas A&M University, College of Agriculture and Life Sciences, Department of Nutrition and Food Science, College Station, TX 77843. Offers food science and technology (M Agr); nutrition (MS, PhD). *Students:* 56 full-time (42 women), 10 part-time (5 women); includes 11 minority (3 Asian, non-Hispanic/Latino; 7 Hispanic/Latino; 1 Two or more races, non-Hispanic/Latino), 17 international. Average age 27. 149 applicants, 13% accepted, 13 enrolled. In 2015, 12 master's, 1 doctorate awarded. *Degree requirements:* For master's, thesis; for doctorate, thesis/dissertation. *Entrance requirements:* For master's and doctorate, GRE General Test. Additional exam requirements/recommendations for international students: Required—TOEFL (minimum score 550 paper-based; 80 iBT), IELTS (minimum score 6), PTE (minimum score 53). *Application deadline:* For fall admission, 12/1 priority date for domestic students, 12/1 for international students; for spring admission, 8/1 for domestic and international students; for summer admission, 12/1 priority date for domestic students, 12/1 for international students. Applications are processed on a rolling basis. Application fee: $50 ($90 for international students). Electronic applications accepted. *Expenses:* Contact institution. *Financial support:* In 2015–16, 56 students received support, including 5 fellowships with tuition reimbursements available (averaging $6,964 per year), 21 research assistantships with tuition reimbursements available (averaging $5,592 per year), 16 teaching assistantships with tuition reimbursements available (averaging $5,260 per year); career-related internships or fieldwork, institutionally sponsored loans, scholarships/grants, traineeships, health care benefits, tuition waivers (full and partial), and unspecified assistantships also available. Support available to part-time students. Financial award application deadline: 3/15; financial award applicants required to submit FAFSA. *Faculty research:* Food safety, microbiology, product development. *Unit head:* Dr. Boon Chew, Department Head, 979-862-6655, E-mail: boon.chew@tamu.edu. *Application contact:* Graduate Admissions, 979-845-1044, E-mail: admissions@tamu.edu.
Website: http://nfs.tamu.edu

Texas Tech University, Graduate School, College of Agricultural Sciences and Natural Resources, Department of Animal and Food Sciences, Lubbock, TX 79409-2141. Offers animal science (MS, PhD); food science (MS). *Faculty:* 28 full-time (10 women). *Students:* 56 full-time (30 women), 17 part-time (8 women); includes 6 minority (5 Hispanic/Latino; 1 Two or more races, non-Hispanic/Latino), 20 international. Average age 27. 56 applicants, 20% accepted, 7 enrolled. In 2015, 14 master's, 11 doctorates awarded. *Degree requirements:* For master's, thesis or alternative; for doctorate, thesis/dissertation. *Entrance requirements:* For master's and doctorate, GRE. Additional exam requirements/recommendations for international students: Required—TOEFL (minimum score 550 paper-based; 79 iBT). *Application deadline:* For fall admission, 6/1 priority date for domestic students, 1/15 priority date for international students; for spring admission, 9/1 priority date for domestic students, 6/15 priority date for international students. Applications are processed on a rolling basis. Application fee: $60. Electronic applications accepted. *Expenses:* Tuition, state resident: full-time $6477; part-time $269.89 per credit hour. Tuition, nonresident: full-time $15,837; part-time $659.89 per credit hour. *Required fees:* $2751; $36.50 per credit hour. $937.50 per semester. Tuition and fees vary according to course level. *Financial support:* In 2015–16, 69 students received support, including 53 fellowships (averaging $2,744 per year), 59 research assistantships (averaging $11,622 per year), 6 teaching assistantships (averaging $14,378 per year); scholarships/grants and unspecified assistantships also available. Financial award applicants required to submit FAFSA. *Faculty research:* Nutrition, welfare and behavior, physiology and reproduction, muscle and meat biology, food safety, food security, companion animal, health and well-being. *Total annual research expenditures:* $3.6 million. *Unit head:* Dr. Michael Orth, Chair and Professor, 806-834-5653, Fax: 806-742-0898, E-mail: michael.orth@ttu.edu. *Application contact:* Sandra Gellner, Administrative Business Assistant, 806-834-0608, Fax: 806-742-0898, E-mail: sandra.gellner@ttu.edu.
Website: http://www.depts.ttu.edu/afs

Texas Woman's University, Graduate School, College of Health Sciences, Department of Nutrition and Food Sciences, Denton, TX 76201. Offers exercise and sports nutrition (MS); food science (MS); nutrition (MS, PhD). *Program availability:* Part-time, evening/weekend. *Degree requirements:* For master's, comprehensive exam, thesis or alternative; for doctorate, comprehensive exam, thesis/dissertation, qualifying exam. *Entrance requirements:* For master's, GRE General Test (preferred minimum score 143 [350 old version] Verbal, 141 [450 old version] Quantitative), minimum GPA of 3.25, resume; for doctorate, GRE General Test (preferred minimum score 150 [450 old version] Verbal, 141 [550 old version] Quantitative), minimum GPA of 3.5 on last 60 undergraduate hours and graduate course work, 2 letters of reference, resume. Additional exam requirements/recommendations for international students: Required—TOEFL (minimum score 550 paper-based; 79 iBT). *Application deadline:* For fall admission, 7/1 priority date for domestic students, 3/1 for international students; for spring admission, 12/1 priority date for domestic students, 7/1 for international students. Applications are processed on a rolling basis. Application fee: $50 ($75 for international students). Electronic applications accepted. *Expenses:* Tuition, state resident: full-time $4380; part-time $243 per credit hour. Tuition, nonresident: full-time $11,400; part-time $633 per credit hour. *International tuition:* $11,465 full-time. *Required fees:* $1778; $99 per credit hour. $283 per semester. One-time fee: $50. Tuition and fees vary according to course load and program. *Financial support:* Research assistantships, teaching assistantships, career-related internships or fieldwork, Federal Work-Study, institutionally sponsored loans, scholarships/grants, traineeships, health care benefits, and unspecified assistantships available. Support available to part-time students. Financial award application deadline: 3/1; financial award applicants required to submit FAFSA. *Faculty research:* Bioactive food components and cancer, nutraceuticals and functional foods in diabetes, obesity and bone health, food safety, dietary modulation of dyslipidemia, childhood obesity prevention. *Unit head:* Dr. K. Shane Broughton, Chair, 940-898-2637, Fax: 940-898-2634, E-mail: nutrfdsci@twu.edu. *Application contact:* Dr. Samuel Wheeler, Assistant Director of Admissions, 940-898-3188, Fax: 940-898-3081, E-mail: wheelersr@twu.edu.
Website: http://www.twu.edu/nutrition-food-sciences/

Tuskegee University, Graduate Programs, College of Agriculture, Environment and Nutrition Sciences, Department of Food and Nutritional Sciences, Tuskegee, AL 36088. Offers MS. *Degree requirements:* For master's, thesis. *Entrance requirements:* For master's, GRE General Test. Additional exam requirements/recommendations for international students: Required—TOEFL (minimum score 500 paper-based).

Universidad de las Américas Puebla, Division of Graduate Studies, School of Engineering, Program in Chemical Engineering, Puebla, Mexico. Offers chemical engineering (MS); food technology (MS). *Program availability:* Part-time, evening/weekend. *Degree requirements:* For master's, one foreign language, thesis. *Faculty research:* Food science, reactors, oil industry, biotechnology.

Universidad de las Américas Puebla, Division of Graduate Studies, School of Engineering, Program in Food Sciences, Puebla, Mexico. Offers MS.

Université de Moncton, School of Food Science, Nutrition and Family Studies, Moncton, NB E1A 3E9, Canada. Offers foods/nutrition (M Sc). *Program availability:* Part-time. *Degree requirements:* For master's, one foreign language, thesis. *Entrance requirements:* For master's, previous course work in statistics. Electronic applications accepted. *Faculty research:* Clinic nutrition (anemia, elderly, osteoporosis), applied nutrition, metabolic activities of lactic bacteria, solubility of low density lipoproteins, bile acids.

Université Laval, Faculty of Agricultural and Food Sciences, Department of Food Sciences and Nutrition, Programs in Food Sciences and Technology, Québec, QC G1K 7P4, Canada. Offers M Sc, PhD. Terminal master's awarded for partial completion of doctoral program. *Degree requirements:* For master's, thesis (for some programs); for doctorate, comprehensive exam, thesis/dissertation. *Entrance requirements:* For master's and doctorate, knowledge of French and English. Electronic applications accepted.

University of Arkansas, Graduate School, Dale Bumpers College of Agricultural, Food and Life Sciences, Department of Food Science, Fayetteville, AR 72701-1201. Offers MS, PhD. *Students:* 11 full-time (7 women), 36 part-time (22 women); includes 11 minority (2 Black or African American, non-Hispanic/Latino; 2 American Indian or Alaska Native, non-Hispanic/Latino; 3 Asian, non-Hispanic/Latino; 4 Hispanic/Latino), 18 international. In 2015, 10 master's, 3 doctorates awarded. *Degree requirements:* For master's, thesis; for doctorate, thesis/dissertation. *Application deadline:* For fall admission, 4/1 for international students; for spring admission, 10/1 for international students. Applications are processed on a rolling basis. Application fee: $40 ($50 for international students). Electronic applications accepted. *Financial support:* In 2015–16, 25 research assistantships were awarded; fellowships with tuition reimbursements, teaching assistantships, career-related internships or fieldwork, Federal Work-Study, scholarships/grants, and unspecified assistantships also available. Support available to part-time students. Financial award application deadline: 4/1; financial award applicants required to submit FAFSA. *Unit head:* Dr. Jean-Francois Meullenet, Department Head, 479-575-4605, E-mail: jfmeull@uark.edu. *Application contact:* Graduate Admissions, 479-575-6246, Fax: 479-575-5908, E-mail: gradinfo@uark.edu.
Website: http://www.foodscience.uark.edu/

University of Arkansas, Graduate School, Dale Bumpers College of Agricultural, Food and Life Sciences, Food Safety Program, Fayetteville, AR 72701-1201. Offers MS. *Program availability:* Part-time, evening/weekend, online learning. *Students:* 2 full-time (1 woman), 19 part-time (10 women); includes 2 minority (both Hispanic/Latino), 2 international. In 2015, 3 master's awarded. *Degree requirements:* For master's, thesis optional. *Application deadline:* For fall admission, 4/1 for international students; for spring admission, 10/1 for international students. Applications are processed on a rolling basis. Application fee: $40 ($50 for international students). Electronic applications accepted. *Financial support:* Fellowships, research assistantships, teaching assistantships, career-related internships or fieldwork, and Federal Work-Study available. Support available to part-time students. Financial award application deadline: 4/1; financial award applicants required to submit FAFSA. *Unit head:* Dr. Lona Robertston, Associate Dean, 479-575-2034, E-mail: ljrobert@uark.edu. *Application contact:* Diana Bisbee, Program Coordinator, 479-575-2025, E-mail: dbisbee@uark.edu.
Website: http://bumperscollege.uark.edu/

The University of British Columbia, Faculty of Land and Food Systems, Program in Food Science, Vancouver, BC V6T 1Z1, Canada. Offers M Sc, MFS, PhD. *Degree requirements:* For master's, thesis; for doctorate, comprehensive exam, thesis/dissertation. *Entrance requirements:* Additional exam requirements/recommendations for international students: Required—TOEFL (minimum score 577 paper-based; 90 iBT), IELTS (minimum score 6.5). Electronic applications accepted. *Faculty research:* Food chemistry and biochemistry, food process science, food toxicology and safety, food microbiology, food biotechnology.

University of California, Davis, Graduate Studies, Graduate Group in Food Science, Davis, CA 95616. Offers MS, PhD. Terminal master's awarded for partial completion of doctoral program. *Degree requirements:* For master's, comprehensive exam (for some programs), thesis (for some programs); for doctorate, thesis/dissertation. *Entrance requirements:* For master's and doctorate, GRE General Test, minimum GPA of 3.0. Additional exam requirements/recommendations for international students: Required—TOEFL (minimum score 550 paper-based). Electronic applications accepted.

University of Delaware, College of Agriculture and Natural Resources, Department of Animal and Food Sciences, Newark, DE 19716. Offers animal sciences (MS, PhD); food sciences (MS). *Program availability:* Part-time. Terminal master's awarded for partial completion of doctoral program. *Degree requirements:* For master's, thesis; for doctorate, comprehensive exam, thesis/dissertation. *Entrance requirements:* For master's and doctorate, GRE General Test. Additional exam requirements/recommendations for international students: Required—TOEFL. Electronic applications accepted. *Faculty research:* Food chemistry, food microbiology, process engineering technology, packaging, food analysis, microbial genetics, molecular endocrinology, growth physiology, avian immunology and virology, monogastric nutrition, avian genomics.

University of Florida, Graduate School, College of Agricultural and Life Sciences, Department of Food Science and Human Nutrition, Gainesville, FL 32611. Offers food science (PhD), including toxicology; food science and human nutrition (MS), including nutritional sciences; nutritional sciences (MS, PhD), including clinical and translational science (PhD). *Faculty:* 13 full-time, 1 part-time/adjunct. *Students:* 43 full-time (32 women), 4 part-time (1 woman); includes 7 minority (3 Black or African American, non-Hispanic/Latino; 2 Asian, non-Hispanic/Latino; 2 Hispanic/Latino), 27 international. Average age 27. 150 applicants, 23% accepted, 23 enrolled. In 2015, 22 master's awarded. *Degree requirements:* For master's, thesis optional; for doctorate, thesis/dissertation. *Entrance requirements:* For master's and doctorate, GRE General Test, minimum GPA of 3.0. Additional exam requirements/recommendations for international students: Required—TOEFL. *Application deadline:* For fall admission, 6/1 priority date for domestic students. Applications are processed on a rolling basis. Application fee: $30. Electronic applications accepted. *Financial support:* In 2015–16, 2 fellowships, 16 research assistantships, 23 teaching assistantships were awarded; career-related internships or fieldwork also available. Financial award applicants required to submit FAFSA. *Faculty research:* Pesticide research, nutritional biochemistry and microbiology, food safety and toxicology assessment and dietetics, food chemistry. *Total annual research expenditures:* $7.5 million. *Unit head:* Susan S. Percival, PhD, Chair and Professor, 352-392-1991 Ext. 202, Fax: 352-392-1991, E-mail: percival@ufl.edu.
Website: http://fshn.ifas.ufl.edu/

University of Georgia, College of Agricultural and Environmental Sciences, Department of Food Science and Technology, Athens, GA 30602. Offers food science (MS, PhD); food technology (MFT). *Program availability:* Part-time. *Degree requirements:* For master's, thesis; for doctorate, thesis/dissertation. *Entrance requirements:* For master's and doctorate, GRE General Test. Additional exam requirements/recommendations for international students: Required—TOEFL (minimum score 550 paper-based). Electronic applications accepted.

University of Guelph, Graduate Studies, Ontario Agricultural College, Department of Food Science, Guelph, ON N1G 2W1, Canada. Offers food safety and quality assurance (M Sc); food science (M Sc, PhD). *Degree requirements:* For master's, thesis; for doctorate, comprehensive exam, thesis/dissertation. *Entrance requirements:* For master's, minimum B- average during previous 2 years of honors B Sc degree; for doctorate, minimum B average. Additional exam requirements/recommendations for international students: Required—TOEFL (minimum score 550 paper-based), IELTS (minimum score 6.5). Electronic applications accepted. *Faculty research:* Food chemistry, food microbiology, food processing, preservation and utilization.

University of Hawaii at Manoa, Graduate Division, College of Tropical Agriculture and Human Resources, Department of Human Nutrition, Food and Animal Sciences, Program in Food Science, Honolulu, HI 96822. Offers MS. *Program availability:* Part-time. *Faculty:* 17 full-time (2 women), 1 part-time/adjunct (0 women). *Students:* 4 full-time (2 women); includes 3 minority (2 Asian, non-Hispanic/Latino; 1 Hispanic/Latino), 1 international. Average age 34. 4 applicants, 75% accepted, 1 enrolled. In 2015, 1 master's awarded. *Degree requirements:* For master's, thesis optional. *Entrance requirements:* For master's, GRE General Test. Additional exam requirements/recommendations for international students: Required—TOEFL (minimum score 580 paper-based; 92 iBT), IELTS (minimum score 5). *Application deadline:* For fall admission, 2/1 for domestic and international students; for spring admission, 9/1 for domestic and international students. Application fee: $100. *Financial support:* In 2015–16, 3 students received support, including 1 fellowship (averaging $4,000 per year), 1 research assistantship (averaging $18,198 per year), 1 teaching assistantship (averaging $14,382 per year). *Faculty research:* Biochemistry of natural products, sensory evaluation, food processing, food chemistry, food safety. *Total annual research expenditures:* $10,000. *Unit head:* Douglas Vincent, Chair, 808-956-8393, E-mail: vincent@hawaii.edu. *Application contact:* Yong Li, Graduate Chairperson, 808-956-8356, Fax: 808-956-4024, E-mail: liyong@hawaii.edu.
Website: http://www.ctahr.hawaii.edu/hnfas/degrees/grad/FSHN.html

University of Idaho, College of Graduate Studies, College of Agricultural and Life Sciences, Bistate School of Food Science, Moscow, ID 83844-2312. Offers MS, PhD. *Faculty:* 7 full-time. *Students:* 11 full-time, 3 part-time. Average age 26. In 2015, 1 doctorate awarded. *Entrance requirements:* For master's, minimum GPA of 2.8. Additional exam requirements/recommendations for international students: Required—TOEFL (minimum score 550 paper-based). *Application deadline:* For fall admission, 8/1 for domestic students; for spring admission, 12/15 for domestic students. Applications are processed on a rolling basis. Application fee: $60. Electronic applications accepted. *Expenses:* Tuition, state resident: full-time $6205; part-time $399 per credit hour. Tuition, nonresident: full-time $20,209; part-time $1177 per credit hour. *Required fees:* $2017; $58 per credit hour. Full-time tuition and fees vary according to course load and reciprocity agreements. *Financial support:* Research assistantships and teaching assistantships available. Financial award applicants required to submit FAFSA. *Faculty research:* Food biotechnology, food and environmental toxicology, bio-preservation of food products, conversion of biomass. *Unit head:* Dr. Barbara Rasco, Director, 509-335-1858, E-mail: foodscience@uidaho.edu. *Application contact:* Sean Scoggin, Graduate Recruitment Coordinator, 208-885-4001, Fax: 208-885-4406, E-mail: graduateadmissions@uidaho.edu.
Website: http://sfs.wsu.edu/

University of Illinois at Urbana–Champaign, Graduate College, College of Agricultural, Consumer and Environmental Sciences, Department of Food Science and Human Nutrition, Champaign, IL 61820. Offers food science (MS); food science and human nutrition (MS, PhD), including professional science (MS); human nutrition (MS). *Program availability:* Part-time, online learning.

University of Kentucky, Graduate School, College of Agriculture, Food and Environment, Program in Animal and Food Sciences, Lexington, KY 40506-0032. Offers MS, PhD. Terminal master's awarded for partial completion of doctoral program. *Degree requirements:* For master's, comprehensive exam, thesis optional; for doctorate, comprehensive exam, thesis/dissertation. *Entrance requirements:* For master's, GRE General Test, minimum undergraduate GPA of 2.75; for doctorate, GRE General Test, minimum graduate GPA of 3.0. Additional exam requirements/recommendations for international students: Required—TOEFL (minimum score 550 paper-based). Electronic applications accepted. *Faculty research:* Nutrition of horses, cattle, swine, poultry, and sheep; physiology of reproduction and lactation; food science; microbiology.

University of Maine, Graduate School, College of Natural Sciences, Forestry, and Agriculture, School of Food and Agriculture, Orono, ME 04469. Offers animal sciences (MPS, MS); food and human nutrition (PhD); food science and human nutrition (MS); horticulture (MS); plant science (PhD). *Program availability:* Part-time. *Faculty:* 30 full-time (15 women). *Students:* 50 full-time (29 women), 2 part-time (both women); includes 3 minority (2 American Indian or Alaska Native, non-Hispanic/Latino; 1 Asian, non-Hispanic/Latino), 15 international. Average age 28. 81 applicants, 48% accepted, 20 enrolled. In 2015, 18 master's, 3 doctorates, 3 other advanced degrees awarded. *Degree requirements:* For master's, thesis (for some programs); for doctorate, comprehensive exam, thesis/dissertation. *Entrance requirements:* For master's and doctorate, GRE General Test. Additional exam requirements/recommendations for international students: Required—TOEFL. *Application deadline:* For fall admission, 2/1 priority date for domestic students. Applications are processed on a rolling basis. Application fee: $65. Electronic applications accepted. *Financial support:* In 2015–16, 36 students received support, including 1 fellowship (averaging $20,000 per year), 25 research assistantships with full tuition reimbursements available (averaging $14,600 per year), 7 teaching assistantships with full tuition reimbursements available (averaging $14,600 per year); Federal Work-Study, institutionally sponsored loans, and tuition waivers (full and partial) also available. Financial award application deadline: 3/1. *Faculty research:* Nutrition education for adults and children, food processing, food safety, sustainable crop and soil management, animal health and nutrition. *Total annual research expenditures:* $1.9 million. *Unit head:* Dr. Sue Erich, Chair, 207-581-2947, Fax: 207-581-2770. *Application contact:* Scott G. Delcourt, Assistant Vice President for Graduate Studies and Senior Associate Dean, 207-581-3291, Fax: 207-581-3232, E-mail: graduate@maine.edu.
Website: http://umaine.edu/foodandagriculture

Food Science and Technology

University of Manitoba, Faculty of Graduate Studies, Faculty of Agricultural and Food Sciences, Department of Food Science, Winnipeg, MB R3T 2N2, Canada. Offers food and nutritional sciences (PhD); food science (M Sc); foods and nutrition (M Sc). *Degree requirements:* For master's, thesis.

University of Maryland, College Park, Academic Affairs, College of Agriculture and Natural Resources, Department of Nutrition and Food Science, Program in Food Science, College Park, MD 20742. Offers MS, PhD. *Degree requirements:* For master's, comprehensive exam, research-based thesis or equivalent paper; for doctorate, comprehensive exam, thesis/dissertation. *Entrance requirements:* For master's, GRE General Test, minimum GPA of 3.0, professional experience, 3 letters of recommendation; for doctorate, GRE General Test, minimum GPA of 3.0. Additional exam requirements/recommendations for international students: Required—TOEFL. Electronic applications accepted. *Faculty research:* Food chemistry, engineering, microbiology, and processing technology; quality assurance; membrane separations, rheology and texture measurement.

University of Maryland Eastern Shore, Graduate Programs, Department of Agriculture, Program in Food and Agricultural Sciences, Princess Anne, MD 21853-1299. Offers MS. *Degree requirements:* For master's, comprehensive exam, thesis or alternative, oral exams. *Entrance requirements:* For master's, GRE General Test, minimum GPA of 3.0. Additional exam requirements/recommendations for international students: Required—TOEFL (minimum score 80 iBT). Electronic applications accepted. *Faculty research:* Poultry and swine nutrition and management, soybean specialty products, farm management practices, agriculture technology.

University of Maryland Eastern Shore, Graduate Programs, Department of Agriculture, Program in Food Science and Technology, Princess Anne, MD 21853-1299. Offers PhD. *Degree requirements:* For doctorate, comprehensive exam, thesis/dissertation. *Entrance requirements:* For doctorate, minimum GPA of 3.0, strong background in food science and related fields, intended dissertation research. Additional exam requirements/recommendations for international students: Required—TOEFL (minimum score 80 iBT). Electronic applications accepted. *Faculty research:* Prevalence, growth, survival and control of listeria; microbial models of the effect of storage temperature.

University of Massachusetts Amherst, Graduate School, College of Natural Sciences, Department of Food Science, Amherst, MA 01003. Offers MS, PhD. *Program availability:* Part-time. Terminal master's awarded for partial completion of doctoral program. *Degree requirements:* For master's, thesis or alternative; for doctorate, comprehensive exam, thesis/dissertation. *Entrance requirements:* For master's and doctorate, GRE General Test. Additional exam requirements/recommendations for international students: Required—TOEFL (minimum score 550 paper-based; 80 iBT), IELTS (minimum score 6.5). Electronic applications accepted.

University of Minnesota, Twin Cities Campus, Graduate School, College of Food, Agricultural and Natural Resource Sciences, Program in Food Science, Saint Paul, MN 55108. Offers MS, PhD. *Program availability:* Part-time. *Faculty:* 18 full-time (6 women), 9 part-time/adjunct (4 women). *Students:* 59 full-time (36 women), 15 part-time (10 women); includes 3 minority (1 American Indian or Alaska Native, non-Hispanic/Latino; 2 Hispanic/Latino), 32 international. Average age 25. 123 applicants, 17% accepted, 21 enrolled. In 2015, 10 master's, 1 doctorate awarded. Terminal master's awarded for partial completion of doctoral program. *Degree requirements:* For master's, comprehensive exam, thesis; for doctorate, comprehensive exam, thesis/dissertation. *Entrance requirements:* For master's, GRE General Test, previous course work in general chemistry, organic chemistry, calculus, physics, and biology; for doctorate, GRE General Test, previous course work in general chemistry, organic chemistry, calculus, physics, and biology; MS or demonstrated research capabilities. Additional exam requirements/recommendations for international students: Required—TOEFL (minimum score 550 paper-based; 79 iBT), IELTS (minimum score 6.5). *Application deadline:* Applications are processed on a rolling basis. Application fee: $75 ($95 for international students). Electronic applications accepted. *Financial support:* In 2015–16, fellowships with full tuition reimbursements (averaging $40,000 per year), research assistantships with tuition reimbursements (averaging $40,000 per year), teaching assistantships with tuition reimbursements (averaging $40,000 per year) were awarded; career-related internships or fieldwork, scholarships/grants, traineeships, health care benefits, and unspecified assistantships also available. Support available to part-time students. *Faculty research:* Food chemistry, food microbiology, food technology, grain science, dairy science, food safety. *Total annual research expenditures:* $2 million. *Unit head:* Dr. David E. Smith, Director of Graduate Studies, 612-624-3260, Fax: 612-625-5272, E-mail: desmith@umn.edu. *Application contact:* Nancy L. Toedt, Program Coordinator, 612-624-6753, Fax: 612-625-5272, E-mail: ntoedt@umn.edu.
Website: http://fscn.cfans.umn.edu/graduate-programs/food-science

University of Mississippi, Graduate School, School of Applied Sciences, University, MS 38677. Offers communicative disorders (MS); criminal justice (MCJ); exercise science (MS); food and nutrition services (MS); health and kinesiology (PhD); health promotion (MS); park and recreation management (MA); social work (MSW). *Faculty:* 65 full-time (36 women), 32 part-time/adjunct (23 women). *Students:* 192 full-time (148 women), 43 part-time (23 women); includes 47 minority (37 Black or African American, non-Hispanic/Latino; 2 Asian, non-Hispanic/Latino; 7 Hispanic/Latino; 1 Two or more races, non-Hispanic/Latino), 12 international. In 2015, 99 master's, 3 doctorates awarded. *Entrance requirements:* For master's, GRE General Test, minimum GPA of 3.0. Additional exam requirements/recommendations for international students: Required—TOEFL. *Application deadline:* For fall admission, 4/1 for domestic students; for spring admission, 10/1 for domestic students. Applications are processed on a rolling basis. Application fee: $40. Electronic applications accepted. *Financial support:* Scholarships/grants available. Financial award application deadline: 3/1; financial award applicants required to submit FAFSA. *Unit head:* Dr. Velmer Stanley Burton, Dean, 662-915-1081, Fax: 662-915-5717, E-mail: applsci@olemiss.edu. *Application contact:* Dr. Christy M. Wyandt, Associate Dean of Graduate School, 662-915-7474, Fax: 662-915-7577, E-mail: cwyandt@olemiss.edu.

University of Missouri, Office of Research and Graduate Studies, College of Agriculture, Food and Natural Resources, Department of Food Science, Columbia, MO 65211. Offers MS, PhD. Terminal master's awarded for partial completion of doctoral program. *Degree requirements:* For doctorate, comprehensive exam, thesis/dissertation. *Entrance requirements:* For master's, GRE General Test (minimum score: Verbal and Quantitative 1000 with neither section below 400, 297 combined under new scoring; Analytical 3.5), minimum GPA of 3.0; BS in food science from accredited university; for doctorate, GRE General Test (minimum score: Verbal and Quantitative 1000 with neither section below 400, Analytical 3.5), minimum GPA of 3.0; BS and MS in food science from accredited university. Additional exam requirements/recommendations for international students: Required—TOEFL (minimum score 550 paper-based; 79 iBT). Electronic applications accepted. *Faculty research:* Food chemistry, food analysis, food microbiology, food engineering and process control, functional foods, meat science and processing technology.

University of Nebraska–Lincoln, Graduate College, College of Agricultural Sciences and Natural Resources, Department of Food Science and Technology, Lincoln, NE 68588. Offers MS, PhD. *Degree requirements:* For master's, thesis optional; for doctorate, comprehensive exam, thesis/dissertation. *Entrance requirements:* For master's and doctorate, GRE General Test. Additional exam requirements/recommendations for international students: Required—TOEFL (minimum score 505 paper-based). Electronic applications accepted. *Faculty research:* Food chemistry, microbiology, processing, engineering, and biotechnology.

University of Puerto Rico, Mayagüez Campus, Graduate Studies, College of Agricultural Sciences, Department of Food Science and Technology, Mayagüez, PR 00681-9000. Offers MS. *Program availability:* Part-time. *Degree requirements:* For master's, comprehensive exam, thesis. *Entrance requirements:* For master's, minimum GPA of 2.5. *Faculty research:* Food microbiology, food science, seafood technology, food engineering and packaging, fermentation.

University of Rhode Island, Graduate School, College of the Environment and Life Sciences, Department of Nutrition and Food Sciences, Kingston, RI 02881. Offers dietetic internship (MS); nutrition (MS, PhD). *Program availability:* Part-time. *Faculty:* 6 full-time (5 women), 2 part-time/adjunct (1 woman). *Students:* 11 full-time (7 women), 9 part-time (all women); includes 4 minority (2 Asian, non-Hispanic/Latino; 1 Hispanic/Latino; 1 Two or more races, non-Hispanic/Latino). In 2015, 5 master's awarded. *Degree requirements:* For master's, comprehensive exam (for some programs), thesis optional; for doctorate, thesis/dissertation. *Entrance requirements:* For master's, GRE, 2 letters of recommendation (3 for MS in dietetic internship); for doctorate, GRE, 2 letters of recommendation. Additional exam requirements/recommendations for international students: Required—TOEFL (minimum score 550 paper-based). *Application deadline:* For fall admission, 2/15 for domestic students, 2/1 for international students; for spring admission, 11/15 for domestic students, 7/15 for international students. Application fee: $65. Electronic applications accepted. *Expenses:* Tuition, state resident: full-time $11,796; part-time $655 per credit. Tuition, nonresident: full-time $24,206; part-time $1345 per credit. *Required fees:* $1546; $44 per credit. One-time fee: $155 full-time; $35 part-time. *Financial support:* In 2015–16, 2 research assistantships with tuition reimbursements (averaging $11,883 per year), 1 teaching assistantship (averaging $7,922 per year) were awarded. Financial award application deadline: 2/15; financial award applicants required to submit FAFSA. *Faculty research:* Food safety and quality, marine resource utilization, nutrition in underserved populations, eating behavior, lipid metabolism. *Total annual research expenditures:* $1.6 million. *Unit head:* Dr. Cathy English, Chair, 401-874-5689, Fax: 401-874-5974, E-mail: cathy@uri.edu. *Application contact:* Graduate Admissions, 401-874-2872, E-mail: gradadm@etal.uri.edu.
Website: http://cels.uri.edu/nfs/

University of Saskatchewan, College of Graduate Studies and Research, College of Agriculture, Department of Applied Microbiology and Food Science, Saskatoon, SK S7N 5A2, Canada. Offers M Ag, M Sc, PhD. *Degree requirements:* For master's, thesis; for doctorate, comprehensive exam (for some programs), thesis/dissertation. *Entrance requirements:* Additional exam requirements/recommendations for international students: Required—TOEFL (minimum score 80 iBT); Recommended—IELTS (minimum score 6.5).

University of Southern California, Graduate School, School of Pharmacy, Regulatory Science Programs, Los Angeles, CA 90089. Offers clinical research design and management (Graduate Certificate); food safety (Graduate Certificate); patient and product safety (Graduate Certificate); preclinical drug development (Graduate Certificate); regulatory and clinical affairs (Graduate Certificate); regulatory science (MS, DRSc). *Program availability:* Part-time, evening/weekend, online learning. Terminal master's awarded for partial completion of doctoral program. *Degree requirements:* For master's, thesis optional; for doctorate, comprehensive exam, thesis/dissertation. *Entrance requirements:* For master's, GRE. Additional exam requirements/recommendations for international students: Required—TOEFL (minimum score 603 paper-based; 100 iBT). Electronic applications accepted.

University of Southern Mississippi, Graduate School, College of Health, Department of Nutrition and Food Systems, Hattiesburg, MS 39406-0001. Offers nutrition (MS, PhD). *Program availability:* Part-time. *Degree requirements:* For master's, comprehensive exam, thesis (for some programs); for doctorate, comprehensive exam, thesis/dissertation. *Entrance requirements:* For master's, GRE General Test, minimum GPA of 2.75 on last 60 hours; for doctorate, GRE General Test, minimum GPA of 3.5. Additional exam requirements/recommendations for international students: Required—TOEFL, IELTS.

The University of Tennessee, Graduate School, College of Agricultural Sciences and Natural Resources, Department of Food Science and Technology, Knoxville, TN 37996. Offers food science and technology (MS, PhD), including food chemistry (PhD), food microbiology (PhD), food processing (PhD), sensory evaluation of foods (PhD). *Program availability:* Part-time. *Degree requirements:* For master's, thesis or alternative; for doctorate, thesis/dissertation. *Entrance requirements:* For master's and doctorate, GRE General Test, minimum GPA of 2.7. Additional exam requirements/recommendations for international students: Required—TOEFL. Electronic applications accepted.

The University of Tennessee at Martin, Graduate Programs, College of Agriculture and Applied Sciences, Department of Family and Consumer Sciences, Martin, TN 38238. Offers dietetics (MSFCS); general family and consumer sciences (MSFCS). *Program availability:* Part-time, 100% online. *Faculty:* 8. *Students:* 1 (woman) full-time, 42 part-time (38 women); includes 13 minority (9 Black or African American, non-Hispanic/Latino; 3 Hispanic/Latino; 1 Two or more races, non-Hispanic/Latino). Average age 28. 74 applicants, 74% accepted, 24 enrolled. In 2015, 9 master's awarded. *Degree requirements:* For master's, comprehensive exam, thesis optional. *Entrance requirements:* For master's, GRE General Test, minimum GPA of 2.5. Additional exam requirements/recommendations for international students: Required—TOEFL (minimum score 525 paper-based; 71 iBT). *Application deadline:* For fall admission, 7/27 priority date for domestic and international students; for spring admission, 12/17 priority date for domestic and international students; for summer admission, 5/10 priority date for domestic and international students. Applications are processed on a rolling basis. Application fee: $30 ($130 for international students). Electronic applications accepted. *Expenses:* Tuition, state resident: full-time $8254; part-time $459 per credit hour. Tuition, nonresident: full-time $22,198; part-time $1234 per credit hour. *Required fees:* $79 per credit hour. Part-time tuition and fees vary according to course load and campus/location. *Financial support:* In 2015–16, 7 students received support, including 1 research assistantship (averaging $7,540 per year), 6 teaching assistantships with full tuition reimbursements available (averaging $7,518 per year); scholarships/grants and unspecified assistantships also available. Financial award application deadline: 2/1; financial award applicants required to submit FAFSA. *Faculty research:* Children with developmental disabilities, regional food product development and marketing, parent education. *Unit head:* Dr. Lisa LeBleu, Coordinator, 731-881-7116, Fax: 731-881-7106,

E-mail: llebleu@utm.edu. *Application contact:* Jolene L. Cunningham, Student Services Specialist, 731-881-7012, Fax: 731-881-7499, E-mail: jcunningham@utm.edu.
Website: http://www.utm.edu/departments/caas/fcs/index.php

University of Vermont, Graduate College, College of Agriculture and Life Sciences, Program in Animal, Nutrition and Food Sciences, Burlington, VT 05405. Offers PhD. *Degree requirements:* For doctorate, one foreign language, thesis/dissertation. *Entrance requirements:* For doctorate, GRE General Test. Additional exam requirements/recommendations for international students: Required—TOEFL (minimum score 550 paper-based; 80 iBT). Electronic applications accepted.

University of Vermont, Graduate College, College of Agriculture and Life Sciences, Program in Food Systems, Burlington, VT 05405. Offers MS. *Entrance requirements:* For master's, GRE. Additional exam requirements/recommendations for international students: Required—TOEFL (minimum score 550 paper-based; 80 iBT). Electronic applications accepted.

University of Wisconsin–Madison, Graduate School, College of Agricultural and Life Sciences, Department of Food Science, Madison, WI 53706-1380. Offers MS, PhD. *Program availability:* Part-time. *Degree requirements:* For master's, thesis; for doctorate, thesis/dissertation. *Entrance requirements:* For master's and doctorate, GRE General Test. Additional exam requirements/recommendations for international students: Required—TOEFL. Electronic applications accepted. *Expenses:* Tuition, state resident: full-time $5364. Tuition, nonresident: full-time $12,027. *Required fees:* $571. Tuition and fees vary according to campus/location, program and reciprocity agreements. *Faculty research:* Food chemistry, food engineering, food microbiology, food processing.

University of Wisconsin–Stout, Graduate School, College of Education, Health and Human Sciences, Program in Food and Nutritional Sciences, Menomonie, WI 54751. Offers MS. *Program availability:* Part-time. *Degree requirements:* For master's, thesis. *Entrance requirements:* For master's, minimum GPA of 3.0. Additional exam requirements/recommendations for international students: Required—TOEFL (minimum score 500 paper-based; 61 iBT). Electronic applications accepted. *Faculty research:* Disease states and nutrition, childhood obesity, nutraceuticals, food safety, nanotechnology.

University of Wyoming, College of Agriculture and Natural Resources, Department of Animal Sciences, Program in Food Science and Human Nutrition, Laramie, WY 82071. Offers MS. *Degree requirements:* For master's, thesis. *Entrance requirements:* For master's, GRE General Test, minimum GPA of 3.0. Additional exam requirements/recommendations for international students: Required—TOEFL (minimum score 525 paper-based). Electronic applications accepted. *Faculty research:* Protein and lipid metabolism, food microbiology, food safety, meat science.

Utah State University, School of Graduate Studies, College of Agriculture, Department of Nutrition, Dietetics, and Food Sciences, Logan, UT 84322. Offers dietetic administration (MDA); nutrition and food sciences (MS, PhD). *Program availability:* Online learning. *Degree requirements:* For master's, thesis; for doctorate, comprehensive exam, thesis/dissertation, teaching experience. *Entrance requirements:* For master's, GRE General Test, minimum GPA of 3.0, course work in chemistry, biochemistry, physics, math, bacteriology, physiology; for doctorate, GRE General Test, minimum GPA of 3.2, course work in chemistry, MS or manuscript in referred journal. Additional exam requirements/recommendations for international students: Required—TOEFL (minimum score 550 paper-based). Electronic applications accepted. *Faculty research:* Mineral balance, meat microbiology and nitrate interactions, milk ultrafiltration, lactic culture, milk coagulation.

Washington State University, College of Agricultural, Human, and Natural Resource Sciences, School of Food Science, Pullman, WA 99164-6376. Offers MS, PhD. Programs offered at the Pullman campus. *Program availability:* Part-time. *Degree requirements:* For master's, comprehensive exam, thesis, oral exam, written exam; for doctorate, comprehensive exam, thesis/dissertation, oral exam, written exam. *Entrance requirements:* For master's, GRE General Test, BS; official transcripts; letter of interest; minimum GPA of 3.0; resume; 3 letters of recommendation, 1 from major advisor; for doctorate, GRE General Test, MS demonstrating ability to conduct and report research; minimum GPA of 3.0; resume; 3 letters of recommendation, 1 from major advisor. Additional exam requirements/recommendations for international students: Required—TOEFL (minimum score 550 paper-based; 80 iBT). Electronic applications accepted. *Faculty research:* Food microbiology and chemistry of food; starch and protein chemistry; food processing and engineering; food safety; microbiological, chemical, and quality aspects of food; dairy, wine processes.

Wayne State University, College of Liberal Arts and Sciences, Department of Nutrition and Food Science, Detroit, MI 48202. Offers dietetics (Postbaccalaureate Certificate); food science (PhD); nutrition (PhD); nutrition and food science (MA, MS). Postbaccalaureate Certificate program admits only in Fall with April 1 application deadline. *Faculty:* 10 full-time (7 women), 6 part-time/adjunct (3 women). *Students:* 31 full-time (23 women), 10 part-time (all women); includes 4 minority (2 Asian, non-Hispanic/Latino; 1 Hispanic/Latino; 1 Two or more races, non-Hispanic/Latino), 23 international. Average age 29. 95 applicants, 31% accepted, 13 enrolled. In 2015, 12 master's, 4 doctorates awarded. *Degree requirements:* For master's, thesis (for some programs), essay (for MA); for doctorate, thesis/dissertation. *Entrance requirements:* For master's, GRE General Test, two letters of recommendation; minimum GPA of 3.0; basic courses in nutrition and food science; courses in human nutrition and metabolism, food chemistry, introductory microbiology, anatomy and physiology, and organic chemistry (for MS); for doctorate, GRE, MS in nutrition and/or food science or in a cognate science with a minimum GPA of 3.5; three letters of recommendation; personal statement; interview (live or web-based); for Postbaccalaureate Certificate, bachelor's degree. Additional exam requirements/recommendations for international students: Required—TOEFL (minimum score 550 paper-based; 79 iBT), TWE (minimum score 5.5), Michigan English Language Assessment Battery (minimum score 85); Recommended—IELTS (minimum score 6.5). *Application deadline:* For fall admission, 2/1 priority date for domestic and international students. Application fee: $0. Electronic applications accepted. *Expenses:* Tuition, state resident: full-time $14,165; part-time $590.20 per credit hour. Tuition, nonresident: full-time $30,682; part-time $1278.40 per credit hour. *Required fees:* $1688; $47.45 per credit hour. $274.60 per semester. Tuition and fees vary according to course load and program. *Financial support:* In 2015–16, 17 students received support, including 1 fellowship with tuition reimbursement available (averaging $16,000 per year), 1 research assistantship with tuition reimbursement available (averaging $22,000 per year), 9 teaching assistantships with tuition reimbursements available (averaging $18,801 per year); scholarships/grants, health care benefits, and unspecified assistantships also available. Financial award application deadline: 3/31; financial award applicants required to submit FAFSA. *Faculty research:* Nutrition cancer; mechanisms by which aging increases cancer risk; nutrition and exercise, nutrition, cancer and metabolomics; diet-induced obesity and diabetes; cholesterol and lipoprotein metabolism; dietetics; food microbiology, antimicrobial resistance, microbial detection; food and nutraceutical chemistry. *Total annual research expenditures:* $1 million. *Unit head:* Dr. Ahmad R. Heydari, Professor and Chair, 313-577-2500, E-mail: ahmad.heydari@wayne.edu. *Application contact:* Dr. Pramod Khosla, Graduate Director, 313-577-0448, Fax: 313-577-8616, E-mail: nfsgradprogram@wayne.edu.
Website: http://clas.wayne.edu/nfs/

West Virginia University, Davis College of Agriculture, Forestry and Consumer Sciences, Division of Animal and Nutritional Sciences, Program in Animal and Nutritional Sciences, Morgantown, WV 26506. Offers breeding (MS); food sciences (MS); nutrition (MS); physiology (MS); production management (MS); reproduction (MS). *Program availability:* Part-time. *Degree requirements:* For master's, thesis, oral and written exams. *Entrance requirements:* For master's, GRE, minimum GPA of 2.5. Additional exam requirements/recommendations for international students: Required—TOEFL. *Expenses:* Tuition, state resident: full-time $8568. Tuition, nonresident: full-time $22,140. Tuition and fees vary according to program. *Faculty research:* Animal nutrition, reproductive physiology, food science.

West Virginia University, Davis College of Agriculture, Forestry and Consumer Sciences, Division of Plant and Soil Sciences, Program in Agricultural Sciences, Morgantown, WV 26506. Offers animal and food sciences (PhD); plant and soil sciences (PhD). *Degree requirements:* For doctorate, thesis/dissertation, oral and written exams. *Entrance requirements:* Additional exam requirements/recommendations for international students: Required—TOEFL. *Expenses:* Tuition, state resident: full-time $8568. Tuition, nonresident: full-time $22,140. Tuition and fees vary according to program. *Faculty research:* Ruminant nutrition, metabolism, forage utilization, physiology, reproduction.

Horticulture

Auburn University, Graduate School, College of Agriculture, Department of Horticulture, Auburn University, AL 36849. Offers M Ag, MS, PhD. *Program availability:* Part-time. *Faculty:* 17 full-time (3 women). *Students:* 14 full-time (9 women), 22 part-time (7 women); includes 1 minority (Black or African American, non-Hispanic/Latino), 5 international. Average age 29. 23 applicants, 65% accepted, 15 enrolled. In 2015, 9 master's awarded. *Degree requirements:* For master's, thesis (for some programs); for doctorate, thesis/dissertation. *Entrance requirements:* For master's and doctorate, GRE General Test. *Application deadline:* Applications are processed on a rolling basis. Application fee: $50 ($60 for international students). Electronic applications accepted. *Expenses:* Tuition, state resident: full-time $8802; part-time $489 per credit hour. Tuition, nonresident: full-time $26,406; part-time $1467 per credit hour. *Required fees:* $808 per semester. Tuition and fees vary according to degree level and program. *Financial support:* Research assistantships, teaching assistantships, and Federal Work-Study available. Support available to part-time students. Financial award application deadline: 3/15; financial award applicants required to submit FAFSA. *Faculty research:* Environmental regulators, water quality, weed control, growth regulators, plasticulture. *Unit head:* Dr. Jeffrey L. Sibley, Head, 334-844-3132. *Application contact:* Dr. George Flowers, Dean of the Graduate School, 334-844-2125.
Website: http://www.ag.auburn.edu/dept/hf/index.html

Colorado State University, College of Agricultural Sciences, Department of Horticulture and Landscape Architecture, Fort Collins, CO 80523-1173. Offers horticulture (MS, PhD); landscape architecture (MLA). *Program availability:* Part-time. *Faculty:* 12 full-time (3 women), 5 part-time/adjunct (3 women). *Students:* 26 full-time (9 women), 22 part-time (11 women); includes 3 minority (2 Hispanic/Latino; 1 Two or more races, non-Hispanic/Latino), 12 international. Average age 33. 22 applicants, 50% accepted, 8 enrolled. In 2015, 7 master's, 4 doctorates awarded. *Degree requirements:* For master's, thesis (for some programs); for doctorate, comprehensive exam, thesis/dissertation. *Entrance requirements:* For master's, GRE General Test (minimum score of 300 combined Verbal and Quantitative sections), minimum GPA of 3.0, letters of reference, related bachelor's degree or experience, transcripts, resume/curriculum vitae, statement of purpose; for doctorate, GRE General Test (minimum score of 300 combined Verbal and Quantitative sections), minimum GPA of 3.0, letters of reference, statement of purpose, related bachelor's degree or experience, resume/curriculum vitae, transcripts. Additional exam requirements/recommendations for international students: Required—TOEFL (minimum score 550 paper-based; 80 iBT), IELTS (minimum score 6.5). *Application deadline:* For fall admission, 4/1 for domestic and international students; for spring admission, 9/1 for domestic and international students; for summer admission, 1/1 for domestic and international students. Applications are processed on a rolling basis. Application fee: $60 ($70 for international students). Electronic applications accepted. *Expenses:* Tuition, state resident: full-time $9348. Tuition, nonresident: full-time $22,916. *Required fees:* $2174; $473.72 per credit hour. $236.86 per semester. Tuition and fees vary according to course load and program. *Financial support:* In 2015–16, 15 students received support, including 1 fellowship with full tuition reimbursement available (averaging $42,840 per year), 7 research assistantships with partial tuition reimbursements available (averaging $19,080 per year), 7 teaching assistantships with partial tuition reimbursements available (averaging $12,891 per year); scholarships/grants and unspecified assistantships also available. Financial award application deadline: 2/15; financial award applicants required to submit FAFSA. *Faculty research:* Specialty crops, environmental physiology, water conservation, rhizosphere biology, cancer prevention through dietary intervention. *Total annual research expenditures:* $2.7 million. *Unit head:* Dr. Stephen J. Wallner, Department Head, 970-491-7018, Fax: 970-491-7745, E-mail: stephen.wallner@colostate.edu. *Application contact:* Kathi Nietfeld, Graduate Coordinator, 970-491-7018, Fax: 970-491-7745, E-mail: kathi.nietfeld@colostate.edu.
Website: http://hortla.agsci.colostate.edu

Cornell University, Graduate School, Graduate Fields of Agriculture and Life Sciences, Field of Horticulture, Ithaca, NY 14853-0001. Offers breeding of horticultural crops (MPS); horticultural crop management systems (MPS); human-plant interactions (MPS,

PhD); physiology and ecology of horticultural crops (MPS, MS, PhD). *Degree requirements:* For master's, thesis (MS); for doctorate, comprehensive exam, thesis/dissertation. *Entrance requirements:* For master's and doctorate, GRE General Test, 3 letters of recommendation. Additional exam requirements/recommendations for international students: Required—TOEFL (minimum score 550 paper-based; 77 iBT). Electronic applications accepted. *Faculty research:* Plant selection/plant materials, greenhouse management, greenhouse crop production, urban landscape management, turfgrass management.

Dalhousie University, Faculty of Agriculture, Halifax, NS B3H 4R2, Canada. Offers agriculture (M Sc), including air quality, animal behavior, animal molecular genetics, animal nutrition, animal technology, aquaculture, botany, crop management, crop physiology, ecology, environmental microbiology, food science, horticulture, nutrient management, pest management, physiology, plant biotechnology, plant pathology, soil chemistry, soil fertility, waste management and composting, water quality. *Program availability:* Part-time. *Degree requirements:* For master's, thesis, ATC Exam Teaching Assistantship. *Entrance requirements:* For master's, honors B Sc, minimum GPA of 3.0. Additional exam requirements/recommendations for international students: Required—TOEFL (minimum score 580 paper-based; 92 iBT), IELTS, Michigan English Language Assessment Battery, CanTEST, CAEL. *Faculty research:* Bio-product development, organic agriculture, nutrient management, air and water quality, agricultural biotechnology.

Iowa State University of Science and Technology, Department of Horticulture, Ames, IA 50011. Offers MS, PhD. *Degree requirements:* For master's, thesis; for doctorate, thesis/dissertation. *Entrance requirements:* For master's and doctorate, GRE General Test. Additional exam requirements/recommendations for international students: Required—TOEFL (minimum score 550 paper-based; 79 iBT), IELTS (minimum score 6.5). Electronic applications accepted.

Kansas State University, Graduate School, College of Agriculture, Department of Horticulture, Forestry and Recreation Resources, Manhattan, KS 66506. Offers horticulture (MS, PhD), including horticulture, urban food systems (MS). *Program availability:* Part-time, online learning. *Degree requirements:* For master's, thesis, oral exam; for doctorate, thesis/dissertation, preliminary exams. *Entrance requirements:* For master's and doctorate, GRE General Test. Additional exam requirements/recommendations for international students: Required—TOEFL (minimum score 550 paper-based; 79 iBT); Recommended—IELTS (minimum score 6.5). Electronic applications accepted. *Faculty research:* Environmental stress, phytochemicals and health, postharvest technology, sustainable production, turfgrass science.

Michigan State University, The Graduate School, College of Agriculture and Natural Resources, Department of Horticulture, East Lansing, MI 48824. Offers horticulture (MS, PhD); plant breeding, genetics and biotechnology-horticulture (MS, PhD). *Entrance requirements:* Additional exam requirements/recommendations for international students: Required—TOEFL. Electronic applications accepted.

Mississippi State University, College of Agriculture and Life Sciences, Department of Plant and Soil Sciences, Mississippi State, MS 39762. Offers agriculture (MS, PhD), including agronomy, horticulture, weed science. *Faculty:* 49 full-time (5 women). *Students:* 45 full-time (11 women), 33 part-time (6 women); includes 2 minority (1 American Indian or Alaska Native, non-Hispanic/Latino; 1 Asian, non-Hispanic/Latino), 20 international. Average age 27. 26 applicants, 46% accepted, 11 enrolled. In 2015, 16 master's, 7 doctorates awarded. *Degree requirements:* For master's, comprehensive exam, thesis, oral and/or written exams; for doctorate, comprehensive exam, thesis/dissertation, minimum of 20 semester hours of research for dissertation. *Entrance requirements:* For master's, GRE (for weed science), minimum GPA of 2.75 (agronomy/horticulture), 3.0 (weed science); for doctorate, GRE (for weed science), minimum GPA of 3.0 (agronomy/horticulture), 3.25 (weed science). Additional exam requirements/recommendations for international students: Required—TOEFL (minimum score 500 paper-based; 61 iBT), TOEFL (minimum score 550 paper-based, 79 iBT) or IELTS (minimum score 6.5) for weed science; Recommended—IELTS (minimum score 5.5). *Application deadline:* For fall admission, 7/1 for domestic students, 5/1 for international students; for spring admission, 10/1 for domestic students, 9/1 for international students. Applications are processed on a rolling basis. Application fee: $60. Electronic applications accepted. *Expenses: Tuition, area resident:* Full-time $7502; part-time $833.74 per credit hour. Tuition, nonresident: full-time $20,142; part-time $2238.24 per credit hour. *Financial support:* In 2015–16, 31 research assistantships (averaging $14,967 per year), 3 teaching assistantships (averaging $15,951 per year) were awarded; Federal Work-Study, institutionally sponsored loans, scholarships/grants, and unspecified assistantships also available. Financial award application deadline: 4/1; financial award applicants required to submit FAFSA. *Faculty research:* Bioenergy crops, cotton breeding, environmental plant pathology, row crop weed control, genomics. *Unit head:* Dr. Mike Phillips, Professor and Head, 662-325-2311, Fax: 662-325-8742, E-mail: jmp657@msstate.edu. *Application contact:* Marina Hunt, Admissions Assistant, 662-325-5188, E-mail: mhunt@grad.msstate.edu.
Website: http://www.pss.msstate.edu/

New Mexico State University, College of Agricultural, Consumer and Environmental Sciences, Department of Plant and Environmental Sciences, Las Cruces, NM 88003-8001. Offers horticulture (MS); plant and environmental sciences (MS, PhD). *Program availability:* Part-time. *Faculty:* 18 full-time (4 women). *Students:* 33 full-time (18 women), 13 part-time (4 women); includes 6 minority (5 Hispanic/Latino; 1 Two or more races, non-Hispanic/Latino), 22 international. Average age 30. 18 applicants, 50% accepted, 7 enrolled. In 2015, 7 master's, 4 doctorates awarded. Terminal master's awarded for partial completion of doctoral program. *Degree requirements:* For master's, thesis or alternative; for doctorate, one foreign language, comprehensive exam, thesis/dissertation, qualifying exam, 2 seminars. *Entrance requirements:* For master's, GRE, minimum GPA of 3.0, 3 letters of reference, letter of purpose or intent; for doctorate, GRE, minimum GPA of 3.3, 3 letters of reference, letter of purpose or intent. Additional exam requirements/recommendations for international students: Required—TOEFL (minimum score 550 paper-based; 79 iBT), IELTS (minimum score 6.5). *Application deadline:* For fall admission, 3/15 for domestic and international students; for spring admission, 10/15 for domestic and international students. Applications are processed on a rolling basis. Application fee: $40 ($50 for international students). Electronic applications accepted. *Expenses:* $274.50 per credit hour for in-state students, and all students enrolled in six or fewer credits; $839.30 per credit hour for out-of-state and international students enrolled in at least seven hours. *Financial support:* In 2015–16, 36 students received support, including 1 fellowship (averaging $4,088 per year), 20 research assistantships (averaging $18,593 per year), 9 teaching assistantships (averaging $17,218 per year); career-related internships or fieldwork, Federal Work-Study, scholarships/grants, traineeships, health care benefits, and unspecified assistantships also available. Support available to part-time students. Financial award application deadline: 3/1. *Faculty research:* Plant breeding and genetics, molecular biology, crop physiology, plant physiology, soil science and environmental science, forestry, nursery and greenhouse production, urban horticulture and turfgrass management. *Total annual research expenditures:* $5.1 million. *Unit head:* Dr. Rolston St. Hilaire, Interim Department Head, 575-646-3405, Fax: 575-646-6041, E-mail: rsthilai@nmsu.edu. *Application contact:* Dr. Paul Bosland, Graduate Chair, 575-646-5171, Fax: 575-646-6041, E-mail: pbosland@nmsu.edu.
Website: http://aces.nmsu.edu/academics/pes

North Carolina State University, Graduate School, College of Agriculture and Life Sciences, Department of Horticultural Science, Raleigh, NC 27695. Offers MS, PhD, Certificate. *Program availability:* Online learning. Terminal master's awarded for partial completion of doctoral program. *Degree requirements:* For master's, thesis (for some programs); for doctorate, thesis/dissertation. *Entrance requirements:* For master's and doctorate, GRE General Test, bachelor's degree in agriculture or biology, minimum GPA of 3.0. Electronic applications accepted. *Faculty research:* Plant physiology, breeding and genetics, tissue culture, herbicide physiology, propagation.

The Ohio State University, Graduate School, College of Food, Agricultural, and Environmental Sciences, Department of Horticulture and Crop Science, Columbus, OH 43210. Offers MS, PhD. *Degree requirements:* For master's, thesis optional; for doctorate, thesis/dissertation. *Entrance requirements:* For master's and doctorate, GRE General Test. Additional exam requirements/recommendations for international students: Required—TOEFL (minimum score 550 paper-based; 79 iBT), Michigan English Language Assessment Battery (minimum score 82); Recommended—IELTS (minimum score 7). Electronic applications accepted.

Oklahoma State University, College of Agricultural Science and Natural Resources, Department of Horticulture and Landscape Architecture, Stillwater, OK 74078. Offers crop science (PhD); environmental science (PhD); horticulture (M Ag, MS); plant science (PhD). *Faculty:* 17 full-time (4 women). *Students:* 3 full-time (1 woman), 9 part-time (3 women); includes 2 minority (1 Black or African American, non-Hispanic/Latino; 1 Asian, non-Hispanic/Latino), 5 international. Average age 30. 8 applicants, 63% accepted, 5 enrolled. In 2015, 3 master's awarded. *Degree requirements:* For master's, thesis (for some programs); for doctorate, comprehensive exam, thesis/dissertation. *Entrance requirements:* For master's and doctorate, GRE or GMAT. Additional exam requirements/recommendations for international students: Required—TOEFL (minimum score 550 paper-based; 79 iBT). *Application deadline:* For fall admission, 3/1 priority date for international students; for spring admission, 8/1 priority date for international students. Applications are processed on a rolling basis. Application fee: $40 ($75 for international students). Electronic applications accepted. *Expenses:* Tuition, state resident: full-time $3528; part-time $196 per credit hour. Tuition, nonresident: full-time $14,144; part-time $785.75 per credit hour. *Required fees:* $1895; $105.25 per credit hour. Tuition and fees vary according to campus/location. *Financial support:* In 2015–16, 9 research assistantships (averaging $10,469 per year), 3 teaching assistantships (averaging $12,261 per year) were awarded; career-related internships or fieldwork, Federal Work-Study, scholarships/grants, health care benefits, tuition waivers (partial), and unspecified assistantships also available. Support available to part-time students. Financial award application deadline: 3/1; financial award applicants required to submit FAFSA. *Faculty research:* Stress and postharvest physiology; water utilization and runoff; integrated pest management (IPM) systems and nursery, turf, floriculture, vegetable, net and fruit produces and natural resources, food extraction, and processing; public garden management. *Unit head:* Dr. Janet Cole, Department Head, 405-744-5414, Fax: 405-744-9709. *Application contact:* Dr. Sheryl Tucker, Dean, 405-744-7099, Fax: 405-744-0355, E-mail: gradi@okstate.edu.
Website: http://www.hortla.okstate.edu/

Oregon State University, College of Agricultural Sciences, Program in Horticulture, Corvallis, OR 97331. Offers M Ag, MS, PhD. *Faculty:* 15 full-time (4 women), 2 part-time/adjunct (0 women). *Students:* 33 full-time (14 women), 2 part-time (0 women); includes 5 minority (4 Hispanic/Latino; 1 Two or more races, non-Hispanic/Latino), 9 international. Average age 31. 32 applicants, 22% accepted, 7 enrolled. In 2015, 7 master's, 3 doctorates awarded. *Degree requirements:* For master's, thesis (for some programs); for doctorate, thesis/dissertation. *Entrance requirements:* For master's and doctorate, GRE General Test, minimum GPA of 3.0 in last 90 hours. Additional exam requirements/recommendations for international students: Required—TOEFL (minimum score 80 iBT), IELTS (minimum score 6.5). *Application deadline:* For fall admission, 4/1 for international students; for winter admission, 7/1 for international students; for spring admission, 10/1 for international students; for summer admission, 1/1 for international students. Application fee: $75 ($85 for international students). *Expenses:* Tuition, state resident: full-time $12,150; part-time $450 per credit. Tuition, nonresident: full-time $20,952; part-time $776 per credit. *Required fees:* $1572; $1443 per unit. One-time fee: $350. Tuition and fees vary according to course load, campus/location and program. *Financial support:* Research assistantships, teaching assistantships, career-related internships or fieldwork, Federal Work-Study, and institutionally sponsored loans available. Support available to part-time students. Financial award application deadline: 2/1. *Unit head:* Dr. Bill Braunworth, Department Head, E-mail: bill.braunworth@oregonstate.edu. *Application contact:* John Lambrinos, Horticulture Advisor, 541-737-3484, E-mail: lambrinj@hort.oregonstate.edu.
Website: http://horticulture.oregonstate.edu/content/graduate-students

Penn State University Park, Graduate School, College of Agricultural Sciences, Department of Plant Science, University Park, PA 16802. Offers agronomy (MS, PhD); horticulture (MS, PhD); turfgrass management (MPS). *Unit head:* Dr. Richard T. Roush, Dean, 814-865-2541, Fax: 814-865-3103. *Application contact:* Lori Stania, Director, Graduate Student Services, 814-865-1795, Fax: 814-863-4627, E-mail: l-gswww@lists.psu.edu.
Website: http://plantscience.psu.edu/

Purdue University, Graduate School, College of Agriculture, Department of Horticulture, West Lafayette, IN 47907. Offers M Agr, MS, PhD. *Program availability:* Part-time. Terminal master's awarded for partial completion of doctoral program. *Degree requirements:* For master's, thesis optional; for doctorate, thesis/dissertation. *Entrance requirements:* For master's and doctorate, GRE General Test, minimum undergraduate GPA of 3.0 or equivalent. Additional exam requirements/recommendations for international students: Required—TOEFL (minimum score 550 paper-based; 77 iBT); Recommended—TWE. Electronic applications accepted. *Faculty research:* Floral scent and plant volatile biosynthesis, mineral nutrient utilization from cellular to global scales, hormone signaling and transport, regulation of plant architecture and reproduction, plant cell cycle regulation, water utilization and stress responses, sustainable biofuel production, enhancement of salt tolerance in crop plants, natural genetic variation, plant epigenetics, mechanisms of heterosis, hybridization and species breeding barriers.

Rutgers University–New Brunswick, Graduate School-New Brunswick, Program in Plant Biology, Piscataway, NJ 08854-8097. Offers horticulture and plant technology (MS, PhD); molecular and cellular biology (MS, PhD); organismal and population biology (MS, PhD); plant pathology (MS, PhD). *Program availability:* Part-time. Terminal master's awarded for partial completion of doctoral program. *Degree requirements:* For master's, comprehensive exam, thesis or alternative; for doctorate, comprehensive exam, thesis/dissertation. *Entrance requirements:* For master's and doctorate, GRE General Test, GRE Subject Test (recommended). Additional exam requirements/

recommendations for international students: Required—TOEFL (minimum score 600 paper-based). Electronic applications accepted. *Faculty research:* Molecular biology and biochemistry of plants, plant development and genomics, plant protection, plant improvement, plant management of horticultural and field crops.

Texas A&M University, College of Agriculture and Life Sciences, Department of Horticultural Sciences, College Station, TX 77843. Offers horticulture (M Agr, MS, PhD). *Faculty:* 9. *Students:* 32 full-time (21 women), 16 part-time (7 women); includes 11 minority (3 Asian, non-Hispanic/Latino; 7 Hispanic/Latino; 1 Two or more races, non-Hispanic/Latino), 17 international. Average age 30. 17 applicants, 94% accepted, 13 enrolled. In 2015, 6 master's, 4 doctorates awarded. Terminal master's awarded for partial completion of doctoral program. *Degree requirements:* For master's, thesis (for some programs), professional internship; for doctorate, thesis/dissertation. *Entrance requirements:* For master's and doctorate, GRE General Test. Additional exam requirements/recommendations for international students: Required—TOEFL (minimum score 550 paper-based; 80 iBT), IELTS (minimum score 6), PTE (minimum score 53). *Application deadline:* For fall admission, 12/15 priority date for domestic and international students; for spring admission, 9/1 priority date for domestic and international students; for summer admission, 9/1 priority date for domestic students, 9/1 for international students. Applications are processed on a rolling basis. Application fee: $50 ($90 for international students). Electronic applications accepted. *Expenses:* Contact institution. *Financial support:* In 2015–16, 28 students received support, including 7 fellowships with tuition reimbursements available (averaging $8,757 per year), 17 research assistantships with tuition reimbursements available (averaging $5,488 per year), 5 teaching assistantships with tuition reimbursements available (averaging $5,533 per year); career-related internships or fieldwork, institutionally sponsored loans, scholarships/grants, traineeships, health care benefits, tuition waivers (full and partial), and unspecified assistantships also available. Support available to part-time students. Financial award application deadline: 3/15; financial award applicants required to submit FAFSA. *Faculty research:* Plant breeding, molecular biology, plant nutrition, post-harvest physiology, plant physiology. *Unit head:* Dr. Dan Lineberger, Professor and Head, 979-845-5278, Fax: 979-845-0627, E-mail: dan-lineberger@tamu.edu. *Application contact:* Dr. Patricia Klein, Associate Professor/ Associate Head for Graduate Studies, 979-862-6308, Fax: 979-845-0627, E-mail: pklein@tamu.edu.
Website: http://hortsciences.tamu.edu/

Texas A&M University–Kingsville, College of Graduate Studies, Dick and Mary Lewis Kleberg College of Agriculture, Natural Resources and Human Sciences, Department of Agriculture, Agribusiness, and Environmental Sciences, Kingsville, TX 78363. Offers agribusiness (MS); agricultural science (MS); horticulture (PhD); plant and soil science (MS); ranch management (MS). *Degree requirements:* For master's, variable foreign language requirement, comprehensive exam, thesis (for some programs); for doctorate, variable foreign language requirement, comprehensive exam, thesis/dissertation. *Entrance requirements:* For master's, GRE (minimum combined Math & Verbal score of 290), GMAT, MAT, minimum GPA of 2.5; for doctorate, GRE, GMAT, MAT. Additional exam requirements/recommendations for international students: Required—TOEFL (minimum score 550 paper-based; 79 iBT). Electronic applications accepted.

Texas Tech University, Graduate School, College of Agricultural Sciences and Natural Resources, Department of Plant and Soil Science, Lubbock, TX 79409. Offers horticulture science (MS); plant and soil science (MS, PhD). *Program availability:* Part-time, evening/weekend, 100% online, blended/hybrid learning. *Faculty:* 16 full-time (4 women), 14 part-time/adjunct (4 women). *Students:* 57 full-time (24 women), 34 part-time (6 women); includes 7 minority (1 Black or African American, non-Hispanic/Latino; 1 Asian, non-Hispanic/Latino; 3 Hispanic/Latino; 2 Two or more races, non-Hispanic/ Latino), 33 international. Average age 30. 55 applicants, 51% accepted, 21 enrolled. In 2015, 22 master's, 7 doctorates awarded. Terminal master's awarded for partial completion of doctoral program. *Degree requirements:* For master's, comprehensive exam (for some programs), thesis (for some programs); for doctorate, comprehensive exam, thesis/dissertation. *Entrance requirements:* For master's and doctorate, GRE. Additional exam requirements/recommendations for international students: Required—TOEFL (minimum score 550 paper-based; 79 iBT). *Application deadline:* For fall admission, 6/1 priority date for domestic students, 1/15 priority date for international students; for spring admission, 9/1 priority date for domestic students, 6/15 priority date for international students. Applications are processed on a rolling basis. Application fee: $60. Electronic applications accepted. *Expenses:* Tuition, state resident: full-time $6477; part-time $269.89 per credit hour. Tuition, nonresident: full-time $15,837; part-time $659.89 per credit hour. *Required fees:* $2751; $36.50 per credit hour. $937.50 per semester. Tuition and fees vary according to course level. *Financial support:* In 2015–16, 78 students received support, including 71 fellowships (averaging $2,923 per year), 55 research assistantships (averaging $13,035 per year), 31 teaching assistantships (averaging $4,062 per year); scholarships/grants, health care benefits, and unspecified assistantships also available. Financial award application deadline: 4/15; financial award applicants required to submit FAFSA. *Faculty research:* Crop protection, crop science, fibers and biopolymers, soil science, horticulture. *Total annual research expenditures:* $3 million. *Unit head:* Dr. Eric Hequet, Department Chair, 806-742-2838, Fax: 806-742-0775, E-mail: eric.hequet@ttu.edu. *Application contact:* Christi Chadwell, Communication and Recruiting Coordinator, 806-834-8124, E-mail: christi.chadwell@ttu.edu.
Website: http://www.pssc.ttu.edu

Universidad Nacional Pedro Henriquez Urena, Graduate School, Santo Domingo, Dominican Republic. Offers agricultural diversity (MS), including horticultural/fruit production, tropical animal production; conservation of monuments and cultural assets (M Arch); ecology and environment (MS); environmental engineering (MEE); international relations (MA); natural resource management (MS); political science (MA); project optimization (MPM); project feasibility (MPM); project management (MPM); sanitation engineering (ME); science for teachers (MS); tropical Caribbean architecture (M Arch).

University of Arkansas, Graduate School, Dale Bumpers College of Agricultural, Food and Life Sciences, Department of Horticulture, Fayetteville, AR 72701-1201. Offers MS. *Students:* 1 (woman) full-time, 9 part-time (3 women); includes 1 minority (Asian, non-Hispanic/Latino). In 2015, 5 master's awarded. *Degree requirements:* For master's, thesis. *Application deadline:* For fall admission, 4/1 for international students; for spring admission, 10/1 for international students. Applications are processed on a rolling basis. Application fee: $40 ($50 for international students). Electronic applications accepted. *Financial support:* In 2015–16, 7 research assistantships were awarded; fellowships, teaching assistantships, career-related internships or fieldwork, and Federal Work-Study also available. Support available to part-time students. Financial award application deadline: 4/1; financial award applicants required to submit FAFSA. *Unit head:* Dr. Wayne Mackay, Department Head, 479-575-2603, E-mail: mackay@uark.edu.
Website: http://hort.uark.edu

University of California, Davis, Graduate Studies, Graduate Group in Horticulture and Agronomy, Davis, CA 95616. Offers MS. *Degree requirements:* For master's, comprehensive exam (for some programs), thesis (for some programs). *Entrance requirements:* For master's, GRE General Test. Additional exam requirements/ recommendations for international students: Required—TOEFL (minimum score 550 paper-based). Electronic applications accepted. *Faculty research:* Postharvest physiology, mineral nutrition, crop improvement, plant growth and development.

University of Delaware, College of Agriculture and Natural Resources, Longwood Graduate Program in Public Horticulture, Newark, DE 19716. Offers MS. *Degree requirements:* For master's, thesis, internship. *Entrance requirements:* For master's, GRE General Test, introductory taxonomy course. Additional exam requirements/ recommendations for international students: Required—TOEFL. Electronic applications accepted. *Faculty research:* Management and development of publicly oriented horticultural institutions.

University of Florida, Graduate School, College of Agricultural and Life Sciences, Department of Environmental Horticulture, Gainesville, FL 32611. Offers MS, PhD. *Program availability:* Part-time, online learning. *Faculty:* 20 full-time, 3 part-time/adjunct. *Students:* 27 full-time (11 women), 5 part-time (3 women); includes 2 minority (1 Black or African American, non-Hispanic/Latino; 1 Hispanic/Latino), 9 international. Average age 34. 26 applicants, 54% accepted, 10 enrolled. In 2015, 7 master's, 4 doctorates awarded. Terminal master's awarded for partial completion of doctoral program. *Degree requirements:* For master's, comprehensive exam, thesis optional, teaching experience; for doctorate, comprehensive exam, thesis/dissertation, teaching experience. *Entrance requirements:* For master's and doctorate, GRE General Test, minimum GPA of 3.0. Additional exam requirements/recommendations for international students: Required—TOEFL (minimum score 550 paper-based; 80 iBT), IELTS (minimum score 6). *Application deadline:* For fall admission, 1/15 priority date for domestic students, 1/15 for international students; for spring admission, 9/1 for domestic and international students; for summer admission, 1/1 for domestic and international students. Applications are processed on a rolling basis. Application fee: $30. Electronic applications accepted. *Financial support:* In 2015–16, 4 fellowships, 18 research assistantships, 1 teaching assistantship were awarded; unspecified assistantships also available. Financial award application deadline: 2/1; financial award applicants required to submit FAFSA. *Faculty research:* Breeding and genetics, conservation and restoration horticulture, landscape design and ecology, floriculture, nursery and foliage crop production, turf grasses and urban horticulture, arboriculture. *Total annual research expenditures:* $741,583. *Unit head:* Sandra Wilson, PhD, Professor and Chair, E-mail: sbwilson@ufl.edu. *Application contact:* Laurie Trenholm, PhD, Professor and Graduate Studies Coordinator, 352-273-4524, Fax: 352-392-3870, E-mail: letr@ufl.edu.
Website: http://hort.ifas.ufl.edu/

University of Florida, Graduate School, College of Agricultural and Life Sciences, Department of Horticultural Sciences, Gainesville, FL 32611. Offers horticultural sciences (MS, PhD), including environmental horticulture, horticultural sciences, toxicology (PhD). *Faculty:* 9 full-time, 1 part-time/adjunct. *Students:* 64 full-time (26 women), 1 part-time (0 women); includes 6 minority (all Hispanic/Latino), 42 international. Average age 31. 32 applicants, 47% accepted, 10 enrolled. In 2015, 15 master's, 13 doctorates awarded. *Degree requirements:* For master's, thesis optional; for doctorate, comprehensive exam, thesis/dissertation. *Entrance requirements:* For master's and doctorate, GRE General Test, minimum GPA of 3.0. Additional exam requirements/recommendations for international students: Required—TOEFL (minimum score 550 paper-based; 80 iBT), IELTS (minimum score 6). *Application deadline:* For fall admission, 1/1 priority date for domestic students, 1/1 for international students; for spring admission, 8/1 for domestic and international students. Applications are processed on a rolling basis. Application fee: $30. Electronic applications accepted. *Financial support:* In 2015–16, 4 fellowships, 52 research assistantships were awarded; teaching assistantships and institutionally sponsored loans also available. Financial award application deadline: 6/1; financial award applicants required to submit FAFSA. *Faculty research:* Breeding and genetics, crop production and nutrition, organic/ sustainable agriculture, physiology and biochemistry. *Total annual research expenditures:* $10.2 million. *Unit head:* Rebecca L. Darnell, PhD, Professor and Interim Department Chair, 352-273-4789, Fax: 352-392-5653, E-mail: rld@ufl.edu. *Application contact:* Gloria A. Moore, PhD, Professor/Graduate Coordinator, 352-273-4786, E-mail: gamoore@ufl.edu.
Website: http://www.hos.ufl.edu/

University of Georgia, College of Agricultural and Environmental Sciences, Department of Horticulture, Athens, GA 30602. Offers horticulture (MS, PhD); plant protection and pest management (MPPPM). *Program availability:* Part-time. *Degree requirements:* For master's, thesis (MS); for doctorate, one foreign language, thesis/ dissertation. *Entrance requirements:* For master's and doctorate, GRE General Test. Electronic applications accepted.

University of Guelph, Graduate Studies, Ontario Agricultural College, Department of Plant Agriculture, Guelph, ON N1G 2W1, Canada. Offers M Sc, PhD. *Program availability:* Part-time. *Degree requirements:* For master's, thesis; for doctorate, comprehensive exam, thesis/dissertation. *Entrance requirements:* For master's, minimum B average during previous 2 years of course work; for doctorate, minimum B average. Additional exam requirements/recommendations for international students: Required—TOEFL (minimum score 550 paper-based; 89 iBT), IELTS (minimum score 6.5), Michigan English Language Assessment Battery (minimum score: 85). Electronic applications accepted. *Faculty research:* Plant physiology, biochemistry, taxonomy, morphology, genetics, production, ecology, breeding and biotechnology.

University of Hawaii at Manoa, Graduate Division, College of Tropical Agriculture and Human Resources, Department of Tropical Plant and Soil Sciences, Honolulu, HI 96822. Offers MS, PhD. *Program availability:* Part-time. *Faculty:* 34 full-time (6 women), 10 part-time/adjunct (5 women). *Students:* 15 full-time (5 women), 2 part-time; includes 9 minority (4 Asian, non-Hispanic/Latino; 2 Hispanic/Latino; 2 Native Hawaiian or other Pacific Islander, non-Hispanic/Latino; 1 Two or more races, non-Hispanic/Latino), 2 international. Average age 34. 11 applicants, 55% accepted, 2 enrolled. In 2015, 2 master's awarded. *Degree requirements:* For master's, thesis optional; for doctorate, comprehensive exam, thesis/dissertation. *Entrance requirements:* For master's and doctorate, GRE General Test. Additional exam requirements/recommendations for international students: Required—TOEFL (minimum score 520 paper-based; 79 iBT), IELTS (minimum score 5). *Application deadline:* For fall admission, 3/1 for domestic students, 1/15 for international students; for spring admission, 9/1 for domestic students, 8/1 for international students. Application fee: $100. *Financial support:* In 2015–16, 1 fellowship (averaging $3,500 per year), 17 research assistantships (averaging $17,461 per year) were awarded; tuition waivers (full and partial) also available. *Faculty research:* Genetics and breeding; physiology, culture, and management; weed science; turf grass and landscape; sensory evaluation. *Total annual research expenditures:* $2.5 million. *Unit head:* Sylvia Yuen, Interim Dean, 808-956-8234, Fax: 808-956-9105, E-mail: syuen@hawaii.edu. *Application contact:* Kent Kobayashi, Graduate Chair, 808-956-5900, Fax: 808-956-3894, E-mail: kentko@hawaii.edu.
Website: http://www.agrss.sherman.hawaii.edu/hort/

Horticulture

University of Maine, Graduate School, College of Natural Sciences, Forestry, and Agriculture, School of Food and Agriculture, Orono, ME 04469. Offers animal sciences (MPS, MS); food and human nutrition (PhD); food science and human nutrition (MS); horticulture (MS); plant science (PhD). *Program availability:* Part-time. *Faculty:* 30 full-time (15 women). *Students:* 50 full-time (29 women), 2 part-time (both women); includes 3 minority (2 American Indian or Alaska Native, non-Hispanic/Latino; 1 Asian, non-Hispanic/Latino), 15 international. Average age 28. 81 applicants, 48% accepted, 20 enrolled. In 2015, 18 master's, 3 doctorates, 3 other advanced degrees awarded. *Degree requirements:* For master's, thesis (for some programs); for doctorate, comprehensive exam, thesis/dissertation. *Entrance requirements:* For master's and doctorate, GRE General Test. Additional exam requirements/recommendations for international students: Required—TOEFL. *Application deadline:* For fall admission, 2/1 priority date for domestic students. Applications are processed on a rolling basis. Application fee: $65. Electronic applications accepted. *Financial support:* In 2015–16, 36 students received support, including 1 fellowship (averaging $20,000 per year), 25 research assistantships with full tuition reimbursements available (averaging $14,600 per year), 7 teaching assistantships with full tuition reimbursements available (averaging $14,600 per year); Federal Work-Study, institutionally sponsored loans, and tuition waivers (full and partial) also available. Financial award application deadline: 3/1. *Faculty research:* Nutrition education for adults and children, food processing, food safety, sustainable crop and soil management, animal health and nutrition. *Total annual research expenditures:* $1.9 million. *Unit head:* Dr. Sue Erich, Chair, 207-581-2947, Fax: 207-581-2770. *Application contact:* Scott G. Delcourt, Assistant Vice President for Graduate Studies and Senior Associate Dean, 207-581-3291, Fax: 207-581-3232, E-mail: graduate@maine.edu.
Website: http://umaine.edu/foodandagriculture

University of Manitoba, Faculty of Graduate Studies, Faculty of Agricultural and Food Sciences, Department of Plant Science, Winnipeg, MB R3T 2N2, Canada. Offers agronomy and plant protection (M Sc, PhD); horticulture (M Sc, PhD); plant breeding and genetics (M Sc, PhD); plant physiology-biochemistry (M Sc, PhD). *Degree requirements:* For master's, thesis; for doctorate, one foreign language, thesis/dissertation.

University of Maryland, College Park, Academic Affairs, College of Agriculture and Natural Resources, Department of Plant Science and Landscape Architecture, Plant Science Program, College Park, MD 20742. Offers MS, PhD. *Entrance requirements:* For doctorate, GRE General Test. Additional exam requirements/recommendations for international students: Required—TOEFL. Electronic applications accepted. *Faculty research:* Mineral nutrition, genetics and breeding, chemical growth, histochemistry, postharvest physiology.

University of Missouri, Office of Research and Graduate Studies, College of Agriculture, Food and Natural Resources, Division of Plant Sciences, Columbia, MO 65211. Offers crop, soil and pest management (MS, PhD); entomology (MS, PhD); horticulture (MS, PhD); plant biology and genetics (MS, PhD); plant stress biology (MS, PhD). Terminal master's awarded for partial completion of doctoral program. *Degree requirements:* For master's, thesis; for doctorate, comprehensive exam, thesis/dissertation. *Entrance requirements:* For master's and doctorate, GRE General Test, minimum GPA of 3.0; bachelor's degree from accredited college. Additional exam requirements/recommendations for international students: Required—TOEFL (minimum score 500 paper-based; 61 iBT), IELTS (minimum score 5.5). Electronic applications accepted. *Faculty research:* Crop, soil and pest management; entomology; horticulture; plant biology and genetics; plant microbiology and pathology.

University of Nebraska–Lincoln, Graduate College, College of Agricultural Sciences and Natural Resources, Department of Agronomy and Horticulture, Program in Horticulture, Lincoln, NE 68588. Offers MS, PhD. *Degree requirements:* For master's, thesis optional. *Entrance requirements:* For master's, GRE General Test. Additional exam requirements/recommendations for international students: Required—TOEFL (minimum score 600 paper-based). Electronic applications accepted. *Faculty research:* Horticultural crops: production, management, cultural, and ecological aspects; tissue and cell culture; plant nutrition and anatomy; postharvest physiology and ecology.

University of Puerto Rico, Mayagüez Campus, Graduate Studies, College of Agricultural Sciences, Department of Crops and Agroenvironmental Sciences, Mayagüez, PR 00681-9000. Offers agronomy (MS); crop protection (MS); horticulture (MS); soils (MS). *Program availability:* Part-time. *Degree requirements:* For master's, comprehensive exam, thesis.

University of South Africa, College of Agriculture and Environmental Sciences, Pretoria, South Africa. Offers agriculture (MS); consumer science (MCS); environmental management (MA, MS, PhD); environmental science (MA, MS, PhD); geography (MA,

MS, PhD); horticulture (M Tech); human ecology (MHE); life sciences (MS); nature conservation (M Tech).

University of Vermont, Graduate College, College of Agriculture and Life Sciences, Department of Plant and Soil Science, Burlington, VT 05405. Offers MS, PhD. *Degree requirements:* For master's, thesis; for doctorate, one foreign language, thesis/dissertation. *Entrance requirements:* For master's and doctorate, GRE General Test. Additional exam requirements/recommendations for international students: Required—TOEFL (minimum score 550 paper-based; 80 iBT). Electronic applications accepted. *Faculty research:* Soil chemistry, plant nutrition.

University of Washington, Graduate School, College of the Environment, School of Forest Resources, Seattle, WA 98195. Offers bioresource science and engineering (MS, PhD); environmental horticulture (MEH); forest ecology (MS, PhD); forest management (MFR); forest soils (MS, PhD); restoration ecology (MS, PhD); restoration ecology and environmental horticulture (MS, PhD); social sciences (MS, PhD); sustainable resource management (MS, PhD); wildlife science (MS, PhD); MFR/MAIS; MPA/MS. *Accreditation:* SAF. *Program availability:* Part-time. *Degree requirements:* For master's, thesis; for doctorate, comprehensive exam, thesis/dissertation. *Entrance requirements:* For master's and doctorate, GRE, minimum GPA of 3.0. Additional exam requirements/recommendations for international students: Required—TOEFL. Electronic applications accepted. *Faculty research:* Ecosystem analysis, silviculture and forest protection, paper science and engineering, environmental horticulture and urban forestry, natural resource policy and economics, restoration ecology and environment horticulture, conservation, human dimensions, wildlife, bioresource science and engineering.

University of Wisconsin–Madison, Graduate School, College of Agricultural and Life Sciences, Department of Horticulture, Madison, WI 53706-1380. Offers MS, PhD. *Program availability:* Part-time. Terminal master's awarded for partial completion of doctoral program. *Degree requirements:* For master's, comprehensive exam, thesis (for some programs); for doctorate, comprehensive exam, thesis/dissertation. *Entrance requirements:* For master's and doctorate, minimum GPA of 3.0. Additional exam requirements/recommendations for international students: Required—TOEFL (minimum score 580 paper-based). Electronic applications accepted. *Expenses:* Tuition, state resident: full-time $5364. Tuition, nonresident: full-time $12,027. *Required fees:* $571. Tuition and fees vary according to campus/location, program and reciprocity agreements. *Faculty research:* Biotechnology, crop breeding/genetics, environmental physiology, crop management, cytogenetics.

Virginia Polytechnic Institute and State University, Graduate School, College of Agriculture and Life Sciences, Blacksburg, VA 24061. Offers agricultural and applied economics (MS); agricultural and life sciences (MS); animal and poultry science (MS, PhD); crop and soil environmental sciences (MS, PhD); dairy science (MS); entomology (PhD); horticulture (MS, PhD); human nutrition, foods and exercise (MS, PhD); life sciences (MS, PhD); plant pathology, physiology and weed science (PhD). *Degree requirements:* For master's, comprehensive exam (for some programs), thesis (for some programs); for doctorate, comprehensive exam (for some programs), thesis/dissertation (for some programs). *Entrance requirements:* For master's and doctorate, GRE/GMAT (may vary by department). Additional exam requirements/recommendations for international students: Required—TOEFL (minimum score 550 paper-based). Electronic applications accepted.

Washington State University, College of Agricultural, Human, and Natural Resource Sciences, Department of Horticulture, Pullman, WA 99164. Offers MS, PhD. Programs offered at the Pullman campus. *Program availability:* Part-time. *Degree requirements:* For master's, comprehensive exam (for some programs), thesis (for some programs), oral exam; for doctorate, comprehensive exam, thesis/dissertation, oral exam, written exam. *Entrance requirements:* For master's and doctorate, GRE General Test, GRE Subject Test, minimum GPA of 3.0, 3 letters of recommendation, statement of purpose/intent. Additional exam requirements/recommendations for international students: Required—TOEFL (minimum score 550 paper-based). Electronic applications accepted. *Faculty research:* Post-harvest physiology, genetics/plant breeding, molecular biology.

West Virginia University, Davis College of Agriculture, Forestry and Consumer Sciences, Division of Plant and Soil Sciences, Morgantown, WV 26506. Offers agricultural sciences (PhD), including animal and food sciences, plant and soil sciences; agronomy (MS); entomology (MS); environmental microbiology (MS); horticulture (MS); plant pathology (MS). *Degree requirements:* For master's, thesis. *Entrance requirements:* For master's, GRE, minimum GPA of 2.5. Additional exam requirements/recommendations for international students: Required—TOEFL. *Expenses:* Tuition, state resident: full-time $8568. Tuition, nonresident: full-time $22,140. Tuition and fees vary according to program. *Faculty research:* Water quality, reclamation of disturbed land, crop production, pest control, environmental protection.

Plant Sciences

Alabama Agricultural and Mechanical University, School of Graduate Studies, College of Agricultural, Life and Natural Sciences, Department of Biological and Environmental Sciences, Huntsville, AL 35811. Offers biology (MS, PhD); plant and soil science (MS, PhD). *Program availability:* Evening/weekend. Terminal master's awarded for partial completion of doctoral program. *Degree requirements:* For master's, thesis optional; for doctorate, one foreign language, thesis/dissertation optional. *Entrance requirements:* For master's, GRE General Test, BS in agriculture; for doctorate, GRE General Test, master's degree. Additional exam requirements/recommendations for international students: Required—TOEFL (minimum score 500 paper-based; 61 iBT). Electronic applications accepted. *Faculty research:* Plant breeding, cytogenetics, crop production, soil chemistry and fertility, remote sensing.

American University of Beirut, Graduate Programs, Faculty of Agricultural and Food Sciences, Beirut, Lebanon. Offers agricultural economics (MS); animal sciences (MS); ecosystem management (MSES); food technology (MS); irrigation (MS); nutrition (MS); plant protection (MS); plant science (MS); poultry science (MS); rural community development (MS). *Program availability:* Part-time. *Faculty:* 19 full-time (4 women). *Students:* 13 full-time (5 women), 55 part-time (41 women). Average age 26. 93 applicants, 52% accepted, 25 enrolled. In 2015, 27 master's awarded. *Degree requirements:* For master's, one foreign language, comprehensive exam, thesis (for some programs). *Entrance requirements:* Additional exam requirements/recommendations for international students: Required—TOEFL (minimum score 600 paper-based; 100 iBT), IELTS (minimum score 7.5). *Application deadline:* For fall admission, 2/10 for domestic and international students; for spring admission, 11/2 for

domestic and international students. Application fee: $50. Electronic applications accepted. *Expenses: Tuition, area resident:* Full-time $16,254; part-time $903 per credit. *Required fees:* $699. Tuition and fees vary according to course load and program. *Financial support:* In 2015–16, 1 research assistantship with partial tuition reimbursement (averaging $1,800 per year), 48 teaching assistantships with tuition reimbursements (averaging $1,400 per year) were awarded; scholarships/grants, health care benefits, and unspecified assistantships also available. Financial award application deadline: 2/2. *Faculty research:* Developing skills in the field of integrated energy planning in med landscaper; profiling refugee households in Lebanon; Improving the nutrition of Syrian refugees and host communities though garden walls; monitoring and evaluation of salt iodization in Lebanon; mother and child cohorts: towards curbing the epidemic of non-communicable diseases in Qatar and Lebanon.. *Total annual research expenditures:* $852,730. *Unit head:* Prof. Nahla Hwalla, Dean, 961-1343002 Ext. 4400, Fax: 961-1744460, E-mail: nahla@aub.edu.lb. *Application contact:* Dr. Rabih Talhouk, Director, Graduate Council, 961-1350000 Ext. 4386, Fax: 961-1374374, E-mail: graduate.council@aub.edu.lb.
Website: http://www.aub.edu.lb/fafs/fafs_home/Pages/index.aspx

Brigham Young University, Graduate Studies, College of Life Sciences, Department of Plant and Wildlife Sciences, Provo, UT 84604. Offers environmental science (MS); genetics and biotechnology (MS); wildlife and wildlands conservation (MS, PhD). *Faculty:* 24 full-time (1 woman), 1 (woman) part-time/adjunct. *Students:* 12 full-time (6 women), 31 part-time (9 women); includes 4 minority (1 Asian, non-Hispanic/Latino; 3 Hispanic/Latino). Average age 25. 25 applicants, 40% accepted, 9 enrolled. In 2015, 15

328 www.petersons.com

Peterson's Graduate Programs in the Physical Sciences, Mathematics, Agricultural Sciences, the Environment & Natural Resources 2017

master's awarded. *Degree requirements:* For master's, thesis; for doctorate, comprehensive exam, thesis/dissertation, minimum GPA of 3.2, 54 hours (18 dissertation, 36 coursework). *Entrance requirements:* For master's, GRE General Test, minimum GPA of 3.2; for doctorate, GRE, minimum GPA of 3.2. Additional exam requirements/recommendations for international students: Required—TOEFL (minimum score 580 paper-based; 85 iBT). *Application deadline:* 2/1 for domestic and international students. Applications are processed on a rolling basis. Application fee: $50. Electronic applications accepted. *Financial support:* In 2015–16, 42 students received support, including 64 research assistantships with partial tuition reimbursements available (averaging $19,000 per year), 52 teaching assistantships with partial tuition reimbursements available (averaging $19,000 per year); scholarships/grants and tuition waivers (partial) also available. Financial award application deadline: 2/1. *Faculty research:* Environmental science, plant genetics, plant ecology, plant nutrition and pathology, wildlife and wildlands conservation. *Total annual research expenditures:* $2.8 million. *Unit head:* Brock R. McMillan, Chair, 801-422-3527, Fax: 801-422-0008, E-mail: brock_mcmillan@byu.edu. *Application contact:* Bradley D. Geary, Graduate Coordinator, 801-422-1228, Fax: 801-422-0008, E-mail: bradley_geary@byu.edu.
Website: http://pws.byu.edu/home/

California State University, Fresno, Division of Graduate Studies, College of Agricultural Sciences and Technology, Department of Plant Science, Fresno, CA 93740-8027. Offers MS. *Program availability:* Part-time. *Degree requirements:* For master's, thesis. *Entrance requirements:* For master's, GRE General Test, minimum GPA of 2.5. Additional exam requirements/recommendations for international students: Required—TOEFL. Electronic applications accepted. *Faculty research:* Crop patterns, small watershed management, electronic monitoring of feedlot cattle, disease control, dairy operations.

Clemson University, Graduate School, College of Agriculture, Forestry and Life Sciences, Department of Plant and Environmental Sciences, Program in Plant and Environmental Sciences, Clemson, SC 29634. Offers MS, PhD. *Faculty:* 5 full-time (2 women). *Students:* 30 full-time (9 women), 16 part-time (5 women); includes 1 minority (Two or more races, non-Hispanic/Latino), 21 international. Average age 30. 27 applicants, 33% accepted, 7 enrolled. In 2015, 12 master's, 8 doctorates awarded. *Degree requirements:* For master's, thesis; for doctorate, comprehensive exam, thesis/dissertation. *Entrance requirements:* For master's and doctorate, GRE General Test, unofficial transcripts, letters of recommendation. Additional exam requirements/recommendations for international students: Required—TOEFL (minimum score 550 paper-based; 80 iBT), IELTS (minimum score 6.5), PTE (minimum score 54). *Application deadline:* For fall admission, 4/15 for domestic and international students; for spring admission, 11/15 for domestic and international students. Applications are processed on a rolling basis. Application fee: $80 ($90 for international students). Electronic applications accepted. *Expenses:* $4,060 per semester full-time resident, $8,103 per semester full-time non-resident, $448 per credit hour part-time resident, $898 per credit hour part-time non-resident. *Financial support:* In 2015–16, 33 students received support, including 3 fellowships with partial tuition reimbursements available (averaging $5,000 per year), 20 research assistantships with partial tuition reimbursements available (averaging $17,289 per year), 10 teaching assistantships with partial tuition reimbursements available (averaging $16,581 per year); career-related internships or fieldwork and health care benefits also available. Financial award application deadline: 4/15. *Faculty research:* Agronomy, horticulture, plant pathology, plant physiology, entomology. *Unit head:* Dr. Patricia Zungoli, Department Head, 864-656-5041, Fax: 864-656-4960, E-mail: pzngl@clemson.edu. *Application contact:* Dr. Paula Agudelo, Graduate Program Coordinator, 864-656-5741,
E-mail: pagudel@clemson.edu.
Website: http://www.clemson.edu/graduate/academics/program-details.html?m_id=Plant-Environmental-Sciences

Colorado State University, College of Agricultural Sciences, Department of Bioagricultural Sciences and Pest Management, Fort Collins, CO 80523-1177. Offers entomology (MS, PhD); pest management (MS); plant pathology and weed science (MS, PhD). *Program availability:* Part-time, evening/weekend. *Faculty:* 18 full-time (6 women), 5 part-time/adjunct (2 women). *Students:* 22 full-time (12 women), 13 part-time (7 women); includes 2 minority (both Two or more races, non-Hispanic/Latino), 8 international. Average age 28. 15 applicants, 100% accepted, 13 enrolled. In 2015, 3 master's, 4 doctorates awarded. *Degree requirements:* For master's, comprehensive exam, thesis; for doctorate, comprehensive exam, thesis/dissertation. *Entrance requirements:* For master's and doctorate, GRE General Test, minimum GPA of 3.0, letters of recommendation, essay, transcripts. Additional exam requirements/recommendations for international students: Required—TOEFL (minimum score 550 paper-based; 80 iBT), IELTS (minimum score 6.5). *Application deadline:* For fall admission, 1/15 priority date for domestic and international students; for spring admission, 9/1 priority date for domestic and international students. Applications are processed on a rolling basis. Application fee: $60 ($70 for international students). Electronic applications accepted. *Expenses:* Tuition, state resident: full-time $9348. Tuition, nonresident: full-time $22,916. *Required fees:* $2174; $473.72 per credit hour. $236.86 per semester. Tuition and fees vary according to course load and program. *Financial support:* In 2015–16, 4 fellowships with full tuition reimbursements (averaging $39,950 per year), 20 research assistantships with full tuition reimbursements (averaging $20,192 per year), 8 teaching assistantships with full tuition reimbursements (averaging $16,403 per year) were awarded. Financial award application deadline: 1/15. *Faculty research:* Genomics and molecular biology, ecology and biodiversity, biology and management of invasive species, integrated pest management. *Total annual research expenditures:* $3.3 million. *Unit head:* Dr. Louis Bjostad, Department Head, 970-491-3612, Fax: 970-491-3862, E-mail: louis.bjostad@colostate.edu. *Application contact:* Janet Dill, Graduate Coordinator, 970-491-0402, Fax: 970-491-3862, E-mail: janet.dill@colostate.edu.
Website: http://bspm.agsci.colostate.edu/

Colorado State University, College of Agricultural Sciences, Department of Soil and Crop Sciences, Fort Collins, CO 80523-1170. Offers MS, PhD. *Program availability:* Part-time. *Faculty:* 19 full-time (6 women), 3 part-time/adjunct (2 women). *Students:* 14 full-time (7 women), 30 part-time (20 women); includes 3 minority (all Hispanic/Latino), 15 international. Average age 34. 14 applicants, 79% accepted, 7 enrolled. In 2015, 4 master's, 4 doctorates awarded. Terminal master's awarded for partial completion of doctoral program. *Degree requirements:* For master's, thesis; for doctorate, comprehensive exam, thesis/dissertation, student teaching. *Entrance requirements:* For master's and doctorate, GRE, minimum GPA of 3.0, transcripts, personal statement, resume/curriculum vitae, letters of recommendation. Additional exam requirements/recommendations for international students: Required—TOEFL (minimum score 550 paper-based; 80 iBT); Recommended—IELTS (minimum score 6.5). *Application deadline:* For fall admission, 4/1 priority date for domestic students, 5/1 priority date for international students; for spring admission, 9/1 priority date for domestic students, 10/1 priority date for international students. Application fee: $60 ($70 for international students). Electronic applications accepted. *Expenses:* Tuition, state resident: full-time $9348. Tuition, nonresident: full-time $22,916. *Required fees:* $2174; $473.72 per credit hour. $236.86 per semester. Tuition and fees vary according to course load and program. *Financial support:* In 2015–16, 2 fellowships with full tuition reimbursements (averaging $42,812 per year), 18 research assistantships with full tuition reimbursements (averaging $23,343 per year), 1 teaching assistantship with full tuition reimbursement (averaging $16,380 per year) were awarded; scholarships/grants and unspecified assistantships also available. Financial award application deadline: 2/15; financial award applicants required to submit FAFSA. *Faculty research:* Water quality, soil fertility, agroecosystems management, plant breeding and genetics, soil science and crop systems. *Total annual research expenditures:* $5.4 million. *Unit head:* Dr. Eugene Kelly, Department Head and Professor, 970-491-6501, Fax: 970-491-5676, E-mail: eugene.kelly@colostate.edu. *Application contact:* Karen Allison, Student Coordinator, 970-491-6295, Fax: 970-491-5676, E-mail: karen.allison@colostate.edu.
Website: http://www.soilcrop.colostate.edu/

Cornell University, Graduate School, Graduate Fields of Agriculture and Life Sciences, Field of Plant Breeding, Ithaca, NY 14853-0001. Offers plant breeding (MPS, MS, PhD); plant genetics (MPS, MS, PhD). Terminal master's awarded for partial completion of doctoral program. *Degree requirements:* For master's, thesis (MS), project paper (MPS); for doctorate, comprehensive exam, thesis/dissertation. *Entrance requirements:* For master's and doctorate, GRE General Test, GRE Subject Test (recommended), 3 letters of recommendation. Additional exam requirements/recommendations for international students: Required—TOEFL (minimum score 550 paper-based; 77 iBT). Electronic applications accepted. *Faculty research:* Crop breeding for improved yield, stress resistance and quality; genetics and genomics of crop plants; applications of molecular biology and bioinformatics to crop improvement; genetic diversity and utilization of wild germplasm; international agriculture.

Cornell University, Graduate School, Graduate Fields of Agriculture and Life Sciences, Field of Plant Protection, Ithaca, NY 14853-0001. Offers MPS. *Degree requirements:* For master's, internship, final exam. *Entrance requirements:* For master's, GRE General Test, 3 letters of recommendation. Additional exam requirements/recommendations for international students: Required—TOEFL (minimum score 550 paper-based; 77 iBT). Electronic applications accepted. *Faculty research:* Fruit and vegetable crop insects and diseases, systems modeling, biological control, plant protection economics, integrated pest management.

Delaware State University, Graduate Programs, Department of Agriculture and Natural Resources, Program in Plant Science, Dover, DE 19901-2277. Offers MS. *Entrance requirements:* For master's, GRE. Additional exam requirements/recommendations for international students: Required—TOEFL (minimum score 550 paper-based).

Illinois State University, Graduate School, College of Arts and Sciences, Department of Biological Sciences, Normal, IL 61790-2200. Offers animal behavior (MS); bacteriology (MS); biochemistry (MS); biological sciences (MS); biology (PhD); biophysics (MS); biotechnology (MS); botany (MS, PhD); cell biology (MS); conservation biology (MS); developmental biology (MS); ecology (MS, PhD); entomology (MS); evolutionary biology (MS); genetics (MS, PhD); immunology (MS); microbiology (MS, PhD); molecular biology (MS); molecular genetics (MS); neurobiology (MS); neuroscience (MS); parasitology (MS); physiology (MS, PhD); plant biology (MS); plant molecular biology (MS); plant sciences (MS); structural biology (MS); zoology (MS, PhD). *Program availability:* Part-time. *Degree requirements:* For master's, thesis or alternative; for doctorate, variable foreign language requirement, thesis/dissertation, 2 terms of residency. *Entrance requirements:* For master's, GRE General Test, minimum GPA of 2.6 in last 60 hours of course work; for doctorate, GRE General Test. *Faculty research:* Redoc balance and drug development in schistosoma mansoni, control of the growth of listeria monocytogenes at low temperature, regulation of cell expansion and microtubule function by SPRI, CRUI: physiology and fitness consequences of different life history phenotypes.

Iowa State University of Science and Technology, Program in Plant Breeding, Ames, IA 50011. Offers MS, PhD. *Degree requirements:* For master's, thesis optional. *Entrance requirements:* For master's and doctorate, GRE. Additional exam requirements/recommendations for international students: Required—TOEFL (minimum score 550 paper-based; 79 iBT), IELTS (minimum score 6.5). Electronic applications accepted.

Kansas State University, Graduate School, College of Agriculture, Department of Agronomy, Manhattan, KS 66506. Offers crop science (MS, PhD); plant breeding and genetics (MS); range and forage science (MS, PhD); soil and environmental science (PhD); weed science (MS, PhD). *Program availability:* Part-time. *Degree requirements:* For master's, thesis or alternative, oral exam; for doctorate, thesis/dissertation, preliminary exams. *Entrance requirements:* For master's, minimum GPA of 3.0 in BS; for doctorate, minimum GPA of 3.0 in master's program. Additional exam requirements/recommendations for international students: Required—TOEFL (minimum score 550 paper-based; 79 iBT). Electronic applications accepted. *Faculty research:* Range and forage science; soil and environmental science; weed science; plant breeding and genetics; crop physiology, ecology and production.

Lehman College of the City University of New York, School of Natural and Social Sciences, Department of Biological Sciences, Program in Plant Sciences, Bronx, NY 10468-1589. Offers PhD. *Degree requirements:* For doctorate, 2 foreign languages, thesis/dissertation. *Entrance requirements:* For doctorate, GRE General Test.

McGill University, Faculty of Graduate and Postdoctoral Studies, Faculty of Agricultural and Environmental Sciences, Department of Plant Science, Montréal, QC H3A 2T5, Canada. Offers M Sc, M Sc A, PhD, Certificate.

Michigan State University, The Graduate School, College of Agriculture and Natural Resources, MSU-DOE Plant Research Laboratory, East Lansing, MI 48824. Offers biochemistry and molecular biology (PhD); cellular and molecular biology (PhD); crop and soil sciences (PhD); genetics (PhD); microbiology and molecular genetics (PhD); plant biology (PhD); plant physiology (PhD). Offered jointly with the Department of Energy. *Degree requirements:* For doctorate, comprehensive exam, thesis/dissertation, laboratory rotation, defense of dissertation. *Entrance requirements:* For doctorate, GRE General Test, acceptance into one of the affiliated department programs; 3 letters of recommendation; bachelor's degree or equivalent in life sciences, chemistry, biochemistry, or biophysics; research experience. Electronic applications accepted. *Faculty research:* Role of hormones in the regulation of plant development and physiology, molecular mechanisms associated with signal recognition, development and application of genetic methods and materials, protein routing and function.

Michigan State University, The Graduate School, College of Agriculture and Natural Resources, Program in Plant Breeding and Genetics, East Lansing, MI 48824. Offers MS, PhD. *Entrance requirements:* Additional exam requirements/recommendations for international students: Required—TOEFL. Electronic applications accepted. *Faculty research:* Applied plant breeding and genetics; disease, insect and herbicide resistances; gene isolation and genomics; abiotic stress factors; molecular mapping.

Mississippi State University, College of Agriculture and Life Sciences, Department of Plant and Soil Sciences, Mississippi State, MS 39762. Offers agriculture (MS, PhD),

including agronomy, horticulture, weed science. *Faculty:* 49 full-time (5 women). *Students:* 45 full-time (11 women), 33 part-time (6 women); includes 2 minority (1 American Indian or Alaska Native, non-Hispanic/Latino; 1 Asian, non-Hispanic/Latino), 20 international. Average age 27. 26 applicants, 46% accepted, 11 enrolled. In 2015, 16 master's, 7 doctorates awarded. *Degree requirements:* For master's, comprehensive exam, thesis, oral and/or written exams; for doctorate, comprehensive exam, thesis/dissertation, minimum of 20 semester hours of research for dissertation. *Entrance requirements:* For master's, GRE (for weed science), minimum GPA of 2.75 (agronomy/horticulture), 3.0 (weed science); for doctorate, GRE (for weed science), minimum GPA of 3.0 (agronomy/horticulture), 3.25 (weed science). Additional exam requirements/recommendations for international students: Required—TOEFL (minimum score 500 paper-based; 61 iBT), TOEFL (minimum score 550 paper-based, 79 iBT) or IELTS (minimum score 6.5) for weed science; Recommended—IELTS (minimum score 5.5). *Application deadline:* For fall admission, 7/1 for domestic students, 5/1 for international students; for spring admission, 10/1 for domestic students, 9/1 for international students. Applications are processed on a rolling basis. Application fee: $60. Electronic applications accepted. *Expenses: Tuition, area resident:* Full-time $7502; part-time $833.74 per credit hour. Tuition, nonresident: full-time $20,142; part-time $2238.24 per credit hour. *Financial support:* In 2015–16, 31 research assistantships (averaging $14,967 per year), 3 teaching assistantships (averaging $15,951 per year) were awarded; Federal Work-Study, institutionally sponsored loans, scholarships/grants, and unspecified assistantships also available. Financial award application deadline: 4/1; financial award applicants required to submit FAFSA. *Faculty research:* Bioenergy crops, cotton breeding, environmental plant pathology, row crop weed control, genomics. *Unit head:* Dr. Mike Phillips, Professor and Head, 662-325-2311, Fax: 662-325-8742, E-mail: jmp657@msstate.edu. *Application contact:* Marina Hunt, Admissions Assistant, 662-325-5188, E-mail: mhunt@grad.msstate.edu.
Website: http://www.pss.msstate.edu/

Missouri State University, Graduate College, William H. Darr School of Agriculture, Springfield, MO 65897. Offers plant science (MS); secondary education (MS Ed), including agriculture. *Program availability:* Part-time. *Faculty:* 16 full-time (5 women), 1 part-time/adjunct (0 women). *Students:* 17 full-time (9 women), 26 part-time (17 women); includes 3 minority (1 Black or African American, non-Hispanic/Latino; 1 Hispanic/Latino; 1 Two or more races, non-Hispanic/Latino), 1 international. Average age 27. 28 applicants, 64% accepted, 17 enrolled. In 2015, 21 master's awarded. *Degree requirements:* For master's, comprehensive exam, thesis or alternative. *Entrance requirements:* For master's, GRE (MS in plant science, MNAS), 9-12 teacher certification (MS Ed), minimum GPA of 3.0 (MS plant science, MNAS). Additional exam requirements/recommendations for international students: Required—TOEFL (minimum score 550 paper-based; 79 iBT), IELTS (minimum score 6). *Application deadline:* For fall admission, 7/20 priority date for domestic students, 5/1 for international students; for spring admission, 12/20 priority date for domestic students, 9/1 for international students; for summer admission, 5/20 priority date for domestic students. Applications are processed on a rolling basis. Application fee: $35 ($50 for international students). Electronic applications accepted. *Expenses:* Tuition, state resident: full-time $5500. Tuition, nonresident: full-time $10,108. *Required fees:* $1000. *Financial support:* In 2015–16, 7 research assistantships with full tuition reimbursements (averaging $9,365 per year), 6 teaching assistantships with full tuition reimbursements (averaging $8,450 per year) were awarded; Federal Work-Study, institutionally sponsored loans, scholarships/grants, and unspecified assistantships also available. Financial award application deadline: 3/31; financial award applicants required to submit FAFSA. *Faculty research:* Grapevine biotechnology, agricultural marketing, Asian elephant reproduction, poultry science, integrated pest management. *Unit head:* Dr. W. Anson Elliott, Head, 417-836-5638, E-mail: ansonelliot@missouristate.edu. *Application contact:* Michael Edwards, Coordinator of Graduate Admissions, 417-836-5330, Fax: 417-836-6200, E-mail: michaeledwards@missouristate.edu.
Website: http://ag.missouristate.edu/

Montana State University, The Graduate School, College of Agriculture, Department of Plant Sciences and Plant Pathology, Bozeman, MT 59717. Offers plant pathology (MS); plant sciences (MS, PhD), including plant genetics (PhD), plant pathology (PhD). *Program availability:* Part-time. *Degree requirements:* For master's, comprehensive exam; for doctorate, comprehensive exam, thesis/dissertation. *Entrance requirements:* For master's, GRE General Test, minimum GPA of 3.0; for doctorate, GRE General Test. Additional exam requirements/recommendations for international students: Required—TOEFL (minimum score 550 paper-based). Electronic applications accepted. *Faculty research:* Plant genetics, plant metabolism, plant microbe interactions, plant pathology, entomology research.

New Mexico State University, College of Agricultural, Consumer and Environmental Sciences, Department of Entomology, Plant Pathology and Weed Science, Las Cruces, NM 88003-8001. Offers MS. *Program availability:* Part-time. *Faculty:* 10 full-time (1 woman). *Students:* 8 full-time (3 women), 3 part-time (all women); includes 3 minority (1 American Indian or Alaska Native, non-Hispanic/Latino; 2 Hispanic/Latino), 4 international. Average age 29. 4 applicants, 75% accepted, 3 enrolled. In 2015, 6 master's awarded. *Degree requirements:* For master's, comprehensive exam, thesis. *Entrance requirements:* For master's, GRE General Test. Additional exam requirements/recommendations for international students: Required—TOEFL (minimum score 550 paper-based; 79 iBT), IELTS (minimum score 6.5). *Application deadline:* For fall admission, 7/1 priority date for domestic students; for spring admission, 11/1 priority date for domestic students. Applications are processed on a rolling basis. Application fee: $40 ($50 for international students). Electronic applications accepted. *Expenses:* $274.50 per credit hour for in-state students, and all students enrolled in six or fewer credits; $839.30 per credit hour for out-of-state and international students enrolled in at least seven hours. *Financial support:* In 2015–16, 10 students received support, including 6 research assistantships (averaging $21,962 per year), 3 teaching assistantships (averaging $16,022 per year); career-related internships or fieldwork, Federal Work-Study, scholarships/grants, traineeships, health care benefits, and unspecified assistantships also available. Support available to part-time students. Financial award application deadline: 3/1. *Faculty research:* Entomology, nematology, plant pathology, weed science. *Total annual research expenditures:* $2.3 million. *Unit head:* Dr. Gerald K. Sims, Department Head, 575-646-3225, Fax: 575-646-8087, E-mail: gksims@nmsu.edu. *Application contact:* Belinda Williams, 575-646-3225, Fax: 575-646-8087.
Website: http://eppws.nmsu.edu/

North Carolina Agricultural and Technical State University, School of Graduate Studies, School of Agriculture and Environmental Sciences, Department of Natural Resources and Environmental Design, Greensboro, NC 27411. Offers plant, soil and environmental science (MS). *Program availability:* Part-time, evening/weekend. *Degree requirements:* For master's, comprehensive exam, thesis optional, qualifying exam. *Entrance requirements:* For master's, GRE General Test, minimum GPA of 3.0. *Faculty research:* Soil parameters and compaction of forest site, controlled traffic effects on soil, improving soybean and vegetable crops.

North Dakota State University, College of Graduate and Interdisciplinary Studies, College of Agriculture, Food Systems, and Natural Resources, Department of Plant Sciences, Fargo, ND 58102. Offers horticulture (MS); plant science (MS); plant sciences (PhD). *Program availability:* Part-time. *Degree requirements:* For master's, thesis; for doctorate, thesis/dissertation. *Entrance requirements:* Additional exam requirements/recommendations for international students: Required—TOEFL (minimum score 525 paper-based; 71 iBT). Electronic applications accepted. *Faculty research:* Biotechnology, weed control science, plant breeding, plant genetics, crop physiology.

The Ohio State University, Graduate School, Center for Applied Plant Sciences, Columbus, OH 43210. Offers PhD. *Degree requirements:* For doctorate, thesis/dissertation. *Entrance requirements:* Additional exam requirements/recommendations for international students: Required—TOEFL (minimum score 550 paper-based; 79 iBT), IELTS (minimum score 7), Michigan English Language Assessment Battery (minimum score 82). Electronic applications accepted.

Oklahoma State University, College of Agricultural Science and Natural Resources, Department of Horticulture and Landscape Architecture, Stillwater, OK 74078. Offers crop science (PhD); environmental science (PhD); horticulture (M Ag, MS); plant science (PhD). *Faculty:* 17 full-time (4 women). *Students:* 3 full-time (1 woman), 9 part-time (3 women); includes 2 minority (1 Black or African American, non-Hispanic/Latino; 1 Asian, non-Hispanic/Latino), 5 international. Average age 30. 8 applicants, 63% accepted, 5 enrolled. In 2015, 3 master's awarded. *Degree requirements:* For master's, thesis (for some programs); for doctorate, comprehensive exam, thesis/dissertation. *Entrance requirements:* For master's and doctorate, GRE or GMAT. Additional exam requirements/recommendations for international students: Required—TOEFL (minimum score 550 paper-based; 79 iBT). *Application deadline:* For fall admission, 3/1 priority date for international students; for spring admission, 8/1 priority date for international students. Applications are processed on a rolling basis. Application fee: $40 ($75 for international students). Electronic applications accepted. *Expenses:* Tuition, state resident: full-time $3528; part-time $196 per credit hour. Tuition, nonresident: full-time $14,144; part-time $785.75 per credit hour. *Required fees:* $1895; $105.25 per credit hour. Tuition and fees vary according to campus/location. *Financial support:* In 2015–16, 9 research assistantships (averaging $10,469 per year), 3 teaching assistantships (averaging $12,261 per year) were awarded; career-related internships or fieldwork, Federal Work-Study, scholarships/grants, health care benefits, tuition waivers (partial), and unspecified assistantships also available. Support available to part-time students. Financial award application deadline: 3/1; financial award applicants required to submit FAFSA. *Faculty research:* Stress and postharvest physiology; water utilization and runoff; integrated pest management (IPM) systems and nursery, turf, floriculture, vegetable, net and fruit produces and natural resources, food extraction, and processing; public garden management. *Unit head:* Dr. Janet Cole, Department Head, 405-744-5414, Fax: 405-744-9709. *Application contact:* Dr. Sheryl Tucker, Dean, 405-744-7099, Fax: 405-744-0355, E-mail: gradi@okstate.edu.
Website: http://www.hortla.okstate.edu/

Oklahoma State University, College of Agricultural Science and Natural Resources, Department of Plant and Soil Sciences, Stillwater, OK 74078. Offers crop science (PhD); plant and soil sciences (MS); soil science (M Ag, PhD). *Faculty:* 28 full-time (3 women). *Students:* 13 full-time (6 women), 37 part-time (12 women); includes 5 minority (4 American Indian or Alaska Native, non-Hispanic/Latino; 1 Two or more races, non-Hispanic/Latino), 28 international. Average age 28. 26 applicants, 50% accepted, 8 enrolled. In 2015, 10 master's, 6 doctorates awarded. *Degree requirements:* For master's, thesis; for doctorate, comprehensive exam, thesis/dissertation. *Entrance requirements:* For master's and doctorate, GRE or GMAT. Additional exam requirements/recommendations for international students: Required—TOEFL (minimum score 550 paper-based; 79 iBT). *Application deadline:* For fall admission, 3/1 priority date for international students; for spring admission, 8/1 priority date for international students. Applications are processed on a rolling basis. Application fee: $40 ($75 for international students). Electronic applications accepted. *Expenses:* Tuition, state resident: full-time $3528; part-time $196 per credit hour. Tuition, nonresident: full-time $14,144; part-time $785.75 per credit hour. *Required fees:* $1895; $105.25 per credit hour. Tuition and fees vary according to campus/location. *Financial support:* In 2015–16, 36 research assistantships (averaging $19,087 per year), 2 teaching assistantships (averaging $17,400 per year) were awarded; career-related internships or fieldwork, Federal Work-Study, scholarships/grants, health care benefits, tuition waivers (partial), and unspecified assistantships also available. Support available to part-time students. Financial award application deadline: 3/1; financial award applicants required to submit FAFSA. *Faculty research:* Crop science, weed science, rangeland ecology and management, biotechnology, breeding and genetics. *Unit head:* Dr. Jeff Edwards, Department Head, 405-744-6130, Fax: 405-744-0354,
E-mail: jeff.edwards@okstate.edu. Website: http://pss.okstate.edu

Oklahoma State University, College of Arts and Sciences, Department of Plant Biology, Ecology, and Evolution, Stillwater, OK 74078. Offers botany (MS); environmental science (MS, PhD); plant science (PhD). *Faculty:* 14 full-time (5 women). *Students:* 8 part-time (3 women); includes 4 minority (1 Asian, non-Hispanic/Latino; 1 Hispanic/Latino; 2 Two or more races, non-Hispanic/Latino). Average age 32. 3 applicants, 67% accepted. In 2015, 3 master's awarded. *Degree requirements:* For master's, thesis; for doctorate, comprehensive exam, thesis/dissertation. *Entrance requirements:* For master's and doctorate, GRE or GMAT. Additional exam requirements/recommendations for international students: Required—TOEFL (minimum score 550 paper-based; 79 iBT). *Application deadline:* For fall admission, 3/1 priority date for international students; for spring admission, 8/1 priority date for international students. Applications are processed on a rolling basis. Application fee: $40 ($75 for international students). Electronic applications accepted. *Expenses:* Tuition, state resident: full-time $3528; part-time $196 per credit hour. Tuition, nonresident: full-time $14,144; part-time $785.75 per credit hour. *Required fees:* $1895; $105.25 per credit hour. Tuition and fees vary according to campus/location. *Financial support:* In 2015–16, 1 research assistantship (averaging $18,504 per year), 12 teaching assistantships (averaging $20,754 per year) were awarded; career-related internships or fieldwork, Federal Work-Study, scholarships/grants, health care benefits, tuition waivers (partial), and unspecified assistantships also available. Support available to part-time students. Financial award application deadline: 3/1; financial award applicants required to submit FAFSA. *Faculty research:* Ethnobotany, developmental genetics of arabidopsis, biological roles of plasmodesmata, community ecology and biodiversity, nutrient cycling in grassland ecosystems. *Unit head:* Dr. Linda Watson, Department Head, 405-744-5559, Fax: 405-744-7074, E-mail: linda.watson10@okstate.edu.
Website: http://plantbio.okstate.edu

Penn State University Park, Graduate School, College of Agricultural Sciences, Department of Plant Science, University Park, PA 16802. Offers agronomy (MS, PhD); horticulture (MS, PhD); turfgrass management (MPS). *Unit head:* Dr. Richard T. Roush, Dean, 814-865-2541, Fax: 814-865-3103. *Application contact:* Lori Stania, Director, Graduate Student Services, 814-865-1795, Fax: 814-863-4627, E-mail: l-gswww@lists.psu.edu.
Website: http://plantscience.psu.edu/

Purdue University, Graduate School, PULSe - Purdue University Life Sciences Program, West Lafayette, IN 47907. Offers biomolecular structure and biophysics (PhD); biotechnology (PhD); chemical biology (PhD); chromatin and regulation of gene expression (PhD); integrative neuroscience (PhD); integrative plant sciences (PhD); membrane biology (PhD); microbiology (PhD); molecular evolutionary and cancer biology (PhD); molecular evolutionary genetics (PhD); molecular virology (PhD). *Entrance requirements:* For doctorate, GRE, minimum undergraduate GPA of 3.0. Additional exam requirements/recommendations for international students: Required—TOEFL (minimum score 550 paper-based; 77 iBT). Electronic applications accepted.

South Dakota State University, Graduate School, College of Agriculture and Biological Sciences, Department of Plant Science, Brookings, SD 57007. Offers agronomy (PhD); biological sciences (PhD); plant science (MS). *Degree requirements:* For master's, thesis (for some programs), oral exam; for doctorate, comprehensive exam, thesis/dissertation, preliminary oral and written exams. *Entrance requirements:* Additional exam requirements/recommendations for international students: Required—TOEFL (minimum score 560 paper-based; 83 iBT).

Southern Illinois University Carbondale, Graduate School, College of Agriculture, Department of Plant, Soil, and General Agriculture, Carbondale, IL 62901-4701. Offers MS. *Faculty:* 12 full-time (1 woman), 8 part-time/adjunct (0 women). *Students:* 3 full-time (0 women), 25 part-time (8 women); includes 1 minority (Asian, non-Hispanic/Latino), 5 international. 11 applicants, 45% accepted, 5 enrolled. In 2015, 8 master's awarded. *Degree requirements:* For master's, thesis. *Entrance requirements:* For master's, minimum GPA of 2.7. Additional exam requirements/recommendations for international students: Required—TOEFL. *Application deadline:* Applications are processed on a rolling basis. Application fee: $65. *Financial support:* In 2015–16, 14 students received support, including 8 research assistantships with full tuition reimbursements available, 6 teaching assistantships with full tuition reimbursements available; fellowships with full tuition reimbursements available, Federal Work-Study, institutionally sponsored loans, and tuition waivers (full) also available. Support available to part-time students. *Faculty research:* Herbicides, fertilizers, agriculture education, landscape design, plant breeding. *Total annual research expenditures:* $2 million. *Unit head:* Dr. Karen Jones, Interim Chair, 618-453-2469, E-mail: kljones@siu.edu. *Application contact:* Mary Dunmyer, Office Support Specialist, 618-453-1770, E-mail: marya@siu.edu.

State University of New York College of Environmental Science and Forestry, Department of Environmental and Forest Biology, Syracuse, NY 13210-2779. Offers applied ecology (MPS); chemical ecology (MPS, MS, PhD); conservation biology (MPS, MS, PhD); ecology (MPS, MS, PhD); entomology (MPS, MS, PhD); environmental interpretation (MPS, MS, PhD); environmental physiology (MPS, MS, PhD); fish and wildlife biology and management (MPS, MS, PhD); forest pathology and mycology (MPS, MS, PhD); plant biotechnology (MPS); plant science and biotechnology (MPS, MS, PhD). *Faculty:* 29 full-time (9 women), 4 part-time/adjunct (3 women). *Students:* 81 full-time (47 women), 57 part-time (24 women); includes 9 minority (1 Black or African American, non-Hispanic/Latino; 2 American Indian or Alaska Native, non-Hispanic/Latino; 1 Asian, non-Hispanic/Latino; 3 Hispanic/Latino; 2 Two or more races, non-Hispanic/Latino), 15 international. Average age 28. 47 applicants, 49% accepted, 15 enrolled. In 2015, 15 master's, 7 doctorates awarded. *Degree requirements:* For master's, thesis (for some programs), capstone seminar; for doctorate, comprehensive exam, thesis/dissertation, capstone seminar. *Entrance requirements:* For master's and doctorate, GRE General Test, minimum GPA of 3.0. Additional exam requirements/recommendations for international students: Required—TOEFL (minimum score 550 paper-based; 80 iBT), IELTS (minimum score 6). *Application deadline:* For fall admission, 2/1 priority date for domestic and international students; for spring admission, 11/1 priority date for domestic and international students. Applications are processed on a rolling basis. Application fee: $60. *Expenses:* Tuition, state resident: full-time $10,870; part-time $453 per credit. Tuition, nonresident: full-time $22,210; part-time $925 per credit. *Required fees:* $1075; $89.22 per credit. *Financial support:* In 2015–16, 4 fellowships with tuition reimbursements, 36 research assistantships with tuition reimbursements, 39 teaching assistantships with tuition reimbursements (averaging $11,490 per year) were awarded; Federal Work-Study, institutionally sponsored loans, scholarships/grants, health care benefits, and unspecified assistantships also available. Financial award application deadline: 6/30. *Faculty research:* Ecology, conservation biology, fish and wildlife biology and management, plant science, entomology. *Total annual research expenditures:* $4.1 million. *Unit head:* Dr. Donald J. Leopold, Chair, 315-470-6760, Fax: 315-470-6934,
E-mail: djleopold@esf.edu. *Application contact:* Dr. Danilo D. Fernando, Director, Graduate Program/Associate Professor, 315-470-6746, Fax: 315-470-6934,
E-mail: dfernando@esf.edu.
Website: http://www.esf.edu/efb/grad/default.asp

Tennessee State University, The School of Graduate Studies and Research, College of Agriculture, Human and Natural Sciences, Nashville, TN 37209-1561. Offers agricultural sciences (MS), including agribusiness, agricultural and extension education, animal science, plant and soil science; biological sciences (MS, PhD); biotechnology (PhD); chemistry (MS). *Program availability:* Part-time, evening/weekend. *Degree requirements:* For master's, thesis. *Entrance requirements:* For master's, GRE General Test, GRE Subject Test, MAT. *Faculty research:* Small farm economics, ornamental horticulture, beef cattle production, rural elderly.

Texas A&M University–Kingsville, College of Graduate Studies, Dick and Mary Lewis Kleberg College of Agriculture, Natural Resources and Human Sciences, Department of Agriculture, Agribusiness, and Environmental Sciences, Program in Plant and Soil Science, Kingsville, TX 78363. Offers MS. *Degree requirements:* For master's, variable foreign language requirement, comprehensive exam, thesis (for some programs). *Entrance requirements:* For master's, GRE (minimum combined Math & Verbal score of 290), MAT, GMAT, minimum GPA of 2.5. Additional exam requirements/recommendations for international students: Required—TOEFL (minimum score 550 paper-based; 79 iBT). Electronic applications accepted.

Texas Tech University, Graduate School, College of Agricultural Sciences and Natural Resources, Department of Plant and Soil Science, Lubbock, TX 79409. Offers horticulture science (MS); plant and soil science (MS, PhD). *Program availability:* Part-time, evening/weekend, 100% online, blended/hybrid learning. *Faculty:* 16 full-time (4 women), 14 part-time/adjunct (4 women). *Students:* 57 full-time (24 women), 34 part-time (6 women); includes 7 minority (1 Black or African American, non-Hispanic/Latino; 1 Asian, non-Hispanic/Latino; 3 Hispanic/Latino; 2 Two or more races, non-Hispanic/Latino), 33 international. Average age 30. 55 applicants, 51% accepted, 21 enrolled. In 2015, 22 master's, 7 doctorates awarded. Terminal master's awarded for partial completion of doctoral program. *Degree requirements:* For master's, comprehensive exam (for some programs), thesis (for some programs); for doctorate, comprehensive exam, thesis/dissertation. *Entrance requirements:* For master's and doctorate, GRE. Additional exam requirements/recommendations for international students: Required—TOEFL (minimum score 550 paper-based; 79 iBT). *Application deadline:* For fall admission, 6/1 priority date for domestic students, 1/15 priority date for international students; for spring admission, 9/1 priority date for domestic students, 6/15 priority date for international students. Applications are processed on a rolling basis. Application fee: $60. Electronic applications accepted. *Expenses:* Tuition, state resident: full-time $6477; part-time $269.89 per credit hour. Tuition, nonresident: full-time $15,837; part-time $659.89 per credit hour. *Required fees:* $2751; $36.50 per credit hour. $937.50 per semester. Tuition and fees vary according to course level. *Financial support:* In 2015–16, 78 students received support, including 71 fellowships (averaging $2,923 per year), 55 research assistantships (averaging $13,035 per year), 31 teaching assistantships (averaging $4,062 per year); scholarships/grants, health care benefits, and unspecified assistantships also available. Financial award application deadline: 4/15; financial award applicants required to submit FAFSA. *Faculty research:* Crop protection, crop science, fibers and biopolymers, soil science, horticulture. *Total annual research expenditures:* $3 million. *Unit head:* Dr. Eric Hequet, Department Chair, 806-742-2838, Fax: 806-742-0775, E-mail: eric.hequet@ttu.edu. *Application contact:* Christi Chadwell, Communication and Recruiting Coordinator, 806-834-8124,
E-mail: christi.chadwell@ttu.edu.
Website: http://www.pssc.ttu.edu

Tuskegee University, Graduate Programs, College of Agriculture, Environment and Nutrition Sciences, Department of Agricultural and Environmental Sciences, Program in Plant and Soil Sciences, Tuskegee, AL 36088. Offers MS. *Degree requirements:* For master's, thesis. *Entrance requirements:* For master's, GRE General Test. Additional exam requirements/recommendations for international students: Required—TOEFL (minimum score 500 paper-based).

University of Arkansas, Graduate School, Dale Bumpers College of Agricultural, Food and Life Sciences, Interdepartmental Program in Plant Science, Fayetteville, AR 72701-1201. Offers PhD. *Students:* 13 part-time (6 women); includes 1 minority (Asian, non-Hispanic/Latino), 4 international. In 2015, 1 doctorate awarded. *Degree requirements:* For doctorate, thesis/dissertation. *Application deadline:* For fall admission, 4/1 for international students; for spring admission, 10/1 for international students. Applications are processed on a rolling basis. Application fee: $40 ($50 for international students). Electronic applications accepted. *Financial support:* In 2015–16, 9 research assistantships were awarded; fellowships with tuition reimbursements, teaching assistantships, career-related internships or fieldwork, and Federal Work-Study also available. Support available to part-time students. Financial award application deadline: 4/1; financial award applicants required to submit FAFSA. *Unit head:* Dr. Wayne Mackay, Department Head, 479-575-2445, E-mail: mackay@uark.edu. *Application contact:* Dr. Ken Korth, Graduate Coordinator, 479-575-2445, E-mail: kkorth@uark.edu.
Website: http://plantpathology.uark.edu/

The University of British Columbia, Faculty of Land and Food Systems, Plant Science Program, Vancouver, BC V6T 1Z1, Canada. Offers M Sc, PhD. *Program availability:* Part-time. *Degree requirements:* For master's, thesis; for doctorate, comprehensive exam, thesis/dissertation. *Entrance requirements:* Additional exam requirements/recommendations for international students: Required—TOEFL (minimum score 577 paper-based; 90 iBT), IELTS (minimum score 6.5). Electronic applications accepted. *Faculty research:* Plant physiology and biochemistry, biotechnology, plant protection (insect, weeds, and diseases), plant breeding, plant-environment interaction.

University of California, Riverside, Graduate Division, Department of Botany and Plant Sciences, Riverside, CA 92521-0102. Offers plant biology (MS, PhD), including plant cell, molecular, and developmental biology (PhD), plant ecology (PhD), plant genetics (PhD). *Program availability:* Part-time. Terminal master's awarded for partial completion of doctoral program. *Degree requirements:* For master's, comprehensive exams or thesis; for doctorate, thesis/dissertation, qualifying exams. *Entrance requirements:* For master's and doctorate, GRE General Test, minimum GPA of 3.2. Additional exam requirements/recommendations for international students: Required—TOEFL (minimum score 550 paper-based; 80 iBT). Electronic applications accepted. *Faculty research:* Agricultural plant biology; biochemistry and physiology; cellular, molecular and developmental biology; ecology, evolution, systematics and ethnobotany; genetics, genomics and bioinformatics.

University of Connecticut, Graduate School, College of Agriculture and Natural Resources, Department of Plant Science, Storrs, CT 06269. Offers plant and soil sciences (MS, PhD). Terminal master's awarded for partial completion of doctoral program. *Degree requirements:* For master's, comprehensive exam; for doctorate, thesis/dissertation. *Entrance requirements:* For master's and doctorate, GRE General Test, GRE Subject Test. Additional exam requirements/recommendations for international students: Required—TOEFL (minimum score 550 paper-based). Electronic applications accepted.

University of Delaware, College of Agriculture and Natural Resources, Department of Plant and Soil Sciences, Newark, DE 19716. Offers MS, PhD. *Program availability:* Part-time. Terminal master's awarded for partial completion of doctoral program. *Degree requirements:* For master's, thesis; for doctorate, thesis/dissertation. *Entrance requirements:* For master's and doctorate, GRE General Test. Additional exam requirements/recommendations for international students: Required—TOEFL (minimum score 550 paper-based). Electronic applications accepted. *Faculty research:* Soil chemistry, plant and cell tissue culture, plant breeding and genetics, soil physics, soil biochemistry, plant molecular biology, soil microbiology.

University of Florida, Graduate School, College of Agricultural and Life Sciences, Program in Plant Medicine, Gainesville, FL 32611. Offers plant medicine (DPM); tropical conservation and development (DPM). *Program availability:* Part-time. *Degree requirements:* For doctorate, comprehensive exam. *Entrance requirements:* For doctorate, GRE General Test (minimum combined score 300), minimum GPA of 3.0, BS or BA. Additional exam requirements/recommendations for international students: Required—TOEFL (minimum score 550 paper-based; 80 iBT), IELTS (minimum score 6).

University of Georgia, College of Agricultural and Environmental Sciences, Institute of Plant Breeding, Genetics and Genomics, Athens, GA 30602. Offers MS, PhD.

University of Hawaii at Manoa, Graduate Division, College of Tropical Agriculture and Human Resources, Department of Plant and Environmental Protection Sciences, Honolulu, HI 96822. Offers entomology (MS, PhD); tropical plant pathology (MS, PhD). *Program availability:* Part-time. *Faculty:* 48 full-time (9 women), 12 part-time/adjunct (6 women). *Students:* 14 full-time (4 women), 3 part-time (1 woman). Average age 33. 23 applicants, 52% accepted, 10 enrolled. In 2015, 2 master's awarded. Terminal master's awarded for partial completion of doctoral program. *Degree requirements:* For master's, thesis optional; for doctorate, comprehensive exam, thesis/dissertation. *Entrance requirements:* For master's and doctorate, GRE General Test. Additional exam requirements/recommendations for international students: Required—TOEFL (minimum score 500 paper-based; 61 iBT), IELTS (minimum score 5). *Application deadline:* For fall admission, 3/1 for domestic and international students; for spring admission, 10/1 for domestic and international students. Application fee: $100. *Financial support:* In 2015–16, 7 fellowships, 24 research assistantships were awarded; teaching assistantships and tuition waivers (full) also available. *Faculty research:* Nematology, virology,

mycology, bacteriology, epidemiology. *Unit head:* Dr. J. Kenneth Grace, Chair, 808-956-7076, Fax: 808-956-2428. *Application contact:* Graduate Division, 808-956-8544.
Website: http://www.ctahr.hawaii.edu/peps/

University of Idaho, College of Graduate Studies, College of Agricultural and Life Sciences, Department of Plant, Soil, and Entomological Sciences, Moscow, ID 83844-2339. Offers entomology (MS, PhD); plant science (MS, PhD); soil and land resources (MS, PhD). *Faculty:* 30 full-time. *Students:* 28 full-time (9 women), 19 part-time (9 women). Average age 32. In 2015, 5 master's, 2 doctorates awarded. *Degree requirements:* For doctorate, thesis/dissertation. *Entrance requirements:* For master's and doctorate, GRE General Test, minimum GPA of 3.0. *Application deadline:* For fall admission, 7/1 for domestic students; for spring admission, 11/1 for domestic students. Applications are processed on a rolling basis. Application fee: $60. Electronic applications accepted. *Expenses:* Tuition, state resident: full-time $6205; part-time $399 per credit hour. Tuition, nonresident: full-time $20,209; part-time $1177 per credit hour. *Required fees:* $2017; $58 per credit hour. Full-time tuition and fees vary according to course load and reciprocity agreements. *Financial support:* Research assistantships and teaching assistantships available. Financial award applicants required to submit FAFSA. *Faculty research:* Entomological sciences, crop and weed science, horticultural science, soil and land resources. *Unit head:* Dr. Paul McDaniel, Department Head, 208-885-6274, Fax: 208-885-7760, E-mail: pses@uidaho.edu. *Application contact:* Sean Scoggin, Graduate Recruitment Coordinator, 208-885-4001, Fax: 208-885-4406, E-mail: graduateadmissions@uidaho.edu.
Website: http://www.uidaho.edu/cals/pses/

University of Kentucky, Graduate School, College of Agriculture, Food and Environment, Program in Plant and Soil Science, Lexington, KY 40506-0032. Offers integrated plant and soil sciences (MS, PhD). *Degree requirements:* For master's, comprehensive exam, thesis optional. *Entrance requirements:* For master's, GRE General Test, minimum undergraduate GPA of 2.75, graduate 3.0. Additional exam requirements/recommendations for international students: Required—TOEFL (minimum score 550 paper-based). Electronic applications accepted.

University of Maine, Graduate School, College of Natural Sciences, Forestry, and Agriculture, School of Biology and Ecology, Orono, ME 04469. Offers biological sciences (PhD); botany and plant pathology (MS); ecology and environmental science (MS, PhD); entomology (MS); plant science (PhD); zoology (MS, PhD). *Program availability:* Part-time. *Faculty:* 24 full-time (12 women), 34 part-time/adjunct (13 women). *Students:* 64 full-time (36 women), 1 part-time (0 women); includes 4 minority (1 American Indian or Alaska Native, non-Hispanic/Latino; 1 Asian, non-Hispanic/Latino; 1 Hispanic/Latino; 1 Two or more races, non-Hispanic/Latino), 8 international. Average age 29. 52 applicants, 25% accepted, 11 enrolled. In 2015, 7 master's, 8 doctorates awarded. Terminal master's awarded for partial completion of doctoral program. *Degree requirements:* For master's, thesis (for some programs); for doctorate, comprehensive exam, thesis/dissertation. *Entrance requirements:* For master's and doctorate, GRE General Test. Additional exam requirements/recommendations for international students: Required—TOEFL. *Application deadline:* For fall admission, 2/1 priority date for domestic students. Applications are processed on a rolling basis. Application fee: $65. Electronic applications accepted. *Financial support:* In 2015–16, 14 students received support, including 6 research assistantships with full tuition reimbursements available (averaging $14,600 per year), 8 teaching assistantships with full tuition reimbursements available (averaging $14,600 per year); career-related internships or fieldwork, Federal Work-Study, institutionally sponsored loans, and tuition waivers (full and partial) also available. Financial award application deadline: 3/1. *Faculty research:* Ecology and evolution (aquatic, terrestrial, paleo); development and genetics; biomedical research; ecophysiology and stress; invasion ecology and pest management. *Total annual research expenditures:* $3.2 million. *Unit head:* Dr. Andrei Aloykhin, Director, 207-581-2977, Fax: 207-581-2537. *Application contact:* Scott G. Delcourt, Assistant Vice President for Graduate Studies and Senior Associate Dean, 207-581-3291, Fax: 207-581-3232, E-mail: graduate@maine.edu.
Website: http://sbe.umaine.edu/

University of Maine, Graduate School, College of Natural Sciences, Forestry, and Agriculture, School of Food and Agriculture, Orono, ME 04469. Offers animal sciences (MPS, MS); food and human nutrition (PhD); food science and human nutrition (MS); horticulture (MS); plant science (PhD). *Program availability:* Part-time. *Faculty:* 30 full-time (15 women). *Students:* 50 full-time (29 women), 2 part-time (both women); includes 3 minority (2 American Indian or Alaska Native, non-Hispanic/Latino; 1 Asian, non-Hispanic/Latino), 15 international. Average age 28. 81 applicants, 48% accepted, 20 enrolled. In 2015, 18 master's, 3 doctorates, 3 other advanced degrees awarded. *Degree requirements:* For master's, thesis (for some programs); for doctorate, comprehensive exam, thesis/dissertation. *Entrance requirements:* For master's and doctorate, GRE General Test. Additional exam requirements/recommendations for international students: Required—TOEFL. *Application deadline:* For fall admission, 2/1 priority date for domestic students. Applications are processed on a rolling basis. Application fee: $65. Electronic applications accepted. *Financial support:* In 2015–16, 36 students received support, including 1 fellowship (averaging $20,000 per year), 25 research assistantships with full tuition reimbursements available (averaging $14,600 per year), 7 teaching assistantships with full tuition reimbursements available (averaging $14,600 per year); Federal Work-Study, institutionally sponsored loans, and tuition waivers (full and partial) also available. Financial award application deadline: 3/1. *Faculty research:* Nutrition education for adults and children, food processing, food safety, sustainable crop and soil management, animal health and nutrition. *Total annual research expenditures:* $1.9 million. *Unit head:* Dr. Sue Erich, Chair, 207-581-2947, Fax: 207-581-2770. *Application contact:* Scott G. Delcourt, Assistant Vice President for Graduate Studies and Senior Associate Dean, 207-581-3291, Fax: 207-581-3232, E-mail: graduate@maine.edu.
Website: http://umaine.edu/foodandagriculture

The University of Manchester, Faculty of Life Sciences, Manchester, United Kingdom. Offers adaptive organismal biology (M Phil, PhD); animal biology (M Phil, PhD); biochemistry (M Phil, PhD); bioinformatics (M Phil, PhD); biomolecular sciences (M Phil, PhD); biotechnology (M Phil, PhD); cell biology (M Phil, PhD); cell matrix research (M Phil, PhD); channels and transporters (M Phil, PhD); developmental biology (M Phil, PhD); Egyptology (M Phil, PhD); environmental biology (M Phil, PhD); evolutionary biology (M Phil, PhD); gene expression (M Phil, PhD); genetics (M Phil, PhD); history of science, technology and medicine (M Phil, PhD); immunology (M Phil, PhD); integrative neurobiology and behavior (M Phil, PhD); membrane trafficking (M Phil, PhD); microbiology (M Phil, PhD); molecular and cellular neuroscience (M Phil, PhD); molecular biology (M Phil, PhD); molecular cancer studies (M Phil, PhD); neuroscience (M Phil, PhD); ophthalmology (M Phil, PhD); optometry (M Phil, PhD); organelle function (M Phil, PhD); pharmacology (M Phil, PhD); physiology (M Phil, PhD); plant sciences (M Phil, PhD); stem cell research (M Phil, PhD); structural biology (M Phil, PhD); systems neuroscience (M Phil, PhD); toxicology (M Phil, PhD).

University of Manitoba, Faculty of Graduate Studies, Faculty of Agricultural and Food Sciences, Department of Plant Science, Winnipeg, MB R3T 2N2, Canada. Offers agronomy and plant protection (M Sc, PhD); horticulture (M Sc, PhD); plant breeding and genetics (M Sc, PhD); plant physiology-biochemistry (M Sc, PhD). *Degree requirements:* For master's, thesis; for doctorate, one foreign language, thesis/dissertation.

University of Massachusetts Amherst, Graduate School, Interdisciplinary Programs, Program in Plant Biology, Amherst, MA 01003. Offers biochemistry and metabolism (MS, PhD); cell biology and physiology (MS, PhD); environmental, ecological and integrative biology (MS, PhD); genetics and evolution (MS, PhD). *Degree requirements:* For master's, thesis; for doctorate, 2 foreign languages, comprehensive exam, thesis/dissertation. *Entrance requirements:* For master's and doctorate, GRE General Test. Additional exam requirements/recommendations for international students: Required—TOEFL (minimum score 550 paper-based; 80 iBT), IELTS (minimum score 6.5). Electronic applications accepted.

University of Minnesota, Twin Cities Campus, Graduate School, College of Food, Agricultural and Natural Resource Sciences, Program in Applied Plant Sciences, St. Paul, MN 55108. Offers MS, PhD. *Program availability:* Part-time. Terminal master's awarded for partial completion of doctoral program. *Degree requirements:* For master's, comprehensive exam, thesis; for doctorate, comprehensive exam, thesis/dissertation. *Entrance requirements:* For master's and doctorate, GRE General Test. Additional exam requirements/recommendations for international students: Required—TOEFL (minimum score 550 paper-based; 79 iBT), IELTS (minimum score 6.5). Electronic applications accepted. *Faculty research:* Weed science, horticulture, crop management, sustainable agriculture, biotechnology, plant breeding.

University of Missouri, Office of Research and Graduate Studies, College of Agriculture, Food and Natural Resources, Division of Plant Sciences, Columbia, MO 65211. Offers crop, soil and pest management (MS, PhD); entomology (MS, PhD); horticulture (MS, PhD); plant biology and genetics (MS, PhD); plant stress biology (MS, PhD). Terminal master's awarded for partial completion of doctoral program. *Degree requirements:* For master's, thesis; for doctorate, comprehensive exam, thesis/dissertation. *Entrance requirements:* For master's and doctorate, GRE General Test, minimum GPA of 3.0; bachelor's degree from accredited college. Additional exam requirements/recommendations for international students: Required—TOEFL (minimum score 500 paper-based; 61 iBT), IELTS (minimum score 5.5). Electronic applications accepted. *Faculty research:* Crop, soil and pest management; entomology; horticulture; plant biology and genetics; plant microbiology and pathology.

University of Saskatchewan, College of Graduate Studies and Research, College of Agriculture, Department of Plant Sciences, Saskatoon, SK S7N 5A2, Canada. Offers M Sc, PhD. *Degree requirements:* For master's, thesis; for doctorate, comprehensive exam (for some programs), thesis/dissertation. *Entrance requirements:* Additional exam requirements/recommendations for international students: Required—TOEFL (minimum score 80 iBT); Recommended—IELTS (minimum score 6.5).

The University of Tennessee, Graduate School, College of Agricultural Sciences and Natural Resources, Department of Plant Sciences, Knoxville, TN 37996. Offers floriculture (MS); landscape design (MS); public horticulture (MS); turfgrass (MS); woody ornamentals (MS). *Program availability:* Part-time. *Degree requirements:* For master's, thesis or alternative. *Entrance requirements:* For master's, minimum GPA of 2.7. Additional exam requirements/recommendations for international students: Required—TOEFL. Electronic applications accepted.

University of Vermont, Graduate College, College of Agriculture and Life Sciences, Department of Plant and Soil Science, Burlington, VT 05405. Offers MS, PhD. *Degree requirements:* For master's, thesis; for doctorate, one foreign language, thesis/dissertation. *Entrance requirements:* For master's and doctorate, GRE General Test. Additional exam requirements/recommendations for international students: Required—TOEFL (minimum score 550 paper-based; 80 iBT). Electronic applications accepted. *Faculty research:* Soil chemistry, plant nutrition.

University of Wisconsin–Madison, Graduate School, College of Agricultural and Life Sciences, Department of Agronomy, Madison, WI 53706-1380. Offers agronomy (MS, PhD); plant breeding and plant genetics (MS, PhD). *Degree requirements:* For master's, thesis or alternative; for doctorate, thesis/dissertation. *Entrance requirements:* For master's and doctorate, GRE, minimum GPA of 3.0. Additional exam requirements/recommendations for international students: Required—TOEFL (minimum score 580 paper-based). Electronic applications accepted. *Expenses:* Tuition, state resident: full-time $5364. Tuition, nonresident: full-time $12,027. *Required fees:* $571. Tuition and fees vary according to campus/location, program and reciprocity agreements. *Faculty research:* Plant breeding and genetics, plant molecular biology and physiology, cropping systems and management, weed science.

University of Wisconsin–Madison, Graduate School, College of Agricultural and Life Sciences, Plant Breeding and Plant Genetics Program, Madison, WI 53706-1380. Offers MS, PhD. *Program availability:* Part-time. Terminal master's awarded for partial completion of doctoral program. *Degree requirements:* For master's, comprehensive exam, thesis; for doctorate, comprehensive exam, thesis/dissertation, formal exit seminar. *Entrance requirements:* For master's and doctorate, GRE, minimum GPA of 3.0. Additional exam requirements/recommendations for international students: Required—TOEFL (minimum: 550 paper, 80 iBT), IELTS (minimum: 6) or Michigan English Language Assessment Battery (minimum: 77). Electronic applications accepted. *Expenses:* Tuition, state resident: full-time $5364. Tuition, nonresident: full-time $12,027. *Required fees:* $571. Tuition and fees vary according to campus/location, program and reciprocity agreements. *Faculty research:* Plant improvement, classical and molecular genetics, quantitative and statistical genetics, cytogenetics, stress and pest resistances.

Utah State University, School of Graduate Studies, College of Agriculture, Department of Plants, Soils, and Biometeorology, Logan, UT 84322. Offers biometeorology (MS, PhD); ecology (MS, PhD); plant science (MS, PhD); soil science (MS, PhD). *Program availability:* Part-time. Terminal master's awarded for partial completion of doctoral program. *Degree requirements:* For master's, thesis; for doctorate, thesis/dissertation. *Entrance requirements:* For master's, GRE General Test, BS in plant, soil, atmospheric science, or related field; minimum GPA of 3.0; for doctorate, GRE General Test, minimum GPA of 3.0. Additional exam requirements/recommendations for international students: Required—TOEFL. Electronic applications accepted. *Faculty research:* Biotechnology and genomics, plant physiology and biology, nutrient and water efficient landscapes, physical-chemical-biological processes in soil, environmental biophysics and climate.

West Texas A&M University, College of Agriculture, Science and Engineering, Department of Agricultural Sciences, Emphasis in Plant, Soil and Environmental Science, Canyon, TX 79016-0001. Offers MS. *Program availability:* Part-time. *Degree requirements:* For master's, comprehensive exam, thesis optional. *Entrance requirements:* For master's, GRE General Test. Additional exam requirements/recommendations for international students: Required—TOEFL (minimum score 550 paper-based). Electronic applications accepted. *Faculty research:* Crop and soil disciplines.

West Virginia University, Davis College of Agriculture, Forestry and Consumer Sciences, Division of Plant and Soil Sciences, Program in Agricultural Sciences, Morgantown, WV 26506. Offers animal and food sciences (PhD); plant and soil sciences (PhD). *Degree requirements:* For doctorate, thesis/dissertation, oral and written exams.

Entrance requirements: Additional exam requirements/recommendations for international students: Required—TOEFL. Expenses: Tuition, state resident: full-time$8568. Tuition, nonresident: full-time $22,140. Tuition and fees vary according to program. Faculty research: Ruminant nutrition, metabolism, forage utilization, physiology, reproduction.

Viticulture and Enology

California State University, Fresno, Division of Graduate Studies, College of Agricultural Sciences and Technology, Department of Viticulture and Enology, Fresno, CA 93740-8027. Offers MS. *Program availability:* Part-time, evening/weekend. *Degree requirements:* For master's, comprehensive exam (for some programs), thesis (for some programs). *Entrance requirements:* For master's, GRE General Test, minimum GPA of 2.5. Additional exam requirements/recommendations for international students: Required—TOEFL. Electronic applications accepted. Faculty research: Ethel carbonate formation, clinical an physiological characterization, grape and wine quality.

University of California, Davis, Graduate Studies, Graduate Group in Viticulture and Enology, Davis, CA 95616. Offers MS, PhD. *Degree requirements:* For master's, comprehensive exam (for some programs), thesis (for some programs). *Entrance requirements:* Additional exam requirements/recommendations for international students: Required—TOEFL (minimum score 550 paper-based).

Peterson's Graduate Programs in the Physical Sciences, Mathematics, Agricultural Sciences, the Environment & Natural Resources 2017

www.petersons.com **333**

ACADEMIC AND PROFESSIONAL PROGRAMS IN THE ENVIRONMENT AND NATURAL SCIENCES

Section 9
Environmental Sciences and Management

This section contains a directory of institutions offering graduate work in environmental sciences and management, followed by an in-depth entry submitted by an institution that chose to prepare a detailed program description. Additional information about programs listed in the directory but not augmented by an in-depth entry may be obtained by writing directly to the dean of a graduate school or chair of a department at the address given in the directory.

For programs offering related work, see also in this book *Natural Resources*. In the other guides in this series:

Graduate Programs in the Humanities, Arts & Social Sciences

See *Political Science and International Affairs* and *Public, Regional, and Industrial Affairs*

Graduate Programs in the Biological/Biomedical Sciences & Health-Related Medical Professions

See *Ecology, Environmental Biology, and Evolutionary Biology*

Graduate Programs in Engineering & Applied Sciences

See *Management of Engineering and Technology*

CONTENTS

Program Directories

Featured School: Display and Close-Up

Environmental Management and Policy

Adelphi University, College of Arts and Sciences, Program in Environmental Studies, Garden City, NY 11530-0701. Offers MS. *Degree requirements:* For master's, thesis optional. *Entrance requirements:* For master's, GRE General Test, 2 letters of recommendation; course work in microeconomics, political science, statistics/calculus, and either chemistry or physics; computer literacy. Additional exam requirements/recommendations for international students: Required—TOEFL (minimum score 550 paper-based; 80 iBT). Electronic applications accepted. *Faculty research:* Contaminates sites, workplace exposure level of contaminants, climate change and human health.

Air Force Institute of Technology, Graduate School of Engineering and Management, Department of Systems and Engineering Management, Dayton, OH 45433-7765. Offers cost analysis (MS); environmental and engineering management (MS); environmental engineering science (MS); information resource/systems management (MS). *Accreditation:* ABET. *Program availability:* Part-time. *Degree requirements:* For master's, thesis. *Entrance requirements:* For master's, GRE, GMAT, minimum GPA of 3.0.

American Public University System, AMU/APU Graduate Programs, Charles Town, WV 25414. Offers accounting (MBA, MS); criminal justice (MA), including business administration, emergency and disaster management, general (MA, MS); educational leadership (M Ed); emergency and disaster management (MA); entrepreneurship (MBA); environmental policy and management (MS), including environmental planning, environmental sustainability, fish and wildlife management, general (MA, MS), global environmental management; finance (MBA); general (MBA); global business management (MBA); history (MA), including American history, ancient and classical history, European history, global history, public history; homeland security (MA), including business administration, counter-terrorism studies, criminal justice, cyber, emergency management and public health, intelligence studies, transportation security; homeland security resource allocation (MBA); humanities (MA); information technology (MS), including digital forensics, enterprise software development, information assurance and security, IT project management; information technology management (MBA); intelligence studies (MA), including criminal intelligence, cyber, general (MA, MS), homeland security, intelligence analysis, intelligence collection, intelligence management, intelligence operations, terrorism studies; international relations and conflict resolution (MA), including comparative and security issues, conflict resolution, international and transnational security issues, peacekeeping; legal studies (MA); management (MA), including defense management, general (MA, MS), human resource management, organizational leadership, public administration; marketing (MBA); military history (MA), including American military history, American Revolution, civil war, war since 1945, World War II; military studies (MA), including joint warfare, strategic leadership; national security studies (MA), including general (MA, MS), homeland security, regional security studies, security and intelligence analysis, terrorism studies; nonprofit management (MBA); political science (MA), including American politics and government, comparative government and development, general (MA, MS), international relations, public policy; psychology (MA); public administration (MPA), including disaster management, environmental policy, health policy, human resources, national security, organizational management, security management; public health (MPH); reverse logistics management (MA); school counseling (M Ed); security management (MA); space studies (MS), including aerospace science, general (MA, MS), planetary science; sports and health sciences (MS); teaching (M Ed), including curriculum and instruction for elementary teachers, elementary reading, English language learners, instructional leadership, online learning, special education; transportation and logistics management (MA), including general (MA, MS), maritime engineering management, reverse logistics management. Programs offered via distance learning only. *Program availability:* Part-time, evening/weekend, online learning. *Faculty:* 431 full-time (241 women), 1,839 part-time/adjunct (865 women). *Students:* 531 full-time (233 women), 9,094 part-time (3,735 women); includes 3,140 minority (1,679 Black or African American, non-Hispanic/Latino; 55 American Indian or Alaska Native, non-Hispanic/Latino; 252 Asian, non-Hispanic/Latino; 773 Hispanic/Latino; 75 Native Hawaiian or other Pacific Islander, non-Hispanic/Latino; 306 Two or more races, non-Hispanic/Latino), 111 international. Average age 37. In 2015, 3,391 master's awarded. *Degree requirements:* For master's, comprehensive exam or practicum. *Entrance requirements:* For master's, official transcript showing earned bachelor's degree from institution accredited by recognized accrediting body. Additional exam requirements/recommendations for international students: Required—TOEFL (minimum score 550 paper-based), IELTS (minimum score 6.5). *Application deadline:* Applications are processed on a rolling basis. Application fee: $0. Electronic applications accepted. *Expenses: Tuition, area resident:* Part-time $350 per credit hour. *Financial support:* Applicants required to submit FAFSA. *Unit head:* Dr. Karan Powell, Executive Vice President and Provost, 877-468-6268, Fax: 304-724-3780. *Application contact:* Terry Grant, Vice President of Enrollment Management, 877-468-6268, Fax: 304-724-3780, E-mail: info@apus.edu.
Website: http://www.apus.edu

American University, College of Arts and Sciences, Department of Environmental Science, Washington, DC 20016-8070. Offers environmental assessment (Graduate Certificate); environmental science (MS); professional science: environmental assessment (MS). *Faculty:* 8 full-time (4 women), 3 part-time/adjunct (1 woman). *Students:* 14 full-time (6 women), 3 part-time (all women); includes 2 minority (1 Black or African American, non-Hispanic/Latino; 1 Asian, non-Hispanic/Latino), 3 international. Average age 25. 17 applicants, 100% accepted, 6 enrolled. In 2015, 4 master's awarded. *Degree requirements:* For master's, comprehensive exam, thesis (for some programs). *Entrance requirements:* For master's, GRE General Test, GRE Subject Test, one year of calculus, lab science, statement of purpose, transcripts, 2 letters of recommendation, resume; for Graduate Certificate, statement of purpose, transcripts, resume. Additional exam requirements/recommendations for international students: Required—TOEFL (minimum score 100 iBT), IELTS (minimum score 7), PTE (minimum score 68). *Application deadline:* For fall admission, 2/1 for domestic students; for spring admission, 11/1 for domestic students. Application fee: $55. *Expenses: Tuition, area resident:* Full-time $27,468; part-time $1526 per credit hour. *Required fees:* $430. Tuition and fees vary according to course level and program. *Financial support:* Application deadline: 2/1. *Unit head:* Dr. Kiho Kim, Department Chair, 202-885-2181, Fax: 202-885-1752, E-mail: acheh@american.edu. *Application contact:* Kathleen Clowery, Associate Director, Graduate Admissions, 202-885-3620, Fax: 202-885-1344, E-mail: clowery@american.edu.
Website: http://www.american.edu/cas/environmental/

American University, School of International Service, Washington, DC 20016-8071. Offers comparative and regional studies (Certificate); cross-cultural communication (Certificate); development management (MS); ethics, peace, and global affairs (MA); European studies (Certificate); global environmental policy (MA, Certificate); global information technology (Certificate); international affairs (MA), including comparative and international disability policy, comparative and regional studies, international economic relations, international politics, natural resources and sustainable development, U.S. foreign policy; international arts management (Certificate); international communication (MA, Certificate); international development (MA); international economic policy (Certificate); international economic relations (Certificate); international economics (MA); international media (MA); international peace and conflict resolution (MA, Certificate); international politics (Certificate); international relations (MA, PhD); international service (MIS); peacebuilding (Certificate); social enterprise (MA); the Americas (Certificate); United States foreign policy (Certificate); JD/MA. *Program availability:* Part-time, evening/weekend, 100% online. *Faculty:* 118 full-time (53 women), 60 part-time/adjunct (24 women). *Students:* 578 full-time (351 women), 502 part-time (295 women); includes 268 minority (96 Black or African American, non-Hispanic/Latino; 9 American Indian or Alaska Native, non-Hispanic/Latino; 59 Asian, non-Hispanic/Latino; 89 Hispanic/Latino; 1 Native Hawaiian or other Pacific Islander, non-Hispanic/Latino; 14 Two or more races, non-Hispanic/Latino), 140 international. Average age 28. 1,810 applicants, 80% accepted, 415 enrolled. In 2015, 399 master's, 7 doctorates, 7 other advanced degrees awarded. Terminal master's awarded for partial completion of doctoral program. *Degree requirements:* For master's, one foreign language, comprehensive exam, thesis or alternative; for doctorate, one foreign language, comprehensive exam, thesis/dissertation. *Entrance requirements:* For master's, GRE, transcripts, resume, 2 letters of recommendation, statement of purpose; for doctorate, GRE, transcripts, resume, 3 letters of recommendation, statement of purpose. Additional exam requirements/recommendations for international students: Required—TOEFL (minimum score 600 paper-based; 100 iBT). *Application deadline:* For fall admission, 1/15 for domestic students; for spring admission, 10/1 for domestic students, 9/15 for international students. Application fee: $55. Electronic applications accepted. *Expenses:* $27,468 per year full-time tuition, $1,526 per credit hour; $1,930 per year full-time fees. *Financial support:* Application deadline: 1/15. *Unit head:* Dr. James Goldgeier, Dean, 202-885-1603, Fax: 202-885-2494, E-mail: goldgeier@american.edu. *Application contact:* Jia Jiang, Associate Director, Graduate Education Enrollment, 202-885-1689, Fax: 202-885-1109, E-mail: jiang@american.edu.
Website: http://www.american.edu/sis/

American University of Beirut, Graduate Programs, Faculty of Arts and Sciences, Beirut, Lebanon. Offers anthropology (MA); Arab and Middle Eastern history (PhD); Arabic language and literature (MA, PhD); archaeology (MA); biology (MS); cell and molecular biology (PhD); chemistry (MS); clinical psychology (MA); computational sciences (MS); computer science (MS); economics (MA); English language (MA); English literature (MA); environmental policy planning (MS); financial economics (MAFE); geology (MS); history (MA); mathematics (MA, MS); media studies (MA); Middle Eastern studies (MA); physics (MS); political studies (MA); psychology (MA); public administration (MA); sociology (MA); statistics (MA, MS); theoretical physics (PhD); transnational American studies (MA). *Program availability:* Part-time. *Faculty:* 114 full-time (36 women), 4 part-time/adjunct (2 women). *Students:* 258 full-time (190 women), 207 part-time (142 women). Average age 27. 241 applicants, 71% accepted, 98 enrolled. In 2015, 47 master's, 3 doctorates awarded. *Degree requirements:* For master's, one foreign language, comprehensive exam, thesis (for some programs); for doctorate, one foreign language, comprehensive exam, thesis/dissertation. *Entrance requirements:* For master's, GRE (for some MA, MS programs), letter of recommendation; for doctorate, GRE, letters of recommendation. Additional exam requirements/recommendations for international students: Required—TOEFL (minimum score 600 paper-based; 97 iBT), IELTS (minimum score 7). *Application deadline:* For fall admission, 4/1 for domestic and international students; for spring admission, 11/1 for domestic and international students. Application fee: $50. Electronic applications accepted. *Expenses: Tuition, area resident:* Full-time $16,254; part-time $903 per credit. *Required fees:* $699. Tuition and fees vary according to course load and program. *Financial support:* Research assistantships, career-related internships or fieldwork, institutionally sponsored loans, scholarships/grants, health care benefits, and unspecified assistantships available. Financial award application deadline: 2/4; financial award applicants required to submit FAFSA. *Faculty research:* Analysis and algebra; software engineering; machine learning and big data analysis; philosophy of mind and political philosophy; anthropology of art, anthropology of migration and medical anthropology; sociology of knowledge, sociology of migration, critical theory; sociology of education; hybrid solid materials; photocatalysis; human creativity. *Total annual research expenditures:* $680,360. *Unit head:* Dr. Patrick McGreevy, Dean, 961-1374374 Ext. 3800, Fax: 961-1744461, E-mail: pm07@aub.edu.lb. *Application contact:* Dr. Salim Kanaan, Director, Admissions Office, 961-1350000 Ext. 2590, Fax: 961-1750775, E-mail: sk00@aub.edu.lb.
Website: http://www.aub.edu.lb/fas/

Antioch University New England, Graduate School, Department of Environmental Studies, Doctoral Program in Environmental Studies, Keene, NH 03431-3552. Offers PhD. *Degree requirements:* For doctorate, thesis/dissertation, practicum. *Entrance requirements:* For doctorate, master's degree and previous experience in the environmental field. Additional exam requirements/recommendations for international students: Required—TOEFL (minimum score 550 paper-based). Electronic applications accepted. *Expenses:* Contact institution. *Faculty research:* Environmental history, green politics, ecopsychology.

Antioch University New England, Graduate School, Department of Environmental Studies, Program in Resource Management and Conservation, Keene, NH 03431-3552. Offers MS. *Degree requirements:* For master's, thesis optional, practicum. *Entrance requirements:* For master's, previous undergraduate course work in science and math. Additional exam requirements/recommendations for international students: Required—TOEFL (minimum score 550 paper-based). Electronic applications accepted. *Expenses:* Contact institution.

Antioch University New England, Graduate School, Department of Environmental Studies, Self-Designed Studies Program, Keene, NH 03431-3552. Offers MS. *Degree requirements:* For master's, practicum, seminar, thesis or project. *Entrance requirements:* For master's, detailed proposal. Additional exam requirements/recommendations for international students: Required—TOEFL (minimum score 550 paper-based).

Antioch University New England, Graduate School, Department of Management, Program in Sustainability (Green MBA), Keene, NH 03431-3552. Offers MBA. *Program availability:* Part-time. *Entrance requirements:* For master's, GRE, resume, 3 letters of recommendation. Additional exam requirements/recommendations for international students: Required—TOEFL (minimum score 600 paper-based).

Antioch University Seattle, Graduate Programs, Center for Creative Change, Seattle, WA 98121-1814. Offers environment and community (MA); organizational development (MA); whole systems design (MA). *Program availability:* Evening/weekend. *Faculty:* 3 full-time (all women), 6 part-time/adjunct (all women). *Students:* 26 full-time (17 women), 4 part-time (all women); includes 2 minority (both Black or African American, non-Hispanic/Latino). Average age 40. *Application deadline:* For fall admission, 8/15 priority date for domestic students; for spring admission, 2/3 priority date for domestic students. Applications are processed on a rolling basis. Electronic applications accepted. *Expenses:* Contact institution. *Financial support:* Research assistantships, Federal Work-Study, institutionally sponsored loans, and unspecified assistantships available. Financial award application deadline: 6/15. *Unit head:* Betsy Geist, Director, 206-268-4904, E-mail: bgeist@antioch.edu. *Application contact:* Eileen Knight, Recruitment and Admissions Director, 206-268-4200, E-mail: eknight@antioch.edu.
Website: http://www.antiochseattle.edu/academics/ma-programs-in-leadership-change

Appalachian State University, Cratis D. Williams Graduate School, Department of Government and Justice Studies, Boone, NC 28608. Offers criminal justice (MS); political science (MA), including American government, environmental politics and policy analysis, international relations; public administration (MPA), including public management, town, city and county management. *Program availability:* Part-time, online learning. *Degree requirements:* For master's, variable foreign language requirement, comprehensive exam, thesis optional. *Entrance requirements:* For master's, GRE General Test, 3 letters of recommendation. Additional exam requirements/recommendations for international students: Required—TOEFL (minimum score 570 paper-based; 79 iBT), IELTS (minimum score 6.5). Electronic applications accepted. *Faculty research:* Campaign finance, emerging democracies, bureaucratic politics, judicial behavior, administration of justice.

Aquinas College, School of Management, Grand Rapids, MI 49506-1799. Offers health care administration (MM); marketing management (MM); organizational leadership (MM); sustainable business (MM, MSB). *Program availability:* Part-time, evening/weekend. *Entrance requirements:* For master's, GMAT, minimum undergraduate GPA of 2.75, 2 years of work experience. Additional exam requirements/recommendations for international students: Required—TOEFL (minimum score 550 paper-based). *Expenses:* Contact institution.

Arizona State University at the Tempe campus, Ira A. Fulton Schools of Engineering, The Polytechnic School, Programs in Technology Management, Mesa, AZ 85212. Offers aviation management and human factors (MS); environmental technology management (MS); global technology and development (MS); graphic information technology (MS); management of technology (MS). *Program availability:* Part-time, evening/weekend, online learning. *Degree requirements:* For master's, thesis or applied project and oral defense; interactive Program of Study (iPOS) submitted before completing 50 percent of required credit hours. *Entrance requirements:* For master's, GRE, minimum GPA of 3.0 or equivalent in last 2 years of work leading to bachelor's degree. Additional exam requirements/recommendations for international students: Required—TOEFL, IELTS, or PTE. Electronic applications accepted. *Faculty research:* Digital imaging, digital publishing, Internet development/e-commerce, information aviation human factors, pilot selection, databases, multimedia, commercial digital photography, digital workflow, computer graphics modeling and animation, information design, sociotechnology, visual and technical literacy, environmental management, quality management, project management, industrial ethics, hazardous materials, environmental chemistry.

Ball State University, Graduate School, College of Sciences and Humanities, Department of Natural Resources and Environmental Management, Muncie, IN 47306. Offers emergency management and homeland security (Certificate); natural resources and environmental management (MA, MS). *Program availability:* Part-time. *Faculty:* 5 full-time (2 women). *Students:* 7 full-time (3 women), 12 part-time (7 women); includes 3 minority (1 Black or African American, non-Hispanic/Latino; 1 Asian, non-Hispanic/Latino; 1 Two or more races, non-Hispanic/Latino), 4 international. Average age 32. 14 applicants, 86% accepted, 6 enrolled. In 2015, 4 master's awarded. *Degree requirements:* For master's, thesis (for some programs). *Entrance requirements:* For master's, GRE General Test, minimum baccalaureate GPA of 2.75 or 3.0 in latter half of baccalauareate, two letters of reference. Additional exam requirements/recommendations for international students: Required—TOEFL (minimum score 550 paper-based; 79 iBT), IELTS (minimum score 6.5). *Application deadline:* For fall admission, 3/1 priority date for domestic students. Applications are processed on a rolling basis. Application fee: $60. Electronic applications accepted. *Expenses: Tuition, area resident:* Full-time $6948; part-time $2316 per semester. Tuition, state resident: full-time $10,422; part-time $3474 per semester. Tuition, nonresident: full-time $19,062; part-time $6354 per semester. *Required fees:* $651 per semester. Tuition and fees vary according to campus/location, program and reciprocity agreements. *Financial support:* In 2015–16, 8 students received support, including 1 research assistantship with partial tuition reimbursement available (averaging $12,000 per year), 6 teaching assistantships with partial tuition reimbursements available (averaging $12,276 per year); unspecified assistantships also available. Financial award application deadline: 3/1; financial award applicants required to submit FAFSA. *Faculty research:* Acid rain, indoor air pollution, land reclamation. *Unit head:* Dr. Amy Gregg, Interim Chairperson, 765-285-5781, Fax: 765-285-2606, E-mail: algregg2@bsu.edu.
Website: http://www.bsu.edu/nrem/

Bard College, Bard Center for Environmental Policy, Annandale-on-Hudson, NY 12504. Offers climate science and policy (MS, Professional Certificate), including agriculture (MS), ecosystems (MS); environmental policy (MS, Professional Certificate); sustainability (MBA); MS/JD; MS/MAT. *Program availability:* Part-time. *Degree requirements:* For master's, thesis, 4-month, full-time internship. *Entrance requirements:* For master's, GRE, coursework in statistics, chemistry and one other semester of college science; personal statement; curriculum vitae; 3 letters of recommendation; sample of written work. Additional exam requirements/recommendations for international students: Required—TOEFL (minimum score 600 paper-based; 100 iBT). Electronic applications accepted. *Expenses:* Contact institution. *Faculty research:* Climate and agriculture, alternative energy, environmental economics, environmental toxicology, EPA law, sustainable development, international relations, literature and composition, human rights, agronomy, advocacy, leadership.

Baylor University, Graduate School, College of Arts and Sciences, Department of Environmental Science, Waco, TX 76798. Offers MES, MS. *Degree requirements:* For master's, thesis. *Entrance requirements:* For master's, GRE General Test. *Faculty research:* Renewable energy/waste management policies, Third World environmental problem solving, ecotourism.

Bemidji State University, School of Graduate Studies, Bemidji, MN 56601. Offers biology (MS); education (MS); English (MA, MS); environmental studies (MS); mathematics (MS); mathematics (elementary and middle level education) (MS); special education (M Sp Ed). *Program availability:* Part-time, online learning. *Degree requirements:* For master's, comprehensive exam, thesis (for some programs). *Entrance requirements:* For master's, GRE; GMAT, letters of recommendation, letters of interest. Additional exam requirements/recommendations for international students: Required—TOEFL (minimum score 550 paper-based; 80 iBT). Electronic applications accepted. *Expenses:* Contact institution. *Faculty research:* Human performance, sport, and health: physical education teacher education, continuum models, spiritual health, intellectual health, resiliency, health priorities; psychology: health psychology, college student drinking behavior, micro-aggressions, infant cognition, false memories, leadership assessment; biology: structure and dynamics of forest communities, aquatic and riverine ecology, interaction between animal populations and aquatic environments, cellular motility.

Boise State University, School of Public Service, Department of Public Policy and Administration, Boise, ID 83725-1935. Offers public policy and administration (MPA, PhD, Graduate Certificate), including environmental and natural resources policy and administration (MPA), general public administration (MPA), state and local government policy and administration (MPA). *Accreditation:* NASPAA. *Program availability:* Part-time. *Faculty:* 16. *Students:* 38 full-time (19 women), 85 part-time (56 women); includes 15 minority (1 American Indian or Alaska Native, non-Hispanic/Latino; 1 Asian, non-Hispanic/Latino; 12 Hispanic/Latino; 1 Two or more races, non-Hispanic/Latino), 1 international. Average age 37. 81 applicants, 43% accepted, 29 enrolled. In 2015, 22 master's awarded. Terminal master's awarded for partial completion of doctoral program. *Degree requirements:* For master's, comprehensive exam, thesis optional, directed research project, internship; for doctorate, thesis/dissertation. *Entrance requirements:* For master's, GRE General Test, minimum GPA of 3.0. Additional exam requirements/recommendations for international students: Required—TOEFL (minimum score 550 paper-based; 80 iBT), IELTS (minimum score 6). *Application deadline:* For fall admission, 2/1 for domestic and international students; for spring admission, 10/1 for domestic and international students. Application fee: $65 ($95 for international students). Electronic applications accepted. *Expenses:* Tuition, state resident: full-time $6058; part-time $358 per credit hour. Tuition, nonresident: full-time $20,108; part-time $608 per credit hour. *Required fees:* $2108. Tuition and fees vary according to program. *Financial support:* In 2015–16, 41 students received support, including 2 research assistantships (averaging $4,083 per year); scholarships/grants and unspecified assistantships also available. Financial award application deadline: 2/1; financial award applicants required to submit FAFSA. *Unit head:* Dr. Gregory Hill, Department Chair, 208-426-2917, E-mail: greghill@boisestate.edu. *Application contact:* Dr. Elizabeth Fredericksen, MPA Director, 208-426-1078, E-mail: efreder@boisestate.edu.
Website: http://sps.boisestate.edu/publicpolicy/

Boston University, Graduate School of Arts and Sciences, Department of Earth and Environment, Boston, MA 02215. Offers earth sciences (MA, PhD); energy and environment (MA); geography (MA, PhD); global development policy (MA); international relations and environmental policy (MA); remote sensing and geospatial sciences (MA). *Students:* 57 full-time (25 women), 5 part-time (1 woman); includes 5 minority (2 Asian, non-Hispanic/Latino; 3 Hispanic/Latino), 23 international. Average age 28. 234 applicants, 51% accepted, 27 enrolled. In 2015, 4 master's, 12 doctorates awarded. Terminal master's awarded for partial completion of doctoral program. *Degree requirements:* For master's, comprehensive exam (for some programs), thesis (for some programs); for doctorate, comprehensive exam, thesis/dissertation. *Entrance requirements:* For master's and doctorate, GRE General Test, 3 letters of recommendation, official transcripts, personal statement, writing sample (for geography). Additional exam requirements/recommendations for international students: Required—TOEFL (minimum score 550 paper-based; 84 iBT). *Application deadline:* For fall admission, 1/31 for domestic and international students; for winter admission, 10/15 for domestic and international students. Application fee: $95. Electronic applications accepted. *Financial support:* In 2015–16, 43 students received support, including 5 fellowships with full tuition reimbursements available (averaging $21,000 per year), 17 research assistantships with full tuition reimbursements available (averaging $21,000 per year), 12 teaching assistantships with full tuition reimbursements available (averaging $21,000 per year); Federal Work-Study, scholarships/grants, traineeships, and health care benefits also available. Financial award application deadline: 1/31. *Faculty research:* Biogeosciences, climate and surface processes; energy, environment and society; geographical sciences; geology, geochemistry and geophysics. *Unit head:* David Marchant, Chair, 617-353-3236, E-mail: marchant@bu.edu. *Application contact:* Nora Watson, Graduate Program Coordinator, 617-353-2529, Fax: 617-353-8399, E-mail: norala31@bu.edu.
Website: http://www.bu.edu/earth/

Boston University, Graduate School of Arts and Sciences, Frederick S. Pardee School of Global Studies, Boston, MA 02215. Offers global development policy (MA); international affairs (MA); international relations and environmental policy (MA); international relations and international communication (MA); international relations and religion (MA); international relations, mid-career (MA); Latin American studies (MA); MA/JD; MBA/MA. *Faculty:* 33 full-time (8 women), 10 part-time/adjunct (4 women). *Students:* 74 full-time (43 women), 12 part-time (9 women); includes 10 minority (3 Black or African American, non-Hispanic/Latino; 2 Asian, non-Hispanic/Latino; 4 Hispanic/Latino; 1 Two or more races, non-Hispanic/Latino), 29 international. Average age 26. 295 applicants, 72% accepted, 26 enrolled. In 2015, 41 master's awarded. *Degree requirements:* For master's, one foreign language, capstone. *Entrance requirements:* For master's, GRE General Test, 3 letters of recommendation, transcript of all prior college coursework, personal statement, resume or curriculum vitae (recommended). Additional exam requirements/recommendations for international students: Required—TOEFL (minimum score 550 paper-based; 84 iBT). *Application deadline:* For fall admission, 4/15 for domestic and international students; for spring admission, 10/15 for domestic and international students. Applications are processed on a rolling basis. Application fee: $95. Electronic applications accepted. *Financial support:* In 2015–16, 29 students received support. Federal Work-Study, scholarships/grants, and unspecified assistantships available. Financial award application deadline: 1/15. *Faculty research:* International relations, area studies, political economy, global development policy, global climate. *Unit head:* Adil Najam, Dean, Fax: 617-353-9290, E-mail: anajam@bu.edu. *Application contact:* Michael Williams, Graduate Program Administrator, 617-353-9349, Fax: 617-353-9290, E-mail: psgsgrad@bu.edu.
Website: http://www.bu.edu/PardeeSchool

California State University, Fullerton, Graduate Studies, College of Humanities and Social Sciences, Program in Environmental Studies, Fullerton, CA 92834-9480. Offers MS. *Program availability:* Part-time. *Degree requirements:* For master's, thesis. *Entrance requirements:* For master's, minimum GPA of 2.5 in last 60 units of course work.

Central European University, Graduate Studies, Department of Environmental Sciences and Policy, Budapest, Hungary. Offers MS, PhD. *Program availability:* Part-time. *Faculty:* 12 full-time (4 women), 4 part-time/adjunct (2 women). *Students:* 89 full-time (63 women), 8 part-time (6 women). Average age 29. 500 applicants, 16% accepted, 43 enrolled. In 2015, 41 master's, 3 doctorates awarded. Terminal master's

awarded for partial completion of doctoral program. *Degree requirements:* For master's, one foreign language, thesis; for doctorate, one foreign language, comprehensive exam, thesis/dissertation. *Entrance requirements:* For master's and doctorate, essay, interview, statement of purpose. Additional exam requirements/recommendations for international students: Required—TOEFL (minimum score 570 paper-based); Recommended—IELTS (minimum score 6.5). *Application deadline:* For fall admission, 2/4 for domestic and international students. Application fee: $40. Electronic applications accepted. *Expenses: Tuition, area resident:* Full-time 12,000 euros. Tuition and fees vary according to degree level, program and student level. *Financial support:* Fellowships, career-related internships or fieldwork, institutionally sponsored loans, scholarships/grants, health care benefits, and tuition waivers (full and partial) available. Financial award application deadline: 2/4. *Faculty research:* Management of ecological systems, environmental impact assessment, energy conservation, climate change policy, forest policy in countries in transition. *Unit head:* Dr. Ruben Mnatsakanian, Head of Department, 36 1 327-3021, Fax: 36-1-327-3031, E-mail: envsci@ceu.hu. *Application contact:* Zsuzsanna Jaszberenyi, Head of Admissions Services, 361-327-3009, E-mail: admissions@ceu.edu.
Website: http://www.ceu.hu/unit/envsci

Clarkson University, Graduate School, Institute for a Sustainable Environment, Program in Environmental Politics and Governance, Potsdam, NY 13699. Offers MS. *Program availability:* Part-time. *Students:* 1 full-time (0 women). Average age 23. 6 applicants, 67% accepted, 1 enrolled. In 2015, 2 master's awarded. Terminal master's awarded for partial completion of doctoral program. *Degree requirements:* For master's, thesis. *Entrance requirements:* For master's, GRE, transcripts of all college coursework, resume, personal statement, three letters of recommendation. Additional exam requirements/recommendations for international students: Required—TOEFL (minimum score 550 paper-based, 80 iBT) or IELTS (minimum score 6.5). *Application deadline:* For fall admission, 1/30 priority date for domestic and international students; for spring admission, 9/1 priority date for domestic and international students. Applications are processed on a rolling basis. Application fee: $25 ($35 for international students). Electronic applications accepted. *Financial support:* In 2015–16, fellowships with full tuition reimbursements (averaging $24,510 per year), research assistantships with full tuition reimbursements (averaging $24,510 per year), teaching assistantships with full tuition reimbursements (averaging $24,510 per year) were awarded; scholarships/grants, tuition waivers (partial), and unspecified assistantships also available. *Unit head:* Dr. Susan Powers, Interim Director of the Institute for a Sustainable Environment/Associate Director of Sustainability, 315-268-6542, Fax: 315-268-4291, E-mail: spowers@clarkson.edu. *Application contact:* Carmen Camp, Administrative Assistant, 315-268-2318, Fax: 315-268-4291, E-mail: isegrad@clarkson.edu.
Website: http://www.clarkson.edu/epg/

Clark University, Graduate School, Department of International Development, Community, and Environment, Program in Environmental Science and Policy, Worcester, MA 01610-1477. Offers MS, MBA/MS. *Program availability:* Part-time. *Students:* 28 full-time (18 women), 2 part-time (0 women); includes 2 minority (1 American Indian or Alaska Native, non-Hispanic/Latino; 1 Hispanic/Latino), 8 international. Average age 27. 68 applicants, 75% accepted, 20 enrolled. In 2015, 22 master's awarded. *Degree requirements:* For master's, thesis. *Entrance requirements:* For master's, 3 references, resume or curriculum vitae. Additional exam requirements/recommendations for international students: Required—TOEFL (minimum score 575 paper-based; 90 iBT) or IELTS (minimum score 6.5). *Application deadline:* For fall admission, 1/15 for domestic students. Application fee: $75. *Expenses: Tuition, area resident:* Full-time $41,590; part-time $1300 per credit hour. *Required fees:* $80. Tuition and fees vary according to course load and program. *Financial support:* Fellowships with partial tuition reimbursements, research assistantships with partial tuition reimbursements, teaching assistantships with partial tuition reimbursements, institutionally sponsored loans, and scholarships/grants available. *Faculty research:* Environmental justice, children's health and risk assessment, smart grids and energy technology transitions, uncertainty-risk analysis, climate variability modeling. *Unit head:* Dr. Ed Carr, Director, 508-793-7201, Fax: 508-793-8820, E-mail: idce@clarku.edu. *Application contact:* Erika Paradis, Student and Academic Services Director, 508-793-7201, Fax: 508-793-8820, E-mail: eparadis@clarku.edu.
Website: http://www.clarku.edu/departments/idce/programs/esp/default.cfm

Clark University, Graduate School, Department of International Development, Community, and Environment, Program in Geographic Information Science for Development and Environment, Worcester, MA 01610-1477. Offers MS. *Students:* 50 full-time (24 women), 2 part-time (1 woman); includes 5 minority (1 Black or African American, non-Hispanic/Latino; 2 Asian, non-Hispanic/Latino; 2 Two or more races, non-Hispanic/Latino), 28 international. Average age 26. 96 applicants, 69% accepted, 22 enrolled. In 2015, 17 master's awarded. *Degree requirements:* For master's, thesis. *Entrance requirements:* For master's, 3 references, resume or curriculum vitae. Additional exam requirements/recommendations for international students: Required—TOEFL (minimum score 575 paper-based; 90 iBT) or IELTS (minimum score 6.5). *Application deadline:* For fall admission, 1/15 for domestic students. Application fee: $75. *Expenses: Tuition, area resident:* Full-time $41,590; part-time $1300 per credit hour. *Required fees:* $80. Tuition and fees vary according to course load and program. *Financial support:* Fellowships with partial tuition reimbursements, research assistantships with partial tuition reimbursements, teaching assistantships with partial tuition reimbursements, institutionally sponsored loans, and scholarships/grants available. *Faculty research:* Land-use change, the effects of environmental influences on child health and development, quantitative methods, watershed management, brownfields redevelopment, human/environment interactions, biodiversity conservation, climate change. *Unit head:* Dr. Ed Carr, Director, 508-793-7201, Fax: 508-793-8820. *Application contact:* Erika Paradis, IDCE Graduate Admissions Office, 508-793-7201, Fax: 508-793-8820, E-mail: eparadis@clarku.edu.
Website: http://clarku.edu/departments/idce/academicsGradGISDE.cfm

Clemson University, Graduate School, College of Agriculture, Forestry and Life Sciences, Department of Plant and Environmental Sciences, Program in Plant and Environmental Sciences, Clemson, SC 29634. Offers MS, PhD. *Faculty:* 5 full-time (2 women). *Students:* 30 full-time (9 women), 16 part-time (5 women); includes 1 minority (Two or more races, non-Hispanic/Latino), 21 international. Average age 30. 27 applicants, 33% accepted, 7 enrolled. In 2015, 12 master's, 8 doctorates awarded. *Degree requirements:* For master's, thesis; for doctorate, comprehensive exam, thesis/dissertation. *Entrance requirements:* For master's and doctorate, GRE General Test, unofficial transcripts, letters of recommendation. Additional exam requirements/recommendations for international students: Required—TOEFL (minimum score 550 paper-based; 80 iBT), IELTS (minimum score 6.5), PTE (minimum score 54). *Application deadline:* For fall admission, 4/15 for domestic and international students; for spring admission, 11/15 for domestic and international students. Applications are processed on a rolling basis. Application fee: $80 ($90 for international students). Electronic applications accepted. *Expenses:* $4,060 per semester full-time resident, $8,103 per semester full-time non-resident, $448 per credit hour part-time resident, $898 per credit hour part-time non-resident. *Financial support:* In 2015–16, 33 students received support, including 3 fellowships with partial tuition reimbursements available (averaging $5,000 per year), 20 research assistantships with partial tuition reimbursements available (averaging $17,289 per year), 10 teaching assistantships with partial tuition reimbursements available (averaging $16,581 per year); career-related internships or fieldwork and health care benefits also available. Financial award application deadline: 4/15. *Faculty research:* Agronomy, horticulture, plant pathology, plant physiology, entomology. *Unit head:* Dr. Patricia Zungoli, Department Head, 864-656-5041, Fax: 864-656-4960, E-mail: pzngl@clemson.edu. *Application contact:* Dr. Paula Agudelo, Graduate Program Coordinator, 864-656-5741, E-mail: pagudel@clemson.edu.
Website: http://www.clemson.edu/graduate/academics/program-details.html?m_id=Plant-Environmental-Sciences

Cleveland State University, College of Graduate Studies, Maxine Goodman Levin College of Urban Affairs, Program in Environmental Studies, Cleveland, OH 44115. Offers environmental nonprofit management (MAES); environmental planning (MAES); geographic information systems (Certificate); policy and administration (MAES); sustainable economic development (MAES); urban economic development (Certificate); urban real estate development and finance (Certificate); JD/MAES. *Program availability:* Part-time, evening/weekend. *Faculty:* 16 full-time (8 women), 13 part-time/adjunct (5 women). *Students:* 1 full-time (0 women), 3 part-time (all women). Average age 29. 4 applicants, 75% accepted, 2 enrolled. In 2015, 3 master's awarded. *Degree requirements:* For master's, thesis or alternative, exit project. *Entrance requirements:* For master's, GRE General Test (minimum score: verbal and quantitative combined 40th percentile, analytical writing 4.0), minimum GPA of 3.0. Additional exam requirements/recommendations for international students: Required—TOEFL (minimum score 550 paper-based; 78 iBT), IELTS (6.0), or International Test of English Proficiency (iTEP). *Application deadline:* For fall admission, 7/1 priority date for domestic students, 5/15 for international students; for spring admission, 11/15 for domestic students, 11/1 for international students; for summer admission, 4/1 for domestic students, 3/15 for international students. Applications are processed on a rolling basis. Application fee: $30. Electronic applications accepted. *Expenses:* Contact institution. *Financial support:* In 2015–16, 4 students received support, including research assistantships with tuition reimbursements available (averaging $7,200 per year), 1 teaching assistantship with partial tuition reimbursement available (averaging $2,400 per year); scholarships/grants, tuition waivers (full and partial), and unspecified assistantships also available. Support available to part-time students. Financial award application deadline: 3/1; financial award applicants required to submit FAFSA. *Faculty research:* Environmental policy and administration, environmental planning, geographic information systems (GIS), urban sustainability planning and management, energy policy, land re-use. *Unit head:* Dr. Sanda Kaufman, Professor/Program Director, 216-687-2367, Fax: 216-687-9239, E-mail: s.kaufman@csuohio.edu. *Application contact:* David Arrighi, Graduate Academic Advisor, 216-523-7522, Fax: 216-687-5398, E-mail: d.arrighi@csuohio.edu.
Website: http://urban.csuohio.edu/academics/graduate/maes/

Cleveland State University, College of Graduate Studies, Maxine Goodman Levin College of Urban Affairs, Program in Urban Planning, Design, and Development, Cleveland, OH 44115. Offers economic development (MUPDD); environmental sustainability (MUPDD); geographic information systems (MUPDD, Certificate); historic preservation (MUPDD); housing and neighborhood development (MUPDD); urban economic development (Certificate); urban real estate development and finance (MUPDD, Certificate); JD/MUPDD. *Accreditation:* ACSP. *Program availability:* Part-time, evening/weekend. *Faculty:* 16 full-time (8 women), 13 part-time/adjunct (5 women). *Students:* 22 full-time (11 women), 28 part-time (12 women); includes 14 minority (9 Black or African American, non-Hispanic/Latino; 4 Asian, non-Hispanic/Latino; 1 Hispanic/Latino). Average age 28. 48 applicants, 56% accepted, 14 enrolled. In 2015, 14 master's awarded. *Degree requirements:* For master's, thesis or alternative, exit project. *Entrance requirements:* For master's, GRE General Test (minimum score: 50th percentile combined verbal and quantitative, 4.0 analytical writing), minimum GPA of 3.0. Additional exam requirements/recommendations for international students: Required—TOEFL (minimum score 550 paper-based; 78 iBT), IELTS (6.0), or International Test of English Proficiency (iTEP). *Application deadline:* For fall admission, 7/1 priority date for domestic students, 5/15 for international students; for spring admission, 11/15 for domestic students, 11/1 for international students; for summer admission, 4/1 for domestic students, 3/15 for international students. Applications are processed on a rolling basis. Application fee: $30. Electronic applications accepted. *Expenses:* Contact institution. *Financial support:* In 2015–16, 10 students received support, including 5 research assistantships with full tuition reimbursements available (averaging $7,200 per year), 3 teaching assistantships with partial tuition reimbursements available (averaging $2,400 per year); scholarships/grants, tuition waivers (full and partial), and unspecified assistantships also available. Support available to part-time students. Financial award application deadline: 3/1; financial award applicants required to submit FAFSA. *Faculty research:* Housing and neighborhood development, urban housing policy, environmental sustainability, economic development, GIS and planning decision support. *Unit head:* Dr. Stephanie Ryberg-Webster, Assistant Professor/Director of MUPD Program, 216-802-3386, Fax: 216-687-2013, E-mail: s.ryberg@csuohio.edu. *Application contact:* David Arrighi, Graduate Academic Advisor, 216-523-7522, Fax: 216-687-5398, E-mail: d.arrighi@csuohio.edu.
Website: http://urban.csuohio.edu/academics/graduate/mupdd/

College of the Atlantic, Program in Human Ecology, Bar Harbor, ME 04609-1198. Offers M Phil. *Degree requirements:* For master's, thesis. *Faculty research:* Conservation of endangered species, public policy/community planning, environmental education, history, philosophy.

Colorado Heights University, Program in International Business, Denver, CO 80236-2711. Offers accounting (MBA); corporate finance (MBA); environmental management (MBA); healthcare management (MBA). *Entrance requirements:* For master's, official transcripts, resume or curriculum vitae, two reference letters, interview.

★ **Columbia University,** School of International and Public Affairs, Program in Environmental Science and Policy, New York, NY 10027. Offers MPA. Program admits applicants for late May/early June start only. *Degree requirements:* For master's, workshops. *Entrance requirements:* For master's, GRE, previous course work in biology and chemistry, earth sciences (recommended), economics (strongly recommended). Additional exam requirements/recommendations for international students: Required—TOEFL. Electronic applications accepted. *Faculty research:* Ecological management of enclosed ecosystems vegetation dynamics, environmental policy and management, energy policy, nuclear waste policy, environmental and natural resource economics and policy, carbon sequestration, urban planning, environmental risk assessment/toxicology, environmental justice.

See Display on page 362 and Close-Up on page 381.

Columbus State University, Graduate Studies, College of Letters and Sciences, Department of Political Science, Columbus, GA 31907-5645. Offers public administration (MPA), including criminal justice, environmental policy, government administration, health services administration, political campaigning, urban policy. *Program availability:* Part-time, evening/weekend, 100% online, blended/hybrid learning. *Faculty:* 8 full-time (2 women), 2 part-time/adjunct (0 women). *Students:* 34 full-time (15 women), 96 part-time (45 women); includes 63 minority (46 Black or African American, non-Hispanic/Latino; 2 American Indian or Alaska Native, non-Hispanic/Latino; 2 Asian, non-Hispanic/Latino; 9 Hispanic/Latino; 4 Two or more races, non-Hispanic/Latino). Average age 33. 75 applicants, 36% accepted, 23 enrolled. In 2015, 47 master's awarded. *Degree requirements:* For master's, comprehensive exam. *Entrance requirements:* For master's, GRE General Test, minimum GPA of 2.75, three letters of recommendation. Additional exam requirements/recommendations for international students: Required—TOEFL (minimum score 550 paper-based; 79 iBT). *Application deadline:* For fall admission, 6/30 for domestic students, 5/1 for international students; for spring admission, 11/1 for domestic and international students; for summer admission, 3/1 for domestic and international students. Applications are processed on a rolling basis. Application fee: $50. Electronic applications accepted. *Expenses:* Tuition, state resident: full-time $4804; part-time $2412 per semester hour. Tuition, nonresident: full-time $19,218; part-time $9612 per semester hour. *Required fees:* $1830; $1830 per unit. Tuition and fees vary according to program. *Financial support:* In 2015–16, 59 students received support, including 8 research assistantships with partial tuition reimbursements available (averaging $3,000 per year); career-related internships or fieldwork, Federal Work-Study, institutionally sponsored loans, scholarships/grants, tuition waivers (partial), and unspecified assistantships also available. Support available to part-time students. Financial award application deadline: 5/1; financial award applicants required to submit FAFSA. *Unit head:* Dr. Frederick Gordon, Director, 706-565-7875, E-mail: gordon_frederick@colstate.edu. *Application contact:* Kristin Williams, Director of International and Graduate Recruitment, 706-507-8848, Fax: 706-568-5091, E-mail: williams_kristin@columbusstate.edu.

Website: http://politicalscience.columbusstate.edu/

Concordia University, School of Graduate Studies, Faculty of Arts and Science, Department of Geography, Planning and Environment, Montréal, QC H3G 1M8, Canada. Offers environmental assessment (M Env, Diploma); geography, urban and environmental studies (M Sc, PhD). *Application deadline:* For fall admission, 3/1 for domestic students; for winter admission, 8/31 for domestic students. Application fee: $50. Tuition and fees vary according to course load, degree level and program. *Unit head:* Monica E. Mulrennan, Chair, 514-848-2424 Ext. 2055, Fax: 514-848-2057. *Application contact:* Jochen A.G. Jaeger, Graduate Program Director, 514-848-2424 Ext. 5481, Fax: 514-848-2057.

Website: http://www.concordia.ca/artsci/geography-planning-environment.html

Cornell University, Graduate School, Graduate Fields of Agriculture and Life Sciences, Field of Natural Resources, Ithaca, NY 14853-0001. Offers community-based natural resources management (MS, PhD); conservation biology (MS, PhD); ecosystem biology and biogeochemistry (MPS, MS, PhD); environmental management (MPS); fishery and aquatic science (MPS, MS, PhD); forest science (MPS, MS, PhD); human dimensions of natural resources management (MPS, MS, PhD); policy and institutional analysis (MS, PhD); program development and evaluation (MPS, MS, PhD); quantitative ecology (MS, PhD); wildlife science (MPS, MS, PhD). *Degree requirements:* For master's, thesis (MS), project paper (MPS); for doctorate, comprehensive exam, thesis/dissertation. *Entrance requirements:* For master's and doctorate, GRE General Test, 2 letters of recommendation. Additional exam requirements/recommendations for international students: Required—TOEFL (minimum score 550 paper-based; 77 iBT). Electronic applications accepted. *Faculty research:* Ecosystem-level dynamics, systems modeling, conservation biology/management, resource management's human dimensions, biogeochemistry.

Cornell University, Graduate School, Graduate Fields of Agriculture and Life Sciences, Field of Soil and Crop Sciences, Ithaca, NY 14853-0001. Offers agronomy (MS, PhD); environmental information science (MS, PhD); environmental management (MPS); field crop science (MS, PhD); soil science (MS, PhD). *Degree requirements:* For master's, thesis (MS); for doctorate, comprehensive exam, thesis/dissertation. *Entrance requirements:* For master's and doctorate, GRE General Test, 2 letters of recommendation. Additional exam requirements/recommendations for international students: Required—TOEFL (minimum score 550 paper-based; 77 iBT). Electronic applications accepted. *Faculty research:* Soil chemistry, physics and biology; crop physiology and management; environmental information science and modeling; international agriculture; weed science.

Cornell University, Graduate School, Graduate Fields of Architecture, Art and Planning, Field of Regional Science, Ithaca, NY 14853-0001. Offers environmental studies (MA, MS, PhD); international spatial problems (MA, MS, PhD); location theory (MA, MS, PhD); multiregional economic analysis (MA, MS, PhD); peace science (MA, MS, PhD); planning methods (MA, MS, PhD); urban and regional economics (MA, MS, PhD). Terminal master's awarded for partial completion of doctoral program. *Degree requirements:* For master's, thesis; for doctorate, comprehensive exam, thesis/dissertation. *Entrance requirements:* For master's and doctorate, GRE General Test, 2 letters of recommendation. Additional exam requirements/recommendations for international students: Required—TOEFL (minimum score 600 paper-based; 77 iBT). Electronic applications accepted. *Faculty research:* Urban and regional growth, spatial economics, formation of spatial patterns by socioeconomic systems, non-linear dynamics and complex systems, environmental-economic systems.

Cornell University, Graduate School, Graduate Fields of Arts and Sciences, Field of Archaeology, Ithaca, NY 14853-0001. Offers environmental archaeology (MA); historical archaeology (MA); Latin American archaeology (MA); medieval archaeology (MA); Mediterranean and Near Eastern archaeology (MA); Stone Age archaeology (MA). *Degree requirements:* For master's, one foreign language, thesis. *Entrance requirements:* For master's, GRE General Test, 3 letters of recommendation, sample of written work. Additional exam requirements/recommendations for international students: Required—TOEFL (minimum score 550 paper-based; 77 iBT). Electronic applications accepted. *Faculty research:* Anatolia, Lydia, Sardis, classical and Hellenistic Greece, science in archaeology, North American Indians, Stone Age Africa, Mayan trade.

Dalhousie University, Faculty of Agriculture, Halifax, NS B3H 4R2, Canada. Offers agriculture (M Sc), including air quality, animal behavior, animal molecular genetics, animal nutrition, animal technology, aquaculture, botany, crop management, crop physiology, ecology, environmental microbiology, food science, horticulture, nutrient management, pest management, physiology, plant biotechnology, plant pathology, soil chemistry, soil fertility, waste management and composting, water quality. *Program availability:* Part-time. *Degree requirements:* For master's, thesis, ATC Exam Teaching Assistantship. *Entrance requirements:* For master's, honors B Sc, minimum GPA of 3.0. Additional exam requirements/recommendations for international students: Required—TOEFL (minimum score 580 paper-based; 92 iBT), IELTS, Michigan English Language Assessment Battery, CanTEST, CAEL. *Faculty research:* Bio-product development, organic agriculture, nutrient management, air and water quality, agricultural biotechnology.

Dalhousie University, Faculty of Management, School for Resource and Environmental Studies, Halifax, NS B3H 3J5, Canada. Offers MES, MREM, MLIS/MREM. *Program availability:* Part-time. *Degree requirements:* For master's, thesis. *Entrance requirements:* For master's, honors degree. Additional exam requirements/recommendations for international students: Required—TOEFL, IELTS, CANTEST, CAEL, or Michigan English Language Assessment Battery. Electronic applications accepted. *Faculty research:* Resource management and ecology, aboriginal resource rights, management of toxic substances, environmental impact assessment, forest management, policy, coastal zone management.

Drexel University, College of Arts and Sciences, Program in Environmental Policy, Philadelphia, PA 19104-2875. Offers MS. *Program availability:* Part-time, evening/weekend. *Degree requirements:* For master's, thesis optional. Electronic applications accepted.

Duke University, Graduate School, University Program in Environmental Policy, Durham, NC 27708. Offers PhD. *Degree requirements:* For doctorate, comprehensive exam, thesis/dissertation. *Entrance requirements:* For doctorate, GRE General Test. Additional exam requirements/recommendations for international students: Required—TOEFL (minimum score 577 paper-based; 90 iBT) or IELTS (minimum score 7). Electronic applications accepted.

Duke University, Nicholas School of the Environment, Durham, NC 27708. Offers environment (PhD); environmental management (MEM); forestry (MF); JD/AM. Application deadline for PhD program is December 8. *Program availability:* Online learning. *Degree requirements:* For doctorate, variable foreign language requirement, thesis/dissertation. *Entrance requirements:* For master's, GRE General Test, previous course work in natural or social sciences relevant to environmental interests, college calculus, college statistics, and microeconomics or ecology. Additional exam requirements/recommendations for international students: Required—TOEFL (minimum score 577 paper-based; 90 iBT) or IELTS (minimum score 7). Electronic applications accepted. *Faculty research:* Climate change, energy, water quality, ecosystem management and conservation, human and environmental health.

Duquesne University, Bayer School of Natural and Environmental Sciences, Environmental Science and Management Program, Pittsburgh, PA 15282-0001. Offers MS, Certificate, JD/MS, MBA/MS. *Program availability:* Part-time, evening/weekend. *Faculty:* 2 full-time (0 women), 9 part-time/adjunct (1 woman). *Students:* 19 full-time (10 women), 13 part-time (8 women); includes 1 minority (Two or more races, non-Hispanic/Latino), 2 international. Average age 27. 37 applicants, 59% accepted, 14 enrolled. In 2015, 13 master's awarded. *Degree requirements:* For master's, thesis (for some programs), minimum of 37 credit hours (for conservation biology); for Certificate, minimum of 18 credit hours. *Entrance requirements:* For master's, GRE General Test, course work in biology, chemistry, and calculus or statistics; 3 letters of reference; official transcripts; statement of purpose; for Certificate, undergraduate degree, 3 letters of reference, official transcripts, statement of purpose. Additional exam requirements/recommendations for international students: Required—TOEFL (minimum score 90 iBT) or IELTS. *Application deadline:* For fall admission, 4/1 priority date for domestic students, 4/1 for international students; for spring admission, 10/1 priority date for domestic students, 10/1 for international students. Applications are processed on a rolling basis. Application fee: $0. Electronic applications accepted. *Expenses:* $1,218 per credit. *Financial support:* In 2015–16, 25 students received support, including 1 fellowship with full tuition reimbursement available (averaging $18,000 per year), 7 research assistantships (averaging $14,488 per year), 3 teaching assistantships with partial tuition reimbursements available; career-related internships or fieldwork, scholarships/grants, tuition waivers (partial), and unspecified assistantships also available. Financial award application deadline: 5/31. *Faculty research:* Watershed management systems, environmental analytical chemistry, environmental endocrinology, environmental microbiology, aquatic biology. *Total annual research expenditures:* $167,230. *Unit head:* Dr. John Stolz, Director, 412-396-6333, Fax: 412-396-5907, E-mail: stolz@duq.edu. *Application contact:* Heather Costello, Senior Graduate Academic Advisor, 412-396-6339, E-mail: costelloh@duq.edu.

Website: http://www.duq.edu/academics/schools/natural-and-environmental-sciences/academic-programs/environmental-science-and-management

The Evergreen State College, Graduate Programs, Program in Environmental Studies, Olympia, WA 98505. Offers MES. *Program availability:* Part-time, evening/weekend. *Faculty:* 5 full-time (4 women), 5 part-time/adjunct (2 women). *Students:* 66 full-time (47 women), 25 part-time (19 women); includes 13 minority (3 American Indian or Alaska Native, non-Hispanic/Latino; 2 Asian, non-Hispanic/Latino; 6 Hispanic/Latino; 2 Two or more races, non-Hispanic/Latino), 1 international. Average age 30. 95 applicants, 80% accepted, 45 enrolled. In 2015, 38 master's awarded. *Degree requirements:* For master's, thesis. *Entrance requirements:* For master's, GRE, BA or BS; minimum GPA of 3.0 in last 90 quarter hours; 15 quarter hours in social science and in natural science; college-level courses in social science, natural science and statistics; 3 letters of recommendation; evidence of writing, analytical and general communication skills of high quality and at level appropriate for graduate study. Additional exam requirements/recommendations for international students: Required—TOEFL (minimum score 600 paper-based; 100 iBT) or IELTS (minimum score 7.5). *Application deadline:* For fall admission, 2/15 priority date for domestic and international students. Applications are processed on a rolling basis. Application fee: $50. Electronic applications accepted. *Expenses:* $9,750 in-state; $22,113 out-of-state. *Financial support:* In 2015–16, 48 students received support, including 8 fellowships with partial tuition reimbursements available (averaging $4,733 per year); career-related internships or fieldwork, Federal Work-Study, institutionally sponsored loans, scholarships/grants, and tuition waivers (partial) also available. Support available to part-time students. Financial award application deadline: 3/1; financial award applicants required to submit FAFSA. *Faculty research:* Economics, political economy, statistics, history of science and technology, chemical oceanography, biogeochemistry, freshwater ecology, conservation biology, wildlife/natural resources management, energy policy, climate justice, climate policy/politics, political ecology, environment and development, restoration of riparian forests, headwater streams, wetlands, environmental education, water resources engineering, conservation and restoration of biodiversity, mapping, global development, and o. *Unit head:* Dr. Kevin Francis, Director, 360-867-5831, Fax: 360-867-5430, E-mail: francisk@evergreen.edu. *Application contact:* Gail Wootan, Assistant Director, 360-867-6225, Fax: 360-867-5430, E-mail: wootang@evergreen.edu.

Website: http://www.evergreen.edu/mes/

Florida Atlantic University, Dorothy F. Schmidt College of Arts and Letters, Department of History, Boca Raton, FL 33431-0991. Offers environmental studies (Certificate); history (MA). *Program availability:* Part-time. *Degree requirements:* For master's, one foreign language, thesis optional. *Entrance requirements:* For master's, GRE General Test, minimum GPA of 3.0. Additional exam requirements/recommendations for international students: Required—TOEFL (minimum score 500 paper-based; 61 iBT), IELTS (minimum score 6). Electronic applications accepted. *Faculty research:* Twentieth-century America, U.S. urban history, Florida history, history of socialism, Latin America.

Environmental Management and Policy

Florida Gulf Coast University, College of Arts and Sciences, Program in Public Administration, Fort Myers, FL 33965-6565. Offers environmental policy (MPA); management (MPA). *Accreditation:* NASPAA. *Program availability:* Part-time. *Faculty:* 235 full-time (96 women), 142 part-time/adjunct (60 women). *Students:* 16 full-time (13 women), 48 part-time (30 women); includes 21 minority (8 Black or African American, non-Hispanic/Latino; 13 Hispanic/Latino), 1 international. Average age 36. 30 applicants, 90% accepted, 23 enrolled. In 2015, 24 master's awarded. *Degree requirements:* For master's, thesis. *Entrance requirements:* For master's, GRE General Test, MAT, minimum GPA of 3.0. Additional exam requirements/recommendations for international students: Required—TOEFL (minimum score 550 paper-based). *Application deadline:* For fall admission, 7/1 priority date for domestic students; for spring admission, 10/15 for domestic students. Applications are processed on a rolling basis. Application fee: $30. Electronic applications accepted. *Expenses:* Tuition, state resident: full-time $6974. Tuition, nonresident: full-time $28,170. *Required fees:* $1987. One-time fee: $10 full-time. Tuition and fees vary according to course load and degree level. *Financial support:* In 2015–16, 11 students received support, including 5 research assistantships; career-related internships or fieldwork and tuition waivers (full and partial) also available. Support available to part-time students. Financial award application deadline: 6/30; financial award applicants required to submit FAFSA. *Faculty research:* Personnel, public policy, public finance, housing policy. *Unit head:* Dr. Roger Green, Chair, 239-590-7838, E-mail: rgreen@fgcu.edu. *Application contact:* Dr. Margaret Banyan, Assistant Professor/Director of MPA Program, 239-590-7850, Fax: 239-590-7846, E-mail: mbanyan@fgcu.edu.

Florida Institute of Technology, College of Engineering, Program in Environmental Resource Management, Melbourne, FL 32901-6975. Offers MS. *Program availability:* Part-time. *Students:* 2 full-time (1 woman), 1 (woman) part-time. Average age 28. 9 applicants, 22% accepted, 2 enrolled. In 2015, 1 master's awarded. *Degree requirements:* For master's, thesis or alternative, internship and oral presentation of internship. *Entrance requirements:* For master's, GRE General Test, minimum GPA of 3.0, 3 letters of recommendation, resume, statement of objectives. Additional exam requirements/recommendations for international students: Required—TOEFL (minimum score 550 paper-based; 79 iBT). *Application deadline:* Applications are processed on a rolling basis. Application fee: $50. Electronic applications accepted. *Expenses: Tuition, area resident:* Full-time $21,690; part-time $1205 per credit hour. *Required fees:* $500. Tuition and fees vary according to degree level, campus/location and program. *Financial support:* Research assistantships, teaching assistantships, career-related internships or fieldwork, and tuition remissions available. Financial award application deadline: 3/1; financial award applicants required to submit FAFSA. *Faculty research:* Coastal management issues, environmental policy, land use, impacts of growth, managing aquatic resources. *Unit head:* Dr. John Windsor, Program Chair, 321-674-7300, E-mail: jwindsor@fit.edu. *Application contact:* Cheryl A Brown, Associate Director of Graduate Admissions, 321-674-7581, Fax: 321-723-9468, E-mail: cbrown@fit.edu.

Website: http://coe.fit.edu/dmes/

Florida International University, College of Arts, Sciences, and Education, Department of Earth and Environment, Program in Environmental Studies, Miami, FL 33199. Offers MS. *Program availability:* Part-time. *Faculty:* 3 full-time (0 women), 1 part-time/adjunct (0 women). *Students:* 19 full-time (10 women), 9 part-time (7 women); includes 15 minority (13 Hispanic/Latino; 2 Two or more races, non-Hispanic/Latino), 3 international. Average age 31. 22 applicants, 32% accepted, 3 enrolled. In 2015, 15 master's awarded. *Degree requirements:* For master's, thesis or alternative. *Entrance requirements:* For master's, GRE General Test, minimum GPA of 3.0, 3 letters of recommendation, letter of intent. Additional exam requirements/recommendations for international students: Required—TOEFL (minimum score 550 paper-based; 80 iBT). *Application deadline:* For fall admission, 3/1 for domestic and international students; for spring admission, 10/1 for domestic students, 9/1 for international students. Applications are processed on a rolling basis. Application fee: $30. Electronic applications accepted. *Expenses:* Tuition, state resident: full-time $10,708; part-time $455.64 per credit hour. Tuition, nonresident: full-time $23,816; part-time $1001.69 per credit hour. *Required fees:* $390; $195 per semester. Tuition and fees vary according to program. *Financial support:* Institutionally sponsored loans and scholarships/grants available. Financial award application deadline: 3/1; financial award applicants required to submit FAFSA. *Unit head:* Dr. Rene Price, Chair, 305-348-3119, Fax: 305-348-6497, E-mail: rene.price@fiu.edu. *Application contact:* Dr. Krishnaswamy Jayachandran, Director, 305-348-6553, E-mail: jayachan@fiu.edu.

George Mason University, College of Science, Department of Environmental Science and Policy, Fairfax, VA 22030. Offers aquatic ecology (MS). *Faculty:* 20 full-time (10 women), 6 part-time/adjunct (0 women). *Students:* 58 full-time (37 women), 73 part-time (49 women); includes 21 minority (8 Black or African American, non-Hispanic/Latino; 7 Asian, non-Hispanic/Latino; 5 Hispanic/Latino; 1 Native Hawaiian or other Pacific Islander, non-Hispanic/Latino), 9 international. Average age 35. 40 applicants, 70% accepted, 14 enrolled. In 2015, 22 master's, 13 doctorates awarded. *Degree requirements:* For doctorate, comprehensive exam, thesis/dissertation, internship; seminar. *Entrance requirements:* For master's, GRE, bachelor's degree with minimum GPA of 3.0 in related field; 3 letters of recommendation; expanded goals statement; 2 official copies of transcripts; for doctorate, GRE, bachelor's degree with minimum GPA of 3.0; 3 letters of recommendation; current resume; expanded goals statement; 2 official copies of transcripts. Additional exam requirements/recommendations for international students: Required—TOEFL (minimum score 575 paper-based; 88 iBT), IELTS (minimum score 6.5), PTE (minimum score 59). Application fee: $75 ($80 for international students). Electronic applications accepted. *Financial support:* In 2015–16, 54 students received support, including 6 fellowships (averaging $7,149 per year), 13 research assistantships with tuition reimbursements available (averaging $15,186 per year), 36 teaching assistantships with tuition reimbursements available (averaging $14,546 per year); career-related internships or fieldwork, Federal Work-Study, scholarships/grants, unspecified assistantships, and health care benefits (for full-time research or teaching assistantship recipients) also available. Support available to part-time students. Financial award application deadline: 3/1; financial award applicants required to submit FAFSA. *Faculty research:* Wetland ecosystems, comparative physiology, systematics, molecular phylogenetics, conservation genetics, estuarine and oceanic systems, biodiversity of fungi, environmental and resource management, human ecology. *Total annual research expenditures:* $751,706. *Unit head:* Dr. Robert B. Jonas, Chair, 703-993-7590, Fax: 703-993-1066, E-mail: rjonas@gmu.edu. *Application contact:* Sharon Bloomquist, Graduate Program Coordinator, 703-993-3187, Fax: 703-993-1066, E-mail: sbloomqu@gmu.edu.

Website: http://esp.gmu.edu/

The George Washington University, Columbian College of Arts and Sciences, Program in Environmental and Resource Policy, Washington, DC 20052. Offers MA. *Students:* 20 full-time (9 women), 6 part-time (all women); includes 6 minority (3 Asian, non-Hispanic/Latino; 1 Hispanic/Latino; 2 Two or more races, non-Hispanic/Latino), 5 international. Average age 26. 47 applicants, 94% accepted, 13 enrolled. In 2015, 10 master's awarded. *Degree requirements:* For master's, capstone course. *Entrance requirements:* For master's, GRE General Test, minimum GPA of 3.0, two letters of recommendation. Additional exam requirements/recommendations for international students: Required—TOEFL (minimum score 600 paper-based; 100 iBT). *Application deadline:* For fall admission, 4/1 priority date for domestic and international students; for spring admission, 10/1 priority date for domestic students, 9/1 priority date for international students. Applications are processed on a rolling basis. Application fee: $60. Electronic applications accepted. *Financial support:* In 2015–16, 2 students received support. Fellowships with tuition reimbursements available, institutionally sponsored loans, and tuition waivers available. Financial award application deadline: 1/15. *Unit head:* Prof. Peter Linquiti, Chair, 202-994-0112, E-mail: linquiti@gwu.edu. *Application contact:* 202-994-6210, Fax: 202-994-6213, E-mail: askccas@gwu.edu.

Website: http://www.gwu.edu/~tspppa/academics/affiliated_environment_policy.cfm

Georgia Institute of Technology, Graduate Studies, College of Architecture, School of City and Regional Planning, Atlanta, GA 30332-0001. Offers city and regional planning (PhD); economic development (MCRP); environmental planning and management (MCRP); geographic information systems (MCRP); land and community development (MCRP); land use planning (MCRP); transportation (MCRP); urban design (MCRP); MCP/MSCE. *Accreditation:* ACSP. *Degree requirements:* For master's, thesis, internship. *Entrance requirements:* For master's, GRE General Test, minimum GPA of 2.7. Additional exam requirements/recommendations for international students: Required—TOEFL. Electronic applications accepted.

Georgia State University, Andrew Young School of Policy Studies, Department of Economics, Atlanta, GA 30303. Offers economics (MA); environmental economics (PhD); experimental economics (PhD); labor economics (PhD); policy (MA); public finance (PhD); urban and regional economics (PhD). MA offered through the College of Arts and Sciences. *Program availability:* Part-time. *Faculty:* 26 full-time (4 women). *Students:* 101 full-time (37 women), 16 part-time (8 women); includes 18 minority (5 Black or African American, non-Hispanic/Latino; 4 Asian, non-Hispanic/Latino; 7 Hispanic/Latino; 2 Two or more races, non-Hispanic/Latino), 61 international. Average age 29. 146 applicants, 41% accepted, 27 enrolled. In 2015, 20 master's, 12 doctorates awarded. Terminal master's awarded for partial completion of doctoral program. *Degree requirements:* For master's, thesis optional; for doctorate, comprehensive exam, thesis/dissertation. *Entrance requirements:* For master's and doctorate, GRE. Additional exam requirements/recommendations for international students: Required—TOEFL (minimum score 603 paper-based; 100 iBT) or IELTS (minimum score 7). *Application deadline:* For fall admission, 1/15 for domestic and international students. Application fee: $50. Electronic applications accepted. *Expenses:* Tuition, state resident: full-time $6876; part-time $382 per credit hour. Tuition, nonresident: full-time $22,374; part-time $1243 per credit hour. *Required fees:* $2128; $2128 per term. $1064 per term. Part-time tuition and fees vary according to course load and program. *Financial support:* In 2015–16, fellowships with full tuition reimbursements (averaging $11,333 per year), research assistantships with full tuition reimbursements (averaging $9,788 per year), teaching assistantships with full tuition reimbursements (averaging $3,000 per year) were awarded; career-related internships or fieldwork also available. Financial award application deadline: 2/15; financial award applicants required to submit FAFSA. *Faculty research:* Public, experimental, urban/environmental, labor, and health economics. *Unit head:* Dr. Rusty Tchernis, Director of the Doctoral Program, 404-413-0154, Fax: 404-413-0145, E-mail: rtchernis@gsu.edu.

Website: http://economics.gsu.edu/

Georgia State University, Andrew Young School of Policy Studies, Department of Public Management and Policy, Atlanta, GA 30303. Offers criminal justice (MPA); disaster management (Certificate); disaster policy (MPA); environmental policy (PhD); health policy (PhD); management and finance (MPA); nonprofit management (MPA, Certificate); nonprofit policy (MPA); planning and economic development (MPP, Certificate); policy analysis and evaluation (MPA), including planning and economic development; public and nonprofit management (PhD); public finance and budgeting (PhD), including science and technology policy, urban and regional economic development; public finance policy (MPA), including social policy; public health (MPA). *Accreditation:* NASPAA (one or more programs are accredited). *Program availability:* Part-time. *Faculty:* 15 full-time (8 women). *Students:* 128 full-time (80 women), 78 part-time (48 women); includes 78 minority (61 Black or African American, non-Hispanic/Latino; 4 Asian, non-Hispanic/Latino; 11 Hispanic/Latino; 2 Two or more races, non-Hispanic/Latino), 31 international. Average age 30. 262 applicants, 63% accepted, 74 enrolled. In 2015, 92 master's, 2 doctorates, 6 other advanced degrees awarded. Terminal master's awarded for partial completion of doctoral program. *Degree requirements:* For master's, thesis optional; for doctorate, comprehensive exam, thesis/dissertation. *Entrance requirements:* For master's and doctorate, GRE. Additional exam requirements/recommendations for international students: Required—TOEFL (minimum score 603 paper-based; 100 iBT) or IELTS (minimum score 7). *Application deadline:* For fall admission, 1/15 for domestic and international students. Application fee: $50. Electronic applications accepted. *Expenses:* Tuition, state resident: full-time $6876; part-time $382 per credit hour. Tuition, nonresident: full-time $22,374; part-time $1243 per credit hour. *Required fees:* $2128; $2128 per term. $1064 per term. Part-time tuition and fees vary according to course load and program. *Financial support:* In 2015–16, fellowships (averaging $8,194 per year), research assistantships (averaging $8,068 per year), teaching assistantships (averaging $3,600 per year) were awarded; institutionally sponsored loans, scholarships/grants, health care benefits, and unspecified assistantships also available. Financial award application deadline: 2/1. *Faculty research:* Public budgeting and finance, public management, nonprofit management, performance measurement and management, urban development. *Unit head:* Dr. Carolyn Bourdeaux, Chair and Professor, 404-413-0013, Fax: 404-413-0104, E-mail: cbourdeaux@gsu.edu.

Website: http://aysps.gsu.edu/pmap/

Goucher College, MA and MFA Programs, Baltimore, MD 21204-2794. Offers arts administration (MA); creative nonfiction (MFA); cultural sustainability (MA); digital arts (MA, MFA); environmental studies (MA); historic preservation (MA); management (MA). *Program availability:* Part-time, evening/weekend, blended/hybrid learning. *Faculty:* 6 full-time (4 women), 100 part-time/adjunct (56 women). *Students:* 70 full-time (50 women), 69 part-time (52 women); includes 15 minority (7 Black or African American, non-Hispanic/Latino; 1 American Indian or Alaska Native, non-Hispanic/Latino; 1 Asian, non-Hispanic/Latino; 4 Hispanic/Latino; 2 Two or more races, non-Hispanic/Latino), 2 international. 74 applicants, 88% accepted, 42 enrolled. In 2015, 83 master's awarded. *Degree requirements:* For master's, thesis, e-portfolio completion. *Entrance requirements:* For master's, digital portfolio (for MA, MFA in digital arts); writing sample (for MFA in creative nonfiction). Additional exam requirements/recommendations for international students: Required—TOEFL (minimum score 550 paper-based; 80 iBT). *Application deadline:* Applications are processed on a rolling basis. Application fee: $75. Electronic applications accepted. *Expenses:* $825 per credit hour; $125 technology fee per semester. *Financial support:* Scholarships/grants and unspecified assistantships available. Financial award application deadline: 4/15; financial award applicants required to submit FAFSA. *Unit head:* Tiffany Espinosa, Assistant Provost, 410-337-6296, E-mail: tiffany.espinosa@goucher.edu. *Application contact:* Kathea Smith, Director of

Admissions and Recruitment, 410-337-6163, Fax: 410-337-6085, E-mail: kathea.smith@goucher.edu.
Website: http://www.goucher.edu/grad

Green Mountain College, Program in Environmental Studies, Poultney, VT 05764-1199. Offers MS. Distance learning only. *Program availability:* Part-time, evening/weekend, online learning. *Entrance requirements:* For master's, portfolio, curriculum vitae, 3 recommendations. Electronic applications accepted. *Faculty research:* Herbarium specimen, solar electricity's value, environmental politics.

Hardin-Simmons University, Graduate School, Holland School of Sciences and Mathematics, Program in Environmental Management, Abilene, TX 79698-0001. Offers MS. *Program availability:* Part-time. *Faculty:* 5 full-time (2 women). *Students:* 5 full-time (2 women), 3 part-time (1 woman); includes 2 minority (1 Hispanic/Latino; 1 Two or more races, non-Hispanic/Latino). Average age 31. In 2015, 4 master's awarded. *Degree requirements:* For master's, comprehensive exam, thesis or alternative, internship. *Entrance requirements:* For master's, minimum undergraduate GPA of 3.0 in major, 2.7 overall; 2 semesters of course work each in biology, chemistry, and geology; interview; writing sample; occupational experience. Additional exam requirements/recommendations for international students: Required—TOEFL (minimum score 550 paper-based; 75 iBT). *Application deadline:* For fall admission, 8/15 priority date for domestic students, 4/1 for international students; for spring admission, 1/5 priority date for domestic students, 9/1 for international students. Applications are processed on a rolling basis. Application fee: $50. Electronic applications accepted. *Expenses: Tuition, area resident:* Full-time $12,060; part-time $670 per credit hour. *Required fees:* $325; $110 per semester. *Financial support:* In 2015–16, 11 students received support. Fellowships, career-related internships or fieldwork, and scholarships/grants available. Support available to part-time students. Financial award application deadline: 6/30; financial award applicants required to submit FAFSA. *Faculty research:* South American history, herpetology, geology, environmental education, petroleum biodegradation, environmental ecology and microbiology. *Unit head:* Dr. Mark Ouimette, Director, 325-670-1383, Fax: 325-670-1391, E-mail: ouimette@hsutx.edu. *Application contact:* Dr. Nancy Kucinski, Dean of Graduate Studies, 325-670-1298, Fax: 325-670-1564, E-mail: gradoff@hsutx.edu.
Website: http://www.hsutx.edu/academics/holland/graduate/environmental

Harvard University, Extension School, Cambridge, MA 02138-3722. Offers applied sciences (CAS); biotechnology (ALM); educational technologies (ALM); educational technology (CET); English for graduate and professional studies (DGP); environmental management (ALM, CEM); information technology (ALM); journalism (ALM); liberal arts (ALM); management (ALM, CM); mathematics for teaching (ALM); museum studies (ALM); premedical studies (Diploma); publication and communication (CPC). *Program availability:* Part-time, evening/weekend. *Degree requirements:* For master's, thesis. *Entrance requirements:* For master's, 3 completed graduate courses with grade of B or higher. Additional exam requirements/recommendations for international students: Required—TOEFL (minimum score 600 paper-based), TWE (minimum score 5). *Expenses:* Contact institution.

Humboldt State University, Academic Programs, College of Natural Resources and Sciences, Programs in Environmental Systems, Arcata, CA 95521-8299. Offers environmental systems (MS), including energy, environment and society, environmental resources engineering, geology, math modeling. *Degree requirements:* For master's, thesis. *Entrance requirements:* For master's, GRE, appropriate bachelor's degree, minimum GPA of 2.5, 3 letters of recommendation. Additional exam requirements/recommendations for international students: Required—TOEFL. *Faculty research:* Mathematical modeling, international development technology, geology, environmental resources engineering.

Idaho State University, Office of Graduate Studies, College of Science and Engineering, Civil and Environmental Engineering Department, Pocatello, ID 83209-8060. Offers civil engineering (MS); environmental engineering (MS); environmental science and management (MS). *Program availability:* Part-time. *Degree requirements:* For master's, comprehensive exam (for some programs), thesis optional, thesis project, 2 semesters of seminar. *Entrance requirements:* For master's, GRE. Additional exam requirements/recommendations for international students: Required—TOEFL (minimum score 550 paper-based; 80 iBT). Electronic applications accepted. *Faculty research:* Floor vibration investigations, earthquake engineering, base isolation systems and seismic risk assessment, infrastructure revitalization (building foundations and damage, bridge structures, highways, and dams), slope stability and soil erosion, pavement rehabilitation, computational fluid dynamics and flood control structures, microbial fuel cells, water treatment and water quality modeling, environmental risk assessment, biotechnology, nanotechnology.

Illinois Institute of Technology, Stuart School of Business, Program in Environmental Management and Sustainability, Chicago, IL 60661. Offers MS, JD/MS, MBA/MS. *Program availability:* Part-time, evening/weekend. *Entrance requirements:* For master's, GRE (minimum score 298) or GMAT (500), one semester of general chemistry and mathematics through calculus. Additional exam requirements/recommendations for international students: Required—TOEFL (minimum score 600 paper-based; 85 iBT); Recommended—IELTS (minimum score 7). Electronic applications accepted. *Expenses:* Contact institution. *Faculty research:* Wind energy, carbon footprint reduction, critical asset management, solar energy, water quality management.

Indiana University Bloomington, School of Public and Environmental Affairs, Public Affairs Programs, Bloomington, IN 47405. Offers economic development (MPA); energy (MPA); environmental policy (PhD); environmental policy and natural resource management (MPA); information systems (MPA); international development (MPA); local government management (MPA); nonprofit management (MPA, Certificate); policy analysis (MPA); public budgeting and financial management (Certificate); public finance (PhD); public financial administration (MPA); public management (MPA, PhD, Certificate); public policy analysis (PhD); social entrepreneurship (Certificate); specialized public affairs (MPA); sustainability and sustainable development (MPA); JD/MPA; MPA/MA; MPA/MIS; MPA/MLS; MSES/MPA. *Accreditation:* NASPAA (one or more programs are accredited). *Program availability:* Part-time. *Degree requirements:* For master's, capstone, internship; for doctorate, comprehensive exam, thesis/dissertation. *Entrance requirements:* For master's, GRE General Test or GMAT, official transcripts, 3 letters of recommendation, resume, personal statement; for doctorate, GRE General Test, official transcripts, 3 letters of recommendation, statement of purpose. Additional exam requirements/recommendations for international students: Required—TOEFL (minimum score 600 paper-based; 96 iBT); Recommended—IELTS (minimum score 7). Electronic applications accepted. *Faculty research:* International development, environmental policy and resource management, policy analysis, public finance, public management, urban management, nonprofit management, energy policy, social policy, public finance.

Indiana University Northwest, School of Public and Environmental Affairs, Gary, IN 46408-1197. Offers criminal justice (MPA); environmental affairs (Graduate Certificate); health services (MPA); nonprofit management (Certificate); public management (MPA). *Accreditation:* NASPAA (one or more programs are accredited). *Program availability:* Part-time. *Entrance requirements:* For master's, GRE General Test or GMAT, letters of recommendation. *Faculty research:* Employment in income security policies, evidence in criminal justice, equal employment law, social welfare policy and welfare reform, public finance in developing countries.

Indiana University of Pennsylvania, School of Graduate Studies and Research, College of Humanities and Social Sciences, Department of Geography and Regional Planning, Environmental Planning Track, Indiana, PA 15705-1087. Offers MS. *Program availability:* Part-time. *Faculty:* 10 full-time (1 woman). *Students:* 8 full-time (3 women), 1 international. Average age 26. 7 applicants, 57% accepted, 4 enrolled. *Degree requirements:* For master's, thesis optional. *Entrance requirements:* Additional exam requirements/recommendations for international students: Required—TOEFL (minimum score 550 paper-based). *Application deadline:* Applications are processed on a rolling basis. Application fee: $50. Electronic applications accepted. *Financial support:* In 2015–16, 5 research assistantships with tuition reimbursements (averaging $3,867 per year) were awarded; career-related internships or fieldwork, Federal Work-Study, scholarships/grants, and unspecified assistantships also available. Financial award application deadline: 4/15; financial award applicants required to submit FAFSA. *Unit head:* Dr. Richard Hoch, Graduate Coordinator, 724-357-5990, E-mail: richard.hoch@iup.edu.

Instituto Tecnologico de Santo Domingo, Graduate School, Area of Basic And Environmental Sciences, Santo Domingo, Dominican Republic. Offers environmental science (M En S), including environmental education, environmental management, marine resources, natural resources management; mathematics (MS, PhD); renewable energy technology (MS, Certificate).

Instituto Tecnológico y de Estudios Superiores de Monterrey, Campus Estado de México, Professional and Graduate Division, Estado de Mexico, Mexico. Offers administration of information technologies (MITA); architecture (M Arch); business administration (GMBA, MBA); computer sciences (MCS, PhD); education (M Ed); educational institution administration (MAD); educational technology and innovation (PhD); electronic commerce (MEC); environmental systems (MS); finance (MAF); humanistic studies (MHS); information sciences and knowledge management (MISKM); information systems (MS); manufacturing systems (MS); marketing (MEM); quality systems and productivity (MS); science and materials engineering (PhD); telecommunications management (MTM). *Program availability:* Part-time, online learning. *Degree requirements:* For master's, one foreign language, thesis (for some programs); for doctorate, one foreign language, thesis/dissertation. *Entrance requirements:* For master's, E-PAEP 500, interview; for doctorate, E-PAEP 500, research proposal. Additional exam requirements/recommendations for international students: Required—TOEFL (minimum score 550 paper-based). *Faculty research:* Surface treatments by plasmas, mechanical properties, robotics, graphical computing, mechatronics security protocols.

Instituto Tecnológico y de Estudios Superiores de Monterrey, Campus Irapuato, Graduate Programs, Irapuato, Mexico. Offers administration (MBA); administration of information technology (MAIT); administration of telecommunications (MAT); architecture (M Arch); computer science (MCS); education (M Ed); educational administration (MEA); educational innovation and technology (DEIT); educational technology (MET); electronic commerce (MBA); environmental administration and planning (MEAP); environmental systems (MES); finances (MBA); humanistic studies (MHS); international management for Latin American executives (MIMLAE); library and information science (MLIS); manufacturing quality management (MMQM); marketing research (MBA).

Inter American University of Puerto Rico, Metropolitan Campus, Graduate Programs, Program in Environmental Evaluation and Protection, San Juan, PR 00919-1293. Offers MS.

Johns Hopkins University, Engineering Program for Professionals, Part-time Program in Environmental Planning and Management, Baltimore, MD 21218. Offers MS, Post-Master's Certificate. *Program availability:* Part-time, evening/weekend, online learning.

Johns Hopkins University, G. W. C. Whiting School of Engineering, Master of Science in Engineering Management Program, Baltimore, MD 21218. Offers biomaterials (MSEM); civil engineering (MSEM); communications science (MSEM); computer science (MSEM); environmental systems analysis, economics and public policy (MSEM); fluid mechanics (MSEM); materials science and engineering (MSEM); mechanical engineering (MSEM); mechanics and materials (MSEM); nanobiotechnology (MSEM); nanomaterials and nanotechnology (MSEM); operations research (MSEM); probability and statistics (MSEM); smart product and device design (MSEM). *Entrance requirements:* For master's, GRE, 3 letters of recommendation, resume. Additional exam requirements/recommendations for international students: Required—TOEFL (minimum score 600 paper-based; 100 iBT) or IELTS (minimum score 7). Electronic applications accepted.

Johns Hopkins University, Zanvyl Krieger School of Arts and Sciences, Advanced Academic Programs, Program in Environmental Sciences and Policy, Washington, DC 20036. Offers energy policy and climate (MS); environmental sciences (MS); geographic information systems (MS, Certificate). *Program availability:* Part-time, evening/weekend, online learning. *Degree requirements:* For master's, thesis (for some programs). *Entrance requirements:* For master's, minimum GPA of 3.0, coursework in chemistry and calculus. Additional exam requirements/recommendations for international students: Required—TOEFL (minimum score 100 iBT). Electronic applications accepted.

Kentucky State University, College of Agriculture, Food Science and Sustainable Systems, Frankfort, KY 40601. Offers aquaculture (MS); environmental studies (MS). *Program availability:* Part-time, evening/weekend. *Faculty:* 11 full-time (1 woman). *Students:* 24 full-time (10 women), 9 part-time (6 women); includes 9 minority (6 Black or African American, non-Hispanic/Latino; 1 Asian, non-Hispanic/Latino; 1 Hispanic/Latino; 1 Two or more races, non-Hispanic/Latino), 1 international. Average age 30. 25 applicants, 84% accepted, 17 enrolled. In 2015, 12 master's awarded. *Degree requirements:* For master's, comprehensive exam, thesis. *Entrance requirements:* For master's, GRE, GMAT. Additional exam requirements/recommendations for international students: Required—TOEFL (minimum score 525 paper-based). *Application deadline:* Applications are processed on a rolling basis. Application fee: $30 ($100 for international students). Electronic applications accepted. *Expenses:* Tuition, state resident: full-time $7524; part-time $418 per credit hour. Tuition, nonresident: full-time $11,322; part-time $629 per credit hour. Tuition and fees vary according to course load. *Financial support:* In 2015–16, 11 students received support, including 24 research assistantships (averaging $21,061 per year); scholarships/grants, tuition waivers (partial), and unspecified assistantships also available. Financial award application deadline: 4/15; financial award applicants required to submit FAFSA. *Faculty research:* Nutritional requirements of fish and shrimp dex manipulation and ploidy manipulation of fishes. development of alternative aquaculture species. development of

alternative aquaculture production system, genetics and molecular markers. *Total annual research expenditures:* $4.5 million. *Unit head:* Dr. Kirk Pomper, Interim Director of Land Grant Programs, 502-597-5942, E-mail: kirk.pomper@kysu.edu. *Application contact:* Dr. James Obielodan, Director of Graduate Studies, 502-597-4723, E-mail: james.obielodan@kysu.edu.
Website: http://www.kysu.edu/academics/CAFSSS/

Lake Forest College, Graduate Program in Liberal Studies, Lake Forest, IL 60045. Offers American studies (MLS); environmental studies (MLS); history (MLS); Medieval and Renaissance art (MLS); philosophy (MLS); writing (MLS). *Program availability:* Part-time, evening/weekend. *Faculty:* 9 full-time (4 women). *Students:* 41 part-time (20 women); includes 5 minority (2 Asian, non-Hispanic/Latino; 3 Hispanic/Latino). Average age 37. 23 applicants, 52% accepted, 8 enrolled. In 2015, 5 master's awarded. *Degree requirements:* For master's, thesis optional, 8 courses, including at least 3 interdisciplinary seminars. *Entrance requirements:* For master's, transcript, essay, interview. Additional exam requirements/recommendations for international students: Required—TOEFL (minimum score 550 paper-based; 83 iBT); Recommended—IELTS (minimum score 6.5). *Application deadline:* For fall admission, 7/15 priority date for domestic students, 6/1 priority date for international students; for spring admission, 12/1 priority date for domestic students, 10/1 priority date for international students. Applications are processed on a rolling basis. Application fee: $30. *Expenses:* $2,500 per course. *Financial support:* In 2015–16, 6 students received support. Partial tuition grants (for full-time teachers) available. *Faculty research:* World War I and the peace movement; sprawling American cities; Renaissance women artists; postwar British intellectual history; contemporary American art. *Unit head:* Prof. D. L. LeMahieu, Director, 847-735-5133, Fax: 847-735-6291, E-mail: lemahieu@lakeforest.edu. *Application contact:* Prof. Carol Gayle, Associate Director, 847-735-5083, Fax: 847-735-6291, E-mail: gayle@lakeforest.edu.
Website: http://www.lakeforest.edu/academics/programs/mls/

Lamar University, College of Graduate Studies, College of Engineering, Department of Civil and Environmental Engineering, Beaumont, TX 77710. Offers civil (ME, MES); environmental engineering (MS); environmental studies (MS, DE). *Program availability:* Part-time. *Faculty:* 8 full-time (1 woman). *Students:* 63 full-time (17 women), 18 part-time (5 women); includes 5 minority (1 Black or African American, non-Hispanic/Latino; 1 American Indian or Alaska Native, non-Hispanic/Latino; 3 Asian, non-Hispanic/Latino), 69 international. Average age 26. 111 applicants, 40% accepted, 19 enrolled. In 2015, 20 master's, 1 doctorate awarded. *Degree requirements:* For master's, thesis optional; for doctorate, thesis/dissertation. *Entrance requirements:* For master's and doctorate, GRE General Test. Additional exam requirements/recommendations for international students: Required—TOEFL (minimum score 550 paper-based; 79 iBT), IELTS (minimum score 6.5). *Application deadline:* For fall admission, 8/1 for domestic students, 7/1 for international students; for spring admission, 1/5 for domestic students, 12/1 for international students. Applications are processed on a rolling basis. Application fee: $25 ($50 for international students). Electronic applications accepted. *Expenses: Tuition, area resident:* Full-time $6720; part-time $4032. Tuition, nonresident: full-time $14,880; part-time $8928. *Required fees:* $1900; $950 $784. *Financial support:* Fellowships with partial tuition reimbursements, research assistantships with partial tuition reimbursements, teaching assistantships with partial tuition reimbursements, scholarships/grants, and tuition waivers (partial) available. Financial award application deadline: 4/1; financial award applicants required to submit FAFSA. *Faculty research:* Environmental remediations, construction productivity, geotechnical soil stabilization, lake/reservoir hydrodynamics, air pollution. *Unit head:* Dr. Robert Yuan, Chair, 409-880-8759, Fax: 409-880-8121. *Application contact:* Melissa Gallien, Director, Admissions and Academic Services, 409-880-8888, Fax: 409-880-7419, E-mail: gradmissions@lamar.edu.
Website: http://engineering.lamar.edu/civil

Lehigh University, College of Arts and Sciences, Environmental Policy Design Program, Bethlehem, PA 18015. Offers environmental policy and law (Graduate Certificate); environmental policy design (MA); sustainable development (Graduate Certificate); urban environmental policy (Graduate Certificate). *Program availability:* Part-time. *Faculty:* 11 full-time (4 women). *Students:* 3 full-time (2 women), 3 part-time (2 women); includes 2 minority (both Hispanic/Latino). Average age 32. 7 applicants, 100% accepted, 2 enrolled. In 2015, 6 master's awarded. *Degree requirements:* For master's, thesis or additional course work. *Entrance requirements:* For master's, GRE, minimum GPA of 2.75, 3.0 for last two undergraduate semesters; essay; 2 letters of recommendation. Additional exam requirements/recommendations for international students: Required—TOEFL (minimum score 85 iBT). *Application deadline:* For fall admission, 1/1 for domestic and international students; for spring admission, 12/1 for domestic and international students. Applications are processed on a rolling basis. Application fee: $75. *Financial support:* Fellowships, scholarships/grants, tuition waivers (partial), and community fellowship and tuition remission available. Financial award application deadline: 1/1. *Faculty research:* Environmental policy, environmental law, urban policy, urban politics, urban environmental policy, sustainability, sustainable development, international environmental law, international environmental policy, environmental justice, social justice. *Unit head:* Dr. Donald P. Morris, Director, 610-758-5175, E-mail: dpm2@lehigh.edu. *Application contact:* Gary Burgess, Academic Coordinator, 610-758-4281, Fax: 610-758-6232, E-mail: glb215@lehigh.edu.
Website: http://ei.cas2.lehigh.edu/

Long Island University–LIU Post, College of Liberal Arts and Sciences, Brookville, NY 11548-1300. Offers applied mathematics (MS); behavior analysis (MA); biology (MS); criminal justice (MS); earth science (MS); English (MA); environmental studies (MS); environmental sustainability (MS); genetic counseling (MS); gerontology (Advanced Certificate); health care administration (MPA); history (MA); interdisciplinary studies (MA, MS); mathematics for secondary school teachers (MS); mobile GIS application development (Advanced Certificate); non-profit management (Advanced Certificate); political science (MA); psychology (MA); public administration (MPA). *Program availability:* Part-time, evening/weekend, online learning. *Faculty:* 77 full-time (35 women), 36 part-time/adjunct (17 women). *Students:* 254 full-time (178 women), 177 part-time (134 women); includes 104 minority (40 Black or African American, non-Hispanic/Latino; 27 Asian, non-Hispanic/Latino; 28 Hispanic/Latino; 1 Native Hawaiian or other Pacific Islander, non-Hispanic/Latino; 8 Two or more races, non-Hispanic/Latino), 44 international. Average age 31. 686 applicants, 47% accepted, 138 enrolled. In 2015, 135 master's awarded. *Degree requirements:* For master's, comprehensive exam (for some programs), thesis (for some programs). *Entrance requirements:* Additional exam requirements/recommendations for international students: Required—TOEFL (minimum score 550 paper-based; 79 iBT), IELTS (minimum score 6.5). *Application deadline:* Applications are processed on a rolling basis. Application fee: $50. Electronic applications accepted. *Expenses:* $1155 per credit; $934 full-time fees; $442 part-time fees. *Financial support:* In 2015–16, 48 fellowships (averaging $12,637 per year), 5 research assistantships with full tuition reimbursements were awarded; Federal Work-Study and institutionally sponsored loans also available. Support available to part-time students. Financial award application deadline: 2/15; financial award applicants required to submit FAFSA. *Faculty research:* Biology, criminal justice, earth and environmental science, English, health care and public administration, history, mathematics, political science, psychology, Spanish. *Unit head:* Dr. Nicholas J. Ramer, Acting Dean, 516-299-2233, Fax: 516-299-4140, E-mail: nicholas.ramer@liu.edu. *Application contact:* Carol Zerah, Director of Graduate Admissions, 516-299-2900 Ext. 3952, Fax: 516-299-2137, E-mail: enroll@cwpost.liu.edu.
Website: http://liu.edu/CWPost/Academics/Schools/CLAS

Louisiana State University and Agricultural & Mechanical College, Graduate School, School of the Coast and Environment, Department of Environmental Sciences, Baton Rouge, LA 70803. Offers environmental planning and management (MS); environmental science (PhD); environmental toxicology (MS).

McGill University, Faculty of Graduate and Postdoctoral Studies, Faculty of Agricultural and Environmental Sciences, Department of Natural Resource Sciences, Montréal, QC H3A 2T5, Canada. Offers entomology (M Sc, PhD); environmental assessment (M Sc); forest science (M Sc, PhD); microbiology (M Sc, PhD); micrometeorology (M Sc, PhD); neotropical environment (M Sc, PhD); soil science (M Sc, PhD); wildlife biology (M Sc, PhD).

Michigan Technological University, Graduate School, College of Sciences and Arts, Department of Social Sciences, Houghton, MI 49931. Offers environmental and energy policy (MS, PhD); industrial archaeology (MS); industrial heritage and archeology (PhD). *Program availability:* Part-time. *Faculty:* 21 full-time (10 women). *Students:* 24 full-time (10 women), 10 part-time (3 women); includes 4 minority (1 Black or African American, non-Hispanic/Latino; 1 American Indian or Alaska Native, non-Hispanic/Latino; 1 Asian, non-Hispanic/Latino; 1 Hispanic/Latino), 7 international. Average age 31. 31 applicants, 32% accepted, 7 enrolled. In 2015, 12 master's, 1 doctorate awarded. Terminal master's awarded for partial completion of doctoral program. *Degree requirements:* For master's, comprehensive exam (for some programs), thesis (for some programs); for doctorate, comprehensive exam, thesis/dissertation. *Entrance requirements:* For master's and doctorate, GRE, statement of purpose, official transcripts, 3 letters of recommendation, writing sample, resume/curriculum vitae. Additional exam requirements/recommendations for international students: Required—TOEFL (recommended score 100 iBT) or IELTS. *Application deadline:* For fall admission, 2/1 priority date for domestic and international students. Applications are processed on a rolling basis. Application fee: $0. Electronic applications accepted. *Expenses:* Tuition, state resident: full-time $15,507; part-time $861.50 per credit. Tuition, nonresident: full-time $15,507; part-time $861.50 per credit. *Required fees:* $248; $248. Tuition and fees vary according to course load and program. *Financial support:* In 2015–16, 15 students received support, including 1 fellowship with full tuition reimbursement available (averaging $15,000 per year), 10 research assistantships with full tuition reimbursements available (averaging $30,000 per year), 13 teaching assistantships with full tuition reimbursements available (averaging $30,000 per year); career-related internships or fieldwork, scholarships/grants, health care benefits, unspecified assistantships, and cooperative program also available. *Faculty research:* Industrial archeology, mining history, environmental and energy policy, land-use policy, environmental decision-making, sustainability. *Total annual research expenditures:* $746,000. *Unit head:* Dr. Hugh S. Gorman, Chair, 906-487-2116, Fax: 906-487-2284, E-mail: hsgorman@mtu.edu. *Application contact:* Amy Spahn, Office Assistant, 906-487-2113, Fax: 906-487-2284, E-mail: gradadms@mtu.edu.
Website: http://www.mtu.edu/social-sciences/

Middlebury Institute of International Studies at Monterey, Graduate School of International Policy and Management, Program in International Environmental Policy, Monterey, CA 93940-2691. Offers MA. *Degree requirements:* For master's, one foreign language. *Entrance requirements:* For master's, minimum GPA of 3.0, proficiency in a foreign language. Additional exam requirements/recommendations for international students: Required—TOEFL (minimum score 550 paper-based; 80 iBT). Electronic applications accepted. *Expenses: Tuition, area resident:* Full-time $37,100; part-time $1776 per credit. *Required fees:* $78 per semester.

Millersville University of Pennsylvania, College of Graduate Studies and Adult Learning, College of Science and Technology, Department of Earth Sciences, Program in Integrated Scientific Applications: Environmental Systems Management Option, Millersville, PA 17551-0302. Offers MS. *Program availability:* Part-time. *Faculty:* 11 full-time (2 women), 2 part-time/adjunct (0 women). *Students:* 1 full-time (0 women), 4 part-time (2 women); includes 1 minority (Asian, non-Hispanic/Latino). 4 applicants, 100% accepted, 4 enrolled. In 2015, 2 master's awarded. *Degree requirements:* For master's, thesis optional, internship, applied research. *Entrance requirements:* For master's, GRE, MAT or GMAT (if cumulative GPA is lower than 3.0), three professional letters of recommendation, academic and professional goals statement, current resume. Additional exam requirements/recommendations for international students: Required—TOEFL (minimum score 600 paper-based), IELTS (minimum score 6). *Application deadline:* Applications are processed on a rolling basis. Application fee: $40. Electronic applications accepted. *Expenses:* Tuition, state resident: full-time $8460; part-time $470 per credit. Tuition, nonresident: full-time $12,690; part-time $705 per credit. *Required fees:* $2471; $133.75 per credit. Tuition and fees vary according to course load, degree level and program. *Financial support:* Application deadline: 3/15; applicants required to submit FAFSA. *Faculty research:* Environmental science, sustainability, environmental economics, applied environmental chemistry. *Unit head:* Dr. Richard D. Clark, Chair, 717-872-7434, Fax: 717-871-7918, E-mail: richard.clark@millersville.edu. *Application contact:* Dr. Victor S. DeSantis, Dean of College of Graduate Studies and Adult Learning/Associate Provost for Civic and Community Engagement, 717-871-7619, Fax: 717-871-7954, E-mail: victor.desantis@millersville.edu.
Website: http://www.millersville.edu/esci/msisa/esm.php

Missouri State University, Graduate College, Interdisciplinary Program in Administrative Studies, Springfield, MO 65897. Offers administrative studies (Certificate); applied communication (MS); criminal justice (MS); environmental management (MS); homeland security (MS); individualized (MS); screenwriting and producing (MS); sports management (MS). *Program availability:* Part-time, evening/weekend, 100% online, blended/hybrid learning. *Students:* 34 full-time (25 women), 50 part-time (33 women); includes 9 minority (5 Black or African American, non-Hispanic/Latino; 4 Two or more races, non-Hispanic/Latino), 21 international. Average age 33. 76 applicants, 58% accepted, 38 enrolled. In 2015, 30 master's awarded. *Degree requirements:* For master's, comprehensive exam, thesis or alternative. *Entrance requirements:* For master's, GRE, GMAT (if GPA less than 3.0). Additional exam requirements/recommendations for international students: Required—TOEFL (minimum score 550 paper-based; 79 iBT), IELTS (minimum score 6). *Application deadline:* For fall admission, 7/15 priority date for domestic students; for spring admission, 12/1 priority date for domestic students; for summer admission, 5/1 for domestic students. Applications are processed on a rolling basis. Application fee: $35 ($50 for international students). Electronic applications accepted. *Expenses:* Tuition, state resident: full-time $5500. Tuition, nonresident: full-time $10,108. *Required fees:* $1000. *Financial support:* Career-related internships or fieldwork, Federal Work-Study, institutionally sponsored loans, scholarships/grants, and unspecified assistantships available. Support available to part-time students. Financial award application deadline: 3/31; financial award

applicants required to submit FAFSA. *Unit head:* Dr. Gerald Masterson, Program Coordinator, 417-836-5251, Fax: 417-836-6888, E-mail: msas@missouristate.edu. *Application contact:* Michael Edwards, Coordinator of Graduate Admissions, 417-836-5330, Fax: 417-836-6200, E-mail: michaeledwards@missouristate.edu.
Website: http://msas.missouristate.edu

Montclair State University, The Graduate School, College of Science and Mathematics, PhD Program in Environmental Management, Montclair, NJ 07043-1624. Offers PhD. *Students:* 35 full-time (15 women), 2 part-time (both women); includes 6 minority (2 Black or African American, non-Hispanic/Latino; 4 Hispanic/Latino), 16 international. Average age 32. 14 applicants, 36% accepted, 4 enrolled. In 2015, 3 doctorates awarded. *Degree requirements:* For doctorate, thesis/dissertation. *Entrance requirements:* For doctorate, GRE General Test, 3 letters of recommendation, essay. Additional exam requirements/recommendations for international students: Required—TOEFL (minimum score 83 iBT) or IELTS (minimum score 6.5). *Application deadline:* For fall admission, 2/1 for domestic students. Application fee: $60. Electronic applications accepted. *Expenses:* Tuition, state resident: part-time $553 per credit. Tuition, nonresident: part-time $854 per credit. *Required fees:* $91 per credit. Tuition and fees vary according to program. *Financial support:* In 2015–16, 15 research assistantships with full tuition reimbursements (averaging $15,000 per year) were awarded; tuition waivers (full) and unspecified assistantships also available. Financial award application deadline: 3/1; financial award applicants required to submit FAFSA. *Faculty research:* Environmental geochemistry/remediation/forensics, environmental law and policy, regional climate modeling, remote sensing, Cenozoic marine sediment records from polar regions, sustainability science. *Unit head:* Dr. Michael Kruge, Director, 973-655-5423, Fax: 973-655-6810. *Application contact:* Amy Aiello, Director of Graduate Admissions and Operations, 973-655-5147, Fax: 973-655-7869, E-mail: graduate.school@montclair.edu.
Website: http://www.montclair.edu/csam/doctoral-environment-management/

Montclair State University, The Graduate School, College of Science and Mathematics, Program in Environmental Studies, Montclair, NJ 07043-1624. Offers environmental education (MA); environmental management (MA); environmental science (MA). *Program availability:* Part-time, evening/weekend. *Students:* 8 full-time (3 women), 14 part-time (8 women); includes 3 minority (1 Asian, non-Hispanic/Latino; 2 Hispanic/Latino). Average age 27. 13 applicants, 69% accepted, 9 enrolled. In 2015, 8 master's awarded. *Degree requirements:* For master's, thesis. *Entrance requirements:* For master's, GRE General Test, 2 letters of recommendation, essay. Additional exam requirements/recommendations for international students: Required—TOEFL (minimum score 83 iBT), IELTS (minimum score 6.5). *Application deadline:* Applications are processed on a rolling basis. Application fee: $60. Electronic applications accepted. *Expenses:* Tuition, state resident: part-time $553 per credit. Tuition, nonresident: part-time $854 per credit. *Required fees:* $91 per credit. Tuition and fees vary according to program. *Financial support:* In 2015–16, 10 research assistantships with full tuition reimbursements (averaging $7,000 per year) were awarded; Federal Work-Study, scholarships/grants, and unspecified assistantships also available. Support available to part-time students. Financial award application deadline: 3/1; financial award applicants required to submit FAFSA. *Faculty research:* Environmental geochemistry/remediation/forensics, environmental law and policy, regional climate modeling, remote sensing, Cenozoic marine sediment records from polar regions, sustainability science. *Unit head:* Dr. Matthew Goring, Chairperson, 973-655-5409. *Application contact:* Amy Aiello, Executive Director of The Graduate School, 973-655-5147, Fax: 973-655-7869, E-mail: graduate.school@montclair.edu.
Website: http://www.montclair.edu/csam/earth-environment-studies/

Morehead State University, Graduate Programs, College of Science and Technology, Department of Biology and Chemistry, Morehead, KY 40351. Offers biology (MS); biology regional analysis (MS). *Program availability:* Part-time. *Degree requirements:* For master's, comprehensive exam, thesis optional, oral and written final exams. *Entrance requirements:* For master's, GRE General Test, minimum GPA of 3.0 in biology, 2.5 overall; undergraduate major/minor in biology, environmental science, or equivalent. Additional exam requirements/recommendations for international students: Required—TOEFL (minimum score 525 paper-based). Electronic applications accepted. *Faculty research:* Atherosclerosis, RNA evolution, cancer biology, water quality/ecology, immunoparasitology.

Naropa University, Graduate Programs, Program in Environmental Leadership, Boulder, CO 80302-6697. Offers MA. *Faculty:* 2 full-time (both women), 4 part-time/adjunct (1 woman). *Students:* 8 full-time (4 women), 4 part-time (all women); includes 1 minority (Two or more races, non-Hispanic/Latino). Average age 32. 18 applicants, 94% accepted, 8 enrolled. In 2015, 7 master's awarded. *Degree requirements:* For master's, applied leadership project. *Entrance requirements:* For master's, interview; letter of interest; resume/curriculum vitae with pertinent academic, employment and volunteer activity; 2 letters of recommendation; transcripts. Additional exam requirements/recommendations for international students: Required—TOEFL (minimum score 550 paper-based; 80 iBT). *Application deadline:* For fall admission, 1/15 priority date for domestic and international students. Applications are processed on a rolling basis. Application fee: $60. Electronic applications accepted. *Expenses: Tuition, area resident:* Full-time $23,880; part-time $995 per credit hour. *Required fees:* $335 per semester. Tuition and fees vary according to course load. *Financial support:* In 2015–16, 9 students received support, including 1 research assistantship (averaging $3,000 per year); career-related internships or fieldwork, Federal Work-Study, scholarships/grants, tuition waivers (partial), and unspecified assistantships also available. Support available to part-time students. Financial award application deadline: 3/1; financial award applicants required to submit FAFSA. *Unit head:* Dr. Jeanine Canty, Chair, Environmental Studies, 303-245-4735, E-mail: jcanty@naropa.edu. *Application contact:* Office of Admissions, 303-546-3572, Fax: 303-546-3583, E-mail: rregnery@naropa.edu.
Website: http://www.naropa.edu/academics/masters/environmental-leadership/index.php

The New School, Schools of Public Engagement, Program in Environmental Policy and Sustainability Management, New York, NY 10011. Offers environmental policy and sustainability management (MS); sustainability strategies (Certificate). *Program availability:* Part-time, evening/weekend. *Faculty:* 3 full-time (2 women), 3 part-time/adjunct (2 women). *Students:* 49 full-time (36 women), 19 part-time (12 women); includes 23 minority (7 Black or African American, non-Hispanic/Latino; 3 Asian, non-Hispanic/Latino; 10 Hispanic/Latino; 3 Two or more races, non-Hispanic/Latino), 5 international. Average age 29. 66 applicants, 98% accepted, 21 enrolled. In 2015, 38 master's, 3 other advanced degrees awarded. *Entrance requirements:* For master's, two letters of recommendation, statement of purpose, resume, transcripts. Additional exam requirements/recommendations for international students: Required—TOEFL (minimum score 100 iBT), IELTS (minimum score 7), PTE (minimum score 68). *Application deadline:* For fall admission, 5/5 for domestic and international students; for spring admission, 10/15 priority date for domestic and international students. Applications are processed on a rolling basis. Application fee: $50. Electronic applications accepted. *Expenses:* $1,530 per credit plus $100 maintenance of status fee. *Financial support:* Research assistantships, career-related internships or fieldwork, Federal Work-Study, scholarships/grants, and unspecified assistantships available. Support available to part-time students. Financial award application deadline: 3/1; financial award applicants required to submit FAFSA. *Faculty research:* Climate change and cities, corporate sustainability and social responsibility, environmental justice and policy (waste, air quality, etc.), infrastructure economics (transport, water, energy), community based participatory research. *Unit head:* Sharon Greenidge, Assistant Director of Admission, 212-229-5150 Ext. 1103, E-mail: greenids@newschool.edu. *Application contact:* Sharon Greenidge, Assistant Director of Admission, 212-229-5150 Ext. 1103, E-mail: greenids@newschool.edu.
Website: http://www.newschool.edu/

New York Institute of Technology, School of Engineering and Computing Sciences, Department of Energy Management, Old Westbury, NY 11568-8000. Offers energy management (MS); energy technology (Advanced Certificate); environmental management (Advanced Certificate); facilities management (Advanced Certificate); infrastructure security management (Advanced Certificate). *Program availability:* Part-time, evening/weekend, 100% online, blended/hybrid learning. *Faculty:* 1 full-time (0 women), 8 part-time/adjunct (1 woman). *Students:* 61 full-time (8 women), 68 part-time (14 women); includes 26 minority (10 Black or African American, non-Hispanic/Latino; 7 Asian, non-Hispanic/Latino; 7 Hispanic/Latino; 2 Two or more races, non-Hispanic/Latino), 68 international. Average age 29. 274 applicants, 58% accepted, 43 enrolled. In 2015, 53 master's, 3 other advanced degrees awarded. *Degree requirements:* For master's, thesis or alternative. *Entrance requirements:* For master's, minimum undergraduate GPA of 2.85. Additional exam requirements/recommendations for international students: Required—TOEFL (minimum score 550 paper-based; 79 iBT), IELTS (minimum score 6). *Application deadline:* For fall admission, 6/1 for domestic and international students; for spring admission, 11/1 for domestic and international students. Applications are processed on a rolling basis. Application fee: $50. Electronic applications accepted. *Expenses: Tuition, area resident:* Full-time $20,790; part-time $1155 per credit. *Required fees:* $95; $75 per credit. Full-time tuition and fees vary according to degree level, campus/location and program. Part-time tuition and fees vary according to course load and campus/location. *Financial support:* Research assistantships with partial tuition reimbursements, career-related internships or fieldwork, scholarships/grants, health care benefits, tuition waivers (full and partial), and unspecified assistantships available. Support available to part-time students. Financial award application deadline: 3/1; financial award applicants required to submit FAFSA. *Unit head:* Dr. Robert Amundsen, Department Chair, 516-686-7578, E-mail: ramundse@nyit.edu. *Application contact:* Alice Dolitsky, Director, Graduate Admissions, 516-686-7520, Fax: 516-686-1116, E-mail: nyitgrad@nyit.edu.
Website: http://www.nyit.edu/degrees/energy_management_ms

New York University, School of Continuing and Professional Studies, Center for Global Affairs, New York, NY 10012-1019. Offers global affairs (MS), including environment/energy policy, human rights and international law, international development and humanitarian assistance, international relations, peace building, private sector, transnational security; global energy (Advanced Certificate); peacebuilding (Advanced Certificate); transnational security (Advanced Certificate). *Program availability:* Part-time, evening/weekend. *Degree requirements:* For master's, thesis. *Entrance requirements:* For master's, GRE or GMAT (only upon request), bachelor's degree, resume with relevant professional work, internship or volunteer experience, two letters of recommendation, statement of purpose. Additional exam requirements/recommendations for international students: Required—TOEFL (minimum score 600 paper-based; 100 iBT), IELTS (minimum score 7). Electronic applications accepted.

Northeastern Illinois University, College of Graduate Studies and Research, College of Arts and Sciences, Program in Geography and Environmental Studies, Chicago, IL 60625-4699. Offers MA. *Program availability:* Part-time, evening/weekend. *Degree requirements:* For master's, comprehensive exam, thesis optional. *Entrance requirements:* For master's, undergraduate minor in geography or environmental studies, minimum GPA of 2.75. Additional exam requirements/recommendations for international students: Required—TOEFL (minimum score 550 paper-based; 79 iBT). Electronic applications accepted. *Faculty research:* Segregation and urbanization of minority groups in the Chicago area, scale dependence and parameterization in nonpoint source pollution modeling, ecological land classification and mapping, ecosystem restoration, soil-vegetation relationships.

Northeastern State University, College of Business and Technology, Program in Environmental, Health, and Safety Management, Tahlequah, OK 74464-2399. Offers MEHS. *Program availability:* Part-time, evening/weekend. *Faculty:* 6 full-time (2 women). *Students:* 5 full-time (3 women), 18 part-time (4 women); includes 14 minority (3 Black or African American, non-Hispanic/Latino; 7 American Indian or Alaska Native, non-Hispanic/Latino; 1 Asian, non-Hispanic/Latino; 1 Hispanic/Latino; 2 Two or more races, non-Hispanic/Latino), 2 international. Average age 35. In 2015, 5 master's awarded. *Degree requirements:* For master's, synergistic experience. *Entrance requirements:* For master's, GRE, MAT, minimum GPA of 2.5. Additional exam requirements/recommendations for international students: Required—TOEFL. *Application deadline:* For fall admission, 6/1 priority date for domestic students. Applications are processed on a rolling basis. Application fee: $25. Electronic applications accepted. *Expenses:* Tuition, state resident: part-time $189.60 per credit hour. Tuition, nonresident: part-time $462.60 per credit hour. *Required fees:* $37.40 per credit hour. *Financial support:* Teaching assistantships and Federal Work-Study available. Financial award application deadline: 3/1. *Unit head:* Dr. Benjamin Ofili, Department Chair, 918-444-2940, E-mail: ofili@nsuok.edu. *Application contact:* Robin Hunter, Department Secretary, 918-444-3086, E-mail: hixrr@nsouk.edu.
Website: http://academics.nsuok.edu/businesstechnology/Graduate/MEHS.aspx

Northern Arizona University, Graduate College, College of Engineering, Forestry, and Natural Sciences, School of Earth Sciences and Environmental Sustainability, Flagstaff, AZ 86011. Offers climate science and solutions (MS); earth sciences and environmental sustainability (PhD); environmental sciences and policy (MS); geology (MS). *Degree requirements:* For master's, comprehensive exam (for some programs), thesis (for some programs). *Entrance requirements:* Additional exam requirements/recommendations for international students: Required—TOEFL (minimum score 550 paper-based; 80 iBT), IELTS (minimum score 7). *Application deadline:* For fall admission, 2/1 priority date for domestic and international students. Applications are processed on a rolling basis. Application fee: $65. Electronic applications accepted. *Expenses: Tuition, area resident:* Full-time $8710. Tuition, nonresident: full-time $20,350. *Required fees:* $896. *Financial support:* Fellowships, research assistantships with full tuition reimbursements, teaching assistantships with full tuition reimbursements, career-related internships or fieldwork, Federal Work-Study, scholarships/grants, health care benefits, tuition waivers (full and partial), and unspecified assistantships available. Financial award applicants required to submit FAFSA. *Unit head:* Dr. Paul Umhoefer, Director, 928-523-6464, E-mail: paul.umhoefer@nau.edu. *Application contact:* SESES Support, 928-523-9333, Fax: 928-523-7432, E-mail: seses_admin_support@nau.edu.
Website: http://nau.edu/cefns/natsci/seses/

Environmental Management and Policy

The Ohio State University, Graduate School, College of Food, Agricultural, and Environmental Sciences, School of Environment and Natural Resources, Columbus, OH 43210. Offers ecological restoration (MS, PhD); ecosystem science (MS, PhD); environment and natural resources (MENR); environmental social sciences (MS, PhD); fisheries and wildlife science (MS, PhD); forest science (MS, PhD); rural sociology (MS, PhD); soil science (MS, PhD). *Degree requirements:* For master's, thesis; for doctorate, thesis/dissertation. *Entrance requirements:* For master's and doctorate, GRE. Additional exam requirements/recommendations for international students: Required—TOEFL (minimum score 550 paper-based; 79 iBT), Michigan English Language Assessment Battery (minimum score 82); Recommended—IELTS (minimum score 7). Electronic applications accepted.

Ohio University, Graduate College, College of Arts and Sciences, Department of Geological Sciences, Athens, OH 45701-2979. Offers environmental geochemistry (MS); environmental geology (MS); environmental/hydrology (MS); geology (MS); geology education (MS); geomorphology/surficial processes (MS); geophysics (MS); hydrogeology (MS); sedimentology (MS); structure/tectonics (MS). *Program availability:* Part-time. *Degree requirements:* For master's, thesis. *Entrance requirements:* Additional exam requirements/recommendations for international students: Required—TOEFL (minimum score 550 paper-based; 80 iBT) or IELTS (minimum score 6.5). Electronic applications accepted. *Faculty research:* Geoscience education, tectonics, fluvial geomorphology, invertebrate paleontology, mine/hydrology.

Ohio University, Graduate College, Voinovich School of Leadership and Public Affairs, Program in Environmental Studies, Athens, OH 45701-2979. Offers MS. *Program availability:* Part-time. *Degree requirements:* For master's, comprehensive exam (for some programs), written exams or thesis, research project. *Entrance requirements:* For master's, minimum GPA of 3.0. Additional exam requirements/recommendations for international students: Required—TOEFL (minimum score 600 paper-based; 100 iBT) or IELTS (minimum score 7). Electronic applications accepted. *Faculty research:* Air quality modeling, conservation biology, environmental policy, geographical information systems, land management and watershed restoration.

Oregon State University, College of Liberal Arts, Program in Environmental Arts and Humanities, Corvallis, OR 97331. Offers environmental action (MA); environmental imagination (MA); environmental thinking (MA). *Degree requirements:* For master's, fieldwork, thesis/project. *Application deadline:* For fall admission, 3/1 for domestic and international students. Application fee: $75 ($85 for international students). *Expenses:* Tuition, state resident: full-time $12,150; part-time $450 per credit. Tuition, nonresident: full-time $20,952; part-time $776 per credit. *Required fees:* $1572; $1443 per unit. One-time fee: $350. Tuition and fees vary according to course load, campus/location and program. *Unit head:* Dr. Jacob Hamblin, Director, 541-737-3503, E-mail: jacob.hamblin@oregonstate.edu.

Oregon State University, College of Liberal Arts, Program in Public Policy, Corvallis, OR 97331. Offers energy policy (MPP, PhD); environmental policy (MPP, PhD); international policy (MPP, PhD); law, crime, and policy (MPP, PhD); rural policy (MPP, PhD); science and technology policy (MPP, PhD); social policy (MPP, PhD). *Program availability:* Part-time. *Faculty:* 32 full-time (13 women), 3 part-time/adjunct (1 woman). *Students:* 72 full-time (47 women), 1 part-time (0 women); includes 13 minority (2 Asian, non-Hispanic/Latino; 7 Hispanic/Latino; 1 Native Hawaiian or other Pacific Islander, non-Hispanic/Latino; 3 Two or more races, non-Hispanic/Latino), 25 international. Average age 29. 90 applicants, 47% accepted, 27 enrolled. In 2015, 34 master's awarded. *Entrance requirements:* For master's and doctorate, GRE. Additional exam requirements/recommendations for international students: Required—TOEFL, IELTS (minimum score 6.5). *Application deadline:* For fall admission, 8/1 for domestic students, 4/1 for international students; for winter admission, 12/1 for domestic students, 7/1 for international students; for spring admission, 2/1 for domestic students, 10/1 for international students; for summer admission, 5/1 for domestic students, 1/1 for international students. Application fee: $75 ($85 for international students). *Expenses:* Tuition, state resident: full-time $12,150; part-time $450 per credit. Tuition, nonresident: full-time $20,952; part-time $776 per credit. *Required fees:* $1572; $1443 per unit. One-time fee: $350. Tuition and fees vary according to course load, campus/location and program. *Financial support:* Application deadline: 1/15. *Unit head:* Dr. Denise Lach, Director. *Application contact:* Dr. Brent Steel, Professor and Director, Public Policy Graduate Program, 541-737-6133, E-mail: schoolofpublicpolicy@oregonstate.edu. Website: http://oregonstate.edu/cla/spp/

Pace University, Dyson College of Arts and Sciences, Department of Environmental Studies and Science, New York, NY 10038. Offers environmental science (MS). Offered at Pleasantville, NY location only. *Program availability:* Part-time, evening/weekend. *Students:* 7 full-time (5 women), 20 part-time (15 women); includes 7 minority (2 Black or African American, non-Hispanic/Latino; 3 Hispanic/Latino; 2 Two or more races, non-Hispanic/Latino), 3 international. Average age 28. 15 applicants, 73% accepted, 6 enrolled. In 2015, 6 master's awarded. *Degree requirements:* For master's, thesis, research project. *Entrance requirements:* For master's, GRE, two letters of recommendation, resume, personal statement, all official transcripts. Additional exam requirements/recommendations for international students: Required—TOEFL (minimum score 88 iBT), IELTS (minimum score 7) or PTE (minimum score 60). *Application deadline:* For fall admission, 8/1 priority date for domestic students, 6/1 for international students; for spring admission, 12/1 priority date for domestic students, 10/1 for international students. Applications are processed on a rolling basis. Application fee: $70. Electronic applications accepted. *Expenses: Tuition, area resident:* Part-time $1195 per credit. *Required fees:* $260 per semester. Tuition and fees vary according to degree level, campus/location and program. *Financial support:* Scholarships/grants and unspecified assistantships available. Financial award application deadline: 2/15; financial award applicants required to submit FAFSA. *Unit head:* Dr. E. Melanie DuPuis, Chair, Environmental Studies and Science program, 914-773-3522, E-mail: edupuis@pace.edu. *Application contact:* Susan Ford-Goldschein, Director of Graduate Admissions, 914-422-4283, Fax: 212-346-1585, E-mail: graduateadmission@pace.edu. Website: http://www.pace.edu/dyson/departments/environmental-studies-science

Penn State University Park, Graduate School, Intercollege Graduate Programs, Intercollege Program in Environmental Pollution Control, University Park, PA 16802. Offers environmental pollution control (MEPC, MS). *Unit head:* Dr. Regina Vasilatos-Younken, Dean, 814-865-2516, Fax: 814-863-4627. *Application contact:* Lori Stania, Director, Graduate Student Services, 814-865-1795, Fax: 814-863-4627, E-mail: l-gswww@lists.psu.edu.

Plymouth State University, College of Graduate Studies, Graduate Studies in Education, Program in Science, Plymouth, NH 03264-1595. Offers applied meteorology (MS); biology (MS); clinical mental health counseling (MS); environmental science and policy (MS); science education (MS).

Point Park University, School of Arts and Sciences, Department of Natural Science and Engineering Technology, Pittsburgh, PA 15222-1984. Offers engineering management (MS); environmental studies (MS). *Program availability:* Part-time, evening/weekend. *Degree requirements:* For master's, comprehensive exam (for some programs), thesis or alternative. *Entrance requirements:* For master's, minimum QPA of 2.75, 2 letters of recommendation, minimum B average in engineering technology or a related field, official undergraduate transcript, statement of intent, resume. Additional exam requirements/recommendations for international students: Required—TOEFL. Electronic applications accepted.

Polytechnic University of Puerto Rico, Graduate School, Hato Rey, PR 00919. Offers business administration (MBA), including computer information systems, general management, management of information systems, management of international enterprises; civil engineering (ME, MS); computer engineering (ME, MS); computer science (MCS, MS); electrical engineering (ME, MS); engineering management (MEM); environmental management (MEM); landscape architecture (M Land Arch); manufacturing competitiveness (MMC, MS); manufacturing engineering (ME, MS); mechanical engineering (M Mech E). *Program availability:* Part-time, evening/weekend. *Entrance requirements:* For master's, 3 letters of recommendation.

Polytechnic University of Puerto Rico, Miami Campus, Graduate School, Miami, FL 33166. Offers accounting (MBA); business administration (MBA); construction management (MEM); environmental management (MEM); finance (MBA); human resources management (MBA); logistics and supply chain management (MBA); management of international enterprises (MBA); manufacturing management (MEM); marketing management (MBA); project management (MBA). *Program availability:* Part-time, evening/weekend, online learning. *Entrance requirements:* For master's, minimum GPA of 3.0. Electronic applications accepted.

Polytechnic University of Puerto Rico, Orlando Campus, Graduate School, Orlando, FL 32825. Offers accounting (MBA); business administration (MBA); construction management (MEM); engineering management (MEM); environmental management (MEM); finance (MBA); human resources management (MBA); management of international enterprises (MBA); management of technology (MBA); manufacturing management (MEM). *Program availability:* Part-time, evening/weekend, online learning. *Entrance requirements:* For master's, minimum GPA of 3.0. Additional exam requirements/recommendations for international students: Recommended—TOEFL. Electronic applications accepted.

Portland State University, Graduate Studies, College of Liberal Arts and Sciences, Program in Environmental Sciences and Management, Portland, OR 97207-0751. Offers environmental management (MEM); environmental sciences/biology (PhD); environmental sciences/chemistry (PhD); environmental sciences/civil engineering (PhD); environmental sciences/geography (PhD); environmental sciences/geology (PhD); environmental sciences/physics (PhD); environmental studies (MS); science/environmental science (MST). *Program availability:* Part-time. *Faculty:* 24 full-time (11 women), 10 part-time/adjunct (4 women). *Students:* 52 full-time (32 women), 41 part-time (23 women); includes 11 minority (1 Black or African American, non-Hispanic/Latino; 1 American Indian or Alaska Native, non-Hispanic/Latino; 2 Asian, non-Hispanic/Latino; 2 Hispanic/Latino; 1 Native Hawaiian or other Pacific Islander, non-Hispanic/Latino; 4 Two or more races, non-Hispanic/Latino), 4 international. Average age 34. 93 applicants, 51% accepted, 29 enrolled. In 2015, 10 master's, 2 doctorates awarded. *Degree requirements:* For master's, thesis or alternative; for doctorate, variable foreign language requirement, comprehensive exam, thesis/dissertation, oral and qualifying exams. *Entrance requirements:* For master's, GRE General Test, 3 letters of recommendation; for doctorate, minimum GPA of 3.0 in upper-division course work or 2.75 overall. Additional exam requirements/recommendations for international students: Required—TOEFL (minimum score 550 paper-based; 80 iBT), IELTS (minimum score 6.5). *Application deadline:* For fall admission, 2/1 for domestic and international students. Applications are processed on a rolling basis. Application fee: $50. *Expenses:* $11,490 per year. *Financial support:* In 2015–16, 5 research assistantships with full tuition reimbursements (averaging $16,120 per year), 15 teaching assistantships with full tuition reimbursements (averaging $15,000 per year) were awarded; Federal Work-Study, scholarships/grants, tuition waivers (partial), and unspecified assistantships also available. Support available to part-time students. Financial award application deadline: 3/1; financial award applicants required to submit FAFSA. *Faculty research:* Environmental aspects of biology, chemistry, civil engineering, geology, physics. *Total annual research expenditures:* $2 million. *Unit head:* Dr. John Rueter, Chair, 503-725-8308, Fax: 503-725-3888, E-mail: rueterj@pdx.edu. *Application contact:* Dr. Robert Scheller, Chair, Graduate Admissions, 503-725-4982, Fax: 503-725-9040, E-mail: rmschell@pdx.edu.
Website: http://www.esr.pdx.edu/

Prescott College, Graduate Programs, Program in Environmental Studies, Prescott, AZ 86301. Offers environmental studies (MA); student-directed independent study (MA). *Program availability:* Part-time, online learning. *Degree requirements:* For master's, thesis, fieldwork or internship, practicum. *Entrance requirements:* For master's, 2 letters of recommendation, resume. Additional exam requirements/recommendations for international students: Required—TOEFL (minimum score 500 paper-based). Electronic applications accepted.

Purdue University, Graduate School, College of Agriculture, Department of Forestry and Natural Resources, West Lafayette, IN 47907. Offers fisheries and aquatic sciences (MS, MSF, PhD); forest biology (MS, MSF, PhD); natural resource social science (MS, PhD); natural resources social science (MSF); quantitative ecology (MS, MSF, PhD); wildlife science (MS, MSF, PhD); wood products and wood products manufacturing (MS, MSF, PhD). *Degree requirements:* For master's, thesis; for doctorate, thesis/dissertation. *Entrance requirements:* For master's and doctorate, GRE General Test (minimum score: verbal 50th percentile; quantitative 50th percentile; analytical writing 4.0), minimum undergraduate GPA of 3.2 or equivalent. Additional exam requirements/recommendations for international students: Required—TOEFL (minimum score 550 paper-based; 77 iBT). Electronic applications accepted. *Faculty research:* Wildlife management, forest management, forest ecology, forest soils, limnology.

Rice University, Graduate Programs, Wiess School–Professional Science Master's Programs, Professional Master's Program in Environmental Analysis and Decision Making, Houston, TX 77251-1892. Offers MS. *Program availability:* Part-time. *Degree requirements:* For master's, internship. *Entrance requirements:* For master's, GRE General Test, letters of recommendation (4). Additional exam requirements/recommendations for international students: Required—TOEFL (minimum score 600 paper-based; 90 iBT). Electronic applications accepted. *Faculty research:* Environmental biotechnology, environmental nanochemistry, environmental statistics, remote sensing.

Royal Roads University, Graduate Studies, Environment and Sustainability Program, Victoria, BC V9B 5Y2, Canada. Offers environment and management (M Sc, MA); environmental education and communication (MA, G Dip, Graduate Certificate); MA/MS. *Program availability:* Online learning. *Degree requirements:* For master's, thesis. *Entrance requirements:* For master's, 5-7 years of related work experience. Electronic applications accepted. *Faculty research:* Sustainable development, atmospheric processes, sustainable communities, chemical fate and transport of persistent organic pollutants, educational technology.

Sacred Heart University, Graduate Programs, College of Arts and Sciences, Department of Biology, Fairfield, CT 06825. Offers environmental systems analysis and management (MS). *Program availability:* Part-time, evening/weekend. *Faculty:* 4 full-time (all women). *Students:* 7 full-time (4 women), 1 part-time (0 women); includes 1 minority (Hispanic/Latino). Average age 29. 6 applicants, 67% accepted, 2 enrolled. In 2015, 8 master's awarded. *Degree requirements:* For master's, comprehensive exam (for some programs), thesis (for some programs). *Entrance requirements:* For master's, minimum GPA of 3.0; one year of each major level general biology and general chemistry; one semester each of organic chemistry, pre-calculus, and elementary statistics; bachelor's degree in a natural science. Additional exam requirements/recommendations for international students: Required—PTE; Recommended—TOEFL (minimum score 570 paper-based; 80 iBT), IELTS (minimum score 6.5). *Application deadline:* Applications are processed on a rolling basis. Application fee: $75. Electronic applications accepted. *Expenses: Tuition, area resident:* Part-time $654 per credit hour. *Financial support:* Unspecified assistantships available. Financial award applicants required to submit FAFSA. *Unit head:* Dr. Mark Jareb, Chair/Associate Professor, 203-365-7782, E-mail: jarebb@sacredheart.edu. *Application contact:* William Sweeney, Director of Graduate Admissions Operations, 203-365-7619, Fax: 203-365-4732, E-mail: gradstudies@sacredheart.edu.
Website: http://www.sacredheart.edu/academics/collegeofartssciences/academicdepartments/biology/pre-graduateschooladvisement/biologicaldegreesoffered/

St. Cloud State University, School of Graduate Studies, College of Science and Engineering, Department of Environmental and Technological Studies, St. Cloud, MN 56301-4498. Offers MS. *Degree requirements:* For master's, thesis or alternative. *Entrance requirements:* For master's, minimum GPA of 2.75. Additional exam requirements/recommendations for international students: Required—TOEFL (minimum score 550 paper-based), Michigan English Language Assessment Battery; Recommended—IELTS (minimum score 6.5). Electronic applications accepted.

St. Edward's University, School of Behavioral and Social Sciences, Austin, TX 78704. Offers environmental management and sustainability (PSM). *Students:* 38 full-time (28 women); includes 8 minority (1 Asian, non-Hispanic/Latino; 7 Hispanic/Latino), 1 international. Average age 26. 67 applicants, 58% accepted, 21 enrolled. In 2015, 15 master's awarded. *Degree requirements:* For master's, 36 hours of coursework with minimum cumulative GPA of 3.0. *Entrance requirements:* For master's, GRE or GMAT, 2 letters of recommendation, resume or curriculum vitae, essay, minimum GPA of 3.0 in last 60 hours of course work. Additional exam requirements/recommendations for international students: Required—TOEFL (minimum score 79 iBT) or IELTS (minimum score 6). *Application deadline:* For fall admission, 2/15 priority date for domestic and international students. Applications are processed on a rolling basis. Application fee: $50. Electronic applications accepted. *Expenses:* $27,741 per year (summer not included); $100 technology fee per year. *Unit head:* Dr. Peter Beck, Program Director, 512-428-1249, Fax: 512-233-1664, E-mail: peterab@stedwards.edu. *Application contact:* Jane Hamann, Graduate Admission Counselor, 512-326-7333, Fax: 512-464-8877, E-mail: jhamann1@stedwards.edu.
Website: http://www.stedwards.edu

Samford University, Howard College of Arts and Sciences, Birmingham, AL 35229. Offers energy management and policy (MSEM); JD/MSEM. *Program availability:* Part-time, evening/weekend. *Faculty:* 8 full-time (2 women), 4 part-time/adjunct (0 women). *Students:* 21 full-time (7 women), 2 part-time; includes 4 minority (all Black or African American, non-Hispanic/Latino), 14 international. Average age 25. 20 applicants, 80% accepted, 8 enrolled. In 2015, 33 master's awarded. *Entrance requirements:* For master's, GRE General Test (minimum score 295 combined) or MAT (minimum score 396), minimum GPA of 2.5 with 3 years of work experience or 3.0 for a recent college graduate. Additional exam requirements/recommendations for international students: Required—TOEFL (minimum score 90 iBT); Recommended—IELTS (minimum score 6.5). *Application deadline:* For fall admission, 8/1 for domestic and international students; for winter admission, 12/1 for domestic and international students; for spring admission, 12/1 for domestic and international students; for summer admission, 5/1 for domestic and international students. Applications are processed on a rolling basis. Application fee: $35. *Expenses: Tuition, area resident:* Full-time $18,673; part-time $766 per credit hour. *Required fees:* $550. Tuition and fees vary according to course load, degree level and student level. *Financial support:* In 2015–16, 1 student received support. Application deadline: 3/1; applicants required to submit FAFSA. *Faculty research:* Mosquito fish as an environmental model for pollutants, PCB contamination, environmental epidemiology and toxicology, geographic information systems, geology and natural resource management, energy management, chemical and biological analysis of water, aquatic biomonitoring. *Application contact:* Dr. Ronald N. Hunsinger, Professor/Chair, Biological and Environmental Sciences, 205-726-2944, Fax: 205-726-2479, E-mail: rnhunsin@samford.edu.
Website: http://howard.samford.edu/

San Francisco State University, Division of Graduate Studies, College of Health and Social Sciences, Public Administration Program, San Francisco, CA 94132-1722. Offers criminal justice administration (MPA); environmental administration and policy (MPA); nonprofit administration (MPA); public management (MPA); public policy (MPA); urban administration (MPA). *Accreditation:* NASPAA. *Expenses:* Tuition, state resident: full-time $6738. Tuition, nonresident: full-time $15,666. *Required fees:* $1004 per year. *Unit head:* Dr. Elizabeth Brown, Director of the School of Public Affairs and Civic Engagement, 415-817-4455, Fax: 415-817-4464, E-mail: mpa@sfsu.edu. *Application contact:* Dr. Sheldon Gen, Graduate Coordinator, 415-817-4458, Fax: 415-817-4464, E-mail: sgen@sfsu.edu.
Website: http://mpa.sfsu.edu/

San Francisco State University, Division of Graduate Studies, College of Science and Engineering, Department of Geography and Environment, San Francisco, CA 94132-1722. Offers geographic information science (MS); geography and environment (MA); resource management and environmental planning (MA). *Expenses:* Tuition, state resident: full-time $6738. Tuition, nonresident: full-time $15,666. *Required fees:* $1004 per year. *Unit head:* Dr. Jerry Davis, Chair, 415-338-2983, Fax: 415-338-6243, E-mail: jerry@sfsu.edu. *Application contact:* Dr. Nancy Wilkinson, Graduate Coordinator, 415-338-1439, Fax: 415-338-6243, E-mail: nancyw@sfsu.edu.
Website: http://geog.sfsu.edu/

San Jose State University, Graduate Studies and Research, College of Social Sciences, San Jose, CA 95192-0001. Offers applications of technology in planning (Certificate); applied anthropology (MA); communication studies (MS); community design and development (Certificate); economics (MA), including applied economics, social sciences; environmental planning (Certificate); geographic information science (Certificate); geography (MA); global citizenship (Certificate); history (MA), including history education, social sciences; Mexican American studies (MA); psychology (MA, MS), including clinical psychology (MS), industrial/organizational psychology (MS), research and experimental psychology (MA); public administration (MA); real estate development (Certificate); social sciences (MPA, MS); sociology (MA); transportation and land use planning (Certificate). *Program availability:* Part-time, evening/weekend. *Students:* 108 full-time (74 women), 51 part-time (28 women); includes 188 minority (16 Black or African American, non-Hispanic/Latino; 1 American Indian or Alaska Native, non-Hispanic/Latino; 56 Asian, non-Hispanic/Latino; 112 Hispanic/Latino; 3 Native Hawaiian or other Pacific Islander, non-Hispanic/Latino), 60 international. Average age 29. 517 applicants, 54% accepted, 158 enrolled. In 2015, 144 master's awarded. *Entrance requirements:* For master's, minimum GPA of 3.0. *Application deadline:* For fall admission, 6/29 for domestic students; for spring admission, 11/30 for domestic students. Applications are processed on a rolling basis. Application fee: $55. Electronic applications accepted. *Financial support:* Teaching assistantships, career-related internships or fieldwork, Federal Work-Study, institutionally sponsored loans, scholarships/grants, and tuition waivers (partial) available. Support available to part-time students. Financial award applicants required to submit FAFSA. *Unit head:* Walt Jacobs, Dean, 408-924-5306, Fax: 408-924-5303. *Application contact:* 408-924-2480, Fax: 408-924-2477.
Website: http://www.sjsu.edu/socialsciences/

Shippensburg University of Pennsylvania, School of Graduate Studies, College of Arts and Sciences, Department of Geography and Earth Science, Shippensburg, PA 17257-2299. Offers geoenvironmental studies (MS). *Program availability:* Part-time, evening/weekend. *Faculty:* 10 full-time (2 women), 1 part-time/adjunct (0 women). *Students:* 17 full-time (10 women), 11 part-time (7 women); includes 2 minority (1 Black or African American, non-Hispanic/Latino; 1 Hispanic/Latino). Average age 29. 28 applicants, 71% accepted, 8 enrolled. In 2015, 14 master's awarded. *Degree requirements:* For master's, comprehensive exam, thesis (6 credits) or 1 semester research project (3 credits) and internship (6 credits); practicum exam. *Entrance requirements:* For master's, GRE (if GPA less than 2.75), 12 credit hours in geography or earth sciences, a combined total of 18 credit hours in the two fields, or 15 credit hours in social sciences including 6 credit hours in geography plus 15 credit hours in the natural sciences including 6 credit hours in the earth sciences. Additional exam requirements/recommendations for international students: Required—TOEFL (minimum score 580 paper-based; 70 iBT); Recommended—IELTS (minimum score 6). *Application deadline:* For fall admission, 3/30 for international students; for spring admission, 9/30 for international students. Applications are processed on a rolling basis. Application fee: $45. Electronic applications accepted. *Expenses:* Tuition, state resident: part-time $470 per credit. Tuition, nonresident: part-time $705 per credit. *Required fees:* $137 per credit. *Financial support:* In 2015–16, 8 students received support. Research assistantships, career-related internships or fieldwork, scholarships/grants, unspecified assistantships, and resident hall director and student payroll positions available. Support available to part-time students. Financial award application deadline: 3/1; financial award applicants required to submit FAFSA. *Unit head:* Dr. Tim W. Hawkins, Professor and Program Coordinator, 717-477-1685, Fax: 717-477-4029, E-mail: twhawk@ship.edu. *Application contact:* Jeremy R. Goshorn, Assistant Dean of Graduate Admissions, 717-477-1231, Fax: 717-477-4016, E-mail: jrgoshorn@ship.edu.
Website: http://www.ship.edu/geo-ess/

Shippensburg University of Pennsylvania, School of Graduate Studies, College of Arts and Sciences, Department of Sociology and Anthropology, Shippensburg, PA 17257-2299. Offers organizational development and leadership (MS), including business, communications, environmental management, higher education structure and policy, historical administration, individual and organizational development, management information systems, public organizations, social structures and organizations. *Program availability:* Part-time, evening/weekend. *Faculty:* 3 full-time (all women). *Students:* 12 full-time (6 women), 31 part-time (16 women); includes 15 minority (10 Black or African American, non-Hispanic/Latino; 1 Asian, non-Hispanic/Latino; 1 Hispanic/Latino; 3 Two or more races, non-Hispanic/Latino). Average age 30. 42 applicants, 64% accepted, 15 enrolled. In 2015, 30 master's awarded. *Degree requirements:* For master's, capstone experience including internship. *Entrance requirements:* For master's, interview (if GPA less than 2.75), resume, personal goals statement. Additional exam requirements/recommendations for international students: Required—TOEFL (minimum score 580 paper-based; 70 iBT); Recommended—IELTS (minimum score 6). *Application deadline:* For fall admission, 4/30 for international students; for spring admission, 9/30 for international students. Applications are processed on a rolling basis. Application fee: $45. Electronic applications accepted. *Expenses:* Tuition, state resident: part-time $470 per credit. Tuition, nonresident: part-time $705 per credit. *Required fees:* $137 per credit. *Financial support:* In 2015–16, 9 students received support. Research assistantships, career-related internships or fieldwork, scholarships/grants, unspecified assistantships, and resident hall director and student payroll positions available. Support available to part-time students. Financial award application deadline: 3/1; financial award applicants required to submit FAFSA. *Unit head:* Dr. Barbara J. Denison, Departmental Chair and Program Coordinator, 717-477-1735, Fax: 717-477-4011, E-mail: bjdeni@ship.edu. *Application contact:* Jeremy R. Goshorn, Assistant Dean of Graduate Admissions, 717-477-1231, Fax: 717-477-4016, E-mail: jrgoshorn@ship.edu.
Website: http://www.ship.edu/odl/

Simon Fraser University, Office of Graduate Studies, Faculty of Environment, School of Resource and Environmental Management, Burnaby, BC V5A 1S6, Canada. Offers quantitative methods in fisheries management (Graduate Diploma); resource and environmental management (MRM, PhD); resource and environmental planning (MRM). *Degree requirements:* For master's, thesis (for some programs); for doctorate, comprehensive exam, thesis/dissertation. *Entrance requirements:* For master's and Graduate Diploma, minimum GPA of 3.0 (on scale of 4.33), or 3.33 based on last 60 credits of undergraduate courses; for doctorate, minimum GPA of 3.5 (on scale of 4.33). Additional exam requirements/recommendations for international students: Recommended—TOEFL (minimum score 580 paper-based; 93 iBT), IELTS (minimum score 7), TWE (minimum score 5). Electronic applications accepted. *Faculty research:* Climate, coastal marine ecology and conservation, environmental toxicology, fisheries science and management, forest ecology.

Slippery Rock University of Pennsylvania, Graduate Studies (Recruitment), College of Health, Environment, and Science, Department of Parks and Recreation, Slippery Rock, PA 16057-1383. Offers environmental education (M Ed); park and resource management (MS). *Program availability:* Part-time, evening/weekend, online only, 100% online. *Faculty:* 3 full-time (2 women). *Students:* 7 full-time (2 women), 108 part-time (69 women); includes 9 minority (5 Black or African American, non-Hispanic/Latino; 1 American Indian or Alaska Native, non-Hispanic/Latino; 1 Asian, non-Hispanic/Latino; 2 Two or more races, non-Hispanic/Latino), 1 international. Average age 31. 66 applicants, 76% accepted, 35 enrolled. In 2015, 48 master's awarded. *Degree requirements:* For master's, comprehensive exam (for some programs), thesis (for some programs), internship. *Entrance requirements:* For master's, official transcripts, minimum GPA of 2.75, personal statement. Additional exam requirements/recommendations for international students: Required—TOEFL (minimum score 550 paper-based; 80 iBT). *Application deadline:* For fall admission, 3/1 priority date for domestic students, 5/1 priority date for international students; for spring admission, 10/1 priority date for domestic students, 9/1 priority date for international students. Applications are processed on a rolling basis. Application fee: $25 ($30 for international

students). Electronic applications accepted. *Expenses:* $629.87 per credit in-state; $912.12 per credit out-of-state. *Financial support:* In 2015–16, 6 students received support. Career-related internships or fieldwork, Federal Work-Study, institutionally sponsored loans, scholarships/grants, tuition waivers (partial), and unspecified assistantships available. Support available to part-time students. Financial award application deadline: 5/1; financial award applicants required to submit FAFSA. *Unit head:* Dr. John Lisco, Graduate Coordinator, 724-738-2596, Fax: 724-738-2938, E-mail: john.lisco@sru.edu. *Application contact:* Brandi Weber-Mortimer, Director of Graduate Admissions, 724-738-2051, Fax: 724-738-2146, E-mail: graduate.admissions@sru.edu.
Website: http://www.sru.edu/academics/colleges-and-departments/ches/departments/parks-and-recreation

Southeast Missouri State University, School of Graduate Studies, Department of Human Environmental Studies, Cape Girardeau, MO 63701-4799. Offers MA. *Program availability:* Part-time, evening/weekend. *Faculty:* 11 full-time (8 women). *Students:* 9 full-time (all women), 19 part-time (all women); includes 3 minority (all Black or African American, non-Hispanic/Latino), 1 international. Average age 31. 11 applicants, 73% accepted, 7 enrolled. In 2015, 4 master's awarded. *Degree requirements:* For master's, comprehensive exam (for some programs), thesis (for some programs), thesis defense. *Entrance requirements:* For master's, minimum undergraduate GPA of 2.75; 15 hours of course work in specialization. Additional exam requirements/recommendations for international students: Required—TOEFL (minimum score 550 paper-based; 79 iBT), IELTS (minimum score 6), PTE (minimum score 53). *Application deadline:* For fall admission, 8/1 for domestic students, 6/1 for international students; for spring admission, 11/21 for domestic students, 10/1 for international students; for summer admission, 5/15 for domestic students. Applications are processed on a rolling basis. Application fee: $30 ($40 for international students). Electronic applications accepted. *Expenses:* Tuition, state resident: part-time $260.80 per credit hour. Tuition, nonresident: part-time $486.80 per credit hour. *Required fees:* $33.70 per credit hour. *Financial support:* In 2015–16, 8 students received support, including 1 teaching assistantship with full tuition reimbursement available (averaging $8,467 per year); career-related internships or fieldwork, Federal Work-Study, scholarships/grants, traineeships, tuition waivers (full), and unspecified assistantships also available. Financial award application deadline: 6/30; financial award applicants required to submit FAFSA. *Faculty research:* Veteran families and relationships, suicide and domestic violence, child abuse and neglect, school system environmental design, obesity and college students. *Unit head:* Dr. Shelba Y. Branscum, Professor/Chair, Human Environmental Studies, 573-651-2729, Fax: 573-651-2949, E-mail: sybranscum@semo.edu.
Website: http://www.semo.edu/hes/

Southeast Missouri State University, School of Graduate Studies, Harrison College of Business, Cape Girardeau, MO 63701-4799. Offers accounting (MBA); entrepreneurship (MBA); environmental management (MBA); financial management (MBA); general management (MBA); health administration (MBA); industrial management (MBA); international business (MBA); organizational management (MS); sport management (MBA). *Accreditation:* AACSB. *Program availability:* Part-time, evening/weekend, online learning. *Faculty:* 27 full-time (7 women), 1 (woman) part-time/adjunct. *Students:* 68 full-time (40 women), 132 part-time (46 women); includes 21 minority (9 Black or African American, non-Hispanic/Latino; 9 Asian, non-Hispanic/Latino; 2 Hispanic/Latino; 1 Two or more races, non-Hispanic/Latino), 60 international. Average age 30. In 2015, 57 master's awarded. *Degree requirements:* For master's, variable foreign language requirement, comprehensive exam (for some programs), thesis or alternative, applied research project, 33 credit hours. *Entrance requirements:* For master's, GMAT or GRE, minimum undergraduate GPA of 2.5, minimum grade of C in prerequisite courses. Additional exam requirements/recommendations for international students: Required—TOEFL (minimum score 550 paper-based; 79 iBT), IELTS (minimum score 6), PTE (minimum score 53). *Application deadline:* For fall admission, 8/1 for domestic students, 6/1 for international students; for spring admission, 11/21 for domestic students, 10/1 for international students; for summer admission, 5/15 for domestic students. Applications are processed on a rolling basis. Application fee: $30 ($40 for international students). Electronic applications accepted. *Expenses:* Tuition, state resident: part-time $260.80 per credit hour. Tuition, nonresident: part-time $486.80 per credit hour. *Required fees:* $33.70 per credit hour. *Financial support:* In 2015–16, 60 students received support. Career-related internships or fieldwork, Federal Work-Study, scholarships/grants, traineeships, tuition waivers (full), and unspecified assistantships available. Financial award application deadline: 6/30; financial award applicants required to submit FAFSA. *Faculty research:* Organizational justice, ethics, leadership, corporate finance, generational differences. *Unit head:* Dr. Kenneth A. Heischmidt, Director, Graduate Business Studies, 573-651-2912, Fax: 573-651-5032, E-mail: kheischmidt@semo.edu. *Application contact:* Gail Amick, Admissions Specialist, 573-651-2590, Fax: 573-651-5936, E-mail: gamick@semo.edu.
Website: http://www.semo.edu/mba

Southern Illinois University Carbondale, Graduate School, College of Liberal Arts, Department of Geography, Carbondale, IL 62901-4701. Offers MS, PhD. *Faculty:* 7 full-time (1 woman), 1 part-time/adjunct (0 women). *Students:* 12 full-time (8 women), 8 part-time (6 women); includes 1 minority (Hispanic/Latino), 9 international. Average age 27. 19 applicants, 42% accepted, 3 enrolled. In 2015, 13 master's awarded. *Degree requirements:* For master's, thesis; for doctorate, thesis/dissertation. *Entrance requirements:* For master's, GRE (recommended), minimum GPA of 2.7; for doctorate, minimum GPA of 3.25. Additional exam requirements/recommendations for international students: Required—TOEFL. *Application deadline:* For fall admission, 2/1 for domestic students; for spring admission, 11/1 for domestic students. Applications are processed on a rolling basis. Application fee: $65. *Financial support:* In 2015–16, 14 students received support, including 5 research assistantships with full tuition reimbursements available, 8 teaching assistantships with full tuition reimbursements available; fellowships with full tuition reimbursements available, career-related internships or fieldwork, Federal Work-Study, institutionally sponsored loans, and tuition waivers (full) also available. Support available to part-time students. Financial award application deadline: 4/1. *Faculty research:* Natural resources management emphasizing water resources and environmental quality of air, water, and land systems. *Unit head:* Dr. Justin Schoof, Chair, 618-453-6019, E-mail: jschoof@siu.edu. *Application contact:* Jennie Absher, Administrative Clerk, 618-536-3375, E-mail: jabsher@siu.edu.
Website: http://cola.siu.edu/geography/graduate/index.php

Southern Illinois University Edwardsville, Graduate School, College of Arts and Sciences, Program in Environmental Science Management, Edwardsville, IL 62026-0001. Offers PSM. *Program availability:* Part-time, evening/weekend. *Students:* 2 part-time (0 women). 5 applicants, 20% accepted, 1 enrolled. *Degree requirements:* For master's, thesis, internship. *Entrance requirements:* For master's, GRE. Additional exam requirements/recommendations for international students: Required—TOEFL (minimum score 550 paper-based; 79 iBT), IELTS (minimum score 6.5). *Application deadline:* For fall admission, 7/22 for domestic students, 7/15 for international students; for spring admission, 12/9 for domestic students, 11/15 for international students; for summer admission, 4/29 for domestic students, 4/15 for international students. Applications are processed on a rolling basis. Application fee: $30. Electronic applications accepted. *Expenses:* Tuition, state resident: full-time $5026; part-time $837 per course. Tuition, nonresident: full-time $12,566; part-time $2094 per course. *Required fees:* $1682; $474 per course. Tuition and fees vary according to course load, campus/location and program. *Financial support:* Fellowships with full tuition reimbursements, research assistantships with full tuition reimbursements, teaching assistantships with full tuition reimbursements, institutionally sponsored loans, scholarships/grants, and unspecified assistantships available. Financial award application deadline: 3/1; financial award applicants required to submit FAFSA. *Unit head:* Dr. Zhiqing Lin, Program Director, 618-650-2650, E-mail: zhlin@siue.edu. *Application contact:* Melissa K. Mace, Coordinator of International and Graduate Recruitment, 618-650-3705, Fax: 618-650-3618, E-mail: graduatestudents@siue.edu.
Website: http://www.siue.edu/artsandsciences/environment/psm.shtml

Southern New Hampshire University, School of Business, Manchester, NH 03106-1045. Offers accounting (MBA, MS, Graduate Certificate); accounting finance (MS); accounting/auditing (MS); accounting/forensic accounting (MS); accounting/taxation (MS); athletic administration (MBA, Graduate Certificate); business administration (IMBA, MBA, Certificate, Graduate Certificate), including accounting (Certificate), business administration (MBA), business information systems (Graduate Certificate), human resource management (Certificate); corporate social responsibility (MBA); entrepreneurship (MBA); finance (MBA, MS, Graduate Certificate); finance/corporate finance (MS); finance/investments and securities (MS); forensic accounting (MBA); healthcare informatics (MBA); healthcare management (MBA); human resource management (Graduate Certificate); information technology (MS, Graduate Certificate); information technology management (MBA); international business (Graduate Certificate); international business and information technology (Graduate Certificate); international finance (Graduate Certificate); international sport management (Graduate Certificate); justice studies (MBA); leadership of nonprofit organizations (Graduate Certificate); marketing (MBA, MS, Graduate Certificate); operations and project management (MS); operations and supply chain management (MBA, Graduate Certificate); organizational leadership (MS); project management (MBA, Graduate Certificate); Six Sigma (MBA); Six Sigma quality (Graduate Certificate); social media marketing (MBA); sport management (MBA, MS, Graduate Certificate); sustainability and environmental compliance (MBA); workplace conflict management (MBA); MBA/Certificate. *Accreditation:* ACBSP. *Program availability:* Part-time, evening/weekend, online learning. Terminal master's awarded for partial completion of doctoral program. *Degree requirements:* For master's, one foreign language, comprehensive exam (for some programs), thesis or alternative. *Entrance requirements:* For master's, minimum GPA of 2.5. Additional exam requirements/recommendations for international students: Required—TOEFL (minimum score 500 paper-based). Electronic applications accepted.

State University of New York College of Environmental Science and Forestry, Department of Environmental Resources Engineering, Syracuse, NY 13210-2779. Offers ecological engineering (MPS, MS, PhD); environmental management (MPS); environmental resources engineering (MPS, MS, PhD); geospatial information science and engineering (MPS, MS, PhD); water resources engineering (MPS, MS, PhD). *Program availability:* Part-time. *Faculty:* 8 full-time (1 woman), 9 part-time/adjunct (3 women). *Students:* 28 full-time (12 women), 10 part-time (6 women); includes 4 minority (1 Black or African American, non-Hispanic/Latino; 2 Asian, non-Hispanic/Latino; 1 Hispanic/Latino), 17 international. Average age 25. 40 applicants, 60% accepted, 5 enrolled. In 2015, 15 master's, 5 doctorates awarded. *Degree requirements:* For master's, thesis (for some programs); for doctorate, comprehensive exam, thesis/dissertation. *Entrance requirements:* For master's and doctorate, GRE General Test, minimum GPA of 3.0. Additional exam requirements/recommendations for international students: Required—TOEFL (minimum score 550 paper-based; 80 iBT), IELTS (minimum score 6). *Application deadline:* For fall admission, 1/15 priority date for domestic and international students; for spring admission, 11/1 priority date for domestic and international students. Applications are processed on a rolling basis. Application fee: $60. *Expenses:* Tuition, state resident: full-time $10,870; part-time $453 per credit. Tuition, nonresident: full-time $22,210; part-time $925 per credit. *Required fees:* $1075; $89.22 per credit. *Financial support:* In 2015–16, 22 students received support, including 8 research assistantships with tuition reimbursements available (averaging $14,000 per year), 14 teaching assistantships with tuition reimbursements available; fellowships with tuition reimbursements available, Federal Work-Study, institutionally sponsored loans, scholarships/grants, health care benefits, and unspecified assistantships also available. Financial award application deadline: 6/30; financial award applicants required to submit FAFSA. *Faculty research:* Ecological engineering, environmental resources engineering, geospatial information science and engineering, water resources engineering, environmental science. *Total annual research expenditures:* $969,347. *Unit head:* Dr. Theodore Endreny, Chair, 315-470-6565, Fax: 315-470-6958, E-mail: te@esf.edu. *Application contact:* Scott Shannon, Dean of the Graduate School, 315-470-6599, Fax: 315-470-6978, E-mail: esfgrad@esf.edu.
Website: http://www.esf.edu/ere

State University of New York College of Environmental Science and Forestry, Department of Environmental Studies, Syracuse, NY 13210-2779. Offers MPS, MS. *Faculty:* 10 full-time (7 women), 7 part-time/adjunct (5 women). *Students:* 16 full-time (11 women), 2 part-time (both women), 3 international. 9 applicants, 89% accepted, 2 enrolled. *Degree requirements:* For master's, thesis (for some programs). *Entrance requirements:* For master's, GRE General Test. Application fee: $60. *Expenses:* Tuition, state resident: full-time $10,870; part-time $453 per credit. Tuition, nonresident: full-time $22,210; part-time $925 per credit. *Required fees:* $1075; $89.22 per credit. *Unit head:* Bennette Whitmore, Chair, 315-470-6636, E-mail: bwhitmor@esf.edu. *Application contact:* Scott Shannon, Associate Provost for Instruction/Dean of the Graduate School, 315-470-6599, Fax: 315-470-6978, E-mail: sshannon@esf.edu.
Website: http://www.esf.edu/es/

State University of New York College of Environmental Science and Forestry, Program in Environmental Science, Syracuse, NY 13210-2779. Offers biophysical and ecological economics (MPS); coupled natural and human systems (MPS); ecosystem restoration (MPS); environmental and community land planning (MPS, MS); environmental and natural resources policy (PhD); environmental communication and participatory processes (PhD); environmental monitoring and modeling (MPS); environmental policy and democratic processes (MPS, MS); water and wetland resource studies (MPS, MS). *Program availability:* Part-time. *Faculty:* 1 full-time (0 women), 1 (woman) part-time/adjunct. *Students:* 56 full-time (33 women), 17 part-time (10 women); includes 6 minority (2 Asian, non-Hispanic/Latino; 3 Hispanic/Latino; 1 Two or more races, non-Hispanic/Latino), 34 international. 85 applicants, 44% accepted, 13 enrolled. *Degree requirements:* For master's, thesis (for some programs); for doctorate, comprehensive exam, thesis/dissertation. *Entrance requirements:* For master's and doctorate, GRE General Test, minimum GPA of 3.0. Additional exam requirements/recommendations for international students: Required—TOEFL (minimum score 550 paper-based; 80 iBT), IELTS (minimum score 6). *Application deadline:* For fall admission, 2/1 priority date for domestic and international students; for spring

admission, 11/1 priority date for domestic and international students. Applications are processed on a rolling basis. Application fee: $60. *Expenses:* Tuition, state resident: full-time $10,870; part-time $453 per credit. Tuition, nonresident: full-time $22,210; part-time $925 per credit. *Required fees:* $1075; $89.22 per credit. *Financial support:* Fellowships with tuition reimbursements, research assistantships with tuition reimbursements, teaching assistantships with tuition reimbursements, career-related internships or fieldwork, Federal Work-Study, institutionally sponsored loans, scholarships/grants, health care benefits, and unspecified assistantships available. Support available to part-time students. Financial award application deadline: 6/30; financial award applicants required to submit FAFSA. *Faculty research:* Environmental education/communications, water resources, land resources, waste management. *Unit head:* Dr. Ruth Yanai, Coordinator, 315-470-6955, Fax: 315-470-6700, E-mail: rdyanai@esf.edu. *Application contact:* Dr. Dudley J. Raynal, Dean, Instruction and Graduate Studies, 315-470-6599, Fax: 315-470-6978, E-mail: esfgrad@esf.edu.
Website: http://www.esf.edu/environmentalscience/graduate/

Stony Brook University, State University of New York, Graduate School, College of Engineering and Applied Sciences, Department of Technology and Society, Program in Energy and Environmental Systems, Stony Brook, NY 11794. Offers MS, Advanced Certificate. *Program availability:* Part-time. *Degree requirements:* For master's, thesis, project. *Entrance requirements:* For master's, GRE. Additional exam requirements/recommendations for international students: Required—TOEFL (minimum score 85 iBT), IELTS (minimum score 6.5). *Application deadline:* For fall admission, 8/2 for domestic students, 4/15 for international students; for spring admission, 12/1 for domestic students, 10/5 for international students. Electronic applications accepted. *Expenses:* $12,421 full-time resident tuition and fees, $453 per credit hour; $23,761 full-time nonresident tuition and fees, $925 per credit hour. *Financial support:* Research assistantships, teaching assistantships, and career-related internships or fieldwork available. *Unit head:* Dr. David Ferguson, Chair, 631-632-8770, E-mail: david.ferguson@stonybrook.edu. *Application contact:* Marypat Taveras, Coordinator, 631-632-8770, Fax: 631-632-7809, E-mail: marypat.taveras@stonybrook.edu.
Website: http://www.stonybrook.edu/est/graduate/msenergyenv.shtml

Stony Brook University, State University of New York, School of Professional Development, Stony Brook, NY 11794. Offers biology (MAT); chemistry (MAT); coaching (Graduate Certificate); earth science (MAT); educational computing (Graduate Certificate); educational leadership (Advanced Certificate); English (MAT); environmental management (MPS, Graduate Certificate); French (MAT); German (MAT); higher education administration (MA, Certificate); human resource management (MS, Graduate Certificate); industrial management (Graduate Certificate); information systems management (Graduate Certificate); Italian (MAT); liberal studies (MA); mathematics (MAT); operations research (Graduate Certificate); physics (MAT); school district business leadership (Advanced Certificate); social studies (MAT); Spanish (MAT). *Program availability:* Part-time, evening/weekend, online learning. *Faculty:* 88 part-time/adjunct (36 women). *Students:* 181 full-time (115 women), 905 part-time (621 women); includes 191 minority (62 Black or African American, non-Hispanic/Latino; 28 Asian, non-Hispanic/Latino; 95 Hispanic/Latino; 6 Two or more races, non-Hispanic/Latino), 6 international. Average age 33. 286 applicants, 87% accepted, 155 enrolled. In 2015, 319 master's, 246 other advanced degrees awarded. *Degree requirements:* For master's, one foreign language, thesis or alternative. *Entrance requirements:* Additional exam requirements/recommendations for international students: Required—TOEFL (minimum score 85 iBT). *Application deadline:* For fall admission, 1/15 for domestic students; for spring admission, 10/1 for domestic students. Applications are processed on a rolling basis. Application fee: $100. *Expenses:* $12,421 full-time resident tuition and fees, $453 per credit hour; $23,761 full-time nonresident tuition and fees, $925 per credit hour. *Financial support:* Fellowships, research assistantships, teaching assistantships, and career-related internships or fieldwork available. Support available to part-time students. *Unit head:* Dr. Ken Lindblom, Interim Dean, 631-632-7993, Fax: 631-632-9046, E-mail: kenneth.lindblom@stonybrook.edu. *Application contact:* Melissa Jordan, Assistant Dean, 631-632-7751, E-mail: melissa.jordan@stonybrook.edu.
Website: http://www.stonybrook.edu/spd/

Tennessee Technological University, College of Graduate Studies, School of Environmental Studies, Professional Science Master's Program, Cookeville, TN 38505. Offers PSM. *Program availability:* Part-time. *Students:* 4 full-time (1 woman), 5 part-time (0 women). 5 applicants, 80% accepted, 3 enrolled. *Degree requirements:* For master's, comprehensive exam, thesis or alternative, internship. *Entrance requirements:* For master's, GRE General Test. Additional exam requirements/recommendations for international students: Required—TOEFL (minimum score 527 paper-based; 71 iBT), IELTS (minimum score 5.5), PTE (minimum score 48), or TOEIC (Test of English as an International Communication). *Application deadline:* For fall admission, 8/1 for domestic students, 5/1 for international students; for spring admission, 2/1 for domestic students, 10/1 for international students; for summer admission, 5/1 for domestic students, 2/1 for international students. Applications are processed on a rolling basis. Application fee: $35 ($40 for international students). Electronic applications accepted. *Expenses:* Tuition, state resident: full-time $8961; part-time $6132 per credit hour. Tuition, nonresident: full-time $23,121; part-time $14,608 per credit hour. *Financial support:* Application deadline: 4/1. *Unit head:* Dr. Hayden Mattingly, Interim Director, 931-372-6246, E-mail: hmattingly@tntech.edu. *Application contact:* Shelia K. Kendrick, Coordinator of Graduate Studies, 931-372-3808, Fax: 931-372-3497, E-mail: skendrick@tntech.edu.
Website: https://www.tntech.edu/is/ses/psm/psmei

Texas Southern University, School of Public Affairs, Program in Urban Planning and Environmental Policy, Houston, TX 77004-4584. Offers MS, PhD. *Accreditation:* ACSP. *Program availability:* Part-time, evening/weekend. *Degree requirements:* For master's, comprehensive exam, thesis optional. *Entrance requirements:* For master's, GRE General Test, minimum GPA of 2.5. Additional exam requirements/recommendations for international students: Required—TOEFL. Electronic applications accepted.

Texas State University, The Graduate College, College of Liberal Arts, Program in Public Administration, San Marcos, TX 78666. Offers human resources in public administration (MPA); international relations (MPA); legal and judicial administration (MPA); public finance administration (MPA); urban and environmental planning (MPA). *Accreditation:* NASPAA. *Program availability:* Part-time, evening/weekend. *Faculty:* 9 full-time (4 women). *Students:* 32 full-time (16 women), 62 part-time (28 women); includes 54 minority (14 Black or African American, non-Hispanic/Latino; 4 Asian, non-Hispanic/Latino; 34 Hispanic/Latino; 2 Two or more races, non-Hispanic/Latino), 1 international. Average age 30. 60 applicants, 87% accepted, 32 enrolled. In 2015, 35 master's awarded. *Degree requirements:* For master's, comprehensive exam, applied research project. *Entrance requirements:* For master's, GRE (minimum preferred score of 297), baccalaureate degree from regionally-accredited university with minimum GPA of 3.0 on last 60 undergraduate semester hours. Additional exam requirements/recommendations for international students: Required—TOEFL (minimum score 550 paper-based; 78 iBT), TWE. *Application deadline:* For fall admission, 6/15 for domestic students, 6/1 for international students; for spring admission, 10/15 for domestic students, 10/1 for international students; for summer admission, 4/15 for domestic students, 3/15 for international students. Applications are processed on a rolling basis. Application fee: $40 ($90 for international students). Electronic applications accepted. *Expenses:* $3,615 in-state tuition for 12 semester credit hours (1 full-time semester), $974 in-state fees. *Financial support:* In 2015–16, 46 students received support, including 6 teaching assistantships (averaging $11,863 per year); research assistantships, career-related internships or fieldwork, Federal Work-Study, institutionally sponsored loans, scholarships/grants, and unspecified assistantships also available. Support available to part-time students. Financial award application deadline: 3/1; financial award applicants required to submit FAFSA. *Unit head:* Dr. Thomas Longoria, Graduate Advisor, 512-245-7582, Fax: 512-245-7815, E-mail: tl28@txstate.edu. *Application contact:* Dr. Andrea Golato, Dean of Graduate School, 512-245-2581, Fax: 512-245-8365, E-mail: gradcollege@txstate.edu.
Website: http://www.polisci.txstate.edu/public_administration/

Texas Tech University, Graduate School, College of Architecture, Lubbock, TX 79409. Offers architecture (M Arch, MS); land use planning, management, and design (PhD); MBA/M Arch. *Program availability:* Part-time. *Faculty:* 43 full-time (12 women), 6 part-time/adjunct (1 woman). *Students:* 86 full-time (23 women), 26 part-time (2 women); includes 50 minority (1 Black or African American, non-Hispanic/Latino; 44 Hispanic/Latino; 1 Native Hawaiian or other Pacific Islander, non-Hispanic/Latino; 4 Two or more races, non-Hispanic/Latino), 19 international. Average age 25. 92 applicants, 65% accepted, 37 enrolled. In 2015, 71 master's, 1 doctorate awarded. *Degree requirements:* For master's, thesis; for doctorate, thesis/dissertation. *Entrance requirements:* For master's, GRE General Test, portfolio; for doctorate, GRE General Test. Additional exam requirements/recommendations for international students: Required—TOEFL (minimum score 550 paper-based; 79 iBT). *Application deadline:* For fall admission, 6/1 priority date for domestic students, 1/15 priority date for international students; for spring admission, 9/1 priority date for domestic students, 6/15 priority date for international students. Applications are processed on a rolling basis. Application fee: $60. Electronic applications accepted. *Expenses:* Tuition, state resident: full-time $6477; part-time $269.89 per credit hour. Tuition, nonresident: full-time $15,837; part-time $659.89 per credit hour. *Required fees:* $2751; $36.50 per credit hour. $937.50 per semester. Tuition and fees vary according to course level. *Financial support:* In 2015–16, 72 students received support, including 73 fellowships (averaging $5,193 per year), 2 research assistantships (averaging $7,800 per year); teaching assistantships, career-related internships or fieldwork, Federal Work-Study, institutionally sponsored loans, scholarships/grants, traineeships, health care benefits, and unspecified assistantships also available. Support available to part-time students. Financial award application deadline: 3/1; financial award applicants required to submit FAFSA. *Faculty research:* Digital design construction and fabrication, community development and design, health care design, historic preservation, visualization, sustainable architecture. *Total annual research expenditures:* $33,200. *Unit head:* Prof. Andrew Vernooy, Dean, 806-742-3136, Fax: 806-742-1400, E-mail: andrew.vernooy@ttu.edu. *Application contact:* Jeff Rammage, Graduate Advisor, 806-742-3169 Ext. 247, Fax: 806-742-1400, E-mail: jeffrey.rammage@ttu.edu.
Website: http://www.arch.ttu.edu/architecture/

Texas Tech University, Graduate School, College of Arts and Sciences, Department of Biological Sciences, Lubbock, TX 79409-3131. Offers biology (MS, PhD); environmental sustainability and natural resources management (PSM); microbiology (MS); zoology (MS, PhD). *Program availability:* Part-time, blended/hybrid learning. *Faculty:* 41 full-time (12 women), 2 part-time/adjunct (1 woman). *Students:* 94 full-time (51 women), 5 part-time (3 women); includes 6 minority (1 American Indian or Alaska Native, non-Hispanic/Latino; 1 Asian, non-Hispanic/Latino; 3 Hispanic/Latino; 1 Two or more races, non-Hispanic/Latino), 53 international. Average age 29. 92 applicants, 39% accepted, 21 enrolled. In 2015, 7 master's, 9 doctorates awarded. *Degree requirements:* For master's, thesis or alternative; for doctorate, thesis/dissertation. *Entrance requirements:* For master's and doctorate, GRE General Test. Additional exam requirements/recommendations for international students: Required—TOEFL (minimum score 550 paper-based; 79 iBT). *Application deadline:* For fall admission, 6/1 priority date for domestic students, 1/15 priority date for international students; for spring admission, 9/1 priority date for domestic students, 6/15 priority date for international students. Applications are processed on a rolling basis. Application fee: $60. Electronic applications accepted. *Expenses:* Tuition, state resident: full-time $6477; part-time $269.89 per credit hour. Tuition, nonresident: full-time $15,837; part-time $659.89 per credit hour. *Required fees:* $2751; $36.50 per credit hour. $937.50 per semester. Tuition and fees vary according to course level. *Financial support:* In 2015–16, 98 students received support, including 79 fellowships (averaging $1,515 per year), 36 research assistantships (averaging $6,272 per year), 98 teaching assistantships (averaging $13,936 per year). Financial award application deadline: 4/15; financial award applicants required to submit FAFSA. *Faculty research:* Biodiversity, genomics and evolution, climate change in arid ecosystems, plant biology and biotechnology, animal communication and behavior, zoonotic and emerging diseases. *Total annual research expenditures:* $1.4 million. *Unit head:* Dr. Ron Chesser, Chair, 806-834-0121, Fax: 806-742-2963, E-mail: ron.chesser@ttu.edu. *Application contact:* Dr. Lou Densmore, Graduate Adviser, 806-834-6479, Fax: 806-742-2963, E-mail: lou.densmore@ttu.edu.
Website: http://www.depts.ttu.edu/biology/

Towson University, Program in Geography and Environmental Planning, Towson, MD 21252-0001. Offers MA. *Program availability:* Part-time, evening/weekend. *Students:* 13 full-time (5 women), 11 part-time (5 women); includes 3 minority (2 Black or African American, non-Hispanic/Latino; 1 Two or more races, non-Hispanic/Latino), 1 international. *Degree requirements:* For master's, thesis optional. *Entrance requirements:* For master's, bachelor's degree with minimum of 9 credits of course work in geography, minimum GPA of 3.0 overall and in all geography courses, 2 letters of recommendation, essay. *Application deadline:* Applications are processed on a rolling basis. Application fee: $45. Electronic applications accepted. *Expenses:* Tuition, state resident: full-time $7440; part-time $372 per unit. Tuition, nonresident: full-time $15,400; part-time $770 per unit. *Required fees:* $2360; $118 per year. $354 per term. *Financial support:* Application deadline: 4/1. *Unit head:* Dr. Charles Schmitz, Graduate Program Director, 410-704-2966, E-mail: cschmitz@towson.edu. *Application contact:* Alicia Arkell-Kleis, University Admissions, 410-704-2113, Fax: 410-704-3030, E-mail: grads@towson.edu.
Website: http://grad.towson.edu/program/master/geog-ma/

Trent University, Graduate Studies, Program in Environmental and Life Sciences, Environmental and Resource Studies Program, Peterborough, ON K9J 7B8, Canada. Offers M Sc, PhD. *Degree requirements:* For master's, thesis; for doctorate, thesis/dissertation. *Entrance requirements:* For master's, honours degree; for doctorate, master's degree. *Faculty research:* Environmental biogeochemistry, aquatic organic contaminants, fisheries, wetland ecology, renewable resource management.

Tropical Agriculture Research and Higher Education Center, Graduate School, Turrialba, Costa Rica. Offers agribusiness management (MS); agroforestry systems (PhD); development practices (MS); ecological agriculture (MS); environmental socioeconomics (MS); forestry in tropical and subtropical zones (PhD); integrated watershed management (MS); international sustainable tourism (MS); management and conservation of tropical rainforests and biodiversity (MS); tropical agriculture (PhD); tropical agroforestry (MS). *Entrance requirements:* For master's, GRE, 2 years of related professional experience, letters of recommendation; for doctorate, GRE, 4 letters of recommendation, letter of support from employing organization, master's degree in agronomy, biological sciences, forestry, natural resources or related field. Additional exam requirements/recommendations for international students: Required—TOEFL (minimum score 550 paper-based). Electronic applications accepted. *Faculty research:* Biodiversity in fragmented landscapes, ecosystem management, integrated pest management, environmental livestock production, biotechnology carbon balances in diverse land uses.

Troy University, Graduate School, College of Arts and Sciences, Program in Environmental and Biological Sciences, Troy, AL 36082. Offers biological science (MS); environmental policy (MS); environmental science (MS). *Program availability:* Part-time, evening/weekend, 100% online, blended/hybrid learning. *Faculty:* 9 full-time (6 women), 1 (woman) part-time/adjunct. *Students:* 14 full-time (7 women), 28 part-time (16 women); includes 10 minority (6 Black or African American, non-Hispanic/Latino; 2 Asian, non-Hispanic/Latino; 1 Hispanic/Latino; 1 Two or more races, non-Hispanic/Latino). Average age 28. 35 applicants, 91% accepted, 9 enrolled. In 2015, 10 master's awarded. *Degree requirements:* For master's, comprehensive exam (for some programs), thesis (for some programs), comprehensive exam or thesis, minimum GPA of 3.0, admission to candidacy. *Entrance requirements:* For master's, GRE (minimum score of 850 on old exam or 290 on new exam), MAT (minimum score of 385) or GMAT (minimum score of 380), bachelor's degree; minimum undergraduate GPA of 2.5 or 3.0 on last 30 semester hours. Additional exam requirements/recommendations for international students: Required—TOEFL (minimum score 523 paper-based; 70 iBT), IELTS (minimum score 6). *Application deadline:* Applications are processed on a rolling basis. Application fee: $50. Electronic applications accepted. *Expenses:* Tuition, state resident: full-time $7146; part-time $397 per credit hour. Tuition, nonresident: full-time $14,292; part-time $794 per credit hour. *Required fees:* $802. Tuition and fees vary according to campus/location and program. *Financial support:* Fellowships, career-related internships or fieldwork, and scholarships/grants available. Support available to part-time students. *Unit head:* Dr. Glenn Cohen, Divisional Chairman, 334-670-3660, Fax: 334-670-3401, E-mail: gcohen@troy.edu. *Application contact:* Jessica A. Kimbro, Director of Graduate Admissions, 334-670-3178, E-mail: jacord@troy.edu.

Tufts University, Graduate School of Arts and Sciences, Department of Urban and Environmental Policy and Planning, Medford, MA 02155. Offers community development (MA); environmental policy (MA); health and human welfare (MA); housing policy (MA); international environment/development policy (MA); public policy (MPP); MA/MS; MALD/MA. *Accreditation:* ACSP (one or more programs are accredited). *Program availability:* Part-time. *Degree requirements:* For master's, thesis, internship. *Entrance requirements:* For master's, GRE General Test. Additional exam requirements/recommendations for international students: Required—TOEFL (minimum score 550 paper-based; 80 iBT), IELTS (minimum score 6.5). Electronic applications accepted. *Expenses:* Contact institution.

Tufts University, Graduate School of Arts and Sciences, Graduate Certificate Programs, Community Environmental Studies Program, Medford, MA 02155. Offers Certificate. *Program availability:* Part-time, evening/weekend. Electronic applications accepted. *Expenses:* Contact institution.

Tufts University, Graduate School of Arts and Sciences, Graduate Certificate Programs, Environmental Management Program, Medford, MA 02155. Offers Certificate. *Program availability:* Part-time, evening/weekend. Electronic applications accepted. *Expenses: Tuition, area resident:* Full-time $48,412; part-time $1210 per credit hour. *Required fees:* $806. Full-time tuition and fees vary according to degree level, program and student level. Part-time tuition and fees vary according to course load.

Tufts University, School of Engineering, Department of Civil and Environmental Engineering, Medford, MA 02155. Offers bioengineering (ME, MS), including environmental technology; civil engineering (ME, MS, PhD), including geotechnical engineering, structural engineering, water diplomacy (PhD); environmental engineering (ME, MS, PhD), including environmental engineering and environmental sciences, environmental geotechnology, environmental health, environmental science and management, hazardous materials management, water diplomacy (PhD), water resources engineering. *Program availability:* Part-time. Terminal master's awarded for partial completion of doctoral program. *Degree requirements:* For master's, thesis or alternative; for doctorate, thesis/dissertation. *Entrance requirements:* For master's and doctorate, GRE General Test. Additional exam requirements/recommendations for international students: Required—TOEFL (minimum score 550 paper-based; 80 iBT), IELTS (minimum score 6.5). Electronic applications accepted. *Expenses: Tuition, area resident:* Full-time $48,412; part-time $1210 per credit hour. *Required fees:* $806. Full-time tuition and fees vary according to degree level, program and student level. Part-time tuition and fees vary according to course load. *Faculty research:* Environmental and water resources engineering, environmental health, geotechnical and geoenvironmental engineering, structural engineering and mechanics, water diplomacy.

Universidad Autonoma de Guadalajara, Graduate Programs, Guadalajara, Mexico. Offers administrative law and justice (LL M); advertising and corporate communications (MA); architecture (M Arch); business (MBA); computational science (MCC); education (Ed M, Ed D); English-Spanish translation (MA); entrepreneurship and management (MBA); integrated management of digital animation (MA); international business (MIB); international corporate law (LL M); internet technologies (MS); manufacturing systems (MMS); occupational health (MS); philosophy (MA, PhD); power electronics (MS); quality systems (MQS); renewable energy (MS); social evaluation of projects (MBA); strategic market research (MBA); tax law (MA); teaching mathematics (MA).

Universidad del Turabo, Graduate Programs, Programs in Science and Technology, Gurabo, PR 00778-3030. Offers environmental analysis (MSE), including environmental chemistry; environmental management (MSE), including pollution management; environmental science (D Sc), including environmental biology. *Entrance requirements:* For master's, GRE, EXADEP, interview.

Universidad Metropolitana, School of Environmental Affairs, Program in Environmental Planning, San Juan, PR 00928-1150. Offers MP. *Program availability:* Part-time. *Degree requirements:* For master's, thesis. *Entrance requirements:* For master's, EXADEP, interview. Electronic applications accepted.

Universidad Metropolitana, School of Environmental Affairs, Program in Environmental Studies, San Juan, PR 00928-1150. Offers MAES. *Program availability:* Part-time. *Degree requirements:* For master's, thesis or alternative. *Entrance requirements:* For master's, EXADEP, interview. Electronic applications accepted.

Université de Montréal, Faculty of Medicine, Programs in Environment and Prevention, Montréal, QC H3C 3J7, Canada. Offers environment, health and disaster management (DESS). Electronic applications accepted. *Faculty research:* Health, environment, pollutants, protection, waste.

Université du Québec à Chicoutimi, Graduate Programs, Program in Renewable Resources, Chicoutimi, QC G7H 2B1, Canada. Offers M Sc. *Program availability:* Part-time. *Degree requirements:* For master's, thesis. *Entrance requirements:* For master's, appropriate bachelor's degree, proficiency in French.

Université du Québec, Institut National de la Recherche Scientifique, Graduate Programs, Research Center–Water Earth Environment, Québec, QC G1K 9A9, Canada. Offers earth sciences (M Sc, PhD); earth sciences - environmental technologies (M Sc); water sciences (M Sc, PhD). *Program availability:* Part-time. *Degree requirements:* For master's, thesis (for some programs); for doctorate, thesis/dissertation. *Entrance requirements:* For master's, appropriate bachelor's degree, proficiency in French; for doctorate, appropriate master's degree, proficiency in French. Electronic applications accepted. *Faculty research:* Land use, impacts of climate change, adaptation to climate change, integrated management of resources (mineral and water).

Université Laval, Faculty of Administrative Sciences, Programs in Business Administration, Québec, QC G1K 7P4, Canada. Offers accounting (MBA); agri-food management (MBA); electronic business (MBA, Diploma); factory management and logistics (MBA); finance (MBA); firm management (MBA); geomatic management (MBA); information technology management (MBA); international management (MBA); management (MBA); management accounting (MBA, Diploma); marketing (MBA); modeling and organizational decision (MBA); occupational health and safety management (MBA); pharmacy management (MBA); social and environmental responsibility (MBA); technological entrepreneurship (Diploma). *Accreditation:* AACSB. *Program availability:* Part-time, evening/weekend, online learning. *Entrance requirements:* For master's and Diploma, knowledge of French and English. Electronic applications accepted.

Université Laval, Faculty of Agricultural and Food Sciences, Department of Soils and Agricultural Engineering, Programs in Agri-Food Engineering, Québec, QC G1K 7P4, Canada. Offers agri-food engineering (M Sc); environmental technology (M Sc). *Degree requirements:* For master's, thesis (for some programs). *Entrance requirements:* For master's, knowledge of French. Electronic applications accepted.

Université Laval, Faculty of Agricultural and Food Sciences, Department of Soils and Agricultural Engineering, Programs in Soils and Environment Science, Québec, QC G1K 7P4, Canada. Offers environmental technology (M Sc); soils and environment science (M Sc, PhD). Terminal master's awarded for partial completion of doctoral program. *Degree requirements:* For master's, thesis (for some programs); for doctorate, comprehensive exam, thesis/dissertation. *Entrance requirements:* For master's and doctorate, knowledge of French and English. Electronic applications accepted.

University at Albany, State University of New York, College of Arts and Sciences, Department of Biological Sciences, Program in Biodiversity, Conservation, and Policy, Albany, NY 12222-0001. Offers MS. *Degree requirements:* For master's, one foreign language. *Entrance requirements:* For master's, GRE General Test. *Faculty research:* Aquatic ecology, plant community ecology, biodiversity and public policy, restoration ecology, coastal and estuarine science.

University of Alaska Fairbanks, College of Engineering and Mines, Department of Civil and Environmental Engineering, Program in Environmental Quality Science, Fairbanks, AK 99775-5900. Offers MS. *Program availability:* Part-time. *Students:* 2 full-time (1 woman). Average age 28. 4 applicants, 75% accepted. In 2015, 1 master's awarded. *Degree requirements:* For master's, comprehensive exam, oral defense of project or thesis. *Entrance requirements:* For master's, BS in science from accredited institution with minimum GPA of 3.0; calculus, chemistry, and basic computer techniques courses. Additional exam requirements/recommendations for international students: Required—TOEFL (minimum score 575 paper-based). *Application deadline:* For fall admission, 6/1 for domestic students, 3/1 for international students; for spring admission, 10/15 for domestic students, 9/1 for international students. Applications are processed on a rolling basis. Application fee: $60. Electronic applications accepted. *Expenses:* Tuition, state resident: full-time $7614; part-time $423 per credit. Tuition, nonresident: full-time $15,552; part-time $864 per credit. *Required fees:* $38 per credit. $187 per semester. Tuition and fees vary according to course level, course load, program and reciprocity agreements. *Financial support:* Fellowships with full tuition reimbursements, research assistantships with full tuition reimbursements, teaching assistantships with full tuition reimbursements, career-related internships or fieldwork, Federal Work-Study, scholarships/grants, health care benefits, and unspecified assistantships available. Support available to part-time students. Financial award application deadline: 7/1; financial award applicants required to submit FAFSA. *Unit head:* Dr. Robert Perkins, Department Chair, 907-474-7241, Fax: 907-474-6087, E-mail: fycee@uaf.edu. *Application contact:* Mary Kreta, Director of Admissions, 907-474-7500, Fax: 907-474-7097, E-mail: admissions@uaf.edu.
Website: http://cem.uaf.edu/cee/environmental-engineering.aspx

University of Alaska Fairbanks, College of Liberal Arts, Department of Arctic and Northern Studies, Fairbanks, AK 99775-6460. Offers arctic policy (MA); environmental politics and policy (MA); Northern history (MA). *Program availability:* Part-time. *Faculty:* 13 full-time (6 women). *Students:* 12 full-time (8 women), 23 part-time (18 women); includes 2 minority (both Two or more races, non-Hispanic/Latino), 5 international. Average age 35. 16 applicants, 69% accepted, 9 enrolled. In 2015, 3 master's awarded. *Degree requirements:* For master's, comprehensive exam, oral defense of project or thesis. *Entrance requirements:* For master's, bachelor's degree from accredited institution with minimum cumulative undergraduate and major GPA of 3.0. Additional exam requirements/recommendations for international students: Required—TOEFL (minimum score 550 paper-based; 79 iBT), IELTS (minimum score 6.5). *Application deadline:* For fall admission, 6/1 for domestic students, 3/1 for international students; for spring admission, 10/15 for domestic students, 9/1 for international students. Applications are processed on a rolling basis. Application fee: $60. Electronic applications accepted. *Expenses:* Tuition, state resident: full-time $7614; part-time $423 per credit. Tuition, nonresident: full-time $15,552; part-time $864 per credit. *Required fees:* $38 per credit. $187 per semester. Tuition and fees vary according to course level, course load, program and reciprocity agreements. *Financial support:* In 2015–16, 1 research assistantship with full tuition reimbursement (averaging $6,236 per year), 10 teaching assistantships with full tuition reimbursements (averaging $9,354 per year) were awarded; fellowships with full tuition reimbursements, career-related internships or fieldwork, Federal Work-Study, scholarships/grants, health care benefits, and unspecified assistantships also available. Support available to part-time students. Financial award application deadline: 1/1; financial award applicants required to submit FAFSA. *Unit head:* Mary Ehrlander, Director, 907-474-7126, Fax: 907-474-5817, E-mail: fynors@uaf.edu. *Application contact:* Mary Kreta, Director of Admissions, 907-474-7500, Fax: 907-474-7097, E-mail: admissions@uaf.edu.
Website: http://www.uaf.edu/northern/

University of Alberta, Faculty of Graduate Studies and Research, Department of Economics, Edmonton, AB T6G 2E1, Canada. Offers economics (MA, PhD); economics and finance (MA); environmental and natural resource economics (PhD). *Program availability:* Part-time. *Degree requirements:* For doctorate, thesis/dissertation. *Entrance* *requirements:* For master's and doctorate, GRE. Additional exam requirements/ recommendations for international students: Required—TOEFL. *Faculty research:* Public finance, international trade, industrial organization, Pacific Rim economics, monetary economics.

The University of Arizona, College of Agriculture and Life Sciences, School of Natural Resources and the Environment, Watershed Resources Program, Tucson, AZ 85721. Offers water, society, and policy (MS); watershed management (MS, PhD). *Degree requirements:* For master's, thesis; for doctorate, comprehensive exam, thesis/ dissertation. *Entrance requirements:* For master's, GRE General Test, minimum GPA of 3.0, 3 letters of recommendation; for doctorate, GRE General Test, minimum GPA of 3.0, 3 letters of recommendation, MA or MS. Additional exam requirements/ recommendations for international students: Required—TOEFL (minimum score 550 paper-based; 79 iBT). Electronic applications accepted. *Faculty research:* Forest fuel characteristics, prescribed fire, tree ring-fire scar analysis, erosion, sedimentation.

University of Calgary, Faculty of Graduate Studies, Interdisciplinary Graduate Programs, Calgary, AB T2N 1N4, Canada. Offers interdisciplinary research (M Sc, MA, PhD); resources and the environment (M Sc, MA, PhD). *Program availability:* Part-time. *Degree requirements:* For master's, thesis; for doctorate, thesis/dissertation, written and oral candidacy exam. *Entrance requirements:* Additional exam requirements/ recommendations for international students: Required—TOEFL (minimum score 600 paper-based).

University of Calgary, Faculty of Graduate Studies, Schulich School of Engineering, Department of Chemical and Petroleum Engineering, Calgary, AB T2N 1N4, Canada. Offers chemical engineering (M Eng, M Sc, PhD); energy and environment engineering (M Eng, M Sc, PhD); energy and environmental systems (M Eng, M Sc, PhD); environmental engineering (M Eng, M Sc, PhD); petroleum engineering (M Eng, M Sc, PhD); reservoir characterization (M Eng, M Sc). *Program availability:* Part-time. *Degree requirements:* For master's, thesis (for some programs); for doctorate, comprehensive exam, thesis/dissertation, candidacy exam. *Entrance requirements:* For master's, minimum GPA of 3.0 or equivalent; for doctorate, minimum GPA of 3.5 or equivalent. Additional exam requirements/recommendations for international students: Required—TOEFL (minimum score 550 paper-based; 80 iBT), IELTS (minimum score 7). Electronic applications accepted. *Faculty research:* Environmental engineering, biomedical engineering modeling, simulation and control, petroleum recovery and reservoir engineering, phase equilibria and transport properties.

University of Calgary, Faculty of Law, Programs in Natural Resources, Energy and Environmental Law, Calgary, AB T2N 1N4, Canada. Offers LL M, Postbaccalaureate Certificate. *Program availability:* Part-time, evening/weekend. *Degree requirements:* For master's, thesis optional. *Entrance requirements:* For master's, JD or LL B. Additional exam requirements/recommendations for international students: Required—TOEFL (minimum score 100 iBT), IELTS (minimum score 7). Electronic applications accepted. *Faculty research:* Natural resources law and regulations; environmental law, ethics and policies; oil and gas and energy law; water and municipal law; Aboriginal law.

University of California, Berkeley, Graduate Division, College of Natural Resources, Department of Environmental Science, Policy, and Management, Berkeley, CA 94720-1500. Offers environmental science, policy, and management (MS, PhD); forestry (MF). Terminal master's awarded for partial completion of doctoral program. *Degree requirements:* For master's, thesis optional; for doctorate, thesis/dissertation, qualifying exam. *Entrance requirements:* For master's and doctorate, GRE General Test, minimum GPA of 3.0, 3 letters of recommendation. Additional exam requirements/ recommendations for international students: Required—TOEFL. Electronic applications accepted. *Faculty research:* Biology and ecology of insects; ecosystem function and environmental issues of soils; plant health/interactions from molecular to ecosystem levels; range management and ecology; forest and resource policy, sustainability, and management.

University of California, Berkeley, UC Berkeley Extension, Certificate Programs in Sustainability Studies, Berkeley, CA 94720-1500. Offers leadership in sustainability and environmental management (Professional Certificate); solar energy and green building (Professional Certificate); sustainable design (Professional Certificate).

University of California, Santa Barbara, Graduate Division, College of Letters and Sciences, Division of Social Sciences, Department of Global Studies, Santa Barbara, CA 93106-7065. Offers global culture, ideology, and religion (MA, PhD); global government, human rights, and civil society (MA, PhD); political economy, sustainable development, and the environment (MA, PhD). *Faculty:* 13 full-time (6 women), 1 part-time/adjunct (0 women). *Students:* 19 full-time (12 women); includes 2 minority (1 Black or African American, non-Hispanic/Latino; 1 Hispanic/Latino), 7 international. Average age 26. 64 applicants, 34% accepted, 12 enrolled. In 2015, 13 master's awarded. *Degree requirements:* For master's, one foreign language, thesis, 2 years of a second language; for doctorate, one foreign language, thesis/dissertation, reading proficiency in at least one language other than English. *Entrance requirements:* For master's, GRE, 2 years of a second language with minimum B grade in the final term, statement of purpose, resume or curriculum vitae, 3 letters of recommendation, transcripts (from all post-secondary institutions attended), writing sample (15-20 pages); for doctorate, GRE, statement of purpose, personal achievements/contributions statement, resume or curriculum vitae, 3 letters of recommendation, transcripts from all post-secondary institutions attended, writing sample (15-20 pages). Additional exam requirements/ recommendations for international students: Required—TOEFL (minimum score 600 paper-based; 94 iBT), IELTS (minimum score 7). *Application deadline:* For fall admission, 12/15 for domestic and international students. Application fee: $90 ($110 for international students). Electronic applications accepted. *Financial support:* In 2015–16, 22 students received support, including 29 fellowships with tuition reimbursements available (averaging $20,000 per year), 10 research assistantships (averaging $1,000 per year), 49 teaching assistantships with partial tuition reimbursements available (averaging $15,000 per year); career-related internships or fieldwork, Federal Work-Study, and scholarships/grants also available. Financial award application deadline: 12/ 15; financial award applicants required to submit FAFSA. *Total annual research expenditures:* $500,000. *Unit head:* Prof. Eve Darian-Smith, Chair, 805-893-4299, Fax: 805-893-8003, E-mail: darian@global.ucsb.edu. *Application contact:* Erika Klukovich, Graduate Program Advisor, 805-893-4668, Fax: 805-893-8003, E-mail: gd-global@global.ucsb.edu.

Website: http://www.global.ucsb.edu/home

University of California, Santa Barbara, Graduate Division, College of Letters and Sciences, Division of Social Sciences, Department of Sociology, Santa Barbara, CA 93106-9430. Offers interdisciplinary emphasis: Black studies (PhD); interdisciplinary emphasis: environment and society (PhD); interdisciplinary emphasis: feminist studies (PhD); interdisciplinary emphasis: global studies (PhD); interdisciplinary emphasis: language, interaction and social organization (PhD); interdisciplinary emphasis: quantitative methods in social science (PhD); interdisciplinary emphasis: technology and society (PhD); sociology (PhD); MA/PhD. *Faculty:* 33 full-time (12 women). *Students:* 52 full-time (34 women); includes 24 minority (5 Black or African American, non-Hispanic/ Latino; 4 Asian, non-Hispanic/Latino; 14 Hispanic/Latino; 1 Native Hawaiian or other Pacific Islander, non-Hispanic/Latino), 3 international. Average age 29. 174 applicants, 10% accepted, 9 enrolled. In 2015, 13 doctorates awarded. Terminal master's awarded for partial completion of doctoral program. *Degree requirements:* For doctorate, comprehensive exam, thesis/dissertation. *Entrance requirements:* For doctorate, GRE General Test. Additional exam requirements/recommendations for international students: Required—TOEFL (minimum score 550 paper-based; 80 iBT), IELTS (minimum score 7). *Application deadline:* For fall admission, 12/1 for domestic and international students. Application fee: $90 ($110 for international students). Electronic applications accepted. *Financial support:* In 2015–16, 51 students received support, including 51 fellowships with tuition reimbursements available (averaging $9,057 per year), 3 research assistantships (averaging $2,000 per year), 48 teaching assistantships with tuition reimbursements available (averaging $17,655 per year); career-related internships or fieldwork, Federal Work-Study, institutionally sponsored loans, scholarships/grants, health care benefits, tuition waivers (full and partial), and unspecified assistantships also available. Financial award application deadline: 12/1; financial award applicants required to submit FAFSA. *Faculty research:* Gender and sexualities, race/ethnicity, social movements, conversation analysis, global sociology. *Unit head:* Prof. Maria Charles, Chair, 805-893-3118, Fax: 805-893-3324. *Application contact:* Sharon Applegate, Graduate Program Advisor, 805-893-3328, Fax: 805-893-3324, E-mail: grad-soc@soc.ucsb.edu.

Website: http://www.soc.ucsb.edu/

University of California, Santa Barbara, Graduate Division, Donald Bren School of Environmental Science and Management, Santa Barbara, CA 93106-5131. Offers economics and environmental science (PhD); environmental science and management (MESM, PhD); technology and society (PhD). *Faculty:* 22 full-time (3 women), 5 part-time/adjunct (1 woman). *Students:* 213 full-time (129 women); includes 33 minority (3 Black or African American, non-Hispanic/Latino; 1 American Indian or Alaska Native, non-Hispanic/Latino; 11 Asian, non-Hispanic/Latino; 16 Hispanic/Latino; 2 Native Hawaiian or other Pacific Islander, non-Hispanic/Latino), 32 international. Average age 27. 404 applicants, 51% accepted, 85 enrolled. In 2015, 70 master's, 7 doctorates awarded. *Degree requirements:* For master's, thesis; for doctorate, thesis/dissertation. *Entrance requirements:* For master's and doctorate, GRE. Additional exam requirements/recommendations for international students: Required—TOEFL (minimum score 550 paper-based; 80 iBT), IELTS (minimum score 7). *Application deadline:* For fall admission, 12/15 priority date for domestic and international students. Application fee: $90 ($110 for international students). Electronic applications accepted. *Financial support:* In 2015–16, 63 students received support, including 23 fellowships with tuition reimbursements available, 3 research assistantships with tuition reimbursements available, 33 teaching assistantships with tuition reimbursements available; career-related internships or fieldwork and tuition waivers (full and partial) also available. Financial award application deadline: 12/15; financial award applicants required to submit FAFSA. *Faculty research:* Coastal marine resources management, conservation planning, corporate environmental management, economics and politics of the environment, energy and climate, pollution prevention and remediation, water resources management. *Unit head:* Dr. Steven Gaines, Dean, 805-893-7363, Fax: 805-893-7611, E-mail: gaines@bren.ucsb.edu. *Application contact:* Kristen Robinson, Director of Admissions and Outreach, 805-893-4886, Fax: 805-893-7612, E-mail: admissions@bren.ucsb.edu.

Website: http://www.bren.ucsb.edu/

University of California, Santa Cruz, Division of Graduate Studies, Division of Social Sciences, Program in Environmental Studies, Santa Cruz, CA 95064. Offers PhD. *Degree requirements:* For doctorate, thesis/dissertation, qualifying exam. *Entrance requirements:* For doctorate, GRE General Test. Additional exam requirements/ recommendations for international students: Required—TOEFL (minimum score 550 paper-based; 83 iBT); Recommended—IELTS (minimum score 8). Electronic applications accepted. *Faculty research:* Political economy and sustainability, conservation biology, agroecology, environmental policy analysis.

University of Central Missouri, The Graduate School, Warrensburg, MO 64093. Offers accountancy (MA); accounting (MBA); applied mathematics (MS); aviation safety (MA); biology (MS); business administration (MBA); career and technical education leadership (MS); college student personnel administration (MS); communication (MA); computer science (MS); counseling (MS); criminal justice (MS); educational leadership (Ed D); educational technology (MS); elementary and early childhood education (MSE); English (MA); environmental studies (MA); finance (MBA); history (MA); human services/ educational technology (Ed S); human services/learning resources (Ed S); human services/professional counseling (Ed S); industrial hygiene (MS); industrial management (MS); information systems (MBA); information technology (MS); kinesiology (MS); library science and information services (MS); literacy education (MSE); marketing (MBA); mathematics (MS); music (MA); occupational safety management (MS); psychology (MS); rural family nursing (MS); school administration (MSE); social gerontology (MS); sociology (MA); special education (MSE); speech language pathology (MS); superintendency (Ed S); teaching (MAT); teaching English as a second language (MA); technology (MS); technology management (PhD); theatre (MA). *Program availability:* Part-time, 100% online, blended/hybrid learning. *Faculty:* 336 full-time (145 women), 39 part-time/adjunct (25 women). *Students:* 2,161 full-time (723 women), 2,077 part-time (1,061 women); includes 188 minority (93 Black or African American, non-Hispanic/ Latino; 4 American Indian or Alaska Native, non-Hispanic/Latino; 15 Asian, non-Hispanic/Latino; 32 Hispanic/Latino; 1 Native Hawaiian or other Pacific Islander, non-Hispanic/Latino; 43 Two or more races, non-Hispanic/Latino), 2,514 international. Average age 28. 3,454 applicants, 68% accepted, 1632 enrolled. In 2015, 1,530 master's, 53 other advanced degrees awarded. *Degree requirements:* For master's and Ed S, comprehensive exam (for some programs), thesis (for some programs). *Entrance requirements:* Additional exam requirements/recommendations for international students: Required—TOEFL (minimum score 550 paper-based; 79 iBT). *Application deadline:* For fall admission, 6/1 priority date for domestic and international students; for spring admission, 10/1 priority date for domestic and international students; for summer admission, 4/1 priority date for domestic and international students. Applications are processed on a rolling basis. Application fee: $30 ($75 for international students). Electronic applications accepted. *Expenses:* Tuition, state resident: full-time $6683; part-time $278.45 per credit hour. Tuition, nonresident: full-time $13,366; part-time $556.90 per credit hour. *Required fees:* $701; $29.20 per credit hour. Tuition and fees vary according to degree level and campus/location. *Financial support:* In 2015–16, 97 students received support, including 146 research assistantships with partial tuition reimbursements available (averaging $7,500 per year), 73 teaching assistantships with partial tuition reimbursements available (averaging $7,500 per year); career-related internships or fieldwork, Federal Work-Study, scholarships/grants, and administrative and laboratory assistantships also available. Support available to part-time students. Financial award application deadline: 3/1; financial award applicants required to submit FAFSA. *Unit head:* Tina Church-Hockett, Director of Graduate School and International Admissions, 660-543-4621, Fax: 660-543-4778, E-mail: church@ucmo.edu. *Application* contact: Brittany Lawrence, Graduate Student Services Coordinator, 660-543-4621, Fax: 660-543-4778, E-mail: gradinfo@ucmo.edu. Website: http://www.ucmo.edu/graduate/

University of Chicago, Harris School of Public Policy, Program in Environmental Science and Policy, Chicago, IL 60637. Offers MS. Offered in partnership with the Argonne National Laboratory. *Entrance requirements:* For master's, GRE General Test. Additional exam requirements/recommendations for international students: Required— IELTS (minimum score 7).

University of Colorado Boulder, Graduate School, College of Arts and Sciences, Program in Environmental Studies, Boulder, CO 80309. Offers MS, PhD. *Faculty:* 13 full-time (5 women). *Students:* 45 full-time (28 women), 3 part-time (2 women); includes 3 minority (1 Hispanic/Latino; 2 Two or more races, non-Hispanic/Latino), 4 international. Average age 31. 160 applicants, 21% accepted, 14 enrolled. In 2015, 10 master's, 4 doctorates awarded. *Entrance requirements:* For master's, minimum undergraduate GPA of 3.0. *Application deadline:* For fall admission, 12/29 for domestic students, 12/1 for international students. Application fee: $50 ($70 for international students). Electronic applications accepted. Application fee is waived when completed online. *Financial support:* In 2015–16, 91 students received support, including 14 fellowships (averaging $3,902 per year), 14 research assistantships with tuition reimbursements available (averaging $36,225 per year), 18 teaching assistantships with tuition reimbursements available (averaging $35,611 per year); institutionally sponsored loans, scholarships/grants, health care benefits, and unspecified assistantships also available. Financial award applicants required to submit FAFSA. *Faculty research:* Environmental planning/policy, environmental studies, environmental conservation, behavioral/social sciences. *Total annual research expenditures:* $1.1 million. *Application contact:* E-mail: envsgrad@colorado.edu. Website: http://www.colorado.edu/envs/prospective-students/graduate-students

University of Colorado Denver, College of Architecture and Planning, Program in Urban and Regional Planning, Denver, CO 80217. Offers economic and community development planning (MURP); land use and environmental planning (MURP); urban place making (MURP). *Accreditation:* ACSP. *Program availability:* Part-time. *Students:* 96 full-time (53 women), 7 part-time (1 woman); includes 24 minority (4 Black or African American, non-Hispanic/Latino; 1 American Indian or Alaska Native, non-Hispanic/Latino; 5 Asian, non-Hispanic/Latino; 10 Hispanic/Latino; 4 Two or more races, non-Hispanic/Latino), 1 international. Average age 30. 144 applicants, 40% accepted, 43 enrolled. In 2015, 36 master's awarded. *Degree requirements:* For master's, thesis, minimum of 51 semester hours. *Entrance requirements:* For master's, GRE (for students with an undergraduate GPA below 3.0), sample of writing or work project; statement of interest; resume; three letters of recommendation. Additional exam requirements/recommendations for international students: Required—TOEFL (minimum score 75 iBT). *Application deadline:* For fall admission, 2/1 priority date for domestic students, 1/1 priority date for international students; for spring admission, 10/1 for domestic students. Application fee: $50 ($75 for international students). Electronic applications accepted. *Expenses:* Contact institution. *Financial support:* In 2015–16, 56 students received support. Fellowships, research assistantships, teaching assistantships, Federal Work-Study, institutionally sponsored loans, scholarships/grants, and traineeships available. Financial award application deadline: 4/1; financial award applicants required to submit FAFSA. *Faculty research:* Physical planning, environmental planning, economic development planning. *Unit head:* Austin Troy, Professor/Chair, 303-315-1006, E-mail: austin.troy@ucdenver.edu. *Application contact:* Rachael Kuroiwa, Manager of Admissions and Outreach, 303-315-2325, E-mail: rachael.kuroiwa@ucdenver.edu. Website: http://www.ucdenver.edu/academics/colleges/ArchitecturePlanning/Academics/DegreePrograms/MURP/Pages/MURP.aspx

University of Colorado Denver, College of Liberal Arts and Sciences, Program in Humanities, Denver, CO 80217. Offers community health science (MSS); humanities (MH); international studies (MSS); philosophy and theory (MH); social justice (MSS); society and the environment (MSS); visual studies (MH); women's and gender studies (MSS). *Program availability:* Part-time, evening/weekend. *Faculty:* 2 full-time (0 women). *Students:* 42 full-time (29 women), 27 part-time (19 women); includes 20 minority (3 Black or African American, non-Hispanic/Latino; 1 American Indian or Alaska Native, non-Hispanic/Latino; 2 Asian, non-Hispanic/Latino; 9 Hispanic/Latino; 5 Two or more races, non-Hispanic/Latino). Average age 35. 19 applicants, 74% accepted, 6 enrolled. In 2015, 13 master's awarded. *Degree requirements:* For master's, 36 credit hours, project or thesis. *Entrance requirements:* For master's, writing sample, statement of purpose/letter of intent, three letters of recommendation. Additional exam requirements/recommendations for international students: Required—TOEFL (minimum score 537 paper-based; 75 iBT); Recommended—IELTS (minimum score 6.5). *Application deadline:* For fall admission, 5/15 for domestic students, 5/15 priority date for international students; for spring admission, 10/15 for domestic students, 10/15 priority date for international students; for summer admission, 3/15 for domestic and international students. Application fee: $50 ($75 for international students). Electronic applications accepted. *Financial support:* In 2015–16, 9 students received support. Fellowships, research assistantships, teaching assistantships, Federal Work-Study, institutionally sponsored loans, scholarships/grants, and traineeships available. Financial award application deadline: 4/1; financial award applicants required to submit FAFSA. *Faculty research:* Women and gender in the classical Mediterranean, communication theory and democracy, relationship between psychology and philosophy. *Unit head:* Margaret Woodhull, Director of Humanities, 303-315-3568, E-mail: margaret.woodhull@ucdenver.edu. *Application contact:* Angela Beale, Program Assistant, 303-315-3565, E-mail: mastershs@ucdenver.edu. Website: http://www.ucdenver.edu/academics/colleges/CLAS/Programs/HumanitiesSocialSciences/Programs/Pages/MasterofHumanities.aspx

University of Colorado Denver, School of Public Affairs, Program in Public Affairs and Administration, Denver, CO 80127. Offers public administration (MPA), including domestic violence, emergency management and homeland security, environmental policy, management and law, homeland security and defense, local government, nonprofit management, public administration; public affairs (PhD). *Accreditation:* NASPAA. *Program availability:* Part-time, evening/weekend, online learning. *Students:* 252 full-time (165 women), 145 part-time (99 women); includes 70 minority (8 Black or African American, non-Hispanic/Latino; 6 American Indian or Alaska Native, non-Hispanic/Latino; 9 Asian, non-Hispanic/Latino; 43 Hispanic/Latino; 2 Native Hawaiian or other Pacific Islander, non-Hispanic/Latino; 2 Two or more races, non-Hispanic/Latino), 17 international. Average age 34. 227 applicants, 70% accepted, 83 enrolled. In 2015, 117 master's, 8 doctorates awarded. *Degree requirements:* For master's, thesis or alternative, 36-39 credit hours; for doctorate, comprehensive exam, thesis/dissertation, minimum of 66 semester hours, including at least 30 hours of dissertation. *Entrance requirements:* For master's, GRE, GMAT or LSAT, resume, essay, transcripts, recommendations; for doctorate, GRE, resume, essay, transcripts, recommendations. Additional exam requirements/recommendations for international students: Required— TOEFL (minimum score 550 paper-based; 80 iBT); Recommended—IELTS (minimum score 6.5). *Application deadline:* For fall admission, 2/1 priority date for domestic students, 1/15 priority date for international students; for spring admission, 10/15 priority

date for domestic students, 10/1 priority date for international students. Application fee: $50 ($75 for international students). Electronic applications accepted. *Expenses:* Contact institution. *Financial support:* In 2015–16, 98 students received support. Fellowships with partial tuition reimbursements available, research assistantships with partial tuition reimbursements available, teaching assistantships with partial tuition reimbursements available, Federal Work-Study, institutionally sponsored loans, scholarships/grants, traineeships, and unspecified assistantships available. Financial award application deadline: 4/1; financial award applicants required to submit FAFSA. *Faculty research:* Housing, education and the social and economic issues of vulnerable populations; nonprofit governance and management; education finance, effectiveness and reform; P-20 education initiatives; municipal government accountability. *Unit head:* Dr. Christine Martell, Director of MPA Program, 303-315-2716, Fax: 303-315-2229, E-mail: christine.martell@ucdenver.edu. *Application contact:* Dawn Savage, Student Services Coordinator, 303-315-2743, Fax: 303-315-2229, E-mail: dawn.savage@ucdenver.edu. Website: http://www.ucdenver.edu/academics/colleges/SPA/Academics/programs/PublicAffairsAdmin/Pages/index.aspx

University of Dayton, Department of Mechanical and Aerospace Engineering, Dayton, OH 45469. Offers aerospace engineering (MSAE, DE, PhD); mechanical engineering (MSME, DE, PhD); renewable and clean energy (MS). *Program availability:* Part-time, online learning. *Faculty:* 15 full-time (3 women), 10 part-time/adjunct (1 woman). *Students:* 158 full-time (33 women), 38 part-time (5 women); includes 6 minority (2 Black or African American, non-Hispanic/Latino; 1 Asian, non-Hispanic/Latino; 2 Hispanic/Latino; 1 Two or more races, non-Hispanic/Latino), 128 international. Average age 27. 340 applicants, 44% accepted, 58 enrolled. In 2015, 66 master's awarded. *Degree requirements:* For master's, thesis optional; for doctorate, variable foreign language requirement, comprehensive exam, thesis/dissertation, departmental qualifying exam. *Entrance requirements:* For master's, BS in engineering, math, or physics. Additional exam requirements/recommendations for international students: Required—TOEFL (minimum score 550 paper-based; 80 iBT), IELTS (minimum score 6.5). *Application deadline:* Applications are processed on a rolling basis. Application fee: $0 ($50 for international students). Electronic applications accepted. *Expenses:* $873 per credit hour for master's programs; $951 per credit hour for PhD programs. *Financial support:* In 2015–16, 3 fellowships with full tuition reimbursements (averaging $25,000 per year), 21 research assistantships with full tuition reimbursements (averaging $13,000 per year), 8 teaching assistantships with full tuition reimbursements (averaging $8,000 per year) were awarded; institutionally sponsored loans, health care benefits, and tuition waivers also available. Support available to part-time students. Financial award application deadline: 3/1; financial award applicants required to submit FAFSA. *Faculty research:* Kinematic synthesis, energy informatics and community sustainability, evaluation of postural control and gait, computational fluid dynamics and surrogate modeling, and control of noise and vibration. *Total annual research expenditures:* $953,406. *Unit head:* Dr. Kelly Kissock, Chair, 937-229-2999, Fax: 937-229-4766, E-mail: jkissock1@udayton.edu. *Application contact:* Dr. Vinod Jain, Graduate Program Director, 937-229-2992, Fax: 937-229-4766, E-mail: vjain1@udayton.edu. Website: https://www.udayton.edu/engineering/departments/mechanical_and_aerospace/index.php

University of Delaware, Center for Energy and Environmental Policy, Newark, DE 19716. Offers energy and environmental policy (MA, MEEP, PhD); urban affairs and public policy (PhD), including technology, environment, and society. *Degree requirements:* For master's, analytical paper or thesis; for doctorate, comprehensive exam, thesis/dissertation. *Entrance requirements:* For master's, GRE General Test, minimum GPA of 3.0; for doctorate, GRE General Test, minimum GPA of 3.5. Additional exam requirements/recommendations for international students: Required—TOEFL. Electronic applications accepted. *Faculty research:* Sustainable development, renewable energy, climate change, environmental policy, environmental justice, disaster policy.

University of Denver, Sturm College of Law, Programs in Environmental and Natural Resources Law and Policy, Denver, CO 80208. Offers environmental and natural resources law and policy (LL M, MLS); natural resources law and policy (Certificate). *Faculty:* 74 full-time (39 women), 69 part-time/adjunct (25 women). *Students:* 8 full-time (4 women), 4 part-time (1 woman); includes 3 minority (1 Hispanic/Latino; 2 Two or more races, non-Hispanic/Latino), 4 international. Average age 32. 28 applicants, 71% accepted, 6 enrolled. In 2015, 24 master's awarded. *Degree requirements:* For master's, internship. *Entrance requirements:* For master's, bachelor's degree (for MRLS), JD (for LL M), transcripts, two letters of recommendation. Additional exam requirements/recommendations for international students: Required—TOEFL (minimum score 550 paper-based; 80 iBT). *Application deadline:* Applications are processed on a rolling basis. Application fee: $65. Electronic applications accepted. *Expenses:* $46,270 full-time; $34,292 3/4 time (evening); $21,884 part-time. *Financial support:* In 2015–16, 5 students received support. Federal Work-Study, institutionally sponsored loans, scholarships/grants, and unspecified assistantships available. Support available to part-time students. Financial award application deadline: 2/15; financial award applicants required to submit FAFSA. *Unit head:* Don Smith, Director, 303-871-6052, E-mail: dcsmith@law.du.edu. *Application contact:* E-mail: gradlegalstudies@law.du.edu. Website: http://www.law.du.edu/index.php/graduate-legal-studies/masters-programs/mls-enrlp

The University of Findlay, Office of Graduate Admissions, Findlay, OH 45840-3653. Offers athletic training (MAT); business (MBA), including health care management, hospitality management, organizational leadership, public management; education (MA Ed), including administration, children's literature, early childhood, human resource development, reading, science, special education, technology; environmental, safety and health management (MSEM); health informatics (MS); occupational therapy (MOT); pharmacy (Pharm D); physical therapy (DPT); physician assistant (MPA); rhetoric and writing (MA); teaching English to speakers of other languages (TESOL) and bilingual education (MA). *Program availability:* Part-time, evening/weekend, online learning. *Degree requirements:* For master's, thesis, cumulative project, capstone project. *Entrance requirements:* For master's, GRE/GMAT, bachelor's degree from accredited institution, minimum undergraduate GPA of 2.5 in last 64 hours of course work; for doctorate, GRE, minimum cumulative GPA of 3.0. Additional exam requirements/recommendations for international students: Required—TOEFL (minimum score 80 iBT). Electronic applications accepted.

University of Guelph, Graduate Studies, Ontario Agricultural College, Department of Land Resource Science, Guelph, ON N1G 2W1, Canada. Offers atmospheric science (M Sc, PhD); environmental and agricultural earth sciences (M Sc, PhD); land resources management (M Sc, PhD); soil science (M Sc, PhD). *Program availability:* Part-time. *Degree requirements:* For master's, thesis (for some programs), research project (non-thesis track); for doctorate, comprehensive exam, thesis/dissertation. *Entrance requirements:* For master's, minimum B- average during previous 2 years of course work; for doctorate, minimum B average during previous 2 years of course work. Additional exam requirements/recommendations for international students: Required—

TOEFL (minimum score 550 paper-based). Electronic applications accepted. *Faculty research:* Soil science, environmental earth science, land resource management.

University of Hawaii at Manoa, Graduate Division, College of Social Sciences, Department of Urban and Regional Planning, Honolulu, HI 96822. Offers community planning and social policy (MURP); disaster preparedness and emergency management (Graduate Certificate); environmental planning and management (MURP); land use and infrastructure planning (MURP); urban and regional planning (PhD, Graduate Certificate); urban and regional planning in Asia and Pacific (MURP). *Accreditation:* ACSP. *Program availability:* Part-time. *Faculty:* 28 full-time (9 women), 11 part-time/adjunct (2 women). *Students:* Average age 33. 45 applicants, 80% accepted, 22 enrolled. In 2015, 30 master's, 3 doctorates, 1 other advanced degree awarded. *Entrance requirements:* For master's, GRE General Test, minimum GPA of 3.0; for doctorate, GRE General Test. Additional exam requirements/recommendations for international students: Required—TOEFL (minimum score 500 paper-based; 61 iBT), IELTS (minimum score 5). *Application deadline:* For fall admission, 3/1 for domestic and international students; for spring admission, 9/1 for domestic and international students. Application fee: $100. *Financial support:* In 2015–16, 11 fellowships (averaging $2,314 per year), 28 research assistantships (averaging $16,718 per year), 2 teaching assistantships (averaging $14,382 per year) were awarded; career-related internships or fieldwork, Federal Work-Study, institutionally sponsored loans, and tuition waivers (full) also available. *Total annual research expenditures:* $423,000. *Unit head:* Richard Dubanoski, Dean, 808-956-6570, Fax: 808-956-2340, E-mail: dickd@hawaii.edu. *Application contact:* Dolores Foley, Graduate Chair, 808-956-7381, Fax: 808-956-6870, E-mail: dolores@hawaii.edu.
Website: http://www.durp.hawaii.edu/

University of Hawaii at Manoa, Graduate Division, College of Tropical Agriculture and Human Resources, Department of Natural Resources and Environmental Management, Honolulu, HI 96822. Offers MS, PhD. *Program availability:* Part-time. *Faculty:* 31 full-time (5 women), 2 part-time/adjunct (1 woman). *Students:* 37 full-time (21 women), 7 part-time (4 women); includes 16 minority (1 American Indian or Alaska Native, non-Hispanic/Latino; 5 Asian, non-Hispanic/Latino; 10 Two or more races, non-Hispanic/Latino), 7 international. Average age 32. 37 applicants, 57% accepted, 6 enrolled. In 2015, 7 master's, 5 doctorates awarded. Terminal master's awarded for partial completion of doctoral program. *Degree requirements:* For master's, thesis optional; for doctorate, comprehensive exam, thesis/dissertation. *Entrance requirements:* For master's and doctorate, GRE General Test, minimum GPA of 3.0 in last 4 semesters of course work. Additional exam requirements/recommendations for international students: Required—TOEFL (minimum score 600 paper-based; 100 iBT), IELTS (minimum score 7). *Application deadline:* For fall admission, 3/1 for domestic students, 1/15 for international students; for spring admission, 9/1 for domestic students, 8/1 for international students. Applications are processed on a rolling basis. Application fee: $100. *Financial support:* In 2015–16, 10 fellowships (averaging $1,822 per year), 22 research assistantships (averaging $19,469 per year), 4 teaching assistantships (averaging $14,820 per year) were awarded; career-related internships or fieldwork and tuition waivers (full and partial) also available. *Faculty research:* Bioeconomics, natural resource management. *Total annual research expenditures:* $3.1 million. *Unit head:* Sylvia Yuen, Interim Dean, 808-956-8234, Fax: 808-956-9105, E-mail: syuen@hawaii.edu. *Application contact:* John Yanagida, Graduate Chair, 808-956-7530, Fax: 808-956-6539, E-mail: jyanagid@hawaii.edu.
Website: http://www.hawaii.edu/graduatestudies/fields/html/departments/mno/nrem/nrem.htm

University of Houston–Clear Lake, School of Business, Program in Administrative Science, Houston, TX 77058-1002. Offers environmental management (MS); human resource management (MA). *Program availability:* Part-time, evening/weekend. *Degree requirements:* For master's, thesis optional. *Entrance requirements:* For master's, GMAT. Additional exam requirements/recommendations for international students: Required—TOEFL (minimum score 550 paper-based). Electronic applications accepted.

University of Illinois at Springfield, Graduate Programs, College of Public Affairs and Administration, Program in Environmental Studies, Springfield, IL 62703-5407. Offers environmental science (MS); environmental studies (MA). *Program availability:* Part-time, evening/weekend, 100% online. *Faculty:* 6 full-time (3 women). *Students:* 16 full-time (11 women), 46 part-time (28 women); includes 9 minority (1 Black or African American, non-Hispanic/Latino; 1 American Indian or Alaska Native, non-Hispanic/Latino; 5 Asian, non-Hispanic/Latino; 2 Hispanic/Latino), 2 international. Average age 33. 63 applicants, 44% accepted, 21 enrolled. In 2015, 25 master's awarded. *Degree requirements:* For master's, thesis, project, or capstone closure course completion. *Entrance requirements:* For master's, minimum undergraduate GPA of 3.0, 2 letters of recommendation, goals essay. Additional exam requirements/recommendations for international students: Required—TOEFL (minimum score 500 paper-based; 61 iBT). *Application deadline:* Applications are processed on a rolling basis. Application fee: $60 ($75 for international students). Electronic applications accepted. *Expenses:* Tuition, state resident: part-time $329 per credit hour. Tuition, nonresident: part-time $675 per credit hour. *Financial support:* In 2015–16, fellowships with full tuition reimbursements (averaging $9,900 per year), research assistantships with full tuition reimbursements (averaging $9,956 per year), teaching assistantships with full tuition reimbursements (averaging $9,956 per year) were awarded; career-related internships or fieldwork, Federal Work-Study, scholarships/grants, health care benefits, and unspecified assistantships also available. Support available to part-time students. Financial award application deadline: 11/15; financial award applicants required to submit FAFSA. *Unit head:* Dr. Dennis Ruez, Jr., Program Administrator, 217-206-8424, E-mail: druez2@uis.edu. *Application contact:* Dr. Lynn Pardie, Office of Graduate Studies, 800-252-8533, Fax: 217-206-7623, E-mail: lpard1@uis.edu.
Website: http://www.uis.edu/environmentalstudies/

University of Maine, Graduate School, College of Liberal Arts and Sciences, Department of Anthropology, Orono, ME 04469. Offers anthropology and environmental policy (PhD). *Faculty:* 12 full-time (4 women), 1 part-time/adjunct (0 women). *Students:* 8 full-time (6 women). Average age 29. 14 applicants, 36% accepted, 2 enrolled. *Degree requirements:* For doctorate, comprehensive exam, thesis/dissertation. *Entrance requirements:* For doctorate, GRE General Test. Additional exam requirements/recommendations for international students: Required—TOEFL. *Application deadline:* For fall admission, 1/15 priority date for domestic students. Application fee: $65. *Financial support:* In 2015–16, 8 students received support, including 6 research assistantships (averaging $24,800 per year), 1 teaching assistantship (averaging $14,600 per year). Financial award application deadline: 3/1. *Faculty research:* Archaeological proxies of past climate, human and climate interactions, environmental policy, human dimensions of natural resource management, environmental risk perception. *Total annual research expenditures:* $1.2 million. *Unit head:* Gregory Zaro, Chair, 207-581-1857, Fax: 207-581-1823, E-mail: gregory.zaro@umit.maine.edu. *Application contact:* Scott G. Delcourt, Assistant Vice President for Graduate Studies and Senior Associate Dean, 207-581-3291, Fax: 207-581-3232, E-mail: graduate@maine.edu.
Website: http://www.umaine.edu/anthropology/

The University of Manchester, School of Environment and Development, Manchester, United Kingdom. Offers architecture (M Phil, PhD); development policy and management (M Phil, PhD); human geography (M Phil, PhD); physical geography (M Phil, PhD); planning and landscape (M Phil, PhD).

University of Maryland, Baltimore County, The Graduate School, College of Arts, Humanities and Social Sciences, Department of Geography and Environmental Systems, Program in Geography and Environmental Systems, Baltimore, MD 21250. Offers MS, PhD. *Program availability:* Part-time. *Faculty:* 15 full-time (5 women), 11 part-time/adjunct (2 women). *Students:* 22 full-time (10 women), 7 part-time (3 women); includes 2 minority (1 Asian, non-Hispanic/Latino; 1 Hispanic/Latino). Average age 30. 33 applicants, 58% accepted, 10 enrolled. In 2015, 6 master's, 3 doctorates awarded. Terminal master's awarded for partial completion of doctoral program. *Degree requirements:* For master's, thesis optional, annual faculty evaluation, research paper; for doctorate, comprehensive exam, thesis/dissertation, annual faculty evaluation, qualifying exams, proposal and dissertation defense. *Entrance requirements:* For master's and doctorate, GRE, minimum GPA of 3.0 overall, 3.3 in major. Additional exam requirements/recommendations for international students: Required—TOEFL (minimum score 550 paper-based; 80 iBT); Recommended—IELTS. *Application deadline:* For fall admission, 2/1 for domestic students, 1/1 for international students. Application fee: $50. Electronic applications accepted. *Expenses:* $21,300 (MS); $31,244 (PhD). *Financial support:* In 2015–16, 18 students received support, including 7 research assistantships with full tuition reimbursements available (averaging $19,700 per year), 11 teaching assistantships with full tuition reimbursements available (averaging $19,700 per year); fellowships, scholarships/grants, traineeships, health care benefits, and unspecified assistantships also available. Financial award application deadline: 2/1. *Faculty research:* Watershed processes; climate and weather systems; ecology and biogeography; landscape ecology and land-use change; human geography, urban sustainability and environmental health; environmental policy; geographic information science and remote sensing. *Unit head:* Dr. Jeffrey Halverson, Graduate Program Director, 410-455-2002, E-mail: jeffhalv@umbc.edu. *Application contact:* Kathryn Nee, Coordinator of Domestic Admissions, 410-455-2944, E-mail: nee@umbc.edu.
Website: http://ges.umbc.edu/graduate/

University of Maryland Eastern Shore, Graduate Programs, Department of Natural Sciences, Princess Anne, MD 21853-1299. Offers chemistry (MS); marine-estuarine-environmental sciences (MS, PhD); quantitative fisheries and resource economics (PMS); toxicology (MS, PhD). *Degree requirements:* For master's, thesis; for doctorate, comprehensive exam, thesis/dissertation. *Entrance requirements:* For master's and doctorate, GRE General Test, minimum GPA of 3.0. Additional exam requirements/recommendations for international students: Required—TOEFL (minimum score 80 iBT). Electronic applications accepted. *Faculty research:* Environmental chemistry (air/water pollution), fin fish ecology.

University of Maryland University College, The Graduate School, Program in Environmental Management, Adelphi, MD 20783. Offers MS, Certificate. Program offered evenings and weekends only. *Program availability:* Part-time, online learning. *Students:* 3 full-time (1 woman), 257 part-time (139 women); includes 86 minority (66 Black or African American, non-Hispanic/Latino; 5 Asian, non-Hispanic/Latino; 11 Hispanic/Latino; 1 Native Hawaiian or other Pacific Islander, non-Hispanic/Latino; 3 Two or more races, non-Hispanic/Latino), 8 international. Average age 34. 83 applicants, 100% accepted, 56 enrolled. In 2015, 87 master's, 13 other advanced degrees awarded. *Degree requirements:* For master's, thesis or alternative, capstone course. *Application deadline:* Applications are processed on a rolling basis. Application fee: $50. Electronic applications accepted. *Financial support:* Federal Work-Study and scholarships/grants available. Support available to part-time students. Financial award application deadline: 6/1; financial award applicants required to submit FAFSA. *Unit head:* Dr. Robert Ouellette, Program Chair, 240-684-2400, Fax: 240-684-2401, E-mail: rana.khan@umuc.edu. *Application contact:* Coordinator, Graduate Admissions, 800-888-8682, Fax: 240-684-2151, E-mail: newgrad@umuc.edu.
Website: http://www.umuc.edu/academic-programs/masters-degrees/environmental-management.cfm

University of Massachusetts Amherst, Graduate School, College of Natural Sciences, Department of Environmental Conservation, Amherst, MA 01003. Offers building systems (MS, PhD); environmental policy and human dimensions (MS, PhD); forest resources (MS, PhD); sustainability science (MS); water, wetlands and watersheds (MS, PhD); wildlife and fisheries conservation (MS, PhD). *Program availability:* Part-time. Terminal master's awarded for partial completion of doctoral program. *Degree requirements:* For master's, thesis or alternative; for doctorate, comprehensive exam, thesis/dissertation. *Entrance requirements:* For master's and doctorate, GRE General Test. Additional exam requirements/recommendations for international students: Required—TOEFL (minimum score 550 paper-based; 80 iBT), IELTS (minimum score 6.5). Electronic applications accepted.

University of Massachusetts Dartmouth, Graduate School, College of Arts and Sciences, Department of Public Policy, North Dartmouth, MA 02747-2300. Offers educational policy (Graduate Certificate); environmental policy (Graduate Certificate); public management (Graduate Certificate); public policy (MPP). *Program availability:* Part-time, 100% online. *Faculty:* 4 full-time (0 women), 1 part-time/adjunct (0 women). *Students:* 10 full-time (3 women), 51 part-time (32 women); includes 15 minority (6 Black or African American, non-Hispanic/Latino; 6 Hispanic/Latino; 3 Two or more races, non-Hispanic/Latino). Average age 36. 47 applicants, 91% accepted, 27 enrolled. In 2015, 16 master's, 21 other advanced degrees awarded. *Degree requirements:* For master's, portfolio of professional work. *Entrance requirements:* For master's, GRE or GMAT (waived with successful completion of environmental policy or public management graduate certificates at UMass Dartmouth), statement of purpose (minimum of 300 words), resume, 2 letters of recommendation, official transcripts; for Graduate Certificate, statement of purpose (minimum of 300 words), resume, official transcripts. Additional exam requirements/recommendations for international students: Required—TOEFL (minimum score 600 paper-based). *Application deadline:* For fall admission, 8/1 priority date for domestic students, 7/1 priority date for international students; for spring admission, 12/15 priority date for domestic students, 11/15 priority date for international students. Applications are processed on a rolling basis. Application fee: $60. Electronic applications accepted. *Expenses:* Tuition, state resident: full-time $2071; part-time $86.29 per credit. Tuition, nonresident: full-time $8099; part-time $337.46 per credit. *Required fees:* $18,074; $762.08 per credit. Tuition and fees vary according to course load and reciprocity agreements. *Financial support:* In 2015–16, 3 research assistantships (averaging $12,900 per year) were awarded; teaching assistantships, career-related internships or fieldwork, scholarships/grants, and unspecified assistantships also available. Financial award application deadline: 3/1; financial award applicants required to submit FAFSA. *Faculty research:* Demographic analysis, legal and regulatory framework, human rights policy, globalization policies, women's public policy issues, educational leadership, environmental law. *Total annual research expenditures:* $8,000. *Unit head:* Chad McGuire, Graduate Program Director, 508-999-8520, Fax: 508-999-8374, E-mail: cmcguire@umassd.edu. *Application contact:* Steven

Environmental Management and Policy

Briggs, Director of Marketing and Recruitment for Graduate Studies, 508-999-8604, Fax: 508-999-8183, E-mail: graduate@umassd.edu.
Website: http://www.umassd.edu/cas/departmentsanddegreeprograms/publicpolicy/

University of Massachusetts Lowell, College of Health Sciences, Department of Work Environment, Lowell, MA 01854. Offers cleaner production and pollution prevention (MS, Sc D); environmental risk assessment (Certificate); epidemiology (MS, Sc D); ergonomics and safety (MS, Sc D); identification and control of ergonomic hazards (Certificate); job stress and healthy job redesign (Certificate); occupational and environmental hygiene (MS, Sc D); radiological health physics and general work environment protection (Certificate); work environment policy (MS, Sc D). *Accreditation:* ABET (one or more programs are accredited). *Program availability:* Part-time. Terminal master's awarded for partial completion of doctoral program. *Degree requirements:* For master's, thesis optional; for doctorate, thesis/dissertation. *Entrance requirements:* For master's and doctorate, GRE General Test. Additional exam requirements/ recommendations for international students: Required—TOEFL.

University of Michigan, School of Natural Resources and Environment, Program in Natural Resources and Environment, Ann Arbor, MI 48109. Offers behavior, education and communication (MS); conservation ecology (MS); environmental informatics (MS); environmental justice (MS); environmental policy and planning (MS); natural resources and environment (PhD); sustainable systems (MS); MS/JD; MS/MBA; MS/MPP; MS/ MSE; MUP/MS. *Students:* 342 full-time (184 women). Average age 27. Terminal master's awarded for partial completion of doctoral program. *Degree requirements:* For master's, practicum or group project; for doctorate, comprehensive exam, thesis/ dissertation, oral defense of dissertation, preliminary exam. *Entrance requirements:* For master's, GRE General Test; for doctorate, GRE General Test, master's degree. Additional exam requirements/recommendations for international students: Required—TOEFL (minimum score 560 paper-based; 84 iBT). *Application deadline:* For fall admission, 4/30 for domestic and international students. Application fee: $75 ($90 for international students). Electronic applications accepted. *Financial support:* Application deadline: 1/6; applicants required to submit FAFSA. *Unit head:* Dr. Marie Lynn Miranda, Interim Dean, 734-764-2550, Fax: 734-763-8965, E-mail: danbrown@umich.edu. *Application contact:* Sondra R. Auerbach, Director of Academic Programs, 734-764-6453, Fax: 734-936-2195, E-mail: sshowen@umich.edu.
Website: http://www.snre.umich.edu/

University of Minnesota, Twin Cities Campus, Graduate School, College of Food, Agricultural and Natural Resource Sciences, Program in Natural Resources Science and Management, St. Paul, MN 55108. Offers assessment, monitoring, and geospatial analysis (MS, PhD); economics, policy, management, and society (MS, PhD); forest hydrology and watershed management (MS, PhD); forest products (MS, PhD); forests: biology, ecology, conservation, and management (MS, PhD); natural resources science and management (MS, PhD); paper science and engineering (MS, PhD); recreation resources, tourism, and environmental education (MS, PhD); wildlife ecology and management (MS, PhD). *Program availability:* Part-time. *Faculty:* 71 full-time (28 women), 55 part-time/adjunct (7 women). *Students:* 80 full-time (45 women), 16 part-time (9 women); includes 5 minority (1 Black or African American, non-Hispanic/Latino; 2 American Indian or Alaska Native, non-Hispanic/Latino; 2 Asian, non-Hispanic/Latino), 8 international. 81 applicants, 52% accepted, 31 enrolled. In 2015, 25 master's, 8 doctorates awarded. Terminal master's awarded for partial completion of doctoral program. *Degree requirements:* For master's, comprehensive exam, thesis; for doctorate, comprehensive exam, thesis/dissertation. *Entrance requirements:* For master's and doctorate, GRE General Test. Additional exam requirements/ recommendations for international students: Required—TOEFL (minimum score 550 paper-based; 79 iBT), IELTS (minimum score 6.5). *Application deadline:* For fall admission, 12/16 priority date for domestic and international students; for spring admission, 10/15 for domestic and international students. Applications are processed on a rolling basis. Application fee: $75 ($95 for international students). Electronic applications accepted. *Financial support:* In 2015–16, fellowships with full tuition reimbursements (averaging $40,000 per year), research assistantships with full tuition reimbursements (averaging $40,000 per year), teaching assistantships with full tuition reimbursements (averaging $40,000 per year) were awarded; scholarships/grants, health care benefits, tuition waivers (full and partial), and unspecified assistantships also available. *Faculty research:* Forest hydrology, biology, ecology, conservation, and management; recreation resources and environmental education; wildlife ecology; economics, policy, and society; geographic information systems (GIS); and forest products and paper science. *Unit head:* Dr. Michael Kilgore, Director of Graduate Studies, 612-624-6298, E-mail: mkilgore@umn.edu. *Application contact:* Toni Wheeler, Graduate Program Coordinator, 612-624-7683, Fax: 612-625-5212, E-mail: twheeler@umn.edu.
Website: http://www.nrsm.umn.edu

University of Minnesota, Twin Cities Campus, Graduate School, Hubert H. Humphrey School of Public Affairs, PhD Program in Public Affairs, Minneapolis, MN 55455. Offers public policy (PhD); public/non-profit management and governance (PhD); science/technology/environmental policy (PhD); urban/regional planning (PhD). *Program availability:* Part-time. *Faculty:* 30 full-time (10 women). *Students:* 16 full-time (8 women); includes 1 minority (Asian, non-Hispanic/Latino), 8 international. Average age 31. 64 applicants, 25% accepted, 9 enrolled. *Degree requirements:* For doctorate, comprehensive exam, thesis/dissertation. *Entrance requirements:* For doctorate, GRE General Test. Additional exam requirements/recommendations for international students: Required—TOEFL (minimum score 650 paper-based; 100 iBT), IELTS (minimum score 7). *Application deadline:* For fall admission, 12/1 priority date for domestic and international students. Application fee: $75 ($95 for international students). Electronic applications accepted. *Expenses:* $16,000 tuition and $2,000 fees per year. *Financial support:* In 2015–16, 16 students received support, including 14 research assistantships with full tuition reimbursements available (averaging $40,000 per year), 2 teaching assistantships with full tuition reimbursements available (averaging $40,000 per year); health care benefits and tuition waivers also available. Financial award application deadline: 12/1. *Faculty research:* Public policy, urban/regional planning, public/nonprofit management and governance, science/technology/ environmental policy. *Unit head:* Laura Bloomberg, Associate Dean, 612-625-0608, Fax: 612-626-0002, E-mail: bloom004@umn.edu. *Application contact:* Edward Goetz, Professor and Director of Graduate Studies, 612-624-8737, E-mail: egoetz@umn.edu.
Website: http://www.hhh.umn.edu/academics/doctor-philosophy-phd-public-affairs

University of Minnesota, Twin Cities Campus, Graduate School, Hubert H. Humphrey School of Public Affairs, Program in Science, Technology, and Environmental Policy, Minneapolis, MN 55455. Offers MS, JD/MS. *Program availability:* Part-time. *Students:* 8 full-time (5 women); includes 3 minority (1 Black or African American, non-Hispanic/Latino; 2 Hispanic/Latino), 1 international. Average age 26. 20 applicants, 70% accepted, 8 enrolled. In 2015, 7 master's awarded. *Degree requirements:* For master's, thesis. *Entrance requirements:* For master's, GRE General Test, undergraduate training in the biological or physical sciences or engineering, minimum undergraduate GPA of 3.0. Additional exam requirements/recommendations for international students: Required—TOEFL (minimum score 600 paper-based; 100 iBT), IELTS (minimum score 7). *Application deadline:* For fall admission, 4/1 for domestic and international students. Applications are processed on a rolling basis. Application fee: $75 ($95 for international students). Electronic applications accepted. *Expenses:* $19,653 state resident full-time; $27,915 nonresident full-time. *Financial support:* In 2015–16, 6 students received support, including fellowships with tuition reimbursements available (averaging $15,000 per year); career-related internships or fieldwork, Federal Work-Study, scholarships/ grants, health care benefits, tuition waivers (full and partial), and unspecified assistantships also available. Financial award application deadline: 1/15; financial award applicants required to submit FAFSA. *Faculty research:* Economics, history, philosophy, and politics of science and technology; organization and management of science and technology. *Unit head:* Laura Bloomberg, Associate Dean, 612-625-0608, Fax: 612-626-0002, E-mail: bloom004@umn.edu. *Application contact:* Dan Cheng, Associate Director of Admissions, 612-624-3800, Fax: 612-626-0002, E-mail: chen0609@umn.edu.
Website: http://www.hhh.umn.edu/degrees/ms_step/

University of Missouri, Office of Research and Graduate Studies, School of Natural Resources, Program in Human Dimensions of Natural Resources, Columbia, MO 65211. Offers MS, PhD.

University of Montana, Graduate School, College of Humanities and Sciences, Program in Environmental Studies (EVST), Missoula, MT 59812-0002. Offers MS, JD/ MS. *Program availability:* Part-time. *Faculty:* 8 full-time (3 women), 2 part-time/adjunct (1 woman). *Students:* 40 full-time (33 women), 12 part-time (5 women); includes 2 minority (both American Indian or Alaska Native, non-Hispanic/Latino). Average age 30. 62 applicants, 71% accepted, 22 enrolled. In 2015, 26 master's awarded. *Degree requirements:* For master's, thesis, portfolio or professional paper. *Entrance requirements:* For master's, GRE General Test (minimum score: 500 verbal on old scoring, 153 new scoring). Additional exam requirements/recommendations for international students: Required—TOEFL (minimum score 580 paper-based; 92 iBT). *Application deadline:* For fall admission, 1/15 priority date for domestic and international students. Application fee: $60. Electronic applications accepted. *Expenses:* $2,783 state resident full-time; $9,790 nonresident full-time. *Financial support:* In 2015–16, 17 students received support, including 3 fellowships with partial tuition reimbursements available (averaging $5,000 per year), 7 teaching assistantships with full tuition reimbursements available (averaging $9,000 per year); scholarships/grants also available. Financial award application deadline: 4/15. *Faculty research:* Pollution ecology, sustainable agriculture, environmental writing, environmental policy, environmental justice, environmental history, habitat-land management, traditional ecological knowledge of Native Peoples. *Total annual research expenditures:* $225,000. *Unit head:* Prof. Phil Condon, Director, 406-243-2904, Fax: 406-243-6090, E-mail: phil.condon@mso.umt.edu. *Application contact:* Karen Hurd, Administrative Assistant, 406-243-6273, Fax: 406-243-6090, E-mail: karen.hurd@mso.umt.edu.
Website: http://www.cas.umt.edu/evst

University of Nevada, Reno, Graduate School, College of Science, Mackay School of Earth Sciences and Engineering, Department of Geography, Program in Land Use Planning, Reno, NV 89557. Offers MS. *Degree requirements:* For master's, thesis. *Entrance requirements:* For master's, GRE General Test, minimum GPA of 3.0. Additional exam requirements/recommendations for international students: Required—TOEFL (minimum score 500 paper-based; 61 iBT), IELTS (minimum score 6). Electronic applications accepted. *Faculty research:* Contemporary planning, environmental planning.

University of New Brunswick Fredericton, School of Graduate Studies, Faculty of Engineering, Department of Chemical Engineering, Fredericton, NB E3B 5A3, Canada. Offers chemical engineering (M Eng, M Sc E, PhD); environmental studies (M Eng). *Program availability:* Part-time. *Faculty:* 14 full-time (3 women). *Students:* 50 full-time (15 women), 9 part-time (3 women). In 2015, 10 master's, 8 doctorates awarded. *Degree requirements:* For master's, thesis; for doctorate, comprehensive exam, thesis/ dissertation, qualifying exam. *Entrance requirements:* For master's and doctorate, minimum GPA of 3.0. Additional exam requirements/recommendations for international students: Required—TOEFL (minimum score 580 paper-based), TWE (minimum score 5), Michigan English Language Assessment Battery (minimum score 85) or CanTest (minimum score 4.5). *Application deadline:* For fall admission, 3/1 for domestic students. Applications are processed on a rolling basis. Application fee: $50 Canadian dollars. Electronic applications accepted. *Financial support:* In 2015–16, 65 fellowships, 65 research assistantships with tuition reimbursements, 47 teaching assistantships were awarded. *Faculty research:* Processing and characterizing nanoengineered composite materials based on carbon nanotubes, enhanced oil recovery processes and oil sweep strategies for conventional and heavy oils, pulp and paper, waste-water treatment, chemistry and corrosion of high and lower temperature water systems, adsorption, aquaculture systems, bioprocessing and biomass refining, nanotechnologies, nuclear, oil and gas, polymer and recirculation. *Unit head:* Dr. Mladen Eic, Director of Graduate Studies, 506-453-4689, Fax: 506-453-3591, E-mail: meic@unb.ca. *Application contact:* Sylvia Demerson, Graduate Secretary, 506-453-4520, Fax: 506-453-3591, E-mail: sdemerso@unb.ca.
Website: http://go.unb.ca/gradprograms

University of New Brunswick Fredericton, School of Graduate Studies, Faculty of Engineering, Department of Civil Engineering, Fredericton, NB E3B 5A3, Canada. Offers construction engineering and management (M Eng, M Sc E, PhD); environmental engineering (M Eng, M Sc E, PhD); environmental studies (M Eng); geotechnical engineering (M Eng, M Sc E, PhD); groundwater/hydrology (M Eng, M Sc E, PhD); materials (M Eng, M Sc E, PhD); pavements (M Eng, M Sc E, PhD); structures (M Eng, M Sc E, PhD); transportation (M Eng, M Sc E, PhD). *Program availability:* Part-time. *Faculty:* 12 full-time (1 woman), 4 part-time/adjunct (0 women). *Students:* 16 full-time (4 women), 15 part-time (5 women). In 2015, 2 master's, 4 doctorates awarded. *Degree requirements:* For master's, thesis; for doctorate, comprehensive exam, thesis/ dissertation, qualifying exam; 27 credit hours of courses. *Entrance requirements:* For master's, minimum GPA of 3.0; B Sc E in civil engineering or related engineering degree; for doctorate, minimum GPA of 3.0; graduate degree in engineering or applied science. Additional exam requirements/recommendations for international students: Required—IELTS (minimum score 7.5), TWE (minimum score 4), Michigan English Language Assessment Battery (minimum score 85) or CanTest (minimum score 4.5); Recommended—TOEFL (minimum score 580 paper-based). *Application deadline:* For fall admission, 5/1 for domestic students; for winter admission, 11/1 for domestic students. Applications are processed on a rolling basis. Application fee: $50 Canadian dollars. Electronic applications accepted. *Financial support:* In 2015–16, 35 fellowships, 48 research assistantships, 35 teaching assistantships were awarded; career-related internships or fieldwork and scholarships/grants also available. *Faculty research:* Construction engineering and management; engineering materials and infrastructure renewal; highway and pavement research; structures and solid mechanics; geotechnical and geoenvironmental engineering; structure interaction; transportation and planning; environment, solid waste management; structural engineering; water and environmental engineering. *Unit head:* Dr. Kerry MacQuarrie, Director of Graduate Studies, 506-453-

5121, Fax: 506-453-3568, E-mail: ktm@unb.ca. *Application contact:* Joyce Moore, Graduate Secretary, 506-452-6127, Fax: 506-453-3568, E-mail: joycem@unb.ca.
Website: http://go.unb.ca/gradprograms

University of New Brunswick Fredericton, School of Graduate Studies, Faculty of Forestry and Environmental Management, Fredericton, NB E3B 5A3, Canada. Offers ecological foundations of forest management (PhD); environmental management (MEM); forest engineering (M Sc FE, MFE); forest products marketing (MBA); forest resources (M Sc F, MF, PhD). *Program availability:* Part-time. *Faculty:* 21 full-time (1 woman), 69 part-time/adjunct (13 women). *Students:* 58 full-time (21 women), 17 part-time (5 women). In 2015, 13 master's, 3 doctorates awarded. *Degree requirements:* For master's, thesis; for doctorate, thesis/dissertation. *Entrance requirements:* For master's and doctorate, minimum GPA of 3.0. Additional exam requirements/recommendations for international students: Required—TOEFL (minimum score 550 paper-based; 80 iBT), IELTS (minimum score 7), TWE (minimum score 4). *Application deadline:* For fall admission, 3/1 for domestic students. Applications are processed on a rolling basis. Application fee: $50 Canadian dollars. Electronic applications accepted. *Financial support:* In 2015–16, 98 research assistantships, 36 teaching assistantships were awarded; fellowships also available. *Faculty research:* Forest machines, soils, and ecosystems; integrated forest management; forest meteorology; wood engineering; stream ecosystems dynamics; forest and natural resources policy; forest operations planning; wood technology and mechanics; forest road construction and engineering; forest, wildlife, insect, bird, and fire ecology; remote sensing; insect impacts; silviculture; LiDAR analytics; integrated pest management; forest tree genetics; genetic resource conservation and sustainable management. *Unit head:* Dr. Marek Krasowski, Director of Graduate Studies, 506-453-4915, Fax: 506-453-3538, E-mail: marek@unb.ca. *Application contact:* Faith Sharpe, Graduate Secretary, 506-458-7520, Fax: 506-453-3538, E-mail: fsharpe@unb.ca.
Website: http://go.unb.ca/gradprograms

University of New Hampshire, Graduate School, College of Life Sciences and Agriculture, Department of Natural Resources and the Environment, Durham, NH 03824. Offers environmental conservation (MS); forestry (MS); integrated coastal ecosystem science, policy and management (MS); natural resources (MS); soil and water resource management (MS); wildlife and conservation biology (MS). *Program availability:* Part-time. *Degree requirements:* For master's, thesis or alternative. *Entrance requirements:* For master's, GRE General Test. Additional exam requirements/recommendations for international students: Required—TOEFL (minimum score 550 paper-based; 80 iBT). Electronic applications accepted.

University of New Haven, Graduate School, College of Arts and Sciences, Program in Environmental Science, West Haven, CT 06516-1916. Offers environmental ecology (MS); environmental education (MS); environmental geoscience (MS); environmental health and management (MS); environmental science (MS); geographical information systems (MS, Graduate Certificate). *Program availability:* Part-time, evening/weekend. *Students:* 20 full-time (10 women), 6 part-time (5 women); includes 2 minority (1 Black or African American, non-Hispanic/Latino; 1 Hispanic/Latino), 5 international. Average age 26. 25 applicants, 88% accepted, 13 enrolled. In 2015, 19 master's awarded. *Degree requirements:* For master's, thesis optional, research project. *Entrance requirements:* Additional exam requirements/recommendations for international students: Required—TOEFL (minimum score 80 iBT), IELTS, PTE. *Application deadline:* For fall admission, 5/31 for international students; for winter admission, 10/15 for international students; for spring admission, 1/15 for international students. Applications are processed on a rolling basis. Application fee: $75. Electronic applications accepted. Application fee is waived when completed online. *Expenses: Tuition, area resident:* Full-time $15,282; part-time $849 per credit hour. *Required fees:* $150; $60 per term. Tuition and fees vary according to program. *Financial support:* Research assistantships with partial tuition reimbursements, teaching assistantships with partial tuition reimbursements, career-related internships or fieldwork, Federal Work-Study, scholarships/grants, and unspecified assistantships available. Support available to part-time students. Financial award applicants required to submit FAFSA. *Unit head:* Dr. Roman Zajac, Coordinator, 203-932-7114, E-mail: rzajac@newhaven.edu. *Application contact:* Michelle Mason, Director of Graduate Enrollment, 203-932-7067, E-mail: mmason@newhaven.edu.
Website: http://www.newhaven.edu/4728/

University of New Mexico, Graduate Studies, College of Arts and Sciences, Program in Geography and Environmental Studies, Albuquerque, NM 87131-2039. Offers MS. *Program availability:* Part-time. *Faculty:* 6 full-time (2 women), 2 part-time/adjunct (both women). *Students:* 11 full-time (5 women), 15 part-time (5 women); includes 7 minority (1 Black or African American, non-Hispanic/Latino; 1 American Indian or Alaska Native, non-Hispanic/Latino; 4 Hispanic/Latino; 1 Two or more races, non-Hispanic/Latino), 1 international. Average age 31. 14 applicants, 71% accepted, 6 enrolled. In 2015, 6 master's awarded. *Degree requirements:* For master's, comprehensive exam (for some programs), thesis (for some programs). *Entrance requirements:* For master's, GRE. Additional exam requirements/recommendations for international students: Required—TOEFL. *Application deadline:* For fall admission, 2/1 priority date for domestic students, 1/1 priority date for international students; for spring admission, 11/15 for domestic and international students. Application fee: $50. Electronic applications accepted. *Financial support:* Research assistantships with full tuition reimbursements, teaching assistantships with full tuition reimbursements, health care benefits, and tuition waivers (full and partial) available. Financial award applicants required to submit FAFSA. *Faculty research:* Geographic information science, environmental management. *Unit head:* Dr. Scott M. Freundschuh, Chair, 505-277-0058, Fax: 505-277-3614, E-mail: sfreunds@unm.edu. *Application contact:* Dr. K. Maria D. Lane, Director of Graduate Studies, 505-277-4075, Fax: 505-277-3614, E-mail: mdlane@unm.edu.
Website: http://geography.unm.edu

University of New Mexico, Graduate Studies, Water Resources Program, Albuquerque, NM 87131-2039. Offers hydroscience (MWR); policy management (MWR). *Program availability:* Part-time. *Faculty:* 2 full-time (1 woman), 4 part-time/adjunct (2 women). *Students:* 17 full-time (11 women), 22 part-time (12 women); includes 13 minority (2 Black or African American, non-Hispanic/Latino; 4 American Indian or Alaska Native, non-Hispanic/Latino; 5 Hispanic/Latino; 2 Two or more races, non-Hispanic/Latino). Average age 34. 21 applicants, 67% accepted, 11 enrolled. In 2015, 5 master's awarded. *Degree requirements:* For master's, professional project. *Entrance requirements:* For master's, minimum GPA of 3.0 during last 2 years of undergraduate work, 3 letters of reference. Additional exam requirements/recommendations for international students: Required—TOEFL (minimum score 550 paper-based). *Application deadline:* For fall admission, 7/15 for domestic students; for spring admission, 11/15 for domestic students. Applications are processed on a rolling basis. Application fee: $50. Electronic applications accepted. *Financial support:* Research assistantships with tuition reimbursements, career-related internships or fieldwork, institutionally sponsored loans, scholarships/grants, and unspecified assistantships available. Financial award application deadline: 3/1; financial award applicants required to submit FAFSA. *Faculty research:* Sustainable water resources, transboundary water resources, economics, water law, hydrology, developing countries, hydrogeology. *Unit head:* Dr. Robert Berrens, Director, 505-277-7759, Fax: 505-277-5226, E-mail: rberrens@unm.edu. *Application contact:* Annamarie Cordova, Administrative Assistant II, 505-277-7759, Fax: 505-277-5226, E-mail: acordova@unm.edu.
Website: http://www.unm.edu/~wrp/

The University of North Carolina at Chapel Hill, Graduate School, Gillings School of Global Public Health, Department of Environmental Sciences and Engineering, Chapel Hill, NC 27599. Offers air, radiation and industrial hygiene (MPH, MS, MSEE, MSPH, PhD); aquatic and atmospheric sciences (MPH, MS, MSPH, PhD); environmental engineering (MPH, MS, MSEE, MSPH, PhD); environmental health sciences (MPH, MS, MSPH, PhD); environmental management and policy (MPH, MS, MSPH, PhD). *Students:* 112 full-time (68 women); includes 20 minority (11 Asian, non-Hispanic/Latino; 4 Hispanic/Latino; 5 Two or more races, non-Hispanic/Latino), 31 international. Average age 28. 178 applicants, 37% accepted, 39 enrolled. Terminal master's awarded for partial completion of doctoral program. *Degree requirements:* For master's, comprehensive exam, thesis (for some programs), research paper; for doctorate, comprehensive exam, thesis/dissertation. *Entrance requirements:* For master's and doctorate, GRE General Test, minimum GPA of 3.0 (recommended). Additional exam requirements/recommendations for international students: Required—TOEFL. *Application deadline:* For fall admission, 12/10 priority date for domestic and international students; for spring admission, 9/10 for domestic students. Applications are processed on a rolling basis. Application fee: $85. Electronic applications accepted. *Financial support:* Fellowships with tuition reimbursements, research assistantships with tuition reimbursements, teaching assistantships with tuition reimbursements, career-related internships or fieldwork, Federal Work-Study, traineeships, health care benefits, and unspecified assistantships available. Support available to part-time students. Financial award application deadline: 12/10; financial award applicants required to submit FAFSA. *Faculty research:* Air, radiation and industrial hygiene, aquatic and atmospheric sciences, environmental health sciences, environmental management and policy, water resources engineering. *Unit head:* Dr. Michael Aitken, Chair, 919-966-1024, Fax: 919-966-7911, E-mail: mike_aitken@unc.edu. *Application contact:* Jack Whaley, Registrar, 919-966-3844, Fax: 919-966-7911, E-mail: jack_whaley@unc.edu.
Website: http://www2.sph.unc.edu/envr/

The University of North Carolina Wilmington, College of Arts and Sciences, Department of Environmental Studies, Wilmington, NC 28403-3297. Offers coastal management, marine and coastal education, environmental education and interpretation, environmental management (MS). *Program availability:* Part-time. *Faculty:* 5 full-time (1 woman). *Students:* 24 full-time (13 women), 6 part-time (4 women); includes 2 minority (1 Hispanic/Latino; 1 Two or more races, non-Hispanic/Latino). Average age 28. 34 applicants, 13 enrolled. In 2015, 20 master's awarded. *Degree requirements:* For master's, comprehensive exam, thesis or alternative, final project, practicum. *Entrance requirements:* For master's, GRE General Test, 3 letters of recommendation, essay, minimum GPA of 3.0 from undergraduate work. Additional exam requirements/recommendations for international students: Required—TOEFL (minimum score 79 iBT), IELTS (minimum score 6.5). *Application deadline:* For fall admission, 4/15 for domestic and international students; for spring admission, 10/15 for domestic and international students. Applications are processed on a rolling basis. Application fee: $60. Electronic applications accepted. *Expenses:* $8,854 in-state full-time per year; $20,945 out-of-state full-time per year. *Financial support:* Scholarships/grants and unspecified assistantships available. Financial award application deadline: 3/15; financial award applicants required to submit FAFSA. *Faculty research:* Coastal management, environmental management, environmental education, environmental law, natural resource management. *Unit head:* Dr. Jeffery Hill, Chair, 910-962-3264, Fax: 910-962-7634, E-mail: hillj@uncw.edu. *Application contact:* Dr. James Rotenberg, Graduate Program Coordinator, 910-962-7549, Fax: 910-962-7634, E-mail: rotenbergj@uncw.edu.
Website: http://www.uncw.edu/evs/academics-MS_Degree.html

University of Northern British Columbia, Office of Graduate Studies, Prince George, BC V2N 4Z9, Canada. Offers business administration (Diploma); community health science (M Sc); disability management (MA); education (M Ed); first nations studies (MA); gender studies (MA); history (MA); interdisciplinary studies (MA); international studies (MA); mathematical, computer and physical sciences (M Sc); natural resources and environmental studies (M Sc, MA, MNRES, PhD); political science (MA); psychology (M Sc, PhD); social work (MSW). *Program availability:* Part-time, evening/weekend, online learning. *Degree requirements:* For master's, thesis; for doctorate, thesis/dissertation. *Entrance requirements:* For master's, GRE, minimum B average in undergraduate course work; for doctorate, candidacy exam, minimum A average in graduate course work.

University of Oregon, Graduate School, College of Arts and Sciences, Environmental Studies Program, Eugene, OR 97403. Offers environmental science, studies, and policy (PhD); environmental studies (MA, MS). *Degree requirements:* For master's, one foreign language, thesis; for doctorate, comprehensive exam, thesis/dissertation. *Entrance requirements:* For master's, GRE General Test, minimum GPA of 3.0; for doctorate, GRE General Test. Additional exam requirements/recommendations for international students: Required—TOEFL (minimum score 550 paper-based). Electronic applications accepted.

University of Pennsylvania, School of Arts and Sciences, College of Liberal and Professional Studies, Philadelphia, PA 19104. Offers applied geosciences (MSAG); applied positive psychology (MAP); chemical sciences (MCS); environmental studies (MES); individualized study (MLA); liberal arts (M Phil); medical physics (MMP); organization dynamics (M Phil). *Students:* 135 full-time (69 women), 329 part-time (203 women); includes 85 minority (27 Black or African American, non-Hispanic/Latino; 23 Asian, non-Hispanic/Latino; 17 Hispanic/Latino; 18 Two or more races, non-Hispanic/Latino), 61 international. Average age 35. 542 applicants, 52% accepted, 173 enrolled. In 2015, 161 master's awarded. *Expenses: Tuition, area resident:* Full-time $31,068; part-time $5762 per course. *Required fees:* $3200; $336 per course. Full-time tuition and fees vary according to degree level, program and student level. Part-time tuition and fees vary according to course load, degree level and program. *Unit head:* Nora Lewis, E-mail: nlewis@sas.upenn.edu.
Website: http://www.sas.upenn.edu/lps/graduate

University of Puerto Rico, Río Piedras Campus, Graduate School of Planning, San Juan, PR 00931-3300. Offers economic planning systems (MP); environmental planning (MP); social policy and planning (MP); urban and territorial planning (MP). *Accreditation:* ACSP. *Program availability:* Part-time. *Degree requirements:* For master's, comprehensive exam, thesis, planning project defense. *Entrance requirements:* For master's, PAEG, GRE, minimum GPA of 3.0, 2 letters of recommendation. *Faculty research:* Municipalities, historic Atlas, Puerto Rico, economic future.

University of Rhode Island, Graduate School, College of the Environment and Life Sciences, Department of Environmental and Natural Resource Economics, Kingston, RI 02881. Offers MESM, MS, PhD. *Program availability:* Part-time. *Faculty:* 6 full-time (1

Environmental Management and Policy

woman), 1 (woman) part-time/adjunct. *Students:* 25 full-time (10 women), 4 part-time (2 women), 13 international. In 2015, 7 master's, 4 doctorates awarded. *Degree requirements:* For master's, comprehensive exam (for some programs), thesis optional; for doctorate, comprehensive exam, thesis/dissertation. *Entrance requirements:* For master's and doctorate, GRE, 3 letters of recommendation. Additional exam requirements/recommendations for international students: Required—TOEFL (minimum score 550 paper-based). *Application deadline:* For fall admission, 7/15 for domestic students, 2/1 for international students; for spring admission, 11/15 for domestic students, 7/15 for international students. Application fee: $65. Electronic applications accepted. *Expenses:* Tuition, state resident: full-time $11,796; part-time $655 per credit. Tuition, nonresident: full-time $24,206; part-time $1345 per credit. *Required fees:* $1546; $44 per credit. One-time fee: $155 full-time; $35 part-time. *Financial support:* In 2015–16, 5 research assistantships (averaging $10,479 per year), 7 teaching assistantships (averaging $9,785 per year) were awarded. Financial award application deadline: 7/15; financial award applicants required to submit FAFSA. *Faculty research:* Policy simulation, policy actions, experimental economics. *Unit head:* Dr. James Opaluch, Chair, 401-874-4590, Fax: 401-874-4766, E-mail: jimo@uri.edu. *Application contact:* Graduate Admission, 401-874-2872, E-mail: gradadm@etal.uri.edu.
Website: http://web.uri.edu/enre/

University of Rochester, Hajim School of Engineering and Applied Sciences, Master of Science in Technical Entrepreneurship and Management Program, Rochester, NY 14642. Offers biomedical engineering (MS); chemical engineering (MS); computer science (MS); electrical and computer engineering (MS); energy and the environment (MS); materials science (MS); mechanical engineering (MS); optics (MS). Program offered in collaboration with the Simon School of Business. *Program availability:* Part-time. *Students:* 43 full-time (14 women), 10 part-time (3 women); includes 7 minority (2 Asian, non-Hispanic/Latino; 3 Hispanic/Latino; 2 Two or more races, non-Hispanic/Latino), 39 international. 168 applicants, 70% accepted, 26 enrolled. In 2015, 23 master's awarded. *Degree requirements:* For master's, comprehensive exam. *Entrance requirements:* For master's, GRE or GMAT, 3 letters of recommendation; personal statement; official transcript; bachelor's degree (or equivalent for international students) in engineering, science, or mathematics. Additional exam requirements/recommendations for international students: Required—TOEFL or IELTS. *Application deadline:* For fall admission, 2/1 for domestic and international students. Applications are processed on a rolling basis. Application fee: $60. Electronic applications accepted. *Expenses:* Tuition, area resident: Full-time $47,450; part-time $1482 per credit hour. *Required fees:* $528. Tuition and fees vary according to program. *Financial support:* Career-related internships or fieldwork and scholarships/grants available. Financial award application deadline: 2/1. *Faculty research:* High efficiency solar cells, macromolecular self-assembly, digital signal processing, memory hierarchy management, molecular and physical mechanisms in cell migration, optical imaging systems. *Unit head:* Duncan T. Moore, Vice Provost for Entrepreneurship, 585-275-5248, Fax: 585-473-6745, E-mail: moore@optics.rochester.edu. *Application contact:* Andrea M. Galati, Executive Director, 585-276-3407, Fax: 585-276-2357, E-mail: andrea.galati@rochester.edu.
Website: http://www.rochester.edu/team

University of South Africa, College of Agriculture and Environmental Sciences, Pretoria, South Africa. Offers agriculture (MS); consumer science (MCS); environmental management (MA, MS, PhD); environmental science (MA, MS, PhD); geography (MA, MS, PhD); horticulture (M Tech); human ecology (MHE); life sciences (MS); nature conservation (M Tech).

University of South Carolina, The Graduate School, School of the Environment, Program in Earth and Environmental Resources Management, Columbia, SC 29208. Offers MEERM, JD/MEERM. *Program availability:* Part-time, online learning. *Degree requirements:* For master's, thesis optional. *Entrance requirements:* For master's, GRE General Test. Additional exam requirements/recommendations for international students: Required—TOEFL. Electronic applications accepted. *Faculty research:* Hydrology, sustainable development, environmental geology and engineering, energy/environmental resources management.

University of South Florida, College of Arts and Sciences, School of Geosciences, Tampa, FL 33620-9951. Offers environmental science and policy (MS); geography (MA), including environmental geography, geographic information science and spatial analysis, human geography; geography and environmental science and policy (PhD); geology (MS, PhD); urban and regional planning (MURP). *Program availability:* Part-time, evening/weekend. *Faculty:* 32 full-time (7 women). *Students:* 87 full-time (41 women), 45 part-time (19 women); includes 18 minority (7 Black or African American, non-Hispanic/Latino; 3 Asian, non-Hispanic/Latino; 7 Hispanic/Latino; 1 Two or more races, non-Hispanic/Latino), 29 international. Average age 34. 39 applicants, 62% accepted, 9 enrolled. In 2015, 10 master's awarded. *Degree requirements:* For master's, comprehensive exam, thesis (for some programs); for doctorate, comprehensive exam, thesis/dissertation. *Entrance requirements:* For master's, GRE General Test, minimum GPA of 3.0 for last 60 credits of undergraduate degree, letter of intent, letters of recommendation; for doctorate, GRE General Test, minimum GPA of 3.0 for all doctorate programs except for ESP/Geography which requires 3.20 GPA for all academic work, letter of intent, letters of recommendation. Additional exam requirements/recommendations for international students: Required—TOEFL (minimum score 550 paper-based; 79 iBT) or IELTS (minimum score 6.5) for MA and MURP; TOEFL (minimum score 600 paper-based) for MS and PhD. *Application deadline:* For fall admission, 2/15 for domestic students, 1/2 for international students; for spring admission, 10/15 for domestic students, 6/1 for international students. Application fee: $30. *Financial support:* In 2015–16, 26 students received support, including 3 research assistantships (averaging $12,345 per year), 25 teaching assistantships with tuition reimbursements available (averaging $12,807 per year); unspecified assistantships also available. Financial award application deadline: 3/1. *Faculty research:* Geography: human geography, environmental geography, geographic information science and spatial analysis, urban geography, social theory; environmental science, policy, and planning: water resources, wildlife ecology, Karst and wetland environments, natural hazards, soil contamination, meteorology and climatology, environmental sustainability and policy, urban and regional planning. *Total annual research expenditures:* $2.3 million. *Unit head:* Dr. Jayajit Chakraborty, Professor and Chair, Geography Division, 813-974-8188, Fax: 813-974-5911, E-mail: jchakrab@usf.edu. *Application contact:* Dr. Jennifer Collins, Associate Professor and Graduate Program Coordinator, 813-974-4242, Fax: 813-974-5911, E-mail: collinsjm@usf.edu.
Website: http://hennarot.forest.usf.edu/main/depts/geosci/

University of South Florida, Innovative Education, Tampa, FL 33620-9951. Offers adult, career and higher education (Graduate Certificate), including college teaching, leadership in developing human resources, leadership in higher education; Africana studies (Graduate Certificate), including diasporas and health disparities, genocide and human rights; aging studies (Graduate Certificate), including gerontology; art research (Graduate Certificate), including museum studies; business foundations (Graduate Certificate); chemical and biomedical engineering (Graduate Certificate), including materials science and engineering, water, health and sustainability; child and family studies (Graduate Certificate), including positive behavior support; civil and industrial engineering (Graduate Certificate), including transportation systems analysis; community and family health (Graduate Certificate), including maternal and child health, social marketing and public health, violence and injury: prevention and intervention, women's health; criminology (Graduate Certificate), including criminal justice administration; educational measurement and research (Graduate Certificate), including evaluation; English (Graduate Certificate), including comparative literary studies, creative writing, professional and technical communication; entrepreneurship (Graduate Certificate); environmental health (Graduate Certificate), including safety management; epidemiology and biostatistics (Graduate Certificate), including applied biostatistics, biostatistics, concepts and tools of epidemiology, epidemiology, epidemiology of infectious diseases; geography, environment and planning (Graduate Certificate), including community development, environmental policy and management, geographical information systems; geology (Graduate Certificate), including hydrogeology; global health (Graduate Certificate), including disaster management, global health and Latin American and Caribbean studies, global health practice, humanitarian assistance, infection control; government and international affairs (Graduate Certificate), including Cuban studies, globalization studies; health policy and management (Graduate Certificate), including health management and leadership, public health policy and programs; hearing specialist: early intervention (Graduate Certificate); industrial and management systems engineering (Graduate Certificate), including systems engineering, technology management; information studies (Graduate Certificate), including school library media specialist; information systems/decision sciences (Graduate Certificate), including analytics and business intelligence; instructional technology (Graduate Certificate), including distance education, Florida digital/virtual educator, instructional design, multimedia design, Web design; internal medicine, bioethics and medical humanities (Graduate Certificate), including biomedical ethics; Latin American and Caribbean studies (Graduate Certificate); mass communications (Graduate Certificate), including multimedia journalism; mathematics and statistics (Graduate Certificate), including mathematics; medicine (Graduate Certificate), including aging and neuroscience, bioinformatics, biotechnology, brain fitness and memory management, clinical investigation, health informatics, health sciences, integrative weight management, intellectual property, medicine and gender, metabolic and nutritional medicine, metabolic cardiology, pharmacy sciences; national and competitive intelligence (Graduate Certificate); psychological and social foundations (Graduate Certificate), including career counseling, college teaching, diversity in education, mental health counseling, school counseling; public affairs (Graduate Certificate), including nonprofit management, public management, research administration; public health (Graduate Certificate), including environmental health, health equity, public health generalist, translational research in adolescent behavioral health; public health practices (Graduate Certificate), including planning for healthy communities; rehabilitation and mental health counseling (Graduate Certificate), including integrative mental health care, marriage and family therapy, rehabilitation technology; secondary education (Graduate Certificate), including ESOL, foreign language education: culture and content, foreign language education: professional; social work (Graduate Certificate), including geriatric social work/clinical gerontology; special education (Graduate Certificate), including autism spectrum disorder, disabilities education: severe/profound; world languages (Graduate Certificate), including teaching English as a second language (TESL) or foreign language. *Unit head:* Kathy Barnes, Interdisciplinary Programs Coordinator, 813-974-8031, Fax: 813-974-7061, E-mail: barnesk@usf.edu. *Application contact:* Karen Tylinski, Metro Initiatives, 813-974-9943, Fax: 813-974-7061, E-mail: ktylinsk@usf.edu.
Website: http://www.usf.edu/innovative-education/

University of South Florida, St. Petersburg, College of Arts and Sciences, St. Petersburg, FL 33701. Offers digital journalism and design (MA); environmental science and policy (MA, MS); Florida studies (MLA); journalism and media studies (MA); liberal studies (MLA); psychology (MA). *Program availability:* Part-time, online learning. *Degree requirements:* For master's, comprehensive exam, thesis or project. *Entrance requirements:* For master's, GRE, LSAT, MCAT (varies by program), letter of intent, 3 letters of recommendation, writing samples, bachelor's degree from regionally-accredited institution with minimum GPA of 3.0 overall or in upper two years. Additional exam requirements/recommendations for international students: Required—TOEFL (minimum score 550 paper-based; 79 iBT); Recommended—IELTS. Electronic applications accepted.

The University of Tennessee, Graduate School, College of Arts and Sciences, Department of Sociology, Knoxville, TN 37996. Offers criminology (MA, PhD); energy, environment, and resource policy (MA, PhD); political economy (MA, PhD). *Program availability:* Part-time. *Degree requirements:* For master's, thesis or alternative; for doctorate, thesis/dissertation. *Entrance requirements:* For master's, GRE General Test, minimum GPA of 3.0; for doctorate, GRE General Test, minimum GPA of 3.5. Additional exam requirements/recommendations for international students: Required—TOEFL. Electronic applications accepted.

The University of Texas at Austin, Graduate School, College of Liberal Arts, Teresa Lozano Long Institute of Latin American Studies, Austin, TX 78712-1111. Offers cultural politics of Afro-Latin and indigenous peoples (MA); development studies (MA); environmental studies (MA); human rights (MA); Latin American and international law (LL M); JD/MA; MA/MA; MBA/MA; MP Aff/MA; MSCRP/MA. LL M offered jointly with The University of Texas School of Law. *Entrance requirements:* For master's, GRE General Test.

University of Washington, Graduate School, Interdisciplinary Graduate Program in Quantitative Ecology and Resource Management, Seattle, WA 98195. Offers MS, PhD. *Degree requirements:* For master's, thesis; for doctorate, thesis/dissertation. *Entrance requirements:* For master's and doctorate, GRE General Test, minimum GPA of 3.0. Additional exam requirements/recommendations for international students: Required—TOEFL. Electronic applications accepted. *Faculty research:* Population dynamics, statistical analysis, ecological modeling and systems analysis of aquatic and terrestrial ecosystems.

University of Waterloo, Graduate Studies, Faculty of Environment, Department of Geography and Environmental Management, Waterloo, ON N2L 3G1, Canada. Offers MA, PhD. MA, PhD offered jointly with Wilfrid Laurier University. *Degree requirements:* For master's, thesis optional; for doctorate, one foreign language, comprehensive exam, thesis/dissertation. *Entrance requirements:* For master's, honors degree, minimum B average; for doctorate, master's degree, minimum A- average. Additional exam requirements/recommendations for international students: Required—TOEFL, IELTS, PTE. *Application deadline:* Applications are processed on a rolling basis. Application fee: $100 Canadian dollars. Electronic applications accepted. *Financial support:* Research assistantships, teaching assistantships, career-related internships or fieldwork, and scholarships/grants available. *Faculty research:* Urban economic geography; physical geography; resource management; cultural, regional, historical geography; spatial data.
Website: https://uwaterloo.ca/geography-environmental-management/

University of Waterloo, Graduate Studies, Faculty of Environment, School of Environment, Resources and Sustainability, Waterloo, ON N2L 3G1, Canada. Offers MES, PhD. *Program availability:* Part-time. *Degree requirements:* For master's, thesis. *Entrance requirements:* For master's, honors degree, minimum B average, resume. Additional exam requirements/recommendations for international students: Required—TOEFL, IELTS, PTE. Application fee: $100 Canadian dollars. Electronic applications accepted. *Financial support:* Research assistantships, teaching assistantships, and scholarships/grants available. *Faculty research:* Applied sustainability; sustainable water policy; food, agriculture, and the environment; biology studies; environment and business; ecological monitoring; soil ecosystem dynamics; urban water demand management; demand response.
Website: https://uwaterloo.ca/environment-resources-and-sustainability/

University of Wisconsin–Green Bay, Graduate Studies, Program in Environmental Science and Policy, Green Bay, WI 54311-7001. Offers MS. *Program availability:* Part-time. *Faculty:* 15 full-time (6 women), 2 part-time/adjunct (0 women). *Students:* 8 full-time (6 women), 17 part-time (10 women); includes 3 minority (1 Asian, non-Hispanic/Latino; 2 Two or more races, non-Hispanic/Latino). Average age 28. 14 applicants, 93% accepted, 9 enrolled. In 2015, 6 master's awarded. *Degree requirements:* For master's, thesis or alternative. *Entrance requirements:* For master's, GRE General Test, minimum GPA of 3.0. *Application deadline:* For fall admission, 8/1 for domestic students; for spring admission, 11/1 for domestic students. Applications are processed on a rolling basis. Application fee: $56. Electronic applications accepted. *Expenses:* Tuition, state resident: full-time $7640; part-time $424 per credit hour. Tuition, nonresident: full-time $16,771; part-time $932 per credit hour. *Required fees:* $1526; $85 per credit hour. $85 per semester. Tuition and fees vary according to program and reciprocity agreements. *Financial support:* In 2015–16, 3 students received support, including 3 research assistantships; career-related internships or fieldwork, Federal Work-Study, institutionally sponsored loans, and unspecified assistantships also available. Financial award application deadline: 7/15; financial award applicants required to submit FAFSA. *Faculty research:* Bald eagle, parasitic population of domestic and wild animals, resource recovery, anaerobic digestion of organic waste. *Unit head:* Dr. Matthew Dornbush, Chair, 920-465-2264, E-mail: dornbusm@uwgb.edu. *Application contact:* Mary Valitchka, Graduate Studies Coordinator, 920-465-2123, E-mail: valitchm@uwgb.edu.
Website: http://www.uwgb.edu/graduate/

Utah State University, School of Graduate Studies, College of Natural Resources, Department of Environment and Society, Logan, UT 84322. Offers bioregional planning (MS); geography (MA, MS); human dimensions of ecosystem science and management (MS, PhD); recreation resource management (MS, PhD). *Degree requirements:* For master's, comprehensive exam, thesis (for some programs). *Entrance requirements:* For master's and doctorate, GRE General Test, minimum GPA of 3.0. Additional exam requirements/recommendations for international students: Required—TOEFL. Electronic applications accepted. *Faculty research:* Geographic information systems/geographic and environmental education, bioregional planning, natural resource and environmental policy, outdoor recreation and tourism, natural resource and environmental management.

Vanderbilt University, School of Engineering, Department of Civil and Environmental Engineering, Program in Environmental Engineering, Nashville, TN 37240-1001. Offers environmental engineering (M Eng); environmental management (MS, PhD). MS and PhD offered through the Graduate School. *Program availability:* Part-time. Terminal master's awarded for partial completion of doctoral program. *Degree requirements:* For master's, thesis or alternative; for doctorate, thesis/dissertation. *Entrance requirements:* For master's and doctorate, GRE General Test. Additional exam requirements/recommendations for international students: Required—TOEFL. Electronic applications accepted. *Faculty research:* Waste treatment, hazardous waste management, chemical waste treatment, water quality.

Vermont Law School, Graduate and Professional Programs, Master's Programs, South Royalton, VT 05068-0096. Offers energy law (LL M); energy regulation and law (MERL); environmental law (LL M); environmental law and policy (MELP); food and agriculture law (LL M); food and agriculture law and policy (MFALP); JD/MELP; JD/MERL; JD/MFALP. *Program availability:* Part-time, online learning. *Entrance requirements:* Additional exam requirements/recommendations for international students: Required—TOEFL. *Faculty research:* Environment and technology; takings; international environmental law; interaction among science, law, and environmental policy; air pollution.

Virginia Commonwealth University, Graduate School, School of Life Sciences, Center for Environmental Studies, Richmond, VA 23284-9005. Offers M Env Sc, MS. *Degree requirements:* For master's, thesis. *Entrance requirements:* For master's, GRE General Test. Additional exam requirements/recommendations for international students: Required—TOEFL (minimum score 600 paper-based; 100 iBT). Electronic applications accepted.

Virginia Polytechnic Institute and State University, Graduate School, College of Architecture and Urban Studies, Blacksburg, VA 24061. Offers architecture (MS Arch); architecture and design research (PhD); building/construction science and management (MS); creative technologies (MFA); environmental design and planning (PhD); landscape architecture (MLA); planning, governance, and globalization (PhD); public administration (MPA); public administration/public affairs (PhD, Certificate); public and international affairs (MPIA); urban and regional planning (MURP); MS/MA. *Accreditation:* ASLA (one or more programs are accredited). *Degree requirements:* For master's, comprehensive exam (for some programs), thesis (for some programs); for doctorate, comprehensive exam (for some programs), thesis/dissertation (for some programs). *Entrance requirements:* For master's and doctorate, GRE/GMAT (may vary by department). Additional exam requirements/recommendations for international students: Required—TOEFL (minimum score 550 paper-based). Electronic applications accepted.

Virginia Polytechnic Institute and State University, VT Online, Blacksburg, VA 24061. Offers advanced transportation systems (Certificate); aerospace engineering (MS); agricultural and life sciences (MSLFS); business information systems (Graduate Certificate); career and technical education (MS); civil engineering (MS); computer engineering (M Eng, MS); decision support systems (Graduate Certificate); eLearning leadership (MA); electrical engineering (M Eng, MS); engineering administration (MEA); environmental engineering (Certificate); environmental politics and policy (Graduate Certificate); environmental sciences and engineering (MS); foundations of political analysis (Graduate Certificate); health product risk management (Graduate Certificate); industrial and systems engineering (MS); information policy and society (Graduate Certificate); information security (Graduate Certificate); information technology (MIT); instructional technology (MA); integrative STEM education (MA Ed); liberal arts (Graduate Certificate); life sciences: health product risk management (MS); natural resources (MNR, Graduate Certificate); networking (Graduate Certificate); nonprofit and nongovernmental organization management (Graduate Certificate); ocean engineering (MS); political science (MA); security studies (Graduate Certificate); software development (Graduate Certificate).

Webster University, College of Arts and Sciences, Department of Biological Sciences, St. Louis, MO 63119-3194. Offers environmental management (MS); science management and leadership (MS); U.S. patent practice (MS). *Program availability:* Part-time, online learning. *Degree requirements:* For master's, comprehensive exam (for some programs), thesis (for some programs). *Entrance requirements:* Additional exam requirements/recommendations for international students: Required—TOEFL. *Expenses: Tuition, area resident:* Full-time $20,550; part-time $685 per credit hour. Tuition and fees vary according to campus/location and program.

Webster University, George Herbert Walker School of Business and Technology, Department of Business, St. Louis, MO 63119-3194. Offers business and organizational security management (MBA); decision support systems (MBA); environmental management (MBA); finance (MBA, MS); forensic accounting (MS); gerontology (MBA); human resources development (MBA); human resources management (MBA); information technology management (MBA); international business (MA, MBA); international relations (MBA); management and leadership (MBA); marketing (MBA); media communications (MBA); procurement and acquisitions management (MBA); Web services (MBA). *Accreditation:* ACBSP. *Program availability:* Part-time, evening/weekend, online learning. *Degree requirements:* For master's, comprehensive exam (for some programs), thesis (for some programs). *Entrance requirements:* Additional exam requirements/recommendations for international students: Required—TOEFL. *Expenses: Tuition, area resident:* Full-time $20,550; part-time $685 per credit hour. Tuition and fees vary according to campus/location and program.

Wesley College, Business Program, Dover, DE 19901-3875. Offers environmental management (MBA); executive leadership (MBA); management (MBA). Executive leadership concentration also offered at New Castle, DE location. *Program availability:* Part-time, evening/weekend. *Entrance requirements:* For master's, GMAT or GRE, minimum undergraduate GPA of 2.75.

Wesley College, Environmental Studies Program, Dover, DE 19901-3875. Offers MS. *Program availability:* Part-time, evening/weekend. *Entrance requirements:* For master's, BA/BSM in science or engineering field, portfolio.

Western State Colorado University, Program in Environmental Management, Gunnison, CO 81231. Offers integrative land management (MEM); sustainable and resilient communities (MEM). *Program availability:* Online learning. *Degree requirements:* For master's, project, portfolio. *Entrance requirements:* Additional exam requirements/recommendations for international students: Required—TOEFL.

West Virginia University, Davis College of Agriculture, Forestry and Consumer Sciences, Division of Resource Management and Sustainable Development, Morgantown, WV 26506. Offers agricultural and extension education (MS, PhD), including agricultural and extension education, teaching vocational-agriculture (MS); agricultural and resource economics (MS); human and community development (PhD); natural resource economics (PhD); resource management (PhD); resource management and sustainable development (PhD). *Program availability:* Part-time. *Degree requirements:* For master's, thesis; for doctorate, comprehensive exam, thesis/dissertation. *Entrance requirements:* For master's, GRE General Test. Additional exam requirements/recommendations for international students: Required—TOEFL. *Expenses:* Tuition, state resident: full-time $8568. Tuition, nonresident: full-time $22,140. Tuition and fees vary according to program. *Faculty research:* Environmental economics, energy economics, agriculture.

West Virginia University, Eberly College of Arts and Sciences, Department of Geology and Geography, Program in Geography, Morgantown, WV 26506. Offers energy and environmental resources (MA); geographic information systems (PhD); geography-regional development (PhD); GIS/cartographic analysis (MA); regional development (MA). *Program availability:* Part-time. *Degree requirements:* For master's, thesis, oral and written exams; for doctorate, comprehensive exam, thesis/dissertation, oral and written exams. *Entrance requirements:* For master's and doctorate, GRE General Test, minimum GPA of 3.0. Additional exam requirements/recommendations for international students: Required—TOEFL. Electronic applications accepted. *Expenses:* Tuition, state resident: full-time $8568. Tuition, nonresident: full-time $22,140. Tuition and fees vary according to program. *Faculty research:* Space, place and development, geographic information science, environmental geography.

Wilfrid Laurier University, Faculty of Graduate and Postdoctoral Studies, Faculty of Arts, Department of Geography and Environmental Studies, Waterloo, ON N2L 3C5, Canada. Offers environmental and resource management (MA, MES, PhD); environmental science (M Sc, MES, PhD); geomatics (M Sc, MES, PhD); human geography (MES, PhD). *Program availability:* Part-time. *Degree requirements:* For master's, thesis optional; for doctorate, thesis/dissertation. *Entrance requirements:* For master's, honors BA in geography, minimum B average in undergraduate course work; honors BSc with minimum B+ or honors BES or BA in physical geography, environmental or earth sciences or the equivalent; for doctorate, MA in geography, minimum A- average. Additional exam requirements/recommendations for international students: Required—TOEFL (minimum score 89 iBT). Electronic applications accepted. *Faculty research:* Resources management, urban, economic, physical, cultural, earth surfaces, geomatics, historical, regional, spatial data handling.

Wilfrid Laurier University, Faculty of Graduate and Postdoctoral Studies, School of International Policy and Governance, International Public Policy Program, Waterloo, ON N2L 3C5, Canada. Offers global governance (MIPP); human security (MIPP); international economic relations (MIPP); international environmental policy (MIPP). Offered jointly with University of Waterloo. *Entrance requirements:* For master's, honours BA with minimum B average. Additional exam requirements/recommendations for international students: Required—TOEFL (minimum score 89 iBT). Electronic applications accepted. *Faculty research:* International environmental policy, international economic relations, human security, global governance.

Wilmington University, College of Business, New Castle, DE 19720-6491. Offers accounting (MBA, MS); business administration (MBA, DBA); environmental stewardship (MBA); finance (MBA); health care administration (MBA, MSM); homeland security (MBA, MSM); human resource management (MSM); management information systems (MBA, MSN); marketing (MSM); marketing management (MBA); military leadership (MSM); organizational leadership (MBA, MSM); public administration (MSM). *Program availability:* Part-time, evening/weekend. *Entrance requirements:* Additional exam requirements/recommendations for international students: Required—TOEFL (minimum score 500 paper-based). Electronic applications accepted.

Yale University, Graduate School of Arts and Sciences, Department of Forestry and Environmental Studies, New Haven, CT 06520. Offers environmental sciences (PhD); forestry (PhD). *Degree requirements:* For doctorate, thesis/dissertation. *Entrance requirements:* For doctorate, GRE General Test.

Yale University, School of Forestry and Environmental Studies, New Haven, CT 06511. Offers environmental management (MEM), including business and the environment, ecosystem and conservation management, energy and the environment, environmental policy analysis; environmental science (MES); forest science (MFS); forestry (MF); forestry and environmental studies (PhD); JD/MEM; MBA/MEM; MBA/MF; MEM/M Arch; MEM/M Div; MEM/MA; MEM/MAR; MEM/MPH. *Accreditation:* SAF (one or more programs are accredited). *Program availability:* Part-time. *Faculty:* 32 full-time, 50 part-time/adjunct. *Students:* 300 full-time. Average age 27. 600 applicants, 150 enrolled. In 2015, 152 master's, 15 doctorates awarded. Terminal master's awarded for partial completion of doctoral program. *Degree requirements:* For master's, internship and capstone project (for MEM and MF); research project and thesis (for MES and MFS); for doctorate, comprehensive exam, thesis/dissertation. *Entrance requirements:* For master's, GRE General Test, GMAT or LSAT; for doctorate, GRE General Test. Additional exam requirements/recommendations for international students: Required—TOEFL (minimum score 600 paper-based; 100 iBT) or IELTS (minimum score 7). *Application deadline:* For fall admission, 12/15 priority date for domestic and international students. Application fee: $80. Electronic applications accepted. *Expenses:* Contact institution. *Financial support:* In 2015–16, 240 students received support. Fellowships, research assistantships, teaching assistantships, career-related internships or fieldwork, Federal Work-Study, institutionally sponsored loans, scholarships/grants, and health care benefits available. Support available to part-time students. Financial award application deadline: 2/15; financial award applicants required to submit FAFSA. *Faculty research:* Environmental policy, social ecology, industrial environmental management, forestry, environmental health, urban ecology, water science policy. *Unit head:* Peter Crane, Dean, School of Forestry and Environmental Studies, 203-432-5109, Fax: 203-432-3051. *Application contact:* Rebecca DeSalvo, Director of Enrollment Management & Diversity Initiatives, 800-825-0330, Fax: 203-432-5528, E-mail: fesinfo@yale.edu.
Website: http://environment.yale.edu

York University, Faculty of Graduate Studies, Program in Environmental Studies, Toronto, ON M3J 1P3, Canada. Offers MES, PhD, MES/LL B, MES/MA. *Program availability:* Part-time. *Degree requirements:* For master's, thesis optional; for doctorate, comprehensive exam, thesis/dissertation, research seminar. Electronic applications accepted.

Youngstown State University, Graduate School, College of Liberal Arts and Social Sciences, Program in Environmental Studies, Youngstown, OH 44555-0001. Offers environmental studies (MS); industrial/institutional management (Certificate); risk management (Certificate). *Degree requirements:* For master's, comprehensive exam, thesis, oral defense of dissertation. *Entrance requirements:* For master's, GRE General Test or minimum GPA of 2.7. Additional exam requirements/recommendations for international students: Required—TOEFL.

Environmental Sciences

Adelphi University, College of Arts and Sciences, Program in Environmental Studies, Garden City, NY 11530-0701. Offers MS. *Degree requirements:* For master's, thesis optional. *Entrance requirements:* For master's, GRE General Test, 2 letters of recommendation; course work in microeconomics, political science, statistics/calculus, and either chemistry or physics; computer literacy. Additional exam requirements/recommendations for international students: Required—TOEFL (minimum score 550 paper-based; 80 iBT). Electronic applications accepted. *Faculty research:* Contaminates sites, workplace exposure level of contaminants, climate change and human health.

Alaska Pacific University, Graduate Programs, Environmental Science Department, Program in Environmental Science, Anchorage, AK 99508-4672. Offers MSES. *Program availability:* Part-time. *Degree requirements:* For master's, thesis. *Entrance requirements:* For master's, GRE General Test, minimum GPA of 3.0. Additional exam requirements/recommendations for international students: Required—TOEFL (minimum score 550 paper-based).

American University, College of Arts and Sciences, Department of Environmental Science, Washington, DC 20016-8070. Offers environmental assessment (Graduate Certificate); environmental science (MS); professional science: environmental assessment (MS). *Faculty:* 8 full-time (4 women), 3 part-time/adjunct (1 woman). *Students:* 14 full-time (6 women), 3 part-time (all women); includes 2 minority (1 Black or African American, non-Hispanic/Latino; 1 Asian, non-Hispanic/Latino), 3 international. Average age 25. 17 applicants, 100% accepted, 6 enrolled. In 2015, 4 master's awarded. *Degree requirements:* For master's, comprehensive exam, thesis (for some programs). *Entrance requirements:* For master's, GRE General Test, GRE Subject Test, one year of calculus, lab science, statement of purpose, transcripts, 2 letters of recommendation, resume; for Graduate Certificate, statement of purpose, transcripts, resume. Additional exam requirements/recommendations for international students: Required—TOEFL (minimum score 100 iBT), IELTS (minimum score 7), PTE (minimum score 68). *Application deadline:* For fall admission, 2/1 for domestic students; for spring admission, 11/1 for domestic students. Application fee: $55. *Expenses: Tuition, area resident:* Full-time $27,468; part-time $1526 per credit hour. *Required fees:* $430. Tuition and fees vary according to course level and program. *Financial support:* Application deadline: 2/1. *Unit head:* Dr. Kiho Kim, Department Chair, 202-885-2181, Fax: 202-885-1752, E-mail: acheh@american.edu. *Application contact:* Kathleen Clowery, Associate Director, Graduate Admissions, 202-885-3620, Fax: 202-885-1344, E-mail: clowery@american.edu.
Website: http://www.american.edu/cas/environmental/

American University of Beirut, Graduate Programs, Faculty of Agricultural and Food Sciences, Beirut, Lebanon. Offers agricultural economics (MS); animal sciences (MS); ecosystem management (MSES); food technology (MS); irrigation (MS); nutrition (MS); plant protection (MS); plant science (MS); poultry science (MS); rural community development (MS). *Program availability:* Part-time. *Faculty:* 19 full-time (4 women). *Students:* 13 full-time (5 women), 55 part-time (41 women). Average age 26. 93 applicants, 52% accepted, 25 enrolled. In 2015, 27 master's awarded. *Degree requirements:* For master's, one foreign language, comprehensive exam, thesis (for some programs). *Entrance requirements:* Additional exam requirements/recommendations for international students: Required—TOEFL (minimum score 600 paper-based; 100 iBT), IELTS (minimum score 7.5). *Application deadline:* For fall admission, 2/10 for domestic and international students; for spring admission, 11/2 for domestic and international students. Application fee: $50. Electronic applications accepted. *Expenses: Tuition, area resident:* Full-time $16,254; part-time $903 per credit. *Required fees:* $699. Tuition and fees vary according to course load and program. *Financial support:* In 2015–16, 1 research assistantship with partial tuition reimbursement (averaging $1,800 per year), 48 teaching assistantships with tuition reimbursements (averaging $1,400 per year) were awarded; scholarships/grants, health care benefits, and unspecified assistantships also available. Financial award application deadline: 2/2. *Faculty research:* Developing skills in the field of integrated energy planning in med landscaper; profiling refugee households in Lebanon; Improving the nutrition of Syrian refugees and host communities though garden walls; monitoring and evaluation of salt iodization in Lebanon; mother and child cohorts: towards curbing the epidemic of non-communicable diseases in Qatar and Lebanon.. *Total annual research expenditures:* $852,730. *Unit head:* Prof. Nahla Hwalla, Dean, 961-1343002 Ext. 4400, Fax: 961-1744460, E-mail: nahla@aub.edu.lb. *Application contact:* Dr. Rabih Talhouk, Director, Graduate Council, 961-1350000 Ext. 4386, Fax: 961-1374374, E-mail: graduate.council@aub.edu.lb.
Website: http://www.aub.edu.lb/fafs/fafs_home/Pages/index.aspx

American University of Beirut, Graduate Programs, Faculty of Engineering and Architecture, Beirut, Lebanon. Offers applied energy (ME); civil engineering (PhD); electrical and computer engineering (PhD); energy studies (MS); engineering management (MEM); environmental and water resources (ME); environmental technology (MSES); mechanical engineering (ME, PhD); urban design (MUD); urban planning and policy (MUPP). *Program availability:* Part-time. *Faculty:* 100 full-time (22 women), 1 part-time/adjunct (0 women). *Students:* 276 full-time (133 women), 58 part-time (26 women). Average age 27. 265 applicants, 66% accepted, 85 enrolled. In 2015, 120 master's, 10 doctorates awarded. Terminal master's awarded for partial completion of doctoral program. *Degree requirements:* For master's, one foreign language, comprehensive exam, thesis (for some programs); for doctorate, one foreign language, comprehensive exam, thesis/dissertation, publications. *Entrance requirements:* For master's, letters of recommendation; for doctorate, GRE, letters of recommendation, master's degree, transcripts, curriculum vitae, interview. Additional exam requirements/recommendations for international students: Required—TOEFL (minimum score 600 paper-based; 100 iBT), IELTS (minimum score 7.5). *Application deadline:* For fall admission, 2/5 priority date for domestic and international students; for spring admission, 11/1 priority date for domestic students, 11/1 for international students. Application fee: $50. Electronic applications accepted. *Expenses: Tuition, area resident:* Full-time $16,254; part-time $903 per credit. *Required fees:* $699. Tuition and fees vary according to course load and program. *Financial support:* In 2015–16, 190 students received support, including 4 fellowships with full tuition reimbursements available (averaging $24,800 per year), 82 research assistantships with full tuition reimbursements available (averaging $24,800 per year), 131 teaching assistantships with full tuition reimbursements available (averaging $9,800 per year); career-related internships or fieldwork, institutionally sponsored loans, scholarships/grants, health care benefits, and unspecified assistantships also available. *Total annual research expenditures:* $1.5 million. *Unit head:* Prof. Makram T. Suidan, Dean, 961-1350000 Ext. 3400, Fax: 961-1744462, E-mail: msuidan@aub.edu.lb. *Application contact:* Dr. Salim Kanaan, Director, Admissions Office, 961-1350000 Ext. 2594, Fax: 961-1750775, E-mail: sk00@aub.edu.lb.
Website: http://staff.aub.edu.lb/~webfea

American University of Beirut, Graduate Programs, Faculty of Health Sciences, Beirut, Lebanon. Offers environmental sciences (MS), including environmental health; epidemiology (MS); epidemiology and biostatistics (MPH); health management and policy (MPH); health promotion and community health (MPH). *Program availability:* Part-time. *Faculty:* 30 full-time (21 women), 3 part-time/adjunct (1 woman). *Students:* 49 full-time (38 women), 99 part-time (81 women). Average age 27. 115 applicants, 71% accepted, 40 enrolled. In 2015, 51 master's awarded. *Degree requirements:* For master's, one foreign language, comprehensive exam (for some programs), thesis (for some programs). *Entrance requirements:* For master's, 2 letters of recommendation, personal statement, transcripts. Additional exam requirements/recommendations for international students: Required—TOEFL (minimum score 583 paper-based; 97 iBT), IELTS (minimum score 7). *Application deadline:* For fall admission, 1/4 priority date for domestic and international students; for spring admission, 11/1 for domestic and international students. Application fee: $50. Electronic applications accepted. *Expenses: Tuition, area resident:* Full-time $16,254; part-time $903 per credit. *Required fees:* $699. Tuition and fees vary according to course load and program. *Financial support:* In 2015–16, 70 students received support. Scholarships/grants, health care benefits, and unspecified assistantships available. Financial award application deadline: 4/1. *Faculty research:* Tobacco control; health of the elderly; youth health; mental health; women's health; reproductive and sexual health, including HIV/AIDS; water quality; health systems; quality in health care delivery; health human resources; health policy; occupational and environmental health; social inequality; social determinants of health; non-communicable diseases; nutrition; refugees health; conflict and health.. *Total annual research expenditures:* $2 million. *Unit head:* Iman Adel Nuwayhid, Dean, 961-1759683, Fax: 961-1744470, E-mail: nuwayhid@aub.edu.lb. *Application contact:* Mitra Tauk, Administrative Coordinator, 961-1350000 Ext. 4687, Fax: 961-1744470, E-mail: mt12@aub.edu.lb.

Antioch University New England, Graduate School, Department of Environmental Studies, Doctoral Program in Environmental Studies, Keene, NH 03431-3552. Offers PhD. *Degree requirements:* For doctorate, thesis/dissertation, practicum. *Entrance requirements:* For doctorate, master's degree and previous experience in the environmental field. Additional exam requirements/recommendations for international students: Required—TOEFL (minimum score 550 paper-based). Electronic applications accepted. *Expenses:* Contact institution. *Faculty research:* Environmental history, green politics, ecopsychology.

Antioch University New England, Graduate School, Department of Environmental Studies, Program in Environmental Education, Keene, NH 03431-3552. Offers MS. *Degree requirements:* For master's, practicum. *Entrance requirements:* For master's, previous undergraduate course work in biology, chemistry, and mathematics; resume; 3 letters of recommendation. Additional exam requirements/recommendations for international students: Required—TOEFL (minimum score 550 paper-based). Electronic applications accepted. *Expenses:* Contact institution. *Faculty research:* Sustainability, natural resources inventory.

Arizona State University at the Tempe campus, College of Liberal Arts and Sciences, School of Human Evolution and Social Change, Tempe, AZ 85287-2402. Offers anthropology (MA, PhD), including anthropology (PhD), archaeology (PhD), bioarchaeology (PhD), evolutionary (PhD), museum studies (MA), sociocultural (PhD); applied mathematics for the life and social sciences (PhD); environmental social science (PhD), including environmental social science, urbanism; global health (MA, PhD), including complex adaptive systems science (PhD), evolutionary global health sciences (PhD), health and culture (PhD), urbanism (PhD); immigration studies (Graduate Certificate). Terminal master's awarded for partial completion of doctoral program. *Degree requirements:* For master's, thesis or alternative, interactive Program of Study (iPOS) submitted before completing 50 percent of required credit hours; for doctorate, comprehensive exam, thesis/dissertation, interactive Program of Study (iPOS) submitted before completing 50 percent of required credit hours. *Entrance requirements:* For master's and doctorate, GRE, minimum GPA of 3.0 or equivalent in last 2 years of work leading to bachelor's degree. Additional exam requirements/recommendations for international students: Required—TOEFL, IELTS, or PTE. Electronic applications accepted.

Arkansas State University, Graduate School, College of Sciences and Mathematics, Program in Environmental Sciences, State University, AR 72467. Offers environmental sciences (MS, PhD). *Program availability:* Part-time. *Faculty:* 1 (woman) full-time. *Students:* 16 full-time (7 women), 16 part-time (12 women); includes 6 minority (3 Black or African American, non-Hispanic/Latino; 1 Asian, non-Hispanic/Latino; 1 Hispanic/Latino; 1 Two or more races, non-Hispanic/Latino), 6 international. Average age 34. 17 applicants, 41% accepted, 5 enrolled. In 2015, 8 master's awarded. *Degree requirements:* For master's, comprehensive exam, thesis (for some programs); for doctorate, comprehensive exam, thesis/dissertation. *Entrance requirements:* For master's, GRE General Test, appropriate bachelor's degree, letters of recommendation, interview, official transcript, immunization records, letter of intent, resume, statement of purpose; for doctorate, GRE, appropriate bachelor's or master's degree, interview, letters of recommendation, personal statement, official transcript, immunization records, resume, statement of purpose. Additional exam requirements/recommendations for international students: Required—TOEFL (minimum score 550 paper-based; 79 iBT), IELTS (minimum score 6), PTE (minimum score 56). *Application deadline:* For fall admission, 2/15 for domestic and international students; for spring admission, 7/15 for domestic and international students. Applications are processed on a rolling basis. Electronic applications accepted. *Expenses:* Tuition, state resident: full-time $4572; part-time $254 per credit hour. Tuition, nonresident: full-time $9144; part-time $508 per credit hour. *International tuition:* $9844 full-time. *Required fees:* $1188; $66 per credit hour. $25 per term. Tuition and fees vary according to course load and program. *Financial support:* In 2015–16, 14 students received support. Fellowships, research assistantships, teaching assistantships, career-related internships or fieldwork, scholarships/grants, and unspecified assistantships available. Financial award application deadline: 7/1; financial award applicants required to submit FAFSA. *Unit head:* Dr. Tanja McKay, Director, 870-972-2007, Fax: 870-972-2008, E-mail: tmckay@astate.edu. *Application contact:* Vickey Ring, Graduate Admissions Coordinator, 870-972-2737, Fax: 870-972-3917, E-mail: vickeyring@astate.edu.
Website: http://www.astate.edu/college/sciences-and-mathematics/doctoral-programs/environmental-science/

Ball State University, Graduate School, College of Sciences and Humanities, Interdepartmental Program in Environmental Sciences, Muncie, IN 47306. Offers environmental science (PhD), including biology, chemistry, geology. *Program availability:* Part-time. *Students:* 3 full-time (0 women), 9 part-time (3 women), 4 international. Average age 31. 4 applicants, 25% accepted, 1 enrolled. In 2015, 2 doctorates awarded. *Degree requirements:* For doctorate, thesis/dissertation. *Entrance requirements:* For doctorate, GRE General Test, minimum cumulative GPA of 3.0 (3.2 for biology and geology concentration), acknowledged arrangement for doctoral environmental sciences research with a faculty mentor (biology, chemistry, or geological sciences), three letters of recommendation. Additional exam requirements/recommendations for international students: Required—TOEFL (minimum score 550 paper-based; 79 iBT), IELTS (minimum score 6.5). *Application deadline:* Applications are processed on a rolling basis. Application fee: $60. Electronic applications accepted. *Expenses: Tuition, area resident:* Full-time $6948; part-time $2316 per semester. Tuition, state resident: full-time $10,422; part-time $3474 per semester. Tuition, nonresident: full-time $19,062; part-time $6354 per semester. *Required fees:* $651 per semester. Tuition and fees vary according to campus/location, program and reciprocity agreements. *Financial support:* In 2015–16, 9 students received support, including 5 research assistantships with partial tuition reimbursements available (averaging $13,866 per year), 4 teaching assistantships with partial tuition reimbursements available (averaging $15,142 per year). Financial award application deadline: 3/1; financial award applicants required to submit FAFSA. *Unit head:* Dr. E. Michael Perdue, Director, 765-285-8096, Fax: 765-285-6505, E-mail: emperdue@bsu.edu.
Website: http://cms.bsu.edu/Academics/CollegesandDepartments/EnvironmentalScience.aspx

Baylor University, Graduate School, College of Arts and Sciences, The Institute of Ecological, Earth and Environmental Sciences, Waco, TX 76798. Offers PhD. *Degree requirements:* For doctorate, variable foreign language requirement, comprehensive exam, thesis/dissertation or alternative. *Entrance requirements:* For doctorate, GRE. Additional exam requirements/recommendations for international students: Required—TOEFL (minimum score 550 paper-based; 80 iBT); Recommended—IELTS (minimum score 6.5). Electronic applications accepted. *Faculty research:* Ecosystem processes, environmental toxicology and risk assessment, biogeochemical cycling, chemical fate and transport, conservation management.

Binghamton University, State University of New York, Graduate School, School of Arts and Sciences, Department of Chemistry, Vestal, NY 13850. Offers analytical chemistry (PhD); chemistry (MA, MS); environmental chemistry (PhD); inorganic chemistry (PhD); organic chemistry (PhD); physical chemistry (PhD). *Program availability:* Part-time. *Faculty:* 21 full-time (4 women). *Students:* 60 full-time (24 women), 1 part-time (0 women); includes 4 minority (2 Black or African American, non-Hispanic/Latino; 1 Asian, non-Hispanic/Latino; 1 Hispanic/Latino), 40 international. Average age 27. 53 applicants, 81% accepted, 16 enrolled. In 2015, 3 master's, 7 doctorates awarded. Terminal master's awarded for partial completion of doctoral program. *Degree requirements:* For master's, thesis; for doctorate, comprehensive exam, thesis/dissertation. *Entrance requirements:* For master's and doctorate, GRE General Test. Additional exam requirements/recommendations for international students: Required—TOEFL (minimum score 90 iBT). *Application deadline:* Applications are processed on a rolling basis. Application fee: $75. Electronic applications accepted. *Financial support:* In 2015–16, 53 students received support, including 8 research assistantships with full tuition reimbursements available (averaging $18,000 per year), 34 teaching assistantships with full tuition reimbursements available (averaging $18,000 per year); career-related internships or fieldwork, Federal Work-Study, institutionally sponsored loans, scholarships/grants, health care benefits, tuition waivers (full and partial), and unspecified assistantships also available. Financial award applicants required to submit FAFSA. *Unit head:* Dr. Wayne E. Jones, Chairperson, 607-777-2421, E-mail: wjones@binghamton.edu. *Application contact:* Kishan Zuber, Recruiting and Admissions Coordinator, 607-777-2151, Fax: 607-777-2501, E-mail: kzuber@binghamton.edu.

Boston University, Graduate School of Arts and Sciences, Department of Earth and Environment, Boston, MA 02215. Offers earth sciences (MA, PhD); energy and environment (MA); geography (MA, PhD); global development policy (MA); international relations and environmental policy (MA); remote sensing and geospatial sciences (MA). *Students:* 57 full-time (25 women), 5 part-time (1 woman); includes 5 minority (2 Asian, non-Hispanic/Latino; 3 Hispanic/Latino), 23 international. Average age 28. 234 applicants, 51% accepted, 27 enrolled. In 2015, 4 master's, 12 doctorates awarded. Terminal master's awarded for partial completion of doctoral program. *Degree requirements:* For master's, comprehensive exam (for some programs), thesis (for some programs); for doctorate, comprehensive exam, thesis/dissertation. *Entrance requirements:* For master's and doctorate, GRE General Test, 3 letters of recommendation, official transcripts, personal statement, writing sample (for geography). Additional exam requirements/recommendations for international students: Required—TOEFL (minimum score 550 paper-based; 84 iBT). *Application deadline:* For fall admission, 1/31 for domestic and international students; for winter admission, 10/15 for domestic and international students. Application fee: $95. Electronic applications accepted. *Financial support:* In 2015–16, 43 students received support, including 5 fellowships with full tuition reimbursements available (averaging $21,000 per year), 17 research assistantships with full tuition reimbursements available (averaging $21,000 per year), 12 teaching assistantships with full tuition reimbursements available (averaging $21,000 per year); Federal Work-Study, scholarships/grants, traineeships, and health care benefits also available. Financial award application deadline: 1/31. *Faculty research:* Biogeosciences, climate and surface processes; energy, environment and society; geographical sciences; geology, geochemistry and geophysics. *Unit head:* David Marchant, Chair, 617-353-3236, E-mail: marchant@bu.edu. *Application contact:* Nora Watson, Graduate Program Coordinator, 617-353-2529, Fax: 617-353-8399, E-mail: norala31@bu.edu.
Website: http://www.bu.edu/earth/

Brigham Young University, Graduate Studies, College of Life Sciences, Department of Plant and Wildlife Sciences, Provo, UT 84604. Offers environmental science (MS); genetics and biotechnology (MS); wildlife and wildlands conservation (MS, PhD). *Faculty:* 24 full-time (1 woman), 1 (woman) part-time/adjunct. *Students:* 12 full-time (6 women), 31 part-time (9 women); includes 4 minority (1 Asian, non-Hispanic/Latino; 3 Hispanic/Latino). Average age 25. 25 applicants, 40% accepted, 9 enrolled. In 2015, 15 master's awarded. *Degree requirements:* For master's, thesis; for doctorate, comprehensive exam, thesis/dissertation, minimum GPA of 3.2, 54 hours (18 dissertation, 36 coursework). *Entrance requirements:* For master's, GRE General Test, minimum GPA of 3.2; for doctorate, GRE, minimum GPA of 3.2. Additional exam requirements/recommendations for international students: Required—TOEFL (minimum score 580 paper-based; 85 iBT). *Application deadline:* 2/1 for domestic and international students. Applications are processed on a rolling basis. Application fee: $50. Electronic applications accepted. *Financial support:* In 2015–16, 42 students received support, including 64 research assistantships with partial tuition reimbursements available (averaging $19,000 per year), 52 teaching assistantships with partial tuition reimbursements available (averaging $19,000 per year); scholarships/grants and tuition waivers (partial) also available. Financial award application deadline: 2/1. *Faculty research:* Environmental science, plant genetics, plant ecology, plant nutrition and pathology, wildlife and wildlands conservation. *Total annual research expenditures:* $2.8 million. *Unit head:* Brock R. McMillan, Chair, 801-422-3527, Fax: 801-422-0008, E-mail: brock_mcmillan@byu.edu. *Application contact:* Bradley D. Geary, Graduate Coordinator, 801-422-1228, Fax: 801-422-0008, E-mail: bradley_geary@byu.edu.
Website: http://pws.byu.edu/home/

Bryant University, College of Arts and Sciences, Smithfield, RI 02917. Offers communication (MA), including general communication; global environmental studies (MS). *Program availability:* Part-time, evening/weekend. *Faculty:* 12 full-time (7 women). *Students:* 2 full-time (1 woman), 13 part-time (9 women); includes 1 minority (Two or more races, non-Hispanic/Latino). Average age 34. 27 applicants, 41% accepted, 4 enrolled. In 2015, 7 master's awarded. *Entrance requirements:* For master's, GRE. Additional exam requirements/recommendations for international students: Required—TOEFL (minimum score 550 paper-based; 80 iBT). *Application deadline:* For fall admission, 8/15 for domestic and international students; for spring admission, 1/15 for domestic and international students; for summer admission, 5/15 for domestic and international students. Applications are processed on a rolling basis. Application fee: $80. Electronic applications accepted. *Expenses:* $932 per credit hour. *Financial support:* Fellowships and research assistantships available. Financial award applicants required to submit FAFSA. *Unit head:* Wendy Samter, Dean, College of Arts and Sciences, 401-232-6944, E-mail: wsamter@bryant.edu. *Application contact:* Jeffrey G. Hunter, Graduate and Professional Studies, 401-480-8148, E-mail: gps@bryant.edu.
Website: http://gradschool.bryant.edu/arts-and-sciences/

California Institute of Technology, Division of Geological and Planetary Sciences, Pasadena, CA 91125-0001. Offers environmental science and engineering (MS, PhD); geobiology (MS, PhD); geochemistry (MS, PhD); geology (MS, PhD); geophysics (MS, PhD); planetary science (MS, PhD). *Degree requirements:* For doctorate, thesis/dissertation. *Entrance requirements:* For doctorate, GRE General Test. Additional exam requirements/recommendations for international students: Required—TOEFL; Recommended—IELTS, TWE. Electronic applications accepted. *Faculty research:* Planetary surfaces, evolution of anaerobic respiratory processes, structural geology and tectonics, theoretical and numerical seismology, global biogeochemical cycles.

California State Polytechnic University, Pomona, John T. Lyle Center for Regenerative Studies, Pomona, CA 91768-2557. Offers MS. *Program availability:* Part-time. *Students:* 10 full-time (8 women), 8 part-time (5 women); includes 10 minority (3 Asian, non-Hispanic/Latino; 5 Hispanic/Latino; 2 Two or more races, non-Hispanic/Latino), 1 international. Average age 28. 14 applicants., 9 enrolled. In 2015, 12 master's awarded. *Application deadline:* For fall admission, 5/1 priority date for domestic students; for winter admission, 10/15 priority date for domestic students; for spring admission, 1/20 priority date for domestic students. Applications are processed on a rolling basis. Application fee: $55. Electronic applications accepted. *Expenses:* Tuition, state resident: full-time $6738. Tuition, nonresident: full-time $13,434. *Required fees:* $1504. Tuition and fees vary according to course load, degree level and program. *Financial support:* Application deadline: 3/2; applicants required to submit FAFSA. *Unit head:* Dr. Denise L. Lawrence, Graduate Coordinator, 909-869-2674, Fax: 909-869-4331, E-mail: dllawrence@cpp.edu.
Website: http://www.cpp.edu/~crs/

California State University, Chico, Office of Graduate Studies, College of Natural Sciences, Department of Geological and Environmental Sciences, Program in Environmental Science, Chico, CA 95929-0722. Offers MS, PSM. *Program availability:* Part-time. *Students:* 1 full-time. *Degree requirements:* For master's, comprehensive exam, thesis. *Entrance requirements:* For master's, GRE, two letters of recommendation, faculty mentor, statement of purpose. Additional exam requirements/recommendations for international students: Required—TOEFL (minimum score 550 paper-based; 80 iBT), IELTS (minimum score 6.5), PTE (minimum score 59). *Application deadline:* For fall admission, 3/1 priority date for domestic students, 3/1 for international students; for spring admission, 9/15 priority date for domestic students, 9/15 for international students. Application fee: $55. Electronic applications accepted. *Expenses: Tuition, area resident:* Full-time $4146; part-time $2730. *Financial support:* Research assistantships, teaching assistantships, and career-related internships or fieldwork available. Financial award application deadline: 3/1; financial award applicants required to submit FAFSA. *Unit head:* Dr. David L. Brown, Chair, 530-898-1995, Fax: 530-898-5234, E-mail: geos@csuchico.edu. *Application contact:* Judy L. Rice, Graduate Admissions Coordinator, 530-898-5416, Fax: 530-898-3342, E-mail: jlrice@csuchico.edu.

Website: http://catalog.csuchico.edu/viewer/15/GEOS/

California State University, East Bay, Office of Graduate Studies Programs, College of Science, Department of Earth and Environmental Sciences, Hayward, CA 94542-3000. Offers geology (MS), including environmental geology, geology. *Program availability:* Part-time, evening/weekend. *Students:* 4 full-time (2 women), 13 part-time (5 women); includes 6 minority (1 American Indian or Alaska Native, non-Hispanic/Latino; 2 Asian, non-Hispanic/Latino; 3 Hispanic/Latino), 2 international. Average age 30. 15 applicants, 73% accepted, 7 enrolled. In 2015, 8 master's awarded. *Degree requirements:* For master's, thesis or project. *Entrance requirements:* For master's, GRE, minimum GPA of 2.75 in field, 2.5 overall; 2 letters of recommendation. Additional exam requirements/recommendations for international students: Required—TOEFL (minimum score 550 paper-based). *Application deadline:* For fall admission, 6/30 for domestic and international students. Application fee: $55. Electronic applications accepted. *Financial support:* Career-related internships or fieldwork, Federal Work-Study, and institutionally sponsored loans available. Support available to part-time students. Financial award application deadline: 3/2; financial award applicants required to submit FAFSA. *Faculty research:* Hydrology, seismic activity; origins of life. *Unit head:* Jean E. Moran, Chair, 510-885-2491, E-mail: jean.moran@csueastbay.edu.

Website: http://www20.csueastbay.edu/csci/departments/earth/

California State University, Northridge, Graduate Studies, College of Science and Mathematics, Department of Chemistry and Biochemistry, Northridge, CA 91330. Offers biochemistry (MS); chemistry (MS), including chemistry, environmental chemistry. *Faculty:* 14 full-time (4 women), 30 part-time/adjunct (10 women). *Students:* 2 full-time (1 woman), 30 part-time (12 women); includes 15 minority (1 Black or African American, non-Hispanic/Latino; 7 Asian, non-Hispanic/Latino; 7 Hispanic/Latino), 3 international. Average age 26. 69 applicants, 23% accepted, 8 enrolled. *Degree requirements:* For master's, thesis. *Entrance requirements:* For master's, GRE General Test or minimum GPA of 3.0. Additional exam requirements/recommendations for international students: Required—TOEFL. *Application deadline:* For fall admission, 11/30 for domestic students. Application fee: $55. Electronic applications accepted. *Financial support:* Teaching assistantships available. Support available to part-time students. Financial award application deadline: 3/1. *Unit head:* Eric Kelson, Chair, 818-677-3381.

Website: http://www.csun.edu/chemistry/

California State University, San Bernardino, Graduate Studies, College of Natural Sciences, Program in Earth and Environmental Sciences, San Bernardino, CA 92407. Offers MS. *Students:* 1 (woman) full-time, 4 part-time (1 woman); includes 1 minority (American Indian or Alaska Native, non-Hispanic/Latino). 7 applicants, 43% accepted, 1 enrolled. In 2015, 8 master's awarded. *Entrance requirements:* Additional exam requirements/recommendations for international students: Required—TOEFL. *Application deadline:* For fall admission, 7/16 for domestic students; for winter admission, 10/16 for domestic students; for spring admission, 1/22 for domestic students. Application fee: $55. *Expenses:* Tuition, state resident: full-time $7843; part-time $5011.20 per year. Tuition and fees vary according to course load, degree level, program and reciprocity agreements. *Unit head:* Dr. Joan E. Frysxell, Graduate Coordinator, 909-537-5311, E-mail: jfryxell@csusb.edu. *Application contact:* Dr. Jeffrey Thompson, Dean of Graduate Studies, 909-537-5058, E-mail: jthompso@csusb.edu.

Carnegie Mellon University, Mellon College of Science, Department of Chemistry, Pittsburgh, PA 15213-3891. Offers atmospheric chemistry (PhD); bioinorganic chemistry (PhD); bioorganic chemistry and chemical biology (PhD); biophysical chemistry (PhD); catalysis (PhD); green and environmental chemistry (PhD); materials and nanoscience (PhD); renewable energy (PhD); sensors, probes, and imaging (PhD); spectroscopy and single molecule analysis (PhD); theoretical and computational chemistry (PhD). *Program availability:* Part-time. Terminal master's awarded for partial completion of doctoral program. *Degree requirements:* For doctorate, thesis/dissertation, departmental qualifying and oral exams, teaching experience. *Entrance requirements:* For doctorate, GRE General Test, GRE Subject Test. Additional exam requirements/recommendations for international students: Required—TOEFL. Electronic applications accepted. *Faculty research:* Physical and theoretical chemistry, chemical synthesis, biophysical/bioinorganic chemistry.

Christopher Newport University, Graduate Studies, Environmental Science Program, Newport News, VA 23606-3072. Offers MS. *Program availability:* Part-time. *Faculty:* 16 full-time (7 women), 1 part-time/adjunct (0 women). *Students:* 8 full-time (7 women), 22 part-time (10 women); includes 1 minority (Hispanic/Latino). Average age 27. 10 applicants, 80% accepted, 7 enrolled. In 2015, 8 master's awarded. *Degree requirements:* For master's, comprehensive exam, thesis (for some programs). *Entrance requirements:* For master's, GRE General Test, minimum GPA of 3.0. Additional exam requirements/recommendations for international students: Required—TOEFL (minimum score 580 paper-based; 92 iBT), IELTS (minimum score 7). *Application deadline:* For fall admission, 7/15 for domestic students, 4/1 for international students; for spring admission, 11/1 for domestic students, 10/1 for international students; for summer admission, 3/15 for domestic students, 3/1 for international students. Applications are processed on a rolling basis. Application fee: $50. Electronic applications accepted. *Expenses:* Tuition, state resident: full-time $6444; part-time $358 per credit hour. Tuition, nonresident: full-time $14,706; part-time $817 per credit hour. *Required fees:* $3690; $205 per credit hour. Tuition and fees vary according to course load. *Financial support:* In 2015–16, 17 students received support, including 9 fellowships with full tuition reimbursements available (averaging $30,000 per year), 3 research assistantships with full tuition reimbursements available (averaging $2,000 per year), 5 teaching assistantships (averaging $1,500 per year); scholarships/grants and unspecified assistantships also available. Financial award application deadline: 3/1; financial award applicants required to submit FAFSA. *Faculty research:* Wetlands ecology and restoration, aquatic ecology, wetlands mitigation, greenhouse gases. *Total annual research expenditures:* $703,453. *Unit head:* Dr. Robert Atkinson, Coordinator, 757-594-7619, Fax: 757-594-7209, E-mail: atkinson@cnu.edu. *Application contact:* Lyn Sawyer, Associate Director, Graduate Admissions and Records, 757-594-7544, Fax: 757-594-7649, E-mail: gradstdy@cnu.edu.

Clarkson University, Graduate School, Institute for a Sustainable Environment, Program in Environmental Science and Engineering, Potsdam, NY 13699. Offers MS, PhD. *Program availability:* Part-time. *Students:* 21 full-time (9 women), 1 part-time (0 women), 13 international. Average age 28. 24 applicants, 50% accepted, 7 enrolled. In 2015, 2 master's, 1 doctorate awarded. Terminal master's awarded for partial completion of doctoral program. *Degree requirements:* For master's, thesis; for doctorate, comprehensive exam, thesis/dissertation, departmental qualifying exam. *Entrance requirements:* For master's and doctorate, GRE, transcripts of all college coursework, resume, personal statement, three letters of recommendation. Additional exam requirements/recommendations for international students: Required—TOEFL (minimum score 550 paper-based, 80 iBT) or IELTS (minimum score 6.5). *Application deadline:* For fall admission, 1/30 priority date for domestic and international students; for spring admission, 9/1 priority date for domestic and international students. Applications are processed on a rolling basis. Application fee: $25 ($35 for international students). Electronic applications accepted. *Financial support:* In 2015–16, 19 students received support, including fellowships with full tuition reimbursements available (averaging $24,510 per year), 10 research assistantships with full tuition reimbursements available (averaging $24,510 per year), 4 teaching assistantships with full tuition reimbursements available (averaging $24,510 per year); scholarships/grants, tuition waivers (partial), and unspecified assistantships also available. *Faculty research:* Biological, chemical, physical and social systems, renewable energy, environmental health. *Unit head:* Dr. Susan Powers, Interim Director of the Institute for a Sustainable Environment/Associate Director of Sustainability, 315-268-6542, Fax: 315-268-4291, E-mail: spowers@clarkson.edu. *Application contact:* Carmen Camp, Administrative Assistant, 315-268-2318, Fax: 315-268-4291, E-mail: isegrad@clarkson.edu.

Website: http://www.clarkson.edu/ese/

Clemson University, Graduate School, College of Agriculture, Forestry and Life Sciences, Department of Plant and Environmental Sciences, Clemson, SC 29634-0310. Offers entomology (MS, PhD); plant and environmental sciences (MS, PhD). *Program availability:* Part-time. *Faculty:* 50 full-time (11 women), 2 part-time/adjunct (1 woman). *Students:* 44 full-time (18 women), 27 part-time (9 women); includes 2 minority (1 Black or African American, non-Hispanic/Latino; 1 Two or more races, non-Hispanic/Latino), 25 international. Average age 29. 75 applicants, 49% accepted, 26 enrolled. In 2015, 20 master's, 11 doctorates awarded. *Degree requirements:* For master's, thesis; for doctorate, comprehensive exam, thesis/dissertation. *Entrance requirements:* For master's and doctorate, GRE General Test, unofficial transcripts, letters of recommendation. Additional exam requirements/recommendations for international students: Required—TOEFL (minimum score 80 iBT), IELTS (minimum score 6.5). *Application deadline:* Applications are processed on a rolling basis. Application fee: $80 ($90 for international students). Electronic applications accepted. *Expenses:* $4,060 per semester full-time resident, $8,103 per semester full-time non-resident, $448 per credit hour part-time resident, $898 per credit hour part-time non-resident. *Financial support:* In 2015–16, 47 students received support, including 3 fellowships with partial tuition reimbursements available (averaging $5,000 per year), 32 research assistantships with partial tuition reimbursements available (averaging $17,587 per year), 12 teaching assistantships with partial tuition reimbursements available (averaging $14,826 per year); health care benefits and unspecified assistantships also available. Financial award application deadline: 2/15. *Total annual research expenditures:* $2.3 million. *Unit head:* Dr. Patricia Zungoli, Interim Department Chair, 864-656-5041, E-mail: pzngl@clemson.edu. *Application contact:* Dr. Alan Johnson, Graduate Program Coordinator, 864-656-6390, E-mail: alanj@clemson.edu.

Website: http://www.clemson.edu/cafls/departments/plant-environmental-sciences/index.html

Clemson University, Graduate School, College of Agriculture, Forestry and Life Sciences, Program in Environmental Toxicology, Clemson, SC 29634. Offers MS, PhD. *Faculty:* 18 full-time (7 women). *Students:* 13 full-time (9 women), 1 part-time (0 women); includes 3 minority (1 Asian, non-Hispanic/Latino; 1 Hispanic/Latino; 1 Two or more races, non-Hispanic/Latino), 2 international. Average age 25. 21 applicants, 14% accepted, 4 enrolled. In 2015, 1 master's, 4 doctorates awarded. *Degree requirements:* For master's, thesis; for doctorate, comprehensive exam, thesis/dissertation. *Entrance requirements:* For master's and doctorate, GRE General Test, unofficial transcripts, letters of recommendation. Additional exam requirements/recommendations for international students: Required—TOEFL (minimum score 80 iBT), IELTS (minimum score 6.5). *Application deadline:* For fall admission, 2/1 for domestic and international students. Application fee: $80 ($90 for international students). Electronic applications accepted. *Expenses:* $4,060 per semester full-time resident, $8,103 per semester full-time non-resident, $448 per credit hour part-time resident, $898 per credit hour part-time non-resident. *Financial support:* In 2015–16, 15 students received support, including 5 research assistantships with partial tuition reimbursements available (averaging $22,200 per year), 10 teaching assistantships with partial tuition reimbursements available (averaging $20,700 per year); health care benefits also available. Financial award application deadline: 2/1. *Faculty research:* Immunotoxicology, mechanistic toxicology, aquatic toxicology, wildlife toxicology, environmental toxicology. *Unit head:* Dr. Joseph Culin, Associate Dean for Research and Graduate Studies, 864-656-2810, E-mail: jculin@clemson.edu. *Application contact:* Dr. Peter van den Hurk, Program Coordinator, 864-656-3594, E-mail: pvdhurk@clemson.edu.

Website: http://www.clemson.edu/entox/

Cleveland State University, College of Graduate Studies, College of Sciences and Health Professions, Department of Biological, Geological, and Environmental Sciences, Cleveland, OH 44115. Offers biology (MS); environmental science (MS); regulatory biology (PhD). *Program availability:* Part-time. *Faculty:* 18 full-time (5 women), 54 part-time/adjunct (22 women). *Students:* 53 full-time (28 women), 15 part-time (10 women); includes 6 minority (2 Black or African American, non-Hispanic/Latino; 4 Asian, non-Hispanic/Latino), 35 international. Average age 30. 40 applicants, 63% accepted, 9 enrolled. In 2015, 6 master's, 12 doctorates awarded. Terminal master's awarded for partial completion of doctoral program. *Degree requirements:* For master's, comprehensive exam (for some programs), thesis (for some programs), thesis defense; for doctorate, comprehensive exam, thesis/dissertation, dissertation defense. *Entrance requirements:* For master's, GRE General Test, 3 letters of recommendation; for doctorate, GRE General Test, 3 letters of recommendation; 1-2 page essay; statement of career goals and research interests. Additional exam requirements/recommendations for international students: Required—TOEFL (minimum score 550 paper-based; 78 iBT), IELTS. *Application deadline:* For fall admission, 7/1 priority date for domestic students, 5/15 priority date for international students; for spring admission, 11/15 priority date for domestic students, 11/1 for international students; for summer admission, 4/1 for domestic students, 3/15 for international students. Applications are processed on a rolling basis. Application fee: $30. Electronic applications accepted. *Expenses:* Tuition, state resident: full-time $9565. Tuition, nonresident: full-time $17,980. Tuition and fees vary according to program. *Financial support:* In 2015–16, 33 students received support, including 1 fellowship with full tuition reimbursement available (averaging $21,000 per year), 16 research assistantships with full tuition reimbursements available (averaging $21,000 per year), 31 teaching assistantships with full tuition reimbursements available (averaging $21,000 per year); tuition waivers and unspecified

assistantships also available. Financial award applicants required to submit FAFSA. *Faculty research:* Cardiopulmonary pathology, signaling pathways and RNA interference, toxoplasmosis, plant ecology, biology and biochemistry of nitric oxide. *Unit head:* Dr. Crystal M. Weyman, Chairperson/Professor, 216-687-6971, Fax: 216-687-6972, E-mail: c.weyman@csuohio.edu. *Application contact:* Dr. Girish C. Shukla, Associate Professor and Graduate Program Director, 216-687-2395, Fax: 216-687-6972, E-mail: g.shukla@csuohio.edu.
Website: http://www.csuohio.edu/sciences/bges

The College at Brockport, State University of New York, School of Science and Mathematics, Department of Environmental Science and Biology, Brockport, NY 14420-2997. Offers MS. *Program availability:* Part-time. *Faculty:* 6 full-time (1 woman), 1 (woman) part-time/adjunct. *Students:* 14 full-time (8 women), 14 part-time (4 women). 16 applicants, 88% accepted, 13 enrolled. In 2015, 8 master's awarded. *Degree requirements:* For master's, comprehensive exam, thesis. *Entrance requirements:* For master's, minimum GPA of 3.0, letters of recommendation, sample of scientific writing, statement of objectives. Additional exam requirements/recommendations for international students: Required—TOEFL (minimum score 550 paper-based; 79 iBT), IELTS (minimum score 6.5). *Application deadline:* For fall admission, 4/15 priority date for domestic and international students; for spring admission, 11/15 priority date for domestic and international students; for summer admission, 4/15 priority date for domestic and international students. Application fee: $50. Electronic applications accepted. *Expenses:* $11,840 per academic year. *Financial support:* In 2015–16, 2 research assistantships with full tuition reimbursements (averaging $6,000 per year) were awarded; Federal Work-Study, scholarships/grants, and unspecified assistantships also available. Support available to part-time students. Financial award application deadline: 3/15; financial award applicants required to submit FAFSA. *Faculty research:* Aquatic and terrestrial ecology/organismal biology, watersheds and wetlands, persistent toxic chemicals, soil-plant interactions, aquaculture. *Unit head:* Dr. James Haynes, Chairperson, 585-395-5975, Fax: 585-395-5969, E-mail: jhaynes@brockport.edu. *Application contact:* Dr. Jaques Rinchard, Graduate Director, 585-395-5750, Fax: 585-395-5969, E-mail: jrinchar@brockport.edu.
Website: http://www.brockport.edu/envsci/grad/

College of Charleston, Graduate School, School of Sciences and Mathematics, Program in Environmental Studies, Charleston, SC 29424-0001. Offers MS. *Program availability:* Part-time, evening/weekend. *Degree requirements:* For master's, thesis optional, thesis or research internship. *Entrance requirements:* For master's, GRE, minimum GPA of 3.0, 3 letters of recommendation. Additional exam requirements/recommendations for international students: Required—TOEFL (minimum score 81 iBT). Electronic applications accepted. *Expenses:* Contact institution.

College of Staten Island of the City University of New York, Graduate Programs, Division of Science and Technology, Program in Environmental Science, Staten Island, NY 10314-6600. Offers MS. *Program availability:* Part-time, evening/weekend. *Faculty:* 2 full-time, 1 part-time/adjunct. *Students:* 24 part-time. Average age 29. 26 applicants, 31% accepted, 5 enrolled. In 2015, 5 master's awarded. Terminal master's awarded for partial completion of doctoral program. *Degree requirements:* For master's, thirty credits in approved courses with minimum GPA of 3.0. *Entrance requirements:* For master's, GRE General Test, 1 year of course work in chemistry, physics, calculus, and ecology; minimum overall average grade of B-, or the equivalent, in undergraduate work and B average, or the equivalent, in undergraduate science and engineering courses; bachelor's degree in a natural science or engineering; interview with faculty. Additional exam requirements/recommendations for international students: Required—TOEFL (minimum score 550 paper-based; 79 iBT), IELTS (minimum score 6.5). *Application deadline:* For fall admission, 4/22 priority date for international students; for spring admission, 11/19 priority date for international students. Applications are processed on a rolling basis. Application fee: $125. Electronic applications accepted. *Expenses:* Tuition, state resident: full-time $10,130; part-time $425 per credit. Tuition, nonresident: full-time $18,720; part-time $780 per credit. *Required fees:* $181.10 per semester. Tuition and fees vary according to program. *Financial support:* Applicants required to submit FAFSA. *Unit head:* Dr. Alfred Levine, Graduate Program Coordinator, 718-982-2822, Fax: 718-982-3923, E-mail: alfred.levine@csi.cuny.edu. *Application contact:* Sasha Spence, Associate Director for Graduate Admissions, 718-982-2019, Fax: 718-982-2500, E-mail: sasha.spence@csi.cuny.edu.
Website: http://www.csi.cuny.edu/catalog/graduate/master-of-science-in-environmental-science-ms.htm

The College of William and Mary, Faculty of Arts and Sciences, Department of Applied Science, Williamsburg, VA 23187-8795. Offers accelerator science (PhD); applied mathematics (PhD); applied mechanics (PhD); applied robotics (PhD); applied science (MS); atmospheric and environmental science (PhD); computational neuroscience (PhD); interface, thin film and surface science (PhD); lasers and optics (PhD); magnetic resonance (PhD); materials science and engineering (PhD); mathematical and computational biology (PhD); medical imaging (PhD); nanotechnology (PhD); neuroscience (PhD); non-destructive evaluation (PhD); polymer chemistry (PhD); remote sensing (PhD). *Program availability:* Part-time. *Faculty:* 7 full-time (1 woman), 1 part-time/adjunct (0 women). *Students:* 26 full-time (9 women), 3 part-time (1 woman); includes 5 minority (2 Black or African American, non-Hispanic/Latino; 1 Asian, non-Hispanic/Latino; 2 Hispanic/Latino), 12 international. Average age 28. 24 applicants, 46% accepted, 6 enrolled. In 2015, 2 master's, 6 doctorates awarded. Terminal master's awarded for partial completion of doctoral program. *Degree requirements:* For master's, comprehensive exam, thesis; for doctorate, comprehensive exam, thesis/dissertation, 4 core courses. *Entrance requirements:* For master's and doctorate, GRE General Test, GRE Subject Test. Additional exam requirements/recommendations for international students: Required—TOEFL, TWE. *Application deadline:* For fall admission, 2/3 priority date for domestic students, 2/3 for international students; for spring admission, 10/15 priority date for domestic students, 10/14 for international students. Applications are processed on a rolling basis. Application fee: $45. Electronic applications accepted. *Expenses:* $6,550 per semester; $13,100 per year. *Financial support:* Fellowships, research assistantships, teaching assistantships, Federal Work-Study, health care benefits, tuition waivers (full), and unspecified assistantships available. Financial award application deadline: 4/15; financial award applicants required to submit FAFSA. *Faculty research:* Computational biology, non-destructive evaluation, neurophysiology, lasers and optics. *Total annual research expenditures:* $1.7 million. *Unit head:* Dr. Christopher Del Negro, Chair, 757-221-7808, Fax: 757-221-2050, E-mail: cadeln@wm.edu. *Application contact:* Lianne Rios Ashburne, Graduate Program Coordinator, 757-221-2563, Fax: 757-221-2050, E-mail: lrashburne@wm.edu.
Website: http://www.wm.edu/as/appliedscience

Columbia University, Graduate School of Arts and Sciences, New York, NY 10027. Offers African-American studies (MA); American studies (MA); anthropology (MA, PhD); art history and archaeology (MA, PhD); astronomy (PhD); biological sciences (PhD); biotechnology (MA); chemical physics (PhD); chemistry (PhD); classical studies (MA, PhD); classics (MA, PhD); climate and society (MA); conservation biology (MA); earth and environmental sciences (PhD); East Asia: regional studies (MA); East Asian languages and cultures (MA, PhD); ecology, evolution and environmental biology (MA), including conservation biology; ecology, evolution, and environmental biology (PhD), including ecology and evolutionary biology, evolutionary primatology; economics (MA, PhD); English and comparative literature (MA, PhD); French and Romance philology (MA, PhD); Germanic languages (MA, PhD); global French studies (MA); global thought (MA); Hispanic cultural studies (MA); history (PhD); history and literature (MA); human rights studies (MA); Islamic studies (MA); Italian (MA, PhD); Japanese pedagogy (MA); Jewish studies (MA); Latin America and the Caribbean: regional studies (MA); Latin American and Iberian cultures (PhD); mathematics (MA, PhD), including finance (MA); medieval and Renaissance studies (MA); Middle Eastern, South Asian, and African studies (MA, PhD); modern art: critical and curatorial studies (MA); modern European studies (MA); museum anthropology (MA); music (DMA, PhD); oral history (MA); philosophical foundations of physics (MA); philosophy (MA, PhD); physics (PhD); political science (MA, PhD); psychology (PhD); quantitative methods in the social sciences (MA); religion (MA, PhD); Russia, Eurasia and East Europe: regional studies (MA); Russian translation (MA); Slavic cultures (MA); Slavic languages (MA, PhD); sociology (MA, PhD); South Asian studies (MA); statistics (MA, PhD); theatre (PhD). Dual-degree programs require admission to both Graduate School of Arts and Sciences and another Columbia school. *Program availability:* Part-time. *Students:* 3,030 full-time, 235 part-time; includes 861 minority (88 Black or African American, non-Hispanic/Latino; 5 American Indian or Alaska Native, non-Hispanic/Latino; 517 Asian, non-Hispanic/Latino; 159 Hispanic/Latino; 4 Native Hawaiian or other Pacific Islander, non-Hispanic/Latino; 88 Two or more races, non-Hispanic/Latino), 1,697 international. 13,288 applicants, 21% accepted, 1162 enrolled. In 2015, 1,061 master's, 553 doctorates awarded. Terminal master's awarded for partial completion of doctoral program. *Degree requirements:* For master's, variable foreign language requirement, comprehensive exam (for some programs), thesis (for some programs); for doctorate, variable foreign language requirement, comprehensive exam (for some programs), thesis/dissertation. *Entrance requirements:* For master's and doctorate, GRE General Test, GRE Subject Test (for some programs). Additional exam requirements/recommendations for international students: Required—TOEFL, IELTS. Application fee: $105. Electronic applications accepted. *Financial support:* Fellowships, research assistantships, teaching assistantships, career-related internships or fieldwork, Federal Work-Study, institutionally sponsored loans, scholarships/grants, traineeships, health care benefits, tuition waivers, and unspecified assistantships available. Support available to part-time students. Financial award application deadline: 12/15. *Unit head:* Carlos J. Alonso, Dean of the Graduate School of Arts and Sciences, 212-854-5177. *Application contact:* GSAS Office of Admissions, 212-854-8903, E-mail: gsas-admissions@columbia.edu.
Website: http://gsas.columbia.edu/

Columbia University, School of International and Public Affairs, Program in Environmental Science and Policy, New York, NY 10027. Offers MPA. Program admits applicants for late May/early June start only. *Degree requirements:* For master's, workshops. *Entrance requirements:* For master's, GRE, previous course work in biology and chemistry, earth sciences (recommended), economics (strongly recommended). Additional exam requirements/recommendations for international students: Required—TOEFL. Electronic applications accepted. *Faculty research:* Ecological management of enclosed ecosystems vegetation dynamics, environmental policy and management, energy policy, nuclear waste policy, environmental and natural resource economics and policy, carbon sequestration, urban planning, environmental risk assessment/toxicology, environmental justice.

See Display on next page and Close-Up on page 381.

Columbus State University, Graduate Studies, College of Education and Health Professions, Department of Teacher Education, Columbus, GA 31907-5645. Offers curriculum and instruction in accomplished teaching (M Ed); early childhood education (M Ed, MAT, Ed S); middle grades education (M Ed, MAT, Ed S); secondary education (M Ed, MAT, Ed S), including biology (MAT), chemistry (MAT), earth and space science (MAT), English/language arts, general science (M Ed), history (MAT), mathematics, science (Ed S), social science (M Ed, Ed S); special education (M Ed, MAT, Ed S), including general curriculum (M Ed, MAT); teacher leadership (M Ed). *Accreditation:* NCATE. *Program availability:* Part-time, evening/weekend, 100% online, blended/hybrid learning. *Faculty:* 15 full-time (10 women), 26 part-time/adjunct (21 women). *Students:* 84 full-time (68 women), 199 part-time (153 women); includes 106 minority (96 Black or African American, non-Hispanic/Latino; 3 Asian, non-Hispanic/Latino; 5 Hispanic/Latino; 2 Two or more races, non-Hispanic/Latino), 6 international. Average age 35. 174 applicants, 62% accepted, 81 enrolled. In 2015, 74 master's, 10 other advanced degrees awarded. *Degree requirements:* For Ed S, thesis or alternative. *Entrance requirements:* For master's, GRE General Test, minimum undergraduate GPA of 2.75; for Ed S, GRE General Test, minimum undergraduate GPA of 2.75, graduate 3.0. Additional exam requirements/recommendations for international students: Required—TOEFL (minimum score 550 paper-based; 79 iBT). *Application deadline:* For fall admission, 6/30 for domestic students, 5/1 for international students; for spring admission, 11/1 for domestic and international students; for summer admission, 3/1 for domestic and international students. Applications are processed on a rolling basis. Application fee: $50. Electronic applications accepted. *Expenses:* Tuition, state resident: full-time $4804; part-time $2412 per semester hour. Tuition, nonresident: full-time $19,218; part-time $9612 per semester hour. *Required fees:* $1830; $1830 per unit. Tuition and fees vary according to program. *Financial support:* In 2015–16, 203 students received support, including 22 research assistantships with partial tuition reimbursements available (averaging $3,000 per year); career-related internships or fieldwork, Federal Work-Study, institutionally sponsored loans, scholarships/grants, tuition waivers (partial), and unspecified assistantships also available. Support available to part-time students. Financial award application deadline: 5/1; financial award applicants required to submit FAFSA. *Unit head:* Dr. Jan Burcham, Department Chair, 706-507-8519, Fax: 706-568-3134, E-mail: burcham_jan@columbusstate.edu. *Application contact:* Kristin Williams, Director of International and Graduate Recruitment, 706-507-8848, Fax: 706-568-5091, E-mail: williams_kristin@columbusstate.edu.
Website: http://te.columbusstate.edu/

Columbus State University, Graduate Studies, College of Letters and Sciences, Department of Earth and Space Sciences, Columbus, GA 31907-5645. Offers natural sciences (MS). *Program availability:* Part-time, evening/weekend. *Faculty:* 4 full-time (0 women), 5 part-time/adjunct (0 women). *Students:* 16 full-time (10 women), 3 part-time (all women); includes 4 minority (1 Black or African American, non-Hispanic/Latino; 1 American Indian or Alaska Native, non-Hispanic/Latino; 1 Asian, non-Hispanic/Latino; 1 Two or more races, non-Hispanic/Latino), 2 international. Average age 27. 22 applicants, 45% accepted, 8 enrolled. In 2015, 7 master's awarded. *Degree requirements:* For master's, thesis. *Entrance requirements:* For master's, GRE General Test, minimum GPA of 3.0. Additional exam requirements/recommendations for international students: Required—TOEFL (minimum score 550 paper-based; 79 iBT). *Application deadline:* For fall admission, 6/30 priority date for domestic students, 5/1 for international students; for spring admission, 11/1 for domestic and international students; for summer admission, 3/1 for domestic and international students. Applications are processed on a rolling basis. Application fee: $50. Electronic applications accepted. *Expenses:* Tuition, state resident: full-time $4804; part-time $2412 per semester hour. Tuition, nonresident: full-time $19,218; part-time $9612 per

Environmental Sciences

semester hour. *Required fees:* $1830; $1830 per unit. Tuition and fees vary according to program. *Financial support:* In 2015–16, 9 students received support, including 12 research assistantships with partial tuition reimbursements available (averaging $3,000 per year); career-related internships or fieldwork, Federal Work-Study, institutionally sponsored loans, scholarships/grants, and unspecified assistantships also available. Support available to part-time students. Financial award application deadline: 5/1; financial award applicants required to submit FAFSA. *Unit head:* Dr. William Frazier, Department Chair, 706-507-8092, E-mail: frazier_bill@columbusstate.edu. *Application contact:* Kristin Williams, Director of International and Graduate Recruitment, 706-507-8848, Fax: 706-568-5091, E-mail: williams_kristin@columbusstate.edu.

Website: http://ess.columbusstate.edu/

Cornell University, Graduate School, Graduate Fields of Agriculture and Life Sciences, Field of Soil and Crop Sciences, Ithaca, NY 14853-0001. Offers agronomy (MS, PhD); environmental information science (MS, PhD); environmental management (MPS); field crop science (MS, PhD); soil science (MS, PhD). *Degree requirements:* For master's, thesis (MS); for doctorate, comprehensive exam, thesis/dissertation. *Entrance requirements:* For master's and doctorate, GRE General Test, 2 letters of recommendation. Additional exam requirements/recommendations for international students: Required—TOEFL (minimum score 550 paper-based; 77 iBT). Electronic applications accepted. *Faculty research:* Soil chemistry, physics and biology; crop physiology and management; environmental information science and modeling; international agriculture; weed science.

Dalhousie University, Faculty of Agriculture, Halifax, NS B3H 4R2, Canada. Offers agriculture (M Sc), including air quality, animal behavior, animal molecular genetics, animal nutrition, animal technology, aquaculture, botany, crop management, crop physiology, ecology, environmental microbiology, food science, horticulture, nutrient management, pest management, physiology, plant biotechnology, plant pathology, soil chemistry, soil fertility, waste management and composting, water quality. *Program availability:* Part-time. *Degree requirements:* For master's, thesis, ATC Exam Teaching Assistantship. *Entrance requirements:* For master's, honors B Sc, minimum GPA of 3.0. Additional exam requirements/recommendations for international students: Required—TOEFL (minimum score 580 paper-based; 92 iBT), IELTS, Michigan English Language Assessment Battery, CanTEST, CAEL. *Faculty research:* Bio-product development, organic agriculture, nutrient management, air and water quality, agricultural biotechnology.

Drexel University, College of Arts and Sciences, Program in Environmental Science, Philadelphia, PA 19104-2875. Offers MS, PhD. *Program availability:* Part-time, evening/weekend. Terminal master's awarded for partial completion of doctoral program. *Degree requirements:* For master's, thesis optional; for doctorate, thesis/dissertation. Electronic applications accepted.

Duke University, Graduate School, Doctoral Program in Environment, Durham, NC 27708-0328. Offers PhD. *Degree requirements:* For doctorate, variable foreign language requirement, thesis/dissertation. *Entrance requirements:* For doctorate, GRE General Test. Additional exam requirements/recommendations for international students: Required—TOEFL (minimum score 577 paper-based; 90 iBT) or IELTS (minimum score 7). Electronic applications accepted.

Duke University, Nicholas School of the Environment, Durham, NC 27708. Offers environment (PhD); environmental management (MEM); forestry (MF); JD/AM. Application deadline for PhD program is December 8. *Program availability:* Online learning. *Degree requirements:* For doctorate, variable foreign language requirement, thesis/dissertation. *Entrance requirements:* For master's, GRE General Test, previous

course work in natural or social sciences relevant to environmental interests, college calculus, college statistics, and microeconomics or ecology. Additional exam requirements/recommendations for international students: Required—TOEFL (minimum score 577 paper-based; 90 iBT) or IELTS (minimum score 7). Electronic applications accepted. *Faculty research:* Climate change, energy, water quality, ecosystem management and conservation, human and environmental health.

Duquesne University, Bayer School of Natural and Environmental Sciences, Environmental Science and Management Program, Pittsburgh, PA 15282-0001. Offers MS, Certificate, JD/MS, MBA/MS. *Program availability:* Part-time, evening/weekend. *Faculty:* 2 full-time (0 women), 9 part-time/adjunct (1 woman). *Students:* 19 full-time (10 women), 13 part-time (8 women); includes 1 minority (Two or more races, non-Hispanic/Latino), 2 international. Average age 27. 37 applicants, 59% accepted, 14 enrolled. In 2015, 13 master's awarded. *Degree requirements:* For master's, thesis (for some programs), minimum of 37 credit hours (for conservation biology); for Certificate, minimum of 18 credit hours. *Entrance requirements:* For master's, GRE General Test, course work in biology, chemistry, and calculus or statistics; 3 letters of reference; official transcripts; statement of purpose; for Certificate, undergraduate degree, 3 letters of reference, official transcripts, statement of purpose. Additional exam requirements/recommendations for international students: Required—TOEFL (minimum score 90 iBT) or IELTS. *Application deadline:* For fall admission, 4/1 priority date for domestic students, 4/1 for international students; for spring admission, 10/1 priority date for domestic students, 10/1 for international students. Applications are processed on a rolling basis. Application fee: $0. Electronic applications accepted. *Expenses:* $1,218 per credit. *Financial support:* In 2015–16, 25 students received support, including 1 fellowship with full tuition reimbursement available (averaging $18,000 per year), 7 research assistantships (averaging $14,488 per year), 3 teaching assistantships with partial tuition reimbursements available; career-related internships or fieldwork, scholarships/grants, tuition waivers (partial), and unspecified assistantships also available. Financial award application deadline: 5/31. *Faculty research:* Watershed management systems, environmental analytical chemistry, environmental endocrinology, environmental microbiology, aquatic biology. *Total annual research expenditures:* $167,230. *Unit head:* Dr. John Stolz, Director, 412-396-6333, Fax: 412-396-5907, E-mail: stolz@duq.edu. *Application contact:* Heather Costello, Senior Graduate Academic Advisor, 412-396-6339, E-mail: costelloh@duq.edu.

Website: http://www.duq.edu/academics/schools/natural-and-environmental-sciences/academic-programs/environmental-science-and-management

Florida Agricultural and Mechanical University, School of the Environment, Tallahassee, FL 32307. Offers MS, PhD. *Degree requirements:* For master's, thesis; for doctorate, comprehensive exam, thesis/dissertation, oral exam. *Entrance requirements:* For master's and doctorate, GRE General Test, minimum GPA of 3.0. Additional exam requirements/recommendations for international students: Required—TOEFL. *Faculty research:* Environmental chemistry, environmental policy and risk management, aquatic and terrestrial ecology, biomolecular sciences.

Florida Atlantic University, Charles E. Schmidt College of Science, Department of Biological Sciences, Boca Raton, FL 33431-0991. Offers biology (MS, MST); business biotechnology (MS); environmental science (MS); integrative biology (PhD). *Program availability:* Part-time. *Degree requirements:* For master's, thesis (for some programs). *Entrance requirements:* For master's, GRE General Test, minimum GPA of 3.0. Additional exam requirements/recommendations for international students: Required—TOEFL (minimum score 500 paper-based; 61 iBT), IELTS (minimum score 6). *Faculty research:* Ecology of the Everglades, molecular biology and biotechnology, marine biology.

362 www.petersons.com

Peterson's Graduate Programs in the Physical Sciences, Mathematics, Agricultural Sciences, the Environment & Natural Resources 2017

Florida Gulf Coast University, College of Arts and Sciences, Program in Environmental Science, Fort Myers, FL 33965-6565. Offers MS. *Program availability:* Part-time. *Faculty:* 235 full-time (96 women), 142 part-time/adjunct (60 women). *Students:* 17 full-time (10 women), 38 part-time (24 women); includes 4 minority (1 Black or African American, non-Hispanic/Latino; 2 Hispanic/Latino; 1 Two or more races, non-Hispanic/Latino), 1 international. Average age 29. 32 applicants, 69% accepted, 17 enrolled. In 2015, 9 master's awarded. *Entrance requirements:* For master's, GRE General Test, minimum GPA of 3.0. Additional exam requirements/recommendations for international students: Required—TOEFL (minimum score 550 paper-based). *Application deadline:* For fall admission, 2/15 priority date for domestic students. Applications are processed on a rolling basis. Application fee: $30. Electronic applications accepted. *Expenses:* Tuition, state resident: full-time $6974. Tuition, nonresident: full-time $28,170. *Required fees:* $1987. One-time fee: $10 full-time. Tuition and fees vary according to course load and degree level. *Financial support:* In 2015–16, 9 students received support. *Faculty research:* Political issues in environmental science, recycling, environmentally-friendly buildings, pathophysiology, immunotoxicology of marine organisms. *Unit head:* Dr. Brian Bovard, Chair, 239-590-7564, Fax: 239-590-7200, E-mail: bbovard@fgcu.edu. *Application contact:* Edwin Everham, Executive Secretary, 239-590-7169, Fax: 239-590-7200, E-mail: eeverham@fgcu.edu.

Florida Institute of Technology, College of Engineering, Program in Environmental Science, Melbourne, FL 32901-6975. Offers MS, PhD. *Program availability:* Part-time. *Students:* 7 full-time (3 women), 2 international. Average age 33. 22 applicants, 27% accepted, 1 enrolled. *Degree requirements:* For master's, thesis or final exam and extra courses; for doctorate, comprehensive exam, thesis/dissertation, comprehensive and departmental qualifying exams, publication of a major portion of the dissertation. *Entrance requirements:* For master's and doctorate, GRE General Test, 3 letters of recommendations, resume, statement of objectives. Additional exam requirements/recommendations for international students: Required—TOEFL (minimum score 550 paper-based; 79 iBT). *Application deadline:* Applications are processed on a rolling basis. Application fee: $50. Electronic applications accepted. *Expenses: Tuition, area resident:* Full-time $21,690; part-time $1205 per credit hour. *Required fees:* $500. Tuition and fees vary according to degree level, campus/location and program. *Financial support:* Career-related internships or fieldwork and tuition remissions available. Financial award application deadline: 3/1; financial award applicants required to submit FAFSA. *Faculty research:* Remote sensing, aquatic systems, pollution abatement, environmental analysis, marine policy, solid and hazardous resource management. *Unit head:* Dr. John Windsor, Chair, 321-674-7300, E-mail: jwindsor@fit.edu. *Application contact:* Cheryl A Brown, Associate Director of Graduate Admissions, 321-674-7581, Fax: 321-723-9468, E-mail: cbrown@fit.edu.
Website: http://coe.fit.edu/dmes/

Florida International University, College of Arts, Sciences, and Education, Department of Earth and Environment, Program in Environmental Studies, Miami, FL 33199. Offers MS. *Program availability:* Part-time. *Faculty:* 3 full-time (0 women), 1 part-time/adjunct (0 women). *Students:* 19 full-time (10 women), 9 part-time (7 women); includes 15 minority (13 Hispanic/Latino; 2 Two or more races, non-Hispanic/Latino), 3 international. Average age 31. 22 applicants, 32% accepted, 3 enrolled. In 2015, 15 master's awarded. *Degree requirements:* For master's, thesis or alternative. *Entrance requirements:* For master's, GRE General Test, minimum GPA of 3.0, 3 letters of recommendation, letter of intent. Additional exam requirements/recommendations for international students: Required—TOEFL (minimum score 550 paper-based; 80 iBT). *Application deadline:* For fall admission, 3/1 for domestic and international students; for spring admission, 10/1 for domestic students, 9/1 for international students. Applications are processed on a rolling basis. Application fee: $30. Electronic applications accepted. *Expenses:* Tuition, state resident: full-time $10,708; part-time $455.64 per credit hour. Tuition, nonresident: full-time $23,816; part-time $1001.69 per credit hour. *Required fees:* $390; $195 per semester. Tuition and fees vary according to program. *Financial support:* Institutionally sponsored loans and scholarships/grants available. Financial award application deadline: 3/1; financial award applicants required to submit FAFSA. *Unit head:* Dr. Rene Price, Chair, 305-348-3119, Fax: 305-348-6497, E-mail: rene.price@fiu.edu. *Application contact:* Dr. Krishnaswamy Jayachandran, Director, 305-348-6553, E-mail: jayachan@fiu.edu.

Florida State University, The Graduate School, College of Arts and Sciences, Department of Earth, Ocean and Atmospheric Science, Program in Oceanography, Tallahassee, FL 32306-4320. Offers aquatic environmental science (MS, PSM); oceanography (MS, PhD). *Faculty:* 16 full-time (4 women). *Students:* 41 full-time (23 women); includes 4 minority (2 Asian, non-Hispanic/Latino; 1 Hispanic/Latino; 1 Two or more races, non-Hispanic/Latino), 10 international. Average age 26. 47 applicants, 23% accepted, 7 enrolled. In 2015, 3 master's, 1 doctorate awarded. *Degree requirements:* For master's, thesis; for doctorate, comprehensive exam, thesis/dissertation. *Entrance requirements:* For master's and doctorate, GRE General Test, minimum upper-division GPA of 3.0. Additional exam requirements/recommendations for international students: Required—TOEFL (minimum score 550 paper-based; 80 iBT). *Application deadline:* For fall admission, 2/15 priority date for domestic and international students; for spring admission, 9/15 priority date for domestic and international students. Applications are processed on a rolling basis. Application fee: $35. Electronic applications accepted. *Expenses: Tuition, area resident:* Full-time $7263; part-time $403.50 per credit hour. Tuition, nonresident: full-time $18,087; part-time $1004.85 per credit hour. *Required fees:* $1365; $75.81 per credit hour. $20 per semester. Tuition and fees vary according to campus/location. *Financial support:* In 2015–16, 28 students received support, including 2 fellowships with full tuition reimbursements available, 20 research assistantships with full tuition reimbursements available, 8 teaching assistantships with full tuition reimbursements available. Financial award application deadline: 2/15; financial award applicants required to submit FAFSA. *Faculty research:* Trace metals in seawater, currents and waves, modeling, benthic ecology, marine biogeochemistry. *Unit head:* Dr. Jeffrey Chanton, Area Coordinator, 850-644-6700, Fax: 850-644-2581, E-mail: jchanton@fsu.edu. *Application contact:* Michaela Lupiani, Academic Coordinator, 850-644-6205, Fax: 850-644-2581, E-mail: admissions@ocean.fsu.edu.
Website: http://www.eoas.fsu.edu

Gannon University, School of Graduate Studies, College of Engineering and Business, School of Engineering and Computer Science, Program in Environmental Science and Engineering, Erie, PA 16541-0001. Offers environmental health and engineering (MS). *Program availability:* Part-time, evening/weekend. *Students:* 6 full-time (3 women), 3 international. Average age 26. 80 applicants, 26% accepted, 4 enrolled. In 2015, 5 master's awarded. *Degree requirements:* For master's, thesis (for some programs), research paper or project (for some programs). *Entrance requirements:* For master's, GRE, bachelor's degree in science or engineering from an accredited college or university. Additional exam requirements/recommendations for international students: Required—TOEFL (minimum score 79 iBT). *Application deadline:* Applications are processed on a rolling basis. Application fee: $25. Electronic applications accepted. Application fee is waived when completed online. *Financial support:* Federal Work-Study and unspecified assistantships available. Financial award application deadline: 7/1; financial award applicants required to submit FAFSA. *Unit head:* Dr. Harry Diz, Chair, 814-871-7633, E-mail: diz001@gannon.edu. *Application contact:* Bridget Philip, Director of Graduate Admissions, 814-871-7412, E-mail: graduate@gannon.edu.

George Mason University, College of Science, Department of Environmental Science and Policy, Fairfax, VA 22030. Offers aquatic ecology (MS). *Faculty:* 20 full-time (10 women), 6 part-time/adjunct (0 women). *Students:* 58 full-time (37 women), 73 part-time (49 women); includes 21 minority (8 Black or African American, non-Hispanic/Latino; 7 Asian, non-Hispanic/Latino; 5 Hispanic/Latino; 1 Native Hawaiian or other Pacific Islander, non-Hispanic/Latino), 9 international. Average age 35. 40 applicants, 70% accepted, 14 enrolled. In 2015, 22 master's, 13 doctorates awarded. *Degree requirements:* For doctorate, comprehensive exam, thesis/dissertation, internship; seminar. *Entrance requirements:* For master's, GRE, bachelor's degree with minimum GPA of 3.0 in related field; 3 letters of recommendation; expanded goals statement; 2 official copies of transcripts; for doctorate, GRE, bachelor's degree with minimum GPA of 3.0; 3 letters of recommendation; current resume; expanded goals statement; 2 official copies of transcripts. Additional exam requirements/recommendations for international students: Required—TOEFL (minimum score 575 paper-based; 88 iBT), IELTS (minimum score 6.5), PTE (minimum score 59). Application fee: $75 ($80 for international students). Electronic applications accepted. *Financial support:* In 2015–16, 54 students received support, including 6 fellowships (averaging $7,149 per year), 13 research assistantships with tuition reimbursements available (averaging $15,186 per year), 36 teaching assistantships with tuition reimbursements available (averaging $14,546 per year); career-related internships or fieldwork, Federal Work-Study, scholarships/grants, unspecified assistantships, and health care benefits (for full-time research or teaching assistantship recipients) also available. Support available to part-time students. Financial award application deadline: 3/1; financial award applicants required to submit FAFSA. *Faculty research:* Wetland ecosystems, comparative physiology, systematics, molecular phylogenetics, conservation genetics, estuarine and oceanic systems, biodiversity of fungi, environmental and resource management, human ecology. *Total annual research expenditures:* $751,706. *Unit head:* Dr. Robert B. Jonas, Chair, 703-993-7590, Fax: 703-993-1066, E-mail: rjonas@gmu.edu. *Application contact:* Sharon Bloomquist, Graduate Program Coordinator, 703-993-3187, Fax: 703-993-1066, E-mail: sbloomqu@gmu.edu.
Website: http://esp.gmu.edu/

Georgia Southern University, Jack N. Averitt College of Graduate Studies, Allen E. Paulson College of Engineering and Information Technology, Department of Mechanical Engineering, Program in Engineering and Information Technology, Statesboro, GA 30458. Offers engineering and manufacturing management, occupational safety and environmental science (Graduate Certificate). *Students:* 2 full-time (1 woman), 5 part-time (1 woman); includes 2 minority (1 Black or African American, non-Hispanic/Latino; 1 Hispanic/Latino), 1 international. Average age 38. 1 applicant, 100% accepted. *Entrance requirements:* Additional exam requirements/recommendations for international students: Required—TOEFL (minimum score 80 iBT). *Application deadline:* For fall admission, 3/1 priority date for domestic students. Application fee: $50. *Expenses:* Tuition, state resident: full-time $7236; part-time $277 per semester hour. Tuition, nonresident: full-time $27,118; part-time $1105 per semester hour. *Required fees:* $2092. *Financial support:* Research assistantships, teaching assistantships, Federal Work-Study, scholarships/grants, and tuition waivers available. Financial award applicants required to submit FAFSA. *Unit head:* Dr. Mohammad S. Davoud, Chair, 912-478-0540, Fax: 912-478-1455, E-mail: mdavoud@georgiasouthern.edu.

The Graduate Center, City University of New York, Graduate Studies, Program in Earth and Environmental Sciences, New York, NY 10016-4039. Offers PhD. *Degree requirements:* For doctorate, one foreign language, comprehensive exam, thesis/dissertation. *Entrance requirements:* For doctorate, GRE General Test. Additional exam requirements/recommendations for international students: Required—TOEFL. Electronic applications accepted.

Harvard University, Cyprus International Institute for the Environment and Public Health in Association with Harvard School of Public Health, Cambridge, MA 02138. Offers environmental health (MS); environmental/public health (PhD); epidemiology and biostatistics (MS). *Entrance requirements:* For master's and doctorate, GRE, resume/curriculum vitae, 3 letters of recommendation, BA or BS (including diploma and official transcripts). Additional exam requirements/recommendations for international students: Required—TOEFL, IELTS (minimum score 7). Electronic applications accepted. *Faculty research:* Air pollution, climate change, biostatistics, sustainable development, environmental management.

Harvard University, Graduate School of Arts and Sciences, Harvard John A. Paulson School of Engineering and Applied Sciences, Cambridge, MA 02138. Offers applied mathematics (ME, SM, PhD); applied physics (ME, SM, PhD); computational science and engineering (ME, SM); computer science (ME, SM, PhD); design engineering (MDE); engineering science (ME), including electrical engineering (ME, SM, PhD); engineering sciences (SM, PhD), including bioengineering, electrical engineering (ME, SM, PhD), environmental science and engineering, materials science and mechanical engineering. MDE offered in collaboration with Graduate School of Design. *Program availability:* Part-time. *Faculty:* 101 full-time (14 women), 10 part-time/adjunct (1 woman). *Students:* 425 full-time (109 women), 12 part-time (1 woman); includes 70 minority (1 Black or African American, non-Hispanic/Latino; 44 Asian, non-Hispanic/Latino; 17 Hispanic/Latino; 8 Two or more races, non-Hispanic/Latino), 207 international. Average age 27. 2,116 applicants, 11% accepted, 132 enrolled. In 2015, 88 master's, 64 doctorates awarded. Terminal master's awarded for partial completion of doctoral program. *Degree requirements:* For master's, thesis (for ME); for doctorate, comprehensive exam, thesis/dissertation. *Entrance requirements:* For master's and doctorate, GRE General Test, GRE Subject Test (recommended), 3 letters of recommendation. Additional exam requirements/recommendations for international students: Required—TOEFL (minimum score 80 iBT). *Application deadline:* For fall admission, 12/15 priority date for domestic and international students. Application fee: $105. Electronic applications accepted. *Expenses:* Contact institution. *Financial support:* In 2015–16, 353 students received support, including 92 fellowships with full tuition reimbursements available (averaging $25,650 per year), 213 research assistantships with tuition reimbursements available (averaging $34,200 per year), 127 teaching assistantships with tuition reimbursements available (averaging $5,775 per year); health care benefits also available. *Faculty research:* Applied mathematics, applied physics, computer science and electrical engineering, environmental engineering, mechanical and biomedical engineering. *Total annual research expenditures:* $38 million. *Unit head:* Francis J. Doyle, III, Dean, 617-495-5829, Fax: 617-495-5264, E-mail: dean@seas.harvard.edu. *Application contact:* Office of Admissions and Financial Aid, 617-495-5315, E-mail: admissions@seas.harvard.edu.
Website: http://www.seas.harvard.edu/

Howard University, Graduate School, Department of Chemistry, Washington, DC 20059-0002. Offers analytical chemistry (MS, PhD); atmospheric (MS, PhD); biochemistry (MS, PhD); environmental (MS, PhD); inorganic chemistry (MS, PhD); organic chemistry (MS, PhD); physical chemistry (MS, PhD). Terminal master's awarded for partial completion of doctoral program. *Degree requirements:* For master's, comprehensive exam, thesis, teaching experience; for doctorate, comprehensive exam, thesis/dissertation, teaching experience. *Entrance requirements:* For master's, GRE General Test, minimum GPA of 2.7; for doctorate, GRE General Test, minimum GPA of 3.0. Additional exam requirements/recommendations for international students: Required—TOEFL. Electronic applications accepted. *Faculty research:* Synthetic organics, materials, natural products, mass spectrometry.

Humboldt State University, Academic Programs, College of Natural Resources and Sciences, Programs in Environmental Systems, Arcata, CA 95521-8299. Offers environmental systems (MS), including energy, environment and society, environmental resources engineering, geology, math modeling. *Degree requirements:* For master's, thesis. *Entrance requirements:* For master's, GRE, appropriate bachelor's degree, minimum GPA of 2.5, 3 letters of recommendation. Additional exam requirements/recommendations for international students: Required—TOEFL. *Faculty research:* Mathematical modeling, international development technology, geology, environmental resources engineering.

Idaho State University, Office of Graduate Studies, College of Science and Engineering, Civil and Environmental Engineering Department, Pocatello, ID 83209-8060. Offers civil engineering (MS); environmental engineering (MS); environmental science and management (MS). *Program availability:* Part-time. *Degree requirements:* For master's, comprehensive exam (for some programs), thesis optional, thesis project, 2 semesters of seminar. *Entrance requirements:* For master's, GRE. Additional exam requirements/recommendations for international students: Required—TOEFL (minimum score 550 paper-based; 80 iBT). Electronic applications accepted. *Faculty research:* Floor vibration investigations, earthquake engineering, base isolation systems and seismic risk assessment, infrastructure revitalization (building foundations and damage, bridge structures, highways, and dams), slope stability and soil erosion, pavement rehabilitation, computational fluid dynamics and flood control structures, microbial fuel cells, water treatment and water quality modeling, environmental risk assessment, biotechnology, nanotechnology.

Idaho State University, Office of Graduate Studies, College of Science and Engineering, Department of Geosciences, Pocatello, ID 83209-8072. Offers geographic information science (MS); geology (MNS, MS); geology with emphasis in environmental geoscience (MS); geophysics/hydrology/geology (MS); geotechnology (Postbaccalaureate Certificate). *Program availability:* Part-time. *Degree requirements:* For master's, comprehensive exam, thesis, oral colloquium; for Postbaccalaureate Certificate, thesis optional, minimum 19 credits. *Entrance requirements:* For master's, GRE General Test (minimum 50th percentile in 2 sections), 3 letters of recommendation; for Postbaccalaureate Certificate, GRE General Test, 3 letters of recommendation, bachelor's degree, statement of goals. Additional exam requirements/recommendations for international students: Required—TOEFL (minimum score 550 paper-based; 80 iBT). Electronic applications accepted. *Faculty research:* Quantitative field mapping and sampling: microscopic, geochemical, and isotopic analysis of rocks, minerals and water; remote sensing, geographic information systems, and global positioning systems: environmental and watershed management; surficial and fluvial processes: landscape change; regional tectonics, structural geology; planetary geology.

Idaho State University, Office of Graduate Studies, Department of Interdisciplinary Studies, Pocatello, ID 83209. Offers general interdisciplinary (M Ed, MA, MNS); waste management and environmental science (MS). *Program availability:* Part-time. *Degree requirements:* For master's, comprehensive exam, thesis optional. *Entrance requirements:* For master's, GRE General Test or MAT, minimum GPA of 3.0. Additional exam requirements/recommendations for international students: Required—TOEFL (minimum score 550 paper-based; 80 iBT).

Indiana University Bloomington, School of Public and Environmental Affairs, Environmental Science Programs, Bloomington, IN 47405. Offers applied ecology (MSES); energy (MSES); environmental chemistry, toxicology, and risk assessment (MSES); environmental science (PhD); hazardous materials management (Certificate); specialized environmental science (MSES); water resources (MSES); JD/MSES; MSES/MA; MSES/MPA; MSES/MS. *Program availability:* Part-time. Terminal master's awarded for partial completion of doctoral program. *Degree requirements:* For master's, capstone or thesis; internship; for doctorate, comprehensive exam, thesis/dissertation. *Entrance requirements:* For master's, GRE General Test or GMAT, official transcripts, 3 letters of recommendation, resume, personal statement; for doctorate, GRE General Test or LSAT, official transcripts, 3 letters of recommendation, resume or curriculum vitae, statement of purpose. Additional exam requirements/recommendations for international students: Required—TOEFL (minimum score 600 paper-based; 96 iBT); Recommended—IELTS (minimum score 7). Electronic applications accepted. *Faculty research:* Applied ecology, bio-geochemistry, toxicology, wetlands ecology, environmental microbiology, forest ecology, environmental chemistry.

Instituto Tecnologico de Santo Domingo, Graduate School, Area of Basic And Environmental Sciences, Santo Domingo, Dominican Republic. Offers environmental science (M En S), including environmental education, environmental management, marine resources, natural resources management; mathematics (MS, PhD); renewable energy technology (MS, Certificate).

Instituto Tecnológico y de Estudios Superiores de Monterrey, Campus Ciudad de México, Virtual University Division, Ciudad de Mexico, Mexico. Offers administration of information technologies (MA); computer sciences (MA); education (MA, PhD); educational technology (MA); environmental engineering (MA); environmental systems (MA); humanistic studies (MA); industrial engineering (MA); international business for Latin America (MA); quality systems (MA); quality systems and productivity (MA). *Program availability:* Part-time, evening/weekend, online learning. *Entrance requirements:* For master's and doctorate, Instituto entrance exam. Additional exam requirements/recommendations for international students: Required—TOEFL.

Inter American University of Puerto Rico, San Germán Campus, Graduate Studies Center, Program in Environmental Sciences, San Germán, PR 00683-5008. Offers MS. *Program availability:* Part-time, evening/weekend. *Degree requirements:* For master's, comprehensive exam, thesis. *Entrance requirements:* For master's, GRE General Test or EXADEP, minimum GPA of 3.0. *Faculty research:* Environmental biology, environmental chemistry, water resources and unit operations.

Iowa State University of Science and Technology, Department of Geological and Atmospheric Sciences, Ames, IA 50011. Offers earth science (MS, PhD); environmental science (MS, PhD); geology (MS, PhD); meteorology (MS, PhD). *Degree requirements:* For master's, thesis (for some programs); for doctorate, thesis/dissertation. *Entrance requirements:* For master's and doctorate, GRE General Test. Additional exam requirements/recommendations for international students: Required—TOEFL (minimum score 550 paper-based; 79 iBT), IELTS (minimum score 6.5). Electronic applications accepted.

Iowa State University of Science and Technology, Program in Environmental Sciences, Ames, IA 50011. Offers MS, PhD. *Degree requirements:* For master's, thesis; for doctorate, thesis/dissertation. *Entrance requirements:* For master's and doctorate, GRE General Test. Additional exam requirements/recommendations for international students: Required—TOEFL (minimum score 550 paper-based; 79 iBT), IELTS (minimum score 6.5). Electronic applications accepted.

Jackson State University, Graduate School, College of Science, Engineering and Technology, Department of Biology, Jackson, MS 39217. Offers environmental science (MS, PhD). *Program availability:* Part-time, evening/weekend. *Degree requirements:* For master's, comprehensive exam, thesis (alternative accepted for MST); for doctorate, comprehensive exam, thesis/dissertation. *Entrance requirements:* For master's, GRE General Test; for doctorate, MAT. Additional exam requirements/recommendations for international students: Required—TOEFL (minimum score 520 paper-based; 67 iBT). *Faculty research:* Comparative studies on the carbohydrate composition of marine macroalgae, host-parasite relationship between the spruce budworm and entomepathogen fungus.

Johns Hopkins University, Zanvyl Krieger School of Arts and Sciences, Advanced Academic Programs, Program in Environmental Sciences and Policy, Washington, DC 20036. Offers energy policy and climate (MS); environmental sciences (MS); geographic information systems (MS, Certificate). *Program availability:* Part-time, evening/weekend, online learning. *Degree requirements:* For master's, thesis (for some programs). *Entrance requirements:* For master's, minimum GPA of 3.0, coursework in chemistry and calculus. Additional exam requirements/recommendations for international students: Required—TOEFL (minimum score 100 iBT). Electronic applications accepted.

Kansas State University, Graduate School, College of Agriculture, Department of Agronomy, Manhattan, KS 66506. Offers crop science (MS, PhD); plant breeding and genetics (MS); range and forage science (MS, PhD); soil and environmental science (PhD); weed science (MS, PhD). *Program availability:* Part-time. *Degree requirements:* For master's, thesis or alternative, oral exam; for doctorate, thesis/dissertation, preliminary exams. *Entrance requirements:* For master's, minimum GPA of 3.0 in BS; for doctorate, minimum GPA of 3.0 in master's program. Additional exam requirements/recommendations for international students: Required—TOEFL (minimum score 550 paper-based; 79 iBT). Electronic applications accepted. *Faculty research:* Range and forage science; soil and environmental science; weed science; plant breeding and genetics; crop physiology, ecology and production.

Laurentian University, School of Graduate Studies and Research, Programme in Chemistry and Biochemistry, Sudbury, ON P3E 2C6, Canada. Offers analytical chemistry (M Sc); biochemistry (M Sc); environmental chemistry (M Sc); organic chemistry (M Sc); physical/theoretical chemistry (M Sc). *Program availability:* Part-time. *Degree requirements:* For master's, thesis or alternative. *Entrance requirements:* For master's, honors degree with minimum second class. *Faculty research:* Cell cycle checkpoints, kinetic modeling, toxicology to metal stress, quantum chemistry, biogeochemistry metal speciation.

Lehigh University, College of Arts and Sciences, Department of Earth and Environmental Sciences, Bethlehem, PA 18015. Offers MS, PhD. *Faculty:* 14 full-time (2 women). *Students:* 21 full-time (9 women), 3 part-time (1 woman), 6 international. Average age 27. 46 applicants, 24% accepted, 8 enrolled. In 2015, 3 master's, 2 doctorates awarded. Terminal master's awarded for partial completion of doctoral program. *Degree requirements:* For master's, thesis; for doctorate, thesis/dissertation. *Entrance requirements:* For master's and doctorate, GRE General Test, transcripts, recommendation letters, research statement, faculty advocates. Additional exam requirements/recommendations for international students: Required—TOEFL (minimum score 85 iBT). *Application deadline:* For fall admission, 1/1 for domestic and international students. Application fee: $75. Electronic applications accepted. *Expenses:* $1,380 per credit. *Financial support:* In 2015–16, 14 students received support, including 5 fellowships with full tuition reimbursements available (averaging $25,377 per year), 6 research assistantships with full tuition reimbursements available (averaging $20,250 per year), 10 teaching assistantships with full tuition reimbursements available (averaging $20,250 per year); scholarships/grants also available. Financial award application deadline: 1/1. *Faculty research:* Tectonics, surficial processes, ecology, environmental change, remote sensing. *Total annual research expenditures:* $1.1 million. *Unit head:* Dr. David J. Anastasio, Chairman, 610-758-5117, Fax: 610-758-3677, E-mail: dja2@lehigh.edu. *Application contact:* Dr. Kenneth Kodama, Graduate Coordinator, 610-758-3663, Fax: 610-758-3677, E-mail: kpk0@lehigh.edu.
Website: http://www.ees.lehigh.edu/

Louisiana State University and Agricultural & Mechanical College, Graduate School, College of Agriculture, School of Renewable Natural Resources, Baton Rouge, LA 70803. Offers fisheries (MS); forestry (MS, PhD); wildlife (MS); wildlife and fisheries science (PhD).

Louisiana State University and Agricultural & Mechanical College, Graduate School, School of the Coast and Environment, Department of Environmental Sciences, Baton Rouge, LA 70803. Offers environmental planning and management (MS); environmental science (PhD); environmental toxicology (MS).

Loyola Marymount University, College of Science and Engineering, Department of Civil Engineering and Environmental Science, Program in Environmental Science, Los Angeles, CA 90045. Offers MS. *Program availability:* Part-time. *Faculty:* 8 full-time (1 woman), 3 part-time/adjunct (1 woman). *Students:* 8 full-time (5 women), 4 part-time (1 woman); includes 7 minority (3 Asian, non-Hispanic/Latino; 3 Hispanic/Latino; 1 Two or more races, non-Hispanic/Latino), 1 international. Average age 31. 11 applicants, 73% accepted, 6 enrolled. In 2015, 2 master's awarded. *Degree requirements:* For master's, comprehensive exam, thesis or alternative. *Entrance requirements:* For master's, 2 letters of recommendation, personal statement. Additional exam requirements/recommendations for international students: Required—TOEFL (minimum score 550 paper-based; 80 iBT). *Application deadline:* Applications are processed on a rolling basis. Application fee: $50. Electronic applications accepted. *Financial support:* In 2015–16, 5 students received support. Scholarships/grants and unspecified assistantships available. Support available to part-time students. Financial award application deadline: 6/30; financial award applicants required to submit FAFSA. *Total annual research expenditures:* $266,759. *Unit head:* Prof. Joe Reichenberger, Graduate Director, 310-338-2830, E-mail: jreichenberger@lmu.edu. *Application contact:* Chake H. Kouyoumjian, Associate Dean of Graduate Studies, 310-338-2721,
E-mail: ckouyoum@lmu.edu.
Website: http://cse.lmu.edu/department/civilengineering/

Marshall University, Academic Affairs Division, College of Information Technology and Engineering, Division of Applied Science and Technology, Program in Environmental Science, Huntington, WV 25755. Offers MS. *Program availability:* Part-time, evening/weekend. *Students:* 19 full-time (10 women), 14 part-time (4 women), 9 international. Average age 30. In 2015, 12 master's awarded. *Degree requirements:* For master's, final project, oral exam. *Entrance requirements:* For master's, GRE General Test or MAT, minimum GPA of 2.5, course work in calculus. Application fee: $40. *Financial*

support: Tuition waivers (full) available. Support available to part-time students. Financial award application deadline: 8/1; financial award applicants required to submit FAFSA. *Unit head:* Dr. D. Scott Simonton, Associate Professor, 304-746-2045, E-mail: simonton@marshall.edu. *Application contact:* Information Contact, 304-746-1900, Fax: 304-746-1902, E-mail: services@marshall.edu.
Website: http://www.marshall.edu/cite/

Massachusetts Institute of Technology, School of Engineering, Department of Civil and Environmental Engineering, Cambridge, MA 02139. Offers biological oceanography (PhD, Sc D); chemical oceanography (PhD, Sc D); civil and environmental engineering (M Eng, SM, PhD, Sc D); civil and environmental systems (PhD, Sc D); civil engineering (PhD, Sc D, CE); coastal engineering (PhD, Sc D); construction engineering and management (PhD, Sc D); environmental biology (PhD, Sc D); environmental chemistry (PhD, Sc D); environmental engineering (PhD, Sc D); environmental fluid mechanics (PhD, Sc D); geotechnical and geoenvironmental engineering (PhD, Sc D); hydrology (PhD, Sc D); information technology (PhD, Sc D); oceanographic engineering (PhD, Sc D); structures and materials (PhD, Sc D); transportation (PhD, Sc D); SM/MBA. *Faculty:* 27 full-time (5 women). *Students:* 183 full-time (59 women); includes 19 minority (1 Black or African American, non-Hispanic/Latino; 7 Asian, non-Hispanic/Latino; 8 Hispanic/Latino; 3 Two or more races, non-Hispanic/Latino), 106 international. Average age 27. 513 applicants, 20% accepted, 56 enrolled. In 2015, 77 master's, 18 doctorates, 1 other advanced degree awarded. *Degree requirements:* For master's, thesis; for doctorate, comprehensive exam, thesis/dissertation; for CE, comprehensive exam, thesis. *Entrance requirements:* For master's and doctorate, GRE General Test; for CE, GRE General Test. Additional exam requirements/recommendations for international students: Required—TOEFL (minimum score 577 paper-based; 100 iBT), IELTS (minimum score 7). *Application deadline:* For fall admission, 12/15 for domestic and international students. Application fee: $75. Electronic applications accepted. *Expenses: Tuition:* Full-time $46,400; part-time $725 per credit. One-time fee: $304 full-time. Full-time tuition and fees vary according to course load and program. *Financial support:* In 2015–16, 150 students received support, including 38 fellowships (averaging $38,000 per year), 111 research assistantships (averaging $35,100 per year), 9 teaching assistantships (averaging $39,900 per year); Federal Work-Study, institutionally sponsored loans, scholarships/grants, traineeships, health care benefits, and unspecified assistantships also available. Support available to part-time students. Financial award application deadline: 4/15; financial award applicants required to submit FAFSA. *Faculty research:* Environmental chemistry, environmental fluid mechanics and coastal engineering, environmental microbiology, geotechnical engineering and geomechanics, hydrology and hydroclimatology, infrastructure systems, mechanics of materials and structures, transportation systems. *Total annual research expenditures:* $24.8 million. *Unit head:* Prof. Markus Buehler, Department Head, 617-253-7101. *Application contact:* Graduate Admissions Coordinator, 617-253-7119, E-mail: cee-admissions@mit.edu.
Website: http://cee.mit.edu/

McNeese State University, Doré School of Graduate Studies, College of Science, Dripps Department of Agricultural Sciences, Program in Environmental and Chemical Sciences, Lake Charles, LA 70609. Offers agricultural sciences (MS); environmental science (MS). *Program availability:* Evening/weekend. *Degree requirements:* For master's, comprehensive exam, thesis or alternative. *Entrance requirements:* For master's, GRE.

Memorial University of Newfoundland, School of Graduate Studies, Interdisciplinary Program in Environmental Science, St. John's, NL A1C 5S7, Canada. Offers M Env Sc, M Sc, PhD. *Program availability:* Part-time. *Degree requirements:* For master's, thesis (MSc), project (M Env Sci). *Entrance requirements:* For master's, 2nd class honours bachelor's degree; for doctorate, master's degree. *Application deadline:* For fall admission, 2/1 for domestic and international students; for winter admission, 4/1 for domestic and international students. Applications are processed on a rolling basis. Application fee: $50 Canadian dollars ($100 Canadian dollars for international students). Electronic applications accepted. *Expenses: Tuition, area resident:* Full-time $2199 Canadian dollars. *International tuition:* $2859 Canadian dollars full-time. *Financial support:* Fellowships, research assistantships, and teaching assistantships available. *Faculty research:* Earth and ocean systems, environmental chemistry and toxicology, environmental engineering. *Unit head:* Dr. Joe Wroblewski, Chair, 709-864-2410. *Application contact:* Gail Kenny, Secretary, 709-864-8154, Fax: 709-864-3316, E-mail: gkenny@mun.ca.

Mercer University, Graduate Studies, Macon Campus, School of Engineering, Macon, GA 31207. Offers biomedical engineering (MSE); computer engineering (MSE); electrical engineering (MSE); engineering management (MSE); environmental engineering (MSE); environmental systems (MS); mechanical engineering (MSE); software engineering (MSE); software systems (MS); technical communications management (MS); technical management (MS). *Program availability:* Part-time-only, evening/weekend, online learning. *Faculty:* 20 full-time (5 women), 2 part-time/adjunct (0 women). *Students:* 35 full-time (8 women), 59 part-time (12 women); includes 18 minority (9 Black or African American, non-Hispanic/Latino; 6 Asian, non-Hispanic/Latino; 1 Hispanic/Latino; 2 Two or more races, non-Hispanic/Latino), 5 international. Average age 30. In 2015, 69 master's awarded. *Degree requirements:* For master's, thesis or alternative. *Entrance requirements:* For master's, GRE (minimum score 300), minimum undergraduate GPA of 3.0. Additional exam requirements/recommendations for international students: Required—TOEFL (minimum score 550 paper-based; 80 iBT). *Application deadline:* For fall admission, 4/1 priority date for domestic and international students; for spring admission, 11/1 priority date for domestic and international students. Applications are processed on a rolling basis. Application fee: $75. Electronic applications accepted. Application fee is waived when completed online. *Expenses:* Contact institution. *Financial support:* Federal Work-Study available. *Faculty research:* Designing prostheses and orthotics, oxygen transfer and limitations in biological systems, low-cost groundwater development, lung airway and transport, autonomous mobile robots. *Unit head:* Dr. Wade H. Shaw, Dean, 478-301-2459, Fax: 478-301-5593, E-mail: shaw_wh@mercer.edu. *Application contact:* Dr. Richard O. Mines, Jr., Program Director, 478-301-2347, Fax: 478-301-5433, E-mail: mines_ro@mercer.edu.
Website: http://engineering.mercer.edu/

Miami University, Institute for the Environment and Sustainability, Oxford, OH 45056. Offers M Env. *Program availability:* Part-time. *Students:* 44 full-time (25 women), 3 part-time (1 woman); includes 6 minority (4 Hispanic/Latino; 2 Two or more races, non-Hispanic/Latino), 2 international. Average age 28. In 2015, 16 master's awarded. *Entrance requirements:* For master's, curriculum vitae; letter of intent; 3 reference letters. Additional exam requirements/recommendations for international students: Recommended—TOEFL (minimum score 80 iBT), IELTS (minimum score 6.5), TSE (minimum score 54). *Application deadline:* For fall admission, 2/1 for domestic and international students. Application fee: $50. Electronic applications accepted. *Expenses:* Tuition, state resident: full-time $12,888; part-time $537 per credit hour. Tuition, nonresident: full-time $29,022; part-time $1209 per credit hour. *Required fees:* $530; $24 per credit hour. $30 per semester. Part-time tuition and fees vary according to course load and program. *Financial support:* Application deadline: 2/15; applicants required to submit FAFSA. *Unit head:* Dr. Jonathan Levy, Director/Associate Professor of Geology and Environmental Earth Science, 513-529-1947, E-mail: levyj@miamioh.edu. *Application contact:* 513-529-5811, E-mail: ies@miamioh.edu.
Website: http://www.MiamiOH.edu/ies/

Michigan State University, The Graduate School, College of Natural Science, Department of Geological Sciences, East Lansing, MI 48824. Offers environmental geosciences (MS, PhD); environmental geosciences-environmental toxicology (PhD); geological sciences (MS, PhD). *Degree requirements:* For master's, thesis (for those without prior thesis work); for doctorate, thesis/dissertation. *Entrance requirements:* For master's, GRE General Test, minimum GPA of 3.0, course work in geoscience, 3 letters of recommendation; for doctorate, GRE General Test, 3 letters of recommendation. Additional exam requirements/recommendations for international students: Required—TOEFL (minimum score 550 paper-based), Michigan State University ELT (minimum score 85), Michigan English Language Assessment Battery (minimum score 83). Electronic applications accepted. *Faculty research:* Water in the environment, global and biological change, crystal dynamics.

Minnesota State University Mankato, College of Graduate Studies and Research, College of Science, Engineering and Technology, Department of Biological Sciences, Program in Environmental Sciences, Mankato, MN 56001. Offers MS. *Degree requirements:* For master's, one foreign language, comprehensive exam, thesis or alternative. *Entrance requirements:* For master's, minimum GPA of 3.0 during previous 2 years. Additional exam requirements/recommendations for international students: Required—TOEFL. Electronic applications accepted.

Montana State University, The Graduate School, College of Agriculture, Department of Land Resources and Environmental Sciences, Bozeman, MT 59717. Offers land rehabilitation (interdisciplinary) (MS); land resources and environmental sciences (MS), including land rehabilitation (interdisciplinary), land resources and environmental sciences. *Program availability:* Part-time. *Degree requirements:* For master's, comprehensive exam. *Entrance requirements:* For master's, GRE General Test. Additional exam requirements/recommendations for international students: Required—TOEFL (minimum score 550 paper-based). Electronic applications accepted. *Faculty research:* Soil nutrient management and plant nutrition, isotope biogeochemistry of soils, biodegradation of hydrocarbons in soils and natural waters, remote sensing, GIS systems, managed and natural ecosystems, microbial and metabolic diversity in geothermally heated soils, integrated management of weeds, diversified cropping systems, insect behavior and ecology, river ecology, microbial biogeochemistry, weed ecology.

Montana State University, The Graduate School, College of Letters and Science, Department of Ecology, Bozeman, MT 59717. Offers ecological and environmental statistics (MS); ecology and environmental sciences (PhD); fish and wildlife biology (PhD); fish and wildlife management (MS). *Program availability:* Part-time. *Degree requirements:* For master's, comprehensive exam, thesis (for some programs); for doctorate, comprehensive exam, thesis/dissertation. *Entrance requirements:* For master's and doctorate, GRE, minimum GPA of 3.0, letters of recommendation, essay. Additional exam requirements/recommendations for international students: Required—TOEFL (minimum score 550 paper-based). Electronic applications accepted. *Faculty research:* Community ecology, population ecology, land-use effects, management and conservation, environmental modeling.

Montclair State University, The Graduate School, College of Science and Mathematics, Program in Environmental Studies, Montclair, NJ 07043-1624. Offers environmental education (MA); environmental management (MA); environmental science (MA). *Program availability:* Part-time, evening/weekend. *Students:* 8 full-time (3 women), 14 part-time (8 women); includes 3 minority (1 Asian, non-Hispanic/Latino; 2 Hispanic/Latino). Average age 27. 13 applicants, 69% accepted, 9 enrolled. In 2015, 8 master's awarded. *Degree requirements:* For master's, thesis. *Entrance requirements:* For master's, GRE General Test, 2 letters of recommendation, essay. Additional exam requirements/recommendations for international students: Required—TOEFL (minimum score 83 iBT), IELTS (minimum score 6.5). *Application deadline:* Applications are processed on a rolling basis. Application fee: $60. Electronic applications accepted. *Expenses:* Tuition, state resident: part-time $553 per credit. Tuition, nonresident: part-time $854 per credit. *Required fees:* $91 per credit. Tuition and fees vary according to program. *Financial support:* In 2015–16, 10 research assistantships with full tuition reimbursements (averaging $7,000 per year) were awarded; Federal Work-Study, scholarships/grants, and unspecified assistantships also available. Support available to part-time students. Financial award application deadline: 3/1; financial award applicants required to submit FAFSA. *Faculty research:* Environmental geochemistry/remediation/forensics, environmental law and policy, regional climate modeling, remote sensing, Cenozoic marine sediment records from polar regions, sustainability science. *Unit head:* Dr. Matthew Goring, Chairperson, 973-655-5409. *Application contact:* Amy Aiello, Executive Director of The Graduate School, 973-655-5147, Fax: 973-655-7869, E-mail: graduate.school@montclair.edu.
Website: http://www.montclair.edu/csam/earth-environment-studies/

Murray State University, College of Health Sciences and Human Services, Program in Occupational Safety and Health, Murray, KY 42071. Offers environmental science (MS); industrial hygiene (MS); safety management (MS). *Accreditation:* ABET. *Program availability:* Part-time. *Degree requirements:* For master's, comprehensive exam, thesis optional, professional internship. Electronic applications accepted. *Faculty research:* Light effects on plant growth, ergonomics, toxic effects of pets' pesticides, traffic safety.

New Jersey Institute of Technology, College of Science and Liberal Arts, Newark, NJ 07102. Offers applied mathematics (MS); applied physics (M Sc, PhD); applied statistical models (Certificate); applied statistics (MS); biology (MS, PhD); biostatistics (MS); biostatistics essentials (Certificate); chemistry (MS, PhD); computational biology (MS); environmental science (MS, PhD); history (MA, MAT); materials science and engineering (MS, PhD); mathematical and computational finance (MS); mathematics science (PhD); pharmaceutical chemistry (MS); professional and technical communications (MS); technical common essentials (Certificate). *Program availability:* Part-time, evening/weekend. *Faculty:* 153 full-time (35 women), 100 part-time/adjunct (40 women). *Students:* 212 full-time (82 women), 94 part-time (37 women); includes 72 minority (22 Black or African American, non-Hispanic/Latino; 25 Asian, non-Hispanic/Latino; 19 Hispanic/Latino; 6 Two or more races, non-Hispanic/Latino), 164 international. Average age 29. 519 applicants, 62% accepted, 104 enrolled. In 2015, 98 master's, 21 doctorates, 3 other advanced degrees awarded. Terminal master's awarded for partial completion of doctoral program. *Degree requirements:* For master's, thesis optional; for doctorate, thesis/dissertation. *Entrance requirements:* For master's, GRE General Test; for doctorate, GRE General Test, minimum graduate GPA of 3.5. Additional exam requirements/recommendations for international students: Required—TOEFL (minimum score 550 paper-based; 79 iBT). *Application deadline:* For fall admission, 6/1 priority date for domestic students, 5/1 priority date for international students; for spring admission, 11/15 priority date for domestic and international

students. Applications are processed on a rolling basis. Application fee: $75. Electronic applications accepted. *Expenses:* $28,800 per year non-resident full-time. *Financial support:* In 2015–16, 56 research assistantships with full tuition reimbursements (averaging $17,711 per year), 52 teaching assistantships with full tuition reimbursements (averaging $17,914 per year) were awarded; fellowships with full tuition reimbursements also available. Financial award application deadline: 1/15. *Total annual research expenditures:* $23.1 million. *Unit head:* Dr. Kevin Belfield, Dean, 973-596-3676, Fax: 973-565-0586, E-mail: kevin.d.belfield@njit.edu. *Application contact:* Stephen Eck, Director of Admissions, 973-596-3300, Fax: 973-596-3461, E-mail: admissions@njit.edu.
Website: http://csla.njit.edu/

New Mexico State University, College of Agricultural, Consumer and Environmental Sciences, Department of Plant and Environmental Sciences, Las Cruces, NM 88003-8001. Offers horticulture (MS); plant and environmental sciences (MS, PhD). *Program availability:* Part-time. *Faculty:* 18 full-time (4 women). *Students:* 33 full-time (18 women), 13 part-time (4 women); includes 6 minority (5 Hispanic/Latino; 1 Two or more races, non-Hispanic/Latino), 22 international. Average age 30. 18 applicants, 50% accepted, 7 enrolled. In 2015, 7 master's, 4 doctorates awarded. Terminal master's awarded for partial completion of doctoral program. *Degree requirements:* For master's, thesis or alternative; for doctorate, one foreign language, comprehensive exam, thesis/dissertation, qualifying exam, 2 seminars. *Entrance requirements:* For master's, GRE, minimum GPA of 3.0, 3 letters of reference, letter of purpose or intent; for doctorate, GRE, minimum GPA of 3.3, 3 letters of reference, letter of purpose or intent. Additional exam requirements/recommendations for international students: Required—TOEFL (minimum score 550 paper-based; 79 iBT), IELTS (minimum score 6.5). *Application deadline:* For fall admission, 3/15 for domestic and international students; for spring admission, 10/15 for domestic and international students. Applications are processed on a rolling basis. Application fee: $40 ($50 for international students). Electronic applications accepted. *Expenses:* $274.50 per credit hour for in-state students, and all students enrolled in six or fewer credits; $839.30 per credit hour for out-of-state and international students enrolled in at least seven hours. *Financial support:* In 2015–16, 36 students received support, including 1 fellowship (averaging $4,088 per year), 20 research assistantships (averaging $18,593 per year), 9 teaching assistantships (averaging $17,218 per year); career-related internships or fieldwork, Federal Work-Study, scholarships/grants, traineeships, health care benefits, and unspecified assistantships also available. Support available to part-time students. Financial award application deadline: 3/1. *Faculty research:* Plant breeding and genetics, molecular biology, crop physiology, plant physiology, soil science and environmental science, forestry, nursery and greenhouse production, urban horticulture and turfgrass management. *Total annual research expenditures:* $5.1 million. *Unit head:* Dr. Rolston St. Hilaire, Interim Department Head, 575-646-3405, Fax: 575-646-6041, E-mail: rsthilai@nmsu.edu. *Application contact:* Dr. Paul Bosland, Graduate Chair, 575-646-5171, Fax: 575-646-6041, E-mail: pbosland@nmsu.edu.
Website: http://aces.nmsu.edu/academics/pes

New York University, Polytechnic School of Engineering, Department of Civil and Urban Engineering, Major in Environmental Science, New York, NY 10012-1019. Offers MS. *Program availability:* Part-time, evening/weekend. *Degree requirements:* For master's, comprehensive exam (for some programs), thesis (for some programs). *Entrance requirements:* Additional exam requirements/recommendations for international students: Required—TOEFL (minimum score 550 paper-based; 80 iBT); Recommended—IELTS (minimum score 6.5). Electronic applications accepted.

North Carolina Agricultural and Technical State University, School of Graduate Studies, School of Agriculture and Environmental Sciences, Greensboro, NC 27411. Offers MAT, MS. *Program availability:* Part-time, evening/weekend. *Degree requirements:* For master's, comprehensive exam, qualifying exam. *Entrance requirements:* For master's, GRE General Test. *Faculty research:* Aid for small farmers, agricultural technology, housing, food science, nutrition.

North Dakota State University, College of Graduate and Interdisciplinary Studies, Interdisciplinary Program in Environmental and Conservation Sciences, Fargo, ND 58102. Offers MS, PhD. *Degree requirements:* For master's, comprehensive exam, thesis. *Entrance requirements:* Additional exam requirements/recommendations for international students: Required—TOEFL (minimum score 550 paper-based; 79 iBT).

Northern Arizona University, Graduate College, College of Engineering, Forestry, and Natural Sciences, School of Earth Sciences and Environmental Sustainability, Flagstaff, AZ 86011. Offers climate science and solutions (MS); earth sciences and environmental sustainability (PhD); environmental sciences and policy (MS); geology (MS). *Degree requirements:* For master's, comprehensive exam (for some programs), thesis (for some programs). *Entrance requirements:* Additional exam requirements/recommendations for international students: Required—TOEFL (minimum score 550 paper-based; 80 iBT), IELTS (minimum score 7). *Application deadline:* For fall admission, 2/1 priority date for domestic and international students. Applications are processed on a rolling basis. Application fee: $65. Electronic applications accepted. *Expenses: Tuition, area resident:* Full-time $8710. Tuition, nonresident: full-time $20,350. *Required fees:* $896. *Financial support:* Fellowships, research assistantships with full tuition reimbursements, teaching assistantships with full tuition reimbursements, career-related internships or fieldwork, Federal Work-Study, scholarships/grants, health care benefits, tuition waivers (full and partial), and unspecified assistantships available. Financial award applicants required to submit FAFSA. *Unit head:* Dr. Paul Umhoefer, Director, 928-523-6464, E-mail: paul.umhoefer@nau.edu. *Application contact:* SESES Support, 928-523-9333, Fax: 928-523-7432, E-mail: seses_admin_support@nau.edu.
Website: http://nau.edu/cefns/natsci/seses/

Nova Southeastern University, Halmos College of Natural Sciences and Oceanography, Fort Lauderdale, FL 33314-7796. Offers biological sciences (MS); coastal studies (Certificate); coastal zone management (MS); marine and coastal climate change (Certificate); marine and coastal studies (MA); marine biology (MS); marine biology and oceanography (PhD), including marine biology, oceanography; marine environmental sciences (MS). *Program availability:* Part-time, evening/weekend, 100% online, blended/hybrid learning. *Faculty:* 17 full-time (3 women), 22 part-time/adjunct (11 women). *Students:* 100 full-time (57 women), 114 part-time (76 women); includes 32 minority (6 Black or African American, non-Hispanic/Latino; 1 American Indian or Alaska Native, non-Hispanic/Latino; 6 Asian, non-Hispanic/Latino; 10 Hispanic/Latino; 9 Two or more races, non-Hispanic/Latino), 5 international. Average age 30. 85 applicants, 60% accepted, 39 enrolled. In 2015, 47 master's, 2 doctorates, 9 other advanced degrees awarded. *Degree requirements:* For master's, thesis; for doctorate, comprehensive exam, thesis/dissertation, departmental qualifying exam. *Entrance requirements:* For master's, GRE General Test, 3 letters of recommendation, BS/BA in natural science (for marine biology program), BS/BA in biology (for biological sciences program), minor in the natural sciences or equivalent (for coastal zone management and marine environmental sciences); for doctorate, GRE General Test, master's degree. Additional exam requirements/recommendations for international students: Required—TOEFL (minimum score 550 paper-based). *Application deadline:* Applications are processed on a rolling basis. Application fee: $50. Electronic applications accepted. *Expenses:* $34,749 per year (for PhD); $3,738 per course (for MS and Graduate Certificate). *Financial support:* In 2015–16, 157 students received support, including 14 fellowships with tuition reimbursements available (averaging $25,000 per year), 42 research assistantships with tuition reimbursements available (averaging $19,000 per year); teaching assistantships, career-related internships or fieldwork, Federal Work-Study, scholarships/grants, health care benefits, tuition waivers (full and partial), and unspecified assistantships also available. Support available to part-time students. Financial award application deadline: 4/15; financial award applicants required to submit FAFSA. *Faculty research:* Physical oceanography, biological oceanography, molecular and microbiology, ecology and evolution, coral reefs. *Total annual research expenditures:* $5 million. *Unit head:* Dr. Richard Dodge, Dean, 954-262-3600, Fax: 954-262-4020, E-mail: dodge@nsu.nova.edu. *Application contact:* Dr. Bernhard Riegl, Chair, Department of Marine and Environmental Sciences, 954-262-3600, Fax: 954-262-4020, E-mail: rieglb@nova.edu.
Website: http://cnso.nova.edu

Oakland University, Graduate Study and Lifelong Learning, College of Arts and Sciences, Department of Chemistry, Rochester, MI 48309-4401. Offers biomedical sciences: health and environmental chemistry (PhD); chemistry (MS). *Faculty:* 13 full-time (5 women). *Students:* 15 full-time (5 women), 26 part-time (9 women); includes 2 minority (1 Black or African American, non-Hispanic/Latino; 1 Asian, non-Hispanic/Latino), 6 international. Average age 29. 33 applicants, 39% accepted, 10 enrolled. In 2015, 5 master's, 2 doctorates awarded. *Degree requirements:* For master's, thesis; for doctorate, thesis/dissertation. *Entrance requirements:* For master's, minimum GPA of 3.0; for doctorate, GRE Subject Test, minimum GPA of 3.0. Additional exam requirements/recommendations for international students: Required—TOEFL (minimum score 550 paper-based). *Application deadline:* Applications are processed on a rolling basis. Application fee: $0. Electronic applications accepted. *Expenses: Tuition, area resident:* Part-time $655 per credit. Tuition and fees vary according to program. *Financial support:* Federal Work-Study, institutionally sponsored loans, and tuition waivers (full) available. Financial award application deadline: 3/1; financial award applicants required to submit FAFSA. *Unit head:* Dr. Roman Dembinski, Department Chair/Professor, 248-370-2248, Fax: 248-370-2321, E-mail: dembinsk@oakland.edu. *Application contact:* Katherine Z. Rowley, Director, Graduate Admissions, 248-370-3167, Fax: 248-370-4114, E-mail: kzrowley@oakland.edu.
Website: http://www2.oakland.edu/chemistry/

The Ohio State University, Graduate School, College of Food, Agricultural, and Environmental Sciences, Program in Environmental Science, Columbus, OH 43210. Offers MS, PhD. *Degree requirements:* For master's, one foreign language, thesis optional; for doctorate, one foreign language, thesis/dissertation. *Entrance requirements:* For master's and doctorate, GRE General Test. Additional exam requirements/recommendations for international students: Required—TOEFL (minimum score 550 paper-based; 79 iBT), IELTS (minimum score 7), Michigan English Language Assessment Battery (minimum score 82). Electronic applications accepted.

The Ohio State University, Graduate School, College of Food, Agricultural, and Environmental Sciences, School of Environment and Natural Resources, Columbus, OH 43210. Offers ecological restoration (MS, PhD); ecosystem science (MS, PhD); environment and natural resources (MENR); environmental social sciences (MS, PhD); fisheries and wildlife science (MS, PhD); forest science (MS, PhD); rural sociology (MS, PhD); soil science (MS, PhD). *Degree requirements:* For master's, thesis; for doctorate, thesis/dissertation. *Entrance requirements:* For master's and doctorate, GRE. Additional exam requirements/recommendations for international students: Required—TOEFL (minimum score 550 paper-based; 79 iBT), Michigan English Language Assessment Battery (minimum score 82); Recommended—IELTS (minimum score 7). Electronic applications accepted.

Oklahoma State University, College of Agricultural Science and Natural Resources, Department of Horticulture and Landscape Architecture, Stillwater, OK 74078. Offers crop science (PhD); environmental science (PhD); horticulture (M Ag, MS); plant science (PhD). *Faculty:* 17 full-time (4 women). *Students:* 3 full-time (1 woman), 9 part-time (3 women); includes 2 minority (1 Black or African American, non-Hispanic/Latino; 1 Asian, non-Hispanic/Latino), 5 international. Average age 30. 8 applicants, 63% accepted, 5 enrolled. In 2015, 3 master's awarded. *Degree requirements:* For master's, thesis (for some programs); for doctorate, comprehensive exam, thesis/dissertation. *Entrance requirements:* For master's and doctorate, GRE or GMAT. Additional exam requirements/recommendations for international students: Required—TOEFL (minimum score 550 paper-based; 79 iBT). *Application deadline:* For fall admission, 3/1 priority date for international students; for spring admission, 8/1 priority date for international students. Applications are processed on a rolling basis. Application fee: $40 ($75 for international students). Electronic applications accepted. *Expenses:* Tuition, state resident: full-time $3528; part-time $196 per credit hour. Tuition, nonresident: full-time $14,144; part-time $785.75 per credit hour. *Required fees:* $1895; $105.25 per credit hour. Tuition and fees vary according to campus/location. *Financial support:* In 2015–16, 9 research assistantships (averaging $10,469 per year), 3 teaching assistantships (averaging $12,261 per year) were awarded; career-related internships or fieldwork, Federal Work-Study, scholarships/grants, health care benefits, tuition waivers (partial), and unspecified assistantships also available. Support available to part-time students. Financial award application deadline: 3/1; financial award applicants required to submit FAFSA. *Faculty research:* Stress and postharvest physiology; water utilization and runoff; integrated pest management (IPM) systems and nursery, turf, floriculture, vegetable, net and fruit produces and natural resources, food extraction, and processing; public garden management. *Unit head:* Dr. Janet Cole, Department Head, 405-744-5414, Fax: 405-744-9709. *Application contact:* Dr. Sheryl Tucker, Dean, 405-744-7099, Fax: 405-744-0355, E-mail: gradi@okstate.edu.
Website: http://www.hortla.okstate.edu/

Oklahoma State University, College of Arts and Sciences, Department of Plant Biology, Ecology, and Evolution, Stillwater, OK 74078. Offers botany (MS); environmental science (MS, PhD); plant science (PhD). *Faculty:* 14 full-time (5 women). *Students:* 8 part-time (3 women); includes 4 minority (1 Asian, non-Hispanic/Latino; 1 Hispanic/Latino; 2 Two or more races, non-Hispanic/Latino). Average age 32. 3 applicants, 67% accepted. In 2015, 3 master's awarded. *Degree requirements:* For master's, thesis; for doctorate, comprehensive exam, thesis/dissertation. *Entrance requirements:* For master's and doctorate, GRE or GMAT. Additional exam requirements/recommendations for international students: Required—TOEFL (minimum score 550 paper-based; 79 iBT). *Application deadline:* For fall admission, 3/1 priority date for international students; for spring admission, 8/1 priority date for international students. Applications are processed on a rolling basis. Application fee: $40 ($75 for international students). Electronic applications accepted. *Expenses:* Tuition, state resident: full-time $3528; part-time $196 per credit hour. Tuition, nonresident: full-time $14,144; part-time $785.75 per credit hour. *Required fees:* $1895; $105.25 per credit hour. Tuition and fees vary according to campus/location. *Financial support:* In 2015–16, 1 research assistantship (averaging $18,504 per year), 12 teaching assistantships (averaging $20,754 per year) were awarded; career-related internships or fieldwork,

Federal Work-Study, scholarships/grants, health care benefits, tuition waivers (partial), and unspecified assistantships also available. Support available to part-time students. Financial award application deadline: 3/1; financial award applicants required to submit FAFSA. *Faculty research:* Ethnobotany, developmental genetics of arabidopsis, biological roles of plasmodesmata, community ecology and biodiversity, nutrient cycling in grassland ecosystems. *Unit head:* Dr. Linda Watson, Department Head, 405-744-5559, Fax: 405-744-7074, E-mail: linda.watson10@okstate.edu.
Website: http://plantbio.okstate.edu

Oklahoma State University, Graduate College, Stillwater, OK 74078. Offers aerospace security (Graduate Certificate); bioenergy and sustainable technology (Graduate Certificate); business data mining (Graduate Certificate); business sustainability (Graduate Certificate); environmental science (MS); international studies (MS); non-profit management (Graduate Certificate); teaching English to speakers of other languages (Graduate Certificate); telecommunications management (MS). Programs are interdisciplinary. *Faculty:* 4 full-time (2 women), 3 part-time/adjunct (0 women). *Students:* 59 full-time (26 women), 130 part-time (65 women); includes 38 minority (3 Black or African American, non-Hispanic/Latino; 7 American Indian or Alaska Native, non-Hispanic/Latino; 9 Asian, non-Hispanic/Latino; 9 Hispanic/Latino; 10 Two or more races, non-Hispanic/Latino), 53 international. Average age 31. 358 applicants, 87% accepted, 70 enrolled. In 2015, 45 master's, 9 doctorates awarded. *Degree requirements:* For master's, thesis (for some programs); for doctorate, comprehensive exam, thesis/dissertation. *Entrance requirements:* For master's and doctorate, GRE or GMAT. Additional exam requirements/recommendations for international students: Required—TOEFL (minimum score 550 paper-based; 79 iBT). *Application deadline:* For fall admission, 3/1 priority date for domestic and international students; for spring admission, 8/1 priority date for domestic and international students. Applications are processed on a rolling basis. Application fee: $40 ($75 for international students). Electronic applications accepted. *Expenses:* Tuition, state resident: full-time $3528; part-time $196 per credit hour. Tuition, nonresident: full-time $14,144; part-time $785.75 per credit hour. *Required fees:* $1895; $105.25 per credit hour. Tuition and fees vary according to campus/location. *Financial support:* In 2015–16, 10 research assistantships (averaging $15,876 per year) were awarded; career-related internships or fieldwork, Federal Work-Study, scholarships/grants, health care benefits, tuition waivers (partial), and unspecified assistantships also available. Support available to part-time students. Financial award application deadline: 3/1; financial award applicants required to submit FAFSA. *Unit head:* Dr. Sheryl Tucker, Dean, 405-744-6368, Fax: 405-744-0355, E-mail: gradi@okstate.edu. *Application contact:* Dr. Susan Mathew, Assistant Director of Graduate Admissions, 405-744-6368, Fax: 405-744-0355,
E-mail: gradi@okstate.edu.
Website: http://gradcollege.okstate.edu/

Old Dominion University, College of Sciences, Program in Chemistry, Norfolk, VA 23529. Offers analytical (MS, PhD); biochemistry (MS, PhD); environmental (MS, PhD); inorganic (MS, PhD); organic (MS, PhD); physical (MS, PhD). *Program availability:* Part-time, evening/weekend. *Faculty:* 19 full-time (5 women). *Students:* 35 full-time (17 women), 6 part-time (2 women); includes 5 minority (4 Black or African American, non-Hispanic/Latino; 1 Two or more races, non-Hispanic/Latino), 16 international. Average age 27. 20 applicants, 55% accepted, 4 enrolled. In 2015, 9 master's, 9 doctorates awarded. *Degree requirements:* For master's, comprehensive exam, thesis (for some programs); for doctorate, comprehensive exam, thesis/dissertation. *Entrance requirements:* For master's and doctorate, GRE General Test, minimum GPA of 3.0 in major, 2.5 overall, transcripts, essay, three letters of recommendation, resume. Additional exam requirements/recommendations for international students: Required—TOEFL. *Application deadline:* For fall admission, 7/1 for domestic students, 1/15 for international students; for spring admission, 11/1 for domestic students, 8/15 for international students. Applications are processed on a rolling basis. Application fee: $50. Electronic applications accepted. *Expenses:* $464 per credit in-state tuition; $1,160 per credit out-of-state tuition. *Financial support:* In 2015–16, 42 students received support, including 2 fellowships with full tuition reimbursements available (averaging $18,000 per year), 10 research assistantships with full tuition reimbursements available (averaging $18,000 per year), 33 teaching assistantships with full tuition reimbursements available (averaging $18,000 per year); career-related internships or fieldwork, institutionally sponsored loans, scholarships/grants, health care benefits, and unspecified assistantships also available. Financial award application deadline: 2/15; financial award applicants required to submit FAFSA. *Faculty research:* Biogeochemistry, materials chemistry, computational chemistry, organic chemistry, biofuels. *Total annual research expenditures:* $2.6 million. *Unit head:* Dr. John R. Donat, Graduate Program Director, 757-683-4098, Fax: 757-683-4628,
E-mail: chemgpd@odu.edu. *Application contact:* Kristi Rehrauer, Graduate Program Assistant, 757-683-6979, Fax: 757-683-4628, E-mail: krehraue@odu.edu.

Oregon Health & Science University, School of Medicine, Graduate Programs in Medicine, Department of Environmental and Biomolecular Systems, Portland, OR 97239-3098. Offers biochemistry and molecular biology (MS, PhD); environmental science and engineering (MS, PhD). *Program availability:* Part-time. *Faculty:* 13 full-time (4 women). *Students:* 19 full-time (16 women), 2 part-time (1 woman); includes 8 minority (2 Black or African American, non-Hispanic/Latino; 3 Asian, non-Hispanic/Latino; 2 Hispanic/Latino; 1 Two or more races, non-Hispanic/Latino), 4 international. Average age 26. 42 applicants, 33% accepted, 7 enrolled. In 2015, 10 master's, 5 doctorates awarded. Terminal master's awarded for partial completion of doctoral program. *Degree requirements:* For master's, thesis (for some programs); for doctorate, comprehensive exam, thesis/dissertation, qualifying exam. *Entrance requirements:* For master's and doctorate, GRE General Test (minimum scores: 153 Verbal/148 Quantitative/4.5 Analytical) or MCAT (for some programs). Additional exam requirements/recommendations for international students: Required—TOEFL. *Application deadline:* For fall admission, 7/15 for domestic students, 5/15 for international students; for winter admission, 10/15 for domestic students, 9/15 for international students; for spring admission, 1/15 for domestic students, 12/15 for international students. Applications are processed on a rolling basis. Application fee: $70. Electronic applications accepted. *Financial support:* Health care benefits and full tuition and stipends (for PhD students) available. *Faculty research:* Metalloprotein biochemistry, molecular microbiology, environmental microbiology, environmental chemistry, biogeochemistry. *Unit head:* Dr. Bradley Tebo, Program Director, 503-346-3438, E-mail: tebob@ohsu.edu. *Application contact:* Vanessa Green, Program Coordinator, 503-346-3411, E-mail: greenva@ohsu.edu.

Oregon State University, Interdisciplinary/Institutional Programs, Program in Environmental Sciences, Corvallis, OR 97331. Offers biogeochemistry (MS, PhD); ecology (MS, PhD); environmental education (MS, PhD); environmental sciences (PSM); natural resources (MS, PhD); quantitative analysis (MS, PhD); social science (MS, PhD); water resources (MS, PhD). *Program availability:* Part-time. *Students:* 17 full-time (12 women), 12 part-time (6 women); includes 7 minority (1 Black or African American, non-Hispanic/Latino; 2 Asian, non-Hispanic/Latino; 2 Hispanic/Latino; 2 Two or more races, non-Hispanic/Latino), 3 international. Average age 34. 42 applicants, 19% accepted, 3 enrolled. In 2015, 6 master's, 4 doctorates awarded. *Entrance requirements:* For master's and doctorate, GRE. Additional exam requirements/recommendations for international students: Required—TOEFL (minimum score 80 iBT), IELTS (minimum score 6.5). *Application deadline:* For fall admission, 1/15 for domestic students. Application fee: $75 ($85 for international students). *Expenses:* Contact institution. *Unit head:* Dr. Carolyn Fonyo Boggess, Interim Director,
E-mail: carolyn.fonyo@oregonstate.edu.
Website: http://envsci.science.oregonstate.edu/

Pace University, Dyson College of Arts and Sciences, Department of Environmental Studies and Science, New York, NY 10038. Offers environmental science (MS). Offered at Pleasantville, NY location only. *Program availability:* Part-time, evening/weekend. *Students:* 7 full-time (5 women), 20 part-time (15 women); includes 7 minority (2 Black or African American, non-Hispanic/Latino; 3 Hispanic/Latino; 2 Two or more races, non-Hispanic/Latino), 3 international. Average age 28. 15 applicants, 73% accepted, 6 enrolled. In 2015, 6 master's awarded. *Degree requirements:* For master's, thesis, research project. *Entrance requirements:* For master's, GRE, two letters of recommendation, resume, personal statement, all official transcripts. Additional exam requirements/recommendations for international students: Required—TOEFL (minimum score 88 iBT), IELTS (minimum score 7) or PTE (minimum score 60). *Application deadline:* For fall admission, 8/1 priority date for domestic students, 6/1 for international students; for spring admission, 12/1 priority date for domestic students, 10/1 for international students. Applications are processed on a rolling basis. Application fee: $70. Electronic applications accepted. *Expenses: Tuition, area resident:* Part-time $1195 per credit. *Required fees:* $260 per semester. Tuition and fees vary according to degree level, campus/location and program. *Financial support:* Scholarships/grants and unspecified assistantships available. Financial award application deadline: 2/15; financial award applicants required to submit FAFSA. *Unit head:* Dr. E. Melanie DuPuis, Chair, Environmental Studies and Science program, 914-773-3522,
E-mail: edupuis@pace.edu. *Application contact:* Susan Ford-Goldschein, Director of Graduate Admissions, 914-422-4283, Fax: 212-346-1585,
E-mail: graduateadmission@pace.edu.
Website: http://www.pace.edu/dyson/departments/environmental-studies-science

Penn State Harrisburg, Graduate School, School of Science, Engineering and Technology, Middletown, PA 17057-4898. Offers computer science (MS); electrical engineering (M Eng, MS); engineering management (MPS); engineering science (M Eng); environmental engineering (M Eng); environmental pollution control (MEPC, MS); structural engineering (Certificate). *Program availability:* Part-time, evening/weekend. *Unit head:* Dr. Mukund S. Kulkarni, Chancellor, 717-948-6105, Fax: 717-948-6452. *Application contact:* Robert W. Coffman, Jr., Director of Enrollment Management, Admissions, 717-948-6250, Fax: 717-948-6325, E-mail: hbgadmit@psu.edu.
Website: https://harrisburg.psu.edu/science-engineering-technology

Penn State University Park, Graduate School, Intercollege Graduate Programs, Intercollege Program in Environmental Pollution Control, University Park, PA 16802. Offers environmental pollution control (MEPC, MS). *Unit head:* Dr. Regina Vasilatos-Younken, Dean, 814-865-2516, Fax: 814-863-4627. *Application contact:* Lori Stania, Director, Graduate Student Services, 814-865-1795, Fax: 814-863-4627,
E-mail: l-gswww@lists.psu.edu.

Pontifical Catholic University of Puerto Rico, College of Sciences, Department of Biology, Ponce, PR 00717-0777. Offers environmental sciences (MS). *Degree requirements:* For master's, thesis. *Entrance requirements:* For master's, GRE, 2 letters of recommendation, interview, minimum GPA of 2.75.

Portland State University, Graduate Studies, College of Liberal Arts and Sciences, Department of Geology, Portland, OR 97207-0751. Offers environmental sciences and resources (PhD); geology (MA, MS); science/geology (MAT, MST). *Program availability:* Part-time. *Faculty:* 10 full-time (2 women), 6 part-time/adjunct (3 women). *Students:* 19 full-time (7 women), 17 part-time (11 women); includes 5 minority (1 Asian, non-Hispanic/Latino; 4 Hispanic/Latino), 2 international. Average age 32. 33 applicants, 61% accepted, 12 enrolled. In 2015, 7 master's awarded. *Degree requirements:* For master's, comprehensive exam, thesis or alternative, field comprehensive; for doctorate, thesis/dissertation. *Entrance requirements:* For master's, GRE General Test, GRE Subject Test, BA/BS in geology, minimum GPA of 3.0 in geology-related and allied sciences, resume, statement of intent, 2 letters of recommendation. Additional exam requirements/recommendations for international students: Required—TOEFL (minimum score 550 paper-based; 80 iBT). *Application deadline:* 1/31 priority date for domestic and international students. Application fee: $50. Electronic applications accepted. *Expenses:* $11,490 per year. *Financial support:* In 2015–16, 2 research assistantships with tuition reimbursements (averaging $2,651 per year), 8 teaching assistantships with full tuition reimbursements (averaging $15,000 per year) were awarded; career-related internships or fieldwork, Federal Work-Study, scholarships/grants, and unspecified assistantships also available. Support available to part-time students. Financial award application deadline: 3/1; financial award applicants required to submit FAFSA. *Faculty research:* Sediment transport, volcanic environmental geology, coastal and fluvial processes. *Total annual research expenditures:* $1.3 million. *Unit head:* Dr. Martin Streck, Chair, 503-725-3379, Fax: 503-725-3025, E-mail: streckm@pdx.edu. *Application contact:* Dr. Andrew Fountain, Graduate Committee Chair, 503-725-3386, Fax: 503-725-3025, E-mail: andrew@pdx.edu.
Website: http://geology.pdx.edu/

Portland State University, Graduate Studies, College of Liberal Arts and Sciences, Program in Environmental Sciences and Management, Portland, OR 97207-0751. Offers environmental management (MEM); environmental sciences/biology (PhD); environmental sciences/chemistry (PhD); environmental sciences/civil engineering (PhD); environmental sciences/geography (PhD); environmental sciences/geology (PhD); environmental sciences/physics (PhD); environmental studies (MS); science/environmental science (MST). *Program availability:* Part-time. *Faculty:* 24 full-time (11 women), 10 part-time/adjunct (4 women). *Students:* 52 full-time (32 women), 41 part-time (23 women); includes 11 minority (1 Black or African American, non-Hispanic/Latino; 1 American Indian or Alaska Native, non-Hispanic/Latino; 2 Asian, non-Hispanic/Latino; 2 Hispanic/Latino; 1 Native Hawaiian or other Pacific Islander, non-Hispanic/Latino; 4 Two or more races, non-Hispanic/Latino), 4 international. Average age 34. 93 applicants, 51% accepted, 29 enrolled. In 2015, 10 master's, 2 doctorates awarded. *Degree requirements:* For master's, thesis or alternative; for doctorate, variable foreign language requirement, comprehensive exam, thesis/dissertation, oral and qualifying exams. *Entrance requirements:* For master's, GRE General Test, 3 letters of recommendation; for doctorate, minimum GPA of 3.0 in upper-division course work or 2.75 overall. Additional exam requirements/recommendations for international students: Required—TOEFL (minimum score 550 paper-based; 80 iBT), IELTS (minimum score 6.5). *Application deadline:* For fall admission, 2/1 for domestic and international students. Applications are processed on a rolling basis. Application fee: $50. *Expenses:* $11,490 per year. *Financial support:* In 2015–16, 5 research assistantships with full tuition reimbursements (averaging $16,120 per year), 15 teaching assistantships with full tuition reimbursements (averaging $15,000 per year) were awarded; Federal Work-Study, scholarships/grants, tuition waivers (partial), and unspecified assistantships also available. Support available to part-time students. Financial award application deadline: 3/1; financial award applicants required to submit FAFSA. *Faculty research:* Environmental aspects of biology, chemistry, civil engineering, geology, physics. *Total annual research expenditures:* $2 million. *Unit head:* Dr. John Rueter, Chair, 503-725-8308, Fax: 503-725-3888, E-mail: rueterj@pdx.edu. *Application contact:* Dr. Robert Scheller, Chair, Graduate Admissions, 503-725-4982, Fax: 503-725-9040, E-mail: rmschell@pdx.edu.

Website: http://www.esr.pdx.edu/

Queens College of the City University of New York, Mathematics and Natural Sciences Division, School of Earth and Environmental Sciences, Flushing, NY 11367-1597. Offers applied environmental geoscience (MS); geological and environmental science (MA). *Program availability:* Part-time, evening/weekend. *Faculty:* 17 full-time (3 women), 9 part-time/adjunct (2 women). *Students:* 14 part-time (6 women); includes 2 minority (1 Black or African American, non-Hispanic/Latino; 1 Hispanic/Latino), 2 international. Average age 27. 11 applicants, 55% accepted, 3 enrolled. In 2015, 6 master's awarded. *Degree requirements:* For master's, comprehensive exam, thesis. *Entrance requirements:* For master's, previous course work in calculus, physics, and chemistry; minimum GPA of 3.0. Additional exam requirements/recommendations for international students: Required—TOEFL, IELTS. *Application deadline:* For fall admission, 4/1 for domestic students; for spring admission, 11/1 for domestic students. Applications are processed on a rolling basis. Application fee: $125. Electronic applications accepted. *Expenses:* Tuition, state resident: full-time $5065; part-time $425 per credit. Tuition, nonresident: part-time $780 per credit. *Required fees:* $522. Part-time tuition and fees vary according to course load and program. *Financial support:* Career-related internships or fieldwork and unspecified assistantships available. Financial award application deadline: 4/1; financial award applicants required to submit FAFSA. *Unit head:* Dr. George Hendrey, Chairperson, 718-997-3300, E-mail: george.hendrey@qc.cuny.edu.

Rice University, Graduate Programs, George R. Brown School of Engineering, Department of Civil and Environmental Engineering, Houston, TX 77251-1892. Offers civil engineering (MCE, MS, PhD); environmental engineering (MEE, MES, MS, PhD); environmental science (MEE, MES, MS, PhD). *Program availability:* Part-time. *Degree requirements:* For master's, thesis (for some programs); for doctorate, thesis/dissertation. *Entrance requirements:* For master's and doctorate, GRE General Test, GRE Subject Test, minimum GPA of 3.25. Additional exam requirements/recommendations for international students: Required—TOEFL (minimum score 600 paper-based; 90 iBT). Electronic applications accepted. *Faculty research:* Biology and chemistry of groundwater, pollutant fate in groundwater systems, water quality monitoring, urban storm water runoff, urban air quality.

Rice University, Graduate Programs, Wiess School–Professional Science Master's Programs, Houston, TX 77251-1892. Offers MS.

Rochester Institute of Technology, Graduate Enrollment Services, College of Science, School of Life Sciences, MS Program in Environmental Science, Rochester, NY 14623. Offers MS. *Program availability:* Part-time. *Students:* 12 full-time (10 women), 9 part-time (6 women); includes 2 minority (1 Black or African American, non-Hispanic/Latino; 1 Hispanic/Latino), 3 international. Average age 25. 21 applicants, 48% accepted, 8 enrolled. In 2015, 1 master's awarded. *Degree requirements:* For master's, thesis or alternative. *Entrance requirements:* For master's, GRE, minimum GPA of 3.0 (recommended). Additional exam requirements/recommendations for international students: Required—PTE (minimum score 58), TOEFL (minimum score 550 paper-based, 79 iBT) or IELTS (minimum score 6.5). *Application deadline:* For fall admission, 2/15 priority date for domestic and international students; for spring admission, 12/15 priority date for domestic and international students. Applications are processed on a rolling basis. Application fee: $60. Electronic applications accepted. *Expenses: Tuition, area resident:* Full-time $41,084; part-time $1742 per credit hour. *Required fees:* $274. Tuition and fees vary according to course load and program. *Financial support:* In 2015–16, 10 students received support. Research assistantships with partial tuition reimbursements available, teaching assistantships with partial tuition reimbursements available, career-related internships or fieldwork, scholarships/grants, and unspecified assistantships available. Support available to part-time students. Financial award applicants required to submit FAFSA. *Faculty research:* Habitat loss, global climate change, water and air pollution, ozone depletion, species invasions, loss of biodiversity, the accumulation of toxic wastes. *Unit head:* Dr. Christy Tyler, Graduate Program Director, 585-475-5042, Fax: 585-475-5000, E-mail: actsbi@rit.edu. *Application contact:* Diane Ellison, Associate Vice President, Graduate Enrollment Services, 585-475-2229, Fax: 585-475-7164, E-mail: gradinfo@rit.edu.

Website: https://www.rit.edu/science/programs/ms/environmental-science

Royal Military College of Canada, Division of Graduate Studies and Research, Engineering Division, Program in Environmental Science, Kingston, ON K7K 7B4, Canada. Offers M Sc, PhD. *Degree requirements:* For master's, thesis; for doctorate, comprehensive exam, thesis/dissertation. *Entrance requirements:* For master's, honours degree with second-class standing; for doctorate, master's degree. Electronic applications accepted.

Rutgers University–Newark, Graduate School, Program in Environmental Science, Newark, NJ 07102. Offers MS, PhD. MS, PhD offered jointly with New Jersey Institute of Technology. *Entrance requirements:* For master's and doctorate, GRE, minimum B average.

Rutgers University–New Brunswick, Graduate School-New Brunswick, Department of Environmental Sciences, Piscataway, NJ 08854-8097. Offers air pollution and resources (MS, PhD); aquatic biology (MS, PhD); aquatic chemistry (MS, PhD); atmospheric science (MS, PhD); chemistry and physics of aerosol and hydrosol systems (MS, PhD); environmental chemistry (MS, PhD); environmental microbiology (MS, PhD); environmental toxicology (PhD); exposure assessment (PhD); fate and effects of pollutants (MS, PhD); pollution prevention and control (MS, PhD); water and wastewater treatment (MS, PhD); water resources (MS, PhD). Terminal master's awarded for partial completion of doctoral program. *Degree requirements:* For master's, comprehensive exam, thesis or alternative, oral final exam; for doctorate, comprehensive exam, thesis/dissertation, thesis defense, qualifying exam. *Entrance requirements:* For master's and doctorate, GRE General Test. Additional exam requirements/recommendations for international students: Required—TOEFL. Electronic applications accepted. *Faculty research:* Biological waste treatment; contaminant fate and transport; air, soil and water quality.

Rutgers University–New Brunswick, Graduate School of Biomedical Sciences, Program in Exposure Science and Assessment, Piscataway, NJ 08854-5635. Offers PhD, MD/PhD. PhD offered jointly with Rutgers, The State University of New Jersey, New Brunswick. *Entrance requirements:* Additional exam requirements/recommendations for international students: Required—TOEFL. Electronic applications accepted.

Sitting Bull College, Program in Environmental Science, Fort Yates, ND 58538-9701. Offers MS. *Entrance requirements:* For master's, GRE, official transcripts from all previous colleges and universities, three letters of recommendation, curriculum vitae, letter of intent.

South Dakota School of Mines and Technology, Graduate Division, PhD Program in Atmospheric and Environmental Sciences, Rapid City, SD 57701-3995. Offers PhD. Program offered jointly with South Dakota State University. *Program availability:* Part-time. *Degree requirements:* For doctorate, comprehensive exam, thesis/dissertation. *Entrance requirements:* For doctorate, GRE General Test, GRE Subject Test. Additional exam requirements/recommendations for international students: Required—TOEFL (minimum score 520 paper-based; 68 iBT), TWE. Electronic applications accepted.

Southeast Missouri State University, School of Graduate Studies, Program in Environmental Science, Cape Girardeau, MO 63701-4799. Offers MS. *Program availability:* Part-time. *Faculty:* 12 full-time (2 women). *Students:* 16 full-time (10 women), 9 part-time (4 women); includes 1 minority (American Indian or Alaska Native, non-Hispanic/Latino), 18 international. Average age 29. 18 applicants, 56% accepted, 7 enrolled. In 2015, 9 master's awarded. *Degree requirements:* For master's, comprehensive exam (for some programs), thesis (for some programs). *Entrance requirements:* For master's, GRE General Test, 30 hours of natural science, minimum GPA of 3.0. Additional exam requirements/recommendations for international students: Required—TOEFL (minimum score 550 paper-based; 79 iBT), IELTS (minimum score 6), PTE (minimum score 53). *Application deadline:* For fall admission, 8/1 for domestic students, 6/1 for international students; for spring admission, 11/21 for domestic students, 10/1 for international students; for summer admission, 5/15 for domestic students. Applications are processed on a rolling basis. Application fee: $30 ($40 for international students). Electronic applications accepted. *Expenses:* Tuition, state resident: part-time $260.80 per credit hour. Tuition, nonresident: part-time $486.80 per credit hour. *Required fees:* $33.70 per credit hour. *Financial support:* In 2015–16, 8 students received support, including 1 teaching assistantship with full tuition reimbursement available (averaging $8,467 per year); career-related internships or fieldwork, Federal Work-Study, scholarships/grants, traineeships, tuition waivers (full), and unspecified assistantships also available. Financial award application deadline: 6/30; financial award applicants required to submit FAFSA. *Faculty research:* Asthma and indoor air, mussels and water quality, metals in wildlife, paths in environmental samples, genesis of arctic soils. *Total annual research expenditures:* $40,000. *Unit head:* Dr. John Kraemer, Director of Environmental Science, 573-651-2355, E-mail: jkraemer@semo.edu. *Application contact:* Dr. John Kraemer, Graduate Coordinator, 573-651-2355, E-mail: jkraemer@semo.edu.

Southern Connecticut State University, School of Graduate Studies, School of Arts and Sciences, Department of Environment, Geography and Marine Sciences, New Haven, CT 06515-1355. Offers environmental education (MS); science education (MS, Diploma). *Accreditation:* NCATE. *Program availability:* Part-time, evening/weekend. *Faculty:* 1 part-time/adjunct (0 women). *Students:* 4 full-time (1 woman), 32 part-time (15 women); includes 5 minority (2 Black or African American, non-Hispanic/Latino; 1 Asian, non-Hispanic/Latino; 1 Hispanic/Latino; 1 Two or more races, non-Hispanic/Latino), 1 international. Average age 33. 36 applicants, 36% accepted, 7 enrolled. In 2015, 13 master's awarded. *Degree requirements:* For master's, thesis or alternative. *Entrance requirements:* For master's, interview; for Diploma, master's degree. *Application deadline:* For fall admission, 7/15 priority date for domestic students. Applications are processed on a rolling basis. Application fee: $50. Electronic applications accepted. *Expenses:* Tuition, state resident: full-time $4968; part-time $494 per credit hour. Tuition, nonresident: full-time $16,078; part-time $509 per credit hour. *Required fees:* $4632; $55 per semester. Tuition and fees vary according to program. *Financial support:* Career-related internships or fieldwork, scholarships/grants, and unspecified assistantships available. Financial award application deadline: 4/15; financial award applicants required to submit FAFSA. *Unit head:* Dr. Patrick Heidkamp, Chairman, 203-392-5919, Fax: 203-392-5834, E-mail: heidkampc1@southernct.edu. *Application contact:* Lisa Galvin, Director of Graduate Admissions, 203-392-5240, Fax: 203-392-5235, E-mail: galvinl1@southernct.edu.

Southern Illinois University Carbondale, Graduate School, College of Science, Department of Geology and Department of Geography, Program in Environmental Resources and Policy, Carbondale, IL 62901-4701. Offers PhD. *Students:* 3 full-time (2 women), 22 part-time (10 women); includes 3 minority (2 Black or African American, non-Hispanic/Latino; 1 Native Hawaiian or other Pacific Islander, non-Hispanic/Latino), 13 international. 6 applicants, 17% accepted, 14 enrolled. In 2015, 2 doctorates awarded. *Degree requirements:* For doctorate, thesis/dissertation. *Entrance requirements:* For doctorate, GRE, minimum GPA of 3.25. Application fee: $65. *Financial support:* In 2015–16, 7 students received support, including 7 teaching assistantships; fellowships, research assistantships, and unspecified assistantships also available. *Unit head:* Dr. Steven Esling, Chair, 618-453-3351, Fax: 618-453-7393, E-mail: esling@geo.siu.edu. *Application contact:* Dana Wise, Office Specialist, 618-453-7328, E-mail: dwise@siu.edu.

Southern Illinois University Edwardsville, Graduate School, College of Arts and Sciences, Program in Environmental Sciences, Edwardsville, IL 62026-0001. Offers MS. *Program availability:* Part-time, evening/weekend. *Faculty:* 6. *Students:* 9 full-time (4 women), 27 part-time (19 women); includes 4 minority (3 Black or African American, non-Hispanic/Latino; 1 Asian, non-Hispanic/Latino), 10 international. 30 applicants, 63% accepted, 10 enrolled. *Degree requirements:* For master's, thesis (for some programs), final exam, oral exam. *Entrance requirements:* For master's, GRE. Additional exam requirements/recommendations for international students: Required—TOEFL (minimum score 550 paper-based; 79 iBT), IELTS (minimum score 6.5). *Application deadline:* For fall admission, 7/22 for domestic students, 7/15 for international students; for spring admission, 12/9 for domestic students, 11/15 for international students; for summer admission, 4/29 for domestic students, 4/15 for international students. Applications are processed on a rolling basis. Application fee: $30. Electronic applications accepted. *Expenses:* Tuition, state resident: full-time $5026; part-time $837 per course. Tuition, nonresident: full-time $12,566; part-time $2094 per course. *Required fees:* $1682; $474 per course. Tuition and fees vary according to course load, campus/location and program. *Financial support:* In 2015–16, 11 students received support, including 1 research assistantship with full tuition reimbursement available, 10 teaching assistantships with full tuition reimbursements available; fellowships with full tuition reimbursements available, institutionally sponsored loans, scholarships/grants, and unspecified assistantships also available. Financial award application deadline: 3/1; financial award applicants required to submit FAFSA. *Unit head:* Dr. Zhiqing Lin, Program Director, 618-650-2650, E-mail: zhlin@siue.edu. *Application contact:* Bob Skorczewski, Coordinator of International and Graduate Recruitment, 618-650-3705, Fax: 618-650-3618, E-mail: graduatestudents@siue.edu.

Website: http://www.siue.edu/academics/programs/graduate/environmental-sciences/

Southern Methodist University, Bobby B. Lyle School of Engineering, Department of Environmental and Civil Engineering, Dallas, TX 75275-0340. Offers air pollution control and atmospheric sciences (PhD); civil engineering (MS); environmental engineering

(MS); environmental science (MS); structural engineering (PhD); sustainability and development (MA); water and wastewater engineering (PhD). *Program availability:* Part-time, evening/weekend, online learning. Terminal master's awarded for partial completion of doctoral program. *Degree requirements:* For master's, thesis optional; for doctorate, thesis/dissertation, oral and written qualifying exams. *Entrance requirements:* For master's, GRE General Test, minimum GPA of 3.0 in last 2 years; bachelor's degree in engineering, mathematics, or sciences; for doctorate, GRE, BS and MS in related field, minimum GPA of 3.3. Additional exam requirements/recommendations for international students: Required—TOEFL. Electronic applications accepted. *Faculty research:* Human and environmental health effects of endocrine disrupters, development of air pollution control systems for diesel engines, structural analysis and design, modeling and design of waste treatment systems.

Southern University and Agricultural and Mechanical College, Graduate School, College of Sciences, Department of Chemistry, Baton Rouge, LA 70813. Offers analytical chemistry (MS); biochemistry (MS); environmental sciences (MS); inorganic chemistry (MS); organic chemistry (MS); physical chemistry (MS). *Degree requirements:* For master's, thesis. *Entrance requirements:* For master's, GMAT or GRE General Test. Additional exam requirements/recommendations for international students: Required—TOEFL (minimum score 525 paper-based). *Faculty research:* Synthesis of macrocyclic ligands, latex accelerators, anticancer drugs, biosensors, absorption isotheums, isolation of specific enzymes from plants.

Stanford University, School of Earth, Energy and Environmental Sciences, Stanford, CA 94305-9991. Offers MS, PhD, Eng. Terminal master's awarded for partial completion of doctoral program. *Degree requirements:* For doctorate, thesis/dissertation; for Eng, thesis. *Entrance requirements:* For master's, doctorate, and Eng, GRE General Test. Additional exam requirements/recommendations for international students: Required—TOEFL. Electronic applications accepted. *Expenses: Tuition, area resident:* Full-time $45,729. *Required fees:* $591.

Stanford University, School of Humanities and Sciences, Department of Anthropology, Stanford, CA 94305-9991. Offers anthropology (MA); archaeology (PhD); culture and society (PhD); ecology and environment (PhD). Terminal master's awarded for partial completion of doctoral program. *Degree requirements:* For master's, thesis; for doctorate, one foreign language, thesis/dissertation. *Entrance requirements:* For master's and doctorate, GRE General Test. Additional exam requirements/recommendations for international students: Required—TOEFL. Electronic applications accepted. *Expenses: Tuition, area resident:* Full-time $45,729. *Required fees:* $591.

State University of New York College of Environmental Science and Forestry, Department of Chemistry, Syracuse, NY 13210-2779. Offers biochemistry (MPS, MS, PhD); environmental chemistry (MPS, MS, PhD); organic chemistry of natural products (MPS, MS, PhD); polymer chemistry (MPS, MS, PhD). *Faculty:* 17 full-time (2 women), 1 part-time/adjunct (0 women). *Students:* 33 full-time (13 women), 5 part-time (2 women); includes 2 minority (1 Black or African American, non-Hispanic/Latino; 1 Asian, non-Hispanic/Latino), 10 international. 55 applicants, 67% accepted, 12 enrolled. In 2015, 4 master's, 7 doctorates awarded. *Degree requirements:* For master's, thesis; for doctorate, comprehensive exam, thesis/dissertation. *Entrance requirements:* For master's and doctorate, GRE General Test, GRE Subject Test, minimum GPA of 3.0. Additional exam requirements/recommendations for international students: Required—TOEFL (minimum score 550 paper-based; 80 iBT), IELTS (minimum score 6). *Application deadline:* For fall admission, 2/1 priority date for domestic and international students; for spring admission, 11/1 priority date for domestic and international students. Applications are processed on a rolling basis. Application fee: $60. Electronic applications accepted. *Expenses:* Tuition, state resident: full-time $10,870; part-time $453 per credit. Tuition, nonresident: full-time $22,210; part-time $925 per credit. *Required fees:* $1075; $89.22 per credit. *Financial support:* In 2015–16, 40 students received support, including 5 fellowships with full tuition reimbursements available (averaging $4,000 per year), 19 research assistantships with full tuition reimbursements available (averaging $20,000 per year), 44 teaching assistantships with full tuition reimbursements available (averaging $21,300 per year); Federal Work-Study, institutionally sponsored loans, scholarships/grants, health care benefits, unspecified assistantships, and departmental tuition assistance also available. Financial award application deadline: 6/30; financial award applicants required to submit FAFSA. *Faculty research:* Polymer chemistry, biochemistry, environmental chemistry, natural products chemistry. *Total annual research expenditures:* $1.8 million. *Unit head:* Prof. Ivan Gitsov, Chair, 315-470-6851, Fax: 315-470-6856, E-mail: igivanov@syr.edu. *Application contact:* Scott Shannon, Associate Provost for Instruction/Dean of the Graduate School, 315-470-6599, Fax: 315-470-6978, E-mail: sshannon@esf.edu.
Website: http://www.esf.edu/chemistry

State University of New York College of Environmental Science and Forestry, Department of Environmental and Forest Biology, Syracuse, NY 13210-2779. Offers applied ecology (MPS); chemical ecology (MPS, MS, PhD); conservation biology (MPS, MS, PhD); ecology (MPS, MS, PhD); entomology (MPS, MS, PhD); environmental interpretation (MPS, MS, PhD); environmental physiology (MPS, MS, PhD); fish and wildlife biology and management (MPS, MS, PhD); forest pathology and mycology (MPS, MS, PhD); plant biotechnology (MPS); plant science and biotechnology (MPS, MS, PhD). *Faculty:* 29 full-time (9 women), 4 part-time/adjunct (3 women). *Students:* 81 full-time (47 women), 57 part-time (24 women); includes 9 minority (1 Black or African American, non-Hispanic/Latino; 2 American Indian or Alaska Native, non-Hispanic/Latino; 1 Asian, non-Hispanic/Latino; 3 Hispanic/Latino; 2 Two or more races, non-Hispanic/Latino), 15 international. Average age 28. 47 applicants, 49% accepted, 15 enrolled. In 2015, 15 master's, 7 doctorates awarded. *Degree requirements:* For master's, thesis (for some programs), capstone seminar; for doctorate, comprehensive exam, thesis/dissertation, capstone seminar. *Entrance requirements:* For master's and doctorate, GRE General Test, minimum GPA of 3.0. Additional exam requirements/recommendations for international students: Required—TOEFL (minimum score 550 paper-based; 80 iBT), IELTS (minimum score 6). *Application deadline:* For fall admission, 2/1 priority date for domestic and international students; for spring admission, 11/1 priority date for domestic and international students. Applications are processed on a rolling basis. Application fee: $60. *Expenses:* Tuition, state resident: full-time $10,870; part-time $453 per credit. Tuition, nonresident: full-time $22,210; part-time $925 per credit. *Required fees:* $1075; $89.22 per credit. *Financial support:* In 2015–16, 4 fellowships with tuition reimbursements, 36 research assistantships with tuition reimbursements, 39 teaching assistantships with tuition reimbursements (averaging $11,490 per year) were awarded; Federal Work-Study, institutionally sponsored loans, scholarships/grants, health care benefits, and unspecified assistantships also available. Financial award application deadline: 6/30. *Faculty research:* Ecology, conservation biology, fish and wildlife biology and management, plant science, entomology. *Total annual research expenditures:* $4.1 million. *Unit head:* Dr. Donald J. Leopold, Chair, 315-470-6760, Fax: 315-470-6934,
E-mail: djleopold@esf.edu. *Application contact:* Dr. Danilo D. Fernando, Director, Graduate Program/Associate Professor, 315-470-6746, Fax: 315-470-6934,
E-mail: dfernando@esf.edu.
Website: http://www.esf.edu/efb/grad/default.asp

State University of New York College of Environmental Science and Forestry, Program in Environmental Science, Syracuse, NY 13210-2779. Offers biophysical and ecological economics (MPS); coupled natural and human systems (MPS); ecosystem restoration (MPS); environmental and community land planning (MPS, MS); environmental and natural resources policy (PhD); environmental communication and participatory processes (PhD); environmental monitoring and modeling (MPS); environmental policy and democratic processes (MPS, MS); water and wetland resource studies (MPS, MS). *Program availability:* Part-time. *Faculty:* 1 full-time (0 women), 1 (woman) part-time/adjunct. *Students:* 56 full-time (33 women), 17 part-time (10 women); includes 6 minority (2 Asian, non-Hispanic/Latino; 3 Hispanic/Latino; 1 Two or more races, non-Hispanic/Latino), 34 international. 85 applicants, 44% accepted, 13 enrolled. *Degree requirements:* For master's, thesis (for some programs); for doctorate, comprehensive exam, thesis/dissertation. *Entrance requirements:* For master's and doctorate, GRE General Test, minimum GPA of 3.0. Additional exam requirements/recommendations for international students: Required—TOEFL (minimum score 550 paper-based; 80 iBT), IELTS (minimum score 6). *Application deadline:* For fall admission, 2/1 priority date for domestic and international students; for spring admission, 11/1 priority date for domestic and international students. Applications are processed on a rolling basis. Application fee: $60. *Expenses:* Tuition, state resident: full-time $10,870; part-time $453 per credit. Tuition, nonresident: full-time $22,210; part-time $925 per credit. *Required fees:* $1075; $89.22 per credit. *Financial support:* Fellowships with tuition reimbursements, research assistantships with tuition reimbursements, teaching assistantships with tuition reimbursements, career-related internships or fieldwork, Federal Work-Study, institutionally sponsored loans, scholarships/grants, health care benefits, and unspecified assistantships available. Support available to part-time students. Financial award application deadline: 6/30; financial award applicants required to submit FAFSA. *Faculty research:* Environmental education/communications, water resources, land resources, waste management. *Unit head:* Dr. Ruth Yanai, Coordinator, 315-470-6955, Fax: 315-470-6700,
E-mail: rdyanai@esf.edu. *Application contact:* Dr. Dudley J. Raynal, Dean, Instruction and Graduate Studies, 315-470-6599, Fax: 315-470-6978, E-mail: esfgrad@esf.edu.
Website: http://www.esf.edu/environmentalscience/graduate/

Stephen F. Austin State University, Graduate School, College of Sciences and Mathematics, Division of Environmental Science, Nacogdoches, TX 75962. Offers MS. *Degree requirements:* For master's, comprehensive exam. *Entrance requirements:* For master's, GRE General Test, minimum GPA of 2.8 in last 60 hours, 2.5 overall. Additional exam requirements/recommendations for international students: Required—TOEFL.

Stockton University, Office of Graduate Studies, Program in Environmental Science, Galloway, NJ 08205-9441. Offers PSM. *Program availability:* Part-time, evening/weekend. *Faculty:* 1 (woman) full-time, 5 part-time/adjunct (0 women). *Students:* 11 full-time (6 women), 19 part-time (5 women); includes 1 minority (Hispanic/Latino). Average age 28. 19 applicants, 84% accepted, 14 enrolled. In 2015, 5 master's awarded. *Degree requirements:* For master's, thesis optional, project. *Entrance requirements:* For master's, GRE. Additional exam requirements/recommendations for international students: Required—TOEFL. *Application deadline:* For fall admission, 7/1 for domestic and international students; for spring admission, 12/1 for domestic students, 11/1 for international students. Applications are processed on a rolling basis. Application fee: $50. Electronic applications accepted. *Expenses:* Tuition, state resident: full-time $13,968; part-time $582 per credit. Tuition, nonresident: full-time $21,502; part-time $895 per credit. *Required fees:* $4200; $175 per credit. $90. Tuition and fees vary according to degree level. *Financial support:* In 2015–16, 5 students received support, including 7 research assistantships; fellowships with partial tuition reimbursements available, career-related internships or fieldwork, Federal Work-Study, scholarships/grants, and unspecified assistantships also available. Financial award application deadline: 3/1; financial award applicants required to submit FAFSA. *Unit head:* Dr. Kathy Sedia, Program Director, 609-626-3640, E-mail: gradschool@stockton.edu. *Application contact:* Tara Williams, Assistant Director of Graduate Enrollment Management, 609-626-3640, Fax: 609-626-6050, E-mail: gradschool@stockton.edu.
Website: http://www.stockton.edu/grad

Tennessee Technological University, College of Graduate Studies, School of Environmental Studies, Department of Environmental Sciences, Cookeville, TN 38505. Offers biology (PhD); chemistry (PhD). *Program availability:* Part-time. *Students:* 4 full-time (0 women), 12 part-time (5 women), 7 international. 13 applicants, 38% accepted, 2 enrolled. In 2015, 5 doctorates awarded. *Degree requirements:* For doctorate, comprehensive exam, thesis/dissertation. *Entrance requirements:* For doctorate, GRE. Additional exam requirements/recommendations for international students: Required—TOEFL (minimum score 527 paper-based; 71 iBT), IELTS (minimum score 5.5), PTE (minimum score 48), or TOEIC (Test of English as an International Communication). *Application deadline:* For fall admission, 8/1 for domestic students, 5/1 for international students; for spring admission, 12/1 for domestic students, 10/2 for international students; for summer admission, 5/1 for domestic students, 2/1 for international students. Applications are processed on a rolling basis. Application fee: $35 ($40 for international students). Electronic applications accepted. *Expenses:* Tuition, state resident: full-time $8961; part-time $6132 per credit hour. Tuition, nonresident: full-time $23,121; part-time $14,608 per credit hour. *Financial support:* In 2015–16, 5 research assistantships (averaging $10,000 per year), 3 teaching assistantships (averaging $10,000 per year) were awarded; fellowships also available. Financial award application deadline: 4/1. *Unit head:* Dr. Hayden Mattingly, Interim Director, 931-372-6246,
E-mail: hmattingly@tntech.edu. *Application contact:* Shelia K. Kendrick, Coordinator of Graduate Studies, 931-372-3808, Fax: 931-372-3497, E-mail: skendrick@tntech.edu.

Texas A&M University–Corpus Christi, College of Graduate Studies, College of Science and Engineering, Program in Environmental Science, Corpus Christi, TX 78412-5503. Offers MS. *Program availability:* Part-time, evening/weekend. *Students:* 24 full-time (15 women), 9 part-time (5 women); includes 9 minority (8 Hispanic/Latino; 1 Two or more races, non-Hispanic/Latino), 3 international. Average age 30. 22 applicants, 50% accepted, 8 enrolled. In 2015, 8 master's awarded. *Degree requirements:* For master's, comprehensive exam, thesis (for some programs), thesis or project. *Entrance requirements:* For master's, GRE General Test, essay (minimum of 300 words), 3 letters of evaluation. Additional exam requirements/recommendations for international students: Required—TOEFL (minimum score 550 paper-based; 79 iBT), IELTS (minimum score 6.5). *Application deadline:* For fall admission, 7/15 priority date for domestic students, 5/1 priority date for international students; for spring admission, 11/15 priority date for domestic students, 9/1 priority date for international students; for summer admission, 5/15 priority date for domestic students, 2/1 priority date for international students. Applications are processed on a rolling basis. Application fee: $50 ($70 for international students). Electronic applications accepted. *Financial support:* Research assistantships, career-related internships or fieldwork, Federal Work-Study, institutionally sponsored loans, scholarships/grants, health care benefits, and unspecified assistantships available. Support available to part-time students. Financial award application deadline: 3/15; financial award applicants required to submit FAFSA. *Unit head:* Dr. Jennifer Smith-Engle, Assistant to the Chair, 361-825-2436,

E-mail: jennifer.smith-engle@tamucc.edu. *Application contact:* Graduate Admissions Coordinator, 361-825-2177, Fax: 361-825-2755, E-mail: gradweb@tamucc.edu.
Website: http://esci.tamucc.edu/

Texas Christian University, College of Science and Engineering, School of Geology, Energy and the Environment, Fort Worth, TX 76129. Offers environmental science (MA, MEM, MS); geology (MS). *Program availability:* Part-time. *Faculty:* 13 full-time (4 women), 1 part-time/adjunct (0 women). *Students:* 32 full-time (10 women), 3 part-time (0 women); includes 5 minority (1 Black or African American, non-Hispanic/Latino; 2 Asian, non-Hispanic/Latino; 2 Hispanic/Latino), 3 international. Average age 27. 56 applicants, 25% accepted, 10 enrolled. In 2015, 15 master's awarded. *Degree requirements:* For master's, comprehensive exam (for some programs), thesis. *Entrance requirements:* For master's, GRE. Additional exam requirements/recommendations for international students: Required—TOEFL (minimum score 550 paper-based; 80 iBT). *Application deadline:* For fall admission, 2/1 for domestic and international students; for spring admission, 9/1 for domestic and international students. Application fee: $60. Electronic applications accepted. *Expenses: Tuition, area resident:* Full-time $26,640; part-time $1480 per credit hour. *Required fees:* $48; $48 per unit. Tuition and fees vary according to program. *Financial support:* In 2015–16, 15 teaching assistantships with full tuition reimbursements (averaging $16,000 per year) were awarded; unspecified assistantships also available. Financial award application deadline: 2/1. *Faculty research:* Structural geology, sedimentology, physical volcanology, geomorphology, planetary geology. *Unit head:* Dr. Helge Alsleben, Graduate Advisor, 817-257-7270, Fax: 817-257-7789, E-mail: h.alsleben@tcu.edu.
Website: http://sgee.tcu.edu

Texas Tech University, Graduate School, College of Arts and Sciences, Department of Environmental Toxicology, Lubbock, TX 79409. Offers MS, PhD, JD/MS, MBA/MS. *Program availability:* Part-time. *Faculty:* 12 full-time (2 women). *Students:* 37 full-time (23 women), 1 (woman) part-time; includes 8 minority (3 Black or African American, non-Hispanic/Latino; 2 Hispanic/Latino; 3 Two or more races, non-Hispanic/Latino), 10 international. Average age 30. 32 applicants, 53% accepted, 11 enrolled. In 2015, 10 master's, 7 doctorates awarded. Terminal master's awarded for partial completion of doctoral program. *Degree requirements:* For master's, thesis; for doctorate, comprehensive exam, thesis/dissertation. *Entrance requirements:* For master's and doctorate, GRE. Additional exam requirements/recommendations for international students: Required—TOEFL (minimum score 550 paper-based; 79 iBT); Recommended—IELTS (minimum score 6.5), TSE (minimum score 60). *Application deadline:* For fall admission, 6/1 priority date for domestic students, 1/15 priority date for international students; for spring admission, 9/1 priority date for domestic students, 6/15 priority date for international students. Applications are processed on a rolling basis. Application fee: $60. Electronic applications accepted. *Expenses:* Tuition, state resident: full-time $6477; part-time $269.89 per credit hour. Tuition, nonresident: full-time $15,837; part-time $659.89 per credit hour. *Required fees:* $2751; $36.50 per credit hour. $937.50 per semester. Tuition and fees vary according to course level. *Financial support:* In 2015–16, 49 students received support, including 40 fellowships (averaging $2,617 per year), 48 research assistantships (averaging $12,456 per year), 2 teaching assistantships (averaging $13,050 per year); Federal Work-Study, institutionally sponsored loans, scholarships/grants, and health care benefits also available. Financial award application deadline: 4/15; financial award applicants required to submit FAFSA. *Faculty research:* Wildlife toxicology; molecular epidemiology and genomics; endangered species toxicology; reproductive, molecular, and developmental toxicology; environmental chemistry. *Total annual research expenditures:* $1.4 million. *Unit head:* Dr. Todd Anderson, Chair, 806-834-1587, Fax: 806-885-2132,
E-mail: todd.anderson@ttu.edu. *Application contact:* Dr. Jaclyn Canas-Carrell, Graduate Officer, 806-834-6217, E-mail: jaclyn.e.canas@ttu.edu.
Website: http://www.tiehh.ttu.edu/

Thompson Rivers University, Program in Environmental Science, Kamloops, BC V2C 0C8, Canada. Offers MS. *Entrance requirements:* For master's, personal resume, 2 letters of recommendation. Additional exam requirements/recommendations for international students: Required—TOEFL.

Towson University, Program in Environmental Science, Towson, MD 21252-0001. Offers MS, Postbaccalaureate Certificate. *Program availability:* Part-time, evening/weekend. *Students:* 8 full-time (6 women), 21 part-time (12 women); includes 3 minority (2 Black or African American, non-Hispanic/Latino; 1 Two or more races, non-Hispanic/Latino). *Entrance requirements:* For master's, 3 letters of recommendation, bachelor's degree in related field, minimum GPA of 3.0, personal statement; for Postbaccalaureate Certificate, 3 letters of recommendation, bachelor's degree in related field, minimum GPA of 3.0. *Application deadline:* Applications are processed on a rolling basis. Application fee: $45. Electronic applications accepted. *Expenses:* Tuition, state resident: full-time $7440; part-time $372 per unit. Tuition, nonresident: full-time $15,400; part-time $770 per unit. *Required fees:* $2360; $118 per year. $354 per term. *Financial support:* Application deadline: 4/1. *Unit head:* Dr. David Ownby, Graduate Program Director, 410-704-2946, E-mail: downby@towson.edu. *Application contact:* Alicia Arkell-Kleis, University Admissions, 410-704-2113, Fax: 410-704-3030,
E-mail: grads@towson.edu.
Website: http://grad.towson.edu/program/master/envs-ms/

Troy University, Graduate School, College of Arts and Sciences, Program in Environmental and Biological Sciences, Troy, AL 36082. Offers biological science (MS); environmental policy (MS); environmental science (MS). *Program availability:* Part-time, evening/weekend, 100% online, blended/hybrid learning. *Faculty:* 9 full-time (6 women), 1 (woman) part-time/adjunct. *Students:* 14 full-time (7 women), 28 part-time (16 women); includes 10 minority (6 Black or African American, non-Hispanic/Latino; 2 Asian, non-Hispanic/Latino; 1 Hispanic/Latino; 1 Two or more races, non-Hispanic/Latino). Average age 28. 35 applicants, 91% accepted, 9 enrolled. In 2015, 10 master's awarded. *Degree requirements:* For master's, comprehensive exam (for some programs), thesis (for some programs), comprehensive exam or thesis, minimum GPA of 3.0, admission to candidacy. *Entrance requirements:* For master's, GRE (minimum score of 850 on old exam or 290 on new exam), MAT (minimum score of 385) or GMAT (minimum score of 380), bachelor's degree; minimum undergraduate GPA of 2.5 or 3.0 on last 30 semester hours. Additional exam requirements/recommendations for international students: Required—TOEFL (minimum score 523 paper-based; 70 iBT), IELTS (minimum score 6). *Application deadline:* Applications are processed on a rolling basis. Application fee: $50. Electronic applications accepted. *Expenses:* Tuition, state resident: full-time $7146; part-time $397 per credit hour. Tuition, nonresident: full-time $14,292; part-time $794 per credit hour. *Required fees:* $802. Tuition and fees vary according to campus/location and program. *Financial support:* Fellowships, career-related internships or fieldwork, and scholarships/grants available. Support available to part-time students. *Unit head:* Dr. Glenn Cohen, Divisional Chairman, 334-670-3660, Fax: 334-670-3401, E-mail: gcohen@troy.edu. *Application contact:* Jessica A. Kimbro, Director of Graduate Admissions, 334-670-3178, E-mail: jacord@troy.edu.

Tufts University, School of Engineering, Department of Civil and Environmental Engineering, Medford, MA 02155. Offers bioengineering (ME, MS), including environmental technology; civil engineering (ME, MS, PhD), including geotechnical engineering, structural engineering, water diplomacy (PhD); environmental engineering (ME, MS, PhD), including environmental engineering and environmental sciences, environmental geotechnology, environmental health, environmental science and management, hazardous materials management, water diplomacy (PhD), water resources engineering. *Program availability:* Part-time. Terminal master's awarded for partial completion of doctoral program. *Degree requirements:* For master's, thesis or alternative; for doctorate, thesis/dissertation. *Entrance requirements:* For master's and doctorate, GRE General Test. Additional exam requirements/recommendations for international students: Required—TOEFL (minimum score 550 paper-based; 80 iBT), IELTS (minimum score 6.5). Electronic applications accepted. *Expenses: Tuition, area resident:* Full-time $48,412; part-time $1210 per credit hour. *Required fees:* $806. Full-time tuition and fees vary according to degree level, program and student level. Part-time tuition and fees vary according to course load. *Faculty research:* Environmental and water resources engineering, environmental health, geotechnical and geoenvironmental engineering, structural engineering and mechanics, water diplomacy.

Tuskegee University, Graduate Programs, College of Agriculture, Environment and Nutrition Sciences, Department of Agricultural and Environmental Sciences, Program in Environmental Sciences, Tuskegee, AL 36088. Offers MS. *Degree requirements:* For master's, thesis. *Entrance requirements:* For master's, GRE General Test. Additional exam requirements/recommendations for international students: Required—TOEFL (minimum score 500 paper-based).

Universidad del Turabo, Graduate Programs, Programs in Science and Technology, Gurabo, PR 00778-3030. Offers environmental analysis (MSE), including environmental chemistry; environmental management (MSE), including pollution management; environmental science (D Sc), including environmental biology. *Entrance requirements:* For master's, GRE, EXADEP, interview.

Universidad Nacional Pedro Henriquez Urena, Graduate School, Santo Domingo, Dominican Republic. Offers agricultural diversity (MS), including horticultural/fruit production, tropical animal production; conservation of monuments and cultural assets (M Arch); ecology and environment (MS); environmental engineering (MEE); international relations (MA); natural resource management (MS); political science (MA); project optimization (MPM); project feasibility (MPM); project management (MPM); sanitation engineering (ME); science for teachers (MS); tropical Caribbean architecture (M Arch).

Université de Sherbrooke, Faculty of Sciences, Centre Universitaire de Formation en Environnement, Sherbrooke, QC J1K 2R1, Canada. Offers M Sc, Diploma. *Program availability:* Online learning. Electronic applications accepted. *Faculty research:* Environmental studies.

Université du Québec à Montréal, Graduate Programs, Program in Environmental Sciences, Montréal, QC H3C 3P8, Canada. Offers M Sc, PhD, Certificate. *Program availability:* Part-time. *Degree requirements:* For master's, research report; for doctorate, thesis/dissertation. *Entrance requirements:* For master's, appropriate bachelor's degree or equivalent, proficiency in French; for doctorate, appropriate master's degree or equivalent, proficiency in French.

Université du Québec à Trois-Rivières, Graduate Programs, Program in Environmental Sciences, Trois-Rivières, QC G9A 5H7, Canada. Offers M Sc, PhD. *Program availability:* Part-time. *Degree requirements:* For master's, thesis. *Entrance requirements:* For master's, appropriate bachelor's degree, proficiency in French.

Université du Québec en Abitibi-Témiscamingue, Graduate Programs, Program in Environmental Sciences, Rouyn-Noranda, QC J9X 5E4, Canada. Offers biology (MS); environmental sciences (PhD); sustainable forest ecosystem management (MS).

Université Laval, Faculty of Sciences and Engineering, Department of Geology and Geological Engineering, Programs in Earth Sciences, Québec, QC G1K 7P4, Canada. Offers earth sciences (M Sc, PhD); environmental technologies (M Sc). Offered jointly with INRS-Géressources. Terminal master's awarded for partial completion of doctoral program. *Degree requirements:* For master's, thesis (for some programs); for doctorate, comprehensive exam, thesis/dissertation. *Entrance requirements:* For master's and doctorate, knowledge of French. Electronic applications accepted.

University at Albany, State University of New York, College of Arts and Sciences, Department of Biological Sciences, Program in Biodiversity, Conservation, and Policy, Albany, NY 12222-0001. Offers MS. *Degree requirements:* For master's, one foreign language. *Entrance requirements:* For master's, GRE General Test. *Faculty research:* Aquatic ecology, plant community ecology, biodiversity and public policy, restoration ecology, coastal and estuarine science.

University at Buffalo, the State University of New York, Graduate School, College of Arts and Sciences, Department of Geography, Buffalo, NY 14261. Offers Canadian studies (Certificate); earth systems science (MA, MS); economic geography and business geographics (MS); environmental modeling and analysis (MA); geographic information science (MA, MS); geography (MA, PhD); GIS and environmental analysis (Certificate); health geography (MS); international trade (MA); transportation and business geographics (MA); urban and regional analysis (MA). *Program availability:* Part-time. *Faculty:* 19 full-time (9 women), 1 part-time/adjunct (0 women). *Students:* 42 full-time (21 women), 58 part-time (18 women); includes 66 minority (1 Black or African American, non-Hispanic/Latino; 63 Asian, non-Hispanic/Latino; 2 Hispanic/Latino), 2 international. Average age 29. 163 applicants, 32% accepted, 32 enrolled. In 2015, 44 master's, 6 doctorates awarded. Terminal master's awarded for partial completion of doctoral program. *Degree requirements:* For master's, thesis (for some programs), project or portfolio; for doctorate, thesis/dissertation. *Entrance requirements:* For master's, GRE General Test, minimum GPA of 2.9; for doctorate, GRE General Test, minimum GPA of 3.0. Additional exam requirements/recommendations for international students: Required—TOEFL (minimum score 550 paper-based; 79 iBT). *Application deadline:* For fall admission, 5/1 priority date for domestic students, 3/10 priority date for international students; for spring admission, 11/1 priority date for domestic students, 9/1 priority date for international students. Applications are processed on a rolling basis. Application fee: $75. Electronic applications accepted. *Expenses:* $6,582 per semester in-state. *Financial support:* In 2015–16, 13 students received support, including 8 fellowships with full tuition reimbursements available (averaging $5,500 per year), 10 research assistantships with full tuition reimbursements available (averaging $13,000 per year), 13 teaching assistantships with full tuition reimbursements available (averaging $13,800 per year); career-related internships or fieldwork, Federal Work-Study, institutionally sponsored loans, traineeships, health care benefits, and unspecified assistantships also available. Financial award application deadline: 1/10. *Faculty research:* International business and world trade, geographic information systems and cartography, transportation, urban and regional analysis, physical and environmental geography. *Total annual research expenditures:* $2.6 million. *Unit head:* Dr. Sharmistha Bagchi-Sen, Chairman, 716-645-0473, Fax: 716-645-2329,

E-mail: geosbs@buffalo.edu. *Application contact:* Betsy Crooks, Graduate Secretary, 716-645-0471, Fax: 716-645-2329, E-mail: babraham@buffalo.edu.
Website: http://www.geog.buffalo.edu/

The University of Alabama in Huntsville, School of Graduate Studies, College of Science, Department of Atmospheric Science, Huntsville, AL 35899. Offers atmospheric science (MS, PhD); earth system science (MS). *Program availability:* Part-time, evening/weekend. *Degree requirements:* For master's, comprehensive exam, thesis or alternative, oral and written exams; for doctorate, comprehensive exam, thesis/dissertation, oral and written exams. *Entrance requirements:* For master's, GRE General Test, minimum GPA of 3.0; sequence of courses in calculus (including the calculus of vector-valued functions); courses in linear algebra and ordinary differential equations; two semesters each of chemistry and calculus-based physics; proficiency in at least one high-level computer programming language; for doctorate, GRE General Test, minimum GPA of 3.0. Additional exam requirements/recommendations for international students: Required—TOEFL (minimum score 550 paper-based; 80 iBT), IELTS (minimum score 6.5). Electronic applications accepted. *Faculty research:* Severe weather, climate, satellite remote sensing, numerical modeling, air pollution.

University of Alaska Anchorage, School of Engineering, Program in Applied Environmental Science and Technology, Anchorage, AK 99508. Offers M AEST, MS. *Program availability:* Part-time, evening/weekend. *Degree requirements:* For master's, comprehensive exam, thesis (for some programs). *Entrance requirements:* For master's, GRE General Test. Additional exam requirements/recommendations for international students: Required—TOEFL (minimum score 550 paper-based). *Faculty research:* Wastewater treatment, environmental regulations, water resources management, justification of public facilities, rural sanitation, biological treatment process.

University of Alaska Fairbanks, College of Engineering and Mines, Department of Civil and Environmental Engineering, Program in Environmental Quality Science, Fairbanks, AK 99775-5900. Offers MS. *Program availability:* Part-time. *Students:* 2 full-time (1 woman). Average age 28. 4 applicants, 75% accepted. In 2015, 1 master's awarded. *Degree requirements:* For master's, comprehensive exam, oral defense of project or thesis. *Entrance requirements:* For master's, BS in science from accredited institution with minimum GPA of 3.0; calculus, chemistry, and basic computer techniques courses. Additional exam requirements/recommendations for international students: Required—TOEFL (minimum score 575 paper-based). *Application deadline:* For fall admission, 6/1 for domestic students, 3/1 for international students; for spring admission, 10/15 for domestic students, 9/1 for international students. Applications are processed on a rolling basis. Application fee: $60. Electronic applications accepted. *Expenses:* Tuition, state resident: full-time $7614; part-time $423 per credit. Tuition, nonresident: full-time $15,552; part-time $864 per credit. *Required fees:* $38 per credit. $187 per semester. Tuition and fees vary according to course level, course load, program and reciprocity agreements. *Financial support:* Fellowships with full tuition reimbursements, research assistantships with full tuition reimbursements, teaching assistantships with full tuition reimbursements, career-related internships or fieldwork, Federal Work-Study, scholarships/grants, health care benefits, and unspecified assistantships available. Support available to part-time students. Financial award application deadline: 7/1; financial award applicants required to submit FAFSA. *Unit head:* Dr. Robert Perkins, Department Chair, 907-474-7241, Fax: 907-474-6087, E-mail: fycee@uaf.edu. *Application contact:* Mary Kreta, Director of Admissions, 907-474-7500, Fax: 907-474-7097, E-mail: admissions@uaf.edu.
Website: http://cem.uaf.edu/cee/environmental-engineering.aspx

University of Alberta, Faculty of Graduate Studies and Research, Department of Civil and Environmental Engineering, Edmonton, AB T6G 2E1, Canada. Offers construction engineering and management (M Eng, M Sc, PhD); environmental engineering (M Eng, M Sc, PhD); environmental science (M Sc, PhD); geoenvironmental engineering (M Eng, M Sc, PhD); geotechnical engineering (M Eng, M Sc, PhD); mining engineering (M Eng, M Sc, PhD); petroleum engineering (M Eng, M Sc, PhD); structural engineering (M Eng, M Sc, PhD); water resources (M Eng, M Sc, PhD). *Program availability:* Part-time, online learning. *Degree requirements:* For master's, thesis (for some programs); for doctorate, thesis/dissertation. *Entrance requirements:* For master's, minimum GPA of 3.0 in last 2 years of undergraduate studies; for doctorate, minimum GPA of 3.0. Additional exam requirements/recommendations for international students: Required—TOEFL (minimum score 550 paper-based). Electronic applications accepted. *Faculty research:* Mining.

The University of Arizona, College of Agriculture and Life Sciences, Department of Soil, Water and Environmental Science, Tucson, AZ 85721. Offers MS, PhD, Graduate Certificate. *Degree requirements:* For master's, thesis; for doctorate, comprehensive exam, thesis/dissertation. *Entrance requirements:* For master's, GRE (recommended), minimum GPA of 3.0, letter of interest, 3 letters of recommendation; for doctorate, GRE (recommended), MS, minimum GPA of 3.0, letter of interest, 3 letters of recommendation. Additional exam requirements/recommendations for international students: Required—TOEFL (minimum score 550 paper-based; 80 iBT). *Application deadline:* For fall admission, 6/1 for domestic students, 12/1 for international students; for spring admission, 10/1 for domestic students, 6/1 for international students. Applications are processed on a rolling basis. Application fee: $75. Electronic applications accepted. *Financial support:* Fellowships, research assistantships, teaching assistantships, Federal Work-Study, institutionally sponsored loans, scholarships/grants, health care benefits, tuition waivers (full and partial), and unspecified assistantships available. Financial award application deadline: 5/1. *Faculty research:* Plant production, environmental microbiology, contaminant flow and transport, aquaculture. *Unit head:* Dr. Jonathan D. Chorover, Department Head, E-mail: chorover@cals.arizona.edu.
Website: http://swes.cals.arizona.edu/

The University of Arizona, College of Agriculture and Life Sciences, Graduate Interdisciplinary Program in Arid Lands Resource Sciences, Tucson, AZ 85721. Offers PhD. *Degree requirements:* For doctorate, one foreign language, comprehensive exam, thesis/dissertation. *Entrance requirements:* For doctorate, GRE. Additional exam requirements/recommendations for international students: Required—TOEFL (minimum score 550 paper-based; 79 iBT). Electronic applications accepted. *Faculty research:* International development; famine, famine early warning systems, and food security; land use, history, change, degradation, desertification, management, and policy; sustainable agriculture and farming systems; remote sensing and spatial analysis; carbon sequestration; political-ecology of natural resources; ethnoecology and other ethno-sciences; economic and agricultural policy and development; economic botany; borderlands issues; globalization; civil conflict; urban development.

University of California, Berkeley, Graduate Division, College of Natural Resources, Department of Environmental Science, Policy, and Management, Berkeley, CA 94720-1500. Offers environmental science, policy, and management (MS, PhD); forestry (MF). Terminal master's awarded for partial completion of doctoral program. *Degree requirements:* For master's, thesis optional; for doctorate, thesis/dissertation, qualifying exam. *Entrance requirements:* For master's and doctorate, GRE General Test, minimum GPA of 3.0, 3 letters of recommendation. Additional exam requirements/recommendations for international students: Required—TOEFL. Electronic applications accepted. *Faculty research:* Biology and ecology of insects; ecosystem function and environmental issues of soils; plant health/interactions from molecular to ecosystem levels; range management and ecology; forest and resource policy, sustainability, and management.

University of California, Davis, Graduate Studies, Graduate Group in Soils and Biogeochemistry, Davis, CA 95616. Offers MS, PhD. Terminal master's awarded for partial completion of doctoral program. *Degree requirements:* For master's, comprehensive exam (for some programs), thesis (for some programs); for doctorate, thesis/dissertation. *Entrance requirements:* For master's, minimum GPA of 3.3; for doctorate, GRE, minimum GPA of 3.3. Additional exam requirements/recommendations for international students: Required—TOEFL (minimum score 550 paper-based). Electronic applications accepted. *Faculty research:* Rhizosphere ecology, soil transport processes, biogeochemical cycling, sustainable agriculture.

University of California, Los Angeles, Graduate Division, Institute of the Environment and Sustainability, Los Angeles, CA 90095-1496. Offers environmental science and engineering (D Env). *Degree requirements:* For doctorate, thesis/dissertation, oral and written qualifying exams. *Entrance requirements:* For doctorate, GRE General Test, minimum undergraduate GPA of 3.0, master's degree or equivalent in a natural science, engineering, or public health. *Faculty research:* Toxic and hazardous substances, air and water pollution, risk assessment/management, water resources, marine science.

University of California, Los Angeles, Graduate Division, School of Public Health, Department of Environmental Health Sciences, Los Angeles, CA 90095. Offers environmental health sciences (MS, PhD); environmental science and engineering (D Env); molecular toxicology (PhD); JD/MPH. *Accreditation:* ABET (one or more programs are accredited). *Degree requirements:* For master's, comprehensive exam or thesis; for doctorate, thesis/dissertation, oral and written qualifying exams. *Entrance requirements:* For master's, GRE General Test, minimum GPA of 3.0; for doctorate, GRE General Test, minimum undergraduate GPA of 3.0. Electronic applications accepted.

University of California, Riverside, Graduate Division, Materials Science and Engineering Program, Riverside, CA 92521. Offers MS, PhD. *Entrance requirements:* For master's and doctorate, GRE. Additional exam requirements/recommendations for international students: Required—TOEFL (minimum score 550 paper-based; 80 iBT). Electronic applications accepted.

University of California, Santa Barbara, Graduate Division, Donald Bren School of Environmental Science and Management, Santa Barbara, CA 93106-5131. Offers economics and environmental science (PhD); environmental science and management (MESM, PhD); technology and society (PhD). *Faculty:* 22 full-time (3 women), 5 part-time/adjunct (1 woman). *Students:* 213 full-time (129 women); includes 33 minority (3 Black or African American, non-Hispanic/Latino; 1 American Indian or Alaska Native, non-Hispanic/Latino; 11 Asian, non-Hispanic/Latino; 16 Hispanic/Latino; 2 Native Hawaiian or other Pacific Islander, non-Hispanic/Latino), 32 international. Average age 27. 404 applicants, 51% accepted, 85 enrolled. In 2015, 70 master's, 7 doctorates awarded. *Degree requirements:* For master's, thesis; for doctorate, thesis/dissertation. *Entrance requirements:* For master's and doctorate, GRE. Additional exam requirements/recommendations for international students: Required—TOEFL (minimum score 550 paper-based; 80 iBT), IELTS (minimum score 7). *Application deadline:* For fall admission, 12/15 priority date for domestic and international students. Application fee: $90 ($110 for international students). Electronic applications accepted. *Financial support:* In 2015–16, 63 students received support, including 23 fellowships with tuition reimbursements available, 3 research assistantships with tuition reimbursements available, 33 teaching assistantships with tuition reimbursements available; career-related internships or fieldwork and tuition waivers (full and partial) also available. Financial award application deadline: 12/15; financial award applicants required to submit FAFSA. *Faculty research:* Coastal marine resources management, conservation planning, corporate environmental management, economics and politics of the environment, energy and climate, pollution prevention and remediation, water resources management. *Unit head:* Dr. Steven Gaines, Dean, 805-893-7363, Fax: 805-893-7611, E-mail: gaines@bren.ucsb.edu. *Application contact:* Kristen Robinson, Director of Admissions and Outreach, 805-893-4886, Fax: 805-893-7612, E-mail: admissions@bren.ucsb.edu.
Website: http://www.bren.ucsb.edu/

University of Chicago, Harris School of Public Policy, Program in Environmental Science and Policy, Chicago, IL 60637. Offers MS. Offered in partnership with the Argonne National Laboratory. *Entrance requirements:* For master's, GRE General Test. Additional exam requirements/recommendations for international students: Required—IELTS (minimum score 7).

University of Cincinnati, Graduate School, College of Engineering and Applied Science, Department of Biomedical, Chemical and Environmental Engineering, Program in Environmental Sciences, Cincinnati, OH 45221. Offers MS, PhD. *Program availability:* Part-time. *Degree requirements:* For master's, thesis or alternative; for doctorate, one foreign language, thesis/dissertation. *Entrance requirements:* For master's and doctorate, GRE General Test. Additional exam requirements/recommendations for international students: Required—TOEFL (minimum score 580 paper-based; 92 iBT). Electronic applications accepted. *Faculty research:* Environmental microbiology, solid-waste management, air pollution control, water pollution control, aerosols.

University of Colorado Colorado Springs, College of Letters, Arts and Sciences, Department of Geography and Environmental Studies, Colorado Springs, CO 80918. Offers MA. *Program availability:* Part-time. *Faculty:* 13 full-time (4 women), 1 (woman) part-time/adjunct. *Students:* 6 full-time (5 women), 16 part-time (8 women); includes 7 minority (1 Asian, non-Hispanic/Latino; 6 Hispanic/Latino). Average age 31. 15 applicants, 60% accepted, 6 enrolled. In 2015, 2 master's awarded. *Degree requirements:* For master's, comprehensive exam (for some programs), thesis (for some programs). *Entrance requirements:* For master's, GRE (recommended minimum combined score for the verbal and quantitative tests of 1000), minimum undergraduate GPA of 3.0, statement of intent (essay). Additional exam requirements/recommendations for international students: Recommended—TOEFL (minimum score 550 paper-based; 80 iBT), IELTS (minimum score 6.5). *Application deadline:* For fall admission, 2/1 priority date for domestic and international students. Applications are processed on a rolling basis. Application fee: $60 ($100 for international students). *Expenses:* Tuition, state resident: full-time $9914. Tuition, nonresident: full-time $19,330. Tuition and fees vary according to course load, degree level, program and reciprocity agreements. *Financial support:* In 2015–16, 11 students received support. Federal Work-Study, scholarships/grants, health care benefits, and unspecified assistantships available. Support available to part-time students. Financial award application deadline: 3/1; financial award applicants required to submit FAFSA. *Faculty research:* Socio-ecological implications of conservation strategies, cultural geography, militarized spaces, geovisualization, geographic information systems, hydrology,

biogeography, human-environment interactions, geomorphology, population. *Total annual research expenditures:* $155,832. *Unit head:* Dr. Kelli Klebe, Dean of the Graduate School, 719-255-3779, Fax: 719-255-3045, E-mail: kklebe@uccs.edu. *Application contact:* Emily Skop, Program Assistant, 719-255-3789, E-mail: eskop@uccs.edu.
Website: http://www.uccs.edu/geography/

University of Colorado Denver, College of Liberal Arts and Sciences, Department of Geography and Environmental Sciences, Denver, CO 80217. Offers environmental sciences (MS), including air quality, ecosystems, environmental health, environmental science education, geo-spatial analysis, hazardous waste, water quality. *Program availability:* Part-time, evening/weekend. *Faculty:* 12 full-time (4 women), 2 part-time/adjunct (1 woman). *Students:* 46 full-time (26 women), 12 part-time (5 women); includes 11 minority (1 Black or African American, non-Hispanic/Latino; 1 Asian, non-Hispanic/Latino; 6 Hispanic/Latino; 3 Two or more races, non-Hispanic/Latino), 3 international. Average age 30. 75 applicants, 61% accepted, 24 enrolled. In 2015, 11 master's awarded. *Degree requirements:* For master's, thesis or alternative, 30 credits including 21 of core requirements and 9 of environmental science electives. *Entrance requirements:* For master's, GRE General Test, BA in one of the natural/physical sciences or engineering (or equivalent background); prerequisite coursework in calculus and physics (one semester each), general chemistry with lab and general biology with lab (two semesters each); three letters of recommendation. Additional exam requirements/recommendations for international students: Required—TOEFL (minimum score 537 paper-based; 75 iBT); Recommended—IELTS (minimum score 6.5). *Application deadline:* For fall admission, 1/20 for domestic and international students; for spring admission, 10/1 for domestic and international students. Application fee: $50 ($75 for international students). Electronic applications accepted. *Financial support:* In 2015–16, 8 students received support. Fellowships, research assistantships, teaching assistantships, Federal Work-Study, institutionally sponsored loans, scholarships/grants, and traineeships available. Financial award application deadline: 4/1; financial award applicants required to submit FAFSA. *Faculty research:* Air quality, environmental health, ecosystems, hazardous waste, water quality, geo-spatial analysis and environmental science education. *Unit head:* Anne Chinn, Director of MS in Environmental Sciences Program, 303-556-3958, E-mail: ges@ucdenver.edu. *Application contact:* Sue Eddleman, Program Assistant, 303-352-3698, E-mail: sue.eddleman@ucdenver.edu.
Website: http://www.ucdenver.edu/academics/colleges/CLAS/Departments/ges/Programs/MasterofScience/Pages/MasterofScience.aspx

University of Guam, Office of Graduate Studies, College of Natural and Applied Sciences, Program in Environmental Science, Mangilao, GU 96923. Offers MS. *Program availability:* Part-time. *Degree requirements:* For master's, thesis. *Entrance requirements:* For master's, GRE General Test. Additional exam requirements/recommendations for international students: Required—TOEFL. *Faculty research:* Water resources, ecology, karst formations, hydrogeology, meteorology.

University of Guelph, Graduate Studies, Ontario Agricultural College, Department of Land Resource Science, Guelph, ON N1G 2W1, Canada. Offers atmospheric science (M Sc, PhD); environmental and agricultural earth sciences (M Sc, PhD); land resources management (M Sc, PhD); soil science (M Sc, PhD). *Program availability:* Part-time. *Degree requirements:* For master's, thesis (for some programs), research project (non-thesis track); for doctorate, comprehensive exam, thesis/dissertation. *Entrance requirements:* For master's, minimum B- average during previous 2 years of course work; for doctorate, minimum B average during previous 2 years of course work. Additional exam requirements/recommendations for international students: Required—TOEFL (minimum score 550 paper-based). Electronic applications accepted. *Faculty research:* Soil science, environmental earth science, land resource management.

University of Hawaii at Hilo, Program in Tropical Conservation Biology and Environmental Science, Hilo, HI 96720-4091. Offers MS. *Entrance requirements:* Additional exam requirements/recommendations for international students: Required—TOEFL, IELTS. Electronic applications accepted.

University of Houston–Clear Lake, School of Science and Computer Engineering, Program in Environmental Science, Houston, TX 77058-1002. Offers MS. *Program availability:* Part-time, evening/weekend. *Entrance requirements:* For master's, GRE General Test. Additional exam requirements/recommendations for international students: Required—TOEFL (minimum score 550 paper-based).

University of Idaho, College of Graduate Studies, College of Natural Resources, Environmental Science Program, Moscow, ID 83844-1142. Offers MS, PhD. *Faculty:* 32 full-time, 2 part-time/adjunct. *Students:* 31 full-time, 62 part-time. Average age 33. In 2015, 23 master's, 12 doctorates awarded. *Entrance requirements:* Additional exam requirements/recommendations for international students: Required—TOEFL. *Application deadline:* For fall admission, 8/1 for domestic students; for spring admission, 12/15 for domestic students. Applications are processed on a rolling basis. Application fee: $60. Electronic applications accepted. *Expenses:* Tuition, state resident: full-time $6205; part-time $399 per credit hour. Tuition, nonresident: full-time $20,209; part-time $1177 per credit hour. *Required fees:* $2017; $58 per credit hour. Full-time tuition and fees vary according to course load and reciprocity agreements. *Financial support:* Research assistantships and teaching assistantships available. Financial award applicants required to submit FAFSA. *Unit head:* Dr. Paul McDaniels, Department Head, 208-885-6113, Fax: 208-885-4674, E-mail: envs@uidaho.edu. *Application contact:* Sean Scoggin, Graduate Recruitment Coordinator, 208-885-4723, Fax: 208-885-4406, E-mail: graduateadmissions@uidaho.edu.
Website: http://www.uidaho.edu/cnr/environmental-science?

University of Illinois at Springfield, Graduate Programs, College of Public Affairs and Administration, Program in Environmental Studies, Springfield, IL 62703-5407. Offers environmental science (MS); environmental studies (MA). *Program availability:* Part-time, evening/weekend, 100% online. *Faculty:* 6 full-time (3 women). *Students:* 16 full-time (11 women), 46 part-time (28 women); includes 9 minority (1 Black or African American, non-Hispanic/Latino; 1 American Indian or Alaska Native, non-Hispanic/Latino; 5 Asian, non-Hispanic/Latino; 2 Hispanic/Latino), 2 international. Average age 33. 63 applicants, 44% accepted, 21 enrolled. In 2015, 25 master's awarded. *Degree requirements:* For master's, thesis, project, or capstone closure course completion. *Entrance requirements:* For master's, minimum undergraduate GPA of 3.0, 2 letters of recommendation, goals essay. Additional exam requirements/recommendations for international students: Required—TOEFL (minimum score 500 paper-based; 61 iBT). *Application deadline:* Applications are processed on a rolling basis. Application fee: $60 ($75 for international students). Electronic applications accepted. *Expenses:* Tuition, state resident: part-time $329 per credit hour. Tuition, nonresident: part-time $675 per credit hour. *Financial support:* In 2015–16, fellowships with full tuition reimbursements (averaging $9,900 per year), research assistantships with full tuition reimbursements (averaging $9,956 per year), teaching assistantships with full tuition reimbursements (averaging $9,956 per year) were awarded; career-related internships or fieldwork, Federal Work-Study, scholarships/grants, health care benefits, and unspecified assistantships also available. Support available to part-time students. Financial award application deadline: 11/15; financial award applicants required to submit FAFSA. *Unit head:* Dr. Dennis Ruez, Jr., Program Administrator, 217-206-8424, E-mail: druez2@uis.edu. *Application contact:* Dr. Lynn Pardie, Office of Graduate Studies, 800-252-8533, Fax: 217-206-7623, E-mail: lpard1@uis.edu.
Website: http://www.uis.edu/environmentalstudies/

University of Illinois at Urbana–Champaign, Graduate College, College of Agricultural, Consumer and Environmental Sciences, Department of Natural Resources and Environmental Science, Champaign, IL 61820. Offers MS, PhD, MS/JD. *Program availability:* Part-time, online learning.

The University of Kansas, Graduate Studies, School of Engineering, Program in Environmental Science, Lawrence, KS 66045. Offers MS, PhD. *Program availability:* Part-time. *Students:* 3 full-time (1 woman), 1 part-time (0 women); includes 1 minority (Two or more races, non-Hispanic/Latino). Average age 29. 5 applicants, 60% accepted, 2 enrolled. In 2015, 1 master's awarded. *Entrance requirements:* For master's, GRE, minimum GPA of 3.0; for doctorate, GRE, minimum GPA of 3.5. Additional exam requirements/recommendations for international students: Required—TOEFL. *Application deadline:* For fall admission, 3/1 priority date for domestic and international students; for spring admission, 12/1 priority date for domestic students, 8/15 priority date for international students. Application fee: $65 ($85 for international students). Electronic applications accepted. *Financial support:* Fellowships, research assistantships, teaching assistantships, and career-related internships or fieldwork available. Financial award application deadline: 2/7. *Faculty research:* Water quality, water treatment, wastewater treatment, air quality, air pollution control, solid waste, hazardous waste, water resources engineering, water resources science. *Unit head:* David Darwin, Chair, 785-864-3827, Fax: 785-864-5631, E-mail: daved@ku.edu. *Application contact:* Susan Scott, Administrative Assistant, 785-864-3826, E-mail: sbscott@ku.edu.
Website: http://ceae.ku.edu/overview-8

University of Lethbridge, School of Graduate Studies, Lethbridge, AB T1K 3M4, Canada. Offers addictions counseling (M Sc); agricultural biotechnology (M Sc); agricultural studies (M Sc, MA); anthropology (MA); archaeology (M Sc, MA); art (MA, MFA); biochemistry (M Sc); biological sciences (M Sc); biomolecular science (PhD); biosystems and biodiversity (PhD); Canadian studies (MA); chemistry (M Sc); computer science (M Sc); computer science and geographical information science (M Sc); counseling (MC); counseling psychology (M Ed); dramatic arts (MA); earth, space, and physical science (PhD); economics (MA); education (MA, PhD); educational leadership (M Ed); English (MA); environmental science (M Sc); evolution and behavior (PhD); exercise science (M Sc); French (MA); French/German (MA); French/Spanish (MA); general education (M Ed); geography (M Sc, MA); German (MA); health sciences (M Sc); individualized multidisciplinary (M Sc, MA); kinesiology (M Sc, MA); management (M Sc), including accounting, finance, human resource management and labor relations, information systems, international management, marketing, policy and strategy; mathematics (M Sc); music (M Mus, MA); Native American studies (MA); neuroscience (M Sc, PhD); new media (MA, MFA); nursing (M Sc, MN); philosophy (MA); physics (M Sc); political science (MA); psychology (M Sc, MA); religious studies (MA); sociology (MA); theatre and dramatic arts (MFA); theoretical and computational science (PhD); urban and regional studies (MA); women and gender studies (MA). *Program availability:* Part-time, evening/weekend. *Students:* 448 full-time (249 women), 110 part-time (64 women). Average age 32. 285 applicants, 36% accepted, 96 enrolled. In 2015, 154 master's, 11 doctorates awarded. *Degree requirements:* For master's, thesis (for some programs); for doctorate, comprehensive exam, thesis/dissertation. *Entrance requirements:* For master's, GMAT (for M Sc in management), bachelor's degree in related field, minimum GPA of 3.0 during previous 20 graded semester courses, 2 years' teaching or related experience (M Ed); for doctorate, master's degree, minimum graduate GPA of 3.5. Additional exam requirements/recommendations for international students: Required—TOEFL (minimum score 580 paper-based; 93 iBT). Application fee: $100 Canadian dollars ($140 Canadian dollars for international students). Electronic applications accepted. *Financial support:* Fellowships, research assistantships, teaching assistantships, scholarships/grants, health care benefits, and unspecified assistantships available. *Faculty research:* Movement and brain plasticity, gibberellin physiology, photosynthesis, carbon cycling, molecular properties of main-group ring components. *Unit head:* Kathleen Schrage, Manager, School of Graduate Studies, 403-329-2121, E-mail: schrage@uleth.ca. *Application contact:* School of Graduate Studies, 403-329-5194, E-mail: sgsinquiries@uleth.ca.
Website: http://www.uleth.ca/graduate-studies/

University of Maine, Graduate School, College of Natural Sciences, Forestry, and Agriculture, School of Biology and Ecology, Orono, ME 04469. Offers biological sciences (PhD); botany and plant pathology (MS); ecology and environmental science (MS, PhD); entomology (MS); plant science (PhD); zoology (MS, PhD). *Program availability:* Part-time. *Faculty:* 24 full-time (12 women), 34 part-time/adjunct (13 women). *Students:* 64 full-time (36 women), 1 part-time (0 women); includes 4 minority (1 American Indian or Alaska Native, non-Hispanic/Latino; 1 Asian, non-Hispanic/Latino; 1 Hispanic/Latino; 1 Two or more races, non-Hispanic/Latino), 8 international. Average age 29. 52 applicants, 25% accepted, 11 enrolled. In 2015, 7 master's, 8 doctorates awarded. Terminal master's awarded for partial completion of doctoral program. *Degree requirements:* For master's, thesis (for some programs); for doctorate, comprehensive exam, thesis/dissertation. *Entrance requirements:* For master's and doctorate, GRE General Test. Additional exam requirements/recommendations for international students: Required—TOEFL. *Application deadline:* For fall admission, 2/1 priority date for domestic students. Applications are processed on a rolling basis. Application fee: $65. Electronic applications accepted. *Financial support:* In 2015–16, 14 students received support, including 6 research assistantships with full tuition reimbursements available (averaging $14,600 per year), 8 teaching assistantships with full tuition reimbursements available (averaging $14,600 per year); career-related internships or fieldwork, Federal Work-Study, institutionally sponsored loans, and tuition waivers (full and partial) also available. Financial award application deadline: 3/1. *Faculty research:* Ecology and evolution (aquatic, terrestrial, paleo); development and genetics; biomedical research; ecophysiology and stress; invasion ecology and pest management. *Total annual research expenditures:* $3.2 million. *Unit head:* Dr. Andrei Aloykhin, Director, 207-581-2977, Fax: 207-581-2537. *Application contact:* Scott G. Delcourt, Assistant Vice President for Graduate Studies and Senior Associate Dean, 207-581-3291, Fax: 207-581-3232, E-mail: graduate@maine.edu.
Website: http://sbe.umaine.edu/

The University of Manchester, School of Earth, Atmospheric and Environmental Sciences, Manchester, United Kingdom. Offers atmospheric sciences (M Phil, M Sc, PhD); basin studies and petroleum geosciences (M Phil, M Sc, PhD); earth, atmospheric and environmental sciences (M Phil, M Sc, PhD); environmental geochemistry and cosmochemistry (M Phil, M Sc, PhD); isotope geochemistry and cosmochemistry (M Phil, M Sc, PhD); paleontology (M Phil, M Sc, PhD); physics and chemistry of minerals and fluids (M Phil, M Sc, PhD); structural and petrological geosciences (M Phil, M Sc, PhD).

University of Manitoba, Faculty of Graduate Studies, Clayton H. Riddell Faculty of Environment, Earth, and Resources, Department of Environment and Geography, Winnipeg, MB R3T 2N2, Canada. Offers environment (M Env); environment and geography (M Sc); geography (MA, PhD). *Degree requirements:* For master's, thesis; for doctorate, one foreign language, thesis/dissertation.

University of Maryland, Baltimore, Graduate School, Program in Marine-Estuarine-Environmental Sciences, College Park, MD 20742. Offers MS, PhD. *Program availability:* Part-time. Terminal master's awarded for partial completion of doctoral program. *Degree requirements:* For master's, thesis, oral defense; for doctorate, comprehensive exam, thesis/dissertation, proposal defense, oral defense. *Entrance requirements:* For master's and doctorate, GRE General Test, minimum GPA of 3.0. Additional exam requirements/recommendations for international students: Required—TOEFL. Electronic applications accepted. Tuition and fees vary according to program.

University of Maryland, Baltimore County, The Graduate School, Marine-Estuarine-Environmental Sciences Graduate Program, College Park, MD 20742. Offers MS, PhD. *Program availability:* Part-time. *Degree requirements:* For master's, thesis, oral defense; for doctorate, comprehensive exam, thesis/dissertation, proposal defense, oral defense. *Entrance requirements:* For master's and doctorate, GRE General Test, minimum GPA of 3.0. Additional exam requirements/recommendations for international students: Required—TOEFL. Electronic applications accepted. *Expenses:* Tuition, state resident: full-time $12,816. Tuition, nonresident: full-time $19,710.

University of Maryland, College Park, Academic Affairs, College of Agriculture and Natural Resources, Department of Environmental Science and Technology, College Park, MD 20742. Offers MS, PhD. Electronic applications accepted.

University of Maryland, College Park, Academic Affairs, College of Computer, Mathematical and Natural Sciences, Program in Marine-Estuarine-Environmental Sciences, College Park, MD 20742. Offers MS, PhD. *Program availability:* Part-time. Terminal master's awarded for partial completion of doctoral program. *Degree requirements:* For master's, thesis, oral defense; for doctorate, comprehensive exam, thesis/dissertation, proposal defense, oral defense. *Entrance requirements:* For master's and doctorate, GRE General Test, minimum GPA of 3.0. Additional exam requirements/recommendations for international students: Required—TOEFL. Electronic applications accepted. *Faculty research:* Ecology, environmental chemistry, environmental molecular biology/biotechnology, environmental sciences, fisheries science, oceanography.

University of Maryland Eastern Shore, Graduate Programs, Department of Natural Sciences, Princess Anne, MD 21853-1299. Offers chemistry (MS); marine-estuarine-environmental sciences (MS, PhD); quantitative fisheries and resource economics (PMS); toxicology (MS, PhD). *Degree requirements:* For master's, thesis; for doctorate, comprehensive exam, thesis/dissertation. *Entrance requirements:* For master's and doctorate, GRE General Test, minimum GPA of 3.0. Additional exam requirements/recommendations for international students: Required—TOEFL (minimum score 80 iBT). Electronic applications accepted. *Faculty research:* Environmental chemistry (air/water pollution), fin fish ecology.

University of Maryland Eastern Shore, Graduate Programs, Program in Marine-Estuarine-Environmental Sciences, College Park, MD 20742. Offers MS, PhD. *Program availability:* Part-time. *Degree requirements:* For master's, thesis; for doctorate, comprehensive exam, thesis/dissertation, proposal defense. *Entrance requirements:* For master's and doctorate, GRE General Test, minimum GPA of 3.0. Additional exam requirements/recommendations for international students: Required—TOEFL. Electronic applications accepted.

University of Massachusetts Boston, College of Science and Mathematics, Program in Environmental Sciences, Boston, MA 02125-3393. Offers MS, PhD. *Program availability:* Part-time, evening/weekend. *Students:* 30 full-time (15 women), 14 part-time (8 women); includes 5 minority (4 Hispanic/Latino; 1 Two or more races, non-Hispanic/Latino), 7 international. 23 applicants, 43% accepted, 7 enrolled. In 2015, 9 master's, 2 doctorates awarded. *Degree requirements:* For doctorate, comprehensive exam, thesis/dissertation, oral exams. *Entrance requirements:* For doctorate, GRE General Test, minimum GPA of 2.75. *Application deadline:* For fall admission, 2/1 for domestic students; for spring admission, 10/15 for domestic students. *Expenses:* Tuition, state resident: full-time $2590. Tuition, nonresident: full-time $9758. *Required fees:* $13,525. *Financial support:* Research assistantships with full tuition reimbursements, teaching assistantships with full tuition reimbursements, career-related internships or fieldwork, Federal Work-Study, and unspecified assistantships available. Support available to part-time students. Financial award application deadline: 3/1; financial award applicants required to submit FAFSA. *Faculty research:* Polychoets biology, predator and prey relationships, population and evolutionary biology, neurobiology, biodiversity. *Unit head:* Dr. Greg Beck, Director, 617-287-6600. *Application contact:* Peggy Roldan Patel, Graduate Admissions Coordinator, 617-287-6400, Fax: 617-287-6236, E-mail: bos.gadm@dpc.umassp.edu.

University of Massachusetts Lowell, College of Health Sciences, Department of Work Environment, Lowell, MA 01854. Offers cleaner production and pollution prevention (MS, Sc D); environmental risk assessment (Certificate); epidemiology (MS, Sc D); ergonomics and safety (MS, Sc D); identification and control of ergonomic hazards (Certificate); job stress and healthy job redesign (Certificate); occupational and environmental hygiene (MS, Sc D); radiological health physics and general work environment protection (Certificate); work environment policy (MS, Sc D). *Accreditation:* ABET (one or more programs are accredited). *Program availability:* Part-time. Terminal master's awarded for partial completion of doctoral program. *Degree requirements:* For master's, thesis optional; for doctorate, thesis/dissertation. *Entrance requirements:* For master's and doctorate, GRE General Test. Additional exam requirements/recommendations for international students: Required—TOEFL.

University of Massachusetts Lowell, College of Sciences, Department of Chemistry, Lowell, MA 01854. Offers analytical chemistry (PhD); biochemistry (PhD); chemistry (MS, PhD); environmental studies (PhD); green chemistry (PhD); inorganic chemistry (PhD); organic chemistry (PhD); polymer science (MS). Terminal master's awarded for partial completion of doctoral program. *Degree requirements:* For master's, thesis; for doctorate, 2 foreign languages, thesis/dissertation. *Entrance requirements:* For master's and doctorate, GRE General Test. Electronic applications accepted.

University of Massachusetts Lowell, Francis College of Engineering, Department of Civil and Environmental Engineering and College of Sciences, Program in Environmental Studies, Lowell, MA 01854. Offers environmental engineering (MSES); environmental studies (PhD, Certificate). *Program availability:* Part-time. *Degree requirements:* For master's, thesis optional. *Entrance requirements:* For master's, GRE General Test. *Faculty research:* Remote sensing of air pollutants, atmospheric deposition of toxic metals, contaminant transport in groundwater, soil remediation.

University of Michigan, Rackham Graduate School, College of Literature, Science, and the Arts, Department of Earth and Environmental Sciences, Ann Arbor, MI 48109-1005. Offers MS, PhD. *Faculty:* 28 full-time (9 women), 6 part-time/adjunct (3 women). *Students:* 59 full-time (28 women), 1 part-time (0 women); includes 6 minority (1 Asian, non-Hispanic/Latino; 3 Hispanic/Latino; 2 Two or more races, non-Hispanic/Latino), 12 international. 131 applicants, 17% accepted, 14 enrolled. In 2015, 3 master's, 9 doctorates awarded. Terminal master's awarded for partial completion of doctoral program. *Degree requirements:* For master's, thesis; for doctorate, comprehensive exam, thesis/dissertation, oral defense of dissertation. *Entrance requirements:* For master's and doctorate, GRE General Test. Additional exam requirements/recommendations for international students: Required—TOEFL (minimum score 100 iBT). *Application deadline:* For fall admission, 1/5 for domestic and international students; for winter admission, 11/1 for domestic and international students. Application fee: $75 ($90 for international students). Electronic applications accepted. *Financial support:* Fellowships with full tuition reimbursements, research assistantships with full tuition reimbursements, teaching assistantships with full tuition reimbursements, career-related internships or fieldwork, scholarships/grants, health care benefits, and unspecified assistantships available. Financial award application deadline: 1/5; financial award applicants required to submit FAFSA. *Faculty research:* Isotope geochemistry, paleoclimatology, mineral physics, tectonics, paleontology. *Unit head:* Dr. Christopher Poulsen, Chair, 734-764-1435, Fax: 734-763-4690, E-mail: michiganearth@umich.edu. *Application contact:* Anne Hudon, Graduate Program Coordinator, 734-615-3034, Fax: 734-763-4690, E-mail: michiganearth@umich.edu.
Website: http://lsa.umich.edu/earth

University of Michigan, School of Natural Resources and Environment, Program in Natural Resources and Environment, Ann Arbor, MI 48109. Offers behavior, education and communication (MS); conservation ecology (MS); environmental informatics (MS); environmental justice (MS); environmental policy and planning (MS); natural resources and environment (PhD); sustainable systems (MS); MS/JD; MS/MBA; MS/MPP; MS/MSE; MUP/MS. *Students:* 342 full-time (184 women). Average age 27. Terminal master's awarded for partial completion of doctoral program. *Degree requirements:* For master's, practicum or group project; for doctorate, comprehensive exam, thesis/dissertation, oral defense of dissertation, preliminary exam. *Entrance requirements:* For master's, GRE General Test; for doctorate, GRE General Test, master's degree. Additional exam requirements/recommendations for international students: Required—TOEFL (minimum score 560 paper-based; 84 iBT). *Application deadline:* For fall admission, 4/30 for domestic and international students. Application fee: $75 ($90 for international students). Electronic applications accepted. *Financial support:* Application deadline: 1/6; applicants required to submit FAFSA. *Unit head:* Dr. Marie Lynn Miranda, Interim Dean, 734-764-2550, Fax: 734-763-8965, E-mail: danbrown@umich.edu. *Application contact:* Sondra R. Auerbach, Director of Academic Programs, 734-764-6453, Fax: 734-936-2195, E-mail: sshowen@umich.edu.
Website: http://www.snre.umich.edu/

University of Michigan–Dearborn, College of Arts, Sciences, and Letters, Master of Science in Environmental Science Program, Dearborn, MI 48128. Offers MS. *Program availability:* Part-time, evening/weekend. *Faculty:* 15 full-time (6 women), 1 part-time/adjunct (0 women). *Students:* 1 full-time (0 women), 22 part-time (17 women); includes 3 minority (all Black or African American, non-Hispanic/Latino), 1 international. 13 applicants, 69% accepted, 3 enrolled. In 2015, 10 master's awarded. *Degree requirements:* For master's, thesis optional. *Entrance requirements:* For master's, 3 letters of reference, minimum GPA of 3.0. Additional exam requirements/recommendations for international students: Required—TOEFL (minimum score 560 paper-based; 84 iBT), IELTS (minimum score 6.5). *Application deadline:* For fall admission, 8/1 priority date for domestic students, 5/1 priority date for international students; for winter admission, 12/1 priority date for domestic students, 9/1 priority date for international students; for spring admission, 4/1 priority date for domestic students, 1/1 priority date for international students. Applications are processed on a rolling basis. Application fee: $60. Electronic applications accepted. *Expenses:* $633 per credit hour in-state; $363 per credit hour for ninth credit hour and beyond in-state; $1,133 per credit hour out-of-state; $736 per credit hour for ninth credit hour and beyond out-of-state; $277 fees per term part-time, $342 fees per term full-time. *Financial support:* In 2015–16, 4 students received support. Scholarships/grants and non-resident tuition scholarships available. Financial award application deadline: 3/1; financial award applicants required to submit FAFSA. *Faculty research:* Fate and transport of heavy metals; land use and impact on ground water and surface water quality; ecosystems and management; natural resources; plant, animal and microbial diversity. *Unit head:* Dr. Sonia Tiquia-Arashiro, Director, 313-593-5148, E-mail: smtiquia@umich.edu. *Application contact:* Carol Ligienza, Coordinator, CASL Graduate Programs, 313-593-1183, Fax: 313-583-6700, E-mail: caslgrad@umich.edu.
Website: http://umdearborn.edu/casl/envsci_ms/

University of Montana, Graduate School, College of Humanities and Sciences, Program in Environmental Studies (EVST), Missoula, MT 59812-0002. Offers MS, JD/MS. *Program availability:* Part-time. *Faculty:* 8 full-time (3 women), 2 part-time/adjunct (1 woman). *Students:* 40 full-time (33 women), 12 part-time (5 women); includes 2 minority (both American Indian or Alaska Native, non-Hispanic/Latino). Average age 30. 62 applicants, 71% accepted, 22 enrolled. In 2015, 26 master's awarded. *Degree requirements:* For master's, thesis, portfolio or professional paper. *Entrance requirements:* For master's, GRE General Test (minimum score: 500 verbal on old scoring, 153 new scoring). Additional exam requirements/recommendations for international students: Required—TOEFL (minimum score 580 paper-based; 92 iBT). *Application deadline:* For fall admission, 1/15 priority date for domestic and international students. Application fee: $60. Electronic applications accepted. *Expenses:* $2,783 state resident full-time; $9,790 nonresident full-time. *Financial support:* In 2015–16, 17 students received support, including 3 fellowships with partial tuition reimbursements available (averaging $5,000 per year), 7 teaching assistantships with full tuition reimbursements available (averaging $9,000 per year); scholarships/grants also available. Financial award application deadline: 4/15. *Faculty research:* Pollution ecology, sustainable agriculture, environmental writing, environmental policy, environmental justice, environmental history, habitat-land management, traditional ecological knowledge of Native Peoples. *Total annual research expenditures:* $225,000. *Unit head:* Prof. Phil Condon, Director, 406-243-2904, Fax: 406-243-6090, E-mail: phil.condon@mso.umt.edu. *Application contact:* Karen Hurd, Administrative Assistant, 406-243-6273, Fax: 406-243-6090, E-mail: karen.hurd@mso.umt.edu.
Website: http://www.cas.umt.edu/evst

University of Nevada, Las Vegas, Graduate College, Greenspun College of Urban Affairs, School of Environmental and Public Affairs, Las Vegas, NV 89154-4030. Offers crisis and emergency management (MS), including crisis and emergency management; environmental and public affairs (MPA); environmental science (MS, PhD); non-profit management (Certificate); public affairs (PhD); public management (Certificate); urban leadership (MA); workforce development and organizational leadership (PhD). *Program availability:* Part-time. *Faculty:* 12 full-time (6 women), 9 part-time/adjunct (1 woman). *Students:* 89 full-time (58 women), 119 part-time (64 women); includes 83 minority (25 Black or African American, non-Hispanic/Latino; 2 American Indian or Alaska Native, non-Hispanic/Latino; 6 Asian, non-Hispanic/Latino; 32 Hispanic/Latino; 4 Native

Hawaiian or other Pacific Islander, non-Hispanic/Latino; 14 Two or more races, non-Hispanic/Latino), 9 international. Average age 37. 62 applicants, 90% accepted, 42 enrolled. In 2015, 60 master's, 6 doctorates, 19 other advanced degrees awarded. *Degree requirements:* For master's, comprehensive exam (for some programs), thesis (for some programs); for doctorate, comprehensive exam, thesis/dissertation. *Entrance requirements:* For master's, GRE General Test or GMAT; for doctorate, GRE General Test. Additional exam requirements/recommendations for international students: Required—TOEFL (minimum score 550 paper-based; 80 iBT), IELTS (minimum score 7). *Application deadline:* For fall admission, 4/1 for domestic students, 5/1 for international students; for spring admission, 11/1 for domestic students, 10/1 for international students. Application fee: $60 ($95 for international students). Electronic applications accepted. *Expenses:* $264 per credit state resident full-time and part-time; $6,955 per semester, $264 per credit nonresident full-time; $555 per credit nonresident part-time. *Financial support:* In 2015–16, 28 students received support, including 1 fellowship with full tuition reimbursement available (averaging $25,000 per year), 10 research assistantships with partial tuition reimbursements available (averaging $13,360 per year), 17 teaching assistantships with partial tuition reimbursements available (averaging $13,362 per year); institutionally sponsored loans, scholarships/grants, health care benefits, and unspecified assistantships also available. Financial award application deadline: 3/1. *Faculty research:* Community and organizational resilience; environmental decision-making and management; budgeting and human resource/workforce management; urban design, sustainability, and governance; public and non-profit management, public policy, governance, economic development, and urban planning. *Total annual research expenditures:* $20,066. *Unit head:* Dr. Christopher Stream, Chair/Associate Professor, 702-895-5120, Fax: 702-895-4436, E-mail: chris.stream@unlv.edu. *Application contact:* Graduate College Admissions Evaluator, 702-895-3367, Fax: 702-895-4180, E-mail: gradadmissions@unlv.edu.
Website: http://sepa.unlv.edu/

University of Nevada, Reno, Graduate School, College of Agriculture, Biotechnology and Natural Resources, Department of Natural Resources and Environmental Sciences, Reno, NV 89557. Offers MS. *Degree requirements:* For master's, thesis optional. *Entrance requirements:* For master's, GRE, minimum GPA of 2.75. Additional exam requirements/recommendations for international students: Required—TOEFL (minimum score 500 paper-based; 61 iBT), IELTS (minimum score 6). Electronic applications accepted. *Faculty research:* Range management, plant physiology, remote sensing, soils, wildlife.

University of Nevada, Reno, Graduate School, Interdisciplinary Program in Environmental Sciences and Health, Reno, NV 89557. Offers MS, PhD. Terminal master's awarded for partial completion of doctoral program. *Degree requirements:* For master's, thesis; for doctorate, thesis/dissertation. *Entrance requirements:* For master's, GRE General Test, minimum GPA of 2.75; for doctorate, GRE General Test, minimum GPA of 3.0. Additional exam requirements/recommendations for international students: Required—TOEFL (minimum score 500 paper-based; 61 iBT), IELTS (minimum score 6). Electronic applications accepted. *Faculty research:* Environmental chemistry, environmental toxicology, ecological toxicology.

University of New Haven, Graduate School, College of Arts and Sciences, Program in Environmental Science, West Haven, CT 06516-1916. Offers environmental ecology (MS); environmental education (MS); environmental geoscience (MS); environmental health and management (MS); environmental science (MS); geographical information systems (MS, Graduate Certificate). *Program availability:* Part-time, evening/weekend. *Students:* 20 full-time (10 women), 6 part-time (5 women); includes 2 minority (1 Black or African American, non-Hispanic/Latino; 1 Hispanic/Latino), 5 international. Average age 26. 25 applicants, 88% accepted, 13 enrolled. In 2015, 19 master's awarded. *Degree requirements:* For master's, thesis optional, research project. *Entrance requirements:* Additional exam requirements/recommendations for international students: Required—TOEFL (minimum score 80 iBT), IELTS, PTE. *Application deadline:* For fall admission, 5/31 for international students; for winter admission, 10/15 for international students; for spring admission, 1/15 for international students. Applications are processed on a rolling basis. Application fee: $75. Electronic applications accepted. Application fee is waived when completed online. *Expenses: Tuition, area resident:* Full-time $15,282; part-time $849 per credit hour. *Required fees:* $150; $60 per term. Tuition and fees vary according to program. *Financial support:* Research assistantships with partial tuition reimbursements, teaching assistantships with partial tuition reimbursements, career-related internships or fieldwork, Federal Work-Study, scholarships/grants, and unspecified assistantships available. Support available to part-time students. Financial award applicants required to submit FAFSA. *Unit head:* Dr. Roman Zajac, Coordinator, 203-932-7114, E-mail: rzajac@newhaven.edu. *Application contact:* Michelle Mason, Director of Graduate Enrollment, 203-932-7067, E-mail: mmason@newhaven.edu.
Website: http://www.newhaven.edu/4728/

University of New Orleans, Graduate School, College of Sciences, Department of Earth and Environmental Sciences, New Orleans, LA 70148. Offers MS. *Program availability:* Evening/weekend. *Degree requirements:* For master's, thesis. *Entrance requirements:* For master's, GRE General Test. Additional exam requirements/recommendations for international students: Required—TOEFL (minimum score 550 paper-based; 79 iBT), IELTS. Electronic applications accepted. *Faculty research:* Continental margin structure and seismology, burial diagenesis of siliclastic sediments, tectonics at convergent plate margins, continental shelf sediment stability, early diagenesis of carbonates.

The University of North Carolina at Chapel Hill, Graduate School, Gillings School of Global Public Health, Department of Environmental Sciences and Engineering, Chapel Hill, NC 27599. Offers air, radiation and industrial hygiene (MPH, MS, MSEE, MSPH, PhD); aquatic and atmospheric sciences (MPH, MS, MSPH, PhD); environmental engineering (MPH, MS, MSEE, MSPH, PhD); environmental health sciences (MPH, MS, MSPH, PhD); environmental management and policy (MPH, MS, MSPH, PhD). *Students:* 112 full-time (68 women); includes 20 minority (11 Asian, non-Hispanic/Latino; 4 Hispanic/Latino; 5 Two or more races, non-Hispanic/Latino), 31 international. Average age 28. 178 applicants, 37% accepted, 39 enrolled. Terminal master's awarded for partial completion of doctoral program. *Degree requirements:* For master's, comprehensive exam, thesis (for some programs), research paper; for doctorate, comprehensive exam, thesis/dissertation. *Entrance requirements:* For master's and doctorate, GRE General Test, minimum GPA of 3.0 (recommended). Additional exam requirements/recommendations for international students: Required—TOEFL. *Application deadline:* For fall admission, 12/10 priority date for domestic and international students; for spring admission, 9/10 for domestic students. Applications are processed on a rolling basis. Application fee: $85. Electronic applications accepted. *Financial support:* Fellowships with tuition reimbursements, research assistantships with tuition reimbursements, teaching assistantships with tuition reimbursements, career-related internships or fieldwork, Federal Work-Study, traineeships, health care benefits, and unspecified assistantships available. Support available to part-time students. Financial award application deadline: 12/10; financial award applicants required to submit FAFSA. *Faculty research:* Air, radiation and industrial hygiene, aquatic and atmospheric sciences, environmental health sciences, environmental management and policy, water resources engineering. *Unit head:* Dr. Michael Aitken, Chair, 919-966-1024, Fax: 919-966-7911, E-mail: mike_aitken@unc.edu. *Application contact:* Jack Whaley, Registrar, 919-966-3844, Fax: 919-966-7911, E-mail: jack_whaley@unc.edu.
Website: http://www2.sph.unc.edu/envr/

University of North Texas, Robert B. Toulouse School of Graduate Studies, Denton, TX 76203-5459. Offers accounting (MS); applied anthropology (MA, MS); applied behavior analysis (Certificate); applied geography (MA); applied technology and performance improvement (M Ed, MS); art education (MA); art history (MA); art museum education (Certificate); arts leadership (Certificate); audiology (Au D); behavior analysis (MS); behavioral science (PhD); biochemistry and molecular biology (MS); biology (MA, MS); biomedical engineering (MS); business analysis (MS); chemistry (MS); clinical health psychology (PhD); communication studies (MA, MS); computer engineering (MS); computer science (MS); counseling (M Ed, MS), including clinical mental health counseling (MS), college and university counseling, elementary school counseling, secondary school counseling; creative writing (MA); criminal justice (MS); curriculum and instruction (M Ed); decision sciences (MBA); design (MA, MFA), including fashion design (MFA), innovation studies, interior design (MFA); early childhood studies (MS); economics (MS); educational leadership (M Ed, Ed D); educational psychology (MS, PhD), including family studies (MS), gifted and talented (MS), human development (MS), learning and cognition (MS), research, measurement and evaluation (MS); electrical engineering (MS); emergency management (MPA); engineering technology (MS); English (MA); English as a second language (MA); environmental science (MS); finance (MBA, MS); financial management (MPA); French (MA); health services management (MBA); higher education (M Ed, Ed D); history (MA, MS); hospitality management (MS); human resources management (MPA); information science (MS); information systems (PhD); information technologies (MBA); interdisciplinary studies (MA, MS); international studies (MA); international sustainable tourism (MS); jazz studies (MM); journalism (MA, MJ, Graduate Certificate), including interactive and virtual digital communication (Graduate Certificate), narrative journalism (Graduate Certificate), public relations (Graduate Certificate); kinesiology (MS); linguistics (MA); local government management (MPA); logistics (PhD); logistics and supply chain management (MBA); long-term care, senior housing, and aging services (MA); management (PhD); marketing (MBA); mathematics (MA, MS); mechanical and energy engineering (MS, PhD); music (MA), including ethnomusicology, music theory, musicology, performance; music composition (PhD); music education (MM Ed, PhD); nonprofit management (MPA); operations and supply chain management (MBA); performance (MM, DMA); philosophy (MA); political science (MA); professional and technical communication (MA); radio, television and film (MA, MFA); rehabilitation counseling (Certificate); sociology (MA); Spanish (MA); special education (M Ed); speech-language pathology (MA); strategic management (MBA); studio art (MFA); teaching (M Ed); MBA/MS. *Program availability:* Part-time, evening/weekend, online learning. Terminal master's awarded for partial completion of doctoral program. *Degree requirements:* For master's, variable foreign language requirement, comprehensive exam (for some programs), thesis (for some programs); for doctorate, variable foreign language requirement, comprehensive exam (for some programs), thesis/dissertation; for other advanced degree, variable foreign language requirement, comprehensive exam (for some programs). *Entrance requirements:* For master's and doctorate, GRE, GMAT. Additional exam requirements/recommendations for international students: Required—TOEFL (minimum score 550 paper-based; 79 iBT). Electronic applications accepted.

University of Oklahoma, College of Architecture, Division of Architecture, Norman, OK 73019. Offers architectural urban studies (MS), including environmental technology, human resources, urban studies; architecture (M Arch). *Faculty:* 41 full-time (16 women), 1 part-time/adjunct (0 women). *Students:* 25 full-time (11 women), 11 part-time (2 women); includes 6 minority (1 Black or African American, non-Hispanic/Latino; 1 American Indian or Alaska Native, non-Hispanic/Latino; 1 Asian, non-Hispanic/Latino; 1 Hispanic/Latino; 2 Two or more races, non-Hispanic/Latino), 10 international. Average age 31. 32 applicants, 47% accepted, 7 enrolled. In 2015, 9 master's awarded. *Degree requirements:* For master's, capstone thesis. *Entrance requirements:* For master's, portfolio, letters of recommendation, letter of intent. Additional exam requirements/recommendations for international students: Required—TOEFL (minimum score 79 iBT) or IELTS (minimum score 6.5). *Application deadline:* For fall admission, 11/1 for domestic and international students; for spring admission, 3/1 for domestic and international students. Application fee: $50 ($100 for international students). Electronic applications accepted. *Expenses:* Tuition, state resident: full-time $4577; part-time $190.70 per credit hour. Tuition, nonresident: full-time $17,758; part-time $739.90 per credit hour. *Required fees:* $3060; $115.70 per credit hour. $141.50 per semester. *Financial support:* In 2015–16, 25 students received support, including 1 research assistantship with partial tuition reimbursement available (averaging $10,372 per year), 2 teaching assistantships with partial tuition reimbursements available (averaging $10,372 per year); fellowships, career-related internships or fieldwork, scholarships/grants, and unspecified assistantships also available. Financial award application deadline: 6/1; financial award applicants required to submit FAFSA. *Faculty research:* Digital fabrication and design; middle eastern architecture and culture; real estate and urbanism; sustainable and resilient buildings. *Total annual research expenditures:* $150,655. *Unit head:* Dr. Stephanie Pilat, Interim Director, Division of Architecture, 405-325-9352, Fax: 405-325-2444, E-mail: spilat@ou.edu. *Application contact:* Marjorie Callahan, Graduate Liaison, Division of Architecture, 405-325-3866, Fax: 405-325-2444, E-mail: mcallahan@ou.edu.
Website: http://arch.ou.edu

University of Oklahoma, Gallogly College of Engineering, School of Civil Engineering and Environmental Science, Program in Environmental Science, Norman, OK 73019. Offers M Env Sc, PhD. *Program availability:* Part-time. *Students:* 8 full-time (4 women), 4 part-time (3 women); includes 1 minority (Two or more races, non-Hispanic/Latino), 5 international. Average age 29. 3 applicants, 100% accepted, 3 enrolled. In 2015, 2 master's, 1 doctorate awarded. Terminal master's awarded for partial completion of doctoral program. *Degree requirements:* For master's, comprehensive exam, thesis; for doctorate, comprehensive exam, thesis/dissertation. *Entrance requirements:* For master's and doctorate, GRE, statement of goals, 2 letters of recommendation, minimum GPA of 3.0. Additional exam requirements/recommendations for international students: Required—TOEFL (minimum score 79 iBT) or IELTS (minimum score 6.5). *Application deadline:* For fall admission, 1/15 for domestic and international students; for spring admission, 5/15 for domestic and international students. Application fee: $50 ($100 for international students). Electronic applications accepted. *Expenses:* Tuition, state resident: full-time $4577; part-time $190.70 per credit hour. Tuition, nonresident: full-time $17,758; part-time $739.90 per credit hour. *Required fees:* $3060; $115.70 per credit hour. $141.50 per semester. *Financial support:* In 2015–16, 10 students received support. Scholarships/grants available. Financial award application deadline: 6/1; financial award applicants required to submit FAFSA. *Faculty research:* Constructed wetlands, sustainable water treatment technologies, subsurface transport and fate of chemicals. *Unit head:* Dr. Randall Kolar, Director, 405-325-4267, Fax: 405-325-4217,

E-mail: kolar@ou.edu. *Application contact:* Susan Williams, Graduate Programs Assistant, 405-325-2344, Fax: 405-325-4147, E-mail: srwilliams@ou.edu.
Website: http://cees.ou.edu

University of Pennsylvania, School of Arts and Sciences, Graduate Group in Earth and Environmental Science, Philadelphia, PA 19104. Offers MS, PhD. *Program availability:* Part-time. *Faculty:* 9 full-time (3 women), 4 part-time/adjunct (0 women). *Students:* 14 full-time (10 women); includes 5 minority (2 Black or African American, non-Hispanic/Latino; 3 Two or more races, non-Hispanic/Latino), 3 international. Average age 27. 40 applicants, 10% accepted, 3 enrolled. In 2015, 4 doctorates awarded. *Expenses: Tuition, area resident:* Full-time $31,068; part-time $5762 per course. *Required fees:* $3200; $336 per course. Full-time tuition and fees vary according to degree level, program and student level. Part-time tuition and fees vary according to course load, degree level and program.
Website: http://www.sas.upenn.edu/graduate-division

University of Pittsburgh, Dietrich School of Arts and Sciences, Department of Geology and Environmental Science, Pittsburgh, PA 15260. Offers geographical information systems and remote sensing (Pro-MS); geology and environmental science (MS, PhD). *Program availability:* Part-time. *Faculty:* 9 full-time (3 women). *Students:* 36 full-time (15 women), 2 part-time (both women); includes 6 minority (1 Black or African American, non-Hispanic/Latino; 4 Asian, non-Hispanic/Latino; 1 Two or more races, non-Hispanic/Latino). Average age 29. 67 applicants, 36% accepted, 12 enrolled. In 2015, 7 master's, 3 doctorates awarded. *Degree requirements:* For master's, thesis, thesis defense; for doctorate, comprehensive exam, thesis/dissertation, thesis defense, public presentation. *Entrance requirements:* Additional exam requirements/recommendations for international students: Required—TOEFL (minimum score 90 iBT), IELTS (minimum score 7). *Application deadline:* For fall admission, 1/15 for domestic and international students. Applications are processed on a rolling basis. Application fee: $50. Electronic applications accepted. Tuition and fees vary according to program. *Financial support:* In 2015–16, 26 students received support, including 7 fellowships with full tuition reimbursements available (averaging $18,219 per year), 15 research assistantships with tuition reimbursements available (averaging $14,893 per year), 12 teaching assistantships with tuition reimbursements available (averaging $17,130 per year); scholarships/grants and tuition waivers (full and partial) also available. Financial award application deadline: 1/15. *Faculty research:* Tectonic, volcanic and surface processes; planetary science and astrobiology; paleoclimate and environmental change; environmental geochemistry and biogeochemistry; hydrologic processes. *Total annual research expenditures:* $1.8 million. *Unit head:* Dr. Mark Abbott, Chair, 412-624-8783, Fax: 412-624-3914, E-mail: mabbott1@pitt.edu. *Application contact:* Annemarie Vranesevic, Academic Coordinator, 412-624-8779, Fax: 412-624-3914, E-mail: alv36@pitt.edu.
Website: http://geology.pitt.edu/

University of Puerto Rico, Río Piedras Campus, College of Natural Sciences, Department of Environmental Sciences, San Juan, PR 00931-3300. Offers MS, PhD.

University of Rhode Island, Graduate School, College of the Environment and Life Sciences, Department of Fisheries, Animal and Veterinary Science, Kingston, RI 02881. Offers animal health and disease (MS); animal science (MS); aquaculture (MS); aquatic pathology (MS); environmental sciences (PhD), including animal science, aquacultural science, aquatic pathology, fisheries science; fisheries (MS). *Faculty:* 10 full-time (3 women). *Degree requirements:* For master's, comprehensive exam (for some programs), thesis optional; for doctorate, comprehensive exam, thesis/dissertation. *Entrance requirements:* For master's and doctorate, GRE, 2 letters of recommendation. Additional exam requirements/recommendations for international students: Required—TOEFL (minimum score 550 paper-based). *Application deadline:* For fall admission, 7/15 for domestic students, 2/1 for international students; for spring admission, 11/15 for domestic students, 7/15 for international students. Application fee: $65. Electronic applications accepted. *Expenses:* Tuition, state resident: full-time $11,796; part-time $655 per credit. Tuition, nonresident: full-time $24,206; part-time $1345 per credit. *Required fees:* $1546; $44 per credit. One-time fee: $155 full-time; $35 part-time. *Financial support:* Application deadline: 2/1; applicants required to submit FAFSA. *Total annual research expenditures:* $1.2 million. *Unit head:* Dr. Marta Gomez-Chiarri, Chair, 401-874-2917, Fax: 401-874-7575, E-mail: gomezchi@uri.edu. *Application contact:* Graduate Admissions, 401-874-2872, E-mail: gradadm@etal.uri.edu.
Website: http://www.uri.edu/cels/favs/

University of Saskatchewan, College of Graduate Studies and Research, School of Environment and Sustainability, Saskatoon, SK S7N 5A2, Canada. Offers MES.

University of South Africa, College of Agriculture and Environmental Sciences, Pretoria, South Africa. Offers agriculture (MS); consumer science (MCS); environmental management (MA, MS, PhD); environmental science (MA, MS, PhD); geography (MA, MS, PhD); horticulture (M Tech); human ecology (MHE); life sciences (MS); nature conservation (M Tech).

University of South Florida, College of Arts and Sciences, School of Geosciences, Tampa, FL 33620-9951. Offers environmental science and policy (MS); geography (MA), including environmental geography, geographic information science and spatial analysis, human geography; geography and environmental science and policy (PhD); geology (MS, PhD); urban and regional planning (MURP). *Program availability:* Part-time, evening/weekend. *Faculty:* 32 full-time (7 women). *Students:* 87 full-time (41 women), 45 part-time (19 women); includes 18 minority (7 Black or African American, non-Hispanic/Latino; 3 Asian, non-Hispanic/Latino; 7 Hispanic/Latino; 1 Two or more races, non-Hispanic/Latino), 29 international. Average age 34. 39 applicants, 62% accepted, 9 enrolled. In 2015, 10 master's awarded. *Degree requirements:* For master's, comprehensive exam, thesis (for some programs); for doctorate, comprehensive exam, thesis/dissertation. *Entrance requirements:* For master's, GRE General Test, minimum GPA of 3.0 for last 60 credits of undergraduate degree, letter of intent, letters of recommendation; for doctorate, GRE General Test, minimum GPA of 3.0 for all doctorate programs except for ESP/Geography which requires 3.20 GPA for all academic work, letter of intent, letters of recommendation. Additional exam requirements/recommendations for international students: Required—TOEFL (minimum score 550 paper-based; 79 iBT) or IELTS (minimum score 6.5) for MA and MURP; TOEFL (minimum score 600 paper-based) for MS and PhD. *Application deadline:* For fall admission, 2/15 for domestic students, 1/2 for international students; for spring admission, 10/15 for domestic students, 6/1 for international students. Application fee: $30. *Financial support:* In 2015–16, 26 students received support, including 3 research assistantships (averaging $12,345 per year), 25 teaching assistantships with tuition reimbursements available (averaging $12,807 per year); unspecified assistantships also available. Financial award application deadline: 3/1. *Faculty research:* Geography: human geography, environmental geography, geographic information science and spatial analysis, urban geography, social theory; environmental science, policy, and planning: water resources, wildlife ecology, Karst and wetland environments, natural hazards, soil contamination, meteorology and climatology, environmental sustainability and policy, urban and regional planning. *Total annual research expenditures:* $2.3 million. *Unit head:* Dr. Jayajit Chakraborty, Professor and Chair, Geography Division, 813-974-8188, Fax: 813-974-5911, E-mail: jchakrab@usf.edu. *Application contact:* Dr. Jennifer Collins, Associate Professor and Graduate Program Coordinator, 813-974-4242, Fax: 813-974-5911, E-mail: collinsjm@usf.edu.
Website: http://hennarot.forest.usf.edu/main/depts/geosci/

University of South Florida, St. Petersburg, College of Arts and Sciences, St. Petersburg, FL 33701. Offers digital journalism and design (MA); environmental science and policy (MA, MS); Florida studies (MLA); journalism and media studies (MA); liberal studies (MLA); psychology (MA). *Program availability:* Part-time, online learning. *Degree requirements:* For master's, comprehensive exam, thesis or project. *Entrance requirements:* For master's, GRE, LSAT, MCAT (varies by program), letter of intent, 3 letters of recommendation, writing samples, bachelor's degree from regionally-accredited institution with minimum GPA of 3.0 overall or in upper two years. Additional exam requirements/recommendations for international students: Required—TOEFL (minimum score 550 paper-based; 79 iBT); Recommended—IELTS. Electronic applications accepted.

The University of Tennessee at Chattanooga, Program in Environmental Science, Chattanooga, TN 37403. Offers environmental science (MS). *Program availability:* Part-time. *Faculty:* 9 full-time (2 women), 1 (woman) part-time/adjunct. *Students:* 18 full-time (12 women), 14 part-time (8 women); includes 5 minority (2 Black or African American, non-Hispanic/Latino; 1 Asian, non-Hispanic/Latino; 1 Hispanic/Latino; 1 Two or more races, non-Hispanic/Latino), 1 international. Average age 28. In 2015, 8 master's awarded. *Degree requirements:* For master's, thesis optional. *Entrance requirements:* For master's, GRE General Test, minimum undergraduate GPA of 2.75; undergraduate course work in ecology or knowledge equivalent. Additional exam requirements/recommendations for international students: Required—TOEFL (minimum score 550 paper-based; 79 iBT), IELTS (minimum score 6). *Application deadline:* For fall admission, 6/13 priority date for domestic students, 6/1 for international students; for spring admission, 10/15 priority date for domestic students, 10/1 for international students. Applications are processed on a rolling basis. Application fee: $30 ($35 for international students). Electronic applications accepted. *Expenses:* Tuition, state resident: full-time $7938; part-time $441 per credit hour. Tuition, nonresident: full-time $24,056; part-time $1336 per credit hour. *Required fees:* $1732; $253 per credit hour. *Financial support:* Research assistantships, teaching assistantships, career-related internships or fieldwork, scholarships/grants, and unspecified assistantships available. Support available to part-time students. Financial award applicants required to submit FAFSA. *Faculty research:* Bioremediation, stream fish ecology and conservation, environmental law and policy, avian conservation and management. *Total annual research expenditures:* $373,232. *Unit head:* Dr. John Tucker, Department Head, 423-425-4341, Fax: 423-425-2285, E-mail: john-tucker@utc.edu. *Application contact:* Dr. J. Randy Walker, Interim Dean of Graduate Studies, 423-425-4478, Fax: 423-425-5223, E-mail: randy-walker@utc.edu.
Website: http://www.utc.edu/biology-geology-environmental-science/

The University of Texas at Arlington, Graduate School, College of Science, Department of Earth and Environmental Sciences, Program in Environmental and Earth Sciences, Arlington, TX 76019. Offers environmental science (MS, PhD); geology (MS, PhD). *Program availability:* Part-time, evening/weekend. Terminal master's awarded for partial completion of doctoral program. *Degree requirements:* For master's, thesis optional; for doctorate, comprehensive exam, thesis/dissertation. *Entrance requirements:* For master's, GRE General Test. Additional exam requirements/recommendations for international students: Required—TOEFL (minimum score 550 paper-based). Electronic applications accepted.

The University of Texas at El Paso, Graduate School, College of Engineering, Department of Mechanical Engineering, El Paso, TX 79968-0001. Offers environmental science and engineering (PhD); mechanical engineering (MS). *Program availability:* Part-time. *Degree requirements:* For master's, thesis optional; for doctorate, thesis/dissertation. *Entrance requirements:* For master's, GRE, minimum GPA of 3.0, letter of reference; for doctorate, GRE, minimum GPA of 3.5, letters of reference, BS or equivalent. Additional exam requirements/recommendations for international students: Required—TOEFL; Recommended—IELTS. Electronic applications accepted. *Faculty research:* Aerospace, energy, combustion and propulsion, design engineering, high temperature materials.

The University of Texas at El Paso, Graduate School, College of Science, Environmental Science Program, El Paso, TX 79968-0001. Offers MS. *Program availability:* Part-time, evening/weekend. *Degree requirements:* For master's, thesis. *Entrance requirements:* For master's, GRE, bachelor's degree in a science or engineering discipline, 3 letters of recommendation. Additional exam requirements/recommendations for international students: Required—TOEFL.

The University of Texas at El Paso, Graduate School, Interdisciplinary Program in Environmental Science and Engineering, El Paso, TX 79968-0001. Offers PhD. *Program availability:* Part-time, evening/weekend. *Degree requirements:* For doctorate, thesis/dissertation. *Entrance requirements:* For doctorate, GRE, letters of recommendation. Additional exam requirements/recommendations for international students: Required—TOEFL; Recommended—IELTS. Electronic applications accepted.

The University of Texas at San Antonio, College of Engineering, Department of Civil and Environmental Engineering, San Antonio, TX 78249. Offers civil engineering (MCE, MSCE); environmental science and engineering (PhD). *Program availability:* Part-time. *Faculty:* 12 full-time (1 woman), 1 part-time/adjunct (0 women). *Students:* 38 full-time (8 women), 33 part-time (6 women); includes 18 minority (4 Black or African American, non-Hispanic/Latino; 4 Asian, non-Hispanic/Latino; 9 Hispanic/Latino; 1 Two or more races, non-Hispanic/Latino), 32 international. Average age 30. 77 applicants, 65% accepted, 24 enrolled. In 2015, 6 master's, 5 doctorates awarded. *Degree requirements:* For master's, comprehensive exam, thesis (for some programs); for doctorate, comprehensive exam, thesis/dissertation, written qualifying exam, dissertation proposal. *Entrance requirements:* For master's, GRE General Test, BS in civil engineering or related field from accredited institution, statement of research/specialization interest, favorable recommendation by the Civil Engineering Master's Program Admissions Committee; for doctorate, GRE, BS and MS from accredited institution, minimum GPA of 3.0 in upper-division and graduate courses, three letters of recommendation, letter of research interest, resume/curriculum vitae. Additional exam requirements/recommendations for international students: Required—TOEFL (minimum score 550 paper-based; 79 iBT), IELTS (minimum score 6.5). *Application deadline:* For fall admission, 7/1 for domestic students, 4/1 for international students; for spring admission, 11/1 for domestic students, 9/1 for international students. Application fee: $45 ($80 for international students). Electronic applications accepted. *Expenses:* Contact institution. *Financial support:* In 2015–16, 42 students received support, including 28 research assistantships with full tuition reimbursements available (averaging $20,000 per year), 14 teaching assistantships (averaging $4,680 per year); scholarships/grants also available. Financial award application deadline: 2/1. *Faculty research:* Structures, application of geographic information systems in water resources,

geotechnical engineering, pavement traffic loading, hydrogeology. *Total annual research expenditures:* $774,040. *Unit head:* Dr. Heather Shipley, Department Chair, 210-458-7517, Fax: 210-458-6475, E-mail: heather.shipley@utsa.edu. *Application contact:* Jessica Perez, Administrative Associate I, 210-458-4428, Fax: 210-458-7469, E-mail: jessica.perez@utsa.edu.
Website: http://engineering.utsa.edu/CE/

The University of Texas at San Antonio, College of Sciences, Department of Geological Sciences, San Antonio, TX 78249-0617. Offers MS. *Program availability:* Part-time. *Faculty:* 10 full-time (3 women), 1 part-time/adjunct (0 women). *Students:* 22 full-time (5 women), 19 part-time (4 women); includes 12 minority (1 Black or African American, non-Hispanic/Latino; 1 American Indian or Alaska Native, non-Hispanic/Latino; 2 Asian, non-Hispanic/Latino; 6 Hispanic/Latino; 2 Two or more races, non-Hispanic/Latino), 1 international. Average age 27. 32 applicants, 75% accepted, 17 enrolled. In 2015, 12 master's awarded. *Degree requirements:* For master's, comprehensive exam, thesis (for some programs). *Entrance requirements:* For master's, GRE General Test, three letters of recommendation, statement of research interest, undergraduate transcripts. Additional exam requirements/recommendations for international students: Required—TOEFL (minimum score 550 paper-based; 79 iBT), IELTS (minimum score 6.5). *Application deadline:* For fall admission, 7/1 for domestic students, 4/1 for international students; for spring admission, 11/1 for domestic students, 11/1 priority date for international students; for summer admission, 4/1 for domestic students, 4/1 priority date for international students. Application fee: $60 ($80 for international students). *Financial support:* In 2015–16, 6 teaching assistantships (averaging $10,578 per year) were awarded. *Faculty research:* Hydrogeology, sedimentary and stratigraphy, structure, paleontology, geographic information science. *Unit head:* Dr. Lance L. Lambert, Department Chair, 210-458-5447,
E-mail: lance.lambert@utsa.edu.
Website: http://www.utsa.edu/geosci/

University of the Virgin Islands, Graduate Programs, Division of Science and Mathematics, Program in Environmental and Marine Science, Saint Thomas, VI 00802-9990. Offers MS. *Entrance requirements:* For master's, GRE. Additional exam requirements/recommendations for international students: Required—TOEFL (minimum score 550 paper-based).

The University of Toledo, College of Graduate Studies, College of Natural Sciences and Mathematics, Department of Environmental Sciences, Toledo, OH 43606-3390. Offers biology (MS, PhD), including ecology; geology (MS), including earth surface processes. *Program availability:* Part-time. *Degree requirements:* For master's, thesis or alternative. *Entrance requirements:* For master's, GRE General Test, minimum cumulative point-hour ratio of 2.7 for all previous academic work, three letters of recommendation, statement of purpose, transcripts from all prior institutions attended. Additional exam requirements/recommendations for international students: Required—TOEFL (minimum score 550 paper-based; 80 iBT). Electronic applications accepted. *Faculty research:* Environmental geochemistry, geophysics, petrology and mineralogy, paleontology, geohydrology.

University of Toronto, School of Graduate Studies, Department of Physical and Environmental Sciences, Toronto, ON M5S 1A1, Canada. Offers environmental science (M Env Sc, PhD). *Entrance requirements:* For master's, bachelor's degree (B Sc or B Eng), minimum B average in last two years of undergraduate program, two half-courses or one full-course each in chemistry, physics, calculus and biology. Additional exam requirements/recommendations for international students: Required—TOEFL (minimum score 580 paper-based; 93 iBT), TWE (minimum score 4). Electronic applications accepted.

University of Utah, Graduate School, Professional Master of Science and Technology Program, Salt Lake City, UT 84112. Offers biotechnology (PSM); computational science (PSM); environmental science (PSM); science instrumentation (PSM). *Program availability:* Part-time. *Students:* 21 full-time (9 women), 35 part-time (12 women); includes 3 minority (2 Asian, non-Hispanic/Latino; 1 Two or more races, non-Hispanic/Latino), 2 international. Average age 32. 55 applicants, 67% accepted, 23 enrolled. In 2015, 11 master's awarded. *Degree requirements:* For master's, internship. *Entrance requirements:* For master's, GRE (recommended), minimum undergraduate GPA of 3.0, bachelor's degree from accredited university or college. Additional exam requirements/recommendations for international students: Required—TOEFL (minimum score 550 paper-based; 80 iBT), IELTS (minimum score 6.5). *Application deadline:* For fall admission, 2/1 for domestic and international students. Application fee: $55 ($65 for international students). Electronic applications accepted. *Expenses:* Contact institution. *Financial support:* Fellowships, research assistantships, teaching assistantships, and unspecified assistantships available. *Unit head:* Ray Hoobler, Program Director, 801-585-5630, E-mail: ray.hoobler@utah.edu. *Application contact:* Jay Derek Payne, Project Coordinator, 801-585-3650, E-mail: derek.payne@gradschool.utah.edu.
Website: http://pmst.utah.edu/

University of Virginia, College and Graduate School of Arts and Sciences, Department of Environmental Sciences, Charlottesville, VA 22903. Offers MA, MS, PhD. *Degree requirements:* For master's, thesis; for doctorate, comprehensive exam, thesis/dissertation. *Entrance requirements:* For master's and doctorate, GRE General Test, 2 letters of recommendation. Additional exam requirements/recommendations for international students: Required—TOEFL (minimum score 600 paper-based; 90 iBT), IELTS (minimum score 7). Electronic applications accepted.

University of Waterloo, Graduate Studies, Faculty of Science, Department of Earth and Environmental Sciences, Waterloo, ON N2L 3G1, Canada. Offers M Sc, PhD. *Program availability:* Part-time. *Degree requirements:* For master's, research paper or thesis; for doctorate, comprehensive exam, thesis/dissertation. *Entrance requirements:* For master's, GRE, honors degree, minimum B average; for doctorate, GRE, master's degree, minimum B average. Additional exam requirements/recommendations for international students: Required—TOEFL, IELTS, PTE. *Application deadline:* Applications are processed on a rolling basis. Application fee: $100 Canadian dollars. Electronic applications accepted. *Financial support:* Research assistantships, teaching assistantships, career-related internships or fieldwork, and institutionally sponsored loans available. *Faculty research:* Environmental geology, soil physics.
Website: https://uwaterloo.ca/earth-environmental-sciences/

The University of Western Ontario, Faculty of Graduate Studies, Physical Sciences Division, Department of Earth Sciences, London, ON N6A 5B8, Canada. Offers environment and sustainability (MES); geology (M Sc, PhD); geology and environmental science (M Sc, PhD); geophysics (M Sc, PhD); geophysics and environmental science (M Sc, PhD). *Degree requirements:* For master's, thesis; for doctorate, thesis/dissertation, qualifying exam. *Entrance requirements:* For master's, honors in B Sc; for doctorate, M Sc. Additional exam requirements/recommendations for international students: Required—TOEFL. *Faculty research:* Geophysics, geochemistry, paleontology, sedimentology/stratigraphy, glaciology/quaternary.

University of West Florida, College of Science and Engineering, Department of Earth and Environmental Sciences, Pensacola, FL 32514-5750. Offers MS. *Program availability:* Part-time. *Entrance requirements:* For master's, GRE (minimum score: 50th percentile for verbal; 40th percentile for quantitative), official transcripts; formal letter of interest, background, and professional goals; three letters of recommendation by individuals in professionally-relevant fields (waived for graduates of UWF Department of Environmental Sciences); current curriculum vitae/resume. Additional exam requirements/recommendations for international students: Required—TOEFL (minimum score 550 paper-based).

University of Windsor, Faculty of Graduate Studies, GLIER-Great Lakes Institute for Environmental Research, Windsor, ON N9B 3P4, Canada. Offers environmental science (M Sc, PhD). *Degree requirements:* For master's, thesis; for doctorate, thesis/dissertation. *Entrance requirements:* For master's, minimum B+ average; for doctorate, M Sc degree, minimum B+ average. Additional exam requirements/recommendations for international students: Required—TOEFL (minimum score 560 paper-based). Electronic applications accepted. *Faculty research:* Environmental chemistry and toxicology, conservation and resource management, iron formation geochemistry.

University of Wisconsin–Green Bay, Graduate Studies, Program in Environmental Science and Policy, Green Bay, WI 54311-7001. Offers MS. *Program availability:* Part-time. *Faculty:* 15 full-time (6 women), 2 part-time/adjunct (0 women). *Students:* 8 full-time (6 women), 17 part-time (10 women); includes 3 minority (1 Asian, non-Hispanic/Latino; 2 Two or more races, non-Hispanic/Latino). Average age 28. 14 applicants, 93% accepted, 9 enrolled. In 2015, 6 master's awarded. *Degree requirements:* For master's, thesis or alternative. *Entrance requirements:* For master's, GRE General Test, minimum GPA of 3.0. *Application deadline:* For fall admission, 8/1 for domestic students; for spring admission, 11/1 for domestic students. Applications are processed on a rolling basis. Application fee: $56. Electronic applications accepted. *Expenses:* Tuition, state resident: full-time $7640; part-time $424 per credit hour. Tuition, nonresident: full-time $16,771; part-time $932 per credit hour. *Required fees:* $1526; $85 per credit hour. $85 per semester. Tuition and fees vary according to program and reciprocity agreements. *Financial support:* In 2015–16, 3 students received support, including 3 research assistantships; career-related internships or fieldwork, Federal Work-Study, institutionally sponsored loans, and unspecified assistantships also available. Financial award application deadline: 7/15; financial award applicants required to submit FAFSA. *Faculty research:* Bald eagle, parasitic population of domestic and wild animals, resource recovery, anaerobic digestion of organic waste. *Unit head:* Dr. Matthew Dornbush, Chair, 920-465-2264, E-mail: dornbusm@uwgb.edu. *Application contact:* Mary Valitchka, Graduate Studies Coordinator, 920-465-2123,
E-mail: valitchm@uwgb.edu.
Website: http://www.uwgb.edu/graduate/

Vanderbilt University, Department of Earth and Environmental Sciences, Nashville, TN 37240-1001. Offers MAT, MS. *Faculty:* 10 full-time (2 women). *Students:* 7 full-time (4 women), 4 part-time (3 women); includes 1 minority (Black or African American, non-Hispanic/Latino). Average age 23. 54 applicants, 15% accepted, 5 enrolled. In 2015, 8 master's awarded. *Degree requirements:* For master's, thesis. *Entrance requirements:* For master's, GRE General Test, GRE Subject Test (recommended). Additional exam requirements/recommendations for international students: Required—TOEFL (minimum score 570 paper-based; 88 iBT). *Application deadline:* For fall admission, 1/15 for domestic and international students. Application fee: $0. Electronic applications accepted. *Financial support:* Fellowships with tuition reimbursements, research assistantships with tuition reimbursements, teaching assistantships with full tuition reimbursements, career-related internships or fieldwork, Federal Work-Study, institutionally sponsored loans, and health care benefits available. Financial award application deadline: 1/15; financial award applicants required to submit CSS PROFILE or FAFSA. *Faculty research:* Geochemical processes, magmatic processes and crustal evolution, paleoecology and paleoenvironments, sedimentary systems, transport phenomena, environmental policy. *Unit head:* Dr. Guil Gualda, Director of Graduate Studies, 615-322-2976, E-mail: g.gualda@vanderbilt.edu. *Application contact:* Teri Pugh, Office Assistant, 615-322-2976, E-mail: teri.pugh@vanderbilt.edu.
Website: http://www.vanderbilt.edu/ees/

Virginia Polytechnic Institute and State University, Graduate School, College of Engineering, Blacksburg, VA 24061. Offers aerospace engineering (ME, MS, PhD); biological systems engineering (ME, MS, PhD); biomedical engineering (MS, PhD); chemical engineering (ME, MS, PhD); civil engineering (ME, MS, PhD); computer engineering (ME, MS, PhD); computer science (MS, PhD); electrical engineering (ME, PhD); engineering education (PhD); engineering mechanics (ME, MS, PhD); environmental engineering (MS); environmental science and engineering (MS); industrial and systems engineering (ME, MS, PhD); materials science and engineering (ME, MS, PhD); mechanical engineering (ME, MS, PhD); mining and minerals engineering (PhD); mining engineering (ME, MS); nuclear engineering (MS, PhD); ocean engineering (MS); systems engineering (ME, MS). *Accreditation:* ABET (one or more programs are accredited). *Degree requirements:* For master's, comprehensive exam (for some programs), thesis (for some programs); for doctorate, comprehensive exam (for some programs), thesis/dissertation (for some programs). *Entrance requirements:* For master's and doctorate, GRE/GMAT (may vary by department). Additional exam requirements/recommendations for international students: Required—TOEFL (minimum score 550 paper-based). Electronic applications accepted.

Virginia Polytechnic Institute and State University, Graduate School, College of Natural Resources and Environment, Blacksburg, VA 24061. Offers fisheries and wildlife (MS, PhD); forestry and forest products (MF, MS, PhD); geography (MS); geospatial and environmental analysis (PhD); natural resources (MNR). *Degree requirements:* For master's, comprehensive exam (for some programs), thesis (for some programs); for doctorate, comprehensive exam (for some programs), thesis/dissertation (for some programs). *Entrance requirements:* For master's and doctorate, GRE/GMAT (may vary by department). Additional exam requirements/recommendations for international students: Required—TOEFL (minimum score 550 paper-based). Electronic applications accepted.

Virginia Polytechnic Institute and State University, VT Online, Blacksburg, VA 24061. Offers advanced transportation systems (Certificate); aerospace engineering (MS); agricultural and life sciences (MSLFS); business information systems (Graduate Certificate); career and technical education (MS); civil engineering (MS); computer engineering (M Eng, MS); decision support systems (Graduate Certificate); eLearning leadership (MA); electrical engineering (M Eng, MS); engineering administration (MEA); environmental engineering (Certificate); environmental politics and policy (Graduate Certificate); environmental sciences and engineering (MS); foundations of political analysis (Graduate Certificate); health product risk management (Graduate Certificate); industrial and systems engineering (MS); information policy and society (Graduate Certificate); information security (Graduate Certificate); information technology (MIT); instructional technology (MA); integrative STEM education (MA Ed); liberal arts (Graduate Certificate); life sciences: health product risk management (MS); natural resources (MNR, Graduate Certificate); networking (Graduate Certificate); nonprofit and nongovernmental organization management (Graduate Certificate); ocean engineering (MS); political science (MA); security studies (Graduate Certificate); software development (Graduate Certificate).

Washington State University, College of Agricultural, Human, and Natural Resource Sciences, School of the Environment, Pullman, WA 99164. Offers environmental and natural resource sciences (PhD); natural resource sciences (MS). Program applications must be made through the Pullman campus. *Degree requirements:* For master's, comprehensive exam (for some programs), thesis (for some programs), oral exam; for doctorate, comprehensive exam, thesis/dissertation, oral exam. *Entrance requirements:* For master's, GRE General Test, official copies of all college transcripts, three letters of recommendation. Additional exam requirements/recommendations for international students: Required—TOEFL, IELTS. *Faculty research:* Environmental and natural resources conservation and sustainability; earth sciences: earth systems and geology; wildlife ecology and conservation sciences.

Washington State University, College of Arts and Sciences, School of the Environment, Pullman, WA 99164. Offers environmental and natural resource sciences (PhD); environmental science (MS); geology (MS, PhD); natural resource science (MS). *Degree requirements:* For master's, comprehensive exam (for some programs), thesis (for some programs), oral exam; for doctorate, comprehensive exam, thesis/dissertation, oral exam, written exam. *Entrance requirements:* For master's, 3 undergraduate semester hours each in sociology or cultural anthropology, environmental science, biological sciences, and calculus or statistics; 4 in general ecology; and 6 in general chemistry or general physics; for doctorate, minimum GPA of 3.0. Additional exam requirements/recommendations for international students: Required—TOEFL, IELTS.

Wesleyan University, Graduate Studies, Department of Earth and Environmental Sciences, Middletown, CT 06459. Offers MA. *Faculty:* 11 full-time (4 women). *Students:* 5 full-time (1 woman). Average age 24. In 2015, 3 master's awarded. *Degree requirements:* For master's, thesis. *Entrance requirements:* For master's, GRE General Test, official transcripts, three recommendation letters, essay. Additional exam requirements/recommendations for international students: Required—TOEFL; Recommended—IELTS. *Application deadline:* For fall admission, 2/15 priority date for domestic and international students. Applications are processed on a rolling basis. Application fee: $0. Electronic applications accepted. *Financial support:* In 2015–16, 2 teaching assistantships with full tuition reimbursements were awarded; scholarships/grants and tuition waivers (full and partial) also available. Financial award application deadline: 4/15; financial award applicants required to submit FAFSA. *Faculty research:* Tectonics, volcanology, stratigraphy, coastal processes, geochemistry. *Unit head:* Dr. Martha Gilmore, Chair, 860-685-3129, E-mail: mgilmore@wesleyan.edu. *Application contact:* Ginny Harris, Administrative Assistant, 860-685-2244,
E-mail: vharris@wesleyan.edu.
Website: http://www.wesleyan.edu/ees/

Western Connecticut State University, Division of Graduate Studies, Maricostas School of Arts and Sciences, Department of Biological and Environmental Sciences, Danbury, CT 06810-6885. Offers MAT. *Program availability:* Part-time. *Degree requirements:* For master's, comprehensive exam or thesis, completion of program in 6 years. *Entrance requirements:* For master's, minimum GPA of 2.5. Additional exam requirements/recommendations for international students: Recommended—TOEFL (minimum score 550 paper-based; 79 iBT), IELTS (minimum score 6). *Expenses:* Contact institution. *Faculty research:* Biology, taxonomy and evolution of aquatic flowering plants; aquatic plant reproductive systems, the spread of invasive aquatic plants, aquatic plant structure, and the taxonomy of water starworts (Callitrichaceae) and riverweeds (Podostemaceae).

Western Illinois University, School of Graduate Studies, College of Arts and Sciences, Program in Environmental Science: Large River Ecosystems, Macomb, IL 61455-1390. Offers PhD. *Students:* 1 full-time (0 women), 2 part-time (both women). Average age 35. 3 applicants, 33% accepted, 1 enrolled. *Degree requirements:* For doctorate, thesis/dissertation. *Entrance requirements:* For doctorate, GRE, three letters of recommendation, official transcripts, statement of research intent, curriculum vitae. Additional exam requirements/recommendations for international students: Required—TOEFL. *Application deadline:* Applications are processed on a rolling basis. Application fee: $30. *Financial support:* In 2015–16, 1 student received support, including 1 research assistantship with full tuition reimbursement available (averaging $7,544 per year). *Unit head:* Dr. Roger Viadero, Director, Institute for Environmental Sciences, 309-298-2040. *Application contact:* Dr. Nancy Parsons, Associate Provost and Director of Graduate Studies, 309-298-1806, Fax: 309-298-2345, E-mail: grad-office@wiu.edu.
Website: http://wiu.edu/graduate_studies/programs_of_study/environsci_profile.php

Western Washington University, Graduate School, Huxley College of the Environment, Department of Environmental Sciences, Bellingham, WA 98225-5996. Offers environmental science (MS); marine and estuarine science (MS). *Program availability:* Part-time. *Degree requirements:* For master's, thesis. *Entrance requirements:* For master's, GRE General Test, minimum GPA of 3.0 in last 60 semester hours or last 90 quarter hours. Additional exam requirements/recommendations for international students: Required—TOEFL (minimum score 567 paper-based). Electronic applications accepted. *Faculty research:* Landscape ecology, climate change, watershed studies, environmental toxicology and risk assessment, aquatic toxicology, toxic algae, invasive species.

Western Washington University, Graduate School, Huxley College of the Environment, Department of Environmental Studies, Bellingham, WA 98225-5996. Offers environmental education (M Ed); geography (MS). *Program availability:* Part-time. *Degree requirements:* For master's, thesis. *Entrance requirements:* For master's, GRE General Test, minimum GPA of 3.0 in last 60 semester hours or last 90 quarter hours. Additional exam requirements/recommendations for international students: Required—TOEFL (minimum score 567 paper-based). Electronic applications accepted. *Faculty research:* Geomorphology; pedogenesis; quaternary studies and climate change in the western U.S. landscape ecology, biogeography, pyrogeography, and spatial analysis.

West Texas A&M University, College of Agriculture, Science and Engineering, Department of Agricultural Sciences, Emphasis in Plant, Soil and Environmental Science, Canyon, TX 79016-0001. Offers MS. *Program availability:* Part-time. *Degree requirements:* For master's, comprehensive exam, thesis optional. *Entrance requirements:* For master's, GRE General Test. Additional exam requirements/recommendations for international students: Required—TOEFL (minimum score 550 paper-based). Electronic applications accepted. *Faculty research:* Crop and soil disciplines.

West Texas A&M University, College of Agriculture, Science and Engineering, Department of Life, Earth, and Environmental Sciences, Program in Environmental Science, Canyon, TX 79016-0001. Offers MS. *Program availability:* Part-time. *Degree requirements:* For master's, comprehensive exam, thesis optional. *Entrance requirements:* For master's, GRE General Test. Additional exam requirements/recommendations for international students: Required—TOEFL (minimum score 550 paper-based). Electronic applications accepted. *Faculty research:* Degradation of presistant pesticides in soils and ground water, air quality.

Wichita State University, Graduate School, Fairmount College of Liberal Arts and Sciences, Department of Geology, Wichita, KS 67260. Offers earth, environmental, and physical sciences (MS). *Program availability:* Part-time. *Unit head:* Dr. William Parcell, Chair, 316-978-3140, E-mail: william.parcell@wichita.edu. *Application contact:* Jordan Oleson, Admissions Coordinator, 316-978-3095, Fax: 316-978-3253,
E-mail: jordan.oleson@wichita.edu.
Website: http://www.wichita.edu/geology

Wilfrid Laurier University, Faculty of Graduate and Postdoctoral Studies, Faculty of Arts, Department of Geography and Environmental Studies, Waterloo, ON N2L 3C5, Canada. Offers environmental and resource management (MA, MES, PhD); environmental science (M Sc, MES, PhD); geomatics (M Sc, MES, PhD); human geography (MES, PhD). *Program availability:* Part-time. *Degree requirements:* For master's, thesis optional; for doctorate, thesis/dissertation. *Entrance requirements:* For master's, honors BA in geography, minimum B average in undergraduate course work; honors BSc with minimum B+ or honors BES or BA in physical geography, environmental or earth sciences or the equivalent; for doctorate, MA in geography, minimum A- average. Additional exam requirements/recommendations for international students: Required—TOEFL (minimum score 89 iBT). Electronic applications accepted. *Faculty research:* Resources management, urban, economic, physical, cultural, earth surfaces, geomatics, historical, regional, spatial data handling.

Wright State University, School of Graduate Studies, College of Science and Mathematics, Department of Biological Sciences, Dayton, OH 45435. Offers biological sciences (MS); environmental sciences (MS). *Degree requirements:* For master's, thesis optional. *Entrance requirements:* Additional exam requirements/recommendations for international students: Required—TOEFL.

Wright State University, School of Graduate Studies, College of Science and Mathematics, Department of Chemistry, Dayton, OH 45435. Offers chemistry (MS); environmental sciences (MS). *Program availability:* Part-time, evening/weekend. *Degree requirements:* For master's, oral defense of thesis, seminar. *Entrance requirements:* Additional exam requirements/recommendations for international students: Required—TOEFL. *Faculty research:* Polymer synthesis and characterization, laser kinetics, organic and inorganic synthesis, analytical and environmental chemistry.

Wright State University, School of Graduate Studies, College of Science and Mathematics, Program in Environmental Sciences, Dayton, OH 45435. Offers PhD.

Yale University, Graduate School of Arts and Sciences, Department of Forestry and Environmental Studies, New Haven, CT 06520. Offers environmental sciences (PhD); forestry (PhD). *Degree requirements:* For doctorate, thesis/dissertation. *Entrance requirements:* For doctorate, GRE General Test.

Yale University, School of Forestry and Environmental Studies, New Haven, CT 06511. Offers environmental management (MEM), including business and the environment, ecosystem and conservation management, energy and the environment, environmental policy analysis; environmental science (MES); forest science (MFS); forestry (MF); forestry and environmental studies (PhD); JD/MEM; MBA/MEM; MBA/MF; MEM/M Arch; MEM/M Div; MEM/MA; MEM/MAR; MEM/MPH. *Accreditation:* SAF (one or more programs are accredited). *Program availability:* Part-time. *Faculty:* 32 full-time, 50 part-time/adjunct. *Students:* 300 full-time. Average age 27. 600 applicants, 150 enrolled. In 2015, 152 master's, 15 doctorates awarded. Terminal master's awarded for partial completion of doctoral program. *Degree requirements:* For master's, internship and capstone project (for MEM and MF); research project and thesis (for MES and MFS); for doctorate, comprehensive exam, thesis/dissertation. *Entrance requirements:* For master's, GRE General Test, GMAT or LSAT; for doctorate, GRE General Test. Additional exam requirements/recommendations for international students: Required—TOEFL (minimum score 600 paper-based; 100 iBT) or IELTS (minimum score 7). *Application deadline:* For fall admission, 12/15 priority date for domestic and international students. Application fee: $80. Electronic applications accepted. *Expenses:* Contact institution. *Financial support:* In 2015–16, 240 students received support. Fellowships, research assistantships, teaching assistantships, career-related internships or fieldwork, Federal Work-Study, institutionally sponsored loans, scholarships/grants, and health care benefits available. Support available to part-time students. Financial award application deadline: 2/15; financial award applicants required to submit FAFSA. *Faculty research:* Environmental policy, social ecology, industrial environmental management, forestry, environmental health, urban ecology, water science policy. *Unit head:* Peter Crane, Dean, School of Forestry and Environmental Studies, 203-432-5109, Fax: 203-432-3051. *Application contact:* Rebecca DeSalvo, Director of Enrollment Management & Diversity Initiatives, 800-825-0330, Fax: 203-432-5528, E-mail: fesinfo@yale.edu.
Website: http://environment.yale.edu

Marine Affairs

American Public University System, AMU/APU Graduate Programs, Charles Town, WV 25414. Offers accounting (MBA, MS); criminal justice (MA), including business administration, emergency and disaster management, general (MA, MS); educational leadership (M Ed); emergency and disaster management (MA); entrepreneurship (MBA); environmental policy and management (MS), including environmental planning, environmental sustainability, fish and wildlife management, general (MA, MS), global environmental management; finance (MBA); general (MBA); global business management (MBA); history (MA), including American history, ancient and classical

history, European history, global history, public history; homeland security (MA), including business administration, counter-terrorism studies, criminal justice, cyber, emergency management and public health, intelligence studies, transportation security; homeland security resource allocation (MBA); humanities (MA); information technology (MS), including digital forensics, enterprise software development, information assurance and security, IT project management; information technology management (MBA); intelligence studies (MA), including criminal intelligence, cyber, general (MA, MS), homeland security, intelligence analysis, intelligence collection, intelligence management, intelligence operations, terrorism studies; international relations and conflict resolution (MA), including comparative and security issues, conflict resolution, international and transnational security issues, peacekeeping; legal studies (MA); management (MA), including defense management, general (MA, MS), human resource management, organizational leadership, public administration; marketing (MBA); military history (MA), including American military history, American Revolution, civil war, war since 1945, World War II; military studies (MA), including joint warfare, strategic leadership; national security studies (MA), including general (MA, MS), homeland security, regional security studies, security and intelligence analysis, terrorism studies; nonprofit management (MBA); political science (MA), including American politics and government, comparative government and development, general (MA, MS), international relations, public policy; psychology (MA); public administration (MPA), including disaster management, environmental policy, health policy, human resources, national security, organizational management, security management; public health (MPH); reverse logistics management (MA); school counseling (M Ed); security management (MA); space studies (MS), including aerospace science, general (MA, MS), planetary science; sports and health sciences (MS); teaching (M Ed), including curriculum and instruction for elementary teachers, elementary reading, English language learners, instructional leadership, online learning, special education; transportation and logistics management (MA), including general (MA, MS), maritime engineering management, reverse logistics management. Programs offered via distance learning only. *Program availability:* Part-time, evening/weekend, online learning. *Faculty:* 431 full-time (241 women), 1,839 part-time/adjunct (865 women). *Students:* 531 full-time (233 women), 9,094 part-time (3,735 women); includes 3,140 minority (1,679 Black or African American, non-Hispanic/Latino; 55 American Indian or Alaska Native, non-Hispanic/Latino; 252 Asian, non-Hispanic/Latino; 773 Hispanic/Latino; 75 Native Hawaiian or other Pacific Islander, non-Hispanic/Latino; 306 Two or more races, non-Hispanic/Latino), 111 international. Average age 37. In 2015, 3,391 master's awarded. *Degree requirements:* For master's, comprehensive exam or practicum. *Entrance requirements:* For master's, official transcript showing earned bachelor's degree from institution accredited by recognized accrediting body. Additional exam requirements/recommendations for international students: Required—TOEFL (minimum score 550 paper-based), IELTS (minimum score 6.5). *Application deadline:* Applications are processed on a rolling basis. Application fee: $0. Electronic applications accepted. *Expenses: Tuition, area resident:* Part-time $350 per credit hour. *Financial support:* Applicants required to submit FAFSA. *Unit head:* Dr. Karan Powell, Executive Vice President and Provost, 877-468-6268, Fax: 304-724-3780. *Application contact:* Terry Grant, Vice President of Enrollment Management, 877-468-6268, Fax: 304-724-3780, E-mail: info@apus.edu.
Website: http://www.apus.edu

Dalhousie University, Faculty of Management, Marine Affairs Program, Halifax, NS B3H 3J5, Canada. Offers MMM. *Degree requirements:* For master's, project. *Entrance requirements:* For master's, minimum GPA of 3.0. Additional exam requirements/recommendations for international students: Required—TOEFL, IELTS, CANTEST, CAEL, or Michigan English Language Assessment Battery. Electronic applications accepted. *Faculty research:* Coastal zone management, sea use planning, development of non-living resources, protection and preservation of the coastal and marine environment, marine law and policy, fisheries management, maritime transport, conflict management.

Louisiana State University and Agricultural & Mechanical College, Graduate School, School of the Coast and Environment, Department of Oceanography and Coastal Sciences, Baton Rouge, LA 70803. Offers MS, PhD.

Memorial University of Newfoundland, School of Graduate Studies, Department of Sociology, St. John's, NL A1C 5S7, Canada. Offers gender (PhD); maritime sociology (PhD); sociology (M Phil, MA); work and development (PhD). *Program availability:* Part-time. *Degree requirements:* For master's, comprehensive exam, thesis optional, program journal (M Phil); for doctorate, one foreign language, comprehensive exam, thesis/dissertation, oral defense of thesis. *Entrance requirements:* For master's, 2nd class degree from university of recognized standing in area of study; for doctorate, MA, M Phil, or equivalent. *Application deadline:* For fall admission, 2/1 priority date for domestic and international students. Applications are processed on a rolling basis. Application fee: $50 Canadian dollars ($100 Canadian dollars for international students). Electronic applications accepted. *Expenses: Tuition, area resident:* Full-time $2199 Canadian dollars. *International tuition:* $2859 Canadian dollars full-time. *Financial support:* Fellowships, research assistantships, and teaching assistantships available. *Faculty research:* Work and development, gender, maritime sociology. *Unit head:* Dr. Ailsa Craig, Head, 709-864-2686, Fax: 709-864-2075. *Application contact:* Liam Swiss, Graduate Coordinator, 709-864-4467, Fax: 709-864-2075, E-mail: lswiss@mun.ca.
Website: http://www.mun.ca/soc/

Memorial University of Newfoundland, School of Graduate Studies, Interdisciplinary Program in Marine Studies, St. John's, NL A1C 5S7, Canada. Offers fisheries resource management (MMS, Graduate Diploma); marine spatial planning and management (MMS). *Program availability:* Part-time. *Degree requirements:* For master's, report. *Entrance requirements:* For master's, high 2nd class degree from a recognized university; demonstrated commitment to the fishery through employment or experience in a sector of the fishery, in a regulatory agency or government department connected to the fisheries, in a non-governmental agency, or through self-employment or relevant professional consulting activities; for Graduate Diploma, high 2nd class degree from a recognized university. *Application deadline:* For fall admission, 5/15 for domestic and international students; for winter admission, 10/15 for domestic and international students. Applications are processed on a rolling basis. Application fee: $50 Canadian dollars ($100 Canadian dollars for international students). Electronic applications accepted. *Expenses: Tuition, area resident:* Full-time $2199 Canadian dollars. *International tuition:* $2859 Canadian dollars full-time. *Faculty research:* Biological, ecological and oceanographic aspects of world fisheries; economics; political science; sociology. *Unit head:* Keith Rideout, Graduate Officer, 709-778-0675, Fax: 709-778-0346, E-mail: keith.rideout@mi.mun.ca.
Website: http://www.mi.mun.ca/programsandcourses/programs/

Nova Southeastern University, Halmos College of Natural Sciences and Oceanography, Fort Lauderdale, FL 33314-7796. Offers biological sciences (MS); coastal studies (Certificate); coastal zone management (MS); marine and coastal climate change (Certificate); marine and coastal studies (MA); marine biology (MS); marine biology and oceanography (PhD), including marine biology, oceanography; marine environmental sciences (MS). *Program availability:* Part-time, evening/weekend, 100% online, blended/hybrid learning. *Faculty:* 17 full-time (3 women), 22 part-time/adjunct (11 women). *Students:* 100 full-time (57 women), 114 part-time (76 women); includes 32 minority (6 Black or African American, non-Hispanic/Latino; 1 American Indian or Alaska Native, non-Hispanic/Latino; 6 Asian, non-Hispanic/Latino; 10 Hispanic/Latino; 9 Two or more races, non-Hispanic/Latino), 5 international. Average age 30. 85 applicants, 60% accepted, 39 enrolled. In 2015, 47 master's, 2 doctorates, 9 other advanced degrees awarded. *Degree requirements:* For master's, thesis; for doctorate, comprehensive exam, thesis/dissertation, departmental qualifying exam. *Entrance requirements:* For master's, GRE General Test, 3 letters of recommendation, BS/BA in natural science (for marine biology program), BS/BA in biology (for biological sciences program), minor in the natural sciences or equivalent (for coastal zone management and marine environmental sciences); for doctorate, GRE General Test, master's degree. Additional exam requirements/recommendations for international students: Required—TOEFL (minimum score 550 paper-based). *Application deadline:* Applications are processed on a rolling basis. Application fee: $50. Electronic applications accepted. *Expenses:* $34,749 per year (for PhD); $3,738 per course (for MS and Graduate Certificate). *Financial support:* In 2015–16, 157 students received support, including 14 fellowships with tuition reimbursements available (averaging $25,000 per year), 42 research assistantships with tuition reimbursements available (averaging $19,000 per year); teaching assistantships, career-related internships or fieldwork, Federal Work-Study, scholarships/grants, health care benefits, tuition waivers (full and partial), and unspecified assistantships also available. Support available to part-time students. Financial award application deadline: 4/15; financial award applicants required to submit FAFSA. *Faculty research:* Physical oceanography, biological oceanography, molecular and microbiology, ecology and evolution, coral reefs. *Total annual research expenditures:* $5 million. *Unit head:* Dr. Richard Dodge, Dean, 954-262-3600, Fax: 954-262-4020, E-mail: dodge@nsu.nova.edu. *Application contact:* Dr. Bernhard Riegl, Chair, Department of Marine and Environmental Sciences, 954-262-3600, Fax: 954-262-4020, E-mail: rieglb@nova.edu.
Website: http://cnso.nova.edu

Oregon State University, College of Earth, Ocean, and Atmospheric Sciences, Program in Marine Resource Management, Corvallis, OR 97331. Offers MA, MS. *Program availability:* Part-time. *Students:* 22 full-time (18 women), 4 part-time (1 woman); includes 4 minority (1 Asian, non-Hispanic/Latino; 1 Hispanic/Latino; 2 Two or more races, non-Hispanic/Latino), 3 international. Average age 28. 30 applicants, 30% accepted, 9 enrolled. In 2015, 9 master's awarded. *Degree requirements:* For master's, thesis optional. *Entrance requirements:* For master's, GRE, minimum GPA of 3.0 in last 90 hours of course work. Additional exam requirements/recommendations for international students: Required—TOEFL (minimum score 575 paper-based). *Application deadline:* For fall admission, 1/5 for domestic students. Application fee: $75 ($85 for international students). *Expenses:* Tuition, state resident: full-time $12,150; part-time $450 per credit. Tuition, nonresident: full-time $20,952; part-time $776 per credit. *Required fees:* $1572; $1443 per unit. One-time fee: $350. Tuition and fees vary according to course load, campus/location and program. *Financial support:* Fellowships, research assistantships, teaching assistantships, career-related internships or fieldwork, Federal Work-Study, and institutionally sponsored loans available. Support available to part-time students. *Faculty research:* Ocean and coastal resources, fisheries resources, marine pollution, marine recreation and tourism. *Unit head:* Dr. Flaxen Conway, Director/Professor. *Application contact:* Lori Hartline, Marine Resource Management Advisor, 541-737-5188,
E-mail: student_advisor@coas.oregonstate.edu.
Website: http://ceoas.oregonstate.edu/mrm/

Stevens Institute of Technology, Graduate School, Charles V. Schaefer Jr. School of Engineering, Department of Civil, Environmental, and Ocean Engineering, Program in Maritime Systems, Hoboken, NJ 07030. Offers MS. *Program availability:* Part-time, evening/weekend. *Students:* 7 full-time (1 woman), 4 part-time (1 woman); includes 2 minority (1 Black or African American, non-Hispanic/Latino; 1 Asian, non-Hispanic/Latino), 3 international. Average age 25. 18 applicants, 89% accepted, 4 enrolled. In 2015, 4 master's awarded. *Entrance requirements:* Additional exam requirements/recommendations for international students: Required—TOEFL (minimum score 74 iBT). *Application deadline:* For fall admission, 6/1 for domestic students, 4/15 for international students; for spring admission, 11/30 for domestic students, 11/1 for international students. Applications are processed on a rolling basis. Application fee: $60. Electronic applications accepted. *Expenses: Tuition, area resident:* Full-time $32,200; part-time $1450 per credit. *Required fees:* $1150; $550 per unit. $275 per semester. *Financial support:* Fellowships, research assistantships, teaching assistantships, career-related internships or fieldwork, Federal Work-Study, scholarships/grants, and unspecified assistantships available. Financial award application deadline: 2/15; financial award applicants required to submit FAFSA. *Unit head:* Dr. David A. Vaccari, Director, 201-216-5570, Fax: 201-216-8739,
E-mail: dvaccari@stevens.edu. *Application contact:* Graduate Admission, 888-783-8367, Fax: 888-511-1306, E-mail: graduate@stevens.edu.

Stony Brook University, State University of New York, Graduate School, School of Marine and Atmospheric Sciences, Program in Marine Conservation and Policy, Stony Brook, NY 11794. Offers MA. *Students:* 16 full-time (11 women), 3 part-time (all women); includes 2 minority (both Black or African American, non-Hispanic/Latino), 5 international. Average age 26. 25 applicants, 88% accepted, 13 enrolled. In 2015, 15 master's awarded. *Degree requirements:* For master's, capstone project or internship. *Entrance requirements:* For master's, GRE General Test, minimum GPA of 3.0; one semester of college-level biology and three additional semester courses in college-level math or science; personal statement; 3 letters of reference; official transcripts. Additional exam requirements/recommendations for international students: Required—TOEFL. *Application deadline:* For fall admission, 1/15 for domestic students; for spring admission, 10/1 for domestic students. Application fee: $100. Electronic applications accepted. *Expenses:* $12,421 full-time resident tuition and fees, $453 per credit hour; $23,761 full-time nonresident tuition and fees, $952 per credit hour. *Unit head:* Dr. Larry Swanson, Interim Dean, 631-632-8700, Fax: 631-632-8820,
E-mail: larry.swanson@stonybrook.edu. *Application contact:* Carol Dovi, Coordinator, 631-632-8681, Fax: 631-632-8915, E-mail: carol.dovi@stonybrook.edu.
Website: http://you.stonybrook.edu/somas/education/graduate/

Université du Québec à Rimouski, Graduate Programs, Program in Management of Marine Resources, Rimouski, QC G5L 3A1, Canada. Offers M Sc, Diploma. *Program availability:* Part-time. *Entrance requirements:* For master's, appropriate bachelor's degree, proficiency in French.

University of Delaware, College of Earth, Ocean, and Environment, School of Marine Science and Policy, Newark, DE 19716. Offers marine policy (MMP); marine studies (MS, PhD), including marine biosciences, oceanography, physical ocean science and engineering; oceanography (PhD).

University of Maine, Graduate School, College of Natural Sciences, Forestry, and Agriculture, School of Marine Sciences, Orono, ME 04469. Offers marine bio-resources (MS, PhD); marine biology (MS, PhD); marine policy (MS); oceanography (MS, PhD).

Program availability: Part-time. *Faculty:* 26 full-time (9 women), 11 part-time/adjunct (0 women). *Students:* 57 full-time (38 women); includes 2 minority (1 American Indian or Alaska Native, non-Hispanic/Latino; 1 Asian, non-Hispanic/Latino), 8 international. Average age 28. 95 applicants, 19% accepted, 16 enrolled. In 2015, 9 master's, 5 doctorates awarded. *Degree requirements:* For master's, thesis; for doctorate, comprehensive exam, thesis/dissertation. *Entrance requirements:* For master's and doctorate, GRE General Test. Additional exam requirements/recommendations for international students: Required—TOEFL. *Application deadline:* Applications are processed on a rolling basis. Application fee: $65. Electronic applications accepted. *Financial support:* In 2015–16, 54 students received support, including 2 fellowships (averaging $22,400 per year), 41 research assistantships with tuition reimbursements available (averaging $14,600 per year), 10 teaching assistantships with tuition reimbursements available (averaging $14,600 per year); career-related internships or fieldwork, Federal Work-Study, and tuition waivers (full and partial) also available. Support available to part-time students. Financial award application deadline: 3/1. *Faculty research:* Oceanography, marine biology, marine policy, aquaculture and fisheries. *Total annual research expenditures:* $12 million. *Unit head:* Dr. Fei Chai, Director, 207-581-3321, Fax: 207-581-4388. *Application contact:* Scott G. Delcourt, Assistant Vice President for Graduate Studies and Senior Associate Dean, 207-581-3291, Fax: 207-581-3232, E-mail: graduate@maine.edu.
Website: http://www.umaine.edu/marine/

University of Massachusetts Dartmouth, Graduate School, School for Marine Science and Technology, New Bedford, MA 02744-1221. Offers coastal and ocean administration science and technology (MS). *Program availability:* Part-time. *Faculty:* 13 full-time (1 woman). *Students:* 22 full-time (9 women), 34 part-time (17 women); includes 3 minority (1 Hispanic/Latino; 2 Two or more races, non-Hispanic/Latino), 15 international. Average age 31. 28 applicants, 93% accepted, 11 enrolled. In 2015, 4 master's, 10 doctorates awarded. Terminal master's awarded for partial completion of doctoral program. *Degree requirements:* For master's, thesis or research paper; for doctorate, comprehensive exam, thesis/dissertation. *Entrance requirements:* For master's and doctorate, GRE, statement of intent (minimum of 300 words), statement of interest (minimum of 300 words), resume, 3 letters of recommendation, official transcripts. Additional exam requirements/recommendations for international students: Required—TOEFL (minimum score 533 paper-based; 72 iBT), IELTS (minimum score 6). *Application deadline:* For fall admission, 2/15 priority date for domestic students, 1/15 priority date for international students; for spring admission, 11/15 priority date for domestic students, 10/15 priority date for international students. Applications are processed on a rolling basis. Application fee: $60. Electronic applications accepted. *Expenses:* Tuition, state resident: full-time $2071; part-time $86.29 per credit. Tuition, nonresident: full-time $8099; part-time $337.46 per credit. *Required fees:* $18,074; $762.08 per credit. Tuition and fees vary according to course load and reciprocity agreements. *Financial support:* In 2015–16, 24 research assistantships with full tuition reimbursements (averaging $17,721 per year), 3 teaching assistantships with full tuition reimbursements (averaging $24,667 per year) were awarded; Federal Work-Study and unspecified assistantships also available. Support available to part-time students. Financial award application deadline: 3/1; financial award applicants required to submit FAFSA. *Faculty research:* Physical oceanography, marine and environmental chemistry, ocean circulation, ocean internal waves, ocean acoustics. *Total annual research expenditures:* $9 million. *Unit head:* Steven Lohrenz, Graduate Program Director, 508-910-6550, Fax: 508-999-8197, E-mail: slohrenz@umassd.edu. *Application contact:* Steven Briggs, Director of Marketing and Recruitment for Graduate Studies, 508-999-8604, Fax: 508-999-8183, E-mail: graduate@umassd.edu.
Website: http://www.umassd.edu/smast

University of Miami, Graduate School, Rosenstiel School of Marine and Atmospheric Science, Division of Marine Affairs and Policy, Coral Gables, FL 33124. Offers MA, MS, JD/MA. *Program availability:* Part-time. *Degree requirements:* For master's, comprehensive exam, thesis (for some programs), internship, paper. *Entrance requirements:* For master's, GRE General Test. Additional exam requirements/recommendations for international students: Required—TOEFL (minimum score 550 paper-based). Electronic applications accepted.

University of Rhode Island, Graduate School, College of the Environment and Life Sciences, Department of Marine Affairs, Kingston, RI 02881. Offers MA, MESM, MMA,

PhD, JD/MMA. *Program availability:* Part-time. *Faculty:* 8 full-time (3 women). *Students:* 37 full-time (21 women), 3 part-time (1 woman); includes 4 minority (1 Black or African American, non-Hispanic/Latino; 1 American Indian or Alaska Native, non-Hispanic/Latino; 2 Asian, non-Hispanic/Latino), 4 international. In 2015, 16 master's awarded. *Degree requirements:* For master's, comprehensive exam (for some programs), thesis optional; for doctorate, comprehensive exam, thesis/dissertation. *Entrance requirements:* For master's, GRE (for MA), 2 letters of recommendation; graduate degree or 5 years of experience in the field (for MMA); for doctorate, GRE, 2 letters of recommendation, writing sample. Additional exam requirements/recommendations for international students: Required—TOEFL (minimum score 550 paper-based). *Application deadline:* For fall admission, 4/1 for domestic students, 2/1 for international students. Application fee: $65. Electronic applications accepted. *Expenses:* Tuition, state resident: full-time $11,796; part-time $655 per credit. Tuition, nonresident: full-time $24,206; part-time $1345 per credit. *Required fees:* $1546; $44 per credit. One-time fee: $155 full-time; $35 part-time. *Financial support:* In 2015–16, 5 research assistantships (averaging $10,479 per year), 7 teaching assistantships (averaging $9,785 per year) were awarded. Financial award application deadline: 2/1; financial award applicants required to submit FAFSA. *Faculty research:* Assessing change in coastal ecosystems and its impact to society. *Total annual research expenditures:* $74,493. *Unit head:* Dr. Robert Thompson, Chair, 401-874-4485, Fax: 401-874-2156, E-mail: rob@uri.edu. *Application contact:* Graduate Admissions, 401-874-2872,
E-mail: gradadm@etal.uri.edu.
Website: http://cels.uri.edu/maf/

University of San Diego, College of Arts and Sciences, Marine Sciences Graduate Program, San Diego, CA 92110-2492. Offers MS. *Program availability:* Part-time. *Faculty:* 2 full-time (both women), 2 part-time/adjunct (0 women). *Students:* 9 full-time (5 women), 10 part-time (6 women); includes 4 minority (1 Black or African American, non-Hispanic/Latino; 2 Asian, non-Hispanic/Latino; 1 Two or more races, non-Hispanic/Latino). Average age 26. 35 applicants, 29% accepted, 6 enrolled. In 2015, 3 master's awarded. *Degree requirements:* For master's, thesis. *Entrance requirements:* For master's, GRE General Test, minimum GPA of 3.0; 1 semester each of biology with lab, physics with lab, and calculus; 1 year of chemistry with lab. Additional exam requirements/recommendations for international students: Required—TOEFL (minimum score 580 paper-based; 83 iBT), TWE. *Application deadline:* For fall admission, 4/1 for domestic and international students. Applications are processed on a rolling basis. Application fee: $45. Electronic applications accepted. *Financial support:* In 2015–16, 13 students received support. Teaching assistantships, career-related internships or fieldwork, Federal Work-Study, institutionally sponsored loans, and unspecified assistantships available. Support available to part-time students. Financial award application deadline: 4/1; financial award applicants required to submit FAFSA. *Faculty research:* Marine ecology, environmental geology and geochemistry, climatology, physiological ecology, fisheries and aquaculture. *Unit head:* Dr. Ronald S. Kaufmann, Director, 619-260-4795, Fax: 619-260-6874, E-mail: andrewsk@sandiego.edu. *Application contact:* Monica Mahon, Associate Director of Graduate Admissions, 619-260-4524, Fax: 619-260-4158, E-mail: grads@sandiego.edu.
Website: http://www.sandiego.edu/cas/marine_science_ms/

University of Washington, Graduate School, College of the Environment, School of Marine and Environmental Affairs, Seattle, WA 98195. Offers MMA, Graduate Certificate. *Degree requirements:* For master's, thesis. *Entrance requirements:* For master's, GRE General Test, minimum GPA of 3.0. Additional exam requirements/recommendations for international students: Required—TOEFL. Electronic applications accepted. *Faculty research:* Marine pollution, port authorities, fisheries management, global climate change, marine environmental protection.

University of West Florida, College of Science and Engineering, School of Allied Health and Life Sciences, Department of Biology, Pensacola, FL 32514-5750. Offers biological chemistry (MS); biology (MS); biology education (MST); biotechnology (MS); coastal zone studies (MS); environmental biology (MS). *Degree requirements:* For master's, thesis. *Entrance requirements:* For master's, GRE (minimum score: verbal 450, quantitative 550), official transcripts; BS in biology or related field; letter of interest; relevant past experience; three letters of recommendation from individuals who can evaluate applicant's academic ability. Additional exam requirements/recommendations for international students: Required—TOEFL (minimum score 550 paper-based).

Peterson's Graduate Programs in the Physical Sciences, Mathematics, Agricultural Sciences, the Environment & Natural Resources 2017

www.petersons.com   **379**

COLUMBIA UNIVERSITY
Master of Public Administration in Environmental Science and Policy

 For more information, visit http://petersons.to/columbiau_environsci

Columbia MPA-ESP

Programs of Study

The Master of Public Administration in Environmental Science and Policy program at Columbia University trains sophisticated managers and policymakers who apply innovative, systems-based thinking to environmental issues. The program challenges students to think systemically and act pragmatically. To meet this challenge, the University offer a high-quality graduate program in management and policy analysis that emphasizes practical skills and is enriched by ecological and planetary science.

Students enrolled in the Master of Public Administration in Environmental Science and Policy program are awarded an M.P.A. degree from Columbia University's School of International and Public Affairs (SIPA) after a single year of intensive study. The program is affiliated with The Earth Institute, a Columbia University research institution dedicated to finding solutions for sustainable development and addressing some of the world's most difficult problems. The curriculum, designed by The Earth Institute and SIPA, requires students to complete a total of 54 points over three semesters, starting the day after Memorial Day. This twelve-month program offers students a unique educational experience at Columbia University's Morningside Campus in New York City.

Two fundamental insights shape this master's program: the realization that institutional, social, and economic processes interconnect to both sustain and endanger the planet and the need for professionals who can maintain the health of this interconnected system. Only by combining an understanding of earth systems issues with management strategies will it be possible to cope with the threats to planetary sustainability.

Students who wish to apply for admission or financial aid should apply online and take the GRE (the Subject Test in physics is strongly recommended), and have a cumulative grade point average of at least 3.0 on a 4.0 scale. Applicants should upload copies of their undergraduate transcripts and when applicable, graduate transcripts, with their online application. Include translations if applicable. Certified transcripts (with final grades and degrees posted) of all undergraduate and graduate study are required no later than time of enrollment. Three letters of recommendation are required for admission with aid. Unless English is the applicant's native language, the TOEFL (IBT) or IELTS exam is required, except in cases in which an international applicant has received an advanced degree from a U.S. institution. Acceptable minimum scores are listed in the application instructions. The final application deadline is February 15. The application fee is waived for U.S. citizens and permanent residents (refer to instructions). Through early March, late applications are accepted on the basis of space availability.

M.P.A. Program Curriculum

To train effective earth systems professionals, the program focuses on the practical skills necessary to understand the formulation and management of public policy. The teaching of public policy and administration is the core of the program. This set of classes focuses on specific professional and vocational skills, such as memo writing, oral briefings, group process and team building, leadership, strategic thinking, spreadsheet and other forms of financial analysis, and the use of computer programs, case studies of earth systems issues, and various internet resources. The principal goal of the core curriculum is to provide students with the analytic, communication, and work skills required to be problem-solving earth systems professionals.

The intensive study begins in the summer term with natural science courses, including Ecology and Urban Ecology, Climatology, Risk Assessment and Toxicology, Environmental Chemistry, and Hydrology. In addition, students enroll in an earth systems and environmental policy course as an introduction to the field of environmental policy. In the fall and spring, students take the core curriculum which focuses on sustainability management, financial management, microeconomics, and quantitative techniques, all of which provides the skills for developing policy and managing public organizations. Physical and social sciences are also linked throughout the program so that students gain an integrated understanding of earth systems and sustainable development.

Two workshops, in Applied Earth Systems Management and in Applied Earth Systems Policy Analysis, are a key part of the curriculum in the program. The summer and fall semester workshops emphasize management issues. Students explore a piece of proposed, but not yet enacted, state, federal, or local environmental law (or a treaty or U.N. resolution), and develop a plan to implement and manage the new program. In the summer, the workshop focuses on the science aspects of the management problem, while in the fall, students work to complete the operational plan for implementing the program. In the spring semester, new groups are formed and students work on projects for real-world governmental or nonprofit clients. The students complete the workshop by writing a report that analyzes an actual environmental policy or managerial problem faced by their client.

Career Opportunities

Upon graduating from the M.P.A. program in Environmental Science and Public Policy, students are prepared to excel in a variety of professional positions in government, private, and nonprofit sectors to address the environmental issues that threaten the long-term sustainability of life on Earth.

Since 2002, the M.P.A. in Environmental Science and Policy program has given 682 graduates the hands-on experience and the analytical and decision-making tools to implement effective environmental and sustainable management policies. Alumni have advanced to jobs in domestic and international environmental policy arenas, and work in the government, private, and nonprofit sectors. Their work focuses on issues of sustainability, resource use, and global change, and their fields include air, water, climate, energy efficiency, food, agriculture, transportation, and waste management. They work as consultants, advisers, project managers, program directors, policy analysts, teachers, researchers, and environmental scientists and engineers.

Research Facilities

Columbia University's wide array of academic resources includes a comprehensive library system and computer services. Its library system—one of the tenth-largest academic libraries in the country—includes 22 libraries, 7.5 million volumes, and 84,000 serials as well as broad collections of electronic resources, manuscripts, rare books, microforms, and other nonprint formats.

Faculty and Research

The M.P.A. in Environmental Science and Policy program faculty members are experts in their fields of study and come from a variety of professional backgrounds, such as management, consulting, and government work. Their research spans an extensive range of subjects including development of environmental movements, ecology, economic and political development, energy and nuclear waste policy, environmental justice, global climate change, marine science, plant community ecology, and urban policy and politics.

A complete listing of faculty profiles and their areas of research can be found at http://mpaenvironment.ei.columbia.edu/faculty/program-faculty/.

Peterson's Graduate Programs in the Physical Sciences, Mathematics, Agricultural Sciences, the Environment & Natural Resources 2017

www.petersons.com **381**

Columbia University

Financial Assistance

Program Fellowships: The program awards the Dean's Fellowship in Environmental Science and Policy—a full-tuition grant and Earth Institute Internship, valued at about $80,000. The program also awards numerous partial-tuition fellowships, which typically range from $5,000 to $20,000. In rare cases, partial fellowships may be as high as $40,000. In 2016, the average fellowship was nearly $16,000. All fellowship awards are based on academic merit and financial need. A fellowship application is included in the application for admission. Students who apply by one of the two fellowship deadlines—November 1 and January 15—automatically qualify for fellowship funding. The program awards this funding without regard to citizenship.

Earth Institute Internships: Students may apply for paid internships in the Earth Institute and in environmental organizations that participate in the Earth Institute's Internship Program. The hourly rate of internships within the Earth Institute is $15, and students may work up to 20 hours a week. Hourly rates and the number of work hours vary for internships at organizations off campus. Students should express an interest in Earth Institute internships as part of their application.

Course Grading Assistantships: Students may also apply for a limited number of course grading assistantships. Students in these positions perform administrative functions associated with the instruction of courses, including the grading of homework assignments and exams. Students in these positions earn $5,000–$6,000 per semester.

Federal Financial Aid: Program applicants who are U.S. citizens or permanent residents are typically eligible for federal Stafford student loans up to $41,000 for the length of the program as well as Work Study. All interested applicants must complete the Free Application for Federal Student Aid (FAFSA), which is available online at www.fafsa.gov. The School's Title IV code is 002707. Students are strongly encouraged to submit their FAFSA forms at the beginning of January. For more information, please contact SIPA's Office of Financial Aid.

Information about additional sources of financial aid to international students, including external fellowship support and private educational loans, is available on the website of the School of International and Public Affairs.

Cost of Study

Tuition for 2016–17 academic year is approximately $23,000 per semester. Total costs, including room, board, and medical insurance, are estimated to be $107,880. Please visit the School's website for a more complete list of tuition and fees.

The Graduate Student Experience

Columbia University offers a wide variety of student organizations, a well-equipped fitness center, and graduate student housing. New York City offers an extensive array of cultural, recreational, and entertainment options such as Central Park, Broadway, and the Lincoln Center of Performing Arts.

The University

Established in 1754, Columbia University in the City of New York is the oldest institution of higher learning in the state of New York and the fifth-oldest in the United States. With over 250 years of experience in higher learning, this esteemed university is the academic home to over 4,000 faculty members and more than 24,000 students who originate from 150 countries.

The University emphasizes cutting-edge research and first-rate academics and includes 3 undergraduate colleges, 14 graduate and professional schools, and 4 affiliated schools. Because of its unyielding commitment to scholarship and diversity, students gain the knowledge, abilities, and confidence needed to excel professionally and contribute to the global community.

Columbia University consistently ranks among the top universities according to *U.S. News & World Report* (#4 in 2014–15). The Environmental Science and Policy Program was ranked third for graduate programs in environmental policy and management within the category of Public Affairs.

Admissions Requirements

Prospective students apply online to the School of International and Public Affairs, selecting the "Summer" term option and the "MPA-ESP" program. Applicants must have a bachelor's degree or evidence of equivalent preparation. Some math and science preparation is helpful, but it is not required to succeed in the program. Applicants who lack basic knowledge of calculus, chemistry, and biology are advised to make up these deficiencies before entering the program.

Application materials must include a statement of purpose, an academic resume, a standard CV, transcripts from each undergraduate and graduate institution attended, an application fee of $95, the completed online application form, three letters of recommendation, and GRE and TOEFL (if applicable) scores. Additional information, including a link to the online application, can be found at http://mpaenvironment. ei.columbia.edu/admissions/how-to-apply/.

Correspondence and Information

Laura Piraino, Assistant Director
Master of Public Administration in Environmental Science and Policy
Columbia University
420 West 118th Street, Room 1404
New York, New York 10027
United States
Phone: 212-851-0261
Fax: 212-864-4847
E-mail: lpiraino@ei.columbia.edu
Website: http://mpaenvironment.ei.columbia.edu/

SIPA Office of Admissions and Financial Aid
Columbia University
514 West 113th Street
New York, New York 10025
Phone: 212-854-6216 (office)
Fax: 212.854.3010

Columbia's campus shines as a beacon of higher education in New York City.

A group of students during the workshop in Applied Earth Systems Management briefing.

382 www.petersons.com

Peterson's Graduate Programs in the Physical Sciences, Mathematics, Agricultural Sciences, the Environment & Natural Resources 2017

Section 10
Natural Resources

This section contains a directory of institutions offering graduate work in natural resources. Additional information about programs listed in the directory may be obtained by writing directly to the dean of a graduate school or chair of a department at the address given in the directory.

For programs offering related work, see also in this book *Environmental Sciences and Management* and *Meteorology and Atmospheric Sciences*. In the other guides in this series:

Graduate Programs in the Humanities, Arts & Social Sciences

See *Architecture (Landscape Architecture)* and *Public, Regional, and Industrial Affairs*

Graduate Programs in the Biological/Biomedical Sciences & Health-Related Medical Professions

See *Biological and Biomedical Sciences; Botany and Plant Biology; Ecology, Environmental Biology, and Evolutionary Biology; Entomology; Genetics, Developmental Biology, and Reproductive Biology; Nutrition; Pathology and Pathobiology; Pharmacology and Toxicology; Physiology; Veterinary Medicine and Sciences;* and *Zoology*

Graduate Programs in Engineering & Applied Sciences

See *Agricultural Engineering and Bioengineering; Civil and Environmental Engineering; Geological, Mineral/Mining, and Petroleum Engineering; Management of Engineering and Technology;* and *Ocean Engineering*

CONTENTS

Program Directories

Fish, Game, and Wildlife Management

American Public University System, AMU/APU Graduate Programs, Charles Town, WV 25414. Offers accounting (MBA, MS); criminal justice (MA), including business administration, emergency and disaster management, general (MA, MS); educational leadership (M Ed); emergency and disaster management (MA); entrepreneurship (MBA); environmental policy and management (MS), including environmental planning, environmental sustainability, fish and wildlife management, general (MA, MS), global environmental management; finance (MBA); general (MBA); global business management (MBA); history (MA), including American history, ancient and classical history, European history, global history, public history; homeland security (MA), including business administration, counter-terrorism studies, criminal justice, cyber, emergency management and public health, intelligence studies, transportation security; homeland security resource allocation (MBA); humanities (MA); information technology (MS), including digital forensics, enterprise software development, information assurance and security, IT project management; information technology management (MBA); intelligence studies (MA), including criminal intelligence, cyber, general (MA, MS), homeland security, intelligence analysis, intelligence collection, intelligence management, intelligence operations, terrorism studies; international relations and conflict resolution (MA), including comparative and security issues, conflict resolution, international and transnational security issues, peacekeeping; legal studies (MA); management (MA), including defense management, general (MA, MS), human resource management, organizational leadership, public administration; marketing (MBA); military history (MA), including American military history, American Revolution, civil war, war since 1945, World War II; military studies (MA), including joint warfare, strategic leadership; national security studies (MA), including general (MA, MS), homeland security, regional security studies, security and intelligence analysis, terrorism studies; nonprofit management (MBA); political science (MA), including American politics and government, comparative government and development, general (MA, MS), international relations, public policy; psychology (MA); public administration (MPA), including disaster management, environmental policy, health policy, human resources, national security, organizational management, security management; public health (MPH); reverse logistics management (MA); school counseling (M Ed); security management (MA); space studies (MS), including aerospace science, general (MA, MS), planetary science; sports and health sciences (MS); teaching (M Ed), including curriculum and instruction for elementary teachers, elementary reading, English language learners, instructional leadership, online learning, special education; transportation and logistics management (MA), including general (MA, MS), maritime engineering management, reverse logistics management. Programs offered via distance learning only. *Program availability:* Part-time, evening/weekend, online learning. *Faculty:* 431 full-time (241 women), 1,839 part-time/adjunct (865 women). *Students:* 531 full-time (233 women), 9,094 part-time (3,735 women); includes 3,140 minority (1,679 Black or African American, non-Hispanic/Latino; 55 American Indian or Alaska Native, non-Hispanic/Latino; 252 Asian, non-Hispanic/Latino; 773 Hispanic/Latino; 75 Native Hawaiian or other Pacific Islander, non-Hispanic/Latino; 306 Two or more races, non-Hispanic/Latino), 111 international. Average age 37. In 2015, 3,391 master's awarded. *Degree requirements:* For master's, comprehensive exam or practicum. *Entrance requirements:* For master's, official transcript showing earned bachelor's degree from institution accredited by recognized accrediting body. Additional exam requirements/recommendations for international students: Required—TOEFL (minimum score 550 paper-based), IELTS (minimum score 6.5). *Application deadline:* Applications are processed on a rolling basis. Application fee: $0. Electronic applications accepted. *Expenses: Tuition, area resident:* Part-time $350 per credit hour. *Financial support:* Applicants required to submit FAFSA. *Unit head:* Dr. Karan Powell, Executive Vice President and Provost, 877-468-6268, Fax: 304-724-3780. *Application contact:* Terry Grant, Vice President of Enrollment Management, 877-468-6268, Fax: 304-724-3780, E-mail: info@apus.edu.
Website: http://www.apus.edu

Arkansas Tech University, College of Natural and Health Sciences, Russellville, AR 72801. Offers fisheries and wildlife biology (MS); health informatics (MS); nursing (MSN). *Program availability:* Part-time. *Students:* 7 full-time (4 women), 49 part-time (29 women); includes 9 minority (6 Black or African American, non-Hispanic/Latino; 1 Asian, non-Hispanic/Latino; 2 Two or more races, non-Hispanic/Latino), 1 international. Average age 36. In 2015, 15 master's awarded. *Degree requirements:* For master's, thesis (for some programs), project. *Entrance requirements:* For master's, GRE General Test. Additional exam requirements/recommendations for international students: Required—TOEFL (minimum score 550 paper-based; 79 iBT), IELTS (minimum score 6). *Application deadline:* For fall admission, 3/1 priority date for domestic students, 5/1 priority date for international students; for spring admission, 10/1 priority date for domestic and international students. Applications are processed on a rolling basis. Application fee: $25 ($75 for international students). Electronic applications accepted. *Financial support:* In 2015–16, research assistantships with full tuition reimbursements (averaging $4,800 per year), teaching assistantships with full tuition reimbursements (averaging $4,800 per year) were awarded; career-related internships or fieldwork, Federal Work-Study, scholarships/grants, health care benefits, and unspecified assistantships also available. Support available to part-time students. Financial award application deadline: 4/15; financial award applicants required to submit FAFSA. *Unit head:* Dr. Jeff Robertson, Dean, 479-968-0498, E-mail: jrobertson@atu.edu. *Application contact:* Dr. Mary B. Gunter, Dean of Graduate College, 479-968-0398, Fax: 479-964-0542, E-mail: gradcollege@atu.edu.
Website: http://www.atu.edu/nhs/

Auburn University, Graduate School, College of Agriculture, Department of Fisheries and Allied Aquacultures, Auburn University, AL 36849. Offers M Aq, MS, PhD. *Program availability:* Part-time. *Faculty:* 19 full-time (2 women). *Students:* 46 full-time (19 women), 47 part-time (17 women); includes 3 minority (1 Hispanic/Latino; 2 Two or more races, non-Hispanic/Latino), 51 international. Average age 28. 31 applicants, 55% accepted, 15 enrolled. In 2015, 18 master's, 8 doctorates awarded. *Degree requirements:* For master's, thesis (for some programs); for doctorate, 2 foreign languages, thesis/dissertation. *Entrance requirements:* For master's and doctorate, GRE General Test. *Application deadline:* Applications are processed on a rolling basis. Application fee: $50 ($60 for international students). Electronic applications accepted. *Expenses:* Tuition, state resident: full-time $8802; part-time $489 per credit hour. Tuition, nonresident: full-time $26,406; part-time $1467 per credit hour. *Required fees:* $808 per semester. Tuition and fees vary according to degree level and program. *Financial support:* Fellowships, research assistantships, teaching assistantships, and Federal Work-Study available. Support available to part-time students. Financial award application deadline: 3/15; financial award applicants required to submit FAFSA. *Faculty research:* Channel catfish production; aquatic animal health; community and population ecology; pond management; production hatching, breeding and genetics. *Total annual research expenditures:* $8 million. *Unit head:* Dr. John Jensen, Interim Director/Professor, 334-844-4786. *Application contact:* Dr. George Flowers, Dean of the Graduate School, 334-844-2125.
Website: http://www.ag.auburn.edu/fish/

Auburn University, Graduate School, School of Forestry and Wildlife Sciences, Auburn University, AL 36849. Offers forest economics (PhD); forestry (MS, PhD); natural resource conservation (MNR); wildlife sciences (MS, PhD). *Accreditation:* SAF. *Program availability:* Part-time. *Faculty:* 30 full-time (7 women), 2 part-time/adjunct (1 woman). *Students:* 36 full-time (15 women), 30 part-time (11 women); includes 2 minority (both Black or African American, non-Hispanic/Latino), 26 international. Average age 28. 27 applicants, 52% accepted, 11 enrolled. In 2015, 13 master's, 4 doctorates awarded. *Degree requirements:* For master's, thesis (MS); for doctorate, thesis/dissertation. *Entrance requirements:* For master's and doctorate, GRE General Test. *Application deadline:* Applications are processed on a rolling basis. Application fee: $50 ($60 for international students). Electronic applications accepted. *Expenses:* Tuition, state resident: full-time $8802; part-time $489 per credit hour. Tuition, nonresident: full-time $26,406; part-time $1467 per credit hour. *Required fees:* $808 per semester. Tuition and fees vary according to degree level and program. *Financial support:* Fellowships, research assistantships, teaching assistantships, and Federal Work-Study available. Support available to part-time students. Financial award application deadline: 3/15; financial award applicants required to submit FAFSA. *Faculty research:* Forest nursery management, silviculture and vegetation management, biological processes and ecological relationships, growth and yield of plantations and natural stands, urban forestry, forest taxation, law and policy. *Unit head:* Dr. Graeme Lockaby, Dean, 334-844-4000, Fax: 334-844-1084, E-mail: brinker@forestry.auburn.edu. *Application contact:* Dr. George Flowers, Dean of the Graduate School, 334-844-2125.
Website: http://www.forestry.auburn.edu/

Brigham Young University, Graduate Studies, College of Life Sciences, Department of Plant and Wildlife Sciences, Provo, UT 84604. Offers environmental science (MS); genetics and biotechnology (MS); wildlife and wildlands conservation (MS, PhD). *Faculty:* 24 full-time (1 woman), 1 (woman) part-time/adjunct. *Students:* 12 full-time (6 women), 31 part-time (9 women); includes 4 minority (1 Asian, non-Hispanic/Latino; 3 Hispanic/Latino). Average age 25. 25 applicants, 40% accepted, 9 enrolled. In 2015, 15 master's awarded. *Degree requirements:* For master's, thesis; for doctorate, comprehensive exam, thesis/dissertation, minimum GPA of 3.2, 54 hours (18 dissertation, 36 coursework). *Entrance requirements:* For master's, GRE General Test, minimum GPA of 3.2; for doctorate, GRE, minimum GPA of 3.2. Additional exam requirements/recommendations for international students: Required—TOEFL (minimum score 580 paper-based; 85 iBT). *Application deadline:* 2/1 for domestic and international students. Applications are processed on a rolling basis. Application fee: $50. Electronic applications accepted. *Financial support:* In 2015–16, 42 students received support, including 64 research assistantships with partial tuition reimbursements available (averaging $19,000 per year), 52 teaching assistantships with partial tuition reimbursements available (averaging $19,000 per year); scholarships/grants and tuition waivers (partial) also available. Financial award application deadline: 2/1. *Faculty research:* Environmental science, plant genetics, plant ecology, plant nutrition and pathology, wildlife and wildlands conservation. *Total annual research expenditures:* $2.8 million. *Unit head:* Brock R. McMillan, Chair, 801-422-3527, Fax: 801-422-0008, E-mail: brock_mcmillan@byu.edu. *Application contact:* Bradley D. Geary, Graduate Coordinator, 801-422-1228, Fax: 801-422-0008, E-mail: bradley_geary@byu.edu.
Website: http://pws.byu.edu/home/

Clemson University, Graduate School, College of Agriculture, Forestry and Life Sciences, Department of Forestry and Environmental Conservation, Program in Wildlife and Fisheries Biology, Clemson, SC 29634-0317. Offers MS, PhD. *Faculty:* 15 full-time (0 women). *Students:* 30 full-time (17 women), 6 part-time (3 women); includes 3 minority (1 Hispanic/Latino; 2 Two or more races, non-Hispanic/Latino), 4 international. Average age 30. 19 applicants, 53% accepted, 9 enrolled. In 2015, 5 master's, 4 doctorates awarded. *Degree requirements:* For master's, thesis; for doctorate, thesis/dissertation. *Entrance requirements:* For master's and doctorate, GRE General Test, unofficial transcripts, letters of recommendation. Additional exam requirements/recommendations for international students: Required—TOEFL (minimum score 80 iBT), IELTS (minimum score 6.5). *Application deadline:* For fall admission, 4/15 for domestic and international students; for spring admission, 9/15 for domestic and international students. Applications are processed on a rolling basis. Application fee: $80 ($90 for international students). Electronic applications accepted. *Expenses:* $4,060 per semester full-time resident, $8,103 per semester full-time non-resident, $448 per credit hour part-time resident, $898 per credit hour part-time non-resident. *Financial support:* In 2015–16, 2 fellowships with partial tuition reimbursements (averaging $5,000 per year), 27 research assistantships with partial tuition reimbursements (averaging $16,856 per year), 7 teaching assistantships with partial tuition reimbursements (averaging $14,433 per year) were awarded; health care benefits also available. Financial award application deadline: 4/15. *Faculty research:* Intensive freshwater culture systems, conservation biology, stream management, applied wildlife management. *Unit head:* Dr. Gregg Yarrow, Department Chair, 864-656-3302, Fax: 864-656-3304, E-mail: gyarrow@clemson.edu. *Application contact:* Dr. Robert Baldwin, Graduate Program Coordinator, 864-656-3302, E-mail: baldwi6@clemson.edu.
Website: http://www.clemson.edu/cafls/departments/fec/index.html

Colorado State University, Warner College of Natural Resources, Department of Fish, Wildlife, and Conservation Biology, Fort Collins, CO 80523-1474. Offers MFWCB, MS, PhD. *Program availability:* Part-time, blended/hybrid learning. *Faculty:* 12 full-time (2 women), 3 part-time/adjunct (1 woman). *Students:* 8 full-time (5 women), 18 part-time (6 women); includes 2 minority (1 Hispanic/Latino; 1 Two or more races, non-Hispanic/Latino). Average age 29. 5 applicants, 20% accepted, 1 enrolled. In 2015, 7 master's, 2 doctorates awarded. Terminal master's awarded for partial completion of doctoral program. *Degree requirements:* For master's, comprehensive exam, thesis; for doctorate, comprehensive exam, thesis/dissertation. *Entrance requirements:* For master's, GRE General Test (minimum 70th percentile), minimum GPA of 3.0, BA or BS in related field, letters of recommendation, resume, transcripts; for doctorate, GRE General Test (minimum 70th percentile), minimum GPA of 3.0, MS in related field, letters of recommendation, resume, transcripts. Additional exam requirements/recommendations for international students: Required—TOEFL (minimum score 550 paper-based; 80 iBT), IELTS (minimum score 6.5). *Application deadline:* For fall admission, 2/1 for domestic and international students. Applications are processed on a rolling basis. Application fee: $60 ($70 for international students). Electronic applications accepted. *Expenses:* Tuition, state resident: full-time $9348. Tuition, nonresident: full-time $22,916. *Required fees:* $2174; $473.72 per credit hour. $236.86 per semester.

Tuition and fees vary according to course load and program. *Financial support:* In 2015–16, 26 students received support, including 8 fellowships with tuition reimbursements available (averaging $49,625 per year), 8 research assistantships with tuition reimbursements available (averaging $25,168 per year), 6 teaching assistantships with tuition reimbursements available (averaging $14,123 per year); career-related internships or fieldwork, scholarships/grants, tuition waivers (full and partial), and unspecified assistantships also available. Financial award application deadline: 2/15; financial award applicants required to submit FAFSA. *Faculty research:* Quantitative, spatio-temporal ecological methods applied to management; behavioral ecology; aquatic, avian, wildlife ecology; management and protection of biodiverse populations; fish ecology, physiology, dynamics. *Total annual research expenditures:* $3.4 million. *Unit head:* Dr. Kenneth R. Wilson, Professor/Department Head, 970-491-5020, Fax: 970-491-5091, E-mail: kenneth.wilson@colostate.edu. *Application contact:* Joyce Pratt, Assistant to Department Head, 970-491-5020, Fax: 970-491-5091, E-mail: joyce.pratt@colostate.edu.
Website: http://warnercnr.colostate.edu/fwcb-home/

Cornell University, Graduate School, Graduate Fields of Agriculture and Life Sciences, Field of Natural Resources, Ithaca, NY 14853-0001. Offers community-based natural resources management (MS, PhD); conservation biology (MS, PhD); ecosystem biology and biogeochemistry (MPS, MS, PhD); environmental management (MPS); fishery and aquatic science (MPS, MS, PhD); forest science (MPS, MS, PhD); human dimensions of natural resources management (MPS, MS, PhD); policy and institutional analysis (MS, PhD); program development and evaluation (MPS, MS, PhD); quantitative ecology (MS, PhD); wildlife science (MPS, MS, PhD). *Degree requirements:* For master's, thesis (MS), project paper (MPS); for doctorate, comprehensive exam, thesis/dissertation. *Entrance requirements:* For master's and doctorate, GRE General Test, 2 letters of recommendation. Additional exam requirements/recommendations for international students: Required—TOEFL (minimum score 550 paper-based; 77 iBT). Electronic applications accepted. *Faculty research:* Ecosystem-level dynamics, systems modeling, conservation biology/management, resource management's human dimensions, biogeochemistry.

Cornell University, Graduate School, Graduate Fields of Agriculture and Life Sciences, Field of Zoology and Wildlife Conservation, Ithaca, NY 14853-0001. Offers animal cytology (PhD); comparative and functional anatomy (PhD); developmental biology (PhD); ecology (PhD); histology (PhD); wildlife conservation (PhD). *Degree requirements:* For doctorate, comprehensive exam, thesis/dissertation, 2 semesters of teaching experience. *Entrance requirements:* For doctorate, GRE General Test, GRE Subject Test (biology), 2 letters of recommendation. Additional exam requirements/recommendations for international students: Required—TOEFL (minimum score 550 paper-based; 77 iBT). Electronic applications accepted. *Faculty research:* Organismal biology, functional morphology, biomechanics, comparative vertebrate anatomy, comparative invertebrate anatomy, paleontology.

Frostburg State University, Graduate School, College of Liberal Arts and Sciences, Department of Biology, Program in Fisheries and Wildlife Management, Frostburg, MD 21532-1099. Offers MS. *Program availability:* Part-time, evening/weekend. *Degree requirements:* For master's, thesis. *Entrance requirements:* For master's, GRE General Test, resume. Additional exam requirements/recommendations for international students: Required—TOEFL. Electronic applications accepted. *Faculty research:* Evolution and systematics of freshwater fishes, biochemical mechanisms of temperature adaptation in freshwater fishes, wildlife and fish parasitology, biology of freshwater invertebrates, remote sensing.

Humboldt State University, Academic Programs, College of Natural Resources and Sciences, Programs in Natural Resources, Arcata, CA 95521-8299. Offers natural resources (MS), including fisheries, forestry, natural resources planning and interpretation, rangeland resources and wildland soils, wastewater utilization, watershed management, wildlife. *Degree requirements:* For master's, thesis or alternative. *Entrance requirements:* For master's, GRE, appropriate bachelor's degree, minimum GPA of 2.5, 3 letters of recommendation, resume. Additional exam requirements/recommendations for international students: Required—TOEFL (minimum score 500 paper-based). *Faculty research:* Spotted owl habitat, pre-settlement vegetation, hardwood utilization, tree physiology, fisheries.

Iowa State University of Science and Technology, Department of Natural Resource Ecology and Management, Ames, IA 50011. Offers forestry (MS, PhD); wildlife ecology (MS). *Entrance requirements:* For master's and doctorate, GRE General Test. Additional exam requirements/recommendations for international students: Required—TOEFL (minimum score 550 paper-based; 79 iBT), IELTS (minimum score 6.5). Electronic applications accepted.

Iowa State University of Science and Technology, Program in Fisheries Biology, Ames, IA 50010. Offers MS, PhD. *Entrance requirements:* For master's and doctorate, GRE. Additional exam requirements/recommendations for international students: Required—TOEFL (minimum score 550 paper-based; 79 iBT), IELTS (minimum score 6.5). Electronic applications accepted.

Louisiana State University and Agricultural & Mechanical College, Graduate School, College of Agriculture, School of Renewable Natural Resources, Baton Rouge, LA 70803. Offers fisheries (MS); forestry (MS, PhD); wildlife (MS); wildlife and fisheries science (PhD).

McGill University, Faculty of Graduate and Postdoctoral Studies, Faculty of Agricultural and Environmental Sciences, Department of Natural Resource Sciences, Montréal, QC H3A 2T5, Canada. Offers entomology (M Sc, PhD); environmental assessment (M Sc); forest science (M Sc, PhD); microbiology (M Sc, PhD); micrometeorology (M Sc, PhD); neotropical environment (M Sc, PhD); soil science (M Sc, PhD); wildlife biology (M Sc, PhD).

Memorial University of Newfoundland, School of Graduate Studies, Interdisciplinary Program in Marine Studies, St. John's, NL A1C 5S7, Canada. Offers fisheries resource management (MMS, Graduate Diploma); marine spatial planning and management (MMS). *Program availability:* Part-time. *Degree requirements:* For master's, report. *Entrance requirements:* For master's, high 2nd class degree from a recognized university; demonstrated commitment to the fishery through employment or experience in a sector of the fishery, in a regulatory agency or government department connected to the fisheries, in a non-governmental agency, or through self-employment or relevant professional consulting activities; for Graduate Diploma, high 2nd class degree from a recognized university. *Application deadline:* For fall admission, 5/15 for domestic and international students; for winter admission, 10/15 for domestic and international students. Applications are processed on a rolling basis. Application fee: $50 Canadian dollars ($100 Canadian dollars for international students). Electronic applications accepted. *Expenses: Tuition, area resident:* Full-time $2199 Canadian dollars. *International tuition:* $2859 Canadian dollars full-time. *Faculty research:* Biological, ecological and oceanographic aspects of world fisheries; economics; political science; sociology. *Unit head:* Keith Rideout, Graduate Officer, 709-778-0675, Fax: 709-778-0346, E-mail: keith.rideout@mi.mun.ca.
Website: http://www.mi.mun.ca/programsandcourses/programs/

Michigan State University, The Graduate School, College of Agriculture and Natural Resources, Department of Fisheries and Wildlife, East Lansing, MI 48824. Offers fisheries and wildlife (MS, PhD); fisheries and wildlife - environmental toxicology (PhD). *Entrance requirements:* Additional exam requirements/recommendations for international students: Required—TOEFL (minimum score 550 paper-based), Michigan State University ELT (minimum score 85), Michigan English Language Assessment Battery (minimum score 83). Electronic applications accepted.

Mississippi State University, College of Forest Resources, Department of Wildlife, Fisheries and Aquaculture, Mississippi State, MS 39762. Offers forest resources (PhD), including wildlife, fisheries and aquaculture; wildlife, fisheries and aquaculture (MS). *Program availability:* Part-time. *Faculty:* 26 full-time (4 women). *Students:* 42 full-time (8 women), 12 part-time (7 women), 6 international. Average age 29. 19 applicants, 53% accepted, 9 enrolled. In 2015, 12 master's, 3 doctorates awarded. *Degree requirements:* For master's, thesis, comprehensive oral or written exam; for doctorate, comprehensive exam, thesis/dissertation. *Entrance requirements:* For master's, GRE, bachelor's degree, minimum GPA of 3.0 on last 60 hours of undergraduate courses; for doctorate, GRE, master's degree, minimum GPA of 3.2 on prior graduate studies. Additional exam requirements/recommendations for international students: Required—TOEFL (minimum score 550 paper-based; 79 iBT); Recommended—IELTS (minimum score 6.5). *Application deadline:* For fall admission, 7/1 for domestic students, 5/1 for international students; for spring admission, 11/1 for domestic students, 9/1 for international students. Applications are processed on a rolling basis. Application fee: $60. Electronic applications accepted. *Expenses: Tuition, area resident:* Full-time $7502; part-time $833.74 per credit hour. Tuition, nonresident: full-time $20,142; part-time $2238.24 per credit hour. *Financial support:* In 2015–16, 34 research assistantships with partial tuition reimbursements (averaging $15,362 per year) were awarded; Federal Work-Study, institutionally sponsored loans, and unspecified assistantships also available. Financial award application deadline: 4/1; financial award applicants required to submit FAFSA. *Faculty research:* Spatial technology, habitat restoration, aquaculture, fisheries, wildlife management. *Unit head:* Dr. Andrew Kouba, Professor and Head, 662-325-7494, Fax: 662-325-8726, E-mail: ak260@msstate.edu. *Application contact:* Nathan Drake, Admissions Assistant, 662-325-3804, E-mail: ndrake@grad.msstate.edu.
Website: http://www.cfr.msstate.edu/wildlife/index.asp

Montana State University, The Graduate School, College of Letters and Science, Department of Ecology, Bozeman, MT 59717. Offers ecological and environmental statistics (MS); ecology and environmental sciences (PhD); fish and wildlife biology (PhD); fish and wildlife management (MS). *Program availability:* Part-time. *Degree requirements:* For master's, comprehensive exam, thesis (for some programs); for doctorate, comprehensive exam, thesis/dissertation. *Entrance requirements:* For master's and doctorate, GRE, minimum GPA of 3.0, letters of recommendation, essay. Additional exam requirements/recommendations for international students: Required—TOEFL (minimum score 550 paper-based). Electronic applications accepted. *Faculty research:* Community ecology, population ecology, land-use effects, management and conservation, environmental modeling.

New Mexico State University, College of Agricultural, Consumer and Environmental Sciences, Department of Fish, Wildlife and Conservation Ecology, Las Cruces, NM 88003. Offers MS. *Program availability:* Part-time. *Faculty:* 7 full-time (4 women). *Students:* 16 full-time (10 women), 9 part-time (2 women); includes 3 minority (all Hispanic/Latino), 1 international. Average age 27. 10 applicants, 60% accepted, 6 enrolled. In 2015, 7 master's awarded. *Degree requirements:* For master's, thesis (for some programs). *Entrance requirements:* For master's, GRE General Test, minimum GPA of 3.0. Additional exam requirements/recommendations for international students: Required—TOEFL (minimum score 550 paper-based; 79 iBT), IELTS (minimum score 6.5). *Application deadline:* For fall admission, 4/1 priority date for domestic and international students; for spring admission, 11/1 priority date for domestic and international students. Applications are processed on a rolling basis. Application fee: $40 ($50 for international students). Electronic applications accepted. *Expenses:* $274.50 per credit hour for in-state students, and all students enrolled in six or fewer credits; $839.30 per credit hour for out-of-state and international students enrolled in at least seven hours. *Financial support:* In 2015–16, 23 students received support, including 16 research assistantships (averaging $19,497 per year), 3 teaching assistantships (averaging $16,964 per year); career-related internships or fieldwork, Federal Work-Study, scholarships/grants, traineeships, health care benefits, and unspecified assistantships also available. Support available to part-time students. Financial award application deadline: 3/1. *Faculty research:* Ecosystems analyses; aquatic, landscape and wildlife ecology; wildlife and fish population dynamics; avian ecology and conservation; wildlife and fish habitat relationships. *Total annual research expenditures:* $2.2 million. *Unit head:* Dr. Kathryn E. Stoner, Department Head, 575-646-7051, Fax: 575-646-1281, E-mail: kstoner@nmsu.edu. *Application contact:* Doris J. Morgan, Graduate Application Committee Chair, 575-646-7051, Fax: 575-646-1281, E-mail: domorgan@nmsu.edu.
Website: http://aces.nmsu.edu/academics/fws/

North Carolina State University, Graduate School, College of Natural Resources, Program in Fisheries and Wildlife Sciences, Raleigh, NC 27695. Offers MFWS, MS, PhD. *Degree requirements:* For master's, thesis optional. *Entrance requirements:* For master's, GRE General Test. Additional exam requirements/recommendations for international students: Required—TOEFL. Electronic applications accepted. *Faculty research:* Fisheries biology; ecology of marine, estuarine, and anadromous fishes; aquaculture pond water quality; larviculture of freshwater and marine finfish; predator/prey interactions.

The Ohio State University, Graduate School, College of Food, Agricultural, and Environmental Sciences, School of Environment and Natural Resources, Columbus, OH 43210. Offers ecological restoration (MS, PhD); ecosystem science (MS, PhD); environment and natural resources (MENR); environmental social sciences (MS, PhD); fisheries and wildlife science (MS, PhD); forest science (MS, PhD); rural sociology (MS, PhD); soil science (MS, PhD). *Degree requirements:* For master's, thesis; for doctorate, thesis/dissertation. *Entrance requirements:* For master's and doctorate, GRE. Additional exam requirements/recommendations for international students: Required—TOEFL (minimum score 550 paper-based; 79 iBT), Michigan English Language Assessment Battery (minimum score 82); Recommended—IELTS (minimum score 7). Electronic applications accepted.

Oregon State University, College of Agricultural Sciences, Program in Fisheries and Wildlife Administration, Corvallis, OR 97331. Offers PSM. *Program availability:* Part-time, online learning. *Faculty:* 33 full-time (10 women), 11 part-time/adjunct (5 women). *Students:* 2 full-time (0 women), 6 part-time (4 women); includes 1 minority (Hispanic/Latino). Average age 36. 6 applicants, 33% accepted, 2 enrolled. In 2015, 2 master's awarded. *Entrance requirements:* For master's, GRE. Additional exam requirements/

recommendations for international students: Required—TOEFL (minimum score 80 iBT), IELTS (minimum score 6.5). *Application deadline:* For fall admission, 6/1 for domestic students; for spring admission, 12/31 for domestic students. Application fee: $75 ($85 for international students). *Expenses:* Tuition, state resident: full-time $12,150; part-time $450 per credit. Tuition, nonresident: full-time $20,952; part-time $776 per credit. *Required fees:* $1572; $1443 per unit. One-time fee: $350. Tuition and fees vary according to course load, campus/location and program. *Unit head:* Dr. Selina Heppell, Department Head/Professor of Fisheries.
Website: http://fw.oregonstate.edu/content/psm-fisheries-wildlife-administration

Oregon State University, College of Agricultural Sciences, Program in Fisheries Science, Corvallis, OR 97331. Offers MAIS, MS, PhD. *Program availability:* Part-time. *Faculty:* 33 full-time (10 women), 11 part-time/adjunct (5 women). *Students:* 41 full-time (22 women), 3 part-time (2 women); includes 9 minority (2 Black or African American, non-Hispanic/Latino; 6 Hispanic/Latino; 1 Two or more races, non-Hispanic/Latino), 4 international. Average age 33. 16 applicants, 38% accepted, 4 enrolled. In 2015, 13 master's, 2 doctorates awarded. *Degree requirements:* For master's, thesis (for some programs); for doctorate, thesis/dissertation. *Entrance requirements:* For master's and doctorate, GRE, minimum GPA of 3.0 in last 90 hours. Additional exam requirements/recommendations for international students: Required—TOEFL (minimum score 80 iBT), IELTS (minimum score 6.5). *Application deadline:* For fall admission, 6/1 for domestic students; for spring admission, 12/31 for domestic students. Application fee: $75 ($85 for international students). *Expenses:* Tuition, state resident: full-time $12,150; part-time $450 per credit. Tuition, nonresident: full-time $20,952; part-time $776 per credit. *Required fees:* $1572; $1443 per unit. One-time fee: $350. Tuition and fees vary according to course load, campus/location and program. *Financial support:* Fellowships, research assistantships, teaching assistantships, career-related internships or fieldwork, Federal Work-Study, and institutionally sponsored loans available. Support available to part-time students. Financial award application deadline: 2/1. *Faculty research:* Fisheries ecology, fish toxicology, stream ecology, quantitative analyses of marine and freshwater fish populations. *Unit head:* Dr. Selina Heppell, Department Head/Professor of Fisheries, 541-737-9039, Fax: 541-737-3590,
E-mail: selina.heppell@oregonstate.edu. *Application contact:*
E-mail: lisa.pierson@oregonstate.edu.
Website: http://fw.oregonstate.edu/content/graduate

Oregon State University, College of Agricultural Sciences, Program in Wildlife Science, Corvallis, OR 97331. Offers M Ag, MS, PhD. *Program availability:* Part-time. *Faculty:* 32 full-time (10 women), 11 part-time/adjunct (5 women). *Students:* 44 full-time (27 women), 5 part-time (2 women); includes 5 minority (1 American Indian or Alaska Native, non-Hispanic/Latino; 2 Hispanic/Latino; 2 Two or more races, non-Hispanic/Latino), 6 international. Average age 32. 32 applicants, 19% accepted, 6 enrolled. In 2015, 10 master's, 5 doctorates awarded. *Degree requirements:* For master's, thesis (for some programs); for doctorate, thesis/dissertation. *Entrance requirements:* For master's and doctorate, GRE, minimum GPA of 3.0 in last 90 hours. Additional exam requirements/recommendations for international students: Required—TOEFL (minimum score 80 iBT), IELTS (minimum score 6.5). *Application deadline:* For fall admission, 5/1 for domestic students, 4/1 for international students. Application fee: $75 ($85 for international students). *Expenses:* Tuition, state resident: full-time $12,150; part-time $450 per credit. Tuition, nonresident: full-time $20,952; part-time $776 per credit. *Required fees:* $1572; $1443 per unit. One-time fee: $350. Tuition and fees vary according to course load, campus/location and program. *Financial support:* Fellowships, research assistantships, teaching assistantships, career-related internships or fieldwork, Federal Work-Study, and institutionally sponsored loans available. Financial award application deadline: 2/1. *Unit head:* Dr. Selina Heppell, Department Head/Professor of Fisheries, 541-737-9039,
E-mail: selina.heppell@oregonstate.edu.
Website: http://fw.oregonstate.edu/content/graduate

Penn State University Park, Graduate School, College of Agricultural Sciences, Department of Ecosystem Science and Management, University Park, PA 16802. Offers forest resources (MS, PhD); soil science (MS, PhD); wildlife and fisheries science (MS, PhD). *Unit head:* Dr. Richard T. Roush, Dean, 814-865-2541, Fax: 814-865-3103. *Application contact:* Lori Stania, Director, Graduate Student Services, 814-865-1795, Fax: 814-863-4627, E-mail: l-gswww@lists.psu.edu.
Website: http://ecosystems.psu.edu/

Purdue University, Graduate School, College of Agriculture, Department of Forestry and Natural Resources, West Lafayette, IN 47907. Offers fisheries and aquatic sciences (MS, MSF, PhD); forest biology (MS, MSF, PhD); natural resource social science (MS, PhD); natural resources social science (MSF); quantitative ecology (MS, MSF, PhD); wildlife science (MS, MSF, PhD); wood products and wood products manufacturing (MS, MSF, PhD). *Degree requirements:* For master's, thesis; for doctorate, thesis/dissertation. *Entrance requirements:* For master's and doctorate, GRE General Test (minimum score: verbal 50th percentile; quantitative 50th percentile; analytical writing 4.0), minimum undergraduate GPA of 3.2 or equivalent. Additional exam requirements/recommendations for international students: Required—TOEFL (minimum score 550 paper-based; 77 iBT). Electronic applications accepted. *Faculty research:* Wildlife management, forest management, forest ecology, forest soils, limnology.

Simon Fraser University, Office of Graduate Studies, Faculty of Environment, School of Resource and Environmental Management, Burnaby, BC V5A 1S6, Canada. Offers quantitative methods in fisheries management (Graduate Diploma); resource and environmental management (MRM, PhD); resource and environmental planning (MRM). *Degree requirements:* For master's, thesis (for some programs); for doctorate, comprehensive exam, thesis/dissertation. *Entrance requirements:* For master's and Graduate Diploma, minimum GPA of 3.0 (on scale of 4.33), or 3.33 based on last 60 credits of undergraduate courses; for doctorate, minimum GPA of 3.5 (on scale of 4.33). Additional exam requirements/recommendations for international students: Recommended—TOEFL (minimum score 580 paper-based; 93 iBT), IELTS (minimum score 7), TWE (minimum score 5). Electronic applications accepted. *Faculty research:* Climate, coastal marine ecology and conservation, environmental toxicology, fisheries science and management, forest ecology.

South Dakota State University, Graduate School, College of Agriculture and Biological Sciences, Department of Wildlife and Fisheries Sciences, Brookings, SD 57007. Offers MS, PhD. *Program availability:* Part-time. *Degree requirements:* For master's, thesis, oral exam; for doctorate, comprehensive exam, thesis/dissertation, interim exam, oral and written comprehensive exams. *Entrance requirements:* For master's and doctorate, GRE. Additional exam requirements/recommendations for international students: Required—TOEFL (minimum score 525 paper-based; 71 iBT). *Faculty research:* Agriculture interactions, wetland conservation, biostress, wildlife and fisheries ecology and techniques.

State University of New York College of Environmental Science and Forestry, Department of Environmental and Forest Biology, Syracuse, NY 13210-2779. Offers applied ecology (MPS); chemical ecology (MPS, MS, PhD); conservation biology (MPS, MS, PhD); ecology (MPS, MS, PhD); entomology (MPS, MS, PhD); environmental interpretation (MPS, MS, PhD); environmental physiology (MPS, MS, PhD); fish and wildlife biology and management (MPS, MS, PhD); forest pathology and mycology (MPS, MS, PhD); plant biotechnology (MPS); plant science and biotechnology (MPS, MS, PhD). *Faculty:* 29 full-time (9 women), 4 part-time/adjunct (3 women). *Students:* 81 full-time (47 women), 57 part-time (24 women); includes 9 minority (1 Black or African American, non-Hispanic/Latino; 2 American Indian or Alaska Native, non-Hispanic/Latino; 1 Asian, non-Hispanic/Latino; 3 Hispanic/Latino; 2 Two or more races, non-Hispanic/Latino), 15 international. Average age 28. 47 applicants, 49% accepted, 15 enrolled. In 2015, 15 master's, 7 doctorates awarded. *Degree requirements:* For master's, thesis (for some programs), capstone seminar; for doctorate, comprehensive exam, thesis/dissertation, capstone seminar. *Entrance requirements:* For master's and doctorate, GRE General Test, minimum GPA of 3.0. Additional exam requirements/recommendations for international students: Required—TOEFL (minimum score 550 paper-based; 80 iBT), IELTS (minimum score 6). *Application deadline:* For fall admission, 2/1 priority date for domestic and international students; for spring admission, 11/1 priority date for domestic and international students. Applications are processed on a rolling basis. Application fee: $60. *Expenses:* Tuition, state resident: full-time $10,870; part-time $453 per credit. Tuition, nonresident: full-time $22,210; part-time $925 per credit. *Required fees:* $1075; $89.22 per credit. *Financial support:* In 2015–16, 4 fellowships with tuition reimbursements, 36 research assistantships with tuition reimbursements, 39 teaching assistantships with tuition reimbursements (averaging $11,490 per year) were awarded; Federal Work-Study, institutionally sponsored loans, scholarships/grants, health care benefits, and unspecified assistantships also available. Financial award application deadline: 6/30. *Faculty research:* Ecology, conservation biology, fish and wildlife biology and management, plant science, entomology. *Total annual research expenditures:* $4.1 million. *Unit head:* Dr. Donald J. Leopold, Chair, 315-470-6760, Fax: 315-470-6934,
E-mail: djleopold@esf.edu. *Application contact:* Dr. Danilo D. Fernando, Director, Graduate Program/Associate Professor, 315-470-6746, Fax: 315-470-6934,
E-mail: dfernando@esf.edu.
Website: http://www.esf.edu/efb/grad/default.asp

Sul Ross State University, Division of Agricultural and Natural Resource Science, Programs in Natural Resource Management, Alpine, TX 79832. Offers range and wildlife management (M Ag, MS). *Program availability:* Part-time. *Students:* 20 full-time (5 women), 7 part-time (0 women); includes 4 minority (1 Asian, non-Hispanic/Latino; 2 Hispanic/Latino; 1 Two or more races, non-Hispanic/Latino), 3 international. Average age 32. *Degree requirements:* For master's, thesis (for some programs). *Entrance requirements:* For master's, GRE General Test, minimum undergraduate GPA of 2.5 in last 60 hours. *Application deadline:* Applications are processed on a rolling basis. Application fee: $0 ($50 for international students). *Financial support:* Research assistantships, teaching assistantships, career-related internships or fieldwork, Federal Work-Study, and institutionally sponsored loans available. Support available to part-time students. Financial award application deadline: 5/1; financial award applicants required to submit FAFSA. *Unit head:* Dr. Bonnie Warnock, Chair, 432-837-8706, Fax: 432-837-8822, E-mail: bwarnock@sulross.edu. *Application contact:* Kelsey Slater, Department Secretary, 432-837-8488, Fax: 432-837-8822, E-mail: kelsey.slater@sulross.edu.
Website: http://www.sulross.edu/natural-resource-management

Tennessee Technological University, College of Graduate Studies, College of Arts and Sciences, Department of Biology, Cookeville, TN 38505. Offers fish, game, and wildlife management (MS). *Program availability:* Part-time. *Faculty:* 22 full-time (2 women). *Students:* 4 full-time (3 women), 17 part-time (9 women); includes 2 minority (1 Black or African American, non-Hispanic/Latino; 1 Hispanic/Latino). Average age 25. 19 applicants, 16% accepted, 3 enrolled. In 2015, 6 master's awarded. *Degree requirements:* For master's, thesis. *Entrance requirements:* For master's, GRE. Additional exam requirements/recommendations for international students: Required—TOEFL (minimum score 527 paper-based; 71 iBT), IELTS (minimum score 5.5), PTE (minimum score 48), or TOEIC (Test of English as an International Communication). *Application deadline:* For fall admission, 8/1 for domestic students, 5/1 for international students; for spring admission, 12/1 for domestic students, 10/1 for international students; for summer admission, 5/1 for domestic students, 2/1 for international students. Applications are processed on a rolling basis. Application fee: $35 ($40 for international students). Electronic applications accepted. *Expenses:* Tuition, state resident: full-time $8961; part-time $6132 per credit hour. Tuition, nonresident: full-time $23,121; part-time $14,608 per credit hour. *Financial support:* In 2015–16, 17 research assistantships (averaging $9,000 per year), 8 teaching assistantships (averaging $7,500 per year) were awarded. Financial award application deadline: 4/1. *Faculty research:* Aquatics, environmental studies. *Unit head:* Dr. Robert Kissell, Chairperson, 931-372-3134, Fax: 931-372-6257, E-mail: rkissell@tntech.edu. *Application contact:* Shelia K. Kendrick, Coordinator of Graduate Studies, 931-372-3808, Fax: 931-372-3497,
E-mail: skendrick@tntech.edu.

Texas A&M University, College of Agriculture and Life Sciences, Department of Wildlife and Fisheries Sciences, College Station, TX 77843. Offers wildlife and fisheries sciences (MS, PhD); wildlife science (MWSc). *Program availability:* Part-time, blended/hybrid learning. *Faculty:* 22. *Students:* 74 full-time (41 women), 46 part-time (24 women); includes 30 minority (2 Black or African American, non-Hispanic/Latino; 1 Asian, non-Hispanic/Latino; 26 Hispanic/Latino; 1 Two or more races, non-Hispanic/Latino), 19 international. Average age 33. 27 applicants, 78% accepted, 18 enrolled. In 2015, 12 master's, 8 doctorates awarded. Terminal master's awarded for partial completion of doctoral program. *Degree requirements:* For master's, thesis, final oral defense; for doctorate, thesis/dissertation, final oral defense. *Entrance requirements:* For master's and doctorate, GRE General Test, minimum GPA of 3.0. Additional exam requirements/recommendations for international students: Required—TOEFL (minimum score 550 paper-based; 80 iBT), IELTS (minimum score 6), PTE (minimum score 53). *Application deadline:* For fall admission, 5/1 for domestic students, 2/1 for international students; for spring admission, 9/1 for domestic and international students. Applications are processed on a rolling basis. Application fee: $50 ($90 for international students). Electronic applications accepted. *Expenses:* Contact institution. *Financial support:* In 2015–16, 78 students received support, including 19 fellowships with tuition reimbursements available (averaging $15,484 per year), 21 research assistantships with tuition reimbursements available (averaging $7,109 per year), 20 teaching assistantships with tuition reimbursements available (averaging $6,126 per year); career-related internships or fieldwork, institutionally sponsored loans, scholarships/grants, traineeships, health care benefits, tuition waivers (full and partial), and unspecified assistantships also available. Support available to part-time students. Financial award application deadline: 3/15; financial award applicants required to submit FAFSA. *Faculty research:* Wildlife ecology and management, fisheries ecology and management, aquaculture, biological inventories and museum collections, biosystematics and genome analysis. *Unit head:* Dr. Michael Masser, Professor and Department Head, 979-845-6295, Fax: 979-845-3786, E-mail: mmasser@tamu.edu. *Application contact:* Dr. Delbert Gatlin, Professor/Associate Department Head for Research and Graduate Programs, 979-847-9333, Fax: 979-845-3786,
E-mail: d-gatlin@tamu.edu.
Website: http://wfsc.tamu.edu/

Texas A&M University–Kingsville, College of Graduate Studies, Dick and Mary Lewis Kleberg College of Agriculture, Natural Resources and Human Sciences, Department of Animal, Rangeland, and Wildlife Sciences, Program in Range and Wildlife Management, Kingsville, TX 78363. Offers MS. *Degree requirements:* For master's, variable foreign language requirement, comprehensive exam, thesis (for some programs). *Entrance requirements:* For master's, GRE (minimum of 150 for each of the math and verbal sections), MAT, GMAT, minimum GPA of 3.0 for coursework from previous degree. Additional exam requirements/recommendations for international students: Required—TOEFL (minimum score 550 paper-based; 79 iBT). Electronic applications accepted.

Texas A&M University–Kingsville, College of Graduate Studies, Dick and Mary Lewis Kleberg College of Agriculture, Natural Resources and Human Sciences, Department of Animal, Rangeland, and Wildlife Sciences, Program in Wildlife Science, Kingsville, TX 78363. Offers PhD. *Degree requirements:* For doctorate, variable foreign language requirement, comprehensive exam, thesis/dissertation. *Entrance requirements:* For doctorate, GRE, MAT, GMAT, 3 letters of recommendation. Additional exam requirements/recommendations for international students: Required—TOEFL (minimum score 550 paper-based; 79 iBT). Electronic applications accepted.

Texas State University, The Graduate College, College of Science and Engineering, Program in Wildlife Ecology, San Marcos, TX 78666. Offers MS. *Program availability:* Part-time. *Faculty:* 7 full-time (2 women). *Students:* 24 full-time (14 women), 7 part-time (4 women); includes 6 minority (1 Black or African American, non-Hispanic/Latino; 1 Asian, non-Hispanic/Latino; 4 Hispanic/Latino), 1 international. Average age 28. 14 applicants, 50% accepted, 6 enrolled. In 2015, 11 master's awarded. *Degree requirements:* For master's, comprehensive exam, thesis. *Entrance requirements:* For master's, GRE General Test (recommended minimum score in at least the 50th percentile on both the verbal and quantitative portions), baccalaureate degree in biology or related discipline from regionally-accredited university with minimum GPA of 3.0 on last 60 undergraduate semester hours, current resume, statement of purpose, 3 letters of recommendation, letter of intent to mentor from a biology department faculty member. Additional exam requirements/recommendations for international students: Required—TOEFL (minimum score 550 paper-based; 78 iBT). *Application deadline:* For fall admission, 2/1 priority date for domestic and international students; for spring admission, 10/15 for domestic students, 10/1 for international students; for summer admission, 4/15 for domestic students, 3/15 for international students. Applications are processed on a rolling basis. Application fee: $40 ($90 for international students). Electronic applications accepted. *Expenses:* $3,615 in-state tuition for 12 semester credit hours (1 full-time semester), $974 in-state fees. *Financial support:* In 2015–16, 21 students received support, including 5 research assistantships (averaging $13,119 per year), 22 teaching assistantships (averaging $13,878 per year); Federal Work-Study and institutionally sponsored loans also available. Support available to part-time students. Financial award application deadline: 3/1; financial award applicants required to submit FAFSA. *Faculty research:* Contribution of bridge dwelling birds to bacterial water quality impairments, survey of small mammals and herpetofauna of Bracken Cave Preserve, linking drought-related tree mortality to plant-available water, correlates of drought-related tree mortality during 2011 Texas drought, population genetic structure of ixodes scapularis and disease transmission, examining species diversity and abundance of butterfly community in La Cypress Swamp. *Total annual research expenditures:* $149,340. *Unit head:* Dr. Floyd Weckerly, Graduate Advisor, 512-245-3353, Fax: 512-245-8713, E-mail: fw11@txstate.edu. *Application contact:* Dr. Andrea Golato, Dean of the Graduate School, 512-245-2581, Fax: 512-245-8365, E-mail: jw02@swt.edu.
Website: http://www.bio.txstate.edu/Graduate-Programs/M-S—Wildlife-Ecology-Program-.html

Texas Tech University, Graduate School, College of Agricultural Sciences and Natural Resources, Department of Natural Resources Management, Lubbock, TX 79409. Offers wildlife, aquatic, and wildlands science and management (MS, PhD). *Program availability:* Part-time. *Faculty:* 17 full-time (4 women), 1 part-time/adjunct (0 women). *Students:* 62 full-time (26 women), 12 part-time (6 women); includes 10 minority (1 Black or African American, non-Hispanic/Latino; 7 Hispanic/Latino; 2 Two or more races, non-Hispanic/Latino), 9 international. Average age 30. 25 applicants, 56% accepted, 12 enrolled. In 2015, 18 master's, 3 doctorates awarded. *Degree requirements:* For master's, comprehensive exam, thesis (for some programs); for doctorate, comprehensive exam, thesis/dissertation. *Entrance requirements:* For master's and doctorate, GRE General Test, formal approval from departmental committee. Additional exam requirements/recommendations for international students: Required—TOEFL (minimum score 550 paper-based; 79 iBT). *Application deadline:* For fall admission, 6/1 priority date for domestic students, 1/15 priority date for international students; for spring admission, 9/1 priority date for domestic students, 6/15 priority date for international students. Applications are processed on a rolling basis. Application fee: $60. Electronic applications accepted. *Expenses:* Tuition, state resident: full-time $6477; part-time $269.89 per credit hour. Tuition, nonresident: full-time $15,837; part-time $659.89 per credit hour. *Required fees:* $2751; $36.50 per credit hour. $937.50 per semester. Tuition and fees vary according to course level. *Financial support:* In 2015–16, 77 students received support, including 49 fellowships (averaging $3,226 per year), 66 research assistantships (averaging $12,159 per year), 9 teaching assistantships (averaging $10,276 per year); Federal Work-Study, scholarships/grants, and unspecified assistantships also available. Financial award application deadline: 4/15; financial award applicants required to submit FAFSA. *Faculty research:* Applying new ecological knowledge in decision-making about sustainable resource use, community (plant or animal) response to disturbances, population dynamics, habitat restoration, climate change, integrated management, game management, fire ecology, aquatic systems. *Total annual research expenditures:* $2.2 million. *Unit head:* Dr. Mark Wallace, Professor and Chair, 806-834-6979, Fax: 806-742-2280, E-mail: mark.wallace@ttu.edu. *Application contact:* Maggie Zebracka, Senior Business Assistant, 806-834-4550, Fax: 806-742-2280, E-mail: maggie.zebracka@ttu.edu.
Website: http://www.nrm.ttu.edu/

Université du Québec à Rimouski, Graduate Programs, Program in Wildlife Resources Management, Rimouski, QC G5L 3A1, Canada. Offers biology (PhD); wildlife resources management (M Sc, Diploma). PhD offered jointly with Université du Québec à Montréal, Université du Québec à Trois-Rivières, and Université du Québec en Abitibi-Témiscamingue. *Entrance requirements:* For degree, appropriate bachelor's degree, proficiency in French.

University of Arkansas at Pine Bluff, School of Agriculture, Fisheries and Human Sciences, Pine Bluff, AR 71601-2799. Offers aquaculture and fisheries (MS).

University of Delaware, College of Agriculture and Natural Resources, Department of Entomology and Wildlife Ecology, Newark, DE 19716. Offers entomology and applied ecology (MS, PhD), including avian ecology, evolution and taxonomy, insect biological control, insect ecology and behavior (MS), insect genetics, pest management, plant-insect interactions, wildlife ecology and management. *Program availability:* Part-time. *Degree requirements:* For master's, comprehensive exam, thesis, oral exam, seminar; for doctorate, comprehensive exam, thesis/dissertation, qualifying exam, seminar. *Entrance requirements:* For master's, GRE General Test, minimum GPA of 3.0 in field, 2.8 overall; for doctorate, GRE General Test, GRE Subject Test (biology), minimum GPA of 3.0 in field, 2.8 overall. Additional exam requirements/recommendations for international students: Required—TOEFL. Electronic applications accepted. *Faculty research:* Ecology and evolution of plant-insect interactions, ecology of wildlife conservation management, habitat restoration, biological control, applied ecosystem management.

University of Florida, Graduate School, College of Agricultural and Life Sciences, Department of Wildlife Ecology and Conservation, Gainesville, FL 32611. Offers environmental education and communications (Certificate); wildlife ecology and conservation (MS, PhD), including geographic information systems, tropical conservation and development, wetland sciences. *Faculty:* 58. *Students:* Average age 32. 33 applicants, 30% accepted, 9 enrolled. In 2015, 15 master's, 4 doctorates awarded. *Degree requirements:* For master's, comprehensive exam, thesis optional; for doctorate, comprehensive exam, thesis/dissertation. *Entrance requirements:* For master's and doctorate, GRE General Test (minimum 34th percentile for Quantitative), minimum GPA of 3.3. Additional exam requirements/recommendations for international students: Required—TOEFL (minimum score 550 paper-based; 80 iBT), IELTS (minimum score 6). *Application deadline:* For fall admission, 12/15 priority date for domestic students, 12/15 for international students; for spring admission, 12/1 for domestic students. Applications are processed on a rolling basis. Application fee: $30. Electronic applications accepted. *Financial support:* In 2015–16, 4 fellowships, 36 research assistantships, 11 teaching assistantships were awarded; institutionally sponsored loans also available. Financial award applicants required to submit FAFSA. *Faculty research:* Conservation biology, spatial ecology, wildlife conservation and management, wetlands ecology and conservation, human dimensions in wildlife conservation. *Total annual research expenditures:* $4.8 million. *Unit head:* Eric C. Hellgren, PhD, Professor and Department Chair, 352-846-0552, E-mail: hellgren@ufl.edu. *Application contact:* Katie Sieving, PhD, Professor and Graduate Coordinator, 352-846-0569, Fax: 352-846-0841, E-mail: chucao@ufl.edu.
Website: http://www.wec.ufl.edu/

University of Maine, Graduate School, College of Natural Sciences, Forestry, and Agriculture, Department of Wildlife, Fisheries, and Conservation Biology, Orono, ME 04469. Offers wildlife conservation (MWC); wildlife ecology (MS, PhD). *Program availability:* Part-time. *Faculty:* 7 full-time (2 women), 5 part-time/adjunct (2 women). *Students:* 24 full-time (9 women), 3 international. Average age 29. 18 applicants, 56% accepted, 3 enrolled. In 2015, 1 master's, 3 doctorates awarded. *Degree requirements:* For master's, thesis (for some programs); for doctorate, one foreign language, comprehensive exam, thesis/dissertation. *Entrance requirements:* For master's and doctorate, GRE General Test. Additional exam requirements/recommendations for international students: Required—TOEFL. *Application deadline:* For fall admission, 2/1 priority date for domestic students. Applications are processed on a rolling basis. Application fee: $65. Electronic applications accepted. *Financial support:* In 2015–16, 26 students received support, including 20 research assistantships with full tuition reimbursements available (averaging $16,000 per year), 5 teaching assistantships; career-related internships or fieldwork, Federal Work-Study, institutionally sponsored loans, and tuition waivers (full and partial) also available. Financial award application deadline: 3/1. *Faculty research:* Forest wildlife ecology, landscape ecology, freshwater fish ecology, wetland ecology, population biology. *Total annual research expenditures:* $1 million. *Unit head:* Dr. Daniel Harrison, Chair, 207-581-2867, Fax: 207-581-2858. *Application contact:* Scott G. Delcourt, Assistant Vice President for Graduate Studies and Senior Associate Dean, 207-581-3291, Fax: 207-581-3232, E-mail: graduate@maine.edu.
Website: http://umaine.edu/wle/

University of Maryland Eastern Shore, Graduate Programs, Department of Natural Sciences, Princess Anne, MD 21853-1299. Offers chemistry (MS); marine-estuarine-environmental sciences (MS, PhD); quantitative fisheries and resource economics (PMS); toxicology (MS, PhD). *Degree requirements:* For master's, thesis; for doctorate, comprehensive exam, thesis/dissertation. *Entrance requirements:* For master's and doctorate, GRE General Test, minimum GPA of 3.0. Additional exam requirements/recommendations for international students: Required—TOEFL (minimum score 80 iBT). Electronic applications accepted. *Faculty research:* Environmental chemistry (air/water pollution), fin fish ecology.

University of Massachusetts Amherst, Graduate School, College of Natural Sciences, Department of Environmental Conservation, Amherst, MA 01003. Offers building systems (MS, PhD); environmental policy and human dimensions (MS, PhD); forest resources (MS, PhD); sustainability science (MS); water, wetlands and watersheds (MS, PhD); wildlife and fisheries conservation (MS, PhD). *Program availability:* Part-time. Terminal master's awarded for partial completion of doctoral program. *Degree requirements:* For master's, thesis or alternative; for doctorate, comprehensive exam, thesis/dissertation. *Entrance requirements:* For master's and doctorate, GRE General Test. Additional exam requirements/recommendations for international students: Required—TOEFL (minimum score 550 paper-based; 80 iBT), IELTS (minimum score 6.5). Electronic applications accepted.

University of Miami, Graduate School, Rosenstiel School of Marine and Atmospheric Science, Division of Marine Biology and Fisheries, Coral Gables, FL 33124. Offers MA, MS, PhD. Terminal master's awarded for partial completion of doctoral program. *Degree requirements:* For master's, comprehensive exam, thesis; for doctorate, comprehensive exam, thesis/dissertation. *Entrance requirements:* For master's and doctorate, GRE General Test. Additional exam requirements/recommendations for international students: Required—TOEFL (minimum score 550 paper-based). Electronic applications accepted. *Faculty research:* Biochemistry, physiology, plankton, coral, biology.

University of Minnesota, Twin Cities Campus, Graduate School, College of Food, Agricultural and Natural Resource Sciences, Program in Natural Resources Science and Management, St. Paul, MN 55108. Offers assessment, monitoring, and geospatial analysis (MS, PhD); economics, policy, management, and society (MS, PhD); forest hydrology and watershed management (MS, PhD); forest products (MS, PhD); forests: biology, ecology, conservation, and management (MS, PhD); natural resources science and management (MS, PhD); paper science and engineering (MS, PhD); recreation resources, tourism, and environmental education (MS, PhD); wildlife ecology and management (MS, PhD). *Program availability:* Part-time. *Faculty:* 71 full-time (28 women), 55 part-time/adjunct (7 women). *Students:* 80 full-time (45 women), 16 part-time (9 women); includes 5 minority (1 Black or African American, non-Hispanic/Latino; 2 American Indian or Alaska Native, non-Hispanic/Latino; 2 Asian, non-Hispanic/Latino), 8 international. 81 applicants, 52% accepted, 31 enrolled. In 2015, 25 master's, 8 doctorates awarded. Terminal master's awarded for partial completion of doctoral program. *Degree requirements:* For master's, comprehensive exam, thesis; for doctorate, comprehensive exam, thesis/dissertation. *Entrance requirements:* For master's and doctorate, GRE General Test. Additional exam requirements/recommendations for international students: Required—TOEFL (minimum score 550 paper-based; 79 iBT), IELTS (minimum score 6.5). *Application deadline:* For fall

admission, 12/16 priority date for domestic and international students; for spring admission, 10/15 for domestic and international students. Applications are processed on a rolling basis. Application fee: $75 ($95 for international students). Electronic applications accepted. *Financial support:* In 2015–16, fellowships with full tuition reimbursements (averaging $40,000 per year), research assistantships with full tuition reimbursements (averaging $40,000 per year), teaching assistantships with full tuition reimbursements (averaging $40,000 per year) were awarded; scholarships/grants, health care benefits, tuition waivers (full and partial), and unspecified assistantships also available. *Faculty research:* Forest hydrology, biology, ecology, conservation, and management; recreation resources and environmental education; wildlife ecology; economics, policy, and society; geographic information systems (GIS); and forest products and paper science. *Unit head:* Dr. Michael Kilgore, Director of Graduate Studies, 612-624-6298, E-mail: mkilgore@umn.edu. *Application contact:* Toni Wheeler, Graduate Program Coordinator, 612-624-7683, Fax: 612-625-5212,
E-mail: twheeler@umn.edu.
Website: http://www.nrsm.umn.edu

University of Missouri, Office of Research and Graduate Studies, School of Natural Resources, Department of Fisheries and Wildlife Sciences, Columbia, MO 65211. Offers conservation biology (Certificate); fisheries and wildlife (MS, PhD). *Degree requirements:* For doctorate, thesis/dissertation. *Entrance requirements:* For master's and doctorate, GRE General Test, minimum GPA of 3.0. Additional exam requirements/recommendations for international students: Required—TOEFL (minimum score 550 paper-based; 79 iBT). Electronic applications accepted. *Faculty research:* Limnology; conservation biology; landscape ecology; natural resource policy and management; rare species conservation; avian ecology; behavior and conservation; large river ecology; native fish ecology and restoration ecology; wildlife disease ecology; behavioral, population and community ecology; conservation biology; mammalian carnivores; fish bioenergetics; compensatory growth; fish population dynamics and aquaculture; endangered species recovery; wildlife stress physiology.

University of Montana, Graduate School, College of Forestry and Conservation, Missoula, MT 59812-0002. Offers fish and wildlife biology (PhD); forest and conservation sciences (PhD); forestry (MS); recreation management (MS); resource conservation (MS); systems ecology (MS, PhD); wildlife biology (MS). *Degree requirements:* For doctorate, thesis/dissertation. *Entrance requirements:* For master's and doctorate, GRE General Test. Additional exam requirements/recommendations for international students: Required—TOEFL (minimum score 575 paper-based).

University of New Hampshire, Graduate School, College of Life Sciences and Agriculture, Department of Natural Resources and the Environment, Durham, NH 03824. Offers environmental conservation (MS); forestry (MS); integrated coastal ecosystem science, policy and management (MS); natural resources (MS); soil and water resource management (MS); wildlife and conservation biology (MS). *Program availability:* Part-time. *Degree requirements:* For master's, thesis or alternative. *Entrance requirements:* For master's, GRE General Test. Additional exam requirements/recommendations for international students: Required—TOEFL (minimum score 550 paper-based; 80 iBT). Electronic applications accepted.

University of North Dakota, Graduate School, College of Arts and Sciences, Department of Biology, Grand Forks, ND 58202. Offers botany (MS, PhD); ecology (MS, PhD); entomology (MS, PhD); environmental biology (MS, PhD); fisheries/wildlife (MS, PhD); genetics (MS, PhD); zoology (MS, PhD). Terminal master's awarded for partial completion of doctoral program. *Degree requirements:* For master's, thesis, final exam; for doctorate, comprehensive exam, thesis/dissertation, final exam. *Entrance requirements:* For master's, GRE General Test, GRE Subject Test, minimum GPA of 3.0; for doctorate, GRE General Test, GRE Subject Test, minimum GPA of 3.5. Additional exam requirements/recommendations for international students: Required—TOEFL (minimum score 550 paper-based; 79 iBT), IELTS (minimum score 6.5). Electronic applications accepted. *Faculty research:* Population biology, wildlife ecology, RNA processing, hormonal control of behavior.

University of Rhode Island, Graduate School, College of the Environment and Life Sciences, Department of Fisheries, Animal and Veterinary Science, Kingston, RI 02881. Offers animal health and disease (MS); animal science (MS); aquaculture (MS); aquatic pathology (MS); environmental sciences (PhD), including animal science, aquacultural science, aquatic pathology, fisheries science; fisheries (MS). *Faculty:* 10 full-time (3 women). *Degree requirements:* For master's, comprehensive exam (for some programs), thesis optional; for doctorate, comprehensive exam, thesis/dissertation. *Entrance requirements:* For master's and doctorate, GRE, 2 letters of recommendation. Additional exam requirements/recommendations for international students: Required—TOEFL (minimum score 550 paper-based). *Application deadline:* For fall admission, 7/15 for domestic students, 2/1 for international students; for spring admission, 11/15 for domestic students, 7/15 for international students. Application fee: $65. Electronic applications accepted. *Expenses:* Tuition, state resident: full-time $11,796; part-time $655 per credit. Tuition, nonresident: full-time $24,206; part-time $1345 per credit. *Required fees:* $1546; $44 per credit. One-time fee: $155 full-time; $35 part-time. *Financial support:* Application deadline: 2/1; applicants required to submit FAFSA. *Total annual research expenditures:* $1.2 million. *Unit head:* Dr. Marta Gomez-Chiarri, Chair, 401-874-2917, Fax: 401-874-7575, E-mail: gomezchi@uri.edu. *Application contact:* Graduate Admissions, 401-874-2872, E-mail: gradadm@etal.uri.edu.
Website: http://www.uri.edu/cels/favs/

The University of Tennessee, Graduate School, College of Agricultural Sciences and Natural Resources, Department of Forestry, Wildlife, and Fisheries, Program in Wildlife and Fisheries Science, Knoxville, TN 37996. Offers MS. *Degree requirements:* For master's, thesis. *Entrance requirements:* For master's, GRE General Test, minimum GPA of 2.7. Additional exam requirements/recommendations for international students: Required—TOEFL. Electronic applications accepted.

University of Washington, Graduate School, College of the Environment, School of Aquatic and Fishery Sciences, Seattle, WA 98195. Offers MS, PhD. *Degree requirements:* For master's, thesis; for doctorate, thesis/dissertation. *Entrance requirements:* For master's and doctorate, GRE General Test, minimum GPA of 3.0. Additional exam requirements/recommendations for international students: Required—TOEFL. Electronic applications accepted. *Faculty research:* Fish and shellfish ecology, fisheries management, aquatic ecology, conservation biology, genetics.

University of Washington, Graduate School, College of the Environment, School of Forest Resources, Seattle, WA 98195. Offers bioresource science and engineering (MS, PhD); environmental horticulture (MEH); forest ecology (MS, PhD); forest management (MFR); forest soils (MS, PhD); restoration ecology (MS, PhD); restoration ecology and environmental horticulture (MS, PhD); social sciences (MS, PhD); sustainable resource management (MS, PhD); wildlife science (MS, PhD); MFR/MAIS; MPA/MS. *Accreditation:* SAF. *Program availability:* Part-time. *Degree requirements:* For master's, thesis; for doctorate, comprehensive exam, thesis/dissertation. *Entrance requirements:* For master's and doctorate, GRE, minimum GPA of 3.0. Additional exam requirements/recommendations for international students: Required—TOEFL. Electronic applications accepted. *Faculty research:* Ecosystem analysis, silviculture and forest protection, paper science and engineering, environmental horticulture and urban forestry, natural resource policy and economics, restoration ecology and environment horticulture, conservation, human dimensions, wildlife, bioresource science and engineering.

University of Wisconsin–Madison, Graduate School, College of Agricultural and Life Sciences, Department of Forest and Wildlife Ecology, Program in Wildlife Ecology, Madison, WI 53706-1380. Offers MS, PhD. *Expenses:* Tuition, state resident: full-time $5364. Tuition, nonresident: full-time $12,027. *Required fees:* $571. Tuition and fees vary according to campus/location, program and reciprocity agreements.

Utah State University, School of Graduate Studies, College of Natural Resources, Department of Watershed Sciences, Logan, UT 84322. Offers ecology (MS, PhD); fisheries biology (MS, PhD); watershed science (MS, PhD). *Degree requirements:* For master's, thesis (for some programs); for doctorate, thesis/dissertation. *Entrance requirements:* For master's and doctorate, GRE General Test, minimum GPA of 3.2. Additional exam requirements/recommendations for international students: Required—TOEFL. Electronic applications accepted. *Faculty research:* Behavior, population ecology, habitat, conservation biology, restoration, aquatic ecology, fisheries management, fluvial geomorphology, remote sensing, conservation biology.

Utah State University, School of Graduate Studies, College of Natural Resources, Department of Wildland Resources, Logan, UT 84322. Offers ecology (MS, PhD); forestry (MS, PhD); range science (MS, PhD); wildlife biology (MS, PhD). *Program availability:* Part-time. *Degree requirements:* For master's, thesis; for doctorate, comprehensive exam, thesis/dissertation. *Entrance requirements:* For master's and doctorate, GRE General Test, minimum GPA of 3.0. Additional exam requirements/recommendations for international students: Required—TOEFL. *Faculty research:* Range plant ecophysiology, plant community ecology, ruminant nutrition, population ecology.

Virginia Polytechnic Institute and State University, Graduate School, College of Natural Resources and Environment, Blacksburg, VA 24061. Offers fisheries and wildlife (MS, PhD); forestry and forest products (MF, MS, PhD); geography (MS); geospatial and environmental analysis (PhD); natural resources (MNR). *Degree requirements:* For master's, comprehensive exam (for some programs), thesis (for some programs); for doctorate, comprehensive exam (for some programs), thesis/dissertation (for some programs). *Entrance requirements:* For master's and doctorate, GRE/GMAT (may vary by department). Additional exam requirements/recommendations for international students: Required—TOEFL (minimum score 550 paper-based). Electronic applications accepted.

West Virginia University, Davis College of Agriculture, Forestry and Consumer Sciences, Division of Forestry, Program in Wildlife and Fisheries Resources, Morgantown, WV 26506. Offers MS. *Program availability:* Part-time. *Degree requirements:* For master's, comprehensive exam, thesis. *Entrance requirements:* For master's, GRE, minimum GPA of 3.0. Additional exam requirements/recommendations for international students: Required—TOEFL. Electronic applications accepted. *Expenses:* Tuition, state resident: full-time $8568. Tuition, nonresident: full-time $22,140. Tuition and fees vary according to program. *Faculty research:* Managing habitat for game, nongame, and fish; fish ecology; wildlife ecology.

Forestry

Auburn University, Graduate School, School of Forestry and Wildlife Sciences, Auburn University, AL 36849. Offers forest economics (PhD); forestry (MS, PhD); natural resource conservation (MNR); wildlife sciences (MS, PhD). *Accreditation:* SAF. *Program availability:* Part-time. *Faculty:* 30 full-time (7 women), 2 part-time/adjunct (1 woman). *Students:* 36 full-time (15 women), 30 part-time (11 women); includes 2 minority (both Black or African American, non-Hispanic/Latino), 26 international. Average age 28. 27 applicants, 52% accepted, 11 enrolled. In 2015, 13 master's, 4 doctorates awarded. *Degree requirements:* For master's, thesis (MS); for doctorate, thesis/dissertation. *Entrance requirements:* For master's and doctorate, GRE General Test. *Application deadline:* Applications are processed on a rolling basis. Application fee: $50 ($60 for international students). Electronic applications accepted. *Expenses:* Tuition, state resident: full-time $8802; part-time $489 per credit hour. Tuition, nonresident: full-time $26,406; part-time $1467 per credit hour. *Required fees:* $808 per semester. Tuition and fees vary according to degree level and program. *Financial support:* Fellowships, research assistantships, teaching assistantships, and Federal Work-Study available. Support available to part-time students. Financial award application deadline: 3/15; financial award applicants required to submit FAFSA. *Faculty research:* Forest nursery management, silviculture and vegetation management, biological processes and ecological relationships, growth and yield of plantations and natural stands, urban forestry, forest taxation, law and policy. *Unit head:* Dr. Graeme Lockaby, Dean, 334-844-4000, Fax: 334-844-1084, E-mail: brinker@forestry.auburn.edu. *Application contact:* Dr. George Flowers, Dean of the Graduate School, 334-844-2125.
Website: http://www.forestry.auburn.edu/

California Polytechnic State University, San Luis Obispo, College of Agriculture, Food and Environmental Sciences, Department of Natural Resources Management and Environmental Sciences, San Luis Obispo, CA 93407. Offers forestry sciences (MS). *Program availability:* Part-time. *Faculty:* 9 full-time (4 women). *Students:* 3 full-time (2 women), 6 part-time (2 women). Average age 26. 6 applicants, 83% accepted, 4 enrolled. In 2015, 3 master's awarded. *Degree requirements:* For master's, comprehensive exam, thesis. *Application deadline:* For fall admission, 4/1 for domestic and international students; for winter admission, 10/1 for domestic students, 6/30 for international students; for spring admission, 10/1 for domestic students. Applications are processed on a rolling basis. Application fee: $55. Electronic applications accepted. *Expenses:* Tuition, state resident: full-time $6738; part-time $3906 per year. Tuition, nonresident: full-time $15,666; part-time $8370 per year. *Required fees:* $3528; $3075 per unit. $1025 per term. *Financial support:* Fellowships, research assistantships, career-related internships or fieldwork, Federal Work-Study, institutionally sponsored loans, scholarships/grants, and unspecified assistantships available. Support available to part-time students. Financial award application deadline: 3/2; financial award applicants required to submit FAFSA. *Faculty research:* Hydrology, biometrics, forest health and management, fire science, urban and community forestry. *Unit head:* Dr. Richard Thompson, Department Head, 805-756-2898, E-mail: rpthomps@calpoly.edu. Website: http://nres.calpoly.edu/

Clemson University, Graduate School, College of Agriculture, Forestry and Life Sciences, Department of Forestry and Environmental Conservation, Program in Forest Resources, Clemson, SC 29634-0317. Offers MFR, MS, PhD. *Program availability:* Part-time. *Faculty:* 23 full-time (3 women), 2 part-time/adjunct (0 women). *Students:* 20 full-time (6 women), 1 part-time (0 women); includes 2 minority (1 Hispanic/Latino; 1 Two or more races, non-Hispanic/Latino), 4 international. Average age 30. 7 applicants, 71% accepted, 3 enrolled. In 2015, 5 master's awarded. *Degree requirements:* For master's, thesis; for doctorate, thesis/dissertation. *Entrance requirements:* For master's and doctorate, GRE General Test, unofficial transcripts, letters of recommendation. Additional exam requirements/recommendations for international students: Required—TOEFL (minimum score 80 iBT), IELTS (minimum score 6.5). *Application deadline:* For fall admission, 3/1 priority date for domestic students, 4/15 for international students; for spring admission, 10/1 for domestic students, 9/15 for international students. Applications are processed on a rolling basis. Application fee: $80 ($90 for international students). Electronic applications accepted. *Expenses:* $3,715 per semester full-time resident, $7,411 per semester full-time non-resident, $400 per credit hour part-time resident, $803 per credit hour part-time non-resident. *Financial support:* In 2015–16, 15 students received support, including 1 fellowship with partial tuition reimbursement available (averaging $5,000 per year), 10 research assistantships with partial tuition reimbursements available (averaging $17,940 per year), 2 teaching assistantships with partial tuition reimbursements available (averaging $9,350 per year); health care benefits and unspecified assistantships also available. Financial award application deadline: 3/1. *Faculty research:* Wetlands management, wood technology, forest management, silviculture, economics. *Unit head:* Dr. Gregg Yarrow, Department Chair, 864-656-3302, Fax: 864-656-3304, E-mail: gyarrow@clemson.edu. *Application contact:* Dr. Robert Baldwin, Graduate Program Coordinator, 864-656-3302, E-mail: baldwi6@clemson.edu.
Website: http://www.clemson.edu/graduate/academics/program details.html?m_id=Forest-Resources

Colorado State University, Warner College of Natural Resources, Department of Forest and Rangeland Stewardship, Fort Collins, CO 80523-1472. Offers forest sciences (MS, PhD); natural resources stewardship (MNRS); rangeland ecosystem science (MS, PhD). *Program availability:* Part-time, evening/weekend, 100% online. *Faculty:* 10 full-time (2 women), 2 part-time/adjunct (1 woman). *Students:* 28 full-time (10 women), 63 part-time (29 women); includes 13 minority (9 Hispanic/Latino; 4 Two or more races, non-Hispanic/Latino), 5 international. Average age 32. 62 applicants, 69% accepted, 37 enrolled. In 2015, 22 master's, 2 doctorates awarded. *Degree requirements:* For master's, thesis (for some programs), professional paper; for doctorate, comprehensive exam, thesis/dissertation. *Entrance requirements:* For master's, GRE General Test, minimum GPA of 3.0, 3 letters of recommendation, curriculum vitae; for doctorate, GRE General Test, minimum GPA of 3.0, 3 letters of recommendation, statement of research interest, curriculum vitae. Additional exam requirements/recommendations for international students: Required—TOEFL (minimum score 550 paper-based; 80 iBT), IELTS (minimum score 6.5). *Application deadline:* For fall admission, 2/1 priority date for domestic and international students; for spring admission, 10/1 priority date for domestic and international students. Applications are processed on a rolling basis. Application fee: $60 ($70 for international students). Electronic applications accepted. *Expenses:* Tuition, state resident: full-time $9348. Tuition, nonresident: full-time $22,916. *Required fees:* $2174; $473.72 per credit hour. $236.86 per semester. Tuition and fees vary according to course load and program. *Financial support:* In 2015–16, 4 fellowships with full tuition reimbursements (averaging $38,750 per year), 30 research assistantships with tuition reimbursements (averaging $21,847 per year), 6 teaching assistantships with tuition reimbursements (averaging $12,540 per year) were awarded; scholarships/grants and unspecified assistantships also available. Financial award application deadline: 2/1; financial award applicants required to submit FAFSA. *Faculty research:* Rangelands, forestry, natural resources economics, natural resources policy, riparian areas, fire effects. *Total annual research expenditures:* $3.1 million. *Unit head:* Dr. Linda Nagel, Department Head and Professor, 970-491-2840, Fax: 970-491-6754, E-mail: linda.nagel@colostate.edu. *Application contact:* Simone Short, Administrative Assistant III, 970-491-6911, Fax: 970-491-6754, E-mail: wcnr_frs_deptadmin@mail.colostate.edu.
Website: http://warnercnr.colostate.edu/frws-home/

Cornell University, Graduate School, Graduate Fields of Agriculture and Life Sciences, Field of Natural Resources, Ithaca, NY 14853-0001. Offers community-based natural resources management (MS, PhD); conservation biology (MS, PhD); ecosystem biology and biogeochemistry (MPS, MS, PhD); environmental management (MPS); fishery and aquatic science (MPS, MS, PhD); forest science (MPS, MS, PhD); human dimensions of natural resources management (MPS, MS, PhD); policy and institutional analysis (MS, PhD); program development and evaluation (MPS, MS, PhD); quantitative ecology (MS, PhD); wildlife science (MPS, MS, PhD). *Degree requirements:* For master's, thesis (MS), project paper (MPS); for doctorate, comprehensive exam, thesis/dissertation. *Entrance requirements:* For master's and doctorate, GRE General Test, 2 letters of recommendation. Additional exam requirements/recommendations for international students: Required—TOEFL (minimum score 550 paper-based; 77 iBT). Electronic applications accepted. *Faculty research:* Ecosystem-level dynamics, systems modeling, conservation biology/management, resource management's human dimensions, biogeochemistry.

Duke University, Nicholas School of the Environment, Durham, NC 27708. Offers environment (PhD); environmental management (MEM); forestry (MF); JD/AM. Application deadline for PhD program is December 8. *Program availability:* Online learning. *Degree requirements:* For doctorate, variable foreign language requirement, thesis/dissertation. *Entrance requirements:* For master's, GRE General Test, previous course work in natural or social sciences relevant to environmental interests, college calculus, college statistics, and microeconomics or ecology. Additional exam requirements/recommendations for international students: Required—TOEFL (minimum score 577 paper-based; 90 iBT) or IELTS (minimum score 7). Electronic applications accepted. *Faculty research:* Climate change, energy, water quality, ecosystem management and conservation, human and environmental health.

Harvard University, Graduate School of Arts and Sciences, Department of Forestry, Cambridge, MA 02138. Offers forest science (MFS). *Degree requirements:* For master's, thesis. *Entrance requirements:* For master's, GRE General Test, bachelor's degree in biology or forestry. Additional exam requirements/recommendations for international students: Required—TOEFL. *Faculty research:* Forest ecology, planning, and physiology; forest microbiology.

Humboldt State University, Academic Programs, College of Natural Resources and Sciences, Programs in Natural Resources, Arcata, CA 95521-8299. Offers natural resources (MS), including fisheries, forestry, natural resources planning and interpretation, rangeland resources and wildland soils, wastewater utilization, watershed management, wildlife. *Degree requirements:* For master's, thesis or alternative. *Entrance requirements:* For master's, GRE, appropriate bachelor's degree, minimum GPA of 2.5, 3 letters of recommendation, resume. Additional exam requirements/recommendations for international students: Required—TOEFL (minimum score 500 paper-based). *Faculty research:* Spotted owl habitat, pre-settlement vegetation, hardwood utilization, tree physiology, fisheries.

Iowa State University of Science and Technology, Department of Natural Resource Ecology and Management, Ames, IA 50011. Offers forestry (MS, PhD); wildlife ecology (MS). *Entrance requirements:* For master's and doctorate, GRE General Test. Additional exam requirements/recommendations for international students: Required—TOEFL (minimum score 550 paper-based; 79 iBT), IELTS (minimum score 6.5). Electronic applications accepted.

Iowa State University of Science and Technology, Program in Forestry, Ames, IA 50011. Offers MS, PhD. *Entrance requirements:* For master's and doctorate, GRE. Additional exam requirements/recommendations for international students: Required—TOEFL (minimum score 550 paper-based; 79 iBT), IELTS (minimum score 6.5). Electronic applications accepted.

Lakehead University, Graduate Studies, Faculty of Natural Resources Management, Thunder Bay, ON P7B 5E1, Canada. Offers forest sciences (PhD); forestry (M Sc F). *Program availability:* Part-time. *Degree requirements:* For master's, thesis. *Entrance requirements:* For master's, minimum B average. Additional exam requirements/recommendations for international students: Required—TOEFL. *Faculty research:* Soils, silviculture, wildlife, ecology, genetics.

Louisiana State University and Agricultural & Mechanical College, Graduate School, College of Agriculture, School of Renewable Natural Resources, Baton Rouge, LA 70803. Offers fisheries (MS); forestry (MS, PhD); wildlife (MS); wildlife and fisheries science (PhD).

McGill University, Faculty of Graduate and Postdoctoral Studies, Faculty of Agricultural and Environmental Sciences, Department of Natural Resource Sciences, Montréal, QC H3A 2T5, Canada. Offers entomology (M Sc, PhD); environmental assessment (M Sc); forest science (M Sc, PhD); microbiology (M Sc, PhD); micrometeorology (M Sc, PhD); neotropical environment (M Sc, PhD); soil science (M Sc, PhD); wildlife biology (M Sc, PhD).

Michigan State University, The Graduate School, College of Agriculture and Natural Resources, Department of Forestry, East Lansing, MI 48824. Offers forestry (MS, PhD); forestry-environmental toxicology (PhD); plant breeding, genetics and biotechnology-forestry (MS, PhD). *Entrance requirements:* Additional exam requirements/recommendations for international students: Required—TOEFL (minimum score 550 paper-based), Michigan State University ELT (minimum score 85), Michigan English Language Assessment Battery (minimum score 83). Electronic applications accepted.

Michigan Technological University, Graduate School, School of Forest Resources and Environmental Science, Houghton, MI 49931. Offers applied ecology (MS); forest ecology and management (MS); forest molecular genetics and biotechnology (MS, PhD); forest science (PhD); forestry (MF, MS); geographic information science (MGIS). *Accreditation:* SAF. *Program availability:* Part-time. *Faculty:* 41 full-time (11 women), 52 part-time/adjunct (18 women). *Students:* 58 full-time (24 women), 23 part-time (6 women); includes 2 minority (both Two or more races, non-Hispanic/Latino), 19 international. Average age 31. 92 applicants, 51% accepted, 32 enrolled. In 2015, 16 master's, 5 doctorates awarded. Terminal master's awarded for partial completion of doctoral program. *Degree requirements:* For master's, thesis (for some programs), comprehensive exam (for non-research degrees); for doctorate, comprehensive exam, thesis/dissertation. *Entrance requirements:* For master's and doctorate, GRE, statement of purpose, personal statement, official transcripts, 3 letters of recommendation, resume/curriculum vitae. Additional exam requirements/recommendations for international students: Required—TOEFL (recommended score 79 iBT) or IELTS. *Application deadline:* Applications are processed on a rolling basis. Electronic applications accepted. *Expenses:* Tuition, state resident: full-time $15,507; part-time $861.50 per credit. Tuition, nonresident: full-time $15,507; part-time $861.50 per credit. *Required fees:* $248; $248. Tuition and fees vary according to course load and program. *Financial support:* In 2015–16, 51 students received support, including 6 fellowships with tuition reimbursements available (averaging $14,516 per year), 17 research assistantships with tuition reimbursements available (averaging $14,516 per year), 6 teaching assistantships with tuition reimbursements available (averaging $14,516 per year); career-related internships or fieldwork, Federal Work-Study, scholarships/grants, health care benefits, unspecified assistantships, and cooperative program also available. Financial award applicants required to submit FAFSA. *Faculty research:* Forest ecology and management, forest molecular genetics and biotechnology, forest biomaterials, restoration ecology, wildlife ecology and management. *Total annual research expenditures:* $3.7 million. *Unit head:* Dr. Terry Sharik, Dean, 906-487-2352, Fax: 906-487-2915, E-mail: tlsharik@mtu.edu. *Application contact:* Dr. Andrew J. Storer, Associate Dean, 906-487-3470, Fax: 906-487-2915, E-mail: storer@mtu.edu.
Website: http://www.mtu.edu/forest/

Mississippi State University, College of Forest Resources, Department of Forestry, Mississippi State, MS 39762. Offers forest resources (PhD); forestry (MS). *Program availability:* Part-time. *Faculty:* 22 full-time (5 women). *Students:* 22 full-time (6 women), 29 part-time (6 women); includes 4 minority (1 Black or African American, non-Hispanic/Latino; 1 American Indian or Alaska Native, non-Hispanic/Latino; 1 Asian, non-Hispanic/Latino; 1 Two or more races, non-Hispanic/Latino), 14 international. Average age 31. 23 applicants, 61% accepted, 12 enrolled. In 2015, 7 master's, 6 doctorates awarded. *Degree requirements:* For master's, thesis optional, comprehensive oral or written exam; for doctorate, comprehensive exam, thesis/dissertation. *Entrance requirements:* For master's, GRE, BS with minimum GPA of 3.0 on last 60 hours of undergraduate study; for doctorate, minimum GPA of 3.1 on prior graduate courses or 3.25 on last 60 hours of undergraduate study. Additional exam requirements/recommendations for international students: Required—TOEFL (minimum score 550 paper-based; 79 iBT); Recommended—IELTS (minimum score 6.5). *Application deadline:* For fall admission, 7/1 for domestic students, 5/1 for international students; for spring admission, 11/1 for domestic students, 9/1 for international students. Applications are processed on a rolling basis. Application fee: $60. Electronic applications accepted. *Expenses: Tuition, area resident:* Full-time $7502; part-time $833.74 per credit hour. Tuition, nonresident: full-time $20,142; part-time $2238.24 per credit hour. *Financial support:* In 2015–16, 21 research assistantships with full tuition reimbursements (averaging $13,762 per year) were awarded; Federal Work-Study, institutionally sponsored loans, and unspecified

assistantships also available. Financial award application deadline: 4/1; financial award applicants required to submit FAFSA. *Faculty research:* Forest hydrology, forest biometry, forest management/economics, forest biology, industrial forest operations. *Unit head:* Dr. Andrew Ezell, Professor and Head, 662-325-1688, Fax: 662-325-8126, E-mail: a.w.ezell@cfr.msstate.edu. *Application contact:* Nathan Drake, Admissions Assistant, 662-325-3804, E-mail: ndrake@grad.msstate.edu.
Website: http://www.cfr.msstate.edu/forestry/

Mississippi State University, College of Forest Resources, Department of Sustainable Bioproducts, Mississippi State, MS 39762. Offers forest products (MS); forest resources (PhD), including forest products. *Faculty:* 12 full-time (4 women), 2 part-time/adjunct (0 women). *Students:* 29 full-time (16 women), 2 part-time (1 woman); includes 2 minority (1 Black or African American, non-Hispanic/Latino; 1 Asian, non-Hispanic/Latino), 20 international. Average age 29. 14 applicants, 50% accepted, 6 enrolled. In 2015, 4 master's, 5 doctorates awarded. *Degree requirements:* For master's, thesis optional; for doctorate, comprehensive exam, thesis/dissertation. *Entrance requirements:* For master's, GRE (if undergraduate GPA of last two years less than 3.0); for doctorate, GRE if undergraduate GPA of last two years is below 3.0. Additional exam requirements/recommendations for international students: Required—TOEFL (minimum score 550 paper-based; 79 iBT); Recommended—IELTS (minimum score 6.5). *Application deadline:* For fall admission, 7/1 for domestic students, 5/1 for international students; for spring admission, 11/1 for domestic students, 9/1 for international students. Applications are processed on a rolling basis. Application fee: $60. Electronic applications accepted. *Expenses: Tuition, area resident:* Full-time $7502; part-time $833.74 per credit hour. Tuition, nonresident: full-time $20,142; part-time $2238.24 per credit hour. *Financial support:* In 2015–16, 100 students received support, including 27 research assistantships with full tuition reimbursements available (averaging $15,818 per year); Federal Work-Study, institutionally sponsored loans, and unspecified assistantships also available. Financial award application deadline: 4/1; financial award applicants required to submit FAFSA. *Faculty research:* Wood property enhancement and durability, environmental science and chemistry, wood-based composites, primary wood production, furniture manufacturing and management. *Unit head:* Dr. Rubin Shmulsky, Professor/Head/Associate Director, 662-325-2116, Fax: 662-325-8126, E-mail: rshmulsky@cfr.msstate.edu. *Application contact:* Nathan Drake, Admissions Assistant, 662-325-3804, E-mail: ndrake@grad.msstate.edu.
Website: http://www.cfr.msstate.edu/forestp//index.asp

Mississippi State University, College of Forest Resources, Department of Wildlife, Fisheries and Aquaculture, Mississippi State, MS 39762. Offers forest resources (PhD), including wildlife, fisheries and aquaculture; wildlife, fisheries and aquaculture (MS). *Program availability:* Part-time. *Faculty:* 26 full-time (4 women). *Students:* 42 full-time (8 women), 12 part-time (7 women), 6 international. Average age 29. 19 applicants, 53% accepted, 9 enrolled. In 2015, 12 master's, 3 doctorates awarded. *Degree requirements:* For master's, thesis, comprehensive oral or written exam; for doctorate, comprehensive exam, thesis/dissertation. *Entrance requirements:* For master's, GRE, bachelor's degree, minimum GPA of 3.0 on last 60 hours of undergraduate courses; for doctorate, GRE, master's degree, minimum GPA of 3.2 on prior graduate studies. Additional exam requirements/recommendations for international students: Required—TOEFL (minimum score 550 paper-based; 79 iBT); Recommended—IELTS (minimum score 6.5). *Application deadline:* For fall admission, 7/1 for domestic students, 5/1 for international students; for spring admission, 11/1 for domestic students, 9/1 for international students. Applications are processed on a rolling basis. Application fee: $60. Electronic applications accepted. *Expenses: Tuition, area resident:* Full-time $7502; part-time $833.74 per credit hour. Tuition, nonresident: full-time $20,142; part-time $2238.24 per credit hour. *Financial support:* In 2015–16, 34 research assistantships with partial tuition reimbursements (averaging $15,362 per year) were awarded; Federal Work-Study, institutionally sponsored loans, and unspecified assistantships also available. Financial award application deadline: 4/1; financial award applicants required to submit FAFSA. *Faculty research:* Spatial technology, habitat restoration, aquaculture, fisheries, wildlife management. *Unit head:* Dr. Andrew Kouba, Professor and Head, 662-325-7494, Fax: 662-325-8726, E-mail: ak260@msstate.edu. *Application contact:* Nathan Drake, Admissions Assistant, 662-325-3804, E-mail: ndrake@grad.msstate.edu.
Website: http://www.cfr.msstate.edu/wildlife/index.asp

North Carolina State University, Graduate School, College of Natural Resources, Department of Forestry and Environmental Resources, Raleigh, NC 27695. Offers MF, MS, PhD. *Program availability:* Part-time. *Degree requirements:* For master's, thesis (for some programs), teaching experience; for doctorate, thesis/dissertation, teaching experience. *Entrance requirements:* For master's and doctorate, GRE General Test. Additional exam requirements/recommendations for international students: Required—TOEFL. Electronic applications accepted. *Faculty research:* Forest genetics, forest ecology and silviculture, forest economics/management/policy, international forestry, remote sensing/geographic information systems.

Northern Arizona University, Graduate College, College of Engineering, Forestry, and Natural Sciences, School of Forestry, Flagstaff, AZ 86011. Offers forest science (PhD); forestry (MF, MSF). *Program availability:* Part-time. *Faculty:* 8 full-time. *Students:* 18 full-time. *Degree requirements:* For master's, thesis optional; for doctorate, comprehensive exam, thesis/dissertation. *Entrance requirements:* For master's and doctorate, GRE General Test. Additional exam requirements/recommendations for international students: Required—TOEFL (minimum score 550 paper-based; 80 iBT), IELTS (minimum score 7). *Application deadline:* For fall admission, 3/15 priority date for domestic and international students; for spring admission, 10/15 priority date for domestic and international students. Applications are processed on a rolling basis. Application fee: $65. Electronic applications accepted. *Expenses: Tuition, area resident:* Full-time $8710. Tuition, nonresident: full-time $20,350. *Required fees:* $896. *Financial support:* Research assistantships, teaching assistantships, career-related internships or fieldwork, Federal Work-Study, scholarships/grants, traineeships, health care benefits, tuition waivers (full and partial), and unspecified assistantships available. Financial award applicants required to submit FAFSA. *Faculty research:* Multisource management, ecology, entomology, recreation, hydrology. *Unit head:* Dr. James Allen, Executive Director, 928-523-5894, Fax: 928-523-1080, E-mail: james.allen@nau.edu. *Application contact:* Karen Blalock, Administrative Associate, 928-523-8810, E-mail: forestrygraduatestudies@xdl.nau.edu.
Website: http://nau.edu/cefns/forestry/

The Ohio State University, Graduate School, College of Food, Agricultural, and Environmental Sciences, School of Environment and Natural Resources, Columbus, OH 43210. Offers ecological restoration (MS, PhD); ecosystem science (MS, PhD); environment and natural resources (MENR); environmental social sciences (MS, PhD); fisheries and wildlife science (MS, PhD); forest science (MS, PhD); rural sociology (MS, PhD); soil science (MS, PhD). *Degree requirements:* For master's, thesis; for doctorate, thesis/dissertation. *Entrance requirements:* For master's and doctorate, GRE. Additional exam requirements/recommendations for international students: Required—TOEFL (minimum score 550 paper-based; 79 iBT), Michigan English Language Assessment Battery (minimum score 82); Recommended—IELTS (minimum score 7). Electronic applications accepted.

Oklahoma State University, College of Agricultural Science and Natural Resources, Department of Natural Resource Ecology and Management, Stillwater, OK 74078. Offers M Ag, MS, PhD. *Faculty:* 24 full-time (5 women), 1 part-time/adjunct (0 women). *Students:* 5 full-time (1 woman), 53 part-time (17 women); includes 9 minority (1 American Indian or Alaska Native, non-Hispanic/Latino; 1 Hispanic/Latino; 7 Two or more races, non-Hispanic/Latino), 8 international. Average age 29. 6 applicants, 83% accepted, 5 enrolled. In 2015, 13 master's, 6 doctorates awarded. *Degree requirements:* For master's, comprehensive exam (for some programs), thesis; for doctorate, comprehensive exam, thesis/dissertation. *Entrance requirements:* For master's and doctorate, GRE or GMAT. Additional exam requirements/recommendations for international students: Required—TOEFL (minimum score 550 paper-based; 79 iBT). *Application deadline:* For fall admission, 3/1 priority date for international students; for spring admission, 8/1 priority date for international students. Applications are processed on a rolling basis. Application fee: $40 ($75 for international students). Electronic applications accepted. *Expenses:* Tuition, state resident: full-time $3528; part-time $196 per credit hour. Tuition, nonresident: full-time $14,144; part-time $785.75 per credit hour. *Required fees:* $1895; $105.25 per credit hour. Tuition and fees vary according to campus/location. *Financial support:* In 2015–16, 43 research assistantships (averaging $17,488 per year), 7 teaching assistantships (averaging $15,958 per year) were awarded; career-related internships or fieldwork, Federal Work-Study, scholarships/grants, health care benefits, tuition waivers (partial), and unspecified assistantships also available. Support available to part-time students. Financial award application deadline: 3/1; financial award applicants required to submit FAFSA. *Faculty research:* Forest ecology, upland bird ecology, forest ecophysiology, urban forestry, molecular forest genetics/biotechnology/tree breeding. *Unit head:* Dr. Jim Ansley, Department Head, 405-744-5438, Fax: 405-744-3530, E-mail: jim.ansley@okstate.edu.
Website: http://nrem.okstate.edu/

Oregon State University, College of Forestry, Program in Forest Ecosystems and Society, Corvallis, OR 97331. Offers forest biology (MF); forest, wildlife and landscape ecology (MF, MS, PhD); genetics and physiology (MF, MS, PhD); integrated social and ecological systems (MF, MS, PhD); restoration and sustainable management (MF, MS, PhD); science of conservation (MF, MS, PhD); silviculture (MF); social science, policy, and natural resources (MF, MS, PhD); soil-plant-atmosphere continuum (MF, MS, PhD); sustainable recreation and tourism (MF, MS). *Program availability:* Part-time. *Faculty:* 28 full-time (12 women), 6 part-time/adjunct (0 women). *Students:* 58 full-time (31 women), 5 part-time (all women); includes 5 minority (1 Black or African American, non-Hispanic/Latino; 1 Asian, non-Hispanic/Latino; 1 Hispanic/Latino; 2 Two or more races, non-Hispanic/Latino), 10 international. Average age 32. 47 applicants, 43% accepted, 12 enrolled. In 2015, 7 master's, 1 doctorate awarded. *Degree requirements:* For master's, thesis (for some programs); for doctorate, thesis/dissertation. *Entrance requirements:* For master's and doctorate, GRE. Additional exam requirements/recommendations for international students: Required—TOEFL (minimum score 80 iBT), IELTS (minimum score 6.5). *Application deadline:* For fall admission, 8/1 for domestic students, 4/1 for international students; for winter admission, 12/1 for domestic students, 7/1 for international students; for spring admission, 2/1 for domestic students, 10/1 for international students; for summer admission, 5/1 for domestic students, 1/1 for international students. Application fee: $75 ($85 for international students). *Expenses:* Tuition, state resident: full-time $12,150; part-time $450 per credit. Tuition, nonresident: full-time $20,952; part-time $776 per credit. *Required fees:* $1572; $1443 per unit. One-time fee: $350. Tuition and fees vary according to course load, campus/location and program. *Financial support:* Fellowships, research assistantships, career-related internships or fieldwork, Federal Work-Study, and institutionally sponsored loans available. Support available to part-time students. *Faculty research:* Ecosystem structure and function, nutrient cycling, biotechnology, vegetation management, integrated forest protection. *Unit head:* Dr. Troy Hall, Department Head, 541-737-8954. *Application contact:* Jessica Bagley, Advisor, 541-737-6556, E-mail: jessica.bagley@oregonstate.edu.
Website: http://fes.forestry.oregonstate.edu/

Oregon State University, College of Forestry, Program in Sustainable Forest Management, Corvallis, OR 97331. Offers engineering for sustainable forestry (MF, MS, PhD); forest biometrics and geomatics (MF, MS, PhD); forest operations planning and management (MF, MS, PhD); forest policy analysis and economics (MF, MS, PhD); forest watershed management (MF, MS, PhD); silviculture, fire, and forest health (MF, MS, PhD). *Program availability:* Part-time. *Faculty:* 16 full-time (2 women), 2 part-time/adjunct (1 woman). *Students:* 42 full-time (8 women), 3 part-time (0 women); includes 1 minority (Hispanic/Latino), 12 international. Average age 31. 40 applicants, 58% accepted, 16 enrolled. In 2015, 15 master's awarded. *Entrance requirements:* For master's and doctorate, GRE. Additional exam requirements/recommendations for international students: Required—TOEFL (minimum score 80 iBT), IELTS (minimum score 6.5). *Application deadline:* For fall admission, 8/1 for domestic students, 4/1 for international students; for winter admission, 12/1 for domestic students, 7/1 for international students; for spring admission, 2/1 for domestic students, 10/1 for international students; for summer admission, 5/1 for domestic students, 1/1 for international students. Application fee: $75 ($85 for international students). *Expenses:* Tuition, state resident: full-time $12,150; part-time $450 per credit. Tuition, nonresident: full-time $20,952; part-time $776 per credit. *Required fees:* $1572; $1443 per unit. One-time fee: $350. Tuition and fees vary according to course load, campus/location and program. *Unit head:* Dr. Claire Montgomery, Professor and Department Head. *Application contact:* Dr. John Sessions, Professor/Chair of Forest Operations Management, 541-737-2818, E-mail: john.sessions@oregonstate.edu.
Website: http://ferm.forestry.oregonstate.edu/academic-programs/graduate-degree

Oregon State University, College of Forestry, Program in Wood Science, Corvallis, OR 97331. Offers biodeterioration and materials protection (MS, PhD); chemistry and chemical processing (MS, PhD); forest products business and marketing (MS, PhD); physics and moisture relations (MS, PhD); process modeling and analysis (MS, PhD); renewable materials sciences and engineered composites (MS, PhD); wood anatomy and quality (MS, PhD); wood engineering and mechanics (MS, PhD). *Program availability:* Part-time. *Faculty:* 12 full-time (0 women), 2 part-time/adjunct (1 woman). *Students:* 30 full-time (10 women), 1 part-time (0 women); includes 4 minority (1 Asian, non-Hispanic/Latino; 1 Hispanic/Latino; 2 Two or more races, non-Hispanic/Latino), 14 international. Average age 29. 15 applicants, 53% accepted, 6 enrolled. In 2015, 6 master's, 2 doctorates awarded. *Degree requirements:* For master's, thesis (for some programs); for doctorate, thesis/dissertation. *Entrance requirements:* For master's and doctorate, GRE General Test, minimum GPA of 3.0 in last 90 hours. Additional exam requirements/recommendations for international students: Required—TOEFL (minimum score 575 paper-based; 93 iBT), IELTS (minimum score 7). *Application deadline:* For fall admission, 8/1 for domestic students, 4/1 for international students; for winter admission, 12/1 for domestic students, 7/1 for international students; for spring admission, 2/1 for domestic students, 10/1 for international students; for summer admission, 5/1 for domestic students, 1/1 for international students. Application fee: $75 ($85 for international students). *Expenses:* Tuition, state resident: full-time $12,150; part-time $450 per credit. Tuition, nonresident: full-time $20,952; part-time $776 per credit. *Required fees:* $1572; $1443 per unit. One-time fee: $350. Tuition and fees vary

according to course load, campus/location and program. *Financial support:* Fellowships, research assistantships, career-related internships or fieldwork, Federal Work-Study, and institutionally sponsored loans available. Support available to part-time students. Financial award application deadline: 12/17. *Faculty research:* Biodeterioration and preservation, timber engineering, process engineering and control, composite materials science, anatomy, chemistry and physical properties. *Unit head:* Dr. Laurence Schimleck, Professor and Department Head. *Application contact:* Jessica King, Graduate Program Coordinator, 541-737-5723, E-mail: woodscience@oregonstate.edu.
Website: http://woodscience.oregonstate.edu/future-graduate-students

Penn State University Park, Graduate School, College of Agricultural Sciences, Department of Ecosystem Science and Management, University Park, PA 16802. Offers forest resources (MS, PhD); soil science (MS, PhD); wildlife and fisheries science (MS, PhD). *Unit head:* Dr. Richard T. Roush, Dean, 814-865-2541, Fax: 814-865-3103. *Application contact:* Lori Stania, Director, Graduate Student Services, 814-865-1795, Fax: 814-863-4627, E-mail: l-gswww@lists.psu.edu.
Website: http://ecosystems.psu.edu/

Purdue University, Graduate School, College of Agriculture, Department of Forestry and Natural Resources, West Lafayette, IN 47907. Offers fisheries and aquatic sciences (MS, MSF, PhD); forest biology (MS, MSF, PhD); natural resource social science (MS, PhD); natural resources social science (MSF); quantitative ecology (MS, MSF, PhD); wildlife science (MS, MSF, PhD); wood products and wood products manufacturing (MS, MSF, PhD). *Degree requirements:* For master's, thesis; for doctorate, thesis/dissertation. *Entrance requirements:* For master's and doctorate, GRE General Test (minimum score: verbal 50th percentile; quantitative 50th percentile; analytical writing 4.0), minimum undergraduate GPA of 3.2 or equivalent. Additional exam requirements/recommendations for international students: Required—TOEFL (minimum score 550 paper-based; 77 iBT). Electronic applications accepted. *Faculty research:* Wildlife management, forest management, forest ecology, forest soils, limnology.

Southern Illinois University Carbondale, Graduate School, College of Agriculture, Department of Forestry, Carbondale, IL 62901-4701. Offers MS. *Program availability:* Part-time. *Faculty:* 9 full-time (0 women). *Students:* 5 full-time (3 women), 22 part-time (6 women); includes 1 minority (Asian, non-Hispanic/Latino), 5 international. Average age 24. 5 applicants, 60% accepted, 3 enrolled. In 2015, 4 master's awarded. *Degree requirements:* For master's, thesis. *Entrance requirements:* For master's, GRE, minimum GPA of 2.7. Additional exam requirements/recommendations for international students: Required—TOEFL. *Application deadline:* For fall admission, 7/9 for domestic students; for spring admission, 11/26 for domestic students; for summer admission, 3/26 for domestic students. Applications are processed on a rolling basis. Application fee: $65. *Financial support:* In 2015–16, 15 students received support, including 7 research assistantships with full tuition reimbursements available, 8 teaching assistantships with full tuition reimbursements available; fellowships with full tuition reimbursements available, career-related internships or fieldwork, Federal Work-Study, institutionally sponsored loans, and tuition waivers (full) also available. Support available to part-time students. *Faculty research:* Forest recreation, forest ecology, remote sensing, forest management and economics. *Unit head:* Dr. Jim Zaczek, Chair, 618-453-7465, E-mail: zaczek@siu.edu. *Application contact:* Patti Cludray, Administrative Clerk, 618-453-3341, E-mail: plc1@siu.edu.

Southern University and Agricultural and Mechanical College, Graduate School, College of Agricultural, Family and Consumer Sciences, Department of Urban Forestry, Baton Rouge, LA 70813. Offers MS. *Degree requirements:* For master's, thesis. *Entrance requirements:* For master's, GRE, minimum GPA of 3.0. Additional exam requirements/recommendations for international students: Required—TOEFL (minimum score 525 paper-based). *Faculty research:* Biology of plant pathogen, water resources, plant pathology.

State University of New York College of Environmental Science and Forestry, Department of Environmental and Forest Biology, Syracuse, NY 13210-2779. Offers applied ecology (MPS); chemical ecology (MPS, MS, PhD); conservation biology (MPS, MS, PhD); ecology (MPS, MS, PhD); entomology (MPS, MS, PhD); environmental interpretation (MPS, MS, PhD); environmental physiology (MPS, MS, PhD); fish and wildlife biology and management (MPS, MS, PhD); forest pathology and mycology (MPS, MS, PhD); plant biotechnology (MPS); plant science and biotechnology (MPS, MS, PhD). *Faculty:* 29 full-time (9 women), 4 part-time/adjunct (3 women). *Students:* 81 full-time (47 women), 57 part-time (24 women); includes 9 minority (1 Black or African American, non-Hispanic/Latino; 2 American Indian or Alaska Native, non-Hispanic/Latino; 1 Asian, non-Hispanic/Latino; 3 Hispanic/Latino; 2 Two or more races, non-Hispanic/Latino), 15 international. Average age 28. 47 applicants, 49% accepted, 15 enrolled. In 2015, 15 master's, 7 doctorates awarded. *Degree requirements:* For master's, thesis (for some programs), capstone seminar; for doctorate, comprehensive exam, thesis/dissertation, capstone seminar. *Entrance requirements:* For master's and doctorate, GRE General Test, minimum GPA of 3.0. Additional exam requirements/recommendations for international students: Required—TOEFL (minimum score 550 paper-based; 80 iBT), IELTS (minimum score 6). *Application deadline:* For fall admission, 2/1 priority date for domestic and international students; for spring admission, 11/1 priority date for domestic and international students. Applications are processed on a rolling basis. Application fee: $60. *Expenses:* Tuition, state resident: full-time $10,870; part-time $453 per credit. Tuition, nonresident: full-time $22,210; part-time $925 per credit. *Required fees:* $1075; $89.22 per credit. *Financial support:* In 2015–16, 4 fellowships with tuition reimbursements, 36 research assistantships with tuition reimbursements, 39 teaching assistantships with tuition reimbursements (averaging $11,490 per year) were awarded; Federal Work-Study, institutionally sponsored loans, scholarships/grants, health care benefits, and unspecified assistantships also available. Financial award application deadline: 6/30. *Faculty research:* Ecology, conservation biology, fish and wildlife biology and management, plant science, entomology. *Total annual research expenditures:* $4.1 million. *Unit head:* Dr. Donald J. Leopold, Chair, 315-470-6760, Fax: 315-470-6934, E-mail: djleopold@esf.edu. *Application contact:* Dr. Danilo D. Fernando, Director, Graduate Program/Associate Professor, 315-470-6746, Fax: 315-470-6934, E-mail: dfernando@esf.edu.
Website: http://www.esf.edu/efb/grad/default.asp

State University of New York College of Environmental Science and Forestry, Department of Forest and Natural Resources Management, Syracuse, NY 13210-2779. Offers ecology and ecosystems (MPS, MS, PhD); economics, governance and human dimensions (MPS, MS, PhD); forest and natural resources management (MPS, MS, PhD); monitoring, analysis and modeling (MPS, MS, PhD). *Accreditation:* SAF. *Faculty:* 34 full-time (9 women), 7 part-time/adjunct (0 women). *Students:* 40 full-time (24 women), 5 part-time (0 women); includes 6 minority (2 American Indian or Alaska Native, non-Hispanic/Latino; 1 Asian, non-Hispanic/Latino; 2 Hispanic/Latino; 1 Two or more races, non-Hispanic/Latino), 10 international. 41 applicants, 68% accepted, 16 enrolled. *Degree requirements:* For master's, thesis (for some programs); for doctorate, comprehensive exam, thesis/dissertation. *Entrance requirements:* For master's and doctorate, GRE General Test, minimum GPA of 3.0. Additional exam requirements/recommendations for international students: Required—TOEFL (minimum score 550 paper-based; 80 iBT), IELTS (minimum score 6). *Application deadline:* For fall admission, 2/1 priority date for domestic and international students; for spring admission, 11/1 priority date for domestic and international students. Applications are processed on a rolling basis. Application fee: $60. *Expenses:* Tuition, state resident: full-time $10,870; part-time $453 per credit. Tuition, nonresident: full-time $22,210; part-time $925 per credit. *Required fees:* $1075; $89.22 per credit. *Financial support:* Fellowships with tuition reimbursements, research assistantships with tuition reimbursements, teaching assistantships with tuition reimbursements, career-related internships or fieldwork, Federal Work-Study, institutionally sponsored loans, scholarships/grants, health care benefits, and unspecified assistantships available. Financial award application deadline: 6/30; financial award applicants required to submit FAFSA. *Faculty research:* Silviculture recreation management, tree improvement, operations management, economics. *Unit head:* Dr. David Newman, Chair, 315-470-6534, Fax: 315-470-6535. *Application contact:* Scott Shannon, Dean, Instruction and Graduate Studies, 315-470-6599, Fax: 315-470-6978, E-mail: esfgrad@esf.edu.
Website: http://www.esf.edu/fnrm/

State University of New York College of Environmental Science and Forestry, Department of Sustainable Construction Management and Engineering, Syracuse, NY 13210-2779. Offers construction management (MPS, MS, PhD); sustainable construction (MPS, MS, PhD); wood science (MPS, MS, PhD). *Students:* 7 full-time (3 women), 4 part-time (2 women); includes 1 minority (Hispanic/Latino), 4 international. 12 applicants, 42% accepted, 2 enrolled. *Degree requirements:* For master's, thesis (for some programs); for doctorate, comprehensive exam, thesis/dissertation. *Entrance requirements:* For master's and doctorate, GRE General Test, minimum GPA of 3.0. Additional exam requirements/recommendations for international students: Required—TOEFL (minimum score 550 paper-based; 80 iBT), IELTS (minimum score 6). *Application deadline:* For fall admission, 2/1 priority date for domestic and international students; for spring admission, 11/1 priority date for domestic and international students. Applications are processed on a rolling basis. Application fee: $60. *Expenses:* Tuition, state resident: full-time $10,870; part-time $453 per credit. Tuition, nonresident: full-time $22,210; part-time $925 per credit. *Required fees:* $1075; $89.22 per credit. *Financial support:* Fellowships with full tuition reimbursements, research assistantships with full tuition reimbursements, teaching assistantships with full tuition reimbursements, career-related internships or fieldwork, Federal Work-Study, institutionally sponsored loans, scholarships/grants, health care benefits, and unspecified assistantships available. Financial award application deadline: 6/30; financial award applicants required to submit FAFSA. *Unit head:* Dr. Susan E. Anagnost, Chair, 315-470-6880, Fax: 315-470-6879, E-mail: seanagno@esf.edu. *Application contact:* Dr. Dudley J. Raynal, Dean, Instruction and Graduate Studies, 315-470-6599, Fax: 315-470-6879, E-mail: esfgrad@esf.edu.
Website: http://www.esf.edu/scme/

Stephen F. Austin State University, Graduate School, College of Forestry and Agriculture, Department of Forestry, Nacogdoches, TX 75962. Offers MF, MS, PhD. *Program availability:* Part-time. *Degree requirements:* For master's, thesis; for doctorate, thesis/dissertation. *Entrance requirements:* For master's and doctorate, GRE General Test. Additional exam requirements/recommendations for international students: Required—TOEFL. *Faculty research:* Wildlife management, basic plant science, forest recreation, multipurpose land management.

Texas A&M University, College of Agriculture and Life Sciences, Department of Ecosystem Science and Management, College Station, TX 77843. Offers ecosystem science and management (M Agr, MS, PhD); forestry (MS, PhD); rangeland ecology and management (M Agr, MS, PhD). *Program availability:* Part-time. *Faculty:* 23. *Students:* 51 full-time (26 women), 24 part-time (12 women); includes 17 minority (1 Black or African American, non-Hispanic/Latino; 4 Asian, non-Hispanic/Latino; 9 Hispanic/Latino; 3 Two or more races, non-Hispanic/Latino), 21 international. Average age 32. 16 applicants, 94% accepted, 10 enrolled. In 2015, 10 master's, 6 doctorates awarded. Terminal master's awarded for partial completion of doctoral program. *Degree requirements:* For master's, thesis (for some programs); for doctorate, thesis/dissertation. *Entrance requirements:* For master's and doctorate, GRE General Test. Additional exam requirements/recommendations for international students: Required—TOEFL (minimum score 550 paper-based; 80 iBT), IELTS (minimum score 6), PTE (minimum score 53). *Application deadline:* For fall admission, 3/1 priority date for domestic students; for spring admission, 10/15 priority date for domestic students. Applications are processed on a rolling basis. Application fee: $50 ($90 for international students). Electronic applications accepted. *Expenses:* Contact institution. *Financial support:* In 2015–16, 65 students received support, including 12 fellowships with tuition reimbursements available (averaging $14,063 per year), 26 research assistantships with tuition reimbursements available (averaging $7,800 per year), 24 teaching assistantships with tuition reimbursements available (averaging $7,517 per year); career-related internships or fieldwork, institutionally sponsored loans, scholarships/grants, traineeships, health care benefits, tuition waivers (full and partial), and unspecified assistantships also available. Support available to part-time students. Financial award application deadline: 3/15; financial award applicants required to submit FAFSA. *Faculty research:* Expert systems, geographic information systems, economics, biology, genetics. *Unit head:* Dr. Kathleen Kavanagh, Professor and Department Head, 979-845-5000, Fax: 979-845-6049, E-mail: katyk@tamu.edu. *Application contact:* Heather Haliburton Janke, Senior Academic Advisor II, 979-862-8993, Fax: 979-845-6049, E-mail: hjanke@tamu.edu.
Website: http://essm.tamu.edu

Tropical Agriculture Research and Higher Education Center, Graduate School, Turrialba, Costa Rica. Offers agribusiness management (MS); agroforestry systems (PhD); development practices (MS); ecological agriculture (MS); environmental socioeconomics (MS); forestry in tropical and subtropical zones (PhD); integrated watershed management (MS); international sustainable tourism (MS); management and conservation of tropical rainforests and biodiversity (MS); tropical agriculture (PhD); tropical agroforestry (MS). *Entrance requirements:* For master's, GRE, 2 years of related professional experience, letters of recommendation; for doctorate, GRE, 4 letters of recommendation, letter of support from employing organization, master's degree in agronomy, biological sciences, forestry, natural resources or related field. Additional exam requirements/recommendations for international students: Required—TOEFL (minimum score 550 paper-based). Electronic applications accepted. *Faculty research:* Biodiversity in fragmented landscapes, ecosystem management, integrated pest management, environmental livestock production, biotechnology carbon balances in diverse land uses.

Université du Québec en Abitibi-Témiscamingue, Graduate Programs, Program in Environmental Sciences, Rouyn-Noranda, QC J9X 5E4, Canada. Offers biology (MS); environmental sciences (PhD); sustainable forest ecosystem management (MS).

Université Laval, Faculty of Forestry, Geography and Geomatics, Department of Wood and Forest Sciences, Programs in Forestry Sciences, Québec, QC G1K 7P4, Canada. Offers M Sc, PhD. Terminal master's awarded for partial completion of doctoral program. *Degree requirements:* For master's, thesis (for some programs); for doctorate, comprehensive exam, thesis/dissertation. *Entrance requirements:* For master's and doctorate, knowledge of French. Additional exam requirements/recommendations for international students: Required—TOEIC or TOEFL. Electronic applications accepted.

Université Laval, Faculty of Forestry, Geography and Geomatics, Department of Wood and Forest Sciences, Programs in Wood Sciences, Québec, QC G1K 7P4, Canada. Offers M Sc, PhD. Terminal master's awarded for partial completion of doctoral program. *Degree requirements:* For master's, thesis; for doctorate, comprehensive exam, thesis/dissertation. *Entrance requirements:* For master's and doctorate, knowledge of French. Electronic applications accepted.

Université Laval, Faculty of Forestry, Geography and Geomatics, Program in Agroforestry, Québec, QC G1K 7P4, Canada. Offers M Sc. *Degree requirements:* For master's, thesis (for some programs). *Entrance requirements:* For master's, English exam (comprehension of English), knowledge of French, knowledge of a third language. Electronic applications accepted.

University of Alberta, Faculty of Graduate Studies and Research, Department of Rural Economy, Edmonton, AB T6G 2E1, Canada. Offers agricultural economics (M Ag, M Sc, PhD); forest economics (M Ag, M Sc, PhD); rural sociology (M Ag, M Sc); MBA/M Ag. *Program availability:* Part-time. *Degree requirements:* For doctorate, thesis/dissertation. *Entrance requirements:* Additional exam requirements/recommendations for international students: Required—TOEFL. *Faculty research:* Agroforestry, development, extension education, marketing and trade, natural resources and environment, policy, production economics.

The University of Arizona, College of Agriculture and Life Sciences, School of Natural Resources and the Environment, Watershed Resources Program, Tucson, AZ 85721. Offers water, society, and policy (MS); watershed management (MS, PhD). *Degree requirements:* For master's, thesis; for doctorate, comprehensive exam, thesis/dissertation. *Entrance requirements:* For master's, GRE General Test, minimum GPA of 3.0, 3 letters of recommendation; for doctorate, GRE General Test, minimum GPA of 3.0, 3 letters of recommendation, MA or MS. Additional exam requirements/recommendations for international students: Required—TOEFL (minimum score 550 paper-based; 79 iBT). Electronic applications accepted. *Faculty research:* Forest fuel characteristics, prescribed fire, tree ring-fire scar analysis, erosion, sedimentation.

University of Arkansas at Monticello, School of Forest Resources, Monticello, AR 71656. Offers MS. *Program availability:* Part-time. *Degree requirements:* For master's, comprehensive exam, thesis. *Entrance requirements:* For master's, GRE General Test, minimum GPA of 2.7. Additional exam requirements/recommendations for international students: Required—TOEFL (minimum score 550 paper-based). Electronic applications accepted. *Faculty research:* Geographic information systems/remote sensing, forest ecology, wildlife ecology and management.

The University of British Columbia, Faculty of Forestry, Vancouver, BC V6T 1Z1, Canada. Offers M Sc, MA Sc, MF, MSFM, PhD. *Degree requirements:* For master's, thesis (for some programs); for doctorate, comprehensive exam, thesis/dissertation. *Entrance requirements:* Additional exam requirements/recommendations for international students: Required—TOEFL (minimum score 100 iBT). Electronic applications accepted. *Faculty research:* Forest and conservation sciences, forest resources management, forest operations, wood science, sustainable forest management.

University of California, Berkeley, Graduate Division, College of Natural Resources, Department of Environmental Science, Policy, and Management, Berkeley, CA 94720-1500. Offers environmental science, policy, and management (MS, PhD); forestry (MF). Terminal master's awarded for partial completion of doctoral program. *Degree requirements:* For master's, thesis optional; for doctorate, thesis/dissertation, qualifying exam. *Entrance requirements:* For master's and doctorate, GRE General Test, minimum GPA of 3.0, 3 letters of recommendation. Additional exam requirements/recommendations for international students: Required—TOEFL. Electronic applications accepted. *Faculty research:* Biology and ecology of insects; ecosystem function and environmental issues of soils; plant health/interactions from molecular to ecosystem levels; range management and ecology; forest and resource policy, sustainability, and management.

University of Florida, Graduate School, College of Agricultural and Life Sciences, School of Forest Resources and Conservation, Gainesville, FL 32611. Offers fisheries and aquatic sciences (MFAS, MS, PhD), including ecological restoration (MFAS, MFRC, MS, PhD), geographic information systems (MFAS, MFRC, MS, PhD), natural resource policy and administration (MFAS, MFRC, MS, PhD), wetland sciences (MFAS, MFRC, MS, PhD); forest resources and conservation (MFRC, MS, PhD), including agroforestry, ecological restoration (MFAS, MFRC, MS, PhD), geographic information systems (MFAS, MFRC, MS, PhD), geomatics, hydrologic sciences (MS, PhD), natural resource policy and administration (MFAS, MFRC, MS, PhD), toxicology (PhD), tropical conservation and development, wetland sciences (MFAS, MFRC, MS, PhD); JD/MFRC; JD/MS; JD/PhD. *Program availability:* Part-time, evening/weekend, online learning. *Faculty:* 38 full-time, 10 part-time/adjunct. *Students:* 60 full-time (24 women), 57 part-time (31 women); includes 13 minority (5 Black or African American, non-Hispanic/Latino; 1 American Indian or Alaska Native, non-Hispanic/Latino; 1 Asian, non-Hispanic/Latino; 6 Hispanic/Latino), 33 international. Average age 33. 64 applicants, 59% accepted, 32 enrolled. In 2015, 25 master's, 5 doctorates awarded. Terminal master's awarded for partial completion of doctoral program. *Degree requirements:* For master's, comprehensive exam, thesis optional, project (for MFRC); for doctorate, comprehensive exam, thesis/dissertation. *Entrance requirements:* For master's, GRE General Test, minimum GPA of 3.0, curriculum vitae, 3 letters of recommendation; for doctorate, GRE General Test, minimum GPA of 3.25, curriculum vitae, 3 letters of recommendation. Additional exam requirements/recommendations for international students: Required—TOEFL (minimum score 550 paper-based; 80 iBT), IELTS (minimum score 6). *Application deadline:* For fall admission, 1/1 priority date for domestic students, 1/1 for international students; for spring admission, 9/1 for domestic and international students. Applications are processed on a rolling basis. Application fee: $30. Electronic applications accepted. *Financial support:* In 2015–16, 2 fellowships, 71 research assistantships, 1 teaching assistantship were awarded; Federal Work-Study and institutionally sponsored loans also available. Support available to part-time students. Financial award application deadline: 1/3; financial award applicants required to submit FAFSA. *Faculty research:* Quantitative and integrative fisheries science, ecology and management of aquatic systems, finfish, invertebrate and ornamental aquaculture, aquatic animal health, geomatics and GIS, natural resource conservation, tropical forestry, economics and policy, environmental education, forest biology and ecology, forest management, hydrology, silviculture. *Total annual research expenditures:* $17 million. *Unit head:* Tim White, PhD, School of Forest Resources and Conservation Director, 352-846-0850, Fax: 352-392-1707, E-mail: tlwhite@ufl.edu. *Application contact:* Bill Linberg, PhD, Graduate Coordinator for Fisheries and Aquatic Sciences, 352-273-3616, Fax: 352-392-1707, E-mail: wjl@ufl.edu.
Website: http://www.sfrc.ufl.edu/

University of Georgia, School of Forestry and Natural Resources, Athens, GA 30602. Offers MFR, MS, PhD. *Degree requirements:* For master's, thesis (MS); for doctorate, one foreign language, thesis/dissertation. *Entrance requirements:* For master's and doctorate, GRE General Test. Electronic applications accepted.

University of Kentucky, Graduate School, College of Agriculture, Food and Environment, Program in Forestry, Lexington, KY 40506-0032. Offers MSFOR. *Degree requirements:* For master's, comprehensive exam, thesis optional. *Entrance requirements:* For master's, GRE General Test, minimum undergraduate GPA of 2.75. Additional exam requirements/recommendations for international students: Required—TOEFL (minimum score 550 paper-based). Electronic applications accepted. *Faculty research:* Forest ecology, silviculture, watershed management, forest products utilization, wildlife habitat management.

University of Maine, Graduate School, College of Natural Sciences, Forestry, and Agriculture, School of Forest Resources, Orono, ME 04469. Offers forest resources (MS, PhD); forestry (MF). *Accreditation:* SAF (one or more programs are accredited). *Program availability:* Part-time. *Faculty:* 28 full-time (7 women), 37 part-time/adjunct (8 women). *Students:* 42 full-time (15 women), 1 part-time (0 women); includes 4 minority (1 Black or African American, non-Hispanic/Latino; 2 American Indian or Alaska Native, non-Hispanic/Latino; 1 Hispanic/Latino), 9 international. Average age 30. 35 applicants, 86% accepted, 12 enrolled. In 2015, 10 master's, 3 doctorates awarded. Terminal master's awarded for partial completion of doctoral program. *Degree requirements:* For master's, thesis; for doctorate, one foreign language, comprehensive exam, thesis/dissertation. *Entrance requirements:* For master's and doctorate, GRE General Test. Additional exam requirements/recommendations for international students: Required—TOEFL. *Application deadline:* For fall admission, 1/15 priority date for domestic students; for spring admission, 10/15 for domestic students; for summer admission, 4/15 for domestic students. Applications are processed on a rolling basis. Application fee: $65. Electronic applications accepted. *Financial support:* In 2015–16, 34 students received support, including 28 research assistantships with full tuition reimbursements available (averaging $14,600 per year), 6 teaching assistantships with full tuition reimbursements available (averaging $14,600 per year); career-related internships or fieldwork, Federal Work-Study, and institutionally sponsored loans also available. Financial award application deadline: 3/1. *Faculty research:* Silviculture, forest ecology, climate change, sustainable tourism, Nano cellulose composites. *Total annual research expenditures:* $3.2 million. *Unit head:* Dr. Stephen Shaler, Director, 207-581-4737. *Application contact:* Scott G. Delcourt, Assistant Vice President for Graduate Studies and Senior Associate Dean, 207-581-3291, Fax: 207-581-3232,
E-mail: graduate@maine.edu.
Website: http://www.forest.umaine.edu/

University of Massachusetts Amherst, Graduate School, College of Natural Sciences, Department of Environmental Conservation, Amherst, MA 01003. Offers building systems (MS, PhD); environmental policy and human dimensions (MS, PhD); forest resources (MS, PhD); sustainability science (MS); water, wetlands and watersheds (MS, PhD); wildlife and fisheries conservation (MS, PhD). *Program availability:* Part-time. Terminal master's awarded for partial completion of doctoral program. *Degree requirements:* For master's, thesis or alternative; for doctorate, comprehensive exam, thesis/dissertation. *Entrance requirements:* For master's and doctorate, GRE General Test. Additional exam requirements/recommendations for international students: Required—TOEFL (minimum score 550 paper-based; 80 iBT), IELTS (minimum score 6.5). Electronic applications accepted.

University of Minnesota, Twin Cities Campus, Graduate School, College of Food, Agricultural and Natural Resource Sciences, Program in Natural Resources Science and Management, St. Paul, MN 55108. Offers assessment, monitoring, and geospatial analysis (MS, PhD); economics, policy, management, and society (MS, PhD); forest hydrology and watershed management (MS, PhD); forest products (MS, PhD); forests: biology, ecology, conservation, and management (MS, PhD); natural resources science and management (MS, PhD); paper science and engineering (MS, PhD); recreation resources, tourism, and environmental education (MS, PhD); wildlife ecology and management (MS, PhD). *Program availability:* Part-time. *Faculty:* 71 full-time (28 women), 55 part-time/adjunct (7 women). *Students:* 80 full-time (45 women), 16 part-time (9 women); includes 5 minority (1 Black or African American, non-Hispanic/Latino; 2 American Indian or Alaska Native, non-Hispanic/Latino; 2 Asian, non-Hispanic/Latino), 8 international. 81 applicants, 52% accepted, 31 enrolled. In 2015, 25 master's, 8 doctorates awarded. Terminal master's awarded for partial completion of doctoral program. *Degree requirements:* For master's, comprehensive exam, thesis; for doctorate, comprehensive exam, thesis/dissertation. *Entrance requirements:* For master's and doctorate, GRE General Test. Additional exam requirements/recommendations for international students: Required—TOEFL (minimum score 550 paper-based; 79 iBT), IELTS (minimum score 6.5). *Application deadline:* For fall admission, 12/16 priority date for domestic and international students; for spring admission, 10/15 for domestic and international students. Applications are processed on a rolling basis. Application fee: $75 ($95 for international students). Electronic applications accepted. *Financial support:* In 2015–16, fellowships with full tuition reimbursements (averaging $40,000 per year), research assistantships with full tuition reimbursements (averaging $40,000 per year), teaching assistantships with full tuition reimbursements (averaging $40,000 per year) were awarded; scholarships/grants, health care benefits, tuition waivers (full and partial), and unspecified assistantships also available. *Faculty research:* Forest hydrology, biology, ecology, conservation, and management; recreation resources and environmental education; wildlife ecology; economics, policy, and society; geographic information systems (GIS); and forest products and paper science. *Unit head:* Dr. Michael Kilgore, Director of Graduate Studies, 612-624-6298, E-mail: mkilgore@umn.edu. *Application contact:* Toni Wheeler, Graduate Program Coordinator, 612-624-7683, Fax: 612-625-5212,
E-mail: twheeler@umn.edu.
Website: http://www.nrsm.umn.edu

University of Missouri, Office of Research and Graduate Studies, School of Natural Resources, Department of Forestry, Columbia, MO 65211. Offers MS, PhD. Terminal master's awarded for partial completion of doctoral program. *Degree requirements:* For master's, thesis; for doctorate, thesis/dissertation. *Entrance requirements:* For master's and doctorate, GRE General Test, minimum GPA of 3.0. Additional exam requirements/recommendations for international students: Required—TOEFL (minimum score 500 paper-based; 61 iBT). Electronic applications accepted. *Faculty research:* Spatial analysis of natural resource-based industries; forest industry corporate responsibility and environmental stewardship programs; consumer preferences for forest products; forest sector economic development; development of improved nut tree cultivars for use in agroforestry-based systems; hardwood tree improvement; tree growth-wood quality interactions; evaluation and development of forest management guidelines to improve forest health, sustainability and value; agroforestry.

University of Missouri, Office of Research and Graduate Studies, School of Natural Resources, Program in Agroforestry, Columbia, MO 65211. Offers MS, Certificate.

University of Montana, Graduate School, College of Forestry and Conservation, Missoula, MT 59812-0002. Offers fish and wildlife biology (PhD); forest and conservation sciences (PhD); forestry (MS); recreation management (MS); resource conservation (MS); systems ecology (MS, PhD); wildlife biology (MS). *Degree requirements:* For doctorate, thesis/dissertation. *Entrance requirements:* For master's and doctorate, GRE General Test. Additional exam requirements/recommendations for international students: Required—TOEFL (minimum score 575 paper-based).

University of New Brunswick Fredericton, School of Graduate Studies, Faculty of Forestry and Environmental Management, Fredericton, NB E3B 5A3, Canada. Offers ecological foundations of forest management (PhD); environmental management (MEM); forest engineering (M Sc FE, MFE); forest products marketing (MBA); forest resources (M Sc F, MF, PhD). *Program availability:* Part-time. *Faculty:* 21 full-time (1 woman), 69 part-time/adjunct (13 women). *Students:* 58 full-time (21 women), 17 part-time (5 women). In 2015, 13 master's, 3 doctorates awarded. *Degree requirements:* For master's, thesis; for doctorate, thesis/dissertation. *Entrance requirements:* For master's and doctorate, minimum GPA of 3.0. Additional exam requirements/recommendations for international students: Required—TOEFL (minimum score 550 paper-based; 80 iBT), IELTS (minimum score 7), TWE (minimum score 4). *Application deadline:* For fall admission, 3/1 for domestic students. Applications are processed on a rolling basis. Application fee: $50 Canadian dollars. Electronic applications accepted. *Financial support:* In 2015–16, 98 research assistantships, 36 teaching assistantships were awarded; fellowships also available. *Faculty research:* Forest machines, soils, and ecosystems; integrated forest management; forest meteorology; wood engineering; stream ecosystems dynamics; forest and natural resources policy; forest operations planning; wood technology and mechanics; forest road construction and engineering; forest, wildlife, insect, bird, and fire ecology; remote sensing; insect impacts; silviculture; LiDAR analytics; integrated pest management; forest tree genetics; genetic resource conservation and sustainable management. *Unit head:* Dr. Marek Krasowski, Director of Graduate Studies, 506-453-4915, Fax: 506-453-3538, E-mail: marek@unb.ca. *Application contact:* Faith Sharpe, Graduate Secretary, 506-458-7520, Fax: 506-453-3538, E-mail: fsharpe@unb.ca.
Website: http://go.unb.ca/gradprograms

University of New Hampshire, Graduate School, College of Life Sciences and Agriculture, Department of Natural Resources and the Environment, Durham, NH 03824. Offers environmental conservation (MS); forestry (MS); integrated coastal ecosystem science, policy and management (MS); natural resources (MS); soil and water resource management (MS); wildlife and conservation biology (MS). *Program availability:* Part-time. *Degree requirements:* For master's, thesis or alternative. *Entrance requirements:* For master's, GRE General Test. Additional exam requirements/recommendations for international students: Required—TOEFL (minimum score 550 paper-based; 80 iBT). Electronic applications accepted.

The University of Tennessee, Graduate School, College of Agricultural Sciences and Natural Resources, Department of Forestry, Wildlife, and Fisheries, Program in Forestry, Knoxville, TN 37996. Offers MS. *Degree requirements:* For master's, thesis or alternative. *Entrance requirements:* For master's, GRE General Test, minimum GPA of 2.7. Additional exam requirements/recommendations for international students: Required—TOEFL. Electronic applications accepted.

University of Toronto, School of Graduate Studies, Faculty of Forestry, Toronto, ON M5S 1A1, Canada. Offers M Sc F, MFC, PhD. *Degree requirements:* For master's, comprehensive exam, thesis, oral thesis/research paper defense; for doctorate, thesis/dissertation, oral defense of thesis. *Entrance requirements:* For master's, bachelor's degree in a related area, minimum B average in final year (M Sc F), final 2 years (MFC); resume, 3 letters of reference; for doctorate, writing sample, minimum A- average, master's in a related area, 3 letters of reference, resume. Additional exam requirements/recommendations for international students: Required—TOEFL (minimum score 580 paper-based; 93 iBT), TWE (minimum score 5). Electronic applications accepted.

University of Vermont, Graduate College, The Rubenstein School of Environment and Natural Resources, Program in Natural Resources, Burlington, VT 05405. Offers natural resources (MS, PhD), including aquatic ecology and watershed science (MS), environment thought and culture (MS), environment, science and public affairs (MS), forestry (MS). *Degree requirements:* For master's, thesis or alternative; for doctorate, thesis/dissertation. *Entrance requirements:* For master's and doctorate, GRE General Test. Additional exam requirements/recommendations for international students: Required—TOEFL (minimum score 550 paper-based; 80 iBT). Electronic applications accepted.

University of Washington, Graduate School, College of the Environment, School of Forest Resources, Seattle, WA 98195. Offers bioresource science and engineering (MS, PhD); environmental horticulture (MEH); forest ecology (MS, PhD); forest management (MFR); forest soils (MS, PhD); restoration ecology (MS, PhD); restoration ecology and environmental horticulture (MS, PhD); social sciences (MS, PhD); sustainable resource management (MS, PhD); wildlife science (MS, PhD); MFR/MAIS; MPA/MS. *Accreditation:* SAF. *Program availability:* Part-time. *Degree requirements:* For master's, thesis; for doctorate, comprehensive exam, thesis/dissertation. *Entrance requirements:* For master's and doctorate, GRE, minimum GPA of 3.0. Additional exam requirements/recommendations for international students: Required—TOEFL. Electronic applications accepted. *Faculty research:* Ecosystem analysis, silviculture and forest protection, paper science and engineering, environmental horticulture and urban forestry, natural resource policy and economics, restoration ecology and environment horticulture, conservation, human dimensions, wildlife, bioresource science and engineering.

University of Wisconsin–Madison, Graduate School, College of Agricultural and Life Sciences, Department of Forest and Wildlife Ecology, Program in Forestry, Madison, WI 53706-1380. Offers MS, PhD. *Expenses:* Tuition, state resident: full-time $5364. Tuition, nonresident: full-time $12,027. *Required fees:* $571. Tuition and fees vary according to campus/location, program and reciprocity agreements.

Utah State University, School of Graduate Studies, College of Natural Resources, Department of Wildland Resources, Logan, UT 84322. Offers ecology (MS, PhD); forestry (MS, PhD); range science (MS, PhD); wildlife biology (MS, PhD). *Program availability:* Part-time. *Degree requirements:* For master's, thesis; for doctorate, comprehensive exam, thesis/dissertation. *Entrance requirements:* For master's and doctorate, GRE General Test, minimum GPA of 3.0. Additional exam requirements/recommendations for international students: Required—TOEFL. *Faculty research:* Range plant ecophysiology, plant community ecology, ruminant nutrition, population ecology.

Virginia Polytechnic Institute and State University, Graduate School, College of Natural Resources and Environment, Blacksburg, VA 24061. Offers fisheries and wildlife (MS, PhD); forestry and forest products (MF, MS, PhD); geography (MS); geospatial and environmental analysis (PhD); natural resources (MNR). *Degree requirements:* For master's, comprehensive exam (for some programs), thesis (for some programs); for doctorate, comprehensive exam (for some programs), thesis/dissertation (for some programs). *Entrance requirements:* For master's and doctorate, GRE/GMAT (may vary by department). Additional exam requirements/recommendations for international students: Required—TOEFL (minimum score 550 paper-based). Electronic applications accepted.

West Virginia University, Davis College of Agriculture, Forestry and Consumer Sciences, Division of Forestry, Program in Forest Resource Science, Morgantown, WV 26506. Offers PhD. *Degree requirements:* For doctorate, comprehensive exam, thesis/dissertation. *Entrance requirements:* For doctorate, GRE, minimum GPA of 3.0. Additional exam requirements/recommendations for international students: Required—TOEFL. *Expenses:* Tuition, state resident: full-time $8568. Tuition, nonresident: full-time $22,140. Tuition and fees vary according to program. *Faculty research:* Impact of management on wildlife and fish, forest sampling designs, forest economics and policy, oak regeneration.

West Virginia University, Davis College of Agriculture, Forestry and Consumer Sciences, Division of Forestry, Program in Forestry, Morgantown, WV 26506. Offers MSF. *Degree requirements:* For master's, thesis. *Entrance requirements:* For master's, GRE, minimum GPA of 3.0. Additional exam requirements/recommendations for international students: Required—TOEFL. *Expenses:* Tuition, state resident: full-time $8568. Tuition, nonresident: full-time $22,140. Tuition and fees vary according to program. *Faculty research:* Health and productivity on Appalachian forests, wood industries in Appalachian forests, role of forestry in regional economics.

Yale University, Graduate School of Arts and Sciences, Department of Forestry and Environmental Studies, New Haven, CT 06520. Offers environmental sciences (PhD); forestry (PhD). *Degree requirements:* For doctorate, thesis/dissertation. *Entrance requirements:* For doctorate, GRE General Test.

Yale University, School of Forestry and Environmental Studies, New Haven, CT 06511. Offers environmental management (MEM), including business and the environment, ecosystem and conservation management, energy and the environment, environmental policy analysis; environmental science (MES); forest science (MFS); forestry (MF); forestry and environmental studies (PhD); JD/MEM; MBA/MEM; MBA/MF; MEM/M Arch; MEM/M Div; MEM/MA; MEM/MAR; MEM/MPH. *Accreditation:* SAF (one or more programs are accredited). *Program availability:* Part-time. *Faculty:* 32 full-time, 50 part-time/adjunct. *Students:* 300 full-time. Average age 27. 600 applicants, 150 enrolled. In 2015, 152 master's, 15 doctorates awarded. Terminal master's awarded for partial completion of doctoral program. *Degree requirements:* For master's, internship and capstone project (for MEM and MF); research project and thesis (for MES and MFS); for doctorate, comprehensive exam, thesis/dissertation. *Entrance requirements:* For master's, GRE General Test, GMAT or LSAT; for doctorate, GRE General Test. Additional exam requirements/recommendations for international students: Required—TOEFL (minimum score 600 paper-based; 100 iBT) or IELTS (minimum score 7). *Application deadline:* For fall admission, 12/15 priority date for domestic and international students. Application fee: $80. Electronic applications accepted. *Expenses:* Contact institution. *Financial support:* In 2015–16, 240 students received support. Fellowships, research assistantships, teaching assistantships, career-related internships or fieldwork, Federal Work-Study, institutionally sponsored loans, scholarships/grants, and health care benefits available. Support available to part-time students. Financial award application deadline: 2/15; financial award applicants required to submit FAFSA. *Faculty research:* Environmental policy, social ecology, industrial environmental management, forestry, environmental health, urban ecology, water science policy. *Unit head:* Peter Crane, Dean, School of Forestry and Environmental Studies, 203-432-5109, Fax: 203-432-3051. *Application contact:* Rebecca DeSalvo, Director of Enrollment Management & Diversity Initiatives, 800-825-0330, Fax: 203-432-5528, E-mail: fesinfo@yale.edu.
Website: http://environment.yale.edu

Natural Resources

American University, School of International Service, Washington, DC 20016-8071. Offers comparative and regional studies (Certificate); cross-cultural communication (Certificate); development management (MS); ethics, peace, and global affairs (MA); European studies (Certificate); global environmental policy (MA, Certificate); global information technology (Certificate); international affairs (MA), including comparative and international disability policy, comparative and regional studies, international economic relations, international politics, natural resources and sustainable development, U.S. foreign policy; international arts management (Certificate); international communication (MA, Certificate); international development (MA); international economic policy (Certificate); international economic relations (Certificate); international economics (MA); international media (MA); international peace and conflict resolution (MA, Certificate); international politics (Certificate); international relations (MA, PhD); international service (MIS); peacebuilding (Certificate); social enterprise (MA); the Americas (Certificate); United States foreign policy (Certificate); JD/MA. *Program availability:* Part-time, evening/weekend, 100% online. *Faculty:* 118 full-time (53 women), 60 part-time/adjunct (24 women). *Students:* 578 full-time (351 women), 502 part-time (295 women); includes 268 minority (96 Black or African American, non-Hispanic/Latino; 9 American Indian or Alaska Native, non-Hispanic/Latino; 59 Asian, non-Hispanic/Latino; 89 Hispanic/Latino; 1 Native Hawaiian or other Pacific Islander, non-Hispanic/Latino; 14 Two or more races, non-Hispanic/Latino), 140 international. Average age 28. 1,810 applicants, 80% accepted, 415 enrolled. In 2015, 399 master's, 7 doctorates, 7 other advanced degrees awarded. Terminal master's awarded for partial completion of doctoral program. *Degree requirements:* For master's, one foreign language, comprehensive exam, thesis or alternative; for doctorate, one foreign language, comprehensive exam, thesis/dissertation. *Entrance requirements:* For master's, GRE, transcripts, resume, 2 letters of recommendation, statement of purpose; for doctorate, GRE, transcripts, resume, 3 letters of recommendation, statement of purpose. Additional exam requirements/recommendations for international students:

Natural Resources

Required—TOEFL (minimum score 600 paper-based; 100 iBT). *Application deadline:* For fall admission, 1/15 for domestic students; for spring admission, 10/1 for domestic students, 9/15 for international students. Application fee: $55. Electronic applications accepted. *Expenses:* $27,468 per year full-time tuition, $1,526 per credit hour; $1,930 per year full-time fees. *Financial support:* Application deadline: 1/15. *Unit head:* Dr. James Goldgeier, Dean, 202-885-1603, Fax: 202-885-2494, E-mail: goldgeier@american.edu. *Application contact:* Jia Jiang, Associate Director, Graduate Education Enrollment, 202-885-1689, Fax: 202-885-1109, E-mail: jiang@american.edu.
Website: http://www.american.edu/sis/

Auburn University, Graduate School, School of Forestry and Wildlife Sciences, Auburn University, AL 36849. Offers forest economics (PhD); forestry (MS, PhD); natural resource conservation (MNR); wildlife sciences (MS, PhD). *Accreditation:* SAF. *Program availability:* Part-time. *Faculty:* 30 full-time (7 women), 2 part-time/adjunct (1 woman). *Students:* 36 full-time (15 women), 30 part-time (11 women); includes 2 minority (both Black or African American, non-Hispanic/Latino), 26 international. Average age 28. 27 applicants, 52% accepted, 11 enrolled. In 2015, 13 master's, 4 doctorates awarded. *Degree requirements:* For master's, thesis (MS); for doctorate, thesis/dissertation. *Entrance requirements:* For master's and doctorate, GRE General Test. *Application deadline:* Applications are processed on a rolling basis. Application fee: $50 ($60 for international students). Electronic applications accepted. *Expenses:* Tuition, state resident: full-time $8802; part-time $489 per credit hour. Tuition, nonresident: full-time $26,406; part-time $1467 per credit hour. *Required fees:* $808 per semester. Tuition and fees vary according to degree level and program. *Financial support:* Fellowships, research assistantships, teaching assistantships, and Federal Work-Study available. Support available to part-time students. Financial award application deadline: 3/15; financial award applicants required to submit FAFSA. *Faculty research:* Forest nursery management, silviculture and vegetation management, biological processes and ecological relationships, growth and yield of plantations and natural stands, urban forestry, forest taxation, law and policy. *Unit head:* Dr. Graeme Lockaby, Dean, 334-844-4000, Fax: 334-844-1084, E-mail: brinker@forestry.auburn.edu. *Application contact:* Dr. George Flowers, Dean of the Graduate School, 334-844-2125.
Website: http://www.forestry.auburn.edu/

Ball State University, Graduate School, College of Sciences and Humanities, Department of Natural Resources and Environmental Management, Muncie, IN 47306. Offers emergency management and homeland security (Certificate); natural resources and environmental management (MA, MS). *Program availability:* Part-time. *Faculty:* 5 full-time (2 women). *Students:* 7 full-time (3 women), 12 part-time (7 women); includes 3 minority (1 Black or African American, non-Hispanic/Latino; 1 Asian, non-Hispanic/Latino; 1 Two or more races, non-Hispanic/Latino), 4 international. Average age 32. 14 applicants, 86% accepted, 6 enrolled. In 2015, 4 master's awarded. *Degree requirements:* For master's, thesis (for some programs). *Entrance requirements:* For master's, GRE General Test, minimum baccalaureate GPA of 2.75 or 3.0 in latter half of baccalaureate, two letters of reference. Additional exam requirements/recommendations for international students: Required—TOEFL (minimum score 550 paper-based; 79 iBT), IELTS (minimum score 6.5). *Application deadline:* For fall admission, 3/1 priority date for domestic students. Applications are processed on a rolling basis. Application fee: $60. Electronic applications accepted. *Expenses:* Tuition, area resident: Full-time $6948; part-time $2316 per semester. Tuition, state resident: full-time $10,422; part-time $3474 per semester. Tuition, nonresident: full-time $19,062; part-time $6354 per semester. *Required fees:* $651 per semester. Tuition and fees vary according to campus/location, program and reciprocity agreements. *Financial support:* In 2015–16, 8 students received support, including 1 research assistantship with partial tuition reimbursement available (averaging $12,000 per year), 6 teaching assistantships with partial tuition reimbursements available (averaging $12,276 per year); unspecified assistantships also available. Financial award application deadline: 3/1; financial award applicants required to submit FAFSA. *Faculty research:* Acid rain, indoor air pollution, land reclamation. *Unit head:* Dr. Amy Gregg, Interim Chairperson, 765-285-5781, Fax: 765-285-2606, E-mail: algregg2@bsu.edu.
Website: http://www.bsu.edu/nrem/

Boise State University, School of Public Service, Department of Public Policy and Administration, Boise, ID 83725-1935. Offers public policy and administration (MPA, PhD, Graduate Certificate), including environmental and natural resources policy and administration (MPA), general public administration (MPA), state and local government policy and administration (MPA). *Accreditation:* NASPAA. *Program availability:* Part-time. *Faculty:* 16. *Students:* 38 full-time (19 women), 85 part-time (56 women); includes 15 minority (1 American Indian or Alaska Native, non-Hispanic/Latino; 1 Asian, non-Hispanic/Latino; 12 Hispanic/Latino; 1 Two or more races, non-Hispanic/Latino), 1 international. Average age 37. 81 applicants, 43% accepted, 29 enrolled. In 2015, 22 master's awarded. Terminal master's awarded for partial completion of doctoral program. *Degree requirements:* For master's, comprehensive exam, thesis optional, directed research project, internship; for doctorate, thesis/dissertation. *Entrance requirements:* For master's, GRE General Test, minimum GPA of 3.0. Additional exam requirements/recommendations for international students: Required—TOEFL (minimum score 550 paper-based; 80 iBT), IELTS (minimum score 6). *Application deadline:* For fall admission, 2/1 for domestic and international students; for spring admission, 10/1 for domestic and international students. Application fee: $65 ($95 for international students). Electronic applications accepted. *Expenses:* Tuition, state resident: full-time $6058; part-time $358 per credit hour. Tuition, nonresident: full-time $20,108; part-time $608 per credit hour. *Required fees:* $2108. Tuition and fees vary according to program. *Financial support:* In 2015–16, 41 students received support, including 2 research assistantships (averaging $4,083 per year); scholarships/grants and unspecified assistantships also available. Financial award application deadline: 2/1; financial award applicants required to submit FAFSA. *Unit head:* Dr. Gregory Hill, Department Chair, 208-426-2917, E-mail: greghill@boisestate.edu. *Application contact:* Dr. Elizabeth Fredericksen, MPA Director, 208-426-1078, E-mail: efreder@boisestate.edu.
Website: http://sps.boisestate.edu/publicpolicy/

California Polytechnic State University, San Luis Obispo, College of Agriculture, Food and Environmental Sciences, Department of Natural Resources Management and Environmental Sciences, San Luis Obispo, CA 93407. Offers forestry sciences (MS). *Program availability:* Part-time. *Faculty:* 9 full-time (4 women). *Students:* 3 full-time (2 women), 6 part-time (2 women). Average age 26. 6 applicants, 83% accepted, 4 enrolled. In 2015, 3 master's awarded. *Degree requirements:* For master's, comprehensive exam, thesis. *Application deadline:* For fall admission, 4/1 for domestic and international students; for winter admission, 10/1 for domestic students, 6/30 for international students; for spring admission, 10/1 for domestic students. Applications are processed on a rolling basis. Application fee: $55. Electronic applications accepted. *Expenses:* Tuition, state resident: full-time $6738; part-time $3906 per year. Tuition, nonresident: full-time $15,666; part-time $8370 per year. *Required fees:* $3528; $3075 per unit. $1025 per term. *Financial support:* Fellowships, research assistantships, career-related internships or fieldwork, Federal Work-Study, institutionally sponsored loans, scholarships/grants, and unspecified assistantships available. Support available

to part-time students. Financial award application deadline: 3/2; financial award applicants required to submit FAFSA. *Faculty research:* Hydrology, biometrics, forest health and management, fire science, urban and community forestry. *Unit head:* Dr. Richard Thompson, Department Head, 805-756-2898, E-mail: rpthomps@calpoly.edu.
Website: http://nres.calpoly.edu/

Central Washington University, Graduate Studies and Research, College of the Sciences, Program in Resource Management, Ellensburg, WA 98926. Offers MS. *Degree requirements:* For master's, thesis. *Entrance requirements:* For master's, GRE, minimum GPA of 3.0. Additional exam requirements/recommendations for international students: Required—TOEFL (minimum score 550 paper-based; 79 iBT). Electronic applications accepted.

Colorado State University, Warner College of Natural Resources, Department of Forest and Rangeland Stewardship, Fort Collins, CO 80523-1472. Offers forest sciences (MS, PhD); natural resources stewardship (MNRS); rangeland ecosystem science (MS, PhD). *Program availability:* Part-time, evening/weekend, 100% online. *Faculty:* 10 full-time (2 women), 2 part-time/adjunct (1 woman). *Students:* 28 full-time (10 women), 63 part-time (29 women); includes 13 minority (9 Hispanic/Latino; 4 Two or more races, non-Hispanic/Latino), 5 international. Average age 32. 62 applicants, 69% accepted, 37 enrolled. In 2015, 22 master's, 2 doctorates awarded. *Degree requirements:* For master's, thesis (for some programs), professional paper; for doctorate, comprehensive exam, thesis/dissertation. *Entrance requirements:* For master's, GRE General Test, minimum GPA of 3.0, 3 letters of recommendation, curriculum vitae; for doctorate, GRE General Test, minimum GPA of 3.0, 3 letters of recommendation, statement of research interest, curriculum vitae. Additional exam requirements/recommendations for international students: Required—TOEFL (minimum score 550 paper-based; 80 iBT), IELTS (minimum score 6.5). *Application deadline:* For fall admission, 2/1 priority date for domestic and international students; for spring admission, 10/1 priority date for domestic and international students. Applications are processed on a rolling basis. Application fee: $60 ($70 for international students). Electronic applications accepted. *Expenses:* Tuition, state resident: full-time $9348. Tuition, nonresident: full-time $22,916. *Required fees:* $2174; $473.72 per credit hour. $236.86 per semester. Tuition and fees vary according to course load and program. *Financial support:* In 2015–16, 4 fellowships with full tuition reimbursements (averaging $38,750 per year), 30 research assistantships with tuition reimbursements (averaging $21,847 per year), 6 teaching assistantships with tuition reimbursements (averaging $12,540 per year) were awarded; scholarships/grants and unspecified assistantships also available. Financial award application deadline: 2/1; financial award applicants required to submit FAFSA. *Faculty research:* Rangelands, forestry, natural resources economics, natural resources policy, riparian areas, fire effects. *Total annual research expenditures:* $3.1 million. *Unit head:* Dr. Linda Nagel, Department Head and Professor, 970-491-2840, Fax: 970-491-6754, E-mail: linda.nagel@colostate.edu. *Application contact:* Simone Short, Administrative Assistant III, 970-491-6911, Fax: 970-491-6754, E-mail: wcnr_frs_deptadmin@mail.colostate.edu.
Website: http://warnercnr.colostate.edu/frws-home/

Colorado State University, Warner College of Natural Resources, Department of Human Dimensions of Natural Resources, Fort Collins, CO 80523-1480. Offers conservation leadership (MS); human dimensions of natural resources (MS, PhD); tourism management (MTM). *Program availability:* Part-time, 100% online. *Faculty:* 15 full-time (7 women). *Students:* 45 full-time (28 women), 92 part-time (45 women); includes 18 minority (3 Black or African American, non-Hispanic/Latino; 1 American Indian or Alaska Native, non-Hispanic/Latino; 13 Hispanic/Latino; 1 Two or more races, non-Hispanic/Latino), 19 international. Average age 30. 125 applicants, 86% accepted, 80 enrolled. In 2015, 47 master's, 2 doctorates awarded. *Degree requirements:* For master's, thesis or alternative; for doctorate, comprehensive exam, thesis/dissertation. *Entrance requirements:* For master's, GRE General Test (minimum combined score of 300), minimum GPA of 3.0, 3 letters of recommendation, statement of interest, transcripts; for doctorate, GRE General Test (minimum combined score of 300), minimum GPA of 3.0, 3 letters of recommendation, copy of master's thesis or professional paper, interview, statement of interest, transcripts. Additional exam requirements/recommendations for international students: Required—TOEFL (minimum score 550 paper-based; 80 iBT). *Application deadline:* For fall admission, 2/15 priority date for domestic students, 2/15 for international students. Application fee: $60 ($70 for international students). Electronic applications accepted. *Expenses:* $727 per credit hour (for online Master of Tourism Management). *Financial support:* In 2015–16, 15 students received support, including 1 fellowship (averaging $40,000 per year), 6 research assistantships with partial tuition reimbursements available (averaging $24,326 per year), 8 teaching assistantships with partial tuition reimbursements available (averaging $13,680 per year); career-related internships or fieldwork, scholarships/grants, and unspecified assistantships also available. Financial award application deadline: 2/15. *Faculty research:* Conservation and sustainable development, environmental communication and governance, human dimensions of wildlife conservation, protected areas, social aspects of wildfire. *Total annual research expenditures:* $553,555. *Unit head:* Dr. Michael J. Manfredo, Professor and Department Head, 970-491-6591, Fax: 970-491-2255, E-mail: michael.manfredo@colostate.edu. *Application contact:* Jacqie Hasan, Graduate Contact, 970-491-6591, Fax: 970-491-2255, E-mail: jacqie.hasan@colostate.edu.
Website: http://warnercnr.colostate.edu/hdnr-home

Cornell University, Graduate School, Graduate Fields of Agriculture and Life Sciences, Field of Natural Resources, Ithaca, NY 14853-0001. Offers community-based natural resources management (MS, PhD); conservation biology (MS, PhD); ecosystem biology and biogeochemistry (MPS, MS, PhD); environmental management (MPS); fishery and aquatic science (MPS, MS, PhD); forest science (MPS, MS, PhD); human dimensions of natural resources management (MPS, MS, PhD); policy and institutional analysis (MS, PhD); program development and evaluation (MPS, MS, PhD); quantitative ecology (MS, PhD); wildlife science (MPS, MS, PhD). *Degree requirements:* For master's, thesis (MS), project paper (MPS); for doctorate, comprehensive exam, thesis/dissertation. *Entrance requirements:* For master's and doctorate, GRE General Test, 2 letters of recommendation. Additional exam requirements/recommendations for international students: Required—TOEFL (minimum score 550 paper-based; 77 iBT). Electronic applications accepted. *Faculty research:* Ecosystem-level dynamics, systems modeling, conservation biology/management, resource management's human dimensions, biogeochemistry.

Dalhousie University, Faculty of Management, Centre for Advanced Management Education, Halifax, NS B3H 3J5, Canada. Offers financial services (MBA); information management (MIM); management (MPA); natural resources (MBA). *Program availability:* Part-time, online learning. *Entrance requirements:* For master's, GMAT, minimum GPA of 3.0, resume. Additional exam requirements/recommendations for international students: Required—TOEFL, IELTS, CANTEST, CAEL, or Michigan English Language Assessment Battery. Electronic applications accepted.

Delaware State University, Graduate Programs, Department of Agriculture and Natural Resources, Program in Natural Resources, Dover, DE 19901-2277. Offers MS.

Entrance requirements: For master's, GRE. Additional exam requirements/recommendations for international students: Required—TOEFL (minimum score 550 paper-based).

Duke University, Nicholas School of the Environment, Durham, NC 27708. Offers environment (PhD); environmental management (MEM); forestry (MF); JD/AM. Application deadline for PhD program is December 8. *Program availability:* Online learning. *Degree requirements:* For doctorate, variable foreign language requirement, thesis/dissertation. *Entrance requirements:* For master's, GRE General Test, previous course work in natural or social sciences relevant to environmental interests, college calculus, college statistics, and microeconomics or ecology. Additional exam requirements/recommendations for international students: Required—TOEFL (minimum score 577 paper-based; 90 iBT) or IELTS (minimum score 7). Electronic applications accepted. *Faculty research:* Climate change, energy, water quality, ecosystem management and conservation, human and environmental health.

Humboldt State University, Academic Programs, College of Natural Resources and Sciences, Programs in Natural Resources, Arcata, CA 95521-8299. Offers natural resources (MS), including fisheries, forestry, natural resources planning and interpretation, rangeland resources and wildland soils, wastewater utilization, watershed management, wildlife. *Degree requirements:* For master's, thesis or alternative. *Entrance requirements:* For master's, GRE, appropriate bachelor's degree, minimum GPA of 2.5, 3 letters of recommendation, resume. Additional exam requirements/recommendations for international students: Required—TOEFL (minimum score 500 paper-based). *Faculty research:* Spotted owl habitat, pre-settlement vegetation, hardwood utilization, tree physiology, fisheries.

Instituto Tecnologico de Santo Domingo, Graduate School, Area of Basic And Environmental Sciences, Santo Domingo, Dominican Republic. Offers environmental science (M En S), including environmental education, environmental management, marine resources, natural resources management; mathematics (MS, PhD); renewable energy technology (MS, Certificate).

Iowa State University of Science and Technology, Program in Biorenewable Resources and Technology, Ames, IA 50011. Offers MS, PhD. *Degree requirements:* For master's, thesis or alternative; for doctorate, thesis/dissertation. *Entrance requirements:* For master's and doctorate, GRE General Test. Additional exam requirements/recommendations for international students: Required—TOEFL (minimum score 550 paper-based; 79 iBT), IELTS (minimum score 6.5). Electronic applications accepted.

Laurentian University, School of Graduate Studies and Research, School of Engineering, Sudbury, ON P3E 2C6, Canada. Offers mineral resources engineering (M Eng, MA Sc); natural resources engineering (PhD). *Program availability:* Part-time. *Faculty research:* Mining engineering, rock mechanics (tunneling, rockbursts, rock support), metallurgy (mineral processing, hydro and pyrometallurgy), simulations and remote mining, simulations and scheduling.

Louisiana State University and Agricultural & Mechanical College, Graduate School, College of Agriculture, School of Renewable Natural Resources, Baton Rouge, LA 70803. Offers fisheries (MS); forestry (MS, PhD); wildlife (MS); wildlife and fisheries science (PhD).

McGill University, Faculty of Graduate and Postdoctoral Studies, Faculty of Agricultural and Environmental Sciences, Department of Natural Resource Sciences, Montréal, QC H3A 2T5, Canada. Offers entomology (M Sc, PhD); environmental assessment (M Sc); forest science (M Sc, PhD); microbiology (M Sc, PhD); micrometeorology (M Sc, PhD); neotropical environment (M Sc, PhD); soil science (M Sc, PhD); wildlife biology (M Sc, PhD).

Michigan State University, The Graduate School, College of Agriculture and Natural Resources, Department of Community, Agriculture, Recreation, and Resource Studies, East Lansing, MI 48824. Offers MS, PhD. *Entrance requirements:* Additional exam requirements/recommendations for international students: Required—TOEFL. Electronic applications accepted.

Montana State University, The Graduate School, College of Agriculture, Department of Land Resources and Environmental Sciences, Bozeman, MT 59717. Offers land rehabilitation (interdisciplinary) (MS); land resources and environmental sciences (MS), including land rehabilitation (interdisciplinary), land resources and environmental sciences. *Program availability:* Part-time. *Degree requirements:* For master's, comprehensive exam. *Entrance requirements:* For master's, GRE General Test. Additional exam requirements/recommendations for international students: Required—TOEFL (minimum score 550 paper-based). Electronic applications accepted. *Faculty research:* Soil nutrient management and plant nutrition, isotope biogeochemistry of soils, biodegradation of hydrocarbons in soils and natural waters, remote sensing, GIS systems, managed and natural ecosystems, microbial and metabolic diversity in geothermally heated soils, integrated management of weeds, diversified cropping systems, insect behavior and ecology, river ecology, microbial biogeochemistry, weed ecology.

New Mexico Highlands University, Graduate Studies, College of Arts and Sciences, Department of Natural Resources Management, Las Vegas, NM 87701. Offers natural science (MS), including chemistry.

North Carolina State University, Graduate School, College of Natural Resources, Department of Parks, Recreation and Tourism Management, Raleigh, NC 27695. Offers natural resource management (MPRTM, MS); park and recreation management (MPRTM, MS); parks, recreation and tourism management (PhD); recreational sport management (MPRTM, MS); spatial information science (MPRTM, MS); tourism policy and development (MPRTM, MS). *Degree requirements:* For master's, thesis (for some programs); for doctorate, thesis/dissertation. *Entrance requirements:* For master's and doctorate, GRE General Test. Additional exam requirements/recommendations for international students: Required—TOEFL. Electronic applications accepted. *Faculty research:* Tourism policy and development, spatial information systems, natural resource management, recreational sports management, park and recreation management.

North Carolina State University, Graduate School, College of Natural Resources and College of Agriculture and Life Sciences, Program in Natural Resources, Raleigh, NC 27695. Offers MNR, MS. *Degree requirements:* For master's, thesis optional. *Entrance requirements:* For master's, GRE. Electronic applications accepted.

North Dakota State University, College of Graduate and Interdisciplinary Studies, Interdisciplinary Program in Natural Resources Management, Fargo, ND 58102. Offers MS, PhD. *Program availability:* Part-time. *Degree requirements:* For master's, thesis; for doctorate, comprehensive exam, thesis/dissertation. *Entrance requirements:* Additional exam requirements/recommendations for international students: Required—TOEFL (minimum score 525 paper-based; 71 iBT). Electronic applications accepted. *Faculty research:* Natural resources economics, wetlands issues, wildlife, prairie ecology, range management.

Northeastern State University, College of Science and Health Professions, Department of Natural Sciences, Program in Natural Sciences, Tahlequah, OK 74464-2399. Offers MS. *Faculty:* 14 full-time (9 women). *Students:* 9 full-time (4 women), 5 part-time (3 women); includes 8 minority (4 American Indian or Alaska Native, non-Hispanic/Latino; 1 Asian, non-Hispanic/Latino; 3 Two or more races, non-Hispanic/Latino). Average age 28. In 2015, 2 master's awarded. *Degree requirements:* For master's, thesis, project. *Application deadline:* For fall admission, 3/1 for domestic students; for spring admission, 10/1 for domestic students. *Expenses:* Tuition, state resident: part-time $189.60 per credit hour. Tuition, nonresident: part-time $462.60 per credit hour. *Required fees:* $37.40 per credit hour. *Unit head:* Dr. Chris Burba, Program Chair, 918-444-3835, E-mail: burba@nsuok.edu.
Website: http://academics.nsuok.edu/naturalsciences/Degrees/Graduate/MSNaturalScience.aspx

The Ohio State University, Graduate School, College of Food, Agricultural, and Environmental Sciences, School of Environment and Natural Resources, Columbus, OH 43210. Offers ecological restoration (MS, PhD); ecosystem science (MS, PhD); environment and natural resources (MENR); environmental social sciences (MS, PhD); fisheries and wildlife science (MS, PhD); forest science (MS, PhD); rural sociology (MS, PhD); soil science (MS, PhD). *Degree requirements:* For master's, thesis; for doctorate, thesis/dissertation. *Entrance requirements:* For master's and doctorate, GRE. Additional exam requirements/recommendations for international students: Required—TOEFL (minimum score 550 paper-based; 79 iBT), Michigan English Language Assessment Battery (minimum score 82); Recommended—IELTS (minimum score 7). Electronic applications accepted.

Oklahoma State University, College of Agricultural Science and Natural Resources, Stillwater, OK 74078. Offers M Ag, MS, PhD. *Program availability:* Online learning. *Faculty:* 220 full-time (51 women), 8 part-time/adjunct (0 women). *Students:* 136 full-time (63 women), 351 part-time (170 women); includes 64 minority (3 Black or African American, non-Hispanic/Latino; 14 American Indian or Alaska Native, non-Hispanic/Latino; 3 Asian, non-Hispanic/Latino; 14 Hispanic/Latino; 30 Two or more races, non-Hispanic/Latino), 149 international. Average age 29. 265 applicants, 57% accepted, 95 enrolled. In 2015, 114 master's, 36 doctorates awarded. *Degree requirements:* For master's, thesis (for some programs); for doctorate, comprehensive exam, thesis/dissertation. *Entrance requirements:* For master's and doctorate, GRE or GMAT. Additional exam requirements/recommendations for international students: Required—TOEFL (minimum score 550 paper-based; 79 iBT). *Application deadline:* For fall admission, 3/1 priority date for domestic and international students; for spring admission, 8/1 priority date for domestic and international students. Applications are processed on a rolling basis. Application fee: $40 ($75 for international students). Electronic applications accepted. *Expenses:* Tuition, state resident: full-time $3528; part-time $196 per credit hour. Tuition, nonresident: full-time $14,144; part-time $785.75 per credit hour. *Required fees:* $1895; $105.25 per credit hour. Tuition and fees vary according to campus/location. *Financial support:* In 2015–16, 246 research assistantships (averaging $17,794 per year), 51 teaching assistantships (averaging $15,582 per year) were awarded; fellowships, career-related internships or fieldwork, Federal Work-Study, scholarships/grants, health care benefits, tuition waivers (partial), and unspecified assistantships also available. Support available to part-time students. Financial award application deadline: 3/1; financial award applicants required to submit FAFSA. *Unit head:* Dr. Thomas Coon, Vice President/Dean, 405-744-5395, E-mail: thomas.coon@okstate.edu.
Website: http://casnr.okstate.edu

Oregon State University, College of Forestry, Program in Natural Resources, Corvallis, OR 97331. Offers fisheries management (MNR); geographic information science (MNR); sustainable natural resources (MNR); water conflict management and transformation (MNR). *Program availability:* Part-time, online only, 100% online. *Students:* 8 full-time (5 women), 45 part-time (24 women); includes 9 minority (2 American Indian or Alaska Native, non-Hispanic/Latino; 1 Asian, non-Hispanic/Latino; 4 Hispanic/Latino; 2 Two or more races, non-Hispanic/Latino). Average age 37. 18 applicants, 67% accepted, 12 enrolled. In 2015, 14 degrees awarded. *Entrance requirements:* For master's, GRE. Additional exam requirements/recommendations for international students: Required—TOEFL (minimum score 80 iBT), IELTS (minimum score 6.5). *Application deadline:* For fall admission, 5/1 for domestic students; for winter admission, 9/1 for domestic students; for spring admission, 1/1 for domestic students; for summer admission, 3/1 for domestic students. Application fee: $75 ($85 for international students). *Expenses:* $18,876 full-time tuition. *Unit head:* Dr. Badege Bishaw, Director, Master of Natural Resources and Sustainable Natural Resource Graduate Program, 541-737-9495, E-mail: badege.bishaw@oregonstate.edu.
Website: http://ecampus.oregonstate.edu/online-degrees/graduate/natural-resources/

Oregon State University, Interdisciplinary/Institutional Programs, Program in Environmental Sciences, Corvallis, OR 97331. Offers biogeochemistry (MS, PhD); ecology (MS, PhD); environmental education (MS, PhD); environmental sciences (PSM); natural resources (MS, PhD); quantitative analysis (MS, PhD); social science (MS, PhD); water resources (MS, PhD). *Program availability:* Part-time. *Students:* 17 full-time (12 women), 12 part-time (6 women); includes 7 minority (1 Black or African American, non-Hispanic/Latino; 2 Asian, non-Hispanic/Latino; 2 Hispanic/Latino; 2 Two or more races, non-Hispanic/Latino), 3 international. Average age 34. 42 applicants, 19% accepted, 3 enrolled. In 2015, 6 master's, 4 doctorates awarded. *Entrance requirements:* For master's and doctorate, GRE. Additional exam requirements/recommendations for international students: Required—TOEFL (minimum score 80 iBT), IELTS (minimum score 6.5). *Application deadline:* For fall admission, 1/15 for domestic students. Application fee: $75 ($85 for international students). *Expenses:* Contact institution. *Unit head:* Dr. Carolyn Fonyo Boggess, Interim Director, E-mail: carolyn.fonyo@oregonstate.edu.
Website: http://envsci.science.oregonstate.edu/

Purdue University, Graduate School, College of Agriculture, Department of Forestry and Natural Resources, West Lafayette, IN 47907. Offers fisheries and aquatic sciences (MS, MSF, PhD); forest biology (MS, MSF, PhD); natural resource social science (MS, PhD); natural resources social science (MSF); quantitative ecology (MS, MSF, PhD); wildlife science (MS, MSF, PhD); wood products and wood products manufacturing (MS, MSF, PhD). *Degree requirements:* For master's, thesis; for doctorate, thesis/dissertation. *Entrance requirements:* For master's and doctorate, GRE General Test (minimum score: verbal 50th percentile; quantitative 50th percentile; analytical writing 4.0), minimum undergraduate GPA of 3.2 or equivalent. Additional exam requirements/recommendations for international students: Required—TOEFL (minimum score 550 paper-based; 77 iBT). Electronic applications accepted. *Faculty research:* Wildlife management, forest management, forest ecology, forest soils, limnology.

State University of New York College of Environmental Science and Forestry, Department of Environmental Resources Engineering, Syracuse, NY 13210-2779.

Natural Resources

Offers ecological engineering (MPS, MS, PhD); environmental management (MPS); environmental resources engineering (MPS, MS, PhD); geospatial information science and engineering (MPS, MS, PhD); water resources engineering (MPS, MS, PhD). *Program availability:* Part-time. *Faculty:* 8 full-time (1 woman), 9 part-time/adjunct (3 women). *Students:* 28 full-time (12 women), 10 part-time (6 women); includes 4 minority (1 Black or African American, non-Hispanic/Latino; 2 Asian, non-Hispanic/Latino; 1 Hispanic/Latino), 17 international. Average age 25. 40 applicants, 60% accepted, 5 enrolled. In 2015, 15 master's, 5 doctorates awarded. *Degree requirements:* For master's, thesis (for some programs); for doctorate, comprehensive exam, thesis/dissertation. *Entrance requirements:* For master's and doctorate, GRE General Test, minimum GPA of 3.0. Additional exam requirements/recommendations for international students: Required—TOEFL (minimum score 550 paper-based; 80 iBT), IELTS (minimum score 6). *Application deadline:* For fall admission, 1/15 priority date for domestic and international students; for spring admission, 11/1 priority date for domestic and international students. Applications are processed on a rolling basis. Application fee: $60. *Expenses:* Tuition, state resident: full-time $10,870; part-time $453 per credit. Tuition, nonresident: full-time $22,210; part-time $925 per credit. *Required fees:* $1075; $89.22 per credit. *Financial support:* In 2015–16, 22 students received support, including 8 research assistantships with tuition reimbursements available (averaging $14,000 per year), 14 teaching assistantships with tuition reimbursements available; fellowships with tuition reimbursements available, Federal Work-Study, institutionally sponsored loans, scholarships/grants, health care benefits, and unspecified assistantships also available. Financial award application deadline: 6/30; financial award applicants required to submit FAFSA. *Faculty research:* Ecological engineering, environmental resources engineering, geospatial information science and engineering, water resources engineering, environmental science. *Total annual research expenditures:* $969,347. *Unit head:* Dr. Theodore Endreny, Chair, 315-470-6565, Fax: 315-470-6958, E-mail: te@esf.edu. *Application contact:* Scott Shannon, Dean of the Graduate School, 315-470-6599, Fax: 315-470-6978, E-mail: esfgrad@esf.edu.
Website: http://www.esf.edu/ere

State University of New York College of Environmental Science and Forestry, Department of Forest and Natural Resources Management, Syracuse, NY 13210-2779. Offers ecology and ecosystems (MPS, MS, PhD); economics, governance and human dimensions (MPS, MS, PhD); forest and natural resources management (MPS, MS, PhD); monitoring, analysis and modeling (MPS, MS, PhD). *Accreditation:* SAF. *Faculty:* 34 full-time (9 women), 7 part-time/adjunct (0 women). *Students:* 40 full-time (24 women), 5 part-time (0 women); includes 6 minority (2 American Indian or Alaska Native, non-Hispanic/Latino; 1 Asian, non-Hispanic/Latino; 2 Hispanic/Latino; 1 Two or more races, non-Hispanic/Latino), 10 international. 41 applicants, 68% accepted, 16 enrolled. *Degree requirements:* For master's, thesis (for some programs); for doctorate, comprehensive exam, thesis/dissertation. *Entrance requirements:* For master's and doctorate, GRE General Test, minimum GPA of 3.0. Additional exam requirements/recommendations for international students: Required—TOEFL (minimum score 550 paper-based; 80 iBT), IELTS (minimum score 6). *Application deadline:* For fall admission, 2/1 priority date for domestic and international students; for spring admission, 11/1 priority date for domestic and international students. Applications are processed on a rolling basis. Application fee: $60. *Expenses:* Tuition, state resident: full-time $10,870; part-time $453 per credit. Tuition, nonresident: full-time $22,210; part-time $925 per credit. *Required fees:* $1075; $89.22 per credit. *Financial support:* Fellowships with tuition reimbursements, research assistantships with tuition reimbursements, teaching assistantships with tuition reimbursements, career-related internships or fieldwork, Federal Work-Study, institutionally sponsored loans, scholarships/grants, health care benefits, and unspecified assistantships available. Financial award application deadline: 6/30; financial award applicants required to submit FAFSA. *Faculty research:* Silviculture recreation management, tree improvement, operations management, economics. *Unit head:* Dr. David Newman, Chair, 315-470-6534, Fax: 315-470-6535. *Application contact:* Scott Shannon, Dean, Instruction and Graduate Studies, 315-470-6599, Fax: 315-470-6978, E-mail: esfgrad@esf.edu.
Website: http://www.esf.edu/fnrm/

State University of New York College of Environmental Science and Forestry, Department of Sustainable Construction Management and Engineering, Syracuse, NY 13210-2779. Offers construction management (MPS, MS, PhD); sustainable construction (MPS, MS, PhD); wood science (MPS, MS, PhD). *Students:* 7 full-time (3 women), 4 part-time (2 women); includes 1 minority (Hispanic/Latino), 4 international. 12 applicants, 42% accepted, 2 enrolled. *Degree requirements:* For master's, thesis (for some programs); for doctorate, comprehensive exam, thesis/dissertation. *Entrance requirements:* For master's and doctorate, GRE General Test, minimum GPA of 3.0. Additional exam requirements/recommendations for international students: Required—TOEFL (minimum score 550 paper-based; 80 iBT), IELTS (minimum score 6). *Application deadline:* For fall admission, 2/1 priority date for domestic and international students; for spring admission, 11/1 priority date for domestic and international students. Applications are processed on a rolling basis. Application fee: $60. *Expenses:* Tuition, state resident: full-time $10,870; part-time $453 per credit. Tuition, nonresident: full-time $22,210; part-time $925 per credit. *Required fees:* $1075; $89.22 per credit. *Financial support:* Fellowships with full tuition reimbursements, research assistantships with full tuition reimbursements, teaching assistantships with full tuition reimbursements, career-related internships or fieldwork, Federal Work-Study, institutionally sponsored loans, scholarships/grants, health care benefits, and unspecified assistantships available. Financial award application deadline: 6/30; financial award applicants required to submit FAFSA. *Unit head:* Dr. Susan E. Anagnost, Chair, 315-470-6880, Fax: 315-470-6879, E-mail: seanagno@esf.edu. *Application contact:* Dr. Dudley J. Raynal, Dean, Instruction and Graduate Studies, 315-470-6599, Fax: 315-470-6879, E-mail: esfgrad@esf.edu.
Website: http://www.esf.edu/scme/

Sul Ross State University, Division of Agricultural and Natural Resource Science, Programs in Natural Resource Management, Alpine, TX 79832. Offers range and wildlife management (M Ag, MS). *Program availability:* Part-time. *Students:* 20 full-time (5 women), 7 part-time (0 women); includes 4 minority (1 Asian, non-Hispanic/Latino; 2 Hispanic/Latino; 1 Two or more races, non-Hispanic/Latino), 3 international. Average age 32. *Degree requirements:* For master's, thesis (for some programs). *Entrance requirements:* For master's, GRE General Test, minimum undergraduate GPA of 2.5 in last 60 hours. *Application deadline:* Applications are processed on a rolling basis. Application fee: $0 ($50 for international students). *Financial support:* Research assistantships, teaching assistantships, career-related internships or fieldwork, Federal Work-Study, and institutionally sponsored loans available. Support available to part-time students. Financial award application deadline: 5/1; financial award applicants required to submit FAFSA. *Unit head:* Dr. Bonnie Warnock, Chair, 432-837-8706, Fax: 432-837-8822, E-mail: bwarnock@sulross.edu. *Application contact:* Kelsey Slater, Department Secretary, 432-837-8488, Fax: 432-837-8822, E-mail: kelsey.slater@sulross.edu.
Website: http://www.sulross.edu/natural-resource-management

Texas A&M University, College of Agriculture and Life Sciences, Department of Ecosystem Science and Management, College Station, TX 77843. Offers ecosystem science and management (M Agr, MS, PhD); forestry (MS, PhD); rangeland ecology and management (M Agr, MS, PhD). *Program availability:* Part-time. *Faculty:* 23. *Students:* 51 full-time (26 women), 24 part-time (12 women); includes 17 minority (1 Black or African American, non-Hispanic/Latino; 4 Asian, non-Hispanic/Latino; 9 Hispanic/Latino; 3 Two or more races, non-Hispanic/Latino), 21 international. Average age 32. 16 applicants, 94% accepted, 10 enrolled. In 2015, 10 master's, 6 doctorates awarded. Terminal master's awarded for partial completion of doctoral program. *Degree requirements:* For master's, thesis (for some programs); for doctorate, thesis/dissertation. *Entrance requirements:* For master's and doctorate, GRE General Test. Additional exam requirements/recommendations for international students: Required—TOEFL (minimum score 550 paper-based; 80 iBT), IELTS (minimum score 6), PTE (minimum score 53). *Application deadline:* For fall admission, 3/1 priority date for domestic students; for spring admission, 10/15 priority date for domestic students. Applications are processed on a rolling basis. Application fee: $50 ($90 for international students). Electronic applications accepted. *Expenses:* Contact institution. *Financial support:* In 2015–16, 65 students received support, including 12 fellowships with tuition reimbursements available (averaging $14,063 per year), 26 research assistantships with tuition reimbursements available (averaging $7,800 per year), 24 teaching assistantships with tuition reimbursements available (averaging $7,517 per year); career-related internships or fieldwork, institutionally sponsored loans, scholarships/grants, traineeships, health care benefits, tuition waivers (full and partial), and unspecified assistantships also available. Support available to part-time students. Financial award application deadline: 3/15; financial award applicants required to submit FAFSA. *Faculty research:* Expert systems, geographic information systems, economics, biology, genetics. *Unit head:* Dr. Kathleen Kavanagh, Professor and Department Head, 979-845-5000, Fax: 979-845-6049, E-mail: katyk@tamu.edu. *Application contact:* Heather Haliburton Janke, Senior Academic Advisor II, 979-862-8993, Fax: 979-845-6049, E-mail: hjanke@tamu.edu.
Website: http://essm.tamu.edu

Texas Tech University, Graduate School, College of Agricultural Sciences and Natural Resources, Department of Natural Resources Management, Lubbock, TX 79409. Offers wildlife, aquatic, and wildlands science and management (MS, PhD). *Program availability:* Part-time. *Faculty:* 17 full-time (4 women), 1 part-time/adjunct (0 women). *Students:* 62 full-time (26 women), 12 part-time (6 women); includes 10 minority (1 Black or African American, non-Hispanic/Latino; 7 Hispanic/Latino; 2 Two or more races, non-Hispanic/Latino), 9 international. Average age 30. 25 applicants, 56% accepted, 12 enrolled. In 2015, 18 master's, 3 doctorates awarded. *Degree requirements:* For master's, comprehensive exam, thesis (for some programs); for doctorate, comprehensive exam, thesis/dissertation. *Entrance requirements:* For master's and doctorate, GRE General Test, formal approval from departmental committee. Additional exam requirements/recommendations for international students: Required—TOEFL (minimum score 550 paper-based; 79 iBT). *Application deadline:* For fall admission, 6/1 priority date for domestic students, 1/15 priority date for international students; for spring admission, 9/1 priority date for domestic students, 6/15 priority date for international students. Applications are processed on a rolling basis. Application fee: $60. Electronic applications accepted. *Expenses:* Tuition, state resident: full-time $6477; part-time $269.89 per credit hour. Tuition, nonresident: full-time $15,837; part-time $659.89 per credit hour. *Required fees:* $2751; $36.50 per credit hour. $937.50 per semester. Tuition and fees vary according to course level. *Financial support:* In 2015–16, 77 students received support, including 49 fellowships (averaging $3,226 per year), 66 research assistantships (averaging $12,159 per year), 9 teaching assistantships (averaging $10,276 per year); Federal Work-Study, scholarships/grants, and unspecified assistantships also available. Financial award application deadline: 4/15; financial award applicants required to submit FAFSA. *Faculty research:* Applying new ecological knowledge in decision-making about sustainable resource use, community (plant or animal) response to disturbances, population dynamics, habitat restoration, climate change, integrated management, game management, fire ecology, aquatic systems. *Total annual research expenditures:* $2.2 million. *Unit head:* Dr. Mark Wallace, Professor and Chair, 806-834-6979, Fax: 806-742-2280, E-mail: mark.wallace@ttu.edu. *Application contact:* Maggie Zebracka, Senior Business Assistant, 806-834-4550, Fax: 806-742-2280, E-mail: maggie.zebracka@ttu.edu.
Website: http://www.nrm.ttu.edu/

Texas Tech University, Graduate School, Interdisciplinary Programs, Lubbock, TX 79409. Offers arid land studies (MS); biotechnology (MS); heritage management (MS); interdisciplinary studies (MA, MS); museum science (MA); wind science and engineering (PhD); JD/MS. *Program availability:* Part-time. *Faculty:* 9 full-time (4 women), 1 part-time/adjunct (0 women). *Students:* 105 full-time (60 women), 102 part-time (56 women); includes 65 minority (17 Black or African American, non-Hispanic/Latino; 3 American Indian or Alaska Native, non-Hispanic/Latino; 4 Asian, non-Hispanic/Latino; 36 Hispanic/Latino; 1 Native Hawaiian or other Pacific Islander, non-Hispanic/Latino; 4 Two or more races, non-Hispanic/Latino), 38 international. Average age 31. 136 applicants, 63% accepted, 50 enrolled. In 2015, 65 master's, 6 doctorates awarded. Terminal master's awarded for partial completion of doctoral program. *Degree requirements:* For master's, comprehensive exam (for some programs), thesis (for some programs); for doctorate, comprehensive exam, thesis/dissertation (for some programs). *Entrance requirements:* Additional exam requirements/recommendations for international students: Required—TOEFL (minimum score 550 paper-based; 79 iBT), IELTS, PTE, Cambridge Advanced (B), Cambridge Proficiency (C), ELS English for Academic Purposes (Level 112). *Application deadline:* For fall admission, 6/1 priority date for domestic students, 1/15 priority date for international students; for spring admission, 9/1 priority date for domestic students, 6/15 priority date for international students. Applications are processed on a rolling basis. Application fee: $60. Electronic applications accepted. *Expenses:* Tuition, state resident: full-time $6477; part-time $269.89 per credit hour. Tuition, nonresident: full-time $15,837; part-time $659.89 per credit hour. *Required fees:* $2751; $36.50 per credit hour. $937.50 per semester. Tuition and fees vary according to course level. *Financial support:* In 2015–16, 147 students received support, including 126 fellowships (averaging $4,063 per year), 27 research assistantships (averaging $10,182 per year), 3 teaching assistantships (averaging $8,073 per year); scholarships/grants and unspecified assistantships also available. Financial award application deadline: 4/15; financial award applicants required to submit FAFSA. *Total annual research expenditures:* $421,608. *Unit head:* Dr. Mark Sheridan, Vice Provost for Graduate and Postdoctoral Affairs/Dean of the Graduate School, 806-742-2787, Fax: 806-742-1746, E-mail: mark.sheridan@ttu.edu. *Application contact:* Cynthia Lopez, Academic Program Review Coordinator, 806-834-0916, Fax: 806-742-1746, E-mail: gradschool@ttu.edu.
Website: http://www.depts.ttu.edu/gradschool/about/INDS/index.php

Universidad Metropolitana, School of Environmental Affairs, Program in Environmental Management, San Juan, PR 00928-1150. Offers MSEM. *Program availability:* Part-time. *Degree requirements:* For master's, thesis. Electronic applications accepted.

Universidad Nacional Pedro Henriquez Urena, Graduate School, Santo Domingo, Dominican Republic. Offers agricultural diversity (MS), including horticultural/fruit production, tropical animal production; conservation of monuments and cultural assets (M Arch); ecology and environment (MS); environmental engineering (MEE);

international relations (MA); natural resource management (MS); political science (MA); project optimization (MPM); project feasibility (MPM); project management (MPM); sanitation engineering (ME); science for teachers (MS); tropical Caribbean architecture (M Arch).

Université du Québec à Montréal, Graduate Programs, Program in Earth Sciences, Montreal, QC H3C 3P8, Canada. Offers earth sciences (M Sc); mineral resources (PhD); non-renewable resources (DESS). *Program availability:* Part-time. Terminal master's awarded for partial completion of doctoral program. *Degree requirements:* For master's, thesis (for some programs); for doctorate, thesis/dissertation. *Entrance requirements:* For master's, appropriate bachelor's degree or equivalent, proficiency in French. *Faculty research:* Economic geology, structural geology, geochemistry, Quaternary geology, isotopic geochemistry.

Université du Québec en Abitibi-Témiscamingue, Graduate Programs, Program in Environmental Sciences, Rouyn-Noranda, QC J9X 5E4, Canada. Offers biology (MS); environmental sciences (PhD); sustainable forest ecosystem management (MS).

University of Alaska Fairbanks, School of Natural Resources and Extension, Fairbanks, AK 99775-7140. Offers natural resources and sustainability (PhD); natural resources management (MS). *Program availability:* Part-time. *Faculty:* 16 full-time (4 women), 2 part-time/adjunct (both women). *Students:* 23 full-time (17 women), 25 part-time (15 women); includes 2 minority (1 Hispanic/Latino; 1 Two or more races, non-Hispanic/Latino), 3 international. Average age 36. 21 applicants, 38% accepted, 7 enrolled. In 2015, 7 master's, 1 doctorate awarded. *Degree requirements:* For master's, comprehensive exam, thesis (for some programs), oral defense of project or thesis; for doctorate, comprehensive exam, thesis/dissertation, defense of the dissertation. *Entrance requirements:* For master's, GRE General Test, bachelor's degree from accredited institution with minimum cumulative undergraduate and major GPA of 3.0; for doctorate, minimum cumulative GPA of 3.0. Additional exam requirements/recommendations for international students: Required—TOEFL (minimum score 550 paper-based; 89 iBT), IELTS (minimum score 6.5). *Application deadline:* For fall admission, 6/1 for domestic students, 3/1 for international students; for spring admission, 10/15 for domestic students, 9/1 for international students. Applications are processed on a rolling basis. Application fee: $60. Electronic applications accepted. *Expenses:* Tuition, state resident: full-time $7614; part-time $423 per credit. Tuition, nonresident: full-time $15,552; part-time $864 per credit. *Required fees:* $38 per credit. $187 per semester. Tuition and fees vary according to course level, course load, program and reciprocity agreements. *Financial support:* In 2015–16, 11 research assistantships with full tuition reimbursements (averaging $10,656 per year), 4 teaching assistantships with full tuition reimbursements (averaging $8,551 per year) were awarded; fellowships with full tuition reimbursements, career-related internships or fieldwork, Federal Work-Study, scholarships/grants, health care benefits, and unspecified assistantships also available. Support available to part-time students. Financial award application deadline: 2/15; financial award applicants required to submit FAFSA. *Faculty research:* Conservation biology, soil/water conservation, land use policy and planning in the arctic and subarctic, forest ecosystem management, subarctic agricultural production. *Total annual research expenditures:* $2.8 million. *Unit head:* Stephen Sparrow, Interim Dean, 907-474-9450, Fax: 907-474-6268,
E-mail: fysnras@uaf.edu. *Application contact:* Mary Kreta, Director of Admissions, 907-474-7500, Fax: 907-474-7097, E-mail: admissions@uaf.edu.
Website: http://www.uaf.edu/snre/

University of Alberta, Faculty of Graduate Studies and Research, Department of Renewable Resources, Edmonton, AB T6G 2E1, Canada. Offers agroforestry (M Ag, M Sc, MF); conservation biology (M Sc, PhD); forest biology and management (M Sc, PhD); land reclamation and remediation (M Sc, PhD); protected areas and wildlands management (M Sc, PhD); soil science (M Ag, M Sc, PhD); water and land resources (M Ag, M Sc, PhD); wildlife ecology and management (M Sc, PhD); MBA/M Ag; MBA/MF. *Program availability:* Part-time. *Degree requirements:* For master's, thesis (for some programs); for doctorate, comprehensive exam, thesis/dissertation. *Entrance requirements:* For master's, minimum 2 years of relevant professional experiences, minimum GPA of 3.0; for doctorate, minimum GPA of 3.0. Additional exam requirements/recommendations for international students: Required—TOEFL (minimum score 550 paper-based). Electronic applications accepted. *Faculty research:* Natural and managed landscapes.

University of Alberta, Faculty of Graduate Studies and Research, Program in Business Administration, Edmonton, AB T6G 2E1, Canada. Offers international business (MBA); leisure and sport management (MBA); natural resources and energy (MBA); technology commercialization (MBA); MBA/LL B; MBA/M Ag; MBA/M Eng; MBA/MF; MBA/PhD. *Accreditation:* AACSB. *Program availability:* Part-time, evening/weekend. *Degree requirements:* For master's, thesis or alternative. *Entrance requirements:* For master's, GMAT. Additional exam requirements/recommendations for international students: Required—TOEFL (minimum score 600 paper-based). Electronic applications accepted. *Faculty research:* Natural resources and energy/management and policy/family enterprise/international business/healthcare research management.

University of Arkansas at Monticello, School of Forest Resources, Monticello, AR 71656. Offers MS. *Program availability:* Part-time. *Degree requirements:* For master's, comprehensive exam, thesis. *Entrance requirements:* For master's, GRE General Test, minimum GPA of 2.7. Additional exam requirements/recommendations for international students: Required—TOEFL (minimum score 550 paper-based). Electronic applications accepted. *Faculty research:* Geographic information systems/remote sensing, forest ecology, wildlife ecology and management.

The University of British Columbia, Program in Resource Management and Environmental Studies, Vancouver, BC V6T 1Z4, Canada. Offers M Sc, MA, PhD. *Degree requirements:* For master's, thesis; for doctorate, comprehensive exam, thesis/dissertation. *Entrance requirements:* Additional exam requirements/recommendations for international students: Required—TOEFL (minimum score 600 paper-based; 100 iBT). Electronic applications accepted. *Faculty research:* Land management, water resources, energy, environmental assessment, risk evaluation.

University of California, Berkeley, Graduate Division, Group in Energy and Resources, Berkeley, CA 94720-1500. Offers MA, MS, PhD. *Degree requirements:* For master's, project or thesis; for doctorate, one foreign language, thesis/dissertation, qualifying exam. *Entrance requirements:* For master's and doctorate, GRE General Test, minimum GPA of 3.0, 3 letters of recommendation. *Faculty research:* Technical, economic, environmental, and institutional aspects of energy conservation in residential and commercial buildings; international patterns of energy use; renewable energy sources; assessment of valuation of energy and environmental resources pricing.

University of Connecticut, Graduate School, College of Agriculture and Natural Resources, Department of Natural Resources Management and Engineering, Storrs, CT 06269. Offers MS, PhD. Terminal master's awarded for partial completion of doctoral program. *Degree requirements:* For master's, comprehensive exam. *Entrance requirements:* For master's, GRE General Test, GRE Subject Test. Additional exam requirements/recommendations for international students: Required—TOEFL (minimum score 550 paper-based). Electronic applications accepted. *Faculty research:* Forest management, forest protection, water resources, biometeorology.

University of Delaware, College of Agriculture and Natural Resources, Department of Bioresources Engineering, Newark, DE 19716. Offers MS.

University of Florida, Graduate School, College of Agricultural and Life Sciences, School of Forest Resources and Conservation, Gainesville, FL 32611. Offers fisheries and aquatic sciences (MFAS, MS, PhD), including ecological restoration (MFAS, MFRC, MS, PhD), geographic information systems (MFAS, MFRC, MS, PhD), natural resource policy and administration (MFAS, MFRC, MS, PhD), wetland sciences (MFAS, MFRC, MS, PhD); forest resources and conservation (MFRC, MS, PhD), including agroforestry, ecological restoration (MFAS, MFRC, MS, PhD), geographic information systems (MFAS, MFRC, MS, PhD), geomatics, hydrologic sciences (MS, PhD), natural resource policy and administration (MFAS, MFRC, MS, PhD), toxicology (PhD), tropical conservation and development, wetland sciences (MFAS, MFRC, MS, PhD); JD/MFRC; JD/MS; JD/PhD. *Program availability:* Part-time, evening/weekend, online learning. *Faculty:* 38 full-time, 10 part-time/adjunct. *Students:* 60 full-time (24 women), 57 part-time (31 women); includes 13 minority (5 Black or African American, non-Hispanic/Latino; 1 American Indian or Alaska Native, non-Hispanic/Latino; 1 Asian, non-Hispanic/Latino; 6 Hispanic/Latino), 33 international. Average age 33. 64 applicants, 59% accepted, 32 enrolled. In 2015, 25 master's, 5 doctorates awarded. Terminal master's awarded for partial completion of doctoral program. *Degree requirements:* For master's, comprehensive exam, thesis optional, project (for MFRC); for doctorate, comprehensive exam, thesis/dissertation. *Entrance requirements:* For master's, GRE General Test, minimum GPA of 3.0, curriculum vitae, 3 letters of recommendation; for doctorate, GRE General Test, minimum GPA of 3.25, curriculum vitae, 3 letters of recommendation. Additional exam requirements/recommendations for international students: Required—TOEFL (minimum score 550 paper-based; 80 iBT), IELTS (minimum score 6). *Application deadline:* For fall admission, 1/1 priority date for domestic students, 1/1 for international students; for spring admission, 9/1 for domestic and international students. Applications are processed on a rolling basis. Application fee: $30. Electronic applications accepted. *Financial support:* In 2015–16, 2 fellowships, 71 research assistantships, 1 teaching assistantship were awarded; Federal Work-Study and institutionally sponsored loans also available. Support available to part-time students. Financial award application deadline: 1/3; financial award applicants required to submit FAFSA. *Faculty research:* Quantitative and integrative fisheries science, ecology and management of aquatic systems, finfish, invertebrate and ornamental aquaculture, aquatic animal health, geomatics and GIS, natural resource conservation, tropical forestry, economics and policy, environmental education, forest biology and ecology, forest management, hydrology, silviculture. *Total annual research expenditures:* $17 million. *Unit head:* Tim White, PhD, School of Forest Resources and Conservation Director, 352-846-0850, Fax: 352-392-1707, E-mail: tlwhite@ufl.edu. *Application contact:* Bill Linberg, PhD, Graduate Coordinator for Fisheries and Aquatic Sciences, 352-273-3616, Fax: 352-392-1707, E-mail: wjl@ufl.edu.
Website: http://www.sfrc.ufl.edu/

University of Florida, Graduate School, School of Natural Resources and Environment, Gainesville, FL 32611. Offers interdisciplinary ecology (MS, PhD). *Faculty:* 265. *Students:* 93 full-time (57 women), 12 part-time (8 women); includes 11 minority (3 Black or African American, non-Hispanic/Latino; 1 American Indian or Alaska Native, non-Hispanic/Latino; 2 Asian, non-Hispanic/Latino; 5 Hispanic/Latino), 32 international. Average age 32. 42 applicants, 62% accepted, 24 enrolled. In 2015, 9 master's, 13 doctorates awarded. *Degree requirements:* For master's, comprehensive exam, thesis; for doctorate, comprehensive exam, thesis/dissertation. *Entrance requirements:* For master's and doctorate, GRE General Test, minimum GPA of 3.0. Additional exam requirements/recommendations for international students: Required—TOEFL (minimum score 550 paper-based; 80 iBT), IELTS (minimum score 6). *Application deadline:* For fall admission, 2/1 priority date for domestic students, 2/1 for international students. Applications are processed on a rolling basis. Application fee: $30. Electronic applications accepted. *Financial support:* Applicants required to submit FAFSA. *Faculty research:* Natural sciences, social sciences, sustainability studies, research design and methods. *Total annual research expenditures:* $11,475. *Unit head:* Dr. Thomas K. Frazer, Director, 352-392-9230, Fax: 352-392-9748, E-mail: frazer@ufl.edu. *Application contact:* Office of Graduate Admissions, 352-392-1365,
E-mail: webrequests@admissions.ufl.edu.
Website: http://www.snre.ufl.edu/

University of Georgia, School of Forestry and Natural Resources, Athens, GA 30602. Offers MFR, MS, PhD. *Degree requirements:* For master's, thesis (MS); for doctorate, one foreign language, thesis/dissertation. *Entrance requirements:* For master's and doctorate, GRE General Test. Electronic applications accepted.

University of Guelph, Graduate Studies, Ontario Agricultural College, Department of Land Resource Science, Guelph, ON N1G 2W1, Canada. Offers atmospheric science (M Sc, PhD); environmental and agricultural earth sciences (M Sc, PhD); land resources management (M Sc, PhD); soil science (M Sc, PhD). *Program availability:* Part-time. *Degree requirements:* For master's, thesis (for some programs), research project (non-thesis track); for doctorate, comprehensive exam, thesis/dissertation. *Entrance requirements:* For master's, minimum B- average during previous 2 years of course work; for doctorate, minimum B average during previous 2 years of course work. Additional exam requirements/recommendations for international students: Required—TOEFL (minimum score 550 paper-based). Electronic applications accepted. *Faculty research:* Soil science, environmental earth science, land resource management.

University of Hawaii at Manoa, Graduate Division, College of Tropical Agriculture and Human Resources, Department of Natural Resources and Environmental Management, Honolulu, HI 96822. Offers MS, PhD. *Program availability:* Part-time. *Faculty:* 31 full-time (5 women), 2 part-time/adjunct (1 woman). *Students:* 37 full-time (21 women), 7 part-time (4 women); includes 16 minority (1 American Indian or Alaska Native, non-Hispanic/Latino; 5 Asian, non-Hispanic/Latino; 10 Two or more races, non-Hispanic/Latino), 7 international. Average age 32. 37 applicants, 57% accepted, 6 enrolled. In 2015, 7 master's, 5 doctorates awarded. Terminal master's awarded for partial completion of doctoral program. *Degree requirements:* For master's, thesis optional; for doctorate, comprehensive exam, thesis/dissertation. *Entrance requirements:* For master's and doctorate, GRE General Test, minimum GPA of 3.0 in last 4 semesters of course work. Additional exam requirements/recommendations for international students: Required—TOEFL (minimum score 600 paper-based; 100 iBT), IELTS (minimum score 7). *Application deadline:* For fall admission, 3/1 for domestic students, 1/15 for international students; for spring admission, 9/1 for domestic students, 8/1 for international students. Applications are processed on a rolling basis. Application fee: $100. *Financial support:* In 2015–16, 10 fellowships (averaging $1,822 per year), 22 research assistantships (averaging $19,469 per year), 4 teaching assistantships (averaging $14,820 per year) were awarded; career-related internships or fieldwork and tuition waivers (full and partial) also available. *Faculty research:* Bioeconomics, natural resource management. *Total annual research expenditures:* $3.1 million. *Unit head:*

Natural Resources

Sylvia Yuen, Interim Dean, 808-956-8234, Fax: 808-956-9105, E-mail: syuen@hawaii.edu. *Application contact:* John Yanagida, Graduate Chair, 808-956-7530, Fax: 808-956-6539, E-mail: jyanagid@hawaii.edu.
Website: http://www.hawaii.edu/graduatestudies/fields/html/departments/mno/nrem/nrem.htm

University of Idaho, College of Graduate Studies, College of Natural Resources, Moscow, ID 83844-1142. Offers MNR, MS, PSM, PhD. *Faculty:* 61 full-time (17 women). *Students:* 148 full-time (82 women), 146 part-time (68 women). Average age 36. In 2015, 62 master's, 29 doctorates awarded. *Degree requirements:* For doctorate, thesis/dissertation. *Entrance requirements:* For master's, minimum GPA of 2.8; for doctorate, minimum undergraduate GPA of 2.8, 3.0 graduate. Additional exam requirements/recommendations for international students: Required—TOEFL. *Application deadline:* For fall admission, 8/1 for domestic students; for spring admission, 12/15 for domestic students. Applications are processed on a rolling basis. Application fee: $60. Electronic applications accepted. *Expenses:* Tuition, state resident: full-time $6205; part-time $399 per credit hour. Tuition, nonresident: full-time $20,209; part-time $1177 per credit hour. *Required fees:* $2017; $58 per credit hour. Full-time tuition and fees vary according to course load and reciprocity agreements. *Financial support:* Fellowships, research assistantships, teaching assistantships, and Federal Work-Study available. Support available to part-time students. Financial award applicants required to submit FAFSA. *Faculty research:* Aquaculture, forest nursery and seedling research, remote sensing and GIS research, wilderness research, conservation and ecological genetics. *Unit head:* Dr. Kurt Scott Pregitzer, Dean, 208-885-8981, Fax: 208-885-5534, E-mail: cnr@uidaho.edu. *Application contact:* Sean Scoggin, Graduate Recruitment Coordinator, 208-885-4723, Fax: 208-885-4406, E-mail: graduateadmissions@uidaho.edu.
Website: http://www.uidaho.edu/cnr

University of Illinois at Urbana–Champaign, Graduate College, College of Agricultural, Consumer and Environmental Sciences, Department of Natural Resources and Environmental Science, Champaign, IL 61820. Offers MS, PhD, MS/JD. *Program availability:* Part-time, online learning.

University of Maine, Graduate School, College of Natural Sciences, Forestry, and Agriculture, School of Forest Resources, Orono, ME 04469. Offers forest resources (MS, PhD); forestry (MF). *Accreditation:* SAF (one or more programs are accredited). *Program availability:* Part-time. *Faculty:* 28 full-time (7 women), 37 part-time/adjunct (8 women). *Students:* 42 full-time (15 women), 1 part-time (0 women); includes 4 minority (1 Black or African American, non-Hispanic/Latino; 2 American Indian or Alaska Native, non-Hispanic/Latino; 1 Hispanic/Latino), 9 international. Average age 30. 35 applicants, 86% accepted, 12 enrolled. In 2015, 10 master's, 3 doctorates awarded. Terminal master's awarded for partial completion of doctoral program. *Degree requirements:* For master's, thesis; for doctorate, one foreign language, comprehensive exam, thesis/dissertation. *Entrance requirements:* For master's and doctorate, GRE General Test. Additional exam requirements/recommendations for international students: Required—TOEFL. *Application deadline:* For fall admission, 1/15 priority date for domestic students; for spring admission, 10/15 for domestic students; for summer admission, 4/15 for domestic students. Applications are processed on a rolling basis. Application fee: $65. Electronic applications accepted. *Financial support:* In 2015–16, 34 students received support, including 28 research assistantships with full tuition reimbursements available (averaging $14,600 per year), 6 teaching assistantships with full tuition reimbursements available (averaging $14,600 per year); career-related internships or fieldwork, Federal Work-Study, and institutionally sponsored loans also available. Financial award application deadline: 3/1. *Faculty research:* Silviculture, forest ecology, climate change, sustainable tourism, Nano cellulose composites. *Total annual research expenditures:* $3.2 million. *Unit head:* Dr. Stephen Shaler, Director, 207-581-4737. *Application contact:* Scott G. Delcourt, Assistant Vice President for Graduate Studies and Senior Associate Dean, 207-581-3291, Fax: 207-581-3232, E-mail: graduate@maine.edu.
Website: http://www.forest.umaine.edu/

The University of Manchester, School of Materials, Manchester, United Kingdom. Offers advanced aerospace materials engineering (M Sc); advanced metallic systems (PhD); biomedical materials (M Phil, M Sc, PhD); ceramics and glass (M Phil, M Sc, PhD); composite materials (M Sc, PhD); corrosion and protection (M Phil, M Sc, PhD); materials (M Phil, PhD); metallic materials (M Phil, M Sc, PhD); nanostructural materials (M Phil, M Sc, PhD); paper science (M Phil, M Sc, PhD); polymer science and engineering (M Phil, M Sc, PhD); technical textiles (M Sc); textile design, fashion and management (M Phil, M Sc, PhD); textile science and technology (M Phil, M Sc, PhD); textiles (M Phil, PhD); textiles and fashion (M Ent).

University of Manitoba, Faculty of Graduate Studies, Clayton H. Riddell Faculty of Environment, Earth, and Resources, Natural Resources Institute, Winnipeg, MB R3T 2N2, Canada. Offers natural resources and environmental management (PhD); natural resources management (MNRM).

University of Maryland, College Park, Academic Affairs, College of Agriculture and Natural Resources, Department of Plant Science and Landscape Architecture, Natural Resource Sciences Program, College Park, MD 20742. Offers MS, PhD. *Faculty research:* Wetland soils, acid mine drainage, acid sulfate soil.

University of Michigan, School of Natural Resources and Environment, Program in Natural Resources and Environment, Ann Arbor, MI 48109. Offers behavior, education and communication (MS); conservation ecology (MS); environmental informatics (MS); environmental justice (MS); environmental policy and planning (MS); natural resources and environment (PhD); sustainable systems (MS); MS/JD; MS/MBA; MS/MPP; MS/MSE; MUP/MS. *Students:* 342 full-time (184 women). Average age 27. Terminal master's awarded for partial completion of doctoral program. *Degree requirements:* For master's, practicum or group project; for doctorate, comprehensive exam, thesis/dissertation, oral defense of dissertation, preliminary exam. *Entrance requirements:* For master's, GRE General Test; for doctorate, GRE General Test, master's degree. Additional exam requirements/recommendations for international students: Required—TOEFL (minimum score 560 paper-based; 84 iBT). *Application deadline:* For fall admission, 4/30 for domestic and international students. Application fee: $75 ($90 for international students). Electronic applications accepted. *Financial support:* Application deadline: 1/6; applicants required to submit FAFSA. *Unit head:* Dr. Marie Lynn Miranda, Interim Dean, 734-764-2550, Fax: 734-763-8965, E-mail: danbrown@umich.edu. *Application contact:* Sondra R. Auerbach, Director of Academic Programs, 734-764-6453, Fax: 734-936-2195, E-mail: sshowen@umich.edu.
Website: http://www.snre.umich.edu/

University of Minnesota, Twin Cities Campus, Graduate School, College of Food, Agricultural and Natural Resource Sciences, Program in Natural Resources Science and Management, St. Paul, MN 55108. Offers assessment, monitoring, and geospatial analysis (MS, PhD); economics, policy, management, and society (MS, PhD); forest hydrology and watershed management (MS, PhD); forest products (MS, PhD); forests: biology, ecology, conservation, and management (MS, PhD); natural resources science and management (MS, PhD); paper science and engineering (MS, PhD); recreation resources, tourism, and environmental education (MS, PhD); wildlife ecology and management (MS, PhD). *Program availability:* Part-time. *Faculty:* 71 full-time (28 women), 55 part-time/adjunct (7 women). *Students:* 80 full-time (45 women), 16 part-time (9 women); includes 5 minority (1 Black or African American, non-Hispanic/Latino; 2 American Indian or Alaska Native, non-Hispanic/Latino; 2 Asian, non-Hispanic/Latino), 8 international. 81 applicants, 52% accepted, 31 enrolled. In 2015, 25 master's, 8 doctorates awarded. Terminal master's awarded for partial completion of doctoral program. *Degree requirements:* For master's, comprehensive exam, thesis; for doctorate, comprehensive exam, thesis/dissertation. *Entrance requirements:* For master's and doctorate, GRE General Test. Additional exam requirements/recommendations for international students: Required—TOEFL (minimum score 550 paper-based; 79 iBT), IELTS (minimum score 6.5). *Application deadline:* For fall admission, 12/16 priority date for domestic and international students; for spring admission, 10/15 for domestic and international students. Applications are processed on a rolling basis. Application fee: $75 ($95 for international students). Electronic applications accepted. *Financial support:* In 2015–16, fellowships with full tuition reimbursements (averaging $40,000 per year), research assistantships with full tuition reimbursements (averaging $40,000 per year), teaching assistantships with full tuition reimbursements (averaging $40,000 per year) were awarded; scholarships/grants, health care benefits, tuition waivers (full and partial), and unspecified assistantships also available. *Faculty research:* Forest hydrology, biology, ecology, conservation, and management; recreation resources and environmental education; wildlife ecology; economics, policy, and society; geographic information systems (GIS); and forest products and paper science. *Unit head:* Dr. Michael Kilgore, Director of Graduate Studies, 612-624-6298, E-mail: mkilgore@umn.edu. *Application contact:* Toni Wheeler, Graduate Program Coordinator, 612-624-7683, Fax: 612-625-5212, E-mail: twheeler@umn.edu.
Website: http://www.nrsm.umn.edu

University of Missouri, Office of Research and Graduate Studies, School of Natural Resources, Natural Resources Master's Program, Columbia, MO 65211. Offers MNR.

University of Montana, Graduate School, College of Forestry and Conservation, Missoula, MT 59812-0002. Offers fish and wildlife biology (PhD); forest and conservation sciences (PhD); forestry (MS); recreation management (MS); resource conservation (MS); systems ecology (MS, PhD); wildlife biology (MS). *Degree requirements:* For doctorate, thesis/dissertation. *Entrance requirements:* For master's and doctorate, GRE General Test. Additional exam requirements/recommendations for international students: Required—TOEFL (minimum score 575 paper-based).

University of Nebraska–Lincoln, Graduate College, College of Agricultural Sciences and Natural Resources, Department of Agricultural Economics, Lincoln, NE 68588. Offers agribusiness (MBA); agricultural economics (MS, PhD); community development (M Ag). *Degree requirements:* For master's, thesis optional; for doctorate, comprehensive exam, thesis/dissertation. *Entrance requirements:* For master's and doctorate, GRE General Test. Additional exam requirements/recommendations for international students: Required—TOEFL (minimum score 550 paper-based). Electronic applications accepted. *Faculty research:* Marketing and agribusiness, production economics, resource law, international trade and development, rural policy and revitalization.

University of Nebraska–Lincoln, Graduate College, College of Agricultural Sciences and Natural Resources, School of Natural Resources, Lincoln, NE 68588. Offers geography (PhD); natural resources (MS, PhD). *Degree requirements:* For master's, thesis optional. *Entrance requirements:* For master's, GRE General Test. Additional exam requirements/recommendations for international students: Required—TOEFL. Electronic applications accepted. *Faculty research:* Wildlife biology, aquatic sciences, landscape ecology, agroforestry.

University of New Brunswick Saint John, Faculty of Business, Saint John, NB E2L 4L5, Canada. Offers administration (MBA); electronic commerce (MBA); international business (MBA); natural resource management (MBA). *Program availability:* Part-time. *Faculty:* 14 full-time (2 women), 15 part-time/adjunct (3 women). *Students:* 68 full-time (27 women), 15 part-time (7 women). In 2015, 91 master's awarded. *Entrance requirements:* For master's, GMAT (minimum score of 550) or GRE (minimum 54th percentile), minimum GPA of 3.0. Additional exam requirements/recommendations for international students: Required—TOEFL (minimum score 580 paper-based; 93 iBT), TWE (minimum score 4.5). *Application deadline:* For fall admission, 5/31 for domestic students, 7/15 for international students. Application fee: $100. Electronic applications accepted. *Expenses:* Contact institution. *Financial support:* In 2015–16, 4 students received support. Career-related internships or fieldwork and scholarships/grants available. *Faculty research:* International business, project management, innovation and technology management; business use of Weblogs and podcasts to communicate; corporate governance; high-involvement work systems; international competitiveness; supply chain management and logistics. *Unit head:* Dr. Shelley Rinehart, Director of Graduate Studies, 506-648-5902, Fax: 506-648-5574, E-mail: rinehart@unb.ca. *Application contact:* Tammy Morin, Secretary, 506-648-5746, Fax: 506-648-5574, E-mail: tmorin@unbsj.ca.
Website: http://go.unb.ca/gradprograms

University of New Hampshire, Graduate School, College of Life Sciences and Agriculture, Department of Natural Resources and the Environment, Durham, NH 03824. Offers environmental conservation (MS); forestry (MS); integrated coastal ecosystem science, policy and management (MS); natural resources (MS); soil and water resource management (MS); wildlife and conservation biology (MS). *Program availability:* Part-time. *Degree requirements:* For master's, thesis or alternative. *Entrance requirements:* For master's, GRE General Test. Additional exam requirements/recommendations for international students: Required—TOEFL (minimum score 550 paper-based; 80 iBT). Electronic applications accepted.

University of New Hampshire, Graduate School, College of Life Sciences and Agriculture, Program in Resource Administration, Durham, NH 03824. Offers MS. *Program availability:* Part-time. *Degree requirements:* For master's, thesis or alternative. *Entrance requirements:* For master's, GRE General Test. Additional exam requirements/recommendations for international students: Required—TOEFL (minimum score 550 paper-based; 80 iBT). Electronic applications accepted.

University of New Hampshire, Graduate School, Interdisciplinary Programs, Doctoral Program in Natural Resources and Earth Systems Science, Durham, NH 03824. Offers earth and environmental science (PhD), including geology, oceanography; natural resources and environmental studies (PhD). *Degree requirements:* For doctorate, thesis/dissertation. *Entrance requirements:* For doctorate, GRE (if from a non-U.S. university). Additional exam requirements/recommendations for international students: Required—TOEFL (minimum score 550 paper-based; 80 iBT). Electronic applications accepted. *Faculty research:* Environmental and natural resource studies and management.

University of New Mexico, Graduate Studies, College of Arts and Sciences, Program in Economics, Albuquerque, NM 87131-2039. Offers econometrics (MA); economic theory (MA); environmental/natural resource economics (MA, PhD); international/development and sustainability economics (MA, PhD); public economics (MA, PhD). *Program availability:* Part-time. *Faculty:* 10 full-time (6 women). *Students:* 35 full-time (12 women), 13 part-time (6 women); includes 8 minority (1 Black or African American, non-Hispanic/Latino; 5 Hispanic/Latino; 2 Two or more races, non-Hispanic/Latino), 24 international. Average age 30. 69 applicants, 33% accepted, 12 enrolled. In 2015, 7 master's, 4 doctorates awarded. Terminal master's awarded for partial completion of doctoral program. *Degree requirements:* For master's, comprehensive exam, thesis (for some programs); for doctorate, comprehensive exam, thesis/dissertation. *Entrance requirements:* For master's and doctorate, GRE General Test, 3 letters of recommendation, letter of intent, curriculum vitae. Additional exam requirements/recommendations for international students: Required—TOEFL (minimum score 520 paper-based; 68 iBT). *Application deadline:* For fall admission, 3/1 priority date for domestic students, 3/1 for international students. Applications are processed on a rolling basis. Application fee: $50. Electronic applications accepted. *Financial support:* Fellowships with tuition reimbursements, research assistantships with tuition reimbursements, teaching assistantships with tuition reimbursements, career-related internships or fieldwork, Federal Work-Study, scholarships/grants, health care benefits, and unspecified assistantships available. Support available to part-time students. Financial award application deadline: 3/1; financial award applicants required to submit FAFSA. *Faculty research:* Core theory, econometrics, public finance, international/development economics, labor/human resource economics, environmental/natural resource economics. *Total annual research expenditures:* $167,690. *Unit head:* Dr. Janie Chermak, Chair, 505-277-2037, Fax: 505-277-9445, E-mail: jchermak@unm.edu. *Application contact:* Jeff Newcomer Miller, Academic Advisor, 505-277-3056, Fax: 505-277-9445, E-mail: econgrad@unm.edu.
Website: http://econ.unm.edu

University of Northern British Columbia, Office of Graduate Studies, Prince George, BC V2N 4Z9, Canada. Offers business administration (Diploma); community health science (M Sc); disability management (MA); education (M Ed); first nations studies (MA); gender studies (MA); history (MA); interdisciplinary studies (MA); international studies (MA); mathematical, computer and physical sciences (M Sc); natural resources and environmental studies (M Sc, MA, MNRES, PhD); political science (MA); psychology (M Sc, PhD); social work (MSW). *Program availability:* Part-time, evening/weekend, online learning. *Degree requirements:* For master's, thesis; for doctorate, thesis/dissertation. *Entrance requirements:* For master's, GRE, minimum B average in undergraduate course work; for doctorate, candidacy exam, minimum A average in graduate course work.

University of Rhode Island, Graduate School, College of the Environment and Life Sciences, Department of Environmental and Natural Resource Economics, Kingston, RI 02881. Offers MESM, MS, PhD. *Program availability:* Part-time. *Faculty:* 6 full-time (1 woman), 1 (woman) part-time/adjunct. *Students:* 25 full-time (10 women), 4 part-time (2 women), 13 international. In 2015, 7 master's, 4 doctorates awarded. *Degree requirements:* For master's, comprehensive exam (for some programs), thesis optional; for doctorate, comprehensive exam, thesis/dissertation. *Entrance requirements:* For master's and doctorate, GRE, 3 letters of recommendation. Additional exam requirements/recommendations for international students: Required—TOEFL (minimum score 550 paper-based). *Application deadline:* For fall admission, 7/15 for domestic students, 2/1 for international students; for spring admission, 11/15 for domestic students, 7/15 for international students. Application fee: $65. Electronic applications accepted. *Expenses:* Tuition, state resident: full-time $11,796; part-time $655 per credit. Tuition, nonresident: full-time $24,206; part-time $1345 per credit. *Required fees:* $1546; $44 per credit. One-time fee: $155 full-time; $35 part-time. *Financial support:* In 2015–16, 5 research assistantships (averaging $10,479 per year), 7 teaching assistantships (averaging $9,785 per year) were awarded. Financial award application deadline: 7/15; financial award applicants required to submit FAFSA. *Faculty research:* Policy simulation, policy actions, experimental economics. *Unit head:* Dr. James Opaluch, Chair, 401-874-4590, Fax: 401-874-4766, E-mail: jimo@uri.edu. *Application contact:* Graduate Admission, 401-874-2872, E-mail: gradadm@etal.uri.edu.
Website: http://web.uri.edu/enre/

University of Rhode Island, Graduate School, College of the Environment and Life Sciences, Department of Natural Resources Science, Kingston, RI 02881. Offers MESM, MS, PhD. *Program availability:* Part-time. *Faculty:* 11 full-time (2 women), 1 part-time/adjunct (0 women). *Students:* 47 full-time (25 women), 13 part-time (9 women); includes 5 minority (1 Black or African American, non-Hispanic/Latino; 3 Asian, non-Hispanic/Latino; 1 Hispanic/Latino), 6 international. In 2015, 18 master's, 2 doctorates awarded. *Degree requirements:* For master's, comprehensive exam (for some programs), thesis optional; for doctorate, comprehensive exam, thesis/dissertation. *Entrance requirements:* For master's and doctorate, GRE, 2 letters of recommendation. Additional exam requirements/recommendations for international students: Required—TOEFL (minimum score 550 paper-based). *Application deadline:* For fall admission, 7/15 for domestic students, 2/1 for international students; for spring admission, 11/15 for domestic students, 7/15 for international students. Application fee: $65. Electronic applications accepted. *Expenses:* Tuition, state resident: full-time $11,796; part-time $655 per credit. Tuition, nonresident: full-time $24,206; part-time $1345 per credit. *Required fees:* $1546; $44 per credit. One-time fee: $155 full-time; $35 part-time. *Financial support:* In 2015–16, 5 research assistantships with tuition reimbursements (averaging $10,479 per year), 7 teaching assistantships (averaging $9,785 per year) were awarded. Financial award application deadline: 7/15; financial award applicants required to submit FAFSA. *Faculty research:* Spatial data modeling, ecological mapping, data integration for environmental applications. *Total annual research expenditures:* $3.7 million. *Unit head:* Dr. Arthur Gold, Chair, 401-874-2903, Fax: 401-874-4561, E-mail: agold@uri.edu. *Application contact:* Dr. Peter August, Co-Director of the CELS Master of Environmental Science and Management Graduate Program, 401-874-4794, Fax: 401-874-4561, E-mail: pete@edc.uri.edu.
Website: http://web.uri.edu/nrs/

University of San Francisco, College of Arts and Sciences, Program in Environmental Management, San Francisco, CA 94117-1080. Offers MS. *Program availability:* Evening/weekend. *Faculty:* 8 full-time (4 women), 7 part-time/adjunct (2 women). *Students:* 80 full-time (57 women), 19 part-time (11 women); includes 40 minority (3 Black or African American, non-Hispanic/Latino; 12 Asian, non-Hispanic/Latino; 19 Hispanic/Latino; 1 Native Hawaiian or other Pacific Islander, non-Hispanic/Latino; 5 Two or more races, non-Hispanic/Latino), 6 international. Average age 29. 121 applicants, 75% accepted, 45 enrolled. In 2015, 36 master's awarded. *Degree requirements:* For master's, thesis, project. *Entrance requirements:* For master's, 3 semesters of course work in chemistry, minimum GPA of 2.7, work experience in environmental field. Additional exam requirements/recommendations for international students: Required—TOEFL, IELTS, PTE. *Application deadline:* For fall admission, 2/15 for domestic and international students. Applications are processed on a rolling basis. Application fee: $55 ($65 for international students). Electronic applications accepted. *Expenses: Tuition, area resident:* Full-time $22,410; part-time $1245 per credit. Tuition and fees vary according to course load, degree level and campus/location. *Financial support:* In 2015–16, 45 students received support. Teaching assistantships and career-related internships or fieldwork available. Financial award application deadline: 3/2; financial award applicants required to submit FAFSA. *Faculty research:* Problems of environmental managers, water quality, hazardous materials, environmental health. *Unit head:* Dr. Maggie Winslow, Chair, 415-422-6553, Fax: 415-422-6387. *Application contact:* Mark Landerghini, Information Contact, 415-422-5101, Fax: 415-422-2217, E-mail: asgraduate@usfca.edu.
Website: http://www.usfca.edu/artsci/msem/

University of South Africa, College of Agriculture and Environmental Sciences, Pretoria, South Africa. Offers agriculture (MS); consumer science (MCS); environmental management (MA, MS, PhD); environmental science (MA, MS, PhD); geography (MA, MS, PhD); horticulture (M Tech); human ecology (MHE); life sciences (MS); nature conservation (M Tech).

The University of Texas at Austin, Graduate School, Cockrell School of Engineering, Department of Petroleum and Geosystems Engineering, Program in Energy and Earth Resources, Austin, TX 78712-1111. Offers MA. *Degree requirements:* For master's, thesis, seminar. *Entrance requirements:* For master's, GRE General Test. Additional exam requirements/recommendations for international students: Required—TOEFL. Electronic applications accepted.

University of Vermont, Graduate College, The Rubenstein School of Environment and Natural Resources, Program in Natural Resources, Burlington, VT 05405. Offers natural resources (MS, PhD), including aquatic ecology and watershed science (MS), environment thought and culture (MS), environment, science and public affairs (MS), forestry (MS). *Degree requirements:* For master's, thesis or alternative; for doctorate, thesis/dissertation. *Entrance requirements:* For master's and doctorate, GRE General Test. Additional exam requirements/recommendations for international students: Required—TOEFL (minimum score 550 paper-based; 80 iBT). Electronic applications accepted.

University of Washington, Graduate School, College of the Environment, School of Forest Resources, Seattle, WA 98195. Offers bioresource science and engineering (MS, PhD); environmental horticulture (MEH); forest ecology (MS, PhD); forest management (MFR); forest soils (MS, PhD); restoration ecology (MS, PhD); restoration ecology and environmental horticulture (MS, PhD); social sciences (MS, PhD); sustainable resource management (MS, PhD); wildlife science (MS, PhD); MFR/MAIS; MPA/MS. *Accreditation:* SAF. *Program availability:* Part-time. *Degree requirements:* For master's, thesis; for doctorate, comprehensive exam, thesis/dissertation. *Entrance requirements:* For master's and doctorate, GRE, minimum GPA of 3.0. Additional exam requirements/recommendations for international students: Required—TOEFL. Electronic applications accepted. *Faculty research:* Ecosystem analysis, silviculture and forest protection, paper science and engineering, environmental horticulture and urban forestry, natural resource policy and economics, restoration ecology and environment horticulture, conservation, human dimensions, wildlife, bioresource science and engineering.

University of Wisconsin–Madison, Graduate School, Gaylord Nelson Institute for Environmental Studies, Environment and Resources Program, Madison, WI 53706-1380. Offers MS, PhD. *Program availability:* Part-time. *Degree requirements:* For master's, thesis; for doctorate, comprehensive exam, thesis/dissertation. *Entrance requirements:* For master's and doctorate, GRE General Test. Additional exam requirements/recommendations for international students: Required—TOEFL (minimum score 550 paper-based; 80 iBT). Electronic applications accepted. *Expenses:* Tuition, state resident: full-time $5364. Tuition, nonresident: full-time $12,027. *Required fees:* $571. Tuition and fees vary according to campus/location, program and reciprocity agreements. *Faculty research:* Land use, soil science/watershed management, geographic information systems, environmental law/justice, waste management, restoration ecology, agroecology, energy resources, sustainability.

University of Wisconsin–Stevens Point, College of Natural Resources, Stevens Point, WI 54481-3897. Offers MS. *Program availability:* Part-time. *Degree requirements:* For master's, thesis or alternative. *Entrance requirements:* For master's, GRE. *Faculty research:* Wildlife management, environmental education, fisheries, forestry, resource policy and planning.

University of Wyoming, College of Agriculture and Natural Resources, Department of Renewable Resources, Laramie, WY 82071. Offers agroecology (MS); entomology (MS, PhD); entomology/water resources (MS, PhD); rangeland ecology and watershed management (MS, PhD), including soil sciences (PhD), soil sciences and water resources (MS); rangeland ecology and watershed management/water resources (MS, PhD); soil science (MS); soil science/water resources (PhD). *Program availability:* Part-time. *Degree requirements:* For master's, comprehensive exam, thesis, oral examination; for doctorate, comprehensive exam, thesis/dissertation, preliminary oral and written exam, oral final exam. *Entrance requirements:* For master's and doctorate, GRE General Test, minimum GPA of 3.0. Additional exam requirements/recommendations for international students: Required—TOEFL. Electronic applications accepted. *Faculty research:* Plant control, grazing management, riparian restoration, riparian management, reclamation.

University of Wyoming, College of Arts and Sciences, Department of Geography, Program in Rural Planning and Natural Resources, Laramie, WY 82071. Offers community and regional planning and natural resources (MP). *Degree requirements:* For master's, thesis or alternative. *Entrance requirements:* For master's, GRE General Test, minimum GPA of 3.0. Additional exam requirements/recommendations for international students: Required—TOEFL. *Faculty research:* Rural and small town planning, public land management.

Utah State University, School of Graduate Studies, College of Natural Resources, Interdisciplinary Program in Natural Resources, Logan, UT 84322. Offers MNR. *Entrance requirements:* For master's, GRE General Test, minimum GPA of 3.0. Additional exam requirements/recommendations for international students: Required—TOEFL. *Faculty research:* Ecosystem management, human dimensions, quantitative methods, informative management.

Virginia Polytechnic Institute and State University, Graduate School, College of Natural Resources and Environment, Blacksburg, VA 24061. Offers fisheries and wildlife (MS, PhD); forestry and forest products (MF, MS, PhD); geography (MS); geospatial and environmental analysis (PhD); natural resources (MNR). *Degree requirements:* For master's, comprehensive exam (for some programs), thesis (for some programs); for doctorate, comprehensive exam (for some programs), thesis/dissertation (for some programs). *Entrance requirements:* For master's and doctorate, GRE/GMAT (may vary by department). Additional exam requirements/recommendations for international students: Required—TOEFL (minimum score 550 paper-based). Electronic applications accepted.

Virginia Polytechnic Institute and State University, VT Online, Blacksburg, VA 24061. Offers advanced transportation systems (Certificate); aerospace engineering (MS); agricultural and life sciences (MSLFS); business information systems (Graduate Certificate); career and technical education (MS); civil engineering (MS); computer engineering (M Eng, MS); decision support systems (Graduate Certificate); eLearning leadership (MA); electrical engineering (M Eng, MS); engineering administration (MEA); environmental engineering (Certificate); environmental politics and policy (Graduate Certificate); environmental sciences and engineering (MS); foundations of political analysis (Graduate Certificate); health product risk management (Graduate Certificate); industrial and systems engineering (MS); information policy and society (Graduate Certificate); information security (Graduate Certificate); information technology (MIT); instructional technology (MA); integrative STEM education (MA Ed); liberal arts (Graduate Certificate); life sciences: health product risk management (MS); natural resources (MNR, Graduate Certificate); networking (Graduate Certificate); nonprofit and nongovernmental organization management (Graduate Certificate); ocean engineering (MS); political science (MA); security studies (Graduate Certificate); software development (Graduate Certificate).

Washington State University, College of Agricultural, Human, and Natural Resource Sciences, School of the Environment, Pullman, WA 99164. Offers environmental and natural resource sciences (PhD); natural resource sciences (MS). Program applications must be made through the Pullman campus. *Degree requirements:* For master's, comprehensive exam (for some programs), thesis (for some programs), oral exam; for doctorate, comprehensive exam, thesis/dissertation, oral exam. *Entrance requirements:* For master's, GRE General Test, official copies of all college transcripts, three letters of recommendation. Additional exam requirements/recommendations for international students: Required—TOEFL, IELTS. *Faculty research:* Environmental and natural resources conservation and sustainability; earth sciences: earth systems and geology; wildlife ecology and conservation sciences.

Washington State University, College of Arts and Sciences, School of the Environment, Pullman, WA 99164. Offers environmental and natural resource sciences (PhD); environmental science (MS); geology (MS, PhD); natural resource science (MS). *Degree requirements:* For master's, comprehensive exam (for some programs), thesis (for some programs), oral exam; for doctorate, comprehensive exam, thesis/dissertation, oral exam, written exam. *Entrance requirements:* For master's, 3 undergraduate semester hours each in sociology or cultural anthropology, environmental science, biological sciences, and calculus or statistics; 4 in general ecology; and 6 in general chemistry or general physics; for doctorate, minimum GPA of 3.0. Additional exam requirements/recommendations for international students: Required—TOEFL, IELTS.

West Virginia University, College of Business and Economics, Division of Economics and Finance, Morgantown, WV 26506. Offers business analysis (MA); developmental financial economics (PhD); environmental and resource economics (PhD); international economics (PhD); mathematical economics (MA); monetary economics (PhD); public finance (PhD); public policy (MA); regional and urban economics (PhD); statistics and economics (MA). Terminal master's awarded for partial completion of doctoral program. *Degree requirements:* For master's, thesis optional; for doctorate, comprehensive exam, thesis/dissertation. *Entrance requirements:* For master's and doctorate, GRE General Test, minimum GPA of 3.0; course work in intermediate microeconomics, intermediate macroeconomics, calculus, and statistics. Additional exam requirements/recommendations for international students: Required—TOEFL. Electronic applications accepted. *Expenses:* Tuition, state resident: full-time $8568. Tuition, nonresident: full-time $22,140. Tuition and fees vary according to program. *Faculty research:* Financial economics, regional/urban development, public economics, international trade/international finance/development economics, monetary economics.

West Virginia University, Davis College of Agriculture, Forestry and Consumer Sciences, Division of Resource Management and Sustainable Development, Program in Resource Management and Sustainable Development, Morgantown, WV 26506. Offers PhD. *Program availability:* Part-time. *Degree requirements:* For doctorate, thesis/dissertation. *Entrance requirements:* For doctorate, GRE General Test. Additional exam requirements/recommendations for international students: Required—TOEFL. *Expenses:* Tuition, state resident: full-time $8568. Tuition, nonresident: full-time $22,140. Tuition and fees vary according to program.

Range Science

Colorado State University, Warner College of Natural Resources, Department of Forest and Rangeland Stewardship, Fort Collins, CO 80523-1472. Offers forest sciences (MS, PhD); natural resources stewardship (MNRS); rangeland ecosystem science (MS, PhD). *Program availability:* Part-time, evening/weekend, 100% online. *Faculty:* 10 full-time (2 women), 2 part-time/adjunct (1 woman). *Students:* 28 full-time (10 women), 63 part-time (29 women); includes 13 minority (9 Hispanic/Latino; 4 Two or more races, non-Hispanic/Latino), 5 international. Average age 32. 62 applicants, 69% accepted, 37 enrolled. In 2015, 22 master's, 2 doctorates awarded. *Degree requirements:* For master's, thesis (for some programs), professional paper; for doctorate, comprehensive exam, thesis/dissertation. *Entrance requirements:* For master's, GRE General Test, minimum GPA of 3.0, 3 letters of recommendation, curriculum vitae; for doctorate, GRE General Test, minimum GPA of 3.0, 3 letters of recommendation, statement of research interest, curriculum vitae. Additional exam requirements/recommendations for international students: Required—TOEFL (minimum score 550 paper-based; 80 iBT), IELTS (minimum score 6.5). *Application deadline:* For fall admission, 2/1 priority date for domestic and international students; for spring admission, 10/1 priority date for domestic and international students. Applications are processed on a rolling basis. Application fee: $60 ($70 for international students). Electronic applications accepted. *Expenses:* Tuition, state resident: full-time $9348. Tuition, nonresident: full-time $22,916. *Required fees:* $2174; $473.72 per credit hour. $236.86 per semester. Tuition and fees vary according to course load and program. *Financial support:* In 2015–16, 4 fellowships with full tuition reimbursements (averaging $38,750 per year), 30 research assistantships with tuition reimbursements (averaging $21,847 per year), 6 teaching assistantships with tuition reimbursements (averaging $12,540 per year) were awarded; scholarships/grants and unspecified assistantships also available. Financial award application deadline: 2/1; financial award applicants required to submit FAFSA. *Faculty research:* Rangelands, forestry, natural resources economics, natural resources policy, riparian areas, fire effects. *Total annual research expenditures:* $3.1 million. *Unit head:* Dr. Linda Nagel, Department Head and Professor, 970-491-2840, Fax: 970-491-6754, E-mail: linda.nagel@colostate.edu. *Application contact:* Simone Short, Administrative Assistant III, 970-491-6911, Fax: 970-491-6754, E-mail: wcnr_frs_deptadmin@mail.colostate.edu.
Website: http://warnercnr.colostate.edu/frws-home/

Kansas State University, Graduate School, College of Agriculture, Department of Agronomy, Manhattan, KS 66506. Offers crop science (MS, PhD); plant breeding and genetics (MS); range and forage science (MS, PhD); soil and environmental science (PhD); weed science (MS, PhD). *Program availability:* Part-time. *Degree requirements:* For master's, thesis or alternative, oral exam; for doctorate, thesis/dissertation, preliminary exams. *Entrance requirements:* For master's, minimum GPA of 3.0 in BS; for doctorate, minimum GPA of 3.0 in master's program. Additional exam requirements/recommendations for international students: Required—TOEFL (minimum score 550 paper-based; 79 iBT). Electronic applications accepted. *Faculty research:* Range and forage science; soil and environmental science; weed science; plant breeding and genetics; crop physiology, ecology and production.

Montana State University, The Graduate School, College of Agriculture, Department of Animal and Range Sciences, Bozeman, MT 59717. Offers MS, PhD. *Program availability:* Part-time. *Degree requirements:* For master's, comprehensive exam; for doctorate, comprehensive exam, thesis/dissertation. *Entrance requirements:* For master's, GRE, minimum GPA of 3.0; undergraduate coursework in animal science, range science or closely-related field; faculty adviser; for doctorate, GRE. Additional exam requirements/recommendations for international students: Required—TOEFL (minimum score 550 paper-based; 80 iBT). Electronic applications accepted. *Faculty research:* Rangeland ecology, wildlife habitat management, residual feed intake, post-partum effect of bulls, increasing efficiency of sheep production systems.

New Mexico State University, College of Agricultural, Consumer and Environmental Sciences, Department of Animal and Range Sciences, Las Cruces, NM 88003. Offers animal science (MS, PhD). *Program availability:* Part-time. *Faculty:* 16 full-time (4 women). *Students:* 28 full-time (21 women), 6 part-time (4 women); includes 6 minority (all Hispanic/Latino), 6 international. Average age 28. 34 applicants, 38% accepted, 11 enrolled. In 2015, 6 master's, 3 doctorates awarded. *Degree requirements:* For master's, thesis, seminar, experimental statistics; for doctorate, thesis/dissertation, research tool. *Entrance requirements:* For master's, minimum GPA of 3.0 in last 60 hours of undergraduate course work (MS), 3 reference letters, personal statement, resume, BS in animal science; for doctorate, minimum graduate GPA of 3.2, MS with thesis, 3 reference letters, personal statement, resume, BS in animal science. Additional exam requirements/recommendations for international students: Required—TOEFL (minimum score 550 paper-based; 79 iBT), IELTS (minimum score 6.5). *Application deadline:* For fall admission, 2/15 priority date for domestic and international students; for spring admission, 10/1 priority date for domestic and international students. Applications are processed on a rolling basis. Application fee: $40 ($50 for international students). Electronic applications accepted. *Expenses:* $274.50 per credit hour for in-state students, and all students enrolled in six or fewer credits; $839.30 per credit hour for out-of-state and international students enrolled in at least seven hours. *Financial support:* In 2015–16, 28 students received support, including 1 fellowship (averaging $4,088 per year), 5 research assistantships (averaging $18,803 per year), 19 teaching assistantships (averaging $17,702 per year); career-related internships or fieldwork, Federal Work-Study, scholarships/grants, traineeships, health care benefits, and unspecified assistantships also available. Support available to part-time students. Financial award application deadline: 3/1. *Faculty research:* Reproductive physiology, ruminant nutrition, nutrition toxicology, range ecology, land use hydrology. *Total annual research expenditures:* $3.4 million. *Unit head:* Dr. Glenn Duff, Department Head, 575-646-2515, Fax: 575-646-5441, E-mail: glennd@nmsu.edu. *Application contact:* Jenny Castillo, Graduate Advising, 575-646-2515, Fax: 575-646-5441,
E-mail: cjenny@nmsu.edu.
Website: http://aces.nmsu.edu/academics/anrs

Oregon State University, College of Agricultural Sciences, Program in Rangeland Ecology and Management, Corvallis, OR 97331. Offers M Ag, MS, PhD. *Program availability:* Part-time. *Faculty:* 6 full-time (2 women), 1 part-time/adjunct (0 women). *Students:* 3 full-time (1 woman). 1 applicant, 100% accepted, 1 enrolled. In 2015, 5 master's, 1 doctorate awarded. Terminal master's awarded for partial completion of doctoral program. *Degree requirements:* For master's, thesis (for some programs); for doctorate, thesis/dissertation. *Entrance requirements:* Additional exam requirements/recommendations for international students: Required—TOEFL (minimum score 80 iBT), IELTS (minimum score 6.5). *Application deadline:* For fall admission, 8/1 for domestic students, 4/1 for international students; for winter admission, 1/1 for domestic students, 7/1 for international students; for spring admission, 2/1 for domestic students, 10/1 for international students; for summer admission, 5/1 for domestic students, 1/1 for international students. Application fee: $75 ($85 for international students). *Expenses:* Tuition, state resident: full-time $12,150; part-time $450 per credit. Tuition, nonresident: full-time $20,952; part-time $776 per credit. *Required fees:* $1572; $1443 per unit. One-time fee: $350. Tuition and fees vary according to course load, campus/location and program. *Financial support:* Research assistantships, career-related internships or fieldwork, Federal Work-Study, and institutionally sponsored loans available. Support available to part-time students. Financial award application deadline: 2/1. *Faculty research:* Range ecology, watershed science, animal grazing, agroforestry. *Unit head:* Dr. Michael M. Borman, Department Head and Extension Specialist, E-mail: michael.borman@oregonstate.edu. *Application contact:* Dodi Reesman, Rangeland Ecology and Management Advisor, 541-737-4761,
E-mail: dodi.reesman@oregonstate.edu.
Website: http://gradschool.oregonstate.edu/programs/6220

Sul Ross State University, Division of Agricultural and Natural Resource Science, Programs in Natural Resource Management, Alpine, TX 79832. Offers range and wildlife management (M Ag, MS). *Program availability:* Part-time. *Students:* 20 full-time (5 women), 7 part-time (0 women); includes 4 minority (1 Asian, non-Hispanic/Latino; 2 Hispanic/Latino; 1 Two or more races, non-Hispanic/Latino), 3 international. Average age 32. *Degree requirements:* For master's, thesis (for some programs). *Entrance requirements:* For master's, GRE General Test, minimum undergraduate GPA of 2.5 in last 60 hours. *Application deadline:* Applications are processed on a rolling basis. Application fee: $0 ($50 for international students). *Financial support:* Research assistantships, teaching assistantships, career-related internships or fieldwork, Federal Work-Study, and institutionally sponsored loans available. Support available to part-time

students. Financial award application deadline: 5/1; financial award applicants required to submit FAFSA. *Unit head:* Dr. Bonnie Warnock, Chair, 432-837-8706, Fax: 432-837-8822, E-mail: bwarnock@sulross.edu. *Application contact:* Kelsey Slater, Department Secretary, 432-837-8488, Fax: 432-837-8822, E-mail: kelsey.slater@sulross.edu.
Website: http://www.sulross.edu/natural-resource-management

Texas A&M University, College of Agriculture and Life Sciences, Department of Ecosystem Science and Management, College Station, TX 77843. Offers ecosystem science and management (M Agr, MS, PhD); forestry (MS, PhD); rangeland ecology and management (M Agr, MS, PhD). *Program availability:* Part-time. *Faculty:* 23. *Students:* 51 full-time (26 women), 24 part-time (12 women); includes 17 minority (1 Black or African American, non-Hispanic/Latino; 4 Asian, non-Hispanic/Latino; 9 Hispanic/Latino; 3 Two or more races, non-Hispanic/Latino), 21 international. Average age 32. 16 applicants, 94% accepted, 10 enrolled. In 2015, 10 master's, 6 doctorates awarded. Terminal master's awarded for partial completion of doctoral program. *Degree requirements:* For master's, thesis (for some programs); for doctorate, thesis/dissertation. *Entrance requirements:* For master's and doctorate, GRE General Test. Additional exam requirements/recommendations for international students: Required—TOEFL (minimum score 550 paper-based; 80 iBT), IELTS (minimum score 6), PTE (minimum score 53). *Application deadline:* For fall admission, 3/1 priority date for domestic students; for spring admission, 10/15 priority date for domestic students. Applications are processed on a rolling basis. Application fee: $50 ($90 for international students). Electronic applications accepted. *Expenses:* Contact institution. *Financial support:* In 2015–16, 65 students received support, including 12 fellowships with tuition reimbursements available (averaging $14,063 per year), 26 research assistantships with tuition reimbursements available (averaging $7,800 per year), 24 teaching assistantships with tuition reimbursements available (averaging $7,517 per year); career-related internships or fieldwork, institutionally sponsored loans, scholarships/grants, traineeships, health care benefits, tuition waivers (full and partial), and unspecified assistantships also available. Support available to part-time students. Financial award application deadline: 3/15; financial award applicants required to submit FAFSA. *Faculty research:* Expert systems, geographic information systems, economics, biology, genetics. *Unit head:* Dr. Kathleen Kavanagh, Professor and Department Head, 979-845-5000, Fax: 979-845-6049, E-mail: katyk@tamu.edu. *Application contact:* Heather Haliburton Janke, Senior Academic Advisor II, 979-862-8993, Fax: 979-845-6049, E-mail: hjanke@tamu.edu.
Website: http://essm.tamu.edu

Texas A&M University–Kingsville, College of Graduate Studies, Dick and Mary Lewis Kleberg College of Agriculture, Natural Resources and Human Sciences, Department of Agriculture, Agribusiness, and Environmental Sciences, King Ranch Institute for Ranch Management, Kingsville, TX 78363. Offers MS. *Degree requirements:* For master's, variable foreign language requirement, comprehensive exam, thesis (for some programs). *Entrance requirements:* For master's, GRE (minimum combined Math & Verbal score of 290), GMAT, MAT, minimum GPA of 2.5. Additional exam requirements/recommendations for international students: Required—TOEFL (minimum score 550 paper-based; 79 iBT). Electronic applications accepted.

Texas A&M University–Kingsville, College of Graduate Studies, Dick and Mary Lewis Kleberg College of Agriculture, Natural Resources and Human Sciences, Department of Animal, Rangeland, and Wildlife Sciences, Program in Range and Wildlife Management, Kingsville, TX 78363. Offers MS. *Degree requirements:* For master's, variable foreign language requirement, comprehensive exam, thesis (for some programs). *Entrance requirements:* For master's, GRE (minimum of 150 for each of the math and verbal sections), MAT, GMAT, minimum GPA of 3.0 for coursework from previous degree. Additional exam requirements/recommendations for international students: Required—TOEFL (minimum score 550 paper-based; 79 iBT). Electronic applications accepted.

The University of Arizona, College of Agriculture and Life Sciences, School of Natural Resources and the Environment, Tucson, AZ 85721. Offers ecology and management of rangelands (MS, PhD). *Degree requirements:* For master's, thesis; for doctorate, comprehensive exam, thesis/dissertation. *Entrance requirements:* For master's, GRE General Test, minimum GPA of 3.0, 3 letters of recommendation, letter of intent; for doctorate, GRE General Test, minimum GPA of 3.0, MS or MA, 3 letters of recommendation, letter of intent. Additional exam requirements/recommendations for international students: Required—TOEFL (minimum score 550 paper-based; 79 iBT). *Application deadline:* For fall admission, 6/1 for domestic students, 12/1 for international students; for spring admission, 10/1 for domestic students, 6/1 for international students. Application fee: $75. Electronic applications accepted. *Financial support:* Fellowships, research assistantships, teaching assistantships, career-related internships or fieldwork, scholarships/grants, health care benefits, tuition waivers (full and partial), and unspecified assistantships available. *Faculty research:* Natural resource policy and management, rangeland ecology and management, wildlife/fish ecology, watershed aquaculture. *Unit head:* Dr. Stuart Marsh, Director, E-mail: smarsh@email.arizona.edu. *Application contact:* 520-621-7255.
Website: http://www.snr.arizona.edu/

University of California, Berkeley, Graduate Division, College of Natural Resources, Group in Range Management, Berkeley, CA 94720-1500. Offers MS. *Degree requirements:* For master's, thesis. *Entrance requirements:* For master's, GRE General Test, minimum GPA of 3.0, 3 letters of recommendation. Additional exam requirements/recommendations for international students: Required—TOEFL. *Faculty research:* Grassland and savannah ecology, wetland ecology, oak woodland classification, wildlife habitat management.

University of Wyoming, College of Agriculture and Natural Resources, Department of Renewable Resources, Laramie, WY 82071. Offers agroecology (MS); entomology (MS, PhD); entomology/water resources (MS, PhD); rangeland ecology and watershed management (MS, PhD), including soil sciences (PhD), soil sciences and water resources (MS); rangeland ecology and watershed management/water resources (MS, PhD); soil science (MS); soil science/water resources (PhD). *Program availability:* Part-time. *Degree requirements:* For master's, comprehensive exam, thesis, oral examination; for doctorate, comprehensive exam, thesis/dissertation, preliminary oral and written exam, oral final exam. *Entrance requirements:* For master's and doctorate, GRE General Test, minimum GPA of 3.0. Additional exam requirements/recommendations for international students: Required—TOEFL. Electronic applications accepted. *Faculty research:* Plant control, grazing management, riparian restoration, riparian management, reclamation.

Utah State University, School of Graduate Studies, College of Natural Resources, Department of Wildland Resources, Logan, UT 84322. Offers ecology (MS, PhD); forestry (MS, PhD); range science (MS, PhD); wildlife biology (MS, PhD). *Program availability:* Part-time. *Degree requirements:* For master's, thesis; for doctorate, comprehensive exam, thesis/dissertation. *Entrance requirements:* For master's and doctorate, GRE General Test, minimum GPA of 3.0. Additional exam requirements/recommendations for international students: Required—TOEFL. *Faculty research:* Range plant ecophysiology, plant community ecology, ruminant nutrition, population ecology.

Water Resources

Albany State University, College of Arts and Humanities, Albany, GA 31705-2717. Offers English education (M Ed); public administration (MPA), including community and economic development administration, criminal justice administration, general administration, health administration and policy, human resources management, public policy, water resources management; social work (MSW). *Program availability:* Part-time. *Degree requirements:* For master's, comprehensive exam, professional portfolio (for MPA), internship, capstone report. *Entrance requirements:* For master's, GRE, MAT, minimum GPA of 3.0, official transcript, pre-medical record/certificate of immunization, letters of reference. Electronic applications accepted. *Faculty research:* HIV prevention for minority students.

California State University, Monterey Bay, College of Science, Program in Applied Marine and Watershed Science, Seaside, CA 93955-8001. Offers MS. *Program availability:* Part-time. *Degree requirements:* For master's, thesis, thesis defense. *Entrance requirements:* For master's, GRE, recommendations, interview. Additional exam requirements/recommendations for international students: Required—TOEFL (minimum score 525 paper-based; 71 iBT). Electronic applications accepted. *Faculty research:* Remote sensing and geospatial technology, efficacy and management, marine science and ecology, watershed process, hydrology, restoration, sedimentology, ecosystem modeling.

Colorado State University, Warner College of Natural Resources, Department of Geosciences, Fort Collins, CO 80523-1482. Offers earth sciences (PhD), including geosciences, watershed science; geosciences (MS). *Program availability:* Part-time. *Faculty:* 11 full-time (3 women), 4 part-time/adjunct (2 women). *Students:* 25 full-time (10 women), 48 part-time (24 women); includes 6 minority (1 Asian, non-Hispanic/Latino; 3 Hispanic/Latino; 2 Two or more races, non-Hispanic/Latino), 9 international. Average age 31. 91 applicants, 31% accepted, 17 enrolled. In 2015, 13 master's awarded. *Degree requirements:* For master's, thesis; for doctorate, comprehensive exam, thesis/dissertation. *Entrance requirements:* For master's and doctorate, GRE General Test, minimum GPA of 3.3, letters of recommendation. Additional exam requirements/recommendations for international students: Required—TOEFL (minimum score 550 paper-based; 80 iBT); Recommended—IELTS (minimum score 6). *Application deadline:* For fall admission, 1/1 priority date for domestic and international students; for spring admission, 9/1 for domestic and international students. Applications are processed on a rolling basis. Application fee: $60 ($70 for international students). Electronic applications accepted. *Expenses:* Tuition, state resident: full-time $9348. Tuition, nonresident: full-time $22,916. *Required fees:* $2174; $473.72 per credit hour. $236.86 per semester. Tuition and fees vary according to course load and program. *Financial support:* In 2015–16, 4 fellowships (averaging $45,000 per year), 16 research assistantships with full tuition reimbursements (averaging $20,208 per year), 10 teaching assistantships with full tuition reimbursements (averaging $14,310 per year) were awarded; scholarships/grants also available. Financial award application deadline: 1/1; financial award applicants required to submit FAFSA. *Faculty research:* Applied geophysics, hydrogeology and hydrogeophysics, sedimentary petrology and geochemistry, seismology and tectonics, economic geology. *Total annual research expenditures:* $1.9 million. *Unit head:* Dr. Richard Aster, Professor and Department Head, 970-491-7606, Fax: 970-491-6307, E-mail: rick.aster@colostate.edu. *Application contact:* Sharon Gale, Graduate Contact, 970-491-5661, Fax: 970-491-6307, E-mail: sharon.gale@colostate.edu.
Website: http://warnercnr.colostate.edu/geosciences-home/

Cornell University, Graduate School, Graduate Fields of Agriculture and Life Sciences and Graduate Fields of Engineering, Field of Biological and Environmental Engineering, Ithaca, NY 14853-0001. Offers bioenergy and integrated energy systems (M Eng, MPS, MS, PhD); biological engineering (M Eng, MPS, MS, PhD); bioprocess engineering (M Eng, MPS, MS, PhD); ecohydrology (M Eng, MPS, MS, PhD); environmental engineering (M Eng, MPS, MS, PhD); environmental management (MPS); food engineering (M Eng, MPS, MS, PhD); industrial biotechnology (M Eng, MPS, MS, PhD); nanobiotechnology (M Eng, MPS, MS, PhD); sustainable systems (M Eng, MPS, MS, PhD); synthetic biology (MS); syntheticbiology (M Eng, MPS, PhD). Terminal master's awarded for partial completion of doctoral program. *Degree requirements:* For master's, thesis (MS); for doctorate, comprehensive exam, thesis/dissertation. *Entrance requirements:* For master's, letters of recommendation (3 for MS, 2 for M Eng and MPS); for doctorate, GRE General Test, 3 letters of recommendation. Additional exam requirements/recommendations for international students: Required—TOEFL (minimum score 550 paper-based; 77 iBT). Electronic applications accepted. *Faculty research:* Biological and food engineering, environmental, soil and water engineering, international agricultural engineering, structures and controlled environments, machine systems and energy.

Dalhousie University, Faculty of Agriculture, Halifax, NS B3H 4R2, Canada. Offers agriculture (M Sc), including air quality, animal behavior, animal molecular genetics, animal nutrition, animal technology, aquaculture, botany, crop management, crop physiology, ecology, environmental microbiology, food science, horticulture, nutrient management, pest management, physiology, plant biotechnology, plant pathology, soil chemistry, soil fertility, waste management and composting, water quality. *Program availability:* Part-time. *Degree requirements:* For master's, thesis, ATC Exam Teaching Assistantship. *Entrance requirements:* For master's, honors B Sc, minimum GPA of 3.0. Additional exam requirements/recommendations for international students: Required—TOEFL (minimum score 580 paper-based; 92 iBT), IELTS, Michigan English Language Assessment Battery, CanTEST, CAEL. *Faculty research:* Bio-product development, organic agriculture, nutrient management, air and water quality, agricultural biotechnology.

Water Resources

Eastern Michigan University, Graduate School, College of Arts and Sciences, Department of Biology, Ypsilanti, MI 48197. Offers cell and molecular biology (MS); community college biology teaching (MS); ecology and organismal biology (MS); general biology (MS); water resources (MS). *Program availability:* Part-time, evening/weekend, online learning. *Faculty:* 26 full-time (8 women). *Students:* 15 full-time (9 women), 33 part-time (19 women); includes 8 minority (3 Black or African American, non-Hispanic/Latino; 2 Asian, non-Hispanic/Latino; 2 Hispanic/Latino; 1 Two or more races, non-Hispanic/Latino), 3 international. Average age 27. 47 applicants, 51% accepted, 19 enrolled. In 2015, 14 master's awarded. *Entrance requirements:* For master's, GRE General Test, GRE Subject Test. Additional exam requirements/recommendations for international students: Required—TOEFL. *Application deadline:* Applications are processed on a rolling basis. Application fee: $45. *Financial support:* Fellowships, research assistantships with full tuition reimbursements, teaching assistantships with full tuition reimbursements, career-related internships or fieldwork, Federal Work-Study, institutionally sponsored loans, scholarships/grants, tuition waivers (partial), and unspecified assistantships available. Support available to part-time students. Financial award applicants required to submit FAFSA. *Unit head:* Dr. Daniel Clemans, Department Head, 734-487-4242, Fax: 734-487-9235, E-mail: dclemans@emich.edu. *Application contact:* Dr. David Kass, Graduate Coordinator, 734-487-4242, Fax: 734-487-9235, E-mail: dkass@emich.edu. Website: http://www.emich.edu/biology

Eastern Michigan University, Graduate School, College of Arts and Sciences, Department of Geography and Geology, Ypsilanti, MI 48197. Offers earth science education (MS); geographic information systems (MS, Graduate Certificate), including geographic information systems (MS), GIS educator (Graduate Certificate), GIS planning (MS), GIS professional (Graduate Certificate); geography and geology (Graduate Certificate), including water resources; historic preservation (MS, Graduate Certificate), including heritage interpretation and museum practice (MS), historic preservation (Graduate Certificate), preservation planning and administration (MS), recording, documentation and digital cultural heritage (MS); urban and regional planning (MS, Graduate Certificate), including transportation planning and modeling (Graduate Certificate), urban and regional planning (MS). *Program availability:* Part-time, evening/weekend, online learning. *Faculty:* 20 full-time (7 women). *Students:* 35 full-time (23 women), 76 part-time (42 women); includes 12 minority (5 Black or African American, non-Hispanic/Latino; 5 Hispanic/Latino; 2 Two or more races, non-Hispanic/Latino), 14 international. Average age 32. 75 applicants, 63% accepted, 35 enrolled. In 2015, 31 master's, 5 other advanced degrees awarded. *Entrance requirements:* Additional exam requirements/recommendations for international students: Required—TOEFL. *Application deadline:* Applications are processed on a rolling basis. Application fee: $45. *Financial support:* Fellowships, research assistantships with full tuition reimbursements, teaching assistantships with full tuition reimbursements, career-related internships or fieldwork, Federal Work-Study, institutionally sponsored loans, scholarships/grants, tuition waivers (partial), and unspecified assistantships available. Support available to part-time students. Financial award applicants required to submit FAFSA. *Unit head:* Dr. Richard Sambrook, Department Head, 734-487-0218, Fax: 734-487-6979, E-mail: rsambroo@emich.edu. Website: http://www.emich.edu/geo/

Humboldt State University, Academic Programs, College of Natural Resources and Sciences, Programs in Natural Resources, Arcata, CA 95521-8299. Offers natural resources (MS), including fisheries, forestry, natural resources planning and interpretation, rangeland resources and wildland soils, wastewater utilization, watershed management, wildlife. *Degree requirements:* For master's, thesis or alternative. *Entrance requirements:* For master's, GRE, appropriate bachelor's degree, minimum GPA of 2.5, 3 letters of recommendation, resume. Additional exam requirements/recommendations for international students: Required—TOEFL (minimum score 500 paper-based). *Faculty research:* Spotted owl habitat, pre-settlement vegetation, hardwood utilization, tree physiology, fisheries.

Marquette University, Graduate School, College of Engineering, Department of Civil and Environmental Engineering, Milwaukee, WI 53201-1881. Offers construction engineering and management (MS, PhD, Certificate); environmental engineering (MS, PhD); structural design (Certificate); structural engineering and structural mechanics (MS, PhD); transportation (Certificate); transportation engineering and materials (MS, PhD); waste and wastewater treatment processes (Certificate); water resources engineering (Certificate). *Program availability:* Part-time, evening/weekend. *Faculty:* 14 full-time (2 women). *Students:* 31 full-time (10 women), 8 part-time (0 women); includes 3 minority (2 Hispanic/Latino; 1 Two or more races, non-Hispanic/Latino), 19 international. Average age 27. 69 applicants, 65% accepted, 9 enrolled. In 2015, 14 master's awarded. Terminal master's awarded for partial completion of doctoral program. *Degree requirements:* For master's, comprehensive exam (for some programs), thesis or alternative; for doctorate, thesis/dissertation. *Entrance requirements:* For master's, GRE General Test (recommended), minimum GPA of 3.0, official transcripts from all current and previous colleges/universities except Marquette, three letters of recommendation; for doctorate, GRE General Test, minimum GPA of 3.0, official transcripts from all current and previous colleges/universities except Marquette, three letters of recommendation, brief statement of purpose, submission of any English language publications authored by applicant (strongly recommended). Additional exam requirements/recommendations for international students: Required—TOEFL (minimum score 530 paper-based). *Application deadline:* For fall admission, 6/1 priority date for domestic students. Applications are processed on a rolling basis. Application fee: $50. Electronic applications accepted. *Financial support:* In 2015–16, 21 students received support, including 6 fellowships with partial tuition reimbursements available (averaging $9,177 per year), 1 research assistantship with full tuition reimbursement available (averaging $13,745 per year), 7 teaching assistantships with full tuition reimbursements available (averaging $13,902 per year); scholarships/grants, health care benefits, tuition waivers (partial), and unspecified assistantships also available. Support available to part-time students. Financial award application deadline: 2/15. *Faculty research:* Highway safety, highway performance, and intelligent transportation systems; surface mount technology; watershed management. *Total annual research expenditures:* $489,576. *Unit head:* Dr. Christopher Foley, Chair, 414-288-5741. *Application contact:* Dr. Stephen M. Heinrich, Director of Graduate Studies, 414-288-5466, E-mail: stephen.heinrich@marquette.edu. Website: http://www.marquette.edu/civil-environmental-engineering/

Michigan Technological University, Graduate School, Interdisciplinary Programs, Houghton, MI 49931. Offers atmospheric sciences (PhD); biochemistry and molecular biology (PhD); computational science and engineering (PhD); data science (MS, Graduate Certificate); engineering (M Eng); environmental engineering (PhD); international profile (Graduate Certificate); nanotechnology (Graduate Certificate); sustainability (Graduate Certificate); sustainable water resources systems (Graduate Certificate). *Program availability:* Part-time. *Faculty:* 118 full-time (26 women), 12 part-time/adjunct. *Students:* 53 full-time (22 women), 10 part-time; includes 2 minority (1 Asian, non-Hispanic/Latino; 1 Two or more races, non-Hispanic/Latino), 44 international. Average age 30. 300 applicants, 19% accepted, 17 enrolled. In 2015, 3 master's, 7

doctorates, 4 other advanced degrees awarded. Terminal master's awarded for partial completion of doctoral program. *Degree requirements:* For master's, comprehensive exam (for some programs), thesis (for some programs); for doctorate, comprehensive exam, thesis/dissertation. *Entrance requirements:* For master's, doctorate, and Graduate Certificate, GRE, statement of purpose, personal statement, official transcripts, 2-3 letters of recommendation. Additional exam requirements/recommendations for international students: Required—TOEFL or IELTS. *Application deadline:* Applications are processed on a rolling basis. Electronic applications accepted. *Expenses:* Tuition, state resident: full-time $15,507; part-time $861.50 per credit. Tuition, nonresident: full-time $15,507; part-time $861.50 per credit. *Required fees:* $248; $248. Tuition and fees vary according to course load and program. *Financial support:* In 2015–16, 41 students received support, including 7 fellowships with tuition reimbursements available (averaging $14,516 per year), 16 research assistantships with tuition reimbursements available (averaging $14,516 per year), 9 teaching assistantships with tuition reimbursements available (averaging $14,516 per year); career-related internships or fieldwork, Federal Work-Study, scholarships/grants, health care benefits, unspecified assistantships, and cooperative program also available. Financial award applicants required to submit FAFSA. *Faculty research:* Big data, atmospheric sciences, bioinformatics and systems biology, molecular dynamics, environmental studies. *Unit head:* Dr. Jacqueline E. Huntoon, Provost and Vice President for Academic Affairs, 906-487-2440, Fax: 906-487-2284, E-mail: jeh@mtu.edu. *Application contact:* Carol T. Wingerson, Administrative Aide, 906-487-2328, Fax: 906-487-2284, E-mail: gradadms@mtu.edu.

Missouri University of Science and Technology, Graduate School, Department of Geological Sciences and Engineering, Rolla, MO 65409. Offers geological engineering (MS, DE, PhD); geology and geophysics (MS, PhD), including geochemistry, geology, geophysics, groundwater and environmental geology; petroleum engineering (MS, DE, PhD). *Program availability:* Part-time. *Faculty:* 18 full-time (4 women), 1 part-time/adjunct (0 women). *Students:* 249 full-time (51 women), 93 part-time (17 women); includes 37 minority (10 Black or African American, non-Hispanic/Latino; 3 American Indian or Alaska Native, non-Hispanic/Latino; 6 Asian, non-Hispanic/Latino; 18 Hispanic/Latino), 169 international. Average age 31. 296 applicants, 58% accepted, 97 enrolled. In 2015, 17 master's, 6 doctorates awarded. *Degree requirements:* For master's, thesis optional; for doctorate, comprehensive exam, thesis/dissertation. *Entrance requirements:* For master's, GRE General Test (minimum score 600 quantitative, writing 3.5), minimum GPA of 3.0 in last 4 semesters; for doctorate, GRE General Test (minimum scores: Quantitative 600, Writing 3.5). Additional exam requirements/recommendations for international students: Required—TOEFL (minimum score 550 paper-based). *Application deadline:* For fall admission, 7/1 for domestic students; for spring admission, 12/1 for domestic students. Applications are processed on a rolling basis. Application fee: $55 ($175 for international students). Electronic applications accepted. *Expenses:* Tuition, state resident: full-time $10,536. Tuition, nonresident: full-time $27,015. Full-time tuition and fees vary according to course load. *Financial support:* In 2015–16, fellowships with full tuition reimbursements (averaging $11,250 per year), 9 research assistantships with partial tuition reimbursements (averaging $1,814 per year), 3 teaching assistantships with partial tuition reimbursements (averaging $1,814 per year) were awarded; Federal Work-Study and institutionally sponsored loans also available. Support available to part-time students. Financial award application deadline: 3/1; financial award applicants required to submit FAFSA. *Faculty research:* Digital image processing and geographic information systems, mineralogy, igneous and sedimentary petrology-geochemistry, sedimentology groundwater hydrology and contaminant transport. *Total annual research expenditures:* $2.1 million. *Unit head:* Dr. Robert Laudon, Chairman, 573-341-4466, Fax: 573-341-6935, E-mail: rlaudon@mst.edu. *Application contact:* Debbie Schwertz, Admissions Coordinator, 573-341-6013, Fax: 573-341-6271, E-mail: schwertz@mst.edu. Website: http://gse.umr.edu/geologicalengineering.html

Montclair State University, The Graduate School, College of Science and Mathematics, Water Resource Management Certificate Program, Montclair, NJ 07043-1624. Offers Certificate. *Program availability:* Part-time, evening/weekend. *Students:* 1 part-time (0 women); minority (Hispanic/Latino). Average age 32. In 2015, 2 Certificates awarded. *Entrance requirements:* Additional exam requirements/recommendations for international students: Required—TOEFL (minimum score 550 paper-based). *Application deadline:* For fall admission, 6/1 for international students; for spring admission, 11/1 for international students. Applications are processed on a rolling basis. Application fee: $60. *Expenses:* Tuition, state resident: part-time $553 per credit. Tuition, nonresident: part-time $854 per credit. *Required fees:* $91 per credit. Tuition and fees vary according to program. *Financial support:* In 2015–16, research assistantships with full tuition reimbursements (averaging $5,000 per year) were awarded; Federal Work-Study, scholarships/grants, and unspecified assistantships also available. Support available to part-time students. Financial award application deadline: 3/1; financial award applicants required to submit FAFSA. *Unit head:* Dr. Matthew Goring, Advisor, 973-655-5409, E-mail: gorringm@mail.montclair.edu. *Application contact:* Amy Aiello, Director of Graduate Admissions and Operations, 973-655-5147, Fax: 973-655-7869, E-mail: graduate.school@montclair.edu.

New Mexico State University, Graduate School, Program in Water Science Management, Las Cruces, NM 88003-8001. Offers MS, PhD. *Program availability:* Part-time. *Faculty:* 3 full-time (0 women). *Students:* 22 full-time (6 women), 8 part-time (3 women); includes 7 minority (1 Black or African American, non-Hispanic/Latino; 6 Hispanic/Latino), 12 international. Average age 34. 22 applicants, 59% accepted, 8 enrolled. In 2015, 4 master's awarded. *Degree requirements:* For master's, comprehensive exam, thesis; for doctorate, thesis/dissertation, written and oral comprehensive exams. *Entrance requirements:* For master's, letter of intent or personal statement; resume or curriculum vitae; 3 letters of recommendation; minimum GPA of 3.0; for doctorate, letter of intent or personal statement; resume or curriculum vitae; 3 letters of recommendation; minimum GPA of 3.5. Additional exam requirements/recommendations for international students: Required—TOEFL (minimum score 550 paper-based; 79 iBT), IELTS (minimum score 6.5). *Application deadline:* For fall admission, 3/15 for domestic and international students; for spring admission, 10/1 for domestic and international students. Application fee: $40 ($50 for international students). Electronic applications accepted. *Expenses:* $274.50 per credit hour for in-state students, and all students enrolled in six or fewer credits; $839.30 per credit hour for out-of-state and international students enrolled in at least seven hours. *Financial support:* In 2015–16, 20 students received support, including 1 fellowship (averaging $4,088 per year), 10 research assistantships (averaging $19,019 per year), 4 teaching assistantships (averaging $12,723 per year); career-related internships or fieldwork, Federal Work-Study, scholarships/grants, traineeships, health care benefits, and unspecified assistantships also available. Support available to part-time students. Financial award application deadline: 3/1. *Unit head:* Desa Daniel, Program Coordinator, 575-646-4198, Fax: 575-646-6418, E-mail: wsm@nmsu.edu. *Application contact:* 575-646-4197, Fax: 575-646-6418, E-mail: wsm@nmsu.edu.

Website: http://wsm.research.nmsu.edu

Old Dominion University, Frank Batten College of Engineering and Technology, Program in Civil Engineering, Norfolk, VA 23529. Offers civil engineering (ME, MS), including coastal engineering, geotechnical, hydraulics and water resources, structures, transportation. *Program availability:* Part-time, evening/weekend, blended/hybrid learning. *Faculty:* 15 full-time (1 woman), 5 part-time/adjunct (0 women). *Students:* 9 full-time (3 women), 37 part-time (5 women); includes 11 minority (5 Black or African American, non-Hispanic/Latino; 3 Asian, non-Hispanic/Latino; 1 Hispanic/Latino; 2 Two or more races, non-Hispanic/Latino), 11 international. Average age 29. 23 applicants, 96% accepted, 8 enrolled. In 2015, 23 master's awarded. *Degree requirements:* For master's, comprehensive exam, thesis optional. *Entrance requirements:* For master's, GRE, minimum GPA of 3.0. Additional exam requirements/recommendations for international students: Required—TOEFL (minimum score 550 paper-based, 80 iBT) or IELTS (6.5). *Application deadline:* For fall admission, 6/1 priority date for domestic students, 4/15 priority date for international students; for spring admission, 11/1 priority date for domestic students, 10/1 priority date for international students. Applications are processed on a rolling basis. Application fee: $50. Electronic applications accepted. *Expenses:* $464 per credit in-state tuition plus $297 fees per year; $1,160 per credit out-of-state tuition plus $367 fees per year. *Financial support:* In 2015–16, 27 students received support, including 1 fellowship with full tuition reimbursement available (averaging $18,000 per year), 12 research assistantships with tuition reimbursements available (averaging $14,950 per year), 7 teaching assistantships with tuition reimbursements available (averaging $14,829 per year); scholarships/grants and health care benefits also available. Financial award application deadline: 4/1; financial award applicants required to submit FAFSA. *Faculty research:* Structural engineering, coastal engineering, environmental engineering, geotechnical engineering, water resources, transportation engineering. *Total annual research expenditures:* $735,060. *Unit head:* Dr. Isao Ishibashi, Graduate Program Director, 757-683-4641, Fax: 757-683-5354, E-mail: cegpd@odu.edu. *Application contact:* Dr. Linda Vahala, Associate Dean, 757-683-3789, Fax: 757-683-4898, E-mail: lvahala@odu.edu.
Website: http://eng.odu.edu/cee/

Oregon State University, Interdisciplinary/Institutional Programs, Program in Environmental Sciences, Corvallis, OR 97331. Offers biogeochemistry (MS, PhD); ecology (MS, PhD); environmental education (MS, PhD); environmental sciences (PSM); natural resources (MS, PhD); quantitative analysis (MS, PhD); social science (MS, PhD); water resources (MS, PhD). *Program availability:* Part-time. *Students:* 17 full-time (12 women), 12 part-time (6 women); includes 7 minority (1 Black or African American, non-Hispanic/Latino; 2 Asian, non-Hispanic/Latino; 2 Hispanic/Latino; 2 Two or more races, non-Hispanic/Latino), 3 international. Average age 34. 42 applicants, 19% accepted, 3 enrolled. In 2015, 6 master's, 4 doctorates awarded. *Entrance requirements:* For master's and doctorate, GRE. Additional exam requirements/recommendations for international students: Required—TOEFL (minimum score 80 iBT), IELTS (minimum score 6.5). *Application deadline:* For fall admission, 1/15 for domestic students. Application fee: $75 ($85 for international students). *Expenses:* Contact institution. *Unit head:* Dr. Carolyn Fonyo Boggess, Interim Director, E-mail: carolyn.fonyo@oregonstate.edu.
Website: http://envsci.science.oregonstate.edu/

Oregon State University, Interdisciplinary/Institutional Programs, Program in Water Resources Engineering, Corvallis, OR 97331. Offers groundwater engineering (MS, PhD); surface water engineering (MS, PhD); watershed engineering (MS, PhD). *Program availability:* Part-time. *Students:* 21 full-time (8 women), 2 part-time (1 woman); includes 3 minority (1 Asian, non-Hispanic/Latino; 2 Hispanic/Latino), 1 international. Average age 31. 42 applicants, 21% accepted, 4 enrolled. In 2015, 8 master's, 1 doctorate awarded. *Entrance requirements:* For master's and doctorate, GRE. Additional exam requirements/recommendations for international students: Required—TOEFL (minimum score 80 iBT), IELTS (minimum score 6.5). *Application deadline:* For fall admission, 1/5 for domestic students. Application fee: $75 ($85 for international students). *Expenses:* Tuition, state resident: full-time $12,150; part-time $450 per credit. Tuition, nonresident: full-time $20,952; part-time $776 per credit. *Required fees:* $1572; $1443 per unit. One-time fee: $350. Tuition and fees vary according to course load, campus/location and program. *Financial support:* Application deadline: 1/5. *Unit head:* Dr. Mary Santelmann, Director, Water Resources Graduate Program, 541-737-1215, E-mail: santelmm@oregonstate.edu.
Website: http://oregonstate.edu/gradwater/

Oregon State University, Interdisciplinary/Institutional Programs, Program in Water Resources Policy and Management, Corvallis, OR 97331. Offers MS. *Students:* 12 full-time (8 women), 3 part-time (1 woman); includes 1 minority (Two or more races, non-Hispanic/Latino), 2 international. Average age 28. 23 applicants, 43% accepted, 4 enrolled. In 2015, 8 master's awarded. *Entrance requirements:* For master's, GRE. Additional exam requirements/recommendations for international students: Required—TOEFL (minimum score 80 iBT), IELTS (minimum score 6.5). *Application deadline:* For fall admission, 1/5 for domestic students. Application fee: $75 ($85 for international students). *Expenses:* Tuition, state resident: full-time $12,150; part-time $450 per credit. Tuition, nonresident: full-time $20,952; part-time $776 per credit. *Required fees:* $1572; $1443 per unit. One-time fee: $350. Tuition and fees vary according to course load, campus/location and program. *Financial support:* Application deadline: 1/5. *Unit head:* Dr. Mary Santelmann, Director, Water Resources Graduate Program, 541-737-1215, Fax: 541-737-1200, E-mail: gradwater_support@oregonstate.edu.
Website: http://oregonstate.edu/gradwater/

Oregon State University, Interdisciplinary/Institutional Programs, Program in Water Resources Science, Corvallis, OR 97331. Offers MS, PhD. *Students:* 17 full-time (8 women), 4 part-time (3 women); includes 6 minority (1 American Indian or Alaska Native, non-Hispanic/Latino; 1 Asian, non-Hispanic/Latino; 2 Hispanic/Latino; 2 Two or more races, non-Hispanic/Latino). Average age 34. 51 applicants, 25% accepted, 5 enrolled. In 2015, 4 master's awarded. *Entrance requirements:* For master's and doctorate, GRE. Additional exam requirements/recommendations for international students: Required—TOEFL (minimum score 80 iBT), IELTS (minimum score 6.5). *Application deadline:* For fall admission, 1/5 for domestic students. Application fee: $75 ($85 for international students). *Expenses:* Tuition, state resident: full-time $12,150; part-time $450 per credit. Tuition, nonresident: full-time $20,952; part-time $776 per credit. *Required fees:* $1572; $1443 per unit. One-time fee: $350. Tuition and fees vary according to course load, campus/location and program. *Financial support:* Application deadline: 1/5. *Unit head:* Dr. Mary Santelmann, Director, Water Resources Graduate Program, 541-737-1215, E-mail: gradwater_support@oregonstate.edu.
Website: http://oregonstate.edu/gradwater/

Rutgers University–New Brunswick, Graduate School-New Brunswick, Department of Environmental Sciences, Piscataway, NJ 08854-8097. Offers air pollution and resources (MS, PhD); aquatic biology (MS, PhD); aquatic chemistry (MS, PhD); atmospheric science (MS, PhD); chemistry and physics of aerosol and hydrosol systems (MS, PhD); environmental chemistry (MS, PhD); environmental microbiology (MS, PhD); environmental toxicology (PhD); exposure assessment (PhD); fate and effects of pollutants (MS, PhD); pollution prevention and control (MS, PhD); water and wastewater treatment (MS, PhD); water resources (MS, PhD). Terminal master's awarded for partial completion of doctoral program. *Degree requirements:* For master's, comprehensive exam, thesis or alternative, oral final exam; for doctorate, comprehensive exam, thesis/dissertation, thesis defense, qualifying exam. *Entrance requirements:* For master's and doctorate, GRE General Test. Additional exam requirements/recommendations for international students: Required—TOEFL. Electronic applications accepted. *Faculty research:* Biological waste treatment; contaminant fate and transport; air, soil and water quality.

State University of New York College of Environmental Science and Forestry, Program in Environmental Science, Syracuse, NY 13210-2779. Offers biophysical and ecological economics (MPS); coupled natural and human systems (MPS); ecosystem restoration (MPS); environmental and community land planning (MPS, MS); environmental and natural resources policy (PhD); environmental communication and participatory processes (PhD); environmental monitoring and modeling (MPS); environmental policy and democratic processes (MPS, MS); water and wetland resource studies (MPS, MS). *Program availability:* Part-time. *Faculty:* 1 full-time (0 women), 1 (woman) part-time/adjunct. *Students:* 56 full-time (33 women), 17 part-time (10 women); includes 6 minority (2 Asian, non-Hispanic/Latino; 3 Hispanic/Latino; 1 Two or more races, non-Hispanic/Latino), 34 international. 85 applicants, 44% accepted, 13 enrolled. *Degree requirements:* For master's, thesis (for some programs); for doctorate, comprehensive exam, thesis/dissertation. *Entrance requirements:* For master's and doctorate, GRE General Test, minimum GPA of 3.0. Additional exam requirements/recommendations for international students: Required—TOEFL (minimum score 550 paper-based; 80 iBT), IELTS (minimum score 6). *Application deadline:* For fall admission, 2/1 priority date for domestic and international students; for spring admission, 11/1 priority date for domestic and international students. Applications are processed on a rolling basis. Application fee: $60. *Expenses:* Tuition, state resident: full-time $10,870; part-time $453 per credit. Tuition, nonresident: full-time $22,210; part-time $925 per credit. *Required fees:* $1075; $89.22 per credit. *Financial support:* Fellowships with tuition reimbursements, research assistantships with tuition reimbursements, teaching assistantships with tuition reimbursements, career-related internships or fieldwork, Federal Work-Study, institutionally sponsored loans, scholarships/grants, health care benefits, and unspecified assistantships available. Support available to part-time students. Financial award application deadline: 6/30; financial award applicants required to submit FAFSA. *Faculty research:* Environmental education/communications, water resources, land resources, waste management. *Unit head:* Dr. Ruth Yanai, Coordinator, 315-470-6955, Fax: 315-470-6700, E-mail: rdyanai@esf.edu. *Application contact:* Dr. Dudley J. Raynal, Dean, Instruction and Graduate Studies, 315-470-6599, Fax: 315-470-6978, E-mail: esfgrad@esf.edu.
Website: http://www.esf.edu/environmentalscience/graduate/

Tropical Agriculture Research and Higher Education Center, Graduate School, Turrialba, Costa Rica. Offers agribusiness management (MS); agroforestry systems (PhD); development practices (MS); ecological agriculture (MS); environmental socioeconomics (MS); forestry in tropical and subtropical zones (PhD); integrated watershed management (MS); international sustainable tourism (MS); management and conservation of tropical rainforests and biodiversity (MS); tropical agriculture (PhD); tropical agroforestry (MS). *Entrance requirements:* For master's, GRE, 2 years of related professional experience, letters of recommendation; for doctorate, GRE, 4 letters of recommendation, letter of support from employing organization, master's degree in agronomy, biological sciences, forestry, natural resources or related field. Additional exam requirements/recommendations for international students: Required—TOEFL (minimum score 550 paper-based). Electronic applications accepted. *Faculty research:* Biodiversity in fragmented landscapes, ecosystem management, integrated pest management, environmental livestock production, biotechnology carbon balances in diverse land uses.

University of Alaska Fairbanks, College of Engineering and Mines, Department of Civil and Environmental Engineering, Fairbanks, AK 99775-5900. Offers arctic engineering (MS); civil engineering (MCE, MS); design and construction management (Graduate Certificate); engineering and science management (MS), including engineering management, science management; environmental engineering (MS, PhD); environmental quality science (MS), including environmental contaminants, environmental science and management, water supply and waste treatment. *Program availability:* Part-time. *Faculty:* 12 full-time (3 women). *Students:* 9 full-time (4 women), 14 part-time (7 women); includes 6 minority (1 Black or African American, non-Hispanic/Latino; 1 American Indian or Alaska Native, non-Hispanic/Latino; 1 Asian, non-Hispanic/Latino; 2 Hispanic/Latino; 1 Two or more races, non-Hispanic/Latino), 2 international. Average age 31. 17 applicants, 47% accepted, 5 enrolled. In 2015, 9 master's, 1 other advanced degree awarded. *Degree requirements:* For master's, comprehensive exam, thesis (for some programs), oral defense of project or thesis; for doctorate, comprehensive exam, thesis/dissertation. *Entrance requirements:* For master's, bachelor's degree from accredited institution with minimum cumulative undergraduate and major GPA of 3.0. Additional exam requirements/recommendations for international students: Required—TOEFL, IELTS. *Application deadline:* For fall admission, 6/1 for domestic students, 3/1 for international students; for spring admission, 10/15 for domestic students, 9/1 for international students. Applications are processed on a rolling basis. Application fee: $60. Electronic applications accepted. *Expenses:* Tuition, state resident: full-time $7614; part-time $423 per credit. Tuition, nonresident: full-time $15,552; part-time $864 per credit. *Required fees:* $38 per credit. $187 per semester. Tuition and fees vary according to course level, course load, program and reciprocity agreements. *Financial support:* In 2015–16, 4 research assistantships with full tuition reimbursements (averaging $10,632 per year), 6 teaching assistantships with full tuition reimbursements (averaging $6,390 per year) were awarded; fellowships with full tuition reimbursements, career-related internships or fieldwork, Federal Work-Study, scholarships/grants, health care benefits, and unspecified assistantships also available. Support available to part-time students. Financial award application deadline: 7/1; financial award applicants required to submit FAFSA. *Faculty research:* Soils, structures, culvert thawing with solar power, pavement drainage, contaminant hydrogeology. *Unit head:* Dr. Robert Perkins, Department Chair, 907-474-7241, Fax: 907-474-6087, E-mail: fycee@uaf.edu. *Application contact:* Mary Kreta, Director of Admissions, 907-474-7500, Fax: 907-474-7097, E-mail: admissions@uaf.edu.
Website: http://cem.uaf.edu/cee

The University of Arizona, College of Agriculture and Life Sciences, Department of Soil, Water and Environmental Science, Tucson, AZ 85721. Offers MS, PhD, Graduate Certificate. *Degree requirements:* For master's, thesis; for doctorate, comprehensive exam, thesis/dissertation. *Entrance requirements:* For master's, GRE (recommended), minimum GPA of 3.0, letter of interest, 3 letters of recommendation; for doctorate, GRE (recommended), MS, minimum GPA of 3.0, letter of interest, 3 letters of recommendation. Additional exam requirements/recommendations for international students: Required—TOEFL (minimum score 550 paper-based; 80 iBT). *Application deadline:* For fall admission, 6/1 for domestic students, 12/1 for international students; for spring admission, 10/1 for domestic students, 6/1 for international students. Applications are processed on a rolling basis. Application fee: $75. Electronic applications accepted. *Financial support:* Fellowships, research assistantships,

teaching assistantships, Federal Work-Study, institutionally sponsored loans, scholarships/grants, health care benefits, tuition waivers (full and partial), and unspecified assistantships available. Financial award application deadline: 5/1. *Faculty research:* Plant production, environmental microbiology, contaminant flow and transport, aquaculture. *Unit head:* Dr. Jonathan D. Chorover, Department Head,
E-mail: chorover@cals.arizona.edu.
Website: http://swes.cals.arizona.edu/

The University of Arizona, College of Agriculture and Life Sciences, School of Natural Resources and the Environment, Watershed Resources Program, Tucson, AZ 85721. Offers water, society, and policy (MS); watershed management (MS, PhD). *Degree requirements:* For master's, thesis; for doctorate, comprehensive exam, thesis/dissertation. *Entrance requirements:* For master's, GRE General Test, minimum GPA of 3.0, 3 letters of recommendation; for doctorate, GRE General Test, minimum GPA of 3.0, 3 letters of recommendation, MA or MS. Additional exam requirements/recommendations for international students: Required—TOEFL (minimum score 550 paper-based; 79 iBT). Electronic applications accepted. *Faculty research:* Forest fuel characteristics, prescribed fire, tree ring-fire scar analysis, erosion, sedimentation.

The University of British Columbia, Faculty of Land and Food Systems, Program in Soil Science, Vancouver, BC V6T 1Z1, Canada. Offers land and water systems (MLWS); soil science (M Sc, PhD). *Degree requirements:* For master's, thesis; for doctorate, comprehensive exam, thesis/dissertation. *Entrance requirements:* Additional exam requirements/recommendations for international students: Required—TOEFL (minimum score 577 paper-based; 90 iBT), IELTS (minimum score 6.5). Electronic applications accepted. *Faculty research:* Soil and water conservation, land use, land use and land classification, soil physics, soil chemistry and mineralogy.

University of Calgary, Faculty of Graduate Studies, Schulich School of Engineering, Department of Civil Engineering, Calgary, AB T2N 1N4, Canada. Offers avalanche mechanics (M Sc, PhD); civil engineering (M Eng, M Sc, PhD); energy and environment engineering (M Eng, M Sc, PhD); environmental engineering (M Eng, M Sc, PhD); geotechnical engineering (M Eng, M Sc, PhD); materials science (M Eng, M Sc, PhD); project management (M Eng, M Sc, PhD); structures and solid mechanics (M Eng, M Sc, PhD); transportation engineering (M Eng, M Sc, PhD); water resources (M Eng, M Sc, PhD). *Program availability:* Part-time. *Degree requirements:* For master's, thesis; for doctorate, thesis/dissertation, written and oral candidacy exam. *Entrance requirements:* For master's, minimum GPA of 3.0; for doctorate, minimum GPA of 3.5. Additional exam requirements/recommendations for international students: Required—TOEFL (minimum score 580 paper-based; 93 iBT), IELTS (minimum score 7). Electronic applications accepted. *Faculty research:* Geotechnical engineering, energy and environment, transportation, project management, structures and solid mechanics.

University of California, Riverside, Graduate Division, Environmental Sciences Department, Riverside, CA 92521-0102. Offers MS, PhD. *Degree requirements:* For doctorate, thesis/dissertation. *Entrance requirements:* For master's and doctorate, minimum GPA of 3.2. Additional exam requirements/recommendations for international students: Required—TOEFL (minimum score 550 paper-based; 80 iBT). Electronic applications accepted. *Faculty research:* Environmental chemistry and ecotoxicology, environmental microbiology, environmental and natural resource economics and policy, soil and water science, environmental sciences and management.

University of Colorado Denver, College of Liberal Arts and Sciences, Department of Geography and Environmental Sciences, Denver, CO 80217. Offers environmental sciences (MS), including air quality, ecosystems, environmental health, environmental science education, geo-spatial analysis, hazardous waste, water quality. *Program availability:* Part-time, evening/weekend. *Faculty:* 12 full-time (4 women), 2 part-time/adjunct (1 woman). *Students:* 46 full-time (26 women), 12 part-time (5 women); includes 11 minority (1 Black or African American, non-Hispanic/Latino; 1 Asian, non-Hispanic/Latino; 6 Hispanic/Latino; 3 Two or more races, non-Hispanic/Latino), 3 international. Average age 30. 75 applicants, 61% accepted, 24 enrolled. In 2015, 11 master's awarded. *Degree requirements:* For master's, thesis or alternative, 30 credits including 21 of core requirements and 9 of environmental science electives. *Entrance requirements:* For master's, GRE General Test, BA in one of the natural/physical sciences or engineering (or equivalent background); prerequisite coursework in calculus and physics (one semester each), general chemistry with lab and general biology with lab (two semesters each); three letters of recommendation. Additional exam requirements/recommendations for international students: Required—TOEFL (minimum score 537 paper-based; 75 iBT); Recommended—IELTS (minimum score 6.5). *Application deadline:* For fall admission, 1/20 for domestic and international students; for spring admission, 10/1 for domestic and international students. Application fee: $50 ($75 for international students). Electronic applications accepted. *Financial support:* In 2015–16, 8 students received support. Fellowships, research assistantships, teaching assistantships, Federal Work-Study, institutionally sponsored loans, scholarships/grants, and traineeships available. Financial award application deadline: 4/1; financial award applicants required to submit FAFSA. *Faculty research:* Air quality, environmental health, ecosystems, hazardous waste, water quality, geo-spatial analysis and environmental science education. *Unit head:* Anne Chinn, Director of MS in Environmental Sciences Program, 303-556-3958, E-mail: ges@ucdenver.edu. *Application contact:* Sue Eddleman, Program Assistant, 303-352-3698,
E-mail: sue.eddleman@ucdenver.edu.
Website: http://www.ucdenver.edu/academics/colleges/CLAS/Departments/ges/Programs/MasterofScience/Pages/MasterofScience.aspx

University of Florida, Graduate School, College of Agricultural and Life Sciences, Department of Soil and Water Science, Gainesville, FL 32611. Offers soil and water science (MS, PhD), including agroecology (MS), geographic information systems, hydrologic sciences, tropical conservation and development, wetland sciences. *Program availability:* Part-time, evening/weekend, online learning. *Faculty:* 24 full-time, 7 part-time/adjunct. *Students:* 58 full-time (28 women), 51 part-time (25 women); includes 15 minority (1 Black or African American, non-Hispanic/Latino; 2 Asian, non-Hispanic/Latino; 12 Hispanic/Latino), 37 international. Average age 32. 29 applicants, 66% accepted, 17 enrolled. In 2015, 16 master's, 12 doctorates awarded. Terminal master's awarded for partial completion of doctoral program. *Degree requirements:* For master's, thesis optional; for doctorate, comprehensive exam, thesis/dissertation. *Entrance requirements:* For master's and doctorate, GRE General Test, minimum GPA of 3.0. Additional exam requirements/recommendations for international students: Required—TOEFL (minimum score 550 paper-based; 80 iBT), IELTS (minimum score 6). *Application deadline:* For fall admission, 2/1 priority date for domestic students, 2/1 for international students; for spring admission, 10/1 for domestic and international students; for summer admission, 2/1 for domestic and international students. Applications are processed on a rolling basis. Application fee: $30. Electronic applications accepted. *Financial support:* In 2015–16, 5 fellowships, 38 research assistantships, 14 teaching assistantships were awarded; career-related internships or fieldwork, Federal Work-Study, institutionally sponsored loans, and unspecified assistantships also available. Support available to part-time students. Financial award applicants required to submit FAFSA. *Faculty research:* Carbon dynamics and ecosystem services; landscape analysis and modeling; nutrient pesticide and waste management; soil, water, and aquifer remediation; wetlands and aquatic ecosystems. *Total annual research expenditures:* $4.4 million. *Unit head:* K. Ramesh Reddy, PhD, Graduate Research Professor and Department Chairman, 352-294-3154, Fax: 352-392-3399, E-mail: krr@ufl.edu. *Application contact:* Max Teplitski, PhD, Associate Professor and Graduate Coordinator, 352-273-8189 Ext. 211, Fax: 352-392-3902,
E-mail: maxtep@ufl.edu.
Website: http://soils.ifas.ufl.edu/

University of Idaho, College of Graduate Studies, College of Agricultural and Life Sciences, Water Resources Program, Moscow, ID 83844-1130. Offers engineering and science (PhD); engineering and science (MS); law, management and policy (MS, PhD); science and management (MS, PhD). *Faculty:* 13 full-time. *Students:* 22 full-time, 7 part-time. Average age 34. In 2015, 2 master's, 5 doctorates awarded. *Entrance requirements:* Additional exam requirements/recommendations for international students: Required—TOEFL. *Application deadline:* Applications are processed on a rolling basis. Application fee: $60. Electronic applications accepted. *Expenses:* Tuition, state resident: full-time $6205; part-time $399 per credit hour. Tuition, nonresident: full-time $20,209; part-time $1177 per credit hour. *Required fees:* $2017; $58 per credit hour. Full-time tuition and fees vary according to course load and reciprocity agreements. *Financial support:* Applicants required to submit FAFSA. *Faculty research:* Water resource systems, biological wastewater treatment and water reclamation, invasive species, aquatics ecosystem restoration, watershed science and management. *Unit head:* Dr. Mark David Solomon, Associate Director, 208-885-6430,
E-mail: iwrri@uidaho.edu. *Application contact:* Sean Scoggin, Graduate Recruitment Coordinator, 208-885-4723, Fax: 208-885-4406,
E-mail: graduateadmissions@uidaho.edu.
Website: http://www.uidaho.edu/cogs/envs/water-resources

University of Maine, Graduate School, College of Natural Sciences, Forestry, and Agriculture, School of Earth and Climate Sciences, Orono, ME 04469. Offers MS, PhD. *Program availability:* Part-time. *Faculty:* 21 full-time (5 women). *Students:* 27 full-time (14 women); includes 1 minority (Hispanic/Latino), 4 international. Average age 31. 43 applicants, 30% accepted, 9 enrolled. In 2015, 6 master's, 2 doctorates awarded. Terminal master's awarded for partial completion of doctoral program. *Degree requirements:* For master's, thesis; for doctorate, one foreign language, comprehensive exam, thesis/dissertation. *Entrance requirements:* For master's and doctorate, GRE General Test. Additional exam requirements/recommendations for international students: Required—TOEFL (minimum score 80 iBT). *Application deadline:* For fall admission, 2/20 priority date for domestic and international students. Applications are processed on a rolling basis. Application fee: $65. Electronic applications accepted. *Financial support:* In 2015–16, 27 students received support, including 19 research assistantships with tuition reimbursements available (averaging $14,600 per year), 7 teaching assistantships with full tuition reimbursements available (averaging $14,600 per year); Federal Work-Study, institutionally sponsored loans, and tuition waivers (full and partial) also available. Financial award application deadline: 3/1. *Faculty research:* Climate change, environmental geosciences, marine geology, geodynamics and solid earth geology. *Total annual research expenditures:* $2.5 million. *Unit head:* Dr. Scott Johnson, Chair, 207-581-2142, Fax: 207-581-2202. *Application contact:* Scott G. Delcourt, Assistant Vice President for Graduate Studies and Senior Associate Dean, 207-581-3291, Fax: 207-581-3232, E-mail: graduate@maine.edu.
Website: http://umaine.edu/earthclimate/

University of Massachusetts Amherst, Graduate School, College of Natural Sciences, Department of Environmental Conservation, Amherst, MA 01003. Offers building systems (MS, PhD); environmental policy and human dimensions (MS, PhD); forest resources (MS, PhD); sustainability science (MS); water, wetlands and watersheds (MS, PhD); wildlife and fisheries conservation (MS, PhD). *Program availability:* Part-time. Terminal master's awarded for partial completion of doctoral program. *Degree requirements:* For master's, thesis or alternative; for doctorate, comprehensive exam, thesis/dissertation. *Entrance requirements:* For master's and doctorate, GRE General Test. Additional exam requirements/recommendations for international students: Required—TOEFL (minimum score 550 paper-based; 80 iBT), IELTS (minimum score 6.5). Electronic applications accepted.

University of Minnesota, Twin Cities Campus, Graduate School, College of Food, Agricultural and Natural Resource Sciences, Program in Natural Resources Science and Management, St. Paul, MN 55108. Offers assessment, monitoring, and geospatial analysis (MS, PhD); economics, policy, management, and society (MS, PhD); forest hydrology and watershed management (MS, PhD); forest products (MS, PhD); forests: biology, ecology, conservation, and management (MS, PhD); natural resources science and management (MS, PhD); paper science and engineering (MS, PhD); recreation resources, tourism, and environmental education (MS, PhD); wildlife ecology and management (MS, PhD). *Program availability:* Part-time. *Faculty:* 71 full-time (28 women), 55 part-time/adjunct (7 women). *Students:* 80 full-time (45 women), 16 part-time (9 women); includes 5 minority (1 Black or African American, non-Hispanic/Latino; 2 American Indian or Alaska Native, non-Hispanic/Latino; 2 Asian, non-Hispanic/Latino), 8 international. 81 applicants, 52% accepted, 31 enrolled. In 2015, 25 master's, 8 doctorates awarded. Terminal master's awarded for partial completion of doctoral program. *Degree requirements:* For master's, comprehensive exam, thesis; for doctorate, comprehensive exam, thesis/dissertation. *Entrance requirements:* For master's and doctorate, GRE General Test. Additional exam requirements/recommendations for international students: Required—TOEFL (minimum score 550 paper-based; 79 iBT), IELTS (minimum score 6.5). *Application deadline:* For fall admission, 12/16 priority date for domestic and international students; for spring admission, 10/15 for domestic and international students. Applications are processed on a rolling basis. Application fee: $75 ($95 for international students). Electronic applications accepted. *Financial support:* In 2015–16, fellowships with full tuition reimbursements (averaging $40,000 per year), research assistantships with full tuition reimbursements (averaging $40,000 per year), teaching assistantships with full tuition reimbursements (averaging $40,000 per year) were awarded; scholarships/grants, health care benefits, tuition waivers (full and partial), and unspecified assistantships also available. *Faculty research:* Forest hydrology, biology, ecology, conservation, and management; recreation resources and environmental education; wildlife ecology; economics, policy, and society; geographic information systems (GIS); and forest products and paper science. *Unit head:* Dr. Michael Kilgore, Director of Graduate Studies, 612-624-6298, E-mail: mkilgore@umn.edu. *Application contact:* Toni Wheeler, Graduate Program Coordinator, 612-624-7683, Fax: 612-625-5212,
E-mail: twheeler@umn.edu.
Website: http://www.nrsm.umn.edu

University of Minnesota, Twin Cities Campus, Graduate School, College of Food, Agricultural and Natural Resource Sciences, Program in Water Resources Science, St. Paul, MN 55108. Offers MS, PhD. *Program availability:* Part-time. *Faculty:* 104 full-time (29 women), 10 part-time/adjunct (3 women). *Students:* 37 full-time (22 women), 17 part-time (8 women); includes 4 minority (2 Asian, non-Hispanic/Latino; 2 Hispanic/Latino), 5 international. Average age 29. 37 applicants, 38% accepted, 13 enrolled. In

2015, 11 master's, 3 doctorates awarded. *Degree requirements:* For master's, comprehensive exam, thesis or project; for doctorate, comprehensive exam, thesis/dissertation. *Entrance requirements:* For master's, GRE, minimum GPA of 3.0 and bachelor's degree in physical, chemical, biological, or environmental science or engineering (preferred); at least two courses each in calculus, chemistry, and physics, and one course in the biological sciences (recommended); for doctorate, GRE, minimum GPA of 3.0 and master's degree in water resources, or physical, chemical, biological, or environmental science or engineering (preferred); at least two courses each in calculus, chemistry, and physics, and one course in the biological sciences (recommended). Additional exam requirements/recommendations for international students: Required—TOEFL (minimum score 550 paper-based; 79 iBT), IELTS (minimum score 6.5), Michigan English Language Assessment Battery (minimum score 80). *Application deadline:* For fall and spring admission, 12/15 priority date for domestic and international students. Applications are processed on a rolling basis. Application fee: $75 ($95 for international students). Electronic applications accepted. *Expenses:* $32,438 resident tuition and mandatory fees per year, $41,102 non-resident. *Financial support:* In 2015–16, 2 students received support, including 1 fellowship with full tuition reimbursement available (averaging $23,500 per year), research assistantships with tuition reimbursements available (averaging $15,210 per year), teaching assistantships with tuition reimbursements available (averaging $15,210 per year); scholarships/grants and unspecified assistantships also available. Financial award application deadline: 12/15. *Faculty research:* Hydrologic science, limnology, water quality, environmental chemistry, aquatic biology. *Unit head:* Dr. John Nieber, Director of Graduate Studies, 612-625-6724, E-mail: nieber@umn.edu. *Application contact:* Alison Frank-Quick, Graduate Program Coordinator, 612-624-7456, Fax: 612-625-1263, E-mail: wrs@umn.edu.
Website: http://wrs.umn.edu/

University of Missouri, Office of Research and Graduate Studies, School of Natural Resources, Program in Water Resources, Columbia, MO 65211. Offers MS, PhD.

University of Nevada, Las Vegas, Graduate College, College of Sciences, Program in Water Resources Management, Las Vegas, NV 89154-4029. Offers MS. *Program availability:* Part-time. *Students:* 3 full-time (all women), 3 part-time (1 woman), 2 international. Average age 31. 2 applicants, 50% accepted, 1 enrolled. In 2015, 3 master's awarded. *Degree requirements:* For master's, comprehensive exam, thesis (for some programs), oral exam. *Entrance requirements:* For master's, GRE General Test. Additional exam requirements/recommendations for international students: Required—TOEFL (minimum score 550 paper-based; 80 iBT), IELTS (minimum score 7). *Application deadline:* For fall admission, 2/1 for domestic students, 5/1 for international students; for spring admission, 10/1 for domestic and international students. Application fee: $60 ($95 for international students). Electronic applications accepted. *Expenses:* $264 per credit state resident full-time and part-time; $6,955 per semester, $264 per credit nonresident full-time; $555 per credit nonresident part-time. *Financial support:* In 2015–16, 4 students received support, including 2 research assistantships with partial tuition reimbursements available (averaging $10,000 per year), 2 teaching assistantships with partial tuition reimbursements available (averaging $12,000 per year); institutionally sponsored loans, scholarships/grants, health care benefits, and unspecified assistantships also available. Financial award application deadline: 3/1. *Faculty research:* Hydrogeology, water conservation, environmental chemistry, invasive species control, ecosystem management and restoration. *Unit head:* Dr. Michael Nicholl, Chair/Associate Professor, 702-895-4616, Fax: 702-895-4064,
E-mail: michael.nicholl@unlv.edu. *Application contact:* Graduate College Admissions Evaluator, 702-895-3367, Fax: 702-895-4180, E-mail: gradadmissions@unlv.edu.
Website: http://www.unlv.edu/sciences/wrm/

University of New Brunswick Fredericton, School of Graduate Studies, Faculty of Engineering, Department of Civil Engineering, Fredericton, NB E3B 5A3, Canada. Offers construction engineering and management (M Eng, M Sc E, PhD); environmental engineering (M Eng, M Sc E, PhD); environmental studies (M Eng); geotechnical engineering (M Eng, M Sc E, PhD); groundwater/hydrology (M Eng, M Sc E, PhD); materials (M Eng, M Sc E, PhD); pavements (M Eng, M Sc E, PhD); structures (M Eng, M Sc E, PhD); transportation (M Eng, M Sc E, PhD). *Program availability:* Part-time. *Faculty:* 12 full-time (1 woman), 4 part-time/adjunct (0 women). *Students:* 16 full-time (4 women), 15 part-time (5 women). In 2015, 2 master's, 4 doctorates awarded. *Degree requirements:* For master's, thesis; for doctorate, comprehensive exam, thesis/dissertation, qualifying exam; 27 credit hours of courses. *Entrance requirements:* For master's, minimum GPA of 3.0; B Sc E in civil engineering or related engineering degree; for doctorate, minimum GPA of 3.0; graduate degree in engineering or applied science. Additional exam requirements/recommendations for international students: Required—IELTS (minimum score 7.5), TWE (minimum score 4), Michigan English Language Assessment Battery (minimum score 85) or CanTest (minimum score 4.5); Recommended—TOEFL (minimum score 580 paper-based). *Application deadline:* For fall admission, 5/1 for domestic students; for winter admission, 11/1 for domestic students. Applications are processed on a rolling basis. Application fee: $50 Canadian dollars. Electronic applications accepted. *Financial support:* In 2015–16, 35 fellowships, 48 research assistantships, 35 teaching assistantships were awarded; career-related internships or fieldwork and scholarships/grants also available. *Faculty research:* Construction engineering and management; engineering materials and infrastructure renewal; highway and pavement research; structures and solid mechanics; geotechnical and geoenvironmental engineering; structure interaction; transportation and planning; environment, solid waste management; structural engineering; water and environmental engineering. *Unit head:* Dr. Kerry MacQuarrie, Director of Graduate Studies, 506-453-5121, Fax: 506-453-3568, E-mail: ktm@unb.ca. *Application contact:* Joyce Moore, Graduate Secretary, 506-452-6127, Fax: 506-453-3568, E-mail: joycem@unb.ca.
Website: http://go.unb.ca/gradprograms

University of New Hampshire, Graduate School, College of Life Sciences and Agriculture, Department of Natural Resources and the Environment, Durham, NH 03824. Offers environmental conservation (MS); forestry (MS); integrated coastal ecosystem science, policy and management (MS); natural resources (MS); soil and water resource management (MS); wildlife and conservation biology (MS). *Program availability:* Part-time. *Degree requirements:* For master's, thesis or alternative. *Entrance requirements:* For master's, GRE General Test. Additional exam requirements/recommendations for international students: Required—TOEFL (minimum score 550 paper-based; 80 iBT). Electronic applications accepted.

University of New Mexico, Graduate Studies, Water Resources Program, Albuquerque, NM 87131-2039. Offers hydroscience (MWR); policy management (MWR). *Program availability:* Part-time. *Faculty:* 2 full-time (1 woman), 4 part-time/adjunct (2 women). *Students:* 17 full-time (11 women), 22 part-time (12 women); includes 13 minority (2 Black or African American, non-Hispanic/Latino; 4 American Indian or Alaska Native, non-Hispanic/Latino; 5 Hispanic/Latino; 2 Two or more races, non-Hispanic/Latino). Average age 34. 21 applicants, 67% accepted, 11 enrolled. In 2015, 5 master's awarded. *Degree requirements:* For master's, professional project. *Entrance requirements:* For master's, minimum GPA of 3.0 during last 2 years of undergraduate work, 3 letters of reference. Additional exam requirements/recommendations for international students: Required—TOEFL (minimum score 550 paper-based). *Application deadline:* For fall admission, 7/15 for domestic students; for spring admission, 11/15 for domestic students. Applications are processed on a rolling basis. Application fee: $50. Electronic applications accepted. *Financial support:* Research assistantships with tuition reimbursements, career-related internships or fieldwork, institutionally sponsored loans, scholarships/grants, and unspecified assistantships available. Financial award application deadline: 3/1; financial award applicants required to submit FAFSA. *Faculty research:* Sustainable water resources, transboundary water resources, economics, water law, hydrology, developing countries, hydrogeology. *Unit head:* Dr. Robert Berrens, Director, 505-277-7759, Fax: 505-277-5226, E-mail: rberrens@unm.edu. *Application contact:* Annamarie Cordova, Administrative Assistant II, 505-277-7759, Fax: 505-277-5226,
E-mail: acordova@unm.edu.
Website: http://www.unm.edu/~wrp/

University of Southern California, Graduate School, Viterbi School of Engineering, Sonny Astani Department of Civil Engineering, Los Angeles, CA 90089. Offers applied mechanics (MS); civil engineering (MS, PhD); computer-aided engineering (ME, Graduate Certificate); construction management (MCM); engineering technology commercialization (Graduate Certificate); environmental engineering (MS, PhD); environmental quality management (ME); structural design (ME); sustainable cities (Graduate Certificate); transportation systems (MS, Graduate Certificate); water and waste management (MS). *Program availability:* Part-time, evening/weekend. Terminal master's awarded for partial completion of doctoral program. *Degree requirements:* For master's, thesis optional; for doctorate, thesis/dissertation. *Entrance requirements:* For master's and doctorate, GRE General Test. Additional exam requirements/recommendations for international students: Recommended—TOEFL. Electronic applications accepted. *Faculty research:* Geotechnical engineering, transportation engineering, structural engineering, construction management, environmental engineering, water resources.

University of the District of Columbia, College of Agriculture, Urban Sustainability and Environmental Sciences, Program in Water Resources Management, Washington, DC 20008-1175. Offers PSM.

University of the Pacific, McGeorge School of Law, Sacramento, CA 95817. Offers advocacy (JD); international water resources law (JSD); public policy and law (LL M); JD/MBA; JD/MPPA. *Accreditation:* ABA. *Program availability:* Part-time, evening/weekend. *Degree requirements:* For master's, thesis (for some programs); for doctorate, thesis/dissertation (for some programs). *Entrance requirements:* For master's, JD; for doctorate, LSAT (for JD), LL M (for JSD). Additional exam requirements/recommendations for international students: Required—TOEFL (minimum score 600 paper-based; 100 iBT). Electronic applications accepted. *Expenses:* Contact institution. *Faculty research:* International legal studies, public policy and law, advocacy, intellectual property law, taxation, criminal law.

University of Wisconsin–Madison, Graduate School, Gaylord Nelson Institute for Environmental Studies, Water Resources Management Program, Madison, WI 53706-1380. Offers MS. *Program availability:* Part-time. *Degree requirements:* For master's, summer group practicum workshop. *Entrance requirements:* For master's, GRE General Test. Additional exam requirements/recommendations for international students: Required—TOEFL (minimum score 550 paper-based; 80 iBT). Electronic applications accepted. *Expenses:* Tuition, state resident: full-time $5364. Tuition, nonresident: full-time $12,027. *Required fees:* $571. Tuition and fees vary according to campus/location, program and reciprocity agreements. *Faculty research:* Geology, hydrogeology, hydrology, fluvial geography, water chemistry, limnology, oceanography, aquatic ecology, rural sociology, water law and policy.

University of Wisconsin–Milwaukee, Graduate School, School of Freshwater Sciences, Milwaukee, WI 53201-0413. Offers freshwater sciences (PhD); freshwater sciences and technology (MS). *Students:* 29 full-time (11 women), 22 part-time (6 women); includes 1 minority (Asian, non-Hispanic/Latino), 2 international. Average age 30. 35 applicants, 57% accepted, 8 enrolled. In 2015, 8 master's, 2 doctorates awarded. Application fee: $56 ($96 for international students). *Financial support:* Fellowships, research assistantships, teaching assistantships, and unspecified assistantships available. Financial award applicants required to submit FAFSA. *Unit head:* David Garman, Founding Dean, 414-382-1700, E-mail: garmand@uwm.edu. *Application contact:* General Information Contact, 414-229-4982, Fax: 414-229-6967,
E-mail: gradschool@uwm.edu.
Website: http://www4.uwm.edu/freshwater/

University of Wyoming, College of Agriculture and Natural Resources, Department of Renewable Resources, Laramie, WY 82071. Offers agroecology (MS); entomology (MS, PhD); entomology/water resources (MS, PhD); rangeland ecology and watershed management (MS, PhD), including soil sciences (PhD), soil sciences and water resources (MS); rangeland ecology and watershed management/water resources (MS, PhD); soil science (MS); soil science/water resources (PhD). *Program availability:* Part-time. *Degree requirements:* For master's, comprehensive exam, thesis, oral examination; for doctorate, comprehensive exam, thesis/dissertation, preliminary oral and written exam, oral final exam. *Entrance requirements:* For master's and doctorate, GRE General Test, minimum GPA of 3.0. Additional exam requirements/recommendations for international students: Required—TOEFL. Electronic applications accepted. *Faculty research:* Plant control, grazing management, riparian restoration, riparian management, reclamation.

Utah State University, School of Graduate Studies, College of Natural Resources, Department of Watershed Sciences, Logan, UT 84322. Offers ecology (MS, PhD); fisheries biology (MS, PhD); watershed science (MS, PhD). *Degree requirements:* For master's, thesis (for some programs); for doctorate, thesis/dissertation. *Entrance requirements:* For master's and doctorate, GRE General Test, minimum GPA of 3.2. Additional exam requirements/recommendations for international students: Required—TOEFL. Electronic applications accepted. *Faculty research:* Behavior, population ecology, habitat, conservation biology, restoration, aquatic ecology, fisheries management, fluvial geomorphology, remote sensing, conservation biology.

APPENDIXES

Institutional Changes
Since the 2016 Edition

Following is an alphabetical listing of institutions that have recently closed, merged with other institutions, or changed their names or status. In the case of a name change, the former name appears first, followed by the new name.

American Baptist College of American Baptist Theological Seminary (Nashville, TN): *no longer offers graduate degrees*

American College of Traditional Chinese Medicine (San Francisco, CA): *merged with California Institute of Integral Studies (San Francisco, CA)*

Augustana College (Sioux Falls, SD): *name changed to Augustana University*

Bainbridge Graduate Institute (Bainbridge Island, WA): *name changed to Pinchot University*

Benedictine University at Springfield (Springfield, IL): *degree programs now offered through Benedictine University's National Moser Center for Adult Learning*

The Boston Conservatory (Boston, MA): *merged with Berklee College of Music (Boston, MA)*

Burlington College (Burlington, VT): *closed*

Cabrini College (Radnor, PA): *name changed to Cabrini University*

Carolina Evangelical Divinity School (High Point, NC): *name changed to Carolina Graduate School of Divinity*

Castleton State College (Castleton, VT): *name changed to Castleton University*

Charles Drew University of Medicine and Science (Los Angeles, CA): *name changed to Charles R. Drew University of Medicine and Science*

The Chicago School of Professional Psychology at Westwood (Los Angeles, CA): *closed*

Concordia University (Irvine, CA): *name changed to Concordia University Irvine*

Concordia University College of Alberta (Edmonton, AB, Canada): *name changed to Concordia University of Edmonton*

The Criswell College (Dallas, TX): *name changed to Criswell College*

DeVry University (Louisville, KY): *closed*

DeVry University (Bethesda, MD): *closed*

DeVry University (Sandy, UT): *closed*

Doane College (Crete, NE): *name changed to Doane University*

Dowling College (Oakdale, NY): *closed*

Emmanuel Christian Seminary (Johnson City, TN): *merged with Milligan College (Milligan College, TN)*

Everest University (Jacksonville, FL): *closed*

Everest University (Melbourne, FL): *closed*

Everest University (Orlando, FL): *closed*

Everest University (Pompano Beach, FL): *closed*

Felician College (Lodi, NJ): *name changed to Felician University*

Five Branches University: Graduate School of Traditional Chinese Medicine (Santa Cruz, CA): *name changed to Five Branches University*

Georgia Regents University (Augusta, GA): *name changed to Augusta University*

Golden Gate Baptist Theological Seminary (Mill Valley, CA): *name changed to Gateway Seminary*

Gooding Institute of Nurse Anesthesia (Panama City, FL): *closed*

Hawaii College of Oriental Medicine (Kamuela, HI): *closed*

Institut Franco-Européen de Chiropratique (94200 Ivry-sur-Seine, France): *name changed to Institut Franco-Européen de Chiropraxie*

King's University (Southlake, TX): *name changed to The King's University*

Lakeland College (Plymouth, WI): *name changed to Lakeland University*

Laurel University (High Point, NC): *name changed to John Wesley University*

Lutheran Theological Southern Seminary (Columbia, SC): *merged with Lenoir-Rhyne University (Hickory, NC)*

Massachusetts School of Professional Psychology (Boston, MA): *name changed to William James College*

Middlebury Institute of International Studies (Monterey, CA): *name changed to Middlebury Institute of International Studies at Monterey*

Midway College (Midway, KY): *name changed to Midway University*

Nashotah House (Nashotah, WI): *name changed to Nashotah House Theological Seminary*

The New England College of Optometry (Boston, MA): *name changed to New England College of Optometry*

New England School of Acupuncture (Newton, MA): *merged with MCPHS University (Boston, MA)*

Northern Baptist Theological Seminary (Lombard, IL): *name changed to Northern Seminary*

Northwest Institute of Literary Arts (Freeland, WA): *closed*

Our Lady of Holy Cross College (New Orleans, LA): *name changed to University of Holy Cross*

Penn State Dickinson School of Law (University Park, PA): *name changed to Penn State University–Dickinson Law*

Purdue University Calumet (Hammond, IN): *name changed to Purdue University Northwest*

Purdue University North Central (Westville, IN): *name changed to Purdue University Northwest*

Rutgers, The State University of New Jersey, Camden (Camden, NJ): *name changed to Rutgers University–Camden*

Rutgers, The State University of New Jersey, Newark (Newark, NJ): *name changed to Rutgers University–Newark*

Rutgers, The State University of New Jersey, New Brunswick (Piscataway, NJ): *name changed to Rutgers University–New Brunswick*

St. Catharine College (St. Catharine, KY): *closed*

Samra University of Oriental Medicine (Los Angeles, CA): *closed*

The School of Professional Psychology at Forest Institute (Springfield, MO): *closed*

Skidmore College (Saratoga Springs, NY): *no longer offers graduate degrees*

Southern Baptist Theological Seminary (Louisville, KY): *name changed to The Southern Baptist Theological Seminary*

Southern Polytechnic State University (Marietta, GA): *merged with Kennesaw State University (Kennesaw, GA)*

South Texas College of Law (Houston, TX): *name changed to Houston College of Law*

Stevens-Henager College–Salt Lake City/Murray (Salt Lake City, UT): *name changed to Stevens-Henager College*

Taft Law School (Santa Ana, CA): *merged into a single entry for Taft University System (Denver, CO)*

Temple Baptist Seminary (Chattanooga, TN): *merged with Piedmont International University (Winston-Salem, NC)*

Texas A&M Health Science Center (College Station, TX): *merged into a single entry for Texas A&M University (College Station, TX)*

Thomas Edison State College (Trenton, NJ): *name changed to Thomas Edison State University*

Thunderbird School of Global Management (Glendale, AZ): *merged with Arizona State University at the Tempe campus (Tempe, AZ)*

Touro University (Vallejo, CA): *name changed to Touro University California*

Toyota Technological Institute of Chicago (Chicago, IL): *name changed to Toyota Technological Institute at Chicago*

Trinity International University, South Florida Campus (Davie, FL): *name changed to Trinity International University Florida*

Union Graduate College (Schenectady, NY): *merged with Clarkson University (Potsdam, NY)*

United States International University (Nairobi, Kenya): *name changed to United States International University–Africa*

United States University (Cypress, CA): *closed*

University of Massachusetts Worcester (Worcester, MA): *name changed to University of Massachusetts Medical School*

The University of Montana (Missoula, MT): *name changed to University of Montana*

University of Phoenix–Austin Campus (Austin, TX): *closed*

University of Phoenix–Birmingham Campus (Birmingham, AL): *closed*

University of Phoenix–Boston Campus (Braintree, MA): *closed*

University of Phoenix–Chicago Campus (Schaumburg, IL): *closed*

University of Phoenix–Cleveland Campus (Beachwood, OH): *closed*

University of Phoenix–Columbia Campus (Columbia, SC): *closed*

University of Phoenix–Des Moines Campus (Des Moines, IA): *closed*

University of Phoenix–Idaho Campus (Meridian, ID): *closed*

University of Phoenix–Indianapolis Campus (Indianapolis, IN): *closed*

University of Phoenix–Kansas City Campus (Kansas City, MO): *closed*

University of Phoenix–Little Rock Campus (Little Rock, AR): *closed*

University of Phoenix–Louisville Campus (Louisville, KY): *closed*

University of Phoenix–Maryland Campus (Columbia, MD): *closed*

University of Phoenix–Memphis Campus (Cordova, TN): *closed*

University of Phoenix–Milwaukee Campus (Milwaukee, WI): *closed*

University of Phoenix–Minneapolis/St. Paul Campus (St. Louis Park, MN): *closed*

University of Phoenix–Nashville Campus (Nashville, TN): *closed*

University of Phoenix–Oklahoma City Campus (Oklahoma City, OK): *closed*

University of Phoenix–Oregon Campus (Tigard, OR): *closed*

University of Phoenix–Philadelphia Campus (Wayne, PA): *closed*

University of Phoenix–Puerto Rico Campus (Guaynabo, PR): *closed*

University of Phoenix–Richmond-Virginia Beach Campus (Glen Allen, VA): *closed*

University of Phoenix–St. Louis Campus (St. Louis, MO): *closed*

University of Phoenix–Savannah Campus (Savannah, GA): *closed*

University of Southernmost Florida (Jacksonville, FL): *closed*

The University of Texas at Brownsville (Brownsville, TX): *merged with The University of Texas–Pan American to become The University of Texas Rio Grande Valley (Edinburg, TX)*

The University of Texas–Pan American (Edinburg, TX): *merged with The University of Texas at Brownsville to become The University of Texas Rio Grande Valley (Edinburg, TX)*

Washington College (Chestertown, MD): *no longer offers graduate degrees*

Weill Cornell Medical College (New York, NY): *name changed to Weill Cornell Medicine*

Western Michigan University Cooley Law School (Lansing, MI): *name changed to Western Michigan University Thomas M. Cooley Law School*

William Howard Taft University (Santa Ana, CA): *merged into a single entry for Taft University System (Denver, CO)*

William Mitchell College of Law (St. Paul, MN): *merged with Hamline University School of Law, a unit of Hamline University (St. Paul, MN)*

Abbreviations Used in the Guides

The following list includes abbreviations of degree names used in the profiles in the 2017 edition of the guides. Because some degrees (e.g., Doctor of Education) can be abbreviated in more than one way (e.g., D.Ed. or Ed.D.), and because the abbreviations used in the guides reflect the preferences of the individual colleges and universities, the list may include two or more abbreviations for a single degree.

DEGREES

A Mus D	Doctor of Musical Arts
AC	Advanced Certificate
AD	Artist's Diploma
	Doctor of Arts
ADP	Artist's Diploma
Adv C	Advanced Certificate
AGC	Advanced Graduate Certificate
AGSC	Advanced Graduate Specialist Certificate
ALM	Master of Liberal Arts
AM	Master of Arts
AMBA	Accelerated Master of Business Administration
AMRS	Master of Arts in Religious Studies
APC	Advanced Professional Certificate
APMPH	Advanced Professional Master of Public Health
App Sc	Applied Scientist
App Sc D	Doctor of Applied Science
AstE	Astronautical Engineer
ATC	Advanced Training Certificate
Au D	Doctor of Audiology
B Th	Bachelor of Theology
BN	Bachelor of Naturopathy
CAES	Certificate of Advanced Educational Specialization
CAGS	Certificate of Advanced Graduate Studies
CAL	Certificate in Applied Linguistics
CAPS	Certificate of Advanced Professional Studies
CAS	Certificate of Advanced Studies
CASPA	Certificate of Advanced Study in Public Administration
CASR	Certificate in Advanced Social Research
CATS	Certificate of Achievement in Theological Studies
CBHS	Certificate in Basic Health Sciences
CCJA	Certificate in Criminal Justice Administration
CCTS	Certificate in Clinical and Translational Science
CE	Civil Engineer
CEM	Certificate of Environmental Management
CET	Certificate in Educational Technologies
CGS	Certificate of Graduate Studies
Ch E	Chemical Engineer
Clin Sc D	Doctor of Clinical Science

CM	Certificate in Management
CMH	Certificate in Medical Humanities
CMM	Master of Church Ministries
CMS	Certificate in Ministerial Studies
CNM	Certificate in Nonprofit Management
CPASF	Certificate Program for Advanced Study in Finance
CPC	Certificate in Professional Counseling
	Certificate in Publication and Communication
CPH	Certificate in Public Health
CPM	Certificate in Public Management
CPS	Certificate of Professional Studies
CScD	Doctor of Clinical Science
CSD	Certificate in Spiritual Direction
CSS	Certificate of Special Studies
CTS	Certificate of Theological Studies
CURP	Certificate in Urban and Regional Planning
D Admin	Doctor of Administration
D Arch	Doctor of Architecture
D Be	Doctor in Bioethics
D Com	Doctor of Commerce
D Couns	Doctor of Counseling
D Des	Doctorate of Design
D Div	Doctor of Divinity
D Ed	Doctor of Education
D Ed Min	Doctor of Educational Ministry
D Eng	Doctor of Engineering
D Engr	Doctor of Engineering
D Ent	Doctor of Enterprise
D Env	Doctor of Environment
D Law	Doctor of Law
D Litt	Doctor of Letters
D Med Sc	Doctor of Medical Science
D Min	Doctor of Ministry
D Miss	Doctor of Missiology
D Mus	Doctor of Music
D Mus A	Doctor of Musical Arts
D Phil	Doctor of Philosophy
D Prof	Doctor of Professional Studies
D Ps	Doctor of Psychology
D Sc	Doctor of Science
D Sc D	Doctor of Science in Dentistry
D Sc IS	Doctor of Science in Information Systems
D Sc PA	Doctor of Science in Physician Assistant Studies
D Th	Doctor of Theology
D Th P	Doctor of Practical Theology
DA	Doctor of Accounting
	Doctor of Arts

DAH	Doctor of Arts in Humanities
DAOM	Doctorate in Acupuncture and Oriental Medicine
DAT	Doctorate of Athletic Training
	Professional Doctor of Art Therapy
DBA	Doctor of Business Administration
DBH	Doctor of Behavioral Health
DBL	Doctor of Business Leadership
DC	Doctor of Chiropractic
DCC	Doctor of Computer Science
DCD	Doctor of Communications Design
DCL	Doctor of Civil Law
	Doctor of Comparative Law
DCM	Doctor of Church Music
DCN	Doctor of Clinical Nutrition
DCS	Doctor of Computer Science
DDN	Diplôme du Droit Notarial
DDS	Doctor of Dental Surgery
DE	Doctor of Education
	Doctor of Engineering
DED	Doctor of Economic Development
DEIT	Doctor of Educational Innovation and Technology
DEL	Doctor of Executive Leadership
DEM	Doctor of Educational Ministry
DEPD	Diplôme Études Spécialisées
DES	Doctor of Engineering Science
DESS	Diplôme Études Supérieures Spécialisées
DET	Doctor of Educational Technology
DFA	Doctor of Fine Arts
DGP	Diploma in Graduate and Professional Studies
DH Ed	Doctor of Health Education
DH Sc	Doctor of Health Sciences
DHA	Doctor of Health Administration
DHCE	Doctor of Health Care Ethics
DHL	Doctor of Hebrew Letters
DHPE	Doctorate of Health Professionals Education
DHS	Doctor of Health Science
DHSc	Doctor of Health Science
Dip CS	Diploma in Christian Studies
DIT	Doctor of Industrial Technology
	Doctor of Information Technology
DJS	Doctor of Jewish Studies
DLS	Doctor of Liberal Studies
DM	Doctor of Management
	Doctor of Music
DMA	Doctor of Musical Arts
DMD	Doctor of Dental Medicine
DME	Doctor of Manufacturing Management
	Doctor of Music Education
DMEd	Doctor of Music Education
DMFT	Doctor of Marital and Family Therapy

DMH	Doctor of Medical Humanities
DML	Doctor of Modern Languages
DMP	Doctorate in Medical Physics
DMPNA	Doctor of Management Practice in Nurse Anesthesia
DN Sc	Doctor of Nursing Science
DNAP	Doctor of Nurse Anesthesia Practice
DNP	Doctor of Nursing Practice
DNP-A	Doctor of Nursing Practice - Anesthesia
DNS	Doctor of Nursing Science
DO	Doctor of Osteopathy
DOT	Doctor of Occupational Therapy
DPA	Doctor of Public Administration
DPDS	Doctor of Planning and Development Studies
DPH	Doctor of Public Health
DPM	Doctor of Plant Medicine
	Doctor of Podiatric Medicine
DPPD	Doctor of Policy, Planning, and Development
DPS	Doctor of Professional Studies
DPT	Doctor of Physical Therapy
DPTSc	Doctor of Physical Therapy Science
Dr DES	Doctor of Design
Dr NP	Doctor of Nursing Practice
Dr OT	Doctor of Occupational Therapy
Dr PH	Doctor of Public Health
Dr Sc PT	Doctor of Science in Physical Therapy
DrAP	Doctor of Anesthesia Practice
DRSc	Doctor of Regulatory Science
DS	Doctor of Science
DS Sc	Doctor of Social Science
DSJS	Doctor of Science in Jewish Studies
DSL	Doctor of Strategic Leadership
DSS	Doctor of Strategic Security
DSW	Doctor of Social Work
DTL	Doctor of Talmudic Law
	Doctor of Transformational Leadership
DV Sc	Doctor of Veterinary Science
DVM	Doctor of Veterinary Medicine
DWS	Doctor of Worship Studies
EAA	Engineer in Aeronautics and Astronautics
EASPh D	Engineering and Applied Science Doctor of Philosophy
ECS	Engineer in Computer Science
Ed D	Doctor of Education
Ed DCT	Doctor of Education in College Teaching
Ed L D	Doctor of Education Leadership
Ed M	Master of Education
Ed S	Specialist in Education
Ed Sp	Specialist in Education
EDB	Executive Doctorate in Business
EDBA	Executive Doctor of Business Administration
EDM	Executive Doctorate in Management

412 www.petersons.com

Peterson's Graduate Programs in the Physical Sciences, Mathematics, Agricultural Sciences, the Environment & Natural Resources 2017

EE	Electrical Engineer	LL D	Doctor of Laws
EJD	Executive Juris Doctor	LL M	Master of Laws
EMBA	Executive Master of Business Administration	LL M in Tax	Master of Laws in Taxation
EMFA	Executive Master of Forensic Accounting	LL M CL	Master of Laws in Common Law
EMHA	Executive Master of Health Administration	M Ac	Master of Accountancy
EMIB	Executive Master of International Business		Master of Accounting
EML	Executive Master of Leadership		Master of Acupuncture
EMPA	Executive Master of Public Administration	M Ac OM	Master of Acupuncture and Oriental Medicine
EMPL	Executive Master in Public Leadership	M Acc	Master of Accountancy
EMS	Executive Master of Science		Master of Accounting
EMTM	Executive Master of Technology Management	M Acct	Master of Accountancy
Eng	Engineer		Master of Accounting
Eng Sc D	Doctor of Engineering Science	M Accy	Master of Accountancy
Engr	Engineer	M Actg	Master of Accounting
Exec M Tax	Executive Master of Taxation	M Acy	Master of Accountancy
Exec MAC	Executive Master of Accounting	M Ad	Master of Administration
Exec Ed D	Executive Doctor of Education	M Ad Ed	Master of Adult Education
Exec MBA	Executive Master of Business Administration	M Adm	Master of Administration
Exec MPA	Executive Master of Public Administration	M Adm Mgt	Master of Administrative Management
Exec MPH	Executive Master of Public Health	M Admin	Master of Administration
Exec MS	Executive Master of Science	M ADU	Master of Architectural Design and Urbanism
Executive Fellows MBA	Executive Fellows Master of Business Administration	M Adv	Master of Advertising
G Dip	Graduate Diploma	M AEST	Master of Applied Environmental Science and Technology
GBC	Graduate Business Certificate	M Ag	Master of Agriculture
GDM	Graduate Diploma in Management	M Ag Ed	Master of Agricultural Education
GDPA	Graduate Diploma in Public Administration	M Agr	Master of Agriculture
GDRE	Graduate Diploma in Religious Education	M Anesth Ed	Master of Anesthesiology Education
GEMBA	Global Executive Master of Business Administration	M App Comp Sc	Master of Applied Computer Science
GMBA	Global Master of Business Administration	M App St	Master of Applied Statistics
GP LL M	Global Professional Master of Laws	M Appl Stat	Master of Applied Statistics
GPD	Graduate Performance Diploma	M Aq	Master of Aquaculture
GSS	Graduate Special Certificate for Students in Special Situations	M Arc	Master of Architecture
IEMBA	International Executive Master of Business Administration	M Arch	Master of Architecture
		M Arch I	Master of Architecture I
IMA	Interdisciplinary Master of Arts	M Arch II	Master of Architecture II
IMBA	International Master of Business Administration	M Arch E	Master of Architectural Engineering
		M Arch H	Master of Architectural History
IMES	International Master's in Environmental Studies	M Bioethics	Master in Bioethics
		M Biomath	Master of Biomathematics
Ingeniero	Engineer	M Ch E	Master of Chemical Engineering
JCD	Doctor of Canon Law	M Chem	Master of Chemistry
JCL	Licentiate in Canon Law	M Cl D	Master of Clinical Dentistry
JD	Juris Doctor	M Cl Sc	Master of Clinical Science
JM	Juris Master	M Comp	Master of Computing
JSD	Doctor of Juridical Science	M Comp Sc	Master of Computer Science
	Doctor of Jurisprudence	M Coun	Master of Counseling
	Doctor of the Science of Law	M Dent	Master of Dentistry
JSM	Master of the Science of Law	M Dent Sc	Master of Dental Sciences
L Th	Licenciate in Theology	M Des	Master of Design
LL B	Bachelor of Laws	M Des S	Master of Design Studies
LL CM	Master of Comparative Law		

Peterson's Graduate Programs in the Physical Sciences, Mathematics, Agricultural Sciences, the Environment & Natural Resources 2017

www.petersons.com **413**

M Div	Master of Divinity
M E Sci	Master of Earth Science
M Ec	Master of Economics
M Econ	Master of Economics
M Ed	Master of Education
M Ed T	Master of Education in Teaching
M En	Master of Engineering
M En S	Master of Environmental Sciences
M Eng	Master of Engineering
M Eng Mgt	Master of Engineering Management
M Engr	Master of Engineering
M Ent	Master of Enterprise
M Env	Master of Environment
M Env Des	Master of Environmental Design
M Env E	Master of Environmental Engineering
M Env Sc	Master of Environmental Science
M Fin	Master of Finance
M FSc	Master of Fisheries Science
M Geo E	Master of Geological Engineering
M Geoenv E	Master of Geoenvironmental Engineering
M Geog	Master of Geography
M Hum	Master of Humanities
M IDST	Master's in Interdisciplinary Studies
M Kin	Master of Kinesiology
M Land Arch	Master of Landscape Architecture
M Litt	Master of Letters
M Mat SE	Master of Material Science and Engineering
M Math	Master of Mathematics
M Mech E	Master of Mechanical Engineering
M Med Sc	Master of Medical Science
M Mgmt	Master of Management
M Mgt	Master of Management
M Min	Master of Ministries
M Mtl E	Master of Materials Engineering
M Mu	Master of Music
M Mus	Master of Music
M Mus Ed	Master of Music Education
M Music	Master of Music
M Nat Sci	Master of Natural Science
M Pet E	Master of Petroleum Engineering
M Pharm	Master of Pharmacy
M Phil	Master of Philosophy
M Phil F	Master of Philosophical Foundations
M Pl	Master of Planning
M Plan	Master of Planning
M Pol	Master of Political Science
M Pr Met	Master of Professional Meteorology
M Prob S	Master of Probability and Statistics
M Psych	Master of Psychology
M Pub	Master of Publishing
M Rel	Master of Religion
M Sc	Master of Science
M Sc A	Master of Science (Applied)

M Sc AC	Master of Science in Applied Computing
M Sc AHN	Master of Science in Applied Human Nutrition
M Sc BMC	Master of Science in Biomedical Communications
M Sc CS	Master of Science in Computer Science
M Sc E	Master of Science in Engineering
M Sc Eng	Master of Science in Engineering
M Sc Engr	Master of Science in Engineering
M Sc F	Master of Science in Forestry
M Sc FE	Master of Science in Forest Engineering
M Sc Geogr	Master of Science in Geography
M Sc N	Master of Science in Nursing
M Sc OT	Master of Science in Occupational Therapy
M Sc P	Master of Science in Planning
M Sc Pl	Master of Science in Planning
M Sc PT	Master of Science in Physical Therapy
M Sc T	Master of Science in Teaching
M SEM	Master of Sustainable Environmental Management
M Serv Soc	Master of Social Service
M Soc	Master of Sociology
M Sp Ed	Master of Special Education
M St	Master of Studies
M Stat	Master of Statistics
M Sys E	Master of Systems Engineering
M Sys Sc	Master of Systems Science
M Tax	Master of Taxation
M Tech	Master of Technology
M Th	Master of Theology
M Tox	Master of Toxicology
M Trans E	Master of Transportation Engineering
M U Ed	Master of Urban Education
M Urb	Master of Urban Planning
M Vet Sc	Master of Veterinary Science
MA	Master of Accounting
	Master of Administration
	Master of Arts
MA Comm	Master of Arts in Communication
MA Ed	Master of Arts in Education
MA Ed/HD	Master of Arts in Education and Human Development
MA Ext	Master of Agricultural Extension
MA Min	Master of Arts in Ministry
MA Past St	Master of Arts in Pastoral Studies
MA Ph	Master of Arts in Philosophy
MA Psych	Master of Arts in Psychology
MA Sc	Master of Applied Science
MA Sp	Master of Arts (Spirituality)
MA Th	Master of Arts in Theology
MA-R	Master of Arts (Research)
MAA	Master of Administrative Arts
	Master of Applied Anthropology
	Master of Applied Arts

Peterson's Graduate Programs in the Physical Sciences, Mathematics, Agricultural Sciences, the Environment & Natural Resources 2017

	Master of Arts in Administration	MADR	Master of Arts in Dispute Resolution
MAAA	Master of Arts in Arts Administration	MADS	Master of Animal and Dairy Science
MAAAP	Master of Arts Administration and Policy		Master of Applied Disability Studies
MAAD	Master of Advanced Architectural Design	MAE	Master of Aerospace Engineering
MAAE	Master of Arts in Art Education		Master of Agricultural Economics
MAAPPS	Master of Arts in Asia Pacific Policy Studies		Master of Agricultural Education
MAAS	Master of Arts in Aging and Spirituality		Master of Applied Economics
MAASJ	Master of Arts in Applied Social Justice		Master of Architectural Engineering
MAAT	Master of Arts in Applied Theology		Master of Art Education
	Master of Arts in Art Therapy		Master of Arts in Education
MAB	Master of Agribusiness		Master of Arts in English
MABC	Master of Arts in Biblical Counseling	MAEd	Master of Arts Education
MABE	Master of Arts in Bible Exposition	MAEL	Master of Arts in Educational Leadership
MABL	Master of Arts in Biblical Languages	MAEM	Master of Arts in Educational Ministries
MABM	Master of Agribusiness Management	MAEP	Master of Arts in Economic Policy
MABS	Master of Arts in Biblical Studies		Master of Arts in Educational Psychology
MABT	Master of Arts in Bible Teaching	MAES	Master of Arts in Environmental Sciences
MAC	Master of Accountancy	MAET	Master of Arts in English Teaching
	Master of Accounting	MAF	Master of Arts in Finance
	Master of Arts in Communication	MAFE	Master of Arts in Financial Economics
	Master of Arts in Counseling	MAFLL	Master of Arts in Foreign Language and Literature
MACC	Master of Arts in Christian Counseling	MAFM	Master of Accounting and Financial Management
	Master of Arts in Clinical Counseling		
MACCT	Master of Accounting	MAFS	Master of Arts in Family Studies
MACD	Master of Arts in Christian Doctrine	MAG	Master of Applied Geography
MACE	Master of Arts in Christian Education	MAGS	Master of Arts in Global Service
MACH	Master of Arts in Church History	MAGU	Master of Urban Analysis and Management
MACI	Master of Arts in Curriculum and Instruction	MAH	Master of Arts in Humanities
MACIS	Master of Accounting and Information Systems	MAHA	Master of Arts in Humanitarian Assistance
		MAHCM	Master of Arts in Health Care Mission
MACJ	Master of Arts in Criminal Justice	MAHG	Master of American History and Government
MACL	Master of Arts in Christian Leadership		
	Master of Arts in Community Leadership	MAHL	Master of Arts in Hebrew Letters
MACM	Master of Arts in Christian Ministries	MAHN	Master of Applied Human Nutrition
	Master of Arts in Christian Ministry	MAHR	Master of Applied Historical Research
	Master of Arts in Church Music	MAHS	Master of Arts in Human Services
	Master of Arts in Counseling Ministries	MAHSR	Master in Applied Health Services Research
MACN	Master of Arts in Counseling	MAIA	Master of Arts in International Administration
MACO	Master of Arts in Counseling		
MAcOM	Master of Acupuncture and Oriental Medicine		Master of Arts in International Affairs
MACP	Master of Arts in Christian Practice	MAIDM	Master of Arts in Interior Design and Merchandising
	Master of Arts in Church Planting		
	Master of Arts in Counseling Psychology	MAIH	Master of Arts in Interdisciplinary Humanities
MACS	Master of Applied Computer Science		
	Master of Arts in Catholic Studies	MAIOP	Master of Applied Industrial/Organizational Psychology
	Master of Arts in Christian Studies		
MACSE	Master of Arts in Christian School Education	MAIPCR	Master of Arts in International Peace and Conflict Management
MACT	Master of Arts in Communications and Technology	MAIS	Master of Arts in Intercultural Studies
			Master of Arts in Interdisciplinary Studies
MAD	Master in Educational Institution Administration		Master of Arts in International Studies
		MAIT	Master of Administration in Information Technology
	Master of Art and Design	MAJ	Master of Arts in Journalism

Peterson's Graduate Programs in the Physical Sciences, Mathematics, Agricultural Sciences, the Environment & Natural Resources 2017

www.petersons.com   **415**

MAJ Ed	Master of Arts in Jewish Education
MAJCS	Master of Arts in Jewish Communal Service
MAJE	Master of Arts in Jewish Education
MAJPS	Master of Arts in Jewish Professional Studies
MAJS	Master of Arts in Jewish Studies
MAL	Master in Agricultural Leadership
MALA	Master of Arts in Liberal Arts
MALD	Master of Arts in Law and Diplomacy
MALER	Master of Arts in Labor and Employment Relations
MALL	Master of Arts in Language Learning
MALP	Master of Arts in Language Pedagogy
MALS	Master of Arts in Liberal Studies
MAM	Master of Acquisition Management
	Master of Agriculture and Management
	Master of Applied Mathematics
	Master of Arts in Management
	Master of Arts in Ministry
	Master of Arts Management
	Master of Avian Medicine
MAMB	Master of Applied Molecular Biology
MAMC	Master of Arts in Mass Communication
	Master of Arts in Ministry and Culture
	Master of Arts in Ministry for a Multicultural Church
	Master of Arts in Missional Christianity
MAME	Master of Arts in Missions/Evangelism
MAMFC	Master of Arts in Marriage and Family Counseling
MAMFT	Master of Arts in Marriage and Family Therapy
MAMHC	Master of Arts in Mental Health Counseling
MAMS	Master of Applied Mathematical Sciences
	Master of Applied Meditation Studies
	Master of Arts in Ministerial Studies
	Master of Arts in Ministry and Spirituality
MAMT	Master of Arts in Mathematics Teaching
MAN	Master of Applied Nutrition
MANT	Master of Arts in New Testament
MAOL	Master of Arts in Organizational Leadership
MAOM	Master of Acupuncture and Oriental Medicine
MAOT	Master of Arts in Old Testament
MAP	Master of Applied Politics
	Master of Applied Psychology
	Master of Arts in Planning
	Master of Psychology
	Master of Public Administration
MAP Min	Master of Arts in Pastoral Ministry
MAPA	Master of Arts in Public Administration
MAPC	Master of Arts in Pastoral Counseling
MAPE	Master of Arts in Physics Education
	Master of Arts in Political Economy
MAPM	Master of Arts in Pastoral Ministry

	Master of Arts in Pastoral Music
	Master of Arts in Practical Ministry
MAPP	Master of Arts in Public Policy
MAPS	Master of Arts in Pastoral Studies
	Master of Arts in Public Service
MAPT	Master of Practical Theology
MAPW	Master of Arts in Professional Writing
MAR	Master of Arts in Reading
	Master of Arts in Religion
Mar Eng	Marine Engineer
MARC	Master of Arts in Rehabilitation Counseling
MARE	Master of Arts in Religious Education
MARL	Master of Arts in Religious Leadership
MARS	Master of Arts in Religious Studies
MAS	Master of Accounting Science
	Master of Actuarial Science
	Master of Administrative Science
	Master of Advanced Study
	Master of Aeronautical Science
	Master of American Studies
	Master of Animal Science
	Master of Applied Science
	Master of Applied Statistics
	Master of Archival Studies
MASA	Master of Advanced Studies in Architecture
MASD	Master of Arts in Spiritual Direction
MASE	Master of Arts in Special Education
MASF	Master of Arts in Spiritual Formation
MASJ	Master of Arts in Systems of Justice
MASLA	Master of Advanced Studies in Landscape Architecture
MASM	Master of Aging Services Management
	Master of Arts in Specialized Ministries
MASP	Master of Applied Social Psychology
	Master of Arts in School Psychology
MASPAA	Master of Arts in Sports and Athletic Administration
MASS	Master of Applied Social Science
	Master of Arts in Social Science
MAST	Master of Arts in Science Teaching
MAT	Master of Arts in Teaching
	Master of Arts in Theology
	Master of Athletic Training
	Master's in Administration of Telecommunications
Mat E	Materials Engineer
MATCM	Master of Acupuncture and Traditional Chinese Medicine
MATDE	Master of Arts in Theology, Development, and Evangelism
MATDR	Master of Territorial Management and Regional Development
MATE	Master of Arts for the Teaching of English
MATESL	Master of Arts in Teaching English as a Second Language

Peterson's Graduate Programs in the Physical Sciences, Mathematics, Agricultural Sciences, the Environment & Natural Resources 2017

MATESOL	Master of Arts in Teaching English to Speakers of Other Languages
MATF	Master of Arts in Teaching English as a Foreign Language/Intercultural Studies
MATFL	Master of Arts in Teaching Foreign Language
MATH	Master of Arts in Therapy
MATI	Master of Administration of Information Technology
MATL	Master of Arts in Teacher Leadership
	Master of Arts in Teaching of Languages
	Master of Arts in Transformational Leadership
MATM	Master of Arts in Teaching of Mathematics
MATS	Master of Arts in Theological Studies
	Master of Arts in Transforming Spirituality
MATSL	Master of Arts in Teaching a Second Language
MAUA	Master of Arts in Urban Affairs
MAUD	Master of Arts in Urban Design
MAURP	Master of Arts in Urban and Regional Planning
MAW	Master of Arts in Worship
MAWSHP	Master of Arts in Worship
MAYM	Master of Arts in Youth Ministry
MB	Master of Bioinformatics
MBA	Master of Business Administration
MBA-AM	Master of Business Administration in Aviation Management
MBA-EP	Master of Business Administration–Experienced Professionals
MBAA	Master of Business Administration in Aviation
MBAE	Master of Biological and Agricultural Engineering
	Master of Biosystems and Agricultural Engineering
MBAH	Master of Business Administration in Health
MBAi	Master of Business Administration–International
MBAICT	Master of Business Administration in Information and Communication Technology
MBATM	Master of Business Administration in Technology Management
MBC	Master of Building Construction
MBE	Master of Bilingual Education
	Master of Bioengineering
	Master of Bioethics
	Master of Biomedical Engineering
	Master of Business Economics
	Master of Business Education
MBEE	Master in Biotechnology Enterprise and Entrepreneurship
MBET	Master of Business, Entrepreneurship and Technology
MBID	Master of Biomedical Innovation and Development

MBIOT	Master of Biotechnology
MBiotech	Master of Biotechnology
MBL	Master of Business Law
	Master of Business Leadership
MBLE	Master in Business Logistics Engineering
MBME	Master's in Biomedical Engineering
MBMSE	Master of Business Management and Software Engineering
MBOE	Master of Business Operational Excellence
MBS	Master of Biblical Studies
	Master of Biological Science
	Master of Biomedical Sciences
	Master of Bioscience
	Master of Building Science
	Master of Business and Science
MBST	Master of Biostatistics
MBT	Master of Biomedical Technology
	Master of Biotechnology
	Master of Business Taxation
MBV	Master of Business for Veterans
MC	Master of Communication
	Master of Counseling
	Master of Cybersecurity
MC Ed	Master of Continuing Education
MC Sc	Master of Computer Science
MCA	Master in Collegiate Athletics
	Master of Commercial Aviation
	Master of Criminology (Applied)
MCAM	Master of Computational and Applied Mathematics
MCC	Master of Computer Science
MCD	Master of Communications Disorders
	Master of Community Development
MCE	Master in Electronic Commerce
	Master of Christian Education
	Master of Civil Engineering
	Master of Control Engineering
MCEM	Master of Construction Engineering Management
MCHE	Master of Chemical Engineering
MCIS	Master of Communication and Information Studies
	Master of Computer and Information Science
	Master of Computer Information Systems
MCIT	Master of Computer and Information Technology
MCJ	Master of Criminal Justice
MCL	Master in Communication Leadership
	Master of Canon Law
	Master of Comparative Law
MCM	Master of Christian Ministry
	Master of Church Music
	Master of City Management

Peterson's Graduate Programs in the Physical Sciences, Mathematics, Agricultural Sciences, the Environment & Natural Resources 2017

www.petersons.com 417

	Master of Communication Management
	Master of Community Medicine
	Master of Construction Management
	Master of Contract Management
MCMin	Master of Christian Ministry
MCMP	Master of City and Metropolitan Planning
MCMS	Master of Clinical Medical Science
MCN	Master of Clinical Nutrition
MCOL	Master of Arts in Community and Organizational Leadership
MCP	Master of City Planning
	Master of Community Planning
	Master of Counseling Psychology
	Master of Cytopathology Practice
	Master of Science in Quality Systems and Productivity
MCPC	Master of Arts in Chaplaincy and Pastoral Care
MCPD	Master of Community Planning and Development
MCR	Master in Clinical Research
MCRP	Master of City and Regional Planning
	Master of Community and Regional Planning
MCRS	Master of City and Regional Studies
MCS	Master of Chemical Sciences
	Master of Christian Studies
	Master of Clinical Science
	Master of Combined Sciences
	Master of Communication Studies
	Master of Computer Science
	Master of Consumer Science
MCSE	Master of Computer Science and Engineering
MCSL	Master of Catholic School Leadership
MCSM	Master of Construction Science and Management
MCTM	Master of Clinical Translation Management
MCTP	Master of Communication Technology and Policy
MCTS	Master of Clinical and Translational Science
MCVS	Master of Cardiovascular Science
MD	Doctor of Medicine
MDA	Master of Dietetic Administration
MDB	Master of Design-Build
MDE	Master of Developmental Economics
	Master of Distance Education
	Master of the Education of the Deaf
MDH	Master of Dental Hygiene
MDM	Master of Design Methods
	Master of Digital Media
MDP	Master in Sustainable Development Practice
	Master of Development Practice
MDR	Master of Dispute Resolution
MDS	Master of Dental Surgery

	Master of Design Studies
	Master of Digital Sciences
ME	Master of Education
	Master of Engineering
	Master of Entrepreneurship
ME Sc	Master of Engineering Science
ME-PD	Master of Education–Professional Development
MEA	Master of Educational Administration
	Master of Engineering Administration
MEAE	Master of Entertainment Arts and Engineering
MEAP	Master of Environmental Administration and Planning
MEB	Master of Energy Business
MEBD	Master in Environmental Building Design
MEBT	Master in Electronic Business Technologies
MEC	Master of Electronic Commerce
Mech E	Mechanical Engineer
MED	Master of Education of the Deaf
MEDS	Master of Environmental Design Studies
MEE	Master in Education
	Master of Electrical Engineering
	Master of Energy Engineering
	Master of Environmental Engineering
MEEM	Master of Environmental Engineering and Management
MEENE	Master of Engineering in Environmental Engineering
MEEP	Master of Environmental and Energy Policy
MEERM	Master of Earth and Environmental Resource Management
MEH	Master in Humanistic Studies
	Master of Environmental Health
	Master of Environmental Horticulture
MEHS	Master of Environmental Health and Safety
MEIM	Master of Entertainment Industry Management
	Master of Equine Industry Management
MEL	Master of Educational Leadership
	Master of English Literature
MELP	Master of Environmental Law and Policy
MEM	Master of Engineering Management
	Master of Environmental Management
	Master of Marketing
MEME	Master of Engineering in Manufacturing Engineering
	Master of Engineering in Mechanical Engineering
MENR	Master of Environment and Natural Resources
MENVEGR	Master of Environmental Engineering
MEP	Master of Engineering Physics
MEPC	Master of Environmental Pollution Control
MEPD	Master of Environmental Planning and Design

MER	Master of Employment Relations
MERE	Master of Entrepreneurial Real Estate
MERL	Master of Energy Regulation and Law
MES	Master of Education and Science
	Master of Engineering Science
	Master of Environment and Sustainability
	Master of Environmental Science
	Master of Environmental Studies
	Master of Environmental Systems
	Master of Special Education
MESM	Master of Environmental Science and Management
MET	Master of Educational Technology
	Master of Engineering Technology
	Master of Entertainment Technology
	Master of Environmental Toxicology
METM	Master of Engineering and Technology Management
MEVE	Master of Environmental Engineering
MF	Master of Finance
	Master of Forestry
MFA	Master of Fine Arts
MFALP	Master of Food and Agriculture Law and Policy
MFAM	Master's of Food Animal Medicine
MFAS	Master of Fisheries and Aquatic Science
MFAW	Master of Fine Arts in Writing
MFC	Master of Forest Conservation
MFCS	Master of Family and Consumer Sciences
MFE	Master of Financial Economics
	Master of Financial Engineering
	Master of Forest Engineering
MFES	Master of Fire and Emergency Services
MFG	Master of Functional Genomics
MFHD	Master of Family and Human Development
MFM	Master of Financial Management
	Master of Financial Mathematics
MFPE	Master of Food Process Engineering
MFR	Master of Forest Resources
MFRC	Master of Forest Resources and Conservation
MFRE	Master of Food and Resource Economics
MFS	Master of Food Science
	Master of Forensic Sciences
	Master of Forest Science
	Master of Forest Studies
	Master of French Studies
MFST	Master of Food Safety and Technology
MFT	Master of Family Therapy
	Master of Food Technology
MFWB	Master of Fishery and Wildlife Biology
MFWCB	Master of Fish, Wildlife and Conservation Biology
MFWS	Master of Fisheries and Wildlife Sciences

MFYCS	Master of Family, Youth and Community Sciences
MG	Master of Genetics
MGA	Master of Global Affairs
	Master of Government Administration
	Master of Governmental Administration
MGC	Master of Genetic Counseling
MGD	Master of Graphic Design
MGE	Master of Geotechnical Engineering
MGEM	Master of Global Entrepreneurship and Management
MGIS	Master of Geographic Information Science
	Master of Geographic Information Systems
MGM	Master of Global Management
MGP	Master of Gestion de Projet
MGPS	Master of Global Policy Studies
MGREM	Master of Global Real Estate Management
MGS	Master of Gerontological Studies
	Master of Global Studies
MGsc	Master of Geoscience
MH	Master of Humanities
MH Sc	Master of Health Sciences
MHA	Master of Health Administration
	Master of Healthcare Administration
	Master of Hospital Administration
	Master of Hospitality Administration
MHB	Master of Human Behavior
MHC	Master of Mental Health Counseling
MHCA	Master of Health Care Administration
MHCD	Master of Health Care Design
MHCI	Master of Human-Computer Interaction
MHCL	Master of Health Care Leadership
MHE	Master of Health Education
	Master of Human Ecology
MHE Ed	Master of Home Economics Education
MHEA	Master of Higher Education Administration
MHHS	Master of Health and Human Services
MHI	Master of Health Informatics
	Master of Healthcare Innovation
MHIHIM	Master of Health Informatics and Health Information Management
MHIIM	Master of Health Informatics and Information Management
MHIS	Master of Health Information Systems
MHK	Master of Human Kinetics
MHM	Master of Healthcare Management
MHMS	Master of Health Management Systems
MHP	Master of Health Physics
	Master of Heritage Preservation
	Master of Historic Preservation
MHPA	Master of Heath Policy and Administration
MHPE	Master of Health Professions Education
MHR	Master of Human Resources
MHRD	Master in Human Resource Development

Peterson's Graduate Programs in the Physical Sciences, Mathematics, Agricultural Sciences, the Environment & Natural Resources 2017

www.petersons.com **419**

MHRIR	Master of Human Resources and Industrial Relations
MHRLR	Master of Human Resources and Labor Relations
MHRM	Master of Human Resources Management
MHS	Master of Health Science
	Master of Health Sciences
	Master of Health Studies
	Master of Hispanic Studies
	Master of Human Services
	Master of Humanistic Studies
MHSA	Master of Health Services Administration
MHSE	Master of Health Science Education
MHSM	Master of Health Systems Management
MI	Master of Information
	Master of Instruction
MI Arch	Master of Interior Architecture
MIA	Master of Interior Architecture
	Master of International Affairs
MIAA	Master of International Affairs and Administration
MIAM	Master of International Agribusiness Management
MIAPD	Master of Interior Architecture and Product Design
MIB	Master of International Business
MIBA	Master of International Business Administration
MICM	Master of International Construction Management
MID	Master of Industrial Design
	Master of Industrial Distribution
	Master of Interior Design
	Master of International Development
MIDA	Master of International Development Administration
MIDC	Master of Integrated Design and Construction
MIDP	Master of International Development Policy
MIE	Master of Industrial Engineering
MIHTM	Master of International Hospitality and Tourism Management
MIJ	Master of International Journalism
MILR	Master of Industrial and Labor Relations
MIM	Master in Ministry
	Master of Information Management
	Master of International Management
MIMLAE	Master of International Management for Latin American Executives
MIMS	Master of Information Management and Systems
	Master of Integrated Manufacturing Systems
MIP	Master of Infrastructure Planning
	Master of Intellectual Property
	Master of International Policy
MIPA	Master of International Public Affairs

MIPD	Master of Integrated Product Design
MIPM	Master of International Policy Management
MIPP	Master of International Policy and Practice
	Master of International Public Policy
MIPS	Master of International Planning Studies
MIR	Master of Industrial Relations
	Master of International Relations
MIRHR	Master of Industrial Relations and Human Resources
MIS	Master of Imaging Science
	Master of Industrial Statistics
	Master of Information Science
	Master of Information Systems
	Master of Integrated Science
	Master of Interdisciplinary Studies
	Master of International Service
	Master of International Studies
MISE	Master of Industrial and Systems Engineering
MISKM	Master of Information Sciences and Knowledge Management
MISM	Master of Information Systems Management
MISW	Master of Indigenous Social Work
MIT	Master in Teaching
	Master of Industrial Technology
	Master of Information Technology
	Master of Initial Teaching
	Master of International Trade
	Master of Internet Technology
MITA	Master of Information Technology Administration
MITM	Master of Information Technology and Management
MJ	Master of Journalism
	Master of Jurisprudence
MJ Ed	Master of Jewish Education
MJA	Master of Justice Administration
MJM	Master of Justice Management
MJS	Master of Judicial Studies
	Master of Juridical Studies
MK	Master of Kinesiology
MKM	Master of Knowledge Management
ML	Master of Latin
ML Arch	Master of Landscape Architecture
MLA	Master of Landscape Architecture
	Master of Liberal Arts
MLAS	Master of Laboratory Animal Science
	Master of Liberal Arts and Sciences
MLAUD	Master of Landscape Architecture in Urban Development
MLD	Master of Leadership Development
	Master of Leadership Studies
MLE	Master of Applied Linguistics and Exegesis
MLER	Master of Labor and Employment Relations

Peterson's Graduate Programs in the Physical Sciences, Mathematics, Agricultural Sciences, the Environment & Natural Resources 2017

MLI Sc	Master of Library and Information Science
MLIS	Master of Library and Information Science
	Master of Library and Information Studies
MLM	Master of Leadership in Ministry
MLPD	Master of Land and Property Development
MLRHR	Master of Labor Relations and Human Resources
MLS	Master of Leadership Studies
	Master of Legal Studies
	Master of Liberal Studies
	Master of Library Science
	Master of Life Sciences
MLSCM	Master of Logistics and Supply Chain Management
MLSP	Master of Law and Social Policy
MLT	Master of Language Technologies
MLTCA	Master of Long Term Care Administration
MLW	Master of Studies in Law
MLWS	Master of Land and Water Systems
MM	Master of Management
	Master of Ministry
	Master of Missiology
	Master of Music
MM Ed	Master of Music Education
MM Sc	Master of Medical Science
MM St	Master of Museum Studies
MMA	Master of Marine Affairs
	Master of Media Arts
	Master of Ministry Administration
	Master of Musical Arts
MMAL	Master of Maritime Administration and Logistics
MMAS	Master of Military Art and Science
MMB	Master of Microbial Biotechnology
MMC	Master of Manufacturing Competitiveness
	Master of Mass Communications
	Master of Music Conducting
MMCM	Master of Music in Church Music
MMCSS	Master of Mathematical Computational and Statistical Sciences
MME	Master of Manufacturing Engineering
	Master of Mathematics Education
	Master of Mathematics for Educators
	Master of Mechanical Engineering
	Master of Mining Engineering
	Master of Music Education
MMF	Master of Mathematical Finance
MMFT	Master of Marriage and Family Therapy
MMH	Master of Management in Hospitality
	Master of Medical Humanities
MMI	Master of Management of Innovation
MMIS	Master of Management Information Systems
MML	Master of Managerial Logistics
MMM	Master of Manufacturing Management

	Master of Marine Management
	Master of Medical Management
MMP	Master of Management Practice
	Master of Marine Policy
	Master of Medical Physics
	Master of Music Performance
MMPA	Master of Management and Professional Accounting
MMQM	Master of Manufacturing Quality Management
MMR	Master of Marketing Research
MMRM	Master of Marine Resources Management
MMS	Master of Management Science
	Master of Management Studies
	Master of Manufacturing Systems
	Master of Marine Studies
	Master of Materials Science
	Master of Mathematical Sciences
	Master of Medical Science
	Master of Medieval Studies
MMSE	Master of Manufacturing Systems Engineering
MMSM	Master of Music in Sacred Music
MMT	Master in Marketing
	Master of Music Teaching
	Master of Music Therapy
	Master's in Marketing Technology
MMus	Master of Music
MN	Master of Nursing
	Master of Nutrition
MN NP	Master of Nursing in Nurse Practitioner
MNA	Master of Nonprofit Administration
	Master of Nurse Anesthesia
MNAL	Master of Nonprofit Administration and Leadership
MNAS	Master of Natural and Applied Science
MNCM	Master of Network and Communications Management
MNE	Master of Nuclear Engineering
MNL	Master in International Business for Latin America
MNM	Master of Nonprofit Management
MNO	Master of Nonprofit Organization
MNPL	Master of Not-for-Profit Leadership
MNpS	Master of Nonprofit Studies
MNR	Master of Natural Resources
MNRD	Master of Natural Resources Development
MNRES	Master of Natural Resources and Environmental Studies
MNRM	Master of Natural Resource Management
MNRMG	Master of Natural Resource Management and Geography
MNRS	Master of Natural Resource Stewardship
MNS	Master of Natural Science
MO	Master of Oceanography

Peterson's Graduate Programs in the Physical Sciences, Mathematics, Agricultural Sciences, the Environment & Natural Resources 2017

www.petersons.com 421

MOD	Master of Organizational Development
MOGS	Master of Oil and Gas Studies
MOL	Master of Organizational Leadership
MOM	Master of Organizational Management
	Master of Oriental Medicine
MOR	Master of Operations Research
MOT	Master of Occupational Therapy
MP	Master of Physiology
	Master of Planning
MP Ac	Master of Professional Accountancy
MP Acc	Master of Professional Accountancy
	Master of Professional Accounting
	Master of Public Accounting
MP Aff	Master of Public Affairs
MP Th	Master of Pastoral Theology
MPA	Master of Performing Arts
	Master of Physician Assistant
	Master of Professional Accountancy
	Master of Professional Accounting
	Master of Public Administration
	Master of Public Affairs
MPAC	Master of Professional Accounting
MPAID	Master of Public Administration and International Development
MPAP	Master of Physician Assistant Practice
	Master of Public Administration and Policy
	Master of Public Affairs and Politics
MPAS	Master of Physician Assistant Science
	Master of Physician Assistant Studies
MPC	Master of Professional Communication
	Master of Professional Counseling
MPD	Master of Product Development
	Master of Public Diplomacy
MPDS	Master of Planning and Development Studies
MPE	Master of Physical Education
MPEM	Master of Project Engineering and Management
MPH	Master of Public Health
MPHE	Master of Public Health Education
MPHM	Master in Plant Health Management
MPHS	Master of Population Health Sciences
MPHTM	Master of Public Health and Tropical Medicine
MPI	Master of Product Innovation
MPIA	Master of Public and International Affairs
MPM	Master of Pastoral Ministry
	Master of Pest Management
	Master of Policy Management
	Master of Practical Ministries
	Master of Project Management
	Master of Public Management
MPNA	Master of Public and Nonprofit Administration

MPNL	Master of Philanthropy and Nonprofit Leadership
MPO	Master of Prosthetics and Orthotics
MPOD	Master of Positive Organizational Development
MPP	Master of Public Policy
MPPA	Master of Public Policy Administration
	Master of Public Policy and Administration
MPPAL	Master of Public Policy, Administration and Law
MPPM	Master of Public and Private Management
	Master of Public Policy and Management
MPPPM	Master of Plant Protection and Pest Management
MPRTM	Master of Parks, Recreation, and Tourism Management
MPS	Master of Pastoral Studies
	Master of Perfusion Science
	Master of Planning Studies
	Master of Political Science
	Master of Preservation Studies
	Master of Prevention Science
	Master of Professional Studies
	Master of Public Service
MPSA	Master of Public Service Administration
MPSG	Master of Population and Social Gerontology
MPSIA	Master of Political Science and International Affairs
MPSL	Master of Public Safety Leadership
MPSRE	Master of Professional Studies in Real Estate
MPT	Master of Pastoral Theology
	Master of Physical Therapy
	Master of Practical Theology
MPVM	Master of Preventive Veterinary Medicine
MPW	Master of Professional Writing
	Master of Public Works
MQM	Master of Quality Management
MQS	Master of Quality Systems
MR	Master of Recreation
	Master of Retailing
MRA	Master in Research Administration
MRC	Master of Rehabilitation Counseling
MRCP	Master of Regional and City Planning
	Master of Regional and Community Planning
MRD	Master of Rural Development
MRE	Master of Real Estate
	Master of Religious Education
MRED	Master of Real Estate Development
MREM	Master of Resource and Environmental Management
MRLS	Master of Resources Law Studies
MRM	Master of Resources Management
MRP	Master of Regional Planning

MRRD	Master in Recreation Resource Development
MRS	Master of Religious Studies
MRSc	Master of Rehabilitation Science
MRTP	Master of Rural and Town Planning
MS	Master of Science
MS Cmp E	Master of Science in Computer Engineering
MS Kin	Master of Science in Kinesiology
MS Acct	Master of Science in Accounting
MS Accy	Master of Science in Accountancy
MS Aero E	Master of Science in Aerospace Engineering
MS Ag	Master of Science in Agriculture
MS Arch	Master of Science in Architecture
MS Arch St	Master of Science in Architectural Studies
MS Bio E	Master of Science in Bioengineering
MS Bm E	Master of Science in Biomedical Engineering
MS Ch E	Master of Science in Chemical Engineering
MS Cp E	Master of Science in Computer Engineering
MS Eco	Master of Science in Economics
MS Econ	Master of Science in Economics
MS Ed	Master of Science in Education
MS El	Master of Science in Educational Leadership and Administration
MS En E	Master of Science in Environmental Engineering
MS Eng	Master of Science in Engineering
MS Engr	Master of Science in Engineering
MS Env E	Master of Science in Environmental Engineering
MS Exp Surg	Master of Science in Experimental Surgery
MS Mat E	Master of Science in Materials Engineering
MS Mat SE	Master of Science in Material Science and Engineering
MS Met E	Master of Science in Metallurgical Engineering
MS Mgt	Master of Science in Management
MS Min	Master of Science in Mining
MS Min E	Master of Science in Mining Engineering
MS Mt E	Master of Science in Materials Engineering
MS Otol	Master of Science in Otolaryngology
MS Pet E	Master of Science in Petroleum Engineering
MS Sc	Master of Social Science
MS Sp Ed	Master of Science in Special Education
MS Stat	Master of Science in Statistics
MS Surg	Master of Science in Surgery
MS Tax	Master of Science in Taxation
MS Tc E	Master of Science in Telecommunications Engineering
MS-R	Master of Science (Research)
MSA	Master of School Administration
	Master of Science in Accountancy
	Master of Science in Accounting
	Master of Science in Administration
	Master of Science in Aeronautics
	Master of Science in Agriculture

	Master of Science in Analytics
	Master of Science in Anesthesia
	Master of Science in Architecture
	Master of Science in Aviation
	Master of Sports Administration
	Master of Surgical Assisting
MSAA	Master of Science in Astronautics and Aeronautics
MSAAE	Master of Science in Aeronautical and Astronautical Engineering
MSABE	Master of Science in Agricultural and Biological Engineering
MSAC	Master of Science in Acupuncture
MSACC	Master of Science in Accounting
MSACS	Master of Science in Applied Computer Science
MSAE	Master of Science in Aeronautical Engineering
	Master of Science in Aerospace Engineering
	Master of Science in Applied Economics
	Master of Science in Applied Engineering
	Master of Science in Architectural Engineering
MSAEM	Master of Science in Aerospace Engineering and Mechanics
MSAF	Master of Science in Aviation Finance
MSAG	Master of Science in Applied Geosciences
MSAH	Master of Science in Allied Health
MSAL	Master of Sport Administration and Leadership
MSAM	Master of Science in Applied Mathematics
MSANR	Master of Science in Agriculture and Natural Resources
MSAPM	Master of Security Analysis and Portfolio Management
MSAS	Master of Science in Applied Statistics
	Master of Science in Architectural Studies
MSAT	Master of Science in Accounting and Taxation
	Master of Science in Advanced Technology
	Master of Science in Athletic Training
MSB	Master of Science in Biotechnology
	Master of Sustainable Business
MSBA	Master of Science in Business Administration
	Master of Science in Business Analysis
MSBAE	Master of Science in Biological and Agricultural Engineering
	Master of Science in Biosystems and Agricultural Engineering
MSBC	Master of Science in Building Construction
	Master of Science in Business Communication
MSBCB	Master's in Bioinformatics and Computational Biology
MSBE	Master of Science in Biological Engineering
	Master of Science in Biomedical Engineering

Peterson's Graduate Programs in the Physical Sciences, Mathematics, Agricultural Sciences, the Environment & Natural Resources 2017

www.petersons.com   423

MSBENG	Master of Science in Bioengineering
MSBH	Master of Science in Behavioral Health
MSBIT	Master of Science in Business Information Technology
MSBM	Master of Sport Business Management
MSBME	Master of Science in Biomedical Engineering
MSBMS	Master of Science in Basic Medical Science
MSBS	Master of Science in Biomedical Sciences
MSBTM	Master of Science in Biotechnology and Management
MSC	Master of Science in Commerce
	Master of Science in Communication
	Master of Science in Computers
	Master of Science in Counseling
	Master of Science in Criminology
	Master of Strategic Communication
MSCC	Master of Science in Community Counseling
MSCD	Master of Science in Communication Disorders
	Master of Science in Community Development
MSCE	Master of Science in Civil Engineering
	Master of Science in Clinical Epidemiology
	Master of Science in Computer Engineering
	Master of Science in Continuing Education
MSCEE	Master of Science in Civil and Environmental Engineering
MSCF	Master of Science in Computational Finance
MSCH	Master of Science in Chemical Engineering
MSChE	Master of Science in Chemical Engineering
MSCI	Master of Science in Clinical Investigation
MSCIS	Master of Science in Computer and Information Science
	Master of Science in Computer and Information Systems
	Master of Science in Computer Information Science
	Master of Science in Computer Information Systems
MSCIT	Master of Science in Computer Information Technology
MSCJ	Master of Science in Criminal Justice
MSCJA	Master of Science in Criminal Justice Administration
MSCJS	Master of Science in Crime and Justice Studies
MSCLS	Master of Science in Clinical Laboratory Studies
MSCM	Master of Science in Church Management
	Master of Science in Conflict Management
	Master of Science in Construction Management
	Master of Supply Chain Management
MSCNU	Master of Science in Clinical Nutrition
MSCP	Master of Science in Clinical Psychology
	Master of Science in Community Psychology

	Master of Science in Computer Engineering
	Master of Science in Counseling Psychology
MSCPE	Master of Science in Computer Engineering
MSCPharm	Master of Science in Pharmacy
MSCR	Master of Science in Clinical Research
MSCRP	Master of Science in City and Regional Planning
	Master of Science in Community and Regional Planning
MSCS	Master of Science in Clinical Science
	Master of Science in Computer Science
	Master of Science in Cyber Security
MSCSD	Master of Science in Communication Sciences and Disorders
MSCSE	Master of Science in Computer Science and Engineering
MSCTE	Master of Science in Career and Technical Education
MSD	Master of Science in Dentistry
	Master of Science in Design
	Master of Science in Dietetics
MSE	Master of Science Education
	Master of Science in Economics
	Master of Science in Education
	Master of Science in Engineering
	Master of Science in Engineering Management
	Master of Software Engineering
	Master of Special Education
	Master of Structural Engineering
MSECE	Master of Science in Electrical and Computer Engineering
MSED	Master of Sustainable Economic Development
MSEE	Master of Science in Electrical Engineering
	Master of Science in Environmental Engineering
MSEH	Master of Science in Environmental Health
MSEL	Master of Science in Educational Leadership
MSEM	Master of Science in Engineering Management
	Master of Science in Engineering Mechanics
	Master of Science in Environmental Management
MSENE	Master of Science in Environmental Engineering
MSEO	Master of Science in Electro-Optics
MSEP	Master of Science in Economic Policy
MSES	Master of Science in Embedded Software Engineering
	Master of Science in Engineering Science
	Master of Science in Environmental Science
	Master of Science in Environmental Studies
	Master of Science in Exercise Science
MSET	Master of Science in Educational Technology

	Master of Science in Engineering Technology	MSIDM	Master of Science in Interior Design and Merchandising
MSEV	Master of Science in Environmental Engineering	MSIE	Master of Science in Industrial Engineering
MSF	Master of Science in Finance		Master of Science in International Economics
	Master of Science in Forestry	MSIEM	Master of Science in Information Engineering and Management
	Master of Spiritual Formation		
MSFA	Master of Science in Financial Analysis	MSIID	Master of Science in Information and Instructional Design
MSFCS	Master of Science in Family and Consumer Science	MSIM	Master of Science in Information Management
MSFE	Master of Science in Financial Engineering		Master of Science in International Management
MSFM	Master of Sustainable Forest Management		
MSFOR	Master of Science in Forestry	MSIMC	Master of Science in Integrated Marketing Communications
MSFP	Master of Science in Financial Planning	MSIR	Master of Science in Industrial Relations
MSFS	Master of Science in Financial Sciences	MSIS	Master of Science in Information Science
	Master of Science in Forensic Science		Master of Science in Information Studies
MSFSB	Master of Science in Financial Services and Banking		Master of Science in Information Systems
MSFT	Master of Science in Family Therapy		Master of Science in Interdisciplinary Studies
MSGC	Master of Science in Genetic Counseling		
MSH	Master of Science in Health	MSISE	Master of Science in Infrastructure Systems Engineering
	Master of Science in Hospice		
MSHA	Master of Science in Health Administration	MSISM	Master of Science in Information Systems Management
MSHCA	Master of Science in Health Care Administration	MSISPM	Master of Science in Information Security Policy and Management
MSHCI	Master of Science in Human Computer Interaction	MSIST	Master of Science in Information Systems Technology
MSHCPM	Master of Science in Health Care Policy and Management	MSIT	Master of Science in Industrial Technology
MSHE	Master of Science in Health Education		Master of Science in Information Technology
MSHES	Master of Science in Human Environmental Sciences		Master of Science in Instructional Technology
MSHFID	Master of Science in Human Factors in Information Design	MSITM	Master of Science in Information Technology Management
MSHFS	Master of Science in Human Factors and Systems	MSJ	Master of Science in Journalism
MSHI	Master of Science in Health Informatics		Master of Science in Jurisprudence
MSHP	Master of Science in Health Professions	MSJC	Master of Social Justice and Criminology
	Master of Science in Health Promotion	MSJE	Master of Science in Jewish Education
MSHR	Master of Science in Human Resources	MSJFP	Master of Science in Juvenile Forensic Psychology
MSHRL	Master of Science in Human Resource Leadership	MSJJ	Master of Science in Juvenile Justice
MSHRM	Master of Science in Human Resource Management	MSJPS	Master of Science in Justice and Public Safety
MSHROD	Master of Science in Human Resources and Organizational Development	MSJS	Master of Science in Jewish Studies
		MSL	Master of School Leadership
MSHS	Master of Science in Health Science		Master of Science in Leadership
	Master of Science in Health Services		Master of Science in Limnology
	Master of Science in Homeland Security		Master of Strategic Leadership
MSI	Master of Science in Information		Master of Studies in Law
	Master of Science in Instruction	MSLA	Master of Science in Legal Administration
	Master of System Integration	MSLFS	Master of Science in Life Sciences
MSIA	Master of Science in Industrial Administration	MSLP	Master of Speech-Language Pathology
		MSLS	Master of Science in Library Science
	Master of Science in Information Assurance	MSLSCM	Master of Science in Logistics and Supply Chain Management
MSIB	Master of Science in International Business	MSLT	Master of Second Language Teaching
		MSM	Master of Sacred Ministry

Peterson's Graduate Programs in the Physical Sciences, Mathematics, Agricultural Sciences, the Environment & Natural Resources 2017

www.petersons.com **425**

	Master of Sacred Music
	Master of School Mathematics
	Master of Science in Management
	Master of Science in Medicine
	Master of Science in Organization Management
	Master of Security Management
MSMA	Master of Science in Marketing Analysis
MSMAE	Master of Science in Materials Engineering
MSMC	Master of Science in Mass Communications
MSME	Master of Science in Mathematics Education
	Master of Science in Mechanical Engineering
MSMFT	Master of Science in Marriage and Family Therapy
MSMHC	Master of Science in Mental Health Counseling
MSMIS	Master of Science in Management Information Systems
MSMIT	Master of Science in Management and Information Technology
MSMLS	Master of Science in Medical Laboratory Science
MSMOT	Master of Science in Management of Technology
MSMP	Master of Science in Medical Physics
MSMS	Master of Science in Management Science
	Master of Science in Marine Science
	Master of Science in Medical Sciences
MSMSE	Master of Science in Manufacturing Systems Engineering
	Master of Science in Material Science and Engineering
	Master of Science in Mathematics and Science Education
MSMT	Master of Science in Management and Technology
MSMus	Master of Sacred Music
MSN	Master of Science in Nursing
MSNA	Master of Science in Nurse Anesthesia
MSNE	Master of Science in Nuclear Engineering
MSNED	Master of Science in Nurse Education
MSNM	Master of Science in Nonprofit Management
MSNS	Master of Science in Natural Science
	Master of Science in Nutritional Science
MSOD	Master of Science in Organization Development
	Master of Science in Organizational Development
MSOEE	Master of Science in Outdoor and Environmental Education
MSOES	Master of Science in Occupational Ergonomics and Safety
MSOH	Master of Science in Occupational Health
MSOL	Master of Science in Organizational Leadership
MSOM	Master of Science in Operations Management

	Master of Science in Oriental Medicine
MSOR	Master of Science in Operations Research
MSOT	Master of Science in Occupational Technology
	Master of Science in Occupational Therapy
MSP	Master of Science in Pharmacy
	Master of Science in Planning
	Master of Speech Pathology
MSPA	Master of Science in Physician Assistant
	Master of Science in Professional Accountancy
MSPAS	Master of Science in Physician Assistant Studies
MSPC	Master of Science in Professional Communications
MSPE	Master of Science in Petroleum Engineering
MSPH	Master of Science in Public Health
MSPHR	Master of Science in Pharmacy
MSPM	Master of Science in Professional Management
	Master of Science in Project Management
MSPNGE	Master of Science in Petroleum and Natural Gas Engineering
MSPO	Master of Science in Prosthetics and Orthotics
MSPPM	Master of Science in Public Policy and Management
MSPS	Master of Science in Pharmaceutical Science
	Master of Science in Political Science
	Master of Science in Psychological Services
MSPT	Master of Science in Physical Therapy
MSpVM	Master of Specialized Veterinary Medicine
MSR	Master of Science in Radiology
	Master of Science in Reading
MSRA	Master of Science in Recreation Administration
MSRE	Master of Science in Real Estate
	Master of Science in Religious Education
MSRED	Master of Science in Real Estate Development
	Master of Sustainable Real Estate Development
MSRLS	Master of Science in Recreation and Leisure Studies
MSRM	Master of Science in Risk Management
MSRMP	Master of Science in Radiological Medical Physics
MSRS	Master of Science in Radiological Sciences
	Master of Science in Rehabilitation Science
MSS	Master of Security Studies
	Master of Social Science
	Master of Social Services
	Master of Software Systems
	Master of Sports Science
	Master of Strategic Studies
	Master's in Statistical Science
MSSA	Master of Science in Social Administration

Peterson's Graduate Programs in the Physical Sciences, Mathematics, Agricultural Sciences, the Environment & Natural Resources 2017

MSSCM	Master of Science in Supply Chain Management
MSSD	Master of Arts in Software Driven Systems Design
	Master of Science in Sustainable Design
MSSE	Master of Science in Software Engineering
	Master of Science in Special Education
MSSEM	Master of Science in Systems and Engineering Management
MSSI	Master of Science in Security Informatics
	Master of Science in Strategic Intelligence
MSSL	Master of Science in School Leadership
	Master of Science in Strategic Leadership
MSSLP	Master of Science in Speech-Language Pathology
MSSM	Master of Science in Sports Medicine
MSSP	Master of Science in Social Policy
MSSPA	Master of Science in Student Personnel Administration
MSSS	Master of Science in Safety Science
	Master of Science in Systems Science
MSST	Master of Science in Security Technologies
MSSW	Master of Science in Social Work
MSSWE	Master of Science in Software Engineering
MST	Master of Science and Technology
	Master of Science in Taxation
	Master of Science in Teaching
	Master of Science in Technology
	Master of Science in Telecommunications
	Master of Science Teaching
MSTC	Master of Science in Technical Communication
	Master of Science in Telecommunications
MSTCM	Master of Science in Traditional Chinese Medicine
MSTE	Master of Science in Telecommunications Engineering
	Master of Science in Transportation Engineering
MSTL	Master of Science in Teacher Leadership
MSTM	Master of Science in Technology Management
	Master of Science in Transfusion Medicine
MSTOM	Master of Science in Traditional Oriental Medicine
MSUASE	Master of Science in Unmanned and Autonomous Systems Engineering
MSUD	Master of Science in Urban Design
MSUS	Master of Science in Urban Studies
MSW	Master of Social Work
MSWE	Master of Software Engineering
MSWREE	Master of Science in Water Resources and Environmental Engineering
MT	Master of Taxation
	Master of Teaching
	Master of Technology
	Master of Textiles

MTA	Master of Tax Accounting
	Master of Teaching Arts
	Master of Tourism Administration
MTCM	Master of Traditional Chinese Medicine
MTD	Master of Training and Development
MTE	Master in Educational Technology
MTESOL	Master in Teaching English to Speakers of Other Languages
MTHM	Master of Tourism and Hospitality Management
MTI	Master of Information Technology
MTID	Master of Tangible Interaction Design
MTL	Master of Talmudic Law
MTM	Master of Technology Management
	Master of Telecommunications Management
	Master of the Teaching of Mathematics
MTMH	Master of Tropical Medicine and Hygiene
MTMS	Master in Teaching Mathematics and Science
MTOM	Master of Traditional Oriental Medicine
MTPC	Master of Technical and Professional Communication
MTR	Master of Translational Research
MTS	Master of Theatre Studies
	Master of Theological Studies
MTWM	Master of Trust and Wealth Management
MTX	Master of Taxation
MUA	Master of Urban Affairs
MUCD	Master of Urban and Community Design
MUD	Master of Urban Design
MUDS	Master of Urban Design Studies
MUEP	Master of Urban and Environmental Planning
MUP	Master of Urban Planning
MUPDD	Master of Urban Planning, Design, and Development
MUPP	Master of Urban Planning and Policy
MUPRED	Master of Urban Planning and Real Estate Development
MURP	Master of Urban and Regional Planning
	Master of Urban and Rural Planning
MUS	Master of Urban Studies
MUSA	Master of Urban Spatial Analytics
MVP	Master of Voice Pedagogy
MVPH	Master of Veterinary Public Health
MVS	Master of Visual Studies
MWC	Master of Wildlife Conservation
MWM	Master of Water Management
MWPS	Master of Wood and Paper Science
MWR	Master of Water Resources
MWS	Master of Women's Studies
	Master of Worship Studies
MWSc	Master of Wildlife Science
MZS	Master of Zoological Science
Nav Arch	Naval Architecture

Peterson's Graduate Programs in the Physical Sciences, Mathematics, Agricultural Sciences, the Environment & Natural Resources 2017

www.petersons.com   **427**

Naval E	Naval Engineer	Psya D	Doctor of Psychoanalysis
ND	Doctor of Naturopathic Medicine	S Psy S	Specialist in Psychological Services
NE	Nuclear Engineer	Sc D	Doctor of Science
Nuc E	Nuclear Engineer	Sc M	Master of Science
OD	Doctor of Optometry	SCCT	Specialist in Community College Teaching
OTD	Doctor of Occupational Therapy	ScDPT	Doctor of Physical Therapy Science
PBME	Professional Master of Biomedical Engineering	SD	Doctor of Science
			Specialist Degree
PC	Performer's Certificate	SJD	Doctor of Juridical Sciences
PD	Professional Diploma	SLPD	Doctor of Speech-Language Pathology
PGC	Post-Graduate Certificate	SM	Master of Science
PGD	Postgraduate Diploma	SM Arch S	Master of Science in Architectural Studies
Ph L	Licentiate of Philosophy	SMACT	Master of Science in Art, Culture and Technology
Pharm D	Doctor of Pharmacy		
PhD	Doctor of Philosophy	SMBT	Master of Science in Building Technology
PhD Otol	Doctor of Philosophy in Otolaryngology	SP	Specialist Degree
PhD Surg	Doctor of Philosophy in Surgery	Sp Ed	Specialist in Education
PhDEE	Doctor of Philosophy in Electrical Engineering	Sp LIS	Specialist in Library and Information Science
PMBA	Professional Master of Business Administration	SPA	Specialist in Arts
		Spec	Specialist's Certificate
PMC	Post Master Certificate	Spec M	Specialist in Music
PMD	Post-Master's Diploma	Spt	Specialist Degree
PMS	Professional Master of Science	SSP	Specialist in School Psychology
	Professional Master's	STB	Bachelor of Sacred Theology
Post-Doctoral MS	Post-Doctoral Master of Science	STD	Doctor of Sacred Theology
Post-MSN Certificate	Post-Master of Science in Nursing Certificate	STL	Licentiate of Sacred Theology
PPDPT	Postprofessional Doctor of Physical Therapy	STM	Master of Sacred Theology
Pro-MS	Professional Science Master's	TDPT	Transitional Doctor of Physical Therapy
Professional MA	Professional Master of Arts	Th D	Doctor of Theology
Professional MBA	Professional Master of Business Administration	Th M	Master of Theology
		TOTD	Transitional Doctor of Occupational Therapy
Professional MS	Professional Master of Science		
PSM	Professional Master of Science	VMD	Doctor of Veterinary Medicine
	Professional Science Master's	WEMBA	Weekend Executive Master of Business Administration
Psy D	Doctor of Psychology		
Psy M	Master of Psychology	XMA	Executive Master of Arts
Psy S	Specialist in Psychology		

428 www.petersons.com

Peterson's Graduate Programs in the Physical Sciences, Mathematics, Agricultural Sciences, the Environment & Natural Resources 2017

INDEXES

Displays and Close-Ups

Directories and Subject Areas

Following is an alphabetical listing of directories and subject areas. Also listed are cross-references for subject area names not used in the directory structure of the guides, for example, "City and Regional Planning (*see* Urban and Regional Planning)."

Graduate Programs in the Humanities, Arts & Social Sciences

Addictions/Substance Abuse Counseling
Administration (*see* Arts Administration; Public Administration)
African-American Studies
African Languages and Literatures (*see* African Studies)
African Studies
Agribusiness (*see* Agricultural Economics and Agribusiness)
Agricultural Economics and Agribusiness
Alcohol Abuse Counseling (*see* Addictions/Substance Abuse Counseling)
American Indian/Native American Studies
American Studies
Anthropology
Applied Arts and Design—General
Applied Behavior Analysis
Applied Economics
Applied History (*see* Public History)
Applied Psychology
Applied Social Research
Arabic (*see* Near and Middle Eastern Languages)
Arab Studies (*see* Near and Middle Eastern Studies)
Archaeology
Architectural History
Architecture
Archives Administration (*see* Public History)
Area and Cultural Studies (*see* African-American Studies; African Studies; American Indian/Native American Studies; American Studies; Asian-American Studies; Asian Studies; Canadian Studies; Cultural Studies; East European and Russian Studies; Ethnic Studies; Folklore; Gender Studies; Hispanic Studies; Holocaust Studies; Jewish Studies; Latin American Studies; Near and Middle Eastern Studies; Northern Studies; Pacific Area/Pacific Rim Studies; Western European Studies; Women's Studies)
Art/Fine Arts
Art History
Arts Administration
Arts Journalism
Art Therapy
Asian-American Studies
Asian Languages
Asian Studies
Behavioral Sciences (*see* Psychology)
Bible Studies (*see* Religion; Theology)
Biological Anthropology
Black Studies (*see* African-American Studies)
Broadcasting (*see* Communication; Film, Television, and Video Production)
Broadcast Journalism
Building Science
Canadian Studies
Celtic Languages
Ceramics (*see* Art/Fine Arts)
Child and Family Studies
Child Development
Chinese
Chinese Studies (*see* Asian Languages; Asian Studies)
Christian Studies (*see* Missions and Missiology; Religion; Theology)
Cinema (*see* Film, Television, and Video Production)
City and Regional Planning (*see* Urban and Regional Planning)
Classical Languages and Literatures (*see* Classics)
Classics

Clinical Psychology
Clothing and Textiles
Cognitive Psychology (*see* Psychology—General; Cognitive Sciences)
Cognitive Sciences
Communication—General
Community Affairs (*see* Urban and Regional Planning; Urban Studies)
Community Planning (*see* Architecture; Environmental Design; Urban and Regional Planning; Urban Design; Urban Studies)
Community Psychology (*see* Social Psychology)
Comparative and Interdisciplinary Arts
Comparative Literature
Composition (*see* Music)
Computer Art and Design
Conflict Resolution and Mediation/Peace Studies
Consumer Economics
Corporate and Organizational Communication
Corrections (*see* Criminal Justice and Criminology)
Counseling (*see* Counseling Psychology; Pastoral Ministry and Counseling)
Counseling Psychology
Crafts (*see* Art/Fine Arts)
Creative Arts Therapies (*see* Art Therapy; Therapies—Dance, Drama, and Music)
Criminal Justice and Criminology
Cultural Anthropology
Cultural Studies
Dance
Decorative Arts
Demography and Population Studies
Design (*see* Applied Arts and Design; Architecture; Art/Fine Arts; Environmental Design; Graphic Design; Industrial Design; Interior Design; Textile Design; Urban Design)
Developmental Psychology
Diplomacy (*see* International Affairs)
Disability Studies
Drama Therapy (*see* Therapies—Dance, Drama, and Music)
Dramatic Arts (*see* Theater)
Drawing (*see* Art/Fine Arts)
Drug Abuse Counseling (*see* Addictions/Substance Abuse Counseling)
Drug and Alcohol Abuse Counseling (*see* Addictions/Substance Abuse Counseling)
East Asian Studies (*see* Asian Studies)
East European and Russian Studies
Economic Development
Economics
Educational Theater (*see* Theater; Therapies—Dance, Drama, and Music)
Emergency Management
English
Environmental Design
Ethics
Ethnic Studies
Ethnomusicology (*see* Music)
Experimental Psychology
Family and Consumer Sciences—General
Family Studies (*see* Child and Family Studies)
Family Therapy (*see* Child and Family Studies; Clinical Psychology; Counseling Psychology; Marriage and Family Therapy)
Filmmaking (*see* Film, Television, and Video Production)
Film Studies (*see* Film, Television, and Video Production)
Film, Television, and Video Production
Film, Television, and Video Theory and Criticism
Fine Arts (*see* Art/Fine Arts)
Folklore
Foreign Languages (*see* specific language)
Foreign Service (*see* International Affairs; International Development)
Forensic Psychology
Forensic Sciences
Forensics (*see* Speech and Interpersonal Communication)
French

Gender Studies
General Studies (*see* Liberal Studies)
Genetic Counseling
Geographic Information Systems
Geography
German
Gerontology
Graphic Design
Greek (*see* Classics)
Health Communication
Health Psychology
Hebrew (*see* Near and Middle Eastern Languages)
Hebrew Studies (*see* Jewish Studies)
Hispanic and Latin American Languages
Hispanic Studies
Historic Preservation
History
History of Art (*see* Art History)
History of Medicine
History of Science and Technology
Holocaust and Genocide Studies
Home Economics (*see* Family and Consumer Sciences—General)
Homeland Security
Household Economics, Sciences, and Management (*see* Family and Consumer Sciences—General)
Human Development
Humanities
Illustration
Industrial and Labor Relations
Industrial and Organizational Psychology
Industrial Design
Interdisciplinary Studies
Interior Design
International Affairs
International Development
International Economics
International Service (*see* International Affairs; International Development)
International Trade Policy
Internet and Interactive Multimedia
Interpersonal Communication (*see* Speech and Interpersonal Communication)
Interpretation (*see* Translation and Interpretation)
Islamic Studies (*see* Near and Middle Eastern Studies; Religion)
Italian
Japanese
Japanese Studies (*see* Asian Languages; Asian Studies; Japanese)
Jewelry (*see* Art/Fine Arts)
Jewish Studies
Journalism
Judaic Studies (*see* Jewish Studies; Religion)
Labor Relations (*see* Industrial and Labor Relations)
Landscape Architecture
Latin American Studies
Latin (*see* Classics)
Law Enforcement (*see* Criminal Justice and Criminology)
Liberal Studies
Lighting Design
Linguistics
Literature (*see* Classics; Comparative Literature; specific language)
Marriage and Family Therapy
Mass Communication
Media Studies
Medical Illustration
Medieval and Renaissance Studies
Metalsmithing (*see* Art/Fine Arts)
Middle Eastern Studies (*see* Near and Middle Eastern Studies)
Military and Defense Studies
Mineral Economics
Ministry (*see* Pastoral Ministry and Counseling; Theology)
Missions and Missiology
Motion Pictures (*see* Film, Television, and Video Production)
Museum Studies
Music
Musicology (*see* Music)
Music Therapy (*see* Therapies—Dance, Drama, and Music)

National Security
Native American Studies (*see* American Indian/Native American Studies)
Near and Middle Eastern Languages
Near and Middle Eastern Studies
Northern Studies
Organizational Psychology (*see* Industrial and Organizational Psychology)
Oriental Languages (*see* Asian Languages)
Oriental Studies (*see* Asian Studies)
Pacific Area/Pacific Rim Studies
Painting (*see* Art/Fine Arts)
Pastoral Ministry and Counseling
Philanthropic Studies
Philosophy
Photography
Playwriting (*see* Theater; Writing)
Policy Studies (*see* Public Policy)
Political Science
Population Studies (*see* Demography and Population Studies)
Portuguese
Printmaking (*see* Art/Fine Arts)
Product Design (*see* Industrial Design)
Psychoanalysis and Psychotherapy
Psychology—General
Public Administration
Public Affairs
Public History
Public Policy
Public Speaking (*see* Mass Communication; Rhetoric; Speech and Interpersonal Communication)
Publishing
Regional Planning (*see* Architecture; Urban and Regional Planning; Urban Design; Urban Studies)
Rehabilitation Counseling
Religion
Renaissance Studies (*see* Medieval and Renaissance Studies)
Rhetoric
Romance Languages
Romance Literatures (*see* Romance Languages)
Rural Planning and Studies
Rural Sociology
Russian
Scandinavian Languages
School Psychology
Sculpture (*see* Art/Fine Arts)
Security Administration (*see* Criminal Justice and Criminology)
Slavic Languages
Slavic Studies (*see* East European and Russian Studies; Slavic Languages)
Social Psychology
Social Sciences
Sociology
Southeast Asian Studies (*see* Asian Studies)
Soviet Studies (*see* East European and Russian Studies; Russian)
Spanish
Speech and Interpersonal Communication
Sport Psychology
Studio Art (*see* Art/Fine Arts)
Substance Abuse Counseling (*see* Addictions/Substance Abuse Counseling)
Survey Methodology
Sustainable Development
Technical Communication
Technical Writing
Telecommunications (*see* Film, Television, and Video Production)
Television (*see* Film, Television, and Video Production)
Textile Design
Textiles (*see* Clothing and Textiles; Textile Design)
Thanatology
Theater
Theater Arts (*see* Theater)
Theology
Therapies—Dance, Drama, and Music
Translation and Interpretation
Transpersonal and Humanistic Psychology

434 www.petersons.com

Peterson's Graduate Programs in the Physical Sciences, Mathematics, Agricultural Sciences, the Environment & Natural Resources 2017

Urban and Regional Planning
Urban Design
Urban Planning (*see* Architecture; Urban and Regional Planning; Urban Design; Urban Studies)
Urban Studies
Video (*see* Film, Television, and Video Production)
Visual Arts (*see* Applied Arts and Design; Art/Fine Arts; Film, Television, and Video Production; Graphic Design; Illustration; Photography)
Western European Studies
Women's Studies
World Wide Web (*see* Internet and Interactive Multimedia)
Writing

Graduate Programs in the Biological/ Biomedical Sciences & Health-Related Medical Professions

Acupuncture and Oriental Medicine
Acute Care/Critical Care Nursing Administration (*see* Health Services Management and Hospital Administration; Nursing and Healthcare Administration; Pharmaceutical Administration)
Adult Nursing
Advanced Practice Nursing (*see* Family Nurse Practitioner Studies)
Allied Health—General
Allied Health Professions (*see* Clinical Laboratory Sciences/Medical Technology; Clinical Research; Communication Disorders; Dental Hygiene; Emergency Medical Services; Occupational Therapy; Physical Therapy; Physician Assistant Studies; Rehabilitation Sciences)
Allopathic Medicine
Anatomy
Anesthesiologist Assistant Studies
Animal Behavior
Bacteriology
Behavioral Sciences (*see* Biopsychology; Neuroscience; Zoology)
Biochemistry
Bioethics
Biological and Biomedical Sciences—General Biological Chemistry (*see* Biochemistry)
Biological Oceanography (*see* Marine Biology)
Biophysics
Biopsychology
Botany
Breeding (*see* Botany; Plant Biology; Genetics)
Cancer Biology/Oncology
Cardiovascular Sciences
Cell Biology
Cellular Physiology (*see* Cell Biology; Physiology)
Child-Care Nursing (*see* Maternal and Child/Neonatal Nursing)
Chiropractic
Clinical Laboratory Sciences/Medical Technology
Clinical Research
Community Health
Community Health Nursing
Computational Biology
Conservation (*see* Conservation Biology; Environmental Biology)
Conservation Biology
Crop Sciences (*see* Botany; Plant Biology)
Cytology (*see* Cell Biology)
Dental and Oral Surgery (*see* Oral and Dental Sciences)
Dental Assistant Studies (*see* Dental Hygiene)
Dental Hygiene
Dental Services (*see* Dental Hygiene)
Dentistry
Developmental Biology Dietetics (*see* Nutrition)
Ecology
Embryology (*see* Developmental Biology)
Emergency Medical Services
Endocrinology (*see* Physiology)
Entomology
Environmental Biology

Environmental and Occupational Health
Epidemiology
Evolutionary Biology
Family Nurse Practitioner Studies
Foods (*see* Nutrition)
Forensic Nursing
Genetics
Genomic Sciences
Gerontological Nursing
Health Physics/Radiological Health
Health Promotion
Health-Related Professions (*see* individual allied health professions)
Health Services Management and Hospital Administration
Health Services Research
Histology (*see* Anatomy; Cell Biology)
HIV/AIDS Nursing
Hospice Nursing
Hospital Administration (*see* Health Services Management and Hospital Administration)
Human Genetics
Immunology
Industrial Hygiene
Infectious Diseases
International Health
Laboratory Medicine (*see* Clinical Laboratory Sciences/Medical Technology; Immunology; Microbiology; Pathology)
Life Sciences (*see* Biological and Biomedical Sciences)
Marine Biology
Maternal and Child Health
Maternal and Child/Neonatal Nursing
Medical Imaging
Medical Microbiology
Medical Nursing (*see* Medical/Surgical Nursing)
Medical Physics
Medical/Surgical Nursing
Medical Technology (*see* Clinical Laboratory Sciences/Medical Technology)
Medical Sciences (*see* Biological and Biomedical Sciences)
Medical Science Training Programs (*see* Biological and Biomedical Sciences)
Medicinal and Pharmaceutical Chemistry
Medicinal Chemistry (*see* Medicinal and Pharmaceutical Chemistry)
Medicine (*see* Allopathic Medicine; Naturopathic Medicine; Osteopathic Medicine; Podiatric Medicine)
Microbiology
Midwifery (*see* Nurse Midwifery)
Molecular Biology
Molecular Biophysics
Molecular Genetics
Molecular Medicine
Molecular Pathogenesis
Molecular Pathology
Molecular Pharmacology
Molecular Physiology
Molecular Toxicology
Naturopathic Medicine
Neural Sciences (*see* Biopsychology; Neurobiology; Neuroscience)
Neurobiology
Neuroendocrinology (*see* Biopsychology; Neurobiology; Neuroscience; Physiology)
Neuropharmacology (*see* Biopsychology; Neurobiology; Neuroscience; Pharmacology)
Neurophysiology (*see* Biopsychology; Neurobiology; Neuroscience; Physiology)
Neuroscience
Nuclear Medical Technology (*see* Clinical Laboratory Sciences/ Medical Technology)
Nurse Anesthesia
Nurse Midwifery
Nurse Practitioner Studies (*see* Family Nurse Practitioner Studies)
Nursing Administration (*see* Nursing and Healthcare Administration)
Nursing and Healthcare Administration
Nursing Education
Nursing—General
Nursing Informatics
Nutrition

Peterson's Graduate Programs in the Physical Sciences, Mathematics, Agricultural Sciences, the Environment & Natural Resources 2017

www.petersons.com **435**

Occupational Health (*see* Environmental and Occupational Health; Occupational Health Nursing)
Occupational Health Nursing
Occupational Therapy
Oncology (*see* Cancer Biology/Oncology)
Oncology Nursing
Optometry
Oral and Dental Sciences
Oral Biology (*see* Oral and Dental Sciences)
Oral Pathology (*see* Oral and Dental Sciences)
Organismal Biology (*see* Biological and Biomedical Sciences; Zoology)
Oriental Medicine and Acupuncture (*see* Acupuncture and Oriental Medicine)
Orthodontics (*see* Oral and Dental Sciences)
Osteopathic Medicine
Parasitology
Pathobiology
Pathology
Pediatric Nursing
Pedontics (*see* Oral and Dental Sciences)
Perfusion
Pharmaceutical Administration
Pharmaceutical Chemistry (*see* Medicinal and Pharmaceutical Chemistry)
Pharmaceutical Sciences
Pharmacology
Pharmacy
Photobiology of Cells and Organelles (*see* Botany; Cell Biology; Plant Biology)
Physical Therapy
Physician Assistant Studies
Physiological Optics (*see* Vision Sciences)
Podiatric Medicine
Preventive Medicine (*see* Community Health and Public Health)
Physiological Optics (*see* Physiology)
Physiology
Plant Biology
Plant Molecular Biology
Plant Pathology
Plant Physiology
Pomology (*see* Botany; Plant Biology)
Psychiatric Nursing
Public Health—General
Public Health Nursing (*see* Community Health Nursing)
Psychiatric Nursing
Psychobiology (*see* Biopsychology)
Psychopharmacology (*see* Biopsychology; Neuroscience; Pharmacology)
Radiation Biology
Radiological Health (*see* Health Physics/Radiological Health)
Rehabilitation Nursing
Rehabilitation Sciences
Rehabilitation Therapy (*see* Physical Therapy)
Reproductive Biology
School Nursing
Sociobiology (*see* Evolutionary Biology)
Structural Biology
Surgical Nursing (*see* Medical/Surgical Nursing)
Systems Biology
Teratology
Therapeutics
Theoretical Biology (*see* Biological and Biomedical Sciences)
Therapeutics (*see* Pharmaceutical Sciences; Pharmacology; Pharmacy)
Toxicology
Transcultural Nursing
Translational Biology
Tropical Medicine (*see* Parasitology)
Veterinary Medicine
Veterinary Sciences
Virology
Vision Sciences
Wildlife Biology (*see* Zoology)
Women's Health Nursing
Zoology

Graduate Programs in the Physical Sciences, Mathematics, Agricultural Sciences, the Environment & Natural Resources

Acoustics
Agricultural Sciences
Agronomy and Soil Sciences
Analytical Chemistry
Animal Sciences
Applied Mathematics
Applied Physics
Applied Statistics
Aquaculture
Astronomy
Astrophysical Sciences (*see* Astrophysics; Atmospheric Sciences; Meteorology; Planetary and Space Sciences)
Astrophysics
Atmospheric Sciences
Biological Oceanography (*see* Marine Affairs; Marine Sciences; Oceanography)
Biomathematics
Biometry
Biostatistics
Chemical Physics
Chemistry
Computational Sciences
Condensed Matter Physics
Dairy Science (*see* Animal Sciences)
Earth Sciences (*see* Geosciences)
Environmental Management and Policy
Environmental Sciences
Environmental Studies (*see* Environmental Management and Policy)
Experimental Statistics (*see* Statistics)
Fish, Game, and Wildlife Management
Food Science and Technology
Forestry
General Science (*see* specific topics)
Geochemistry
Geodetic Sciences
Geological Engineering (*see* Geology)
Geological Sciences (*see* Geology)
Geology
Geophysical Fluid Dynamics (*see* Geophysics)
Geophysics
Geosciences
Horticulture
Hydrogeology
Hydrology
Inorganic Chemistry
Limnology
Marine Affairs
Marine Geology
Marine Sciences
Marine Studies (*see* Marine Affairs; Marine Geology; Marine Sciences; Oceanography)
Mathematical and Computational Finance
Mathematical Physics
Mathematical Statistics (*see* Applied Statistics; Statistics)
Mathematics
Meteorology
Mineralogy
Natural Resource Management (*see* Environmental Management and Policy; Natural Resources)
Natural Resources
Nuclear Physics (*see* Physics)
Ocean Engineering (*see* Marine Affairs; Marine Geology; Marine Sciences; Oceanography)
Oceanography
Optical Sciences
Optical Technologies (*see* Optical Sciences)
Optics (*see* Applied Physics; Optical Sciences; Physics)
Organic Chemistry

Peterson's Graduate Programs in the Physical Sciences, Mathematics, Agricultural Sciences, the Environment & Natural Resources 2017

Paleontology
Paper Chemistry (*see* Chemistry)
Photonics
Physical Chemistry
Physics
Planetary and Space Sciences
Plant Sciences
Plasma Physics
Poultry Science (*see* Animal Sciences)
Radiological Physics (*see* Physics)
Range Management (*see* Range Science)
Range Science
Resource Management (*see* Environmental Management and Policy;
    Natural Resources)
Solid-Earth Sciences (*see* Geosciences)
Space Sciences (*see* Planetary and Space Sciences)
Statistics
Theoretical Chemistry
Theoretical Physics
Viticulture and Enology
Water Resources

Graduate Programs in Engineering & Applied Sciences

Aeronautical Engineering (*see* Aerospace/Aeronautical Engineering)
Aerospace/Aeronautical Engineering
Aerospace Studies (*see* Aerospace/Aeronautical Engineering)
Agricultural Engineering
Applied Mechanics (*see* Mechanics)
Applied Science and Technology
Architectural Engineering
Artificial Intelligence/Robotics
Astronautical Engineering (*see* Aerospace/Aeronautical Engineering)
Automotive Engineering
Aviation
Biochemical Engineering
Bioengineering
Bioinformatics
Biological Engineering (*see* Bioengineering)
Biomedical Engineering
Biosystems Engineering
Biotechnology
Ceramic Engineering (*see* Ceramic Sciences and Engineering)
Ceramic Sciences and Engineering
Ceramics (*see* Ceramic Sciences and Engineering)
Chemical Engineering
Civil Engineering
Computer and Information Systems Security
Computer Engineering
Computer Science
Computing Technology (*see* Computer Science)
Construction Engineering
Construction Management
Database Systems
Electrical Engineering
Electronic Materials
Electronics Engineering (*see* Electrical Engineering)
Energy and Power Engineering
Energy Management and Policy
Engineering and Applied Sciences
Engineering and Public Affairs (*see* Technology and Public Policy)
Engineering and Public Policy (*see* Energy Management and Policy;
    Technology and Public Policy)
Engineering Design
Engineering Management
Engineering Mechanics (*see* Mechanics)
Engineering Metallurgy (*see* Metallurgical Engineering and
    Metallurgy)
Engineering Physics
Environmental Design (*see* Environmental Engineering)
Environmental Engineering
Ergonomics and Human Factors
Financial Engineering

Fire Protection Engineering
Food Engineering (*see* Agricultural Engineering)
Game Design and Development
Gas Engineering (*see* Petroleum Engineering)
Geological Engineering
Geophysics Engineering (*see* Geological Engineering)
Geotechnical Engineering
Hazardous Materials Management
Health Informatics
Health Systems (*see* Safety Engineering; Systems Engineering)
Highway Engineering (*see* Transportation and Highway Engineering)
Human-Computer Interaction
Human Factors (*see* Ergonomics and Human Factors)
Hydraulics
Hydrology (*see* Water Resources Engineering)
Industrial Engineering (*see* Industrial/Management Engineering)
Industrial/Management Engineering
Information Science
Internet Engineering
Macromolecular Science (*see* Polymer Science and Engineering)
Management Engineering (*see* Engineering Management; Industrial/
    Management Engineering)
Management of Technology
Manufacturing Engineering
Marine Engineering (*see* Civil Engineering)
Materials Engineering
Materials Sciences
Mechanical Engineering
Mechanics
Medical Informatics
Metallurgical Engineering and Metallurgy
Metallurgy (*see* Metallurgical Engineering and Metallurgy)
Mineral/Mining Engineering
Modeling and Simulation
Nanotechnology
Nuclear Engineering
Ocean Engineering
Operations Research
Paper and Pulp Engineering
Petroleum Engineering
Pharmaceutical Engineering
Plastics Engineering (*see* Polymer Science and Engineering)
Polymer Science and Engineering
Public Policy (*see* Energy Management and Policy; Technology and
    Public Policy)
Reliability Engineering
Robotics (*see* Artificial Intelligence/Robotics)
Safety Engineering
Software Engineering
Solid-State Sciences (*see* Materials Sciences)
Structural Engineering
Surveying Science and Engineering
Systems Analysis (*see* Systems Engineering)
Systems Engineering
Systems Science
Technology and Public Policy
Telecommunications
Telecommunications Management
Textile Sciences and Engineering
Textiles (*see* Textile Sciences and Engineering)
Transportation and Highway Engineering
Urban Systems Engineering (*see* Systems Engineering)
Waste Management (*see* Hazardous Materials Management)
Water Resources Engineering

Graduate Programs in Business, Education, Information Studies, Law & Social Work

Accounting
Actuarial Science
Adult Education

Peterson's Graduate Programs in the Physical Sciences, Mathematics, Agricultural Sciences, the Environment & Natural Resources 2017

www.petersons.com   **437**

Advertising and Public Relations
Agricultural Education
Alcohol Abuse Counseling (*see* Counselor Education)
Archival Management and Studies
Art Education
Athletics Administration (*see* Kinesiology and Movement Studies)
Athletic Training and Sports Medicine
Audiology (*see* Communication Disorders)
Aviation Management
Banking (*see* Finance and Banking)
Business Administration and Management—General
Business Education
Communication Disorders
Community College Education
Computer Education
Continuing Education (*see* Adult Education)
Counseling (*see* Counselor Education)
Counselor Education
Curriculum and Instruction
Developmental Education
Distance Education Development
Drug Abuse Counseling (*see* Counselor Education)
Early Childhood Education
Educational Leadership and Administration
Educational Measurement and Evaluation
Educational Media/Instructional Technology
Educational Policy
Educational Psychology
Education—General
Education of the Blind (*see* Special Education)
Education of the Deaf (*see* Special Education)
Education of the Gifted
Education of the Hearing Impaired (*see* Special Education)
Education of the Learning Disabled (*see* Special Education)
Education of the Mentally Retarded (*see* Special Education)
Education of the Physically Handicapped (*see* Special Education)
Education of Students with Severe/Multiple Disabilities
Education of the Visually Handicapped (*see* Special Education)
Electronic Commerce
Elementary Education
English as a Second Language
English Education
Entertainment Management
Entrepreneurship
Environmental Education
Environmental Law
Exercise and Sports Science
Exercise Physiology (*see* Kinesiology and Movement Studies)
Facilities and Entertainment Management
Finance and Banking
Food Services Management (*see* Hospitality Management)
Foreign Languages Education
Foundations and Philosophy of Education
Guidance and Counseling (*see* Counselor Education)
Health Education
Health Law
Hearing Sciences (*see* Communication Disorders)
Higher Education
Home Economics Education
Hospitality Management
Hotel Management (*see* Travel and Tourism)
Human Resources Development
Human Resources Management
Human Services
Industrial Administration (*see* Industrial and Manufacturing Management)
Industrial and Manufacturing Management
Industrial Education (*see* Vocational and Technical Education)
Information Studies
Instructional Technology (*see* Educational Media/Instructional Technology)
Insurance
Intellectual Property Law
International and Comparative Education
International Business
International Commerce (*see* International Business)

International Economics (*see* International Business)
International Trade (*see* International Business)
Investment and Securities (*see* Business Administration and Management; Finance and Banking; Investment Management)
Investment Management
Junior College Education (*see* Community College Education)
Kinesiology and Movement Studies
Law
Legal and Justice Studies
Leisure Services (*see* Recreation and Park Management)
Leisure Studies
Library Science
Logistics
Management (*see* Business Administration and Management)
Management Information Systems
Management Strategy and Policy
Marketing
Marketing Research
Mathematics Education
Middle School Education
Movement Studies (*see* Kinesiology and Movement Studies)
Multilingual and Multicultural Education
Museum Education
Music Education
Nonprofit Management
Nursery School Education (*see* Early Childhood Education)
Occupational Education (*see* Vocational and Technical Education)
Organizational Behavior
Organizational Management
Parks Administration (*see* Recreation and Park Management)
Personnel (*see* Human Resources Development; Human Resources Management; Organizational Behavior; Organizational Management; Student Affairs)
Philosophy of Education (*see* Foundations and Philosophy of Education)
Physical Education
Project Management
Public Relations (*see* Advertising and Public Relations)
Quality Management
Quantitative Analysis
Reading Education
Real Estate
Recreation and Park Management
Recreation Therapy (*see* Recreation and Park Management)
Religious Education
Remedial Education (*see* Special Education)
Restaurant Administration (*see* Hospitality Management)
Science Education
Secondary Education
Social Sciences Education
Social Studies Education (*see* Social Sciences Education)
Social Work
Special Education
Speech-Language Pathology and Audiology (*see* Communication Disorders)
Sports Management
Sports Medicine (*see* Athletic Training and Sports Medicine)
Sports Psychology and Sociology (*see* Kinesiology and Movement Studies)
Student Affairs
Substance Abuse Counseling (*see* Counselor Education)
Supply Chain Management
Sustainability Management
Systems Management (*see* Management Information Systems)
Taxation
Teacher Education (*see* specific subject areas)
Teaching English as a Second Language (*see* English as a Second Language)
Technical Education (*see* Vocational and Technical Education)
Transportation Management
Travel and Tourism
Urban Education
Vocational and Technical Education
Vocational Counseling (*see* Counselor Education)

Peterson's Graduate Programs in the Physical Sciences, Mathematics, Agricultural Sciences, the Environment & Natural Resources 2017

Directories and Subject Areas in This Book

NOTES

NOTES

NOTES

NOTES

NOTES

NOTES

NOTES

NOTES

NOTES

NOTES